P9-ARR-871

Education in the States: **Historical Development and Outlook**

A project of the Council of Chief State School Officers

Edited by
Jim B. Pearson and Edgar Fuller

Published by
NATIONAL EDUCATION ASSOCIATION OF THE UNITED STATES
1201 SIXTEENTH STREET, N.W. WASHINGTON, D.C. 20036

Library of Congress Catalog Card Number 70-81973

The research by the Council of Chief State School Officers reported herein was performed pursuant to Contract No. OEC-2-6-000991-0686 with the U.S. Department of Health, Education, and Welfare, Office of Education.

Foreword

Provision of education of broad scope and high quality to serve all the people is a major responsibility of the states. Standing in a strategic position between the local school agencies on the one hand and the federal government on the other, the state department of education is an important factor in making such educational opportunities available in each state.

This is the first of two volumes reporting a nationwide study of state departments of education, a project conducted since June 1966 by the Council of Chief State School Officers and financed in part under a contract with the U.S. Office of Education. It traces the historical development since 1900 of each of the 50 state departments of education and the central school agencies of Puerto Rico, American Samoa, Guam, the Panama Canal Zone, and the Virgin Islands. The second volume of this report, *Education in the States: Nationwide Development Since 1900,* deals with 16 areas of educational concern to all state departments of education. Both volumes fill voids in existing literature in education as related to the state level.

Each state chapter was written independently, dealing with whatever phases of departmental development the author may have selected for his own state. Most chapters reflect distinctive characteristics of the environments in which their respective state departments operate. The authors go far to explain present practices and often clarify promising lines for future development.

Perceptive readers of several state chapters will be able to compare departments in terms such as size, structure, functions, policy directions, and rate of development. Much can be inferred about each department's situation in regard to its responsibility to the people, its position within the state government, and its relationships within the educational community. Questions may occur: Do a department's basic structure and internal organization appear to operate in ways that facilitate achievement of its purposes?; Do its working relationships within the state capitol and throughout the state reinforce its effectiveness?; and, Are the legislative policies of the state concerning education clear and appropriate for our times?

Readers who evaluate the historical development and current status of several departments in such terms may discover implications for constructive improvements in their own state department of education. Such purposeful readers could well include members of legislatures and state boards of education, chief state school officers, departmental staff leaders, other officers of the state government, and numerous citizens who support effective state leadership in education. The most obvious function of these publications will be their nationwide use by teachers, administrators, scholars, and students, for whom they will be resources for study and research at the state level of education not heretofore available.

February 15, 1969

Jim B. Pearson, *Project Director*

Edgar Fuller, *Project Administrator*

Acknowledgments

A large number of organizations and individuals have contributed generously to the project. We shall first identify the organizations, and then name many of the individuals. We gratefully acknowledge the encouragement and assistance of all.

The U.S. Office of Education

Approximately one-half the total financing of the project—originally scheduled for 18 months but which required a period of more than 2 years—was supplied by the U.S. Office of Education. The project would not have been launched without this substantial contribution of funds, nor would it have proceeded so well without the helpful encouragement and splendid cooperation of the Office of Education personnel.

The Project Advisory Committee

This committee held only a small number of meetings, but these were extremely helpful in giving direction to the project in its early development.

The Chief State School Officers and Their Council

The chief state school officers directly or indirectly supplied almost one-half the financial support for the project and in numerous ways ensured its successful completion. The Study Commission of the Council of Chief State School Officers contributed its 1966 annual workshop to the early development of the state histories, and the authors of 28 chapters were drawn from the Commission's membership. These and other authors within the departments were generously supported by their respective chiefs in developing their chapters. Resource materials also were made available to authors outside the state agencies. The officers and directors of the Council appropriated substantial funds and authorized their Washington office to spend the necessary staff time and resources. We recognize especially the work of Assistant Executive Secretary Blanche E. Crippen in coordinating the preparation and organization of the materials of both volumes prior to publication.

The Publications Division of the National Education Association

The two volumes of the project report have been published and distributed on a nationwide basis by this division of the National Education Association. Its assumption of responsibility for these services makes certain that the results of the project will be made available nationwide and abroad. We gratefully acknowledge the perfect cooperation and generous contributions made by Director Sidney Dorros and his colleagues in the NEA Publications Division.

Contributors

The U.S. Office of Education

Harold Howe II
Wayne O. Reed
Arthur S. Harris
Harry L. Selden
Robert L. Hopper
F. H. Hundemer, Jr.

Project Committee

M. F. Peterson, Chairman
Terrel H. Bell
Sam M. Lambert
John R. Mayor
J. R. Rackley
Walter Rundell, Jr.
Harry M. Sparks
Joseph R. Strayer
Wendell H. Pierce
Harry L. Selden

Council of Chief State School Officers

General Officers

Byron W. Hansford
E. E. Holt
Owen B. Kiernan
M. F. Peterson
J. M. Tubb
Hubert Wheeler

Directors

Terrel H. Bell
Louis Bruno
Floyd T. Christian
J. W. Edgar
Martin W. Essex
Paul F. Johnston
Leon P. Minear
Jack P. Nix
Ray Page
Angus Rothwell
William J. Sanders
James A. Sensenbaugh
J. Howard Warf

Project Staff

Jim B. Pearson
Betsy S. Turvene
Mary O. Clampitt
Katherine C. Clark

Council Staff

Edgar Fuller
Blanche E. Crippen
Lori J. Blevins
Jamie E. Pinn

Publications Division, National Education Association

Sidney Dorros
Anne Marie Zahary
Kirsten H. Carter
Kenneth B. Frye
Charles E. Ford

Authors

Alabama	*Austin R. Meadows
Alaska	*William R. Marsh
Arizona	John E. Sinclair
Arkansas	*Frank W. Cannaday
California	State Department Bureau of Publications
Colorado	H. Edgar Williams
Connecticut	*William H. Flaharty
Delaware	*Paul H. Johnston
Florida	*John W. Seay
Georgia	Walter E. Wade
Hawaii	James R. Hunt
Idaho	*Harold Farley
Illinois	*Warren L. Evenson
Indiana	*Harold H. Negley
Iowa	*Richard N. Smith
Kansas	Adel F. Throckmorton
Kentucky	Louise Combs
	Kern Alexander
Louisiana	James S. Cookston
	R. L. Frye
	Louis Nicolosi
	Charles E. Sutton
	Ralph P. Whitehead
Maine	*Kermit S. Nickerson
Maryland	Robert Moyer
	*David W. Zimmerman
Massachusetts	Franklin P. Hawkes
	*Thomas J. Curtin
Michigan	State Department of Education Staff
Minnesota	T. C. Engum
Mississippi	*R. W. Griffith
Missouri	Raymond A. Roberts
Montana	Lyle L. Berg
Nebraska	Ginger Jensen
Nevada	Harold Brown
New Hampshire	William H. Mandrey
New Jersey	Robert F. Palmer
New Mexico	Tom Wiley
New York	Edmund H. Crane
	Esther C. Smith
	Kathryn Sue Updike
North Carolina	Vester M. Mulholland
North Dakota	E. J. Taylor, Jr.
Ohio	R. Merle Eyman
	*Earl Metz
Oklahoma	Guy H. Lambert
	Guy M. Rankin
Oregon	*Jesse V. Fasold
Pennsylvania	Patricia L. Rosenbaum
Puerto Rico	*Angel M. Mergal
Rhode Island	*Arthur R. Pontarelli
South Carolina	*Frank M. Kirk
South Dakota	*James C. Schooler
Tennessee	Sam Smith
Texas	E. D. Yoes, Jr.
Utah	*Lerue W. Winget
Vermont	Marshall True
	Judith Cyronak
	*Leon H. Bruno
Virginia	*Fendall R. Ellis
	Harry L. Smith
	C. J. Watkins
Washington	Robert G. Wark
West Virginia	State Department of Education Staff
Wisconsin	Walter B. Senty
	*Robert C. Van Raalte
Wyoming	*Paul Graves
American Samoa	*William B. Banks
Canal Zone	Francis A. Castles
Guam	*Harley G. Jones
	Trubee Joy Jones
Virgin Islands	*Alexander Henderson

*CCSSO Study Commission member

Contents

1 Alabama

DEPARTMENT OF EDUCATION

Austin R. Meadows

Contents

EARLY PERIOD TO THE 1920'S

The Beginning

Any education of historical importance evolves out of the reactions of people to their environment over a period of time. The cultural and political aspects of the Renaissance were carefully nurtured like seedlings in a rich garden plot in northern Italy for two centuries before being carried northward across the Alps in 1475 to enrich the lives of all the people it touched (1). Learning started long before then, but its revival after the Dark Ages prompted refinements in economic, social, and political criteria from which we greatly benefit to this day.

Our own immediate beginning was rooted in the explorations, colonizations, and trade of some of the most enlightened leaders in the world who represented three of the most celebrated royal houses in history (2). In 1540, while Charles I was king of Spain, Hernando de Soto led a band of Spanish noblemen across the Alabama Country in search for gold. Later, Spain colonized part of the Gulf Coast-Mobile area eastward, from whence Spanish Fort in Baldwin County on Mobile Bay gets its name.

In 1702, the French, led by Bienville in the reign of Louis XIV, started colonizing Mobile to be their capital of half a continent reaching from the Gulf of Mexico to the Great Lakes and beyond. Their names adorn public parks, streets, and waters: Bienville Square, with its giant oaks; Dauphin Street, with its famous Protestant churches; Dauphin Island, with Fort Gaines; and Bon Secour River, the French name for good succor and the home of the Bon Secour oyster. The early French influence on public education was indirect. In the 1763 Treaty of Paris, during the reign of George III, the British won the French possessions in America, and the Alabama Country was made a royal colony subject to the rule of the king and his royal privy council.

While under the French and Spanish influences, education in the Alabama territory was dominated by the Catholic policy of church schools rather than public schools. The British influence favored private tutoring and private schools or laissez-faire. Out of this background of royalty, monarchy, aristocracy, Catholicism with its chants and foreign tongues, Protestantism from the English with songs set to be sung by all, nature-loving tribes of savage Indians, and American pioneers from adjacent states evolved the State of Alabama in 1819.

For the first half of the nineteenth century the people of Alabama maintained the ideas they brought with them about the type of schools they wanted, without any state leadership or state school system. There was no county or local school system except the Mobile County school system, which started legally in 1826. Apparently the non-Catholic citizens of Mobile County saw the need for uniting to provide public schools comparable to the Catholic church-controlled education in that area.

In 1854, the state public school system was established, with a state superintendent of education to be elected by the voters of the state to be the chief state school officer. However, during the last half of the nineteenth century education below the college level continued to be primarily a private matter because substantial provisions were not made for financing public schools.

From the time of the early settlements in the state until 1900, cotton was the main money crop, and the population was overwhelmingly rural. Until recently cotton was produced by manpower and horsepower and was harvested by manpower. Mass education was not considered necessary to the economy of the times. In 1856, out of a total school census of 171,073, only 89,160 pupils were enrolled in public schools. Available state public school funds in 1856 were $267,690, and they did not reach $1 million until the twentieth century. The assessed valuation of property of the state increased from $110,992,000 in 1856 to only $270,408,000 in 1901 (3).

The tragic era of the pyramided catastrophes of the Civil War and Reconstruction left the state devastated economically, destitute of school building facilities, and with newly freed homeless citizens who had been sold as slaves previously by slave traders. Out of this lost cause, the loss of many of its men, 4 years of war devastation, 7 years of Reconstruction, the state was left alone to rehabilitate itself economically, educationally, and spiritually.

Through all of this difficult time the state superintendent crusaded to develop sentiment for mass education. He published annual or biennial reports on school funds, enrollment, and school conditions and needs, except for the years 1859 through 1868—the Civil War and Reconstruction era. The superintendent was a one-man department with little or no clerical assistance and no professional staff. Despite these limitations, he was placed on all public state education boards including those of the University of Alabama, which opened in 1831, Auburn University, which opened in 1872 as the "Agricultural and Mechanical College," and the State Board of Education that existed during the Reconstruction era of 1868-75.

The state board of the Reconstruction era established a state normal school at Florence in 1872; a state normal school and university for Negroes in 1873 at Marion, which was later moved to Montgomery by the General Assembly; and the Alabama Agricultural and Mechanical College near Huntsville as a normal school in 1873.

The Reconstruction state board had legislative authority on educational matters, and the state superintendent, under authority of the board, appointed all of the county superintendents of schools. The university and other colleges were placed under the state board. Although the state superintendent was not given any assistance for professional services, he was furnished clerical assistance to record laws passed while the board was in legislative session. The one-man department continued to publicize the need for better schools and to make annual reports, but that was not enough.

Throughout the century Alabama produced many highly educated citizens through private tutoring, private schools, and the state colleges. One of the U.S. Commissioners of Education, N. H. R. Dawson, appointed in 1885, had lived in Selma. William Rufus King, also from Selma, was Vice-President of the United States. J. L. M. Curry of Talledega won national fame in directing the Peabody Educational Funds, and he was one of the three cofounders of the public school system created in 1854. None of these or of the other highly educated citizens succeeded in ensuring adequate state educational leadership for public schools.

This left the state without the leadership necessary to lead the people into taking steps to either establish or operate public schools for the masses. Economic conditions were no better than public school conditions. In 1899, only half the children of school census age were enrolled in school, and the total assessed valuation of the state was only $260,201,000 (4). Poor economic conditions accompanied poor education then as now. One man just could not do the school job. In the language of his many farmer constituents, the state superintendent had "a tough row to hoe."

The One-Man Department Turns the Twentieth Century

John W. Abercrombie, who became state superintendent of education in 1898, launched a new tide of public sentiment for public schools through his many speeches, his outstanding printed annual reports, and his notable success in getting the Legislature to levy a 1-mill state school property tax. His report of September 1900 states that he had made addresses in more than 50 of the 66 (now 67) counties of the state in 2 years, while simultaneously attending state, Southern, and national educational gatherings to keep abreast of the times. He believed that great interest in the cause of public education had been aroused and, further, that hope had replaced discouragement, concluding, only partially correctly, that indifference among the people had vanished. Dr. Abercrombie stated that it was impossible to do the work satisfactorily without a stenographer, an assistant to the chief clerk, a typewriter, and postage. He further reported the Department of Education as "fast becoming recognized as the most important department in the government, and the State cannot afford any longer to refuse such assistance as is necessary to properly conduct the affairs of the Department" (5).

Dr. Abercrombie included in his 1900 report short, informative narratives and pertinent statistics from county superintendents and each normal school. A lengthy report was included from Booker T. Washington, president of Tuskegee Normal and Industrial Institute, which noted the visit of the Alabama Legislature and its unanimous high commendation of the work at the institute. Booker T. Washington also reported the gift of 25,000 acres of land by Congress, philanthropic gifts from 16 donors in amounts ranging from $500 to $24,000, and an increase in the annual appropriation from the John F. Slater Fund from $8,000 to $10,000. Dr. Abercrombie knew that local reports of progress and needs would support his own exhortations for public education and for the Legislature to levy a 1-mill state school tax. He persuaded county superintendents and township trustees to increase the public school term from 3 to 4 months and requested extension to four and a half months for the next year because of the additional revenue from the state 1-mill school tax. He made 27 specific recommendations to the Legislature for educational improvement. The new State Constitution of 1901 expanded the state 1-mill school tax to 3 mills and authorized the voters in each county to levy a 1-mill school tax. Dr. Abercrombie's leadership was so outstanding that he was appointed president of the University of Alabama before his term expired, but he returned to the state superintendency in 1920.

Dr. Abercrombie's successors continued to publish annual reports containing state and local school finance and enrollment statistics, as well as narrative statements from state and local public school officials. Issac W. Hill, state superintendent of education from 1903 to 1907, reported in 1906 that he had spoken for education in 65 counties and that the Peabody Board had provided funds for the employment of a full-time experienced teacher to work with the State Federation of Women's Clubs in assisting him in the task of organizing the state counties and districts into school improvement associations. The one-man department received no funds from the state for professional assistants but obtained philanthropic financing of one assistant for a specific school organizational project. Hill's 1906 report is noteworthy partly because he recommended financing a system of high schools with at least one in each county (6).

In 1910, the Department of Education published the first course of study for the public elementary schools of Alabama, which was widely used by elementary teachers. Although there was no law authorizing such a manual and no provision for a course of study committee, the state superintendent of education secured the services of leading educators in its preparation. The materials were edited and arranged for publication by professors of education at Auburn Polytechnic Institute and the University of Alabama.

The first decade of the twentieth century ended with improvement in specific phases of public education, and department reports indicated an increasing statewide sentiment for public schools. However, there still was no vigorous, unified, organized state effort for education.

Unified Public School Action Begins 40 Years After Reconstruction

In 1915, a brilliant, energetic, and forceful state superintendent of education, William F. (Bill) Feagan, drafted and sponsored through the Legislature 15 bills that revolutionized the public school structure of the state. He had served 6 years as chief clerk in the department when he was appointed superintendent in 1913 to complete the unexpired term of Henry J. Willingham, who resigned to become president of Florence State Normal School. Feagan was elected to succeed himself. He used his 2 appointive years and his knowledge gained as chief clerk to plan and build strong county and local school improvement associations throughout the state. The community organization revolved around observance of 4 special days in which school patrons of each school were urged to attend. Feagan designated the school days to be as follows:

School Improvement Day – October 30, 1914
Good Roads Day – January 15, 1915
Health Day – February 12, 1915
Better Farming Day – March 12, 1915.

He gave suitable observance programs to the teachers for each special day so that they could hold successful meetings. Feagan knew that the four different type meetings would bring people of all interests to the school and that, by being better informed and a part of the school-community organization, they would help him get his bills ratified by the Legislature and his two constitutional amendments ratified by the voters at the polls. Two of his 15 bills would authorize constitutional amendments to levy property ad valorem school taxes. These had to be ratified first by a statewide vote; second, by a majority vote in each county for a 3-mill county tax; and after that, by the voters in each school district for the 3-mill district school tax. Because of his careful preparation, he was successful on all counts.

Feagan later called members of county boards of education to meet with him at the capital in December 1916, at which time he emphasized their legal duty to appoint the county superintendent of education along with other duties. Feagan resigned a year before his term expired to accept the superintendency of Montgomery County, Alabama, and the Governor appointed one of his chief assistants, Spright Dowell, to succeed him.

Another outstanding educational achievement of this decade was a comprehensive survey in 1919 of all education in the state, which was recommended by Spright Dowell and authorized by the Legislature with an appropriation therefor. Under legislative authority, the Governor appointed a five-man commission empowered to employ assistants to make the survey (7). The commission contracted with the U.S. Commissioner of Education, P. P. Claxton, for the U.S. Bureau of Education to make the study and report back to the commission. The Bureau of Education detailed 16 of its foremost men and women and procured the services of eminent specialists from other states to make the study. Federal relations in education are of such national and local concern that it is important to note here that Spright Dowell included in his 1919 annual report the opinion that the value of the survey service of the U.S. Bureau of Education to the state exceeded any other service to the state in its entire history.

Following the 1919 survey recommendations, the State Board of Education was created to include the Governor as chairman, the state superintendent of education as executive officer and secretary, and six other members appointed by the Governor and approved by the Senate. The state board, on the recommendations of the state superintendent of education, established policies for the department and public schools.

Ten divisions, with a head of each division and a suitable number of assistants, were provided as follows:

1. Executive and business management
2. Teacher training, certification, and placement
3. Statistics
4. Rural schools
5. Elementary schools
6. Secondary education
7. Physical education
8. Vocational education
9. Exceptional education
10. School and community betterment.

After 100 years of statehood, Alabama created a full department to furnish leadership, consultative services, adequate reporting of school progress and needs, and statistics on school finance and attendance. During the decade, the one-man department had increased first to two field assistants; then up to nine under Feagan, including Spright Dowell as chief clerk and later as director of institutes; and finally up to 10 divisions.

The department first furnished leadership under Feagan in developing local community organizations to support educational progress, and then under Dowell in providing a comprehensive, scientific, educational survey of all education in the state. The state superintendent served as chairman of the vocational education state board, appointed by the Governor in 1917; and he proceeded to wisely use the federal funds under the 1917 Smith-Hughes Law for vocational education. Dowell appointed J. B. Hobdy as vocational education director and appointed an agriculture, home economics, and trade and industrial education supervisor. Spright Dowell was elected to succeed himself for a 4-year term beginning in January 1919, but he resigned 3 years before expiration of his term to accept the presidency of Alabama Polytechnic Institute (now Auburn University).

Departmental Organization and Functions in the Twenties

In 1920, John W. Abercrombie returned to the state superintendency to serve 7 years—3 years by appointment of the Governor and 4 by election. During the 18-year interim he had served as president of the University of Alabama and a term in Congress. He inherited an expanded and reorganized department professional staff, which he proceeded to further expand and direct. He made R. E. Tidwell assistant state superintendent and kept him on as teacher-training director. Seven years later, Tidwell succeeded Dr. Abercrombie to become a great state superintendent also. Dr. Abercrombie recruited the best educational talent in the nation to round out the department as it had been recommended in the U.S. Office of Education 1919 survey.

A new periodic bulletin, "Alabama School Progress," was prepared by the department and published by the Alabama Education Association first as its official organ, and later as part of the *Alabama State Journal* that was mailed to all teachers belonging to AEA. Dr. Abercrombie reported that the bulletin was being used as an example of progressive educational propaganda at Columbia Teachers College, Harvard University, and Chicago University.

The 1920 annual report of the Alabama Department of Education presented the "Index Number Study of Rural Elementary Schools" by counties, with white and Negro schools considered separately, and an effective chart showing the rank of the counties in descending order according to ranking score on 10 items. The eight most important items were school-holding power, length of school term, literacy from 10 to 21 years of age, grade of teaching certificates held by teachers, teachers' salaries, value of teaching equipment per teacher, percent of available school taxes (7 mills) levied locally, and percent of schools consolidated. This gave department field staff people a new medium for encouraging adequate provisions for quality education. The 1921 annual report carried the conclusion, measured by the Ayer's number for state school systems, that Alabama's public schools gained 74 percent as many points from 1918 to 1921 as previously gained from 1890 to 1918. A table in the report portrayed what Alabama had to do to meet the national average of 1918 on Ayer's 10 index components (8). The department continued thereafter to inform the teachers and the public, through the *AEA Journal,* of school achievements, school needs, and how these needs might be met.

Dr. Abercrombie continued to use his outstanding ability to encourage the people to make maximum efforts for education. He had able support from the department employees. In his 1926 annual report he urged expanding the state revolving fund of $100,000 into an "Equalization Fund" of $2.5 million to $3 million. He started educational exhibits at the Alabama State Fair representing the work of the 10 divisions in the department. He reported that the visitors at the state fair were so impressed with the exhibits that many of them called at the department to express their approval. His annual reports included narrative and statistical reports by the directors of the divisions. All of this helped develop public opinion favorable to school improvement.

The department produced and published a *Course of Study for Elementary Schools* in 1921 and a revised issue in 1924 for which the demand was so great that it was reprinted in 1926. The 1924 revision presented a plan for meeting the state law to expand from 11 to 12 grades in 1924-25 (9). The 7-4 state plan was reorganized into the 6-3-3 plan. The *Course of Study* was furnished to each school official, supervisor, and teacher. It proved to be a remarkable guide to teachers, for it included detailed suggestions for planning the first day of school; a review of the school laws to be observed by the teacher; the program for each subject in each grade as related to general aims for the grade; specific aims for the subject; suggestions for attaining the aims; textbooks and reference books; results to be attained; and requirements for promotion. Tentative suggestions were given for short-term schools.

This *Course of Study* was a great aid to the growing number of new teachers required for the increasing enrollment, many of whom lacked a college education. R. E. Tidwell, director of institutes, and Spright Dowell reported in 1919 that of 9,495 teachers attending institutes that fall, 2,049 held 2-year normal school diplomas, 854 were college graduates, 3,940 were high school graduates only, leaving 2,652 teachers who had not finished high school.

In the elections of 1926 the people moved ahead on all fronts and elected Bibb Graves as Governor and R. E.

Tidwell as state superintendent of education. This excellent team developed the 1927 educational equalization program for all the children of all the people. This program was modeled after the Paul Mort plan of equalization, except that the teacher unit was used as a factor of need instead of the weighted pupil factor used by Mort. It provided a 7-month minimum school term with provisions for teachers' salaries, school transportation, and other current expenses. This was a new beginning—the beginning of state responsibility for financing a minimum educational offering for all children. Dr. Tidwell's 7 years of experience as assistant state superintendent paid the people rich dividends through his creative educational planning and through the cooperation he gained from the Governor and the Legislature. The minimum program included provisions for county supervisors of instruction and county joint school attendance-child welfare supervisors. Outstanding elementary educators were employed as state instructional supervisors and stationed at the normal schools located in southeast, northeast, northwest, and west-central Alabama. They were assigned to work with the county and city supervisors in the school systems served by the normal schools and to assist in updating teacher training in the institutions.

Dr. Tidwell created a new and outstanding department service beginning in 1928—a comprehensive educational survey of county and city school systems, with a 10-year plan for economy and efficiency in school operation. He created the administration division to direct the survey service and placed it under the direction of A. F. Harman, who was later state superintendent of education and, after that, president of Alabama College.

Tidwell created a research and information division of which Dale S. Young, a brilliant Ph.D. from Columbia University, was made director in July 1927. Young had studied under Paul Mort and developed the 1927 state equalization program regulations that were later expanded into the 1935 state minimum program.

Dr. Tidwell filled his former position of director of teacher training and certification with B. L. Parkinson, who later became president of Mississippi State College for Women. Clyde Pearson, employed first as architectural draftsman, later became the chief state school architect. Norma Smith, a supervisor of instruction, was appointed first as director of school and community organization and later to direct elementary supervision. N. R. Baker, who had served as high school supervisor at one time and had been superintendent of the Jefferson County school system for several years, was employed to head the state program for improving junior high schools.

The department was staffed with able, well-educated, professional people who wielded great influence in promoting progress in education through the twenties and until partially cut down by the Depression.

THE DEPARTMENT AND THE DEPRESSION

The department entered the Depression under the leadership of one of its most courageous chief state school officers, A. F. Harman. He was an outstanding scholar with administrative qualities, and he marshaled all of his ability and strength to keep schools going.

The first local uniform school child accounting system was developed and installed in 1930 by Austin R. Meadows, who was appointed as a member of the department in November 1929. In 1930, the department, under Dr. Harman, published and distributed an outstanding state course of study for elementary grades that was started under Dr. Tidwell.

Dr. Harman led his staff to work with WPA and PWA during the Depression to keep schools running on federal relief funds. The 1931 Legislature cut educational appropriations and did nothing to prevent heavy proration of appropriations to the department and to other educational needs. In July 1931, Senator Harlan, an elderly distinguished physician, stated that the 1931 Legislature was the worst since Reconstruction (10). Department appropriations were cut 22 percent in 1932-33.

Dr. Harman kept the school survey service going in full force with the collaboration of the University of Alabama College of Education under Dean John R. McLure in furnishing survey field staff people to assist in the school surveys without cost to the department. The General Education Board of the Rockefeller Foundation financed the divisions of research and Negro education for a time, but the research division was lost finally. The administration division was eliminated because of lack of funds.

In 1934, the voters turned again to Bibb Graves for Governor and elected J. A. Keller as state superintendent of education. The two worked with department personnel to get a 1.5-percent gross receipt tax, later changed to a 2-percent sales tax, levied and earmarked for public education, except for the first one-fourth of the proceeds and finally $1,700,000. This restored the 1927 equalization program under the name of the minimum program. The 1935 minimum program continued the teacher-unit as the basic factor in calculating the need except for transportation. The teacher-unit factor for calculating the state minimum program was not originated or developed by either Paul Mort, Edgar L. Morphet, or R. L. Johns. Johns directed the development of a crude and difficult local effort formula in the minimum program but included freezing assessed valuation of property at the 1938 level in determining the total amount of local effort. This practically destroyed local effort in the minimum program because the freezing factor decreased local effort to 1.1 mills instead of the original 5 mills.

Local effort was, in 1967, 2.58 percent of the total state minimum program, and this percentage will decrease as state aid increases. The freezing of the assessed valuation of property taxes to the 1938 level is depriving the state minimum program of at least $16 million annually, which would be enough to provide a 10-percent increase in allotments for teachers' salaries. Morphet and Johns each contributed much to state education in Alabama; but they also learned much from the 1927 state equalization program and the state survey program, which were already in successful operation before they came into the department—Morphet in 1934 and Johns in 1936. They both took to Florida successful working equalization and survey programs about which they had learned much in Alabama. One of the fascinating developments of public education in America has been the innovations developed by state and local school systems based on programs originated in other places.

Morphet, as administration and finance director under Keller, calculated the state minimum program needs for legislative consideration in 1935. But when Keller presented the figures to the State Senate Finance and Taxation Committee, the committee requested a recalculation and the elimination of $800,000 calculated in the program for school nurses. Meadows proposed to Keller the recalculation of the program on the basis of current and defensible data rather than data used by Morphet, who was in Atlantic City attending an educational convention. The new program, recalculated with the help of Audrey Brown and 14 other assistants, used current number of teachers employed, and current expenses and capital outlay were calculated on the basis of average expenditures for the state as a whole during the 4 Depression years. The recalculated program eliminated the $800,000 for nurses but increased the budget request by $900,000. Keller counseled with his professional staff, and they unanimously endorsed the recalculated budget.

In the Senate committee rehearing the chairman asked Keller what kind of finance he was proposing for an increase of $900,000 when he was asked to reduce the appropriation request by $800,000. Keller replied that the recalculated program was his program rather than the previous program, which he had inherited. Three times the chairman asked Keller to reduce his request. Each time Keller stated that he would do the best he could with what the Legislature gave him, but that it would not do the job the Legislature wanted done nor the job that needed to be done. Finally, the chairman, the late Senator Shelby Fletcher, a millionaire, said, "Keller, I am not going to try to beat you down on your figures anymore: I am going to help you get this appropriation." And he did. This recalculated program was what justified Governor Bibb Graves and the Legislature's levying a 2-percent sales tax in 1937 with the first three-fourths of the tax and later all but $1,700,000 earmarked for education.

This is reported in detail because progress in education has often hinged on a stalwart educator like Keller and a defensible department calculation of educational needs. Not a single legislator asked Keller to reduce his request below the current teachers' salaries and the 4-year Depression average expenditures for other items. Keller put through a school budget act, designed to prevent local school budget deficits in the future, and a School Warrant (bond) Act that enabled local school boards to secure long-term bonds at the lowest interest rate in the nation. His administrative ability prompted the state board to make him president of Florence State College before his term as superintendent expired.

After 1935, the department, through official action of the state superintendent, approved all local school budgets before they could receive state funds. Approval, however, was limited to prohibiting estimated expenditure from exceeding estimated revenue and requiring state minimum program allotments for teachers' salaries to be budgeted as allotted in order to be received. A school system was penalized in state funds one-fourth of any excess of current expenditures over the approved estimated receipts. The state superintendent was required to approve all issues of school warrants (bonds) of indebtedness of local school systems before they could be sold. But his approval was limited to ascertaining that the annual schedule of payment of principal and interest neither jeopardized the state minimum program nor exceeded 80 percent of the estimated annual revenue of the tax pledged, and further that the use of such funds was to be spent at survey-approved school centers or on school buses meeting state specifications.

This combination of budget control, issuance of school warrants of indebtedness, and capital outlay investments only at survey-approved school centers enabled local school boards to get the best possible interest rates on long-term indebtedness and prevented waste of school funds on school centers that would otherwise be abandoned because they would be either too small or not located in or near the centers of the school population to be served. The school survey service advanced from recommending a minimum of three teachers or more for a permanent school center to a minimum six-teacher school. Department staff members presented survey findings to local school boards and, with their approval, to citizen groups in the school system. In this way school consolidation was accelerated.

County-wide action was possible because of a newly developed plan of school board ownership and operation of school buses based on research by Meadows in fulfillment of the partial requirement for a Ph.D. degree at Columbia University (11). Meadows developed the first Alabama state uniform school financial accounting system. The department furnished research findings which were used by the 1939 National School Bus Conference of department representatives from the 48 states in which national school bus specifications were adopted. The research findings included data by health officers from Indiana and Alabama that gave the average dimensions of school-age children. From this information bus body width and length could be determined for a given number of passengers. National school bus body specifications permitted mass production of safe and economical school buses. The contribution of the Alabama department to the 1939 Conference on School Bus Specification Standards contributed to safety and economy in school bus transportation throughout the United States. It also enabled Alabama local school systems to change over from unsafe, dilapidated school bus firetraps to all-steel school buses with forward-facing seats because of the lower prices secured through mass production of school bus bodies.

The department, with approval of the State Board of Education, developed a formula for allocating state minimum program funds for school transportation to local school systems. This was based on cost of transportation per pupil per day of the previous year by density of transportable pupils, using 11 density groupings. Johns, as director of administration and finance, developed this formula.

The federal PWA officials were persuaded by the department to follow the school survey recommendations on school centers after having made the mistake of approving constructing a small building in Morgan County that was later abandoned because of its smallness and proximity to a survey-approved permanent school center. Under Keller the department instructor positions in elementary education stationed at Troy, Jacksonville, Florence, and Livingston State Colleges were eliminated, as were the high school supervisor positions at Auburn, University of Alabama, and Alabama College.

In 1939 state employees were placed under a separate state personnel board for employment, tenure, and salary schedules, including the professional staff of the department. Albert Collins, as state superintendent of education, and Meadows vigorously opposed placing professional staff members of the department who were college graduates under the state personnel board. The state personnel board procedures continued to be a handicap in the selection of outstanding educators and especially of young, promising educators, in that they limited recruitment of professional educators, and especially young, promising educators who lacked statistical measures of experience to push them up to the top priority list of applicants.

Governor Bibb Graves appointed A. H. Collins to succeed Keller. Collins had been an able department consultant in secondary education and was elected for a full term as superintendent without opposition. He resigned after all legislation had been completed to become director of the office of price administration, and E. B. Norton was appointed to succeed him. Dr. Norton was elected without opposition for a full term, but he in turn resigned 7 months before his term expired to become U.S. Deputy Commissioner of Education in 1946.

THE DEPARTMENT IN DEFENSE OF THE NATION

The *Narrative Report 1937-1942* declared that it was always wartime for public education–

> Because public education from its very beginning has been engaged in a pitched battle with ignorance, injustice, intolerance, selfishness, poverty, crime, and all of their allies .... Public education did not wait for the Atlantic Charter to join in the battle for the "four freedoms" because those four freedoms have been a part of the basic philosophy of American public education since the days of Horace Mann. On Sunday, December 7, 1941, our Nation was attacked by the armed forces of its enemies. On Monday, December 8, 1941, one million school teachers and thirty million school children dedicated themselves anew to the defense of their country with a unanimity of spirit unparalleled in any other segment of the American people. It did not take an act of Congress or a plea from the President to enlist this support. Our public schools are local institutions not legally subject to Federal control. Nevertheless, the leadership of public education immediately recognized the emergency needs of the Nation as of paramount importance (12).

Paul V. McNutt, Director of National Mobilization for World War II, in 1942 declared Alabama to be the best balanced war state in the Union; certainly the department did everything possible to help the state merit this commendation. It provided leadership and workable plans to local school systems for selective service registration, rationing registration, civilian defense training, control of inflation, sales of war stamps and bonds, collection of scrap, conservation programs, school transportation to meet wartime needs, consumer education, the building of public morale, and many other phases of the war effort.

The Alabama School of Trades, under the direction of the department, converted to a program especially for the Air Force and trained students from propeller specialists to airplane mechanics. Daily school schedules were modified in order to fit into wartime schedules. School buses were used to transport defense workers. By the end of 1944, 296,253 individuals had received war production training, including supplementary courses, preemployment courses, and food production war training administered under the supervision of the vocational education division.

The department met with federal officials and developed cooperative plans for providing school facilities for pupils in national defense areas in the state. This involved getting representatives of the Army, the Air Force, and the maritime agencies to approve needed construction in the defense areas for the influx of school population. This service included meeting with U.S. Office of Education officials and local school officials to develop and execute plans toward applications for federal funds for school building construction and school operation. The cooperation between the U.S. Office of Education and the department was excellent. Alabama's war effort was increased by the willingness of employees to move into the war centers when assured they would have schools for their children.

School transportation, a serious problem in wartime, was aided by the cooperative efforts of representatives of 15 state education departments; a representative of the U.S. Office of Education; representatives of other federal agencies; representatives of the American Automobile Association, Automotive Safety Foundation, National Education Association, National Safety Council; Frank W. Cyr of Teachers College, Columbia University; and Amos E. Neyhart of Pennsylvania State College. The Alabama Department of Education furnished the representative who had published the research study on *Safety and Economy in School Bus Transportation* for the work conferences at Yale University and in Washington, D.C., in which a special handbook was developed, entitled *School Transportation in Wartime* (13).

The production of the handbook was preceded by a meeting of Meadows of Alabama, Morphet of Florida, and Henry F. Alves of the U.S. Office of Education with Joseph B. Eastman, Director of the U.S. Office of Defense Transportation, and his assistant, C. D. Hutchins. A policy was approved at this time to route all school transportation wartime applications and regulations relating thereto through each state education department. The handbook was approved by the National Council of Chief State School Officers and carried a letter from Joseph B. Eastman, "To those interested in wartime uses of school buses," stating that—

> National Council of Chief State School Officers and those associated in the preparation of this handbook have made a notable contribution . . . and I urge that all concerned work vigorously and effectively toward attaining these objectives as a patriotic part of the total war effort (14).

John Studebaker, U.S. Commissioner of Education, included in the handbook a letter to all school authorities responsible for school transportation urging that the handbook procedures be followed and pledging that the U.S. Office of Education would lend every possible assistance to state departments of education in planning and executing this urgently needed program.

The cooperative efforts on *School Transportation in Wartime*, as published in 1942, and the minimum standard for school buses developed by the 48 states with the assistance of Frank W. Cyr, professor of education at Teachers College, Columbia University, in 1939 are reported in some detail because these two developments of national significance were made with the complete cooperation of state education departments, the U.S. Office of Education, other federal agencies concerned, and private enterprise. Moreover, effective action was taken with a minimum of red tape, no waste of funds, and in a manner which engendered the finest possible respect and appreciation for all individuals and agencies concerned.

The entire program of *School Transportation in Wartime*, involving the daily transportation of over four million children to and from school and approximately 93,000 school buses in daily service, was cleared and approved by the relatively small staff of the school bus transportation section of the Office of Defense Transportation. This pattern of local, state, and national cooperation for the greatest possible national efforts proves that the same type pattern could be operated successfully in any peacetime operation.

There was practically no school building construction during this period except in national-defense-connected school systems. Because of the federal spending program in Alabama, a surplus of over $12 million was collected in the educational trust fund, which was appropriated to education for capital outlay. The Legislature created a State Building Commission, with the superintendent of education as one of its members along with the Governor, the state health officer, and legislative members elected by the Legislature. The state superintendent, as executive secretary of the State Board of Education, directed department staff members to check requests for building construction and to submit them for his approval in terms of approved survey school centers and state school building regulations. The department supervised the letting of school construction contracts on bids and made final inspection on all contracts before contractors received complete payment for both the public schools and all educational institutions under the supervision of the state board. The department followed a similar procedure with all WPA and PWA school building projects.

The department assumed full responsibility for state administration policy formulation and administration of the national school lunch program of assistance to local schools. It scheduled regional workshops for lunchroom managers in the local schools, presenting the best recommendations and procedures for school lunches to offer adequate nutrition for one meal, maximum educational values, and all within a framework of economy.

Veterans education was administered at the national level by the Veterans Administration, and on the state level through the department. The administration and finance division and the vocational education division were those specifically involved. The department organized and developed the plan of education of veterans by local school systems and reimbursed local school systems for the total cost of veterans education. In the fall of 1946, the department held an official meeting, called by Meadows, with all county and city superintendents of education and worked out an agreement for the local officials to expand the program of educating veterans which they had started. It was understood that the department would speed up the reimbursement of federal funds by installing data-processing equipment to expedite the statistical work involved in checking the 26 items required on each veteran at that time. This was done. In 1949, 48,429 veterans cleared through the department for on-the-job training in industry and agriculture and continuation schools.

The department, by working through local school officials, equipped veterans with enough know-how to continue full time on the jobs in which they were training or to get new jobs immediately after World War II. This economic pump priming enabled Alabama to make the greatest percentage increase in per-capita income from 1950 to 1960 of any state in the Union (15). Federal funds financed the necessary increase in department personnel to adequately develop and administer the veterans program. As the department expanded its services through increased employees, the economic welfare of the people expanded. People were ready to invest more in public education through public taxes.

Superintendent E. B. Norton joined the other chief state school officers in creating a Study Commission, and within that a Planning Committee, the former consisting of a member from each state education department to make studies and recommendations to their chiefs. Meadows served 2 years during wartime (1943-44) as chairman of the Planning Committee, which recommended that an office be established in Washington by the chief state school officers. In 1947, the National Council of Chief State School Officers was incorporated under the leadership of its executive committee, secured a grant from the General Education Board of the Rockefeller Foundation to assist in financing its central office, and appointed E. B. Norton as its first executive secretary.

Norton had contributed greatly to the establishment of the office and took charge when it was established in July 1948. He resigned in December 1948, however, to assume the presidency of Alabama State Teachers College at Florence and was succeeded on the same day by Edgar Fuller, former New Hampshire Commissioner of Education and director of the Division of School Administration of the U.S. Office of Education.

THE DEPARTMENT IN THE IMMEDIATE POSTWAR PERIOD

A new and entirely different state political figure arrived on the scene in 1947 to greatly affect the department and all education in Alabama. James E. Folsom was elected Governor in 1946 on a platform of providing a minimum teacher's salary of $1,800 annually and a constitutional convention to write a new constitution. Meadows was appointed June 1946 by Governor Chauncey M. Sparks to complete the unexpired term of Norton and was elected for a 4-year term without opposition in the special 1946 Democratic primary. Meadows worked with outgoing Governor Sparks in securing a 5-percent increase in teachers' salaries for 1946-47. He then worked out a compromise with the Governor-Elect to support an educational program of 9 months as the minimum school term and an average teacher salary of $1,800 rather than a minimum salary of $1,800 including untrained teachers. The actual salary requested by the department, which the Legislature made possible, ranged from $1,200 for the lowest certificated teacher with 1 year of college training or none, with $300 allotment for each additional year of college training, to $2,400 for the highest trained teacher. The average annual salary was actually increased from $1,239 in 1946 to $2,127 in 1950-51, but it was the Governor who set the stage for the increase in his campaign for the minimum of $1,800.

Appropriation bills were submitted by the department to include funds for teachers' salaries on the sliding scale outlined above, with the explanation that such a salary schedule would encourage high school graduates and teachers to continue their college education in order to receive higher salaries. It was clearly pointed out that this plan would cost the state more money every year but that the taxpayers would be obtaining better educated teachers in return for their tax dollar. This program met the overwhelming approval of the Legislature.

The Legislature was so enthusiastic about the proposed new program that it agreed to recess early in the regular session so that Governor Folsom might call a special session for the purpose of raising revenue to finance the educational program. The Legislature created a Joint House and Senate Educational Committee under the chairmanship of the late Edward Miller, representative from Etowah County, and cochairmanship of the late Senator Albert L. Patterson. The joint committee, with department representatives, visited representative counties, cities, and institutions of higher learning to get facts firsthand. This committee, working with the department, became a tremendous driving force in creating the educational program which followed. The Legislature recessed and was called back into special session. It met for 5 consecutive days and authorized a constitutional amendment, which was submitted to the voters of Alabama, to earmark for teachers' salaries future state income tax collections in excess of the amount needed to provide annual homestead exemptions of the state 6.5-mill ad valorem tax on homesteads assessed up to $2,000.

Meadows worked closely with the state Parent-Teacher Association, under the leadership of Mrs. Ellen Walker as president, and with the Alabama Citizens Committee for Schools under its president, Milton Fies, in getting the State Citizens Committee to sponsor the campaign for the passage of the state income tax amendment. The department, working with the PTA, the late C. B.

Gilmore, and Karl Harrison of the State Citizens Committee, raised funds to finance the campaign. Organizations were set up in the counties of the state to campaign for the amendment. The Governor wanted part of the tax earmarked for old-age pensions, but he did not campaign against the amendment. The amendment passed by over 2 to 1 majority, whereas a similar amendment for general purposes rather than for teachers' salaries had failed by over 2 to 1 during the previous administration. Leaders of the opposition to the amendment congratulated the department on the victory and on the fine manner in which the campaign was waged (16).

The 1947 Legislature reconvened after the 90 days required for passage of the state income tax constitutional amendment. It then passed the appropriations sponsored by the department for the first minimum 9-month school term in the state and for a salary schedule that prompted teachers to continue their college education. More than 95 percent of Alabama's teachers have at least a bachelor's degree today.

In 1950, the department published a new course of study for grades 1-12 (17), which presented education in a democracy from the national viewpoint as well as the state viewpoint. Educational purposes were clearly stated. The best references available at that time were given in the extensive bibliography. Suggested high school programs were presented in terms of the state accreditation requirements.

W. J. Terry, the incoming superintendent in 1951, divided the instruction division into the elementary and secondary education divisions, which had been consolidated in 1935. In 1954, he published a new course of study (18). Terry had never served in any position of state leadership before being elected superintendent of education. For 50 years prior to that time, superintendents, before beginning an elective 4-year term, had either served in the department or in a position of state service, with the exception of Issac W. Hill. Terry's executive actions disturbed the professional educators in the department. C. P. Nelson, director of the administration and finance division, resigned in 1951. Terry forced N. F. Greenhill out of the department, where he had done an outstanding job under Norton and Meadows in supervising the textbook program. The centennial of the establishment of the public school system in 1854 was ignored by this administration, but the incoming administration joined the AEA in proper observance of it in 1955. Teachers received a small bonus in state funds during the last 2 years of this administration, but no regular salary increase. The statewide TV program was started, but the department was eliminated from the administration or coordination of the programs.

James E. Folsom as Governor and Meadows as superintendent of education were returned by the voters of the State of Alabama to their respective positions in 1954 elections. After that, education began to move forward again. The exceptional education division, created in 1951, was consolidated under the secondary education division in 1955, and J. C. Blair was made director. N. F. Greenhill was made director of the administration and finance division. Frank R. Stewart was made administrative assistant to the state superintendent of education and was later elected as state superintendent of education.

A new division was created by combining the sections of rehabilitation and crippled children in 1955, and O. F. Wise was appointed director, in which position he has made an outstanding contribution both to the state and to the nation. Later, another able educator, R. B. Bagley, was made assistant director of the division, in charge of the crippled children section, and George M. Hudson became assistant director in rehabilitation.

The department organized and developed an annual workshop of school administrators, with local school superintendents serving as chairmen and recorders of committees and with the other superintendents selecting the committee of their choice for program development. During the workshop, local teacher salary schedules were developed, and procedures were developed for improving school administration. The workshop program was later continued in some degree by the state organization of school administrators. The department led educational leaders to join together in a unified legislative program with success, and there was an era of good feeling throughout the state.

The 1954 U.S. Supreme Court decision reversed the previous 1898 decision of equal but separate educational facilities for the races. In 1955, the State Legislature passed the pupil placement law recommended by the department. This law gives local school officials full and final authority to place pupils in the schools in terms of available school facilities and nearness to school centers with available facilities. This was followed in 1956 by the constitutional amendment providing freedom of choice of pupils to attend school with certain limitations. The principle of freedom of choice was established in the minds of the people as a beginning for meeting the 1954 U.S. Supreme Court decision outlawing equal but separate provisions for the races.

In 1958, the State Board of Education approved the department state plan, which was later approved by federal officials for state participation in the National Defense Education Act. In 1959, the Alabama department developed, organized, and processed statewide testing of all pupils in the eighth, ninth, and eleventh grades. The department contracted with the University of Alabama to machine-score the test answers and rank by percentiles over 140,000 pupils in the spring of 1959. After that, the testing program was applied to the eighth and eleventh grades with tests given in October and scored by the department. A guidance counselor was employed in the department to assist with the counseling and testing program. One score card for each pupil in the seventy-fifth percentile or above in the eleventh grade is furnished to each college in the state, and a score card for each eleventh-grade pupil in the fiftieth percentile or above is furnished to the trade school that serves the area in which the pupil lives. The scoring, the tests, and the score cards are provided by the department.

Under Title III of the NDEA, personnel were employed to develop and take all possible advantage of the acquisition of equipment for the subjects covered in the act and for counseling with local school personnel engaged in teaching subjects included in the act.

The NDEA department consultants were decentralized. One of the science consultants was stationed at Florence State College, and another consultant was stationed at Jacksonville State College. A mathematics consultant was stationed at the University Center in Birmingham.

THE DEPARTMENT IN THE SOARING SIXTIES

The department entered the soaring sixties under a heavy proration of state appropriations to all education totaling $11,608,825 in 1959-60 and $19,791,255 in 1960-61. This heavy proration was due to the failure of the Legislature to provide the revenue for the appropriations which they unanimously voted as needed and justified. When the Legislature met in the second regular session in 1961, trust fund appropriations to education were reduced $13,113,932 below the 1960-61 appropriations in spite of anticipated school enrollment increases. The total accumulated reduction for 3 years was $44,514,013 below what the Legislature voted as needed in 1960-61. The department, through courageous Superintendent Frank R. Stewart, prevailed upon the state board not to pass a resolution proposed by the Governor to cut the annual minimum program allotment of teachers' salaries 10 percent after the teachers had taught approximately 7 months of the school term. School terms were completed on local deficits and by curtailment of other needed current expenses.

During proration the Alabama Society for Crippled Children increased its allotments to the department for adult rehabilitation and for crippled children, which were used to match increased federal funds for the two services and to expand the services to the crippled children and crippled adults in the state. State appropriation and local donations were not adequate to match all of the federal funds for these two services.

The state had for many years overmatched federal funds for vocational education, and the increased federal appropriations during the proration period were used to provide additional services in this field. Expansions were made in the state staff in agriculture, home economics, and trade and industrial education.

The 1963-65 Breakthrough Programs

In 1962, Meadows, the incoming state superintendent of education, prior to taking office in January 1963, recommended a breakthrough program which was approved by a unified agreement of officials of the public schools, the trade schools, the state-supported colleges, the Alabama Education Association, and the state Parent-Teacher Association. Meadows was elected without opposition after the May Democratic primary on a platform to increase teachers' salaries to the national average and to improve education at all levels.

After the 1962 Democratic party nomination, the Alabama Congress of Parents and Teachers scheduled Meadows to meet with parent-teacher representatives in eight district meetings attended by 1,000 parents representing 225,000 PTA members to explain the breakthrough program. All eight district PTA meetings approved the program. Members returned to their respective districts and developed the greatest roadbed of public opinion for this program that had ever been developed for any educational program. After taking office, in company with Frank Rose, president of the University of Alabama, Ralph Draughon, president of Auburn University, and C. P. Nelson, executive secretary of the AEA, Meadows informed the Governor of the tremendous roadbed of public opinion developed by the members of the Alabama Congress of Parents and Teachers through their representatives for the breakthrough program. Governor Wallace agreed to adopt the program.

The department presented the program in appropriation bills to the Legislature. Governor Wallace and legislative administrative leaders put through bills which reduced the appropriations requested below those agreed on by the Department of Education, the AEA, and the PTA, but the appropriations were increased enough to justify being classified as a breakthrough program. Teacher salary allotments were increased 53.9 percent; appropriations to education were increased 95 percent; the annual teacher salary allocation was increased an average of 42.7 percent per teacher; the pending proration inherited from the previous administration was circumvented by tax levies; state capital outlay school bond revenue totaling $146,000,000 was provided; and a $23,217,000 cushion was created in the educational trust fund for the next administration.

During this administration 14 new state junior colleges and 26 state trade schools were in operation with publicly owned school buses routed to blanket the state with free transportation to either a junior college or a trade school. The junior college-trade school programs covering the entire state, together with the remainder of the breakthrough program if continued, could be the means of placing Alabama among the leading states in the nation economically. As a result of its studies, the department recommended the location of all of the new trade schools, except Walker County, and all of the 14 state junior colleges. Alabama is the only state in the Union that offers free transportation for all qualified pupils to attend either a trade school or a junior college.

In 1965, on the recommendation of the state superintendent of education and data furnished by the department, Governor Wallace successfully sponsored legislative appropriations for furnishing state-owned textbooks through all 12 grades for the first time in the history of the state. Under legislative authority, usable, secondhand, state-adopted textbooks were bought from parents for half price or less, and the procedures and reimbursement for such purchases were processed by the department. All requisitions, bids to furnish state-owned textbooks, and contracts for purchasing them were processed by the department. By action of the department through the state superintendent of education, all textbook companies furnished state-owned textbooks for the opening of schools for the scholastic year beginning July 1, 1965, with the understanding that state purchase orders under the law would necessarily have to be dated October 1, 1965, or thereafter. The cooperation of all the textbook publishing companies with the department in getting the books delivered to the local schools in time for their opening was one of the greatest examples of cooperation of private enterprise with a public agency in the history of the state. Another notable example, in 1959, was that of the California Testing Bureau's furnishing all the testing materials through the department by requisitions without state purchase orders in time to test over 142,000 pupils for mental maturity and achievement.

Through the 1965 signing of the required federal compliance agreement by Meadows as state superintendent of education and approved plans for eligibility for federal funds, the department handled $69,207,000 in federal funds for public education for the scholastic year beginning July 1, 1965, that would not have been received otherwise. This included $40,551,274 from Title I, Public Law 89-10, for elementary and high schools. The State Board of Education held in abeyance any action on the federal compliance agreement pending federal court action on the Bessemer school system court case (19). Commissioner Francis Keppel accepted the compliance agreement signed by the state superintendent charged under the state constitution as being responsible for the supervision of the public schools. Alabama was the only state in the Union so accepted. The agreement was signed on the basis of freedom of choice of pupil enrollment in schools where classrooms and other school facilities were available for the grade to be attended. The department fulfilled the requirement of the compliance agreement, and all schools opened and operated effectively in 1965.

Harold Howe, who succeeded Keppel as U.S. Commissioner of Education, insisted on quota and/or percentage enrollment of pupils instead of freedom of choice. He scheduled and held four regional meetings with local school officials without the approval of state educational authorities and changed the local compliance agreement accordingly. The department believed Howe usurped its authority by taking over the state regulatory functions and duties regarding federal funds to be received by the state, including vocational funds that the department had administered for half a century.

SERVICES OF DEPARTMENT DIVISIONS

There were no divisions of the department, as such, listed in the annual reports of the Alabama Department of Education until 1919-20. In 1920-21, Abercrombie reported 10 divisions. In 1925-26, teacher training, certification, and placement were consolidated with elementary education, leaving only nine divisions. In 1928-29, the new school administration division and the Negro education division were created, making 11 divisions. In 1932-33, the school administration division was consolidated with the research and information division, leaving only 10 divisions. In 1933-34, the exceptional education division was abolished, leaving only nine divisions.

In 1935, Keller reorganized the department into four divisions. The school administration division was reinstated under administration and finance, which also included research, rural schools, and/or schoolhouse planning and business management. Elementary education, secondary education, and teacher certification and placement were consolidated into the instruction division. The vocational education and Negro education divisions remained unchanged.

Rehabilitation and Crippled Children

Rehabilitation and crippled children were a part of the vocational division before being organized as a separate division. Key personnel in the overall administration of these programs, together with clerical assistants, originally were stationed in the central office. The services and personnel therefore greatly expanded, and the assistant personnel have been decentralized through 15 district offices.

The state appropriations have not been sufficient to match available federal funds for rehabilitation, and the Alabama Society for Crippled Children has donated many thousands of dollars to match federal funds. The Society has cooperated with the department in agreeing on legislative budget requests and in acquainting legislators with the advantages of the program economically for the state and individually for the clients.

One of the outstanding phases of the department program for rehabilitation and crippled children has been through clinic services by outstanding surgeons and orthopedic doctors who have served on stipends that amounted to little more than actual travel expense. The state advisory medical staff met periodically with the state superintendent of education, the director of rehabilitation, and the head of the crippled children section in planning clinics, supervision of hospitals used for clinical work, and rehabilitative work with reference to policies for admitting and discharging clients. Three eminent surgeons, Dr. John D. Sherrill of Birmingham, the late Dr. Marcus Skinner of Selma, and Dr. W. C. Hannon of Mobile, combined, served over one hundred years in holding periodic clinics, in which crippled children were diagnosed for remedial treatment, and in state meetings as a committee. Dr. H. E. Conwell of Birmingham early became a fourth member of the famous staff. Other doctors were added later to meet the demands. The department personnel make arrangements for scheduling the clinics, transportation of children to the clinics, office space for the examinations, and personnel to assist the examining doctor. A copy of the complete record of each crippled child and adult is filed either with the state central office or with the office for the district in which the child resides. The department has had good working relations with federal officials connected with this service.

Division of Administration and Finance

The Division of Administration and Finance services all other divisions on all financial matters for the department. All budgets are reviewed and recommended for revision or approval by the director of this division. All department requisition purchase orders must clear through this division before they are used. All county and city school budgets and annual reports must be reviewed by this division before being approved by the superintendent. The quadrennial school census made by the local school systems is processed through this division. It also compiles and edits the annual statistical report of the department, which gives child/teacher personnel, and financial accounting by school systems. The issuance of all local school warrants (bonds) of long-term indebtedness are processed by the division for approval by the superintendent.

The number of different funds handled by the department through the finance division increased from 22 in 1940-41, totaling $15,815,593, to 60 in 1965-66, totaling $266,900,160–the largest being the state minimum program fund of $164,466,870.

This division calculates the teacher units, the transportation formula by density of transportable pupils, and the other factors that make up the state minimum program allocation to each local school system.

Vocational Education

Vocational education in the department operated from its inception with the director and section heads of home economics and vocational agriculture stationed in the central office, and with other staff members stationed at the college approved for teacher training for each section. The vocational agriculture field staff was located at Alabama Polytechnic Institute, Auburn, in the east-central part of the state. The home economics staff was located at Alabama College, Montevallo, which is in the center of the state. Trade and industrial education staff members and section heads were located at the University of Alabama in the west-central part of the state at first, but later the head of the section was stationed at the central office. Staff members for vocational agriculture, home economics, and trade and industrial education also were stationed later at Tuskegee Institute, as well as at A & M, near Huntsville, for agriculture. The department contracted with respective colleges to pay salaries and travel of such employees and to furnish office facilities just as if they were employed by the college. The teacher trainers were employed by the colleges.

Division of Elementary Education

The Division of Elementary Education has always functioned primarily through consultants working with groups of teachers and school officials, rather than on an individual school visitation schedule. The concept of the elementary education division has always been to help teachers and school officials in the full development of the well-rounded pupil. This division did outstanding work in helping to plan the education of elementary teachers in the state normal schools, which later became state teachers colleges. The late George D. Strayer commented that the Alabama teachers colleges "made brick without straw," but did an outstanding job in teacher education (20). This division did an equally fine job in assisting in the development of courses of study and in in-service education to use them to the fullest advantage.

Except for short periods, this division has processed state certification of teachers since 1924. Recently the division started the accreditation of elementary schools. In the Alabama statewide annual testing program, started in the spring of 1959, the department found that eighth-grade pupils were equal to or above the national norms, except in spelling. Much of this can be attributed to the state teachers colleges and the services of the elementary division, starting with the leadership of Tidwell, who came to the department with superintendency experience in administering the well-staffed and well-equipped elementary schools provided by the Tennessee Coal and Iron Company in the Birmingham area.

Division of Secondary Education

The Division of Secondary Education, which started in 1920 with major emphasis on the development of high schools and their accreditation on the basis of academic education to meet college entrance requirements, has expanded in recent years into education for the maximum development of all pupils.

After the junior high schools were established in 1924-25, this division broadened its emphasis to include the practical arts and exploratory courses for grades 7, 8, and 9, which were never adequately developed because of lack of funds to provide the necessary facilities. The junior high schools meeting state standards were approved but were not accredited until recently, except where they were included as a part of the senior high school.

In a staff meeting, some consultants expressed concern that one of the largest senior high schools in the state was using an 1898 edition of a physiology textbook instead of a modern textbook. T. W. Smith, a philosopher and former county superintendent, replied that he was far more concerned about high school pupils' having to put up with an outdated teacher who would require the use of such an outdated textbook than he was with the textbook itself. All of the consultants except Smith were discontinued by Keller when he consolidated the division with the elementary education division in 1935. The division was reinstated in 1951. J. C. Blair, the director from 1955 to the present time, has done an outstanding job in working with high school principals in the annual workshop on plans to improve education, in helping to improve the high school course of study, in processing applications for out-of-state aid to Negro college students, in encouraging state participation in the regional compact for college education, and in developing programs to eliminate high school dropouts.

Division of Instruction

The Division of Instruction was created by consolidation in 1935 and remained until 1951. The consolidation was justified for the purpose of broadening the viewpoint on secondary education with new leadership and for coordinating elementary and secondary education. The instruction division promoted the educational viewpoint that had always been held by the elementary division. Consultants of the division worked with supervisors and principals in organizing curriculum workshop programs at Peabody College during the summer and at the state institutions of higher learning.

C. B. Smith directed the newly created division until he was made president of Troy State College in 1937. He was followed by Morrison W. McCall, who became a national authority on teacher certification and teacher education.

Research Division

The Research Division was established in 1927 with Dale S. Young as director until January 1934. Young, a native of Illinois, who studied for his doctorate under Mort at Columbia University, revamped the statistical report of the department and greatly improved information service on all education in the state. He was followed as director by Edgar L. Morphet, who served until the division was consolidated with the division of administration and finance in 1935. The division was financed by the General Education Board of the Rockefeller Foundation up to 1935, but it was not continued because of the Depression and resulting lack of state funds.

The division was reinstated in 1965 through the use of Public Law 89-10, Title V, federal funds.

Executive Division

The Executive Division had existed as a section under the title of chief clerk or clerk; but it was not organized into a division until 1920, when it was listed under executive and business management, with a chief clerk, a filing clerk, two bookkeepers, and a stenographer. This division has expanded by the addition of sections placed in charge of new and developing programs.

NDEA–Title III Section. This section was created in 1959 and operates in terms of the purposes of Title III. One of the consultants is stationed in Huntsville, one at Jacksonville State College, and one in Birmingham. The section performed a valuable service, including processing the acquirement of equipment and the services of consultants in holding regional or district workshops with teachers in science, mathematics, modern foreign language throughout the state, and in working with teacher groups in county and city school systems.

English Consultative Section. The English section was really started by one consultant in 1965 and was thereafter expanded into a section. This section has done an outstanding job in holding English workshops at the state-supported colleges in Alabama during the summer. The workshops were rated as highly successful by English teachers and colleges throughout the state.

Exceptional Education. Exceptional education was reinstated by state law in 1955, and Mrs. Alpha Brown started directing the services in 1956. Mrs. Brown, who has earned national prominence in her field, has formulated quality standards and given creative supervision to the program through annual workshops with teachers of exceptional children and consultations with individual teachers. Two psychologists and a consultant have been added to the staff to help meet the great demand for this type of service.

Adult Basic Education. The adult basic education section includes much of the work done by the illiteracy division that existed in the twenties. It is financed by a state appropriation of $100,000, matching federal funds on the ratio of 1 state dollar to 9 federal dollars. Under the assistant state superintendent of education, it has made a fine contribution in developing standards and in processing applications for adult basic education classes. The local program is channeled through county and city school systems.

School Library Section. This section was created through the use of Public Law 89-10, Title II, federal funds, with the chief educational consultant stationed at the University of South Alabama in Mobile and another consultant stationed at Florence State College. This program has been most helpful toward meeting Alabama's great deficit in school libraries, especially in elementary school libraries. Maximum use has been made of federal funds for this program, which is channeled through local county and city school systems.

Civil Defense Section. This section was started in 1963 through the use of federal funds in the beginning, which were later matched by a small state appropriation. It has a staff of four consultants and two clerical assistants. The consultants teach classes approved by county and city superintendents of education.

International Education. This program operates as a part of the Texas State Education Department project financed entirely from federal funds. It is operated in accordance with the purpose of the program and by working with a state committee in the planning of the Alabama program.

Higher Education. The program of this section, operated entirely from federal funds, has been of great help in securing money for urgently needed buildings for private and public colleges. The program has been of special help to the junior colleges that qualified for federal funds.

Textbook Section. This section, as the name implies, processes all applications for state-owned textbooks, keeps records, and reports on all state matters dealing with textbooks and textbook needs.

DEPARTMENT PIONEERS IN SCHOOL BUS TRANSPORTATION

The department, through surveys and observations from 1935 to 1944, found that the overwhelming majority of Alabama school buses were dilapidated, potential firetraps, with side-facing seats on homemade wooden bodies mounted on trucks. At that time the department was recommending consolidating schools, which meant more transportation without safe school bus standards. As compulsory education required transportable children to ride the school buses, the department assumed responsibility for developing a state plan for safe and economical transportation.

In 1938, Meadows joined representatives from two bordering states in going to the nationally known school bus body manufacturing companies in Indiana and Ohio to persuade them to construct lightweight, all-steel school bus bodies with forward-facing seats and with gas tanks vented outside the bus. The Wayne Works in Richmond, Indiana, constructed such a bus at a reasonable price, and other companies met this competition.

The department, through the cooperation of the state director of finance, submitted invitations to all of the chassis manufacturing companies in the United States to bid on school buses by wheelbase length and common specifications. The bids were satisfactory, and the school buses were purchased at the state price. Local school systems reimbursed the state or paid the manufacturing company directly for the chassis to be delivered to the body manufacturing company chosen by the local school board. On the fleet-purchase basis the state bought the chassis at $100 per unit cheaper than what the local state dealer or distributor paid for the same unit. The state then set up a test case in 1939 for chassis bids to the state one day and to Fayette County on a local basis the next day for the same wheelbase length and the same specifications. The bids were actually lower to Fayette County than to the state. Thereafter, state bids were continued in order to safeguard counties that could not get favorable local bids.

The 48-seating-capacity bus body mounted on a 191-inch wheelbase chassis with dual rear wheels and tires meeting state specifications was bought at an approximate cost of $1,250 per unit price for the complete bus. The entire state started rapidly changing to county-owned buses meeting state specifications. North Carolina, in emerging from the Depression, set up a system of state purchase and ownership of school buses; but Alabama secured the same advantages through department leadership in securing state bids with local school board ownership. Local school board ownership encourages local initiative and local responsibility for the pupils transported. A department representative attended all of the bids for school buses, and bids were submitted on forms approved by the department.

The state created an adjustment board, which was used to compensate individuals who were injured or suffered property damages in school bus collisions in which the school bus driver or school bus was at fault, thereby eliminating premium payments to insurance companies. The department furnishes accident report forms, processes all applications for damages, and recommends that payments be made or not paid, according to evidence available.

The department conducted special courses whereby local school bus driver instructors were trained to teach individuals who were to be employed as bus drivers to drive the buses safely, economically, and efficiently. Many high school students were trained and employed to drive school buses.

TEXTBOOKS

In 1924, Dr. Abercrombie reported that since 1903 the state had maintained uniform textbook requirements for all public schools and that the Governor and state superintendent of education were ex officio members of the textbook committees. He further reported that the 1919 law required the State Board of Education, upon the recommendation of the state superintendent, to appoint not more than seven well-known educators engaged in public school work to select uniform textbooks for the state in the elementary schools and in all high schools, except those located in cities and towns of 2,000 or more population.

The department, under policies adopted by the state board, developed forms for publishers to bid on textbooks and processed textbook contracts to be approved by the state board.

In 1935, the department presented to Governor Bibb Graves a study directed by Meadows outlining progress of pupils through the grades. It showed that over 60 percent of the rural schoolchildren made slow progress through the first six grades and were overage according to national standards. When the Governor wanted to know the major causes of this situation, Superintendent J. A. Keller advised him that much of the difficulty lay in the failure of pupils to have textbooks in the lower grades because too many parents spent money for other things, including snuff and tobacco. The Governor successfully sponsored a tax on snuff for state-owned textbooks. The state staggered the state-owned textbooks by purchasing books for the first grade for the first year, for the second grade for the second year, and for the third grade for the third year, and on through the first six grades. The department prepared the statistics and the plan for purchasing and distributing the state-owned textbooks.

In 1965, the Legislature passed a law and appropriations for state-owned textbooks through the 12 grades, to be allocated and processed by the department under policies approved by the state board.

STATE COURSES OF STUDY AND THE DEPARTMENT

Through its elementary and secondary divisions, the department made great contributions to the public schools, particularly the elementary schools, by giving leadership in developing, publishing, and distributing state courses of study. Although they were designed as guides, with suggestions and recommendations, they also included legal requirements that governed the schools.

The department generated the development of a state course of study, which it had printed and distributed in 1910. Special subject materials were developed either by or through the leadership of the department. One of the outstanding department bulletins was the 1931 *Course of Study in Physical and Health Education*, which was reprinted in 1934 and again in 1935.

The 1950 and 1954 state courses of study have already been detailed to some extent.

In the 1963-67 administration, the following state courses of study were developed:

Alabama Course of Study for Grades 7-12—Vol. I, Bulletin 7, 1964. Developed by the state course of study committee members engaged in high school education, and edited by Ben A. Forrester, as assistant state superintendent of education, and Mrs. Betty (Adams) Wilborn.

Alabama Course of Study for Grades 1-6—Vol. V, Bulletin 23, 1965. Developed by the state course of study committee with the guidance of Lulu Palmer and Erline Curlee of the department.

Alabama Course of Study for Home Economics—Vol. III, 1964. Developed and edited under the guidance of Ruth Stovall, head of the home economics section of the vocational education division.

Alabama Course of Study for Vocational Agriculture—Vol. II, 1964. Developed and edited under the supervision of T. L. Faulkner, state supervisor of agricultural education.

Alabama Course of Study for Trade and Industrial Education—Vol. IV, 1965. Developed and edited under the guidance of J. F. Ingram, director of the vocational education division, and H. F. Worthy, state supervisor of trade and industrial education.

The high school course of study is one of the most complete handbooks ever developed and incorporates accreditation requirements. The course of study for home economics has received a "dress parade review" by the Montgomery *Advertiser* society editor, Madera Spencer.

Valuable bulletins in science, mathematics, and modern foreign languages have been developed by the department through National Defense Education Act funds. Recently special bulletins have been developed in the communicative arts by the English section of the department (21).

Superior course of study materials have been repeatedly developed and published under the direction of Mrs. Alpha Brown, educational consultant and supervisor of exceptional children and youth, who is recognized as a national authority.

Guideline materials for adult education, along with statements of state and federal regulations, were developed by W. Bemon Lyon, assistant state superintendent of education succeeding Ben A. Forrester, who was appointed president of the junior college at Enterprise, Alabama.

Outstanding guideline materials were developed in testing and counseling from the beginning, and this service is now functioning through Clifton Nash, guidance consultant, and J. C. Blair, secondary education director.

The vocational education division has produced excellent materials for vocational teachers since the beginning of federal aid for that purpose in 1917. The materials have included plans for successful functioning of FFA and FHA programs.

LONG-TERM PLANS FOR LOCAL SCHOOLS

In 1928, the state board approved comprehensive educational surveys of county and city school systems by the department. The division of research and information and the division of schoolhouse planning cooperated with the division of educational administration in the surveys. The field studies division of the University of Alabama College of Education under its dean, John R. McLure, collaborated with the department from the beginning in this service.

The comprehensive educational survey not only provides a 10-year plan for educational development, but also furnishes the school administrator and the local board of education with defensible data to justify to the public the policies adopted in accordance with the survey. Maps are used to show recommended school centers by exact locations, recommended school bus routes, and pupil residence locations. The local superintendent displays the maps so that inquiring parents and citizens can see the plans for future school centers and school transportation.

The survey serves as a stimulant to county officials to consolidate schools. The one-teacher schools were consolidated, and local school officials said they had the most harmonious school program throughout the county that had ever existed. The school survey was the catalyzer for courageous, progressive educational action.

The department assisted the Florida department in setting up county school survey services. Moe Stone and Joe Hall, then of the Florida department, worked with Meadows on the survey of an Alabama county school system. Johns and Meadows then assisted in the survey of two Florida county school systems in 1939.

One of the outstanding contributions growing out of the survey was the research study developed by J. W. Letson of the department, and now superintendent of Atlanta city school system. This bulletin, entitled *Better School Buildings for Alabama* (22), was published and distributed by the department to provide specific guides for planning and financing a school building program.

The state survey service tied in with the issuance of county and city capital outlay building warrants (bonds) in that proceeds from sales of such warrants could be used only at approved centers where schools could be expected to remain in operation beyond the term of the indebtedness. These and other safeguards permitted bonds to be sold at par value as low as 1.25-percent annual interest. The double economy of low interest rates on school bonds and construction at permanent school centers made the Alabama school construction dollar purchase the maximum benefits for taxpayers and schoolchildren.

Television

In July 1952, when the Federal Communications Commission allotted 268 TV channels exclusively for educational purposes, it granted 7 to Alabama. One year later, the Legislature established the Alabama Educational Television Commission and appropriated $500,000 to get the program under way. The Alabama ETV network, the nation's first large-scale, state-owned and -operated ETV network, was soon utilized by the state's leading educators to improve the quality of instruction in the public schools. The organized in-school ETV program went on the air in September 1957 with only 48 schools pledged to use it.

J. H. Hadley, assistant state superintendent of education, was elected chairman of the ETV Project's executive committee in 1957, and Meadows furnished free office space for the coordinator. The state board authorized the use of certain high school TV courses for credit, and the ETV program grew steadily.

In 1960, the department took over the coordination and general supervision of the in-school ETV program. It also assumed responsibility for publishing the ETV program schedule in booklet form and continues to carry out this responsibility. This booklet, now called the *Instructional Television Teacher's Guide*, has developed into a teacher's handbook and is distributed at the annual meetings of the AEA and the Alabama State Teachers Association.

It appears that the major weakness in the state ETV network at the present time is the absence of any agency with final authority for the program. More effective use of the network potentialities could be realized if the department had administrative authority and responsibility for the public school programs. Because of vested interests, however, it has been impossible to get the necessary legislative action to clear up this problem.

THE DEPARTMENT AS A WHOLE IN ACTION

The 1934 annual report, quoting from a survey by the Brookings Institution on the organization and administration of Alabama's state government, states:

> The Department of Education is staffed with qualified professional men and women; it appears on the whole to be functioning efficiently; the morale of the personnel seems notably high. The various divisions are well coordinated; the direction and supervision exercised by the Superintendent and Assistant Superintendent are adequate and effective.

The most satisfactory accounts kept anywhere in the county are those of the county superintendent of education, who is guided by uniform accounting instructions, forms, and report blanks prescribed by the State Department of Education under the authority of Section 43 of the School Code (23).

All state educational surveys have appraised the department as meeting its responsibilities in a highly successful manner. Since the turn of the century, it has had to fight for legislative support for education on two fronts—one front for public schools and higher education, and the other front for appropriations to adequately staff itself to meet the state responsibility for education. The department has always placed major emphasis on the first front and in so doing has never been able to secure adequate appropriations for itself.

The salary of the state superintendent of education has been notoriously low. The department entered the Depression with the salary of the superintendent at $6,000 annually, but the Legislature cut the salary of the next superintendent to $3,600. And in 1946 the salary was increased to $5,400, with part of it paid from federal funds.

In 1947, at the request of Meadows, the salary of the state superintendent was paid entirely from state funds, rather than partly from federal funds, so the position would not be subject to federal control on the basis of the old adage, "The agent that pays the fiddler calls the tune." Under constitutional provisions the salary of constitutional officers cannot be raised during the term of office, but the salary was raised to $10,000 annually starting with 1955. In 1965, Meadows sponsored a bill to set the salary of the incoming superintendent at $22,000, but it was cut to $18,000 in the House and to $15,000 in the Senate before final passage. The maximum salary range in the department in 1965 was $12,000, which was far below the salaries of deans in the state-supported colleges and much less than many county and city superintendents of education in the state serving under the supervision of the state department. The chief state school officer is responsible for overall state supervision of the public schools, which in 1965-66 enrolled 862,041 pupils and carried on their payroll approximately 40,000 employees, including 30,433 teachers, and for 571 department employees.

The state superintendent of education's annual salary of $15,000 is ridiculously low by any measure of responsibility for either the $275 million plus spent annually for education, the 40,000 employees for 889,570 public school and college students, or the 571-plus employees of the department in 1965-66.

Every state survey has recommended the following: The head of the State Department of Education as a chief state school officer should be appointed by a State Board of Education. The professional personnel of the department should be removed from the state personnel board jurisdiction and placed under the state board on salary schedules comparable to professional positions of equal responsibilities in the colleges. Divisional directors should be paid as much as college deans. Clerical assistants might well remain under the state personnel board, provided adequate compensation is given to meet competition from federal employees and private enterprise.

Such salaries now do not compete with salaries for federal personnel for similar type positions and do not begin to compete with private enterprise.

During the last 70 years all state superintendents of education except Hill, Gunnels, Terry, Harman, and Meadows have resigned because of nonsuccession in office and to accept better-paying positions before their elective terms expired. Alabama should gear its education department to meet current and anticipated future needs and should authorize the legal structure to make possible necessary changes for the future. The department must be the bulwark against encroachment by federal agencies, either judicial or executive, that would destroy state and local control of public education. The department must lead in developing vigorous education to ward off destructive deterioration from within. The Legislature and the people of Alabama should make sure that this state has a strong, able State Department of Education dedicated to serve all the children and all the people.

The major developments that have been discussed have helped education, but they are not enough to enable Alabama's potential human resources to make maximum use of its natural resources.

FOOTNOTES

1. Arnold J. Toynbee, *A Study of History*, Abridgement of Vols. I-VI by D. C. Somervall (New York and London: Oxford University Press, 1947), p. 2.
2. A. B. Moore, *History of Alabama and Her People* (Chicago and New York: American Historical Society, 1927), pp. 57, 65, 72, 75.
3. Austin Ruel Meadows, "The Progress of School Attendance in the Public Schools of Alabama Since 1900" (unpublished master's thesis, University of Alabama, 1932), pp. 124, 128.
4. *Ibid.*, p. 124.
5. Department of Education, *Annual Report* (1900), p. v.
6. Department of Education, *Annual Report* (1906), p. 14.
7. U.S. Department of the Interior, Bureau of Education, *An Educational Study of Alabama*, Bulletin 1919, No. 41 (Washington, D.C.: Government Printing Office, 1919).
8. Department of Education, *Annual Report* (1921), p. 14.

9. Department of Education, *Course of Study for Elementary Schools*, Bulletin No. 35 (Birmingham, Ala.: Birmingham Printing Co., 1926).
10. Author's Interview with Senator A. L. Harlan, July 25, 1931.
11. Austin Ruel Meadows, *Safety and Economy in School Bus Transportation* (Wetumpka, Ala.: Wetumpka Printing Co., 1940).
12. Superintendent of Education, *Narrative Report 1937-1942* (Montgomery: The Department, 1942), p. 11.
13. National Council of Chief State School Officers, *School Transportation in Wartime* (Washington, D.C.: The Council and the Traffic Engineering and Safety Department of the American Automobile Association, 1942).
14. *Ibid.*
15. Alabama Business Research Council, *Transition in Alabama* (University: University of Alabama Press, 1962), p. 13.
16. The AEA, with Frank L. Grove as executive secretary and under first Mrs. Norma (Bristow) Salter followed by Ernest Stone as president, cooperated in the campaign and in the legislative program.
17. Department of Education, *Alabama Course of Study*, Bulletin No. 3 (Wetumpka, Ala.: Wetumpka Printing Co., 1950).
18. Department of Education, *Alabama Course of Study*, Bulletin No. 8 (Alexander City, Ala.: Outlook Publishing Co., 1954).
19. The Bessemer, Alabama, city board of education, later joined by adjacent local boards of education, filed a case in federal courts testing the constitutionality of HEW regulations made under Title VI of the Civil Rights Act.
20. George D. Strayer, Professor Emeritus, Columbia University, in conversation with A. R. Meadows in 1960.
21. These were developed by Mrs. Annie Mae Turner, Mrs. Lois Miller, and the late Mrs. Albert P. Lowman.
22. J. W. Letson, *Better School Buildings for Alabama, A Planning Manual*, Bulletin 1950, No. 3 (Montgomery: Department of Education, 1950).
23. Department of Education, *Annual Report* (1934), pp. 18, 19, 20.

BIBLIOGRAPHY

Public Documents

Alabama. *Alabama Board of Education Laws with Blank Forms and Instruction, 1870*. Montgomery: J. G. Stokes and Co., 1870.

--*Alabama Board of Education Acts, Session of 1872*. Montgomery: Arthur Bingham, 1873.

--*Alabama Board of Education Acts, Session November 17, 1873*. Montgomery: Arthur Bingham, 1874.

--*Constitution* (1901).

--*School Laws*. Montgomery: Department of Education, 1854-1966.

--*Title 52, Code of Alabama (1940)*. Especially see Minimum Program Fund, Sections 208-215, art. 4 on school warrants, and art. 5 on the budget system. Montgomery: Department of Education, 1940.

Books and Pamphlets

Alabama Business Research Council. *Transition in Alabama*. University: University of Alabama Press, 1962.

Belser, Danylu. *Elementary Education in Alabama*. Birmingham: Birmingham Printing Co., 1930.

Bowers, Claude G. *The Tragic Era*. Cambridge, Mass.: Literary Guild of America, 1929.

Boyd, Minnie C. *Alabama in the Fifties*. New York: Columbia University Press, 1931.

Brown, W. G. *History of Alabama*. New York and New Orleans: University Publishing Co., 1900.

Clark, Willis G. *History of Education in Alabama*. Washington, D.C.: Government Printing Office, 1889.

Covert, Timon. *Financing of Schools as a Function of State Departments of Education*. Washington, D.C.: Government Printing Office, 1940.

Department of Education. *Alabama Courses of Study*. The state department has issued courses of study since 1910. Devoted to a wide range of subjects, many of these have been published by the department itself, with others being published by private printing firms.

Harper, Cliff, ed. *Our Alabama Government*. Prepared under the supervision of the State Department of Education for the Alabama Boys State. Second edition. Montgomery: Luther Skinner Co., 1958.

Jackson, Walter M., and Owen, Marie B. *History of Alabama for Junior High Schools*. Montgomery: Dixie Book Co., 1938.

Johns, R. L. *An Index of the Financial Ability of Local School Systems To Support Public Education*. Montgomery: Department of Education, 1938.

Letson, J. W. *Better School Buildings for Alabama, A Planning Manual*. Bulletin 1950, No. 3. Montgomery: Department of Education, 1950.

Meadows, Austin Ruel. *Safety and Economy in School Bus Transportation*. Wetumpka, Ala.: Wetumpka Printing Co., 1940.

Moore, A. B. *History of Alabama and Her People*. Chicago and New York: American Historical Society, 1927.

National Council of Chief State School Officers. *School Transportation in Wartime*. Washington, D.C.: The Council and the Traffic Engineering and Safety Department of the American Automobile Association, 1942.

Owen, Marie B. *The Story of Alabama*. 5 vols. New York: Lewis Historical Publishing Co., 1949.

Owen, Thomas M. *History of Alabama and Dictionary of Alabama Biography*. 4 vols. Chicago: S. J. Clarke Publishing Co., 1921.

Pannell, Henry C. *The Preparation and Work of Alabama High School Teachers*. New York: Teachers College, Columbia University, 1933.

Pickett, Albert J. *History of Alabama*. 2 vols. Birmingham: Webb Book Co., 1900.

Toynbee, Arnold J. *A Study of History*. Abridgement of Vols. I-VI by D. C. Somervall. New York and London: Oxford University Press, 1947.

Weeks, Stephen B. *History of Public Education in Alabama.* Bulletin 1915, No. 12. Washington, D.C.: Government Printing Office, 1915.

Periodicals

The Alabama School Journal, XXXVII-XLVII. Montgomery: Alabama Education Association, 1921-1947.

The Educational Exchange, I-XXXVI. Montgomery: Alabama Education Association, 1885-1921.

Reports

Alabama Education Commission. *Report*. Montgomery: The Department, 1959.

Alabama Education Survey Commission. *Public Education in Alabama*. Hubert Searcy, chairman; Maurice F. Seay, director. Washington, D.C.: The American Council on Education, 1945.

Institute for Government Research. *Report on a Survey of the Organization and Administration of the State Government of Alabama,* Vol. III, Part 2, Vol. V, Part 4. Washington, D.C.: Brookings Institution, 1932.

Superintendent of Education. *Annual Reports*. Montgomery: Department of Education, 1900-1949.

––*Narrative Report 1937-1942.* Montgomery: The Department of Education, 1942.

U.S. Department of the Interior, Bureau of Education. *An Educational Study of Alabama*. Bulletin 1919, No. 41. Washington, D.C.: Government Printing Office, 1919.

Unpublished Material

Department of Education. Selected releases. Since 1955, the Department has prepared a number of papers, some for the Department, others for special groups, and a number for statewide distribution. These topics include almost every facet of education. In 1966 alone, there were 39 special releases including such topics as "Federal Funds for Summer School Operation."
"Head Start for Young Alabamians and Freedom of Education Beyond the High School."
"State-Wide Vocational Occupational Survey."
"First New Elementary Course of Study in 35 Years."
"Report on Research Findings on Teachers Pupil Overload."
"Giant Steps for Alabama Education on State-Wide ETV Network Schedule."

––Surveys and resurveys of county and city school systems, No. 2-235. These surveys are mimeographed, with photostatic copies of maps, and filed in numerical order according to date of completion in Montgomery, the Department, 1929-68.

––Minutes of the Alabama State Board of Education, 1919-66, in Montgomery, the Department.

Meadows, Austin Ruel. "The Progress of School Attendance in the Public Schools of Alabama since 1900." Unpublished master's thesis, University of Alabama, 1932.

Other Sources

Harlan, A.L. Author's interview with Senator Harlan, July 25, 1931.

Strayer, George D. Author's conversation with Dr. Strayer in 1960.

Appendix A

ALABAMA CHIEF STATE SCHOOL OFFICERS

1854-58	William F. Perry
1858-64	Gabriel B. Duval
1864-65	W. C. Allen
1865-66	John B. Taylor
1866-68	John B. Ryan
1868-70	N. B. Cloud
1870-72	Joseph Hodgson
1872-74	Joseph H. Speed
1874-76	John M. McKleroy
1876-80	Leroy F. Box
1880-84	Henry Clay Armstrong
1884-90	Solomon Palmer
1890-94	John Gideon Harris
1894-98	John O. Turner
1898-1902	John William Abercrombie (Resigned June 30, 1902, to accept the presidency of the University of Alabama)
1902-1903	Harry Cunningham Gunnels
1903-1907	Issac W. Hill
1907-11	Harry Cunningham Gunnels
1911-14	Henry Jones Willingham (Resigned to accept presidency of Florence State Normal School)
1914-18	William Francis Feagan (Resigned to accept superintendency of Montgomery County, Alabama, schools)
1918-20	Spright Dowell (Resigned to accept presidency of Alabama Polytechnic Institute)
1920-27	John William Abercrombie
1927-29	Robert Earl Tidwell
1929-35	Arthur Fort Harman
1935-37	James Albert Keller
1937-42	Albert Hamilton Collins (Resigned to become director of OPA for Alabama)
1942-46	Ethelbert Brinkley Norton (Resigned in 1946 to accept position of Assistant Commissioner of Education, Washington, D.C.)
1946-51	Austin Ruel Meadows (Appointed to fill unexpired term and elected to full term)
1951-55	William J. Terry
1955-59	Austin Ruel Meadows
1959-61	Frank R. Stewart (Resigned to accept the presidency of Troy State Teachers College)
1961-63	W. A. LeCroy
1963-67	Austin Ruel Meadows
1967-	Ernest Stone

Appendix B

Chart I.—ALABAMA DEPARTMENT OF EDUCATION (38 EMPLOYEES), 1920

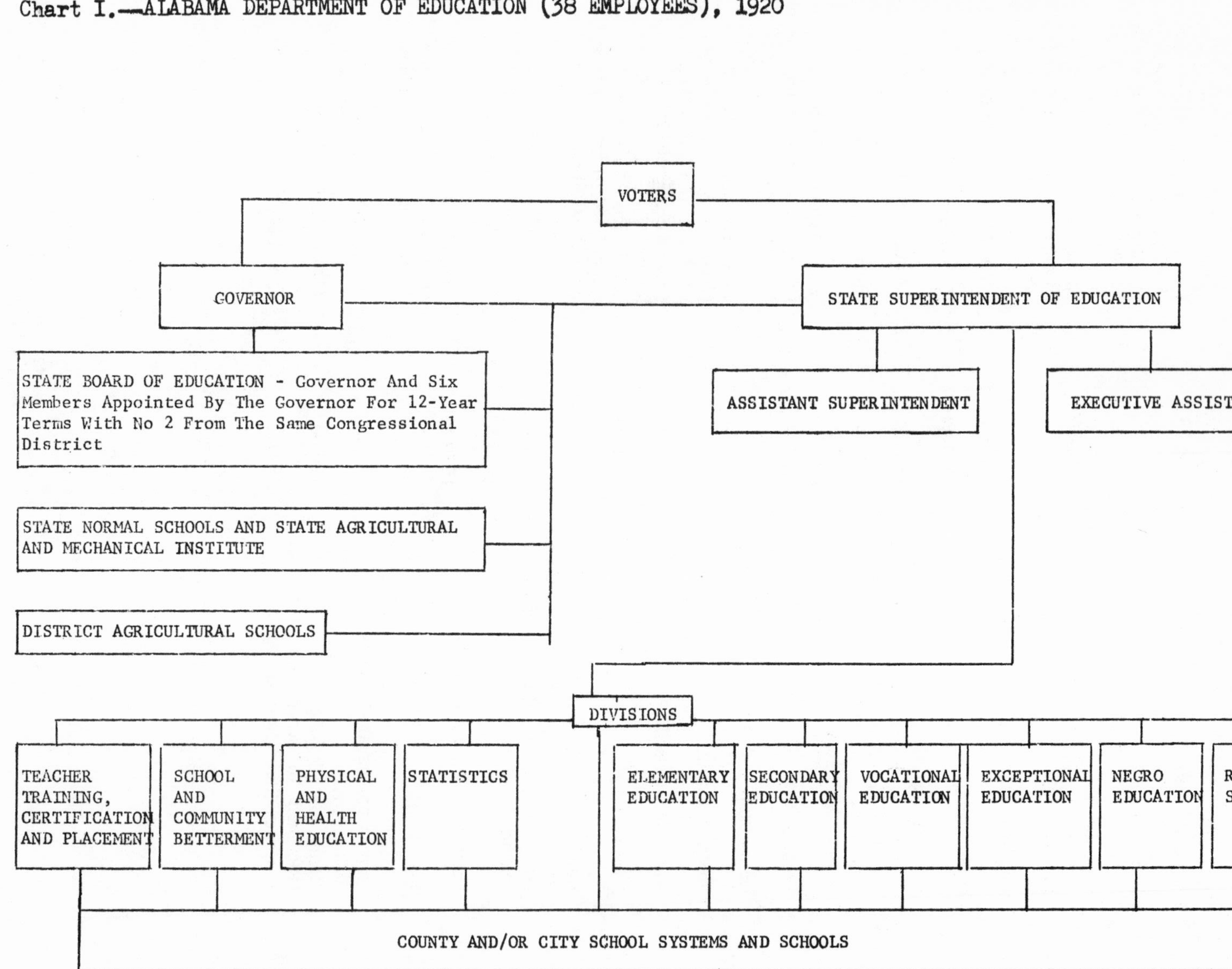

Chart II.—ALABAMA DEPARTMENT OF EDUCATION (TOTAL EMPLOYEES, 571), 1966

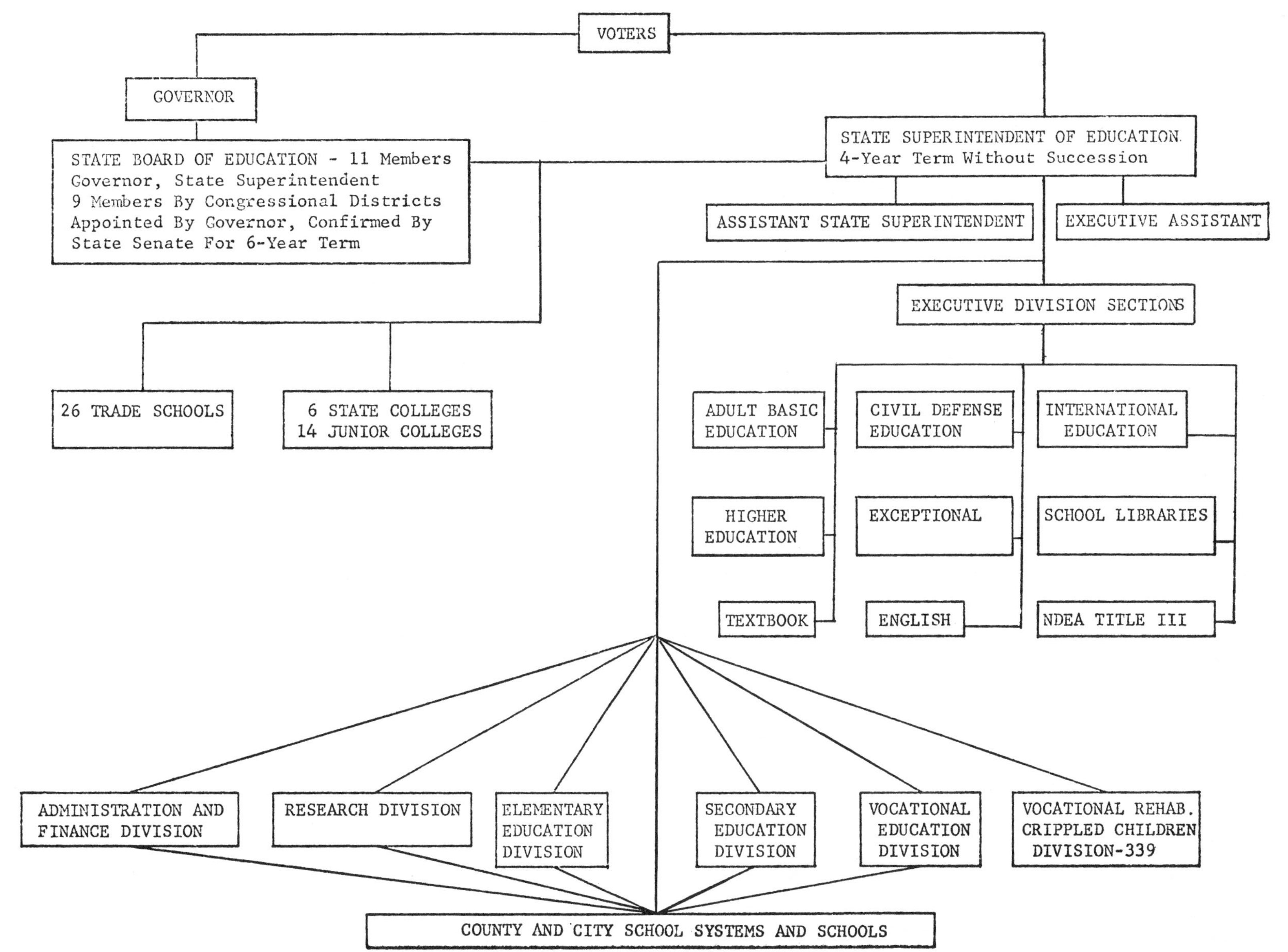

2 Alaska

DEPARTMENT OF EDUCATION

William R. Marsh

Contents

INTRODUCTION

: a map of Alaska were superimposed on a map of the Inited States, Ketchikan, in Southeast Alaska, would be ocated in Florida; the extreme western portion of the leutians would be in the southern part of California; Point arrow, in the extreme north, would be located in linnesota near the Canadian border; the island chain at its earest point to the mainland of Alaska would be extended own below the panhandle in Texas.

This land, formerly owned by the Russians and purhased by the United States in 1867, is not, contrary to opular belief, a land of continuous ice and snow. It does ave nearly insurmountable mountain ranges that impede avel to the interior, and it is a land of thousands of miles f rugged coastline with narrow fjords that are fed by lacial streams flowing down steep mountainsides. Many of ie mountain ranges rise directly from the sea to heights of iousands of feet, and travel between the various localities restricted to sea and air.

The people, dependent as they were on sea transportation, located their villages along the shoreline and devised elatively efficient craft for traveling the waters. The ocean nd streams not only provided means for transportation, hey also were a main source of food and economic suport. Fish, clam, crab, walrus, seal, whale, and fur-bearing nimals were abundant in the waters. At the time of the urchase, nearly every village in Alaska was located near the vater's edge, whether on a bay, an ocean, a river, or a lake.

Before the coming of the Russians, four distinct thnic groups inhabited the country the Russians chose to all Russian-America. Each group had separate languages, haracteristics, and customs. There were, however, many ialects that provided some commonality of language.

In the north and west lived the Eskimo. Theirs was a omewhat common language, for they traveled widely and ommunicated freely in their search for subsistence; veather was often severe and nearly every activity was of a fe-preserving nature. The Aleuts on the island chain fared nuch better because of a more temperate climate and a nore abundant food supply. It was this group that the ruel, barbaric, Russian Promyshleniki encountered as they earched for furs in the late 1700's.

The last group to experience the influence of the white man was the Athabascan Indians of central Alaska. A nomadic, poverty-stricken people, in continuous search of food that was mainly migrating salmon or caribou, they roved through the interior.

The Indians of the southern coast and the southeastern panhandle were mostly Thlingit or Koloshes, as the Russians called them. They had permanently located villages, a highly developed form of art, a complex political-social-cultural system, and an abundant food supply. However, they were divided into various clans, and as there were other small tribes in the area, a warlike atmosphere prevailed.

While no accurate census was taken in the 1800's, it was estimated in 1887 that there were 5,000 to 6,000 children of school age in a total population of over 35,000. In the area westward of Kodiak Island, a reported 25,000 lived, with about 4,000 being Aleuts and people of mixed blood having a highly civilized and educated society. Southeastern Alaska held an Indian population of 7,000 to 8,000 and a Caucasian group of 2,000 residing principally at Sitka, Juneau, Douglas Island, Wrangell, and Killisnoo.

HISTORICAL BACKGROUND

Despotism drove many Cossacks and Russians from their homes in the sixteenth century and started them across the Siberian wastes on a journey that was ultimately to terminate in what is now Alaska. They reached the shores of the Pacific and founded Okhotsk in 1638. In the next half-century, the Kamchatka Peninsula was discovered, and expeditions to the North American continent were launched. Under the sponsorship of Peter the Great, Vitus Bering explored eastward, discovering St. Lawrence Island and the Bering Strait. Further expeditions by Bering and Alexei Chirikof established the principal discoveries on which Russia based her claim to Alaska.

Actual colonization was not begun until 1783, when Grigor Ivanovich Shelikof established a settlement on Kodiak Island. The land in which colonization was thus started was eventually to comprise an area of approximately 586,000 square miles, one-fifth the size of the contiguous United States, extending 1,400 miles from north to south, 2,500 miles from east to west, and having a coastline of 25,000 miles. The climate ranged from temperate to frigid; waters were uncharted; the native population was widely scattered and uncivilized. The central government in Russia was 10,000 miles from the local capital, established at Sitka, with the vast Siberian wastes intervening. Under such conditions, the work accomplished by the Russians is in striking contrast to the first century of American administration.

Education in the Russian Period

Prior to the coming of the Russians, we may only conjecture concerning education in Alaska. That there was some attention given to this subject, as is the case with all aboriginal people, is doubtlessly true. The accumulated knowledge of the race–its traditional heritage, the provision of food and shelter, the practice of native arts, the observance of laws and customs regarding marriage, religion, and the general conduct of the individual in his relation to society as a whole–was, without doubt, transmitted from one generation to another by means of an informal and yet more or less definite system of education.

As a result of the temporary settlements founded by the pioneer Russian fur traders and explorers on the Aleutian Islands and the inevitable fraternization with native population, the number of children of mixed blood gradually increased until a need for formal education was recognized. Consequently, Shelikof established the first school in Alaska at Three Saints Bay (Kodiak) in 1785 and personally provided instruction in language, arithmetic, and religion. His work, and that of Fathers Juvenal and German, marked the beginning of the educational activities of the Graeco-Russian Church, which terminated only with the close of the two orphanages for boys at Sitka and Unalaska in 1911 and of the girls' boarding school at Kodiak in 1916. The other agency responsible for the conduct of education in Russian-America was the Russian-American Company, organized under imperial charter in 1799 to become Russia's agent for the government of the province. By the terms of its charter, the company was required to establish schools in conjunction with its trading posts. Such schools were usually under the supervision of the local trader or agent and were open to children of both sexes.

The educational activities of both the church and the company were so closely blended that it is difficult to treat them separately, especially in view of the limited information available. Neither made any real attempt to bring education to the masses of people except in isolated instances. The church schools were maintained principally for the children of the clergy and as a means of preparing a few Creoles (children with native mothers and Russian fathers) for the priesthood or as lay readers for the missions where no regular priest was stationed.

The Russian-American Company, while ostensib complying fully with the requirements of its charter, a parently arranged all educational facilities offered to th natives of Alaska with the sole object of benefiting itsel Graduates from some of the more advanced courses we required to remain in the service of the company for period of 15 years. In view of the vast expanse of th Siberian waste and the stretch of tempestuous sea th separated the company from the home base, it is n remarkable that an effort was made to serve its own intere and provide employees who were not only familiar with th country, but also bound to it by ties of home and famil Many competent clerks, copyists, bookkeepers, shi builders, and navigators were trained in the compan schools, the most notable of which was located at Sitka an known as the Colonial Academy. Creole girls also we trained to be housekeepers and frequently married th minor employees.

Although some years prior to the transfer of Alask to the United States, the Russian-American Company di continued its schools as a result of increasing expenses an diminishing income, during the height of company activit Sitka was the center of education in Alaska with fiv schools in session: two elementary schools conducted fo the benefit of the children of minor employees; on boarding school for girls, maintained by the coloni government; one for the children of company officials; an a theological seminary.

Some concept of the magnitude of educational wor of the Graeco-Russian Church may be obtained by notir that in 1887, 17 schools were in operation, 11 of whic were taught by the clergy and 6 by secular teachers. Th church expended $40,000 annually for church work an $20,000 for schools.

First American Schools

For a time after the purchase of Alaska, educatio languished. There was danger that even the few traces o enlightenment that the Russians had left behind would b obliterated in the reign of disorder that followed the departure. The military rule organized in 1867, whic continued for 10 years, was not conducive to education progress.

Since it was apparent that nothing was being don the residents of Sitka, then by far the largest and mo important city in Alaska, took matters in their own hand in 1867, they organized a city government, elected tw trustees, and made the mayor ex officio chairman of th school board. This government lasted 6 stormy years an was then discontinued, the school expiring with it.

During the first decade of American sovereignty, tw other American schools were maintained. These, on th Pribilofs, were more a continuation of Russian policy tha any great desire of the government to provide education acilities for the residents of Alaska. Furthermore, the operation of the schools was without cost to the government or in 1870 a contract was entered into between the nited States and the Alaska Commercial Company whereby the latter received certain concessions in the Pribilof slands. Schools were established on St. Paul and St. George slands in 1870.

ission Schools

y 1888, educational efforts had expanded so that there ere 13 government schools, 2 Alaska Commercial Company schools, and 17 Graeco-Russian and 11 other church chools.

The Presbyterian denomination was first to establish n American church school, setting up a boarding and ndustrial school for natives at Wrangell in 1877. Others ollowed at Sitka in 1878, and later at Haines, Jackson, oonah, and Point Barrow. Of these, the most important as the Sheldon Jackson School at Sitka. While many of e others had been transferred to the Bureau of Education, heldon Jackson High School was still operating in 1965, ith 134 students. In addition, a junior college had been stablished at the same location.

The Moravians established schools at Bethel, Carmel, nd Inigillingok. These schools were eventually taken over y the Bureau of Education, although the State Department of Education now operates the Bethel school with an nrollment of nearly 700 students.

The educational work of the Roman Catholic Church egan in 1886 with the establishment of a school for white hildren at Juneau. In 1896, a school for white children was t up in Douglas, only to close in 1920. Other schools were pened at Nome, Holy Cross, Akularek, Nulato, and Hot prings.

The educational work of the Protestant Episcopal hurch was confined entirely to schools established for the atives of Alaska. Among these were St. Thomas at Point ope, Fortella Hall at Nenana, St. John's-in-the-Wilderness Allakaket, St. John's at Ketchikan, St. James's at Tanana, t. Stephen's at Fort Yukon, and St. Paul's at Eagle. Others ere located at Anvik, Circle City, Tanana Crossing, alchaket, and Chena. All these schools were established etween 1887 and 1900.

The Methodist Episcopal Church established schools n the Seward Peninsula and at Unalaska. The church by 920 also maintained an orphanage, the Jesse Lee Home, ith the children attending the government school at nchorage. An early site at Sinuk was abandoned and established at Nome.

Other denominations establishing schools included e Friends' Society and the Swedish Evangelical Church. he former set up a school in Douglas, while the latter perated one at Yakutat and one at Unalakleet, which was aken over by the Bureau of Education.

One of the most important missionary enterprises in Alaska was undertaken in 1887 by William Duncan, an independent working among the Tsimpsean Indians of British Columbia. Father Duncan, who had formerly been connected with the Church of England, became dissatisfied and brought between 800 and 1,000 Indians from the old town of Metlakatla in British Columbia to Annette Island in Alaska, where he established the new town of Metlakatla. Within a short time, a thriving community was developed, with Father Duncan as teacher, guide, and counselor of young and old.

By legislative act in 1891, Congress set aside Annette Island for the use and occupancy of the Father Duncan colony of natives under such rules and regulations and subject to such restrictions as might be prescribed from time to time by the Secretary of the Interior. In 1913, the Bureau of Education established a school at Metlakatla and operated it until the State Department of Education assumed control in the early 1960's.

Federal Schools

For 17 years after the purchase of Alaska from Russia, the United States made no provision for education there through either appropriation of funds or enactment of legislation that would permit residents to help themselves. Such a condition prevailed, despite the fact that many interested persons laid the problem before Congress and the heads of various departments.

Much credit is due the Reverend Sheldon Jackson, superintendent of Presbyterian Missions in Alaska, for stirring the federal government to action. His close acquaintance with Commissioner of Education John Eaton produced more activity than otherwise might have been expected. During the winters of the years 1877 through 1883, Dr. Jackson delivered a series of lectures on Alaska in most of the larger cities throughout the United States. He also enlisted the aid of the National Education Association, state teacher associations, the Baptist, Methodist, and Presbyterian Mission Boards, and he appeared before the Forty-Sixth, Forty-Seventh, and Forty-Eighth Congresses.

Finally, in 1884, the Harrison Bill, known as the "Organic Act," was passed by Congress, providing a civil government for Alaska. In the next year the commissioner of education was assigned to carry out provisions of the legislation affecting education.

The task was one of great magnitude and beset with many difficulties. The schools to be established would be 4,000 to 6,000 miles from Washington; of the 36,000 people in Alaska, not more than 2,000 could speak English—and these were mainly in the three settlements of Juneau, Sitka, and Wrangell. In addition to the three "R's," it was necessary that children be taught the basic principles of health, dwelling improvements, housekeeping, as well as a means of living in the newly established civil order. To construct and equip schoolhouses, it would be necessary to ship materials from 1,500 to 4,500 miles. Further, teachers must be found who would be willing to exile themselves from society and to render services for the limited remuneration it would be possible to give them.

In 1885, the Reverend Sheldon Jackson was appointed to be general agent of education in Alaska. The work of establishing schools began in the southeastern region, since that was the only area then readily accessible. The school service was extended to the North Pacific and Aleutian regions in 1886 by means of a chartered schooner.

The plan of making contracts with the various missionary societies for schools in the vicinity of their stations was adopted early. Under this arrangement, it was possible to extend the educational system much more rapidly. The practice was discontinued in 1895.

A code of rules and regulations for the conduct of schools in Alaska was approved by the U.S. Commissioner in 1887. The code created a territorial board of education, consisting of the Governor, the judge of the U.S. District Court, and the general agent. Two more members were added in 1888, but because of the difficulties of communication, the central board was abolished, and local school communities were established. By 1903, experience indicated that the most effective type of supervision could be exercised by the district superintendent, and the local communities were discontinued.

The activities of the Bureau of Education included the formal education of native children; social services in native villages; medical services in the villages; establishment and maintenance of cooperative stores; and the reindeer service, which provided a stable supply of meat and made it possible to establish a more permanent settlement of natives, from which the government could dispense its services.

Up to the year 1890, only two schools for nonnative children had been established, and these were not considered adequate by the nonnative population. The population influx prompted by the discovery of gold and the increase in numbers of white children further complicated the situation. Although there were 10,000 more people in the area by 1898, the annual school appropriation was still only $30,000. Governor Brady in 1899 suggested that legislation be passed to allow larger communities to organize a municipal government and support their own schools. Congress accordingly passed such legislation in 1900 and provided that 50 percent of the license money collected within the corporate limits of such communities could be used for school purposes.

Juneau and Skagway were the first communities to incorporate and maintain their own schools for nonnative children under the legislation, doing so in 1900. Ketchikan and Treadwell followed in 1902; Douglas, Eagle, Valdez, and Wrangell in 1908; Cordova in 1909; Haines and Petersburg in 1910; Iditarod in 1911; Tanana in 1912; Anchorage and Sitka in 1920. Some idea of the importance of th legislation may be gathered from the fact that Juneau an Skagway each had revenues of $15,000 annually for th support of schools; the combined amount was equal to th total sum available to the bureau for the rest of Alaska.

In 1903, Senator Knute Nelson of Minnesota visite Alaska and became interested in the cause of education the territory. Due to his interest Congress passed th "Nelson School Law" in 1905, under which any com munity outside incorporated towns having a school popul tion of 20 white children and "children of mixed bloo who lead a civilized life" could petition the clerk of th court and secure establishment of a school district. Reven for the support was provided by 25 percent of the mone derived from liquor licenses and occupation or tra licenses outside incorporated towns. This legislation, pl that of 1900 mentioned above, relieved the bureau of th responsibility for education of other than natives of Alask

Summary

The four stages of education development in Alaska pri to 1917 may be summarized as follows:

1. The period of Russian control, from 1785 t 1867.

2. The period of governmental neglect, extendin from 1867 to 1885. During that time, the various churche including the Graeco-Russian, were responsible for wha ever educational work was accomplished.

3. The period of cooperative effort between th government and the various religious denominations, whic began in 1885 and terminated in 1895, when the Bureau o Education discontinued the practice of granting contrac to church organizations for the maintenance of schools.

4. The period during which local control of schoo for nonnative children was provided, and assistance to suc schools was definitely established; this period began wit the 1900 legislation permitting the incorporation of tow and providing for school revenues, and culminated in 190 when the Nelson Act, with its provision for schools fo nonnative children in communities outside incorporate towns, was passed.

A fifth distinctive period is that beginning in 191 when Congress removed the restrictions formerly place around the Territorial Legislature and permitted the peop of Alaska to control their own schools. It was in that ye that the Alaska Department of Education was establishe

THE UNIQUE STRUCTURE OF EDUCATION IN ALASKA

Establishment of the Department

Alaska was without a delegate to Congress until 1906. Th first delegate, Frank Waskey, was elected in August 190 and served until March 1907. Although he had no vote, he had the right to speak before Congressional committees, was entitled to membership on House committees, and could bring the affairs of Alaska to the attention of various officials. This representation resulted in greater attention to Alaska's needs.

In August 1912, delegate James Wickersham secured the enactment of Congressional legislation making provision for an Alaskan Territorial Legislature, which held its first session in Juneau in March 1913. After that date, sessions were convened biennially until the change to an annual session was made following statehood. The Territorial Legislature, by the terms of the "Organic Act" creating it, was prohibited from passing any laws affecting schools insofar as their establishment and maintenance were concerned and from appropriating territorial money for the support of schools. That restriction was removed through an act approved in March 1917 authorizing the Legislature of Alaska to establish and maintain schools.

The third session of the Legislature convened in March 1917 and, among its many actions, passed the Uniform School Act. The principal provision of this legislation was the activation of the Territorial Board of Education, consisting of the Governor and the four senior Senators, one from each judicial division. The board's main duties included the appointment of a commissioner of education at an annual salary not to exceed $4,000; the appointment of clerks and other office employees on the recommendation of the commissioner; and the exercise of general supervision over the policies of the commissioner. The latter was invested with broad powers for the general supervision of all territorial education institutions, the preparation of general rules and regulations regarding the conduct of schools, formulation of courses of study, examination and certification of teachers, authorization of all school expenditures, auditing of the accounts of all school boards, and general responsibility for standardization and coordination of educational activities in the territory (1).

Changing Structure of the Department

When the commissioner of education assumed charge of the Territorial Department of Education in May 1917, the department existed in name only. At that time, schools were maintained in 15 incorporated towns and in 40 communities outside incorporated towns. Schools were scattered from Kiana and Eagle, in the north, to Unga and Ketchikan, on the southern coast. Information regarding the schools was confined to the rather limited statistics appearing in the reports of the Governor. The matter of securing further information was the work of months because of the inadequate mail service in some parts of the territory and the great distances involved. Several school boards had no knowledge of the appointment of a commissioner until he visited them in September and October of that year. Slow and uncertain transportation facilities made the inspection of schools difficult and resulted in considerable wasted time. It was nearly impossible for one official, with a limited travel allowance, a very limited office staff, and a field embracing 586,000 square miles, to visit the various schools more than once in 2 or 3 years. These conditions resulted in supervision of an indirect type, still provided in many of the schools throughout Alaska.

When the department was created and Commissioner Lester D. Henderson took office, he had one secretary to help him. During the 1921-22 school year, he gained a stenographer, and the staff remained the same size for 12 years until a clerk was added. By 1935-36, vocational education had forced an organizational addition, and a supervisor and an assistant in that area were added (2). In 1939-40, vocational education per se was dropped by the department, although it was to be added again in later years. However, a deputy commissioner was employed in 1935-36, and it is assumed that the deputy took over many of the supervisory responsibilities vacated.

Commissioner James C. Ryan initiated the Superintendents' Advisory Commission in the period between 1941 and 1951. The commission began the work that resulted in establishment of the tobacco tax, dedicated to school construction and revision of the administrative manual.

By 1945-46, a health education position had been created, and the supply function became a specific position. The functions covered by the staff included instruction supervision; child accounting; records and reports; correspondence study; filing, clerical, and stenographic work; school inspection and visitation; school plant construction and repairs; finance; transportation; purchasing; accounting; research; and public relations (3). From this point, the same functions were to be carried on, but with an ever–increasing staff.

The organizational pattern by 1951-52 showed two education supervisors, a study coordinator, and a development that had begun in 1946–the on-base school operating program, which was a separate division with its own accounting and secretarial services. A divisional unit for administrative services was also set up and included bookkeeping, vouchering, purchasing, and clerical services (4).

By 1957-58, the pattern of organization had altered considerably, with new units in curriculum and instruction, secretarial services, accounting, and vocational education (5).

Commissioner Don M. Dafoe had continued the practice of utilizing the superintendents' commission to originate and comment on legislation during his 6-year tenure from 1953 to 1959.

The organizational structure had changed to show assistant commissioners by 1959-60–one in instruction and one in administration. The positions of director of vocational education and the director of the Anchorage field office had been set up, and the on-base schools system was a unit in its own right. Further actions were taken in succeeding years to establish various directorships and divisions to parallel functions assumed by department personnel. The organizational pattern is shown for the middle of 1966, as it was the subject of much work in the 2 years before its implementation (6).

The State Board of Education

Under the legislation establishing the Territorial Board of Education, the board consisted of the Governor as ex officio president, plus the four senior Senators, one from each judicial division. It was empowered to make its own rules and regulations and to assign and direct the commissioner of education in the performance of his duties.

There are three major high points in the history of the territorial and state boards. The first came with the establishment of the territorial board; the second, in 1933, concerned the creation of a new type of board by the Legislature. The new law provided for a continuous board consisting of five members, one from each judicial division and one at large, appointed by the Governor and approved by the Legislature. The members held office for 6 years, and no more than two were new at any time. The board met twice each year.

Under the old law, the members were not selected because of their particular fitness for serving the educational needs of the territory. The Governor, appointed by the President of the United States, was sometimes from one of the states and knew little about the educational needs of Alaska; or, if he were an Alaskan, he was not selected because of his interest in education. The other members were elected as Senators because of their fitness. The only time they met was during sessions of the Legislature, and then they were busy on other matters.

The third major change occurred with the creation of the State of Alaska. Article VII, Section I, of the state constitution established a system of public schools, and the 1959 state organization act established the State Department of Education. A six-member Board of Education was created to confirm programing actions of the commissioner and to approve all rules and regulations. However, the board was given no administrative, budgeting, or fiscal powers, and the commissioner became the administrator of the education program (7).

Functions and Responsibilities of the Department

In administering the duties delegated to it under law, the Alaska Department of Education serves a threefold purpose. It is a leadership-regulatory agency for the state system of public education; it is a governing agency for specific programs operated on a statewide basis; and a third duty assigned covers the actual operation and administration of School District No. 1 (state-operated schools).

Leadership and Regulatory Functions. Effective leadership contributes significantly to the improvement of state and local education programs. Each program conducted by the department must have the resources needed to provide leadership throughout the state. Leadership activities and services provided include planning, research, consultation, public relations, demonstration, in-service training, and dissemination of information.

In the Alaska department, leadership in development of elementary and secondary programs lies with the Division of Instructional Services, which is responsible for ensuring a continuing program of curriculum revision and development. Activity in this area may include stimulation of curriculum study groups or preparation of guides, bulletins, and journals. All such efforts are designed to improve the efficiency of classroom instruction in all schools of the state. General supervision is concerned with improving not only instruction, but also those practices within school organization and administration that make better teaching possible. Consultative services to local school districts are provided to aid administrators and teachers in planning programs, organizing materials of instruction, improving instruction, and evaluating pupil and teacher progress through study groups, conferences, workshops, and discussion groups.

In addition to these two main responsibilities, the division works to promote the use of instructional facilities and materials including laboratories, shops, audiovisual aids, textbooks, educational media, and school library services. The division offers services to local programs to promote growth and adjustment of the child in closely related programs of instruction and guidance. Although the classroom teacher is the key to operation of guidance programs at the elementary level and is of vital importance in guidance work in secondary schools, specially trained resource people and counselors also are necessary. The division also provides consultative services in the selection of textbooks to promote a well-rounded program of instruction.

Regulatory responsibilities are a direct consequence of state authority for education. The establishment of standards and the accompanying power to enforce compliance with them are commonly termed the *regulatory function.* In the instruction division, the accreditation and licensing of public and private schools, as well as the approval of programs for the education of school personnel in preparation programs, constitute a specific function. The certification of local school personnel and attempts to increase such personnel resources become part of the cooperative effort with higher education institutions. These programs include preparation of teacher training requirements, promotion of in-service activities, and the advancement of statewide practices in personnel selection.

Operational programs in the instructional services division include responsibility for institution of federally funded programs, correspondence study for students in isolated areas having no elementary or secondary schools, and adult and preschool programs.

The Division of Administrative Services is involved in the leadership function by its responsibility for finance and business administration, pupil transportation, school attendance, and census. The division's involvement includes development and administration of a financial plan ensuring an adequate foundation program for support of education in the state, development of plans and procedures for promoting economy and efficiency, and establishment of prudential safeguards for educational funds.

The division provides such services in pupil transportation as can best be performed at the state level and those of most assistance to local schools in the development of an efficient, economical, and safe system of school bus operation.

Many aspects of the education program utilize the information obtained through child accounting procedures and the school census. These data supply the basic information for projecting future educational needs. The statistical services section of administrative services is responsible for these functions.

Two major functions of the division are those of internal management and supporting services. Internal management encompasses the activities in personnel management, budget development and execution, and program management. Supporting services include research, statistical services, state museum, printing and publications, and such supporting services as mail, central files, and space allocations.

The instructional and administrative services divisions form, with the immediate functions of the commissioner's office, the staff level of the State Department of Education in Alaska. In addition to these are two other main divisions with leadership and regulatory responsibilities. The divisions of vocational education and vocational rehabilitation are mentioned here as operating programs because of their more specific program functions. Each has responsibility for development and supervision of statewide programs of a highly skilled, technical, or scientific nature.

The State Department as an Operating School District. In some states the department of education operates certain special schools, classes, or programs of direct service to individuals or groups. These direct governing functions are quite different in character from leadership-regulatory functions. When a state department of education exercises the leadership-regulatory function, it deals with another agency which is charged with the operation of a particular institution or program. When exercising the governing function, the department is the agency charged with operating the institution or program. In the one instance there is an agency between the department and the program of operation. In the other there is no such agency. In Alaska, the department acts in its leadership-regulatory functions through local educational agencies. However, it also has the governmental function over what is referred to as State School District No. 1: the schools outside incorporated areas, the schools on military bases, regional-vocational schools, regional groupings of schools, and those operated under special contracts, as is the instance in the Pribilofs, where a contract exists with the Bureau of Commercial Fisheries.

In past years, such schools have been operated by staff members of the instructional and administrative services divisions, usually at the expense of the leadership and regulatory functions. Commencing in 1965, the organizational pattern was altered to support a balanced concept among the functions of leadership, regulation, and operation. Such a reorganization will provide for clearer lines of responsibility and an increased ability to meet new programs. In many cases, personnel in the past were less effective because of the many different types of responsibilities being assigned to a single individual. Operation thus received the greatest percentage of effort with a resultant lessening of time devoted to the other two functions (8).

The Dual System

In 1905, with the passage of the Nelson Act, Alaska joined the U. S. Bureau of Education in the task of operating schools in the unorganized areas. Each, by 1965, operated some 80 schools, varying from large boarding schools to small one-room schools. This two-headed enterprise has come to be known as the "Dual System."

Background of the System. The beginning of a dual system in Alaska came about unofficially as resentment grew among the relatively few whites over emphasis on education for natives and a belief that integrated schools would provide only inferior education. In such towns as Juneau and Sitka, where there were proportionately greater white populations, separate schools were established. With the increased population resulting from the Gold Rush in the late 1890's, agitation grew for the establishment of a separate system of schools for the nonnative. In 1900, Congress provided for the establishment of independent schools for whites within incorporated towns. The Nelson Act of 1905 clarified this previous legislation and extended it to rural areas.

The Nelson Act was an important point in the history of education in Alaska. The territorial government was to be responsible for the education of white children and children of mixed blood who lived "civilized lives" in the areas outside of town, and for the education of white children in towns. The Bureau of Education (or Bureau of Indian Affairs, as it came to be known) was to be responsible for the education of all other natives. It is important to note, however, that the Nelson Act did extend to the territorial government responsibility for natives of mixed blood. As the years passed, more and more children of mixed and sometimes full native blood have come into the territorial and state schools. Actually, the Territory of Alaska, for the decade preceding statehood, was responsible for the education of more native children than the Bureau of Indian Affairs (BIA).

For nearly 30 years following the 1905 act, little consideration was given to unification of the two systems. Some officials openly discouraged it on the grounds that there would be friction between the two races and that the natives were irregular in attendance, were unable to conform to white standards in matters of health and sanitation, and generally would represent an unfair cost to the territory.

During the 1930's, territorial officials began to recognize the need for unification of the systems. This recognition may have been, in part, stimulated by the reaction of some native leaders against the paternalism of the BIA in the 1920's. A review of correspondence does indicate that some overtures were made by the education department, but with a clear emphasis on the need for increased federal funds. The BIA attitude, as shown in the correspondence, reflected a paternalistic policy and doubted the ability of the department to meet the native needs.

Since World War II, the BIA has shown a departure from its previous paternalistic attitude and has adopted a policy of gradual elimination of its educational functions in Alaska, as well as in the United States proper. The Eighty-Third Congress gave specific recognition to this policy in 1953 in Concurrent Resolution 108. In Alaska, implementation of this policy is based on a recognition of population shifts and cultural transition. The increased acceptance of the native population was evidenced by the passage of antidiscrimination laws in the territory in 1945 and by increased participation of native peoples in governmental affairs.

It also is evident that the territory was showing increased willingness to take over functions that are traditionally those of state governments. Although neither the Statehood Act nor the Omnibus Bill mentioned the transfer of school functions from the BIA, there was a strong feeling in Alaskan governmental circles that, with statehood, attention was to be given to unification of the two systems, or that the alternative might be a natural withdrawal from school operations by the BIA regardless of Alaskan consent.

Some progress was made, particularly after 1945. The unification of school operations in communities where there were separate schools is one example. Between 1945 and 1955, a number of communities of predominantly native population incorporated as cities and thereby also became school districts. This incorporation was protested on grounds that it shifted financial burdens to territorial funds for school support purposes. Others argued that their villages were not ready for incorporation from the standpoint of either taxable wealth or willingness to tax themselves. This latter contention was borne out in the early 1950's when several of these communities were involved in financial difficulties.

The Department of Education also contended that these districts should be given financial assistance under the Johnson-O'Malley Act, but the BIA refused to consider this. There was a feeling on the part of the department that this refusal was being used as a lever to force the territory into an overall Johnson-O'Malley plan that would speed up the transfer of all schools to the department. In the case of two villages incorporated in the 1950's, Angoon and Hydaburg, the BIA did enter into modified JOM agreements and did assume some financial responsibility. The territory itself, however, cannot disclaim responsibility for the failure of some villages since the territory had no agency to give assistance in organizing local governments or tax programs. One of the favorable features of the Organization Act for the new state was the provision for a local affairs agency to render such service.

An Overall Educational Plan for Rural Alaska. The concept of two systems of education clearly is inconsistent with the tenets of democracy. More specifically, it is in conflict with the state constitution, which places responsibility for education with the state. However, with little tax base in the rural areas and the high costs involved in educating a scattered population, assuming complete control of all schools now under the BIA would create a financial burden that the state cannot support at present.

The continued operation of two school systems creates a very real danger that differing educational programs and a disparate philosophy will result in further obstacles to consolidation. With full recognition of this danger, a joint meeting of officials of the BIA, the State of Alaska, the University of Alaska, and the U.S. Office of Education was held in Washington, D.C., in March 1962. An agreement was developed commissioning the State of Alaska to formulate an overall plan with local participation for expansion of secondary school facilities and transfer of bureau-operated schools to state management and operation.

Following the Washington agreement, Governor William A. Egan appointed a state education committee comprised of the area director of BIA, the secretary of state, the commissioner of education, the dean of the College of Behavioral Sciences at the University of Alaska, and a member of the State Board of Education. The committee was directed to prepare an overall plan for rural school operation and ultimate consolidation of the two systems.

A document entitled "An Overall Education Plan for Rural Alaska" was developed by the committee. It included the elements of long-range planning for rural education, a schedule for gradual consolidation of schools operated by the two agencies, and provisions for continued study and revision so that the plan might be adjusted to changing conditions.

The Continuing Committee on Education. As a result of the early meetings of the committee, a continuing committee was established to review and suggest modifications of agency procedures, to direct further research and investigations, and to make recommendations to the two agencies. The following recommendations were developed and continue to be the basis of action on the part of the two agencies:

1. The criteria set forth for establishing new schools should be adhered to as closely as possible.

2. Every effort should be made to provide an elementary and secondary school education for all Alaska's children through local schools and boarding high schools, or by placement of children in approved homes where schools are located.

3. The highest priority should be given to establishing and improving elementary schools where adequate education is not now being provided, with the second priority being given to the construction of local high schools in communities that can support them. Third priority should go to regional boarding schools to accommodate students for whom a high school program is not available locally.

4. The Alaska Department of Education and the BIA should jointly determine where additional high school facilities can and should be established for eligible pupils and should investigate the feasibility of providing strong junior high schools in locations where enrollment does not justify a full high school program.

5. The Alaska Department and BIA should cooperate closely in developing emergency and long-range plans to educate all children in the state. This includes those students for whom boarding school space in local high schools is not available and students needing special education.

6. Adequacy of educational programs in the local and boarding schools should be under continuous review. In particular, the department should investigate the adequacy of educational programs in very small high schools and compare the achievement and adjustment of their students with that of boarding high school students.

7. Careful studies should be made of per pupil costs at the boarding schools. The possibility of increasing enrollments should be investigated as an alternative to establishing new boarding schools.

8. Where possible the state should carry out a continuing program of prevocational and occupationally oriented education that will realistically take into account the availability of job opportunities in Alaska.

9. A coordinating committee should be organized to develop joint state-federal and village planning prior to relocation of villages. All requests for assistance from such villages should be referred to the coordinating committee.

10. Postgraduate technical or vocational training at high school sites, particularly at the boarding school locations, should be considered.

11. The possibility of assisting uneducated youth and adults through additional education and training should be explored.

12. The state and BIA should continue to arrange for an orderly transfer of BIA schools to state administration on a region-by-region basis under Johnson-O'Malley contracts.

13. Transfer of BIA schools to state operation should be effected as quickly as practicable, supplementary financial support for operation of schools by the state to be obtained under applicable federal laws.

14. The state, through its political subdivisions, should assume the financial burden of all elementary and secondary day schools when the areas in which these schools are located are incorporated into boroughs.

15. The possibility of locating suitable living accommodations in cities for students who cannot attend local or regional boarding high schools should be explored.

Local School Agencies

In addition to the efforts of the state and the Bureau of Indian Affairs, there are two other major units of school operational authority through which the department is called upon for services. Twenty-seven borough and city school districts currently (1965-66) serve 53,872 students. There are 2,132 professional personnel in these local education agencies. The department exercises leadership and regulatory functions and provides financial support under the foundation program.

Statutes and regulations also invest certain supervisory and regulatory powers in the state department with reference to private and denominational schools. Some supervision and coordination is necessary to maintain some comparability of educational standards and to ensure good working relationships among all educational institutions in the state. Statistics gathered in the department indicate that there were 28 private and denominational schools, serving 2,439 students, in 1965-66 (9).

CONDITIONS INFLUENCING EDUCATION IN ALASKA

The States of Maine and Hawaii are the only others whose operational procedures approach the unique situation of education in Alaska. The State Department of Education in Maine operates some schools in isolated sections of its northern area; all of Hawaii's schools are operated by its state department. Alaska's department, however, must exercise its leadership and regulatory functions with the local district and private schools (where there are specific regulatory responsibilities); must cooperate with the Bureau of Indian Affairs system; and, in addition, must operate a large number of schools in isolated rural areas spread over 586,000 square miles, as well as serve relatively large systems on military bases.

Growth and Costs of Alaskan Schools

The student population in Alaska during the 1965-66 school year in the four major systems of the Alaskan educational structure totaled 69,628 (10). In comparing growth, enrollments, and costs, attention is drawn to the much more rapid growth in city and borough school districts than in the unincorporated areas. Although the cost per pupil in average daily attendance for the year 1917-18 indicates that city districts were spending $102 per pupil, those schools outside incorporated areas were spending only slightly more. By 1965-66, however, the per-pupil expenditure in rural areas was much higher. In that year, nearly 54,000 students were in city or borough districts, with only 5,000 in rural areas (ignoring for the moment approximately 10,000 pupils in schools on military bases); small numbers, high shipping costs, low pupil/teacher ratios, and high operational costs all contributed to the disparity in per-pupil expenditures.

The military on-base school system had its beginning in 1946-47 with four schools and had doubled in number by 1965-66. The total enrollment grew from 158 to over 10,000 in a 20-year period (11).

Problems of Alaskan Rural Schools

The native student of today who returns to his village home finds little in the way of common discussion grounds with his parents, for they had little opportunity for education in earlier years. The policy of both the state and BIA is to establish an elementary school only when sufficient numbers of students are present in a location to make it economically feasible. The state uses a minimum figure of 10, while the BIA uses 12. Otherwise, the children must use correspondence courses (Calvert courses in earlier years, but now the state has developed its own). The compulsory education law was nearly impossible to enforce in rural areas, and, in any case, those who lived more than 2 miles from the schools were not required to attend.

Education can be a determining factor in the process of acculturation, but the high incidence of dropout must be lowered if it is to do so. Problems of home background, especially bilingualism, contribute to the dropout rate, as well as lack of materials and instructional techniques adapted to the environmental and cultural handicaps of the student.

The level of education is gradually rising in the villages, but it has been a very slow process. The mixing of the two cultures is necessary to improve the ability of village people to compete with those of the dominant culture. Contrastingly, the two worlds the villagers face are that of the majority—urbanized, Western European, English-speaking peoples—and their own minority—isolated village, Eskimo-Indian, dialect-speaking groups.

Of paramount importance to the department in its operation of schools, then, is the problem inherent in the existence of two cultures, both of which impinge on the student daily as he faces one at home and the other at school. Villages will form and grow where an economic base is present to supply resources to meet the needs and wants of the people. Others, where the economic base has shifted or vanished, exist mainly through welfare support and tend to be static or may eventually disappear. Educators must consider these factors and provide the means whereby children may gain an education that will enable them to compete in the modern world, whether the village remains or disappears or whether the children eventually end up in urban or rural areas.

The following points represent some of the major problems that must be considered by the Department of Education in the establishment of a meaningful program of education for rural peoples:

1. It has been said that the typical Alaskan village family consists of the mother, the father, one grandparent, six children, and one anthropologist. Many specialists from educational, economic, governmental, and social institutions could appear in one village to answer one plea for help. The forces available should coordinate their efforts to avoid duplication and waste.

2. It has been assumed that what is good for one group may also be good for another. The problems in education of the village people are not limited to the concept of the majority versus the minority culture. Rather, the problem is of many subgroups within any one group.

3. The primary point of attack should be the insufficient background of language and reading skills.

4. Some variations must be allowed for the teaching of English as a second language, whereas now promotion is based on the individual's ability in the English language only.

5. Most of the existing instructional materials, designed for Midwestern, middle class, English-speaking children, are not appropriate for use in remote Alaskan villages.

6. Evaluation techniques, testing programs, and psychological services need to be improved and adapted. In testing across cultural lines, tests must be revised to take into account nonverbal skills.

7. There is inadequate motivation to pursue long-range educational careers because of the failure to recognize the peculiar characteristics of the village populations.

8. Many village students have a poor self-concept when mixed with nonvillage groups. Sullivan's "Mirror Effect," as well as the school's lack of provision for individual success, may contribute to the problem. A restructuring of grade-placement systems is needed to provide for the variation in student abilities. There is also a lack of an "educational tradition" in the home.

9. Health problems are common, especially those of the eye and ear. In some areas the numbers of students affected are estimated at 50 percent.

10. Over past years inadequate opportunities have been provided for education of students beyond the eighth-grade level. A program of adult education is necessary.

11. Teacher attitudes toward the minority culture, their lack of specialized training in the problems of teaching in village schools, large classes, and excessive teacher responsibilities contribute to the many problems. The lack of adequate staff housing in many villages does not aid in the attraction of competent, highly skilled teachers.

12. Costs of school facilities in rural areas are far higher than any place else in the country. Some years ago it cost nearly $27 per square foot to build in the southeastern area, $35 in the central, $55 in the northern. Costs have risen since then.

To overcome these problems, Alaskan educators must prepare students by increasing their perceptivity, reasoning ability, knowledge, understanding, and respect for the heritage of their own people and others. Motivation may then be increased toward the attainment of appropriate objectives and goals.

Anthropologists, sociologists, economists, and educators must combine to effect change in the villages and in educational programs, for the largest problems to be faced are cultural in nature.

It should be pointed out that the most urgent need lies in defining desirable ultimate goals for native children and youth and the development of immediate curriculum objectives that will lead toward those ultimate goals.

A third need which must be fulfilled is the development of appropriate Alaska-adapted instructional materials. Above all else, the teaching of English as a second language, especially in the primary years, through the medium of an oral situational approach should be developed and implemented through in-service training programs.

Fourth, techniques for recruitment and selection of teachers for the village schools must be improved. Face-to-face contacts (rather than mail selection) are a costly process, and the state Legislature must be convinced of the need to obtain qualified personnel before they will fund such recruitment programs. Once contracted, instructional and administrative personnel must be involved in a continual in-service program.

Charles K. Ray, dean at the University of Alaska, directed a study during the years immediately before and after statehood. The following two paragraphs set forth his comments relative to planning programs for the village people:

> Regardless of the rate of development of the Alaskan economy, the native people are committed to the task of finding their way in a new culture in a new way of life which will involve the development of new values and the dropping of many vestiges of their own culture. Such a process must be a voluntary one; still, there are myriad evidences to support the claim that the people themselves desire the change. No longer do these people want to settle for a lower standard of living than is maintained by the average citizen, nor do they wish to be wards of the government. The desire on the part of the people for prestige, self-respect, and economic independence has been demonstrated in numerous intangible, yet emphatic ways.
>
> Education can serve as one vital influencing force designed to increase the differences in attainment and opportunity which exist at the present time between native and nonnative groups. Therefore, the long-range objectives of the schools must be pointed toward an eventual common education for all, regardless of race. Yet the immediate instructional program must be planned to account for the enormous differences in the background, values, and orientation of the native students in the diverse regions of the territory. An intelligent understanding by the teachers of the problems faced by those "caught between two worlds" is essential (12).

Problems of Education in the Boroughs

The Borough Act of 1961 (13), as amended, restructured the grouping of schools in Alaska to borough-operated, city-operated, and state-operated. At that time, about 62 percent of the 60,000 schoolchildren in the state were enrolled in borough schools.

On January 1, 1964, there were nine boroughs in the state. One of these, Bristol Bay, assumed control over three state schools within its boundaries. The other eight acceded to all powers over former city independent school districts and state-operated schools within these boundaries. Each such borough was thus made a school district; first- and second-class boroughs were required to establish, maintain, and operate a system of public schools on an area-wide basis. The borough assembly could, by ordinance, require that all school money be deposited in a central treasury with all other borough money; the borough chairman then would have custody of all money in the centralized treasury. The borough assembly could, however, with the consent of the borough school board, delegate to the borough school board responsibility for a decentralized treasury. One major change through this legislation required the borough assembly to review the school budget and approve the total amount–only appropriating, however, the local share.

In the matter of school buildings the borough assembly was to determine such sites from the recommendations of the borough school board. The latter had responsibility for the design of school buildings, but again this was with the approval of the assembly. The board provides custodial services and routine maintenance; the assembly provides for all major rehabilitation and construction.

In the years since the passage of the Borough Act and its implementation in 1964, a number of arguments have grown over the centralized treasury, budget review and approval by the assembly, design and construction of school buildings, and bonding procedures. Undoubtedly some will be settled through legal interpretations, either by opinions from the office of the attorney general, or by final resort to the courts.

DEVELOPMENT OF THE SCHOOL SUPPORT SYSTEM

Early Basis for Support

Commencing in 1919, 75 percent of the total amount expended for the maintenance of schools within the limits of incorporated towns, cities, or school districts was refunded by the territory. No money was included for construction, and not more than 10 percent of the total amount could be used for repairs or improvements. No district was to receive more than $15,000 during any school year.

Total refund amounts at the 75 percent level were raised to $20,000 in 1921 and remained there until 1931, when a new refund schedule was set up according to the number of pupils in school. With less than 150 pupils, 80 percent was refunded; with 150 to 300, 75 percent; with 300 pupils and over, 70 percent. In 1955 this was changed to the following: 0 to 200 pupils, 85 percent; 200 to 500, 80 percent; and 500 and over, 75 percent.

The commissioner received the budget prior to January 1. He then designated those expenditures acceptable for refund; his decision was final.

Taxation for School Purposes

In 1919 a $5 school tax was levied on each male person between 21 and 50 years of age, excluding military personnel and paupers. In 1943 the age was changed to 21 to 55, and in 1960 to 19 years and up. The amount rose to $7.50 in 1955, and to $10 in 1957. In 1960 the tax ceased to be dedicated for school purposes and went to the general fund.

In 1951, an act was passed allowing the assessment, levying, and collection of a tax for school and municipal purposes not to exceed 3 percent of the assessed valuation of all real or personal property. An exemption was provided for those below $200 in property holdings, and for property held by religious, educational, or charitable institutions and by nonprofit organizations.

Revenue collected from the tobacco tax, passed by the Legislature in 1951, was to go into a territorial "school fund" to be used for rehabilitation, construction, insurance, and repairs of facilities.

A consumers sales tax was authorized in 1953 and allowed school districts, on approval by referendum, to levy a tax not to exceed 2 percent of all retail sales, rents, and services within the district.

In 1960, the bonding capacity of the districts was set at 10 percent of the aggregate value of the real and personal property subject to taxation. Such funds could be used to construct, improve, repair, reconstruct, acquire, and operate any and all types of public utilities, school buildings, and facilities connected to such authority.

The Public School Foundation Program

The present program of school support began in 1962 with the establishment of a foundation program that recognized a level of "basic need" and then equalized this according to the taxing resources of the district. Three elements of support are used: (a) a per-pupil allotment of $140, $150, or $160 (depending on geographic area); (b) a teacher unit allowance based on average daily membership and the state minimum salary scale; and (c) $1,000 for each attendance center. The sum of these allowances constitutes the "basic need." From this is subtracted an amount equivalent to that which would be raised by a 3.5-mill levy on the full value of all real and personal property in the district, and one-half of the P.L. 874 entitlement for the preceding year. This subtractive element is called the "required local effort."

A special education schedule for teacher units was set up in 1963, establishing one teacher unit for the first 5 to 10 students, and adding one teacher for each 10 students.

The foundation program provides basic support for education in grades 1 through 12 (14).

Importance of Federal Aid

Chapter 27, Session Laws of Alaska, 1959, assented to federal aid to education in the state under the National Defense Education Act of 1958. The commissioner of education was authorized to cooperate with the federal government and to participate under that act or any acts amendatory or supplementary to it, subject to prior concurrence of the Governor.

From 1959 to the present, the percentage of federal funds in total expenditures has varied only slightly (15). Amounts have certainly changed and show an increase well over 150 percent between 1959 and 1965, from over $6 million to nearly $15 million.

CHANGES IN EDUCATION THROUGH LEGISLATION

The following material is an attempt to describe the more important legislation which has changed education in Alaska since the inception of the department (16). Due to limited space and previous discussions of legislation, only a few major topics have been chosen.

School Boards and District Organization

In 1919, power to establish a school district was awarded to the clerk of the district court for those areas where resided 10 children of white or mixed blood leading a "civilized life" and between the ages of 6 and 17 years. For the clerk to perform this act eight adult citizens of the United States had to file a petition. After approval, the voters of the district were allowed to vote on a three-member board. The board was empowered to build or rent the necessary facilities and equipment, provide utilities, employ teachers, and do anything else necessary for the maintenance of public schools.

Independent school districts were authorized by legislation in 1947 but were limited to a total of 1,000 square miles of territory in 1953. The limitation of territory was removed in 1964, when the borough system was implemented.

Where the Territorial Board of Education operated schools, it could discontinue such operation when the average daily membership in the district reached 100 students and the community was able to provide local school support in accordance with territorial law; such a decision was at the board's discretion. Following such action, the territory was to pay for the support of the schools up to 100 percent for the first 2 fiscal years; 90 percent for the third; for the fourth and successive years, the schools were to be placed in the appropriate reimbursement group.

A 1960 act provided that there were to be five members of local boards in independent districts with average daily membership of less than 5,000 students. Over that number, a board of seven members was provided. Officers were to include a president, treasurer, and clerk. The board could appoint an assessor and place an assessed evaluation on all real and personal property outside the city and within the district so long as it was comparable to valuations of similar property within the city.

Legislation in 1960 established advisory school boards of three members in each community served by a rural school operated by the State Department of Education. Powers of such boards were limited to advising and assisting the state board and the department.

In 1963, advisory boards in rural areas were set at three members if the average daily membership was less than 250 pupils; beyond that figure a board of five members was created. In both instances, the term of office was 3 years.

Compulsory Attendance

In Alaska, attendance at school is compulsory for children between the ages of 7 and 16 years or until the child has completed the twelfth grade. School age is defined as being 6 years of age on or before November 2 of the school year, being under 20, and not having completed the twelfth grade. Such children may attend public school without payment of tuition in the district of which they are residents. A person over school age may be admitted at the discretion of the governing body of the district, but he may be charged tuition. A child under school age may be admitted at the discretion of the governing body if he meets minimum standards prescribed by the board related to his mental, physical, and emotional capacify.

A child 5 years of age on or before November 2 following the beginning of the school year, and who is under school age, may enter a public kindergarten. A child under school age shall be admitted to school in the district of which he is a resident if immediately before he became a resident he was legally enrolled in the public schools of another district or state.

If a physician is available, a physical examination is required of every child upon entrance to school and thereafter at regular intervals considered advisable by the governing body of the district. Where no physician is available, an examination is required at the earliest date possible.

Accreditation and Approval of Secondary Schools

In 1929, a section of the statutes defined accredited high schools as those equal to the standards set by the commissioner of education, who was to be guided by the practices employed by the University of Washington in accrediting State of Washington secondary schools In later years, the Northwest Association of Secondary and Higher Education has become the accrediting agency for Alaskan schools. The three-member state committee processes applications in advance of association meetings.

The education department is presently considering standards for approval of secondary and elementary schools on a state basis.

Transportation

The department provides for the transportation of all pupils who reside more than 1.5 miles from established schools. It may require districts to enter into contracts with the department for administration, supervision, operation, or subcontracting of transportation systems. An annual report is required, including a financial statement and operational data. Each district is entitled to receive full reimbursement from the state for such operations.

Although made ineffective by a court decision in 1959, it is notable that legislation once provided for transportation of nonpublic school students at public expense. Where children, in order to reach nonpublic schools, had to travel distances comparable with, and over routes the same as, the distances and routes over which children attending public schools were transported, this legislation allowed for such combined service.

Vocational Education

Legislation in 1935 established the territory's right to carry out the provisions of acts relating to vocational education from the federal level. The act provided for the promotion of vocational education and for cooperation with states in promotion of educational programs in agriculture, home economics, and trades and industries. Section 3 of the act gave the territorial board full and complete authority and power to cooperate with federal units in vocational education and in administration of the provisions of the acts of Congress. In 1935, $30,000 was appropriated for the 1935-37 biennium.

Vocational Rehabilitation

The Alaska Board of Education, by legislation of 1960, was directed to act as the Board of Vocational Rehabilitation and to administer its program. It was empowered to cooperate with federal agencies as required by federal statutes.

The board appoints a director who serves as the executive officer of the board. All rules and regulations for the operation of the vocational rehabilitation unit originate with the commissioner of education and become effective when approved by a majority of the board.

State Textbook Commission

Legislation in 1919 created a Textbook Commission consisting of the commissioner of education and two legally qualified teachers to be appointed by him with the advice and consent of the Governor. Members were to serve for 4 years, or until successors were appointed. It was the duty of the commission to select and adopt a uniform set of textbooks for use in all branches of study in the elementary school and for each of the subjects in the high school. Adoptions were made for a period of 4 years and required a majority vote of the members of the commission.

The membership of the commission was changed periodically and had reached seven by 1965-66. Districts were required to follow the adoptions unless special approval for variation was received from the commissioner. Any other variation was required to be funded from local district sources (17).

Provisions for Exceptional Children

Competent special services for exceptional children in Alaska between the ages of 5 and 18 for whom regular school facilities are inadequate or not available was the subject of Chapter 120, SLA 1959. The term special services was interpreted to include transportation, special teaching in the curriculum, corrective teaching, and provision of special books, teaching supplies, and equipment required for the education of physically handicapped and mentally retarded children. Section 8 gave the commissioner the right to appoint a supervisor or to delegate duties to an existing staff member.

An act in 1965 made it mandatory that special education be established in a district for each classification of exceptional children represented by not less than five children living in the area served by the program. A program could be offered at local expense for less than the five.

The Department of Health and Welfare was directed in 1965 to establish by regulation certain standards for the evaluation and classification of exceptional children. This legislation augmented the provisions of Chapter 70, SLA 1963, which increased the allowable number of teacher units allowed for special education in the school foundation program.

Teacher Welfare Legislation

Salary. A minimum schedule for teachers was established in 1939 setting salaries in the first division at $1,800, the third division at $1,980, and the second and fourth divisions at $2,100. Local districts could pay higher salaries, but state reimbursement was based on the established minimums.

In 1946, legislation established a superintendents salary scale by divisions: in the first, $3,000 to $4,000; in the third, $3,300 to $4,300; in the second and fourth, $3,500 to $4,500. By 1957, an act was passed providing for the setting of salaries, qualifications, and numbers of teachers, principals, vice-principals, head-teachers, teachers-in-charge, and superintendents allowed to schools in the territory. Salary scales were set for 3 years' training, a bachelor's degree, and a master's degree. The department was allowed to pay salaries above the scale. In 1961, the department was directed to pay a salary not less than $500 above the scale.

The state minimum scale was changed to an index system in 1963, with yearly increments of 0.04 percent. Superintendents' salaries were set at 20 percent above teacher scales in schools with an average daily membership of less than 500 and at 25 percent for 500 or more. Principals drew 15 percent above base, and vice-principals 10 percent.

Retirement. A retirement system for Alaskan teachers was first established in 1929 although it was repealed 4 years later when it was found to be actuarially unsound. Reactivated in 1945, it was subsequently changed several times. At present, benefits are computed on an average of the highest 3 years of salary earned within the last 10 years prior to leaving service. A 10 percent cost of living is added if a retired teacher resides in Alaska. A disability provision and survivor's benefit are included in the plan.

The commissioner of administration is responsible for the administration of the retirement system, with an advisory board meeting annually to review investments of the fund.

Tenure. Although a form of tenure existed earlier, a law passed in 1960 granted tenure to those who had been employed 2 years or more in a school system and were holders of standard teaching certificates; it specifically excluded all temporary certificates. Causes for nonretention were listed as incompetency, immorality, or substantial noncompliance with school laws of the state, regulations of the department, or other governmental agency. Necessary reduction of staff occasioned by a decrease in school attendance also could warrant nonretention. In any of these instances hearings were to be provided within 10 days if requested.

Contracts could be issued at any time after January 1, but teachers were required to be notified of nonretention in writing, on or before March 15. The section on notification was added by the 1957 Legislature. In 1965, tenure was further defined, and a section was added providing that such rights could be forfeited upon transfer from a district. Approved leaves of absence were not considered a break in service for tenure or retirement purposes.

Sabbatical Leave. There have been several variations in the sabbatical leave laws passed by the Legislature, primarily in the numbers of teachers who could be on leave at any one time. In 1962, eight leaves at state expense were authorized, and the department was directed to develop rules and regulations for selecting participants. A teacher was eligible to apply for leave after 7 consecutive years of service to a single district and, if selected, receive half his base salary. A proviso was included requiring a teacher to serve at least 1 full year after his return, unless his inability to complete the year was attributable to sickness, injury, or death.

A teacher must submit information regarding his qualifications and educational plans to be eligible. Only one year is allowable, and it may be approved for educational purposes only.

Right To Criticize. An act prohibiting restriction on the right of a teacher to comment or criticize public officials and employees was passed in 1965. Thus, a teacher has the right to engage in comment and criticism, outside school hours, of school administrators, members of the governing body of the district or any other public official, or any school employee.

GROUPS AND INDIVIDUALS INFLUENTIAL IN EDUCATIONAL CHANGE

Three groups will be discussed in this section: the Department of Education, including commissioners and their Superintendents' Advisory Commission; the Alaska Education Association; and the Alaska School Boards Association.

Comments from those who were district superintendents during the 1940's and 1950's indicate that these groups worked well together in those years. It is probably due to this spirit of cooperation that the era produced much significant legislation.

Individual legislators, powerful in their own right and interested in education, have contributed a measure of influence on educational legislation. However, lack of documentation makes it difficult to establish the degree of such influence.

The Department of Education and the Superintendents' Advisory Commission

As the commissioner's staff has grown through the years, he has had access to more and more professional advice in specific areas of education. Perhaps the most important source of aid, however, has been obtained through judicious use of advisory groups, particularly the Superintendents' Advisory Commission. It appears that the most productive periods, in terms of educational advance through legislation, occurred when the office of the commissioner was filled by strong individuals, who in turn made wide use of the advisory commission; and there was a high degree of cooperation between these and the State or Territorial Board of Education. When these efforts converged, a greater degree of unity was apparent to legislators, who then became more amenable to changes in educational legislation.

Two names were presented to the writer by interviewers as being the strongest commissioners from 1917 to present: James C. Ryan, who is credited as the initiator of the advisory commission and who later moved to the superintendency at Fairbanks; and Don M. Dafoe, who assumed the office after service at Anchorage and later returned there as superintendent. All persons interviewed indicated that these two made most effective use of the advisory commission and thus involved more people in the process of educational change.

Also among those reported as influential through the 1940's, 1950's, and into the 1960's were Theron J. Cole of Sitka, Sterling Sears of Juneau (now at Kenai), Lester Wingard at Petersburg, A. W. Morgan of Anchorage, and J. E. Danielson of Ketchikan.

L. R. Joy of Fairbanks and Keith Lesh of Anchorage were pointed out as having been influential members of the Alaska School Boards Association. Both served as board members over a period of many years and were members of the White House Conference on Education in 1956.

The State Activities Association also provided opportunities for meetings of administrators. Athletic events, music festivals, or some other activity where students were involved in sponsored travel usually offered an opportunity to get together. Since such travel was costly in terms of school time and money, administrators usually took full advantage of it to hold their meetings. Individual superintendents became somewhat influential due to their holding officerships in the Activities group.

The Alaska Education Association

The association began its activities in 1922 and endorsed national legislation in 1924-25 calling for a cabinet post in education at the federal level as well as federal aid to education. These two points were within the program of the National Education Association, with which the AEA became affiliated. The meetings of the AEA were generally held in conjunction with the teacher institutes until 1926, when the latter were discontinued. Thereafter, meetings were scattered and poorly attended due to the cost and difficulty of travel until the middle 1950's (18).

In 1941, when George V. Beck and Lester L. Wingard were elected president and secretary-treasurer, respectively, a policy was begun which has continued to the present—that both officers be from the same locality so that each could reinforce the other. Slow mail service and travel problems enhanced the arrangement.

Commencing in 1939, the AEA has worked primarily for legislation in two teacher benefit areas: salary increases and a strong retirement program. These were first presented to the Legislature in 1941. Although not successful, they marked the first active effort on the part of the AEA to influence legislation. The names of Beck, Wingard, Ryan, Marjorie Tillotson of Juneau, and A. B. Phillips, superintendent at Juneau, were especially influential in the education of legislators relative to the need for strong programs in the two areas.

Following these first efforts, the leadership of the AEA has been very active in securing changes in the retirement program, salary increases, provision of adequate funds for support of territorial and state schools, fiscal independence for school boards, activation and reactivation of the vocational education program, provisions for a stronger professional organization, and provisions for protection of the state department from political influence.

From 1922 to 1950, the AEA officers were school administrators and were probably more effective due to the combination of offices with those positions on the Superintendents' Advisory Commission. One person interviewed indicated that superintendents (until the 1950's) and the commissioner saw themselves as responsible for teacher welfare programs. With the growth of the AEA, this function was assumed by that group, and leadership in the organization was gradually taken over by teachers. The 1950 election of Marjorie Tillotson, a classroom teacher from Juneau, as president marked the transfer of power from administrator-officers to teacher-officers.

When Everett R. Erickson became commissioner in 1951, he requested the removal of the position from the executive committee of the AEA, reasoning that a conflict of interest was possible should the Board of Education and the association disagree.

By the later 1950's, the AEA became capable of supporting an executive secretary and formulating a legislative program acceptable to its membership. Prior to this time only a few members had carried on the work, but with the establishment of the delegate assembly in 1956 (the last such representative group to be established in the various states and territories), the working basis was broadened to include teacher representatives from the various communities throughout Alaska.

John M. Poling was appointed the first executive secretary and took up his duties in 1957. He was followed in office by Haze Bergeron, Frank Darnell, and Robert Van Houte, the latter still serving.

The Alaska School Boards Association

This association appears to have been gaining in influence over the past few years. Organized in 1954-55, the group early provided moral support as it worked with the commissioners and the Superintendents' Advisory Commission. Some interviewers expressed the opinion that the ASBA could be much more influential if, following their meetings, individual members would work more closely with their area legislators. However, it was also pointed out that the main strength lay in being an organized body.

FOOTNOTES

1. The terms of office and the names of the various commissioners are set forth in Appendix A.
2. See Appendix B, Chart I, for organization by 1935-36.
3. See Appendix B, Chart II, for organization by 1945-46.
4. See Appendix B, Chart III, for organization by 1951-52.
5. See Appendix B, Chart IV, for organization by 1957-58.
6. For graphic presentation of the organizational structure of the department from 1959 to 1966, see Appendix B, Charts V, VI, and VII.
7. A fourth major change was made by the 1967 Legislature when it created a Board of Education of seven members to head the department. As mentioned above, the commissioner had been responsible for initiating rules and regulations in accordance with the political belief that a strong central administration should control each department. With the advent of the new board structure, control over approval of the rules and regulations and the appointment of the commissioner will lie with the board. The Governor will appoint the board members, with approving authority over the board's choice for commissioner. Terms of office for members will be 5 years, overlapping; one member will be from each of the four judicial districts; the board selects its own chairman; all members serve at the pleasure of the Governor. See Appendix B, Chart VIII.
8. Chart VII, Appendix B, indicates the reorganization of April 1966, completed in conjunction with these statements. That effort resulted in the addition of more personnel to provide consultative services, an emphasis on curriculum development and revision, and the setting out of the division of state-operated schools as a third major division of the commissioner's staff. It effectively divided the three functions and provided the balanced concept discussed previously.
9. See Appendix C, Table 1, for a chart of the multiagency educational system in Alaska.
10. Also see Appendix C, Table 1, for a comparison of the student enrollments, sources of funding, and numbers of schools in the various types of schools.
11. See Appendix C, Table 2, for a statistical comparison of the various types of schools in a cost and growth summary.
12. Charles K. Ray, *A Program of Education for Alaskan Natives* (College: University of Alaska Press, 1959), p. 269.
13. Alaska's *Session Laws* (1961), ch. 146.
14. Legislation in 1966 included kindergarten in the program.
15. See Appendix C, Tables 3 and 4, for comparison of federal-state fund sources and expenditures.
16. Revision of the Education Code commenced in 1957 and culminated in passage of a revised Title 14 in the 1966 legislative session.
17. Under the revised Education Code of 1966, districts were freed to choose their own textbooks, and the commission adoptions were for state-operated schools only.
18. Hollis P. Harrison, "A Historical Study of the Alaska Education Association" (unpublished master's thesis, University of Alaska, 1962). This thesis is an excellent source of material.

BIBLIOGRAPHY

Public Documents

Alaska. *Constitution* (1959).

——*Session Laws* (1961).

Books

Andrews, C. L. *The Story of Alaska.* Caldwell, Idaho: The Caxton Printers, Ltd., 1942.

Gruening, Ernest Henry. *The State of Alaska.* New York: Random House, 1954.

Hulley, Clarence. *Alaska: Past and Present.* Portland, Oreg.: Binfords and Mort, 1958.

Nichols, Jeannette Paddock. *Alaska.* New York: Russell and Russell, 1963.

Ray, Charles K. *A Program of Education for Alaskan Natives.* College: University of Alaska, 1959.

Reports

Commissioners of Education. *Biennial Reports.* Juneau: Department of Education, 1920-62.

Department of Education. *Alaska Educational Directory.* Juneau: The Department, 1961-65.

Lindman, Erick L. *A Foundation for Alaska's Public Schools.* Juneau: Alaska State Board of Education, 1961.

Ray, Charles K. *Report of Alaska White House Conference on Education.* Juneau: Alaska Committee, White House Conference on Education, 1956.

Cummiskey, J. K., and Garcia, J. D. *State of Alaska Regional Secondary School Systems.* Falls Church, Va: Training Corporation of America, 1967.

Unpublished Material

Dafoe, Don M. "Some Problems in the Education of Native Peoples in Alaska," Stanford University, June 1959.

Harrison, Hollis P. "A Historical Study of the Alaska Education Association." Unpublished master's thesis, University of Alaska, College, 1962.

Appendix A

ALASKA CHIEF STATE SCHOOL OFFICERS

1917-29	Lester D. Henderson	1953-59	Don M. Dafoe
1929-31	Leo W. Breuer	1959	Howard A. Matthews (Apr.–Oct.)
1931-33	William K. Keller	1959-62	Theo J. Norby
1933-40	Anthony E. Karnes	1962-63	Robert P. Isaac (acting)
1941-51	James C. Ryan	1963-67	William T. Zahradnicek
1951-53	Everett R. Erickson	1967-	Clifford R. Hartman

Appendix B

Chart I.--ALASKA DEPARTMENT OF EDUCATION, 1935-36

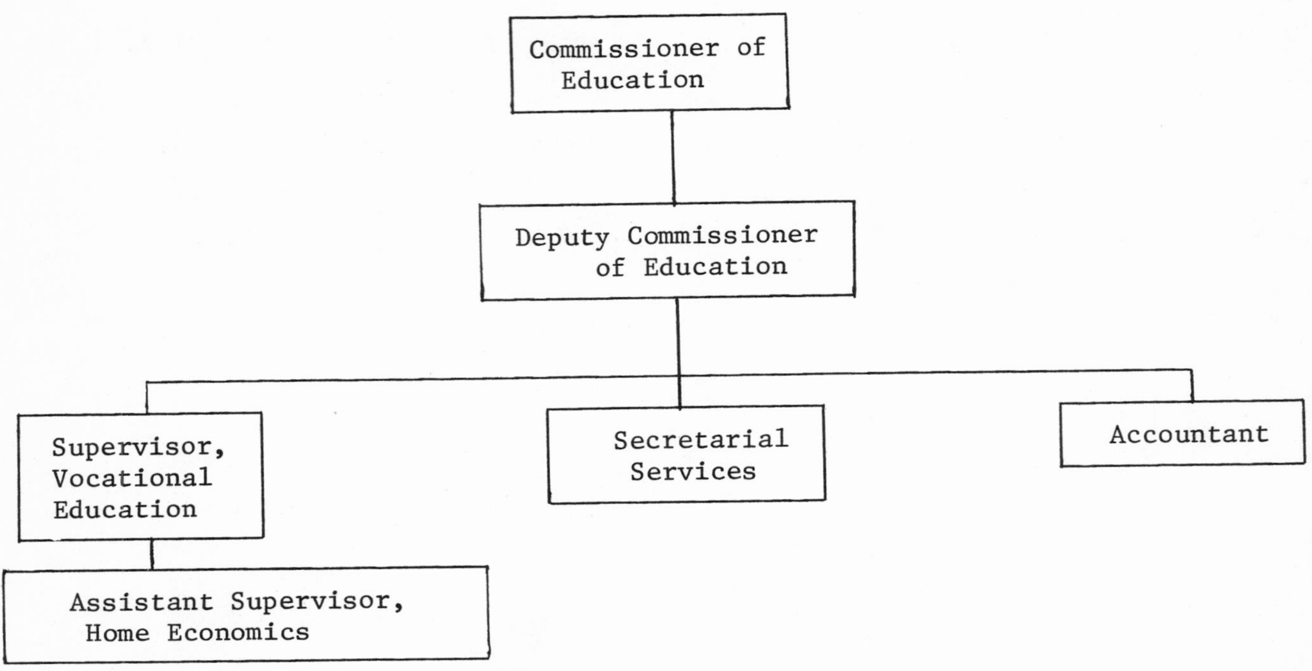

Source: Commissioner's Report, 1936.

Chart II.--ALASKA DEPARTMENT OF EDUCATION, 1945-46

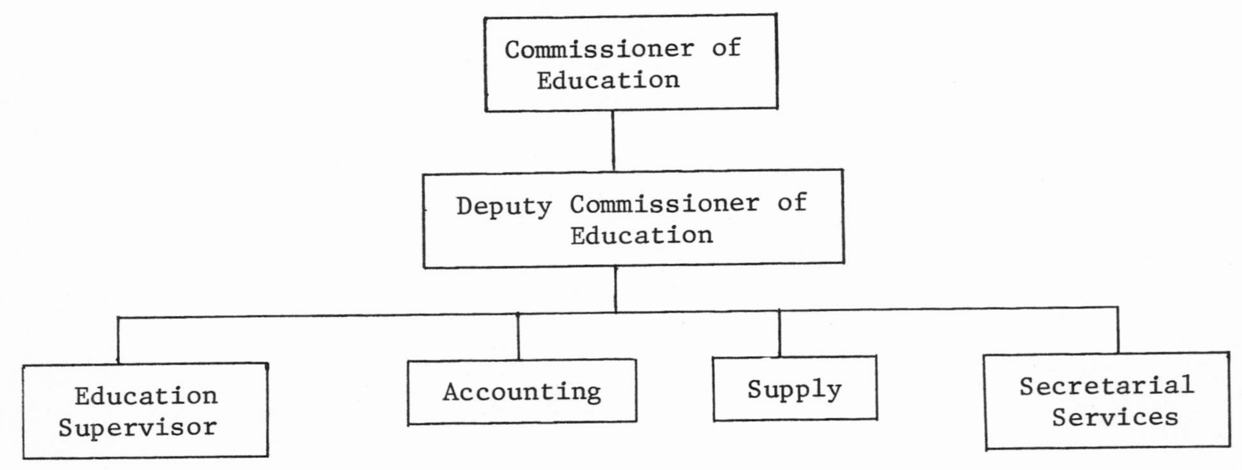

Source: Commissioner's Report, 1946.

Appendix B

Chart III.--ALASKA DEPARTMENT OF EDUCATION, 1951-52

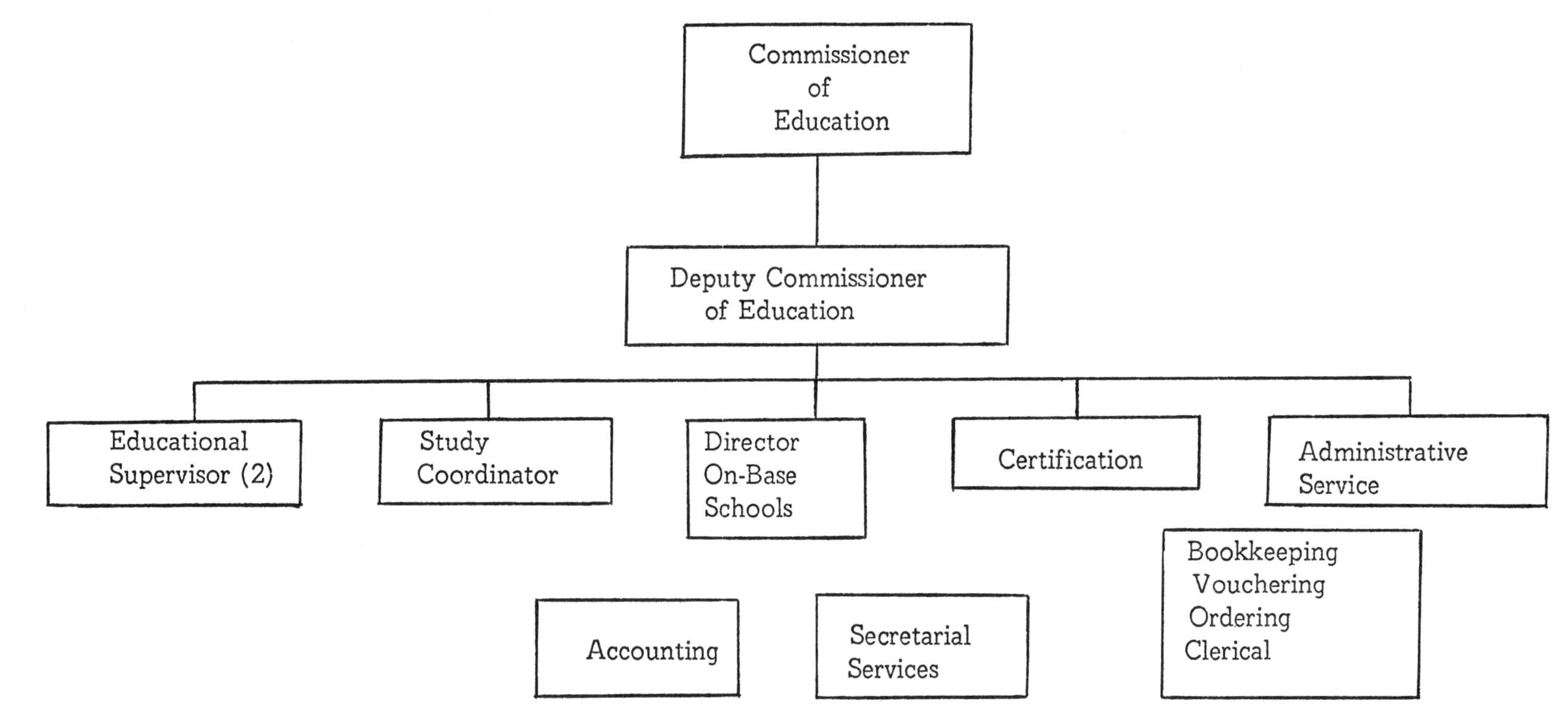

Source: Commissioner's Report, 1952.

Appendix B

Chart IV.--ALASKA DEPARTMENT OF EDUCATION, 1957-58

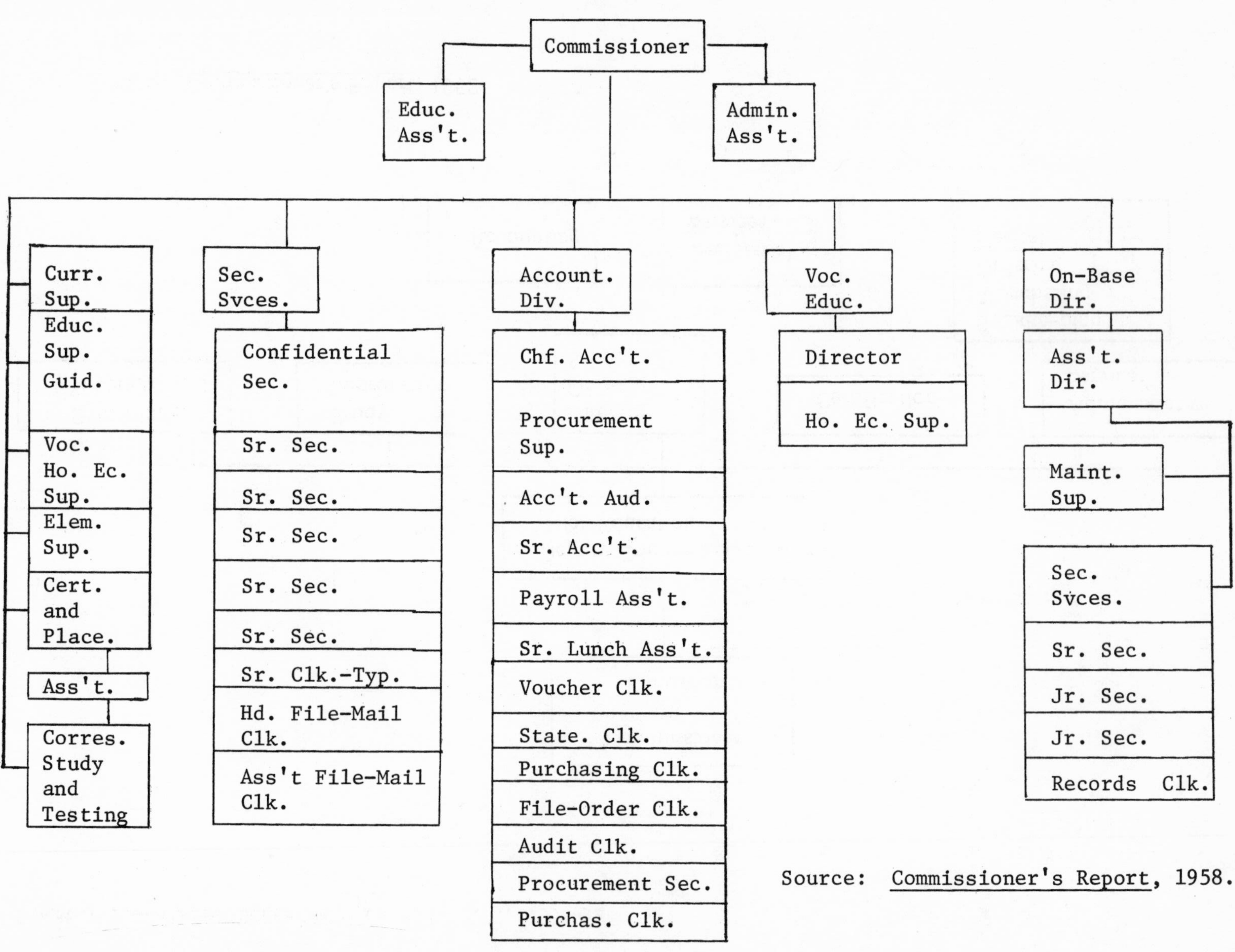

Source: Commissioner's Report, 1958.

Appendix B

Chart V.--ALASKA DEPARTMENT OF EDUCATION, 1959-60

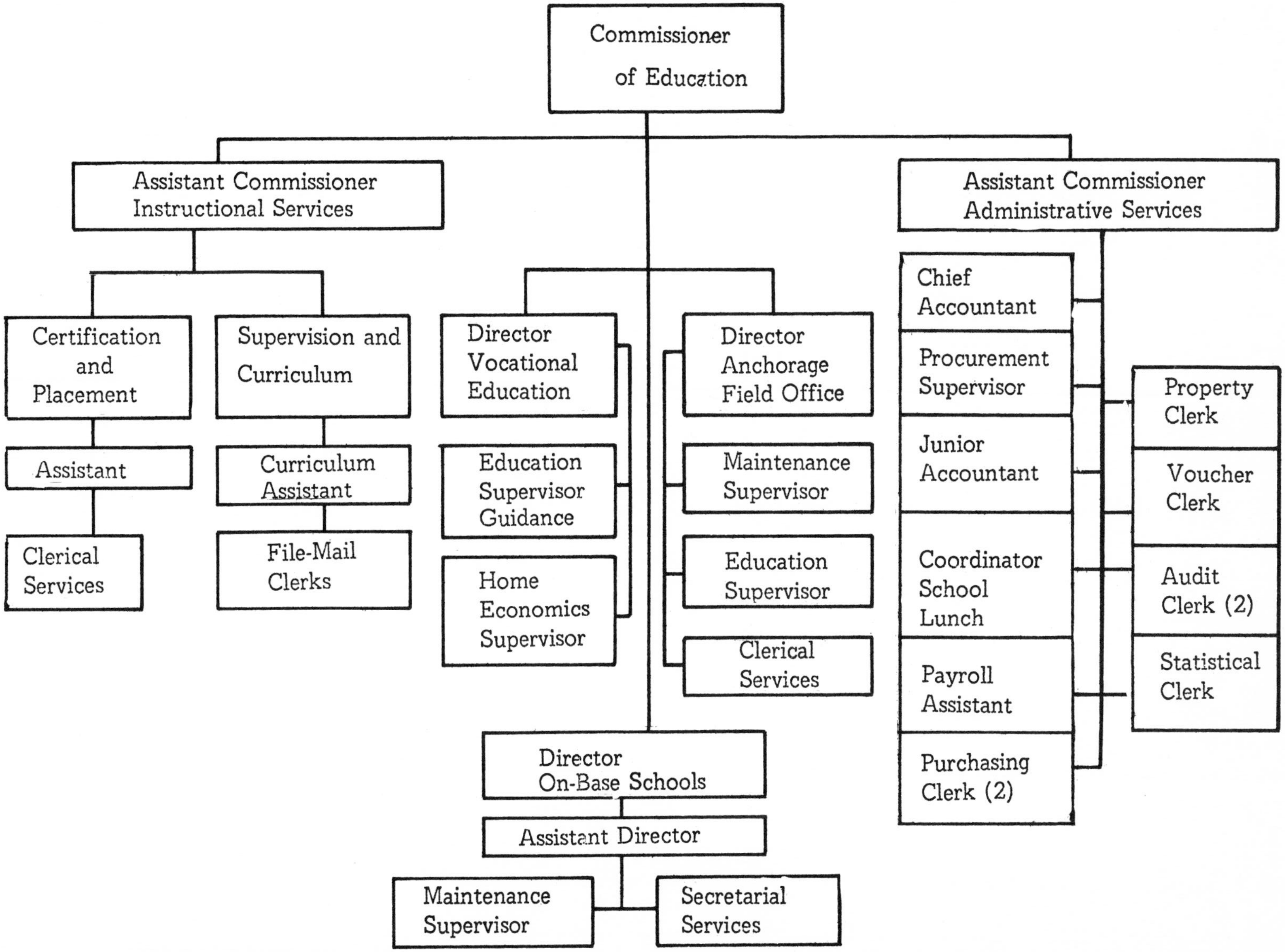

Commissioner of Education

Assistant Commissioner Instructional Services

Certification and Placement

Assistant

Clerical Services

Supervision and Curriculum

Curriculum Assistant

File-Mail Clerks

Director Vocational Education

Education Supervisor Guidance

Home Economics Supervisor

Director Anchorage Field Office

Maintenance Supervisor

Education Supervisor

Clerical Services

Director On-Base Schools

Assistant Director

Maintenance Supervisor

Secretarial Services

Assistant Commissioner Administrative Services

Chief Accountant

Procurement Supervisor

Junior Accountant

Coordinator School Lunch

Payroll Assistant

Purchasing Clerk (2)

Property Clerk

Voucher Clerk

Audit Clerk (2)

Statistical Clerk

Source: Commissioner's Report, 1960.

Appendix B

Chart VI.--ALASKA DEPARTMENT OF EDUCATION, 1964

Governor
Textbook Commission
Certif. Committee
Curriculum Committee
Board of Education
Board For Voc. Ed.
Board For Voc. Rehabilitation
Supt. Advisory Commission
Advisory Committee Voc. Ed.
Commissioner of Education
Executive Officer Board of Education
Executive Officer Board of Vocational Ed.
Curriculum Development
Special Education
Educational Materials: Audio-Visual Ed.
Teacher Certification
Civil Defense Education
Extension Services
Textbook Adoption (Textbook Commission)
Testing and Guidance
School Accreditation and Approval
Supervision of Schools
Assistant Commissioner Division of Instructional Services
Assistant Commissioner Division of Administrative Services
State and District Budget Analysis and Management
P. L. 815-874 Administration
School Design and Construction
Record Management
Legislative Research
Departmental Business Services (Accounting, Purchasing, Property Accounting, Audit Serv.)
School Bus Transportation
Administrative Assistant
Alaska On-Base Schools Director
Alaska Rural Schools Director
Library Services Director
Alaska State Museum Curator
Vocational Rehabilitation Director Executive Officer of Bd.
Vocational Ed. Director
Boroughs:
Greater Sitka
Greater Juneau
Election Dist. #7 (Palmer)
Election Dist. #8 (Anchorage)
Election Dists. #9-10 (Kenai)
Kodiak Island
Gateway (Ketchikan)
Fairbanks
Bristol Bay
Cities:
Cordova
Craig
Hoonah
Hydaburg
Kake
King Cove
Klawock
Nenana
Nome
North Pole
Pelican
Petersburg
Skagway
Unalaska
Wrangell
Yakutat
Independent School District : Haines

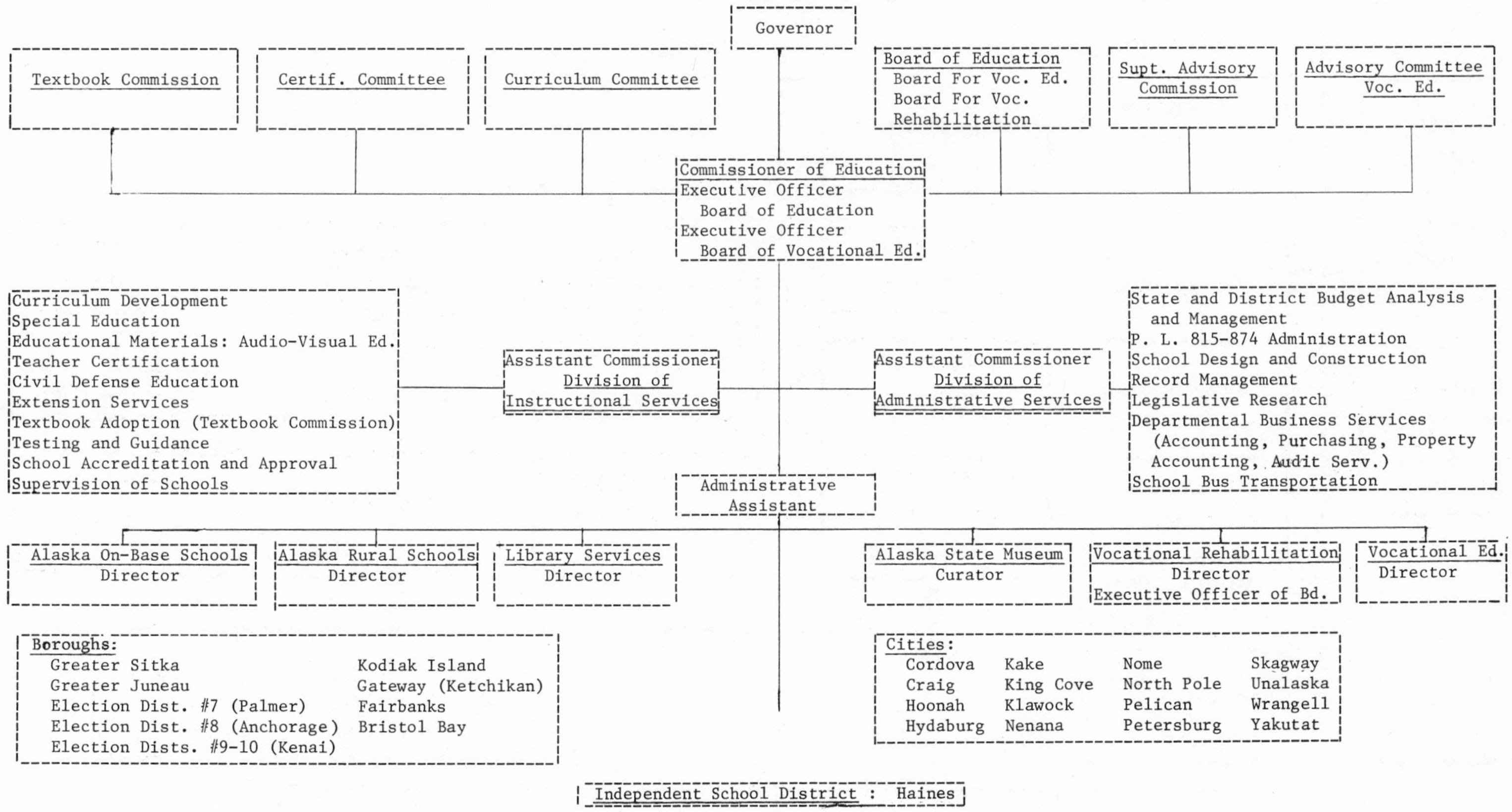

Source: Commissioner's Report, 1964, and existing Chart.

Appendix B

Chart VII.--ALASKA "LEVELS OF ORGANIZATION" CONCEPTS, 1966

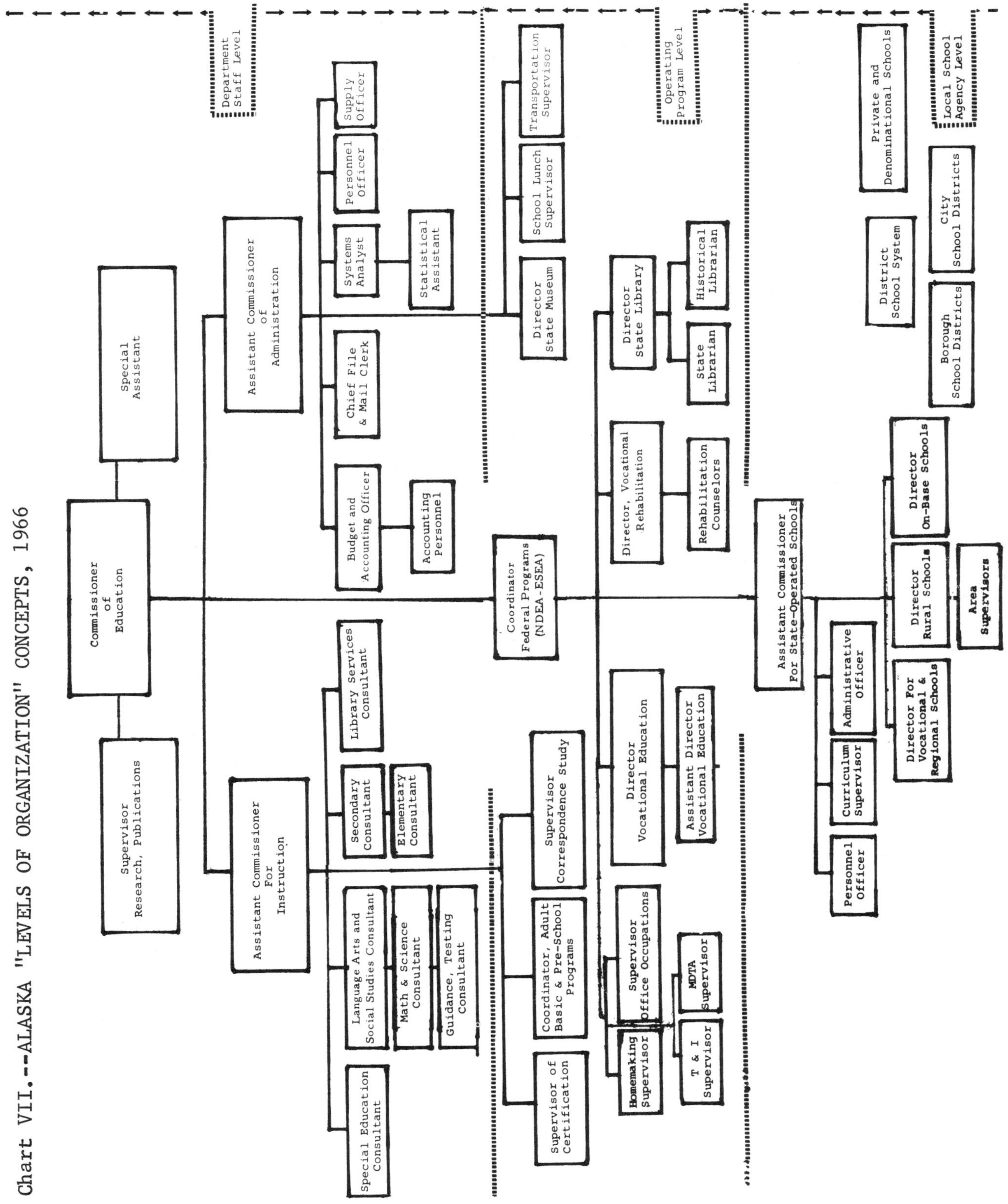

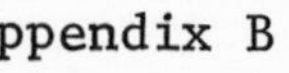

Appendix B

Chart VIII.--ALASKA DEPARTMENT OF EDUCATION, 1968

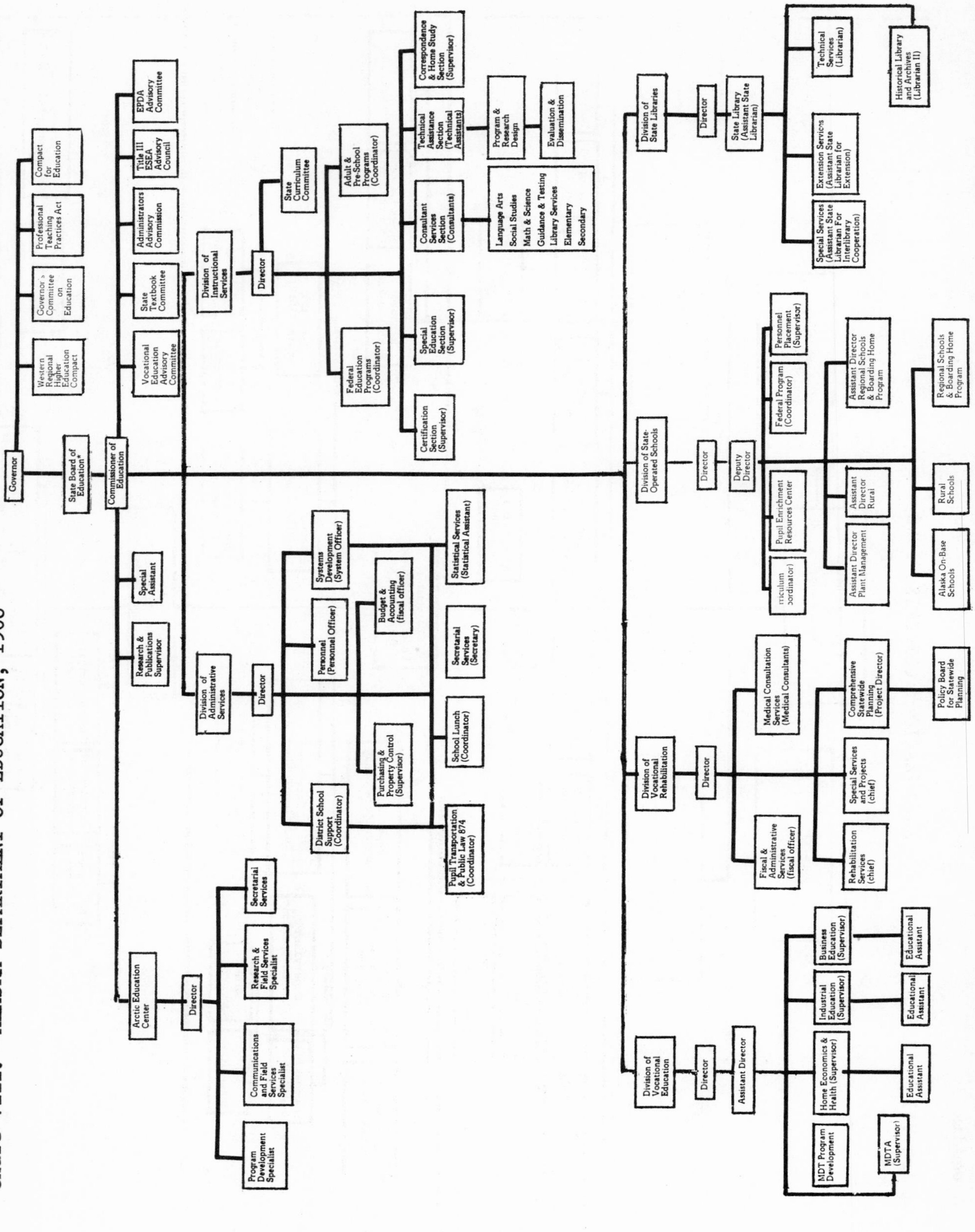

Governor
Western Regional Higher Education Compact
Governor's Committee on Education
Professional Teaching Practices Act
Compact for Education
State Board of Education*
Commissioner of Education
Arctic Education Center
Research & Publications Supervisor
Special Assistant
Vocational Education Advisory Committee
State Textbook Committee
Administrators Advisory Commission
Title III ESEA Advisory Council
EPDA Advisory Committee
Director
Program Development Specialist
Communications and Field Services Specialist
Research & Field Services Specialist
Secretarial Services
Division of Administrative Services
Director
District School Support (Coordinator)
Personnel (Personnel Officer)
Systems Development (System Officer)
Purchasing & Property Control (Supervisor)
Budget & Accounting (fiscal officer)
Pupil Transportation & Public Law 874 (Coordinator)
School Lunch (Coordinator)
Secretarial Services (Secretary)
Statistical Services (Statistical Assistant)
Division of Instructional Services
Director
State Curriculum Committee
Federal Education Programs (Coordinator)
Adult & Pre-School Programs (Coordinator)
Certification Section (Supervisor)
Special Education Section (Supervisor)
Consultant Services Section (Consultants)
Technical Assistance Section (Technical Assistants)
Correspondence & Home Study Section (Supervisor)
Language Arts
Social Studies
Math & Science
Guidance & Testing
Library Services
Elementary
Secondary
Program & Research Design
Evaluation & Dissemination
Division of Vocational Education
Director
Assistant Director
MDT Program Development
Home Economics & Health (Supervisor)
Industrial Education (Supervisor)
Business Education (Supervisor)
MDTA (Supervisor)
Educational Assistant
Educational Assistant
Educational Assistant
Division of Vocational Rehabilitation
Director
Fiscal & Administrative Services (fiscal officer)
Medical Consultation Services (Medical Consultants)
Rehabilitation Services (chief)
Special Services and Projects (chief)
Comprehensive Statewide Planning (Project Director)
Policy Board for Statewide Planning
Division of State-Operated Schools
Director
Deputy Director
rriculum ordinator)
Pupil Enrichment Resources Center
Federal Program (Coordinator)
Personnel Placement (Supervisor)
Assistant Director Plant Management
Assistant Director Rural
Assistant Director Regional Schools & Boarding Home Program
Alaska On-Base Schools
Rural Schools
Regional Schools & Boarding Home Program
Division of State Libraries
Director
State Library (Assistant State Librarian)
Special Services (Assistant State Librarian For Interlibrary Cooperation)
Extension Services (Assistant State Librarian for Extension)
Technical Services (Librarian)
Historical Library and Archives (Librarian II)

Appendix C

Table 1.—ALASKA SCHOOL SYSTEM STRUCTURE, SPRING 1966

Type of school	Number of schools	Number of pupils	Source of income	Source of supervision and administration
Borough and city school districts	30	45,503 (20,408 in Anchorage)	Local, state, federal	Local: Includes incorporated cities and boroughs
On-base schools: Eielson, Fort Richardson, Elmendorf, Fort Wainwright, Adak, Kodiak, Fort Greely, Whittier	8	10,328	Supported by federal and state funds approved by Legislature	State Department of Education: high schools on Adak, Fort Greely, and Eielson
State-operated rural schools; established for minimum of 10 pupils	73	3,979	Supported by state and federal funds approved by Legislature	State Department of Education: includes "Gildersleeve," a school on a raft, movable, operational, very expensive; commissioner is acting director
Johnson-O'Malley	13	356	U.S. Government federal funds under J.O.M. contract	State Department of Education, formerly BIA
Bureau of Indian Affairs (BIA)		6,880	Department of Interior	U.S. Government "teacher," also radio operator, nurse, troubleshooter
Day	80			
Boarding	2			
Fish and Wildlife	2	143	Bureau of Federal Fisheries	State Department of Education Pribilof Islands, including St. George and St. Paul
Private and denominational	28[a] registered	2,439	Private funds	Especially Seventh Day Adventist and Roman Catholic; unregistered may have substandard teachers

Source:

Alaska Department of Education, Statistical Services.

[a]Registered are with standard equipment and teachers.

Appendix C

Table 2.–GROWTH OF SCHOOLS IN ALASKA, 1917-66

Year	Schools	Professional workers	Total enrollment	Expense exclusive of capital outlay and debt service	Cost per pupil enrolled	ADA	Cost per pupil ADA
			City and district schools				
1917-18	18	87	2,161	172,858	79.98	1,696	101.92
1920-21	17	101	2,286	241,961	105.84	1,813	133.45
1930-31	17	163	3,613	385,170	106.60	3,074	125.29
1940-41	18	208	5,054	573,032	113.38	4,051	141.45
1950-51	26	516	12,658	3,025,426	239.01	9,639	313.87
1960-61	29	1,437	34,399	15,016,988	436.55	29,299	512.54
1965-66	27	2,132	53,872	31,219,445	579.51	42,677	731.70
			Schools outside incorporated towns and districts				
1917-18	46	58	1,180	92,350	78.26	905	102.04
1920-21	51	64	1,186	127,976	107.90	917	139.55
1930-31	64	88	1,642	195,484	119.05	1,351	144.69
1940-41	48	98	1,699	198,711	116.95	1,358	146.32
1950-51	62	110	1,969	509,237	258.62	1,527	333.48
1960-61	113	316	6,115	2,876,661	470.42	5,317	541.03
1965-66	86	240	5,071	3,907,770	770.61	4,019	972.32
			On-base schools				
1946-47	4	7	158	28,222	178.62	114	247.56
1950-51	6	43	1,179	175,767	149.08	892	197.04
1960-61	9	339	8,766	2,990,324	341.12	7,624	392.22
1965-66	8	453	11,978	5,920,349	494.26	9,819	602.95

Source:

Alaska Department of Education, Statistical Services.

Appendix C

Table 3.—FEDERAL CONTRIBUTIONS TO EDUCATION IN ALASKA, 1949-67

Year	P.L. 874	Vocational education	Vocational rehabilitation	School lunch	Civil Defense	Adult education	NDEA	ESEA
1949-50	Law not in effect until 1951	NA	...	11,684	...	...	...	...
1954-55	NA 1951-59 receipts totaled 20,093,427	19,539	39,900	30,612	...	...	...	...
1959-60	5,836,702	90,805	125,451	71,406	...	...	...	...
1960-61	6,469,113	85,470	120,049	113,758	...	...	126,653	...
1961-62	7,464,254	155,411	140,975	121,670	7,222	...	87,455	...
1962-63	8,344,864	194,865	149,246	123,467	19,507	...	117,807	...
1963-64	9,535,918	397,194	204,298	139,692	20,617	...	119,066	...
1964-65	9,320,606	992,947	300,354	161,104	11,833	...	209,795	...
1965-66	10,618,955	1,732,512	426,935	176,212	18,369	28,396	174,529	1,610,222
1966-67	11,907,725	695,047	480,362	200,878	...	40,078	223,386	2,058,300

Table 4.—RELATIONSHIP OF FEDERAL-STATE FUNDS FOR EDUCATION IN ALASKA, 1949-67

Year	Total of federal funds from preceding table	State-local expenditures beyond federal contributions	Total expenditure for education in Alaska	Percent of federal contribution of total expended
1949-50	61,684 (Includes $50,000 from "Alaska Fund")	3,064,724	3,126,408	1.97%
1954-55	90,051[a]	10,165,784	10,255,835	.88
1959-60	6,124,364	13,688,522	19,812,886	30.91
1960-61	6,915,043	14,038,269	20,953,312	33.00
1961-62	7,976,987	16,902,919	24,879,906	32.06
1962-63	8,949,756	19,480,329	28,430,085	31.48
1963-64	10,416,785	21,815,353	32,232,138	32.31
1964-65	10,996,639	26,049,772	37,046,411	29.68
1965-66	14,786,130	26,928,356	41,714,486	35.44
1966-67	15,605,776	...	...	...

[a]P.L. 874 contribution not available.

3 Arizona

DEPARTMENT OF EDUCATION
John E. Sinclair

Contents

ARIZONA TERRITORIAL EDUCATION

Public education in Arizona first received formal attention in 1864, when Governor John N. Goodwin apprised the first Legislative Assembly of the importance of providing for public elementary, secondary, and college education. However, the problems of a post-Civil War period, ravaging Indian attacks, and organization for a vast, sparsely settled area being foremost in the minds of the legislators, they decided that it was not yet time to establish a system of schools for the territory. Still, appropriations were made for education grants of $250 each to the towns of Prescott, Mohave, and La Paz. A $500 grant was provided for Tuscon, and $250 was pledged to the San Xavier Mission School "as a fitting compliment to the first school opened in Arizona" (1). In order to receive the funds as provided, the towns were required to raise an equal amount. It was further stipulated for the Tucson grant that English was to be the language used for instruction.

Unfortunately, this first legislation offered little motivation for the establishment of public schools, and Prescott was the only town to take advantage of the grant. The 1867 Assembly made provisions for towns to establish tax-supported schools, but no real progress in public education was accomplished until 1871, when Governor Anson Peacely Killen Safford, "The Father of Arizona's Public Schools" (2), began his dedicated effort to establish a system of schools.

Safford was a warm and humane person, a thinker, a statesman, and a gentleman. Born in New England, he grew up in Illinois under impoverished conditions and went to California during the Gold Rush. There he worked in mining camps and began a political career when he was elected to the California Legislature at the age of 26. After spending some time in Nevada, both in business and politics, Safford was appointed by President Grant as Governor of the Arizona Territory in 1869.

The situation in Arizona at the time demanded a strong administrator. Civil officers were neglecting their duties; citizens were refusing to pay taxes; it was claimed that the Legislature just previous to Safford's coming was illegally convened; the Apaches were on the rampage; and the territory had no public schools.

Safford's personal education having been mainly self-acquired, he particularly sensed the need for a public school system. Finding that little effort had been given to organizing educational opportunities for the nearly 2,000 school-age children then residing in the territory, he set about to secure enactment of school legislation by the 1871 Territorial Legislative Assembly.

Safford drafted a bill that proposed territorial and county cooperation in the support of public schools. This bill, approved as presented except for some of the important fiscal clauses, created a framework within which Safford could begin an organizational program on a territory-wide basis.

The 1871 school law made provision for a territorial superintendent of public instruction, which position the Governor served ex officio. A Territorial Board of Education, composed of the superintendent, the territorial treasurer, and the secretary of the territory, was created to serve as the highest authority in implementing the law. Since the Governor appointed the treasurer of the territory and the probate judges who served as ex officio county superintendents, Safford indirectly had complete control of school matters. Because of his extreme dedication to education, this arrangement proved to be most advantageous during the time he was attempting to organize schools.

The 1871 law also prescribed some of the duties of the superintendent and levied a territorial tax of 10¢ per $100 of assessed valuation. The proceeds of this tax were to be apportioned first to the schools through the counties according to the number of resident children between the ages of 6 and 21 and subsequently distributed on the basis of attendance. The duties of the superintendent were to prescribe forms and registers, appoint boards of examiners to test applicants for teacher's certificates, provide a budget estimate detailing anticipated revenues from the territorial fund, visit each county, and prescribe and cause to be adopted a uniform series of texts.

Local control of education was vested in boards of trustees to serve as bodies corporate. A county tax levy of 50¢ per $100 of assessed valuation for the support of schools, a school census, and a minimum school term of 3 months per year were requirements made on the local agency. The intent to provide a nonsectarian education was clearly set forth: no tracts, papers, or instruction of a religious nature were to be used in the schools, and no public funds were to go to schools organized for religious purposes. This stipulation seems especially noteworthy in view of the fact that the territory's first act of support of schools was a grant to the San Xavier Mission School. But the battle to keep the public schools free from sectarian influence was not over. Safford and other officials were to again be confronted with the issue in 1875.

Safford was not paid for his work as superintendent, but a small appropriation of $500 for expenses was provided. Notwithstanding the lack of financial support, he traveled extensively to discuss education with citizens throughout the territory. In performing what today would be called public relations, he promoted widespread enthusiasm for schools among citizens. As a result, schools were established, legislators became conscious of popular support for education, and later legislative sessions worked in a climate conducive to progress.

In 1873, the Legislature considerably increased fiscal support for education. The new legislation provided for a territorial tax of 25¢ per $100 of assessed valuation and a uniform county tax of the same amount. Safford apparently was pleased that schools would have adequate financial backing; but he could hardly have been heartened by the repeal of parts of the 1871 law which stipulated that territorial funds would be distributed, after the first apportionment, on the basis of attendance.

Even after 4 years of administering the government and schools of the new territory, Safford continued to hold education in the most prominent position. His recommendations for strengthening the school laws were more closely followed by the 1875 Legislature. This assembly again apportioned school funds on the basis of attendance beginning in 1876, enacted a compulsory attendance law, returned authority for textbook adoption to the superintendent's office, and established easier procedures for creating or changing school districts.

The 1875 Legislature was also the scene of a struggle to provide funds for parochial schools. That Safford was successful in thwarting this movement is an example of his influence on this Legislature. The forces to be met were strong. Many prominent settlers were in sympathy with the movement; the population of the territory was then about three-fifths Mexican, and the Catholic Church itself was exerting its power. Although the issue was great, its settlement in that session ended the vigorous activities of sectarian groups seeking control of public education.

Not the least of Safford's many contributions to Arizona's early schools was his effort to secure good teachers. He made attempts to recruit competent female teachers. Although he was briefly successful, the bride shortage much impeded his teacher-recruitment endeavor. Two men of the profession who came to Arizona during Safford's tenure were W. B. Horton and Moses H. Sherman, each of whom later served as superintendent of public instruction. Sherman came from Vermont in 1873 to head the school at Prescott, and Horton arrived in 1875 to serve as principal of the Tucson public school. Both towns were then the leaders in developing schools.

Secretary of the Territory John P. Hoyt became Acting Governor in 1877 on the resignation of Governor Safford. Hoyt had little time to fulfill the duties of superintendent, and neither he nor the next Governor, John C. Frémont, gave much attention to education. The chief contribution of Frémont was his appointment of Moses Sherman to serve as superintendent beginning in 1878 (3). By such action, coordination of territorial schools became the responsibility of a professional educator. Although Sherman remained in his post with the Prescott schools throughout most of his tenure as superintendent and was thus unable to give as much of his time as might have been desired, his appointment to some degree filled the void created by Governor Safford's resignation.

The 1879 Legislative Assembly enacted a new school law which separated the positions of Governor and superintendent of public instruction. The superintendent was to be appointed by the Governor for a 2-year term beginning in 1879 and was to be elected in 1880 for a term beginning in 1881. The composition of the Territorial Board of Education was changed so that the Governor, the superintendent, and the territorial treasurer were members, and the superintendent was president and secretary of the board.

Sherman was reappointed by Governor Frémont for the term 1879-81 and was subsequently elected for another 2-year period. During his tenure the schools were growing rapidly and needed greater fiscal support. The Legislature gave some consideration to the problems of school finance in 1879 but developed no real solutions. A new law did place more support of schools at the county level by requiring of the counties a tax of not less than 50¢ nor more than 80¢ per $100 of assessed valuation. A territorial lottery scheme was approved which was to use 10 percent of all prizes for the territorial school fund (4). The salary of the superintendent was set at $1,000, and salaries of ex officio county superintendents, the probate judges, were $250. It is somewhat uncertain what compensation Sherman received as superintendent before the 1879 Legislature approved the $1,000 amount, but he apparently was paid the $500 authorized for expenses.

In 1881, the lottery was discontinued while, at the same time, the salaries of the superintendent and probate judges were increased. The superintendent was now paid $2,000 a year, and salaries varying from $250 to $1,000 were approved for the probate judges.

Sherman resigned as head of the Prescott school shortly before the end of his third term as superintendent. Thus, for a brief period, in addition to being the first superintendent other than a governor, he was also the first full-time superintendent.

It is difficult to evaluate Sherman's contributions to Arizona education. He, like others to follow him, occupied the office during a period of great economic and cultural expansion in the territory. Thus the growth of the schools cannot be attributed to his leadership in the same way that Safford may be given credit for his organizational work. One historian is quite reserved in giving Sherman credit as a strong leader, stating that his most important contribution was to select the two townships of land by which Congress endowed the university. Another, writing at a later date, noted that Arizona had, in 1882, uniform textbooks, uniform examinations for teachers, and a manual of schoolwork. He accords Sherman with having been an effective superintendent. "Indeed, the progress, which was soon apparent, following the appointment of Sherman, seems to prove that there was at least some supervision, for the slump of 1876-77 was soon overcome . . . " (5).

Sherman was succeeded by William B. Horton, who served only one term. Horton's concern for the educational program rather than his own political status or financial welfare made him an able administrator. He was the first man willing and able to give his full energies to the office. Although the 2-year term did not allow time either for Horton to develop a great program or for his influence to be directly realized, it appears that his work and the favorable attitude of Governor Frederick A. Tritle had some effect on the passage of strong school legislation by the 1885 Legislative Assembly.

In 1885, R. L. Long assumed the office for a 2-year term, the first of three periods he served. Long, another of the true professionals to serve the position, generally continued the line of work Horton had been pursuing. He also devoted much time to drafting a new or amended school code. From these efforts came the School Law of 1885, which continued as the basic framework for education in Arizona during its remaining time as a territory.

Governor Tritle challenged the authority of the Legislature to have made the office of superintendent elective. He asserted his authority by appointing the elected Long. From that time until statehood the superintendency remained an appointive position. This situation created much difficulty in 1889 when two men claimed the office. Charles M. Strauss was elected and appointed for the 1887-89 term and had again been elected for the 1889 term. However, Governor Lewis Wolfley appointed George W. Cheyney, who also claimed the office (6). The resultant muddle was such that the problems of the schools were almost completely neglected during the 1889-91 term.

The frequently changing political scene had its effects on the superintendency. One education historian states that "the last year of Long's administration seems to mark the crest of the wave of progress; with the incoming of Strauss retrogression became more and more marked" (7). Despite this confusion, the school system continued to grow, the territorial board adopted policies for the operation of schools, and progress was not retarded for the full period that was characterized as one of "retrogression and advance, reaction and progress" (8).

The Rules and Regulations for the Government of Public Schools in Arizona, as adopted by the board in 1887, were the most comprehensive directions from the territorial office to that date. These rules covered such subjects as schedule of hours, discipline, classroom physical environment, instructional materials, vandalism, teacher reports, and instructional methods. Two areas were covered in very modern fashion: Preparation and instruction were to be characterized by motivation, animation, and in such a manner "as not to be constantly confined to the textbook" (9); corporal punishment was specifically prohibited. This latter rule apparently received much criticism and was removed in 1890. Then, in 1893, a new regulation required that if a teacher were to administer corporal punishment, a parent and one member of the board of trustees must be invited, 24 hours in advance, to witness the act. This restriction was again removed in 1896, and the subject has not been directly covered by policy or statute.

With R. L. Long's return to the superintendency in 1898, the office again achieved a measure of stability. For the most part, Long resumed the job about where it was interrupted in 1887. He began anew to develop effective courses of study, better examinations for teacher certification, and systematic organization of the office. In addition, he and the board were involved in the many details of textbook adoptions, apportionment of funds, and certification.

Although Arizona had not yet attained a great degree of centralization in its school system, the board exerted its authority on occasion through its power to revoke certificates. An example was the charge against I. Ruthrauff, supervising principal of the Tucson schools, for failing to use prescribed texts and for using unauthorized supplementary books. Ruthrauff defended his actions on the ground that he was attempting to provide a program to meet local needs; but he agreed to comply with the board's direction when it threatened to revoke his certificate.

The superintendent had no clerical or other assistance until 1911, when the board finally authorized the employment of a secretary and a part-time assistant to help with textbooks.

The pattern of education constructed during the territorial period was the foundation on which the state's program was to be built. Progess was achieved as the result of actions by legislators, superintendents, governors, territorial boards, and individuals throughout the territory; all played some role which either directly or indirectly affected the system. Retrogression caused reaction; reaction sooner or later resulted in positive movements; and Arizona, on reaching statehood, had developed a reasonably strong educational program.

THE DEPARTMENT DURING STATEHOOD, 1912 TO 1967

In the words of Charles O. Case, first state superintendent of public instruction, "the old Territorial trail, picturesque and appealing in the dim light of pioneer campfires, comes to an end, and the trail of Statehood, crowded and dramatic with action, begins" (10). It is somewhat disappointing after over a half century of statehood that this "action" has not been more "dramatic" and successful in the organization of the State Department of Public Instruction. Perhaps the fact that Case held the state superintendency for 19 years without exerting any great influence on the development of a strong department had some bearing on the matter. But the legal framework of the system, the ever-present political maneuverings, and the problems of general state growth have been primarily responsible for the less-than-optimum maturation.

The functions of the state board and state superintendent did not differ greatly from that of the territorial board and superintendent. An examination of board minutes shows hardly any evidence of change. Although the office of superintendent became elective rather than appointive, its powers and duties were not outlined in any greater detail. The composition of the board was changed to five ex officio and three appointed members: the Governor, the state superintendent, presidents of the three state institutions of higher education, a city superintendent, a county superintendent, and a principal of a high school. Thus, the state board was a professional unit until changed by constitutional amendment in 1965.

Despite Case's indifferent record, described as "everlasting performance of duties assigned" (11), his political skill enabled him to hold the office for a long period and to provide some continuity previously unknown. Born in Illinois, the son of a preacher-teacher, he was orphaned while young. After graduating from Hillsdale College in Michigan, he came to Arizona in 1889, where he became acquainted with George W. P. Hunt while teaching in Globe. Possibly from this association with Hunt, who was later to become Governor, but also from his own aspirations, Case became widely known and politically prepared for his election as superintendent in 1911. Throughout his tenure in office he "seldom overlooked the political angle of any question" (12). There appears to have been a continual conflict in his life between rigid honesty and political ambition.

During Case's administration Arizona's school enrollment grew from 31,782 students in 1912 to almost double that by the end of 1918. The board's authorization for an assistant in 1919 was by no means premature.

Case believed that the state superintendent should be elected. But from shortly after his assumption of the office until the present, attempts have been to change the constitution to free the superintendency from politics. It was only natural for Case to hold such conviction; popular opinion apparently has agreed with his view.

Arizona gave much attention to Americanization during Case's term. Because of the high percentage of Mexican and Indian population, the schools emphasized holidays and the American way of life. Primarily for this purpose, the state tried to give adults basic educational opportunities prior to 1920. Appropriations were never adequate at this early date.

Elsie Toles was elected superintendent for the term 1921-23. During her tenure the issue of an appointive superintendent first came to a vote. In the last days of the session, the 1921 Legislature approved a constitutional amendment to be placed on the ballot in the general election of 1922. But the same Legislature changed its mind—the records do not reveal why—and voted to repeal it during a special session the following April. The State Teachers Association then spearheaded a drive to place it on the ballot by an initiative petition. Essentially, its amendment differed from the legislative amendment in the provisions for controlling the University of Arizona and educational programs in penal institutions. The State Teachers Association's measure, providing for a state board of seven members who would in turn appoint the superintendent, did find a place on the ballot and was defeated.

Miss Toles was credited with changing the state superintendency from an office of clerical and certification responsibilities to one of educational leadership (13). Having previously served as a county superintendent and a member of the state board, she was in a position to see some of the state's educational needs. She established an office of research and took a statistical survey of the state school system. Her administration also developed a long-range program for teacher certification and conducted teachers institutes. Not until her term did the board have enough authority to take these actions. In her biennial report, Miss Toles said that the most pressing problem was the need for attention to the long-neglected rural schools. But neither she nor her successors accomplished much in this regard until some four decades later.

Case was reelected to succeed Miss Toles in 1923. By this time the department had a staff of six. It is difficult to follow the organization of the department into divisions, but Case's report for the biennium ending in 1924 mentions a division of certification, a division of free textbooks, and a statistical and accounting division. The department of vocational education had attained some autonomy by 1923.

The state made a renewed effort to provide Americanization and night school classes, since the Legislature had made a more adequate appropriation. Case's report for the period ending in 1926, however, refers to this problem as one definite need. In 1923, a survey of the Arizona school system was begun by C. Ralph Tupper. This survey was reported to the board in 1925 with several recommendations for more efficient organization of the department. The board went on record as supporting these recommendations, but they were not implemented. The standards for teacher certification that had been developed in 1921 were revised and adopted in 1925, to become effective in 1929. Essentially, these revisions ended the issuance of certificates on the basis of examinations or previously held certificates; they would now be awarded on the basis of training and institutional recommendation.

The Board of Education passed a resolution in 1929 calling for improvements in the compulsory teaching of the effects of alcohol and narcotics. This action was the result of an appearance by a committee from the Women's Christian Temperance Union. In the same year, the board heard from other lay groups that sought endorsement and implementation of their proposals. The Laymen's Civic League of Arizona requested a program of released time for religious instruction. A committee of The American Legion, which had previously been interested in the physical education program, began to agitate for the employment of a state director. The disposal of these and other matters indicates that the board was beginning to function in a rather independent manner.

Case's biennial reports give attention to proposed legislation and review of the Legislature's enactments. Because of his political power, Case was reasonably influential in this realm of his responsibility as a state officer. That he could have exerted greater influence in the matter of school legislation had he not considered the "political angle" is certainly doubtful. It is probably a valid generalization that state superintendents and state departments are not notably effective in such an endeavor.

Case was well beyond retirement age when he was succeeded by H.E. Hendrix in 1933. Hendrix was born in Germany, grew up in Minnesota, and came to Arizona in 1917. Before being elected, he had been superintendent within the state at Miami and Mesa. Although not holding such strong political ties as his predecessor, Hendrix was well known in political circles, and it has been said that "in choosing his staff and in organizing his office, Dr. Hendrix used good political judgment. . ." (14).

The Depression had forced the state to reduce drastically appropriations for education at both the state and county levels. Teachers were unable to secure renewal credit for certification, so 1-year extensions were granted. Compulsory attendance laws were hard to enforce, and a general lack of public enthusiasm was evident. Perhaps because of these conditions, but also because he had a message to convey, Hendrix conducted a successful program of public relations through various media. In the early part of 1934, he divided his staff into two groups that toured the state to meet with civic organizations and to discuss the educational situation. In later years Hendrix used newspapers and radio to present his educational picture. Thus, he renewed interest in education, and as the economy improved, so did the schools.

By 1934, the department had divisions of curriculum, certification, research, and tests and measurements; a statistician; and a textbook depository. This structure generally followed previous plans but gave more emphasis to testing. Hendrix, aware of the growing testing movement, presented a different approach to testing. He felt that the eighth-grade tests then being used primarily for promotion should more properly be considered as indicators of the quality of the instructional program. A statewide plan for achievement testing was therefore instituted.

Other evidences of Hendrix' instructional leadership were his proposal for using radio in the classroom, his promotion of audiovisual education through the purchase of a small library of films, and his efforts to cover every high school subject by a revised or new course of study. During his administration modern ideas were at least considered, even if their ultimate implementation was not to come until later.

In the Depression years and continuing through World War II, the department continued to grow. The budget administered through the state superintendent's office more than doubled, and more employees were added. At the close of the war, the teacher shortage that had been felt for several years became more acute. Superintendent E. D. Ring reported that it was the exception rather than the rule to find a high school in the state without one or more teachers who failed to meet the requirements for teaching in high school. He suggested that housing facilities might be provided in the more isolated areas to attract teachers to such positions. The inadequate supply of teachers was to persist through 1953, at which time it was reported that "from all indications the future supply of available teachers is exhausted. Shortages are imminent" (15). Fortunately, this difficulty was shortly overcome, except in the more remote areas, by attractive salaries and the lure of the land.

Notwithstanding a general trend of progress and improvement, the department's activities during the forties and fifties were no more dramatic or earthshaking than during earlier years. In 1946, a Curriculum Coordinating Committee was appointed to assist in the development of courses of study and the evaluation of textbooks. This committee, while important for the state's instructional program, was subject to considerable change in membership and reorganization.

Superintendent N. D. Pulliam, who resigned in 1947 to accept a position with the U.S. Office of Education, had proposed an organizational scheme of three divisions: education, vocational education, and vocational rehabilitation. He sought to establish vacation and sick-leave policies for departmental employees, and after some delay these were completed. Pulliam suggested that an assistant superintendent might be appointed on a 10-month basis, thereby making it possible to secure a professionally expert person who could supplement his income by summer school teaching in a college or university.

L. D. Klemmedson was appointed to serve Pulliam's unexpired term. Klemmedson criticized the outmoded method of adoption and purchase of textbooks in 1948. The next year, a motion before the board that the curriculum committee be authorized to make a complete evaluation of the method for book adoptions was lost for want of a second. Klemmedson had been mainly interested in securing multiple adoptions, but it was not until 1960 that this was achieved.

Klemmedson's successor, M. L. Brooks, reorganized the curriculum committee to include 16 members who would serve staggered 4-year terms. He also issued an organization order for the department which called for three assistant superintendents, each of whom was to head various divisions. The office of comptroller was created to handle all accounting procedures. This innovation did not meet with favor from vocational education, so the accounting duties of that department were removed from the responsibilities of the comptroller. Brooks's reports reflect the tremendous increase in school population due to emigration to Arizona and the postwar birth rate. These reports were begun on an annual basis in 1953, due in part to improvements in accounting and statistics.

In 1949, the Special Legislative Committee on State Operations commissioned a comprehensive survey of the public school system by Griffenhagen and Associates. This study was reported in great detail in 1952 and clearly stated areas of weakness (16). Neither the Department of Education nor the Legislature paid much heed to this accurate and critical analysis of existing problems.

The Griffenhagen report did have some influence on another move to change the method of selection of the superintendent and the composition of the board. The 1953 Legislature passed a law abolishing the office of superintendent and the state board with companion legislation to establish a department of public schools, a commissioner of education, and a new board. These measures required an amendment of the constitution, which the voters defeated at the polls. An editorial urging defeat of the proposal, appearing in the *Arizona Daily Star*, listed some factors that voters may have considered. The editorial claimed that support for the amendment by the Arizona school administrators implied some intent to remove control of the schools from the general public. It further asserted that the Arizona Education Association had sponsored legislation to create a separate teachers' certification board and had thereby shown its distrust of the new plan (17). A later editorial in the same paper opposed the plan on the ground that it created two boards to do the job that one was then performing in a satisfactory manner (18).

C. L. Harkins served one term as superintendent between the third and fourth terms of Brooks. Under Harkins, the department was organized under two divisions—administration and instruction. Harkins was much concerned about the political atmosphere and the problems of securing and maintaining a good staff. He noted that the professional staff had dropped from six to three since 1939 and that salaries were inadequate. After the attorney general ruled that the board and the superintendent had the authority and responsibility for regulating private schools, Harkins said that the departmental staff was inadequate to do such supervision.

After Brooks's fourth term, W. W. Dick assumed the post for three terms. Dick's experience as a former teacher, principal, and county superintendent showed more promise than was realized. Perhaps the political influences that continued to hold sway were too restrictive. Dick strongly supported electing the superintendent. He was quoted as saying: "An appointed superintendent could become a dictator if extremists got control of the board. The board and superintendent ought to answer to somebody" (19).

His awareness of the political nature of the position likely retarded the development of educational opportunities. In 1960, when appearing before the Senate Appropriations Committee, Dick refused to take a stand on a budget item for the state's participation in Title III of the National Defense Education Act (20). Even though it cannot be definitely stated that the advantages of Title III could have then been realized had Dick strongly supported the budget item, this incident is a good example of the reluctance of state superintendents to push for programs that might be somewhat controversial.

It is interesting to note that when the state's plan for Title III was approved in 1964, quite an issue was raised over technicalities involved in the board's approval of the plan. In May 1964, in order to get quick approval for long-delayed action on Title III, Dick arranged a telephone conference which did not include Governor Fannin or board member Sarah Folsom. The plan was approved by the participants in the phone conference but was protested by Mrs. Folsom in the October meeting of the board. Her objection was based on the legality of the telephone meeting and the status of the Title III situation wherein local schools had already encumbered funds. The earlier action was ratified by the board, and the question of telephone conferences was directed to the attorney general (21). Mrs. Folsom, who defeated Dick in his bid for a fourth term, stated in the annual report for 1964-65 that the Title III program was approved in May 1964 and implemented in July 1964.

Sarah Folsom's ascendancy to the office of state superintendent in 1965 was accompanied by a new state board. A constitutional amendment approved by the voters had changed the composition of the board and had increased the number of members to nine. Under the new plan, membership included laymen, and the Governor no longer was a member.

Mrs. Folsom's experience prior to election as state superintendent included being a county superintendent and member of the state board. She was elected on a platform stressing the "3 R's" and equal opportunities for all children. She also had indicated that the political atmosphere in the department would be lessened.

After more than 2 years in office, Mrs. Folsom's leadership is encouraging. A handbook for departmental employees has been prepared, federal programs have been approved and staffed, great effort has been expended to secure state aid for kindergarten, and there has been a creditable fulfillment of campaign promises.

Other areas of growth have been noted in the employment of specialists in the fields of music, health and physical education, foreign languages, guidance, vocational education, science, audiovisual media, and reading. These people have aided the local school districts, as well as the county school offices, in the development of educational programs. State, county, and regional workshops dealing with the many facets of the educational programs have been held as a result of these improvements within the structure of the state department. The development of several outstanding teacher guides in several areas of education and the strong emphasis on the dissemination of information have improved the overall status of the department. Love of country, respect for law and order, and patriotism have received a fair share of attention from the present superintendent. Curriculum guides, attorney general's opinions dealing with the pledge of allegiance, and other facets dealing with patriotism have been strongly advocated by Mrs. Folsom.

From an overall point of view, the development of the department during the 1960's suggests a definite forward movement. The increasing complexity of its organization, its new affiliations with federal projects, the installation of a computer and data-processing equipment, and the activities of divisional offices all indicate a more prominent agency.

FRAMEWORK FOR ARIZONA EDUCATION

The Arizona constitution provides that the conduct and supervision of the state public school system shall be vested in a State Board of Education, a state superintendent of public instruction, county superintendents, and such governing boards for the state's educational institutions as provided by law. The arrangements for local control of schools depend on the statutes.

The State Board of Education

Since 1965 the board has had nine members: the state superintendent, the president of a state university or state college, three lay members, a member of the state junior college board, a superintendent of a high school district, a classroom teacher, and a county superintendent. Each member other than the state superintendent is appointed by the Governor with the advice and consent of the senate. Appointed members serve staggered terms of 4 years. The member who is a president of an institution of higher learning cannot succeed himself. Members serve without compensation although their expenses are reimbursed.

The powers and duties of the board are generally ministerial and supervisory. The most important powers are lodged in the board's authority to prescribe courses of study, to adopt textbooks, and to control the certification of teachers. The general authority to "exercise general supervision over and regulate the conduct of the public school system" (22) implies more power than actually exists, since the real authority rests with the Legislature.

The State Superintendent of Public Instruction

The superintendent is one of the six members of the executive department and is fourth in succession to the Governor. He is elected for a 2-year term on a partisan ballot to "superintend the public schools of the state" (23). His civic qualifications for office are that he must be at least 25 years of age, an American citizen of at least 10 years' standing, and a legal resident of Arizona for the 5 years immediately prior to election. His salary is fixed by statute. The present annual salary is $13,000 plus travel expenses.

The powers and duties of the superintendent are poorly defined by statute. The laws mostly detail his reporting duties and the clerical aspects of the office. The power lies in his authority as executive officer of the board and in his voting membership in it.

The County Superintendent

The county superintendent of schools is primarily a clerical manager for the schools in each county. He is elected to office under the same civic qualifications as other county officers, but with the additional requirement that he must hold a regular certificate to teach in the schools of Arizona. Perhaps the most important functions of the office are the details of finance. School funds are apportioned through this office in accordance with the budgetary and apportionment measures for the various school districts. Vouchers for claims and salaries are paid by his warrant drawn on the county treasurer and charged to the appropriate school fund. His other clerical functions include maintaining records of teachers' certificates and teachers' health examinations.

Local School Districts

The state's schools are organized into local elementary and high school districts. The control of these local units is vested in boards of trustees elected by the voters. In areas where the elementary and high school districts are coterminous, the same board serves both districts. In union high school districts—those composed of more than one elementary school district—a separate board of trustees is organized, and members of the boards of trustees of the component districts are ineligible for the high school board.

Within statutory limitations and controls of the state board, local boards are granted rather broad powers. School districts may hire professional administrators, provide funds for the operation and maintenance of schools, provide free textbooks to elementary students, provide school transportation, expel students for misconduct, and perform other duties.

Teachers

In addition to holding the proper certificates, a teacher in Arizona must pass a physical examination, must take a loyalty oath, and must be able to pass an examination in United States and Arizona Constitutions after no more than 1 year's service in the state schools. A teacher is granted tenure as a continuing teacher on signing his fourth consecutive contract. Under penalty of suspension or revocation of certification, a teacher may not resign after signing a contract without permission of the local board. Teachers are covered by a combination Social Security and state retirement plan to which contributions are made by both the teacher and the state. Salaries of teachers are fixed by the local district.

School Attendance

Arizona's public schools are open to children between the ages of 6 and 21. Compulsory attendance is required of children between the ages of 8 and 16.

Textbooks

The adoption of textbooks and the furnishing of free textbooks to elementary students have been major responsibilities of the state. Originally, single-text adoptions were made and the books were purchased by the state. Later developments have placed the purchasing responsibility at the local level and have increased the number of adoptions. No free textbooks are provided for high school students.

School Finance

Since 1871, fiscal support of the Arizona public schools has been borne primarily by property taxation. Federal aid, income from state lands, and other state revenues provide some support of local schools, but the problem of paying for public education is basically that of the property owners.

The local school district prepares an annual budget based on estimated expenditures. This budget is funded by a special school district levy made by the county supervisors for the school district, by state funds, and by a county levy. From the beginnings of the public school system to the present, the territory or state has participated in the financing of schools with varying degrees of assistance. The earliest plans called for a fixed tax levy, the proceeds of which were to be apportioned to each county on an equal basis. Later, revenue from the fixed levy was apportioned on the basis of attendance. Further progress resulted in the state's making an appropriation equal to the product of a per-pupil figure times the number of students in average daily attendance. A tax sufficient to raise this total appropriation was then levied. This system of state taxation has provided some equalization throughout the state, although assessments have been described as grossly inequitable.

Arizona does not have an abundance of industry, and it is one of the states in which a high percentage of the land is under public ownership. In 1960, only 12 percent of the total acreage was privately owned (24). Fortunately, the area of the state is large, the population is small, and the effect is not as severe as it might be. Also, federal aid for Indian education and for education in federally impacted areas helps the financial picture.

The income from school lands is relatively insignificant when taken as a percentage of the total cost of schools. The territorial superintendents and legislators had attempted to sell public lands to endow a permanent common school fund. Congress did not approve the requests for sale of the lands but granted permission shortly before the turn of the century to lease them. Despite evidence of mismanagement of the public lands, receipts for state schools were approximately $22 million between 1912 and 1960.

The state appropriations for public schools, the earnings from the permanent school fund, and all other receipts for the benefit of the public schools are placed in the state school fund. This money, except for the expenses of the department, is subsequently apportioned to the school districts through the counties. Thus the department is quite involved in school finance through its distributive functions.

At this writing, the Legislature is in special session considering tax reforms, especially with reference to school finance. A reevaluation of the entire state has been completed by the division of appraisal and assessment standards of the State Tax Commission. Changes are expected in the levels of assessment and the structure of school finance.

Junior Colleges

Between 1927 and 1960, junior colleges were under the supervision of the State Board of Education. In 1927, the

Legislature enacted provisions for school districts of sufficient size to establish junior colleges. The state provided financial aid beginning in 1935. The level of state support has increased through the years and has been distributed according to various formulas. Concurrently, the state pays $115 per student in equivalent full-time attendance. Also the state participates in capital outlay to the extent of 50 percent or a maximum of $500,000 after approval of the college's plan by the Legislature.

Due to the increasing interest in and need for junior colleges, a board of directors separate from the state board was created in 1960. This board consists of 17 members: one from each of the 14 counties, a representative from the Board of Regents, the director of vocational education, and the superintendent of public instruction.

Higher Education

The University of Arizona at Tucson, Arizona State University at Tempe, and Northern Arizona University at Flagstaff are the three state institutions for higher education. All three are under the jurisdiction of one Board of Regents composed of eight appointive members, the Governor, and the state superintendent. Tempe and Flagstaff have laboratory schools for the training of teachers. These schools are considered a branch of the public school system but are controlled by the Board of Regents.

A FUNCTIONAL VIEW OF THE DEPARTMENT

Since the Arizona Department of Public Instruction is not provided for in the statutes, its organization has been at the discretion of the superintendents and has not followed any definite evolutionary process.

Certification of Teachers

The examination and licensing of teachers was the duty solely of county boards of examiners in 1871. By the time of Superintendent Horton's administration, the Territorial Board of Education was issuing diplomas which were valid in any county and was giving close supervision to the work of the boards of examiners. In 1885, a Territorial Board of Examiners was created to supervise the county boards and to issue territorial certificates on the basis of examinations and/or credentials. Shortly thereafter, all territorial certificates were recalled in a general housecleaning. This action resulted in some improvement, but evidence of the use of incompetent teachers necessitated another recall in 1893. From these early beginnings until 1921, the method of certifying teachers was essentially the same. During this period refinements were made, professional training was recognized, and the Legislature empowered the board to handle certification.

By 1921, the first definite and specific rules for teacher certification were adopted by the board. These rules were revised in 1925, and in 1928, the requirement of 3 years of post-high school training was added. In 1936, all teachers holding valid certificates were given until 1946 to qualify under new regulations that required a bachelor's degree for elementary certificates and a master's degree or the equivalent for high school teaching. Special certificates for administrators were first required in 1933.

Recent years have seen numerous technical changes and specialization, and the completion of 5 years' training has become the minimum requirement for standard certification. The recommendations of state teacher training institutions are followed for the issuance of certificates to their graduates. Out-of-state applicants are granted certificates according to comparable levels of training on review of their credentials by the division of teacher certification. Permanent or life certificates are not issued.

Elementary Education

The Division of Elementary Education has participated in statewide curriculum development for the elementary schools. Through its diverse activities the department has provided a measure of coordination for curriculum development projects being conducted by local schools. Some of the division's specific activities are disseminating information on changing curriculums, revising policies for textbook adoption, visiting local school districts, developing a curriculum materials center, planning statewide workshops, and supervising the basic education program for the inmates of the state prison.

Secondary Education

The first high school was authorized by the Territorial Board of Education in 1888. From that time until the present, much endeavor has been directed toward the development of strong courses of study. In 1909, the board developed a minimum course of study for high school graduation, and in 1915, the unit of credit was specifically defined as a requirement for high school records.

Considering all the effort made by the state to develop strong high school programs, it is rather surprising to note that a request of one school to include Latin and modern foreign language in its program was denied in 1907. The board's concern over foreign influence evidently was the reason for the denial.

The director of the Division of Secondary Education is an ex officio member of the State Committee on Accreditation. This committee evaluates and classifies the high schools. Other functions of the division of secondary education are curriculum development activities, supervision of the high school equivalency certificate program, and coordination of consultant services for high school subject areas.

Special Education

The territorial board made arrangements to educate deaf and blind students at institutions outside the state. An Arizona school for the deaf and blind was established in 1929. Initially, this school was a part of the University of Arizona, but it later became a separate institution with its own governing board.

Provisions for the education of crippled children were made in 1947. In 1949, the Arizona Children's Colony was established to provide care and training for mentally deficient children. Aid for the instruction of homebound students was approved in 1951. Comprehensive legislation for the education of educable and trainable mentally retarded children was enacted in 1961. This legislation inaugurated financial aid to local districts that have approved programs of special education and established by statute a division of special education.

Adult Education

Adult education in Arizona had its beginnings prior to 1920 under the terms of the Smith-Hughes Act and the state's own program of Americanization classes. Through the years, and especially in the 1960's, offerings in adult education have increased, and the department has shown some definite leadership in this area. At the present, Civil Defense adult education is administered under one division, and adult basic education under a separate division of the department. Adult programs of vocational education and vocational rehabilitation are the responsibilities of those divisions.

Indian Education

The distribution of funds to the public schools under the terms of the Johnson-O'Malley Act is the responsibility of the Division of Indian Education. The funds are made available for Indian children who live on reservations and attend public schools. The amount to which each district is entitled is equal to what the local share of educational costs for such children would be if they were living on private property.

Vocational Education

High school programs in vocational education have been authorized since statehood, but these programs were rather insignificant until the Smith-Hughes Act made substantial federal support available. Under the Arizona plan to qualify for federal aid, the state board also served as the State Board for Control of Vocational Education. The state superintendent was assigned the responsibility for administering the program by being named executive officer for vocational education. The state board was reluctant to employ a director and to pay such an officer from state funds. However, after an attorney general's opinion that the board could legally make such an appointment, Professor I. Colodny was appointed as the first director of vocational education in 1918.

Within a few months, Colodny had implemented the program to the point that he reported 15 of the 30 high schools in the state were establishing programs under the vocational act. There was then, as there is now, the problem of hiring competent vocational education instructors. The director's position was subject to the effects of political patronage. Colodny was not reappointed in 1919 and was succeeded by R. H. Blome, whose tenure was also of short length.

In 1920, the director's salary was increased from $3,000 to $3,600, which may have had some bearing on the fact that the office of director was abolished in 1921. It is more likely, however, that the change in superintendents was responsible for the reorganization. The new plan called for the superintendent to serve as director of vocational education and for the supervisor of trade and industrial education to serve as assistant director.

When C. O. Case returned to office in 1923, he effected an almost complete turnover in the vocational staff. The state having made arrangements to participate in the federal Industrial Rehabilitation Act, Case appointed A. M. Davis as acting director of vocational education and director of vocational rehabilitation, research, and Americanization. Friction between Case and Davis occurred over the relative authority of each's position, so much so that the chairman of the House Committee on Education appeared at a state board meeting requesting the board to harmonize the relationship between the director of vocational education and the Department of Public Instruction. The strained relationship continued for some time, particularly since some budgets included a director's salary higher than that of the superintendent. By 1928, the differences were apparently resolved; at least, Davis and seven other members of his staff were reappointed on the recommendation of Case.

The next year, 1929, when the Governor requested that a new director be appointed, Davis needed more than the support Case could give, and he lost his position. The position of director was again relegated to a part-time office. Halbert W. Miller was hired as part-time director and as supervisor of agricultural education. In 1930, the board decided to increase the director's and supervisor's terms from 1 year to 2 years. Case opposed this decision and submitted a letter to the attorney general requesting an opinion as to the board's authority to make appointments for a 2-year period. The opinion stated that the board could legally contract for the extended period and that the superintendent, although also an executive officer, had no more authority than any other member of the board.

On Miller's resignation in 1931, Davis was again made director until his resignation was requested 2 years later. For the next 7 years, the superintendent served as vocational director. In 1940, Superintendent Hendrix recommended that a director be appointed.

At the close of World War II, vocational education was designated as the agency to handle the distribution of surplus property. In this function the department incurred some notoriety after a federal and state investigation into fraudulent handling of surplus property.

There was further controversy about the authority of the superintendent in vocational matters during the administration of M. L. Brooks. Brooks reported in 1949 that he had been unable to get cooperation from the vocational department in carrying out the operations which he, as executive officer, considered to be the intent of the board. It was the consensus of board members that the superintendent-executive officer was the one through whom recommendations should come to the board and who would be responsible for the functioning of the Department of Vocational Education. This situation was primarily one of conflicting personalities, and some reconciliation was later achieved. It was necessary, however, 10 years later, for the board to reaffirm the authority of the executive officer.

Notwithstanding the several incidents of friction and the organizational problems, the need for a state plan that was acceptable to the federal government appears to have resulted in the creation of a unit successful in carrying out the intended purposes of vocational education. The department's efforts in helping schools establish programs, in supervising these programs, and in working in the area of teacher training deserve commendation. Currently, the vocational education department exists as a unit separate from the Department of Public Instruction, but its activities are coordinated through the superintendent and board.

Vocational Rehabilitation

The Department of Vocational Rehabilitation has developed under somewhat less stormy conditions than the vocational education department. Beginning in 1923, the department has grown to one which was, in late 1966, handling approximately 1,500 active cases and administering a budget of over $2 million. This department also exists separately under the board and superintendent.

Recent Federal Programs

The full benefits of the National Defense Education Act (NDEA) were not fully available in Arizona until 1964, when the long-delayed Title III plan was approved. Earlier participation in Title V was administered through the vocational education department until recently when a separate division in the Department of Public Instruction was created.

Nothing has been more helpful to the state department than the Elementary and Secondary Education Act of 1965 (ESEA). Although the effects of this assistance have not yet been fully realized, the department is now being strengthened through the implementation of Title V.

Some delay occurred in getting approval for local schools' projects under Title I because of staff shortages in the department. These problems were overcome, however, and local agencies were able to use almost the entire state allocation of over $10 million for the first year.

Title II, providing funds for library and instructional materials, has been directed by the department's library division. The activities of this division in implementing Title II have produced marked improvement in many school libraries.

Various experimental projects funded by Title III have been undertaken by the state's school districts. Some cooperative projects among districts were organized, but the legality of such ventures was challenged. Legislative effort has permitted these projects to continue but has restricted further cooperative plans.

Research and Finance

The activities of the research and finance division have, for the most part, been statistical and clerical. The research function has not been highly developed to date. This division handles fiscal procedures and student accounting for the department, except for the accounting details handled by the Indian education division and the school lunch division.

School Lunch

School lunch has been a function of the department since 1947, and the duties in this matter have been discharged by a division of school lunch. The statutes permit using tax funds for the support of lunch programs, but not directly for the purchase of food.

Western States Small Schools Project

The Western States Small Schools Project was established in 1962 as the result of a $105,000 grant from the Ford Foundation to study improvement practices in small schools. Initially funded for the period 1962 to 1965, it has since been extended through 1968. This project supports teacher in-service education programs, publications, workshops, and consultations.

Designing Education for the Future

A cooperative eight-state project, funded by Title V, ESEA, works as a division within the department. The purpose of this project is to anticipate educational needs for the next 10 or 15 years and to plan programs to fulfill the expected needs.

PROBLEMS THAT HAVE AFFECTED THE DEPARTMENT

The department's failure to be a strong and vital force in Arizona education is not necessarily the fault of those who have headed it. Rather, it would appear that the legal structure has restricted the department's influence. Through the years, various individuals and groups have surveyed the work of the department and have submitted recommendations for improvements. Even though these efforts may have had some effect, very little change resulting in a stronger department has occurred.

In 1917, a survey of education in Arizona criticized the state school system as being too decentralized and suggested a constitutional amendment making the state superintendency an appointive position. It was also recommended that the Legislature enlarge and clearly define the functions of the board and the superintendent.

The survey by Tupper, in 1925, recommended an appointive superintendent, a lay board, and reorganization of the department to include directors for each of several functions (25).

A combined report of the Arizona Lay Advisory Council and the Arizona Professional Advisory Council, in 1949, noted a very apparent need for reorganization of the department. It further stated that the department was "handicapped by an unsuitable framework within which the central educational enterprise has been forced to operate" (26). These groups believed that the board was too much involved with such things as certification and textbook adoption details. The organization of separate vocational education and vocational rehabilitation departments, for which state plans were approved that eliminated such detail, was given as an example of a more efficient arrangement. The composition of the board and the method of selecting the superintendent were judged to be definite shortcomings. The report even said that budgetary limitations were evidence that the Legislature had lost confidence in the board and superintendent. What appeared to have been votes against education was actually discontent with an ex officio professional board and a politically elected superintendent (27).

The comprehensive Griffenhagen report also proposed an appointive superintendent and lay board. This report expressed the need for greater financial support to enable the department to give statewide leadership. It recommended that the department provide better interpretation of its needs and school problems to the Legislature. The state should become, through the department, more active in pupil transportation, perhaps by establishing a central agency for procurement of buses and in providing financial aid for transportation (28).

Such were the findings of some of the professionals who took a close look at the school system and the Department of Public Instruction. In addition to these professional groups, lay organizations have reviewed the problems and have made similar proposals, especially concerning the board and superintendent.

The ex officio duties of the state superintendent have necessitated his spending much time on matters not directly connected to the functions of the department. The first Legislature created a board of pardons and parole which was composed of the attorney general, the state superintendent, and one other member appointed by these two. Because of the nature of the duties and because these duties were not related to education, state superintendents repeatedly advocated changes in the composition of this board. It was not until 1966 that the Legislature made the changes and discharged the superintendent from this responsibility. His service on other boards as an ex officio member relates more directly to education.

Having the superintendent on the State Board of Education may not be administratively sound. Since the superintendent serves as executive officer of the board, it might be better if he were not a voting member but were given sufficient administrative authority to perform broader duties.

The problems of inadequate salaries and political atmosphere as they affect the departmental staff have been mentioned previously. The present $13,000 annual salary of the superintendent, although not mandating lower salaries for other professional employees, has the practical effect of limiting all salaries. The most recent increase in the superintendent's salary was in 1962, when it was raised from $12,000. The superintendent's pay seems unrealistic when compared to salaries of teachers and public school administrators.

Working under the handicap of not being able to offer appointees high salaries and job security, the superintendents have nevertheless been able to hire highly competent people for staff positions. If these two problems could be eliminated, the efficiency of the department would surely increase, and more and better people would consider future appointments.

Aside from a few incidents of personality conflict on issues or how best to organize the department, most of the operational problems have been of structural origin. The department often has been hampered by lack of authority, insufficient funds, or both. For example, the superintendent has little authority to require reports or to demand accuracy in the reports of county superintendents. Also, the board has not had the authority to determine the classification of students for ADA distribution. Funds have not been adequate to provide leadership in school transportation, schoolhouse planning services, and consultants in the many areas of curriculum.

Through ESEA, the department's advisory capacities will improve. But the problems of proper authority and adequate funds must be solved by the Legislature. The solutions do not seem to be immediately forthcoming.

Some citizens argue that limitations on the authority of the board and the superintendent are as they should be—that control of the schools should rest with the Legislature. This premise is easily accepted. However, it would seem to follow that the limitations and powers should be more specifically outlined in the statutes. The department would then have sufficient authority to fulfill whatever duties the Legislature expects to be performed.

FOOTNOTES

1. Samuel P. McCrea, "Establishment of the Arizona School System," *Biennial Report* (Phoenix: Superintendent of Public Instruction, 1908), p. 78.
2. Frank C. Lockwood, *Arizona Characters* (Los Angeles: The Times Mirror Press, 1928), p. 125. Lockwood credits John Spring, master of the first school in Tucson, as responsible for Safford's title, "Father of Arizona's Public Schools."
3. According to McCrea, Sherman was appointed in 1878 to fulfill the duties of superintendent which were actually the responsibility of the Governor until the positions were separated in 1879. Therefore, Sherman is not listed as superintendent until 1879.
4. It may be assumed that the lottery provisions were more of an effort to legalize gambling than to support schools. Some of the proceeds were also to be used for the construction of a capitol.
5. Stephen B. Weeks, *History of Public School Education in Arizona* (Washington, D.C.: Government Printing Office, 1918), p. 41.
6. *Ibid.*, p. 61. This situation was further complicated by the fact that the location of the office was left to the discretion of the superintendent, the only requirement being that it must be located where there was a post office. Strauss held the records and seal, refusing to return them over to the board or to Cheyney. He finally released the records and relinquished claim to the office in 1890.
7. *Ibid.*, p. 60.
8. *Ibid.*, p. 61.
9. Minutes of the Territorial Board of Education, Prescott, Arizona, May 16, 1887.
10. Superintendent of Public Instruction, *Biennial Report* (1912), p. 3.
11. J. Morris Richards, "Biography of Dr. Charles O. Case," p. 1. (Typewritten.) This paper was prepared by the author in 1935 while at the University of Arizona and is now located in the State Library and Archives. Case's doctorate was an honorary degree.
12. *Ibid.*, p. 6.
13. Delta Kappa Gamma, "Miss Elsie Toles: First Woman State Superintendent of Public Instruction in Arizona." This manuscript was prepared for Delta Kappa Gamma's record of pioneer teachers and does not include either the date or name of the author. It is located in the library of the Arizona Pioneers' Historical Society in Tucson.
14. J. Morris Richards, "Biography of Dr. H. E. Hendrix," (1936), p. 18. (Typewritten.) This biography was prepared while the author was at the University of Arizona and is now in the State Library and Archives. Hendrix held an earned doctorate.
15. State Superintendent of Public Instruction, *Annual Report* (1953), p. 1.
16. Griffenhagen & Associates, *A Report on a Study of the Public School System of Arizona,* prepared for the Special Legislative Committee on State Operations. (3 vols.; Los Angeles: Griffenhagen & Associates, 1952), I, pp. 2-33.
17. Editorial, *Arizona Daily Star* (Tucson), May 18, 1953, p. 10.
18. *Ibid.*, September 14, 1953, p. 6.
19. *Ibid.*, January 17, 1963, p. 8.
20. *Ibid.*, January 13, 1960, p. 4.
21. Minutes of the State Board of Education, Phoenix, Arizona, October 9, 1964. There are also recorded minutes of the telephone conference in May 1964.
22. Arizona, *Revised Statutes,* (1960 as amended) Title 15, Education, art. 1, 15-102.
23. *Ibid.*, art. 2, 15-121.
24. Frank H. Gladen, Jr., "An Historical Survey of Public Land and Public Education in the State of Arizona from 1863 to 1960" (unpublished Ph.D. dissertation, University of Arizona, Tucson, 1965), p. 190.
25. C. Ralph Tupper, *A Survey of the Arizona Public School System* (Phoenix: State Board of Education, 1925), pp. 9-12.
26. Arizona Advisory Councils on Education, *Improving Education in Arizona* (Phoenix: The Councils, 1949), p. 7.
27. *Ibid.*, p. 36.
28. Griffenhagen & Associates, *op. cit.,* I, pp. 4, 18, 31; II, pp. 2, 4.

BIBLIOGRAPHY

Public Documents

Arizona. *Acts* (1871-1911).

--*Constitution* (1912, as amended).

——*Revised Statutes* (1960, as amended). Title 15, Education.

Books

Arizona Advisory Councils on Education, *Improving Education in Arizona.* Phoenix: The Councils, 1949.

Arizona State College. *Elementary and Secondary Education in Arizona.* Phoenix: Arizona Academy, 1963.

Larson, Emil. *Arizona School Law.* Tucson: University of Arizona Press, 1964.

Lockwood, Frank C. *Arizona Characters.* Los Angeles: The Times Mirror Press, 1928.

McClintock, James H. *Arizona: The Youngest State.* Vol. II. Chicago: S. J. Clarke Publishing Co., 1916.

Martin, Douglas D. *The Lamp in the Desert.* Tucson: University of Arizona Press, 1960.

Murdock, John R. *Constitutional Development of Arizona.* Phoenix: Privately printed by John Ben Murdock, 1933.

Pare, Madeline, and Fireman, Bert M. *Arizona Pageant.* Phoenix: Arizona Historical Foundation, 1965.

Pickering, Robert L. *Some Significant Events in the History of Arizona Education.* Phoenix: Superintendent of Public Instruction, 1966.

Tupper, C. Ralph. *A Survey of the Arizona Public School System.* Phoenix: Board of Education, 1925.

U.S. Bureau of Education. *Educational Conditions in Arizona.* Bulletin No. 44. Washington, D.C.: Government Printing Office, 1917.

Weeks, Stephen B. *History of Public School Education in Arizona.* Washington, D.C.: Government Printing Office, 1918.

Periodicals

Arizona Daily Star (Tucson), February 20, April 25, May 18, 25, June 19, and September 14, 1953; June 13, 1956; January 13, 1960; January, 17, 1963; July 2, 1964.

Arizona Republic (Phoenix), November 5, 1967.

Tucson Citizen, December 7, 1907.

Reports

Griffenhagen & Associates. *A Report on a Study of the Public School System of Arizona.* Prepared for the Special Legislative Committee on State Operations. 3 vols. Los Angeles: Griffenhagen & Associates, 1952.

McCrea, Samuel P. "Establishment of the Arizona School System," *Biennial Report.* Phoenix: Superintendent of Public Instruction, 1908. p. 78.

Superintendents of Public Instruction. *Annual* and *Biennial Reports.* Phoenix: The Superintendents, 1898-1966.

Unpublished Material

Arizona Tax Research Association. "Research Report of the Office of the State Superintendent of Public Instruction." Phoenix: The Association, 1942. (Mimeographed.)

Arizona White House Conference on Education. "The Oncoming Tide." Phoenix: The Conference, 1955.

Blackburn, Richard Leroy. "The Development of the Arizona Public School System." Unpublished Ph.D. dissertation, University of Southern California, Los Angeles, 1932.

Delta Kappa Gamma. "Miss Elsie Toles: First Woman Superintendent of Public Instruction in Arizona." A manuscript prepared for Delta Kappa Gamma's record of pioneer teachers. Library of the Arizona Pioneer's Historical Society, Tucson. (Typewritten.)

Gladen, Frank H., Jr. "An Historical Survey of Public Land and Public Education in the State of Arizona from 1863 to 1960." Unpublished Ph.D. dissertation, University of Arizona, Tucson, 1965.

Minutes of the State Board of Education, 1912-67.

Minutes of the State Board of Vocational Education, 1918-51.

Minutes of the Territorial Board of Education, 1887-1911.

Richards, J. Morris. "Biography of Dr. Charles O. Case." A paper prepared by the author while at the University of Arizona, 1935. State Library and Archives. (Typewritten.)

—— "Biography of Dr. H. E. Hendrix." A paper prepared by the author while at the University of Arizona, 1936. State Library and Archives. (Typewritten.)

Zimmerman, Ralph H. "Trends in the School Law of Arizona Since Statehood." Unpublished master's thesis, University of Arizona, Tucson, 1934.

Appendix A

ARIZONA CHIEF STATE SCHOOL OFFICERS

Territorial Superintendents

1871-77	A. P. K. Safford (Governor)
1877-78	John P. Hoyt
1878-79	John C. Frémont (Governor)
1879-83	Moses H. Sherman
1883-85	W. B. Horton
1885-87	R. L. Long
1887-90	Charles W. Strauss
1890-93	George W. Cheyney
1893-96	F. J. Netherton
1896-97	Thomas E. Dalton
1897-98	A. P. Sherman
1898-1902	R. L. Long
1902-1906	Nelson G. Layton
1906-10	R. L. Long
1910-12	Kirke T. Moore

State Superintendents

1912-21	Charles O. Case
1921-23	Elsie Toles
1923-33	Charles O. Case
1933-41	Herman E. Hendrix
1941-47	E. D. Ring
1947-47	N. D. Pulliam
1947-49	L. D. Klemmedson
1949-55	M. L. Brooks
1955-57	C. L. Harkins
1957-59	M. L. Brooks
1959-65	W. W. "Skipper" Dick
1965-	Sarah Folsom

Appendix B

Chart I.--ARIZONA DEPARTMENT OF PUBLIC INSTRUCTION, 1956

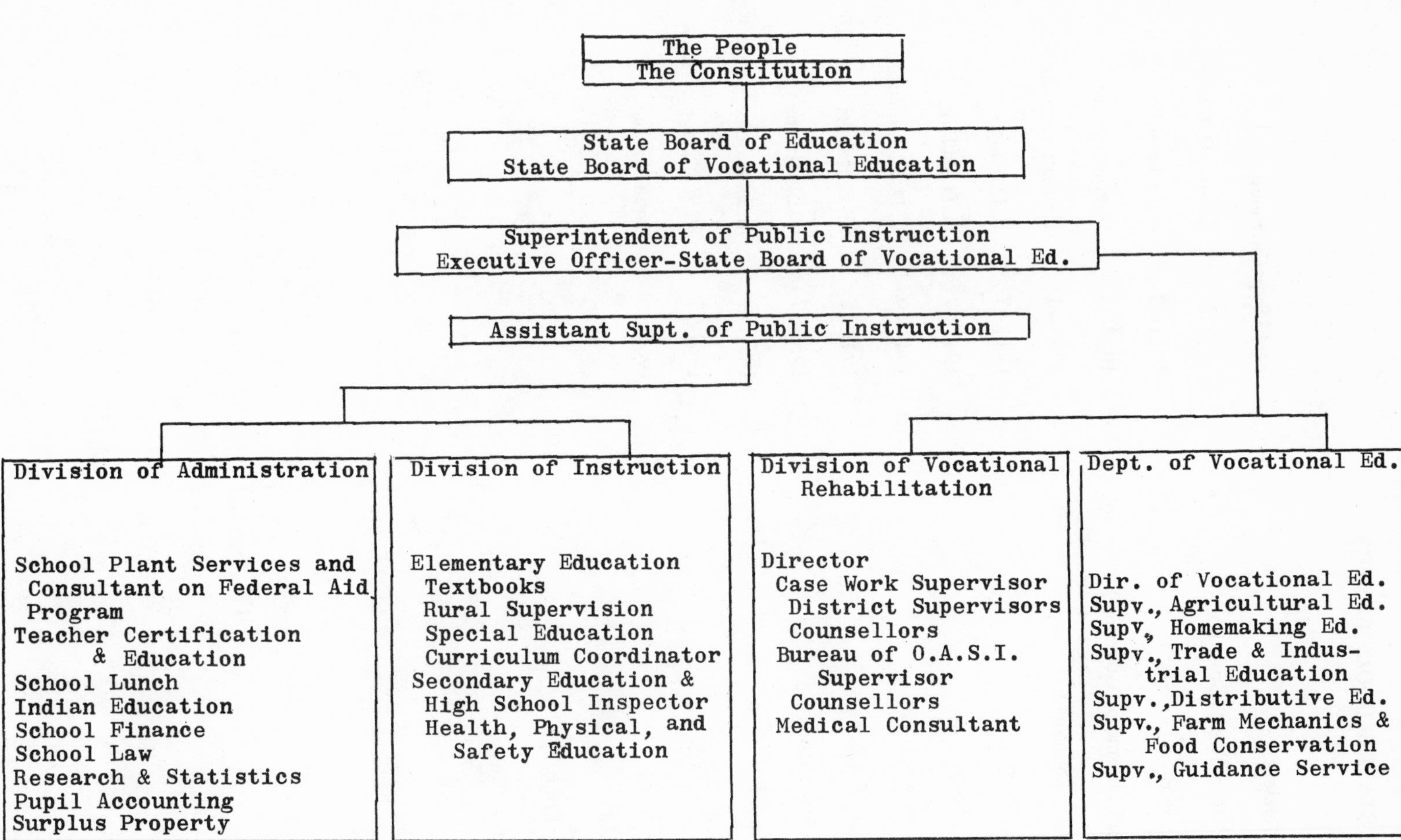
The People
The Constitution
State Board of Education
State Board of Vocational Education
Superintendent of Public Instruction
Executive Officer-State Board of Vocational Ed.
Assistant Supt. of Public Instruction
Division of Administration
School Plant Services and Consultant on Federal Aid Program
Teacher Certification & Education
School Lunch
Indian Education
School Finance
School Law
Research & Statistics
Pupil Accounting
Surplus Property
Division of Instruction
Elementary Education
Textbooks
Rural Supervision
Special Education
Curriculum Coordinator
Secondary Education &
High School Inspector
Health, Physical, and Safety Education
Division of Vocational Rehabilitation
Director
Case Work Supervisor
District Supervisors
Counsellors
Bureau of O.A.S.I.
Supervisor
Counsellors
Medical Consultant
Dept. of Vocational Ed.
Dir. of Vocational Ed.
Supv., Agricultural Ed.
Supv., Homemaking Ed.
Supv., Trade & Industrial Education
Supv., Distributive Ed.
Supv., Farm Mechanics & Food Conservation
Supv., Guidance Service

Appendix B

Chart II.-- ARIZONA DEPARTMENT OF PUBLIC INSTRUCTION, 1967

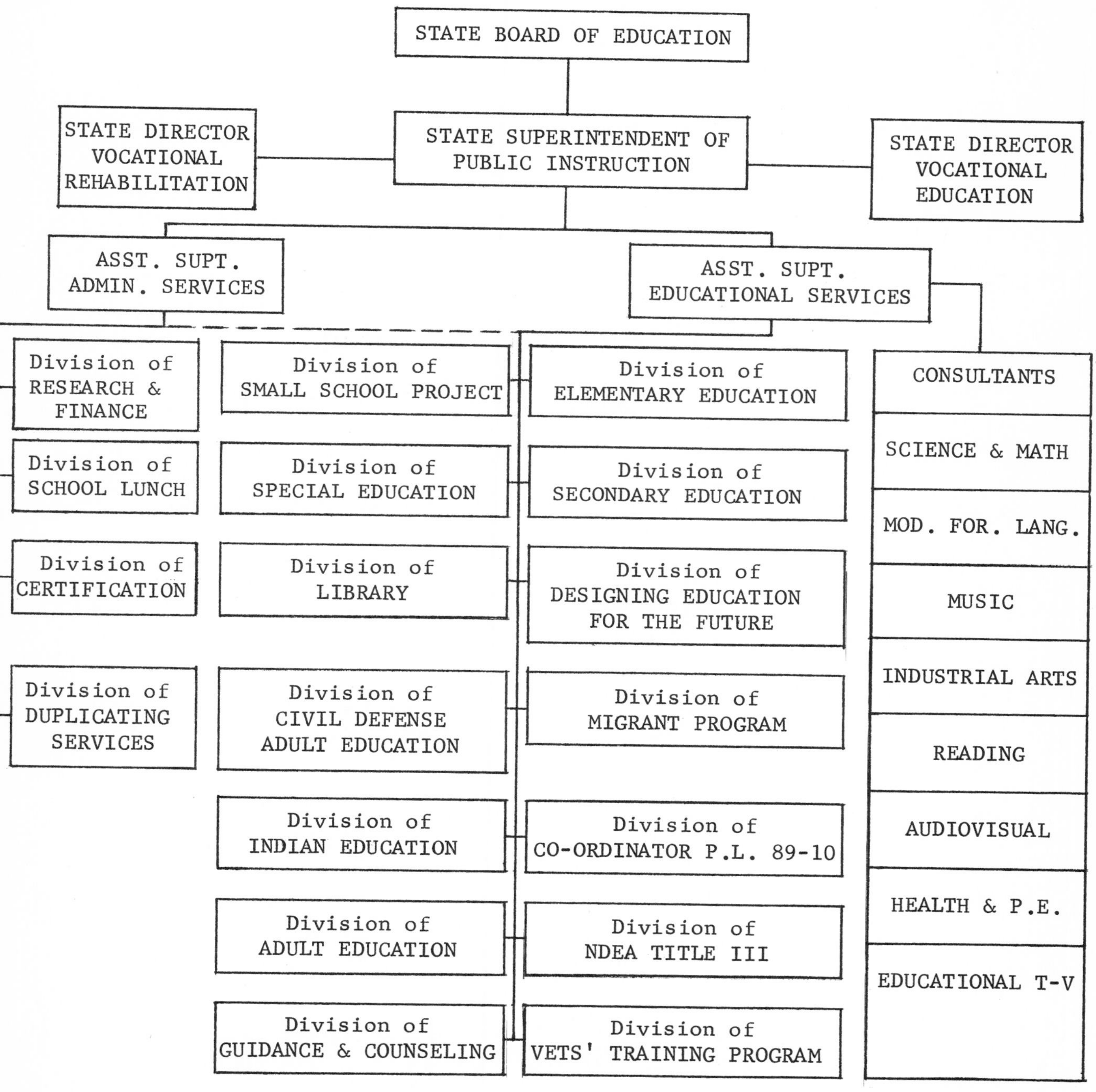

4 Arkansas

DEPARTMENT OF EDUCATION

Frank W. Cannaday

Contents

BEFORE 1900

Establishing a Public School System

Arkansas was so sparsely populated during territorial days and early statehood that schools were organized only with difficulty. Many pupils rode horseback, while others walked 8 or 10 miles, to poorly constructed log cabins without heating or lighting. Books were scarce, accommodations few, and the schools offered only an elementary curriculum: reading, writing, arithmetic, spelling, geography, and history. Teachers' salaries were meager, and many teachers had to accept produce for part of their pay and take turns at boarding with their pupils (1).

In 1829, the Territorial Legislature passed the first law on public education by requiring county judges to appoint a trustee for the sixteenth section of land in each township granted to Arkansas when the territory was organized in 1819. At the same time, each township was to select three trustees responsible for maintaining a school building and for hiring a teacher. The teacher was expected to know everything, to have a good reputation, and to be able to discipline the students as well as develop their character. Children who could afford it were to pay tuition–or subscription, as it was called–to attend schools that were run at least 5 months of the year. The trustees were required to visit the schools once a month.

In 1836, the year Arkansas was admitted into the Union, Congress passed an act presenting to Arkansas' General Assembly the sixteenth section of each township for educational purposes. The act also granted 72 sections of so-called Saline Lands and 72 sections (two townships) known as the Seminary Lands. The Saline Lands were areas set aside by the federal government because salt springs were located on these lands; the Seminary Lands were sections granted by Congress to Arkansas in 1827 for the purpose of establishing a seminary or university. Ten years later, Congress modified the Seminary Land Grant by authorizing the General Assembly to add these 72 sections to the section 16 lands for use by the public schools (2).

County and State Administration

From 1829 to 1853, the Legislature left with the county courts (county judges) the general jurisdiction, supervision, and control of all matters concerning the public schools. But a definite trend toward centralization arose during this period. For instance, in 1851 the Legislature attempted to unify and simplify the school system by providing for a township organization, but with some county supervision (3). Two years later the Legislature passed a school act creating the office of county common school commissioner to further unify the schools, establishing a pattern for the county school official that has existed in one form or another until present day, despite seven changes in the title itself (4). The duties and responsibilities of this official remained similar during each of the major turning points in the history of the office.

Following the Civil War, Governor Isaac Murphy, a former school teacher from Madison County, urged the Legislature to make education a responsibility of the state. As a result of Murphy's untiring efforts, the 1867 Legislature passed an act providing for a 2-mill state tax for the public schools. The act also created the office of state superintendent of public instruction, to be elected first by the General Assembly, but later by qualified electors. His duties were specifically outlined. The act further required the elected county school commissioners to examine all persons applying for teaching positions and made it illegal for anyone to teach without a license.

The 1867 Legislature also enacted other school laws. One stipulated that a tax of 20¢ on each $100 worth of taxable property should be levied to support schools for white children. The school districts would be coterminous with the political township. Another law required the trustees to operate a school in each district at least 3 months a year and warned that if they failed to do so they would forfeit their state revenues. Many people associated free schools with pauper schools, but the first state superintendent of public instruction, Thomas Smith, attempted to change this attitude with slogans such as "schools free to all," "equal rights and privileges to all," and "separate schools for whites and blacks"(5).

At the end of 1867 the carpetbaggers began an effective campaign to gain control of the state government. They had already begun to educate the Negroes and then used Negroes to help them elect Powell Clayton Governor in 1868. From 1868 to 1874, when the carpetbaggers reigned in Arkansas, they appointed many Negroes to offices for which they were not qualified. This was particularly true of J. C. Corbin, a Negro from Ohio, who became state superintendent in 1873 and was serving when the office was abolished the following year (6).

The carpetbag government vested general control of educational affairs in a State Board of Education in 1868. This same year, 10 district or circuit superintendencies were established, and under this system all of the Permanent School Fund was squandered or lost. In 1874, after a hard, bitter struggle, the Democrats regained control of the government by electing Augustus H. Garland as Governor. Shortly after taking office, Governor Garland said: "There is not enough money in the treasury to buy sufficient firewood to build a fire in the Governor's office" (7). Disenchanted by the Reconstruction experience, the state turned against school centralization. When the new constitution was written in 1874, it abolished the office of state superintendent of public instruction, and Arkansas was without a state superintendent for more than a year.

The local township system had worked well when most townships had only one settlement or neighborhood, but as soon as additional communities were founded, they began to demand local school districts to correspond to them. This led directly to the adoption of the common school district system in 1874 (8). Under this system, there was no uniformity in the number of pupils in each district, the size of the districts, or the quality or scope of the available educational program.

As communities grew, the people found that these school districts were incapable of meeting educational needs. Frequently, citizens sought membership on district school boards for selfish purposes. Too often they merely wanted to secure a place for a friend or hoped to escape working on the roads and highways (a school board member was not required to work on the roads), and they spent little time or thought on school matters. In many instances, the directors needed education as much as the children. Not until each district could elect a better-qualified school board and hire a well-qualified school superintendent and a dedicated teaching staff could the state provide adequate schools for its children.

In 1875, the Legislature abolished the office of circuit superintendent and created an elective county superintendency. Two years later this office was eliminated, and the county court established the office of county examiner, whose duties were to conduct teacher examinations and issue teachers' licenses, conduct teacher institutes, and make statistical reports to the state superintendent of public instruction.

To give the schools financial stability, the 1899 General Assembly created a Permanent School Fund by consolidating the three separate funds derived from lands: the Sixteenth Section Fund, the Seminary Land Fund, and the Saline Land Fund. The General Assembly increased this permanent fund in 1919 and passed an act directing that all money derived from the sale of state lands be credited to the common school fund. Only the interest could be spent.

REORGANIZATION AND FINANCE

Early Attempts To Consolidate

At the turn of the century, the schools were so widely scattered that it was necessary for each local district to exercise as much authority as possible. The incumbent superintendent of public instruction, J. J. Doyne, advocated, however, that a county office be created that would exercise stronger control over the school districts. The importance he attached to this office is evident in his annual report for 1900:

> The claims of intelligent supervision are so pronounced that they need no comments. In all lines of activity where system, progress, and well-defined results are sought, it has proven indispensible. . . . The patrons, the director, the teacher, all have a common end in view . . . the culture and development of the child . . . yet as long as there is no one to see that, notwithstanding the diversity of influence, there shall be a unity of purpose, the work of these will be more or less faulty. . . . The State has gone into the business of educating children; . . . educate the children, says the State, and yet it leaves to the school directors and the teachers the privilege of directing this important work according to any plan or no plan, as the importance of the same may impress them. In other words, instead of having at the head of the system in each county a person whose business it shall be to see that well thought out plans shall be executed in every classroom and every director shall have the benefit of such aid and counsel as the importance of the work demands, who shall be under the direction of the State Department of Education and receive in general such instruction from the same as may be necessary to render most efficient the provisions of the school law, thus forming a well organized and effective school system, we have each board of directors exercising its own pleasure in all school matters, and each teacher having the same privilege, so long as he is able to keep on good terms with his board. The saving of the . . . expenses of the district, the increased efficiency of the teacher, the gradation and advancement of the pupil will more than compensate for the expense attached to such office (9).

It was 1907 before the people were given the option of voting in an annual school election whether or not they wanted an elective county superintendent of schools. The number of counties taking advantage of this plan increased steadily until 1919. In that year the Legislature provided each county with a board of education composed of five members elected by popular vote in the annual school election, which then appointed the county superintendent of schools.

As new communities continued to spring up throughout the state, the number of school districts increased from slightly less than 1,500 in 1874 to 5,118 by 1920. A growing demand arose for highway and road improvements to connect these schools, as each community sought to benefit from relations with its neighboring towns. Immediately after World War I, local improvement districts financed the building of highways in many sections of the state. The state assumed the debts of local districts in 1927 and at the same time began financing highway and secondary road building. The expanding network of highways and roads made the people increasingly aware of the advantages of larger school districts and led to numerous consolidations.

Another important factor that prompted school districts to reorganize was the increasing demand for public high schools. At the turn of the century, only the city special school districts had the legal power to maintain public high schools; most secondary education was offered by private academies. In 1899, the state had six 4-year public high schools, and in 1909 there were still only 31. But in 1911, the General Assembly made the high school a part of the public school system. By 1915, the number had increased to 116, with a total enrollment of 8,948 pupils. During the next decade, the number of high schools rose to 290, with an enrollment of 27,255 (10).

During these early years no reorganization plan existed. With the local boards and county superintendents in charge of the schools, what little consolidation did take place resulted from expediency and local whims. The Consolidated District Act, passed by the General Assembly in 1911, did provide for districts to include parts or all of two or more counties, and to form common, consolidated, or special school districts by election. It was this act that made the high school a part of the public school system and resulted in a rapid increase in the number of new high schools. It provided an annual appropriation of $40,000 for state aid to high schools. Another act in 1919 provided for rural special school districts with the same powers as those granted incorporated cities and towns. This also aided the rapid establishment and growth of educational programs for grades 1 through 12.

Governor McRae Creates Financial Stability

When Thomas C. McRae was elected Governor in 1921, the state's finances were in a muddle. World War I had brought the construction of new school buildings to a standstill. The quality of educational programs had been greatly reduced, the better-qualified teachers had left the schoolrooms to serve in the armed forces or work in the plants producing war materials, and the school terms were cut short. The schools suffered in particular from inadequate financial support. From 1874 to 1922, the schools were financed by revenues from state and local general property taxes. In 1906, a constitutional amendment increased the state property tax rate from 1 mill to 3 mills and the permissive local district tax rate from 5 mills to 7 mills. Ten years later the local rate limit was increased to 12 mills, and again to 18 mills in 1926. In 1947 the General Assembly proposed an amendment to the state constitution, which was approved by voters at the polls in the general election in November 1948. This amendment, among other things, removed the ceiling on the local school millage levy and left it to the local school district to determine the number of mills needed. If the voters approved the proposed rate at a regular school election, it became the rate on which local school taxes would be collected. If the proposed tax rate failed to pass, taxes were to be collected at the rate approved in the preceding annual school election. Unfortunately, many of the local laws considerably handicapped the State Legislature.

Governor McRae called two extra sessions of the Legislature, but a crisis developed between the Governor and the Senate. C. P. Newton, the Governor's administrative assistant, described it as follows:

> The Senate refused to function further unless and until Governor McRae agreed to "roll logs" to some political bargaining. . . . The Senate could obstruct measures and refuse to confirm appointments made by the Governor. They indicated a determination to stop the Chief Executive's Program, midstream, if he would not "play ball." The Governor managed to make his answer clear. It was to the effect that the days of such collusion between the Legislature and the Governor were over . . . for the period of his stewardship (11).

In the second session, the Governor advocated an income tax and a privilege or franchise tax to provide better financial support for the schools. Big businessmen induced the farmers to line up against the proposal, and it was defeated.

The Governor finally persuaded the Legislature to pass a cigar and cigarette tax, but the State Supreme Court declared it unconstitutional on a technicality. As soon as the court's decision reached Governor McRae, he made the boldest move of his administration: He called the Legislature for a third extraordinary session to correct the flaws the court had found in the cigar and cigarette law. This call came as a bolt out of the blue to both the public and the legislators. Rumors spread that the Legislature would ignore the call. However, it did meet and, under the Governor's leadership, passed an educational program that attracted the attention of leading educators throughout the nation.

Governor McRae was one of the public schools' greatest friends up to this time. His program strengthened the compulsory school attendance law, established a free library service, and deserves praise for the businesslike manner in which he managed the entangled state finances. His motto was: "Make no appropriation until funds are in sight to meet it." When he retired from office in 1926, there was a cash balance in every fund, and the public school system had been reorganized and strengthened.

The Legislature again attempted to improve the Arkansas schools in 1927 by enacting a law permitting counties having 75,000 or more population to organize all schools–exclusive of first-class city schools–into county school districts if the majority of the citizens voted to do so. This law actually applied only to Pulaski County, which did vote to organize a county district. In 1929 the General Assembly enacted an optional county-unit law under which the people, by a majority vote, could form a county school district under the county board of education and the county superintendent. It further provided–

> That every school district except those in which there is a city of not less than 10,000 inhabitants as aforesaid, whether created by County Courts, County Boards of Education or by special Act of the Legislature, shall cease to exist when a County School District as herein provided for has been created. Said district shall be a special, single school district with all the powers and responsibilities of a Special District organized in cities of the first class (12).

Because this act exempted two counties and one special district, the State Supreme Court invalidated it on grounds that it contravened a constitutional amendment prohibiting local legislation.

In keeping with the trend in other states, the Arkansas Legislature passed a State Equalizing Fund Law (Act 28) in 1927 to assist in equalizing educational opportunities in the public schools by authorizing the State Board of Education to grant aid to needy districts. The board determined the approximate amount of money each district needed and then forwarded requisitions to the State Debt Board. The debt board sold the number of state bonds necessary to build an equalizing fund sufficient to do the job. Since there was an immediate need for new buildings and other facilities, the board of education was permitted to borrow money and issue negotiable coupon bonds.

Survey for Reorganization

To get the best results from this school financing plan, the State Board of Education decided to determine the kind of school that could give adequate service at the lowest cost. A preliminary study showed the need for larger schools and a larger local tax unit. In fact, the state's experience with consolidated schools, established in a more or less haphazard manner during the preceding decade, proved that most were quite satisfactory, particularly in providing a more adequate high school program.

Unfortunately, evidence showed that some campaigns for reorganization had been carried out by overenthusiastic supporters who exaggerated the advantages and quality of such a program, thus selling a number of people on the idea that a larger unit could be operated at considerable savings to the taxpayers. In communities where the citizens failed to provide adequate funds for operating the newly created school districts, the consolidation movement was condemned as a failure. In a few cases where two or more districts had formed a new district, they secured special legislation permitting them to revert back to their original organization. These experiences indicated a need to avoid superconsolidations and to plan a school system that would consider the needs of all the children in every area and community in the state.

In 1928, the State Department of Education made extensive surveys to outline for each of the 75 counties a program of reorganization and consolidation. With the approval of the State Board of Education and a financial grant from the General Education Board, a research staff was placed under the direction of the department's division of research and surveys (13). The survey staff worked closely with the director of school plant services, other members of the department, and four graduate students in education administration from Peabody College in making its study.

The state department also cooperated with its survey staff in determining reorganization standards for the county schools. The school system was to be organized on the basis of a 6-year elementary school leading to a 6-year high school or a 3-year junior high school and a 3-year senior high school. These schools would be planned for a minimum number of pupils in the elementary school and 150 in the 6-year high schools, or 100 each in the junior and senior high schools if maintained separately. Larger school districts would be planned where feasible, but smaller school districts would be proposed where transport conditions, community life, or strong neighborhood ties seemed to justify doing so. The survey staff established the pupil-teacher ratios and agreed that transportation should be provided for all pupils living more than 2 miles from the school and that no pupil should spend more than 2 hours per day traveling to and from school.

The survey team agreed that school districts should be planned to provide 12 years of instruction. The boundary of each district would be determined by the area from which pupils would attend the senior high school, but the district would have as many elementary schools as the neighborhood structure demanded. A local board of education would be in charge of all schools in the district. The county board of education and the county superintendent of schools would then constitute an intermediary between the local district and the state department. The program for each county would be planned so that it might legally reorganize on a county-unit basis without relocating any schools. Whenever the community structure warranted it, the district would include territory in more than one county.

The survey group prepared maps showing topography, highways, district boundary lines, location of schools, and distribution of the school population. It analyzed all data relating to the schools, the community neighborhood structure of each county, and population trends. It consulted with the county board of education in deciding on the district boundaries, where the schools should be located, and the disposition of the existing buildings and property. In many instances, the county superintendent selected committees of lay citizens and educators to advise him, and open community meetings were held frequently to discuss various proposals. When the boundaries and the locations of the school districts were decided, the survey group prepared a map, wrote a descriptive report, and made plans for pupil transportation, school buildings, and the district's budget.

In 1927, the Legislature also had passed Act 156, giving county boards the discretionary power to create new school districts, alter district boundaries, and consolidate school districts when petitioned to do so by a majority of the qualified electors in the area affected. These actions were usually initiated by interested citizens and encouraged by the county superintendent. On receiving the petition, the county board would post notices describing the proposal in each affected district and would set a date within 30 days for a public hearing. After the hearing, the board could then reject the proposal or ratify it by issuing orders establishing the district.

When the surveys began, most of the county boards resolved to approve only reorganization proposals that complied substantially with the countywide plans developed by the survey group. In practically all cases, the county boards refused to approve consolidations that ran counter to the countywide plan or did not progress toward completion of the plan in the future.

Each new district had a board of six directors with the powers usually exercised by school board members in the city school district. The new district assumed all financial liabilities as well as the assets of the old districts. Where school districts were divided, the county board divided the assets and liabilities in proportion to the assessed valuation of taxable property in each district, except that the school buildings became the property of the new district in which they were located. The board of the new district had the power to issue bonds to finance new buildings or to refinance outstanding indebtedness when authorized to do so by a majority vote of the electors voting at an election held for that purpose.

Financing Education

As stated above, the State Equalizing Fund established by the Legislature under Act 28 of 1927 provided the new district sufficient funds to operate the schools in accord with state standards. Whenever the estimated revenue from customary state sources and from the 18-mill local property tax was insufficient to maintain these standards (including pupil transportation), the district received the difference between this revenue and the cost from the equalizing fund. The State Board of Education would aid only those districts that conformed to its regulations and to certain requirements stated in the law. Thus, the state board gave first—although not exclusive—consideration to reorganized districts set up according to the countywide plan.

At this time the state department was confronted with a serious financial problem. The majority of the 4,734 school districts were heavily in debt; most of them had issued bonds for constructing new buildings and for purchasing equipment. In many instances nearly all the current annual revenue of these districts was required to pay the principal and interest on the bonds already outstanding, and their buildings and equipment were already antiquated and in a bad state of repair.

In March 1927 the General Assembly passed Act 119, creating a Revolving Loan Fund to further relieve the needy school districts. The act directed the State Debt Board to make the assets of the Permanent School Fund available to the revolving fund so that it could make loans to various school districts for repairing, erecting, or equipping the school buildings, and to pay off the outstanding indebtedness already incurred. The State Debt Board could authorize the funds to be transferred from the Permanent School Fund to the Revolving Loan Fund as the cash balance accumulated.

This Permanent School Fund has been developed over a period of many years from revenues received from the sale of the federal land grants. As mentioned earlier, it is loaned to various state agencies, chief of which is the Revolving Loan Fund, which in turn provides income for the State Common School Fund. The State Common School Fund, the general school fund for Arkansas, is distributed quarterly to the various counties on the basis of the school census (enumeration) after the funds have been appropriated and certain deductions have been made.

Probably no other legislation has been more beneficial to Arkansas' school system than the Revolving Loan Fund. All payments are current, and there have been no defaults. The state board consistently refused, as in the case of the equalizing funds, to lend money for constructing buildings that did not conform in location and type to the countywide plan of school reorganization.

The equalizing fund reserved 25 percent of its money for new school buildings. If a district that could not pay for a state-standard plan approved by the director of the department's division of schoolhouse planning borrowed enough money to equal 7 percent of the assessed valuation of its taxable property, the state board could grant the additional amount needed.

The proposal, for the state as a whole, called for establishing 307 local administrative units, an average of four districts per county. Each district was to have a senior high school, one or more junior high schools (or a junior-senior high school), and one or more elementary schools. In all, the plan called for 1,784 elementary schools, 270 of which were to be isolated eight-grade schools; 560 separate junior high schools; and 307 senior or junior-senior high schools, a large majority to be the latter. The surveys did not try in all cases to make a final recommendation on the exact type of organization. The plan called for the number of one-teacher schools to be reduced from 2,495 to 473, two-teacher schools from 920 to 478, and three- and four-teacher schools from 371 to 256; the number of schools having five or more teachers was to be increased from 412 to 577. The equalizing fund would provide about $2.8 million annually to finance the new program, but the estimated enrollment expansion called for an additional $3,666,000 annually.

From the 1927-28 to the 1931-32 school years, more than 350 consolidated districts were formed, 173 in 1929-30 alone. These new districts provided 660 school centers with new, improved facilities. The number of districts decreased from 4,711 in 1926-27 to 3,086 in 1932-33–a total reduction of 1,625. The major reductions occurred in 1929-30 (664) and 1930-31 (591). The number of one-teacher schools for white pupils decreased during this same period from 3,106 to 1,990. This brought corresponding increases in the number of pupils transported to schools: 3,136 in 1926; 9,694 in 1928; 25,563 in 1930; and 52,654 in 1932 (14).

Both enrollments and size of the high schools increased immediately following the reorganization program. In 1926, the high schools enrolled approximately 31,000 students; by 1931 they had 47,274. The surveys indicated that the average enrollment would increase to 153 pupils per high school, with only two senior high schools in the entire state having fewer than 40 pupils.

Impact of the Depression

As in other states, the Depression hit Arkansas schools hard, and the decline in both state and local revenues contributed heavily to bringing the entire reorganization program to a halt. In 1931, the General Assembly changed the reorganization law to require a majority vote or a petition signed by the majority of the electors in *each* district–rather than a majority in the proposed district–in order to consolidate two or more districts. This change was not the result of an all-out movement against reorganization, but was rather an innocent-looking bill that was hotly contested. The General Assembly also abolished the distinction between the various types of school districts and declared all districts to have the same powers and privileges as the city special districts. (In 1937, as a result of another reorganization study financed by the Works Progress Administration, districts were classified according to size in order to determine the number of board members each should have.)

Despite this legislation, which effectively stopped district reorganization, the state school system was strengthened by another act passed by the 1931 Legislature. Governor Harvey Parnell persuaded the legislators that the State Department of Education could function more efficiently if the elective office of state superintendent were abolished and the State Board of Education empowered to select a commissioner of education. This act enabled the board to organize and control the state department, and it has gradually strengthened its power and expanded its duties. As a result, the state board's prestige has increased tremendously.

In 1941, the General Assembly passed Act 127, which reorganized both the State Board of Education and the State Department of Education. It required the state board to be composed of nine members appointed by the Governor, subject to the confirmation of the Senate, one from each congressional district and the remainder at large. The Governor was given the power to remove members of the board for sufficient reasons after a formal hearing and a majority vote by the board. This enabled the board and the department staff to reach a high degree of professional standards and stability (15). Under the dynamic leadership of Commissioner A. W. Ford, who has served under three Governors continuously since 1953, the professional staff of the department has attained a high degree of stability, accounting for the rapid expansion and development of a quality educational program never before achieved in the history of this state.

Finding New Revenues

The General Assembly also attempted to provide stability to the schools by passing an act in 1941 earmarking for the Common School Fund 50 percent of the net returns from a 2-percent sales tax. Another piece of legislation gave to this fund 39.2 percent of the net proceeds from an excise tax of $2.50 per thousand on the sale of cigarettes.

Prior to 1945, when the General Assembly enacted the Revenue Stabilization Law sponsored by Governor Ben Laney, deficit spending was permitted under certain circumstances, and each assembly was faced with the problem of taking care of the resulting debts. Under this law, certain revenues, including sales tax, income tax, cigarette tax, and taxes on alcoholic beverages, were grouped into a category designated as General Revenues. It is from this General Revenue Fund that the public school funds were appropriated (16).

One major source of revenue for supporting the schools was lost when the General Assembly abolished the state ad valorem property tax, a 6.5-mill levy that produced an average of $4 million annually for the General Revenue Fund. The 1947 Legislature reenacted this levy for 1948, but only on sand and gravel (17). The citizens voted down a proposed amendment to the State Constitution which would have removed the state permanently from the property tax field; however, an amendment proposed by the General Assembly and accepted by the voters at the general election in November 1958 prohibits the General Assembly from levying an ad valorem tax on property.

An amendment was added to the constitution in 1949 which removed the ceiling on the local tax rate, providing that–

> The Board of Directors shall prepare, approve, and make public, not less than sixty days in advance of the annual school election, a proposed Budget of expenditures deemed necessary to provide for the foregoing purposes, together with a rate of tax levy sufficient to provide the funds therefor, including the rate under any continuing levy for the retirement of indebtedness. If a majority of qualified electors in the district voting in the annual school election shall approve a proposed tax rate, then the tax on the proposed tax rate shall be collected. In the event a majority shall disapprove the proposed tax rate, then the tax shall be collected at the rate approved in the preceding annual school election (18).

AEA's Reorganizational Efforts

The reorganization problem was always closely connected with the efforts to finance the schools. The Arkansas Education Association, with the support of the State Department of Education, initiated a proposal under the initiative and referendum amendment to the state constitution providing for the dissolution of all districts having fewer than 350 residents between the ages of 6 and 17, inclusive. It also called for these districts to be organized into county rural school districts under the superintendency of the county school supervisors. The county boards of education could annex the territory of their county school districts to other districts if the latter's boards also consented. The proposal, submitted to the electors of the state in the November general election of 1946, was defeated by a narrow margin of 1,301 votes (19).

Two years later, the AEA and the State Department of Education placed a similar measure, known as the School District Reorganization Bill, on the ballot. Initiated Act No. 1 of 1948 was approved by the voters by a margin of about three to one. Under its provisions, the number of school districts was immediately reduced to 426, and has gradually decreased to only 395 in 1967 (20).

In 1965, when the Arkansas Education Association proposed another initiated act, it aroused aggressive opposition from a group known as the Arkansas Rural Education Association (AREA). Although its officers represented the smaller rural school districts, its membership was drawn from medium and even larger school districts as well. It slowly gained strength so that later in 1965, when the AEA introduced this proposed initiated act to further reorganize the school districts by abolishing all having fewer than 400 pupils, the AREA was able to offer formidable opposition. The battle lines were so tightly drawn that the AEA's Council on Education amended the original proposal to read that all districts with less than 2,000 pupils would be dissolved and annexed to other existing districts.

The council sent letters to each delegate asking how many petitions he wanted and how many signatures he could secure. Of those who responded, an overwhelming majority objected to the 2,000 provision. The executive committee of the AEA unanimously voted to drop this figure, and a few days later the original 400 proposal was revived by Joshua K. Shepherd, a Little Rock insurance executive and a long-time friend of public education. He organized a statewide committee and personally raised the money to cover the expenses of initiating a petition for the proposed act.

By early July the petitions had a sufficient number of signatures to get the proposal on the ballot. When the Council on Education held a special meeting on October 1, it voted to endorse this plan. Despite all these efforts, the plan was overwhelmingly defeated at the general election in November 1966.

TEACHER EDUCATION, CERTIFICATION, AND INSTRUCTIONAL SERVICES

Teacher Certification

Junius Jordon, the state superintendent of public instruction from 1894 to 1898, described the improvements in the competence and proficiency of Arkansas teachers due to the Peabody Fund as "fantastic." He stated:

> The trustees of the Peabody Fund still continue their beneficent donations annually in favor of Summer Normal Schools. In addition to this, they gave to this State seventeen free scholarships to the Peabody Normal University at Nashville, Tennessee. The benefits that have accrued to all will be a perpetual monument to the memory of Mr. Peabody who has enabled Arkansas to arouse the pride and improve the professional power of every teacher within the borders (21).

Dr. Jordon persuaded the Legislature to pass an act providing for teacher institutes to run 4 months each year, but it was an appropriation by the Peabody Board in 1899–1 year after Jordon had left office–that made these institutes possible. By 1900, 53 institutes were providing professional training for 2,034 students. At this time, the county examiner administered the teacher examination quarterly, based on the following requirements:

> Nothing below fifty per cent to be considered; for a first grade certificate, eighty-five per cent of the examination must be passed; for a second grade, seventy-five per cent; and for a third grade, sixty per cent. The examination included tests in written arithmetic, mental arithmetic, grammar, and orthography. An average of the above percentages must be made upon all of the other tests combined (22).

All teachers who passed the examination received county certificates classified as third-grade county licenses good for 6 months, second-grade county licenses valid for 1 year, or first-grade county licenses good for 2 years.

In 1900, the Legislature invested the state superintendent with power to grant a state certificate valid for life. The law stated: "Applicants for State Certificates must bear in mind that the school law, section 6974, requires an examination. The statute does not recognize diplomas from colleges, normals, or universities" (23). The act required the applicants to be examined in the same subjects as for county licenses: algebra, geometry, physics, rhetoric, mental philosophy, history, Latin, the Constitutions of the United States and Arkansas, natural history, and the theory and art of teaching.

There were no changes in the certification laws until 1941, when the Arkansas Legislature delegated sole certificating authority to the State Board of Education. The law stipulated that to be eligible for a teacher's license, the applicant had to be at least 18 years of age and not over 72, to be of good moral character, and believe in a supreme being (24). Although an applicant could now receive a certificate by submitting a college transcript, the 1941 Legislature continued the policy of allowing individuals desiring to teach in a particular county to be certified by passing an examination given twice each year by the county supervisor. However, the county supervisor could issue only one type of county certificate: the state board county certificate. Holders of county second- and third-grade certificates were required to convert these to state board county certificates on or before September 1, 1941. Holders of county first-grade certificates could retain them or convert them to statewide certificates.

In its 1941 reorganization of the certification laws, the Legislature stipulated that an administrator's certificate valid for 6 years could be issued to a person holding a bachelor's degree from an approved institution. This was changed in 1946 to a minimum of a master's degree in an approved institution, with at least 14 semester hours in education, including 8 semester hours in graduate work in school administration.

The law also stated that to earn the 6-year high school certificate, an applicant had to be a graduate from an approved 4-year college with certain minimum requirements. A 4-year junior high school certificate would be issued on a minimum of 60 semester hours from an approved college if this included specific areas of study. The 6-year elementary certificate required a bachelor's degree, but a 4-year elementary certificate would be issued to a person who had completed 2 years of college, and a 3-year elementary certificate could be issued after 1 year of college work.

These legal requirements were not changed during the Depression or World War II. But during these periods of national turmoil, the requirements were not strictly enforced.

In 1956, Commissioner A. W. Ford appointed a subcommittee of seven from the Arkansas Advisory Council on Teacher Education and Certification to initiate the most comprehensive study ever made in the state on the board's responsibility for certification. The council specifically directed that this study should include the role of the colleges. With the state department's assistant commissioner for instructional services as chairman (25), the Committee of Seven in representing public and private schools, the University of Arkansas, the public schools, and the State Department of Education spent more than 3 years researching, analyzing, and writing recommendations.

On the basis of the subcommittee's report, the state board wrote new requirements for certification, to become effective September 1, 1963. The 6-year superintendent certificate now required a master's degree with a minimum of 20 semester hours of graduate education courses in at least five areas. The 6-year secondary school principal certificate required a master's degree with a minimum of 20 semester hours of graduate credit in administration and supervision of secondary schools, and at least five 3-hour courses in specified areas. The 6-year elementary school principal certificate required a master's degree, including at least 18 semester hours of graduate credit in administration and supervision of elementary education in a minimum of four specified areas.

A person desiring a 6-year high school certificate according to the new certification requirements should have a bachelor's degree with 18 hours in education, along with certain courses in the various teaching fields. A 5-year high school permit could be issued to a candidate with 90 credit hours, if 15 hours were in education and the total included special requirements in the teaching fields. The board allowed a 4-year high school permit to be issued on 60 semester hours, including specified work in the teaching fields and 12 hours in education. Similar prerequisites applied to 5-year and 4-year elementary certificates.

The State Department of Education, following the recommendations of the Committee of Seven and its own staff, adopted a regulation requiring all beginning teachers to possess certificates based on a minimum of a bachelor's degree after September 1, 1963. It no longer allowed permits to be issued, and teachers holding such permits were given a reasonable time to earn additional hours (an average of 6 hours per year) to qualify for regular certificates. At present, less than 3 percent of Arkansas' teachers have less than a bachelor's degree.

The Department of Education's certification division, which is a part of the instructional services division, not only analyzes transcripts and issues proper certificates, but works closely with the colleges and universities to plan and develop teacher education programs. At present, it has approved teacher training programs in 18 institutions of higher education.

School Accreditation

In 1909, when V. W. Tarryson joined the faculty of the State University of Arkansas at Fayetteville, he became the first professor of secondary education in the state. From his office in the State Department of Education, he led a movement to standardize the state's high schools. This resulted in the General Assembly's passing legislation making the high schools a part of the public school system and providing for a system of supervision by the department staff, which developed the criteria for minimum standards. This first attempt to accredit high schools according to A, B, or C ratings ended with 20 A-, 44 B-, and 10 C- rated high schools in 1909. Within a decade there were 84 A's, 38 B's, and 38 C's.

From 1909 to 1924, a number of high schools were accredited by the Southern Association. In 1924, 28 Arkansas high schools, all members of the Southern Association, transferred their membership to the North Central Association of Secondary Colleges (NCA). By the 1966-67 school term, NCA had granted membership to 156 schools in the state, and there were 187 high schools with an A rating, 95 with a B rating, and 51 with a C rating.

With the great emphasis on the secondary schools, Arkansas' elementary schools suffered. Receiving little attention and less help, they grew around the high schools instead of into them. Weaker teachers were assigned to the elementary grades, classrooms were crowded, and the schools were almost completely lacking in libraries and equipment. As educators and the public alike finally realized that the school system's ultimate success depended in large measure on the efficiency of the elementary schools, a movement to improve them gradually gained ground. In 1931, the assembly authorized the State Department of Education to standardize the elementary schools.

To provide proper supervision for standardizing all the schools, the department began to employ more elementary and high school supervisors and add supervisors of special programs such as agriculture, home economics, and guidance. The department coordinated these services so that it could influence the total educational program. Although it has maintained its special program supervisors, in 1945, the department changed the duties of its elementary and high school supervisors by making each responsible for both elementary and secondary schools in his particular supervisory area.

In 1954, Commissioner A. W. Ford reorganized the State Department of Education to give more emphasis to supervising special programs such as speech therapy, special education, and vocational education. Federal programs, such as the National Defense Education Act of 1958 (NDEA) and the Elementary and Secondary Education Act of 1965 (ESEA), have accelerated this trend toward specialized supervision.

Supervisors in the instructional services division have a multiplicity of duties and responsibilities. Each general supervisor is assigned to the elementary and secondary council or to one area, such as English, health and physical education, science, dramatics, social studies, library science, economics, modern foreign language, reading, general education, and economic education. Special education has become a full-time assignment.

The supervisor represents the department in upholding standards and reports on conditions and progress in the schools. But much more important than his regulatory function is his leadership role in developing understanding and a genuine desire to improve instructional programs. This requires him to have considerable information on all phases of the school program and to be tactful, persuasive, sincere, and dedicated. Real leadership cannot be imposed—the supervisor must earn the local school people's respect and admiration.

The associate commissioner in charge of the instructional services division is chairman of the North Central Association's state committee. Each supervisor is a member of the State Accreditation Committee and thus participates in the annual review and accreditation of schools. After reviewing the annual report of each North Central Association secondary school, the general supervisor abstracts his findings for the state committee. Following the state committee's session, he makes separate abstracts for each school and attaches one to the report for the annual meeting in Chicago. Each general supervisor recommends the secondary schools that are to conduct self-evaluations during the year, and he is responsible for these plans and preparations. A self-evaluation of each NCA member high school must be made at least every 7 years.

Accreditation of the elementary and secondary schools also is required by the law, which says: "The State Board of Education shall have general supervision of the Public Schools of the State . . . qualify and standardize public schools of the State" (26). The Division of Instructional Services has prepared a set of policies, regulations, and criteria, which the board has adopted, outlining the minimum standards a school must meet before it can be accredited. The policies are guiding principles followed by the department; the regulations are the minimum requirements for accreditation; the criteria are guideposts pointing to goals of excellence. The extent to which a school conforms to the policies, regulations, and criteria determines whether it will be accredited as a Class A, Class B, or Class C elementary or secondary school.

Adult Education

The Division of Instructional Services is responsible for a general adult education program initiated by the department in 1961. Its purpose is to raise the educational level of adults at both the elementary and secondary levels and to provide dropouts the opportunity to earn a high school diploma or a certificate of equivalency. Any Arkansas resident 18 years or older who has less than a high school education and who has been out of school 6 months or longer may enroll in a variety of courses (27) including language, arts, mathematics, social studies, science, and foreign languages.

A local or county board is eligible to sponsor classes in adult education. School districts participating in the program are then reimbursed 100 percent of the amount paid to teachers. With the financial assistance now available through Titles I and II of ESEA, Public Law 89-10, nearly all the schools in the state are strengthening their programs by adding teachers, teacher aides, counselors, librarians, remedial teachers in various subject areas, and many other specialists whom they could not afford in the past.

The Department of Education established a General Educational Development (GED) testing program in 1945 for young men drafted out of high school during World War II. When the general adult education program began during the 1961-62 school year, nonveteran adults who had completed a minimum of 120 hours of instruction in an approved general adult education program were eligible to take these tests to earn the equivalency of a high school diploma, but veterans with 90 or more days of military service were exempt from this requirement.

At present, the education department can issue certificates of equivalency of high school graduation to both veterans and nonveterans 20 years of age or older who have successfully completed the GED test. However, if an employer writes the assistant commissioner of instructional services stating that he will employ an applicant if he passes the GED test, the applicant will not be required to complete the 120 hours of instruction in adult classes. During the 1965-66 school year, 1,790 GED applicants were processed, including 630 who had taken the general adult education program, 700 who had completed U.S. Armed Forces Institute courses, 260 veterans not required to take the 120 hours of instruction, and 200 nonveterans tested for employment (28).

The associate commissioner for instructional services also administers an adult basic education program authorized under the federal Economic Opportunity Act of 1964. Its objectives are to raise the educational level of adults 18 years or older who have less than a sixth-grade education and need more training or retraining to secure jobs commensurate with their ability, and to make them less dependent on others.

Handicapped Children

The Division of Educational Personnel Training of the U.S. Office of Education has general responsibility for operating and financing a program for handicapped children under the terms of Public Law 85-926. This program awards grants to institutions of higher education and to state education agencies for preparing persons to teach handicapped children and to be supervisors of teachers, speech therapists, and other specialists. The program is administered by the special education supervisors of the state agency.

This program is expanding due to the additional funds made available under the provisions of Public Law 88-164, which supplements the state appropriation for this program. Public Law 88-164 provides funds for the preparation of professional personnel in the education of the handicapped. This program is also being supplemented by a planning grant under the provisions of Title VI of ESEA, Public Law 89-10.

The director of this program provides leadership and consultative services to the public school, the Childrens Colony, and similar institutions and agencies of the state.

PROGRAMS IN VOCATIONAL AND REHABILITATION EDUCATION

In 1917, Congress passed the Smith-Hughes Act, which appropriated funds for promoting vocational education in agriculture, trades and industry, and home economics, and for training teachers in these fields. The law required the State Department of Education to allocate these federal funds to local school districts to defray as much as 50 percent of their instructional costs. The George-Reed Act of 1929 extended the provisions of the act by authorizing more funds for vocational agriculture and home economics. The George-Deen Act of 1936, the George-Ellzey Act of 1934, and the George-Barden Act of 1946 all provided additional federal financial support and widened the scope of these programs. By 1947, federal funds were providing a high percentage of the costs of these programs.

Within 11 days after Congress approved the Smith-Hughes Act, the Arkansas Legislature enacted legislation to qualify the state for federal aid and set up a program of vocational education. A. B. Hill (29), the first state director of vocational education, worked with community leaders to organize vocational training schools that would prepare every individual in the state to enter the world of work and advance in his chosen occupation.

Agriculture

The vocational agriculture programs were organized primarily for boys 14 years of age or older in rural areas who were enrolled in regular high school subjects or who had reached the ninth grade. Each student was required to enroll in a supervised farming program in addition to his regular agricultural classes, all under the direct supervision of the regular vocational agriculture teacher. Each of these vocational agriculture teachers conducted at least two classes for adult farmers—one consisting of boys who had completed or dropped out of school and were becoming established in farming, and the other for adults who had already become farmers.

In 1923, the vocational agriculture pupils at Bruno High School organized the Lincoln Aggie Club, believed to be the first organization of its kind in the nation (30). When the National Future Farmers of America was organized in 1928, Arkansas received the second FFA charter (31). The Danville chapter was the first chapter in the state (32). Throughout the history of the FFA, Arkansas chapters and members have been active at all levels; John Haid of Siloam Springs served as national president during the 1956-57 school year.

The State Department of Education employed two specialists in 1959, one to supervise and assist high schools in developing a program of livestock improvement, and one to assist high schools in teaching the selection, operation, and maintenance of farm facilities and equipment.

Technical and Industrial Education

World War I not only revealed the need to improve techniques in agriculture, but brought an increasing demand for industrial products, requiring thousands of new industrial workers. One of the major purposes of the 1917 Smith-Hughes Act was to prepare youth and adults for industry and help those already employed gain advancement.

In 1918 the trade and industrial program in Arkansas consisted only of a drafting class for adults at Little Rock High School and a high school printing class at Hot Springs. It was 1927 before the General Assembly implemented this part of the Smith-Hughes Act and provided for establishing and maintaining public school vocational training. The state was divided into four districts, each authorized to establish two state vocational schools. The Governor appointed a three-man board of trustees charged with selecting the locations of the schools. A community wishing to be considered as a site for one of these vocational schools was required to donate land, buildings, and equipment, and raise at least $15,000. The only two state vocational schools established under this act, one at Huntsville in Madison County and the other at Clinton in Van Buren County, continued to operate until the Legislature discontinued them in 1955.

Governor Orval E. Faubus worked untiringly to organize the Arkansas Industrial Development Commission in 1955. Under the leadership of its chairman, Winthrop Rockefeller, this commission attempted to sell the advantages of Arkansas to industrialists looking for sites for new industry or to expand their present business. It was evident to the members of the commission that to attract industry—especially new industry—Arkansas would have to supply technically trained employees. Faubus convinced the 1957 Legislature of the real need for Act 328, authorizing the State Board for Vocational Education to create vocational-technical schools for persons 16 years of age and over.

The first plant constructed with state funds was the Pines Vocational-Technical School at Pine Bluff. The Petit Jean Vocational-Technical School, also constructed from state funds, opened at Morrilton in 1963. At present, additional classroom and shop space has been provided at both the Pine Bluff and Morrilton Schools. In September 1966, schools opened at Ozark, Searcy, Hope, and Burdett in plants constructed with federal-state matching funds, and schools were under construction at Harrison, Marked Tree, Forrest City, and El Dorado.

The state's objective is to make vocational and technical courses available to all its citizens 16 years of age or older, and to provide new industry and industrial development with skilled workers. The courses offered by the 10 vocational-technical schools include welding, tailoring, sheet-metal fabrication, masonry, horticulture and landscaping, forestry, cabinetmaking, air conditioning, auto mechanics, body repair, cooking, machine shop, office practice, practical nursing, radio-television service, cosmetology, electronics, and data processing. In addition to these resident courses, mobile units move into areas where such training is needed. When the federal Vocational Education Act of 1963 was passed, business and office education was added to the program. Neither the resident nor the mobile units give high school or college credit.

Distributive Education

Arkansas also has a distributive education program for high school students in grades 11 and 12. Little Rock Senior High School (now Little Rock Central High School) started a program known as "retail selling" in 1929, 7 years prior to the passage of the George-Deen Act in 1936. Arkansas is a charter member of Distributive Education Clubs of America, organized in 1947, composed of students enrolled in distributive education and trade and industrial subjects. In 1966, the future tradesmen disbanded, and the club adopted the name "Arkansas Association of DECA."

Twenty-seven high schools offer distributive education programs, employing coordinators who teach the students two periods per day and work with them in their employing firms in the afternoon. The distributive education section also maintains three programs at the state level for adults, including retail selling, petroleum industry training, commercial food service, management training, human relations, and tourist service.

The trade and industry division offers preparatory courses for specific occupations to students at least 16 years of age, including on-the-job training, applied mathematics, science, and blueprint reading. It offers extension courses to those who cannot attend organized classes and provides supervised training in how to train employees on the job, employee relationships, and safety; it conducts regional schools for firemen in cooperation with local fire departments. This division also offers free employment training for new industries.

Home Economics

The home economics program offers courses in foods and nutrition, clothing selection and sewing, child care and development, personal and family relationships, housing equipment, and home furnishings, as well as home management to the students in grades 8 through 12 enrolled in a regularly organized high school. Adult education is an integral part of the vocational homemaking program. It informs homemakers about new trends, developments, and techniques. The first high school programs established on a continuing basis were initiated in the 1920-21 school year at Newport, Hazen, Hope, Dermott, and Arkadelphia.

In 1945, representatives from Arkansas attended the organizational meeting of the Future Homemakers of America in Chicago. A group organized an Arkansas affiliate the same year and at the same time chartered the New Homemakers of America for Negro girls. The home economics teachers served as advisors to the local chapters, which were affiliated with state and national associations. The Future Homemakers of America and the New Homemakers of America were merged July 15, 1965, to be known as the Arkansas Association, Future Homemakers of America.

In 1959, the state department employed a clothing specialist to work with teachers and adult homemakers through workshops, conferences, and visits to local schools.

Nursing Education

In 1947, the Legislature passed the Nurse Practice Act, which stipulated that persons engaged in nursing without a license would have to submit proof of their qualifications and register for a license by waiver before May 1, 1948. Approximately 1,400 women without formal training were licensed in this way. In 1948, the state department's vocational division allocated funds to employ a registered nurse to conduct extension courses for women who had no formal training, and 655 licensed practical nurses enrolled in the first course. After the waiver period had elapsed, it was evident that schools were still needed to train practical nurses. Since the law required practical nurses to graduate from an approved school and successfully complete a state board examination before they could obtain a license, the Division of Vocational Education set aside funds for a practical nursing school, which opened in Little Rock in 1948. Four years later, the Kellogg Foundation provided funds to purchase equipment and hire three additional registered nurses. At the same time, the number of instruction hours was increased to 150.

The success of the Little Rock School prompted the Kellogg Foundation to open other schools. Under its plan, the new schools were financed by Kellogg fully the first year, two-thirds the second year, and one-third the third year. After this, the Kellogg Foundation support was terminated, and the vocational education funds had to provide full support. The department's vocational division now administers 16 practical nurse education schools using 46 affiliated hospitals for clinical experiences, all approved by the Arkansas State Board of Nursing and State Board of Education (33). After completing a year of instruction, the graduates are eligible to take the examination for a license as practical nurses.

The vocational division now receives federal funds under the Vocational Education Act of 1963 for practical nurse education programs and other health occupation education. It offers courses in practical nursing, organized in local school districts for adults between the ages of 19 and 50. It also has programs at the secondary level for health occupations, adult classes for continuing education, and postsecondary level programs for medical laboratory assistants and dental assistants. These classes run for 1 year. They include instruction in theory and practice and provide hospital-learning experiences under the supervision of a graduate nurse.

After a thorough study of occupational needs, the employment security division recommended training medical assistants. The Metropolitan High School in Little Rock started such a course for eleventh- and twelfth-grade girls and boys in 1965, consisting of techniques in nursing, the terminology of health occupations, background, medical aid, health record keeping, and field trips. The students are also required to learn office practices and typing. After completing the course, the students are prepared to become medical assistants in doctors' offices or hospitals, or to enter the regular training programs in hospitals. It is the only course of its kind offered in the Arkansas public high schools.

In the first year the public schools offered training under the Smith-Hughes Act, they included training only in agriculture, home economics, printing, and mechanical drawing. In the 1966-67 school year, preemployment instruction was provided in almost 100 occupational classifications. The Arkansas program includes 297 agricultural departments, 384 home economics departments, 27 distributive education programs, 13 office occupations programs, 15 practical nursing programs, 70 high school trade and industrial programs, and 10 area vocational-technical schools operated by the State Board for Vocational Education.

Rehabilitation Education

The federal Vocational Rehabilitation Act of 1954, Public Law 565, allotted funds to the state agencies for establishing and operating centers, workshops, small-business enterprises, and other facilities which could be integral parts or supplements to a regular program of rehabilitation. In 1955, the Arkansas Legislature authorized the state to participate. However, it was not until Congress gave the Army-Navy Hospital at Hot Springs to the state that the State Board for Vocational Education was able to administer such a center. The Legislature passed an act in 1959 making the Rehabilitation Center an integral part of the Arkansas Rehabilitation Service, although the business and financial operations are separate from the regular program. It provides medical, psychological, social, and vocational evaluation and services needed by the disabled—particularly the severely disabled.

The Rehabilitation Center provides basic services for medical evaluation and supervision, physical therapy, occupational therapy, and speech therapy. The emphasis is on building up physical tolerance and developing muscles, strength, and coordination, and in fitting and using prostheses. It is staffed by psychologists, social workers, and counselors to provide services relating to student personnel activities. It employs a number of doctors on a part-time consultative basis and maintains a staff of physical therapists, occupational therapists, speech therapists, nurses, aids, and attendant and student trainees. The center has approximately 50 beds for individuals who need active nursing care.

The center provides high-quality vocational evaluation, as well as training in 20 or more trades or vocations in which handicapped persons can find employment. The vocations are selected from a survey of the industrial needs of Arkansas and the Southwest, and there is space for training 300 or more persons at one time. The center directs workshops in other activities in which clients are evaluated for employment in particular work situations, and they are trained in acceptable work habits as well as motivation for work. The latter two are particularly useful for persons handicapped by social and emotional factors which have destroyed their motivation or adjustment for work.

An integral part of the total project is research, demonstration, and experimentation in problems of rehabilitation. The center engages in special projects to solve these problems, and it has become a principal research facility, engaging in projects in which other states are interested. At full capacity, it can serve 500 persons at one time in the basic program, and approximately 100 persons can be employed in the workshops and 50 in the work evaluation and training programs. The Rehabilitation Center's services are available to clients of the rehabilitation agencies of other states, public and private agencies and organizations, labor unions, and insurance companies. The fees charged for these services defray most of the operating expenses.

In 1959, the Legislature turned over the Rehabilitation Service duties connected with the Disability Determination Bureau of Old Age and Assistance Insurance, which deals with persons who are disabled and covered by Social Security. The Rehabilitation Service, by state law, is also the sole agency to administer services to the blind. The service operates programs for other public agencies, such as the rehabilitation facilities of the State Hospital, the State Sanatorium, the McRae Sanatorium, the School for the Deaf, the School for the Blind, and the Training School for Girls. In cooperation with private agencies, it also operates a vending stand program for the blind and sheltered workshops in the homebound industries program.

The trend in rehabilitation services in recent years has been more and more for health and welfare services. Educational services remain as a function of the agency, but they no longer constitute the major phase of its work. The cooperative arrangements of the Arkansas Rehabilitation Service with other institutions or agencies have increased personnel and services. Such arrangements supplement the programs of the various institutions and agencies, but the State Board for Vocational Education in no way interferes with the administration of the institutions concerned (34). For example, although it assists the School for the Deaf, the School for the Blind, the State Tuberculosis Sanatorium, and others, the Rehabilitation Service has no control over their operations.

SERVICES TO THE SCHOOLS

School Lunch Program

The first school lunch programs in Arkansas, as in most other states, were started by dedicated teachers who cooked the food brought in by children to make hot soup or stew as a supplement to the cold lunches they brought from home. The Depression provided the impetus that firmly established school lunches. As early as 1932 surplus foods were distributed on a limited basis for free lunches. In 1935, Congress provided a permanent annual appropriation to the Department of Agriculture, enabling it to institute a direct purchase and distribution program to help farmers with the surplus problem, and the nonprofit school lunch program received a portion of these commodities. At the same time, when the Works Progress Administration was created in 1936, it provided funds to employ cooks and servers in schools throughout the United States. Arkansas schools immediately took advantage of both of these programs and began feeding children with improvised equipment provided by local Parent-Teachers Associations.

In 1939, the Department of Agriculture announced an expanded lunch program to distribute surplus foods on the basis of the number of needy children served. Gradually the initial relief aspect of the program blended into one with a twofold objective: improving the children's health and encouraging an increased consumption of surplus agricultural commodities. Most of the Arkansas schools were happy to participate in the WPA program. The cash reimbursement program, which paid for part of the food purchased locally by schools, was begun in the spring of 1943. The following year, Congress authorized a specific amount for operating the school lunch and penny milk programs, permitting them to operate whether or not foods were at a surplus.

In 1945, Congress appropriated funds for a school lunch program and specified for the first time the conditions under which it could be provided. This act served as a basic authority for the present National School Lunch Program, passed in 1946. The Legislature gave the State Department of Education the authority to administer the funds under the National School Lunch Act, and the state board created this service in its vocational division in July 1947. The staff, under an agreement between the State Department of Education and the U.S. Department of Agriculture, was made responsible for distributing federal funds to local school districts based on the number of lunches served. The department's supervisory staff was then responsible for reviewing the program to determine if the lunches met the Secretary of Agriculture's minimum requirements. During these reviews, the department could provide consultative services in management, equipment, menu planning, food purchasing, food preparation, and record keeping. The administration of this program is now under the vocational education services division.

The auditors carry out audits on approximately 20 percent of the programs in operation during each fiscal year, not only to account for the federal funds, but also to determine whether they have been used in accordance with the regulations. The staff processes the school lunch claims made by local districts on a monthly basis. During the 1946-47 school year, the state received $271,257 in federal funds to assist the local districts in purchasing school lunch equipment. The Special School Milk Program was authorized by the Agriculture Act of 1954 and was initiated in Arkansas in 1955 by 888 schools. During its years of operation, this program has increased to the point where 1,034 schools are operating special milk programs.

In the 1965-66 school year, Arkansas schoolchildren consumed 30,916,413 type A lunches. A great increase in the number of children participating during the last half of the 1965-66 school year has been due to the special attention given to the disadvantaged children with funds provided by ESEA, Public Law 89-10, and the provision in the 1966 appropriation implementing Section 11 of the National School Lunch Act. Many schools in low-income areas are now able to construct school lunch facilities, purchase equipment, and provide free meals with funds available through Title I of Public Law 89-10. In 1964-65, Arkansas ranked ninth with 51 percent of its public elementary and secondary school enrollment participating in the School Lunch Program.

Under the provisions of Public Law 89-642, the Child Nutrition Act of 1966, several schools are participating in the Breakfast Program, which is designed primarily for underprivileged schoolchildren.

Guidance and Counseling

The State Department of Education took its first step in developing a guidance program for public schools in July 1942 by appointing Dolph Camp as the first state supervisor of occupational information and guidance services in the department's vocational education division (35). The emphasis was on vocational preparation and job placement, but it was based on the idea that each teacher in a school would do some counseling, with advice and assistance from the state supervisor. This plan was soon abandoned, as it became evident that counseling should be done by a trained counselor who could devote full time to his duties. No funds were available for reimbursing the local guidance programs at first, but the vocational division pledged some federal funds for the operating expenses of the guidance program in 1943.

Congress passed the George-Barden Act August 1, 1946, allotting state departments of education funds for guidance. These funds could be used to support local guidance programs and to encourage counselor training. Since the program developed because educators and businessmen became convinced that more effective job placement and occupational training should be developed, the term *vocational guidance* was generally used. With $75,000 from state vocational funds, 28 schools operated programs during the 1945-46 school year. The following year, the state's plan stipulated that 5 percent of the federal vocational funds and 5 percent of the state vocational funds would be devoted to the guidance program.

Under the new state program, the colleges were entitled to half salaries for counselor trainers, with the state paying travel expenses. In 1946, Henderson State Teachers College employed the first counselor trainer, and three other state-supported colleges had followed by 1951. A committee composed of the state supervisor of occupational information and guidance services and at least two counselor trainers spent two days in each school having a guidance program from January 1952 to December 1954. Although the committee's purpose was to evaluate the state's programs, perhaps the most important result was that the visits provided in-service training for the staff, students, school board members, and parents. When the state department was reorganized in 1954, the state board withdrew its support for counselor training, and the program ended the following year. However, institutions that had employed counselors on a half-time basis continued to offer the courses in guidance counseling.

In 1958, in order to participate in Title V of NDEA, the State Department of Education made the guidance services independent of the vocational division. Since then, the director of guidance has added two supervisors to his staff—one to assist the elementary schools and the other to work with the secondary schools. By 1960, 91 of the 151 counselors serving in reimbursed guidance programs held master's degrees, 52 held bachelor's degrees, 69 had more than 15 hours (a semester) in guidance, 31 had 15 hours in guidance, and only 51 had less than 15 hours. Those not certified were allowed 1 year to meet the state's requirements. By 1966-67, there were 240 counselors.

When the state department was reorganized in 1966, this service area was placed in the instructional services division.

Budgets and Loans

In 1931, the peak of the Depression, the Legislature authorized all school districts to borrow money and issue negotiable coupon bonds for building and equipping school buildings, making additions and repairs, purchasing sites, and funding any indebtedness for these purposes. It further stipulated that no bonds should be issued that would make the total outstanding indebtedness of a district exceed 7 percent of the assessed valuation (36). This law required any district desiring to borrow money or issue bonds to furnish the commissioner of education a statement of the amount and the maturity of indebtedness, a description of the property to be mortgaged, a financial statement, and a certificate from the county clerk showing the assessed valuation of the district's real and personal property. The district was required to sell the bonds to the highest bidder (lowest rate of interest) at a public sale advertised in at least one of the county's newspapers. A 1953 law authorized the school districts to borrow money from the State Revolving Loan Fund and set up the procedures for securing such loans. The department processes all loans with the prior approval of the State Board of Education.

The budgets and loans division, founded by an act passed in 1949 (37), was required to make an annual report on the public schools' outstanding indebtedness, showing the nature of the debts and the borrowing power of each district. It also computes the legal 40 percent of local revenue (based on the assessed valuation and the millage voted in each district) retained by each school district. In the meantime, the local districts must publish their budget and tax rates, along with the required procedures for holding the annual school election. The division prepares the bulletins and forms each district must use for these purposes.

One of the division's primary responsibilities is to determine the amount of state aid to be distributed to each local school district. This minimum foundation program aid was based on the level of professional training of the teachers employed for the 1951-52 school year (38). The number of teachers was determined by dividing by 28 the average daily attendance for grades 1 through 6 for the 1950-51 year, and dividing by 24 the average daily attendance grades 7 through 12. One additional teacher was allowed for a total of the remainders above 14 but less than 33. Two teachers were allowed if the total of these remainders was 34 or more.

The laws of 1949 and 1951 established a schedule of teacher salaries based on the type of certificate multiplied by the number of teachers employed, but not exceeding the teacher units allowed. The schedule is as follows: emergency certificate issued on less than 30 semester hours, \$1,050; certificates issued on 30 semester hours or more, \$1,260; certificates issued on 60 semester hours or more, \$1,470; certificates issued on 90 semester hours or more, \$1,750; certificates issued on bachelor's degrees, \$2,100; and certificates issued on master's degrees or higher, \$2,540.

In 1957, the Legislature provided a new method for distributing state public school funds to the districts. The formula was now based on the weighted average daily attendance in a school district, the elementary schools being weighted from 1.0 to 1.5 and the secondary schools weighted from 1.2 to 1.7. The formula took into account the county ability index, which was based on two-sevenths of the county's proportion of the total sales tax return, two-sevenths of its proportion of the state's gainfully employed workers, and one-seventh times its proportion of the state's total assessed valuation of public utilities. The local school district's contribution was then determined by its ability index times the state's total contributions, one-third of the amount it received from the National Forest Reserve Fund, and one-third of its receipts from the severance tax.

Under this 1957 law, the state's contribution to the minimum foundation program was determined by the product of the state's total number of weighted average daily attendance units times \$114, minus the local district's contribution. This amount could not be less than 165 percent of the minimum foundation program aid received the previous year nor more than 230 percent of it. The budgets and loans division processes all applications for minimum foundation law aid. Act 153 of 1955 has been responsible for reappraising all property (personal and real estate) and assessing it at 20 percent of its market value. A penalty is assessed against any school district whose county assessment ratio is less than 18 percent of true and market value.

The personnel of the budgets and loans division work on school district budgets and county board budgets, applications for state financial aid, state district audits, statistical reports, and fiscal planning and reporting. They do not budget school money, but check local budgets for compliance with various laws and act as a clearinghouse for local school district budgets. This enables the department to offer professional counseling services, but the division has no authority to plan or control school district budgets except that granted by the Legislature—these are the responsibility of the local school boards. Nor does the division issue funds to the local districts; it merely certifies to the Division of Disbursement and Accounting that certain funds should be allocated to the local school districts of the state.

As the General Assembly approved additional legislation requiring more statistics to be collected, the duties of the budgets and loans division expanded. In 1957, a school census law called for an enumeration every other year (Act 103 of 1967 amends Section 1 of Act 217 of 1957 to permit school districts to make an enumeration every 2 years or every 5 years at the option of each local board of education), the reports from the county school supervisor's office to be filed with the division and compiled into a state report. The Classroom Teacher Minimum Salary Law of 1957 placed additional responsibilities on the division. A 1965 act provided for a minimum beginning salary of $3,600 for a teacher with a bachelor's degree, and $4,000 for a teacher with a master's degree, with an increase of $400 per biennium for each.

When Congress passed NDEA in 1958, the State Department of Education created a statistical service subdivision to the budgets and loans division under Title X. The subdivision developed a complete new set of accounting forms for the local districts in compliance with the U.S. Office of Education's regulations. It has developed many other forms to conform with the requirements for electronic data processing. In fact, an evaluation program continuously determines what reports should be eliminated or revised.

The division performs an important service in providing consultative and technical assistance on financial accounting procedures to beginning superintendents and their staffs. The school audit division of the state comptroller's office is responsible for auditing the local school districts, but districts may employ approved certified public accounting firms to audit their accounts if they wish. In either case, the state department receives a copy of the audit, which is reviewed and analyzed by the budget and loans division (now the Division of Administrative Services). It then uses these audits as a basis for giving professional counsel in budget planning to the local school authorities. Practically all the districts use the services of the comptroller's school audit division, although 10 or 12 of the larger school districts use public accounting firms, primarily because they can make a more detailed breakdown of expenditures.

Disbursements and Accounting

The State Board of Education established a division of disbursements and accounting to centralize its payments. The division functions very much like a comptroller's office, accounting to the commissioner and the various federal and state agencies that audit the department's books. The commissioner of education is given the authority to designate one or more purchasing agents, the funds are allocated by the various divisions of the department, and the invoices are then submitted to the director. Thus, a system of checks and balances is maintained by the department before requisitions go to the comptroller's office for approval of expenditures or disbursements to local school districts.

The department classifies its moneys as cash funds, state-appropriated funds, and federal funds. The State Public School Fund, the largest of these, is used for administering the department of education, for audiovisual services, handicapped children services, textbooks, transportation aid, county board budgets, state apportionment, minimum foundation program aid, vocational education aid, vocational-technical schools, school lunch commodity distributions, vocational rehabilitation, the library commission, Social Security and state employees' retirement, and teacher retirement matching programs. All these purposes are defined by the legislative appropriations.

Previously, federal receipts were deposited in the state treasury and disbursed to local districts according to the state and federal laws and state plans. This procedure has now been replaced by the use of a letter of credit. The federal receipts include vocational education aid, NDEA aid, the Forest Reserve Fund, the Flood Control Fund, the Mineral Lease Fund, and public domain land sales. Beginning in 1965, they included funds from ESEA, Public Law 89-10. The 1966 reorganization changed the name of this division to the Division of Finance.

Instructional Materials

When an overwhelming majority of the people approved Initiated Act No. 1 in 1936, the state was obligated to furnish free textbooks to all public schools for grades 1 through 8. The department immediately created an instructional materials division to carry out this responsibility. From the beginning, the division did not have enough money to furnish free textbooks for each pupil. The director of the program had to secure the cooperation of local school administrators in collecting and redistributing usable textbooks that had been purchased previously by the pupils themselves.

The 1936 act did not provide specific procedures for purchasing and distributing free textbooks, but left this to the discretion of the state board. In 1951, the Legislature established procedures for selecting, purchasing, and distributing the textbooks, but for the most part allowed the state board to administer the programs with its own regulations.

At its March quarterly meeting (39), the board calls for written bids from all publishers listed with the state department (40). The office of instructional materials examines these bids to see that the prices meet the regulations, and they are presented to the board at its June meeting. These bids and sample textbooks are referred to selecting committees composed of five teachers or supervisors of elementary subjects in which the adoption is to be made. The 1966 reorganization of the state department placed this service in the instructional services division.

The members of the selecting committees must have had 4 years of college training before they can be nominated by the commissioner. The board approves them at its June meeting for only one adoption. The selecting committees examine the samples of the textbooks and interview the publishers' representatives at a state hearing in Little Rock during the latter part of August. At this time, the committees decide on the series of books—a minimum of four or a maximum of six series—that will be recommended to the State Board of Education. The law directs that the board must execute contracts with all publishers recommended by the selecting committees.

The local schools make adoptions only in basal subjects. Local selecting committees composed of three teachers or supervisors in the elementary grades are appointed by local administrators subject to the approval of the local boards of directors. These local selecting committees have until December 20 to adopt textbooks from the state's multiple list. On the other hand, there are no state adoption of high school textbooks or regulations governing adoption or prices. The superintendents and their boards of education have full authority to adopt high school textbooks whenever they need to do so.

The 1951 Arkansas Textbook Law requires publishers having state contracts to maintain a depository in Little Rock at their own expense. The state owns no textbooks in the depository; it purchases textbooks only on requisitions from schools.

The textbook budget depends on the average number of pupils reported annually by the county school supervisors. Approximately $35,000 is deducted from the total textbook appropriation to take care of emergency budgets and office expense. The balance is then divided by the total average number of pupils to determine the per-capita allotment. In general, there has been little modification of these procedures in selecting, purchasing, and distributing free textbooks since the beginning of the program.

Act 334 of 1967 permits the state to provide free textbooks in all basic subjects for pupils attending public schools of this state in grades 9 through 12, as funds are available therefor—as determined by the State Board of Education.

The state initiated an audiovisual program in July 1947 with funds the Legislature appropriated to the department's vocational education division. The division operated on a small budget for 2 years, but in 1949 the Legislature appropriated $150,000 to the program as a line item in the public school fund budget. Subsequent appropriations have varied, however, dropping to a low of $60,000 in 1961.

In 1949, a series of film libraries were set up in the eight state-supported colleges and the University of Arkansas, primarily for teacher education. Although this program was discontinued in 1953, 6 years later the board authorized the establishment of five county film or filmstrip centers. These centers were located in the offices of the county school supervisor. If proven valuable, the centers were to be increased to meet the needs of the entire state.

Thus far, the film experimental centers have failed, mainly because of a lack of funds at both the state and county levels. Several centers have continued to operate on funds available through Title III of NDEA. The audiovisual program is now operating on a state appropriation of $80,000, supplemented by funds from Title III to provide a total of approximately $140,000 annually.

Research indicates that students show a 55 percent increase in learning when audiovisual materials are properly used in the instructional program (41). Since the success of the program depends in a large measure on the teacher's judgment in wisely selecting materials, the state department attempts to encourage wise selection among the schools.

Educational Television

In 1961, the Legislature created an agency known as the Arkansas Educational Televison Commission, composed of seven members appointed by the Governor with the consent of the Senate. This commission attempts to help educators and laymen understand the benefits of educational television (ETV) and promote its use. It is responsible for surveying, studying, and appraising the need for an overall plan for using TV facilities available for noncommercial use. It also is charged with controlling and supervising the channels reserved by the Federal Communications Commission to Arkansas for noncommercial educational use.

The Legislature reorganized the Educational Television Commission in 1963 and increased its membership to eight. A station was opened at Conway after Arkansas State Teachers College gave the commission a 99-year lease on a 3-acre site and the Conway Chamber of Commerce donated $61,000. The commission is now operating on a full-time basis, licensed by the FCC, with a director and 30 full-time employees. Act 5 of 1967 changed the name of Arkansas State Teachers College to State College of Arkansas.

ETV in Arkansas is still in its infancy, but the department is considering plans for expansion. A survey completed by Jansky and Bailey, a division of the Atlantic Research Corporation in Washington, D.C., found that it will take at least four additional ETV stations, plus several translators, to completely cover the state. Three additional production studios will be necessary in addition to the one now located at Conway. The transmitter at Bay with the production studio at Jonesboro will reach the northeast part of the state as well as part of Missouri.

A director of instructional materials coordinates the activities of the Educational Television Commission with the department's instructional programs. In this capacity he is a liaison among the ETV Commission, the State Department of Education, and the local school districts.

School Plant

The 1931 General Assembly made the State Department of Education responsible for school plant services. A section of the Arkansas laws, as recodified in 1957, states:

> The Board shall have general supervision of the schools of the state; prepare and distribute plans and specifications for the construction and equipment of school buildings, and approve plans and expenditures of public school funds for all new school buildings; . . . take such other action as it may deem necessary to promote the physical welfare of school children and promote the organization and increase the efficiency of the Public Schools of the state; . . . (42).

Given this authority, the state board established the Division of School Plant Services.

At the request of local school authorities, the division makes local school building surveys and studies enrollment trends and the development of long-range housing programs. These studies and surveys are always made in cooperation with other department sections that might be concerned, such as the instructional services, accounting disbursements, and budgets and loans divisions, and the school lunch services. The plans and specifications for all local school buildings are reviewed cooperatively to assist the local schools and architectural firms and secure the most desirable facilities for the money spent. When the State Department of Education was reorganized in 1966, this area of service was placed in the administrative services division.

The division also organizes and conducts, in cooperation with other agencies, workshops on the proper care and maintenance of school facilities for local school plant personnel.

Transportation

The Arkansas General Assembly gave the school districts the legal authority to provide transportation in 1919.

In 1927, the General Assembly ordered the State Board of Education to develop a formula for distributing state aid for school transportation based on the number of pupils transported, the number and size of school buses, and the size of the school district. The Division of School Plant Services was also given responsibility for seeing that all the safety laws and regulations pertaining to the standards are enforced. This division passes on all applications for transportation aid; conducts training programs for local personnel, drivers, and mechanics; and supervises the annual school bus inspection. It also assists the local schools in purchasing buses, setting up routes, and establishing safety programs.

The reorganization of the State Department of Education placed pupil transportation service in the administrative services division.

RECORD OF SCHOOL TRANSPORTATION (43)

School Year	Number of buses operated	Average daily attendance transported pupils	Expenditures for transportation by local school dist.
1925-26	108	3,136	. . .
1929-30	655	24,173	. . .
1948-49	2,505	145,284	$4,233,037
1958-59	3,133	187,292	6,286,431
1964-65	3,534	207,013	8,055,098

Surplus Property

In 1949, the Eighty-First Congress passed Public Law 152, the Federal Property and Administrative Services Act, making available certain federal properties to eligible health, educational, and Civil Defense units. The Arkansas General Assembly passed an act in 1951 placing full responsibility on the State Board of Education for handling the properties. The board has distributed this surplus property to 700 claimants. The average cost of these properties to the federal government was over $2 million per year, while the average cost to the receiving units has been approximately 6.8 percent of this original cost, including moving, storing, and securing them.

The state department's disbursing officer handles the physical aspects of this surplus property program. All accounts are subject to audit by the State Legislative Audit Committees and by appropriate federal authorities.

The administration of the surplus property program was placed in the finance division when the state department was reorganized in 1966.

Federally Affected Areas

Congress passed Public Law 815 in 1950 providing for construction assistance to local school districts that experience a 3.5-percent non-federal increase per year in the number of children in their schools where the number of federally connected children is equal to 5 percent or more of the total school enrollment. The amount of funds varies in accordance with the average state cost of school facilities. The amount allowed is established for each child whose parents both work and live on federal property; one-half of this amount is allowed per child whose parents live off but work on federal property.

Public Law 874, also passed in 1950, provides assistance to school districts where federally connected students account for at least 3 percent of the total average daily attendance. Payments under this program vary from an established amount per child for those whose parents both live and work on federal property to one-half that amount per child for those whose parents live off but work on federally owned property.

Under these laws the federal government makes payments directly to the school districts concerned, but applications for this aid must be reviewed, processed, and approved by the State Department of Education. The Arkansas schools have received an average of approximately $1 million per year in maintenance and operating aid under Public Law 874 since 1950, and a total of approximately $13 million in construction aid during this same period.

This service has been in the Division of Administrative Services since the state department reorganization in 1966.

Fire Safety

In 1948, the State Department of Education joined with other agencies concerned with school safety to start a junior fire marshall training program. In 1959, the General Assembly made a fire prevention program mandatory in every school district in the state. The department was given full responsibility to see that the necessary checks are maintained. The junior fire marshall program is being expanded so as to include every local school district. The program, under the provisions of Act 61 of 1959, is being expanded to make full participation by every school district mandatory. State board policies implementing this act place the full responsibility for compliance upon the local superintendents, with the penalty of a forfeit of state aid if a satisfactory monthly report showing full compliance is not received.

This program is a cooperative program which includes many agencies of the state (44).

SUMMARY

The Arkansas public schools have made notable progress since 1900. At the beginning of the twentieth century the state had very few public high schools. From 1900 to 1925 the department's major tasks were founding and developing good elementary schools and high schools; but since 1925 there has been a marked trend for all communities to look on the public schools as a unitary system including grades 1 through 12. Some of the improvements in the public school programs are as follows (45):

1. At the beginning of the century, there were 4,903 school districts; these have been reduced to 395 in 1967.

2. School buses and public transportation of pupils to school centers were practically unknown in 1900. Now, almost every school district in the state provides free bus transportation.

3. In 1900, most school districts did not envisage serving school lunches. Now, nearly all school systems have well-equipped lunchrooms and employ staffs to prepare hot lunches as well as to administer a special milk program for the students.

4. At the turn of the century, public school buildings and equipment were crude and very poorly adapted. During recent years the people have spent millions of dollars building school plants and installing equipment that compare favorably with the best in the nation.

5. The instructional program has been greatly enriched to meet the needs of the students. There are marked improvements in library facilities, better textbooks, and free textbooks for the first eight grades. Radio, television, recordings, and an array of other audiovisual aids are also available. On the secondary level the offerings have been expanded to include vocational agriculture, home economics, business education, shop, industrial arts, mechanics or trade training, training for sales service jobs, and guidance and counseling.

6. In music, the school programs include band, orchestra, public school music, choral work, and music appreciation. While little was done in public school art in 1900, today it is considered an integral part of the elementary and secondary curriculum. Physical education, virtually unknown in 1900, is now a state requirement. The State Department of Education provides two supervising specialists in this area.

7. In 1900, no school district was permitted to vote a levy in excess of 5 mills for public school support. The limit was set at 18 mills in 1926, and in 1949 the ceiling was removed, so that each district may vote whatever levy it needs to maintain a satisfactory program. At present, a school district must levy a *minimum* of 18 mills to qualify for state minimum foundation program aid and transportation aid. At least one school district levies only 18

mills and at least one levies 60 mills. The average for the state is 42.8 mills.

8. In 1900, the total assessed valuation of the state was $201,908,783; in 1966, it was $1,802,265,097.

9. The average length of the school term has increased from 69 days in 1900 to 175 days in 1965. A minimum term of 9 months for all children was attained by all districts for the first time in the 1958-59 school year and has been maintained ever since.

10. The number of classroom teachers has increased from 6,959 in 1900 to 19,098 in 1967-68; the average salary for the classroom teacher has increased from $166 to $5,580 during this same period.

11. In 1900, the amount of state revenue for public elementary and secondary programs was $446,558, compared to $96,142,955 in 1967-68; the amount of local revenue for all the public schools was $988,089, compared to $77,907,604 in 1967-68.

12. The total current expenditure by the local school districts in 1967-68 amounted to $157,527,154 compared to $1,124,497 in 1900; this represented an average expenditure per pupil of $441 compared to $6 in 1900.

Looking Ahead

The State Department of Education is in a process of self-analysis and adjustment as a result of recent developments, including the expanding role of the federal government. There are an increasing emphasis on programs for the disadvantaged and community junior colleges, plans for establishment of a kindergarten program, and an ever-increasing demand for vocational-technical schools. There is also an intense interest in experimental and innovative programs in the local schools. These developments, coupled with the department's efforts to improve its internal operations, have created new complexities, but at the same time have begun to point in new directions.

The state's educational advancement continues to be characterized by cooperation between local school personnel and department staff members. The ultimate results will be measured in terms of how they affect the work and achievement of the teachers and pupils. Progress is being made in developing an adequate educational data-processing system, which, when fully implemented, should provide valid and timely data on professional staff, pupils, curriculums, facilities, and finance.

The department must develop various decision-making mechanisms and ways of analyzing problems to keep abreast with rapid advancements in almost all aspects of life. The challenges of poverty and totalitarianism, and the difficult, complex, and courageous decisions necessary for urban and rural development must be dealt with if the department is to promote education toward the moral and humanistic values that are fundamental to democracy and freedom. The state's and the nation's greatness, their near greatness, or their mediocrity will depend upon how well the Department of Education meets these challenges.

FOOTNOTES

1. For more information on these early schools, see O. E. McKnight and Boyd W. Johnson, *The Arkansas Story* (Oklahoma City: Harlow Publishing Corp., 1956), p. 144.
2. For further information, see Josiah H. Shinn, *History of Arkansas* (Richmond, Va.: B. F. Johnson Publishing Co., 1900), p. 141.
3. Arkansas County Supervisors Association, *Arkansas County Supervisor Handbook* (Little Rock: The Association, 1955), p. 8.
4. The changes in the title of county common school officials are as follows:
   1853-68 Common school commissioner
   1868-73 Circuit superintendent
   1873-75 County superintendent
   1875-1907 County examiner
   1907-19 Optional country superintendent and county examiner
   1919-33 County superintendent
   1933-41 County examiner
   1941 to date County school supervisor
5. McKnight and Johnson, *op. cit.* p. 236.
6. W. S. McNutt, *et al., A History of Arkansas* (Little Rock: Democrat Printing and Lithographing Co., 1932), pp. 516-17.
7. Fay Hempstead, *Pictorial History of Arkansas* (St. Louis and New York: N. D. Thompson Publishing Co., 1890), p. 650.
8. Superintendent of Public Instruction, *Sixteenth Biennial Report, 1898-1900,* p 12.
9. *Ibid.*, pp. 11-12.
10. National Commission on School District Reorganization, *Your School District: The Report of the National Commission on School District Reorganization,* Howard A. Dawson and Floyd W. Reeves, cochairmen (Washington, D.C.: Department of Rural Education, National Education Association, 1948), p. 147.
11. *Journal of the Arkansas Education Association,* III (January 1925), 7.
12. Arkansas, *Laws* (1929), 48th General Assembly, 1st sess., Act 152.
13. Howard A. Dawson was the director of the division of research and surveys.
14. National Commission on School District Reorganization, *op. cit.*, p. 152.
15. This was evident by the fact that the present commissioner, A. W. Ford, has served continuously since 1953.

16. The Legislature appropriated $74,650,000 from this fund for the public schools in the 1965-66 school year.

17. This tax on sand and gravel is still in effect, but it produces less than $14,000 annually.

18. Arkansas, *Constitution* (1874, as amended in 1949), Amendment XL, art. 14, sec. 1.

19. National Commission on School District Reorganization, *op cit.*, p. 153.

20. The number of school districts dropped from 1,600 in 1948 to 423 in 1949, the first year Initiated Act No. 1 went into effect, and to 410 in 1965.

21. Superintendent of Public Instruction, *Sixteenth Biennial Report, 1898-1900*, p. 65.

22. *Ibid.*, p. 121.

23. Superintendent of Public Instruction, *Fourteenth Biennial Report, 1894-1896,* p. 37.

24. A 1943 act requires members of the teacher retirement system to automatically retire on July 1 following their seventy-second birthday.

25. Ed McCuiston was the chairman of the subcommittee and the assistant commissioner for instructional services.

26. Arkansas, *Laws* (1941), 54th General Assembly, 1st sess., Act 127, sec. 6.

27. These adult courses do not include commercial and vocational subjects.

28. Approximately two-thirds of the applicants passed the test.

29. Hill is still a resident of Little Rock, Arkansas.

30. J. B. Ewart, the local teacher who helped organize the club, later served as the supervisor of vocational agriculture in the State Department of Education.

31. Virginia received the first.

32. J. W. Hull, now president of Arkansas Polytechnic College at Russellville, was the local teacher.

33. All but four were administered by the area vocational-technical schools.

34. The term *vocational* has been deleted from the Arkansas law. It is still a part of the federal law, but the term is interpreted to include mental deficiencies and maladjustments of various kinds. Such an interpretation has vastly broadened the scope of the agency.

35. George Harrod, "The Origin, Growth and Development of the Guidance Services in the Public Schools of Arkansas" (unpublished Ed.D dissertation, Michigan State University, East Lansing, 1963), pp. 44-45.

36. This has been raised to 15 percent at present.

37. The budgets and loans division was a part of the school finance division from 1949 until 1954, when Commissioner A. W. Ford reorganized the department.

38. The type of valid certification held by these teachers on September 1, 1951, was recorded in the certification division.

39. The state board meets the second Monday of March each year.

40. The contracts expire July 1 of the following year. A request for bids is issued approximately 15 months prior to the expiration of the contracts, and publishers are given until May 15 to file bids.

41. Department of Education, *A Manual, Organization, Function and Services of the State Department of Education* (Little Rock: The Department, 1961), p. 23.

42. Arkansas, *Laws* (1931, recodified in 1957), 49th General Assembly, 1st sess., Act 169, sec. 14.

43. These figures are from the transportation division's records.

44. This program is a cooperative program including the following agencies: Office of the Governor, State Department of Education, Fire Marshall's Division, State Police Department, Fire Prevention Division, Arkansas Inspection and Rating Bureau, Arkansas State Fire Prevention Association, Boiler Safety, Inspection Division, State Department of Labor, State Firemen's Association, Arkansas Association of Insurance Agents, Arkansas Fire Chiefs' Association, and Arkansas Junior Chamber of Commerce.

45. Department of Education, *Statistical Summary for the Public Schools of Arkansas, for 1964-1965 and 1965-1966* (Little Rock: The Department, 1966), pp. 34-39.

BIBLIOGRAPHY

Public Documents

Arkansas. *Constitution* (1874, as amended in 1949).

——*Laws* (1929), 48th General Assembly, 1st sess.

——*Laws* (1931), 49th General Assembly, 1st sess.

——*Laws* (1941), 54th General Assembly, 1st sess.

U.S. Congress. Senate. *Arkansas 1836-1936*. S. Doc. 191, 74th Cong., 2d sess., 1936.

Books

Arkansas County Supervisors Association. *Arkansas County Supervisor Handbook.* Little Rock: The Association, 1955.

Arkansas Education Association. *The Arkansas Cooperative Program To Improve Instruction.* Vol. III, Bulletin No. 5. Little Rock: The Association.

Arkansas History Commission. *Publications of the Arkansas Historical Association, 1906-1917.* Vols. I-III. Little Rock: The Commission.

Blocher, S. J. *A Practical Treatise on the Civil Government of Arkansas and the United States.* Richmond, Va.: B. F. Johnson Publishing Co., 1900.

Board of Vocational Education. *Arkansas State Plan for Vocational Education for the Five-Year Period, July 1, 1947, to June 30, 1952.* Little Rock: Department of Education, 1952.

Brown, Walter L. *Our Arkansas.* Revised edition. Austin, Tex.: The Steck Co., 1958.

Davis, C. B. *Arkansas.* New York: Rinehart and Co., 1940.

Department of Education. *A Manual, Organization, Function and Services of the State Department of Education.* Little Rock: The Department, 1961.

—— *Study of the Local School Units in Arkansas.* Little Rock: The Department, 1937.

Department of Public Instruction. *Digest of School Laws Relating to Free Schools in the State of Arkansas,* 1907, 1910, 1923, 1931. Little Rock: The Department.

Donahgey, George W. *Building a State Capitol.* Little Rock: Parke-Harper Co., 1937.

Fletcher, John Gould. *Arkansas.* Chapel Hill: University of North Carolina Press, 1947.

Furguson, John Lewis. *Arkansas and the Civil War.* Little Rock: Parke-Harper Co., 1965.

Grant, James R. *The Life of Thomas C. McRae.* Russellville, Ark.: Russellville Printing Co., 1932.

Hall, C. G. *Historical Report of the Secretary of State, 1958.* Edited by C. Armitage Harper, D. D. Glover, Jr., and Larry Curry. Little Rock: Democrat and Lithographing Co., 1958.

Hallum, John. *Biographical and Pictorial History of Arkansas.* Albany, N.Y.: Week, Parsons and Co., Printers, 1887.

Harrell, John M. *The Brooks and Baxter War.* St. Louis: Slawson Printing Co., 1893.

Hempstead, Fay. *Historical Review of Arkansas: Its Commerce, Industry and Modern Affairs.* Chicago: The Lewis Publishing Co., 1911.

—— *Pictorial History of Arkansas.* St. Louis and New York: N. D. Thompson Publishing Co., 1890.

Herndon, Dallas T. *Annals of Arkansas.* Vol. I of 7 vols. Hopkinsville, Ky., and Little Rock: The Historical Records Association, 1947.

—— *Centennial History of Arkansas.* Deluxe supplement. 3 vols. Chicago and Little Rock: The S. J. Clark Publishing Co., 1922.

—— *Highlights of Arkansas History.* Little Rock: Arkansas History Commission, 1922.

—— *Outline of Executive and Legislative History of Arkansas.* Little Rock: Arkansas History Commission, 1922.

—— *The Arkansas Handbook.* Little Rock: Parke-Harper Co., 1936.

Hill, A. B. *Four Years with the Public Schools in Arkansas.* Little Rock: Department of Education, 1927.

Irby, N. M. *Program for the Equalization of Educational Opportunities in the State of Arkansas.* Nashville, Tenn.: Cullom and Ghertner Co., 1930.

Knoop, F. Y., and Grant, J. R. *Arkansas Yesterday and Today.* Chicago and Philadelphia: J. B. Lippincott Co., 1935.

McKnight, O. E. *Living in Arkansas.* 2d and 3d eds. Revised by Amy Jean Green. Oklahoma City: Harlow Publishing Corp., 1957 and 1963.

McKnight, O. E., and Johnson, Boyd W. *The Arkansas Story.* Oklahoma City: Harlow Publishing Corp., 1956.

McNutt, W. S.; McKnight, Olin Eli; and Hubbell, George A. *A History of Arkansas.* Little Rock: Democrat Printing and Lithographing Co., 1932.

Moore, Johnathan H. *A School History of Arkansas.* Little Rock: Democrat Printing and Lithographing Co., 1924.

Nuttall, Thomas. *A Journal of Travels into Arkansas in the Year 1819.* Edited by Reubin Gold Thwaites. Cleveland, Ohio: The Arthur H. Clark Co., 1905.

Price, John G. *Arkansas Constitutional Convention.* Little Rock: J. G. Price, Printer to the Convention, 1868.

Reed, E. W. *Comparative Analysis of the Arkansas Tax System.* Fayetteville: University of Arkansas Press, 1950.

Reynolds, John High. *Makers of Arkansas History.* Little Rock: R & R Publishing Co., 1930.

Rhoton, Lewis, and Galbraith, William J. *Arkansas and the Nation.* Little Rock: Wilson and Webb Book and Stationery Co., 1898.

Rothrock, Thomas. *From Wilderness to Statehood.* Eureka Springs, Ark.: Times-Echo Press, 1961.

Shinn, Josiah H. *History of Arkansas.* Richmond, Va.: B. F. Johnson Publishing Co., 1900.

—— *Pioneers and Makers of Arkansas.* Little Rock: Democrat Printing and Lithographing Co., 1908.

Thomas, D. Y. *Arkansas and Its People. A History, 1541-1930.* 4 vols. New York: The American Historical Society, 1930.

—— *Arkansas in War and Reconstruction.* Little Rock: Central Printing Co., 1926.

Weeks, S. B. *History of Public School Education in Arkansas.* Bound in the Charles H. Brough Collection, Little Rock Public Library. Washington, D.C.: Government Printing Office, 1912.

William, Fay. *Arkansas of the Year.* Little Rock: C. C. Allard and Associates, 1951.

Worley, Ted R. *At Home in Confederate Arkansas*. Edited by Margaret Smith Ross. Little Rock: Pulaski County Historical Society, 1955.

Periodical

Journal of the Arkansas Education Association, III (January 1925), 7.

Reports

Arkansas Expenditure Council. *Taxes in Arkansas: A Survey*. Little Rock: Democrat Printing and Lithographing Co., 1948.

Arkansas Legislative Council. *Special Education Survey*. Conway, Ark.: Log Cabin Democrat, 1952.

Department of Education. *Statistical Summary for the Public Schools of Arkansas.* Little Rock: The Department, 1966.

National Commission on School District Reorganization. *Your School District: The Report of the National Commission on School District Reorganization.* Howard A. Dawson and Floyd W. Reeves, cochairmen. Washington, D.C.: Department of Rural Education, National Education Association, 1948.

Superintendents of Public Instruction. *Biennial Reports*, 1893-1940. Little Rock: Department of Public Instruction.

Unpublished Material

Harrod, George. "The Origin, Growth and Development of the Guidance Services in the Public Schools of Arkansas." Unpublished Ed.D. dissertation, Michigan State University, East Lansing, 1963.

Other Sources

Arkansas Historical Records Survey. *Inventory of the County Archives of Arkansas*. The Survey, 1939. Bound in the Charles H. Brough Collection, Little Rock Public Library, Little Rock, Arkansas.

—— *Arkansas State Teachers Association Proceedings*. Vols. I-III. Proceedings of the Association from 1905-21. Bound in the Charles H. Brough Collection, Little Rock Public Library, Little Rock, Arkansas.

—— *Education in Arkansas*. Miscellaneous education reports, periodicals, and speeches bound together in the Charles H. Brough Collection, Little Rock Public Library, Little Rock, Arkansas.

Appendix A

ARKANSAS CHIEF STATE SCHOOL OFFICERS

State Superintendents of Public Instruction

1868-73	Thomas Smith
1873-74	J. C. Corbin
1875-78	G. W. Hill
1878-82	J. L. Denton
1882	Dunbar H. Pope (Oct.)
1882-90	W. E. Thompson
1890-94	J. H. Shinn
1894-98	Junius Jordon
1898	J. W. Kuykendall (Sept.–Oct.)
1898-1902	J. J. Doyne
1902-1906	John H. Hinemor
1906-1908	J. J. Doyne
1908-16	George B. Cook
1916-23	J. L. Bond
1923-27	A. B. Hill
1927-29	J. P. Womack
1929-31	C. M. Hirst

State Commissioners of Education

1931-33	C. M. Hirst
1933-38	W. E. Phipps
1938-41	T. H. Alford
1941-49	Ralph B. Jones
1949-53	A. B. Bond
1953-	A. W. Ford

Appendix B

Chart I.—ARKANSAS DEPARTMENT OF EDUCATION, 1946

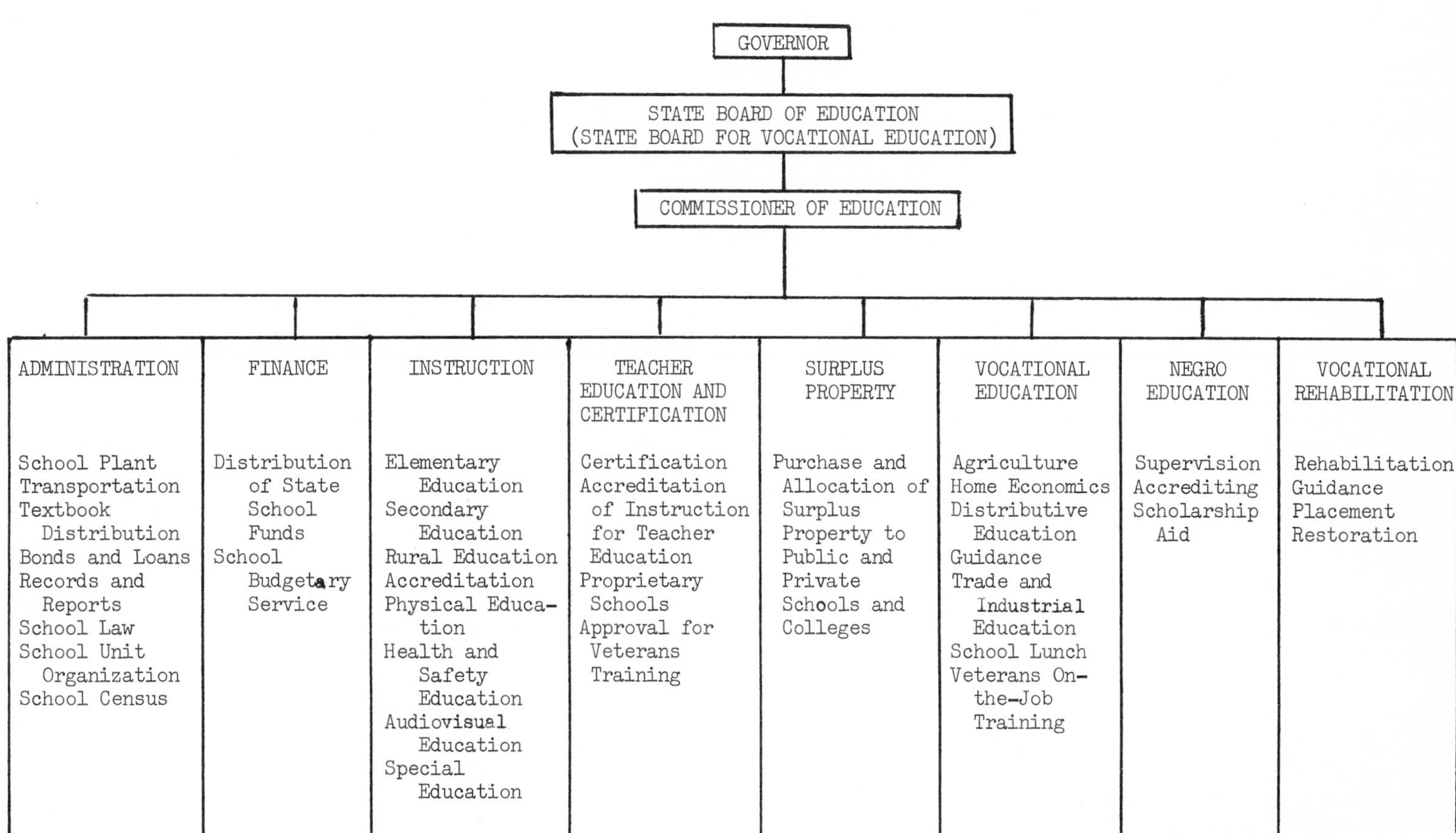

GOVERNOR
STATE BOARD OF EDUCATION (STATE BOARD FOR VOCATIONAL EDUCATION)
COMMISSIONER OF EDUCATION
ADMINISTRATION
School Plant
Transportation
Textbook Distribution
Bonds and Loans
Records and Reports
School Law
School Unit Organization
School Census
FINANCE
Distribution of State School Funds
School Budgetary Service
INSTRUCTION
Elementary Education
Secondary Education
Rural Education
Accreditation
Physical Education
Health and Safety Education
Audiovisual Education
Special Education
TEACHER EDUCATION AND CERTIFICATION
Certification
Accreditation of Instruction for Teacher Education
Proprietary Schools
Approval for Veterans Training
SURPLUS PROPERTY
Purchase and Allocation of Surplus Property to Public and Private Schools and Colleges
VOCATIONAL EDUCATION
Agriculture
Home Economics
Distributive Education
Guidance
Trade and Industrial Education
School Lunch
Veterans On-the-Job Training
NEGRO EDUCATION
Supervision
Accrediting
Scholarship Aid
VOCATIONAL REHABILITATION
Rehabilitation
Guidance
Placement
Restoration

Appendix B

Chart II.--ARKANSAS DEPARTMENT OF EDUCATION, 1954

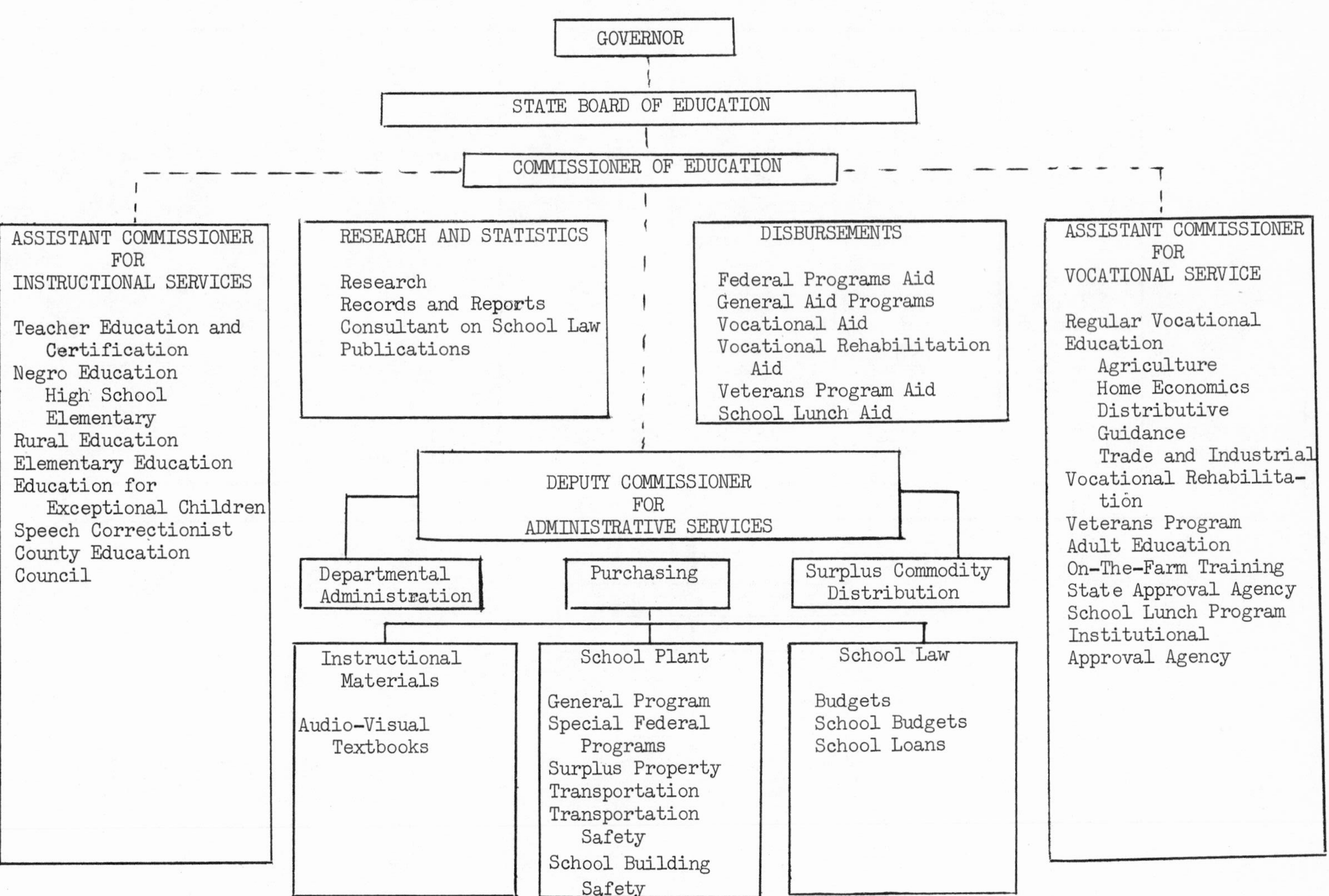
GOVERNOR
STATE BOARD OF EDUCATION
COMMISSIONER OF EDUCATION
ASSISTANT COMMISSIONER FOR INSTRUCTIONAL SERVICES
Teacher Education and Certification
Negro Education
High School
Elementary
Rural Education
Elementary Education
Education for Exceptional Children
Speech Correctionist
County Education Council
RESEARCH AND STATISTICS
Research
Records and Reports
Consultant on School Law
Publications
DISBURSEMENTS
Federal Programs Aid
General Aid Programs
Vocational Aid
Vocational Rehabilitation Aid
Veterans Program Aid
School Lunch Aid
ASSISTANT COMMISSIONER FOR VOCATIONAL SERVICE
Regular Vocational Education
Agriculture
Home Economics
Distributive
Guidance
Trade and Industrial
Vocational Rehabilitation
Veterans Program
Adult Education
On-The-Farm Training
State Approval Agency
School Lunch Program
Institutional Approval Agency
DEPUTY COMMISSIONER FOR ADMINISTRATIVE SERVICES
Departmental Administration
Purchasing
Surplus Commodity Distribution
Instructional Materials
Audio-Visual
Textbooks
School Plant
General Program
Special Federal Programs
Surplus Property
Transportation
Transportation Safety
School Building Safety
School Law
Budgets
School Budgets
School Loans

Appendix B

Chart III.--ARKANSAS DEPARTMENT OF EDUCATION, 1958

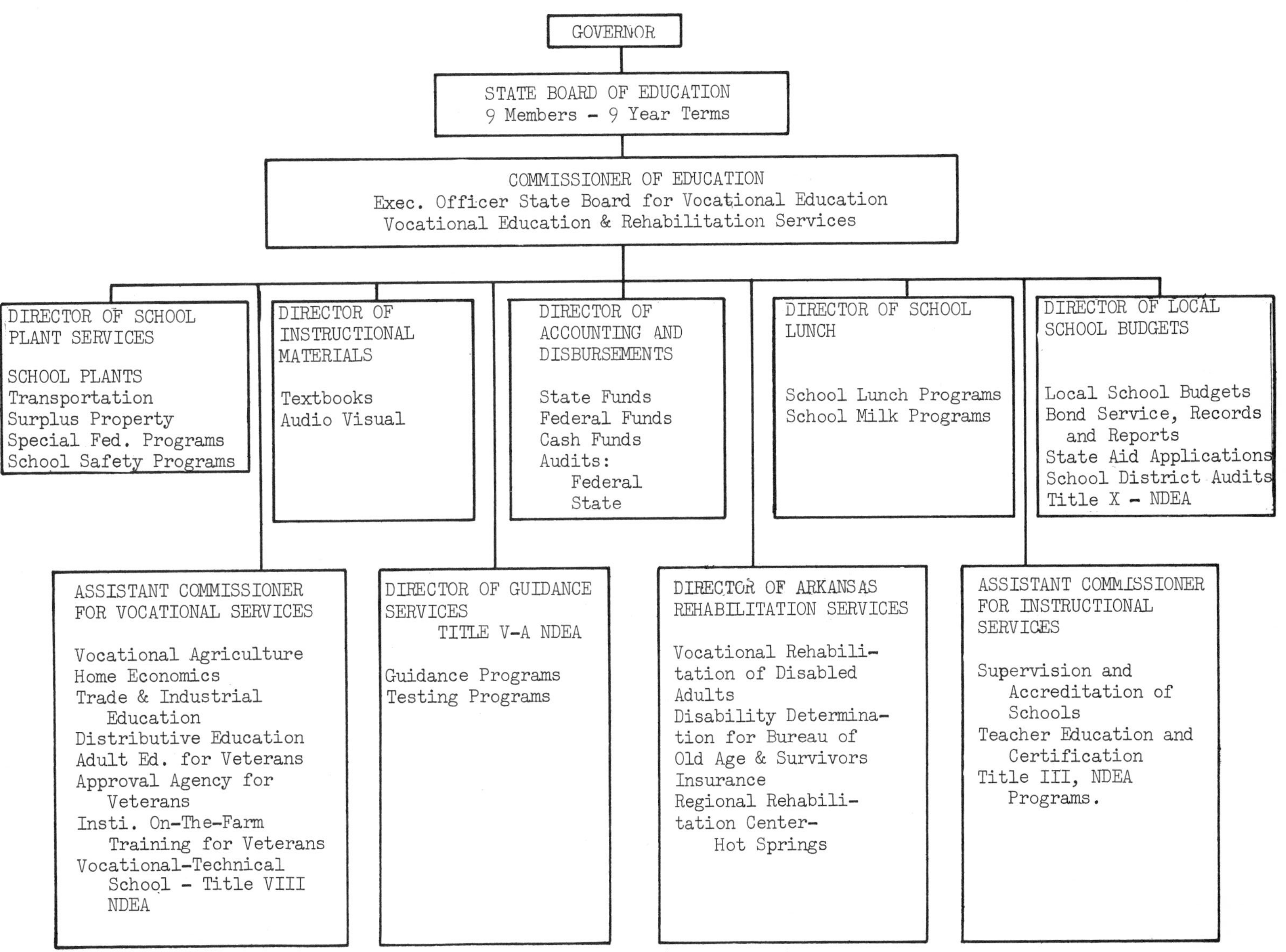

Appendix B

Chart IV.--ARKANSAS DEPARTMENT OF EDUCATION, 1963

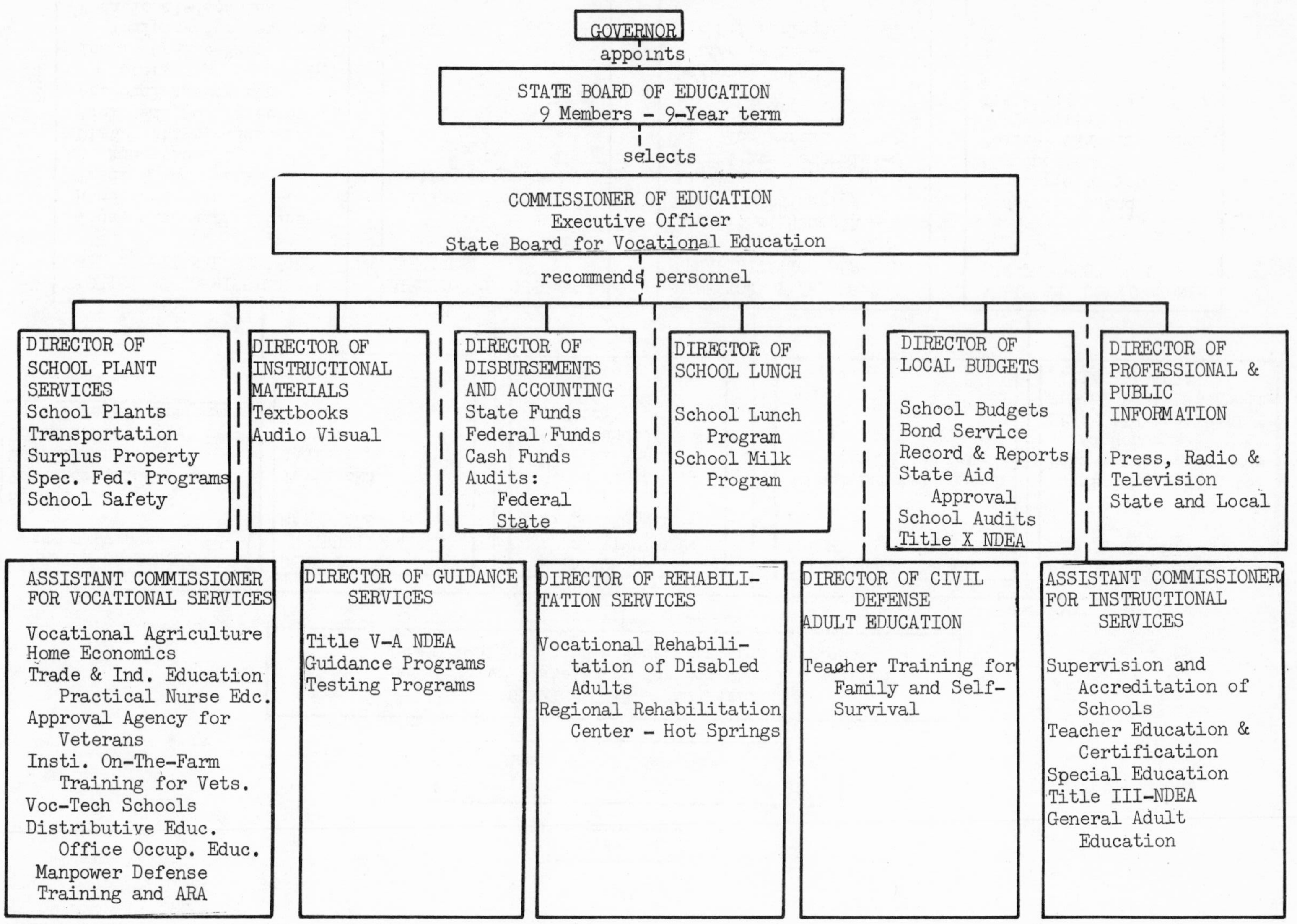

Appendix B

Chart V.--ARKANSAS DEPARTMENT OF EDUCATION, 1966

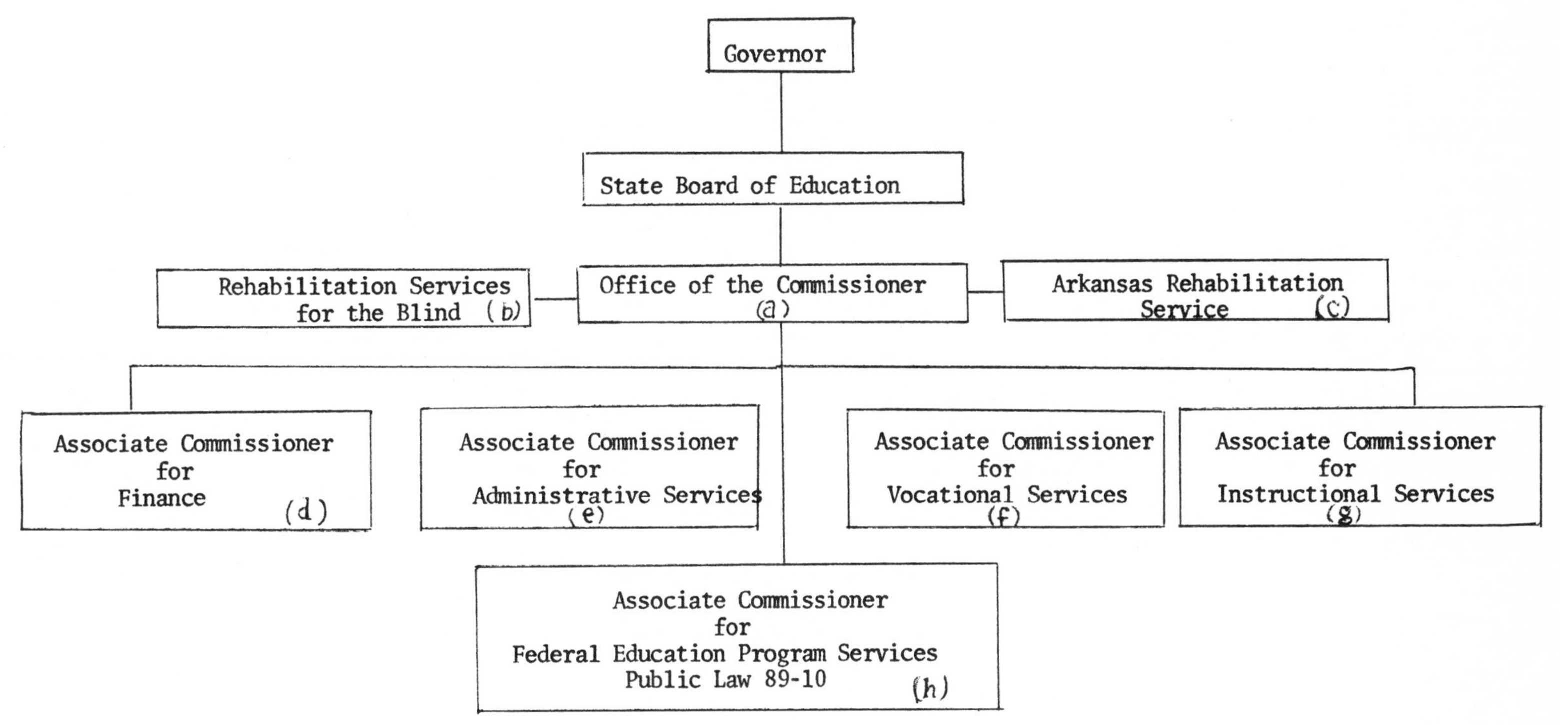

Seven (7) people responsible directly to the Commissioner

See Charts V(a) through V(h) for details of organization.

Appendix B

Chart V(a)

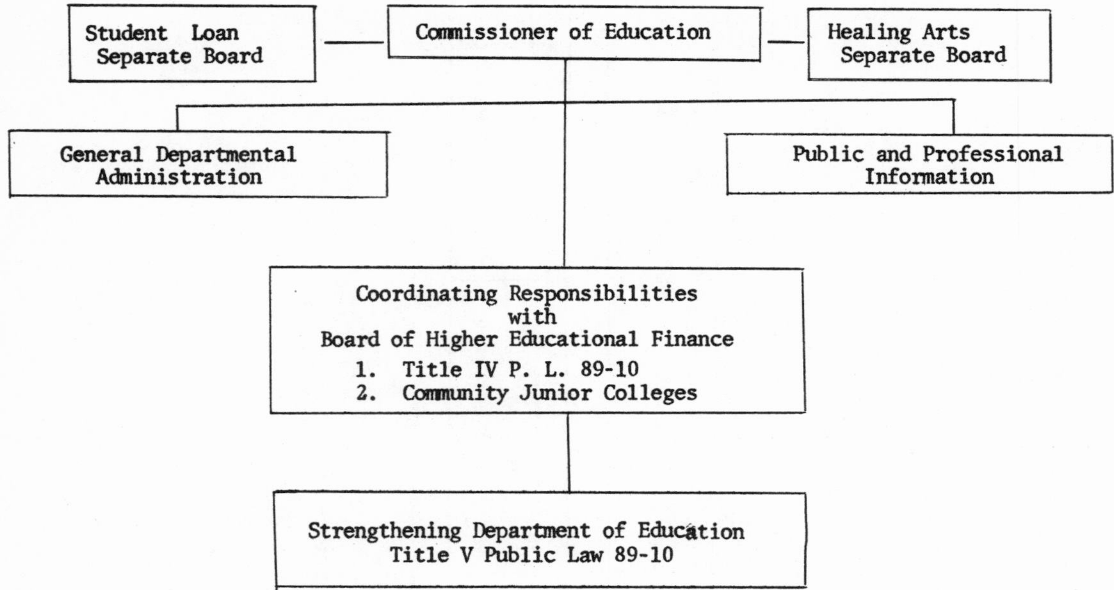

Chart V(b)

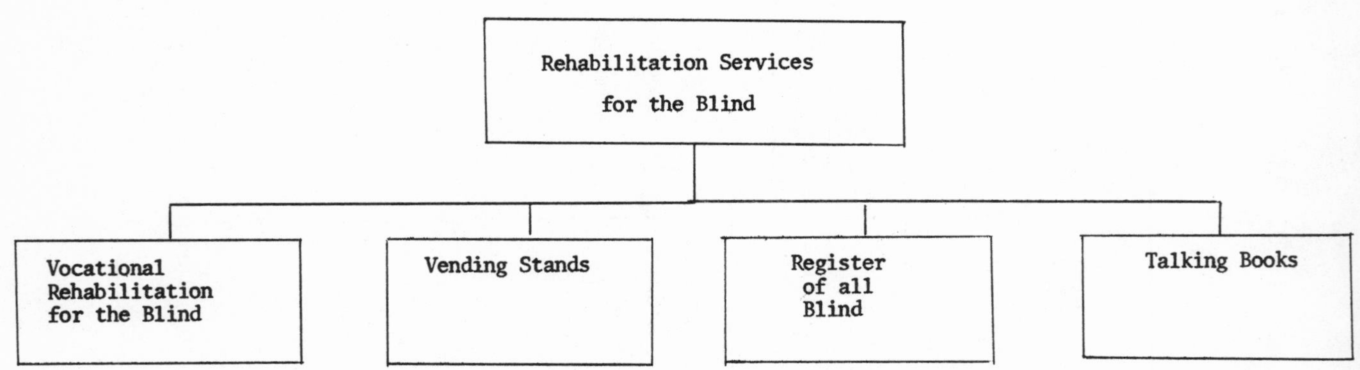

NOTE:
Act 180 of 1965 established a "Division of Rehabilitation Services for the Blind" in the State Department of Education with a Director responsible directly to the Commissioner of Education, and with the Commissioner serving as Executive Officer of the Board. All personnel and structure of services in the "Division of Rehabilitation Services for the Blind" are subject to the will of the Board as is true in all aspects of the Department of Education.

Appendix B

Chart V(c)

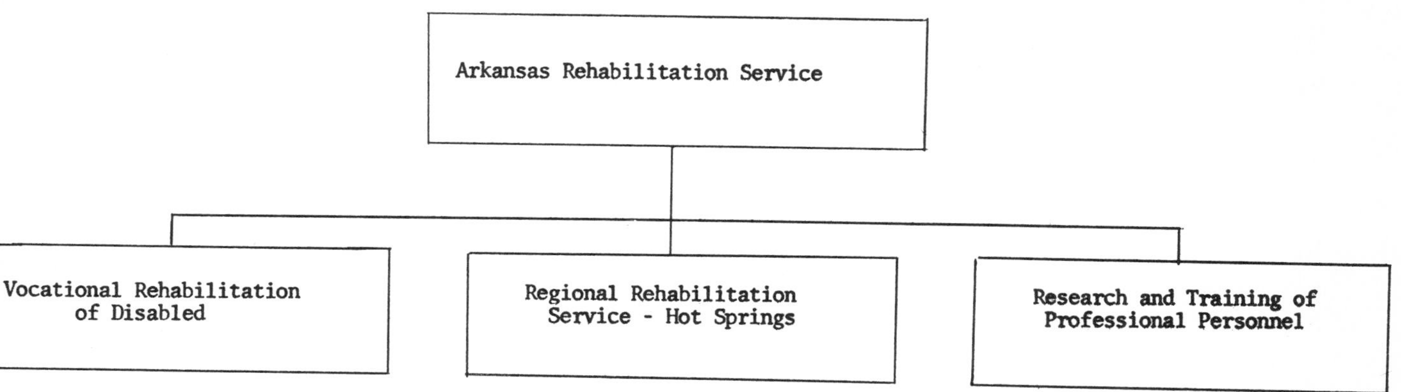

NOTE:
Act 34 of 1959 established the "Arkansas Rehabilitation Service" in the State Department of Education with a Director. The Commissioner of Education serves as Executive Officer of the Board for the administration of the "Arkansas Rehabilitation Service." All personnel and structure of services within the "Arkansas Rehabilitation Service" are subject to the will of the Board as is true in all aspects of the Department of Education.

Chart V(d)

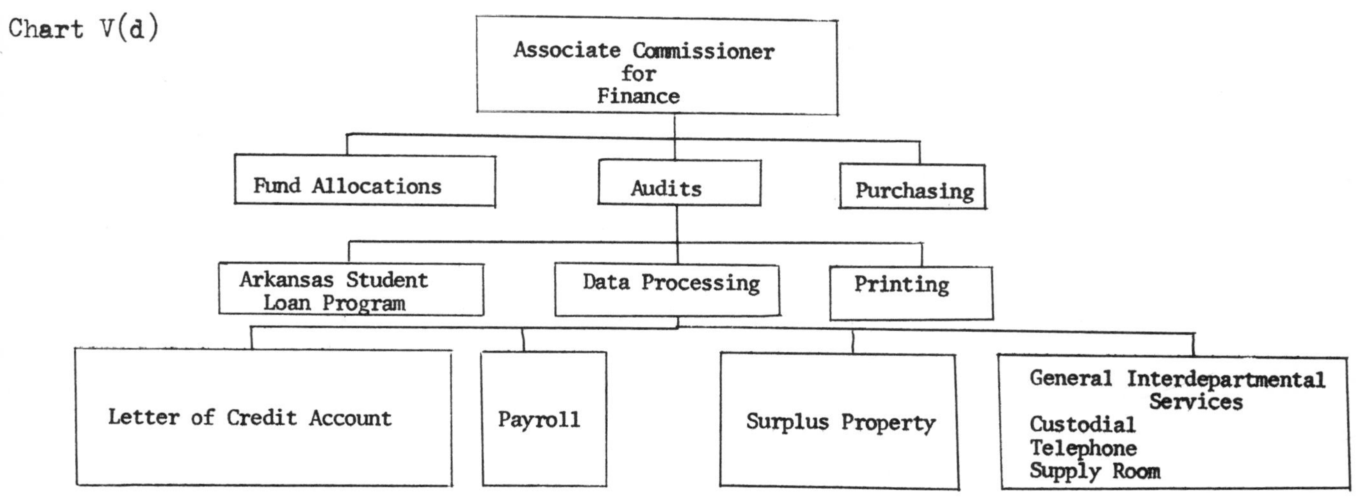

Appendix B

Chart V(e)

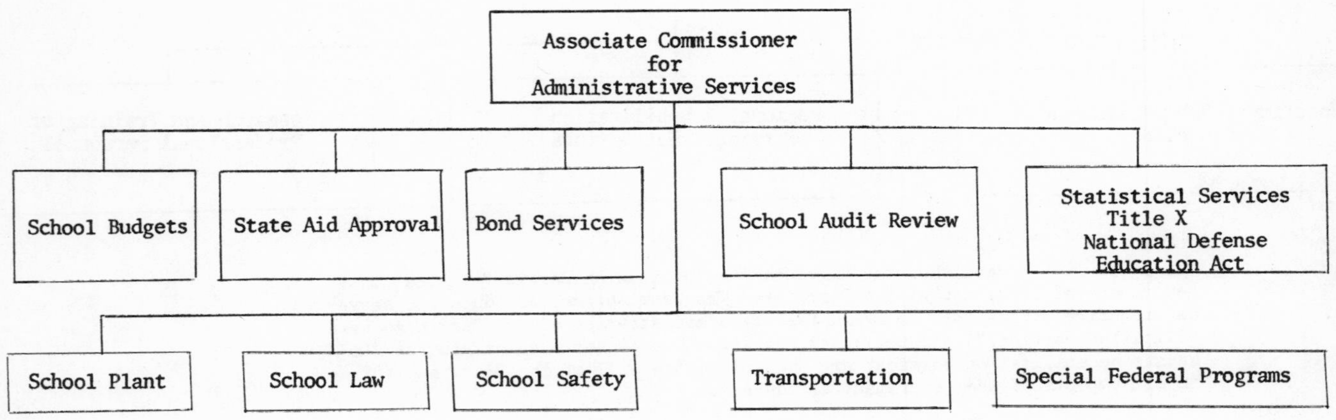

Chart V(f)

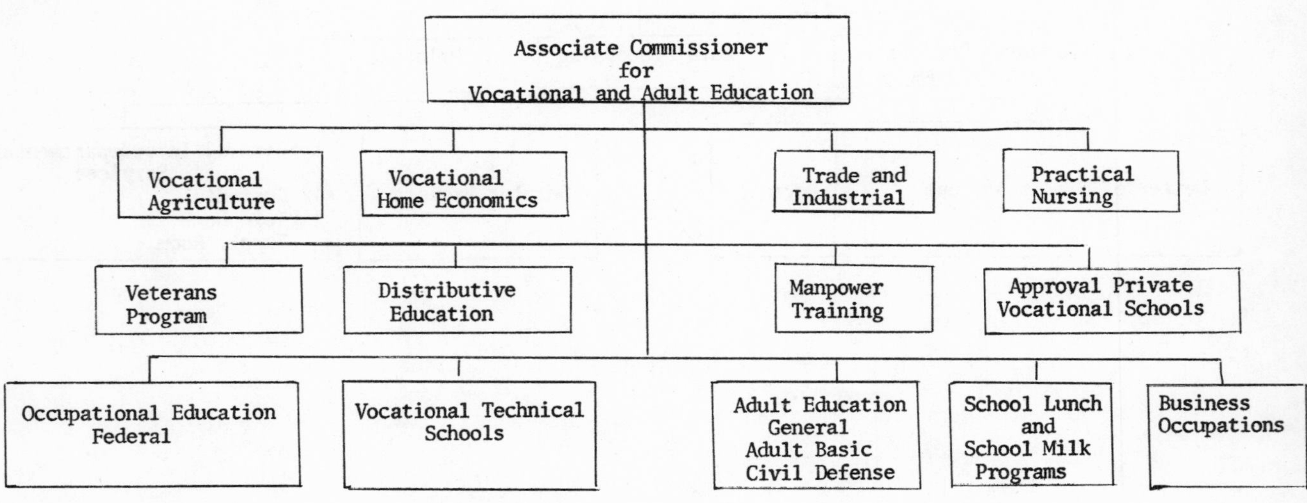

Appendix B

Chart V(g)

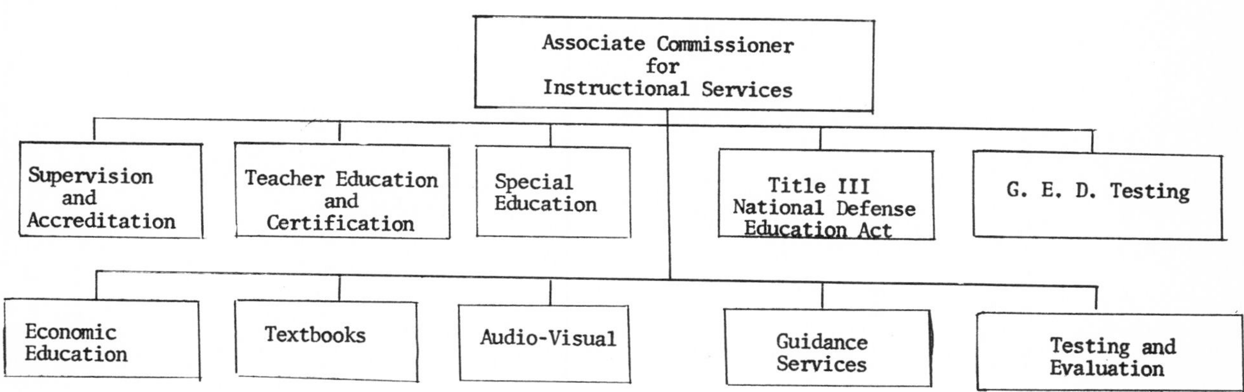

Chart V(h)

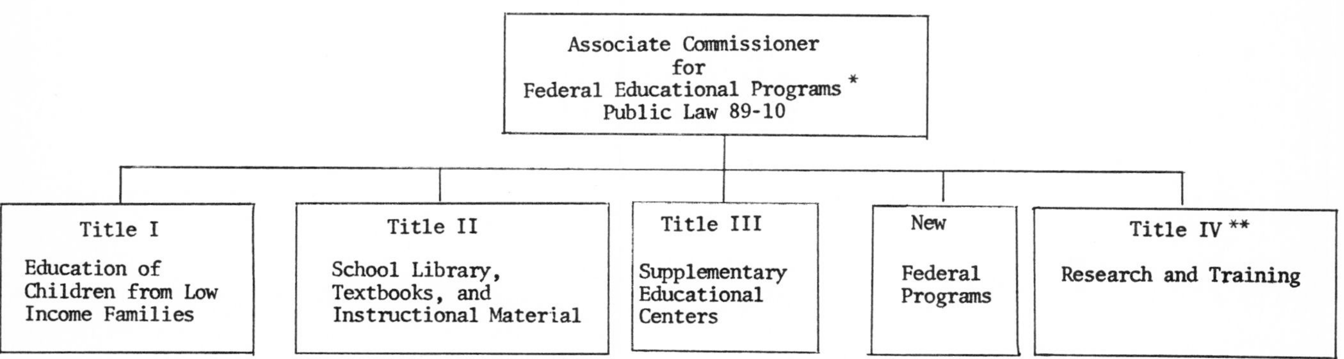

*Commissioner and Associate Commissioner for Federal Educational Programs have a coordinating function.

**This program administered by Board of Higher Educational Finance.

Appendix C

Table 1. – PUBLIC SCHOOL STATISTICS, 1900-66

Year ending June 30	Assessed valuation	Enumeration	Enrollment	Average daily attendance	No. of days in the term	No. of clrm. teach.	Average clrm. teach. salary
1900	$ 201,908,783	484,619	314,662	195,401	69	6,959	$ 166
1905	299,730,877	527,524	335,765	207,440	88	7,826	189
1910	380,520,823	573,842	395,978	255,135	107	9,522	273
1915	447,020,270	626,032	476,663	281,236	117	10,039	288
1920	612,426,084	676,009	483,172	326,053	124	10,947	476
1925	604,832,174	635,139	504,324	368,714	135	12,015	459
1930	608,238,521	620,572	456,174	330,824	149	12,960	691
1935	411,427,405	646,881	464,924	357,499	148	12,543	497
1940	444,953,450	624,811	472,014	373,356	159	13,173	584
1945	531,164,443	451,950	401,662	315,742	163	12,770	937
1950	678,516,852	456,943	425,173	355,031	173	13,740	1,801
1955	876,715,958	430,052	420,139	363,580	173	14,106	2,332
1960	1,366,688,564	435,933	424,206	372,591	173	15,273	3,293
1965	1,687,307,755	459,355	449,607	404,874	175	17,211	4,070
1966	1,802,265,097	457,737	452,370	409,398	175	17,939	4,619

Source:
Statistical Summary-Public Schools of Arkansas, State Department of Education.

Table 2. – PUBLIC SCHOOL FINANCES, 1900-66, RECEIPTS

Year ending June 30	RECEIPTS OF LOCAL SCHOOL DISTRICTS				
	Federal	State	Local	Nonrevenue	Total
1900	$ . . .	$ 446,558	$ 988,089	$ 570,595	$ 2,005,242
1905	. . .	593,514	1,448,421	938,518	2,980,453
1910	. . .	1,040,773	2,209,159	1,280,198	4,530,130
1915	. . .	1,394,953	2,648,365	1,206,826	5,250,144
1920	48,254	1,681,975	5,975,507	1,652,574	9,358,315
1925	101,215	3,124,549	6,842,005	3,019,466	13,087,235
1930	133,793	4,146,690	9,447,387	5,666,842	19,394,712
1935	1,213,238	2,203,060	7,537,605	397,072	11,350,975
1940	390,178	5,423,971	7,349,154	2,017,172	15,180,475
1945	781,516	10,560,595	9,020,677	831,379	21,194,167
1950	946,378	24,395,969	15,161,963	2,462,987	42,962,297
1955	1,670,460	27,212,820	27,323,811	993,835	57,200,916
1960	2,763,374	43,291,090	43,102,470	1,115,585	90,272,519
1965	2,716,499	62,276,375	62,446,975	16,399,036	143,838,885
1966	3,699,727	73,779,758	66,599,753	1,234,438	145,313,676

Source:
Statistical Summary-Public Schools of Arkansas, State Department of Education.

Appendix C

Table 3. – PUBLIC SCHOOL FINANCES, 1900-66, EXPENDITURES

Year ending June 30	EXPENDITURES OF LOCAL SCHOOL DISTRICTS				
	Current	Capital outlay debt service	Total	Current expenditure per ADA	Number of districts
1900	$ 1,124,497	$ 105,865	$ 1,230,362	6	4,903
1905	1,732,202	186,071	1,918,273	8	4,989
1910	3,163,479	451,188	3,614,667	12	5,110
1915	3,830,719	403,444	4,234,163	14	5,039
1920	6,494,496	1,008,235	7,502,731	20	5,112
1925	8,488,838	1,731,290	10,220,128	23	4,919
1930	11,512,252	5,109,614	16,621,866	35	3,703
1935	8,356,712	2,415,635	10,772,347	23	3,151
1940	10,807,980	3,024,749	13,832,729	29	2,920
1945	17,045,137	3,430,816	20,475,953	54	2,345
1950	34,847,999	6,811,725	41,659,724	98	421
1955	47,334,059	9,170,927	56,504,986	130	423
1960	77,288,133	12,740,285	90,028,418	207	422
1965	110,627,227	16,795,812	127,423,039	281	412
1966	126,317,797	17,941,190	144,258,987	293	410

Source:

Statistical Summary-Public Schools of Arkansas, State Department of Education.

5 California

DEPARTMENT OF EDUCATION
Prepared by the
Bureau of Publications of the Department

Contents

INTRODUCTION

The California State Department of Education is the agency through which the public school system—except the state university, the junior colleges, and the state colleges—is regulated and controlled at the state level as required by law. The department is governed by the State Board of Education whose 10 members are appointed by the Governor to serve 4-year terms. It is administered by the superintendent of public instruction, elected for a 4-year term, who acts as director of education. The department is located in Sacramento, but maintains an office in Los Angeles which provides services required by the public schools in the southern part of the state.

The superintendent of public instruction is assisted by a cabinet composed of two deputy superintendents, two associate superintendents, one assistant superintendent, and one director. Each member of his cabinet also serves as the chief administrative officer of a division or office of the department. And each of these divisions or offices provides certain services required for the department to carry out the provisions of legislation pertaining to the public schools, to futher educational policies and regulations of the State Board of Education, and to provide the educational guidance and leadership needed to keep the public school education program modern, functioning as necessary to meet existing needs, and geared to meet new needs promptly and effectively.

The State Department of Education was established in 1921. However, the public school system and a state officer to supervise the schools were provided for in the state's first Constitution of 1849. For many years no very large or complex system of state administration for public schools was needed. But since 1921, rapid growth and change have brought increasingly heavy and diverse responsibilities upon the department.

As in all states, the administration of education at the state level has been under pressures other than population growth and shifting urban-rural patterns. The Depression, two world wars, and the expanding role of the United States in international affairs have brought about substantial changes. The influence of educational leaders with vision and purpose has had impact. Professional personnel in the State Department of Education have fostered progress in particular fields. Federal planning and assistance have materially influenced state educational agencies.

In response to these many pressures and influences on education, many commissions have been appointed over the years by the Legislature, by the department, and by educational organizations to assess the operation of the public school system and the State Department of Education. Certain studies made by these groups brought about significant changes in the organization of the state's educational administration. These studies can be used as dividing lines for the chronicle that follows.

THE DEPARTMENT OF PUBLIC INSTRUCTION BEFORE 1921

A trend toward centralized responsibility for education at the state level characterized legislation in California from the beginning. This trend was reversed abruptly, but not for long, when the second state constitution, adopted in 1879, returned to school district governing boards such duties as selection of textbooks and certification of teachers, previously performed by the state agency. But an amendment in 1884 established the first constitutional State Board of Education and began another movement for increased state responsibility. This tendency toward central control agreed with the thinking of progressive educators throughout the nation. Efforts in this direction culminated in the establishment in 1921 of a State Department of Education to perform the many functions that had previously been assigned by the Legislature and by the State Board of Education to the superintendent of public instruction and his staff.

Early Legal Provisions for Education

Neither Spain nor Mexico provided public schools in California, although scattered attempts had been made to educate Indian children in the missions, and a few short-lived private and parochial schools were established. The first American settlers, therefore, were confronted with many of the same school problems their fellow citizens faced in wilderness territories elsewhere in America. In 1849 the writers of California's first constitution provided for a superintendent of public instruction, so that school districts could be organized, school trustees elected, schoolhouses built, and teachers hired. The superintendent was to be elected for a term of 3 years and was directed to be head of the state school system.

The first state constitution also provided for state school support. The second section of the article on education reads as follows:

> The Legislature shall encourage, by all suitable means, the promotion of intellectual, scientific, moral, and agricultural improvement. The proceeds of all land that may be granted by the United States to this State for the support of schools, which may be sold or disposed of, and the five hundred thousand acres of land granted to the new States, under an act of Congress, distributing the proceeds to the public lands among the several States of the Union, approved A.D. 1841; and all estates of deceased persons who may have died without leaving a will, or heir; and also such per cent, as may be granted by Congress on the sale of lands in this State, shall be and remain a perpetual fund, the interest of which, together with all the rents of the unsold lands, and such other means as the Legislature may provide, shall be inviolably appropriated to the support of common schools throughout the state (1).

Another section established and safeguarded a permanent fund for the support of a state university and its branches. However, the University of California was not established until 1868.

Despite these constitutional provisions, the first session of the Legislature refused to provide for free public schools. John Swett, fourth state superintendent of public instruction and historian of the school system, reports that–

> Near the close of the first session of the Legislature, 1849-50, . . . Mr. Corey, from the Committee on Education, reported that the taxes laid on the people for State, county, and municipal purposes were so heavy the committee did not consider it advisable to report a bill to tax the people still further for the support of public schools, and accordingly, the school bill, of which no record remains, was indefinitely postponed. While the school bill, thus defeated, has been forgotten, the reason advanced by Mr. [Assemblyman Benjamin] Corey has been the standing argument against every school bill which has contained any provision for maintaining by taxation a system of public schools (2).

In 1852 the Legislature adopted the first real school law. It reenacted provisions of 1851 for the organization of school districts to be governed by three trustees and created a State Board of Education to consist of the Governor, the superintendent of public instruction, and the surveyor general.

As John Swett tells us,

> The Surveyor General was included because the law originally proposed to entrust the board with the sales of school lands. This, however, was not done; and the state board remained . . . without powers or duties, except to apportion, annually the state school moneys (3).

First Superintendents of Public Instruction

The first two men elected as superintendent of public instruction, John Marvin (1851-53) and Paul K. Hubbs (1854-56), were lawyers. Besides being unfamiliar with teaching, both had to cope with an apathetic public and legislature. Nevertheless, both men took their responsibilities seriously and helped establish the basis for a school system. Interest on the meager State School Fund was distributed to counties on the basis of the "census child"– that is, the number of children between the ages of 5 and 17 living in the county. Half a century passed before the basis for apportionment changed to average daily attendance. A law of 1855 stipulated that the state money was to be used exclusively for teachers' salaries.

Andrew J. Moulder, third superintendent of public instruction, had been a teacher. He took an aggressive stand during his two terms of office (1857-62) for better public support of the schools. In his annual report of 1858, he declared that three-fourths of the children in the state were not in school and that if the Legislature failed to take instant and effective means to remedy the situation, these children would "grow up into 29,347 benighted men and women; a number nearly sufficient, at ordinary times, to control the vote of the State, and, in consequence, to shape its legislation and destiny!" (4).

Progressive legislation passed during Moulder's terms of office provided for an increase in county school taxes. The superintendent of public instruction was authorized to hold an annual state teachers convention, and $3,000 was appropriated for that purpose. He was authorized to appoint a State Board of Examination, to grant state teachers' certificates. The State Board of Education was authorized to adopt series of textbooks and to compel their adoption. A law was passed by which nearly 200,000 acres of school land were sold and the proceeds applied to the State School Fund. A state normal school was provided for; the members of the State Board of Education were to be members of the new Board of Trustees for the Normal School of the State of California. In 1860 the Legislature established a school for the education of indigent deaf, dumb, and blind children in San Francisco. In 1865, that body appropriated funds to educate blind children and established a combined school for the deaf and blind in Berkeley.

John Swett was the most outstanding and colorful superintendent of public instruction to serve before 1900. Having taught in a "shanty" school in San Francisco, he was warmly enthusiastic about free public education. Many of the schools were not "free" when he took office; parents customarily paid tuition. Facilities were very poor, supplies were inadequate, and teachers' salaries were pitifully small. During his tenure (1863-67) John Swett substantially increased state support. In his report for 1866-67, he stated that–

> The school year ending June 30, 1867, marks the transition period of California from rate bill common schools to an American free school system.
>
> For the first time in the history of the State, every public school was made entirely free for every child to enter (5).

One objective sought by Superintendent Swett was raising standards of professional teaching. He advocated the use of county funds to enable teachers to attend institutes. He saw that the professional journal, the *California Teacher*, was distributed to school trustees and school libraries. He was partially responsible for legislation that provided for life diplomas to teachers, recognized normal diplomas of other states, and required that city, county, and state boards of examination should be composed of professional teachers. Through the teachers institutes and other professional contacts, Swett widely influenced educational thought and progress in California.

Known as the "father of the state school system," Swett built the permanent structure of California's free public school system. By the end of his term, he had won his objectives: free schools for California's children, school funds to meet the greatest need, and examination and certification of teachers by teachers alone.

Each superintendent served with but one clerk until 1875, when a deputy was authorized. In 1890 the staff consisted of the superintendent, a deputy, a statistical clerk, a textbook editor, a textbook clerk, and a porter. With no more assistance than this, the superintendent supervised the schools and several educational agencies, state asylums, and orphanages; prepared forms for school records and gathered information and statistics on public education; apportioned state school funds; made biennial reports to the Governor; and published the school laws. He also attended educators conventions and made addresses at county institutes. As executive officer of the State Board of Education, he carried out the board's policies in regard to textbooks, teacher certification, and investigation of teacher-training institutions.

First State Boards of Education

From 1852 to 1864 the state board consisted of the Governor, the superintendent of public instruction, and the surveyor general. In 1864 the board was changed to include the superintendents of schools of San Francisco, Sacramento, and San Joaquin counties; the surveyor general was dropped. The board was given authority in the same year to adopt textbooks, require a uniform course of study, and make regulations for the schools. In 1866, on the recommendation of John Swett, the Legislature enlarged the State Board of Education to nine–adding the principal of the state normal school, the Santa Clara county superintendent of schools, and two teachers nominated by the state superintendent. The board also was authorized to provide a list of books for school libraries, make regulations for teachers examinations, and grant life diplomas. In 1870 the superintendents of schools of Alameda and Sonoma counties were added; in 1872 the two teachers were omitted.

In 1879, the delegates at a new constitutional convention felt that the danger of graft and corruption was too great regarding attempts to influence the State Board of Education's selection of textbooks and to wrest information from the State Board of Examination. They wanted to shift responsibility from the state to the local level. The second constitution, adopted that year, permitted the county boards of education to select textbooks, certify teachers, prescribe courses of study, and make regulations for the schools. It made no mention of the Board of Education or the Board of Examination.

In 1880 the sections of the Political Code concerning the State Board of Examination were repealed, and that board passed out of existence. The State Board of Education, stripped of most of its powers because of the constitutional shifts, was continued by the amended code; but its membership was reduced to the Governor, the state superintendent of instruction, and the principal of the state normal school. As new normal schools in the state were established, their principals became board members.

The tide turned in 1884, when the State Board of Education was written into the constitution by an amendment. The board's chief duty was to provide textbooks. The system of each county adopting its own had proved inefficient and expensive and was disliked both by the teachers and by the public. The board was therefore given authority "to compile, or cause to be compiled" a uniform series of textbooks, to have them printed at the State Printing Office, and to distribute and sell them at cost. In 1894, another amendment to the constitution added to the board's membership the president and the professor of pedagogy at the University of California.

Until 1912, the State Board of Education was a professional advisory council to the superintendent of public instruction. But instead of advising on general policies, selecting professionals, approving expenditures, and authorizing new programs, the board concerned itself with work that could have been entrusted to professional employees, such as revision and management of the state textbook series. It also issued state diplomas to graduates of normal schools and life diplomas to teachers.

Educators of the time favored a board composed wholly of laymen, rather than a board of professional educators and officeholders. In 1913, Ellwood P. Cubberley, writing for the *Cyclopedia of Education*, said:

> The tendency of legislation, and particularly of the recommendations of the many recent state educational commissions, has been clearly toward the creation of a state board of education, with some powers of supervision and control, and the assignment to this body of the appointment of its expert executive officers. . . . There should be a State Board of Education, neither too large nor too small, composed of citizens of the state, and appointed by the Governor, for reasonably long terms. A board of seven or nine is both small and large enough, and the terms should be arranged so that but one new appointment is to be made each year (6).

In November 1912, another constitutional amendment abolished the ex officio professional State Board of Education and instructed the Legislature to provide for the appointment or election of a State Board of Education. Accordingly, the Legislature of 1913 provided that the Governor should appoint a state board of seven members, none of whom should be actively engaged in educational work. The term of office was to be 4 years, since a section of the constitution prohibited the longer term favored by experts. Because the members of this new board had terms of the same length as the Governor's and because they were appointed by the Governor without any check whatever, it became possible from this time on for the Governor to regard the State Board of Education as he might regard any other executive commission. This made possible the reflection in the state school system of the political attitudes of the Governor's office.

The potential for conflict between the elected superintendent of public instruction and the appointed Board of Education was recognized at the time, but no effort was made to clarify the position of the superintendent. On the one hand, he was charged with carrying out the policies of the board; on the other, he was responsible to the people who elected him. The difficulty of requiring a policy-making board to have its policies carried out by and through an individual elected by the people has been pointed out again and again, but the system has never been changed.

Commissioners of Education

The 1913 Legislature empowered the State Board of Education to employ three commissioners—one for elementary schools, one for secondary schools, and one for vocational education—responsible directly to the board. The first meeting of the board was held in September 1913; after considering many candidates, it appointed the three.

Each commissioner was required to submit a biennial report. Much of each officer's time was occupied with visiting schools, preparing recommendations to legislative committees on education and to the state board, making public addresses, attending educators conferences, and working with other state agencies.

The first commissioners of elementary schools were women. Margaret Schallenberger, long interested in rural education, served from 1913 until 1922. Mrs. Grace Chandler Stanley succeeded her. When Mrs. Stanley resigned in 1925, she was followed by Mamie B. Lang, who died shortly afterward. Helen Heffernan served in this position until 1927, when she became chief of the department's rural education division. Duties assigned to the commissioner of elementary schools were outlined in the Political Code: to visit the elementary day and evening schools and investigate the course of study; to enforce the use of the state textbooks; to make recommendations to the State Board of Education; and to perform any other duties assigned by the superintendent of public instruction under the direction of the board.

The first commissioner of secondary schools was Will C. Wood, an educator well known for his interest in the state high schools. His first report to the State Board of Education states very well the principal basis for the creation of such a commission:

> The office was created in order that the state department might undertake a closer supervision of the secondary schools, which have increased in number until they have reached a total of two hundred and fifty-seven. When the constitution of 1879 was adopted provision was made for the Superintendent of Public Instruction and the various county superintendents of schools. At that time the high school was not fully recognized as an integral part of the state school system. There were a few public institutions of secondary grade but these were supported entirely by district taxation. Owing to the fact that they were locally supported, the inspection of high schools by county superintendents was only casual and perfunctory. Since that time the growth of the elementary schools has been so great that the county superintendent has been kept busy supervising the work of the grades (7).

Wood was interested also in the rapidly growing junior college movement. A 1911 act of the Legislature enabled school boards to prescribe postgraduate courses of study approximating the studies that had been prescribed for the first 2 years of university courses. By March 1914 public junior colleges had been established in nine cities with an enrollment of 722 students. Including those students taking postgraduate courses in high schools, the total was 1,331.

Edwin Snyder, the first commissioner of industrial and vocational education, had to define his own duties. One of his first acts was to make a statistical survey of manual, domestic, and vocational arts in the public schools of the state. And then the Smith-Hughes Act, providing federal funds to support vocational education, was passed in 1917. At once state legislation was passed designating the State Board of Education as the Board of Vocational Education required by the federal act and providing for apportionments to school districts by the state so that they could participate in the federal program.

The Smith-Hughes Act and the beginning of World War I stimulated much interest in industrial and vocational education. Hundreds of new classes were added, teacher training in vocational fields increased in colleges and normal schools, and many part-time and cooperative plans were set up in California schools. The commissioner of industrial and vocational education's office was reorganized, and three supervisors were added—one for agricultural instruction, one for teacher-training courses in home economics, and one for trade and industrial instruction.

The Staff and Increasing Responsibilities

From an early date the superintendent of public instruction and the State Board of Education had referred to the "Department of Public Instruction," though in fact no such department existed. Increasing responsibilities and activities of the superintendent, commissioners, and other members of the educational staff, however, called for some type of state-level organization to handle the state's educational business. A few developments of this period deserve brief mention.

Certification and Retirement of Teachers. In 1913, a new state-controlled system of retirement salaries for teachers was set up, and the State Board of Education constituted the Teachers' Retirement Salary Fund Board. Certification of teachers tended to become once again centralized in the state agency. In 1917, the state board was authorized by the Legislature to establish a Commission of Credentials, consisting of three commissioners of education, who were to consider applications for regular and special credentials and arrange for examinations of candidates.

Development of Normal Schools. The San Jose Normal School was the first state educational institution to be established in California. Opened as a normal school in San Francisco in 1862, it was moved to San Jose in 1871. Following the adoption of the 1879 Constitution, other normal schools were opened throughout the state: in Chico (1889), San Diego (1898), San Francisco (1899), Santa Barbara (1909), Fresno (1911), and Arcata (Humboldt Normal School, 1914). A branch of the San Jose Normal School established in Los Angeles in 1882 became the Los Angeles Normal School in 1887, which operated as an independent normal school until 1919 when it became the southern branch of the University of California. In 1921 the Legislature changed the state normal schools to state teachers colleges and centralized their control, formerly under local boards of trustees, under the state board and the state director of education (8).

Beginning of the Polytechnic School. Before the turn of the century, sentiment had been growing among educators for a school, state-sponsored if necessary, that would train young people for trades, industries, agriculture, and other occupations. In 1901, the Legislature provided for the establishment of a polytechnic school, and in 1903, the California Polytechnic School was opened at San Luis Obispo.

Early Publications. One of the superintendent of public instruction's duties was to supply school districts with the necessary books, forms, and report sheets. As time went on, more publications were added, including the biennial reports of the superintendent, the commissioners, and the state board. The *California Teacher*, published by the Department of Public Instruction, appeared from 1863 to 1876. This was followed by the *Pacific School and Home Journal*, described as an "Organ of the Department of Instruction," published from 1877 to 1883. Other journals followed, sometimes functioning as official publications of the department and at other times as private ventures. Edward Hyatt, superintendent of public instruction from 1907 to 1918, issued small pamphlets called "Blue Bulletins"; these were circulated to school people at irregular intervals from 1911 to 1914. From 1915 to 1921 the *California Blue Bulletin* was issued quarterly; it was edited by the superintendent of public instruction and the three commissioners of education and was sent to teachers, school clerks, superintendents, and others.

Staff Leadership and Development. Edward Hyatt, who served as state superintendent from 1907 to 1918, was greatly concerned with the schools under his care and how they could be best served. An unusual facet of Hyatt's tenure was that he was constantly traveling up and down the state on friendly visits to principals, teachers, and students.

In 1917, a State Board of Education office was established in Los Angeles. In the same year California became the second state in the Union to establish state supervision of physical education and the seventh to make physical education compulsory. In the spring of 1920, three assistant supervisors of physical education were employed by the board.

In 1918, Will C. Wood, having served as commissioner of secondary schools for 5 years, was elected state superintendent of public instruction. His practical experience stood him well. He formed an unofficial body known as the cabinet, consisting of himself and the three commissioners. He also reorganized the entire staff (that is, the employees of the board) to prevent overlapping of functions and duplication of efforts. In 1920, he secured the cooperation of the state commissioner of immigration and housing to supply the services of an assistant superintendent of public instruction in charge of Americanization. Similarly, when he needed a school attendance agent and funds were short, he arranged to have the Industrial Welfare Commission pay half the salary for the attendance officer. Because of Wood's tireless efforts, the Department of Education began to operate as a unified organization.

Vigorous leadership by Superintendent Wood, activities of the war years, and rapid growth of the state and its schools focused increasing attention on problems of public education in California. In 1919, the Legislature provided, by means of Senate Concurrent Resolution No. 21, for a legislative investigation of the problem of meeting the needs and furnishing support for the state schools and educational institutions.

THE JONES REPORT AND THE DEPARTMENT OF EDUCATION, 1921-27

On the basis of the 1919 legislation, the Special Legislative Committee on Education held meetings on California education. Every effort was made to have representatives of taxpayers associations, labor union personnel, laymen, and people directly interested in public education attend these meetings. The final report was drafted by Ellwood P. Cubberley, dean of the School of Education, Stanford University, and published by the Legislature in 1920 as the *Report of the Special Legislative Committee on Education*; it was referred to as the Jones Report because of the chairmanship of Senator Herbert C. Jones. Particularly pertinent here are the views of the committee on "State Educational Organization," Chapter I of the report.

The report criticized the vulnerable "doubleheaded" system, uncorrected in 1913 when a lay board of education succeeded the ex officio professional board. Any breach between the superintendent and the board could cripple the work of both. The report recommended that the present California educational organization be superseded at the earliest opportunity by a more rational form of state educational organization (9).

As evidence of a lack of logical, efficiently planned organization in the state agency, the report enumerated a number of "more or less unrelated boards, commissions, and other agencies having charge of some part of the educational work of the state" (10). In supervision and control, educational work was scattered among 23 boards and commissions, with a membership of about 160 persons; these agencies acted with little or no relation to one another.

Reasons for such a lack of sensible organization were found in the long-standing principle of decentralization and in the old pre-1913 State Board of Education, composed of busy men, hardly able to organize an educational department.

Committee Recommendations on Organization

The committe recommended, first, a constitutional amendment to abolish the election of a superintendent of public instruction and provide, rather, for the State Board of Education to appoint a commissioner of education to act as the chief executive officer of the board.

Second, the committee recommended that educational functions being exercised elsewhere should gradually be reassigned to the new State Department of Education.

The committee listed 16 divisions to be included in the new Department of Education. Seven already existed while nine either would be considered new divisions or would be the result of transferring responsibilities and defining new functions. Those in operation were: (1) a business division—to keep books and records, make purchases, pay bills, apportion school funds, and act as secretary to the State Board of Education; (2) a publication, information, and statistical division—to collect statistics, prepare forms and registers, prepare the biennial report and other publications, and answer public inquiries; (3) an examining, certificating, and pensioning division—to have charge of examinations for teacher certification (such certification to be a uniform state function); (4) a vocational education division—to add to its duties supervision of the California Polytechnic School and the State Nautical School, and to include, possibly, a new rehabilitation division; (5) a secondary education division—to take over from the University of California the inspection and accrediting of high schools and to supervise junior colleges; (6) an elementary education division—to supervise elementary schools, including kindergartens; and (7) a health and physical welfare division—to take on the duties of supervising health instruction and making studies of the health, physical welfare, nutrition, and abnormalities of schoolchildren.

The additional nine divisions and their duties were suggested as follows:

1. A legal division, headed by an attorney well versed in school law, to edit and publish a school code, advise the Legislature as to needed legislation, and interpret school laws.

2. A research division to act as a center for the dissemination of educational information and supply or select educational tests and scales.

3. A teacher-training division to supervise the teacher-training work in all state institutions and possibly for a time combined with the examining, certificating, and pensioning division.

4. A buildings and sanitation division to study the needs and suggest plans for improving schoolhouse construction and sanitation, prepare plans to be loaned to school corporations, approve plans for new school buildings, and assist counties in making sanitary surveys of school buildings.

5. A special education division to supervise and conduct studies to improve education for the blind, deaf and dumb, feebleminded and mentally defective, truant and incorrigible, and dependent and delinquent children. It was to supervise educational work in charitable, penal, and reformatory institutions and orphan asylums supported by the state.

6. A rehabilitation division to take over from the Industrial Accident Commission work provided for by the Legislature of 1919 to rehabilitate persons crippled in industry and to become the agent of the federal government for such work. Education of crippled children would also come under the jurisdiction of this division.

7. An adult education division to have charge of immigrant education, Americanization, and other adult education. This had already begun under the State Commission on Immigration and Housing. Combined with this division would be certain responsibilities in visual education.

8. An art and music division to study the needs of the state in pure and applied art and in music to improve the instruction in these fields.

9. A library division could be formed, mainly to improve county library work.

Organization of the State Department of Education

In May 1921, the Legislature created a State Department of Education under the control of an executive officer to be known as the director of education; the superintendent of public instruction was to be ex officio director. Powers and duties of the boards of trustees of the normal schools, henceforth to be called "state teachers colleges," were transferred to the new department. Similarly, the department took over the powers and duties of the board of trustees of the California Polytechnic School and of the board of directors of the School for the Deaf and Blind.

Formation of the department was in line with recommendations of the Jones Report. However, other sections of the law of May 1921 continued the anomalous organizational features the report had objected to. The State Board of Education was continued, along with its previous responsibilities. One new division of the department—textbooks, certification, and trust funds—would be under the state board. The new normal and special schools division would be under the director of education, although the appointment of principals and faculty members was subject to approval by the board, which also could enact regulations for these schools. The three commissioners of education were unaffected by the new legislation and were to continue with the status of assistant superintendents, appointed by and responsible to the state board.

Several positions were added: A deputy director of education to represent the director of education in the Division of Normal and Special Schools. The statistician became an assistant superintendent, with general research duties added to his former responsibilities. Provisions of the Federal Vocational Rehabilitation Act were accepted by the Legislature in 1921, and a supervisor of vocational rehabilitation and an assistant in rehabilitation were added to the office of commissioner of industrial and vocational education.

Although the offices constituting the new department were based on the functions of the superintendent's office or on appointment by the state board, Superintendent Wood organized the department into a remarkably unified body considering the double-headed nature of the agency.

With a real State Department of Education in Sacramento, education became more centralized. School people were encountering increasingly complex problems, and they brought to the state department their questions about school law, federal vocational education, compulsory attendance, compulsory physical education, and education of immigrants. The three commissioners of education closely supervised the schools. Courses in elementary and secondary schools had to be approved by the department. The department published the state series of elementary school textbooks and the official list of approved high school textbooks. The department also directly influenced the conduct of the teachers colleges.

The department's leadership was in part due to the cooperative spirit and long experience of several persons in key positions. Will C. Wood had served the department for 5 years as commissioner of secondary schools before his election to two terms as superintendent of public instruction. Edwin Snyder, commissioner of vocational education, served for 10 years. Job Wood, Jr., who was statistician for 20 years, served as deputy superintendent from 1919 to 1923. Helen Heffernan, commissioner of elementary schools, served the department for 40 years.

Political Action and Educational Change

In 1923, Will C. Wood began his second term of office as superintendent of public instruction, and Friend W. Richardson began his term as Governor. Richardson was a conservative who denounced extravagance in education. His policies were immediately criticized by educational associations, but were endorsed by taxpayers associations.

Meanwhile, important changes were taking place in the state department. In 1924, the title of assistant superintendent in charge of "immigrant" education was changed to "adult." In 1925, Superintendent Wood appointed Mrs. Mabel Gifford to be the first assistant superintendent of public instruction in charge of speech correction. The appointment was made possible through a grant of funds from the California Speech Foundation.

On the darker side, because of severe cutbacks in appropriations, the 51 positions in Wood's department had been reduced to 39 by 1925. A disparate salary situation came about when the salaries of the assistant superintendents employed by the state board were increased to $5,000, while the salaries of assistant superintendents in the Office of the Superintendent of Public Instruction remained at $3,000. The superintendent was still paid $5,000.

The situation foreseen by the Jones Report became a reality in 1924 when a majority of the State Board of Education, appointed by Richardson, sided with the Governor in opposition to the superintendent of public instruction, refusing to confirm the superintendent's appointments of the presidents of the San Jose and San Francisco state teachers colleges. The resulting impasse, lasting several years, dramatically pointed up the shortcomings of the existing organization. In his last biennial report, Wood recommended legislation to define the powers of the board—to be legislative and regulatory—and those of the superintendent—to be executive and supervisory (11).

During this period the California Teachers Association's Committee on Duties and Functions of Public School Administrative Authorities studied the organization of other state boards of education. In a second study it traced the trends in organization of such boards and recommended a constitutional amendment to change the California State Board of Education. The committee recommended a larger board, its members to be elected by the people; it defined the board's functions and recommended that the agency's professional work be done by professionally trained persons.

Superintendent Wood made several legislative recommendations affecting the Board of Education and the Department of Education. One was to create a division of school planning, for which he had long felt the need; another, to establish a state curriculum commission to "adopt minimum standards for elementary school courses of study" and "succeed to the powers of the State Board of Education in reference to approved courses of study in high schools and junior high schools. . ." (12); still another, to codify school laws. He also urged legislation to provide better education for physically handicapped children.

The 1927 Legislature took note of Wood's suggestions and those of the California Teachers Association. Legislation affecting the organization of the State Department of Education was introduced, and much of it was passed.

CHANGE AND GROWTH THROUGH THE DEPRESSION AND WAR, 1927 TO 1945

Because Clement C. Young, elected governor in 1926, regarded education quite differently than did Richardson, new educational legislation prepared by Superintendent Wood and others had a friendly reception. In 1927, Senator H. C. Jones introduced a bill to unify the state department with members of the state board appointed to 10-year terms, and an appointive director of education who would take over the duties, powers, and responsibilities of the superintendent of public instruction. This bill was approved overwhelmingly by the Legislature, but it required an amendment to the constitution, which failed to pass in the general election of 1928. However, changes in the Political Code provided for a new state board and a reorganized state department. Despite the continuance of the old double-headed responsibility, the newly organized department served satisfactorily through the trying days of the Depression and World War II.

Amendments to the Political Code, effective July 29, 1927, launched the following changes: (a) creation of a new State Board of Education of 10 members, appointed by the Governor with Senate approval; (b) abolishment of the three commissionerships established in 1913; (c) full power for the board "to establish upon recommendation of the Superintendent, such divisions in the State Department of Education as appear advisable for the efficient transaction of the business" (13); and (d) election of the chiefs of these divisions by the board, on nomination of the superintendent.

Reorganization of the Department of Education

Governor Young immediately appointed the 10 new members of the State Board of Education for 4-year terms—three expiring in 1928, two in 1929, three in 1930, and two in 1931. The board met in August 1927 and, acting on the recommendation of the superintendent, established 10 divisions in the State Department of Education:

1. Rural Education provided administrative and supervisory services to the rural schools, both elementary and secondary.

2. City Secondary Schools administered city high schools and junior colleges. Its chief concern was to supervise vocational education, except agriculture (which was under the rural schools division).

3. Adult Education promoted adult education in high schools and junior colleges, carrying out research and developing courses in parent education and child study, and education of immigrants.

4. Health and Physical Education supervised health education and physical education of boys and girls in the public schools.

5. Special Education supervised programs for the education of physically handicapped, mentally retarded, and otherwise exceptional children, and mental hygiene.

6. Research and Statistics was to compile statistics; draft official records and report forms; conduct educational research; and apportion state school funds.

7. Teacher Training and Certification supervised teacher training in institutions approved by the state department and issued teachers' certificates.

8. Publications and Textbooks was responsible for editorial and clerical activities in connection with all publications compiled, listed, or distributed by the department.

9. Schoolhouse Planning, created to give advice concerning planning and construction of school buildings, had the responsibility for establishing standards, conducting surveys, and checking and approving plans and specifications for new buildings.

10. Libraries was created by special legislation that brought the State Library (established in 1850) into the Department of Education. It performed library services for the people of the state, the schools, and school officials, and supervised the county library system and libraries of the state teachers colleges.

Acting on recommendations of the superintendent, the State Board of Education appointed chiefs for all divisions except two. All state officers, including the three commissioners of education, were appointed to appropriate positions in the new organizational structure, with the result that there was little or no disruption.

Although reelected superintendent of public instruction in 1926, Wood resigned in 1927 to become state superintendent of banks. Governor Young appointed William J. Cooper to fill out Wood's unexpired term. Cooper, then, became responsible for inaugurating the legislative changes. In his first report to the Governor in 1928, Cooper spoke of the smoothness with which the changes had been effected and expressed appreciation for the work of the members of the state department, who "have given themselves wholeheartedly to the service of the State" (14).

Departmental Changes, 1927 to 1931

Reorganization of the department and other educational legislation brought about further changes in the following years. A Curriculum Commission, set up in July 1927, had been earlier recommended after a thorough study of the public schools' instructional program. Under a subvention of the Commonwealth Fund of New York, the study was begun in 1923 and its results published in 1926 under the title, *The California Curriculum Study* (15). After its publication, only 12 subjects were prescribed by law for elementary schools instead of 32. The Curriculum Commission was a second result of the study. It was to outline minimum courses for use in elementary and secondary schools and to study textbooks in elementary subjects before they were adopted. The commission soon expanded its activities to include preparation of guides for teachers.

A School Code was enacted by the Legislature in 1929 to unify the provisions of the several codes and general laws relative to public education. An expanded publications program followed the appointment, in 1931, of a chief of the textbooks and publications division. Even before, a monthly educational journal, *California Schools*, had been inaugurated as an official organ of the department. In January 1932, a numbered series known as the Department of Education "Bulletin" replaced the division or bureau publications. In 1932 the department began publishing the *California Journal of Elementary Education*.

In 1929, the Legislature established the California Nautical School (later renamed the California Maritime Academy) which began operation in 1931. The legislation was based on an act of Congress in 1911 which provided that, on request of the governor of a state, the U.S. Navy would furnish a ship for training officers for the merchant marine. A board of governors for the school, created within the state department, consisted of the superintendent of public instruction and four other members to be appointed by the Governor.

In August 1927, the State Board of Education became the trustees of the California State Historical Association. It was administered by a part-time director. In 1928 a new home for the State Library, the Library and Courts Building, was completed, and the State Department of Education moved its headquarters there.

Depression and Earthquake

Governor Young's annual message to the Legislature in January 1929 included recommendations for a comprehensive survey of the school system. But Young's successor, Governor James Rolph, who took office in 1931, showed little interest in the schools. One reason, of course, was the Depression. Governor Rolph asked the Legislature to cut costs everywhere, and specifically to amend the constitution to reduce the fixed sums for schools. Although this was not done, it did cut drastically the budget for the schools and the state department.

School districts felt the Depression keenly; they cut educational services to the bone. In March 1933, Vierling Kersey, then superintendent of public instruction, published an article entitled "Shall Public Schools in California Be Closed?" (16) in which he pointed out that demands for tax relief, strengthened by local taxpayers associations, resulted in a decrease of almost $10 million in public school spending for 1931-32 compared with the previous year.

The total reduction for 1932-33 was a staggering $49 million. This, said the superintendent, would make it impossible for many districts to maintain schools through the year. In hundreds of other districts, children would receive very little schooling. Kersey called for the restoration of funds insofar as possible, and also for a radical revision of the state tax system.

The Legislature slashed the superintendent's budget and tried to reduce the department's services. But Kersey handled his meager funds so astutely that he was able to continue all the services which the Legislature had hoped to eliminate.

At the time that Kersey's pleas for support to keep the schools open were being presented, a disaster further increased the financial burden of the schools—the Long Beach earthquake of March 1933. School buildings were destroyed, and others so damaged as to be unsafe. Fortunately, school was not in session at the time of the earthquake, but the frightening prospect of a recurrence focused attention on the safety of school buildings throughout the state. The Field Act, passed as an emergency measure, provided that school construction be supervised by the state. The federal Reconstruction Finance Corporation loaned funds to impoverished school districts that suffered building losses in the earthquake.

In June 1933, the voters passed a constitutional amendment which radically changed the method of financing public schools. Compulsory county school taxes for school support were eliminated, and the amounts previously required to be raised by county taxes were provided as apportionments from the State General Fund.

Recovery of the Schools

The federal government, through the Federal Emergency Education Program, gave much assistance to the schools through the Depression years. Starting January 1934, a certain portion of the federal relief funds was earmarked for educational purposes (17).

Under the Civil Works Administration, and later under the Federal Emergency Relief Administration and the Works Project Administration, money was allocated nationwide to provide employment to unemployed teachers; to restore normal school facilities in the areas of greatest depression; and to supplement existing school facilities, especially in the field of adult education. In California, where state and district support was adequate to maintain the public schools (although with curtailed services), federal funds were utilized to supplement ordinary activities. Under the WPA program several thousamd teachers and allied workers who could find no other work were employed as teachers of special adult education classes, of classes for the retraining of unemployed workers, and of children in nursery schools. Public schools also were improved through development of radio programs, provision for school health services, extension of library facilities, promotion of museum projects and visual instruction aids, and construction and rehabilitation of school plants and equipment (18).

By 1936, with the help of state and federal agencies, school districts were recovering from the effects of the Depression. Superintendent Kersey was able to report that—

> In spite of all evils resulting from the depression, at least one benefit resulted. This benefit, which applies to education as well as to other social agencies, came from the reexamination of purpose and procedures which took place in all fields of social planning during this period, and gave immediate promise of more efficient planning for the future (19).

Superintendent Kersey resigned in 1937. During his term of office, no additional divisions were created in the state department, but the vocational education bureaus were placed under the Commission for Vocational Education, independent of the city secondary schools division. A few additions were made to the administrative staff, including an assistant superintendent in Los Angeles, but several administrative staff offices were discontinued. The Commission for Special Education was organized; its members were the superintendent and the chiefs of bureaus of the education of the blind, education of the deaf, correction of speech defects, mental hygiene, and vocational rehabilitation.

State teachers colleges became state colleges and were thus legalized as regional 4-year collegiate institutions not limited to teacher training. A Public School Teachers Retirement Investment Board was established to invest the funds of the teachers retirement system.

In 1937, Governor Frank F. Merriam appointed Walter Dexter superintendent of public instruction. The Governor was friendly to education, and his lieutenant governor, George J. Hatfield, strongly supported the schools. Hatfield said: "I prefer to spend thousands today for better education . . . than to spend millions tomorrow for bigger prisons, . . . and bigger pensions for unemployables" (20). The 1937 Legislature voted for a minimum salary of $1,320 per year for teachers in public schools; this action meant a substantial raise for almost every rural teacher. In 1939, bonus funds were provided for educating physically handicapped children, and an additional appropriation allowed spastic children to enter school at age 3.

A concientious man with a warm personality, Dexter had served as president of Whittier College and as executive secretary to Governor Merriam before being appointed superintendent. He found that soaring enrollments were straining the capacity of the department to provide adequate services. Obviously the department's obsolete structure needed overhauling. Under Dexter's leadership a committee drew up a constitutional amendment, later approved by the voters, which called for reshaping the department.

Influence of World War II on the Schools

World War II was first felt by the schools in California by an enormous increase in demands for vocational training. The federal government increased its help, which created some anxiety that the public schools would be unduly controlled by Washington.

By November 1940, the schools began to feel the pressure to teach technical skills needed in defense industries and other types of training demanded by the national emergency. In 1941, National Defense Training courses were established with federal funds under the State Department of Education's Commission for Vocational Education. By July, 118,920 students were enrolled in these classes. Rural schools had classes in farm machinery repair and vocational agriculture.

A proliferation of state and federal agencies, designed to supplement the work of the schools, led Assistant Superintendent Aubrey A. Douglass to remind these agencies of their obligations to the department and to the schools of California: (a) they should cooperate with the department in carrying out their programs; and (b) they should not interfere with the programs and administration of the schools (21).

The State Board of Education took note of the problem of federal-state relations and in its meeting of October 1941 provided that each federal agency should "submit to the State Department of Education a statement of the policies under which it operates, a description of its program, and contemplated developments," and that "a member of the State Department of Education shall be assigned to act as a liaison officer between the Department and each of the federal agencies," who shall be aware of questions of jurisdiction "so that there may be no violation of law and no assumption by the schools or by the federal agency of functions recognized as belonging to the other" (22).

Despite difficulties encountered during the war in teacher shortages, postponement of building programs, loss of young people who dropped out of school to enter the defense industries, and shortages of material of all kinds, the schools contributed greatly to the war effort. The state director of vocational training for war production workers, John C. Beswick, was credited with having developed the largest program of vocational training for essential war industries in the United States (23).

Postwar Problems and Solutions

When the war ended, numerous school facilities were needed. The need was also great for retraining workers for peacetime pursuits and aiding veterans and school dropouts to complete their education. A shortage of trained teachers still existed; thousands of teachers held only emergency credentials. In addition, many people had come into the state during the war; few of them left when the war was over.

In 1944, several influential groups of school administrators called upon the State Department of Education to recommend various changes in the school system.

At a meeting in Sacramento in January 1944, the State Education Council reconstituted itself as the state superintendent's Advisory Council. The council defined its purposes: (a) to advise the superintendent of public instruction on matters he may wish to refer to the council and to interpret and present to him problems or conditions concerning the proper functioning of the state's school system; (b) to coordinate the work of the divisions of the State Department of Education, the various state professional organizations and lay groups concerned with educational problems, practices, and support; (c) to assist in implementing the programs of the department and other organizations; and (d) to carry out research needed by the superintendent and his staff.

This group set up committees to consider the following problems: (a) rehabilitation of disabled veterans of the military forces; (b) study of legislative proposals; (c) teacher selection and training; (d) audiovisual education; (e) standards for school buildings and equipment; and (f) post-high school education (24). Each of these committees in turn made specific recommendations.

The Association of California County Superintendents of Schools met in January 1944 and went on record as being strongly in favor of federal aid to equalize educational opportunity and of state aid for more suitable financing of education. The group suggested certain changes in the state department, such as adding an audiovisual division, starting a committee on radio services in education, and making a survey of county library services. It recommended that the department certify teachers in cooperation with county superintendents of schools and repeal the authority of county boards to grant elementary school certificates. The association suggested legislation for more effective school organization and administration, and for better equalization of educational opportunities and costs. It also suggested that the department exercise leadership in developing postwar building plans (25).

Meeting in April 1944, the Association of California Secondary School Principals adopted resolutions touching on the work of the State Department of Education. Among them were a resolution favoring more personnel in the department and the creation of a division of educational research. It also passed resolutions requesting a survey and evaluation of junior high schools and favoring high standards for regular credentials.

The State Board of Education established a Division of Audiovisual Education in April 1944, and a Division of Readjustment Education for the education of veterans in August.

A special legislative session was called in June 1944 to consider educational needs. One bill provided $4.5 million for elementary schools, to be spent on teachers' salaries and school supplies. A teachers' retirement bill was passed; $20,000 was allocated to the State Reconstruction and Reemployment Commission to study the administration, organization, and financial support of the public school system. George D. Strayer, professor emeritus of education, Teachers College, Columbia University, was employed as consultant. Subgroups worked on various aspects: how to equalize the burden of education among the school districts; supply and demand for teachers; and reorganization of district administration. J. N. Mills, head of a firm of management consultants, made an analysis of the organization and administration of the State Department of Education. The Mills study, presented in December 1944, and the Strayer study, in February 1945, resulted in far-reaching changes in the State Department of Education.

THE STRAYER REPORT AND THE REORGANIZATION OF THE DEPARTMENT, 1945 TO 1963

The Strayer Report was a masterly summary of the California public school system, with specific recommendations for solving many of its problems (26). After pointing out the need for overall expansion, the report touched on Department of Education leadership:

> Even a rough sketch of the problems confronting education in California in the postwar period indicates the desirability of taking action now to provide for the best possible organization, administration, and financing of the program of education. The highest type of leadership on the State level will demand the professionalization of the office of the State Superintendent of Public Instruction. This means the need for a constitutional amendment that will provide for the selection of this official by a lay board rather than by popular vote.
>
> There will most certainly be required an expansion of the staff of the State Department of Education in order that significant leadership and general supervision of the expanded program may be furnished. The State office must be in a position to guarantee that whatever program of education is mandated by the State is actually carried out in all local school districts (27).

Recommendations of the Strayer Report

The Strayer Report's first recommendation was that the Governor appoint a State Board of Education consisting of 10 laymen, each with overlapping terms of 10 years, and that the board select an outstanding educator as superintendent of public instruction. Other recommendations called for an expanded and reorganized State Department of Education: hiring specialists for the divisions of elementary and secondary education and appointing a deputy superintendent, an associate commissioner of education, and an associate superintendent in charge of business and administrative services. The report then listed 28 more appointments to the professional staff and recommended employing at least 25 additional stenographic, clerical, and statistical workers.

Aside from the reorganization of the State Department of Education, Strayer proposed that the State Board of Education determine qualifications for the office of county superintendent of schools, and the creation of a state commission on local school districts. He also recommended setting up a bureau to forecast teacher supply and demand and a committee on coordinated teacher training. Strayer believed that kindergartens should be included in the state aid program. And he proposed that state support be distributed to schools on an equalization basis and that state aid be made available to impoverished districts for capital outlay.

Finally, the Strayer Report suggested that the State Department of Education have its own building. In 1945, the department was scattered about the capital city in some six or seven buildings in addition to the main headquarters in the Library and Courts Building. In 8 years it had grown so much that the need for more adequate facilities had become critical. Therefore, in 1953, the State Department of Education moved into its present home, the State Education Building at 721 Capitol Mall in Sacramento.

The Mills Report

A firm of management consultants, J. N. Mills & Company, conducted the departmental study, as required by the 1944 Legislature. Its findings were, briefly, that the department was greatly understaffed, underpaid, and overworked, and that there was general looseness of the management structure within the department. It found many ambiguities in the various sections of the Education Code defining the duties and responsibilities of the superintendent of public instruction, the director of education, and the State Board of Education.

> It would appear appropriate...that the problem be called to the attention of the legislature so that it may, if it deems it proper, clarify the Code sections relative to the respective powers, duties, and functions of the State Board of Education, the State Director of Education, the Superintendent of Public Instruction and the State Department of Education . . . .
>
> If it be the intent of the Legislature to establish a Board of Education as the governing and policy making body of the State Department of Education, the functioning of the Board should be confined strictly to such purpose, and the execution of such policies as may be laid down by the Board should be left to the Director of Education, without further participation or interference by the Board (28).

Legislative Changes

Drafts of three proposed constitutional amendments and bills were included in the Strayer Report as appendixes. One of the amendments pertained to the appointment of the superintendent of public instruction and of the members of the State Board of Education; the second, to qualifications of county superintendents; and the third, to appointment of a deputy superintendent of public instruction and three associate superintendents, all of whom would be exempt from Civil Service.

The first bill set forth a comprehensive system of equalization of state aid for support of elementary schools; the second, supervision of instruction in elementary schools; and the third, optional unification of school districts by vote of electors.

All of these measures were introduced in the assembly in January 1945. The three bills were passed and signed by the Governor. The first amendment to the constitution, calling for the appointment of the superintendent of public instruction, was defeated; however, the other two passed. Other education bills passed by this Legislature established schools and training centers for spastic children and permitted admission of children with speech disorders and blind children to special schools established for handicapped children. The Legislature also appropriated $388,680 to augment the support of the state department.

Department Reorganization

After the Strayer and Mills studies were started, the superintendent of public instruction also appointed a committee to study the organization of the State Department of Education. The committee presented its report to the State Board of Education in October 1945, and the board approved the plan for reorganization drawn up in the report.

After Superintendent Walter Dexter died in October 1945, his successor, Roy E. Simpson, continued the work of reorganization. In November 1946, the voters approved the constitutional amendment allowing for the appointment of a deputy and three associate superintendents, thus clearing the way for the new organization to be completed.

The department was reorganized into six divisions: departmental administration, instruction, public school administration, special schools and services, state colleges and teacher education, and libraries. In addition, seven groups not considered part of the administrative structure of the department were closely connected with the state educational system: the Board of Examiners for Vocational Teachers; the Board of Governors of the State Nautical School; the Commission for Vocational Education; the Commission of Credentials; the Retirement Investment Board; the State Curriculum Commission; and the Teachers' Retirement Board. With but a few changes, this departmental organization is essentially the same today.

During the ensuing years other proposals were made to change the relationship between the State Board of Education and the superintendent of public instruction. In 1955, the Hardesty Report advocated that the superintendent be appointed by the board. It recommended that the board be composed of nine members, one member per year to be nominated by the California School Boards Association and elected by the school districts. In 1958, Proposition 13, to amend the constitution to provide an appointive superintendent, was roundly defeated. Although the Department of Education had vigorously upheld the "grass-roots" philosophy of selection of the superintendent, Roy E. Simpson, superintendent of public instruction from 1945 to 1962, proposed in 1959 that the superintendent be appointed by the board, who should have the power to determine the term of office and salary. He suggested an 11-member board, appointed by the Governor with Senate approval, but without results.

School District Organization Changes

The Strayer Report concluded that the California schools were good, but improvements were necessary. In some communities, the survey team found schools that might have been models for the nation; other schools provided unacceptable education. The chief reasons for this wide variance—that there were too many school districts, and too many were small and had a low tax base—had long been apparent to the department. Efforts to consolidate districts, however, had met much local resistance. Passage in 1945 of the school district bill drafted by the State Reconstruction and Reemployment Commission was a great step toward remedying the situation.

A Commission on School Districts was empowered to conduct surveys throughout the state and make recommendations for school district reorganization. The people might, by majority vote, accept or reject these recommendations. Studies made by the commission focused on district reorganization and brought about a remarkable degree of public understanding regarding problems of school administration. The law stipulated that the commission be discontinued in 1949 and its responsibilities turned over to the State Board of Education. County committees were to carry on the work of district organization. A bureau of school district organization was established in the Department of Education as an advisory group within the public school administration division. When the commission began its work, 2,568 school districts were maintaining schools in the state. By 1950, they were reduced to 2,111; and they have since steadily decreased.

Financial Support for Districts

In addition to unifying school districts, equalizing support by the state had often been suggested as a means of solving problems of the rural districts and the less wealthy urban school districts. Proponents of equalization aid recalled Horace Mann's views on taxing property where it is and spending money where the children are. However, as of 1944, school districts were financed almost wholly in terms of the number of pupils in average daily attendance, with no regard to the need of the school. A variation affecting a relatively small number of school districts was made in providing a teacher or classroom quota for very small schools. According to the Strayer Report,

> The system of state aid represents a piece-meal accumulation of changes, based upon conditions and needs which have arisen during the past fifty years. The process has been one of accretion, and a consideration of separate parts of the total program, rather than a complete and overall review of the basic problem concerning the State's policy in the support of schools (29).

Constitutional amendments were adopted in 1944, 1946, and 1952, increasing and equalizing the state's support of the schools. In 1952, the people mandated that the contributions to the State School Fund from the General Fund, together with annual income from the Permanent School Fund (consisting of lands granted to the state, bonds bought with proceeds of land sold, and oil and mineral royalties) should be not less than $180 per unit of average daily attendance in the public schools for the preceding year. Subsequent legislation increased this to $201.36.

Apportionments are made from the State School Fund for basic aid (at $125 per unit of average daily attendance [ADA] or $2,400, whichever is greater), plus equalization aid, based on the concept of a foundation program. This guarantees that each district will have a specified amount available, provided a specified rate of tax is levied in the district. If the amount of district aid computed by the tax rate, when added to basic aid, is less than the foundation program, the state provides an additional amount equal to the difference.

Apportionments for special aid programs were added from time to time by the Legislature until by 1963 they included (a) excess costs of educating physically and mentally handicapped and mentally gifted minors, and excess costs of transportation of such minors; (b) reimbursement of the costs of home-to-school transportation of pupils; (c) a growth allowance which supplements the initial apportionment due to increase of the current ADA over that of the previous year; (d) excess costs of providing behind-the-wheel driving instruction; and (e) certain costs of operation of offices of county superintendents of schools.

The federal government made funds available for certain programs, such as vocational education, vocational rehabilitation, education of veterans, school food service, and child care centers. Beginning with Public Law 874 in 1950-51, it gave support to local educational agencies to operate and maintain schools where federal activities created serious school problems. Public Law 815, passed in 1950, provided for construction of school buildings in such areas.

Role of the Department in Schoolhouse Planning

School districts had a legally limited ability (5 percent of assessed valuation) to finance needed school facilities. A survey of schoolhousing after the 1933 earthquake showed over 400 small districts, many with very old buildings, that had a legal bonding capacity less than would be required to replace the old buildings. Several later surveys convinced the department that many districts were unable, however willing, to finance adequate facilities.

Efforts to bring about state aid for school construction were successful in 1947 when the Legislature appropriated $20 million for outright grants to impoverished school districts for capital outlay. The well-documented requests by school districts to participate in the program provided decisive evidence of the magnitude of the problem, and the voters have approved bond issues ever since to implement a state-controlled loan and grant program for school construction in financially distressed school districts.

The bureau of school planning had some control over the plans for buildings to qualify for state apportionments, and it was thus able to influence the type of facilities being built. It was instrumental in changing the design of schoolhouses in line with changes in educational programs.

The National Defense Education Act of 1958

In 1957, when the Russians succeeded in orbiting the first satellite, critics of schools complained that children were not being taught enough mathematics and science. As one response to the "emergency," Congress passed the National Defense Education Act (NDEA). The federal government authorized aid of more than $1 billion to education over a 4-year period. The California State Department of Education administered three parts of the act that directly affected the schools: Title III, for strengthening science, mathematics, and modern foreign language instruction; Title V, for guidance, counseling, and testing in secondary schools; and Title VIII, for vocational education. The department administered the funds, for the most part, through a new bureau called the Bureau of NDEA Administration.

In the first 3 years of the program's operation under Title III, the department approved projects to 887 California school districts, which had 81.1 percent of the total average daily attendance of the state. More than half of the approved projects were in science; 24 percent in modern foreign languages; and 14 percent in mathematics. In addition to funds for instruction, schools received funds to buy equipment for minor remodeling and to improve supervisory and related services. Over 65 percent of the expenditures were for specialized equipment and materials of instruction. The greatest change was in science. Increased emphasis was placed on mastering basic scientific relationships and learning laboratory methods. Less change was seen in mathematics, the school districts adopting a "wait and see" attitude in reference to adoption of the "new math." Improvement in teaching skills and in pupil achievement was directly attributable to the new programs.

An assessment of the value of the Title V was made in 1967 after the program had been in operation for 7 years. The difficulty of evaluating programs, particularly in the field of guidance and counseling, made the study rather inconclusive.

Title VIII of the NDEA amended the George-Barden Act of 1946 relating to the training of skilled technicians in California. During the 1962-63 school year, California districts participated in 94 projects under Title VIII at a cost of $1,329,937. Local industrial needs were largely met through the technical education programs.

Vocational Education

Additional federal aid was given to California's already strong vocational education programs by Public Law 87-415, the Manpower Development and Training Act (MDTA). This provided for training unemployed persons so they could take their place in the nation's economy. The law directed that whenever appropriate, the programs should be conducted in the public schools. The State Department of Employment selects and places trainees under the act, and the Department of Education supervises the training through the regional offices of the vocational education section. By the end of October 1963, in the first year of the program's operation, California had 8,255 trainees.

Vocational Rehabilitation

California began to rehabilitate the disabled in 1919 when the Legislature set aside funds for the Industrial Accident Commission to reeducate persons crippled in industry. In 1921, the program was placed under the administration of the State Board of Education to qualify for federal funds. Federal support was expanded until, by 1954, it included assistance to establish rehabilitation facilities, workshops, and business enterprise programs. The scope of the program was widened; state funds were contributed to include persons who needed retraining because of changes in occupational demands. In October 1963, the vocational rehabilitation section "graduated" from the division of special schools and services to become the new State Department of Rehabilitation. Also included were other units providing educational and rehabilitation for blind adults.

Special Education

In 1947, a great deal of legislation relating to handicapped children was passed. One bill made it mandatory for school districts and county school superintendents to maintain classes for mentally retarded minors. In 1951, permissive programs for trainable mentally retarded children were established by the Legislature, and were made mandatory in 1964. In 1961, special programs for intellectually gifted children were established. In that year the bureau of special education was transferred from the Division of Instruction to the Division of Special Schools and Services. In 1963, special programs for the educationally handicapped (children with neurological and behavioral disorders) were established.

Educating outstanding children has been one of the state's most rapidly growing programs during the past 15 years, costing about $65 million in 1967-68.

Higher Education

Since July 1961, the state colleges have been administered by the trustees of the State College System, including the superintendent of public instruction. This change resulted from a study of higher education made by the Liaison Committee of the State Board of Education and the Regents of the University of California. The basic issues studied were the roles of the junior colleges, state colleges, and the University of California in the state's tripartite system and how the three segments should be governed and coordinated to avoid unnecessary duplication.

As one result of the study, *A Master Plan for Higher Education* was published in 1960 (30). In that year the Legislature adopted some recommendations in the plan. The Donahoe Higher Education Act, in addition to placing the state colleges under a board of trustees, defined the California system of higher education as consisting of all public junior colleges, all state colleges, and branches of the University of California. Junior colleges remained under the state board. The University, under the Board of Regents, was defined as the primary state-supported academic agency for research and given sole authority in public education to grant doctoral degrees. The Coordinating Council for Higher Education was created to include three representatives from the University of California, the State College System, the public junior colleges, the private colleges and universities of the state, and the general public. Its primary responsibility was to advise governing boards and state officials in the review of annual budgets and capital outlay requests of the University of California and state colleges. It also was charged with developing plans for the orderly growth of higher education and making recommendations regarding needed facilities and programs.

Certification of Teachers

An important change in teacher training and certification took place in 1964. The Licensing of Certificated Personnel Law of 1961, popularly known as the Fisher bill, made it mandatory for teachers to have an academic major before they could be granted a teaching credential. This change resulted from many studies of the basic certification structure in the state. By 1950, about 60 different types of credentials were used to authorize public school service. Credentials could be granted by the state on any of three bases: direct application, formal recommendation by a teacher training institution, or informal institutional recommendation. Various proposals for remedying this confused system, combined with criticisms of courses in professional education, resulted in the Fisher bill.

Teaching certificates could not be granted by county boards of education after 1945. Emergency credentials, first granted during the war, were discontinued in 1954. But "provisional credentials" have been issued since 1947 on the basis of a statement of need by the employing district. Since 1942, the demand for teachers in California has been greater than the supply, and no solution for the problem of ensuring enough well-qualified teachers is yet in sight.

Time for a Change

In 1962, for the first time in 43 years, an incumbent superintendent of public instruction did not stand for reelection, and a vigorous contest developed among nine candidates. In the general election two candidates carried on a series of public debates, with candidate Max Rafferty finally winning and selecting one of the primary candidates, Everett T. Calvert, as his chief deputy to help implement his program. One result of Dr. Rafferty's first term in office was a public airing of the powers and functions of both the State Board of Education and the superintendent of public instruction. Two bills introduced in the 1963 Legislature to eliminate the superintendent of public instruction suffered the fate of all previous measures to this effect.

Shortly after he took office, Dr. Rafferty asked that the State Department of Education be surveyed to determine how it should be reorganized to provide the required services with maximum efficiency. The State Board of Education also wanted a survey of the department, and in 1963, it appointed a Committee on Department Survey. In laying the groundwork for the survey, the State Board of Education posed the following questions:

> Although the Department has a long history of effectively providing educational services to the State, the question arises: Are the present purposes, goals, and functions most appropriate to provide and render adequate, imaginative, stimulating, and optimum educational services to the State in the 1960's and the decades to follow? Also, is the Department best organized and equipped, or following the best practices, to provide these educational services? (31)

The committee recommended that a management firm, Arthur D. Little, Inc., conduct the survey.

A second major study of the department, "the Governor's Survey on Efficiency and Cost Control," was subsequently made by the Governor's Task Force in 1967 upon the election of Ronald Reagan as Governor. This task force was made up of many outstanding business and professional people.

THE LITTLE SURVEYS, 1963 TO 1967

The results of the first phase of the Little Survey were made available in 1964 (32). It concentrated on examining the role and functions of the State Department of Education and possible changes in department services.

The second phase of this survey was conducted in 1966, and results were published the following year (33). It emphasized a new organization for the state's education administration. While this and other surveys were being made—from approximately 1963 through 1967—the department did make organizational changes, and others are under consideration.

Today's climate for organizational change in California was summarized in the report of the second phase of the Little Survey. It pointed out that America's investment in education is second only to defense in proportion to gross national product and that public interest in education has increased dramatically. This enterprise has become an important instrument of national and state policy in social and economic improvement. Compounding the demands on education in all states are the impact of Sputnik on our instructional programs; new federal support of education; the "knowledge explosion" that is outdating much of what is being taught; research and experimentation in education; burgeoning population; "big city blight"; and increasing costs of education. The educational system of California is regarded as one of the best in the nation. However, educators and the public recognize that improvements can be made.

The Little Report, Phase One

In its 1963-64 study the Arthur D. Little team reached 17 key conclusions. For instance, it stated that California lacks the coordinated leadership needed to solve increasingly serious educational problems. School districts lack the resources necessary to move ahead in educational development. The team also suggested that the State Board of Education and the State Department of Education cooperate in educational planning. It concluded that the state department needs major revamping and should extend its services regionally to help districts plan education development (34).

These conclusions were reached after the survey team interviewed school administrators and their staffs and consulted many persons in and out of the educational professions. The investigators found significant changes taking place in the school. And this alone indicated that the

State Department of Education must change its role to meet the needs of the schools adequately.

The survey team found that, even in the smallest and most remote districts, progress was being made in the use of radically new programs, but the most significant changes were being developed *for* the schools, rather than *by* them. Many of the new courses originated in large-scale, heavily financed projects financed by the National Science Foundation, other foundations, or textbook publishers.

The Legislature's increasing interest in the curriculum was another factor in speeding up change. But many administrators also pointed out that much of the curriculum mandated and controlled at the state level restricted innovation and flexibility.

Conferences with administrators revealed growth in programs for the gifted, mentally retarded, culturally deprived, and physically handicapped; remedial programs; and experiments with multitrack and nongraded programs to meet needs of special groups. Special facilities and equipment and specialized personnel also were increased. Administrators stressed that they needed unbiased information on which they could depend to make wise decisions.

Interviews with administrators also revealed a need for an overall plan to identify national and state educational goals for consideration in local planning. A second need was for information based on careful research to help in planning. Schools will continue to need financial support and general assistance from both state and federal sources to implement plans. The state administration was considered extremely helpful in some areas, less helpful and even old-fashioned in others, and unnecessarily burdensome in the required paper work.

The report recommended that the State Department of Education strengthen its ability to plan and implement educational growth; that project teams be employed on a short-term basis to help the department develop this ability; and that the instruction division coordinate research and communication in curriculum and teaching development. The study also concluded that the department can contribute most effectively by focusing sharply on functions that *support* constructive change and by withdrawing from attempts at *direct* consultation with school districts. The office of the county superintendent of schools or another intermediate unit would be the logical level at which to collaborate with local districts on matters of planning and implementing constructive change.

Some form of intermediate administrative unit, such as the office of the county superintendent of schools, should take over many of the tasks of direct collaboration with districts, the report concluded. In this role it should be made more explicitly an extension of the State Department of Education and should maintain services (e.g., instructional materials centers and educational television) small districts cannot provide for themselves. The intermediate unit would plan area programs and coordinate and implement fiscal procedures. The intermediate unit would also serve as a communication link between the State Department of Education and school districts in interpreting or enforcing policies, laws, and regulations.

The Little Report, Phase Two

In 1966, the Arthur D. Little firm proceeded with the second phase of its study. Certain areas of concern to school administrators that affected the recommended changes were mentioned: need to improve business administration in school districts; confusing and overlapping regulations in the Education Code; slow adoption of new but reasonably proven educational developments; and need for better management of human resources, such as attracting better teachers, using talent more effectively, and maintaining an adequate supply of qualified teachers and administrators.

The study recommended that the state department adopt as its major responsibility "sensing the emerging needs for educational development in the state and for related changes in the state's educational system." The department should assign priorities and allocate resources among areas of need. Three new instruments were suggested: (1) a long-range master plan for public education in California; (2) a comprehensive annual report of recent educational activities in the state; and (3) a state plan for specific actions to be taken in the immediate future. These plans are to clearly state the philosophy of the State Board of Education to justify their adoption by the Legislature as the educational goals of the state.

Other responsibilities concern developing new instructional programs and services and include (a) design, (b) evaluation, (c) informing the public about them, (d) encouraging and supporting their adoption, and (e) seeking to improve their quality.

Specific reorganizational changes at the top of the state-level system and in all units of the state department also were recommended.

As with all studies of California's state education agency, the Little Report recommended fundamental changes in selecting the State Board of Education and the superintendent of public instruction. Unless the present conflicting organization is changed, the report stated, California will continue to lack an effective educational administration in Sacramento. It called for a board of 10 members, nominated by the Legislature and appointed by the Governor, to serve overlapping terms of 10 years. It also recommended that the board appoint the superintendent to serve as its executive officer and secretary and as the chief administration officer of the state department, the board to set his term of employment and pay. And it spelled out in detail the duties of the board, the superintendent, and his cabinet.

The Little Report recommended that the personnel and functions of the department be reassigned to four divisions related to educational programs and three offices related to educational services. Junior colleges would be a separate agency. (In 1966, the State Board of Education called for the creation of a separate community college administrative agency, reporting directly to the state board and headed by its own chancellor.) The recommended units and their assignments are as follows:

1. A Division of General Education to administer elementary and secondary education, as differentiated from special education (such as vocational education) and education for special pupils (such as the handicapped). It would include adult education, counseling services, readjustment education, industrial arts education, as well as consultants on various subjects in the school curriculum.

2. A Division of Vocational Education to identify needs and update the state plan for precollege vocational education, design and guide programs, and do research. It would strengthen intermediate units, help local units, recruit and train instructors, and satisfy requirements for programs under federal funding.

3. A Division of Special Education to ensure that all physically, mentally, educationally handicapped, and otherwise exceptional children could enroll in public schools, get education appropriate to their needs, and be taught by qualified teachers.

4. A Division of Fiscal and Business Management to absorb the present responsibilities for budgeting, accounting, school planning, textbooks, surplus property, and transportation now mainly performed by the Division of Public School Administration.

5. An office of state education personnel to certify teachers, accredit schools, and handle other personnel work within the Department of Education. The office would work closely with the State Personnel Board.

6. An office of educational information to combine data processing and education research.

7. An office of departmental supporting services to include mailing and shipping, supplies, editing, art work, duplicating, handling office space and equipment, and cashiering.

The reorganizational details suggested by the report, however, are less important and less innovative than its general approach to the department's proper functioning as the head and heart of a comprehensive, efficient state-level information system for public education in California. In the words of the report, the department should be regarded as a "collector, compiler, synthesizer, interpreter, disseminator, stimulator, and facilitator of the use of new knowledge" (35).

Study by the Governor's Task Force

In 1967, the Governor's Survey on Efficiency and Cost Control, also known as the Governor's Task Force, after spending hundreds of hours in an intensive study of the State Department of Education over a period of several months, made its report and recommendations. Many of these recommendations were different and perhaps more practical than those in the Little Report. The purposes of the task force were to recommend improvements by which immediate savings could be accomplished by administrative order; to identify areas where further savings could probably be realized after more thorough study; and to make long-term recommendations to the executive and legislative branches of the state government.

The Governor's Task Force made almost 200 recommendations for improving nearly every aspect of departmental organization and operations, including a number of recommendations that would aid the department to further its role of leader, innovator, and disseminator of useful information.

New Directions

When Max Rafferty took office as superintendent of public instruction in January 1963, he headed the largest public school system in the nation, enrolling over 4.5 million pupils. A strong believer in greater autonomy for local districts, Dr. Rafferty made it his business to develop two-way communication with the governing boards of school districts and to respond to what he interpreted as a mandate from the people to change certain educational practices. He announced an end of "life adjustment" and the substitution of "education in depth" as the department's philosophy. He advocated a more thorough grounding in reading skills through the use of phonics in teaching primary pupils and that all pupils be given a better understanding of their American heritage through basic courses in history, geography, civics, and economics. He encouraged the schools to emphasize the harmful effects of alcohol, drugs, and tobacco. He favored stronger school library services, use of children's classics for supplementary reading, and wider use of closed-circuit educational television. In his concern for teachers, he advocated the use of data processing to minimize their clerical work; faster service in issuing credentials; merit pay for outstanding performance; and smaller classes. As one result, legislation passed in 1964 requires that the enrollments in classes in grades 1, 2, and 3 be no more than 30 by the beginning of the 1968-69 school year.

Believing that school districts should have wider choice of teaching materials, Dr. Rafferty favored a wider selection of textbooks for elementary schools. In response, the Curriculum Commission recommended multiple adoptions in certain subjects and gave districts an opportunity to select books for different levels of ability. It also insisted on a more accurate portrayal of minority groups in books submitted by textbook companies.

The following portion of a speech delivered in Sacramento in 1964 is one example of Max Rafferty's strong convictions about education:

> The schools of America are the hope of America–the "last, best hope of men on earth." To those of us in education...the great, soul-shaking opportunity has been given to assist, with God's grace, in the saving of our country. For almost two centuries, the teachers of the United States have kept the American heritage intact, passing it from one generation to another as a rich legacy. What we have done before we can do again (36).

A major responsibility of the superintendent of public instruction is to inform the Legislature about the schools' financial situation. This has involved him and his staff in a constant struggle to find a balance between state and local support. In spite of an ever-increasing amount of state aid (about 10 percent a year in dollars), steady growth of school population has meant a decreasing proportion of state support.

Through the superintendent's efforts, the State Department of Education was reorganized and strengthened, based on the Little studies, a Department of Finance survey, and a Department of Education study.

The junior college staff was reorganized, and the Legislature established a separate governing board for public junior colleges (renamed "community colleges"), effective January 1, 1968.

Editorial staffs and facilities of the department were combined to form a bureau of publications to bring about greater efficiency in producing department publications suggested by a 1963 study (37).

The Bureau of Special Education was reorganized into three bureaus: physically exceptional children; educationally handicapped and mentally exceptional children; and program development and evaluation, special education. A central clearinghouse-depository for the visually handicapped became a reality in December 1964. This agency loans to schools books in Braille and large print, as well as other materials, apparatus, and equipment specifically designed for the visually handicapped.

A regional data-processing center to serve 300,000 students in Northern California opened in Sacramento in July 1964. This was the first of an anticipated network of as many as 10 such centers to be established throughout California. It will minimize clerical work and will also serve as a training center for students in data processing. At the same time, the department enlarged its Los Angeles office and improved its services to Southern California.

To secure maximum coordination the department combined kindergarten through grade 12, the services formerly provided by two bureaus, in the single Bureau of Elementary and Secondary Education.

The McAteer Act, passed in 1963, provided for a 2-year pilot project to determine the most effective way to help children handicapped by lingual, cultural, and economic disadvantages remain in school. In 1965 the Legislature established the position of director of compensatory education to oversee the spending of $73 million in federal funds (under Title I of ESEA) and $1 million in state funds allocated to educating culturally disadvantaged children.

In November 1964, a Bureau of Intergroup Relations was established as the staff for the Commission on Equal Opportunities in Education. Established in 1958 (as the Commission on Equal Employment Opportunity for Teachers), this office was, in 1963, given responsibility to assist and advise schools in problems of de facto segregation. This assignment brought it into action in the summer of 1964, when a boycott was planned to protest segregation in Oakland schools, where 59 percent of the enrollment was made up of minority groups. The boycott was forestalled, partly as a result of timely intervention by the commission. The Bureau of Intergroup Relations later became a unit in the Office of Compensatory Education.

Dr. Rafferty was the first superintendent of public instruction to appoint members of minority groups to top-level cabinet positions. His appointments included two Negroes–one as an associate superintendent, one as the director of compensatory education–and a Mexican-American, first appointed assistant superintendent in charge of the department's Los Angeles office and later as associate superintendent and chief of the Division of Instruction. Many other positions in the department, at all levels, are held by members of minority racial and ethnic groups.

The Future

The studies made by Arthur D. Little, Inc., and by the Governor's Task Force produced numerous recommendations as to how the department should be organized to meet its responsibilities proficiently, effectively, and economically (38). Many of the recommendations in one study were unlike those in the other, and neither provided a detailed outline of how the recommendations might be best implemented. Therefore, the State Board of Education employed a consultant to coordinate and appraise all the recommendations and to present to the board an organizational plan. This consultant, who was employed early in 1968, has worked with the professional staff of the department and with the State Board of Education to secure the best possible appraisal and interpretation of the recommendations presented. The results are reflected in the organization chart in Appendix B. This plan, which has been approved by the State Board of Education, sets the pattern that will be employed in reorganizing the department. Certain phases of the reorganization will be effected at once; however, others must be postponed until the Legislature makes the necessary legal and financial provisions.

FOOTNOTES

1. California, *Constitution* (1849), art. 9, sec. 2.
2. John Swett, *History of the Public School System of California* (San Francisco: A. L. Bancroft and Co., 1876), p. 12.
3. *Ibid.*, p. 170.
4. Superintendent of Public Instruction, *Eighth Annual Report* (1858), p. 6.
5. Superintendent of Public Instruction, *Second Biennial Report* (1867), p. 5.
6. Ellwood P. Cubberley, "State Educational Organization," *A Cyclopedia of Education,* ed. by Paul Monroe (New York: The Macmillan Co., 1913), pp. 409-10.
7. Commissioner of Secondary Schools, "First Annual Report," *First Biennial Report of the State Board of Education,* Part IV (1915), p. 83.
8. Department of Education, *Rules and Regulations Governing the California State Teachers Colleges,* Bulletin No. 12 (Sacramento: The Department, 1934), pp. 1-3.
9. *Report of the Special Legislative Committee on Education,* Herbert C. Jones, chairman. Authorized by Senate Concurrent Resolution No. 21 by the forty-third session of the Legislature of California. (Sacramento: California Legislature, 1920), p. 20.
10. *Ibid.*
11. Superintendent of Public Instruction, *Thirty-Second Biennial Report* (1927), p. 14.
12. *Ibid.*, pp. 14, 18.
13. California, *Statutes* (1927), ch. 453, sec. 5, par. 1520 (a), p. 780. Amends California, *Statutes* (1913), p. 659.
14. Department of Education, *Biennial Report, Including the Thirty-Third Biennial Report of the Superintendent of Public Instruction and the Biennial Report of the Director of Education* (1929), p. 46.
15. William G. Bagley and George C. Kyte, *The California Curriculum Study* (Berkeley: University of California Printing Office, 1926). This study was begun under a grant from the Commonwealth Fund.
16. Vierling Kersey, "Shall Public Schools in California Be Closed?" *California Schools,* IV (March 1933), 119.
17. Department of Education, "Emergency Education Program," *Biennial Report, Including the Thirty-Sixth Biennial Report of the Superintendent of Public Instruction and the Biennial Report of the State Board of Education* (1934), p. 91.
18. "Services Provided in California Public Schools Under the Federal Emergency Education Program," *California Schools,* XI (July 1940), 203, 207.
19. Department of Education, *Biennial Report, Including the Thirty-Seventh Biennial Report of the Superintendent of Public Instruction and the Biennial Report of the State Board of Education* (1937), pp. 15-16.
20. Roy W. Cloud, *Education in California: Leaders, Organizations, and Accomplishments of the First Hundred Years* (Stanford, Calif.: Stanford University Press, 1952), p. 195.
21. Aubrey A. Douglass, "The Policies and Program of the California State Department of Education," *California Schools,* XI (November 1940), 293-97.
22. "State Board of Education Actions," *California Schools,* XII (November 1941), 226.
23. "In Memoriam," *California Schools,* XV (April 1944), 89.
24. "Statement of Organization and Summary of Committee Reports of the State Superintendent's Advisory Council," *California Schools*, XV (March 1944), 47-58. A report of a meeting of State Education Council members in Sacramento, January 28-29, 1944, at which the Council reconstituted itself as the State Superintendent's Advisory Council and adopted a statement of purpose, organization, and procedures.
25. "Resolutions of the Conference of the Association of County Superintendents of Schools," *California Schools,* XV (March 1944), 77-81.
26. Citizens Advisory Committee of Readjustment Education of the State Reconstruction and Reemployment Commission, *The Administration, Organization and Financial Support of the Public School System, State of California* (Sacramento: State Reconstruction and Reemployment Commission, February, 1945). This committee worked under the general direction of George D. Strayer, consultant.
27. *Ibid.*, pp. 7-8.
28. J. N. Mills & Co., "The Internal Organization of the Department of Education, State of California," Sacramento, State Reconstruction and Reemployment Commission, 1944, pp. 11-13. (Mimeographed.)
29. Citizens Advisory Committee of Readjustment Education of the State Reconstruction and Reemployment Commission, *op. cit.*, p. 33.
30. Master Plan Survey Team of the Liaison Committee of the State Board of Education and the Regents of the University of California, Arthur G. Coons, chairman, *A Master Plan for Higher Education in California, 1960-1975* (Sacramento: Department of Education, 1960).
31. William A. Norris, "Invitation To Submit Qualifications To Provide Consulting Advice on the California State Department of Education," Sacramento Board of Education, May 3, 1963, p. 1. (Mimeographed.)

32. Arthur D. Little, Inc., *The Emerging Requirements for Effective Leadership for California Education: A Study To Provide a Basis for Planning the Services and Organization of the California State Department of Education* (Sacramento: Department of Education, November 1964).

33. Arthur D. Little, Inc., *A New Organizational System for State-Level Educational Administration: A Recommended Response to Emerging Requirements for Change in California* (Sacramento: Department of Education, 1967).

34. Arthur D. Little, Inc., *The Emerging Requirements for Effective Leadership for California Education* (Sacramento: Department of Education, November 1964), pp. 1-3.

35. Arthur D. Little, Inc., *A New Organizational System for State-Level Educational Administration* (Sacramento: Department of Education, 1967), pp. 45-46.

36. Max Rafferty, "The Elements of Patriotism," a keynote address delivered at the June, 1964, annual California convention of The American Legion in Sacramento, *California Education,* II (September 1964), 4.

37. Lloyd N. Morrisett, "Appraisal of Communication Facilities, Especially Publications, in the California State Department of Education." A report transmitted to the Superintendent of Public Instruction, Sacramento, California, October 31, 1963. (Mimeographed.)

38. Arthur D. Little, Inc., *A New Organizational System for State-Level Educational Administration* (Sacramento: Department of Education, 1967), pp. xii-xiii.

BIBLIOGRAPHY

Public Documents

California. *Administrative Code, Title 5, Education* (1968). Sacramento: Office of Administrative Procedure, Department of General Services, 1968.

--*Constitution* (1849, 1879).

--*Education Code: Statutes (1967).* Sacramento: Department of General Services, Documents Section, 1967.

--*Education Code,* Vol. XXVI, secs. 1-5000 in *West's Annotated California Codes.* St. Paul, Minn.: West Publishing Co., 1960, with 1967 pocket supplement, 1968.

--*Statutes, Constitution of 1879: General Laws, Amendments to Codes, Resolutions, and Constitutional Amendments.* Sacramento: California Legislature, biennially.

Deering's California Education Code, Annotated. San Francisco: Bancroft Whitney Co., 1960, with 1967 Cumulative Pocket Part, 1968.

Books and Bulletins

Bagley, William G., and Kyte, George C. *The California Curriculum Study.* Berkeley: University of California Printing Office, 1926.

Bulletin of the State Department of Education. 33 vols. Sacramento: Department of Education, 1932-64. A series of bulletins dealing with a variety of specific educational topics.

Cloud, Roy W. *Education in California: Leaders, Organizations, and Accomplishments of the First Hundred Years.* Stanford, Calif.: Stanford University Press, 1952.

Cubberley, Ellwood P. "State Educational Organization." *A Cyclopedia of Education.* Edited by Paul Monroe. New York: The Macmillan Co., 1913.

Department of Education. *California State Department of Education Bulletin No. G-2.* Sacramento: The Department, 1928.

--*Rules and Regulations Governing the California State Teachers Colleges.* Bulletin No. 12. Sacramento: The Department, 1934.

--*The Dynamics of Educational Change,* Vol. XXXII, No. 3. Sacramento: The Department, 1963.

Ferrier, William Warren. *Ninety Years of Education in California, 1846-1936.* Berkeley, Calif.: Sather Gate Book Shop, 1937.

Holy, T. C.; Semans, H. H.; and McConnell, T. R. *A Restudy of the Needs of California in Higher Education.* Sacramento: Department of Education, 1955.

Johnson, Leighton H. *Development of the Central State Agency for Public Education in California, 1849-1949.* University of New Mexico Education Series No. 4. Albuquerque: The University of New Mexico Press, 1952.

Master Plan Survey Team of the Liaison Committee, Board of Education and the Regents of the University of California, Arthur G. Coons, chairman. *A Master Plan for Higher Education in California, 1960-1975.* Sacramento: Department of Education, 1960.

Swett, John. *History of the Public School System of California.* San Francisco: A. L. Bancroft and Co., 1876.

Reports

Citizens Advisory Committee of Readjustment Education of the State Reconstruction and Reemployment Commission. *The Administration, Organization and Financial Support of the Public School System, State of California.* Sacramento: State Reconstruction and Reemployment Commission, February 1945.

Department of Education. *Biennial Reports, Including Reports of the Superintendent of Public Instruction, the Director of Education, and Commissioner of Secondary Schools.* Sacramento: The Department, 1926-68.

Evans, David N., and Johnson, I. T. *The Impact in California of NDEA, Titles III, V, VIII.* Sacramento: Department of Education, 1967.

Governor's Survey on Efficiency and Cost Control: State Department of Education. O. Kenneth Pryor, chairman of the Governor's Committee. Sacramento: State of California, November 1967.

Joint Interim Committee on the Public Education System, Gordon H. Winton, chairman. *Report.* Sacramento: California Senate, 1961.

Little, Arthur D., Inc. *A New Organizational System for State-Level Educational Administration: A Recommended Response to Emerging Requirements for Change in California.* Sacramento: Department of Education, 1967.

—— *The Emerging Requirements for Effective Leadership for California Education: A Study To Provide a Basis for Planning the Services and Organization of the California State Department of Education.* Sacramento: Department of Education, November 1964.

Special Legislative Committee on Education. *Report (The Jones Report).* Authorized by Senate Concurrent Resolution No. 21 by the forty-third session of the Legislature of California. Sacramento: California Legislature, 1920.

Superintendents of Public Instruction. *Annual and Biennial Reports.* Sacramento: Department of Education, 1851-1968.

Articles and Periodicals

California Education (September 1963-June 1966).

California Journal of Elementary Education (August 1932-May 1962).

California Journal of Elementary Education (September 1963-June 1966).

California Schools (1930-63).

Douglass, Aubrey. "The Policies and Program of the California State Department of Education." *California Schools,* XI (November 1940), 293-97.

"In Memoriam." *California Schools,* XV (April 1944), 89.

Journal of Secondary Education (1925-68).

Kersey, Vierling. "Shall Public Schools in California Be Closed?" *California Schools,* IV (March 1933), 119.

Pacific Educational Journal (1887-96).

Pacific School and Home Journal (1879-83).

Rafferty, Max. "The Elements of Patriotism." A keynote address delivered at the June, 1964, annual California convention of The American Legion in Sacramento. *California Education,* II (September 1964), 4.

"Resolutions of the Conference of the Association of County Superintendents of Schools." *California Schools,* XV (March 1944), 77-81.

"Services Provided in California Public Schools Under the Federal Emergency Education Program." *California Schools,* XI (July 1940), 203, 207.

"State Board of Education Actions." *California Schools,* XII (November 1941), 226.

The California Teacher (July 1863-May 1876). Resumed as the *California Teacher and Journal of Home Education* (1883-87).

Western Journal of Education (1898-1910).

Unpublished Material

Assembly Legislative Reference Service. "The State Superintendent of Public Instruction." A report on the history of the office in the State of California, and a review of the recent trends in the other 49 states. State Capitol, Sacramento, March 14, 1963. (Mimeographed.)

Mills, J. N., & Co. "The Internal Organization of the Department of Education, State of California." State Reconstruction and Reemployment Commission, Sacramento, 1944. (Mimeographed.)

Morrisett, Lloyd N. "Appraisal of Communication Facilities, Especially Publications, in the California State Department of Education." A report transmitted to the Superintendent of Public Instruction, Sacramento, October 31, 1963. (Mimeographed.)

Norris, William A. "Invitation To Submit Qualifications To Provide Consulting Advice on the California State Department of Education." Sacramento, Board of Education, May 3, 1963, p. 1. (Mimeographed.)

Appendix A

CALIFORNIA CHIEF STATE SCHOOL OFFICERS

1851-53	John G. Marvin
1854-56	Paul K. Hubbs
1857-62	Andrew J. Moulder
1863-67	John Swett
1867-71	Oscar P. Fitzgerald
1871-75	Henry N. Bolander
1875-79	Ezra S. Carr
1879-83	Frederick M. Campbell
1883-87	William T. Welcker
1887-91	Ira G. Hoitt
1891-95	James W. Anderson
1895-98	Samuel T. Black
1898	Charles T. Meredith
1899-1907	Thomas J. Kirk
1907-19	Edward Hyatt
1919-27	Will C. Wood
1927-29	William John Cooper
1929-37	Vierling Kersey
1937-45	Walter F. Dexter
1945-62	Roy E. Simpson
1962-	Max Rafferty

Appendix B

Chart I.--PROPOSED ORGANIZATION OF CALIFORNIA DEPARTMENT OF EDUCATION, 1968

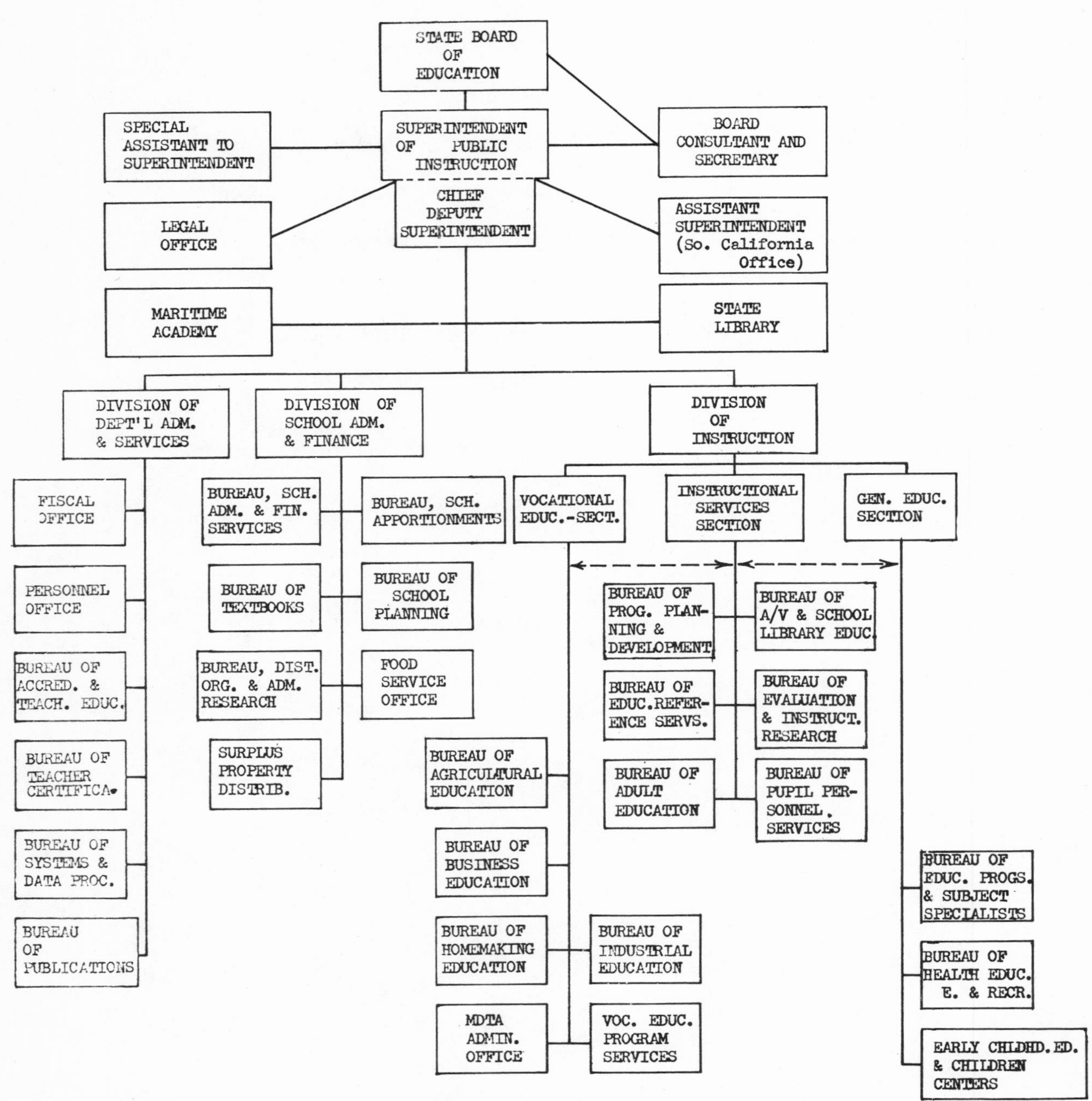

Appendix B

Chart I.--PROPOSED ORGANIZATION OF CALIFORNIA DEPARTMENT OF EDUCATION, 1968 (Continued)

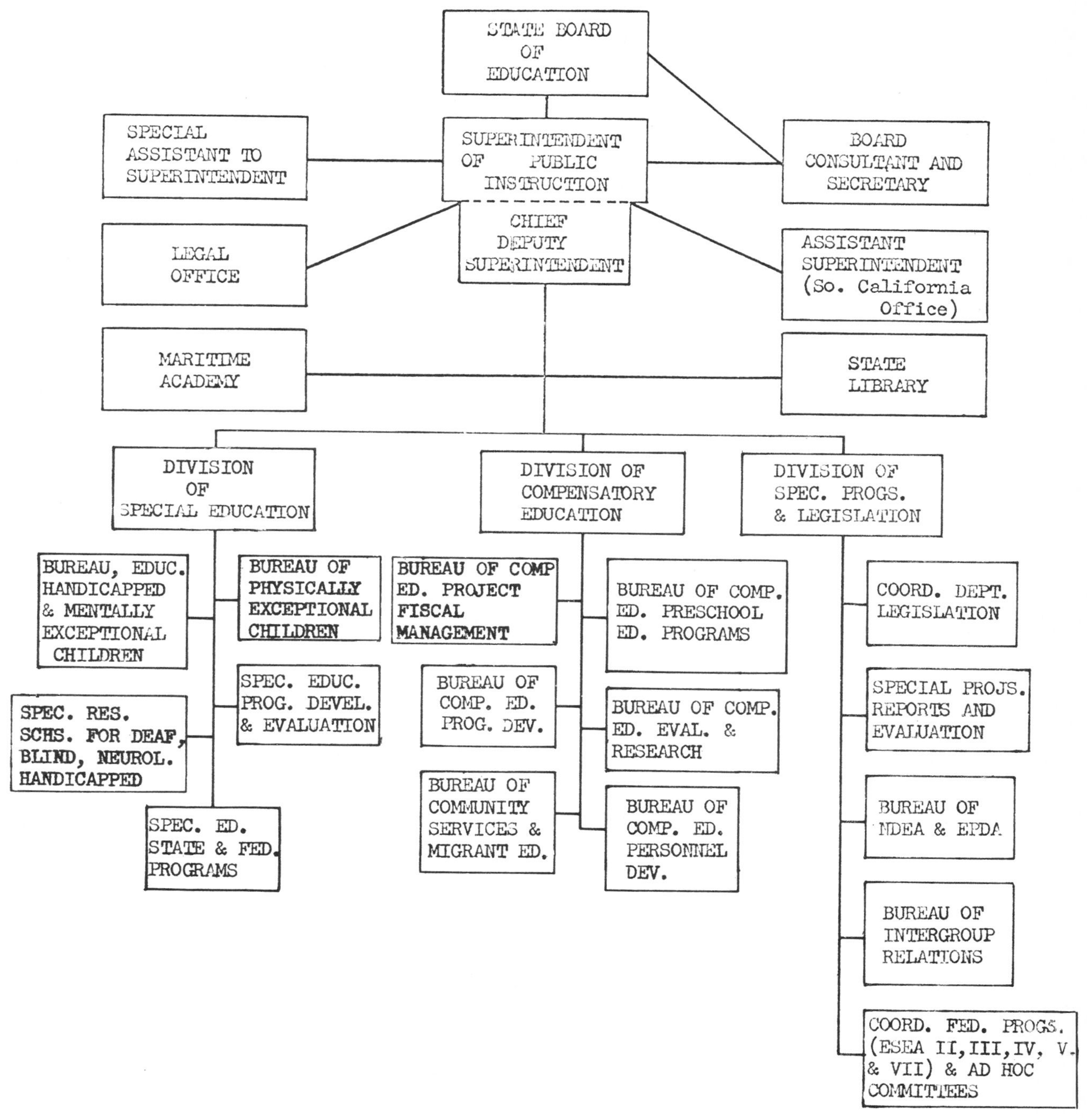

6 Colorado

DEPARTMENT OF EDUCATION
H. Edgar Williams

Contents

THE STATE DEPARTMENT OF EDUCATION BEFORE 1900 (1)

Except for widely scattered Spanish and Mexican settlements in the southern part, the first permanent settlers of Colorado were miners and others supporting mining enterprises. Among these people, rugged individualism and self-reliance were highly valued characteristics. As a consequence, education was for many years viewed as primarily a local concern. Although this point of view prevailed in all states in their early history, it received exaggerated emphasis in Colorado. A prime educational problem, therefore, has been to establish the concept of a wider responsibility for education than that of the local district or even of the county.

In a 1963 study, the Denver Research Instititute divides Colorado's economic growth into three periods: (1) the era of mining, from 1880 to 1900; (2) the era of agriculture, from 1900 to 1940; and (3) the era of defense, from 1940 to 1960 (2). In 1880, mining accounted for 20 percent of Colorado's employment and 26 percent of the state's personal income. Manufacturing, agriculture, and the railroads were developed principally to serve the mining industry. The population of the state increased from 194,000 in 1880 to 540,000 in 1900.

During the second period, agriculture and food-processing industries dominated the economy. Agricultural employment reached its peak in the 1920's and began to recede substantially by 1940. In 1920, agriculture contributed 20 percent of Colorado's income, as compared to 14 percent nationally. During these two decades, the food-processing industries accounted for two-thirds of manufacturing employment. During the same period, mining employment declined from 540,000 to 16,000; and the population increased from 939,629 in 1920 to 1,123,196 – a natural increase, in contrast to the influx of workers during the mining era.

The picture began to change by 1940. In particular, World War II influenced Colorado's economic development. Spending for defense continued to grow, until by 1960 it accounted for 18 percent of the state's manufacturing employment, against 7.3 percent for the country as a whole. Meanwhile, employment in mining and in agriculture continued to decline.

This increase in manufacturing resulted in concentrating much of the state's population in areas suited to industry, particularly around Denver and along the eastern slope of the Rocky Mountains. Obviously, Colorado was emerging from a predominantly rural economy into a business and industrial one.

Before and During the Territorial Period

Little was known of the general geographic area that included Colorado prior to 1859. "A very large portion of the country was, as late as 1840, described in the school atlases of the day as the Great American Desert" (3). A few fur traders visited the area, and Pike, Long, Bonneville, and Frémont explored it. Spanish-speaking people visited the southern and southwestern part of the state from time to time. Some historians claim that soldiers and explorers were in the San Luis Valley of southern Colorado prior to 1700. Spanish explorers did enter the San Luis and Arkansas River Valleys around 1700, as did a few French explorers some years later (4). It is known that pioneer Mexican settlers of Spanish descent were in the San Luis Valley around 1820.

In 1859, the year following the discovery of gold in the Denver area, thousands of adventurers trekked across the plains in search of the precious metal. Although many intended to make their fortunes and then return to their homes, within 3 years a stable population was developing, consisting principally of miners with profitable claims and of tradesmen who catered to the needs of the miners.

The Territory of Colorado was organized in February 1861. In one of its first acts the Territorial Council passed a set of school laws, modeled after those of Illinois, which provided for a territorial superintendent of common schools. Governor William Gilpin appointed W. J. Curtice as the first superintendent, at an annual salary of $500.

An amendment to the school law in 1865 transferred the superintendent's duties to the state treasurer, who was allowed $100 per year for this added responsibility. Two years later, Columbus Nuckrolls, the first treasurer serving in that capacity to issue a state school report, emphasized the difficulty in realizing operating funds from "school mining claims," the predecessor of federally provided public school lands. This was the first in a long series of references by state school officers to inadequacies in funds derived from public school lands.

The Territorial Council of 1870 reestablished an independent state school officer with the title of superintendent of public instruction, who was appointed by the Governor at a salary of $1,000 annually.

The Mining Era, 1876-1900

Settlers who had come to Colorado in search of gold instead of homes had left the gold fields after missing their "strikes," and many had settled in this beautiful part of the country. The major Indian wars had been won by 1868, and railways began to make the region accessible to people from other parts of the country. While the nation was suffering the Panic of '73, Colorado was faring somewhat better with its mining and agricultural wealth, rapidly developing business centers, and new rail ties to the East.

In the meantime, although some schools closed down when mining communities became ghost towns, new strikes and the developing industry and agriculture brought others. In 1873, Denver turned out to hear speeches, watch parades, and attend various other ceremonies which took place during the dedication of its first high school, the Arapahoe School. The Arapahoe School was unusual for its time in that boys and girls attended classes together, which many considered questionable educational procedure at the time. The school also housed a library, which was open daily to the general public.

Despite these advances, school facilities across the territory were poor, and the average salary for a teacher was $20 per month. There were virtually no standards for teachers or for education. But Colorado was on the brink of progress and prosperity.

The superintendent of public instruction was Horace M. Hale, the son of a New England manufacturer and inventor, who had first come to Colorado for his health. A graduate of Union College, New York, he had held a number of teaching assignments and had been admitted to the bar in Michigan. At one time he had held four jobs at once: regent of the University of Colorado, superintendent of schools at Gilpin County, mayor of Central City, and principal of the public schools in Central City. Concerned about the state of education in Colorado, Superintendent Hale called for the teachers to meet at the Arapahoe School in Denver during the Christmas vacation of 1875. The 58 men and 41 women who attended the meeting organized a Colorado Teachers Association and elected Horace Hale as the first president.

In the meantime, the way had already been paved for Colorado to attain statehood. Territorial Governor John L. Routt called for a constitutional convention to meet in December 1875, almost coinciding with the first meeting of the CTA. In fact, the teachers appointed a committee of seven members, with Hale as chairman, to work with the convention and the Legislature in writing the laws. The constitution was ratified by the people in July 1876, and President Grant proclaimed Colorado a state a month later. John L. Routt was then elected as the first state Governor.

Colorado's new constitution provided for a state superintendent of public instruction to be elected in the general elections every 2 years (5). It also established an ex officio State Board of Education, consisting of the state superintendent, the secretary of state, and the attorney general, with the superintendent designated as chairman. The Legislature set the salary for the state superintendent at $2,000 annually.

Joseph C. Shattuck was elected superintendent of public instruction in the first state election in 1876. Born and educated in Marlborough, New Hampshire, he attended Wesleyan University and then went to Missouri to teach. Later, in Greeley, Colorado, he organized the first grade school. Shattuck was seriously interested in educational development and progress in his adopted state and was elected the third president of the Colorado Teachers Association. In his presidential address in January 1878, he came out strongly against compulsory education laws, preferring instead to make education more readily available to American youth so that there would be schools enough for all.

Shattuck was reelected twice as state superintendent. He was later elected dean of the academic department of the University of Denver in 1885, and thus became head of all the business affairs for the university.

The superintendent during these years usually (but not always) had one clerical assistant; but he had no professional staff until 1895, when an assistant superintendent was added. The responsibilities of the superintendent's office were relatively simple and principally regulatory and operational. "Its earliest functions were primarily to gather and report financial and statistical data" (6). The superintendent also was required to visit and inspect schools, but since he received little or no travel appropriation, these visits frequently were made possible through the courtesy of the railroads (7).

Throughout this period, the state superintendents were continually concerned with the problem of getting adequate financial support for the schools. Several complained that not enough funds were derived from the state school lands and that even this amount was poorly managed. Most of the support at this time, and in the early 1900's, came from county and district levels. By 1889, superintendents were recommending a state tax for the support of schools, but it was to be many years before these recommendations were carried out.

During this entire period, the state superintendents gave considerable attention to county and state teachers examinations; the questions used were fully published in biennial reports. The superintendents frequently criticized the qualifications of members of local boards of education and the services they rendered and sometimes charged misuse or misappropriation of funds. For example, in 1885 the superintendent of public instruction stated:

> A well-known citizen and banker, who has been the treasurer of his county for a number of terms, tells me he has repeatedly seen three district officers come to his office, and, after receiving the district funds from the county treasurer, divide the money between themselves before leaving the room, making no pretense of accounting for it. This is, of course, an extreme case, but every year money was lost to the schools, at different points (8).

And the superintendent, in his Ninth Biennial Report (for 1893-94), makes the following recommendation:

> It is high time the legislature should appoint a committee to examine into the results of our present district school system, regarding the acts of school boards, and see if some methods of control cannot be devised by which existing evils can be remedied (9).

When county and regional normal training institutes became popular, the state superintendents vigorously supported them. They were quite concerned about the quality of the programs offered in the numerous ungraded schools, and some reported efforts to improve these schools by providing statewide courses of study (10).

These early superintendents were industrious and were dedicated to the services of education, with special attention to the local school districts. However, they depended to a great extent on county superintendents for statistical and financial information about the schools. Further, subject to election every 2 years, they complained of a lack of continuity in the office, and at least one recommended to the General Assembly that the method of selection be changed to appointment by the Governor for a 4-year term. Although they demonstrated leadership on occasion, they had neither the time nor the means to extend their duties much beyond the merely regulatory and operational.

By the turn of the century, Colorado's educational progress was remarkable. Its education association (CEA) was host to the National Education Association in 1895, when the latter had only 1,000 members, and again in 1909, when its membership was around 6,000.

THE STATE DEPARTMENT FROM 1900 TO 1965

The Agricultural Era, 1900 to 1940

There is no dividing line to distinguish the Colorado State Department of Public Instruction before and after 1900. Until the Colorado State Board of Education and the department were reorganized by the constitutional amendment of 1948, only a very slight and gradual change is evident. The department from 1900 to 1948 had a limited staff headed by a politically chosen state superintendent. But choosing the superintendent every 2 years by popular vote and delegating to him duties and responsibilities that were essentially operational and custodial fitted the state's economic and social pattern during this period.

From 1900 to 1940, state services, and in particular those from the office of the state superintendent, were developed for a rural economy. Small rural school districts dominated the educational scene, except for Denver and a few other metropolitan areas, and the county superintendents were expected to provide most of the leadership for the local schools. Since secondary school programs were comparatively slow in developing, the state superintendent gave a major emphasis to standardization of rural schools and courses of study adapted to their needs.

The state department's staff reflected this predominantly rural economy. In 1900, it consisted of three persons in addition to the superintendent—an assistant superintendent, an assistant state librarian (then as now, the superintendent served as state librarian, ex officio), and a clerk. By 1910, the only change was the addition of two clerks. A decade later, in 1920, the department added a state supervisor of rural schools, a teacher of the adult blind, and an educational statistician. As Chart I of Appendix B shows, even as late as 1940 the total staff consisted of only 15, including 8 clerks.

Although state superintendents were elected every 2 years, only six different persons occupied the office from 1900 to 1940. One of these, Inez Johnson Lewis, won election five times in a row during this period. Another person, Mary C. C. Bradford, was elected to the office six times. (She was also elected president of NEA in 1918.) Katherine L. Craig was elected five times. Despite considerable continuity in office during this time, there is some question as to whether the superintendents could give continuous attention to their duties when they had to campaign every 2 years.

All those who filled the office during this period were women, usually former county superintendents. The state superintendents frequently recommended in their biennial reports that the salary, which continued to be $3,000 annually, be increased to a level on par with that of the chief state school officers in other states. One superintendent presented her case in these strong terms:

> I recommend for the fifth time what every state superintendent for the past sixteen years has recommended, an increase in the salary of the superintendent . . . . The salary . . . has not been increased since that office was created in 1876. That one of the six Executive Constitutional officers of the Commonwealth should receive a

less salary than many holding merely appointive positions has become, in the eyes of thousands of thinking citizens of Colorado, little less than a scandal (11).

The recommendations, however, were apparently ignored.

Superintendents were aware of the need for a larger professional staff, particularly supervisors of elementary and secondary schools. Especially interested in upgrading rural schools, one superintendent recommended the addition to the department staff of "no less than three, or as many as six" rural school supervisors (12). However, the General Assembly was slow in providing for such services.

Certification of Teachers. From its inception, one of the state department's principal responsibilities was certification of teachers. It issued state diplomas for teaching, on the basis of both an examination and a "distinguished service" record. At the same time, county superintendents also had the authority to examine prospective teachers. But by 1900, the county examination questions were prepared by the state department and sent to county superintendents, who in turn administered them on previously announced dates. They required only limited preparation. The law stated that—

> The county superintendent shall meet all persons, of not less than eighteen years of age, desirous of passing an examination as teachers, at which time he shall examine all such applicants in orthography, reading, writing, arithmetic, English grammar, geography, history and Constitution of the United States and the Constitution of Colorado, civil government, physiology and the natural sciences, theory and practice of teaching and the school law of the state . . . (13).

The state superintendents' biennial reports published the examination questions in full until the eighteenth report (for 1911-12). The county examinations continued until the assembly abolished them by law in 1937 and at the same time gave the state department complete authority for granting certificates, with the exception of those issued by the state teachers colleges.

School Consolidation. As early as 1900, educators realized that many of the numerous small school districts were inadequate and inefficient. The state superintendent at that time remarked that "the chief evils of our country schools are unequal taxation, short and unequal terms, unequal equipment, untrained and poorly paid teachers, small schools, lax supervision." She went on to recommend that "a method of administration patterned as clearly as practicable after that of the city would result in some measure of relief" (14). In conclusion, she recommended the county as a unit of school administration.

For a number of years, the state department promoted school district consolidation. In 1919, the superintendent reported that "the twenty-one consolidated schools of two years ago have grown to the encouraging number of sixty-six. . ." (15). In the next report (1919-20), the superintendent was able to claim that there were now 130 centralized and consolidated schools. The 1927-28 report referred to the "large number of consolidated schools" (16), and the next reported that the consolidation process was continuing. Of course, urbanization prompted much of this consolidation, but the reports do show the state education officials' interest in the formation of districts sufficiently large to maintain adequate school programs.

In the 1930-32 biennial report, this problem is best summarized as follows:

> It is generally conceded that we are burdened with too many school districts in the various counties of the state. The Legislature can render a great service to education, from the standpoint of efficiency and economy, if it will pass a comprehensive statute under which the number of school districts in the state will be greatly reduced.
>
> It is sometimes contended that the maintenance of schools is the exclusive responsibility of local districts. This is not in accordance with the spirit of either the Constitution of the United States or the Constitution of the State of Colorado (17).

The difficulty in providing efficiently organized school districts continued to plague the state superintendents and has not been completely solved to this day.

Standardizing Schools. Superintendent of Public Instruction Mary C. C. Bradford gained a wide reputation, extending outside the state, for her program of school standardization.

> On June 18, 1914, she sent out the first Standardization Proclamation, laying her plan of scoring the schools of Colorado before the county superintendents. At the next meeting of the State Association of County Superintendents, the plan, as outlined by her, was formally adopted . . . and christened by her as the "Colorado Plan of Standardization." This has been called by various school authorities throughout the nation the sanest and most practical plan of standardization yet adopted in the country (18).

In her report for 1915-16, Mrs. Bradford claimed that the Colorado Plan of Standardization had already made history, earning the compliment of imitation in seven other states since its adoption. As in other states, this plan of developing levels of standardized schools through inspection and grading made a very substantial contribution to the upgrading of elementary schools. The state department continued to provide leadership for standardization.

Superintendent Bradford had been a county superintendent for 6 years before becoming state superintendent in 1913. She held office in many organizations and was an ardent supporter of women's suffrage.

The Normal Institutes. For many years the state department exercised leadership in organizing normal institutes for training teachers in the summer. By 1900, these institutes were being conducted in 13 regions of the state. The department appropriated $50 to each region to help defray the expenses, but the General Assembly had never actually earmarked money for the institutes. In 1901, the assembly passed a special act stipulating that candidates taking the county teachers examination pay a $1 fee and that the money collected be apportioned equally among the 13 regional normal institutes.

At this time, normal institutes were apparently the principal means for stimulating and upgrading teachers. One superintendent explained:

> The purpose of these institutes is not to cram applicants for a teachers certificate, but to present by high class educators such matters in such form as will inspire the common school teacher with high ideals and noble purposes, and to instruct him in the methods whereby such ideals may be approached and such purposes attained. It may safely be said that no single line of endeavour is doing more to professionalize the vocation of the common school teacher than the effort put forth in the direction of the normal institute (19).

The state superintendents reported regularly on these institutes and continually stressed the need to improve them.

By 1928, normal institutes were still held in the 13 regions, and, in addition to money collected from teachers examinations, they were supported by registration fees and appropriations from county commissioners. Nevertheless, in the next (1929) legislative session, the General Assembly repealed the law providing for normal institutes. The subsequent records contain nothing further about them.

The Depression. The biennial reports for the postwar period 1918 to 1921 do not indicate any serious disruptions of the state department services or any major increase in educational problems. This was not true, however, during the Depression of the thirties. Schools were hard pressed to continue operating, and the department was forced to curtail its staff. The State Library would have had to close had it not received assistance from the federally supported Works Projects Administration. In fact, it did close for a short time in 1938.

The state superintendent reported for 1930-32 that the schools had shortened their terms and reduced teachers' salaries. In many districts teachers were unable to cash school warrants, and some teachers had not been paid at all. Despite these setbacks, the superintendent summed up the situation as follows:

> Due to the careful planning of the boards of education in charge of our schools, to the attitude of our people toward public schools, and in many cases, to the personal sacrifice of both our citizens and our public school teachers, the wholesale discontinuance of schools has not yet occurred in Colorado. The future is not clear, but with the careful consideration of constructive measures by the Governor and the Legislature, I believe by the united efforts of state, county and school districts, we may be able to protect, during these trying times, the educational interests of the growing children of our State (20).

In the succeeding biennial report, the effects of the Depression were evident. The superintendent lamented that "at no other time within the history of Colorado has the administration of educational affairs been attended by such precarious situations in regard to its finances" (21).

In both reports, she made strong pleas for more adequate state support for the schools.

The Defense Era, 1940 to 1960

Prior to 1940, a number of state superintendents were aware of the need to increase the state department's services. Gradually, several superintendents, various groups, and educational leaders concluded that only by completely reorganizing the department, including the State Board of Education, could it provide the leadership needed for a twentieth-century educational system.

As it stood, the board was composed of the state superintendent, the attorney general, and the secretary of state. Although such ex officio state boards were common, there was a national trend to change to a board of laymen, chosen by popular election. In 1928, the Colorado Education Association, with the support of the Colorado Parent-Teachers Association, spearheaded a drive to establish an elective State Board of Education with the authority to appoint a state commissioner of education. They argued that such a board would eliminate the necessity for a chief state school officer to engage in a political campaign every 2 years and would be more likely to provide professional leadership in solving educational problems. When this proposal was submitted to the people at the general election, however, it received only 35 percent of the vote.

The CEA, backed by the PTA, submitted a similar proposal as a constitutional amendment in 1930, but it only received 32 percent of the vote. The *Colorado School Journal* charged that the proposal was defeated because the powers of the proposed board were not specific enough, and that a board appointed by the Governor would not eliminate politics. It also stated that the onset of the economic crisis had created a strong reaction, and some people feared that education would be dominated by professional educators. In fact, some people even expressed the fear that if the amendment passed, Colorado's educational system would be dominated by the Teachers College of Columbia University (22).

The educational programs of the Depression years and World War II so absorbed the state's time and effort that scant attention was given to reorganization. But shortly after the war, the CEA and the PTA, joined by the Colorado School Board Association and the Colorado County Superintendents Association, began to plan more carefully an effort to reorganize the educational structure. These associations also had the support of Governor W. Lee Knous and State Superintendent Nettie S. Freed.

In her successful campaign of 1946, Mrs. Freed had definitely committed her support to such an amendment. In addition, she promised to step aside after the amendment passed to permit the board to select a new commissioner of education. A large majority of the state's school leaders favored this reorganization and worked actively in her campaign and later for the amendment. The following statement sums up their attitude toward the reorganization of the state department.

> The organizational structure . . . in its extreme weakness has so limited the possibilities of the state department that the legislature has not seen fit to delegate adequate responsibility nor funds which would allow significant activities beyond those of teacher certification, record keeping, the distribution of state funds, the interpretation of school laws, miscellaneous advisory activities and an extra curricular type of educational leadership between election campaigns (23).

Such a large number of educators and leading lay people supported the amendment that it is not surprising that both political parties endorsed it. Both the House and Senate, by a practically unanimous vote, placed it on the general election ballot as amendment number 1. This time, in 1948, the people approved the amendment.

The new amendment provided for a State Board of Education to consist of one member from each congressional district, and one additional member to be elected at large if there were an even number of districts. A state commissioner of education, appointed by the state board, replaced the state superintendent of instruction. The amendment specifically excluded the commissioner from the state's Civil Service.

Following the amendment's adoption, the Legislature enacted a law to clarify and implement it. Subsequent legislation provided for board members to be nominated and elected for 6-year terms in the same manner as Colorado Representatives to Congress—they were to be political party nominees. The law stipulated that the board would appoint a commissioner of education, formulate policies for the department, adopt rules and regulations for supervising the public schools, and distribute funds to the schools. It also authorized the board to approve newly created divisions, appraise the work of the commissioner and the department, approve salary schedules, and submit the department's biennial budget request to the General Assembly.

The law stated that the commissioner of education was to be the "administrative and executive head" of the Department of Education, but he would serve at the pleasure of the Board of Education at a salary determined by the board. In brief, his duties were to act as executive officer of the board, to keep the board advised concerning the public schools, to keep financial and statistical records, and to provide a program of research. He was to prescribe the financial and statistical forms, distribute state and federal funds, direct the preparation of courses of study and recommend their use, evaluate qualifications and issue teachers certificates, and render technical and expert assistance in school building construction. He was also required to submit to the Governor and General Assembly a biennial report, prepare and execute—with the board's approval—a budget for the department, and establish and maintain a system of personnel administration. He was directed to carry out other legal duties and responsibilities, including those of state librarian.

This reorganization of the state board and the department marked a high point in the history of Colorado's State Department of Education. However, setting up the constitution and legal background were merely enabling actions. Implementing these provisions and redirecting the policies and procedures provided a great challenge to the board, the appointed commissioners, the department's personnel, and the state's educational and lay leaders.

Staffing and Reorganization, 1940 to 1955

By 1942, there were 26 persons on the staff of the department, including the State Library (see Appendix B, Chart II). These employees were organized by areas of service: general office, accounting and records, elementary education and curriculum, certification, and bureau of home and school services. Employees of the Colorado State Board for Vocational Education and the State Historical Society were listed on the departmental chart, but only as subsidiary agencies of the state department. By law they were designated as belonging to the department, but in practice their relationship was tenuous. Until the 1962-63 school year, the vocational education board was identified as one of the three "offices" of the department, but this was a purely voluntary arrangement that broke down in practice. Actually, the vocational education board was entirely separate from the state board, and almost completely autonomous in its relation to the latter.

When the constitutional amendment on reorganization was adopted in 1948, the department's staff, in addition to the positions listed above, included four employees in the school lunch program and a finance and research director. The state superintendent exercised administrative control with the assistance of a deputy superintendent in charge of internal office management.

The transition from the old to the reorganized state department began when the first commissioner of education was appointed in January 1951. Mrs. Nettie S. Freed, elected to a second term as state superintendent in 1948, continued at the end of her term to hold the office in order to give the new State Board of Education time to select a new commissioner. The board finally selected J. Burton Vasche, and the new commissioner was inducted into office that July.

Vasche served as commissioner for approximately a year before leaving to accept a position in California. After an interim of 9 months, the board chose H. Grant Vest, but he held the position only until November 1959. After another interim, Byron W. Hansford was appointed commissioner and holds the office at present.

One of the new State Board of Education's first acts was to authorize a study of the proposed reorganization of the department. Under the leadership of Dr. Vest, an intensive study was conducted for 3 years, with both the board and the commissioner fully aware of its significance. It finally reported:

> Three years of conscientious study of this problem by the members of the State Board of Education has clearly revealed the need for fundamental improvements in departmental organization and administration. These needs were anticipated in the legislation which brought the board into existence. In arriving at this conclusion, the board members have received and studied the suggestions of its staff. The help of leaders in the educational profession of the state and of leaders in the Colleges and Universities of the state has been solicited. The help of the Colorado Expenditures Council has been most significant. Members of the board have visited in other states observing and studying their programs. Out-of-state leaders have been consulted. The board collaborated with surrounding states in sponsoring a study of the emerging role of state departments of education (24).

The board declared that it was imperative to secure the Legislature's support in its 1954 session—particularly financial support for new positions. It recommended above all other improvements the merger of vocational education with the state department. It pointed out the "obvious limitations" in the instructional services program, especially in the supervision and leadership in elementary education. Having four people involved in the hot lunch program and only two in special education seemed to indicate an imbalance. Similarly, secondary education had only one supervisor, but vocational education had seven. The report also pointed to other areas of insufficient staffing and services.

The General Assembly did not give its support to these proposals immediately, but in the regular session of 1955, it did vote a sufficient special appropriation for reorganization to enable the department to expand considerably. During 1955, the commissioner was able to add two assistant commissioners (as proposed) and two people each in elementary and secondary education. He also was able to secure additional personnel in eight new areas of service: school plant, transportation, district organization, conservation education, audiovisual instruction, adult education, guidance services, and publications.

At this time, as the department was being reorganized and its services expanded, efforts were made in two principal directions. First, the department exerted leadership in assisting the schools to meet the challenge of the "atomic age." It stated: "The main problems which challenge us in this mid-century decade are those of adjusting our educational system and programs to the needs of a new kind of civilization based upon technology, automation and atomic energy . . ." (25). Second, the department had to awaken the citizens of the state to the importance of education in general, and to the leadership role of the state department in particular: "There is also a need for a rebirth of citizen understanding of the role and importance of education to society. If our civilization is to endure, it must use the united insights and judgments of our people collectively" (26).

During the next several years, the Department of Education directed considerable attention to lay citizen participation in educational planning. It worked closely with the White House Conference on Education, the Colorado Congress of Parents and Teachers, the Citizens Council for Public Schools, the Colorado Association of School Boards, the Colorado Education Association, and the High School Activities Association.

The general plan of the White House Conference on Education, provided for by Public Law 530 of the Eighty-Third Congress in 1955, was to hold a national conference on education, preceded by local and state conferences. Reflecting general criticism and unrest, the basic assumption was that critical problems faced the nation's schools and needed attention. Preceding the national conference, held in Washington, D.C., from November 30 to December 2, 1955, Colorado carried on a yearlong program.

The Governor appointed a committee of 60 distinguished citizens to work with the state department in planning and conducting local conferences and a statewide conference. This committee developed plans to encourage the local communities to share in the program, and to follow these local meetings with five regional meetings. At the final state conference, the deliberations of local and regional conferences were summarized and a state report prepared.

A Decade of Growing Services, 1955-65

The substantial expansion of department personnel and services inaugurated in 1955 continued throughout the decade. Further impetus was given by the National Defense Education Act of 1958 (NDEA) and the Elementary and Secondary Education Act of 1965 (ESEA). Thus, the

Colorado State Department of Education has developed into a strikingly different agency since its reorganization in 1949.

Differences are evident in the number of employees and in the organization of the education department. The number of employees increased from 30 in 1948 to 149 in 1965. The organization developed into a threefold pattern: (a) office of administrative services; (b) office of instructional services; and (c) divisions responsible directly to the commissioner. The department was offering new and timely services with the addition of consultants for automatic data processing, urban educational affairs, and designing education for the future in the Rocky Mountain Area States Project.

The department expanded services in the instructional areas in general, and in all its divisions. With the assistance of federal funds, it expanded considerably the library and school lunch programs. Federal funds also supported expansion of services in science, mathematics, and modern foreign languages under Title III of NDEA, and in guidance and counseling under its Title V. NDEA's Title X gave financial support to stimulate services in research and statistical programs.

Several special projects undertaken during the decade helped thrust the department into an increasingly important educational leadership role. A high-level group made up of selected education leaders from both in and outside the state were named to the Colorado Council on Instruction. This advisory group was charged with the responsibility of advising the department and the state board on all matters relating to curriculum and instruction in the state's public schools. It has functioned well, and one of its most valuable contributions was the development in 1962 of the publication *Goals for Education in Colorado.*

During this decade, the department also initiated a regional approach to instructional improvement. The state was divided into multicounty, multischool-district regions, represented by cooperative associations, whose purpose was to share ideas and pursue solutions to common problems in instruction. At the same time, the Rocky Mountain Area States Project, designed to give special help to small, rural, isolated schools, and supported by the Ford Foundation, expanded into the Western States Small Schools Project, which was also supported by grants from the Ford Foundation. This multistate effort, under the leadership of the chief state school officers of five participating states, has become nationally known for its new approaches to rural education.

The department also undertook the recodification of the school laws, and this was largely implemented by the General Assembly during the 1963, 1964, and 1965 sessions. Stimulated by Commissioner Hansford, a project was undertaken to study the role of state departments of education. Funded under Title V of ESEA, it eventually resulted in an eight-state project, titled "Designing Education for the Future."

The department found it difficult to attract able personnel and establish status because of the uncertainty concerning the classification of professional personnel. The State Civil Service Commission exerted considerable effort to bring them under Civil Service classification. As the result of a test case, the Colorado Supreme Court ruled in 1960 that the State Department of Education was in effect an educational institution. Therefore, its professional personnel were employees of an educational institution, comparable to employees of state colleges and universities, and thus were exempt from Civil Service.

The state board and the commissioner immediately set about raising the salaries of those positions exempted from Civil Service classification. In addition to raising and maintaining competitive salaries for the professional staff, the commissioner began to upgrade its quality by hiring relatively young and aggressive people, many holding earned doctorates.

One of the significant undertakings of the early 1960's was "Project School Child," cooperatively sponsored by the Colorado Association of School Boards, the Colorado Congress of Parents and Teachers, the Coloradc Education Association, and the State Department of Educa tion. During the first 5 months of 1964, more than 20,00(Colorado citizens participated in discussions on the schools They displayed an intense interest in securing more infor mation about public education and expressed opinions tha may be useful in future years. Of particular significance, lay persons directed and guided all phases of the project, wit occasional assistance from state and local educators, an this was one of its basic purposes—to involve many citizen at the local level in finding facts; in discussing goals, pro grams, facilities, and finances; and in making known thei wishes regarding future educational planning.

A variety of activities undertaken by the departmen contributed to a major breakthrough in state-level financin of Colorado public education in the 1960's. These activitie included special reports describing the financial conditio of the schools and numerous regional and statewid meetings to call the attention of citizens, educators, an legislators to the financial plight of the local systems Through such activities the department was able to increas state support by more than $20 million.

Perhaps one of the most significant pieces of legisla tion was the handicapped children's law passed in 195 Primarily, through the leadership of department staff mem bers, the proportion of public school enrollment receivin special education services increased from 2.9 percent i 1959 to 4.7 percent in 1965.

Other significant accomplishments include the cre tion of the research and development division to encourag research at the local level, the Teacher Certification Act c 1961, and the reduction in the number of school distric from 478 in 1960 to 184 in 1965. There was increasing recognition on the part of the state board and the commissioner of their major responsibilities in the areas of urban education. Legislation also was passed to establish boards of cooperative services. These accomplishments all contributed to greater prestige and leadership by the Colorado State Department of Education.

THE DEPARTMENT ORGANIZED FOR SERVICE

The Department's Basic Design

From its beginning, the State Department of Public Instruction, later to become known as the State Department of Education, attempted to render a limited service to the Colorado schools that was typical of what state departments of education offered in the early 1900's. Superintendents visited school districts, issued reports, and rendered semilegal decisions. The department issued teaching certificates and initiated a system of standardization of school districts. By means of biennial reports and personal conferences, the superintendents and the department presented the interests of the schools to the Governor and the Legislature. Moneys from the public school income fund were distributed. Despite these efforts, it cannot truly be said that these leadership and service functions covered all that is implied in the accepted concept of the state's ultimate responsibility for education.

Early Colorado superintendents, aware of the need to extend more adequate services to the schools, called for additional professional staffing, particularly for supervisors in elementary and secondary education. They pointed out the need to organize school districts more adequately to meet the growing demands of American education. But they could not have conceived of the many programs and kinds of services provided today by modern state departments of education.

As already stated, change was evident in the early 1940's; there was an increase in the staff, and the department provided a few specialized services (see Appendix B, Chart II). Nevertheless, there was no wholehearted effort to exercise leadership through such services until about 1951, after the state department reorganization. In fact, it was about 1955 before adequate legislative support for increased appropriations enabled the department to effectively offer these services.

The new basic design of the Colorado State Department of Education consisted of having two principal "offices," each composed of divisions and sections. (The Office of Vocational Education was a part of the department for only a brief period.) The Office of Administrative Services (27) established in 1955, initially included only one formally organized division—that of finance and research. Consultants, rather than division directors, had rendered other services (28). In 1955, divisions were formally organized for school district organization, school plant and transportation, legal services, and school lunch. Four years later the teacher education and certification division was created. In 1964, the department placed school district organization and school plant and transportation in the new organization and management division and changed the finance and research division to the finance and statistics division.

The Office of Administrative Services served the schools in both a consultative and an initiatory capacity. It provided consultative services to local school boards and administrators and provided leadership in developing certain education topics. It conducted workshops and individual visits to help local schools institute new and desirable practices. The office offered direct services in finance and legislation to the local agencies and served as the legislative liaison between the department and the Colorado General Assembly.

In the summer of 1955, the department established the Office of Instructional Services to implement the new instructional services program. Following the appointment of Leo P. Black as assistant commissioner in charge (29), the office organized a staff of consultants in elementary education, secondary education, and accreditation and appointed a director and a consultant in special education. During the next few months, four directors were employed to direct divisions of curriculum development, elementary education, guidance services, and junior colleges and adult education (initially financed by private funds). The following year, the department appointed a director of secondary education and a director of mental health and state institutions. Concerned with improving instruction from kindergarten through junior college and in the broad area of adult education as well, the Office of Instructional Services finally included nine divisions, including the State Library for a time.

In 1957, the Office of Instructional Services was reorganized. The State Library was withdrawn to report directly to the commissioner of education, who, legally, is the state librarian. The divisions of elementary education, secondary education, and curriculum development consolidated to form a new elementary and secondary education division, and the divisions of special education and of mental health and state institutions consolidated into a new special education division.

Both the staff and services received an impetus for expansion when Congress passed the National Defense Education Act in 1958. The department organized a new section for Title III in the elementary and secondary education division to strengthen instruction in science, mathematics, and modern foreign languages. Title V-A (guidance, conseling, and testing) prompted the addition of several staff members to the guidance services division.

The Colorado State Department of Education had used advisory committees composed of educators and lay leaders even before the reorganization of the State Board of Education. Before 1955, there were state advisory committees working on school health services and on problems of special education for handicapped children. After 1955, many such advisory groups were organized, but two of the principal ones were (1) the Colorado Council on Instruction, charged with advising the board and the department on problems relating to curriculum development and instructional improvement, and (2) the Colorado Council on Educational Research, which had a comparably broad responsibility in research. During succeeding years, the department appointed numerous subject matter advisory bodies, as well as advisory committees to assist in operating programs, such as those under Title III and Title V-A of the NDEA.

Since the instructional services staff was relatively small, wherever possible it worked with the school districts on a regional basis. In the midfifties, one successful experience of this kind involved the department's participation in the Cooperative Project on Educational Administration program, funded by the Kellogg Foundation. In the 1960-61 school year, the department organized several regional instructional improvement associations. That fall (1961), the Colorado Council on Instruction developed a statewide plan entitled the Colorado Instructional Improvement Program. One of its major facets involved developing more regional associations for improving instruction—to facilitate sharing ideas and experiences and to utilize more effectively the department's leadership. Subsequently, it organized about two new regional associations each year.

After the state board reorganization, it was generally understood that the department no longer would attempt to develop courses of study except in emerging areas, such as driver education. This policy was based on the premise that the schools needed various instructional guides to assist teachers and supervisors but which would not necessarily outline the course content.

Colorado's constitution makes it impossible for the State Board of Education or the Legislature to prescribe textbooks for the schools. Thus, the state has never had a state adoption program or selected any instructional materials. The department does, however, assist local schools in making selections by suggesting ways of evaluating materials and even by preparing suggested lists of instructional materials in certain areas.

From 1955 to 1965, about every other spring the department sponsored a series of regional conferences emphasizing "Problems of Instructional Improvement." This enabled the department's representatives to contact the instructional leaders throughout the state and inform them of trends, major problems, and issues, and of some of the means for improving curriculum development and instruction (30).

After the 1955 reorganization, certain divisions were established or maintained outside the two principal "offices" described above because of their unique relationship to the state commissioner or the state board. It has already been mentioned that in 1957 the library services division was again made directly responsible to the commissioner. The departmental administration division, which served as the center for internal management, was left directly responsible to the commissioner. The publications and public information division was so directly involved in serving the entire department that, after a period in the Office of Instructional Services, it also was placed directly under the commissioner. The adult education division, set up in 1955 as part of the Office of Instructional Services, became the education beyond high school division in 1962 and was placed in the commissioner's area of responsibility by legislative edict.

Internal Management

During the early history of the State Department of Education, the state superintendent was principally responsible for managing the business and budgetary matters. By 1942, however, internal management had become the responsibility of a newly established deputy superintendent (see Appendix B, Chart II). The departmental administration division was then established as part of the state department after the 1948 reorganization, and a professional educator was appointed as commissioner. The assistant commissioner no longer had time for the "housekeeping" duties, so a division director (previously a deputy superintendent), Helen H. Downing, was appointed to supervise the division. Mrs. Downing has continued to serve in this capacity through 1965.

When the department decided that the division director should be a professional staff member and not fall under the classified Civil Service, the Civil Service Commission protested. The dispute finally was resolved in the Colorado Supreme Court in favor of the Department of Education.

In 1965, the Legislature specifically wrote the legal authority for this division's functions into law in the following terms: "(d) to prepare and submit to the state board a budget for the department and to properly execute the approved budget in accordance with appropriations; (e) to establish and maintain a system of personnel administration within the department" (31).

The Division of Departmental Administration was made responsible for all business activities and for preparing the annual budget for presentation to the Governor and the Legislature. Purchase orders and vouchers must originate in the division, which maintains the records of such transactions. The division also was made responsible for keeping records of appropriations and other funds available to the department and of expenditures. The law required all departmental and accounting records to be reconciled with records in the State Division of Accounts and Controls.

The division also is responsible for preparing periodic reports, maintaining and furnishing operating supplies for other divisions, maintaining the department's stock of publications, and providing a mailing service for the department. The division is responsible for administering the department's personnel, and it maintains the records of all employees. It also has responsibility for administering and interpreting Civil Service rules and regulations and for recruiting and assigning support personnel. In addition, it purchases equipment, maintains a comprehensive inventory of all departmental property, and is in charge of two emeritus retirement programs: one for public school teachers and one for personnel from institutions of higher learning.

The influx of federal funds for various programs greatly increased the need for more detailed fiscal accounting and for inventories of the department's property. The large numbers of new employees in all areas of the department incrased the division's paper work. Thus, the division's staff increased from 6 in 1952 to 15 in 1965, but its activity increased many more times in the same period (32).

Instructional Services in Elementary and Secondary Education

The Colorado Department of Public Instruction gave early attention to the need for particular supervisory service by adding to its staff supervisors of rural schools or elementary schools and, somewhat later, supervisors of secondary schools. During the 1940's, the department staff included a supervisor of elementary education and curriculum and a supervisor of secondary education (see Appendix B, Chart III). The division of curriculum improvement and that of elementary education were among the first divisions established after the 1955 reorganization. The following year the department added a secondary education division.

In 1957, these three divisions were combined into a single Division of Elementary and Secondary Education under Clifford Bebell. The division consisted of these six sections: elementary education; secondary education; Title III, National Defense Education Act; Western States Small Schools Project; migrant education; and conservation education. In 1964, the Western States Small Schools Project and migrant education were transferred to the new research and development division, and Raymond A. McGuire became the division director. At the same time, Title III of the NDEA was expanded to include, in addition to its services in mathematics, science, and modern foreign languages, services in English, reading, and the social studies.

Obviously, the Division of Elementary and Secondary Education provided services basic to the schools' instructional program. In a sense, these services in the various subject matter areas constituted the focus of the state's entire educational endeavor. In recognition of this situation, reorganization gradually evolved a pattern of services of significantly broad scope in this departmental division which reflected a statewide, evolving program in the state's public schools.

With state department leadership and cooperation, subject matter programs continued to develop. In his forty-fourth biennial report (for 1962-64), the state commissioner mentioned advances in individual reading, spelling, and English; developmental reading in secondary schools; and team teaching in high school English. He pointed to the organization of the Colorado Language Arts Society, as well as to the Language Arts Advisory Committee, which would assist the department. In social studies, he reported that a Social Studies Advisory Committee was giving attention to a statement of goals for a K-12 program. This committee also prepared a position statement, "Teaching About Controversial Issues," for distribution in 1964.

Schools participated in experimental mathematics programs of local design, as well as in programs developed by the National Science Foundation and some of the colleges and universities. "Twenty percent of Colorado pupils study SMSG (School of Mathematics Study Group) secondary mathematics; 6 percent study UICSM (University of Illinois Committee on School Mathematics); and about 1 percent studies programed mathematics "(33).

In science, the state department fostered the use of such programs as the physical science study committee physics, biological sciences curriculum study, chemical education materials study, and chemical band approach chemistry, all developed by national groups and sponsored by the National Science Foundation. The department initiated a "science guide" for use in grades 1 through 6, utilizing a child-centered approach. For several years the department operated a "Science Lab-Mobile" to help improve the science programs.

From 1958 to 1964, total high school enrollments increased by 40 percent, while students taking foreign languages in Colorado's public secondary schools increased by 88 percent. This was in part due to the state department's leadership in implementing Title III of the National Defense Education Act. At the same time, there were increased enrollments in foreign languages in elementary schools.

Some progress was reported in physical education and health instruction. A State Advisory Committee on Physical Education prepared a statement on teacher certification for physical education teachers, as well as a pamphlet titled "Competition in the Elementary Schools." The State

Advisory Committee on School Health prepared a statement on the "Effects of Smoking."

The Division of Elementary and Secondary Education has provided instructional leadership through conferences, visitations, and consultations in art education, conservation education, and driver education. It has directed considerable attention to kindergarten education, the use of the "continuous progress school," individual instruction, computer scheduling, and "electronic learning laboratories."

While these activities indicate that the state department gradually geared itself for effective leadership and service to the elementary and secondary schools, it is recognized that these steps are only beginnings and much remains to be done. The National Defense Education Act has rendered strong support to many of the programs. But perhaps it is fair to say that the department is effectively organized to keep pace with the ever-increasing demands of the "atomic" educational age.

Finance

From the beginning of Colorado's history as a state, the responsibility for apportioning money from the state school fund–later known as the Public School Income Fund–was assigned to the state superintendent of public instruction. This function has continued to be a departmental responsibility to the present. Among the powers and duties of the reorganized State Board of Education (1949), it was directed "to make and adopt such rules and regulations as are necessary ... for the equitable distribution of funds as are available to the State Department of Education for distribution . . . "(34).

Until 1935, state support for local schools was limited to the Public School Income Fund, derived from state-owned school lands. Major school support, up to this time, came from local property taxes, although the General Assembly made a small appropriation in 1917 to match the federal funds available under the Smith-Hughes Act, "an act to provide for the promotion of vocational education "(35).

In 1935, the General Assembly made a token appropriation of $500 to replace local and county property taxes for school support, and as a test case to determine whether or not the state had constitutional authority to finance the public schools. In a 1937 decision, the Colorado Supreme Court ruled: "We hold that the establishment and financial maintenance of the public schools of the state is the carrying out of a state, and not a local or municipal purpose . . . "(36).

In November 1936, the state's voters approved at a general election a constitutional amendment permitting the General Assembly to levy either graduated or proportioned income taxes "for the support of the State, or any political subdivision thereof, or for the public schools" (37). The amendment's main purpose was to provide support for the public schools, but after a year the income tax funds were used for a variety of purposes. The first allocation under the amendment, amounting to approximately $878,000, was used to replace county and local property taxes. But the principle of state financing had been established, and state appropriations for the public schools increased steadily. "By 1945, approximately $3,000,000 (including $800,000 from the Public School Income Fund) was being distributed to the public schools annually. By 1950, the amount had increased to approximately $10,000,000" (38).

By the 1946-47 school year, state support amounted to about 19 percent of Colorado's total school costs. Following the report of a Governor's Committee, appointed in 1950 to study school finances, the assembly enacted the 1952 Public School Finance Act. This law established classroom units as the basis for school support and defined a classroom unit as 25 pupils in average daily attendance for a school year of 172 days. Amendments to the act in 1953 and 1955 placed the distribution of funds on an average daily attendance basis.

The Public School Foundation Act, passed in 1957, incorporated the 1955-56 Legislative Council's recommendations. Classroom unit values were increased to $4,500 for nongraduates and $5,200 for graduates. Average daily attendance was continued as a basis for the method of distribution, and an objectionable "sparsity factor," which favored small schools, was eliminated. The assembly amended the Foundation Act in 1960 to include a "sales ratio factor," the ratio of assessed valuation to the actual sales price of a piece of property. Again, in 1961 and 1962, it added an "adjusted gross income factor," or amount of personal income reported to the state revenue office after withholdings. The adjusted gross income factor was added to the assessed valuation to compute a part of the Foundation Act formula until the sales ratio factor was eliminated in 1963. The assembly approved legislation establishing a "Property Tax Relief Fund" in 1965 to provide an appropriation for the relief of "school district general fund property taxes "(39).

During the fiscal year 1965-66, total state aid amounted to a little more than $69,500,000–approximately 29 percent of the total operating costs of local schools, contrasted with about 40 percent nationally (40).

Just as the assembly increased financial support to the schools, its appropriations for the state department grew from $7,750 in 1901 to $994,100 in 1965. Undoubtedly, some of this increase was due to rising costs and inflation, but most of it came through the expansion of the department's services. As Appendix C, Table 1, shows, there was a steady increase in moneys available to the department, decade by decade, until the sharp jump from 1941 to 1951. This reflects the increase in departmental responsibilities. The increase was even more striking from 1951 to 1961, principally because of the General Assembly's appropriations for the 1955 reorganization. This increase clearly reveals the citizens' recognition of the department's educational leadership.

Until 1935, when the Legislature first appropriated funds for distribution to local school districts, the Public School Income Fund provided the only state money available to the schools. Throughout the early years, the superintendent of public instruction easily discharged this duty with the assistance of whatever clerical help he had. It was not until the early 1940's that the department appointed a director of finance and research. Charles E. Hathaway, employed as director in 1947, continued by that title until the 1950-51 reorganization. Hathaway made substantial contributions to the development of records and controls for the distribution of state school funds during this period. In 1964, the division was reorganized as the finance and statistics division with Charles L. Bostrom as director.

Teacher Certification

In common with many states during the early period, Colorado relied on the counties to issue teaching certificates. In 1879, the assembly passed a law authorizing county superintendents to certificate teachers who successfully passed county examinations in prescribed subjects. In 1887, it created the State Board of Examiners to issue state diplomas (teaching certificates) based on written examination and on an "honorary basis"(41). It defined the honorary basis as "good moral character," "scholarly attainment," and "rendering eminent service" in the state for at least 6 years. However, they were sometimes issued at least partially on the basis of political expediency. Two years later, legislation authorized state colleges to certificate their own graduates.

The General Assembly modified the State Board of Examiners several times, and then in 1961 changed it to the State Board of Teacher Certification. At present, it consists of the state commissioner of education as chairman and 10 persons appointed by the State Board of Education, 2 representing educational institutions, 2 lay persons, 1 superintendent of schools, and 5 classroom teachers.

Beginning in 1881, the department prepared teacher examinations and distributed them to county superintendents. The questions were subsequently published in the state superintendent's biennial reports.

In 1917, Colorado's first-class districts were authorized to prescribe their own requirements and certificate vocational, music, and art teachers. Thus, at this time there were four certificating agencies in Colorado: county superintendents, state educational institutions, the large first-class districts, and the State Department of Education.

The department's certification personnel were first mentioned in the biennial report for 1921-22 under the title, "Secretary of Certification." Apparently, the State Board of Examiners and state department personnel cooperated in issuing certificates, as the report states that "all the work of the State Board of Education, State Board of Examiners, . . . is done in this office, including . . . issuance of certificates"(42). The 1923-24 biennial report lists a "supervisor of certification," and a certification stenographer had been added by the next biennial report.

In 1923, the General Assembly passed a state certification law authorizing the State Department of Education to issue certificates on the basis of the State Board of Examiners' recommendations. The entire certification procedure also was overhauled in 1923, to give Colorado one of its biggest steps forward in the history of certification. Long-sought reforms in county certification were finally enacted, but the law did permit persons holding county certificates to continue using them. The law established academic requirements for persons wishing to renew their certificates and was so designed that it required an elementary teacher to continue working toward a permanent elementary certificate, based on 2 years of college education. The law allowed only professionally trained graduates to teach in the secondary schools.

Although the 1923 law phased out county superintendents, thus ending some of the confusion caused by four different certificating agencies, many problems still remained. The situation was further confounded by the necessity to issue "war emergency" and "dire emergency" certificates during World War II and shortly thereafter, because of the shortage of qualified teachers. The state had to lower the standards for certificating both elementary and secondary teachers.

The state law under which the State Department of Education was reorganized in 1948 stated that the "State Board of Education shall make and adopt rules and regulations . . . for the proper certification of all school personnel"(43). Rules and regulations were formulated and adopted in 1953 for certifying teachers of exceptional children, school psychologists, and speech correctionists; and in 1960 for school nurses. Certification of school administrators was established in 1957.

In 1961, the General Assembly passed an act effecting a sweeping reorganization of certification in Colorado. This law placed all certification exclusively in the hands of the state department. It was at this time that the State Board of Examiners became the State Board of Teacher Certification, responsible for examining and approving teacher preparation programs in institutions of higher learning, subject to review by the State Board of Education.

This 1961 act raised considerably the standards for teacher certification. The bachelor's degree, with the proper professional preparation, became the minimum basis for certifying elementary as well as secondary teachers. The life certificates were discontinued in favor of "professional certificates" based on at least 3 years of teaching experience and "one or more years of study and preparation beyond the bachelor's degree . . . ." The law provided various types of "special services certificates" and provided for endorsements showing proficiencies in certain specialized areas. Similarly, the act set out the procedures for annulling, suspending, and revoking certificates for cause.

Otto G. Ruff became director of the Division of Teacher Education and Certification in 1959, but his assistant, Eleanor Casebolt, has served the division in a professional capacity since January 1950. The division examines credentials and issues certificates, and it works closely with the teacher training institutions in assisting the State Board of Teacher Certification in "examining and approving teacher preparation programs."

School Accreditation

Prior to 1952, the University of Colorado, like many other state universities, accredited high schools, mainly to uphold the standards of students who would enroll in the university. In 1952, at the request of the university, the state department assumed responsibility for accreditation. In its policy statement that August, the state board declared:

> The State Board of Education in assuming the state program of accreditation anticipates no major change in the program in the immediate future. The policies contained in this bulletin (on accreditation) are tentative criteria to be used during the interim in which plans are being developed for a program of broadened services to entire school systems (44).

The board took a step toward broadening the program in 1955 when "it passed a resolution to the effect that the programs in the elementary grades must measure up to reasonable standards if the high schools are to be accredited "(45). Following this, it decided to make a general evaluation of elementary programs when new high schools were added to the accredited list.

In 1958, the superintendent appointed an advisory committee on accreditation, composed of 17 persons representing schools, colleges, and some of the major educational organizations of the state "to assist the state department in the expansion and further development of the accreditation program" (46). It was expected to make recommendations concerning the accreditation status of all the schools in the state.

The staff of the Division of Accreditation hoped to visit annually as many schools as possible, but definitely hoped to visit each school district every other year. These visitations were considered necessary, since the reports were inadequate.

In 1964, the accredited list included 1,172 schools, 164 unified school districts, 1 county high school district, 2 special public schools, and 25 nonpublic schools. Only 19 unified public school districts were not accredited.

District Organization and Reorganization

From the beginning of statehood, Colorado placed the responsibility for organizing school districts on the local communities. The Constitution of 1876 stated that "the General Assembly shall, by law, provide for organization of school districts of convenient size, in each of which shall be established a board of education, to consist of three or more directors to be elected by the qualified electors of the district" (47).

In 1877, the first Colorado General Assembly then delegated this responsibility to the people in the scattered neighborhoods of the raw, undeveloped wilderness. The law states that—

> For the purpose of organizing a new district, the parents of at least ten children of school age residing within the limits of the proposed new district shall petition the county superintendent in writing . . . that a meeting shall be held . . . to determine the question of such organization (48).

The early settlers of Colorado were quite eager to establish schools for their children. By 1880, there were over 800 school districts in the state, and by 1935, there were more than 2,200 districts. In many instances, mining and agricultural communities developed, thrived, and declined in a few years or a decade. As a result, schools were founded, grew to considerable size, and were abandoned, leaving the districts with no schools or very small schools supported by a limited population.

Although the people recognized the need for education in the high school grades, it was very difficult to maintain grades 9 through 12 in the small rural schools. A number of the small districts found it necessary to combine to offer high school work. The law authorized "union high school districts" to organize in 1889 and "county high school districts" in 1909. These were established in numerous areas. Union high school districts, in contrast to high schools organized on a countywide basis, were formed by cooperating districts in a smaller area. By 1957, there were 41 of these special high school districts in the state.

The situation was further confused by numerous but separate legislative provisions, "governing boundary changes, dissolution and annexation of districts, organization of unorganized territory, and reorganization of districts." The state established a system of classifying districts into first, second, and third class, according to the pupil population.

By the 1940's, there was a general awareness that the state's district organization was chaotic and unplanned. A number of bills were introduced in the General Assembly to correct the problem. In 1947, a "county unit" bill passed the Senate but failed in the House. Two years later, the assembly passed a sweeping reorganization act providing for the election of county committees to study district organization and recommend plans for reorganization. Vigorous opposition to the law by the Colorado School Protective Association and affiliated rural groups finally prompted the 1951 Legislature to amend it to such an extent that it was made virtually inoperative. In the meantime, at least 29 counties had reorganized.

The continuing need for more instructionally effective administrative units made it impossible to let the matter rest. In 1957 a new reorganization bill was introduced in the General Assembly. Despite opposition so strong that deadlock nearly resulted, the bill eventually was passed and provided the basis for reorganizing districts throughout the state. By the end of 1965, the total number of districts had been reduced to 184, as indicated in Appendix C, Table 2. There are still many districts too small to offer effective programs, but the state has made much progress.

Both reorganization acts of 1949 and 1957 required the department to exercise leadership. Although the responsibility for planning and implementing reorganization rested in the hands of local county committees, the organization and management division provided consultation and encouragement. The state department had a direct responsibility in only one respect: the law required all reorganization plans to be submitted to the commissioner for his approval before elections to consider them could be held.

Guidance Services

The State Board for Vocational Education initiated state guidance services in Colorado for a brief period in 1945 and 1946, when it employed a supervisor of vocational guidance, partially supported by federal funds available under the George-Barden Act.

The position then lapsed until 1949. The new supervisor changed the emphasis from vocational guidance to guidance services in general. Only a small number of schools—no more than 30 outside of Denver—employed counselors, and few of those assigned were qualified by special training.

By establishing a vigorous program of visitation and consultation, the supervisor and his staff contacted nearly all high schools within a 3-year period. He conducted regional conferences and commenced publishing the *Colorado Guidance Newsletter.* In cooperation with the state's teacher training institutions, an in-service training program was taken to the high schools. At the same time, George-Barden funds were used to provide a limited number of pilot programs. Progress in developing formal guidance programs in the high schools was slow, but steady.

In 1955, by agreement with the vocational education board, the state department assumed responsibility for guidance services. The transfer was based on the assumption that guidance services should continue to be broader than helping students with vocational choices and that these services logically belonged with the newly reorganized Department of Education's instructional services. H. Edgar Williams, supervisor since 1949, was transferred along with the services and continued as director of the Division of Guidance Services until his retirement in 1966.

Following the transfer, the vocational education board continued to use George-Barden funds for 2 years to support an in-service training program directed by Clarence W. Failor, a staff member of the University of Colorado.

Until 1958, guidance services continued essentially as they were before the transfer, the division consisting of the director and one clerical assistant. With the enactment of NDEA, these services expanded substantially, and the staff increased to five professional and four clerical persons. A plan was inaugurated for apportioning Title V-A, NDEA, funds to approved school guidance programs. These approved programs were selected according to standards written into the state plan, and after personal visitation and inspection. Beginning with 25 approved programs, the plan expanded to a total of 60 in 1965. At the same time, stimulated by NDEA, teacher education institutions expanded their counselor preparation programs, and the number of qualified counselors increased rapidly.

In 1951, there were less than 100 secondary school counselors in Colorado. By 1965, there were more than a thousand in Colorado high schools; of this number, 600 held counseling certificates. The overall ratio of qualified counselors to pupils was 1 counselor to each 408 pupils.

A unique feature of the department's guidance program is a test-scoring service. Initiated with funds under the National Defense Education Act, the department purchased a test-scoring machine and offered its services to all of the state's schools.

Although marked progress is evident from 1958 to 1965, a number of problems have had to be overcome, such as that of finding an adequate supply of trained counselors and developing programs of guidance services in elementary schools. Particularly, it was difficult to serve the small school systems, where qualified counselors were seldom available—

> While in districts with enrollments of 5,000 or more, 97 per cent of secondary school students were enrolled in schools with counselors (in 1964) . . . only 21 per cent were enrolled in schools with counselors in districts with secondary enrollments of less than 300 (49).

Special Education

Special education services now provided in the State Department of Education's Division of Special Education Services are a continuation of earlier state efforts that began formally when the State Child Welfare Bureau was established in 1919. This "Act To create and establish a

Child Welfare Bureau" was designed to carry out the provisions of the Sheppard-Towner Act, passed by Congress in 1921. These state-federal matching funds "enabled the bureau to carry out a generalized public health nursing program, traveling health clinics, etc., from 1922 to 1929" (50).

The Sheppard-Towner funds were withdrawn in 1929, but a limited state appropriation continued to maintain the Bureau through 1932. In 1936, following Congress' enactment of the Social Security Act, the State Department of Public Welfare created a Division of Child Welfare. In the same year, at an extraordinary session, the General Assembly passed a law changing the Child Welfare Bureau to the Bureau of Home and School Services and placing it as a division in the State Department of Education.

The functions of the bureau did not change significantly. It continued to be primarily concerned with educating the physically handicapped children, but it also stressed parent and safety education. In 1937, the first school for crippled children, St. Anthony's Neighborhood House, was begun in Denver under the auspices of the State Department of Education. In 1945, the General Assembly increased appropriations for physically handicapped children. In 1948, the Evans School in Denver began two classes for mentally handicapped children. The following year, mainly through the efforts of legislator Betty Pellett, the General Assembly passed another enabling act strengthening special education by reimbursing for mentally handicapped as well as physically handicapped.

In 1953, the assembly reached a high point in its efforts to improve special education in Colorado by passing House Bill 108. This law provided "for reimbursement to local districts for excess cost of special education classes and for reimbursement of 80 per cent of the salaries of speech correctionists" (51). At that time, the assembly voted an annual appropriation of $200,000 for special education.

In particular, Mrs. Dorothy Craig Tynar, first a consultant and in 1950 the head of the new special education services division, deserves special mention for her many years of yeoman service in stimulating special education programs in the state. Miss Carey J. Downing, supervisor of the division, pioneered survey work on the need for special education. The Division of Mental Health and Institutions combined with the Division of Special Education in 1958. E. Ellis Graham, the director, provided strong leadership in expanding the services and in securing increasing legislative support for special education (see Appendix C, Table 3).

While special education appropriations have climbed steadily during recent years, they have not been sufficient to keep pace with the state's needs, according to the claims submitted by local districts. John A. Ogden, who became director of the division in 1964, stressed this need:

> But we have a long way to go. The total of 18,412 children served by some kind of special education program during the 1963-64 school year constitutes only 4.05 per cent of the approximately 500,000 children enrolled in public schools last year. Only 84 of the operating school districts in Colorado provided some kind of special education. Twenty-three of the 63 counties in the state provided no service whatever. The $1,200,000 appropriations last year allowed the state to reimburse only 53.7 per cent of the total claims of $2,230,601.41 (52).

In 1965, the General Assembly, in recodifying the school laws, wrote the Handicapped Children's Education Act. This law effected two major changes: (1) it added the "educationally handicapped" as another category of handicapped children; and (2) it specified that reimbursement from the state would be 80 percent of the salaries paid approved personnel. The educationally handicapped, defined as those children "emotionally handicapped or perceptually handicapped, or both," was the one large group of handicapped children not being served, so this was considered a major breakthrough. The change in the reimbursement procedures from excess costs to 80 percent of the salaries facilitated less complicated administrative procedures.

School Lunch Program

For 4 years prior to the enactment of the National School Lunch Act by Congress in 1946, the Colorado office of the U.S. Department of Agriculture's Division of Food Distribution contracted directly with school districts for operating the food services in about 250 schools. Immediately following the federal legislation, the Colorado State Department of Education signed an agreement with the U.S. Department of Agriculture to administer the school lunch program. The department then established in October 1946 a School Lunch Division. The following year, the General Assembly passed an enabling act to allow the state to participate in the new program (53).

When the state department took over the school lunch program from the State Office of Food Distribution in the fall of 1946, 206 schools were serving an average of 24,824 Type A lunches; by 1948, 257 schools were in the program. The school food service continued to expand as most new schools included food service facilities, and many older schools either provided makeshift facilities or added to the old.

In 1965, 936 participating schools served 189,628 Type A lunches daily. At this time, all but three districts were participating, and these three were mountain districts with very few students.

Although federal appropriations for the National School Lunch Act increased from approximately $62 million to $165 million in 1965, federal cash assistance did not keep pace with the program's growth. Thus, the federal per-pupil contribution in Colorado decreased from 9¢ to less than 4¢ during this period. In addition to cash assistance, the Department of Agriculture donated commodities to schools, and these commodities constituted approximately 20 percent of the total food costs for the Type A lunch.

Adult Education

As in many other states, the Colorado adult education programs began in a few public school districts. The most notable was organized in 1916 at the Emily Griffith Opportunity School, the public school adult education unit for the Denver public schools.

Prior to World War II, the elected state superintendents did not feel that the department had any responsibility for educating adults in public schools. But shortly after the war, Marguerite Juchem, a consultant in secondary education, was charged with the task of relating the work of the department to adult education. However, her duties tended to be limited to writing reports relating to the activities of the Council of Adult Education and the Adult Education Council of Denver.

In the early 1950's, the staff of the State Board for Vocational Education, which already handled federally subsidized programs in trade and industry, was interested in promoting adult education in homemaking, but there was little contact with the Department of Education in its operation. There was also little or no participation by the department in the state's largest adult education program, administered by the Cooperative Extension Service of Colorado State College of Agriculture and Mechanical Arts at Ft. Collins. The University of Denver offered the only graduate program for preparing professional adult educators, except for one or two courses available at the University of Colorado and the Agriculture and Mechanical Arts College.

When H. Grant Vest became commissioner of education, he secured approval from the state board to study the adult education programs in Colorado and get the opinions of educational and civic leaders concerning the development of adult education programs sponsored by the public schools. At his suggestion, the board appointed an Adult Education Committee to conduct the study. Upon this committee's recommendation, the state board acquired the services of two University of Denver doctoral students to work under the direction of Roy B. Minnis, professor of adult education.

Dr. Minnis and the students collected the field data for the state committee, which in turn recommended to the state board and the commissioner that they establish a division of adult education and secure a professional staff. In 1955, the Colorado State Department of Education then became the first recipient of a National Association for Public School Adult Education (NAPSAE) grant, funded by the Ford Foundation to create a position in adult education. That same year the state board hired Dr. Minnis to be director of adult education.

The state received another grant from NAPSAE to provide moneys to local institutions for innovative projects in adult education. Among the projects approved was one for community development in Cortez, a great decisions discussion in international understanding at Mesa Junior College in Grand Junction, and a community problems and social issues discussion program at Limon. The grant also sponsored a survey of adult education needs in Lamar, community involvements for adult education programs in the newly organized Cherry Creek district, and a two-county adult education service project at Otero Junior College at La Junta.

In the midfifties, the department of education began collecting statistical data on the kinds of programs and the number of adults engaged in continuing education offered by the public schools. It was found that the school districts providing such services increased substantially, and the number of persons participating tripled or quadrupled.

During the same period, the Colorado Education Association organized the very active Adult Education Committee. It, in turn, helped develop a state organization known as the Colorado Association for Public School Adult Education, an affiliate of the National Association for Public School Adult Education.

Dr. Minnis accepted a position in adult education with the U.S. Office of Education in 1958, and the supervisor of the junior college section doubled as consultant in adult education until 1962, when Calvin Orr was appointed section head for adult education in the newly organized Division of Education Beyond High School. Orr was instrumental in obtaining funds from the U.S. Office of Education in the spring of 1964 for a cooperative research project, involving Texas, Colorado, Arizona, and New Mexico, to assess the educational needs of agricultural migrants. The staff would then make recommendations to meet the educational needs of these workers.

In 1964, the Economic Opportunity Act provided moneys to state departments of education for conducting adult basic education. In March 1965, the department developed the Colorado State Plan for Adult Basic Education, enabling the state to participate in these funds (54).

State Library

Since territorial days, the Colorado State Library has been considered part of the Department of Education. In 1861, the Territorial Legislature designated the territorial superintendent of common schools as ex officio state librarian (55). And, except for a period from 1865 to 1877, the chief state school officer has continued to hold this title. Actually, no state library was established until Colorado became a state in 1877, and, at this time—

> It did not offer traditional public library services. Its small staff was engaged in the collection and processing of local, state, and federal documents, and in the distribution of Colorado publications to public agencies . . . outside the state and to offices of government, both local and state, within Colorado (56).

The General Assembly created a State Board of Library Commissioners in 1899, to strengthen and stimulate library service throughout Colorado. The commissioners, appointed by the Governor for 5-year terms, were responsible for providing counseling services to "all free libraries," helping establish new libraries, assisting in library management and control, and reporting biennially to the Governor. All libraries supported by public funds were required to report to the commission.

Through the influence of the State Federation Women's Clubs, in 1903, the General Assembly passed a law establishing a Colorado Traveling Library Commission to make, for the first time, quantity book loans. The 1929 General Assembly merged the library commissioners with the Colorado Traveling Library Commission to form the Colorado Library Commission. In 1933, however, when a new administrative code went into effect, this commission's functions were transferred to the Colorado State Library. This code also extended the State Library program to include general and extension library services.

New legislation in 1947 repealed all previous library statutes and provided for modern library services. Subsequent amendments merely changed the financing of county libraries and dealt with the State Library's advisory and financial assistance to local programs. An amendment in 1961 specifically provided bookmobile services for distributing materials. Later in the same year the assembly appropriated $100,000 for public library grants to be distributed to qualifying local units.

The services of the State Library increased substantially from 1955 to 1965 and, although not adequate in all areas, made a marked contribution to the libraries of Colorado. For instance, the State Library loaned materials to public libraries and public schools, contracted with libraries for services in specific areas, rendered reference and advisory assistance to state institutions, and offered services to state officials and departments. However, the staff considered its "consultation and advice to schools, public and state-supported libraries, and to individuals or groups of persons desiring to establish libraries . . . . the most important service available from the State Library" (57).

Mobile units, for both service and demonstration, constituted one of the State Library's important contributions to the state, beginning with one improvised unit shortly after World War II. A unit was added in 1955, and within 5 years four units were in use throughout the state. The use of these mobile units resulted in regional and multicounty units' operating their own.

The Library Services Act, passed by Congress in 1956 to promote public libraries in rural areas, greatly influenced the State Library's activities. Colorado initiated its program in April 1957, and the State Library attempted to secure personnel and facilities to serve libraries in rural areas all over the state. Involvement in the federal program did force it to make some curtailments in its services to schools and libraries in communities with populations in excess of 10,000. Although the gains are difficult to assess statistically, on the whole, the program met with substantial success with its on-the-job training, conferences and institutes, and intensive work with local and state officials.

Publications and Public Information

Throughout its history, the Colorado State Department of Education attempted to inform the public through letters, announcements, and releases to news media. Prior to the reorganization movement in the early 1950's, most of its publications were mimeographed aids and reports. No one was specifically assigned to oversee the editing and production of these materials. For many years, the superintendent undertook these publications chores personally, usually with limited clerical assistance. Later, they were performed by personnel in the various divisions.

In 1952, the department published its first newsletter, called "ADES." The brainchild of Mrs. Helen Downing, administrative assistant to the commissioner, "ADES" first appeared in mimeographed form, but was commercially printed the next year. Following closely the department's reorganization in 1951, the newsletter helped show the need to disseminate more news to the state's school districts.

Marcus Eimas, employed part time in May 1955 to assist with publications, was the department's first person in this field. The position became full time that July, and the following March, Ray E. Petersen, an Ohio newspaper reporter, replaced Eimas with the title "supervisor of publications." His duties were as follows:

> Public relations and news releases are the responsibility of the Commissioner, but he is being assisted at his discretion by the supervisor of publications and others, so that educational information is more timely and complete in reaching the several news media in the state . . . . Departmental publications have mounted in stature and significance, and the supervisor of publications has developed into a fulltime job for the preparation and assembling of copy, editing, proofreading, and layouts necessary to put materials into printed form (58).

When E. Dean Coon succeeded Petersen in 1961, he became director of the new Division of Publications and Public Information. Four years later, funds from the Elementary and Secondary Education Act enabled the division to employ another professional person, K. Douglas Bassett.

As the division developed, it assumed broader responsibilities: facilitating communication between the department and public schools, and using a variety of media to inform the general public of the status and needs of the public schools. These functions, discharged through publications of instructional guides, statistical reports, and periodicals, are designed to improve the schools' educational program.

The division assists and instructs department staff members and administrators in planning, writing, and editing materials. Its staff also handles printing jobs, edits a biweekly newspaper, and writes news and feature articles. In addition, the staff also assumes some responsibility for helping school people improve publications and public information, and tries to inform journalism teachers of trends, current practices, innovations, and curriculum materials in the field (59).

Research and Development

The state department first used the word *research* for a staff title in 1945, when it employed a director of finance and research. In 1954, following the reorganization, a Division of School Finance was created, but research did not share in the title. The Division of Research was officially established 2 years later, but its work was almost entirely statistical. Three years later, a department reorganization resulted in a Division of Research and Statistics.

By 1955, educational leaders were expressing a concern for improved educational research. Representatives of institutions of higher education, school administrators, school boards, teachers, and the state department discussed the matter and finally agreed that some kind of cooperative research council should be organized. It was 4 years later, however, before a committee representing these groups met with the State Board of Education to propose that such an educational research council be established through the initiative of the Department of Education, which would serve as its official home. The committee further recommended that the department's research and statistics division be expanded to engage in more statewide educational research. The board agreed to consider the matter fully.

By April 1960, the committee formally drafted a proposal calling for the establishment of a Colorado Council on Educational Research to be "an official organization, the members of which will be appointed by the State Board of Education to serve as an advisory committee to the State Department of Education on matters relating to educational research" (60). Appointments to the council were made from a list of persons nominated by agencies, institutions, and professional organizations interested in educational research, including all institutions of higher learning, all legitimate professional groups, certain school districts, and appropriate state agencies. In the same month, the state board agreed to appoint members to the council upon receipt of nominations from groups planning to participate.

Four years later, the functions of research and statistics were separated and the research and development division established. Two cooperative research projects and the Western States Small Schools Project were assigned to this division. At the same time, the Colorado Council on Educational Research was disbanded, and a Research and Development Advisory Committee was established.

The Division of Research and Development assumed more and more tasks. Following the enactment of the Elementary and Secondary Education Act in 1965, it became responsible for the administration of Titles III and IV. It also became responsible for stimulating state research activity in all areas of education, helping determine the areas in which research was needed, and encouraging local districts and teachers to undertake research and experimental activities. It encourages statewide coordination and cooperation with all educational agencies. Division members write research proposals and assist others in doing so, seek funds for research, present proposals to the U.S. Office of Education and to foundations, analyze and evaluate educational research, and disseminate its findings (61).

Legal Functions

State superintendents have always been expected to give answers to legal questions about educational matters. Since the attorney general was a member ex officio of the state board in its early history, involved legal questions were referred to his office, and the same is true today. However, the state superintendent was specifically designated to answer legal questions, and more often he personally handled them during the early days of the department.

The Division of Legal Services was created in 1932, when Lucy C. Auld joined the department as deputy superintendent of instruction. Mrs. Auld, later administrative assistant to the commissioner, handled these problems for the commissioner and in 1958 became director of school legal services.

The legal division was created to provide information found in the statutes, in case law, and in administrative rulings to any person or entity requiring it. This division also interprets the law.

The legal division gives information and advice by letter or telephone, and indirectly through department personnel, school district and county offices, and publications. Its staff also assists other department personnel to serve school districts. In addition, the division compiles educational legislation annually and assists with legislation in which the department is interested (62).

State-Federal Relations

The federal government's increasing participation in education has had marked effects on the Colorado State Department of Education. While the department recognized the great need for statewide leadership in curriculum development and in instructional improvement, sufficient state funds were not available. Furthermore, the overwhelming need for district reorganization from 1945 to 1965 overshadowed these curricular and instructional needs. But funds under the National Defense Education Act enabled the department to employ staff specialists in critical subject areas, in guidance and counseling, and in statistical services. With increasing momentum, the department became a leader in curriculum reform and was able to assist local school districts in their instruction.

The Library Services and Construction Act enabled the State Library to give more help to public libraries and local school districts in developing comprehensive library programs.

The unique history of the state, with particular reference to its intense commitment to independence and individualism, caused many of its citizens to question the increasing participation of the federal government in education. The need for a clarification and understanding of the proper roles of local, state, and federal agenies was pointed out by State Commissioner of Education Byron W. Hansford as follows:

> We need a true partnership of local, state, and national interests to bring about the dramatic improvements that are urgently needed in American education; but this partnership *must* be based on mutual respect and goodwill. The partnership must not be dominated by one level (63).

FOOTNOTES

1. The Department of Education was known as the Department of Public Instruction until its name was changed in 1932.
2. University of Denver, Denver Research Institute, *Economic Growth in Colorado* (Denver: The University, 1963), p. 7.
3. Horace Morrison Hale, *et al., Education in Colorado, 1861-1865* (Denver: Colorado News Printing Co., 1885), p. 7.
4. Leroy R. Hafen, *Colorado and Its People,* I (4 vols.; New York: Lewis Historical Publishing Co., 1948), 9-31.
5. Colorado, *General Laws* (1877), art. 4, sec. 1, p. 33; art. 9, sec. 1, p. 54. Colorado, *Constitution* (1877), p. 54. This copy of the Constitution is in the back of the first volume titled *General Laws.*
6. Commissioner of Education, *Report of Regional Conferences of Colorado School Superintendents, 1956-1957* (Denver: Department of Education, March 1957), p. 23.
7. Superintendent of Public Instruction, *First Biennial Report, 1877-1878,* p. 29.
8. Superintendent of Public Instruction, *Fourth Biennial Report, 1883-1885,* p. 28.
9. Superintendent of Public Instruction, *Ninth Biennial Report, 1893-1894,* p. 18.
10 Superintendent of Public Instruction, *Second Biennial Report, 1879-1880,* pp. 27-34; *Third Biennial Report, 1881-1882,* pp. 17-23; *Fifth Biennial Report, 1885-1886,* pp. 20-25.
11. Superintendent of Public Instruction, *Twenty-Fourth Biennial Report, 1923-1924,* p. 5.
12. Superintendent of Public Instruction, *Biennial Report, 1921-1922,* p. 11. Superintendent Lewis omitted ordinal numbers from her biennial reports.
13. Superintendent of Public Instruction, *Thirty-Third Biennial Report, 1940-1942,* p. 8.
14. Superintendent of Public Instruction, *Twelfth Biennial Report, 1899-1900,* p. 16.
15. Superintendent of Public Instruction, *Twenty-Second Biennial Report, 1917-1918,* p. 81.
16. Superintendent of Public Instruction, *Biennial Report, 1927-1928,* p. 40. Superintendent Lewis omitted ordinal numbers from her biennial reports.
17. Superintendent of Public Instruction, *Twenty-Eighth Biennial Report, 1930-1932,* pp. 4-5.
18. Superintendent of Public Instruction, *Twenty-First Biennial Report, 1915-1916,* p. 16.
19. Superintendent of Public Instruction, *Twelfth Biennial Report, 1899-1900,* p. 13.
20. Superintendent of Public Instruction, *Twenty-Eighth Biennial Report, 1930-1932,* p. 6.
21. Superintendent of Public Instruction, *Twenty-Ninth Biennial Report, 1933-1934,* p. 135.
22. *Colorado School Journal,* XVI, No. 6 (February 1931), 28.
23. John R. Little, "Reorganization of State Department: A Fundamental Issue," *Colorado School Journal,* LXIII, No. 6 (March 1948), 9.
24. Commissioner of Education, *State School Board Readies Plan for Reorganization of the State Department of Education* (Denver: Department of Education, 1951), p. 1.
25. Commissioner of Education, *Thirty-Ninth Biennial Report, 1952-1954,* p. 16.
26. *Ibid.,* p. 17.
27. The assistant commissioner over this office was Burtis E. Taylor.
28. According to Leo P. Black, assistant commissioner of education, the desire to render leadership and service to the schools resulted in the use of the term *consultant,* rather than that of *supervisor.*
29. Dr. Black has continued to serve in that capacity to the present time.

30. Much of the information for the section on "The Department's Basic Design" was secured from Raymond A. McGuire, assistant commissioner for the office of administrative services, and from Leo P. Black, assistant commissioner for instructional services.

31. Colorado, *Revised Statutes* (1965), ch. 123, art. 1, sec. 13.

32. Material for this section was secured directly from Mrs. Helen H. Downing, director of the Division of Departmental Administration.

33. Commissioner of Education, *Forty-Fourth Biennial Report, 1962-1964,* p. 1.

34. Colorado, *Session Laws* (1949), ch. 153, sec. 5c, p. 365.

35. Colorado Legislative Council, "State Aid to Schools," Research Bulletin No. 117, Denver, The Council, 1966, p. 1. (Mimeographed.)

36. Wilmore *v.* Annear, auditor, *et al.,* 100 Colo. 106, 65 pp. 2d 1433 (1937).

37. Colorado, *Session Laws* (1937), ch. 174, sec. 17, p. 676.

38. Colorado Legislative Council, *op. cit.,* p. 2.

39. *Ibid.,* p. 18. The Property Tax Relief Fund was the flat grant amount appropriated by the state in an effort to halt local property tax increases for 1 year. The fund has continued, and state money was added in 1966, 1967, and 1968.

40. Estimates provided by the Division of Finance and Statistics, Department of Education.

41. Much of the information on certification in Colorado was secured from a report, "A Systematic Approach to Intelligent Change–Certification Reform in Colorado," by Otto G. Ruff, director of Teacher Education and Certification, Department of Education, January 8, 1962. (Mimeographed.)

42. Superintendent of Public Instruction, *Twenty–Third Biennial Report, 1921-1922,* p. 8.

43. Lucy C. Auld, *Constitutional Amendment Reorganizing School Laws of the State of Colorado* (Denver: Department of Education, 1956), ch. 123, art. 1, sec. 5, p. 19.

44. Department of Education, *Accreditation of Colorado Schools, Criteria and Procedures* (Denver: The Department, 1959), p. 4.

45. *Ibid.,* p. 4.

46. *Ibid.,* p. 5.

47. Colorado, *General Laws (1877), Constitution,* art. 9, sec. 15, p. 57.

48. Stanley A. Leftwich, "The Colorado Story of District Organization," an address prepared for the Conference on School District Organization at Harrisburg, Pennsylvania, on April 21-22, 1966. Leftwich is director of the Division of Organization and Management of the Department of Education.

49. Commissioner of Education, *Forty-Fourth Biennial Report, 1962-1964,* p. 12.

50. John A. Ogden, quotations from an address delivered to a section of the Colorado Education Association in October 1964, p. 7. Ogden is director of the Division of Special Education Services, Department of Education.

51. *Ibid.,* p. 12.

52. *Ibid.,* p. 14.

53. Information for this section was secured directly from Charles Lilley, director of School Lunch, Department of Education.

54. The information for this section was secured from an unpublished statement by Gary A. Eyre and Roy B. Minnis, "A History of Adult Education in the Colorado State Department of Education," November 1967. (Mimeographed.)

55. Gordon L. Bennett, "Colorado State Library – Self Survey," unpublished work at the Department of Education, Denver, 1961, p. 3.

56. *Ibid.,* pp. 3-4.

57. *Ibid.,* p. 15.

58. Commissioner of Education, *Fortieth Biennial Report, 1954-1956,* p. 139.

59. Information for this section was secured from K. Douglas Bassett, director of the Division of Publications and Public Information, Department of Education.

60. Commissioner of Education, *Forty-Second Biennial Report, 1958-1960,* p. 220.

61. Information for this section was secured from Russell B. Vlaanderen, director of the Division of Research and Development, Department of Education.

62. Information for this section was secured from D. Reese Miller, director of the Division of Legal Services, Department of Education.

63. Byron W. Hansford, address to the Council of Chief State School Officers and U.S. Office of Education personnel at a Conference on Federal-State Cooperation in American Education, Washington, D.C., June 23, 1967.

BIBLIOGRAPHY

Public Documents

Colorado. *Constitution.* (1876).

——*General Laws, Session Laws, Revised Statutes* (1877-1965).

Wilmore *v.* Annear, auditor, *et al.,* 100 Colo. 106, 65, p. 2d, 1433.

Books

Auld, Lucy C. *Constitutional Amendment Reorganizing*

School Laws of the State of Colorado. Denver: Department of Education, 1956.

Department of Education, *Accreditation of Colorado Schools, Criteria and Procedures.* Denver: The Department, 1959.

Hafen, Leroy R. *Colorado and Its People.* 4 vols. New York: Lewis Historical Publishing Co., 1948.

Hale, Horace Morrison, *et al. Education in Colorado, 1861-1865.* Denver: Colorado News Printing Co., 1885.

Reports

Commissioner of Education. *Report of Regional Conferences of Colorado School Superintendents, 1956-1957.* Denver: Department of Education, 1957.

—— *State School Board Readies Plan for Reorganization of the State Department of Education.* Denver: Department of Education, 1951.

Department of Education. *Our Schools Are the Cornerstone of Democracy.* Denver: The Department, 1955.

Department of Education, Division of Guidance Services. *Annual Report to the U.S. Office of Education.* Denver: The Department, 1966.

Superintendents of Public Instruction and Commissioners of Education. *Biennial Reports,* 1877-1964. Denver: Department of Education.

University of Denver, Bureau of Research, School of Education. *Teacher Certification.* Denver: The University, 1959.

University of Denver, Denver Research Institute. *Economic Growth in Colorado.* Denver: The University, 1963.

Articles and Periodicals

Colorado School Journal, Vol. XVI, No. 6 (February, 1931); Vol. LXV (October 1949).

Little, John R. "Reorganization of State Department: A Fundamental Issue." *Colorado School Journal,* LXIII, No. 6 (March 1948), 9.

Unpublished Material

Bennett, Gordon L. "Colorado State Library: Self Survey." Unpublished work at the Department of Education, Denver, 1961. (Mimeographed.)

Colorado Legislative Council. "State Aid to Schools." Research Bulletin No. 117, Denver, The Council, 1966. (Mimeographed.)

Eyre, Gary A., and Minnis, Roy B. "A History of Adult Education in the Colorado State Department of Education." Denver, Department of Education, 1967. (Mimeographed.)

Ruff, Otto G. "A Systematic Approach to Intelligent Change: Certification Reform in Colorado." A Report at the Department of Education, Denver, January 8, 1962. (Mimeographed.)

Other Sources

Freed, Nettie S. Personal interview, April 25, 1967.

Hansford, Byron W. Address to the Council of Chief State School Officers and U.S. Office of Education personnel at a Conference on Federal-State Cooperation in American Education, Washington, D.C., June 23, 1967.

Leftwich, Stanley. "The Colorado Story of District Organization." Address prepared for the Conference on School District Organization at Harrisburg, Pennsylvania, on April 21-22, 1966.

Ogden, John A. Address delivered to a section of the Colorado Education Association in October 1964.

Staff, Department of Education. Personal interviews with various members, May to December 1967.

Appendix A

COLORADO CHIEF STATE SCHOOL OFFICERS

Territorial School Superintendents

1861-63	W. J. Curtice
1863-65	William S. Walker
1865-67	A. W. Atkins
1867-69	Columbus Nuckrolls
1869-73	William C. Lothrop
1873-76	Horace M. Hale

State Superintendents of Public Instruction

1877-80	Joseph C. Shattuck
1881-82	L. S. Cornell
1883-84	Joseph C. Shattuck
1885-88	L. S. Cornell
1889-90	Fred Dick
1891-92	Nathan B. Coy
1893-94	J. F. Murray
1895-96	Mrs. A. J. Peavey
1897-98	Grace Espey Patton
1899-1904	Mrs. Helen L. Grenfell
1905-1908	Katherine L. Craig
1909-10	Katherine M. Cook
1911-12	Helen Marsh Wixson
1913-20	Mary C. C. Bradford
1921-22	Katherine L. Craig
1923-26	Mary C. C. Bradford
1927-30	Katherine L. Craig
1931-46	Inez Johnson Lewis
1947-48	Nettie S. Freed

(Mrs. Freed was the last of the state superintendents and the first commissioner of education in Colorado.)

State Commissioners of Education

1949-51	Nettie S. Freed
1951-52	J. Burton Vasche
1952-53	Burtis E. Taylor (Interim)
1953-59	H. Grant Vest
1959-60	John H. Swenson (Interim)
1960-	Byron W. Hansford

Appendix B

Chart I.--COLORADO DEPARTMENTAL PERSONNEL, 1900-40

Position	1900	1910	1920	1930	1940
State Superintendent	1	1	1	1	1
Deputy Superintendent[a]	1	1	1	1	1
Assistant State Librarian[b]	1	1	1	1	...
State Supervisor of Rural Schools	...	...	1	...	...
Director of Elementary Education[c]	...	...	...	...	1
State Teacher of Adult Blind	...	...	1	...	...
Supervisor of Certification	...	...	...	1	1
Assistant to Supervisor of Certification	...	...	...	1	...
Special Examiner and Grader	...	...	...	1	...
Director of Correspondence and Records	...	...	...	...	1
Bookkeeper and Traveling Auditor	...	...	...	...	1
Educational Statistician[d]	...	...	1	1	1
Clerical	1	3	3	6	8
Total	4	6	9	13	15

Source:

Table developed from Biennial Reports of the State Superintendents of Public Instruction.

[a] Designated as "Assistant Superintendent" in 1900.

[b] Superintendent of Public Instruction served as State Librarian, ex officio.

[c] Full title, "Director of Elementary Education and Curricula."

[d] Designated simply as "Statistician" in 1940.

Appendix B

Chart II.--COLORADO DEPARTMENT OF EDUCATION, 1942

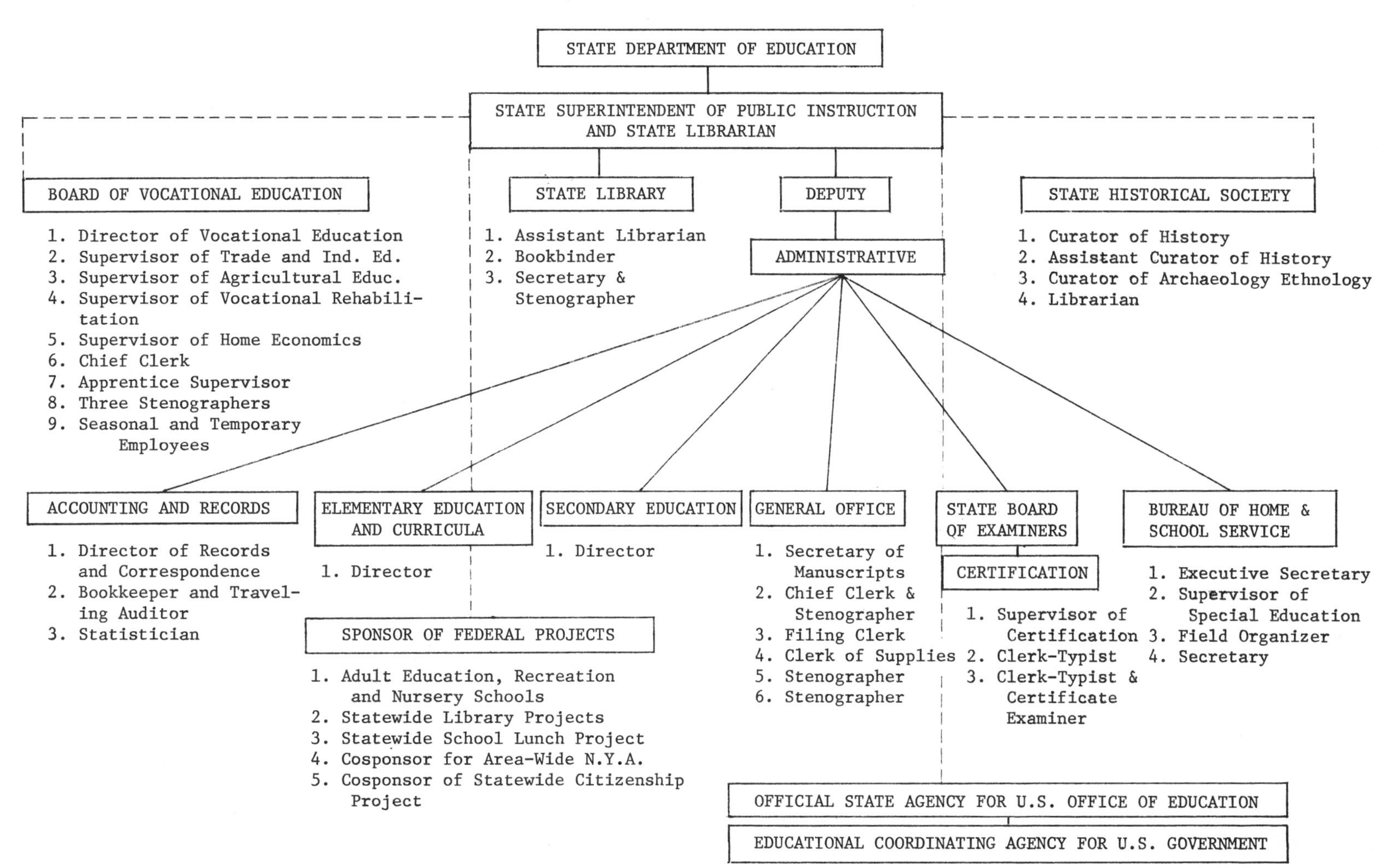

Appendix B

Chart III.--COLORADO DEPARTMENTAL PERSONNEL, 1948 (Just prior to reorganization)

			Total
Official Staff			
State Superintendent	1		
Deputy Superintendent	1		
Administrative Assistant	1		
Supervisor of Secondary Education	1		
Supervisor of Elementary Education	1		
Director of Finance and Research	1		
Accountant	1		
Clerical		8	
	7	8	15
Teacher Certification			
Supervisor	1		
Clerical		2	
	1	2	3
School Lunch			
Supervisor	1		
Auditor	1		
Clerical		2	
	2	2	4
Bureau of Home and School Service			
Supervisor of Special Education	1		
Teacher	1		
Clerical		1	
	2	1	3
State Library			
Deputy State Librarian	1		
Library Assistant	2		
Clerical		2	
	3	2	5
Total Professional	15		
Total Clerical		15	
Total Personnel			30

Appendix B

Chart IV.--COLORADO DEPARTMENT OF EDUCATION, EARLY 1950'S

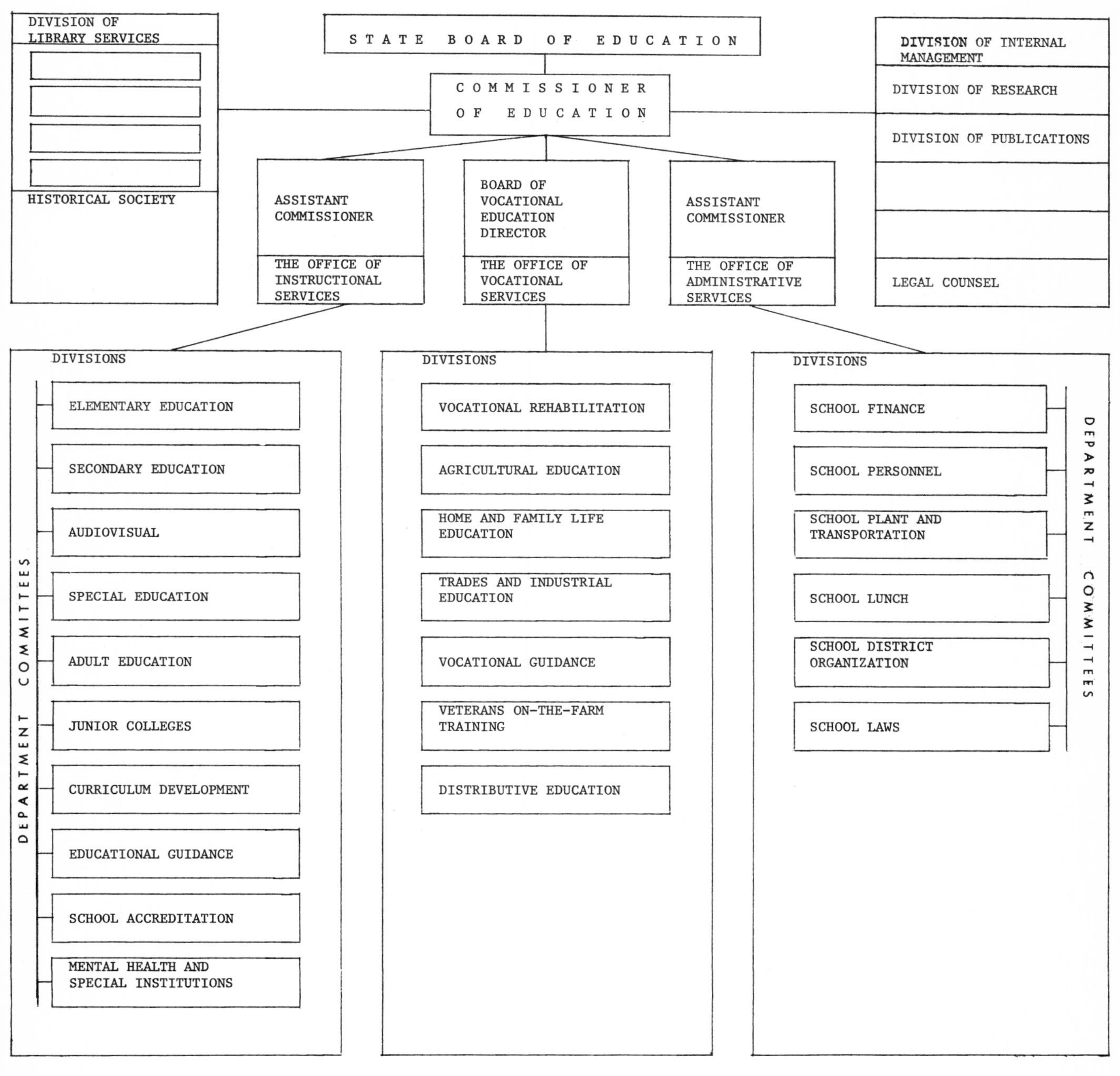

DIVISION OF LIBRARY SERVICES
HISTORICAL SOCIETY
STATE BOARD OF EDUCATION
COMMISSIONER OF EDUCATION
DIVISION OF INTERNAL MANAGEMENT
DIVISION OF RESEARCH
DIVISION OF PUBLICATIONS
LEGAL COUNSEL
ASSISTANT COMMISSIONER
THE OFFICE OF INSTRUCTIONAL SERVICES
BOARD OF VOCATIONAL EDUCATION DIRECTOR
THE OFFICE OF VOCATIONAL SERVICES
ASSISTANT COMMISSIONER
THE OFFICE OF ADMINISTRATIVE SERVICES
DIVISIONS
DEPARTMENT COMMITTEES
ELEMENTARY EDUCATION
SECONDARY EDUCATION
AUDIOVISUAL
SPECIAL EDUCATION
ADULT EDUCATION
JUNIOR COLLEGES
CURRICULUM DEVELOPMENT
EDUCATIONAL GUIDANCE
SCHOOL ACCREDITATION
MENTAL HEALTH AND SPECIAL INSTITUTIONS
DIVISIONS
VOCATIONAL REHABILITATION
AGRICULTURAL EDUCATION
HOME AND FAMILY LIFE EDUCATION
TRADES AND INDUSTRIAL EDUCATION
VOCATIONAL GUIDANCE
VETERANS ON-THE-FARM TRAINING
DISTRIBUTIVE EDUCATION
DIVISIONS
SCHOOL FINANCE
SCHOOL PERSONNEL
SCHOOL PLANT AND TRANSPORTATION
SCHOOL LUNCH
SCHOOL DISTRICT ORGANIZATION
SCHOOL LAWS
DEPARTMENT COMMITTEES

Appendix B

Chart V.--COLORADO DEPARTMENT OF EDUCATION, MID-1950'S

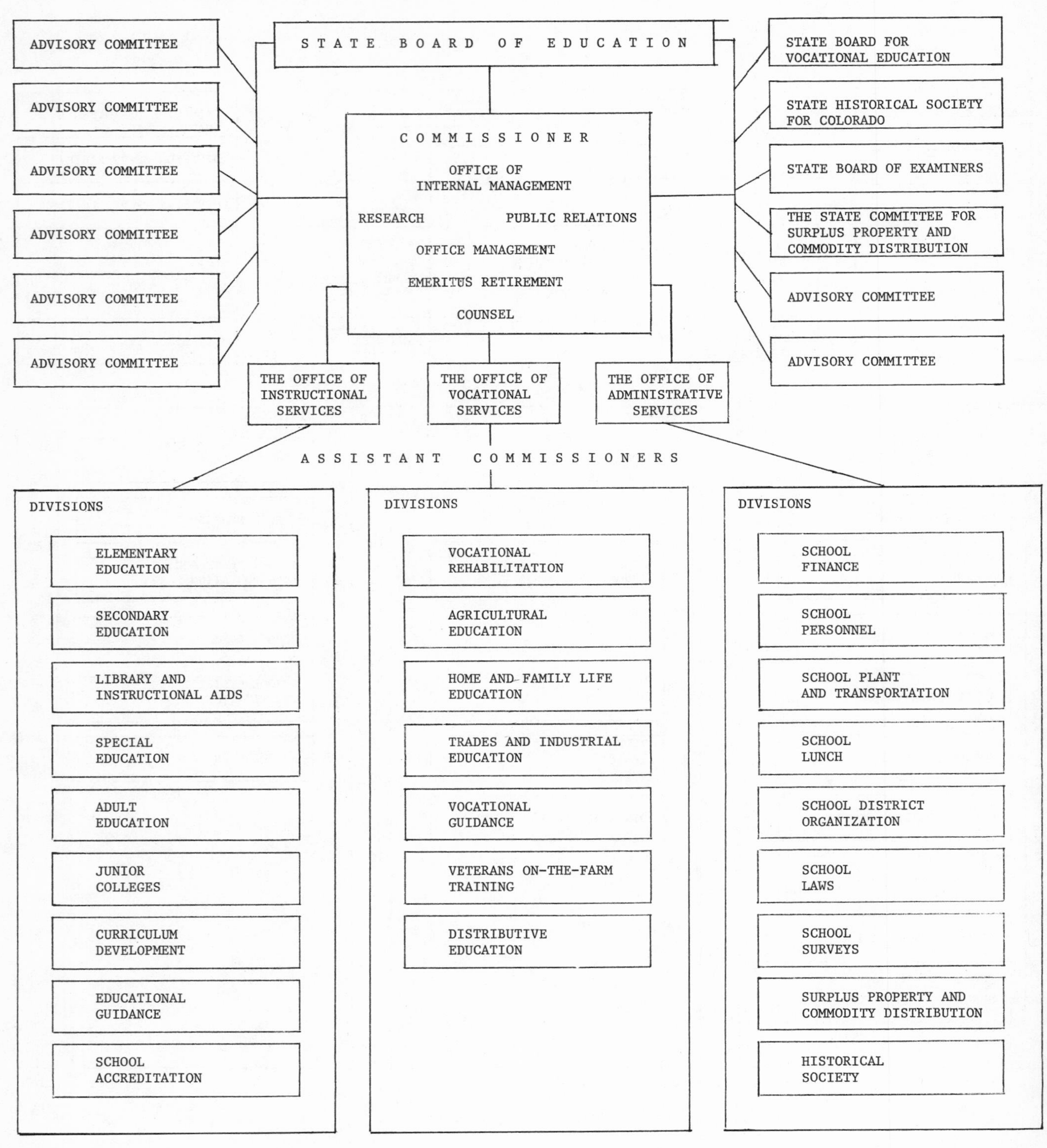

Appendix B

Chart VI.--COLORADO DEPARTMENT OF EDUCATION, 1968

COMMISSIONER OF EDUCATION

OFFICE OF ADMINISTRATIVE SERVICES

Assistant Commissioner

- Division of Accreditation
- Division of Adult Education
  - Adult Basic Education
  - Adult Education for Civil Defense
- Division of Legal Services
- Division of Organization and Management
  - Boards of Cooperative Services
  - Fiscal Planning
  - School Buildings and Transportation
  - School Finance
  - School Food Services
  - Intercommunity Cultural Relations
- Division of Teacher Education and Certification
  - Teacher Certification

OFFICE OF INSTRUCTIONAL SERVICES

Assistant Commissioner

- Division of Elementary and Secondary Education
  - Conservation Education
  - Driver Education and Traffic Safety
  - Elementary Education
  - English
  - Gifted and Creative Student Programs
  - Health, Physical Education
  - Industrial Arts
  - Mathematics
  - Modern Foreign Languages
  - Science
  - Secondary Education
  - Social Studies
- Division of Guidance Services
- Division of Research and Development
- Colorado Western States Small Schools Project
- Designing Education for the Future Project
- Division of Special Education Services
- Educationally Handicapped
  - Mentally Handicapped
  - Public Law 88-164
  - Title VI ESEA
  - Aurally and Speech Handicapped
  - Instructional Materials
  - Visually Handicapped and Crippled
- Division of Title I ESEA and P.L. 815-874
- Education of Migratory Children

OFFICE OF PLANNING SERVICES

Assistant Commissioner

Consultant in Planning

- Division of Departmental Administration
  - Senior Accountant
  - Junior Buyer
- Division of Publications and Public Information
  - Publications
- Division of Statistics and Data Processing
  - Data Processing
  - Statistical Analyses
  - Planning and Analysis
  - Data Base Management
- Division of Urban Education
  - Urban Education Project
- Interstate Project for Planning and Program Consolidation

  (Project terminates September 30, 1968)

Division of Library Services--State Library

- General Administration
  - Institutional Libraries
  - Audiovisual and Adult Education
  - Public Library Building
  - Public Library Fiscal
  - Public Library Grants
- General Services
  - Reference and Documents Librarian
  - Cataloger
  - Loans Librarian
  - Young Adult Librarian
- Public Library Services
- School Library Services and Title II ESEA
  - Instructional Materials Center
  - Computerized Instruction
  - Educational Television Librarian
- Special and Institutional Libraries
  - Title III LSCA
  - Title IV LSCA
  - Title IVA LSCA
  - Services in Correctional and Penal Institutions
  - Services in State Institutions Serving Youth
  - Services in Hospitals and Health Institutions
  - Title IVB LSCA
  - Talking Book Program

Designing Education for the Future: An Eight-State Project

(This is a semiautonomous unit with operations governed by a separate policy board.)

Appendix C

Table 1. – ANNUAL APPROPRIATIONS, COLORADO STATE DEPARTMENT OF EDUCATION BY DECADES, 1900-65

1901	$ 7,750
1911	10,700
1921	16,300
1931	23,134
1941	50,227
1951	175,154
1961	737,872[a]
1965	994,108[b]

Source:

This table was developed from Session Laws of Colorado–Long Bill Appropriations.

[a]Including State Library; excluding State Historical Society.

[b]Including relatively small amounts of money distributed locally under Title V-A, NDEA, and from school reorganization funds.

Table 2. – NUMBER OF PUBLIC ELEMENTARY AND SECONDARY SCHOOL DISTRICTS AND END-OF-YEAR ENROLLMENTS, 1900-65

School year ending on June 30	Number of school districts	End-of-year enrollment
1900	1,485	117,555
1910	1,726	168,798
1920	1,306	220,232
1930	2,041	240,175
1935	2,105	238,726
1940	2,037	212,283
1945	1,884	190,518
1950	1,759	220,840
1955	1,064	234,756
1960	415	364,583
1961	340	386,265
1962	312	407,547
1963	228	429,833
1964	204	451,918
1965	184	465,621

Source:

Division of Organization and Management, Colorado State Department of Education.

Table 3. – SPECIAL EDUCATION APPROPRIATIONS AND CLAIMS, 1956 TO 1965

Year	Appropriations	Claim amounts
1956-57	$ 400,000	$ 512,570
1957-58	400,000	568,357
1958-59	424,000	654,323
1959-60	475,000	771,978
1960-61	650,000	841,579
1961-62	800,000	1,431,601
1962-63	1,200,000	1,927,147
1963-64	1,200,000	2,230,601
1964-65	1,300,000	2,473,025
1965-66	1,884,000	2,699,804

Source:

Division of Special Education, Colorado State Department of Education.

7 Connecticut

DEPARTMENT OF EDUCATION

William H. Flaharty

Contents

ORIGIN AND EARLY DEVELOPMENT OF PUBLIC SCHOOL EDUCATION

> For the better trayning up of youth in this towne, that through God's blessings they may be fitted for publique service hereafter, either in church or comonweale, it is ordered, that a free schoole be set up, & the magistrates, with the teaching elders are entreated to consider what rules & orders are meete to be observed & what allowance may be convenient for the schoolemrs care & pajnes, wch shalbe paid out of the townes stocks (1).

Thus the New Haven Colony Records of 1641 describe the origin of the first free school in America. The Hartford Colony took similar action soon after.

In 1650, this "town" action was followed by "state" action when the Connecticut Colony adopted provisions for education as follows:

> Forasmuch as the good Education of Children is of singular behoofe and benefitt to any Common wealth, and whereas many parents and masters are too indulgent and negligent of theire duty in that kinde;–*It is therefore ordered by this Courte and Authority thereof,* That the Selectmen of every Towne, in the severall precincts and quarters where they dwell, shall have a vigilant eye over theire brethren and neighbours, to see first, that none of them shall suffer so much Barbarisme in any of theire familyes as not to endeavor to teach by themselves or others theire Children and Apprentices so much Learning as may inable them perfectly to read the Inglish tounge, and knowledge of the Capitall Lawes, uppon penalty of twenty shillings for each neglect therein; . . . (2).

The order continued with the stipulation that each town with 50 or more families should establish an "elementary" (common) school and that towns with 100 or more families should add a "secondary" (grammar) school.

By 1700, the system of public instruction embraced these elements:

> a tax of "forty shillings on every thousand pounds of the lists of estates" was collected in every town with the annual tax of the Colony, and payable proportionately to those towns only which should keep their schools according to law;
>
> A school in every town having over seventy families, kept eleven months in the year, and in every town with less than seventy families, kept for at least six months in the year,
>
> A grammar school in each of the four 'head county towns' to fit youth for college, two of which grammar schools must be free, and
>
> A collegiate school, toward which the General Court made an annual appropriation (3).

The evolution of the school district is interesting to trace during the next century and a half. Schools were established, provided for, and regulated by town governments until 1712. Parishes or societies were then recognized, but only as subdivisions–or virtually school districts–of the towns. In 1750, societies and towns were given almost equal powers in conducting school affairs. By the close of the century, the school societies superseded the towns and took entire charge of the schools. In 1856, the societies were abolished and the towns (as school districts) restored to their original place in the school system. Thus, school districts existed for all practical purposes as early as 1725 but were not recognized by law until 1766. They were given corporate existence in 1794 but were not fully endowed as bodies corporate until 1839.

The earliest mention of state supervision appears in a committee report to the House of Representatives in 1826. It stated:

> With a view to invigorate and improve the system, *the committee recommends the appointment of a superintendent of Common Schools,* whose duty it shall be to recommend suitable books to the adoption of school visitors, and such modes of instruction and government as he may deem most expedient; and from the reports of the several school societies, to prepare and present to the Legislature, annually, a report, so far as he may obtain information, showing the actual condition of every common school in the State, together with his proceedings for the year (4).

But 12 years elapsed before such a provision became a reality. In 1838, the General Assembly passed "An Act for the Better Supervision of Common Schools," creating a "Board of Commissioners of Common Schools"—in effect, the first state board of education, but not so designated until 1865. The act had been introduced by a 26-year-old member of the assembly, Henry Barnard, who supported it with brilliant speeches based upon firsthand information. Authorized to appoint its own secretary, who was to be in fact the state commissioner of education, the board selected Barnard. The wisdom of this choice is now legend in Connecticut, in the United States, and, indeed, in much of the civilized world.

In his new job, he worked without letup—especially in his search for facts. His first report to the Legislature in 1839 was based on inspections of more than 200 schools, attendance at school conventions of every county in the state, and correspondence or interviews with two-thirds of the state's teachers. The report itself gave a depressing picture of conditions—including poor schoolhouses, short school terms, low pay scale for teachers, no fixed courses of study, and poor supervision of teachers. As the need for reforms became apparent, town after town upgraded its school system. Connecticut began to gain attention as a state interested in educational improvement, and Henry Barnard became known throughout the land as a crusader for popular education. He and Horace Mann of Massachusetts (1796-1859) share the credit for laying the foundation of the public school system.

However, the trial-and-error period which characterized the board's early years antagonized a great many people. After 4 years, a reactionary state legislature abolished the board and the office of secretary. No board existed for 23 years. Barnard moved into Rhode Island and a better job as state commissioner of public schools. For the next 5 years he performed the most concentrated work of his life, holding more than 1,100 meetings, making over 1,500 speeches, and organizing numerous training institutes for teachers.

In 1845, the need for state leadership became so apparent in Connecticut that the position of superintendent of common schools was created to exercise general supervision over the common schools, to collect information from "school visitors" (5) and other sources, to prepare and submit an annual report to the General Assembly about the condition of the common schools, to plan and make suggestions for improving the common schools, and to handle all matters relating to the interest of education. The statute provided for the position to be held by the commissioner of the school fund, an office established in 1795.

Meanwhile, Barnard's labors in Rhode Island had not passed unnoticed in Connecticut. When he resigned in 1849 after working himself to the brink of collapse, Connecticut offered him two jobs—as state superintendent of schools and as principal of the new state normal school in New Britain. Barnard accepted readily. His own state now seemed ripe for some real educational reforms, and the normal school had been one of his long-time dreams. He had recommended its establishment in his report to the Legislature in 1841.

During his second tour of duty on the educational firing line in Connecticut, this compelling orator, whose keen intellect was backed by a formidable arsenal of facts based on firsthand study of school conditions, launched the most extensive drive that had yet been made for the betterment of public education in his state. He spoke out for kindergartens, a radical idea at the time. He pushed for reforms that gave the educational profession new stature and urged the consolidation of school districts.

In 1855, Barnard resigned as state superintendent to found and edit the *American Journal of Education,* a periodical designed to offer the best educational thought, both past and present. He had established a pattern that kept his successors busy, so busy, in fact, that it was difficult for the principal of the state normal school to continue as superintendent of common schools, the heavy duties limiting the efficiency of both. Dissatisfaction became so widespread by 1865 that the General Assembly, in effect, re-created the board of commissioners, calling it the Board of Education, and provided for the appointment of its own secretary as in the original 1838 statue. The assembly also reenacted the board's policy-making power.

While changes in the number and method of selecting its members have occurred over the years, the board has existed continuously since that time, and its scope of activity has widened to include such responsibilities as the selection of personnel necessary for administering its programs (6). The board's broad duties as described in the statutes today reflect the committee report of 1826:

> Sec. 10-4. Duties of board. Reports. Said board shall have general supervision and control of the interests of the state in elementary and secondary education; may direct what books shall be used in all of its schools, but shall not direct any book to be changed oftener than once in five years; shall prescribe the form of registers to be kept in said schools and the form of blanks and inquiries for the returns to be made by the various boards of education; shall keep informed as to the condition and progress of said schools and shall seek to improve the methods and promote the efficiency of teaching therein by holding at convenient places in the state, meetings of teachers and school officers for the purpose of instructing in the best modes of administering, governing and teaching public schools and by such other means as it deems appropriate and shall perform such other duties as are specifically imposed upon it by law. Said board shall submit to the governor, as provided in section 4-60, a report containing an abstract of the returns made to it by the various boards of education, a

detailed statement of the doings of the board and an account of the condition of the public schools and of the amount and quality of instruction therein and such other information as will apprise the general assembly of the true condition, progress and needs of elementary and secondary public education, and may publish such reports and information concerning the educational interests of the state within its jurisdiction as it deems advisable (7).

Early decisions have had a profound effect on the way public education evolved in this century. Because the schools were established for all children, greatly increased enrollments have been accepted without serious challenge. Even the establishment of new programs and the extension of the privilege of free education to older youth have been accomplished within the original philosophy of education in a democracy. Also, the provision for both state and local responsibility has strengthened the system.

Local control of education, a policy established in the colonial period, has been both salutary and harmful. It has encouraged support and initiative by keeping education close to the people. Also, curriculum by statute has been avoided largely because of this concept. On the other hand, lack of local vision has resulted in the rejection or delay of many desirable innovations. Connecticut's relatively low rank among the states in state financial support of the schools is due in no small measure to the tradition of local autonomy. Only in recent years has the state share of the cost increased to any considerable amount. Likewise, state accreditation of elementary and secondary schools, both public and private, has never become mandatory; the State Board of Education has established standards, but their use is entirely voluntary. This, too, is a reflection of the independence of the people.

Other such effects of early decisions on the educational scene are still to be found on every hand. To a considerable extent, they condition the policies of the state board and the activities of its staff.

PATTERNS OF ORGANIZATION

The State Board of Education supervises a complex State Department of Education, composed of 5 administrative divisions and 13 bureaus, and employing a full-time staff of 1,555 persons. The board operates 14 high-school–level vocational-technical schools and 4 college-level technical institutes, with a combined enrollment of 9,000 full-time students, as well as a school for the deaf.

Through these facilities and staff, the board provides educational services to the state's public schools, which currently enroll 600,000 elementary and secondary school youngsters. This was not always the case, however. In 1900, when the total public school enrollment was only 155,000 students, the board had much more limited functions. The report made by the secretary of the board to the Governor in 1900 dealt with statistics, attendance, law enforcement, teacher certification, elements of a common school education, normal schools, high schools, kindergartens, school libraries, town management of schools, eyesight tests, conveyance of children, and free textbooks.

No complete roster of employees has been found, but documents refer to seven "agents," known legally as "compelling officers," whose principal duty was to enforce the compulsory attendance law. Although probably not listed as such in a pattern of organization, at least four departmental units were operating under the secretary's supervision: attendance; county homes; normal schools at New Britain, Willimantic, and New Haven; and public libraries. By the end of the decade, responsibility for teacher certification and for the New Britain and Bridgeport trade schools had been added.

The records indicate a new pattern after 1920 (8). The board organized its functions and services into larger units, such as elementary and secondary education, and added others not listed earlier: Americanization, transportation, employment certificates, vocational agriculture, and finance. It also created new titles, such as director and inspector, and employed 23 supervisors for specialized services. A more refined structure was apparent by 1930, and, as the charts in Appendix B indicate (9), by the end of the next 10 years the state board and its secretary were clearly attempting to develop a functional organization. There was a definite division between administration and instruction. When the Council of Chief State School Officers published in 1952 *The State Department of Education*, "a statement of some guiding principles for its legal status, its functions and the organization of its service areas" (10), Connecticut's department used it as a guide to effect a major reorganization the following year. In most cases, it designated broad responsibility areas as divisions, subdividing these into bureaus. It substantiated the position of deputy commissioner (assistant secretary of the state board) authorized by an earlier statute but not filled until 1946, and it listed technical institutes which were formed as early as 1946 in response to demands from World War II veterans.

Changes in the professional titles clearly indicate that the reorganization also recognized the shift in emphasis from regulation to advice or consultation which had taken place from 1940 to 1953. For instance, titles such as senior supervisor, junior supervisor, and interviewer were replaced by consultant, associate consultant, and service specialist, respectively. Bureau heads became chiefs, and division heads became directors (11).

By 1960, the reorganization had been refined to include most of the recommendations in the Chief State School Officers' bulletin. Vocational rehabilitation still retained its bureau status, but had been separated from vocational education. The Mystic Oral School for the Deaf, transferred to the state board in 1959, is listed in the organization chart as a separate unit, not as a division or bureau. The divisions created in 1953 still operate, but the bureaus within them had been modernized, new bureaus added, and a number of names changed. For instance, the administrative services division now consisted of a school buildings bureau, a federal-state-local relations bureau, a research, statistics, and finance bureau, and a rural services bureau.

The General Assembly enacted laws in 1965 affecting the department in a major way. It transferred the jurisdiction of the state colleges from the Board of Education to a newly created Board of Trustees of State Colleges under a new Commission for Higher Education. It also transferred the Public Library Service to the State Library Committee and elevated the Bureau of Vocational Rehabilitation to division status. At the same time, it appropriated $10 million for a 2-year period for the education of disadvantaged children. One significant change resulting from this new organization was the creation of an Office of Program Development to administer the state act for disadvantaged children and Titles I and III of Public Law 89-10, the Elementary and Secondary Education Act of 1965.

During the many years that the four state colleges were under the jurisdiction of the state board and department, they had grown remarkably, their enrollment topping 9,000 full-time students by 1965. All had started as normal schools, later became teachers colleges, and finally were transformed by the 1959 General Assembly into state colleges with liberal arts programs. In creating a new agency to coordinate all public higher education activities, the General Assembly of 1965 followed the recommendations of a U.S. Office of Education study team which suggested that Connecticut conform to the practices of other states, such as Arkansas, California, Illinois, Missouri, Pennsylvania, and South Carolina, which had in recent years set up organizational structures apart from their departments of education to coordinate higher education. With these changes, the department took on a new look, as revealed in Appendix B.

STATE PROGRAMS AND SERVICES

Many activities have characterized the work of the department in this century. Some of the early programs diminished in importance, some expanded dramatically, many new ones have been added. The following brief descriptions of the individual programs, the department's contributions to strengthening public education, reflect these changes. They are arranged by the major categories of administrative services, instructional services, vocational education, and vocational rehabilitation.

Division of Administrative Services

Interpretation of Statutes. In an era when there was little financial assistance from the state, communities determined their own school policies, adjusted curriculum to the extent of their own resources, expanded as they were able, and gave little attention to the Legislature or its regulatory arm. With the increase in state support, the expansion of population, the growing classroom shortage, the increasing need for more transportation in consolidated districts, rising costs, and greater curriculum demands by parents, people became increasingly aware of legislative activities. Pressure groups, unwilling to accept sterile, conventional patterns of schooling, sought state support for expanded and expensive services. Youth, compelled by law to stay in school, found the ordinary college entrance programs ill adapted to their requirements.

Mass education and the development of group testing pointed to many deficiencies in the pre-1910 selective schooling. Slow to catch on, the schools were forced by the Depression of the 1930's to reappraise their whole outlook and practice. World War II gave an awakened and disillusioned GI the determination to make a place for himself and his children in the new technical civilization. The laissez-faire attitude of the community was forced to give way before unprecedented pressures. The hortatory statements of commissioners and other departmental leaders appear to have resulted in legal citations that evidenced more direction but little compulsion. Also, in the 1940's and early 1950's, there were actual legal opinions reflecting not only the law but the position of the courts.

Increasing financial support by the State Legislature forced more attention to the local boards' legal duties and powers and relations to their municipal governments, especially to the finance committees. Legal questions were raised as teachers sought support from the state in their efforts to exercise more influence. Legal considerations also were involved as the state began subsidizing and exercising more and more authority for school buildings. Adult education strained for legal and financial support, and school attendance became a legal problem rather than a matter of family cooperation. Nonpublic schools found federal court rulings troublesome.

The commissioners' writings, succeeded by the legal opinions of department members competent to give them, were replaced by reports of experts in school administration who "interpreted" the statutes, searched and relayed the court judgments, and advised on practices where the law was not specific. More commonly in the last 15 years, a state assistant attorney general has been assigned to legal matters affecting education, and his services have been readily available to the department. His interpretations and advisory letters have been compiled since 1953 and serve as sources for much of the guidance now furnished local districts (12).

Educational Finance. The enumeration grant, established in 1871 when all towns were paid 50 cents per enumerated child, applied to all towns generally and has had the longest operation span of any, continuing into recent times. The amount was originally set at $2.25 per child, and it remained at this figure until 1945 when it was increased substantially. The teachers' salaries grant, instituted in 1903, was probably the most important during the early 1900's. Until discontinued in 1947, it was related to the fiscal condition of the town as measured by its assessed property valuation. The pattern of state aid for pupil transportation is noteworthy in that the present provisions are very much the same as they were in the early years of this century. In general, the state has provided one-half the transportation cost within certain specified limits.

The modern history of the state's aid to education began in 1947. Nine of the old specific grants were abolished, and a new general one established, based on a sliding scale from $110 per pupil for the first 100 to $30 per pupil in excess of 750. The significance of this new act is reflected in an increased cost for the first year of nearly 70 percent.

Numerous changes have been made since the aid formula was first adopted, and the amount per child expanded dramatically. For example, the 1965 General Assembly set up a formula under which each town received $170 for each of the first 300 pupils in average daily membership, $150 for each of the second 300 pupils, and $120 for each pupil above 600. Concern for the plight of "bedroom towns," where heavy growth in school enrollments resulted in unusual increases in school costs, prompted legislators to add a new factor to the formula: an extra grant for the growth in school enrollments during a 10-year period. As a result, the state aid, which ran to about $11 million in 1947, was up to $75 million by 1965.

There has been considerable discussion—but so far no definite action—about a system of state aid related to the fiscal resources of the individual school districts. In 1907, 1927, and 1954, commissions were appointed to draw up such a plan, and the State Board of Education and legislative committees have undertaken several studies. The department's 1963 proposal to tie major support for local education to an equalized grand list failed for a variety of reasons. For one thing, it referred to public school pupils only, and, in large cities where some 30 percent of the pupils are in nonpublic schools, the grand list for public schools was inflated. Furthermore, while larger towns were providing a variety of costly municipal services, smaller towns were not, thereby enabling the latter to devote their property taxes largely to education. Towns with any type of fiscal advantage were fearful that the equalized grand list concept would be extended to other services. And lastly, the plan was part of an omnibus state support bill, which meant that opponents of any part took aim at the whole bill.

In recent years, the trend has been to bring the upper and lower limits of the grant formula closer together while increasing the amounts. The 1965 action, creating no more than three pupil categories and a difference of only $55 between the top and bottom amounts, illustrates this. Support for educating exceptional children has grown extensively as the General Assembly has continued to place new responsibilities on the towns. Local boards must now provide opportunities for physically handicapped and mentally retarded children and, beginning in 1967, will be required to do so for children who are emotionally or socially handicapped. The grant for the physically handicapped amounts to two-thirds of the cost, and for the other categories the school district is paid an additional 150 percent of the established grant.

Research and Statistics. A new research unit was established in 1930, staffed by a director and a research associate. Up until 1938, research was actually considered a minor function in the department and was assigned to the office of finance and research since most of it was statistical. When the department was reorganized in 1955, the administrative services division included a research bureau. Four years later, a reorganization broadened the bureau to include statistics and finance.

The department's services in research increased when federal funds became available. This money made it possible to use data processing for more extensive activities, and by 1965 the professional staff had grown to four. The department's research is supplemented by research related to vocational agriculture conducted by a division of vocational services which established such a unit in 1953.

School Buildings. In the early 1900's the state board maintained a bureau of building construction and maintenance, whose chief concern appears to have been matters of health and safety. An inspector checked on lighting and heating arrangements for schoolhouses and made sure they were sanitary. The law provided that when further or different sanitary provisions, or means of lighting or ventilation, were required, they may be achieved "without unreasonable expense," and the state board may have the local health authority order the necessary changes.

In its 1924 annual report, the state board noted that the majority of towns were anxious to cooperate with it and that sanitary conditions showed marked improvement. The board was attempting to furnish leadership by working with the school districts on a voluntary basis through its survey unit, which studied local school systems, considered school building needs, and encouraged some towns to make plans for new buildings. Progress was rather slow, however, as indicated in the board's 1928 report: "As a result of the constant urging of this bureau (building construction and maintenance) we have a new school in Niantic. In this case we have labored for ten years. The result is good" (13).

The law provided that no new schoolhouse could be built except according to a plan approved by the board of school visitors and by the district's building committee, the state board having no authority to require state approval. It was amended in 1931, however, to require that a copy of plans and specifications for any new construction be filed and approved by the state board, thus necessitating the employment of a supervisor of school buildings. In 1941, a building code was adopted. In the foreword to the code, the director of supervision bureau noted: "Not only have requirements for approval been included but also many suggestions concerning desirable practices. The department regards its activities under this law as primarily a service rather than as a regulatory function" (14).

Although responsibility for supervising construction remained with the state board until 1949, when the General Assembly initiated a system of state aid for school buildings 4 years earlier, it created a separate agency, the Public School Building Commission, to handle it. From 1945 until 1953, therefore, new construction had to be approved by both this commission and the state board.

Finding it cumbersome for two state agencies to share responsibility, the assembly abolished the Public School Building Commission in 1953 and transferred its functions to the board. Six years later it passed a law establishing a School Construction Economy Service to work with a board-appointed advisory committee in providing districts more services designed to promote economy and efficiency in constructing new school buildings. This law also required that the board establish standards, review the plans and specifications in the light of these standards, and then report directly to the districts.

School building grants were substantially increased during this period, reaching their highest point in 1965 when, based on building capacity, per-pupil grants were set at $700 in the elementary school and at $1,100 in the secondary school. In the 20 years following passage of the first school construction aid law in 1945, over 1,300 school building projects were completed at a cost, exclusive of sites, of nearly $600 million, the state assuming a liability of more than $200 million.

Public School Transportation. Connecticut has transported students to its schools at public expense for over 70 years, the first act in 1893 stating that when a school was discontinued, the school visitors might provide transportation of children to and from another school. Ten years later, the Legislature put teeth into the law by setting age limits and approving the phrase "illegally and unreasonably deprived of schooling." The law also established appeal machinery, making this phrase the basis for an appeal to the State Board of Education. After the board eliminated the limitation to discontinued schools in 1909 and applied the law to all schools, the transportation statutes remained virtually unchanged until 1931. In that year, the age limit was lowered from "over seven" to "over six" to accommodate 6-year-olds for whom the local board was required to provide an educational program, the "over seven" conforming to the compulsory school age (15). At the same time, the law allowed the superior courts to receive appeals from the state board's findings.

During World War II, the state board responded to an Office of Defense Transportation order to conserve mileage and gasoline by ruling that in hearing appeals for school transportation it would require 1.5 miles for grades 1 through 8 and 2 miles for grades 9 through 12 as reasonable walking distances. When the war ended, this ruling was terminated, and each case is now considered individually.

Prior to 1957, the board issued findings in transportation hearings based on distance only, but since that date it has ruled that the element of hazard must be taken into consideration. Under Public Act 547, the General Assembly enacted legislation in 1957 wherein by referendum any municipality or school district could provide transportation for children attending private schools. Electors in several towns have voted on this issue and in most cases have approved it.

Teacher Certification. Prior to 1923, local school boards examined, licensed, and employed teachers, giving certificates (later recognized by law) valid only in the districts issuing them. In an era of local control and largely immobile population, this had been acceptable; but schools became ingrown, teaching parochial, standards lax, and school board practices capricious if not chaotic. There were many arguments for greater state control to improve the schools by centralizing the certification of teachers. Finally impressed, the Legislature enacted a law in the early 1920's with a basic normal school standard of education as the criterion for professional preparation and efficiency.

A teacher surplus during the Depression created an excellent excuse to raise standards, and many predicted that in the near future the bachelor of arts degree would be required of all public school teachers. Normal schools were rapidly becoming teachers colleges. Proponents of a college degree for teachers continued to gain strength, so that by 1940 such a requirement had been added to the certification standards. Following World War II, during a period of teacher shortage, there were efforts to reduce standards, but education interest groups stoutly maintained pressures to keep them at a high level. The administration of these regulations enabled the state to attract more good teachers than would have been the case if lower standards had been adopted.

The original legislation requiring the state board to establish rules for teacher certification is essentially unchanged, but the regulations have developed both to provide leadership and to reflect improvements in teacher preparation and the needs of local schools. As patterns of preparation and school usages become more complex in our modern society, regulations need a continuing study revision and proper administration in order for the state to enable professional personnel to perform a high caliber of work in good schools.

School Lunch Program. In reflecting on the experiences of his childhood, Mark Twain concluded with perfect childish delight that the best part of his school day was the lunch recess. Whether his lunch recess had any educational values may be open to question, but Twain has no trouble stimulating the reader's nostalgia, and we withhold any condemnation of the good ol' days.

The prices of foodstuff rose during the First World War; farmers opened vast new lands to feed our own troops and to support our allies, and Hoover was able to rescue millions in Europe and the Near East from starvation. This "war boom" so expanded the capacity for agricultural production that surpluses accumulated. In the aftermath of the war and following the 1921 depression, the country began a long era of prosperity.

While city children lived only a few blocks from school and walked home for lunch, children in the country were watching their "consolidated schools" rising some distance from their farms, diminshing the customary conveniences of the old local schools. As more and more children went to school by bus, toting a sandwich and apple became a familiar practice. As the central schools grew larger, children came to them from greater distances, the hours spent away from home were longer, and the time from breakfast to lunch became a matter of considerable importance to the appetites and health of growing children.

The public's growing concern for the nutritional needs of rural schoolchildren was not lost on the Legislature, which not only looked at the conditions in the schools, but also kept in mind the agriculture surpluses. Among the laws passed in 1923, one empowered the local boards of education to provide "lunches for school teachers and children." Ironically, the cities took advantage of this to a greater extent than the rural areas.

Connecticut did not employ a state lunch supervisor until 1943, but was still one of the first states to prepare for the inevitable National School Lunch Program 3 years later. From an initial 125 programs, the number increased to 350 by 1948, requiring the employment of an assistant supervisor. Within 7 years, the state board published a notable guide specifying directions, menu suggestions, accounting procedures, and a broad suggestion that this growing business was not for amateurs (16). The number of programs had doubled by 1965.

The spring following Congress' enacting of the 1955 Special Milk Program, Connecticut began an experimental program to study the effect of price on participation. It decided to take part, and this project has grown until there are nearly 1,200 of the special milk programs in operation. During the past quarter century, the department has attempted to upgrade food-service workers, train leaders, systemize accounting and reporting, and has conducted experiments in group purchasing. It is developing automatic data processing, menus are continually revised, food-service rooms and equipment are being improved, and the program continues to expand with no end in sight.

Public Information. In the 1930's an editor was employed and attached to the office of the commissioner to assist in the secretarial work and publish a monthly newsletter of four to eight pages, entitled "The Board of Education." A publicist, mainly concerned with the preparation of news releases, was added in 1949. Although the department did not have a program broad enough to respond to the great increase in public interest in education, it did develop a news service, publications, and a general informational service.

When Title V of the Elementary and Secondary Education Act of 1965 provided funds for improving services in communications, the department established an Office of Communications with a staff of four persons. This unit developed a planned, continuing method for supplying news on education to the newspapers throughout the state and improved the format of the department's publications. Procedures are under way to assist staff members to produce more effective publications. Title V also has enabled the department to purchase large quantities of equipment to assist in developing stronger communication among the staff, local school systems, and the public.

Teacher-Board of Education Mediation. The department's mediation activities originated about 1946 when the commissioner intervened in several salary disputes between teachers organizations and local boards, some involving strikes or threatened strikes. The Connecticut Supreme Court of Errors, in the case of Norwalk Teachers Association *v.* Board of Education of the City of Norwalk, ruled in 1951 that teachers as well as other public employees could not strike (17). A committee was appointed to study the working relationships between boards and teachers organizations. This committee issued a preliminary report in 1952, which was approved by the State Board of Education 5 years later after several revisions. It established principles and procedures for dealing with situations where teachers and boards could not reach agreements (originally referred to as "impasses" and later as "persistent disagreements").

The General Assembly approved Public Act 298 in 1965, requiring boards to negotiate with individuals chosen by teachers to be their exclusive representatives, naming the commissioner as the mediator, and calling for nonbinding arbitration if the issue could not be resolved any other way (18). During the school year 1965-66, teacher organizations sought recognition under the law in 101 of the 177 districts, 76 being "designated" by action of the board of education, 25 by means of a referendum. The secretary also received requests and mediated in 16 cases. This developing function of state boards of education may become a significant force in teacher-board relations.

Rural Supervisory Services. The state board has provided special administrative and supervisory services to local boards for many years. As early as 1903, the General Assembly authorized supervising agents (superintendents of schools) for districts of two or more towns employing not more than 25 teachers each. They were paid by the state, but subject to direction from the local board. At first, there were only four superintendents to visit eight towns, but by 1910, 33 superintendents served 73 towns enrolling 17,000 students. The high point came in 1920, with a staff of 35 superintendents and an enrollment of 25,000 students in 97 towns. The following year, the department began providing elementary supervisors as well as supervising agents.

By sharply reducing the number of towns and slightly reducing the number of teachers, the consolidation movement enabled the board to employ the same number of superintendents in 1965, 12, to cover 42 districts and five regional high schools that it had assigned to 90 districts and one regional high school 25 years earlier. The first 10 years the department was responsible for these services, its staff developed a curriculum that received statewide adoption and exercised considerable influence. It continued to develop and promote curriculum materials, resulting in a uniformly high-quality program of studies.

Division of Instructional Services

Elementary and Secondary Education. Concern for elementary and secondary education at the state level is focused through the Bureau of Elementary and Secondary Education, established following a departmental reorganization in 1955. The bureau began with a professional staff consisting of a bureau chief and 10 consultants; today there are 19 consultants, 1 each for early childhood, elementary, business and driver education; English and reading; foreign languages; industrial arts; mathematics; school libraries; science; social studies; art; and music; with 2 consultants each for health and physical education, school library services, and school administration (19). Each consultant is concerned with the entire educational program and, as a specialist, deals with his particular area from the time it is introduced in the elementary school through the senior high school.

The staff is mainly involved in assisting local school personnel to improve their educational programs by identifying the significant problems, developing ways of solving them, and evaluating them in terms of the objectives. Implicit in this approach is the necessity for consultants to be abreast of all new developments and to have close working relationships with groups and individuals affecting school programs. In particular, there is an effort to design programs in terms of the future.

The state board authorized curriculum guides to be prepared in 1957 for the various subject areas, but lack of funds, staff, and time has made it possible to develop only a few, and, with the exception of art, for grades 7 through 12 only. Federal funds are beginning to help this effort.

Although the bureau itself is of recent origin, its functions have been carried on for many years despite a tradition of strong local autonomy. Actually, the school districts are empowered by the General Assembly to build and operate elementary and secondary schools without the state board's approval. To enable school districts without high schools to acquire public funds to send their students to those in nearby towns on a tuition basis, the state board does approve high schools for tuition purposes. This approval, however, is based on the fact that they operate according to law and does not involve an evaluation of their programs.

The department initiated a program of high school evaluation in 1949 in connection with a cooperative study of secondary school standards. Closely following the procedures and "evaluative criteria" prepared and distributed by the National Study of Secondary School Evaluations, each senior high school is evaluated every 10 years. A few junior high schools have been examined on a similar basis.

Since 1900, two legal provisions—one calling for the approval of pupils and tuitions from towns without high schools, and the other pointing to "duties of parents" in securing public school instruction or the equivalent for their children—have empowered the state board to approve academic private schools. In 1941, the licensing of private schools that give trade instruction also became the board's responsibility.

With little attention from the state, local schools began giving high school equivalency tests in 1925. Finally, on the basis of a law passed in 1905, providing for a "qualifying academic certficate" determined by examination rather than other academic records for professional preparation (including high school completion), the department did assume responsibilities for both tests and a state diploma in 1947, and drew up regulations for each.

Historically, developments in elementary education and secondary education have been somewhat different. Reference has been made earlier to the Rural Supervisory Service established in 1903. This was an exclusive service to elementary schools, although in recent years a few regional secondary schools came under its aegis. Three persons have served as elementary education consultants, the first being employed in 1923. Each has worked mainly with elementary schools not under the rural service.

In earlier years, the department was a mosaic of rather separate and discrete specialists, each going his own way without too much interest in his colleagues' activities. This situation, which undoubtedly reflected the extreme degree of local control that has had a long and strong history in the state, has, however, been changing over the years. As a reflection of the times and what is happening locally, more effort is being spent attempting to develop a comprehensive, consistent, unified approach to education.

Many school districts are joining forces to secure programs and services they cannot achieve alone. It seems apparent that there will be much more agreement and cooperation on a statewide basis in the future, which in turn will set the pattern for many of the Bureau of Elementary and Secondary Education's activities.

Pupil Personnel and Special Educational Services. In 1915, Connecticut became the first state to have a school psychologist appointed to its education department. Although the directory listed the position as dealing with "defective and deficient" children, the needs of both the handicapped and the gifted were given attention from the beginning. Although 23 classes were established for the retarded and 7 for the physically handicapped in 1919, the need for 125 such classes was reported.

A legislative commission on child welfare appointed in 1919 resulted in legislation 2 years later requiring the state board to appoint a "director of special education and standards." This law established the principle of both the public schools' and the board's responsibility for educating exceptional children, including those in institutions. With major attention given to surveying the number of children requiring special education and to demonstrating projects for training them, much of the staff's time during the 1920's was spent in testing for special educational placement and operating clinics in various parts of the state. By 1930, there were six persons employed in special education and psychological testing.

Specialists in various aspects of this work have been appointed on a full-time basis over the years, Connecticut scoring a "first" in employing a health supervisor in 1921, a guidance consultant in 1940, and a school social work consultant in 1949. Other consultants have been added from 1940-65, including those dealing with guidance, the physically handicapped, the handicapped in speech and hearing, the mentally retarded, school social work, the socially and emotionally maladjusted, the perceptually handicapped, and the gifted (20). Also, a project was started in 1965 to demonstrate vocational rehabilitation counseling of retarded children in the public secondary schools. At first the staff included only a project director and 3 counselors, but both state and federal legislation made possible an increase to 20 by the end of the year. It represents one of the department's fastest growing service areas.

The emphasis on particular services has changed from time to time, reflecting in part the national trend. For example, during World War II, there was much emphasis on guidance, particularly to prepare young men for the armed services as well as for employment and work experiences. The publications reflect a concern for the total community organization of guidance and its related services. Guidance has been particularly involved in the dropout problem. Perhaps at first, this "looking toward guidance" reflected a failure to appreciate the complex nature of the problem, which more recently has involved many aspects of both curriculum and special services as well as other community effort. When the State Scholarship Commission was established in 1963, guidance consultants assumed a major role as sources of information on scholarships and assisted in administering the state scholarship program until it was transferred to the Commission on Higher Education.

School social work has been closely identified with special efforts in dealing with delinquents and school attendance problems, as well as with special services for the socially and emotionally maladjusted. It was an interest in these problems that prompted the employment of a school social worker. Along with the guidance and psychological personnel, the social workers have attempted to resolve some of the interprofessional problems interfering with the effectiveness of these services at the local level during the early 1950's. They published a bulletin entitled "The Team Approach in Pupil Personnel Services" (21) and, when this attracted nationwide attention, followed it with other publications which have been favorably received in other states.

Connecticut has led in the development of certification requirements in several special fields. The 1922 regulations covered teachers of exceptional children, including the retarded, blind, and deaf. Three years later, the board began certifying school nurses. By 1934, regulations also included certification for vocational guidance instructors, teachers of the below-normal, visiting teachers, school nurses, and dental hygienists. In the early 1940's, the state separated the classification for elementary and secondary special education and adopted regulations for certifying school psychologists and psychological examiners. Connecticut was among the first in the nation to require the professional master's degree for school social workers and school counselors, and a doctorate for school psychologists' permanent cerificates in 1955.

Adult Education. Connecticut began its public school adult education program well before 1900 by establishing evening schools for students over 14, and including literacy and Americanization courses. Legislation in 1930 provided for supervisors, classes, rooms, personnel, and financial support. A full-time professional supervisor had been employed since 1920; from 1929 to 1951 he was given a full-time assistant. The basic adult education program, supported by federal funds, is increasing its scope at a rapid rate.

Veteran education became the board's responsibility after 1944 when several federal laws provided for educating veterans. This program has been ably administered, and regardless of the level of education approved, no breath of scandal has been associated with it.

After experimenting for 3 years in a small but increasing number of states, the U.S. Office of Education initiated Civil Defense education. By 1952, all states were encouraged to conduct such programs; Connecticut's plan was approved that year, requiring a full-time professional staff member from 1952 to 1957. At that time, it ended as an experiment and became the responsibility of the local public schools, requiring little if any attention from the department thereafter.

The basic education provisions of the Economic Opportunity Act of 1964 introduced a new factor in adult education by making funds available through local boards to improve adults' "communicational and occupational skills" to at least the eighth-grade level. The state department designed a state plan and supervised its implementation, employing a full-time director in 1965.

Manufacturers were required by the child labor laws dating back to 1813 to file working papers showing that they were providing some schooling for the children they employed. At the beginning of the twentieth century, persons hiring boys under 16 in any mechanical, mercantile, or manufacturing establishment had to file papers proving the boys were not under 14. The basic present law was passed in 1911, requiring an agent of the state board to sign certificates for minor employees showing them to be over 18, literate, and in "apparent" good health. By numerous amendments, the law now requires certificates for leaving school and gives detailed regulations for employment in agriculture, manufacturing, mechanical, and mercantile establishments. In 1957, the Legislature delegated this responsibility for issuing certificates to school superintendents under supervision of the State Board of Education.

Audiovisual Services. During the late 1920's and early 1930's, the department's art consultant spent much time attempting to interest teachers in using visual aids. But in 1952, when the audiovisual program was integrated with the vocational education program (because its consultants were particularly interested), only two cities reported full-time audiovisual directors. Two years later, the department appointed an audiovisual consultant and began collecting a film library, which now serves a majority of the school systems and is one of its major activities. The consultant's responsibilities were expanded in 1945 to implement a plan "to extend the program of audiovisual aids . . . to cover all schools in the state to an effective depth." A second consultant was added in 1949, and an extensive survey of the state's audiovisual education was conducted the following year.

During the years following the audiovisual consultant's recommendation in 1951 for a study of educational television, there was a marked interest in its development. Within 2 years, Bloomfield and Danbury were demonstrating closed-circuit television, and the state board had received permission from the Federal Communications Commission to construct three stations. But following a report by a Governor's Commission on Educational Television in 1954 (22), the state board rejected its plan for a separate agency, and there was a period of uncertainty as to how Connecticut would develop educational television. The Legislature established the Connecticut Educational Television Corporation in 1959, and 2 years later, the state board created a Telecast Council to recommend educational TV programs for the schools. The state's first station (WEDH) went on the air in October 1962. The department's staff has used commercial television for several series in fields of guidance, elementary education, and Far Eastern cultures, as well as for lectures on topics of current interest.

Federal legislation created an increased demand for consultant services in the field. The department is developing an educational media laboratory and is attempting to broaden its staff's professional interest to include many types of educational media.

Public Libraries. Following legislative action in 1893, the State Board of Education appointed the Public Library Committee to assist in developing the state's free public libraries. Approved public libraries were granted $100 annually after 1895, and additional grants of $200 were available for several years to encourage communities to found new ones. Both grants were paid in the form of approved books purchased by the state. The committee's reports, published until 1918, reveal that its original activities were mainly to make book loans to clubs and small public libraries, to provide a traveling book collection to different parts of the state, and (with Works Progress Administration aid) to sponsor a bookmobile to serve several eastern Connecticut towns from 1939 to 1942. The Legislature empowered the board to assume the committee's duties in 1947, and it became an agency within the libraries bureau.

Although the board employed its first professional—the visitor and inspector of libraries—as early as 1902, it was 1947 before regional library services were authorized. Eight years were to elapse before the establishment of the Regional Library Service Center in Middletown to serve the public libraries in Middlesex County. Four years later, the board opened another center in Willimantic for the public libraries in Windham and Tolland Counties.

Another state agency, the State Library Committee, charged with administering the State Library, was created in 1854. The State Library has been concerned chiefly with legislative reference, law reference, Connecticut history and genealogy, archives, and museum activities. With the increase in federal aid, gradually a feeling developed that administratively it made sense to combine this agency and the libraries bureau. This was done by the Legislature in 1965 under a new State Library Committee appointed by the Governor.

Higher Education. The Board of Education's first concern for higher education other than normal schools began when the Legislature passed an act in 1931 requiring licenses for institutions claiming to be of college level or offering degrees. The Legislature strengthened this law in 1943, 1947, and 1950, but set up a new Commission for Higher Education in 1965 limiting the department's responsibilities in higher education to the administration of the state technical institutes, to high school educational guidance, and to teacher education programs leading to certification (23).

Teacher education had become a state function in the early nineteenth century. The New Britain Normal School, the first in Connecticut and the sixth in the United States, was established in 1849, and three similar institutions were founded at Danbury, New Haven, and Willimantic at later dates, all operated by the State Board of Education (24). The New Britain Normal School became the Teachers College of Connecticut in 1933, granting its first baccalaureate degrees to some sixty graduates the following year. A few years later, the other normal schools became 4-year colleges.

Because of an acute shortage of teachers after World War II, the four colleges developed a program to prepare and certify graduates of liberal arts colleges to become elementary teachers. It was started in the summer of 1949 with an enrollment of about 150 students. A plan for graduate work was approved in January 1954, and the following summer, it was initiated with a total enrollment of 310. Over 6,000 students have been admitted to these graduate programs, comprising almost one-third of the teachers in Connecticut.

The General Assembly enacted a statute in 1959 requiring the state colleges to offer baccalaureate degree programs in the liberal arts, and these were launched in the fall of 1961. By the fall of 1965, there were over 9,000 full-time students in the various programs offered by the colleges. As pointed out earlier, the General Assembly in 1965 created a Commission for Higher Education to coordinate all public higher education activities. As a part of the legislation, a new Board of Trustees was charged with the operation of the state colleges. The long and fruitful stewardship of the state colleges by the State Board of Education came to an end.

Mystic Oral School. In 1921, the state purchased the Mystic Oral School, a private residential school for deaf children established at the turn of the century. Until it was transferred to the State Board of Education in 1959, it operated as a separate state agency with its own board of trustees. The board, although responsible for implementing a 1959 law allowing it to send aphasic children to out-of-state schools, decided that Connecticut should inaugurate its own program for these children through its newly acquired school. Because of a dearth of teachers, the board found it necessary to sponsor teacher preparation in this field and secured scholarship aid from the Legislature in 1961 for all prospective teachers of deaf and aphasic children. The following year, it enrolled pupils in this program. By the close of 1965, a total of 169 deaf and aphasic children, age 2 to 20, were enrolled.

Division of Vocational Education

Trade and Industrial Education. The state's interest in trade and industrial education dates back to 1808 when a compilation of statutes included one pertaining to apprenticeship. The pattern for establishing schools for trade education and training, however, was not set by the General Assembly until 100 years later, 1907, when it enacted legislation for founding two trade schools, one in New Britain and the other in Bridgeport. Under the direction of the state board, they began operating 3 years later as state trade education shops, later to be known as state trade schools.

The first trade education shops emphasized industrial apprenticeship training—the teaching of shop skills. Students were admitted at any time during the year and graduated individually upon completing 4,800 hours of satisfactory work, receiving a "trade apprentice certificate." The school operated 6 days a week, 9 hours a day except on Saturday, the school year consisting of 50 weeks. The success of these first two schools provided the foundation upon which Connecticut built 14 state-operated, regional vocational-technical schools.

A major change in trade and industrial education evolved by 1944, when the state and industry recognized the need for a "more balanced training program" to meet the requirements of the rapidly changing technical economy. The trend was toward the general high school pattern, but the main objective continued to be preparing youth for immediate employment as advanced apprentices in skilled trades. By 1965, there were more than 30 offerings, ranging from a minimum of 7 in all schools to 18 in the larger schools. Connecticut took another step forward in 1947 when the Legislature passed a multimillion-dollar 10-year construction program to erect 14 modern buildings on new, spacious sites to give youth a high school education with an emphasis on trade skills.

Stimulated by federal and state legislation, another new direction was taken in 1965 to meet industry's demand for semiskilled and operative-type workers. For the first time, industrial educational programs on the "less than career" level were introduced and developed in local public high schools to prepare youth for immediate employment in occupations not generally classified as professional, technical, or skilled trade.

The vocational-technical schools began offering professional counseling when the department appointed a consultant in 1940; the larger schools immediately employed full-time counselors. This phase of the program developed substantially in high schools and state-operated vocational-technical schools, with students being channeled through their own counseling services in their local districts in regional vocational-technical schools. This counseling, along with research, in-service teacher education, and curriculum development, have all been integral parts of the growth in the vocational education programs.

Agricultural Education. The year 1906 marked the beginning of vocational agriculture when the Manual Training School, a private institution which became known as the Chapman Technical Institute and later the New London High School, added agriculture to its curriculum. The New Milford High School organized the first public school agriculture program on an experimental basis in 1912, supporting it entirely from local funds.

The Smith-Hughes Act of 1917, allocating federal funds for promoting vocational education, related agriculture to "meeting the needs of persons over fourteen years of age who have entered or who are preparing to enter upon the work of the farm or farm home" (25). The state adopted a plan whereby it paid the salary of agriculture teachers, and the towns contributed the facilities, necessary equipment, and supplies. From 1917 through 1956, nearly all of the agriculture programs followed this plan. They were not completely satisfactory, however, as the local centers were serving only a limited area with inadequate facilities and little or no equipment.

In 1954, a statewide Vocational Agriculture Consulting Committee proposed that regional vocational agriculture centers be formed to give training to any student who might find it profitable. The Legislature appropriated state funds in 1955 to local school boards for constructing such centers. Since Woodrow Wilson High School at Middletown opened the first regional center in 1956, 11 additional centers have been constructed.

Distributive Education. With support from the George-Barden Act, distributive education was introduced in 1942 in Middletown, Meriden, Norwich, and Waterbury, to an enrollment of 72 students. At the same time, 18 towns began offering adult education courses for upgrading retail store personnel.

During the next decade, seven high schools offering distributive education programs enrolled 187 pupils. By 1960, the curriculum had expanded and improved, youth clubs had been organized, and specific certification standards had been established for distributive education coordinators. Five years later, 29 high schools offered programs for 1,600 students. A group of businessmen, interested in giving both advisory and financial assistance, established the Distributive Education Foundation of Connecticut. It is anticipated that within the next decade every secondary school will offer this program as well as adult courses.

Home Economics Education. Hartford High School first introduced home economics in 1898, but 8 years passed before another school, New London's Manual Training School, became interested in such courses. Then, in 1916, New Britain introduced domestic science for its students. Most of these early courses concentrated on sewing, and it was not until 1920 that the elementary programs added cooking.

With impetus from the Smith-Hughes Act in 1917, it was possible to expand the curriculum, to include courses in foods, nutrition, clothing, and textiles. The scope was further broadened in the next 30 years to encompass interior decorating, home nursing, consumer education, and home management. The Home Economics Education Service issued resource units in eight areas from 1947 to 1962, the entire program from the seventh to the twelfth grades providing a sequence of instruction designed to meet the needs of students.

The Vocational Education Act of 1963 placed new emphasis on programs leading to gainful employment, which in turn has led to new courses in food services and child care. Five-year agreements worked out with local schools have pointed to the need for better physical facilities, changes in curriculum, and materials for instruction.

Adult home economics education has flourished since 1945. In the beginning, the emphasis was on homemaking skills, but before long there were courses in child development, parental interest, and training occupations such as food care and child service. The program has attracted many disadvantaged persons and is providing them with essential skills and understandings.

Vocational Health Services Programs. The State Board of Education and the Board of Examiners for Nursing instituted a 1-year trained-attendant course in the fall of 1942. Offered at the trade school in New Britain, it consisted of 3 months of classroom instruction and 9 months of clinical experience at two cooperating hospitals. Fourteen students completed the course, successfully passing the examination for licensure a year later. In 1953, the original title of trained attendant was officially changed to licensed practical nurse. This program, offered by 9 vocational-technical schools and 16 affiliated hospitals, graduates 400 nurses annually. The state also initiated a dental assistant program in 1960, and two additional programs are planned for the immediate future. Several junior and senior high schools are offering nurse's aide training under the Vocational Education Act of 1963; additional ones are in the developmental stage.

State Technical Institutes. As Connecticut's industry expanded rapidly after World War II, incorporating the technical advances stimulated by war, the demand for employees with technical education beyond high school level grew rapidly. In March 1946, the state board authorized the Hartford Trade School to offer 2-year, postsecondary education to fill the widening gap between the skilled craftsman and the graduate engineer, thus inaugurating the

Connecticut Engineering Institute, later known as the Hartford State Technical Institute.

The institute, offering curriculum in electrical and mechanical technology, operated as the upper technical division of the Hartford Trade School from its start in April 1946 until December 1957 when it was separated from the parent institution. Within a year after it opened, it inaugurated an adult education program designed to upgrade technical employees and prepare technicians. It added tool technology to the day school curriculum in 1948, and when the institute moved into its new building in September 1960, it was again expanded to include civil technology and data processing. At the same time, the evening school enrollment had continued to climb to an all-time high.

The success of the institute's graduates and the evergrowing need for more technicians generated demands for additional institutes. The Legislature responded with funds for three more, opening them in quick succession in Norwalk (1961), Thames Valley (1963), and Waterbury (1964). An original enrollment of 22 students grew to 1,700 in 1965, and the curriculum from two offerings to eight. A fifth institute is planned for 1967. The evening school program has kept pace with the day school, serving over 5,000 adults with 250 courses in 1965, with 1,600 adults working toward their associate degrees.

The Engineering Council for Professional Development recognized the excellence of the Hartford Institute program by accrediting its curriculum in 1955 (26). The state board extended recognition in June 1962, when it authorized the awarding of the associate degree in applied science. Since they have become degree-granting institutions, there has been a growing desire that the institutes be designated as technical colleges. Appropriate legislation has been prepared to effect this change.

Vocational Rehabilitation

The Legislature accepted the Vocational Rehabilitation Act in 1929 and appropriated a small amount to initiate the program. It functioned as a one-man operation until temporary emergency funds from the federal government enabled it to employ five counselors in 1934. By the end of the following year, however, these funds were no longer available, and it returned to its one-man status.

In 1935, Connecticut inaugurated the first program in the nation to rehabilitate tuberculosis patients with funds from the federal government pooled with money collected from the sale of Christmas seals. One supervisor was immediately employed, and another was added in 1940. The following year, the vocational rehabilitation bureau pioneered the "team approach" which led to the inauguration of the Rehabilitation Clinic, widely known as the Man-Salvage Clinic.

Funds were gradually increased during the next 3 years, and rehabilitation offices were opened in New Haven, Bridgeport, Hartford, Norwich, and Waterbury. When the vocational rehabilitation bureau celebrated its twenty-fifth anniversary in 1955, it had rehabilitated 14,000 patients; the annual number of handicapped served had increased from 160 in 1930 to 3,400; and eight local offices were operating in the state's key communities.

Congress increased the allotments to the states in 1956, adding more funds by enacting the Social Security Freeze and Cash Benefits Program, enabling Connecticut to expand its activities. The General Assembly gave the program further impetus by passing an act the following year requiring that services provided by the vocational rehabilitation unit include mentally handicapped as well as physically handicapped individuals and provide for workshops (27).

A Division of Vocational Rehabilitation, consisting of the bureaus of rehabilitation services, disability determination services, and community and institutional services, was established in 1965. At various times from 1954 to 1965, Congress enacted legislation to protect the old age and survivors insurance benefits of persons covered by Social Security who became disabled for long periods. These programs were administered through the disability determination bureau, comprising a chief, a service specialist, and 10 counselors. With increased state and federal funds, there is every promise that greatly expanded services will be available for the handicapped.

RELATIONSHIPS WITH OTHER AGENCIES

Through the years, the effectiveness of the department has been increased materially by a close working relationship with other state government units. Similarly, through this cooperative approach to common problems, the department has attempted to be of assistance to other groups. Moreover, it has provided opportunities for private citizens to offer advice and give assistance. For example, the department organized regional citizen councils in 1938, and effective dialogue ensued until interrupted by World War II; beginning in 1948, the department sponsored annual citizens' conferences on education to deal with a wide variety of topics representing current concerns (28).

The department-sponsored Connecticut Council on Education began meeting in 1945 to serve as a sounding board for new ideas and help secure progressive legislation. Its membership consisted of representatives from 20 statewide lay and professional organizations with major interests in education. Specifically, the department hoped to bring to these member organizations a broader understanding of its problems and encourage more participation by lay citizens in public education. The Council was dissolved in 1960 because its objectives had been adopted by other organizations.

The department has always had a close working relationship with the Parent-Teachers Association of Connecticut.

Its staff serves on the board of managers; the deputy commissioner has been a member since 1960. Occasionally, joint studies have been made and published. At the local level, hundreds of PTA groups have been served by department personnel.

Among the several interdepartmental state committees, the most active are those involving health, development, welfare, labor, and mental health. The Division of Vocational Education would find it difficult to function without cooperating closely with the labor department, and much the same feeling exists within other divisions in their relations with other departments.

From time to time, temporary state commissions are created, such as the commissions on state government formed in 1929 and 1949. In the latter year, the Governor's Fact-Finding Commission on Education probed the state's responsibility to education in considerable depth, and again by a State Personnel Study Commission created in 1965. In these and all other studies, the department has been an active participant.

Since 1945, a great deal of effort has been directed to coordinating the department's work with that of the University of Connecticut. A subcommittee of the state board and the university trustees formed in 1949, known as the Liaison Committee after 1953, concerned itself with preventing unnecessary duplication of services and planning an orderly growth in public higher education. It held regular meetings, issued reports, and made an official study of higher education at the Governor's request in 1955. It did stellar work in coordinating many of the programs, particularly the preparation of teachers and administrators, until the board's responsibilities in higher education were transferred in 1965. The department created two other groups—the Council on Higher Education and the Council on Teacher Education—which complemented the work of the Liaison Committee. Composed of members designated by the department and one representative for each higher education institution, they will continue to meet despite the department's new relationship to higher education.

The department attempts to demonstrate the effectiveness of this cooperative approach in meeting educational problems in its relations with local school systems. Since 1940, the emphasis has been on leadership rather than regulation. Requests for advice, consultation, and direct service come from every town in the state. The department's orientation programs, offered for many years to new school board members, have given hundreds of these interested citizens a better grasp of educational problems and a clearer understanding of their duties and responsibilities. In more recent years, the Connecticut Association of Boards of Education has cooperated with the department in conducting this activity. And, as mentioned earlier, the department cooperates with the attorney general's staff in assisting boards to interpret the school laws.

Evidence of mutual confidence and professional respect can be found in the many requests from school staffs for assistance in organizing and carrying on local educational studies and research. Dozens of high schools request and receive aid in evaluating their programs and resources. In addition, there is a constant demand from local school systems for materials for self-surveys; some communities have requested the department to conduct complete educational surveys. The department's consultants are always available to assist in locally sponsored group conferences, and they respond to calls from classroom teacher groups, from principals and supervisors, and from school superintendents. They participate in workshops and serve as speakers, striving always to maintain wholesome working relationships and to offer a superior professional service.

The department has tried to utilize to the fullest all educational resources of the state, public and private, in solving problems. Its units—such as the teachers colleges and bureaus in the central office—have constantly cooperated through committees and research projects with teachers and administrators organizations in developing and evaluating programs. Staff members meet regularly with regional groups of superintendents and work with such organizations as the secondary school principals, the elementary school principals, the elementary school supervisors, and organized groups in special subject areas. In recent years, curriculum consultants have led in organizing statewide specialized curriculum groups.

For nearly 20 years, the chief state school officers of New England, New York, and New Jersey have held regular meetings to develop programs of common interest and seek ways and means of increasing cooperation and reciprocity. In recent years, Pennsylvania has been added to the group. Committees from several special areas within each state have worked together to develop common standards in such areas as teacher certification, accreditation of institutions, citizenship education, and improvement of vocational schools.

Increasingly, states have become involved with many federal agencies in discharging their functions, starting with almost no involvement in 1900 and reaching a climax with the adoption of Public Law 89-10, Elementary and Secondary Education Act of 1965. Although the U.S. Office of Education and the Social and Rehabilitation Service remain the agencies the department deals with most frequently, it also has dealings with other federal agencies, such as the Department of Agriculture, the Department of Labor, the Public Health Service, and the National Science Foundation. The department also maintains a liaison with Washington through other channels, among them the Council of Chief State School Officers, the American Council on Education, the Joint Council on Educational Television, the American Association of School Administrators, and the National Education Association.

MAJOR EFFORTS AND ACCOMPLISHMENTS

> The time was when the suggestion that schools could do no more than they are doing was met with incredulity, with denial, and often with personal abuse. That they can do more has been repeated, in some cases tried, and in others illustrated and proved, so that now many people believe it and even teachers admit it (29).

This conviction that "schools can do more," found in the annual report of the secretary of the state board at the beginning of this century, has been the keystone to the progress which has been made since it was written. To prove the point, the State Board of Education declared in its 1900 report to the Governor that certain improvements in public education were desperately needed: the introduction of skilled supervision, the substitution of complete town for small district management, a change in high school education, and a required standard of teaching qualifications. It also pointed out that it was necessary to adjust and balance the studies so as to form a well-founded and planned whole, extending throughout the entire period of school life. It called for an examination of the educational values of different subjects, the introduction of well-defined usefulness into all schoolwork, and an adaptation of instruction to people's needs, such as elementary technical education.

That these goals were taken seriously is illustrated by the action taken on many of them in the ensuing years. For instance, a state system of supervision and administration for rural schools was established in 1903 and continues to this day. The obsolete, small school districts existing in 1900 within larger towns and numbering more than 1,000 were abolished in all but a few large towns and cities in 1909. By 1965, with only 179 districts remaining, the transition was complete, and small town districts had extended the concept by agreeing to combine for specific purposes, such as secondary education. State teaching certificates representing certain minimum qualifications were required by statute in 1923. Although "adjustment and balance of studies" is broad and fundamental as a concept, it has characterized the majority of changes introduced during this 65-year period as education has been extended to include nursery schools, kindergartens, junior colleges, and technical institutes.

The state board's influence in promoting these objectives is evident in the growth of its education department. For example, the first trade school was opened in 1907 and expanded by 1965 to encompass 14 secondary technical schools and 4 collegiate technical institutes, all actually operated by the board and unique in the nation. Additional shortcomings had been recognized and ciscussed widely by 1910, some having considerable importance: the responsibility of parents for their children's education, the abuse of child labor, and the supply of teachers. The General Assembly helped to alleviate some unhealthy practices. One statute stated:

> No certificate of age (working paper) . . . shall be given to any child under 16 years of age unless such child shall be able to read with facility, to write legibly simple sentences in the English language, and to perform the operations of the fundamental rules of arithmetic up to and including fractions; . . . (30).

This law's enforcement, particularly the compulsory attendance section, occupied the department's attention in a major way. Indeed, the 1920 records state that achievement of universal education was one of the greatest contributions of state leadership since the turn of the century. Having succeeded in this, more attention could now be directed toward the solution of other problems.

The affluence of the 1920's, the depression of the thirties, the war during the forties, and the scientific revolution of the fifties and sixties all profoundly affected education. Thus, the board's responsibilities, as in other states, expanded rapidly after the first quarter of the twentieth century in response to society's demands. For one thing, financing education gradually shifted from a legal responsibility to encompass both the state and federal governments, with the Department of Education playing an ever more important role. Research became necessary, and the public information function grew increasingly important. Vocational education, vocational rehabilitation, and teacher education, all major responsibilities of the board, expanded tremendously. Public libraries needed help and received marked attention from the department until the General Assembly transferred this function to the State Library Commission in 1965. As mentioned earlier, it also transferred the operation of the state colleges to the newly created Board of Trustees. Both transfers were due mainly to the heavy and divergent duties assumed by the rapidly expanding state board, which made it seem best to shift these responsibilities elsewhere.

The expansion of curriculum and specialized pupil services characterizes this period, with the greatest advances taking place in the last decade. The most dramatic change among the services occurred in guidance and among the instructional areas in science and mathematics, both inspired by federal funds available under the National Defense Education Act of 1958.

The popular designation of Connecticut as the Constitution State is one of which its citizens are justly proud. John Fiske stated that the Funadmental Orders of 1638-39 was "the first written constitution known to history that created a government and it marked the beginning of American democracy" (31). Students of education regret that this document made no reference to the function of public education in specific terms, but since it referred to the guidance and government of civil affairs, it can be assumed that education was considered one of these.

Public education fared better, but only slightly so, in the next constitution adopted in 1818. Reference was made to the school fund which shall be used perpetually for "the support and encouragement of the public, or common schools throughout the state, and for the equal benefit of all the people thereof" (32). To be sure, this is an oblique way to effect the constitutionality of public schools, but the provision was never challenged. It should be recorded to the everlasting credit of the citizens of Connecticut that by statute, and with meager support from the constitution, they have fashioned a strong, effective system of public education. A new constitution was adopted in December 1965, and progress for education can be noted in the addition of two new sections (33):

> Sec. 1. There shall always be free public elementary and secondary schools in the state. The general assembly shall implement this principle by appropriate legislation.
>
> Sec. 2. The state shall maintain a system of higher education including The University of Connecticut, which shall be dedicated to excellence in higher education. The general assembly shall determine the size, number, terms and methods of appointment of the governing boards of The University of Connecticut and of such constituent units or coordinating bodies in the system as from time to time may be established.

Connecticut, the land of steady habits, persists; and Connecticut, the Constitution State, endures.

FOOTNOTES

1. New Haven Colony, *Records,* I (1641), 210.
2. *Annual Report of the Board of Education* (1876), p. 95.
3. *Ibid.,* pp. 95-97, 102.
4. *Report of the Committee on Common Schools to the General Assembly* (May 1826), p. 6.
5. "School visitors" or overseers are to "examine the in structors, and to displace such as may be found deficient in any requisite qualification, or who will not conform to the regulations by them adopted; to superintend and direct the general instruction of scholars. . . ." Connecticut, *General Statutes* (1824-26), Title 86, ch. 1, sec. 9.
6. See Appendix A.
7. Connecticut, *Supplement to the General Statutes* (1965), Vol. II, ch. 163, sec. 10-4, p. 56.
8. For further information, see *Report of the Board of Education to the Governor, 1918-1920.*
9. See organizational charts for 1930 and 1940 in Appendix B, and *Report of the Board of Education to the Governor, 1928-1930.*
10. National Council of Chief State School Officers, *The State Department of Education* (Washington, D.C.: Government Printing Office, 1952).
11. No provision has ever been made in Connecticut for the title of assistant commissioner. Under the 1953 reorganization, the divisions included Teachers Colleges, Instructional Services, Administrative Services, and Vocational Services. For a breakdown of these divisions, see Appendix B.
12. Willis H. Umberger, comp., "Compilation of Legal Opinions, 1953--," Hartford, Connecticut, State Department of Education. (Typewritten.)
13. *Report of the Board of Education to the Governor, 1926-1928,* p. 48.
14. Department of Education, *School Building Code* (1941), foreword.
15. For further information, see Connecticut, *General Statutes* (1949), ch. 67, sec. 1349, p. 512.
16. Department of Education, *Connecticut School Lunch Guide,* Bulletin 60. (Hartford: The Department, 1955).
17. Norwalk Teachers Association *v.* Board of Education of the City of Norwalk, 138 Conn. 269, 83A. 2d 482 (1951).
18. Connecticut, *Supplement to the General Statutes* (1965), Vol. II, ch. 166, sec. 10-153b and 10-153f, pp. 80-83.
19. There were no consultants available in 1955 for art, music, mathematics, science, and school administration.
20. The years these full-time specialists were added are as follows: guidance (1940), physically handicapped (1944), speech and hearing handicapped (1945), mentally retarded (1946 and a second position in 1960), school social work (1949), socially and emotionally maladjusted (1965), perceptually handicapped (1965), and gifted (1965).
21. Department of Education, *The Team Approach in Pupil Personnel Services,* Bulletin No. 69 (Hartford: The Department, Reprinted June 1958).
22. Connecticut State Commission on Educational Television, "Report to the Honorable John Davis Lodge, Governor of Connecticut," May 1954.
23. Connecticut, *Supplement to the General Statutes* (1965), Vol. II, ch. 178, secs. 10-322 through 10-334, pp. 106-13.
24. Normal schools founded: New Haven, 1893; Willimantic, 1889; Danbury, 1903.
25. U.S. Department of Health, Education, and Welfare, Office of Education, *Administration of Vocational Education, Rules and Regulations,* Vocational Education Bulletin No. 1 (Revised edition; Washington D.C.: Government Printing Office, 1967), p. 43.
26. Norwalk was accredited in 1965; Thames Valley and Waterbury in 1967.

27. Connecticut, *General Statutes* (1958), ch. 164, sec. 10-100.

28. A sampling of conference themes proves this assertion: Community Teamwork for Better Education (1950); Implications of the 1955 White House Conference on Education (1955); Educational Services for Those Beyond High School Age (1957); The School Staff (1960); The Role of the State Department of Education in the Evaluation, Approval, and Accreditation of Public Schools (1961); and The Elementary and Secondary Education Act of 1965 (1965).

29. *Report of Board of Education to the Governor, Together with the Report of the Secretary of the Board* (1900), p. 145.

30. Connecticut, *General Statutes* (1918 revision), ch. 283, sec. 5323, p. 1491.

31. John Fiske, *The Beginnings of New England or the Puritan Theocracy in Its Relation to Civil and Religious Liberty* (Boston: Houghton Mifflin & Co., 1889), p.127.

32. Connecticut, *Journal of the Proceedings of the Convention of Delegates Convened at Hartford, August 26, 1818* (Hartford: The Comptroller, 1901).

33. Connecticut, *Constitution and Historical Antecedents* (1966).

BIBLIOGRAPHY

Public Documents

Connecticut. *Constitution and Historical Antecedents* (1966).

--*General Statutes* (18-1926, 1918 revision, 1949, 1958 revision, 1959).

--*Journal of the Proceedings of the Convention of Delegates Convened at Hartford, August 26, 1818.* Hartford: The Comptroller, 1901.

--*Supplement to the General Statutes.* Vol. II. (1965).

Connecticut Council on Education. *Constitution of the Council* (1943), art. 2, sec.1.

Connecticut State Department of Education. *Laws Relating to Education* (1964).

--*School Building Code* (1941).

New Haven Colony. *Records.* Vol. I (1641).

Norwalk Teachers Association *v.* Board of Education of the City of Norwalk. 138 Conn. 269, 83A. 2d 482 (1951).

Books

Allen, D. C. *Three Centuries of North Haven School History.* Winsted, Conn.: The Dowd Printing Co., 1956.

Fiske, John. *The Beginnings of New England or the Puritan Theocracy in its Relation to Civil and Religious Liberty.* Boston: Houghton Mifflin & Co., 1889.

Governor's Fact-Finding Commission on Education. *Do Citizens and Education Mix?* Naugatuck, Conn.: O'Brien Suburban Press, 1950.

Griffin, Orwin B. *The Evolution of the Connecticut State School System.* Teachers College, Columbia University, Contributions to Education Series, No. 293. New York: J.J. Little and Ives Co., 1928.

Hertzler, Silas. *The Rise of the Public High School in Connecticut.* Baltimore,Md.: Warwick and York, 1930.

James, May Hall. *The Educational History of Old Lyme, Connecticut, 1639-1935.* New Haven: Yale University Press, 1939.

Larson, Emil L. *One-Room and Consolidated Schools of Connecticut.* New York: Teachers College, Columbia University, 1925.

National Council of Chief State School Officers. *The State Department of Education.* Washington, D.C.: Government Printing Office, 1952.

Bulletins

Board of Education. *List of Town School Committees, Board of School Visitors, Boards of Education.* No. 8-1919. Hartford: The Board, 1920.

-- *List of Town School Committees, Board of School Visitors, Boards of Education.* No. 1-1930. Hartford: The Board, 1930.

Connecticut Normal-Training School. *Catalogue 1922-1923.* New Britain: The School.

Department of Education. *Connecticut School Lunch Guide.* Bulletin No. 60. Hartford: The Department, 1955.

-- *The Organization and Functions of the State Department of Education.* Bulletin 3. Hartford: The Department, August 1940.

-- *The Team Approach in Pupil Personnel Services.* Bulletin No. 69. Hartford: The Department, June, 1958.

U.S. Department of Health, Education, and Welfare, Office of Education. *Administration of Vocational Education, Rules and Regulations.* Vocational Education Bulletin No. 1. Revised edition. Washington, D.C.: Government Printing Office, 1967.

Reports

Board of Commissioners of Common Schools. *Report Together with the Annual Report Of the Secretary of the Board.* Hartford: The State of Connecticut, 1839-42.

Board of Education. *Annual Reports.* Hartford: The Board, 1876-1967.

Commissioner of Education. *Annual Report to the Governor.* Hartford: The State of Connecticut, 1949-52.

Committee on Common Schools. *Report to the General Assembly.* New Haven: The Committee, May 1826.

National Study of Secondary School Evaluations (formerly, Cooperative Study of Secondary School Standards). *Evaluative Criteria.* Washington, D.C.: National Study of Secondary School Evaluations, 1960.

Unpublished Material

Connecticut State Commission on Educational Television, "Report to the Honorable John Davis Lodge, Governor of Connecticut." May 1954.

Umberger, Willis H., comp. "Compilation of Legal Opinions, 1953–." Hartford, Connecticut, State Department of Education. (Typewritten.)

Appendix A

CONNECTICUT STATE BOARD OF EDUCATION AND CHIEF STATE SCHOOL OFFICERS

Year	Number of board members	Composition of board	Length of term	Title of chief state school officer	Name of chief state school officer
1838	10, Board of Commissioners of Common Schools	Governor, School Fund Commissioner ex officio; 8 others–1 from each county appointed by Governor with consent of Senate	1 Year	Secretary of the Board of Commissioners	Henry Barnard, 1838-42
1842	Board abolished	. . .		. . .	. . .
1845	. . .	Commissioner of School Fund, ex officio, appointed by legislation		Superintendent of Common Schools	Seth P. Beers, 1845-49
1849	8, Board of Trustees	8 Trustees (1 from each county), appointed by Legislature, 2 in each year (overlapping terms)	4 years	Superintendent of Common Schools (Principal of State Normal School, ex officio)	Henry Barnard, 1849-55 John D. Philbrick, 1855-56 David N. Camp, 1856-65
1865	6, State Board of Education	Governor, Lieutenant Governor, 4 members–1 from each congressional district	4 years	Secretary of the Board	Daniel C. Gilman, 1865-67 Birdsey G. Northrop, 1867-83 Charles D. Hine, 1883-1895
1895	7, State Board of Education	Governor, Lieutenant Governor, Secretary of the State Board of Education ex officio, 4 members–1 from each congressional district	4 years	Secretary of the Board	Charles D. Hine, 1895-1919
1919	11, State Board of Education	Governor, Lieutenant Governor, ex officio 9 others, 1 from each county, 1 at large	6 years	Secretary of the Board (Commissioner of Education)	Charles D. Hine, 1919-1920 Albert B. Meredith, 1920-30
1931	9, State Board of Education	1 from each county, 1 at large, appointment by Governor	6 years	Secretary of the Board (Commissioner of Education)	Ernest W. Butterfield, 1930-38 Alonzo G. Grace, 1938-48 Finis E. Engleman, 1948-56 William J. Sanders, 1956-

Appendix B

Chart I.--CONNECTICUT DEPARTMENT OF EDUCATION, 1900

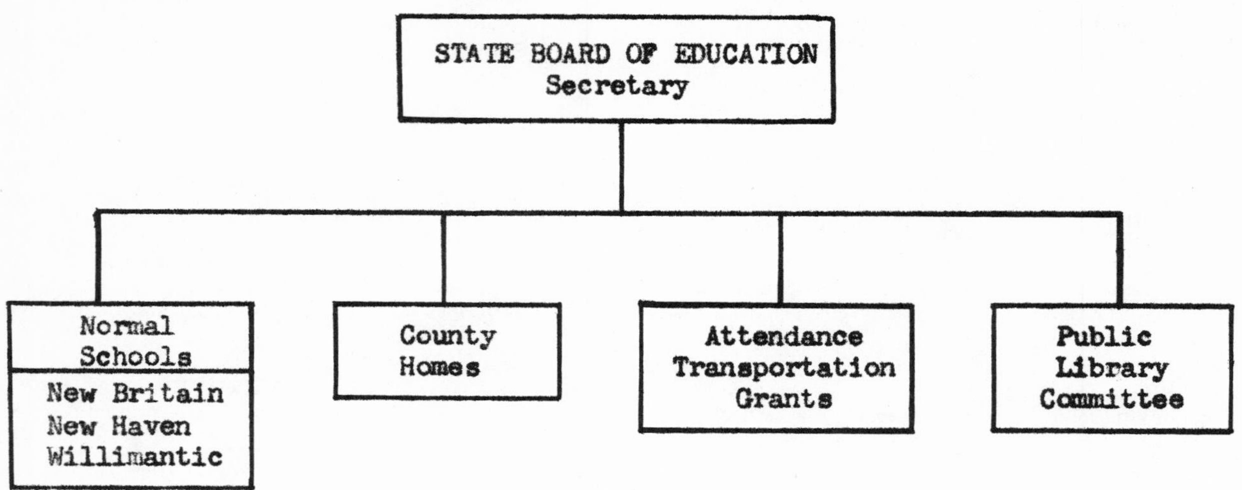

Chart II.--CONNECTICUT DEPARTMENT OF EDUCATION, 1910

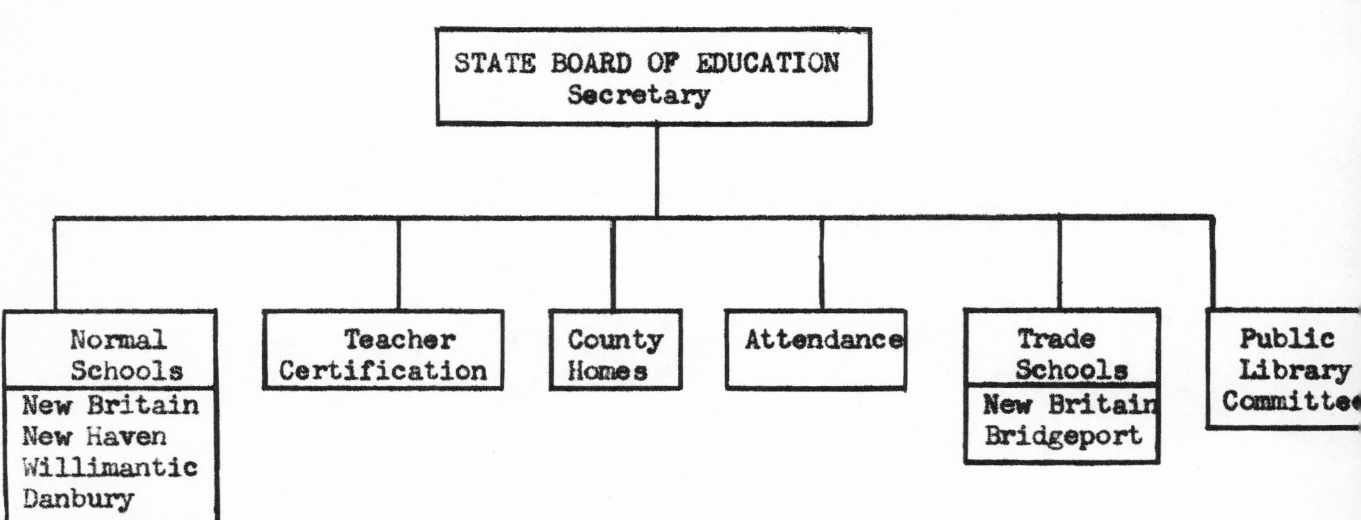

Appendix B

Chart III.--CONNECTICUT DEPARTMENT OF EDUCATION, 1920

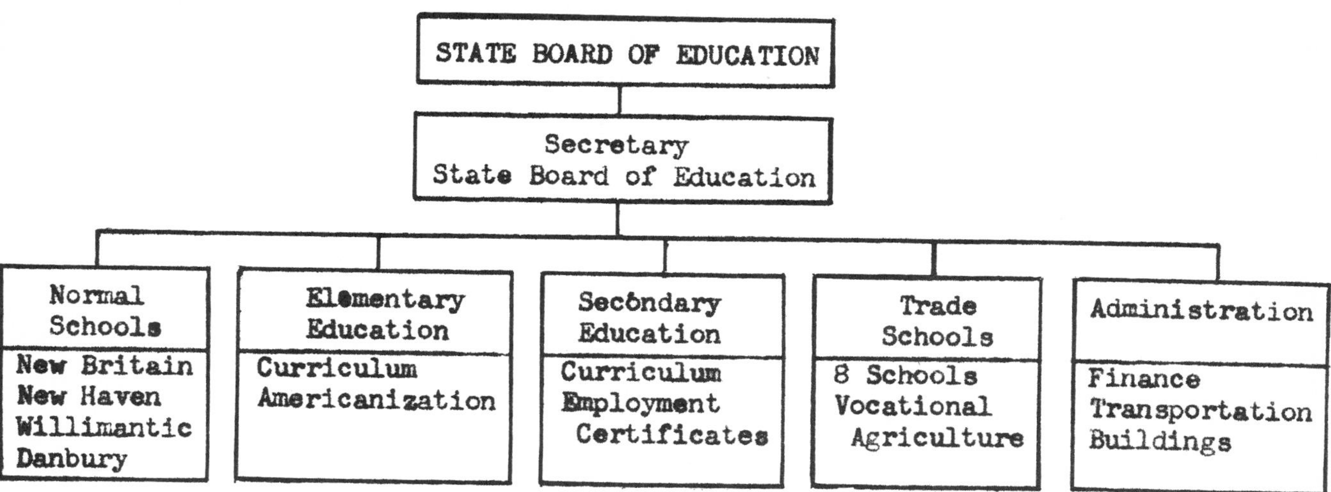

Chart IV.--CONNECTICUT DEPARTMENT OF EDUCATION, 1930

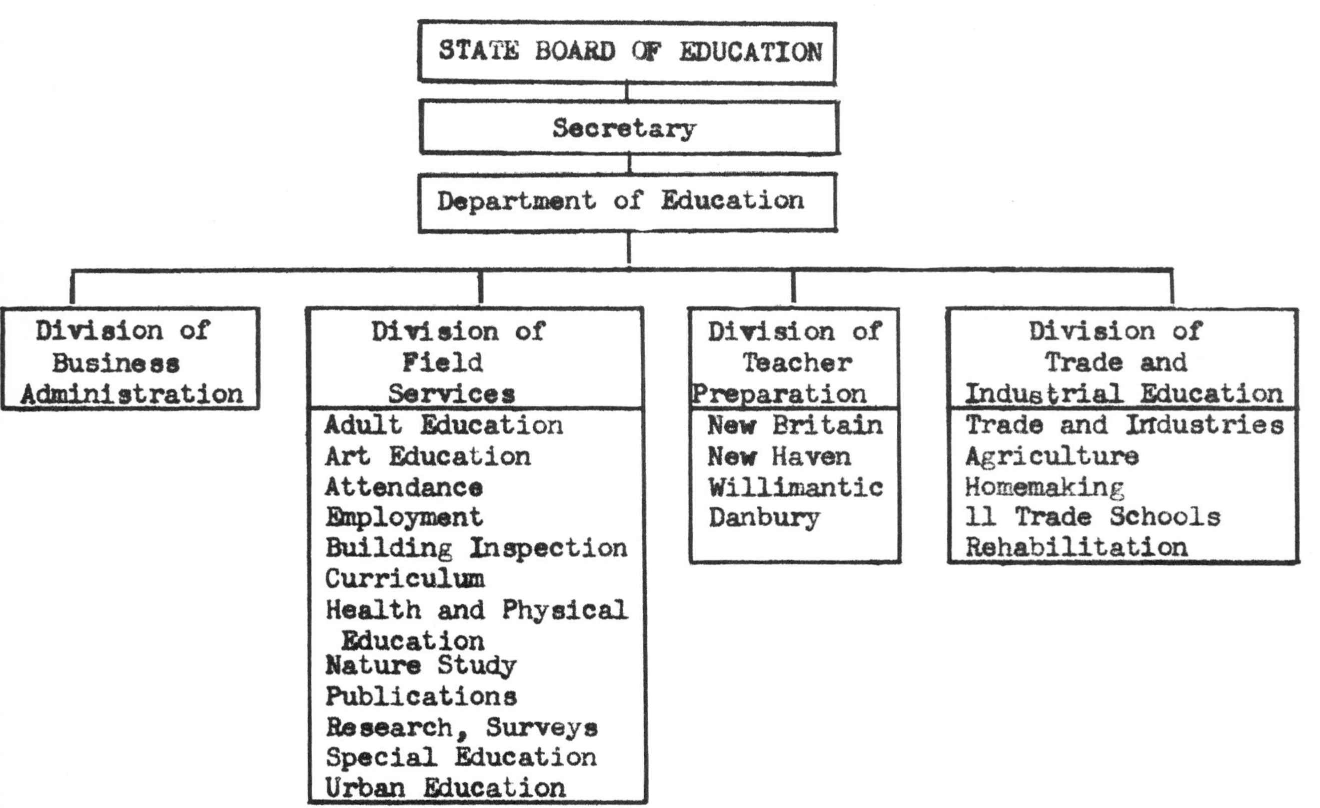

Appendix B

Chart V.--CONNECTICUT DEPARTMENT OF EDUCATION, 1940

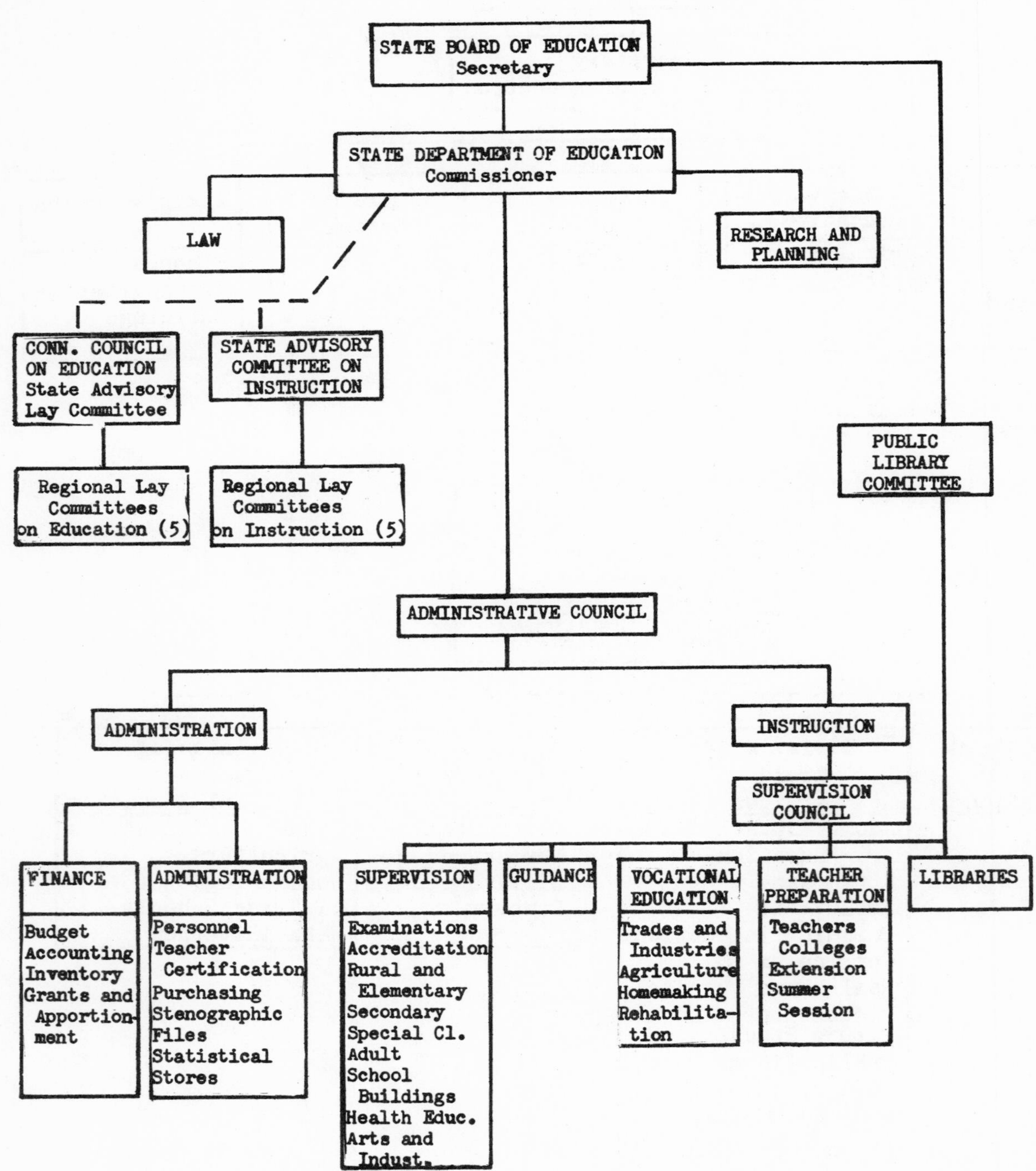

Appendix B

Chart VI.--CONNECTICUT DEPARTMENT OF EDUCATION, 1953

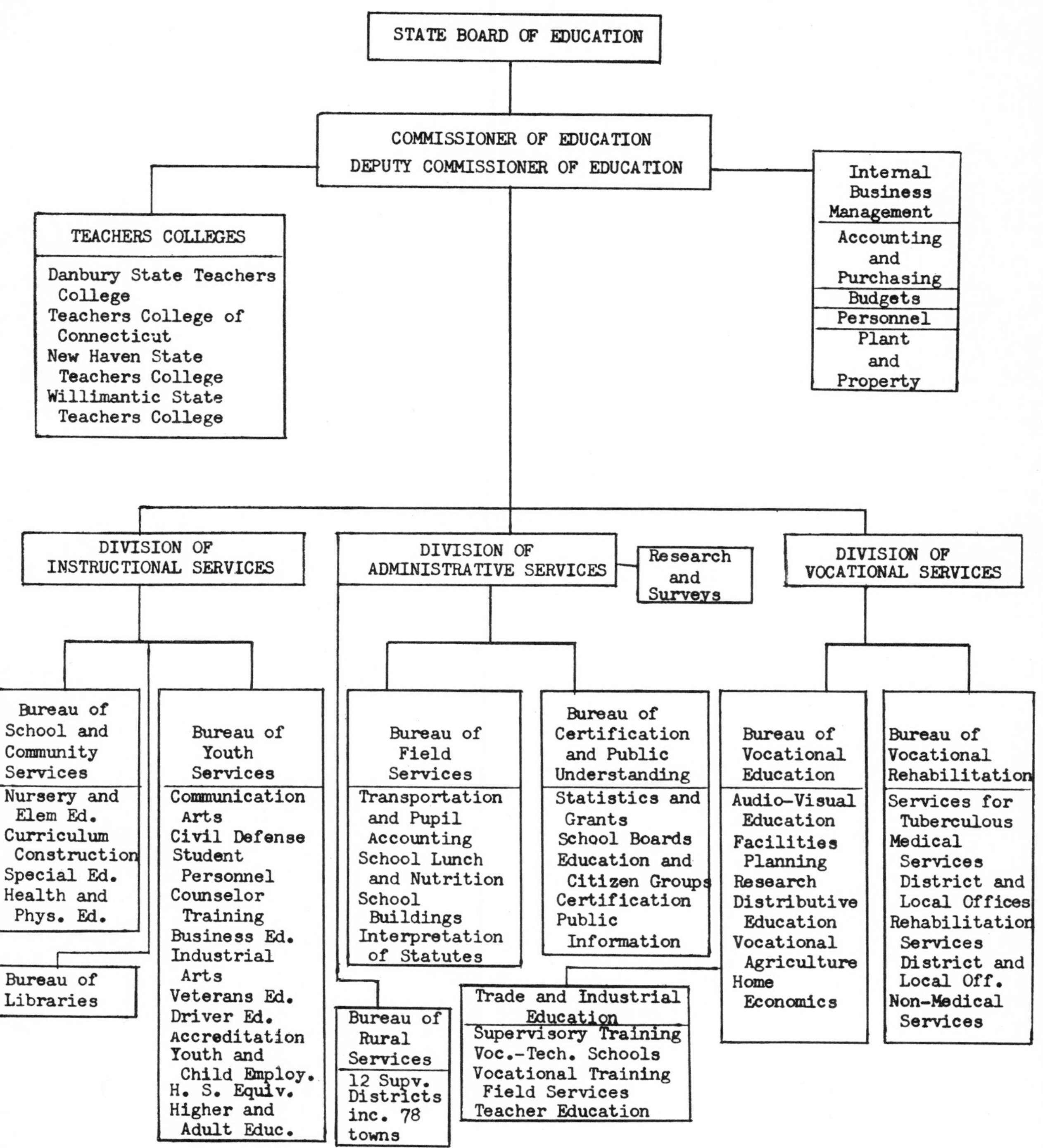

Appendix B

Chart VII.—CONNECTICUT DEPARTMENT OF EDUCATION, 1960

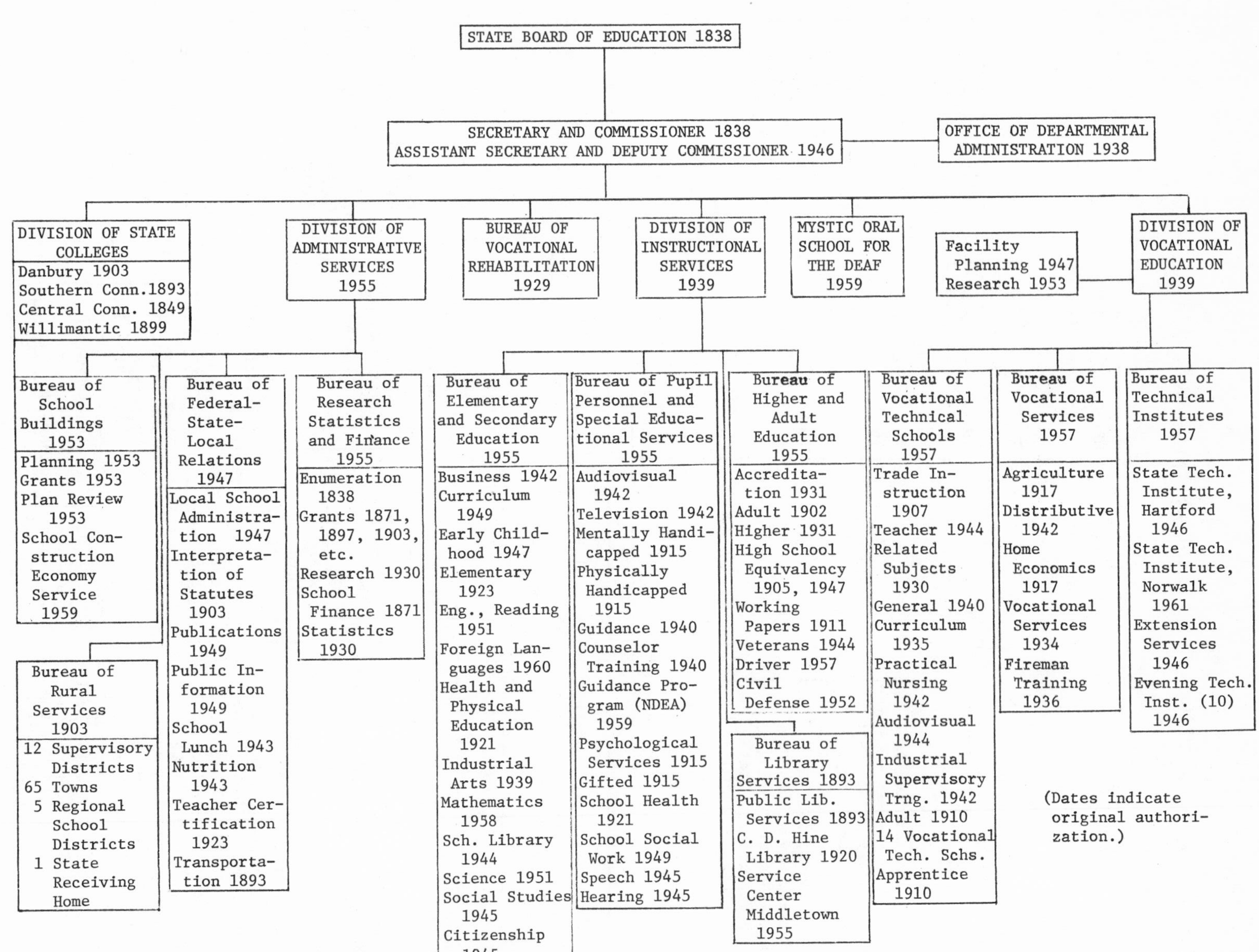
STATE BOARD OF EDUCATION 1838
SECRETARY AND COMMISSIONER 1838
ASSISTANT SECRETARY AND DEPUTY COMMISSIONER 1946
OFFICE OF DEPARTMENTAL ADMINISTRATION 1938
DIVISION OF STATE COLLEGES
Danbury 1903
Southern Conn. 1893
Central Conn. 1849
Willimantic 1899
DIVISION OF ADMINISTRATIVE SERVICES 1955
BUREAU OF VOCATIONAL REHABILITATION 1929
DIVISION OF INSTRUCTIONAL SERVICES 1939
MYSTIC ORAL SCHOOL FOR THE DEAF 1959
Facility Planning 1947 Research 1953
DIVISION OF VOCATIONAL EDUCATION 1939
Bureau of School Buildings 1953
Planning 1953
Grants 1953
Plan Review 1953
School Construction Economy Service 1959
Bureau of Rural Services 1903
12 Supervisory Districts
65 Towns
5 Regional School Districts
1 State Receiving Home
Bureau of Federal-State-Local Relations 1947
Local School Administration 1947
Interpretation of Statutes 1903
Publications 1949
Public Information 1949
School Lunch 1943
Nutrition 1943
Teacher Certification 1923
Transportation 1893
Bureau of Research Statistics and Finance 1955
Enumeration 1838
Grants 1871, 1897, 1903, etc.
Research 1930
School Finance 1871
Statistics 1930
Bureau of Elementary and Secondary Education 1955
Business 1942
Curriculum 1949
Early Childhood 1947
Elementary 1923
Eng., Reading 1951
Foreign Languages 1960
Health and Physical Education 1921
Industrial Arts 1939
Mathematics 1958
Sch. Library 1944
Science 1951
Social Studies 1945
Citizenship 1945
Bureau of Pupil Personnel and Special Educational Services 1955
Audiovisual 1942
Television 1942
Mentally Handicapped 1915
Physically Handicapped 1915
Guidance 1940
Counselor Training 1940
Guidance Program (NDEA) 1959
Psychological Services 1915
Gifted 1915
School Health 1921
School Social Work 1949
Speech 1945
Hearing 1945
Bureau of Higher and Adult Education 1955
Accreditation 1931
Adult 1902
Higher 1931
High School Equivalency 1905, 1947
Working Papers 1911
Veterans 1944
Driver 1957
Civil Defense 1952
Bureau of Library Services 1893
Public Lib. Services 1893
C. D. Hine Library 1920
Service Center Middletown 1955
Bureau of Vocational Technical Schools 1957
Trade Instruction 1907
Teacher 1944
Related Subjects 1930
General 1940
Curriculum 1935
Practical Nursing 1942
Audiovisual 1944
Industrial Supervisory Trng. 1942
Adult 1910
14 Vocational Tech. Schs.
Apprentice 1910
Bureau of Vocational Services 1957
Agriculture 1917
Distributive 1942
Home Economics 1917
Vocational Services 1934
Fireman Training 1936
Bureau of Technical Institutes 1957
State Tech. Institute, Hartford 1946
State Tech. Institute, Norwalk 1961
Extension Services 1946
Evening Tech. Inst. (10) 1946
(Dates indicate original authorization.)

Appendix B

Chart VIII.—CONNECTICUT DEPARTMENT OF EDUCATION, 1965

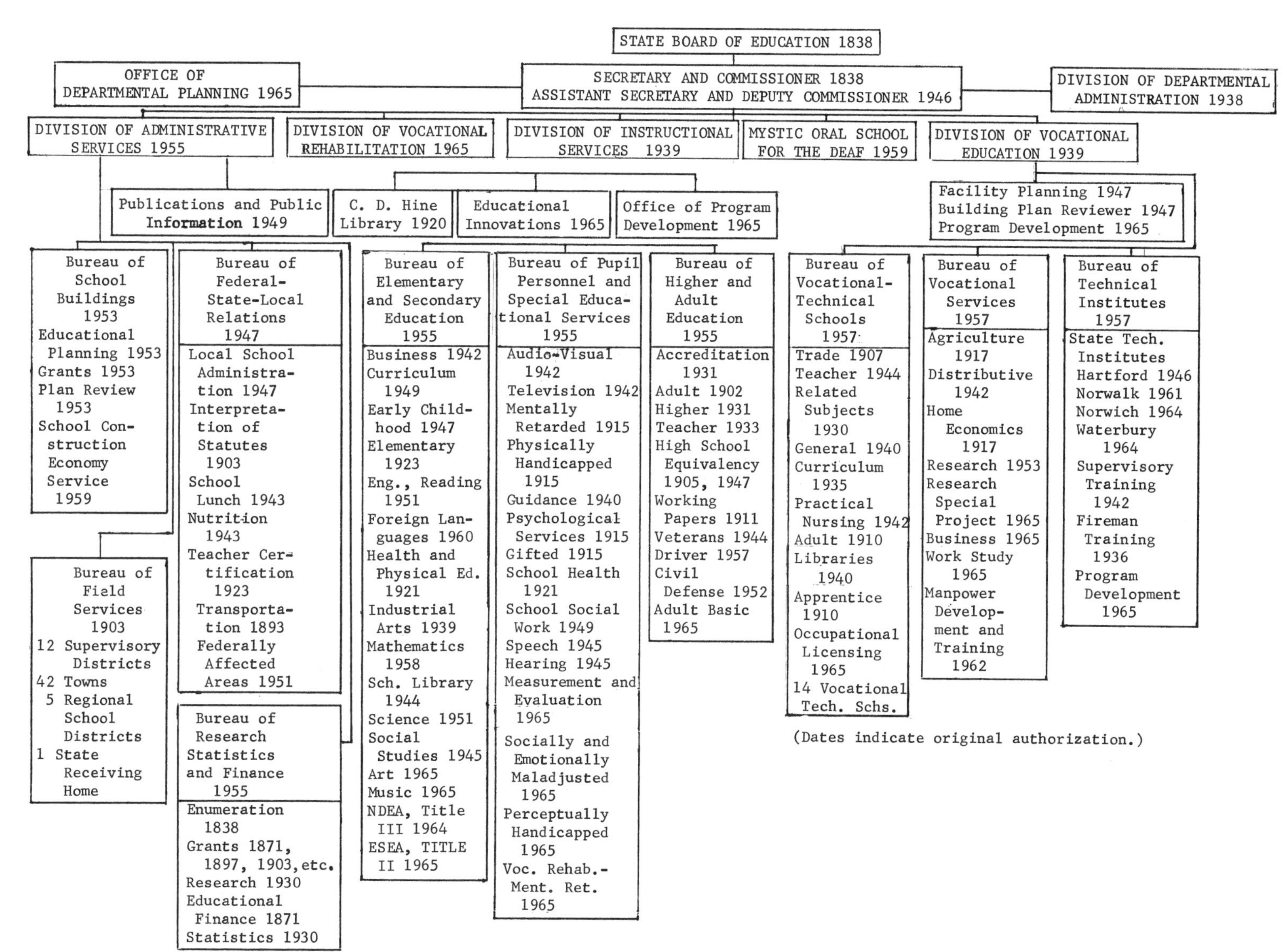

STATE BOARD OF EDUCATION 1838
SECRETARY AND COMMISSIONER 1838
ASSISTANT SECRETARY AND DEPUTY COMMISSIONER 1946
OFFICE OF DEPARTMENTAL PLANNING 1965
DIVISION OF DEPARTMENTAL ADMINISTRATION 1938
DIVISION OF ADMINISTRATIVE SERVICES 1955
DIVISION OF VOCATIONAL REHABILITATION 1965
DIVISION OF INSTRUCTIONAL SERVICES 1939
MYSTIC ORAL SCHOOL FOR THE DEAF 1959
DIVISION OF VOCATIONAL EDUCATION 1939
Publications and Public Information 1949
C. D. Hine Library 1920
Educational Innovations 1965
Office of Program Development 1965
Facility Planning 1947
Building Plan Reviewer 1947
Program Development 1965
Bureau of School Buildings 1953
Educational Planning 1953
Grants 1953
Plan Review 1953
School Construction Economy Service 1959
Bureau of Field Services 1903
12 Supervisory Districts
42 Towns
5 Regional School Districts
1 State Receiving Home
Bureau of Federal-State-Local Relations 1947
Local School Administration 1947
Interpretation of Statutes 1903
School Lunch 1943
Nutrition 1943
Teacher Certification 1923
Transportation 1893
Federally Affected Areas 1951
Bureau of Research Statistics and Finance 1955
Enumeration 1838
Grants 1871, 1897, 1903, etc.
Research 1930
Educational Finance 1871
Statistics 1930
Bureau of Elementary and Secondary Education 1955
Business 1942
Curriculum 1949
Early Childhood 1947
Elementary 1923
Eng., Reading 1951
Foreign Languages 1960
Health and Physical Ed. 1921
Industrial Arts 1939
Mathematics 1958
Sch. Library 1944
Science 1951
Social Studies 1945
Art 1965
Music 1965
NDEA, Title III 1964
ESEA, TITLE II 1965
Bureau of Pupil Personnel and Special Educational Services 1955
Audio-Visual 1942
Television 1942
Mentally Retarded 1915
Physically Handicapped 1915
Guidance 1940
Psychological Services 1915
Gifted 1915
School Health 1921
School Social Work 1949
Speech 1945
Hearing 1945
Measurement and Evaluation 1965
Socially and Emotionally Maladjusted 1965
Perceptually Handicapped 1965
Voc. Rehab.-Ment. Ret. 1965
Bureau of Higher and Adult Education 1955
Accreditation 1931
Adult 1902
Higher 1931
Teacher 1933
High School Equivalency 1905, 1947
Working Papers 1911
Veterans 1944
Driver 1957
Civil Defense 1952
Adult Basic 1965
Bureau of Vocational-Technical Schools 1957
Trade 1907
Teacher 1944
Related Subjects 1930
General 1940
Curriculum 1935
Practical Nursing 1942
Adult 1910
Libraries 1940
Apprentice 1910
Occupational Licensing 1965
14 Vocational Tech. Schs.
Bureau of Vocational Services 1957
Agriculture 1917
Distributive 1942
Home Economics 1917
Research 1953
Research Special Project 1965
Business 1965
Work Study 1965
Manpower Development and Training 1962
Bureau of Technical Institutes 1957
State Tech. Institutes
Hartford 1946
Norwalk 1961
Norwich 1964
Waterbury 1964
Supervisory Training 1942
Fireman Training 1936
Program Development 1965
(Dates indicate original authorization.)

8 Delaware

DEPARTMENT OF PUBLIC INSTRUCTION

Paul H. Johnston

Contents

INTRODUCTION

Delaware is at the upper end of the Del-Mar-Va Peninsula, which separates the Delaware and Chesapeake Bays. The state is not quite 100 miles long and, at its widest point, is 35 miles across. Its land area of 1,965 square miles makes Delaware next to the smallest state in size. Its 1965 population was 512,000, ranking it forty-sixth among the states (1). Delaware has but three counties, each of which extends the entire width of the state; from north to south they are New Castle, Kent, and Sussex. Because of its shape Delaware is called the Diamond State. The first of the 13 original colonies to ratify the federal Constitution, it is also known as the First State.

The Dutch, thought to be the first Europeans to arrive in what is now Delaware, settled in the southeastern area near Lewes in 1625 (2). The Swedes arrived a decade later, followed by the English in 1666. The English ruled the region from the time of their arrival until the American Revolution.

During the nineteenth century, Delaware was mostly agricultural, and the people held a conservative philosophy of government. Located on a peninsula, they were undisturbed by east-to-west migration and were involved but little in urbanization. During the Civil War, Delaware, as a border state, was divided, the north being loyal to the Union and the south loyal to the Rebels. Since the state accepted slavery, it was slow to ratify the Thirteenth, Fourteenth, and Fifteenth Amendments. Negroes remained politically subjugated well into the twentieth century.

Although largely rural before the Civil War, Delaware slowly acquired industry and urban characteristics thereafter. Following World War I, it changed from an agricultural to an urban society. These economic and social changes are reflected in Delaware's evolving system of education.

EDUCATION BEFORE 1917

Although the Dutch were on the banks of the Delaware River earlier, in 1638 the Swedes and a few Finns founded the first permanent settlement when they erected Christina Fort near the mouth of Christina Creek. At this time, since Sweden had no public education, it depended on the church and the home to educate the children. The church was a state institution and thus was able to control education. The duties of ministers and schoolmasters were frequently combined, or the schoolmaster held a position in the church in addition to his teaching duties. This was the educational system Sweden transplanted to its settlements.

The church congregation at Christina established the first school in Delaware when in October 1699 it engaged Swen Colsberg to act as both bellringer and schoolmaster. Since the Swedes regarded education as very important, as the settlers founded other communities they organized more new schools. The church usually served as the schoolhouse and the minister as the schoolmaster, although a few nonministerial schoolmasters came over from time to time, and private homes sometimes served as schoolhouses. These schools emphasized reading and arithmetic.

The Dutch, who began to found their own settlements in 1656, sent schoolmaster Evert Pietersen from Amsterdam to organize a school in what is now New Castle, Delaware. As in Holland, the church served as a schoolhouse and the minister as schoolmaster.

The English began moving into Delaware in 1664, and they soon outnumbered the earlier settlers. They brought with them from England a system of education that can hardly be called public or universal, since their schools were private and admitted few who were not wealthy. William Penn laid plans for universal education, but they were not carried out. In fact, the English did very little to further education other than to grant charters to a few schools and in 1683 to enact legislation enabling certain religious societies to hold property and to raise funds by lottery for school purposes.

As the English settlers became more numerous, the Swedes elected English-speaking clergymen to preach to them and began abandoning their own tongue. Gradually the children began to learn the English language before Swedish. By the Revolution, the distinctive Swedish and Dutch schools were abandoned and merged with those operated by the Lutheran and Episcopal churches.

From 1638 to 1776, the history of Delaware was closely identified with that of Pennsylvania (3). In fact, from 1703 to 1776, Delaware and Pennsylvania had the same governor, although Delaware was considered a separate colony. William Penn and the Friends Society were intelligent and aggressive, and made their imprint on Delaware society. The legislative provisions Penn presented to the colonists included the establishment of public schools. However, it was 1748 before the Friends organized a school at Wilmington.

Universal education was still far away, in Delaware, but there was an increasing interest. Delaware's first constitution in 1776 failed to mention education, but the Constitution of 1792 stated: "The legislature shall, as soon as conveniently may be, provide by law...for establishing schools, and promoting arts and sciences" (4).

Acting on constitutional authority, in 1792, the state Legislature passed a school fund law which became the basis of financing a public school system. This law stipulated that money accruing from marriage and tavern licenses, gifts, donations, and bequests should be placed in a special fund for establishing schools in Delaware. The act designated the state treasurer as the trustee for the fund, and he was authorized to invest the income in shares of various bank stocks until they were needed for school purposes.

In 1817, the Legislature appropriated the first money for public education in the history of Delaware by providing for the education of poor children. Undoubtedly, the act was a mistake as it delayed the development of effective, universal public education by providing only for paupers, thus identifying public education as a pauper system. Citizens did not relish the idea of the pauper schools; they believed free education to be of little worth and only for those who could not help themselves.

Most property owners in early Delaware did not favor public education because they did not like the necessary taxation. Despite this opposition, in 1821 the Legislature passed an act to support Sunday schools for teaching reading, writing, and morality.

It was only through the persistence of Judge Willard Hall that the state progressed in creating free public schools. Hall, a lawyer from Massachusetts, came to Delaware in 1803 and devoted half a century to public education. He served as secretary of state, a member of the state Senate, and later as a federal judge. Through his efforts the Governor and finally the Legislature were persuaded to support a bill in 1829 providing free schools for all children.

This school law provided for the funds to come in part from the state school fund and in part from private, local contributions. School districts were to extend for a radius of 2 miles from the centers of population, with an adequate number of pupils the sole criterion for creating a new district. The law required the state to provide as much money for each school district as was raised by private contributions. The following year the law was amended to permit local school districts to levy taxes by a vote of the majority of taxpayers and protected the taxpayers by limiting the amount each district could raise to \$300. The \$300 in turn was matched by a state contribution.

The school law of 1830 provided for the voters of a district to have full control of the schools. They were to hold meetings to determine their schools' operation and could decide how much money they would raise to support schools. In 1833, 133 school districts were drawing state aid; 61 districts in New Castle County, 36 in Kent, and 36 in Sussex.

Judge Hall's ideas on democracy, incorporated in the school laws of 1829 and 1830, influenced Delaware's education for the next half century. As he feared central government, the legislation permitted local school districts to do as they pleased, but it also allowed them to do nothing if they so desired. The schools were too loosely organized, and depended too much on private contributions, to meet their costs. Hall wanted to see education as a voluntary activity with no state compulsion and with little or no state supervision. But the two school laws proved unsatisfactory because poor families, who would benefit most, refused to vote in favor of school taxes, and the districts had to depend on private contributions to meet their costs. As a result, teachers were poorly paid and poorly prepared.

From 1829 to 1875, two forces developed representing the conservative and liberal elements among the citizens. The liberals, known as the "friends of education," were increasingly dissatisfied and sought at least a minimum of central control. In 1861, they were influential in revising the school law of 1829 to overcome some of the negative effects of centralization by requiring school districts to levy a minimum tax for school purposes. The law provided that each district could vote increases in this minimum requirement. Six years later, after the Legislature failed to provide for a state superintendent of education, the "friends of education" planned a campaign for greater state control.

The "friends," under the leadership of J.E.Clawson and supported by groups of teachers, continued to point out the weaknesses in the educational system and the need for state leadership. Again, in 1875, they were influential in getting the Legislature to pass a free school law. This act created the position of state superintendent of Delaware Free Schools and a State Board of Education, consisting of the president of Delaware College, the secretary of state, the state auditor, and the state superintendent.

The Governor appointed James H. Groves as the first state superintendent for a 1-year term in 1875. Although he was empowered to visit schools and examine and certify teachers, the law gave him little other authority to administer the public schools. Subject to appointment by the Governor on a yearly basis, his position was considerably weakened. Local taxpayers continued to have the final say as to the extent they would support education, and for the most part they refused to tax themselves enough to develop a strong system.

Taxpayers' opposition to more authority in the hands of the state superintendent was supported by the growing independence of the incorporated towns, particularly Wilmington and New Castle. New Castle's influence grew to the point that in 1879 they were able to persuade the Legislature to exempt schools in incorporated towns and cities from the authority of the state superintendent and state board.

Thomas N. Williams succeeded State Superintendent Groves in 1883, only to face a legislature growing increasingly hostile to state control. The "local control" forces gained enough power by 1887 to abolish the office of state superintendent and return to the county system of education. The State Board of Education now consisted of the secretary of state, the president of Delaware College, and three county superintendents. The state board had little authority, however, and three county boards of education administered the school system. Each county board administered its system independently, with separate, parallel systems operating for Negro and poor white pupils. Within each county, certain independent school districts were not required to operate under the laws of the county unless they so desired and made "special requests."

Conditions in the schools became increasingly chaotic. Within a decade it became clear that this completely decentralized system was unworkable. Many of the local districts contained small, uneconomical units with wide variations in length of school years. Teacher certification also varied greatly among school districts, and there was a rapid teacher turnover. Very few statistical records were kept, and these lacked uniformity.

There appeared to be less hostility toward taxation for schools; more revenues were raised than spent. But it was even more evident that the views held in the Constitutions of 1792 and 1831 were outdated and that better administration was necessary. When the state decided to write a new constitution, there was an effort to incorporate more modern concepts for education. The Constitution of 1897 required the Legislature to establish and maintain a general and efficient school system. It continued to allow separate schools for white and nonwhite pupils, but it generally required all children to attend.

The Constitution of 1897 also provided a financial basis for public education, designating the public school fund for educational purposes only. It also stipulated that the state would provide a minimum of $100,000 for the public schools from any available source. These funds were to be allocated to white and Negro pupils separately, but on the same proportional basis. Also, they could not be used for nonpublic school purposes.

The following year, the Legislature changed the school laws to give the state board authority to control the white and nonwhite schools in each county. The Governor appointed county commissions of three members to 3-year terms, and a county superintendent for a 2-year term. The 1898 school law charged the county commissions with direct supervision of the schools; the commissioners would examine the county superintendents' reports and investigate operation of the school systems.

The 1898 law also reorganized the Board of Education. When the new board first met, it found such a lack of educational data that it decided its most important task was to compile reliable statistics. It sent out questionnaires and collected data for a report, finally printed in 1900.

One problem, caused in part by the poor statistics and in part by political considerations, was the inequitable distribution of school funds. The new state board learned that certain districts were getting twice as much financial aid as others in proportion to the number of pupils. To remedy the situation, it recommended, and in 1901 the Legislature enacted into law, a requirement that these funds be distributed according to the number of teachers employed for a minimum of 140 days the previous year. The Constitution of 1897 required attendance of physically able pupils, but since it gave no further details, pupils attended school more or less on a voluntary basis. Attendance varied widely among the districts, as did the length of the school year. In 1907, the Legislature enacted a law requiring compulsory attendance for at least 5 months of the year, with penalties for those who failed to comply.

Another problem centered on the composition of the board itself and the administration of its responsibilities. Since senior members of the county school commissions made up part of the board's membership, continuity of the board's action was broken because they were able to serve only for 1 year. This deprived the board of experienced members. The board itself recommended a change, and the 1911 Legislature abolished the old Board of Education and created a new one composed of seven members, appointed by the Governor for staggered terms of 7 years each.

The new Board of Education faced such problems as a lack of graded schools, little or no supervision of teachers, no uniformity in teacher certification, and poor schoolhousing. The board, composed of laymen, quickly realized that it needed professional leadership. With the support of the Governor, it persuaded the 1913 Legislature to permit the Governor to appoint a state commissioner of education, who would serve for a 2-year term. The law required the new commissioner to be a graduate of a reputable college or normal school and have 5 years teaching experience. But when the Governor appointed Charles W. Wagner, Ph.D., to be the first commissioner, there was considerable opposition from people who still felt that this was merely another useless state office and a waste of taxpayers' money.

EDUCATIONAL CHANGE, 1917 TO 1925

From 1917 to 1925, Delaware experienced a greater change in education than at any other time in its history. This was due to a number of forces, but the impetus stemmed from a group of lay leaders, educational organizations, and parent-teacher groups who wanted to bring about better education. They were in large measure responsible for the School Codes of 1919 and 1921 and the subsequent reorganization of the public school system.

The Service Citizens of Delaware

In 1914, a group of citizens organized the General Service Board to study and publicize social conditions in Delaware. A little later, they combined with another organization known as the Council for Defense. In 1918, under the guidance of Pierre S. duPont, the combined groups organized the Service Citizens of Delaware to bring together men and women interested in improving social conditions in the state. The group was incorporated for 5 years–later extended to 9 years–with duPont as the elected president.

DuPont, president of E. I. duPont de Nemours and Company and chairman of the board of directors of the General Motors Corporation, had recently been appointed by Governor John G. Townsend to the State Board of Education. From his personal fortune, duPont donated to the Service Citizens an annual working fund of $90,000. The association elected the most competent and experienced men and women in the state to the board of managers, which in turn appointed Joseph H. Odell as director. The organization then set about collecting reliable information, disseminating the facts to the people, and conducting demonstrations which hopefully would lead to improved conditions. It brought to Delaware the country's most experienced advisers to survey the school buildings, public health, taxation, and many other aspects of the economy and society. Thus, it was able to piece together a scientific description of conditions in the state.

Particularly interested in education, the Service Citizens joined forces with local boards of education. Made up largely of people who thought in statewide terms, this group also worked closely with top administrators and official policy-building groups, including the State Board of Education.

Along with the efforts of duPont and the Service Citizens, the U.S. Bureau of Education played a positive role in creating a climate for educational change. In line with his policy of cooperating with state agencies requesting help, the U.S. Commissioner of Education requested a Bureau of Education staff member, Stephen B. Weeks, to study the condition of education in Delaware. In 1917, Weeks published his study, entitled *The History of Public Education in Delaware*, and it proved to be most effective in further arousing the citizenry concerning educational deficiencies.

Weeks encouraged State Commissioner of Education Wagner to use his influence in working for changes he recommended. Wagner inaugurated a statewide compaign with the support of leading educational and social organizations and, with assistance from the press, the pulpit, and a variety of public forums, vigorously insisted that something be done.

This widespread interest in education prompted the 1917 Legislature to appoint a survey commission of five members to make its own study. In turn, the commission delegated to the General Education Board, founded in New York by John D. Rockefeller, the authority to conduct the survey. The results exposed "to public view a motley collection of laws which had been accumulating, haphazardly, for more than a century" (5). It further revealed that those responsible for developing schools had been given "plenty of nominal power but little or no means of implementing it" (6).

The General Education Board survey found some of the same deficiencies that the Service Citizens of Delaware had pointed up in their studies: poor condition of school buildings; lack of uniformity in teacher certification, supervision, and curriculum; poorly defined administrative authority; and too little financial assistance. It concluded that –

> On the whole, therefore, public education in Delaware is at a low ebb. Public opinion is unaroused; professional standards are as yet unformed; the state organization, despite certain good features, is ill-jointed, and ineffective. The laws need to be rounded out, so as to give the state an organization, the various parts of which play into each other effectively; policies must be framed on larger lines; cooperation between the state and the county unit must be brought out; proper provisions for teacher training must be made; the state, the county and the local community must join in raising the larger sums required to sustain creditable schools, adapted to the needs, capacity, and opportunities of the school children of Delaware (7).

The reports were distributed throughout the state, newspapers presented the findings, and speakers explained and discussed the report before many lay groups.

The Delaware State Education Association agreed wholeheartedly with the General Education Board's recommendations for a central program. Teachers were particularly concerned with the problems of inadequate buildings and one-room schools, malnutrition among the pupils, reading problems, and teacher qualifications. The association had been trying to improve the training and certification of teachers, as well as teacher benefits such as salaries, tenure, and pensions. Thus, the important educational surveys, with support from lay and professional groups, created an excellent climate for legislative change in Delaware's education.

School Codes of 1919 and 1921

The commission appointed by the Legislature to study school conditions accepted the General Education Board's report as a basis for proposing drastic changes in the School Code. In 1919, the Legislature adopted a new code vesting administrative authority for operating the school system in the State Board of Education, with a commissioner of education as it executive officer. This was in sharp contrast to the previous system where local school districts still operated completely independent of each other with limited central authority.

The 1919 School Code also provided for boards and superintendents for Delaware's three counties. County boards were authorized to raise taxes, appoint teachers, supervise instruction, standardize teacher certification, and increase teacher salaries. They were responsible for providing transportation for elementary school pupils living over 2 miles from a school and for high school pupils living over 3 miles from a school. They could require pupils up to the eighth grade and under 16 to attend school for 180 days per year, and they were authorized to consolidate schools upon the recommendation of the county superintendents. The law eliminated the elected local school officials in the rural schools, but the school officials of Wilmington and 13 of the largest communities continued to operate their systems independently of the 1919 School Code.

The code was passed with considerable opposition, mainly centering around the loss of local control and centralization of authority, the longer school year, and higher real estate taxes. Most of this opposition came from the downstate rural elements of Kent and Sussex Counties where the schools were small and attendance irregular. Two years later, in 1921, the opposition finally succeeded in persuading the Legislature to enact a modified school code.

The School Code of 1921 eliminated the county system of education and replaced the county boards and superintendents with local boards authorized to appoint their own teachers. At the same time, it strengthened the State Board of Education by assigning to it some of the county boards' functions, such as budget making and teacher supervision. The state board also would make budget requests to the Legislature for Wilmington, the special school districts, and the rural school districts.

As a compromise to the rural areas, the 1921 Legislature reduced compulsory school attendance from 180 to 160 days. It compromised with property owners, particularly farmers, by introducing a graduated income tax, ranging from 1 to 3 percent of net income, as a replacement for the high tax on real estate. It did continue a modest real estate tax to be levied by the state, and it permitted the state to provide further funds by levying corporation franchise and corporation income taxes. The schools were to receive additional revenue from the state school fund and occasional appropriations from the Legislature.

State Board of Education. The school laws of 1921 authorized the State Board of Education to administer Delaware's public schools. The Governor was to appoint four board members to serve 5-year terms, no more than two belonging to the same political party. In 1931, the Legislature increased the board to six members, who would serve 3-year terms, no more than three belonging to the same political party.

Under the law, the Board of Education was made responsible for appointing a state superintendent of public instruction for a 1-year term, but subject to reappointment indefinitely. It required the state superintendent to serve as executive secretary to the board and chief administrator of the state's school system, with duties prescribed by the board. However, the board would determine the educational policies of the state. It would consult and cooperate with local school boards, school officials, and citizens concerning education, and appoint professional and clerical assistants to carry out its policies. The law required the state board to adopt regulations concerning such matters as apportionment of revenues, salaries, school buildings, health of the pupils, program grading and standardization, certificates and diplomas, courses of study, textbooks, qualifications in certification of teachers, and pupil attendance.

The law made the board responsible for submitting to the Governor and General Assembly a state budget indicating the nature and amount of expenditures for operating the total centralized state school system. Instructional spending was to include the basic teacher salary schedule and other such costs. Matching funds were established for vocational education. The board also would establish spending for school construction, particularly to encourage consolidation of small schools. It also would make expenditures for debt services and for maintaining a state school tax department. The law required the board to submit to the Governor an annual report covering its operation, conditions, and progress.

Department of Public Instruction. The Department of Public Instruction served as the administrative organization for executing the policies of the Board of Education, with the state superintendent as its chief officer. Shortly after the Legislature created the office of state superintendent in 1921, the board appointed H. V. Holloway to the position. Dr. Holloway stated that his philosophy was in keeping with the "cardinal principles" of education, which had as general objectives character development, command of fundamental processes, health and physical efficiency, good citizenship, training for worthy home membership, vocational efficiency, worthy use of leisure, and general mental efficiency.

During 1921, in addition to the state superintendent, the department included a professional staff with the following titles: assistant superintendent of elementary education, assistant superintendent of secondary education, business manager, director of research, director of vocational education, director of adult education and Americanization, supervisor of agriculture, supervisor of home economics, and supervisor of trades and industries. There were seven rural supervisors, four visiting teachers, and three supervisors of handicrafts to work with Negro schools. Fourteen of these 23 professional staff members were working closely with local rural school districts and consequently cannot be considered part of the central administration. In other words, during this first year the department created positions that met special needs.

When the State Department of Public Instruction was organized, there were already divisions of elementary and secondary education. These were each headed by an assistant superintendent, whose chief responsibilities were curriculum development, teacher improvement and certification, and enforcement of laws pertaining to elementary and secondary education. At this time, 1921, four supervisors worked with the assistant superintendent for elementary education and three with the assistant superintendent for secondary education.

Trend Toward Centralization

During the period of reorganization, 1917 to 1925, when Delaware was searching for a system of education that would offer the greatest benefits, the Legislature decided to move toward a centralized, state-financed system. Paul Mort described the trend as follows:

> Delaware embarked upon a fiscal policy for public education that diverged markedly from the plan generally followed in the United States. It moved from the plan of local fiscal responsibility, supplemented in some degree by state aid, to all but complete state fiscal responsibility for operating expenses. It did not remove, however, the legal arrangements by which individual communities could provide supplemental financing. . . (8).

In determining the type of system to be developed, educators and laymen alike were determined that all children should have an equal opportunity for education. Superintendent H. V. Holloway expressed this concern in his report on "One Hundred Years of Public Education in Delaware," when he stated: "No equalization of educational opportunity is possible in a State when educational opportunity is in the hands of the local school district. Democracy defeats itself when small, remote local committees must determine and wholly finance their improvements" (9).

Enactment of the school laws of 1921 acknowledged the principle that education was a function of state government. As mentioned above, county boards were eliminated and a state department of education created. Also created was a state school tax department "to collect the revenue needed for the schools, and all funds for the use of (State Board Unit Districts) were placed in the custody of the state treasurer" (10). This principle of government was also reflected in the fact that the Legislature provided a means of developing a well-organized system of school administration with a professionally trained staff to plan and administer an effective program of education. In other words, although the Constitution of 1897 required the Legislature to provide for this additional system (11), it was not until 1921 that the constitutional mandate was taken seriously.

Pierre S. duPont

In addition to his leadership in obtaining the school laws of 1921, Pierre S. duPont continued to make significant contributions in school construction and finance. Although he was an industrial leader with heavy responsibilities, he nevertheless devoted much of his time to public education and from 1918 to 1937 served as a member of the State Board of Education and the Service Citizens of Delaware, and as state tax commissioner.

DuPont and his Service Citizens were responsible for the General Education Board's study of Delaware's public education in 1917, and a part of the study was a survey of school buildings. When it revealed that they were in unsatisfactory condition, he felt compelled to initiate a statewide program of construction. To carry out the program, in 1919, he organized the Delaware School Auxiliary Association and personally contributed \$2 million to start the construction.

From 1919 to 1944, the Delaware School Auxiliary Association assumed major responsibility for school construction. For instance, with a personal contribution from duPont it erected and equipped 89 school buildings, equal to those for the white pupils, which housed the entire Negro enrollment of 8,000. DuPont also assisted in time and money to construct and equip 81 school buildings for white pupils. In brief, he was instrumental in reconstructing the entire system of school buildings in Delaware, with a total of 170 buildings to house 44,000 pupils.

DuPont was the driving force in building consolidated schools and eliminating one-room buildings. By 1944, the number of schools had been reduced from over 400 to 188, and the one-room schools decreased from 294 to 74. DuPont accepted the position of state tax commissioner at the request of the Governor in 1925, to establish a sound state tax structure. The school laws of 1921 stipulated that the schools' cost should be paid by state taxes. The funds, distributed on a per-pupil basis, were to provide enough money both to operate the schools and to pay for a building program to be carried out in cooperation with the Delaware School Auxiliary Association. Three years later, the Board of Education became aware that the taxes were yielding very little revenue.

DuPont investigated and found that only a small portion of taxes was collected because the Legislature did not provide enough personnel and equipment. For instance, he discovered that only about half the taxpayers owing income tax actually paid it. DuPont reorganized the tax office, collected all back taxes, and reported a surplus for the following 2 years. By the time he left the position in 1937, the state had collected over $63 million for public education, and of this amount $45 million was spent for operating the schools, $15 million was for new buildings, and $3 million remained as a surplus in the school fund (12).

THE DEPARTMENT FROM 1926 TO 1965

The Department of Public Instruction's development from 1926 to 1965 can be divided into two periods: one of slow growth and one of rapid growth. The first extended from about 1926 to 1949 and includes the years of the Depression and World War II. Pupil enrollments remained almost constant and even declined slightly during World War II, while the number of teachers increased very slowly, with salaries at a low level.

The second period extends from 1950 to 1965. During 1950 to 1959, pupil enrollments for grades 1 through 12 increased 71 percent, and by 1965 increased another 37 percent. This rapid growth in pupil enrollment posed serious problems, particularly for the state's financial structure (13).

Elementary and Secondary Education

Art. From 1921 to 1929, art was taught by regular classroom teachers only in the elementary schools, but art education had been provided for adults by the division of adult education. This enabled parents to better understand the art expressions of their children, and also gave impetus for more art education in the public schools. The department appointed a director of art in 1929 and then employed a supervisor and four teachers to develop a program for the state. Two years later, art was introduced as an elective subject in the high schools.

In 1933, the Legislature tried to remove "fads and frills" from education and hotly debated a bill to drop art, music, and physical education from the curriculum. School patrons objected so strenuously that the bill was withdrawn. By 1936, most school districts containing both elementary and secondary schools employed art teachers, but schools with fewer than three teachers depended on the traveling teachers.

In 1940, county supervisors replaced the traveling art teachers. From 1941 to 1945, the schools sponsored "war-inspired" art. Delaware pupils contributed work to a metropolitan exhibition of "Children's Paintings and the War" at the Museum of Modern Art in New York City and to an exhibition sent to several South American republics, titled "Portrait of the U.S.A. by Its Children."

Since World War II, local school districts have gradually taken over art education and receive less direct supervision from the state. In 1967, the department employed only one supervisor for art education.

Music. The Department of Public Instruction did not recognize music as a school subject until 1930, when the state superintendent appointed a director and supervisor of music. Several large schools had begun a variety of musical programing, but this marked the beginning of the music education division on the state level.

A visit to the schools by the director and supervisor showed that there was much to be done. Within a year, the department increased its music staff to include a supervisor for each county, in addition to a number of traveling teachers. Not only did the supervisors help establish programs, they furnished materials to the schools and occasionally taught classes.

The supervisor of music also made an important contribution by organizing an all-state orchestra and chorus, which since 1951 has met in Dover at the Delaware Music Camp on the Campus of Wesley College every summer to study and perform for a statewide audience. The students have received some of the finest instruction available in the East. Districts gradually accepted responsibility for a music program, and the department cut its supervisory staff to two in 1957. By 1960, it was reduced to one, and it continues at this level today.

Health. Health services were initiated in the state for public school pupils in 1919, in keeping with the legal mandate that the state agency encourage medical inspection of schoolchildren. To initiate such a program, it requested $50,000, but the Legislature refused to make the appropriation. The Service Citizens of Delaware stepped in and donated the necessary funds.

In cooperation with the State Board of Health, in March 1920, the Department of Public Instruction cooperated in inaugurating physical examinations in the schools. The following year, the Delaware School Auxiliary Association financed a dental unit. Then in 1924, all secondary schools in the state required pupils to take noncredit courses in health education two or three periods per week for 4 years.

Health education did not become a part of the education department until 1927, when it was combined with physical education. Two years later the Legislature enacted a law requiring all elementary and high school pupils to take courses in physiology and hygiene, with special focus on the effects of alcoholic drinks, stimulants, and narcotics.

Since 1932, Delaware schools have kept both health and medical records on each pupil, and these forms have been improved through the years. The education department and the health board cooperated in 1937 in screening and examining crippled children. And in 1949, the state superintendent recommended to the Board of Education that all school personnel should have chest X-rays beginning with the following year.

Although the schools have offered nursing services since the early twenties, it was 1949 before the state adopted a salary schedule and certification standards for school nurses. The following year, a state committee composed of members of the Department of Public Instruction, State Board of Health personnel, school nurses, and administrators prepared a school nurses guide entitled "The School Nurse–Her Duties and Responsibilities."

Driver Education. In 1934, the Delaware Safety Council inaugurated driver education by offering classroom instruction in several schools. An automobile dealer made available eight cars, and the following school year behind-the-wheel instruction was introduced for the first time in the United States. This traffic safety program continued from that time with both classroom and road instruction. By 1945, 555 pupils from 17 Delaware high schools were enrolled in driver education. A study of 300 drivers, one-half having completed the training, revealed that the 150 nontrained drivers were charged with 46 percent more violations (14).

In 1947, with 94 percent of the state's high schools offering driver education, the Legislature appropriated $50,000 to help the state board expand the program. The superintendent appointed a State Driver Education Advisory Committee and held a 1-week conference for teachers. The program continued to expand, and 2 years later the first adult driver education course was conducted at Newark for 34 enrollees. By this time the department had expanded to seven full-time teachers and one supervisor.

Delaware's driver education program continued to gain prestige and expand. In 1954, a staff member conducted a study revealing that individuals having driver education had, statistically, a significantly superior performance over those who had not. By 1967, every public high school in the state offered a course in driver education, with 45 full-time teachers handling 6,300 pupils.

Modern Foreign Languages. Although educational directories of Delaware schools reveal that Latin, French, and Spanish were taught in 1921, it was not until 1959, under impetus of the National Defense Education Act, Title III, that the state board approved the creation of a position of supervisor of modern foreign languages.

The first supervisor, appointed in 1960, provided leadership in conducting workshops and conferences to train teachers of modern foreign languages. Courses were improved, in part, through installation of electronically equipped classrooms. From 1959 to 1964, enrollments in French, Spanish, German, and Russian doubled from 6,889 to 13,581 (15).

Science. Supervision of science teaching benefited from federal funds from the National Defense Education Act of 1958. Before this, Delaware had not provided funds to the state agency for this service. With federal aid, the state board employed a supervisor in 1960 for the first time. At the same time, federal and state dollars were matched to upgrade science laboratory equipment.

The science supervisor has cooperated with the University of Delaware in establishing in-service training programs for teachers in science education. A major focus in training is on the Biological Science Curriculum Study (BSCS). Other trends in training and in teaching are increases in use of the Physical Science Study Committee (PSSC) physics courses, the Chemical Education Materials Study (CHEM), and the Chemical Bond Approach (CBA). Junior high schools are teaching life science and earth science. Elementary schools are initiating programs with use of materials from the American Association for the Advancement of Science, K-3 Science Program, and the Science Curriculum Improvement Study.

Adult Education

In 1919, through the efforts of the Service Citizens of Delaware and with the leadership and financial assistance of Pierre S. duPont, a bureau was established to serve the foreign-born population. These citizenship classes formalized adult education for the first time. Today, adult education consists of six divisions: adult basic education, education for foreign born, general education, high school extension, Civil Defense education, and manpower development and training.

Basic Education. Citizenship education, offered in the cities since about 1900, developed into adult basic education. In 1910, 17,000 foreign-born persons were living in the state, with about two-thirds from non-English-speaking countries.

Immigration, particularly heavy from 1910 to 1915, concentrated around Wilmington. In 1919, the Service Citizens of Delaware took over the Delaware State Council of Defense's Americanization program and created a service bureau to assume the task of financing and developing it until public funds could be appropriated. At least the Service Citizens demonstrated the value of preparing foreign-born persons for participation in American life.

After World War I, literacy classes were established for native as well as foreign-born soldiers returning to Delaware, and this program became an important part of the state's overall adult education program. The Department of Public Instruction accepted responsibility and appointed a director of adult education in 1922, when state funds were provided.

In 1927, the Legislature appropriated money for operating the Service Bureau for Foreign-Born People, and the Service Citizens transferred control of the program to the education department. Thus, from 1927 to 1959, the service bureau and the adult education division operated as two divisions under the Department of Public Instruction. In the meantime, the state reduced its appropriations to the adult education program so that classes for foreign-born persons were limited to citizenship and English. Since 1959, both divisions have been under the direction of the supervisor of adult education.

In 1964, the federal government, under the Equal Opportunity Act, authorized Delaware to spend $50,000 annually to eliminate illiteracy, particularly among the disadvantaged.

High School Extension. Public pressure by many persons wanting to complete their education finally convinced the State Board of Education in 1963 to establish the James H. Groves Adult Evening High School as part of adult education. Its purpose was to provide adults and out-of-state youth with an opportunity to earn a diploma. The usual high school subjects are now offered in Wilmington, Dover, Georgetown, and Seaford under the department's supervisor of adult education.

The high school extension program was an outgrowth of this program. In 1964, the Legislature provided funds to establish high school extension classes under the supervision of the state board. The program was established so that adults could earn high school credits three ways: extension classes, achievement tests for high school credit, and correspondence studies. That year there were 700 enrollees. Courses were offered in English, history, civics, government, health, general mathematics, algebra, geometry, general science, biology, Spanish, French, typewriting, shorthand, general business, and bookkeeping.

Civil Defense. The department added education for Civil Defense to its program in 1963 with federal funds. During the academic year ending June 30, 1965, 1,025 adults received training in Civil Defense education, of whom 980 were trained in personal and family survival and 45 were trained in radiological monitoring.

Manpower Development and Training. The Manpower Development and Training Act, enacted by Congress in 1962, provided the impetus to institute a multitraining program in Wilmington, sponsored by the Department of Public Instruction (16). Three years later the program enrolled 368 trainees, 257 being trained in Wilmington and 111 in downstate Delaware. Training was provided in auto body repair, building maintenance, clerk-typist, nurse's aide, salesclerk, service station attendant, farm mechanic, and welder.

Vocational Education

The Smith-Hughes Act of 1917 gave an impetus to vocational education in Delaware. The 1919 Legislature accepted the federal terms and designated the State Board of Education to administer the act. The department created supervisory positions in agriculture, home economics, and trades and industries. To implement the program, the department got the approval of the state and federal boards for a state plan calling for vocational training in agriculture, trades and industries, and home economics; vocational rehabilitation of the physically handicapped; and service and distributive occupations. The plan specified the physical facilities, courses of study, teaching methods and materials, and teacher qualifications.

Under the law, the state was supposed to match the $30,000 in federal funds given annually to Delaware, but the Legislature failed to vote a sufficient appropriation. Consequently, Pierre S. duPont, member of the State Board of Vocational Education (1917-21) made up the state's share of the matching funds so the program could begin. At the same time, the Delaware Manufacturers Association donated funds and equipment to initiate a strong program in trades and industries.

Agriculture programs were designed not only for high school students, but for young out-of-school and adult farmers as well. From 1918 to the present, the basic course continues to center on crop and livestock production. However, to meet the changing needs of the state's agriculture, current emphasis is on management, ornamental horticulture, and agriculture business; a county vocational-technical high school offers specialized programs.

By the end of the first year, 1918, the department employed a supervisor in home economics, and five high schools offered the first home economics classes in Delaware. The following year, the Legislature required that the subject be a part of the state curriculum. Most of these early classes were taught in makeshift facilities, including churches, school basements, fire halls, and large halls, with the cooking done on two-burner gas plates and kerosene ranges.

Since the late thirties, food rooms have been constructed with kitchens closely resembling those in the home, laundry areas have been added, and most departments contain a family living area. Sewing machines are now electric, and even electric shears are used by more advanced pupils. While the early courses were centered around the family's producing its own food and clothing—with courses in preserving, preparing, and serving foods or constructing garments—today, the emphasis is on the study of foods and clothing available in the stores.

Each time the home economics curriculum has been revised, committees of teachers have worked with state supervisors and consultants. In 1965, the University of Delaware and the Department of Public Instruction sponsored a new curriculum project in five subjects: foods and nutrition; clothing and textiles; housing, home furnishing, and household equipment; management and family economics; and human development. The Vocational Act of 1963 provided funds for teaching occupations using home economics skills. Today there is a course for training child care workers at the Camp County Vocational-Technical Center where students study and work with children aged 3 to 6 in a well-equipped nursery-classroom. Enrollment has increased to the point that two full-time teachers were needed in 1968.

With the aid of cash and equipment donated by the Delaware Manufacturers Association, trade classes were organized in 1919 under the provisions of the Smith-Hughes Act. The Wilmington High School conducted day and evening and part-time classes for industrial apprentices.

In 1921, all children between 14 and 16 had to have work permits issued by the department's vocational division before being employed to attend continuation school 4 hours per week. Within a short time, 500 boys and girls were attending continuation school.

In 1926, Wilmington High School's commercial department was placed on a vocational basis, and cooperative, part-time instruction in the senior year was subsidized under the part-time continuation program until 1950. At the same time, in 1926, the classes in five different trades held for 120 pupils in the attic of Wilmington High School were transferred to an old school renamed the Wilmington Trade School. It was 1938 before the Brown Vocational School was opened in Wilmington, built by private funds at no cost to the taxpayers, to offer a program of 12 skill trades and occupations.

In 1940, the war production program pressed new responsibilities on the vocational education division. With the department's director of trades and industries in charge, within 2 weeks several classes were organized, and enrollment increased so rapidly that the school was forced to operate on a 24-hour a day schedule, 7 days a week, until all unemployed persons in the area were in training. When the enrollment grew beyond the capacity of the school, extra classes were organized in the plants. When the program ended in 1945, it had enrolled 38,766 men and women in 45 courses. The federal government paid the entire cost of $1,727,464.

Gradually, the state agency's responsibilities in trade and industrial education increased, and it added supervisors for training of foremen, apprentices, trade extension students, teachers, and in other occupations. By 1950, there were 31 trade and industrial education classes, of which 27 were in Wilmington. It was not until 1957 that the Legislature decided to provide trade and industrial education for Kent and Sussex Counties. The Sussex County Vocational-Technical Center opened in 1961 and was followed by the Kent County Vocational-Technical Center in 1965.

Distributive Education. Although the Smith-Hughes Act provided cooperative state and federal efforts for vocational education, it was not until Congress passed the George-Deen Act of 1937 and the George-Barden Act of 1946 that the law provided specifically for those employed in distributive occupations. The department appointed the first supervisor of distributive education in 1938, with responsibilities for supervising business education as well. It was not until a decade later, in 1949, that cooperative programs in distributive education had been established in six local high schools for 143 students. A year later, four centers were opened to offer evening programs for adults in supervision, management, and merchandising. During the 1950's, the Delaware Association of Distributive Education Clubs of America affiliated with the National DECA movement, thus giving the state's students chance to participate in an organized program conducted on local, state, and national levels.

The department appointed a full-time state supervisor in 1960 to be solely responsible for development, promotion, and supervision of all distributive education. The program doubled in size over the next 4 years; student enrollment in secondary classes numbered 150, and adult classes went well beyond 1,000.

With passage of the Vocational Education Act of 1963, Delaware immediately reorganized its curriculum and concentrated on the secondary programs for unemployed persons of high school age. The program continued to grow, again doubling student enrollment in the secondary programs. It has been a tremendous success, reflected in the large number of graduates who are enjoying successful careers in marketing, merchandising, and management.

Vocational Rehabilitation. The Department of Public Instruction accepted responsibility for vocational rehabilitation in 1939. When the Legislature refused to appropriate enough funds to match the federal appropriations, H. Fletcher Brown, a former member of the State Board of Vocational Education, contributed the money to initiate the program. Since 1941, the Legislature has appropriated the matching funds, and the program continues to grow.

The vocational rehabilitation division provides a variety of services to physically and mentally disabled persons, to prepare them for employment. This is a joint state-federal program, including diagnosis, surgery, treatment, prosthetic appliances, hospitalization, training, maintenance, and transportation.

In the 1965-66 fiscal year, over $497,000 was spent for vocational rehabilitation in Delaware, of which $270,000 came from federal funds. Case service costs amounted to $321,000 including physical rehabilitation and training. Guidance and placement costs amounted to $153,000. In the fiscal year ending June 30, 1966, 640 disabled persons were rehabilitated, and 1,226 others received services from the program.

Occupational Information and Career Services. In 1964, the department created the position of supervisor of occupational information and career services, to determine employment opportunities for young people. The supervisor, employed in 1965, also was expected to make recommendations for necessary training programs, plan them, and see that they operated.

The supervisor has emphasized vocational training in all of the state's educational plans. He has been in large measure responsible for the program's growth, so that at present adult high schools have vocational courses as part of their curriculum. Sussex and Kent programs have been enlarged to serve 1,600 youth, and in 1967 the New Castle County Vocational-Technical High School was under construction.

Planning and Research in Vocational Education. Under provisions of the Vocational Act of 1963, the Legislature created the position of planning and research in 1965, emphasizing pilot and experimental programs, curriculum research, in-service education, new types of occupational programs, and programs to serve persons with special needs. The office develops state plans and reports for the various programs under vocational-technical education and the extended services.

Also in 1965, the University of Delaware, in cooperation with the department's vocational-technical division, offered an Institute for Teachers of Rural Low-Achieving Disadvantaged Junior High School Youth under a grant from the U.S. Office of Education. The Institute developed 10 occupational booklets and prepared a detailed report. These materials have been circulated to all states by the Office of Education.

Migrant Education

The migrant education program began in 1961, when the state superintendent assigned two staff members to develop a pilot summer school program. The Council of Churches agreed to cooperate. The program was conducted cooperatively with a day care program under the auspices of the Migrant Ministry of the State, with $5,000 in private funds.

The first class began in the summer of 1962 in Dover with 33 pupils. It met 5 days a week for 6 weeks. Hot lunches were served, and reading, writing, music, and art were taught by a master teacher and an assistant teacher.

In 1965, the Office of Economic Opportunity (OEO) granted some $95,000 for a cooperative interagency program for migrant children. In the same year, another federal grant of $11,500 was provided to train 21 seasonal welfare workers in an intensive day care course to prepare them for work in the migrant program as day care attendants. In 1967, elementary education was added with funds from Title I, ESEA. The elementary education program was in addition to the existing OEO-funded preschool program consisting of day care, nursery school, and auxiliary services.

Education for Handicapped Children

Although the Legislature had made special appropriations to educate physically handicapped children as early as 1841, it was not until 1932 that legislation was passed to establish a special division within the Department of Public Instruction to serve such children. Unfortunately, the 1932 Legislature failed to grant funds.

Three years later, private agencies donated money to establish this program in the public school system. For instance, the Women's Club of the Trinity Episcopal Church of Wilmington made it possible to employ the first audiometrician. The Delaware Citizens Association enabled the department to employ a psychological examiner in 1935, particularly to set up classes for mentally retarded children. Eight years later, a program in lip reading was initiated and an additional psychological examiner and audiometrician employed.

It was 1953 before the Legislature modified the School Code to provide more funds to educate handicapped children. Following this act, the Wilmington School District established classes for a wide variety of handicapped children. Other school districts, such as Alfred I. duPont, Middletown, Stanton, Caeser Rodney, Smyrna, and Seaford, offered programs for the trainable mentally retarded. The orthopedically handicapped are educated in De La Warr and Dover, in addition to Wilmington. Classes for mentally retarded are provided in most public school districts having grades 1 through 12.

Pupil Transportation

Shortly after World War I, when the department became interested in consolidating small schools, it became involved in transportation problems. The annual report of 1926 pointed out that Delaware was the only state in which transportation was paid entirely from state funds. The state board either arranged for transportation or contracted with railroads, trolleys, or buses. In 1931, the department employed a supervisor of transportation and placed him under the direction of the business manager.

The state agency has continued to administer pupil transportation. The supervisor arranges for contracting of all schoolbuses operated by private contractors and for employing drivers to operate state-owned buses. He organizes and lays out the routes, supervises the operation of the buses, and has developed a set of regulations on safety education. His schedule is becoming increasingly difficult as the number of pupils eligible for transportation rapidly increases. In recent years, however, several larger school districts have assumed the responsibility for routing buses.

School Lunch Program

As early as 1912, Wilmington pupils were able to obtain lunches at the schools, and 6 years later Wilmington opened the first cafeteria. Although there was usually a small charge for lunches, the Kiwanis Club, American Legion, student councils, and other organizations donated funds for free meals. The state agency became involved in 1929 when several home economics rooms began serving lunches.

The program developed slowly, however, until Congress passed the National School Lunch Act, and the Legislature authorized the state agency to employ a supervisor of school lunches. The program then developed so rapidly that all school districts and nearly all schools in the state were participating in the special milk and type A school lunch programs. Average daily participation today is about 40 percent; 2 percent of the school lunches are served free to needy pupils (17).

Research

When the Department of Public Instruction was reorganized in 1921, it created a position of director of research primarily to gather statistics, particularly for the state superintendent's annual report. He was also responsible for preparing forms, supervising attendance, supervising visiting teachers, directing publicity, and supervising athletics. A decade later, he became responsible for the state testing program.

From 1940 to 1960, the research office assumed the responsibility for gathering educational statistics and publishing the department's reports. In recent years, this office has employed staff personnel in data processing and has moved toward a more detailed analysis of educational data. It also plans, designs, and evaluates research projects, which affect nearly all divisions.

School Construction

Although the research division and several of the other professional staff members have been involved for many years in planning for school construction, it was not until 1964 that the agency created a separate school construction division. Since the Delaware School Auxiliary Association headed by duPont provided personnel and finances for supervising school construction, the agency itself simply didn't need to become involved until this date.

Departmental Organization in 1965

From 1963 to 1965, the state agency reorganized, mainly by regrouping and expanding the number of positions. At present, the state superintendent and five professional staff members—an administrative assistant, a section for research and publication, and a section for public information—comprise one division. The assistant superintendent for administrative services has 12 professional staff members, responsible for school finance, school construction, state-federal programs, pupil transportation, school lunch, and data processing. The assistant superintendent for instructional services and his 33 professional staff members are responsible for all phases of the instructional program except vocational-technical education. This division includes services for libraries, audiovisual education, and certain federal programs.

The assistant superintendent for vocational-technical education heads a division with 23 professional staff members. It is responsible for certain types of adult education, Civil Defense education, education of the foreign born, vocational rehabilitation, migrant education, and vocational research. The director of educational television, appointed in 1965, has a staff of 41 professional and technical persons responsible for a schedule of closed-circuit programs transmitted to every school district in the state. The state superintendent is the chief administrative officer.

IMPORTANT ISSUES

Negro Education

Before the Civil War, Delaware did little to educate its Negroes. But in 1867, several philanthropists formed the Delaware Association for the Moral Improvement and Education of the Colored People. They contributed funds to organize 15 schools for Negroes—7 in New Castle County, 4 in Kent, and 4 in Sussex. The association supervised these schools and donated heavily to their operation, but it did receive voluntary subscriptions from other sources.

In 1869, Wilmington established the Howard School as the first elementary school for Negroes in Delaware. It developed into a 3-year high school in 1888, but it was 23 years before it added a fourth year to its high school program. Not only did it have a course in normal training, but it included a normal department for educating Negro teachers.

By 1875, the association was supervising 28 Negro schools without financial support from the state. In that year, however, the Legislature enacted a law taxing the citizens for educating Negroes, but stipulated that the association would administer the revenues. The taxes proved to be insufficient, and the Negroes themselves gave the additional support necessary. Within 6 years, 1881, state financial aid amounted to $2,400 annually. Two years later, the Legislature delegated supervision of the Negro schools to the state superintendent, but in 1887 it decided to turn the operation over to the county superintendents. At the same time, it provided a legal basis for separating the races in the public schools and established a parallel system for Negro pupils, with both state and county officials responsible for each system.

Although the law levied a uniform tax for each system, independently incorporated schools could still receive state funds directly from the state treasury.

In the mideighties, few schoolhouses for Negroes existed, and the children usually were taught in private houses, churches, and society halls. In 1889, the state provided $500 to help erect a schoolhouse in Lewes. Two years later, the Legislature increased the annual appropriation for Negro schools from $6,000 to $9,000 and directed that $500 be used to repair schoolhouses if the local citizens contributed half as much as the state (18).

In 1895, the Legislature recognized the legal existence of separate school districts for Negroes and stipulated that these separate schools would be based on financial equality with the schools for white pupils. At this time, there were 25 districts for Negro schools in New Castle County, 32 in Kent, and 33 in Sussex. There were about 3,400 pupils, nearly all enrolled in elementary one-teacher schools.

All Negro pupils were taught by Negro teachers, although after 1895 the county superintendents exercised general supervision. In 1891, the Legislature initiated teacher training for Negroes by chartering and financing a state college for Negro students at Dover.

When public school systems were reorganized under the school laws of 1919 and 1921, the Legislature instituted a system of full state support for education. It eliminated the separate tax on Negro property and appropriated funds to Negro schools on the basis of net enrollments, in the same manner as schools for white pupils.

In 1919, duPont and the Service Citizens of Delaware sponsored a number of surveys, with particular attention given to the condition of the buildings. Two years later, they concluded that Negro pupils could be served better by constructing one- and two-room schools throughout the state. The Department of Public Instruction accepted this as a recommendation, and in 1926 duPont personally financed the construction of 86 school buildings for Negro pupils. The survey committee on school buildings further recommended constructing a high school for Negroes at Dover, pointing out that enrollments were increasing on the secondary level, and it would be impossible to establish a high school for Negro pupils in each county.

It was 1948, over 20 years later, before another survey focused on Negro education. At this time, the American Council on Education pointed out that in the 1945-46 school year there were over 60 schools for Negro pupils, most very small, with few Negro administrative and supervisory personnel. Thirty-four were one-teacher schools, and few Negro pupils outside Wilmington had access to a school with a 12-year program. However, it did point out that in 1947 the Legislature had appropriated funds so that Negro pupils could either board or be transported to high schools in Wilmington or to the State College High School near Dover.

Among other things, the survey committee recommended that small schools be eliminated by consolidation and Negro children be given the opportunity to attend a 12-year program. It further recommended that the state establish a centrally located junior and senior high school in New Castle County, that the Department of Public Instruction add a Negro staff member to interpret the needs of Negro schools, and that the state organize a parents program for Negroes. It recommended medical services and standards to encourage Negro pupils to graduate instead of dropping out of school.

As a result of the commission's recommendations, the Legislature voted to construct high schools for Negroes. By 1950, three—one for each county— were completed: the L. L. Redding Comprehensive High School for New Castle, the William Henry Comprehensive High School for Kent, and the William Jason High School for Sussex. Thus, with the Howard High School in Wilmington, there were four Negro high schools in the state.

The concept of separate but equal schools for white and Negro pupils remained unchallenged in Delaware until 1947, when Negro students sought admission to the University of Delaware. They contended that the instructional program at Delaware State College, which had been established for Negroes, was inadequate and did not meet the equal protection provisions of the Fourteenth Amendment to the federal Constitution. Trustees of the

University of Delaware then passed a resolution admitting Negroes to the university if they met the admission requirements and wished to pursue a program of study not offered in the state's Negro college.

In 1950, a number of students once again demanded the right to attend the University of Delaware, with proper qualifications, regardless of whether Delaware State College offered courses they desired. Although their demands were challenged by the university, they were upheld by the state's courts. As a result of this court decision to end segregation in higher education, a number of civic associations started a movement to remove segregation from the public schools at both the elementary and secondary levels.

The move for desegregation immediately expanded. By 1952, the parents of several Negro pupils at Claymont and Hockessin Elementary Schools challenged the dual system of education, contending that educational facilities available to their children were not equal to white facilities. After a series of appeals from state to federal courts, in 1954 the U. S. Supreme Court declared segregation to be unconstitutional. The Court ruled that where separate educational facilities were provided for Negroes, the education was not equal to that for white pupils.

Following the 1954 Supreme Court decision, the State Board of Education developed a plan for integrating Negro and white pupils at the rate of one grade per year, commencing in 1957. However, in 1961, the U.S. District Court set aside the grade-a-year plan on the basis that it would not accomplish integration rapidly enough. Thus, in February 1965, the state board adopted a resolution to end segregation of the races in the public schools by voluntary agreements on the part of the school boards of Negro school districts to dissolve and close their schools. At the same time, school boards of the neighboring white districts were to voluntarily agree to accept the pupils from these closed districts. The state board was prepared to cut off state aid for any school district that failed to reach a voluntary agreement or refused to comply (19).

As a final step to force complete integration, the state board was prepared to seek further legislation. However, the voluntary system worked. The boards did close all the school districts for Negro pupils and integrated with the neighboring white school districts. Twenty-three elementary schools were closed in 1965. At the end of the 1965-66 school year, the high schools for Negroes in New Castle and Kent Counties were closed, and the Sussex County High School was closed at the end of the following year. By June 30, 1967, all Negro high schools in Delaware were phased out: 26 Negro schools were closed, 307 Negro teachers were transferred to school districts for white pupils, and 8,912 Negro pupils integrated in the white schools.

Reorganization

By 1919, out of 450 school districts in Delaware 300 were one-teacher schools. In that year, the school laws created "special school districts" in the urban areas, requiring them to maintain schools for elementary and high school pupils and permitting them to establish from local revenues kindergartens, schools for handicapped children, evening schools, and vocational schools. All other school districts were designated as "state board districts" in 1921. These districts, usually small and in the rural areas, depended on the Department of Public Instruction for supervison of instruction, preparation of budgets, hiring of teachers, and other assistance. Gradually, the state board districts increased in enrollments and became more independent of the state agency for services, until today there is very little distinction between the state board districts and special districts.

In addition to the special and state board districts, the Legislature created two area high school districts, each comprising several elementary districts, and one area vocational school district for each of the three counties. Two are already operating area vocational high schools, and the third county is preparing to do so at present.

The state superintendents raised the question of school district reorganization from time to time and occasionally mentioned it in their annual reports. In 1946, a school survey recommended redistricting (20), and this prompted the first comprehensive study and report on reorganization since 1921. This report, issued in 1951, recommended that 12 administrative units replace the existing 117 districts (21). Although these recommendations were not followed, there has been a gradual reduction in the number of school districts through consolidation.

In 1965, the Governor's Committee on Education inaugurated another study, with considerable emphasis on reorganization. In its first report, issued the following October, it recommended a reduction from the present 51 school districts to 25 (including vocational districts), as well as changes in staffing and financing.

Teacher Certification and Education

Securing well-trained teachers for Delaware schools has long been a problem, but it has become critical as pupil enrollments have rapidly increased. Since 1950, Delaware has had to recruit four out of five new teachers from other states.

Certification. Delaware passed, in 1829, its first law concerning certification to provide for a county superintendent, who would serve without remuneration and issue teacher certificates on examination. No professional qualifications were written into the law itself. It was 1880 before the Legislature enacted a law requiring teachers to attend the County Institute for Teachers and established three grades of certificates for candidates taking examinations: first grade, second grade, and third grade. The kind of certificate a candidate received depended on his examination grade. Applicants for first-grade or life certificates had to make a grade of 90 percent, have 10 years teaching experience, and furnish five testimonials of good moral character.

After the state adopted the Constitution of 1897, the Legislature enacted a law providing for one set of examinations for white teachers, another for Negro teachers, and a third for teachers in certain "graded schools" (22). In 1903, the law authorized the county superintendent to grant any person holding a diploma or certificate of graduation from a respectable normal school or college a certificate to teach in any of the free schools of the county in which the superintendent held office, without requiring him to take an examination. The certificate was to be good for 1 year only. In 1911, the law was amended to create a board of seven members to establish rules and regulations and determine when and how the county superintendents should issue these certificates.

The School Code of 1919 permitted the State Board of Education to require a certificate of "good health and of sound physical condition." It also stated that 1 year's teaching experience would be considered equivalent to practice teaching and agreed to accept other states' certificates if the qualifications were equal to or superior to Delaware's. Standard certificates were granted to normal school, college, and university graduates without examination, if their credentials were satisfactory. The certificates were renewable if the teacher completed a successful year of experience and had the proper professional "spirit." The regulations also provided for examinations for second- and third-grade certificates for teaching in the elementary school.

From the reorganization in 1921 to 1957, the state superintendent certified teachers. Before this, the Department of Public Instruction had only one special secretary to the state superintendent responsible for evaluating credentials for teacher certification. Since there was no one else working on teacher education, the secretary was called the state supervisor of certification from 1947.

In 1957, the state board approved establishing a teacher education and professional standards division with a director and supervisor. It was now possible to begin a comprehensive study of certification regulations. In 1961, over 200 people, representing all levels and areas of teaching and various lay and professional organizations, participated in this 3-year study. The result was an increased emphasis on general education, increased requirements in the subject matter areas, a 60-hour graduate program for superintendents, a broadened reciprocity policy, and expansion of special education. At the same time, a State Advisory Committee on Teacher Education and Professional Standards was organized to be responsible for finally reviewing all certification policies and major program changes or new courses in programs of teacher education.

Four years later, in 1965, representatives of the 1961 committee were called back to review the earlier regulations and in particular study reciprocity and certification. Since Delaware must import 80 percent of its new teachers, this is most important. The immediate outcome is that, although reciprocity is accepted as a matter of principle, it is still necessary to study credentials and count course credits before granting certification.

Teacher Education. Prior to 1921, state and county boards of education were directly responsible for training teachers through the summer county institutes, which were tied to certification. Once the University of Delaware and Delaware State College developed programs of teacher education, the state agency stopped training teachers. However, in the 1921 school laws, the state board was charged with the responsibility of approving all their courses of teacher education. For many years the state board approved the teacher education programs informally. In fact, the only state control was the requirement that these college and university programs meet state certification requirements. In 1957, with the creation of the teacher education and professional standards division, there was a renewed effort to coordinate all phases of teacher education. Both Delaware State College and the University of Delaware have been involved in all phases of the work relating to both certification and teacher education.

In 1957, Delaware initiated a state in-service program and developed guidelines for setting up local and state in-service projects, in preparation for a time when this training could be counted toward salary increments. Progress has been made in coordinating these projects with the university extension program and the state educational television network's in-service offerings to avoid overlapping and to ensure a balanced state program.

Finance

Delaware's financial history dates back to 1796 when the Legislature enacted a law stating that all money received by the state treasurer for tavern and marriage licenses should be set apart to provide for a school fund. The revenues accumulating in the fund were unused until 1817, when the Legislature appropriated \$80,000 to \$100,000 from the fund to each of Delaware's three counties and directed that this money be used for instructing the children of poor parents in reading, writing, and arithmetic.

In 1829, the first free school law stipulated that voters should determine how much money was to be raised for education in their own districts during the year. The schools would then be able to spend the money raised locally, plus an equal amount provided by the state from the school fund. In 1861, the Legislature amended the law of 1829 to require each school district to raise a minimum sum from local assessment for education. Fourteen years later, the law set a fixed tax to be raised annually in each district. Those in New Castle and Kent Counties were to raise \$100, and each Sussex County district was to raise \$75.

In 1897, the constitution required the Legislature to contribute to the cost of public education and the General Assembly to appropriate for the schools the income from the investments of the public school fund. The Legislature also was to appropriate at least \$100,000 for such costs as teacher salaries and textbooks. It was not until 1921, however, that it actually required that the state school fund revenues be used for public schools. At that time, all revenues derived from personal income taxes, corporation income and franchise taxes, real estate taxes, and other appropriations were required to be used for maintenance and support of public schools.

State Support. After the reorganization of 1921, Delaware developed a state-supported system of education in which the major portion of the revenue is derived from the state government. Pierre S. duPont implemented this system by organizing and placing in operation a state tax department. The Delaware system is unique—no other state has this type of educational organization to obtain financial support for the schools. The Legislature appropriates moneys biennially for all school districts, although additional revenues are raised by local taxation. Even though local districts depend on the state, they do have a fair degree of local autonomy, and there is a definite feeling of local responsibility and authority. In 1965, the state contributed 75 percent of the revenues for current expenses of the public school system, local school districts 16.5 percent, and the federal government 8.5 percent.

Although duPont contributed much of his time and money to organize public education for Delaware, he apparently had no desire to relieve the citizens of their responsibility in this connection. It was through his efforts that thousands of individuals were placed on the tax rolls and additional millions were collected in personal income taxes. Delaware continues to be one of the high income tax states, with 37.7 percent of state revenues in 1965-66 derived from the personal income tax. Of the entire state budget in 1965-66, 37.3 percent was spent for public education (23).

The 1949 unit allocation law is the basis for apportioning the state's revenues for education. The Legislature makes its appropriation for all operational expense on the basis of the number of pupil "units" enrolled in the school districts on September 30 of each year. The law defines this unit to be 25 elementary pupils, grades 1 through 6, or 20 secondary pupils, grades 7 through 12. It uses other figures for handicapped and vocational pupils (24).

The number of units allocated to a school district determines the number of teachers and other personnel each is entitled to. These salaries are paid for by the state according to the state salary schedule. However, local districts may increase the number of personnel at salaries above the state level through local taxation. The state revenues provide educational supplies and equipment and all other costs of operating the school system on the basis of the number of units allocated to the various school districts. Furthermore, the state contributes, in most cases, 60 percent of the cost of school construction, and 100 percent for vocational schools and pupil transportation is paid from state revenues.

The Budget. From a legal standpoint, the Legislature has delegated to the executive branch authority to initiate the financial budget. The Budget Act of 1939 created a Permanent Budget Commission, consisting of the Governor, the secretary of state, the auditor of accounts, the state treasurer, and the state tax commissioner. The Governor serves as chairman, and since he appoints the secretary of state and the tax commissioner, he controls the commission. The budget commission requires all state agencies to submit statements of estimated expenditures for the coming biennium. It then investigates and holds hearings and makes suggestions for modifications. The Governor, upon receipt of the commission's report, may make additional changes before he submits the budget to the Legislature.

When the Governor submits copies of his proposed appropriation measures to the Legislature, this budget appropriation bill is referred to a joint legislative finance committee, consisting of five members of the house appropriations committee and five members of the state finance committee. But the main task is to move the budget through the legislative process, as pointed out by one authority on Delaware state government:

> The Joint Finance Committee usually has full responsibility for legislative action upon the governor's budget. At times, rather drastic changes are made by it in the executive proposals, but if the governor stands firm, he will generally prevail.
>
> The power of the governor arises, in part, from his item veto. If the legislature has added to the budget he may cut out certain of the items in the appropriation. On the other hand, if his estimates have been drastically reduced by the lawmakers, he may effect retaliation by use of the regular veto on some measure that they want

enacted. Inasmuch as most of the appropriation bills reach his desk toward the end of the legislative session, he has great opportunity to bring much of the spending into line with his own desires (25).

Due to the difficulty in accurately estimating all financial requirements for a biennium, there is a frequent need for supplementary appropriations. In fact, this type of legislation has been enacted with such frequency that it alters to some extent the purposes of the original budget bill.

Sources of Revenue. As stated previously, the state government provides about 75 percent of the revenue for public education. In 1965, the sources of this revenue were: personal income tax, 35 percent; corporation franchise tax, 12 percent; motor fuel tax, 10 percent; corporation income tax, 8.4 percent; motor vehicle registration, 4 percent; pari-mutual, 4 percent; alcoholic beverage tax, 2 percent; cigarette tax, 3 per cent; inheritance and estate tax, 14 percent; other taxes, 8 percent (26).

The 16.5 percent of the revenue provided by local taxes comes from real estate and capitations. From 1921 to 1950, local taxation for public education was used primarily for debt service, but since 1950 an increasing number of districts have levied taxes to increase the salaries beyond the minimum state schedule and to buy educational supplies, equipment, and other services beyond those provided by the state. Before a local tax is levied, it must be authorized by a voter referendum.

Federal Programs. The fact that Delaware is a small state has enabled the state agency to operate largely in the manner characteristic of the "horse and buggy" days until the end of World War II. With such a small staff the department could not specialize its efforts.

Since World War II, school population has nearly tripled. The rapid increase in pupil enrollments and the demand for quality education have placed tremendous strains on the public education system, particularly on the state education agency. Although its staff had increased from 1921 to 1960, the rate of growth was far too slow to keep pace with the rate of growth in school population and the demands for state leadership.

Since 1960, federal funds, particularly under NDEA's Title X and ESEA's Title V, have aided in strengthening the department's efforts in planning. A program of automatic data processing, initiated in 1960 under Title X of NDEA, has made a noticeable impact in providing timely, accurate, and detailed information. A growing need for more complete and speedy dissemination of information has been aided by funds under Title V of ESEA. A public information division, created in 1965, has operated under the office of the state superintendent in close cooperation with the research and publications division. Federal funds also have made possible improvement and expansion of publications by the state agency.

Administration of federal programs by the state agency has been facilitated by employing a coordinator of federal funds in 1963 and a supervisor of federal programs the following year. The agency employed a coordinator of Title I, ESEA, programs and added a supervisor of finance. The state superintendent appointed a deputy superintendent as of July 1, 1968.

The state agency's instructional programs area has been augmented and strengthened in a variety of ways. In 1960, under provision of NDEA's Title III, supervisory positions were created in mathematics, science, and modern foreign languages; a supervisory position for testing programs was created under Title V-A. Supervisory positions were filled in English in 1963, in social studies in 1964, and in reading in 1965 under Title III, NDEA. Other federally financed positions within the state agency created in 1963 were supervisors for Civil Defense education, occupational information, and manpower training. This addition of supervisory personnel has resulted in upgrading the level of instruction through in-service training programs and conferences, improved curriculum, and more equipment and instructional aids.

The impact of federal aid has speeded the tempo of educational change in Delaware, especially the increasing leadership role afforded the state agency. Specific areas of thrust are better collection, analysis, and dissemination of education data; a training program of greater scope and depth for education personnel; extensive planning to provide more effective administrative services and better programs of instruction; and increasing use of evaluation techniques.

FOOTNOTES

1. National Education Association, *Rankings of the States* (Washington, D.C.: The Association, 1967), p. 10.
2. Paul Dolan, *The Government and Administration in Delaware,* Vol. VII of the American Commonwealth Series, ed. by W. Brooke Graves (48 vols.; New York: Thomas Y. Crowell Co., 1956), pp. 2-4.
3. Stephen B. Weeks, *History of Public School Education in Delaware,* Department of the Interior, Bureau of Education, Bulletin No. 18 (Washington, D.C.: Government Printing Office, 1917), pp. 7-14.
4. Delaware, *Constitution* (1792), art. 8, sec. 12.
5. Etta J. Wilson, "Delaware's Educational Progess, 1917-1945," *Delaware: A History of the First State, II,* ed. by H. Clay Reed (3 vols.; New York: Lewis Historical Publishing Co., 1947).
6. *Ibid.*

7. Jacquelin Hayden Smith, "Education in Delaware Since 1917" (unpublished master's thesis, University of Delaware, Newark, 1942), p. 21.

8. Paul R. Mort, *A Fiscal Survey of the Public School System of Delaware* (Newark, Del.: School Study Council, 1960), p. 75.

9. Department of Public Instruction, *Annual Report, 1929,* p. 22.

10. Dolan, *op. cit.,* p. 183.

11. Delaware, *Constitution* (1897), art. 10, secs. 1, 2, 3.

12. Wilson, *op. cit.,* p. 707.

13. After a brief survey of the state agency's growth from 1926 to 1965, a few of these problems will be treated separately.

14. Robert A. Massaferi, "Driver and Safety Education" (unpublished manuscript, Department of Public Instruction, Dover, 1967).

15. Department of Public Instruction, *Annual Report, 1965,* p. 70.

16. Board for Vocational Education, *Thirty Years of Vocational Education in Delaware, 1919-1949* (Dover: The Board, 1950), pp. 1-51.

17. Martha Bonar, "School Lunch Program" (unpublished manuscript, Department of Public Instruction, Dover, 1967).

18. Weeks, *op. cit.,* p. 106.

19. Department of Public Instruction, *Annual Report, 1965,* p. 15.

20. American Council of Education, *A Survey of Education in Delaware* (Washington, D.C.: The Council, 1946), p. 257.

21. Robert C. Stewart, *Report on the Reorganization of School Districts in Delaware* (Dover: Department of Public Instruction, 1951).

22. Apparently, considerable flexibility was permitted for county superintendents to select teachers according to the type of school involved. Requirements for the "graded schools" were the most severe.

23. Office of the Budget Director, *General Fund Revenue and Disbursements for Fiscal Year 1966* (Dover: The Director, 1966).

24. The basis for unit allocation of handicapped pupils is as follows: educable mentally retarded, one unit for 15 pupils; trainable mentally handicapped, 6 pupils; socially and emotionally maladjusted, 10 pupils; partially sighted, 10 pupils; orthopedically handicapped, 10 pupils; partially deaf or hard of hearing, 8 pupils; and blind, 8 pupils. The pupils in vocational programs are counted once as secondary pupils on the basis of one unit for every 20 pupils, plus an extra unit for every 30 pupils in the vocational program.

25. Dolan, *op. cit.,* p. 125.

26. *Budget and Financial Report of the State of Delaware for the Fiscal Year Ending June 30, 1965* (Dover: Office of the Governor, 1966).

BIBLIOGRAPHY

Public Documents

Delaware. *Constitution* (1792; 1897, amended).

--*Laws* (1921).

--*Laws* (1929).

Books

American Council of Education. *A Survey of Education in Delaware.* Washington, D.C.: The Council, 1946.

Bevan, Wilson Lloyd, and Williams, E. Melvin, eds. *History of Delaware, Past and Present,* 4 vols. New York: Lewis Historical Publishing Co., 1929.

Board for Vocational Education. *Thirty Years of Vocational Education in Delaware, 1919-1949.* Dover: The Board, 1950.

Dolan, Paul. *The Government and Administration of Delaware.* American Commonwealth Series, Vol. VII. Edited by W. Brooke Graves. 48 vols. New York: Thomas Y. Crowell Co., 1956.

Powell, Lyman P. *The History of Education in Delaware.* University of Pennsylvania, Bureau of Education Circular of Information, No. 3. Contributions to American Educational History, No. 15. Edited by Herbert B. Adams. Washington, D.C.: Government Printing Office, 1893.

Reed, H. Clay, ed., *Delaware: A History of the First State.* 3 vols. New York: Lewis Historical Publishing Co., 1947.

Weeks, Stephen B. *History of Public School Education in Delaware.* Department of the Interior, Bureau of Education, Bulletin No. 18. Washington, D.C.: Government Printing Office, 1917.

Wilson, Etta J. "Delaware's Educational Progress, 1917-1945," *Delaware: A History of the First State,* Vol. II. Edited by H. Clay Reed, 3 vols. New York: Lewis Historical Publishing Co., 1947.

Reports

Budget and Financial Report of the State of Delaware for the Fiscal Years Ending June 30, 1965, 1966, and 1967. Dover: Office of the Governor.

Department of Public Instruction. *Annual Reports 1918-1965.* Dover: The Department.

Mort, Paul R. *A Fiscal Survey of the Public School System of Delaware.* Newark, Del.: School Study Council, 1960.

National Education Association. *Rankings of the States.* Washington, D.C.: The Association, 1967.

National Industrial Conference Board, Inc. *The Fiscal Problem in Delaware: Studies in Taxation and Public Finance.* New York: The Board, 1927.

School Survey Commission. *Report on System and Standards of Public Education in Delaware with Recommendations for Their Improvement.* Dover: The Commission, 1948.

Stewart, Robert C. *Report on the Reorganization of School Districts in Delaware.* Dover: Department of Public Instruction, 1951.

Unpublished Material

Aird, Mildred V. "Health Occupations." Unpublished manuscript, Department of Public Instruction, Dover, 1967.

Ayars, George W. "Health and Physical Education." Unpublished manuscript, Department of Public Instruction, Dover, 1967.

Board of Education. Minutes of August 13, 1925, and September 16, 1949, meetings, Dover.

Bonar, Martha. "School Lunch Program." Unpublished manuscript, Department of Public Instruction, Dover, 1967.

Department of Public Instruction, Adult Education Section. "History and Recent Developments in Adult Education." Unpublished manuscript, Dover, 1967.

Division of Trade and Industrial Education. "History of Trade and Industrial Education in Delaware, 1949-1967." Unpublished manuscript, Dover, 1967.

Gervan, James R. "Art Education Division Historical Résumé." Unpublished manuscript, Department of Public Instruction, Dover, 1967.

Hart, Floyd T. "History of Music Education in Delaware." Unpublished manuscript, Department of Public Instruction, Dover, 1967.

Laws, Ruth M. "Planning and Research in Vocational Education." Unpublished manuscript, Department of Public Instruction, Dover, 1967.

——"Progress Report on Migrant Education, 1961-1967." Unpublished manuscript, Department of Public Instruction, Dover, 1967.

Lloyd, Elizabeth C., and Jones, Ruth S. "Teacher Education and Professional Standards." Unpublished manuscript, Department of Public Instruction, Dover, 1967.

Massaferi, Robert A. "Driver and Safety Education." Unpublished manuscript, Department of Public Instruction, Dover, 1967.

McGorman, George B. "History of Distributive Education in Delaware." Unpublished manuscript, Department of Public Instruction, Dover, 1967.

Myer, Fredric E. "Agriculture Education." Unpublished manuscript, Department of Public Instruction, Dover, 1967.

Schweet, Ray G. "Business and Office Education." Unpublished manuscript, Department of Public Instruction, Dover, 1967.

Smith, Jacquelin Hayden. "Education in Delaware Since 1917." Unpublished master's thesis, University of Delaware, Newark, 1942.

Snowberger, Mildred H. "Home Economics Education in Delaware 1917-1967." Unpublished manuscript, Department of Public Instruction, Dover, 1967.

Stewart, Robert C. "A Proposed Plan for the Reorganization of Administrative Units in the State of Delaware." Unpublished Ph.D. dissertation, University of Pennsylvania, Philadelphia, 1949.

Wallin, J. E. W. "The Early Development of Special Educational Facilities for Handicapped Children in the Delaware Public Schools." Unpublished manuscript, Wilmington, Delaware, 1966.

Wilson, John C. "Occupational Information and Career Services." Unpublished manuscript, Department of Public Instruction, Dover, 1967.

Appendix A

DELAWARE CHIEF STATE SCHOOL OFFICERS

State Superintendents

1875-83 James H. Groves

1883-87 Thomas N. Williams

The Office of State Superintendent was discontinued in April 1887, and three county superintendents were appointed, one for each county.

State Commissioners

1913-17 Charles W. Wagner

1917-21 Arthur R. Spaid

State Superintendents

1921-46 Harry V. Holloway

1946-64 George R. Miller, Jr.

1964-67 Richard P. Gousha

1967- Kenneth C. Madden

Appendix B

Chart I.--DELAWARE DEPARTMENT OF PUBLIC INSTRUCTION, 1921*

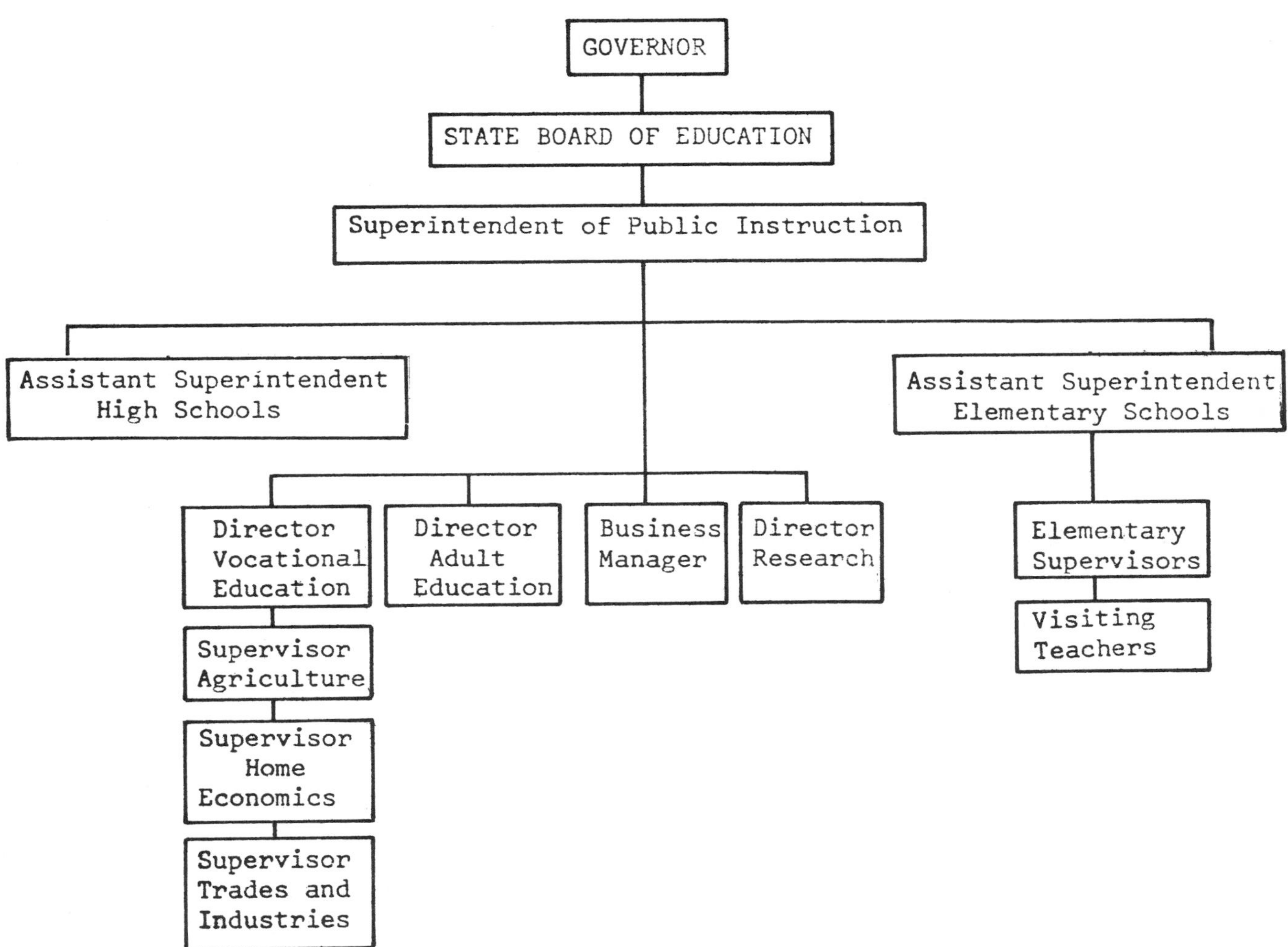

*This is a schematic of the organization set up by the State Board of Education for carrying into effect the School Law of 1921.

Appendix B

Chart II.--DELAWARE DEPARTMENT OF PUBLIC INSTRUCTION, 1966

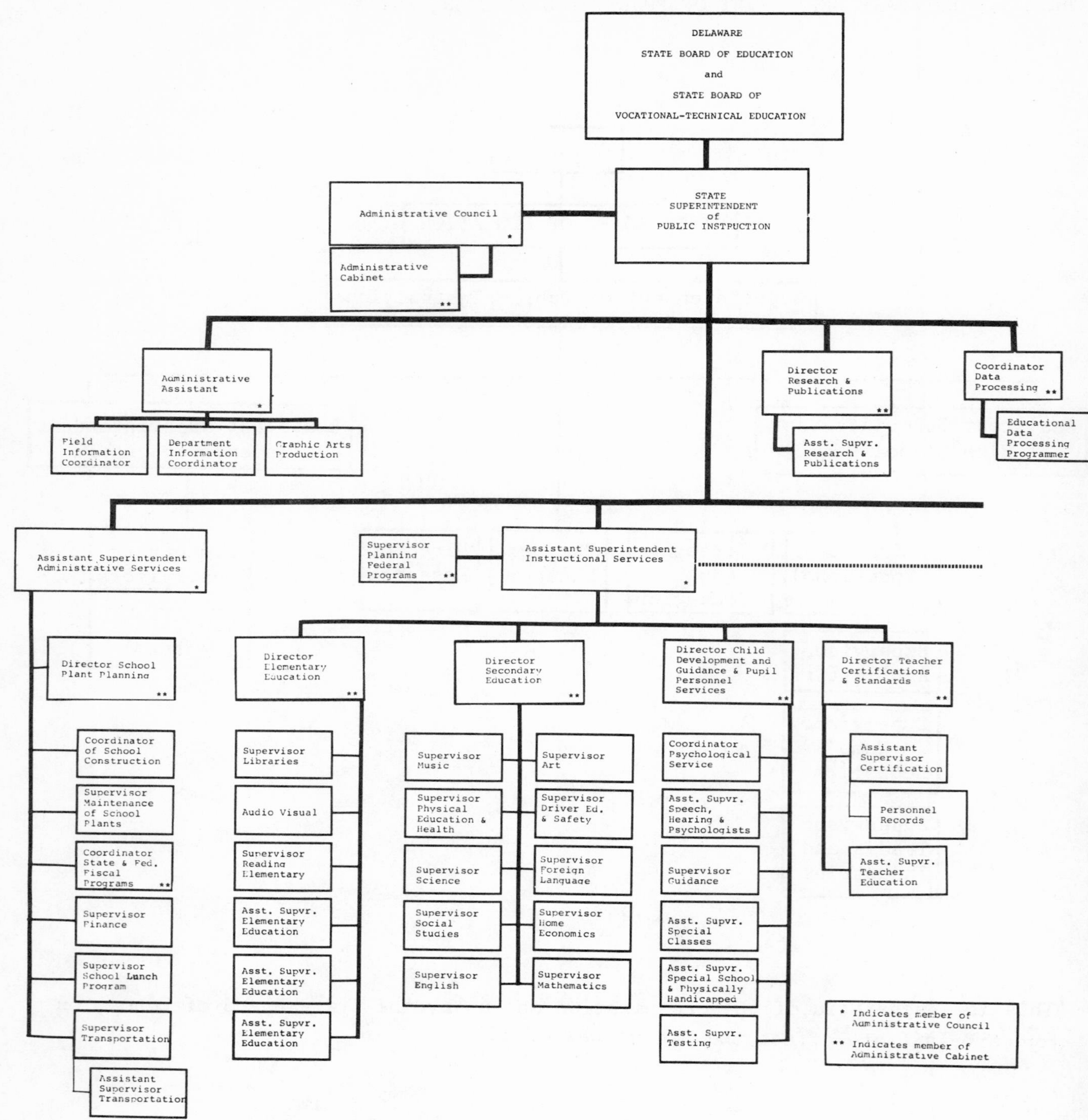

Appendix B

Chart II.--DELAWARE DEPARTMENT OF PUBLIC INSTRUCTION, 1966 (Continued)

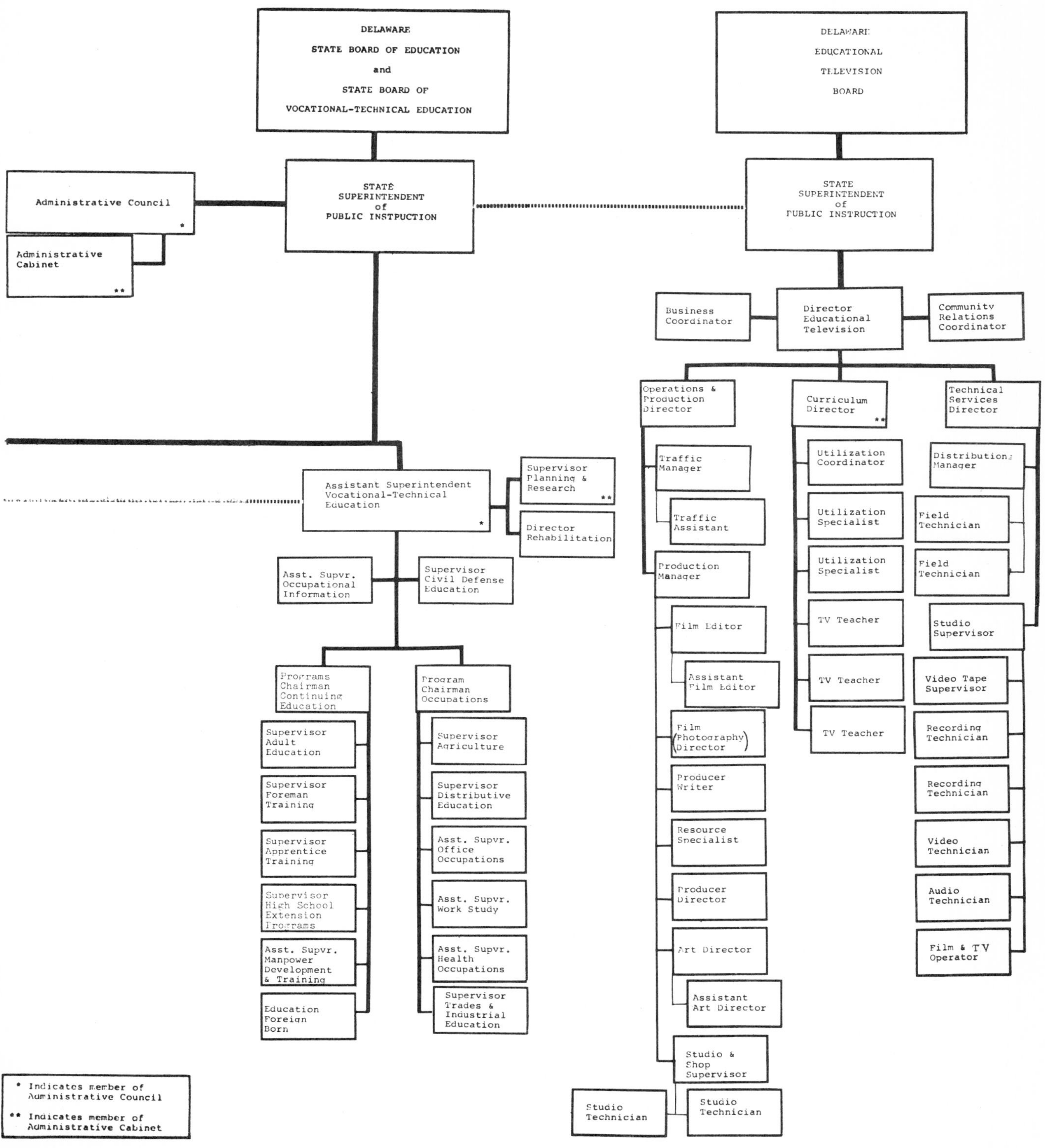

Appendix B

Supplement 1. – DATES OF ORIGIN OF POSITIONS IN STATE DEPARTMENT OF PUBLIC INSTRUCTION

1875 State Superintendent

1918 Supervisors: Agriculture, Home Economics, Trades and Industries

1919 Director, Vocational Education

1921 Assistant Superintendent, Elementary Education; Assistant Superintendent, Secondary Education; Business Manager; Director, Research; Director, Medical Inspection; Rural Elementary Supervisor (4); Visiting Teacher (4)

1922 Director, Adult Education and Immigrant Education

1925 Director, Physical Education

1927 Director, Health and Physical Education (Health combined with Physical Education)

1929 Director, Art Education; Supervisor, Art Education

1930 Director, Music; Supervisor, Music

1931 Supervisor, Transportation

1932 Director, Special Education

1934 Supervisor, Driver Education

1938 Supervisor, Distributive Education

1939 Director, Rehabilitation

1941 Psychologist

1943 Speech and Hearing Therapist

1946 Supervisor, School Lunch; Assistant Superintendent, Business Administration

1947 Supervisors: Certification; Guidance

1948 Assistant Supervisor, Trades and Industries

1951 Supervisor, Child Development

1954 Coordinator, Apprentice Training

1955 Assistant Superintendent, Vocational Education; Assistant Supervisor, Pupil Transportation

1957 Director, Teacher Education and Professional Standards; Supervisor, Research and Publications

1958 Supervisor, Special Classes

1960 Supervisors: Science; Mathematics; Modern Languages; Group Testing Program

1961 Supervisor, Industrial Education

1962 Data Processing Programmer; Supervisors: Personnel Records; School Libraries

1963 Coordinator of Civil Defense Adult Education; Film Librarian; Supervisors: Occupational Information and Career Service; Manpower Development Training; Trades, Industry, and Teacher Training

1964 Administrative Assistant to the State Superintendent; Assistant Superintendent, Administrative Serivces; Director, School Plant Planning; Specialist, Public Information; Coordinators: School Plant Construction; Data Processing; Public Information; State and Federal Funds; Supervisors: Maintenance of School Plants; English Education; Planning and Vocational Technical Research; Office Occupations; Work Study and Diversified Programs; Special Schools and Physically Handicapped

1965 Coordinator, State Leadership for Migrant Education; Supervisors: Finance; Planning-Federal Programs; Social Studies; High School Extension Programs; Reading Education; Teacher Education

Appendix B

Supplement 2. – CHRONOLOGICAL FACT SHEET

1792 The second constitution of Delaware provided for the establishment of public schools and the promotion of arts and sciences.

1796 A public school fund was created, and the first fees were received from marriage and tavern licenses.

1817 The first appropriation by the Legislature was made for the education of poor children, and the funds were received from state and county revenues.

1821 The first tax law for education provided public funds for the support of Sunday schools and was used for the teaching of reading, writing, and religious morals.

1829 Free education was provided for all children by law. School districts and school boards were created by law.

1843 First State Educational Convention was held in Dover.

1861 The Legislature mandated that school districts levy a minimum tax for education, with voter option to go beyond the minimum.

1867 The Delaware Association for the Moral Improvement and Education of the Colored People was formed for the purpose of organizing a program of Negro education in the state.

1875 The position of State Superintendent of Education was created by law. The State Board of Education was created by law. The State Teachers' Association was organized at a meeting held in Wilmington. Teacher certification was required by law. Tax law for Negroes was enacted providing for the maintenance of Negro schools.

1881 First state aid was extended to Negro schools.

1891 Free textbooks were provided by law.

1897 A new state constitution was adopted in which detailed provisions were made for the financing of public education.

1898 State funds were provided for the education for Negroes on an equal basis with white pupils.

1901 A State Library Commission was created to provide for school libraries, and the law required that the state pay for one-half of the cost.

1907 The first compulsory attendance law was enacted.

1919 The State Department of Immigrant Education, which later became a part of the State Department of Public Instruction, was created by an act of the Legislature. A program of vocational education was inaugurated in the areas of agriculture, home economics, and trades and industries. Special school districts were created by law. The School Code provided for the transportation of elementary pupils living more than 2 miles from school and for high school pupils living over 3 miles from school. The Delaware School Auxiliary Association was organized for the purpose of constructing new school buildings. Pierre S. duPont provided an initial contribution of $2 million to start this program.

1921 The revised school law eliminated the county system of education and authorized the State Board of Education to assume the functions of the county board, which included financial budgeting and supervision of instruction. The State Board of Education was required by law to maintain separate schools for white and Negro children and to make both types of schools equally effective.

1935 The first area high school was created and known as the Henry C. Conrad School District.

1936 Standard high schools were established under the rules and regulations of the State Board of Education.

1941 A school construction formula was established wherein the state was to contribute 60 percent and the local school district 40 percent for the construction of school buildings.

1945 Teacher pension system was established by the Legislature.

1947 A uniform state-supported salary schedule and classification for teachers and other educational personnel was authorized by the Legislature. Legislation dealing with delayed repairs to school buildings was authorized.

1949 The unit allocation law which provided the basis for financing public education in Delaware was enacted to become effective July 1, 1951. The unit allocation law provided that appropriations should be based on units of 20 secondary pupils, 25 elementary pupils, and varying figures for special categories. A school construction act was passed which appropriated money for said purposes, authorized the issuance of bonds of the state and by contributions from school districts. Redistricting: The General Assembly of 1949 took an important step in school district reorganization by passing a consolidation enabling act.

1950 The Legislature provided for the establishment of three comprehensive high schools for Negroes: L. L. Redding Comprehensive High School, William Henry Comprehensive High School, and W. C. Jason Comprehensive High School.

1952 Measures enacted by the Legislature provided an increase in age of compulsory school attendance from 14 to 16 years of age.

1953 The Legislature modified the unit allotment system for calculating the number of units of pupils classified as exceptional, or handicapped, providing smaller classes for handicapped pupils than for normal pupils. The Educational Code was revised providing clarification of legal purposes and providing a ready reference and index to educational statues.

1957 The 1957 General Assembly provided funds for the construction of vocational facilities in Kent and Sussex Counties.

1960 A school constuction formula was adopted by members of the Department of Public Instruction.

1964 The State Board of Education passed a resolution which resulted in the consolidation of 26 Negro schools with adjoining districts for white pupils, thus abolishing segregation in the state. An Educational Television Board was created by the Legislature, with authorization to establish and maintain an educational TV network.

9 Florida DEPARTMENT OF EDUCATION
John W. Seay

Contents

THE HISTORICAL BACKGROUND

Florida was officially transferred from Spain to the United States in ceremonies at Pensacola on July 17, 1821, and was recognized as a territory by Congress the following March. That same year, 1822, the federal government established the basis for a permanent state school fund by reserving the income from every sixteenth section of land specifically for this purpose. Five years later, Congress turned the control of these school lands over to the Governor and the Territorial Legislature. In 1828, the Legislature authorized the Governor and legislative council to appoint three trustees of school lands in each county. Although the law remained in force for 4 years, the school land rents netted only $101.50 during this time.

The Territorial Legislature passed a law in 1832 empowering the people in each township to elect three commissioners to take charge of the public school lands of the county. Two years later, the Legislature changed the law to authorize the county judges to appoint two commissioners of school lands for each county. However, little attention was given to this law, so the Legislature in 1835 authorized the register of the state land office to supervise all school lands. The following February, it transferred this supervision to the territorial treasurer. As the territory grew, the treasurer could not give sufficient time to the school lands, so little or nothing was accomplished except to lend an element of centralization that had been lacking (1).

In 1839, the Legislature again enacted a law providing for the election of three trustees in each township to be responsible for leasing school lands and using the proceeds to establish and support the common schools. This act directed each county tax assessor to prepare a census of the orphans in his county, and it made the county judge responsible for supervising the school fund expenditures.

The officials responsible for education and controlling school money continued to change rapidly. In 1843, the Legislature directed the county sheriffs to take charge of the school lands and arrange for educating the poor children. This lasted only 1 year, when the electors were again empowered to elect three trustees and a treasurer to carry out this responsibility. Two years later, the Legislature designated each county judge as the county superintendent of common schools. At the same time, the trustees of each county were required to report to the judge, who would then write a county school report. In other words, the Legislature delegated some of the responsibilities and duties of the present-day county superintendent of public instruction to the county judge, and the secretary of the territory served somewhat in the capacity of a state superintendent.

Florida was admitted into the Union as a state in March 1845. Two years later, control of the school lands again passed into the hands of the state registrar of public lands. In 1848, for the first time, rather than only lease the lands as in the past, the state was authorized to sell them and establish a permanent state school fund. With this financial source, the new state passed a law the next year providing for a state system of public education open to all white children between the ages of 5 and 19. This law also directed the registrar of the land office to act as state superintendent of schools, the county probate judges to serve as county superintendents, and the taxpayers of the various districts to elect the local board of trustees.

In 1851, the Legislature attempted to further strengthen the state educational system by starting an equalization program of state support. This law stated that in all counties where interest on the school fund did not provide at least $2 per child per year, the state would make up the deficiency from state funds. The eligibility for this state aid was calculated on the number of children required to attend school at least 3 months the previous year.

Since the income from the state's school fund was so small, when the Legislature established the equalization program, it authorized the counties, for the first time, to levy a tax on real and personal property "not to exceed four dollars for each child of school age" (2). As only two counties—Franklin and Monroe—supplemented school funds from the general county treasury, the 1853 Legislature attempted to increase school receipts by authorizing the county commissioners "to add to the sum apportioned to the county by the State any sum which they may deem proper to be paid out of the county treasury" (3). No limit was put on the commissioners' discretion; they could make the county school fund as large as they desired. At the same time, the law attempted to strengthen county organization by designating the commissioners in each county as the board of education. The probate judge continued to be the county superintendent and served as president of the board.

Unfortunately, during the 1850's, there was apparently little general interest in public education, and only meager sums were voted to support it. The fault was not with the law; if any child was deprived of the opportunity to attend a good common school, the fault was almost entirely with the school officers, especially the probate judges and county commissioners on whom the welfare of the public school system primarily depended. David S. Walker, the first aggressive state superintendent of schools (4), stated in his 1853-54 report: "Hitherto, the judges of probate and county commissioners have not, I fear, given to this subject the consideration it deserves . . ." (5). The evidence indicates that during this period most of the money received from public funds was used in many counties to subsidize favored private schools already in operation rather than to establish public schools.

Virtually no provision was made for the support of the public schools other than revenue from federal land grants. Of even greater significance, the state had not really provided for a centralized administration and state direction of the public system. This is understandable in view of the great distances between population centers and the lack of communication and transportation facilities in the early 1800's. The present system of public schools in Florida was made possible by the State Constitution of 1868 and the state school law of 1869.

Under the Constitution of 1868 and the school law enacted the following year, the state superintendent was no longer the registrar of the land office, but a separate state officer appointed by the Governor. The state superintendent, the secretary of state, and the attorney general comprised an ex officio State Board of Education.

The new laws also stipulated that the Governor would appoint the superintendent of public instruction in each county, a practice that prevailed until the constitution was revised in 1885. Appointment by the Governor did open the office to abuses during the Reconstruction period, and this may account in part for a great deal of the difficulty Florida's public school system had in winning the support of the general public. The people, often with good cause, had little confidence in local and state officials appointed by the carpetbag regime (6). Secretary of State Samuel B. McLin, who served as acting state superintendent from August 1874 to March 1875, commented on the county superintendents in general in his 1873–74 report:

> While a few of our county superintendents are in every way worthy, qualified, and efficient officers, a large majority of them are notoriously unfit for the position, and utterly incapable of performing their duties. The literary qualifications of some of them, if we may be permitted to judge from the letters and annual reports sent to this office, are of a very primitive type, and some of them are so indolent, incompetent, or uninterested, as to omit the making of an annual report at all. The truth is that this and all other offices in any way connected with the educational interests of the State must be entirely and forever divorced from party politics. Too frequently has the county superintendency fallen into the hands of men who have prostituted it to their political advancement, or made use of it for the pecuniary gain it brought. This should not be (7).

This analysis of the county superintendents by McLin is particularly interesting, because he was one of the "hateful imports" then in the control of the state government. He had succeeded Jonathan C. Gibbs, Florida's only Negro state superintendent, and was referring to the appointees of his own party. Superintendent Gibbs served as secretary of state in the same administration and presumably had considerable influence in appointing the county superintendents–at least, a number of "conservatives" (Democrats) were removed from office when he was appointed state superintendent.

Superintendent Gibbs, an 1852 graduate of Dartmouth College, moved from Pennsylvania to Florida in 1866 during the Reconstruction period. He was appointed state superintendent in January 1873 but died suddenly in August 1874. A later state superintendent wrote about his administration:

> While it is regarded as exceedingly unfortunate that a Negro should have been put at the head of educational affairs in a Southern State at that particular juncture, when the system needed above everything else popularizing with the white population, and their cooperation to make it a success–it is folly to undertake to force the prejudices of any people, especially of a Florida "Cracker"–still justice must be done Mr. Gibbs, without regard to his color, his politics, or his birthplace. He is reputed to have been a man of integrity, culture, an orator, and quite a gentleman. He was generally conceded to be far superior in all that constitutes a man of worth to the great majority of his white partisans who held office in the State at that time (8).

During this period, from June 1868 to January 1877, when the government was in the hands of a political party that was neither elected nor favored by the majority of the intelligent voters and property-owning people, there was little continuity in the offices of the superintendent of schools at either the state or county levels. State and county superintendents were appointed by the Governor, who was tempted to play politics at the expense of the schools. Too often, men were chosen, not on the basis of fitness for service, but according to their party affiliation. A number of Florida's citizens did not cooperate to improve education as they would have had they been in sympathy with the party in power. The result was disaster for the education of the state's youth.

From 1870 to 1876, five state superintendents held office, and from 1871 to 1874, only five counties did not have a turnover in county superintendents. From the beginning of the administration of Governor George F. Drew in 1877, the first "conservative" Governor after the Civil War, the public school system made increasing progress. Governor Drew removed or accepted the resignations of well over half of the county superintendents appointed by his Republican predecessor. He restored these offices to the party representing the majority of the people, who began to show evidence of greater interest in the schools (9). The Constitution of 1885, which went into effect in January 1887, provided for the state superintendent to be elected and for each county to elect its own county superintendent. This constitution placed the schools under a county-unit organization and authorized a district school tax to be added to the county school tax for their administration. Between 1884 and 1892, the Governor and state treasurer were added to the state board.

By 1884, a few high schools and more than 1,500 common schools had been established, serving about 42 percent of the school population of the state. By 1901, approximately 2,500 schools were operating, with almost 112,000 pupils attending average terms of 96 days. Almost 3,000 teachers taught in the schools of the state, some in more than one school during the year. The average monthly salary for teachers was approximately $35, ranging from a high of $150 (for principals) to a low of $15. The state's school property was valued at $970,815, and the total expenditures for schools in 1901 amounted to $774,870 (10).

PERSONNEL AND ORGANIZATION OF THE STATE DEPARTMENT (11)

At the turn of the century, the Department of Public Instruction consisted of three people: the state superintendent, a clerk, and a typewriter-stenographer. By the end of the 1904-1906 biennium, the clerk was designated as a chief clerk and had an assistant chief clerk to help him with his duties. Superintendent W. N. Sheats attempted to get the Legislature to provide a state high school inspector. But the $1,500 in salary and appropriation for travel was eliminated by a penny-wise and pound-foolish policy. Sheats reported that–

> The labor of inspection was assigned to the State Superintendent, an office with more duties than he could well discharge. After trial, it was demonstrated that the State Superintendent could not find the time to visit and properly inspect all of these schools and perform the other duties placed upon him by law (12).

The need for a high school inspector increased, but no further expansion took place until 1908, when the General Education Board of New York employed a professor of secondary education to inspect and supervise high schools under the joint authority of the state university at Gainesville and the state superintendent. The inspector was not paid by the state, but from his headquarters in Gainesville he performed a valuable service to Florida high school teachers.

The Southern Education Board, a philanthropic foundation organized to help Southern states improve education, provided Florida with an elementary rural school inspector in 1911, with duties and responsibilities similar to those of the high school inspector. Within 3 years, the elementary rural school inspector's services had proven so valuable that the Legislature passed an act providing for two rural school inspectors to be appointed by the Governor on the state superintendent's nomination. They were to work directly under the state superintendent (13).

Except for the addition of a clerk in 1916, the department staff did not grow until 1919, when the General Education Board, founded by John D. Rockefeller in 1902, agreed to pay the entire expense for a state supervisor of Negro schools. The following year, Congress appropriated money for Florida to employ three vocational education supervisors–one for agriculture, one for trades and industries, one for home economics–under the Smith-Hughes Act, passed by Congress in 1917 to promote vocational education. Also, the General Education Board placed a full-time high school supervisor in the field in 1920 with the explicit understanding that its appropriation for this work would be discontinued in 1925. The Legislature agreed to continue the two rural school inspectors at increased salaries and created a new position–state supervisor of elementary schools. The General Education Board contributed $1,250 to defray the traveling expenses of one state rural school inspector, in addition to the $5,300 for salary and traveling expenses it had donated for the supervisor of Negro schools. Thus, by 1920 the department's staff had expanded to include a three-man state board of examiners for teacher education and 14 full-time staff members.

Only minor changes occurred in the department's staff until 1926, though a few titles changed. For example, the high school supervisor now was called the state supervisor of high schools. The clerical staff had expanded, so that some were performing semiprofessional duties. Superintendent W. S. Cawthon (14) described his staff in his 1926 biennial report:

> There are now nine supervisory positions, four of them being maintained by the general revenue fund of the State, three by the joint appropriations of the State and Federal Governments, one by the Florida Public Health Association, and one by the General Education Board. The incumbents of all these positions except the

Supervisor of Negro Education now have their offices in that part of the Capitol allotted to the State Department of Education. The intimate relationship existing between any phase of education and every other phase of it renders this arrangement highly desirable; and the benefits resulting from the consolidation are already being noted (15).

By 1932, Florida, along with the rest of the nation, was in the throes of the Depression. The department found it difficult to hold the ground it had gained, much less expand its services. In 1933, the Legislature abolished several positions and authorized a reorganization, but it did not appropriate sufficient funds to carry it out. Even though the financial picture was even darker in 1934, the state board did add a state director of instruction and a state director of school finance. By the end of 1934, the department was composed of 21 persons.

The period between 1934 and 1938 was a trying one for education in Florida. Superintendent W. S. Cawthon, who served from 1922 to 1937, worked under the handicap of severely limited funds and an insufficient staff. He devoted his energies primarily to carrying out the administrative rather than the instructional leadership functions of his office. His role was more one of carrying out the legislative mandates than promoting educational progress. His conception of democracy was that of the idealist: Everything was supposed to be done by the book.

Superintendent Cawthon took great pride in the fact that he had never asked anyone to vote for him, and, in spite of this, he was elected three times after his original appointment. His son stated:

> He refused to spend any money campaigning and screamed to high heaven about the injustice of the qualifying fee. It really hurt him to dig down every four years for the $250 or $300, as the case might be. When he ran in 1936 and was faced with a second primary, some of his friends persuaded him to change his attitude about campaigning and he did; but I think he always regretted it.
>
> As I recall, the State Superintendent was paid $5,000 a year when he took office and when the question of a raise came up, he refused to join the rest of the Cabinet in requesting it, saying, "I knew what the job paid when I took it."
>
> He did not fall in with the demands of the teachers in the latter part of his administration for more pay even though I think he knew that they deserved it. He always thought that the local governmental body should bear the larger part of the school expense (16).

Superintendent Cawthon was almost miserly in the conduct of his office. He believed that a man with an expense account should only eat and sleep as well as he did at home and that was all—no luxuries. He always stayed at the Aragon Hotel in Jacksonville for $2 a night, although most of the members of his staff refused to join in this sacrificial gesture. The fact that the U. S. government owed so much money always frightened him. When his son suggested that he keep a more accurate account of his medical expenses so that he could deduct them from his income tax, he took a dim view, saying: "They need it worse than I do. They owe a hundred billion dollars and I don't owe a damn cent . . ." (17).

Florida not only suffered from the Depression but had the additional problem of recovering from the shock caused by the collapse of a "land boom." During the late 1920's, extravagant advertising and wild land speculation lured large numbers of new residents to Florida, and most were unable to leave when tropical storms sent prices plummeting and the Depression followed 2 years later. Many schools were operating curtailed terms, teachers were paid in script, and counties were defaulting on school building bond payments.

The change in population, plus a general dissatisfaction with the school system, combined to create a public demand for change. The agitation was particularly evident at the county level, especially among the county school superintendents. In response to this general feeling of dissatisfaction, in January 1936 Governor David Sholtz appointed a special committee, the Florida School Code Committee, to examine the entire field of education and make recommendations to ensure better planning and direction. The committee was composed of state officials, university personnel, board members, county officials, and representatives from organizations such as labor, women's clubs, The American Legion, the state bar association, chambers of commerce, and the Parent-Teachers Association. Although this effort was initiated by laymen rather than the education department, the department's staff did play an active role in the committee's work.

In March 1937, the committee completed a very extensive 220-page report covering almost every phase of education in Florida. It recognized the State Department of Public Instruction (which was renamed the State Department of Education in 1938) as an important agency for maintaining a liberal system of public schools, and that it was "probably desirable for this Department to be created and recognized directly in the school code" (18). The report further stated that the department, operating under the direction of the state superintendent, should—

> Assist the Superintendent in carrying out the policies, procedure, and powers authorized by law or by regulation of the State Board of Education; in assembling, explaining and making available data for the intelligent appraisal and operation of the state system of public education; in formulating, revising and executing plans and programs for the system of public education; in arranging, in interpreting and publishing the laws and regulations for the organization and management of

schools and educational institutions; in providing professional leadership, guidance, stimulation, for the public school personnel; and in promulgating educational information for the people of the state (19).

In the 1936 election for state superintendent, Colin English, a former county superintendent from Lee County, campaigned on a platform demanding that the department take a more active and dynamic role in promoting education in Florida. The electors agreed, and English took office in January 1937. He served 12 years before resigning to run unsuccessfully for governor.

The period from 1940 to 1946 was a trying one for the department, with six regular staff members on military leave. The two state universities, the University of Florida at Gainesville and the Florida State College for Women at Tallahassee (now Florida State University), did provide part-time assistance to the department. The staff members' assignments were doubled, and despite the fact that a considerable number of employees were new to the department, assignments were made on the basis of their personalities and talents rather than following a formal pattern. For example, the director of the division of instruction also served as supervisor of teacher certification and consultant in physical and health education. Travel had to be curtailed due to wartime restrictions and rationing, materials were in short supply, and some services had to be curtailed.

Besides the personnel shortages and travel restrictions, the war presented other problems. Large numbers of recruits were sent to the many military posts and bases located in the state, and whole communities grew up around them. Schools had to be built, staffed, and equipped at a time when materials, labor, and equipment were in short supply. Families with diverse educational backgrounds moved into Florida from all over the country, and pupils were constantly moving from place to place in and out of the state. At the same time, the curriculum had to keep up with new needs and demands.

In 1946, the department was reorganized to better handle the problems brought about by the war and the influx of people by placing its staff members in functional areas. There remained the two primary divisions: the administration and finance division, and the instruction division. However, separate sections or subdivisions had developed under the instruction division, such as veteran education, vocational services, and Negro education, each with its own director.

The vocational rehabilitation services, formerly a part of the vocational services section, expanded so dramatically that it was designated a separate section in 1948. While agricultural education, home economics, and trade and industrial education also emerged as separate sections, they were nominally part of the instruction division, although each operated with a considerable degree of autonomy, reporting directly to the state superintendent on many matters.

By the end of the 1948-50 biennium, the department had added a deputy superintendent to relieve the state superintendent of some of his time-consuming administrative functions. The new deputy superintendent, J. K. Chapman, a former principal and state department consultant, assumed responsibility for much of the internal management, enabling his chief to devote much more time to educational leadership.

When Superintendent Thomas D. Bailey took office in January 1949, new residents were still pouring into Florida from all over the nation, bringing thousands of pupils to swell the schools. This was the beginning of Florida's greatest growth, and the department was truly forced to develop its leadership and expand its services. County school officials were increasingly turning to the department for guidance and help in such areas as curriculum development, budget control, in-service education, school construction, transportation, research, and school law. Rendering these services required the department to add additional personnel. Superintendent Bailey explained this new role of the Department of Education in an address to the Chief State School Officers at Sault Ste. Marie, Michigan, on June 21, 1955:

> Only a few years ago it was commonly believed that the chief functions of the state department of education were to gather and disseminate data; to enforce regulations; to inspect and accredit schools; and to issue certificates. These are still, for the most part, functions and responsibilities of state departments of education, but they are no longer matters of primary importance. They have been reduced to established routines, and the energies of staffs at the state level have been channeled into new directions . . . .
>
> State school administration must be based upon the generally approved policy of cooperation between local, state, and federal authorities, with the responsibility shared in terms of (1) local operation, (2) state responsibility, and (3) federal assistance. The most desirable situation is one in which there is a maximum of local freedom and initiative, aided and supported by extensive and intelligent state services. It should be noted here that state services should be of such character that local leadership will be encouraged and developed rather than discouraged and usurped . . . .
>
> Quality in a state department staff is much more to be sought after than quantity—and is regarded by many as the essential ingredient in the development of a successful state department of education . . . (20).

By 1952, the department was much more efficiently organized. The instruction division was divided to create a new instructional field services division. Textbooks, formerly the responsibility of the administration and finance division, were now under a new publications and textbook services division. But it was 1954 before the major reorganization was completed. No longer was the department's structure dictated primarily by the strengths and abilities of individual staff members—now there was a formal classification of responsibilities. A special executive services unit headed by the deputy superintendent, similar in many ways to an operating division, not only exercised general business control over the department's internal operations, but it also included the managers of central services, purchasing, duplicating, mail, supply, and the editor of the *Florida School Bulletin.* The school lunch section was transferred from the instruction division to this unit.

The administration and finance division changed very little under the reorganization. It had added considerably more personnel, especially in school plant services and school survey services. While somewhat informally organized, it comprised the following sections: capital outlay and debt service, finance, records and reports, research and statistics, school law and information, school plant, survey, and transportation. These sections worked closely together, with some overlapping of duties and responsibilities.

The former instruction division was abandoned entirely, and the following divisions were created or continued: teacher education, certification, and accreditation; vocational rehabilitation; vocational and adult education; instructional field services; and publications and textbook services. Thus, by 1954 the department had six operating divisions and a special executive services unit. The vocational and adult education division now contained all of the adult and vocational programs in a unified division, eliminating some overlapping and duplication of effort and services that had occurred in the independent sections.

Minor expansion continued to occur. By the end of 1956, the department added consultants in music education and driver education to the instructional field services division and employed a full-time curriculum consultant and a curriculum librarian. The central services branch was moved from special executive services to directly under the state superintendent. By the biennium ending in 1958, the publications and textbooks services division had been abolished when its director retired and the functions transferred to the special executive services unit.

The teacher education, certification, and accreditation division had added a research section, and the vocational rehabilitation division had added a substantial number of counselors to its district offices. At the same time, since Florida's rapidly expanding junior college system needed supervising, regulating, and coordinating, a community junior colleges division was created. This later proved to be one of the greatest forward steps taken by Superintendent Bailey's administration.

The administration and finance division, which had remained virtually unchanged since its establishment in the mid-thirties, had been divided into three separate divisions. By January 1963, the department's organization consisted of eight operating divisions, each under a director (21), with a clear delineation of duties and responsibilities.

During the next 2 years, the coordinator of the National Defense Education Act (NDEA) was moved from the special executive services branch to work directly under the state superintendent. Federal legislation made it necessary to add the higher education facilities program to the administration division. The former school plant section was divided into two sections—school plant management and school plant planning. The vocational and adult education division was renamed the vocational, technical, and adult education division, a more appropriate title since the work had expanded in the technical education areas. Within this division, the division services section was expanded to include manpower development and training, and business education was added to the old distributive and cooperative education section. Technical education was separated from industrial education and made into a new section.

Later in 1965, as a result of the increasing number of new federal programs, a legal aide, an accountant, and a coordinator of federal-state relations were added to the special executive services branch. The department also appointed a fiscal administrator of federal programs to promote a more uniform approach to the solution of accounting problems, both for the county school systems and for the reports required by the U.S. Office of Education. Superintendent Bailey resigned in October 1965 after working for 17 years to give every child in Florida an adequate educational opportunity. One newspaper stated that he had "become a legend in his time. . ." (22). He received the plaudits of educators, politicians, newspapers, and the public in general. One editorial stated:

> Bailey has devoted much of his time to correct inequities in the educational system of the state, so much, that today the child in the smallest county of the state has equal educational opportunities with one residing in the largest county in Florida.
>
> All of this and much more has been made possible through the inspirational leadership of Thomas D. Bailey and his own dedication to his highly responsible position.
>
> Tom refuses to take all the credit for the accomplishments he has brought to education in Florida. Being the humble man he is, he turns and states the news media of Florida deserve as much credit as does he for the

> tremendous stride the state has made in education in the past decade and a half. He says the same of educators with whom he has rubbed elbows over the years.
>
> Tom Bailey is a man who will be sorely missed by the people of Florida when he walks out of his office for the last time next Thursday. The people of this sunshine paradise owe him a debt only true thanks can repay.
>
> Farewells are always sad, but they border on the tragic when they are said to a great man and a distinguished citizen and educator (23).

The Florida Education Association also paid high tribute to Bailey; he had been the director of its public relations when he was asked to take the state superintendent's job. In fact, he had been tagged to succeed James Richards as the full-time FEA executive secretary. He had served as president of the organization and held life memberships in the FEA, the NEA, and the Florida Congress of Parents and Teachers. He had won many awards for his distinguished service, plus a national reputation as president of the Council of Chief State School Officers. He also served as chairman of the council's legislative committee, a member of its board of directors, and a council representative to the National Council for Accreditation of Teacher Education.

Educators were particularly proud of his battle against the "overly zealous do-gooders who, for a short time, stirred the state (and the nation) with the battle cry to 'burn the books and clean the library shelves' " (24). He was a real champion of academic freedom. He left the school systems in the hands of the county superintendents and principals, but helped direct legislative action which made teaching in Florida a legally recognized profession. One man states that in the 20 years he had known and worked with Bailey, he had never known him to be malicious, vindictive, jealous, or to lose his temper.

> He often questioned the judgement of state politicians, and he sparred verbally on dozens of occasions with governors and Cabinet members when he felt the welfare of Florida's school children was at stake. But he always came away with respect and appreciation for the talents of those with whom he had to work (25).

Present Activities

Effective July 1, 1966, the board appointed an associate superintendent of public instruction to coordinate instructional activities as part of a two-man team with the deputy superintendent, who continues to coordinate administrative and fiscal functions. The Elementary and Secondary Education Act of 1965 (ESEA) prompted the department to add substantially to its staff, particularly since the beginning of 1966. The department has studied the organization and assignment of duties during 1966, and a new organization is now in effect.

IMPORTANT ISSUES FACED BY THE DEPARTMENT

Problems in the Early 1900's

A great many problems faced by the state department—and the entire public school system—in 1900 have been solved, some are no longer important, and still others are unresolved after 65 years. Many evoked heated controversies and political battles. For instance, considerable difference of opinion existed among educators regarding the need for a statewide compulsory attendance law in the early 1900's. Some county officials felt that it was impractical, while others doubted if teachers and classroom space could be provided. Those who spoke in favor of such a law generally felt that it should be reasonable and moderate. It is apparent from his reports that State Superintendent William N. Sheats, who served from 1893 to 1905, was a man of positive opinions, and he did not hesitate to make his position known in forthright and colorful terms (26). Sheats not only spoke for the state department—for all practical purposes he was the department. He stated:

> It would seem that the compulsory attendance is a natural concomitant of the public school system. All of the people are forced to pay taxes to build houses and pay teachers, then why higgle at compelling a few of the people to give their children the benefit of that which is provided for them? (27)

Superintendent Sheats was very critical of the unequal preparation of students applying for admittance to the state colleges and normal schools. He charged that these institutions were dissipating their efforts because of this deficient preparation. The difficulty, he explained, arose because more than 80 percent of Florida's youth were taught in rural schools. They passed into the so-called high schools and were taught by incompetent teachers for short terms with completely inadequate curriculums. But even with these shortcomings, the high schools were far too demanding for the preparation most of the pupils had received in the elementary grades. To make matters worse, the rural elementary schools depended on these high schools for teachers. Thus, Superintendent Sheats argued that a standard grade of high school instruction should be made mandatory in at least one school in every county for a minimum of 8 months each year.

In his biennial report of 1902, Superintendent Sheats stated that numerous investigations and experiments pointed to greater support than ever before for solving the rural school problem by concentrating the numerous small schools into fewer and better ones. This would be accomplished by transporting pupils in wagons from their homes to the central schools. He declared that it had been shown conclusively that all small schools within a radius of 5 or 6 miles could be concentrated into one central school, usually with an actual saving in cost and certainly with a marked improvement in structural facilities, attendance, health, moral influence, and safety. He added: "In this State where the rural pupils of so many sections are compelled to go miles through forests frequented only by nomadic Negroes, their protection is an especially strong argument in favor of transportation" (28).

The state superintendent realized that if these schools were to improve, the teaching and administrative staffs would have to be upgraded. Teacher examinations were conducted at the county level with the many abuses such a system invited. Although opinion was divided, most county superintendents seemed to favor the local examination despite Superintendent Sheats' opposition. He charged that numerous fraudulent examinations had been reported to his office, and his personal investigations of them in one or more counties completely convinced him that in many instances they were worse than farcical—they were criminal. He added that they plainly indicated either the utter want of ability on the part of the officers holding the examinations or a conspiracy between the examiner and the examinees to bring the law into contempt.

At the turn of the century many county superintendents argued for uniformity of textbooks throughout the state. On the other hand, Sheats countered that it was "a most undemocratic and offensive proposition to mold all the minds of the State by means of the state textbooks, and it passes my comprehension how it is expected to crush a trust by creating a state monopoly" (29). He claimed that his own investigations clearly revealed no advantage in state uniformity comparable to the disadvantages and dangers. He reported that this was the opinion of the educational experts, including the U.S. Commissioner of Education and practically all of the educators of Florida and elsewhere who had expressed themselves on it. He said he found it difficult to understand why this perennial agitation for state uniformity of textbooks should receive any consideration at the hands of the Legislature.

Although a majority of school people recognized the necessity of providing free textbooks to children if the state required attendance, Sheats contended that they should not be furnished at the expense of other parts of the educational program. Since the average school term was only 94 days, he seriously questioned the wisdom of reducing this "ruinously short term" to gain the benefits of free books. In other words, if the cost of the books were to be taken from the already inadequate funds, this would reduce this term by an average of at least 10 days—considerably more in some counties. Sheats added:

> Whether or not I would favor free textbooks depends almost wholly upon the size of the school fund, whether the maximum county levy is to be raised, and the school term, now far too short, is to be still further shortened (30).

On the other hand, Superintendent Sheats supported the mothers' and women's clubs in their campaign for free public kindergartens in Florida. Interest in public kindergartens had revived around the beginning of the century, and a strong demand for them cropped up in many parts of the state, stimulated in part by the success of private kindergartens. Sheats explained to the Legislature that children properly taught in kindergarten were better prepared to pursue the second-year course in the public schools than those spending 1 year in the ordinary schools. They also continued to show the advantages of their kindergarten training in other grades.

Changing the School Laws

Almost every recent session of the Legislature has appointed committees or indicated the need for reforms in school law in one field or another. In fact, this desire to update and clarify the school laws has been prevalent since the early 1900's, when Superintendent Sheats called attention to a number of defects in them. He believed that the general outline of the laws was admirable but that parts were not always in harmony nor always connected and explicit. In other words, they represented too many patchwork efforts that had left many parts vague, meaningless, superfluous, or obsolete, and he recommended to the Legislature that they be "recast, perfected, codified, and enacted as one whole . . ." (31).

Sheats stated that a commission of wise men was needed to formulate such legislation—not only to cope with the complexities involved, but to give it weight so that it would pass both houses. He realized that it would be cast aside without due consideration unless it received a strong endorsement but that each branch of the Legislature had men who were familiar with its purpose in every detail and who could explain and defend the measure. He stated:

> Too much school legislation has been attempted by novices, often at the instigation of persons whose range of vision in educational affairs was circumscribed, and oftener under the incitement of those with a personal axe to grind, little caring who was injured so that a present personal advantage was gained. To the latter class belong those seeking the right to teach by special legislation, or by retrograde laws prescribing long terms and small qualifications for low grade licenses (32).

Traditionally, Florida's educators have made full use of the energies, talents, and interests of lay citizens. Many of the most progressive ideas resulted directly from lay participation in educational affairs. For instance, in September 1909, county superintendents, school boards, principals, college presidents, and other "friends of education" organized to inaugarate an effective educational campaign to inspire the public to raise more money for the schools. County school boards contributed from $25 to

$100, for a total of $1,220, and the Southern Education Board contributed $1,000, so the campaign fund had a total of $2,220 available. The first meeting was held at Mariana in October 1909, and the last was held at Leesburg in February 1910. After the close of the regular campaign, however, special meetings were held at Plant City, Tampa, St. Petersburg, Clearwater, Dover, Sopchoppy, Altha, Bristol, Blountstown, and Umatilla. The campaigners covered 3,500 miles by rail, 200 by automobile, and 40 by horse and buggy to hold 196 meetings in 46 of the state's 47 counties. Levy County was omitted only because of a measles-diphtheria epidemic.

According to Superintendent W. M. Holloway, the campaign resulted in increasing the millage assessments in 40 of the counties. In fact, only one county failed to assess a tax of less than 6 mills. More than 60,000 persons attended the rallies, and the campaign aroused enough public interest that 50 School Improvement Associations were organized with memberships totaling more than 10,000. All members pledged to use their influence to get the Legislature to pass a compulsory education law and establish at least one high school in each county. At its state convention in August 1910, the powerful Farmers' Union, representing over 30,000 farmers, unanimously adopted a resolution to endorse the same program.

School Financing

Financing, as in all states, has been one of the most important issues educators have faced in Florida. In 1910, Superintendent Holloway complained that the $500 appropriated for travel in 1909 had not been increased in 25 years and that he had to spend one-fifth of his $2,500 annual salary in representing the interests of education (33). In 1918, when the department again called on the county boards of public instruction to help develop a state course of study, the Legislature failed to appropriate the funds to carry it out. Finally, at the request of the Conference of County Superintendents, State Superintendent Sheats solicited contributions from the county boards of public instruction. Fifty-three of the 54 boards responded, and with the $990 donated, the commission was to prepare a course of study and distribute 5,000 copies before the 1918-19 school term opened.

During the early 1920's, the special-tax school districts, organized in an effort to raise sorely needed funds for the schools, threatened the existing school organization when they attempted to move toward full control of the local schools. In his 1920-22 biennial report to the Legislature, Superintendent Cawthon pointed out that Florida had about the purest county system of administration in the Union and should jealously preserve it. He admitted that the development of districts had been a prominent and effective factor in the great educational progress of the past 20 years. The special-tax school districts, now numbering nearly 1,000, covered almost the entire state and were growing stronger. As these districts realized their increasing importance, they inevitably tended to exercise greater influence and control. He considered it dangerous that they might, either legally or by political pressure, gradually take over many of the counties' powers and thus impair the simple but forceful county management. In fact, he observed that something like this had already occurred in some of the counties. He concluded:

> These districts are doubtless proper, vital, and very valuable units, and the people of the districts, through their trustees, should have a voice in district measures. Perhaps our law is approximately or quite correct in this. We merely suggest the advisability of closely adhering to the law and to the principles indicated by it. We believe the boards of trustees, and county boards also, do well to leave the selection of teachers and many other matters largely to the superintendents. . . (34).

Enriching Instruction

When the 1917 Legislature failed to pass a bill providing for a state course of study as recommended by the state superintendent, the county superintendents, high school principals, and other school officers adopted resolutions at their Gainesville conference in May 1918, requesting the state superintendent to prepare as speedily as possible a state course of study for both elementary and high schools. Superintendent Sheats, as directed by the conference, requested voluntary contributions from each board to raise $1,000 to meet the expenses involved. By prorating this amount among the boards on the basis of their county's assessable property, he was able to raise $990–only one county failed to contribute–and appointed a commission of leading educators to begin work. The commission met in Tallahassee late in June and prepared the Course of Study for Elementary and High Schools in Florida in time to distribute 5,000 copies to the schools during the 1918-19 school year.

The course developed in 1918 proved to be of great value, but by the middle of the 1920's it needed to be revised. Again, the initiative for rewriting the state course of study came from the field–a joint resolution voted in April 1929 by a conference of high school principals and elementary supervisors. The state was divided into districts, and committees of teachers were appointed to prepare courses of study in their subject fields. Actual production was under way by the 1930-31 school year. The General Education Board granted the project $7,300 for expenses in the spring of 1931, enabling the state superintendent to appoint a director. The new state course of study was completed during the 1931-32 school year.

During the 1920's, most of the schools lacked well-trained teachers. In 1925, the Legislature tried to solve the problem in part by creating teacher training departments in the high schools. Students flocked into these departments because, as graduates, they were virtually assured of jobs as teachers. The program did help to meet the teacher shortage, but, at the same time, it tended to "dry up" the regular high schools in some counties and at least held back their development in others.

Toward the end of the decade, the state also tried to improve instruction by changing the concept of the supervisor. Originally, supervision was synonymous with inspection rather than improvement of instruction, and this conception of the state department's function as one of inspection found its way into the Florida laws. The department now, however, made an effort to have the schools think of the supervisor's duties not as inspectoral, but as cooperative and helpful.

As the state department attempted to change its philosophy, functions, and image, it also was forced to wrestle with problems created by the Depression which followed the crash of 1929. Logically, it turned its attention to school business management. In 1933, the Legislature required the county boards to adopt a uniform system of accounting, budgets, audits, and reports, which would then be reviewed by the state superintendent. The submission of county school budgets to the state superintendent was an important milestone in school business relations in Florida. The state auditor and his assistants, representatives of the office of the state comptroller, the state department, and the county boards formed a committee to develop the uniform accounting system. The state board employed a number of special accountants to help the auditor and his men install the new system, and by January 1934, practically every county in the state had adopted the new procedures.

During World War II, the department faced many problems of an emergency nature, such as work-experience programs for youth, Americanization programs, general adult education, vocational and occupational retraining programs, nursery schools and kindergartens, and recreation and physical education programs. Florida's entire educational program was in a period of transition, and important decisions had to be made regarding it. At the same time, the schools found it necessary to employ thousands of unqualified emergency teachers to remain open.

It was evident by the end of the war that Florida was on the threshold of the era of its greatest growth, and the schools faced a crisis. Former teachers returning from the services and new prospects alike found salaries so low they would not accept positions. The school buildings were in poor repair because of the wartime shortage of materials and skilled workmen.

With the approval of the 1945 Legislature, the Governor appointed a Florida Citizen's Committee on Education to make an intensive study of the schools. Its 2-year study recognized at the outset that "Florida has made a great many improvements in its educational program during recent years, and some features of this program compare very favorably with corresponding features found in other states" (35). The final report, however, pointed out the deficiencies and problems, such as great differences in the level of support among counties, inadequate school buildings, low salaries for teachers, lack of instructional materials, and need for more school buses.

Minimum Foundation Program

As a result of the Citizen's Committee's important study and leadership and pressure exerted by outstanding Florida lay and educational leaders, the 1947 Legislature enacted a comprehensive school plan: a minimum foundation program. The credit for this significant forward step must go to many people. Edgar Morphet of the Florida State Department of Education and R.L. Johns, now on the faculty of the University of Florida, provided the technical leadership. LeRoy Collins, then Senator and later Governor, helped steer the bills through the Legislature with only one dissenting vote.

The minimum foundation program adopted in 1947 was much more complex than the legislators who voted for it realized. Actually, it was based on the premise that each child in Florida, regardless of the wealth of his county, deserves an equal opportunity for an adequate education and that the state and county have a joint responsibility to provide this opportunity. The plan had built-in flexibility: It varied the state financial support according to the school population, the professional training levels of instructional personnel, and the breadth of the program maintained by the county—such as vocational education, adult education, kindergartens, summer programs, classes for exceptional children, supervision, junior colleges, and length of employment.

Governor Millard Caldwell insisted that if money was to be collected from where it could be found in the state and spent on children wherever they were to be found, the same philosophy had to be followed at the county level. At this time the state was operating under a county system. The Governor insisted that the Legislature eliminate all district lines, which it then did. This meant that all local money raised at the county level could be expended for all the children in the county irrespective of the former school districts. The entire county's wealth could be placed behind all of its children. Thomas D. Bailey, who took over the state superintendency in January 1949, stated:

> I doubt if it is matched anywhere in the United States, when a Governor insisted, in spite of great opposition from the Legislature, that if they didn't want him to veto the foundation program, these districts had to be eliminated so that all local money could be expended for

all the children in the respective counties. This, I think, is to his credit (36).

The schools were in a financial dilemma 2 years later. When the minimum foundation program was enacted in 1947, Governor Caldwell had tried to persuade the Legislature to increase taxes to take care of the necessary increased spending. But since the state treasury had surplus funds, this money was used for the program, and no new taxes were enacted. The surplus was gone by 1949, when Fuller Warren became Governor.

The 1949 Legislature passed an act giving the cigarette tax to the cities and cutting off this source of funds to the general revenue without replacing it. Because of Governor Warren's stand against new taxes, none was passed. The budget commission (state cabinet) found itself in a dilemma: The state had appropriations to be financed and insufficient funds to do the job. The only possible solution the budget commission could reach, since there was no constitutional provision for the state to incur indebtedness for current operating expenses, was to reduce the appropriations for all state agencies by 25 percent for the first quarter of the new fiscal year beginning July 1, 1949, and 10 percent each subsequent quarter.

During this economy move, the Legislature eliminated support for kindergartens, driver education, summer enrichment programs, and financial support for additional junior colleges. Superintendent Bailey used his influence with Governor Warren to get him to veto removal of these items so that they were retained as a part of the foundation program. In only a few years, great strides were made in developing each of these particular programs, and additional money was appropriated.

At the end of June, Superintendent Bailey appealed to the budget commission for additional funds on the grounds that contracts had been entered into with teachers by their respective county school boards, school bus drivers had been given legal contracts, and it was imperative that funds be provided to meet these obligations. Superintendent Bailey stated:

> As a result of my pleadings, the Budget Commission agreed to do some fast bookkeeping and released all of the money that had been withheld from the public schools in June of that year so that the funds would not be lost permanently. With the beginning of the new fiscal year, July 1, this money was again withheld from the schools in the new fiscal year for the next quarter. I have at least saved the schools from losing their money on a permanent basis (37).

In the meantime, Governor Warren found it necessary to call a special session of the Legislature to increase taxes to support the state government and the public schools. The Legislature enacted a limited sales tax program—including some provisions to which the Governor objected. The tax money, which began to come into the state treasury fairly early the following year, began accumulating in the treasury, enabling the schools to meet all of their obligations in the latter part of the year. Other state agencies suffered a 10-percent reduction for the fiscal year, but at least the public schools received the funds that had been definitely appropriated to them and were saved great embarrassment. Superintendent Bailey concluded:

> This experience was one of the great virtues of our Cabinet system of government, where five members of the Budget Commission compose the State Board of Education. I realize that in some quarters where the Cabinet system of government in Florida is not understood, this type of ex-officio board of education is not considered as in the best interests of education. In Florida, particularly, the experts have never recommended, in every White House Conference we held, that the state superintendent be appointed or that the state board of education be other than the type of board that we have at the present time. Because of the involvement in the State Cabinet system where we wear different hats on the different boards, I am confident that by reason of a majority of the seven members of the Cabinet being on the state board of education, we were able to save the public schools that particular year from financial embarrassment and a great crisis (38).

The Legislature improved the Minimum Foundation Program Law in almost every subsequent session, largely as a result of the state department's and the professional education associations' determined and coordinated efforts. At the same time, due to the urgings of Superintendent Bailey, the Legislature advanced the educational program with other legislation. For example, in 1952, a constitutional amendment strengthened the provision for capital outlay and debt service by guaranteeing the allocation of motor vehicle license revenues to these purposes and authorizing the State Board of Education to issue bonds on behalf of the counties to build school buildings. The following year, the Legislature increased the allocation per transportation unit from $1,100 to $1,250. Again, in 1955, the Legislature increased the allocation for operating costs from $300 per instruction unit to $325. At the same time, it initiated a program in driver education which was later extended to all public secondary schools in the state.

In 1957, the Legislature passed several significant measures affecting education. It began by providing $200 for each additional pupil in average daily attendance per year to be matched by sums from the counties' funds for capital outlay. It also liberalized the minimum foundation program teacher allocations and started a program of rebating part of the state tax collections to the counties in proportion to the number of instruction units.

Following an intensive 2-year study by the Community College Council, the Legislature in 1957 embarked on a full-scale statewide plan for community junior colleges. Superintendent Bailey stated on numerous occasions that the development of the state-supported junior colleges afforded him the greatest satisfaction of any educational endeavor during his 47 years in education. The program attempted to bring the advantages of higher education and the opportunities of terminal and technical education to the doorsteps of all youth and adults in Florida.

Florida also experimented with four-quarter, year-round schools, with staggered pupil attendance. When the Department of Education studied the results in 1957, it found that they failed principally because starting new groups of pupils each 3 months created the equivalent of four small schools within each school. Such a division sacrificed almost all the benefits of large school attendance units. It would have reversed the results of decades of rapid consolidation of both school districts and attendance units, which made possible the complete programs required by modern conditions.

The state department's study revealed that only a few of the largest attendance units could remain educationally efficient with these four staggered schedules. The elementary schools would need 24 more teachers to provide one teacher per grade for six grades operating on four staggered schedules. Junior high schools would require 50 or more teachers, and senior high schools 80 or more, before they could be scheduled without sacrificing the offerings.

By 1957, Florida had 205 elementary schools in 35 counties that were not large enough to use this plan, although there was none in the other 32 counties. Only 22 junior high schools in 7 counties were of the necessary size, along with 10 senior high schools in 5 of the 67 counties. The principal proponents of this plan hoped to save money, but a careful analysis showed that it would seriously reduce educational opportunities and increase costs if it were installed in all Florida schools (39).

The Future

Many problems remain to be solved, and not all will be met successfully in the immediate future. Among these are the need for extending a statewide kindergarten program, increased salaries for teachers, the impact of integration on the public school system, curriculum revision, vocational education, and the improvement of instruction. In any growing educational system there will always be problems—such as raising enough money. There must be an adequate supply of teachers, and the curriculum must change to meet new conditions. If these overall problems were ever solved, there would no longer be a need for a state department of education staff—only a few clerks and bookkeepers.

The Florida school system and state department are facing up to these issues. Floyd T. Christian, who assumed the office of state superintendent of public instruction when Superintendent Thomas D. Bailey retired in October 1965, recently stated: "The climate for education is progress. The technique is innovation. The dedication is to provide an educational program which meets the individual needs of each individual student. The watchword is quality" (40).

INTERAGENCY RELATIONS

Traditionally, the Florida State Department of Education has exhibited a willingness and desire to cooperate with other agencies—local, state, and national—in programs and activities designed to improve the public schools. In 1872, the state took advantage of the Morrill (Land-Grant) Act of 1862. In 1891, it received money from the Hatch Act to establish agricultural experiment stations as a department of the Florida Agricultural College. As mentioned earlier, the state cooperated fully with the General Education Board of New York and the Southern Education Board in providing supervision of common schools, and with the Peabody Educational Fund for maintaining summer schools for teachers and erecting and equipping a building for the Teachers College and Normal School at the University of Florida in Gainesville.

The Florida Legislature moved promptly in 1914 to participate in the Smith-Lever Act, which provided for cooperative agricultural extension work. Again, in 1917, the Legislature quickly authorized the state to take full advantage of the provisions of the Smith-Hughes Act, enacted by Congress to promote vocational education. At the time Superintendent Cawthon wrote his 1920-22 biennial report, he discussed Florida's attitude toward federal aid:

> The largest unit is the nation. It is fortunate that we southerners are overcoming our squeamishness toward federal revenue for public school,—that we have begun to reconcile our cherished doctrine of state's rights with some practical basis upon which the nation, as such, may be permitted to contribute to public education. The justice of this lies in admitting to the children and youth benefits a right to which is inherent in their citizenship in the nation, whose burdens they will be called upon to bear in adult life. The profit to the nation lies in the consequent preparation of these young people for bearing ably those burdens. The rural schools, more than any others, need national aid, because they get least financial support from local taxation (41).

Actually, as Superintendent Colin English pointed out, federal funds originally were indirectly used as practically the sole source of support for the state's school system. For instance, when Florida was admitted to the Union, the state and federal governments set aside section 16 in each township for public school purposes, and this constituted approximately one-thirty-sixth of the land area of each township. Due to inadequate records, lack of attention, and occasional mismanagement, the proceeds from these federal land grants did not meet expectations. The funds were rapidly dissipated and were inadequate to support the schools, even though there were very few public free schools.

Although these funds have been derived from federal land grants to aid the schools during the entire history of Florida, federal funds as such were not directly appropriated for public elementary and high schools until 1918. Since that time, appropriation has been greatly increased and expanded until, in the 1937-38 school year, $240,764 was received from federal sources. The federal appropriations for vocational education, supplemented by the state and local funds, were now sufficient to provide vocational training in most secondary schools. In fact, this phase of the program had been developing and expanding even more rapidly than many other phases.

During the 1940's, the department cooperated with the federal government to meet needs resulting from the war effort. The department assigned a staff member to direct the development of materials to assist teachers in preparing students for work in defense and war projects. Special courses were introduced at the senior high school level to prepare people for the defense industries.

The National School Lunch Program of 1946 (amended in 1954) had a considerable impact on the lunch programs in Florida, as well as serving its original purpose of encouraging the consumption of surplus agricultural commodities. At the federal level, the program was administered by the U.S. Department of Agriculture rather than the U.S. Office of Education. Although federal-state cooperation in administering the program has generally been quite successful, the state has found a primary problem in the year-to-year appropriation rather than in any unduly restrictive regulation.

In the years following World War II, the federal government moved to provide categorical aid in many areas. The Florida department cooperated to the fullest extent possible with these programs, a few of which will be mentioned.

In September 1950, the Eighty-First Congress enacted Public Laws 815 and 874 to help school districts provide facilities and operating costs for systems having excessive increase in pupils as a result of federal activities within or near their boundaries (42). The philosophy behind the two laws was that the federal government has removed lands from the tax rolls, and its activities had brought an increase in the number of pupils in school. Therefore, it was deemed only right that it should assume the role of a taxpayer within the state and assist in constructing buildings and operating the school system. The laws made substantial contributions to education in many Florida counties. Neither of the programs has proven to be unduly restrictive, and the school systems have made effective use of the federal funds—probably more so than in any other federal aid program.

Congress passed the National Defense Education Act (NDEA) in 1958 and amended and extended it in 1963, 1964, and 1965. The state department incorporated this program into its structure so that it could be carried out essentially by the divisions and sections already operating, but an NDEA coordinator and a few additional personnel were added. Four advisory committees were formed to assist in planning and coordination. Admittedly, some problems developed in implementing NDEA. In a desire to move ahead quickly, the department made commitments in some cases prior to receiving written regulations; under such circumstances, as can be expected, misunderstandings and misinterpretations developed. When the written regulations were finally promulgated, they did not always agree with what had been anticipated from oral communications between the department and U.S. Office of Education. This caused confusion and expensive backtracking in several instances to provide supporting documentation for expenditures already made. Still, the funds provided under the NDEA materially improved the program of instruction in Florida's schools at a time when such help was badly needed.

Some school people, legislators, and members of the business community have feared a developing specter of federal control over public schools, despite assurances to the contrary by federal aid proponents. Some of the developments in federal-state relations have done little to lay the fears to rest. The report "A Federal Agency for the Future," published in 1961 by the Office of Education's Committee on Mission and Organization, added no reassurances.

In June 1965, Superintendent Bailey expressed to his fellow chief state school officers meeting in Washington his concern about some of the U.S. government reports:

> After two days of considering regulations and guidelines implementing the Federal Acts of Education, I feel somewhat indisposed this morning. I have diagnosed my affliction as "Feducationitis." The symptoms which have led me to this diagnosis can best be defined as "Creeping Paralysis of Conscience on Basic Educational Philosophy." This organization has policy statements on the Church- State issue and State responsibility and local control of education which leave no doubt about intent or allow for no variance in interpretation. In the Federal Acts we have discussed the past two days it is obvious that our policy positions will be as many idle words in the administration of these acts of Congress. Large sums of money will be available for education and for expanding state departments of education. With restrictions of law, regulations and administrative decrees the trend appears that state departments of education may well become administrative arms of the Federal government . . . .
>
> We cannot afford to discard our fundamental beliefs for a price in the form of large sums of money, however

> worthy the objective may appear on the surface. We are the leaders of American education in our respective states and territories. Let us not fail to act the part of leaders in representing our citizens and public education as our conscience dictates . . . (43).

In Superintendent Bailey's last official address to the county superintendents in Gainesville, Florida, in September 1965, he again warned that the federal government was usurping the strength of the states. He quoted David Brinkley, the National Broadcasting Company news commentator, who was reported in the press to have told Ohio University students that July: "The decline and fall of the fifty state governments will be completed within our lifetime. The movement of political power from state capitals to Washington, D.C., is inevitable and unstoppable, whether we like it or not " (44).

Bailey particularly criticized the categorical character of the aid provided, which tended to give the federal government considerable influence over the educational policies and programs of the states. He agreed with James E. Allen, Jr., the New York State commissioner of education, who said: "In no small degree, educational policy in America today is being shaped by the Federal government" (45). He predicted that increased federal financing of education would make possible increased federal control–these two influences being inseparable. Thus, federal control in large measure would continue to increase with the federal government's financing education through piecemeal legislation as opposed to general aid, and he felt this was being deliberately done. He saw a declining influence of elected state and local officials in the administration of public education, and he lamented that a number of people had lost faith in the local and state governments. He continued:

> What is not possible to accomplish by national legislation is being readily facilitated by administrative decrees with regulations from the U.S. Office of Education. Whoever controls public education in the world of tomorrow will control, for the most part, the affairs of men. Public education has been and should continue to be the people's main tool of freedom. Therefore, if we want people to govern themselves in the long stretch ahead, we must be willing for the people themselves to control public education. The American traditions of education are based on this valid assumption. Although I am willing to accept change when justified by fact, logic, and reason, I do not wish to be a party to changes which will undermine the basic foundations of American culture (46).

The Elementary and Secondary Education Act of 1965 (ESEA) introduced massive federal aid to the states for the first time. It brought along with it some onerous problems as well as solutions to educational needs, and these problems still have not all been resolved. In spite of the political and social climate which, in some communities, did not allow the schools to change as fast as others, the state had committed itself to eliminating the dual school system in full compliance with the Civil Rights Act. The Department of Education held conferences throughout the state to help the school systems interpret the guidelines and prepare compliance plans. It invited USOE consultants to participate in conferences for superintendents and school board members. An in-service training program for county personnel engaged in education for the disadvantaged was held in Jacksonville in the spring of 1966, and regional meetings were organized throughout the state during the fall on the theme "Education for All."

During the summer of 1966, the U.S. Office of Education sent teams to Florida to discuss the plans of compliance which several counties had filed. The state department did not know the teams were coming until the news appeared in the newspapers. In all cases, the county superintendents called the state department to ask the staff to attend the meetings and to give them assistance.

Superintendent Christian stated in a report to the Florida congressional delegation in August 1966 that he was sure the U.S. Office of Education faced a shortage of personnel and had little choice, but he added:

> I speak now not critically, but a little sadly. Because to send into a Florida county, as the U.S. Office did last week in north Florida, four young men and women with a total school experience for the four of them of one year in second grade teaching, is not to give us the kind of help we need.
>
> These four youngsters–and that's what they are, youngsters, the oldest being 26–are obviously not prepared or qualified by experience to understand or to appreciate the economic and political and social problems of the communities in which they are working. Frankly, I don't think youngsters with such little training and background have had enough experience to recognize the progress which is being made in the counties they visited (47).

Christian went on to say that this team told the superintendents and the school board *what they had to do* to comply with the guidelines on staff desegregation.

Christian also pointed to similar experiences in other counties–specifically Taylor, Columbia, and Gadsden. In Gadsden, the team left two college sophomores to discuss this highly sensitive issue with the county superintendent and his representatives. Christian charged that in every case these young people had "overstepped their authority and acted contrary to the assurances given to us by the Commissioner of Education that the guidelines were just that–guidelines–and not rigid and unbending formulas to be applied indiscriminately and without reason."

The state superintendent chided the U.S. Office of Education for attempting to measure the good faith of the school system by numbers or the progress of desegregation in a community by arbitrary percentages. He stated that it was wrong to apply the same yardstick in every situation or to hold the public schools accountable for parental or community attitudes beyond their control. He explained to the congressional delegates that a majority of the state's people were proud of the law-abiding and honorable manner in which the schools had worked to meet the requirements of the Civil Rights Act and that every responsible public official had lent his support and endorsement to it. But he felt that the recent contracts between USOE personnel and some of the counties, and the lack of communication with responsible state authorities, made it increasingly difficult for the counties to continue to work in the same spirit of cooperation they had shown in the past. He added:

> Frankly, they feel they are being frustrated by arbitrary and unfeeling decisions which ignore both the problems and the progress. I fear that, if this continues, many of them may just throw up their hands and quit. More and more of them will turn toward resistance ... (48).

Christian pointed out that USOE dealt directly with county superintendents, bypassing the Department of Education. The county superintendents looked to the state department for advice and recommendations—the department and the superintendents had a good working relationship—but the state was not informed about many matters except indirectly. Christian also was concerned about federal officials' wanting fiscal audits so detailed and exhaustive as to provide an evaluation of programs' effectiveness, whereby he felt that program evaluations should be done by program-approving personnel familiar with their objectives. He also called attention to Washington program administrators' changing signals in midyear, keeping the local school people in a state of uncertainty as to the direction the program would take.

There were many other problems disturbing to Superintendent Christian; one was the difficulty of obtaining positive answers to direct questions. The arbitrary administrative decisions that seemed to go beyond the language of the law itself have led many Florida educators to believe that the national welfare of the child has been neglected in the interest of forcing social change. The state superintendent said that, for the first time, he felt the county school systems of Florida had been placed in the position of being "guilty" regardless of what they did and what progress they made. But he still asserted that the Florida department desired to maintain a cooperative relationship with the U.S. Office of Education and other federal agencies. He ended his report by saying:

> The foregoing statement is not meant to be unduly critical of the U.S. Office of Education. It is a candid appraisal of some of the problems being faced. With improved communication and a willingness to reason together, these problems can be resolved as have others in the past (49).

FOOTNOTES

1. For further information on this period, see Thomas Everette Cochran, *History of Public School Education in Florida,* Department of Education Bulletin 1921, No. 1 (Lancaster, Pa.: New Era Printing Company, 1921), pp. 7-8.
2. *Ibid.,* p. 19.
3. Florida, *Laws,* (1852-1853), ch. 510, sec. 4.
4. Officially, his title was Register of the Land Office.
5. Florida, *House Journal, 1854-1855,* pp. 6-8; also *Senate Journal, 1854-1855,* pp. 6-8.
6. A carpetbagger was a Northerner in the South after the War Between the States, seeking private gain under the Reconstruction government.
7. Superintendent of Public Instruction, *Report, 1873-1874,* p. 53.
8. *Biennial Report of the Superintendent of Public Instruction, 1892-1894,* pp. 14-16. W. N. Sheats served as county superintendent of schools in Alachua County from 1881 to 1893, at which time he became state superintendent. He served as state superintendent from 1893 to 1905, and again from 1913 until his death on July 19, 1922.
9. For further information, see Cochran, *op. cit.,* pp. 58-59.
10. Superintendent of Public Instruction, *Report, 1900-1902,* pp. 3-10.
11. The data for this part are derived primarily from the state superintendent's biennial reports. The narrative sections were discontinued with the 1940-42 report; after this they became purely statistical.
12. Superintendent of Public Instruction, *Biennial Report, 1902-1904,* p. 229.
13. Thus, by 1912, the staff of the State Department of Public Instruction was composed of the state superintendent, the chief clerk, an assistant chief clerk, a typewriter-stenographer, a part-time high school inspector, and a full-time elementary rural school inspector, both of the latter being paid from other than state funds.
14. Cawthon served as state high school inspector for 6 years prior to becoming state superintendent in 1922. He had been a member of the faculty at the old East Florida Seminary in Lake City and the University of Florida in Gainesville, and school principal at Quincy, Madison, De Funiak Springs, and Pensacola.
15. Superintendent of Public Instruction, *Biennial Report, 1924-1926,* pp. 12-13.
16. Letter from Joe A. Cawthon, son of W. S. Cawthon, to Mrs. Dorothy Sauls, April 28, 1967.
17. *Ibid.*
18. *Florida School Code Committee Report* (March 1937), pp. 22-23. W. S. Cawthon, the original chairman, was succeeded by Colin English.

19. *Ibid.*

20. Thomas D. Bailey, *Trials in Florida Education* (Tallahassee: Department of Education, 1963), pp. 54-55.

21. See Appendix B for the Organization Table.

22. *Orlando Sentinel,* September 26, 1965.

23. *Ibid.*

24. "An Old Pro Steps Down," *Florida Education,* XLIII, No. 1 (September 1965), p. 24.

25. *Ibid.*

26. He was defeated for reelection in 1904 by William M. Holloway in a bitter campaign. Holloway held the office until January 1913, when Sheats was reelected to serve until July 1922.

27. Superintendent of Public Instruction, *Biennial Report, 1900-1902,* p. 422.

28. *Ibid.,* pp. 445-46.

29. *Ibid.,* p. 426.

30. *Ibid.,* p. 428.

31. *Ibid.,* p. 452.

32. *Ibid.,* pp. 452-55.

33. Superintendent of Public Instruction, *Biennial Report, 1908-1910,* p. 20.

34. Superintendent of Public Instruction, *Biennial Report, 1920-1922,* p. 188.

35. Florida Citizens' Committee on Education, *Education and the Future of Florida: A Report of the Comprehensive Study of Education in Florida* (Tallahassee: Rose Printing Co., 1947), p. 32.

36. Letter from Thomas D. Bailey to Mrs. Dorothy Sauls, April 5, 1967. Mrs. Sauls retired in January 1966 after more than 35 years with the state department. She served as administrative assistant to Superintendent Bailey and in the same capacity to Superintendent Christian until her retirement. In all, Mrs. Sauls served under four state superintendents during her employment, which began with a temporary position in 1927.

37. *Ibid.*

38. *Ibid.*

39. Edgar Fuller, "A Report: Should Schools Be Used the Year Around?" *The Rotarian,* June 1964.

40. Floyd T. Christian, "Where the Action Is," (unpublished manuscript, Tallahassee, Florida, Department of Education, 1966).

41. Superintendent of Public Instruction, *Biennial Report, 1920-1922,* p. 189.

42. These original laws have been extended from time to time in subsequent years.

43. Thomas D. Bailey, an informal statement to Council of Chief State School Officers, Washington, D.C., June 26, 1965.

44. Thomas D. Bailey, Address to the Conference of County Superintendents at Gainesville, Florida, on September 30, 1965.

45. *Ibid.*

46. *Ibid.*

47. Floyd T. Christian, "Report to Florida Congressional Delegation," speech delivered on August 5, 1966.

48. *Ibid.*

49. *Ibid.*

BIBLIOGRAPHY

Public Documents

Florida. *Constitution* (1887).

—— *House Journal, 1854-1855.*

—— *Law* (1852-53).

—— *Senate Journal, 1854-1855.*

Books

Bailey, Thomas D. *Trails in Florida Education.* Tallahassee: Department of Education, 1963.

Cawthon, W. S. *A Semi-Centennial View of Public Education in Florida and Other Addresses.* Tallahassee: Department of Education, 1936.

Cochran, Thomas Everette. *History of Public School Education in Florida.* Department of Education Bulletin, No. 1. Lancaster, Pa.: New Era Printing Co., 1921.

Pyburn, Nita Katherine. *Documentary History of Education in Florida, 1822-1860.* Tallahassee: Florida State University Press, 1951.

Articles and Periodicals

"An Old Pro Steps Down." *Florida Education,* XLIII, No. 1 (September 1965).

Fuller, Edgar. "A Report: Should Schools Be Used the Year Around?" *The Rotarian,* June 1964.

Orlando Sentinel. September 26, 1965.

"State Department of Public Instruction Changes." *Florida Education, XIV,* No. 1 (January 1937).

Williams, D. E. "A Brief Review of the Growth and Improvement of Education for Negroes in Florida, 1927-1962." Published as an "Occasional Paper" by the Southern Education Foundation, Inc., Atlanta, Georgia, 1963.

Reports

Committee on Mission and Organization. *A Federal Education Agency for the Future.* Washington, D.C.: U.S. Office of Education, 1961.

Department of Education, Community Junior College Division. *The Community Junior College in Florida's Future.* A report to the Board of Education. Tallahassee: The Department, 1957.

Florida Citizens' Committee on Education. *Education and the Future of Florida: Report of the Comprehensive Study of Education in Florida.* Tallahassee: Rose Printing Co., 1947.

Florida School Code Committee. *Report.* Tallahassee: Department of Education, March 1937.

Superintendents of Public Instruction. *Reports.* Tallahassee: Department of Education, 1874-1960.

Unpublished Material

Bailey, Thomas D. An informal statement to Council of Chief State School Officers, Washington, D.C., June 26, 1965.

——"Florida Schools Under the Administration of Thomas D. Bailey." Department of Education, Tallahassee, 1965. (Typewritten.)

Christian, Floyd T. "Where the Action Is." Unpublished manuscript, Department of Education, Tallahassee, 1966.

Other Sources

Bailey, Thomas D. Address to the Conference of County Superintendents at Gainesville, Florida, on September 30, 1965.

Christian, Floyd T. "Report to Florida Congressional Delegation." Speech delivered on August 5, 1966.

Letter from Thomas D. Bailey to Mrs. Dorothy Sauls, April 5, 1967.

Letter from Joe A. Cawthon, son of Superintendent W. S. Cawthon, to Mrs. Dorothy Sauls, dated April 28, 1967.

Sauls, Dorothy. Personal interview with Thomas D. Bailey, Tallahassee, April 5, 1967.

Appendix A

FLORIDA CHIEF STATE SCHOOL OFFICERS

State Superintendents

1868-71	C. Thurston Chase
1871-73	Rev. Charles Beecher
1873-74	Jonathan C. Gibbs
1874-75	Samuel B. McLin, Secretary of State and Acting Superintendent
1875-77	Rev. William Watkin Hicks
1877-81	William P. Haisley
1881-84	Eleazer K. Foster
1884-93	Albert J. Russell
1893-1905	William N. Sheats
1905-13	William M. Holloway
1913-22	William N. Sheats
1922-37	W. S. Cawthon
1937-49	Colin English
1949-65	Thomas D. Bailey
1965-	Floyd T. Christian

NOTE:

Prior to 1869, there was no state official with primary responsibility for public schools. Generally, such duties were added responsibilities carried by the registrar of the land office.

Appendix B

Chart I.--FLORIDA DEPARTMENT OF EDUCATION, 1926

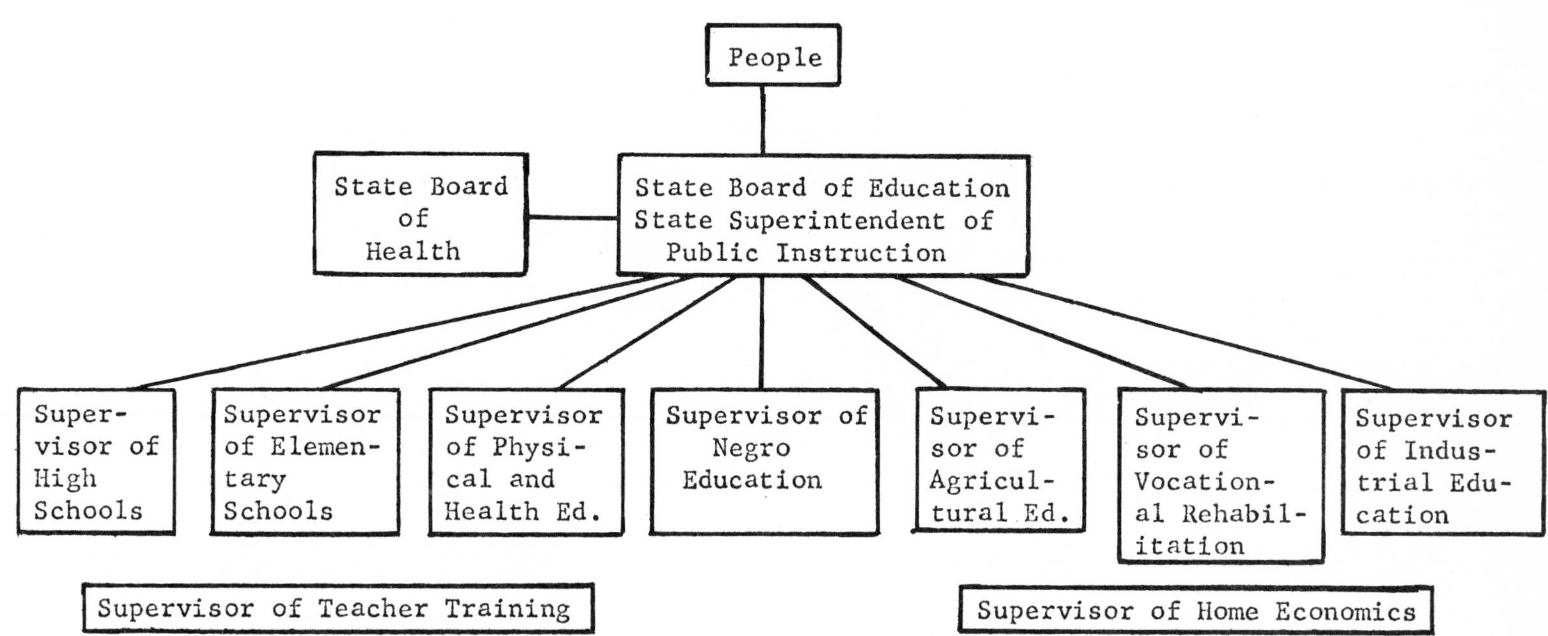

Appendix B

Chart II.—FLORIDA DEPARTMENT OF EDUCATION, 1963

State Superintendent
- Administrative Assistant
- Manager of Central Services
- General Auditor
- Special Executive Services, Deputy Superintendent
  - Editor, *Florida School Bulletin*
  - Coordinator of National Defense Education Act
  - Coordinator of Systems
  - Coordinator of Data Processing
  - Personnel Officer
  - Publications and Textbook Services
- Division of Administration
  - Capital Outlay and Debt Service
  - School Law
  - School Plant
  - School Surveys
  - Transportation
- Division of Community Junior Colleges
- Division of Finance
  - Financial Accounting and Reports
  - School Lunch
- Division of Instructional Services
  - Titles varied, and various sections generally operated in close cooperation. Services were offered in the following general areas:
    - General Consultants in Instruction
    - Secondary Education

Division of Instructional Services *(Contd.)*
- Elementary Education
- Exceptional Child Education
- Guidance and Testing
- Instructional Systems
- Physical Education, Health, and Recreation
- Driver Education
- Music Education
- Language Arts
- Social Studies
- Library Services
- Audiovisual Education
- Science Education
- Modern Foreign Languages
- Curriculum

Division of Research

Division of Teacher Education, Certification, and Accreditation
- Accreditation
- Certification
- Scholarships

Division of Vocational and Adult Education
- Division Services
- Adult and Veteran Education
- Agriculture Education
- Distributive and Cooperative Education
- Home Economics Education
- Industrial Education

Division of Vocational Rehabilitation

Appendix B

Chart III.--FLORIDA DEPARTMENT OF EDUCATION, 1968

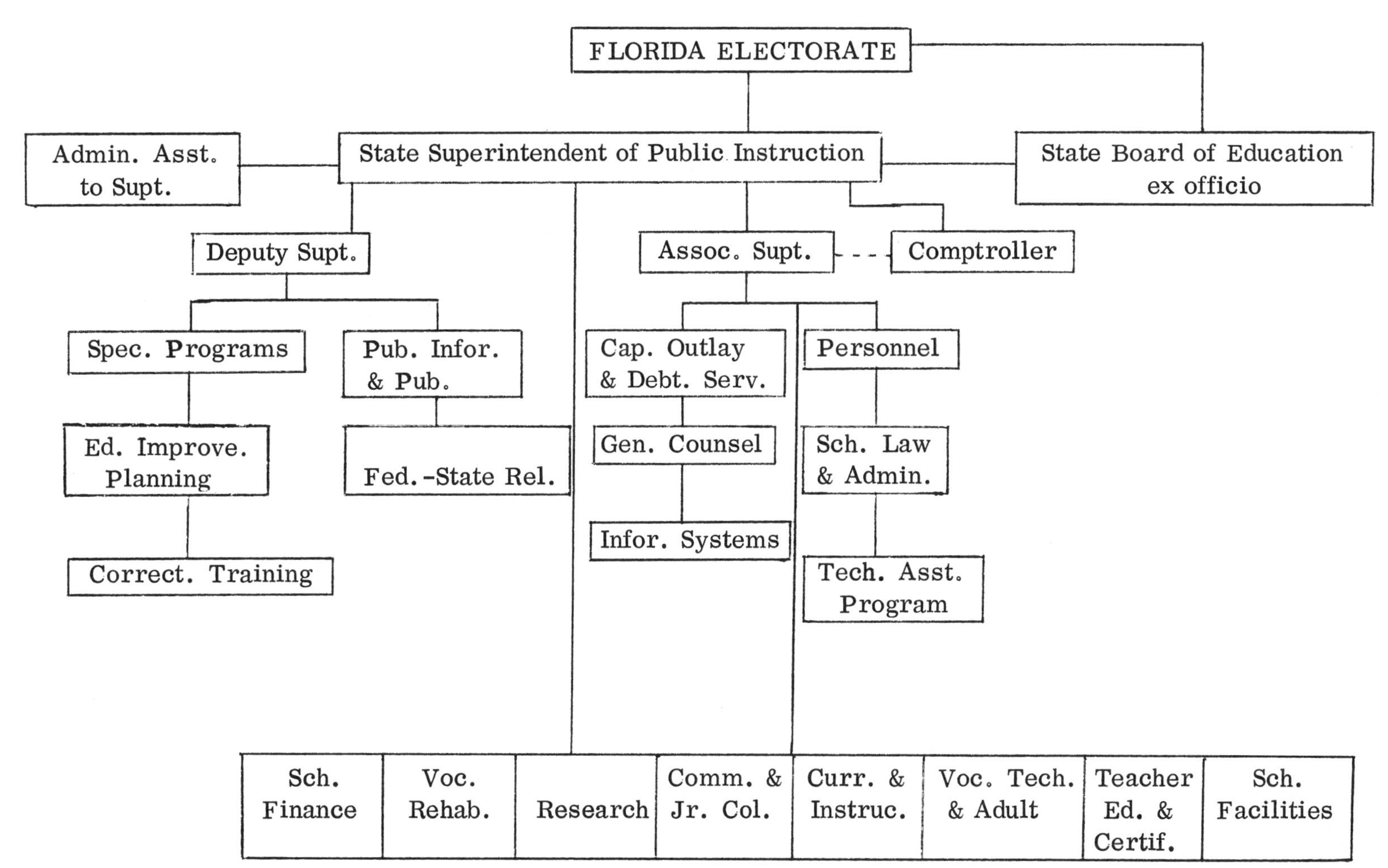

10 Georgia

DEPARTMENT OF EDUCATION
Walter E. Wade

Contents

EDUCATION IN GEORGIA PRIOR TO 1900

Georgia's first constitution in 1777 mentioned schools to be built in each county and supported by appropriations from the State Legislature. But the Legislature did not provide adequate funds, and the few communities that were able to establish free common schools had to struggle to maintain them. And although several religious denominations displayed considerably more interest in setting up schools, academies, and colleges, most suffered from a lack of both funds and capable teachers.

In 1820, a group of liberal legislators, frustrated in their efforts to create common schools, pushed through an appropriation for educating the children of the poor. The law required the justices of the peace to report the names of all children whose parents or estates did not pay a tax of at least 51¢ but not more than the poll tax (1). The plan failed because (a) not more than three-fourths of the children were reported, (b) only a little more than half of these were sent to school, and (c) they attended no more than 4 months in the year (2). The plan also was handicapped by the stigma of "poor people" attached to these children attending schools supported by the "poor-school" funds.

During the 1830's, a number of religious and educational leaders contended that the mind influenced the body and physical condition affected the mind and that, therefore, the body and mind should be educated together. Since manual labor would furnish natural exercise, equip students with practical knowledge, make education less expensive, and work to break down class distinctions, they advocated using these poor-school funds to establish manual labor schools. Their plan called for each county to attach a workshop or farm to each county academy.

The manual labor school idea spread, in large measure due to its support by the major religious denominations. (The Presbyterians, Methodists, and Baptists founded manual labor schools that eventually developed into Oglethorpe University, Mercer University, and Emory University, respectively.) Eventually, this interest—and pressure—led to the Legislature's voting state support for agricultural and mechanical schools in each of the 12 congressional districts. However, public funds were no longer used in developing manual labor schools on the common-school level after 1900.

As early as 1831, a group of educators organized the Teachers Society and Board of Education of the State. Despite the implications in the title, this was no legal board of education in any sense, and the organization lasted only 3 years. Four years later, the Methodists and Baptists joined the Presbyterians in the Georgia Education Society, which the latter had created in 1823 to promote better education. Although it was also short-lived, many of its leaders became active in the Georgia Teachers' Association, organized in Atlanta in August 1867 by 25 educators from various colleges and private schools (3). The association changed its name in 1900 to the Georgia Educational Association and again in 1922 to the Georgia Education Association.

At the time the state's leading educators were organizing a teachers association, Georgia was culturally, economically, and socially devastated. Not only had the Civil War destroyed its resources and freed its slaves, but a new generation of illiterates was growing up throughout the South. Funds appropriated for the schools were being used to pay other state expenses. The state was under military law, and most of the carpetbaggers running the state made few efforts to establish a state school system. Public confidence in the future of education was badly shaken.

When George Peabody granted money in 1867 for a study of the state's educational needs, the Georgia Teachers' Association formed a committee to work with the George Peabody Fund trustees to develop a state system of public schools. After working diligently for more than 2 years, the committee presented a sound report, and the Georgia Teachers' Association proposed that it be drafted into law.

The association's bill, containing its committee's recommendations, passed on October 13, 1870. That same day, the Governor carried out one provision of the act by appointing the first state school commissioner. But since this was a carpetbag administration, Georgians were considerably hostile toward its officials, and this undoubtedly presented a serious obstacle in developing a state system. The superintendent was further hampered by having a staff consisting of only one clerk employed for 10 months. The law provided for a State Board of Education, but the board lacked the authority to do a proper job.

The 1870 law did not provide for local taxation; cities and towns could levy taxes for schools, but counties could not do so without special legislation. A few populous counties that enjoyed able leadership convinced the Legislature that they could support their own schools and secured the legal authority to levy school taxes. Chatham, Bibb, Richmond, and Glynn Counties provide outstanding examples of counties where this local option worked.

The major portion of the schools' state funds came from rentals paid by the state-owned Western and Atlantic Railroad. In 1878, the Legislature added the liquor tax revenues to the state school fund (4). For the most part, these funds, appropriated for school purposes, were handled in an irresponsible manner, and many communities were unable to open their schools.

When Georgia adopted a new State Constitution in 1877, it limited public education to the elementary levels of education. In other words, the common schools could teach only basic courses, such as reading, writing, arithmetic, grammar, and spelling. The constitution made the rentals from the Western and Atlantic Railroad part of the public school support plan and specifically prohibited any of this money to be used for teaching courses beyond the elementary level. Secondary schools in the state were privately owned, and the new laws protected the owners in their monopoly of secondary education.

Numerous Georgia educators had long recognized the need to establish teacher-training institutes throughout the state, and with assistance from the George Peabody Fund the effort was gaining momentum by 1887. Institutes were established in 1888 at Salt Spring; in 1889 at Milledgeville, Lithia Springs, and Waycross; in 1892 at Athens, Savannah, and Americus; and in 1893 at Marietta and Thomasville. The state superintendent and his three associates spent a considerable portion of their time and efforts in working to establish these institutes. As new teachers were graduated, the public schools expanded to the point that by 1900 a number of private schools had closed.

As the public schools increased, so did the duties of the state school superintendent. To help him carry out these new tasks, the Legislature approved an act in 1893 directing him to appoint three state school supervisors and authorizing him to hire additional staff as he deemed necessary.

EDUCATION IN GEORGIA, 1900-65

In the 1890's, the Grange and the Farmers' Alliance developed a serious interest in promoting public education and found an ally in the Georgia Teachers' Association. Together these groups inaugurated a campaign to increase the state's support of all education. As a result, in 1903 the Legislature passed a tax measure, called the McMichael Bill after a former teacher-legislator, which was to be submitted to the people as a constitutional amendment. Though limited to a tax of 1 mill, this was the first legislation to authorize local taxation throughout the state for school purposes. Unfortunately, it contained a weakness–it permitted county boards of education to map out local tax districts within the counties. Thus, the richer parts of a county were often gerrymandered into separate school districts, leaving poorer sections with meager tax resources.

Before 1900, although Georgia provided limited state support for its elementary schools and colleges, the academies and high schools supported privately in the urban centers offered the only secondary school program in the state. Numerous attempts had been made to get the General Assembly to pass legislation permitting local communities to support high schools, but these had been defeated. Not until 1912 did the assembly finally pass a constitutional amendment deleting the limitation of support to elementary education alone, thereby opening the door to permissive support for public secondary schools. Based on a study conducted by the University of Georgia on the need for high school accreditation, the Legislature passed a bill in 1925 authorizing the superintendent to appoint a state high school supervisor.

During the years just prior to World War I, educators were joined by both the city and rural press in urging the assembly to write a new school code and uniform tax laws. Editorializing on a survey of the Tattnall County schools by State School Supervisor M. L. Duggan, the *Tattnall Journal*, a rural weekly paper, pointed out that local financial support for schools usually came from such sources as box suppers and other forms of entertainment. The editor concluded: "The survey points out that a different method of maintaining the schools must be adopted if greater efficiency is to be had and suggests local taxation for this purpose" (5). In an article 2 years later, the *Tattnall Journal* reported that a principal had resigned his position because there was no tax money to repair the Reidsville School's sanitary facilities, damaged by freezing weather the preceding winter. The editor argued that local tax money was necessary for maintaining and operating the rural schools.

One of the men most aware of the needs of Georgia schools was a vigorous young attorney practicing in Tattnall County, Herschel Elders, who had served several terms in the General Assembly. In 1919, he was chairman of the Senate Education Committee and the administration floor leader for Governor Hugh Dorsey. With his thorough, first-hand knowledge of school needs, and perhaps prompted by the *Journal's* editorials, Elders sponsored an education reform bill.

In the lower House, George Carswell of Wilkinson County took the lead in writing the new education proposals. Carswell had served several years on the Wilkinson

County board of education and was personally acquainted with the rural schools' struggle to survive (6). He had served several terms in both the lower and upper Houses of the General Assembly, but during the 1919 session he was the administration's floor leader in the House.

Elders and Carswell together prepared a bill that they introduced the first day of the assembly's 1919 session (7). The state's leading educators and legislators, who favored stronger education bills, had long been frustrated in their efforts to secure the adoption of a new school code and faced in this session the usual opposition against a new tax. Nevertheless, they had high hopes that the Elders-Carswell Bills would alleviate many school problems, so they gave them their support. The state superintendent, M. L. Brittain, speaking before the General Assembly in favor of this new school code, said:

> The importance of this legislation is seen in view of the fact that there has never been a school code in the state. In consequence, there are dozens of laws interfering with each other. Some of them partially overlap laws passed years ago; others nullify some parts of the law and leave in force others, and again legislation has passed occasionally which left other conflicting laws on the subject still in force. Such, for instance, is the case with the State Board of Education. The regular state code of general laws prepared in 1914 shows in one place the professional State Board of Education provided by the laws of 1911 and in another the old ex-officio board which served prior to that time.
>
> Besides correcting old troubles and making a code which superintendents, boards, and parents may definitely and clearly understand, the new school code makes needed suggestions and recommendations as required by law. For instance, the recommendation is made by the codifying committee that the compulsory education law be amended by the employment of an attendance officer to secure the attendance of pupils from 8 to 14 years. There has never been proper enforcement of compulsory laws without an official. This legislation is further strengthened by the recommendation of six months instead of four months attendance, requiring completion of the seventh instead of the fourth grade.
>
> The suggestion is made that appropriations to the public schools shall be made on a definite scale of 3½ mills and providing that it shall never be less than $3,500,000 per annum. This gives stability and certainty instead of leaving it to the uncertainty of legislative passing yearly.
>
> The right to establish junior high schools of vocational or other character is given to boards of education where there are sufficient local funds to provide same.
>
> The construction of public school buildings no matter how small must be approved by the county and city school authorities.
>
> Changes in the laws are also made so that the state law will not conflict with the use of the Smith-Hughes funds for vocational education. This is needed because there is no provision for part time and evening schools at present.
>
> There are many other helpful suggestions in this new code besides the elimination of laws which are no longer in force and impossible of enforcement under present circumstances.
>
> The code is the result of careful preparation by the Committee. For the good of the schools and those interested in education, it is hoped that it will pass without delay (8).

The county school superintendents had worked diligently for years to secure the type of legislation proposed in the new school code. On July 17, at a meeting held at the University of Georgia, they agreed to send the Legislature the following resolutions:

> *Resolved:* That we fully endorse and urge the speedy passage of the Elders-Carswell Bill, providing for statewide local taxation for public schools.
>
> That we especially urge the importance of the adoption by passing legislation of a school code, which will give to us and the general public the school laws of the state in such logical order as will make them clear and definite, instead of the present confused and confusing shape.
>
> That we ask the strengthening of the compulsory attendance laws in order that we may properly enforce the same.
>
> That we would welcome and encourage legislation to facilitate the consolidation of schools.
>
> That the salary of the State School Superintendent be increased.
>
> That the number of School Supervisors be increased—three is too few (9).

People throughout the state were studying the bill and voicing their opinions. While the Legislature was still considering the measure, 100 Negroes appeared before the State Board of Education to request consideration of the following items: (a) larger salaries for Negro teachers, (b) longer school terms, (c) better school buildings, (d) help in securing a normal school for training Negro teachers, (e) more district agricultural schools for Negroes, (f) a more equitable share for Negroes of federal funds coming to Georgia, (g) a Negro to be assistant state supervisor of Negro schools, and (h) appropriations for training Negro teachers in summer schools (10).

The Elders-Carswell Bills, the most far-reaching laws for education enacted in Georgia up to this time, passed overwhelmingly. They provided for levying local taxes to maintain and operate schools and for issuing schoolhouse bonds, defined the duties of local boards of education, and placed some budgetary responsibilities on state and local officials. They also set up grants to school systems that consolidated their small schools, permitted districts to provide transportation, and placed the licensing of teachers in the hands of the state board.

While the 1919 acts corrected many educational problems, they still lacked several provisions necessary for a good school system. The maximum of 5 mills the laws allowed the counties to levy pointed up dramatically the inequality existing in the state's 160 counties. True, many of the cities operated fairly adequate public schools in grades 1 through 11, but too many were poorly supported.

One of the most important of several studies concerning this inequality of education was conducted by Gordon G. Singleton of Columbia University's Teachers College (11). In 1925, he analyzed the tax support programs in Georgia and concluded that, despite a permissive 5-mill tax levy, property in various counties was not assessed uniformly. For example, teachers' average salaries in the 160 counties, comprising about 80 percent of the state's total educational cost, ranged from $292 to $1,418 annually. To provide a minimum program, he advocated an equalization plan that would require the following:

> (1) That every county levy a uniform tax to provide its contribution to the minimum offering on equalized valuation; (2) that the amount of this tax rate be determined by the tax rate it would be necessary for the wealthiest county in the state to levy in order to provide the minimum educational offering the state agrees to equalize; (3) that the state supply the difference between the amount thus raised by each county and the total amount necessary to finance the minimum offering; (4) that the state set up administrative conditions for participation in the state fund which will (a) provide adequate information for the accurate determination of the state's financial responsibility, and (b) insure economical expenditure of all funds necessary to provide the minimum offering the state assumes to equalize. These elements...are accepted as the elements of the proposed plan of school support for Georgia (12).

On the basis of Dr. Singleton's recommendations, an equalization bill was presented to the Legislature. The Georgia Education Association, the state school superintendent, and Governor Clifford Walker all backed it vigorously. There was no apparent organized opposition to the bill. The Equalization Act, finally passed in March 1926, earmarked certain gasoline taxes to equalize educational opportunities in the poor districts and made it the state board's responsibility to develop the formula by which these funds would be distributed.

Despite progress under these important school laws, college professors, school superintendents, public school teachers, the Georgia Education Association, the Georgia Press Association, The American Legion, and the Georgia Laymen's Educational Convention continued to work on plans to improve the state's educational structure. Many interested business and professional leaders in these groups held a Georgia Educational Convention in Macon in April 1934. They proposed that the Legislature adopt laws to ensure (a) a state-supported minimum 9-month school term, (b) the proper minimum preparation of teachers, (c) a state minimum salary schedule for teachers, and (d) a sound taxation program for the schools.

When the General Assembly convened in 1935, it was faced with conflicting information. Governor Eugene Talmadge, in his State of the State address, indicated that he anticipated a substantial reduction in revenue and directed all department heads to reduce their budget requests by 20 percent (13). However, the state auditor's report showed a greater balance in the treasury than at any other time in the state's history (14). Less than 2 months later, the Governor again cautioned legislators to go slow in spending the money, warning: "Heads of the common school system, the university system and the eleemosynary system agreed they could operate on funds recommended by the budget committee. To increase funds would encourage extravagance and affect other departments" (15).

Although the Depression forced all government officials to proceed with caution in projecting their future needs, the 1935 session, famous as the "no appropriation session," did pass a series of education bills sponsored by House Speaker E. D. Rivers embodying the provisions of the resolutions drafted at the Macon convention the previous year. The Governor vetoed the first bill, stating: "This bill appropriates no funds for free textbooks. It would put an idle gesture on the statute books" (16). In a bill designed to let the state superintendent fix the salary schedule for teachers (which could be supplemented by local pay if money was available), the Governor stated his opposition to a uniform school law: "It proposes to change the law. The superintendent of schools would draw a warrant on the treasury and disburse instead of the governor drawing thc warrant" (17).

When Rivers became Governor in 1937, he supported another bill similar to the 1935 bill Governor Talmadge had vetoed. Again, the assembly passed it, and the act, this time known both as "The Seven-Months School Law" and the "Equalization of Educational Opportunities Law," was signed by the Governor. It required all schools to have a 7-month term with provisions for this to be extended by counties, independent school systems, or local tax districts with local tax funds. It set a minimum state salary for teachers, with provisions for local units' paying supplements. The state agreed to pay a given number of teachers in each system from state funds, based on a formula involving the average daily attendance of pupils and the pupil-density ratio. The law also provided for free textbooks for all students, state support for pupil transportation services, minimum courses of study, and revision of the curriculum.

During the 1940's, a number of lay groups, such as the Georgia Congress of Parents and Teachers, the Lion's Club, the Georgia Federation of Women's Clubs, and the Georgia Farm Bureau, assisted the Georgia Education Association in drawing up legislation to increase the standards for public education and provide additional state support. In particular, the Farm Bureau campaigned for a 3-percent sales tax in every county where it had a chapter, arguing that this was the only way a minimum program could be financed throughout the state.

In its 1946 session, the Legislature authorized a special committee to study Georgia's educational needs. The committee submitted its report, "A Survey of Public Education of Less Than College Grade in Georgia," to the Legislature in January 1947. State Superintendent M. D. Collins coordinated the efforts of all lay and professional groups to press for the enactment of the Georgia Minimum Foundation Act it recommended. The proposal finally passed 2 years later but was not put into action until 1951 because the state lacked the necessary funds.

The Minimum Foundation Act of 1949 contained many improvements over previous laws. For instance, it increased the minimum school term to 9 months, liberalized the teacher allotment plan, and established standards for school transportation. It also improved and strengthened the federal programs and provided a plan for determining the minimum amount of local financial support for each school system. It forced the State Department of Education to reorganize in order to provide all of the services needed to operate the schools.

In its 1951 session, the General Assembly adopted the Farm Bureau's 3-percent sales tax proposal to finance its minimum foundation program. At the same time, the Legislature passed an act establishing the state school building authority. Since the foundation law provided for the state board to allocate funds for capital outlay purposes, this authority was now established to finance capital improvements in the school systems on a long-term basis.

It was 1963 before the Legislature again authorized a special committee, the Governor's Commission on Education, to study Georgia's public education. All of its recommendations to the Governor and the state board were included in a bill which the Legislature enacted in 1964.

With authorization from the new law, the state board, in consultation with the state school superintendent, completely reorganized the state department in 1964 (18). The law itself, called a new "foundation program for education," required an adjusted tax digest for determining the local effort. It contained a more liberal plan for allotting teachers and other professional personnel and used an index for establishing a teacher salary schedule. It set up a state-supported sick-leave plan for teachers and bus drivers, furnished state money for purchasing instructional materials, appropriated funds for a statewide educational TV network, expanded the state support for capital outlay, and provided state support for a 12-month school program. The new law also included money for a Governor's Honors Program for gifted students, state support for school lunch programs, an expansion of vocational education, new area vocational-technical schools, schools operating within correctional institutions, a budget audit and a financial review section of local school systems, and an educational research division. It gave permission for students to cross school system lines to attend school.

STRENGTHENING INSTRUCTION

Teacher Education

During the nineteenth century and the early part of the twentieth, certification of teachers was almost completely in the hands of the county and city school superintendents. Wide differences existed in the standards required by the various local systems, some localities securing highly qualified teachers while others saved money by employing poorly prepared teachers. Educators were becoming more and more insistent that the state establish some sort of control over standards. In 1911, the State Board of Education designated, for the first time, various teacher classifications based on examinations.

The movement for higher standards continued to gain momentum and finally influenced the Legislature to pass a law in 1919 requiring the state board to certificate teachers. Almost immediately, the colleges, the public schools, and the state department became more concerned with the standards for certification. It was not long, however, before Georgians began to assume that the 1919 school code had solved the problem, and only moderate progress was made in improving teacher qualifications during the next few years—save for summer and Saturday teachers institutes. The various colleges were allowed to take the responsibility for training teachers according to their own philosophies and concepts with little interference from the state. A number of leading educators, however, recognized that many students were being deprived of an adequate education because of poorly trained teachers, and although at first these leaders were voices in the wilderness, they gradually gained influence. By 1924, they were able to institute state certification of teachers based on a 4-year college program.

Some of Georgia's educational leaders were as dissatisfied with the school curriculum as with the caliber of teachers, but for the most part they were unheeded until the early thirties. State Superintendent M. D. Collins and Philip Weltner, chancellor of the University of Georgia, took the lead in a movement to develop clear-cut ideas of school objectives and the program needed to train teachers on the job to obtain these objectives. They assumed that the movement's progress would require the cooperative effort of many lay people concerned with the quality of public education.

Their efforts bore first fruit in 1932 when the requirement for a 4-year teaching certificate was changed to include a college degree based on more functional courses than previously. But more important, in December of the following year, they secured the cooperation of the Georgia Education Association in holding a conference which started the movement to develop a statewide public school curriculum. L. M. Lester was designated as director of the curriculum program, and Paul Morrow of the University of Georgia was named the curriculum advisor. Nine persons representing the public schools and the public and private colleges formed a committee to serve in an advisory capacity. In turn, they formed the Georgia Council on Teacher Education, which was expected to develop a Georgia program for improving instruction (19).

Study groups of classroom teachers and parents throughout the state began considering ways of providing curriculum improvements on the local level. Approximately 3,000 of Georgia's 20,000 teachers in 1934-35 voluntarily enrolled in these study groups. The movement subsequently expanded until approximately 8,000 persons–parents, teachers, members of civic clubs, and representatives of the press–were participating in one way or another, devoting many hours to educational study and planning. The groups also wrote several guides that were of great importance.

The State Department of Education published Bulletin No. 1, "Organization and Conduct of Teacher Study Groups," in September 1935. At the same time, the Georgia Congress of Parents and Teachers published "Parent Cooperation in the Georgia Program for the Improvement of Instruction in the Public Schools."

By 1937, the study groups were ready to recommend a curriculum designed for all the public schools of Georgia, and the state department published this as Bulletin No. 2, the "Georgia Program for the Improvement of Instruction," more commonly known as the "Red Book." Although an interest in improving the curriculum had inspired the organization of these white and Negro teacher councils, it is obvious that the leaders developed the feeling that the key to curriculum improvement was teacher education.

In 1938, M. E. Thompson, director of the teacher education and certification division, formally organized the State Advisory Committee on Teacher Education and Curriculum. This committee originally consisted of one member from each junior and senior college, the seven state school supervisors, the secretary of the Georgia Education Association, the university high school inspector (a position since abolished), and three public school supervisors.

From 1938 to 1940, the National Commission on Teacher Education, an ad hoc commission of the American Council on Education, operated a project that worked with and gave financial assistance to selected state programs for improving teacher education. In January 1940, the Georgia Advisory Committee requested that the state be admitted as one of the units in the commission's project. Michigan and New York had already been accepted, and Georgia was approved as the third state, with the understanding that the white and Negro councils would operate separately, but that the commission's work would concern itself with both the white and Negro activities.

The commission's consultative and financial help during the period 1940 to 1943 was interrupted for a short time in 1941 due to political interference. Governor Eugene Talmadge and the University System Board of Regents were critical of some individuals in the university system connected with teacher training. They withdrew financial support until these men were removed. Commission help to Georgia resumed the same year, this time with an increased emphasis on in-service teacher education in both the white and Negro councils. The Georgia Advisory Committee (white) reorganized in July 1943 as the Georgia Council on Teacher Education, with an official membership of 17 persons. The steering committee became the executive committee, each member serving from 1 to 4 years on a staggered basis; later it was composed of representatives from the state department and the larger teacher education institutions. The following January, the Georgia Advisory Council (Negro) modified its structure and took the name, Georgia Committee on Cooperation in Teacher Education.

Although the council's major emphasis continued until 1946 to be on details of certification and in-service education, the group did give some attention to other aspects of the school program. In February 1946, L. M. Lester prepared a summary of the council's activities in which he wrote that it had clarified the goals of education and had unified both the teacher preparation and school programs. It had helped teachers with their problems, especially those who had been recruited after their retirement for the war emergency, and had ensured an adequate supply of new teachers to replace those leaving the profession. It also had developed leadership on the local and state levels (20).

The first National Clinic on Teacher Education was held in Georgia in November 1946. Sponsored by the National Council on Cooperation in Teacher Education, it was attended by representatives from 34 states. Its chief value to Georgia was in modifying points of view and creating greater understanding of the state's educational problems. The Georgia council's committees made significant contributions to teacher education, particularly after 1946. The council, in its fall meeting that year, classified its work into four general areas: teacher recruitment selection, preservice education, in-service education, and leadership education.

Perhaps the most important result of the council's efforts in preservice education was the development of a new certification plan, which the state board subsequently approved (21). The new plan for certificating teachers required each teacher education institution to plan its own preservice program to conform with criteria developed by the state councils. These programs were then evaluated by a visiting committee appointed by the director of the teacher education and certification division and approved by the state board. This new plan was approved by the state board in February 1948 and became effective in September 1950.

Since the beginning, the in-service education committee has been concerned with finding better ways to help teachers. After considerable experimentation, it developed two effective instruments: the "educational clinic" or planning conference, where attention is focused on problems in improving instruction, and the "school system workshop," which provides an opportunity for group study of curriculum and other aspects of school improvement.

When the new certification plan became effective in 1950, the council again concentrated its efforts on a study of the preservice education of teachers. In addition to the work of its regular standing committees, the council organized other committees to study preparation programs for the preschool and primary level, the middle grades (4-9), and selected special fields programs of the upper secondary level. All of these committees worked within an overall special fields committee.

In the fall of 1953, the council appointed a committee on criteria for the teaching fields to review studies made by former committees and to develop guides for preparing teachers in different fields. As a result, specific criteria were agreed on for evaluating programs in health, music, and art, and for preparing supervising teachers. Other committee reports offered recommendations or general criteria for developing and evaluating programs in elementary education, science, mathematics, English, social studies, homemaking, industrial arts, and business education.

Emphasis on preservice training focused on student teaching. Since colleges were not equipped to provide facilities for this training, many public schools were selected as off-campus centers. The colleges helped train a number of outstanding teachers as supervising teachers, and the state department supplemented their salaries.

In addition to the committees' work on current problems in teacher education, from 1955 to 1957 the council was concerned with its own organization and function. It found that it needed to keep better records of its activities and establish more effective communication with its member institutions and agencies. Although the council had had a very constructive impact on Georgia schools, its program also had some shortcomings. For instance, the personnel of the council and its committees changed too often to ensure adequate continuity; separate white and Negro organizations caused too much duplication of time and effort; the political interruption in 1941 discouraged many participants who might have served for longer periods; and research was either lacking or weak during the early years of its studies.

On the positive side, the teacher education council had stimulated the state department and teacher-training institutions to develop 6-year specialist and doctoral programs, not only for classroom teachers but also for leadership personnel, such as administrators, curriculum directors, visiting teachers, librarians, counselors, and school psychologists. The state minimum salary schedules now provided wider differentials between professional and provisional certificates. (While higher certificates warrant higher salaries, it is also evident that the higher salaries do affect certification [22].)

Training of Instructional Supervisors

In 1936, Marvin S. Pittman, president of South Georgia Teachers College, received a grant from the Rosenwald Foundation to begin a program for training instructional supervisors on the undergraduate level. He named Jane Franseth and Kate Hauk directors of the training program and recruited several excellent teachers by paying them a small stipend with Rosenwald Foundation funds while they were enrolled.

It was apparent that appropriate training to meet technical certification requirements could best be obtained on the graduate level. Since South Georgia Teachers College did not have a graduate school at the time, it was agreed that the University of Georgia would assume responsibility for training these instructional supervisors in 1939-40. Dr. Franseth and Dr. Hauk moved to the University of Georgia to continue the program (23).

The Rosenwald Fund continued to contribute to the program after the move to the University of Georgia, but after some years it discontinued the stipend for trainees. Recruitment and screening became the program's important features, and John Cook of the Department of Education became the coordinator of recruitment, selection, and training, and cooperated closely with the staff at the University of Georgia. The state department encouraged school systems to employ instructional supervisors by allotting additional teacher units to those who did and by paying a state supplement to personnel certificated by the state department.

This program received wide recognition, mainly due to the intense recruitment and screening process, the state-directed specialized training program, and the state support for certificated personnel.

> In summary it may be said that the Georgia program for the education of supervisors attempts to prepare the prospective supervisors for the kind of work which they will be expected to do by giving them as much of it to do in their education program as possible. The program at-

> tempts through cooperative leadership to help supervisors to develop competencies of "good" teachers, of resource persons, and of leaders in educational planning (24).

A great many people still felt that the title of instructional supervisor did not convey a clear picture of the office, so the title was changed in 1960 to director of curriculum. Special allotments were included in the school law of 1964 for school systems employing these curriculum directors.

Visiting Teacher Services

The Georgia Education Association played a vital role in developing the Georgia Association of Visiting Teachers from an idea first presented in 1944 into an effective compulsory school attendance law. J. Harold Saxon, former executive secretary of the Georgia Education Association, states:

> A committee was appointed by the Georgia Education Association Board of Directors in 1944, for the purpose of making research on the need for a compulsory (school) attendance law in Georgia....This committee met many times during the year and made the necessary research for the basis for writing the preliminary draft of the Compulsory Attendance Bill. This preliminary Bill was cleared through the Georgia Education Association Legislative Committee and approved by the Georgia Education Association Board of Directors before being introduced in the Legislature (25).

The only vocal opposition to compulsory school attendance came from those who felt it might hurt the labor market and thereby affect the war effort. One legislator even introduced a resolution asking that it not be rigidly enforced (26); the resolution did not pass.

When the new compulsory school attendance law passed in 1945, it provided that each school system would employ a visiting teacher "whose duty it shall be to act as attendance officer to enforce the compulsory school attendance laws of the State and to discharge such other duties as are usually performed by, or delegated to, visiting teacher (sic)" (27).

Georgia presents a good example of a statewide program based on legislation motivated by concern over the state's high illiteracy rate. This legislation differed from that of most states because it provided for a compulsory statewide program that had to be set up immediately in each school system. State funds were allotted to the school superintendents for the salaries of these visiting teachers, one visiting teacher to each system having a minimum of 75 state-paid classroom teachers, and the cost of travel was shared by both state and local authorities on a matching basis. When the minimum foundation program for education was started in 1950, the state assumed full responsibility for travel expenses. Some school systems employed additional workers at their own expense.

Claude Purcell, the state department's assistant director of administration, was mainly responsible for recognizing the need for a social work approach to removing the causes of nonattendance. Although he had the strong support of both State School Superintendent M. D. Collins and Assistant Superintendent John I. Allman, it was Dr. Purcell's understanding and foresight that was the deciding factor in shaping the visiting teacher services as an integral part of the school program. The initial focus of the services was on the enrollment of all children. As this goal was accomplished, it became evident that many children were unable to use the school effectively, so the visiting teacher's function expanded to not only getting the children to school but helping them make the maximum use of school experiences.

Training for the visiting teacher position included from the beginning a graduate program with a professional 4-year college certificate as a prerequisite (28). The education department staff worked with the University of Georgia in developing the training and certification procedures for these visiting teachers. Fortunately, the local school systems usually selected experienced classroom teachers for this training.

Many economy-minded legislators have attempted to reduce or eliminate the visiting teacher program, but schoolmen have prevented reductions thus far. In fact, the school acts of 1964 provided for special allotments to school systems to improve the services. The state department employed a full-time coordinator of visiting teacher work in 1954 to assist visiting teachers, colleges, and school administrators in promoting better services. The coordinator worked in the administration and finance division for 10 years, but the reorganization of the department in 1964 placed him in the instruction division under the pupil personnel services unit. At present, approximately 90 percent of the school systems in the state use visiting teacher services.

Guidance, Counseling, and Testing Services

In 1944, the state department established a program of vocational guidance in the vocational education division. When the first minimum foundation program was established in 1951, this service was transferred to the instruction division and was enlarged to provide some testing services. Four years later, a state appropriation permitted allotments to school systems for testing materials.

The National Defense Education Act of 1958 provided federal funds to supplement the state funds in this area. The state's staff for guidance, counseling, and testing now consists of six professionals (one program coordinator, five consultants) and seven stenographic and clerical staff members. For the 1964-65 school year, 530 schools had approved guidance and counseling programs handling approximately 339,000 students. At present Georgia has 446 counselors, 108 of whom work at counseling more than half but less than full time, 103 half time, and 41 less than half time. This is 50 more counselors than the 396 reported in the 1964-65 school year, and plans are under way to extend the elementary guidance programs. New programs have been started for training additional counselors to meet the growing needs of both elementary and secondary schools throughout the state, and statewide in-service conferences are being conducted for those already in the field.

The state department's guidance and counseling service has published books, brochures, and material on professional consultative services and program improvement at local and state levels. These have been distributed to schools throughout the state. It also has conducted statistical studies on the activities of ninth-grade students, seniors, high school graduates, and dropouts.

BETTER FACILITIES AND ENRICHED CURRICULUM

Accrediting Service

In July 1903, on the recommendation of Chancellor Walter B. Hill, the University of Georgia undertook a program of cooperating with the high schools to promote secondary education throughout the state. With financial assistance from George Foster Peabody of New York, the university engaged Joseph S. Stewart as professor of secondary education (29). Professor Stewart stated in his first address at the university's summer school:

> It will be our duties to study the education conditions in the several counties, to encourage the establishment of high schools by local support, to bring these courses into some system and relate these to the common schools and to the institutions of higher learning above. . . . By a system of accredited schools, passed upon after examination, having approved courses of study, suitable laboratories, libraries and skilled teachers, we may hope in a few years to see a system of high schools established (30).

From 1904 to 1929, authority for school accreditation was vested in the University of Georgia Committee on Accrediting, with the State Department of Education represented by a state high school supervisor. The name of the committee was changed to the Georgia Accrediting Commission in 1929, with its headquarters still at the university. Despite the state's financial woes during the Depression, when the 1937 school laws were enacted and accreditation became more important in the plans for improving schools, the number of state school supervisors was increased.

The commission's staff continually requested that consideration be given to moving its headquarters from the university to the state department. The constitution was amended to include the president and secretary of the Georgia High School Association on the commission, but it was 1941 before the office of the commission's secretary was transferred to the State Department of Education in Atlanta.

In 1944, the accrediting commission's constitution was changed again to give it authority to accredit elementary schools and to increase the membership of the commission by two representatives from the Georgia Education Association's department of elementary principals. The chairman of the Georgia Committee of the Southern Association, an advisory group composed of school personnel appointed by the Southern Association of Colleges and Secondary Schools, was designated as an ex officio member. The constitution was subsequently amended to provide for an additional representative from the Department of Education, two representatives from the High School Principals' Association, and one from the Georgia Association of Independent Schools. It also designated the Georgia High School Association representatives as elected rather than ex officio members. In 1958, the constitution was again amended to authorize an increase in the commission membership to include two representatives from the Georgia Education Association's department of classroom teachers and two from the Georgia Association of School Administrators.

Though unique in organization, this plan of making accreditation the responsibility of an independent body has permitted school accreditation to be conducted on a professional basis, free from political pressures, legislative statutes, and government interference. The state department has always worked closely with the Georgia Accrediting Commission and continues to do so.

Transportation Service

Despite the fact that the department operated during most of the years prior to 1937 on the theory that its functions were primarily regulatory, it did offer several services to the local school systems (31). The state department's thirtieth annual report (1901) to the General Assembly contained a very interesting but crude statement on the subject of school transportation. In describing the process of providing transportation for the students of Jefferson County, the report said:

> We had some difficulty in getting somebody to furnish the horse. They said you furnish the wagon, and now you furnish the horse. We told them, no, sir, that we would give it out by contract to any man who would bring the children for five cents a day. We had to change

one of these wagons three times. The two-horse wagon is successfully run now by a widow lady, who keeps a horse to plow her garden and go visiting. When we asked her to let her children go to the school, she said, "No, sir, they might fall out and break their necks." She was so well pleased with the wagon that when the man who had been running it quit, she said, "I'll run it." She is very much pleased with the job, and says she will never give it up (32).

The school law of 1919 specifically permitted districts to provide school transportation, and a law in 1926 referred to pupil transportation, but not until the assembly enacted the Seven Month School Law in 1937 were state funds earmarked for this service. Since school consolidations were gaining momentum, transportation was becoming one of the most important local administrative problems.

During the following years, the service became important enough for school bus drivers (mostly white male adults) to form a state association to strengthen their welfare and bargaining position. Although they did not affiliate with a labor union, they exercised influence in political campaigns on impending legislation.

The 1946 General Assembly authorized its committee on education to conduct the first major study of school transportation service. In its report, the committee pointed to a comprehensive analysis of the transportation system completed 2 years earlier by the Agricultural and Industrial Development Board's education panel, and then went on to say: "The transportation program has grown to such an extent that it can no longer be considered a local function of the schools .... The committee recommends a state-owned and operated system ..." (33). However, the assembly refused to act on the recommendation.

During the early 1950's, a $632 million school program gave considerable impetus to the school consolidation movement. As the state's 3,906 schools were consolidated into 1,800 schools, more and more pupils were forced to ride buses. Correspondingly, both the state board and the state department exercised more positive leadership in developing adequate transportation facilities. For instance, the state board began calculating allotments to school systems on the basis of the county-owned buses' operating costs, producing a decided trend toward county-owned buses.

Through close cooperation over the years among the Governors, legislatures, the state board, and the school bus drivers association, pupil transportation services advanced to the point where there is competitive bidding on equipment purchases, construction specifications on equipment, state regulations on bus routes and schedules, and periodic surveys for determining needs and costs. The department holds statewide clinics for transportation personnel and pays the basic salaries of certificated supervisory personnel. It provides bus drivers with annual medical examinations, a state minimum salary, Social Security coverage, and a sick-leave plan.

School Plant Services

The state first stepped into the area of school plant services when the 1919 Legislature enacted legislation authorizing the sale of schoolhouse bonds. School buildings throughout the state were obsolete or in a dismal condition by the end of World War I, especially in the rural areas. Many educators–particularly Negroes–were calling for assistance to provide better buildings.

The Chief State School Officers and State Agents for Negro Education in the South, meeting at Gulfport, Mississippi, in January 1925 under the auspices of the General Education Board, asked for help from either the board or the Julius Rosenwald Fund to establish divisions of schoolhouse planning under trained directors. The general board officials responded by agreeing to consider the state's applications for funds to set up such a division over a 5-year period. It was agreed that the state directors would be carefully selected and sent to Peabody College for at least a year of graduate work in school plant problems on scholarships given by both the General Education Board and the Julius Rosenwald Fund.

Georgia took advantage of this opportunity to establish an office of school plant services. The unit now has 10 staff members, consisting of 2 secretaries, 3 maintenance consultants, 2 architects, 2 engineers, and the unit head. It is responsible for school plant surveys and offers consultative services to school architects.

When the foundation program was established in 1951, it included a State School Building Authority, an agency for constructing school buildings on a lease-purchase plan, and an appropriation for capital-outlay funds for constructing buildings in each of the state's school systems. The State Board of Education developed firm policies concerning the rules and regulations for allotting these funds. Through this building authority, Georgia has embarked on a long-range financing plan based on bonds; the state appropriates the funds as needed. These bonds are issued by the authority, to be retired eventually by leases whereby the school systems pay a stipulated rent on the projects built. The school plant services office, working closely with the education department and the building authority, has assisted in planning over $300 million worth of buildings financed by the state (34).

Library Services

School Libraries. The State Board of Education approved a program to expand and improve Georgia's school library services in 1937 and employed a library supervisor. The Legislature had already passed a law in 1935 stating that the revenue derived from a tax on beer and wine would be used for purchasing textbooks. The attorney general ruled in 1938 that libraries could be defined as instructional materials and that it was legal to spend this textbook money for library books. Early in 1939, the board made the first state funds available to elementary schools for expanding their libraries. This first state aid, amounting to $50,000, was allotted to the systems on a matching basis according to the state-paid teacher allotment. The following year, when high schools were made eligible to participate, the amount was increased to a total of $100,000.

The Legislature continued this state aid for purchasing school library materials by writing it into the first minimum foundation law (35). State aid to libraries again was included in the new minimum foundation law of 1964 (36), but this time it was changed so that the funds were sent directly to the systems to pay their bills instead of the state department's handling the accounts. The law also changed the allocation from a per-teacher to a per-pupil basis and changed the matching proportion from two-thirds state and one-third local to the same formula by which local participation was calculated for other educational expenditures.

The figures for the amounts spent were either nonexistent or inaccurate during the early years of the program. Almost no elementary schools had libraries, and those that did used mainly branches of the public libraries in the cities. By the 1953-54 school year, all of the high schools and more than a quarter of the elementary schools had centralized libraries. The number of elementary libraries continued to grow, and 1,198 schools (88.5 percent) had libraries by 1966.

The number of certificated school librarians increased from 436 in 1954 to 1,217 in 1966, not including supervisors or additional professional staff members. The state had only two system-wide library supervisors in 1944, but by 1966, 15 systems had library supervisors. The professional staff at the state level increased from one person in 1937 to three in 1948; it has not increased since that time.

The School Building Authority regulations included libraries as one of its eligible areas, and the agency deserves commendation for its fine job in improving library facilities. But the growth of collections and the implementation of new instructional programs have made it necessary to replan and expand many of the existing school libraries.

Despite these important improvements, more money, more personnel, and expanded facilities are still needed at all levels if the school library program in Georgia is to meet the needs of schools moving toward excellence in education.

Library for the Blind. In 1936, an independent agency, the Kreigshaber Memorial Library, was established in Atlanta to serve the blind with reading materials. Although supported by public subscriptions, it had some connection with the Atlanta Carnegie Library. The State Department of Education had become responsible for managing this school for the blind by the time the state superintendent made his 1951 report. It still serves all visually impaired readers in Georgia and Florida with talking books (books on records), books in braille, tapes, and small portable record players.

Over 3,000 readers use the talking-book service today, and 342 are reading braille and listening to the tapes. The library staff sponsors a summer reading program for blind students in Georgia and Florida that usually attracts over 200 participants. The staff, composed of a librarian, a secretary, two clerks, and two men in the mailing department, takes care of about 50 new readers each month.

Public Library Services. The Georgia Library Commission operated as an independent state agency under a law passed by the General Assembly in 1933. However, in 1943, the assembly repealed the act creating the commission and, through subsequent legislation in the same session, placed this public library service under the State Board of Education. The department operated the unit of public library services as a part of a textbook and library services division from 1943 to 1964. When the department was reorganized that year, the unit was placed under the administrative services division.

The Library Services and Construction Act, passed in 1963, allocated $714,375 to the state in 1964 and $680,700 in 1965. These funds have been matched by $1,620,000 in local funds. It is evident from the data in the table below that Georgia has made considerable progress in its public library program.

	1943-44	1965-66
Population served	1,782,216	3,943,116
Counties receiving state aid for purchase of library materials	55	159
Number of independent libraries	32	11
Per-capita support	$0.17	$1.41
Number of regional (multi-county) library systems	6	34
Counties in regional (multi-county) library systems	14	127
Number of books in libraries	.4 per capita	1.3 per capita
Number of books circulated	1.3 per capita	5.23 per capita
Number of bookmobiles	29	89

	1943-44	1965-66
Number of library systems using State Public Library film service	0	32
Number of staff members in local public libraries	353	847
Number of staff members at state agency	6	35

Curriculum Development

A state committee has been concerned with curriculum revision continuously since 1933. As mentioned previously, under the leadership of L. M. Lester, director of curriculum, M. E. Thompson, director of certification, and Paul Morrow, the Georgia Council on Teacher Education and the education department organized curriculum study groups throughout the state (37). The interest aroused by the groups prompted the 1937 Legislature to pass a law entitled "Rules and Regulations Prescribing Courses of Study; Curriculum Revision; Administration of School Funds." In part, it reads as follows:

> The State Board of Education shall provide rules and regulations prescribing a course of study for all common and high schools receiving State aid and may, in their discretion, approve additional courses of study set up by the local units of administration; provide for curriculum revisions and for the classification and certification of teachers. They shall make such rules and regulations as may be necessary for the administration of the common school fund (38).

In keeping with the law, the state board in 1938 adopted the curriculum designed for Georgia by the study groups and published by the department, commonly known as the "Red Book."

The state department continued to give attention to curriculum improvement and organized an economy and efficiency committee in 1939 to consider other revisions. Special committees of this kind did most of the work rather than the director of teacher education and curriculum development, because the director was primarily concerned with teacher education. The teacher shortage during World War II curtailed consistent progress in curriculum development. However, in many instances curriculum offerings were altered to meet the needs of the war effort where qualified staff was available.

When the 1947 Legislature passed a law permitting the state board to spend state money for the twelfth grade, the department attempted to give leadership to local systems making the transition from 11- to 12-grade schools. In actual practice, this again led to the establishment of a revision committee concerned with curriculum development, and the committee became an official part of the department when the latter was reorganized in 1953. This committee's recommendations, published as a "Curriculum Framework for Georgia Schools," was distributed throughout the state and was finally adopted by the state board. It has been amended several times, the first major change occurring in 1958 when the state department's curriculum unit recommended additional requirements in line with the national trend to provide more depth and dimension to public school offerings. The state board raised the graduation requirements from 16 Carnegie units to 18 and required all public high schools to offer foreign languages, physics, chemistry, human biology, and 2 years of vocational education, in addition to its previous offerings.

The curriculum unit staff works closely with the local superintendents in developing curriculum, and they have participated in all of the elementary and secondary school evaluations. The surveys to determine school plant needs have used the curriculum unit's standard of educational adequacy as a major criterion. The movement has had a constructive impact throughout Georgia.

Vocational Education

The Federal Program in Georgia. Vocational education in Georgia had its real beginning when the Sixty-Fourth Congress approved the Smith-Hughes Act in 1917, providing grants to the states for promoting vocational training in agriculture, home economics, and trade and industrial education. It received another impetus when Congress approved the Vocational Education Act of 1946 (the George-Barden Act), technically an amendment to the George-Deen Act, broadening the offerings of the previous legislation and authorizing additional funds.

The programs in Georgia were again stimulated by Title II of the George-Barden Act, enacted in August 1956. Known as the Health Amendments Act, it specifically authorized the training of practical nurses and has since been extended and made permanent. Two years later, NDEA appropriated funds for turning out highly skilled technicians in occupations necessary to the national defense. The Manpower Development and Training Act, approved by Congress in 1962, provided essentially new methods of federal assistance for vocational education, enabling this training to be offered in all occupational service areas in cooperation with the Department of Labor. It even paid students subsistence allowances while in training.

The Vocational Education Act of 1963 granted additional funds to the states and emphasized vocational training as an area concept, as well as providing funds for construction and equipment. Georgia took full advantage of these funds: the Legislature immediately passed an act authorizing the establishment of area trade, vocational, and industrial schools. The program developed quickly, the citizens eagerly accepting the area idea. By the end of 1966, the state had 23 of these vocational schools in operation. Additional area schools will be developed in the near future. Enrollment in vocational training increased from 2,541 in 1918 to 197,517 in 1965. The Division of Vocational Education now has a staff of 113, and the Department of Education expects the staff will have to be increased to maintain and extend its supervisory and leadership role in Georgia's vocational education.

Area Technical Schools. Since 1946, the Georgia Department of Education has operated two residential vocational-technical schools, one in the northern part of the state at Clarkesville and the other in the south at Americus. Within a few years after their opening, it became evident that these could not serve the state adequately and that drive-in schools were badly needed. It was 1957 before the Legislature appropriated funds for this purpose, but within 4 years 17 new area vocational-technical schools had been completed and 11 more were under contract. By 1965, 359 teachers were training over 12,000 students in more than 50 occupations, including every major technical skilled occupation existing in the state. It is estimated that by 1970 these schools will enroll more than 43,000 students.

Vocational Rehabilitation Service

When Congress passed an act initiating the vocational rehabilitation program for the nation in 1920, Georgia passed an enabling act the same year in order to participate. The state program did not grow much prior to 1940, but it has expanded constantly since that time, primarily due to the passage of Public Law 113 by the Seventy-Eighth Congress in 1943, Public Law 565 in 1954 by the Eighty-Third Congress, and Public Law 333 by the Eighty-Ninth Congress in 1965.

For 5 consecutive years, from 1956 to 1960, Georgia led the nation in the number of persons rehabilitated per capita. For 3 consecutive years and 1 other, Georgia led the nation in absolute total number of persons rehabilitated, and for approximately 20 years, from 1947 to 1966, it was never lower than fourth in the total number of disabled citizens rehabilitated for employment.

Georgia's excellent record in providing vocational rehabilitation services had been due principally to the Legislature's willingness to appropriate 100 percent of the money required to match all federal funds. The state has enjoyed the complete cooperation of related agencies and the medical profession. Since 1940, the program has increased to approximately 700 staff members, and such excellent service could not have been provided without a high caliber of personnel.

At present, the vocational rehabilitation program is administered through the State Board of Education. It operates under the Georgia Vocational Rehabilitation Laws, which first passed the assembly in 1951 and were amended in 1956, 1957, and 1959.

Health Education

In the late thirties and early forties, the nationwide trend in health education had an impact on the curriculum of many states, including Georgia (39). The Department of Education and the Georgia Education Association cooperated in a 3-year project to study health education needs throughout the Southern states. Their report indicated that revisions were needed in teaching methods, concepts, and the scope of health education if the program was to meet the needs of the people (40).

In the spring of 1944, representatives from the state departments of education and health of nine Southern states met in Atlanta under the sponsorship of the U.S. Office of Education and the U.S. Public Health Service to discuss possibilities for closer cooperation, particularly through the schools. Following this meeting, the Georgia education and health departments held a similar conference. The local public school and public health officials and representatives from the university system who participated formed a Joint Health Education Committee composed of three members from each of the two departments and the university system.

Through the efforts of this joint committee, the education department secured grants for 1945, 1946, and 1947 from the W. K. Kellogg Foundation of Battle Creek, Michigan, to sponsor and promote special health projects in four counties. The department employed both a coordinator of health education to work with the committee and a Negro health educator to serve the Negro schools. Approximately 80 teachers, half of them Negroes, from Cobb, Crisp, Spalding, and Walton Counties attended health education workshops for 6 weeks to receive instruction in creating a healthful school-community environment. These workshops also presented instruction in nutrition, physical education, recreation, safety, dental hygiene, social hygiene, and health habits. Participants were taught to use the services offered by public health workers, dentists, private physicians, and agencies having educational programs with special emphasis on the public health services. The program attempted to cover the whole personality—physical, mental, emotional, and social—and was adapted to the abilities, needs, and interests of the learners. It was considered a vital part of the total school program, not merely an addition to it. Since the participants assumed leadership in their own county-wide health education programs, the programs placed the department in a leadership role in promoting better health education programs in all the school systems (41).

The improvements in health education pointed up a need for temperance or alcohol education. The Women's Christian Temperance Union, working closely with several church groups, sought legislation to require this instruction in all public schools. The Legislature finally passed a bill in 1951 authorizing the state board to set up a program in alcohol education. Nothing was done, however, until Governor Talmadge, who had often publicly advocated the need for an alcohol education program in the public schools, made $25,000 available to the department 2 years later. The department employed a full-time person in September 1953 to promote the program.

In the summer of 1954, the department conducted two workshops to train teachers in the correct method of presenting alcohol education, a highly controversial subject in Georgia. Each subsequent summer, similar workshops have been held for teachers in different subject matter areas at different grade levels, attending from all parts of the state. In turn, these teachers have inaugurated alcohol education programs in their respective schools.

SPACE-AGE EDUCATION–NEW SERVICES IN THE SIXTIES

Financial Review Service

The Department of Education established a school financial review section in September 1964 as a result of Senate Bill 180, which the General Assembly passed that January. This section's staff has spent about 75 percent of its time instructing local school officials in using the *Georgia Handbook for Local School Systems.* The other 25 percent of their time has been devoted to auditing and reviewing the financial operations of the local systems.

A great deal of progress has been made in establishing uniform systems and training people in financial responsibility. Most of the local fiscal operations now comply with the state board's policies and the state department's audit regulations. In fact, school systems failing to meet these legal requirements can lose their state funds.

At present, the department's staff is preparing additional handbook materials as well as sample ledgers, cash books, and various other forms for use by the local schools. The present staff, consisting of a chief budget analyst, three auditors, and three clerks, has the responsibility of reviewing local systems having difficulty with deficit financing or their required local foundation support.

Educational Television

The Georgia education department participated in the 1956 Southern States Work Conference, which assessed the potentialities and problems of educational television. By 1960, the department had accumulated sufficient data to begin broadcasting courses on a regular basis from commercial stations and station WGTV-TV, owned by the University of Georgia. To expand its telecourses, the department secured a construction permit from the Federal Communications Commission to erect a station, WXFA-TV, at Waycross. The station began its first broadcast in the summer of 1961.

The department has continued to study ways in which ETV can be used in the state. In 1963, the Governor's Commission To Improve Education recommended that the department establish sufficient in-school ETV programing to involve all of the state's public schools. The General Assembly accepted the commission's recommendations and passed an act in 1964 which designated the state board as Georgia's ETV authority. This act empowered the board to own and operate the state's ETV and all related facilities and required the board to furnish schedules, consultative services, and teacher aids, as well as to perform all other tasks necessary in programing, producing, and transmitting TV programs to Georgia's citizens. It designated the state board as the proper state agency to receive all federal funds and any other funds that might be appropriated, granted, or made available to the state for ETV at all levels, and to use or distribute these funds in accordance with their intent.

The state board is now operating five TV stations and has five more under construction to complete its statewide network. The department has adequate personnel consisting of 92 professionals and technicians and will continue to add more as they are needed.

Operation Bootstrap

Claude Purcell, the state department's assistant director of administration, advocated a program whereby local superintendents could improve their professional competence while on the job and at the same time earn college credit for intensive work in specific fields. In 1961, Dr. Purcell arranged the first conference for local superintendents at the state FFA-FHA Camp. It was so successful that the University of Georgia and the state department have since jointly sponsored three "Operation Bootstrap" conferences.

The conferences usually devote 2 or 3 days each to professional studies in the areas of instruction, school laws, proposed legislation, school plant construction, school finance, and innovations in education. Nationally known consultants, including college professors, U.S. Office of Education staff, representatives of other state departments, and professionals in other fields have been invited to participate in this unique project. A special feature of all sessions is a question-and-answer period in which the consultants are interrogated closely by a panel of superintendents and others who wish to enter the discussions. The department and the university, as well as the superintendents, have concluded that one of the project's best features is that the conferences are held at a camp where there are no distracting influences and sessions can be held continuously.

Operation Bootstrap does not replace the regular meetings of the association of the school superintendents with its work sessions devoted entirely to self-improvement. Approximately 150 of the 195 local superintendents have participated, with about 60 percent enrolled for college credit.

Governor's Honors Program

Several members of the state department wanted summer residential programs organized for Georgia's gifted and talented students. Their hopes were fulfilled when Governor Carl E. Sanders personally requested that provisions for a summer honors program be written into Georgia's Minimum Foundation Program of Education bill in 1964. Section 51 authorized the state board to establish such a program for pupils in public high schools who show exceptional ability, unique potential, or who have attained exceptional academic achievement. The first Governor's Honors Program, an 8-week summer residential program for 400 highly gifted secondary students, was held on the Wesleyan College Campus in Macon in the summer of 1964.

The purpose of this program has been to provide students with an opportunity to participate in educational experiences not usually available in the regular school year. It attempts to assist students in recognizing both their potential and their role in society. The state's public school teachers nominate students in any of eight major areas of instruction where the students have shown an intense interest as well as exceptional ability.

In addition to supplying academic instruction and direction, the specially selected faculty and staff for the honors program provide additional experiences for the students by conducting seminars on contemporary issues and ideas, a physical education program, a series of special events, and special-interest study and counseling services. Thus, the entire program not only extends each student's awareness in his particular area of interest, but also provides knowledge in other fields.

The Governor's Honors Program, now in its third year of operation, has created an increased interest in the education of the gifted and the need for special programing. This has resulted in the addition of a second staff member in the area of the gifted within the division for exceptional children. It has also increased the number of summer honors programs operated by public school systems and by private schools, increased the number of gifted secondary students who enter college a year early, and has heightened the interest of the teacher education personnel in the colleges. It seems evident from the number of students nominated in these academic areas and those who qualify for consideration by the final selection committee that the public school personnel are now better able to identify gifted students. In 1964, the Governor's Honors Program staff included 41 professional and nonprofessional people and was increased to 52 in 1965.

Public Information Services

Prior to the implementation of the first minimum foundation program, the Georgia education department did not have a department-wide unit for public information services. The vocational education division employed two staff members for public relations, and the vocational rehabilitation division had its own unit. The directors of other divisions assumed some responsibility for public information. But the arrangement did not prove very satisfactory for the department as a whole.

When the department was reorganized in 1951, the state board and the state superintendent decided to create a public information unit to serve the entire department. It operated for some time under the assistant state superintendent for staff services but in 1961 was placed under the direction of the state school superintendent, where it has operated ever since.

The Present

The State Board of Education is responsible for developing policies, rules, and regulations for implementing the many services specified by the Legislature. Therefore, with the advice and consultation of the state superintendent, the state board organizes and develops the staff that performs the duties designated by law. Since 1900, the state funds for education have increased from $1,440,642 to $233,786,836 in 1965.

When the Legislature enacted the 1964 Foundation Law, the state board assigned the George Peabody College division of surveys and fields services the responsibility of studying the public schools in Georgia and developing the criteria that should be applied throughout the state. It also directed the Department of Education to establish and enforce minimum standards for operating all phases of public education in Georgia.

The Peabody report in 1965 stated that dissatisfaction with the status quo had been the key to Georgia's progress (42). It contained sweeping recommendations for school district reorganization. Even though the state reduced the number of the districts in 1945 from 1,454 to 197, the report stated that the state needed no more than 50 school districts, each with a minimum of 10,000 students. While these recommendations have not yet been implemented, their publication has had a dramatic impact on Georgians.

The application of minimum standards in all schools by the department is excellent evidence that the quality of education has been upgraded. From its beginning, this movement has shown unusual potential. Most Georgians agree with Governor Carl E. Sanders' speech of October 11, 1966, when he dedicated the state's fifth educational TV station:

> The single most important job of State and local government is the education of our children. Georgia can have splendid highways, ultra-modern physical and mental health services, unlimited natural resources, and a stubborn determination to improve, yet unless our children receive the finest education obtainable, then our State will founder in a quagmire of failure and despair (43).

FOOTNOTES

1. Dorothy Orr, *A History of Education in Georgia* (Chapel Hill: University of North Carolina Press, 1950), pp. 76-77.
2. C. E. Jones, *Education in Georgia* (Washington, D.C.: Government Printing Office, 1889), p. 27.
3. Haygood S. Bowden, *The Building of the Empire State* (Savannah: Braid and Hutton, 1925), pp. 40-44.
4. Table 1, Appendix C, shows the annual state appropriations for public schools from 1871 to 1924.
5. Editorial, *Tattnall Journal,* June 15, 1916.
6. For further information, see Victor Davidson, *The History of Wilkinson County* (Macon: J. W. Burke Co., 1930), p. 479.
7. *Atlanta Constitution,* June 27, 1919, p. 9.
8. *Ibid.,* July 3, p. 9.
9. *Ibid.,* July 18, p. 6.
10. *Ibid.,* July 3, p. 9.
11. Gordon G. Singleton, *State Responsibility for the Support of Education in Georgia,* Contributions to Education No. 181 (New York: Teachers College, Columbia University, 1925), p. 20.
12. *Ibid.,* pp. 40-41.
13. *Atlanta Constitution,* January 11, 1935, p. 1.
14. *Ibid.,* January 12.
15. *Ibid.,* March 4.
16. *Ibid.,* March 29.
17. *Ibid.*
18. See charts of this reorganization in Appendix B.
19. For the story of this statewide cooperative study and the organization of both white and Negro teacher education councils in Georgia, see Sam P. Wiggins, "Georgia Teacher Education Councils and Pre-Service Education: 1933-1951" (unpublished Ph.D. dissertation, George Peabody College for Teachers, Nashville, Tenn., 1952).
20. *Ibid.,* pp. 77-78.
21. Department of Education, Division of Instruction, *Georgia Council on Teacher Education* (Atlanta: The Department, 1961).
22. Carl G. Renfroe, "The Growth and Development of Teacher Certification in Georgia" (unpublished Ph.D. dissertation, University of Georgia, Athens, 1964), p. 180.
23. Dr. Franseth accepted a position with the U.S. Office of Education and was replaced by Johnnye V. Cox. Dr. Hauk accepted another position several years later.
24. Southern States Work Conference on Educational Problems, *Educational Supervision–A Leadership Service* (Tallahassee, Fla.: State Department of Education, 1954), p. 82.
25. Florrie Still, "Georgia Association of Visiting Teachers–A Brief History," *Georgia Education Journal,* LX (October 1966), 18.
26. *Atlanta Constitution,* February 9, 1945, p. 6.
27. Georgia, *Acts* (1945), p. 343.
28. Renfroe, *op. cit.,* p. 183.
29. The program was subsidized later by the General Education Board.
30. Georgia Accrediting Commission, *Official Bulletin,* XIV, No. 1 (September 1965), p. 33.
31. See Appendix B Supplement.
32. Department of Education, *Thirtieth Annual Report* (1901), p. 105.
33. Education Panel, *A Survey of Public Education of Less Than College Grade in Georgia,* report of the Bureau of Education Research and Field Service, O. C. Aderhold, chairman (Athens: College of Education, University of Georgia, 1947), pp. 154, 162-63.
34. See Appendix C for the amount of Building Authority bond sales, as well as local school bond issues.
35. Georgia, *Acts* (1949), p. 1406.
36. Georgia, *Acts* (1964), pp. 3, 14.
37. Wiggins, *op. cit.,* p. 31.
38. Georgia, *Acts* (1937), pp. 864, 866; (1961), pp. 39, 40.
39. Advisory Committee on Education, *Education in the Forty-Eight States* (Washington, D.C.: Government Printing Office, 1939), pp. 80-86.
40. Southern States Work Conference on School Administrative Problems, *Building a Better South Through Education, Improving Education in the Southern States,* Bulletin No. 3 (Tallahassee, Fla.: State Department of Education, 1943), p. 60.
41. O. C. Aderhold, *School Leaders Manual, Program of Educational Development for Georgia* (Atlanta: State Department of Education, 1947), p. 67.

42. W. C. McClurkin, *A Survey Report Organization of School Systems in Georgia* (Nashville, Tenn.: George Peabody College for Teachers, 1965), p. 13.

43. Carl E. Sanders, paper read at the dedication of educational TV station, Wrens, Georgia, October 11, 1966.

BIBLIOGRAPHY

Public Documents

Georgia. *Acts* (1937, 1945, 1949, 1961, 1964).

—— *Constitution* (1945).

—— *School Laws* (1948, 1955, 1958, 1961).

—— *State School Items–Georgia School Laws* (1933).

—— *Minimum Foundation Program of Education Act* (1964).

Books

Bowden, Haygood S. *The Building of the Empire State.* Savannah, Ga.: Braid and Hutton, 1925.

Coulter, E. Merton. *A Short History of Georgia.* Chapel Hill: University of North Carolina Press, 1950.

Davidson, Victor. *The History of Wilkinson County.* Macon, Ga.: J. W. Burke Co., 1930.

Department of Education. *Area Vocational-Technical Schools.* Atlanta: Division of Vocational Education, 1966.

—— *Educational Progress in Georgia 1955-1965.* Atlanta: Research and Statistical Services Division, 1966.

—— *Handbook, Georgia Council on Teacher Education.* Atlanta: Division of Instruction, 1961.

—— *How Georgia Operates Its Schools.* Atlanta: Division of Public Information, 1961.

—— *Imagination at Work.* Atlanta: Division of Public Information, 1962.

—— *Requirements and Regulations for Certification of Teachers and School Leaders.* Atlanta: Division of Instruction, 1962.

—— *Schoolhouse Story.* Atlanta: Division of Administration, 1955.

—— *Time for a New Breakthrough in Education in Georgia.* Atlanta: Division of Administration, 1963.

Department of Education, Division of Instruction. *Georgia Council on Teacher Education.* Atlanta: The Department, 1961.

Jones, C. E. *Education in Georgia.* Washington, D.C.: Government Printing Office, 1889.

Knight, Lucian Lamar. *A Standard History of Georgia and Georgians.* 6 vols. Chicago and New York: The Lewis Publishing Co., 1917.

Orr, Dorothy. *A History of Education in Georgia.* Chapel Hill: University of North Carolina Press, 1950.

Singleton, Gordon G. *State Responsibility for the Support of Education in Georgia.* Contributions to Education No. 181. New York: Teachers College, Columbia University, 1925.

Reports

Aderhold, O. C. *School Leaders Manual, Program of Educational Development for Georgia.* Atlanta: State Department of Education, 1947.

Advisory Committee on Education. *Education in the Forty-Eight States.* Washington, D.C.: Government Printing Office, 1939.

Department of Education. *Annual and Biennial Reports of the State Department of Education, 1876-1964.* Atlanta: The Department.

Education Panel. *A Survey of Public Education of Less Than College Grade in Georgia.* O. C. Aderhold, chairman. Report of the Bureau of Education Research and Field Service. Athens: College of Education, University of Georgia, 1947.

Georgia Accrediting Commission. *Official Bulletin.* Vol. XIV, No. 1. Atlanta: Curtis Printing Co., September 1965.

Governor's Commission To Improve Education. *Educating Georgia's People: Investment in the Future.* Atlanta: Bryant Lithographing Co., 1963.

McClurkin, W. C. *A Survey Report: Organization of School Systems in Georgia.* Nashville: George Peabody College for Teachers, 1965.

Southern States Work Conference on Educational Problems. *Educational Supervision–A Leadership Service.* Tallahassee: Florida Department of Education, 1954.

Southern States Work Conference on School Administrative Problems. *Building a Better South Through Education, Improving Education in the Southern States.* Bulletin No. 3. Tallahassee: Florida Department of Education, 1943.

State School Building Authority, State of Georgia. *A Progress Report with Facts and Figures.* Atlanta: Foote & Davies, 1957.

Articles and Periodicals

Allman, J. I. "Financing a Minimum Term and a Minimum Salary." *Georgia Education Journal,* XXIX, No. 4 (December 1936), 21.

Atlanta Constitution. June 27, July 3, 18, 1919; January 11, 12, March 4, 29, 1935; February 9, 1945.

Atlanta Journal. January 12, February 15, 1937; February 24, March 4, 1945.

Owens, Ted R. "Certification and the Teacher." *Georgia Education Journal,* LVI (January 1963), 9.

Perkins, Mary Ellen. "The Georgia Council on Teacher Education." *Georgia Education Journal,* LVI (November 1962), 14.

Schreiber, Daniel. "School Dropout." *Georgia Education Journal,* LV (April 1962), 17.

Stephens, Jerome. "Politics and the Teacher." *Georgia Education Journal,* LV (May 1962), 12.

Still, Florrie. "Georgia Association of Visiting Teachers–A Brief History." *Georgia Education Journal,* LX (October 1966), 18.

Tattnall Journal. Editorial, June 15, 1916; September 19, 1918.

Unpublished Material

Hodges, Carl V. "A Study of Concepts of the Role of the Board of Education." Unpublished Ph.D. dissertation, University of Georgia, Athens, 1966.

Renfroe, Carl G. "The Growth and Development of Teacher Certification in Georgia." Unpublished Ph.D. dissertation, University of Georgia, Athens, 1964.

Steelman, Peggy S. "Growth and Development of the Georgia Education Association." Unpublished Ph.D. dissertation, University of Georgia, Athens, 1966.

Usher, George Ephriam. "Development of the Georgia Education Association." Unpublished master's thesis, Duke University, Durham, North Carolina, 1935.

Wiggins, Sam P. "Georgia Teacher Education Councils and Pre-Service Education: 1933-1951." Unpublished Ph.D. dissertation, George Peabody College for Teachers, Nashville, Tennessee, 1952.

Williams, Joseph A. "A Proposed Method of Distributing State School Funds for Public Education of Less Than College Grade for the Purpose of More Nearly Equalizing Educational Opportunities in Georgia." Unpublished Ph.D. dissertation, University of Georgia, Athens, 1948.

Other Sources

Georgia State Department of Education. Personal interviews with state school superintendent and division directors, December 1965 and February 1966.

Sanders, Carl E. Paper read at the dedication of educational TV station, Wrens, Georgia, October 11, 1966.

Appendix A

GEORGIA CHIEF STATE SCHOOL OFFICERS

1871-72	John R. Lewis
1872-86	Gustavus J. Orr
1887-90	James S. Hook
1891-93	Samuel D. Bradwell
1894-1901	Gustavus R. Glenn
1902-1906	William B. Merritt
1907-10	Jere M. Pound
1910-22	Marion L. Brittain
1922-23	Marvin M. Parks
1923-24	Nathaniel H. Ballard
1925-27	Fort E. Land
1927-33	Mell L. Duggan
1933-58	Mauney D. Collins
1958-65	Claude L. Purcell
1966-	Jack P. Nix

Appendix B

Chart I.--GEORGIA DEPARTMENT OF EDUCATION, 1959

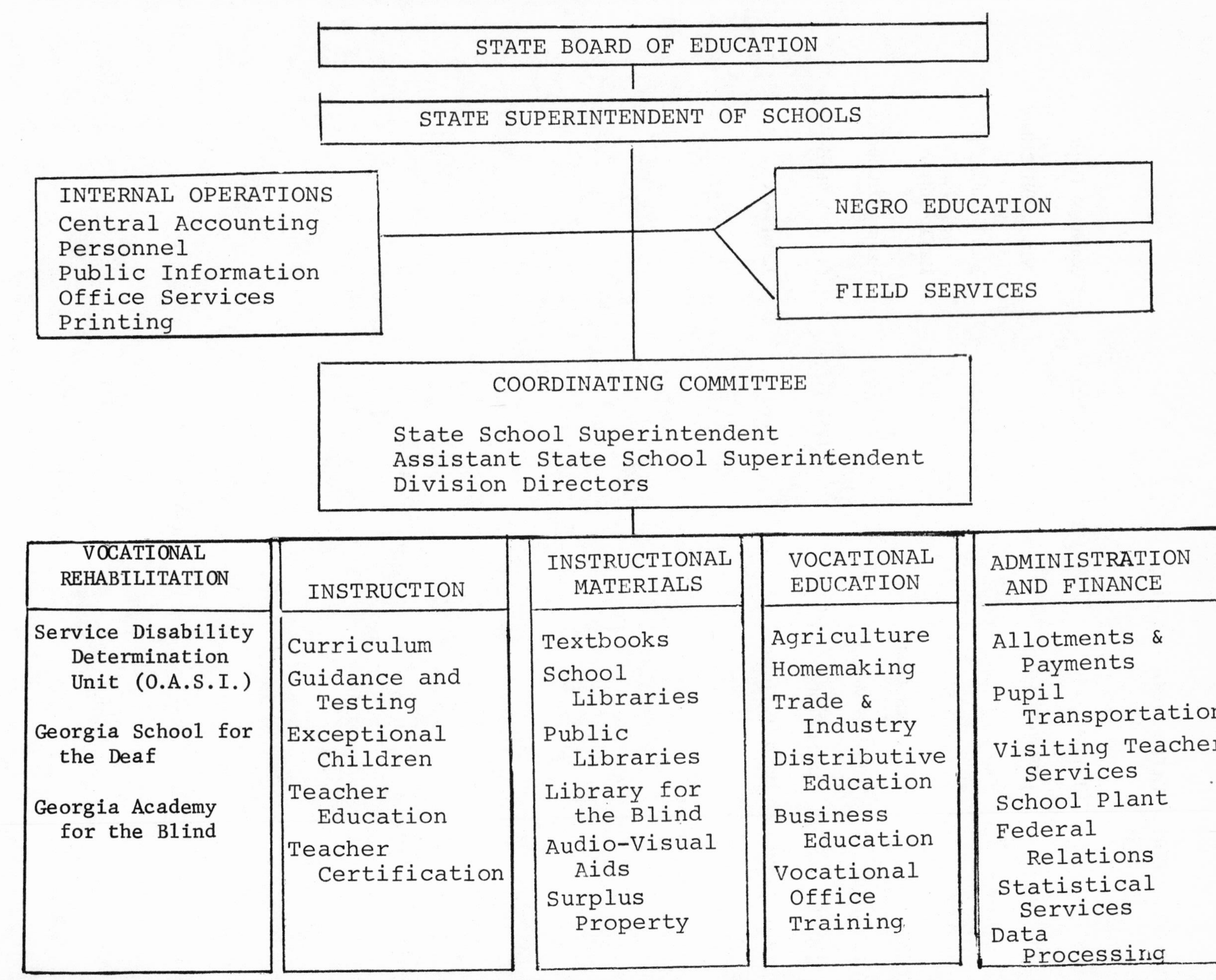

Appendix B

Chart II.--GEORGIA DEPARTMENT OF EDUCATION, CIRCA 1967

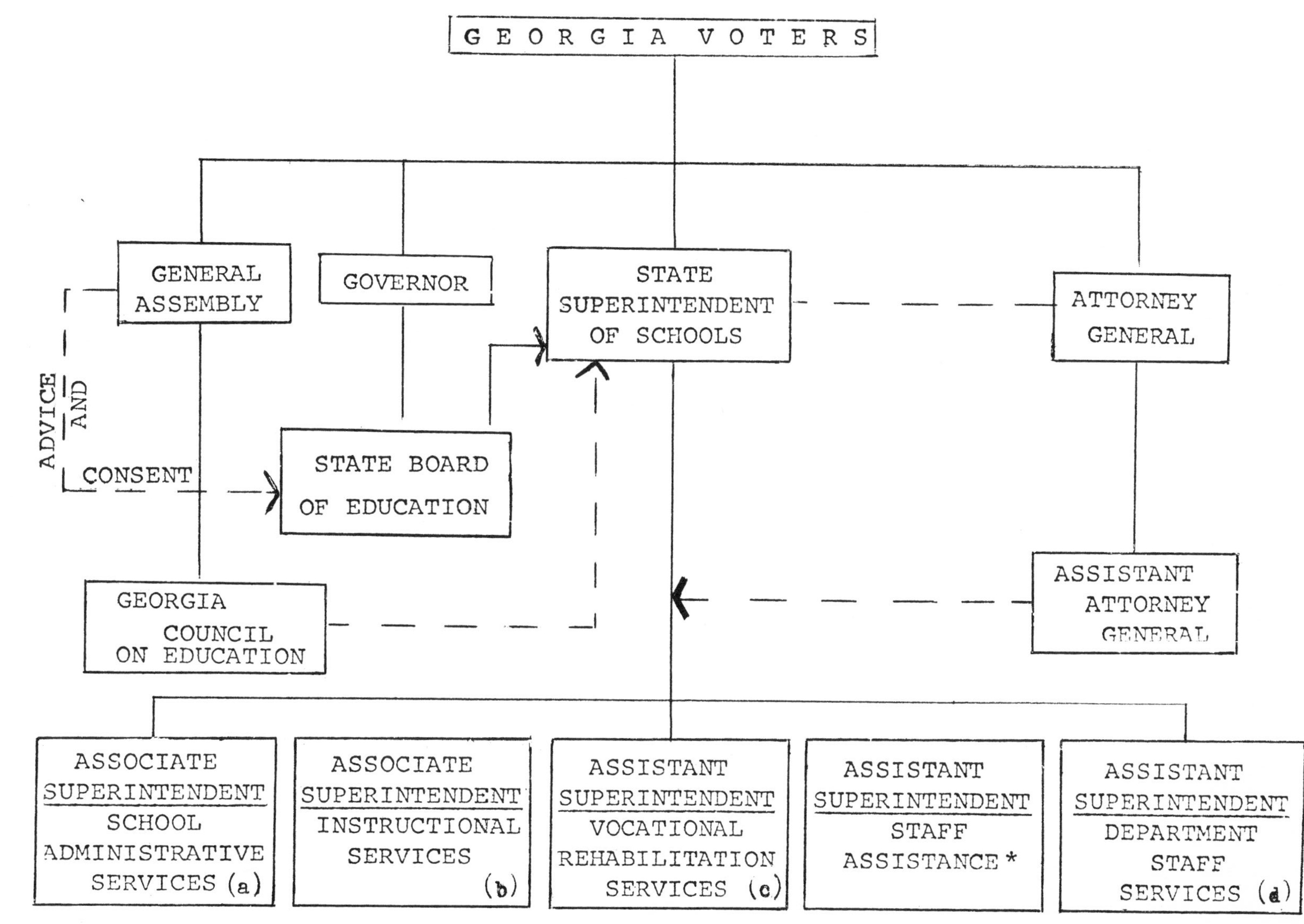

*The Office of the Assistant Superintendent is the only unit under this Office at the present time.

See Charts II(a) through II(d) for details of organization.

Appendix B

Chart II(a)

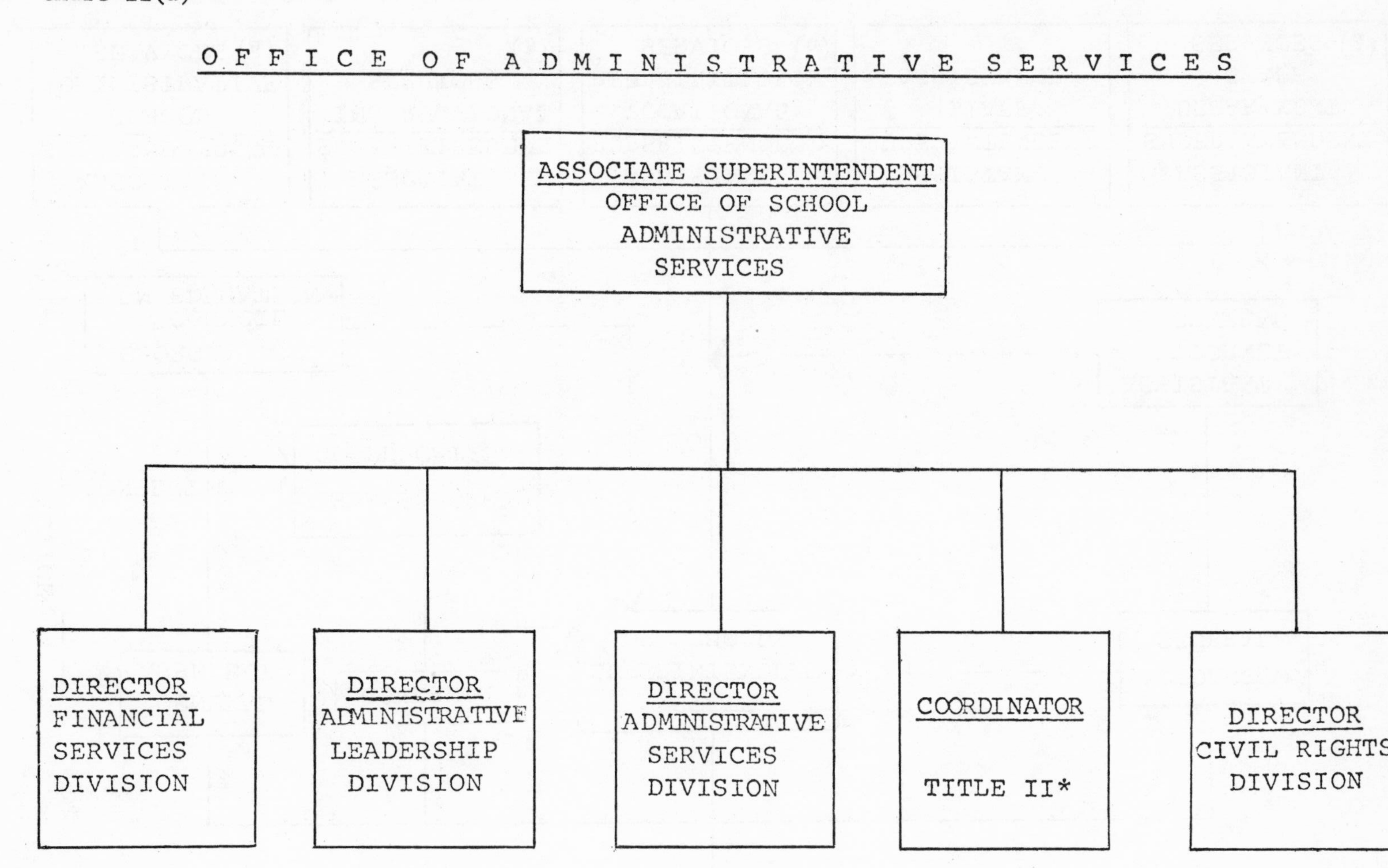

*Of the National Elementary and Secondary Education Act of 1965 (P.L. 89-10).

Appendix B

Chart II(b)

OFFICE OF INSTRUCTIONAL SERVICES

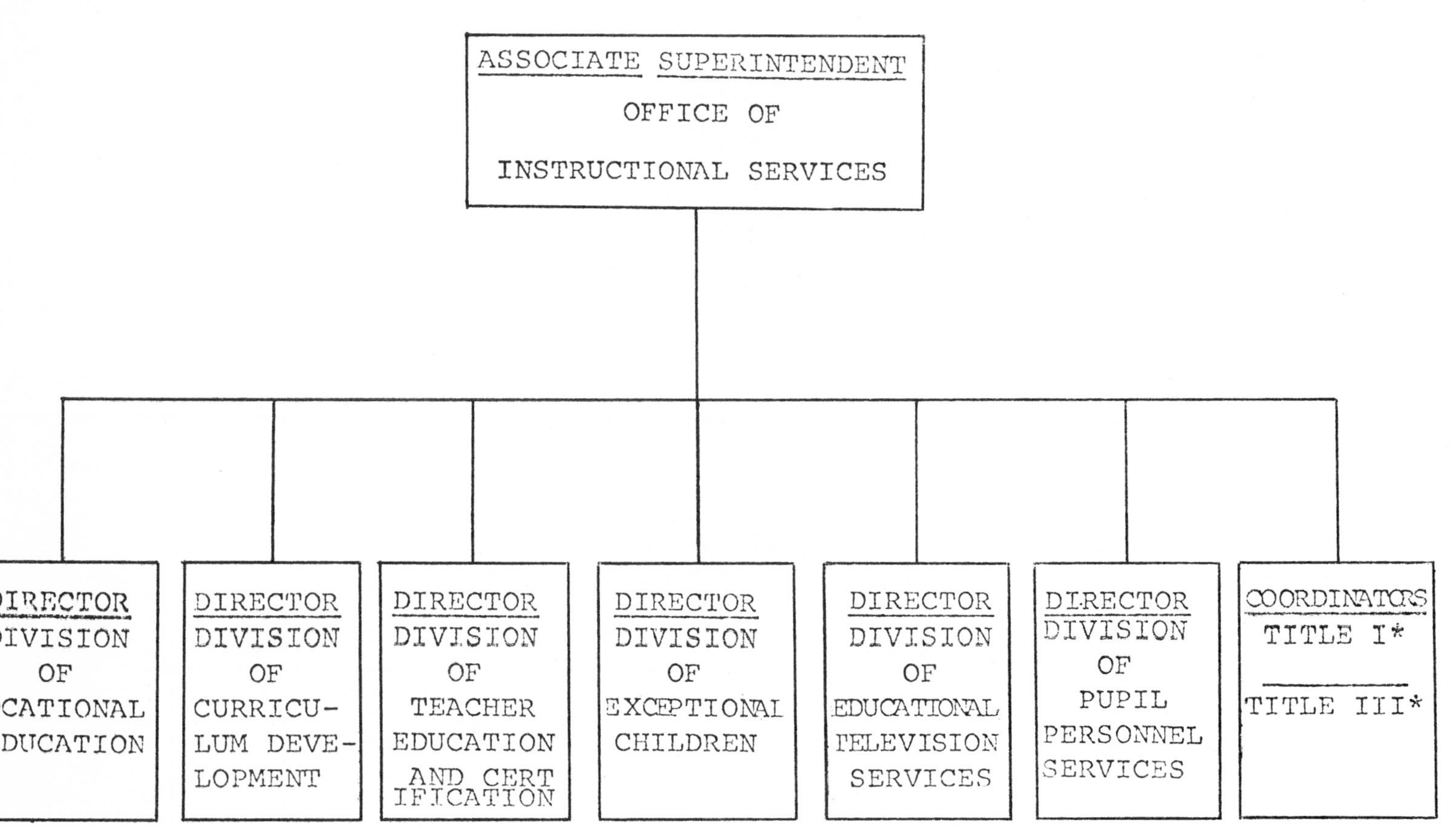

*Of National Elementary and Secondary Education Act of 1965 (P.L. 89-10).

Appendix B

Chart II(c)

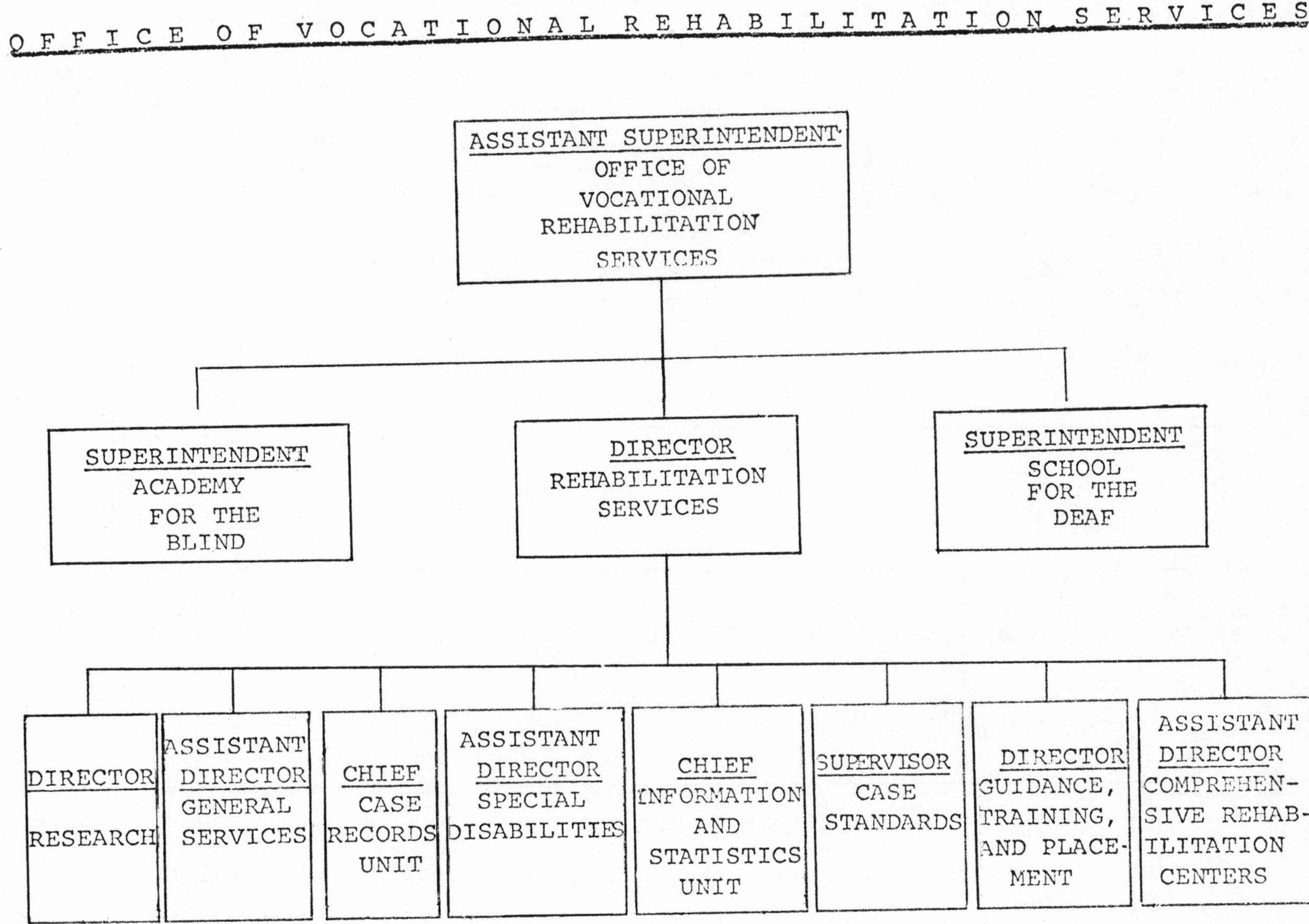

Appendix B

Chart II(d)

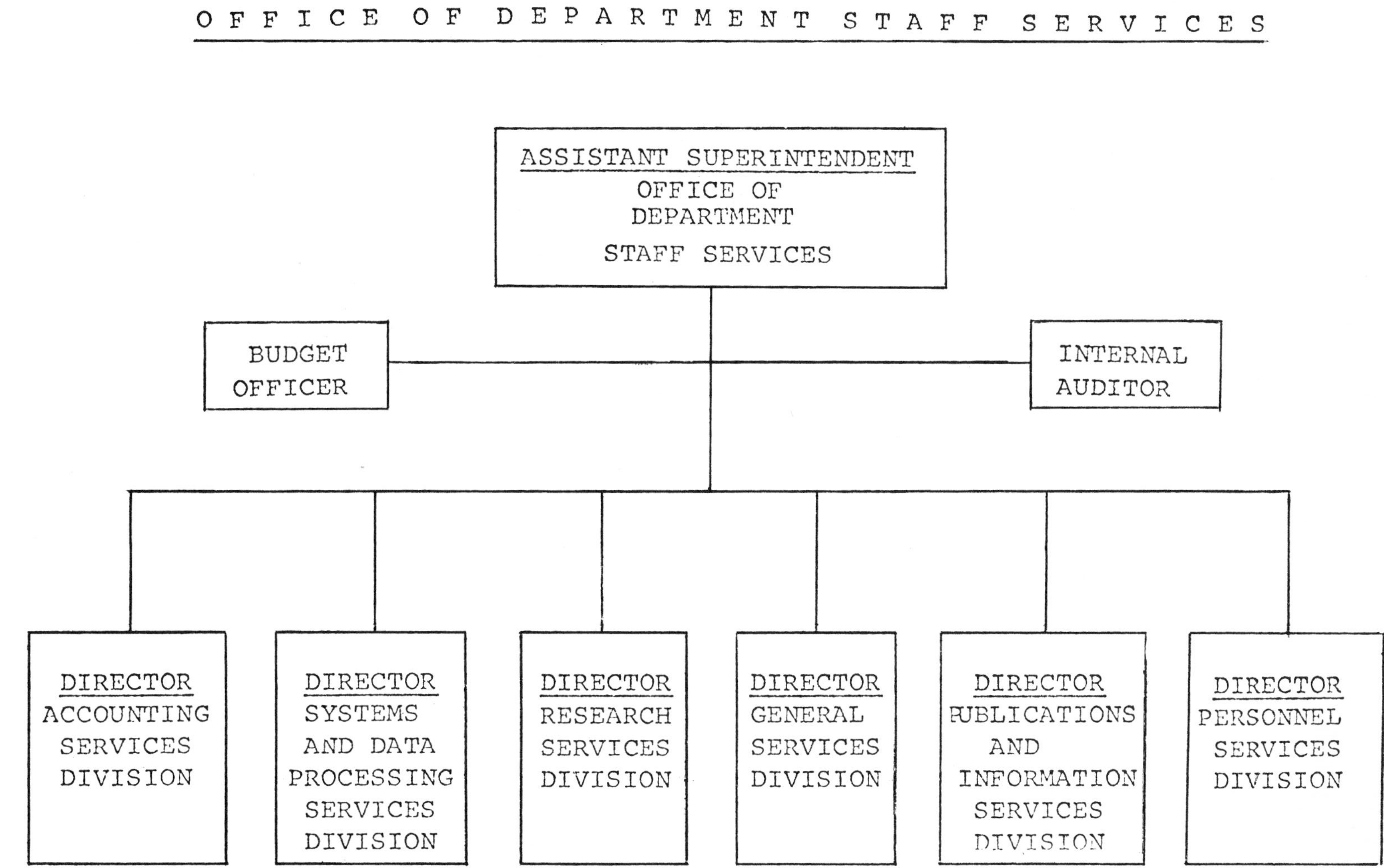

Appendix B

Supplement 1.--SIGNIFICANT SERVICES OFFERED BY GEORGIA DEPARTMENT OF EDUCATION

Unit or Service	Date Begun	Authorization
Pupil Transportation	1919	Legislative Act
School Plant Services	1919	Legislative Act
Vocational Rehabilitation	1920	State and Federal Legislation
Curriculum Development	1933	State Board of Education policy
Textbooks	1936	Acts 1931
State Teachers Salary Schedule	1937	Legislative Act
School Library Services	1937	Legislative Act
Public Library Services	1943	Legislative Act
School Food Services	1943	State Board of Education policy
Guidance, Counseling & Testing	1944	State and Federal Legislation
Visiting Teacher Services	1945	Legislative Acts
Surplus Property	1945	Public Law 91, 1919
Health Education Services	1945	Legislative Act
Exceptional Children's Services	1951	State Board of Education policy
Public Information Service	1951	State Board of Education policy
Adult Education Services	1951	Legislative Act
Alcohol Education	1951	Legislative Act
Library for the Blind	1951	State Board of Education policy
Educational Television	1956	State Board of Education policy
Teacher Scholarship Program	1959	State Constitution
Data-Processing Services	1960	State Board of Education policy
Governor's Honors Program	1964	Legislative Act
School Audit and Review Services	1964	Legislative Act

Appendix C

Table 1.–GEORGIA PUBLIC SCHOOLS: STATE APPROPRIATION FOR EDUCATION, 1871-1924

Year	Amount	Year	Amount
1871	$ 174,107.00	1898	$1,640,361.00
1872	0	1899	1,398,122.00
1873	250,000.00	1900	1,440,642.00
1874	265,000.00	1901	1,505,127.00
1875	151,304.00	1902	1,615,052.00
1876	149,464.99	1903	1,538,955.00
1877	150,225.00	1904	1,591,471.00
1878	154,378.00	1905	1,735,713.00
1879	155,264.00	1906	1,711,844.00
1880	150,789.00	1907	1,786,688.00
1881	196,317.00	1908	2,000,000.00
1882	272,754.00	1909	2,250,000.00
1883	282,221.00	1910	2,250,000.00
1884	305,520.00	1911	2,500,000.00
1885	502,115.00	1912	2,550,000.00
1886	312,292.00	1913	2,550,000.00
1887	489,008.00	1914	2,550,000.00
1888	330,113.00	1915	2,550,000.00
1889	490,708.00	1916	2,700,000.00
1890	638,656.00	1917	2,700,000.00
1891	935,611.00	1918	3,200,000.00
1892	951,700.00	1919	3,500,000.00
1893	1,021,512.00	1920	4,000,000.00
1894	937,874.00	1921	4,500,000.00
1895	1,266,707.00	1922	4,250,000.00
1896	1,161,052.00	1923	4,250,000.00
1897	1,169,945.00	1924	4,500,000.00

Appendix C

Table 2. – GEORGIA PUBLIC SCHOOLS, 1925-65

Year	State Appropriation For Education	Enrollment	ADA	Number Teachers	Number Schools	Pupils Transported	Maintenance and Operation				Capital Outlay Local Sale of Bonds
							Local	State	Federal	Total	
1925-26	$ 4,502,000.00	694,545	489,586	17,756	7,317	46,607	$	$	$	$	$
1926-27	5,003,000.00	692,907	513,017	17,881	7,158	52,382	...	...	...	...	...
1927-28	5,003,200.00	720,087	544,093	19,231	6,977	65,255	...	...	...	...	...
1928-29	6,562,334.00	714,394	535,196	19,263	6,855	69,760	...	...	...	...	...
1929-30	6,597,198.00	723,005	543,637	19,449	6,600	77,762	...	...	...	...	...
1930-31	7,458,002.00	737,755	549,062	19,994	6,508	81,147	...	...	...	...	...
1931-32	7,537,271.00	751,397	577,353	20,019	6,464	103,178	...	...	...	...	...
1932-33	7,037,970.27	757,830	580,979	20,255	6,406	---	...	...	...	...	...
1933-34	6,987,032.40	781,477	589,297	20,056	6,269	124,696	...	...	...	...	...
1934-35	7,123,921.01	759,596	595,692	19,967	6,194	---	...	...	...	...	...
1935-36	7,392,073.46	741,170	580,691	20,783	6,149	---	...	...	...	...	...
1936-37	12,448,803.20	772,613	595,131	20,999	6,072	---	...	...	...	...	...
1937-38	14,457,132.80	789,511	572,386	22,276	5,903	144,793	...	...	...	...	...
1938-39	14,448,420.64	807,522	604,745	22,852	5,730	173,931	...	...	...	...	...
1939-40	14,713,587.06	779,918	587,543	22,779	5,554	174,684	9,207,873.23	14,505,091.07	698,214.90	24,411,179.20	...
1940-41	20,303,120.00	782,929	582,654	22,172	5,470	170,781	8,505,397.04	14,899,568.80	1,576,829.99	24,981,795.83	...
1941-42	15,506,400.00	769,835	577,875	21,912	5,221	177,734	8,703,578.94	14,435,566.35	1,346,433.58	24,485,578.87	...
1942-43	18,893,893.05	757,216	546,633	22,871	5,121	179,361	9,758,282.86	17,585,242.62	1,470,277.57	28,813,803.05	...
1943-44	17,995,210.50	728,457	516,463	22,754	5,015	168,135	10,775,369.86	17,233,162.70	2,316,780.29	30,325,312.85	...
1944-45	21,348,000.00	718,208	546,480	22,344	4,862	---	11,270,407.29	19,833,840.36	3,256,889.59	34,361,137.24	...
1945-46	21,968,000.00	745,892	563,653	22,484	4,745	188,733	13,670,477.97	18,518,773.20	4,160,445.07	36,349,696.24	303,654.12
1946-47	31,656,681.65	746,299	579,618	22,664	4,622	202,403	17,049,440.16	31,121,582.16	4,391,749.60	52,562,771.92	3,918,452.40
1947-48	37,250,000.00	743,201	582,255	22,481	4,299	215,768	19,259,656.45	34,553,622.48	4,416,472.63	58,229,751.56	2,352,384.38
1948-49	41,508,500.00	752,046	597,895	23,500	4,239	226,826	20,309,695.35	36,915,869.21	4,320,235.28	61,545,799.84	7,378,275.96
1949-50	50,100,000.00	769,961	619,846	23,766	3,906	246,903	24,326,758.18	46,129,291.65	5,208,920.53	75,664,970.36	7,332,500.36
1950-51	50,300,000.00	787,580	628,186	24,362	3,572	263,415	26,947,341.00	49,976,807.15	4,770,643.53	81,694,791.68	8,659,504.16
1951-52	86,863,804.00	806,243	637,529	26,153	3,290	290,537	30,187,383.40	65,162,776.73	5,689,194.04	101,039,354.17	2,569,701.32
1952-53	93,842,967.00	834,236	671,016	27,358	3,113	317,992	32,052,016.54	75,961,406.67	5,771,227.55	113,784,650.76	11,104,162.48
1953-54	95,153,704.60	863,761	705,712	28,081	2,998	336,205	33,576,361.72	77,436,040.12	5,547,055.99	116,559,457.83	5,433,303.36
1954-55	104,979,418.72	892,467	737,678	28,735	2,864	356,721	35,806,118.80	81,239,637.61	5,442,577.98	122,488,334.39	6,743,777.35
1955-56	117,102,091.35	917,265	747,012	29,687	2,480	374,933	38,150,315.32	95,881,073.10	5,514,369.70	139,545,758.12	4,634,722.29
1956-57	124,170,000.00	939,104	761,953	30,714	2,177	396,184	44,071,978.25	101,623,151.96	7,669,373.99	153,364,504.20	13,214,185.02
1957-58	134,733,509.73	960,411	770,959	31,326	2,119	408,701	50,181,992.76	109,677,585.36	8,336,533.03	168,196,111.15	14,975,745.43
1958-59	143,536,915.45	981,223	807,915	32,281	1,940	425,942	52,597,177.06	120,497,976.90	8,752,083.01	181,847,236.97	13,737,416.88
1959-60	151,910,000.00	1,000,759	820,995	33,302	1,930	436,079	59,950,326.30	126,444,175.07	11,029,805.53	197,424,306.90	17,247,591.12
1960-61	170,926,323.88	1,023,241	847,516	34,102	1,938	444,903	62,202,719.47	138,941,893.01	12,355,917.72	213,500,530.20	8,236,910.51
1961-62	183,045,000.00	1,045,316	871,773	35,209	1,929	456,597	69,944,266.82	150,889,936.93	11,852,479.62	232,686,683.37	8,737,473.92
1962-63	196,192,976.82	1,076,200	897,847	36,504	1,929	471,019	76,710,734.14	163,105,791.66	14,151,775.33	253,968,301.13	40,390,006.99
1963-64	208,955,410.88	1,107,470	930,723	37,822	1,942	484,313	86,403,974.80	174,831,714.77	15,522,510.13	276,758,199.70	14,781,685.59
1964-65	233,786,836.65	1,127,046	952,691	39,635	1,944	495,275	91,277,036.00	194,479,945.12	18,433,971.36	304,190,952.48	15,356,793.00
1965-66	262,139,555.58	1,142,544	966,737	42,237	1,926	505,888					

Appendix C

Table 3. – GEORGIA PUBLIC SCHOOLS: SCHOOL BOND ELECTIONS, 1959 THROUGH 1966

Year	"Amount passed"
1959-60	$ 15,422,000
1960-61	20,610,000
1961-62	15,863,000
1962-63	45,496,000
1963-64	18,586,600
1964-65	16,852,000
1965-66	46,025,000
7-year total	$178,854,600

NOTES:

1. The total outstanding school bonds as of June 30, 1966, amounted to $237,349,046, or 57.7 percent total bonding capacity ($411,136,394).

2. Of all outstanding school bonds ($237,349,046) as of June 30, 1966, 75.4 percent ($178,854,600) have been passed in the last 7 years.

Table 4. – GEORGIA PUBLIC SCHOOLS: STATE SCHOOL BUILDING AUTHORITY, SCHOOL BOND ISSUES

Year	Date	Amount
1952-A	October 1952	$ 32,097,000
1953-A	September 1953	63,300,000
1954-A	March 1954	32,512,000
1955	May 1955	29,238,000
1961	October 1961	31,452,000
1962	June 1962	26,600,000
1964	November 1964	27,905,000
1965	April 1965	27,030,000
1966	September 1966	32,125,000
	Total	$302,259,000

Table 5. – GEORGIA PUBLIC SCHOOLS: FEDERAL FUNDS, 1957-65

For current operation (P. L. 874)	Year	For construction (P. L. 815)
$ 3,557,308.79	1957-58	$ 807,057.48
3,605,111.81	1958-59	473,505.37
4,576,471.71	1959-60	1,057,247.00
5,088,384.38	1960-61	1,251,883.90
5,200,616.58	1961-62	1,015,588.15
6,851,640.82	1962-63	245,067.82
6,830,276.14	1963-64	598,907.56
7,793,236.00	1964-65	1,907,177.00
$43,503,046.23	Total	$7,356,434.28

Appendix C

Table 6. – GEORGIA PUBLIC SCHOOLS: CAPITAL OUTLAY, 1949-65

Year	Local capital outlay (S-18)	State dept. outlay	SSBA construction fund	Total capital outlay
1949-50	$10,602,988.52	$ . . .	$ . . .	$10,602,988.52
1950-51	16,030,370.82	. . .	. . .	16,030,370.82
1951-52	14,486,866.34	. . .	36,754.19	14,523,620.53
1952-53	16,996,427.54	. . .	3,355,808.72	20,352,236.26
1953-54	20,400,601.95	. . .	20,111,247.74	40,511,849.69
1954-55	14,482,743.02	20,624.08	41,733,310.68	56,236,677.78
1955-56	17,625,450.45	73,642.04	43,226,790.19	60,925,882.68
1956-57	16,555,141.98	79,318.67	32,452,373.69	49,086,834.34
1957-58	21,729,736.98	155,803.83	17,656,162.39	39,541,703.20
1958-59	17,914,230.85	112,324.44	4,919,480.90	22,946,036.19
1959-60	20,042,224.49	445,228.88	1,465,500.14	21,952,953.51
1960-61	24,025,845.43	60,685.23	650,377.86	24,736,908.52
1961-62	21,906,419.37	561,725.79	2,959,608.09	25,427,753.25
1962-63	25,111,814.19	24,486.87	23,817,360.55	48,953,661.61
1963-64	36,223,780.49	716,607.19	17,209,004.55	54,149,392.23
1964-65	44,131,658.00	512,065.65	18,562,149.08	63,205,872.73

11 Hawaii

DEPARTMENT OF EDUCATION
James R. Hunt

Contents

INTRODUCTION

A brief history of education in Hawaii is a formidable task. In any consideration of Hawaii's educational history, one must trace its centralization from the days of the monarchy to the present, when Hawaii is a sovereign state of the United States of America. The approach taken in this paper has been to review the accomplishments of the various administrators under the monarchy, the 18 territorial superintendents of education, and the 5 superintendents since Hawaii achieved statehood (see Appendix A). In some cases, the acting superintendents have been included when they continued an administration's policies so that they are essentially and historically one.

THE MONARCHICAL PERIOD

Beginnings of Public Education

Christian missionaries initiated in 1820 the first attempts to bring formal education to the people of Hawaii. The missionaries possessed an unbounded zeal for education, the primary goal of which, they believed, was to serve God. They worked diligently and produced the first textbook with a Hawaiian alphabet in 1822. "Four years later, there were 400 native teachers, and by 1830, one third of the population was enrolled in schools" (1). Formal public education in Hawaii in terms of codified law had been launched.

The period from 1820 to 1840 was one of a loosely organized school system operated by the missionaries, but none the less a school system. After much development and refinement, it provided the basis for the statewide school system. Hawaii is and has been unique, and it follows that its institutions are and have been unique. Thus, the central administering of schools in the entire kingdom was the result "of the slow building upon foundations already laid by the American Protestant missionaries" (2).

The islands of Hawaii have been a monarchy, a republic, a territory, and a state, each with a highly centralized form of government. Formal educational policies and practices were directed and disseminated from the central hub of government. Although local educationists have influenced the central authority, the existence of a highly centralized administration of schools and the educational enterprise is a basic consideration in understanding the uniqueness of educational institutions in Hawaii.

The fact of central administration and control did not diminish the growth and development of democratic education in Hawaii. In fact, it created a school system which provides a high degree of equal opportunity for education and an integration that has not been achieved by any of the other states. While local educational interests are indistinct at one period of educational history and quite distinct at another, no attempt has been made to separate state issues from local issues because the constitution was adopted many decades later. Before 1840, all laws, including school laws, were enacted somewhat informally in the main by the missionaries and ruling chiefs. The king and the nobles enacted the *fundamental law* of Hawaii, but these were not formally codified. The first laws printed in the Hawaiian language appeared in 1822 and related to the harbor of Honolulu. Other laws, relating to murder, theft, and other crimes, were published in 1824.

The period from 1840 to 1845 saw the beginning of formal public education in Hawaii in terms of codified laws. In October 1840, King Kamehameha III enacted the first public school laws. The previous year, on June 7, the king and nobles approved a general law which included a section on schools under the title of "The Business of Females," but this law was simply an expression that it was the business of females to teach children to read, understand, and write, and to teach other subjects to guide children in good behavior. This expression was later incorporated into the law as reenacted in November 1840 as follows:

> This is the appropriate business of all the females of these islands; to teach the children to read, cipher, and write, and other branches of learnings, to subject the children to good parental and school laws, to guide the children to right behavior, and place them in schools, that they may do better than their parents. But if the parents do not understand reading, then let them commit the instruction of their children to those who do understand it, and let the parents support the teacher, inasmuch as they feel an interest in their children, let them feel an

> interest in the teacher too. But if any woman do not conduct according to the requirements of this section, then let her return to the labor of her landlord as in former times, to such labor however as is appropriate to women. The tax officers will look to and manage this business (3).

The missionaries, in a further effort to give a firmer base to education, urged the king to adopt a constitution for the kingdom. This would not only provide the foundation for a stabilized political society, but would include educational laws as part of the social and political framework. The first public school laws of October 1840, which followed the Constitution of 1840, imposed compulsory attendance on all children through the age of 14 years. This provided the basis for a modern statewide school system—an American school system established long before many existed on the mainland. An "extraordinary feature of the Hawaiian educational plan is that in a land far removed in the Pacific it did become typically American and the transformation was achieved even before the islands themselves became American soil" (4).

The public school laws of 1840 further provided that a school was to be established in any village where there were 15 or more children. "Each community was to select a school committee of three, which would act with the local missionary—interpreted by officials as Protestant—and the tax collector in the selection of a suitable teacher" (5). The committee was given the authority to set the teachers' salaries and establish the tax in the community to support the school. Land was to be set aside, and the teachers and parents would work this land to meet the taxes required. "Parents failing to meet their obligations were to be fined. Attendance was made compulsory for children from four to fourteen years of age. Dismissal of a teacher was the prerogative of the school committee and the missionary" (6).

The public school law enacted in May 1841 repealed the provisions of the school laws enacted in October 1840, preserving some of the original sections but rewriting others. For instance, the law continued to require villages with 15 or more children to procure a teacher and inaugurate a school. If there were less than 15 children in the village, the law required their fathers to unite with another company nearby.

To select the teacher for a school, the parents of a village were to choose a committee of three from their number. The law was not definite as to how many teachers would be selected, stating that if there were but "few" children, there would be one; if "more," then two teachers; and if the children were "numerous," there should be three or more teachers as the committee "should think best."

The committee was responsible for negotiating with the teacher the wages to be paid. The teacher could be given land instead of wages or to supplement his wages, but he was to have use of it only as long as he remained on the job. When he ceased to serve as teacher, the land reverted to the government. If he did receive additional support, it was to be paid from the yearly tax, but not from the poll tax.

The 1841 law further provided for the Legislature to appoint annually "certain men of intelligence" as general school agents, one for Hawaii, one for Maui, one for Molokai, one for Oahu, one for Kauai ,and one superintendent of the whole. It was the general school agent's responsibility to certify the teachers. The criteria were specified as follows:

> Furthermore, it shall not be proper for the general school agent to give the teacher's certificate to ignorant persons, nor to persons known to be vicious or immoral. If a man can read, write and understands geography and arithmetic, and is a quiet and moral man, and desires a teacher's certificate, it shall be the duty of the school agent to give him one, and not refuse (7).

Comparing the 1840 and 1841 laws, Wist says that "the word 'missionary' was replaced by the word 'school agent.' Employment and dismissal of teachers were hereafter to be the responsibility of the school committee and the school agent. Teachers' certificates were to be issued by the agent instead of by Lahainaluna" (8).

The role and responsibility of the school agent was in a very real way the forerunner of the inspector general of the schools and the district superintendents, who were to appear later. Amendments made to the basic school laws in 1842 restated the philosophy of the kingdom regarding education:

> In the estimation of the Nobles and of the Representative Body, schools for the instruction of children in letters are of vast importance. We are firmly determined to give protection to the schools, and also to teachers of good character, and also to treat with great severity all those who oppose schools, or throw hindrances in the way of that business (9).

These amendments gave the school agents additional authority in securing land and regulating the schools, and exhorted that more care be given to administering the school laws of 1841.

These first school laws laid the basis for a superintendent of schools who was to become both the state and local authority. A system of public education had been established in the kingdom that permitted the community to support two types of common schools: one for Protestant children and one for Catholic children.

Actually, when supervision did exist in a school, it was provided somewhat extralegally by the Protestant missionary or the Catholic priest. Besides the three R's, the curriculum included geography and considerable time for religious instruction. The schoolhouses generally were ordinary grass huts, with little or no equipment, and the pupils sat on mats spread over the earthen floor. The tools of learning consisted of a small number of slates and a few books from the mission press (10).

THE SUPERINTENDENCY

In May 1841, under an amendment to the school laws passed the previous year, the Legislature appointed David Malo school agent for Maui and superintendent for the kingdom. A colorful and versatile Hawaiian, Malo was the first to serve as head of the central educational authority. Although he proved to be an excellent school agent and brought about rapid improvement in the schools of Maui, his leadership as a general superintendent was not conspicuous. The school laws gave him "little opportunity for service beyond receiving reports from other agents and making reports annually to the legislature" (11).

By 1842, the school system had been shaped by additional laws. In conjunction with the previous laws, it had established certain basic characteristics, such as the concept of universal education as essential to the well-being of the state, the right of government to legislate for local school organization, and a tax structure to support education. The system acknowledged the right of the state to appoint educational officers and parental responsibility for educating their children. It provided for overall state and district control and supervision of schools. The school system required compulsory school attendance for children. At the same time, it asserted the right of the state to certificate teachers and the right of the state to require an accounting for the educational program. It also acknowledged the right of the state to punish those who do not comply with educational laws, and defined education as a requirement for marriage and holding certain public offices.

The Organic Law, passed in October 1845, established the minister of public instruction as one of five major departments of government. William Richards, who held this position for only 1 year due to his untimely death, was the first appointed to the position. In the first annual report, read before His Majesty to the Hawaiian Legislature, August 1, 1846, Richards summarized the educational effort from 1822 to August 1, 1846. The following chart shows the number of students out of the total population who were enrolled in the schools, although Richards admitted it was based on imperfect returns.

Islands	Learners	Writing	Reading	Arithmetic	Geography
Hawaii	6,319	3,312	1,517	2,926	1,537
Maui	4,897	2,587	1,234	2,287	1,004
Oahu	2,974	1,761	793	1,513	788
Kauai	1,203	625	350	642	317
Total	15,393	3,285	3,894	7,368	3,666

In the various Catholic schools throughout the islands, according to returns furnished by the Reverend Abbé Maigret, there were 1,800 readers, 1,000 additional learners, and 600 enrolled not attending school, making in the whole 3,400 (12).

In his report to the king the following year, 1847, Richards pointed to the Organic Act of 1846, which took effect the previous September and organized the department (see Appendix D). The act conferred on the minister of public instruction the power to administer oaths and to "superintend the moral and intellectual well being of all who reside within the jurisdiction of this kingdom, and in an especial manner of all children within the age of legal majority" (13). He was appointed the guardian and protector of the youth and pupils attending the legalized schools, and charged with seeing that they enjoyed all of the privileges under the laws. He also was made responsible for seeing that parents and guardians performed certain duties prescribed in regard to education and good morals. He was to inform those guilty of improprieties set forth in the law that they might be punished as prescribed by the criminal code.

The Organic Act specifically forbade the minister from interfering in the religious beliefs or mode of Christian worship of individuals in the kingdom. He was directed to avoid official interference with the parents or guardians in relation to the doctrinal opinions of the children. He could not show "official partiality towards one denomination of Christians to the prejudice of another in the conferring of offices or of licenses to teach" (14). However, Section VI stated:

> The religion of our Lord and Saviour Jesus Christ shall continue to be the established national religion of the Hawaiian Islands. The laws of Kamehameha III, orally proclaimed, abolishing all idol worship and ancient heathenish customs are hereby continued in force, and said worship and customs are forbidden to be practiced in this kingdom upon the pains and penalties to be prescribed in the criminal code (15).

Chapter III of the Organic Act provided for dividing the Hawaiian Islands into school districts and for the appointment of general district superintendents, and it established certification of teachers by these district superintendents. The minister of public instruction was to recommend to His Majesty an individual for appointment as a general superintendent of schools. It further provided for 24 subagents to supervise the public and private schools. Parents were to participate in the selection of the subagents by making their wishes known to the minister of public instruction, who was directed to consider them (16).

The section of the Organic Act dealing with certification of teachers was the first legal provision for certification of teachers in Hawaii. The law empowered the superintendents to license teachers within their districts, after they had been examined on the principles and branches of education, and according to the rules established by the council. But the law conferred on the minister of public instruction the power to disallow the licenses for good cause, and to order them revoked. Section IV of the law gave the precise form to be followed:

TEACHER'S CERTIFICATE

Island of ________________
District No. ____ Hawaiian Islands.

________ having exhibited evidence of good moral character, and having been duly examined and found to be versed in the rudiments of general education, and particularly versed in (here insert the particular branches in which he is versed) I do hereby license him to teach any of said branches of education within this district so long as he conforms to the requirements of the law and observes the general rules laid down by the minister of public instruction.

Given under my hand this__day of__, 18_

________________________,
General superintendent for the district No.__ (17).

Since this law was so detailed and was to provide legal precedents for education in years to come, the remaining sections, dealing with finances, school building (repair and maintenance), and supervision, are included in Appendix D.

In reviewing the administration of the law in his annual report of 1847, Richards pointed out that the general superintendents had appointed their subagents, according to law, and the schools had been "organized under the direction of these agents and under newly licensed teachers" (18). He reported the enrollment of students, divided as follows: Hawaii, 6,805; Maui, 5,308; Molokai, 1,243; Oahu, 3,790; Kauai, 1,401; Niihau, 47. Total expenses for operating the schools (including schoolhouses) from April 1846 to the end of April 1847 amounted to $40,000.

Richards ended his 1847 report by summarizing his views on education:

> Schools constitute one of the great instrumentalities in raising up the people. All enlightened nations now take this view of the subject. So great importance do they attach to the subject that committees are appointed in one nation to visit another and report the improvements made. The amount of property expended in support of the schools is immense: in the State of Massachusetts there is annually expended more than a million dollars for education. . . . In the State of New York, the amount is much more than this.
>
> We may, therefore, rest assured, that in our exertions to improve, multiply and support schools, we are but imitating the example of all enlightened nations (19).

William Richards died in November 1847, and Keoni Ana (John Young, Jr.) became the acting minister of public instruction the following April. Another missionary, Richard Armstrong, who had assisted Keoni Ana, accepted appointement as the new minister in May 1848. In his report in 1850 to the Hawaiian Legislative Council, he asserted that it was important that the head of the department be neutral and "have as little to do as possible, with the general politics of the nation, standing aloof from party strife, should any exist, and devoting his whole time to the one great, good, and noble cause of moral, physical, and intellectual education" (20).

Armstrong reported that in 1849 the Hawaiian school system cost $21,989. Each teacher taught an average of 164 days for an average salary of $31.57, or an average daily wage of slightly over 13¢. "Computing from the same data the average cost of education of each scholar in the common schools was $1.37-1/2 for the year 1849" (21). This amounted to about 8 mills per day for teaching 15,620 native children in the common schools. (See Appendix C for costs of education from 1846 to 1967.)

Armstrong was particularly pleased with the efforts to connect manual labor with the schools. For instance, he pointed out to the legislators that a coffee planter on Kauai, G. Rhodes, Esq., had expressed his gratitude for the minister's request to employ schoolchildren in the gathering of coffee. A letter from Rhodes, dated December 17, 1849, stated that these children had been employed for several hours each day, and had earned a considerable sum of money, which he divided equally among them. Rhodes was particularly pleased that due to the employment of the children, the old coffee pickers, who had struck for higher wages, had all returned (22).

Armstrong continued to encourage this combination of labor and scholarship. He focused on the advantages of this program in his addresses to parents, in instructions to both superintendents and teachers, and in talking to students. Premiums were granted to the most deserving scholars.

The program worked extremely well. In the high schools at Lahainaluna, Hilo, and Waioli, Kauai, and Kohala, students devoted time to labor, thus earning a large portion of their support. Armstrong's pride in the program was evident. When an epidemic of measles, whooping cough, and influenza struck, killing many people, the minister credited the lack of deaths in the schools to the regular daily labor, wholesome food, and rugged constitutions of these students.

Armstrong admitted, however, that the task of inculcating industrious habits in native children was slow and difficult. Unfortunately, the parents did not appreciate industry, and training their children in love of labor proved doubly difficult and necessarily slow. He added, however, that he did not feel discouraged, as his greatest interest was in this field, and he was convinced that, with the help of God, he would persevere (23).

When Richard Armstrong took the census in January 1849 and 1850, he listed the total population of the Islands as 84,165. He stated that "the sum total of the population in January 1849 was 3,861 less than in January 1850" (24).

Armstrong reported in May 1851 that instruction in the Islands was still in the Hawaiian language. But he was responsible for introducing English as the medium of instruction in public education. English schools were established in 1854 under an act of August 10, 1854. Armstrong spoke with pride of the new era in Hawaii's educational history. He was confident that the introduction of the English language to the native race would be one of the distinguishing glories of His Majesty's reign. He reported that "the progress of English schools, under the new Act, has been quite equal if not greater, than the highest expectations of its friends . . . " (25).

In 1855, the ministry of education was abolished and the Board of Education established as the governing body. A Reorganization Act of 1855 gave the Board of Education complete responsibility for the Hawaiian Department of Public Instruction. The act designated the minister of the interior as the chief official through whom reports were to be made to the Legislature and placed education in a subordinate position to other governmental functions. The new board was to be composed of three members—a president and two directors. Richard Armstrong was appointed president of the board, which was to make its own bylaws under its own authority. The powers formerly given to the minister of public instruction and certain powers of the district superintendent were conferred on the new department. The board also was granted the right to fix the salaries of the superintendents, which had formerly been the right of the Legislature.

The Reorganization Act of 1855 set new precedents for education in Hawaii. It separated education from other functions of government, and it established the Board of Education and gave it certain responsibilities that had been vested in the Legislature and to subordinate officials in education. The act provided for a dual board and overall superintendents. One danger inherent in the new organizational structure was that it did not always guarantee professional leadership in the presidency of the board.

In particular, the Reorganization Act empowered the president of the board to report the department's actions to the Legislature each year, through the minister of interior. He was responsible for keeping an office of business at the seat of government, signing all official documents of the board, and employing a clerk. The president promoted the interests of education and morality in the Islands and the general objects of the department (26).

Four years after passing the Reorganization Act, in 1859, the Legislature again made important changes in the codified laws. For one thing, the Legislature itself assumed the right to determine the content of curriculum and took a step toward establishing secondary schools. The codification of the laws in 1859 also included the first codification of education laws. Although previous education laws were repealed, the Legislature provided for most of them to be reenacted, including the administrative reorganization accomplished by the Reorganization Act of 1855.

By 1856, 10,076 scholars were attending the Hawaiian schools. The new Board of Education entered at once upon its duties, held weekly meetings, and, according to Armstrong, "imposed no trifling task upon my colleagues, who are sufficiently burdened by the cares of their respective departments" (27). For one thing, the department expected to begin immediate publication of *Hae Hawaii (Hawaiian Banner)* "devoted to news, politics, moral literature and especially to agriculture" (28), but this was delayed until March 1856.

Armstrong, who continued in the office as minister of education and president of the Board of Education until 1860, earned the title of "Father of American Education in Hawaii." His 12 years of service ended with his death in September 1860.

King Kamehameha V, who had been a member of the three-man Board of Education since its origin in 1855, appointed his father, Mataio Kekuanaoa, as the new president of the Board of Education. Although a man of character and ability, he was an unfortunate choice. Kekuanaoa was handicapped in dealing with the issues because he knew little English, and the pro-British king was able to dominate the board. The lack of professional leadership hindered progress in the public schools (29).

Four years after assuming office, Kekuanaoa advocated that the Legislature establish an inspector general for the school system, who would also serve as chief clerk to the Department of Public Instruction. Kekuanaoa's plan called for this officer to be a practical person, well acquainted with the public schools, who would personally inspect the schools throughout the kingdom. He would assume the president's duties, such as examining teachers, and recommend for certification those whose qualifications met the standard required by the board. In other words, the inspector general of schools would superintend the system under the direction of the Board of Education. The board would remain the same: a president and two honorary members, appointed by the king (30).

This request, and a general realization that the system needed stronger leadership, resulted in the passage of the Reorganization Act of 1865. This act created a Bureau of Public Instruction in place of the Department of Public Instruction, increased the Board of Education from three to five members, reorganized school districts to correspond to taxation divisions, and empowered the Board of Education to appoint a school agent for each district. However, the most important feature of the act permitted the appointment of a professional educator as inspector general of schools.

Kekuanaoa remained as president of the board for 3 more years, but in 1865, Abraham Fornander was appointed as the first inspector general of schools. Fornander, an excellent historian and journalist, did not have the qualifications to be a professional educator. The result was vacillation and little progress. A reformatory school was established at Kapalama, and by 1868, 51 boys and 4 girls had attended.

Period of Transition, 1865 to 1894

The period from 1865 to 1894 was a transitional period in which Hawaii's education system established precedents which made it a truly American system.

In 1869, William P. Kamakau succeeded Kekuanaoa as president of the board, and the board appointed H. Rexford Hitchcock to the position of inspector general of schools. After little progress, Kamakau was replaced by Charles R. Bishop as president of the board in 1872. Bishop, a man imbued with ideals of service, believed in Hawaii and in public education as a means of promoting its social and economic welfare. He held the confidence of both the native Hawaiian and the leading industrialists. While not belonging to the missionary group, he was in no way inimical to its purposes.

Hitchcock was an educator, primarily interested in the improvement of the public school program. In his first official act, he thoroughly investigated the educational system and reported some glaring deficiencies. Particularly, he attacked the inefficiency of the school personnel and the resulting weakness in classroom procedures. He issued a manual of directions to the staff and revived the conventions of Armstrong's time to improve the background and instructional methods of teachers. Under the leadership of these two men, Bishop and Hitchcock, public education in Hawaii, so ably planned and begun by Richard Armstrong, again took on new life (31).

When Hitchcock accepted the principalship of Lahainaluna in 1877, D. Dwight Baldwin, an Island-born educator, succeeded him as inspector general. Like Hitchcock, he deplored the incompetency of the teachers and the difficulties in recruiting able ones, poor attendance, the inadequate supervision, and the indifference of parents—factors which had virtually doomed the manual labor program. He was particularly interested in improving the program of work in the public schools and Americanizing the entire program.

Baldwin visited the United States to familiarize himself with modern educational practices. He substituted American textbooks for those published by the Board of Education in Hawaii. As English became more and more the basic school language, American books naturally replaced the materials in Hawaiian. And during the 1880's, the people began to develop a greater appreciation of the importance of education.

Unfortunately, in 1883, Charles R. Bishop was forced to resign from the Board of Education by political pressures, and the education system again began to lag. He returned as president 4 years later at the same time Alatau T. Atkinson, the former principal of St. Albans College and editor of the *Honolulu Star*, became inspector general. Atkinson proved to be an excellent organizer, and he and Bishop began bringing order to the schools.

In 1887, the Hawaiian system was legally set up with some similarity to American patterns. The law established a lay board of five members, selected at large. The board members, who were to serve without pay, were charged with the responsibility for setting policy and employing an executive officer as the professional head of the system.

By 1890, the Legislature had eliminated the tuition in the public English language schools. This was in part responsible for an increase of 1,236 pupils during the following 2 years, but it also resulted from better accommodations and the growth in number of children of school age (32).

One of the big problems still facing the schools was the shortage of able teachers, particularly in the English language. Bishop, as president of the board, pointed out in his report of 1890 that as English became more commonly used, the difficulties of learning it would diminish. But out of the many who would be fairly well educated in it, only a few would be competent and willing to teach. A knowledge that might well serve in the shop, plantation, or ranch would not be adequate for a teacher.

The work of the inspector had increased as the schools improved. The president's 1890 report included a plea for a deputy inspector. He stated:

> The improvement in the schools during the last two years is apparent to anyone having a knowledge of the facts, and is owing to several causes; better facilities for teaching in the new and well furnished schoolhouses; a larger proportion of competent teachers; and, I think, very largely, if not mainly, to the frequent visits and thorough work of the Inspector. At no time since the reorganization of the Bureau of Education in 1865, has the Inspector made so many visits to, and spent so large a part of his time in the schoolrooms.
>
> It is almost, if not quite impossible for one man to visit all the schools of the Kingdom twice in each year, and give the necessary attention to them. I am of the opinion that provision for a Deputy Inspector, so that the schools could be visited at least three times a year, either by the chief or the deputy, would be money wisely spent. The visits could be longer, and more time given to inspection of schools and of school property than is possible without such additional help (33).

The president of the Board of Education's 1892 biennial report was the last one made during the kingdom, as political events sounded the death knell for the monarchy. The period from 1890 to 1900, one of the most dramatic periods in Hawaiian history, witnessed the overthrow of the monarchy in 1893 and the Islands' annexation as a territory by the United States 5 years later.

The precise American character of public education undoubtedly contributed to these events. The public school system had changed its instruction from the Hawaiian language to an almost complete adoption of English. American ideals in government, taught from the very beginning, eventually contributed to the annexation on August 12, 1898.

The Legislature reorganized the Board of Education by an act passed in January 1894, and the board was commissioned the following month. In its first report to the president and members of the executive and advisory councils of the Provisional Government of the Hawaiian Islands in 1894, the board noted that "pupils in both Government and Independent schools increased from 8,770 to 11,307" (34).

THE INTERIM OF THE REPUBLIC

During the existence of the republic—from January 17, 1893, when the Hawaiian monarchy came to an end, until President McKinley approved the Organic Act on April 30, 1900, which designated the Hawaiian Islands as a Territory—the basic educational system which had existed since 1865 continued. Its basic structure consisted of a board of control comprised of five appointed laymen who selected the professional executive officer and a centralized system subject to the board. There were, however, two significant changes. As a result of a provision in the Constitution of 1894, no public aid could be appropriated to sectarian or private schools after the end of 1895 (35). Second, the Legislature passed an act in 1896 placing the public schools under the direction of an executive department, with the minister of public instruction a member of the cabinet. It thus nullified that part of the reorganization of 1855 whereby the Department of Public Instruction had been made subordinate to the Department of the Interior.

It is not clear from the reports and other records why the republic restored education to its earlier status. Probably, the local leaders regarded this in accordance with American precedents. At any rate, as part of the cabinet, the Department of Public Instruction (re-created by the act) had intimate relations with the general government. The act did not provide for a separate official to serve as minister of public instruction; the minister of interior was given the new portfolio, ex officio, and served as president of the board, consisting of six commissioners of education appointed for 3-year terms. Henry E. Cooper served in the dual ministerial capacity from 1896 to 1899, followed by Ernest A. Mott-Smith (36).

Another important provision of the 1896 School Act was that English be the required language of instruction.

Francis M. Damon, the founder of Mills School, a private school, introduced the kindergarten movement to Hawaii in 1892, when he established the first one in connection with the Chinese Mission under his charge. While the kindergarten movement was not adopted by the public educational system at this time, it did influence the primary-grade program. Alatau T. Atkinson, inspector general of schools, reported in 1894 that "this is not carried on by the Board of Education, though many of the kindergarten methods are used in the primary rooms . . . . " He further stated that "it is a question at present whether the Board would be justified in using funds in this direction" (37).

Atkinson, who had replaced D. D. Baldwin as inspector general of schools in 1886, continued in this office until 1896. He was known as an educational formalist but also as a competent administrator. With the help of his associates, he revised the curriculum of the common schools but did not materially enrich the courses of study.

Henry S. Townsend succeeded Alatau Atkinson as inspector general of schools in 1896. Townsend, a man of bursting energies, was not always understood. Often referred to as Hawaii's first progressive educator, Townsend believed in education that was experience centered. Indeed, Townsend was ahead of his times and aroused the ire of his predecessor, who decried the reforms in his *Honolulu Star.* Nevertheless, Townsend's administration was responsible for such notable firsts as starting a periodical called *The Progressive Educator,* opening the first evening school in Honolulu, holding the first summer school for teachers (John Dewey was invited to conduct a session in 1899), and providing the schools a systemized course of study. There was increased attention to the various branches of vocational education and to art and music.

It was under Townsend's administration that a committee of 12, appointed by the National Education Association in 1895, studied the condition of rural schools. Its report prompted Townsend to request that five deputy inspector general positions be created to help supervise the 344 teachers "whose work ought to be inspected and supervised" (38).

On April 27, 1900, the Congress of the United States passed the Organic Act formally approving of Hawaii's status as a territory and containing the legal basis for this relationship. Section 27 stated "that there shall be a superintendent of public instruction who shall have the powers and perform the duties conferred upon and required of the minister of public instruction by the laws of Hawaii as amended by this Act, and subject to modification by the legislature" (39).

Townsend expected to be appointed the first superintendent of public instruction as soon as the territorial government was established. But Atkinson, who had a considerable following among the businessmen and other nonteaching groups, was also eager for the appointment. The majority of the board found Townsend too advanced, and Atkinson stepped into the office.

THE TERRITORIAL PERIOD

Alatau Atkinson, the veteran Hawaiian educator now serving as superintendent of the public schools, was assisted by Thomas H. Gibson, the deputy superintendent, who received the title of inspector general of schools. Gibson's service to education dated back to the 1880's, and, like Atkinson, he well understood the need for improving the quality of teaching.

The reports of the superintendent and inspector general throw considerable light on the public school situation at the turn of the century. Atkinson cited the great need for better supervision of teaching and in one of his first acts established positions for three normal instructors. He assigned each to a supervisory district with the task of improving the quality of teaching. These were the forerunners of the supervising principals.

Atkinson also recommended a uniform salary schedule. This had been requested by previous administrators but had never been implemented. The Legislature adopted the uniform salary schedule, and Atkinson reported in 1902 that it had worked in a fairly satisfactory manner.

James C. Davis, ultraconservative and cautious, succeeded Atkinson on an interim basis in 1905, remaining less than a year before Winifred H. Babbitt replaced him as the new superintendent. In his first report, Babbitt noted that enrollment in the schools had increased by 1,828, for a total of 16,651. He also pointed to the congestion in new schoolhouses, advising that "the practice of building one and two room schools should be discouraged as far as practicable" (40). Babbitt urged adoption of a policy of consolidation "whereby several schools could be merged in one and the Department provide transportation" (41).

Babbitt also reported that there was a definite need for medical examination every 2 years because of the prevalence of sore eyes, skin diseases, and other physical defects in public school children. He is credited with the initial planning that led to the establishment of a state school for the blind and the deaf. At the same time, he inaugurated a policy of medical inspections in cooperation with the Board of Health.

Willis T. Pope, who succeeded Babbitt in 1910, found that during the period from 1908 to 1910, there was a great reduction in the more common diseases among public school children. Pope, who served as superintendent until 1913, was particularly concerned about the short supply of teachers, due mainly to the increase in public school enrollments.

In reviewing Pope's reports, his problems do not seem unlike those that beset superintendents of schools today. The normal school was unable to train sufficient teachers to meet the shortage, and recruitment trips to the mainland failed to supply the demand. Pope also was plagued with the necessity of using uncertificated teachers. Summer schools were devised to upgrade teachers but "there was little of professional emphasis in the courses pursued" (42).

Summer schools for teachers continued until 1922, when the normal school began its first collegiate summer session. Although Atkinson had appointed normal instructors to supervisory districts, it was Pope's administration that established the position of supervising principal. Principals of larger schools, centrally located, were designated as supervising principals. Modification of the original plan took place until 18 supervising principals were operating by 1912.

This expansion of supervising principals resulted in part because enrollment continued to increase rapidly during Pope's administration; in December 1912, public school enrollment reached 24,993, an increase of 4,738 over the 20,245 of December 31, 1910. The total school population —public and private—of the entire territory was 32,300, "or about 16% of the entire population," Pope reported, and "the last census taken (1910) gives the population of the territory as 191,909" (43). Pope's report for 1910-12 also mentioned, for the first time, a "cost of living" increase for teachers.

The inspector general of schools' title was shortened to inspector of schools in September 1910, replacing the normal inspectors instituted previously.

The duties and responsibilities of the supervising principals were prescribed in the Rules and Regulations published in 1911. Pope stated in his report that the schools are "pursuing a comparatively uniform system of instruction which makes the work of both pupils and teachers fare more satisfactory" (44) because of the supervision system.

Pope's administration was responsible for starting the *Hawaii Educational Review,* a territorial school journal published under the auspices of the Hawaii Education Association "for the comprehensive treatment of Hawaii's very creditable educational institutions and progress" (45).

Inspector of Schools Thomas Gibson followed Pope in 1913 as an interim appointment of 1 year. Henry Walsworth Kinney succeeded Gibson as the new superintendent of public instruction in 1914, shortly before the outbreak of World War I. The appointment of Kinney, a newspaper editor, was unusual, although he had been "one of the severest critics of public educational practices, using his newspaper to that end" (46). Despite his lack of professional experience, he went to work with a will. He made a valiant effort to purify the curriculum by emphasizing simplicity—the three R's. Kinney's educational philosophy was based on a complete understanding and mastery of the fundamental tools of learning.

Despite many mistakes, there were some notable beginnings during his tenure which have since become sound educational practice. For instance, he was interested in a supported development of school cafeterias. He prepared the citizens of Hawaii to accept the Smith-Hughes Act and its federal aid for vocational education. He made a definite place in the curriculum for shop and agricultural classes and gave his firm support to vocational education. He also recommended establishing a trade school.

Kinney established two new public high schools on Maui and Kauai and developed a bungalow style of building as a prototype of school building to relieve the shortage of classrooms. He introduced the practice of requiring teachers to first gain experience in rural schools before being appointed to teaching positions in Honolulu, a practice that endured until 1964. Kinney established a school for the deaf, dumb, and blind children, which also served as a school for mentally defectives. He also recommended transferring the responsibility for reform schools to an independent board. Kinney remained in office until 1919, when he was replaced by Vaughan MacCaughey, professor of botany and horticulture at the College of Hawaii. MacCaughey opposed the formalism characteristic of the Kinney regime which, except for Townsend's brief attempts, had marked Hawaiian education for many years. Although MacCaughey was an extreme liberal, he was not a progressive educator as we understand today. But Wist concludes that "the extreme, but disassociated and disorganized liberalism of the MacCaughey regime was in no small part necessary as a prelude to clearer thinking and more productive results later on" (47).

Superintendent MacCaughey immediately eliminated the examination-grading procedure instituted under Kinney and relaxed the letter-of-the-law interpretation of the regulatory provisions. He attempted to develop a new curriculum, but it failed somewhat because he did not take into consideration the teachers' lack of preparation for their new freedom. "Neither his training nor his experience had given him real insight into the purposes and workings of a dynamic school curriculum. His tendencies, however, were pragmatic, and he almost leaned over backwards in his zeal to be democratic" (48).

Perhaps the most significant event during MacCaughey's administration was the survey of the Hawaiian schools conducted by the Bureau of Education of the federal Department of the Interior. The results were published in 1920, and the major recommendations included lengthening the school day from 7 to 8 hours; abolishing all foreign language schools; appointing county boards of education; organizing junior high schools; providing better supervision of private schools (excluding foreign language schools); reorganizing the Territorial Normal School; and organizing kindergarten classes in every public school. These recommendations eventually had a definite impact on education in Hawaii.

Willard E. Givens succeeded Vaughan MacCaughey in 1923. Givens, the principal of Kamehameha Boys' School and former principal of McKinley High School, was primarily interested in the field of secondary education. His administration did, however, see notable developments in the retirement system and in the establishment of the so-called English standard schools.

In 1916, the Legislature had established provisions for an expanded and actuarially sound pension plan as the Hawaii Retirement System. As first established, however, it was not compulsory; its members were but a small portion of the total teachers, and the retirement allowance was very small. But this was a first step toward a more inclusive system. In 1926, it was made compulsory and applied not to teachers alone, but to all government employees. After a decade of work and pressure, the Legislature adopted a system that was nationally recognized as one of the best in the country (49).

The second development, the English standard schools, stemmed from the department's policy of designating certain schools as such where admission was based on a child's ability to use and to speak the English language. This was in part precipitated by the federal survey conducted in 1920 under the MacCaughey administration. One historian stated that "the suggestion made in the federal survey to segregate pupils in the public schools according to their ability to use English correctly reminded old timers of the effort made toward the close of the century to establish separate public schools for children of Chinese ancestry" (50).

The English standard schools existed until 1947, when the Department of Public Instruction decided to phase them out. From the time that Lincoln School became the first English standard school in 1928 until they were phased out in 1947, the schools of Hawaii had become completely integrated.

Givens' tenure as superintendent ended in 1925, and Will C. Crawford began one of the longest and most difficult administrations. The Depression struck Hawaii in 1929, along with the rest of the nation, and the birthrate in the Islands dropped drastically from 41.57 to 27.4 per thousand in Crawford's last year in office. Nevertheless, during this period, junior high schools, begun as a result of the federal survey's recommendations under MacCaughey, continued to expand until 1930 there were 15, with nearly 10,000 students.

Like the rest of the nation, Hawaii experienced a reduction in occupational opportunity and employment for its senior high school graduates. Governor Lawrence M. Judd appointed an advisory committee to conduct a survey "to suggest policies and recommend changes which it believes will improve the service that the schools are rendering to the Territory and thereby contribute more to the welfare of all the youth of Hawaii" (51).

In its 1931 report, the committee recommended that the Legislature set up a strong lay board of education with full power and authority to administer the Department of Public Instruction. Since the territory's financial resources were at a low ebb, it suggested that the schools be financed on a basis showing the total amount of money involved, but without sacrificing the advantages of the salary schedule as fixed by law. At the same time, it recommended that the program of instruction in the elementary schools be modified and expanded. It also recommended that a director of health education be created in the department.

The committee showed a definite interest in preparing young people for the world of work. For instance, it called for expanding prevocational and vocational training, particularly in agriculture, in the elementary and junior high schools. It would limit to the present figure for 5 years the enrollment in, and expenditure for, full-time academic courses in the senior high schools; but at the same time, it would provide funds for the creation of courses in part-time and continuation schooling for employed youth. The committee called upon the employers of the territory to organize placement bureaus to place the maturing youth of Hawaii in available employments in industry.

In its concern for higher education, the committee concluded that the enrollment of candidates for the bachelor's degree in the University of Hawaii should be limited for 5 years to the present number, and the construction of new buildings should be restricted to a minimum. It further recommended that the Legislature merge the Territorial Normal School into the School of Education of the University of Hawaii and require a bachelor's degree for all elementary school teachers. It then added that the addition of kindergartens to the public school system should be postponed until more urgent educational needs had been satisfied (52).

The survey utilized several committees operating under one general advisory committee, but some educators felt that the committee had been stacked by forces wanting to control and restrict educational authority, seeing an ulterior motive in the recommendation to strengthen the Board of Education, perhaps aimed at Superintendent Crawford. They defeated this change, except for the addition of one person to the board, but many of the recommendations did result in action (53).

One impact of the survey was that textbooks were utilized to better achieve the aims of the curriculum. School libraries were developed to a greater degree than in the past. The recommendation concerning the appointment of a director of health education was implemented. A better atmosphere and attitude between educators and leaders in industry developed. It is obvious now that the recommendation concerning the limiting of high school enrollment was the result of the hysteria of industrial leaders who were frightened at the prospect of seeing all of Hawaii's youth educated. Fortunately, contrary to the committee's recommendations, high schools were established in rural areas.

Oren E. Long, who became superintendent in 1934, enjoyed the longest tenure of any educational leader in Hawaii; he continues to hold this distinction today. President Truman appointed Long Governor of the territory in May 1951, and he won election as U.S. Senator in 1960.

Under Long's guidance, from 1934 to 1946, the schools of Hawaii increased both in number and in quality. The Department of Education, both at the central administrative level and at the local level, was greatly expanded. During Long's 12 years as superintendent, school costs, including capital outlay, increased from $4,905,519 (including $154,664 for capital outlay) to $12,700,930 (including $36,420 for capital outlay).

Long can be credited with leading the school system in Hawaii to a place of excellence it had not achieved before. In his report to the Legislature in 1935, he stated:

> For a period of almost a century, Hawaii has had a public school tradition. The organized educational effort had its origin in the days of the Monarchy, received new emphasis at the time of the Republic and has been a major interest since the beginning of the Territory. It has been based on the concept that enlightenment is basic in government and that progress is possible only with an educated citizenry (54).

Enrollment increased by 3,487 to 83,961 during the 1933-34 school year, the lowest increase in 20 years. But Long pointed out to the Legislature that the ideal of equal opportunity for all children was not being realized; children, at their own expense, had to travel as much as 8 to 10 miles to attend school. True, the curriculum had been enriched, but spoken English remained one of the major problems.

During Long's first years in office, the commissioners authorized the publication of a school code. Additional sites for schools were acquired, new schools were established in rural areas, and additional benefits for teachers were implemented. Thus, by the 1935-36 school year, Long was able to point to the general survey completed under MacCaughey's administration and assert that "every major recommendation of the committee has been carried out. There is general agreeement that the survey was of unusual value to the schools" (55).

In reviewing the educational needs and objectives in 1936, Long requested repeal of the 1933 Emergency Tuition Law, adoption of a single salary schedule, extension of the compulsory school age to the fifteenth or sixteenth birthday, extension of the vocational education program, and extension of the guidance and placement program. He called for the attainment of—

> The public school ideal as defined by the Commissioners in their statement of educational policy: namely that of providing "for every normal child such free

education as well as prepare him to perform his duties as a citizen and to live usefully and wholesomely under the conditions of life in these Islands" (56).

In 1938, Long reported that the total number of children actually in schools was more than ever before—a total of 88,885.

> Only a few years ago schooling above the eighth grade was confined to Honolulu and Hilo and few other communities. There are now thirty-four rural districts where work above the eighth grade is offered. Ten of these are senior high schools. Fourteen others are intermediate schools. Under present plans at least five of these will become high schools within the next two years (57).

Long stated that outlook for education in 1938 was "practical" in that—

> Hawaii is committed to the principle of education that the schools, as far as possible, should fit boys and girls for the professional or vocational careers of their choice. It is especially important that they have an educational background and an understanding of occupational opportunities that will enable them to choose wisely. On the basis of varying interests and abilities, they will elect to spend their lives as teachers, preachers, lawyers, physicians, engineers, plumbers, carpenters, electricians, mill hands, workers of the soil or in other occupations. They should have received in school the educational foundations, ideals of living and specific training required to enable them to achieve success and render a worth while service in the work of their choice.
>
> Much of the basis for attaining this ideal is found in the general program of the school. In a specific way, it is furthered by the work of the Vocational Division which offers classes in homemaking, agriculture and the trades. Obviously, a great majority of youth in this community or any other American community must find their life work in agriculture and the trades rather than in the professions. All school girls are potential housewives and will either do the work in the home or will direct it. Regardless of what the boy or the girl may ultimately do, experiences offered in the vocational courses have sound educational values. . .(58).

The Senate of the 1939 Territorial Legislature created a Holdover Committee of the Legislature to survey the schools, and Long reported in 1940 that the survey was not an investigation of the schools but "a study of the educational problems which the school and the community face together" (59). Assistance was given to the Holdover Committee by a special Committee on Education of the Chamber of Commerce and the Department of Public Instruction. The study was completed in March 1941 and was published as the *Community Survey of Education in Hawaii* (60). Long notes in his annual report of 1941 that—

> Some of the most important immediate results of the survey are:
>
> 1. A wider community interest in the schools and an understanding of their efficiencies and deficiencies, of what they are accomplishing and what they should accomplish.
>
> 2. An increased awareness on the part of teachers and principals of existing problems and a realization that the lay public desires to cooperate in improving the schools.
>
> 3. An excellent analysis of the problems and needs of the schools. Some of the improvements recommended can be realized only through enlarged appropriations. Until economic conditions make these possible, there is a disposition to find those points at which improvements can be made with appropriations and equipment now available and to work for those improvements.
>
> 4. A better basis for evaluating the work of the schools. Judgment must be based on facts, with sympathetic understanding, appreciation and tolerance. The findings of the Survey Committee are above hearsay and opinion. They represent constructive criticism and afford a basis for cooperative effort in preserving all that is good in the present program and in bringing about improvements (61).

Long remained at the helm of education during the difficult years of World War II, and his report of 1941 reflects concerns and problems created by the conflict. It was during 1941 that Hawaii was notified that the Department of Public Instruction could participate in the Adult National Defense Program. Hawaii was granted $81,794 for carrying on a national defense program under Public Law 812. The department cooperated with a Defense Training Advisory Committee of 20 men named by the chairman of the Territorial Board of Vocational Education.

The many challenges presented to education in Hawaii are a recurrent theme in Long's reports of 1942 and 1943. In 1942, Long stated that "the adjustments and readjustments made necessary by conditions in a battle zone of the war have been made in a satisfactory way" (62). The impact of the war on school enrollment was substantial. In June 1942, the enrollment decreased by 10,801 from the 91,121 reported in June 1941.

However, even under war conditions advances were being made.

Long reports that in 1943—

> The opening of twelve kindergarten centers as a regular part of the public school program was authorized by the 1943 Session of the Legislature. The understanding is

> that additional centers will be established each biennium until every community in the Territory is served. This development is viewed as one of the most important in the entire history of public school education in Hawaii. It should have an important bearing on the problem of speech, the formation of proper health habits and the process of social growth (63).

Also in 1943, the Legislature enacted a law (Act 7) which directed the department to establish a division of pupil guidance. A new program known as "Business Education" was planned in cooperation with the U.S. Office of Education. A program administered by the Vocational Division of the U.S. Office of Education, titled "Occupational Information and Guidance," was also planned.

In his last report to the Legislature, Long reviewed the impact of World War II on the Hawaii school system and strongly urged that after victory had been won, those in education become acutely aware of the "new age of transport, of television, and of freezing units. . ." (64).

W. Harold Loper replaced Long as superintendent in 1946. He used as a guide, in general, the recommendations of two surveys conducted during the Long administration: *Community Survey of Education in Hawaii,* previously mentioned as completed in 1941, and *Hawaiian Schools: A Curriculum Survey* 1944-45, completed in 1946 (65). This second study is sometimes referred to as the Draper-Hayden Survey.

In the first biennial report under his signature, Loper claimed considerable progress had been made in reorganizing the school system according to the recommendations of the surveys and reports. For instance, the department's plan had grouped all educational services represented in the personnel of the central office into four divisions, each headed by a deputy superintendent. It had reduced the number of school districts to provide for one district in each county under the direction of a district superintendent and a staff of field assistants. And it had added specialized personnel in each school district and in the central office.

> The recommended reduction in the number of school districts is nearly complete, but only a beginning has been made in the addition of Field Assistants. On the Island of Hawaii, the number of districts has been reduced from three to two; for the County of Maui, we now have one district instead of two; and on Oahu, the single school district plan has been inaugurated. Kauai has always been organized as a single school district (66).

Post-World War II

Loper continued to complete the reorganization measures started under Long's administration. In his 1947 report to the Legislature, he asserted that further reorganization had been carried out to implement the Community Survey and the Draper-Hayden Survey. An assistant superintendent had been appointed to work directly under the superintendent (67).

The matter of spoken English and its influence on the curriculum and organization of the schools remained a major educational problem during Loper's administration. "Pidgin" English was still the common tongue of a great portion of the populace. Marked increases in enrollment and the concomitant need for additional teachers were of great concern. And there was a continuing demand for expansion in the vocational educational program by organized labor, students, parents, and employees.

An important achievement during Loper's administration was the publication in 1946 of *A Handbook for Elementary Teachers in Hawaii.* The *Handbook* comprised three separate volumes and dealt with general directions for elementary school teachers and specific directions for teachers in the areas of social studies, English, and mathematics. The *Handbook* was the product of the tremendous efforts of professional educators of the department and lay advisors. A newly established position called the director of elementary education was charged with directing the production of the *Handbook.*

Loper and his staff continued to lay a well-stated program for curriculum development during the next several years. His biennial report for 1947-48 reflects achievements of the department in areas that were the result of "public demand for new services and of a better understanding of conditions affecting the learning process."

In 1948, a Guidance Service Committee was organized to coordinate the work of pupil guidance and vocational guidance, which operated as two separate divisions. The implementation of this coordination was strongly supported by the work of the chief of the occupational information and guidance services of the U.S. Office of Education.

Because of great public interest in kindergartens in every community, the kindergarten program was greatly expanded in 1948-51. Funds were appropropriated by the Legislature to establish 136 new kindergarten teachers during this period. Vocational education programs also continued to increase, particularly on the neighbor islands.

In 1951, a school building services division was established, which qualified the department to apply for and receive federal aid under Public Laws 815 and 874.

Also under Loper, work was begun with mentally handicapped children in 1952, and efforts were made to combat a growing narcotics menace. The adult education program, which had begun operation in 1946 with an enrollment of 3,000, had increased to 11,228 by 1950. The curriculum expanded considerably in other areas as well to "provide experiences for children and youth that will help them develop into the kinds of young citizens most parents and teachers would like them to be." Loper added: "This important task is not that of the school alone. It is shared with homes, churches and the communities in which children live and play" (68).

Following Loper's resignation in 1952, Clayton J. Chamberlin accepted the superintendency and faced the same questions and problems that had plagued Loper. A shortage of teachers and of school buildings was of major concern, followed by the need for a curriculum that would meet the student needs for the contemporary world.

Chamberlin had served as deputy superintendent in charge of the special services division. When he assumed the leadership of the department, four deputy superintendents administered the programs under divisions of instruction, special services, vocational education, and administrative affairs. In addition, there was an administrator of schools' personnel, and the assistant superintendent served as the second man under the superintendent. The territory was organized in five administrative districts, each headed by a district superintendent.

Chamberlin directed the Department of Education under a seven-man board, serving as an ex officio member, until the "eve" of statehood. He strongly emphasized in-service training for teachers and principals during his term of office. Increasing enrollments still plagued the department, along with the resulting shortage of classrooms. A Governor's Conference on Education attempted to involve citizens in a discussion of these problems and other needs of education.

By 1957, the department had been expanded both at the central administrative level and at the local level. The administrator of schools' personnel became a deputy superintendent in 1954, and a deputy superintendent of school building services was added 3 years later.

The department contracted for a comprehensive survey of the administrative organization and operation of the Hawaiian public school system in July 1956. Conducted by William R. Odell and Associates of Stanford University, it was the fifth education survey since 1920. Completed in June 1957, the survey gives, perhaps, one of the most succinct statements of Hawaii's education growth. It summarized the past, pointing out that government support of the schools began in 1849, but it was not until 1888 that the public schools were "free." The report continued:

> During the period of 175 years, the Islands have changed even more dramatically than the United States. From a primitive Polynesian society, through a feudalistic monarchy, they have emerged as a modern democracy. From a hand-labor economy to a highly mechanized industrial society, and from a single culture, through a pluralistic society as waves of Chinese, Japanese, Koreans, Portuguese, Scotch and Philippinos have immigrated the Islands, it is today an international culture of an order that seems to anticipate the world of tomorrow (69).

On the eve of statehood, expansion in education continued to be made. In 1958, because of the recurring problem of obtaining qualified teachers for Hawaii's public schools, Superintendent Chamberlin appointed a committee to study teachers' salaries. A program for gifted students was begun on a pilot basis, and a new foundation program for public secondary schools was established that required a minimum of 2 years of math and science. James MacConnell of Stanford University held a workshop on educational specifications, out of which grew the document called *Educational Specifications for Public School Buildings in Hawaii*, published by the department in 1959 (70).

During Chamberlin's tenure, considerable increases in federal funds under Public Laws 815 and 874 continued to be an important factor in the expansion of schools. For example, total federal funds received by the department for the 3-year period 1956-58 are as follows:

Fiscal period ending June 30, 1956	$2,702,931
Fiscal period ending June 30, 1957	4,974,106
Fiscal period ending June 30, 1958	3,252,588

STATEHOOD

Chamberlin resigned in late 1958, to be replaced by Walton M. Gordon the following January, 6 months before Hawaii became a state. Thus, Gordon, the first superintendent of education of the State of Hawaii, was in office during the transition on August 21, 1959.

The new state immediately implemented a new constitution, which had been drawn up in 1950. The constitutional provision for education in Article IX, Section I, states:

> The State shall provide for the establishment, support and control of a statewide system of public schools free from sectarian control, a state university, public libraries and such other educational institutions as may be deemed desirable, including physical facilities therefor. There shall be no segregation in public educational institutions because of race, religion or ancestry; nor shall public funds be appropriated for the support or benefit of any sectarian or private educational institution (71).

Hawaii's legislators began studying the needs of the new state government, and this resulted in the Reorganization Act of 1959—which in turn was implemented by executive orders in 1960 and 1961. At this time, the Department of Public Instruction became the Department of Education, and the superintendent of public instruction became the superintendent of education.

Five superintendents of education have occupied the top position of educational leadership under the Reorganization Act. Gordon continued to occupy the superintendency, and his first annual report issued after June 1959 notes that Hawaii is a state, although the department is still referred to as the Department of Public Instruction.

Gordon reports that *Educational Specifications for Public School Buildings in Hawaii* has been issued and that–

> While most mainland building specifications are designed for a single school in a specific community, those for Hawaii were developed as a guide for architects, school staffs and lay people planning school construction anywhere in the islands.
>
> The Guide points out the importance of planning for facilities in terms of the curriculum and suggests the relationship of classrooms to playgrounds, library, cafeteria, administrative units, etc. (72).

He also indicates that Hawaii had begun to participate in receiving federal aid under the National Defense Education Act. Federal funds for the fiscal year ending June 30, 1959, are reported as $5,452,953, out of a total budget of $40,819,117.

In the first annual report of the department issued by the newly created State Department of Education for the year 1960-61, Gordon states that further reorganization of the department was taking place. The report, issued under the title of "Our Island Schools," notes that experiments were begun in team teaching and that better library services and audiovisual education were instituted. Experiments in educational television were also begun during 1960-61.

It was at this time that several studies for the reorganization and management of the government of Hawaii were completed by the firm of Booz, Allen and Hamilton, Inc. These studies had many implications for the state department. The most significant of the reports and studies was the *Report on Survey of Organization Structure* submitted to the Governor in February 1961. The report made recommendations for implementing the Reorganization Act of 1959 which recast the entire executive branch of the state government of Hawaii into 18 branches of which the Department of Education was one.

The Hawaii State Government Reorganization Act was passed as Act I by the First State Legislature, Second Special Session, in 1959. It was approved in November 1959. Under Section 18 of the act, the Department of Education was to be headed by an executive board, and under policies established by the board the superintendent would administer the functions of the former department of public instruction which were transferred to the new Department of Education. Vocational rehabilitation programs were to be transferred to the Department of Social Services as soon as the transfer could be made without jeopardizing any federal aid, and some other adjustments were made, such as the transfer of the library of Hawaii and certain other libraries to the new Department of Education. (For the text of the law, see Appendix F.)

The constitution required that local school advisory councils be established by law and that the superintendent of public instruction be appointed by the state board and serve as an ex officio voting member. It is interesting to note that the superintendent was also made an ex officio member of the Board of Regents of the University of Hawaii under the constitution. (For text of constitutional provisions, see Appendix E.) Some of the basic functions of the department were to be changed in the next few years, however.

Gordon did not remain to see the reorganization of the department completed. In his annual report for 1961-62, he referred to the great progress that has been made because of reorganization and cited the expansion of the programs for the gifted, foreign languages, school counseling, and the mentally retarded. He noted that great stimulation was given to the foreign language program by the National Defense Education Act passed by Congress in 1959. He emphasized the need for flexible scheduling and evinced strong belief in the importance of educational television. In September 1962, Gordon was succeeded by R. Burl Yarberry.

Yarberry's tenure began what might be called the transition period of the sixties. The educational structure has undergone tremendous change during the past 6 years. This change continued during Lowell Jackson's tenure as interim superintendent, February 1966 to January 1967, and is still ongoing under the direction of Ralph H. Kiyosaki, who became superintendent on June 1, 1967.

The directions in which the department has been going during this 6-year period is, in the minds of many, a sound one. It is difficult to assess the impact of change as it relates to directions since the writer is intimately involved in these directions. For the reader it may suffice to simply summarize the structure of the Department of Education at the present time.

SUMMARY, 1968

At this writing, and in summary, the State Department of Education administers programs of public educational services to the children, youth, and adults of the state and renders statewide library services. The department continues its unique state system-one system concept.

The state is divided into seven school administrative districts. There are four districts on the island of Oahu, and one each on the islands of Hawaii, Kauai, and Maui. The division of library services provides statewide library service in each of the counties through the Oahu Public Library in the City and County of Honolulu, and the Hawaii, Kauai, and Maui county libraries. In addition, there are several divisions or offices within the department: business administration; personnel; research, statistics, and data processing; curriculum, instruction, and guidance; and library services. The vocational rehabilitation division was transferred to the Department of Social Services by Act 274, approved June 1967, and the Board of Regents assumed the responsibility for vocational education under Act 716, effective May 1968. This act transferred to the University of Hawaii responsibility for the administration of that part of the Manpower Development and Training Act of 1962 formerly administered by the Department of Education. It should be noted that by Act 39, approved April 1964, the Board of Regents also has the responsibility for administering the community college program.

Board of Education

The State Department of Education is headed by an executive Board of Education which formulates policy and exercises control over the public school system through its executive officer, the superintendent of education.

Formerly the members of the Board of Education were appointed by the Governor, by and with the consent of the Senate, from panels submitted by the local school advisory councils. However, at the 1964 elections, an amendment to Section 2, Article IX, of the constitution, providing for an elective rather than appointive Board of Education, was approved by the electorate. Act 50, Session Laws of Hawaii 1966, implemented the amendment and provided for an 11-member board to be elected from school board districts and at large as follows: first school board district (Hawaii County), two members; second school board district (Maui County), one member; third school board district (Honolulu), one member; fourth school board district (Central Oahu), one member; fifth school board district (Leeward Oahu), one member; sixth school board district (Windward Oahu), one member; seventh school board district (Kauai County), one member; and one at-large district (Oahu - City and County of Honolulu), three members. Each member must be a registered voter of the school board district or at-large district from which he seeks election and is prohibited from holding public office under state or county governments. Members of the Board of Education serve for 4 years. Vacancies on the board are filled by the Governor, and the appointee must be of the same political party as the person he succeeds.

The elected Board of Education succeeds to all rights and powers exercised and all duties and obligations incurred by the previously appointed Board of Education.

District School Advisory Councils

With the ratification of the constitutional amendment providing for an elective Board of Education by the electorate in 1964 and the subsequent enactment of Act 50, Session Laws of Hawaii 1966, the elective local school advisory councils were replaced by appointive district school advisory councils. There is a district school advisory council for each school board district, and the size of membership of each council is as follows: first school board district (Hawaii County), seven members; second school board district (Maui County), five members; third school board district (Honolulu), five members; fourth school board district (Central Oahu), five members; fifth school board district (Leeward Oahu), five members; sixth school board district (Windward Oahu), five members; and seventh school board district (Kauai County), five members. The members of the school advisory council are appointed by the Governor and serve for terms commencing upon their appointment and ending upon the expiration of the term of office of the Governor. Not more than a bare majority of the members of each district school advisory council may belong to the same political party or shall be nonpartisan. Each councillor appointed by the Governor must be a registered voter of his school board district. Each member of the Board of Education is an ex officio, nonvoting member of the district school advisory council of his board district, provided that all of the at-large members of Oahu shall be ex officio, nonvoting members of each of the district school advisory councils on Oahu. The district school advisory councils serve in an advisory capacity to the Board of Education and to its board district member or an at-large district member, if any.

Library Advisory Commissions

There is a Library Advisory Commission in each of the four counties. Each commission consists of not less than 7 nor more than 11 members appointed for 4-year terms by the Governor with the advice and consent of the Senate. The commissions sit in an advisory capacity to the Board of Education on matters relating to public library services in their respective county.

The Future

Education in Hawaii faces a brilliant future. There is no government official–Governor, legislator, or citizen–who does not seem to be vitally interested in its progress. This interest currently is manifesting itself in increased appropriations for both operating and capital improvement budgets. In addition, the impact of federal legislation has permitted growth and expansion in many areas of the educational structure. Our people have high hopes that this interest will remain at this level to propel Hawaii at an even faster rate into the twenty-first century. Hawaii is and has been unique in its educational organization. Its simplicity of organization gives it a great advantage–an advantage of moving quickly and expeditiously to see that our children will be the best educated in the world.

FOOTNOTES

1. Lawrence H. Fuchs, *Hawaii Pono: A Social History* (New York: Harcourt, 1961), p. 263.

2. Benjamin O. Wist, *A Century of Public Education in Hawaii* (Honolulu: Hawaii Educational Review, 1940), p. 34.

3. Lorrin A. Thurston, *The Fundamental Law of Hawaii* (Honolulu: The Hawaiian Gazette Co., Ltd., 1904), p. 26.

4. Wist, *op.cit.*, p. 36.

5. *Ibid.*, p. 50.

6. *Ibid.*

7. Thurston, *op. cit.*, pp. 38-42.

8. Wist, *op. cit.*, p. 51.

9. Thurston, *op. cit.*, p. 131.

10. Wist, *op. cit.,*, pp. 52-54.

11. *Ibid.*, p. 51.

12. Minister of Public Instruction (Kingdom), *Report* (1846), pp. 24-25.

13. Hawaii(Kingdom), *Statute Laws of His Majesty Kamehameha III* (1846), I, 204.

14. *Ibid.*

15. *Ibid.*

16. *Ibid.*

17. *Ibid.*, p. 205.

18. Minister of Public Instruction (Kingdom), *Report* (1847), p. 4.

19. *Ibid.*, p. 28.

20. Minister of Public Instruction (Kingdom)., *Report* (1850), pp. 3-4.

21. *Ibid.*, pp. 8-9.

22. *Ibid.*, pp. 19-20.

23. *Ibid.*, pp. 20-22.

24. *Ibid.*, p. 44.

25. Minister of Public Instruction (Kingdom), *Report* (1855), pp. 23-24.

26. Hawaii (Kingdom), *Session Laws* (1855), p. 9.

27. President of the Board of Education (Kingdom), *Report* (1856), p. 28.

28. *Ibid.*, p. 12.

29. Wist, *op. cit.*, pp. 75-76.

30. President of the Board of Education (Kingdom), *Biennial Report to the Legislature of 1864* (1864), p. 5.

31. Wist, *op. cit.*, p. 78.

32. President of the Board of Education (Kingdom), *Biennial Report to the Legislature of the Hawaiian Kingdom* (1890), pp. 1-2.

33. *Ibid.*, p. 3.

34. President of the Board of Education (Republic), *Biennial Report to the President and Members of the Executive and Advisory Councils of the Provisional Government of the Hawaiian Islands* (1894), pp. 1-2.

35. Thurston, *op. cit.*, p. 238.

36. Wist, *op. cit.*, p. 130.

37. President of the Board of Education (Republic), *Report* (1894), pp. 33-34.

38. Minister of Public Instruction (Republic), *Report to the President of the Republic of Hawaii - Biennial Period Ending December 31, 1897* (1898), p. 68.

39. Thurston, *op. cit.*, pp. 279-80.

40. Superintendent of Public Instruction (Territory), *Report of the Superintendent of Public Instruction to the Governor of the Territory of Hawaii from December 31st, 1904 to December 31st, 1906* (1907), p. 1.

41. *Ibid.*, p. 2.

42. Wist, *op. cit.*, p. 151.

43. Superintendent of Public Instruction (Territory), *Report of the Superintendent of Public Instruction to the Governor of the Territory of Hawaii from December 31st, 1910 to December 31st, 1912* (1913), p. 14.

44. *Ibid.*, p. 26.

45. T. H. Gibson and Vaughan MacCaughey, "The Mission of the *Review,*" *Hawaii Educational Review*, I, No. 1 (1913), 1.

46. Wist, *op. cit.*, p. 154.

47. *Ibid.*, p. 158.

48. *Ibid.*, p. 156.

49. *Ibid.*,p. 160.

50. Fuchs, *op. cit.*, p. 274.

51. Governor's Advisory Committee on Education, *Survey of Schools and Industry in Hawaii* (Honolulu: The Printshop Co., Ltd., 1931), p. 3.

52. *Ibid.*, p. 51.

53. Wist, *op. cit.*, p. 164.

54. Department of Public Instruction (Territory), *Report, 1933-34,* p. 1.

55. Department of Public Instruction (Territory), *Report, 1935-36,* p. 14.

56. *Ibid.*, p. 49.

57. Department of Public Instruction (Territory), *Annual Report, 1938,* p. 1.

58. *Ibid.*, p. 4.

59. Department of Public Instruction (Territory), *Annual Report, 1940,* p. 5.

60 Complete citation is Committee of Fifteen (Territory), *Community Survey of Education in Hawaii* (Honolulu: The Committee, 1941).

61. Department of Public Instruction (Territory), *Annual Report, 1941,* p. 1.
62. Department of Public Instruction (Territory), *Annual Report, 1942,* p. 4.
63. Department of Public Instruction (Territory), *Annual Report, 1942-43,* p. 9.
64. Department of Public Instruction (Territory), *Biennial Report, 1943-44,* p. 2.
65. Edgar M. Draper and Alice H. Hayden, *Hawaii Schools: A Curriculum Survey, 1944-45* (Washington, D.C.: American Council on Education, 1946).
66. Department of Public Instruction (Territory), *Biennial Report, 1945-46,* p. 1.
67. Department of Public Instruction (Territory), *Annual Report, 1947,* pp. 2-3.
68. Department of Public Instruction (Territory), *Biennial Report, 1949-50,* p. 1.
69. William R. Odell and Associates, *Organization and Administration of the Public Schools, Territory of Hawaii: Social Setting* (Stanford, Calif.: Stanford University, 1957), pp. 8-9.
70. Department of Public Instruction (Territory), *Educational Specifications for Public School Buildings in Hawaii,* Vols. I, II (Honolulu: The Department, 1959).
71. Hawaii, *School Laws* (1966), p. 1.
72. Department of Public Instruction (Territory), *Annual Report, 1958-59,* p. 3.

BIBLIOGRAPHY

Public Documents

Hawaii. *School Laws* (1966).

Hawaii (Kingdom). *Session Laws* (1855).

--*Statute Laws of His Majesty Kamehameha III* (1846).

Books

Draper, Edgar M., and Hayden, Alice H. *Hawaii Schools: A Curriculum Survey, 1944-45.* Washington, D.C.: American Council on Education, 1946.

Fuchs, Lawrence H. *Hawaii Pono: A Social History.* New York: Harcourt, 1961.

Odell, William R., and Associates. *Organization and Administration of the Public Schools, Territory of Hawaii: Social Setting.* Stanford, Calif.: Stanford University, 1957.

Thurston, Lorrin A. *The Fundamental Law of Hawaii.* Honolulu: The Hawaiian Gazette Co., Ltd., 1904.

Wist, Benjamin O. *A Century of Public Education in Hawaii.* Honolulu: Hawaii Educational Review, 1940.

Reports

Committee of Fifteen (Territory). *Community Survey of Education in Hawaii.* Honolulu: The Committee, 1941.

Department of Public Instruction (Territory). *Annual and Biennial Reports.* Honolulu: The Department, 1933-50.

Department of Public Instruction (State). *Annual Report.* Honolulu: The Department 1964-65.

Governor's Advisory Committee on Education. *Survey of Schools and Industry in Hawaii.* Honolulu: The Printshop Co., Ltd., 1931.

Minister of Public Instruction (Republic). *Reports.* Honolulu: Office of the Minister, 1846-97.

President of the Board of Education (Kingdom). *Biennial Reports.* Honolulu: The Board, 1864-94.

Superintendent of Public Instruction (Territory). *Reports.* Honolulu: Department of Public Instruction, 1904-13.

Article and Periodical

Gibson, T. H., and MacCaughey, Vaughan. "The Mission of the *Review.*" *Hawaii Educational Review,* I, No. 1 (1913), 1.

Appendix A

HAWAII CHIEF STATE SCHOOL OFFICERS

1820-41	Missionary Supervision
School Agent and Luna	
1841-45	David Malo
Ministers of Public Instruction	
1845-47	William Richards
1848	Keoni Ana (John Young, Jr.)
1848-55	Richard Armstrong
President, Department of Public Instruction	
1855-60	Richard Armstrong
Inspectors General of Schools	
1860-74	Abraham Fornander
1874-77	H. Radford Hitchcock
1877-86	D. Dwight Baldwin
1886-87	Vacant
1887-96	Alatau T. Atkinson
1896-1900	Henry S. Townsend
Superintendents of Public Instruction	
1900-1905	Alatau T. Atkinson
1905-1906	James C. Davis
1906-10	Winifred H. Babbitt
1910-13	Willis T. Pope
1913-14	T. H. Gibson (acting)
1914-18	Henry W. Kinney
1919-23	Vaughan MacCaughey
1923-25	Willard E. Givens
1925-34	Will C. Crawford
1934-46	Oren E. Long
1946-52	W. Harold Loper
1952-58	Clayton J. Chamberlin
Superintendents of Education	
1959-62	Walton M. Gordon
1962-66	R. Burl Yarberry
1966-67	Lowell D. Jackson
1967	E. E. Hawkins (acting, Feb.–May)
1967-	Ralph H. Kiyosaki

Appendix B

Chart I.--HAWAII DEPARTMENT OF EDUCATION PLAN, 1962

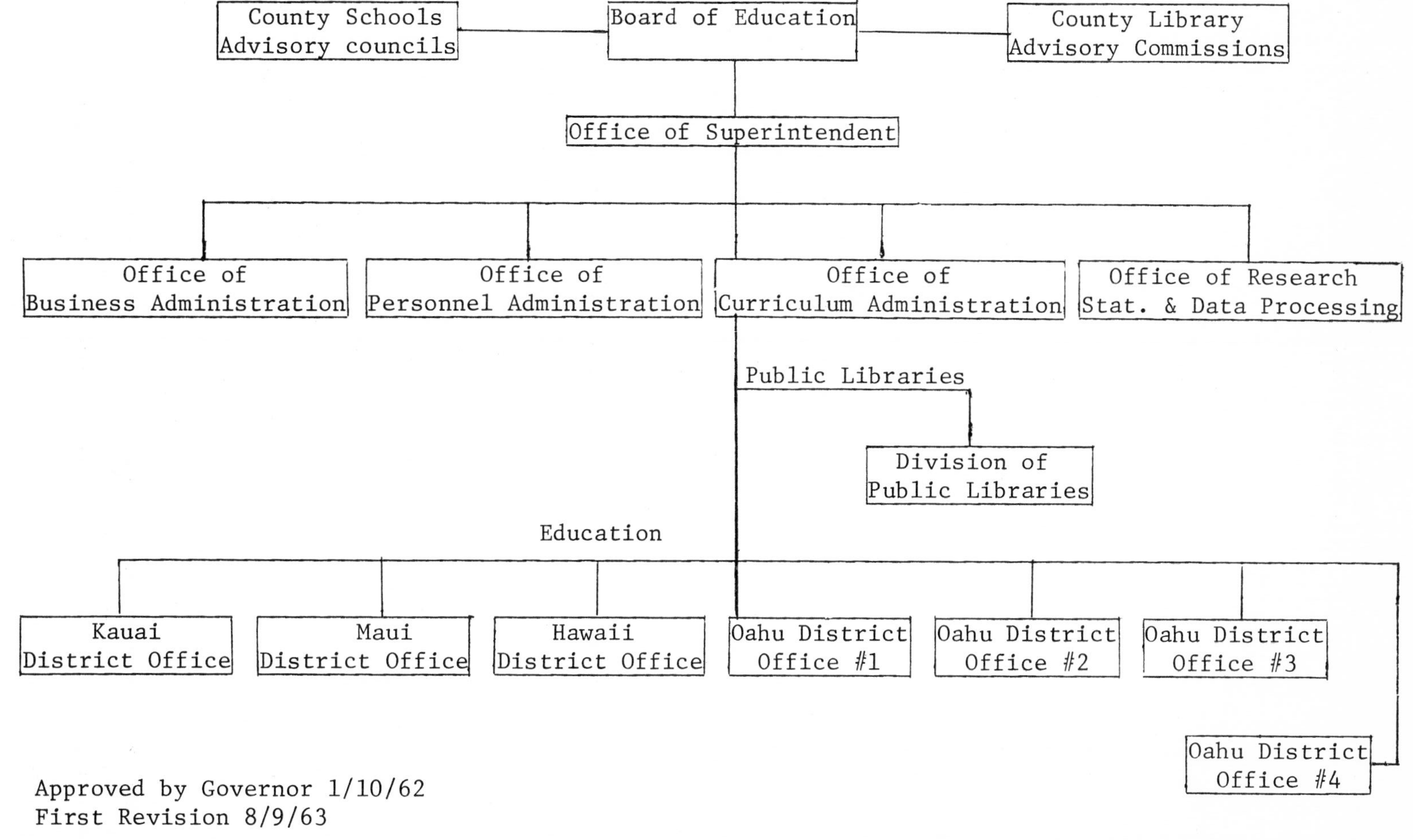

Approved by Governor 1/10/62
First Revision 8/9/63

Appendix C

Table 1.– SUMMARY OF ENROLLMENT AND TOTAL EXPENDITURES (APPROPRIATED) FOR GOVERNMENT, COMMON, AND PUBLIC SCHOOLS (PRIVATE SCHOOLS EXCLUDED), 1846-1967

Date	Enrollment		Total expenditure	Fiscal period
1846	18,793[a]		$ 27,442.75[a]	...
1850	15,620		21,989.84	...
1855	10,076		18,851.21	...
1860	8,771		31,528.21	...
1865	7,367		26,732.38	(p. 31, 1866 report)
1870	5,938		31,379.38	...
1875	4,799		44,629.38	...
1880	5,917[a]		46,872.00	...
1885	6,432[a]		33,892.54	...
1890	7,343	(10,006)	391,438.73	For biennial period ending March 31, 1890
1895	7,361	(12,616)	324,000.00	For 21-month period ending December 31, 1895
1900	11,501	(15,537)	717,100.00	For biennial period ending December 31, 1900
1906	14,591		342,228.00	For 12 months ending June 30, 1905
1910	20,245	(25,770)	876,440.00	For biennial period 1909-11
1916	32,278	(39,024)	1,568,362.24	For biennial period 1915-16
1920	41,350	(48,923)	2,671,908.00	For biennial period ending December 31, 1920
1926	62,460		4,962,610.00	For calendar year 1926
1930	76,634		5,587,670.00	For calendar year 1930
1936	87,276	(99,447)	5,795,553.00	For calendar year 1936
1940	92,424		7,507,657.00	For calendar year 1940
1945	79,927		10,709,338.00	For fiscal year ending June 30, 1946

NOTE:

Figures have been taken from biennial or annual reports of the department of education for that year. Unless otherwise noted, expenditures include capital outlay where this information was indicated in the report. Figures for years after 1900 are for the year indicated. In some cases, enrollment figures are for December of the preceding year where this has been noted in the annual report.

[a]Includes government common schools and government select schools.

Appendix C

Table 1. – SUMMARY OF ENROLLMENT AND TOTAL EXPENDITURES (APPROPRIATED) FOR GOVERNMENT, COMMON, AND PUBLIC SCHOOLS (PRIVATE SCHOOLS EXCLUDED), 1846-1967 (Continued)

Date	Enrollment	Total expenditure	Fiscal period
1950	89,656	16,583,714.00	For fiscal year ending June 30, 1950
1951	93,903	$ 16,848,257.00	For fiscal year ending June 30, 1951, exclusive of capital outlay
1952	96,837	18,489,816.00	For fiscal year ending June 30, 1952, exclusive of capital outlay
1953	106,464	19,496,720.00	For fiscal year ending June 30, 1953
1954	113,544	22,497,847.00	For fiscal year ending June 30, 1954, inclusive of capital outlay
1955	119,054	28,820,615.00	For fiscal year ending June 30, 1955, inclusive of capital outlay
1956	124,857	28,979,897.00	For fiscal year ending June 30, 1956, inclusive of capital outlay
1957	130,158	35,813,969.00	For fiscal year ending June 30, 1957, inclusive of capital outlay
1958	130,158	36,297,334.00	For fiscal year ending June 30, 1958
1959	134,129	40,819,117.00	For fiscal year ending June 30, 1959
1960	140,331	53,345,220.00	For fiscal year ending June 30, 1960
1961	144,764	56,355,091.00	For fiscal year ending June 30, 1961
1962	149,156	58,790,453.00	For fiscal year ending June 30, 1962
1963	152,748	71,498,484.00	For fiscal year ending June 30, 1963
1964	155,051	76,636,595.00	For fiscal year ending June 30, 1964
1965	158,787	92,181,679.00[b]	For fiscal year ending June 30, 1965
1966	160,617	118,908,403.00	For fiscal year ending June 30, 1966
1967	165,734	141,276,467.00	For fiscal year ending June 30, 1967

NOTE:

Figures have been taken from biennial or annual reports of the department of education for that year. Unless otherwise noted, expenditures include capital outlay where this information was indicated in the report. Figures for years after 1900 are for the year indicated. In some cases, enrollment figures are for December of the preceding year where this has been noted in the annual report.

[b]Includes public libraries for first time.

Appendix D

ORGANIC ACT OF 1846

Section V. No person shall be so licensed to teach without having first exhibited satisfactory evidence of good moral character and qualifications to instruct, particularly in the rudiments of reading, writing, arithmetic and geography; and no person having been so licensed shall be entitled to the benefits of the law relating to the support of schools after having exhibited a want of aptitude to teach or a want of that industry and faithfulness necessary to the successful discharge of his duties, nor after having become of immoral character or habits. Neither shall a license granted in one district qualify nor authorize the holder to teach in another, without new examination, although it may be considered by every other general superintendent as prima facie evidence of the holder's qualifications.

Section VI. The general superintendent of each school district in concert with the sub-agent of any sub-division, shall have full power to erect, alter, modify and repair school houses, also to contract with and employ teachers, and to this end he may require of the tax gatherer and overseers of the labor tax any amount of labor, or in lieu thereof, the commutation therefor in money or in property. When labor is so required by the superintendent of schools, he shall always indicate the place and manner in which it shall be performed. Whenever the labor tax or its avails prove inadequate to the support of any school established by the general superintendent or by any of his sub-agents, it shall then be lawful for the agent or the superintendent who has pledged such support, to draw on the tax gatherer of the district in accordance with instructions from the department of public instruction for the payment of the residue in any government property in his hands, other than the poll tax. Said general superintendent shall also have power to allot land, not otherwise appropriated, to the teachers and to the schools of their respective district sub-divisions. Such land shall not however be allotted to the use of any teacher of youth not duly licensed by the general superintendent of the district in which he designs to teach, as herein provided. Neither shall any land set apart by the general superintendent of the district, in concert with the sub-agents thereof, be considered validly appropriated to that object until the said general superintendent shall have notified the same, in location, quality and quantity to the minister of public instruction, and received from said minister the certificate of the minister of the interior to that effect. All land so set apart shall be registered as school lands in the interior department, and shall be considered as set apart to eleemosynary uses, not given to the teacher or temporary occupant thereof, who only while continuing to hold the teacher's license, and to teach statedly in the district sub-division, shall have the private use, occupancy and usufruct of such land. When for any cause he is dismissed, or voluntarily retires or dies, the land shall pass to his successor in said school, with all the tenements erected thereon, unless erected from his own private means, with the written approbation of the minister of public instruction.

Section VII. The sub-agents of the several districts, as far as practicable, shall on the first day of January in each year report to the general superintendent for their respective districts the number of schools established therein, the number of families residing in their sub-divisions, the number of children between the ages of four and fourteen years, the number of children actually scholars in the schools of their districts, the number of children dependent upon adoption or guardianship, and the number of parents dependent upon filial support.

Section VIII. It shall be the duty of the several general superintendents of districts, annually, on the first day of January in each year, to report in like manner to the minister of public instruction the aggregate of the statistics in the last section required for their respective districts, and the number of teachers by them respectively licensed, also the number of school houses established in the district, how and at what expense supported.

Section IX. The general superintendent of each district shall, under the minister of public instruction, have the nominal ownership and be the trustee of all school property for his district. He shall have power to sue and be sued on account of the same in any court of this kingdom. He, in concert with the local sub-agent, shall, under direction of said minister, indicate the site for all school houses in his district. The sub-agent may, under this direction, superintend the erection thereof, and may make contracts for that purpose. The buildings so erected shall be under his immediate guardianship. He shall preserve them from decay and deterioration, and when requisite in his opinion, shall cause them to be repaired or altered at the expense of the district, giving due notice of all his acts to the minister of public instruction for approval.

Section X. The labor tax imposed by article third of chapter second of the third part of this act shall be specially devoted, so far as need be, to the support of schools established on the foundation of this part and to the maintenance and support of teachers licensed and teaching in some district pursuant to the provisions thereof: Provided that the several superintendents shall annually account to the minister of the public instruction for the manner in which it has been appropriated by them, and the minister of public instruction shall certify to the king, through the minister of finance, what deficit ought to appear in the tax gatherer's reports for each taxation district.

Section XI. The minister of public instruction from time to time, as the wants of the district may require, shall furnish to the respective superintendents any requisite amount and kind of books and stationery which, in his opinion, may be needed by the district to be paid on audit by special appropriation from the resources of the labor or other taxes set apart for the support of schools: Provided, however, that such books and stationery shall, when practicable, be sold at cost in the districts.

Section XII. The minister of public instruction, in concert with the minister of the interior and with the approbation of His Majesty in privy council, shall have power to set apart for the use of specific schools attached to the respective districts or to the endowment of select schools or seminaries of learning, incorporated as hereinbefore provided, any quantity of the unappropriated land which being rented or otherwise rendered productive, under his instruction by the general superintendent of the district, if set apart for district schools, or of the trustee of the select school or seminary, if set apart to select school purposes, shall be applied to their support in the manner to be by said minister indicated in each case.

Section XIII. The minister of public instruction shall, from time to time, make a tour of the respective islands to inquire into the condition of the public schools, when it shall be his duty to hold public examinations of the pupils attached thereto, and when in his estimation the merits of any pupil will warrant it, he shall have power, by way of special encouragement, to give a certification of honor to such pupil, which may in his discretion, with the after ratification of His Majesty, extend to exemption from future taxes of any particular kind therein to be specified, or to a general teacher's license for the islands. Pupils thus distinguished shall be eligible on arrival at a proper age and retaining their pre-eminent character to employment in the government service, if found by His Majesty otherwise qualified: Provided, however, that in case of immorality, subsequent to the date of said certificate, it shall be considered as no longer of any force or value.

Section XIV. The general superintendent of schools for the district, upon complaint that a designated pupil is refractory or disorderly to the detriment of the school, shall have power to suspend such pupil from the school, and report the same to the minister of public instruction, who may confirm or revoke the order of suspension at his discretion, and such pupil, being over the age of twelve years, shall, while so suspended, be liable to the labor tax and to the other taxes for the support of government, and be liable to impressment into the public service as a vagrant.

SectionXV. It shall be lawful for any licensed teacher in actual employment in any sub-division of any of said districts to administer correctional punishment to the pupils of his school when, in his judgment, necessary, and the teacher so acting shall not be in any way amenable therefor: Provided such correctional punishment shall in no case exceed reasonable flagellation; and provided that in case a pupil shall be immoderately or unreasonably or cruelly beaten by his teacher, or wounded or maimed, the teacher shall be liable in private damages to the parent, adopter or guardian of such pupil, and may, on complaint and satisfactory proof to the general superintendent of the district, be deprived of his license to teach: Provided that such teacher may at any time appeal from the decision of the general superintendent to the minister of public instruction who may affirm or reverse the sentence of suspension.

Appendix E

CONSTITUTION • STATE OF HAWAII

ARTICLE IX

EDUCATION

Public Education

Section 1. The State shall provide for the establishment, support and control of a statewide system of public schools free from sectarian control, a state university, public libraries and such other educational institutions as may be deemed desirable, including physical facilities therefor. There shall be no segregation in public educational institutions because of race, religion or ancestry; nor shall public funds be appropriated for the support or benefit of any sectarian or private educational institution.

Board of Education

Section 2. There shall be a board of education, the members of which shall be nominated and, by and with the advice and consent of the senate, appointed by the governor from panels submitted by local school advisory councils to be established by law. At least part of the membership of the board shall represent geographic subdivisions of the State.

Powers of the Board of Education

Section 3. The board of education shall have power, in accordance with law, to formulate policy, and to exercise control over the public school system through its executive officer, the superintendent of public instruction, who shall be appointed by the board and shall be ex officio a voting member thereof.

University of Hawaii

Section 4. The University of Hawaii is hereby established as the state university and constituted a body corporate. It shall have title to all the real and personal property now or hereafter set aside or conveyed to it, which shall be held in public trust for its purposes, to be administered and disposed of according to law.

Board of Regents; Powers

Section 5. There shall be a board of regents of the University of Hawaii, the members of which shall be nominated and, by and with the advice and consent of the senate, appointed by the governor. At least part of the membership of the board shall represent geographic subdivisions of the State. The president of the university and the superintendent of public instruction shall be ex officio voting members of the board. The board shall have power, in accordance with law, to formulate policy, and to exercise control over the university through its executive officer, the president of the university, who shall be appointed by the board.

Appendix F

HAWAII STATE GOVERNMENT REORGANIZATION ACT OF 1959

ACT I

Section 18. Department of education. The department of education shall be headed by an executive board to be known as the board of education.

Under policies established by the board, the superintendent shall administer programs of education and public instruction throughout the state, including education at the pre-school, primary and secondary school levels, post high school vocational and adult education, library services, vocational rehabilitation (subject to the proviso hereinafter set forth), health education and instruction (not including dental health treatment transferred to the department of health), and such other programs as may be established by law.

The function of vocational rehabilitation shall be transferred to the department of social services as soon as such transfer may be made without jeopardizing any federal aid.

The functions and authority heretofore exercised by the department of public instruction (except dental health treatment transferred to the department of health), library of Hawaii, Hawaii county library and Maui county library as heretofore constituted are hereby transferred to the department of education established by this Act.

The management contract between the board of supervisors of the county of Kauai and the Kauai public library association entered into under the provisions of section 45-13 of the Revised Laws of Hawaii 1955, as amended, shall be terminated at the earliest time after the effective date of this Act permissible under the terms of such contract and the provisions of this paragraph shall constitute notice of such termination, and the functions and authority heretofore exercised by the Kauai county library as heretofore constituted and the Kauai public library association over the public libraries in the county of Kauai shall thereupon be transferred to the department of education established by this Act.

The management contracts between the trustees of the library of Hawaii and the friends of the library of Hawaii entered into under the provisions of section 45-1 of the Revised Laws of Hawaii 1955, as amended, and between the library of Hawaii and the Hilo library and reading room association entered into under the provisions of section 45-11 of the Revised Laws of Hawaii 1955, as amended, shall be terminated at the earliest time after the effective date of this Act permissible under the terms of such contracts, and the provisions of this paragraph shall constitute notice of such termination.

Upon the termination of such contracts, the state or the counties shall not enter into any library management contracts with any private association; provided, that in providing library services the board of education may enter into contracts approved by the governor for the use of lands, buildings, equipment and facilities owned by any private association.

There shall be within the department of education a commission in each county to be known as the library advisory commission for such county which shall in each case sit in an advisory capacity to the board of education on matters relating to public library services in the respective county. Each commission shall consist of not less than seven and no more than eleven members .

12 Idaho

DEPARTMENT OF EDUCATION

Harold Farley

Contents

THE TERRITORIAL PERIOD, 1863 TO 1890

Establishing the Territorial Schools

Some time after 1825, three young Nez Percé Indians attended the Red River Mission School in Canada. Their experiences so impressed the tribe's elders that they decided to send representatives to St. Louis in 1831 to request help from the Governor, General William Clark, in receiving more instruction of this kind. The story, slightly distorted, excited the Eastern religious press (1). Reverend Jason W. Lee journeyed to the "Oregon Country" in 1834 to establish an Indian school. When he reached Fort Hall in the southern part of what became Idaho Territory, he delivered a sermon to the trappers–probably the first sermon in the Northwest area west of the Rocky Mountains.

Two years after Lee, Dr. Marcus Whitman and Reverend H. H. Spaulding, a Presbyterian minister, followed for the same purpose. A year after he arrived, in 1837, the Reverend Spaulding established Idaho's first school near the junction of Lapwai Creek and the Clearwater River. Except for a few missions set up for the Indians by passing missionaries, the only other school on record prior to Idaho's becoming a territory was established for white children at Franklin, Idaho, in 1860 by the Latter-Day Saints.

These missions opened the heavy immigration to Oregon during the next decade, though most of the people who settled in the Idaho Territory were lured by the discovery of minerals. The communities developed around mining properties. The Chinese, who did a little truck farming near the mining camps, were the only settlers interested in agriculture. Florence, a thriving mining town, established in 1864 the first common school in the territory with six pupils and a teacher, Mrs. Statira Robinson, the wife of a pioneer from Ohio. Other communities followed suit.

Since the majority of the early settlers came from California, where the public school system was fairly well established, there was a strong sentiment for public education. In 1863, when Idaho was organized as a separate territory, laws passed in the first Legislative Assembly provided for a territorial superintendent of public instruction. When the second Legislative Assembly met the following year, it adopted a complete school code modeled after the California code as the legal basis for the territory's public school system (2).

The first Territorial Board of Education consisted of the superintendent, acting as president; the territorial auditor, acting as secretary; and the territorial treasurer. In its second session, the Territorial Legislature changed the board so that it was composed of the Governor, the superintendent of public instruction, and the territorial controller. The board's duties were not stipulated, but the territorial superintendent was charged with preparing instruction and forms for subordinate divisions; apportioning school money; exercising general supervision over the schools; reporting educational conditions and his official actions, together with suggestions relating to construction of schoolhouses, improvement and better management of common schools, qualification of teachers, and ways and means for raising funds; and having to "disseminate intelligence among the people in relation to the method and value of education" (3).

In 1864, J. R. Chittenden took office as the first territorial superintendent. In his first report, he showed that by the close of 1865 the territory had 12 schools, 4 private and 8 public, to educate 427 white children out of the 1,239 between 5 and 21 years of age estimated to be in the territory (4). The private schools mentioned in the superintendent's report were in reality pseudopublic schools or "subscription schools," such as existed in all pioneer territories. They were financed by fixed sums (subscriptions), assessed by the citizens–usually the parents–to maintain schools in the mining camps. An early Lewiston pioneer described the first subscription school, established in Lewiston in 1863:

> Late in the fall of 1863 a middle-aged man of professional appearance and quiet demeanor appeared in Lewiston and proceeded to organize a small school. He wore a tall silk hat, a suit of blackest broadcloth, and a white tie, all bearing unmistakable signs of long usage and giving the impression that their proprietor was a broken down sport. They did not belie him, as events proved, but for the time the ability of the man was all

that was inquired into. After diligent canvassing, he secured a few pupils and opened his school. Everything progressed satisfactorily until the teacher drew his first month's pay, whereupon the sporting proclivities of the pedagogue manifested themselves. He set out to double his money at the gambling table, but, unfortunately for him, the fickle Dame played him false at the most critical juncture, and his wages passed into other hands. Not desiring to remain longer in Lewiston in face of his ignominious downfall he quietly departed whence he came and the school was left teacherless (5).

Conditions of the Territorial Schools

Conditions in the new territory were not favorable to establishing a dynamic school system. The first white inhabitants were miners who followed the gold rushes and men without families who did not stay long. But on their heels came farmers, stockmen, and small businessmen who required some kind of schooling for their families. The people were ordinary pioneers, poor in purse and education, accustomed to the hard toil necessary to clear the wilderness, and though most believed in education for their children, they were too hard pressed providing themselves with a meager living to give schooling considerable attention. Except for an occasional temporary private school in the more populous centers, only the traditional American "district" schools were established to serve students within designated areas.

School Buildings. The territorial laws did not provide for constructing school buildings, and these were rare in the early history. Only three buildings were constructed by 1865, all financed by subscription. Until the school code was revised in 1879 to provide for construction, classes were held in private homes, old store buildings, dance halls, church buildings, or any place where sufficient room could be found. One county superintendent reported in 1882:

> The first school houses erected are unworthy of the name, and as yet there are but a few in the county that deserve the title of school house. Heretofore there has been entire disregard of everything except ventilation, which is applied as freely as the wind that blows (6).

The rapidly growing towns found the revised School Code of 1879 inadequate to provide funds for building and maintaining their schools. Boise and Lewiston in 1881 and Emmetsville in 1883 secured charters from the Territorial Legislature granting their districts and school authorities complete independence from the school code. The mining town of Bellevue did not secure a special charter, but it did get the 1885 Legislative Assembly to permit it to sell bonds to erect "a brick structure at a cost not to exceed eight thousand dollars" (7).

Despite these difficulties, by 1889, Idaho had 386 school districts and 296 schoolhouses, attended by 12,457 children an average of 4.4 months each year. A law enacted 2 years earlier required parents to send children from 8 to 14 years of age to school at least 12 weeks each year, 8 of them consecutive. Some of the children could get education beyond the eighth grade: Boise established its first high school in 1881, and a few of the populated districts followed suit.

Teacher Qualifications. In 1864, the second Territorial Legislature permitted school trustees to issue teacher certificates, and these were changed six times by 1885. Until 1880, all certificates were issued through examinations by trustees and county superintendents, the laws allowing the local school boards or districts to set the qualifications. After 1880, the examinations were prepared by the state superintendent or a person designated as superintendent when the office was not filled.

Although the teachers in the territory represented varying degrees of preparation, many were from Yale, Princeton, the University of Maine, and Bowdoin. Perhaps these men were better equipped mentally than morally, because it was not uncommon for them to be "tipplers" and card players, whose love of adventure or some misfortune inspired them to "go West." In 1874, Superintendent Joseph Perrault reported that "almost every day complaints are made that our teachers are incompetent" (8). Two years later he declared:

> One cause of so many incompetent teachers in Idaho is the mistaken policy of letting the contract of school keeping to the lowest bidder.... Another cause is the absence, in most cases, of any competent and responsible authority for the examination of those offering to teach. The present law authorizes the trustees of the school districts to examine and employ teachers. The first person who comes along wanting a situation, who can gain the good will of the trustees, and guardians, need entertain no fears from any trying ordeal in the shape of an examination; more especially, if he or she is willing to enter upon the task for a salary so low as to defy competition (9).

These complaints about the quality of teachers continued throughout the territorial period.

Financial Problems

During the early territorial period, funds were so scarce that the schools ran an average of only 2 months per year. Private property was respected and almost immune from invasion by a law officer, so the bridge and ferry tax of 1 percent of income was often not collected. Five percent of the taxes collected on county assessed valuation was provided for schools by law, but little of it was set aside for the schools. Since the county superintendent's salary was paid from the county school fund rather than from the county general funds, as was the case with other county officers, this reduced the money available for schools. The county superintendent's salary did not become a county obligation until 1895, after Idaho became a state. As a result, many early county superintendencies were not filled because the pay was so indefinite.

Until the late 1880's, the state superintendent received little money—scarcely enough to print the required forms. When the Legislature attempted to reduce expenditures in 1868, it dropped the superintendent as an officer and transferred his duties to the controller. In 1887, it once again designated the superintendent of public instruction as a territorial officer and assigned him the following new duties: to decide disputed points of law; to visit counties during 3 months of the year in order to inspect the schools, consult with county superintendents, and perfect titles to school property; to hold teachers examinations for territorial certificates; and to deliver lectures to institutes.

School superintendents constantly complained about the "selfishness and ignorance" of the territory's settlers. Isolated and lacking culture, these were generally indifferent to education; homes, better means of travel and communication, and public buildings had priority over schoolhouses and playgrounds. Legislators and county commissioners heeded the taxpayers' demands for economy in public expenditures. Although Governors as well as superintendents argued that the infancy of a new civil society was the time for the general government to give a special lift to the schools, they had little success in arousing interest.

The first "Act To Establish a Common School System" set up a territorial school fund composed of (a) the "principal of all moneys accruing to this Territory from the sale of land heretofore given, or which may be given by Congress for school purposes," and (b) legacies. This fund was declared to be "irreducible and indivisible," the interest on its investment to be divided among common school districts "proportionally to the number of children in each, between the ages of four to twenty-one years" (10).

Territorial Legislatures never established machinery for selling the 3.5 million acres of land in sections 16 and 36, and apparently the legacies were never received. The second legislative session made escheated estates part of the fund, but the total amounted to only $12,464. The last Territorial Legislature finally passed in 1889 an act for investing the money in the territorial general fund. The controller was authorized to draw warrants on the general school fund to pay for the care of prisoners, but there was no provision for him to use the funds to operate the schools. To enable the schools to operate immediately, the Legislature passed an act in 1864 stipulating that 5 percent of the tax money received by the county treasurer should be apportioned to the school districts on the per-capita principles stated in the previous act. The same Legislature passed another act giving the schools 1 percent of the gross receipts of toll roads, bridges, and ferries—the only public utilities at the time—and all of the fines and forfeitures for breach of penal laws.

In place of the 5 percent of tax collections, the third Legislature authorized a county school levy of 1.5 to 2 mills and provided for district levies for general support. This county levy was fixed at 4 to 10 mills in 1883, where it remained for a decade. This same year, the limit on special school district levies was placed at 10 mills, and it remained so until statehood. The law limited the right to vote on district taxes to actual resident taxpayers, but widows or unmarried women age 21 or more who resided in, held, or owned property subject to the special tax were entitled to vote. County commissioners did not make full use of their levying powers, and in general the assessments were approximately one-third of true valuations.

The apportionment of funds to school districts was proportional to the number of children of school age until 1871, when the law was changed to require that two-thirds of the fund be divided equally among the school districts and one-third by the per-capita principle. In the same session, the Legislature amended this act to read that one-half would be divided evenly among the districts and one-half according to per capita. Later Legislatures made some variations among counties, but the revised statutes of 1887 made the 50-50 division uniform throughout the territory, and it remained so until statehood.

The distribution of available resources among districts was essentially inequitable during the territorial period. Superintendent Silas W. Moody reported to Governor Edward A. Stevenson in 1886:

> Some system should be devised for the assistance of poor and thinly populated districts. Under the present laws one-half of the school money is distributed per capita and "to him that hat shall be given" finds a practical illustration in the method. The feebler districts are forced to be content with but a few months' school (11).

Some years later, Moody's successor, Charles C. Stevensen, referring to the small, crude, and overcrowded schoolhouses, stated:

> I would suggest that the proceeds of the General School Fund, with what may be added to it from time to time, be used largely for the purpose of building and equipping proper school-houses for the smaller and poorer districts. The wealthier districts can look out for themselves more properly for in this free land of ours the poor man's child is as much entitled to a common school education as the rich man's (12).

Since the general school fund consisted almost entirely of the proceeds from the escheated estates and was irreducible and indivisible, with only the interest usable,

Stevensen was proposing very slight assistance. However, it stands as one of the first suggestions to establish equalization among school districts.

Records indicate that the Territorial Legislature paid scant attention to the requests of school officials. The maximum levy by counties was gradually increased, and since trustees of local districts were in complete control of the school systems, any advances the schools made were directly related to their progressive thinking.

EARLY STATEHOOD, 1890 TO 1913

Organizing a State Department of Education

The people of Idaho greeted statehood in 1890 with great expectations–especially educators and those interested in education for their children. In January 1891, the first State Legislature met in Boise and adopted a complete school code. It established a State Board of Public Instruction composed of the state superintendent, who served as president; the secretary of state; and the attorney general. The state superintendent was given equal status with other state officials.

When the first state superintendent, Joseph Harroun, took office in 1891, the Department of Education came into existence. By the end of the decade it consisted of the superintendent, one staff member, and a part-time secretary. The superintendent and his staff were responsible for summarizing reports from 21 county superintendents, granting state certificates and life diplomas for teachers who passed the state examinations or otherwise qualified, and preparing examination questions for the first-, second-, and third-grade certificates. The 1891 law also required the superintendent to meet with the county superintendents, print lists of textbooks adopted by the Board of Textbook Commissioners and regulations for textbook care, distribute income from the state school fund to the county superintendents, and prepare a course of study in all public schools. The superintendent assumed general supervision of the county superintendents and the state's public schools. Not only did he serve as president of the State Board of Education, but also as a member of the Board of Trustees of the Lewiston and Albion normal schools and the State Library Commission.

Since the state superintendent and his staff had neither the funds nor the professional assistance to carry out all of these duties, his work mainly consisted of inspecting the schools and collecting meager statistics. The boards of trustees of the independent school districts had the right, by law, to determine the number and qualifications of teachers they employed; many hired teachers who did not hold certificates or diplomas. Although districts were supposed to use textbooks listed for use by a State Textbook Commission established in 1899, many did not, much to the chagrin of professional people, county superintendents, and common schools who did not have this right. Superintendent Permeal French requested the state attorney general to render an opinion on this practice, and in May 1900, he ruled that all districts would have to employ teachers with certificates and use books selected by the textbook commission.

This ruling settled another problem. The law said that the school board should have the power to determine the number and qualifications of its teachers, but the independent school district trustees were employing teachers who did not hold certificates from either the state or the county superintendent. When the attorney general ruled that all school districts must employ teachers with certificates, most of these certificates were issued only by the superintendent at the county level. In 1905, the Legislature changed the law so that the certificates could be issued to graduates of state normal schools and chartered colleges empowered to grant degrees.

The problems of education in Idaho were no different from those in other states during their early history, but they were made more acute by its topography, sparse population, and great distances, magnified by the lack of transportation and other communication facilities. In 1898, the superintendent reported:

> A general view of the Idaho system shows at once its strength and weakness. The county district schools, the independent district schools, the normal schools and the State University are the component parts of the State system. Some of these parts taken separately are doing strong and efficient work, but the weakness of the system is manifest when we come to study the articulation of its elements. The country schools are not in touch with the graded schools of the independent districts, nor are the graded schools yet in touch with the University. . . .The teachers of the State have worked well, but each in his separate field with hardly a definite idea as to the general condition of the schools round about him and with hardly a thought as to his relation to the general trend of education in the State or his place in the State system. After two years' time taken to survey the educational field in the state it is my opinion that the best lines of progress possible for our schools lie in an effort tending to centralize and unify the educational forces of the State (13).

At this time, the superintendent was working with the new state university, founded at Moscow in 1889, on a plan of unity. The president of the university outlined the plan as a set of uniform examinations for admission to the university. The university would then issue a report card certifying the branches the student could enter.

The plan failed because the two normal schools, established by the Legislature in 1893 at Lewiston and

Albion, had adjusted their courses to appeal to more students and meet the needs of graduates from both public and private schools. The normal schools and the districts having high schools were against having the University of Idaho determine who could attend the university and what course offerings there could be. The Legislature, as well as the people, were against the "university plan," and this accounts in part for the failure of the state superintendent in his bid for reelection.

The schools continued to grow, however, and by 1900 there were 722 districts. Schools operated an average of 5.3 months each year for 35,329 students, out of a total of 54,839 children between the ages of 5 and 21. The 1,067 teachers received an average monthly salary of slightly over $48. Despite an expenditure of $499,839 in the 1899-1900 school year, 99 of the 756 school buildings were without suitable outhouses.

Setting the Stage for Progress

Rivalry Among Schools. At the end of the first decade of the twentieth century, much to the distress of most educators, the higher institutions were fighting over shares of the tax dollar. Long after the need ceased to exist, the normal schools continued to maintain large preparatory programs and duplicated the offerings of the university. The institutions' separate boards and their presidents spent considerable time at legislative sessions lobbying for appropriations.

Not only did the relationships with the colleges fail to improve, but rivalry also sprang up between the state department and the city schools. Since the city school systems had developed independent of the state department, the department's relations to them were extended only through the various county superintendents. Students transferring from one school to another or coming from outside the state were caught in a "web of distrust," and they usually found they had fewer credits than they had been led to believe, or they had to repeat courses after they transferred. The situation was compounded because the law provided for the organization of independent school districts, and the state superintendent was unable to get support for controlling laws from a state board whose members were extremely busy with their regular duties as elected state officials.

The "Idaho Plan." In 1911, Governor James H. Hawley outlined the major problems to the Legislature. He then recommended that the Legislature levy a fixed tax to put the higher educational institutions on a more stable financial basis. His second recommendation, which eventually laid the foundation for Idaho's educational structure, called for the creation of a single governing body responsible for the general supervision of the state's schools. The Legislature supported these recommendations and submitted the following constitutional amendment to the electors at the next general election:

> 'Shall Section 2 of Article 9 of the Constitution of the State of Idaho be so amended that the general supervision of the educational institutions and public school system of the State of Idaho shall be vested in a State Board of Education, the membership, powers and duties of which shall be prescribed by law?' The State Superintendent of Public Instruction shall be ex-officio member of said Board (14).

Both political parties accepted the single-board concept and included it in their platforms. The amendment carried by a wide majority—33,045 to 14,796—and set the stage for newly elected Governor John M. Haines to carry out the mandate of the people.

On Governor Haines's recommendations, the 1913 Legislature established one board to be in charge of all phases of public education and prescribed its membership, power, and duties. Officially titled the State Board of Education and Board of Regents of the University of Idaho, it was also later designated as the State Board for Vocational Education. The law stipulated that this single governing body was to be composed of six members, five to be appointed by the Governor, with the state superintendent of public instruction as an ex officio member (15). The law provided for 5-year terms for each of the appointed members, the first terms staggered from 1 to 5 years so that one expired annually. To counteract the existing animosities, the law forbade any person who had been a board member of a higher educational institution or connected with a state educational institution, either as an instructor or a student, to be appointed to the State Board of Education. Members were to be selected by ability, without reference to locality, occupation, party affiliation, or religion.

The law also empowered the board to appoint a commissioner of education, his term and salary to be set by the board, which could terminate the appointment by a two-thirds vote. It further provided for the appointment of "specialists, assistants, clerks or other executive officers . . . upon recommendation of the Commissioner of Education" (16). This established the legal basis for the State Department of Education.

The "Idaho Plan" placed the state's entire school system under the direction of the State Board of Education and the Board of Regents of the University of Idaho, with the commissioner of education serving as an adviser to the board. The state superintendent acted as the assistant to the commissioner of education except when performing his duties as a member of the State Land Board.

Thus, Idaho was in a unique position as it set the stage for educational progress. The superintendent's biennial report for 1913-14 stated: "Several states have undertaken to unify their education system, but none have gone so far as the new law in Idaho. The best educational authorities have approved the Idaho plan, however, and are watching its operation with interest" (17).

As the governing authority for the state's educational institutions, the new board was responsible for the efficient operation of 1,278 school districts located in 33 counties. These districts employed 3,144 teachers to instruct 92,437 pupils, with 392 of the teachers responsible for 6,105 students enrolled in high schools. These districts were under the jurisdiction of 4,236 school trustees. Thus, in the rural schools the ratio of trustees to teachers was almost three to one.

A PERIOD OF GROWTH, 1913 TO 1933

In April 1913, the new State Board of Education assumed the task of directing the affairs of the six state institutions and the public schools. The board selected E. O. Sisson as commissioner of education to work with public school administrators and heads of the higher educational institutions in making the transition from the old system to what became known as the "Idaho System."

Progress Under the Commissioners of Education

After organizing his staff, Dr. Sisson conducted a survey of the public schools to determine the conditions and revenue. His reports prompted the state board to standardize the high schools in 1915 and the Legislature to enact a law requiring free high school instruction for pupils in home districts without high schools. The Legislature also raised the limit of the levy from 5 mills to 10 mills. In 1915, it also enacted the first comprehensive certification law. In addition to county certificates, which were limited to the elementary grades, the law created "state" certificates valid in all grades and for secondary subjects. They were based on certain minimum requirements and could be renewed and converted to "life" certificates.

State Superintendent Grace M. Shepherd launched a vigorous campaign to bring about school consolidation. The commissioner's survey had revealed inequities and inefficiency in the operation of the schools, and Miss Shepherd recommended the county unit for school government. Miss Shepherd made a good argument for consolidation by pointing to the rural communities, where the problems were worse and where there were more trustees than teachers. But the state board opposed any law making the county unit compulsory, so no bill was introduced. Miss Shepherd decided not to seek reelection.

Bernice McCoy, assistant to Miss Shepherd, was elected state superintendent on a platform of eliminating the duplicate offices and responsibilities. In April 1915, she presented the state board with a resolution, which it accepted unanimously, requesting the Legislature to give the people an opportunity to eliminate the constitutional office of state superintendent of public instruction. The Legislature submitted such a constitutional amendment to the people, but they rejected it.

During his years of service to the state board, Commissioner Sisson instituted many changes. When he resigned in 1917, the school laws had been consolidated, simplified, and clarified by the Legislature; the apportionment of school funds from the state land earnings had been simplified; and there was more flexibility and simplification of teacher certification. The school term had been increased from 5 to 7 months. The department had released many publications, including pamphlets. Some were designed to help rural teachers or to improve purchasing procedures. One outlined the study of Idaho history, and others assisted in organizing and planning high school programs of instruction to comply with standards adopted by the state board. The state board adopted standard methods for gathering statistical data from the schools, and those statistics were used frequently in presentations to the Legislature. In fact, the education committee of the Legislature met in the commissioner's office, where the information was readily available.

Enoch A. Bryan, retired president of the State College of Washington, was appointed to succeed Dr. Sisson in July 1917. He continued ongoing activities and broadened them. The state board had the responsibility for prescribing a minimum course of study for schools and determining how and under what regulation textbooks were to be adopted. The commissioner appointed advisory committees, and identical sets of textbooks were adopted for use in all districts except Class A independent districts. A course of study covering the minimum 7 months of school was adopted and published.

In the meantime, Superintendent McCoy, as a member of the Board of Land Commissioners, spent considerable time studying the school accounts. Income from the state lands was deposited in the general fund, and this money, when invested, drew interest to the general fund. The money invested from the sale of lands did not go into the school fund, thus it could earn no profit for the schools. The State Supreme Court ruled in 1918 that the funds should be kept separate and that the interest earned be credited to the school fund.

Until 1918, the state department conducted its many duties with three principal staff members. The commissioner was head of the department, the state superintendent served as his assistant, and a business agent supervised the business of the department, the state institutions, and the public schools.

The commissioner's duties were expanded as a result of the Smith-Hughes Act, passed by Congress in February 1917. A bill was immediately introduced in the Idaho Legislature to accept the provisions; it passed the House unanimously, but the Senate overlooked it. However,

Congress amended the bill to authorize the Governor to accept the provisions of the act on behalf of the state, and Idaho was permitted to participate. The Governor designated the State Board of Education as the State Board for Vocational Education. The board appointed the commissioner of education as director of vocational education. The Legislature appropriated the matching funds for operating the program in 1919, and by July a state director and three supervisors were operating the program under the direction of the commissioner of education.

As a result of the 1921 Depression, the Legislature in 1923 decided to economize by eliminating the appropriation for a commissioner from the state board's budget. Dr Bryan resigned, but the department's administrative staff remained at three persons, and a director and two supervisors administered the vocational education programs. The elected state superintendent and the appointed director of vocational education assumed the duties of the business manager. The following year in November, the State Board of Education requested the Legislature to renew the appropriation for a commissioner of education. The Legislature granted the request, and in 1925, Idaho once more had a dual administration in the Department of Education.

Upgrading the High Schools

When the Legislature created the State Board of Education in 1913, it directed the board to "grade and classify" high schools and to "adopt and publish standards and requirements" for their operation. Moving promptly, at its June meeting the Legislature provided for four classes of high schools based on the number of years of work offered to meet the needs of a pioneer state with a wide variation in the maturity of its communities. Class I schools were those offering 4 years and 15 units, Class II were schools of 3 years and 12 units, Class III were schools of 2 years and 8 units, and Class IV schools offered 1 year and 4 units.

The state board also recognized as early as 1913 the need for inspecting the high schools. It postponed action in the interest of economy until July 1915, when the state board approved such a recommendation by the commissioner of education. The inspection was to be performed by a team consisting of the commissioner, state superintendent, and representatives from the four state schools. Although the standards adopted in 1915 to assist the inspectors have been revised a number of times, they still contain some of the elements in the original draft.

In 1923, the state board approved a resolution providing for cooperation with the University of Idaho to inspect the high schools. A university instructor was charged with inspecting as many of the schools as possible during a 5-month period each year. This arrangement continued until 1941, when the state department was given responsibility for inspecting the high schools.

Under the laws, every child in Idaho was entitled to a free high school education, and in those districts where it was not available, the districts were to pay tuition to a school outside the home district. Only accredited or approved high schools were permitted to collect tuition. The accredited high schools were the responsibility of the high school inspector. The approved high schools, usually those offering less than 4 years of high school, were under the county superintendents, who recommended their approval to the state superintendent. These approved schools could be accredited when they offered 4 years of high school work and met the requirements for accreditation, which closely followed the Northwest Accreditation Association standards.

Teacher Certification

Establishing the Idaho Professional Association. Prior to 1918, graduation from high school was not a prerequisite for certification, but 3 years later, with the exception of provisional and county certificates, Idaho ranked with three other states at the top of the list in the professional preparation of its teachers. The new law, enacted in 1921, discontinued the many forms of state certificates and provided for those previously issued to be converted into 5-year state elementary and state high school certificates. Teachers had to graduate from a 4-year high school and take professional courses varying from 6 weeks to 1 year. The county superintendent and the higher education institutions did continue to issue certificates, and most of these issued as state certificates were endorsements of out-of-state certificates.

Despite the profession's efforts to increase the standards over the years, too often the Legislature tended to block the raised requirements just when it appeared that progress was being made. The repeated recommendations by state superintendents frequently had little effect.

In 1919, a teachers organization was established to form a closer liaison among teachers and between the teachers and the Department of Education. When the seventeenth session of the Legislature used the excuse of a teacher shortage to lower the standards for teacher certification, the association protested vigorously. In 1924, experienced teachers could not secure teaching positions, so the state superintendent urged the Legislature to restore the former standards.

The deep concern among teachers gave life to the organization. It commenced publishing *The Idaho Teacher* to mold its 3,800 members—about 88 percent of the state's teachers—into a tighter organization. In July 1926, the association employed an executive secretary and established its headquarters in Boise. It worked closely with the state board and pledged its support to make the Idaho system effective in all divisions of public education. It promised to promote the general educational welfare of the state, to advance the educational standards, to encourage and develop the educational field, to cooperate with other organizations, and to bring the people of Idaho to an understanding and appreciation of the state's education system.

Upgrading Teaching Qualifications

Despite the efforts of the teachers association, there was an extensive teacher turnover in Idaho schools. In her 1923-24 report, State Superintendent Elizabeth Russum estimated the average turnover to be nearly 50 percent. She found that only 50 percent of the state's teachers had been employed in Idaho the previous year. The schools lacked adequate accommodations, and the communities gave little recognition for good service, so the teachers shifted within the state and moved out in large numbers. The state superintendent solicited help from the school trustees and the Parent-Teachers Association to secure annual salary increases for the teachers, and she suggested to the Legislature that it enact an effective teacher retirement law. She received no support from the legislators.

Superintendent Russum also pointed out that most of Idaho's undertrained teachers were in the rural schools, and they had little supervision. In 1927, the Legislature raised the requirements for a teaching certificate to not less than 2 years of professional training, with the provision that no person could teach in the Idaho schools after September 1929 who had not received this training. The following year, only 60 county certificates were issued compared to 409 during the previous 4 years.

In 1933, the state board decided to grant state certificates to applicants who held comparable certificates from states in which they received their training. It also stipulated 6 semester hours of practice teaching for the elementary certificates and required all out-of-state applicants to attend an Idaho school for at least a summer term to receive elementary or secondary certificates. By 1933, only 10 county certificates were issued.

Elected Superintendent Becomes Chief State School Officer

Considerable duplication existed between the offices of the state superintendent of public instruction and the commissioner of education, and there was a lack of harmony between the offices. Perhaps this was due in large measure to the appointment of State Superintendent Ethel E. Redfield to the office of commissioner of education when the Legislature restored the funds to operate the latter office in 1925.

W. D. Vincent, superintendent of the Industrial Training School, replaced Miss Redfield as commissioner. Mrs. Myrtle R. Davis, the assistant state superintendent, was elected state superintendent in 1928. Idaho Attorney General Bert Miller commented on the relationship:

> It is a known fact that during the existence of the office of said commissioner and the personnel thereof, the constitutional office of State Superintendent of Public Instruction was relegated to the point of innocuous desuetude (18).

After 2 years in office, Superintendent Davis appealed to Governor H. C. Baldridge to eliminate duplication in the state's school office. She pointed out that although many people wanted a single state board, the Legislature had established the commissioner of education and named him secretary of the state board. She stated that the tendency of the state board had been to delegate more power to the commissioner by taking duties from the state superintendent until the commissioner assumed authority and control over public education.

Superintendent Davis also pointed to other problems. Idaho ranked third highest in the salaries it paid its two executive officers, but eighth lowest in total pupil enrollment and teachers employed. There were no specialists in either elementary or secondary education and no unification of educational programing. She claimed that the budget she proposed would provide for two assistants to supervise elementary and secondary schools, a business manager, a certification clerk, and three secretaries, and that the budget would still save over $17,000 per biennium, an amount equal to over 24 percent of the total requested for each office. The Governor and the 1931 Legislature did not heed her request, but the groundwork had been laid. In the following session, the Legislature eliminated the office of commissioner of education and in 1933 named the state superintendent as the executive secretary of the State Board of Education. For the first time the state superintendent was in a key position with respect to the total educational program in Idaho.

THE DEPRESSION AND WORLD WAR II, 1933 TO 1947

Idaho, like other states, struggled in the early thirties to free itself from the grip of the Depression. While many states were closing their schools for lack of funds, Idaho was fortunate in not having to shut down any school for this reason after 1932. This was partially due to better payment of taxes–people did not want their property to be put into the hands of county officials because of nonpayment. But local school boards deserved a great deal of credit for their close attention to financial accounting. Although most school districts paid with warrants, and in many places teachers were forced to take discounts for cashing the warrants, the schools continued to operate.

Idaho's First Foundation Program

In 1933, the Legislature passed a bill providing for a more equitable distribution of state funds to the school districts that took into consideration the varying ability of the districts to finance education. For the first time the state recognized an obligation to contribute to the schools' operations from its general fund. This money, although meager in the beginning, was eventually to be combined with the public land investment earnings and forest funds and be distributed by an adopted formula. The Legislature also taxed beer and chain stores more than $155,000 and combined this sum with $556,417 earned by the endowment funds to help the schools during the 1933-34 terms. This state aid enabled nearly 80 percent of the school districts to operate on a cash basis.

The new equalization formula was actually the product of years of work by educators and interested citizens. Various proposals had been presented as early as 1927, but it was difficult to reach an agreement on all parts of the formula. The final compromises established a formula based on classroom units determined by student average daily attendance, with the high school units weighted. School districts making a 3-mill levy would receive state funds appropriated by the Legislature, and the balance needed for a "minimum program" would come from a flexible county levy. School districts deciding to offer more than the "minimum program" could raise the funds needed by levying a special district tax.

During the first year under the new school formula, the county levies ranged from a low of 2.65 mills to a high of 14.97 mills. The assessed valuation of county wealth for each classroom unit ranged from $54,055 to $182,959. The districts' special levies for funds above the minimum ranged from 5 mills to 12 mills. When the valuation of the districts decreased the next year, the counties raised the levies to make up the difference in funds available from the state and district minimum levies.

Education Improvement

State Superintendent John W. Condie labeled the biennial 1935-36 as one of real educational accomplishment. Enrollments in both the elementary and high schools increased, and the higher education institutions grew beyond predictions. Many schools found it difficult to provide adequate facilities.

Economies forced by the Depression, such as the elimination of four rural supervisors from the state normal schools' budgets, placed an added burden on the county superintendents and the education department. Condie, who had served as executive secretary of the Idaho Education Association prior to his election, did secure the cooperation of the public schools, the higher institutions, and county superintendents in maintaining standards. For instance, the University of Idaho held a 2-week training session for county superintendents to assist them in assuming the responsibilities of the elementary supervisors. The regional teacher institutions assisted classroom teachers.

The department also took on other activities. The federal government apportioned emergency education funds to provide part-time jobs for college students, emergency employment of teachers in nursery schools and adult education, and assistance to the rural school districts that needed funds or whose warrants were impaired. In the fall of 1933, the department assumed the entire supervision of these projects for Idaho. The following year, the state board appointed a director of emergency education and employed a supervisor for each of the adult education and nursery school programs. This gave the department eight persons to fulfill its responsibilities and offer services to the public schools.

In 1934, the department, to improve classroom instruction, held a curriculum conference to which it invited teachers, administrators, and representatives from institutions of higher education. Paul R. Hanna of Stanford University and Edgar M. Draper of the University of Washington were visiting participants. The conference resulted in a request to the Legislature for funds to continue a study of the state's education needs, but the request was not granted.

The department also conducted surveys to determine how many different textbooks were used by the state's 195 high schools and whether there should be more uniformity. It made a statewide library survey to chart standards for elementary and high school libraries and to compare Idaho school libraries with those in other states. In cooperation with institutions of higher education, the department conducted curriculum studies that resulted in revisions and the production of numerous subject guides and curriculum bulletins. With a grant from the federal government and the assistance of WPA personnel, the state department supervised a complete survey of school district organization and finance.

The information from these studies enabled Superintendent Condie to make many recommendations to educators, the general public, and the Legislature. He called attention to the school districts' outdated financial reporting and accounting system. Since some schools carried no insurance, he recommended that school property be evaluated, the actual need for insurance coverage be determined, and this information be made available to the public. Specifically, he recommended–

1. Increased state support for schools to pay the total of the minimum program to achieve equalization of educational opportunity.
2. A plan for more economical and efficient organization of school districts with the hint that the Legislature should require, rather than permit, consolidation of districts.
3. A careful investigation of small schools before allowing any of them to continue to operate.

4. Replacement of rural high schools by independent districts encompassing a number of the present rural organizations.
5. Rejection of a county unit plan of reorganization of schools (19).

Condie also urged giving considerable attention to transportation. He described the conditions:

> School children are being transported to school in any sort of conveyance from a trailer, an open 'pickup' body or a bob sleigh, to the most modern trucks with safety school bus bodies. The cost per child per year ranges from $11.00 to over $100.00. The distances traveled per day range from 3 to 90 miles. The conditions of buses are in many cases unsafe under normal conditions and absolutely hazardous under other circumstances. By this we mean such conditions as noted in the following incomplete list:
>
> 1. Poor brakes
> 2. Poor lights
> 3. Poor tires
> 4. Loose drivers' seats
> 5. Wooden framework
> 6. Breakable glass
> 7. Only one small door in the front of a closed bus (20).

Condie recommended that the state establish minimum transportation standards and qualifications for bus drivers and special bus driving rules.

Financial Problems Emerge

During the 1936-37 school year, revenue from the endowment earnings; the taxes on beer, chain stores, and liquor; and the sales tax provided only 30 percent of the minimum program. To make matters worse, the sales tax was discontinued by a referendum in 1936 and did not provide funds the following year. A mine profits tax, which had been before the courts for 4 years, was added to provide some funds, but since it was estimated that it would bring in only about 50 percent of the sales tax revenues, it was a poor replacement.

In the meantime, with the state paying more, the county levies decreased to less than half the mill levies for the first year of operation under the new school formula. The distribution formula was not changed, and, as the county levies decreased and school costs rose, the need for greater local district levies caused a number of legislators to question the effectiveness of the formula. Districts were paying the total costs for more than 500 teachers who were not part of the formula's minimum program classroom unit allowance. In fact, the minimum program provided only 50 percent of the total funds spent by the public schools. State Superintendent Condie recommended a reduction in the average daily attendance of students, which determined the classroom units for both elementary and high schools. This would decrease the district support, increase the county support, and spend the money available from the state.

The Legislature did not accept the superintendent's recommendation. In 1939, the revenue from different taxes used for the public school fund—with the exception of the endowment earnings—was deposited in the general fund. To replace the revenue lost by education, the Legislature placed an ad valorem tax on the assessed valuation of the state to raise $1 million a year for distribution to the schools. County levies increased, state funds decreased, classroom size increased, and average teacher salaries increased only slightly.

Despite the growing problems faced by the schools, the 1939 Legislature turned a deaf ear to Superintendent Condie's recommendations for increasing state funds, consolidating school districts, regulating transportation, and improving curriculum. Condie again emphasized the need to consider the problems of finance, reorganization, teacher salaries, transportation, insurance, and upgrading of the schools and instructional offerings in his recommendations to the 1941 Legislature.

The curriculum committees busied themselves updating guides and bulletins. The department continued to administer and account for the Works Progress Administration programs. When the Legislature passed laws which permitted the two private junior colleges at Coeur d'Alene and Boise to become public junior colleges, they were placed under the jurisdiction of the state board. The department also established adult education classes at the state penitentiary and correspondence courses for enrollees in the Civilian Conservation Corps. Although the department's work load increased, the staff remained constant, except for personnel added under the federally financed vocational education and rehabilitation services (21).

Superintendent Condie, whose 8-year tenure exceeded all other continuous terms of elected state superintendents, decided not to run for reelection and was succeeded by his assistant, C. E. Roberts. Roberts appointed Condie state high school inspector, thus removing this position from the University of Idaho and placing it in the state department. By 1942, the department's administrative staff consisted of an assistant state superintendent, a high school supervisor (the name was changed from inspector), a supervisor of elementary education, an accountant-auditor, a certification clerk, and an insurance clerk.

World War II

Gearing for the War Effort. It was invaluable for the department to have a state superintendent with Roberts' experience to cope with the mounting problems during World War II. In addition to the regular vocational education program, the department used federal funds to train over 14,000 workers for defense industries, agriculture, and technical fields serving the military. Both the state board and Superintendent Roberts emphasized the need for continuing this vocational educational training—both terminal vocational training and vocational retraining for adjustment—once peace was achieved. Roberts pointed out that such a program would be impossible without the help of wise legislative planning and action (22).

In his report to the Governor and the 1943 Legislature, Superintendent Roberts called attention to earlier recommendations by Condie and presented statistical information to emphasize the critical problems facing the schools. The $2.5 million appropriated by the Legislature for the 1941-42 year fell short in meeting financial needs, and the county tax again paid the largest share for the minimum program. As people left Idaho for war industry employment, student enrollments decreased, and additional state funds provided during the second year of the biennium caused state support to exceed county support. Even so, state funds provided less than 25 percent of the current expenditures; the greatest contribution came from the local school districts.

Groups Organized for Education. The 1943 legislative session was disappointing to education. School district trustees from all parts of the state came to the capital to support regular and emergency appropriations to prevent a continuing exodus of teachers from Idaho. Their requests were not heeded, but their trip to Boise was not entirely futile. While there, they perfected the organization of the Idaho State Trustees Association under the able leadership of Charles T. Whittaker of Rupert.

The association immediately launched a statewide campaign for education and joined others in calling for a second extraordinary session of the Legislature. The Legislature responded, but the acts passed to provide emergency aid for teachers' salaries were declared unconstitutional in the Canyon County District Court (23). The laws were corrected early in the 1945 regular session and made retroactive for the 1944-45 school year to protect the districts that had already provided funds under the act.

Representatives of the Idaho Education Association, the state's Chamber of Commerce, and the State Department of Education met with the presidents of the Idaho Congress of Parents and Teachers and the Idaho State Trustees Association in the summer of 1943 . They became the nucleus of a new organization known as the Idaho Education Council, which also included the state's Junior Chamber of Commerce, Federated Women's Clubs, State Federation of Labor, American Legion, County Superintendents Association, and the Idaho State Grange and Idaho State Farm Bureau. The Governor's Interim School Committee, appointed after the second extraordinary legislative session in 1944, participated in the council's meetings.

In March 1944, State Superintendent C. E. Roberts resigned to devote full time to this newly formed council. Because of his knowledge of the problems and his insistance on reliable statistical data, he provided the council with ideal leadership for developing plans to present to the Legislature.

By the fall of 1944, the Idaho Education Council had developed two major recommendations for the Legislature's consideration: a plan for reorganizing school districts and a school finance program. State Superintendent Acel H. Chatburn, appointed by Governor C. A. Bottolfsen to complete Roberts' term, outlined both proposals to the Governor. The State Board of Education supported the plan and actively assisted in its presentation to the Legislature.

The finance program recommended by the council called for an increase in the minimum program by (a) reducing the size of the classroom unit for both elementary and high schools, (b) increasing the financial allowance for elementary and high school units, (c) providing a minimum transportation program, (d) increasing the minimum district levy, and (e) increasing the minimum county levy. The council estimated that this program would require approximately $1.5 million above the previous appropriation, but the Legislature appropriated only $3,025,000, an increase of only $525,000.

The plan for reorganization proposed a minimum size for districts and suggested that the Governor appoint a state school reorganization commission of seven members, which would include the state superintendent and a state board member. The commission, which would be empowered to appoint a director and staff, would pass on reorganization plans. Each county would establish a seven-member committee to develop and present plans to the state reorganization committee. The superintendent asked the Legislature to appropriate $60,000 to operate the study commission the first 2 years. Despite strong support for the measures, the 1945 Legislature postponed the problem by providing $50,000 for a commission to conduct a complete study of the state's schools. Peabody College agreed to make this survey.

After turning down the state superintendent's recommendations, the Legislature ordered the state board to initiate programs that had not been requested. In 1943, the Legislature enabled the state board to employ staff to supervise a program on the harmful effects of narcotics and stimulants. In 1945, it appropriated funds, separate from the department's budget, to hire personnel to develop a program in guidance and to distribute occupational information.

The state superintendent made no recommendations in his 1945-46 biennial report, but Asher B. Wilson, member of the state board and chairman of the Idaho Education Survey Commission, presented the results of the "Peabody Survey" and its recommendations to the 1947 Legislature (24). The study's recommendations for school district reorganization were nearly identical to those made earlier by Superintendent C. E. Roberts and in 1944 by the Idaho Education Council. The survey committee praised the accomplishments that had been made, particularly the 12-month salary schedule for teachers, the 9-month school term, the method of selecting textbooks, the minimum program principles, and the increased holding power of the schools.

The survey did recommend that the state increase the minimum program by taking into consideration (a) a teacher salary allotment, (b) a transportation allotment, and (c) other current expenses based on classroom units. It would equalize the ability to finance school facilities by providing variable state support and would increase the support for school operation from the counties as well as the state. It pointed to a need for competent school plant consulting services with prior approval of school construction plans, an up-to-date transportation code with transportation supervision, and an increase in the requirements for teacher preparation with a minimum teacher salary schedule. It further recommended that the school curriculum be upgraded through studies of the needs of students relative to the subject matter content, vocational training, and a unified program of curriculum development.

The Peabody Survey also recommended raising the qualifications and salary of an appointed state superintendent, who would serve as executive secretary of the board of education. It recommended that the law recognize and establish officially the State Department of Education. The department, organized into divisions with staff salaries comparable to those paid for similar positions in the public schools, would be expected to expand its services.

The stage was set for the Legislature to perform a great educational service to the state. Educators, organizations, and citizens who had been close to educational problems for the past 5 years had every reason to believe that this was to be the year of accomplishment.

THE PRESENT ERA, 1947 TO 1966

Legislative Action on the Peabody Recommendations

The year 1947 did herald a new era in education for Idaho. The Legislature enacted into law over 30 educational bills, including many of the major and some of the minor Peabody Survery recommendations. One act based the minimum program payments on five factors, including an allowance for teacher training and experience. Another upgraded teacher qualifications through a new certification program. A new transportation code was established with provisions for the state board to provide standards for equipment. The Legislature adopted a minimum salary schedule for teachers, provided for sick leave, and required all instructional personnel to have health examinations. One act charged the state board with administration of the school lunch program.

The new legislation also affected higher education. The 2-year school at Pocatello was permitted to become a 4-year liberal arts school and was renamed Idaho State College. The two normal schools were renamed and their offerings expanded so they could grant bachelor degrees in both elementary and secondary education. The appropriations for both public schools and the higher educational institutions were quite liberal compared to previous appropriations.

The job of initiating these new programs was tremendous, and the state board, State Superintendent Alton B. Jones, and the department's staff faced the task with the addition of only one person: a school lunch accountant. The Legislature had neglected to increase the department's budget adequately; it added a mere $7,500 to help operate the entire school lunch program.

School Lunch Program

The school lunch program came under the jurisdiction of the education department when Congress passed the National School Lunch Act in 1946. Until the Legislature appropriated $7,500 for a clerk, the department administered the program with its regular staff and absorbed these costs. The Department of Health cooperated by providing sanitarians for inspections, and the Department of Public Assistance distributed commodities. The education department was able to assume the entire operation of the program in July 1949 after the Legislature appropriated enough money to pay most of its administration.

Organization other than the district boards of trustees sponsored over 50 percent of the 272 lunch programs operated in the schools, with the Parent-Teachers Associations the most active in various communities. But the basic responsibility for the programs rested with the individual boards of trustees, even though this was not finally assumed by the districts until 1965, when the state board ruled that only local boards could sign the agreements. The department's efficient operation has made the school lunch program easily available to the districts and has increased participation from 30 percent at the beginning to 40 percent of the students attending schools in 1965-66.

School Reorganization

The new reorganization law provided for a nine-member state reorganization committee appointed by the state board and composed of a state board member and four persons from each of the two congressional districts, with no more than three of the appointed persons actively engaged in education. The committee selected Kenneth F. Dean, a school superintendent, as director of school reorganization, and he worked tirelessly for the program.

The department faced a particularly thorny task in attempting to combine the state's 1,082 school districts into workable consolidated units. Many communities had built all of their social activities around their small school, and they were sentimentally attached to the "little red schoolhouse." Furthermore, many people believed that "what was good enough for me is good enough for my child." The reorganization committee therefore held 35 meetings during its first 18 months of existence to explain and sell the program to the people.

Asher B. Wilson, chairman of the State Board of Education, personally accepted the responsibility for the state board to reorganize school districts. He attended most of the reorganization committee's meetings and did not hesitate to speak out for better education. He became well-known throughout the state for his "God, country, and motherhood" speeches. Wilson's dedication and personal appeal to the people to accept this program–so necessary to achieve the goals for Idaho's children set by the school survey and the Legislature–made him the cherished friend of all educators.

As required by law, the county committees were selected by July 1, 1947, and 2 weeks later they held their first organizational meeting. Each county committee was required to submit to the state committee a comprehensive plan for reorganizing its districts and unorganized territory into the classes created by the Legislature. The state committee would either approve or disapprove each plan and return it to the county with recommendations. Within 10 days after the state committee had approved the plan, the county commissioners were required to hold an election in the area to be reorganized. If no component district had a majority of the total votes, then a single majority could carry the proposal. If a component district had a majority, two favorable majorities were required–one in the district having the majority and another in the remaining area. Defeated proposals could be voted on again after 60 days.

Dean developed procedural guides for the state committee and prepared a bulletin outlining procedures for county committees. He also provided the counties with statistical information from state records showing pupil enrollment by schools, pupil costs, assessed valuations, and other information.

The first reorganization election, held in October 1947, resulted in a county unit district. By the end of the year, 11 reorganized districts–5 of them county units–had been created. By September 1950, the 1,082 districts had been reduced to 301 by consolidating 781 districts into 85 reorganized districts. Only 2 of the state's 45 counties had not participated in reorganization; 13 counties had formed county unit plans. These reorganized districts contained 87.2 percent of the school population and 82.04 percent of the state's land area (25).

The term of the state committee expired in July 1951, and its functions were transferred to the State Board of Education. Staff members within the department now were responsible for carrying out the reorganization program, and within the first 6 months the number of districts was reduced from 301 to 276. By the end of 1952, all counties had approved a reorganization proposal, and by the following July the number of districts had been reduced to 190. In 1954, 96 percent of the pupils attended schools in reorganized districts, and 30 of the 44 counties were completely reorganized. Despite legislative amendments which delayed reorganization, by 1956 there were 162 school districts, including 12 nonoperating districts and 109 reorganized ones. After 12 years of agonizing compromise, final reorganization was completed with 116 school districts.

Since 1961, several districts have combined and others have divided, so that in 1966 there were 117 school districts. An amendment to the state foundation program in 1965 called for a reduction in funds to adjacent school districts maintaining schools within 10 miles of each other by all-weather roads. Thus, districts with a small number of students in school will lose funds and will be forced to reorganize. However, many educators believe this is not a correct approach, because schools losing funds must reduce their educational offerings, and this affects the children's opportunity for learning. The Legislature agreed with educators and eliminated this requirement in 1967.

School Transportation

The reorganization program required more attention to school transportation. The 1947 Legislature passed a school transportation act requiring school districts to furnish transportation to every pupil living over 1.5 miles from a school. Although the county board of education approved the routes established by the local districts, the state department, with the state board's approval, established the school bus rules, regulations, and purchase procedures. The law also established specifications for buses and provided for safety inspection of all buses by law enforcement officials.

The Legislature did not provide funds for a school bus supervisor, so this responsibility was first assumed by the state superintendent. The job was then turned over in November 1947 to the director of guidance, who had a budget separate from the department's funds. It remained in the director's office until he resigned from the department in March 1951. The staff person in charge of school reorganization was then named school bus supervisor 3 months later.

Under the 1947 law, the state assisted the districts with funds based on the average per-pupil cost for the students they transported. In 1951, on the basis of transportation costs maintained for 4 years, the state board adopted a formula which included in the minimum education program

65 percent of the actual cost of district transportation. It also adopted the national school bus standards and required liability insurance. The department staff inaugurated conferences for school bus drivers and sponsored driver schools.

Although the transportation formula has been changed a number of times, it has remained a part of the school foundation program; thus, it does not take funds from the actual education program. The districts transport nearly half the students enrolled each year, and buses travel over 60,000 miles daily at an annual cost of $3.5 million. The ratio of accidents to miles traveled is small, and only one student death by bus accident was recorded from 1964 to 1966.

Teacher Certification

Prior to 1947, teacher certification remained a prerogative of the Legislature. The law required a minimum base training of 4 years for certification, but provisional certificates could be issued in an emergency. The act also set three general requirements for a teacher: citizenship, minimum age of 18, and graduation from a 4-year high school. In 1945, the Legislature gave the state board responsibility for setting the specific minimum prerequisites for a certificate within this framework.

Under the direction of Executive Secretary John Booth, the Idaho Education Association had studied certification requirements for a number of years. When it finally presented a program, the state board adopted it, thus greatly assisting the department in getting the program under way. The requirements recommended by the state board became effective in January 1948.

Rising school enrollments placed an increasing load on the department's teacher certification section. Although the department issued over 2,000 certificates and 2,400 emergency permits during 1947 and 1948–more than any other previous period–teacher preparation was not adequate. Over half the authorizations were granted to teachers who could not meet the minimum requirements for state certificates, and the state certificate requirements were lower than in a number of other states. Thus, Idaho attracted many persons not qualified to teach in other states.

It was assumed that the principal reason for the large number of temporary permits issued was the increase in certification requirements from 2 years of training to a B.A. degree for elementary teachers. A survey showed, however, that 678 elementary permits were issued in 1946-47 and 780 in 1947-48, while in the year following the increased requirements, 1948-49, there were only 716 elementary permits issued. The number dropped to 671 the following year. The percentage of permit teachers dropped from 29 percent of the total number of teachers in 1947-48 to 22 percent between July 1948 and June 1950, even though more certificates and permits were issued. Many of the teachers had completed the 4 years of training but had not completed the minimum teacher-training requirements.

In July 1954, the State Board of Education modified the certification requirements according to recommendations by members of the State Trustee Association, State Congress of PTA, and the Idaho Education Association. This practice of using an advisory committee composed of educators, lay people, and the department's director of certification continued and resulted in minor changes from 1954 to 1961. The board adopted a major revision in 1961, effective the following September.

In 1965, the teacher certification program expanded to include teacher education. A permanent professional standards board representing professional and lay groups was appointed to replace the advisory committee. This board not only advises but also assists the higher education institutions in planning programs in teacher education. At the same time, the State Employment Agency assumed responsibility for the department's teacher placement program to avoid a duplication of services.

The education department's teacher certification section is within the instructional services division. It issues new certificates to applicants with the proper credentials, issues renewals, and determines if the teachers employed are properly certificated so the districts can be approved for state funds. It consults with teacher-training institutions regarding curriculums, advises applicants on how to meet the requirements, assembles statistical data, cooperates with other states in endorsing or revoking certificates, and maintains records of certificates issued. It also furnishes each school district with a list of its teachers and when their certificates will lapse.

Reorganization has helped, but staffing the smaller and more isolated schools continues to be a basic problem in most of Idaho's districts because they cannot compete financially for qualified teachers.

Curriculum Development

In 1949, the state board created the State Curriculum Development and Textbook Committee as an advisory body to evaluate textbooks, improve both curriculums and classroom instruction, and develop materials and guides. The Legislature appropriated $50,000 and employed as director an Idaho State University professor, Buford F. Minor. Actually, this continued officially the program that Superintendent John Condie had started in the early 1930's–without a legal requirement or special appropriation–and that had been interrupted by World War II.

Minor organized the advisory committee, appointed subcommittees to develop guides for each subject area, and inaugurated a study of textbook adoptions on a 5-year cycle. By 1950, over 1,500 educators were working on these guides and courses. They completed their findings and recommendations in workshops sponsored during the summer months at Idaho's higher education institutions. Many of these guides and their revisions received national recognition from educators, colleges, and departments of education.

In 1953, the budget for the curriculum development program was incorporated into that of the education department, and the program was placed under the instruction division, thus ensuring better continuity and a greater uniformity in the base schools' offerings and enabling students transferring within or outside the state to find classes similar to those previously attended.

The launching of the Russian Sputnik prompted Idaho, like other states, to evaluate its programs of education. Superintendent Alton B. Jones organized the Idaho Task Force Conference on the Educational Implications of Sputnik and presided over its meeting in Boise in January 1958. The participants recommended to the state board that the course content for high school graduation be strengthened, stressed the importance of guidance and counseling programs, requested more emphasis on education for a democracy, and suggested that the schools provide programs for the exceptional child. Three months later, a Governor's Conference on Education reached the same conclusions but also stressed the need for a high school multitrack program, improved school facilities, ability grouping, and a greater emphasis on fundamentals.

The state board acted on these recommendations by establishing local school textbook and instruction committees, adopting a wide range of foreign language textbooks in high schools, and urging the elementary schools to offer foreign language courses. It also established a committee to examine the mathematics and science program for the first grade through college, raised graduation requirements for high schools, and sponsored a conference for teachers of migrant children.

Since Sputnik seemed to result in greater focus on secondary education programs, the elementary supervisors battled for more attention to their schools. Gertrude Eastman, one of Idaho's most respected and loved elementary supervisors, warned:

> We should continue to alert ourselves, however, to the danger that the critics may destroy the very strength of American Education—an education for all children....The assignment to schools is clear. We develop the potentialities in all children, emphasizing the talents in every child.
>
> We must resist the trend to educate children for the immediate national goals, rather than for the contributions of individuals (26).

Such influence did much to strengthen the total program of education in the public schools.

By 1963, the tasks of writing new study guides, revising adopted guides, and establishing the scope and sequence of subject areas were being accomplished by the director of curriculum, the department's supervisors, and specially appointed committees from public schools and higher institutions of learning. The state textbook and improvement of instruction committee worked primarily on textbook adoption and recommended to the state board studies to be performed by the department.

Funds from Title V of the Elementary and Secondary Education Act, approved by Congress in 1965, have enabled the department to employ competent supervisors in all major subject areas. The curriculum program is up-to-date in nearly all areas, and Idaho has led the way in developing revisions in some of the new programs—especially in mathematics. The in-service teacher-training programs have been very successful in updating instructional methods using new media, techniques of new subjects instruction, and knowledge of subject areas. There is an emphasis on developing excellent library services in both the elementary and secondary schools.

The Department's Growth and Reorganization

Alton B. Jones, elected state superintendent for a 4-year term in November 1946, took office the following January. In 1947, the big legislative year for Idaho education, the department had eight staff members (27). With the addition of the curriculum construction and reorganization programs, the staff increased to 10 in 1950 and to 13 by 1954; it dropped to 9 in 1956, but was up to 10 by 1958.

The changes in the staff from 1948 to 1958 directly reflect the Legislature's acceptance of the state superintendents' budget requests. Jones, a Republican, serving with Republican Governors and a Republican Legislature, was quite conservative and never spent all of his appropriations, so the succeeding Legislatures reduced his request by an amount approximating what had been returned to the general fund at the end of the biennial period.

By 1958, Jones had completed three terms (12 years), a longer period of continual service than any other chief state school officer in Idaho up to that time. He chose not to run in 1958, and Delbert F. Engelking was elected to the position. Jones brought his successor into the department soon after his election in November so he could present recommendations to the Legislature in January.

Superintendent Jones sponsored one last conference at Pocatello, Idaho, soon after the passage of the National Defense Education Act of 1958, for the state departments of the northern Rocky Mountain states and the U.S. Office of Education. This conference gave the departments firsthand information about the act and enabled them to develop state plans. They became among the first to receive funds and to participate in the programs for the public schools.

During the Jones term of office, the Legislature appropriated $8 million to public schools in 1947,

$7,160,000 in 1949, and $8,250,000 in 1951. The foundation program was redefined and adjusted to utilize $12 million in 1953, and $15 million 2 years later. An adjustment in the foundation program in 1957, increasing the liable amounts of two factors, called for the Legislature to appropriate $22 million.

Departmental Changes Under Superintendent Delbert F. Engelking

At the time Superintendent Engelking assumed office, it was obvious that the foundation program was a limiting factor in providing funds from the state. Since the formula had not been studied sufficiently to give an accurate estimate of how the adjustments would affect particular schools, Engelking recommended that such a study be made. The Legislature granted his request. The study resulted in a new formula, which used a weighted average daily attendance in relation to school size and permitted an allowance per average daily attendance in relation to funds available from state, county, and local sources.

The new formula brought the state appropriations to $28 million in 1959, $33 million in 1961, $40 million in 1963, and over $57 million in 1965. In 1965, an "average increase" and a "floor" allowance were added to the formula to satisfy particular school districts and provide a favorable atmosphere for passage of a sales tax. This special provision granted funds from the state appropriation to certain school districts when they (a) had an above-normal assessed valuation increase and/or (b) received no increase in state funds for each pupil. Funds received by qualifying districts for each student were greater than in many other districts, and the 1967 Legislature discontinued this program because they thought it unfair.

The federal programs available to the states in 1959 required the new superintendent to reorganize and expand his staff. The National Defense Education Act required five additional persons, and increased activities in finance and curriculum added two more. By 1960, for the first time since the beginning of the state's vocational education and vocational rehabilitation programs, the department had a larger staff than those departments.

In the early 1960's, the department added personnel for programs in Civil Defense education, driver education, special education, and junior high supervision. The lay organizations interested in education, special-interest groups, school administrators, and trustees all were demanding these additional services. The Elementary and Secondary Education Act required four more persons, so that by 1966 the department totaled 26, not counting those who retired during the fiscal year. However, it was the following year, when personnel became available for employment under the Elementary and Secondary Education Act, that the department enjoyed its greatest single increase. By the end of fiscal 1967, the department numbered 74–36 staff persons and 38 secretaries, clerks, bookkeepers, and keypunch operators.

Finding space to house the department's many activities posed problems. Although it was necessary to rent space outside of the State House, no state funds were available to pay for rent. Personnel working in federal programs had to be stationed away from the department's headquarters office. Lacking space large enough to hold a meeting for all regular staff members, Superintendent Engelking meets regularly with the division heads to keep all personnel informed. A state office building large enough to house the entire department is now on the drawing board.

When Engelking first became superintendent, he organized the department into five divisions: curriculum, finance, certification, school lunch, and state-federal programs. This proved to be quite cumbersome for the department's size and resulted in overlapping services. In 1964, he combined the services and established three divisions: finance and administration, instruction, and general services. Two years later he divided each of these into two sections, one for consultative services and the other for program services. Each division operates federal programs, and all programs and services are coordinated by the assistant state superintendent (28).

The 1965 Legislature presented a joint resolution to again provide the people an opportunity to eliminate the state superintendent as a constitutional officer, elected on a partisan ticket. The House approved the measure, but the Senate Democrats rejected it on a partisan vote. A bill was then passed changing the state board membership from five to seven, all still appointed by the Governor to 5-year terms. The bill also provided for the appointment by the board of an executive director of the State Board of Education, who also would be an ex officio member of the board and an ex officio member of the University of Idaho Board of Regents. His duties were confined to supervising and administering all state institutions having instruction above the twelfth grade.

Under the law, the state superintendent remained an ex officio member of the State Board of Education but was removed as ex officio member of the Board of Regents and as the executive officer of the regents. His duties changed to the enforcement of the rules and regulations of the state board only as they related to public schools.

This is the first time the state superintendent's duties have been removed by legislative action. However, the single state board provides an opportunity to coordinate the programs of public elementary and secondary schools, junior colleges, and the higher institutions of education. The state superintendent now has more time to devote to the elementary and secondary schools and is better able to live up to his commitment to serve the people of the state through enlightening its youngest citizens.

State Superintendent Engelking repeatedly requested larger appropriations than the Legislature granted, as the chart below indicates.

Although the superintendent attempted to get the Legislature to study the financial needs, both the 1963 and 1965 Legislatures refused. With limited funds available from all sources, the public school education program approaches a crisis.

The local school trustees are limited to a 30-mill levy for their operations. Since any additional levy has to be approved by two-thirds vote of the people, it is almost impossible to secure. Despite repeated requests, the Legislature has not permitted the local boards of trustees to levy beyond the 30 mills, nor can such a levy be passed by a majority vote of the people. The people have thus been "saved from themselves" by their representatives, and Idaho children are losing improved educational offerings. The silent prayer of neighboring states, "thank God for Idaho," is poor consolation for the school districts that are losing their experienced teachers as well as their best trained young teachers or instructors.

State-Federal Relations

Idaho used federal funds early in its history when it was endowed with public lands. The Morrill Land Grant Act of 1862 provided public land for the University of Idaho. The state received funds for vocational education under the Smith-Hughes Act in 1917 and vocational rehabilitation funds in 1921. A school survey conducted in the early thirties used federal funds, and the school districts received assistance from the federal government for school construction during the Depression years. The department accepted school lunch funds in 1946, for the Indian education program in 1949, and the following year, Public Laws 817 and 874 granted funds to Idaho for school construction and school operation in federally impacted areas.

In 1959, the Legislature voted for the school districts and the State Department of Education to participate in the programs under the National Defense Education Act, but it did not approve the request for matching the funds available to the school districts. Instead, it left to each local district the decision whether or not to participate in the funds available for guidance counseling and the purchase of equipment in science, mathematics,and modern foreign languages. Only 64 percent of the high school districts participated in the Title III program during the 1959-60 school year. The money available to Idaho was not completely used—in part because school districts rejected the federal funds for specific program areas or because there was no adequate planning for the expenditure. In fact, until the 1965-66 school year, school districts did not fully use federal funds available to Idaho.

The 1959 Legislature appropriated matching funds for administering the NDEA programs, but in 1961, 1963, and 1965, it failed to provide the state funds requested. Without these matching funds, federal funds still were not completely used.

Without the money, the department could not offer the services or employ the personnel it needed. It had to operate the entire Title V-A program of NDEA with only one person from 1959 to 1965. The department was unable to initiate data-processing programs with federal funds under Title X of NDEA; less than 50 percent of Title X funds available have been matched by state funds in any fiscal year since 1959.

The careful operation of NDEA Titles III and V programs has done much to eliminate Idahoans' reluctance to use federal funds for general programs. Even though school trustees and responsible citizens never really opposed the use of federal funds for vocational education programs, they did view with suspicion what they considered to be a federal invasion of their public school general program. As school trustees used the Title III funds and participated in the reviews before the payments were made, their fear of federal controls gradually disappeared. Prior to 1960, the Idaho School Trustees Association passed resolutions against federal funds for programs in school subject areas, and beginning in 1960, it passed resolutions opposing general federal aid. But, since 1965, its attitude has again

Year	Amount required for formula	Amount requested by state supt.[a]	Amount recommended by Governor	Amount approved by Legislature
1959	$ 23,575,000	$ 23,575,000[a]	$ 24,575,000	$ 27,000,000
1961	30,818,559	30,818,559[a]	32,000,000	33,000,000
1963	40,487,243	40,487,243[a]	36,200,000	40,000,000
1965	Amount provided	67,270,450	56,300,000	57,100,000
1967	Amount provided	71,400,000	58,600,000	59,742,000

[a] Required to request an amount to provide for formula.

changed. Its resolutions do not suggest federal aid, but they do approve general aid programs if the state education agency operates and has jurisdiction over these programs.

The principal opposition to federal support for schools had disappeared by the time Congress passed the Elementary and Secondary Education Act in 1965. Since Idaho's Legislature holds its regular sessions every 2 years, there was no opportunity to approve the state's participation in this act's programs. On Superintendent Engelking's request, however, Governor Robert E. Smylie granted permission for the state board and state department to participate. Thus, the state was able to operate many excellent programs under Title I during the 1965-66 school year. School districts were able to plan for spending all Title II funds available, and the department strengthened its services to the public schools through five projects under Title V—including a program of data processing. School districts were quite active in the Title III program. By 1966, the department was operating all programs available to the public schools and the state agency (29).

The Idaho Department of Education and the State Board of Education have had to face several problems in connection with the federal programs. They are deeply concerned about the tendency of Congress to appropriate funds after the beginning of a fiscal year. The Legislature approves departmental budgets on a biennial basis. The department's quarterly operation funds (6 months) are submitted to the Board of Examiners 45 days prior to the beginning of a quarterly period. Program needs are not known, and the estimates are often not too realistic in terms of the final maximum appropriations possible within the programs. Budget planning by the school districts also becomes little more than a very rough estimate. School personnel are usually employed before or during the first 2 months of a fiscal year, and not knowing what funds are available prohibits effective planning.

One other practice disturbing to the department is Congress' failure to approve program extensions prior to their expiration date, thus prohibiting prior planning. For example, Public Law 815, which provides federal funds for public school construction in federally impacted areas, expired for single connected students. The school districts cannot make applications for these students without an extension. Because of this, one Idaho district will be on double shifts in the lower grades in 1967.

The Idaho department also is greatly concerned about the separate accounting it and the school districts must keep when using federal funds. These detailed reports require a great amount of personnel time that could otherwise be spent on more effective planning. At the end of fiscal year 1966, the department was keeping 29 separate accounts, including the commodity program and the separate administration funds for the different programs. The department is willing to do it this way but believes that it should be possible to combine the accounting of some programs.

The Idaho Department of Education has become critical of the U.S. Office of Education's attitude in recent years concerning some federal funds and programs. Any program that bypasses the state agency without its approval arouses the suspicions of local educational agencies and provides an opportunity for criticism by citizens who do not approve of the program. The authority and responsibility for education lies with the state, and the state delegates specific responsibilities to the local school districts.

The department is in full accord with the principle of federal support for education. State Superintendent Engelking has remarked favorably on the federal government as a junior partner in education, but he is determined that the junior partner shall not take the role of the senior partner—the state. Education within a state will be only as strong as the strength of the state educational agency. Thus, it must be kept strong, and efforts to bypass it are injustices to all education.

FOOTNOTES

1. Alvin M. Josephy, Jr., ed., *The American Heritage Book of Indians* (New York: American Heritage Publishing Co., 1961), p. 309.
2. Idaho Territorial Assembly, *Laws,* 2d sess. (1864), art. 2, ch. 6, sec. 1, p. 378.
3. Idaho Territorial Assembly, *Laws,* 4th sess. (1867), art. 2, sec. 2, p. 20.
4. These schools were located in the following places:

County	*Number*	*Location*
Ada	2 public schools	Boise and Boise City
Alturus	1 private school	Atlanta
Boise	4 (1 private) schools	Idaho City
Idaho	1 public school	Florence
Owyhee	3 (1 public) schools	Silver City
Nez Percé	1 public school	Lewiston

The school established by the Latter Day Saints at Franklin in 1860 had evidently closed by this time. Territorial Superintendent of Public Instruction, *Biennial Report* (1865).

5. C. P. Coburn, *Illustrated History of North Idaho, Embracing Nez Percés, Idaho, Latah, Kootenai, and Shoshone Counties, State of Idaho* (n.p.: Western Historical Publishing Co., 1903), p. 115.
6. Territorial Superintendent of Public Instruction, *Eighth Biennial Report* (1882), p. 25.
7. Idaho Territorial Assembly, *Laws,* 13th sess. (1885), sec. 1, p. 38.
8. Territorial Superintendent of Public Instruction, *Fourth Biennial Report* (1874), p. 9.

9. Territorial Superintendent of Public Instruction, *Fifth Biennial Report* (1876), p. 7.

10. Idaho Territorial Assembly, *Laws*, 2d sess. (1864), art. 1, sec. 1, p. 377.

11. Governor, *Report to the Secretary of the Interior;* Vol. IX of *Executive Documents of the House of Representatives*, 49th Cong., 2d sess. (Washington, D.C.: Government Printing Office, 1887), p. 843.

12. Superintendent of Public Instruction, *Biennial Report* (1891), p. 6.

13. Superintendent of Public Instruction, *Biennial Report* (1898).

14. Idaho, *Laws* (1911), H.R. 30, pp. 791-92.

15. The state superintendent was still an elected official. Idaho, *Laws* (1913), ch. 77, sec. 2, pp. 328-29.

16. Idaho, *Laws* (1913), art. 1. ch. 77, sec. 6, p. 330.

17. Superintendent of Public Instruction, *Biennial Report* (1914), p. 3.

18. Letter from Bert H. Miller to State Superintendent C. E. Roberts, May 9, 1941.

19. Board of Education, *Twelfth Biennial Report* (1936), pp. 24-27.

20. *Ibid.*, p. 26.

21. The vocational education and rehabilitation services increased the department's personnel from 5 to 8 persons in 1940 and to 11 in 1942.

22. Board of Education, *Fifteenth Biennial Report* (1942), p. 6.

23. District Court Records, Canyon County (1944). The bills were declared unconstitutional because they provided funds for teachers' salaries only, and not for the operation of schools, as stated in the Governor's proclamation for calling the Legislature. E. N. Hanson *v.* T. M. DeCoursey, 8766 Idaho Book 19, p. 365 (1944). Idaho, *Journal of the State Senate*, 2d extraord. sess., 27th leg., 1944, p. 3.

24. These findings and recommendations made by Peabody College were completed and accepted by the Idaho Education Survey Commission in October 1946. *Public Education in Idaho: A Report of the Idaho Education Survey Commission* (Nashville, Tenn.: George Peabody College for Teachers, 1946), pp. 70-76.

25. Board of Education, *Nineteenth Biennial Report* (1950), pp. G5-G9. After completing the major portion of the district reorganization, Kenneth Dean resigned as director to accept the superintendency of a county unit which needed consolidation within the district and a major building program. The state board then appointed George Denman, a veteran educator, to replace Dean as director.

26. Board of Education, *Twenty-Third Biennial Report* (1958), p. 55.

27. For many years, the Department of Education's duties had been in the hands of the superintendent, an assistant superintendent, an auditor, and a teacher certification clerk. When the two normal schools received budget cuts during the Depression, eliminating four elementary supervisors, the department added an elementary supervisor. When the University of Idaho discontinued the inspection of secondary schools, the Department of Education added a high school supervisor. Another staff member was added when the 1943 Legislature required the public schools to teach the harmful effects of stimulating narcotics, and another in 1945 when the department assumed the school lunch payments. A field supervisor was added later, and when the Legislature required guidance supervision in 1945, the department employed a director and assistant director of guidance.

28. See Appendix B for the organization of the department in 1966.

29. On the state superintendent's suggestion, the state board approved the Department of Education's operating the following programs: (a) school lunch programs—commodity distribution, special milk, and equipment purchases; (b) Indian education; (c) Public Laws 874 and 815; (d) Title III, Title V-A, and Title X of the NDEA; (e) Civil Defense Adult Education; (f) Adult Basic Education; (g) training program for teachers in special education; (h) Head Start (program discontinued when the department was informed that no project would be approved by the Kansas City Office) and Neighborhood Youth Projects; (i) Higher Education Facilities Act; and (j) Titles I, II, III, IV, and V of ESEA.

BIBLIOGRAPHY

Public Documents

Idaho. *Attorney General Opinions.*

--*Code.* Vol. VIA.

--*Constitution* (1890).

--*Laws* (1890-1965).

--*Revised Statutes* (1887).

--*School Laws.*

Idaho, Canyon County. *District Court Records* (1944).

Idaho Territorial Assembly. *Laws* (1863–89).

Books

Coburn, C. P. *Illustrated History of North Idaho, Embracing Nez Percés, Idaho, Latah, Kootenai, and Shoshone Counties, State of Idaho.* n.p.: Western Historical Publishing Co., 1903.

Josephy, Alvin M., Jr., ed. *The American Heritage Book of Indians.* New York: American Heritage Publishing Co., 1961.

Reports

Board of Education. *Biennial Reports.* Boise: Department of Education, 1913-66.

Governor. *Report to the Secretary of the Interior.* Vol. IX of *Executive Documents of the House of Representatives.* 49th Cong., 2d sess. Washington, D.C.: Government Printing Office, 1887.

Governor's Biennial Message to the Eleventh State Legislature. Boise, 1911.

Hyatt, Byron E. *Federal Land Grants and Endowment Funds of the State of Idaho.* Boise: Bureau of Public Accounts, 1930.

Idaho Education Survey Commission. *Public Education in Idaho.* Nashville, Tenn.: George Peabody College for Teachers, 1946.

State Auditor's Report on Endowments. Boise: State of Idaho, 1918.

Superintendents of Public Instruction. *Biennial Reports.* Boise: Department of Education, 1891-1913.

Territorial Superintendents of Public Instruction. *Biennial Reports.* Boise: The Territory of Idaho, 1863-89.

Periodical

Idaho Education News, 1947-50.

Unpublished Material

Banta, Donald Marion. "A Statistical Evaluation of Inspection Method of Accrediting High Schools in the State of Idaho." Unpublished master's thesis, University of Idaho, Moscow, 1925.

Booth, John M. "State School Administration in Idaho." Unpublished Ph.D. dissertation, Leland Stanford Jr. University, Palo Alto, California, 1946.

Curtis, George Henry. "The Influence of the Teaching Profession of Idaho upon the Course of Legislation for Public Schools." Unpublished master's thesis, University of Idaho, Moscow, 1951.

Fridley, Don E. "Some Effects of the Depression on Public Education." Unpublished master's thesis, University of Idaho, Moscow, 1934.

Hinskey, Kenneth Robert. "An Analysis of Major Tax Problems as Discussed and Set Forth by Forty-Four State Governors in Their Recent Messages to Their Respective State Legislatures." Unpublished master's thesis, University of Idaho, Moscow, 1933.

Johnson, Lloyd Gilmore. "A Treatise on Rural School Consolidation." Unpublished master's thesis, University of Idaho, Moscow, 1932.

Kail, Kenneth Edwin. "An Analysis of Federal Aid to Education in Idaho from Statehood to June 1938." Unpublished master's thesis, University of Idaho, Moscow, 1940.

McCoy, Bernice. "Educational Progress in Idaho as Shown by the Development of the Public School System, 1863-1923." Unpublished master's thesis, University of Idaho, Moscow, 1923.

Ruiz, Fred. "Idaho Court Decision on Public School Problems." Unpublished master's thesis, University of Idaho, Moscow, 1935.

Thomas, Lewis Ambrey. "The Organization of State Departments of Education." Unpublished master's thesis, University of Idaho, Moscow, 1935.

Thompson, James M. "The Effect of Supreme Court Decisions upon Education in Idaho." Unpublished master's thesis, University of Idaho, Moscow, 1935.

Other Source

Miller, Bert H. Letter to State Superintendent C. E. Roberts, May 9, 1941.

Appendix A

IDAHO CHIEF STATE SCHOOL OFFICERS

Territorial Superintendents of Public Instruction

1864-66	J. R. Chittenden
1866	W. R. Bishop
1867	Horace B. Lane, ex officio
1868-73	Daniel Cram, ex officio
1873-81	Joseph Perrault, ex officio
1881-85	James L. Onderdonk, ex officio
1885-87	Silas W. Moody, ex officio
1887-89	Silas W. Moody
1889-90	Charles C. Stevensen

State Superintendents of Public Instruction

1890-93	Joseph E. Harroun
1893-95	B. Byron Lower
1895-97	Charles A. Foresman
1897-99	L. N. B. Anderson
1899-1903	Permeal French
1903-1907	May L. Scott
1907-11	S. Belle Chamberlain
1911-15	Grace M. Shepherd
1915-17	Bernice McCoy
1917-23	Ethel E. Redfield
1923-27	Elizabeth Russum
1927-29	Mabelle McConnel Allen
1929-33	Myrtle Ramey Davis
1933-41	John W. Condie
1941-44	C. Elmer Roberts
1944	Acel H. Chatburn
1945-47	G. C. Sullivan
1947-59	Alton B. Jones
1959-	D. F. Engelking

Commissioners of Education

1913-17	Edward O. Sisson
1917-23	Enoch A. Bryan
1925-29	Ethel E. Redfield
1929-33	Wilbur D. Vincent

Appendix B

Chart I.--IDAHO DEPARTMENT OF EDUCATION, 1890

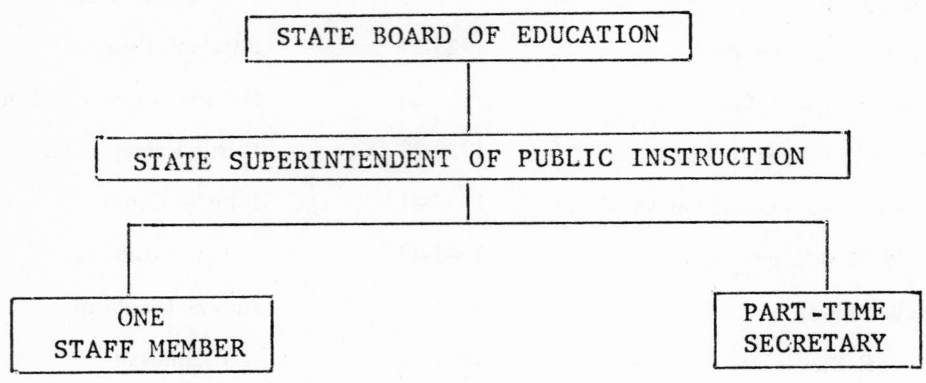

Chart II.--IDAHO DEPARTMENT OF EDUCATION, 1918

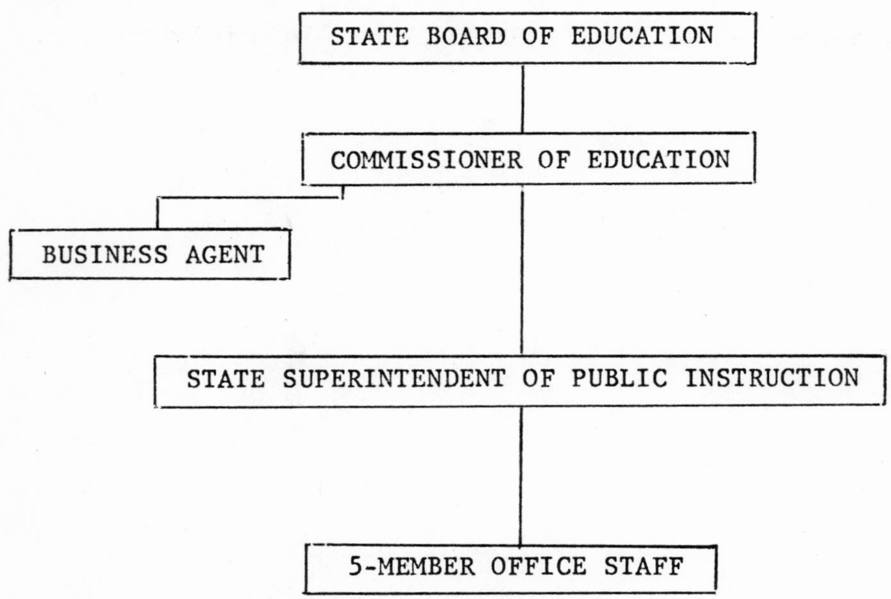

Appendix B

Chart III.--IDAHO DEPARTMENT OF EDUCATION, 1966

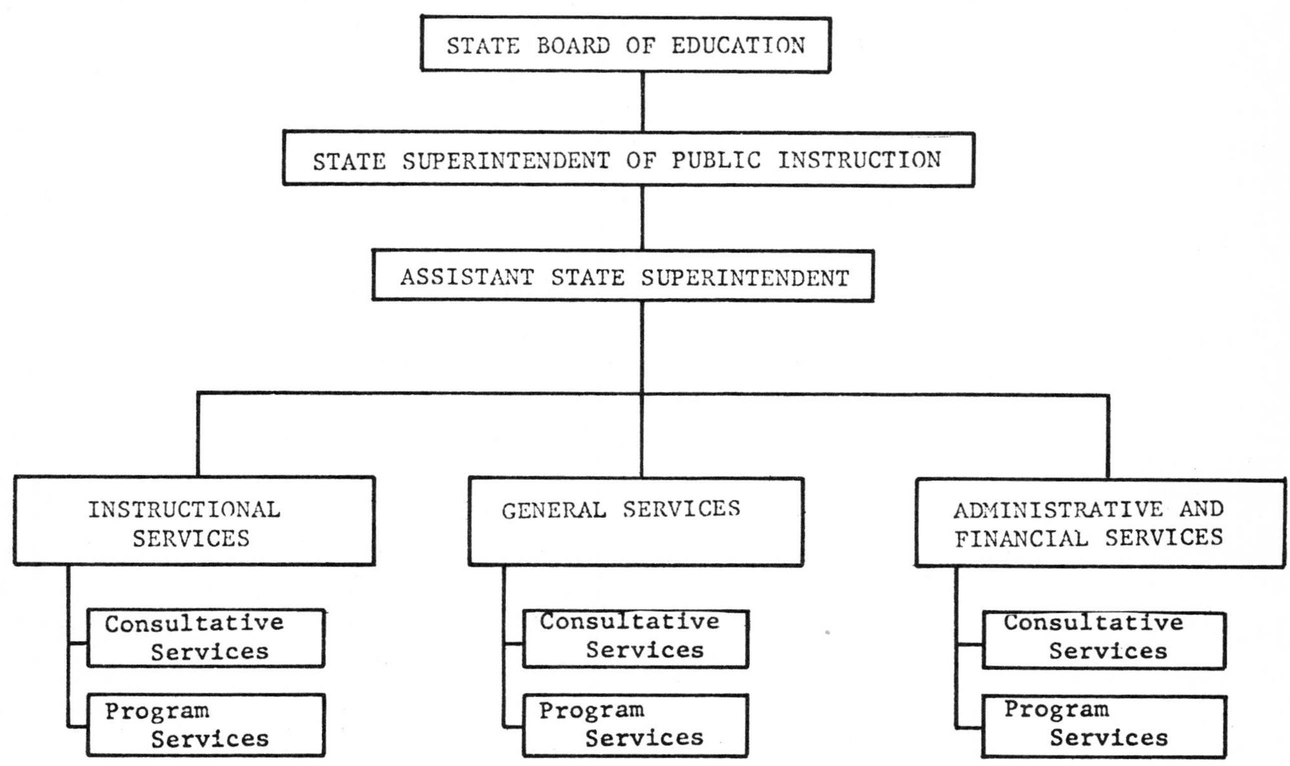

Appendix C

Table 1. – IDAHO STATE APPROPRIATIONS FOR PUBLIC SCHOOLS, 1933-67

Biennial period	Amount	Source
1933-35	$ 328,959.86	Chain store and beer tax
1935-37	1,392,959.60	Chain store, beer, liquor and sales tax
1937-39	1,950,073.68	Chain store, beer, liquor, mine profit and sales tax
1939-41	2,104,360.73	General fund
1941-43	2,776,145.10	General fund
1943-45	2,441,629.71	General fund
1945-47	3,025,000.00	General fund
1947-49	8,000,000.00	General fund
1949-51	7,160,000.00	General fund
1951-53	8,250,000.00	General fund
1953-55	12,000,000.00	General fund
1955-57	15,000,000.00	General fund
1957-59	22,000,000.00	General fund
1959-61	27,000,000.00	General fund
1961-63	33,000,000.00	General fund
1963-65	40,000,000.00[a]	General fund
1965-67	57,100,000.00	General fund

[a]Appropriation reduced 4.8 percent with the difference made up by a county levy.

Table 2. – IDAHO PUBLIC SCHOOL ENDOWMENT FUNDS BY YEARS, 1891-1966

Date	Endowment fund total	Earnings of endownment fund
1891-1892	$ 81,922.49	$ 19,386.65
1893-1894	98,412.75	52,481.23
1895-1896	113,255.60	29,328.22
1897-1898	130,229.80	48,996.25
1899-1900	164,300.49	66,660.03
1901-1902	325,798.70	93,194.48
1903-1904	529,852.73	145,987.02
1905-1906	997,007.93	227,160.92
1907-1908	1,371,524.39	315,478.98
1909-1910	1,891,777.34	413,329.53
1911-1912	2,472,554.31	499,537.75
1913-1914	2,986,036.75	615,987.24
1915-1916	3,464,804.39	749,393.55
1917-1918	4,085,228.98	1,041,453.27
1919-1920	5,214,721.47	1,158,361.89
1921-1922	5,781,895.54	1,162,444.21
1923-1924	6,722,790.49	1,155,564.59
1925-1926	7,120,543.13	1,272,705.04
1927-1928	7,370,493.94	1,214,219.69
1929-1930	7,549,586.49	1,297,934.53
1931-1932	7,619,641.23	891,639.19
1932-1934	7,811,540.15	683,639.53
1934-1936	8,060,627.35	757,339.79
1936-1938	8,407,983.75	666,049.15
1938-1940	8,262,170.61	631,499.41
1940-1942	9,947,149.39	552,011.02
1942-1944	11,014,987.03	620,708.64
1944-1946	12,007,276.68	592,982.91
1946-1948	13,145,322.24	613,529.87
1948-1950	15,996,470.84	645,399.64
1950-1952	19,938,485.33	812,357.04
1952-1954	23,710,396.61	1,115,915.90
1954-1956	28,240,090.27	1,308,962.35
1956-1958	30,228,615.01	1,508,449.36
1958-1960	34,404,107.81	1,758,806.77
1960-1962	38,166,755.78	1,999,173.58
1962-1964	41,516,661.59	2,307,208.56
1964-1966	45,666,972.32	2,631,872.48
Total Receipts		$31,677,150.26

Appendix C

Table 3. – RELATED SCHOOL INFORMATION, 1870-1965

School year	Number of districts	School census, ages 5 - 21	School enrollment
1870	29	888	345
1875	81	3,852	2,093
1880	149	6,698	2,740 (1881)
1885	263	15,399	9,873 (1886)
1890	410	25,741	14,311
1895	614	39,570	29,709
1900	772	54,839	35,329
1905	Not available	72,025	57,377
1910	1,165	94,393	76,168
1915	1,508 (1916)	119,898	98,161 (1916)
1920	1,771	137,756	115,192
1925	1,461 (1923-24)	137,256	117,904
1930	1,406	143,322	124,947
1935	1,211	144,840	119,397
1940	1,195	142,288	120,987
1945	1,110	116,137	110,936
1950	301	142,961	127,031
1955	189	Census not taken	140,918
1960	150	205,000 (ages 5-19)	162,839
1965	117	Not known	178,728

Appendix D

CHRONOLOGICAL TABLE OF EDUCATIONAL EVENTS IN IDAHO

1837 First school in Idaho was opened for Indian children at Lapwai.

1860 Hannah Cornish started first school for white children at Franklin, established by L.D.S. Church.

1863 By action of the Territorial Legislature the office of territorial superintendent of schools was created. First "subscription" school established at Lewiston.

1864 First public school established at Florence with Statira Robinson as the teacher.

1865 The superintendent of schools reported 1,239 school-age children in the territory and 12 schools in operation.

1877 Fielding Academy at Paris established by the L.D.S. Church began operation.

1880 Boise and Lewiston independent school districts were created by action of the Territorial Legislature.

1881 Idaho's first high school began operation at Boise.

1888 Ricks Academy, now known as Ricks College, was established at Rexburg.

1889 The establishment of the University of Idaho was authorized by the last session of the Territorial Legislature.

1891 The College of Idaho was established at Caldwell.

1892 The Idaho Education Association was organized.

1899 Fifth session of the Idaho Legislature established two normal schools, one at Albion and the other at Lewiston.

1901 The Academy of Idaho, now known as Idaho State University, was established at Pocatello.

1903 A bonded indebtedness limit of 8 percent of the total assessed valuation of a school district was set by the Legislature. Ten 4-year high schools were in operation.

1905 By legislative action, special funds were created for the perpetuation of the University of Idaho, the normal schools, and the Academy of Idaho.

1906 The first state school for the deaf and blind was established in Boise.

1908 A total of 356 students were enrolled in Idaho's two normal schools; 214 students were enrolled at the Academy of Idaho; 484 students were enrolled at the University of Idaho; and 65 students were enrolled at the College of Idaho. There were 2,052 teachers in the public schools of Idaho.

1909 The Legislature made provisions for the establishment of rural high school districts. There were 75 high schools in the state.

1910 A State Land Board, consisting of the Governor, superintendent of public instruction, secretary of state, attorney general, and state auditor, was constituted. Gooding was designated as the permanent site for the state school for the deaf and blind.

1911 Expenditures for public schools amounted to $2,926,250. The Legislature enacted compulsory attendance laws.

1912 There were 1,540 schools in the state, 117 of which were high schools. The unified State Board of Education was established by constitutional change.

1915 Free high school tuition for pupils residing in elementary school districts was provided by legislative action. The Idaho Academy became the Idaho Technical Institute. The minimum school year was extended from 5 to 7 months.

1917 A law providing for a voluntary district-level teacher retirement program was enacted.

1919 The State Board of Education was also designated as the State Board for Vocational Education by the Legislature.

1921 A teacher retirement law was enacted which provided a $700 annual retirement benefit and was financed by a charge of one-half of 1 percent of the salary of each teacher. (Later declared unconstitutional.)

1923 Legislation requiring instruction in the U.S. Constitution in grades 6 and 8, in high school, Idaho State College, and the University of Idaho was enacted–the extent of such instruction to be determined by the State Board of Education.

1925 The State Board of Education was required by law to authorize normal schools, junior colleges, and colleges and universities to issue elementary teaching certificates valid for 1 year and reissuable for 2 years. The State Board of Education was also made responsible for establishing courses to be required of the colleges in leading to teaching certification.

1927 A minimum of 2 years of training for elementary teachers was established to become effective September 1929.

1929 The salary of the state superintendent of public instruction was set at $2,400 annually.

1933 The office of commissioner of education was abolished and his duties transferred to the state superintendent. A minimum program education law, commonly referred to as the School Equalization Act, was passed by the Legislature.

1935 Maximum interest rate for school warrants was set by the Legislature at 6 percent.

1937 Legislation allowing trustees of school districts to assist parents in providing board and room in lieu of district transportation was passed.

1939 Legislation providing for the creation, organization, and maintenance of junior college districts was passed.

1941 Legislation providing for the education of children from migratory labor camps was enacted.

1943 Biennial appropriation to the public school income fund was $2,500,000.

1945 The Idaho Education Survey Commission, more commonly known as the Peabody Survey, was created.

1946 The Idaho teacher retirement law was enacted. The direct appropriation to public schools for 1946-47 was $2,174,000.

1947 In March, the School Reorganization Act became law. The State Board of Education revised the certification standards for teachers and authorized the issuance of adminstrator's certificates.

1948 All Indian schools in the state were closed, and the State Board of Education entered into a contract with the federal government for the provision of education of Indian children in the public schools.

1949 The Legislature redefined Idaho's compulsory school attendance age.

1951 The Legislature prohibited the sale of public school lands for less than $10 per acre. The Legislature approved permissive programs for handicapped children.

1953 Legislation providing that all school board meetings be public was enacted. County boards of education were abolished, as was the office of county superintendent in all counties where reorganization was completed.

1955 The Legislature increased the bonding limits for school districts.

1957 The State Board of Education adopted a new manual of regulations and recommendations for school buildings constructed in the state. The 1957-58 direct appropriation to the public schools was $11,903,474. The Legislature authorized the inclusion of teachers for coverage under the Federal Social Security Act. Handicapped education laws were strengthened.

1959 Biennial appropriation to the public school income fund was $27,000,000. Education laws for the handicapped were amended to obligate school districts to provide this type of education program.

1961 The Legislature enacted into law provisions for absentee voting in school elections. The Legislature provided for the recodification of all school laws. Driver education program was established.

1963 Provision was established for the creation and regulation of library districts. Property tax exemption was given certain products manufactured and in transit (free-port provisions).

1965 School foundation program was amended with an appropriation of $55,300,000 to the public schools for the 1965-67 biennium.

1967 Teacher retirement system was discontinued and all teachers transferred to the State Employee Retirement Program.

13 Illinois

OFFICE OF THE SUPERINTENDENT
OF PUBLIC INSTRUCTION
Warren L. Evenson

Contents

STATEWIDE INVOLVEMENT

One manifestation of the widespread involvement of citizens in Illinois education is found in the 50 councils and committees which in 1965 advised the superintendent of public instruction. Additional evidence of extensive public participation in improving educational opportunities for all children is revealed by discussion of organized bodies. The efforts of the State Legislature, the School Problems Commission, and the Task Force on Education to improve education provide further evidence of public participation. Certain mandates of the people before 1900 show that Illinoisans have long been concerned with educational matters.

The First Free School Law, 1825

Less than 7 years after attaining statehood, influential leaders with an intense interest in education brought about the enactment of the first Free School Law in Illinois. One hundred years later, Superintendent Francis G. Blair called this law "the most advanced and forward looking law on public education which had ever been presented in any of the commonwealths" (1). Superintendent Blair was disappointed that the Fifty-Fourth General Assembly had not made provisions for a centennial observance of the law. He invited every public official to do all within his power "to arouse an appreciation of the heroic, courageous efforts of the men who were responsible for this law" (2). Evidently, the new law was too advanced for its time; the succeeding General Assembly repealed all the law's main provisions. Despite repeal, the law and those who had vigorously supported it had made an indelible impression upon the course of education in the state.

In 1777, when Illinois was a county of Virginia, Thomas Jefferson presented to the Virginia House of Burgesses a bill on free schools that he had worked out in great detail. Despite limited reception of Jefferson's plan, he persisted and presented a similar bill to the Virginia lawmakers in 1824. Illinois was now a separate state, and although its Free School Law was not patterned after Virginia law, it probably was influenced by Jefferson's thinking. Jefferson also was influential in selling the land, now Illinois, to the federal government and including this land in the ordinances of 1785 and 1787, which provided that the sixteenth section in each township be set aside for the benefit of the public schools.

Other persons also deserve credit for their roles in shaping Illinois attitudes toward public education. Nathaniel Pope, territorial delegate in 1818, was largely responsible for two acts that helped make possible the Free School Law. Originally, the northern boundary of Illinois was on a line running east and west through the southernmost tip of Lake Michigan. Pope managed to get this northern boundary extended 60 miles up the west coast of the lake. He argued that Illinois would in this manner be joined with all the Middle Atlantic and New England states through the Great Lakes, and to the south through a canal and the Mississippi River, and that "when the war between the North and South shall come, Illinois will help to hold the Union together" (3). Pope's move attracted many Easterners who brought high standards of education to Illinois and helped establish and maintain public schools. The area

---

The writer is grateful to Superintendent Page for this assignment and indebted to Verne E. Crackel, Sherwood Dees, and John H. O'Neill for their many constructive suggestions from the superordinate level. Fellow Assistant Superintendents Reave Evans, William Bealmer, and Wayne Newlin have proved exceptionally helpful. For the specific parts of this paper dealing with financing Illinois education, conservation education, educational television, curriculum programs, school lunch, gifted children programs, handicapped children, adult education, and statutory duties, the writer expresses his appreciation for the help of Reave Evans, Robert Ring, Robert Shultz, Woodson Fishback, Ray Suddarth, Herbert Baker, Vernon Frazee, Tom Mann, and Everett Nicholas, respectively. Frank Santarelli, Juanita Jenkins, and Rosella Lancaster were especially helpful in locating the needed references. Lee McCulley deserves a special note of thanks for her patience and skill in preparing the typed copy. Ed Bydalek's skill and effort in preparing the graphs are deeply appreciated.

added to the state includes practically all of the 14 northernmost counties, including Chicago; in 1965, approximately 65 percent of the state's population lived in this area. Twenty years after Illinois attained statehood, Abraham Lincoln raised his voice to protect Pope's contribution. While Lincoln was serving his fourth term as a state legislator, he joined with the Whigs and Democrats and, by a vote of 70 to 11 in the Twelfth General Assembly, defeated a bill to return the 14 counties to the Territory of Wisconsin. Thus, Illinois kept in its borders the vital and growing Great Lakes port of Chicago.

Pope's second contribution was equally unusual and provided a financial impetus to establish free public schools. Congress granted Indiana 5 percent of the proceeds from the sale of public lands for building roads. Pope argued that Illinois imperatively needed education and urged that 3 of the 5 percent should be given to Illinois for public schools. Congress made such a provision in the Enabling Act.

Edward Coles, who had come to Illinois from Virginia, was elected Governor in 1822. He contended that universal education was essential to perpetual freedom. Although his first educational message to the General Assembly caused little legislative response, in 1824 he had more success—Senator Joseph Duncan responded to his message and worked enthusiastically for passage of a free school bill. Largely through his efforts, the Legislature, in January 1825, enacted Illinois' first Free School Law.

The General Assembly, 1854

The second Illinois constitution, in 1848, was remarkable because of the powers it entrusted to the people, both in the election of officers and in the decision making left to the localities. In 1854, the General Assembly created the Office of Superintendent of Public Instruction and provided that the superintendent be elected by the people in a general election.

The first superintendent, however, was not an elected official. Ninian W. Edwards, who was appointed by the Governor to serve in the interim until the election could be held, served longer than the assembly had anticipated. There was no general election in 1855, so Edwards had well over 2 years to work on the backlog of educational matters which had prompted the Legislature to provide for the position.

William H. Powell, member of the newly organized Republican party, was the first elected superintendent. He won office in the general election of 1856 and assumed his duties in January 1857.

Since superintendents have always been elected on a partisan basis, they usually have held strategic positions of educational leadership and exerted much political influence on the course of education in Illinois.

During the 112-year period through 1968, 9 of the 14 Illinois superintendents have been Republicans, serving a total of 83 years; 5 were Democrats, serving a total of 26 years. The tenure of the Republican Superintendent Francis G. Blair exceeded the combined tenures of all the Democrats.

Today, 22 states still elect their superintendent. But Illinois has never had a state board of education, although 48 states do. It may be that the Illinois state education agency has more freedom and flexibility than the boards of education of other states to interact in the dynamic field of education with the various elements of its working environment. One measure of the effectiveness of any state education agency is its ability to work effectively, not only with its own organization, but with local school authorities, the Governor, legislators, special advisory councils, universities, and professional and political organizations, including those at the federal level.

To understand the role and function of the Illinois state education agency, one must study the scope and depth of its relationships with other agencies, such as the School Problems Commission, which may have resulted from the absence of a state board.

The Constitution of 1870

Illinois' present constitution, its third, has been in force since August 1870. Justifiable praise has been accorded this document, which encompasses the best features of the Constitution of 1818, the Constitution of 1848, and certain recommendations in the 1860's of the third and fourth constitutional conventions. Despite rejection by the voters in 1862, the contributions of the third constitutional convention should not be minimized; much serious consideration was given to investigations of the branches of government, and many of the proposals were incorporated into the document presented in May 1870 by the fourth constitutional convention.

The present constitution further enhanced the stature and prestige of the superintendent of public instruction by elevating him to the position of a state official in the executive branch of government. The constitution maintained the provision that the superintendent be elected to a 4-year term in a general election. A precedent for the extended term was established earlier; Newton Bateman had served three 2-year terms and then was elected in 1866 to the first 4-year term.

The first seven articles in the constitution refer to boundaries, a bill of rights, distribution of powers, the legislative department, the executive department, the judicial department, and suffrage. By devoting the eighth article to education, members of the constitutional conventions served notice that their enthusiasm for education was equal to that of the leaders who had preceded them. Section I of Article VIII, entitled "Free Schools," contains a mandate that the General Assembly shall provide an efficient system of free schools in which all children of this state may receive a good common school education.

Structures for Interaction

The State Legislature. The constitutional mandate concerning schools has been taken so seriously by the Legislature that, in one sense, the Legislature itself may be viewed as a very large state board of education elected by the people. A lively dialogue has endured between the Legislature and the superintendent since the early day of Superintendent Powell (4). In addition to the efforts of the individual legislators and the internal legislative committees to deal with educational matters, the General Assembly also has created numerous commissions to improve education in the state. The research staff of the School Finance and Tax Commission found that between 1907 and 1947 no less than 14 governmental commissions had dealt with this important subject.

The relationship between the special legislative commissions and the state education agency is best illustrated by the creation in 1907 of the Educational Commission, consisting of seven members: the state superintendent, as ex officio chairman, and six appointed by the Governor. Superintendent Bayliss had recommended establishing such a commission in his last biennial report. The Governor included this recommendation in his message of 1907, and it received the support of the State Teachers Association. Perhaps the commission made its most significant contribution in codifying the school laws, which were approved by the General Assembly in 1909.

From the time it created the office in 1854, the Legislature has dealt directly with the state superintendent by specifying his powers and duties. They have continued to expand. Thus, in 1901, Superintendent Bayliss was guided by 18 duties and 9 powers; by 1965 there were 34 (5).

Superintendent Blair, in 1907, had 19 duties. Where Bayliss had one duty, to address circular letters to the county superintendents advising them on school matters, Blair had two: to be the general adviser of the county superintendents and to address circulars to county superintendents, giving advice on matters including, among others, school construction. Perhaps it was this second duty which prompted Blair in 1908 to address the builders and janitors on the matter of safety with a scare approach. He referred to children struggling, fighting, gasping, dying on crowded, crumbling stairways and to writhing, strangling children piled high against the doors. As a result, an item was added to the school code making the superintendent responsible for preparing building specifications. Blair continued his efforts in the 1920's; however, this mandate was largely ineffective until George Wilkins became superintendent in 1958. One of Wilkins' campaign pledges was to enforce the law, but even before he took office, a tragic fire swept through a parochial school in Chicago, killing 92 children and 3 nuns. Though the code did not apply to this school, no greater catalyst was needed to develop a sufficient safety code. After 6 years of intensive study and discussion, two documents were developed, one applying to existing schools and the other to new buildings to be constructed.

The School Problems Commission. The School Problems Commission, appointed by the General Assembly in 1949, included W. O. Edwards, as chairman, and 13 other members: the superintendent of public instruction, the director of finance, three senators appointed by the president pro tempore, three representatives appointed by the speaker, and five members appointed by the Governor. The law stipulated eight areas of study and, in addition, provided that the commission determine the improvements necessary to raise the level of public education.

To become better acquainted with school problems as experienced by the people of the state, the commission chose the "grass-roots" approach. Eight days of public hearings were held during January and February of 1950 in Chicago, Dekalb, Galesburg, Normal, Mattoon, Carbondale, and East St. Louis. The estimated attendance was 1,165, and 118 presentations were made by 172 participants. Seven more meetings were held, during which various groups presented problems for consideration. Over 200 formal proposals were presented. At the same time, a research staff, assisted by Superintendent Vernon L. Nickell and his staff, analyzed these proposals and attempted to present a clearer picture of Illinois education.

In its final report, the School Problems Commission stated:

> The suggestions received were so numerous and were presented in such a haphazard and disorganized fashion as to be somewhat bewildering–problems were unearthed that most members of the Commission had not known to exist. Much light was thrown on the solution to some of these (6).

The comprehensive nature of its first report alone indicates that the School Problems Commission has been of inestimable value to the cause of public education in Illinois. With modifications, the commission continues to exist and has earned the respect of schoolmen. Members of the commission, such as Representative Charles Clabaugh, have become more knowledgeable about school problems than most professional educators.

The Task Force on Education. The state's concern for education nurtures developments such as the Illinois Task Force on Education with its three sponsors: the Democratic Governor, the Republican superintendent of public instruction, and the School Problems Commission. In 1965, the General Assembly appropriated $105,250 to pay for 13 staff research assistants, materials, and travel expenses of members of the task force, who served without pay. In general, the task force had two purposes: to consider long-range goals for elementary and secondary education in Illinois and to recommend plans to attain these goals.

Professor William P. McLure, University of Illinois, served as chairman; Paul J. Misner, Western Michigan University, as vice-chairman; and State Superintendent Ray Page as honorary chairman. Among the 54 distinguished members, 13 were identified with universities of the state, 12 were state legislators, and 8 were superintendents or assistant superintendents of local school districts. Also included were five school board members, five representatives of industry or commerce, two classroom teachers, two union representatives, one attorney, and three representatives of the Office of the Superintendent of Public Instruction. The Governor's Office, the Illinois Education Association, and the Congress of Parents and Teachers each had one representative.

The group assembled in Chicago on May 1, 1965, for a 2-day session to begin the 18-month study. There were subsequent meetings of the entire membership, but most of the work was done in meetings of the subcommittees on elementary schools, junior and senior high schools, vocational and adult continuing education, nonpublic educational agencies, innovations, administrative structure, and finance. In addition to the members, 56 individuals and 32 groups assisted in the preparation of position papers and other written materials.

After the tentative findings and recommendations were established, public hearings were scheduled throughout the state. In December 1966, the study report with its 60 recommendations was published.

Summary

So far, the focus of this brief history has been on the people, organizations, and circumstances that have contributed monumentally to education in Illinois. The Free School Law of 1825, which "was from 25 to 50 years in advance of a school enactment in any of the commonwealths of the Union" (7), was passed at a time when education was considered an enemy of slavery and the proslavery element was strong. Pope's victory 6 years earlier in obtaining money for schools from the sale of public lands was won against similar odds. Even before statehood, Illinoisans had placed a priority on education. They reaffirmed this position in 1870 by placing the superintendent of public instruction, as a constitutional state official, in the executive branch of government and indicating that, after suffrage, education was the first work of their time.

SPECIAL PROGRAMS

Throughout its history, the Office of the Superintendent of Public Instruction has exercised positive leadership and counsel through special programs. In one sense, these programs, such as those in conservation, adult education, and educational television, tend to expand the powers and duties beyond those just outlined. These programs also are characterized by widespread public involvement.

School Lunch

By 1900, school lunch programs had been established in large cities to ensure that children from poor families were provided with needed food. It is interesting to note that, like our program today, these earlier programs were designed to provide one-third of the child's daily food requirements. Rapid growth in the program did not occur until after 1909.

The National School Lunch Program was established in 1946 when Congress enacted Public Law 396. Although Illinois had had school lunch programs since 1900, the national program gave impetus to the overall program and to better record keeping. It is reasonable to assume that the 1946 program was developed through experiences in the Depression under the auspices of the Works Progress Administration.

In Illinois, the number of school lunch programs has steadily increased, and the state now ranks among the leaders in number and volume of school lunch activities.

Education of Handicapped Children

A more complete response to the constitutional mandate for a good education for all children dictated that certain children be provided with more specialized services. In 1942, Superintendent John A. Wieland named J. Roy Byerly as director of the education of handicapped children. In 1945, the departmental designation referred to exceptional children rather than handicapped children. Ray Graham, during the Nickell administration, earned the title of "Mr. Special Education" in Illinois. Vernon Frazee, no less dedicated to the field than Graham, carried on the work, and in the third year of the Page administration, the 1965 General Assembly responded by passing one of the most important laws in educational history, ensuring handicapped children an opportunity for a good education.

The law, Article 14 of the school code, makes special education services to handicapped children in the public schools mandatory after July 1, 1969. This means that the mentally handicapped will be educated to the limits of their potential through academic and vocational training; the physically handicapped, including the blind and partially seeing, the deaf and hard of hearing, will receive added help which has been so desperately needed in the past; and the socially and emotionally maladjusted will have access to services that should enable them to reach the peak of their academic potential.

One important provision of Article 14 establishes a special education advisory committee in each of Illinois' 102 counties. In 1967, in accordance with the law, the county committees determined the needs of handicapped children in each county, wrote academically and financially sound plans for special education, and presented the plans to local school districts and to the state advisory council for approval.

Prior to 1943, some 3,000 children were receiving special education services; by 1945, almost 40,000; and by 1961, 118,646. At the end of the 1964-65 school year, special education services had reached 171,236 pupils. With services provided to only one-third of those children who need them, Illinois still has a big job to do. Article 14 is evidence that Illinois intends to meet the challenge.

Program for Gifted Children

Use of the term *exceptional children* in lieu of *handicapped children* focused attention on the exceptionally able child. Educators had long felt concern for improved programs for the more able children, but Sputnik I increased the acceptance of schools as instruments of national defense and led to emphasis on programs for gifted children. Public officials became more sensitive to the need. In 1959, both Superintendent Wilkins and the Governor were equally receptive to the idea of a statewide program. The School Problems Commission recommended a special study, and the 1959 General Assembly appropriated $150,000 for this purpose. The Seventy-Second General Assembly extended the study with an additional appropriation of $150,000. In 1962, the School Problems Commission voted to approve the recommendations of the study group, and in 1963, Superintendent Page made the proposed plan a part of his legislative recommendation. The Seventy-Third General Assembly passed the bill to establish the program by unanimous vote.

Section 14A of the school code calls for a program to assist and encourage local school districts in increasing educational services for gifted children. An appropriation of $7,750,000 was approved by the Seventy-Fourth General Assembly for the 1965-67 biennium.

The Illinois plan, a comprehensive effort to improve educational services for gifted children, consists of five parts. The first part provides for reimbursement to the districts of the cost of services and materials to improve their services to gifted children up to a maximum amount determined by a formula based on the number of students enrolled in the program and the assessed valuation of the district. The second part provides for demonstration centers to enable educators to see approaches to the education of gifted children. In its third part, the plan makes funds available to conduct significant experimentation in practical programs for the gifted. The fourth part enables field consultants at the state level to develop programs in the schools. The plan's fifth part offers state support for programs to increase the number of specially trained personnel. The training program includes summer and in-service institutes and a fellowship program to help meet the great need for specially trained consultants, directors, and teachers.

The effect of the program during its relatively brief existence is most encouraging. The attention paid to teachers is producing more results than any other effort. In the 1965-66 school year, approximately 3,000 teachers participated in teacher-training programs. The following summer, 476 teachers were enrolled in eight institutes conducted by people trained in the 1964 program.

The Illinois Curriculum Program

The largest of the 50 advisory councils which serve the Office of the Superintendent is the Illinois Curriculum Council, made up of representatives of more than 50 statewide professional and civic organizations having special interest in educational programing (8). The council meets twice a year to formulate suggestions and recommendations to the superintendent regarding curriculum. One of its central responsibilities is to advise the Illinois Curriculum Program, launched in 1947.

The Secondary School Principals Association of Illinois appointed a committee to study high school curricular problems. When the 1956 General Assembly responded to a request from Superintendent Nickell with an appropriation of $35,000 to advance the study, the Illinois Secondary School Curriculum Program was set up under the sponsorship of the superintendent. Thirty-two organizations cooperated in this program. In addition to Nickell, James Blue, past president of the principals' group, and C. W. Sanford, University of Illinois, who served as the director, rendered valuable services to the program.

When the curriculum study expanded to include elementary education, it became the Illinois Curriculum Program. It is central to the Department of Curriculum Development, and, essentially, the department's responsibilities are consistent with the objectives of the Illinois Curriculum Program. These responsibilities include providing consultative services to local school districts interested in curriculum revision, developing in-service programs, and upgrading teaching practices (K-14). The department offers leadership in the development of statewide curriculum publications to assist teachers, curriculum coordinators, and administrators. It assists school staffs in research studies, with particular emphasis on the teaching-learning process. The department uses both state and federal funds to organize and direct educational conferences and curriculum workshops for professional staff members of elementary schools, secondary schools, and institutions of higher learning. And it cooperates in developing and interpreting curriculum policies formulated in the Office of the Superintendent of Public Instruction.

Under the direction of the Illinois Curriculum Council, made up of representatives of statewide professional, civic, and educational organizations, the program operates with a director and six regional curriculum consultants. With the implementation of the Elementary and Secondary Education Act (ESEA) of 1965, the curriculum development department greatly expanded in personnel, publications, and in-service projects.

Despite 100 publications and numerous workshops, much remains to be done in the Illinois Curriculum Program. The challenge is best revealed in the findings of an evaluation of the Illinois Curriculum Council and the Illinois Curriculum Program by Thomas Barrett Goodkind. Among his observations and conclusions are these: The publications were regarded to be of high quality by those who used them; elementary school publications were used more often than secondary school publications; teachers did not use the publications as much as supervisory and administrative personnel believed; less than one-half of the districts included in the survey had their own curriculum guides; and the impact of the program on the local school district curriculum had been limited.

Goodkind recommended that the council reconsider its functions with a view toward assisting and directing the superintendent to introduce and implement state programs at the local level.

Conservation Education

In 1957, the General Assembly established the Department of Conservation Education in the Office of the Superintendent. This act served as a prime example of interagency cooperation at the state level. From 1943, when Superintendent Nickell had appointed a committee on teaching conservation, the conservation and agriculture departments had worked with the superintendent to promote the teaching of conservation. Universities and colleges had joined the endeavor as the early efforts were directed toward teacher education. Nickell had assigned Robert Ring to direct the first committee, and by 1955, the movement had gained sufficient momentum to justify the employment of a full-time staff member. B. K. Burton, Eastern Illinois University, had accepted the appointment as an employee of the three state agencies.

Continued cooperation among the agencies was ensured in 1957 by the provision for an advisory council to consist of the superintendent, the directors of the conservation and agriculture departments, and two members to be appointed by the Governor. One of the appointive members must represent institutions of higher education, and one must be a member of a soil conservation district.

The conservation education department cooperates with the federal government and state agencies engaged in adult education, and it promotes and aids schools and classes within the state to teach how to conserve wildlife, forests, timberlands, minerals, and scenic and recreational areas. It also is responsible for establishing courses in conservation education programs, with the advice of the advisory board.

In 1964, the staff, while continuing the programs previously initiated, assumed another responsibility—that of cooperating with the supervisory teams in the school visitation program, which includes classroom visits, conferences with administrators and teachers, and suggestion of materials and methods for informing students about the importance of natural resources to the individual and to society.

Adult Basic Education

The present adult basic education program in Illinois, perhaps the most extensive in the United States today, originated from a series of studies by Denton Brooks of the Cook County Department of Public Aid. In March 1962, Benjamin Willis, superintendent of Chicago city schools, announced jointly with Raymond Hilliard, director of the Cook County Department of Public Aid, the beginning of basic adult education classes for able-bodied adults receiving public assistance. Early evaluation of the program in Chicago indicated the program to be a sound educational approach to combating illiteracy.

At about the same time, Congress passed Public Law 87-543 making federal funds available under "The Community Work Aid Training Program." Two state agencies worked together to formulate the plan. Superintendent Ray Page and Harold O. Swank, director of the Illinois Department of Public Aid, asked the Seventy-Third General Assembly for legislation to make it possible for Illinois to take full advantage of this law. The bill passed in both Houses and was signed by the Governor in July 1963. Thus, Illinois became the first state to require adult basic education and vocational training for those least able and in greatest need—public aid recipients.

The Illinois law provides for a dual responsibility: The public aid department selects and assigns students to classes, checks attendance, and does follow-up after the students have completed their classwork; and the Office of the Superintendent establishes standards for courses and supervises administration of the program. Local districts are reimbursed for the total costs of providing this program from funds allocated to the Office of the Superintendent from the Department of Public Aid. Of the $4 million appropriated for the 1963-64 biennium, 75 percent came from federal funds and 25 percent came from state funds. The Seventy-Fourth General Assembly in 1965 appropriated $6 million for the program and amended the school code to allow for the costs of transporting the students to and from classes. Further provision was made to allow for child care for enrolled mothers.

Because of this successful pioneering effort, the Illinois state education agency was in a position to continue in a cooperative partnership when Congress passed Public Law 88-452, the Economic Opportunity Act of 1964.

Educational/Instructional Television

The development of educational television (ETV) in Illinois is marked by the growth of station and closed-circuit (cable) television for this purpose alone. But the state's commercial stations have donated many hours of air time to ETV. Instructional television (ITV) is also offered at Bradley University, New Trier Township High School East, and Sterling Township High School.

The growth of these endeavors is shown by the development of area ETV/ITV associations made up of school representatives. The oldest and most extensive organization of this type in Illinois is Chicago Area School Television, Inc. (CAST), now in its eighth year. This group, like the others in the state, supports efforts to obtain program production or rental and the use of station time for school purposes.

The outlook for ETV/ITV expansion into a state network is good. The 1965 General Assembly passed a bill authorizing Southern Illinois University to build and operate a new UHF station at Olney in association with its present operation at Carbondale. The bill carried an appropriation of $400,000 and attracted matching funds from the federal government. WTTW in Chicago now has two channels, with the addition of WXXW during the early autumn of 1963. Also, facilities at the University of Illinois, Station WILL, have been expanded with a higher tower, greater power, and a new location for the tower.

Development of the ETV department within the Office of the Superintendent has included hiring a director and secretary, a temporary staff engineer, and a director of special projects with an assistant. The Office is supplying consultant and demonstration services to schools with a portable TV unit. These are used in workshop sessions with teachers and administrators practicing on-camera production. Taped materials also are used to show what is available in instructional television and for practice in classroom use.

The Office likely will carry its share of responsibility in preparing and recommending legislation centered around the theme of network development for statewide distribution and signal coverage for ETV.

ORGANIZATION AND PERSONNEL

This section focuses on the state education agency without direct reference to the larger environment, tracing developments chronologically from 1907 through 1965. Recognition is given to the superintendents and their appointees who have stimulated the development of a dynamic and effective state agency.

Superintendents Blair, Wieland, Nickell, Wilkins, and Page had much in common. Each had administrative training and had served in administrative and leadership positions before election to the state post. Through example and appointments, each tried to inculcate a higher level of professional administration in the Office. Blair's unbounded energy was matched by that of Page, although a description of the sincerity and intense dedication of these two men would apply equally to Wieland, Nickell, and Wilkins.

Blair issued the earliest annual school directory for the 1907-1908 school year. Since 1909, all of the directories issued by Blair have included an opening statement alluding to the difficulty of publishing such a document. Blair's final directory in 1934 appealed to schoolmen to notify the Office if the data were not correct. He also gave credit to W. A. Spence for "whatever excellence in matter and form this directory may have" (9). Despite inaccuracies in other portions of the directories, the lists of state agency personnel served as the basis for this part of the overview.

Organizational charts did not appear in the directory until 1959; apparently, none was needed during Blair's tenure. In 1907, the total office force included the superintendent, three assistants, one stenographer, and one messenger-clerk. In 1908, the departments of country schools, law, and publicity were staffed by U. J. Hoffman, J. C. Thompson, and H. T. Swift, respectively. The team of Blair, Hoffman, Thompson, and Swift remained intact until 1931; only Swift, then chief clerk, was with the superintendent when he completed his final year in office.

The professional positions remained constant from 1907 through 1911. In 1912, two new departments were added: W. S. Booth led the new country and village schools department, and A. L. Whittenburg, the statistics department. The new high schools department was created under John Calvin Hanna in 1913. The superintendent's staff of 1916 included D. F. Nichols, secretary of the Teachers Pension Board, and A. L. Whittenburg, secretary of the State Examining Board. The 1916 directory listed nine advisers: one for schools of art and drawing, three examiners for entrance into dental and medical colleges, three advisers on recognition of colleges and universities, an adviser on recognition of kindergartens, and an adviser on recognition of schools of music.

In 1919, the Office added its second supervisor of high schools and employed F. J. Muhlig to establish and maintain a section on textbooks. Vocational education appeared in the 1921 directory. The eight professional and five nonprofessional employees were listed under four educational units: home economics, agriculture, industrial education, and industrial rehabilitation.

In the same directory, Blair referred more accurately to his office as the Office of the Superintendent of Public Instruction rather than the Department of Public Instruction, as in previous directories. The 1921 directory listed Gladys Walsh, state examining board stenographer, and J.

E. Hill, assistant supervisor, agricultural education. With the exception of Hill's absence in 1922 and 1923, these two served with distinction throughout the remaining portion of the period covered in this study.

In 1923, supervision of high schools was increased with the addition of Ray L. Moore as supervisor of 2- and 3-year high schools. Hanna and H. M. Thrasher continued as supervisors of 4-year high schools, W. S. Booth was designated supervisor of city elementary schools, and U. J. Hoffman devoted his time to the country and village elementary schools.

The industrial rehabilitation staff was sharply increased with the introduction of field agents: five in 1923 and three more in 1924. In 1925, industrial rehabilitation with a supervisor, an assistant supervisor, and nine field agents equaled in number the total professional staff in the Office of the Superintendent. Throughout the remainder of the Blair administration, the number of professionals in vocational education, including industrial rehabilitation, exceeded the number of other Office staff members.

The addition of L. L. Blair in 1927 increased to four the number of supervisors serving high schools; however, the distinction between supervisors of 4-year high schools and supervisors of 2- and 3-year high schools continued until 1929.

Louis Kulinski, the first supervisor of a special subject, was named supervisor of physical education in 1929. Rosella Lancaster, hired in 1930 as stenographer, served throughout all the subsequent administrations included in this report and serves at present as a highly valued administrative secretary in the legal department.

When U. J. Hoffman was replaced by three supervisors in 1931, the title of supervisor of country and village elementary schools was changed to supervisor of rural and village elementary schools. The new supervisors were T. A. Simpson, J. E. W. Miller, and Charles H. Watts.

With two exceptions (Floyd T. Goodier replaced Booth in 1933 and S. S. DuHammel became the law assistant in 1934), the organization and professional personnel remained constant for the final 3 years of the Blair administration. At the close of Blair's tenure, the 1934-35 school directory refers to these five components of the Illinois education agency: Office of the Superintendent of Public Instruction; State Examining Board; State Teachers Pension Board; Board for Vocational Education, including industrial, agriculture, and home economics education; and Division of Rehabilitation. The relationship among these various groups is revealed in the titles bestowed upon Francis G. Blair: superintendent, Office of the Superintendent of Public Instruction; executive officer, Vocational Education; executive officer, Division of Rehabilitation; member, Board of Trustees of the Teachers Pension and Retirement Fund; and chairman, Illinois State Examining Board.

Figure 1 indicates the number of professional and nonprofessional employees of the Office of the State Superintendent of Public Instruction during the Blair administration as revealed in the school directories. It does not include the personnel, activities, or expenditures of the Board for Vocational Education. It also does not include advisers. For example, Margaret E. Lee, who served as the official adviser on the recognition of kindergartens from 1916 to 1932, was not listed. One limitation placed on a graph of

Figure 1. – EMPLOYEES IN THE OFFICE OF THE SUPERINTENDENT OF PUBLIC INSTRUCTION, 1907-34

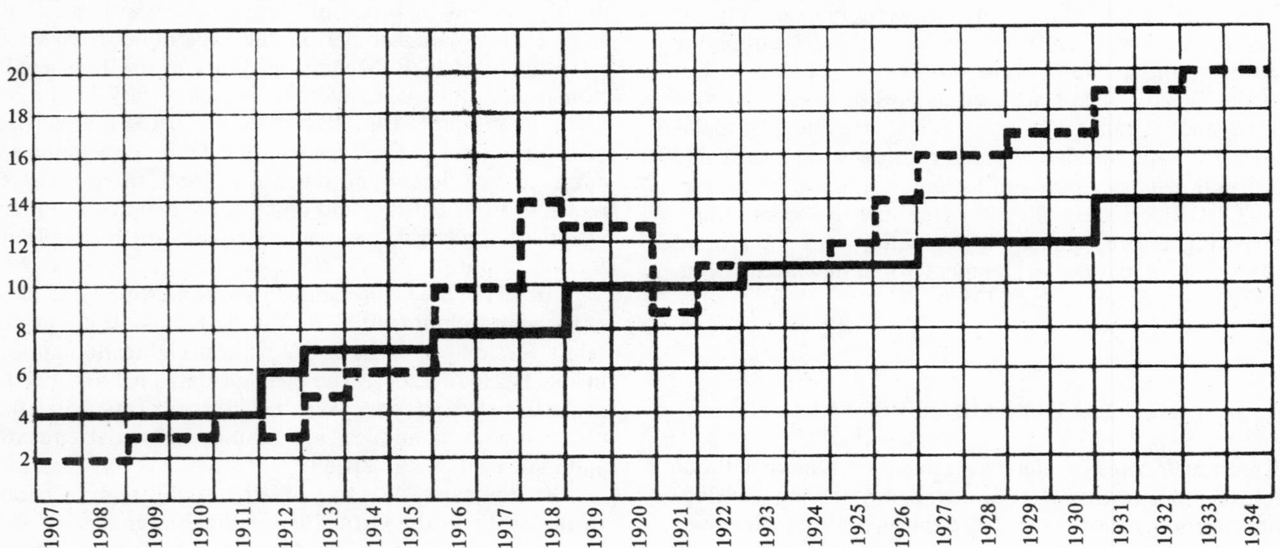

Solid line indicates number of professional employees; broken line indicates number of support staff members.

personnel employed by the Office results from the inherent difficulty of classifying people into professional and nonprofessional categories. For example, H. T. Swift was employed in 1908 as assistant superintendent in charge of publicity and was named chief clerk in 1929. Objection could be raised to the classification of Swift as one of the four professionals in 1908, or as one of the 20 nonprofessionals in 1934.

For comparison with other states, Figure 2 indicates the total personnel employed by the Office of the Superintendent of Public Instruction, Teachers Pension Board, State Examination Board, and Board for Vocational Education, including the rehabilitation division.

Wieland designated Charles C. Stadtman as first assistant superintendent in 1935 and T. A. Reynold, legal adviser, as a second assistant superintendent in 1937. The following year, Stadtman became coordinator of the supervision department, a title which he held until he was named assistant superintendent for the final year of the Wieland administration. Apparently, there was no loss of prestige in the changing titles for Stadtman; his name was listed immediately below Wieland's name throughout their 8-year association.

As coordinator, Stadtman brought about an important organizational change in the Office. The positions of high school supervisor and elementary school supervisor disappeared as a three-regional pattern emerged. The northern district, the southeastern district, and the southwestern district were staffed by a total of seven general supervisors. Of these seven, Claude Vick, Otis Keeler, Paul Belting, E. S. Simmonds, and J. Roy Byerly served with Wieland during his 8 years in office.

Wieland's second directory, in 1936, listed a new unit: the Board of Education for Blind, Deaf, and Dumb. The 1938 directory included only the employees of the Office of the Superintendent of Public Instruction.

The omission of the Board for Vocational Education and other boards in the 1938 directory breaks the continuity in the graph showing the number of professional and nonprofessional employees in the state education agency as revealed in the state school directories. The 1939 directory returned to the more established format with a noteworthy exception; the rehabilitation division was not reinstated. The same year, distributive education made its appearance under the Board for Vocational Education.

In 1941, occupational information and guidance became a unit under vocational education, and a supervisor of handicapped children was appointed on the Office staff. The following year, J. Roy Byerly was named the first director of education of handicapped children.

Vernon Nickell began his 16-year administration during World War II with a more definitive departmental structure. In 1944, a directory reference to the school lunch program appeared for the first time. The following year, the concept of education of handicapped children yielded to the more encompassing program – the education of exceptional children. In 1946, a director of audiovisual education was appointed. The director of school libraries appeared in 1950, and music education and teacher recruitment made their appearances the following year. The coordinator for Civil Defense was appointed in 1952. William Bealmer, in 1954, was the first art education coordinator. The same year, the State Agency on Surplus Property was established in the Office. Conservation education appeared in 1955.

Figure 2. – TOTAL PERSONNEL EMPLOYED IN OFFICE OF THE SUPERINTENDENT OF PUBLIC INSTRUCTION 1907-19; TOTAL PERSONNEL EMPLOYED BY OFFICE OF THE SUPERINTENDENT OF PUBLIC INSTRUCTION, TEACHERS PENSION BOARD, STATE EXAMINATION BOARD, BOARD FOR VOCATIONAL EDUCATION, AND DIVISION OF REHABILITATION, 1920-34

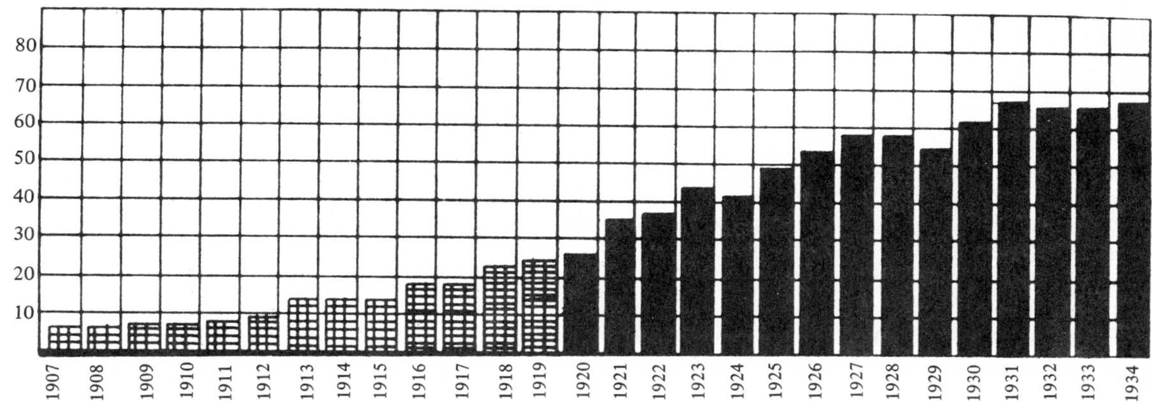

Two years later, nine field offices for exceptional children were listed. Field supervisors of safety and driver education appeared in 1958.

The first organization chart appeared in the 1959 directory as George Wilkins introduced the divisional approach to the organization of the Office and the allied boards.

In 1960, vocational education was listed in the instructional services division; 2 years later, vocational education regained its separate identity. About this time, a department of guidance, testing, and counseling began to take shape. Educational research appeared the following year with Ralph Marty as coordinator. The 1962 directory included two commissions: the State Scholarship Commission and the State School Building Commission.

The first directory prepared by Superintendent Page in 1963 was noteworthy in three ways: It showed six regional supervisory districts that coincided with the regional organization of the county superintendents of schools (10); relationships of the Office of the Superintendent, the Board of Vocational Education and Rehabilitation, the State Teachers Retirement System, and Teacher Certification were made clear; and an administrative line and staff organization was established. Page designated two administrative assistants. Roy Clark was appointed first assistant superintendent; the five assistant superintendents were Sherwood Dees, John H. O'Neill, John L. Kirby, Carl H. Wilson, and N. R. Hutson. In this same directory, the Department of Program Development for Gifted Children made its first appearance.

In 1964, Roy Clark was the first person to be named deputy superintendent, and two special assistant superintendents were named. The following year, Verne E. Crackel was appointed deputy superintendent to fill a vacancy created by Clark's death.

The uniqueness of the 1965 directory is its early and detailed presentation of Superintendent Page's response to the educational acts of the Eighty-Ninth Congress. Effective on October 1, 1965, the organization chart and personnel lists reveal the Office structure and personnel assignments for implementing the new federal programs at the local level and also plans for the use of federal funds in strengthening the state educational agency. Noah Neace was named director of Title I, ESEA, programs; his unit, with special education, was placed in the pupil personnel services division. James Boula was named supervisor of Title II, ESEA, activities as his unit was placed in the instructional materials department in the instruction division. Robert Shultz, Dale Kaiser, and Frank Santarelli were designated directors, respectively, of activities relating to Title III, Title IV, and Title V, ESEA. These three directors were placed in a newly created planning and development division established under the provisions of ESEA, Title V. Thomas W. Mann, director of adult education, assumed the responsibility for implementing the Economic Opportunity Act. William Elam was assigned to develop the new instructional areas of history, geography, and civics included under the National Defense Education Act. Gloria Calovini and Lenore Powell were named to supervise, respectively, the educational materials coordinating unit for the visually handicapped and the educational materials center for handicapped children. Sherwood Dees and John H. O'Neill occupied the newly created posts of associate superintendents; vacancies were created for the appointment of six curriculum consultants, one for each of the six supervisory regions; a data information center was established in the finance and statistics division; and a materials center was established for the use of the office personnel.

Figure 3 indicates the number of professional employees in the Office for the second half of the period covered by the overview. This graph differs from the preceding graph in three ways: (1) It does not show the number of employees under the Board for Vocational Education and other boards; (2) the 1959 directory and subsequent directories did not list personnel previously included in the nonprofessional category, thereby providing an added restriction; and (3) the scale was changed to accommodate the increase in number of professional personnel. The professional staff was increased by 10 during the 1907-33 period and by 172 from 1934 through 1965.

ISSUES

Four central questions emerged by 1900, continued throughout the period of this overview, and apparently are more challenging today than ever before: What quality programs would ensure a good education for all children? What is the best way to organize and administer these programs? How shall these programs be financed? Shall Illinois have a state board of education? Continuous responses to these naggingly persistent questions have served to shape the Office of the Superintendent of Public Instruction.

Curriculum and Supervision

At the turn of the century, Superintendent Bayliss expressed great concern about the disparities between urban and rural education. He emphasized the deplorable conditions which existed in many rural schools and pledged a crusade until every school in the state had a library. He placed emphasis also on the need for high schools, primarily to develop the well-educated citizenry necessary to deal with the social problems of the day.

Superintendent Blair equaled Bayliss in his enthusiasm for rural schools; his top assistant dealt with country schools. Blair did not support the Bayliss position that consolidation was the solution to the problem. Instead, he stated that conditions had much improved in the rural schools and inferred that the quality of education was

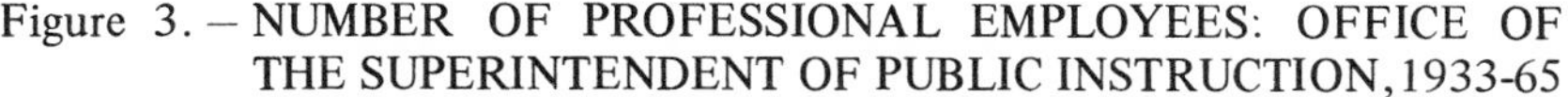

Figure 3. – NUMBER OF PROFESSIONAL EMPLOYEES: OFFICE OF THE SUPERINTENDENT OF PUBLIC INSTRUCTION, 1933-65

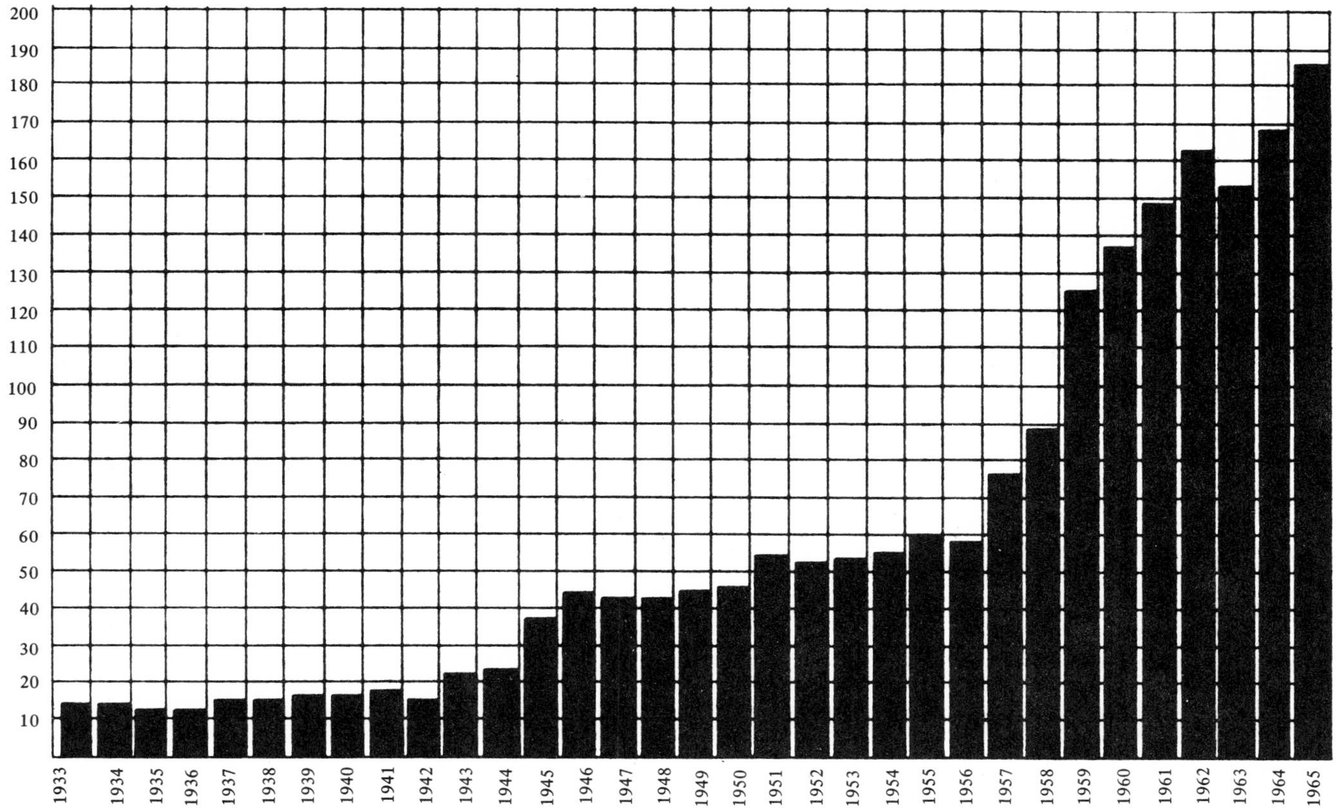

better when the schools remained close to the people. Interestingly, none of the nine bulletins issued in 1910 by the Illinois Educational Commission, chaired and greatly influenced by Blair, dealt directly with curriculum. Although Blair reminded the public in his 1912 report that his duties included the improvement of instruction, his criteria were sufficiently relaxed to allow one-room schools to qualify for "superior" ratings. The criteria for a "standard school" were divided into five categories: yard and outbuildings, schoolhouse, furnishings and supplies, organization, and the teacher.

Blair was fully aware in 1912 that during the preceding 25-year period the number of Illinois high schools had increased from 179 to 531, but he wondered if some high schools were being built unnecessarily and to the detriment of the elementary schools. His request for a high school supervisor had been denied twice by the General Assembly. He continued to criticize high schools for paying too much attention to college accreditation. The situation provided the impetus for a direct confrontation, the outcome of which was to affect extensively the role of the Office and its development. Prompted by a jealous normal school, the Illinois State Teachers Association passed a resolution at its 1911 convention calling for the Legislature to provide that the superintendent appoint one or more inspectors of high schools to inspect, classify, and standardize high schools under rules drawn by the superintendent.

This resolution brought about a discussion between Blair and H. A. Hollister, the University of Illinois high school visitor. Hollister proposed a dual system to allow continuance of university inspection and university standards for accrediting. Blair replied that the resolution did not deny the right or power of the university to establish standards and inspect schools for accreditation, but that the university had no legal right to be in the schools for any other purpose except by invitation of the local authorities. Furthermore, it had no legal power to enforce the findings. Blair ruled out the double system of inspection by stating that there are as many systems of inspection as there are universities and colleges desiring and able to make such inspections.

Hollister, emphasizing his 9 years of experience as a visitor, pointed out that the university had already established a system of standardization. He made comparisons with other states and praised the university-controlled systems. In contrast, he stated that "the situation in Wisconsin is too notoriously bad to need further mention" (11). Blair, citing major contributions made by state departments, replied that the question related to "supervision" and not to "inspection." In this respect, the school law made it the duty of the superintendent to supervise all the common and public schools, and he maintained that the high school was the last four grades of the common school. In answer to the visitor's contention that the teachers' proposal would lead toward political control of education, he stated: "If the political character of the Department of Public Instruction renders it unfit to supervise the high schools of this State, it is for the same reason unfit to supervise any of the schools" (12). The superintendent further pointed out that the university was controlled by a board of trustees, nominated in political conventions, who ran as candidates of a political party and had as much inclination and opportunity to administer along political lines as did the superintendent of public instruction. Even the visitor would have had to agree that the high school was the last four grades of the common school, and its supervision and direction should be the responsibilities of the same office which supervised and directed the first eight grades. Blair contended that the weakest feature of the township high school was that, as a "floating kidney," it had very loose connections with the elementary schools and no local supervision other than its own faculty.

At this time, the Illinois Educational Commission specifically mentioned curriculum in a report to the Forty-Seventh General Assembly:

> An ideal school with a fair faculty should provide a curriculum broader and more extensive than necessary for the needs of any single individual and until it does this, it has not gone far in meeting the varied needs of the many individuals that make up its constituency (13).

The report contained an example of how the school adjusts its program, following a section devoted to a general course in domestic science. To offer vocational courses for some people in cooking, sewing, dressmaking, and millinery, it suggested the school allow a doubling up so that courses such as sewing and cooking could be taken together. The school would arrange extra work specially designed for the purpose, or, better yet, put students on a part-time plan by which they should spend perhaps half their time with families, in stores, or in shops, actually practicing these arts. The report strongly advocated a plan allowing students who felt a need to earn money to do so and receive credit and thus, before leaving the school, acquire some actual business experience without severing connections with the school.

This plan was deemed better than preparing separate definitive courses which would divide pupils into two classes, one labeled in advance as the serving class. Blair stated: "Let mistress and maid be educated side by side, for both should be wives of American men and mothers of American citizens" (14).

In 1913, the Legislature authorized the appointment of a high school supervisor who immediately tackled the problem of preparing curriculums for the various high schools. By 1923, there were three high school supervisors and an abundance of ideas as to how schools could reorganize their instructional programs. The University of Illinois and the Office of the Superintendent of Public Instruction established a spirit of cooperation. They divided the state into an eastern and a western division, and in the first year of the cooperative endeavor, all western division schools requesting inspections addressed the superintendent; eastern schools, the university. The assignments were alternated annually.

During the later twenties, progress in the state's education was marked by an expansion of vocational education and instructional pattern variations due to the John Dewey influence. The first years of the Depression were devoted to the search for money to keep the instructional programs in operation; school terms were shortened, student-teacher ratios increased, and courses discontinued. Deterioration of the schools became so critical that the superintendent requested the Governor to call a special session of the Legislature, which responded by making one-third of the fuel tax revenues available to the Common School Fund.

Charles C. Stadtman is credited with a major contribution toward curriculum improvement, but because of their close personal relationship and similar attitudes toward education, equal credit should go to Stadtman's superior, Superintendent Wieland. Though Wieland and Stadtman opposed each other for the Democratic nomination in 1934, after the general election they joined forces in the state office. Stadtman emphasized the need for involving all units of the public school system in curriculum development. In 1936, a committee of educators met for a curriculum conference. Teacher colleges and other institutions of higher education followed the lead and included the subject of curriculum in their summer conferences. In 1938, Stadtman stated with pride that a rural curriculum guide was ready for the printer.

Apparently, Wieland believed in 1940 that radio should be used far more effectively as a teaching tool. He established the State Radio Committee, which advocated the use of radio programs carefully planned in advance and articulated with units of class work. It encouraged individual listening to enhance pupils' appreciation and understanding of drama, music, and art. By the following year, the major stations, such as WENR, WMAQ, WLS, WCIL, WIND, WJJD, and WAIT, were transmitting educational programs. Wieland pledged his continued support of radio education.

When Vernon L. Nickell took office in 1943, he emphasized cognitive objectives of the curriculum: "Actual education is the attainment of the ability to think and act for one's self. What the student should consider and how he may best be equipped to increase his knowledge is the immediate concern of modern-day leaders of education" (15).

In the midst of the many activities related to the war effort, curriculum efforts steadily continued: Ray Graham announced the Illinois plan for speech correction; a revision of the state course of study was being considered; the importance of visual aids in education was noted; and the Office conducted demonstration clinics. When the atomic bomb ended the war, Nickell believed that education faced its greatest challenge as all people had to be rehabilitated to the postwar reconversion.

The General Assembly in 1945 placed the entire responsibility for special education on the Office instead of on the several state agencies. The *Illinois Curriculum and Course of Study* came off the press in 1946.

The Illinois Curriculum Program, established in 1947, and its evaluation in 1965 were treated in the Special Programs section, but the excellent leadership and extensive activities deserve elaboration. The Illinois Curriculum Council had three chairmen: Mathew Gaffney, later a senior associate of James B. Conant in the study of the American high schools, served from 1947 to 1955; Gerald W. Smith, past president of the Illinois Association of Secondary School Principals, served from 1955 to 1962; and Darrell Blodgett, superintendent of schools in Wheaton, Illinois, served through the remainder of the period covered in this report.

The superintendent of public instruction appoints the director of the Illinois Curriculum Program. Four men have served with distinction: C. W. Sanford, recently retired as dean at the University of Illinois; Eric Johnson, now vice-president of Illinois State University, Normal; Fred P. Barnes, professor at the University of Illinois; and Woodson Fishback, the present director. Activities of the program include over 100 publications, special projects in schools, and a continuing series of workshops.

In 1963, Superintendent Page gave the Division of Instruction additional responsibilities. He divided the state into six regions to carry out the work of the Division of Recognition and Supervision. Teamwork developed between the instructional and recognition personnel to improve local educational programs. Local, county, regional, and state personnel assisted local schools to assess the extent to which the program met the needs of all pupils.

School District Reorganization

At the close of World War II, professors of educational administration were pointing a disapproving finger at Illinois for having approximately 12,000 school districts. Although it required legislative action to change dramatically this condition, efforts to decrease the number of districts had been initiated much earlier.

As early as 1909, the Legislature passed an act requiring districts which did not maintain a high school to pay tuition for their eighth-grade graduates in some 4-year high school. This law provided that the district must pay the tuition only if the parent or guardian were unable to pay. The principle was tested in the Illinois Supreme Court, which ruled that the board was not competent to decide who was able and who was not able to pay tuition. The Forty-Seventh General Assembly then made the necessary statutory provisions effective July 1, 1913. The effect was most noticeable during the 1915-16 school year, as the high school enrollment increased by 15 percent, while the elementary school enrollment increased by only 1 percent.

The extension of a "good, common school education" to include a high school education for all children was becoming generally accepted. However, the rapid increase in the number of high school pupils brought rapid increases in the total cost of education. Concern for economic efficiency gave impetus to the movement to reorganize schools.

A matter of greater concern to a lesser number of people was the problem of providing a high school curriculum suited to all children. In 1911, the Educational Commission appointed a special committee to study industrial education and preparation of teachers who were to teach the subjects. Concern for curriculum improvement was not limited to the high schools. As may have been expected, the grade schools were chastised for not preparing pupils for high school.

Early in the 1920's, the phenomenal growth of the American high school had its admirers and its critics. The movement for district reorganization had gained momentum with a twofold purpose: to provide more efficient schools and to provide a broader, better, and more equitable program for boys and girls.

The law providing for consolidation had been passed in 1919; however, the immediate response was limited. The purposes of consolidation remained constant, and the efforts to obtain reorganization were persistent. The General Assembly, in 1939, for the first time provided state aid for transporting pupils. Although this act did not greatly hasten consolidation, it did help. Perhaps Illinoisans were too enamored with their one-room schools.

The Sixty-Fourth General Assembly enacted a new school survey law providing for the creation of a state advisory commission of nine members to be appointed by the superintendent. Only two of the nine members were to be professional educators. The commission was required to report to the Legislature no later than January 1950.

County survey committees of nine members each were set up to study and plan school reorganization and to make final reports by January 1948. County committees were particularly effective for several reasons: The county superintendent was named the executive secretary of each county committee (most of the superintendents favored reorganization); school boards were advocating reorganization; taxpayers federations had considered the advisability of reorganization; and a minimum salary law for teachers caused a new concern for schools with small enrollments. The Illinois Agriculture Association School Committee reported the need for equalized educational opportunities, equitable distribution of costs, and maintenance of freedom.

The success of the reorganization effort is shown by statistics. In 1945, Illinois supported 11,955 school districts; at the close of the 1964-65 school year, Illinois had 1,363 school districts—a decrease of 10,592. The dramatic change in the number of school districts is best revealed by Figure 4.

Figure 4. – ELIMINATION OF 10,592 SCHOOL DISTRICTS IN ILLINOIS, 1945-65

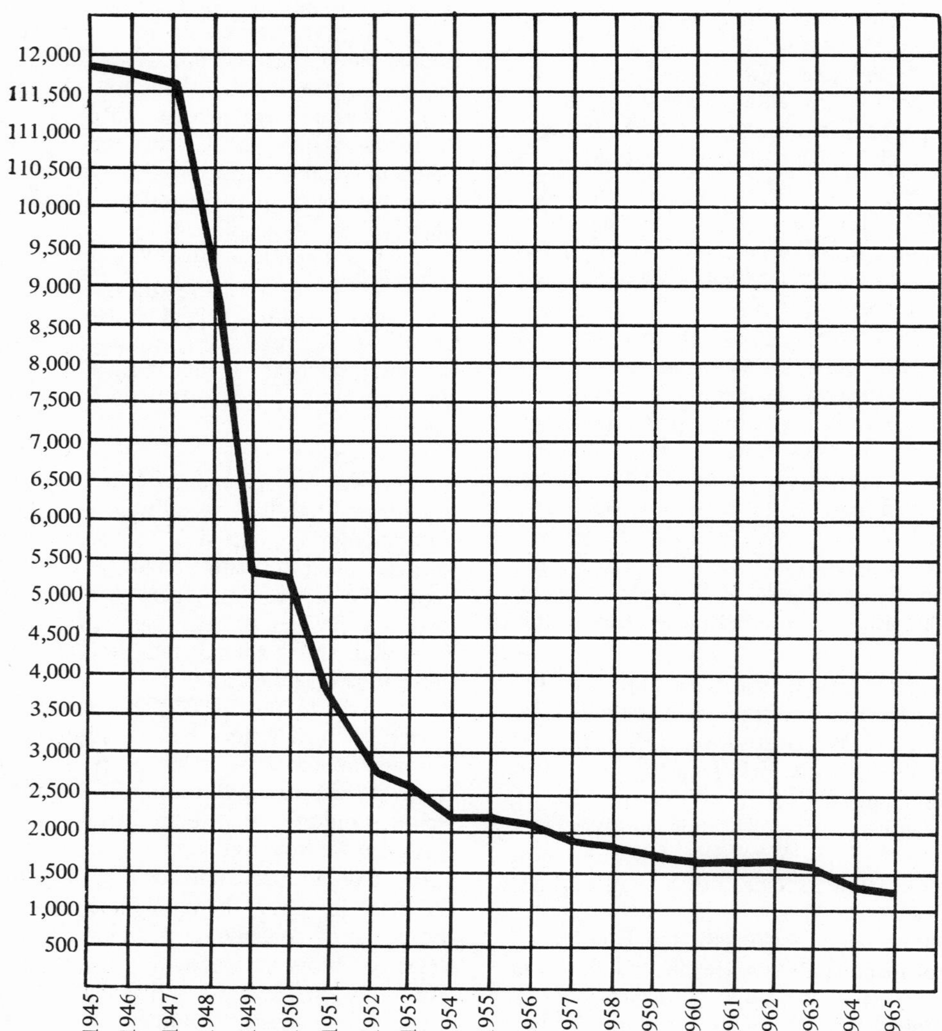

Financing Illinois Education

Article VIII of the Illinois Constitution states: "The General Assembly shall provide a thorough and efficient system of free schools, whereby all children of this State may receive a good, common school education" (16). In the main, the Legislature reflected the extent to which the state aided in financing education by a biennial appropriation to the Common School Fund.

The Illinois Free School Law of 1825 appropriated 2 percent of state treasury receipts to encourage free schools. In 1827, this act was amended to read "by consent of taxpayers" and in 1829 repealed entirely. The Free School Law of 1855 provided a levy of 2 mills per dollar of assessed valuation for support of common schools. This produced approximately $607,000 in 1856 and only $600,000 in 1862. The amount had risen to $900,000 per year just before the change in law in 1873, when a flat appropriation was substituted for the 2-mill tax. The taxes brought in about $1,067,000 for each year from 1873 to 1911. Such an appropriation resulted in a decline in the percent of education costs borne by the state: In 1874, state funds provided 13 percent of the total cost of the common schools; in 1911, the state's share was only 2. 6 percent.

Effective July 1913, local school districts which did not maintain a high school were required to pay tuition for their eighth-grade graduates in some 4-year high school. High schools were conducted without benefit of general state aid until the 1930's.

In the 1920's, the "smart" schoolman, in order to provide the varied programs needed for an increasing number of children in the high schools, turned to funds provided for vocational courses. In the elementary school, the "smart" schoolman took advantage of the state formula which included the number of teachers employed; by having a larger number of teachers, he obtained ample money for supplies.

The forerunner to the modern plan for distributing general state aid became operational in 1927, when provisions were made for flat grants and a guaranteed foundation level: a flat grant of $9 and a foundation of $34 per elementary pupil.

In 1939, high schools received general state aid for the first time as funds were received under a special equalization formula. High schools began receiving flat grants 4 years later. In 1947, the foundation levels became the same for elementary and high schools, and flat grants for these two groups became identical in 1965.

Figure 5 shows the changes in appropriation to the Common School Fund as it rose from $2 million in 1909 to $443 million in the biennial appropriation for the 1963-65 period. This fund includes the claims from local school districts for state aid, compensation of county superintendents and assistant superintendents, state payment to the teachers retirement system, tax-equivalent grants to districts where state institutions are located, and tuition for children from orphanages and children's homes, in veterans hospital areas, in military encampment areas, and in state-owned housing units.

Figure 5. – STATE BIENNIAL APPROPRIATIONS FOR THE COMMON SCHOOL FUND, 1909-65

Biennium	Amount	Biennium	Amount
1909-11	$ 2,114,000	1937-39	$ 26,114,000
1911-13	4,114,000	1939-41	29,494,000
1913-15	6,114,000	1941-43	31,380,000
1915-17	8,114,000	1943-45	35,160,000
1917-19	8,114,000	1945-47	44,087,000
1919-21	12,114,000	1947-49	65,753,000
1921-23	16,114,000	1949-51	100,419,000
1923-25	16,114,000	1951-53	124,438,000
1925-27	16,114,000	1953-55	144,266,865
1927-29	16,114,000	1955-57	201,076,850
1929-31	20,114,000	1957-59	227,000,000
1931-33	21,114,000	1959-61	337,600,000
1933-35	21,114,000	1961-63	393,396,000
1935-37	26,114,000	1963-65	433,090,000

Biennial appropriations for the Common School Fund are difficult to analyze, especially in making comparisons with the appropriations of other states. Primarily, too often faulty analysis and misinterpretation have stemmed from the mistaken belief that the appropriation is the only financial assistance provided by the state to the local school districts for a 2-year period and from failure to recognize that the property tax is reserved to the local government. In addition to the sum for the Common School Fund, the Legislature appropriates separate sums for special education, transportation, vocational education, driver education, and adult education. In 1965, the General Assembly appropriated $559 million for the Common School Fund for 1965-67 and voted an additional total of $135 million for special programs. In case the application of prescribed formulas yields too little, the Legislature may vote deficiency appropriations before the end of the biennium.

Illinois school districts receive the major share of their income from local assessments on real and personal property, since the state, with no income tax, empowers local units of government to levy the property tax. In the 1964-65 school year, school support was divided as follows: state aid, 20 percent; federal aid, 2 percent; and local support, 78 percent. In 1965, the General Assembly ensured a rise in state support to approximately 24 percent. The same year, Congress ensured that the federal level of support would rise to approximately 6 percent. Figure 6 shows the growth of total expenditures in the common schools of Illinois.

Figure 6. – GROWTH OF EDUCATIONAL EXPENDITURES, 1900-60

Year	State population	School enrollment	Educational expenditures	Per-capita costs
1900	4,821,550	958,911	$ 12,584,620.46	$ 13.12
1910	5,638,591	1,002,687	35,259,197.47	35.16
1920	6,485,280	1,127,560	57,899,160.81	51.35
1930	7,630,654	1,395,907	123,582,996.20	88.53
1940	7,897,241	1,287,085	117,493,670.74	91.28
1950	8,712,176	1,214,237	253,599,314.63	208.85
1960	10,081,158	1,787,869	640,190,189.42	358.07

By 1965, Superintendent Page's position on state aid was clear to the members of his policy staff. He presented his legislative program to the School Problems Commission in December 1966. While recognizing that local support was high and desirable, he maintained that the property tax, the base for local revenues, could not in the future be expected to bear so large a percentage of the cost of a quality program for all children. The state share, he said, should be increased to 45-48 percent by 1973.

He further recommended increasing the guaranteed foundation level to $400; the preceding General Assembly had raised this component of the state aid formula from $252 to $330, a figure which had remained unchanged through several bienniums. The superintendent emphasized that the 1973 support level would include all programs financed by the state for the common schools, instead of only those presently encompassed by the Common School Fund.

Elected *v.* Appointed Superintendents

Although the 1854 General Assembly provided for an elected superintendent of public instruction, it did not provide for a state board of education. The situation remains unchanged today. The Constitution of 1848 had expressed confidence in the people by giving them broad powers to elect officials. Since the establishment of the Office of the State Superintendent, the policy in Illinois has been that the people maintain control through the election of school boards and county superintendents as well as of the state superintendent. Illinoisans generally do not believe that the chief state school officer would remain a true servant of the people if he were not elected by public ballot. The Constitution of 1870, in force today, provided added protection for maintaining an elected superintendent.

There was little evidence of disagreement with the 1854 ruling until the time of Bayliss' tenure (1898-1906), when he recommended the creation of a nonpartisan state board of education with the superintendent as the executive officer. What influenced Bayliss' recommendation? The relationship may be coincidental rather than causal, but Bayliss' assistant was J. H. Freeman, who had been the only appointed superintendent in the history of the Office since Powell's election in 1856. The two may have had considerable discussion about how convenient it was not to be forced to face the people directly with the issues of the day. Then, too, the recommendation came at a time when the endorsement of the Republican party turned in 1906 in favor of Francis G. Blair.

The Educational Commission of 1907 continued the discussion and developed a plan for a state board.

At the time of the fifth constitutional convention, after World War I, Blair convincingly defended electing the superintendent, saying that it was then less necessary to have an appointed superintendent than it had been earlier. He referred to the fact that at the time of the Educational Commission's report, the superintendent had been nominated by political conventions and that the adoption of the direct primary should eliminate any objections. He countered the charge that the direct primary did not eliminate political malpractice with the statement that there was no method of selection to ensure choice of the right man. He pointed to Iowa, which had changed from the elective to the appointive plan and then back to the elective.

The state board of education is still an issue today. The need for such a board was recognized by both candidates for the superintendency in 1966. There are two central questions: Would the members be appointed or elected, and what would be the duties of the board? School administrators throughout Illinois, including Superintendent Page, agree that Illinois needs a state board of education with regulatory and supervisory powers to coordinate the functions of education on a state level. After studying the experiences of other states, Superintendent Page concluded that Illinois should adopt an elective state board system. He stated:

> Many members of that Council have become aware, as I have, of the inequities which can exist when one man is given the power to make each and every selection to a board of such grave importance. For example, the present Illinois Governor recently made the appointments to the newly created Illinois Junior College Board. No members on that appointive board come from south of Bloomington. More than one-half of the area of Illinois is thus without representation on that board. Very probably metropolitan and suburban members of that board

will have little understanding of the unique problems found in Southern Illinois, just as a board entirely from Southern Illinois would have little understanding of urban problems (17).

Page further pointed out that an elected board would have the advantage of making the members responsible directly to the districts rather than to the man who appointed them. He suggested that because of the great diversity in social and cultural attitudes in the state, and to ensure that all areas and attitudes are represented in a policy-making state board, an elected board is necessary.

A bill introduced in the 1965 General Assembly to create a state board of education took the superintendent by surprise. It was his understanding that the Governor's Office, his Office, and the Illinois School Problems Commission would hold off on legislative proposals for educational reorganization until 1967. They could then use the Illinois Task Force on Education recommendations as the basis for a so-called master plan. The bill was defeated because it did not clarify the method by which the board members would be selected.

Even though he was an elected superintendent, Page urged that the proposed new board appoint the superintendent. He stated:

> I see the great need for an Illinois Board of Education. And when such a board is created, it should be given the power to appoint the state school superintendent, the man who will be directly responsible to the board. We must work toward such a board, but it must be an elective board if we are to preserve representation for all sections of the State (18).

FOOTNOTES

1. Francis G. Blair, "Centennial of the First Free School Law of Illinois," *Blue Book of the State of Illinois, 1925-1926* (Springfield: Illinois State Journal Co., 1925), p. 422.
2. *Ibid.*, p. 415.
3. *Ibid.*, p. 416.
4. The series of biennial reports which all elected superintendents have submitted as required by the General Assembly now serve as a highly valued primary source of information. Victor H. Sheppard, a historian of the Office (see Bibliography), with no less than 100 footnotes relating to these biennial reports, refers to these documents more frequently than any other source, including the numerous references to the laws of Illinois and the Educational Press bulletins.
5. In the 1945 revision of the school code, the distinction between powers and duties was eliminated, for it was felt that the powers should also be considered duties.
6. Illinois School Problems Commission, *Illinois School Problems* (Springfield: State of Illinois, 1951), p. 32.
7. Francis G. Blair, *Educational Addresses, 1906-1920* (Danville: Illinois Printing Co., 1921), p. 77.
8. To emphasize the widespread network of relationships which the Office has with its organizational environment, a complete listing of the organizations represented on the Illinois Curriculum Council is attached as Appendix C.
9. Superintendent of Public Instruction, *Illinois School Directory, 1934-1935* (Springfield: State of Illinois, 1934), p. 4.
10. In the opinion of the writer, Superintendent Page's decision during his first year in office to establish six regional supervisory districts will eventually prove to be one of the most important in the history of the Office to date. The same year, the county superintendents organized on a coterminous basis, thereby establishing relationships leading to a vastly improved program for the supervision and recognition of schools.
11. Superintendent of Public Instruction, *Twenty-Ninth Biennial Report* (1912), p. 39.
12. *Ibid.*, p. 45.
13. *Ibid.*, p. 317.
14. *Ibid.*, p. 349.
15. Superintendent of Public Instruction, *Educational Press Bulletin*, XXXIV, No. 2 (February 1943), 2.
16. Illinois, *Constitution* (1870), art. 8.
17. Ray Page, "A State Board of Education and Its Chief Officer," a position statement, 1966, p. 1. (Mimeographed.) May be found in the files of the Department of Public Instruction, Springfield, Illinois.
18. *Ibid.*, p. 3.

BIBLIOGRAPHY

Public Documents

Illinois. *Blue Book*. Springfield: Illinois State Journal Co., 1861-1966. Biennial publication issued by the state since 1861. The first edition listed only legislative officers. The 1965-66 volume, containing 896 pages, presents a comprehensive view of Illinois government, including a copy of the constitution.

—— *Constitution* (1848, 1870).

Superintendent of Public Instruction. *The School Code of Illinois with Additional Acts Affecting Schools* (1965).

Books

Blair, Francis G. *Educational Addresses, 1906-1920.* Danville: Illinois Printing Co., 1921.

Sandburg, Carl. *Abraham Lincoln.* Vol. I: *The Prairie Years.* New York: Dell Publishing Co., 1959.

Sheppard, Victor H. *A Brief History of the Office of Public Instruction.* Springfield: State of Illinois, 1957.

-- *A Brief History of the Office of Public Instruction: Supplement Number One Covering the Period 1955-1963.* Springfield: State of Illinois, 1962.

Superintendent of Public Instruction. *Guide to Supervision, Evaluation, and Recognition of Illinois Schools.* Springfield: State of Illinois, September 1, 1958.

-- *Illinois School Directory, 1934-1935.* Springfield: State of Illinois, 1934.

Articles and Periodicals

Blair, Francis G. "Centennial of the First Free School Law of Illinois." *Blue Book of the State of Illinois, 1925-1926.* Springfield: Illinois State Journal Co., 1925.

Educational Press Bulletin, I, No. 1 (1907); XXXIV, No. 2 (February 1943); and LII, No. 3 (May 1961). This is a monthly bulletin issued until May 1961.

Fishback, Woodson W. "The Illinois Curriculum Program Moves Forward." *Illinois Educational Press Bulletin,* LI, No. 3 (May 1960), 5-13.

Illinois Journal of Education, LVII, No. 1 (February 1966). This entire issue, written by various members of the Office of the Superintendent of Public Instruction, focuses on "Federal Programs." This is one issue in a series which began in September 1961.

Sanford, C. W., and Spalding, Willard. "The Illinois Secondary School Curriculum Program." *The California Journal of Secondary Education* (January 1952), pp. 28-35.

Reports

Illinois School Problems Commission. *Illinois School Problems.* Springfield: State of Illinois, 1951. This is the first of a series of biennial reports by the School Problems Commission.

Superintendent of Public Instruction. *Annual Statistical Report for the Year Ending June 30, 1962.* Circular Series A, No. 154. Springfield: State of Illinois, 1962. This is one of a series of biennial statistical reports covering the years 1855-1967.

Superintendents of Public Instruction. *Biennial Reports.* Springfield: State of Illinois, 1855-1967.

Unpublished Material

Goodkind, Thomas B. "The Impact of the Illinois Curriculum Program upon Local School District Curriculum Operations." Unpublished Ph.D. dissertation, Northwestern University, Evanston, Illinois, 1965.

Page, Ray. "A State Board of Education and Its Chief Officer." A position statement, 1966. (Mimeographed.)

Appendix A

ILLINOIS CHIEF STATE SCHOOL OFFICERS

1856-58	William H. Powell, Republican	1890-94	Henry Raab, Democrat
1858-62	Newton Bateman, Republican	1894-98	Samuel M. Englis, Republican
1862-64	John P. Brooks, Democrat	1898-1906	Alfred Bayliss, Republican
1864-74	Newton Bateman, Republican	1906-34	Francis G. Blair, Republican
1874-78	Samuel M. Etter, Democrat	1934-42	John A. Wieland, Democrat
1878-82	James P. Slade, Republican	1942-58	Vernon L. Nickell, Republican
1882-86	Henry Raab, Democrat	1958-62	George T. Wilkins, Democrat
1886-90	Richard Edwards, Republican	1962-	Ray Page, Republican

Appendix B

Chart I.--ILLINOIS OFFICE OF THE SUPERINTENDENT OF INSTRUCTION, 1967-68

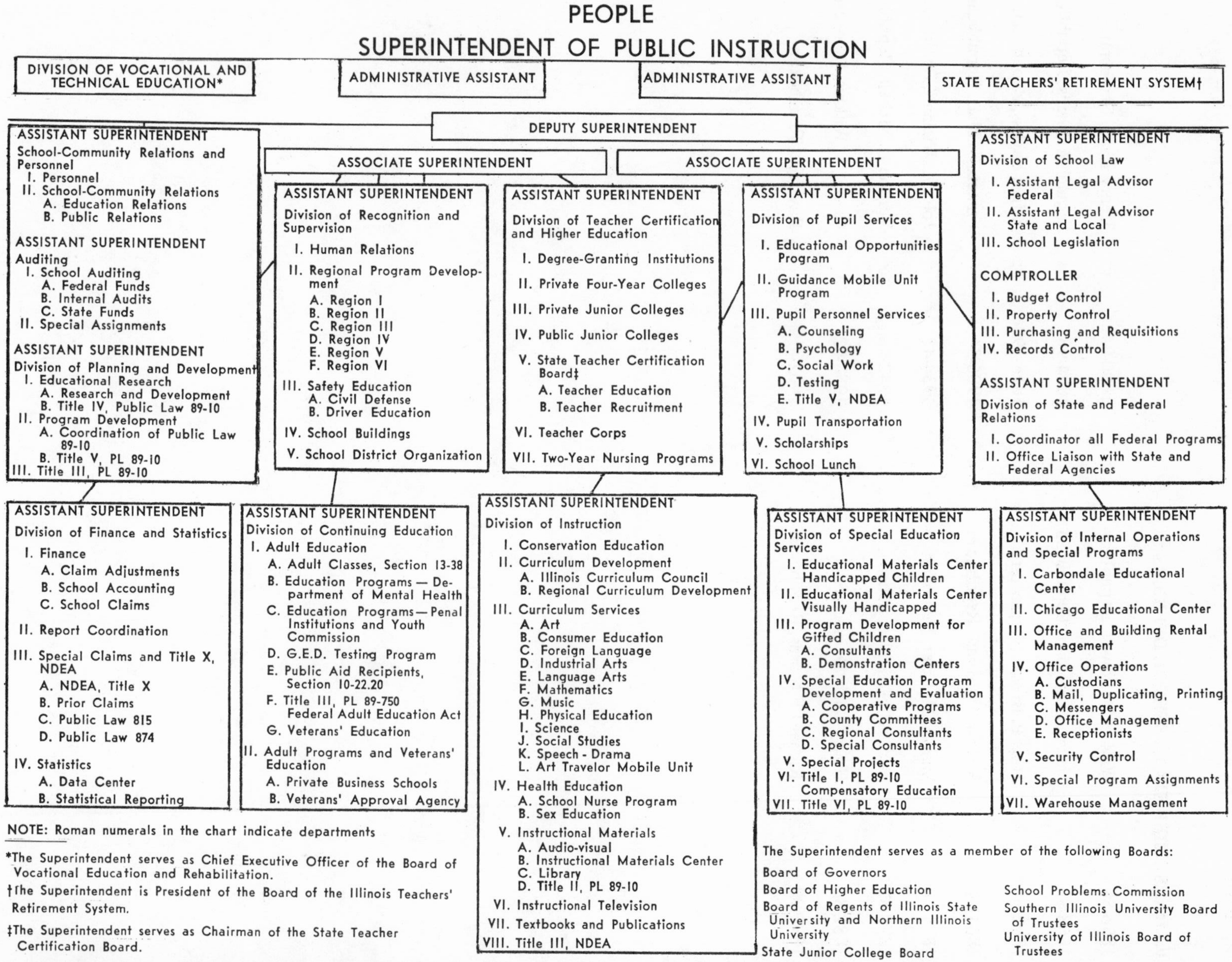

PEOPLE

SUPERINTENDENT OF PUBLIC INSTRUCTION

DIVISION OF VOCATIONAL AND TECHNICAL EDUCATION*

ADMINISTRATIVE ASSISTANT

ADMINISTRATIVE ASSISTANT

STATE TEACHERS' RETIREMENT SYSTEM†

DEPUTY SUPERINTENDENT

ASSISTANT SUPERINTENDENT
School-Community Relations and Personnel
I. Personnel
II. School-Community Relations
A. Education Relations
B. Public Relations

ASSISTANT SUPERINTENDENT
Auditing
I. School Auditing
A. Federal Funds
B. Internal Audits
C. State Funds
II. Special Assignments

ASSISTANT SUPERINTENDENT
Division of Planning and Development
I. Educational Research
A. Research and Development
B. Title IV, Public Law 89-10
II. Program Development
A. Coordination of Public Law 89-10
B. Title V, PL 89-10
III. Title III, PL 89-10

ASSOCIATE SUPERINTENDENT

ASSISTANT SUPERINTENDENT
Division of Recognition and Supervision
I. Human Relations
II. Regional Program Development
A. Region I
B. Region II
C. Region III
D. Region IV
E. Region V
F. Region VI
III. Safety Education
A. Civil Defense
B. Driver Education
IV. School Buildings
V. School District Organization

ASSISTANT SUPERINTENDENT
Division of Teacher Certification and Higher Education
I. Degree-Granting Institutions
II. Private Four-Year Colleges
III. Private Junior Colleges
IV. Public Junior Colleges
V. State Teacher Certification Board‡
A. Teacher Education
B. Teacher Recruitment
VI. Teacher Corps
VII. Two-Year Nursing Programs

ASSOCIATE SUPERINTENDENT

ASSISTANT SUPERINTENDENT
Division of Pupil Services
I. Educational Opportunities Program
II. Guidance Mobile Unit Program
III. Pupil Personnel Services
A. Counseling
B. Psychology
C. Social Work
D. Testing
E. Title V, NDEA
IV. Pupil Transportation
V. Scholarships
VI. School Lunch

ASSISTANT SUPERINTENDENT
Division of School Law
I. Assistant Legal Advisor Federal
II. Assistant Legal Advisor State and Local
III. School Legislation

COMPTROLLER
I. Budget Control
II. Property Control
III. Purchasing and Requisitions
IV. Records Control

ASSISTANT SUPERINTENDENT
Division of State and Federal Relations
I. Coordinator all Federal Programs
II. Office Liaison with State and Federal Agencies

ASSISTANT SUPERINTENDENT
Division of Finance and Statistics
I. Finance
A. Claim Adjustments
B. School Accounting
C. School Claims
II. Report Coordination
III. Special Claims and Title X, NDEA
A. NDEA, Title X
B. Prior Claims
C. Public Law 815
D. Public Law 874
IV. Statistics
A. Data Center
B. Statistical Reporting

ASSISTANT SUPERINTENDENT
Division of Continuing Education
I. Adult Education
A. Adult Classes, Section 13-38
B. Education Programs — Department of Mental Health
C. Education Programs — Penal Institutions and Youth Commission
D. G.E.D. Testing Program
E. Public Aid Recipients, Section 10-22.20
F. Title III, PL 89-750 Federal Adult Education Act
G. Veterans' Education
II. Adult Programs and Veterans' Education
A. Private Business Schools
B. Veterans' Approval Agency

ASSISTANT SUPERINTENDENT
Division of Instruction
I. Conservation Education
II. Curriculum Development
A. Illinois Curriculum Council
B. Regional Curriculum Development
III. Curriculum Services
A. Art
B. Consumer Education
C. Foreign Language
D. Industrial Arts
E. Language Arts
F. Mathematics
G. Music
H. Physical Education
I. Science
J. Social Studies
K. Speech - Drama
L. Art Travelor Mobile Unit
IV. Health Education
A. School Nurse Program
B. Sex Education
V. Instructional Materials
A. Audio-visual
B. Instructional Materials Center
C. Library
D. Title II, PL 89-10
VI. Instructional Television
VII. Textbooks and Publications
VIII. Title III, NDEA

ASSISTANT SUPERINTENDENT
Division of Special Education Services
I. Educational Materials Center Handicapped Children
II. Educational Materials Center Visually Handicapped
III. Program Development for Gifted Children
A. Consultants
B. Demonstration Centers
IV. Special Education Program Development and Evaluation
A. Cooperative Programs
B. County Committees
C. Regional Consultants
D. Special Consultants
V. Special Projects
VI. Title I, PL 89-10 Compensatory Education
VII. Title VI, PL 89-10

ASSISTANT SUPERINTENDENT
Division of Internal Operations and Special Programs
I. Carbondale Educational Center
II. Chicago Educational Center
III. Office and Building Rental Management
IV. Office Operations
A. Custodians
B. Mail, Duplicating, Printing
C. Messengers
D. Office Management
E. Receptionists
V. Security Control
VI. Special Program Assignments
VII. Warehouse Management

NOTE: Roman numerals in the chart indicate departments

*The Superintendent serves as Chief Executive Officer of the Board of Vocational Education and Rehabilitation.

†The Superintendent is President of the Board of the Illinois Teachers' Retirement System.

‡The Superintendent serves as Chairman of the State Teacher Certification Board.

The Superintendent serves as a member of the following Boards:

Board of Governors
Board of Higher Education
Board of Regents of Illinois State University and Northern Illinois University
State Junior College Board
School Problems Commission
Southern Illinois University Board of Trustees
University of Illinois Board of Trustees

Appendix C

ORGANIZATIONS REPRESENTED ON THE ILLINOIS CURRICULUM COUNCIL

Fifty advisory councils serve the Office of the Superintendent of Public Instruction; the largest of these, the Illinois Curriculum Council, has representatives from over 50 organizations. The superintendent also invites individuals to serve as representatives-at-large. An organization or institution not represented on the council may request the superintendent to approve its organization for council membership.

Membership of the Council

American Association of University Women, Illinois Division
American Civil Liberties Union
Chicago Public Schools
Federation of Illinois Colleges
Illinois Adult Education Association
Illinois Aerospace Education Committee
Illinois Agricultural Association
Illinois Art Education Association
Illinois Association of Chemistry Teachers
Illinois Association of Classroom Teachers
Illinois Association of County Superintendents of Schools
Illinois Association of Community and Junior Colleges
Illinois Association for Health, Physical Education and Recreation
Illinois Association of School Administrators
Illinois Association of School Boards
Illinois Association of School Librarians
Illinois Association of Secondary School Principals
Illinois Association for Supervision and Curriculum Development
Illinois Association for Teacher Education in Private Colleges
Illinois Association of Teachers of English
Illinois Association of Vocational Agricultural Teachers
Illinois Association of Women Deans and Counselors
Illinois Business Education Association
Illinois Catholic Secondary School Principals Conference
Illinois Classical Conference
Illinois Congress of Parents and Teachers
Illinois Council for the Social Studies
Illinois Council for Teachers of Mathematics
Illinois Education Association
Illinois Elementary School Principals Association
Illinois Federation of Business and Professional Women's Clubs Incorporated
Illinois Geographical Society
Illinois Guidance and Personnel Association
Illinois Home Economics Association
Illinois Industrial Education Association
Illinois Joint Committee on School Health
Illinois Modern Language Teachers Association
Illinois Music Educators' Association
Illinois Speech Association
Illinois State Academy of Science
Illinois State Advisory Council of Outdoor Education
Illinois State Association for Childhood Education
Illinois State Chamber of Commerce
Illinois Vocational Association
Illinois Vocational Homemaking Teachers Association
Junior High School Association of Illinois
Junior High School Principals Association
Liberal Arts Disciplines
North Central Association of Secondary Schools and Colleges
Office of the Superintendent of Public Instruction
Private Schools
State-Supported Universities
- Chicago State College
- Eastern Illinois University
- Illinois State University
- Northeastern Illinois State College
- Northern Illinois University
- Southern Illinois University
- University of Illinois
- Western Illinois University

Representatives-at-Large (Appointed by Superintendent of Public Instruction)

14 Indiana

DEPARTMENT OF PUBLIC INSTRUCTION
Compiled by Harold H. Negley

Contents

DEVELOPMENT OF THE INDIANA PUBLIC SCHOOL SYSTEM TO 1900

First Efforts To Establish a Public School System

As early as 1816, Indiana citizens recognized that the general diffusion of knowledge and learning was essential to the preservation of free government and the well-being of the state. The first state constitution authorized the General Assembly "to provide, by law, as soon as circumstances will permit, for a general system of education, ascending in regular gradation, from township schools to a state university, wherein tuition shall be gratis and equally open to all" (1). Although the legislators accepted the general diffusion of knowledge and learning in principle, they did little to provide the legal means necessary to implement the constitution. In fact, the phrase "as soon as circumstances will permit" may have enabled them to avoid the often sensitive issue of a general system of education (2).

Although the schools were to be tuition-free, the assembly did not appropriate funds to develop a system. In 1824, the legislators enacted a law authorizing householders of a district to levy a tax for school construction. This levy was optional on the part of the voters of each district, and there was general reliance on the scant revenue from congressional land grants to support schools.

The system that developed during this period was both public and private. Some districts constructed school buildings but had no funds available to pay teachers. In most instances, parents paid a fixed amount based on the length of time their children attended school. Consequently, education was available only to those children whose parents could afford the tuition charges.

Most functions relating to the general system were administered at the local level, but the state assumed a minor supervisory role in school finance. The constitution made it the duty of the General Assembly to provide for the sale of school lands and the maintenance of revenue derived from the sale of such lands. School lands included the sixteenth section of land in each township as prescribed by the Ordinance of 1787, land granted to schools or seminaries, and any additional land granted to the State of Indiana by the U.S. government. Through the years, the General Assembly enacted numerous laws to provide for the administration and preservation of school lands and revenues at the local level. But most local officials showed little or no interest in their duties; consequently, much of the revenue was lost.

To remedy this situation, an act passed by the General Assembly in 1843 declared the state treasurer to be ex officio superintendent of common schools. The main duties of the superintendent included preparing an instruction manual for local officials and presenting an annual report to the General Assembly.

Educational Reform in Indiana

After the work of the Legislature in 1843, interest in public education subsided. It is possible that popular education would not have received further attention for some time, had it not been for the efforts of one man–Caleb Mills.

Shortly after his graduation from Dartmouth College, Mills came to the "Wabash Country" to study the effectiveness of religious education. He was dismayed at the lack of interest shown by Indiana residents in providing schools and education. As principal of the Presbyterian School (later Wabash College), Caleb Mills dedicated himself to the cause of popular education in the state.

Concurrent with the opening session of the General Assembly in December 1846, an article addressed to the members of the assembly and signed "one of the people" appeared in the *Indiana State Journal.* In this article, Mills reprimanded the legislators and other state officials for their neglect of education and pointed out some rather startling facts about the public school system. The decennial census of 1840 showed that Indiana ranked sixteenth on the national scale of literacy–only one in seven persons could read or write. This was the lowest rate among the Northern states. Mills stressed the lack of school buildings, the poor training of teachers, and the need for funds as factors contributing to the low literacy rate.

The Establishment of a State-Supervised System of Public Education

Many citizens ignored Mills, but the General Assembly of 1846, by joint resolution, recommended "to the friends of education" that a state common school convention be held at Indianapolis in May 1847 "for the purpose of consulting and devising the best course to be pursued to promote Common School Education in our State." The convention proposed to draft a school bill to be presented, along with an address to the people "on the subject of Common Schools," to the General Assembly in December.

The address contained three general conclusions with respect to a common school system:

1. A proper education for the citizens cannot be obtained without an efficient system of common schools.
2. Such a system must be a free system, where all children of the state may obtain an elementary education.
3. It is time for the General Assembly to fulfill its duty to provide for a system of township schools.

The convention recommended that the system be administered by a general superintendent and a superintendent for each county. In order to provide the necessary funds, it recommended that a tax levy be established to keep school for at least 3 months each year. Other important recommendations pertained to teacher qualifications, teacher education, and cooperation between the common schools and the private seminaries.

In the years that followed, opposition was directed more toward the state's paying for the system than toward a general system itself. In 1848 and again in 1849, the "free school" question was voted on by the people of Indiana at the general election. Each time, the majority vote was cast for free schools.

In 1851, a constitutional convention was held, and the basis for a general system of education was incorporated into the new constitution. The first section authorized the General Assembly to provide for the development of a " general and uniform system of common schools." Second, the Common School Fund was established as a permanent fund from the following sources: Congressional Township Fund, a fund derived from the sale of the sixteenth section of land; the Surplus Revenue Fund; the Saline Fund; the Bank Tax Fund, derived from a levy on state banks; the Seminary Fund, consisting of the revenue from the sale of county seminaries and properties; fines and forfeitures, a fund derived from breaches in penal law; escheated estates, or those lands and moneys which revert to the state for want of heirs; and the Swamp Lands Fund, derived from the congressional grant after deducting the expense of selecting and draining. In addition, the Office of State Superintendent of Public Instruction was established on an elective basis (3).

Experience had proved that if a public school system were to succeed in Indiana, supplemental legislation would have to be provided immediately. The General Assembly accomplished this task a year later. Under the new school law, the civil township became the basic administrative unit, with a board of three township trustees serving as school administrators. At the state level, the office of state superintendent became separate and distinct from any other elected office, and the State Board of Education was defined.

The Role of the State Superintendent

In addition to performing the administrative and clerical chores necessary for the operation of his office, the superintendent supervised the purchase of library books, ruled on appeals made by township trustees, maintained the Common School Fund, and licensed common school teachers. It was further required upon his induction into office that he address the State Board of Education on the most efficient ways and means to develop popular education. Also, he served as ex officio president of this body. He presented an annual report of his "labors and observations" to the General Assembly, and, perhaps most important, he spent at least 10 days in each judicial district conferring with local officials and teachers on school matters. For these tasks, the superintendent received an annual salary of $1,300 and an additional sum (not to exceed $500) for travel, postage, stationery, and other miscellaneous expenses. Should the business of the office so require, the superintendent might hire a clerk (but not for more than 6 months each year) at a salary of $2 per day.

From that time until the turn of the century, the duties of the superintendent were only slightly modified. Instead of visiting each judicial district, he was required to visit each county. Collection of data on teacher salaries, number of teachers, licenses issued, tax rates, and school facilities became the main function of the office. While this information had little value, accurate student enumeration figures were essential to make an equitable distribution of state school funds. During this time (1851-1900), the only additions to the staff were a deputy superintendent and two full-time clerks.

The State Board of Education

The first State Board of Education was created by Section 147 of the School Law of 1852. As prescribed by law, the state superintendent, the auditor, the treasurer, the secretary of state, and the Governor served as members of the board. This group may have made some notable contributions to the development of public education, but the state superintendent, as the only professional member, was largely responsible for the two functions of the board—establishment of township libraries and adoption of uniform textbooks.

In the revised School Law of 1865, the membership of the newly designated "Indiana State Board of Education" was changed to include the Governor, the state superintendent, the president of the state university, the president of the state normal college, and the superintendents of common schools from the state's three largest cities (then Evansville, Indianapolis, and Fort Wayne). Although the responsibility for the adoption of textbooks was transferred to township trustees, the revised law authorized the board to examine applicants and grant state certificates of qualification to teachers who possessed eminent training and professional ability. Very few state licenses were issued, but the board did assume the responsibility for preparation and distribution of teacher examinations to county examiners and later to county superintendents.

With the exception of the law of 1889, which returned the responsibility for adoption of texbooks to the Indiana State Board of Education, the group acted primarily in an advisory capacity. An 1875 law extended the membership to include the president of Purdue University. Under pressures exerted by rural citizens, who argued that the board represented only large city systems and the state colleges and universities, an 1899 law provided for three additional members to be appointed by the Governor, one of whom must be a county superintendent.

Deterrents to Tuition-Free Schools

New laws did not bring about immediate acceptance of the idea that a state system was superior to a district system. Opposition was expressed in many ways, in particular, toward local tax levies for schools. "In this respect," said State Historian Logan Esarey, "the congressional fund had been a misfortune in that it caused the citizens of the state to believe that schools should be provided with no effort on their part (4).

Legally, the General Assembly had exclusive legislative authority—it was the duty of the assembly to provide the legal means for a general and uniform system of common schools. To this end, all local and special laws for the support of schools and the preservation of school funds were prohibited.

Supplemental legislation of 1852 consolidated the revenue would then be applied to the support of schools and the revenue from Common School Funds, including the Congressional Township Fund, into a general fund. This revenue would then be applied to the support of schools throughout the state on a per-pupil basis. This brought immediate outcries from many citizens in the state who argued that Congressional Township Fund revenues were for the support of local schools and could not be distributed on a statewide basis. In 1854, the Indiana Supreme Court upheld this view. Unlike the procedure in other states, land grants had been given not to the state but to the inhabitants of the townships exclusively for the purpose of maintaining schools. With this decision, Congressional Township Funds were returned to local units. Two weeks later, the court invalidated that section of the 1852 law which authorized township voters to impose a levy on taxable property to continue schools after state funds had been expended. This section conflicted with constitutional provisions against local and special laws for the support of schools. Although these decisions brought about the near collapse of the system, it was said that they established the state's responsibility for providing tuition and the township's responsibility for school construction.

In 1865, township trustees were given the power to levy a special tax for construction, rentals, repairs, furniture, equipment, fuel, and the payment of other necessary expenses of the school *except tuition.* Two years later, trustees were further authorized to levy a special tuition tax. In 1885, the supreme court upheld the use of local levies by stating that such levies were general laws for school support rather than special laws.

The Office of the County Superintendent

Under the provisions of the School Law of 1852, there were two administrative units—the state department and the civil township. In theory, the trustees and the state superintendent were responsible for supervising the system. In practice, local trustees did not have the training or experience to provide effective supervision. On the other hand, the state superintendent did not have enough time to provide adequate supervision to all local officials. To fill the gap between state and local administrative units, the office of county superintendent was created in 1873.

Prior to that time, some degree of supervision had been provided by county examiners and commissioners. Their duties included the examination of teachers, grading examinations, issuing licenses, accounting for license fees, and encouraging the use of teacher institutes to improve the quality of teaching.

In effect, the legislation of 1873 did not establish a new office, but merely extended the duties of an old one. The county superintendent performed the same basic duties as the examiner and commissioner; however, the new law made school visitations and teacher institutes mandatory. In addition, the superintendent examined school records and established a closer working relationship with township officials. There was one distinct difference between the offices. With extended responsibility and authority to act, the county superintendent could provide effective supervision at the local level.

The Establishment of a General System of Education

The general education system, as described by the Constitution of 1816, included graded schools from the elementary through the university level. However, in the Constitution of 1851, revisions limited the General Assembly to providing a general and uniform system of common schools, tuition-free and open to all. A year later, the assembly provided the legal framework for that system. At about the same time, by a separate act, legislators recognized Indiana University as a state-endowed institution and therefore a part of the public school system. Before the rulings against local school levies, a few high schools were established, but since there was very limited revenue available, elementary schools took priority.

From the early part of 1860, private academies provided secondary education. The acceptance of the academy was due in part to the emphasis placed on a classical curriculum by the state colleges and universities. In order to be admitted to these schools, the student had to pass a rigid entrance examination, a substantial portion of which consisted of readings in classical languages, especially Greek, a subject offered only in the academies.

Many citizens opposed tax-supported secondary schools. Superintendent James H. Smart noted that many who took this position were men of more than ordinary intelligence; hence, their opinions deserved consideration. Recognizing the general diffusion of knowledge and learning throughout a community as a prerequisite to the preservation of free government, opponents argued that the state's authority to educate extended to the level where good citizenship was ensured and that for this purpose an elementary education would suffice. Moreover, they concluded that a general tax levied on all citizens to support high schools could not be justified since a select few would benefit. By the same reasoning, a general tax levy imposed on all citizens of a county to support high schools (then limited to cities and towns) was considered discriminatory.

In the 1870's, it had been pointed out by the state board that, in practice, Indiana had three educational systems: the common schools, the private secondary schools, and the university. In the opinion of the board, these systems should be connected; common schools should prepare pupils for the high schools, and the latter should constitute a preparatory department for the state university.

At about the same time, the state university shifted from a classical to a more liberal curriculum, discontinuing the classical language requirement. Cyrus Nutt, president of the state university and a member of the state board, recommended that students who held certificates from commissioned high schools be admitted to the university without examination. In 1873, the board completed a survey of the 78 existing high schools, evaluating the extent of courses, number of pupils enrolled, and teacher qualifications in each. On the basis of this study, the board commissioned 15 high schools.

In the 1880's, secondary education was not a popular idea; but the number of high schools continued to increase in cities and towns. In rural areas, high school education was almost nonexistent, and elementary schools were poorly attended. In 1896, the Legislature passed the state's first compulsory education law establishing mandatory attendance to age 14. At the turn of the century, the public school system was still legally an elementary system.

THE DEPARTMENT OF PUBLIC INSTRUCTION IN THE TWENTIETH CENTURY

Legal Background and Developments

Article 8 of Indiana's 1851 constitution consists of eight sections, the longest of which deals with the Common School Fund. There is no mention of a state board of education, but Section 8 has the following key provision: "The General Assembly shall provide for the election, by the voters of the State, of a State Superintendent of Public Instruction; who shall hold his office for two years, and whose duties and compensation shall be prescribed by law" (5).

Thus Indiana established a pattern of electing the superintendent, a practice followed by 33 states, most in the South, Midwest, and West. The process of amending the constitution is so complex that change was quite difficult, particularly prior to the supreme court decision in the Todd case, when it was assumed that ratification required a majority of votes in favor rather than a mere plurality (6). Even so, Hoosier voters have thus far rejected amendments to make the office of superintendent appointive. The vote in 1921 was 46,023 in favor and 117,479 against. Again, in 1957, two amendments failed, one of which would have given the power to appoint the state superintendent to the state board.

State Superintendents of Public Instruction

Eighteen men have served as superintendent during the first 7 decades of the twentieth century—10 Republicans and 8 Democrats. Two terms, or 4 years, has been the average tenure in office, but five men served three or four terms, as follows:

Fassett A. Cotton	1903-1909
Charles A. Greathouse	1910-17
Clement T. Malan	1941-47
Wilbur E. Young	1951-59
William E. Wilson	1959-67

All but four were native Hoosiers. Their ages when they assumed office varied from 27 for Frank L. Jones to 62 for Wilson; the average age has been 47. The incumbent, Richard D. Wells, 39, is the second youngest. Typically, they were principals or local superintendents at the time of their election, although a few came from high school or college classrooms. Several became college presidents after leaving the superintendency.

The salary has never been attractive, a condition lamented by one of the most eminent superintendents, Fassett A. Cotton, who thought that the salary of the office should be equal to the salaries of the presidents of the state colleges and universities. An annual salary of $1,300, set in 1852, reached $6,000 in 1945. Paradoxically, William E. Wilson left the position of superintendent of Clark County in 1959 with a salary of $11,700 to receive $200 less as state superintendent. However, the General Assembly voted in 1963 to increase the salary to $18,000; this became effective in 1965 during Wilson's final term in office. This is still the figure today, plus travel allowance.

In 1865, the General Assembly outlined the superintendent's basic responsibilities, authorizing him to employ two clerks. Almost every session has seen the addition of other responsibilities, with the implicit understanding that his staff would be augmented. Typical legislation has included:

1913–Appointment of a high school inspector

1921–Appointment of the high school and elementary school inspectors

1923–Maintenance of a complete record of licenses issued to teachers

1939–Membership on the New Harmony Memorial Commission (The superintendent could devote a major portion of his time to attendance and participation in the activities of the numerous boards and commissions of which he is an ex officio member.)

1951–Secretary of the Indiana State School Survey Commission.

One of the most interesting subjects is the relationship of the superintendent and the state board, of which the superintendent became a member with full voting rights in 1913. He served as president until the board's reorganization in 1945, and since 1949, he has been called chairman in his annual report to the Governor.

As a part of the reorganization of state government promoted by Governor Paul V. McNutt in 1933, the Department of Education was one of eight administrative departments created. Upon the return of the Republican party to control of the General Assembly, the Department of Education was abolished in 1941 and the old title of Department of Public Instruction resumed. The superintendent's full voting rights on the state board were confirmed.

By 1960, it became increasingly apparent that many overlapping responsibilities had developed in the department as a result of legislative enactments. Hence the General Commission of the State Board of Education and the state superintendent initiated a study which led to a reorganization as approved by the General Assembly in 1961. The superintendent was authorized to appoint an administrative assistant (designated "deputy superintendent" by the present state superintendent) and three assistant superintendents for administration, instructional services, and field services. A tentative organization chart (which has undergone several revisions) appeared in the first issue of the valuable departmental publication inaugurated in September 1961–*The Hoosier Schoolmaster of the Sixties.*

The State Board of Education

In 1865, the General Assembly passed legislation setting forth the composition, powers, and duties of a State Board of Education, allowing members a per diem of $5, plus 5¢ per mile for travel. One of the first major additions of authority occurred in 1889 when the board was empowered to select textbooks for use in the public schools. Other extensions of authority included:

1907–Definition of "high school" and "equivalent"

1917–Power to function as a state board of vocational education

1919–Prescription of suitable courses in physical education

1921–Power to function as a state rehabilitation board

1923–Responsibility to certify school employees.

During the first few decades of the twentieth century, the board consisted of 13 members, 8 of whom were ex officio, including the state superintendent of public instruction, the presidents of the four state institutions of higher learning, and the superintendent of the three largest city school systems (Indianapolis, South Bend, and Evansville, until the latter was supplanted by Gary). The Governor appointed a representative of a private college, a county superintendent, and three members at large. Under the 1933 reorganization, membership declined to nine, largely at the expense of the original ex officio members. Memberships of three college presidents and two city superintendents were eliminated, and the Governor and lieutenant governor became ex officio members. Lay people had more representation for a brief period than had been true previously or is true today. Later came the major reorganization in 1945, resulting in part from wide dissatisfaction with policies in the adoption of textbooks.

In 1945, the General Assembly terminated the State Board of Education, as constituted, replacing it with the Indiana State Board of Education, a bipartisan body consisting of the state superintendent and 18 members appointed by the Governor. "The term of office is for four years at the pleasure and discretion of the Governor and until a successor is duly appointed and qualified" (7).

The present board functions through three commissions, with the state superintendent serving as chairman and a voting member. Each commission consists of six members, in addition to the state superintendent, and not more than four of the six may be members of the same political party. Presumably the three commissions may meet periodically as a state board, with the state superintendent presiding. Such action, however, is rare.

The Commission on Textbook Adoptions and the Commission on Teacher Training and Licensing have highly specialized duties. All other responsibilities of the old state board were assigned to the Commission on General Education, which meets regularly on the second Friday of each month in the office of the state superintendent.

Perennial Subjects of Legislation

Ideally, the needs of the pupils have resulted eventually in either formal or informal action, usually the latter in the nineteenth century. In the twentieth century, however, with the problems of mass education, centralization of government, and efforts to equalize educational opportunity both within the state and nationally, there has come to be almost complete reliance on statutory enactments and administrative regulations. As a matter of fact, rules adopted by the commissions of the state board have the effect of law if they are in conformity with Section 120 of the Acts of 1945 of the General Assembly.

Fourteen problem areas seem increasingly to be beyond local capacities for effective solution. In each case, an effort has been made to cite several of the early state or national legislative enactments. Probably the constitution makers of 1851 would have been astounded if a seer had predicted many of these developments. These perennial subjects of legislation are—

Adoption of textbooks (1889, 1891, 1893, 1905, 1907, 1913, 1921, 1935, 1939, 1943, 1945)

Compulsory attendance (1899, 1907, 1919, 1921)

Transportation of pupils (1913, 1917, 1927, 1935)

Equal educational opportunity (1905, 1907, 1921, 1933)

Minimum wage laws for teachers (1899, 1907, 1921, 1941, 1945, 1967)

School inspection (1913, 1921)

Teacher qualifications (1907, 1919, 1921, 1923, 1935, 1943)

Transfer of pupils (1903, 1911, 1919, 1921, 1933, 1935, 1945)

Curriculum (1901, 1907, 1911, 1913, 1917, 1919, 1925, 1931, 1933, 1935, 1937, 1945)

Federal aid (1862, 1917, 1923, 1946, 1950, 1958, 1964, 1965)

Consolidation (1873, 1877, 1907, 1915, 1917, 1921, 1929)

Vocational education (1913, 1919, 1963)

Schoolhouse planning (1949, 1955, 1959)

Reorganization (1947, 1949, 1951, 1959, 1961).

School Reorganization

Some 9,000 school districts, established under the Constitution of 1816, underwent merging in 1852 as a result of the first reorganization act passed under the Constitution of 1851, reducing the total of city, town, and township school districts to 1,033. School boards controlled all of these units until the creation of the unique township trustee system in 1859. Limited only by advisory boards (which met infrequently) and public opinion, the trustees had almost complete autonomy for 70 years in the control of education, welfare, and local roads. They served terms of 4 years and were eligible for reelection not to exceed two terms out of three, as contrasted with the Governor, who also had a 4-year term but might not serve successive terms.

Quite early it was perceived that many of the units lacked the financial resources to provide adequate schools, particularly for grades 9 to 12. Although permissive legislation was passed to alleviate this condition, the township trustees long were able to prevent any fundamental change in the system. The Indiana Township Trustees Association, with more than 1,000 members, had one of the most powerful lobbies at Indianapolis during the 61-day session of the General Assembly, which met biennially unless called into special session by the Governor.

State superintendents deplored the situation. Benjamin J. Burris, in 1924, urged the establishment of a county unit system. He made this comment regarding those states still employing the township or district as the chief local unit:

> Nowhere do traditions developed under pioneer conditions persist more tenaciously, nowhere is there greater lack of confidence in the people, lack of faith in the integrity of public officials, and lack of appreciation of expert knowledge than in the management of the rural schools of the United States . . . (8).

It is outside the scope of this chapter to trace the legislation of the 1930's by which the General Assembly placed road building and welfare under county administration. However, the first major innovation in local school organization came in 1929. (Early legislation, which permitted transfer of pupils but did not require legal consolidation, had many drawbacks. An act passed in 1917 and amended in 1921 permitted a consolidated school district, although participating school corporations remained separate corporate bodies.) Voluntary merger of certain school townships and towns now legalized larger tax and administrative units, of which three were established before the law was repealed and a similar one enacted in 1937 (9). By 1951, 49 cities and towns had united with neighboring townships in various forms of school consolidation, and several rural townships had consolidated their schools. In Floyd and Brown Counties, county units had been established as a result of a law passed in 1949, although there were still more than 1,000 township administrative units (10).

There is little evidence that the state department played a dynamic part in bringing about school reorganization. However, a number of private organizations, particularly the Indiana State Chamber of Commerce, through its education department, were quite aggressive. The Indiana State Teachers Association, under its able executive secretary, Robert H. Wyatt, exercised its usual potent influence on school legislation. It employed Edgar L. Morphet, then of the Florida Department of Education, to prepare a survey of the Hoosier school system, which was published in 1949 (11). Space is lacking to comment on all of the significant studies, but at least the following four should be listed:

Report of the Indiana State Committee on Governmental Economy (1935)
An Evaluation of the Indiana Public Schools (1949)
A Re-evaluation of the Organization and Financing of the Indiana Public Schools (1950)
Report of the Indiana State School Survey Commission to the Governor of Indiana (1952)

The last publication, one of the most significant in Indiana educational history, merits more than passing reference. The School Survey Commission was created by House Concurrent Resolution 18, approved in March 1951. It provided for a bipartisan commission of eight members, with State Superintendent Wilbur Young as ex officio secretary.

After extensive research, its members concluded that 11,440 additional classrooms would be needed by 1957, costing $343 million. It was estimated that $218 million could be raised in 369 corporations by means of bonds and a cumulative building fund tax. However, 396 other corporations lacked the ability to employ these methods, and 436 had no pressing needs. It was recognized that the final solution to the problem depended on school reorganization. The commission also concluded that the state department could not conduct local reorganization until it, too, was overhauled.

The School Survey Commission's recommendations, appearing on pages 70-72 of the 1952 report, may be summarized under schoolhousing and school reorganization.

With respect to housing, it was proposed that the state should participate in financing public school buildings in local school administrative units. Seven conditions were stipulated for participation by the state. The report pointed out how imperative it was to make building funds available immediately and suggested that corporations transferring pupils should "pay a building transfer cost applicable to capital outlay in the corporation receiving such transfer pupils" (12).

Two recommendations were made regarding school reorganization. The first asked the General Assembly to create a bipartisan state commission on school reorganization empowered to establish local committees to work out suggestions for reorganization and to provide technical assistance to these committees. The second declared that the General Assembly—

> Should give attention to the desirability of provisions for a greater length of term for the State Superintendent of Public Instruction, more adequate facilities for the department, additional permanent professional personnel for the performance of the various duties, and a budget adequate to meet the necessary expansions of the Department of Public Instruction (13).

An account of legislative developments which were a sequel to this report was prepared by the education department of the Indiana State Chamber of Commerce, entitled "Four Years of Indiana School Reorganization." In 1957, a major school reorganization bill was introduced in the General Assembly, which had "powerful support, but the traditional resistance was strong also and the measure, after passing the Senate, was defeated in the House." Nine minor measures were passed, "mostly dealing with specific localities or situations" (14). Although notable advance was made under the 1955 Metropolitan School Consolidation Law, none of the nine laws passed in 1957 hastened to any marked degree the elimination of the hundreds of small school corporations.

With bipartisan authorship and legislative support, the Legislature enacted six laws in 1959 that affected school reorganization, one of which was of great significance in launching a movement that has continued to the present. The most important (Chapter 202) was passed in the Senate by a vote of 44 to 4, and in the House of Representatives by a vote of 62 to 32. Numerous amendments were added in 1961, 1963, and 1965.

Space does not permit a detailed statement of developments as a result of the legislation outlined above. However, the 1967 report of the State Commission for the Reorganization of School Corporations pointed out that there has been an 80-percent reduction in the number of school corporations "too small to provide a minimum educational program," and that more than 90 percent of the public school pupils "now reside in school corporations which have been reorganized" (15). There has been a reduction of about 60 percent in the number of school corporations (966 to 402). In only 10 of the 92 counties has there been no reorganization. It has been completed in 63 counties and partially completed in 19. Eventually, the state commission may exercise its statutory authority to develop a plan where little or nothing is being done locally.

Curriculum

Curriculum (16) was interpreted narrowly in the nineteenth century and was largely a matter of local policy, although college entrance requirements were beginning to affect offerings of high schools as they came into being. By the twentieth century, however, courses of study were being published in the state superintendents' biennial reports to the General Assembly. (These volumes often exceeded 1,000 pages in length, quite a contrast to the largely statistical reports published from 1917 to 1950, as a part of the *Indiana Year Book.*) Moreover, a virtual textbook monopoly was established under the aegis of the State Board of Education and remained until multiple adoptions by courses became mandatory in the 1940's.

Court cases involving curriculum, as well as opinions of the attorney general, were virtually nonexistent because of the paucity of state laws. As a matter of fact, the General Assembly undoubtedly reflected the feelings of most Hoosiers by adopting laws like the following:

1907–Minimum lists of courses stipulated for high school offerings, subject to revision by the State Board of Education

1909–Provision for the singing of the "Star Spangled Banner"

1911–Teaching of hygiene and sanitary science prescribed for grade 5

1919–English language only to be employed to conduct classes in the elementary school

1925–Teaching of the constitutions of Indiana and the United State required in public, private, and parochial schools, grades 6 to 12 (This stipulation was made very specific at the high school level in 1935 and so remains to this day.)

1933–Teaching of the effects of alcoholic drinks and narcotics required for 5 years in the elementary school and 2 years in high school

1937–Instruction in morals prescribed for all grades; in safety education for grade 8.

This list, of course, does not reflect the unsuccessful efforts to tamper with the curriculum by legislative fiat, such as the effort in the 1967 session of the General Assembly to add Indiana history as an elective subject in high school. In general, however, the lawmakers appear to have been more reasonable than many college and university curriculum committees.

There is no evidence that the state superintendent exerted sustained leadership in curriculum prior to 1940. Courses of study, published periodically, appear to have been ignored by the majority of classroom teachers. A central coordinating committee, appointed by the state superintendent, was authorized in 1931 to revise the curriculum for the elementary grades. The result was a new course of study, announced in 1935.

I. Owen Foster, a member of the School of Education faculty, Indiana University, from 1926 to 1961, influenced curriculum both as a teacher and as an appointee of the state superintendent (he served as director of curriculum from 1951 until 1961). A newspaper account regarding his activities, published in 1940, declared that he "largely wrote the elementary school course of study in social studies, and the high school course . . . was prepared by him and his graduate students . . . "(17). During the 1940's, he served as consultant for further revisions, one of which, for world history, was published in 1949 as Bulletin No. 211 by the Department of Public Instruction. He appears to have had considerable responsibility for the curriculums as revised and published periodically in the *Digest of Courses of Study for Secondary Schools,* including the editions of 1944, 1949, 1954, and 1961.

The current *Administrative Handbook* lists four functions for the Division of Curriculum, the first of which warrants being cited in its entirety:

> To study the curriculum needs at the state level, to organize personnel from the various school systems to work on state curriculum reconstruction, to develop curriculum conferences and workshops both in the public schools, and in the state institutions of higher education, and to produce state curriculum bulletins and courses of study (18).

As a result of federal programs in education, particularly the National Defense Education Act (NDEA), Title III, and the Elementary and Secondary Education Act (ESEA), Title V, it has been possible to employ consultants in most subject areas. Former State Superintendent W.E. Wilson considered the greatest accomplishment of his 8 years in office to be the upgrading of the professional staff of the Department of Public Instruction.

The Social Studies: An Example of Curriculum Problems

One of the most ambitious curriculum projects in Indiana educational history was initiated in 1961 with the appointment of a state committee for social studies. Wholehearted cooperation was given not only by the public schools but also by institutions of higher learning, particularly Indiana University and Indiana State University. A curriculum for kindergarten through grade 12, based on a conceptual approach to teaching, was reported to the General Commission of the State Board in 1964 and adopted, with modifications at the high school level, in 1965 (19). Eleven curriculum guides, published in the latter part of 1965, received favorable comments by Hoosier social studies teachers and national educators.

Meanwhile, the Commission on Textbooks, following a cycle established in the 1940's, adopted social studies textbooks in December 1963, for the period 1964-69. The lack of synchronization of the activities of the two commissions was most unfortunate for social studies teachers, especially in grades 5, 6, 7, and 8. It became virtually impossible to comply with decisions of the two commissions of the state board without considerable financial loss on the part of local school corporations because large supplies of textbooks became outmoded. The problem will be resolved when social studies textbooks are adopted for another 5-year period in December 1968.

Conclusion

An effort has been made to outline the principal statutory changes affecting the state superintendent of public instruction and the state board during the past 100 years. There has been a listing of some of the laws involving perennial subjects of legislation. Two of these have been described in some detail–curriculum and school reorganization. These changes indicate that the Constitution of 1851 is flexible enough except for the provision that the office of state superintendent be elective for a term of only 2 years.

There are several possibilities for future action to be considered:

1. Preserving the status quo. On several occasions, people have rejected amendments making the superintendent's position appointive and lengthening the term of office.

2. Renewing efforts to amend the constitution as simply as possible; for example, providing for election for a term of 4 years.

3. Amending the constitution to make the office completely statutory–as is true of the State Board of Education.

Shortly after taking office, State Superintendent Richard D. Wells appointed a committee to study possible courses of action. Their findings may be reported in time for the 1969 General Assembly.

SCHOOL FINANCE SINCE 1900

Not much school financing was provided by the state until the turn of the century. It was accepted that local moneys would provide for the schools and that school costs were the responsibility of those who had children attending school. In 1865, a tax for the operation of schools was created; in 1867, the power to tax in order to pay teachers was given to local units, normally townships, cities, and towns.

In the early 1900's, most money for schools came from property taxes and fell into a special school tax for operation of schools and a tuition tax for paying teachers' salaries. These two funds have remained in existence; in 1967, they still provide about two-thirds of the moneys used to support the public schools.

The School Relief Law

The idea of using state money for local schools first developed as schools trying to keep up educational standards in their own localities became "needy." In 1905, a School Relief Law was passed, levying 7¢ per $100 valuation, money collected to be distributed only to those schools that could show that the funds they were collecting from local revenue were inadequate.

Development of the School Relief Law

1905–School corporations with a 0.40 tax levy could draw from the state fund (created by the 7¢ tax) an amount sufficient to extend their school term to 6 months and meet the provisions of the minimum teachers salary of $300.
1907–An amendment required a 0.25 tax levy to extend schools for a 6-month term and a 0.40 tax levy to extend schools for a 7-month term.
1919–100-percent valuation of taxable property established, with the State Tax Board given the power of enforcement.
1927–Private holding companies were legalized for school construction, but mounting tax delinquencies (16 percent in Indiana) brought about repeal of the measure in 1933.
1933–Gross income tax established.
Rules were adopted by the State Board of Education for reporting attendance of pupils enrolled in grades 1-12 in the public schools of Indiana for the purpose of determining the number of elementary and high school units for which a school corporation could receive support.

The public schools of Indiana suffered financial setbacks in the late 1920's and 1930's. Many local attempts were made to solve that problem. The concept of school consolidation and reorganization actually started in Indiana during the Depression years when townships joined forces as a means of survival. The Depression not only affected the schools immediately, but also had a prolonged effect on the next two decades of school operation and progress. For example, no building could be started, teachers' salaries were kept down, repairs and maintenance were neglected, and many other items were curtailed or omitted, resulting in financial problems for the post-Depression period.

The Tuition Support Law

Attempting to help schools, the Legislature passed a tuition support law in 1933. Previously the state had never provided more than 10 percent of the revenue needed for the operation of a local school. As its obligations increased, it was necessary to add the Indiana gross income tax and also establish a law limiting the property tax. In 1933, the state became an official partner, providing an average of 36 percent of total school revenue. The distribution of funds under the 1933 act was made to each school on the same basis, with no regard for difference in ability to pay or for high and low assessed valuation. This concept of state distribution of money continued up to 1949 and was known as relief grants.

In 1949, the Indiana Legislature developed a concept of equalization of resources which has endured to the present. Industrial growth, agricultural prosperity, and "bedroom" community status were considered along with the other factors in distributing tax funds. A criterion was developed for each school corporation receiving state funds so that tuition, current expenses, and transportation all were accounted for. From 1949 until the present, each Legislature has used the concept of distributing state support to public schools through a Minimum Foundation Program, with changes being made in qualifications for the support and total amounts of money. In addition, some categorical distributions also are made on a per-pupil basis.

During the 1967 General Assembly, the Minimum Foundation Program was funded for the fiscal year 1968 (July 1, 1967, to June 30, 1968) with $189,227,460 for instructional salaries and other current expense (equalization) and $14,190,713 for transportation. For the fiscal year 1969, $193,808,888 was funded for instructional salaries and other current expense and $14,173,750 for transportation.

The distribution formula is worded so as to provide more for greater numbers of students and better trained and more experienced teachers. It also encompasses additional administrative, supervisory, guidance, and auxiliary personnel at the rate of one for each 400 students; at the same time, it required the richer corporations (defined according to assessed valuations) to contribute a greater local share. The base pay per pupil is $185. The average factor for teachers according to state average is 1.04, which increases the per-pupil average to $194 per student in average daily attendance or 30 times the number of classroom teachers, whichever is less. Administrative, supervisory, guidance, and auxiliary personnel employment is compensated for on the basis of the value of 30 students or on the average of $5,820 for the corporation's entitlement. Each corporation that has an average daily attendance of at least 750 students is entitled to receive for its superintendent the unit value of 30 students or another $5,820. The total becomes the school corporation's share under the Minimum Foundation Program, and from this is subtracted the local charge, which is 65¢ per $100 adjusted assessed valuation for corporations receiving support for students in grades 1 through 12 only, and 70¢ per $100 adjusted assessed valuation for corporations receiving state support for students in grades kindergarten through 12. The formula allows $60 per student in grades 1 to 12 as a maximum for other current expense (equalization) but requires a corporation to make a local share charge of 75¢ per $100 adjusted assessed valuation so that no equalization is received by a corporation with an $8,000 per-pupil adjusted assessed valuation.

The base rate for transportation is $20 per student multiplied by a sparsity factor (determined by finding the relationship of pupils transported more than 1.5 miles to total miles traveled). Larger amounts are provided to corporations with few children and to those in poorer communities. The authors of the formula for distribution of state support for school corporations, as can be seen, have attempted to put the state money where the students are located but have required the corporations that have greater wealth to provide more, locally, in order to qualify.

The formula worked well throughout the 1940's and the 1950's, as the legislative sessions raised maximum tax rates as school costs increased. Levies to pay for buildings constructed, plus cumulative building funds, provided in advance of construction, brought in funds to make possible great educational strides in Indiana during these two decades.

As mentioned previously, some state money outside the formula is provided for each corporation based on a categorical per-pupil distribution. Some background information on assessed valuations is needed to understand why the Indiana General Assembly provided these funds. Indiana was the first state to establish a group charged with establishing assessed valuations, official appropriations, and the tax rates necessary to provide needed moneys– the State Tax Commission, established in 1891 and still operating.

Establishing the assessment of personal and real property on a basis that is equitable to all taxpayers is most difficult. In 1929, property was to be assessed at 100 percent of its value for taxation purposes, but in 1949 a law required that property be assessed at not more than one-third of its *real value,* that is, value received through sale of the property. The person charged with the assessment of property is either the township trustee or, in larger areas, an elected assessor. Because of overassessing in some areas and underassessing in others, the State Tax Commission has established a system of determining equalizing factors in order to place the ratio between actual assessed valuation and sale valuation in proper relationship to the one-third concept. If local assessing is done at too low a level, a one plus factor is used; if, on the other hand, local assessing is done at a rate of higher than one-third sale value, a factor of less than one is used. Even though factors have been applied, some areas, due to their physical makeup, have found it most difficult to maintain educational standards without overburdening the local property owner.

The late 1950's and 1960's have seen efforts made to put in the hands of local school corporations additional funds, outside the formula, to be used as property tax relief. One fund, called the Property Tax Relief Fund, is an actual appropriation of about $31 per pupil per year, distributed regardless of wealth. The second distribution, a corporate net tax distribution determined by moneys collected, amounts to about $16 per student. A third distribution, the intangible tax distribution, is based on the amount collected and on an assessed valuation ratio with 65 percent of the total amount collected being distributed to schools.

Special programs for special students provide additional state funds. Mentally retarded students or tuberculosis patients, evening school and summer school students taking courses for credit, students whose parents work for the state and live on state property, vocational students, and other groups all fall in a category with separate formulas for distributing funds.

A crisis exists in Indiana in the 1960's due to many factors. Young people are a precious investment, and everyone wants to provide the best for them in educational opportunities. Despite the benefits of consolidating many school corporations, with new and beautiful buildings under construction, higher teachers' salaries to maintain professionalism, and new subject areas being offered, even to maintain the status quo costs approximately 10 percent more each year. Moreover, the relocation of people away from the industrial areas has resulted in an overburdening of the property tax to meet the gap between state funds provided and total costs of local schools. Prelegislative committees are working on the problem at the present time, and Indiana has reached the point in financing schools at which a different approach to financing with a greater obligation on the part of the state and less reliance on local property taxes probably will be the necessary result.

BENEFITS AND PROBLEMS OF THE DEPARTMENT'S RELATIONS WITH OUTSIDE ORGANIZATIONS

The explicit constitutional provisions for the office of Superintendent of Public Instruction in Article 8, Section 8, of the Indiana Constitution of 1851 have already been discussed. The constitutional provisions include those powers and duties stemming from statutes of the Indiana General Assembly, and from the quasi-legislative and quasi-judicial actions taken by the Indiana State Board of Education, an 18-member organization divided into three commissions of 6 members each. The three commissions are separately concerned with teacher training and certification, textbook adoptions, and general educational affairs. The department is represented through the superintendent, who is chairman of each of the commissions.

Relations with Other Governmental Entities

The Indiana Governor is responsible for appointing the 18 members of the state board at staggered intervals. Each appointment is for 4 years or at the pleasure of the Governor. Through his control over the state budget agency, the Governor also can exercise considerable influence in procuring equipment and in repair and construction expenditures within the department itself. In addition, he may apply inflexible economy rules to the department's requests for new personnel, in effect influencing the rate of growth and the areas of instructional emphasis at any time.

The treasurer of Indiana may also influence the efficiency and reputation of the department by the alacrity or slowness with which he sends checks to school corporations for the amounts called for in the state support program. The treasurer may experience some temptation to extend the interest time as a service to the public and the banks.

The attorney general of Indiana is the officer responsible for furnishing legal opinions when they are sought. In addition, he defends in suits brought against the department's officers and checks each commission decision for constitutionality and conformity to law before it is promulgated.

The Department and the Indiana Vocational College

Since 1965, money for post-high school and high school vocational training has been allocated both to the autonomous Indiana Vocational Technical College and to the Department of Education. The allocating agency is the State Board of Vocational Education, whose members are appointed by the Governor. Thus, the orientation of the vocational board and ultimately of the Governor tends to enhance or impoverish the regular vocational program of the public schools. The department's officers view this as a major obstacle to be overcome in the interest of effective vocational education for all pupils. The number served by Indiana Vocational Technical College is disproportionately smaller than the number of persons served by Indiana's public high schools, the ratio being approximately 1 IVTC enrollee for each 80 high school pupils. Despite the disparity, funds are now allocated on an equal basis.

Local units of government have very little contact with the state department, other than through local school districts.

The State Library

The library cooperates by furnishing a large supply of books, pamphlets, and other materials to schools; and it is hoped that the State Library also will furnish a "bookmobile" service for art work displays in the schools of sparsely populated areas.

The Department's Relations with Professional Organizations

In the last 4 or 5 years, professional organizations have come to furnish much in inspiration and assistance to specialists within the department. Various groups are a source of recruitment when department openings occur, and the membership of the department's study committees is partly drawn from lists of persons active in these organizations. Committees of professional people meet periodically to prepare recommendations concerning school accreditation, departmental tenure of office, school finance, administrators' salaries, and Title III, ESEA.

Since 1960, the department has had cooperation from the Indiana Language Program in sponsorship of foreign language area workshops. Also the department has gained advice from FLES, the Foreign Language Elementary Section, in revising certification requirements.

The music consultant has organized a state music education council which consists of the presidents of all the music organizations in the state. Through this organization, the department's curriculum and cultural arts staff effects improvement in communication and coordination. During 1967-68, the department has been able to establish the same rapport with the State Art Teachers Association, which selected the first art consultant in the history of the Department of Public Instruction.

There continues to be close cooperation between the department's curriculum representatives and such organizations as the International Reading Association and the Indiana Council of Teachers of Mathematics. This cooperation is improving particularly in the in-service training activities which have been instituted since March 1967.

Departmental Relations with Lay Groups

The department's use of lay groups as sources of assistance is increasing, especially in the implementing of curriculum activities. Currently, department specialists are cooperating with the American Red Cross in developing and/or trying out five pilot programs. It also is assisting the League of Women Voters in the distribution of materials about state and local government. Another cooperative endeavor with a lay group includes a 1967-68 project with migratory pupils in a church community center. In a different vein, the department is now also cooperating with the John Herron Art Institute in a series of exhibitions at Indiana colleges. Individual lay persons also are members of the several study committees created by the current state superintendent to reexamine the main issues facing the department and Indiana's educators.

A unique program of economic education has been under way privately under the joint sponsorship of labor, farm organizations, and business, joined together as the Purdue Economic Education Advisory Board. Now, after some 15 years of this group's existence, the department has entered into a joint sponsorship with the advisory board in an effort to advance a reasonable economic education program on a statewide basis.

Pressure Groups

Several nationally active interest groups are periodically represented in confrontation or cooperation with the superintendent or the commissions. The National Association for the Advancement of Colored People has shown an interest in the distribution of supplemental materials concerning the Negro heritage. The Chamber of Commerce and the Indiana Farm Bureau have taken part in discussions about school finance, and the Parent-Teacher Association has been keenly interested in reorganization.

The Indiana State Teachers Association has at times held a special relationship to the Department of Public Instruction. Under earlier leadership, the department's administrative assistants and division heads sometimes seemed to be drawn almost entirely from the ranks of those very active in the ISTA. At present, the relationship is good, but there is no dependence upon the teachers association to furnish departmental leadership.

In summary, it can be said that other government officers and agencies, particularly the Governor of Indiana, have more immediate influence on the Department of Public Instruction than on lay and professional groups. However, the department does look to these latter sources for steady assistance and support.

EFFECT OF FEDERAL FUNDS ON EDUCATION IN INDIANA

As early as the Land Ordinance of 1785, enacted by the Continental Congress, the sixteenth section of each township in the Northwest Territory was reserved for the maintenance of public schools. Moreover, the Northwest Ordinance of 1787 provided that "schools and the means of education shall forever be encouraged." In the preconstitutional era, national interest in education seemed to be predicated on the idea that a literate, informed, and educated citizenry must be the basic foundation for American democracy.

When the U.S. Constitution was adopted in 1789, education was not listed as one of the enumerated powers of the new federal government. Nor was the subject of education mentioned. Therefore, powers concerning education were reserved to the states and have been considered throughout our national history as primarily a state responsibility. However, from time to time, the federal government in exercising its power to provide for the common defense and to promote the general welfare has legislated concerning education and has appropriated funds to support certain educational enterprises which were considered to be of national concern.

Until early in the twentieth century, most legislation was related to the establishment of military schools and institutions of higher learning such as land grant colleges, provided for in 1862. It was not until the early part of the twentieth century that the federal government began to concern itself with vocational education at the secondary level. An initial act passed in 1917 provided aid to the states on a contribution basis for vocational training in specified areas. It was the development of this program which resulted in the establishment of the Division of Vocational Education in the State Department of Public Instruction.

Vocational Education

Vocational education has always been recognized as an important part of Indiana's total educational program. Although the words *vocational education* have not always been used, a significant provision was made for job training in the 1851 constitution. From 1859 to 1913, the public came to appreciate the type of training that would prepare youth for the industrial employment market. Many articles were published on vocational training, and Indiana governors, superintendents of public instruction, professional teaching organizations, and lay citizens heartily endorsed it as a part of the total school curriculum.

In 1891, the Legislature authorized large school systems to levy taxes to establish manual and industrial training as part of their programs. Governor Thomas R. Marshall appointed a commission in 1911 to develop a course of action for Indiana. The report of the Commission on Industrial and Agricultural Education contained recommendations including a vocational law which was enacted and approved in February 1913. The 1913 Indiana Vocational Education Act contemplated that all Indiana public schools would provide definite helpful vocational training for the young people who would work in the shops, homes, and farms during their adult lives.

As a result of the shortage of qualified agricultural and industrial workers for employment during World War I, the U. S. Congress enacted the Smith-Hughes Act in 1917 to provide cooperation with the states in the promotion of education in agriculture, trade and industries, and home economics. The law provided for cooperation with the states in preparation of teachers of vocational subjects and appropriated money and regulated its expenditures. With the passage of this act, vocational agriculture and vocational home economics classes were started in many of the rural schools. However, by 1920-21, only 341 of Indiana's 1,256 school corporations were participating in vocational education. The enrollment of approximately 23,000 pupils represented about one-fourth of the student population of Indiana. Up to 1935, the enrollment in vocational education remained at approximately 25,000 students, with Indiana receiving a federal appropriation from the Smith-Hughes Act of $265,162. In 1940, the appropriation from the Smith-Hughes Act increased to $545,749. This resulted in an increased enrollment of 65,796 students and at this time included students taking distributive education.

Another milestone for vocational education in Indiana was the passage of the George-Barden Act of 1946, which resulted in a total enrollment of 72,063 students and an appropriation of $664,484 of federal funds for Indiana by 1950. This act, passed near the close of World War II, was designed to provide qualified technical workers and nurses.

Additional acts passed by the federal government were the Practical Nurse Act of 1956, NDEA, the Area Redevelopment Act of 1961, and the Manpower Development and Training Act of 1962—none of which increased total appropriations or enrollment for students in the public high schools. However, these acts added emphasis and increased the appropriations and enrollment for the adult classes conducted by the public schools.

Indiana received $1,298,509 in federal funds from the Smith-Hughes and George-Barden Acts in 1960, and this increased the enrollment to 75,866 students.

The greatest impetus for vocational education came with the passage of the Vocational Education Act of 1963. This opened the door to new areas such as health, business, and office occupations and stressed the importance of on-the-job occupational training for vocational agriculture, home economics, trade and industry, and distributive education. The 1963 act also encouraged the development of the area vocational schools, emphasized vocational guidance and research, and strengthened the vocational teacher training programs in all state universities.

Since the passage of the Smith-Hughes Act, and with an early appropriation of $265,162 for vocational education, the state is now receiving a combined total of $5,538,925 from the Smith-Hughes, George-Barden, and Vocational Education Acts. With this increase in federal appropriations, the 1967 General Assembly appropriated $2,400,000 from state funds for 1967 and 1968.

The public schools are now training approximately 85,000 students in vocational education, and this number will increase rapidly with the construction of the area vocational schools and increased federal and state allocations for vocational education, plus interest from legislators and school administrators.

Vocational Rehabilitation

Federal concern with vocational education for secondary school students was extended in 1919 to a concern with vocational rehabilitation of the educable handicapped person over 16 years of age. The impetus for action was the need of handicapped veterans of World War I for job training. Persons with a substantial job handicap due to physical or mental disability and with a reasonably good chance of becoming employable may get a more suitable job through the rehabilitation service. This program is supported by the federal government on a 75-percent basis and is administered by the Vocational Rehabilitation Division, established in 1923. Special matching funds are available at higher rates of federal participation to the rehabilitation division for projects involving innovations, statewide planning to meet rehabilitation needs, and expansion of vocational rehabilitation services. Also, grants-in-aid for special projects in vocational rehabilitation are administered by this division.

As a result of the regular vocational rehabilitation. program, case service reports of the division for the year ending June 30, 1967, show 1,955 clients rehabilitated. More than three-fourths of those rehabilitated became industrial, clerical, sales, and service workers, while 295 entered professional, technical, or managerial occupations. Clients in training at division expense in October 1967 numbered 2,660. The projected budget for the division for fiscal year 1968 amounts to $3,200,000–$2,400,000 from the federal government and $800,000 from the state. Federal financial assistance to education in the years before World War II was primarily for vocational education, preparing high school students and the handicapped for jobs. These programs have been supported by the federal government with increased funds since their inception.

School Lunch

The National School Lunch Act of 1946 established the school lunch program, primarily to use farm surpluses. Basically, the program rested on the reduction of the food surplus at home or abroad by feeding the surplus to schoolchildren, particularly to those children who were malnourished. Despite the fact that many school districts had instituted school lunch programs before the national program (for example, at Frankfort, Indiana, a lunch program was started in December 1917), impetus for the expansion of the program was provided by the National School Lunch Act. To administer the program the School Lunch Division was created in the State Department of Public Instruction.

Of the 2,345 public schools in Indiana, 1,785 participated in the program in the 1966-67 school year, serving 44.9 percent of the students in these schools. In that year, local food purchases amounted to $22,466,000, and federal contribution to the program amounted to $3,167,000.

The school lunch program was extended by the Children's Nutrition Act of 1965 to provide breakfast to underprivileged children. Indiana has six pilot schools in this program, to be paid for out of the Indiana allocation for the total program.

Impacted Areas

Federal funds to relieve school districts from the additional burden of educating children brought into the districts because of national defense activities during and after World War II are provided for by two public laws. Both laws provide federal funds to qualified school districts on a formula basis. Public Law 874 provides federal funds for the operation of the schools in these districts, and Public Law 815 provides financial aid for construction of school buildings in extremely needy areas.

This program, inaugurated in Indiana in September 1950, is administered by the Division of Finance. From this program, Indiana school corporations have received millions of dollars. For example, in the period 1961-66, $7,975,749 was received under Public Law 874 and $456,720 under Public Law 815. In the fiscal year ending June 30, 1967, $3,016,892 was received from 874 and $44,364 from 815.

National Defense Education Act of 1958

While U. S. scientists were working on the conquest of space, Russia placed Sputnik in orbit around the earth. The news shocked the nation into enactment of the National Defense Education Act of 1958. The purpose of the act was "to provide substantial assistance in various forms to individuals, and to states and their subdivisions, in order to insure trained manpower of sufficient quantity and quality to meet the national defense needs of the United States." Title III of the Act provided for 50-50 matching grants of federal funds to states to help remodel and equip laboratories and classrooms and to assist in expanding and improving their supervisory services in science, mathematics, and modern foreign languages. In 1964, five additional subjects were added–history, civics, geography, English, and reading–and later, economics and industrial arts were added. So closely related to Title III of NDEA was the provision for purchase of materials and equipment in the 1965 National Foundation on the Arts and the Humanities Act that the administration of Section 12 of the latter act was brought under Title III.

At the inception of the program in 1959, an NDEA division was created in the Department of Public Instruction under the supervision of the assistant superintendent for field services. At this time, both the acquisition and supervisory phases of the program were included in this division, and as additional subjects were included, they were added to the responsibility of the division.

From the beginning of the program in Indiana in 1959, to June 30, 1966, the state had used $8,239,864 of the $11,468,424 available to it. During this time, local school districts had requested in approved projects $20,393,286, one-half of which they expected to pay from local funds. During the year July 1, 1966, to June 30, 1967, expenditures of federal funds in Indiana amounted to $1,449,347, of which $1,391,729 was used for acquisition and $57,618 for supervision and administration. Of 398 eligible agencies in Indiana, 325 participated in the program.

In 1967, the acquisition phase of NDEA Title III was transferred to a newly created Federal Projects Division, and the supervision phase was transferred to the Division of Curriculum.

Civil Defense

Directly related to national defense but not a part of the education of schoolchildren, the Civil Defense Adult Education Program was established in 1958 by the federal government and lodged in the U.S. Office of Education. The responsibility for this program was transferred to the Division of Civil Defense Adult Education within the State Department of Public Instruction in February 1962 and was expanded by the federal government in 1965, 1966, and 1967. The program includes a personal and family survival course, a radiological monitoring course, and a shelter management training course, each supported solely by the federal government.

Since the beginning of the program, 1,420 teachers for the survival course have been trained, and 36,756 adult students have been graduated from the course itself; 917 have been graduated from the radiological course, and 80 have been graduated from the management course. During this period, $475,740 has been invested in all three courses.

Adult Basic Education

Adult basic education orginally was provided for in the Economic Opportunity Act of 1964, and responsibility for its administration assigned to the U.S. Office of Education. To administer the program, an adult education division was created in the state department in February 1966. The program is designed to teach elementary-level education skills to individuals 18 years of age and over who are unable because of educational deficiencies to meet adult responsibilities and profit from occupational training. It is designed to bring the uneducated and the undereducated to the eighth-grade level or as near to this level as possible, with a view to breaking the poverty cycle. Actual operation of the program is delegated to local school districts on the basis of an application submitted to the Division of Adult Education and approved by it.

In fiscal year 1967, 22 local school districts had adult basic education programs with an enrollment of over 5,000 students. Federal assistance to the program in that year was $397,489, and the amount expected from the federal government for fiscal year 1968 is $488,728.

Elementary and Secondary Education

The Elementary and Secondary Education Act of 1965 (Public Law 89-10) represents the largest single commitment by the federal government to the elementary and secondary schools of the nation. The act became law in April 1965 and was funded in September 1965. It provided for federal financial assistance in the following categories:

Title I—Education of educationally disadvantaged children of the poor and the handicapped
Title II—Procurement of library books and other printed or published materials
Title III—Creation of supplementary centers and services with emphasis on innovative and exemplary practices
Title IV—Establishment of regional research laboratories
Title V—Stengthening of state departments of education.

In anticipation of the comparatively massive amount of money involved and the need for "crash" implementation of the act, a special administrative office, popularly known as the "P.L. 89-10 Administration," was created in the State Department of Public Instruction.

An amendment to the basic act in 1966 added Title VI, providing for special financial assistance for the education of the handicapped. This program was assigned to the special education division for administation. Also, this amendment included in Title I the education of neglected and delinquent children and the children of migrant agricultural workers.

A new division of the State Department of Public Instruction, the Federal Projects Division, was established in March 1967 to administer Titles I, II, and III of ESEA and the acquisition phase of Title III of NDEA.

In the first year of operation of ESEA (actually only 9 months), $20,911,423 was made available to Indiana school districts through Titles I, II, and III. Almost every school district in the state took advantage of one or more of the titles.

In the second year of the operation of the act, July 1966 to June 1967, 383 Indiana school corporations were allocated $14,580,135 for Title I projects; 374 Title II applications were funded for $2,510,238; 15 Title III proposals were approved for approximately $1,800,000; and under Title III, NDEA distributed $2,080,000 to 325 school districts.

Projected federal funds to be administered by the Federal Projects Division for the State of Indiana for the year July 1967 to June 1968 amount to:

Title I	$15,092,249
Title II	2,605,381
Title III ESEA	5,200,000
Title III NDEA	2,330,000
	$25,227,630

These programs, as well as the federal aspects of the vocational education program of the State Department of Public Instruction, will be discussed in more detail in connection with the history of the development of the appropriate state program.

ESEA Title V Funds Intensify Activity

The development of the Department of Public Instruction during the twentieth century has been marked by late-blooming areas of activity, many during the 1960's, and steadily growing activities, some of which have expanded as the population has expanded. Prototypes of both kinds of activities will be discussed.

Part of the very recent escalation in the intensity of departmental activity emanates from the help received through ESEA Title V funds.

Appropriately entitled "Grants To Strengthen State Departments of Education," Title V is designed as a program for making grants to stimulate and assist states in strengthening the leadership resources of their state educational agencies, and to assist those agencies in the establishment and improvement of programs to identify and meet the educational needs of states. Congress authorized this program for a 5-year period ending June 30, 1970, and it is expected that with progressively more responsibility resting on state departments, the program will be extended.

Prior to the creation of Title V, funds granted to state departments for their own use were related to the administration of specific federal programs and to that extent were categorical in nature. While Title V may also be defined as categorical in that the act stipulated the purposes for which federal funds are to be used, the criteria are sufficiently broad to allow the states great flexiblity in planning and designing activities for using these funds.

The state department, in designing applications for the use of Title V funds, has emphasized activities which cover these aspects of programing: state agency planning and information, internal administration, educational information and research, school finance, teacher education and certification, curriculum, schoolhouse planning, school traffic safety.

The major thrust in strengthening leadership services of the state agency was provided through the establishment of a curriculum division as a separate operating activity of the department. With expanded activities under the fiscal 1968 application for Title V funds, this division is now staffed by 14 professional personnel and provides consultant and planning services to local schools for all major subject areas. By working in coordination with other divisions of the department, this division also evaluates applications by local schools under other federal programs so that the department shall approve only those projects that are consistent with sound educational programs and that meet the educational needs of children in the state's elementary and secondary schools.

Activities in other areas listed above were not as significant in terms of personnel involved, but they were as significant in terms of providing and/or strengthening leadership in their respective areas. Title V projects under these areas were not established as separate entities within the department but were integrated into other operating activities. Public information and administrative personnel were added to the state superintendent's staff; research and data-processing specialists were brought into the educational information division; fiscal and field consultants were employed by the school finance division; and other professional and nonprofessional personnel were added to the teacher education, schoolhouse planning, and school traffic safety divisions.

In addition to providing personnel, Title V significantly strengthened a supportive service of the department by providing funds for the acquisition and installation of electromechanical filing and retrieval equipment in the teacher education division. Conversion to this system of filing and retrieval has reduced the time required for processing and issuing licenses from weeks or months to days.

Without question, the leadership capabilities and services of the Department of Public Instruction have been substantially improved under programs supported by Title V funds. All of the activities described here provide sound rationale for this conclusion.

It is easy to identify examples of long-term stability among the programs now being carried on by the department. Those programs and activities which began in the 1920's or earlier include vocational education, special education for handicapped children, and teacher certification.

Summary

A trickle of federal financial assistance to Indiana for education appears to be growing into an ever-enlarging stream, until the federal government has become junior partner in the educational enterprise in the state.

To recapitulate, the major federal financial assistance programs administered by the department are listed chronologically:

Vocational education	1917
Vocational rehabilitation	1923
School lunch	1946
Impacted areas	1950
National Defense Education Act, Titles III and V	1959
Civil Defense education	1964
Adult basic education	1964
Elementary and Secondary Education Act, Titles I, II, III, V, VI	1965

In practically all cases, establishment of each of the federal programs has resulted in addition of personnel to administer the program. In some cases, the new program was added to an existing division of the state department, and personnel were added to take care of the increased work load, as in the case of the pupil personnel and guidance division, when Title V, NDEA, was made the responsibility of this division. In the case of Title V of ESEA, personnel were added in many areas of the department in order to strengthen new divisions to administer the programs. Examples of this development are the vocational education, federal projects, and vocational rehabilitation divisions.

Because of their categorical nature, federal programs have placed great pressures upon the State Department of Public Instruction in certain areas in order to meet the requirements of the various acts and have thus complicated the operation of the department. Also, these categorical programs have, in some cases, caused an uneven development of the total educational programs; other aspects of the total educational program tend to be overshadowed.

A look into the future suggests overall planning to meet the total educational needs of the state and general federal financial aid to help meet these needs. Upon the speed with which these two developments take place depends the balance which the educational program of the state will have. This is the challenge for the future so far as the effect of federal funds on education in Indiana is concerned.

SPECIAL ACTIVITIES

Education for Handicapped Children

Indiana public schools have operated programs for handicapped children on a minimal basis for nearly three-quarters of a century. The first program on record within an Indiana public school for handicapped children was a special class for disturbed and delinquent adolescent boys initiated by the Indianapolis public schools in 1897. Prior to that time, however, the State of Indiana had established state residential public schools for deaf children (1844) and for blind children (1847). Responsibility for the operation and maintenance of these residential schools was vested in the Indiana State Board of Health by the Indiana General Assembly, although the educational programs of these institutions, like other public school programs, were required to meet standards of curricular offerings and teacher certification adopted by the state board and the state department.

Legislative Developments Affecting Education of the Handicapped

The first special education legislation for nonresidential schools in Indiana was passed in 1927 (20). This law enabled public schools, on a permissive basis, to establish programs for physically handicapped children. A 1931 law was passed which permitted public schools to establish special education programs for pupils "retarded in mental development" (21). As a result of these two laws, a few of the larger Indiana cities began to serve the crippled child through special schools. In addition, children with intelligence quotients of approximately 50-75 (now termed the educable mentally retarded) began to receive services through special class placement. Growth in the statewide program was negligible, however, since neither the 1927 nor the 1931 law provided funds which could be used for state financial support of the program.

In 1947, a law was passed which provided state reimbursement to local schools which operated approved special education programs (22). This law also created a special education division in the department and provided salaries for a director and a secretary. The 1947 law further established the duties of the director, as follows:

1. To supervise all classes and schools for handicapped children and to coordinate the work of these schools
2. To make, with the approval of the State Board of Education, rules and regulations governing the curriculum and the instruction, including licensing of personnel in the field of education as provided by law
3. To inspect and rate all schools or classes for handicapped children in order to maintain proper standards of personnel, buildings, equipment, and supplies
4. With the consent of the state superintendent of public instruction, to appoint and fix salaries for any assistants and other personnel needed to enable him to accomplish the duties of his office.

A 1955 law provided that programs for trainable mentally retarded children could be established by public school corporations (23). This broadened the provisions of the previous program to include children with intelligence quotients below 50 and extending downward to approximately 35. Also, the 1955 law made day-school programs for deaf and blind children possible in public school corporations.

Two supervisors were added to the staff of the special education division in 1958 through funds provided by legislation in 1957, one in the area of the mentally retarded and the other in the area of speech and hearing (24).

The duties of these supervisors were as follows:

1. General supervision of state-approved programs
2. Assistance to local school authorities in the organization and improvement of programs
3. Improvement of instruction, training, and therapy through working with therapists and teachers, both individually and in workshop situations
4. Administration of the technical aspects of approval and reimbursement of programs.

The 1961 Legislature passed a bill providing for reimbursement to public school corporations for the excess cost of psychological services and of special education administration, and for the securing of more meaningful diagnostic information concerning exceptional children (25).

The 1965 Legislature changed the formula of state support for special education of the handicapped to percentages of salaries of teachers and therapists and other approved costs (26). The purposes of the change were to provide for a greater financial incentive to public schools and to eliminate certain inequities present in the 1947 support formula.

Contribution of Rules and Regulations to Growth of Special Education

The operation of special education programs in Indiana public schools has been regulated in two ways: legislation and rules and regulations. Legislation is passed by the biennial sessions of the Indiana General Assembly, while the rules and regulations implementing the legislation have been adopted by the Commission on General Education of the Indiana State Board of Education. Rules and regulations have been established which permit the development of the following additional types of programs not specifically delineated in the previous section setting forth Indiana legislation.

1. Itinerant teachers for speech and hearing therapy programs
2. Special programs for the emotionally disturbed and socially maladjusted
3. Special experimental programs for brain-injured children
4. Homebound and school-to-home telephone programs for physically handicapped children
5. Occupational therapy programs
6. Physical therapy programs
7. Supervisory and consultative specialists
8. Multiply handicapped children.

Contribution of Federal Programs to the Education of Handicapped Children

In 1879, Congress passed a law designed to improve the lot of school pupils who had visual handicaps serious enough to qualify as "legal blindness" (visual acuity of 20/200 or worse in the better eye after correction). This law, as amended and incorporated into Title VI of the 1964 Civil Rights Act, provided funds for the purchase from the American Printing House for the Blind of text materials and tangible aids in braille or large print for Indiana children who are registered with the Federal Quota Plan for the Blind. The special education division instituted this program immediately after passage of the law and has conducted a survey each January among all Indiana school corporations to identify all pupils and register them with the Federal Quota Plan. Materials purchased through this program, when no longer needed by the particular child for which they were purchased, have been returned to the Textbook Library for the Blind, operated by the Department of Public Instruction with the cooperation of the Indiana School for the Blind. These materials are then loaned free of charge to all visually handicapped pupils in the state who may need them. Nearly 7,000 volumes have been accumulated, and about three-quarters of these are in use by students at any given time during the school year.

The Eighty-Fifth Congress passed a grant program for the development of professional personnel in the education of mentally retarded children. This law, which was broadened by the Eighty-Eighth Congress to include other handicapping conditions, was intended as a measure to increase the supply of trained manpower available to educate the handicapped. As a result of its involvement in this program, the state department has markedly increased its in-service training programs for practitioners in local schools who are working with, or plan to work with, handicapped children.

Title VI of ESEA Amendments of 1966

This provided authorization of funds through the state department to local schools for the initiation of new programs specifically to benefit handicapped children and youth. Funds were not appropriated until the 1968 fiscal year, however. The department used this opportunity to infuse much-needed funds into the state's special education program. A state plan was developed for using these funds by establishing priorities based on the state's greatest unmet needs. Local schools were subsequently invited to submit proposals for the development of projects based on these priority categories:

Exceptionality Areas of Greatest Need

1. Multiply handicapped
2. Minimal brain dysfunctioning
3. Emotionally disturbed
4. Deaf and hard of hearing
5. Trainable mentally retarded
6. Visually handicapped
7. Educable mentally retarded
8. Physically handicapped
9. Speech handicapped.

Programing Priority

1. Joint school service program
2. Creative administration and supervision
3. Creative programing
4. Preschool programing
5. Secondary school programing
6. Creative rural area programing
7. Services for multiply handicapped.

Recent Developments: Projects and Programs

Experimentation in programing for handicapped children was given impetus by the state department in 1965 when it permitted local schools to obtain state support for innovation and flexible programing possibilities for one or more handicapped children.

Provision of additional specialist consultant assistance services has been made during recent years as follows: a supervisor of programs for emotionally disturbed children was added during the 1965-66 school year; a coordinator of special projects was added to the staff for the 1967-68 school year; a supervisor of programs for the deaf and hard of hearing was approved for the 1967-68 school year; and a Title VI, ESEA, coordinator and six regional consultants were approved for the second semester of the 1967-68 school year.

A visual aids reproduction center was established in 1967 with the cooperation of the Indiana Department of Corrections and a private association to provide otherwise unavailable teaching and instructional materials in large print and braille to visually handicapped children. This program incorporated the services of some 26 inmates of the Pendleton Reformatory and provided the means to begin to meet the special needs of all Indiana blind and partially seeing youngsters for textbooks reproduced in braille or greatly enlarged print. The program was soon expanded to include a pilot project in producing conceptual-understanding aids for deaf children.

An Instructional Materials and Media Repository and Evaluation Center was established during 1967 for the collection of commercially prepared materials for use with handicapped children. Evaluation procedures through field testing were set up by the department with the primary aim of serving Indiana schools through continual feeding of evaluational information concerning the utility of special products and equipment in actual use in the schools.

Teacher Certification

In 1921, an act of the Indiana General Assembly defined the powers of the State Board of Education to license teachers and administrators (27). Prior to this act, applicants for teaching and administrative licenses qualified by passing examinations covering the subjects or grades to be taught, or by a combination of examination and credit. Licenses were then issued by a local official, or optionally for a few years by the State Department of Public Instruction.

After 1923, examinations no longer were given, and licenses were issued on the basis of credit earned in institutions approved for teacher education. Minimum requirements for licenses in elementary school teaching were set as graduation from a commissioned high school or equivalent and 1 year of special preparation. For licenses for high school teaching, minimum requirements were set at graduation from a commissioned high school or the equivalent and 3 years of special preparation. Definite requirements for administrative licenses also were set. The pattern of preparation for each license was announced, and institutions of higher learning were instructed to adapt their curriculums in accordance with the standards for licensing if they wished their credits to become acceptable for teacher licensing.

Teachers holding valid licenses in December 1923 were required to exchange them. Some of the licenses issued on exchange carried statements of the additional credit needed to qualify for the next higher grade, but some did not. If the notation made by the state was "consult college," the license holder was expected to meet the new licensing requirements prescribed by the college. If the specific requirement for the new license was stated, the holder could, and can still, qualify by satisfying the requirement stated.

The grades of licenses issued under the 1923 law were, in ascending order, third grade, second grade, first grade, and life. Another type of license issued as the lowest grade of exchange license was the permit which was issued to the teacher holding a valid license in December 1923 who had had a specified minimum of experience and credit but could not meet the new standards for the lowest grade of the license he was holding in 1922-23.

First-grade licenses could be converted to life licenses at the close of their period of validity (5 years) by presentation of evidence of at least 3 years of successful experience earned within the period of validity of the first-grade license. If the experience necessary for conversion had not been obtained, and if the applicant still met current requirements for the issuance of the first-grade license, the first-grade license could be renewed for a second 5-year period merely on application, and this pattern of renewal could be followed until the license could be converted to life.

The permit, the second-grade license (excluding those marked valid for life), and the third-grade license each were valid for a 2-year period and renewable thereafter on evidence of 1 year of successful experience (which requirement was waived if the applicant for renewal could not meet it) and 12 weeks of work (10 semester-hours or 16 quarter-hours of credit) specified for the next grade of license, except that if fewer than 12 weeks of work were required for conversion to first grade, the license had to be converted to first grade rather than renewed.

Exchange licenses still exist, and those lower than first grade may be converted to higher grade under specified terms.

First-grade licenses issued after December 1923 and prior to September 1946, including exchange licenses, may be renewed and converted to life licenses on the terms specified for their renewal and conversion under the 1923 law, except that the experience required for conversion since January 1935 has been 5 years, 2 of which shall have been in Indiana (28).

In the beginning of the operation of the 1923 law, elementary licensing was highly diversified among the various levels such as kindergarten, primary, intermediate, and grammar grades, and rural. These were gradually combined into kindergarten, lower elementary, and upper elementary, and finally into kindergarten, general elementary, and junior high school and ninth-grade subjects.

An extensive revision of certification regulations became effective September 9, 1946. A candidate for a certificate who matriculated before that date on the level (undergraduate or graduate) specified for the certificate may under certain conditions elect to meet the requirements in effect on September 8, 1946 (29). Institutions of higher learning contact the teacher training and licensing division with respect to these older requirements and advise candidates for certificates regarding their eligibility. The following paragraphs describe generally the latest revisions of teacher certification which were effective September 1963.

Teacher certification in Indiana has as its major purpose the guaranteeing of qualified professional personnel for the public schools. Attainment of this aim is based on definition of minimum requirements in preparatory programs leading to certification for the various instructional, administrative, and school service personnel positions. It is always assumed that institutions of higher education engaging in the preparation of teachers may choose to submit programs to the Teacher Training and Licensing Commission that exceed the minimum requirements.

Teacher education consists of a balanced program of general education, professional education, and subject matter concentration. It is understood that, although a common core of educational experience is desirable for teachers, differentiation in preparatory programs is essential for elementary, junior high, and secondary school teachers, as well as for other areas of educational specialization.

Teacher education in Indiana consists of an integrated 5-year program of preparation. Four years of study on a teacher education program culminating in a baccalaureate degree and recommendation by the institution of higher education awarding the degree are prerequisite to granting of a provisional license to teach. A provisional certificate is valid for 5 years from date of issue. Qualification for a professional certificate is based on completion of a master's degree in teacher education and 3 years of public school teaching experience. The undergraduate program of study constitutes only the minimum preparation for a beginning teacher and in no case is terminal in nature or intent. The fifth year of study, a continuation of the undergraduate program, completes the basic preparation for a professional position in the public schools of Indiana. Although subject matter concentration and professional specialization are emphasized in graduate-level programs, continuation of study in general education is expected. Administrative and school service personnel certification requires preparation beyond the master's degree and is based on a professional teaching certificate.

Institutions wishing to be accredited by the Teacher Training and Licensing Commission must meet minimum requirements set forth in the rules for each area in which accreditation is sought.

SUMMARY

The superintendent of public instruction is the official upon whom Indiana's constitution places the greatest responsibility for public education. During the 117-year history of the office, there has been a change from a single incumbent, acting alone, to a department of 395 persons, several of whom hold statutory positions. The growth in responsibility that this increased size reflects has come largely in the last 10 years, although several functions were in existence in some form in the 1920's or earlier.

Indiana was a leader in creating institutions and programs for handicapped children and adults. The state was also one of the first to establish a system of certification for teachers, although the earliest efforts were by separate localities rather than through the Department of Public Instruction.

Among the activities which had gone on for a long time without emphasis, curriculum stands out, for a curriculum division was not created until the incumbent superintendent took office in March 1967. However, during the past year, a division of 14 people has been established and is assuming an increasing number of functions. Other growing divisions concern themselves with research, library and audiovisual media, traffic safety, and increasing specialization in educating the handicapped.

The Department of Public Instruction in Indiana is among those institutions at every government level that are moving steadily into positions of greater leadership and responsibility.

FOOTNOTES

1. Indiana, *Constitution* (1816), art. 9, sec. 2.
2. Fassett A. Cotton, *Education in Indiana, 1793-1934* (Bluffton, Ind.: The Progress Publishing Co., 1934), p. 24.
3. Indiana, *Constitution* (1851), art. 8, secs. 2-8.
4. Logan Esarey, *History of Indiana* (3rd ed.; Fort Wayne: The Hoosier Press, 1924), II, 693.
5. Indiana, *Constitution* (1851), art. 8, secs. 2-8.
6. *In re* Todd 193 N.E. 865, 208 Indiana 168 (A35) (1935).

7. Charles E. Rochelle, "The Commission on General Education of the Indiana State Board of Education," *The Teachers College Journal,* XXXI, No. 6 (May 1960), 135. For the complete text of the law, consult Indiana, *Acts of the Indiana General Assembly* (1945), ch. 330, p. 1529.

8. Benjamin J. Burris, comp.,*County School System: How Organized and Administered,*Indiana Department of Public Instruction, Bulletin No. 73 (Indianapolis: The Department, 1924), p.55.

9. W.Monfort Barr,*et al.,School District Reorganization in Indiana,* Bulletin of the School of Education, Indiana University, Vol. XXXV, No. 6 (Bloomington: Division of Research and Field Services, Indiana University, 1959), p. 5.

10. *Report of the Indiana State School Survey Commission to the Governor of Indiana* (Indianapolis: The Commission, 1952), p. 62.

11. The source for this episode is a veteran staff member of the Indiana State Teachers Association, Borden R. Purcell, who served as publicity director. Burley V. Bechdolt, also an ISTA staff member, acted as study director. Edgar Morphet, a 1918 graduate of the Indiana State Normal School, served for almost two decades as a professor of school administration at the University of California (Berkeley).

12. *Report of the Indiana State School Survey Commission to the Governor of Indiana* (Indianapolis: The Commission, 1952), p. 54.

13. *Ibid.*, p. 70.

14. Robert B. Weaver, "Four Years of Indiana School Reorganization," *A Special Report of the Indiana State Chamber of Commerce* (Indianapolis: The Indiana State Chamber of Commerce, n.d.), p. 4.

15. Arthur Campbell, *Report of the State Commission for the Reorganization of School Corporations* (Indianapolis: The Commission, 1967), p. i.

16. A summary of curriculum legislation can be found in Otto T. Hamilton and Margaret T. Fisher, comps., *School Law of Indiana,*Department of Public Instruction, Bulletin No. 154 (Indianapolis: The Department, 1946), ch. 11. C. T. Malan, state superintendent from 1941 to 1947, a graduate of the Indiana University Law School, wrote extensively in this field.

17. *Indianapolis Star*, October 19, 1939, p. 20, col. 2, found in the *Indiana Biography Series* (clippings collected by the Indiana State Library). This interesting set of clippings contains biographical data that would not otherwise be available except by perusal of newspaper files.

18. Department of Public Instruction, *The Administative Handbook for Indiana Schools* (Indianapolis: The Department, 1967), pp. 8-9. This invaluable publication first appeared in 1929 under the title, *Administrative Handbook for Indiana High Schools,* but "High" did not appear in the issues published in 1930, 1937, 1948, 1958, 1961, and 1967.

19. A conceptual approach emphasizes induction to or from general statements and involves efforts by pupils to gain varying levels of abstract visualized situations or concrete artifacts.

20. Indiana, *Laws* (1927), ch. 211.

21. Indiana, *Laws* (1931), ch. 129.

22. Indiana, *Laws* (1947), ch. 276.

23. Indiana, *Laws* (1955), ch. 81.

24. Indiana, *Laws* (1957). ch. 317.

25. Indiana, *Laws* (1961), ch. 4.

26. Indiana, *Laws* (1965), ch. 272.

27. Indiana, *Laws* (1921), ch. 110., p. 265.

28. Department of Public Instruction, *Teacher Training and Licensing,* Bulletin 192 (Indianapolis: The Department, 1946), p. 90.

29. *Ibid.*

BIBLIOGRAPHY

Public Documents

Indiana. *Acts of the General Assembly* (1816-50; 1852-1967).

-- *Constitution* (1816, 1851).

-- *Laws* (1927-65).

Books and Pamphlets

Barnhart, John D., and Carmony, Donald F. *Indiana: From Frontier to Industrial Commonwealth.* 4 vols. New York: Lewis Historical Publishing Co., 1954.

Barr, W. Monfort; Church, Harold H.; Stapley, Maurice E.; and McGhehey, Marion A. *School District Reorganization in Indiana.* Bulletin of the School of Education, Indiana University, Vol. XXXV, No. 6. Bloomington: Division of Research and Field Services, Bloomington University, 1959.

Boone, Richard G. *A History of Education in Indiana.* New York: D. Appleton Century Co., 1892.

Burris, Benjamin J., comp. *County School System: How Organized and Administered.* Department of Public Instruction, Bulletin No. 73. Indianapolis: The Department, 1924.

Cotton, Fassett A. *Education in Indiana, 1793-1934.* Bluffton, Ind.: The Progress Publishing Co., 1934.

Department of Public Instruction. *The Administrative Handbook for Indiana Schools.* Indianapolis: The Department, 1st edition 1929, revised periodically; latest edition, 1968.

—— *Education in Indiana.* Indianapolis: Wm. B. Burford, 1904.

—— *Teacher Training and Licensing in Indiana.* Department of Public Instruction, Bulletin No. 192. Indianapolis: The Department, 1946.

Esarey, Logan. *History of Indiana.* 3d edition, 2 vols. Fort Wayne: The Hoosier Press, 1924.

Hamilton, Otto T., and Fisher, Margaret T., comps. *School Law of Indiana.* Department of Public Instruction, Bulletin No. 154. Indianapolis: The Department, 1946.

Reports

Campbell, Arthur. *Report of the State Commission for the Reorganization of School Corporations.* Indianapolis: The Commission, 1967.

Report of the Indiana State School Survey Commission to the Governor of Indiana. Indianapolis: The Commission, 1952.

Weaver, Robert B. "Four Years of Indiana School Reorganization." *A Special Report of the Indiana State Chamber of Commerce.* Indianapolis: Indiana State Chamber of Commerce, n.d.

Articles and Periodicals

Indianapolis Star, October 19, 1939. p. 20, col. 2. Collected by the Indiana State Library in *Indiana Biography Series.*

Rochelle, Charles E. "The Commission on General Education of the Indiana State Board of Education." *The Teachers College Journal,* XXXI, No. 6 (May 1960), 135.

Unpublished Material

Dean, C. Ross. "The Development of State Control of Secondary Education in Indiana." Unpublished Ph.D. dissertation, Indiana University, Bloomington, 1947.

Finley, Daniel D. "An Evaluation of State Control of Public School Finance in Indiana." Unpublished Ph.D. dissertation, Indiana University, Bloomington, 1942.

Stoneburner, William E. "A History of Public School Finance in Indiana." Unpublished Ph.D. dissertation, Indiana University, Bloomington, 1940.

Swalls, Fred. "An Evaluation of the Indiana State Board of Education and Its Functions." Unpublished Ph.D. dissertation, Indiana University, Bloomington, 1950.

Other Source

Indiana State Teachers Association. Personal interview with Borden R. Purcell, professional relations administrator with Indiana State Teachers Association.

Appendix A

INDIANA CHIEF STATE SCHOOL OFFICERS

State Superintendents

1852-54	William C. Larrabee
1854-57	Caleb Mills
1857-59	William C. Larrabee
1859-61	Samuel L. Rugg
1861-62	Miles J. Fletcher
1862	Samuel K. Hoshour (May-Nov.)
1862-65	Samuel L. Rugg
1865-68	George W. Hoss
1868-71	Barnabas C. Hobbs
1871-74	Milton B. Hopkins
1874-75	Alexander C. Hopkins
1875-81	James H. Smart
1881-83	John M. Bloss
1883-87	John W. Holcombe
1887-91	Harvey M. LaFollette
1891-95	Hervey D. Vories
1895-99	David M. Geeting
1899-1903	Frank L. Jones
1903-1909	Fassett A. Cotton
1909-10	Robert J. Aley
1910-17	Charles A. Greathouse
1917-19	Horace D. Ellis
1919-21	Linnaeus N. Hines
1921-24	Benjamin J. Burris
1925-27	Henry N. Sherwood
1927	Charles F. Miller (March–Sept.)
1927-31	Roy P. Wisehart
1931-33	George C. Cole
1934-41	Floyd I. McMurray
1941-47	Clement T. Malan
1947-49	Ben H. Watt
1949-51	Deane E. Walker
1951-59	Wilbur E. Young
1959-67	William E. Wilson
1967-	Richard D. Wells

Appendix B

Chart I.--INDIANA DEPARTMENT OF PUBLIC INSTRUCTION, 1917

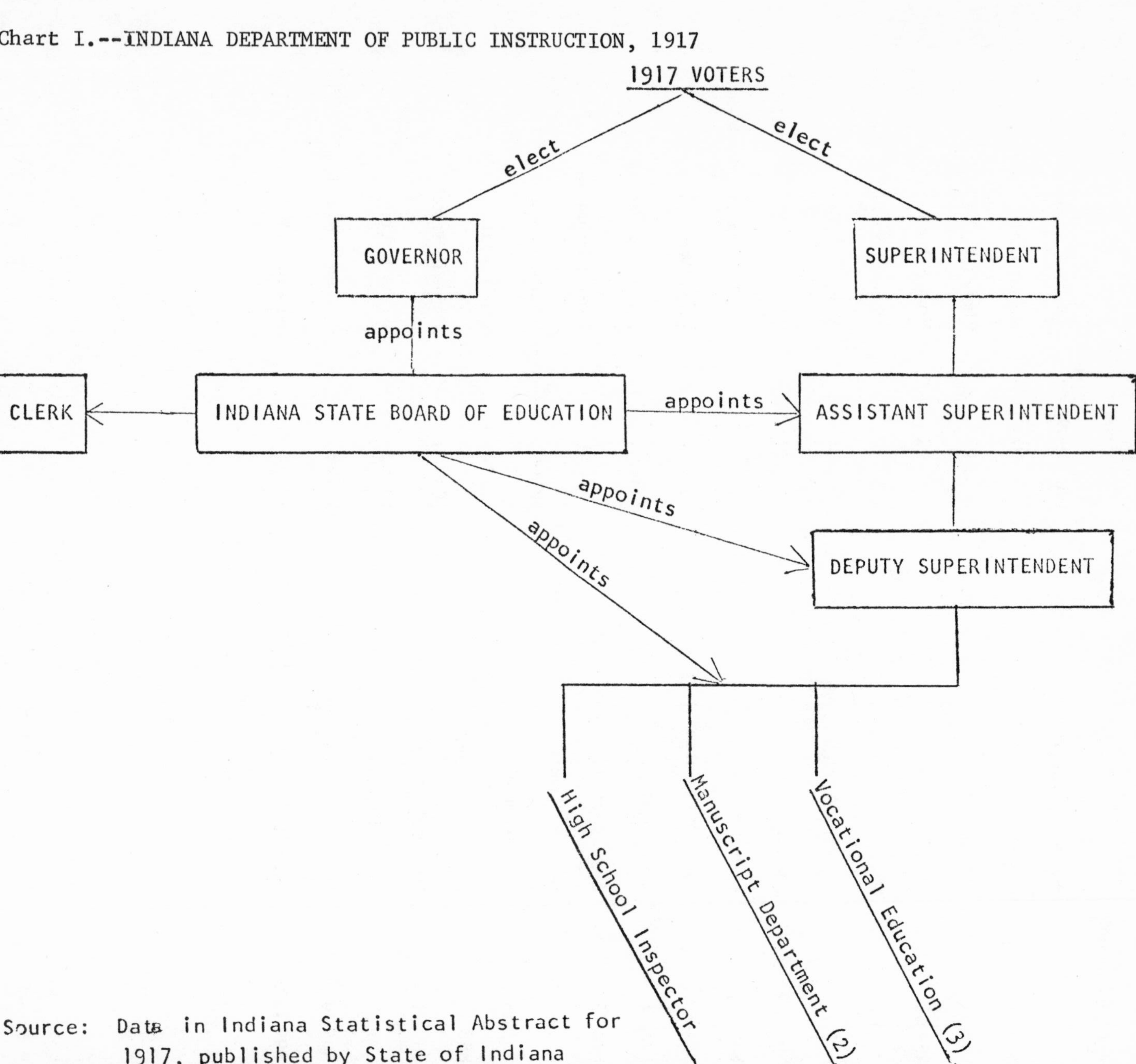

Source: Data in Indiana Statistical Abstract for 1917, published by State of Indiana

Appendix B

Chart II.--INDIANA DEPARTMENT OF PUBLIC INSTRUCTION, 1968

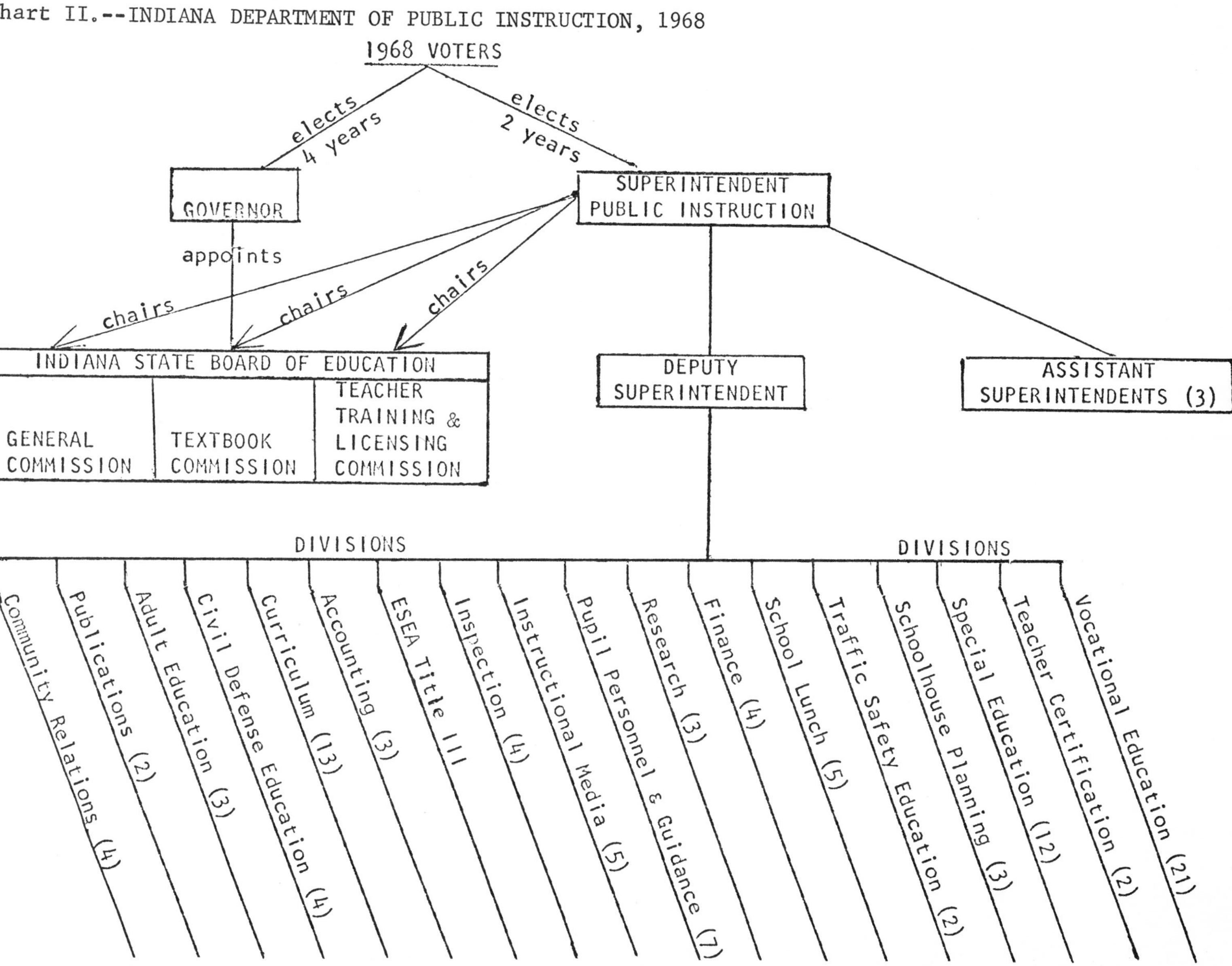

Source: Directory in Hoosier Schoolmaster, Oct., 1968, published by Department of Public Instruction

15 Iowa

DEPARTMENT OF PUBLIC INSTRUCTION
Richard N. Smith

Contents

DEVELOPMENTS AND CONDITIONS PRIOR TO 1900

Because the Iowa country was attached to the territory of Michigan, any legislation dealing with education in the Iowa country was found in the laws of Michigan. The Territorial General Assembly actually took over the Michigan School Law of 1838 and adopted it section for section (1). It would seem that the Legislature did not give very serious consideration to the Michigan law, for the first attempt to establish a state educational agency was not made until 1841. The Territorial Law of 1841 created the Office of State Superintendent of Public Instruction, but it appears that this was done to satisfy the requirements of the earlier law rather than because of a need.

The Law of 1841 assigned the Iowa state superintendent two tasks, both financial rather than educational. He was to administer the permanent school fund and to sell the public lands. It is obvious that the title of the office had little in common with its function. The territorial leaders clearly were feeling their way, and after only 1 year, the office of state superintendent was abolished by legislative act in February 1842.

William Reynolds, the first state superintendent, urged that the superintendent give his entire time to the office so that he might give effective assistance to developing a strong school system. He cited the right of a child to a free school, the enlisting of popular support through a full publication of plans, and provision for the care of the school lands as of special importance in his first report to support his recommendation (2).

However, in the middle 1800's, Iowa was a fairly large territory, and transportation was limited. A state superintendent was handicapped in determining what was going on in the various parts of the territory, and he had an even more difficult time supervising the school system. It was, therefore, the feeling that such matters must wait until Iowa had become an independent commonwealth, and it was anticipated that the fundamental law of the state would contain such a provision.

In 1846, Iowa became a state, and the Office of Superintendent of Public Instruction was set forth in the State Constitution. The first General Assembly provided for the election of a state superintendent whose major duties were administration of the permanent school fund, general supervision of the schools, and interpretation of school law. Thus was established a pattern which exists to the present day. The office existed in this manner until 1857, when a second State Constitution was ratified by the people of Iowa.

The new state had hardly come into being when it began experiencing political unrest because of problems caused by the prohibition of banks and corporations. Many Iowa Democrats became dissatisfied with their party, and, because of the strong Quaker element and New England background of many, both Whigs and Democrats joined the new Republican party. This new party elected a Governor and immediately began the work to make changes in the government. The political upheaval also resulted in a constitutional convention called in 1857 (3).

Three propositions relative to education were presented to the constitutional convention. The first dealt with the reorganization of the public school system; the second was concerned with the withdrawal of the school fund from its distribution through small loans and its reinvestment in some permanent securities; and the third proposition was a provision that would confine the state university to one location (4).

Thus, early in the convention, work began on the creation of a board of education that would consist of 10 to 12 persons from different parts of the state. The majority of those present at the convention agreed that the Legislature had neglected the problems of education and that some radical change was indicated. Out of this belief grew a demand for a legislative body independent of the General Assembly.

Another factor of importance was the opposition to the Office of State Superintendent of Public Instruction. The problem was to provide for the continuance of the functions carried on by the office while eliminating the one-man power concept.

Thus was created a State Board of Education consisting of 11 members—one from each of the judicial districts in the state. The lieutenant governor presided over this board. The secretary of the board was appointed by this body and served as its executive officer, assuming the duties of the state superintendent. The constitution also included the power given to the General Assembly to abolish or reorganize the board at any time after the year 1863.

The Constitution of 1857, which is the fundamental law of the State of Iowa to the present day, created a division of legislative authority. In their zeal to ensure adequate attention to educational matters, which they felt the General Assembly had not done, the framers of the constitution gave the board of education full power and authority to legislate on education. This placed educational matters in a somewhat questionable relationship. The board had the power to legislate, but the Legislature had the power of the purse.

It is the unusual law with which everyone will agree. The educational laws of the state board were no exception, and from the beginning efforts were made to get the board to change some of its laws. By 1860, there was a move to abolish the board, and a bill was passed by the General Assembly to do just that. Governor Kirkwood vetoed the bill, for the constitution gave the assembly power to abolish or reorganize the board, but not until after 1863. The State Board of Education was abolished in March 1864, with provision made for the election of a superintendent of public instruction by popular vote. The system had failed because of the division of authority between the board and the Legislature and because there was little opportunity to make it work before the clamor for change set in.

The superintendent of public instruction carried on the work of the office alone until 1865, when a clerk was provided. A deputy was added in 1868. However, the responsibilities and powers of the superintendent in those days were limited. His principal function was still the supervision and distribution of the school fund, which was almost nonexistent.

It was in 1861 that a board of examiners was created by the State Board of Education. This came about through the influence of leading teachers and the recommendation of the secretary of the education board. The new board was given authority to issue certificates good for life and in any school in the state. It also was given the power to revoke a certificate. The board consisted of the faculty of the state university, and the professor of the normal department served as secretary.

Written examinations were introduced at this time. These and the methods used were patterned after those in use in the East and particularly those used in Cincinnati. However, it was still possible to teach with a lesser certificate, and very few persons presented themselves to the examining board. In the 11 years from 1862 to 1873, only 17 did so (5). Certificates issued by a county superintendent were much easier to obtain.

The statute providing for the State Board of Examiners, of little value to teachers, was repealed to clear the right of way for the creation of a law that would be more comprehensive in nature. In 1874, the Iowa State Teachers Association recommended the appointment of a board of examiners to consist of the state superintendent and four professional teachers, but the request was not granted.

The teachers did not give up. They continued their efforts for a new board, and a petition was circulated among the teachers of the state prior to the 1882 legislative session requesting a board of examiners. The General Assembly heeded this request, and a Board of Educational Examiners was established, with the superintendent of public instruction serving as president of the board. The presidents of the state university and the state normal school also served on the board along with two persons appointed by the State Executive Council.

This body was required to hold at least two public examinations of teachers each year. As the law did not provide for the employment of staff, the work for the board, which involved a large volume of correspondence, was conducted by the state superintendent and the clerk of his office. This arrangement existed until 1907, when the General Assembly empowered the board to employ a secretary and prescribe his duties.

Thus, at the turn of the century the department of public instruction as such did not exist. The rudiments of its makeup were found in the Office of the Superintendent of Public Instruction and the Board of Educational Examiners. The total staff consisted of three: the state superintendent, his deputy, and one stenographer. From such a beginning the department was destined to grow into a single agency encompassing numerous and varied responsibilities and employing a professional staff of 199 and a nonprofessional staff of 195 on December 31, 1965.

Iowa was clearly a rural state in 1900. The one-room school had been developed to meet the need for providing some education to boys and girls in an isolated rural population. Moreover, it was necessary that the schools be located so that children could walk to them, for the roads of the period defied any type of vehicular traffic other than horse-drawn wagons or carts.

The schools of the state were manned by poorly educated and poorly trained teachers. Only 4,202 teachers could be considered as experienced or well trained, as evidenced by the holding of first-grade county or state certificates. The majority of the remaining teachers—in excess of 20,000—had no education beyond the eighth grade and a few weeks at a county normal institute (6).

The school district structure also was inadequate at the beginning of the twentieth century. Its decentralization and lack of state direction or attention resulted in a limited ability to adjust to change. Prior to 1872, Iowa had township districts. Not heeding the advice of the state's ablest educators, the Fourteenth General Assembly passed a law permitting subdistricts within the township districts to become independent school districts. Between 1872 and

1874, the number of independent districts grew from 400 to 2,026, and the number increased to 3,686 by 1900 (7). Schoolhouses as a rule were only 2 miles apart as late as 1910.

The conditions were poor, and the problems were much too numerous for a staff of two professional educators and one stenographer. But progress or change had taken place. Writing in 1903, State Superintendent Richard C. Barrett stated:

> Fifty years ago the average annual school session for the state was 72 days, today it is 160. Then there was not a single graded school, now there are thousands; then the total enrollment was 42,442, now it is 550,202; then the total value of schoolhouses was $144,979, now it is more than $20,000,000 (8).

Gradually, Iowa began to face up to the issues and to take corrective action, although often after other states had done so. As this happened, a Department of Public Instruction slowly evolved. Road conditions were improved, reorganization of school districts took place in two different periods of history, standards for teachers were gradually raised, and instructional programs were enriched.

GROWTH AND STRUCTURAL CHANGES OF THE DEPARTMENT

The Iowa Department of Public Instruction came into existence as such in 1913. Prior to this time, the work of public education was carried on by the Office of the Superintendent of Public Instruction. Modifications in the structure of the department came as a result of the pressures of the time reflected in legislative acts and because the state superintendent and his staff saw a need for a new structure in order to accomplish the task assigned.

The Administration of Richard C. Barrett, 1898-1904

Two pages of the code of Iowa were devoted to the position held by Superintendent Barrett. His responsibilities were basically in the areas of record keeping, officiating at and assisting with teachers institutes, advising as to the school laws, making reports, and the general supervision of county superintendents and the common schools of the state. The state superintendent had no specific powers and duties with regard to supervision at this time.

The structure of the department has been to a great extent dictated by law. Figure 1 depicts the organizational structure for the state supervision of public schools as it existed at the beginning of the period when there were very few responsibilities.

The certification of teachers was not a responsibility of the Office of Superintendent of Public Instruction in 1900 but was under the province of the Board of Educational Examiners. This body consisted of the superintendent of public instruction, the president of the State University of Iowa at Iowa City, the principal of the normal school, and two additional persons appointed by the Governor. The superintendent of public instruction served as president of the board.

The authority of the state superintendent was increased somewhat by the General Assembly with the passage of Senate File 178 in 1900. This law gave him the power to collect, publish, and distribute information relative to public schools and education in general. It also authorized him to promote the cause of education by delivering addresses and publishing and distributing leaflets and circulars. More important, it empowered him to "make tours of inspection among the common schools and other institutions of learning in the state. . . " (9). He had no authority to do anything about the conditions he might have found other than to publish information on them or talk to groups about his findings.

Because the state superintendent's staff was limited to a deputy and a stenographer, he obviously had little time for inspection. However, the law was important because it established inspection of public schools as a responsibility of the state superintendent. This initiated the pattern that was to exist for many decades, and it was to become a handicap to the department in performing its leadership

Figure 1. – ORGANIZATION OF THE IOWA DEPARTMENT OF PUBLIC INSTRUCTION, 1900

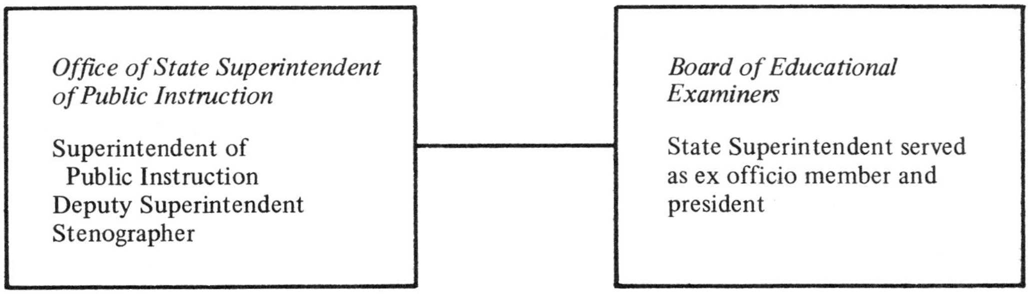

Office of State Superintendent of Public Instruction

Superintendent of Public Instruction
Deputy Superintendent
Stenographer

Board of Educational Examiners

State Superintendent served as ex officio member and president function in the period following 1950 and specifically in the 1960's.

The Administration of John F. Riggs, 1904-11

During the administration of John F. Riggs, legislation was enacted that somewhat broadened the authority of the state superintendent. In 1906, the General Assembly passed the Teachers' Uniform State Certificate Law, which transferred the licensing of teachers from county to state authority. By this time, the teachers of Iowa had become desirous of the status that came with a certificate issued by the state, and the people wanted greater assurance of more uniform quality in the preparation of teachers.

As early as 1840, educators in the United States had known and pointed out that the one-room school, even at its best, was ineffective and should continue only where it was impracticable to provide anything better (10). Although Iowa was not a leader in the consolidation of schools, it did fit into the pattern that had evolved nationally.

The consolidation of schools received powerful help from the State Department of Public Instruction. Since Henry Sabin's administration (1888-92), most of the superintendents gave their support to consolidation (11).

In the first decade of this century the rural school buildings were in a deplorable condition, so shocking, in fact, that one writer stated that the provision for clean, supervised indoor toilets alone justified the cost of new consolidated schools (12). Conditions such as these, coupled with all the efforts to consolidate schools, resulted in the passage of a law in 1906 providing for the organization of consolidated independent districts. Although this act did not immediately extend the authority of the state superintendent, it did provide the first legal step to later extension of the responsibilities of the state office.

Iowa had few well-educated or professionally prepared teachers at the turn of the century. As indicated previously, most of the teachers of this period had received no preparation beyond the eighth grade and what they received in a few weeks at county normal institutes.

The structure of the Iowa department has reflected the grants of funds to public schools, both state and federal. In the early years, the various state funds were the cause of the gradual growth of the department staff and the extension of authority, and they determined the department structure.

Superintendent Barrett recommended in 1901 the discontinuance of the normal institutes. In 1903, he recommended the establishment of county schools, which were to have as their main purpose the teaching of agriculture, manual training, domestic science, and the training of teachers. However, it was not until 8 years later, in 1911, that this concept was partially enacted into law.

In 1911, the General Assembly enacted legislation providing for the approval of normal courses of study to prepare rural school teachers. The law also provided for the inspection and supervision of such schools and the appointment of an inspector of normal training in high school and private and denominational schools at a salary not to exceed $2,000 per year plus necessary traveling expenses. An appropriation of $25,000 for the first year of the biennium and $50,000 annually thereafter was made to carry out the provisions of this act.

The General Assembly also authorized the transportation of pupils in consolidated school districts. This act did not result in expansion of the authority and responsibility of the state office, and it was not until 34 years later that this authority was increased because of pupil transportation. However, the state superintendents throughout the first few decades of the century did give leadership in this area because of its important role in the consolidation of school districts.

The Administration of Albert M. Deyoe, 1911-19

Albert M. Deyoe must be classed as a particularly effective educational leader. During his term of office there was considerable educational progress and much school legislation.

F. L. Mahannah, president of the Iowa State Teachers Association, and Superintendent Deyoe, at the 1911 annual meeting of the association, asked that a committee be established to study the conditions of the rural, graded, and high schools of the state.

The Better Iowa Schools Commission of 1911-12 was created. Mr. Deyoe appointed 22 people to the commission, with the membership almost equally divided between educators and laymen from all parts of the state.

The commission functioned well and had great success. That its work resulted in the enactment of a considerable number of its recommendations can be attributed to two factors. The first was the technique of preparing separate bills for each recommendation, and the second was an exceptionally effective legislative committee. Superintendent Deyoe had done his work well and exercised wisdom in his appointments. The legislative committee of the Better Iowa Schools Commission of 1911-12 was composed of a former Governor as chairman, state legislators, and a prominent newspaperman of the time.

The Legislature passed all of the important bills proposed by the commission. One of these was an appropriation for state aid to consolidated schools. As recommended, this was an incentive aid. It went only to those consolidated schools which taught agriculture and home economics or other industrial subjects. This law resulted in the addition in 1913 of a new staff member, an inspector of rural and consolidated schools.

Another important recommendation enacted into law was the Savage Bill, which provided for reorganization of the state education agency and the creation of a State Department of Public Instruction. The bill created the department with a state superintendent of public instruction appointed for a 4-year term by the Governor, with the consent of two-thirds of the Senate.

There was not much heat generated over this proposal. Possibly this was because it had the full support of the profession and the commission. Attention also may have been diverted to other matters dealing with education. The state board, which operated the three state institutions of higher learning, had been attempting to develop coordination to provide a balanced program. There were inter-institutional rivalries involved in this, and the clash erupted in the General Assembly.

The arrangement of an appointed state superintendent did not have a long tenure, and the office was placed back in partisan politics beginning with the general election of 1918, and every 4 years thereafter. M. G. Clark, president of the Iowa State Teachers Association, gave the following reasons for this in his address in 1918:

> A few years ago found Iowa making splendid progress toward educational freedom. The departments of both state and county school supervision were removed from party political control. The lost party plums, however, proved too great for our legislature to contemplate with any degree of complacency. Politics needed these for teaching purposes. Fortunately the legislature awakened before the office of county superintendent was prostituted. Our state superintendent, however, . . . must become a political diplomat rather than an educational expert. Politics must be placated before educational efficiency can be demanded (13).

Another factor that apparently contributed to the return of the state superintendent to partisan politics was the political situation of the time. Certain enemies of Governor Harding desired to deprive him of the privilege of appointing a successor to Superintendent Deyoe (14).

Even though the 1918 law returned the state superintendency to an elective office, this did not materially affect the powers of the department, for the 1913 law had not changed the legal authority of the state education agency. Because of an enlarged appropriation, Superintendent Deyoe was able to increase his professional staff by four; this made it possible to make a better determination of school conditions in the state and to bring these to the attention of the people and governmental authorities.

The State Board for Vocational Education was created in 1917 to enable Iowa to participate in the Smith-Hughes Vocational Act. The state superintendent of public instruction was designated as chairman of this board. On the board with the state superintendent was the president of the State Board of Education (now the State Board of Regents) and the commissioner of the Bureau of Labor Statistics.

The Administration of P. E. McClenahan, 1919-23

P. E. McClenahan served as state superintendent for one 4-year term. During his administration, a number of laws were enacted as a result of the accumulation of several years of work that had taken place prior to his administration.

Superintendent Deyoe had recommended special aid to mining camp schools in his 1916 and 1918 reports. Such aid was appropriated in 1919 to help upgrade the educational opportunity in these depressed areas. Superintendent McClenahan recommended that an inspector of the mining camp schools be appointed, and in August 1921 the executive council acted on the recommendation and made such an appointment.

In April 1919, the Governor approved an act providing for state aid to encourage the standardization of rural schools. Superintendent McClenahan gave the work of standardization his support, but he was handicapped by a shortage of staff. Although the Legislature had added to the responsibilities and authority of the department, it did not make provision for adequate implementation of the law.

The standardization law added considerably to the legal authority of the state superintendent. It gave him the duty to "prescribe and promulgate the requirements he shall deem necessary" for the standard schools (15). In order to get the work started, a state inspector was taken from another duty temporarily. The position of inspector of rural schools was added in 1924.

There was little opposition to the standardization of the one-room schools. This can possibly be attributed to the poor conditions that had prompted the law. It may also have been an outgrowth of the consolidation movement of this period. People resisted the loss of their one-room country school, and standardization gave them some support for retaining it if they could say that it met state standards and was considered an approved school.

In 1919, an act of the General Assembly directed the state superintendent to assist in the placement or employment of teachers in the public schools. Irving H. Hart, a contemporary of the period writing about this service, states that it was considered ineffective by some school administrators and that its operation incurred considerable hostility from private teacher placement agencies and also among laymen (16). The act was repealed 12 years later, in 1931.

World War I gave the impetus necessary for the inauguration of the federal-state program of vocational rehabilitation in the United States. The federal vocational rehabilitation legislation passed by Congress in June 1920 made funds available to the states on a 50-50 matching basis provided there was state legislative acceptance that gave the State Board of Vocational Education authority to cooperate with the federal board.

Charles A. Prosser, formerly head of the Dunwoody Institute, was director of the Federal Board for Vocational Education. He believed rehabilitation of the handicapped was a vocational education task. It thus became a responsibility of the federal board and, as a result, was placed under the state board in 1921. Willis W. Grant, an instructor at Dunwoody, was selected as state supervisor.

The Administration of May E. Francis, 1923-27

May E. Francis had served as inspector of rural schools for 2 years immediately prior to her election to one term as state superintendent. She had campaigned vigorously and had formed her philosophy after "due consideration and after a period of travel of the State of Iowa." She was for "progress and advance of the smallest school unit—the rural school" (17). During her tenure of office the regulations for the standardizing of one-room rural schools were developed, and in 1926 an inspector of rural schools was added to the staff to implement the standards. This was 7 years after enactment of the law providing for these standards.

The Administration of Agnes Samuelson, 1927-39

During the administration of Miss Samuelson the department's responsibilities and authority continued to grow. The organizational structure experienced considerable change. Miss Samuelson became a recognized leader in education and served on various national boards and commissions. She received special recognition in the summer of 1935: She was awarded an honorary degree of doctor of letters from Augustana College, and she was elected president of the National Education Association.

The first Iowa public junior college was initiated in Mason City in 1918, and there were 12 existing in the state by 1926. The Forty-Second General Assembly repealed the law under which junior colleges could be established by resolution of the local board and made provision for their establishment with the approval of the state superintendent and the voters of the district.

The supervision of these institutions was made the responsibility of the supervisor of the normal training high schools. The Legislature over the years had established the pattern for staffing the department by specifically providing for individual positions. Positions had been added by the Legislature for specific inspectoral purposes as categorical aids were added (18). However, no provision was made for staff members to work with the junior colleges of the state, and this assignment was therefore given to a person who already had a full-time responsibility.

Prior to the passage of the 1927 law, which called for preparation by the state superintendent of standards for junior colleges, an intercollegiate standing committee had inspected the junior colleges and acted as an accrediting agency. This committee was composed of two people from each of the three state institutions of higher learning. Thus, the Legislature turned over to the department a responsibility that had been cared for by six people without making provision for adequate staffing. The committee, therefore, continued to function, and there was some duplication of effort although the department gave only partial attention to this responsibility.

Various arrangements, all makeshift, were utilized for the supervision of the junior colleges for a number of years. A regional supervisor carried the responsibility from 1954 to 1961, when funds were made available to employ a consultant for community and junior colleges.

In 1922, the Educational Finance Inquiry Commission of the American Council on Education selected Iowa as a state in which to study educational finance. The commission had previously conducted similar research in the State of New York. Iowa was chosen because of its contrast in economic conditions to an industrial state such as New York and because it had men especially qualified to do the work (19). This study pointed up a need for the comparability of data and for a state aid plan that would help financially weak school districts.

State Superintendent Samuelson followed up the finance inquiry study with a recommendation that a commission be authorized to study the needs of the public school system. The Forty-Third General Assembly heeded this recommendation and authorized the superintendent to employ a statistician and such clerical help as needed to make a survey. The sum of $8,000 was appropriated for this purpose.

The department at this time, as in other periods, was organized to attack the problems existing as interpreted by the state superintendent. Superintendent Samuelson was evidently not satisfied with the structure of the department, for in 1930 she allocated the work of the department in eight "divisions," a definite change in structure. However, while she could experiment with the structure of the department, she was limited considerably in what she could accomplish with a staff of only seven professional people to assist her.

The Legislature in 1931 took action on a recommendation of the state superintendent and authorized the continued employment of a director of research. This provided the impetus for additional legislation. The financial accounting systems in the state were so varied that it was extremely difficult to make any meaningful financial studies. The pressure to conduct such research grew out of the condition of the Iowa economy at this time. Therefore, the Forty-Third General Assembly ordered the establishment of a uniform cost accounting and financial record system in all public schools. This was to be under the supervision of the state superintendent and gave the superintendent considerable authority.

By 1935, Miss Samuelson was still not satisfied with the manner in which the department was organized. Up to this time the field work of the state education agency, not including vocational education, which for all intents and purposes was a separate department, had been handled by five persons. A substantial increase in the department appropriation made it possible for her to appoint two additional professional staff members. Thus, by 1935 the professional staff had grown to nine in the department, nine in vocational education including rehabilitation, and two under the Board of Educational Examiners—a grand total of 20.

In 1935, Miss Samuelson proceeded to reorganize the department. Because of the nature of the work, no change was made in the supervision of standard rural schools and the normal training high schools. However, it was felt that the characteristics of the consolidated and approved schools were of such nature that both could be adequately supervised by the same personnel. The state was, therefore, divided into four regions and a staff member assigned to supervise all the consolidated and approved schools in each region. Thus was established a pattern of the generalist responsible for the supervision of a certain number of schools in an area. This continues to the present day in the department through its division of supervision.

Financial recognition of the need for special education programs for handicapped children began in 1935 with an appropriation of $10,000. This did not immediately result in extending the authority of the department, and no provision was made for staff to work in this area.

The department did give considerable attention to special education during the late thirties and early forties, but it was not until the 1945-46 school year that the department had a professional staff member with a specific responsibility for the education of the handicapped. The Legislature created a division of special education in 1945.

In 1937, the Legislature designated the state superintendent of public instruction as the chief educational authority of the state where federal moneys for education were concerned. This act authorized the state superintendent to adopt such rules and regulations as were necessary and proper for the administration of the law.

The Administration of Jessie M. Parker, 1939-55

Jessie M. Parker, the seventh person to serve in the position of state superintendent in the 1900's, had the longest tenure of any of Iowa's state superintendents. Miss Parker worked well with people; as a teacher and principal she had always gotten along with the "bad boys." Miss Parker was a person of hearty and enjoyable laughter, and she found much at which to laugh. She was also a fighter and was not afraid to "take on" the Governor or groups such as the Iowa State Teachers Association.

A number of significant changes in the legal authority of the department took place during Miss Parker's administration. These alterations came about as a result of the work of two code commissions created by the Legislature acting on the recommendation of Miss Parker. The Iowa State Education Association had adopted a six-point legislative program that reinforced the recommendations made by the state superintendent.

A commission was established in 1941 to prepare a proposed revision of the school laws. The law creating this commission reiterated the purposes stated by Miss Parker and directed that a complete report be filed with the Governor not later than 60 days preceding the convening of the Fiftieth General Assembly. The state superintendent was designated as the ex officio chairman of the commission.

Unfortunately, the act creating this commission called for the preparation of a "proposed new school code which shall consist in a complete revision and codification" of the laws relating to education (20). The commission, therefore, submitted a report to the Fiftieth General Assembly, and that body found itself confronted by "The School Code Act" consisting of 437 pages. Moreover, the report was not submitted prior to the session as required and was not in the hands of the Legislature until approximately 1 month after it had begun its work. No action was taken on the recommendations of the code commission, therefore, but a second commission was authorized by the Legislature in 1943.

J. P. Street, deputy state superintendent of public instruction from 1939 to 1954, writing in 1950, listed 10 recommendations of the 1943 commission that resulted in school legislation. Two of these dealt with the department: One created state funds for the transportation of children and a division within the department to administer the law; the other established a division within the department for the special education of handicapped children. The remaining eight recommendations were concerned with county school administration, school district reorganization, teacher qualifications and contracts, school finance, and the closing of schools by boards of education (21).

Street also summarized three additional recommendations that had not been enacted into law by 1950. Two of these dealt with the Department of Public Instruction. The first called for a State Board of Public Instruction of seven members which would appoint the state superintendent, a deputy, and other personnel. The second recommended the discontinuance of the then existing State Board for Vocational Education and the transferring of its duties and powers to the new state board.

For many years the education profession in Iowa had been working to remove state education administration from politics. Back in 1910, State Superintendent John F. Riggs urged not only that such a change be made but also that the state superintendent be appointed. Iowa had an appointed state superintendent from 1913 to 1917, when the position was returned to partisan politics. However, the profession, under the leadership of the Iowa State Teachers Association (later the Iowa State Education Association), made continuous efforts to obtain the appointment of the state superintendent by a lay board.

There was also influential support for such an arrangement outside of the education profession. The Brookings Institution was engaged by the Legislature to make a comprehensive study of state government in the early 1930's. These experts favored a lay board of education to represent all the education policies of the public. This board, the Institution said, should delegate the professional aspects of education and the administration of policies established by the board to an appointive state superintendent or commissioner. The recommendation was to abolish the educational examiners board, the vocational education board, the vocational rehabilitation board and to transfer their duties to the State Board of Education. As this board already was operating the state institutions, it was recommended that it should take over the public schools as well (22).

State Superintendent Parker, in 1948, gave support to such a reorganization of the three boards into one and the appointment of the state superintendent. She stated as her reason the danger of the lack of coordination among the separate boards and divisions. As early as 1942, Miss Parker had said that "the department of public instruction includes the state board for vocational education and the board of educational examiners" (23).

The concept of an appointed superintendent also was given support by another governmental reorganization commission in 1950. However, this commission made no recommendation for a state board. Reflecting the opinion of political scientists for a strong executive, it therefore recommended a commissioner of education appointed by the Governor, with all phases of education the responsibility of this one commissioner. The recommendation was that the commissioner should appoint the superintendent of public instruction (24).

The School Code Commissions of 1941 and 1943 made many recommendations for the improvement of education in Iowa. As the effecting and implementing of these would require a strong state education agency, the recommendations for a State Board of Education and the consolidation of the boards into one were enacted into law by the Legislature in somewhat modified form in April 1953. This law gave extensive and broad powers to a State Board of Public Instruction and to the state superintendent of public instruction. It made the state board responsible for vocational education as well as for the work of the educational examiners. The state superintendent was to be appointed by the board.

The Fifty-First General Assembly enacted several important items of legislation that were recommended by the commissions and that materially affected the legal authority of the department. The act creating the special education division has been mentioned. A transportation division was also established by law. This accompanied the reimbursement to school districts for transportation costs. An appropriation of $2 million annually was made in 1945. Such aid was designed to remove one of the obstacles to school district reorganization, which was another recommendation of the school code commissions.

Equalized educational opportunity, as recommended by the school code commissions' supplementary aid to schools, also was provided by the General Assembly. This resulted in the creation of the administration and finance division within the department and in the extension of the authority of the state education agency, as school officials were required to keep accurate financial and attendance records. The department also set forth regulations that required uniformity in the computation of average daily attendance.

In 1947, the General Assembly strengthened the reorganization law and placed additional responsibilities with the state superintendent. Responsibilities and authority also were added in 1947 with the initiation of general aid to school districts. The law providing for general aid authorized the state superintendent to adopt necessary and proper rules and regulations for the administration of the chapter in the code that created the aid.

The newly created State Board of Public Instruction held its initial meeting in January 1954 at the Hotel Kirkwood in Des Moines. Jessie M. Parker continued as state superintendent to complete her term as prescribed in Chapter 257 of the code, thereby becoming the state board's first executive officer.

Almost immediately the new state education agency clashed with another branch of government when the office of the state personnel director asserted its authority over the department. However, at its meeting of January 1954, the board received an opinion of Assistant Attorney General Oscar Strauss that the Department of Public Instruction did not come under the state personnel director. This was an important ruling, for it enabled the department to remain free from any possible political appointments, and it strengthened the state board's authority as an independent agency.

In June 1954, the state board met in executive session and elected J. C. Wright as state superintendent. Wright, superintendent of schools at Keokuk, Iowa, was subsequently employed as a consultant to the board for the period July 1, 1954, to January 1, 1955. This action provided for a smoother transition in the change of superintendents.

The budget and financial control committee, a powerful interim committee of the Legislature, in an attempt to obtain greater efficiency, employed Griffenhagen and

Associates to do four management improvement studies. The Office of the Superintendent of Public Instruction was one of the four state agencies included in the study which began in 1952. This work resulted in a recommendation for a greatly expanded state education agency: an increase from 11 divisions to 16, and the creation of two assistant superintendents to supervise the work of these divisions.

The Griffenhagen report pointed up the influence of the form of financial support for education on the organization of the state department. Although over three-fourths of the state aid to local school districts was for general education purposes in 1952, two of the special fields of instruction (vocational education and instruction of handicapped children) received the exclusive attention of 48 percent of the professional staff of the department (25). This made it difficult to provide a balanced system of instruction. However, it may have been equally difficult to obtain the emphasis needed to develop these special programs in the public schools without this accent at that particular time in history.

The Administration of J. C. Wright, 1955-60

J. C. Wright saw six major problem areas facing the department and the State of Iowa at the time he was appointed state superintendent of public instruction. These were –

1. The need for more adequate organization of school districts.
2. Upgrading of the preparation of teachers in Iowa and the development of a more efficient method of processing certificates.
3. The need to increase and improve consultative services to local and county school systems.
4. The need for a substantial increase in state funds for the support of local public schools.
5. The accreditation of schools and the establishment of standards for state approval of school districts.
6. The clarification of the relationship between the department and the colleges and universities in the preparation of teachers (26).

The administration of J. C. Wright was marked by the vigorous promotion of school district reorganization. Chapter 275 of the Iowa Code, which is concerned with the reorganization of school districts, had been rewritten by the General Assembly in 1953. Superintendent Wright used the techniques of personal appearance, publications, research, standards, and staff utilization to conduct this program.

The Legislature, recognizing that strong and positive measures were needed to accomplish the improvement of education in Iowa, delegated considerable authority to the state superintendent.

During the school years 1955-56 to 1960-61, the school districts of Iowa were reduced from 4,142 to 1,575. The number of non-high school districts was lowered from 3,334 to 1,013, and the reduction in high school districts was from 808 to 562. Standards for the approval of school districts were introduced in 1958, and the momentum of reorganization reached its peak in the 1959-60 school year.

The division of curriculum was created in 1958. However, it was in reality only a "paper" division for it had no new staff members. The division was created because of the recognition of a need for some special attention to curriculum. During the 1940's the state agency had published a number of curriculum guides for secondary schools. The creation of this division was an attempt to set up enough structure to enable the department to develop new handbooks.

In 1958, the department began preparation for involvement in the National Defense Education Act. Participation in this act resulted in a substantial increase in the authority of the department through implementation of the state plan that involved approval of projects. A substantial increase in staff took place in 1959. Eleven professional staff members, all of whom had responsibilities under the National Defense Education Act, were added to a professional staff of 51 the previous year, exclusive of vocational rehabilitation.

The Administration of Paul F. Johnston, 1961-

The period of Superintendent Johnston's tenure of office as the chief state school officer during the years 1961 through 1965 was also quite significant with respect to the legal authority of the department, the state superintendent, and the state board.

The newly appointed state superintendent outlined his proposed program to the state board in January 1961. In this report Johnston recommended the development of a long-range plan for the state system of public education in Iowa, which included vocational education, community colleges, adult education, and technical schools. In April 1961, House Resolution 6 was adopted by the Iowa House of Representatives. The resolution directed the Department of Public Instruction to study community colleges and vocational-technical education in Iowa and to make recommendations to the General Assembly in 1963. The sum of $12,000 was appropriated to finance the study.

Superintendent Johnston saw a need for combining the functions of the intermediate unit and the community college into a single district structure so that only one taxing unit and one governing board would be created. This actually would have resulted in no additional tax unit, but rather the replacement of the existing county board of education, which had taxing powers, with an area board. The department committee and the state advisory committee established to review and react to the work of the department committee concurred after deliberation over the pros and cons of combining the two functions under one board. The department report submitted to the

Sixtieth General Assembly subsequently recommended 16 such districts for the state.

Property tax supported the great bulk of the cost of public elementary and secondary education in Iowa in 1963. There were, therefore, those who opposed the department proposal because it contained the recommendation for part of the support of the area districts to be borne by a property tax. It was the position of the state education agency that an area community college should be responsive to the needs of the people of the area and should, therefore, be dependent on the area for at least part of the funds needed. The department also assumed that the burden on local property taxes for the support of public elementary and secondary education would be relieved and that its recommendation for such relief would not be ignored. The department recommendation was for the assumption of the building construction costs by the area district. It further recommended the sharing of the current operation expenditures by the state and the districts in proportions to be determined from time to time by the Legislature. The state agency also recommended the inclusion of the area districts in the foundation program when adopted by the General Assembly.

The department believed that the pattern of local area responsibility for capital outlay and state support for operation would be in the best interest of the state. This reasoning was explained in the following way:

> The fact that the voters in an area education district are willing to assume the responsibility for capital outlay for their community college should constitute sufficient evidence of their belief in the value of this institution to warrant the state in making substantial contributions to operating costs (27).

The feeling against any additional property tax was quite strong in the rural-dominated Sixtieth General Assembly. There was also considerable opposition to the concept of combining the service functions of an intermediate unit and the education functions of a community college. This objection was given strong support by the junior college people in the state. Because of these objections and the conservative nature of the Sixtieth General Assembly, the recommendations of the department were not acted on in 1963. Had the assembly been in favor of reorganizing the county administrative units and the establishment of community colleges serving a number of counties, bills could have been drafted that would have separated the two and provided for state financing of the schools.

The proposal was reintroduced in the reapportioned Sixty-First General Assembly as two separate bills: one on area community colleges or vocational schools, and the other on merged county school systems. Both of them received a favorable vote and subsequently became law in 1965, thereby adding considerably to the responsibility and authority of the state education agency.

The department initiated automatic data processing in 1953. This service grew in importance, and in 1962 it was given division status. By this time it was making extensive use of its automatic data-processing equipment. The data from the various reports required by law and regulation were available for machine use. This capability, plus the experience and knowledge existing at the State University of Iowa and the Measurement Research Center in Iowa City, made feasible a complete educational information center that could bring the benefits of automatic data processing to bear on the problems of education.

Thus, the Iowa Educational Information Center was formally organized in December 1963 as a joint enterprise of the State Department of Public Instruction and the College of Education of the State University of Iowa. The purpose of the center was to collect and maintain a complete file of information about Iowa students, public schools, personnel, buildings, administrative units, and fiscal records. Paul F. Johnston had envisioned such a service some 4 years before. The center was to process this information, to provide a systematic feedback of it to the individual schools and agencies, and to have information available for research purposes. A coordinating committee was named, consisting of State Superintendent Johnston as chairman, Dean Howard Jones of the College of Education at the university, and Professor E. F. Lindquist, president of the Measurement Research Center.

The Iowa Educational Information Center is financed by the State University of Iowa, the State Department of Public Instruction, grants from the U.S. Office of Education and the Ford Foundation, and service fees paid by schools which voluntarily subscribe for such services as grade reporting and class scheduling.

The rapid reorganization of school districts pushed by the state department under the administration of J. C. Wright was not accomplished without some expression of dissatisfaction and resistance. In 1961, the Legislature mandated the submission of all department rules to it before they could become effective. While this law did not specifically single out any one department, it was the general belief that one of its targets was the Department of Public Instruction. An attempt also was made to again make the position of state superintendent elective, but this did not succeed. The department was taken to court, and in 1964, the Iowa Supreme Court declared Section 257.18 (13) unconstitutional (28).

Thereafter, the schools of Iowa operated without the guiding force of approval standards, and in 1965, the Legislature mandated approval standards to be written by the state board. This law gave much broader power to the board, the state superintendent, and the department than previously because it placed all private and parochial nursery, kindergarten, elementary, junior high, and senior high schools under the jurisdiction of the state board in addition to those operated by public school districts.

The Sixty-First General Assembly added other responsibilities and authority to the state education agency in addition to those described above. Driver education was required to be taught or made available by every public school district in the state. Aid was appropriated, and responsibility for supervision of the law was placed with the department. In addition, legislation attempting to regulate the advertising and selling of courses of instruction was made a responsibility of the state education agency. However, because of numerous exceptions that were added to the bill and became part of the law, it was ineffective; the department's role, therefore, was of little consequence, although the law did require additional work.

The new legislation, both federal and state, passed during the years 1963 through 1965 made further change in the department necessary. A departmental committee was appointed by the state superintendent with the approval of the state board to study the problem and make recommendations. This committee worked for a number of months in late 1963 and early 1965–it did nothing in 1964–studying the organizational structure of the department. Both long- and short-range plans were formulated.

A review of the state board minutes of April 16, 1964, discloses one of the major problems connected with federal legislation dealing with new educational programs. Congress enacts new legislation that requires the drafting of a state plan. However, Congress fails to appropriate funds to be used by state departments of education which would enable them to hire additional personnel to prepare the state plan. This results in loading additional responsibilities on a historically already overloaded staff and the concomitant inadequate preparation of state plans. To this must be added the effect the passage of the new legislation has on the school districts. The minutes point up this problem as follows:

> Mr. Graeber stated that the problems associated with writing a state plan were almost overwhelming. He indicated the office has been deluged by letters and communications from schools asking how they could make application for funds and that it was more than a full-time job of the present staff in trying to maintain some semblance of communication with the schools on current problems. This left no time for the solution of the major problem which was to write the state plan itself (29).

The implications of the Elementary and Secondary Education Act for the structure of the department were evident in the spring of 1965. Because of this legislation and enactments of the Legislature, the state board took up the proposed long-range plan for the organizational structure of the department in its April and May board meetings of that year. There had been two main staffing weaknesses in the past. One of these was that there was more work to be done than there were people available to do it. The second was that because of an overloaded staff there was no one with the time to plan, coordinate, and review the department's operation.

Effective July 1, 1965, the Department of Public Instruction experienced a major reorganization brought about by the rapid growth that had come and that was further necessitated because of the growth foreseen in the near future. The change in structure also was felt necessary because of the two weaknesses discussed above. The new structure provided for seven branches, each of which was headed by an associate superintendent who was not to be responsible for day-to-day operations. The associate superintendents were to have time to work together and coordinate the entire operation of the department. Another key aspect of the new structure was a planning and development staff which was to have the specific responsibility of working with the associate superintendents in the initiation of programs for the department. See Appendix B for the organizational structure effective as of July 1, 1965. It should be noted that important organizational features are lost in this chart. A new publications section was created within the internal services division. A noteworthy position, which does not appear on the 1965 chart, is that of administrative assistant to the state superintendent. This position was included with the planning and development staff.

On July 1, 1965, the Iowa State Department of Public Instruction consisted of 161 professional and 166 nonprofessional staff members. By December 31, 1965, there were a professional staff of 199 and a nonprofessional staff of 195.

FINANCING THE PUBLIC SCHOOLS AND THE STATE DEPARTMENT OF PUBLIC INSTRUCTION

The development of a state school support program in Iowa followed a similar pattern to that which evolved in the nation. Iowa went through the same stages, but it frequently was behind many other states. The efforts of the department to obtain financing for Iowa public schools evolved through three periods:

1900-22– Efforts to obtain and maintain state-distributed funds that would encourage selected programs

1922-36– Preparation and study for implementation of a state support program based on the foundation principle of equalization

1936-65– Repeated attempts to obtain state funds distributed on a basis that would equalize educational opportunity and the taxes necessary to provide such a program.

Superintendent John F. Riggs in 1905 initiated 60 years of effort by the State Department of Public Instruction to obtain state support for public schools. He recognized the possibilities for improving educational opportunity through the use of state funds and recommended their distribution on the basis of average daily attendance as an inducement to increase attendance.

The emphasis for a period of better than 25 years was on the use of state funds to improve the educational opportunities for rural boys and girls. In the period from 1911 to 1919, four different state aids were introduced to provide funds to accomplish this. Three of these were continued through 1948, when they were discontinued and replaced by general and supplemental aid. (See Table 1, Appendix C.)

Iowa could not embark on an equalization program of any magnitude during the 1920's and 1930's because the financial accounting of the schools was neither comprehensive nor uniform enough to make this possible. Iowa was not ready for such a program, and it was therefore necessary to educate the people of the state. Thus approximately 16 years were spent, from 1922 to 1938, in developing the techniques, knowledge, and accounting system necessary for the initiation of a state support plan designed to equalize educational opportunity.

Another 7 years passed, from 1938 to 1945, in which the educational campaign was paramount before supplemental aid in the amount of $1 million was provided by the Iowa Legislature. This marked the beginning of repeated and strong efforts on the part of the department, along with other groups, to obtain more adequate state support. These efforts have continued up to the present. Various plans were developed and pushed with considerable vigor by the department and other organizations, especially the Iowa State Education Association, during the 1950's and 1960's. The department provided the coordination and leadership of these efforts, none of which met with success because of the differences of opinion that existed over how the funds should be distributed.

A state educational agency is a creation of the State Legislature and is, therefore, what the lawmakers want it to be. The Legislature was dominated and controlled by rural Iowa during the first 65 years of the twentieth century. This being the case, the attention given education by the Iowa General Assembly consistently was rural-oriented. The state aids that were provided, although in very negligible amounts, were designed to improve the education of those living in rural Iowa. This was to be expected, not only because of a rural-dominated Legislature, but because the level of education in the rural areas was considered by contemporaries to be of a lesser quality than that in the cities of Iowa.

Because of the rural emphasis placed on state aid, the recruitment of staff was from the ranks of school superintendents and principals in Iowa's smaller school districts. The money provided for these positions was adequate because wage demands were low in this group. Also, Iowa never really recovered from the economic recession of 1920 and 1921.

Following World War II, considerable legislation that changed the department's role was passed by the Iowa General Assembly. New state aids were enacted into law. A state board with broad powers was created to make policy for all public education through the junior college. This board appointed the state superintendent, who also was assigned considerable authority and responsibility. A reorganization law was passed, which assigned the responsibility for accomplishment to local boards, the county superintendent and county board, and the state education agency. Beginning in 1958, Congress began enacting a series of laws that had the effect of changing the state education agency.

These state and federal laws brought about a change in the staffing of the department. No longer could a professional staff be recruited from the ranks of the school administrators in the smaller Iowa school districts.

The economy of the nation was on an almost continuous upward spiral after 1950, and professional staff increasingly became more difficult to obtain at all levels of education. Thus the department found it necessary to hire younger people to fill the new specialist positions. These people were, by and large, highly mobile young men, and the department found itself in competition for professional staff with the better school districts of the nation, colleges and universities, the U.S. Office of Education, other state departments of education, intermediate units, and other agencies.

Political influence had a direct effect on the financing of the department. When the state superintendent was elected, he was treated like any other head of a state agency with regard to salary. (See Table 3, Appendix C, for a comparison of the state superintendent's salary with those of other agency heads.) This, coupled with the fact that for a period of over 30 years Iowa's state superintendents were women, served to hold down the salary of the state superintendent. This condition carried over after the position became appointive and proved to be a real detriment to the department in obtaining staff. Too often its professional staff members were considered to be like any other state government workers by the Legislature and other state department heads. The *Des Moines Register* of April 17, 1959, said in an editorial:

> It would appear that the legislators have made the mistake of regarding these employees of the public instruction department, not as the professional educators that they are, but as just another group of statehouse employees doing routine jobs. This is sadly underrating the work of the department.

It was, therefore, difficult to obtain the funds necessary to adequately finance the department. The department's performance of the duties assigned it by the Legislature also had detrimental effects. As the state education agency worked on school district reorganization, it encountered considerable opposition, and this was reflected in the Legislature. The appropriations for the department were used by the Legislature to discipline the state agency.

Reapportionment somewhat changed the makeup of the Legislature, and increased funds were appropriated for the department in 1965. New federal laws also provided more funds. The National Defense Education Act, the Vocational Education Act of 1963, and the Elementary and Secondary Education Act of 1965 were of special significance in providing funds for the department. In 1965, the Department of Public Instruction found itself in a healthy financial position: Funds were available for its operation, and for the first time in many years it was competitive for professional staff.

LOCAL, STATE, AND FEDERAL RELATIONS

Local School Districts

The Iowa Department of Public Instruction had very limited contact with the school districts of Iowa until the 1950's. The staff was extremely small, and it was impossible to give anything but token service to the public schools of the state. School people of Iowa had very little awareness of the department for a number of years.

The efforts of the state department to bring about an improved school district structure have colored the relationship of the state agency with local school districts to a considerable extent. The consolidation movement in the early decades of this century provided for many people their only contact with the state education agency. This situation continued until 1935, and, while limited because of the large number of schools, these contacts did serve as a narrow bridge to some of the districts of the state.

The school district reorganization efforts of the Department of Public Instruction in the 1950's and 1960's created "the" relationship of the department with local districts. It also set the tone of the support with the Legislature.

The energetic zeal of State Superintendent J.C. Wright and the steady pressure of Paul F. Johnston were greatly responsible for the considerable progress made in school district reorganization. For every action there is a reaction, and the reaction to the department's efforts to bring about a change in school district structure erupted in each session of the assembly after 1957.

There were no special state funds to encourage school district reorganization after World War II. The department did considerable work to educate the people about the need for, and the advantages of, joining school districts together.

Under the leadership of State Superintendent J. C. Wright, approval standards were developed as prescribed by law. Many school districts could not meet these standards, and the disapproval of districts was used to promote reorganization. Considerable opposition developed to this procedure, and the subsection of the Code of Iowa that provided the authority for the standards was declared unconstitutional by the Iowa Supreme Court. The General Assembly subsequently wrote very stringent and detailed standards into law in 1965.

Beginning in the late 1920's, the department embarked on a program of elementary curriculum improvement. This was followed by the development of a series of 20 bulletins devoted to subject matter fields in the high school program. In the middle 1940's, a new secondary school curriculum project was initiated that resulted in the publication of a series of curriculum handbooks. The supply of these materials was exhausted by the late 1950's.

Many new developments and much new knowledge created a need for further work of this type, but the department did not have the funds necessary to finance a new curriculum project. However, the National Defense Education Act of 1958 made it possible to develop needed materials in mathematics, science, modern foreign languages, and guidance.

Over the years, the state department has been able to serve mainly as the initiator and coordinator of committees created to produce curriculum materials. The handbooks that have been published were possible only because of the unselfish and professional efforts of teachers, administrators, and college professors who donated their time and talents to the improvement of education in Iowa.

A state plan for the improvement of education was initiated in 1963. The state was divided into 16 areas in which the school administrators could work together to solve some of the problems facing the school districts. The plan was also designed to provide a closer working relationship between the department and local and county school systems.

The certification of teachers has important public relations implications for the agency assigned this responsibility. Such an assignment was given to the Department of Public Instruction in 1953, when there was a shortage of qualified people willing to teach. This shortage of teachers continues to the present day, and the department has been subjected to pressures to lower the requirements for qualification of teachers. There has been an increasing number of certified personnel to process because of expanding enrollments and because of a requirement that children in private schools be instructed by certified teachers. Additional complications and pressures were created by new federal programs and the growth of the junior and community colleges of the state.

The position of county superintendent of schools has been an important one in Iowa education. Because of its own limited staff, the state education agency has relied on the county superintendents to accomplish what otherwise could not have been done. Constant efforts have, therefore, been made to strengthen the position and to raise the qualifications for it to a professional level. The numerous rural schools in the state retarded the upgrading of the position for a number of years. The county superintendent has been an important factor in setting the tone of the relationship between the department and local school districts.

The department embarked on a rather ambitious data-collection program in 1965. This was called CardPac and was handled for the department by the Iowa Educational Information Center.

CardPac required the completion of forms by both teachers and pupils. Included as a part of CardPac was a student questionnaire. Considerable opposition to CardPac developed because the teachers did not like to work with the system and because some people objected to the student questionnaire. There had been a breakdown in communication in introducing CardPac to the public schools; however, modifications in the experimental plan were made, and CardPac was continued.

The Iowa Department of Public Instruction has had a close relationship with the state organizations representing the teachers of Iowa and local school boards. The state education agency played an important role in the early development of the organizations representing both of these groups.

Relations with the Teachers Association

A state teachers organization held its initial meeting in the courthouse in Muscatine in May 1854. The purposes of the new organization were to promote the educational interests of the state, to improve teaching, and to elevate the profession of teaching. Eleven of the 18 founding fathers of the association were school administrators. One of them, D. Franklin Wells, later became state superintendent during 1867 and 1868. Five of the other presidents of the Iowa State Teachers Association also served as state superintendents before 1900; one exception was Richard C. Barrett, who was president of the ISTA in 1895 and state superintendent from 1898 to 1904.

The control of the Iowa State Teachers Association in its early years by school administrators was important and accounts for the establishment of a close relationship between the ISTA and the state superintendent. This connection was nurtured for a number of years during the time the state association was administrator-dominated.

It is, therefore, not wholly surprising that Henry Sabin, state superintendent of public instruction, suggested in 1893 that the state should recognize the Iowa State Teachers Association and publish its proceedings as a part of the biennial report. Superintendent Sabin's influence resulted in the enactment of a law in 1894 by the General Assembly that authorized the annual publication by the state of 1,500 copies of the proceedings and their free distribution to the membership. The policy of state publication of the annual association meeting proceedings continued until 1931, when it was discontinued because of the economic depression.

Superintendent Barrett worked for the improvement of teacher certification, contracts, salaries, and preparation among other things. The ISTA had similar goals and joined with the state superintendent of public instruction to obtain appropriate legislation. This effort resulted in the Uniform County Certificate Law of 1906. This act replaced a previously chaotic system operated by 99 county superintendents with a uniform system of certification on the county level. The system was supervised by the State Board of Educational Examiners, with the state superintendent serving as chairman of the board.

The state education agency and the association representing the bulk of the teachers of Iowa have, on the whole, worked cooperatively for legislative change. This cooperative effort was especially evident during the first three decades of the twentieth century before new constitutions were adopted to democratize the association and obtain wider membership. A reorganization committee consisting of three superintendents called attention to the fact that in 1928 only 16,000 of the 26,000 teachers in the state were members of the ISTA. As membership increased, and as the association became more democratic, its emphasis shifted more to teacher welfare.

The Iowa State Teachers Association supported Superintendent John F. Riggs in his efforts to obtain a recodification of the school laws. A commission consisting of an educator and two attorneys was authorized by the General Assembly in 1907. A comprehensive report was made but received little attention from the Legislature. All of the recommendations were contained in one large and bulky bill; the Legislature has generally not reacted favorably to such omnibus bills.

The Better Iowa Schools Commission of 1911-12 must be ranked as one of the crowning achievements of the cooperative efforts of the department and the association. The commission was suggested and chaired by Superintendent Deyoe, and it was made possible only through the cooperation and financial contribution of the ISTA. Eighteen recommendations were introduced in bill form in the Legislature, and 13 of them became law.

The association and the department have, on the whole, had common or similar legislative goals in the past 20 years. Both organizations have worked for school district reorganization, improved state financing of public schools, and the strengthening of local and county school administration. Cooperative efforts also were made to obtain improved state school administration in the early 1950's, although the association goal differed from those of the department for many years.

Probably the most notable example of cooperative legislative effort has been in the area of state financing of the public schools. With the exception of one instance, the two organizations have worked almost hand in hand to obtain adequate state financing.

There were strained relations between the department and the ISTA during the administration of May E. Francis. It was stated in *Midland Schools* that opposition in Iowa on the part of the state superintendents to organized teachers had been neither general nor chronic. Rather, it said, the Iowa situation in 1925 was unique among the states and unusual in its own history. It said that instead of offering opposition, most state superintendents in the nation worked harmoniously with teacher groups because the cause of education was of such vital concern to the state and nation that active cooperation between the forces interested in schools was necessary to accomplish their task (30).

Miss Francis had campaigned in 1922 on a platform of economy and improvement of the rural school, but she called for retrenchment in consolidation. She said that if she were elected, "Fads and fadism shall not run rampant like a hungry lion." She was for "progress and advance for the smallest school unit—the rural school" (31). The opponents of Miss Francis spoke of progressive education measures. It follows that Miss Francis did not endear herself to the majority of the members of the ISTA.

Superintendent Francis was investigated during the last week of the special session of the Fortieth General Assembly in April 1924. For many months, charges were circulated around the state concerning alleged illegal and unfair acts by the department. Miss Francis was charged with raising the grades of teachers to permit them to receive certificates, refusing to accredit some consolidated schools, and arbitrarily refusing certificates to some entitled to them.

The Iowa State Teachers Association publicly took no stand on the matter and neither defended nor accused the department. The matter was not settled, and Miss Francis left public office after her term as state superintendent was completed.

The Department of Public Instruction and the Iowa State Teachers Association were not in accord on the method by which the state superintendent should be selected. This situation existed until approximately 1949. The ISTA reiterated its policy in favor of the appointment of the state superintendent by the state board quite consistently over the years. State Superintendent Samuelson avoided conflict by openly refraining from stating a position on the issue until 1938, when she publicly recommended the appointment of the state superintendent of public instruction.

Jessie M. Parker succeeded to the state superintendency in 1939. Whereas Miss Samuelson's administration had been marked by a very smooth and cordial relationship with the ISTA, Miss Parker's was somewhat strained from time to time. During her 16 years in office, education became a highly controversial field. Problems of financing public schools, school district structure, and teacher certification grew during these years. Following World War II, schools came under attack generally as an aftermath of the war and as a result of the uncertainty of the world situation.

Personalities were brought into the fight for an appointive state superintendent in 1945. They were introduced by name in behind-the-scenes maneuvering and by implication. The personalities involved were Agnes Samuelson, executive secretary of the Iowa State Education Association, and Jessie M. Parker, state superintendent of public instruction. The implication was that a "feud" was on between the two and that Miss Samuelson wanted the superintendency back.

In 1945, the *Cedar Rapids Gazette* reported that the two ladies did part company on the appointive bill. Their organizations were, however, in accord on the other school bills. Miss Parker was said to have been working through subordinates to keep the office elective. Miss Samuelson, along with her subordinates, worked to make the office appointive. Miss Samuelson maintained that the stories were not true and that they were circulated to kill the bill. Miss Parker was of the opinion that making the office appointive would open it more widely to politics than under the elective system.

The association dropped its push for an appointive state superintendent until 1949. Miss Parker had begun working for an appointive state superintendent late in 1948. However, the association was still at odds with Miss Parker. Harvey Hill of Des Moines, president of the ISEA, said that a letter opposing the renomination of Jessie Parker had been sent to some association members. Officials of the association "did not deem Miss Parker's attitude satisfactory in regard to either reorganization of the department of public instruction, or cooperation with the ISEA and educational officials in Iowa" (32).

In 1952, the department and the ISEA joined forces in sponsoring a bill for the reorganization of the state education agency with an appointive state superintendent. The superintendent was to be appointed by a board elected by school board members from each congressional district, with one member appointed by the Governor. This was the first time the two organizations had reached agreement on this issue.

The arrangement was a compromise. Miss Parker favored an elected state board that would appoint the state superintendent. Charles F. Martin, then ISEA executive secretary, advocated a board appointed by the Governor, which in turn would appoint the state superintendent. This compromise on the method of selecting the board, as well as the cooperative efforts of the two organizations, resulted in enactment of the measure into law.

The Iowa State Education Association and the State Department of Public Instruction worked very closely together over the years to obtain adequate state sharing in the costs of the public schools. On one occasion this cooperation broke down, and friction temporarily resulted.

The Iowa State Education Association included the minimum foundation program recommended by the committee on educational finance in its legislative program in 1950. In fact, it was given first place in the discussion of legislative goals in *Midland Schools.* However, 2 months later, the ISEA withdrew its support of the program. Charles F. Martin, executive secretary, stated that there was not sufficient time to disseminate information essential to the successful promotion of the program (33).

This created considerable friction within the education profession of the state. It is significant to note that the only increase in the amounts appropriated for state support of schools in the 1951 legislative session was $200,000 for vocational education. No other highly important educational legislation was passed at this time.

Relations with the School Boards Association

The beginning of an organization representing the school boards of Iowa is somewhat hazy. There is evidence that school boards met together in annual sessions as early as 1894, with the proceedings published by the superintendent of public instruction. Such publication ended after 1905.

An association of consolidated school boards was formed in 1920 as a result of a meeting of the National Conference on the Consolidation of Schools held on the campus of Iowa State Teachers College at Cedar Falls.

In 1933, the department began the sponsorship of an annual conference for boards of education. The department was requested to assist in the organization of a state school board association at the fourth annual conference sponsored by the department. Such organizational work did get under way in 1936.

The early conferences for school board members were held in February, but later they were conducted during the last week of March immediately following the reorganization of boards of education. Prior to the 1950's, school board elections were held in March.

By 1938, the Iowa Association of School Boards was holding an annual meeting in Des Moines during the convention of the Iowa State Teachers Association. The state superintendent of public instruction gave recognition to the association for the considerable amount of work that had been done to improve the service of boards of education.

The department was feeling its way in attempts to provide leadership to the school boards of the state in the 1930's. Obviously, a meeting attended by only 350 of over 21,000 school board members was not a very effective way in which to make a great impact. Therefore, the department took the meetings out into the state where the school board members were.

Conferences for school board members and superintendents were organized and promoted in half the counties of the state during the biennium ending in 1940, and they were planned for the other half in the next biennium. The importance of school budgeting was stressed in these conferences, and principles of state support and equalization of tax burdens were discussed.

The Iowa Association of School Boards became an established and permanent organization under the leadership of Don Foster, its first full-time executive director. Generally, it has enjoyed a cordial and cooperative relationship with the Department of Public Instruction because of the efforts of the executive directors and the state superintendents. Regional meetings were cosponsored, and the department furnished considerable talent for the annual meetings.

No major points of disagreement have developed between the two organizations. The one area in which some difference in policy can be found has been in that of the method by which the state should participate in the financing of the public schools. In its representative assembly meeting of November 1962, the IASB voted to work for a minimum of 25 percent of total school costs to be paid directly to school districts from state funds. It also recommended that an equalization feature be incorporated into any plan for the distribution of state moneys.

However, the January 1963 issue of the *Iowa School Board Bulletin* stated that the IASB had not endorsed any one plan for increased state aid to schools, and it was thus left free to evaluate the different proposals made. The minimum foundation plan recommended by a legislative study committee and by the State Department of Public Instruction was described.

Also discussed in this issue was the Nelson Plan for state aid, which provided for payment of state funds on a per-pupil basis with no equalization factor. This plan also included a "bonus," which provided for the payment of more state aid for any reduction in per-pupil expenditures. In addition, those districts that had a smaller increase of expenditures were to receive "bonus" aid. Thus the wealthy district, which had been spending at a high rate, could reduce expenditures or hold the increase to a minimum and receive more state aid. This was the opposite of an equalization factor.

The views of the Iowa Association of School Boards and the Department of Public Instruction differed somewhat 2 years later when a proportionate sharing plan was recommended by the state education agency.

In 1963, when the state board and the state superintendent were under fire in the Legislature because of school district reorganization, the IASB came out against making the position of state superintendent elective, considering such a move as a backward step.

Relations with Agencies of State Government

Although the Department of Public Instruction has maintained amicable relationships with many agencies of state government, the best of these, as would be expected, have been with those departments or boards interested in some phase of the educational program.

There has been a notable relationship with the State Department of Health dating back to at least 1936, when a course outline for health and physical education in the elementary school was prepared. All the agencies of the state having to do with health and physical education cooperated in the production and distribution of the outline under the leadership of the Iowa Physical Education Association. The bulletin produced was printed by the State Department of Health because the Department of Public Instruction did not have the necessary funds. Over the years the two agencies have developed and distributed similar materials.

There has been a close working relationship with the Department of Public Safety. In 1938, the motor vehicle division published and distributed safety education bulletins at the request and with the cooperation of the state department. Safe school bus transportation has been a shared goal. The state highway safety patrol has cooperated since 1937 in a program of school bus inspection and has been helpful in instructing school bus drivers.

Relations with some agencies of state government have not always been smooth. The physical needs of the department must be approved and allocated by the State Executive Council, which at times has been slow to recognize these needs.

The Governors of Iowa have on the whole supported the department, but in at least one instance the friction that existed erupted in the press. Miss Parker had differences with Governor Robert Blue and other department heads over salaries paid to members of her staff in 1948. The conflict began when the executive council attempted to establish a uniform salary schedule for statehouse employees in the summer of 1948.

Superintendent Parker declared that she could not obtain and hold competent staff members if she adhered to the schedule. She, therefore, ignored the schedule and raised the salaries of her staff. The state budget and financial control law provided that the Governor must allocate department appropriations each quarter. In an attempt to enforce the state salary schedule, Governor Blue did not make the allocation. This resulted in the department's staff not getting their checks for a short time. Miss Parker eventually was successful in this confrontation.

Difficulties also developed in 1963 when the State Executive Council approved the transfer of the department's data-processing equipment to the state comptroller's office. The department had been a pioneer in Iowa state government in the use of such equipment. As much of the expenditure for the machines was made from National Defense Education Act, Title X, funds, the department did not look with favor on the move. Moreover, the department has been protected from political patronage pressures since 1953 when Chapter 257, which created the State Board of Public Instruction, was enacted. It has been necessary to remind others of this fact from time to time, as when the data-processing machines of the department temporarily came under the control of the state comptroller's office.

Relations with the Federal Government

Iowa has been hesitant about accepting federal participation in school affairs. A wary Legislature delayed participation in the National School Lunch Program. Once enabling legislation was enacted, it was done in a way that indicated considerable skepticism about continuance of the program by the federal government.

For a number of years, the State Board of Public Instruction took a neutral attitude about federal aid. While it authorized participation in such programs as the National Defense Education Act, it did not come out for or against the program. As to further participation, the department staff was informed that the state board's position was one of neutrality.

The board discussed the pros and cons of federal aid at some length during its February 1960 meeting. It was the consensus of the members that while they did not think federal participation in education was necessarily needed in Iowa, it would probably be authorized by Congress eventually. The board was of the opinion that if this did occur, such funds should take the form of grants to the several states to be administered by the state departments of education.

Iowa has steadfastly maintained the position that there should be a minimum of federal control. It also has taken the position that the state rather than the federal government should supervise the operation of the federal programs. It has insisted that the federal government deal with the state education agency, which in turn would deal with local school districts.

While the department has maintained this position, it also has attempted to meet faithfully the intent of federal legislation. Thus, while some states have allocated federal funds on a per-pupil basis, Iowa has required local school districts to plan and show how the project submitted met the intent of the law and would specifically improve instruction in the particular area concerned.

Under the National Defense Education Act, local school districts have been required to submit projects indicating considerable planning. This has resulted in a certain amount of complaint from local school administrators who have found at national and regional meetings that some other states required little or no such planning.

Thus the department's position has been one of state operation and control within the guidelines and intent of the federal legislation.

FOOTNOTES

1. Clarence Ray Aurner, *History of Education in Iowa,* I (6 vols.; Iowa City: State Historical Society, 1914), 10.
2. *Ibid.,* II, 9.
3. Federal Writers Project for Iowa, *Iowa: A Guide to the Hawkeye State* (New York: Hastings House, 1949), p. 53.
4. Aurner, *op. cit.,* II, 105.
5. *Ibid.,* II, 137.
6. George S. May, "Iowa's Consolidated Schools," *The Palimpset,* XXXVII, No. 1 (January 1956), 8.
7. *Ibid.,* p. 5.
8. Superintendent of Public Instruction, *School Report, 1902-1903,* p. xiv.
9. Iowa, *Laws* (1900), ch. 94.
10. J. F. Abel, *Consolidation of Schools and Transportation of Pupils,* Bulletin No. 41 (Washington, D.C.: Department of Interior, Bureau of Education, 1923), p. 1.
11. May, *op. cit.,* p. 30.
12. *Ibid.,* p. 9.
13. Iowa Teachers Association, *Proceedings of the Sixty-Fourth Annual Session of the Iowa State Teachers Association* (Des Moines: The Association, 1918), pp. 60-61.
14. Irving H. Hart, *Milestones* (Des Moines: Iowa Education Association, 1954), p. 167.
15. Iowa, *Laws* (1919), ch. 364.
16. Hart, *op. cit.,* p. 95.
17. May E. Francis, "Iowa's Three Candidates for State Superintendent of Public Instruction," *Midland Schools,* XXXVI, No. 8 (April 1922), 281-82.
18. See Table 1, Appendix C, for the historical development of aid programs in Iowa.
19. William F. Russell, Thomas C. Holy, and Raleigh W. Stone, *The Financing of Education in Iowa,* a report reviewed and presented under the auspices of the American Council on Education, Washington, D.C., Publication V8 (New York: The Macmillan Co., 1925), p. vii.
20. Iowa, *Laws* (1941), ch. 152.
21. John Purcell Street, "Iowa Department of Public Instruction: Its Origin and Development," *Annals of Iowa,* XXX, No. 6 (October 1950), 427.
22. Institute of Government Research of the Brookings Institution, *Survey of Administration in Iowa* (Des Moines: State of Iowa, 1933), pp. 166-67.
23. Superintendent of Public Instruction, *School Report, 1940-1942,* p. 15.
24. Iowa Governmental Reorganization Commission, *Report of the Governmental Reorganization Commission* (Des Moines: State of Iowa, 1950), p. 54.
25. Griffenhagen and Associates, *Report on a Management Improvement Study of the Office of the Superintendent of Public Instruction* (Des Moines: Iowa Budget and Financial Control Committee, June 1952), p. 4.
26. Letter from J. C. Wright, professor of education, Northeast Missouri State Teachers College, Kirksville, September 29, 1966.
27. Department of Public Instruction, *Education Beyond High School Age: The Community College* (Des Moines: State of Iowa, 1962), p. 16.
28. Lewis Consolidated School District of Cass County *v.* Paul F. Johnston, 1964, 127 NW 2d 118, Iowa, 236.
29. Minutes of the State Board of Public Instruction, meeting of April 16, 1964.
30. Iowa Teachers Association, "The State Superintendent and Teachers Organization," *Midland Schools,* XL, No. 1 (September 1925), 9.
31. Francis, *op. cit.,* pp. 281-82.
32. *Des Moines Tribune,* June 3, 1950, p. 1.
33. Charles F. Martin, "A Supplement to Our 1951 Legislative Goals," *Midland Schools,* LXV, No. 3 (November 1950), 21.

BIBLIOGRAPHY

Public Documents

Iowa. *Code* (1897).

—— *Constitution* (1857).

—— Department of Public Instruction. *School Laws of Iowa,* 1960. Des Moines: The Department, 1960.

—— *Law Reports.* "Durant Community School District," CCLII (1961), 237-48.

—— *Law Reports.* "Lewis Consolidated School District of Cass County *v.* Paul F. Johnston," CCLVI (1964), 236.

—— *Law Reports.* "Silver Lake Consolidated School District *v.* Jessie M. Parker," CCXXXVIII (1947), 984-97.

—— *Journal of the House* (1913, 1961).

-- *Journal of the Senate* (1913, 1917).

-- *Laws* (1846-1965).

McClain, Emlin. *McClain's Annotated Code and Statutes of the State of Iowa.* Chicago: Callaghan and Co., 1888.

Books and Pamphlets

Aurner, Clarence Ray. *History of Education in Iowa.* 6 vols. Iowa City: State Historical Society, 1914.

Church, H. V. *Illinois, History-Geography-Government.* Boston: D. C. Heath and Company, 1925.

Cubberley, Ellwood P. *The History of Education.* Boston: Houghton Mifflin Co., 1920.

-- *School Funds and Their Apportionment.* New York: Bureau of Publications, Teachers College, Columbia University, 1905.

Cubberley, Ellwood P., and Elliott, Edward G. *State and County School Administration.* New York: The Macmillan Co., 1915.

Federal Writers Project for Iowa. *Iowa: A Guide to the Hawkeye State.* New York: Hastings House, 1949.

Hart, Irving H. *Milestones.* Des Moines: Iowa Education Association, 1954.

Hawthorn, Horace B. *The Persistent Case of the Castana Community School District.* Sioux City, Iowa: Verstegen Press, 1966.

Knezevich, Stephen J. *Administration of Public Education.* New York: Harper Brothers, 1962.

McConnell, Robert Ervie. *A History of the Development of the Department of Public Instruction in Iowa.* University of Iowa Studies in Education. Iowa City: University of Iowa, October 1, 1930.

Mort, Paul R. *The Measurement of Educational Need.* New York: Bureau of Publications, Teachers College, Columbia University, 1925.

Peterson, E. T., *et al. Teacher Supply and Demand in Iowa.* University of Iowa Studies in Education, VII, No. 2. Iowa City: University of Iowa, 1932.

Smith, Richard N. *School Business. A Manual for School Officials.* Des Moines: Department of Public Instruction, 1965.

Stone, H. E. *Consolidated Schools in Iowa.* Des Moines: Department of Public Instruction, 1926.

Van Dyke, L. A., *et al. Issues Concerning the Secondary School Curriculum.* Des Moines: Department of Public Instruction, 1945.

Venn, Grant. *Man, Education and Work.* Washington, D.C.: American Council on Education, 1964.

Articles and Periodicals

"Charles F. Martin Is the Logical Candidate." *The Maquoketa Community News* (Maquoketa, Iowa), May 19, 1938.

Clayton, John, and Finks, Lloyd. "Education Is Big Business." *The Iowan*, I, No. 6 (August-September 1953), 7-9.

Department of Public Instruction. *Education Bulletin.* Published monthly September through May, except 1963-1964 and 1964-1965. First issue published February 1, 1930. Published until 1932 as the *News Bulletin.*

Department of Public Instruction. *Iowa Educational Directory.* Des Moines: The Department, 1890-1966.

Des Moines Tribune, June 3, 1950, p. 1.

Francis, May E. "Iowa's Three Candidates for State Superintendent of Public Instruction." *Midland Schools*, XXXVI, No. 8 (April 1922), 281-82.

Hart, Irving H. "The Governors of Iowa as Educational Leaders." *Iowa Journal of History*, III (July 1956), 233-62.

Hogan, Robert. "Department of Education Shakeup Seen." *Ledger* (Fairfield, Iowa), September 11, 1952.

Iowa Teachers Association. "The State Superintendent and Teachers Organization." *Midland Schools*, XL, No. 1 (September 1925), 9.

Martin, Charles F. "A Supplement to Our 1951 Legislative Goals." *Midland Schools,* LXV, No. 3 (November 1950), 21.

May, George S. "Iowa's Consolidated Schools." *The Palimpset* (Iowa City), XXXVII, No. 1 (January 1956), 8.

Nye, Frank. "Personalities Beclouded School Bill Fight." *Gazette* (Cedar Rapids, Iowa), April 1, 1945.

"Representative Assembly Sets Legislative Goals." *The Iowa School Board Bulletin*, XIII, No. 4 (December 1962), 2.

"School Reorganization Discussed." *Independent* (Hawarden, Iowa), February 2, 1950.

Stephens, Richard L. "What Is the Role of the ISEA?" *Wallaces Farmer* (April 15, 1961), 94-95.

Street, John Purcell. "Iowa Department of Public Instruction: Its Origin and Development." *Annals of Iowa*, XXX, No. 6 (October 1950), 427.

Waterloo Courier (Waterloo, Iowa). Editorial, "Too Many Bosses at Statehouse," October 3, 1948.

Waterloo Courier, April 9, 1963.

Reports

Abel, J. F. *Consolidation of Schools and Transportation of Pupils.* U.S. Department of the Interior, Bureau of Education Bulletin No. 41. Washington, D.C.: Government Printing Office, 1923.

Area District IV-A for the Improvement of Education in Iowa Schools. *Northwest Iowa Telewriter Project.* Des Moines: State of Iowa, 1965.

Beach, Fred F. *The Functions of State Departments of Education*. Misc. No. 12. Washington, D.C.: Federal Security Agency, Office of Education, 1950.

Beach, Fred F., and Gibbs, Andrew H. *The Personnel of State Departments of Education*. Misc. No. 16. Washington, D.C.: Federal Security Agency, Office of Education, 1952.

Beach, Fred F., and Hutchins, Clayton D. *The Financing of State Departments of Education*. Misc. No. 15. Washington, D.C.: Federal Security Agency, Office of Education, 1951.

Committee of Educational Finance. *The Financial Equalization of Educational Opportunity in Iowa*. Des Moines: Department of Public Instruction, October 1950.

Department of Public Instruction. *Data on Iowa Schools*. Des Moines: The Department, March 1966.

—— *Education Beyond High School Age: The Community College*. Des Moines: The Department, 1962.

Gibson, Raymond C. *The Junior Colleges of Iowa*. Study No. 4 of *Resources and Needs for Higher Education in Iowa*. 4 studies. Des Moines: Iowa Legislative Research Bureau, 1961.

Griffenhagen and Associates. *Report on a Management Improvement Study of the Office of the Superintendent of Public Instruction*. Des Moines: Iowa Budget and Financial Control Committee, June 1952.

Institute of Government Research of the Brookings Institution. *Survey of Administration in Iowa*. Des Moines: State of Iowa, 1933.

Iowa Association of School Administrators. *Fifth Annual Report*. A Report prepared by the Executive Board, October 20, 1966. Des Moines: The Association, 1966.

Iowa Governmental Reorganization Commission. *Report of the Governmental Reorganization Commission*. Des Moines: The Commission, 1950.

Iowa Research Committee on the Intermediate Unit. *Effective Intermediate Units in Iowa*. Des Moines: Department of Public Instruction, April 1960.

Iowa Research Committee on School Finance. *Minimum Foundation Program for Public School Education*. Des Moines: Department of Public Instruction, 1952.

Iowa Teachers Association. *Proceedings of the Fifty-Eighth Annual Session of the Iowa State Teachers Association*. Des Moines: The Association, 1912.

—— *Proceedings of the Fifty-Seventh Annual Session of the Iowa State Teachers Association*. Des Moines: The Association, 1911.

—— *Proceedings of the Sixty-Fourth Annual Session of the Iowa State Teachers Association*. Des Moines: The Association, 1918.

Monahan, A. C. *Consolidation of Rural Schools and Transportation of Pupils at Public Expense*. Bulletin No. 30, U.S. Bureau of Education. Washington, D.C.: Government Printing Office, 1914.

Munse, Albert R., and McLoone, Eugene P. *Public School Finance Programs of the United States, 1957-1958*. Washington, D.C.: U.S. Department of Health, Education, and Welfare, Office of Education, 1960.

Perry, Hartsel M. *Use of State Funds To Improve Public Education in Iowa*. Publication 161A-309AF. Des Moines: Department of Public Instruction, February 1961.

Report of the Committee on Reduction of Governmental Expenditures. Des Moines: State of Iowa, 1932.

Report of the Iowa School Code Commission. Des Moines: The Department of Public Instruction, November 1, 1942.

Report of the Joint Legislative Committee on Taxation. Des Moines: State of Iowa, 1930.

Report of the Legislative Advisory Committee on the Study of State Aid to Schools. Des Moines: Legislative Research Bureau, January 1963.

Russell, William F.; Holy, Thomas C.; and Stone, Raleigh W. *The Financing of Education in Iowa*. A report reviewed and presented under the auspices of the American Council on Education. Publication V8. New York: The Macmillan Co., 1925.

Samuelson, Agnes, and Williams, R. C. *Public School Finance in Iowa*. Research Bulletin No. 6. Des Moines: State of Iowa, 1930.

Strayer, George D., and Haig, Robert M. *The Financing of Education in the State of New York*. Report of the Educational Finance Inquiry Commission. New York: The Macmillan Co., 1923.

Superintendents of Public Instruction. *Iowa School Reports*. Des Moines: Department of Public Instruction, 1900-65.

Unpublished Material

Cook, Herbert Clare. "The Administrative Functions of the Department of Public Instruction in Iowa." Unpublished Ph.D. dissertation, University of Iowa, Iowa City, 1926.

Cowan, E. E. "History of School Lunch and Its Development in Iowa." Unpublished paper at the Department of Public Instruction, Des Moines, 1949.

Department of Public Instruction. "Adaptation of Project Proposal to Educational Application." Draft No. 2. The Department, Des Moines, August 22, 1966. (Multilithed.)

—— "Departmental Guidelines for Professional Staff Members." Unpublished duplicated staff material, Des Moines, August 30-31, 1965.

—— "Proportionate Sharing of Public School Support." Publication 1264A-1196AF. The Department, Des Moines, December 1964.

—— "State Aid Funds for Improvement of Public Education in Iowa." The Department, Des Moines, August 1960. (Multilithed.)

—— "State Aid Funds for Improvement of Public Education In Iowa." Publication 1062A-698AF. The Department, Des Moines, October 9, 1962. (Multilithed.)

—— "State Distributive Funds for Improvement of Public Education." Publication 758A-1686AF. The Department, Des Moines, August 1958. (Mimeographed.)

Governmental Reorganization Commission. "Departmental Reports, 1950." Iowa State Law Library, Des Moines. (Typewritten.)

Ingle, Marvin. "Reorganization of Iowa School Districts 1954-1955 to 1959-1960." Department of Public Instruction, Des Moines, March 1960. (Multilithed.)

Iowa Teachers Association. "Vocational Education and Vocational Guidance." Department of Public Instruction, Des Moines, November 1914.

Johnston, Paul F. "Report to State Board of Public Instruction: Proposed Program." Publication 1610-410. Department of Public Instruction, Des Moines, January 15, 1961. (Multilithed.)

Knezevich, Stephen J. "Past and Present Problems in Financing Iowa Schools." Special Commission Research Report No. 1. Iowa Center for Research in School Administration, Iowa City, November 1, 1960. (Mimeographed.)

Lancelot, W. H. "Taxable Property per Child in Farm and Non-Farm Communities in Iowa." Iowa State College Agricultural Experiment Station, Ames, May 1943.

Lindquist, E. F. "The Iowa Educational Information Center: A Summary." State University of Iowa, Iowa City, December 18, 1963. (Mimeographed.)

Parker, Jessie M., and Bangs, C. W. "Iowa-National School Lunch Program Outline: State Plan of Operation, 1948-1949." Unpublished report in the files of the Department of Public Instruction, Des Moines, n.d.

Savill, W. K. "Consolidation as Viewed by the Patrons of the Orient, Iowa School District." Unpublished master's field report, Drake University, Des Moines, 1943.

Tope, D. E. "A Proposed Program for the Fiscal Equalization of Educational Opportunity in Iowa." Unpublished Ph.D. dissertation, University of Iowa, Iowa City, 1934.

Truesdell, Wayne P. "A History of School Organization and Superintendence in Iowa." Unpublished Ph.D. dissertation, University of Iowa, Iowa City, 1965.

Wallace, V. C. "A Financial Appraisal of the Present School District Organization in Iowa." Unpublished Ph.D. dissertation, University of Iowa, Iowa City, 1933.

Williams, R. C. "A Check List of Financial Economies for a Local School District." Research Bulletin No. 9. Department of Public Instruction, Des Moines, April 1932. (Mimeographed.)

—— "Distribution of State School Funds in Iowa." Research Bulletin No. 2. Department of Public Instruction, Des Moines, July 1930. (Mimeographed.)

—— "Distribution of State Funds to School Districts in 1934." Research Bulletin No. 17. Department of Public Instruction, Des Moines, December 1934. (Mimeographed.)

—— "Distribution of State Funds to School Districts in 1936." Research Bulletin No. 19. Department of Public Instruction, Des Moines, September 15, 1936. (Mimeographed.)

—— "Public School Finance in Iowa—Preliminary Report." Research Bulletin No. 6. Department of Public Instruction, Des Moines, 1930. (Mimeographed.)

—— "Salaries in the Public Schools of Iowa." Research Bulletin No. 8. Department of Public Instruction, Des Moines, 1952. (Mimeographed.)

—— "State Responsibility for the Support of Public Schools." Research Bulletin No. 20. Department of Public Instruction, Des Moines, September 1936. (Mimeographed.)

—— "Taxes in Consolidated School Districts." Research Bulletin No. 7. Department of Public Instruction, Des Moines, November 1931. (Mimeographed.)

—— "Type of School District as a Factor in High School Attendance in Iowa." Research Bulletin No. 23. Department of Public Instruction, Des Moines, October 1938. (Mimeographed.)

—— "Uniform Financial Accounting for Iowa School Districts." Research Bulletin No. 17. Department of Public Instruction, Des Moines, June 1934. (Mimeographed.)

—— "Unit Levies and Costs, 1930-1932." Research Bulletin No. 11. Department of Public Instruction, Des Moines, March 1933. (Mimeographed.)

Other Sources

"An Organizational Pattern for the Department of Public Instruction." Unpublished report in the files of the Department of Public Instruction, Des Moines, no date. (Duplicated.)

Benshoof, Howard L., consultant, Planning and Development, Department of Public Instruction. Memorandum on December 15, 1966.

Coordinating Committee for the Improvement of Education in Iowa. Minutes of the meeting of October 16, 1963. 10630-9401RP, in the files of the Department of Public Instruction.

Cowan, Elmer, chief, School Lunch Section, Department of Public Instruction, Des Moines. Personal interview on December 6, 1966.

Department of Public Instruction. "Outline of a State Plan for Improvement of Education in Iowa." The Department, Des Moines, April 1963. (Multilithed.)

—— Payroll records for 1965, in the Department, Des Moines.

—— "Thirteen Midwestern States Begin Educational Information Project." Midwestern States Educational Information Project, No. 1. The Midwestern States Educational Information Project Center, Des Moines, September 1966.

Department of Public Instruction and College of Education, University of Iowa. "Iowa Educational Information Center." This is located at the Center in Iowa City, n.d.

Experiences of the writer, Richard N. Smith, as a teacher at Lytton, Iowa, 1949-54; as superintendent of schools at Webb, Iowa, 1955-59; and as a staff member of the Iowa Department of Public Instruction, 1959-69.

Foster, Don, former executive secretary, Iowa Association of School Boards, Des Moines. Personal interview on May 11, 1967.

Iowa CardPac System of Educational Accounting. "Student Questionnaire." Educational Information Center, Iowa City, n.d.

Johnston, Paul F. Letter to Charles F. Martin, January 29, 1957.

Letters from former staff members of the State Department of Public Instruction.

Letters from superintendents with many years experience in Iowa schools: Carl T. Feelhaver, Fort Dodge, Iowa, April 3, 1967; Joe L. Gettys, Oskaloosa, Iowa, April 10, 1967; Fannie G. Howell, Floyd County, Iowa, April 4, 1967; Russel Mourer, Council Bluffs, Iowa, April 16, 1967; W. W. Molsberry, Keokuk County, Iowa, April 8, 1967; M. M. Rogers, Sumner, Iowa, April 11, 1967; Charles S. Whitney, Hancock County, Iowa, April 6, 1967.

Nordstrom, John H. "A Plan for Distributing State Aid to Schools." Iowa Association of School Boards, Des Moines. (Mimeographed.)

Olney, Norris G., Jr. "Dear Fellow Citizen." Circular letter dated March 27, 1964. (Mimeographed.)

Osborn, Wayland W., consultant, Department of Public Instruction; former executive secretary, Iowa Association of School Boards. Personal interview in Des Moines on October 1, 1966, and on May 3, 1967.

Parker, Jessie M. Notes found in the effects of Jessie M. Parker, n.d.

—— "Objectives of S. F. 291." Speech given before a joint meeting of the Iowa State Teachers Association and Department of Public Instruction, no date. (Typewritten.)

—— Radio speech given over Station KSO, Des Moines, on October 25, 1938. (Typewritten.)

—— Radio speech given over Station WOI, Ames, on September 2, 1939. (Typewritten.)

—— "Remarks made by Jessie M. Parker, Superintendent of Public Instruction, to House Committee on Schools and Textbooks." Des Moines, February 1942. (Mimeographed.)

—— "Reorganization of School Districts and Preservation of Local Control as Provided in the New School Code." Radio speech on March 7, 1943. (Typewritten.)

Shultz, John G., former reorganization consultant, Department of Public Instruction. Personal interview in Des Moines on April 30, 1967.

State Board of Public Instruction. Minutes, 1955-65. Department of Public Instruction, Des Moines. (Multilithed.)

Wright, J. C. "How Do Iowa's Schools Rate?" Reprint of exclusive interview published in the *Cedar Rapids Gazette,* February 14, 1960. Publication 3600-176, Department of Public Instruction, Des Moines, March 1960. (Multilithed.)

—— Letter from J. C. Wright, professor of education, Northeast Missouri State Teachers College, Kirksville, September 29, 1966.

Appendix A

IOWA CHIEF STATE SCHOOL OFFICERS

1841-42*	William Reynolds	1888-92	Henry Sabin
1847	James Harlan	1892-94	J. B. Knoepfler
1848-54	Thomas H. Benton	1894-98	Henry Sabin
1854-57	James D. Eads	1898-1904	Richard C. Barrett
1857	Joseph C. Stone	1904-11	John F. Riggs
1857-58*	M. L. Fisher	1911-19	Albert M. Deyoe
1864-67	Oran Faville	1919-23	P. E. McClenahan
1867-69	D. Franklin Wells	1923-27	May E. Francis
1869-72	A. S. Kissell	1927-39	Agnes Samuelson
1872-76	Alonzo Abernethy	1939-55	Jessie M. Parker
1876-82	C. W. von Coelln	1955-61	J. C. Wright
1882-88	J. W. Akers	1961-	Paul F. Johnston

*In 1842, the office of superintendent was abolished. In 1858, it was again abolished and its duties performed by the secretary of the State Board of Education, Thomas H. Benton.

Appendix B

Chart I.--IOWA DEPARTMENT OF PUBLIC INSTRUCTION, 1928

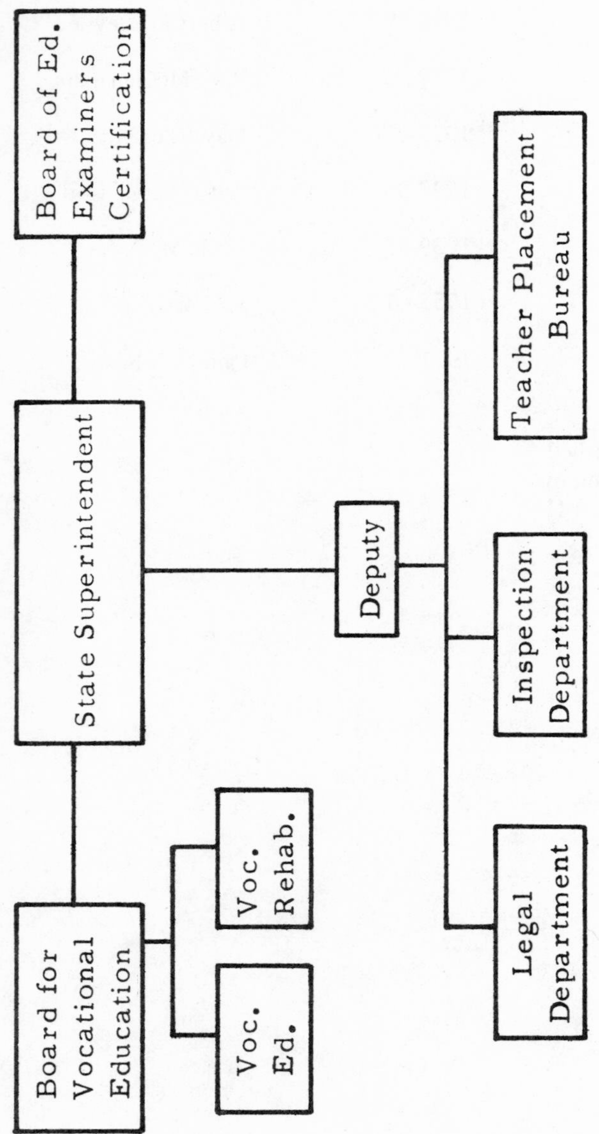

Source: Iowa School Report, 1926-1928.

Appendix B

Chart II.--IOWA DEPARTMENT OF PUBLIC INSTRUCTION, 1940

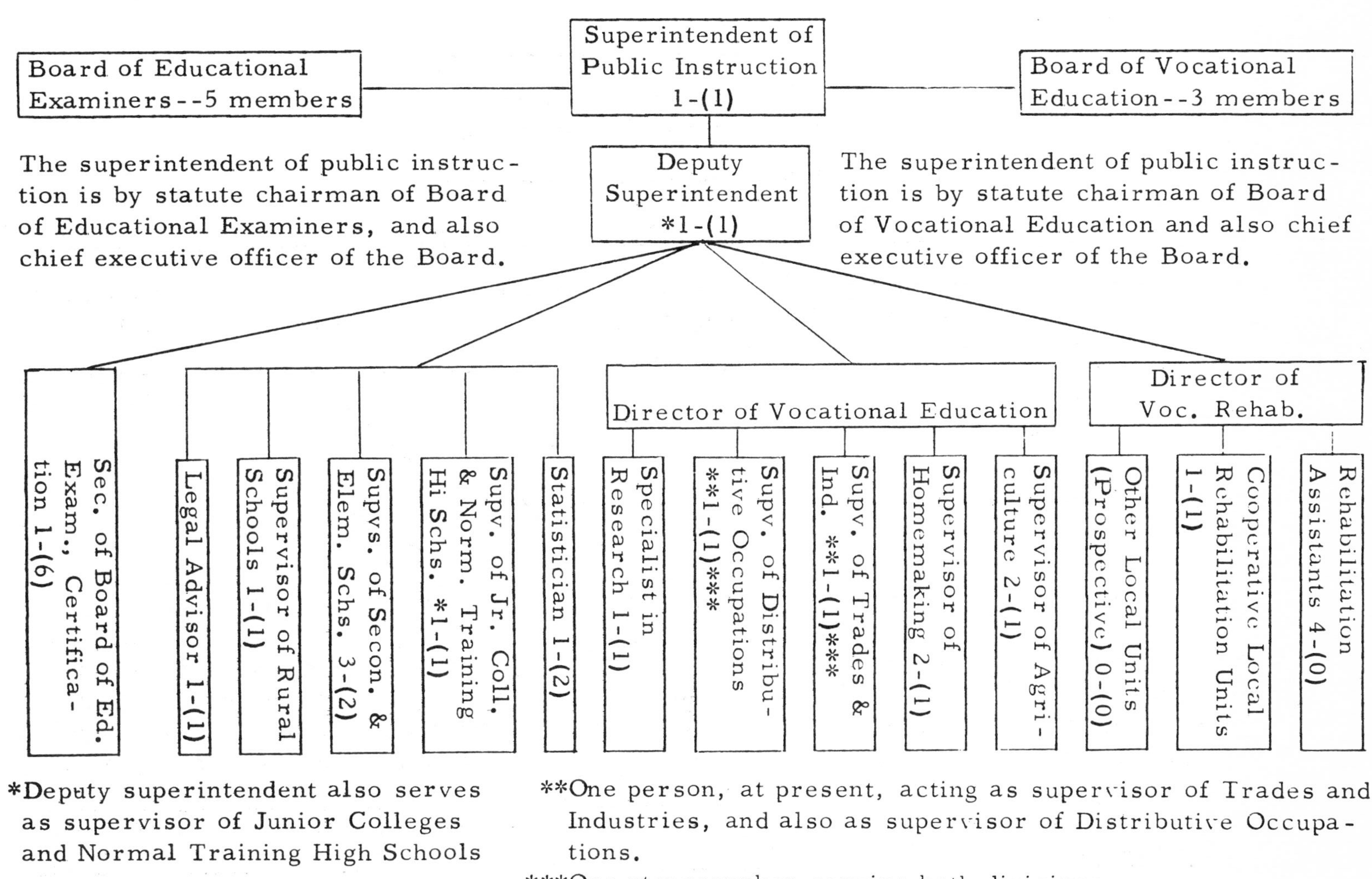

*Deputy superintendent also serves as supervisor of Junior Colleges and Normal Training High Schools

**One person, at present, acting as supervisor of Trades and Industries, and also as supervisor of Distributive Occupations.

***One stenographer serving both divisions

Source: Iowa School Report, 1938-1940, p. 10.

Appendix B

Chart III.--IOWA DEPARTMENT OF PUBLIC INSTRUCTION, 1948

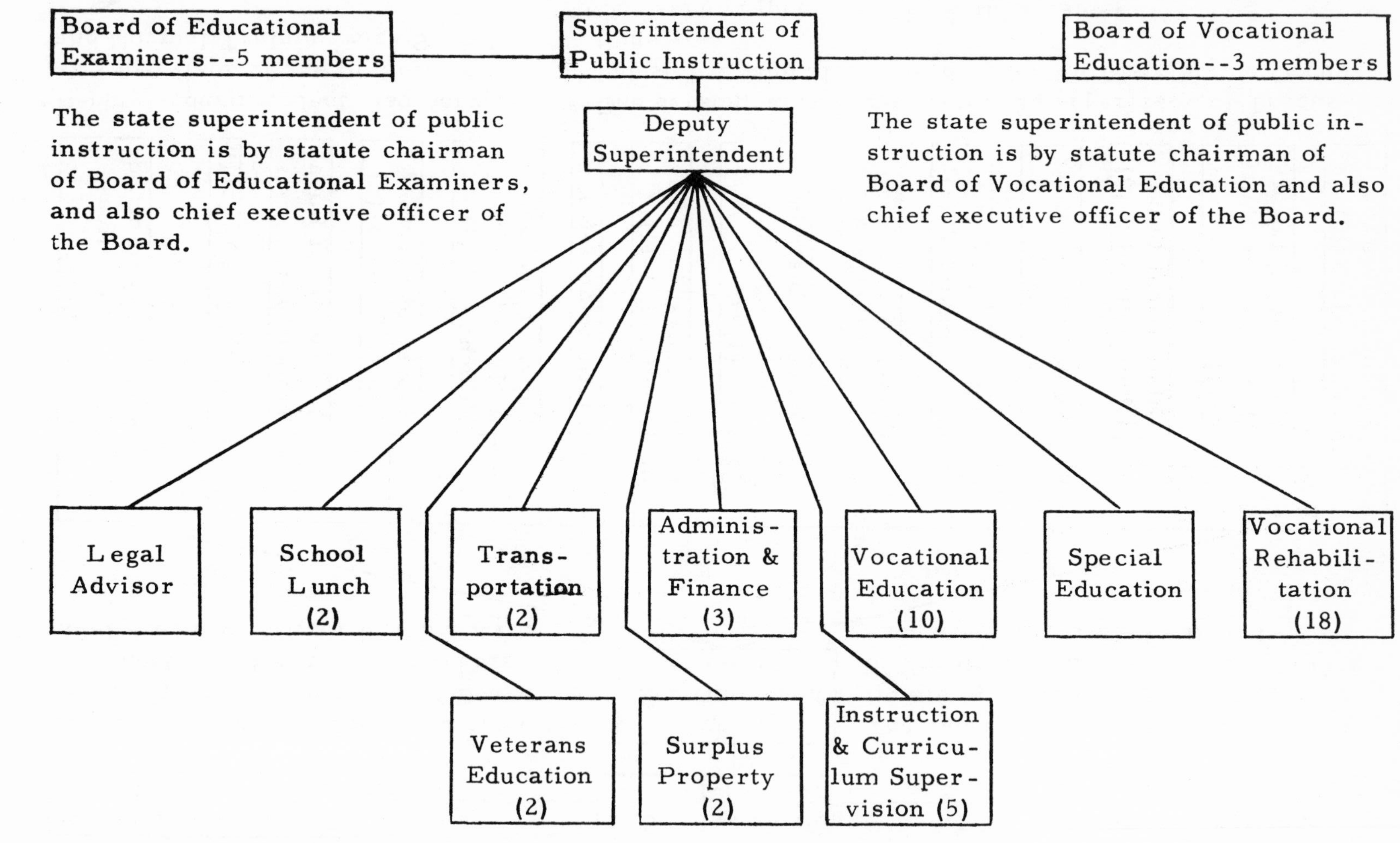

Source: Iowa School Report, 1948, pp. 11-12.
Note: Number in () indicates the number of professional staff members greater than one.

Appendix B

Chart IV.--IOWA DEPARTMENT OF PUBLIC INSTRUCTION, 1952

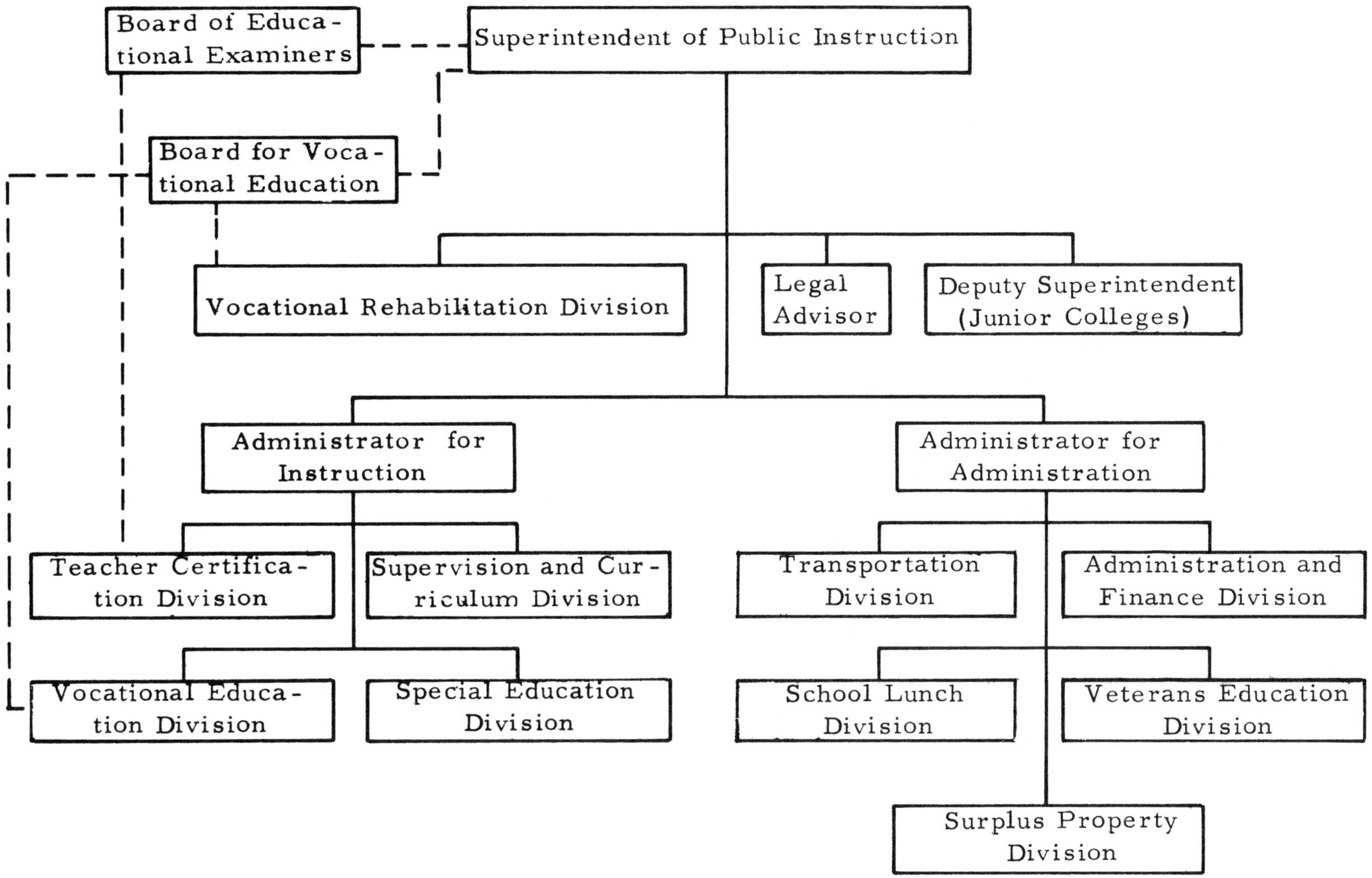

Source: <u>Iowa Educational Directory</u>, 1954-1955.

Appendix B

Chart V.--IOWA DEPARTMENT OF PUBLIC INSTRUCTION, 1955

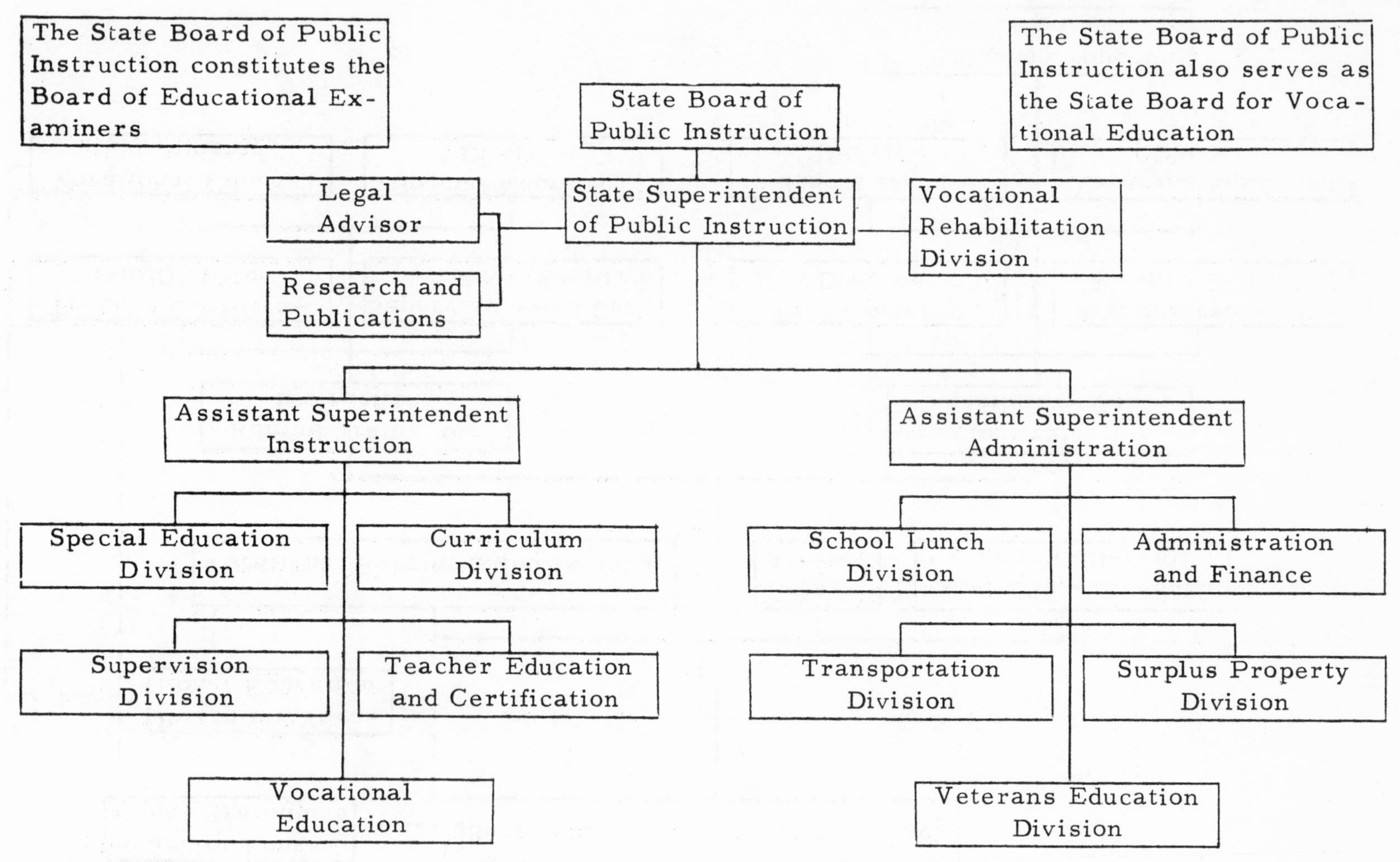

Source: Iowa Educational Directory, 1955-1956

Appendix B

Chart VI.--IOWA DEPARTMENT OF PUBLIC INSTRUCTION, 1965

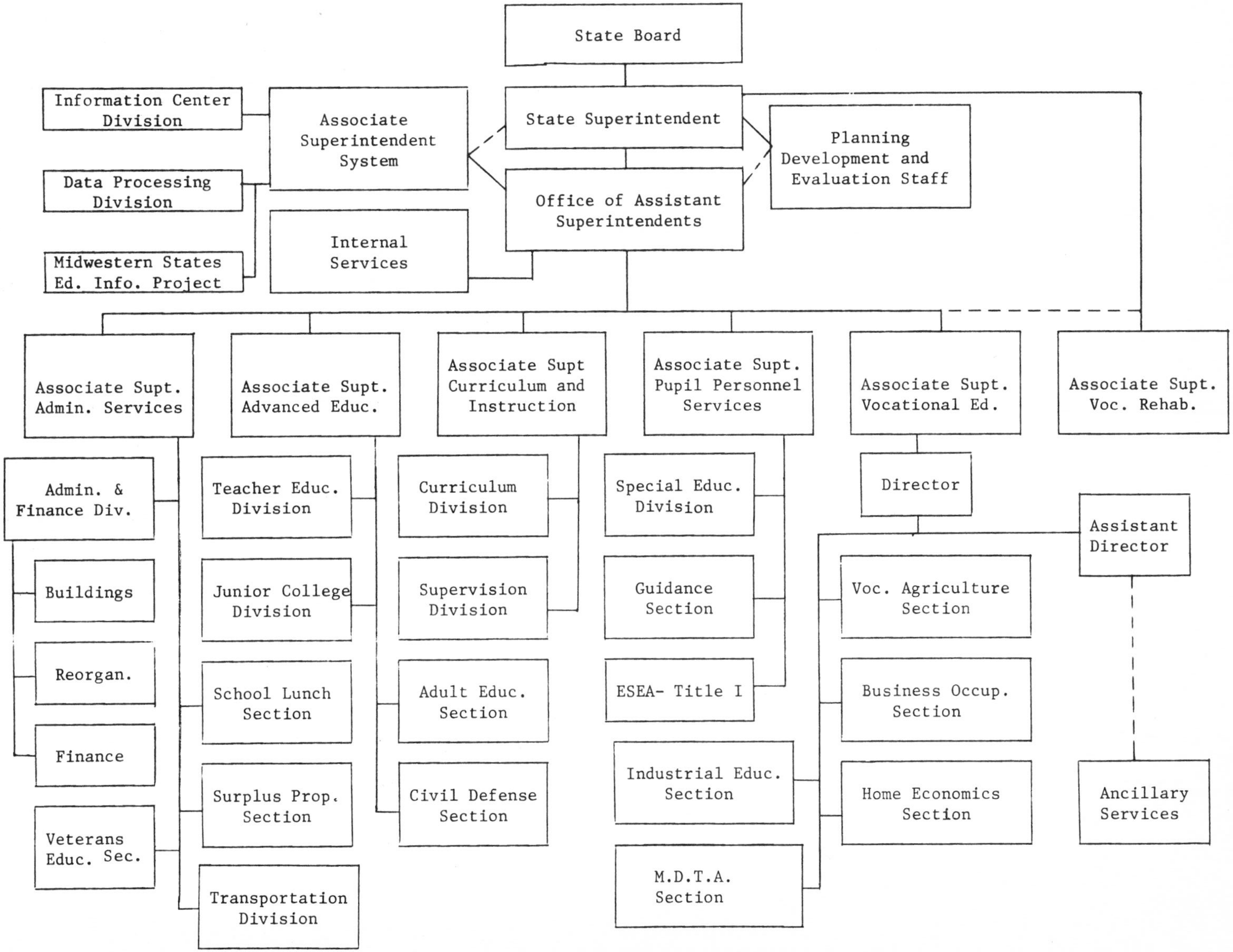

State Board

State Superintendent

Office of Assistant Superintendents

Planning Development and Evaluation Staff

Associate Superintendent System

Information Center Division

Data Processing Division

Midwestern States Ed. Info. Project

Internal Services

Associate Supt. Admin. Services

Admin. & Finance Div.

Buildings

Reorgan.

Finance

Veterans Educ. Sec.

Associate Supt. Advanced Educ.

Teacher Educ. Division

Junior College Division

School Lunch Section

Surplus Prop. Section

Transportation Division

Associate Supt Curriculum and Instruction

Curriculum Division

Supervision Division

Adult Educ. Section

Civil Defense Section

Associate Supt. Pupil Personnel Services

Special Educ. Division

Guidance Section

ESEA- Title I

Associate Supt. Vocational Ed.

Director

Assistant Director

Ancillary Services

Voc. Agriculture Section

Business Occup. Section

Home Economics Section

Industrial Educ. Section

M.D.T.A. Section

Associate Supt. Voc. Rehab.

Source: Mimeographed Material of the Department of Public Instruction.

Appendix C

Table 1.—STATE FUNDS APPROPRIATED BY THE IOWA LEGISLATURE FOR DISTRIBUTION EACH YEAR OF THE BIENNIUM BY THE DEPARTMENT OF PUBLIC INSTRUCTION, 1900-65

Year	Normal Courses	Con-solidated Districts	Standard Schools	Mining Camp	Emerg. Mining Camp	Normal Inst.	Handi-capped Children	Trans-portation	Supple-mental	General Aid	Vocational Education	Driver Education	Voc. Ed. Capital Outlay	Emergency Aid
1911	$25,000	$	$ . . .	$ . . .	$ . . .	$ . . .	$ . . .	$ . . .	$ . . .	$ . . .	$ . . .	$ . . .	$ . . .	$ . . .
1913	100,000	30,000	. . .	. . .	. . .	. . .	. . .	. . .	. . .	. . .	. . .	. . .	. . .	. . .
1915	125,000	100,000	. . .	. . .	. . .	. . .	. . .	. . .	. . .	. . .	. . .	. . .	. . .	. . .
1917	125,000	100,000	. . .	. . .	. . .	. . .	. . .	. . .	. . .	. . .	. . .	. . .	. . .	. . .
1919	150,000	150,000	100,000	25,000	. . .	. . .	. . .	. . .	. . .	. . .	. . .	. . .	. . .	. . .
1921	150,000	150,000	100,000	50,000	. . .	. . .	. . .	. . .	. . .	. . .	. . .	. . .	. . .	. . .
1923	150,000	150,000	100,000	50,000	. . .	. . .	. . .	. . .	. . .	. . .	. . .	. . .	. . .	. . .
1924	150,000	200,000	100,000	50,000	. . .	. . .	. . .	. . .	. . .	. . .	. . .	. . .	. . .	. . .
1925	300,000	300,000	200,000	100,000	. . .	9,900**	. . .	. . .	. . .	. . .	. . .	. . .	. . .	. . .
1927	150,000	150,000	100,000	50,000	10,000	4,950	. . .	. . .	. . .	. . .	. . .	. . .	. . .	. . .
1929	150,000	150,000	100,000	50,000	30,000	4,950	. . .	. . .	. . .	. . .	. . .	. . .	. . .	. . .
1931	150,000	150,000	100,000	50,000	30,000	4,950	. . .	. . .	. . .	. . .	. . .	. . .	. . .	. . .
1933	110,000	125,000	90,000	45,000	27,000	4,450	. . .	. . .	. . .	. . .	. . .	. . .	. . .	. . .
1935	100,000	125,000	90,000	45,000	27,000	4,450	10,000	. . .	. . .	. . .	. . .	. . .	. . .	. . .
1937	100,000	125,000	90,000	45,000	27,000	4,450	10,000	. . .	. . .	. . .	. . .	. . .	. . .	. . .
1939	100,000	125,000	90,000	45,000	27,000	4,450	15,000	. . .	. . .	. . .	. . .	. . .	. . .	. . .
1941	100,000	125,000	90,000	45,000	27,000	4,450	32,000	. . .	. . .	. . .	. . .	. . .	. . .	. . .
1943	100,000	125,000	90,000	45,000	27,000	4,450	30,000	. . .	. . .	. . .	. . .	. . .	. . .	. . .
1945	100,000	125,000	90,000	45,000	27,000	4,450	30,000	2,000,000	1,000,000	. . .	. . .	. . .	. . .	. . .
1947	35,000	125,000	90,000	45,000	27,000	33,000	250,000	2,000,000	1,000,000	7,375,000[1]	. . .	. . .	. . .	. . .
1949	. . .	. . .	. . .	45,000	27,000	49,500	526,000	3,000,000	2,000,000	12,000,000	. . .	. . .	. . .	. . .
1951	. . .	. . .	. . .	45,000	27,000	49,500	526,000	3,000,000	2,000,000	12,000,000	200,000	. . .	. . .	. . .
1953	. . .	. . .	. . .	45,000	27,000	49,500	526,000	3,000,000	3,000,000	12,000,000	300,000	. . .	. . .	. . .
1955	. . .	. . .	. . .	45,000	27,000	49,500	675,000	3,000,000	4,000,000	14,335,000	300,000	. . .	. . .	. . .
1957	. . .	. . .	. . .	45,000	27,000	49,500	800,000	3,000,000	4,000,000	14,610,000	300,000	. . .	. . .	50,000
1959	. . .	. . .	. . .	45,000	27,000	49,500	1,000,000	3,000,000	4,000,000	15,000,000	300,000	. . .	. . .	100,000
1961	. . .	. . .	. . .	45,000	27,000	49,500	1,500,000	4,000,000	4,000,000	19,529,780	650,000	. . .	. . .	200,000
1963	. . .	. . .	. . .	45,000	27,000	49,500	1,500,000	4,000,000	4,000,000	19,529,780	650,000	. . .	. . .	200,000
1965	. . .	. . .	. . .	35,000	20,000	49,500	2,500,000	4,000,000	4,000,000	33,500,000	2,400,000	1,200,000	6,000,000[2]	200,000

[1]Includes $5,000,000 Emergency General Aid

[2]Appropriated for the biennium

**Biennial figures--41st General Assembly did not make annual appropriation, but approved these amounts for use as needed during the biennium.

Source: Laws of the General Assembly, 1900-1965

Appendix C

Table 2. – IOWA DEPARTMENT OF PUBLIC INSTRUCTION STAFF, 1952[a]

Division or unit	Professional	Clerical
General office	4	7
Certification	2	14
Supervision and curriculum	6	7
Administration and finance	7	11
Transportation	2	4
Special education	13	5
School lunch	5	6
Veterans education	5	2
Vocational education	16	16
Total	60	72

[a]These figures did not include the staff of the Vocational Rehabilitation Division which had 34 employees. There was, therefore, a total of 166 people.

Table 3. – COMPARISON OF STATE SUPERINTENDENT OF PUBLIC INSTRUCTION SALARY WITH THAT OF HEADS OF SEVEN OTHER STATE AGENCIES IN IOWA, 1900-65

Year	Secretary of state	Secretary of agriculture	Auditor of state	Treasurer	Attorney general	Commissioner of health	Public safety commissioner	Comp-troller	State superintendent
1900	$ 2,200	...	$ 2,200	$ 2,200	$ 4,000	...	...	...	$ 2,200
1910	2,200[a]	$ 2,400	2,200	2,200	4,000	...	...	...	2,200
1920	4,000	4,000	4,000	4,000	5,000	...	...	...	4,000
1930	5,000	5,000	5,000	5,000	6,000	$ 5,000	...	...	4,000
1940	5,000	5,000	5,000	5,000	6,000	5,000	$ 4,000	$ 6,000	4,500
1950	6,500	6,500	6,500	6,500	7,500	6,500	6,000	6,500	6,500
1960	10,000	10,000	10,000	10,000	11,000	9,500	10,000	12,000	12,000
1965	15,000	15,000	15,000	15,000	16,500	22,500	15,000	18,000	18,000

Source:
Appropriation Acts, *Laws of the General Assembly.*

[a]Including assistants.

Appendix C

Table 4. – COMPARISON OF SUPERINTENDENTS' SALARY IN 10 LARGEST IOWA SCHOOL DISTRICTS WITH THAT OF THE STATE SUPERINTENDENT OF PUBLIC INSTRUCTION, 1900-65

Year	Burlington	Cedar Rapids	Council Bluffs	Davenport	Des Moines	Dubuque	Mason City	Ottumwa	Sioux City	Waterloo	State Supt.	10 Dist. Average	State Supt. as a % of Average
1900-01	$ 1,700	$ 2,400	$ 2,000	$ 2,000	W$ 2,250 E 1,600	$ 2,400	$ 1,500	$ 1,900	$ 2,750	E$ 1,600 W 1,600	$ 2,200	$ 1,975	111.39
1910-11	2,200	3,000	2,600	3,000	5,000	3,200	2,200	2,400	3,000	E 2,700 W 2,200	2,200	2,864	76.82
1920-21	4,000	5,000	4,000	6,250	7,500	N.R.*	5,000	4,500	7,000	E 4,800 W 4,800	4,000	5,285	75.69
1930-31	N.R.	7,500	N.R.	6,800	N.R.	6,000	5,100	4,500	N.R.	E 5,000 W N.R.	4,000	5,629	71.06
1940-41	5,000	7,000	5,948	6,000	6,686	5,800	5,340	5,000	7,500	E 3,500 W 6,000	4,500	5,798	77.61
1950-51	7,500	10,100	7,482	10,220	10,000	10,000	9,958	5,174	12,917	9,840	6,500	9,319	69.75
1960-61	14,500	18,000	11,998	22,500	22,500	15,500	14,917	13,300	17,500	20,000	12,000	17,072	70.29
1965-66	16,900	21,000	14,350	19,750	24,500	17,000	18,000	17,500	19,000	24,000	18,000	19,200	93.75

*Not reported

Source: Salaries of district superintendents for 1900-01, 1910-11, and 1920-21 from Iowa School Report; 1930-31 from Iowa Educational Directory, 1940-41, and 1950-51 from Report of County Superintendent of Schools to State Superintendent of Public Instruction; 1960-61 and 1965-66 from Secretary's Annual Report to County Superintendent of Schools.

16 Kansas

DEPARTMENT OF PUBLIC INSTRUCTION

Adel F. Throckmorton

Contents

EDUCATION IN KANSAS PRIOR TO 1900

Education was wholly unorganized during territorial days under the Kansas-Nebraska Act of 1854. This stormy, unsettled period saw proslavery and antislavery forces fight to control the newly formed territory. First one side and then the other formed a government, the voters adopting three constitutions before approving the "Wyandotte" Constitution under which Kansas became a state.

The curriculum and the quality of instruction for those schools that existed, and whether to establish a school at all, depended entirely on the people in each community. Neither the 1855 nor the 1857 Legislature, each proslavery, provided for territorial supervision, but when the first free-state Legislature met the next year, it created an office officially designated as the "territorial superintendent of common schools." The first superintendent, James H. Noteware, served only 9 months and left no record of his official acts except a recommendation for textbooks. His successor, Samuel Wiley Greer, the first elected territorial superintendent, traveled extensively and recommended improvements in the schools, demonstrating the important task of the new office (1).

Academic achievement played a minor role with the immigrant farmers of the state, but they came determined to build a better future for their children.

> The pioneers brought with them a desire for education and the hope of religion. Schoolhouses of rude pattern, built of logs or sod, sprang up everywhere. They were used for the dual purpose of education during the week, and devotional exercises on Sunday. . . . The building of any schoolhouse in any neighborhood was an event of more than passing interest. They were frequently built before a regular organized district was set apart and any taxes were levied for schools or school buildings (2).

Peter MacVicar, state superintendent from 1867-71, stated in his report on the sanitary conditions found in these schools: "It is evident that very great neglect extensively prevails. Very many of the edifices have no outhouses at all. Only a few have one each, and rarely are schoolhouses provided each with two such conveniences" (3).

MacVicar's successor, Superintendent Hugh D. McCarty, vigorously attacked the primitive conditions of the schools, visiting each county biennially, interpreting school laws, and holding annual teachers institutes in each judicial district. But he found the job too much for one man. In his 1872 annual report, he requested that he be allowed to hire two clerks to assist him in the time-consuming duties of carrying on correspondence with other states, providing blanks and forms for school reports, publishing school laws, and preparing the annual report—particularly since he was also busy interpreting school laws, serving as secretary to the Commission for the Permanent School Fund, and attending State Board of Regents' meetings.

In his report, McCarty further recommended that the Legislature establish a State Board of Education, provide for uniformity in textbooks, and compel every healthy boy and girl to attend school for at least 4 months each year. He deplored the meager financial support provided his office, pointing out that his $1,200 salary compared unfavorably with 14 other states (4).

The 1873 Legislature, acting on the superintendent's recommendations, created a State Board of Education and prescribed its duties. For the most part, the new law limited the board to issuing certificates and diplomas that were to be valid in any school district during the life of the holder. Applicants not qualified for the diploma could take an examination for certificates valid for either 3 years or 5 years. The frugal character of the Legislature was reflected in a concluding limitation: "The provisions of this act shall be carried out without expense to the state" (5). It was to be 20 years before a $300 annual appropriation was voted to cover members' expenses to attend state board meetings. Formerly, the superintendent was by himself the entire state agency for education, making policies and administering them. Under the newly formed State Board of Education, he spent even more time on clerical duties. His success in developing programs depended mainly on his initiative, because the law provided him little authority to exercise leadership.

> Both the Board and the State Superintendent participated in administering such programs as the preparation of courses of study for county institutes and the public schools, and in the accreditation of colleges. In many cases both the Superintendent and the Board seemed

responsible for developing policy. The actual practice for dividing duties and allocating responsibility remains obscured in the informal practices. Coordination of effort was achieved, apparently with success, by the dual role of the Superintendent as the leading member of the State Board of Education and as an independent officer responsible for the Department of Education (6).

Following McCarty's recommendations, the Legislature enacted a Compulsory Attendance Law in 1874 requiring children aged 8 to 14 to attend school. Many schools operated only 3 or 4 months of the year, however, and the law gave school boards the authority to grant children exemptions from attendance. The law was further weakened by a provision allowing home instruction to be substituted for school attendance in preparing the child for his examinations (7).

The first session of the Legislature created a Board of Commissioners, authorized in the constitution, to manage the permanent school fund. Today, as then, the board consists of the state superintendent of public instruction, secretary; the secretary of state, chairman; and the attorney general. The fund itself receives money collected from the estates of persons dying without heirs or wills and from the sale of school lands–mainly sections 16 and 36 in every township–which Congress set aside for the schools. The board had the responsibility of investing the permanent funds wisely since only the interest can be used for the schools. Today all of these lands have been sold, but earlier superintendents worried about speculators' gaining control and diverting the funds from the schools. Superintendent MacVicar uncovered several instances of questionable practices. He also found one serious loophole in the regulations: the authority of county treasurers to hold private sales. Too often, none of the bids equaled the appraised value (8).

The 1897 Legislature exercised a profoundly beneficial effect on education in Kansas for the next 60 years by following the recommendations of several early superintendents and creating a School Textbook Commission to administer a uniform, statewide adoption program. The state superintendent served as ex officio chairman until 1945, when the commission's functions were assigned to a lay state board, leaving the superintendent with no jurisdiction over a most important educational activity. The commission's functions had simply been superannuated by new instructional techniques, better-prepared teachers, and the new availability of a wide variety of materials. The transfer marked virtually the end of statewide textbook adoption.

THE LEGAL FRAMEWORK FOR KANSAS EDUCATION

By 1900, most of the legal structure for Kansas education's next 45 years of development had been established in rudimentary form. The "Wyandotte" Constitution, under which Kansas was admitted to the Union in 1861, had created the Office of State Superintendent of Public Instruction, provided the authority for the Board of School Fund Commissioners, formed a State Board of Education to certify teachers, and established a system of common schools and higher education. Until the mid-1940's, most statutory revisions were evolutionary, though superintendents continuously called for extensive improvements.

The constitution provided for a county superintendent of public instruction in each county, and the Legislature, following a pattern set by the 1858 Territorial Legislature, assigned each superintendent the task of dividing his county into school districts (9). With "convenience" the only stated criterion to guide them, county superintendents tried to found schools within walking distance of most pupils. In general, they tried to establish schools at 2-mile intervals in populated areas, each within a district governed by a three-man board. By 1896, 35 years after Kansas became a state, 9,284 school districts had been created, which until 1945 required a veritable army of more than 24,000 school board members, who outnumbered the state's teachers by several thousand.

Many thousands of New England immigrants familiar with the town-meeting form of government brought to Kansas that statutory framework for their school districts. The districts' electors conducted business in annual meetings on such issues as the election of board members, the spending of school funds, the length of the school year, and the schedule for each term. In turn, the elected boards employed the teachers, kept the building in repair, and purchased supplies.

This form of school government, operating in all districts except those of first- and second-class cities, remained in effect until the school district unification programs of 1963 and 1965 placed unified districts under the jurisdiction of boards of education (10). Usually, only a handful of electors attended most annual meetings, but if controversial issues aroused the citizens, the meetings could, and sometimes did, degenerate into little more than mob scenes at which an unpopular teacher or board member suffered verbal crucifixion. Before this type of government was abandoned, some districts and urban areas with populations running into the thousands found the annual meeting an anachronism that painfully exemplified the difficulty of revising governmental procedures.

In 1876, the Legislature changed the law to allow other types of school districts to organize. Several first- and second-class cities took advantage of the law to form districts differing from those established by county superintendents. These city districts, according to the 1876 legislation, were governed by autonomous boards of education operating outside the jurisdiction of county superintendents. But the district structure still had weaknesses. The superintendent's report in 1895 noted that 390 districts were not operating any schools. Despite a growing demand for high schools, thousands of small common school districts did not have sufficient pupils or financial resources to maintain them. Only 11,508 students were enrolled in public high schools in 1900, but the number more than doubled during the following decade (11).

As high school enrollment increased, the Legislature did not realign existing districts so that they would have sufficient population and financial resources to support 12 grades, but rather formed several types of high school districts. Operating under governing boards separate from those responsible for the first eight grades, these new districts usually included all or parts of several common school districts. The movement finally developed into a double-decked system of districts with diverse boundaries, mainly because citizens had a fierce loyalty to the "home district," were reluctant to relinquish control of their elementary schools, and, in some instances, opposed higher taxes. One state department staff member observed that many taxpayers fought to maintain the school district status quo as though their small inefficient districts had been let down from heaven in a basket.

The first units providing only secondary education were authorized in 1886. Any county with 6,000 or more inhabitants could establish a high school district. Within a few years, an increasing number of common school districts were extending their programs to include high school courses. When this occurred in county high school districts, the residents of the common school districts were faced with double taxation; not only did they have to pay for the county high school, but they also had to support the local high schools—all without outside financial assistance. Quite understandably, county high school patrons resisted any change which threatened to wipe out these tax resources. The issue was not fully resolved until 1923, when the county high schools were designated as community high schools, to be supported by all in the county who were not included in another high school district.

The 1911 Legislature enacted a law authorizing the establishment of township high schools. It was repealed 4 years later in the face of a new act creating rural high school districts. If 40 percent of the area's electors petitioned, the people could call an election to vote whether they should establish a rural high school district. According to the original legislation, high schools formed under districts of this type were governed by annual meetings and school boards similar to the common school districts and were limited to operating grades 9 through 12. Later, the Legislature did authorize a variety of rural high school districts, before the district unification laws of 1963 and 1965 eliminated most districts not offering 12 years of instruction.

Thus, in the course of 100 years, the system of common school districts created by county superintendents became an unwieldy conglomeration of districts governed under scores of general and special laws. Fortunately, good schools developed despite inefficient district organization (12).

The State Education Agency

As pointed out earlier, the state superintendent of public instruction was the state agency for education until the Legislature created the first State Board of Education in 1873. But the relationship between the new state board and the state superintendent was not clearly defined by the law. At times, the board made policy to be administered by the state superintendent. Or the state board would not only decide policy but carry out the department's administrative functions, making the state superintendent its errand boy unless he was able to exert direction, outside his specific statutory authority, as a member of the state board, the school fund commission, and the textbook adoption agency. Perhaps this explains in part why 22 different state superintendents served during the 84-year period from 1861 to 1945, when the present department was organized. These short terms, averaging less than 4 years, handicapped superintendent leadership considerably.

Though strong leadership was rare, it was not entirely absent. W. D. Ross provided vigorous direction, finally persuading the 1915 Legislature to formalize the roles of his office and that of the state board by creating a State Department of Education. After 42 years of confusion, the state department's time had come.

The state's rapidly expanding population demanded an increasing number of high schools, which in turn created a need for more 4-year higher education institutions to prepare more teachers. As in other states, schoolmen and the public realized that better procedures for accrediting high schools and teacher education programs were necessary, as was improved instruction at all levels. The 1915 Legislature authorized the state board to employ a secretary, who, in the words of the law, "shall be an expert in education," to serve as inspector of colleges and universities accredited by the state board and to have charge of all matters relating to teachers' certificates. It also directed the board to prescribe courses for the normal institutes and to act as the sole authority in defining official standards of excellence in all matters relating to the administration, course of study, and instruction in the public schools. It could then accredit schools adhering to these standards. To help the superintendent facilitate these improvements, the legislation enabled him to add two elementary and two high school supervisors to his staff.

Other forward-looking recommendations by Superintendent Ross were not enacted for many years. Only in 1941 were his suggestions for expanding the health and physical education programs and establishing a teacher retirement program heeded. And it was not until 1966 that the Kansas electorate approved a constitutional amendment making the position of state superintendent of public instruction appointive.

When the Legislature created the education department, it failed to take seriously the constitutional provision that "the State Superintendent of Public Instruction shall have the general supervision of the common school funds and educational interest of the state . . . " (13). Instead, it placed such supervision and policy-making powers in the hands of the state board. The constitutionality of giving the state superintendent a minor role in relation to the state board was later challenged. In 1947, and again in 1965, although the Kansas Supreme Court ruled against delegating powers to other boards, it did uphold the Legislature's delegating these powers to the state superintendent of public instruction.

The State Department of Education carried on its activities for the first 30 years with no significant change in its legal structure. Finally, in 1945, the Legislature restructured it as the State Department of Public Instruction, defining it as the state superintendent of public instruction and the State Board of Education. The professional educators, who composed the board since its creation in 1873, were replaced by laymen, and the relationship of the board to the superintendent was radically revised. The Legislature stripped the state board of its direct jurisdiction over teacher certification, elementary and secondary school accreditation, junior college supervision, teacher education programs, curriculum development, and other activities, placing them in the hands of the state superintendent, who would develop policies to be approved by the board. Thus, as an arm of the state department, the state board's dominion was limited to approving or disapproving the superintendent's proposals and serving as an advisory body.

This action was a step in recognizing the constitutional status of the state department, but it was not the paramount reason for changing the legal patterns established in 1915. Superintendent W. T. Markham, who provided outstanding leadership from 1932 to 1939, was esteemed by school leaders throughout the state. A Democrat, he had been swept out of office in the 1938 election on a tide of political change. Friction developed between political leaders and educators strongly represented on the professional state board, which in turn led to differences between the board and the superintendent who succeeded Markham. It was finally apparent to the legislators that this unrest was seriously affecting the department's ability to lead (14).

Other serious problems arose. No clear-cut lines of demarcation separated the functions of the professional board from those of the state superintendent. The department suffered from a poor image and inadequate financial support. It was short of staff members, and the annual budget of less than $40,000, together with the minimal sum collected from teacher certificate fees, could not finance its operations.

In moving from a professional to a lay board, the Legislature prescribed the Governor's limitations in appointing board members (15) and listed the required qualifications for candidates to the superintendency (16). Prior to this, any candidate receiving a plurality in a statewide election became eligible if he met the resident requirements applicable to all elected state officials.

Although the 1945 legislation provided a legal framework for cooperative action between the state board and the state superintendent, the transition from a predominantly professional board to a lay board and the removal of the state superintendent from membership and ex officio chairmanship of the board created unforeseen problems. The lay board had no legally designated professional leadership in the adoption and printing of textbooks. These duties, transferred from the School Book Commission to the professional State Board of Education in 1937, remained in the hands of the lay board and outside the jurisdiction of the superintendent. Thus, the official responsible for developing courses of a study and supervising instructional programs in the public schools had no voice in selecting a major tool with which these activities were carried on.

Another problem arose because the state superintendent was given no official connection with the lay board's administration of vocational programs in secondary schools, junior colleges, or area-vocational schools. The state board is legally the vocational education board, administering these programs under its own budget and appointing its own administrative officer. In effect, this means that Kansas has two state departments.

The Department of Public Instruction's continued growth necessitated an internal reorganization in 1955. Three divisions were established: administrative services, instructional services, and teacher certification and accreditation – each under a director and divided into sections also headed by directors. With the exception of the sections added since 1955, the department was reorganized according to the chart in Appendix B (17).

Since 1945, there have been increasing demands for more services from the department. School administrators, lay organizations interested in education, and special-interest groups concerned with adult education, driver education, and the state scholarship program applied considerable pressure, and federally financed activities led to even more calls for assistance. Perhaps another factor contributing to the department's expansion during this period was its growing prestige and competence in the eyes of legislators and the state and local agencies.

This increased interest in the department gave new impetus to a reorganization calling for an elected lay board, which the Kansas Teachers Association and other organizations had recommended for years. In 1955, the superintendent and his staff published a statement calling for an elected lay board with power to appoint a commissioner of education as its chief administrative officer (18). A report published in 1960 covering the entire Kansas system of public education from kindergarten through the university and conducted by out-of-state personnel aroused further interest (19). Its recommendations pertaining to the state department were similar to those proposed by the superintendent in 1955.

The report didn't have to point up a number of the problems because they were all too obvious. The division of responsibility among several state agencies had become increasingly unsatisfactory as educational programs had expanded and federally sponsored activities multiplied. The Highway Department administered school transportation; the Budget Division handled surplus commodities for the schools; the Kansas State High School Activities Association controlled interscholastic competition in athletics, music, and forensics; and the State Board of Education supervised vocational education and rehabilitation services as a separate agency outside the State Department of Public Instruction. Also, the election of a state superintendent every 2 years on a partisan political ticket often hampered continuity in administrative policies. The Kansas Supreme Court raised questions about the constitutionality of the State Board of Education's administering the vocational programs.

The problems and pressures continued to build, until the 1965 Legislature stripped the board of functions it had performed for 20 years and increased the authority of the state superintendent. The junior colleges were put under his direction, and he could now, without board approval, enter into agreements and develop plans with federal agencies for federally financed programs. The governing body of a newly created state technical institute included the state superintendent and two other persons appointed by the Governor, with no voice given to the state board or any of its members. The following year, the Legislature amended the State Constitution to create a State Board of Education composed of 10 lay persons to be named by the electors of 10 board-member areas as determined by the Legislature (20). The board would then appoint the state commissioner of education. When the amendment was submitted to the electorate in the general election, they not only approved it by a substantial majority, but they elected a state superintendent for a 2-year term, allowing the Legislature that much time to work out the details for electing a board of education. The amendment was to be in full operation not later than January 1969.

In reviewing the legal framework of the State Department of Public Instruction, it is necessary to take a close look at the State Department of Administration, an office that exercises control over all state agencies. This department, created by the Legislature in 1953, includes a finance council, an executive director, a budget division, an accounts and reports division, a purchasing division, a personnel division, the state architect, and other employees. Not only must the state superintendent's clerical and secretarial appointments be made from lists of qualified persons provided by the personnel division, but the division also establishes the standards for professional staff members. The state superintendent's annual budget is submitted and reviewed by the budget division before it is presented to the Legislature. The purchasing division must approve all orders for equipment for the superintendent's office in excess of $50; supplies and materials are generally purchased under open-end contract arrangements made by the purchasing division. New positions can be established by the education department only with the approval of the finance council, a six-member body composed of the Governor, the lieutenant governor, and four legislative leaders. The state department obviously is not an autonomous agency.

Aside from the time required to work through the administration department, however, the system has proven to be quite satisfactory. In fact, personnel in the budget division have testified before the Legislature and its committees about the department's financial needs. For example, it simplifies the process of selecting competent clerical, secretarial, and professional employees. The state department should increasingly benefit from working with the administration department as the latter unit's leaders become familiar with educational problems.

EDUCATIONAL PROGRAMS IN KANSAS AND THE ROLE OF THE STATE DEPARTMENT OF PUBLIC INSTRUCTION

The State Superintendent of Public Instruction

The state superintendent, an arm of the state department, is the chief state school officer with powers granted by the Legislature under authority of the State Constitution. Traditionally, the office in Kansas has been regarded as a minor one and is still so considered, despite the heavy responsibilities assigned to it in recent years. Not only must the superintendent lead the department, but, as pointed out earlier, he has sole responsibility in many areas. He is the state authority for junior colleges, he enters into agreements with federal agencies for administering several government-financed programs, he presents the department's budget for the Legislature's approval, and he makes the final decisions on many issues respecting school district organization and boundary changes. In addition, he appoints staff personnel, addresses numerous educational conferences, keeps in close touch with institutions of higher education, and holds many interviews and informal discussions. The Legislature looks to the superintendent for recommendations for improving the state's educational program. He is subject to a thousand pressures as he backs up staff members who handle school district problems and who administer teacher certification, accreditation activities, distribution of state funds to schools, and other departmental programs.

By law the state superintendent is an ex officio member of several other state agencies. He serves as chairman of the state teacher retirement board; chairman of the budget review committee, which administers expenditure limitations required by the school foundation finance act; and chairman of the governing board of Schilling Institute, a state technical school. He is also secretary of the school fund commission, which administers the permanent school fund, and a member of the executive council, composed of elected state officials. He cooperates with a member of unofficial agencies that work to improve education, such as the Kansas State Teachers Association, the Kansas Association of School Administrators, the Congress of Parents and Teachers, and the State Association of Boards of Education, and is on the executive committee of the Mid-Continent Regional Education Laboratory, which has its headquarters in Kansas City.

W. C. Kampschroeder, who served as assistant state superintendent most of the time after joining the staff in 1951, has been instrumental in developing a spirit of cooperation between the department and other state agencies. He has established good working relations with the State Department of Administration and its subdivisions, since the State Department of Public Instruction's activities are channeled through the assistant superintendent's office. Kampschroeder was appointed state superintendent in September 1966, following the resignation of Adel F. Throckmorton, who had filled the post since January 1949. Kampschroeder was then elected to serve a full 2-year term.

Since federal programs are administered in most segments of the department, a coordinator of federal programs, reporting directly to the state superintendent and his assistant, acts as a central clearing agent and keeps informed about educational developments at the federal level. Other personnel working outside the department's three divisions include a personnel director; a director of what is known as the Iowa Project, a cooperative endeavor involving Midwestern states in the development of a new and unique educational information system for facilities, finance, pupils, instructional programs, and personnel; and a director of information, who edits *Kansas Schools* (the official publication of the department), edits teacher guides, writes news releases to keep the public informed about educational developments, and assists in orienting staff members.

Department Status Improved

The state superintendent, more than any other person, shapes the department's image and constantly appraises the effectiveness of its public relations. In the early days of statehood, the department was either ignored or considered to be a necessary evil, but abundant evidence suggests that legislators and the public in general have learned to appreciate it more, especially in the last 10 years. Perhaps the first Sputnik and the fear that our schools were not as good as Russia's contributed to its new status. Most assuredly did a series of supreme court decisions firmly establishing the state superintendent as the constitutional officer to whom the Legislature can delegate almost unlimited powers in the field of education. One example of this increased confidence is the power granted the state superintendent to administer the 1963 and 1965 school district reorganization laws. He had been bypassed by the 1945 and 1961 acts, both of which were declared unconstitutional by the Kansas Supreme Court.

The Division of Instructional Services

George Cleland, former president of the National Association of Secondary School Principals and director of the Division of Instructional Services (21) since its formation in 1955, heads the staff of 28 professional assistants, divided into five sections, working to upgrade the instructional programs in the Kansas schools.

The development of educational programs and activities from 1900 to 1965 and their relationship to the state department are outlined under the department's appropriate divisions as indicated in this section. In the past, some have been administered by the superintendent, some by the state board, a few under organizational patterns that no longer exist in the department, and others by outside state agencies.

From the time the first Kansas schools opened, the state superintendents have played an important role in certifying teachers, supervising institutes designed to raise teacher qualifications, and publishing course guides. With a few rare exceptions, they have been aware that enriching education is the real purpose of the schools. But, lacking funds and staff, too much of their energy has been required just to keep the schools operating. Comparatively little appears in the record about improving instruction, except as this most important concern is indirectly affected by the preparation of teachers.

It was not until 1915 that the superintendent was able to add elementary and secondary school supervisors to his staff, specialists in curriculum development who could devote full time and effort to helping teachers do a better job. In fact, only four of these assistants were available to cover the state until two more were added in 1945. Despite their small numbers and the inspectorial nature of their assignment, they contributed greatly in uplifting classroom procedures through the dual role of working with teachers and evaluating their schools for accreditation.

Prior to World War II, most instruction was the traditional textbook-oriented method of teaching, with few instructional materials available. State Superintendent W. T. Markham (22) published the first elementary courses not based on textbooks in 1934 – the Unit Program in Social Studies. Prepared by May Hare, a department elementary supervisor, it introduced Kansas teachers to the social studies concept that was replacing courses in history, civics, geography, and some phases of science in other school systems (23). Unfortunately, few elementary teachers had the training or experience needed for this approach. Materials required to carry out the new program were not available in thousands of small elementary schools. Most of Kansas was still rural, and teachers and parents who had been taught by the old textbook method resisted this and any other innovation. For a decade, *social studies* was all but a subversive term.

With the publication of the *Unit Program in Social Studies*, a 5-year curriculum study and research project was introduced, in which all state institutions of higher education participated with the State Department of Public Instruction (24). Results of the curriculum studies were published in a series of bulletins (25), but before the project was completed Markham was defeated in his bid for reelection in 1938. The loss of his leadership, widespread opposition to the social studies guides, and pressures for a return to textbook instruction by subject all but shelved the studies. With aggressive leadership, they could have served as a model for curriculum improvement 30 years ago.

In the decade after World War II, teachers began coming out of college with the preparation and understanding needed for the new social studies approach. Today, Superintendent Markham and Miss Hare receive due credit for courageously breaking with tradition and introducing new concepts that have since been almost universally adopted.

Curriculum. The curriculum section is one of the most important in the Division of Instructional Services. It operates under the philosophy that the curriculum includes all experiences which pupils have in school, and it attempts to project this philosophy through conferences, curriculum guides, and visits by consultants. The department held 46 curriculum conferences for over 7,000 elementary teachers as early as 1951, an indication of the long-standing demand for some kind of consultative service (26). By 1965, the staff included 10 specialists representing as many subject areas. Three additional consultants were added in 1966.

The section holds a series of annual conferences for administrators and their curriculum directors at conveniently located centers throughout the state. It publishes teachers guides, compiles lists of instructional materials, and gives individual help to teachers who come to the state office. The subject matter specialists spend about half of their time in the field with administrators and teachers conferring about local problems. These specialists also serve as consultants for many federally financed programs designed to improve instruction, and they have the major responsibility for administering Title III of the National Defense Education Act, under which school districts are reimbursed for equipment purchased to upgrade programs in specific subject matter areas.

Special Education. The Kansas Society for Exceptional Children, composed of both lay and professional persons, was organized in the mid-1940's to press for legislation that would authorize special services for educating the handicapped and other nontypical children. It gained the support of the Kansas Council for Children and Youth, the Kansas State Teachers' Association, the State Federated Women's Clubs, the Congress of Parents and Teachers, the State Department of Public Instruction, and other groups concerned with the educational welfare of all children. Their activities culminated in legislation in 1949 authorizing the department to create a special section and form special classes in the districts. With a modest appropriation for a director and other staff, the superintendent began searching for personnel. All appointments were subject to the state board's approval.

Progress was dishearteningly slow. The services were available to districts only on a voluntary basis—children were not legally required to enroll in the special education classes. It was 2 years before the Legislature provided funds with which to reimburse districts for organizing special classes. Besides inadequate financing at the district level, the program suffered from a serious lack of space, a shortage of qualified teachers, sparse population areas, too many school districts, public apathy, and even overt opposition in several locales.

The Legislature retained its interest in special education despite this foot-dragging by the local districts and in 1951 expanded the program by agreeing to reimburse school districts that established classes for the mentally retarded or provided instruction for homebound children. Two years later, it again voted funds for the exceptional children—this time defining the term more explicitly and including the intellectually gifted—and by law extended authorization to give these children special full-time or part-time instruction.

In the meantime, numerous organizations had begun working in the field of mental retardation, mainly due to the effective leadership of James Marshall, who has headed the special education activities in the department for 12 years. Marshall and his staff cooperate with universities and colleges in developing teacher education programs and work closely with personnel in the U.S. Office of Education (27).

Textbook Adoptions. The history of instructional programs in Kansas would not be complete without a review of textbook adoption policies and their impact on education over a 60-year period. Textbook adoption has been a controversial issue from the earliest days of statehood. State Superintendent Isaac T. Goodnow joined his school superintendents in urging the Legislature to enact a law providing for uniformity. But his successor, Peter MacVicar, took the opposite view, evincing the same philosophy and same arguments used by those seeking to repeal such a law 88 years later, when he said:

> I presented somewhat at length the impracticability of requiring by law a state uniformity of textbooks, and of giving either to a state superintendent, or to a board, the power of deciding what that uniformity should be for a series of years. . . . A vast system of state monopoly would be created. It is doubtless much better that books, like other products of brain and industry, be left free to a healthy competition (28).

Certainly such powerful opposition delayed the enactment of a textbook law until 1897, 26 years after MacVicar left office.

The 1897 act created a School Textbook Commission, making the state superintendent ex officio chairman and giving him the right to vote on all propositions. It was the commission's responsibility to contract with publishers, adopt uniform series of textbooks, and make bids. One unique provision foreshadowed later unsavory developments: No one except members was to be present or cognizant of the commission's proceedings during its sessions, and no member was permitted to give information to anyone about what was going on during any of the meetings. After all business had been transacted, the proceedings were published. This would never have satisfied people today, who demand "the right to know."

Shifting the responsibility for adopting textbooks from one commission or government agency to another indicates the sensitivity of the issue (29). The most serious problems did not develop, however, until after the 1913 Legislature mandated that all elementary textbooks and some high school books be manufactured in the state printing plant. A punitive provision in the law, remaining in effect for 44 years, stated that any school official convicted of adopting, using, or procuring for use in the public schools any textbook as a substitute for an adopted one could be subjected to a fine of not less than $25 nor more than $100, or be imprisoned in the county jail, or both (30).

The state superintendent remained the ex officio chairman of the commission until the laymen took over the state board in 1945. This reorganization provided for an advisory committee, but the manner in which the board selected the committee's members proved to be one of the major weaknesses of the adoption procedure. Contrary to the state superintendent's recommendation, the board followed a policy whereby each member appointed his proportional share; thus 8 of the 14 advisory committee members in 1954 came from the hometowns of board members (31). The board thereupon tended to disregard the committee's recommendations. Operating outside the education department and without professional leadership, it often made ill-advised adoptions. The Legislature finally realized its mistake and abolished the whole system in 1957.

Under the present law the superintendent, with the approval of the state board, appoints a State Textbook Review Committee which publishes a list of all textbooks suitable for Kansas schools, unless in the committee's judgment they contain subversive material or cannot be classified under one of the subject matter areas. This committee has operated successfully, assisted by a member of the department's staff. The published lists provide a welcome service to school officials who now make their own adoptions at the district level and determine when textbook changes are needed. Following expiration of the 1957 adoptions in 1962, the plan went into full operation, and the demands for statewide uniform adoption and state textbook printing had a peaceful death.

Guidance and Counseling Services. The use of guidance and pupil personnel services in Kansas schools is a recent development. In the 1946-47 school year, only 21 secondary schools had at least one person assigned as much as 1 hour per day for this work (32); 11 years later, only 222 nonadministrative personnel were doing guidance and counseling. The department did not become actively interested until 1956, when it hired one guidance counselor. The following year, the superintendent established the first standards for certifying counselors. Not only were guidance services seldom requested, but schools even opposed the certification standards, so that in the closing hours of the 1959 session, one legislator was persuaded to introduce a resolution revoking them. It was 2 years before this action was repealed.

The National Defense Education Act, which became effective in 1959, gave counseling and guidance real impetus. At the time, only 85 full-time counselors in Kansas were qualified under both the state's standards and the agreement with the U.S. Office of Education. With federal funds under this act, the state department staff was enlarged to include three counselors in addition to the director; the number of full-time counselors increased to 161, the part-time counselors showing a comparable growth.

The department gives consultant services to local schools, holds conferences for their counselors and administrators, studies various problems faced by dropouts and high school students who enter college or go to work, cooperates with institutions of higher education in developing training programs, and publishes and distributes numerous bulletins. Its staff also exercises general supervision over a state testing program administered by Kansas State Teachers College in Emporia. It has given aptitude tests to ninth- and tenth-grade students annually since 1959-60, and the results have been turned over to their schools to be used for research purposes under special arrangements with the department's guidance section.

Elementary and Secondary Education Act, Titles I and II. Appropriations for programs under Titles I and II were not made until late 1965, which made it difficult for the small staff in the instructional services division to plan how best to use them in the schools during the 1965-66 term. The state approved projects to spend about $9.8 million out of the $10.8 million allotted to Kansas, primarily to improve the educational opportunities for culturally deprived children from families living at the poverty level. Securing trained personnel to handle the original projects was not only difficult but impossible in some instances, so the projects had to be replanned with an unfortunate emphasis on equipment and materials. The evaluation of the results under Titles I and II were not completed until late 1966.

The Division of Administrative Services (33)

School Finance Section (34). This section serves as a clearinghouse for the department and for local school officials who need information from the financial and statistical records. Until 1965, it administered the general support funds, but the number of new programs became so heavy that this function was transferred to the statistical services section. It still prepares the department budget and supervises accounting procedures, and because the accounts required by federal agencies differ from state practices, its record keeping has almost doubled.

School Facilities Services. These services were initiated by the department in 1951 to deal with two new aspects of administration: (1) federal activity in school enrollment and its effect on buildings, equipment, and transportation; and (2) a nationwide study of how to alleviate school building shortages created by shifting populations, increasing birthrates, and obsolete buildings that had developed since World War II—each state to make its inventory. Since the Kansas Legislature delayed 3 years before sanctioning the use of federal funds for the survey, the department collected the necessary data with the assistance of the state's 105 county superintendents. While processing the local school districts' applications for building funds, the department began providing consultative services in this field.

School Lunch Programs. The superintendent appointed a school lunch director in 1946, the first year of the National School Lunch Program, to train supervisors and cooks in the schools, conduct field visits, and compute the federal reimbursement rate to the districts on a per-meal basis. In general, the public disliked the program at first, branding it a socialistic venture contrary to the American way of life. Today, it is considered, along with the special milk program established by Congress in 1954, as indispensable in most districts. The school lunch section cooperates with the Department of Social Welfare, which handles the distribution of surplus commodities.

Statistical Services and School Finance. The superintendent's office has always had the task of collecting statistical data and incorporating them into the annual and biennial reports. As the school system expanded, adding new activities and spreading all over the state, the need for statistical services intensified. Until recently, electronic data-processing equipment was used only for teacher certification procedures and related activities. But it has now come into use in finding a new formula for distributing state funds to schools—the basis for a school foundation finance law. The statistical services section's principal duty is now to administer the law.

Before 1937, more than 95 percent of the financial support for Kansas public schools came from district ad valorem taxes. But in that year the Legislature appropriated the first state aid (other than an insignificant amount from the permanent school fund). However, changing conditions and a too-rigid formula for distributing the money resulted in a 46-percent decline from the $2,113,000 allotted in 1937 to the amount of a decade later. Financing the schools gradually changed from a local district responsibility to a joint endeavor by the federal government, the state, and the county (35). Until 1965, when the first school foundation finance law was enacted, these attempts to provide adequate financing included a hodgepodge of at least a dozen funds from county and state sources to supplement revenues from the school districts. The school lunch and milk funds, and money from Public Laws 814 and 874, the National Defense Education Act, and Public Law 89-10 put much-needed funds into the kitty.

Little imagination is needed to envision the complexities involved in administering allotments from so many different sources. Because of inequities in the property tax, inadequate state support, and insufficient revenues from all sources, plus encouragement from legislative leaders, the department decided to conduct studies of its sources of income. It sought a formula to gain substantially more state aid from non-ad valorem sources, consolidate many funds already available, correct educational and tax inequities, and set up incentives for improving instruction in the schools. Carl B. Althaus, the departmental specialist in school finance who had developed the basic formulas in most of the legislation since 1947, commenced work in 1963 and published his reports the following year (36).

The Legislature made a few minor revisions in the formula Althaus submitted, then enacted its significant features as the school foundation finance law in the 1965 session. As a basis for distributing state funds, the formula takes into consideration (a) preparation and experience of teachers, (b) population density, (c) countywide tax levies from ad valorem sources, (d) amounts of state money received, and (e) pupil-teacher ratios. It also includes an economic index to determine the financial ability of each county to support its schools. Another feature is the new limitation on district expenditures: Instead of the old mill levy limits, it restricts spending to 104 percent of the per-pupil expenditures the preceding year.

Civil Defense Adult Education. The federally financed Civil Defense adult education program prepares public school teachers to instruct adults and upper-class high school students in disaster preparedness and cooperates with Civil Defense authorities in a radiological monitoring program. Staff members and public school officials together promote these classes; the teachers brought into the program are paid a nominal fee.

School District Unification. State Superintendent Peter MacVicar undoubtedly made the understatement of his illustrious career when he said: "More difficulties probably arise from organization and changes of school district boundaries than from all other sources" (37). He should have added that no social change is made against more agonized resistance than school district reorganization, only to be accepted with so much satisfaction a year or two afterward.

The 9,284 school districts in Kansas in 1896 met the needs of a pioneer society in which academic achievement was secondary to wresting a living from the soil. The schools served as community centers sponsoring ciphering matches, box suppers, spelling bees, community sings, and other social activities. Under these conditions, people developed sentimental attachments to the one-room schools that persisted long after the educational and economic welfare of the state demanded a new framework for education. As recently as 1950, many people thought of rural education in terms of one-room schools, although no semblance of the uniform system of school districts prescribed by the constitution remained. In fact, only a decade later, no fewer than 18 different kinds of districts were operating. An ever-increasing number of special laws was needed to enable such a variety to carry on.

The Legislature made its first major effort to correct some of the obvious inadequacies of this system in 1945 when it required all elementary districts to reorganize. Public officials – including legislators, county committeemen, county superintendents, and the state superintendent – attempting these reforms were accorded rough treatment.

While a 1947 amendment strengthening the reorganization act was under consideration, a thousand rural citizens including wives and many children appeared before the Senate Education Committee. They protested vociferously, calling for the abolition of the county committees and a return to democracy, charging that they were being forced into town school systems so that farm children would have to travel long distances and be unable to help with the chores. One elderly man testified: "Why in the name of God, common sense, and democracy would anyone want to tear up our system which has brought bleeding Kansas schools from the next to lowest to the next to highest of any state in the Union?" (38). He failed to mention the scale he used to arrive at this evaluation. The bitterness reached a climax when two senators received letters threatening them with death unless they supported a repeal of the law (39), and State Superintendent L. W. Brooks reported he received similar threats.

In spite of the uproar, much was accomplished—the Legislature validated all redistricting completed before the Kansas Supreme Court declared the reorganization acts to be unconstitutional 2 years later. The court ruled that the legislators had no authority to delegate lawmaking powers to the county committees in charge of the program. By March 1947, more than 45 percent of the 8,112 elementary districts in existence 2 years earlier had been affected in some way, with 3,700 either eliminated or their boundaries changed. Approximately 4,300 districts remained the same (40).

If the school district system was bad in 1945, rural-to-urban population shifts made it terrible by 1961. School-finance laws became more discriminatory against urban schools, and special legislation further complicated the situation. The state's welfare and local responsibility was little heeded. In most years, one or several schools operated with only one teacher and one pupil. For a time, four boards of one-room school districts were paying salaries to teachers who had no pupils, and in one instance a board employed two teachers to instruct three pupils, all from the same family. The boards of several closed schools paid exhorbitant sums to transport pupils to other districts, and the law permitted hundreds of schools to operate only 8 months a year. In 1960, 255 of the state's 552 public high schools operated with less than 75 students each; 18 had less than 25 students each.

In an attempt to bring some order out of this chaos, the 1961 Legislature enacted another reorganization law to create unified districts. But opponents, dead-set against any kind of realignment, exerted so much pressure that the bill was rendered ineffective before it was passed. In a test case, the State Supreme Court declared even this law to be unconstitutional on the same ground as the 1945 legislation.

By 1963, the situation begged for action. The legislators, determined to enact a sound law, consulted continually with the attorney general and other lawyers concerning the new bill's constitutionality until it finally passed that year. The role assigned the state superintendent under the new act completely reversed the authority granted him under the 1945 and 1961 laws. To ensure its constitutionality, every significant procedure in the reorganization process required either the superintendent's approval or certification, including action taken by the county planning boards and, in some instances, the results of elections. It provided for all territory in the state to be incorporated into school districts offering instruction from grades 1 through 12 and included authority to operate kindergartens and junior colleges under certain conditions. This act resulted in considerable unification, but unforeseen problems and inequities in it had to be adjusted by amendatory legislation 2 years later.

The staff of the new section created to administer the unification law traveled extensively over the state, consulting with county planning boards, holding hearings, and participating in hundreds of discussions and conferences. They prepared official forms, published instructional bulletins and brochures, and in many other ways contributed to the program's success. The department also assumed many duties formerly handled by the state's 105 county superintendents, such as certifying to county clerks the boundaries of school districts, advising them of all boundary changes, preparing up-to-date maps of all districts, conducting hearings on disputes over boundary changes, and advising local school officials on legal matters. This section even includes a transportation consultant who helps boards of education work out problems resulting from their enlarged districts.

The state superintendent had suffered a storm of unparalleled vilification and abuse when he had tried to administer the new law. So much authority had been delegated to him that opponents of the reorganization leveled a campaign against him as though he had enacted the legislation by dictatorial edict. They filed numerous law suits against him, hoping that the State Supreme Court would invalidate the statutes. Since this had been the fate of the 1945 and 1961 acts, opponents widely believed that the 1963 and 1965 legislation also would be thrown out. But the law stood; unification was upheld in every case (41).

Division of Certification and Accreditation

Teacher Certification. In the spring of 1864, Rosella Honey, a young prospective teacher from the Elm Creek settlement where Clyde is now located, traveled the 30 miles to the seat of Washington County to take the examination for a certificate. She had to make the 60-mile round trip twice because the county superintendent was not at home the first time. The examination itself proved not too difficult. She qualified for her certificate by writing her name, reading a paragraph from a newspaper, and answering oral questions in grammar, geography, and arithmetic. With this evidence of her ability, she began teaching the Elm Creek school the following fall.

From prestatehood days, Kansas required public school teachers to be certified and made certification the principal responsibility of the State Board of Education. The Legislature conferred this authority on the county superintendents during the territorial period, and they continued to exercise it until 1937.

In 1877, the demand for better qualified elementary teachers prompted the formation of county normal institutes to replace the senatorial district institutes conducted by the state superintendent. Closely supervised by the state board—which even certified each instructor—these institutes, usually meeting for about 4 weeks during the summer months, constituted the only professional preparation available for many teachers. After 1915, county superintendents were allowed to run institutes for only 5 to 20 days and then administer one of the four examinations conducted by their office annually. Since 1937, these county institutes have become little more than briefing sessions of from 2 to 5 days' length.

The Legislature took another step to ensure better-prepared elementary teachers in 1909, when it authorized accredited high schools to establish normal training programs. High school graduates who satisfactorily completed work prescribed by the state board became eligible for certification upon passing an examination conducted under the board's supervision. These graduates helped fill the demand for thousands of beginning teachers. But new teachers in rural schools seldom stayed long. Girls hoped to marry after a few years of teaching, and a number of rural boards adopted a policy of not retaining teachers more than 2 or 3 years regardless of their proficiency. Encouraged by a $500 subsidy to each participating high school, the normal training program reached its height in 1924 with 349 schools offering courses (42).

F. Floyd Herr, appointed secretary to the state board in 1943, administered the teacher certification program and the board's policies for accrediting educational institutions until 1945, when he became the director of teacher education and certification in the newly organized State Department of Public Instruction. He has provided state and national leadership in these fields for more than 23 years.

Under the direction of Dr. Herr and State Superintendent L. W. Brooks, the Kansas Advisory Council on Education was formed in 1947 (43), when the department became the only certifying agency in the state. This voluntary, independent agency's members are named by the organizations represented on it, including 4-year colleges and universities, several groups of professional educators, the State Department of Public Instruction, and the Kansas Association of Boards of Education. The Kansas Advisory Council has played an important role in raising standards for teachers and improving teacher education in the colleges and universities (44).

The council's first task was to rewrite certificate regulations and develop a set of standards for evaluating colleges and universities that trained teachers. The result was a dramatic reduction in the kinds of certificates—teachers held no less than 89 different types from 1944 to 1964. Today, the state issues only one type each for elementary, secondary, and junior college teachers, three levels of certificates for administrators, and an original 1-year certificate at each level under certain conditions (45). The council also coordinates teacher education programs in the colleges and universities, conducts studies of current educational issues, and provides a forum for discussing college and public school relations. In its advisory capacity, it facilitates the department's policy-making responsibilities.

Elementary and Secondary School Accreditation. From the 1870's, the University of Kansas served as the first accrediting agency for high schools. When the State Department of Education was formally created in 1915, all of these responsibilities were transferred to it. The move was the climax of long-time criticism of the university by public school officials who charged that it had overemphasized college preparation for accreditation (46). Under the rules and regulations the state board adopted, the department had the power to accredit high schools and standard elementary schools.

Under a kind of ex post facto policy, the department did not accredit high schools until the close of the term. Neither the students nor school officials knew whether they were working in an accredited school until the year ended. Not until 1959 were the schools accredited on June 30 for the coming year.

Classifying accredited high schools as A, B, or C was discontinued that year. This classification system had worked well for a long time, but eventually pressures on the department made it difficult to lower A ratings of the schools that held them for several years, whether they maintained standards or not. Also, since the A rating placed little emphasis on the breadth and variety of curricular offerings, it was not a satisfactory criterion for judging the quality or quantity of instruction. A majority of high schools offered only a few courses outside college preparatory programs, although until 1960 less than one-half of their graduates enrolled in college. Laymen naturally assumed that a class A high school enrolling 75 students offered the same quality of education as a large school teaching a comprehensive diversified program.

A neighboring state approached the same problem in a clever and sensible manner by changing the A, B, and C classifications to A, AA, and AAA, thus offending no one when A became the lowest classification. But rather than attempt to rejuvenate the classification system that had been used for more than 40 years, the department decided to revise the whole accreditation procedure. During 1957, hundreds of administrators, teachers, and college personnel collaborated in revising the standards. After 2 years of work and study, the state board formally approved new standards. It scheduled a 2-year transition from the old to the new plans, the revised standards to be the basis for accrediting all high schools starting with the 1961-62 school year.

The new standards established three categories of high schools: comprehensive, standard, and approved. Distinctions between them are both quantitative and qualitative. The comprehensive high school must offer and teach a minimum of 50 units of balanced courses in addition to meeting the highest requirements for teacher preparation. Standard high schools must meet the same requirements but must teach only 30 units, the minimum permitted by statute. Schools accredited as comprehensive or standard can receive special recognition for meeting the highest standards of excellence if an appraisal by a committee named by the department and the school's own self-evaluation warrants it. Since legislation passed in 1965 requires all high schools to offer and to teach a minimum of 30 units of instruction as defined by the state superintendent, the "approved" category will not be used after 1966-67.

In the early 1920's, the state board adopted standards for accrediting junior high schools, but since the schools have no system of classification and the standards are loosely drawn, practices have been somewhat sketchy until recently. More attention has been given to upgrading these schools since C. W. Rice joined the accreditation section in 1963 as a junior high school consultant. He directed a 2-year study and prepared an evaluation guide which promises to strengthen these schools tremendously (47).

Standards for elementary schools adopted by the state board under the 1915 act were not used for accreditation, but rather to stimulate improvement by issuing certificates and door plates that would recognize schools meeting superior, standard, or approved requirements. In the late 1930's, these designations were changed to A, B, and C, but aside from the difference in terminology the program remained the same until 1945, when a self-rating plan was adopted. At present, elementary schools are accredited under procedures similar to those used in evaluating secondary schools. The standards are published, the administrators must make annual organization reports, and departmental consultants visit schools and cooperate with administrators in evaluating them.

Kansas Junior Colleges. The enabling law of 1917, under which the junior colleges were established, closely followed the national pattern for such laws. Although the Kansas junior colleges were originally organized as high school extension courses and continued as such until 1965, they have almost certainly met the needs of many young people. The demand for higher education increased along with opportunities for educated persons in business and industry, but many prospective students were unable to travel the distances from their homes to colleges. The junior colleges served these students and, by being so easily available, motivated some to continue their schooling. The schools improved significantly under state department supervision and accreditation. In 1960, the standards were revised, and all 2-year institutions conducted evaluation studies which they filed with the state superintendent.

Many Kansas educators hoped that the junior colleges could teach a comprehensive curriculum, including courses that would be acceptable for the first 2 years of a college degree, vocational-technical courses, and terminal courses.

Economics again proved to be the obstacle, preventing many schools from implementing these plans and even forcing some of them into financial crises by 1965. A contributing factor was the policy of the vocation education board, which adopted a recommendation by its executive officer to bypass junior colleges in distributing new federal funds available under the 1963 vocational-technical act. Since the state department supervised the junior colleges but had no jurisdiction over vocational-technical education, its only recourse was to protest to the Legislature. One school threatened suit to test the constitutionality of delegating legislative powers to the vocational board. As a result, the Legislature created a separate board in 1965 to govern the state technical institute and curtailed the state board's jurisidiction over junior colleges. The board then reversed its policy for vocational education so that junior colleges could receive the federal funds.

Anxious to establish junior colleges on a sound basis, the Kansas Legislative Council authorized its education committee to study the colleges' role, function, organization, financing, and supervision. The report, published the following year, served as the blueprint for a law providing for a state system of community junior colleges. This legislation, also passed in 1965, names the state superintendent as the authority over junior colleges and allows him to employ a director, an assistant director, and a secretary for a junior college section in the Division of Teacher Certification and Accreditation. Not only does the law separate these schools from their former high school extension role, but it also allows the junior college districts to expand with additional state support. It calls for the development of a plan under which new community junior colleges can be established and for a state advisory council of 11 members to give them all possible assistance. The community junior colleges have taken on new life since 1964: Three new ones have been organized, and 12 of the present 17 have begun building programs to accommodate expected enrollment increases.

The state superintendent has turned over to the junior college section the administration of 200 annual scholarships created by the Legislature in 1963 for college freshmen with ability and need. They are limited to tuition and fees not to exceed $500 at the college of the applicant's choice and are renewable for 1 year if the student successfully completes his freshman work.

Adult Education. The growing need for more skilled personnel in business and industry not only created the demand for junior colleges, but also resulted in a call for more adult education. Business organizations, university extension divisions, and other groups pointed to the technological advances that created a need for trained workers. Many people with a minimum of schooling became increasingly aware of the need for better training. The department created an adult education section—headed by a director employed under a foundation grant for 1960-61—which received almost unanimous support from the various adult education groups. The Legislature failed to make an appropriation to continue this service but authorized its reestablishment in 1965, when federal funds became available under the adult basic education act.

Under a 90-10 finance agreement with the U.S. Office of Education, the director and his assistant divide their time between the adult basic education program and the services launched in 1960 under the foundation grant. The adult education section conducted 14 programs in basic education during 1965-66, enrolling 1,100 adults under the direction of 75 specially trained teachers. The total expenditures for the first year were $132,000. The 1966-67 expenditure was expected to be $285,000, for a projected enrollment of 2,000.

This section also administers other important programs that meet the needs of adults who have not graduated from high school. It issues annually some 1,200 certificates of academic equivalency to adults who make the required score on the general educational development tests. Most employees accept the certificate in lieu of a high school diploma, and some colleges use it for entrance requirements.

Private, commercial, and trade schools must qualify for permits before they can solicit students, and the adult education section has granted more than 150 such permits since the law was revised in 1961 to include all categories operated for profit.

FEDERAL-STATE RELATIONS

Most Kansans have dramatically changed their attitudes toward federal support of education since 1960. In spite of the nationwide concern following Russia's first Sputnik, Kansas legislative leaders were extremely reluctant to provide funds in 1959 to match federal money appropriated under the National Defense Education Act of 1958. Although Congress enacted the NDEA to improve educational opportunity throughout the nation, the Kansas Legislature appropriated only $20,000 the first year to match the $59,000 in federal funds allocated to Kansas on a 50-50 basis for administering and supervising Title III (purchase of instructional equipment).

Until the Kansas Legislature established the area vocational schools in 1963, financed partly with federal funds from the Vocational Education Act, local chambers of commerce consistently opposed federal support for education. Now, in a reversal of their historic position, they have engaged in a spirited competition to acquire one of the 20 area vocational schools for their communities. This scramble for federal money was amusing to educators who long had sought support from Washington for educational programs; many of the business groups were almost "climbing the walls" to obtain the benefits they realized would accrue from these federally subsidized schools.

When Congress enacted Public Law 89-10, the Elementary and Secondary Education Act of 1965, the traditional Kansas opposition to federal support had mostly disappeared, although a small group of lawmakers tried unsuccessfully to push through legislation that would have deprived the schools of such aid early in 1966. With $1,847,000 in federal money available on a 50-50 matching basis during the first 2.5 years under the NDEA, Kansas districts applied for only $1,568,170, indicating again the reluctance of the citizens to use federal money. But in 1965-66, the applications for NDEA funds exceeded the state's allotment by 25 percent–convincing evidence of the change in attitude.

All of the department's guidance and counseling activities except the director's salary are wholly supported by federal funds under Title V of NDEA. Much has been done with NDEA Title X funds to upgrade the department's statistical services, including the development of an accounting system for schools and partial financing of the studies that led to the 1965 school foundation finance act. A Civil Defense adult education program is wholly supported by federal money, as are activities under Titles I and II of ESEA. School lunch programs have been federally subsidized since 1946. It is the department's policy to use all of the Title V funds to upgrade its services. In fact, most of the department's expansion since 1945 has been federally financed, and at present about half of its payroll is derived from federal sources.

The department's philosophy for many years has been to use whatever funds are available for education, but this money and its sources must first have legislative approval. Thus, some federal appropriations for education have remained unused each year: The Legislature failed to act. A more serious handicap is Congress' tendency to appropriate these funds late in the fiscal year. These delays make advance planning all but impossible at both state and local levels and place undue burdens on state departments of education and the schools.

Another major concern of state education agencies is the increasing mass of administrative detail required by the federal agencies. Much of the red tape injected by the federal agencies seems to defy justification. One example is the administration of federal funds used for upgrading the State Department of Public Instruction under Title V of ESEA. The regulations require the department to submit each project proposal separately to the U.S. Office of Education, rather than submitting one overall plan, as provided in many other federally supported programs. Writing six or eight separate projects to improve one department, together with separate accounting and evaluation for each, involves endless and, in the opinion of many state officials, unnecessary clerical, statistical, and managerial work.

Another basic issue in federal-state relations is the requirement that the state, in addition to maintaining an accounting system of its own as prescribed by state law, account for the federal funds under another system. This means that state agencies must maintain two accounting systems, which are too often incompatible.

The Kansas department is in full accord with the principle of federal support for education but believes that the categorical aid approach has not been properly balanced in several instances. As the federal government increases its support of education, all of its agencies should recognize the role the states play in this field and trust state education agencies to be as effective and competent to handle funds from federal sources as in administering state funds. State department officials are somewhat critical of activities authorized under Title III of Public Law 89-10, because these programs, involving local school districts, are administered directly by the Office of Education, thus violating the philosophy that education is a state function. Department officials also have reservations about the regional educational laboratories established under Title IV of ESEA, believing that the stated objectives of the title could be more effectively achieved by state departments if comparable funds were available to them and at the same time would be consistent with the principle of state control of education.

FOOTNOTES

1. L. E. Wooster, *et al., Columbian History of Education* (Topeka: Kansas State Historical Society, 1893), p. 5.
2. P. J. Wyatt, ed., "School Then and Now," *Heritage of Kansas* (Emporia: Department of English, Kansas State Teachers College, 1963), pp. 9-10.
3. Superintendent of Public Instruction, *Eighth Annual Report* (1868), p. 40.
4. Superintendent of Public Instruction, *Twelfth Annual Report* (1872), p. 13.
5. Kansas, *Laws* (1873), ch. 133, sec. 3.
6. John L. Eberhardt, *Kansas State Department of Public Instruction,* Governmental Research Series No. 14 (Lawrence: University of Kansas, 1955), pp. 1, 6-7.
7. These exemptions were also allowed in a 1903 revision of the law. See Table 1 in Appendix C for listing of compulsory attendance laws.
8. For further instances of fraud, see Superintendent of Public Instruction, *Ninth Annual Report* (1869), p. 35.
9. For the complete story, see: Kansas, *Laws* (1861), ch. 76, art. 2, sec. 2; Territorial Assembly, "Organization Act for the State School System," *Laws* (1859), sec. 15, p. 3.

10. In Kansas, there are three classes of cities: first, second, and third. Communities of 150 or more persons may incorporate as third-class cities. Their only relationship to common school districts is that every third-class city is located in a common school district. When cities reach a population of 2,000, they may, by making application, qualify as second-class cities. The school districts in which second-class cities are located are designated as second-class city districts. When a city reaches a population of 15,000, it may apply to become a city of the first-class, and the school district in which it is located becomes a first-class city school district.

    Each classification of cities and each classification of school districts is governed by codes of laws that differ widely. Except for a small scattering of school districts not yet reorganized under the 1963 and 1965 Unification Acts, all categories of school districts were wiped out in 1965. All reorganized districts are now unified districts; the Legislature provided that unified districts would be governed by laws applicable to school districts of cities of the first class in matters not covered in the skeleton code.

11. Superintendent of Public Instruction, *Twelfth Biennial Report* (1900), pp. 154-59. Dr. Throckmorton questions the accuracy of this enrollment of 11,508, but this is the figure reported. The enrollment in 1910 was 29,933. *Seventeenth Biennial Report* (1910), p. 164.
12. The School District Unification Acts of 1963 and 1965 and the realignment of school districts under their provisions are discussed in section 3. "Educational Programs in Kansas and the Role of the State Department of Public Instruction." See Table 2 in Appendix C for kinds of school districts in 1963.
13. Kansas, *Constitution* (1961), art. 6, sec. 1.
14. Interview with F. Floyd Herr, October 19, 1966.
15. See Appendix B, Supplement 1, for qualifications of State Board of Education members.
16. See Appendix B, Supplement 2, for qualifications of candidates for the state superintendent of public instruction.
17. See Appendix B.
18. For other details, see Department of Public Instruction, *Our Kansas System of Education* (Topeka: The Department, 1960), p. 17.
19. Otto E. Domian and Robert J. Keller, *Comprehensive Educational Survey of Kansas* (5 vols. and a Summary; Topeka: Kansas Legislative Council, 1960).
20. See Appendix B, Supplement 3, for House Concurrent Resolution No. 505.
21. For the structure of this division, see Appendix B.
22. Markham served as state superintendent from 1932 to 1939.
23. W. T. Markham, *Unit Program in Social Studies* (Topeka: Department of Public Instruction, 1934).
24. Superintendent of Public Instruction, *Thirtieth Biennial Report* (1935), p. 7.
25. W. T. Markham, *Study Bulletins 1-6 for the Improvement of Instruction,* Bulletin 15 (Topeka: Kansas State Historical Society, 1939).
26. Superintendent of Public Instruction, *Reports, 1954-56* (1956), p. 10.
27. For further information, see Marguerite Thorsell, "The Education of Educable Mentally Retarded Children in Sparsely Populated Rural Areas," Cooperative Research Project No. 055, Topeka, Department of Public Instruction, 1963. (Mimeographed.)
28. Superintendent of Public Instruction, *Ninth Annual Report* (1869), p. 5.
29. See Appendix C, Table 4, for textbook adoption agencies.
30. Kansas, *Laws* (1913), ch. 288, sec. 13.
31. George L. Frey, "Troublesome Adoptions," *The Kansas Teacher* (December 1954), p. 24.
32. Superintendent of Public Instruction, *Reports, 1951-52* (1952), p. 61.
33. The six sections of this division are headed by Lawrence Simpson, a former superintendent of schools. Its work has become especially heavy because it assists the superintendent in planning policy, now involving new federally financed programs.
34. Fay Kampschroeder, who has held a key position in the department for 18 years, is the director of this section as of this writing, 1967.
35. Carl B. Althaus, *A Quest for Quality* (Topeka: Department of Public Instruction, 1963), pp. 41-57.
36. *Ibid.;* Carl B. Althaus, *An Emphasis on Earnings* (Topeka: Department of Public Instruction, 1964).
37. Superintendent of Public Instruction, *Ninth Annual Report* (1869), p. 6.
38. *Daily Capital* (Topeka), February 18, 1947.
39. *Ibid.*, February 21.
40. Kansas Legislative Council, *School District Reorganization,* Publication No. 150 (Topeka: The Council, September 1947), p. 1.
41. Kansas Supreme Court, *Kansas Reports,* CXCIV (1964-65), 519; CXCV (1965), 144.
42. The High School Normal Training Act was not terminated until 1945.
43. Problems resulting from the multiplicity of certifying agencies from the earliest days of statehood clearly disclosed the need for a group of this kind, and in little more than a decade at least 37 states were functioning with councils or advisory committees.

44. L. Eileen Heinen, "An Analysis of the Kansas Advisory Council on Teacher Education" (unpublished master's thesis, Kansas State Teachers College, Emporia, 1965), chs. 3 and 4.

45. See Floyd F. Herr, *Certification Handbook* (Topeka: Department of Public Instruction, 1966).

46. John L. Eberhardt, *Kansas State Department of Public Instruction*, Governmental Research Series No. 14 (Lawrence: University of Kansas, 1955), pp. 140-41.

47. C. W. Rice, *Evaluation Guide for the Junior High Schools of Kansas* (Topeka: Department of Public Instruction, 1966).

BIBLIOGRAPHY

Public Documents

Kansas. *Constitution* (1861).

-- *House Concurrent Resolution No. 505* (1966).

-- *Session Laws* (1861-1965).

Kansas Secretary of State. *Kansas Directory, 1965-66*.

Kansas Supreme Court. *Kansas Reports*. Vol. CXCIV (1964-65), Vol. CXCV (1965).

Kansas Territorial Assembly. *Session Laws* (1858-60).

Books

Board of Education. *Manual of the State Board of Education, 1894-1913*. Topeka: Kansas State Historical Society. These manuals are on file in the Society's office.

-- *Standardization of Rural Graded Schools*. Topeka: Kansas State Historical Society, 1902.

Department of Public Instruction. *Adult Education in Kansas*. Topeka: The Department, 1961.

-- *Course of Study for Rural Schools of Kansas*. Varied titles. Topeka: The Department, 1913-27.

-- *Educational Kansas*. Topeka: The Department, 1902.

-- *Kansas Educational Directory*. Topeka: The Department, 1907-66.

-- *Kansas Scholarship Program*. Topeka: The Department, 1965.

-- *Kansas Secondary School Handbook*. Topeka: The Department, 1961.

-- *Manual for Cooperative Evaluation of High Schools*. Topeka: The Department, 1965.

-- *Our Kansas System of Education*. Topeka: The Department, 1960.

-- *Pulling Together*. Topeka: The Department, 1960.

Eberhardt, John L. *Kansas State Department of Public Instruction*. Governmental Research Series No. 14. Lawrence: University of Kansas, 1955.

Frey, George L. *A Century of Education in Kansas*. Vol. 2: *Kansas the First Century: A History*. Edited by John D. Bright. New York: Lewis Historical Publishing Co., 1956.

Herr, F. Floyd. *Certification Handbook*. Topeka: Department of Public Instruction, 1966.

Kansas Legislative Council. *School District Reorganization*. Publication No. 150. Topeka: The Council, 1947.

Markham, W. T. *Study Bulletins 1-6 for the Improvement of Instruction*. Bulletin 15. Topeka: Kansas State Historical Society, 1939.

-- *Unit Program in Social Studies*. Topeka: Department of Public Instruction, 1934.

Peach, John R., ed. *Kansas, Its Power and Glory*. Topeka: The Editor, 1966.

Rice, C. W. *Evaluation Guide for the Junior High Schools of Kansas*. Topeka: Department of Public Instruction, 1966.

Throckmorton, Adel F. *The Kansas System of Schools*. Topeka: State Department of Public Instruction, 1962.

Wooster, L. E., *et al. Columbian History of Education*. Prepared under the general supervision of the Board of Directors for the Kansas Educational Exhibit for the Columbian Exposition, 1893, commemorating the four-hundredth anniversary of the discovery of America. L. E. Wooster, Superintendent of the Kansas Educational Exhibit. Topeka: Kansas State Historical Society, 1893.

Wright, C. O. *100 Years in Kansas Education*. Topeka: Kansas State Teachers Association, 1964.

Articles and Periodicals

Daily Capital (Topeka), February 18 and 21, 1947.

Frey, George L. "Troublesome Adoptions." *The Kansas Teacher* (December 1954), p. 24.

--"Textbook Costs." *The Kansas Teacher* (January 1955).

Wyatt, P. J., ed. "School Then and Now." *Heritage of Kansas*. Emporia: Department of English, Kansas State Teachers College, 1963.

Reports

Althaus, Carl B. *A Quest for Quality*. Topeka: Department of Public Instruction, 1963.

-- *An Emphasis on Earnings*. Topeka: Department of Public Instruction, 1964.

Department of Public Instruction. *Report of a Review by the United States Office of Education Under Title V of Public Law 89-10* (1966).

Domian, Otto E., and Keller, Robert J. *Comprehensive Educational Survey*. 5 vols. and a Summary. Topeka: Kansas Legislative Council, 1960.

Kampschroeder, W. C. *School Building Survey Report.* Topeka: Department of Public Instruction, 1952.

Kansas Legislative Council. *Community Junior Colleges.* Topeka: The Council, 1964.

Superintendent of Public Instruction. *Annual and Biennial Reports,* 1868-1935, 1952-58. Topeka: Department of Public Instruction.

Unpublished Material

Heinen, L. Eileen. "An Analysis of the Kansas Advisory Council on Teacher Education." Unpublished master's thesis, Kansas State Teachers College, Emporia, 1965.

Herr, F. Floyd. "History of the Kansas Advisory Council on Teacher Education." State Department of Public Instruction, Topeka, 1954. (Mimeographed.)

Iske, Gladys. "Kansas Teacher Certification Legislation from 1937 Through 1957-58." Unpublished master's thesis, University of Kansas, Lawrence, 1965.

Minutes of the State Board of Education, 1873-1966.

Thorsell, Marguerite. "The Education of Educable Mentally Retarded Children in Sparsely Populated Rural Areas." Cooperative Research Project No. 055. Topeka: State Department of Public Instruction, 1963. (Mimeographed.)

Other Source

Personal interview with F. Floyd Herr, director of certification and accreditation, Kansas State Department of Public Instruction, Topeka, on October 19, 1966.

Appendix A

KANSAS CHIEF STATE SCHOOL OFFICERS

Territorial Superintendents

1858	James H. Noteware (March-Oct.)
1858-61	Samuel Wiley Greer
1861	John C. Douglass (Jan.-Feb.)

State Superintendents of Public Instruction

1861-62	William Riley Griffith
1862-63	Simeon Montgomery Thorp
1863-67	Isaac T. Goodnow
1867-71	Peter MacVicar
1871-75	Hugh DeFrance McCarty
1875-77	John Fraser
1877-81	Allen Borsley Lemmon
1881-85	Henry Clay Speer
1885-89	Joseph Hadden Lawhead
1889-93	George Wesley Winans
1893-95	Henry Newton Gains
1895-97	Edmund Stanley
1897-99	William Stryker
1899-1903	Frank Nelson
1903-1907	Insley L. Dayhoff
1907-12	Edward T. Fairchild
1912-19	Wilbert Davidson Ross
1919-23	Miss L. E. Wooster
1923-27	Jess W. Miley
1927-32	George A. Allen, Jr.
1932-39	W. T. Markham
1939-45	George L. McClenny
1945-49	L. W. Brooks
1949-66	Adel F. Throckmorton
1966-67	W. C. Kampschroeder
1967-	Murle M. Hayden

Appendix B

Chart I.--KANSAS DEPARTMENT OF PUBLIC INSTRUCTION, 1950

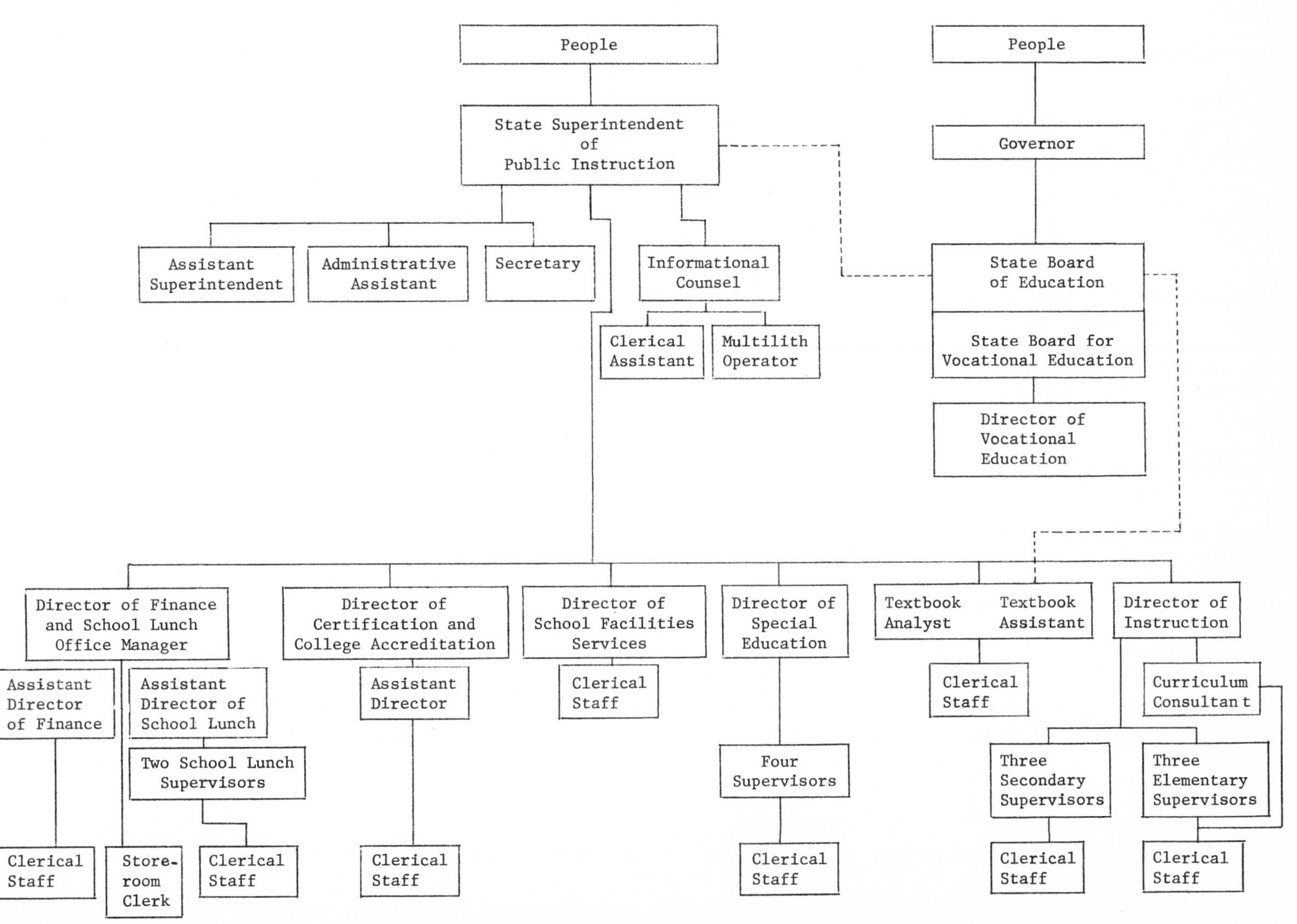

Appendix B

Chart II.--KANSAS DEPARTMENT OF PUBLIC INSTRUCTION, 1966

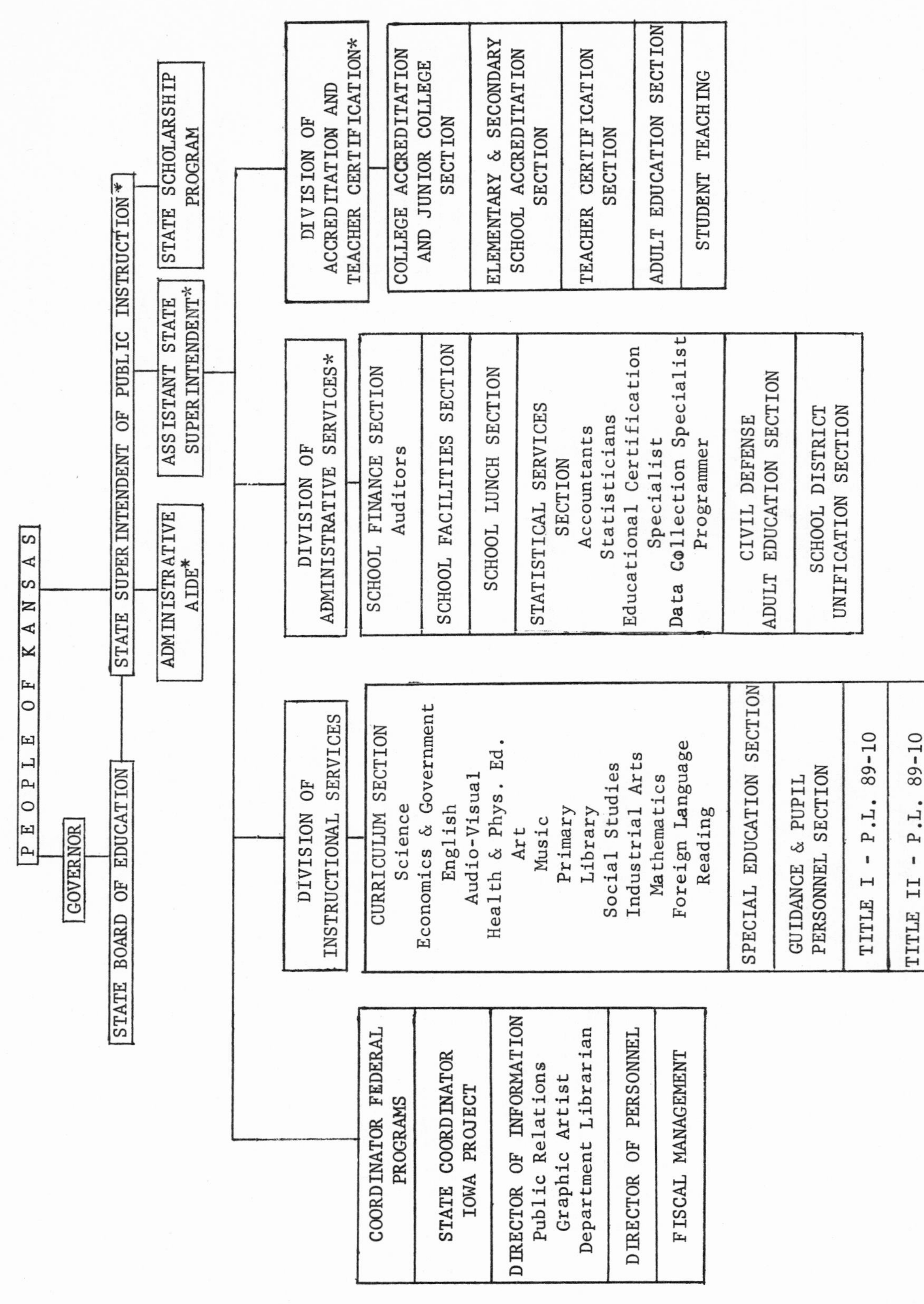

* Key staff members assigned to State Emergency Operation Center.

Appendix B

Chart III.--KANSAS DEPARTMENT OF PUBLIC INSTRUCTION, 1968

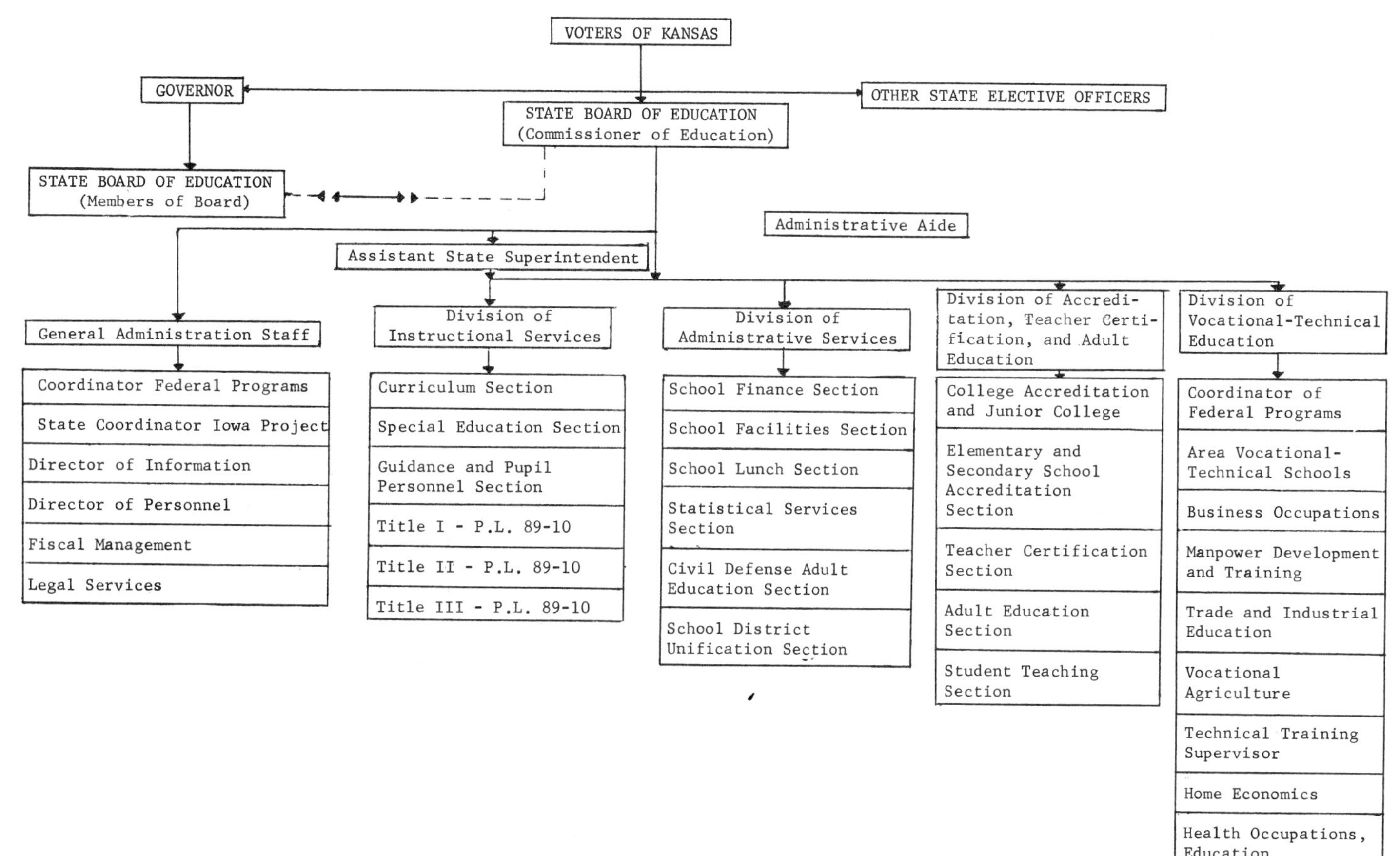

Projected under provisions of revised State Constitution effective in 1969.

Appendix B

Supplement 1. – Qualifications for Membership on State Board of Education

In appointing members to serve on the State Board of Education the Governor–

Is prohibited from appointing anyone who is engaged in school work as teacher, principal, or superintendent.

Must appoint members of the two major political parties with not more than four at the same time from the same party.

May not appoint more than three members who are residents of territory governed by boards of education of school districts in cities of the first or second class.

Must appoint at least one member from each Congressional District.

May not appoint any of the seven members to serve more than two consecutive terms of three years each.

–*Laws of Kansas* (1945), Chapter 282, Section 19

Supplement 2. – Qualifications for State Superintendent of Public Instruction

At the time of filing candidates for the office of State Superintendent of Public Instruction must–

Hold the highest type of teachers certificate prescribed by law.

Be a resident of Kansas for at least 5 years immediately preceding.

Be a graduate of an accredited college or university with at least 30 hours of postgraduate credit.

Have at least 10 years teaching or administrative experience, of which at least 5 years shall have been in the public school systems of Kansas and active in such work within 2 years prior to the date of filing for such office.

–*Laws of Kansas* (1945), Chapter 282, Section 5

Appendix B

Supplement 3.–House Concurrent Resolution No. 505

A Proposition to amend the education article of the constitution of the state of Kansas, being all of article 6 of the constitution.

Be it resolved by the Legislature of the State of Kansas, two-thirds of the members elected to the House of Representatives and two-thirds of the members elected to the Senate concurring therein:

Section 1. The following proposition to amend the constitution of the state of Kansas shall be submitted to the qualified electors of the state for their approval or rejection: Article 6 of the constitution of the state of Kansas is amended to read as follows:

"Article 6.–Education

"Section 1. *Schools and related institutions and activities.* The legislature shall provide for intellectual, educational, vocational and scientific improvement by establishing and maintaining public schools, educational institutions and related activities which may be organized and changed in such manner as may be provided by law.

"Sec. 2. *State board of education and state board of regents. (a)* The legislature shall provide for a state board of education which shall have general supervision of public schools, educational institutions and all the educational interests of the state, except educational functions delegated by law to the state board of regents. The state board of education shall perform such other duties as may be provided by law.

"*(b)* The legislature shall provide for a state board of regents and for its control and supervision of public institutions of higher education. Public institutions of higher education shall include universities and colleges granting baccalaureate or postbaccalaureate degrees and such other institutions and educational interests as may be provided by law. The state board of regents shall perform such other duties as may be prescribed by law.

"*(c)* Any municipal university shall be operated, supervised and controlled as provided by law.

"Sec. 3. *Members of state board of education and state board of regents. (a)* There shall be ten members of the state board of education with overlapping terms as the legislature may prescribe. The legislature shall make provision for ten member districts, each comprised of four contiguous senatorial districts. The electors of each member district shall elect one person residing in the district as a member of the board. The legislature shall prescribe the manner in which vacancies occurring on the board shall be filled.

"*(b)* The state board of regents shall have nine members with overlapping terms as the legislature may prescribe. Members shall be appointed by the governor, subject to confirmation by the senate. One member shall be appointed from each congressional district with the remaining members appointed at large, however, no two members shall reside in the same county at the time of their appointment. Vacancies occurring on the board shall be filled by appointment by the governor as provided by law.

"*(c)* Subsequent redistricting shall not disqualify any member of either board from service for the remainder of his term. Any member of either board may be removed from office for cause as may be provided by law.

"Sec. 4. *Commissioner of education.* The state board of education shall appoint a commissioner of education who shall serve at the pleasure of the board as its executive officer.

"Sec. 5. *Local public schools.* Local public schools under the general supervision of the state board of education shall be maintained, developed and operated by locally elected boards. When authorized by law, such boards may make and carry out agreements for cooperative operation and administration of educational programs under the general supervision of the state board of education, but such agreements shall be subject to limitation.

"Sec. 6. *Finance. (a)* The legislature may levy a permanent tax for the use and benefit of state institutions of higher education and apportion among and appropriate the same to the several institutions, which levy, apportionment and appropriation shall continue until changed by statute. Further appropriation and other provision for finance of institutions of higher education may be made by the legislature.

"*(b)* The legislature shall make suitable provision for finance of the educational interests of the state. No tuition shall be charged for attendance at any public school to pupils required by law to attend such school, except such fees or supplemental charges as may be authorized by law. The legislature may authorize the state board of regents to establish tuition, fees and charges at institutions under its supervision.

"*(c)* No religious sect or sects shall control any part of the public educational funds.

"Sec. 7. *Saving clause. (a)* All laws in force at the time of the adoption of this amendment and consistent therewith shall remain in full force and effect until amended or repealed by the legislature. All laws inconsistent with this amendment, unless sooner repealed or amended to conform with this amendment, shall remain in full force and effect until July 1, 1969.

"*(b)* Notwithstanding any other provision of the constitution to the contrary, no state superintendent of public instruction or county superintendent of public instruction shall be elected after January 1, 1967.

"*(c)* The state perpetual school fund or any part thereof may be managed and invested as provided by law or all or any part thereof may be appropriated, both as to principal and income, to the support of the public schools supervised by the state board of education.

"Sec. 2. This resolution, if concurred in by two-thirds of the members elected to the house of representatives and two-thirds of the members elected to the senate, shall be entered on the journals, together with the yeas and nays. The secretary of state shall cause the proposed amendment to be published and submitted to the electors of the state at the general election in the year 1966 as provided by law. This resolution shall be published by the secretary of state in the Special Session Laws of 1966, and shall be given a chapter number therein.

Appendix C

Table 1. – COMPULSORY ATTENDANCE LAWS

Laws of	Ages applicable	Alternate requirements
1874, chap. 123	8 to 14	None
1903, chap. 123	8 to 15	Complete 8th grade
1919, chap. 272	8 to 16	Complete 8th grade
1923, chap. 182	7 to 16	Complete 8th grade
1965, chap. 409	7 to 16	None

Table 2. – KINDS OF SCHOOL DISTRICTS IN 1963 AND NUMBER OF EACH

Kind of district	Number organized
Cities of the first class	13
Cities of the second class	84
Unified	5
Common school, elementary and high	146
Common school, elementary	753
Common school, grades 1-9	2
Common school, one teacher	330
County board of education	1
Fort Leavenworth board	1
Johnson County special	11
Sedgwick County special	8
Rural high school, regular	267
Rural high school, Russell Plan	12
Rural high school, grades 7-12	3
Sedgwick County special high school	1
Community high school	20
Closed common school districts	169
Closed rural high school districts	14

Table 3. – KINDS OF SCHOOL DISTRICTS IN 1966 AND NUMBER OF EACH

Kind of district		Number organized
Unified under special legislation		2
Greeley county unit		1
Unified under acts of 1963 and 1965		304
Nonunified districts:	rural high school	9
	common school	27
	second-class cities	2
Total districts in Kansas		345

Table 4. – STATE TEXTBOOK AGENCIES

Year	Name of agency	Function
1897	School Textbook Commission [a]	Adopt textbooks, contract with publishers, set prices on textbooks
1913	School Book Commission[a]	Same as in 1897 and administer state printing of textbooks
1937	State Board of Education[a] (Professional)	Same as in 1913
1945	State Board of Education[a] (Lay)	Same as in 1913
1957	Textbook Review Committee [b]	Publish lists of suitable textbooks (adoptions by local school districts)

[a] State superintendent ex officio chairman.

[b] Appointed by state superintendent with State Board of Education approval.

Appendix C

Table 5. – THE STATE BOARD OF EDUCATION: PERSONNEL, DATES AUTHORIZED, AND PRINCIPAL DUTIES

Authorized	Personnel	Principal duties
1873	State superintendent; chancellor, State University; president, Agricultural College; president, Emporia Normal School; president, Leavenworth Normal School	Issue state diplomas and state certificates of two grades upon examination.
1893	Same as in 1873	Same as in 1873, and examine work of colleges and accept college credits in lieu of examination for teachers certificates.
1915	State superintendent became ex officio chairman of state board and some lay representation added	Same as in 1893, and prescribe courses of study, employ a professional secretary to inspect colleges, and administer teacher certification.
1919	Lay representation eliminated from the State Board of Education	Same as in 1915, and serve as Board for Vocational Education.
1933	State superintendent ex officio chairman, one representative from each of five institutions of higher education, one member from faculty of private college, one county superintendent, one high school principal, two citizens in farming or business	Same as in 1919. After 1937, served as textbook adoption agency.
1945	Seven lay members, one from each congressional district, others at large	Approve or disapprove policies of state superintendent, adopt textbooks until 1957, serve as Board for Vocational Education.

NOTE:
All board members except those holding ex officio positions appointed by the Governor.

Appendix C

Table 6. – TEACHER CERTIFICATION PROGRESS AND DATES OF LEGISLATIVE ACTION

Year	Action taken
1858	County superintendents authorized to certify teachers.
1863	State normal schools authorized to certify teachers who meet requirements set by the institution.
1873	State Board of Education created and authorized to certify teachers upon examination.
1876	Boards of education of cities of the first and second class authorized to certify teachers.
1893	State Board of Education authorized to substitute credit from approved colleges for examination in those subjects as qualification for certification of teachers.
1899	Graduates of the University of Kansas and other accredited institutions taking required courses could qualify to be certified by the State Board of Education.
1909	State Board of Education authorized to issue certificates to high school graduates completing high school normal training courses and passing a state examination.
1915	Legislature set bachelor's degree requirement for high school teachers.
1937	The State Board of Education and the three state teachers colleges given exclusive authority to certify teachers.
1945	The state superintendent of public instruction given exclusive authority to certify teachers under rules and regulations approved by the State Board of Education and to graduates of teachers colleges with institutional recommendation.

Table 7. – SUMMARY OF SPECIAL EDUCATION SERVICES, 1965

Reimbursable special classes for educable mentally retarded children	241
Reimbursable special classes for severely mentally retarded children	21
Reimbursable speech and hearing programs	. . .
Programs for the hearing impaired	126
Reimbursable programs of school social work and psychological services	57
Reimbursable programs of city or county directors of special education	9
Reimbursable programs for the gifted	20
Reimbursable programs for the neurologically impaired	1
Reimbursable programs for the emotionally disturbed	22
Reimbursable programs for the visually impaired	8
Reimbursable programs for the orthopedically handicapped	11
Reimbursable programs for the children with physical problems	6
Programs for homebound and hospital (full time)	13
School systems supplied with clear-type books for partially seeing	82

17 Kentucky

DEPARTMENT OF EDUCATION
Louise Combs
Kern Alexander

Contents

EDUCATIONAL PATTERNS BEFORE 1900

The development of Kentucky's system of public education and that of the Kentucky State Department of Education are intertwined. Both developed slowly and haltingly through delayed beginnings. Both have their origins in statutes enacted by the General Assemblies of 1837 and 1838; and both were recognized constitutionally by Kentucky's third constitution, the Constitution of 1850. The evolution of the state department, as its patterns emerged in the nineteenth century, is presented in this first section. Its development in the twentieth century is a story of efforts to build on these early foundations.

The Commonwealth of Kentucky, the Bluegrass State, created out of the westernmost county of Virginia, was admitted as the fifteenth state of the Union on June 1, 1792 (1). The early inhabitants of Virginia held the opinion that education was a private matter and that it was not the business of the state to furnish it free. Following the examples of the constitutions of Virginia and of the United States, which were silent on education, the first and second constitutions of Kentucky, in 1792 and 1799, failed to provide for education. This failure to authorize education as a state function did not mean that early Kentuckians were not interested in the education of their children. The pioneers who came prior to and during the Revolutionary War had an interest in education. As early as 1776, a school was established at Harrodsburg, Kentucky, as an outpost of civilization in the wilderness (2). It was taught by Mrs. Jane Coomes, who crossed the Alleghenies from Pennsylvania. This frontier state, the first west of the Alleghenies, inherited two institutions of higher learning created by the General Assembly of Virginia, including Transylvania Seminary, established in 1783 (3).

Kentucky made several unsuccessful attempts to provide education below the college level throughout the state, beginning shortly after its admission into the Union. The first general plan, in 1794, provided for the establishment of an academy in each county, to be supported by a grant of 6,000 acres of land for each. This plan was soon recognized as a failure because these were secondary schools which charged tuition and were controlled by independent boards of trustees. In 1821, the Legislature adopted a second plan, the Literary Fund, to be supported by profits of the newly created Bank of the Commonwealth. The fund ceased to grow, and the records fail to show that even one penny from it was ever spent for public schools. The third plan, that of private academies, made it legal for five individuals in a community to organize a school. Under this plan, 230 private academies were established, owned, and controlled by religious denominations, stock companies, and private individuals. In the main, only pupils whose parents could pay tuition attended private academies, which tended to produce a cleavage between the wealthy and the poor. In January 1830, the General Assembly enacted an ambitious piece of legislation in its fourth attempt to establish a system of public education. This act allowed counties to establish school districts and levy a local tax for school support. However, since establishment of school districts was entirely voluntary, very few counties took advantage of the act.

In the first quarter century of its statehood, Kentucky had only two Governors who regarded education as a function and responsibility of the state. Governor Christopher Greenup, a well-educated lawyer, included a few lines relative to education in his message to the General Assembly. Governor Gabriel Slaughter spoke out boldly for public education during this period. In pleading for a system of schools administered at the state level, he said, "Every child born in the state should be considered a child of the Republic and educated at public expense . . . " (4). In his second message to the General Assembly, Governor Slaughter made a plea for a wide distribution of schools in order to fulfill the state's obligation, saying that "nothing short of carrying education to the neighborhood of every man in the state would suffice" (5). Because of his political conflicts with members of the Legislature, his recommendations for education were not heeded.

The concept of a unified system of education for the masses, paid for out of the public treasury and administered by a state agency, had not been accepted by early Kentuckians and their political leaders. The slow development of public education during the first half century of Kentucky's statehood was dramatized by McVey in *The Gates Open*

Slowly. A chapter entitled "They Walked in the Dark" emphasizes that "between the two dates 1792 and 1908, there is a period of more than a hundred years filled with the struggle for a living and a place in the wilderness, with political conflict, and religious controversy" (6).

The Common School System by Statute

Governor James Clark's message to the 1836 General Assembly proposed that Kentucky's anticipated share of money from the federal government be set aside for education. Congress passed a law in June 1836 distributing to the states the surplus funds in the U.S. Treasury. In 1837, the General Assembly passed an act declaring that $1,000,000 of the $1,433,757 which Kentucky received should be set apart for the establishment of a general system of public instruction and providing for the custody of the fund until such contemplated system had been devised (7). In February 1838, the Legislature approved an act establishing a system of common schools and creating the position of superintendent of public instruction. Although this was the beginning of a system of common school education, it was not yet a system of "free" education. The act also provided for reduction of the state school fund to $850,000; appointment of the superintendent of public instruction by the Governor, to be confirmed by the Senate, for a period of 2 years; creation of an ex officio State Board of Education including the superintendent, the attorney general, and the secretary of state; apportionment and distribution of the school money by the superintendent of public instruction, with advice of the state board, on the basis of the number of white children on the census; appointment of five commissioners of common schools in each county by the state board; establishment of local school districts as fast as they met the requirements of the law, including the levying of a local tax and establishing a school building; and election of boards of trustees with full control of schools in their districts.

The first superintendent of public instruction, the Reverend J. J. Bullock, was appointed in 1838 (8), the year after the appointment of Horace Mann as secretary to the Massachusetts State Board of Education. Superintendent Bullock's 1839 report to the General Assembly, made in keeping with a provision of the 1838 act requiring such a report, includes a philosophy of universal education consistent with the ideas of Horace Mann, one of the earliest proponents of universal education. Superintendent Bullock's philosophy, expressed as follows, is as challenging today as it was a century and a quarter ago:

> The great object of the Common School law is to give to every child in the Commonwealth the good common school education; to develop the whole intellect of the State. The great principle of the System is that of equality; the rich and the poor are placed on the same footing; . . . . The State has an interest in every child within her limits . . . (9).

The effect of the new school law was gradual. In 1840, only 24 of the 90 counties had been divided into school districts; and 1 year later, only 33 counties had established common schools. Kentucky's depressed economy, weak local government, and lack of interest among the scattered population were barriers to the early success of the common school system.

Constitutional Provisions

An unfortunate situation developed in regard to the use of the school fund. The Sinking Fund Commissioners, entrusted under the 1837 act with the custody of the school fund, had lent much of it to other units of state government for internal improvements in return for bonds on which the principal and interest were to be paid to the State Board of Education. In 1840, Governor Letcher reported that the commissioners were falling behind on their interest payments to the state board. The General Assembly passed an act in 1845 making it mandatory that the state board deliver to the Governor the bonds it held, which were to be burned. The Sinking Fund Commissioners had found it politically expedient to expend the funds for general internal governmental improvement rather than for redemption of bonds of the new and generally misunderstood public school system. Robert J. Breckinridge, the sixth superintendent of public instruction, courageously led the struggle of the State Board of Education with the Sinking Fund Commissioners over the failure to honor their obligations. This was climaxed in a struggle between Superintendent Breckinridge and Governor Helm during the period 1848 to 1850. Under the able leadership of Superintendent Breckinridge, landmark decisions and fundamental changes were made in the common school system and in the Office of the Superintendent of Public Instruction. State support through taxation for the common schools was initiated by vote of the people in 1848 for a state tax of 2¢ on every $100 worth of taxable property for the support of schools. This tax was enacted into law and approved by the Governor in February 1849.

During the conflict between Superintendent Breckinridge and Governor Helm, a constitutional convention was called in 1849; and the support of schools became one of the major issues in the selection of delegates to the convention. The vote of the people for a state plan of taxation to support common schools strengthened Superintendent Breckinridge in his effort to safeguard the public school fund and to establish the system on a permanent basis. The delegates, reflecting the sentiment of the people, supported Superintendent Breckinridge as indicated in the provisions for education in the Constitution of 1850. These provisions included making the Office of the Superintendent of Public

Instruction elective for 4-year periods, with no limit on reelection; making the capital of a perpetual school fund inviolate; and providing that "the interest and dividend together with any sum which may be produced for that purpose by taxation and otherwise may be appropriated in aid to common schools and for no other purpose" (10). Superintendent Breckinridge, who had served one appointed term, was elected by the people in 1850. The Governor took the position that the school fund was not a debt that the state owed itself and that money set apart for schools had never been recognized as a part of the public debt. Superintendent Breckinridge denied this contention with arguments which were accepted by the Legislature. The Legislature, by an act approved in March 1851 (11), required the Sinking Fund Commissioners to pay interest for the benefit of the common schools. With the passage of this act over Governor Helm's veto, the struggle for the establishment of a permanent school fund was ended.

Under Superintendent Breckinridge's leadership, the 1851-52 Legislature provided for a fundamental change in the state system of education by defining a common school as a school "accessible to the poor as to the rich" and a school which "every free white child in the district between the ages of six and eighteen years" might attend (12). Further, the common schools were defined as elementary schools since the course of study was limited to "the elements of plain education in English, including grammar, arithmetic, and geography" (13). This action represents the acceptance of the principle of education for all children at public expense. The idea of universal, rather than private, education, at least at the elementary level, had been accepted. "The change that took place in Breckinridge's time was fundamental; it was so far reaching that it may be said to have influenced greatly every movement toward improving our school system from that day to this" (14).

After the Constitutional Convention of 1849 and the subsequent battle to strengthen public education in the early 1850's, the development of the public schools once again suffered a setback with the outbreak of the Civil War. The deterrent effect of the Civil War on the school system is illustrated in a statement by Superintendent Richardson in 1861 in which he pointed out that the number of children in the public schools was reduced from 165,000 to 90,000 in a 1-year period. As a result of the war, the operation of the common schools was brought to a virtual halt. Funds which had been dedicated and set apart for education were "seized upon and wickedly misappropriated by those who invaded or connived at the invasion of Kentucky" (15).

The Constitution of 1891, Kentucky's fourth and present constitution, retained Section XI, which guarantees a permanent school fund and provides for the election of the superintendent of public instruction by the people for a term of 4 years. Under provisions of the new constitution, the superintendent was included among the state officers who could not succeed themselves and whose salary within a maximum limit of $5,000 should be fixed by the General Assembly. Further, the 1891 constitution contained the following new principles:

1. Section 183: The General Assembly shall, by appropriate legislation, provide for an efficient system of common schools throughout the state;
2. Section 186: Each county in the Commonwealth shall be entitled to its proportion of the school fund on its census of pupil children for each school year; and
3. Section 187: In distributing the school fund, no distinction shall be made on account of race or color; and separate schools for white and colored children shall be maintained.

Implications for Centralized Administration

During the last quarter of the nineteenth century, trends were developing which had implications for centralized administration.

A dual system of schools for white and Negro children had been established in 1874, with the superintendent of public instruction responsible for the administration of the system and the distribution of school funds on a separate basis for white and Negro children. Beginning in 1882, the superintendent had authority to distribute the funds without regard to color (16). State administration relative to range of school age, length of school term, course of study, and qualifications of teachers was provided on a uniform basis.

Selection of textbooks on a uniform and statewide basis was gaining popular support. This controversial question became an issue in the 1899 gubernatorial campaign.

The trend toward uniform standards for the issuance of certificates at the state level appeared with the creation by the Legislature in 1884 of the State Board of Examiners, composed of the superintendent of public instruction and two professional persons he might select.

It had been recommended by superintendents from J. J. Bullock in 1838 to H. V. McChesney in 1899 that the state establish normal schools for preparation of teachers. One unsuccessful attempt was made to establish a normal department at Transylvania University, and then, in 1880, a normal department was established in the Agricultural and Mechanical College (17).

There was a growing demand for high schools as part of the common school system. In 1867, Superintendent Z. F. Smith recommended that free high schools be provided. Public high schools had their origins in the city graded school system, authorized by the Legislature in 1888. High schools were organized in the independent and graded schools prior to 1900; however, authority for establishing high schools as a part of the common school system had to wait until the twentieth century.

Recognition of the failure of the voluntary plan of local taxation for the support of schools and the sentiment against local control of schools by district trustees reflected the need for a more strongly organized state system of common schools. The fact that too few districts were taking advantage of the local tax levies to improve schools led Superintendent Ed Porter Thompson to express the opinion in 1895 that "local taxation by districts, subject to the will of the people, is a failure" (18). The delegates to the constitutional convention also pointed out that the law did not require a single common school to be taught in the whole state (19). Popular sentiment was more favorable, however, toward state taxes for school purposes, first established in 1848 and then raised in 1870 to 20¢ on each $100 worth of taxable property. State taxation for school purposes was consistent with national thinking, as reported by the National Education(al) Association in 1897, to the effect that "units of taxation should be created . . . as will fully develop the sound American principle, that the whole wealth of the state shall be made available for educating all the youth of the state" (20). From 1860 to 1900, state payments to local schools had increased from $342,440 to $1,867,597.

The trustee system was failing because of lack of county and state control. All real control was in the hands of 25,000 district trustees who had jurisdiction over 8,000 school districts. By 1900, the state superintendents were speaking out boldly in criticism of the trustee system.

These attitudes no doubt influenced the 1893 statute wherein the Legislature provided that "there shall be maintained throughout the State of Kentucky a uniform system of common schools . . . " (21). This provision continued to stimulate further legislation increasing the administrative and supervisory responsibility of the State Department of Education.

Emergence of the State Department of Education

After the position of state superintendency was given constitutional basis, this office began to be referred to, generally, as the State Department of Education. In 1875, Governor James B. McCreary, in his gubernatorial message, referred to the Department of Education as one of the coordinate departments of state government. In an 1893 act, the legislators referred to the State Department of Education in connection with the uses of the annual resources of the school fund. It was not until 1924 that the Department of Education was recognized by statute as an organization of state government and defined according to the divisions of services and personnel. In 1942, the Legislature precisely defined by statute the coordinate parts of the State Department of Education as the State Board of Education, the superintendent of public instruction, and his staff.

The attitude of the Legislature toward the office of superintendent was reflected in the salary increases and decreases, beginning with $1,500 in 1838, reaching $3,000, and being reduced to $2,500 by the close of the nineteenth century (22). In 1850, Superintendent Robert J. Breckinridge spoke of the importance of the superintendency as follows:

> During almost the entire period which preceded the adoption of the new Constitution, attacks were made upon the existence of the office itself, or upon its dignity and efficiency; and almost every recent session of the Legislature witnessed attempts to degrade the office, or to abolish it on the part of those who selected this as at once the safest and most effectual method of waging war upon the common school system itself. By the second section of the XIth Article of the Constitution of 1850, this office is made constitutional and permanent, and is to be filled by election by the qualified voters of the Commonwealth every fourth year. Henceforward, he who shall fill it will do so as the representative of the entire people of Kentucky—called by the voice of a great Commonwealth to discharge a great constitutional trust, touching the very greatest interests of the people . . . . The Superintendent of Public Instruction is not the clerk of the board of education, but is the head of one of the most difficult and important enterprises ever undertaken by the State (23).

Until the close of the nineteenth century, the state department was a one-man enterprise except for the brief period at the close of the century when the superintendent was allowed by the Legislature to employ three clerks. His authority included numerous responsibilities: to collect and tabulate statistics on census, attendance, teachers, and finances; to advise as to the law; to visit the counties throughout the Commonwealth; to advise the local school authorities; to encourage the public to establish schools by providing for local taxation; to advise the Legislature on the conditions and needs of the schools; and to apportion and distribute the state school fund to the local school districts.

By tradition and practice, professional preparation and educational experience have been established as qualifications of the men who are elected to the position of superintendent of public instruction. Although academic qualifications have not been fixed by statute, beginning with the election of Ed Porter Thompson in 1891, every man elected to this office has emerged from the leadership of the profession. This is in harmony with an 1897 recommendation of the National Education(al) Association which states: "The Superintendent of Public Instruction should be a person in close touch with the educational spirit of the times and one whom the profession regards as authority in all that constitutes excellence in school matters" (24). Early in the twentieth century, Barksdale Hamlett observed that "a careful study of our school system reveals the fact that it has been built largely by our state superintendents. In the past these men, as a rule, have been able men devoted to the cause of education . . . " (25). The state superintendents of the nineteenth century, however, had demonstrated by the force of their personalities, abilities, and dedication that the Office of the Superintendent of Public Instruction should be one of leadership and authority.

KENTUCKY EDUCATION FROM 1900 TO 1930

Although significant achievements were few and the quality of education was certainly questionable, there had been steady progress toward a desirable public educational system during the 50 years prior to 1900. By the turn of the century, the public education concept had been indelibly imprinted on the mind of the public. In addition, public school enrollment had steadily increased, and the state was making a definite commitment for financing education.

The educational system of Kentucky took an important forward step in 1908 when, under the able leadership of State Superintendent John G. Crabbe, the General Assembly enacted legislation abolishing the local district and setting up the county as the unit of school administration. This was one of the most significant pieces of school legislation in the history of the state. This "county administration" act takes on additional importance when one realizes that most of the Midwestern and Northeastern states are still working toward such legislation. This act specifically provided for division boards within counties, the chairmen of which were to constitute the county board. In addition, each county was required to establish one or more county high schools within 2 years after the passage of the act; and each county was required to levy a tax for school purposes not to exceed 20¢ on each $100 of taxable property (26).

The taxation required at the local level, climaxing 70 years of little or no local fiscal effort for education, was extremely important. This provision alone substantially increased the educational commitment and obligated the local community to supplement state efforts for support of education.

The 1908 Legislature also created a commission to study the educational needs of the state. In the commission's report to the General Assembly in 1910, the major recommendation was that the General Assembly establish a seven-member State Board of Education, consisting of six experienced educators and the state superintendent. This board would supplant the old three-member, ex officio state board. The powers and duties of the state board were to be extended, also. Unfortunately, the 1910 General Assembly did not enact the recommended measures. However, the commission report was important because it helped establish an awareness of public education in the state; and many of its recommendations served as a guide for subsequent Legislatures (27).

Following the 1908 legislation, there was widespread opposition to the "county administration" law and to the required tax at the local level. In order to promote public acceptance of the legislation, State Superintendent Crabbe went to the people in what he called "whirlwind campaigns." Through these campaigns, he and three other speakers made addresses which reached 60,000 citizens. In addition to informing the people concerning the 1908 legislation, a side benefit of Crabbe's effort was a strengthened State Department of Education. During his presentations before the people, Superintendent Crabbe expressed the viewpoint that the state department is "a center of educational thought and activity, a clearing house for educational ideas, a forum for open discussion of legislation affecting the schools. It is the place where educational sentiment is crystallized" (28).

In both 1908 and 1911, the Kentucky Education Association recommended changes to strengthen the state board. This question was presented periodically to the Legislature from 1908 to 1920, but the board remained unchanged.

In 1920, the General Assembly amended the "county administration" law to provide for a county board of education elected from the county at large. The term of office was to be 4 years. This law was again amended in 1922 with the provision that county board members would be selected from five geographical divisions, with one board member from each division.

Again in 1920-21, the question of state board selection came to the forefront. A report by the Kentucky Educational Commission in 1922 maintained that an ex officio state board could not be effective. This commission pointed out that two of the three members of the ex officio board—the attorney general and the secretary of state—could not be effective board members because, as officials elected to serve in capacities other than education, they might not have the interest and seldom the time to serve adequately. The commission also observed that the political nature of the board prevented it from assuming its proper position in educational matters and, to some degree, explained the reluctance of the Legislature to bestow more power and authority in the board. This commission recommended a State Board of Education of nine members, made up of the superintendent of public instruction, an ex officio member, and eight broad-minded laymen appointed by the Governor (29).

Pursuant to this recommendation, a bill was introduced in the General Assembly in 1922, passed the Senate, but failed to receive the approval by the House of Representatives. A similar bill was defeated in 1924, and again in 1928. It was not until 1934 that there was sufficient strength mustered in the General Assembly to change the ex officio board.

The portion of the "county administration" law of 1908 which provided for a mandatory local tax not to exceed 20¢ on each $100 of taxable property and allowed for an additional tax not to exceed 25¢ voted by the people of a subdistrict was followed 10 years later by a law which provided that a county board of education could levy a tax not to exceed 30¢ on $100 of taxable property and a poll tax of $1. "In 1926 the maximum tax rate was raised to 75 cents and the capitation tax was still not to exceed one dollar" (30). This increase in the local tax rate from 20¢ in 1920 to 75¢ in 1926 was a very significant improvement over the previous years of little local support for schools.

During this period, the state school fund was distributed to the counties on a per-capita basis of school population, and the districts within the county having the largest number of children received the most state money. In 1912, the district's school population was dropped as a means of allocating state funds, and "thereafter, each district shared in the funds available, both state and county, according to its needs . . . " (31).

Even though the 1912 legislation was an improvement, there were still many inequities in fund distribution. The primary one was that the fiscal ability of the local district was not taken into account in distributing the funds.

The Legislature of 1920 passed several laws designed to give the state a better public school system. One was an act creating a county board of education with the power to select a county superintendent on the basis of professional training and experience. Another Legislature was to create a commission to survey the public school system of Kentucky. Other legislations provided for certifying teachers on the basis of training, employing attendance officers, and authorizing county boards of education to issue bonds to raise funds for the purchase of grounds and the construction of buildings.

The Kentucky Educational Commission conducted a survey of the public school system and concluded that an ex officio State Board of Education could not be effective. It also reported that the election of the superintendent of public instruction on a partisan ticket reduced the chances of finding a competent man and made continuity of policy impossible. At the same time, it found the office of the county superintendent to be one of the weakest spots in the public school system. It concluded that little or no thought had been given to supervision of instruction; educational conditions were bad in small graded school districts; teachers were poorly trained; school buildings were bad and poorly heated, lighted, and ventilated; attendance in rural schools was poor; and pupils were retarded (32).

The commission commented on equalization of educational opportunity:

> A method of distributing state school funds that thus ignores differences in financial resources, ignores differences in the grade and in the quality of the schools although there is equal willingness on the part of the people to make sacrifices for them, and ignores the state's responsibility to provide equal educational opportunities of a satisfactory standard for all the children of the commonwealth, ought not to be longer tolerated. Sound policy requires that these differences be taken into account in distributing state school funds (33).

In 1922, the General Assembly created the Efficiency Commission to study all functions of the state government and to make recommendations. In this commission's report it was stated that—

> With respect to the distribution of State funds, educators are generally agreed upon the principle that districts (counties, cities, and graded school districts, in the case of Kentucky) should receive aid in inverse proportion to their "ability" to support schools as shown by their deficiencies in true valuations per teacher or per child of school age, and in direct proportion to the amount of effort they make to support schools as shown by their true tax rates (34).

State Department of Education

Beginning in 1908, with the creation of the county unit system of local schools, the Legislature has created an increasingly complex enterprise involving broader powers for the local boards as the school program and the total school system have expanded. Correspondingly, there has been an increased demand for legal advice on school issues, problems, and laws.

Three developmental stages of growth of the State Department of Education are evident in the programs and services provided to the local school systems. Its clerical and statistical services, extending throughout the nineteenth century, continued through the first decade of the twentieth century. Its regulatory and inspectorial services, emerging in the first decade of the twentieth century, extended into the early 1920's. Its administrative leadership services became the firmly established pattern in the 1930's.

The 1912 act provided that the state superintendent, with the help of two assistants, should inspect and examine the fiscal and general management of schools to see if the laws and regulations of the State Board of Education were being enforced and operated in the interest of efficiency (35). In 1924, when the Legislature defined by statute the State Department of Education, an inspection and accounting division was one of the nine divisions of service specified. This division was retained by statute until all divisions were abolished in 1956, leaving the superintendent of public instruction freedom and authority to establish divisions as he deemed necessary.

By 1923, the court of appeals had ruled that members of the local boards of education were not county officials and that the county attorney had no duty to advise them (36). The General Assembly, which constitutionally has power to determine authority of state officials, had provided that the attorney general was the chief law officer of the Commonwealth of Kentucky and of all its departments but had no power to intervene in local matters. Consequently, the Legislature of 1924 expanded the legal responsibility of the superintendent of public instruction by providing that, as executive officer of the State Board of Education, he "shall explain the true intent and meaning of the school laws and of the published regulations of the State Board of Education . . . and in all such matters he shall consult fully with the Attorney General" (37).

The 1924 laws provided that the superintendent of public instruction should prepare regulations for adoption by the State Board of Education in areas including, in addition to the state school budget and census, courses of study, certification, buildings, and classifying and accrediting schools.

1930 TO THE PRESENT

The years 1930 through 1934 marked a very important period in the development of education in the state. Of special significance were the Equalization Act of 1930 and the School Code of 1934.

The General Assembly of 1930 showed its perception of educational needs by providing a financial program which would facilitate equal educational opportunity. The Constitution of 1891 had prevented equalization through its mandate that state fund distributions must be on a per-capita basis.

In an effort to change this pattern, the State Department of Education prepared and submitted to the Legislature of 1930 a bill which provided for appropriation of state school aid on an equalization basis. This bill was enacted into law and became operative in the 1930-31 school year. It provided for an annual appropriation of $1,250,000, which was to be expended under the direction of the state department. The purpose of this fund was described by the statute:

> Equalization of educational opportunities, as used in this Act, means the raising of the level of expenditures per pupil for educational purposes in school districts where the level of educational opportunities is below the level or standard fixed and prescribed by law and the State Board of Education . . . (38).

This act enabled the state board to help local boards in poorer counties to pay their teachers a minimum of $75 per month. Under the provisions of this law, the state distributed $630,005.50 during 1930-31 (39). But in 1932, the constitutionality of the act was questioned because of the constitutional limitations of Section 186. The court of appeals ruled that the act did, in fact, violate the constitution (40). This constitutional limitation greatly handicapped the state department in distributing state funds, and the inequalities caused by wealth differentials were perpetuated for many years.

The General Assembly of 1932 enacted a law providing for a Kentucky Educational Commission consisting of the superintendent of public instruction and eight appointed members. The General Assembly directed this commission to make a study of public education in Kentucky and report the findings to the Governor and the assembly at the opening of the next regular session, "with recommendations of such measures and such revision of the school laws as may be found necessary to increase efficiency and equalize the benefits of public education throughout the Commonwealth" (41). The work of this commission resulted in the adoption of a completely new school code for Kentucky. Several other fundamental educational achievements resulted from its recommendations.

Attempting to clarify the relationship between state and local school districts, the commission stated:

> In America much is made of the doctrine of self-government. . . . Self-government or local self-government, as one may choose to call it, inheres only in the state. It must be borne in mind at all times that all local governmental units—counties, cities, and others—are creatures of the State. All powers, duties, and privileges of local units are delegated to them by the State. Legally, they are but conveniences of the State in carrying its government to the people. They may be discontinued, changed, or modified at the will of the State. The inherent rights of the people are rights of state citizenship and not rights of local citizenship. The conclusion is reached, therefore, . . . that education is a function and responsibility of the State. The part in education played by local school units—county, city, and independent graded school district—is a service rendered by these units as agents of the State (42).

At the time of this report, the State Board of Education was an ex officio board composed of the superintendent of public instruction, the secretary of state, and the attorney general, all politically elected officers. The commission also pointed out that the superintendent of public instruction, a politically elected officer, was unable to succeed himself and that this manner of selecting the chief educational officer was fixed by the constitution and could not be changed except by constitutional amendment. It was recommended, however, that the superintendent of public instruction serve as ex officio member of the State Board of Education as long as he held this position. The commission also recommended that the state board be made up of seven representative laymen appointed by the Governor from the state at large.

These recommendations were enacted into law by the 1934 session of the General Assembly; and from 1934 to 1962, the State Board of Education was composed of seven lay members appointed by the Governor from various locations in the state, and the superintendent of public instruction was ex officio chairman.

The new school code gave the superintendent wide authority and responsibility as the educational leader in Kentucky. Other meaningful provisions enacted in 1934 resulting from the study of the commission gave broad authority, instead of specific duties, to the superintendent and to the state board in the areas of courses of study, curriculum, and instruction. The state department, under this general authority, has made continuing efforts to develop to the fullest the potential of this leadership responsibility. Since 1934, the role of state superintendent has included approval of minimum courses of study and the adoption of rules and regulations describing the scope of the instructional program.

After 1934, the courses of study as set forth by the state board consisted of the subject areas, the name of subjects in each area, and the listing of subjects by grades. The state department's other legal functions had direct influence upon the courses of study. These included adoption of textbooks by the Textbook Commission (a division of the state department), setting of certification standards, adoption of qualifications for teachers assigned to high school subjects, and adoption of accreditation standards covering a broad spectrum of elements having direct bearing on the curriculum and the quality of instruction. It is evident from the reports of the superintendents of public instruction that the goal has been to have in every school curriculum offerings broad and deep enough to meet the varying abilities, achievements, career interests, and aspiration levels of all students.

The 1934 school code provided for only two kinds of districts, county and independent. It abolished subdistricts and provided that independent graded common school districts should have a school census enumeration of at least 250 or more white children. Both types of districts were to be governed by boards of education consisting of five members elected by the people. Further, the 1934 acts made provision for the merger of school districts.

In 1934, the State Department of Education was given the legal responsibility for accrediting schools, as well as approving both elementary and high schools. The 1934 law follows:

> The Superintendent of Public Instruction shall prepare, or cause to be prepared, and submit for approval and adoption by the State Board of Education rules and regulations for grading, classifying, and accrediting of all common schools, and for determining the scope of instruction that may be offered in the different classes of schools, and the minimum requirements for graduation from the courses offered. The Superintendent of Public Instruction shall prepare, or cause to be prepared, and submit for adoption and approval by the State Board of Education, rules and regulations for approving private and parochial schools of elementary or high school grade and commercial schools (43).

Since the responsibility for accrediting high schools was given by the Legislature to the State Board of Education, the accrediting committee of the Kentucky Association of Colleges has served as an advisory body to the supervisory staff of the State Department of Education. With minor changes, the 1934 legal provisions continue to provide the legal basis for accreditation for both elementary and secondary public schools, for private schools, and commercial schools.

By 1939, the state department was organized in eight divisions along the lines of services offered: school buildings and grounds, school census and attendance, school finance, textbooks, school supervision, teacher education and certification, special education, and vocational education.

The Department of Education at this time reported that the state had 494,339 pupils in average daily attendance. This figure represented only 78.5 percent of the public school enrollment. The average annual salary for teachers was only $890.32, and the typical teacher had had but 3.5 years of college. The percentage of certificated teachers who were college graduates had increased from approximately 25 percent in 1935-36 to only about 40 percent in 1938-39 (44).

The problems indicated by these statistics were increased by the outbreak of World War II. John W. Brooker, who was state superintendent from 1940 to 1944, stated:

> National defense is not measured alone by ships, planes, guns and bombs. These can be taken care of by government. We must deal with the problem of making men able to use our physical instruments of defense; but more important is the task of emphasizing the spiritual values which we must defend. Democracy is a way of life. We must work together and reason together (45).

A problem of considerable magnitude during the war years was teacher turnover. In 1943, the state department reported that one-fourth of the men and women had left the teaching profession. The positions vacated were filled chiefly by emergency teachers.

Worker migration from rural areas to industrial centers was greatly accelerated by the war. From 1940 through 1943, county districts lost 46,864 census pupils, and independent districts lost 13,673. Of course, this was not a net loss to the state, since many pupils moved about within the state and were not recounted properly; but the migration did greatly complicate and increase problems in pupil attendance services, school building construction needs, staffing, and instructional services.

The impact of the war on education, felt in all phases of the program, was particularly important to vocational education. Defense training became a standard part of the vocational program; and educators were called upon to organize courses for out-of-school youths in auto mechanics, electricity, metalwork, and woodwork. In many cases the courses were coordinated with the National Youth Administration. In courses involving NYA, there were 6,221 persons enrolled and 162 teachers employed. During the 1940-44 period, nearly all of the trade schools offered part-time and evening extension courses for apprentices. The Kentucky Department of Education cooperated with the federal government in providing trainees with courses which were essentially preemployment training or were of a supplementary nature. In addition, the area trade schools carried on a foremanship training program which was of great value to the war effort.

In 1944, Governor Simeon Willis stated that the commitment to the crisis which faced the nation should not lessen the duty to educate our children and youth. As the obligation to youth is continuous and cannot be postponed, Governor Willis felt that the financial program for the betterment of the common schools must be met.

The 1944 General Assembly responded to the needs of education by enacting legislation which allowed local school districts greater latitude in financing their own educational programs. Under this legislation, city school districts could levy from $1 to $1.50 per $100 of taxable property, depending on the classification of the city. Subdistrict taxes in counties were abolished by this act, and county school districts were given authority to levy a maximum of $1.50 per $100 of taxable property. These levies were for other than sinking fund purposes.

This same General Assembly appropriated $3 million to supplement salaries of teachers. The enactment of this pay increase was important because, as the act stated, "due to the present emergency, there is a great shortage of teachers because of low salaries and the attraction of more lucrative paying positions in war and in private industries" (46).

This same Legislature attempted to ease the school construction problem by authorizing boards of education in county and independent school districts containing second-class cities to establish a building fund. The tax for this fund could be levied for 1¢ to 5¢ on each $100 of property valuation annually in addition to existing taxes. A 1946 amendment to this act allowed the board of education of any district to levy from 4¢ to 20¢ on each $100 of property valuation. The revenues from this tax could be used for the erection, alteration, enlargement, and equipping of school buildings (47).

During 1945 and immediately after the war, there were signs of substantial progress in the public school system of Kentucky. The state common school fund had increased 94 percent between 1942-43 and 1947-48. The median annual teacher's salary in the state had nearly doubled, from $782 in 1942-43 to $1,325 in 1946-47. The 1946 enactment by the General Assembly allowing school districts to levy a tax of up to $1.50 gave local superintendents and boards of education more discretion in preparing an adequate school budget (48). School districts had begun to reduce some of the school building backlog which had accumulated during the war. In 1947, the state department approved 201 projects for new buildings and remodelings, with an estimated cost of $16,232,000.

While Kentucky's educational system as a whole was improving, the state department continued to grow and offer educational services so badly needed by local school districts. It was reorganized during this period into four bureaus: administration, finance, instruction, and vocational education. New divisions included surplus property, Negro education, and library science.

The Foundation Program Law and Implications for Development of the State Department of Education

The Foundation Program Law was enacted by the General Assembly in 1954, initially financed at 70 percent of its estimated cost level, and fully financed by the General Assembly in 1956. The first report of the Commission on Public Education, released December 1961, includes the following observations:

> The enactment of the Minimum Foundation Program for support of public schools in Kentucky has been one of the most phenomenal and historic acts of any state legislature in modern history of American education finance . . . .The Foundation Program is quite effective in sending its funds where there is most need in order to put a nine months school program in every district with a qualified teacher in each classroom. . . . The Foundation Program and more adequate expenditures came none too soon for almost any measure of educational attainment showed Kentucky at the bottom of the list of states at that time. . . . Between 1953-54 and 1960-61 the increase in current expense per pupil in average daily attendance in Kentucky was 1.54 times as great as in the highest neighboring state and 1.7 times as great as the national average (49).

In 1956, Governor Chandler said:

> I have said . . . that the Executive and Legislative branches of the government will furnish the tools to the Department of Education with which it can do a dramatic job and the Department must get its house in order to perform the task which lies ahead of it. The people of Kentucky are entitled to value received for the enormous amount of its tax money which will be spent

> for education during the next four years. The reorganization of the Department is essential to the performance of its important and increased responsibilities (50).

This was in reference to the budget representing a $20 million increase over the previous year and to the 1956 Reorganization Act, through which all divisions were abolished and the superintendent of public instruction was given authority to reorganize the Department of Education.

The enactment of the Foundation Program Law was a culmination of more than a century of effort to provide equal educational opportunities for the children of Kentucky. As early as 1848, Superintendent Breckinridge said:

> The method of distribution has been too complicated. If there be one idea said to be more fatal to the school system than any other, it is that school money be distributed among counties and districts in proportion to the number of children in districts instead of the number of children attending schools in the district. Children who never attend school should no more be considered in distribution of school revenue than the same number of people who are not children. If this method were changed and counties knew they would be paid the State's money on the basis of the number of pupils in school, then everybody, not the teacher only, would have an immediate and a vital interest in getting children into school (51).

Thus, the state was 106 years getting this principle embodied in the Foundation Program Law.

Progress Toward Foundation Program

As early as 1921, Superintendent George Colvin in his biennial report expressed succinctly a concept of a foundation program based on equality of opportunity for children:

> The question of financing schools in Kentucky is complicated by the fact that there is such a great disparity of taxable wealth in different counties and in different communities. . . . It will thus be seen that our financial problem is not merely to raise more money for the support of the schools, but that we must find some way by which we can equalize the sacrifice and the support back of the schools. Left alone and unaided by the state, many of the poorer counties in Kentucky will never be able to establish nor maintain good schools. Supported by the state on a per capita basis only, the prospect of good schools for these counties is equally remote. A better method of distribution must be found if we are to give to all the children of the state equal educational advantage (52).

In his biennial report of June 1939, State Superintendent Peters pointed out that there is "an ever-increasing demand from the people that the schools serve better the needs of children, and we are now facing problems which are preventing the schools from serving the children as they should." As a solution, Superintendent Peters recommended increased state aid and an equalization fund (53).

In 1941, the voters approved an amendment to Section 186 of the Constitution of Kentucky, a section of which had long hampered state aid to local districts because it put distribution of state school funds on a pupil-census basis. The amendment of 1941 authorized the state to distribute 10 percent of the state funds on other than a pupil-census basis. In 1942, the General Assembly authorized an equalization fund, which represented the first step toward the present foundation program. This act stipulated that if the available funds of any district failed to provide an income of $30 per pupil per year, then the equalization fund would bring the total up to $30 per pupil for the district. In case the fund was not sufficient for this, the available amount of the fund was to be distributed on a percentage basis determined by the ratio of the fund to $30 per pupil per year.

As a result of the 1941 amendment, in 1944 the Legislature appropriated $1.5 million for equalization purposes for districts whose total net revenue did not yield as much as $40 per pupil in average daily membership. In 1943-44, 60 counties and 19 independent school districts participated in this equalization program. In 1945-46, 57 county school districts and 12 independent districts shared in the fund. In 1946-47, $1.8 million was distributed to 51 county districts and 39 independent districts.

In 1949, another amendment to Section 186 of the constitution was approved by the voters, changing the percentage that could be used for equalization from 10 to 25 percent.

In 1950, a series of steps were taken which culminated in the enactment of the Foundation Program Law by the General Assembly in 1954. First, the Kentucky Education Association held a leadership conference in August for the purpose of discussing a minimum foundation program for Kentucky. However, the report of the association's Committee on Education recommended that legislation be enacted to provide an efficient system of schools throughout the Commonwealth.

Another step toward a foundation program was taken when the report of the Committee on Functions and Resources of State Government was presented in December 1951 (54). Superintendent-Elect Wendell P. Butler pledged to devote his administration to the removal of the "roadblock" by amending Section 186 of the constitution and to enactment into law of a foundation program of education. In 1952, the Legislature appointed a statewide Advisory Committee on Educational Policy. Through studies involving 5,000 members of local advisory committees and

20,000 interested citizens, some significant conclusions were reached: The distribution of the school fund should be based on ability and need if educational opportunities were to be provided all children on an economical and fair basis; and the pupil-census basis of distribution of school funds perpetuated inequities, rewarded nonattendance, and ignored the need for ensuring a low pupil-teacher ratio (55).

As a result of this painstaking work, Section 186 of the constitution was again amended in November 1953; in 1954, the Legislature enacted the Foundation Program Law. Two years later, the Legislature appropriated funds to implement the foundation program, declaring its intent in enacting Kentucky Statute 157.310 as follows:

> It is the intention of the General Assembly to assure substantially equal public school educational opportunities, through a foundation program for those in attendance in the public schools of the Commonwealth, but not to limit nor to prevent any school district from providing educational services and facilities beyond those assured by the foundation program; and to provide, as additional state funds are made available for the public schools, for the use of such funds for the further equalization of educational opportunities (56).

The foundation program provided for at least a minimum school program for every child in the state, regardless of where he lives, and an opportunity for the people in any school district to go beyond the minimum program whenever they decide to do so. It also demanded that educational responsibility be shared between the state and the local school districts and that the school district's contribution be based on local ability to support an educational program.

The foundation law, as amended in 1956, contains slightly less than 12 printed pages. The Legislature, elected by the people, set the limits and safeguards as to what may be done under the law, but assigned the task of administering the foundation law to the superintendent of public instruction under regulations adopted by the State Board of Education under the laws of the Commonwealth.

The foundation program provided for the distribution of funds, not only for salaries for which all state aid in the past was expended, but for transportation, capital outlay, and materials and supplies. Thus, the State Department of Education has each year, within limits of the available budget, been expanded in order to provide more adequate leadership services in all these facets of the school program.

The Office of the Superintendent of Public Instruction and the State Board of Education

The Office of the State Superintendent of Public Instruction and the State Board of Education are interlocked legally, organizationally, and functionally.

As pointed out earlier, in 1934, climaxing an effort of many decades on the part of the state superintendents and other educational leaders, the General Assembly enacted a law reconstituting the State Board of Education. The statutory provision for a new state board of seven laymen appointed by the Governor, with the state superintendent of public instruction as chairman, was consistent with the recommendation of the 1933 report of the Kentucky Educational Commission, of which Superintendent James H. Richmond was chairman (57).

In 1951, the final report of the Committee on Functions and Resources included the following recommendation:

> The Constitution should be amended to provide that the State Board of Education shall appoint the State Superintendent of Public Instruction on the basis of proven experience and qualifications and that he be eligible to serve for more than a period of four years (58).

The 1961 report of the Kentucky Commission on Public Education made by Booz, Allen and Hamilton, Management Consultants, stated:

> The Administration and leadership of schools throughout the state depends more upon the ability and integrity of the State Superintendent of Public Instruction than on any other single individual .... The position of State Superintendent of Public Instruction should become an appointive position . . . (59).

In 1921, 1953, and 1957, attempts were made, under the leadership of the state superintendent of public instruction and the Kentucky Education Association in conjunction with the various Legislatures, to amend the 1891 constitution in this regard. All three efforts were rejected by the people at the polls. Then, again in 1964, the Legislature took action to give the people an opportunity to vote on a revised constitution. One of the significant revisions related to the election of the superintendent. Harry M. Sparks, a leader in this movement, stated in January 1964, on beginning his limited 4-year term:

> In the last ten years eleven states have adopted the plan to keep public education out of politics as much as possible. Our neighbor state of Ohio is changing now. The new concept puts educational leadership in the hands of truly professional administrators, plus a direct relationship with the representatives responsible to the people (60).

The cochairman of the statewide committee of Kentuckians for a Better Constitution, John Fred Williams, was a former superintendent of public instruction. Although the proposed revised constitution was supported by the State Department of Education, the Kentucky Education Association, the Governor, and many lay organizations, it was overwhelmingly defeated in November 1966.

An amendment to the constitution making it possible for the superintendent of public instruction to succeed himself in office remains an imperative.

The relationship between the superintendent and the State Board of Education has varied. From 1838 to 1908, the superintendent was designated by the law as the president of the board. In 1908, he was designated as chairman and executive officer. In the 1934 acts, when after nearly a century the ex officio board was replaced by a lay board, the superintendent of public instruction was designated as chairman. In describing this relationship in 1961, the survey by Booz, Allen and Hamilton stated that –

> Under the present system, the regulating authority, at the state level, over the state school systems is divided between the elected state superintendent and the appointed state board members. Either can block the action of the other, but the state superintendent has the dominant role (61).

A fundamental change was made in this relationship by the acts of 1962, which removed the superintendent of public instruction from membership and chairmanship of the state board, effective January 1964, and which provided that the state board elect its chairman from its membership. The relationship was further altered by the 1962 acts in that provision was made under Section 156.132 that action on the removal or suspension of any district board member or superintendent of school could be taken by a majority vote of the state board without recommendation from the superintendent of public instruction. Further, under the 1962 acts it was provided that the attorney general, upon the written recommendation of the Governor, the auditor of public accounts, the superintendent of public instruction or the state board, shall institute the necessary actions to recover from any source school funds which he believes have been erroneously or improperly allowed or paid to any person. These two fundamental changes broke the 124-year-old legal procedures and relationship between the state superintendent of public instruction and the State Board of Education. These changes emerged during a period of high tension created by statewide publicity of a local school situation where there were alleged irregularities in the expenditure of public school funds. Out of this situation, uncordial relationships developed between the 1960 General Assembly and the superintendent of public instruction's office. An extremely critical report made by a special legislative committee in response to House Resolution 55, enacted in February 1960, led to the creation of the Commission on Public Education, for which the firm of Cresap, McCormick and Paget, Management Consultants, was engaged to make a study of the State Department of Education. Out of this study, recommendations were made which were enacted into the laws bringing about the changes described.

At present the law provides that the superintendent of public instruction shall be head of the Department of Education, which shall consist of the State Board of Education and the superintendent of public instruction. Further, in the same section of law, the Department of Education, of which the superintendent is the head, shall exercise all the stated administrative functions in relation to the management and control of the public common schools. But then again in another section, the statutes specify that the superintendent shall perform such duties as are assigned by the board. The fact that he is elected by the people raises a question relative to this basic relationship as stated by law.

The State Department of Education Today

In 1924, the State Department of Education was recognized by the General Assembly as a unit of state government, and budget appropriation was made directly to the department for its operation under the administrative direction of the superintendent of public instruction. The Legislature, in the acts of 1924, gave the types of positions needed and the appropriate salaries.

The responsibilities of the department have been increased substantially during four periods since 1924. The adoption of the new school code in 1934, in keeping with the Kentucky Educational Commission recommendations, reflected additional appropriations and responsibilities for the department; in 1944, a substantial increase was made in the state budget appropriation for the department; in 1954 and in 1956, the department was greatly strengthened in order to provide the services demanded for proper administration of the newly enacted Foundation Program Law; and during 1965, the department again significantly increased its staff in order to administer the state's portion of the Elementary and Secondary Education Act of 1965.

The Department of Education today has a total of approximately 500 professional and nonprofessional employees. This number does not include the personnel in vocational schools, School for the Blind, School for the Deaf, Kentucky Industries for the Blind, and clerical and stenographic staff in these special schools and district offices, all of which are under the direct administrative control of the Department of Education. If these personnel are included, the total employee force of the department numbers in excess of 1,500. This figure may be contrasted with a total staff of only 11 in 1915-16, 43 in 1935-36, and 86 in 1945-46 (62).

The Department of Education today is organized into six bureaus made up of 32 divisions: administration and finance, instruction, pupil personnel services, rehabilitation services, state-federal relations, and vocational education. In addition to these bureaus, there are special divisions directly responsible to the state superintendent or the deputy superintendent which provide services in the areas of information, civil rights, school law, and research.

SELECTED PROGRAMS AND THEIR DEVELOPMENT

In order to provide a better view of the historical development and the present operation of the Department of Education, several selected service areas are presented separately. The key dates in the historical progress of these program areas of course correspond with the overall development of the Department of Education; however, a micro-investigation of the internal development of the department may be of added historical interest and significance.

Certification and Teacher Preparation

The act of the Kentucky General Assembly approved in February 1838 providing for a system of common schools prescribed a method of certificating teachers. The only duty assigned by this act to the superintendent of public instruction relative to certification was that of prescribing the form on which the certificate was to be written. The gradual change in authority for certification from local administrative units to the state level was not complete until 1934.

By the acts of the General Assembly in 1914, the state board was empowered for the first time to fix standards for qualifications of teachers in the public high schools, specifying that, to be eligible to teach in the public high schools of Kentucky, persons must give satisfactory evidence of scholarship equivalent to graduation from a 4-year standard high school and, in addition thereto, the equivalent of 2 years of work in a college or normal school (63).

Under the acts of 1920, the General Assembly transferred the certification of teachers from counties to the State Board of Examiners by requiring that this board prepare the questions and grade all the examination papers, which were to be returned to the State Department of Education by the county board of examiners. The State Board of Examiners had been the certifying agency since 1870.

The General Assembly of 1924 passed a different certification law abolishing the different kinds of certificates previously issued by the State Board of Examiners and setting up a new basis, terminology, and validity of certificates. This act inaugurated the issuance of provisional and standard elementary certificates, provisional and standard high school certificates, emergency permits, and the local elementary certificate, which was the only grade of certificate left to be issued upon the basis of examination. By statute, also, the 1924 Legislature created a certification and examination division, to be headed by a director with such assistants and stenographers as were necessary and consistent with the funds available (64). Responsibilities of the state department in the whole area of teacher certification and teacher preparation had been recognized as of such importance that by 1933 the superintendent of public instruction, with funds from the General Education Board, created the teacher-training division. The 1933 report of the Kentucky Educational Commission, of which the superintendent of public instruction was chairman, included teacher education and certification recommendations. Under the impact of this report, a significant change was made in the whole structure of teacher preparation and certification. The 1934 acts, in their reorganization of the state department, combined the teacher education and examinations division with the teacher-training division to form a teacher-training and certification division. Further, the 1934 acts placed all certification authority in the hands of the reorganized State Board of Education and provided that –

> The State Board of Education, upon the recommendation of the Superintendent of Public Instruction, should from time to time publish . . . rules and regulations governing the issuance of each kind and grade of certificate issued, . . . the renewal of certificates, the transfer of certificates to and from other states, the acceptance of credentials from institutions of other states, and such other information relating to the training and certification of teachers as it deems advisable (65).

The 1950 Legislature repealed all certification acts which referred to certificates or standards in terms of college preparation or semester hours. Beginning with the acts of 1950, only two statutes (KRS 161.020 and KRS 161.030) have served as the legal basis for determining types of certificates and the programs and standards under which they are issued. As recommended by Superintendent Boswell B. Hodgkin, all certificates are issued and renewed by the State Board of Education upon curriculums as prescribed by the Council on Public Higher Education and approved by the state board; and all teacher education curriculums offered in any standard college or university of the state for the training of teachers are submitted to the state board for approval.

In 1949-50, the median preparation of elementary teachers was 88.8 semester hours, while in the fall of 1965 the median had reached the bachelor's degree plus 17.3 semester hours. The percentage of elementary teachers with a bachelor's degree increased from 33 percent in 1949-50 to 91.1 percent in the fall of 1965. The percentage of teachers holding a master's degree increased from 23.6 in 1949-50 to 33.3 in the fall of 1965. The percentage of all elementary and secondary teachers holding a bachelor's degree rose from 50.9 percent in 1949-50 to 94.3 percent in the fall of 1965 (66). In addition to raising the quality of teacher education and certification, there has been opportunity under the freedom of the 1950 act to develop standards and programs for additional types of personnel, including guidance counselors, special education teachers in all areas of exceptionality, finance officers, and curriculum consultants.

Pupil Personnel Services

Pupil personnel records and accounting have been vital areas of responsibility from the beginning. Information from these records has been made available to the U.S. Office of Education on an annual basis. Statistics on school census, enrollment, attendance, grade placement, failure, promotion, high school graduation, children transported, and other items have served the Department of Education in planning with local school systems and with the Kentucky Legislatures.

As early as 1873, school attendance was so poor that the county school commissioners advocated compulsory attendance laws – laws regarded by the people as tyrannical. The superintendent of public instruction suggested that comfortable houses and efficient teachers would be magnets of influence to attract parental attention to the advantages of regular attendance in school. The attendance continued to remain so poor that in 1896, 23 years after the 1873 proposals, the General Assembly passed a compulsory attendance act which became a law without the approval of Governor William O. Bradley. However, the law proved so inefficient that in 1904, 1908, 1912, 1920, 1922, and 1928, revised compulsory attendance laws were enacted. These laws attempted to place responsibility for attendance first on the teachers, then on the county commissioners, and, finally, on the parents, providing penalties for parents who failed to keep their children in attendance. In 1934, the present compulsory attendance law was enacted, and the state department was required to employ a staff member who would give services to the local systems in the area of attendance and census (67). Recently, the title of attendance officer was changed to director of pupil personnel.

Records, Reports, Statistics, and Computer Services

In 1956, with the full financing of the foundation program and the reorganization of the state department, the records and reports division, including statistical services, was organized. During the period 1956-60, the work of this division increased tremendously. In calculating the foundation program allotments to each school district, computations were based on an array of data including the attendance of each child in each separate district by schools, as well as the qualifications of teachers and the number of teachers in each classification provided for by law.

In 1959, the Kentucky Department of Education inaugurated a state plan for improvement of statistical services as the first step in implementing Title X of Public Law 85-864, known as the National Defense Education Act. Services in the area of records, reports, and statistics could then be facilitated by the use of automatic processing machines. Information and data are furnished to all divisions of the Department of Education, to local systems, to the U.S. Office of Education, to the Legislature, the Office of Public Information, state universities and colleges, the Departments of Health, Economic Security, and Finance, and to the Governor.

By 1965, a computer services division had been created, staffed by seven professional personnel and eight clerks. This was in addition to the statistical services division.

Supervision and Consultative Services

The present Bureau of Instruction, with approximately 50 professional staff members, is an outgrowth of a program of supervisory services begun in 1910 when two educational supervisors, one for the rural elementary schools and one for the high schools, were appointed by Superintendent Ellsworth Regenstein and supported by funds from philanthropic agencies.

In 1924, the Legislature, recognizing supervision as one of the major functions of the state educational agency, created the rural, high school, and Negro school divisions and appropriated sufficient funds to cover part of the salaries, the remaining part being paid by philanthropic agencies. The new school code in 1934 stated that the establishment of the divisions was for "the successful administration and supervision of the common schools and other educational agencies placed under the management and control of the board" (68). This is the legal authority under which the State Department of Education continues to provide supervision and consultative services.

For a short time beginning in 1923, the services of a supervisor of music were made available with state funds. In the 1930's, a supervisor of library services and an elementary supervisor were added to the staff for a short time. Then, in the latter part of the 1940's, with funds from private agencies, a supervisor of health and, again, a supervisor of library sciences were added; and with state funds, a supervisor of elementary education was employed. It was not until 1956 that the State Department of Education began to provide on a continuing basis supervisors and consultative services in art, music, physical education, and special education. Since the passage of the National Defense Education Act in 1958, supervisors and consultants have been provided in areas of mathematics, science, reading, and guidance. Under the Foundation Program Law, no distinction is made between elementary and secondary schools, and these services are available on a 12-grade basis.

With additional personnel made possible by the Foundation Program Law and the National Defense Education Act, a more comprehensive plan of providing consultative services to the local school systems has been inaugurated. The plan, known as the team approach to system-wide evaluation, was initiated on a voluntary basis. The total staffs of the instruction and vocational education bureaus participated in creating the plan and implementing it in the local districts.

Special Education

Kentucky school leaders in 1934 influenced the Legislature to establish vocational rehabilitation and special education divisions in the department. The program was administered by the State Board of Education in cooperation with local county and independent boards of education. By 1938-39, under state department stimulation, 51 school units were providing some special education to more than 1,800 handicapped children.

In 1948, the Legislature created a Division of Special Education for Handicapped Children and appropriated funds for the State Department of Education for administrative and supervisory services.

The 1948 acts created within the State Department of Education a Division of Special Education and gave to the department responsibility for maintaining a census of handicapped children and authority to approve plans of local school systems for providing special education programs. Further, the acts required that teachers of exceptional children meet standards of preparation and certification adopted by the State Board of Education.

In 1952-53, just prior to the enactment of the Foundation Program Law, 23 school districts under the reimbursement policy act were providing to a limited extent educational opportunities to a number of handicapped children.

The 1954 legislation contained special provisions for the education of exceptional children. In implementing the foundation program, the state board adopted criteria for approving each classroom unit, including teacher qualifications, facilities, and program. The law itself specifies sizes of classes. Since the financing of the foundation program in 1956, the number of classroom units provided for exceptional children has increased from 99.3 to 424 in 1964-65. These 424 classroom units include programs for a variety of exceptionalities: the crippled, the visually handicapped, the speech handicapped, the hearing handicapped, the mentally retarded, and the neurologically impaired. The Department of Education has increased its consultative staff in special education from one supervisor in 1947 to a director and four supervisors.

Legal Services

The very first service performed by the first superintendent of public instruction in 1838 was to order and distribute 1,000 copies of the 1838 act on education, containing 42 sections.

The acts of 1894 placed upon the state superintendent the statutory responsibility for rendering decisions on school law and for collecting, indexing, publishing, and distributing throughout the state biennially the general school laws and abstracts of decisions of the appellate court and the attorney general on points of school law and "construction thereof," as well as decisions and regulations of the State Board of Education.

The 1924 law, when the main provisions of the present statutes concerning legal services were enacted, stated:

> The Superintendent of Public Instruction shall explain the true intent and meaning of the school laws and of the published regulations of the State Board of Education. He shall decide, without expense to the parties concerned, all controversies and disputes involving the proper administration of the public school system, but in all such matters he shall freely consult the Attorney General.
>
> He shall publish biennially school laws of the State, omitting all that have been repealed and inserting in its proper place that which is amendatory or new. There shall also be included and inserted in connection with the proper sections abstracts of the decisions of the appellate court, and the decisions and interpretations of the Attorney General and of the Superintendent of Public Instruction (69).

Increasingly, as local school controversies arose, the superintendent of public instruction and the attorney general were called upon to explain the laws and to render decisions and opinions. The attorney general, in practice, has interpreted the laws for local school officials, usually rendering opinions after consultation with the state superintendent or his representative. The Legislature in 1924 authorized the superintendent to appoint an assistant superintendent. The superintendent designated his assistant to be legal adviser to local school officials. It is significant in the historical development of the State Department of Education that each superintendent has provided these legal services through the assistant superintendent (70). Cooperation between the state department and the attorney general's office has led to a continuity of legal interpretation which has earned the respect and confidence of local school personnel.

Vocational Education

As early as 1908, curriculum offerings now classified as vocational education were recognized as essential to the high school program. The 1908 act of the General Assembly which made mandatory provisions for establishment of at least one county high school in each county also provided that the high school course of study prepared by the State Board of Education "may provide for instruction in manual training, domestic science, and elementary agriculture" (71).

In 1917, a half century ago, the Congress of the United States passed an act signed by President Woodrow

Wilson for the promotion of vocational education. This act provided for annual federal appropriations for salaries of teachers, supervisors, or directors of vocational subjects, including agriculture, home economics, and industrial arts, and for funds to assist in preparing teachers, supervisors, and directors of these subjects. The Governor of Kentucky immediately appointed a State Board of Vocational Education with the state superintendent as chairman. In 1918, the Legislature passed an act accepting the provisions of the acts of Congress and providing for a vocational education board as already established and with the same personnel. It was not until 1934 that the Legislature transferred the responsibility for the administration of vocational education to the State Board of Education.

Under the leadership of the state department, the Legislature, from time to time, has been encouraged to make appropriations on a matching fund basis to enable Kentucky to take full advantage of the additional funds and programs offered under the George-Reed Act of 1929, the Ellzey-Reed Act of 1934, the George-Deen Act of 1936, the George-Barden Act of 1946, the Health Amendments Act of 1956, the NDEA Act of 1958, the Area Redevelopment Act of 1961, the Manpower Development Act of 1962, and the Vocational Education Act of 1963. With these supporting funds, vocational education has been expanded to include distributive education, practical nursing, technological education, industrial arts, business education, education for veterans, the Manpower Development Program, and the Work Study Program. With increased federal funds under the George-Barden Act of 1946, post-secondary preparatory programs in vocational education were established. The Health Amendments Act of 1956 provided for practical nursing. The Vocational Education Act of 1963 provided for more flexibility in the program of vocational education than was possible under previous acts. Programs for unemployed of all age groups are provided. The NDEA Act of 1958, providing for the training of technicians, and the federal Vocational Education Act of 1963 have added new dimensions to vocational training, including programs in health occupations, technician training, office occupations, home economics for gainful employment, and for the academically and socioeconomically disadvantaged. Also, encouragement through funding has been given to occupational guidance, to more effective teacher training, and to local and state supervision.

No doubt, continuity of leadership by the Department of Education in the overall area of vocational education has contributed to the growth of all facets of vocational education as provided for under the various federal acts.

Vocational Rehabilitation Services

The federal government, through the Federal Civilian Rehabilitation Act of 1920, provided matching funds to the states for the purpose of reeducating persons of employable age who had been incapacitated in industry. Governor Morrow worked out an agreement between the State Board of Vocational Education and the Workmen's Compensation authorities, but funds were not available until the Legislature met in 1922 (72). In 1954, Public Law 565, amending the Rehabilitation Act, set up the financial structure under which the State Department of Education provides services to the disabled. The 1956 act authorized the superintendent of public instruction to establish within the department a state rehabilitation agency which should have such powers and duties as were contained in the act and such other functions as might be established by regulations of the state board.

In 1958, the Bureau of Vocational Education was organized around its three distinct programs of services – rehabilitation services, services to the blind, and disability determinations. By an agreement with the U.S. Department of Health, Education, and Welfare, the federal government provides the funds for this program.

The Bureau of Rehabilitation Services is responsible for the administration, supervision, direction, and overall promotion of the state-federal program for the vocational rehabilitation of the disabled in Kentucky. The head of this bureau maintains liaison with the U.S. Department of Health, Education, and Welfare.

The latest report on the study of the State Department of Education points out the following:

> The Bureau operates on a separate budget from the regular budget of the Department of Education. For the 1965-66 fiscal year, the Bureau provided rehabilitation services to 9,554 persons through its eleven district offices and 22 special facilities throughout the state. The Bureau of Rehabilitation Services is one of the fastest growing and most vigorous units of the department. The advancement in number of cases served, the increased use of available federal funds, and the imaginative plans for the future are highly commendable (73).

Adult Education

Adult education has been recognized as an area of need for at least a half century. Superintendent John G. Crabbe, in his report to the 1908 Legislature, pointed out that the federal census showed that of the 52 states and territories, only 3 had a higher percentage of illiterates than Kentucky (74).

The need for a state program in adult and continuing education has become increasingly clear each decade since 1908. According to national census reports in each decade from 1920 to 1960, Kentucky has ranked low in the educational level of adults. From February 1961 until June 1962, a general adult education program, with funds provided by a special appropriation of the Legislature to the state department, was sponsored through the Bureau of Vocational Education. The funds were discontinued in June 1962, but during that brief period 5,051 adults had attended classes in 23 school districts, and the value of such services to both the communities and the schools had become clear (75). When funds were withdrawn, only 9 of the 23 districts could continue the program.

Adult education has now become one of the fastest growing concerns of Kentucky's public school system. A significant forward step was the creation in 1962 of a program for high school equivalency certificates. This program of services is administered and supervised through the Department of Education under regulations authorized by the State Board of Education. This program is not subsidized by federal funds. A dramatic expansion of the program of adult education was sparked by the Economic Opportunity Act of 1964, through which funds are distributed to the states on a 90-10 percent ratio. By the end of 1965, the value of adult education had been recognized by every district.

The success of the adult education program is evidenced by the fact that a substantial number of adults who complete the adult basic program continue their education until they receive the equivalency high school certificates; substantial numbers are promoted to better jobs, secure jobs as a result of their additional schooling, or enroll in vocational and manpower training programs; and a significant number enroll in college. During the 1965-66 and 1966-67 school years, the basic adult program cost $2,400,836, the administration and supervision being provided through the State Department of Education (76).

School Buildings and Grounds

"Next to the Scriptures, I want you to read this bulletin constantly" was the key message by Superintendent of Public Instruction John G. Crabbe in 1909 in an educational bulletin he prepared entitled *School Buildings and Grounds.* He was alarmed over the condition of the buildings in which young Kentuckians were receiving their educations. He was especially concerned over the number and condition of log huts being used as schoolhouses, even though the number had decreased from 2,845 in 1891 to 740 in 1909. As reported in the school report for 1907-1909 by Superintendent Crabbe, there was a great demand among school officers for plans for better country schoolhouses. He said:

> With great care I have prepared this bulletin containing modern plans for one-room school houses, a two-room school house, and a four-room building; instructions for heating, ventilation, lighting, and equipping school buildings and for improving and beautifying the buildings and grounds . . . (77).

Prior to 1908, each district was responsible for its schoolhouses. Under the 1908 county school law, the county became responsible for the rural schools.

In order to achieve the present improved status of school buildings in Kentucky, the Legislature has taken significant action from time to time since 1900; and the state department, in fulfilling the legal and leadership responsibilities delegated to it by the Legislature, has provided significant programs and services. Each development paved the way for the next. Some of these developments follow.

First, an act of 1920 required the state superintendent to approve plans for school buildings in local districts; but these provisions had been ineffective, said the Educational Commission of 1921 (78). In 1921, Superintendent George Colvin reported that although the law required county boards to submit their plans and specifications for school buildings to him for approval, few had.

Second, acting on the basis of the 1921 and 1923 reports of the Efficiency Commission (79), the Legislature in 1924 enacted a law which placed more specifically on the superintendent the responsibility of preparing and submitting for approval by the State Board of Education plans for public school buildings and of providing advice to public school officials on planning and constructing school buildings. Further, the law provided that all plans, specifications, and contracts from the county board of education and boards of trustees of graded schools for new buildings and repair of old buildings should be examined and approved or disapproved by the superintendent of public instruction.

Third, in 1936, Superintendent H. W. Peters secured from the U.S. Office of Education a grant to be used in making a study of school conditions in Kentucky. One of the major goals of the study was to plan a long-time program of improvement, including schoolhouse construction and facilities. Through this study, buildings were identified as permanent or temporary, and school building sites were determined. On the basis of the full study, a plan of school improvement was developed for each school system in the state. This became a guide for two decades or more.

In 1946, the Legislature enacted legislation making it possible for local boards of education to levy up to 20 percent on each $100 valuation of property subject to local taxation, to provide special funds for the purchase of school sites, for erecting and equipping new buildings, and for enlarging existing buildings. By 1947, projects for new buildings and remodeling costing $16,232,000 had been approved by the state department. In 1946, a consulting schoolhouse construction engineer was employed in the buildings and grounds division.

Fourth, the General Assembly in 1950 enacted a "Special Voted School Building Fund Tax," in keeping with a recommendation by Superintendent Boswell B. Hodgkin, who called for this tax as a basis for securing revenue for financing the capital outlay program. Under this new law, school districts could request the authority to submit to the voters of the district the levying of a special school building tax rate of not less than 5¢ but not more than 50¢. The State Board of Education, by judicial interpretation, had been given authority to approve or advise on school bond issues. This represented a major expansion in the functions of the State Department of Education. The state board placed this responsibility upon the superintendent of public instruction; therefore, the state department became responsible for approving all types of school bond issues and determining the fiscal ability of a district to retire this type of indebtedness.

Fifth, the impact of the foundation program enacted into law in 1954 has proved to be the most significant development in stimulating the school building program. The foundation program legislation provided for the first time in the history of Kentucky state funds for capital outlay, up to $400 per classroom unit. This amount was increased to $600 per classroom unit in 1960 on the recommendation of the state department.

State financing of school construction and state assistance in planning school buildings have steadily increased, especially during the past 25 years. The services for planning school facilities are provided by five professional staff members in addition to the assistant superintendent, who has overall responsibility for this and other related divisions. These services focus on five programs: general school plant services; school building planning and engineering; school building maintenance and operation; school property accounting; and school property insurance. The finance division assists local districts in devising schoolhouse financing programs.

Transportation

At the turn of the century, several local superintendents had expressed the desire for legal authority to transport pupils. The state superintendent of public instruction submitted such a program to the Governor in 1907. But the County School District Law enacted in 1908 did not provide for transportation.

As the need for transportation authority increased, one county (Mason County) provided transportation out of funds provided by taxation in the district. When the right of the board to use these funds for transportation was contested in the courts, it became clear that further legislation would be needed. The General Assembly in 1912 passed an act giving county boards authority to transport pupils and to finance their transportation. The amount of money expended for transportation in 1915 was approximately $15,000.

The 1938 General Assembly passed a law requiring the State Board of Education to adopt and enforce regulations governing design and operation of school buses. Upon recommendation of Superintendent H. W. Peters, who gave encouragement and leadership to the transportation movement, the state board adopted in December 1939 rules and regulations relative to safety, comfort, bus equipment, school bus drivers, and the operation of school buses (80). In 1949, the state board revised school bus standards to conform to national standards.

The foundation program legislation provided the first state funds for transportation of school pupils in the amount of $1,600 in 1954. The amount was determined by the number of pupils who lived a mile or more from school and the area in square miles served. This legislation placed increased responsibility on the state department for regulatory, administrative, and consultative services (81).

The transportation division of the state department coordinates school bus purchases by local school districts. The state cooperative purchase plan has resulted in an average price reduction of $1,000 per bus, making Kentucky school bus prices among the lowest in the nation. These reduced prices have enabled the districts to upgrade their school buses faster than otherwise would have been possible (82).

School transportation has grown as districts consolidated schools or merged into larger school centers and as the school population increased. In 1964-65, the number of schools totaled 2,272, while the number of buses totaled 4,814. This represents a decrease during the decade of 42.2 percent in the number of schools and an increase of 31 percent in the number of buses. The number of pupils transported increased from 263,572 in 1954-55 to 379,859 in 1964-65. Expenditures for transportation increased from $6,101,399 in 1954-55 to $11,893,618 in 1964-65. In 1964-65, all of the 120 county districts and 45 of the independent districts had pupil transportation programs. The pupil transportation system continues to grow as the population moves to suburbia, as school systems continue to merge, and as enrollment and attendance increase.

FOOTNOTES

1. Lewis Collins, *History of Kentucky*, I, revised by Richard H. Collins (Frankfort: Kentucky Historical Society, 1966), 23.
2. *Ibid.*, p. 515.
3. M. E. Ligon, *A History of Public Education in Kentucky*, Bulletin of the Bureau of School Services, XIV, No. 4 (Lexington: University of Kentucky, June 1942), 17.
4. Edsel T. Gobey, *The Governors of Kentucky and Education 1780-1852*, Bulletin of the Bureau of School Services, XXXII, No. 4 (Lexington: University of Kentucky, 1960), 39.
5. *Ibid.*

6. Frank McVey, *The Gates Open Slowly* (Lexington: University of Kentucky, 1949), p. 48.
7. Ligon, *op. cit.*, p. 78.
8. *Ibid.*, pp. 79-80.
9. Barksdale Hamlett, *History of Education in Kentucky*, Bulletin of the Department of Education, VII, No. 4 (Frankfort: Department of Education, July 1914), 19.
10. *Ibid.*, p. 53.
11. *Ibid.*
12. *Ibid.*, p. 64.
13. *Ibid.*, p. 78.
14. *Ibid.*, p. 42.
15. Ligon, *op. cit.*, p. 109.
16. Superintendent of Public Instruction, *Biennial Report, 1927-1929*, pp. 54-56.
17. Ligon, *op. cit.*, pp. 288-89.
18. *Ibid.*, p. 116.
19. Kentucky, *Official Report of the Proceedings and Debates of the Constitutional Convention 1890*, III (Frankfort: E. Polk Johnson, 1890), 4454. Referred to hereafter as *Proceedings and Debates.*
20. National Educational Association, *Report of the Committee of Twelve on Rural Schools* (Chicago: University of Chicago Press, 1897), p. 26. Referred to hereafter as the *Committee of Twelve Report.*
21. Kentucky, *Acts* (1893), pp. 1413-14.
22. Kentucky Educational Commission, *Public Education in Kentucky* (New York: General Education Board, 1921), p. 20.
23. Hamlett, *op. cit.*, p. 55.
24. National Educational Association, *op. cit.*, p. 56.
25. Hamlett, *op. cit.*, p. 275.
26. Ligon, *op. cit.*, pp. 141-42.
27. *Ibid.*, pp. 145-46.
28. Superintendent of Public Instruction, *Biennial Report, 1908-1909*, p. 342.
29. Kentucky Educational Commission, *op. cit.*, pp. 151-52.
30. Ligon, *op. cit.*, pp. 155-56.
31. Kentucky Educational Commission, *op. cit.*, p. 139.
32. *Ibid.*, pp. 22-25.
33. Ligon, *op. cit.*, p. 159. Also see Talbott *v.* Kentucky State Board of Education, 244 Ky. 826.525W.2D.727 (1932).
34. Efficiency Commission of Kentucky, *Report*, V (Frankfort: State Journal Co., 1923), p. 37.
35. Kentucky, *Common School Laws* (1912), p. 16.
36. Hoskins *v.* Ramsey, 197 Ky. 465, 247 S.W. 371 (1923).
37. Kentucky, *Common School Laws* (1924), pp. 3-4.
38. Kentucky, *Acts* (1930), p. 98.
39. Superintendent of Public Instruction, *Biennial Report, 1929-1931*, Part I, p. 43.
40. Talbott *v.* Kentucky State Board of Education, 244 Ky. 826.525W.2D.727 (1932).
41. H. W. Peters, *History of Education in Kentucky, 1915-1940*, Bulletin of the Department of Education, VII, No. 10 (Frankfort: Department of Education, December 1939), 90.
42. Kentucky Educational Commission, *Report*, Bulletin of the Department of Education, I, No. 8 (Frankfort: Department of Education, 1933), 38-39.
43. Kentucky, *Common School Laws* (1934), p. 41.
44. Wendell P. Butler, *History of Education in Kentucky, 1939-1964*, Bulletin of the Department of Education, XXXI, No. 11 (Frankfort: Department of Education, November 1963), 15-16.
45. *Ibid.*, pp. 30-31.
46. *Ibid.*, p. 59.
47. *Ibid.*, pp. 57, 61.
48. *Ibid.*, p. 73.
49. Commission on Public Education, *First Report of the Commission* (Frankfort: The Commission, December 1961), p. 7.
50. Kentucky, *Senate Journal: First Extraordinary Session* (1956). The Governor's message to the General Assembly, February 27, 1956, p. 7.
51. Department of Education, *Organization, Growth, and Services of State Department of Education*, Bulletin of the Department of Education, XXIX, No. 3 (Frankfort: The Department, March 1961), 131.
52. Superintendent of Public Instruction, *Biennial Report, 1919-1921*, p. 14.
53. Butler, *op. cit.*, p. 19.
54. Committee on Functions and Resources of State Government, *Final Report, Findings and Recommendations* (Frankfort: Legislative Research Commission, December 1951).
55. Legislative Research Commission, *Kentucky's Education Puzzle* (Frankfort: The Commission, 1953), pp. 4, 10-11.
56. Kentucky, *Common School Laws* (1958), p. 499.
57. Kentucky Educational Commission, *Report*, Bulletin of the Department of Education, Vol. I, No. 8 (Frankfort: Department of Education, October 1933).
58. Committee on Functions and Resources of State Government, *op. cit.*, p. 22.
59. Kentucky Commission on Public Education, *Program Evaluation Survey* (Frankfort: Booz, Allen and Hamilton, Management Consultants, October 1961), pp. 98-99.

60. *School News,* Newsletter of the Kentucky Department of Education, II, No. 5, January 1964, 1-2.
61. Kentucky Commission on Public Education, *op. cit.*, p. 44.
62. These figures exclude the district and special school offices.
63. Superintendent of Public Instruction, *Biennial Report, 1919-1921,* pp. 56-58.
64. Kentucky, *Common School Laws* (1924), pp. 10-15.
65. Kentucky, *Common School Laws* (1934), pp. 125-26.
66. Department of Education, Bureau of Instruction, Division of Teacher Education and Certification, *The Preparation of Public School Personnel Employed in 200 School Districts in Kentucky in 1966-1967,* Teacher Education Circular No. 241 (Frankfort: The Department, March 15, 1967).
67. Kentucky, *Common School Laws* (1934), pp. 115-16.
68. *Ibid.,* p. 35.
69. Kentucky, *Common School Laws* (1924), pp. 3-5.
70. During the period from 1924 through 1968 only four men have served in the statutory capacity of assistant superintendent, two of whom have served a total of 36 years: Gordie Young, 1928-55, and Samuel M. Alexander, 1960 to present.
71. Kentucky, *Common School Laws* (1908), p. 61.
72. Superintendent of Public Instruction, *Biennial Report, 1919-1921,* pp. 43-44.
73. Department of Education, *A Cooperative Study of the Kentucky Department of Education* (Frankfort: The Department, 1966), p. 46.
74. Superintendent of Public Instruction, *Biennial Report, 1907-1909,* p. 14.
75. Butler, *op. cit.,* p. 224.
76. Superintendent of Public Instruction, *Biennial Report, 1965-1967,* p. 173.
77. Superintendent of Public Instruction, *Biennial Report, 1907-1909,* p. 3.
78. Kentucky Educational Commission (1921), *op. cit.,* p. 84.
79. Efficiency Commission of Kentucky, *The Educational System of Kentucky* (Frankfort: State Journal Co., 1923).
80. Peters, *op. cit.,* p. 132.
81. Butler, *op. cit.,* pp. 203-204.
82. *Ibid.,* p. 204.

BIBLIOGRAPHY

Public Documents

Hoskins *v.* Ramsey, 197 Ky. 465, 247 S.W. 371 (1923).

Kentucky. *Acts* (1893, 1930).

——*Constitution* (1850, 1891, 1915).

——*Official Report of the Proceedings and Debates of the Constitutional Convention 1890.* Vol. III. Frankfort: E. Polk Johnson, 1890.

——*Senate Journal: First Extraordinary Session* (1956). The Governor's message to the General Assembly, February 27, 1956.

Kentucky Department of Education. *Kentucky Common School Laws.* Frankfort: The Department, 1912, 1926, 1934, 1958.

Talbott *v.* Kentucky State Board of Education. 244 Ky. 826.525W.2D.727 (1932).

Books and Bulletins

Butler, Wendell P. *History of Education in Kentucky 1939-1964.* Bulletin of the Department of Education. Vol. XXXI, No. 11. Frankfort: Department of Education, November 1963.

Collins, Lewis. *History of Kentucky.* Revised by Richard H. Collins. Frankfort: Kentucky Historical Society, 1966.

Department of Education. *A Cooperative Study of the Kentucky Department of Education.* Frankfort: The Department, 1966.

—— *Organization, Growth, and Services of State Department of Education.* Bulletin of the Department of Education. Vol. XXIX, No. 3. Frankfort: The Department, March 1961.

Department of Education, Bureau of Instruction, Division of Teacher Education and Certification. *The Preparation of Public School Personnel Employed in 200 School Districts in Kentucky in 1966-67.* Teacher Education Circular No. 241. Frankfort: The Department, March 15, 1967.

Efficiency Commission of Kentucky. *The Educational System of Kentucky.* Frankfort: State Journal Co., 1923.

Gobey, Edsel T. *The Governors of Kentucky and Education 1780-1852.* Bulletin of the Bureau of School Services. Vol. XXXII, No. 4. Lexington: University of Kentucky, 1960.

Hamlett, Barksdale. *History of Education in Kentucky.* Bulletin of the Department of Education. Vol. VII, No. 4. Frankfort: Department of Education, July 1914.

Kentucky Educational Commission. *Public Education in Kentucky.* New York: General Education Board, 1921.

—— *Report.* Bulletin of the Department of Education. Vol. I, No. 8. Frankfort: Department of Education, 1933.

Legislative Research Commission. *Kentucky's Education Puzzle*. Frankfort: The Commission, 1953.

Ligon, M. E. *A History of Public Education in Kentucky*. Bulletin of the Bureau of School Services. Vol. XIV, No. 4, Lexington: University of Kentucky, June 1942.

McVey, Frank. *The Gates Open Slowly*. Lexington: University of Kentucky, 1949.

Peters, H. W. *History of Education in Kentucky, 1915-1940*. Bulletin of the Department of Education, Vol. VII, No. 10. Frankfort: Department of Education, December 1939.

Reports

Commission on Public Education. *First Report of the Commission*. Frankfort: The Commission, December 1961.

Committee on Functions and Resources of State Government. *Final Report, Findings and Recommendations*. Frankfort: Legislative Research Commission, December 1951.

Efficiency Commission of Kentucky. *Report*. Vol. V. Frankfort: State Journal Co., 1923.

Kentucky Commission on Public Education. *Program Evaluation Survey*. Frankfort: Booz, Allen and Hamilton, Management Consultants, October 1961.

Kentucky Educational Commission. *Report*. Bulletin of the Department of Education, Vol. I, No. 8. Frankfort: Department of Education, 1933.

National Educational Association. *Report of the Committee of Twelve on Rural Schools*. Chicago: University of Chicago Press, 1897.

Superintendents of Public Instruction. *Biennial Reports*. Frankfort: Department of Education, 1908-67.

Periodical

School News. Newsletter of the Kentucky Department of Education, Vol. II, No. 5, January 1964.

Appendix A

KENTUCKY CHIEF STATE SCHOOL OFFICERS

State Superintendents of Public Instruction

1899-1903	H. V. McChesney	1936-40	Harry W. Peters
1903-1907	James H. Fuqua	1940-44	John W. Brooker
1907-10	John Grant Crabbe	1944-48	John Fred Williams
1910-12	Ellsworth Regenstein	1948-52	Boswell B. Hodgkin
1912-16	Barksdale Hamlett	1952-56	Wendell P. Butler
1916-20	Virgil O. Gilbert	1956-59	Robert R. Martin (to Dec. 1959)
1920-24	George Colvin	1959-60	Ted C. Gilbert (Dec. 1959 - Jan. 1960)
1924-28	McHenry Rhoads	1960-64	Wendell P. Butler
1928-32	W. C. Bell	1964-68	Harry M. Sparks
1932-36	James H. Richmond	1968-	Wendell P. Butler

Appendix B

Chart I.--KENTUCKY DEPARTMENT OF PUBLIC INSTRUCTION, 1933

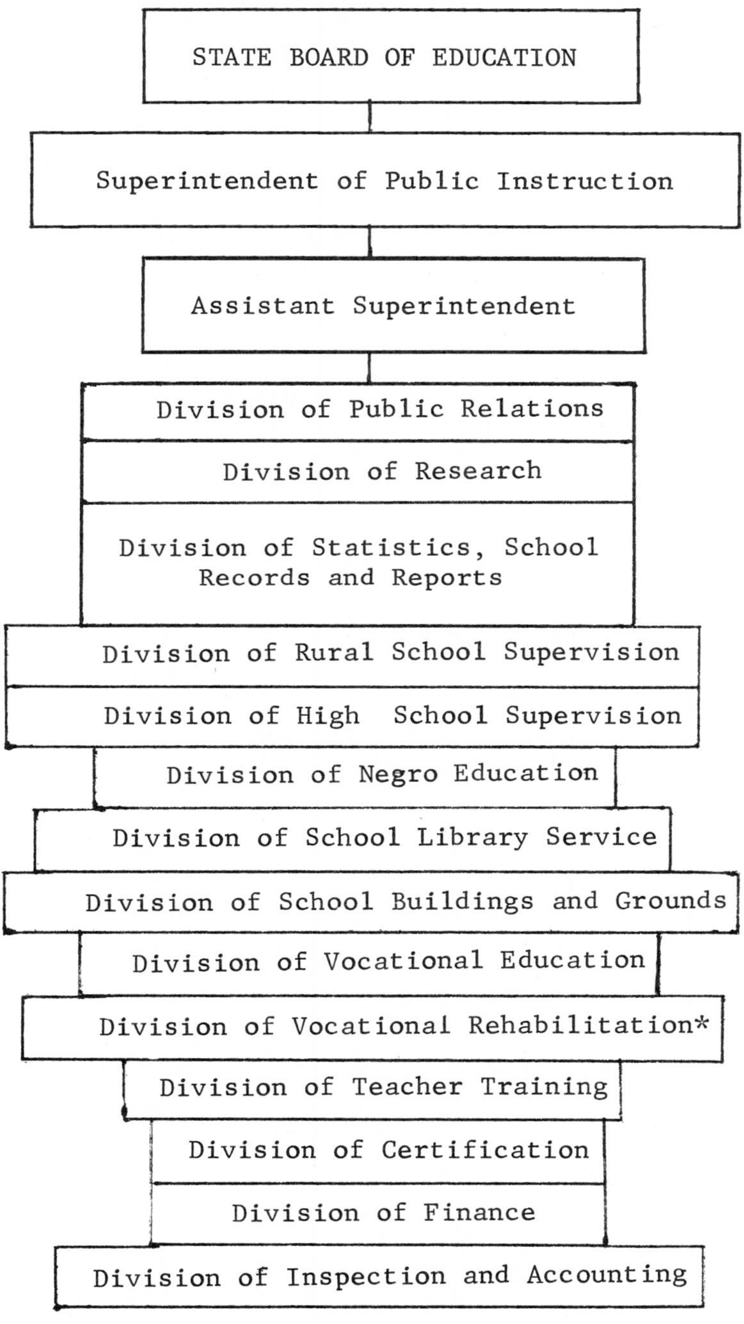

*In September 1933, the name of this division was changed to "Special Education."

Appendix B

Chart II.--KENTUCKY DEPARTMENT OF EDUCATION, 1959

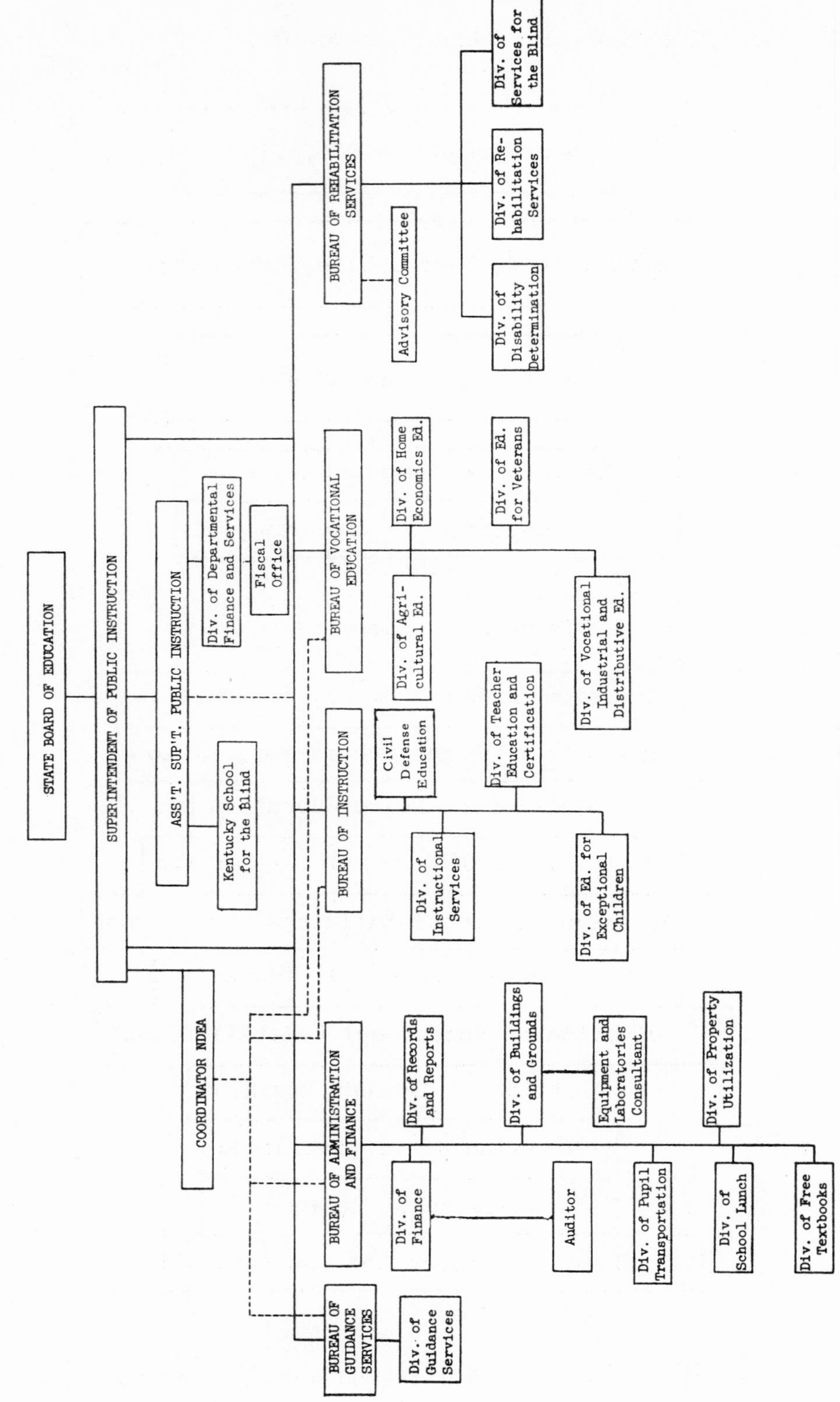

Appendix B

Chart III.--KENTUCKY DEPARTMENT OF EDUCATION, 1967

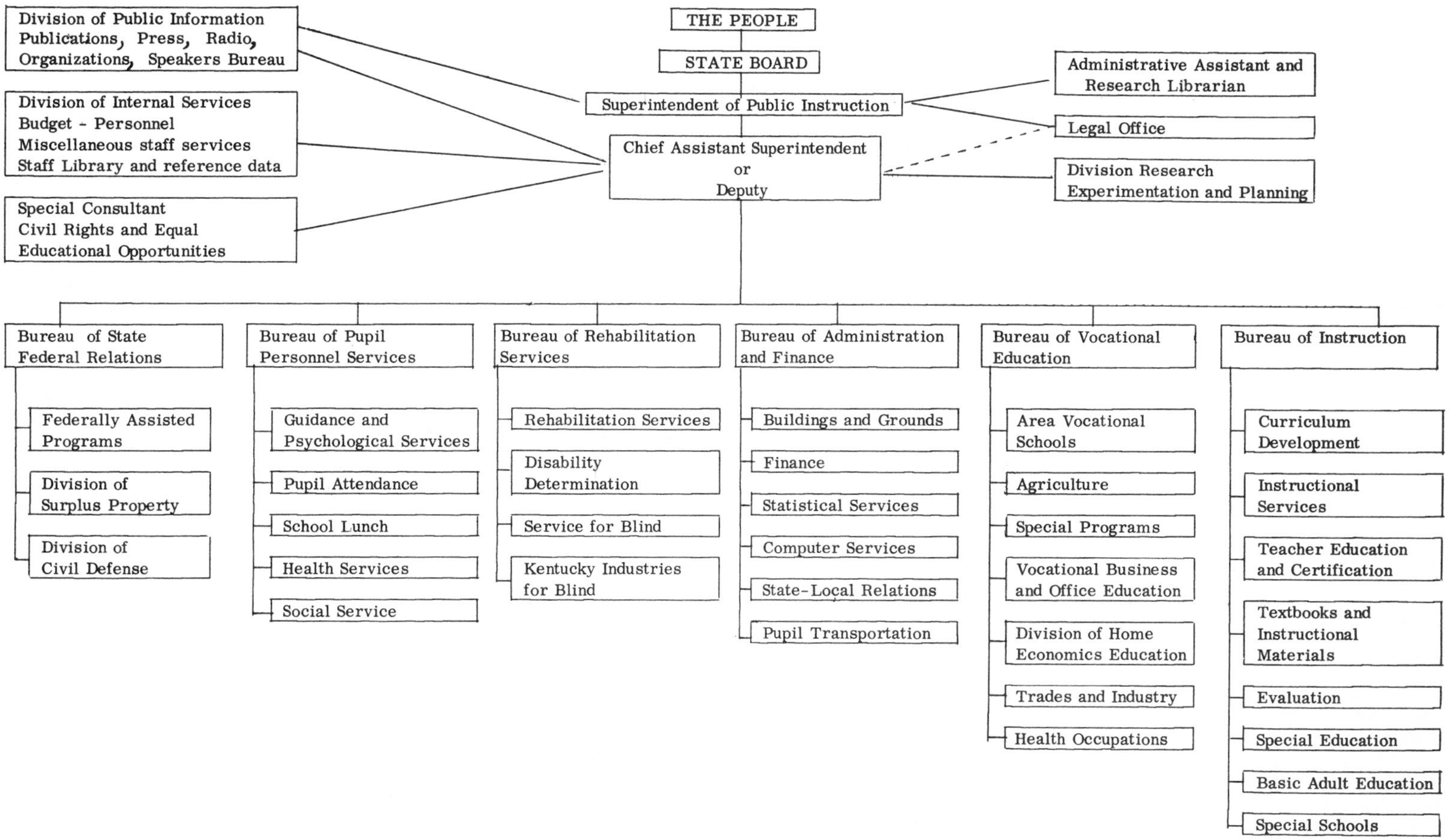

THE PEOPLE

STATE BOARD

Superintendent of Public Instruction

Chief Assistant Superintendent or Deputy

Division of Public Information
Publications, Press, Radio, Organizations, Speakers Bureau

Division of Internal Services
Budget - Personnel
Miscellaneous staff services
Staff Library and reference data

Special Consultant
Civil Rights and Equal Educational Opportunities

Administrative Assistant and Research Librarian

Legal Office

Division Research Experimentation and Planning

Bureau of State Federal Relations
- Federally Assisted Programs
- Division of Surplus Property
- Division of Civil Defense

Bureau of Pupil Personnel Services
- Guidance and Psychological Services
- Pupil Attendance
- School Lunch
- Health Services
- Social Service

Bureau of Rehabilitation Services
- Rehabilitation Services
- Disability Determination
- Service for Blind
- Kentucky Industries for Blind

Bureau of Administration and Finance
- Buildings and Grounds
- Finance
- Statistical Services
- Computer Services
- State-Local Relations
- Pupil Transportation

Bureau of Vocational Education
- Area Vocational Schools
- Agriculture
- Special Programs
- Vocational Business and Office Education
- Division of Home Economics Education
- Trades and Industry
- Health Occupations

Bureau of Instruction
- Curriculum Development
- Instructional Services
- Teacher Education and Certification
- Textbooks and Instructional Materials
- Evaluation
- Special Education
- Basic Adult Education
- Special Schools

18 Louisiana

DEPARTMENT OF EDUCATION
James S. Cookston
R. L. Frye
Louis Nicolosi
Charles E. Sutton
Ralph P. Whitehead

Under the Supervision of
William F. Beyer, Jr.
M. E. Wright

Contents

EARLY BEGINNINGS

Sporadic efforts attempted to establish public education in Louisiana before 1860, and some of these starts had lasting influence on education in the state. Significant among these were provision for a state superintendent of education in 1845; the first statewide public school law of 1847; provision for parish superintendents in 1847; provision to distribute state school funds on a per educable basis in 1847; abolition of the office of parish superintendent in 1852, which continued to 1877; and division of parishes into small school districts.

Early State Educational Efforts

Prior to statehood, the Legislative Council for the territory in 1804 set up a board of regents which was to establish in each parish (county) one or more academies for instruction in the French and English languages, reading, writing, arithmetic, grammar, and geography. The territory also set up academies for females. The council appropriated $50,000 to be raised by lotteries, but indications are that this money never became available in amounts sufficient to implement the program. In 1811, the territory appropriated $39,000; no county was to receive more than $2,000. It also allowed $500 for poorer families. But the parishes did not draw upon the money available, and the parish system was abandoned in 1819 (1).

The Louisiana Constitution of 1812 did not include any provision for education, although each revision since that time has done so. Free schools were of no concern to the members of the convention, who primarily were men of means, able to employ private tutoring or patronize the private schools so firmly entrenched at this time (2). The Legislature of 1812 enacted a law which created crude public school machinery and provided limited funds for financing public schools.

The General School Act, passed by the Legislature in 1821, provided that police juries in each parish – local governing bodies active in administration of schools (especially in calling school tax elections) – should appoint five landowners as school board members. In 1833, the Legislature designated the secretary of state as ex officio state superintendent of public instruction and required parish school boards to report to him. Provisions also were made by the Legislature to allot $2.50–$4.00 per child to schools, based on the number enrolled (3).

In 1847, the Legislature passed the first statewide public school law providing for a public school system at state and parish levels. At this time only a few poorly attended schools had been established, and there is little evidence as to their organization or the type of program they conducted. The people were still largely indifferent toward public schools, due to the entrenchment of private education and the feeling that public schools were for paupers. The Legislature subsidized many private academies if they offered free board and tuition to a certain number of indigents. However, under the 1847 law each parish was to elect a superintendent and pay a salary not to exceed $300 annually. More important, the act provided for a full-time state superintendent of public education appointed by the Governor for 2-year terms. State school funds were to be distributed on a per educable basis, a practice that continues today. The Governor appointed Alexander Dimitry to serve as the first state superintendent of education. Dimitry served two terms, from 1847 through 1851. In 1852, the Legislature felt that the salary paid to parish superintendents was extravagant and abolished the office. For the next 25 years, the schools of Louisiana lacked local administrative leadership. The state superintendent became the administrative leader for the parishes. The additional handicap of the division of parishes into small school districts lingered well into the twentieth century (4).

The Dark Decades, 1860–1900

The War Between the States, beginning in 1861, ushered in four of the darkest decades in public education. Even though the Confederate Legislature in 1862 appropriated $500,000 for this purpose, public education came to a near standstill. The war lessened the little sentiment that had existed for public education in Louisiana and in the South and practically wiped out the financial resources of the section (5).

Shortly after the war, the people of Louisiana gained temporary control of the state government. The mild Reconstruction plan of Presidents Lincoln and Johnson had allowed a large number of ex-Confederates to win election to the Legislature and to parish and municipal offices in 1865. Robert M. Lusher, appointed state superintendent of education, attempted to reorganize the defunct school system, but his efforts were halted by the return of Reconstruction personnel and their Freedman's Bureau. Thus, from 1868 to 1877, Louisiana government was in the firm grip of officials alien to the Southern cause. These officials imported Thomas W. Conway from New England to serve as state superintendent of education from 1868 to 1872. Conway apparently did little, and newspapers at the time labeled him an "ignorant, drunken, incompetent politician." A Negro, William G. Brown, became the state superintendent in 1872, holding the position until the end of the period. Little is known of Brown or of his activities since he apparently had little to do with the schools and employed as his secretary a Northern Baptist minister who did the work and wrote his reports. Many New Orleans teachers later testified that they knew nothing about Brown, and only one could recall ever having seen him (6).

The Reconstruction Convention of 1868 adopted a constitution similar to the preceding one insofar as education was concerned. The new constitution forbade separate schools for the races, thus destroying the schools for that time. One notable provision was instituted that has remained a part of the educational framework until the present time—the establishment of a State Board of Education. The Governor had appointive power over the state superintendent of education and was responsible for appointing all local parish and district school boards, giving his office complete power throughout the educational structure (7).

In 1869, when the Reconstruction Legislature convened, apparently the only concern for education was to provide the largest number of education jobs for those in power. Records reveal that large appropriations were made for schools during this period. Education appropriation bills seldom failed to pass, but most of the moneys appropriated never reached the public schools. The Legislature apportioned school funds on the basis of the number of educables, and the tax assessors – who made the enumerations – seldom agreed with the census takers. For example, in 1870, Plaquemines Parish listed 4,000 educables and had only 100 pupils in school. New Orleans listed 90,000 educables and enrolled only 19,000; and while the 350 teachers were paid an average of only $70 per month, the cost of the city's educational system was $374,000. In 1874, Natchitoches Parish had a school fund of nearly $20,000 yet operated only one three-teacher Negro school; Raford Blunt, an illiterate Negro State Senator, was one of the teachers and was also a member of the parish school board. In 1871, the state superintendent of education reported that most of the $1,193,500 received from the sale of school lands had been stolen by the political machine and diverted to its purposes. An investigation of the Department of Education 6 years later revealed that $2,137,369 had been lost to the public schools by mismanagement and corruption (8).

The educational climate continued to be poor during the period between 1877 and 1900. Ravaged by the war and misconduct of Reconstruction, most of the people of Louisiana were poverty stricken and thus handicapped in their efforts toward rebuilding their educational structure. Other obstacles that blocked their progress were the lack of educational leadership at the state and local levels, the absence of suitable legislation, and fear of the return of forced integration of the races in the schools (9).

When the military forces withdrew in 1877, Francis T. Nicholls was elected Governor and, because of popular demand stemming from Reconstruction experiences, the position of state superintendent became an elective one. Robert M. Lusher, who had served previously as the appointed state superintendent of education, was elected by popular vote in 1877. That same year, in an effort to create more local initiative as well as statewide financial support, the Legislature adopted a general school act which provided for a State Board of Education, parish and district school boards, parish superintendents, and a statewide property tax of 2 mills for school support. In 1879, the state drafted a new constitution leaving the responsibility of separate schools for the races up to local school boards. The constitution required the Legislature to provide for establishment, maintenance, and support of the public schools. It also provided for a state superintendent of education, parish school boards, and parish superintendents (10).

In 1898, the voters of Louisiana adopted a new constitution. It included provisions for a state superintendent of education to be elected every 4 years by popular vote. An annual salary of $2,000 was prescribed along with an additional $2,000 for expenses necessary to performing duties as prescribed for his office by law.

The Turn of the Century

At the turn of the century, the State Department of Education consisted of State Superintendent Joseph V. Calhoun (1896-1904) and his secretary. The $2,000 provided for the expenses of the office was used to pay the secretary's salary, travel, stationery, postage, and other necessary items (11).

When J. B. Aswell became state superintendent in 1904, he initiated the semblance of a staff for the department by moving the state institute conductor from the state normal college in Natchitoches to Baton Rouge. The state institute conductor was responsible for institutes held throughout the state for instructing teachers in methods of procedures and for educating the public in favor of tax-supported schools. This office continued until 1914. In February 1908, the first high school inspector was added, and in November 1909, Superintendent T. H. Harris added a supervisor of rural schools. The salaries and expenses of these new positions came from various funds. The General Education Board, a John D. Rockefeller educational foundation agency which took the lead in promoting and financing educational development in the Southern states, and the Peabody Education Fund for teacher training and scholarships were the mainstays until the state provided additional funds (12).

In conjunction with Louisiana State University, the department also utilized the director of club services in the agricultural extension division as supervisor of agriculture in the state department. In 1910, the department consisted of the state superintendent and his secretarial staff, the state institute conductor, the supervisor of agriculture, the high school inspector, and the supervisor of rural schools. This was an imposing staff compared to that of a few years earlier, but indeed small considering what the future held in store (13).

The Constitution of 1921

The Constitution of 1921, which affects the State Department of Education and public education today, provided for a State Board of Education consisting of 11 members, with 3 members appointed by the Governor for 4-year terms, 1 each from the districts corresponding to the public service commission districts, and 8 members selected by the people, 1 each from the districts corresponding to the congressional districts, with overlapping terms. Since 1948, the three members heretofore appointed by the Governor have been elected by the people for 6-year terms. The State Board of Education was to elect the state superintendent of education for a term of 4 years. Before this provision became effective, however, the election of the state superintendent was placed in the hands of the voters through a constitutional amendment based on Act No. 105 of the 1922 Legislature. (In 1946, a constitutional amendment calling for the appointment of the state superintendent by the State Board of Education was defeated.)

The new constitution gave the State Board of Education general supervision and control of the state's public elementary and secondary schools and direct control of all other state educational institutions, except Louisiana State University and Agricultural and Mechanical College. It authorized the state board to employ such assistance in the state department as was needed. (It was almost 30 years (1950) before the state laws specifically authorized the state superintendent to establish and staff the State Department of Education.) Parish school boards were authorized to elect parish superintendents for terms of 4 years (this has continued since July 1925), fix their salaries, and employ such assistants as might be needed.

The minimum state property tax for schools was set at 2.5 mills, and the parish tax at 3 mills. In addition, at the parish level, special maintenance taxes up to 8 mills, building taxes which would not be funded into bonds up to 5 mills, and building bond issues up to 10 percent of the assessment were permitted. A severance tax of 2 percent on the gross output of national resources, except agriculture, was dedicated to the support of Louisiana State University until January 1925; thereafter, the university was to be supported by the state property tax of 0.5 mill and such additional appropriations as the Legislature would make. The Legislature was required to set aside annually a minimum of $700,000 for the support of state institutions under the control of the State Board of Education. Provision was made for the pensioning of old and incapacitated teachers, but a funded teacher retirement system was not set up in Louisiana until 1936 (14).

EDUCATIONAL PROGRAMS

Elementary Education

Prior to 1908, the department had no functional elementary division; elementary schools were supervised by the superintendent directly, and later by the supervisor of high schools. The state superintendent's responsibilities in elementary education were of a general nature, concerned mainly with distributing state funds to local schools and making recommendations to the state board for improvements.

In 1909, the superintendent appointed a rural school supervisor and charged him with the responsibility of improving the rural elementary schools. This position was created when the Peabody Fund offered to pay salary and expenses. Rural consolidation of one- and two-room schools, a major problem, received the immediate attention of the elementary (rural) supervisor (15). More emphasis on higher education and high schools had created bad conditions in the rural elementary schools. The constitutional provisions of 1898, permitting school tax elections for building and maintenance, were a powerful factor in promoting consolidation. Other factors were the improvement of road building throughout the state, the employment in 1909 of a rural school supervisor, and appropriations from the Legislature with the assistance of the state board to many parishes for consolidation purposes.

Due to the limited support by the people for public education in general and the diversity of Louisiana's rural population, there was no close relationship between the schools and the communities. This made it easier for the department to promote consolidation.

Between 1908 and 1920, the rural (elementary) supervisor made efforts to bring about improvements in buildings, grounds, equipment, teaching procedures, and the program of studies. A report during this period indicated that popular support was increasing for consolidation of schools and pupil transportation as well as for more competent teachers and a better course of study.

In 1920, two additional elementary supervisors were added to the staff, making a total of three, and they assisted in making curriculum improvements as well as in instructional procedures. Several changes were made in the elementary course of study during the 1920's. With outside help, the elementary division issued curriculum bulletins (courses of study) emphasizing the scientific approach to problems in reading, language, spelling, and testing, and containing specific help for teachers (16).

By 1926-27, a definite program for elementary schools was emphasized. Each parish conducted supervising programs which were designed to accentuate the importance of "careful planning for the year's work" and to suggest how the planning might be done. The program also stressed the evaluation and analysis of lessons and listed points to assist teachers in doing their work.

The Depression affected elementary education programs less than others as far as financial matters were concerned. Perhaps most of Louisiana's schools fared better than those of many other states because Louisiana's economic base was a larger, parish-wide system rather than the small, independent district township system common to other states. The department staff actually shows an increase in personnel from 21 in 1929 to 40 in 1940. There was no reduction during any of these years.

A 1936 department bulletin listed major elementary school functions as development of desirable understandings and attitudes that typify the good citizen and preparation of the pupil for satisfactory high school work (17).

Even during the Depression, department officials were interested in upgrading elementary education. The State Department of Education and Louisiana State University cooperated in an all-out effort to improve the educational program in the public schools. For instance, they cooperated in inaugurating curriculum studies in the summer of 1936, which continued for several summers thereafter. As a result of the efforts of the state supervisor of elementary schools, the department published bulletins citing the results of these studies conducted by educators each summer. The State Department of Education published courses of study for the basic programs in reading, math, etc., in an effort to correlate the courses with the latest advances in pedagogy.

During the 1936-37 school session, department supervisors, local supervisors, principals, teachers, and college faculty members promoted the curriculum study. The following year the cooperative meetings showed that the studies had gained tremendous momentum and were clearly indicating a movement toward formulating basic principles and a philosophy for elementary schools.

In summary, the elementary division, in the early beginning, provided very little service to the schools of the state. A course of study for the elementary schools was a very brief statement of subjects to be taught in the different grades. With appointment of an inspector of elementary and rural schools, the services to the schools were increased through better conditions, consolidation, new equipment, and increased length of term. The state department, in an effort to improve elementary schools, published a standards bulletin in 1936. Provision was made that high schools would accept only those students who had completed the grade work in an approved elementary school, and students from unapproved schools only by examination. Students going from one elementary school to another were subject to similar requirements.

Parish school boards were asked to establish such public schools as were deemed necessary, and, at their request, personnel of the state department would visit the schools for approval. The standards for approval were raised and strengthened about 14 years after the first standards bulletin was published.

The curriculum development project during the thirties which involved the department received the interest and attention of elementary supervisors for several years. Elementary schools were definitely influenced in the areas of philosophy, curriculum, supervision, teaching methods, and materials of instruction. In the years that followed, members of the department continued to work on courses of study and methods of teaching. Questionnaires sent to parish superintendents for evaluating the proposals indicated an increase in the teachers' understanding of educational problems, an improvement in the professional attitude and initiative of teachers, extensive use of local materials, encouragement of adventuring and experimenting in teaching, reduced stress on memorizing facts, and promotion of interest in education on the part of parents.

The 1940's saw a general continuation of the basic programs of the thirties. The department's supervisor of elementary schools became director of elementary schools with assistant supervisors of elementary and primary areas. Standards for approval of elementary schools, adopted by the State Board of Education, are used as the basis for the granting of school approvals by the Elementary Section, which functions under the direction of Superintendent William J. Dodd and the assistant superintendent of curriculum and instruction.

The present major role of the Elementary Section is one of service, along with certain regulatory functions and curriculum work.

Secondary Education

Prior to the Louisiana Purchase in 1803 and before Louisiana became a state in 1812, the territory had only a few private and four public schools. The Spanish established in 1771 the first public school, which was a failure because its purpose was to assimilate the French population. In 1811, three public schools, established in Pointe Coupee Parish with the help of Julien Poydras, represented the sum total of public school effort in Louisiana. Because very little had been done toward establishing high schools prior to 1908, a High School Section in the State Department of Education had received only token recognition. Superintendent Calhoun, during his term of office from 1896 to 1904, recognized the need for state accreditation of high schools. In 1902, Calhoun recommended to the state board that an approved diploma be designed and adopted and that all students receiving the diploma be entitled to admittance into any of the advanced state institutions of learning without examination. He felt that this recognition would add prestige to the high school diploma and encourage students to continue in school until graduation (18).

It was highly possible that Calhoun made his recommendation at that time because Louisiana State and Tulane Universities had taken steps to admit without examination students from recognized schools. Although there were then no accredited high schools in Louisiana, the state superintendent listed 35 public schools as high schools, and annual statistical reports showed the attendance in the schools. This, at least, was a measure of affiliation and the beginning of accreditation by the state. In the biennial report for 1904-1905, a list of "Authorized High Schools" appeared, listing names of 43 public schools, most of which were located in the larger towns and parish seats (19).

During 1906, the State Board of Education set up the following requirements for high schools: (a) title to the property on which the school was located had to be vested in the parish board of education; (b) the parish board of education had to pass a resolution establishing such a school as a high school; (c) all schools in the parish where the high school was had to run at least 7 months; and (d) a copy of the property title, parish board resolution establishing the school, a certificate certifying that the schools were operated for 7 months, and a proposed course of study were to be forwarded to the state board. Thus, for the first time the state was assuming responsibility for approving the various high schools throughout the state.

Other than a general listing of subjects prescribed by the state board in 1896, nothing had been done to approve courses of study. There was no follow-up of this general listing until 1904, when Superintendent Aswell recognized, in a report to the board, the need for a more uniform pattern of schools and course offerings (20).

Beginning of the High School Section. The real beginning of a high school section in the state department was made when the state board, in October 1907, created the office of state high school inspector. In February 1908, an inspector was hired to be paid from funds provided by the General Education Board of New York. His duties were to visit some of the approved high schools and aid the state superintendent in his many duties. One of the first recommendations made by the new inspector was that the principal be allowed at least one teacher to help with the high school program (21).

In 1909, upon recommendations by Superintendent Harris and the high school inspector, the state board passed a series of resolutions governing the approval of high schools. These resolutions included (a) following the state course of study; (b) maintaining a 9-month school session; (c) maintaining a minimum 40-minute recitation period; (d) employing at least two high school teachers; (e) providing at least two periods of the principal's time for supervision; (f) acquiring science laboratories at a minimum of $300; (g) purchasing laboratory equipment only after the approval of the state department; (h) requiring students in the inductive sciences to perform and report a minimum of 30 experiments; (i) subsidizing each newly approved school with $500; and (j) subsidizing each previously approved school that continued to meet standards with $500 (22).

To assist in the approval and visitation of rural schools, the state established the position of inspector of rural schools in November 1909. The number of approved high schools increased until nearly one hundred schools had state approval by 1910. The high school inspectors made recommendations early in the century as to requirements for high school teachers. In fact, the early concern for certification of teachers appears to have evolved from the visitation and approval recommendations of the high school inspector.

During the years 1910 to 1920, high school improvements throughout the state continued. Through the inspector's recommendations, teacher certification improved, school facilities progressed, libraries and science laboratories expanded, professional attitudes of principals were developed, and the number of approved high schools increased to 298.

Over the years, the title of high school inspector was changed to supervisor of high schools. An assistant supervisor of high schools was added in 1916-17.

Coordination of High School Work. Until 1939, there was little coordination of the different phases of high school supervision. The state high school supervisor involved himself primarily in standards for approval, buildings, equipment, libraries, requirements for graduation, and numerous other problems of general interest. Supervisors in special fields such as agriculture, home economics, health, and physical education charted their courses with little direction for the high school supervisors. In 1939, Superintendent Harris decided to bring together the different departments of the secondary schools and include the program of elementary instruction as an integral part of supervision under a single head. The supervisor who worked in this capacity also was to perform most of the duties of the assistant state superintendent of education (23).

The first 50 years of the twentieth century saw a tremendous expansion in the responsibilities for the High School Section. During the school year 1905-1906, there were 55 approved high schools with 1,408 high school students and no graduates. Statistics reveal that the session 1949-50 produced 460 approved high schools, 82,199 high school students, and 12,860 graduates.

Early high school inspectors and supervisors contributed considerably to the growth and development of high schools throughout Louisiana. They pointed up the dire need for improvement of teachers, facilities, and instructional materials. They also recommended improvements to the proper policy-making bodies, thus providing needed change and development. The responsibility of the High School Section grew from a regulatory function into a more sophisticated, combined regulatory and instructional service function.

The High School Section Today. In 1964, Superintendent William J. Dodd reorganized the State Department of Education into three administrative divisions, placing the High School Section in the Division of Curriculum and Instruction under the direction of an assistant superintendent. Today, the High School Section – consisting of a director, four supervisors, and six secretaries – administers regulatory responsibilities and instructional services to 812 schools that are composed partially or totally of high school grades. Regulatory responsibilities include school approvals, evaluation of transcripts, issuance of diplomas, and related activities. Instructional services involve workshop participation, consultative services for Southern Association Accreditation, and related high school activities. The number of high school graduates per year now is approaching 50,000 – a considerable increase from the turn of the century. The High School Section also issues diplomas and equivalency certificates to those who can qualify through veteran stipulations and adult education programs. Special area supervisors today cooperate with the High School Section to help develop better instructional services to Louisiana schools.

Negro Education

In 1881, Superintendent of Education Edwin Fay, with the cooperation of the general agent of the Peabody Fund, hired two experienced conductors of teachers institutes to open summer institutes for a short period in several Louisiana towns to instruct teachers in their duties and upgrade their certification and training. These highly successful institutes instructed both white and Negro teachers, stimulating much enthusiasm for education (24).

Nonetheless, prior to 1900, the educational picture for Negroes in Louisiana was bleak. There were very few Negro schools, salaries for Negro teachers were low, teacher training and certification were at a low level, and generally there were minimum opportunities for Negro education. In 1898, Superintendent Calhoun reported that 982 schools for Negro children employed 1,039 teachers at an average annual salary of $140. These schools enrolled 72,021 children and reported an annual daily attendance of 52,217, or 72.5 percent of the enrollment. In all probability, most of the schools operated on a split-session basis of 3 or 4 months in winter and 2 or 3 months in summer after the "crops were laid by" (25).

Factors causing these conditions, particularly in Negro schools, were poverty and lack of leadership and legislation. As is the case in other Southern states, the provision of educational opportunities for Negro children has developed very slowly in Louisiana. The state superintendents of education in their annual and/or biennial reports would point out the need for something to be done for Negro education (26). Local school board members, parish superintendents, and high school principals passed resolutions at their annual conferences to the effect that training for Negro teachers should be provided to help them in teaching agricultural and industrial subjects (27).

The Jeanes Fund – a sizable amount left by Anna T. Jeanes of Philadelphia to be devoted to assisting the Negro rural schools – was incorporated in 1907 and gave assistance by providing Negro teachers and supervisors to work in the various local school systems. There were other grant-type programs that gave assistance to the Negro education work (28).

In the biennial report for 1911-13, the state superintendent stated that the Negro school situation was deplorable. He said that either the schools should be organized to do good work or all efforts to educate the Negro child should be abandoned.

Early Supervision. In August 1916, Superintendent Harris announced that the General Education Board of New York had approved a plan to finance the employment of a state agent of rural schools for Negroes. This supervisor was charged by the superintendent to assist in every way possible in the organization of movements to build up a system of Negro education adapted to the needs of the race. Some of the movements deemed necessary to promote at the time were improvement of reading, writing, and arithmetic skills; teaching of practical skills concerned with homemaking and farming; organization of agricultural clubs to encourage thrift, greater farm production, and interest in farm life; stressing of sanitation and personal hygiene; establishment of industrial and agricultural schools in each parish for older youth; fostering of training of rural teachers; and stress on the erection of substantial school buildings.

In 1917, when the Julius Rosenwald Foundation saw a dire need for improving Negro schools in the South, Louisiana was receptive to any aid for this purpose. Negro schools at this time were housed mainly in cabins, churches, lodge halls, and abandoned structures. In order to promote the construction of better buildings, the Rosenwald Fund paid one-half the salary and expenses for the employment of an assistant to the state agent of Negro schools. The Jeanes supervisor endeavored to arouse interest among Negroes and communities to raise money to qualify for the building of Rosenwald schools and county training schools, for the employment of additional Jeanes supervisors, and for the lengthening of school terms. This Rosenwald Fund money paid part of the expense of each Negro school building erected under certain conditions and also paid the salary and traveling expenses of a Negro agent to interest communities in providing better school facilities.

With the appointment of agents to supervise Negro education from 1916 through 1964, there was noticeable improvement in the Negro schools. The Depression years took their toll on white and Negro schools in Louisiana. Teachers' salaries went down, school terms shortened, and expenditures were cut to the bare minimum. The burden that the schools had to carry was increased while support decreased. At the outbreak of World War II, Negro school plants were generally inferior to white school plants. As the war progressed, there was very little money available for maintaining schools. Since the Negro facilities were generally in worse shape, this lack of maintenance money left many Negro schools in deplorable condition. Also, many white and Negro teachers were drawn away from education during this period by higher-paying industrial positions (29).

Since then, agents supervising Negro education have helped the situation considerably. Eight men have held the position of supervisor of Negro education in the state department. These supervisors helped to create harmony between the races and an atmosphere conducive to good working relationships. They stimulated public sentiment in favor of a sound elementary education for all Negro children and a good program for those wishing to prepare for work in the state's industries. The elementary as well as high schools were given more attention by the local school boards because of the work of the state department supervisors. Attendance in the Negro schools increased, and the teachers began to prepare themselves better for their profession (30).

Upon retirement of the director of Negro education in 1964, Negro education was placed under the supervision of the directors of elementary and secondary education. These supervisors have worked with white citizens, Negro leaders, parish school boards, and superintendents throughout the state. They have rendered a service that would be difficult to duplicate.

The Picture Today. Although the number of schools for Negroes reported for 1965 (527) is considerably smaller than the 1898 figures, it can safely be assumed that this smaller number represents, in quality, a substantial improvement in facilities and personnel. The following statistics for the 1964-65 academic year help to confirm this fact:

	Negro	White
Capital outlay	$ 10,254,637	$ 28,269,320
Inventory of school property	$206,270,151	$498,736,448
Number of teachers	11,805	20,870
Average teacher's salary	$5,438	$5,583
Pupil enrollment	343,386	487,039
Average daily attendance	305,119	444,124
Number of pupils graduated from high school (1963-64)	10,611	24,511
Number of above entering college	4,335	12,944
Teachers with less than bachelor's degree	230	1,560
Teachers with bachelor's degree	9,594	13,580
Teachers with master's degree	1,885	5,412
Teachers with training above master's degree	96	317

Adult Education

When federal funds were made available for the public schools by the Smith-Hughes Act of 1917, classes for adults became an important part of the work of teachers of agriculture and home economics. Two years later, Superintendent Harris asked that parish school boards attack the problem of illiteracy among adults by employing special teachers. A 1920 census showed that Louisiana had the largest percentage of adult illiterates of any state in the nation.

In 1929, the Legislature passed the "malt tax" law and dedicated the receipts for use in eliminating adult illiteracy. A course of lessons, textbooks, and a plan of procedure were recommended by Superintendent Harris and adopted by the state board.

The National Advisory Committee, created by President Hoover, later adopted and revised the Louisiana manual for adult illiteracy for use in other states.

The Depression limited financial support for adult education. The program continued as long as the Federal Education Relief Administration and the Works Progress Administration activities operated in the state. The results of the program cannot be estimated, but it is safe to say that Louisiana kept in step with the progress that was going on in the rest of the United States.

In 1950, the Louisiana Legislature passed Act 252, which appropriated $25,000 to initiate a program for adults at the elementary and secondary school levels. The adult education programs are conducted by the local school systems in addition to regular school year and summer programs.

The adult education program met with immediate success and proved highly popular with persons inside and outside education. Appropriations increased steadily. From 1960 to 1965, the Legislature appropriated almost $250,000 for reimbursement of teachers' salaries for conducting adult academic education classes in the state's 67 school systems.

Adult students attending the classes have the opportunity of advancing themselves from grade 1 through grade 11. If certain qualifications are met, adults may be issued a certificate indicative of the grade level which they have completed. Qualified adults may be given the General Educational Development Test, and if they have completed minimum class requirements and score 13.0 on the test, they are issued a certificate of equivalency.

The Economic Opportunity Act of 1964 provides for adult basic education and makes substantially increased funds available for adult education in Louisiana.

In 1964, State Superintendent William J. Dodd launched the Adult Literacy Testing Program. Over 30,000 adults successfully passed sixth-grade equivalency tests, indicating that Louisiana should occupy a more favorable position with respect to its literacy status.

EDUCATIONAL SERVICES

Teacher Certification

Prior to 1877, certification of teachers was the responsibility of parish police juries, and (during Reconstruction) the parish superintendent. From that date until 1912, the parish school boards assumed the responsibility.

During the period 1877-1907, there were three institutions offering programs in teacher education: Louisiana State Normal College, the New Orleans Normal, and the Department of Education and Philosophy at Louisiana State University. Graduates from these were exempt from the parish board examinations. The parish superintendent gave the examination, graded the papers, and awarded first-, second-, or third-grade certificates. If a teacher was needed in the schools of the parish and had a modest education and the recommendation of local trustees in the community, he usually received a certificate (31).

The state certificates issued in keeping with Act 55 of 1906 were based on a written test given by the State Board of Examiners. In 1910, a committee of five teachers appointed by the state superintendent of education administered and graded teacher examination papers prepared by the state superintendent.

The requirements for third-grade certification stipulated that the applicant must average 75 percent or more and not fall below 40 percent in any area of the test; some of the subjects were spelling, reading, penmanship, arithmetic, and English grammar. Requirements for a second-grade certificate were that the applicant must average 80 percent and not fall below 50 percent on any subject; some of the subject areas were grammatical analysis, physical and political geography, elementary algebra, and agriculture. Requirements for a first-grade certificate required that the applicant average 85 percent and not fall below 50 percent on any subject. Some of the subject areas were advanced algebra, physics, geometry, penmanship and drawing, theory and art of teaching, and English grammar and composition.

Complete state control of teacher certification came with Act 214 of 1912 when the State Board of Education assumed control of certification through an examining committee appointed by the board (32).

A certification division was organized in the department in 1913. Examinations were abolished, and certificates were issued upon the basis of college courses completed. Life certificates were issued to teachers who had earned a college degree, and three lesser grade certificates to those who completed 1, 2, and 3 years of college work. The procedure was altered by 1940, and a degree was required for all classes of certificates.

In 1924, the state board passed regulations which based all future certification of high school teachers on the completion of the baccalaureate degree. After 1925, the preparation of teachers became more specialized due to (a) the expanding program of studies in the high schools; (b) the state approval of elementary schools, which began in 1928; (c) the statewide program of curriculum revision between 1936 and 1940; and (d) state certification regulations, particularly those for high school teachers and administrative and supervisory personnel (33).

Certification of Teachers Today. To be eligible for professional service in the public schools of Louisiana, a teacher must hold a valid teacher's certificate issued by the Louisiana State Department of Education in keeping with standards determined by the Louisiana State Board of Education.

Minimum General, Professional, and Specialized Education for Teacher Education Curriculums. Certificates of types A, B, and C are based on completion of an approved curriculum of 4 years of general, professional, and specialized education. A minimum of 46 semester hours of general education—including 12 in English, 12 in social studies, 12 in science, 6 in mathematics, and 4 in health and physical education—is required. In addition, a minimum of 18 semester hours of professional education is required for high school teachers, and a minimum of 24 semester hours of professional education is required for elementary school teachers. Finally, prospective elementary and high school teachers must complete specific requirements in a specified subject matter area or field in order to be eligible to teach.

From 1948 until 1964, teacher certification was administered through the higher education division. At present, the program for teacher certification is administered by the assistant superintendent of the curriculum and instruction division through a director of teacher education, accreditation, certification, and placement.

Revisions and adoptions of certification requirements were made in 1931, 1936, 1943, and 1952. The 1931 revision gave increased attention to specialization. The 1936 revision set up a 3-year course as a minimum for elementary teachers, and in 1940 the baccalaureate degree became a minimum requirement for elementary teachers. In general, the revisions and adoptions of certification requirements were in keeping with what was happening in the other states and particularly in the Southern states.

The standards adopted in 1943 and put into effect in 1947 were greatly improved. One of the strong features of the standards adopted in 1952 was the requirement that all teachers must graduate in an approved program of general, professional, and specialized education before being certified to teach. No longer could a prospective teacher add a few minimum courses required by the state and be licensed to teach.

Another milestone was reached with adoption, by the state board in October 1956, of Bulletin No. 996, *Louisiana Standards for Accrediting Teacher-Education Institutions.* This is for all institutions preparing teachers. Prior to this time, any institution—regardless of the quality of its staff, library, and other facilities—could prepare teachers if its curriculums were approved by the State Department of Education. These standards were accepted with wholehearted support by all teacher education institutions.

One other development which holds great promise for the teaching profession is the Louisiana unit of the Commission for Teacher Education and Professional Standards. This step was authorized by the Louisiana Teachers Association in November 1956, and its organization was effected in 1957.

School Finances

The Constitution of 1868 set up a State Board of Education through which all state school funds were distributed. For the most part the General Assembly, as directed by the Constitution of 1898, provided that state school funds be apportioned to the parishes on a per educable basis, and specified certain sources of revenue for the state school fund. The sources were designed as a statewide levy of not less than 1.25 mills on the assessed value of property, poll tax, and a provision for local school districts to tax themselves beyond the former limitation of 10 mills on the dollar. An educable was defined as within the age of 6 to 18. Each school system received a variable amount per each educable, depending on the amount of state funds available for schools. The state superintendent of education, in 1935, provided a school census of the number of educables, and from this date forward the department figures of educables have been used in the distribution of state school funds.

Financial and statistical reports from the parish school systems sent to the state superintendent of education were based on a calendar year until 1910, when the Legislature required that parish superintendents prepare reports ending June 30. Gathering information on a calendar year required that the statistics from two fiscal sessions be mixed to make up this report. Reporting on a fiscal year avoided this confusion, and it was felt that the information was much more accurate (34). In 1912, Act 214 placed all public school statistics on a session basis and required that parish school boards adopt, at the beginning of the session, a carefully prepared budget of receipts and expenditures. This act also required that state funds be distributed to the parish as a unit rather than to each school district as in the past. This same act designated the parish superintendent of the public schools as the treasurer of all school funds appropriated by the state to such parish, or raised, collected, or donated therein for the support of free public schools. The parish superintendent, as treasurer, was to draw warrants, and the warrants were to show the school districts they were drawn against (35).

Finance Division, State Department of Education. During 1925, a service and information division was added to the state department. The ensuing years witnessed studies on the inequalities in educational opportunities in Louisiana because of the inability of some parishes to support reasonably good schools. The State Teachers Association, through its research committee and in keeping with its record of service, conducted during 1925-26 an equalization study of the distribution of state school funds among the parishes. It recommended more money and a better plan for distributing funds. John M. Foote, of the department, conducted a study in 1929, and the department published a bulletin setting forth a plan for administering an equalization fund which became the basis of the equalization program that was later established.

In 1928, when the Legislature enacted the malt tax law, it approved the principle of equalization of school facilities. The law stipulated that revenues were to be used by the state board to help weaker parishes provide adequate educational opportunities. However, this tax did not yield sufficient funds to implement equalization, and the first actual distribution of equalization funds was not made until the 1930-31 fiscal year, when the sum of $360,712 was sent to 35 parishes.

By 1920 most parishes had voted taxes for new buildings, longer school terms, and better teachers' salaries. The existence of small taxing districts, however, resulted in unequal school facilities. It was gradually realized that larger taxing units should be used in raising school funds, first on a parish-wide basis, and then at the state level in order to aid the weaker school districts. In 1928, State Superintendent Harris, recognizing that the system then in effect failed to equalize educational opportunity, pointed out that education was a responsibility of the state and that the state should ensure some satisfactory standard or minimum of education for all local units. He also advocated taxing existing economic resources and expending the revenues to meet the needs.

Prior to 1930, the entire public school fund was distributed to parishes on the basis of the number of educable children from 6 to 18 years of age, inclusive. This is still considered the basic source from which parish and city school boards receive state school funds. In 1930, however, an amendment was written into the constitution which provided that one-sixth of the public school fund be apportioned and distributed to the parish and city school boards on the basis of equalization, and five-sixths on the basis of the number of educables. Sources of state funds for equalization in 1930-31 were from the malt tax and any of its derivatives and combinations. Despite the availability of additional state funds during the early thirties, overall support for schools declined due to depressed economic conditions. The major support for public schools came from the property tax; however, property assessments were declining, and land was being adjudicated to the state for nonpayment of taxes. All this had a serious effect on the finances of public education, causing many school systems to operate for shortened terms of 4 to 8 months. In many parishes, special maintenance taxes had expired, and the voters refused to renew the taxes because they were unable to pay them. In an effort to find solutions to the problems of school finances and tax revenues, the Legislature appointed a tax reform commission in 1932. With the assistance of the state department, this commission made extensive studies, and its recommendations to the 1934 Legislature resulted in important changes in state school financing (36).

The constitution was amended in 1934 to provide that three-fourths of the funds be distributed to the parish and city school boards on the basis of the number of educable children and that one-fourth be apportioned and distributed to the parish school boards on the basis of equalization. Thus, it attempted to enable the state board to ensure a minimum educational program in the common public schools for all parishes. It further provided that the state board would administer and regulate this apportionment and distribute this fund to the parish school boards, as well as provide the plans, rules, and regulations for this distribution.

As more and more state and federal funds were added to the support of public education, the state department hired additional personnel to administer these funds for the state board. In 1925, an educational services and information division was added to the department; its one professional staff member had responsibilities in the areas of surveys, reports, budgets, etc. One additional staff member was added in 1929-30. Reorganization of the department in 1940 established an administration and finance division with two professional staff members and three other employees with titles of clerk and auditor specifically assigned to finance.

Reorganization of State Department of Education. The administration and finance division, which was set up by the reorganization of the state department in 1940, was later changed to include administration only, and then went back to its original form. The sole responsibility of one section in this division having to do with finances is to administer school finances for the state superintendent and the state board.

Immediately following the close of World War II, in 1944-45, the public schools of Louisiana added the twelfth grade. The great knowledge explosion and the interest shown in science and mathematics prompted many states to add an extra year to their programs. This entailed an increase in school funds, but the people of the state were inclined to go along with the increased taxes and the transfer of funds to the public school fund.

Division of Administration and Finance Today. Disbursement of school funds from state and federal sources was handled for the state board by the state department's administration and finance division. The division's finance section has capable, experienced personnel with long years of service on the local and state levels.

This section receives certain statistical and most financial reports from the parish and city systems for processing, recording, and future publication, and all requests for payments on special programs are received here. State funds are distributed to the local school systems today on the basis of per educable and equalization. The Louisiana Constitution provides that an amount totaling not less than $10 million per annum be maintained in the public school fund for these two distributions. The cost part of the equalization formula includes five factors: (1)

teachers allotted and employed with salaries, (2) supervisors of instruction allotted and employed with salaries, (3) visiting teachers allotted and employed with salaries, (4) transportation, and (5) other costs. The support part of the equalization formula includes five factors: (1) per educable distribution, (2) 5-mill constitutional tax, (3) severance tax, (4) 50 percent of rent or lease of school lands, and (5) court fines and forfeitures.

State revenues are derived primarily from the 2.5-mill ad valorem tax, which is the property tax, the severance tax, and the state sales tax. Local revenues are derived from the 5-mill parish-wide maintenance tax, 5-mill construction tax, 7-mill maintenance tax for current operation, and 7-mill special leeway tax for maintenance (37).

The division administering finances today performs many services for the parish and city systems. Under the leadership of Superintendent William J. Dodd, this service goes far beyond that performed in previous years, and yet it is the desire of the state department to further expand these services. With the advent of data processing this should advance by great strides.

Curriculum Development

Teacher institute work was turned over to the State Department of Education shortly after the turn of the century. In 1904, State Superintendent J. B. Aswell appointed J. E. Keeny as state institute conductor, the first professional staff member of the state department. In this capacity, Keeny promoted higher qualifications for the classroom teachers and organized institutes at various places throughout the state. Teachers attending these institutes heard lectures, witnessed demonstrations, participated in discussions, and became acquainted with new books and materials.

Many state department divisions and sections were established over the years: high school, elementary, agriculture, home economics, teacher certification, Negro schools, vocational trades and industries, reference and service, library, music, health and physical education, distributive occupations, safety, business education, and higher education.

Since 1940, other sections have been established to meet new needs: Civil Defense, finance, administration and research, school lunch, data processing, school transportation, school attendance, audiovisual aids, veterans education, adult education, federally financially assisted programs, materials of instruction, guidance, industrial arts, manpower development and training, and trade and industrial education (38).

The supervisory staff, appointed in various subject area fields, includes personnel in Baton Rouge, New Orleans, Monroe, and Shreveport. In addition to state supervisors, local school boards employ supervisors to help the local superintendents in improving classroom instruction.

The Legislature established the State Board of Education and gave it control and supervision of all public education. The board has under its direct control and supervision 10 institutions of higher learning, 31 trade and vocational-technical schools, and 5 special schools. The state department performs services to a limited extent for the state board in these areas, such as providing supervisory personnel to work with these institutions in carrying out board policies and regulations.

Educational Surveys and Studies

Six studies of the Louisiana educational system were made after 1940: the Reorganization Study of 1940, commonly known as the Griffenhagen Study; the Louisiana Educational Survey, popularly called the Washburne Survey; the Legislative Committee on Education Survey; the Peabody Survey; the Special Committee on Education Survey; and the Committee of One Hundred.

Surveys generally are performed to help determine the needs and necessities for improvements in one or more areas or institutions of education. Louisiana undertook these studies because its citizens realize that education is an ongoing, dynamic, and changing endeavor, and that to remain static would mean disaster. Louisiana educators have generally provided the leadership for attempting to solve the state's education problems, but persons from outside the state have participated in most of the studies and surveys. The persons participating have shown vision, intelligence, and determination to have a broader, more realistic educational program. Most of the recommendations from the surveys have been implemented.

The Reorganization Study of 1940. An act of the Legislature authorized a survey in 1940, commonly known as the Griffenhagen Study, because the new Governor Sam Jones and the Legislature felt there was a need for general reorganization on a statewide basis. It directed the Governor, with the aid of an advisory committee, to undertake a comprehensive and constructive program of review, reorganization, and improvement in every department, agency, and political subdivision of the state. The study was conducted by a team of professional consultants from Chicago in cooperation with state and local education leaders.

The Louisiana Education Survey. The Louisiana Education Survey was popularly called the Washburne Survey. Authorized by Act 36 of the Louisiana Legislature in 1940, this survey of elementary and secondary education was made by a commission headed by John M. Fletcher of Tulane University as chairman and general director. Carleton Washburne, superintendent of schools in Winnetka, Illinois, was director of the committees that studied the elementary and secondary schools.

Dr. Washburne stated that his function as director was to organize the people of Louisiana to do their own thinking and make their own recommendations. To effect this, he gathered a large staff of highly competent persons—mostly from Louisiana and the rest of the South, but also from the nation at large—who carried out a remarkable group of studies. The recommendations, except for a very few of a technical nature, are those of the committees of Louisiana people.

Washburne organized numerous study groups throughout the state, and his extensive report, submitted in a series of volumes, had a stimulating effect on the schools, improving their organization and teaching methods. The report cited many areas of concern for the schools of Louisiana. It specified that the state should progressively adjust toward a uniform salary schedule and that parishes should assume some responsibility for developing special services for exceptional children. The report also recommended counseling service for high school students, training programs for adolescents in child care, parish ownership and operation of school buses, community use of school plant, an end to public competitions (e.g., to select the brightest academic students, best speakers) known as "rallies," parent education, more practical shop and mechanical work, vocational guidance and vocational training, a state program for exceptional children, a 12-year school program, federal aid to educators, revision of method for distribution of state funds to parishes, and consideration of the desirability of permitting graduate work for the master's degree in teacher education at state colleges.

The Legislative Committee on Education Survey. Six years after the Washburne Study, the Louisiana Legislature set up the Legislative Committee on Education Survey. This survey was authorized in 1946, and its report was submitted by Committee Chairman C. H. Downs, Rapides Parish, in May 1948. The Committee was—

> To make a survey of needs and necessary improvements of the following institutions:
>
> The kindergarten, primary and secondary public schools under the supervision of the parish school boards, the colleges and schools under the supervision of the Louisiana State Board of Education; and the Louisiana State University and Agricultural and Mechanical College and colleges under the supervision of its Board of Supervisors, and to report their findings and recommendations to the Governor and members of the Legislature.

In accordance with the spirit of the act creating it, the Legislative Committee on Education Survey made a study of Louisiana education, but it was not the committee's plan to conduct a "professional" study. It attempted to obtain essential information which would make it possible to make practical recommendations to the Legislature for improving the schools.

Every effort was made to enlist the educational talent of the state to assist with the study. School people at all levels cooperated wholeheartedly, and many individuals gave generously of their time and energy when called upon by the Committee.

The Committee included Representative C. H. Downs, chairman; Senator H. H. Richardson, vice-chairman; Representative Bonnie V. Baker; Representative W. J. Dodd; Senator A. A. Fredericks; Representative W. I. Hair; Senator Gilbert F. Hennigan; Representative Ragan Madden; J. W. Brouillette, coordinator; and Ruth Holland, secretary.

The recommendations of the committee were in two categories—those requiring legislative action and those not requiring legislative action—and suggested steps to be taken by the Legislature, educators, and citizens generally to strengthen education. The committee urged that an independent agency be set up to make a continuous organized study of all levels and types of education in Louisiana.

The report played an important role in setting the stage for school legislation which was passed in 1948 and in subsequent sessions of the Legislature.

The Peabody Survey. The 1952 Louisiana Legislature established a Legislative Council as its fact-finding agency. On the recommendation of its Education Committee, the council engaged the Division of Surveys and Field Services, George Peabody College for Teachers, to conduct a comprehensive study of public education in the elementary, secondary, and special schools of Louisiana. The study was designed to determine the conditions existing in the public schools, to consider the problems identified, and to develop suggestions and recommendations for their solution.

W. D. McClurkin, head of the college's Division of Surveys and Field Services, was chosen as director of the Peabody Survey. E. L. Lindman, professor of school administration at George Peabody College for Teachers, served as the general consultant. An Education Advisory Committee, appointed by the Legislative Council, gave McClurkin and his staff assistance in planning the outline of the study, pointing out unique problems, and suggesting procedures to be followed. The committee represented the major organizations most actively related to the public school enterprise—education committees of the Louisiana House and Senate, State Department of Education, Louisiana Education Association, Louisiana Parent-Teacher Association, Louisiana School Boards Association, and Louisiana State University Extension Division.

The final report constituted a thorough, overall analysis of the problems of public education in Louisiana, with a practical, workable guide to the planning of a long-range program.

The Special Committee on Education Survey. Because of the rise in cost of public education and the many new and expanded programs, it became apparent in 1959 that a source of additional revenue would be needed to meet needs. Educational leaders felt that a statewide committee should seek ways to ensure programs of excellence in all schools of Louisiana. These educators were aware that all schools were not on a par with each other and that many young persons were not completing their education.

The Governor appointed a survey committee in February 1959, consisting of representatives from the Legislature, business, labor, lay groups, and professional educators. The committee was charged with recommending ways and means to provide more adequately for the financial needs of the state's elementary and secondary schools.

The Committee of One Hundred. On the basis of a legislative concurrent resolution, State Superintendent William J. Dodd appointed a Committee of One Hundred in 1965 to conduct a comprehensive study of the educational programs of Louisiana at the elementary and secondary levels. In addition to educators, members of the committee included persons from labor, business, law, medicine, government, agriculture, and other fields. William F. Beyer, Jr., the state department's assistant superintendent of curriculum and instruction, served as general chairman.

After evaluation of existing programs, the committee made 19 recommendations based on identified objectives of Louisiana education. For instance, it recommended that the school curriculum place special emphasis on the academic disciplines to give each person the best possible liberal education consistent with his ability, aptitudes, and interests. It recommended that the state department use the reports from the committee in the several academic disciplines as a basis for improving these areas.

The committee further recommended extending the length of the school day and the length of the school session, and that the schools include kindergartens. It suggested that consideration be given to the advisability of adding grades 13 and 14, particularly in highly populated areas.

At the same time the committee recognized the need to improve certification standards for teachers by strengthening subject matter preparation, the understanding of children, and teaching skills. It recommended expansion and improvement of programs in guidance and testing for children at all levels of instruction; library services for every school, meeting the standards of the Southern Association of Colleges and Schools; and more extensive use of the new instructional media, including development of a statewide educational TV system under the direction of the state department. The committee felt that high schools should be encouraged to move in the direction of multitrack curricular offerings, including adequate programs in the academic disciplines, comprehensive offerings in the various vocational areas, and adequate guidance services.

The committee commended those responsible for inauguration of the recent "crash" program in adult education and literacy testing and recommended it be continued and further developed. It recognized that there are many children and youth in the state needing special education services and recommended that adequate funds be provided to meet the needs of all exceptional children. It stated that interscholastic competitive sports should be eliminated at the elementary level, be discouraged at the junior high school level, and that more emphasis should be placed on health and physical education at the high school level than upon varsity competition. And the committee recommended that the state accept and use to the best advantage all federal funds available for public education.

Because the state felt that adopting these recommendations was important if Louisiana was to gain the maximum from its educational resources and remain abreast of contemporary demands, Superintendent Dodd appointed a Curriculum Advisory Council composed of 25 educators to review the steps necessary to implement the 19 recommendations of the Committee of One Hundred. Several meetings have been held and progress reports made on many of the committee's recommendations.

SCHOOL SERVICES

The State Department of Education has been service motivated since the turn of the century when it became a vital force in Louisiana's educational picture. Of the many services offered by the department to the school systems and citizens, three will be elaborated upon: materials of instruction, school lunch program, and transportation.

Materials of Instruction

In 1928, the Legislature, at the insistence of Governor Huey P. Long, approved a bill providing free textbooks to schoolchildren. Act No. 100 provided that the severance tax fund, a tax on produce or resources severed or separated from soil or water, be distributed for the purchase of school books and that the remaining balance be placed in the state public school fund. During the 1928-29 school year, a total of 2,329,027 books were distributed at a cost of $1,115,297, or an average cost of $2.34 per pupil.

The textbook law was written into the constitution in 1936. As a result, the textbook program was extended and a state printing board established. The same year, a group of citizens from Caddo Parish in northwest Louisiana instituted a suit contesting the free textbook program and maintaining that the textbook law was unconstitutional. The State Supreme Court, in 1936, ruled the law constitutional and further ruled that school books could be furnished free to the schoolchildren of the state attending public, private, and parochial schools, based on what has become known as the "child-benefit" theory. This theory advocates that the purchase of textbooks is made for the benefit of the schoolchildren and the subsequent benefit of the state; the schoolchildren and the state are the sole beneficiaries. The local school board bringing the suit soon recognized the benefits of the program and joined in the distribution of the materials (39).

Act No. 153, of 1936, provided that a part of the revenues from the severance tax be used for the purchase of library books. Funds were used, beginning with the second semester of 1935-36, to buy school supplies such as paper, pencils, and ink. Since their beginning, these funds have continued to be available for materials of instruction. The sum of $6,862,580 was appropriated for textbooks for the 1964-65 school year, and $1,135,000 was appropriated for library books. School libraries have been under the supervision of a professional librarian since 1929, when the General Education Board granted funds to Louisiana to establish this supervisory position, one of four in the United States at that time. During 1964-65, 1,411 libraries were operating in the public and private schools of Louisiana.

School Food Services

During the Depression years of the 1930's, many families were not financially able to provide their children with sufficient school lunches. The PTA often helped in this matter by furnishing sandwiches and milk; the Emergency Relief Administration also provided food, and the Works Progress Administration canning projects aided in supplementing lunches. These various projects developed a sentiment favoring hot lunches for all children. The U.S. Bureau of Indian Affairs, the State Department of Education, and the St. Mary Parish School Board opened the first publicly supported lunch program in Louisiana at the Charenton Indian School in St. Mary Parish in 1932-33 on a cooperative basis.

The first state appropriation for the school lunch program was $250,000 during the 1939-40 school year. After federal legislation for school lunch programs was inaugurated in 1946, there were 165,598 children in Louisiana eating lunch at school daily. This legislation helped to expand lunch programs by enabling local school systems to provide lunchrooms and lunchroom workers in most of the schools, and by making possible a well-coordinated program of food preservation centers for receiving and storing surplus commodities from the federal government. By 1958, 75 percent of the state's schoolchildren were participating in the school lunch program. The program has been expanded through the provision by local school systems of lunchrooms and lunchroom workers in most schools and through food preservation centers for receiving and storing surplus commodities from the federal government. During 1964-65, the Legislature appropriated $11,089,321 for Louisiana's school lunch program.

Transportation

Transportation for Louisiana's schoolchildren had its origin in a 1902 cyclone that destroyed a school in Lafayette Parish. Because of the necessary delay in erecting a new building, members of the parish school board furnished, at their own expense, a wagonette to transfer children to a school 6 miles away. The project was so successful that the board decided not to rebuild the demolished school, but to continue operating the wagonette at public expense. Comparable disasters such as hurricanes, tornadoes, floods, and fires in other sections of the state brought about consolidation of schools and transportation of children. In 1932, the state began to subsidize the transportation of elementary and secondary pupils.

The system of transporting children in sparsely settled districts to consolidated schools rather than multiplying the number of one-teacher schools was generally appreciated by the people. Consolidated schools were found to be far superior to the small, isolated schools, but the transportation of schoolchildren over bad roads to these schools was unsatisfactory. Superintendents of local school systems found that vehicles operating on good roads for distances greater than 4.5 miles did not work well, and they reported that the transportation system would break down unless a responsible man was placed in charge (40). The state superintendent, in his biennial report for 1911-12, stated that many of the parishes had adopted a system of transportation which eliminated the school wagon: Parents would provide transportation for their children, and the school board would reimburse them monthly, based on the average attendance of the child in school (41).

The building of farmers' roads in the period from 1920-50 made it easy to consolidate the country schools and to transport the children to the centers of consolidation (42). The advent of paved highways, improved bus bodies, and steel chassis all have helped to increase the progress of school transportation. In 1920, some 20,000 children were transported; in 1930, 95,000; and in 1940, 159,500. By 1966, there were 479,149 pupils being transported in 5,530 vehicles.

FEDERAL PROGRAMS

The beginning of federal participation and aid to education cannot all be found in one document, nor can it be cited as one dramatic event. The expanding federal influence has developed in different ways, and more frequently by indirect control rather than by the direct assumption of school administration and control.

During 1917, the same year Congress passed the Smith-Hughes Act supporting vocational education, the Louisiana State Department of Education entered into an agreement with the College of Agriculture, Louisiana State University, to conduct the training program for teachers of vocational agriculture and home economics. Part of the salaries was to be paid by the state department with federal vocational funds. In 1918, a vocational trades and industries division was established in the state department to administer some of the vocational programs. The department already had a division established in 1909 to handle agriculture programs. Local schools were able to establish classes in agriculture and home economics and to receive financial support through these programs.

After the close of World War I, Congress passed legislation for rehabilitation of war veterans. In 1920, the Smith-Bankhead Act gave additional grants to states for vocational rehabilitation programs. The Vocational Rehabilitation Act of 1943 provided assistance to disabled veterans. In January 1921, the State Board of Education accepted the Louisiana plan for administering the Vocational Rehabilitation Act of 1920. In the annual report for 1922-23, the state superintendent reported that federal funds were used to pay a part of the cost of artificial limbs and to give instruction to physically handicapped persons who desired to prepare themselves for earning a livelihood. The annual report for 1923-24 reported that 64 persons had been helped with the purchase of artificial limbs and that 52 had received instruction. In 1925, a person was employed with the dual responsibilities of industrial education and rehabilitation. Prior to this, the responsibility was in the hands of the trades and industries section. During this year, 145 cases were handled, with an expenditure of $12,691. Two years later, a section was added to the trades and industrial education division to administer this program. These federal programs were first administered from previously established divisions until 1943, when the programs were consolidated into a separate section in the instruction and supervision division.

During 1964-65, the state staff was composed of 14 professional people. The state was divided into four districts, each district having a supervisor and a number of counselors, instructors, and medical consultants. Most of the medical consultants are on a part-time basis, and the other employees are full-time. The whole section has several hundred employees. The total expenditure for this year was $3,422,802, including regular vocational rehabilitation with state and federal support. The section completed services for well over 2,000 individuals.

During 1919, Congress passed a law authorizing the use of federal surplus property by educational institutions. Again, in 1944, the Surplus Property Act authorized the transfer of surplus property to educational institutions. The Federal Property and Administrative Services Act of 1949 provided for the donation of surplus property to educational institutions and for other public uses. A specific section to handle this program was established after 1944. In 1948, a supervisor in the schoolhousing section was added to handle surplus property. Later, a separate section was established in the department's administration division. Surplus property secured from the armed services and allocated to the schools had grown to the point in 1948 that property exceeding $2 million in value was distributed. Almost every parish participated, and various colleges and other schools acquired 250 buildings with fixtures. In the last year of the Surplus Property Utilization Agency in the State Department of Education–1963–the value of the property distributed to schools and institutions exceeded $3 million.

A number of other federal programs have affected the State Department of Education. The WPA programs, beginning in 1936, added a whole section to the department; these programs were phased out after several years of operation. Federal Aid to Impacted Areas, begun in 1941, still operates in 1968, assisting various parishes with grants to hire additional school personnel and to add classes and build new buildings to cope with the influx of children. It is implemented by the schoolhousing and survey section, composed of a director and one supervisor. The first year of operation, 1941-42, saw three parishes participating and receiving $94,718. During 1964-65, seven parishes participated and received $1,350,000. The Serviceman's Readjustment Act of 1944, known as the "GI Bill of Rights," and the Veterans Adult Education Act in 1949 brought about additions to the department. A section with two supervisors was added in the elementary and secondary education division. The new section soon expanded in this division and also into the vocational education division with veterans training and on-the-job training. At the height of these programs, the department had as many as 15 employees on the professional staff. Thousands of veterans took part, and almost every school system had a program. The institutional part of the program was phased out in 1954.

The National Defense Education Act of 1958 provided assistance to state and local school systems in the purchase of equipment and material in the areas of science, mathematics, and modern foreign languages. These subject areas were later expanded to include social studies, English, and reading. Under this act were a number of titles affecting the department. Two full-time supervisors were first added under Titles III and V (the latter provided assistance in vocational guidance and counseling). This number of personnel was later expanded to eight full-time employees. The balance of the responsibility for these two titles and for Title VIII was given to various staff members already in the department. The expenditure of federal funds for the first year was less than $500,000. During 1964-65, the expenditure for several thousand projects amounted to $1.5 million for NDEA Titles III, V, VIII, and X.

Among other federal programs instrumental in expanding the State Department of Education, the Manpower Development and Training Act of 1962 added a director and seven other professional personnel, and projects accounted for $591,000 in 1964-65. The Vocational Education Act of 1963 increased the present vocational offerings for residential vocational schools and work study programs, and the Adult Basic Education Title under the Economic Opportunity Act of 1964 expanded the services of the adult education program on the local school level. Two additional supervisors were added to the Adult Education Section in 1964-65, and a total expenditure of just under $2 million was made.

One of the most important federal programs covered by this chapter was passed by Congress in 1965–the Elementary and Secondary Education Act. This resulted in establishment of a federally assisted programs section in the curriculum and instruction division, with a director and four supervisors and consultants. Thirty-eight of the 67 school systems were eligible to participate, but at the close of 1965 only one or two projects had been approved, and expenditures for administration only from the state level had been made.

Use of federal funds for education by the Louisiana State Board of Education and the State Department of Education has been a practice for many years. The Louisiana Legislature has accepted these funds but has not always been willing to match them with state funds. Because of this, the local school systems have had to match with local funds, thus leaving some of the federal allocations unused each year. A concern of the department has been that several of the local school systems have not participated recently in the various federal programs. Unless these school systems have the local funds, their schools could be hampered by the resulting lack of equipment and material to carry on a school program equal to the rest of the state. Another major concern and problem of the department is the matter of budgets. The state is not notified in advance of the exact amount of funds it can expect, and Congress has the tendency to appropriate these funds late in the fiscal year. This makes it almost impossible to have advanced planning at both the state and local level. It places a hardship on the State Department of Education and local school systems in employing new personnel and purchasing much needed equipment and material.

The State Department of Education today, under the leadership of Superintendent William J. Dodd, assists in the administration, from the state level, of approximately 17 federal programs. Personnel in the three divisions of the department–administration and finance, curriculum and instruction, and vocational education–work directly or in related areas of one or more of these programs. Support for the various phases of education has been timely and, in all cases, needed. Superintendent Dodd and the State Board of Education are strong advocates of obtaining financial support from all sources as long as the control of education remains in the hands of local and state authorities.

FOOTNOTES

1. Department of Education, *Annual Report,* Session 1855-56.
2. Henry E. Chambers, *A History of Louisiana* (Chicago: The American Historical Society, 1925), p. 565.
3. E. B. Roberts, *et al.,* eds., *Public Education in Louisiana, Yesterday, Today, Tomorrow,* Proceedings of the Centennial Symposium (Baton Rouge: Bureau of Educational Materials and Research, College of Education, Louisiana State University, 1960), pp. 8-9.
4. *Ibid.*
5. C. W. Hilton, Donald E. Shipp, and Berton J. Gremillion, *The Development of Public Education in Louisiana* (Baton Rouge: Bureau of Educational Materials and Research, College of Education, Louisiana State University, 1965), pp. 10-11.
6. Edwin A. Davis, *Louisiana: A Narrative History* (Nashville, Tenn.: Benson Printing Co., 1961), p. 276.
7. Hilton, *op. cit.*, p. 11.
8. *Ibid.,* p. 9.
9. *Ibid.*, p. 12.
10. *Ibid.*, p. 13.
11. M. S. Robertson, *Public Education in Louisiana After 1898* (Baton Rouge: Bureau of Educational Materials and Research, College of Education, Louisiana State University, 1952), p. 204.
12. *Ibid.* See also Appendix B.
13. *Ibid.*
14. Hilton, *op. cit.*, pp. 16-17.
15. Robertson, *op. cit.*, p. 204.
16. *Ibid.*, p. 95.
17. Department of Education, *Standards for Approved Elementary Schools,* Bulletin No. 327 (Baton Rouge: The Department, 1936).
18. Robertson, *op. cit.*, p. 55.
19. *Ibid.*
20. *Ibid.*, p. 57.
21. *Ibid.*, p. 58.
22. *Ibid.*, p. 59.
23. *Ibid.*, p. 74.
24. Department of Education, *Biennial Report,* Session 1882-83.
25. Robertson, *op. cit.*, p. 24.

26. Department of Education, *Biennial Report,* Session 1909-11.
27. *Ibid.*
28. *Ibid.*
29. Department of Education, *Louisiana Education in Wartime,* Official Bulletin, Vol. I, No. 7 (Baton Rouge: The Department, December 1942).
30. Department of Education, *Public School Situation (1914-20)* (Baton Rouge: The Department, 1921).
31. Robertson, *op. cit.*, p. 125.
32. Hilton, *op. cit.*, p. 62.
33. *Ibid.*
34. Department of Education, *Biennial Report,* Session 1909-11.
35. Louisiana, *Acts,* Regular Session (1912), Act. No. 214.
36. Hilton, *op. cit.*, pp. 78-79.
37. D. E. Shipp, C. W. Hilton, and J. B. Gremillion, *School Finance in Louisiana* (Baton Rouge: Louisiana Education Research Association, 1966), pp. 59-70.
38. See Appendix B.
39. Robertson, *op. cit.*, pp. 198-99.
40. Department of Education, *Biennial Report,* Session 1909-11.
41. Department of Education, *Biennial Report,* Session 1911-13.
42. Department of Education, *Annual Report,* 1929-30.

BIBLIOGRAPHY

Public Document

Louisiana. *Acts.* Regular Session (1912 and 1932).

Books

Chambers, Henry E. *A History of Louisiana.* Chicago: The American Historical Society, 1925.

Davis, Edwin A. *Louisiana: A Narrative History.* Nashville, Tenn.: Benson Printing Co., 1961.

Department of Education. *Louisiana Education in Wartime.* Official Bulletin, Vol. I, No. 7. Baton Rouge: The Department, December 1942.

—— *Louisiana Standards for State Certification of School Personnel.* Bulletin No. 746. Baton Rouge: The Department, 1964.

—— *Standards for Approved Elementary Schools.* Bulletin No. 327. Baton Rouge: The Department, 1936.

Harris, T. H. *Memoirs of T. H. Harris.* Baton Rouge: Bureau of Educational Materials and Research, Louisiana State University, 1963.

Hilton, C. W.; Shipp, Donald E.; and Gremillion, J. Berton. *The Development of Public Education in Louisiana.* Baton Rouge: Bureau of Educational Materials and Research, Louisiana State University, 1965.

Ives, C. A. *As I Remember.* Baton Rouge: Bureau of Educational Materials and Research, College of Education, Louisiana State University, 1964.

Robertson, M. S. *Public Education in Louisiana After 1898.* Baton Rouge: Bureau of Educational Materials and Research, College of Education, Louisiana State University, 1952.

Shipp, D. E.; Hilton, C. W.; and Gremillion, J. B. *School Finance in Louisiana.* Baton Rouge: Louisiana Education Research Association, 1966.

Reports

Department of Education. *Annual and Biennial Reports.* Baton Rouge: The Department, 1900-65.

—— *A Blueprint for Progress.* Parts 1-3. Baton Rouge: The Department, 1965.

—— *Circular Letters.* 1964-65.

George Peabody College for Teachers, Division of Surveys and Field Services. *Public Education in Louisiana.* A survey report. Nashville: The Division, 1954.

Legislative Committee on Educational Survey. *Education in Louisiana.* Baton Rouge: The Committee, 1948.

Roberts, E. B.; Hilton, C. W.; Shipp, Donald E.; and DeBlieux, May, eds. *Public Education in Louisiana, Yesterday, Today, Tomorrow.* Proceedings of the Centennial Symposium. Baton Rouge: Bureau of Educational Materials and Research, College of Education, Louisiana State University, 1960.

Washburne, Carleton. *Louisiana Looks at Its Schools.* Baton Rouge: Louisiana Educational Survey Commission, Louisiana State University, 1942.

Appendix A

LOUISIANA CHIEF STATE SCHOOL OFFICERS

State Superintendents

1847-51	Alexander Dimitry
1851-53	Robert Carter Nicholas
1853-55	John N. Carrigan
1855-57	Samuel Bard
1857-59	W. T. Hamilton
1859-61	Henry Avery
1862-65	M. H. N. McGruder
1863-65	John McNair*
1865-68	Robert M. Lusher
1868-72	Thomas W. Conway
1872-76	W. G. Brown
1877-79	Robert M. Lusher
1880-84	Edwin H. Fay
1884-88	Warren Easton
1888-90	Joseph A. Breaux
1890-92	W. H. Jack
1892-96	A. D. Lafargue
1896-1904	Joseph V. Calhoun
1904-1908	James B. Aswell
1908-40	Thomas H. Harris
1940-48	John E. Coxe
1948-64	Shelby M. Jackson
1964-	William J. Dodd

*Appointed by the federal government.

Appendix B

Chart I.--LOUISIANA DEPARTMENT OF EDUCATION, 1900-1904

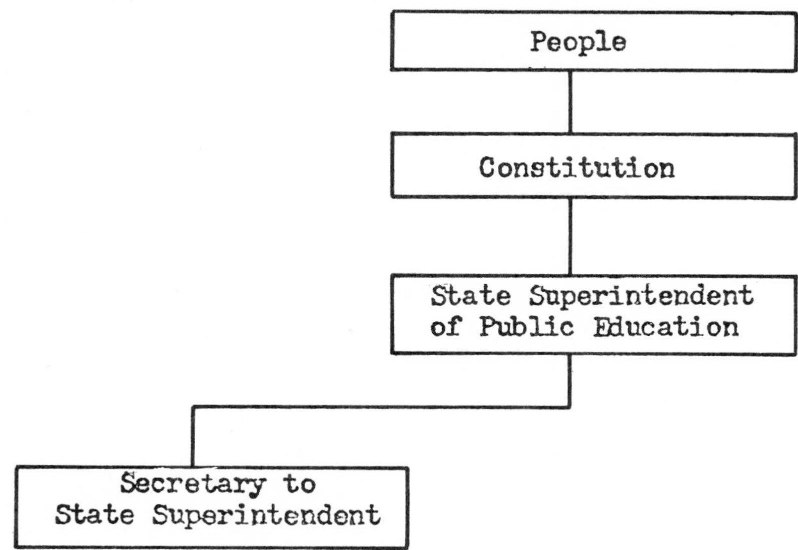

Chart II.--LOUISIANA DEPARTMENT OF EDUCATION, 1904-10

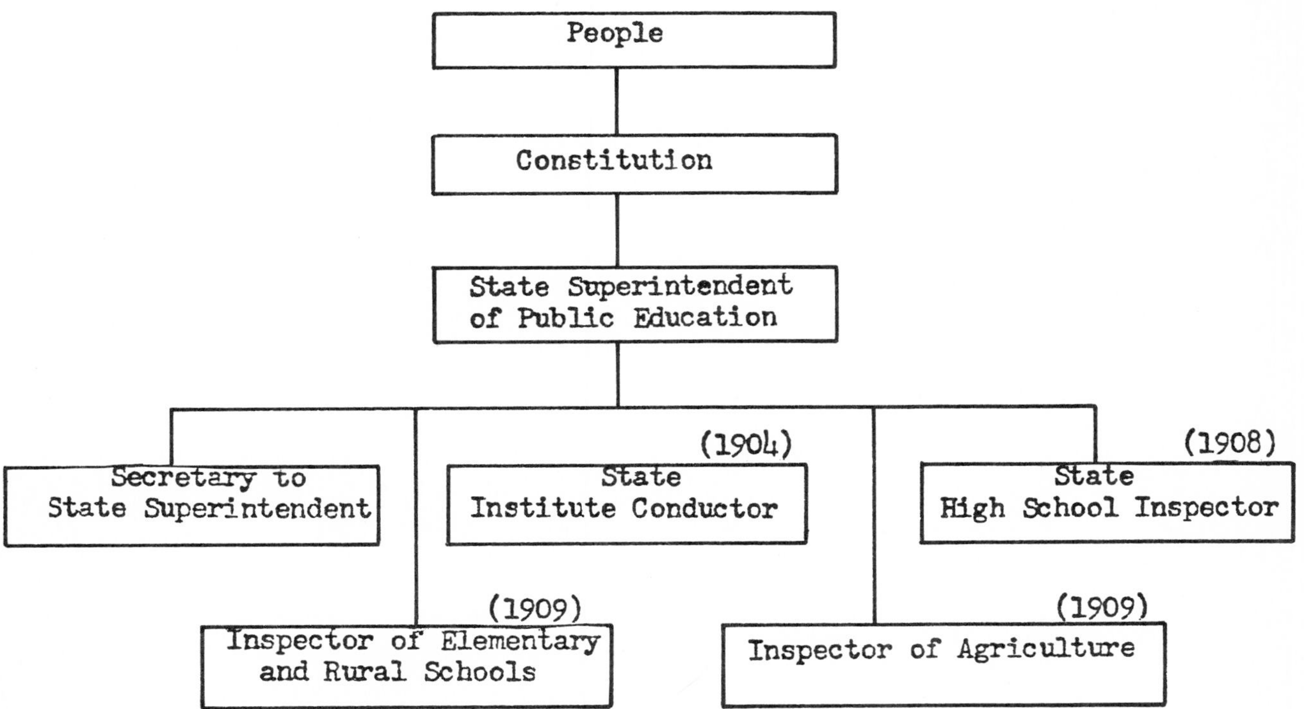

Appendix B

Chart III.--LOUISIANA DEPARTMENT OF EDUCATION, 1968

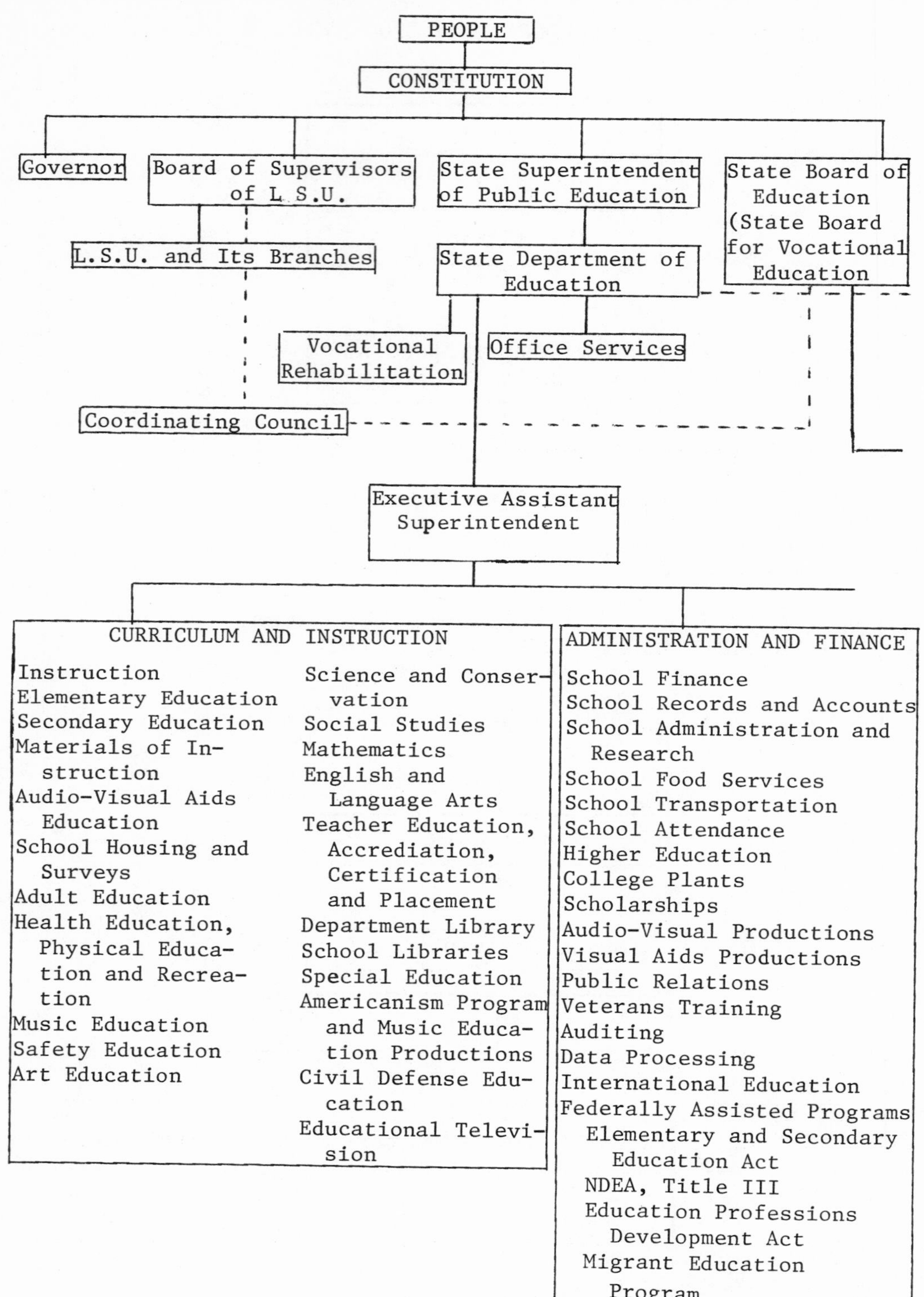

PEOPLE
CONSTITUTION
Governor
Board of Supervisors of L. S.U.
State Superintendent of Public Education
State Board of Education (State Board for Vocational Education
L.S.U. and Its Branches
State Department of Education
Vocational Rehabilitation
Office Services
Coordinating Council
Executive Assistant Superintendent
CURRICULUM AND INSTRUCTION
Instruction
Elementary Education
Secondary Education
Materials of Instruction
Audio-Visual Aids Education
School Housing and Surveys
Adult Education
Health Education, Physical Education and Recreation
Music Education
Safety Education
Art Education
Science and Conservation
Social Studies
Mathematics
English and Language Arts
Teacher Education, Accrediation, Certification and Placement
Department Library
School Libraries
Special Education
Americanism Program and Music Education Productions
Civil Defense Education
Educational Television
ADMINISTRATION AND FINANCE
School Finance
School Records and Accounts
School Administration and Research
School Food Services
School Transportation
School Attendance
Higher Education
College Plants
Scholarships
Audio-Visual Productions
Visual Aids Productions
Public Relations
Veterans Training
Auditing
Data Processing
International Education
Federally Assisted Programs
Elementary and Secondary Education Act
NDEA, Title III
Education Professions Development Act
Migrant Education Program

Appendix B

Chart III.--LOUISIANA DEPARTMENT OF EDUCATION, 1968 (Continued)

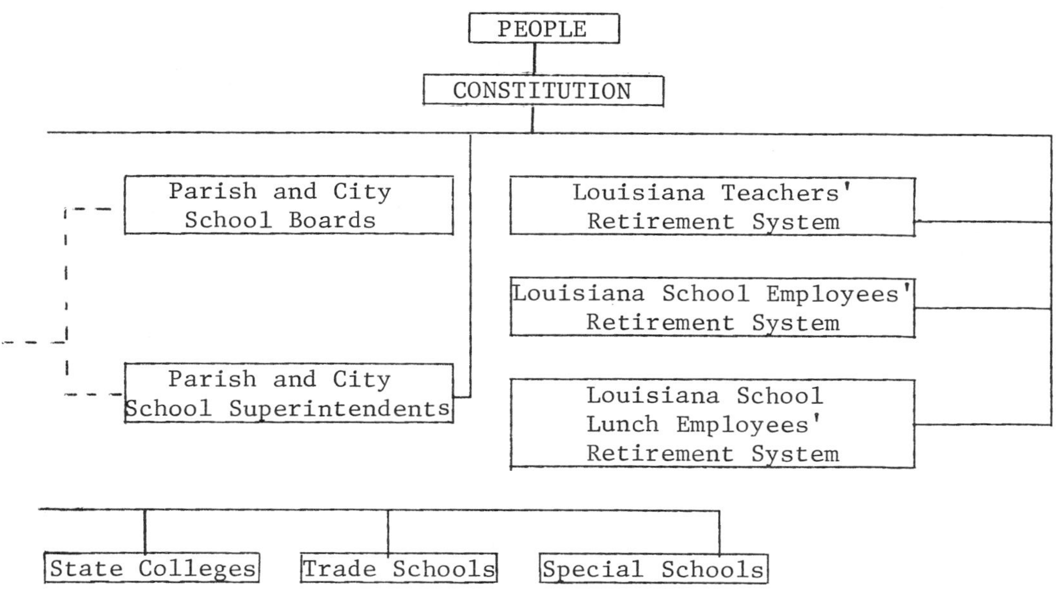

VOCATIONAL EDUCATION

Food Preservation
Youth Camp
Guidance
Trade and Industrial Education
Industrial Arts
Distributive Education
Business Education
Vocational Agriculture
Manpower Training Program
Home Economics
Research Coordinating Unit
Materials Center

19 Maine

DEPARTMENT OF EDUCATION
Kermit S. Nickerson

Contents

EDUCATION IN MAINE PRIOR TO 1900

During the early years of exploration and settlement in the "Province of Main" there was little interest in the establishment of schools. Survival itself was paramount, for the area was settled slowly, and the threat of Indian attacks was ever present. Because children could not go out of sight of their homes with any degree of safety, regularly maintained schools did not appear until about 1700.

Although education was slow in developing, we find in the eighteenth and nineteenth centuries the elements of the system that was to come to fruition in later years. Nearly every aspect of current-day education emerged out of the strivings for an improved program prior to 1900.

The Massachusetts Bay Colony in 1652 claimed the Province of Main under its charter, which stated that the colony had title to all lands "within the space of three English miles to the northward of the River Merrimack and to the northward of any and every part thereof" (1).

The purchase of the Province of Main by Massachusetts in 1677 removed all doubt about the claim and brought it under the Massachusetts Bay Colony laws of 1642 and 1647, which contained the first legal requirements regarding schools. In 1642, the General Court of the Colony and Province of Massachusetts Bay had ordered—

> That the selectmen in every town, shall have a vigilant eye over their bretheren and neighbors, to see, first, that none of them shall suffer so much barbarism in any of their families, as not to endeavor to teach, by themselves or others, their children and apprentices, so much learning as may enable them, perfectly, to read the English tongue and knowledge of the capital laws, upon penalty of twenty shillings for each neglect therein (2).

Thus, in this ancient law we see the first step taken toward compulsory attendance and recognition that neglect of duty was a punishable offense. The legislators of those days seemed to recognize the danger of youth's growing up in ignorance and took positive action to avoid it.

Another enactment followed in 1647 by which public schools as such were first established. This law ordered every township of 50 householders to appoint a person—

> To teach all such children as shall resort to him to write and read, whose wages shall be paid either by the parents or masters of such children or by the inhabitants in general: provided that those who send their children be not oppressed by paying much more than they can have them taught for in other towns (3).

It also directed that when any town increased to 100 families, a grammar school should be set up to instruct youth for the university.

This law is remarkable because it provided the basis for the establishment of schools of a higher grade than the so-called common school. The early grammar schools, however, were not the same as those of today, but were more like high schools and academies. The law actually compelled the establishment of what would now be called a high school in every town of 100 families.

In spite of these basically sound laws, little attention was given to their observance until sometime after the controversies over the Maine territory were settled by the 1677 purchase.

Education was not allowed to be a dead letter, however, for as early as 1671 the penalty for "failure to keep a school" was increased from £5 to £10. Apparently some towns neglected the law, for in 1673 the towns of Kittery and York were presented for not providing a school and schoolmaster as required. In reality, public education as a going concern was not definitely established in Maine until after the turn of the eighteenth century.

Although 161 towns had been incorporated within the territorial limits of Maine by 1800, only 7 had grammar schools. From this it may be assumed that no more than seven towns contained one hundred or more families and that the population was relatively sparse. In theory, at least, the provisions for higher education at public expense were much more extensive than any now existing.

Early Schools

The towns in York County, adjacent to Massachusetts, were the first settled in the state. As most of the early records were destroyed during the Indian wars, there is no reliable history of schools prior to 1700.

In 1701, following a vote of the town, the selectmen of York—

> Indented and bargined with Mr. Nath'l Freeman to ceep a free scool, for which the town to pay said Freeman for one year eight pounds in or as money and three pence per week for taching to reade, and four pence per week for writing and sifering and no moor (4).

The town of Wells had the next oldest record, for in March 1715, it was voted "to procure a schoolmaster at the town's charge." Apparently the selectmen met with no success, because in 1716 the town was indicted for not having a school. This action apparently had the effect of awakening the people to a sense of their duty.

In the beginning, there was not a schoolhouse in a single town, and whatever provision was made for the instruction of children must have been at some of the dwelling houses. The first recorded action was in the town of York in March 1725, when it was voted that "a schoolhouse shall be built at ye lower end of ye town on ye ministerial land this year at ye town cost" (5). In Wells, the first schoolhouse was built in 1731, and in 1734 two were built.

The description given of the first schoolhouse in the town of Kennebunk is a far cry from today's school facilities. It was built of large round logs notched at the ends so as to let into each other, as logging camps are built today. The walls were about 6 feet high, with a roof over the top, though the gable ends were entirely open. There were no windows, the light coming in freely from the ends. The only way of entering, both for masters and scholars, was by climbing up on a stile at the end and jumping down into the house. There is no description of the means of egress.

Teachers

Maine was settled for the most part by Puritan stock from Massachusetts, which accounts for the close connection that existed between the school and the church. Early laws regarding teachers were more concerned with moral character than with educational qualifications. This concern is evidenced in an act of 1671 that directed that the youth be educated not only in good literature, but in sound doctrine, and ordered the selectmen not to allow anyone to teach in the schools or colleges who had manifested themselves unsound in the faith or scandalous in their lives and had not given satisfaction according to the rules of Christ.

For a long period, the church took care of educational affairs, receiving money from the town and disbursing it for parochial purposes in parish meetings. Teachers were given examinations and certified by the settled minister.

The remuneration paid to teachers seems small compared with today's salaries. Yet, considering the hardships and actual poverty of the early settlers, a teacher's salary of £20 per year, plus his "diate," compares quite favorably and probably was more liberal than the salaries of teachers in more recent times.

School Districts

In 1789, Maine, as a part of Massachusetts, adopted the school district plan for operation of schools (6). Each town or plantation was authorized to determine the number and limits of school districts. In some cases, to accommodate the pupils, a school was kept part of the time in one section of a town and part of the time in another.

In the District Act of 1789 are found a number of the principles on which education in the state was to develop in succeeding years. These principles include the requirement that towns support schools; establishment of districts as a part or subsection of a town; teaching of morals; issuance of certificates to teachers; establishment of primary schools; recognition of women as teachers; and rights of towns to manage schools by a committee (7).

The school district plan undoubtedly served an important purpose in the pioneer period, guaranteeing a school wherever there were people. But there were indications that it was beginning to hamper the development of schools rather early in the nineteenth century. As early as 1822, when the city of Portland found the district system, as well as the multiplicity of school officers, committees, and agents, an obstacle to good schools, it asked for and obtained a special act abolishing school districts and granting to the school committee all the powers of district agents (8). Bath and Bangor soon followed Portland's lead, and a general law was enacted in 1834 authorizing towns to discontinue school districts in favor of town organization.

Dissatisfaction with the district system continued to grow and came to the surface in 1843 in the report of a group known as the Friends of Education. This group agreed that many of the defects were due to having over 4,000 independent districts in 450 towns with nearly 7,000 teachers operating without direction, the inevitable result of such a system being chaos and inefficiency. An organization was proposed that would join together the individual parts and serve as a channel of communication from school to school and teacher to teacher.

Legislation was presented to implement the report providing for a board of school commissioners. It passed the House by a close vote but was indefinitely postponed in the Senate without debate. Its significance lies in its initial efforts to improve education on a statewide basis and in that it was followed by other efforts that did bear fruit in later years.

In 1868, State Superintendent Warren Johnson listed the district system as one of the causes of partial failure of the common schools, and it was along this line that a real battle was to be fought. In 1870, a law was passed authorizing any town to abolish districts, since the district system had come to be regarded as an obstacle to progress. Its subsequent demise in 1893 was assisted by the passage of another act in 1870 whereby the town committee, rather than the district agents, was empowered to employ teachers. From 1880 to 1893, when the district system was abolished, the number of towns employing a supervisor of schools increased, and the need for more professional supervision emerged.

State Board of Education

The initial step in an attempt to secure information of a statistical nature came in 1825 when towns were required to make reports to the secretary of state once every 3 years. As these returns were incomplete, they were of doubtful value and obviously a far cry from today's system for data collection. Until the middle of the nineteenth century, few statistics were collected, and no information was available on how the laws were being observed by the towns or how school money was being expended. Teachers had no associations or conventions for mutual improvement.

In January 1846, a convention of teachers and friends of education appointed a committee to "carefully consider the defects in our school system, and to suggest measures for improvement" (9). These defects were identified as the multiplication of school districts, the inefficiency of school committees, the lack of qualification of teachers, the absence of a systematic course of study, and the want of general interest in schools.

This convention is notable in that it recommended for the first time the establishment of a State Board of Education, which was introduced in the Legislature and became a law (10). Maine thereby became a pioneer in establishing a state board. Even though the board lasted only from 1846 to 1852 and a solid basis for a state board was not realized until 1949, this was a significant step and marked an era of reform and advance in schoolwork. The board consisted of one member from each county who was chosen by the school committee of the several towns in the county. Its duties were to collect and disseminate information on the location and construction of schoolhouses, the arrangement of school districts, and the best use of school apparatus; to consult with school committees and school agents on the best and cheapest method of introducing uniform school books and the expediency of establishing school libraries; to inquire and to report on the advantages of normal schools; to devise improvements in teaching in the common schools; and to report to the Governor and the Legislature.

William G. Crosby, who later became Governor, was chosen as the first secretary of the board. The report to the Legislature in 1847 gives the first reliable statistics about the schools of Maine. The average wage for male teachers was $16.71 per month. Female teachers were paid $1.52 per week, exclusive of food, which was an advance of 6¢ per week over the previous year. The average school year was 21 weeks and 1 day. The number of persons of legal school age was 201,992, which is not too different from recent years. The board recommended the establishment of teacher institutes to assist teachers in acquiring some knowledge of their work, and through its influence a law was passed in 1847 establishing such institutes. During that year, 13 institutes were attended by 1,686 teachers: This was the beginning of teacher training and education in the state. Reports indicate that these first institutes aroused professional pride, stimulated an interest in study, and were responsible for the formation of several county teachers associations, some of which are still active today.

Despite the initially unique and timely contributions of the board, it was abolished in 1852. This action is perplexing when viewed in retrospect. William G. Crosby was a talented lawyer, scholar, and speaker; his successor, E. M. Thurston, was an eminent teacher skilled in public affairs. There is little question that the board created an interest in schools never known before and emphasized the importance of education. W. J. Corthell wrote: "It raised the dead corpse of the old school into an active growing life" (11). After such an auspicious beginning, it is difficult to understand the board's demise after 6 years of apparent success. Perhaps the peculiar formation of the board was at the root of the trouble, or possibly it was the fact that the election of the board by school committees was too far removed from the control of the political powers in the state. Corthell, who studied this period closely, says: "It died not because it was a political power but because it was not and whatever power it had educationally could not be used politically" (12).

The Legislature replaced the board with county commissioners who were directed to spend at least 50 days in visiting schools and to report to the Legislature on the character of the teachers and the order and condition of the schools and schoolhouses. The county commissioners were named, but there is no record of any work accomplished, and apparently no reports were ever made. The failure of these county officials to act removed any tendency to establish a county system of education. From that day the county in Maine has had no educational functions.

State Supervision

The abolition of the state board and discontinuance of the position of secretary left the state without a chief state school officer, but this gap was filled in 1854 by passage of an act establishing the Office of State Superintendent of Schools. The superintendent was to be appointed by the Governor, with the approval of the council, and was "to devote his time to the improvement of common schools and the general interests of education" (13). An annual salary of $1,200 was set by statute. The position continued uninterruptedly from that time on, although the title was changed in 1897 to state superintendent of public schools and later, in the twentieth century, to commissioner of education (14).

The first state superintendent was Charles H. Lord of Portland, who served in 1854 and seems to have spent his time visiting various parts of the state and observing the schools. He reported on the lack of punctuality in attendance, absence of parental interest, poor discipline, and incompetence of teachers. As a solution, he proposed the enlightenment of the public and a normal school for the training of teachers.

In 1868, the duties of the state superintendent were set forth more distinctly; the salary was raised to $1,800, exclusive of travel and other necessary expenses. The office was given a "local habitation," which it had not had before, at the capitol in Augusta. The duties of the superintendent were to supervise all the public schools, to advise and direct town committees, to disseminate information, to hold a state teachers convention each year, to prescribe the studies to be taught in the common schools, and to supervise the normal schools.

In the early years, the tenure of the state superintendent was short. In the 46 years between 1854 and 1900, no fewer than 12 persons held the position, although Nelson A. Luce served for 15 years, from 1880 to 1895.

State Financial Assistance

When Maine became a state in 1820, 236 towns had elementary schools supported by public taxation. The constitution emphasized the advantages of education but directed the Legislature to require the towns to support and maintain schools at their own expense (15). This might be interpreted as an intent to delegate responsibility for public schools to local units; but, in actual practice, the state has participated in school financing and has demonstrated by appropriate action that the support of public schools is a joint responsibility of state and local agencies.

The first school law passed in 1821 established the minimum amount of money that a town must raise annually for the support of schools at 40¢ per capita. Interestingly enough, a minimum per-capita requirement continues to the present day; despite inflation and extension of educational opportunities, it has risen in nearly 150 years to only 80¢.

The development of state assistance to local schools was slow and probably reflects a strong prejudice of Maine citizens against anything in governmental affairs that looked like centralization of control. Even in the early years, however, the need for state participation in the support of schools became evident.

The first evidence of state financial support came in 1828 when 20 townships of public lands were sold and the proceeds of approximately $200,000 used to establish a common school fund, the income from which was to be distributed according to the number of scholars. This fund established the principle of state support and was the forerunner and basis for funds of later years for equalization of educational opportunity.

In 1833, the banking corporations were required to pay to the state one-half of 1 percent semiannually on their capital stock. This has significance as it was the first state appropriation from tax money for school aid. The amount was not large compared with present-day sums, for from 1833 to 1849 the revenue averaged only $31,511 per year. The bank tax did not prove for long to be a stable source of revenue because of a tax on state banks imposed by the federal government. It seemed likely that this school resource would disappear entirely. So in 1863, in order to supply the deficiency, the sums to be raised by taxation were increased to 75¢ per inhabitant, and in 1868, to $1.

The Legislature of 1872 provided a broader basis for support by the enactment of a tax for common schools of 1 mill per dollar on all property in the state. The same session reduced the per-capita tax from $1 to 80¢ where it has remained ever since.

Teacher Education

The early standards for teachers seem somewhat out of line with the actual status of teaching, for, according to a law of 1789,

> No person shall be employed as a schoolmaster unless he shall have received an education at some college or university and if he was to teach in a grammar school he must be skilled in the Greek and Latin languages (16).

The teacher institutes established in 1847 by the State Board of Education were the beginning of teacher preparation and filled a need for a time; but these were abolished by the Legislature in 1860 in favor of a so-called normal training program in connection with 18 designated academies. This plan was soon found to be impractical, and the law was repealed in 1862. It was evident that some better means than institutes and academy programs must be found to prepare teachers. The secretary of the state board and later the state superintendents and every teachers convention passed resolutions calling the attention of the Legislature and the people to the need for normal schools. The constant urging at length produced results.

The first normal school was established in Farmington in 1863, when the trustees of Farmington Academy offered its property to the state for a normal school. A second normal school, Eastern State at Castine, was opened in September 1867; and a third at Gorham, known as Western Normal, was opened in 1878 on the site of the Gorham Female Seminary.

The Madawaska Training School, which later became Fort Kent State College, was opened in 1878 to prepare teachers for the French population of the St. John's Valley area of northern Maine. Other normal schools were established at Presque Isle and Machias soon after the turn of the twentieth century, in 1903 and 1909, respectively. In the early years, these normal schools were under the control of the Governor and council, but they were transferred to a board of trustees in 1873. The board of trustees continued to be responsible for the state's normal schools and teacher colleges until 1949, when it was superseded by the State Board of Education.

The condition of the public schools at the end of the nineteenth century resulted more from natural growth and a desire for the advantages of an education than from adherence to a well-developed plan. However, the state succeeded in establishing the foundation for a basically sound school system which has grown and improved with passing years. The organization and structure of public education was well prepared to enter the twentieth century and to move ahead toward the attainment of recognized goals.

THE CHIEF STATE SCHOOL OFFICERS

From the time of the appointment of the first state superintendent of common schools in 1854 to about 1913, the State Department of Education was predominantly a one-man operation. He kept what records were available, visited schools, held an annual conference for local superintendents of schools, and served as secretary of the normal school board of trustees.

In 1899, the superintendent was assigned the responsibility for the education of children residing in the Unorganized Territory, an area comprising nearly one-half the state, with numerous townships sparsely settled and with no local government. This remained his personal responsibility until 1911, when a director for these schools was employed. In making provision for complete state support and control of schooling in the Unorganized Territory, Maine took a step that still stands as a model for other states. Not only has it guaranteed educational opportunities to children in sparsely settled areas, but it has been able to provide an education equivalent to that offered in organized towns and plantations at a cost that is exceedingly low compared with similar services under somewhat similar conditions in other states.

A review of the statutes reveals a gradual growth in the responsibilities assigned to the state superintendent or commissioner from 1900 to 1949 when the State Board of Education was reinstated. At that time the selection of a commissioner was removed from the political realm of appointment by the Governor to election by the Board of Education, and most of the policy-making duties of the commissioner were transferred to the board although he became its executive officer and professional leader.

The scope of legislation extending the chief state school officer's duties and responsibilities ranged from the professional to the ridiculous, with items of the highest educational implications mingled with items of perhaps lesser but practical importance. The authorization of the commissioner to devise and furnish plans for privies is one such item.

The strengthening image of the education department and its services may be attributed, in large measure, to the caliber of men holding the position and the relatively long tenure enjoyed.

The advances made in extension of services and programs were almost universally based on recommendations of the chief state school officer. In some cases, however, it took many years before an idea obtained acceptance. The educational history of the period is closely related to the endeavors of these men and would not be complete without some comment on their achievements. As contrasted with the high turnover in previous years, only eight men regularly occupied the office. From 1900 to 1965, the average term of service was over 8 years.

William W. Stetson, 1895-1907

William W. Stetson spanned the turn of the century, serving as state superintendent from 1895 to 1907. His formal introduction to the profession came when he was appointed as the teacher of a district school at the age of 15. For some years he taught the winter term and worked on his father's farm when not engaged in teaching. Using some accumulated savings, he followed the example of many other Maine boys and went west in search of greater opportunity. With a minimum of education, but evidence of great ability, he became superintendent of schools in Rockford, Illinois. Returning to Maine, he served with conspicuous success for 10 years as superintendent of schools in Auburn and in 1895 was appointed as state superintendent of public schools. Among his accomplishments during his term of office were the establishment of the town system of school administration and the abolition of the district system, the institution of free conveyance for elementary pupils, the adoption of the free textbook system, the extension of free tuition privileges to all pupils, the improvement of courses of instruction in the teacher-training institutions, and the adoption of an optional plan of professional supervision. His annual reports, from 1895 to 1907, are noted for his knowledge and grasp of educational operation in the state and are filled with constructive suggestions (17).

In 1905, he was selected as president of the Department of Superintendence of the National Education Association. He might well be called the Horatio Alger of his day in education, for he proved that a poor farm boy, through his own initiative and effort, could progress from a one-room district school to positions of state and national leadership.

An indication of how close Superintendent Stetson was to the pupils and teachers of the state is found in a report of a visit he made to the schools in northern Aroostook County, where he noted some things with which he was not pleased and some which gave him satisfaction. He wrote:

> I noticed in certain schools that the pupils were idle and listless. You must realize that one of the great advantages which children derive from attending school comes from learning to work, to dig things out for themselves . . . . Do not place upon the walls of your schoolroom advertisements of tobacco or other pictures representing objects with which children should not become familiar. Be sure of your facts and that which you state is true (18).

The printing of these comments in his annual report undoubtedly had a wholesome effect on all of the schools of the state.

As a good teacher should, he did conduct a follow-up inspection, accompanied by the Governor. He noted good results from his suggestions in that—

> Pupils read fluently in French and English; pupils are clean, bright, wholesome looking; dressed neatly and becomingly; manners courteous and easy; prompt and accurate recitations; methods employed by the teacher are such as would be used by our best teachers in cities. There is a marked improvement in calling and dismissing classes. In many schools when the signal is given, the children rise in their places, face in the direction they are to march, keep step as they pass to their places, face the teacher and visitor and bow simultaneously (19).

State administration has changed considerably since 1900, but without a doubt, many of his successors also would like to have time to visit schools.

Payson Smith, 1907-17

During the incumbency of Payson Smith, much constructive legislation was enacted. Dr. Smith was particularly interested in lengthening the school year and was able to increase the minimum from 20 to 30 weeks. He was an ardent champion of adequate salaries for teachers and showed his understanding of human nature by admitting that a solution was not to be reached by legislation, but through public opinion. He believed that certain requirements could be enforced by law, but that the real spirit of educational progress was not to be obtained by statute but to be found only in the people.

Promotion of industrial or vocational education was one of his many endeavors. He saw that too great an emphasis was placed on college preparation while 90 percent of the product of Maine's public schools went into agriculture or the trades. He was a pioneer in the advocacy of vocational schools, which did not come to pass until years later. He was, however, successful in introducing manual training and home economics into the normal schools.

Summer schools were encouraged, and a beginning was made in 1909 when five were held. A report from St. Agatha in northern Maine indicates the value of the summer programs because "many have never heard English spoken outside of the schools, for French still remains the language of the home in much of Northeastern Maine" (20).

Dr. Smith was a champion of good education for the rural sections, believing that the country boys and girls deserved the best teaching and that the course of study for rural schools should not be an imitation of that used in city schools. He recommended state certification of teachers, rather than optional state examination, on the grounds that the state will fail to guarantee a reasonable equality of educational opportunity unless it safeguards entrance to the teaching profession.

During this period, a great effort was made to provide professional supervision of schools. A permissive law allowing towns to join together in unions for the purpose of jointly employing a superintendent of schools had been passed by 1897, and a number of voluntary unions had been formed. During Dr. Smith's term of service, emphasis on union formation was increased, and in 1917 he was authorized to group all towns with less than 50 teachers in school unions (21). This was unprecendented and reflects the confidence of the legislators in Payson Smith.

Dr. Smith moved on to become commissioner of education in the Commonwealth of Massachusetts, and later he returned to become dean of the College of Education at the University of Maine. In his college teaching he had a great influence on teachers and administrators, liberally sharing his philosophy and experience with those who were fortunate enough to attend his classes.

An illustration of his keenness is remembered when one day in a class he was asked to comment on a newspaper article which stated that Maine public schools were godless. He said, in reply, that it was his understanding that God was not subject to the ruling of a school committee or the Legislature, and he thought it would be difficult to keep Him out of the public schools.

Dr. Smith's accomplishments were great, and Maine schools progressed in many directions under his leadership. But he was also a dynamic force toward changes that came about many years later. William H. Soule, in his biography of Smith, says:

> Payson Smith meant more to the education of his time than a person who provided the leadership for translating into accomplishment an impressive number of educational goals . . . he played two important roles in the educational circles in which he moved: he was a conscience for education; and he was a balance wheel for education . . . (22).

To summarize, Payson Smith believed in well-trained and well-paid teachers, adequately equipped schoolhouses, professional supervision, a simple and definite course of study, reasonable consolidation for educational advantages, and community interest and support.

Augustus O. Thomas, 1917-29

Soon after Dr. Thomas assumed office, the United States became involved in World War I. Considering that it was the purpose of the department to safeguard the welfare of schools in the essentials of education, keep up the standards of instruction, and, at the same time, participate in the war effort, he called upon the schools to prepare to meet the conditions that would come with peace. He urged the schools and the people to get ready to accept new ideals and newer concepts of education.

His chief concern was for qualified teachers. In 1918, he warned:

> This is a "making" time and it would be a mistake to lower standards from which the state could not recover for a decade. It is better to close some schools than to supply them with poorly trained teachers. If schools were places for herding of children standards might be lowered, but viewed from the standpoint of professional service, standards should be raised. A teacher shortage will bring this country to a realization of the necessity of an adequate remuneration for trainees of coming men (23).

In September of the same year, he wrote that it would be unwise to lower the minimum qualifications for certification. Two years of post-high school study was considered to be the minimum allowable. He did express a hope that matters would gradually adjust themselves, because "salaries are uniformly higher and will tend to hold teachers from the allurements of lucrative war work and will gradually bring back some who have gone for that purpose" (24).

His optimism was short-lived, for the end of the war did not solve the teacher shortage. An appeal was made by Dr. Thomas for young people to attend normal school or college. The mobility of teachers and their short duration of service were pointed out in 1919, when 4,281 teachers out of a total of 6,554 were new to the positions held. At that time, 2,014, or 31 percent, were normal graduates, with an average experience of only 3.6 years. Commenting on the need for more stability, he said:

> It would seem reasonable to expect a teacher who receives a normal or college education to teach five years. This would make it a profession and a life work and give her a chance to settle down in life at the age of 25 (25).

The shortage continued throughout the 1920's despite the commissioner's constant urging of local units to increase salaries and make teaching an attractive profession. Some advancements were made, and many places were planning improved salaries when the Depression hit, and school officials were forced to retrench.

Dr. Thomas was prophetic of the growth in the leadership roles of the chief state school officer and the state department when he stated in an annual report:

> There is a strong tendency today to make state departments of education more vital to the progress of education. The office is more and more becoming a promotion enterprise susceptible of as high art and technical skill as the engineering profession. It is necessary that the departments of education be brought together into a purposeful whole (26).

Noting the need for what he termed *educational engineering*, he initiated a statewide survey of school conditions so that he could know if the system was progressing or slipping back from year to year. Although Dr. Thomas had strong support from the educators in the state, a change in state administration in 1929 brought his term of office to an end.

Bertram E. Packard, 1929-41

During the difficult Depression years, Bertram E. Packard, formerly deputy commissioner, served as commissioner of education. He was a thickset, practical man not given to hyperbole, but well aware of Maine's educational needs. In his writing and speeches he continually called attention to the need for courses in the fine arts, which many citizens considered "fads and frills."

The effects of the Depression were somewhat slower in affecting Maine than more urban sections of the country, but by 1931, general unemployment had turned many former teachers to seeking positions in schools. This situation is described in the *Maine School Bulletin* of April 1931:

> There is no longer an appreciable shortage of teachers, no superintendents should find it difficult to fill all or nearly all vacancies from the graduating classes of the normal schools. There is an oversupply of teachers of English, Latin, modern language and social studies. There is a demand slightly in excess of supply in mathematics, science, commercial and vocational subjects (27).

The effects of the Depression worsened, and in 1933, many school systems were eliminating special subject offerings that had previously been introduced after much work and effort. The number of regular elementary and secondary positions was also decreased, and over 4,000 teachers received reductions in salary ranging from 5 to 20 percent. Other retrenchments involved transportation of pupils, purchase of textbooks and supplies, and deferment of needed repairs. These cutbacks represented a saving well beyond the half-million mark (28).

Commissioner Packard minced no words in saying to the people in 1933:

> When we consider the fact that the amount expended two years ago was at a very low level, no one can for a moment believe but that a decrease in these expenditures in the two-year period of over $2,000,000 must have resulted in serious impairment of facilities for the children in our schools. It means the schools in our state are being maintained on a starvation diet and if further reductions were to be made it would be preferable to entirely close the public schools. The time is ripe for organized public sentiment to demand that further attempts at chiseling and paring of school appropriations be abandoned and that substantially increased appropriations be made (29).

Again, in 1936, he warned that the day of the $10- or $12-per-week teacher was over and that if municipalities expected to employ teachers at those salaries, they must accept a more or less inefficient and unsatisfactory type of service.

The years of Commissioner Packard's service were difficult ones and might be characterized as a holding operation.

Harry V. Gilson, 1941-47

Maine had barely recovered from the effects of the Depression and regained the ground lost when World War II erupted, and schools became involved with Victory Corps, Victory Gardens, and many other patriotic endeavors. A surplus of teachers soon became a critical shortage.

Harry V. Gilson, who succeeded Bertram E. Packard in 1941, was young, dynamic, and aroused the school systems to greater efforts. He implored teachers to stay on the job as a patriotic duty. Like his successors, he was a defender and an advocate of high standards and adequate salaries. In 1942, however, he was forced to recognize that the war with its various demands on teaching personnel, both on the home front and for defense, had created a serious situation in which, if schools were to open, he must lower the standards for certification. The situation grew steadily worse: Some schools were forced to drop courses because of lack of personnel, and an already heavy pupil load was increased. In 1944, he reported at midyear that some schools had not yet opened. During these years, permits and emergency licenses were granted to persons who lacked the established minimum requirements for certification, and the department was compelled to "sanction" the employment of persons having little or no education beyond the high school level.

Harland A. Ladd, 1947-52

Harland A. Ladd, a former superintendent of schools and department director of curriculum and instruction, was appointed commissioner in 1947. While the emphasis during his term of office was on instructional programs, much constructive legislation was passed. The most important was the reestablishment of the State Board of Education with authority to select the commissioner. Mr. Ladd became the first commissioner appointed by the board.

Other forward steps included authority for the creation of community school districts, the Maine School Building Authority, and the start of Maine's first postsecondary vocational-technical institute. State subsidies were increased, and a more equitable method of distribution was adopted, based on state valuation of local units. Tenure for teachers, which had been a controversial subject for some years, was adopted, and equal pay for women was mandated. Commissioner Ladd literally gave his life in the cause of Maine education, dying from a heart attack brought on by overwork.

Herbert G. Espy, 1952-55

Commissioner Espy's term was relatively short in comparison with that of some of his predecessors. He was an intelligent, scholarly person, noted for his academic achievements as a teacher and author of professional books. He was the first commissioner to hold an earned doctoral degree. During his incumbency, attention was given to safeguarding the integrity of granting degrees, and largely due to his efforts a statute was enacted. An increase in the minimum salary for teachers was adopted, and the school year was extended from 32 to 36 weeks.

Warren G. Hill, 1956-63

From 1956 to 1963, under the leadership of Warren G. Hill, Maine moved ahead rapidly on many educational fronts. Dr. Hill, born in Nova Scotia, came to Buxton, Maine, at an early age and was educated at Gorham State Teachers College and Boston and Columbia Universities. He began his teaching on the tiny island of Islesford on the Maine coast and had progressed to the acting presidency of New Haven State College when he was elected commissioner. He had a kinship with Maine people and Maine ideas that enabled him to capitalize on their strengths and create a desire to overcome their weaknesses.

During this period, the commissioner, state board, and department were active in promoting the acceptance of the Sinclair Bill, a district reorganization act. This piece of legislation has been called the most significant educational law enacted since 1893, when the town school districts were abolished in favor of a townwide school system. It led to the establishment of 65 school administrative districts embracing 238 towns. A revised state foundation program to equalize opportunity and guarantee a minimum program of education was adopted; it provided supplemental operational aid to districts and, for the first time, construction aid to districts and properly organized units. Dr. Hill was recognized outside the state as a leader and impressive speaker, and through his efforts Maine became more and more involved with regional and national educational affairs. He resigned in 1963 to become president of Trenton State College in New Jersey. Dr. Hill was succeeded in 1964 by William T. Logan, Jr., superintendent of schools at Burlington, Vermont.

The men who served in the position of commissioner of education in the twentieth century without exception were men of vision who spared no efforts to discharge their responsibilities and extend education to the children of Maine. Their reports and public utterances indicate the seriousness with which they undertook their duties and their dedication to education. Personalities undoubtedly shaped the course of events.

Leadership was not limited to the chief state school officer, for there were many able members of the state department who served in perhaps a less conspicuous manner but nevertheless made many worthwhile contributions. To single out individuals for mention would be most difficult, but a history of the Maine Department of Education would not be complete without mention of Richard J. Libby and Florence Hale. Mr. Libby served as agent for rural education and in other capacities. He was a respected adviser to commissioners and was revered by all with whom he came in contact. He became known as "Mr. Department of Education" for his broad knowledge and the service he rendered. Although he retired in 1950, he did not lose his interest or perspective as is evidenced by his observation to the writer in 1964 that "it is good to know that this generation is better than we were." Miss Hale served as a rural agent from 1916 to 1932. She was a dynamic leader in the improvement of rural schools and attained national prominence by being elected president of the National Education Association. She resigned as rural agent to become editor of *The Grade Teacher.*

The positions for these rural agents came about in a somewhat curious way as they were financed by the General Education Board, a forerunner of present-day foundations, which was interested in improving schools in rural areas and donated funds for this purpose to be handled by the commissioner. Maine was the only New England state to receive such a grant. The commissioner employed Mr. Libby and Miss Hale and paid them by his personal check from funds advanced by the board. This procedure continued until 1932, when the grants were discontinued, and Commissioner Packard was able to secure state funds to continue the positions.

THE DEPARTMENT AND THE TEACHER

A review of school bulletins, biennial reports, and public addresses of the commissioners and staff indicate continuing concern for an adequate supply of teachers and for their welfare.

Two world wars and a major depression made it difficult to staff Maine schools with well-qualified teachers and to expand the normal schools and colleges to a point of annually preparing enough teachers to fill vacancies. Maine has been handicapped by its location at the northeast corner of the United States and its proximity to states paying the highest salaries in the nation. Maine teachers have been welcomed in other states for their dedication and efficiency; consequently, the drain has been heavy and serious.

Although positive efforts were made to attract young people to teaching and enrollments in the state colleges doubled between 1953 and 1966, shortages persisted in primary grades, English, mathematics, science, and vocational subjects.

Certification

The development of standards for teachers has progressed from the day when certification was voluntary, and the only requirements for being a teacher were to be a good disciplinarian, excellent in penmanship, quick at figures, and a good grammarian, to full certification based on 4 to 5 years of professional study. Teacher examinations leading to state certification were offered in 1895 and became compulsory in 1913.

Standards were revised and strengthened in 1924 under Commissioner Augustus O. Thomas, who stated in a foreword to a manual of information:

> A trained teaching staff is essential to good schools. We do not hope to come at once into the ideal of a trained teacher for every school in the state but it is not too much to expect that by 1930 our teaching staff will be raised to a reasonably satisfactory level (30).

He expressed the hope that the regulations would be conducive to a full professional training in normal school or college.

No particular changes were made in certification laws or regulations until 1931, when the Legislature authorized the commissioner to set up, from time to time, such standards as would seem advisable for the best educational interests of the state. Acting under this statute, the examination plan was abandoned except for the certificate of superintendence grade. In place of teacher examinations, some actual training in an approved institution was required; elementary teachers could not be certified without evidence of completion of at least 1 year of postsecondary work, and secondary teachers with 4 years of college study. It was an opportune time to raise standards, as there was an oversupply of teachers.

In 1949, a summary of regulations was published which updated the changes that had been made since the earlier bulletins had been issued. The philosophy expressed was that Maine must set justifiably high standards while adjusting minimum requirements to a point where a reasonably adequate supply of teachers would be available. Subject matter certification was never prescribed because of the large number of small high schools in isolated areas.

The national trend toward greater participation by the teaching profession in the establishment of standards was recognized in 1958 by Commissioner Warren G. Hill, and through his influence the State Board of Education appointed the Maine Advisory Committee on Teacher Certification. By this action, teachers and lay people for the first time had a formal voice in setting the standards for the profession. The committee recommended that procedures be streamlined and that standards be raised to the bachelor degree level. The recommendations were adopted by the state board. In 1963, after continuing study by the advisory committee, several changes were made with a reduction in emphasis on "how to teach" courses for elementary certification.

In retrospect, the history of certification in Maine has followed the national pattern to a large extent. Some of the modern trends adopted include increased participation by the profession itself, involvement of lay and advisory groups, simplification of procedures with a reduction in the number of certificates issued, a gradual increase in the level of preparation required, the use of proficiency examinations, and the extension of reciprocity among the Northeastern states. An analysis of Maine practices and policies indicates a high degree of conformity with James B. Conant's specific recommendations with the exception of strict subject matter certification (31). In the twentieth century, the teacher became a professional while retaining the qualifications of character, strong discipline, and "know-how."

The role of administering certification and upgrading standards has not been an easy one or without assaults from both within and without the profession. Measures were presented to the Legislature in 1963 that would have eliminated any required professional preparation, but the matter was referred to an interim research committee. A report of the committee was presented to the next session with no action taken, and the matter was left to the commissioner and state board.

Teacher Retirement

The first pension or retirement law for teachers enacted in 1913 was not based on concern for teachers but, in the words of the act, "to increase the efficiency of the public schools by retiring teachers of long service" (32). It provided, at age 60, a pension of $250 per year for 35 years of service, $200 for 30 years, and $150 for 25 years of teaching service. Improvements have been made from time to time, but small as the first pensions now appear, the noncontributory type of pension was never equaled.

The Maine Teachers Retirement Association was organized in 1924 and administered by the commissioner and state department. Membership was voluntary in the first years of its operation, but as so few teachers joined and would be without any benefits in later years, it was made compulsory in 1930. In 1947, the Teachers Retirement Association was merged with the Maine State Employees Retirement System.

An act, passed in 1965, provided substantial adjustments for teachers and other retired state employees according to the length of time retired. More significantly, it provided that on all future adjustments in state salaries made to active employees, the same percent of increase or decrease would be applied to all retired state employees. This measure provided a safeguard against the inroads of inflation and made retirement for teachers more secure.

In all of the changes the commissioner and department staff have been active promoters and supporters of an equitable retirement system.

Minimum Salaries for Teachers

The first annual minimum salary law for teachers was $575. This was increased in 1943 to $720, and in 1945 a state minimum of $1,000 was required.

In the early years, when teachers were neither well organized nor particularly vocal, the commissioner was their spokesman in bringing the need for better salaries to the attention of citizens. He and his staff consistently advocated increased state appropriations for subsidies and equalization measures so that local units could improve teachers' salaries. The words of Commissioner Harry V. Gilson in 1943 are illustrative of these endeavors. He wrote at the time:

> Teachers are being forced out of teaching not because they want a change of vocation but because prices are going up and the dollar is losing its purchasing power. More generous financial support of schools and teachers' salaries is the logical answer (33).

The Legislature in 1947 made additional state funds available to committees to compensate for a substantially increased minimum salary, and Commissioner Harland Ladd hailed the action as the dawn of a new day for schoolteachers. At the same time he cautioned that in spite of the salary increases the teacher was little, if any, better off financially than he was in the prewar period (34). The amounts for various levels of training and experience have been revised upward at nearly every session of the Legislature in recent years until the minimum for those with a bachelor's degree starts at $5,000 and goes to $7,500 with 10 years of experience. The range for teachers with a master's degree is $5,300 to $8,000.

Teachers Associations

The first state convention of teachers was held in Waterville in November 1859. At this meeting an organization was formed under the name of the Maine Educational Association, and provision was made for an annual meeting. In 1882, the association transferred its records and property to the Maine Pedagogical Society, which had organized in 1880.

Another teacher group called the Maine Teachers' Association was formed in 1876, and in 1879 it also merged with the Maine Pedagogical Society. The object of the society was to promote the consideration and discussion of all questions relating to the organization of schools, methods of instruction, and professional standards. In 1901, the name was changed to the Maine Teachers' Association, and a new constitution was adopted.

The relationship between the department and the officers and members of the Maine Teachers' Association has been characterized by a spirit of cooperation in working for common goals. The commissioners and department staff encouraged the teachers association by planning and participating in programs and provided office space and a part-time secretary. From 1920 to 1940, Adelbert W. Gordon, state agent for the Unorganized Territory, also served as secretary for the teachers association. In 1940, the organization established its own headquarters and selected Richard B. Kennan as the first full-time secretary. This action did not affect the cooperative spirit, and a harmonious relationship has continued to exist.

Other Benefits to Teachers

Many other benefits have been achieved by teachers since 1900. The state commissioner and department have operated a teacher placement service that has been mutually advantageous to teachers, superintendents, and school officials. The success of this service, which began in 1917, may be attributed in large part to Margaret (Lewia) Arber, who has served as placement director continuously since 1923. Mrs. Arber has become acquainted with nearly every teacher in the state and is known for her remarkable memory for names and faces. The extent of the service is indicated by more than 2,700 placements made in 1966.

In 1919, in a move to improve supervision and teaching practices in the rural schools, the state initiated a special summer school for 100 teachers and paid their expenses for attendance. These teachers were the forerunner of a group of experienced teachers who had special training at the normal schools to enable them to assist other teachers in the same school system. The plan followed was for them to teach their own class or school on Saturday and to visit another school on one of the regular school days. This was the beginning of state assistance in improving instruction by visitation.

Sabbatical leave was authorized in 1929 at the rate of one-half the annual salary. But worthy as the idea was, there is no indication that it was widely utilized.

In 1959, sick leave of 10 days a year cumulative to 30 days was provided, which was subsequently made cumulative to 90 days. Fringe benefits such as insurance on life, health, accident, liability, major medical expenses, and tax-sheltered annuities were authorized in 1965.

The education department has supported all of these measures and cooperated closely with the teacher associations in bringing them about.

PROGRAMS AND SERVICES FOR EFFICIENT EDUCATION

Curriculum and Instructional Developments

In 1915, the state department was first granted a formal voice in what was to be taught in the public schools, for in that year the Legislature prescribed that courses of study for all schools be approved by the state superintendent of schools. The following year a state course of study was developed and initiated in all elementary schools. The state superintendent's authority to approve courses of study was extended to private schools in 1919, and since that time approval has been required of all private schools receiving public funds for payment of tuition.

An interesting extension of educational opportunity occurred in 1915 when a modicum of school privileges was extended by the state to the children living at the numerous light stations scattered along the coast. The need for providing some education for these children had been considered for some time, and a program was put into active operation early in the summer of 1915. A traveling teacher, who was known as the "lighthouse teacher," was employed to make visits to each light station and remain for several days to a week at a time. She gave the pupils regular instruction and upon her departure left an outline of work, which the pupils were to pursue until she came again. During her absence the pupils were supposed to be taught by their parents or some other person living at the station, and on her return visit the work was reviewed.

Many of the light stations on Maine's extensive and rockbound coast were out of the usual routes of travel, and to reach these places the teacher often had to go some distance in a small boat. The commissioner's report of 1915 indicates that, despite usual hardships of this mode of travel, especially during the stormy season of the year, the teacher was able to follow a reasonably regular schedule of visits. The plan was described as "practicable and bids fair to be a permanent solution to the problem" (35). It was not a permanent solution, however, for the number of light stations and children living at them diminished until the program was discontinued after a few years. Still, the "lighthouse teacher" did serve a real need for a period of time, and her arrival must have been an important event for the children isolated from the mainland.

In 1919, in response to the state superintendent's urging, legislation was enacted requiring the teaching of personal hygiene, sanitation, and physical education.

With the passing years, many laws were enacted affecting the curriculum, some of which stemmed from the commissioner's recommendations and others which were reflections of the times but required implementation by the department. There has been continuing emphasis on the teaching of American history and civil government, the Constitution of the United States, the Declaration of Independence, and the American Freedoms. Special day observances have grown in number, such as Temperance Day, Poetry Day, and John F. Kennedy Day. In each instance, the department has been charged with supplying suitable materials for observance.

The annual reports of the commissioners and department bulletins are replete with suggestions for curricular improvement. As early as 1917, no doubt due to the passage of the federal Smith-Hughes Vocational Education Act, industrial and vocational education were being advocated. Vocational guidance was first proposed in 1918 and received some attention, but it was not until 1940 that a state guidance director was added to the staff. The first director was Dana M. Cotton, who later became placement director at Harvard University and has held other positions of national importance. In 1919, distributive education was recommended, but it did not become a reality until 20 years later when the city of Bangor initiated a program.

Improved libraries were stressed in 1920, when it was reported that "Maine is rated as having the smallest high school libraries," but the report hastened to add that "this position is about to undergo a change" (36). The importance and value of libraries has been emphasized since that time, and today many schools have quite respectable collections. The secondary school accreditation standards of 1955 gave added impetus to library improvement when libraries were made a consideration for accreditation.

A survey entitled *The Financing of the Public Schools of Maine,* made in 1934 by a special commission with Paul R. Mort, director, was very critical of the curricular offerings (37). It classified the schools surveyed into three expenditure levels: high, medium, and low. The author reported that the only attempts to make the curriculum a living thing were on the high-expenditure level. Bangor was cited as an example of a community where the school committee was engaged in revising the curriculum. In the low-level elementary schools, the scope of the curriculum was limited to the mastery of the tool subjects, and the teacher was portrayed as more of a taskmaster than a teacher. The secondary schools on the medium and high levels showed evidence of developing programs to fit the needs of pupils rather than to force all to take a program made for conditions common 50 years earlier. A student had some choice of courses in high-level schools, whereas one program only was offered in the low-level schools. The Mort survey undoubtedly had some beneficial effect in identifying the need for changes, but the times were adverse and progress was slow. In 1940, it was reported in the *Maine School Bulletin* that very little work on the whole was being done to broaden and enrich the curriculum for pupils completing their education in high school. The need for improvement, however, was not forgotten but was delayed until district reorganization was improved. The reorganization of schools after 1957 did much to broaden educational opportunity.

Educational use of the radio was attempted, but, as in other states, it did not develop into an ongoing program. Its most effective use was a series of radio talks on current educational issues by Harrison C. Lyseth, state director for secondary schools.

Educational television has proved to be an effective means of instruction, and by 1966 it was being widely utilized. The establishment of a state station at the University of Maine and authority for the department to contract with WCBB (Colby-Bates-Bowdoin) extended coverage to over 90 percent of the pupils in the state. The department added a specialist in TV instruction to the staff and has produced programs in health, Maine history, and other subject areas in which programs have not been readily available.

Educational Finance

As a basis for comparison with later state appropriations, the total allocated to the state department for all purposes for the 1901-1902 biennium was $2,174,678. Sixty-six years later, the biennial appropriation totaled $74,709,536, an increase of 3,335 percent.

State financial assistance to local education had originated with the sale of public lands in 1828. It was increased in 1872 when the Legislature earmarked 1 mill of tax money for the support of common schools. In 1909, another 1.5 mills of tax money was allocated for the support of education, with 1.5 mills being distributed according to the school census and the other mill on the basis of the town's valuation. This action resulted in increasing the funds available from $869,188 in 1909 to $2,377,684 in 1910, the first year the law was in effect. This was probably the greatest percentage increase in state support ever experienced before or since that time. The state tax was raised to 3.3 mills in 1921 with the establishment of the state school fund. The fund provided first for all department expenses; the balance was distributed to cities and towns on the basis of $100 per teaching position, $3 for each person on the school census between the ages of 5 and 21, and the remainder, if any, on aggregate attendance (38).

The most significant event during the thirties relating to financing of education was the survey by the Maine School Finance Commission. The study concentrated on potential economies in the operation of schools, more equitable sources of revenue for the state school fund, and the distribution of funds on an equalized basis. The commission endeavored to present an accurate portrayal of existing conditions and to improve the financial structure so as to guarantee to all boys and girls a minimum program of educational opportunity.

Among other things, the survey found that the cost of education was a small item in the total expenditures of the citizens of the state and that state government funds going to education had dropped from 39 percent to 16 percent in the period between 1915 and 1931 even though the percentage for highways more than doubled in the same period. It was apparent that Maine must increase its expenditures considerably to reach a satisfactory minimal condition. It was pointed out that the state department had not been sufficiently well supported to permit it to give any extensive guiding standards. The report emphasized the responsibility of the state for setting up an acceptable foundation program and for distributing the burden over the state so that it would fall on the people in accordance with their ability to pay. The commission recognized that it would take time to accomplish its suggestions and stated that under "recovery conditions" the goals could be attained within the next 10 to 20 years.

The study did not lead to many immediate reforms. However, it created more interest in education and did much to establish the principal of state responsibility for providing equal educational opportunity for children in all sections of the state. It undoubtedly contributed to the adoption of a foundation program in 1949 and the Uniform Effort Tax Principle in 1965.

In 1945, the Legislature adopted the policy of making all appropriations from the state's general fund, and the day of "earmarked funds" for education was at an end.

The need for equalization of tax burdens and educational opportunities was a critical issue during the twentieth century. The first effort was made in 1919, when a special fund of $40,000 was appropriated to strengthen small high schools (39). Further acceptance of the state's responsibility for the education of all its children was revealed in two ways in 1920. An equalization fund deducted from the common school fund, plus interest on reserved lands of unorganized townships totaling $55,621, was distributed to towns having tax rates for school and municipal purposes in excess of the state average. In the same year, a somewhat unprecedented action was taken when the Governor and executive council allocated $100,000 to help towns maintain schools and pay teachers' salaries under emergency conditions resulting from the high cost of living following World War I. Funds for equalization purposes were increased from time to time, until in 1949 a new formula for the allocation of subsidies was adopted. This divided the 492 separate school units into nine classifications according to wealth.

Another study, known as the Jacobs Study (40), was authorized in 1955 to examine all expenditures of funds within the jurisdiction of the state department, particularly the distribution of funds to municipalities on an equitable basis. This study led to the enactment of legislation that provided a minimum foundation program and, perhaps more important, the means for reorganizing small units into larger, more efficient school administrative districts embracing all pupils from the kindergarten through high school. Through this act some of the long-sought goals were achieved, such as establishing a basic educational program for every child in the state toward which the state would contribute a greater share of the cost of education.

The per-pupil allowances in the foundation program have been updated at each session of the Legislature in an attempt to keep pace with increased local costs. They, however, have never been realistic in terms of local costs and actually have been approximately 2 years in arrears.

The adoption of the Uniform Effort Principle in 1965 was another forward step in sound financing of education (41). Under this law, each unit was required to make a 20-mill effort on an equalized valuation toward the support of the foundation program, with the state providing the difference between the local assessment and the foundation program.

In the 25-year period from 1940 to 1965, state appropriations for subsidies to local units increased from slightly less than $2 million to nearly $26 million. The percentage of state support, however, did not increase proportionately but remained fairly constant at approximately 27 percent in 1965.

In addition to the foundation program aid, which includes construction aid varying from 18 percent to 66 percent according to the wealth of the unit, there are various special subsidies for driver education, vocational education, special education, adult evening schools, education of island children and children of temporary residents, education of orphans, and professional credits for teachers.

At the conclusion of this period, the state's responsibility in underwriting local school operations has become accepted. While state support in Maine is still much below the national average of state support, it is on the rise.

Extension of Services to Pupils

With the possible exception of financial measures, more laws have been enacted since 1900 for the benefit and extension of services to pupils than on any other educational subject. Educational opportunities were extended from the kindergarten to evening classes for out-of-school youth and adults. Included were programs for physically handicapped and educable mentally retarded youth, practical nursing, vocational and occupational courses, firemanship training, fisheries education, and driver education.

Conveyance was extended for elementary pupils, and towns were authorized to convey secondary pupils. Conveyance of the latter is still optional in the separate towns but is required in the school administrative districts. Board may be paid and subsidized for island children. A rather serious controversy arose in 1959 over the conveyance of pupils to private parochial schools, but this was resolved by permissive legislation allowing a town or city to vote to convey these pupils. No state subsidy is paid on such expenditures.

A shared-time arrangement with private schools was approved in 1965 without opposition. Under this plan, pupils at private schools may attend a public school for a portion of their classes, and their attendance at the public schools is prorated for subsidy purposes.

Compulsory attendance laws were strengthened and truancy made a juvenile offense. The compulsory attendance age was raised from 14 in 1900 to 17 in 1965.

The school year was gradually lengthened from 20 to 26 weeks in 1909, to 30 in 1915, to 32 in 1929, and to 36 in 1953.

Transfer of supervision and operation of the schools on the Penobscot and Passamaquoddy Indian Reservations to the department in 1965 added another assignment. These and many other acts indicate a concern by the state for the individual and especially a desire to extend educational opportunity.

School District Organization

The national trend toward consolidation of small schools into larger and more efficient units has had a successful counterpart in Maine. Prior to 1947, most of the towns had consolidated their elementary schools into central schools with a single grade per teacher, but many small high schools were still in operation. It was recognized for years that these small schools were extremely expensive and inefficient, that they were wasteful of teacher personnel, and that they offered a very limited curriculum.

In 1947, a significant act known as the Community School District Act was passed, allowing towns to join together to operate a secondary school (42). There were no financial incentives or inducements other than that two or more towns might have a better secondary school if they joined together. Much of the leadership in this action was given by the state department ably assisted by Senator Carroll L. McKusick, a former teacher who was chairman of the Joint Legislative Committee on Education and who later served for many years on the State Board of Education. A few districts were formed in which it was mutually beneficial for towns to join together, but because of the lack of financial rewards for operation only 32 towns combined.

The Community School District Act, however, is significant in that it was the forerunner of the Sinclair Act of 1957, which provided additional state assistance when towns joined together. This act included all grades, kindergarten through 12, and Maine was spared the ills of overlapping intermediate districts. The formation of 65 administrative districts embracing 238 towns has reduced the number of small high schools, and the consensus of opinion is that better education has resulted.

The formation of the school administrative districts was not accepted unanimously and wholeheartedly in all sections of the state. In the early history of administrative district formation, many questions were raised, and a few cases were carried through the courts. School Administrative District No. 3 in Waldo County, comprising 11 towns, had more than its share of legal troubles and was the battleground on which the legal problems for all districts were fought to a conclusion. The decisions were generally favorable to the district, and the court was sometimes irked by having the same questions presented repeatedly. In one case, the superior court stated that the issue had been laid to rest and the parties could not litigate it again. The court appeared to be in tune with the space age terminology of the times, for in a 1962 decision Judge Armand DuFresne wrote:

> The pad from which they say their legal rocket ship is now being prepared for launching is Landover vs. Denner. Unless the plaintiffs in their count down realize that their vehicle must be completely overhauled, they shall witness the major fizzle of the century (43).

The complaint was dismissed with prejudice and with costs.

State Standards and Accreditation of Schools

Standards for high schools developed slowly. In 1909, an act designed for the improvement of free high schools established three classes of approval dependent on the number of courses offered, the amount expended for instruction, and the length of the school year. Recognition of the relationship between the curricular offering and level of expenditure is evident for the first time in legal terms. In 1915, the commissioner's authority was strengthened by an act requiring that the course of study prescribed by him be followed. It was some years before truly broad-based standards for curriculum approval were established, for emphasis continued to be placed on the academic studies. As late as 1930, the statutes stated that "the ancient or modern languages and music shall not be taught except by direction of the Superintending School Committee." These barriers were gradually overcome and more flexibility allowed.

In 1955, a system of optional state accreditation of secondary schools was authorized in addition to the basic minimum approval that had been required of all schools (44). Standards for the new level of classification were designed to reflect a high-quality program. The commissioner was assisted in developing criteria by an advisory committee composed of representatives of both public and private schools. These criteria have been reviewed periodically in recent years, and increased emphasis has been placed on quality of instruction rather than facilities.

The accreditation program has been credited with stimulating many worthwhile improvements in local schools, such as a program of studies to better meet the needs of pupils with differing abilities, the expansion of libraries, a reduction in teaching loads to levels that will permit effective teaching, and greater emphasis on the preparation of teachers. Within a decade, 59 schools were accredited out of a total of approximately 125, and the department reported that probably more had been achieved by this program than any other single development in the previous 50 years. Considering the high quality of standards established and the number of necessary small schools due to a sparsity of population, the record is commendable. In 1965, plans were initiated to extend accreditation to elementary schools.

The State and Higher Education

In 1900, the five state normal schools and Madawaska Training School were under the jurisdiction of a Normal School Board of Trustees. The state superintendent was the executive officer for the board and was nominally in charge until 1930, when the deputy commissioner was assigned this responsibility. The annual appropriation in 1900 was only $31,000, as compared with approximately $3,800,000 65 years later, not including nearly $5,000,000 for capital outlay.

In 1949, the normal school board was terminated, and its duties and functions were assumed by the newly created State Board of Education (45). The 2- and 3-year normal schools gradually emerged as state teachers colleges with degree-granting status. In 1965, they became state colleges with authority, subject to state board approval, to offer 5-year programs and to grant appropriate baccalaureate degrees.

The primary function of the state colleges has been to prepare elementary teachers. Other areas of concentration include art, business, health and physical education, home economics, industrial arts, music, and special education for the handicapped and mentally retarded. The board and state colleges have operated on a planned program to meet the need for teachers in the state. An estimated goal of 2,900 students was made in 1958 but was revised to 5,100 by 1975. This projection is in line with one made in 1965 by the Academy for Educational Development, which estimated that higher education enrollments would double by 1975.

Departmental Organization

Growth in the number of professional personnel and accompanying clerical staff has been substantial and has accelerated in recent years. In 1920, the department consisted of a state superintendent, a deputy, two rural educators, and directors of programs for vocational rehabilitation, home economics, industrial education, secondary schools, and schools in the Unorganized Territory. From such a modest beginning has evolved in 1966 a staff of 260 professional and clerical personnel. Positions have been added, from time to time, to meet the demand for services by the schools of the state. All of the department personnel are in the classified service, with the exception of the commissioner, who is selected by the state board and whose salary is set by statute.

The organization of the department is determined by the board, which, on the recommendation of the commissioner, may organize and, from time to time, reorganize the department into divisions, branches, or sections as may be found necessary or desirable.

In 1956, the department had grown to the point at which a reorganization was necessary. On the recommendation of Commissioner Warren G. Hill, the staff was grouped into six major divisions and subdivisions known as bureaus. The major divisions established were administrative services, with responsibility for district reorganization and research; finance, which in the 1965-67 biennium dispensed nearly $75 million; field services, embracing planning of school facilities, transportation, surplus foods, property, and school lunch programs; professional services, with responsibility for higher education, certification, and placement of teachers; instruction, including elementary and secondary school programs and special services; and vocational rehabilitation, whose function is to assist handicapped persons to become self-supporting. The organizational pattern conforms quite closely to national trends, with adaptations to Maine's needs.

The State Department and Federal Aids to Education

The first real impact of federal aid on Maine education came with the passage of the Smith-Hughes Vocational Act of 1917. A state plan for extending vocational education was developed, and thereafter a director of vocational education and supervisors of agriculture, industrial arts, and home economics were employed. The state superintendent served as chairman of the State Board of Vocational Education, which was required under the act. This board was later superseded by the State Board of Education when it was created in 1949. Further funds were provided and programs extended under the George-Barden Act of 1946 and the Vocational Education Act of 1963. The grants of federal funds stimulated local efforts and led to the acceptance and establishment of courses in vocational education in many high schools.

For several years, Public Law 874, providing aid to federally impacted areas, was by far the largest federal program. It provided assistance to 79 separate units amounting to approximately $3 million annually. The largest recipients of this aid were Limestone, Bangor, Presque Isle, Brunswick, and Kittery. The department and local school officials have found the federal administration of this program to be excellent, and oftentimes it has been pointed to as an illustration of federal aid without interference and restrictive controls.

The National Defense Education Act of 1958 brought much-needed funds to strengthen the department's supervisory staff and to provide for the purchase of equipment by local schools. The department had recognized the need for subject matter supervisors for years but, except for vocational education, which was federally assisted, had not been able to convince the Legislature of this necessity. This act made it possible to employ state supervisors in science, mathematics, foreign languages, social studies, and reading and to add a second person in guidance. One unfortunate aspect was encountered in that even though large sums of federal money were available for equipment, the local units were not able to provide sufficient matching money to utilize all the funds available.

The statistical services of the department were expanded under Title X. Procedures for the collection of information and methods of reporting were revised in keeping with federal handbooks, and Maine data were made more reliable and consistent with practices followed elsewhere.

In another program the department served as the agency for coordination and operation of all the Neighborhood Youth Corps Projects of the state, involving nearly 3,000 students. A financial crisis appeared in the making at one time in the early days of Youth Corps Projects when a ruling from the state personnel department required that all students employed on local projects be registered with that department and certified before payrolls could be approved. A call to the Governor soon eliminated the red tape, and the checks were sent on their way to expectant students.

The Elementary and Secondary Education Act of 1965 had the greatest impact on education in Maine. Title I projects amounting to approximately $4 million provided funds for the employment of teacher aides to work with classroom teachers, remedial programs in the basic skill subjects, extension of the school day, evening programs of supervised study and individual help, classes for the mentally retarded, and speech therapy. The programs were designed to assist the underprivileged, and all funds available were utilized. Some clashes occurred between local school officials and Office of Economic Opportunity officials over jurisdiction of programs, but in most sections the issues were resolved amicably. The department and local officials have felt strongly that educational programs should be operated by school officials and that the Congress should transfer such programs as Head Start and adult education to school authorities.

Under Title II of the same act, the state distributed funds to local units for the purchase of library books and materials. The state also served as the agency for the distribution of books to religious and independent schools. This plan was approved by the attorney general on the basis that the funds were federal funds and that federal law allows participation by nonpublic schools.

The state utilized other federal funds available. The state board, serving as the higher education facilities commission, has allotted several millions of federal funds for college classrooms. The Vocational Act of 1963 stimulated vocational courses in secondary schools and expansion of postsecondary vocational-technical institutes. The Manpower Development and Training Act, operated jointly with the Employment Security Commission, made training and retraining possible for members of the labor force. Other programs under which substantial grants have been administered include Head Start, rehabilitation, surplus foods and commodities, school lunch, and Civil Defense.

Although a harmonious relationship has existed between the department and the federal government, there has been a distinct feeling that a more general form of aid would be preferable to such a proliferation of special aids administered through so many federal departments and bureaus.

Advisory Committees

The Maine department has moved from a one-man role to one that has made increasing use of advisory committees composed of lay and professional people. The philosophy that has governed these activities was expressed in 1938 by Commissioner Packard:

> I have a conviction that a better type of educational opportunity for our youth depends on informed public opinion. Any far-sighted school official should lay his plans with the cooperation of teachers, school committees, influential citizens and friends of education (46).

The use of advisory committees appears to have begun with vocational education in 1917 and has been used with excellent results in other fields. A Governor's Advisory Committee on Education, composed of approximately one hundred members, has supported sound and progressive measures. An Educational Conference Board organized during Dr. Espy's commissionership, with representation from organizations having an interest in youth, has devoted much time and study to educational matters and has spoken effectively for the combined membership at legislative hearings. Other advisory committees have been formed as needs have arisen, and their assistance has been beneficial.

Conclusion

The role of the Maine Department of Education has been one of constant effort to provide leadership and services. Progress and change have not been spectacular, but the slow and steady pace has been due largely to the lack of resources. Two world wars, with accompanying shortages of teachers and other personnel, and a major depression had retarding effects. But education as measured by the opportunities to students has emerged in a stronger position than at any other time in the period covered. The leaders and legislative powers have not been ones to rush to embrace every new idea proposed, and perhaps for this reason there are few instances where a program once begun has failed or been discontinued. The department has given top priority at all times to assisting local school officials and citizens and has endeavored to provide the leadership and coordination needed to develop and implement statewide plans for the attainment of desirable goals. The growth of staff and the extension of services in recent years have added much to the department's influence.

This résumé is concluded by reference to a review of the department conducted by the U.S. Office of Education in 1967 at the request of Commissioner William T. Logan, Jr. It was made by nationally prominent educators supplemented by local legislators and citizens. In the report the department is described as one which has grown from a small, service-oriented agency to one providing educational leadership. The report found that the department had attained a higher level of service and leadership while remaining sensitive to the principle of local control. It commended the strategy and philosophy used in dealing with local educational agencies and found that a proper degree of flexibility had been exercised in beginning new programs with federal funds. It considered that the salary schedule for staff members was unsatisfactory and that crowded office conditions threatened its efficiency. However, it concluded that despite these deficiencies the department was "functioning efficiently in mounting the constantly increasing dimensions of an educational program for the state" (47).

FOOTNOTES

1. William D. Williamson, *History of the State of Maine,* I (Hallowell, Maine: Glazier, Masters and Smith, 1839), 334.
2. Massachusetts Bay Colony, *Ancient Charters and Laws* (Boston: T. B. Wait and Co., 1814), p. 73.
3. *Ibid.,* p. 186.
4. *York Town Records,* I, 440.
5. *Ibid.,* II, 2.
6. Massachusetts, *Laws, 1780-1807,* I, sec. 1, 470. Maine became a state in 1820.
7. *Ibid.,* p. 471.
8. Maine, *Public Laws (1822),* ch. 196, sec. 1.
9. *Ibid.* (1846), ch. 195, sec. 9.
10. Superintendent of Common Schools, *Maine School Report, 1876,* p. 32.
11. *Ibid.,* p. 39.
12. *Ibid.,* p. 89.
13. Maine, *Public Laws* (1854), ch. 89, sec. 11.
14. *Ibid.,* 1923, ch. 5, sec. 120.
15. Maine, *Constitution* (1820), art. 8.
16. Massachusetts, *Laws and Resolves* (Boston: Adams and Nourse, 1894), pp. 417-18.
17. Superintendent of Public Schools, *Maine School Reports, 1895-1907.*
18. Superintendent of Public Schools, *Maine School Report, 1903,* p. 56.
19. *Ibid.,* pp. 58-60.
20. Superintendent of Public Schools, *Maine School Report, 1909,* p. 19.
21. Maine, *Public Laws* (1917), ch. 188, sec. 1.
22. William H. Soule, "Payson Smith: His Life and Work in Education" (unpublished dissertation, Boston University, 1967), p. 208. Now being microfilmed by University of Michigan.
23. Maine, *State School Bulletin,* II, No. 1 (1918), 6.
24. *Ibid.,* II, No. 4 (1918), 5.
25. *Ibid.,* III, No. 7 (December 1919), 6.
26. Superintendent of Public Schools, *Maine School Report, 1921,* p. 9.
27. Maine, *State School Bulletin* (April 1931), p. 3.
28. *Ibid.,* II, No. 3 (January 1933), 14-15.
29. *Ibid.,* III, No. 3 (January 1934), 2.
30. Department of Education, *State Certification of Teachers Manual of Information* (Augusta: The Department, 1924), p. 1.
31. James B. Conant, *Education of American Teachers* (New York: McGraw Hill Book Co., 1963), pp. 209-18.
32. Maine, *Public Laws* (1913), ch. 75.
33. Maine, *State School Bulletin,* XIII, No. 2 (November 1943), 2.
34. *Ibid.,* XVII, No. 1 (September 1947), 2.
35. Superintendent of Public Schools, *Maine School Report, 1915,* p. 14.
36. Maine, *State School Bulletin,* IV, No. 5 (October 1920), 4.

37. Public School Finance Commission, *The Financing of the Public Schools of Maine* (Augusta: The Commission, 1934), pp. 64-69.
38. Maine, *Public Laws* (1921), ch. 173, sec. 1.
39. Maine, *Public Laws* (1919), ch. 228, secs. 1-2.
40. Maine Legislative Research Committee, *School Finances and Needs* (Chicago: J. L. Jacobs Co., 1957).
41. Maine, *Public Laws* (1965), ch. 429, secs. 1-7.
42. Maine, *Public Laws* (1947), ch. 357, secs. 92A-92K.
43. Peavey *v.* Nickerson, Maine, Sup. Ct., March 5, 1962.
44. Maine, *Public Laws* (1955), ch. 369, sec. 1.
45. Maine, *Public Laws* (1949), ch. 403, sec. 9.
46. Maine, *State School Bulletin,* VIII, No. 1 (September 1938), 2.
47. U.S. Office of Education and Maine Department of Education, *Report on the Review of the Maine State Department of Education, Under Title V, P. L. 89-10* (Augusta: The Department, 1967), p. 7.

BIBLIOGRAPHY

Public Documents

Maine. *Constitution* (1820).

—— *Biennial and Special Session Laws, 1820-1966.*

Massachusetts. *Laws 1780-1807.*

—— *Laws and Resolves.* Boston: Adams and Nourse, 1894.

Massachusetts Bay Colony. *Ancient Charters and Laws.* Boston: T. B. Wait and Co., 1814.

Peavey *v.* Nickerson. Maine Supreme Court, Waldo County *S.S.,* March 5, 1962.

York Town. *York Town Records.* Minutes of annual town meeting.

Books

Burrage, Henry Sweetser. *Maine History.* Portland, Maine: Marks Printing House, 1914.

Chadbourne, Ava Harriet. *A History of Education in Maine.* Bangor: Furbush Roberts Printing Co., 1936.

Clifford, Harold Burton. *Maine and Her People.* Freeport, Maine: Bond Wheelwright Co., 1963.

Conant, James B. *Education of American Teachers.* New York: McGraw-Hill Book Co., 1963.

McBride, Jack G. *ETV for Maine.* Washington, D.C.: Jansky and Bailey, 1960.

Marriner, Ernest Cummings. *Remembered Maine.* Waterville, Maine: Colby College Press, 1957.

Snow, Charles Augustus. *The History and Development of Public School Supervision in Maine.* Orono, Maine: University Press, 1939.

Starkey, Glenn W. *Maine, Its History, Resources and Government.* Boston: Silver, Burdett and Co., 1947.

Stetson, William Wallace. *History and Civil Government of Maine.* Chicago: Werner School Book Co., 1898.

Williamson, William D. *History of the State of Maine.* 2 vols. Hallowell, Maine: Glazier, Masters and Smith, 1839.

Reports

Advisory Commission for the Higher Education Study. *The First Business of Our Times.* Augusta: The Academy for Educational Development, 1966.

Advisory Committee on Education. *Report of the Sub-Committee on the Sinclair Law.* Augusta: The Committee, 1958.

Board of Education. *Annual Reports, 1847-1852.* Augusta: The Board.

Department of Education. *Maine State School Bulletin.* Augusta: The Department, 1917-65.

—— *State Certification of Teachers Manual of Information.* Augusta: The Department, 1924.

Maine Legislative Research Committee. *School Finances and Needs.* Chicago: J. L. Jacobs Co., 1957.

Public School Finance Commission. *The Financing of the Public Schools of Maine.* Augusta: The Commission, 1934.

School District Commission. *Educational Opportunities Improve Through Consolidation.* Augusta: The Commission, 1961.

Superintendent of Common Schools and Commissioner of Education. *Annual and Biennial Reports, 1853-1965.* Augusta: Board of Education.

U.S. Office of Education and Maine Department of Education. *Report on the Review of the Maine State Department of Education, Under Title V, Pub. L. 89-10.* Augusta: Department of Education, 1967.

Unpublished Material

Soule, William H. "Payson Smith: His Life and Work in Education." Unpublished dissertation, Boston University, 1967. Now being microfilmed by University of Michigan.

Appendix A

MAINE CHIEF STATE SCHOOL OFFICERS

State Commissioners

1854-55	Charles H. Lord	1907-17	Payson Smith
1855-56	Mark H. Dunnell	1917	Glenn W. Starkey
1856-57	J. P. Craig	1917-29	A. O. Thomas
1857-60	Mark H. Dunnell	1929-41	B. E. Packard
1860-65	Edward P. Weston	1941-47	H. V. Gilson
1865-68	Edward Ballard	1947-52	Harland A. Ladd
1868-76	Warren Johnson	1952	William O. Bailey
1876-78	William J. Corthell	1952-55	Herbert G. Espy
1878-79	Nelson A. Luce	1955-56	Kermit S. Nickerson
1879-80	Edward S. Morris	1956-63	Warren G. Hill
1880-95	Nelson A. Luce	1963-64	Kermit S. Nickerson
1895-1907	W. W. Stetson	1964-	William T. Logan, Jr.

Appendix B

Chart I.--MAINE DEPARTMENT OF EDUCATION, 1955

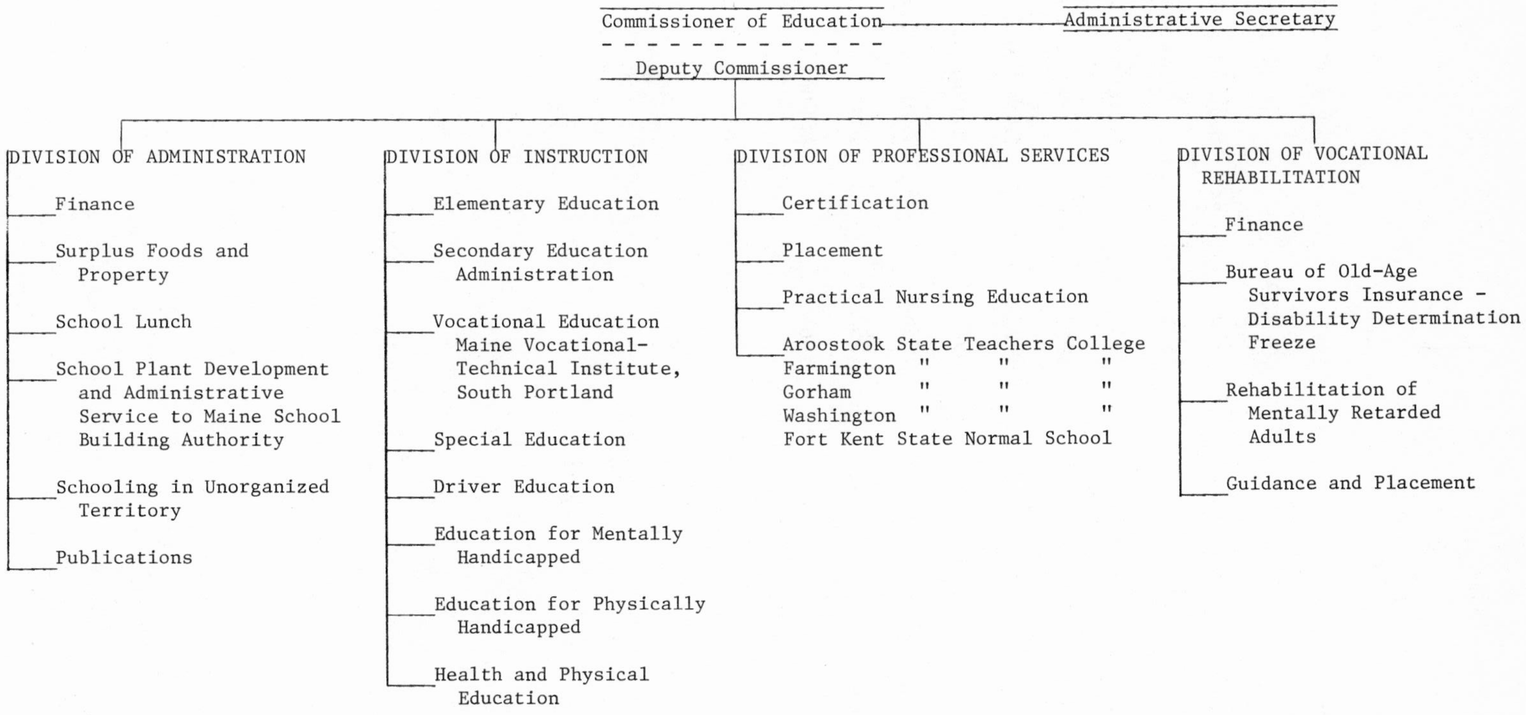

Commissioner of Education — Administrative Secretary

Deputy Commissioner

DIVISION OF ADMINISTRATION
- Finance
- Surplus Foods and Property
- School Lunch
- School Plant Development and Administrative Service to Maine School Building Authority
- Schooling in Unorganized Territory
- Publications

DIVISION OF INSTRUCTION
- Elementary Education
- Secondary Education Administration
- Vocational Education
  Maine Vocational-Technical Institute, South Portland
- Special Education
- Driver Education
- Education for Mentally Handicapped
- Education for Physically Handicapped
- Health and Physical Education

DIVISION OF PROFESSIONAL SERVICES
- Certification
- Placement
- Practical Nursing Education
- Aroostook State Teachers College
  Farmington " " "
  Gorham " " "
  Washington " " "
  Fort Kent State Normal School

DIVISION OF VOCATIONAL REHABILITATION
- Finance
- Bureau of Old-Age Survivors Insurance - Disability Determination Freeze
- Rehabilitation of Mentally Retarded Adults
- Guidance and Placement

Appendix B

Chart II.--MAINE DEPARTMENT OF EDUCATION, 1968

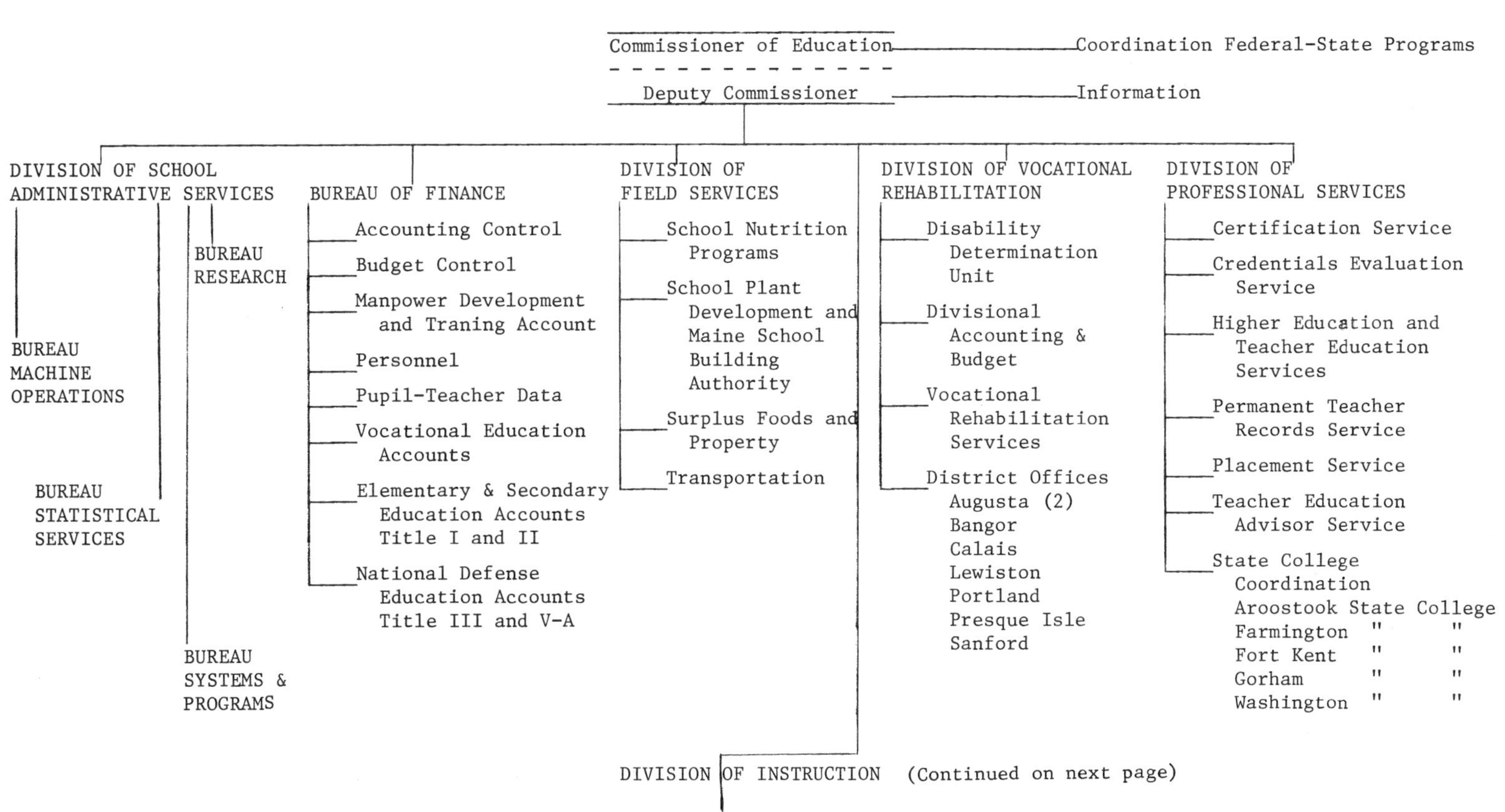

(Continued on next page)

Appendix B

Chart II.--MAINE DEPARTMENT OF EDUCATION, 1968 (Continued)

DIVISION OF INSTRUCTION

- BUREAU OF ELEMENTARY EDUCATION AND SUPERVISION
  - Approval of Public and Private Elementary Schools
  - Art Education
  - Elementary Education
  - Health and Physical Education
  - Music Education
  - Schooling of Children in Unorganized Territory and Indian Children
  - National Defense Education Act - Title III
    - Arts and Humanities
    - English
    - Mathematics
    - Modern Foreign Languages
    - Reading
    - Science
    - Social Studies
- BUREAU OF SECONDARY EDUCATION AND SPECIAL PROJECTS
  - Approval & Accreditation of Public & Private Secondary Schools
  - Driver Education
  - Educational Television
  - High School Equivalency Certificates
  - Newspaper in the Classroom
  - Secondary Supervision
  - Elementary & Secondary Education Act
    - Program for Disadvantaged Children- Title I
    - Library Services - Title II
    - Supplemental Services - Title III
- BUREAU OF GUIDANCE AND SPECIAL EDUCATION
  - Adult Education (General Evening Schools)
  - Civil Defense Adult Education
  - Education for Emotionally Disturbed Children
  - Education for Mentally Retarded Children
  - Education for Physically Handicapped Children
  - Elementary & Secondary Education Act
    - Basic Adult Education Title III
  - National Defense Education Act Title V-A
    - Guidance
  - Maine State Scholarship Board
  - Coordination of Special Education
  - Education for Speech and Hearing Handicapped Children
- BUREAU OF VOCATIONAL EDUCATION
  - Agriculture
  - Business & Distributive Education
  - Fire Service Training
  - Health Occupations
  - Home Economics
  - Industrial Arts Education
  - Manpower Development & Training
  - Trade & Industrial Education
  - Vocational-Technical Institutes (4)
- NEIGHBORHOOD YOUTH CORPS
  - District Offices
    - Auburn
    - Augusta
    - Bangor

20 Maryland

DEPARTMENT OF EDUCATION
Robert Moyer
David W. Zimmerman

Contents

INTRODUCTION

Public education was well organized in Maryland by 1900, but the system's achievements were highly unsatisfactory. The Maryland Department of Education was undermanned and poorly equipped, professionalism was practically non-existent, and politics permeated and controlled the entire system at both the state and local levels. Today, Maryland's public education system is achieving eminently satisfactory results. In large measure, this is due to an increase in staff from 3 to 550 people in nine divisions, the development of professional leadership in all of the department's activities, and the elimination of politics from its operation over the last half century.

In 1916, the State Legislature moved to eliminate the factors that had hampered the Department of Education in the early 1900's by adopting the recommendations made for the Maryland Educational Survey Commission by Abraham Flexner and Frank P. Bachman of the General Education Board of New York. The Maryland General Assembly had created the commission in 1914 to make a comprehensive study of the public school system and had appropriated $5,000 to carry it out. As this amount was insufficient, the commission requested the General Education Board, then conducting educational surveys throughout the country, to undertake the Maryland survey. In consenting to do so, the board agreed to supplement the legislative appropriation with $7,500, or such part as might be needed. To direct the survey, the board employed Flexner, who had been one of its secretaries, and Dr. Bachman, a former assistant superintendent of schools in Cleveland.

BEFORE 1900: DEVELOPING A CENTRALIZED SYSTEM

Between 1671 and 1867, several attempts were made to establish some type of free schooling in Maryland, but they were ineffective. The most notable effort came in 1825, when the General Assembly passed an "act to provide for the public instruction of youth in primary schools throughout the State," subject to a general referendum (1). Based on a report prepared by Littleton Dennis Teackle of Somerset County, the act provided for a state superintendent, appointed by the Governor and council; nine commissioners of primary schools for each county, appointed by the justices of the levy courts; and no more than eighteen inspectors of primary schools, also appointed by the justices. However, the voters rejected the act in 1826, and Maryland continued without a state system of education.

Although the 1825 act marked the General Assembly's acceptance of the principles of modern public education, it had two cardinal defects –

> The first of which was due to the fact that its provisions were largely borrowed from states in which the people were trained in local political action in the township system, while the people of Maryland had no such training .... The second was the want of adequate provisions for raising money sufficient to carry it out even on the fallacious basis of the Lancaster system, in which one teacher was deemed sufficient for the instruction of any number of children up to 400 or 500 that could be brought together in one schoolroom (2).

As a result, this legislation accomplished very little.

The Act of 1825 stipulated that the establishment and regulation of Baltimore's public and private schools be vested in the mayor and city council. If the mayor and city council did not establish a system of public education within 5 years, however, the city would lose this privilege and also be under the full effect of the act. Three years later, Baltimore passed an ordinance appointing commissioners and directing that they establish six male and six female schools, but then failed to provide adequate funds. In 1829, when the commissioners presented their first report, they stated that one female and two male schools had been established on the monitorial (Lancastrian) system, under which a single teacher was responsible for 200 to 300 or more pupils. The teacher selected "clever" pupils to teach as many as 10 other pupils lessons that the teacher previously had taught. These schools, which caught on only slowly at first, never became common throughout the city.

Prior to the Civil War, public education in Maryland was primarily a local responsibility. But the constitution adopted in 1864 provided for the establishment and maintenance of free public schools and created the office of state superintendent. Governor Bradford appointed an Episcopalian minister, the Reverend Libertus Van Bokkelen, rector of St. Timothy's Church at Catonsville, as the first state superintendent. Dr. Van Bokkelen investigated both public and private schools in and out of the state, and he corresponded with college presidents and superintendents where state systems existed. In accordance with the constitutional mandate "that the State Superintendent should within thirty days after the first session of the General Assembly report a uniform system of free public schools" (3), he submitted a comprehensive analysis. The General Assembly then enacted his recommendations into law.

The plan accepted by the assembly provided for a uniform statewide system of common schools that would qualify the pupils for admission into any of its high schools and academies; uniform secondary courses, qualifying high school pupils for admission into any of the colleges; and scientific, classical, and mathematical instruction in the colleges, qualifying every graduate for admission into the state university's law, medical, or mechanical departments. The 1865 assembly established the first state normal school in Baltimore City (now known as Towson State College), which enrolled its first students the following year. The plan concentrated considerable power in the hands of state officials (4).

Dr. Van Bokkelen received national recognition as an educator. In 1866, he was elected a director of the National Teachers' Association, its secretary in 1868, and its president in 1869 (5). Within the state he was recognized as an outstanding leader in promoting the cause of free public education.

During the reactionary period following the Civil War, the majority of the people had no desire to allow a centralized government so much authority over their schools. A public school system headed by a State Board of Education comprised of the Governor, the lieutenant governor, the speaker of the House, and a state superintendent appointed by the Governor was entirely unpalatable to the counties, and especially to Baltimore City. There were immediate outcries. A convention met in 1867 to repeal the Constitution of 1864 and to enact a new one. Thus, a good beginning was doomed to early failure. It should be noted that the Constitution of 1864 was adopted only with great difficulty; without the vote of Maryland soldiers serving in the Union Army, who overwhelmingly supported it, it would never have been approved.

The new constitution provided for free public schools and their maintenance, but it did not retain the office of state superintendent. The essentially conservative document was adopted by a vote of 47,152 to 23,036. The forces for local control were able to muster enough votes in the assembly to pass a new school law in 1868 which, although it retained some of the features of the 1865 act that implemented the 1864 constitution, restored the right of local self-government in school affairs and left the private academies that received state aid in the same position they had occupied previously. The 1868 law gave a board of three trustees the authority to control the normal school, whose principal was granted general supervision over all of the state's public schools.

Two years later, the forces for stronger state control were able to push a bill through the General Assembly reestablishing the Maryland State Board of Education and designating the principal of the normal school as the state superintendent of public instruction. Fortunately, the principal, M. Alexander Newell, was a noted scholar and a man of broad attainment who had organized the Maryland State Normal School 5 years earlier. During the next 20 years, he infused new life into the schools.

E. Barrett Prettyman succeeded Dr. Newell in 1890 and conducted a conservative administration for the next decade. Dr. Prettyman, a forceful public speaker with exceptional general knowledge, gave considerable thought to the processes of public school administration. But rather than introduce change, he concentrated on emphasizing and refining the elements he considered good in the system he had inherited.

In the development of Maryland's governmental structure, the county played a vital role from the beginning. While school districts were established later as "conveniences," the county had always been the administrative unit, with the county school superintendent serving as the head of the local school system. Thus, by the end of the nineteenth century, Maryland had a sound state-county organizational pattern that enabled it from the beginning to provide educational opportunities on a much broader base.

FROM 1900 TO WORLD WAR I

Political Superintendents

In 1900, the General Assembly separated the state superintendent of public instruction's office from the principalship of the normal school, and Governor John Walter Smith appointed M. Bates Stephens as the new superintendent. Governor Smith appointed Dr. Stephens for 4 years by and with the consent of the Senate; he could be removed at the Governor's pleasure when sanctioned by a two-thirds vote of the board. Dr. Stephens, one of Governor Smith's close political associates, had been a school examiner (county superintendent) since 1886. Actually, no professional qualifications were required for appointment as superintendent; the only legal limitation imposed on the Governor's free choice was that the appointee be "competent." As state superintendent, he did not have the strong executive powers that had been proposed in 1864.

In 1915, at the time of the Flexner-Bachman survey, the board consisted of eight members, including the Governor and the superintendent. The other six were appointed by the Governor, subject to Senate confirmation, for 6-year terms staggered so that two terms expired every 2 years; two had to be from the political party defeated at the preceding gubernatorial election. As the Governor controlled the board and as there were no professional requirements for the state superintendent, it was almost certain that the administration of the schools would be based more on politics and less on professionalism than the public interest dictated. As the Flexner-Bachman survey stated, "the arrangement . . . makes the State Department of Education part and parcel of the elected state government and thus exposes it—and with it, public education in general—to the vicissitudes of state politics" (6).

The Flexner-Bachman survey found that the same situation existed in the counties. The school superintendents were selected by the politically constituted county boards, and politicians in most counties regarded the superintendency as "spoils" and occupied it on that basis. The survey found that in the first year of the new Democratic administration in 1900, 16 new county superintendents were appointed in Maryland's 23 counties. Perhaps the most flagrant example of misuse of political power uncovered by the survey involved a county superintendent who actually reclassified teachers in order to lower their salaries and reduce the amount of money needed by the county school board. When a majority of the county commissioners—the elected local governing body—belonged to the same political party, they frequently appealed to the county superintendent to reduce the school budgets on grounds of party loyalty or political expediency.

The statutes established no professional qualifications and no minimum salaries for county superintendents. The Flexner-Bachman survey discovered that 3 of the superintendents in office in 1915 had not finished high school, 4 others had no preparation beyond secondary school, and no more than 6 of the 15 who were college graduates had any special professional preparation. Only 3 of the 23 superintendents received salaries of more than $2,000 per year, and 1 was paid only $800. Under such circumstances, particularly since most county offices and staffs were totally inadequate, only a few superintendents could render skilled leadership.

As state superintendent, Dr. Stephens not only served as a member of the state board, but he also was the executive who carried out the board's orders. At the same time, he had certain supervisory and inspection responsibilities, which included using his discretion to accept or reject normal school and college diplomas issued by other states and defining the qualifications of teachers for teaching high school domestic science, manual training, and other special courses. It was his responsibility to rate the teachers who were not normal school graduates but were offering practical experience and training that they considered equivalent. The state superintendent examined the county school boards' reports and expenditures, and he prepared and distributed pamphlets to teachers on the prevailing methods of instruction in various subjects.

One of Dr. Stephens' first acts was to develop a uniform course of study for both elementary and high schools. Through his efforts, commercial subjects and agriculture were introduced into the secondary schools as electives. Also, he introduced modern methods for handling the schools' business. Stephens was able to secure legislation providing state aid to the high schools, supervision of them, certification of high school teachers, and a minimum standard of professional training for elementary school teachers.

It would have been nearly impossible for the state superintendent to "supervise," "inspect," or "pass upon" schools and to handle other business without a trained staff. Unfortunately, as late as 1915, he had a single assistant and one clerk, paid $2,000 and $1,200 respectively. The superintendent's salary was only $3,000, although he was allowed $500 for expenses; an additional $1,000 for furniture, supplies, and printing; and $3,000 for travel to meetings, printing, and supplies. In other words, the entire state department cost the state only $10,700 per year. With such a meager budget and small staff, the department had to perform many of its tasks only superficially.

The 1915 survey concluded that Maryland's system of public education, though soundly conceived and organized, was producing, on the whole, extremely unsatisfactory results. It stated:

> A few counties possess good and steadily improving schools; a good school may be found here and there in other counties. But the large majority of the schools are poor; teachers are, for the most part, poorly trained; instruction is ineffective and obsolete; children attend school with disastrous irregularity; school buildings are far too often in unsatisfactory condition, school grounds frequently neglected and untidy (7).

At this time, the state had 1,935 schools for 200,783 white pupils with about 5,000 teachers, and about 550 schools for 44,475 Negro students with about 1,000 teachers. The survey reported that only 8 percent of the 500 white and 50 Negro schools visited had satisfactory physical conditions. Nearly 13 percent of the state's white elementary teachers had only an elementary education themselves; more than 20 percent had spent only 1 or 2 years in high school; and only a third had completed a 4-year high school course. Less than 5 percent had received a standard normal school education. Of the remainder, some had briefly attended normal school, others had spent some time in college, and a few had qualified for bachelor degrees. In summary, only about 10 percent of the white elementary teaching staff were normal school or college graduates or had some college work; not quite one-third were fairly well prepared; and at least one-third were practically untrained. Only about 8 percent of the Negro elementary school teachers had a standard normal school education. The high school teachers showed a similar range of inadequacy, with about two-fifths adequately prepared, two-fifths from 1 to 4 years short, and the remaining one-fifth woefully lacking in preparation.

On the basis of the 1910 federal census of children between 6 and 14 years of age, out of each 100 children, 17 white and 29 Negro were not enrolled in 1914. Significantly, of those who were enrolled, 31 percent in the one-room rural schools and 19 percent in the village schools were absent on the average of more than half the time. Under these circumstances, it was difficult to educate the state's pupils even if the instruction were adequate. Small wonder that the 1910 census ranked Maryland thirty-first among the states in literacy.

Financing Education

Paradoxically, Maryland was one of the states that made large contributions for local education, contributing about one-third of the total cost while the counties provided about two-thirds. Together, the state and counties furnished an annual total outlay amounting to about $5 million. But there were wide variations among the counties. In 1914, for example, the expenditures per pupil ranged from $9.17 to $28.21. The school tax rates varied from 17¢ to 45¢ per $100 of assessed valuation, while the taxable wealth back of each child varied from $710 to $3,840. For the state as a whole, the taxable wealth in 1900 was slightly more than $600 million, so that in back of each schoolchild was taxable property valued at just over $1,500. Every $100 of taxable property contributed 42¢ to education in that year. The largest source of money contributed by the state was the state school tax levied against all taxable property. It did not recognize the differences in ability to support education at the local level; in fact, some counties receiving the larger allocation from states funds were themselves making the least effort.

Other money available for the state's distribution came from the Common Free School Fund and the Academic Fund. The common fund, consisting in part of interest from a $278,000 investment derived from taxes on state bank stock, was distributed in equal shares to the counties. It also included $229,000 derived from interest payments made by the U.S. government to Maryland in 1858 in the amount of $169,000 for funds the state had advanced to the federal government during the War of 1812. It was distributed annually to the counties, based on their representation in the General Assembly. The Surplus Revenue Fund constituted the third source for the common fund. Since Maryland had spent the original amount distributed by the federal government in 1837 from surplus revenues, the state was obligated to pay the schools an annual income equal to 5-percent interest. In 1910, it began deducting this amount from the state school tax.

The Academic Fund was a regular annual appropriation from the general treasury to encourage secondary education. By 1831, it had become standard policy to appropriate $1,200 a year to each county, irrespective of size and needs. Although it was a political pork barrel and there were many abuses, political deals kept it going.

Most of the state's funds were intended to support the elementary schools. Only three conditions were attached to this aid: Schools had to be kept open at least 9 months (the Negro schools varied from 4 to 10 months); white teachers had to be paid at least $300; and all allocations for textbooks and supplies had to be spent for those purposes.

The standards for high schools were raised by the state board in 1910, and this stimulated more progress during the ensuing 5 years than had been made in the previous 20. To be eligible for state funds, 4-year high schools now had to have at least 80 students, 4 academic teachers, a 4-year course with at least a 36-week year, an approved course of study, manual training, home economics, a commercial or agricultural course, a library, a laboratory, and $250 worth of science apparatus and material. The principal had to receive at least $1,000 per year, and the teachers–whose qualifications were passed on by the state board–had to receive at least $500 each (8).

EDUCATIONAL REFORM

The increased standards for the high school in 1910 were merely the starting point for a campaign to raise the state to a leading educational position. Leonard Ayers, an acknowledged national authority on tests and measurement, prepared "An Index Number for State School Systems" for use by the U.S. Census, which revealed that in comparison with other states Maryland's system was undergoing a rapid decline: from twelfth in 1890, to nineteenth in 1900, and to thirty-third in 1910 (9). Obviously, there were still many problems that prompted educators throughout the state to demand reforms.

The Reformers

During the nineteenth century, most of the initiative for improvements in the educational system had come from within the profession. Although informed and enlightened citizens played a key role in subsequent developments, the leadership came from the dedicated professionals, men who were experts in the field of education. These men included

Littleton Dennis Teackle, who was appointed state superintendent in 1826 but never served legally because the act establishing his office required that his appointment be ratified by the voters, and they refused to do so. Libertus Van Bokkelen has been mentioned as an early leader. Another was James W. Thompson of Queen Anne's County, the only school examiner (county superintendent) in the early eighties who had been a teacher; most of the others were doctors of divinity or doctors of medicine. One of the outstanding lay leaders who fought for a statewide system of universal education was Joseph M. Cushing, who served as chairman of the education committee of the Constitutional Convention of 1864 (10).

A columnist for the *Baltimore Sun,* writing under the nom de plume of Ezekiel Cheever, through his column-one, front-page discussions of "School Issues," probably was more responsible than any other individual for Maryland's educators' becoming activists in the second decade of the twentieth century. Cheever not only schooled himself in educational administration by extensive reading, but he attended the more important state and national educational conventions and personally contacted recognized authorities. He also was able to deal effectively with school issues in Maryland because of his membership in two relatively small power-structure groups. One consisted of superintendents of schools and certain public and nonpublic professional educators, and the other of individuals in key positions to influence public opinion. These were primarily social groups, meeting in the evening to discuss public issues over dinner.

Educators and interested laymen followed Cheever in exerting considerable pressure on the Legislature to enact the Flexner-Bachman recommendations into law. The legislation enacted by the assembly in 1916 was of marked significance not only to Maryland but to U.S. educational history as well.

The 1916 Legislation

The 1916 school laws divorced the State Board of Education from politics and invested it with reasonable and important responsibilities and authority. They prescribed high academic, professional, and experience qualifications for the state superintendent, named him the executive officer of the board, and stipulated his additional responsibilities. At the same time, the qualifications and duties of the county school superintendents were prescribed. The laws put state aid on a sound basis, provided the basis for an effective statewide attendance law, and set forth regulations for the county boards of education and county superintendents similar to those for the state board and the state superintendent.

Perhaps the most significant accomplishment of the 1916 laws was that they provided a legal basis for professional leadership. In achieving the major objective—taking the schools out of politics—they established the present-day legal structure for the state department. The Governor was authorized to appoint seven members to the board for 7 years without regard to parties and without confirmation by the Senate, the terms staggered to ensure a continuity of membership. Neither the Governor nor the state superintendent was given membership on the board. Under the new laws, the board no longer attempted to administer the schools; it legislated within its power and passed judgment on the efficiency of its paid officers. The board was given authority to appoint the state superintendent and members of his staff and to fix their salaries, within the limits of its appropriation. The laws also provided for an enlarged, adequate staff of administrative, supervisory, and clerical assistants in the state superintendent's office to carry out the board's policies.

Perhaps the most important responsibility conferred on the board by Maryland's new model school code was that of considering the educational needs of the state and, with the advice of the state superintendent, recommending to the Governor and the General Assembly the legislation it deemed desirable. These recommendations were to be in the form of prepared bills. The Senate and the House committees were then obligated to grant the board and the state superintendent a hearing on request. This clearly placed the major responsibility for Maryland's public education on the State Board of Education.

These laws produced a precedent-setting combination of state and local authority in public education. By centralizing the administration at the state level, they made possible a unity of design and uniformity of standards while allowing local authority to manage the details within the general framework. This enabled the local communities to exercise local initiative and ensured the schools of community interest, effort, pride, and sacrifice for their progress. Because of the broad, sweeping organization, these laws have been flexible enough to allow for societal changes, including those produced by two world wars.

Almost as soon as the assembly enacted the new code in 1916, Ezekiel Cheever began an unrelenting attack on the incumbent state superintendent, M. Bates Stephens. His efforts culminated in the publication of a series of charges in the January 4, 1920, edition of the *Baltimore Sun.* The main charges were:

1. The state superintendent was seldom to be found in his office.
2. Someone in the state department overruled the normal school principal's nomination of a teacher of music to serve on the summer school faculty.
3. The state superintendent has looked on his office as one for educational fellowship instead of educational leadership.
4. A large balance of unexpended school appropriations, earning no interest, was carried in a bank in which

the state superintendent was a director and an extensive stockholder.

5. The state superintendent controlled appointments to the State Board of Education.
6. The state department was manipulated to foster political control in the counties, but refused to exert its influence in the counties to solve purely professional problems.
7. The state superintendent had failed to prepare himself fully to meet the legal scholastic requirements of his office, written in the law of 1916 (11).

Rebuttals and further attacks followed.

(In 1934, when it appeared that the Baltimore City public schools were becoming enmeshed in partisan politics, Cheever came out of retirement to attack those who were supposedly using the school system to further their own ambitions. It is possible that certain individuals failed to gain high office because of his exposé (12).)

In April 1920, the newly elected Governor Ritchie announced the reappointment of one member to the state board and replaced two others whose terms had expired. On the same day, the old board in special session reelected Stephens after passing a bylaw providing that the state superintendent be elected not less than 30 days, nor more than 90 days, before the expiration of the incumbent's term. On Friday, April 30, the Governor sent a call for the State Board of Education to meet him at noon on Tuesday, May 4. On the following day, the newspapers announced that the state board had repealed Stephens' election and rescinded the bylaw at the Governor's demand.

On June 4, 1920, for the first time, the new State Board of Education *appointed* a state superintendent of schools when Albert S. Cook agreed to accept the position. Dr. Cook had earned a national reputation both for developing courses of study and for supervising classroom instruction while serving as Baltimore County school superintendent.

Reform Under Superintendent Albert S. Cook

Dr. Cook inherited a school system that had matured considerably in the years preceding his appointment. One writer commenting on progress during the latter part of the nineteenth century stated:

> For the log hut we have the substantial, or it may be the artistic, schoolhouse; for the peripatetic schoolmaster, wandering form county to county and finding no place to rest, we have a teacher firmly established from term to term and from year to year, until legally displaced. In place of teachers working under a permit or without a permit, we have regular examinations and formal certificates. In place of the individual preferences and prejudices of teachers, one being all for Grammar and another all for Arithmetic, we have a regular schedule of studies, the same in principle for all schools of the same grade, but yet elastic enough to accommodate itself to different conditions. In place of the three R's we have a course of instruction which leads to liberal culture in many directions. We have almost abolished the rod – it may linger yet in secluded districts, like the smallpox, but it is no longer the ultima ratio regnum. Physical culture is recognized as a prime necessity and industrial training has made a promising beginning in more than one county (13).

Cook was able to operate from a position of strength that none of his predecessors had enjoyed, for the new school code allowed him a 4-year term and gave him such authority that he could have built a highly regulatory, centralized State Department of Education—as found in other states—had he desired to do so. For instance, it was the superintendent's responsibility to explain the true intent and meaning of the school laws. To enforce these provisions, he could withhold state funds if necessary. It was his responsibility to approve school sites, plans, specifications, and the contracts for constructing school buildings. Subject to the rules and regulations of the state board, he had the responsibility for certificating all public school teachers. The state superintendent also was to prepare for the state board's approval courses of study for the different grades and kinds of elementary schools, high schools, and normal schools, and the college courses for teachers.

Dr. Cook possessed the ability, temperament, and training to develop the highly professional Department of Education that could improve and advance the cause of public education in Maryland. In addition, he was an experienced and competent educator in teaching and administration. He was vitally interested in placing only well-trained and highly qualified superintendents and supervisors as well as teachers in each local school system, which meant mandating adequate state-supported salaries to facilitate recruiting them. He inspired confidence in those outside the school system as well as those in it, and he enjoyed an especially close relationship with Maryland's Governors, particularly Albert C. Ritchie, a personal friend with whom he frequently relaxed and played cards.

An Equalization Program

The outstanding achievement of Dr. Cook's administration was the enactment of an equalization law by the General Assembly. The law constituted one of the major advances of the state's public school system. Based on Cook's philosophy that there should be equal educational opportunity for all children in the state, it provided the legal and financial bases for such a program by guaranteeing a minimum state support behind each child in Maryland, regardless of the financial status of his particular community. Any county that could not carry the state's minimum program on a levy of 67¢ per $100 of assessed evaluation, plus other forms of state aid, received support from the equalization fund.

The Maryland equalization plan required the schools to employ qualified teachers, who were to be paid guaranteed minimum salaries with increments at various intervals for successful experience. It required the public schools for white youth to remain in session at least 180 days per year, and the Negro schools at least 140 days per year. The schools were to maintain an adequate supply of free books and materials, there was to be a competent instructional supervisor in every school unit, and the county superintendents were to furnish effective professional leadership. Professor Fletcher Harper Swift of the University of California described it as "perhaps the most far-reaching and scientific method from the standpoint of equalizing revenues of any state in the Union" (14).

The principle of equalized financial aid as provided in the 1922 act enabled Maryland's counties to employ better-trained and more-experienced teachers, purchase aids for instruction, consolidate the schools more rapidly, and provide transportation for elementary pupils. The entire school system was upgraded, and when Frank P. Bachman returned to study the changes that had taken place since his 1915 survey, he commented that Maryland now had the best legally established, the most unified, the most efficient, and the most professional state school system in America.

The two principal elements in the equalization plan are mandated minimum salary scales for teachers, and the required local tax levy to support the guaranteed minimum program of education. The following chart indicates the changes that have been made in these elements since 1922:

Year	Salary scale	Local tax levy (per $100 assessed valuation)
1922	$ 950 – 1,150 elementary 1,150 – 1,350 secondary	$0.67
1939	1,200 – 1,800 all teachers	0.51
1945	1,500 – 2,250	0.56
1947	2,200 – 3,800	0.65
1953	2,500 – 4,300	0.65
1955	2,800 – 4,600	0.75
1958	3,200 – 5,000	0.75
1960	3,200 – 5,300	0.75
1961	3,600 – 5,700	0.87
1964	4,800 – 7,000	1.20 (calculated)
1967	5,100 – 7,400	1.33 (calculated)

To what extent have these equalized financial efforts resulted in an equal educational opportunity for each child in the state? The wide range of pupil abilities both within and between local school systems requires differentiated programs of instruction and well-prepared, compassionate teachers who are sensitive to the needs of children at various stages of development. The record indicates clearly that equal educational opportunity does not exist in 1968. Thousands of Maryland children with learning disabilities due to handicaps of one kind or another are not receiving an education appropriate to their needs for the simple reason that there are insufficient funds to provide it. It costs significantly more to educate a disadvantaged child than it does a so-called normal, average child. More professional personnel, teachers, specialists in learning disabilities, guidance counselors, psychologists, social workers, and teaching materials are required to individualize instruction. The state has provided certain special categorical financial assistance, in addition to the foundation program, to help solve this problem. The most recent of these aids was enacted in 1967 for the economically disadvantaged (15).

Adult Education

The department's leadership improved and extended the instructional, supervisory, and supporting services essential to a strong school system in several ways. During the nineteenth century, Maryland, like many other states, had recognized that illiteracy existed in certain groups and that the influx of immigrants required action on the part of its educators. The earliest public adult education program in Maryland—indeed, in the entire United States—consisted of evening schools organized in Baltimore City in 1839.

> These were followed by vocational classes in Garrett, Allegany [sic], and Washington Counties. The impetus for a much more comprehensive program came much later—in 1933 when the Federal government provided funds to organize classes for the unemployed. Within a year these programs were statewide. The first state appropriation for general adult education was made in 1939 in the amount of $10,000 (16).

At present, the appropriation is $75,000, supplemented by $585,466 in federal funds for basic and vocational education.

Vocational Education

Since the constitution had made the state fundamentally responsible for education and the state had adopted the thesis that each individual's education should prepare him for a full and effective life, it was the state's philosophy that youth who did not go to college should receive an education that would prepare them for the world of work.

Accordingly, the Maryland Legislature accepted the provisions of the Smith-Hughes Act, passed by Congress in 1917, which made it possible to establish vocational education courses in the state's high schools. The vocational education program received additional funds and expanded considerably between 1919 and 1933. During the Depression years from 1933 to 1937, vocational education remained on a plateau; but following the George-Deen Act in 1937 and the acts of 1946, 1956, and 1958, additional federal appropriations gave the program tremendous impetus. With these increasing federal appropriations, the state was able to organize classes in trade and industry, home economics, distributive education, practical nursing, technical occupations necessary for national defense, and agriculture.

However, the greatest impact in vocational education came as a result of the Vocational Education Act of 1963. This legislation broadened the scope of the program from specialized areas to more generalized areas of need, such as health occupations, technician training, business and office occupations, trades and industry, agriculture and related occupations, home economics with particular emphasis on the wage-earning aspect, and such other programs as may be required from time to time to meet the technology of the world of work.

Education of the Handicapped

In 1929, the Legislature provided financial assistance which stimulated Baltimore City and some of the counties to begin educating handicapped children. This movement heralded the beginning of adapting education to fit the needs of individual children. Classes were organized for crippled children, and, as interest and demand increased, the state provided increased financial assistance for these special classes and for teaching the homebound. The 1940 annual report shows that 441 children were receiving this special education. In later years, special classes were established for the mentally retarded and emotionally handicapped. In 1965, there were 25,196 children enrolled in all special education programs; 80 percent were mentally retarded.

In 1929, the department also established a program in vocational rehabilitation for handicapped youth and adults 14 years of age and older, with federal funds available on a 1-1 matching basis with the state's funds. In 1933, when the Federal Emergency Relief funds were appropriated on a matching basis for this purpose, the program was expanded to include those who were unemployable because of permanent physical disability as a result of injury while employed or because of an accident, disease, congenital defect, or mental disability. Successive changes in the federal law have enabled the program to be expanded in recent years under the dynamic and aggressive leadership of the department and the support and cooperation of local community social agencies.

The Consolidation Movement

The development of the vocational and adult education movement paralleled that of the consolidation movement. Economy often was used as the argument for consolidating ineffective and expensive schools, but the State Department of Education's viewpoint was that the larger schools were able to offer a wider variety of courses that would fit the needs of the individual as well as the community. It also was discovered that the larger, consolidated schools obtained better results academically and created greater public interest. The consolidation movement received an impetus from the progressive urbanization of the state and the increasing number of automobiles and good roads. It was stimulated particularly by the 1916 law and by aid given for transportation by the equalization fund. Maryland was one of the few states that enacted consolidation and transportation laws at the same time. In 1915, nearly 1,500 schools housed almost 245,000 pupils, with 40 percent of the teachers in one-room schools that were generally deplorably inadequate. Forty years later, the number of schools was less than 1,000, only 9 of them one-room schools. At the same time, enrollment had more than tripled.

With the enactment of the Equalization Law in 1922, the state accelerated its efforts to provide pupil transportation at public expense. According to the annual reports of the Maryland State Department of Education, four counties in the state were transporting pupils in 1910. This number had increased to 10 counties in 1915, 18 in 1920, and 22 in 1925. St. Mary's, the last holdout, began providing pupil transportation in 1927. No record of the number of pupils transported is available prior to 1923, when 4,334—or 2.8 percent of the total enrollment in the counties—were reported as receiving transportation. By 1928, the number had increased to 15,907, representing 10 percent of the total enrollment; in 1933, 40,308 pupils, or 23.3 percent; in 1938, 56,268 pupils, or 32.6 percent; and in 1943, 74,711 pupils, or 41 percent of the total enrollment in the counties. In 1967, 336,201 pupils, or 56.2 percent, were transported.

State financial assistance for pupil transportation began in 1928 for elementary pupils as part of the foundation program to be supported by the Equalization Law. Beginning in 1933, 50 percent of the cost of transporting high school pupils was included in state aid. The full cost of high school transportation was included in 1947.

The state developed school transportation very carefully, setting standards for buses, qualifications for bus drivers, and requirements for bus inspections. Maryland's safety record has been excellent, and all pupils now receive free transportation if they do not live within a "reasonable distance," or, in some cases, if the roads they must travel are unusually dangerous.

THE PROFESSIONALIZATION OF TEACHERS

Certification

The groundwork for the professional preparation of teachers was embodied in the 1916 School Code, which placed the certification of teachers and supervisors in the hands of the state superintendent. It also set definite certification requirements for county school officials. Superintendents and high school principals were required to have a year of graduate work, including prescribed academic and professional courses. The elementary school principals had to have 2.5 years of normal and college work, including courses in administration and supervision. The 1916 law also stipulated that administrative and supervisory certificates could be issued only if the candidates had successful teaching experience.

High school teachers of academic subjects were to be college graduates who had taken professional courses and had a minimum of preparation in their particular subjects. High school teachers of special subjects were required to have 2 years of college work, about one-third in general academic subjects and two-thirds in their special subjects, education, and the art of teaching the subject. Four years of normal and college work (or equivalent preparation), with courses in elementary school methods and supervision, were required for an elementary school supervisor's certificate. Before the second- and third-grade certificates (valid for 2 years) could be renewed, the teacher had to take 6 semester hours of academic and professional preparation. However, any certificate could be renewed if the applicant showed evidence of successful experience and professional spirit, which was interpreted to mean a recommendation from the superintendent.

After the summer of 1924, certification by examination was abolished, and the certificates were issued only on the basis of accredited training in approved institutions. The qualifications for admittance into teaching have gradually been raised until at the present time Maryland ranks among those states having the highest certification requirements.

Teacher Education

One of Maryland's most distinguished sons, Francis Scott Key, consistently and eloquently advocated that the state provide teacher education. In 1827, Key delivered the principal commencement address for his alma mater, St. John's College, and he proposed that teachers be given instruction on the university level under competent professors of education. The following statement from his address, delivered more than 140 years ago, is particularly significant:

> That this [education] is a science and a very difficult one, will be admitted. Yet among the numbers engaged in it very few have received any instruction. It is true, there are some good works on the subject, but there are also bad ones. Nor is it true that those so employed seek for instruction on the subject. Every teacher adopts his own system and improves it only by his experience. This cannot be supposed right by any one who considers its importance. The most learned man in science and languages may be utterly unable to excite a desire for learning in his pupils, to form their minds, dispositions, habits, and tastes, and to impart his knowledge to them in a way best suited to their capacities. All this is certainly his business as a teacher (17).

Samuel Knox, a Presbyterian clergyman and the first principal of Frederick Academy, shared the prize offered in 1796 by the American Philosophical Society for a plan for –

> The best system of liberal education and literary instruction adapted to the genius of the Government of the United States; comprehending also a plan for instituting and conducting public schools in this country on principles of the most extensive utility (18).

Knox, a distinguished Marylander who gained a measure of national prominence and advocated the education of teachers–and for a while operated a private academy in Baltimore–was offered the first professorship at the University of Virginia by Thomas Jefferson. He declined.

At the time the United States entered World War I, Maryland had only two normal schools for white teachers and one for Negro teachers. All of these institutions were for training elementary school teachers. Towson had been established in Baltimore in 1865, and Frostburg in 1897. Bowie had been founded in 1911 as the Maryland Normal and Industrial School, and for the first time the state had created an institution for educating teachers for the Negro schools.

Albert S. Cook had worked to develop teacher education long before he was appointed state superintendent. Shortly after his appointment as superintendent of schools in Baltimore County in 1900, he began conducting a 2-week teacher institute each summer. Rather than spend the time giving inspirational lectures–the common practice in those days–Dr. Cook organized professional schools of high quality, which featured programs of instruction and training that were selected with great care and administered with rare skill. The instructors were drawn from various parts of the country and were among the best known in their respective fields. The impact of these institutes was felt throughout the state as other superintendents emulated Baltimore County's experience and organized their own.

Dr. Cook not only provided professional training and stimulation to help his teachers become more efficient from year to year, but he attempted to hire and retain competent teachers in all of his schools. He profoundly influenced the selection and education of teachers in America. By 1910, a decade after he had become the superintendent, educators recognized that the Baltimore County schools were the best county educational system in the United States.

Since the 1916 laws made the state superintendent and the Board of Education members trustees of the state normal schools, Dr. Cook was eager to accept the challenge to concentrate on the professional education of teachers. For more than a decade after the Normal Department at Washington College had been abandoned in 1910, the state had not specifically provided for the education of teachers on the Eastern Shore. In 1924, Superintendent Cook was instrumental in persuading the General Assembly to authorize and to provide the necessary funds for the establishment of a state normal school at Salisbury.

America enjoyed great prosperity during the 1920's and could afford to pay more for teachers. Maryland's 1922 school law guaranteed a minimum salary schedule for teachers who were professionally trained, considerably enhancing the attractiveness of teaching in the state. An unprecedented number of students were seeking training, and teachers were remaining longer in the service of public schools than ever before. Teaching was finally approaching the status of a true profession. Outside of Baltimore, the proportion of teachers with "standard" training increased from 35 percent in 1922 to 85 percent in 1927.

The state found that, by improving its teacher pension and retirement plans, it attracted more prospective teachers into Maryland schools. Before 1916, a public school teacher with 25 years' service who became unable to teach because of physical or mental disability, who was 60 years of age, had a record without reproach, and was without means of comfortable support could apply to the State Board of Education for a pension of $200 per year if the county school commissioners agreed to substantiate the application. In 1923, the General Assembly doubled this pension to $400. Four years later, the assembly passed an actuarially sound retirement law patterned on the system Baltimore City had established for its teachers in January of 1926, providing for contributions from the teachers and the state on a 50-50 basis. Although given the option of joining or not, most of the teachers joined, and the plan proved to be a big gain for the profession.

During the Depression of the thirties, the department and the schools found there were so many teachers seeking employment that it was possible to upgrade the requirements. The normal schools had offered 2-year courses since 1916. In 1931, on the recommendation of the state superintendent and the State Board of Education, the General Assembly enacted legislation stipulating that the normal school courses should require "for graduation a total of not less than three years' work" (19). Again, 3 years later, on Dr. Cook's recommendation, the Legislature increased the graduation requirement to 4 years, and the normal schools became teachers colleges with authority to issue bachelor's degrees.

Compared with many other states, Maryland moved slowly in upgrading its normal schools. But, in line with the state superintendents' careful, long-range planning, the state waited until conditions fully justified advancing the institutions to a higher status. As has been true with other states, Maryland's major economic depressions seem to have initiated major educational advances, gains which have not been lost with the return of prosperity.

In 1939, as the Depression neared its end and competition for well-trained, professional teachers increased, Maryland improved its chances of attracting them by establishing a single salary scale for teachers of both elementary and secondary schools, which was based on preparation and experience. From 1922 to 1939, while a dual salary was in effect, high school teachers were paid more than elementary teachers of equal training and experience. The 8- or 9-year periods in which increments could be earned were too short, and teachers reaching the maximum relatively early in their careers lacked further financial incentive to improve themselves. The 1939 legislation's new minimum salary provided for biennial increments extending over 17 years. The act accomplished its purpose and considerably increased the drawing power of the Maryland schools.

In 1941, the Legislature equalized the salaries of white and Negro teachers as the outgrowth of litigation started in a U.S. District Court in 1939. Although no order requiring equalization was issued, State Superintendent Cook recommended the legislation to correct the discrimination.

WORLD WAR II AND ITS AFTERMATH, 1942 TO 1964

When Dr. Cook stepped into the superintendency in 1920, the department consisted of only 10 professional employees; when he retired in March 1942, there were 34. The man who inherited this expanded department, Thomas G. Pullen, Jr., had been a member of it for 8 years, 6 of them as assistant state superintendent. The Pullen administration spanned the period of World War II, the subsequent population and knowledge explosion, and the renaissance in education at all levels.

Dr. Pullen combined a classical education and training with a pragmatic, philosophical outlook. Educated in the liberal arts tradition, he became a successful Latin teacher before rising through the ranks from classroom teacher to principal, to county superintendent, to state supervisor, to assistant state superintendent, and finally to the state superintendency. In all, he devoted 38 years of his life to the schoolchildren and teachers of Maryland.

Philosophy and Change

Throughout his career, and especially as state superintendent, Dr. Pullen typified the great teacher who ministers to the needs of all with a deep and abiding interest. A kindly and understanding scholar, extremely articulate, knowledgeable, and persuasive, it was the combination of these qualities that enabled him to follow through effectively on creative ideas and to implement plans for carrying them out. His duties were not always easy, and he engaged in many battles in discharging his responsibilities as he saw them, regardless of the personal consequences. Pullen's stature grew along with the state school system; respect for him as a person increased with the passing years well beyond the confines of Maryland. Superintendent Pullen used his knowledge in a scholarly manner to enrich and direct his own life, and, because he was such an inspirational leader, he enriched the lives of his associates—especially the teachers and children. In summary, this visionary and creative educator, who held fast to the philosophy that education should lead to a desirable course of action on the part of the learner, is credited with making a difference in the lives of countless individuals.

At the time Dr. Pullen took office, as a result of both state and national legislation, the state department was rapidly assuming new responsibilities for an ever-broadening educational enterprise. It was fortuitous for Maryland that there was a man with the creative genius and intellectual capacity to cope successfully with these demands. Under Dr. Pullen, the state department was able to develop new and more efficient methods, assuming additional duties with a minimum of additions to the staff.

Dr. Pullen shared his predecessor's belief that the department's main responsibility should be to exert professional leadership and that the local school system should administer the schools with a minimum of regulation by the state. This is contrary to the practice in most states, where new duties brought with them continuously increasing, highly centralized bureaucracy at the state level. This did not mean, however, that the department did not expand. The new needs caused by the tremendous influx of new residents during and after World War II, coupled with an increasing public awareness of education's importance and the emphasis on education that accompanies the inauguration of a technical era, caused the department to increase its staff from 34 in 1942 to 208 at the end of Pullen's 22-year term. It was a period of unprecedented growth.

Through all the growth and changes, an informed and interested citizenry affirmed the state's commitment to support education across a broad front. Consistently throughout this period came a succession of legislative acts increasing the state's financial support and the minimum salaries for teachers and other professional personnel. Thus, Maryland was able to achieve the highest mandated state salary schedule in the United States. The state has given unstinting financial support to school building construction, current expenses and building construction for community colleges, general and teacher education scholarships to institutions of higher education, and current expenses and building construction for public libraries.

The 1939 Legislature showed considerable foresight when it passed an act creating a commission to survey the public schools and the state teachers colleges. It charged the commission to define the public school system's obligations, describe the existing conditions, and make specific recommendations for improving them to Governor Herbert R. O'Conor. The study was to include curriculum offerings; vocational preparation; adult education; recreational, cultural, and aesthetic opportunities; health and social services; and adjustment to higher education. The commission also was to consider the financial implications and the adequacy of the physical plant to perform the services of any proposed revision of programs.

The commission selected Herbert B. Bruner, professor of education at Columbia University's Teachers College, to direct the study. The survey commission decided that the Maryland schools' chief need was for an intensive and continued program development that would help every pupil in the state to realize his full potential as a citizen in a flourishing democracy and to prepare him to meet existing emergencies and those bound to follow the Second World War. In his report early in 1941, Bruner made two major recommendations: One was a proposal for a long-term study of the curriculum, and the other was to extend school systems from 11 to 12 grades. If Maryland's schools were to attain the scope envisioned, the Bruner survey strongly recommended that the 11-grade system, organized in 20 counties as 7 years of elementary and 4 years of secondary schooling, be extended to 12 grades on a 6-6 or 6-3-3 basis.

The Legislature did not act on these recommendations until 1945. But the shift to a 6-3-3 grade organization was gradually effected, so that by 1952, the junior high school had become an integral part of Maryland's unified program of education. The addition of the twelfth grade helped the schools take care of the burgeoning student population and at the same time enabled them to give the students a richer program of instruction.

The Department's Expanding Responsibilities

The state department had to be completely flexible when fast-breaking developments were taking place in education. To a large extent the department shaped these developments and organized quickly to meet the added responsibilities. For instance, one of the most significant accomplishments in this period was the establishment of a statewide system of public libraries, authorized by the Legislature in 1945. The department created a library extension division to provide the direction and supervision necessary to develop a modern and efficient system. By 1967, all of the local political subdivisions had taken steps to establish a countywide library system. Initially, state aid provided only for the books; but later, under a formula similar to that used by the public schools, the state provided general financial aid.

During this same period, school libraries also grew rapidly. In the larger school systems, they developed into instructional material centers. Since 1965, federal funds have provided an added impetus to this growth and development, and Maryland has received $2,645,425 annually from federal sources for this purpose.

During the 22 years prior to 1942, school enrollment had increased by only 41,328; but from 1942 to 1964, it soared from 282,946 to 704,379–a gain of 421,433 pupils. During the first 3 years of this period, the enrollment actually decreased, as the gains from the growth of high schools in the thirties were offset in the forties by the decrease in the birth rate during the Depression years. The upward trend occurring in the late forties was a result of considerable migration of new residents into Maryland because of wartime employment opportunities and increased federal activities. The population explosion that finally hit the schools in the fifties and continued into the sixties, a nationwide phenomenon, brought the largest increase of school population in history. Maryland is still one of the six fastest growing states in the nation.

Another factor contributing to this vast expansion of the public school system was a 1947 amendment to the compulsory school attendance law, which made mandatory the attendance of children between the ages of 7 and 16. The schools' holding power was further strengthened as programs were developed to meet the needs of all pupils, including the handicapped, and the general public became increasingly cognizant of the real need for education in today's world.

Although Dr. Pullen planted and nurtured an abundance of ideas when he was state superintendent, many of them were guided to fruition with help from outside the State Department of Education. In fact, he not only received support from educators but gained the backing of lay leaders representing a broad spectrum of the major statewide groups. For instance, during a 1942 conference held at the University of Maryland to discuss the immediate educational needs in Maryland, the participants decided to form an informal steering committee composed of three representatives each from the Maryland Congress of Parents and Teachers, the Maryland State Teachers' Association, the Maryland Superintendents' Association (composed of local superintendents), and the State Department of Education. This committee, which now includes representatives from other key lay groups as well, still functions. Though not widely known, it has played an important role in advancing public education in Maryland over the last quarter of a century. It is a powerful combination, but it has exercised its power judiciously to gain broad-based support for its proposals.

It was vital to Maryland that the public seriously study the needs of the public schools because of the dramatic changes during the postwar period. To develop quality education, the state encouraged the schools to reduce the size of their classes. It emphasized special classes for handicapped pupils, which required a lower pupil-teacher ratio. Thus, while the school population was more than doubling from 1940 to 1965, the professional staff tripled from nearly 9,000 to almost 30,000 staff members. The schools also added various subject matter specialists, librarians, and counselors.

The state department, supported by the various lay organizations, encouraged these changes and added staff personnel to assist the schools in developing quality programs with lower pupil-teacher ratios. In 1947, the assembly amended the 1922 law, which provided for supervision, to include state support for high school supervision, and at the same time expanded the pupil-personnel services.

In the midst of rapidly changing conditions during this period, leaders in industry, business, and government emphasized that quality education required good physical facilities as well as good teachers. This caused the General Assembly in 1947 to enact the first state aid law for school construction. It provided $10 per pupil enrolled, with a matching requirement of 5¢ on each $100 assessed evaluation. This was increased to $20 per pupil in 1956 and to $22 in 1961. An incentive of $70 per additional pupil was provided for growing school systems.

In 1949, a state grant of $60 million was made available for construction on a 1-3 matching basis, the funds to be allocated on a basis of $60 per pupil enrolled. Also, the local political subdivisions were permitted to borrow through the state.

A significant advance was provided by the legislation of 1967, which placed the state's share for school construction on an equalization basis. The state's share includes both current construction and debt service incurred prior to July 1, 1967. This new program places Maryland in the forefront nationally and will require an annual appropriation by the state of approximately $50 million.

In order to facilitate this vast school construction program and to carry out the provisions of the law requiring the state superintendent to pass on all proposals for the purchase of school sites and all plans and specifications for remodeling old school buildings and constructing new ones, the bureau of school plant planning was added to the department in 1949.

The state department not only assisted the schools in securing qualified teachers for these newly constructed schools, but it also upgraded the certification requirements and improved the retirement system to retain them. Beginning in 1940, the state required all new teachers to have bachelor's degrees and to have taken specified courses from accredited institutions as a minimum for regular certificates. In 1947, the department established the certification and accreditation division, whose main duties were to approve the teacher-training programs in the institutions and to coordinate them with the basic requirements.

In 1961, new requirements were established to provide three approaches to certification. They required more depth in content courses for elementary-level certificates and increased the content requirements in the various subject fields at the secondary level. The new bylaw of the state board established two certificates—professional and advanced professional—to reduce the number of kinds of certificates issued. To achieve the advanced professional certificate, the applicant had to take a fifth year at a college or university. The renewal provisions were changed to allow credit for certain in-service experiences in lieu of college courses, thus making them easier to administer. The certificates also provided for an easier transition from elementary to secondary teaching or from secondary to elementary in an effort to develop equality in the professional training for teachers at both levels.

The retirement system law was amended to provide a fixed benefit plan to guarantee a retirement allowance of one-seventieth of the average final compensation for each year of creditable service. Death benefits were revised to provide a stated pension credit to a spouse (if named as beneficiary) of any deceased member who was eligible for service retirement. The basis for averaging the final compensation was changed from the 10 highest years to 5 consecutive years of highest earnings, and Social Security was added to the members' coverage effective July 1, 1956. The new system increased disability benefits, gave supplemental benefits to teachers without Social Security, and extended the privileges of the system to retired members working part time and to substitute teachers if their combined earnings and retirement income did not exceed the average of the highest 5 years' salary as a teacher. The change made it possible for employees who entered the military service to receive full credit for both the state's and individual's contributions, and it was now possible to transfer credit service from other retirement systems within the state, such as city employees or state employees.

Dr. Pullen believed in involving people in matters affecting their own work and well-being. Thus, he attempted in every way possible to establish a good human relations policy so that both he and his staff would have rapport with the local superintendents or their representatives, and all major efforts toward improving the school program could be undertaken cooperatively. Specifically, he and the department offered conferences and workshops, surveys and studies, supervisory and consultant services, bulletins and reports that kept them in constant touch with the people in the field. As various agencies demanded that the state play a more active role, the department's good relations with the local units enabled it to move quickly and efficiently.

The General Assembly dictated the department's expansion to a certain extent. For instance, a law passed in 1941 enabling high school dropouts to qualify for the Certificate of High School Equivalency made it necessary to establish eight official testing centers about the state (20). Again in 1945, the assembly passed a law to protect citizens against schools not qualified to give the training they claimed; many substandard schools had formed overnight to take advantage of students receiving money under the GI Bill. This law, involving the accreditation of nonpublic schools, and the act providing for the establishment and operation of public libraries required the department to add staff members. A law passed in 1961 permitting the establishment and operation of public and community colleges also required the department to add qualified people. These and other programs required administration and leadership at the state level to implement the provisions, so the department grew.

Federal legislation also accounted for increases in the department's staff. The school lunch, special milk, and surplus commodities programs affected all local school systems in the state, as did the National Defense Education Act of 1958 (NDEA), which strengthened courses in science, mathematics, and modern languages. The department participates in all these programs, along with those related to the Manpower Development and Training Act and the Civil Defense Education Program. The vocational rehabilitation division, formed in 1942 with support from federal funds, employs nearly half of the state department's total employees. It has a central office, a metropolitan Baltimore office, three district offices, and eight branch offices. Thus, the department has grown from a single unit in 1942 to nine divisions today.

Federal-State Relations

A prophetic statement by State Superintendent Albert S. Cook in a commencement address at the University of Maryland in 1925 expresses succinctly the thrust of federal-state relations:

> I am not among those who have been obsessed with the idea of Federal aid to public education; I believe that the respective states, eventually, if and when they desire, can work out their educational destinies; but where we see the wonderful progress of agriculture, of agriculture education, of vocational education and of road building through the impetus of Federal aid, we are confronted with a condition, not a theory. The state that repudiates the idea of Federal aid for public education thereby assumes the responsibility for producing the results by its own efforts, by its own financial and moral support

of its schools, and such assumption of responsibility is necessarily incompatible with a progressively diminishing effort on the part of that state (21).

During the intervening years, Maryland has exercised strong leadership in federal-state relations. The state superintendent and key staff members have been involved with the U.S. Office of Education in the development of policies at the federal level for the administration of various federal grants. Also, Superintendent Thomas G. Pullen, Jr., was one of the key members of a steering committee of chief state school officers which was responsible for making the Council of Chief State School Officers a dominant force in the development of a body of nationally accepted policies for state school administration. These policies have influenced the type of educational legislation enacted by the Congress. The deputy state superintendent has been a member of the Study Commission of the council, which has been the working group responsible for developing policies in areas indicated by the council.

Maryland has a record of accepting federal grants promptly and working well with federal officials in developing guidelines and regulations for effective administration. Its state plans for the acceptance of such grants have been used as models by other states. Maryland is fortunate and unique in that the State Board of Education, the state superintendent, and the staff of the State Department of Education have placed major emphasis on leadership and have exercised the regulatory function only as required by law. Accordingly, the state department has been structured on the basis of broad, well-defined functions. As a result, when federal programs become available, they are integrated into the appropriate units of the existing organization without creating additional units. The only exception was the establishment in 1965 of an additional unit known as the Division of Federal-State Programs to coordinate the various state and federal allocations. It is the position of the State Board of Education that all state and federal grants should be administered through the department in accord with policies of the state board.

Recent federal grants have provided a significant stimulus to increasing the professional staff of the department. Since 1945, the professional staff has grown from 34 to 309, an increase of 809 percent. Of this number, 211 are paid wholly or partially from federal funds. It should be pointed out, however, that the largest increase has been in the Division of Vocational Rehabilitation, which increased its staff from 15 in 1945 to 171 in 1968.

Fiscal authorities and the Legislature have approved almost without exception requests for increased staffing that is federally supported in toto or on a matching basis. Requests for staffing requiring full state funding meet with less success, depending on priorities. Yet, there is a positive attitude across the state for increased financing for education at all levels to improve markedly the quality of education.

EDUCATION FOR A RAPIDLY CHANGING SOCIETY

James A. Sensenbaugh was appointed state superintendent of schools by the State Board of Education on June 1, 1964. A native Marylander who received his elementary and secondary education in the public schools of Frederick and Washington Counties, all of his professional experiences—as teacher, principal, assistant superintendent, and county superintendent prior to becoming state superintendent—have been in Maryland. He is steeped in the educational tradition. His parents were teachers in Frederick County, and six of his eight brothers and sisters also have been teachers.

Dr. Sensenbaugh is a man of strong conviction regarding the challenge of the public schools to provide educational programs to meet the needs of our rapidly changing society. He believes that the schools should be assertive in trying out new curriculums and teaching procedures for which research indicates a high probability of success. He is also an advocate of radical change in school building design to make buildings more functional, more flexible for changing teaching methodology, and more efficient. As superintendent of schools of Frederick County for 8 years, he pioneered in these areas with a high degree of success, notwithstanding the efforts of conservative groups to limit the rapid rise in local taxation to support new and improved educational programs and new school construction. This is the posture he is presently espousing throughout the state and at regional and national conferences across the nation.

Since 1964, the State Department of Education has been affected significantly by the following federal legislation: (1) the Civil Rights Act of 1964, (2) the Economic Opportunity Act of 1964, and (3) the Elementary and Secondary Education Act of 1965 (ESEA).

School desegregation, following the decrees of the U.S. Supreme Court in 1954, proceeded with varying degrees of deliberate speed throughout Maryland. The state board acted promptly by accepting the decision of the court as the supreme law of the land and urged local school systems to take the necessary steps to comply with this decision. None of the 24 local school systems refused to take official action affirming its intent to desegregate. However, only one school system promptly abandoned the dual system for white and Negro pupils. The other 22 systems elected to follow the freedom-of-choice policy. There are no Negro children in one county. By 1964, 15,712 Negro pupils had elected to transfer to former all-white schools. This represented 27 percent of the Negroes enrolled, exclusive of Baltimore City. Meanwhile, the state board took no legal steps to accelerate desegregation. Litigation in Harford and St. Mary's Counties, pressure from the National Association for the Advancement of Colored People, together with persuasion from the state superintendent and the deputy superintendent, were responsible for the limited progress labeled as tokenism in certain counties of Southern Maryland and the Eastern Shore.

In Frederick County, where Dr. Sensenbaugh was superintendent of schools from 1956 to 1964, he had instituted a plan of redistricting geographical boundaries for individual schools as early as 1957 to eliminate the dual system. When he resigned in 1964, there remained but one Negro school to be eliminated when the required new school building construction was completed. Dr. Sensenbaugh brought this same commitment to the state superintendency. The Civil Rights Act of 1964, which required compliance with the federal regulations regarding discriminatory practices in order to receive federal financial assistance, provided the incentive and impetus to accelerate desegregation of the public schools. By September 1967, only three school systems remained on the free-choice plan. In two of them, transfers have taken place at such a rate that the depopulation of the Negro schools will automatically bring about total desegregation. In the single remaining school system, the state board has intervened on the recommendation of the state superintendent and, following a series of conferences with the local and federal authorities, has issued an order directing the local board of education to desegregate the entire school system according to a plan agreed to by all parties concerned.

The Economic Opportunity Act of 1964 contained an educational component that was destined to cause a minor revolution in the public education establishment. This legislation provided for Head Start programs for economically and educationally disadvantaged children, remedial education programs for in-school children possessing the same characteristics, and basic adult education for individuals who did not possess the basic education necessary for employment or training in skills for job upgrading.

Under the leadership of the state department, local school systems, in cooperation with local community agencies, applied for federal grants promptly and inaugurated Head Start and remedial programs to the full extent that funds were available. These programs have been continued and expanded. The basic adult education program was much slower in getting started because of the reluctance of disadvantaged adults to enroll. However, by January 1968 there were 2,900 people enrolled in the 24 local school systems.

The Head Start program, which was gradually absorbed by Title I of ESEA, provided an increased interest in early childhood education and thus assisted the passage of state legislation in 1967 that made kindergartens a part of the state foundation program of education. Also, the compensatory education for disadvantaged children provided by federal funds under Title I added a new dimension to the existing concept of an adequate educational program. The state superintendent promptly endorsed the new concept and hired three additional professional staff members to work with local school systems in instituting these new programs. There was general public acceptance of this educational advance, and the state provided a special appropriation of $5 million in 1967 for Baltimore City for this purpose.

Dr. Sensenbaugh is especially interested in Title III, which provides federal funding for supplementary educational centers and services. Here is an opportunity for innovation and creativity, an opportunity to develop new ideas to be researched, and an opportunity to push forward the frontiers of education. A highly qualified staff member was added to coordinate and provide leadership for this program, and the Maryland projects submitted for approval by federal officials rank among the best in the nation.

The greatest concern of the state superintendent is the recruitment and retention of a highly qualified professional staff in the State Department of Education. Salaries are not competitive with those paid in urban school systems in the state; thus recruitment is difficult. The State Board of Education lacks the legal authority to establish salary scales for professional personnel in the department. The control is placed in the standard salary board, which sets the scales for the state merit system. However, there is hope for a brighter future. Title V of ESEA, for strengthening state departments of education, has made possible advances that would have required a decade at the state level. Fifteen additional staff members, including an associate superintendent for instructional services, were added in areas that were understaffed and of high priority in terms of need. For the first time, sabbatical leave with full salary for half a year or half salary for a full year has been made possible for staff growth and improvement. Also, reimbursement is allowed for tuition for graduate courses that will contribute to the effectiveness of staff members. An annual 3-day workshop institute staffed by highly qualified individuals at the national level constitutes the core of the staff improvement program.

As has been stated earlier, the Vocational Education Act of 1963 expanded greatly the scope of vocational education to meet the changing technology of the world of work. In Maryland, public interest in vocational education reached such proportions that legislation was enacted to provide from state funds not less than 50 percent of the cost of area vocational school construction. The state's share in excess of 50 percent is that percentage which the local political subdivision receives from the state for current expenditures. During the past 5 years, 45 area vocational schools have been established, enrolling 43,664 pupils. The state has contributed $13,108,977 toward the construction of these facilities.

In addition, the community colleges began to offer occupationally oriented courses at the post-high school level. These courses are centered primarily on business studies, engineering technologies, health-related occupations, personal service occupations, and public (government) service. During 1967-68, 57 different occupationally oriented curriculums were offered in the 12 community colleges. And this is only the beginning in this field.

In Retrospect: Fifty Years of Progress and Change

> The historians of the future will, in all probability, record the period 1916 to 1966 in public education in Maryland as the "era of enlightenment" when the citizenry evidenced unusual insight into the importance of education in democratic society. This was not a sudden flash of insight; rather it was the culmination of a series of movements and change dating back as far as 1880. New but steady changes were taking place in the purpose and direction of education along the lines of the new democratic and social forces. The schools were transformed from mere disciplinary institutions into instruments of democracy intended to prepare young people for intelligent participation in the increasingly complex life of the State and Nation.
>
> The creative and progressive legislation which was enacted during this half century resulted from a unified effort by the forces committed to better schools, better government, and a better way of life. The State Superintendent of Schools provided the leadership for marshalling these forces in the direction of new legislation for better schools. During the period following World War II there was a vigorous "grass roots" movement for greater universal education at public expense. The returning war veterans, because of their experiences, were determined to have for themselves and succeeding generations the best education possible to perpetuate the democratic way of live (22).

Maryland has now embarked upon a multifaceted program of education to meet the needs of a rapidly changing society. The department will, in all probability, expand its services to new areas still in the blueprint stage. There will be more innovations and school building construction, with greater uses planned for these buildings, including year-round schools, evening and adult programs, and general community use. The curriculums will change in order to provide more continuity, more challenges to the individual student, and a greater blending of the school and community.

The schools of the future also will include more efficient use of teaching talent. Instructional aids will be added, and more emphasis will be put on research and technology so that new and better ways of doing things will be devised. The firmly established Department of Education, based on a sound legal structure and coordinated with the state government and its internal organizations, with its tradition of statesmanlike leadership, will bring about a greater acceptance of the public schools and a greater respect for education, the teaching profession, and knowledge.

FOOTNOTES

1. Bernard C. Steiner, *History of Education in Maryland* (Washington, D.C.: Government Printing Office, 1894), p. 57.
2. *Ibid.*, p. 61.
3. Maryland, *Constitution* (1864), pp. 65-66.
4. David W. Zimmerman, "The State Suprintendency," *Baltimore Bulletin of Education,* XLII, No. 1 (1964-65), 16-17.
5. Board of Education, *Annual Report, 1909,* p. 154.
6. Abraham Flexner and Frank P. Bachman, *Public Education in Maryland: A Report to the Maryland Education Survey Commission* (New York: The General Education Board, 1916), p. 9.
7. *Ibid.*, p. xvi.
8. *Ibid.*, p. 143.
9. *Ibid.*, p. 12.
10. Anonymously authored, unpublished manuscript dealing with educational efforts during the nineteenth century, the state superintendent's office, Baltimore, Maryland, p. 5. (Typed from original handwritten manuscript.)
11. The *Baltimore Sun,* January 4, 1920.
12. Ezekiel Cheever, "Mr. Cheever Becomes An Ostler," *Ezekiel Cheever's School Issues,* IV, No. 1 (May 1934), 3-5.
13. Anonymously authored, unpublished manuscript dealing with educational efforts during the nineteenth century, the state superintendent's office, Baltimore, Maryland, p. 13.
14. Albert S. Cook, "The Equalizing Principle in State School Support," *Department of Superintendence Official Report,* an address given at the annual meeting of the department held in Boston, Massachusetts, February 26 to March 1, 1928 (Washington, D.C.: The Department of Superintendence, National Education Association, 1928), p. 8.
15. School Law Revision Commission, *Report of the School Law Revision Commission* (Annapolis: State of Maryland, 1968).
16. Department of Education, *Public Adult Education in Maryland,* Maryland School Bulletin, XXXIX, No. 4 (Baltimore: The Department. 1963), 5.

17. Francis Scott Key, *A Discourse on Education* (Annapolis: J. Green, 1827), p. xi.
18. Steiner, *op. cit.*, p. 44.
19. Maryland, *Laws* (1931), ch. 163, p. 457.
20. Maryland, *Laws* (1941), ch. 150, p. 187.
21. Department of Education, *Vocational Education in Maryland County High Schools,* Maryland School Bulletin, Vol. VIII, No. 11 (Baltimore: The Department, 1927).
22. School Law Revision Commission, *op. cit.*, p. 7.

BIBLIOGRAPHY

Public Documents

Maryland. *Constitution* (1776, 1851, 1864, 1867).

—— *Laws* (1931, 1941).

Books and Pamphlets

Cubberley, Ellwood. *Public Education in the United States.* Boston: Houghton Mifflin Co., 1934.

Department of Education. *A Decade of Progress in the Maryland Public Schools, 1939-1949.* Maryland School Bulletin, Vol. XXXI, No. 1. Baltimore: The Department, August 1950.

—— *A Decade of Progress in Education in Maryland, 1949-1959.* Maryland School Bulletin, Vol. XXXVIII, No. 2. Baltimore: The Department, October 1961.

—— *Educating the Highly Able.* Maryland School Bulletin, Vol. XXXIX, No. 1. Baltimore: The Department, December 1962.

—— *The Maryland State Department of Education: A Manual Outlining Its Legal Foundations and Services.* Maryland School Bulletin, Vol. XXXVIII, No. 1. Baltimore: The Department, September 1961.

—— *Progress in Education in Maryland.* Maryland School Bulletin, Vol. XX, No. 2. Baltimore: The Department, October 1938.

—— *A Proposed Program of Education for Maryland.* Maryland School Bulletin, Vol. XXVI, No. 3. Baltimore: The Department, December 1944.

—— *Public Adult Education in Maryland.* Maryland School Bulletin, Vol. XXXIX, No. 4. Baltimore: The Department, 1963.

—— *The Public and Its Schools.* Maryland School Bulletin, Vol. XXVI, No. 1. Baltimore: The Department, November 1944.

—— *The Public School Laws of Maryland: Including the Code of Bylaws of the Maryland State Board of Education.* Maryland School Bulletin, Vol. XLI, No. 1. Charlottesville, Va.: The Michie Co., Law Publishers, May 1965.

—— *The Public School Laws of Maryland: 1965 Supplement.* Maryland School Bulletin, Vol. XLI, No. 3. Charlottesville, Va.: The Michie Co., Law Publishers December 1965.

—— *Redirection of the School Progress in Wartime.* Maryland School Bulletin, Vol. XXIV, No. 2. Baltimore: The Department, December 1942.

—— *Vocational Education in Maryland County High Schools.* Maryland School Bulletin, Vol. VIII, No. 11. Baltimore: The Department, 1927.

Key, Francis Scott. *A Discourse on Education.* Annapolis: J. Green, 1827.

Rhodes, Harry C. *Lay Participation in School Budget Development in Maryland.* Staff Study No. 13: Review of the Fiscal Policy for Public Education in Maryland. Baltimore: Department of Education, 1960.

Stapleton, Edward G. *Educational Progress in Maryland Public Schools Since 1916.* Staff Study No. 1: Review of the Fiscal Policy for Public Education in Maryland. Baltimore: Department of Education, 1959.

Steiner, Bernard C. *History of Education in Maryland.* Washington, D.C.: Government Printing Office, 1894.

Willis, Charles W. *A Program of Financing School Construction Designed To Safeguard the Current Operating Program in Maryland.* Staff Study No. 8: Review of the Fiscal Policy for Public Education in Maryland. Baltimore: Department of Education, 1959.

Zimmerman, David W. *The Nonproperty Tax Potential of Maryland.* Staff Study No. 4: Review of the Fiscal Policy for Public Education in Maryland. Baltimore: Department of Education, 1961.

Reports

American Council on Education. *Higher Education in Maryland: A Report of a Survey by the American Council on Education with Recommendations of the Maryland Commission on Higher Education.* Washington, D.C.: American Council on Education, 1947.

Board of Education. *Annual Reports.* Annapolis: The Board, 1866-1966.

Cook, Albert S. "The Equalizing Principle in State School Support." *Department of Superintendence Official Report.* An address given at the annual meeting of the department held in Boston, Massachusetts, February 26 to March 1, 1928. Washington, D.C.: The Department of Superintendence, National Education Association, 1928.

Cooperative Study Policy Committee. *Education for Our Times: A State Action Program.* Report No. 1. Baltimore: Department of Education, May 1959.

Flexner, Abraham, and Bachman, Frank P. *Public Education in Maryland: A Report to the Maryland Education Survey Commission.* New York: The General Education Board, 1916.

Maryland State School Survey Commission. *The 1941 Survey of the Maryland Public Schools and Teachers Colleges,* Herbert B. Brunner, director. Baltimore: The Commission, 1941.

School Law Revision Commission. *Report of the School Law Revision Commission.* Annapolis: State of Maryland, 1968.

Articles and Periodicals

Cheever, Ezekiel. "Mr. Cheever Becomes An Ostler." *Ezekiel Cheever's School Issues,* IV, No. 1 (May 1934), 3-5.

The *Baltimore Sun,* January 4, 1920.

Zimmerman, David W. "The State Superintendency." *Baltimore Bulletin of Education,* XLII, No. 1 (1964-65), 16-17.

Unpublished Material

Anonymously authored unpublished manuscript dealing with educational efforts during the nineteenth century, the state superintendent's office, Baltimore, Maryland. Typed from original handwritten manuscript.

Appendix A

MARYLAND CHIEF STATE SCHOOL OFFICERS

State School Superintendents

1865-68	Rev. Libertus Van Bokkelen
1870-90	M. Alexander Newell
1890-1900	E. Barrett Prettyman
1900-20	M. Bates Stephens
1920-42	Albert S. Cook
1942-64	Thomas G. Pullen, Jr.
1964-	James A. Sensenbaugh

NOTE:

During the period 1868 to 1870, the principal of the State Normal School, M. Alexander Newell, was given general supervision over all the public schools of the state. The laws of 1870 made the principal of the normal school also state superintendent.

Appendix B

Chart I.--MARYLAND DEPARTMENT OF EDUCATION, 1910

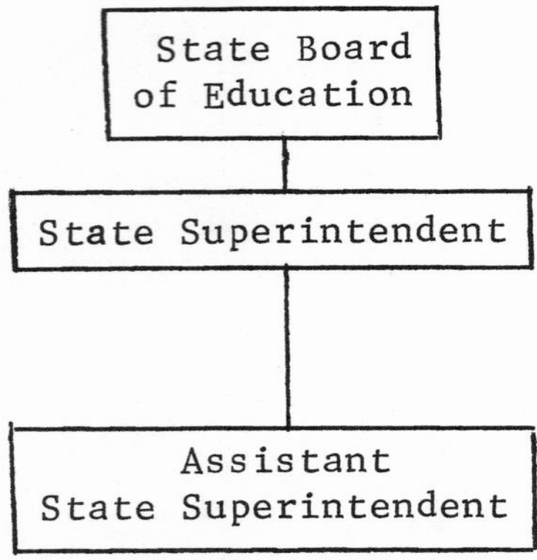

Chart II.--MARYLAND DEPARTMENT OF EDUCATION, 1920

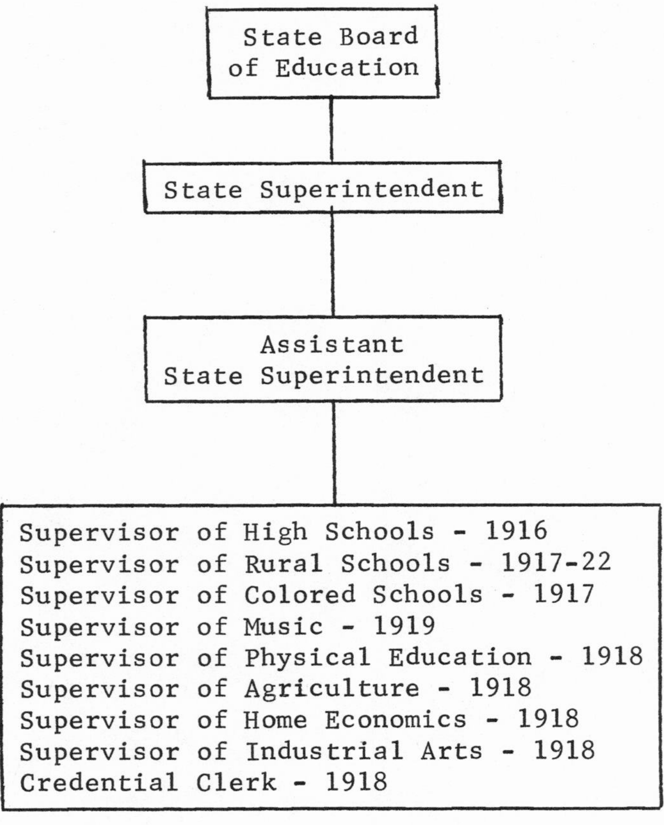

Appendix B

Chart III.--MARYLAND DEPARTMENT OF EDUCATION, 1940

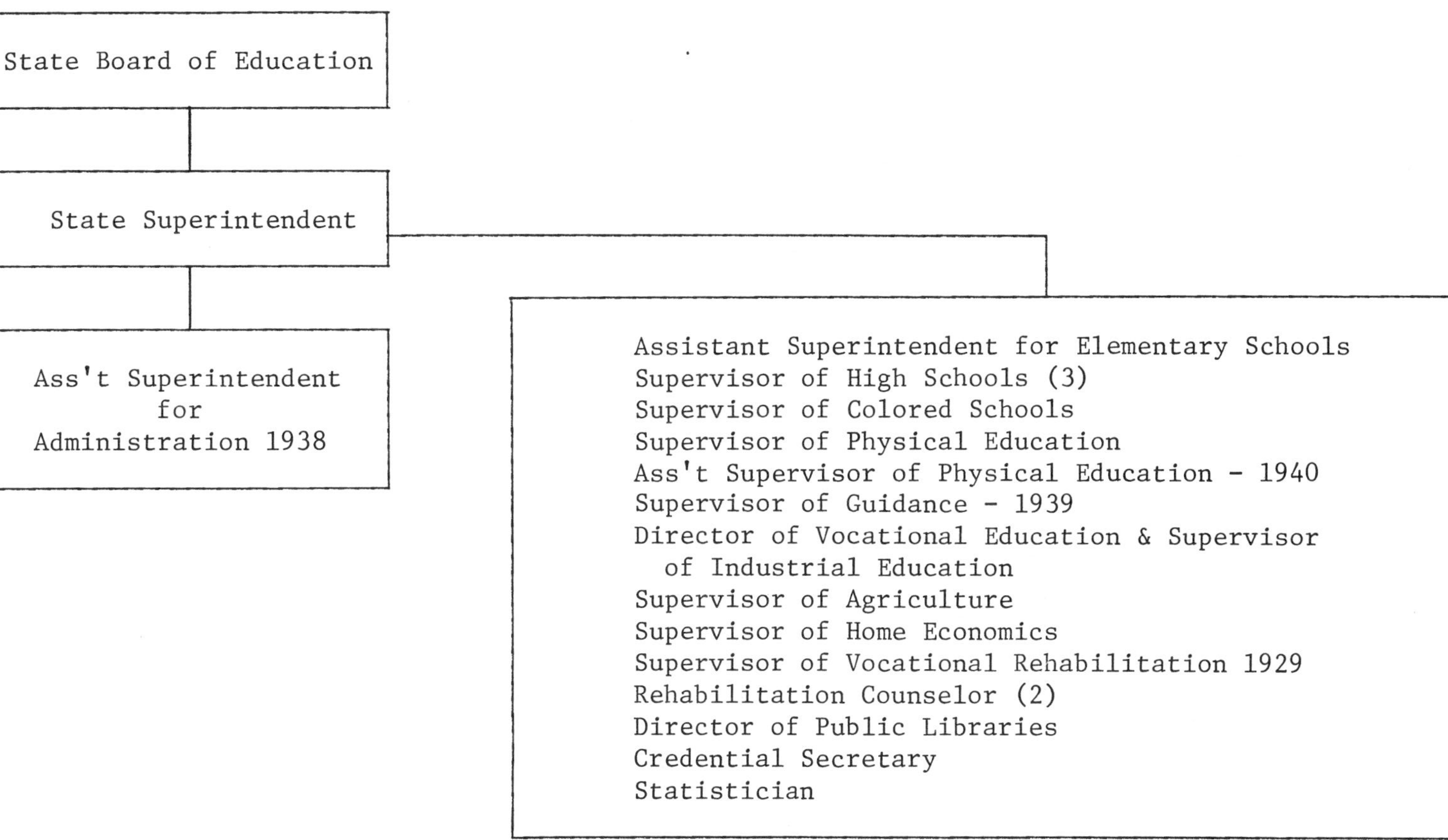
State Board of Education
State Superintendent
Ass't Superintendent for Administration 1938
Assistant Superintendent for Elementary Schools
Supervisor of High Schools (3)
Supervisor of Colored Schools
Supervisor of Physical Education
Ass't Supervisor of Physical Education - 1940
Supervisor of Guidance - 1939
Director of Vocational Education & Supervisor of Industrial Education
Supervisor of Agriculture
Supervisor of Home Economics
Supervisor of Vocational Rehabilitation 1929
Rehabilitation Counselor (2)
Director of Public Libraries
Credential Secretary
Statistician

Appendix B

Chart IV.--MARYLAND DEPARTMENT OF EDUCATION, 1960

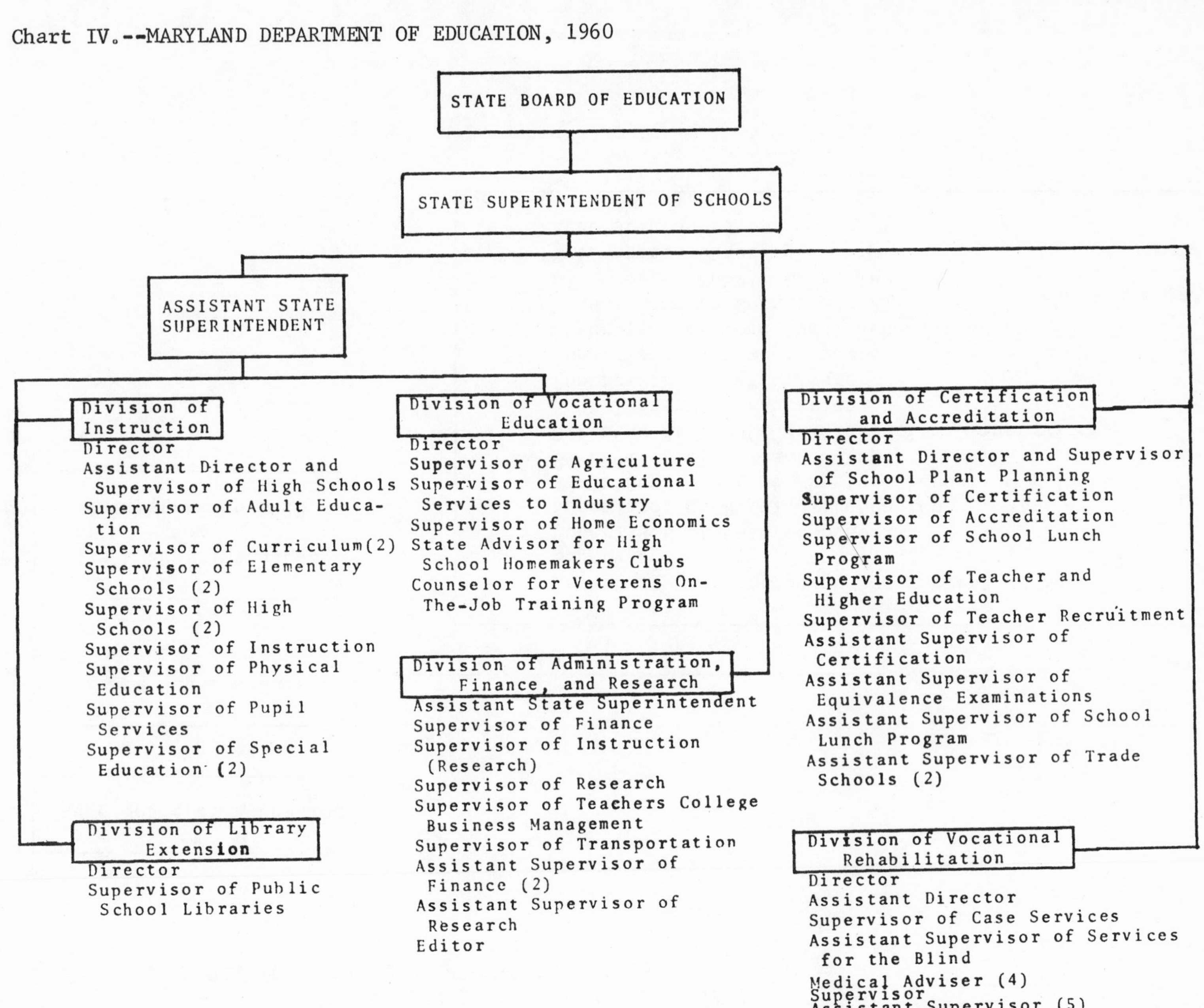
STATE BOARD OF EDUCATION
STATE SUPERINTENDENT OF SCHOOLS
ASSISTANT STATE SUPERINTENDENT
Division of Instruction
Director
Assistant Director and Supervisor of High Schools
Supervisor of Adult Education
Supervisor of Curriculum(2)
Supervisor of Elementary Schools (2)
Supervisor of High Schools (2)
Supervisor of Instruction
Supervisor of Physical Education
Supervisor of Pupil Services
Supervisor of Special Education (2)
Division of Library Extension
Director
Supervisor of Public School Libraries
Division of Vocational Education
Director
Supervisor of Agriculture
Supervisor of Educational Services to Industry
Supervisor of Home Economics
State Advisor for High School Homemakers Clubs
Counselor for Veterens On-The-Job Training Program
Division of Administration, Finance, and Research
Assistant State Superintendent
Supervisor of Finance
Supervisor of Instruction (Research)
Supervisor of Research
Supervisor of Teachers College Business Management
Supervisor of Transportation
Assistant Supervisor of Finance (2)
Assistant Supervisor of Research
Editor
Division of Certification and Accreditation
Director
Assistant Director and Supervisor of School Plant Planning
Supervisor of Certification
Supervisor of Accreditation
Supervisor of School Lunch Program
Supervisor of Teacher and Higher Education
Supervisor of Teacher Recruitment
Assistant Supervisor of Certification
Assistant Supervisor of Equivalence Examinations
Assistant Supervisor of School Lunch Program
Assistant Supervisor of Trade Schools (2)
Division of Vocational Rehabilitation
Director
Assistant Director
Supervisor of Case Services
Assistant Supervisor of Services for the Blind
Medical Adviser (4)
Supervisor
Assistant Supervisor (5)
Counselor(34)

Appendix B

Chart V.--MARYLAND DEPARTMENT OF EDUCATION, 1967

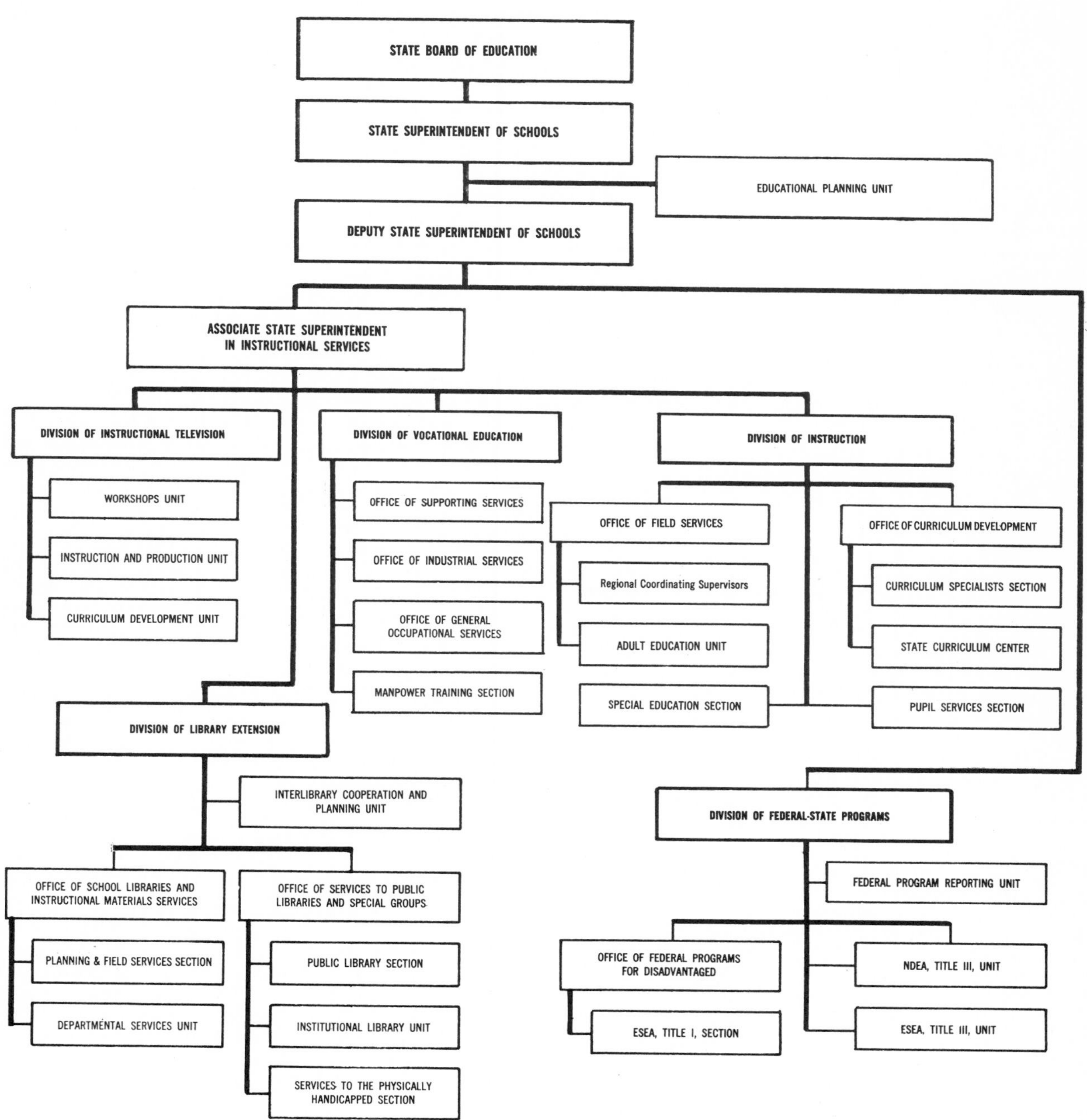

See next page for second half of chart.

Appendix B

Chart V.--MARYLAND DEPARTMENT OF EDUCATION, 1967 (Continued)

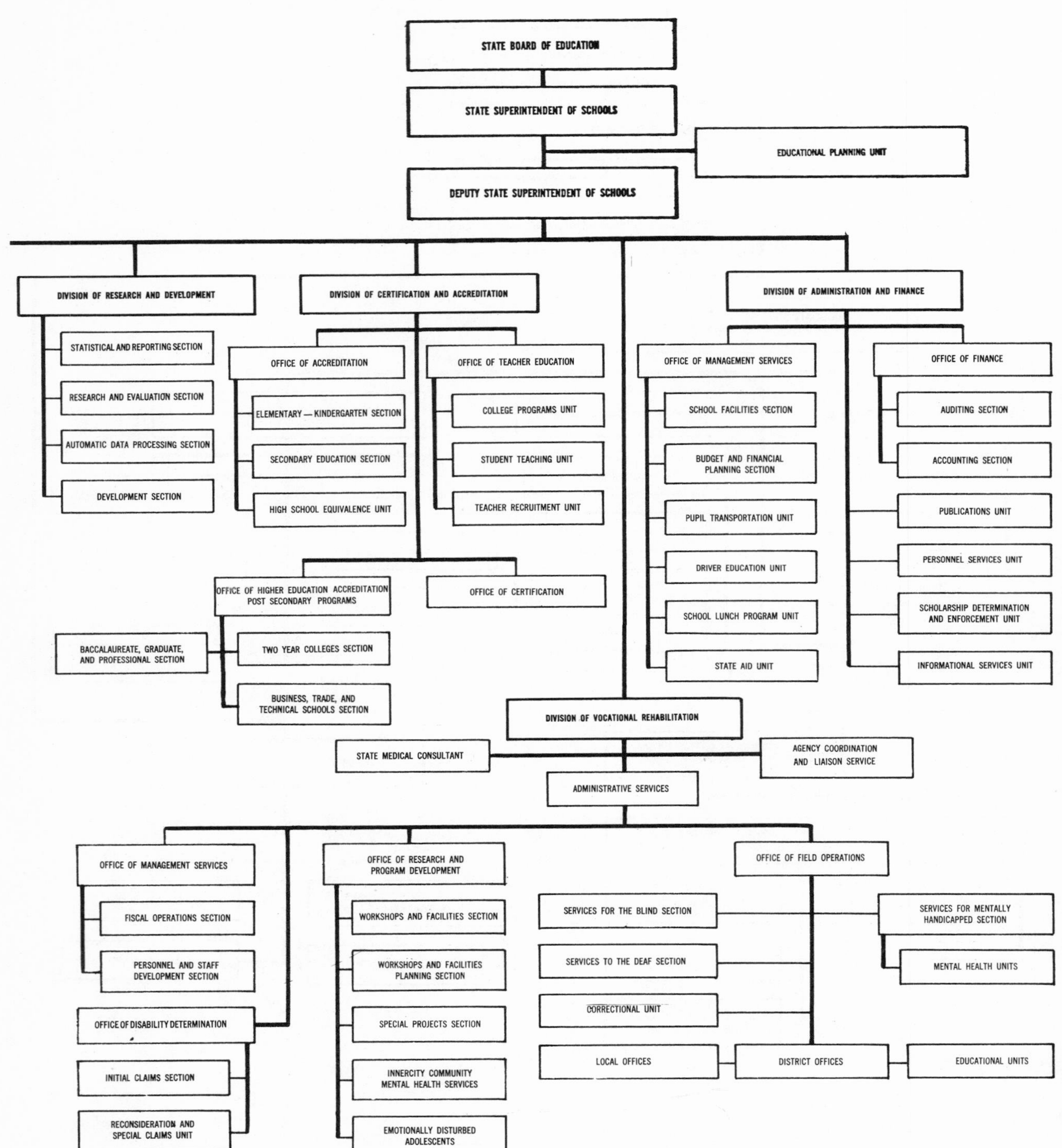

21 Massachusetts

DEPARTMENT OF EDUCATION
Franklin P. Hawkes
Thomas J. Curtin

Contents

THE EARLY YEARS: 1635-1837

The cause of education has been close to the heart of Massachusetts citizens since the coming of the first colonists in the early seventeenth century. One has only to examine the list of Massachusetts firsts (Appendix C) to note the establishment of the country's first public school (Boston Latin School) in 1635, the founding of Harvard College in 1636, as well as the order for the first public school supported by direct taxation in 1639.

One eminent historian wrote that "towns could be founded only by lawful owners or proprietors . . . . " Requirements included the following:

> Approved normal size—36 square miles. Sixty resident families within five to seven years. Besides 60 lots, three were reserved—one for the minister; one to support the ministry; one for the support of education, called the "school lot." A meeting house must be erected near the center of town, and a lot of eight acres laid out for a "Common" (1).

"Each New England settlement thus became a *unit*—called a town," writes Ellwood P. Cubberley. "At the center, facing the town common, were the meeting house, and later the town school, and the town hall" (2). Residents had to live within a half-mile of the meetinghouse, were required to attend meetings, and sent their children to the town school. One wonders how this pattern came about, as well as what the settlers of the New World brought with them as they landed on the shores of Massachusetts.

Cubberley notes that from the Greeks came the emphasis on personal freedom and initiative, with emphasis on art, literature, and philosophy; from the Romans came law and government, which provided common bases for language, dress, manners, religion, and government. Christianity became a connecting link by providing a new ethical force that called for education for all. General education, as a means to salvation, required that ministers who instruct be adequately prepared. The Puritans thus brought to New England three basic concepts: Church membership was required; the young must be educated; a learned ministry must be perpetuated.

The *Tercentenary of the Massachusetts Bay Colony* sums up these developments as follows:

> Not only did the parents work for the education of their children, but the colonists ordered that a school be built where there were enough families and children. In 1647 a law was passed in Massachusetts which ordered that every town of fifty families should provide a school where children could be taught to read and write. Every town of one hundred families was required to have a grammar school. This would be the same as our high school. These were public schools, but they were not always free. They were supported by the parents in many cases.

> The schoolmaster shall faithfully attend his school and do his best to benefit his scholars . . . . From the beginning of the first month until the end of the seventh, he shall begin to teach every day at seven o'clock in the morning. For the other five months he shall begin every day at eight of the clock in the morning and end at four in the afternoon.

One of the men who lived in the early days wrote this story about his life in school:

> When I was three years old, I was sent to school to a mistress, where I learned to read with great dispatch; in my fifth year, I was taken away and put to a writing master. In my seventh year I could flourish a tolerable

---

The authors are particularly indebted to Francis X. Guindon, director, Division of State Colleges, for the section on higher education, and to the following staff members of the Department of Education for their valuable assistance in the preparation of other foundational materials: Everett G. Thistle, William A. Philbrick, Jr., John E. Hodgen, Alice M. Cahill, John P. Morine, and Francis J. Farrenkopf. We are particularly grateful also to Mrs. Evelyn Haddad for clerical assistance in the production of this manuscript.

hand, and began my grammar. By the time I was fourteen I was considerably proficient in the Latin and Greek Languages, and was admitted into Harvard College (3).

Along with this pattern of operation, as Paul H. Hanus has indicated, the following principles were emphasized:

> The State may determine the kind of education and fix the minimum amount of education to be insisted upon for every member of the Commonwealth. Taxes may be assessed and collected to provide such education as the State demands, and these taxes may be general though the school attendance is not (4).

The Massachusetts Law of 1642, the so-called "Satan deluder" law, ordered the officials of the town to ascertain if the parents or masters were attending to their educational duties. Authority was given to selectmen to impose fines for nonobservance or to require regular reporting to officials. Courts were charged with enforcing the law. The licensing of teachers was in the hands of the local minister, who examined the candidate to see that he was "sound in the faith, and knew his Latin." The selectmen, usually accompanied by the minister, gave supervision by recurrent visits to all the schools, especially at the time of promotion.

Throughout this early period, the influence and authority of the Church were quite evident (5). The meetinghouse required for a town was where defense against the Indians was planned—but it was primarily where the Puritans gathered for prayer. Out of this pattern the town meeting developed, establishing a kind of religious republic. In the following 100 years, however, religious interest waned, and the monopoly of the Church ended. Schools became town schools, the town meetings were held in a town hall, and religious activities were arranged for the meetinghouse.

During this period, as towns grew and spread out, sections developed like neighborhoods or suburbs; each wanted its own school under its own control and set up parishes with parish officers and a minister in charge (6). As private schools were organized in an area, the enrollment in the town schools dropped off, even though they were free and supported by taxation. Because of this, the residents of the parish or district demanded that the town school sessions be held for a term of 12 to 16 weeks in each district. This proved costly, and the problem was finally resolved by allowing each parish to have its own parish school and to levy taxes to support it.

By the year 1768, the Commonwealth had recorded seven major educational events, beginning in 1673 with the first private, tuition schools—known as "Dame Schools"—and climaxing with the 1768 legislation authorizing districts and decentralizing the schools. In between were the initiation in 1682 of separate grammar schools teaching the three R's and New England Primer, certification of the Master by a committee of ministers in 1701, moving of the schools into parishes in 1704, and replacement in 1763 of Latin grammar schools by academies which charged tuition.

The Massachusetts School Law of 1789 gave to each town the right to elect school trustees, levy school taxes, and select a teacher for the usual one-room district school. By placing such a school under school trustees, the civil, or public, school was originated. It took another 50 years, however, before the "American school" emerged. The 1789 legislation was the first general state school law in the country (7). It legalized educational practices of the previous 150 years and made them state requirements. Six- and 12-month schools, depending on the town size, were required. All teachers had to be certified, and all grammar school teachers were required to be college graduates, or passed by the minister in Latin. In 1797, the General Court granted land endowments to approved academies as a kind of state aid. Finally, in 1821, the first publicly supported, publicly controlled American high school (English High School, Boston) was established for boys, followed by the first state law for public high schools in 1827. A year earlier, 1826, the first modern school committee was elected.

During these 200 years, it might well be said that the foundations of the American school were laid, as certain milestones were passed: elimination of the pauper school, the rate-bill, and the fuel tax; extension of education through high school and toward college; beginnings of a graded system of instruction; demands for normal schools for training of teachers; extension of schooling opportunities to women; and authorization of taxation to support education.

As Cubberley expresses it, "the road changed from the philosophy that 'Might made Right, and children had no rights that parents need respect' to 'A child shall be cared for and educated for the best welfare of the State, and hence is of first importance' " (8).

The U.S. Constitution states that all matters not specifically mentioned in the Constitution are the function of the states; in other words, education is a function of the state. The Massachusetts Education Study Commission commented that the Massachusetts Bay Colony's interest in learning did not commit the Company to carry on education single-handedly. "The Company took steps to require a literate rising generation, but put no money of their own into the enterprise .... The program was mandated, given teeth, and decentralized to local operating units . . ." (9). Thus the Commonwealth embarked on a policy of encouraging local support of state-mandated education. Such a policy has continued to this day.

Schooling in the public interest was somewhat more than 200 years old in Massachusetts when the first State

Board of Education was created in 1837. One study commission comments:

> Although the Massachusetts Department of Education is the state's—and the nation's—most senior state-wide agency for public education, it is a relative newcomer on the Massachusetts educational scene .... It followed the constitutional injunction in being made an executive arm of state government, financed by and reporting to the legislature (10).

With this brief background of the early years, we will examine what took place in education in Massachusetts as a result of the appointment of the first Board of Education.

THE BOARD OF EDUCATION FROM 1837 TO 1848

Establishment of the Board of Education by the General Court in 1837—

> Created an agency to promote and guide the lasting concern of the State for the education of its inhabitants .... What Horace Mann, as Secretary, and the Board did was to arouse strongly and at length local compliance with school laws (11).

Massachusetts authorized its board to accept grants for educational purposes, to appoint a secretary who shall make abstracts, and to prescribe the forms of school registers and blanks. The board also was to prepare and submit to the Legislature each January an abstract of school returns. Principally, the board collected and diffused information.

With the mandate to "collect and diffuse information" came changes in duties and responsibilities for the Board of Education. Necessary expenses of the board and secretary *were* reimbursed after auditing. Periodic consolidations of statutes and regulations were needed.

Between 1830 and 1850, practically every Northern state created an ex officio state school officer, whose duties were financial, statistical, clerical, and exhortatory. In 1840, Springfield employed the first city superintendent of schools, followed in later years by Boston and Worcester. This trend revealed the need for an executive officer to manage city and town school programs, as well as state school systems, in the interest of strengthening education (12).

The 1836 Child Labor Law, as implemented in 1842, required working permits for those 14 to 16 years of age and the establishment of continuation and evening schools. In 1847, it also brought school grading, with the first separate grading at Quincy School, in Boston.

One of the outstanding developments in this period was the memorial to the Legislature in 1837 regarding the establishment of state normal schools, followed by a report on Prussian and French "normal" schools. The first normal school in America was established at Lexington in 1839, with the next one at Bridgewater in 1840.

Undoubtedly, Horace Mann made one of the greatest contributions during this period when he published and issued annual reports, following his extensive visits to cities and towns as well as throughout the country. These reports, and the *Common School Journal* edited by Mann, had great impact, in particular during the next 50 years, from 1850 to 1900.

The Board from 1848 to 1904

Horace Mann was succeeded as secretary by five different leaders (Barnas Sears, George S. Boutwell, Joseph White, John W. Dickinson, Frank A. Hill) during this period of 56 years, with terms ranging from 4 to 16 years (13).

In order to have adequate information and statistics, the state board was authorized to appoint special agents to make inquiries. In 1859 came the first official compilation of *General Laws Relating to Education.* By 1867, all officers were required to furnish statistics about their pupils, instruction, and schools, as well as the institutions serving the deaf, dumb, and blind (14). Another compilation of *General Laws,* issued in 1882, brought the legislators and the administrators up-to-date on educational legislation.

There was increasing activity on the part of educational associations during the last half of the nineteenth century. The Massachusetts Teachers' Association, founded in 1845, put out the first issue of its *Massachusetts Teacher* in 1848. The National Teachers' Association, formed in 1857, became the National Educational Association in 1870. Seven years later, the Massachusetts Schoolmasters Club came into being, meeting regularly to discuss new movements in education. The conventions, institutes, meetings, and publications of these organizations greatly influenced the development of programs in the field.

It was in this era that Agassiz, Froebel, and Pestalozzi made significant contributions which resulted in improved methods and curriculum in the public schools of the Commonwealth. Emphasis developed in science and nature, in history, geography, physiology, and hygiene. In 1860, Elizabeth Peabody founded the first English-speaking kindergarten in Boston. In 1872, the Legislature passed a law providing for industrial schools to teach industrial and mechanical drawing so that Massachusetts could maintain its position in manufacturing and the arts. The law mandated manual training in high schools of towns with 20,000 population by 1895, and in elementary schools by 1896—a step to prevocational training which has persisted to this day.

Between 1880 and 1892, in accordance with the law, the state board developed and printed many courses of study as guides for school systems. With this greater emphasis on subject matter, departmental teaching developed during the last decade of the century and gradually led into the movement to establish 6-year elementary schools instead of the customary 8- or 9-year schools. A series of studies, by the Committee of Ten on the secondary schools, and the Committee of Fifteen on the elementary schools, all contributed to the ferment for change in the curriculum.

An important trend developed as the result of the Compulsory Education Act of 1852, which required all children ages 8-14 to attend school at least 12 weeks of the year, of which 6 had to be consecutive. This legislation brought into the schools many children not adapted to the usual academic program, such as: "The Truant–The Incorrigible–The Foreign-born unaccustomed to books; The Mentally Retarded–The Crippled–The Tubercular–The Deaf; the Epileptic–The Blind–The Sick–The Needy–The Unfit" (15).

This action reflected somewhat the state's concern during the preceding decade, when it had established a State Reform School and the Massachusetts School for the Feeble-Minded. To implement the Compulsory Education Act, it became necessary for school systems to have personnel, such as an attendance officer, the school nurse, and the visiting teacher–all of which brought into focus the needs of individual children.

The objective became one of salvaging as many as possible, and turning students back into society prepared to do something to serve both the community and self. The Massachusetts Truancy Law in 1862 led to the erection and staffing of county reform schools, county truant schools, and county training schools to give delinquents appropriate education. The first class for the mentally retarded was set up in Springfield in 1898, followed by others in Boston and Worcester. Meanwhile, there were many adults not equipped for a changing civilization. An optional law provided evening schools for those not attending day schools. Later, this included those needing elementary schooling and then the foreign born, as well as native illiterates whose education had been neglected.

Other important developments of the period included the establishment of a new group of normal schools, the development of textile schools, the consolidation of school districts into the union structure, and medical inspection of students.

The Board from 1904 to 1946

The Douglas Commission, set up in 1905 by Governor William Douglas, responded to the mounting concern relating to inadequacies in industrial education by recommending modification of elementary programs to include agriculture and mechanic arts and of secondary schools to include drawing, mathematics, and science; new electives in industrial courses in high schools; evening schools for out-of-school youth and adults; and part-time day programs for the age group 14-16. It also recommended establishing a normal school department at the Massachusetts Agricultural School at Amherst and appointing a Commission on Industrial Education, independent of the Board of Education, with authority to establish independent schools.

Four years later, new legislation abolished the position of secretary to the board, superseding it with the post of commissioner of education. The board appointed David Snedden to the newly created post.

Snedden's period in office (1909-17) coincided with such national developments as individualized instruction, ability grouping, introduction of the junior high school, and promulgation of the Seven Cardinal Principles of Education. In addition to absorbing these advances, Massachusetts was busy on the home front as well. During this period, the Commonwealth authorized state-aided high schools, established the Teachers' Retirement Association, organized junior high schools (beginning in Wellesley in 1914), began state conferences of superintendents of schools and later of principals and instructors, and initiated the Division of University Extension to provide educational advantages to adults and persons in the armed services.

The Acts of 1919 established the Department of Education as one of 20 departments in a general reorganization of state structure. The restructured department incorporated eight separate boards and divisions. The Governor appointed Payson Smith as commissioner (Smith had previously been chosen commissioner by the board in 1917) to administer the department with an Advisory Board of Education comprising six members, with terms of 3 years. At least two board members were to be women, and one was to be appointed from the ranks of the teachers. Hence the leadership was to come from the commissioner rather than the board; this became a burdensome responsibility as the department increased in size and authority. This legal structure continued until the next reorganization of the Board of Education under the Acts of 1947.

During this 38-year period, Payson Smith served as state commissioner until 1935, and he was followed by James G. Reardon (1935-38), Walter F. Downey (1939-43), and Julius E. Warren (1943-46). John J. Desmond, Jr., was appointed by the Governor in 1946 and was reappointed by the new Board of Education in 1947.

The Commonwealth approved participation in the Smith-Hughes Act for the expansion of vocational education in 1917. In 1919, Americanization classes were authorized in order to teach English and citizenship to the foreign born who constituted a substantial segment of the state's population. In this same early postwar period, the state promulgated minimum salaries; mandated compulsory continuation schools; and passed a stronger law governing instruction for the mentally retarded, a program first instituted in 1898. In 1921, degrees were authorized for 4-year courses at the state normal schools. By 1925, state curriculum committees were appointed in several subject disciplines.

Despite the lack of staff and limited department authority, there was progress in such areas as certification of teachers, equal educational opportunity, accreditation of schools and colleges, educational publications, school construction, teacher education, vocational education, and pupil services.

Certification of Teachers. Although certificating teachers was a prime concern in the colonial era, certification by modern statutory provisions came to Massachusetts only after a protracted struggle. The regulations were strengthened in 1924, when all full-time teachers were required to have a minimum of 2 years education beyond high school, but the Commonwealth trailed far behind its sister states. In fact, according to the commissioner's annual report of 1939, Massachusetts was the only state without a teacher certification law. In 1940, the commissioner and the Board of Education recommended qualifying standards for teachers and sponsored regional meetings of superintendents and school committees for voluntary adoption of these recommended standards. Five years later, the Educational Policies Committee of the Massachusetts School Superintendents Association issued a *Digest of Certification Goals* based in part on bills which had been proposed in 1920 and 1939 and the Downey brochure of 1940. The Legislature again attempted to pass a bill in 1947, but it was not until 1951, following reorganization of the Board of Education, that it enacted the first comprehensive certification law.

Equality of Educational Opportunity. Massachusetts took steps to prohibit discrimination based on race or color as early as 1865 and made it a personal liability to indulge in such practices by 1895. Public service employees were guaranteed protection from discriminatory practices in 1920. The Governor's Committee on Racial and Religious Understanding was appointed in 1945. The Fair Employment Practices Act, one of the first in the nation, became law in 1946, followed in 1949, under the new board, by enactment of the Fair Educational Practices Act, which provided for admission to schools and colleges without reference to race, color, creed, or national origin. The present Board of Education and its immediate predecessor have achieved national recognition for their leadership in ensuring equality of educational opportunity.

Accreditation and Licensing. Before 1940, the General Court, through its department of corporations, passed upon the financial structure of institutions of higher education and issued charters for their operation. The Department of Education made only limited recommendations. Secondary schools were evaluated only in terms of whether they were following the statutory requirements.

With the advent of World War II came the need to provide for veterans education. Thus the Legislature established a Board of Collegiate Authority in the Department of Education in 1943 to approve schools and colleges for attendance by returning veterans. Two years earlier, it had created a recess commission on junior colleges and provided for licensing private trade schools and promulgating regulations for correspondence schools. In this same period, the commissioner appointed a planning committee to study the evaluation of secondary schools.

Although the state's role in accreditation was limited throughout these years, it should be noted that the highly respected New England Association of Colleges and Secondary Schools broadened its activities in the 1930's and thereafter and set high standards for its membership.

Educational Publications. The Department of Education continued to strive toward its objective of diffusing information, using largely the system of annual reports; nevertheless, the Legislature did not deem these of sufficient importance to print, and the board, as well as the commissioner, had difficulty getting any material other than statistical reports published. Again and again, "the absence of standardized, reliable, valid, and consistent information" (16) led to the practice of civic and educational organizations' collecting their own data and issuing mimeographed, unofficial material about school systems. Departmental publications from 1921 to the end of World War II included *Manual for Junior High Schools; Manual for High Schools; Tercentenary of the Massachusetts Bay Colony; General Laws Relating to Education; The Development of Education in Massachusetts, 1630-1930; Supervision of Instruction in Junior High Schools; Massachusetts Public School Administration; Massachusetts Youth Study;* and *Primary Curriculum Guide.*

In 1923, the Zook Report (17) had called for the establishment of a research division similar to that found in business and industry. It was not until many years later, however, that this recommendation gained recognition and then implementation by virtue of federal assistance. The department took one important step toward this goal in the 1940's with a School Survey Form, instituted to help school districts examine their educational programs and facilities with the assistance of department staff members.

School Construction. From 1920 to 1930, as prosperity increased and the suburbs expanded, 439 public schools were built. During the Depression, however, practically all construction was seriously curtailed, and only 287 schools were erected. Similarly, in the prewar and war years construction continued to be restricted as cities and towns put off major capital expenditures. It was not until the baby boom and the rapid increase in suburban living of the postwar era that the next big surge in school construction got under way. But in 1962, 40 percent of the school buildings in use in the Commonwealth had been constructed prior to 1920 (18).

Teacher Education. From the time of Horace Mann, the preparation and training of teachers had been a major concern of the Board of Education. The Legislature had assigned the board the responsibility for the normal schools, but the teacher-training programs were largely elementary school oriented. By 1921, degrees were authorized for 4-year courses, as a result of gradual extensions of the curriculum in the colleges.

With the advent of the junior high schools, a new type of teacher training was needed. The Massachusetts Junior High Principals' Association became critical of the college instructors' qualifications to give the training, and the facilities available. The association appointed a committee of five principals in 1937 to cooperate with college administrators in conducting a study of the situation. The report covered such topics as supply and demand, selection and admission, curriculum, faculty, laboratory school, graduation, and follow-up services. While college presidents generally appreciated the report, the department did not act on its recommendations. However, with the appointment in 1946 of a new commissioner who had been a member of the superintendents' policies commission, interest was revitalized and ultimately produced excellent results.

Pupil Services. As the philosophy of the purposes of education and schooling changed from teaching the fundamentals to meeting the needs of individual pupils, there came a demand for various types of pupil services. In 1920, the Commonwealth organized a "High School Equivalency Certificate," based on completion of a 16-unit high school education through a program of correspondence and/or standard courses to be completed with supervised examination. Minimum requirements in English, literature, mathematics, U.S. history, government, and science were specified. Originally intended to assist Massachusetts residents 20 years of age or older in reaching their educational goal, this program was transferred to a Veteran's Service budget in July 1947 and operated under a policies commission subordinate to the new Board of Education (19).

Health services assumed more and more importance as one of the cardinal principles. Physical examinations, physical education, and athletics received increasing attention. To encourage coordination, school health councils were set up, capped by a state interdepartmental Health Council in 1940, which met monthly during the school year and published a number of handbooks and checklists to raise the standards of school health programs.

Concurrent with the national emphasis on ability grouping and meeting of individual needs, junior high schools increased to 170 by 1928. They stressed three important objectives in particular: exploration of abilities, educational and vocational guidance, and inculcation of "how-to-study" habits.

Just prior to World War II, the field of guidance found itself in the midst of a rapid expansion, in keeping with a prime Massachusetts Youth Study recommendation. The Acts of 1941 authorized the appointment of directors of occupational guidance and placement in school systems and a supervisor in the state department. Such a program expanded into Veterans Centers throughout the state and began to bring in- and out-of-school youth and adults into a coordinated program.

More attention also was being given to atypical children. In 1919, the Commonwealth authorized formation of special classes for mentally retarded pupils. Increasingly, attention was given to the deaf, the blind, and other physically handicapped pupils through appropriate legislation and services (20).

Adult Services. In 1915, when the only public institutions of higher education were 2-year normal schools and the Massachusetts Agricultural School, the General Court established the Division of University Extension in the department to offer courses at cost to thousands who wished to enrich their backgrounds. Classes and correspondence courses were set up, and enrollment soon swelled to 40,000 in numerous communities throughout the state.

The year 1919 saw the department instituting Americanization courses in English and American citizenship for the foreign-born noncitizens to attain citizenship. Enrollments ran from 20,000 to 30,000 in the 1920's and from 10,000 to 20,000 in the 1940's. The state reimbursed the communities one-half the cost of instruction.

Another important service for adults came in library extension. In the last part of the nineteenth century, the Governor appointed the first Free Public Library Commission in the United States. At that time, there were only 103 towns without libraries, but the other 248 were in need of assistance both in terms of personnel and standards of service. The first salaried professional staff member in the Department of Education had been appointed in 1910, and this was increased to two in 1912. Interlibrary loans of books were authorized in 1911, and house-to-house delivery of books was carried on. During 1935-39, a statewide regional system of libraries was set up and was materially aided by the Works Progress Administration in 1940.

Vocational Education. In 1921, the General Court established the commissioner and the Advisory Board of Education as the State Board of Vocational Education in order to handle the activities arising from enactment of the Smith-Hughes Act. In the same year, the federal Vocational Rehabilitation Act was passed, and responsibility for extending its related services in Massachusetts was placed in the Department of Education.

Seventeen years later, the work of the department's vocational education division received added impetus with passage by Congress of the George-Deen Act. In 1941, the

Legislature voted to regulate private trade schools. The greatest boon to vocational education in this entire era was the replacement in 1946 of the George-Deen Act by the George-Barden Act whereby Congress extended the basis upon which the expenditure of federal funds could be made.

Like its counterparts in the other states, the Massachusetts Department of Education made a major contribution to the war effort from 1940 to 1946. The reports of the Board of Education in those years contain many references to actions taken. Among the more significant ones were organization of defense training classes in 10 trade schools, around-the-clock utilization of vocational education shops, establishment of high school Victory Corps, training of thousands of boys to assist in war industries, and organization of war ration book distribution.

As the war neared its end, mounting concern for the future of public education led the Massachusetts General Court to appoint a Legislative Research Commission in 1945 to study and report (21) on areas of major importance.

Chapter 652 of the Acts of 1947 resulted from this study, creating a new pattern of organization for the state board which was to last until 1965.

THE DEPARTMENT, 1947-65

The 1947 legislation placed the department under a Board of Education of nine members appointed by the Governor for terms of 9 years each. To the board went the authority to appoint the commissioner of education, who, in turn, received the power to appoint a deputy commissioner. Later legislation provided for the commissioner and deputy commissioner to serve "at the discretion of the Board."

John J. Desmond, Jr., reappointed in 1947, served as commissioner until his retirement in 1957. He was succeeded by Owen B. Kiernan, who continued to hold this position through 1968, serving as president of the Council of Chief State School Officers in 1967.

The period since 1947 has brought expansion of direct personal services by department staff and a marked increase in the number of educational conferences and institutes sponsored, or shared in, by the Board of Education and the Department of Education. The department has sponsored conferences of superintendents of schools, principals, supervisors, and special subject teachers annually with strong and repeated emphasis on new educational objectives, innovative practices, administrative techniques, research findings, policy developments, and new or contemplated legislation. Parallel efforts have been conducted by the Massachusetts Teachers Association and its affiliated county teachers associations, aided by department staff and regional and national leaders.

Each of the Governors of the Commonwealth in this period devoted considerable attention to the needs of the department and of public education in general. Of particular import were Governor Christian A. Herter's calling together the Massachusetts White House Conference on Education at Amherst in September 1955 and the address by Governor Foster Furcolo at the Governor's Conference on Higher Education at Cambridge in November 1957, focusing on the need for a more effective system of post-high school educational coordination.

The Massachusetts White House Conference on Education (22), planned by civic and government leaders (including members of the Board of Education), drew over 1,800 participants to probe the major issues of the day.

Another source of renewed strength in providing educational leadership in the Commonwealth has been the 1960 resumption of the practice of publishing the annual reports of the commissioner of education, a procedure which had been dropped for many years because of the failure of the General Court to provide the necessary funds for printing. Utilizing Title X (Public Law 85-864) funds, Commissioner Kiernan has in each subsequent year disseminated his report to the school systems and to other important makers of public opinion, thereby adding new dimensions to the process of spreading new ideas and of clarifying significant issues.

The most vital issue to achieve public recognition through the medium of Dr. Kiernan's annual reports has been the need to examine the total spectrum of education. This call, issued in 1961, ultimately led to support by the executive and legislative branches with a resultant appropriation of $250,000 to institute what has since become known as the Willis-Harrington Report—the most comprehensive study of public education in the history of the Commonwealth (23). This and other annual reports prepared between 1962 and 1966 have offered policy positions on such crucial matters as regional vocational schools, educational television, federal and state interrelationships, education of the emotionally disturbed, fiscal autonomy, and equality of educational opportunity. Few, if any, controversial subjects relating to public education in this Commonwealth have escaped scrutiny or lacked clarification within the scope of these contemporary reports.

One of the first actions of the newly organized Board of Education was to appoint an executive committee of three officers and one other member to serve with the commissioner and to accompany him to legislative hearings. They were instructed to further legislation on the budget and state aid. Expanding their efforts, board members and department staff representatives worked with, and through, regular committees or special commissions and study groups established by the General Court in the 1950's and early 1960's. Their efforts led to the enactment of a body of important statutes and related programs and facilities, including the Commission on the Structure of State Government (1949), the Commission on State Aid (1952), the Commission on State Medical and Dental Schools (1953), the Commission To Study the Problems of Mental Retardation (1954), the State Youth Commission Relative to Facilities Available for Meeting the Problems of Juvenile Delinquency (1954), and the Special Commission To Audit State Needs (1967).

During the same years, 1947-65, the Board of Education, carrying out its statutory responsibility, also annually filed bills which not only introduced new and desirable facilities, machinery, and programs, but also, in some instances, served to correct or repeal unsatisfactory existing laws. Major changes wrought by these bills include provision for instruction and training of certain emotionally disturbed children and reimbursing cities and towns and school districts for expenses in connection therewith (1960); establishment in the department of an advisory board of higher education policy, the first major step toward centralized reviewing of present and predicted programs for higher education with budgetary recommendations therefor (1962); licensing of correspondence schools to protect Massachusetts citizens from fraudulent promotional efforts (1963); authorization of an advisory committee on disadvantaged children and of special programs for said children in elementary and secondary schools, one of the first state programs in the nation to identify and assist educationally disadvantaged children (1964); authorization of the department to prescribe special programs for academically talented children in elementary and secondary schools and to assist cities, towns, and regional school districts in establishing said programs—a pioneering effort to encourage local school sytems to develop special curriculum approaches to challenge the academically talented (1964); and hiring of aides for assignments in laboratories and classrooms to enable the overburdened regular teacher to focus on prime instructional responsibilities (1965).

Legislative programs of the Board of Education have gained impetus, particularly in recent years, from the cooperation given by the Department of Education's Advisory Council on Legislation comprising representatives of the Massachusetts State Federation of Women's Clubs, Delta Kappa Gamma, Massachusetts Association of School Committees, League of Women Voters, Massachusetts State Labor Council, AFL-CIO, Massachusetts Teachers Association, Massachusetts Association of School Superintendents, Massachusetts Educational Conference Board, Massachusetts Congress of Parents and Teachers, American Association of University Women, Massachusetts Council for Public Schools, National Council of Jewish Women, Massachusetts Federation of Teachers, Massachusetts Committee on Children and Youth, Association of Massachusetts State Colleges Alumni, and Massachusetts League of Cities and Towns. Council representatives not only annually review with the commissioner all pending board bills, but also, in many instances, actively support them before committees of the General Court and in the public arena. In turn, the commissioner, acting with board approval, periodically lends public support to legislation originating with these organizations.

The commissioner, or other department staff members, also regularly appears for or against legislation filed by legislators or others affecting public education. Other significant facets for influencing the lawmaking process are the statutory requirements under which the commissioner, with occasional assistance from the department counsel and the research and development division, presents to the ways and means committee of the General Court and to the Governor his judgments as to the meaningfulness and cost of educational bills being considered by them.

Educational laws and their interpretation and implementation by the Department of Education, school committees, and others are most seriously affected by legal opinions of attorneys general and decisions of the courts. This has been particularly true in this Commonwealth since 1960 in the contentious area of civil liberties and civil rights.

Three opinions of the attorney general were of particular importance to the department in this period. All were requested during the years when the Honorable Edward W. Brooke, now a U.S. Senator, was the chief law officer of the Commonwealth.

The first of these opinions, rendered in August 1963, related to the constitutionality of certain practices, real and hypothetical, of the public schools, as affected by the decisions of the U.S. Supreme Court in the Schempp and Murray cases with respect to reading the Bible and reciting the Lord's Prayer. The questioned practices declared to be permissible were a pause for silent meditation, or gatherings of students before classes on their own initiative for devotional exercises; vocal prayer at functions such as graduation or baccalaureate exercises which are not a part of the regular curricular activities; the teaching and study of the Bible, or religion, or usages in the public schools in connection with the observance of holidays having religious overtones such as Christmas and Easter, or of exercises and songs involving religious beliefs to illustrate the religious history and universal significance of these holidays.

One of the most significant passages in the attorney general's opinion enables school officials and others to make appropriate constitutional distinctions of a state's approval of devotional exercises and its obligation to enhance moral training. This part of the opinion merits reprinting herewith:

> The Court made clear that in its view of the First Amendment, devotional readings and recitations of the type under consideration exceeded the powers of the

state. Accordingly, it was immaterial that the exercises were brief, enjoyed widespread support, and were not mandatory. It was equally immaterial, in the Court's opinion, that the practices may have had beneficial effects on the students. A devotional reading as part of the public school curriculum is simply not within the power of the civil government, in much the same fashion that the passage of a general law, however minor in nature and however beneficial it may be, is not within the power of any church. As a constitutional ruling under the Fourteenth Amendment, these decisions set forth the supreme law of the land, and are binding on the states and all political subdivisions thereof.

But if the moral value of the exercises was not in question, it was made equally clear that within the limits of their jurisdictional competence, the schools have a right and a duty to instill into the minds of the pupils those moral principles which are so necessary to a well-ordered society. It is difficult to conceive of a more compelling function of education than is the molding of the moral strength of the student. Indeed, this function has been a part of the statutory obligations of teachers in Massachusetts since 1789 . . . (24).

In February 1964, the attorney general issued two other opinions of consequence to the public schools in their relationships to the department. One related to the highly controversial matter of a proposed school boycott, directed against the Boston School Committee in connection with charges of de facto segregation; the other pertained to the authority of the Department of Education to seek information concerning color of students, i.e., racial census.

In the instance of the proposed school boycott, the attorney general dealt with a very sensitive situation. On the one hand, many civil rights leaders and some legal experts regarded the boycott as an appropriate method with which to correct alleged injustices. On the other hand, the department felt that, regardless of the worthiness of a cause, school attendance laws could not be violated. The attorney general's opinion (25) supported the department's position.

In order to ascertain vital information with respect to the guaranteeing of equal educational opportunity to all children of the Commonwealth, the commissioner of education, with board approval, took steps to initiate a racial census. In answer to specific questions proposed by the commissioner, the attorney general, in the second of his February 1964 opinions, clearly indicated that the making of a record of color does not violate the Fair Educational Practices Law and, further, that the department or the commissioner has the power to insist that school committees provide information by which a determination could be made concerning the extent to which various racial groups utilized the public school system.

Notwithstanding this opinion, the New Bedford School Committee voted in March 1964 not to take a racial census which was requested by the commissioner to be returned before April 1. The school committee also contended, among other points, that the racial composition of the public school population of New Bedford did not lend itself to realistic distinctions between "white" and "nonwhite" students. Two court cases—one before the Superior Court of the Commonwealth and one, on appeal, before the Supreme Judicial Court of the Commonwealth—resulted. The ultimate decision of the Supreme Judicial Court (26), announced in the summer of 1965, upheld the right of the department to obtain such census information and the form on which it was requested.

Some issues, problem areas, and movements, while already alluded to with varying degrees of emphasis, merit additional consideration. Among these are civic education, equality of educational opportunity, pupil services, school districting, higher education, state and federal aid, vocational education, and, as a culminating feature of the period, reorganization of the Department of Education.

EXPANDING EDUCATIONAL OPPORTUNITY

The Civic Education Movement

From the earliest beginnings of public education, dating back to the 1630's, Massachusetts had placed major emphasis upon the need to prepare its children and youth for the duties of citizenship in addition to maximizing individual excellence. Horace Mann appropriately reflected this objective toward the dual mandate when he wrote about "the high purposes of training an American child to become an American citizen." By the end of World War II, this state already had many laws on the books to this effect, including requirements for the local school systems to teach U.S. history, civics, morality, and the Constitutions of the United States and of the Commonwealth. What became clearly evident by 1950, however, was the need to adopt a more sophisticated and more comprehensive concept of citizenship education, one that advanced beyond a somewhat simplistic preparation for political responsibility.

The modern civic education movement—nationally, as well as within Massachusetts—was considerably influenced by the pioneering efforts of John J. Mahoney, a former president of Lowell Normal School and the first director of the department's Americanization program. Moving to Boston University in the 1920's, Dr. Mahoney evolved an approach to citizenship over the next 20 years which strongly emphasized behavioral goals in relation to economic education, human relations, attitude toward law, practical politics, and international relations. In 1946, in concert with Henry W. Holmes, former dean of the Harvard

Graduate School of Education, Mahoney founded the Civic Education Project (later to become the Filene Center for Citizenship at Tufts University) which had the full support of Commissioner Desmond of Massachusetts and the other Northeastern states' commissioners of education. Two very specific products resulted from this Project-Department of Education relationship: enactment of Chapter 693 of the Acts of 1951–after a campaign by President Karl Compton of the Massachusetts Institute of Technology, Ralph Lowell, and other distinguished trustees of the Civic Education Foundation–setting up an Office of American Citizenship in the department; and publishing of *Education for Citizenship,* a blueprint for civic education by the commissioners of education of the Northeastern states, in 1952–this report was written by a committee headed by Dr. Mahoney.

The Office of American Citizenship, which became the Division of Civic Education in 1957, was the first such office established in the country. Chapter 693 charged the office with–

> Responsibility for leadership in the co-operative study and fuller use, in the public schools and teachers colleges of the Commonwealth, of teaching materials and methods, student activities, and administrative and supervisory procedures directed toward more effective preparation for the duties of citizenship.

Building on the objectives incorporated into *Education for Citizenship* and capitalizing on the contribution to the citizenship movement by the Columbia Citizenship Education Project, the Detroit Citizenship Study, the Civic Education Project at Tufts, the Joint Council on Economic Education, and others, the Office of American Citizenship developed a state program which has achieved regional and national recognition.

This office, or division as it was later called, has stressed the service and leadership function. Among its many accomplishments, this office has provided degree-credit courses and professional improvement courses under the label "Civic Behavior" and "Youth Problems Institute" for approximately 2,500 teachers in service; it also has conducted the state's Student Government Day program which annually involved 500 public and nonpublic schools in the study of state government, the Student Government Exchange Program which annually involves more than 100 high schools in the study of local government through intercommunity invitations, and the State Youth Citizenship Conferences, which for the past several years have annually provided more than 1,100 high school students forums for the discussion of vital civic issues.

In cooperation with the school bureau of the Greater Boston United Community Services, the division organized in 1956 a youth-in-community-services project known as Operation Kindness, which involved thousands of secondary pupils in more than 2,000,000 hours of volunteer work through 1965. (This project served as one of the models for the Peace Corps and VISTA.) In 1960, the division organized the "Freedom Lectures," a series on civil liberties that won first prize in the Freedoms Foundation Awards to governmental agencies. The following year, the division conducted a statewide survey relating to teaching about communism, which, coupled with the issuance of a basic policy statement on teaching controversial subjects and the distribution of the resource unit *Ideology and World Affairs* (prepared in conjunction with Tufts University and other Northeastern states' representatives), had a nationwide impact on coping with this difficult education and public policy issue. The "Education and Race Relations" special course at Boston State College also was a by-product of the division's energies organized and conducted in 1964; the course was the forerunner to the TV course approved for federal funding in the amount of $134,000 under Title IV of the Civil Rights Act of 1964 in the summer of 1965.

Separate from its focus on teacher training and other programs for elementary and secondary schools, the civic education division has, since 1954, also conducted the department's adult civic education program. This has involved the training and certifying of teachers for this activity which is carried on in approximately 70 Massachusetts cities and towns.

Equality of Educational Opportunity

Precedent to the determination to take a race census in March 1964, the Board of Education had issued a statement on racially imbalanced schools and the underprivileged child which clearly and unequivocally sustained the policy position of its predecessors in relation to the goal of equality of educational opportunity and, further, served to strike down new impediments to this objective. On August 19, 1963, the board stated:

> The Massachusetts Board of Education is deeply concerned by the number of American children who are underprivileged, partly because of neighborhood racial imbalance as reflected in some public schools. The Board recognizes its responsibility to call attention to the educational needs of the underprivileged child in the Commonwealth of Massachusetts and will use to the fullest its moral and legal powers to equalize opportunities wherever the need may appear in our schools. The Board, consistent with its role of guiding and assisting school committees–all of which have prime legal responsibility locally–urges each committee to intensify its efforts to identify and to meet the educational needs of any such underprivileged children. The Board urges further that action, consistent with sound educational practices, be taken immediately to eliminate racial imbalance when and where it is ascertained to exist in any school system (27).

In the next several months, the board authorized the 15-week teacher-training course, "Education and Race Relations," at Boston State College under its civic education division and approved distribution of a so-called "Human Relations Kit" to every public school in the Commonwealth. Each kit included the course bibliography, a special bibliography on "The Negro in American Life," and a teacher's unit of study entitled "Discrimination—Danger to Democracy."

In March 1964, concurrent with the race census action, the board appointed a 21-man Advisory Committee on Racial Imbalance to reassess the research data regarding the impact of racial imbalance on minority-group and other children. Assisting the advisory committee—which included five college presidents and an outstanding array of religious and lay leaders—with this major research effort was a task force of nationally and regionally respected educators.

After a year of intensive study, the committee published its findings under the title of *Because It Is Right–Educationally* (28), popularly known as the Kiernan Report. The report has since achieved national recognition. It points out that 55 schools (including 45 Boston schools) contained more than 50-percent nonwhite enrollments and that racial imbalance is harmful on the grounds that it damages the self-confidence and motivation of Negro children, reinforces the prejudices of children regardless of their color, does not prepare the child for integrated life in a multiracial community and world, impairs the opportunities of many Negro children to prepare for the vocational requirements of our technological society, often results in a gap in the quality of educational facilities among schools, and represents a serious conflict in the public schools with the American creed of equal opportunity.

The recommendations and suggestions incorporated into the Kiernan Report have had a marked influence. Among the significant educational advantages have been the awarding of a $134,000 federal grant under Title IV of the Civil Rights Act of 1964 to the Department of Education to make a TV series for state, regional, and national use based on the "Education and Race Relations" course; establishment by the presidents of the Massachusetts state colleges of a Human Rights Committee composed of faculty representatives from 11 institutions to revitalize human relations education offering to all undergraduates; expansion of summer school and camp programs which provided rich interracial learning experiences, in particular for Boston nonwhite children, and served to some extent to influence the formation of the Metropolitan Council for Educational Opportunity, now regarded as one of the nation's most valuable experiments in urban-suburban human relations education; and passage by the General Court, on August 18, 1965, of the Racial Imbalance Act (Chapter 641), the first of its kind in the nation. Following the racial census taken on October 1, the Board of Education notified the school committees of Boston, Springfield, New Bedford, and Cambridge to submit plans for the elimination of racial imbalance in certain of their schools which had been found to be in violation of Chapter 641.

Concurrent with its extensive efforts to deal with the issue of racial imbalance, the Board of Education enhanced the cause of equal educational opportunity further by filing legislation which ultimately became Chapter 650 of the Acts of 1964, an act designed to provide special assistance programs to assist children and youth educationally disadvantaged as a result of home and environmental conditions. Passage of this act had a national impact in that its design served as one of the models for the development in 1965 of what has become known as Title I of the Elementary and Secondary Education Act (Public Law 89-10).

Six school systems (Arlington, Boston, Easton, Holyoke, Sharon, and Springfield) instituted programs to help the disadvantaged during the 1964-65 school year under the state's matching formula.

The introduction in 1965 of Title I, Elementary and Secondary Education Act, with its more attractive funding arrangement, caused a major shift from local involvement in the state programs by the end of 1965. The year or more of state department focus on the needs of the disadvantaged contributed greatly, however, to the development of meaningful Title I proposals when this federal program was introduced in the Commonwealth.

Federal Programs

As has been the case in so many areas of government, the "federal presence" has increasingly pervaded the Department of Education during the past decade. Admittedly, while the advent of major amounts of federal money has brought problems of several kinds, the overall effect has been to provide to local school districts programs and services not available through state funds.

Prior to the orbiting of the first Sputnik in October 1957, the federal influence in the state department was felt chiefly through programs in vocational and school lunch areas. The department staff members added as a result of federal activity were engaged in administering the distribution to the local schools of money and commodities. The National Defense Education Act of 1958 and the amendments thereto have had an increasingly important effect.

For example, Title III of the National Defense Education Act for improving instruction in the critical subjects has grown from its emphasis on science, mathematics, and modern foreign languages to now include, in addition, English, civics, history, geography, reading, economics, and industrial arts. The number of specialists in these areas has grown from none to more than twenty. In addition to the distribution of federal funds to local school districts, the federal support for these supervisory positions has enabled the department to provide greatly expanded services to local educational agencies. During one recent period, the elementary and secondary education bureau had twice as many supervisors supported from federal funds as from state funds.

Recent Congresses have added several educational programs which have essentially involved the distribution of money to local agencies. Most of these programs provided for administrative staff to assist not only in program review but to provide leadership in the specialized areas.

Public Law 88-210, the Vocational Education Act of 1963, following closely on the heels of the Manpower Development and Training Act of 1962, had a revolutionary impact on the area of vocational education. The legislation substantially increased the support of regular programs, broadened research activities, and encouraged work-study programs.

Passage of the Elementary and Secondary Education Act in 1965 gave an added boost to the expansion of federally supported activity at the state level for the broad purposes of channeling federal money to local districts. However, one area of this legislation evidenced a new approach. Title V of the Elementary and Secondary Education Act provided funds for strengthening state departments of education. The Massachusetts Department of Education used these Title V moneys to initiate several department programs for which state funds were not available.

ESEA Title V funds have permitted an expansion into the area of research and development of department activities supported in a minor way by state and NDEA Title X funds. The Research and Development Center in Woburn, with its third-generation computer and highly qualified staff members, was the major project in the department plan for Title V funds.

Similarly, Title V funds were set aside to start the first two regional centers of the department, one in Pittsfield and one in Worcester. With the transfer of the regional center activity to state funding, the federal funds available under Title V will be utilized to initiate other programs for which state funds have not yet been appropriated.

The greatly expanded federal activity affecting the Department of Education is further illustrated by reference to Chapter 572 of the Acts of 1965. This act, resulting from the report of the Massachusetts Education Study Commission, established a state and federal assistance division in view of the "enormous increase in number, size, scope, and complexity of federal programs in aid of education." Further emphasis is contained in Section 1G of General Laws, Chapter 15, as inserted from Chapter 572:

> The board of education shall develop plans for education to meet state needs, and shall be the planning and approving authority for federal programs to be undertaken in the commonwealth . . . . The board may receive allotments for the commonwealth from federal programs in aid of elementary, secondary, and vocational education and may direct the disbursement of such funds and state aid funds in accordance with law.

In summary, the federal impact on the department was relatively minor for many years. However, beginning with 1958, the years have brought a tremendous growth in the amount and kinds of federally related activities carried on within the department. Present conditions foretell a continued growth through the next decade of the federal impact on the programs and policies of the Department of Education.

Higher Education

With the influx of veterans studying under the GI Bill of Rights, male enrollments increased and greater interest was shown in the teachers colleges. In 1948, the Department of Education was authorized to develop 2-year programs leading to the associate in arts degree at the teachers colleges. Tragically, however, funds were not provided in the next decade to implement such programs despite annual budgetary requests for such support.

Meanwhile, the institution originally known as the Massachusetts Agricultural College had become known in 1931 as Massachusetts State College; in 1947 it became the University of Massachusetts and was made solely responsible to a board of trustees rather than to the Department of Education. It, too, began to experience a major influx of veterans and initiated a comprehensive master plan for the physical and academic growth of the university.

In 1950, largely in recognition of the many nonteaching programs offered, the Commonwealth gave the Massachusetts School of Art authority to grant the bachelor of fine arts degree to students completing these programs. Thus the dual role of the college in preparing art teachers and supervisors and in developing persons with a high degree of technical proficiency in various art forms received overdue recognition.

After a prolonged legislative deliberation in 1953, Lowell Textile School, renamed Lowell Technological Institute, was put under the exclusive control of a separate board of trustees and its destiny left in the hands of the trustees—as had been the case with the University of Massachusetts a few years earlier.

Following protracted negotiations between the City of Boston and the Legislature, the transfer to state control and support of the Teachers College of the City of Boston became reality in 1952. Long the target of local political personalities and aspirants, this college had been sadly neglected in the preceding decade. Its entrance into the system of state teachers colleges was destined to coincide with the development of improved facilities and burgeoning enrollments. Its new title was the State Teachers College at Boston. Staff members had the option of accepting other assignments within the city school system or joining the service of the state; most chose the latter alternative.

A little-heralded event in 1954 was to develop into a major aspect of the teachers college program. In the budget for the year beginning July 1, 1954, the state teachers colleges were permitted by the Legislature to undertake a program of courses for teachers and others to be financed out of a revolving fund and "at no expense to the Commonwealth." From a small first-year gross intake of $50,000, the program increased in volume nearly 40-fold in the next dozen years. More significantly, it has provided courses of steadily increasing quality for teachers and others through the master's degree level throughout the Commonwealth.

The year 1959 brought to a close the first six decades of this century with a number of startling and progressive strides in Massachusetts public higher education. The Acts of 1959 recognized the truly collegiate character of the work being done by the Massachusetts School of Art by changing its title to the Massachusetts College of Art, thus completing its evolution from a "normal art" school. Similarly, the Legislature that same year authorized the state teachers colleges to grant "other appropriate baccalaureate degrees" beyond those in education already authorized. This action was closely followed in 1960 by a change in the title of the institutions to "state colleges" in keeping with nationwide developments. Thus the colleges were officially ready to launch into a variety of liberal arts programs and other areas of specialization having no necessary connection to teaching. This action proved to be the necessary precursor to greatly broadened programs in the 1960's.

Almost simultaneously with this basic expansion of the role of the state teachers colleges came authorization for establishment of a number of 2-year community colleges regionally distributed through the Commonwealth. These colleges were under the direction of the Massachusetts Board of Regional Community Colleges in, but not subject to, the Department of Education and were charged with providing technical and terminal forms of collegiate programs as well as 2-year college transfer programs. Rapid implementation of its responsibilities by the Board of Regional Community Colleges added a new and vital dimension to Massachusetts' higher education in the 1960's.

The year 1960 also saw the establishment of a new technologically orientated institution in the southeastern section of the state. Significantly, under the title of Southeastern Massachusetts Technological Institute, it was designed as the ultimate replacement of the two former textile schools established in the nineteenth century and later renamed New Bedford Institute of Technology and Bradford Durfee College of Technology. Its location in South Dartmouth placed it about midway between the two institutions it was destined to replace. Planned also in the program for this new campus is an undergraduate program in the liberal arts and sciences.

The Acts of 1963 provided fiscal autonomy for a new Board of Trustees of State Colleges, slightly expanded in membership from its predecessor, the Board of Education. Composition of the new board included the nine members of the Board of Education, the commissioner of education (ex officio), and one state college president elected annually by his fellow presidents. The provision of fiscal autonomy, a policy already established for the University of Massachusetts, allowed much greater responsibility and flexibility in fiscal and personnel management than had ever been possible under previous regulations by the executive branch of the state government. This act constituted a major step forward in the development of the state colleges.

In 1962, the Legislature created the Massachusetts Education Study Commission. With the appointment of this group and their immediate involvement in a comprehensive study of all levels of public education in the Commonwealth, a new impetus was added to the growth of the state colleges. Through a 2-year period a careful analysis of public higher education was undertaken, with a great deal of attention being paid to the structure and functions of all segments of higher education. The resultant legislation in 1965 created the first overall structure for coordinating all public higher education—a Board of Higher Education—coequal to a new Board of Education whose responsibilities were designated as pertaining to the elementary and secondary schools of the Commonwealth. The Willis-Harrington Act redesigned the structure of higher education, removed the state colleges from the responsibilities of the Board of Education, and established a new 11-member lay Board of Trustees of State Colleges. This action brought to a close a long era of steady progress in teacher education in these institutions and launched another in the midst of rapidly expanding horizons for public higher education in Massachusetts.

School District Reorganization

The union superintendency, an organizational pattern by which two or more towns share the services of a superintendent and some supervisory and auxiliary personnel, was first authorized in 1888. In each instance, however, the member towns retained their own school committees and school buildings. Through 1950, 66 union superintendencies had been formed involving 204 towns. There were 60 local high schools with fewer than 100 students, and 76 local high schools which enrolled between 100 and 300 pupils.

The national movement to consolidate school districts in order to allow for more meaningful educational programs and more efficient management produced a unique post-World War II result in Massachusetts: namely, a positive effect in the development of the regional high school district and at least a numerically negative ending in that the total number of school districts advanced from 352 to 390 by 1965. The explanation lies in the fact that the union structure continued at the elementary level, with only a modest number of dissolutions, while approximately forty regional districts, mostly at the secondary school level, reached the functional stage. (Fifteen more regional districts were in the formative state.) The major current thrust, induced to some degree by the Massachusetts Education Commission Study of 1965, is an all-out drive to establish K-12 regional school districts through the elimination of archaic unions and the consolidation of small independent districts.

The regional school district owed its origin to the passage in 1948 of Chapter 645, "An Act To Encourage the Establishment of Regional and Consolidated Public Schools and To Provide Financial Assistance to Cities and Towns in the Construction of School Buildings." In August 1949, the General Court enacted Chapter 638, which provided the legal machinery for establishing regional school districts. Regional vocational school districts exclusively devoted to this specialized purpose were authorized by the passage of Chapter 650 of the Acts of 1960.

Initially, Chapter 645 of the Acts of 1948 allowed state construction grants ranging from 25 to 55 percent for regional schools. Later amendments to this act extended its terminal date from June 30, 1951, to June 30, 1971, and increased the grant percentage to a range of from 40 to 65 percent for regional projects.

Since the formation of the first regional school district in 1950, approximately 200 of the Commonwealth's 312 towns have taken advantage of the regional school district legislation, and more than $100 million has been invested in the construction of new regional schools and additions thereto. The number of local high schools with less than 100 pupils has diminished to 3, while the total of high schools enrolling 100 to 300 students has been reduced to 23.

PUPIL SERVICES

Guidance

As a result of the High School Victory Corps and its emphasis on guidance from 1941 to 1945, there had been a substantial increase in the number of secondary schools offering such services to youth. This pace accelerated in the postwar period at the local level with a modicum of assistance from the department due to serious staff limitations. By 1958, 232 high schools provided guidance programs. A similar impact was felt at the junior high school level, but very little was done, in a formal sense, in the elementary schools.

A major breakthrough in terms of comprehensive guidance services came in 1958 with passage of Title V-A of the National Defense Education Act and resultant increase in department staffing and related funding. By the end of the end of the 1958-59 school year, the department had added three supervisors, and there were 900 counselors employed in local school systems. One year later, the department's annual report revealed that 141 public school systems and 84 private school systems were formally participating in the Title V-A program. The reimbursements to public schools amounted to $325,904, while an additional $2,029 was paid for private school testing.

Strong leadership by the Department of Education's Office of Guidance and Placement had a salutary effect in the period from 1958 to 1965 with the result that many valuable publications were produced, the Massachusetts School Counselor Association was founded, workshops to train counselors were established, and regular regional conferences were instituted. There was also a marked increase in supervisory services to local school systems. Two other noteworthy achievements were the undertaking in 1963 of a Work-Study Development Program and of a statewide study of the status of guidance in the elementary schools. The statistics contained in the 1964-65 annual report reflected growth since 1958 in that there were 313 more counselors employed at the end of the period, and the number of state supervisors had doubled. At the end of 1965, $406,774 in federal funds was used under Title V-A in public schools, and the reimbursement for private school testing amounted to $9,176.

School Adjustment Counselors

The director of the Division of Youth Service, an autonomous state agency, instituted the School Adjustment Counseling Program by authorization of the Legislature upon the enactment of Chapter 696 of the Acts of 1955. This pioneering effort, whose approving authority includes the division's director and the commissioner of education, recognized the need to assist maladjusted, emotionally disturbed children (kindergarten-grade 8) if they are to avoid serious underachievement and behavioral disorders during later years. As a result, this program deals with these children, their families, and appropriate social agencies in an attempt to help them normally progress in school and to allow them to utilize effectively the resources of the school according to their own abilities.

In the 10-year history of this state-aided program, more than 100 public school systems have engaged school adjustment counselors and thereby contributed substantially to the wholesome development of hundreds of children who might have otherwise been lost to society.

School Lunch

The Office of School Lunch Programs was incorporated into the department as an educational program in 1948 following the earlier enactment in 1946 of the National School Lunch Act by the Congress. This highly efficient operation, which appropriately recognizes the basic need to protect and maintain the individual's strength and health, has had a remarkable growth in the intervening years, going from 26,475,938 lunches in the 1954-55 school year to 78,632,058 in the 1965-66 term.

Special Education

The end of World War II coincided with the one-hundredth anniversary of Massachusetts' initial effort to establish a school for the feeble-minded. These children and those who suffer from other mental and physical handicaps have been, and continue to be, a prime concern of the Commonwealth, particularly as aided by vital legislation, financial support, and department services. The postwar period represents the most dramatic span. The following summarization does not do justice to the basic and comprehensive steps that have been undertaken.

Mental Retardation. The Acts of 1950, as amended, provided a $500 differential for teachers of the mentally retarded. Legislation passed in 1954 mandated classes for the mentally retarded where five or more such pupils were so classified by intelligence quotients, created the special education division and provided for reimbursement of 50 percent of costs for maintaining special classes and for transportation thereto. Later legislation has provided additional services for educable and trainable mentally retarded children. In addition, school psychologists and classroom teachers have been trained in increasing numbers, and summer recreational programs have been introduced.

The Deaf. Deaf children in Massachusetts also have benefited substantially in this interim. The Acts of 1958 permitted these youngsters to go to school outside, as well as within, the Commonwealth. The first supervisor of deaf children was appointed in September 1961. That same year, the board passed certification standards for teachers of the deaf. Public Law 87-276 was passed by Congress in 1961 thereby enhancing the training of more teachers of the deaf in this state.

Partially Seeing Children. The General Laws of 1951 provided for an assistant supervisor to assist in the education of blind and partially seeing children. Legislation 9 years later provided a 50-percent reimbursement to local systems for instruction of these children. And in 1961, a library of large-type books and recorded books was set up for partially seeing children.

Blind Children. Integration of blind children in regular school classes at the local level was made possible under legislation passed in 1951 and 1952 which included substantial state aid. In the period 1952-57, Boston, Malden, Braintree, Medford, and Chicopee launched public school programs. The nation's first course in sensory and mobility training was introduced in this state in 1959.

Physically Handicapped Children. Massachusetts broadened earlier legislation mandating home instruction for physically handicapped children by itinerant teachers in 1945, 1954, 1955, and 1956. The requisite number of children was reduced from five to one, including victims of cerebral palsy. State aid included 50-percent reimbursement for transportation and for the utilization of special audio-visual equipment. The first full-time supervisor of physically handicapped children started work in 1958. Four hours of instruction per week were to be guaranteed to each child. Fifty-percent state reimbursement was provided for home and school instruction. The year 1959 saw adoption of regulations permitting state-aided recreation programs for the physically handicapped.

Speech-Handicapped and Hard-of-Hearing Children. By 1957, when the Commonwealth appointed its first supervisor of speech-handicapped, hard-of-hearing, and deaf children to the department, cities and towns were offering speech and hearing programs to approximately 11,000 children. The Acts of 1960 included children who are speech-handicapped along with children who are hard of hearing. State reimbursement up to 50 percent was voted for communities offering programs in this area. Ninety-six cities and towns now assist 18,000 children with these handicaps.

Aphasic Children. Department staff members attended the nation's first course offered on diagnosis and therapy for aphasic children in 1957 in St. Louis. The same year, new legislation permitted special instruction for these children. With state assistance, the Boston School for the Deaf also opened a program for the aphasic in 1957.

Emotionally Disturbed Children. After 5 years of intensive activity, the Commonwealth enacted legislation in 1960 to provide instruction for the emotionally disturbed. The basic program began in 1962 and includes instruction at the local level and, where approved, in private institutions. As of January 1964, 112 children were being instructed at home, 41 were in regular school programs, and 136 were being taught in special classes for emotionally disturbed children.

Library Extension

The successful experimental project in the Greenfield area, developed by the Western Massachusetts Library Federation between October 1950 and September 1952 with the assistance of the Department of Education's Division of Library Extension, had a lasting effect in that staffing, and funds were obtained shortly thereafter to broaden the services of the division's Greenfield regional office.

The work of the Special Administrative Library Commission, which reported to Governor Herter and the General Court in March 1955, represented a significant step toward long-range planning for libraries. With the passage of the Library Services Act by Congress in 1956, the Commonwealth had a meaningful design in readiness whereby an appropriate plan of implementation could be put into operation. During the period 1957-64, the division expended annually federal funds varying from $40,000 to $122,847 for rural services.

A 13-year struggle to provide state aid for free public libraries culminated in success in 1960 with the passage of legislation providing direct grants to municipalities for library services and money for establishing a series of state-supported regional library systems. In 1961, the Board of Library Commissioners certified 237 of 351 municipalities for grants totaling $974,442. The next year, 277 public libraries received aid. In 1964, 300 libraries received grants. The central and the western regional systems were established by 1963.

Under the Library Services and Construction Act of 1964, further federal funds became available. In 1965, Massachusetts received $658,637 for library services and $810,122 for construction purposes, administered in each instance by the Division of Library Extension.

Vocational Education

The South Shore, in an area from Hull to Plymouth, was the scene in 1955 of Massachusetts' first regional vocational-technical school survey, which culminated in the opening of the South Shore Regional Vocational-Technical School in Hanover in 1962. In 1957, a survey was initiated in Northern Berkshire County, and in 1962, the Northern Berkshire Regional Vocational-Technical School was opened in North Adams.

Dedication of the first two regional vocational-technical schools in 1962 signified a revolutionary breakthrough affecting some of the most pervasive social and psychological issues of the times. Coinciding with the event were three major legislative acts passed by Congress which changed the entire complex of vocational education. Title VIII of the National Defense Education Act (P. L. 85-864), the Manpower Development and Training Act of 1962 (P. L. 87-415), and the National Vocational Education Act of 1963 (P. L. 88-210) expanded instruction in vocational education to both older and younger pupils and broadened the related studies at all levels. Not only was vocational education commissioned to introduce technical education, but also to assist the uneducated and the undereducated, as well as the culturally, socially, economically, and academically disadvantaged.

As a result of surveys conducted by the vocational education bureau and the organization of regional vocational-technical school planning boards in cooperation with the school building assistance bureau according to Chapter 71 of the General Laws for forming school districts, the decade has witnessed the opening of six comprehensive regional vocational-technical schools which, already oversubscribed, offer most diversified programs and eliminate the terminal education status. Many of the students graduate as skilled craftsmen. Many more study to be technicians in industry and hospitals, and others pursue their education at 2- and 4-year colleges.

Never in the history of vocational education in Massachusetts has the vocational education bureau or the state department presented such concise plans for regions and cities to meet the challenge of society and minority groups by offering diverse, comprehensive vocational education for all youth. No city is too large, no town too small for the bureau to offer assistance. When one considers that for the first 50 years only large cities and towns offered vocational education to their youth, an articulation of the need for all to have an education to profit from was unprecedented. Much of this credit should go to foresighted superintendents of schools and directors of vocational education. It was mentioned before that boards of trade initiated two surveys, but superintendents of schools, directors of vocational education, and alert school committees and citizens initiated other requests for surveys. Nearly $100 million of construction is anticipated for improving the offerings for all students in the city schools, and, were some cities to make a serious attempt, this figure would increase.

This period also saw initiation of programs in the health occupations. A State Plan for Practical Nurse Training was approved by the Board of Education in December 1956. During the next 10 years, programs to train licensed practical nurses have expanded throughout the Commonwealth as have courses for medical assistant, medical laboratory assistant, surgical technician, dental assistant, dietary assistant, physical therapy assistant, and geriatric aide. Understanding the elderly, service to the mentally ill, and nurses' aide programs are also available at present.

Research projects included institutes in guidance and the health occupations approved and funded by USOE under 4(c) of the 1963 Vocational Education Act and other institutes funded under 4(b), the state allotment of the grant for research. *An Information System for Vocational Decisions* was submitted to USOE by the Graduate School of Education, Harvard University, and endorsed by the Bureau of Vocational Education and funded under 4(c) of the Vocational Education Act, and *Development of a Career Resource Service,* culminating in a model Career Resource Center at Newton High School, was funded through 4(b) under the Bureau of Vocational Education. The involvement with Quincy in Project ABLE completed more research in vocational education during this decade than was believable during the previous 50 years and symbolized the movement of vocational education to a new parallel of latitude.

State Aid

Although the Commonwealth ranked tenth among the states in total expenditures for public education at the conclusion of World War II, the heaviest support was attributable to the local property tax. The state's own share of the responsibility represented only 9 percent in 1945.

The 1947 Recess Commission of the General Court advanced seven criteria for evaluating school aid: adequacy for a sound school program, certainty of payments, encouragement of sound local organization, equalization of educational opportunity, strengthening of local control, arousing of local initiative, and improved salaries for professionally prepared teachers.

The Acts of 1948 provided a foundation program based on $130 per child aged 7 to 16 enrolled in public schools. State aid to local school systems increased to 14 percent by 1950 when the final commission report was issued. Then, as in 1947, however, the commission urged that the state's share should be 25 to 30 percent to realize the goal of equal educational opportunity. In 1959-60, school revenue receipts by level of government were as follows: federal, 5.3 percent; state, 19.9 percent; and local, 74.8 percent.

Widespread criticism of the 1948 program mounted in the 1950's and into the 1960's based essentially on the belief that the method of determining ability was not truly equalizing. The most penetrating analysis of the existing method was presented in a report entitled *State Aid to Education in Massachusetts,* published in 1962 by the New England School Development Council, with the cooperation of the Department of Education (104 Massachusetts school systems were members of the council at this time). The prime outcome of this study was a strong recommendation for the adoption of a percentage equalizing program based on the measures of ability, need, and effort. It set the goal for the state support at 40 percent of the educational dollar. Based on 1960 figures, the council's percentage equalizing formula would have cost approximately $123 million rather than the then-current state aid amounting to about $48 million.

The Massachusetts Educational Conference Board, composed of delegates from the leading educational organizations of the state, the Board of Education and the commissioner, and a host of citizens, business and labor leaders, legislators, and individual educators worked intensively over the next 3 years to improve the state aid situation.

Concurrent with this concerted effort to increase state aid, the Massachusetts Education Study Commission (the so-called Willis-Harrington Commission) also gave major attention in its total study of public education in the Commonwealth to the marked need to improve financial support at the state level and to lessen, if not eradicate, the obvious educational inequities prevailing in the cities and towns. The final commission report, published in June 1965, recommended that the existing state aid formula should be applied in full rather than only half and that full adjusted equalized valuation should be used as the tax base for aid to education. The proposed costs for 1965-66 totaled $123 million and were as follows: full payment on the state aid formula to meet elementary and secondary school improvements, $91 million; categorical and incentive aids, $7 million; improvements in higher education and expansion of the scholarship programs, $25 million.

The General Court has since passed a limited sales tax of 3 percent, of which four-fifths is credited to education in the distribution of local aid funds. These funds actually go into the city and town treasuries without being earmarked for said purposes. Additionally, a new percentage equalizing distribution formula based on need and effort has been adopted. Thirty-five percent of the education dollar has been set as the state's goal. To date, however, the sales tax returns distributed to the municipalities under the revised Chapter 70 have yet to exceed two-thirds of the entitlements anticipated under the new formula. The drive to achieve full funding and to remove inequities in the distribution formula continues.

The Massachusetts Education Study

Several direct references have already been made to the Massachusetts Education Commission Study (the Willis-Harrington Report), which was launched in September 1962 and concluded in December 1964. The full report of this comprehensive study of public education, ranging from the primary grades through college, was published in June 1965. Chapter 572 of the Acts of 1965 represents the first major piece of legislation designed to implement the commission's recommendations.

In brief, Chapter 572 set up three boards: an 11-member Board of Education responsible for public elementary and secondary education (the Department of Education is the administrative arm of the board and the commissioner of education is its executive officer); an 11-member Board of Higher Education responsible for providing active and effective leadership and coordination for the public higher education institutions (the executive officer of this board is the chancellor); and a 9-member Advisory Council on Education designed to provide a medium for the continuing study of public education essentially through the research activities directed by its executive secretary and small staff.

January 1966 signified not only the beginning of another calendar year, but also the start of a new era for public education in the Commonwealth of Massachusetts. The new boards had been appointed, the legislative prerogatives ascertained, and the sights set. A renewed quest for quality education had been instituted.

FOOTNOTES

1. Albert Bushnell Hart, *Commonwealth History of Massachusetts,* IV (Boston: The State History Co., 1930), 81, 222.
2. Ellwood P. Cubberley, *Public Education in the United States* (Cambridge: Houghton Mifflin Co., 1934), pp. 68-69.
3. *Tercentenary of the Massachusetts Bay Colony, 1630-1930,* Department of Education Committee, Frank P. Morse, chairman (Boston: Department of Education, 1930), p. 81.
4. *Ibid.,* p. 140.
5. Cubberley, *op. cit.,* pp. 56-58.
6. *Ibid.,* p. 70.
7. *Ibid.,* p. 91.
8. *Ibid.,* pp. 1-11.
9. Education Study Commission, *Report of the Special Commission Established To Make an Investigation and Study Relative to Improving and Extending Educational Facilities in the Commonwealth,* Pub. Doc. No. 4300 (Boston: Department of Education, June 1965), p. 126.
10. *Ibid.,* p. 124.
11. *Ibid.,* p. 129.
12. Board of Education, *Fifty-Fourth Annual Report* (1891), p. 16.
13. Department of Education, "Annual Listing: Former Members of the Board of Education," 1966, Boston, Massachusetts, p. 2.
14. Raymond A. Fitzgerald, *History of the Statutory Development of the Board of Education Since Its Inception, 1837-1964* (Boston: Department of Education, 1964), p. 3.
15. Cubberley, *op. cit.,* p. 91.
16. Education Study Commission, *op. cit.,* pp. 98, 154-57.
17. George F. Zook and Associated Specialists, "Report of a Fact Finding Survey of Technical and Higher Education in Massachusetts," *Massachusetts Resolves of 1922,* ch. 43.
18. Education Study Commission, *op. cit.,* pp. 149-50, 372.
19. Department of Education, Division of University Extension, *Annual Report: Fifty Years of University Extension* (1965), pp. 12-13.
20. Department of Education, *Excerpts from Reports of the Board of Education: Five Year Periods.* Compiled by Franklin P. Hawkes from the *Annual Reports, 1900-1965* (Boston: The Department, 1965).
21. Legislative Research Commission, *Report of Special Commission on Educational Matters,* Pub. Doc. No. 1899 (Boston: General Court of Massachusetts, 1948), Massachusetts, *Acts of 1948,* ch. 643, 645.
22. Department of Education, *Massachusetts White House Conference on Education, Final Report* (Boston: The Department, September 1955).
23. Commissioner of Education, *Annual Report* (1961).
24. Massachusetts, Attorney General, *Report, December, 1964.* Pub. Doc. No. 12, p. 85.
25. *Ibid.,* pp. 184-87.
26. School Committee of New Bedford, *et al., v.* Commissioner of Education, *et al.,* Mass. Sup. Ct. 208 N.E. 2d. 814-19 (1966).
27. Board of Education, minutes of the meeting of August 19, 1963.
28. Advisory Committee on Racial Imbalance, *Because It Is Right–Educationally: Report of the Committee* (Boston: Department of Education, April 1965), pp. 1-2.

BIBLIOGRAPHY

Public Documents

Department of Education. *General Laws Relating to Massachusetts Education* (1961, 1962, 1963, 1964, and 1965).

Massachusetts. "An Act To Eliminate Racial Imbalance." *Acts of 1965,* ch. 641.

—— "An Act To Improve and Extend Educational Opportunities in Massachusetts." *Acts of 1965,* ch. 572.

—— "Budgetary Powers of the Trustees of the University of Massachusetts and Other Institutions." *Resolves of 1961.* Resolve 92.

—— *Constitution* (1780).

—— "Establishment of a State-Supported Medical School." *Resolves of 1961.* Resolve 122.

—— *Laws* (1882).

—— Report of the Attorney General. Public Doc. No. 12 (December 1964).

School Committee of New Bedford, *et al., v.* Commissioner of Education, *et al.,* Mass. Sup. Ct. 208 N.E. Rep. 2d. 814-19 (1966).

Massachusetts General Court Publications

Board of Educational Television. *Educational Television.* Boston: Massachusetts General Court, 1952.

Commission on Audit of State Needs. *Needs in Massachusetts Higher Education.* Boston: Massachusetts General Court, 1958.

Commission on Industrial and Technical Education. *Douglas Commission Report.* Senate No. 349. Boston: Massachusetts General Court, 1906.

Committee on Education. *Special Report.* House No. 2520. Boston: Massachusetts General Court, 1952.

Committee on Higher Education. *Higher Education in Greater Boston.* House No. 3007. Boston: Massachusetts General Court, 1964.

Department of Education and Department of Public Health. *Program for Emotionally Disturbed Children.* Boston: Massachusetts General Court, 1960.

Education Study Commission. *Summary Report on Quality Education for Massachusetts.* Boston: Massachusetts General Court, 1964.

Elliot, Thomas H. *Special Commission on the Structure of State Government: Education.* Boston: Massachusetts General Court, 1952.

Establishment of a State Supported Medical School. Boston: Massachusetts General Court, 1961.

Legislative Research Commission, Ralph Mahar, chairman. *Final Report of Recess Commission on Educational Matters.* House No. 2334. Boston: Massachusetts General Court, 1950.

-- *Report of Special Commission on Educational Matters.* House No. 1899. Boston: Massachusetts General Court, 1948.

Massachusetts General Court, Legislative Research Council. *Report on Correspondence Schools.* Boston: Massachusetts General Court, 1962.

Massachusetts State Teachers Colleges. Homer Anderson, director of the study. Boston: Massachusetts General Court. Resolves 47, 82 of 1953, and 64 of 1954.

Problems of Mentally Retarded Children. House No. 2270. Boston: Massachusetts General Court, 1952.

Special Commission Established To Investigate and Study Certain Problems in Education in the Commonwealth. *Final Report.* House No. 2050. Boston: Massachusetts General Court, 1948.

State Youth Commission on the Problem of Juvenile Delinquency. *Report.* Boston: Massachusetts General Court, 1955.

The Chamberlain Report. Senate Document 330. Boston: Massachusetts General Court, 1919.

Reports

Advisory Committee on Racial Imbalance. *Because It Is Right–Educationally: Report of the Committee.* Board of Education, April 1965.

Becker and Becker Associates. *Space Utilization Report: State Colleges and Lowell Technological Institute,* Vols. I and II. Boston: Department of Education, 1960.

Board of Education. *Annual Reports.* Boston: Department of Education, 1837-1965.

Commission on Academically Talented Pupils. *Education of Academically Talented Pupils.* Boston: Department of Education, 1961.

Commission on the Enrichment of Adult Life. *Adult Education in Massachusetts.* Boston: Department of Education, 1932.

Commissioner of Education. *Annual Reports.* Boston: Board of Education, 1961-66.

-- *Massachusetts Youth Study.* Boston: Department of Education, 1940.

Commissioners of Education of the Northeastern States. *Education for Citizenship.* Medford, Mass.: Lincoln Filene Center for Citizenship and Public Affairs, 1952.

Committee on Professional Courses in Junior High Education in State Colleges. *Report.* Boston: Department of Education, 1958.

Conference of School Superintendents. *Structure of School Systems.* Boston: Department of Education, 1961.

Department of Education. *Excerpts from Reports of the Board of Education: Five Year Periods.* Compiled by Franklin P. Hawkes from the *Annual Reports,* 1900-65. Boston: The Department, 1965.

-- *Massachusetts White House Conference on Education: Final Report.* Boston: The Department, September 1955.

Department of Education, Bureau of School Lunch. *February Report on School Lunch Program.* Boston: The Department, 1967.

-- *History and Summary of Program Activities.* Boston: The Department, 1963.

Department of Education, Division of University Extension. *Adult Education: Twenty-Five Years, 1915-1940.* Boston: The Department, 1940.

-- *Annual Report.* Boston: The Department, 1965.

Department of Education, Research and Development Division. *Facts About Education in Massachusetts.* Boston: The Department, 1963 and 1966.

Education Study Commission. *Report of the Special Commission Established To Make an Investigation and Study Relative to Improving and Extending Educational Facilities in the Commonwealth.* Pub. Doc. No. 4300. Boston: Department of Education, June 1965.

Jansky and Bailey Engineering Firm. *Educational Television in Massachusetts.* Boston: Executive Committee for Educational Television, Department of Education, 1966.

Junior High School Principals' Association Delegation, R. J. Dickman, chairman, *et al. Report of the Co-operative Visit Between the Junior High School Principals' Association and the State Teachers Colleges.* Boston:

Massachusetts Junior High Principals' Association, 1937.

Massachusetts, Executive Department. *Annual Report of the Massachusetts Commission Against Discrimination.* Boston: The Department, 1956 and 1957.

New England School Development Council. *State Aid to Education in Massachusetts.* Cambridge: Harvard University, 1962.

Shurcliff, Shurcliff, and Merrill. *Master Plan for the University of Massachusetts.* Boston: Commonwealth of Massachusetts, Commission on Administration and Finance, October 1957; Revision, 1960-61.

Tufts Assembly on Massachusetts Government. *Public Education in Massachusetts: Problems and Challenges.* Medford, Mass.: Lincoln Filene Center for Citizenship and Public Affairs, 1965.

Zook, George F., and Associated Specialists. "Report of a Fact Finding Survey of Technical and Higher Education in Massachusetts." *Resolves of 1922.*

Books, Pamphlets, and Bulletins

Cubberley, Ellwood P. *Public Education in the United States.* Cambridge: Houghton Mifflin Co., 1934.

Curtin, Thomas J. *Educating the Disadvantaged.* Boston: Department of Education, 1964.

Department of Education. *Curriculum Guide: Educable, Trainable, and Mentally Retarded Children.* Boston: The Department, 1962.

-- *Curriculum Guide for Intermediate Grade Teachers.* Boston: The Department, 1950.

-- *Curriculum Guide for Primary Grade Teachers.* Boston: The Department, 1953.

-- *Drop-Out Studies: Massachusetts Secondary Schools.* Boston: The Department, 1964.

-- *Equality of Educational Opportunity* (Massachusetts Fair Educational Practices Act). Boston: The Department, 1954.

-- *Facts and Statistics for Massachusetts White House Conference on Education.* Boston: The Department, 1955.

-- *General Education in State Colleges.* Boston: The Department, 1959.

-- *Guidance Services in the Elementary School.* Boston: The Department, 1964.

-- *Junior High School Manual.* Bulletin No. 5. Boston: The Department, 1921.

-- *Manual for High Schools.* Bulletin No. 5. Boston: The Department, 1924.

-- *Massachusetts Public School Administration.* Bulletin No. 11. Boston: The Department, 1936.

-- *Phonics at Work.* Boston: The Department, 1954.

-- *Policy Statement of the Board of Education.* Boston: The Department, 1961.

-- *School Facilities Survey.* Boston: The Department, 1959.

-- *Supervision of Instruction: Junior High School.* Boston: The Department, 1933.

-- *The Development of Education in Massachusetts, 1630-1930.* Bulletin No. 5. Boston: The Department, 1930.

-- *The Evaluation of Secondary Education in Massachusetts.* Boston: The Department, 1950.

-- *The High School Graduate and Higher Education.* Boston: The Department, 1965.

-- *Vocational Education in Massachusetts.* Boston: The Department, 1952.

Department of Education, Coordinating Council of Presidents. *The Need for Salary Adjustments and Staff Changes in Massachusetts Institutions of Public Higher Education.* Boston: The Department, 1958.

Department of Education, Division of Elementary and Secondary Education. *Studies in Secondary Education.* Boston: The Department, 1958.

Department of Education, Division of State and Federal Assistance. *Federal Aid to Education in Massachusetts.* Boston: The Department, 1966.

Department of Education, University Extension Division. *A Brief History of the Activities of the Committee on University Extension of the Connecticut Valley College, 1914-1958.* Boston: The Department, 1962.

Department of Education and Department of Public Health. *Curriculum Guide for Teaching Health in the Junior High School.* Boston: The Department, 1956.

-- *The Administrator's Guide for the School Health Program.* Boston: The Department, 1957.

Department of Public Health. *Standards for Day Care Schools: Recommended Minimum and Preferred Standards.* Boston: The Department, 1952.

-- *Revised Standards for Day Care Schools: Rules and Regulations–Day Care Services for Children.* Boston: The Department, 1962.

Fitzgerald, Raymond A. *History of the Statutory Development of the Board of Education Since Its Inception, 1837-1964.* Boston: Department of Education, 1964.

Hart, Albert Bushnell. *Commonwealth History of Massachusetts,* IV. Boston: The State History Co., 1930.

League of Women Voters. *Massachusetts State Teachers Colleges.* Ruth Fletcher, chairman. Boston: The League, 1953.

New England Commissioners of Education, Steering Committee. *October Conference on Educational Opinion:*

Historical Account, 1924-1965. Portsmouth, N.H.: The Commissioners, 1965.

Tercentenary of the Massachusetts Bay Colony, 1630-1930. Department of Education Committee, Frank P. Morse, chairman. Boston: The Department, 1930.

Articles and Periodicals

Cahill, Alice M. "Nineteenth Century Library Innovation: The Division from 1890 to 1940." *Bay State Librarian,* Vol. LV, No. 4 (October 1965).

Massachusetts Teacher. Published monthly except June, July, and August.

Wagenknecht, Robert E. "The Massachusetts Division of Library Extension and the Development of Regional Library Service, 1940-1965." *Bay State Librarian,* Vol. LVI, No. 1 (January 1966).

Other Sources

Board of Education. Minutes of the meeting of August 19, 1963. Boston, Massachusetts, Department of Education.

Department of Education. "Annual Listing: Former members of the Board of Education," 1966. Boston, Massachusetts.

Governor's Conference on Education. "Education: An Obligation; An Opportunity." Proceedings of the Conference in Amherst, Massachusetts, Bureau of Government Research, University of Massachusetts, Amherst, 1966.

Appendix A

MASSACHUSETTS CHIEF STATE SCHOOL OFFICERS

Secretaries of the Board of Education

1837-48	Horace Mann
1849-55	Barnas Sears
1856-60	George S. Boutwell
1861-76	Joseph White
1877-93	John W. Dickinson
1894-1902	Frank A. Hill
1903-1904	C. B. Tillinghast
1904-1909	George H. Martin

Commissioners of Education

1909-17	David Snedden
1917-35	Payson Smith
1935-38	James G. Reardon
1939-43	Walter F. Downey
1943-46	Julius E. Warren
1946-57	John J. Desmond, Jr.
1957-68	Owen B. Kiernan

Appendix B

Chart I.--MASSACHUSETTS DEPARTMENT OF EDUCATION, 1948

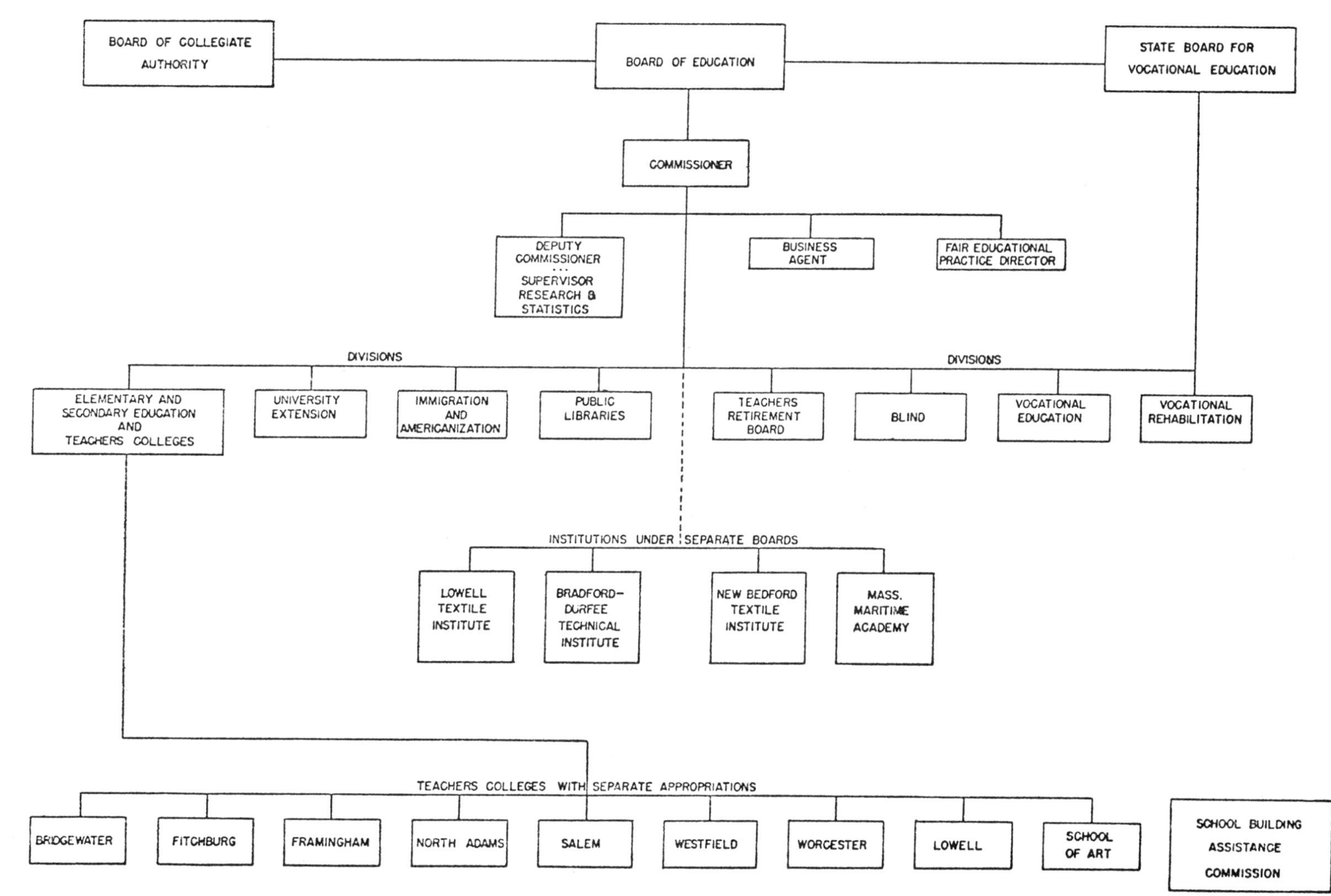

Appendix B

Chart II.--MASSACHUSETTS DEPARTMENT OF EDUCATION, 1965

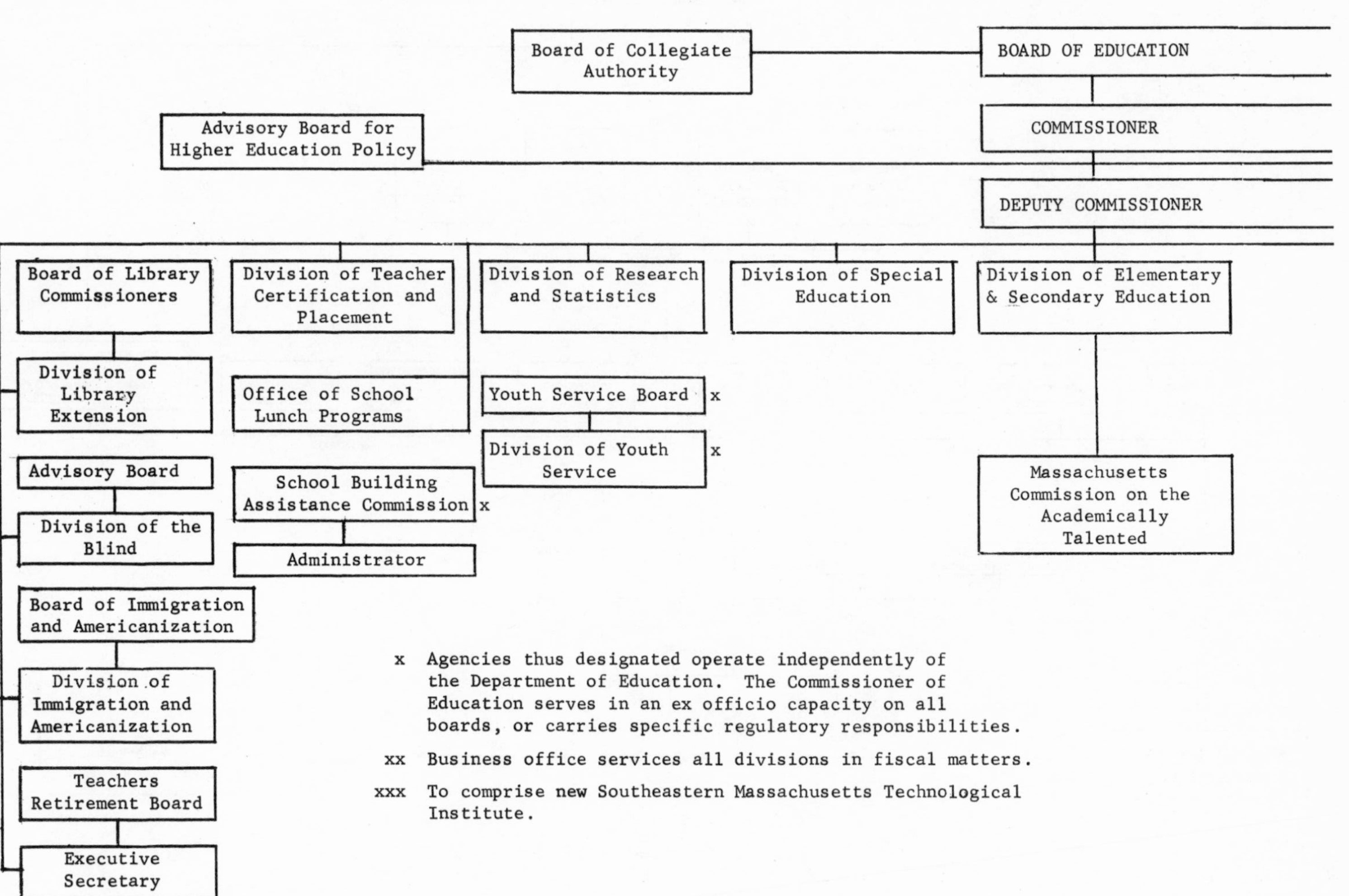

x Agencies thus designated operate independently of the Department of Education. The Commissioner of Education serves in an ex officio capacity on all boards, or carries specific regulatory responsibilities.

xx Business office services all divisions in fiscal matters.

xxx To comprise new Southeastern Massachusetts Technological Institute.

Appendix B

Chart II.--MASSACHUSETTS DEPARTMENT OF EDUCATION, 1965 (Continued)

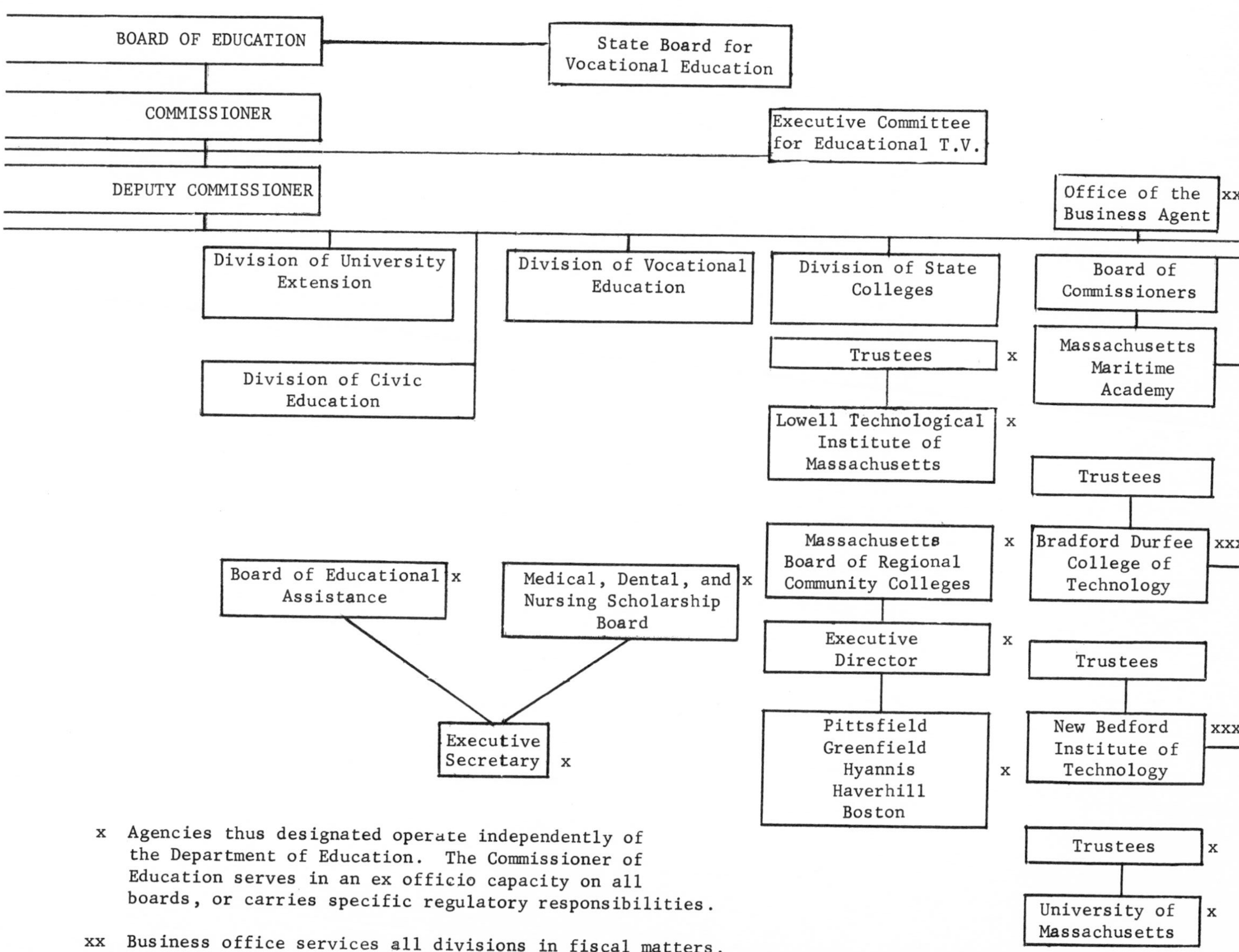

x Agencies thus designated operate independently of the Department of Education. The Commissioner of Education serves in an ex officio capacity on all boards, or carries specific regulatory responsibilities.

xx Business office services all divisions in fiscal matters.

xxx To comprise new Southeastern Massachusetts Technological Institute.

Appendix B

Chart III.--MASSACHUSETTS DEPARTMENT OF EDUCATION, 1967

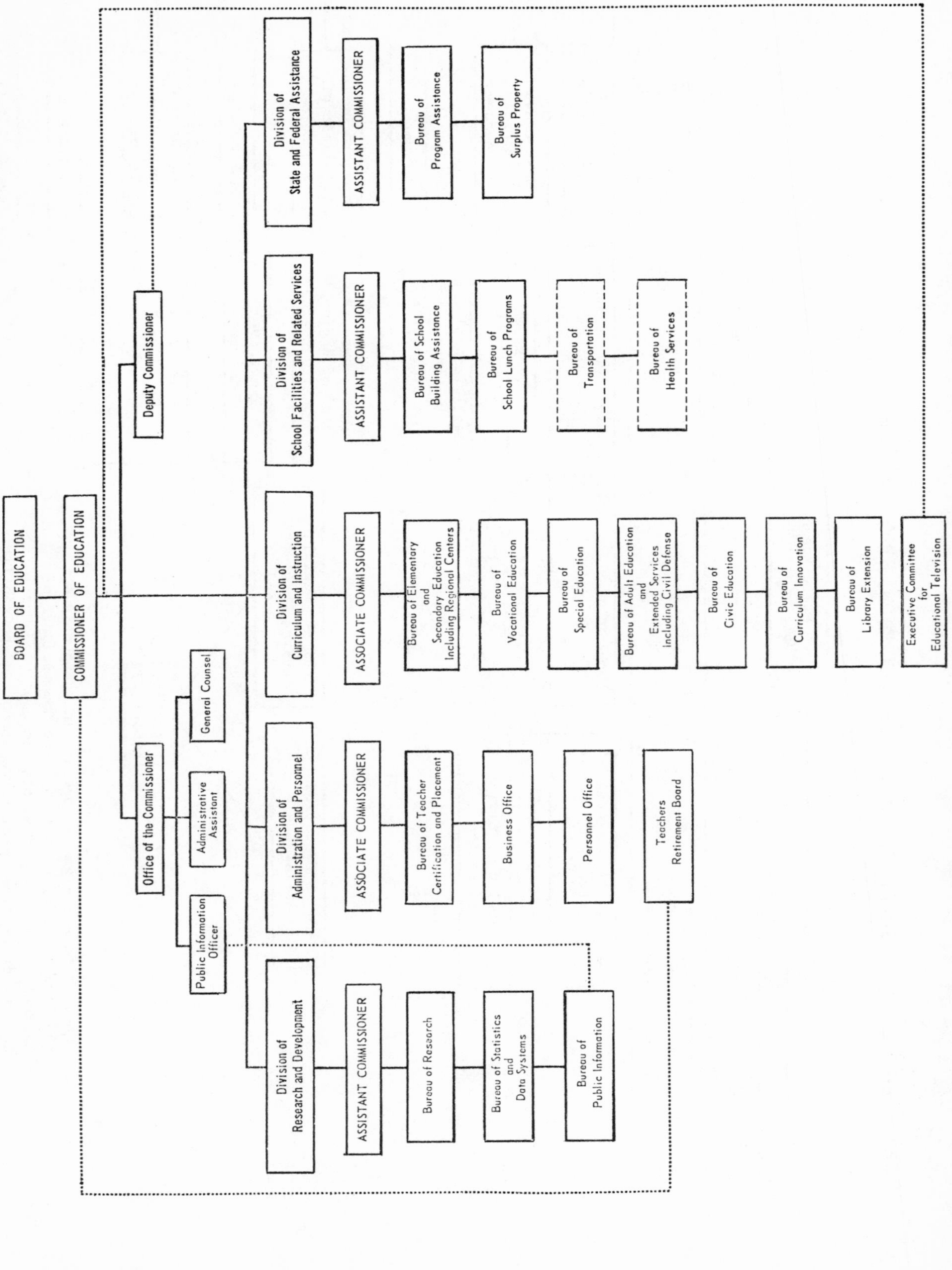

Appendix C

MASSACHUSETTS FIRSTS

CONSTITUTION of the COMMONWEALTH OF MASSACHUSETTS

CHAPTER V

ARTICLE I, Section II - The Encouragement of Literature, etc.

Wisdom and knowledge, as well as virtue, diffused generally among the body of the people, being necessary for the preservation of their rights and liberties: and as these depend on spreading the opportunities and advantages of education in the various parts of the country, and among the different orders of the people, it shall be the duty of legislatures and magistrates, in all future periods of this commonwealth, to cherish the interests of literature and the sciences, and all seminaries of them; especially the university at Cambridge, public schools and grammar schools in the towns; to encourage private societies and public institutions, rewards and immunities, for the promotion of agriculture, arts, sciences, commerce, trades, manufactures, and a natural history of the country; to countenance and inculcate the principles of humanity and general benevolence, public and private charity, industry and frugality, honesty and punctuality in their dealings; sincerity, good humor, and all social affections, and generous sentiments, among the people. (1780)

1635 First public school with a continuous existence–Boston Latin Public School

1636 First college–Harvard College

1639 First public school supported by direct taxation or by assessment on the establishment of the town inhabitants–establishment by a vote of Dorchester

1642 First school law–universal education in homes, enforced by selectmen

1645 First elected school committee in America–again, Dorchester

1647 First compulsory school regulation

1821 First publicly supported, publicly controlled American high school

1837 First State Board of Education, with Horace Mann elected secretary of the board

1839 First normal school in America

1851 First state law regarding public libraries

1890 First State Library Commission

1965 First act by a Legislature to provide for "Elimination of Racial Imbalance in Public Schools."

Men wait until the tide of evil rises and desolates the land, again and again, before they will erect barriers against the deluge . . . . Republics, one after another, – a splendid yet mournful train, – have emerged into being; they have risen to greatness, and surrounding nations have sought protection beneath the shelter of their power; but they have perished through a want of intelligence and virtue in the masses of the people . . . . If we do not prepare children to become good citizens, – if we do not develop their capacities, – if we do not enrich their minds with knowledge, imbue their hearts with love of truth and duty, and a reverence for all things sacred and holy, then our republic must go down to destruction . . . .

–HORACE MANN, 1845
Eighth Report to the Board of Education

22 Michigan

DEPARTMENT OF EDUCATION

Prepared by
Michigan Department of Education Staff

Contents

INTRODUCTION

Michigan historically has been a national educational leader. From the earliest days, its system of education has had the flexibility and resiliency to adapt to change without losing or destroying the basic foundations that have made it outstanding.

The Northwest Ordinance of 1787 laid the keystone: "Religion, morality and knowledge, being necessary to good government and the happiness of mankind, schools and the means of education shall be encouraged" (1). From such encouragement, the concept of free schools quickly emerged. By the time Michigan reached statehood in 1837, it had the nation's first state superintendent and a system of education that served as an example for many other states.

During the past 132 years, the people of Michigan have adopted four different constitutions–in 1835, 1850, 1908, and 1963. The citizens spelled out strongly and clearly their commitment to public education in each of these documents.

THE EARLY YEARS

In 1809, the territorial law directed the overseers of the poor in each judicial district to launch the schools they deemed necessary for their district and to serve as the trustees. It also allowed them to levy a tax for the support of these "free" schools. The law, however, was not enforced, and, consequently, very few schools were established.

Concerned that no one was taking the initiative in establishing schools, a group of Detroit citizens–the Territorial Governor, judges, and lay people–established the University of Michigania in 1817 to provide for public education for all. In the same year, the Territorial Council voted the first tax appropriation for public education: $300 for a university building and $80 for a site. This academic organization, which would serve the entire territory, was to offer courses in at least 13 fields of knowledge.

The University of Michigania prior to 1820 established primary schools in Monroe and Michilimackinac (Mackinac Island) and a primary school and a classical academy in Detroit. In 1821, the latter became the University of Michigan.

Several years later, in 1827, the Territorial Council passed a law requiring every township with 50 families to employ a schoolmaster "of good morals" to teach children "reading, writing, English, French, arithmetic, spelling, and decent behavior" (2). The law required the schools to be in session for 6 months, financed by a township tax. The law also stipulated that townships with 100 families were to provide schools for an entire year, and those with 150 families were to maintain schools for 6 months, with advanced English taught for an entire year. In addition, it directed that each township of 200 families employ a grammar schoolmaster.

In 1829, the council enacted a law making mandatory the division of townships into school districts. It abolished the township tax but left the primary responsibility for operating the schools in the hands of the people. Parents were charged tuition, and each family was required to provide a portion of the firewood used in the schoolhouse. The parents also boarded and fed the schoolmaster, who received part of his salary in this manner.

Although the tuition was waived for the indigent, the children of the poor seldom attended because, in most cases, the parents were too proud to accept the waiver.

During these early years, the pupils ranged from beginners to boys and girls 16 or 17 years of age. In some districts it was the custom to hold school for 2 or 3 months in the winter and 2 or 3 months in the summer. In such cases, the districts hired a female teacher for the summer session, when only those children too small to work attended, and hired a male teacher for the winter term for the older boys. Unless a teacher could whip the biggest boy in his class, he usually resigned.

In the meantime, a number of individuals and groups in Detroit attempted to organize schools or academies where students could prepare themselves for college work. The Territorial Council issued 12 charters for such schools, but few were established until after Michigan became a state. In 1829, one did open in Ann Arbor under the name of Merrill's Select School. In advertising for students in a local paper, a typical ad might read as follows:

> Select school for young gentlemen and ladies in Ann Arbor village. Reading, spelling, mental arithmetic, modern geography and English grammar at $2.50 per quarter (three months); including writing, practical arithmetic, ancient geography, history, philosophy, chemistry, logic, astronomy, the higher branches of mathematics, composition and declamation at $3.00; including the Latin and Greek languages, $4.50.
>
> The instructors pledge themselves to take a lively interest in their pupils' advancement in knowledge, good habits and amiable deportment; and by a general superintendency regarding the intellectual, physical and moral welfare of those committed to their care, while at their boarding houses as well as at their class schoolroom, they hope to merit, as well as receive the patronage of parents and guardians. Boarding may be obtained at $1.00 per week.

For those who could afford it, this appears to have been a bargain even in those territorial days. However, the Merrill's Select School closed its doors after only 2 years of operation.

The early territorial laws pertaining to education in Michigan established certain important principles, and despite the little accomplished, these principles formed the bedrock for the state's public education system of today. For example, they made clear that education was a function of the state and that public education should be nonsectarian. The first officials of the Catholepistemidad (or the University of Michigania) were a Presbyterian minister and a Catholic priest. These laws established that education should be supported by public taxation and that the state would determine what should be taught in the schools. In fact, the statutes of 1817 specifically state the subjects to be taught in the primary schools and the classical academies. The law of 1827 was also definite in providing for the curriculum.

Although these laws firmly established the principle of local control rather than extreme centralization by the creation of a district system in 1829, the state was given the right to inspect and to supervise schools. The state was even given the right to determine the amount of time each school would be open. In other words, it was established that the school system of Michigan would be an organic whole—the "Michigan idea" included an elementary school, a secondary school, and the University of Michigan, all under unified control.

Two young men from Marshall, Michigan—General Isaac Crary and Reverend John D. Pierce—were leaders in the drive to formally establish public education in Michigan. They met in the early 1830's and, with vision beyond their relatively young years, planned and outlined a system of public education for the entire state. Through their efforts and dedication, the first constitution, in 1835, incorporated several educational firsts. For instance, Michigan became the first commonwealth to have an independent department of education with its own administrator—a state superintendent of public instruction. The constitution also included a section providing for the forfeiture of state financial aid in case of failure to maintain a school for 3 months. Indirectly this clause compelled communities to establish school facilities. And Michigan became the first state to provide libraries in its state institutions.

Territorial Governor Stevens T. Mason appointed Reverend Pierce as Michigan's first state superintendent of public instruction in 1836—thus, the first man in the United States to hold such a position under a state constitution. His friend and co-worker, Crary, entered politics and became a representative in the U.S. Congress, where he served for three terms: 1835-40. Together Pierce and Crary laid the groundwork for a system of public education that became an example for the states in the Middle West and even many in the East.

In 1837, Michigan was admitted to the Union. In his first report to the Legislature, Superintendent Pierce outlined a system of education and a plan for organizing primary schools, a university, and its branches. When granting public lands to this state, Congress had set aside Section 16 in each township to be used for the schools, and Pierce presented a plan for their use. Unlike other states in the Northwest Territory, the Michigan Legislature sold the land instead of turning it over to the individual townships. The money received was placed in the state treasury and designated as the Primary School Interest Fund.

Detroit, already a hustling, dynamic city, took the lead in education. In 1842, the first completely free schools were opened, and 2 years later the Board of Education appropriated $150 and fuel to support a high school. The high school was to admit only 85 students: all boys from the age of 11 up who had attended public school for 3 months and passed an examination before the committee of teachers. Unfortunately, the school did not last long.

The Constitution of 1850 incorporated several important changes. It made the state superintendent an elected official instead of an appointee of the Governor, and he was given general supervision of public instruction. The state superintendent became a voting member and secretary of the State Board of Education, which was given general supervision of the State Normal School in Ypsilanti. The constitution also stated that the Legislature should provide free schools by 1855, but that section was deferred until 1869, when all provisions of the rate bill law (passed in 1843) were repealed.

Although the high school, as such, had long been a part of the system developed in Michigan, it was not until the celebrated Kalamazoo Case of 1874 that it became in a true sense free and public. The right of the school district of Kalamazoo to levy taxes in support of a high school was challenged by Charles E. Stuart and others, and the case was appealed all the way to the State Supreme Court.

In its opinion, the court stated:

> We had supposed it had always been understood in this state that education, not merely the rudiments, but in an enlarged sense, was regarded as an important practical advantage to be supplied at their (the peoples') [sic] option to rich and poor alike, and not as something pertaining merely to culture and accomplishment to be brought, as such within the reach of those whose accumulated wealth enabled them to pay for it (3).

The court cited the Territorial Laws of 1817 and 1827, as well as the Constitutions of 1835 and 1850, in reaching its decision upholding the right of school authorities (boards of education) to levy taxes on the general public for the support of high schools. It upheld the right of the district to use these taxes, not only to support a high school, but also to provide free instruction to children in other languages than English; it upheld the district's right to offer instruction in the classics and living modern languages. At the same time, the decision substantiated the right of the district board to appoint a superintendent of schools. This case not only benefited Michigan but set a precedent for the support and aid to public education throughout the United States—it was a giant step forward in America's dream of free, public education.

During these early years, the work of the department was to a great extent a one-man operation, although the superintendent was often aided by a secretary and a janitor. Even obtaining adequate office space often proved difficult. Nevertheless, the department exercised influence in curricular matters. The course of study had to be authorized by the Legislature, and the majority of the state superintendents during the first 100 years either supported this policy or did not fight it.

In 1839, the Legislature directed Superintendent Pierce to recommend a list of textbooks to be used in the common schools. He was further directed to publish this list in the state journal of education and to develop a plan to ensure an adequate supply of these recommended books. There was no legal requirement, however, that the schools use them. Superintendent-Elect John M. Gregory, in 1858, suggested that it was not necessary, and perhaps not even desirable, that textbook uniformity be maintained throughout the state. He did think it would be advantageous if all schools in a township used the same texts, and he thought it was essential that a uniform series be used in the same district. The Legislature incorporated the latter suggestion into the School Laws of 1859 (4).

Superintendent Gregory made the first attempt to establish a course of study for the primary schools in Michigan. He believed this would result in more continuity in the school curriculum, establish a definite point of progress, encourage regular attendance, and set some standards for the length of the school year. The Legislature replied in 1861 that it was the duty of each local board of education to determine which texts should be used in the local schools. It passed a law stating that once the books were selected, however, a change could not be made without a majority vote of the people (5).

For two decades after Gregory's term of office ended in 1865, the state superintendents all favored a state course of study. In 1877, Superintendent Horace S. Tarbell gave his support to a course of study planned by the Michigan Superintendents Association and reported that he hoped to see nine-tenths of the schools working with the uniform curriculum. He suggested that the simplest way to achieve this would be to distribute free, uniform textbooks to all schools. On the other hand, Superintendent Cornelius A. Gower (1878-81) believed that schools with only 10 grades should have a course of study that would prepare them for the common school course of study at the state normal school, and schools with 12 grades should have a course of study to prepare students for the state university. Both Superintendents Varnum B. Cochran, in 1881, and Herschel R. Gass, in 1883, advocated a state course of study to which the student should adjust rather than vice versa. Gass was concerned because less than one-third of the rural schools used the adopted list of books. It was 6 years later before the Legislature allowed school districts to vote on whether textbooks would be furnished free, but the law also specified the subject areas in which these free books would be furnished.

In 1887, the county school examiners pushed for a state manual and course of study, and State Superintendent Ferris S. Fitch incorporated this recommendation and a 30-page manual in his 1890 annual report (6). Seven years later, the Legislature required the state superintendent to prepare a course of study for district schools. At the same time, a bill was passed providing for a state textbook commission, which would designate the books to be used throughout the state except in those districts where books were free or where citizens voted not to come under the law. This law was repealed the following year on the strong recommendation of Superintendent Jason E. Hammond, who believed that textbook lobbies had been responsible for its enactment.

FINANCING AN EXPANDED STATE DEPARTMENT OF EDUCATION

By the turn of the century, the increased responsibilities and demands upon the State Department of Public Instruction were reflected in the additional personnel. In 1900, there were, in addition to the state superintendent, a deputy, a chief clerk, three statisticians, an editor, three stenographers, a shipping clerk, and a janitor, who also served as a messenger. There were no separate bureaus or divisions. The department functioned in areas of teacher education and certification, teacher examinations, consolidation, improvement of rural education, improvements of school buildings and facilities, financing of education, and courses of study.

State Courses of Study

In 1901, Superintendent Delos Fall stated that he believed each district board should specify the studies in local schools. If, however, it failed to do so, he thought the teacher should have the right to follow the state manual and course of study. Like Hammond, he thought people should not be molded to the course of study. Despite his concern, it was 1913 before the Legislature passed two significant bills relating to textbooks. One, Act 315, required book companies to comply with certain regulations dealing with the quality and uniformity of texts before doing business in the state. Act 23 required school boards, except those in city districts, to purchase for libraries only those books on the list compiled by the state superintendent and the state librarian.

In the mid-1930's, the emphasis changed from a legislative-mandated and department-supported course of study to a cooperative venture in curriculum development involving local administrators, teachers, and the department in more positive leadership roles. In 1935, Superintendent Eugene Elliott appointed a curriculum steering committee to cooperate with the department in planning the state curriculum (7). This committee, consisting of leading educators, was chaired by Paul Rankin of Detroit. Specifically, it was charged with developing activities for achieving the goals developed by the Michigan Educational Planning Commission, officially adopted in 1934 as the state educational objectives.

By 1938, the state's pattern of curriculum development seemed to be established. The program was later expanded and more and more persons were involved. Instead of a single committee, like that which started the program in 1935, several committees were appointed by the state superintendent, and many professional organizations and groups were brought into the program. In 1941, after several revisions, the results were published in a department bulletin (8).

Both the department's administrative policy and the Michigan curriculum program explicitly included the community school concept. The program's bulletin stated that the department was "stretching the evaluation of the present curriculum and has adopted a general administrative policy designed to further the development of community school units and also a functional community-connected curriculum . . ." (9). The Michigan Cooperative Curriculum Program today has 28 separate committees, with a total membership of approximately 1,000 including department personnel, teachers, administrators, and representatives from business, labor, the professions, industry, church, and government.

Growing Responsibilities

Just as the State Department of Public Instruction changed its participation in curricular matters from operating a legislative-mandated program to developing one in which the department assumes a leadership and cooperative role, so did its other responsibilities grow and change. From 1900 to 1920, although there were no major organizational changes, the department continually added nonprofessional personnel, such as statisticians and stenographers. In 1917, two assistant superintendents were appointed, though their duties were not specifically stated and there were no divisions or bureaus for them to administer. Four years later, there were six assistant superintendents, four of them administrators in rural education, one in charge of the high schools department, and the other in the physical education department.

The Smith-Hughes Act, passed by Congress in 1917, caused the greatest growth in the department up to that time. Earlier, in 1907, the state, anticipating concepts incorporated by the Smith-Hughes Act, enacted Act 189, paving the way for large-scale vocational education. Since the State Board of Education did not satisfy federal requirements for operating the programs, a special board for vocational education had to be formed. This board was not actually a part of the department at this time, but there was a close working relationship. For the first time, four supervisors of vocational education were listed with the department's employees in the 1920 superintendent's annual report.

In 1922, the department created two divisions: the statistical division and the rural education division, consisting of a superintendent of rural education and four assistant superintendents. This was the first time separate units appeared in the organizational structure. Both were apparently formed for administrative purposes; there is no indication that they were developed in response to a new educational need. At the time, the department's staff consisted of 32 professional and nonprofessional employees.

In 1927, the statistical division was combined with child accounting and statistics. Other units operated as divisions, but they were one-employee units and were not listed separately. These included divisions of public school music, physical education, interscholastic athletics, private and parochial schools, and an editorial division. Two years later, in 1929, five employees were assigned to a high school inspection and supervision division. At the same time, the department launched a school public relations program to keep the people informed (10).

During the 1930's, the Depression forced the department to a status quo position. There was virtually no expansion, and because of rigid budgets services were kept to a minimum. In 1934, the department created a bureau of finance and research and a bureau of curriculum and guidance—the first units called bureaus—and divisions of personnel, public relations, and higher education. In the same year, an elementary and rural education division and a secondary and vocational education division were created, but these disappeared from the organizational chart a year later. At the same time, 1935, the bureau of curriculum and guidance became the curriculum research division, and finance became a separate division. The school board counseling division, the child accounting division, and the school plant division were added. Some of these changes resulted from a 40-percent budget curtailment during this money-scarce era.

By 1937, the department began to develop a somewhat different organizational pattern under two major units: general administration and instruction. New units now dealt with special projects which were functions of the department or were just department-sponsored. For instance, in the late thirties, the department created the secondary study unit, the in-service education project, and the teacher education study.

The impact of World War II was felt in several ways. Department personnel went into active military service; replacements were difficult to come by; and, consequently, services had to be limited. Standards for teacher certification were relaxed, and many more special certificates and war emergency certificates were issued in order that Michigan classrooms would be manned with teachers. Enrollment at the secondary level dropped as students of both sexes moved out of school into the war effort. The inflow of families from all parts of the country and the shifting of population toward centers of industrial production overtaxed school facilities in many cities and suburban communities, while at the same time a large part of rural Michigan was practically depopulated.

Peacetime standards in school health, transportation, nutrition, and instructional materials were difficult to maintain. The lack of qualified school personnel, both in teaching and administration, was keenly felt in the operation of schools.

As educational needs and demands changed—increased services, added curriculum requirements, the advent of the space age—the Department of Public Instruction continued to change its organization to meet them. From 1955 to 1965, when the department experienced its most recent rapid growth, there was a trend away from stricter administrative and regulatory functions toward broad service-type functions. This is evident through the development of such units as research, school board counseling, school plant planning, and the curriculum research group. This trend, which began in the midthirties, has continued up to the reorganization of 1965.

The 1963 constitution states that all executive and administrative offices, agencies and instrumentalities of the executive branch of state government and their respective functions, powers, and duties, except for the office of Governor and lieutenant governor and the governing bodies of institutions of higher education provided for in the constitution, shall be allocated by law among and within not more than twenty principal departments.

Prior to the 1963 constitution, the different state agencies, departments, and boards numbered more than 100. Article VIII of the constitution in effect established the Department of Education as one of the 20 principal departments.

Consequently, in November 1965, the most sweeping organizational change took place. Since the twenties, organizational changes had more or less followed the elections of the state superintendents, who added staff when they felt the need and when funds were available. They shifted divisions and sections when they thought the work of the department would be strengthened, and they created new units as necessary. Still, many of the previous changes were made with the idea of functional units in mind.

It was the Legislature, however, by enacting Act 380 in July 1965, that moved the reorganization. The reorganization created five separate bureaus with an assistant superintendent over each, and vocational education and vocational rehabilitation were placed under one bureau. Research became a separate bureau, whereas it had previously been a part of general education. The department's functions in relation to the universities and colleges were placed in a bureau of higher education. The State Library became a part of the department. And the name of the Department of Public Instruction was changed to the State Department of Education. By the end of the year, when the reorganization was completed, the department had approximately 1,300 employees.

Financing Education

At the turn of the century, the bulk of public school state funds came from the Primary School Interest Fund and the remainder from local taxes. In 1921, as reported in the *Revision of the General School Laws,* the major sources of educational support were the following: income from the Primary School Interest Fund (apportioned on the basis of the number of children over 5 and under 20 years of age); the meal tax; district, township, and county taxes; and state aid. State aid, however, constituted a very small amount.

In addition to the general fund, each district maintaining a school for 9 months received $200 annually from the state treasury when the cost of 7 months required a levy of $12 or more per $1,000 valuation. This money could be used for purchasing textbooks for those who could not afford to buy their own. By majority vote, the department could authorize local boards to use local taxes to furnish free textbooks, to pay tuition and transportation of high school students, and to pay, from the general fund, tuition of pupils in elementary school who were nearer to another schoolhouse than to their own. Money from the general fund could be used to pay for educating the children of the indigent. It also could be used to supplement a county tax for support of county schools of agriculture. The state would apportion two-thirds of the amount actually expended, not to exceed $4,800 for any one school.

The first sizable amount of state aid voted by the Legislature came in 1927 when it passed the Turner Act, appropriating $1 million for poor school districts—the first effort by the state to equalize taxation (11). Two years later, an amendment to the Turner Act provided $2 million out of the general fund to be distributed to school districts having a tax rate of more than 10 mills on each dollar of assessed valuation, and having an average membership in excess of the average for the whole state for each $100,000 of equalized valuation. It stipulated that no district could receive a sum sufficient to bring its tax rate below 10 mills on a dollar.

As already stated, Michigan experienced considerable difficulty in supporting education during the Depression of the 1930's. Some of this was beyond the control of educators and legislators, but part of the trouble can be traced back to an act passed by the Legislature in 1905. At that time, part of the Primary School Interest Fund came from taxes from car-loading companies, express companies, insurance companies, railroad companies, telephone and telegraph companies, and from inheritance and franchise corporation taxes. All this could have been expanded, but the Legislature of 1905 did not do so. By 1930, the interest from the Primary School Interest Fund was paying approximately half the cost of education in the state.

Unfortunately, the local districts were increasingly unable to carry their share of the burden. Enrollments had increased, curriculum had expanded, and during the Depression there was a need for local tax relief. The schools cut back expenses and had to operate with a 15-mill limitation. This in turn cut the Primary School Interest Fund, since much of it was derived from specific taxes that had been reduced. The $24 million available from the Primary School Interest Fund in 1930 had dropped to $14 million in 1934.

The 1933 Legislature attempted to alleviate the schools' financial straits by passing the Thatcher-Sias Act. This legislation directed that two-thirds of the $15 million the act would provide in state aid annually be disbursed on the basis of the number of children on the school census between the ages of 5 and 19. The balance was to be used for equalization purposes. State Superintendent Paul F. Voelker pointed out that this was not enough, since the schools required $25 million above what they received from the Primary School Interest Fund. The schools were already abolishing library services and such subjects as music, home economics, manual training, and health education. They were also having to curtail spending for instructional supplies, teachers' salaries, and capital outlay, and many were forced to cut the school year (12).

When the situation did not change significantly, the 1937 Legislature guaranteed that, beginning with the 1937 school year, $38 million, including the amount from the Primary School Interest Fund, would be appropriated annually. It also ensured $65 in tuition costs for nonresident pupils attending the ninth, tenth, eleventh, and twelfth grades. This mainly benefited those rural students who lived in districts where there were no high schools. The situation was still desperate, so the state aid was increased to $41 million in 1938, and the department asked for an additional $5 million for the next year. This was not realized.

In 1942, Superintendent Eugene B. Elliott requested the state to partially underwrite school building construction. He believed that since the state paid about 50 percent of school operating costs, it should pay something for school construction, especially since the 15-mill tax ceiling made it extremely difficult for schools to finance new buildings.

Four years later, in 1946, Elliott asked the Legislature to examine the entire state program and consider a comprehensive plan that would include all forms of state aid for schools. The following year, the Governor appointed the Michigan Committee on School Appropriation to make a comprehensive study of the program. In May 1948, the Legislature passed Act 26 appropriating $70,291,776, with approximately $14 million earmarked for specific areas and the remaining $46 million to be distributed according to the formula. It stipulated that transportation allowances would be made solely from the state aid appropriations.

During the 1950's, two developments occured that directly affected state school support. In 1954 the citizens voted for a sales tax amendment to the constitution, whereby schools would receive two-thirds of a 3-percent sales tax collected, after the costs of collecting had been deducted. This was omitted 6 years later when the sales tax was increased to 4 percent, but the amount going to the schools remained at 2 percent.

In addition, the State Supreme Court ruled in the Pittsfield School District case that the term *assessed valuation,* used in the Tax Limitation Act, was the local assessment as provided or changed or corrected through the statutory process of county and state equalization. In effect, this tended to equalize some of the glaring inequities that existed in the assessment of local property. There was an immediate impact on state aid to schools. In 1954-55, the total paid to the state public schools was $203, 874,530, and 2 years later it rose to $256,642,338–an increase of nearly $53 million!

By 1952, state aid to the schools amounted to $185 million, with $107,800,000 from appropriated funds according to the State Aid Act–$37 million from the Primary School Interest Fund and $41 million from the Sales Tax Diversion Amendment, the amendment that earmarked a specific amount for schools. For the 1954-55 school year, the appropriation was $200 million. Actually, an additional $20 million had been requested to meet the increased enrollment figures and the rising costs. Again, there were not enough funds to operate adequately in 1956-57, and the state superintendent recommended that the appropriation be over and above the amount set aside.

By the time Lynn M. Bartlett became superintendent in 1957, the situation was critical. In his 1956-58 report to the Legislature, he stated:

> To educate their children, the citizens of Michigan invested approximately $500 million for operating purposes each year during the biennium. Of this amount, the state's share during 1956-57 was $256,642,338. During 1957-58, it amounted to $258,768,735. The state provides approximately 50 percent of the public school operating costs.
>
> If we consider all monies invested in education during the years 1956-57 and 1957-58–operating funds, capital outlay, and debt retirement–the amount for each year of the biennium comes to approximately $700 million. The state's dollar share in this total amount remains the same as listed in the preceding paragraph. However, the percentage figure for the state's share drops to 36 percent when the total is considered (13).

Superintendent Bartlett also pointed out that operating costs all along the line would continue to increase. He charged that the financial support had not been adequate and that the support for public institutions, "particularly those having to do with education, as compared with the rapid growth of our population and economy, has lagged" (14).

The Legislature continued to revise and modify the state aid funding program, particularly to meet growing needs in specific areas, such as transportation and special education. But unfortunately, the patchwork efforts could not fully meet the problems, and there continued to be a burden on local property taxes. In an address in September 1963, Dr. Bartlett stated:

> Two years ago when I spoke to you, I pointed out that if we consider the percentage of all funds (current, building, debt) obtained from local and state tax sources, we would find that during the past several years there has been a definite trend to shift more and more of the financial burden to the local level. This trend has not stopped. In 1950-51 the state was contributing 52 percent. Now we find that this has gone down to some 41 percent. During this same period, local contribution rose sharply from 43.5 percent to more than 55 percent.
>
> During the past year $338 million in school aid, including primary money, was distributed to local school districts by the state for operating purposes. Although this represents an increase of about $34 million over 1961-62, it does not represent an equitable share of the additional revenue needed to accommodate increased enrollments and increasing costs of operation (15).

Again, in his biennial report for 1962-64, Bartlett pointed to the modification in the state school aid formula by the Legislature. Despite these gains, he stated, in most areas the tax rate applied to property had reached the saturation point, and in some places it was almost at the confiscatory level. At the same time, he pointed out that the school-age population was rapidly outgrowing the tax base, resulting in a yearly decrease in valuation per pupil. He pointed to the evolutionary pattern of state support, beginning with the flat grant aid from the Primary School Interest Fund, then the equalizing grant incorporated in the school aid fund, and later some special-purpose grants built into the current school aid formula.

Since the 1963 constitution had discontinued the Primary School Interest Fund, further consideration of the flat grant aid was eliminated. Over the years, the amount school districts received from the Primary School Interest Fund had been incorporated into the total state aid payments. This made a separate payment from the fund unnecessary. In addition, the Primary School Interest Fund money was distributed on a school census basis and not on the actual school membership of the districts. It was argued that this was not realistic, nor did it channel this money into areas of greatest need.

To meet the schools' critical financial needs, Superintendent Bartlett recommended an appropriation of more than $91 million for the 1965-66 school year.

The Legislature, fully aware of the increasing demands throughout the state for additional school support, immediately appropriated $200,000 requested by the State Board of Education for a penetrating study of financing education in Michigan from kindergarten through the twelfth grade. State Superintendent Ira Polley, appointed in 1966, secured the services of J. Alan Thomas, assistant director of the Midwest Administration Center, University of Chicago, who had taken part in recent school studies in Missouri, Illinois, and Ohio. Polley also organized a 40-member statewide citizens advisory committee and a 5-member panel of national consultants to assist him and evaluate the study and its progress (16). The study formally began in September 1966, and a final report and recommendations were presented to the State Board of Education in December 1967.

The study concluded that Michigan students enjoy great variation in educational opportunities, but "critical problems" in financing urban education demand more support from the citizens. Also, compared with many states, vocational education is inadequately supported by state funds; present procedures for financing school construction are costly; and state aid distribution is "overly complex" and not accomplishing the purpose of equalizing educational opportunity. It pointed out that a revenue crisis faces Michigan's nonpublic schools.

The study found that the most favorable educational opportunities were available to students in districts with high per-pupil state equalized valuation, high per-pupil expenditures for education, enrollments of more than 5,000 students, and high social class reflected in incomes, homes, and occupations. Services of well-qualified teachers are not equally available to children throughout the state, the study found; larger school systems have better-qualified teachers, pay higher salaries, and provide more opportunity for teachers to upgrade their knowledge and skills.

To help meet the "severe problems" of urban education where there is a disproportionate degree of low student achievement and high dropout rates, the study recommended setting aside a "sizable amount" of money, perhaps $30 million a year, which could be directed on a specific project basis. Projects should be aimed at such targets as cutting student-teacher ratios, using paraprofessionals, and increasing in-service education programs for teachers. The study said that all such projects should contain a "rigorous evaluatory process."

The Thomas Study also made several recommendations regarding the operation of the State Department of Education. If educational opportunities in Michigan are to be expanded at a reasonable cost, careful short- and long-term planning is needed. This requires the improvement of data gathering, storing, retrieving, and analyzing, since decision making for the present and planning for the future are based on the available information and on careful projections of future requirements.

The Thomas Study recommended that the State Department of Education expand and strengthen its bureau of research, planning, and development. It stated that the department should be provided with the staff and the computer facilities needed to gather and process information. A central information system, in which the interrelationships among programs, finance, and staffing may be examined, should be the goal of this department. Ongoing attempts should be made by school districts and the state to devise standards and means of assessing the effectiveness of educational programs.

In view of the increased usefulness of the computer as a tool in administration and instruction, the study concluded that strategically located computer facilities should eventually be provided throughout the state. The department should continue to evaluate and revise its data-collection procedures. Once collected, information should be processed electronically, thus ensuring rapid reporting and utilization.

The recommendations further suggested that as part of the planning process, attempts should be made to determine the unit costs of educational programs. Efforts should be made, through appropriate accounting and statistical techniques, to determine the factors associated with the costs of educational programs.

Federal Programs

Michigan entered the Union, as did other states formed from the Northwest Territory, with a permanent source of school support in the lands granted by Congress. The principle of federal participation in the support of public schools is a long-established one. Michigan's original sectional grants amounted to 1,148,160 acres with a valuation in 1937 estimated to be almost $6 million.

The Michigan Constitution of 1835 provided that the moneys of all lands that have been or hereafter may be granted by the United States to Michigan for the support of schools that might be sold or disposed of shall be a part of a perpetual fund, the interest from which, together with the rents of all such unsold lands, shall be inviolably appropriated to the support of schools throughout the state. Following this action on the part of Michigan, Congress in 1836 enacted a law which provided that Section 16 in every township of the public lands shall be granted to the state for the use of the schools. When such section has been sold or otherwise disposed of, other lands equivalent thereto and as contiguous as may be shall be granted to the state for the use of the schools.

It was Superintendent Pierce's idea to provide for state ownership and sale of primary school lands and to disburse the funds obtained thereby as equitably as possible for the organization and support of schools.

As early as it was possible, the Department of Education participated in federal programs. However, it was not until congressional action in 1917, passage of the Smith-Hughes Act for vocational education, that the department made significant increases in staff personnel to handle the impact of federal legislation.

Some 41 years later, reacting to Russia's dramatic achievement in space, Congress passed the National Defense Education Act of 1958. The Michigan Legislature, traditionally reluctant to accept federal financing, did not authorize the Michigan schools to accept funds under the various titles of the National Defense Education Act until late in 1959.

Superintendent Bartlett, long an advocate of federal participation in financing education, moved as quickly as money and personnel would permit to be of service to local districts and to establish a close liaison with the U.S. Office of Education.

Anticipating additional federal programs, Bartlett specifically assigned this area to the general education division. Because of limited department funds, a number of staff personnel, in addition to their other duties, also were assigned responsibility for various titles of the NDEA. From 1958 up to and including 1965, increases in staff to handle federal programs were relatively modest.

Immediately after his appointment as state superintendent of public instruction, Ira Polley established the position of assistant superintendent for federal programs. By late 1966, approximately 25 professional staff personnel were involved either full time or part time in administering federal programs. Primary thrust was increased services to local school districts in order to permit greater participation at the local level. Quite naturally, the demand for consultative help did increase.

The consensus is that the funds provided by the federal government have given impetus to new and already established educational programs. They have enabled the department to move into educational areas that needed greater exploration and emphasis. The funds have been used to strengthen the Department of Education and its operations, giving it greater depth and scope. The state is now participating in all current federal educational programs. Realistically, it can be expected that federal participation will increase in the the future and assume a greater share of the support of education at all levels. The department will be prepared to take advantage of the expansion.

SCHOOL DISTRICT ORGANIZATION AND CONSOLIDATION

Consolidation

Until 1900, the organization of the schools revolved around the question of district versus township system. In 1861, the Legislature considered legislation that would have allowed townships to establish school systems. State Superintendent John M. Gregory and his successor in 1865, Oramel Hosford, pointed up the advantages; but it was Superintendent Daniel B. Briggs who discussed the matter in depth. In his 1873 report, under the title "District Versus Township," he pointed out that the only apparent advantage of the smaller district was convenient access, whereas the disavantages were many and great. He argued as follows:

> Why is it desirable to have thirty-nine or more men in a township chosen for a service (as is true in numberless townships of the State), which six, nine, or twelve will do better? We have an army of school officers in the State exceeding twenty thousand; and it is repeatedly and very naturally urged as an objection to our district system, that the average quality of the officers is inferior, and in many districts where intelligence and character are especially needed even tolerably suited men can not be secured to hold the office; the public money is often times misapplied and wasted if not stolen; the law repeatedly violated, and the schools comparatively worthless. But by enlarging the area of the district a wider opportunity of choice is allowed, a superior average of official character is at once obtained, and more vigor, honor and intelligence is infused into the management of school affairs. But perhaps the most serious objection to the existence of small districts, arises from the difficulties necessarily existing in the way of organization, classification and gradation of schools (17).

Superintendent Briggs added that a township board would be responsible for securing equal school privileges for all of the children in the township. There would be no more schoolhouses built and operated than needed, thus enabling the township to construct better buildings. He believed that individual favoritism or nepotism would not be as likely to control the selection of teachers, enabling particular schools to find better teachers. There would be a uniformity of textbooks and a gradation of schools, leading to a better classification. The township plan would facilitate more effective supervision of the schools. Remote from petty neighborhood quarrels, the board would be more influential and could exercise steadier management. The equitable apportionment of school funds, almost impossible under the present system, would be comparatively easy, as the whole amount would come into the hands of a township board, which would expend the funds discreetly, justly, and for the general good.

It was 1887, however, before the Legislature's committee on education reported favorably on a bill providing for the township school district. The bill lost by one vote.

The department continued to work for the township system. Actually, some townships had been allowed to form units, and Superintendent Joseph Estabrook tried to win general support for this plan in 1888. The following year, the Legislature again failed to pass an act. But 2 years later, in 1891, it adopted Act 176, which allowed the organization of township districts in the Upper Peninsula. Because of the relatively large geographical area involved, the township plan was deemed the better plan. It quickly caught on, and by 1898, 92 township units had been formed.

Interest waned somewhat until 1908, when State Superintendent Luther L. Wright suggested that this township or unit system would permit employing better teachers, increase the tax base, make more effective teaching tools possible, and allow more scientific studies of agriculture. Essentially, consolidation was a movement for centralization. Even though there was no direct relationship between the two, in actual practice it happened that wherever the township unit existed, consolidated schools also existed.

In 1901, Superintendent Delos Fall had recommended that the number of schools in each township be reduced to four and that a fifth district, in the center of the township, contain a high school. At the same time, he presented an alternate plan to abandon all district schools in a township and have one central school. The Legislature of 1901 passed legislation making it impossible for rural communities to consolidate contiguous districts.

At the turn of the century, Michigan had 7,163 school districts. In his report for 1900, Superintendent Jason E. Hammond stated: "In the first place there are too many school districts, and therefore too many school houses and too many teachers employed. . . . Our school districts should be reorganized and many of them abandoned" (18).

Three years later, the Legislature amended the School Code so that districts could levy taxes for the transportation of pupils to and from school, and also pay the tuition of pupils who had completed the eighth grade and had to go outside their home districts to continue their education. This legislation aided consolidation in later years, but for the first decade of the century, it did not check the rising number of districts. In fact, the number of school districts reached its peak. Despite the moves toward consolidation, by 1912 there were 7,362 school districts–a gain of 199 since 1900.

Superintendent Patrick H. Kelley attacked the problem and presented his criteria for further consolidation. He stated that "in my judgment, no school in the State of Michigan shoul have less than two departments and two teachers and in each of these schools there should be a course of study of at least ten grades" (19).

Consolidation could be legally conducted under the Graded School Act, the Township Unit Act for the Upper Peninsula, and the General Township Unit Act, passed in 1909. In 1917, the Legislature enacted the Rural Agriculture School Act, which brought about further consolidation. This act stated:

> Three or more rural schools which have been or may hereafter be consolidated and in which the teaching of agriculture, manual training, and home economics shall or may be established as part of the regular courses of study, shall be known as rural agricultural schools and shall be entitled to state aid for the maintenance thereof, if built, equipped, and managed as provided for in this act (20).

As a result, the period from 1912 to 1920 saw the first decline in the number of school districts–7,362 to 7,273. There also was a decrease of 498 districts during the decade ending in 1930: 7,273 to 6,775.

During the Depression, in November 1934, the Federal Emergency Relief Administration sponsored a research project inquiring into the organization of school district government in Michigan. The purpose was to provide data on the ability of the 6,700 school districts to function effectively and to investigate the inequalities of educational opportunities among the children. It also was to investigate the unequal distribution of the property tax for education and to discover effective techniques for reorganizing the school districts. This FERA study prompted Superintendent Eugene B. Elliott to request the Legislature to grant more authority to the state department for reorganizing school districts. The Legislature did not respond.

Elliott's successor, Lee M. Thurston, continued the drive toward consolidation by appealing to educational leaders and lay people interested in education. In his 1946-48 report, he stated:

> Educational leaders in this State feel that we need to have local reorganization studied by lay groups with the help and assistance of local professional educators and of the available State services. The principles of self-determination, equality of opportunity and responsibility, and equalization of local and State fiscal support, need clearer recognition of our school laws. The tendency in Michigan to organize around natural communities has borne good fruit and should be encouraged (21).

The following year, in 1949, the Legislature took action to aid school district reorganization. It passed Act 225 to prevent the formation of more township school districts, but provided for "area studies" to assist in reorganization. Essentially, area studies pinpointed the most feasible school district organization plan and outlined the advantages to be gained by reorganization. The Legislature in 1949 also passed Act 248 detailing the procedure for the annexation of primary districts–less than 75 students, eight or less grades, and no superintendent–to graded districts.

By the end of 1954, Superintendent Taylor reported that reorganization was proceeding slowly but steadily and that he was encouraged by factors he believed would contribute to even further changes. For instance, most people in the state now recognized the need for education through grade 12 for everyone. It was evident that larger districts could offer better and broader educational programs, and since there was a shortage of qualified teachers, the smaller districts found it difficult to attract the necessary personnel. He also believed that the people now understood that reorganization created a broader tax base for financing capital outlay, and there was a growing recognition that the equitable distribution of state aid was dependent on adequate school district reorganization.

When Superintendent Bartlett took office in 1957, he continued to work for consolidation. In his 1956-58 biennial report, he pointed out that one of the most serious deterrents to improving public education in Michigan was the existing pattern of local school district organization. The primary school district organization, conceived more than a century earlier to meet the needs of a frontier society, had long outlived its usefulness. He stated:

> I shall never challenge the contribution of America's rural schools. Rather, I acknowledge the importance of their contribution to our American heritage. But this acknowledgement I make as one who eulogizes that which was important, but has since passed on (22).

Bartlett added that already 88.6 percent of all public school pupils in Michigan lived in 12-grade districts with a total state equalized valuation equaling 90 percent of all school districts. By the end of the decade, the number of school districts had been reduced from 4,918 in 1950 to 2,145.

Superintendent Bartlett realized that if the state was to make a major reduction in the number of school districts, it should make reorganization studies mandatory on an intermediate district basis. There was considerable opposition, particularly from such organizations as the "Friends of the Little Red Schoolhouse" and the Michigan Farm Bureau. They were unhappy with the prospect of losing local control. Despite their efforts, the Legislature did pass an act in 1964 to incorporate all non-high school districts into those operating K-12 programs. The act also intended to combine effective districts into units capable of offering a comprehensive educational program through grade 12. It provided for a state committee on reorganization to develop the guidelines for the intermediate district committees. The law, Public Act 289, was designed to eliminate non-K-12 districts, though it did not provide for the elimination of inadequate high school districts. As a result of the act, there was a dramatic reduction from 2,145 districts in 1960 to 1,241 on June 30, 1965–a reduction of 904 districts. By May 1968, this number had decreased to 718. Certainly this has led to a broader basis for educational opportunities for Michigan's youth.

TEACHER PREPARATION AND CERTIFICATION

The Nineteenth Century

In the early days of statehood and the term of the first state superintendent, Reverend John Pierce, certifying teachers was strictly a local matter. The township school inspectors issued certificates good for 1 year and only in the township in which they were needed. There were no age limitations, no special qualifications with regard to educational background or ability to teach, and there was no uniformity in the questions used to determine competency in subject matter fields. By the 1840's, Superintendent Ira Mayhew objected strongly to this type of certification. He proposed that different grades of certificates be granted as a way of recognizing superior teaching ability and of giving teachers an incentive to upgrade themselves educationally. He further recommended that the state superintendent be authorized to grant certificates valid throughout the state at his discretion.

Superintendent Mayhew was very much interested in improving the quality of teaching by providing opportunities for better preparation. In 1846, he held the first teachers institute in the state at Jackson. At the same time, he attempted to get the Legislature to pass acts providing special schools to prepare teachers. Out of the five attempts to pass legislation during the late 1840's, two were to establish a separate branch or department at the University of Michigan for teacher education, two were to provide for a normal school, and the fifth was to provide for a normal school instructor (23). But in his 1849 report, Mayhew made it clear he preferred teachers institutes over normal schools. He believed that teachers would not travel to Ann Arbor to study the science of education at the University, but they might attend classes near their homes. Nevertheless, the 1849 Legislature did pass an act establishing a state normal school, which provided for instruction in the art of teaching and establishing a model school. The act also provided for a certificate to teach in the common schools after 22 weeks of classes and an examination.

Francis W. Sherman became superintendent in 1849, but in 1855 Ira Mayhew returned to the office and served until 1859. During this second period, he asked the Legislature to allow graduates to be certified by the normal schools, and in 1857 such a measure was adopted. However, his recommendation that the state superintendent be authorized to grant certificates valid throughout the state was rejected.

John M. Gregory, who replaced Mayhew as state superintendent in 1859, believed that most teachers considered their profession as a stopgap occupation and that they were not likely to spend long periods of time in normal schools. In his first report, he recommended that teaching candidates be well grounded in subject matter fields and that they avail themselves of professional classes offered at academies, colleges, and union schools. At the same time, Gregory suggested that the state superintendent be allowed to give an annual examination and certify each candidate who passed and had completed a prescribed course of study.

But the institutes had proven relatively successful. The 1855 Legislature authorized the state superintendent to draw from the treasury up to $200 for each institute, up to $1,800 for the entire year to operate these programs. In 1861, it reduced the length to 5 days and limited state support to $100 for each. Gregory then formally recommended in 1864 that the Legislature provide additional facilities for educating teachers by establishing normal classes under the strict supervision of the State Board of Education and the superintendent of public instruction. Unfortunately, nothing was done.

It was 1867 before the Legislature permitted the state superintendent to have some authority in certification matters. This law authorized the county superintendents to examine teaching candidates in certain subjects, and on the basis of the results, the state superintendent was authorized to grant one of three grades of certificates to teach in any primary or grade school in the state. When in 1895 the Legislature repealed the law providing for the county superintendent, it also disposed of the state superintendent's certification authority.

One answer to the problem of securing better teachers was to open another normal school. In 1875, the Senate passed a bill to organize a normal school in the Upper Peninsula, but the House defeated it. One state representative claimed it failed because a normal school principal and his instructors, along with some influential professors from the university, had lobbied against it (24). They argued that another normal school would weaken the one already existing and ruin both. Two years later, the Legislature did strengthen the institutes by permitting fees to be collected from the participants for their support and by allowing the state superintendent to contribute up to $60 if local funds were insufficient. The state superintendent was authorized to hold an annual state institute, at a cost not to exceed $400, to bring together those who were to operate the county institutes in the summer and fall. In 1879, Superintendent Cornelius A. Gower issued the first manual of institute work.

Unfortunately, by this time teachers were not as interested in attending institutes. In 1879, the university detracted somewhat from the institutes by establishing a chair of science and art of teaching. The Legislature felt that this was a step in the direction of broadening the possibilities of teacher training and, therefore, institutes were not needed. By 1885, less than one-third of the teachers were attending institutes, and these were the ones who needed help the least.

The institutes faced even greater competition from the new normal schools. In 1891, a private normal school was founded in Mount Pleasant, and 4 years later it became a public normal school, mainly to educate teachers for the rural schools. In 1899, a normal school was established in the Upper Peninsula at Marquette.

In 1879, the Legislature authorized the state board to hold meetings, examine candidates, and grant 10-year certificates permitting the holders to teach anywhere in the state. It went a step further in 1887, by making the state superintendent responsible for preparing the county examinations. Superintendent Joseph Estabrook, considerably ahead of his time, in 1889 recommended reciprocity and acceptance of life certificates from other states. The Legislature did not act immediately, but in 1893 it did give the state board the authority to certify teachers who qualified for a degree and who had pursued an approved course of study in the science and art of teaching. Two years later, the Legislature finally acted on Estabrook's original suggestion and enacted legislation permitting the state board to certify teachers holding life certificates from other states that recognized Michigan certificates. At the turn of the century, teaching certificates were granted by local school authorities (county certificates), normal schools, the university, and the state board.

Teacher Preparation, 1900 to Present

The Department of Public Instruction's influence on the normal schools increased in 1902, when the state superintendent was designated chairman of a special committee to study their operations from finance to programs. The committee's scope and influence is difficult to determine, because it seems to have operated in the shadow of the Normal Executive Council, which had been organized in 1901 to advise the state board about courses of study and the needs of each institution.

In 1903, the Legislature further strengthened the department's influence by expanding an act passed in 1897 to give the state board the authority to prescribe courses of study for normal schools, to issue licenses and certificates, and grant diplomas and degrees. The state board, in complying with the act, resolved that there should be uniform courses of study so that reciprocity would be possible without loss of credit. It also declared that it would set definite standards for certain certificates and provide for an advanced course of study.

Despite the higher standards promulgated by the state board, Superintendent Delos Fall estimated that about 3,000 inexperienced and untrained teachers were entering the field each year, especially in the rural schools. Greatly concerned, he recommended that the normal schools be taken to the people. The Legislature responded by passing a law allowing each county to house a normal school. This law permitted each county board, the county commissioner, and the state superintendent to select one school in each county as a training center, determine a course of study, set the requirements for admission, and decide the terms for granting certificates to graduates. If the local board agreed to certain conditions, such as providing space, a minimum school year, capable teachers, and an annual report, a school could be organized by a majority vote. The state would grant funds to partially support these county normal classes.

Since the officials did not want students to lose credits if they transferred, they attempted to develop uniform programs for these county normal classes. Superintendent Fall outlined the pattern of organization and the qualifications for admission and established a course of study for a 1- and/or 2-year program. By October 1903, eight counties had opened normal classes with 97 students; 86 completed the program. By the following September, 20 counties had organized classes, with a total of 300 prospective teachers attending; 267 graduated in June of 1905.

Just as the Legislature centralized authority over the normal schools and the State Board of Education, in 1905 it placed supervision of all county normal classes in the hands of the state superintendent. He could now require the schools to follow his plan of organization, course of study, and various other rules and regulations.

The county normal classes grew at an extraordinary rate. In the fall of 1906, the number of county normal schools had jumped from 20 to 32, with 7 new ones preparing to begin operation. In June 1906, 319 teachers graduated, bringing the total number to 669 who had received 1 year of professional training to take back to the rural schools of the state. This meant that approximately one-eighth of the rural students in Michigan were being taught by teachers trained in the county normal classes and the state normal schools. That same year, Superintendent Patrick H. Kelley reported that the county commissioners were saying, "These classes have improved educational spirit, advanced wages and increased professional spirit . . . (the county training class is one of the greatest educational steps taken in Michigan in recent years)" (25).

Superintendent Kelley supplemented the normal school training with active institutes, and his successor, Luther L. Wright, established the pattern which is still used today. In 1906, Kelley ordered that no institute could be planned without first consulting his office for dates and instructors, and the department set about compiling a list of specialists who could serve on the staffs. When they were in operation, a representative of the department visited each of the institutes. By 1909, 195 institutes were being held throughout the state.

The plan was changed somewhat in 1910, as there was a tendency toward the long-term summer institutes. The state normal schools held institutes in which 3,300 teachers attended, and 5,000 participated in two state institutes, one sponsored by the Upper Peninsula Education Association and the other by the Michigan State Teachers Association (26). The 143 county institutes attracted 11,543 teachers. Thus, about 70 percent of the state's teachers attended institutes in 1910.

Both the institutes and normal schools continued to expand. In June 1912, the county normal schools graduated 638 students, to make a total of 5,245 graduates since they had opened. Four years later, there were 49 separate classes turning out 759 graduates. World War I and the immediate postwar years caused many teachers to go into the service or to other fields, and the normal school classes had decreased to 37 by 1922. By the midtwenties, the number had increased to 47, and 1,063 teachers graduated in 1927, bringing a total of 13,866 graduates for the 24-year period of operation (27).

The state played an increasing role in financing the county institutes. In 1903, it had appropriated $250 for each instructor needed to operate a county normal school, with a maximum of $1,000 for any one school. By 1927, these figures were $1,500 and $3,000, respectively.

During the 1930's, the county normal schools were declining. The Legislature had changed the three state normal schools to state teachers colleges in 1927 (28). As these four teachers colleges, the University of Michigan, Michigan Agricultural College, and a number of private colleges were educating more teachers each year, the need for the county normal classes declined. But more important, during the Depression there was a surplus of teachers. The educational programs were curtailed throughout the state, and this led to strong competition for positions and lower teacher salaries. Thus, in 1931, Superintendent Webster H. Pearce discouraged counties that did not need teachers from continuing normal classes. In 2 years, the county normals decreased by 20, and the enrollment declined by 50 percent; in 1932, there were 51, and in 1937, only 24. The Legislature still appropriated $55,000 for the support of these county normal schools (as a department in the office of the state superintendent) in 1939.

The colleges and state institutes received more support during the postwar period as the county normal schools continued to decline. One educational historian stated:

> The county normal schools were established for one purpose only—to train teachers for the rural schools. They have performed a valuable service, and have contributed much to the educational advancement of the rural schools during the nearly half century of their existence (29).

In 1948, only 19 county normal classes were held in Michigan. The state appropriated $75,000 for them, but this was a small part of the total state aid appropriation of $70 million.

Like the county normal school classes, the county institutes also reached their peak and began to decline during and after World War II. They have almost disappeared, with only a few counties holding them in the spring. On the other hand, the state institutes continue to be held each fall, authorized by the state board and conducted by the Michigan Federation of Teachers, the Detroit Board of Education, and the Michigan Education Association.

By 1965, however, a great many educators were seriously questioning the meaningfulness of teacher institutes. The state board appointed a 12-member committee, consisting of representatives from various educational and professional organizations, to review the purpose and need for these institutes and to make policy recommendations. Many believe that the local school districts should be given the responsibility, with individual districts determining whether time should be used for in-service training or institutes, or whether any such training should be held.

Certification

At the turn of the century, there were numerous ways for a teacher to earn certification in Michigan. For instance, the state issued certificates, on the basis of examinations, to teachers who were successful in completing an approved program in a normal school, the university, or one of the denominational colleges. The counties issued four types of certificates, and the county normal training schools offered county normal certificates. Teachers could be certified by the larger schools in the city, and the state board could issue certificates to holders of life certificates in other states. In 1901, the Legislature permitted the state superintendent to issue kindergarten, music, and drawing certificates.

During these early years of the twentieth century, there was a definite move to broaden certification—to grant more certificates on a statewide basis and eliminate the local types. In 1910, the county certificate, which required little preparation, accounted for 27 percent of all certificates issued. Superintendent Fred L. Keeler, in particular, urged the state to adopt a program establishing various grades of certificates based on the length of the training program. He proposed a 6-week program for a third-grade certificate, 12 weeks for a second-grade certificate, and 24 weeks for a first-grade certificate. A year after this recommendation, in 1915, the Legislature did pass a law stipulating that a county could not grant a certificate unless a candidate had at least 6 weeks of professional training.

The urgent demand for manpower during World War I years made it difficult to recruit teachers. Requirements were somewhat relaxed. During the years immediately following World War I, teaching personnel became more available, and there was for a time a status quo situation.

The Legislature carried out the next major step in certification in 1929—it reduced the number of certifying bodies. Certificates could be conferred now only by the University of Michigan, the state superintendent, the State Board of Education, and the county normal boards. To earn a life certificate, a candidate had to take at least 144 quarter-hours of course work, except in special cases where the demand dictated reducing the requirements to fill vacancies. No life certificates could be conferred after January 1, 1930, however, without the candidate's earning 144 quarter-hours of credit. Those who did not have enough college work to meet degree requirements could obtain 3- and 5-year certificates.

During the Depression years, many qualified teachers could not find jobs, and salaries were declining. State Superintendent Webster H. Pearce recommended that the teachers colleges eliminate their short courses, that professional training be limited to the junior and senior years of college, that scholastic and aptitude requirements be established for admission to professional training, and that legislation provide for a probationary period before a person could be granted a life certificate. He also suggested that an accrediting agent be established for the higher education institutes.

In 1933, certificates ranging from 1 year to life were granted by five authorities: the superintendent of public instruction, the state board, county and normal boards, the university, and the vocational education board. That year, the state board created the Planning Commission on Teacher Training and Certification to study the field and give their advice. The commission recommended that all laws allowing agencies other than the state board to certify teachers be repealed, and it also suggested establishing a central system of accounting for certificates to keep a check on teacher supply.

Two years later, in 1935, the Legislature passed—

> An act to authorize and require the State Board of Education to prescribe courses of study, issue licenses and certificates, and grant diplomas and degrees in connection with several educational institutions of the State, and to repeal all acts and parts of acts in any way contravening the provisions of this act (30).

Now designated as the sole agency for issuing teachers' certificates, the state board appointed an Extra Legal Advisory Commission consisting of representatives from the teaching profession and Michigan's teacher education institutions. This commission proposed a new certification code which was adopted in May 1936. At the same time, the state board appointed an advisory committee on teacher education to supervise an 8-year study of the new code's impact and the laws in general.

During the 1940's, the state advisory committee received numerous complaints about the certification requirements, particularly that not enough preparation was required. There was a general feeling that a change was needed. In 1953, the advisory committee appointed a subcommittee to draft a new certification code.

The subcommittee, in its initial report in April 1954, recommended a complete revision of the 1939 code. The committee held hearings and meetings throughout the state to get the reactions of teachers and other professional people on the proposed revisions. It finally presented the new code to the state board for its approval in December 1956, but the board rejected it on the grounds that too much dissatisfaction with the revisions had been expressed in the hearings.

The original subcommittee was dissolved, but in 1956, the state board appointed an ad hoc committee to develop a revised certification code. This committee made a tentative report to the board in May 1961, and the board gave it tentative approval. The board then combined the ad hoc committee with the state advisory committee on teacher education to form the State Advisory Commission on Teacher Education and Certification.

The commission held meetings throughout the state to explain its proposals and get the reactions of teachers, school administrators, college faculty members, and other people interested in education. After the state board held a final hearing in January 1963, the State Advisory Commission reedited the code. The state board formally adopted it that May, and it was sent to the attorney general for approval. Local interest in the proposed code prompted a number of additional hearings, before the attorney general could give his approval. At the same time, there was some question as to the impact of a new State Constitution and a new eight-member State Board of Education, which was to be elected.

Certainly, the state had progressed, but many problems still had to be solved. In 1950-51, approximately 25 percent of the state's 38,000 teachers had master's degrees or higher, but 27 percent did not hold degrees of any kind. By 1963, only 8 percent of the 75,000 teachers employed did not have degrees, and approximately 31 percent had completed work at the master's level. Despite the fact that Michigan schools were attracting better teachers, State Superintendent Lynn Bartlett pointed out that over 5,000 teachers employed during the 1961-62 school year did not return to their posts the following year and that the state needed some 3,000 new teachers just to meet its enrollment growth. It was estimated that some 6,000 full-time positions would be filled by teachers holding special certificates, indicating that they had not fulfilled all of the educational requirements for full certification (31).

In 1966, Superintendent Ira Polley invited former U.S. Commissioner of Education Francis Keppel and two of the nation's leading authorities on teacher education and certification, Robert J. Schaefer, dean of Columbia's Teachers College, and Donald J. McCardy, dean of education, University of Wisconsin, to assist Michigan in a comprehensive review and appraisal of the new code. The new state board, which took office in January 1965, carefully considered all of the recommendations and adopted the new certification code in June 1967.

SOME EDUCATIONAL PROGRAMS IN MICHIGAN

Special Education

Even during early statehood, Michigan's leaders declared educational opportunity for all children as one of their goals. In keeping with this philosophy, in 1848 the Legislature approved the establishment of a Michigan School for the Deaf in Flint. Funds were finally made available, and in 1854, under the direction of the State Board of Education, it opened. This school also served blind children until 1879, when the Michigan School for the Blind was established in Lansing.

In 1878, the state established an institution at Pontiac to care for feeble-minded children. Fifteen years later, in 1893, the Lapeer Home and Training School was established as the Michigan Home for Feeble Minded and Epileptic, with facilities for 210 children. The Legislature, in 1899, also provided for educating the deaf with special day classes in public schools other than the Flint school.

In 1915, Superintendent Fred L. Keeler approved the first complete survey of the state's towns and cities in regard to the number and types of youth being served by "special classes." He sent a questionnaire to the superintendents of schools in communities of 1,000 or more asking for statistics on classes and pupils who were backward, delinquent, defective in any way, late in entering school, or exceptionally bright. He hoped to learn what was being done for educating these various groups, and to what extent the teachers of backward and defective children had special training for this kind of work. He also hoped to learn from the superintendents the advisability of forming special classes, not only for backward and defective children, but for the exceptionally bright as well. The returns indicated that the state should do more, particularly in emphasizing teacher preparation in the whole area of special education.

In 1923, as a result of the 1915 survey, the Legislature enacted a law providing for the education of all physically handicapped children—the crippled, the deaf and hard of hearing, and the blind or partially sighted. In his 1929 report, Superintendent Webster H. Pearce outlined a plan for training teachers for the deaf and hard of hearing, the blind and partially sighted, the mentally deficient, and the crippled in the department of special education at Michigan State Normal College at Ypsilanti. This training also would include speech reading for adult deaf persons, and instruction for their teachers.

Until the thirties, most of the progress in special education was centered in the cities. In his 1935-37 report, Superintendent Eugene B. Elliott strongly urged that the entire program be expanded. He stated:

> In the case of special education, there has existed for several years an optional program in which the State has reimbursed local districts for the excess costs of conducting classes for certain types of handicapped children, including the blind, partially seeing, deaf, hard of hearing, crippled, cardiopathic, and epileptic. The wording of the Act, however, makes it possible for only the largest cities to avail themselves of its advantages. A change in this law is needed, therefore, (1) to permit the establishment of smaller centers in the less densely populated areas of the State to serve more than one school district; (2) to permit a modified program for isolated cases (the deaf and blind excepted) in which there is an insufficient number of children for a special class; and (3) to extend the benefits as rapidly as possible including speech defectives, those low in vitality, and the mentally retarded (32).

During the next immediate years, special education programs continued to grow, and more and more people became interested. Consequently, during the 1939 session, the Legislature, by amendment, passed a special education act to include crippled children from the fourth birthday, to allow summer programs, and to increase services to rural children by permitting establishment of special education centers to serve surrounding districts.

In line with legislative action, the Department of Public Instruction established a section of special education in 1939.

An extralegal advisory planning commission, in cooperation with the teacher-educating institutes offering training in special education, established policies and requirements for the certification of teachers in the field of special education. These were recommended to the state board for adoption in August 1940.

In 1949, Superintendent Lee M. Thurston broadened the scope of the special education work by inaugurating a visiting teacher program. In establishing this program, Thurston stated that "the term exceptional children is applied to those children, who, because of physical, mental, or emotional deviations, need additional services not required by non-exceptional children" (33).

In 1958, Superintendent Bartlett commented in regard to legislative action and support as follows:

> It provided for the mentally handicapped individual who has enough potential capacity to achieve some success in a school program adapted to his needs and who, within limited expectations, can make reasonably satisfactory adjustment to his job and in the community. For the child with this type of handicap, consultant service in the regular classroom (Type C) or instruction in special classes (Type A) is available. A separate special class program (Type B) is provided for the mentally handicapped individual, who, at best, can assume only partially his responsibilities in the family and community (34).

The special education programs continued to expand. Broader tax bases and supplementary state aid benefits, in accordance with additional local costs, made possible by the County and Special Education Act, increased not only the number but also the quality of the special education programs. In 1962, Superintendent Bartlett's pleas resulted in legislation providing for reimbursement to public school programs for emotionally disturbed children under the provisions of the State School Aid Act. By 1966, the special education programs were serving 105,739 youngsters, and the state was investing $30,289,437–about $286 per pupil. The new eight-member State Board of Education continues to support vigorously increased educational opportunities and training for these youngsters.

Vocational Education

Historically, the early concerns for vocational education in Michigan are lost in obscurity. It is known, however, that a private citizen provided funds for the first manual training school to be established in Muskegon in 1897. Educators must have had considerable interest in such programs, as some 40 pages of the state superintendent's report for 1900 deal with the broadly defined area of manual training. In 1912, Lansing started a cooperative work plan in which the students spent half time in school and half time on the job. And two private gifts made it possible to inaugurate industrial education in Saginaw.

Even before the Smith-Hughes Act of 1917, which gave the real impetus to vocational education, some Michigan schools were offering courses. Lay and professional groups were very much concerned with functional education, particularly in agriculture. Home economics, like agriculture, was a derivative of the manual training movement and resulted from community interest but did not grow as fast as the agricultural programs.

To participate in the funds available under the Smith-Hughes Act, Michigan passed the Tufts Act (Act 189). At its first meeting, held in July 1917, in State Superintendent Fred L. Keeler's office, the State Board of Control for Vocational Education interpreted the act as applying to "any education the controlling purpose of which is to fit for profitable employment" (35). The board appointed a secretary and designated the state superintendent as the board's executive officer, in accordance with the enabling act.

Early experimentation in vocational education made it possible for the state to move rapidly. Most of the local programs were already meeting the requirements set down in the Smith-Hughes law. The Legislature almost immediately appropriated state funds to match federal vocational education funds, and a total of $60,544 was distributed to Michigan schools for the 1917-18 school year, $37,593 of it from the federal government. This provided programs for 7,218 students.

The Legislature revised the Tufts Act in 1919 with Act 149, and this still is the controlling legislation for vocational education in Michigan. The number of school districts taking advantage of the federal and state funds for developing and improving vocational education for both youth and adults grew steadily. The federal programs were expanded considerably by the George-Reed Act in 1929 and the George-Ellzey Act of 1934. In 1937, Congress granted additional aid through the George-Deen Act, which provided funds not only for programs already in existence, but also for distributive education.

From 1917 through the war years, the Department of Public Instruction increased its staff as necessary to meet the growing demands in the vocational education area. During World War II years, primary emphasis was on meeting the needs for war production.

In 1946, the George-Barden Act supplanted the George-Deen Act, and in 1958, the National Defense Education Act provided funds for training highly skilled technicians in the fields essential to national defense. In 1961 and 1962, the Area Redevelopment Act and the Manpower Development Training Act added to the department's employees and responsibilities. Today, area vocational studies are being conducted to determine the need and to plan for area vocational-technical schools.

Federal funding has played an all-important part in the upsurge in vocational education. The Vocational Education Act, enacted by the Eighty-Eighth Congress in 1963, not only increased the amount of federal funds, but again broadened the scope of the programs. Two years later, Superintendent Bartlett emphasized to the Legislature the growing need for expanded vocational and technical training. He stated:

> It is high time that an end be called to the controversy that has existed between those who advocate only the academic side of high school preparation and those who teach in vocational education.
>
> The point of view that looks down upon vocational education and training is unwarranted and detrimental to both kinds of students.
>
> . . . There have been many who have called for an end to traditional and obsolescent approaches in this area of our education program. They have been asking for new programs, ideas, and attitudes. In Michigan we have recognized the fact that this must be done (36).

Recognizing the impact of science and technology on all aspects of educational programing, the Department of Education has acknowledged the critical need for updating, broadening, and expanding programs of vocational-technical education. Schools are urged to meet more realistically these new demands and to break with traditional and stereotyped courses.

Michigan vocational-technical education programs strive to provide occupational preparation for all Michigan citizens who need it, including students in public secondary schools; persons who completed or left high school and are available for full-time study in preparation for entering the labor market; persons who have already entered the labor market and who need training to achieve stability or advancement in employment; and persons who suffer handicaps that prevent them from succeeding in the regular vocational program.

Vocational-technical education programs for the above groups of persons are provided by local educational agencies, largely in local school districts, and community colleges. A limited number of programs of less-than-baccalaureate-degree level are offered in a few 4-year institutions of higher education.

During 1966-67, more than 6,000 students were enrolled in high school cooperative programs leading to employment in sales and related jobs, and 675 were enrolled in similar programs at the post-high school level. In the preparatory program, 8,235 high school students were enrolled, and in post-high school programs, 3,157. In the same period, 6,575 high school and 662 post-high school students were enrolled in cooperative office education programs. In addition to these, 18,677 adults and out-of-school youth were enrolled in adult preparatory programs in sales and marketing, and 5,870 were in preparatory office occupations programs. These programs were operated largely by local school districts.

Home economics education classes enrolled 62,687 high school students, including a small percentage of boys, plus another 17,300 persons in adult programs. Home economics was extended by the Vocational Education Act of 1963 to include the preparation of persons at all educational levels for employment in occupations requiring such knowledge and skills. In 1966-67, 35 communities enrolled 1,390 high school students and 25 adults in wage-earning classes in seven occupational fields.

Programs in agricultural education provide high school and post-high school preparation for production farming and for related occupations which require knowledge and skills in agriculture. In 1966-67, agriculture programs were offered in 198 high schools and 3 post-high school institutions, including Michigan State University. High schools enrolled 11,815 students, 1,113 of whom were in off-farm occupations on a part-time basis during the school year. Some students in this group were employed in off-farm occupations and also conducted farm-based enterprises outside of school hours. Local school districts operated programs for young and adult farmers in which 1,196 persons were enrolled, and two community colleges and Michigan State University offered 1- and 2-year post-secondary programs in eight specialized areas in agriculture.

In 1966-67, 265,480 students participated in various vocational education programs at a cost of $12,242,098, more than 85 percent of which came from the federal government.

Vocational Rehabilitation

In 1920, Congress passed Public Law 236, establishing a vocational rehabilitation program by making funds available to the states on a 50-50 matching basis. In order for Michigan to take part, the following year the Legislature enacted Act 211. Although an independent program, it was placed under the auspices of the State Board for Vocational Education.

From 1920 up through World War II, the vocational rehabilitation division remained as a part of the vocational education operation of the department which was able, with a relatively small staff, to handle the work that was required.

During World War II, in 1943, Congress passed Public Law 113, which essentially broadened the services and eligibility under the rehabilitation programs. Two years later, in 1945, Superintendent Eugene B. Elliott established a vocational rehabilitation section, equal in status to vocational education, and appointed a director.

The Legislature gave increased attention to vocational rehabilitation. In 1954, more funds were voted, and the program was broadened by Public Law 565. In 1965, Public Law 333 enabled the state to participate in a program which upped federal financing to 75 percent (3 federal dollars for every state dollar) and provided funds for constructing facilities, such as sheltered workshops, rehabilitation centers, and community workshops.

During its first year of operation, there were only two employees in the vocational rehabilitation program; in the second year, six. As of 1968, there were nearly 700 professional and staff people engaged in this important work, serving more than 25,000 persons. Almost $13 million is being invested in such programs.

The growing importance of vocational rehabilitation as another means of making a positive investment in our human resources is becoming more obvious each year. It offers a new opportunity and a new lease on a full, productive life for those who have physical or mental restrictions, who might be disabled, who might not have marketable skills, or who may be unemployed.

Future expansion by the Department of Education into this service area will be needed if all who might benefit are to be reached.

CONCLUSION

The State Board of Education believes that education is an investment in people, in social progress, and in scientific, industrial, and economic advancement. It believes education today is the most essential and critical factor for the continuing existence of our free and democratic way of life. It takes the position that our public schools must remain a leading, dynamic force in the development of the kind of society that respects the individual, that has a high regard for humanity, and that has a deep, sincere concern for social problems and issues. Only in such a society can human resources be fully developed, and only if our human resources are ensured maximum development can such a society flourish.

President John F. Kennedy, in his special message to the Congress on education, January 29, 1963, stated:

> In all the years of our national life, the American people – in partnership with their governments–have continued to insist that "the means of education shall forever be encouraged" as the Continental Congress affirmed in the Northwest Ordinance. Fundamentally, education is and must always be a local responsibility . . . in our present era of economic expansion, population growth and technological advance, state, local and private efforts are insufficient. These efforts must be reinforced by national support, if American education is to yield a maximum of individual development and national well-being (37).

For Michigan education, the future holds many promises and tremendous opportunities. There is much that must be done if Michigan is to continue in the forefront of educational leadership. The State Department of Education is dedicated to this goal.

FOOTNOTES

1. *Northwest Ordinance of 1787.* Michigan's present constitution, adopted in 1963, still carries this passage.
2. Territory of Michigan, *Laws,* II (1827), 472-77.
3. Stuart *v.* School District No. 1 of the Village of Kalamazoo, 30 Mich. 69 (1874).
4. Michigan, *Act No. 161* (1859), sec. 3, p. 447.
5. The Legislature passed a similar law 20 years later, giving local boards the power to specify the subjects to be taught and the textbooks to be used in these subjects. The texts had to be uniform and once chosen could not be changed for 5 years without the majority vote of the people.
6. Superintendent of Public Instruction, *Fifty-Fourth Annual Report, 1890,* Appendix L.
7. Department of Public Instruction, *The Michigan Program of Curriculum Revision - Progress Report,* Bulletin No. 305 (Lansing: The Department, 1936).
8. Department of Public Instruction, *The Michigan Curriculum Program, Third Report of Progress* (Lansing: The Department, 1941).
9. *Ibid.,* pp. 4-5.
10. Superintendent of Public Instruction, *Ninetieth Report, 1927-1929,* pp. 9-10.
11. Michigan, *Act No. 293* (1927), secs. 1-2, p. 545.
12. Superintendent of Public Instruction, *Ninety-Second Report, 1931-1933,* pp. 18-20.
13. Superintendent of Public Instruction, *One Hundred and Fourth Report, 1956-1958,* p. 2.
14. *Ibid.,* p. 3.
15. Lynn M. Bartlett, "Education in Michigan Today," an address by Superintendent Bartlett before a meeting of the Michigan Association of School Administrators and the Michigan Association of School Boards, September 11, 1963, included in bound records of Council of Chief State School Officers, "Letters to All Chief State School Officers," XVI, Part 2, p. 372.
16. The five-member panel of national consultants consisted of Kenneth Clark, psychologist, City College of New York, member of the New York State Board of Regents, and a specialist in problems of the inner cities; Steven K. Bailey, political scientist, dean of the

Maxwell School of Citizenship and Public Affairs, Syracuse University, and a member of the New York State Board of Regents; Roald F. Campbell, education administration, dean, College of Education, University of Chicago; H. Thomas James, education administration, dean, College of Education, Stanford University; and Roe L. Johns, education administration, chairman, Department of Education Administration, University of Florida.

17. Superintendent of Public Instruction, *Thirty-Seventh Annual Report, 1873,* pp. 5-7.

18. Superintendent of Public Instruction, *Sixty-Fourth Annual Report, 1900,* p. 6.

19. Superintendent of Public Instruction, *Sixty-Ninth Annual Report, 1905,* p. 5.

20. Michigan, *Act No. 319* (1927), ch. 5, sec. 1.

21. Superintendent of Public Instruction, *Ninety-Ninth Report, 1946-1948,* p. 3.

22. Superintendent of Public Instruction, *One Hundred and Fourth Report, 1956-1958,* p. 49.

23. Normal schools, so designated from the French "Ecole Normale," were usually 2-year institutions for training elementary teachers, while institutes were more or less concentrated, short-term (5 to 10 days) sessions for upgrading teachers already in the field.

24. George Leroy Jackson, *The Development of State Control of Public Instruction in Michigan* (Lansing: Michigan Historical Commission, 1926), p. 168.

25. Superintendent of Public Instruction, *Seventieth Annual Report, 1906,* pp. 18-20.

26. Two years earlier in 1908, Superintendent Luther L. Wright had authorized the Michigan State Teachers Association to conduct institutes.

27. John D. Springman, *The Growth of Public Education in Michigan* (Ypsilanti: Division of Field Services, Michigan State Normal College, 1952), p. 204.

28. In 1941, the teachers colleges became colleges of education.

29. Springman, *op. cit.,* p. 211.

30. Michigan, *Act No. 55* (1935), p. 86.

31. Bartlett, *op. cit.,* p. 371-b.

32. Superintendent of Public Instruction, *Ninety-Fourth Report, 1935-1937,* pp. 12-19.

33. Superintendent of Public Instruction, *Ninety-Ninth Report, 1946-1948,* p. 10.

34. *Superintendent of Public Instruction, One Hundred and Fourth Report, 1956-1958,* p. 22.

35. Michigan Board of Control for Vocational Education, Minutes of Meetings, files of the Vocational Education Division, Department of Education, Lansing, Michigan.

36. Superintendent of Public Instruction, *One Hundred and Seventh Report, 1962-1964.*

37. *Public Papers of the Presidents of the United States: John F. Kennedy, January 1 to November 22, 1963* (Washington, D.C.: Government Printing Office, 1964), p. 115.

BIBLIOGRAPHY

Public Documents

Michigan. *Act No. 161* (1859).

—— *Act No. 293* (1927).

—— *Act No. 319* (1927).

—— *Act No. 55* (1935).

—— *Constitution* (1835, 1837, 1850, 1908, 1963).

Northwest Ordinance of 1787.

Public Papers of the Presidents of the United States: John F. Kennedy, January 1 to November 22, 1963. Washington, D.C.: Government Printing Office, 1964.

Stuart *v.* School District No. 1 of the Village of Kalamazoo, 30 Mich. 69 (1874).

Territory of Michigan. *Laws,* II (1827).

Books

Better Education for Michigan Children and Adults. Lansing: Department of Public Instruction, 1954.

Bigelow, Martha Mitchell. *Michigan, Pioneer in Education.* Michigan Historical Collections Bulletin No. 7. Ann Arbor: University of Michigan, 1955.

Dain, Floyd R. *Education in the Wilderness.* Vol. I: *History of Education in Michigan.* Lansing: Michigan Historical Commission, 1968.

Department of Education. *Education in Michigan.* Lansing: The Department, 1967.

Department of Public Instruction. *Education in Michigan.* Bulletin No. 407. Lansing: The Department, 1944.

——*Education in a Rural School District, 1928-1929.* Parts 1 and 2. Bulletin No. 56. Lansing: The Department, 1929.

—— *Five Years of Change in the Public Elementary and Secondary Schools of Michigan.* Lansing: The Department, 1964.

—— *Five Years of Growth in Michigan Education.* Bulletin No. 528. Lansing: The Department, 1963.

—— *Historical Sketches of Education in Michigan.* Lansing: The Department, 1881.

—— *A Look at Michigan Schools.* Lansing: The Department, 1958.

—— *Michigan Today: Its Human and Physical Resources as They Affect Education.* Bulletin No. 307. Lansing: The Department, 1937.

—— *A Statement of Basic Philosophy Regarding Public Education in Michigan.* Bulletin No. 364. Lansing: The Department, 1960.

Disbrow, Donald W. *Schools for an Urban Society.* Vol. III: *History of Education in Michigan.* Lansing: Michigan Historical Commission, 1968.

Dunbar, Willis F. *The Michigan Record in Higher Education.* Vol. IV: *History of Education in Michigan.* Detroit: Wayne State University Press, 1963.

Hoyt, Charles Oliver, and Ford, R. C. *John D. Pierce, Founder of the Michigan School System: A Study of Education in the Northwest.* Ypsilanti, Mich.: The Scharf Co., 1905.

Jackson, George Leroy. *The Development of State Control of Public Instruction in Michigan.* Lansing: Michigan Historical Commission, 1926.

Michigan Historical Commission. *Records of the Michigan Department of Public Instruction, 1859-1957.* Finding Aid Series, No. 12. Lansing: Department of Public Instruction, 1963.

—— *Michigan History.* Lansing: The Commission, 1917. Approximately 80 articles dealing with the history of education in Michigan.

—— *Michigan Pioneer and Historical Collections, 1874-1876.* Lansing: The Commission, 1929. Numerous articles and reminiscences concerning the history of education in Michigan.

Payne, William Harold. *The Relation Between the University and Our High Schools.* A lecture delivered before the State Teachers' Association at Ypsilanti, Michigan, on December 27, 1890. Adrian, Mich.: Charles Humphrey, 1871.

Putnam, Daniel. *The Development of Primary and Secondary Public Education in Michigan.* Ann Arbor, Mich.: G. Wahr, 1904.

Schmidt, Charles, Jr.; Parker, Hyman; and Pepas, Bob. *Guide to Collective Negotiations in Education.* Prepared for the School of Labor and Industrial Relations, Michigan State University, in cooperation with the Michigan State Board of Education. Lansing: Social Science Research Bureau, Michigan State University, 1967.

Springman, John D. *The Growth of Public Education in Michigan.* Ypsilanti: Division of Field Services, Michigan State Normal College, 1952.

Starring, Charles R., and Knouse, James O. *The Michigan Search for Educational Standards.* Vol. II: *History of Education in Michigan.* Lansing: Michigan Historical Commission, 1968.

Reports

Department of Education. *Annual Reports of Michigan Cooperative Curriculum Program, 1962-1967.* Lansing: The Department, 1962-67.

Department of Public Instruction. *In 151 Communities. First Annual Report.* Lansing: The Department, 1945.

—— *Means of Education: A Report of the Progress of the School Facilities Survey in Michigan.* Lansing: The Department, 1953.

——*The Michigan Curriculum Program: Third Report of Progress.* Lansing: The Department, 1941.

—— *The Michigan Program of Curriculum Revision - Progress Report.* Bulletin No. 305. Lansing: The Department, 1936.

Governor's Citizens Committee on Higher Education. *Report of the Citizens Committee on Higher Education, a Consolidated and Summary Statement of Findings and Recommendations.* Lansing: The Committee, March 1965.

Governor's Constitutional Convention, Citizens Advisory Committee on Education. *Education.* Lansing: The Committee, September 1961.

Higher Education Assistance Authority. *Annual Reports.* Lansing: The Authority, 1962-67.

Legislative Study Committee on Higher Education. *Final Report of the Survey of Higher Education in Michigan.* Lansing: The Committee, 1958.

Michigan Public Education Study Commission. *The Improvement of Public Education in Michigan.* Lansing: The Commission, 1944.

Michigan Senate Education Committee. *Report on Special Education in Michigan.* Lansing: The Committee, 1966.

Michigan White House Conference on Education. *Report.* Lansing: Department of Public Instruction, 1965.

Superintendents of Public Instruction. *Annual and Biennial Reports.* Lansing: Department of Public Instruction, 1837-1967.

Periodicals

Michigan Education Bulletin. Lansing: Michigan Education Association, 1933-35.

Michigan Education News. A newsletter of the Department of Education, 1933-68.

Michigan Journal of Education. Vols. I-IX, published in Lansing, 1854-61.

Michigan School Board Journal. Vols. I-X, 1955-64.

Unpublished Material

Bartlett, Lynn M. "Education in Michigan Today." An address by Superintendent Bartlett before a meeting of the Michigan Association of School Administrators and the Michigan Association of School Boards, September 11, 1963. Included in bound records of the Council of Chief State School Officers, "Letters to All Chief State School Officers," Vol. XVI, Part 2.

Draper, William Burle. "The Activities and Contributions of Walter H. French to Michigan Education." Unpublished master's thesis, Michigan State University, East Lansing, 1959.

Michigan Board of Control for Vocational Education. Minutes of Meetings. Files of the Vocational Education Division, Department of Education, Lansing, Michigan.

Appendix A

MICHIGAN CHIEF STATE SCHOOL OFFICERS

State Superintendents

1836-41	John D. Pierce	1893-97	Henry R. Pattengill
1841-43	Franklin Sawyer, Jr.	1897-1901	Jason E. Hammond
1843-45	Oliver C. Comstock	1901-1905	Delos Fall
1845-49	Ira Mayhew	1905-1907	Patrick H. Kelley
1849-55	Francis W. Sherman	1907-13	Luther L. Wright
1855-59	Ira Mayhew	1913-19	Fred L. Keeler
1859-65	John M. Gregory	1919-26	Thomas E. Johnson
1865-73	Oramel Hosford	1926-27	Wilford L. Coffey
1873-77	Daniel B. Briggs	1927-33	Webster H. Pearce
1877-78	Horace S. Tarbell	1933-35	Paul F. Voelker
1878-81	Cornelius A. Gower		Maurice R. Keyworth*
1881-83	Varnum B. Cochran	1935-48	Eugene B. Elliott
1883-85	Herschel R. Gass	1948-53	Lee M. Thurston
1885-87	Theodore Nelson	1953-57	Clair L. Taylor
1887-90	Joseph Estabrook	1957-65	Lynn M. Bartlett
1890-93	Ferris S. Fitch	1966-	Ira Polley

*Elected in 1935, died before taking office.

Appendix B

Chart I.--MICHIGAN DEPARTMENT OF EDUCATION, 1949

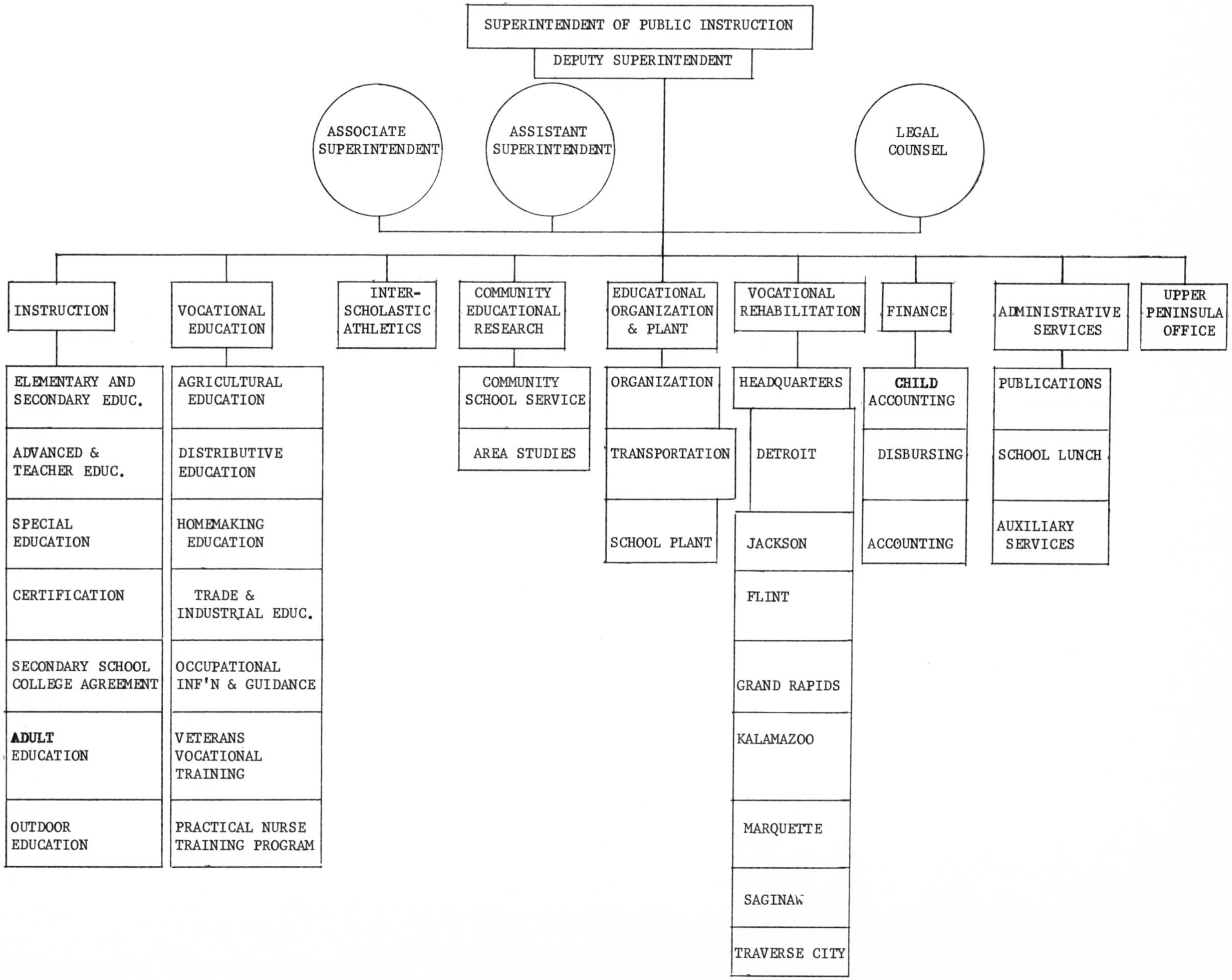

SUPERINTENDENT OF PUBLIC INSTRUCTION
DEPUTY SUPERINTENDENT

ASSOCIATE SUPERINTENDENT
ASSISTANT SUPERINTENDENT
LEGAL COUNSEL

INSTRUCTION
- ELEMENTARY AND SECONDARY EDUC.
- ADVANCED & TEACHER EDUC.
- SPECIAL EDUCATION
- CERTIFICATION
- SECONDARY SCHOOL COLLEGE AGREEMENT
- ADULT EDUCATION
- OUTDOOR EDUCATION

VOCATIONAL EDUCATION
- AGRICULTURAL EDUCATION
- DISTRIBUTIVE EDUCATION
- HOMEMAKING EDUCATION
- TRADE & INDUSTRIAL EDUC.
- OCCUPATIONAL INF'N & GUIDANCE
- VETERANS VOCATIONAL TRAINING
- PRACTICAL NURSE TRAINING PROGRAM

INTER-SCHOLASTIC ATHLETICS

COMMUNITY EDUCATIONAL RESEARCH
- COMMUNITY SCHOOL SERVICE
- AREA STUDIES

EDUCATIONAL ORGANIZATION & PLANT
- ORGANIZATION
- TRANSPORTATION
- SCHOOL PLANT

VOCATIONAL REHABILITATION
- HEADQUARTERS
- DETROIT
- JACKSON
- FLINT
- GRAND RAPIDS
- KALAMAZOO
- MARQUETTE
- SAGINAW
- TRAVERSE CITY

FINANCE
- CHILD ACCOUNTING
- DISBURSING
- ACCOUNTING

ADMINISTRATIVE SERVICES
- PUBLICATIONS
- SCHOOL LUNCH
- AUXILIARY SERVICES

UPPER PENINSULA OFFICE

Appendix B

Chart II.--MICHIGAN DEPARTMENT OF EDUCATION, 1967

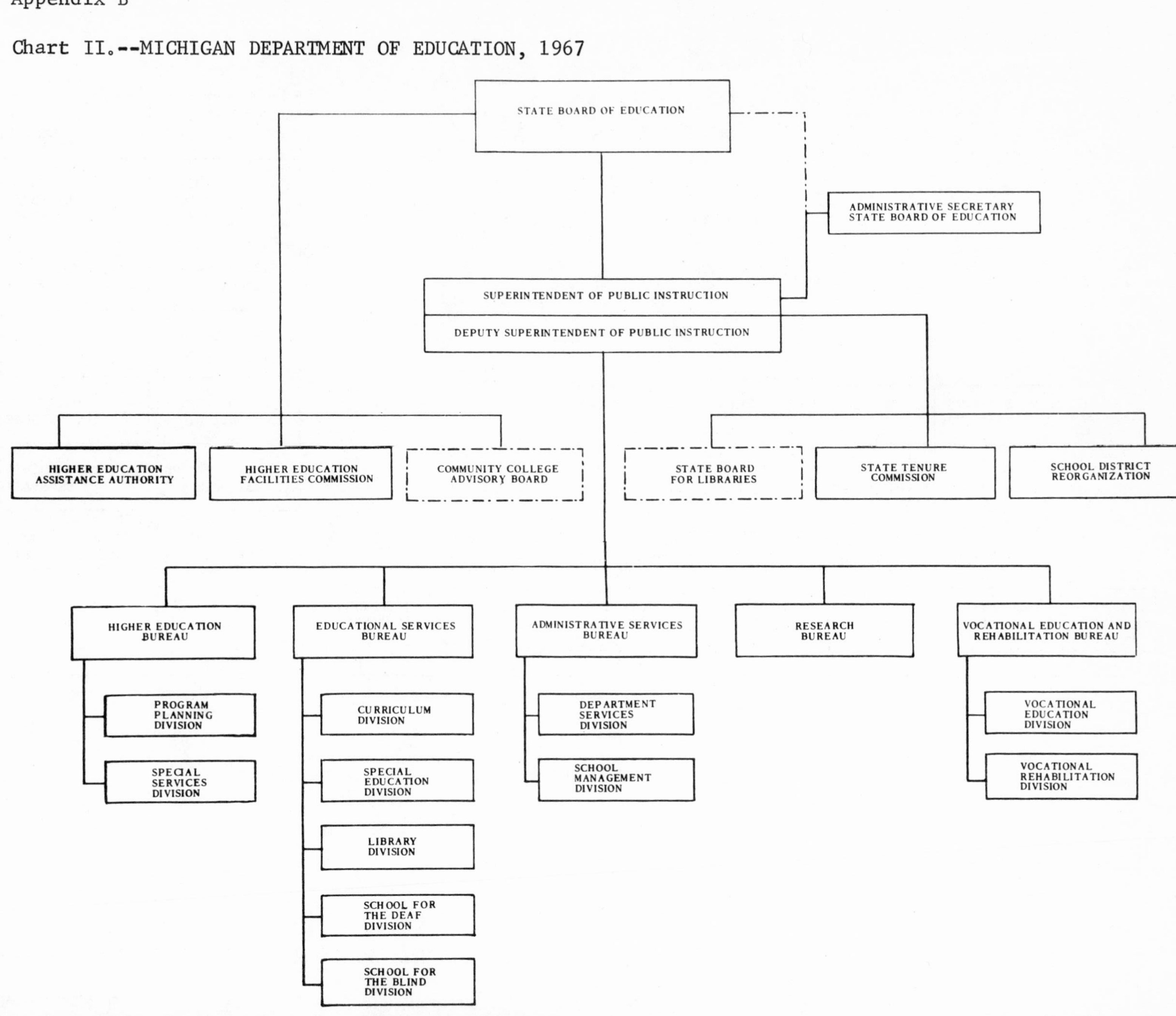

STATE BOARD OF EDUCATION
ADMINISTRATIVE SECRETARY STATE BOARD OF EDUCATION
SUPERINTENDENT OF PUBLIC INSTRUCTION
DEPUTY SUPERINTENDENT OF PUBLIC INSTRUCTION
HIGHER EDUCATION ASSISTANCE AUTHORITY
HIGHER EDUCATION FACILITIES COMMISSION
COMMUNITY COLLEGE ADVISORY BOARD
STATE BOARD FOR LIBRARIES
STATE TENURE COMMISSION
SCHOOL DISTRICT REORGANIZATION
HIGHER EDUCATION BUREAU
PROGRAM PLANNING DIVISION
SPECIAL SERVICES DIVISION
EDUCATIONAL SERVICES BUREAU
CURRICULUM DIVISION
SPECIAL EDUCATION DIVISION
LIBRARY DIVISION
SCHOOL FOR THE DEAF DIVISION
SCHOOL FOR THE BLIND DIVISION
ADMINISTRATIVE SERVICES BUREAU
DEPARTMENT SERVICES DIVISION
SCHOOL MANAGEMENT DIVISION
RESEARCH BUREAU
VOCATIONAL EDUCATION AND REHABILITATION BUREAU
VOCATIONAL EDUCATION DIVISION
VOCATIONAL REHABILITATION DIVISION

23 Minnesota

DEPARTMENT OF EDUCATION
T. C. Engum

Contents

STATE SUPERVISION OF EDUCATION PRIOR TO 1900

The evolution of the role of state supervision was slow and deliberate. To the pioneer, so dependent on his own individual initiative, there was something suspicious about educational supervision from an office far removed from his neighborhood schoolhouse. The eminent Minnesota historian William Folwell stated:

> A study of the subject of state supervision of schools [in the early years of statehood] leaves the impression that for a long time the people of Minnesota wanted as little of it as possible and that they later grudgingly tolerated its expansion as school funds requiring guardianship increased (1).

Territorial Days

In 1849, the Territorial Legislature enacted the first law pertaining to education: Common schools were to be open to all persons between the ages of 4 and 21 years, and townships were to be divided into school districts when the districts contained more than five families. To support the schools, the law levied a general tax of 2.5 mills and supplemented it with 15 percent of the funds collected from liquor licenses and fines for criminal offenses.

This history is the result of extensive help and cooperation from a large number of people, the names of whom are too numerous to mention individually. However, because of assistance well beyond the call of duty, special thanks go to T. C. Engum, retired staff member, who was formerly chief of the elementary and secondary school section; E. Raymond Peterson, assistant commissioner for instruction; August W. Gehrke, assistant commissioner for vocational rehabilitation and special education; members of their staffs; and Dean M. Schweickhard, former commissioner of education. Additional thanks go to staff members at the library of the Minnesota Historical Society and to countless others who kindly volunteered information and advice, both oral and written, to aid in the writing of this document.

But formal education developed slowly—in 1851, there were only three schools in Minnesota, enrolling a total of 250 children. It was not unusual in these early years for the school year to be as short as 3 months. Most schools included courses in reading, writing, geography, and some form of mathematics. The teachers' salaries averaged $13 a month for women and $21 for men (2).

Edward D. Neill, a Presbyterian minister and one of the ablest educators in the territory, was appointed the first of four territorial superintendents of public instruction in 1854. His annual salary of $100 was hardly enough to support a man and his family. When he resigned 2 years later, finding a successor was difficult; the Territorial Governor announced in his 1856 annual message that the superintendent had resigned and that he could not find anyone who would take the office at $100 a year. The following year a St. Paul lawyer agreed to take the position on a part-time basis (3).

From Statehood to 1900

Minnesota became a state in 1858, and 2 years later, the Legislature stipulated that every township would be a school district. The town supervisors were appointed school trustees ex officio, and the town clerks and treasurers were named the school officials. This township plan lasted only a year, however, for, in 1862, the Legislature adopted the so-called neighborhood plan, which firmly established the district system of public schools—a system still in existence today.

Educational progress in the early statehood years was substantial compared to the slow development during territorial days. In 1868, Governor William R. Marshall reported that Minnesota had more school buildings than any other state with comparable population and taxable property (4).

In the first decade of statehood, the emphasis was on two extremes: the common school for those who desired only the basics, and the university for those who desired an extensive education. Since usually only the well-to-do could afford the luxury of a college education, there was a real need to develop a systematic and comprehensive intermediate program. Thus, in 1872, Superintendent Horace B.

Wilson appointed a special committee to plan a course of study for the high school, frequently referred to as "the people's college." Wilson also directed the committee to study a way to establish a curriculum that would provide better preparation for those who would attend a college or university.

Superintendent Wilson's dream of a realistic high school program was realized in 1878 when the Legislature enacted the first law recognizing the need for high schools: It appropriated $400 annually to each high school maintaining a minimum course of study. To enforce these regulations, the act established a high school board consisting of the superintendent of public instruction, the president of the University of Minnesota, and a third member to be appointed by the Governor.

> This was the beginning of state supervision of high schools, although it is to be noted that supervision extended only to schools that desired to be placed on the "accredited list" and to receive state aid. . . . At first there could not be more than three state-aided high schools in any one county, but later this number was increased to five (5).

Originally, the high school board assigned the duties of inspecting these high schools to university faculty members without compensation. However, this was later changed, and a full-time inspector was hired.

The Legislature made another early effort to exert some control over the public schools' curriculum by conferring power on a board to recommend a list of textbooks for the schools. The state had been overrun with book agents in the 1860's, and it was clear that some form of regulation was necessary. To prevent chaos, Superintendent Mark Dunnell urged the Legislature to set up a textbook commission to select books and ensure minimal costs. But prices did not fall substantially. There were charges that a "textbook ring" operated in the state and that textbook profits ran 100 percent or more.

In 1877, at the height of the textbook controversy, Daniel D. Merrill of St. Paul offered to supply the state with textbooks for 15 years at one-half the usual price and to put up bond to ensure his contract. State Superintendent David Burt vetoed the offer, but nonetheless the Legislature enacted it in 1877. It was later charged that the books were cheap in quality as well as price.

Establishment of the Office of State Superintendent of Public Instruction

When Minnesota became a state in 1858, one of the first legislative acts provided for a state superintendent of public instruction. The Legislature named former Territorial Superintendent Edward D. Neill to the position in April 1860; but in May 1861, he resigned to become a chaplain in the First Minnesota Regiment. Neill later became the first president of Macalester College. B. F. Crary, who succeeded Neill, resigned in 1862 to become chaplain of the Third Minnesota Regiment.

When the Civil War began to drain the state financially, there was an effort to economize. The Office of the State Superintendent of Instruction was abolished. His duties were turned over to the secretary of state, who performed them under protest until 1867, when Mark Dunnell was appointed state superintendent. Dunnell served until 1870, and it was during his term that the textbook controversy reached its height.

In 1870, Horace B. Wilson, a professor of mathematics and a former county superintendent of schools, was named superintendent of public instruction. During Wilson's 5-year term, the office expanded greatly in scope and in prestige. He was succeeded by David Burt, who resigned in 1881.

In 1881, David Kiehle, the principal of the state normal school at St. Cloud and a former county superintendent, assumed the office. Kiehle served for seven consecutive terms, the longest period of service of any superintendent up to that time. A foresighted educator, he did much to improve education and to correct some of his office's obvious weaknesses. Among other things, he established a system of summer training schools for teachers. As a regent, a position held by all state superintendents of public instruction in these early years, he formulated the plan for the University of Minnesota's School of Agriculture.

In his biennial report for 1883-84, Kiehle called attention to the large number of children not attending school (6). He recommended specific legislation dealing with this serious situation, and the following year, the Minnesota Legislature enacted a measure requiring every parent or guardian of a child between the ages of 8 and 18 to send him to a public or private school for 12 weeks each year. Disobeying the law was considered a misdemeanor. Its weakness, however, was in the exceptions allowed. In cases where the parent or guardian was too poor to clothe the child, when the child was physically or mentally unable to attend school, when the child was being taught at home or had already acquired the ordinary school training, or where there was no school within 2 miles of the home, school boards could grant excuses. More often than not the children did not attend school. A parent who needed them for work on the farm was usually not reluctant to stretch the truth somewhat to keep the children home. The Act of 1885, therefore, was actually little more than an expression of sentiment.

In 1893, Kiehle resigned, and William Pendergast assumed the duties of state superintendent. Pendergast, a former assistant superintendent of public instruction in the Department of Education, was at the time of his appointment principal of the School of Agriculture of the University of Minnesota.

Under Superintendent John Lewis, who was appointed in 1899 to succeed Pendergast, two significant developments occurred. First, at Lewis' suggestion, the Legislature passed an act designed to strengthen the compulsory attendance law. It authorized school boards in cities and large villages to appoint truant officers with power to arrest truants, take them to school, and file complaints against their parents or guardians. This attendance law also had its weaknesses: It did not affect the smaller villages and rural areas, where the majority of children lived; and the act prescribed no definite procedure for its enforcement. Many children still remained out of school at the turn of the century.

A second significant development in Minnesota education during Lewis' term dealt with teacher qualifications. Prior to 1899, there were no meaningful requirements for the preparation of teachers. Frequently a classroom was staffed by someome with almost no education, and there was little the Office of Public Instruction could do to require much more. But in 1899, the Legislature required that prospective teachers take an examination prepared by the Office of Public Instruction and that, upon satisfactory completion of the test, the teacher be issued one of three certificates, depending on academic and professional preparation.

The primary duty of the state superintendent during the nineteenth century was the annual apportionment of interest from the school fund and the state school tax to the counties. Additionally, he classified schools according to law, regulated the examination of teachers and issued certificates, established specifications for school buildings, and approved all plans for school construction. As a direct result of the general mistrust of state supervision of schools, the state superintendent did not have the duty of supervision of the schools assigned to him. Instead, the duty evolved as a result of state aid to schools.

Financial Aid to Schools

The story of state financial aid to education prior to 1900 was one of sporadic assistance enacted only after it became clear that without such aid education in Minnesota could not progress. The State Constitution provided for a permanent school fund to be derived from the sale of lands granted by the United States for the use of schools within each township, the sale of swamp land, and other cash and investments. The interest from that fund was to be distributed according to the number of school-age children in the district. By 1877, the fund had grown to nearly $3.4 million, the fifth largest school fund in the United States.

In 1885, the Legislature made two important steps toward state financial aid to schools. First, the mode of distribution of funds from the permanent fund was changed: It would be made in proportion to the number of pupils actually in attendance at a school and not according to a census of school-age children in the district. Second, the Legislature proposed a constitutional amendment that would authorize loans from the fund for county and school buildings. The amendment was authorized by the voters in 1887.

As mentioned earlier, the first state aid to education, per se, came in 1878 with the distribution of state moneys to high schools that maintained a minimal program. After that legislation, it was not until 1895 that aid was granted to other schools. Legislation in 1895, 1897, and 1899 provided for grants of some type to practically every public school in the state. However, it must be noted that the aid was initially inadequate to meet the needs of the schools; more substantial aid was to come after the turn of the century.

ORGANIZATION OF STATE SCHOOLS

In the early days of the territory, the Legislature provided that every township with five or more families establish a school district. But because the township was considered too large and cumbersome for operation of a school, and because the early pioneers wished their schools close to their places of residence, the county commissioners in 1851 were allowed to establish smaller school districts, disregarding the formerly used township lines. In retrospect this was an unfortunate move, for the establishment of the so-called "neighborhood common school" brought on a proliferation of school districts, most of which were inefficient, inadequate to the educational task, and financially unable to support education. Today there are many educators who maintain that if the state had continued with the larger township organization, Minnesota would not have experienced as many consolidation and reorganization problems in later years. In general terms, today's common school district in Minnesota is much the same as it was many years ago. It is usually a one-room schoolhouse with an average of about fifteen pupils.

Recognizing that areas of significant population density should have greater control over their schools, the Legislature in 1865 granted incorporated cities, towns, and villages the right to establish independent school districts, a second major form of district organization. Not only were the districts authorized to establish high schools, but they were given greater authority in electing school boards and more direct control over education in their areas.

At the request of several villages and cities, the Minnesota Legislature early in the state's history enacted legislation establishing special school districts, a third major form of district organization. The reasons these areas desired a special classification were numerous. Primarily, however, special district classification provided for closer supervision by the local city government, permitted the districts to rule by their own charters, and gave them a degree of independence not available to other school districts. At one time there were about fifty special charter school districts, and the result was less than effective. Educational progress in these districts was often lacking because legislation regarding them was not uniform. Legislation applying to independent school districts (which constituted the vast majority of districts) did not always apply to the special districts; thus, unless the state lawmakers took special action for them, the special districts were not affected by legislation aimed at educational improvements.

The number of special districts has gradually decreased for several reasons. Most significantly, a special district may not annex property outside the city or village limits. Growth of the school district, therefore, is tied to the often slow expansion of the city boundaries. Additionally, a constitutional amendment ratified by the voters in 1892 prohibited further special charters for school districts. In 1965, only five special districts remained, and this number will decrease further in the next few years.

If one educational issue in Minnesota could be designated as that which stirred up more controversy than most others in the past 20 years, it would be school consolidation. At the turn of the century, there were about 8,000 school districts in the state, a number with which the small staffs in the Office of Public Instruction and the high school board found it difficult to maintain any semblance of contact. Thus, after much urging by several state superintendents, legislation was passed in 1901, 1903, and 1905 enabling various forms of districts to merge. But efforts in these early years of the twentieth century failed. Only a few districts merged, and by 1913, there were still 7,900 districts. One deterrent was the farmers' concern that consolidation would mean higher taxes.

It was left to Governor A. O. Eberhart to exert sufficient influence to obtain meaningful legislation affecting school district consolidation. Eberhart, a product of a one-room schoolhouse, felt that his educational experience was less than adequate.

> He feelingly recalled the old school with its little one-room building, bare walls, benches, wooden bucket and dipper, its narrow course of inferior teaching, its unattractive and unsanitary construction, and pleaded with the legislature for state aid to encourage consolidation (7).

Noting that there were more than 2,000 one-room schools with less than 21 pupils, and another 300 with less than 11 pupils, the Governor contended that unless legislation was soon enacted, educational improvement would continue to be dangerously slow.

In 1911, primarily due to the Governor's urging and backing from the Office of Public Instruction, the Legislature passed a new law offering a financial incentive to newly consolidated districts. They were offered one-fourth of the cost of erecting a building and were granted annual aid up to $1,500 a year if the school met 8 months of the year and supplied transportation for pupils living long distances from the school building. In the next 5 years, 170 districts consolidated, representing a remarkable achievement in light of past progress.

Nonetheless, progress in reducing the number of school districts was not adequate. From 1915 to 1947, there was no legislation of significance aimed at decreasing the number of districts. Undoubtedly such events as World Wars I and II and the Depression preoccupied educators and legislators with more immediate needs. Whatever the case, it was not until 1947 that further consolidation again became a major educational goal. In that year, when there still were 7,679 districts, the Legislature enacted a law that provided for the appointment of a state advisory commission on school reorganization by the state board. The commission was given the power to serve in an advisory capacity to the commissioner of education in conducting a program of district reorganization. In addition, local survey committees were created to formulate recommendations for reorganization to be submitted to the people in a referendum. The first election under this program, held in December 1948, merged nine districts into one administrative unit with offices in Roseville, Minnesota. The primary weakness remained, however, in that reorganization and consolidation were voluntary.

The first mandatory reorganization legislation was enacted in 1963. It provided for the automatic dissolution of all nonoperating school districts that did not join a district maintaining a high school. On the whole, the legislation was a success; most nonoperating districts voluntarily joined a so-called high school district. However, it was not expected that so many nonoperating districts would join common school districts maintaining only elementary schools. This development deferred and often complicated the later establishment of desirable school districts.

By July 1965, there were 1,742 districts, a decrease of more than 5,800 in an 18-year period. Parenthetically, late in 1965, the Department of Education was formulating plans to present a proposal to the 1967 Legislature that would require a district not offering secondary education to merge with a district maintaining secondary schools. Such a plan emanated from recommendations of the state advisory commission in reports to the Legislature in 1961, 1963, and 1965. Despite dissent by supporters of the more than 900 common school districts that would be affected by such legislation, the department became firmly convinced of the importance of this legislation in providing the education needed by Minnesota's pupils.

ORGANIZATION OF STATE DEPARTMENT OF EDUCATION

At the turn of the century, state supervision of education in Minnesota was relatively unorganized and disjointed.

Coordination of effort among the multitudinous agencies was difficult, if not impossible. Duties and powers were divided among the public instruction office, the high school board, the normal school board, the state library commission, the board of special schools, the county superintendent's offices, the local school districts, and others. It was left to Governor Van Zant, a forward-looking chief executive, to propose a remedy. In 1901, the Governor suggested that a State Board of Education be established to achieve a unity of supervision designed to promote greater efficiency and economy. Members of the board, under the proposal, would include the superintendent of public instruction, a representative of the university, a representative from the normal schools, and a person chosen by the rural schools. However, by 1912, the Legislature gave little consideration to the proposal (8).

It was clear that unless a more concerted effort was made to promote the idea of a state board, the proposal would not win the approval of the Legislature. Thus, in 1912, the Minnesota Education Association proposed that the Legislature appoint a committee to study the state school situation and to draft a new school code. The committee was formed the following year and in 1914 it issued its report. The central theme was clear: The state needed unification of its educational effort. As expected, it was recommended that the Legislature create a State Board of Education responsible for the duties and powers held by the public instruction office, the high school board, the normal school board, the state library commission, and the board for the special schools for the deaf and blind (9).

In spite of the report, however, the Legislature did not act for 5 years. In 1919, with only slight opposition, a state board was established consisting of five members. Under its jurisdiction were all educational institutions except the normal schools and the university. To administer and enforce all school laws, the board was empowered to elect a commissioner of education for a 6-year term. This executive officer was given the responsibilities of safeguarding the school funds, administering the education department, and nominating all its officials and employees.

The same Legislature directed the state board to serve as the State Board of Vocational Education. The action came on the heels of the creation of a division designed to train and instruct persons injured in industrial accidents. The new division was to cooperate with the department of labor and industry as well as federal agencies. The initial appropriation for the training and instruction program was $15,000.

Organization of the State Board of Education remained virtually unchanged until 1951, when the Legislature added two members to the board and extended terms to 7 years. Shorter terms tended to leave the board open to undue influence by a governor reelected for several consecutive terms, thus enabling him to appoint a majority of its members.

The State Board of Education has broad powers over the development of education in Minnesota: It administers, through the commissioner and the department, all laws relating to the public schools, libraries, and public educational institutions, including the educational programs throughout the state; supervises the payment of various school aids; submits to the Governor and the Legislature a biennial education budget; and prescribes rules or regulations relating to all plans of education. The Legislature has directed that it meet annually on the first Tuesday in August and hold quarterly meetings and special meetings as it deems necessary; it also meets periodically as the Board of Vocational Education.

Commissioner of Education

The executive secretary of the State Board of Education is the commissioner. His role has evolved from one of general weakness to growing influence on the state's educational effort. The Legislature of the early Civil War years abolished the Office of Public Instruction, claiming that such action would not hinder the educational program of the state. When the office was restored in 1867, it remained one of gathering and reporting statistics, and its powers did not exceed the duty to make recommendations to the Legislature concerning needed improvements. The weakness of the office was not surprising when one considers the diffuse authority delegated to it. With educational responsibilities divided among many agencies, it could hardly be expected that the superintendent could exert significant influence.

It is indeed fortunate for the state department that the first commissioner, under the organization of 1919, was James M. McConnell. Throughout his administration, Mr. McConnell provided the guidance needed to nurse the infant organization to adolescence. He served diligently until his death in 1933.

When McConnell died in the second year of his third 6-year term, the Board of Education elected E. M. Phillips, a staff member who had been with the department since 1911. However, the strains of office made extraordinary demands on his health, and after only 1 year in office he resigned. In August 1934, the state's third commissioner was appointed to complete the still unexpired term of the late Mr. McConnell. By a 3-2 vote, John Gunderson Rockwell, a professor of psychology at the University of Minnesota, was appointed to serve until 1937.

In 1937, Commissioner Rockwell was reappointed to another 6-year term, which he never completed. The next 3 years were the stormiest in the history of relations between a board and a commissioner of education. Primarily because the composition of the board changed, frictions developed. The differences were kept largely in the background until 1940, when the board dismissed the director of vocational education, Eugene Debs Carstater, as not qualified to hold the job. Rockwell protested the action. Moreover, the commissioner felt that the board added insult to injury when it appointed Harry Schmid as acting director. Rockwell maintained that Schmid did not meet his approval, but the board overruled him (10).

Further dissension occurred in November 1940, when the board abolished the position of nursing education analyst in an effort to save money. Rockwell called this false economy as much of the salary was financed through federal funds. Again he made no headway (11).

At several subsequent meetings the schism became deeper as the board and Rockwell clashed over such things as out-of-state travel expenses for department employees, which he thought to be exorbitant, and procedures in reviewing projects, in which he felt he was being bypassed.

The parting of ways came late in November 1940, when, in the presence of Rockwell, board member Mrs. Raymond M. Gould moved the adoption of a resolution suspending the commissioner for actions "inconsistent with the duties of his office" (12). H. E. Flynn was appointed acting commissioner, and a hearing for the suspended commissioner was set for December 1940.

Litigation surrounding the dismissal continued for most of the first half of 1941. In September 1941, after lawyers for both sides had submitted briefs, the board issued its final and formal order of dismissal (13). After unsuccessful appeals to the district court and to the Minnesota Supreme Court, the litigation ended.

It probably will never be fully known what prompted the action against Mr. Rockwell. Certainly some personalities were imcompatible with others. But there are those who claim that the commissioner was the victim of political changes in the statehouse; others claimed that he was "used" by those surrounding him. Whatever the reason, the entire incident is still viewed as an unfortunate blot on the otherwise cordial relations that have existed between the board and its executive officer.

When Commissioner Flynn resigned in 1943, the State Board of Education elected Dean Schweickhard, who had served in the department until 1930 when he left to become assistant superintendent of schools in Minneapolis. He eventually served as commissioner for 18.5 years, the longest term of service of any chief state school officer in Minnesota's history.

Commissioner Schweickhard's years of service are marked by their quality. His wide training, interests, and involvements equipped him to make an indelible impact on education throughout Minnesota and the Midwest. Since his retirement in 1961 at the age of 69, he has received numerous calls to action on the expanding frontiers of education in Minnesota, all of which he has dutifully answered and effectively fulfilled.

E. O. Johnson succeeded Dean Schweickhard as the sixth commissioner. He served until 1964, when he accepted the superintendency of schools at Anoka, Minnesota. The present commissioner, Duane Mattheis, was named to succeed Johnson. Mattheis was superintendent of schools at Owatonna, Minnesota, at the time of his appointment.

Today the commissioner holds a vital position in state education. Through the years he has been given the powers and duties that have provided for an educational system more highly organized and better prepared than ever to meet educational problems. He is administrative head of the State Department of Education, secretary and executive officer of the State Board of Education, member and secretary of the State College Board, member of the Board of Trustees of the Minnesota Teachers Retirement Fund, secretary and executive officer of the State Advisory Commission on School Reorganization, a member of the Equalization Aid Review Committee, member and secretary of the School Loan Committee, member of the board of the Minnesota State High School League, member of the Minnesota Liaison and Facilities Commission for Higher Education, and an adviser to the Youth Conservation Commission.

State Department of Education

Fifteen years ago, Beach and Gibbs described three stages of development of most state departments of education: statistical, inspectorial, and leadership (14). Though the Minnesota State Department of Education still maintains all these functions, it is safe to state that the department has experienced the evolutionary process described by Beach and Gibbs.

During the early years of the department, perhaps until about 1900, the gathering, compilation, and reporting of statistics seemed to be the main preoccupation of the Office of Public Instruction. Unfortunately, lack of an adequate staff prevented the office from doing little more. At the turn of the century, there were only two members on the professional staff, the superintendent and an assistant. The several clerical members of the staff and a multitudinous number of duties related to the gathering of statistics.

Although the compilation of statistics has never ceased to be a function of the state educational agency, it slowly became a secondary function following the turn of the century. With the employment by the high school board of an "inspector," efforts were exerted to enforce rules and regulations. In the early 1900's, the inspector's reputation was one of a dictatorial, uncompromising "snooper," and many administrators in the outlying districts exhibited a negative reaction toward him.

Without discarding the functions of statistical gathering and inspection, the Minnesota Department of Education has gradually assumed its current primary role, leadership. In this stage, the department has become increasingly concerned with not only ensuring minimal standards for schools, but also using its influence and expertise in improving schools to greater levels of excellence. Such a turn of events has necessitated the increased use of experts and specialists in education and within the department.

At the time the Board of Education was organized in 1919, there were six divisions in the new department: rural schools, high and graded schools, building and sanitation and special classes for defectives, libraries, employment bureau, and reeducation and placement of injured persons. The total number of professional staff members was 20, and 10 years later the number had increased to 30.

By 1936, it was clear that some form of reorganization would be needed; the number of divisions had increased to 13, each with a director directly responsible to the commissioner. It was becoming impossible to maintain meaningful contact with these numerous directors (15). By 1938, reorganization had reduced the number of divisions to eight.

From 1943 until 1951, Commissioner Dean Schweickhard instigated numerous changes in the structure and organization of the department, but, by 1951, it was again clear that a major reorganization would be needed to keep pace with the changing structure brought about by major curriculum changes and a rapidly increasing enrollment. The new organization provided for six divisions: ungraded elementary schools, graded elementary and secondary education, business and legal, teacher personnel, vocational education, and vocational rehabilitation. Three years later, the number of divisions was reduced to five by combining the ungraded elementary schools with the graded elementary and secondary education division.

The last reorganization of major significance occurred in 1957. After considerable study by the commissioner and the board, the department was reorganized into three divisions so as to—

1. Give increased emphasis to basic education and the fundamental subjects of English, science, social studies, mathematics, reading, and writing.
2. Provide more effective use of state aid by increasing the amount of high-level management in the department and including positions long recognized in good school administration for all school systems of the state.
3. Give new emphasis to four areas of education: fundamental subjects for a basic education, libraries, handicapped children, and vocational rehabilitation. (See Appendix B.)

Thus, the board requested additional funds from the Legislature to enable it to hire an assistant commissioner for the division of instruction, an assistant commissioner for vocational rehabilitation, a director of research, and a director of program planning. This last reorganization created three divisions: business and legal services, instruction, and vocational rehabilitation and special education.

There were numerous additions following this reorganization with the advent of the National Defense Education Act, which provided for specialists in subject areas, Civil Defense staff, the Minnesota National Laboratory, the Manpower Redevelopment Program, and the expansion of the vocational rehabilitation program (16).

During the past 65 years, and particularly in the past 10 years, there has been a tremendous increase in the number of professional staff. By 1965, there were about 400 employees in the State Department of Education.

The expanding educational program in Minnesota, combined with increased federal influence, has drastically increased appropriations to the state department in the last 10 years. On salaries alone the appropriation jumped $350,000 during this period, excluding the salaries and expenses paid by federal programs.

Table 1. – APPROPRIATIONS FOR DEPARTMENT MAINTENANCE AND ASSOCIATED ACTIVITIES FOR SELECTED YEARS [a]

Account	1957	1959	1961
Salaries	$502,887	$596,808	$ 852,995
Supplies and expense	94,549	92,193	137,276
Curriculum	14,500	14,500	______ [c]
Research	32,500	35,000	______ [c]
Advisory Commission	22,500	23,000	______ [c]
Minnesota National Laboratory	. . .	164,600[b]	100,000[d]
Nurse scholarships	70,000	. . .	______ [e]
Indian scholarships	7,500	12,000	20,000
Total	$774,436	$773,591	$1,010,271

[a] The funds for salaries and expenses of employees on federal programs not included.
[b] Appropriation for 2 years.
[c] Included in the total appropriations.
[d] $195,000 for biennium.
[e] Transferred to Minnesota Board of Nursing.

Despite generally cordial relations between the department and the school districts, there are times when local school authorities and officials of the department find themselves at odds. Such disagreement is to be fully expected when one considers the numerous contacts made between the number of people involved in education. The most notable differences occurred in 1931. When the Depression struck, the state was confronted with a serious shortage of revenue that began to affect numerous programs including education.

Partially as a result of the financial squeeze, many districts were unable to fulfill their duties. The Department of Education, overdiligently attempting to enforce regulations, raised the ire of many school districts across the state. As a result of this dissatisfaction and significant pressures from local school administrators, the House and Senate established a joint committee to investigate the department. It examined a number of witnesses, including members of the state board, the commissioner of education, his assistant, several department inspectors, and members of several of the school boards in the state. In its final report, the committee absolved the department of any malfeasance of office or violation of the law in the conduct of its affairs. However, in a subtle way the committee slapped the wrists of the department. It noted that in attempting to vigorously enforce its regulations, the department caused the people of some school districts to feel dissatisfied with its requirements. It noted that such dissatisfaction was often caused by misunderstandings.

To the accusation that the board had withheld state aid from districts for failure to comply with the laws and regulations of the state, the committee said it could find no evidence of such attempts when the districts had attempted reasonably to find a solution to their problems. The committee recommended that the department be lenient with all districts experiencing financial difficulties because of delinquencies of tax levies.

Finally, the committee noted without comment that it was difficult during the hearings to secure testimony from complaining correspondents. Most frequently they claimed they feared reprisals. It was acknowledged by the committee, however, that the department had assured the prospective witnesses there would be no reprisals, but generally such assurances were to no avail. Though the events leading to the investigation were unfortunate, the investigation itself contributed toward clearing up differences that had developed between the department and many school districts (17).

If the office space allotted the state educational agency was any indication of the importance it had in the state governmental structure, then until a few years ago it was none too encouraging. In 1860, the state superintendent of public instruction conducted the business of the public schools from a single small office in the State Capitol Building. When state school inspectors were appointed, the lack of space forced them to establish offices in their home.

Shortly after the turn of the century, the superintendent's office was moved to the Historical Building where it was located when the State Board of Education was created. Rooms on the first and second floors of the south end of the building and in the basement and sub-basement housed the State Department of Education.

In December 1932, the offices were moved to the third floor of the State Office Building where all but two divisions were located in 30 separate rooms. Two divisions were located elsewhere.

In 1960, the new Centennial Building was constructed, and the education department was established on the entire fourth floor. Although facilities in this building are spacious, they are becoming cramped as new programs and staff positions are added.

SUPERVISORY AND CONSULTATIVE SERVICES OF THE MINNESOTA DEPARTMENT OF EDUCATION

This discussion is divided into three separate parts. Each portion is patterned after the organization of the Department of Education in 1965, although obviously the organization and allocation of services were not always as described here.

Division of Business and Legal Services

In general terms, the function of this division is directing, planning, and coordinating the legal, legislative, administrative, and business activities of the department. It is one of three divisions in the departmental organization and is headed by an assistant commissioner of education.

Legal services became a function of the education department for several reasons. First, the service tended to relieve the attorney general's office of routine legal matters pertaining to education. Second, it provided educators with a legal service administered by a fellow educator who not only was well versed in law but had insight into the educational implications of laws of the Legislature, opinions of the attorney general, and regulations of the state board.

Whenever a question with legal implications arises, it is referred to the assistant commissioner for reply. When there is a legal question not answered by the statutes or a pertinent opinion, a written request is made for an opinion from the office of the attorney general. Upon receipt of the opinion, the interested parties are so informed, and the press is made aware of the new development.

The assistant commissioner also is directly responsible for administrating laws and rules and regulations relating to the sale of textbooks. Minnesota statutes require that before any school textbook may be sold, used, or exchanged in the state, the publisher or dealer must file a copy of the textbooks with the state department. Moreover, a bond and price list of all textbooks sold in the state must be filed by the publisher with the department. These controls have effectively curbed the dubious textbook sales practices mentioned earlier.

State Aids and Statistics Section. As mentioned earlier, the first and primary duty of the Office of Public Instruction was gathering and interpreting statistics. In the first annual report of the superintendent in 1860, the statistics included were extremely meager; inadequate returns from town superintendents and the lack of a systematic plan for gathering statistics by territorial superintendents resulted in a less than desirable report. The enforcement of a penalty or forfeiture of school money if district clerks failed to make reports resulted in more adequate returns by 1867 (18).

Prior to 1882, the state superintendent's annual report was, for the most part, presented in narrative form. Beginning in that year, however, the annual report contained a special section devoted to statistical tables. For educators in the state, the report was the only reliable, comprehensive account of the status of education. Today, to persons interested in the historical aspect of Minnesota education, the reports are a valuable source of information.

In those early years, there was no departmental coordination of effort in gathering statistics; each division was responsible for collecting its own data. To answer the need for some form of central control of this function, the state board established the statistical division in 1929. The one-man division was headed by a statistician, T. J. Berning, who later became the assistant commissioner of education.

Throughout the years, the functions of the statistics division increased significantly. From 1933 to 1938, when the state board examinations were the responsibility of the rural division, the statistical division assisted in the preparation of statistical summaries for the examinations, established passing marks, designed tables indicating the number of pupils who passed and failed in the various school districts, and developed a question reservoir. In 1932, the division was given the responsibility of distributing courses of study. Finally, whenever a special study of education in Minnesota was prepared, the statistical division and later the statistical section played a significant role.

State law provides that—

> The State Board of Education shall supervise distribution of the school fund in accordance with the law. It may make rules and regulations consistent with the law for such distribution . . . including reasonable requirements for such reports and accounts as will assure accurate and lawful apportionment of state aids (19).

The state aids and statistical section was delegated the responsibility for carrying out the above legislation. It is responsible for the calculation and distribution of state and federal aids, collection and analysis of various statistics, calculation of costs per pupil in average daily attendance, preparation of reports, collection and analysis of data on assessed valuation and tax rates, and codification of forms and bulletins.

Administrative Services Section. From a department employing only several professionals and a few clerical workers at the turn of the century, the education department had expanded over the years until, by the midfifties, employees numbered about 300. Obviously, such growth brought growing pains. Such heretofore infant "departments" as bookkeeping, personnel, and procurement were experiencing phenomenal growth. Since all these personnel reported directly to the assistant commissioner of business and legal services, the demands on his time were outstripping his ability to devote the necessary time.

In 1958, at the urging of Commissioner Dean Schweickhard—a strong advocate of departmental reorganization— the Board of Education created the administrative services section and made the supervisor directly responsible to the assistant commissioner of business and legal services. The supervisor was responsible for coordinating activities previously operated independently: departmental budgets, accounting, auditing, disbursements, fiscal reports, payrolls, office supplies, office equipment, and incoming and outgoing mail.

With constant departmental growth there continues to be a substantial increase in duties assigned to this section, particularly in relation to the expanding role of the federal government in educational assistance to the states.

School Plant Planning and Development Section. One of the earliest interests of the Office of Public Instruction was school plant planning. Although a formal division for school construction was not formed until after the turn of the century, concern for adequate facilities received considerable attention. As early as 1860, the first superintendent of public instruction, Edward D. Neill, recommended in his first report to the Legislature the provision for providing suitable school buildings and sites in the state.

That efforts to promote adequate school facilities were unsuccessful in the early years is an understatement. Secretary of State David Blakely, serving as the superintendent of public instruction, remarked in 1864 that "the schoolhouses are the worst that will at all answer to the name, many of them, indeed, being so wretchedly wanting in comfort as to render them unfit asylums in wintry weather even for the beasts of the field" (20). As an example, he reported:

> The Superintendent of Houston County states that of 39 schoolhouses in the county, 20 are built of logs. A few of these are good, but the majority are very poor affairs. Some are built of poles, badly chinked, and not plastered. Some are scarcely fit for barns or stables. One school was held in a straw-covered granary with one door and no windows. In another, the doors and windows were enclosed apertures in the logs. A third was a small barn, fitted with rude seats, while a fourth was held in a dwelling house scarcely fourteen feet square, *with a family of six persons living in the same room.*
>
> From Rice County the Superintendent writes: "The schoolhouses are as a general thing . . . in a wretched condition. Many rich districts have none, and almost every schoolhouse in the county is a mere apology for what it should be" (21).

In the ensuing years, the reports of the state superintendents continued to call attention to the need for providing good physical facilities for housing public school pupils. Periodic bulletins were issued providing guidelines for school districts planning construction or remodeling.

Realizing, however, that the influence of the state could not be effectively exerted until some legal status was conferred on a section or division responsible for school plant planning, the Legislature conferred specific powers on the State Department of Education in 1913. The legislation specifically provided that a buildings division directed by a commissioner of buildings be established in the Office of Public Instruction. The division was directed to prescribe rules for the erection, enlargement, and change of school buildings. Twenty-eight years later, the law was amended to give the department specific authority to prescribe for school sites and mechanical equipment.

As the construction of school facilities has increased, so has the influence of the school plant planning section. Following World War II, the drastic increase in enrollments began to affect school facilities in the early 1950's. As serious classroom shortages appeared, it became clear that if an orderly program of construction were to be carried out, a comprehensive study would be necessary. Thus, from 1951 to 1953, at the urging of the school plant planning section, a school facilities survey was made of all school buildings in the state. Conducted by the bureau of field studies of the University of Minnesota, under the direction of the Department of Education, the two-volume study represented a milestone in providing a comprehensive overview of school building needs in Minnesota. The study and its implementation by the school plant planning section played a major role in accelerated construction across the state; from 1955 through 1961, more than $400 million was expended by local school districts for construction.

School Lunch Section. It is difficult to pinpoint where and when the first school-sponsored lunch program began. Recently discovered records indicate that a lunch program in Minneapolis in 1903 may have been the earliest. Another early program originated shortly after in Clark's Grove, Minnesota, with children bringing a portion of their lunch from home in mason jars. These jars of lunch (warmed in a kettle of hot water just before lunchtime), combined with a hot dish prepared by the teacher, were one of several unsophisticated but significant beginnings in school-sponsored meals (22).

An early pioneer in the development of school lunches in Minnesota was Inez Hobart, a nutritionist at the University of Minnesota, who was most noted in those early years for her role in establishing a breakfast program in a Minneapolis school in the 1920's. Administrators in the school were concerned about the unusually large number of working mothers in the pupils' families who were employed as cleaning women at night in downtown office buildings and often did not return home early enough in the morning to prepare breakfast for their youngsters. To remedy this situation, the school, with the assistance of Miss Hobart, established what came to be known as the "penny breakfast." However, only after the child's family was visited and his eligibility determined could the youngster receive the meal. It was a bargain sought by most parents.

When the Depression struck, school lunch programs reached important proportions in school districts' educational programs. To the youngster whose parents were unemployed, the school lunch was the only meal of sufficient nutrition. Although some of the ingredients used in preparing meals—dry salt pork, sauerkraut juice, dried onions, and raisins—may be unappetizing by today's standards, they were better than what could be served at home.

Primarily as a result of the Depression and the consequent financial strain on smaller units of government, the federal government assumed a role in school lunch programs in 1933 with the allocation of foodstuffs. Distribution of the commodities shipped into Minnesota had to be efficient. As many commodities were fresh, speedy distribution was essential to prevent spoilage. Sometimes distribution was complicated because the food was placed in storage areas in courthouses rather than local warehouses, and those schools desiring the food were compelled to travel to the county seat to obtain it.

Further federal involvement came with the Community School Lunch Program of 1943, the National School Lunch Act of 1946, and the Special Milk Program of 1954. The combination of federal aid and significant amounts of state aid has produced an effective, far-reaching program of school lunch support.

Supervision and control of the school-lunch program in Minnesota was transferred from the State Welfare Department to the Department of Education in 1943, although it did not become a legal entity until June 1946. Since then the department's role has expanded rapidly. It reviews and approves applications and claims from schools, institutions, and welfare agencies for reimbursement aids for school lunch, special school milk, and donated foods programs. It approves school lunch programs and special school milk programs, distributes donated foods, assists in preparation of daily menus, visits schools, and conducts school lunch workshops. In 1964-65, more than 64 million lunches were served.

Pupil Transportation. The role of the education department in the transportation of youngsters to and from school has existed for many years. Minnesota today remains one of the top 10 states in expenditures earmarked for transportation. On the other hand, large geographical areas of population sparsity have resulted in ranking Minnesota well toward the bottom among all states in the actual number of pupils transported at public expense. Thus,

Minnesota retains the dubious honor of having one of the highest per-pupil transportation expenditures in the country.

But despite these expenditures, the transportation program has been markedly successful. The first law on transportation came in 1901 as part of a bill designed to affect school consolidation. It gave consolidated districts authority to provide free transportation to the pupils of the district. In subsequent years, other districts were given the same authorization.

It soon became evident, however, that the heavy costs of transportation were working an undue hardship on many districts, and agitation began for state help. In 1915, the Legislature passed the first statute providing for reimbursement aid for transportation or board and room. The aid, which went to consolidated districts, was limited to $2,000 a year per district. Eventually, reimbursement was granted to other types of districts and specifically to pupils with exceptional needs, such as handicapped children.

As the transportation program expanded, legal problems arose concerning the responsibilities of various school districts to bus pupils located outside their official jurisdiction. In December 1938, the State Board of Education divided the state into high school areas to control the competition for nonresident pupils. Each high school area was to have at least one classified public secondary school and could also serve parts of school districts as could be conveniently served by the secondary school of the area.

In 1964-65, the state department distributed $14,380,000 in state transportation aids, while the local districts expended $22,000,000 of their local funds to finance transportation for 47 percent of the total number of pupils enrolled in the public schools in Minnesota.

The state board and the transportation section oversee a legion of buses, drivers, and pupils. Enforcing qualifications for bus drivers; providing consultative services to school districts; conducting meetings on transportation, school bus inspection clinics, and schools of instruction for school bus drivers; computing and administering the transportation reimbursement aids to school districts; and approving pupil transportation routes—these and other duties constitute the work load of the transportation section today.

Division of Instruction

In general terms, this second of three divisions is responsible for directing, planning, and coordinating the programs of all public schools, from kindergarten through secondary school and including adult education. The division is headed by an assistant commissioner of education.

Elementary and Secondary School Section. The largest section in the Division of Instruction in terms of personnel and the number of units is the elementary and secondary school section. Because the duties of this section are multitudinous, their historical development will be outlined according to sectional units.

1. Elementary and Secondary Units. Although these are two separate units within the elementary and secondary section, they are here considered together because their historical development is closely related.

These sections had their beginning in 1878 when the high school board was established. It was responsible for visiting and inspecting graded schools, classifying them, and approving the aid to be paid to them. Inspection of the common schools remained the responsibility of the Office of Public Instruction.

By 1916-17, the staff of inspectors from the office of the high school board had increased to nine.

When the State Department of Education was established in 1919, the graded and high school division was created. It assumed all the duties of the inspectors and many of the duties of the Office of Public Instruction. For all practical purposes, this entire division handled, at one time or another, most of the responsibilities now handled by the numerous specialized units of the present elementary and secondary section and other divisions and sections in the department.

Today, the elementary unit is headed by two directors: one in charge of graded elementary; the other heading ungraded schools, Indian education, and related duties. In general terms, the staff of the elementary unit provides consultative and advisory services on instructional and operational problems encountered in the elementary schools, provides services to superintendents and county school officers, conducts teacher institutes, visits schools, and prepares material for the use of elementary schools.

The secondary unit also provides advisory and consultative services and additionally visits and recommends classification for secondary schools, assists in the preparation of administrative bulletins and manuals, and aids in-service training workshops for teachers and administrators.

2. Curriculum Development Unit. Upon the establishment of the Department of Education, it was assumed that one of its roles would be to aid districts in curriculum development. In 1921, the state board ordered distributed the completed manuscript of a course of study for elementary schools, the first such course of study to have statewide circulation. A revision was approved by the board in 1928. Unfortunately, subsequent curriculum planning was primarily hit-and-miss. To correct the situation, the department called an educational planning conference in 1944, and the delegates in turn established the Curriculum Policy and Planning Committee. This committee set up procedures for producing a series of guides for curriculum development. Since then, curriculum development efforts have been more organized and have expanded as much as budget, personnel, and time will permit. However, today's curriculum development unit is handicapped by a lack of all three,

and there are those who claim that this factor alone has worked great hardship on efforts of the department to extend its influence regarding curriculum development in school districts throughout the state.

In addition to preparing curriculum guides, the unit directs state testing and examination programs, evaluates elective courses not previously approved, and provides consultative service in general program planning and evaluation.

The Minnesota National Laboratory (23) was created in 1958 to carry out curriculum research on the effectiveness of the "new" mathematics when compared to the more traditional programs. Funds were provided by the Hill Family Foundation of St. Paul. The laboratory carried out its research as an agency of the instruction division of the department. When legislation was passed in 1959 in support of the laboratory, the MNL began to extend its activities, still within the field of mathematics. Over the years, the laboratory has received support from the Legislature through biennial appropriations for base operations and projects and has, in addition, received grants and contracts from such agencies as the U.S. Office of Education, the National Science Foundation, the Office of Economic Opportunity, and the Upper Midwest Regional Educational Laboratory.

The Department of Education and the Legislature have demonstrated their support of MNL and interest in educational innovations. In 1963, both agencies illustrated their broad concern by giving the laboratory freedom to work with agencies outside the state and by encouraging it to extend its research activities to areas of subject matter other than mathematics. The Legislature enabled the realization of a five-state project for the evaluation of secondary mathematics and encouraged the laboratory's broader range of activities, including work with social studies, music, and new approaches in beginning reading instruction. In the future, specialists in other areas may join the staff to carry on research activities, drawing on MNL's experience with various research techniques and the now extensive data collection available.

The MNL serves five states: Iowa, Minnesota, North Dakota, South Dakota, and Wisconsin; the central staff is made up largely of psychologists and subject matter specialists.

3. Adult Education Unit. Classes for adults in general school subjects and Americanization were authorized by the Legislature as early as 1905. For many years, these classes achieved relative success in obtaining their objective—a more literate society. However, when the Depression forced the state to discontinue aid for adult education, the federal government began distributing funds to keep the programs alive. The Depression continued to take its toll, and many districts dropped their adult education programs as economy measures. It should be noted, however, that throughout this period adult vocational education remained substantially intact.

In the early 1950's, the National Association of Public School Educators took note of a department survey indicating that local districts were not eager to reestablish general adult education. In 1956, the association granted $12,000 to the department to initiate a general adult education program at the state level; state funds were subsequently provided for the employment of a director.

In 1964, the Economic Opportunity Act provided funds for undereducated adults, particularly those in poverty stricken areas. Minnesota's allotment for fiscal year 1965 was approximately $150,000. These funds and other federal funds, from the Manpower Development and Training Act, the Vocational Education Act of 1963, the Community Action Program of the Economic Opportunity Act, and the Elementary and Secondary Education Act of 1965, have made the adult education program in Minnesota an example of money wisely spent. In 1965, more than 75 percent of the state's high school districts conducted adult education programs, with enrollments estimated at 112,000 (24).

4. Physical and Health Education Unit. As early as 1878, the Minnesota Legislature required daily instruction in health, purity, temperance, and cleanliness. Subsequent laws made it the duty of local school boards receiving state aids to instruct in physiology and hygiene, with required reference to stimulants and narcotics. Revocation of teacher certificates or withholding of state aids to districts were the penalties imposed on violators.

With the advent of World War I came the revelation that the young men of this country were not physically fit. In 1923, the landmark Physical Education Law was enacted, and a physical and health education division was created in the education department. Formulation of regulations regarding the amount of such education was left to the State Board of Education.

In 1937, the division was assigned the additional duty of working with district recreation programs authorized by legislation of that year and 3 years later was renamed the Division of Physical and Health Education and Recreation. In 1944, the division was given responsibility for safety education in the schools. The driver education program, initiated 3 years later, is undoubtedly the unit's primary contribution to safety education (25).

5. Audiovisual Unit. Although audiovisual programs existed in many schools for a number of years, it was not until 1948 that the education department established a unit for their supervision. The following year, with the assistance of the department, the Audiovisual Coordinators Association of Minnesota was organized. Eleven years later, the teacher certification section, in cooperation with the audiovisual unit, established a set of qualifications to ensure

that there were competent audiovisual leaders in the schools, to become effective in 1962-63.

Today, the audiovisual unit provides consultative and advisory services to schools; conducts several workshops and conferences; and maintains a tape-recording service for education programs, a library of tapes for distribution to schools, and a library of films, filmstrips, and slides.

6. School Reorganization Unit. The role of the Department of Education in district reorganization and the difficulties in creating districts of efficiency and quality have already been noted. Suffice it to say at this point that through departmental efforts in the last 20 years, district reorganization has made marked progress. Since 1947, nearly 6,000 school districts have been merged or dissolved through legislation promoted by this unit and the department as a whole.

7. Subject Matter Specialists Unit. By the midfifties, an increasing number of school district administrators were requesting information and guidance from the department on various academic subjects such as mathematics and science. As there were no specialists in these areas on the staff, the department was unable to provide adequate assistance. Recognizing the desirability and the obligation of the state education agency to provide these specialized services, the department convinced the 1957 Legislature to allot funds for the development of a program for talented and gifted pupils, for which a professional was subsequently employed.

Other specialists added to the department included science, mathematics, language arts, and modern foreign language consultants. They are responsible for reviewing each subject in the curriculums of all schools and for making recommendations to expand and improve the courses offered in elementary and secondary schools. In addition, federal funds from NDEA Title III have enabled these consultants to conduct in-service education programs for teachers in the state.

8. Indian Education Unit. Minnesota is one of several states with unique educational problems related to a relatively substantial Indian population. The first schools for Indian children were under the jurisdictition of the U.S. Army. When the Bureau of Indian Affairs was established in the Department of the Interior, the children were placed in boarding schools. However, the expense and results were unsatisfactory, and the children were then placed in public schools, with the federal government providing the money.

In 1917, the Minnesota Legislature allotted the first state funds for Indians. Assistance went to public schools on Indian reservations where the taxable property was not sufficient to support public schools. The money was to be used only for teachers' wages and for textbooks. For 20 years thereafter, the Legislature made an annual although insignificant appropriation. In 1937, the Legislature turned over the entire program to the department, authorizing it to execute contracts with the federal government and to hire a supervisor whose entire concern was Indian education.

Today, the state works under an agreement with the federal government whereby the Bureau of Indian Affairs provides funds under the Johnson-O'Malley Act to supplement basic state school aids. When Public Law 81-874, providing aid to federally impacted areas, was broadened to include Indian children in 1958, the contribution of the Bureau of Indian Affairs was substantially reduced.

Although much more needs to be done to improve the educational situation for the Minnesota Indian, substantial progress has been made, in large part due to federal assistance. The federal government, under Public Law 815, Title IV, has given aid to local school districts with large concentrations of Indian children. In addition, Indian children receive free lunches, their teachers are better qualified, and scholarships for their higher education have been granted by the Legislature.

9. North Central Association. The North Central Association of Colleges and Secondary Schools is the largest of six regional accrediting agencies in the United States. Geographically, the area covers 19 states and portions of overseas countries containing schools for children of American armed forces personnel. The Minnesota state director of NCA maintains offices in the education department and provides consultative and advisory services to the public and member secondary schools in Minnesota belonging to NCA. Minnesota had a total of 140 member secondary schools in 1965, representing about 25 percent of all secondary schools in the state.

10. Vocational Section. Years before federal legislation was enacted to encourage state supervision of vocational education, Minnesota had taken action, albeit elementary, to provide some form of vocational training. In 1905, the Legislature passed a law authorizing counties to establish county schools of agriculture.

The Putman Act of 1909 and the Benson-Lee Act of 1911 provided for state aids for vocational or prevocational departments offering training in agriculture, manual training, and domestic economy. These two laws were subsequently repealed in 1915 and replaced with more comprehensive legislation.

However, the major incentive for vocational education came in 1917 when Congress passed the Smith-Hughes Act. Without examining subsequent vocational laws in detail, it is sufficient to state that Minnesota took significant advantage of federal legislation designed to improve vocational education in a rapidly changing technological world. The years of greatest growth, from 1940 to 1960, saw the number of agricultural departments almost triple, the business education classes increase by more than 100, the home economics departments expand by almost 200, and the industrial arts classes grow to a total of 385. Distributive education, health education, and trade and industrial education made similar significant strides.

In 1941, Governor Harold Stassen issued an executive order accepting federal funds for defense training and gave to the vocational division the responsibility of administering and supervising the program. To facilitate this effort, the Minnesota Board of Education, acting as the Vocational Board, approved the separation of war production training from the vocational education division and appointed a director for each unit. In June 1945, with the victory of the Allies, the war production program was terminated, and the equipment was ordered transferred to school districts for disposition.

In 1945, the area vocational-technical schools were first authorized. The schools, which granted no degrees, were meant to fill the need of those who needed preparation for jobs in agriculture, home economics, health, office, distributive, trade and industrial, and technical occupations. The education is generally post-high school in nature and is free to qualified persons under 21 years of age. Both graduates and nongraduates qualify, although every effort is made to persuade pupils to complete their high school education. In 1965, there were 19 such schools in operation, and several additional cities had requested approval to operate such an institution.

The section supervises private trade schools and veterans training, the Future Farmers of America, Future Homemakers of America, and the Minnesota Diversified Vocations Club. It prepares standards and plans for each major field of vocational service, assists in the planning and preparation of instructional material, and determines and calculates federal and state vocational aids to schools. The section is divided into nine major units: agricultural education, distributive education, office education, guidance and counseling, homemaking education, trade and industrial education, private trade schools, area vocational-technical schools, and Manpower and Area Redevelopment Act.

Teacher Personnel Section. One of the earliest concerns of the state and local educators was to provide pupils with the best possible teachers. To say that the task in Minnesota has been difficult is to understate the situation. The situation was critical enough in 1864 to prompt State Superintendent David Blakely to remark that "the teachers are the cheapest that can be hired, when hired at all . . . " (26).

For many years, the certification of teachers was decentralized, accounting for numerous difficulties encountered in enforcing regulations. In 1893, the Legislature not only authorized the issuance of certificates by county superintendents, state normal schools, and the state superintendent of public instruction, but also defined qualified teachers. But with the exception of a few modifications, the situation did not change appreciably until 1929. In that year, the Legislature, concluding that it could not effectively continue to set standards for certification, repealed a number of laws regarding certification and vested sole authority for it in the education department. The state board was charged with adopting supplementary regulations to certification laws remaining on the books. The 1949 Legislature went one step further and gave the state board *sole* authority for determining the qualifications of teachers.

The problems directly or indirectly related to certification of teachers have been numerous. The primary concern is usually supply and demand, with the latter usually exceeding the former. Consequently, even today the teacher personnel section is forced to issue certificates to inadequately trained teachers to aid districts, usually small and inefficient, in placing a teacher in each classroom. In 1964-65 alone, 813 such certificates were issued.

Another difficulty has been the increased work load pressed upon this section by certification. Currently, it takes from 3 to 6 months to process a request for certification. However, plans are now under way to hire additional staff and to eventually computerize the entire certification process.

To better serve teachers, the department established in 1913 the State Teachers Employment Bureau. In 1919, the bureau was incorporated with the teachers retirement fund under a single director. The arrangement did not improve efficiency, so the state board established in 1936 the teacher personnel division. At the same time, the employment bureau merged with the certification section to form a single division.

Today the teacher personnel section is divided into three units: certification, placement, and teacher preparation. The certification unit issues, renews, and records all Minnesota teaching certificates and develops regulations relative to issuance and renewal of certificates for adoption by the state board. The teacher preparation unit evaluates teacher preparation programs of colleges and assists in developing such programs as to ensure adequate preparation of teachers. It works closely with the state advisory committee on teacher education in establishing requirements on teacher education and certification to be submitted to the board. The placement unit is responsible for registering and providing placement services to teachers and administrators in schools of the state through the teachers placement bureau. In 1965, 1,992 teachers registered with this unit. A total of 659, or 32 percent, of the registrants were placed in teaching positions.

Library Section. The first record of voiced sentiment for school libraries came in 1861 when Superintendent Neill specifically recommended that the Legislature appropriate $1,000 for the purchase of library books, as "the masses must have an acquaintance with the general facts of history and the progress of events, to prevent them from falling a prey to crafty demagogues" (27). He stated that the schools should be encouraged to use much of their own money to finance libraries. Shortly after Neill's plea, the Legislature permitted the establishment of school libraries and allowed local tax levies for their support.

In 1887, generally viewed as the year of the first major breakthrough in improving school library services in Minnesota, the Legislature passed the first state aid law for school libraries, providing $10,000 annually.

The public instruction office was not given its first control over school libraries until 1911, with the creation of the Office of Supervisor of School Libraries. Although there was no direct authority over school libraries, the first supervisor, Martha Wilson, who was originally an employee of the public library commission, provided guidelines for schools that significantly improved many school libraries.

When the Legislature created the State Board of Education in 1919, the functions of the public library commission were turned over to the state board, and the organization continued as the library division. Through the evolution of numerous reorganizations, the library division has become a section in the instruction division. Today, there are three units in the library section. The school libraries unit is charged with the responsibility of providing consultation, advice, and supervision to all public school libraries regarding materials, programs, equipment, quarters, and personnel. In addition, it is to provide for visitation of schools, develop and issue guides and lists of materials, and assist the teacher personnel section in certification of librarians.

The second unit of the library section is the public library development unit. As indicated earlier, the public libraries commission became a part of the education department in 1919. Today, the unit provides advisory and consultative services to public libraries and encourages local citizens, public officials, and library officials in the establishment, development, and improvement of public library service. Since 1956, it has administered the Minnesota public library development program, under the federal Library Services Act, and the new Library Services and Construction Act, both of which are combined with the correlated program of state aid to public libraries. This program has resulted in the establishment of the first multicounty regional public library systems in Minnesota. It has three bookmobiles for demonstration and loan to help get bookmobile service started quickly in new county and regional libraries.

The third unit, rural libraries extension, is charged with two primary duties. First, it provides references and open-shelf loans to libraries and to individuals without local library service. Second, it provides loans of books in quantity to newly established county and regional libraries to help them begin service.

Division of Vocational Rehabilitation and Special Education

In general terms, this division is to plan, direct, and coordinate the activities of vocational rehabilitation and special education. It is headed by an assistant commissioner.

Vocational Rehabilitation Section (28). In 1919, acting as the State Board of Vocational Education, the State Board of Education adopted a plan of cooperation with the State Department of Labor and Industry for the reeducation and training of persons injured in industrial accidents. The Legislature's initial allocation of $15,000 was less than adequate, but it was an important beginning. The action established Minnesota as a leader in the field of vocational rehabilitation.

The first general vocational rehabilitation act, passed by Congress the following year, was to provide vocational rehabilitation to persons disabled and unable to return to gainful employment. Minnesota was one of eight states to immediately establish rehabilitation agencies as a result of the federal legislation. When the Federal Social Security Act made the Office of Vocational Rehabilitation a permanent federal agency in 1935, the Minnesota Legislature enacted similar legislation at the state level.

In 1943, Congress made it possible for the rehabilitation agency to provide physical restoration services, prosthetic devices, more detailed and comprehensive evaluative procedures, and a limited amount of tools and equipment for use by the handicapped. Moreover, the mentally ill and mentally retarded were classified as handicapped persons who could benefit from vocational rehabilitation services.

The Vocational Rehabilitation Act of 1954 was a major milestone in federal legislation affecting the handicapped. It provided for a broad program of grants to facilities and training agencies, as well as new support to state vocational rehabilitation agencies, and established a program of matching fund grants to community organizations to establish or improve rehabilitation centers of all types; $2 million have been spent in Minnesota under the latter section. In 1954, the vocational rehabilitation division maintained a professional staff of 23 located in six offices and rehabilitating about six hundred persons a year. In 1964-65, 6,297 disabled persons received services from 72 professional staff members.

Statistics alone cannot reveal the true development of rehabilitation in Minnesota. The increased staff, case service appropriations, and rapid expansion of rehabilitation facilities in the state have enabled the section to greatly increase the scope of its service, both in terms of more severely disabled persons who can be served and more extensive services provided to clients. The section is no longer merely a training resource for handicapped persons but the coordinating factor that brings together all of the resources needed to help an individual make a successful social, psychological, and vocational comeback from dependency created by a disability.

Special Education Section. For many years, the Legislature enacted laws granting aids to districts that provided for the education of handicapped children. However, the state department had little control or influence over the direction of special education programs.

In 1915, at the urging of concerned educators and lay citizens, the Legislature encouraged the establishment of special classes for handicapped children by granting fixed amounts of state aid to school districts for each enrolled child. Initial aid went to the deaf, blind, mentally handicapped, and children with impaired speech. Two years later, aid was granted for crippled children. Financial aid was $100 per child per year. In succeeding years, the Legislature broadened the programs by increasing the financial assistance and adding such services as transportation and room and board. However, in spite of increased appropriations for the handicapped, special education remained a "stepchild" in the statewide educational endeavor.

In 1955, a turning point for special education in Minnesota, the Legislature created an interim commission on handicapped children and charged the group with making a comprehensive and detailed investigation of the problems of handicapped children (29). The commission recommended, among other things, the enactment of a law requiring every school district to provide special instruction and services to every handicapped child in need of them and providing for adequate state aid to implement the program. It also strongly suggested the establishment of a division of special education in the education department to assist school districts in the development of special education programs, to establish standards for such programs, to supervise the system of special education for exceptional children in local school districts, and to prescribe curriculum and courses of study for state-operated residential schools. The Legislature of 1957 not only complied with these recommendations but also created an advisory board on handicapped, gifted, and exceptional children consisting of 12 members to be appointed by the Governor. The board was to aid in formulating policies and to encourage programs for exceptional children.

The new special education section in the state department was established under the jurisdiction of the rehabilitation and special education division. By 1965, every county in the state had at least one type of special education program. In that year, there were 4,189 persons teaching the handicapped in Minnesota, compared with 25 teachers in 1915 when the state first passed legislation affecting special education. However, there are still numbers of school districts that have no special education program at all and numbers of handicapped children who are not receiving appropriate instruction and services or who do not have the availability of minimum services.

Old Age and Survivors Insurance Program Section. Twenty-two years after the inception of the federal Social Security program, Congress initiated the payment of monthly disability benefits as part of the old-age survivors and disability insurance program. It was stipulated that the determinations of disability should be made by state agencies under agreements with the Secretary of HEW.

In Minnesota, the contracting agency is the education department, which acts as an agent of the federal government in evaluating disability. Costs of the program are borne entirely by the federal government, thus making the OASI section the only section financed entirely from federal funds. In providing that determinations for disability be made by a state agency, Congress intended that there would be rehabilitation contacts for every applicant and that the advantages of medical and vocational care development would be provided by an agency already working with the medical profession and the disabled.

In 1965, there were 18,196 disabled workers, and benefits for their dependents amounted to $14,378,000 annually. In that same year, the OASI section handled a work load of 8,013, the largest since the program's inception. A total of 292 cases were referred to the vocational rehabilitation section. A staff of 13 professional members, 11 clerical workers, and 6 part-time physicians administered this federal-state program.

FOOTNOTES

1. William Watts Folwell, *A History of Minnesota* (4 vols.; St. Paul: Minnesota Historical Society, 1930), IV, 139.
2. Theodore C. Blegen, *Minnesota: A History of the State* (Minneapolis: University of Minnesota Press, 1963), p. 186.
3. *Ibid.*, p. 183.
4. Theodore Christianson, *Minnesota: A History of the State and Its People* (5 vols.; Chicago: American Historical Society, 1935), I, 411.
5. *Ibid.*, II, 98-99.
6. Superintendent of Public Instruction, *Biennial Report, 1883-84*, p. 32.
7. Christianson, *op. cit.*, II, 322.
8. Folwell, *op. cit.*, IV, 187.
9. *Ibid.*
10. State Board of Education, minutes of July 20, 1940, meeting, p. 1119.
11. *Ibid.*, November 14, 1940, p. 1163.
12. *Ibid.*, November 30, p. 1184.
13. *Ibid.*, September 26, 1941, p. 1268.

14. Fred Beach and Andrew Gibbs, *Personnel of State Departments of Education,* U.S. Office of Education Misc. No. 16 (Washington, D.C.: Government Printing Office, 1952).

15. See Appendix B.

16. State Board of Education, minutes of February 7, 1957, meeting, p. 9.

17. *Ibid.,* April 29, 1931, p. 418.

18. "Special Report to Minnesota House of Representatives Interim Committee on State Administration," St. Paul: Department of Education, 1944. (Mimeographed.)

19. Minnesota, *Statutes* (1965), sec. 124.14.

20. Superintendent of Public Instruction, *Report* (1865), pp. 5-7.

21. *Ibid.*

22. Carl Holt, "Minnesota School Lunch," St. Paul: Minnesota Department of Education, 1967, 3 pp. (Mimeographed.)

23. Minnesota National Laboratory, "Educational Leadership Through Research," St. Paul, 1966; and W. W. Keenan, ed., "Minnesota National Laboratory," August 1966. (Both mimeographed.)

24. Commissioner of Education, *Annual Report to State Board of Education, 1965.*

25. The physical and health education unit became responsible for the nurse scholarship program, enacted by the Legislature in 1951, with an appropriation of $750,000. In 8 years, before it was transferred to the Minnesota Nursing Board, the department awarded scholarships to approximately 1,300 nurses.

26. Superintendent of Public Instruction, *Report* (1865), p. 5.

27. Superintendent of Public Instruction, *Annual Report, 1861,* p. 11.

28. August Gehrke, "History and Philosophy of Rehabilitation," St. Paul: State Department of Education, 1964. (Mimeographed.)

29. Chaired by State Senator Elmer L. Anderson, later Governor, the commission found special classes for handicapped children in only 30 of the state's 87 counties. Only a few counties offered special classes for more than one type of handicap.

BIBLIOGRAPHY

Public Documents

Laws and Rules Governing School Buildings and Sites. St. Paul: Division of Buildings and Sanitation, Department of Education, 1928.

Laws Relating to the Minnesota Public School System. St. Paul: Department of Education, 1966.

Minnesota. *Constitution* (1858).

-- *Statutes* (1965).

Books

Armstrong, Grace, ed. *A Handbook for Minnesota Teachers.* St. Paul: Minnesota Education Association, 1966.

Beach, Fred, and Gibbs, Andrew. *Personnel of State Departments of Education.* U.S. Office of Education Misc. No. 16. Washington, D.C.: Government Printing Office, 1952.

Blegen, Theodore C. *Minnesota: A History of the State.* Minneapolis: University of Minnesota Press, 1963.

Campbell, Roald F.; Sroufe, Gerald E.; and Layton, Donald H. *Strengthening State Departments of Education.* Chicago: Midwest Administration Center, University of Chicago, 1967.

Castle, Henry A. *Minnesota, Its Story and Biography.* 3 vols. New York: Lewis Historical Publishing Co., 1915.

Christianson, Theodore. *Minnesota: A History of the State and Its People.* 5 vols. Chicago: American Historical Society, 1935.

Folwell, William Watts. *A History of Minnesota.* 4 vols. St. Paul: Minnesota Historical Society, 1930.

Kiehle, David L. *Education in Minnesota.* Minneapolis: H. W. Wilson Co., 1903.

Articles and Periodicals

Briggs, Margaret. "The Development of Public School Libraries in Minnesota." *Minnesota Libraries,* XVI (December 1948), 372-75.

Hess, Arthur E. "Five Years of Disability Insurance Benefits: A Progress Report." *Social Security Bulletin* (July 1962), pp. 3-14.

Weerts, I. T. "What Is the Department of Education?" *Minnesota Journal of Education,* XLVI (October 1965), 63-65.

Reports

Commissioner of Education. *Annual Report to State Board of Education.* St. Paul: Department of Education, 1940-68.

Legislative Interim Commission on Handicapped Children. *Report.* St. Paul: State of Minnesota, 1957.

Superintendents of Public Instruction. *Annual and Biennial Reports.* St. Paul: Department of Education, 1860-1940.

Unpublished Material

Brainard, Ben R. "Disability Insurance Benefits and Rehabilitation." St. Paul: Department of Education, 1966. (Mimeographed.)

Gehrke, August. "History and Philosophy of Rehabilitation." St. Paul: Department of Education, 1964. (Mimeographed.)

Holt, Carl. "Minnesota School Lunch." St. Paul: Department of Education, 1967. (Mimeographed.)

Keenan, W. W., ed. "The Minnesota National Laboratory." St. Paul: Department of Education, 1966. (Mimeographed.)

Minnesota National Laboratory. "Educational Leadership Through Research." St. Paul, 1966. (Mimeographed.)

"Policies of the Minnesota State Board of Education." St. Paul: Department of Education, 1963. (Mimeographed.)

Potter, George H. "Special School Districts in the State of Minnesota." Unpublished master's thesis, University of Minnesota, Minneapolis, 1933.

"Report of Department of Education, July 1, 1940, to June 30, 1960." St. Paul: Department of Education, 1960. (Mimeographed.)

"Special Report to Minnesota House of Representatives Interim Committee on State Administration." St. Paul: Department of Education, 1944. (Mimeographed.)

State Board of Education. Minutes. 1919 to present.

"Your State Department of Education." St. Paul: Department of Education, 1963. (Mimeographed.)

Appendix A

MINNESOTA CHIEF STATE SCHOOL OFFICERS

Superintendents of Public Instruction

1860-61	Edward D. Neill
1861-62	Benjamin F. Crary
1862-66	David Blakely*
1866-67	Henry C. Rogers*
1867-70	Mark H. Dunnell
1870-75	Horace B. Wilson
1875-81	David Burt
1881-93	David L. Kiehle
1893-99	William W. Pendergast
1899-1901	John H. Lewis
1901-1909	John W. Olson

Superintendent of Education

1909-19	Carl G. Schulz

Commissioners of Education

1919-33	James M. McConnell
1933-34	Eugene M. Phillips
1934-40	John G. Rockwell
1940-43	Harry E. Flynn
1943-61	Dean M. Schweickhard
1962-64	Erling O. Johnson
1964-	Duane J. Mattheis

*Secretary of state, ex officio superintendent of public instruction.

Appendix B

Chart I.--MINNESOTA DEPARTMENT OF EDUCATION, 1919

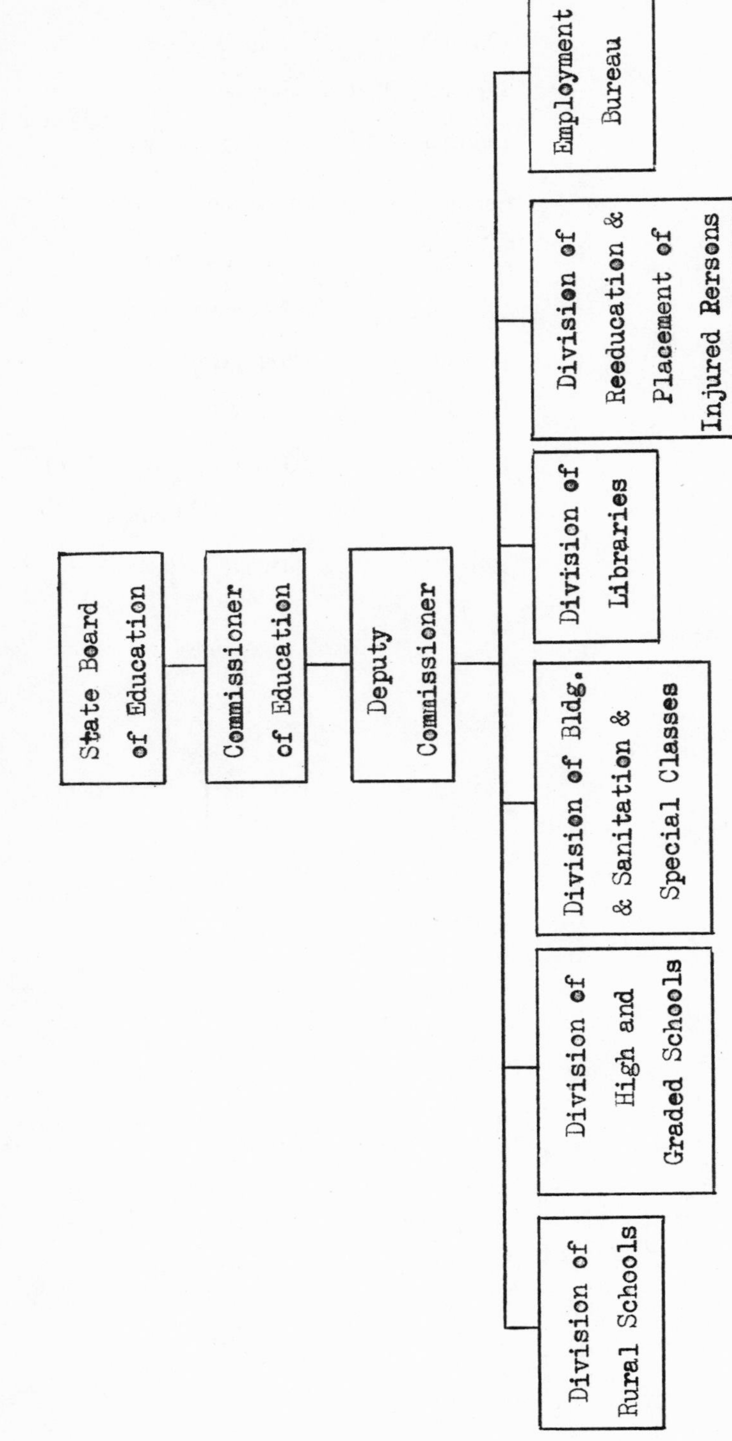

Appendix B

Chart II.--MINNESOTA DEPARTMENT OF EDUCATION, 1936

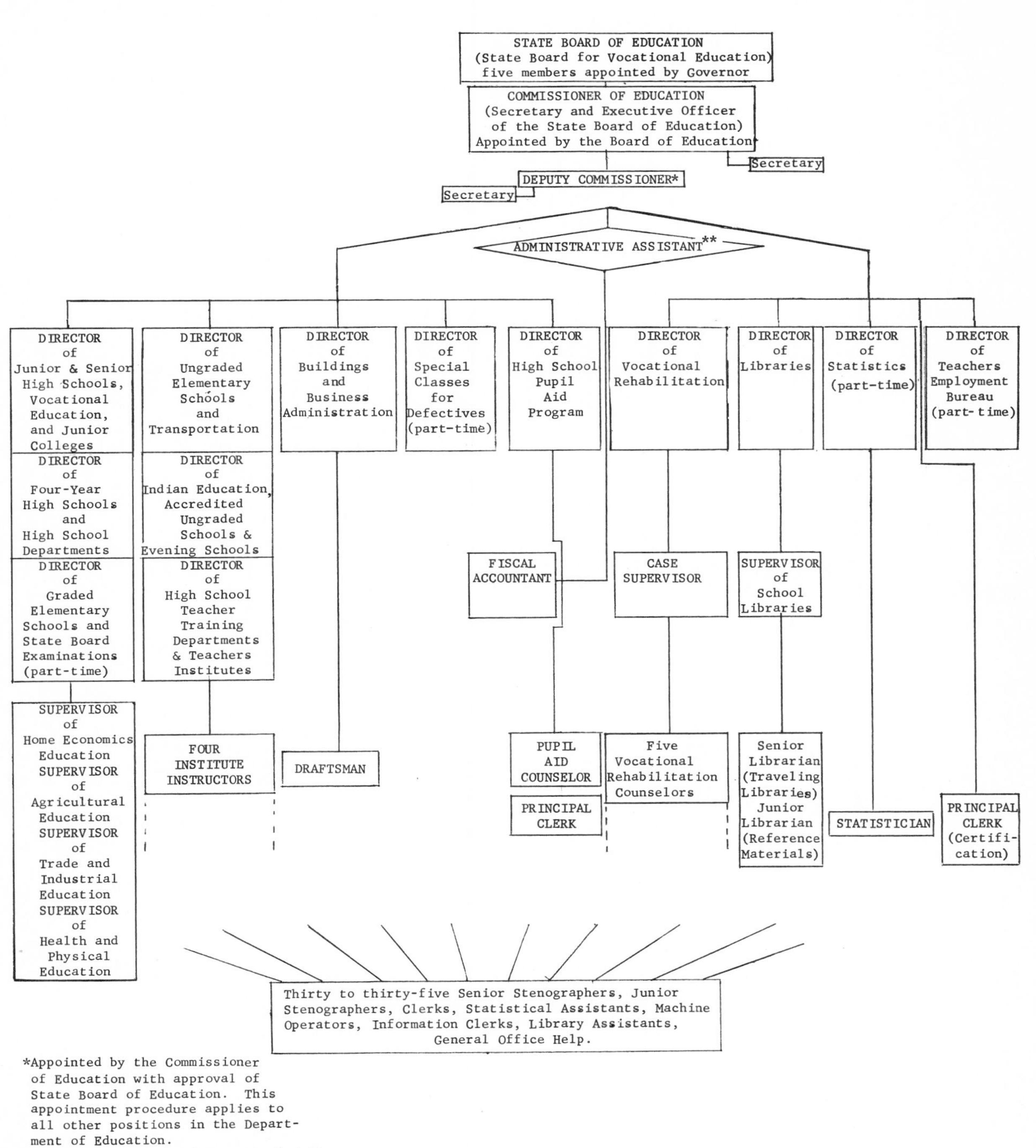

*Appointed by the Commissioner of Education with approval of State Board of Education. This appointment procedure applies to all other positions in the Department of Education.

**In addition to the departmental duties, all federal relief projects are either supervised or cleared through this position.

Appendix B

Chart III.--MINNESOTA DEPARTMENT OF EDUCATION, 1943-44

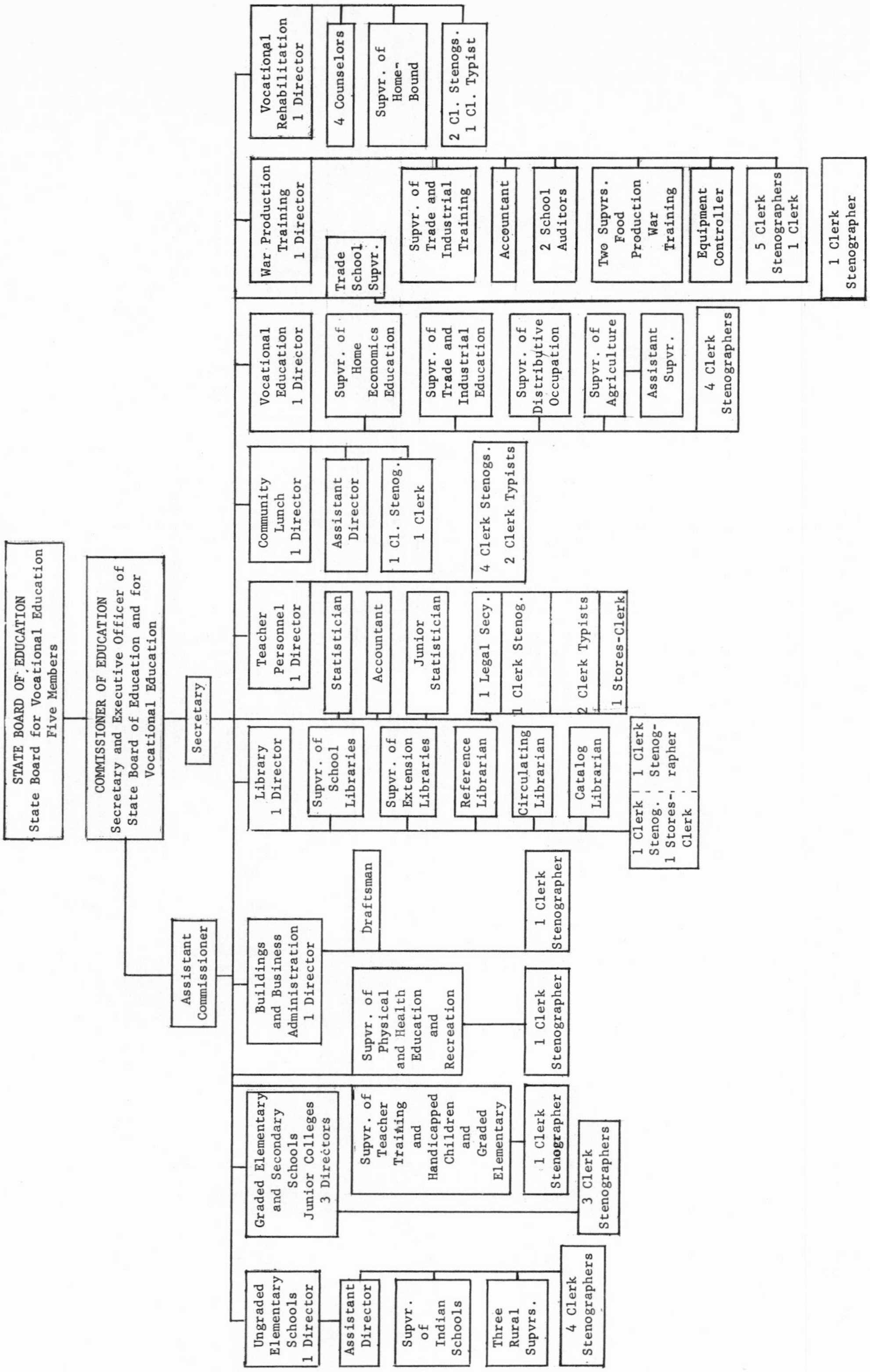

STATE BOARD OF EDUCATION
State Board for Vocational Education
Five Members

COMMISSIONER OF EDUCATION
Secretary and Executive Officer of State Board of Education and for Vocational Education

Assistant Commissioner

Secretary

Ungraded Elementary Schools 1 Director
Assistant Director
Supvr. of Indian Schools
Three Rural Supvrs.
4 Clerk Stenographers

Graded Elementary and Secondary Schools Junior Colleges 3 Directors
Supvr. of Teacher Training and Handicapped Children and Graded Elementary
1 Clerk Stenographer
3 Clerk Stenographers

Buildings and Business Administration 1 Director
Supvr. of Physical and Health Education and Recreation
1 Clerk Stenographer
Draftsman
1 Clerk Stenographer

Library 1 Director
Supvr. of School Libraries
Supvr. of Extension Libraries
Reference Librarian
Circulating Librarian
Catalog Librarian
1 Clerk Stenog. 1 Stores-Clerk
1 Clerk Stenographer

Teacher Personnel 1 Director
Statistician
Accountant
Junior Statistician
1 Legal Secy.
1 Clerk Stenog.
2 Clerk Typists
1 Stores-Clerk

Community Lunch 1 Director
Assistant Director
1 Cl. Stenog. 1 Clerk
4 Clerk Stenogs. 2 Clerk Typists

Vocational Education 1 Director
Supvr. of Home Economics Education
Supvr. of Trade and Industrial Education
Supvr. of Distributive Occupation
Supvr. of Agriculture
Assistant Supvr.
4 Clerk Stenographers

War Production Training 1 Director
Trade School Supvr.
Supvr. of Trade and Industrial Training
Accountant
2 School Auditors
Two Supvrs. Food Production War Training
Equipment Controller
5 Clerk Stenographers 1 Clerk
1 Clerk Stenographer

Vocational Rehabilitation 1 Director
4 Counselors
Supvr. of Home-Bound
2 Cl. Stenogs. 1 Cl. Typist

Appendix B

Chart IV.--MINNESOTA DEPARTMENT OF EDUCATION, 1957

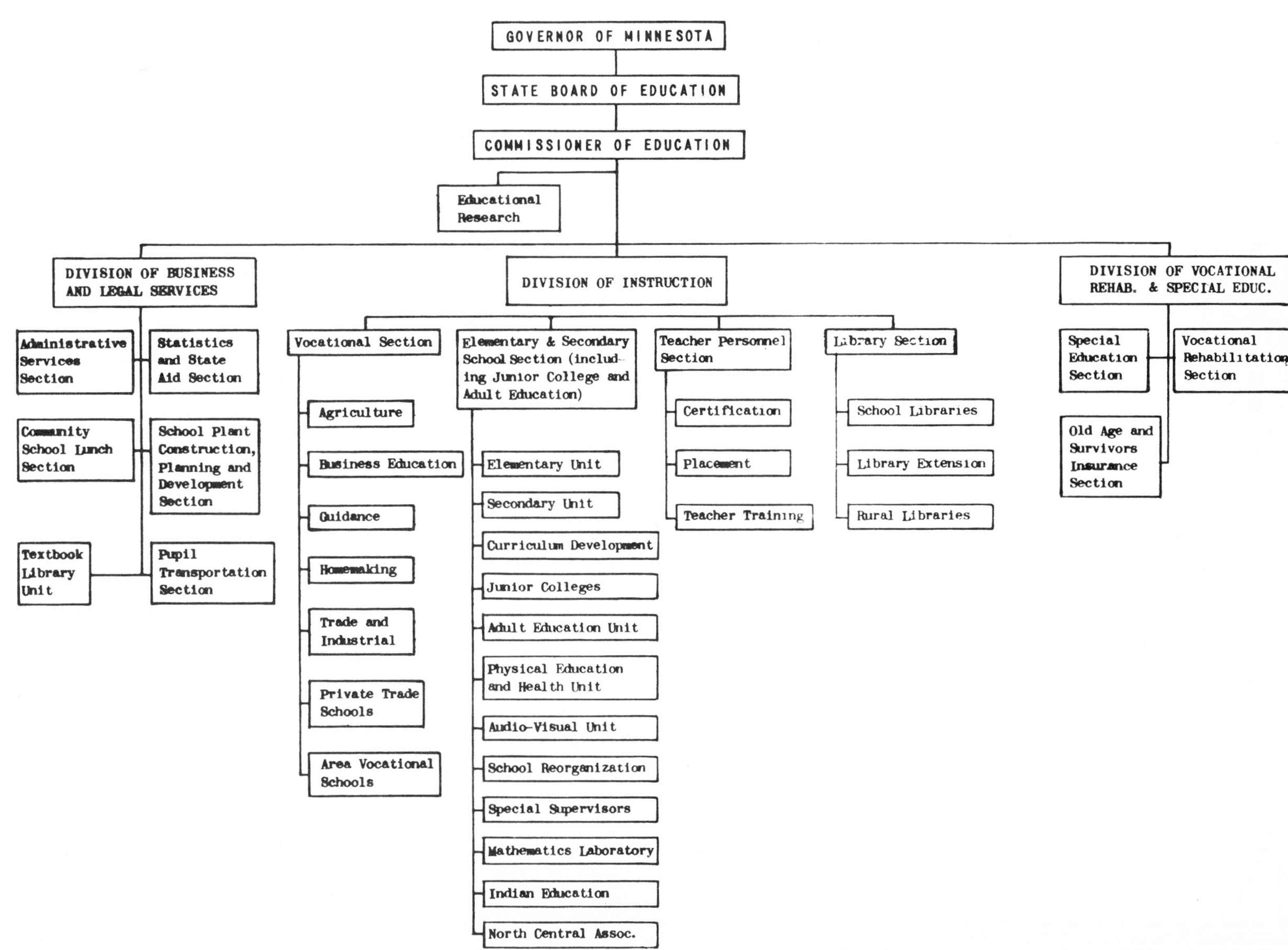

Appendix B

Chart V.--MINNESOTA DEPARTMENT OF EDUCATION, 1966-67

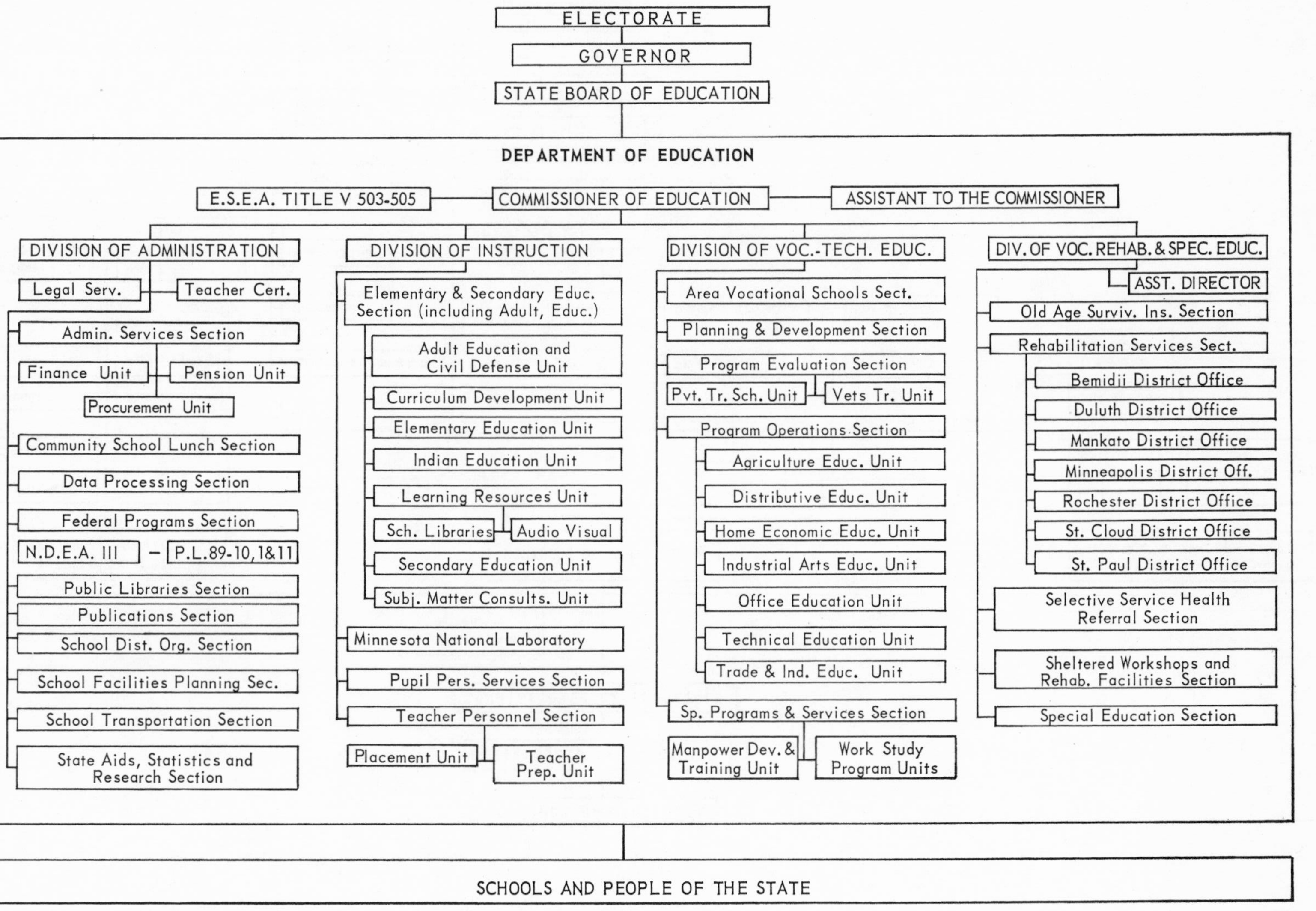

From The Role and Policymaking Activities of State Boards of Education, a special research study under P. L. 89-10, Title V, prepared and edited by Dean M. Schweickhard, September 1967.

24 Mississippi

DEPARTMENT OF EDUCATION

R. W. Griffith

Contents

THE PERIOD PRIOR TO 1860

Hernando de Soto, the famous Spanish explorer, entered the country in 1540 and spent about a year within the present borders of Mississippi. It was the French, however, who planted the first colony on the Bay of Biloxi in 1699. About 20 years later, 300 more French colonists founded Fort Rosalie (now Natchez) on the Mississippi River. This settlement grew until the Natchez Indians massacred the people in 1729. When Mississippi became a part of the British province of West Florida in 1763, many of the French moved to Louisiana.

In 1770, 18 families founded the first permanent settlement in what was to be the Mississippi Territory when they moved to the present site of Natchez. "All of the settlers in the Natchez District during the seventies (1770's) were of English, Scotch, and Irish extraction and practically all were from the colonies along the Atlantic" (1). The Spanish took British West Florida in 1779 and 1780, but they were compelled to give it up to the Americans in 1798.

On June 12, 1797, President John Adams recommended in a special message to Congress the erection of a "government in the district of Natchez, similar to that established for the territory northwest of the Ohio . . ." (2). Congress approved an act April 7, 1798, creating the Mississippi Territory. The sparseness of the population was a serious obstacle to the new territory's growth, and particularly to education. When territorial Governor Claiborne recommended in 1802 a "system of public education and a seminary of learning, he was addressing the representatives of a number of people who would not make a respectable rural county" (3). The territory had a population of only 31,306 in 1817, about half of them slaves, and 75,448 at the end of the next decade.

The increase, due in large measure to immigration, did not much increase population density, because the immigrants did not congregate in the Natchez area but scattered about the state (4). The great bulk of immigrants came from the Carolinas, Georgia, Virginia, and Tennessee, with a sprinkling from the North and East. Imbued with the ideals and customs of the Old South, they were not acquainted with public elementary schools, nor did they conceive public education to be a duty of the state.

> They did believe in education, but they conceived of that as a duty of the parent to his child. To be sure, if the parent were dead or too poor to educate the child, then they thought it was the duty of the state to stand in loco parentis (5).

The settlers brought their families and slaves to the new territory to raise cotton and cattle, requiring broad fields and grazing lands, which aggravated the difficulties of population sparseness. Too, Mississippi was on the frontier until 1840, and a distinctive Western idea of local school supremacy in government affected the people's beliefs about public education.

> This ideal is everywhere evident in legislation on school matters. It manifests itself in the vast amount of permissive legislation which left the final decision on educational questions to local communities. Township control of school was preferred to county control (6).

Marcus Jernigan, an eminent University of Chicago historian, in his introduction to William H. Weathersby's history of educational legislation in Mississippi, stated:

> The history of the educational legislation of Mississippi is of peculiar interest for several reasons. Being one of the states of the New South this legislation was influenced by the two important factors absent in the states of the Old South: first, the original settlers came principally from the back-country regions of the South Atlantic states; and, secondly, they entered an environment which approached that of the New West, the region west of the Alleghanies [sic]. Both of these factors led to the development of a democratic decentralized school system, designed to meet the special needs or demands of individual counties and even smaller units. As a result, we may observe the consequences of local self government in education at the expense of an efficient centralized state system, based on general laws operative over the entire state (7).

Two important factors, however, favored the establishment of common schools. One was the presence of a number of public leaders who strongly favored a public-supported system of schools. In February 1798, two months before the Mississippi Territory was created, John Henderson and others sent the first of many memorials to Congress calling for aid to establish and support "a regular ministry of the Gospel and schools for the education of the youth" (8). Most of the state and territorial Governors' messages from 1802 until the Civil War recommended improvements for the schools. Time and again they requested a state tax for education, and at least one Governor made it an issue in his campaign.

The second important factor favoring common schools was the federal government's extension of its policy of endowing education by granting public lands to "the territory south of the State of Tennessee," reserving the sixteenth section of each township for this purpose. Until the mid-1950's, "in at least one township of the State a free school has been maintained constantly since 1821 by sixteenth section funds" (9).

The entire state was settled by 1840, and the schools had improved distinctly. "The Choctaw Indians had ceded their lands to Mississippi by the Treaty of Dancing Rabbit Creek, September 28, 1830, and the Chickasaws by the Treaty of Pontotoc, October 22, 1832" (10). The frontier had disappeared, several areas becoming densely populated. "In 1830 the population of the state was 136,000; a decade later it had doubled; and in 1850 it stood at 606,500" (11).

As the people connected their villages with railroads, dotted the rivers with boats transporting goods, and chopped out dirt roads, they were drawn closer together. They endured the panic of 1837, rapidly recovered, and enjoyed a period of almost unbroken prosperity from 1840 to 1860. Land values increased, cotton crops were good, and prices were high. Slaves were becoming more numerous. A popular slogan of the day depicts the economic philosophy of Mississippians: "Make more cotton to get more money to buy more Negroes to make more cotton to get more money to buy more Negroes, ad infinitum" (12).

Governor Sargent and others continued to request more money from affluent planters to establish schools. With funds from the sale of the "sixteenth sections," the Reverend David Ker, a Presbyterian minister from Ireland, started "the first public female school" at Natchez in 1801 (13). The next year, the Territorial Legislature charted Jefferson College, which continued to operate in the Natchez area until it closed in 1965. These private, chartered schools continued to grow in number, providing the basis for the public school system.

When Congress approved Mississippi's admission into the Union on December 10, 1817, the State Constitution virtually copied the words of the Northwest Ordinance of 1787. Specifically, it stated: "Religion, morality and knowledge being necessary to good government, the preservation of liberty and the happiness of mankind, schools and the means of education shall forever be encouraged in this State" (14). The following year, the new Legislature enacted a law specifying that the justices of the county courts should–

> Take charge of the lands given by the United States to the State of Mississippi, in their counties respectively, and provide for the erection of one or more schools as they deem right and useful; to lease the lands and guard against waste of soil and timber (15).

In 1824, the county court justices were replaced by a board of township trustees in those townships having rented lands.

Albert Gallatin Brown, the leading advocate of a system of public education during the period from 1832 to 1860, was elected Governor in 1843, and in his inaugural address to the Legislature "pleaded with great eloquence for a general system of common schools which would be open to all and in which the poor should be educated gratis" (16). Brown did succeed in securing the passage of the first statewide school law in 1846. Unfortunately, the new law contained the elements of its own undoing (17). Conforming to a philosophy of local control, it required the consent in writing of the majority of the heads of township families before taxes could be levied. Efforts to strengthen the law or to enact new ones were hampered by a serious division among the legislators. "Under such conditions they drifted along to the period of the Civil War (1860), doing some good, more in some localities than in others, but in all crippled, in many paralyzed, by the want of a uniform and vigorous policy"(18).

Despite strong local control and the overall failure of Governor Brown's legislation, some progress was made. The U.S. Census indicates considerable increases from 1850 to 1860 in the number of schools, teachers, students, and in educational expenditures (19). Although statewide taxation for schools had not been enacted, some township taxes were levied to supplement the tuition that parents paid for their children's instruction. Also, the "sixteenth section" lands had laid the basis for a permanent school fund.

THE PERIOD FROM 1860 TO 1900

The decade of the 1860's could well be styled the "locust years." It reaffirmed the old adage that man can stand adversity better than prosperity, because during these disordered times public education in Mississippi took shape. The Civil War years found Mississippians centering their lives on the war. Most public and private schools were closed. Boys old enough and able to carry a gun were engaged in the fighting, and girls carried out auxiliary duties. Commerce, industry, agriculture, and civil government, except as needed for military operations, were practically paralyzed. When the South was defeated, Mississippi was broken and bankrupt, its interest in education submerged in the misery of the postwar period.

In August 1864, the Legislature by joint resolution authorized the Governor to appoint a committee of 20 persons to canvas the counties and receive donations and subscriptions to a fund for educating the children of soldiers killed or disabled in the war. In its report, the committee responded that–

> No subject could appeal more eloquently and touchingly to the heart of every Mississippian than the education of the children of the noble sires who have perished in this direful struggle for independence, and we only consider one thing more important, and that is to feed and clothe them (20).

Perhaps more than anything else, the need for such a committee indicates the overwhelming economic disaster brought on by the war. The total assessed value of real and personal property for 1860 was $509,472,902; for 1865, it was $134,131,128; and for 1870, it was $177,288,892. During this decade, the value of farm property declined 61.5 percent. The production of cotton, Mississippi's chief source of income, dropped from 1,202,507 bales to 565,559 bales; the federal government had confiscated 8 million bales outright. The levees along the Mississippi, breached during the war, were not repaired until 1870, leaving 4 million acres of fertile land open to floods. Vandals had destroyed many public buildings, and farmers suffered intense labor problems during these unsettled years.

As Mississippians busied themselves with the tasks of rebuilding, they again turned their attention to the schools. In December 1865, the Legislature passed an act calling upon the presidents of county commissions to report the exact status, nature, and availability of all school funds, along with any suggestions they deemed appropriate for establishing a system of common schools by the next legislative session. The act also included a similar request to boards of police, which were asked to collect all money owed to school funds within 12 months. The 1865 Legislature also amended the 1846 and 1848 laws by deleting sections pertaining to certain counties, to put all counties on the same statutory basis as the state school system. Unfortunately, Reconstruction and the era of carpetbag rule began soon after, and the legislators did nothing for the next 4 years.

In the meantime, educators from around the nation, meeting in Philadelphia in August 1866, asked Congress to leave the adjustment of Southern affairs to the Southern states. Mississippi teachers then attempted to follow up with a meeting in Jackson in September, but they held so many different opinions as to what to do that they postponed it twice. A group of the state's leading educators finally did meet in January 1867.

The state teachers association reorganized and adopted resolutions calling for a state school system to meet the needs of all people. It also resolved that the Legislature should establish normal schools to train Negro teachers for the separate Negro schools. The association's president then prepared and distributed to the legislators a pamphlet entitled "A Plea for the Common Schools," which said, in part:

> Lower public education should be made first and foremost. In our opinion, the establishment of high schools by state aid should be abandoned for the present and all the state's attention and resources turned to the perfecting of the common schools, . . . industrial schools should be established where the eye and hand may be trained (21).

This pamphlet undoubtedly was instrumental in shaping subsequent legislation; its ideas are reflected in both the Constitution of 1869 and the statute that inaugurated a statewide school system in July 1870 (22).

The constitutional convention, often called the Black and Tan Convention, met in Jackson in January 1868 to draw up the state's third constitution. When it was submitted to the people in June, they voted it down because it disenfranchised those who had fought and worked for the Confederacy. When the disenfranchisement was removed, the people ratified it in December 1869. This Reconstruction Constitution, the only constitution ever adopted by popular vote in Mississippi, readmitted the state to its proper place in the Union and restored its right of self-government (23).

It had been evident from the beginning that the delegates to the convention would make more definite provisions for education in the new constitution than were contained in those of 1817 and 1832. The state's "reconstructionists" were committed to establishing an elaborate system of public schools for the benefit of both races. Many of the convention members were freedmen or Northern white men "thoroughly embued with the idea of education for the Negro race." The majority were ready to support measures designed to establish a system of public schools for the benefit of "all children between the ages of five and 21 years" (24). Even before the convention met, Governor Humphreys, in an address to a joint session of the Legislature in October 1865, reflected the sentiment of most Mississippians when he said:

> Several hundred thousand of the Negro race, unfitted for political equality with the white race, have been turned loose upon society; and in the guardianship she may assume over this race, she must deal justly with them in all their rights of person and property. The highest degree of elevation in the scale of civilization to which they are capable, morally and intellectually, must be secured to them by their education and religious training (25).

The new Reconstruction Legislature convened in Jackson in January 1866 with a responsibility to effectuate the provisions of the newly adopted constitution and to set up a public school system. Fifty-five of the 116 House members and 9 of the 37 Senators were Negroes, and many of the legislators belonged to what Horace Greeley called the "driftwood brigade." All members of the House Committee on Education, which introduced one of the state's most important school laws, were Northerners except for two Mississippi freedmen. The new Governor, James L. Alcorn, a native of Illinois who had been elected the previous November, appealed for a public school system in his inaugural address, arguing:

> The poor white children of the State who were permitted in the past to grow up like wild flowers, without training, the administration which we are about to inaugurate today is determined to expend a large proportion of its energies in educating. And so, also, will the government which reigns over us from this hour devote a large proportion of its energies to the training of the rising generation of the colored people for the higher duties of life, under an enlightened system of public schools (26).

The law that the Governor finally signed in 1870, perhaps not as innovative as claimed when compared with the Law of 1846 (see Appendix E), did provide a legislative plan for a public school system and for a State Department of Education—an agency new to Mississippi. It authorized State Superintendent Henry R. Pease, a native of Winsted, Connecticut, to name a clerk, and together they comprised the first staff of this embryonic state department.

The constitution made a State Board of Education responsible for the general supervision of the public school system and the management of the school funds and property. The first state board, selected in November 1869, consisted of State Superintendent Pease; Secretary of State James L. Lynch, a Negro Methodist preacher from Pennsylvania; and Attorney General Joshua A. Morris, a native Mississippian. It was required to submit periodic reports, annual or biennial, to the Legislature and was responsible for naming the county superintendents.

The Law of 1870 provided for free public schools in each district, each county constituting a school district, except where incorporated cities with 5,000 or more population organized as separate districts. The law required all children from ages 5 to 21 to have equal advantages—an ambition that has not been fulfilled completely even today. It did not provide for separate schools for the races.

Teachers had to be certificated by county superintendents and were to be trained in institutes held annually in each congressional district under the immediate direction of the state superintendent of education. Teachers who regularly attended were to be granted full pay as if teaching the entire time. The law specifically declared that the Bible should not be excluded from the schools.

Henry R. Pease, 1869-74

The Law of 1870 swung from strong local control to a system of ultracentral control. It was costly—perhaps even extravagant. The direct taxation imposed by the law aroused considerable resentment among people who blamed nontaxpaying legislators and those who feared too much central control. Many of their questions could not be answered immediately, such as what to do with the freedmen, who would teach their children, and who would pay the high costs of education.

Superintendent Pease, who personally disliked several features of the new law, accepted the mandate to activate its provisions in the fall of 1870. In his report to the Legislature for the fiscal year ending December 31,1871, he elaborated on the school situation after the fashion of his day. In showing the department's costs, he stated:

> These expenditures, including the salaries of the Superintendent, Clerk, and Secretary of the Board of Education amount to $10,719.59. . . . One of the largest items of expense in this total is for printing, amounting in the aggregate to $5,039.26, a large part of which was for . . . school registers (27).

Superintendent Pease was a man of unquestioned ability who demonstrated a devotion to his duty. He was not reelected in 1874 because "the demand of the colored race for office in 1873 caused him to be set aside for a Negro named Cardozo" (28).

Cardozo, Gathright, and Bardwell, 1874-78

Thomas W. Cardozo, a native of South Carolina, had come to Mississippi at the close of the war and had served as a circuit court clerk in Vicksburg before becoming the state superintendent of education. He resigned in March 1876, after the state Senate impeached him for crimes and misdemeanors.

Governor John M. Stone then named Thomas S. Gathright, the head of Somerville Institute, a private school he had founded in Gholsen, Mississippi, to the state superintendency in April 1876. He resigned after only 6 months to accept the presidency of Texas A & M College and was replaced by the Reverend Joseph Bardwell, pastor of the First Presbyterian Church of Meridian. Bardwell worked conscientiously, particularly to increase salaries of the teachers and county superintendents. Although he got the 1876 Legislature to pass an education act, it did little to help the school system. These were lean days, and reaction against the Reconstruction acts tended to hurt the state's finances. Bardwell reported that his department spent $4,196 for 1876 and the public schools spent $417,760;

white teachers received an average monthly salary of $43, and Negro teachers received $39.55.

General James Argyle Smith, 1878-85

When Bardwell did not run for reelection, General James Argyle Smith, a native of Tennessee, stepped into the superintendency. An 1854 graduate of the U.S. Military Academy, General Smith served with the U.S. Army until 1861, resigned his commission to join the Confederate Army as a captain, and commanded a division at the end of the war. He farmed in Mississippi until elected state superintendent in 1878.

General Smith deplored the constant change in school laws and the lack of qualified teachers. He insisted that unless he could employ an assistant superintendent he would have to close his office whenever he visited the schools. His report for 1878 showed that the department spent almost $4,000 for the year, including his salary of $2,000.

James R. Preston, 1885-95

James R. Preston, a native Virginian, became the first Mississippi school teacher to be elected state superintendent. In his first report, Superintendent Preston listed several major defects in the state's educational system: "(1) a want of qualified teachers; (2) too many schools; (3) no supervision and inspection of the teaching force; (4) a waste of the school funds by dividing the term into sessions of two months each (29)." The superintendent still only received a $2,000 annual salary, and Preston was forced to pay $53 out of his own pocket for clerical services during the 1888-89 biennium—indicating that he was the state department's total staff.

During Preston's term, a constitutional convention met in Jackson and adopted in November 1890 the present constitution, which has been amended from time to time by popular vote. Its Article VIII, concerning the schools, differed very little from that of the 1869 constitution. The new constitution did provide for a 4-month school term, permitting districts to extend it by levying local taxes, and specifically provided for separate schools for white and Negro children.

Andrew Kincannon, 1896-98

Kincannon, a native of Noxubee County and a graduate of the University of Mississippi, became state superintendent in January 1896. He did not hesitate to comment on the difficulties that beset the people of Mississippi, but, at the same time, he felt that the public school system had steadily prospered. He rejoiced that the University of Mississippi and the Industrial Institute and College at Columbus (now Mississippi State College for Women) provided teacher-training courses, and that a board of examiners was authorized by law to place teacher certification on a statewide, professional basis. He resigned in September 1898 to accept the presidency of the Industrial Institute and College (30).

1900 TO 1946

A New Century

What a contrast in the world before and the world after 1900! Will a normal calm return one day? Probably not in our time. For, as William Alexander Percy has said,

> Ishmael lived one hundred and thirty-seven years. During that time he must have laughed and joked and loved; he must have looked at the sky and sat beneath the cool palm trees; he must have been glad—but he was a wanderer and a stranger all his days. The North destroyed my South; Germany destroyed my world (31).

During the first school year of the new century, the total enrollments included 158,154 whites and 193,588 Negroes, for a total of 351,742 students. The state had 7,806 teachers (4,658 white and 3,148 Negro), who earned average monthly salaries of $30.64 for the whites and $19.39 for the Negroes (32). Henry L. Whitfield, a native of Brandon and a graduate of Mississippi College, succeeded Kincannon as state superintendent in 1898. As in 1870, his department of education still consisted of the superintendent and one clerical worker—even this assistance came and went with the whims of the Legislature. At least Whitfield did not have to spend his time certifying teachers; the Legislature created the State Board of Examiners in 1896 for this purpose. In the board's first biennium, it passed 4 out of 18 applicants for professional licenses and issued 496 state licenses out of 950 applicants examined.

By comparing pupil enrollments, the teachers employed, the number of schools, and the costs in 1850 and 1900, one can see that Mississippi education underwent a great deal of growth during that period. By eliminating those who taught because they were "moved to teach" but lacked other qualifications, the board of examiners began a slow process of developing a program of teacher certification that today places Mississippi among the top states in rigid certification rules and number of teachers with bachelor's and master's degrees. During Whitfield's time, teachers' salaries were pitifully low. In his report to the Legislature, he said: "I submit that teachers who receive no better compensation than this cannot pay their necessary expenses and have sufficient means left to qualify themselves as they should do for their work" (33).

School Buildings. In the same report, Whitfield pointed out that "our school houses as a rule are a disgrace to the State" (34). Commenting on building new schoolhouses, he suggested: "The foundation of the building should be sufficiently high as to permit under ventilation and should be closed to keep out hogs, sheep, and goats" (35). On warm days, the odors from these animals seeped into the schoolhouses, and when commingled with that from sweaty bodies and dirty feet, must have been overpowering for the poor teachers.

Perhaps these miserable facilities explain in part why so many boys were leaving the rural areas (36). To deal with some of the patent weaknesses, particularly in the rural schools, the teachers association named a Committee of Ten which reported in May 1903 at the Vicksburg meeting and substantiated Whitfield's conclusions, declaring: "The greatest need of the rural public schools in Mississippi is better school houses" (37). Schoolmen and laymen now began focusing more attention on buildings, and architects began preparing plans based on suggestions offered by the state board.

During this first decade of the twentieth century, the Legislature appropriated more and more funds for plans, specifications, and blueprints, which were to be prepared by the engineering department of Mississippi Agricultural and Mechanical College (now Mississippi State University). The districts then began erecting buildings with fire escapes, iron ladders, slides, stairways, and outside doors opening outward. Later, beginning in 1920, school buildings also were constructed for Negroes from Julius Rosenwald Fund grants matched by state money. The Department of Education, with the assistance of a grant from the General Education Board of New York—a philanthropic agency which was exceedingly generous to Mississippi—constantly encouraged an accelerated building program and gave direction whenever asked. For the most part, the state gradually eliminated the little, crude, unsightly schoolhouses that were eyesores to their communities.

Rural Education. Since the separate city and town districts were showing more progress, most educational leaders naturally considered rural school improvement their greatest challenge. Through the generosity of the General Education Board, the state board secured funds to employ a supervisor for the rural elementary schools, and the Holmes County superintendent, W. H. Smith, accepted the assignment in July 1910. Smith emphasized repeatedly that the schools could be improved only by consolidation, better transportation, cultural supervision, and a vitalized course of study.

One result of the teacher association's committee report—and the arrival of the Mexican boll weevil—was a recommendation by the state superintendent that agricultural high schools be established. These would help rural students by providing them boarding facilities and work opportunities while teaching them diversified farming and educating them enough to emancipate them from the ranks of unskilled labor. The Legislature responded in 1908, requiring each county agricultural high school to own not less than 20 acres of land and to conduct experiments in farm crops, livestock, and poultry raising.

Fifty county boarding high schools were organized during the next 11 years. The graduates of these schools usually remained in their home communities. Each school strongly supported improved roads and consolidation, backing the teachers association and superintendents who had long argued that consolidating was necessary. In turn, consolidation required county district taxation and a good system of school transportation.

As the consolidated schools grew, the agricultural high schools began to disappear or were converted into junior colleges. In fact, during the period from 1928 to 1953, when most of the junior colleges were founded, they were set out according to the zones in the basic law. Only a few agricultural high schools remain today (38).

District Reorganization. Whitfield, in his 1899-1901 biennial report, stated:

> One of the greatest defects in our school laws is that which makes it mandatory on the County Board of Education to define the boundaries of the school districts and to locate the schools(houses) every year. . . . Such a law has a tendency to discourage their erecting suitable school houses and beautifying school grounds (39).

Also, by modifying the districts so frequently the county board continually stirred up neighborhood dissensions which could not help but impair the efficiency of the school system. These disputes usually centered on the strong desire of many people to maintain as much local control as possible. With the School Law of 1870 permitting any incorporated city of more than 5,000 inhabitants (lowered by subsequent legislation) to constitute itself as a separate school district, these districts appear to have forged ahead, not only in basic stability, but in educational capacities as well (40).

One of the five subtopics of the Committee of Ten's report included a list of benefits to be derived from school consolidation. Convinced that it could save enough money on teacher pay to underwrite the cost of transportation, the Legislature gave school consolidation a considerable boost in its 1910 session. But this was still a weak beginning for what was later to become a vital, integral part of the public school program. In 1914, the law was amended to allow a majority of qualified electors to petition the board of supervisors and, with the approval of the county school board, to levy a property tax in the district to pay for fuel, transportation wagons, construction and repair of school buildings, maintenance of schools, and extra teachers' salaries if the district maintained its schools for at least 7 months. The board of supervisors could also vote bonds for these consolidated districts to erect, repair, and equip buildings. Rural schools were not on a level with separate district schools (41).

Textbooks. One more contribution to education occurred during Superintendent Whitfield's term, when the Legislature, following the recommendations of Governor James K. Vardaman, created a textbook commission. In April 1905, the Governor named eight responsible schoolmen to this commission, with the state superintendent as ex officio member. In its first meeting, the commission resolved not to discuss textbooks with any except authorized representatives, and instructed publishers to file lists of these representatives with the secretary, E. L. Bailey. Whitfield, president of the commission, stated that this "not only lessened the annoyances usually incident to book adoption, but placed the adoption on a high plane" (42).

Beginning a New Era

Governor Vardaman named Joseph Neely Powers as state superintendent in July 1907, when Whitfield resigned to accept the presidency of the Industrial Institute and College at Columbus. The new superintendent's salary was increased to $2,500 in the following session, and he was allowed a clerk at $900 per year, plus $500 for traveling expenses and $250 for office equipment.

Despite considerable progress during this first decade of the twentieth century, many of the recommendations by Superintendents Preston, Whitfield, and Powers, based on sound educational practices in other states, had been ignored.

> As the year 1910 dawned, the Legislature and administrations continued to keep alive a school system based upon a plan thirty to forty years of age. They refused to believe that time had not stood still. A rather stagnant era in the history of the State Department of Education ended (43).

Governor Earl Brewer appointed W. H. Smith, the rural school supervisor, to the state superintendency when Powers resigned in September 1914. Besides the superintendent and his secretary, the department now had seven other people paid for by General Education Board grants. In March 1916, a year after Smith had been elected without opposition to continue in office, the Legislature permitted him to have an assistant state superintendent and an additional secretary. Smith resigned in September 1916 to accept the presidency of Mississippi Agricultural and Mechanical College at Starksville, and Governor Bilbo appointed W. F. Bond, a member of the Mississippi Normal College Faculty, in his place (44).

New Programs. The Legislature continued to show an increasing interest in education and passed a number of acts, for the most part initiated by Senators who had spent years as teachers. For instance, it authorized graduates of the University of Mississippi and other colleges to receive professional licenses when they had taken sufficient professional courses, improved the consolidation laws, fixed the salaries of the county superintendents and required them to have more training, and increased the common school appropriations. At the same time, the General Education Board, the Julius Rosenwald Fund, the Jeanes Fund, and the Slater Fund continued contributing to Negro education, including money for new schoolhouses and for paying teachers to supervise in the Negro elementary schools.

The Mississippi Legislature voted to accept funds for agricultural education from the Smith-Hughes Act in 1917. State Superintendent Smith had advocated this type of education several years earlier, declaring in his biennial report for 1913-15:

> Education for culture is a noble ideal, but it is needless to talk of higher culture for the great mass of humanity until they are better housed, fed, and clothed, and until they have surplus leisure and are taught to use that leisure rationally. Our civilization rests on agriculture and we must learn to gain culture through agriculture or go without culture for the masses (45).

The federal government paid the state $30,850 for the year ending June 30, 1918, and this was matched by state funds. In accordance with the law, Mississippi established a Board of Vocational Education consisting of the state superintendent, the acting supervisor of white rural schools, the acting supervisor of Negro elementary schools, and one citizen appointed by the Governor with the consent of the Senate (46). This was a far cry from the earlier days when the emphasis was on township control–and yet what a paltry sum compared to $33.6 million for the fiscal year 1965! Mississippi education has changed dramatically, and the changes come faster every year.

Mississippi's Legislature had voted funds in 1916 to maintain an industrial and training school for children under 18 who were destitute, abandoned, or delinquent. It further extended the benefits of the public schools when local trustees were permitted to maintain evening or part-time programs if they voted the necessary local taxes to do so. And there were programs to open more schools for Indian children and illiterate adults. Congress enacted the Civilian Vocational Rehabilitation Act on June 2, 1920, and the Legislature accepted its benefits 2 years later. Commenting on this program, a former assistant state superintendent stated: "If you want to know the real joy that must have come to the Son of God as He sent the cripples forth walking and leaping and praising God–then you will want a part in the rehabilitating of these unfortunate ones" (47).

Finances. The public schools received their main financial support in 1900 from the state per-capita fund, poll taxes, interest on the Chickasaw School Fund in the north and northeastern areas, and the "sixteenth section" funds in other parts of the state. The Constitution of 1890 provided that these funds be distributed by the state board to the counties and separate districts according to the population of educable children from 5 to 21 years. The state first authorized an enumeration every 4 years, but after 1923, it was necessary to enumerate biennially because the population fluctuated so much (48).

The people voted an important constitutional amendment in November 1919, authorizing the Legislature to establish an equalizing fund which would provide a minimum school program to all local units in the state. The Legislature then effectuated it the very next year by voting $1,268,720 for the 1920-21 biennium and $2,114,535 for the per-capita fund for the same period. At the same time, the state superintendent's salary was raised to $4,500, and the Legislature authorized $3,000 biennially for the administrative support fund; other money was provided by outside sources. The Slater Fund contributed $76,000 from 1910 to 1923, the Jeanes Fund provided $70,000 from 1909 to 1922, and the Julius Rosenwald Fund contributed $73,000 annually for building schoolhouses for Negroes.

Using General Education Board funds, Superintendent Bond established a model county organization in Pearl River County with a staff composed of a county superintendent, an assistant superintendent, a county health officer, a farm demonstration agent, the agricultural high school principal, and two clerks. This experiment resulted in recommendations to empower an elective county board of education to appoint the county superintendent, give him clerical help, pay his expenses to meetings called by the state superintendent, make his salary commensurate with other county officers, and give every child a physical examination every 3 years.

To further strengthen the position of the county superintendents, J. T. Thomas, a Grenada banker, donated $2,000 for several years to pay the expenses of annual meetings for county superintendents. One county superintendent rode a mule 20 miles to attend one of these meetings. Another, after attending a banquet in a meeting in Greenwood, remarked that he had never been to a banquet before, but "didn't see any harm in it." After the Gulfport meeting in 1919, the state superintendent found a county superintendent in the lobby of the hotel and asked him why he did not go to bed. He replied, "Nobody had said anything about going to bed." Realizing that the man had never been in a hotel before, Bond invited him to sleep in his room.

Much more important than acquainting county superintendents with social amenities, these conferences enlightened them about their responsibilities. Most of the educational issues of the day were discussed in depth with all county officials who dealt with the schools. Many were pleased and others appalled at the information they received. For instance, after the compulsory school law had been explained at a meeting in Lafayette County, one trustee said that he would move out of the county before he would put up with such a law. When he learned the law was statewide, he declared that he would move out of the state. It was pointed out that Mississippi was the last state to have such a law; shaking his fist with considerable emotion, he said that he would go to hell before he would put up with it (49).

Prosperous Twenties

During the affluent decade after World War I, there were many efforts to improve the schools. The department's staff increased from 14 to 25 persons by 1930 and even included a supervisor of music. Although school accreditation had never been under the department's jurisdiction, the superintendent took it upon himself to lay down a full set of rules and regulations schools would have to follow to become accredited. At the same time, he advocated stronger teacher certification laws, a teacher retirement fund, and much greater consolidation of schools.

The Legislature recodified the school laws in 1924 and declared the equalizing fund amendment valid and mandatory, ending the confusion that had resulted by its having been added through the initiative and referendum. At the request of Governor Whitfield, the former state superintendent who defeated Bilbo in a primary election the previous summer, the Legislature voted to allow up to $10,000 to conduct a survey of all public education. Governor Whitfield then selected M. V. O'Shea, professor of education at the University of Wisconsin, to conduct the study of Mississippi's school system. "Many valuable recommendations for the improvement of the school system of the state were made; but like many other surveys, these recommendations were, for the most part, consigned to the archives" (50). About the only concrete result from this O'Shea Survey was the creation of the division of information.

The country as a whole enjoyed an economic boom during these years, but financing schools equitably still posed a problem. The state superintendent pointed out that in some counties over $40,000 of assessed valuations supported each child, while in other counties less than $500 per child was available as a tax base. He also reported that less than 10 percent of the state's white children were attending the old one- and two-teacher schools, a commendation to the tremendous job of consolidation, but he recommended—and the Legislature agreed—that the educable age be changed from 5 to 21 to 6 to 18. At the same time, he recommended that the financial burden be shifted to the county and state to lighten the load on local districts.

The Depression Years

The Depression of the 1930's left the schools' economic plans in chaos. In the first sentence of his 1931-33 biennial report, the state superintendent said:

> The depression came down upon the world like a wolf out of the fold and caused great havoc in every phase of the life of the people . . . . Departing, it is leaving behind a disorganized condition that challenges the heroic spirit and rugged honesty bequeathed to us by our forefathers (51).

A new Legislature, a new Governor, and the same state superintendent (reelected without opposition) began terms in January 1932, as a new President in the White House broadcast in a fireside chat to the nation that there was nothing to fear but fear itself. Catching the spirit of this changing era, a song writer wrote: "There is a new day in view, there is gold in the blue . . . ." An optimistic urge seized many Americans, suffering as they were in the throes of our greatest depression.

Finances. Governor Mike Conner, an able and optimistic state leader, urged the Legislature to pass a retail sales tax. Convinced that this was the only way to keep the schools open, Superintendent Bond presided over a mass meeting in Jackson of more than 5,000 educators, including every county superintendent in the state endorsing such a tax. Governor Conner and a number of legislative leaders pledged their support to the tax measure, which appeared to the great majority to be the only hope for the state as well as the public schools. The Legislature did enact the bill, and it was signed by the Governor in April 1932 (52).

As the Depression reached its nadir in 1933, the state's financial difficulties persisted. Superintendent Bond traveled to Washington to appear before a House Committee on Education to seek federal aid for his schools (53). Although the national government supplied $1,320,000 during the 1933-35 biennium, teachers and bus drivers were unpaid and due $1 million in back salary. The equalizing fund, inadequate for the demands on it and impossible to administer objectively, became the chief issue in the 1935 campaign for the superintendency.

J. Sloan Vandiver and S. L. Stringer entered the race against veteran Superintendent Bond. Charges of favoritism in distributing the equalizing fund made the race a bitter one. When the first primary returns put Bond second to Vandiver, Bond withdrew rather than prolong the struggle into the second primary. The end of his term the following January brought a close to the longest tenure of any state superintendent in Mississippi up to that time (54).

Superintendent Vandiver, a native Mississippian who had served for 18 years as superintendent of the Sunflower County Agricultural High School and president of the Sunflower County Junior College at Moorhead, now wrestled with the same financial problems as his predecessor (55). The Legislature carefully prescribed the distribution of state funds and prohibited deficits by enacting the Kyle-Cook Budget Law in 1936. This law required county and district superintendents to file with the state superintendent detailed budget estimates for each fiscal year, and to regulate their expenditures according to these estimates and within the revenues. The law further authorized boards of supervisors, boards of trustees, and governing authorities of municipalities to borrow money to pay off valid notes, teachers' and school bus drivers' certificates, and other valid obligations at the time the law was adopted. Vandiver said: "We are happy to state that the Kyle-Cook Budget Law . . . has worked wonderfully well. As a result of this, no new deficits have been created; and in most cases, teachers and other school employees have received their pay on time" (56).

More money was still needed for the schools, vocational education, rehabilitation, crippled children's services, and junior colleges. The department itself, which received itemized appropriations for salaries, travel, and other expenses, also needed more money, particularly since a majority of the staff members were supported by state funds rather than by funds from federal and philanthropic sources (57).

School Plants. A Civil Works Administration survey during the 1934-35 school year revealed many serious deficiencies in the state's schoolhouses, with Mississippi's investment averaging only $69 per child against $250 for the nation. The Public Works Administration, the CWA's successor, appropriated $5 million to Mississippi, about half of it for direct grants to aid school plant construction and improvement. The Works Progress Administration also allotted sizable sums to build schoolhouses and improve them. Mississippi's school plant investment increased from $41.1 million in 1934 to $61.6 million in 1941, "by far the most extensive school building program ever accomplished during a similar period in the history of the state (58).

Textbooks. The Mississippi Education Association recommended that free textbooks be provided, after spot checks revealed that many children dropped out of school because their families could not afford books. The state superintendent supported this recommendation, and the Legislature passed a free textbook law in 1940. It established a state textbook rating and purchasing board, prescribed its powers and duties, and detailed how the books were to be selected, adopted, purchased, distributed, cared for, and used in all schools through the first eight grades. Two years later, the law was amended to include all 12 grades.

The Governor named three members to the board, one from each supreme court district, in addition to himself as chairman and the state superintendent as vice chairman. To assist in textbook adoptions, the law provided for the

Governor to appoint rating committees. Later, the state superintendent did the appointing, until finally the law was changed so that the Governor named four members and the state superintendent three members.

A suit enjoined the textbook board from distributing free textbooks to children in parochial schools on grounds of violating the doctrine of separation of church and state. Following appeals, the State Supreme Court denied the injunction, holding that the books were to be distributed to the children as beneficiaries of the state's munificence irrespective of their schools.

The department continued to expand its activities during the latter part of the decade, adding supervision in home economics and distributive education under authorization of federal acts. Its staff held two schools for bus drivers during the summer of 1940 at Mississippi Southern College and Mississippi State College; the counties followed their similar instruction for more than 2,500 bus drivers. The department organized a vocational training school for janitors in Clarksdale in the same year. Climaxing several years of effort, the 1940 Legislature set up a training school for Negro teachers at Jackson College. In arguing for better trained teachers in the Negro schools, the supervisor for Negro education said: "The state owes it to them to give them a chance to become a self-respecting, self-supporting, law-abiding people" (59).

The department's staff continued to grow to include a supervisor of narcotics education, a supervisor of school transportation, and additional staff members for vocational education, rehabilitation, and adult education. By 1943, it had 40 members. Many of these positions were supported initially from outside sources such as the General Education Board, the Julius Rosenwald Fund, the Jeanes Fund, and the Slater Fund. But as these sources of income ceased to be available, the state financed them itself.

World War II

On September 1, 1939, World War II began, and on December 7, 1941, the United States was in it, bringing the heavy demands of war to all agencies, including the administration of the public schools. Superintendent Vandiver remarked:

> We are very proud of the loyalty and patriotism shown by our teachers in the development of the wartime programs in Mississippi schools. Practically all of them have participated in some form of reorganization of their regular school programs to meet the rapidly changing needs of their communities. The schools almost as a unit have cooperated in salvage campaigns, bond and stamp sale drives. The F.F.A. and 4-H Clubs have gone forward with their Food for Victory programs. Health and nutrition have been given added emphasis. Junior Red Cross organizations have taken on new impetus. The "Walk to School" movement, initiated in many of our schools, has received national recognition. Mississippi has led the nation in the number of illiterates prepared for military service and in the total enrollment in OSYA (60).

Transportation. Transportation, always a costly part of the school program, was even more difficult to manage during the war. A committee that studied the problem finally reported "that Mississippi had in 1943-44 the least efficient and most expensive school transportation service of any southern state" (61). It further reported that 2,237 farm trucks were used to transport children, but "were also used in transporting farm produce and in many instances cattle, hogs, and fertilizer" (62). The 1944 Legislature authorized county school boards to develop a system of county-owned school buses. Following this survey, the state made so much progress in school transportation–procuring new buses, operating bus drivers training programs, and so economizing in the maintenance of its program–that Glen Featherston, a specialist for pupil transportation in the U.S. Office of Education, stated: "In view of these accomplishments, it probably can be said that Mississippi is one of the two states that have made the most progress in the last three years in developing a good program in pupil transportation" (63).

THE TUBB ERA, 1946 TO PRESENT

Vandiver resigned his office effective July 15, 1945, to accept the presidency of Chamberlain-Hunt Academy at Port Gibson. Governor Tom Bailey appointed J. M. Tubb to fill the unexpired term, beginning the longest tenure of any man in this office (64). A native of Hatley in Monroe County, Tubb obtained his B.S. degree from Mississippi Southern College and his M.A. from the University of Mississippi. He had represented Monroe County for one term, 1928-32, in the lower House of the Legislature and had taught many years in Prentiss and Perry Counties and at the demonstration school at Mississippi Southern College. He was serving a 6-year term as president of East Mississippi Junior College at Scooba when appointed to the state superintendency. Tubb assumed his duties well prepared by both training and experience, and his personal characteristics have endeared him to thousands of his fellow Mississippians, enabling him to serve with understanding and finesse.

Up to this time, the state department had grown by accretion, more or less Topsy-like, meeting exigencies as they arose. Many educators realized that the time had come for a more functional departmental organization. Superintendent Tubb recommended in his first biennial report that the Legislature give attention to a plan recommended by a committee assigned by the 1944 Legislature to study public education.

The committee filed its report in February 1946 after many conferences with Tubb and his staff, and the Legislature agreed with the reorganization almost *in toto* (see Appendix B). A department of education was set up to consist of the state superintendent, the assistant state superintendent, and directors of the six divisions. A coordinate school-health division was to be jointly administered by the State Department of Education and the State Board of Health. The duties of the superintendent and his officers were spelled out more clearly than before, and responsibility was plainly fixed.

Although the state superintendent was chairman of both the State Board of Education and the State Board for Vocational Education, frequently the lines of administrative control crossed. Sometimes this resulted in bickering on the local level between the school superintendent and the vocational agriculture teacher. To correct this, the Legislature abolished the vocational board and transferred its various duties to the education board, streamlining and centralizing the latter's administrative authority. The crippled children's services and vocational rehabilitation, formerly one unit, are now two divisions under the education board. The crippled children's services inaugurated the first program for spastic children on a statewide basis in the South in 1947. This program is now under a separate board designated by statute as the Mississippi Hospital School for Cerebral Palsy.

District Reorganization

Better transportation, through improved highways and modern vehicles, made it possible to step up the pace of district reorganization to reduce costs and give students richer offerings than the one- and two-teacher schools provided. Superintendent Tubb pointed this out in his 1947-49 biennial report, saying that each boy and girl in the rural areas should have the opportunity of studying vocational agriculture, trades and industrial arts, diversified occupations, music, drama, art, physical education, and other special courses if he or she needed or wanted them. He stated that a committee report from another state summed up his opinion on district reorganization:

> School organizations showed the effects of failure to keep pace with such improvements as transportation and road development. However, the social lag must not be taken up too rapidly by rushing headlong into school district reorganization. If we insist on riding roughshod over attitudes and ideas that now exist in rural areas without trying to bring them into focus with social progress represented in school reorganization, we would be retarding reorganization in some areas perhaps for many years (65).

The Legislature gave impetus to the reorganization in 1953 when it revamped the School Code in large measure and created an Educational Finance Commission of six members, appointed by the Governor and confirmed by the Senate, to reorganize school districts and allocate funds appropriated for school facilities construction. To give the commission a free hand, all school districts were abolished with the proviso that they remain active until replaced, reorganized, or otherwise changed.

The reorganization resulted in 151 districts or administrative units composed of 70 county units, 24 consolidated units, 5 line consolidated units, 47 separate municipal districts, and 5 special municipal separate districts. After further reorganization, 149 districts are in operation today.

Buildings

Consolidation created a need for more school construction under the direction of and partly financed by the state. Recognizing this, the Legislature made a start in 1946 by appropriating $3 million to assist local school districts with their building programs. Not until January 1952 was a complete survey of all the school buildings in the state made. The study revealed that in many rural areas the buildings were not crowded, but in the cities or near the cities they were bulging.

The state's economy was changing rapidly. Cattle raising, mechanized farming, and tree farming reduced the number of laborers needed in agriculture, and new industries attracted an increasing number into the cities. The survey showed that only 224 prereorganization school districts had an assessed valuation of $500,000 or more, and 527 districts had less than $300,000 assessed valuation.

The Legislature appropriated a total of $10 million from 1946 to 1952 to help districts build schoolhouses. These funds were matched or mixed with local and federal funds so that during this same period $53.4 million was spent for school facilities–$35.6 million for white schools and $17.8 for Negro schools. The new classrooms were well lighted, well ventilated, and properly heated.

All school districts began receiving credit for aid in school facilities construction in July 1954, when a minimum program plan of financing the public schools became effective. This program, to be discussed later, gave a tremendous impetus to the building program, which continues to progress according to this plan under the administration of the Educational Finance Commission.

Department Growth and Curriculum

The changing world in which Mississippians found themselves after World War II challenged the department to prepare students for a new era. The state continued to take a more active part, not only by transporting students to large centrally located schools and by assisting them in constructing new plants, but by developing new programs, improving established programs, and adding new supervisory personnel and other professional persons to its staff. With the assistance of various professional committees, the department prepared a number of valuable bulletins (66). It hired a supervisor of music education in 1948 to give the public schools leadership and to assist teachers in using the music textbooks adopted for the first six grades.

The state board entered into a contract with the Veterans Administration in May 1948 to provide elementary academic training to World War II veterans and other adults. In fact, Mississippi was the first state to offer this type of training, which was expanded in its early stages to include high school courses. The board also cooperated with the Veterans Administration to inaugurate on-the-job training and institutional on-the-farm training, two programs administered by the vocational education division. The state board and the state high school accrediting commission jointly authorized high school equivalency certificates to be issued in lieu of high school diplomas based on the results of General Educational Development Tests.

The need for driver education was apparent in most states by the end of World War II, and Mississippi added such courses to its curriculum. It also held a series of conferences in cooperation with the state highway patrol to awaken the people to the need for safety programs. The department purchased 12 simulators with money accumulated in a penalty assessment fund to more effectively teach driver education.

Finance

Improving the physical plants and transportation and enriching the curriculum required increasing amounts of money, and this was, of course, of serious concern to the legislators during the postwar years. The 1946 legislative recess study committee had barely finished its report before another study was under way. The new study, done in 1948, was limited to answering three questions: What kind of education was Mississippi getting for the money spent on its schools? How was the money being spent? Could the financial support be increased? In particular, the study was to analyze the financial support of both elementary and secondary schools so as to give the people a better understanding of just what was involved in adequately supporting an educational system. The study was carried out under the direction of William P. McLure of the University of Mississippi, and a report of it was published in 1948 (67).

Stimulated by the report and guided by its procedures, a Citizens' Council on Education formally organized in Jackson in 1950, sponsored by the Mississippi Education Association, the Mississippi Congress of Parents and Teachers, and the Mississippi State Department of Education. Boyd Campbell, a leading Jackson businessman and later chairman of the U.S. Chamber of Commerce, was the Council's temporary chairman. He opened its first meeting by pointing out that Mississippi's greatest economic frontier was the education of 1 million illiterate whites and Negroes. He added: "It has been apparent for some time that our school structure needs an overhauling. In our changing modern world, more and more demands are made on education and the school structure shows up as more and more inadequate" (68).

Minnie Chesteen, president of the Mississippi Education Association, called for immediate action:

> Tomorrow will be too late to do what should be done today because tomorrow will have its own problems. . . . This is our opportunity to develop education in Mississippi and to present a sound, practical and up-to-minute school program to the 1952 Legislature (69).

Superintendent Tubb added: "This may be a historic day in Mississippi education for the concerted efforts of all citizens can solve any problem" (70).

Under the direction of permanent chairman R. D. Morrow, Jackson businessman and later state treasurer, the council launched a full-scale study to determine what kind of schools the people wanted and whether they were willing to pay the bill. Questionnaires were sent to citizens throughout the state, and more than 20,000 replies were tabulated. The council then submitted recommendations to the Legislature calling for (a) equalization of salaries, (b) equalization of building facilities, (c) organization administration, and (d) curriculum and instruction. Organization administration implied that the schools were to be organized and administered according to the constitution and state laws—which provided for separate schools for the races. The curriculum and instruction recommendation called for courses that would equip youngsters for further education or employment. These observations are read into these expressions out of the voluminous material acquired by the Citizens' Council on Education. It was estimated that the cost of this program would be $34 million a year, exclusive of costly additional buildings and facilities.

The education committees of both the House and Senate held several conferences with Governor White and decided that before additional revenue could be appropriated, a study of the state school system by a legislative committee should be conducted to determine the kind of reorganization necessary to provide equal and adequate opportunities and facilities for all children. After a legislative committee of eight Senators and ten House members had been named, the Governor called its first meeting in his office in May 1952. He "urged the Committee to make a careful study of school attendance, school finance, teachers' salaries, transportation, and building facilities in order to equalize opportunities between the races" (71). He promised the committee that he would accept its recommendations and would work to enact them into law.

The majority of the committee argued for immediate consideration of its proposals, but a minority filed a brief listing certain exceptions to the majority report. One member dissented vigorously, primarily because of the increased cost necessary to put the proposals into effect. The segregation issue also was of great concern to the committee as cases were being heard in 1952 and 1953 by the U.S. Supreme Court on this question. The committee said:

> In the event segregation is declared unconstitutional, the only possibility of maintaining a segregated system in Mississippi is by persuading the Negro to attend of his own volition, schools provided for him; such persuasion can succeed only where adequate, respectable, and equal facilities are provided. The enactment of this program will provide such facilities (72).

The Governor called the Legislature into extraordinary session in November 1953, to consider the committee's report. In December, it approved the recommendations almost exactly as presented, which in effect revamped the School Code. It was in this session that the Legislature created the aforementioned Educational Finance Commission to reorganize districts and allocate funds for constructing school facilities.

The Legislature replaced the old equalizing fund with a minimum program plan effective July 1, 1954, which practically nullified the per-capita fund as it had been known. Disbursements under the minimum program plan are based on an economic index with the burden shared by the state, the county, and the district according to a specified formula and subsequent interpretations of the law.

The Segregation Issue

Superintendent Tubb indicated his own interest in improving the Negro schools in his 1947-49 report, stating:

> Quite a number of counties in Mississippi have put on a special tax levy for the purpose of improving the physical facilities of the Negro schools. State aid through the State Building Commission has enabled counties to meet, in part, their obligations for building better and more comfortable classrooms for Negro children. There is a vital need for the passage of new legislation in Mississippi that will provide a way whereby Negro schools can be conducted and maintained through more public support than is now possible under existing laws. It is imperative that the Legislature enact necessary laws that will insure a greater degree of comparable educational opportunities for all the children of all the people (73).

Later, in supporting a program for the education of spastic children, he held that—

> One of the fundamental principles of the American philosophy of education is that every child, regardless of race, color, creed, social position, physical condition, or native intelligence should have the opportunity for full development of his powers through education (74).

Considerable attention had been given to upgrading the Negro schools, not only in facilities, but also in teacher preparation and pay. This was done, however, under the state's constitutional provision of separate schools for the races and the U.S. Supreme Court's "separate but equal" doctrine.

Following the Supreme Court school desegregation decisions on May 17, 1954, the Mississippi Legislature held an extraordinary session to consider a constitutional amendment to abolish the public school system as a last resort for preserving the segregated schools. It voted to repeal the old statute requiring separate districts for white and Negro children. Under the new law, children of both races were to be in the same district but in separate schools according to the state's constitution. The guidelines set up by the U.S. Office of Education based on the Civil Rights Act of 1964 in effect nullified Mississippi's constitution by their desegregation compliance plans.

The proposal to dismantle the public schools in order to maintain segregation continued to have support among a number of white people. Superintendent Tubb had earlier addressed the seventy-fifth annual convention of the Mississippi Education Association in March 1961 and had referred to this proposal in part, when he said:

> In Mississippi a dual, segregated program of education has been operated for all the children. It is the belief of an overwhelming majority of our people that this type program, considering the background and traditions of our people, is best for us.
>
> If, however, this system of operation is challenged, the solution must be found through the efforts of dedicated leaders who put the welfare of the children and the future of our State and Nation above everything else. In the day of last resort, our people must know that to abolish the public schools would be to close the door of hope for many ambitious youth in this state . . . (75).

This statement was given much publicity and provoked considerable adverse comment. So far "the day of last resort" is not gone, and many classrooms have learned that white and Negro children can work together.

Impact of Federal Programs

The state has used federal funds for its schools since as far back as the Smith-Hughes Act in 1917. Vocational and other programs have been paid for in part by federal moneys. During the Depression, Mississippi, like many other states, sought financial assistance from the federal government to maintain its schools and programs. Also, although school lunch programs had been in existence in Mississippi since 1912, they became an integral and important part of the school day after President Truman signed the National School Lunch Act in June 1946. Following the Mississippi Legislature's action in accepting the school lunch program during a 1947 extraordinary session, the Governor assigned it to the Department of Education.

Superintendent Tubb maintained close liaison with the U.S. Office of Education. When the great White House Conference of November-December 1955 picked education as its central and singular theme for the first time in the nation's history, Governor White named Superintendent Tubb to be state chairman for the conference. Tubb called meetings on the local and state level as a preliminary to the national meeting. Men and women across the state showed an evangelistic fervor as they examined education and how it should meet the needs of their children. The experiences of the previous 5 years paved the way for active and intelligent participation in this historic conference.

More important perhaps than increased citizen interest was the money turned over to the states in both general funds and for special programs. When Superintendent Tubb took office in 1945, only 12 of the 51 staff members of the state department were paid jointly by state and federal funds, and 5 by federal funds alone. Fourteen years later, of the 191 staff members, the state paid 68, the health and education division paid 5, 31 were supported jointly by state and federal funds, and the federal government alone paid the salaries of 87. This increase over a 14-year period from 5 to 87 persons paid entirely by the federal government was due mainly to the expansion of programs in vocational education, rehabilitation, crippled children's services, and the school lunch program. But the full force of the federal government participation was not felt until the 1957-59 biennium.

Congress enacted the National Defense Education Act of 1958 as an emergency measure to undergird the defenses of our country in the face of Sputnik I. Of the act's 10 titles, Mississippi adopted plans in 4: Title III–instruction in natural science, mathematics, and modern foreign languages; Title V–guidance, counseling, and testing; Title VIII–area vocational education programs; and Title X, Section 1009–statistical services of the state department. This meant the department had to employ new personnel to supervise and handle assignments in these areas. Special supervision had to be added in science, mathematics, language, guidance, counseling, and testing to those already available in audiovisual education, alcohol and narcotics education, libraries, music, and special education.

Over the years, general supervision on the elementary and secondary levels has been provided through the instruction division. Activities under Title VIII, planned for area vocational schools, spread into the area of vocational-technical education and resulted in a tremendous program, not only at the secondary level but in the junior colleges as well. Superintendent Tubb later named a nine-member advisory committee to assist the State Board of Education in formulating plans for expanding this very practical and useful program.

Title X enabled the administration and finance division to upgrade its statistical services with IBM data-processing units. When the Eighty-Ninth Congress enacted the Elementary and Secondary Education Act in 1965, Title V of the act accelerated and broadened the services of this unit to aid the entire department. The state also had its plans approved under Titles I, II, and III of this new law. The superintendent and his divisional directors decided to set up an independent administrative unit to handle the far-reaching programs under Title I. This unit, directly responsible to the superintendent, who in turn receives the advice and approval of the directors before forwarding proposals to Washington, has proven very effective. The benefits of the program have been felt over the entire state.

The Civil Rights Act of 1964 contained two sections of significance to public education: Title VI provides for nondiscrimination in federally assisted programs, and Title IV provides for desegregation in public education. Soon after Congress approved the act and the guidelines were published, the Mississippi State Board of Education drew up its proposed plan of compliance, submitted it to the U.S. Commissioner of Education in February 1965 and obtained his approval.

The state board immediately started working with county and district boards to assist them in working out their plans of compliance with Title VI on a voluntary basis, so that federal funds would not be cut off and regular programs of public education could proceed unimpaired and uninterrupted in a given district. The superintendent, department staff members, and other school people made many trips to Washington and elsewhere to attend meetings and obtain information. Professionals from the Office of Education were invited to the state's offices, and the state superintendent arranged for them to meet with school superintendents, their boards of education, and their attorneys to discuss the compliance plans. The local people were grateful for this assistance, and federal officials praised the plan.

Although the Governor did not encourage the school boards to draw up these compliance plans, the state superintendent thought this the soundest procedure, and school leaders continued their efforts to work out desegregation plans. Thus, most of the districts were able to qualify for financial assistance and experienced no unusual difficulties, setting examples of obedience to law and court orders which were distasteful to them. Under these adverse conditions, at variance with the customs and traditions of the past, four school districts were brought under court order for the 1964-65 session. The following year, 107 complied voluntarily and 24 were ordered to by the court; for the 1966-67 sessions, out of 149 districts in the state, 93 complied voluntarily, and 42 obeyed the court orders to do so.

The Department's Growth

The 1960 Legislature authorized a nine-member committee to make another study of public education. In a report it filed in December 1961, the committee recommended that the Governor be empowered to appoint a lay state board which would then name the state superintendent. Superintendent Tubb was not opposed to the idea of an expanded lay board but was opposed to the Governor's being given the authority to name its members. A constitutional amendment was required to make the change, and this was turned down by popular vote. These same controversial proposals had been made before, and in a study authorized in the 1966 session of the Legislature, they have again been introduced. But Mississippi continues at present to support an ex officio board, as set up in 1869, and prefers selecting the state superintendent by popular vote.

The department had a staff of 191 during the 1957-59 biennium. Federal programs and the demand for new services made a tremendous impact on the department, so that by 1966-67 its staff numbered 447. Appropriations increased from $11.5 million for the 1946-47 school year to $80.5 million in 1965-66, including an increase in annual per-pupil costs of from $53.48 to $269.72 during this period. Average annual teacher salaries also have gone up—from $736.95 in 1944-45 to $4,212.58 in 1965-66 (see Appendix C, Table 2). Many present staff members have stayed with the department over the entire period of this phenomenal growth from infancy to maturity.

After 22 years as superintendent of education in Mississippi, J.M. Tubb retired in January 1968. He was succeeded by Garvin H. Johnston, president of Pearl River Junior College, a prominent Mississippi public school educator with background as a teacher and superintendent of schools.

Conclusion

This description comes up to the present on an optimistic note—a note of confidence in the people of the state working together for common causes. Mississippians have long yearned and labored for federal aid to education, conditioned each time "but without objectionable federal control." Federal aid is now available in great quantities, and tied to it are controls that most Mississippians find shocking.

To obtain the aid and adhere to the controls, men and women from the federal, state, and local levels have sat down together to tackle these very difficult problems. They can be solved. The federal aid is joined to civil rights, and civil rights calls for desegregation; desegregation has provoked guidelines which many believe go beyond the law, and certainly they conflict with local customs and traditions. The North, the South, the East, and the West eye each other a bit suspiciously on many counts, yet all of these concerns are alleged to be for children.

Perhaps by tackling these problems and disputes the great American dream will be fulfilled. The expanded—and some say overgrown—departments of education have a real challenge to meet all of the demands. Willa Cather, when looking at Nebraska, observed: "The generation that subdued the wild land and broke up the virgin prairies, inspires respect and compels admiration. We made this, our backs and hands"(76).

Now federal, state, and local governments have an obligation that compels cooperation for the benefit of humanity, and youth in particular. This will have to be done with the heart and mind. Men are too close to continue carrying chips on their weary shoulders. Those same shoulders, rejuvenated, must be put together to push the great load of national concern: education.

FOOTNOTES

1. William H. Weathersby, *History of Educational Legislation in Mississippi from 1798 to 1860,* University of Chicago Monograph No. 16 (Chicago: University of Chicago Press, 1921), p. 2.
2. Robert Lowry and William H. McCardle, *A History of Mississippi* (Jackson: R. A. Henry & Co., 1890), p. 163.
3. Weathersby, *op. cit.,* p. 3.
4. Compared with several other states, the density of the white population per square mile demonstrates the greater difficulty in establishing schools in the Mississippi Territory. *Ibid.,* p. 6.

State	*1849*	*1850*	*1860*
Ohio	38.08	49.55	58.54
Indiana	20.07	29.24	39.94
Illinois	8.52	15.37	30.09
Mississippi	3.82	6.32	8.19

5. Weathersby, *op. cit.,* p. 7.
6. *Ibid.,* p. 9.
7. *Ibid.,* p. vii.
8. *Ibid..,* p. 10.
9. Franklin L. Riley, *School History of Mississippi* (Richmond, Va.: B. F. Johnson Publishing Co., 1900), p. 174. The oldest free school in Mississippi (by 21 years) is Franklin Academy at Columbus, chartered in 1821.
10. Lowry and McCardle, *op. cit.,* p. 420.
11. *Ibid.,* p. 420.
12. Weathersby, *op. cit.,* p. 11.
13. Edward H. Mayes, *Education in Mississippi* (Washington, D.C.: Government Printing Office, 1899), p. 23.

14. Lowry and McCardle, *op. cit.*, p. 418.

15. Mayes, *op. cit.*, p. 23.

16. *Ibid.*, p. 278.

17. Prior to the enactment of the law, in his message to the Legislature on January 6, 1846, in Jackson, Mississippi, Governor Brown said:

What would we think of a man who had built a ship and sent her upon a distant and perilous sea, laden with priceless jewels of liberty and cast it upon the uncertain elements of public opinion untempered as yet by the hallowed influence of education and shall we still refuse the safety of that government by refusing to contribute to the only means that give it safety – to the education of its people. The rich may say, "We have no interest in the education of the poor." There could be no greater or (more) fatal error. Pride, the love of offspring, the ephemeral pleasures of witnessing the tree of youth nurtured by our care as it expands and grows and ripens into manhood – these teach the rich to educate their own children, but the higher consideration of patriotism, the holier cause of religion and morality, the pure and unstained love of human happiness, teach them to educate the poor.

18. Mayes, *op. cit.*, p. 282.

19. The U.S. Census reports in 1850 that there were 756 teachers, 782 common schools, and 18,746 pupils at a cost of $254,159; in 1860, there were 1,215 teachers, 1,116 common schools, and 30,970 pupils at a cost of $385,677 – an increase of approximately 33.3 percent for the decade. Elsie Timberlake, "Did the Reconstruction Regime Give Mississippi Her Public Schools?" *Mississippi Historical Society Publications*, XII (Jackson: The Society, 1912), 75-76.

20. Mississippi, *Senate Journal* (1865), p. 29.

21. Timberlake, *op. cit.*, p. 84. The Reverend Walter Hillman, a native of the Island of Martha's Vineyard, Massachusetts, the president of Central Female Institute in Clinton, was president of the Mississippi State Teachers Association. Lowry and McCardle, *op. cit.*, p. 419.

22. Senator L. Q. C. Lamar of Mississippi considered a public school system so important that he made an eloquent speech in the U.S. Senate on March 28, 1884, requesting federal aid to education. He stated:

In my opinion, it is the first step, and the most important step that this government has ever taken in the direction of the solution of what is called the race problem; and I believe that it will tell more powerfully and decisively upon the future destinies of the colored race in America than any measure or ordinance that has yet been adopted . . . .

Edward Mayes, *L.Q.C. Lamar, His Life, Times, and Speeches, 1825-1893* (2d ed.; Nashville: Publishing House of the Methodist Episcopal Church, 1896), pp. 774-79.

23. For further information, see Mississippi, *Journal of the Constitutional Convention* (1868), p. 1; and Dunbar Rowland, *History of Mississippi: The Heart of the South,* II (4 vols.; Chicago: S. J. Clarke Publishing Co., 1925), 520.

24. Mississippi, *Constitution* (1869), art. 8, sec. 1.

25. Rowland, *op. cit.*, p. 894.

26. Mississippi, *House Journal* (1870), p. 57.

27. Superintendent of Education, *Annual Report, 1871,* p. 7. See Appendix D for the statistics included in this report for 1871.

28. James W. Garner, *Reconstruction in Mississippi* (Gloucester, Mass.: Peter Smith, 1964, Reprint. New York: The Macmillan Co., 1901), p. 366.

29. Superintendent of Education, *Biennial Report, 1886-1887,* p. 4.

30. Kincannon was later named chancellor of the University of Mississippi, and in 1914, he became superintendent of schools in Memphis.

31. William Alexander Percy, *Lanterns on the Levee* (New York: Alfred A. Knopf, 1941), p. 156.

32. Superintendent of Education, *Biennial Report, 1899-1901,* pp. 95-111. These can be compared against the statistics for 1850 and 1860 in footnote 19. See Appendix C, Table 1, for a comparison of salaries, and enrollments from 1871 to 1889.

33. *Ibid.*, p. 5.

34. *Ibid.*

35. *Ibid.*, p. 234.

36. Superintendent Whitfield came to this conclusion, stating:

I am very much of the opinion that the criticism often made that our schools as now conducted are educating our boys out of sympathy with their environments and making them dissatisfied with their surroundings is, in a large measure, true. That our boys are manifesting more and more a disinclination to remain in the country, everyone will admit. Mississippi is a great rural state, and the rural state, and the future happiness and prosperity of her people will be indissolubly connected with rural life. If the State is to be great, we must make our great rural life attractive and remunerative.

Superintendent of Education, *Biennial Report, 1901-1903,* pp. 8-9.

37. *Ibid.*, p. 231.

38. Knox M. Broom, living in busy retirement in Jackson, served 25 years as state supervisor for these schools and had more to do with laying the foundations of the law, the philosophy, and the plans than any other person. Although it was not fulfilled during his tenure, it was his dream to inaugurate a program of vocational and technical education in the junior colleges. Knox M. Broom, *History of Mississippi Public Junior Colleges, 1928-1953* (Raymond, Miss.: Keith Press, 1954), p. 7.

39. Superintendent of Education, *Biennial Report, 1899-1901,* p. 5.

40. Superintendent Whitfield pointed out that the children in rural schools attended 90 days while those in towns averaged 163.3 days, and there were more than nine times as many attending the rural schools as attended the separate school districts. The amount of money spent for rural schools was still less than three times the amount spent at separate school districts. According to the enumeration of educable children in 1900, 89.5 percent lived outside the separate school districts. Whitfield wrote: "The great problem before the people of the State in my opinion is the betterment of the rural schools. Gosh! What a challenge is thrown to the people in 1900 toward equalization . . . ." *Ibid.,* p. 11.

41. W. H. Smith, the state rural school supervisor and later superintendent, wrote: "In Harrison County, in which I spent one week in July with county superintendent, J. J. Dawsey, we consolidated fifteen one-teacher schools and installed seven school wagons – the first school wagons ever used in Mississippi at public expense."

The honor of being the first consolidated school organized in the state is claimed by Woolmarket Consolidated School, whose cornerstone certifies that it was organized July 16, 1910. Willard F. Bond, *I Had a Friend* (Kansas City, Mo.: The Author, 1958), p. 97.

42. The members of this first textbook commission were D. A. Hill, H. L. Jobe, C. E. Saunders, O. A. Shaw, L. Q. C. Williams, T. K. Boggan, H. P. Hughes, E. L. Bailey, and State Superintendent H. L. Whitfield. They were invited by the Governor to meet him in his office where they received official notice of their appointment. Superintendent of Education, *Biennial Report, 1903-1905,* p. 17.

43. William Gibson Butt, "A Documentary History of the Mississippi State Department of Education" (unpublished Ph.D. dissertation, University of Mississippi, 1953), p. 116.

44. Mississippi Normal College later became Mississippi State Teachers College and is now the University of Southern Mississippi at Hattiesburg. Although past 90 years of age, Bond and his wife are very active in Jackson's church, civic, and educational affairs. He still drops by the state department to see old friends and is considered Mississippi's elder educational statesman. The book first mentioned in footnote 41 concerning his experiences is most interesting.

45. Superintendent of Education, *Biennial Report, 1913-1915,* p. 6.

46. This board was reorganized in 1936 to consist of the state superintendent, state commissioner of agriculture and commerce, the executive secretary of the State Board of Health, the president of Mississippi State College, and one white citizen appointed by the Governor with the advice and consent of the Senate. This board was abolished by the Legislature in 1946, and its powers and duties transferred to the State Board of Education.

47. M. E. Moffitt, *Twenty Years of Progress of Public Education, 1910-1930,* Research Bulletin No. 1 (Jackson: Department of Education, 1931), p. 33. Jim Brown, the former assistant state superintendent who made this statement, was the first president of Delta State Teachers College (now Delta State College).

48. Superintendent of Education, *Biennial Report, 1899-1901,* pp. 5–6. The 1966 Legislature left it up to the State Board of Education to decide how often it should make the enumeration. In a special meeting in January 1967, it decided that no enumeration should be made for this year.

49. Superintendent Bond relates that at the conclusion of the program at the Gulfport meeting in 1919, the Jackson County superintendent and the Sharkey County superintendent got into an argument and pulled off a fake pistol duel over the heads of nearly 100 people. Each felt he was about to be shot by a stray bullet. One superintendent looked right at the muzzle of one of the pistols and froze in his seat, never moving a muscle. Another rolled into the aisle and tried to jerk his collar a little higher on his neck. With each shot every head would disappear behind the benches and then slowly reappear. Bond, *op. cit.,* pp. 94-96.

50. Percy H. Easom, "Public School Legislation in Mississippi, 1860 to 1930" (unpublished Ph.D. dissertation, George Peabody College for Teachers, Nashville, Tennessee, 1937), p. 292.

51. Superintendent of Education, *Biennial Report, 1931-1933,* p. 9.

52. One Mississippi historian had this to say about the Honorable Mike Conner, who became Governor in January 1932:

> Beginning his administration amid the stress and strain of the greatest depression in history, Governor Conner in less than two years cut down the debt of the state, balanced the budget, restored Mississippi's credit, placed its revenues upon a solid basis by procuring the passage of the general sales tax, proved the soundness of this new source of revenue, aroused nation-wide interest in the sales tax idea, and made Mississippi a center of study for those interested in financial and economic reform.

Pearl Vivian Guyton, *Our Mississippi* (revised ed.; Austin, Tex.: The Steck Co., 1959), p. 233.

53. This was Bond's first appearance before a congressional committee, and with its permission he began reading an imposing list of the taxes Mississippians were paying at that time. The chairman asked why Mississippi had no tax on chewing tobacco, and Bond replied that he supposed the members of the Legislature were afraid they might hurt the feelings of the

tobacco chewers in the rural areas. When asked if Mississippians chewed much tobacco, he told them that he didn't know whether they outchewed the people of every state or not, but that they did chew right sharply. The chairman observed that very likely the people of Mississippi were in a "state of great expectoration."

In reply to the chairman's question on how much Mississippians were paying on dogs, he told them the tax was $1 on some dogs and $2 on some others. One committee member wanted to know why it varied, why tax one dog $1 and another $2. Bond explained that Mississippi had a $1 tax on the male and a $2 tax on the female or bitch dogs, and it was his personal opinion that this illustrated one of those rare occasions when a son-of-a-bitch got a break. He said he heard someone in the committee room say, "They ought to stop asking him questions." Bond, *op. cit.*, pp. 119-20.

54. During his administration, Bond built the State Department of Education into a potential force for intelligent, aggressive service. He had been largely responsible for establishing the equalization fund and obtaining countywide and district levies for schools. He was particularly proud of his work in consolidation, raising the minimum educable age from 5 to 6 years, organizing the vocational high schools, and extending benefits to crippled children. He had also worked to implement programs in vocational rehabilitation, helped begin services for the blind that finally became second to none in the nation, and added 2 years to the strongest agricultural high schools to start the junior college program. His surveys of both the county and city systems resulted in raising standards of both the schools and teachers. He recognized that denominational and private schools and colleges were a vital part of the educational system. He started a weekly prayer service in the Department of Education that continues until today. *Ibid.*, pp. 132-33.

55. Vandiver attended the Iuka Normal Institute and obtained his bachelor of arts degree from Mississippi College. He had served as superintendent of schools at Nettleton, Ackerman, and New Albany, and in 1916 had been the director of the Model County School System in Pearl River County.

56. Superintendent of Education, *Biennial Report, 1935-1937*, p. 7. The teachers and bus drivers certificates were issued because funds were not available. The Kyle-Cook Budget Law gave the boards the authority to borrow money to pay off their indentures.

57. The 1936 appropriation began a new practice of itemizing salaries, travel, and other expenses. Since 1954, however, the department has received lump sum appropriations which are administered by the state superintendent and the State Board of Education.

58. Superintendent of Education, *Biennial Report, 1941-1943*, p. 49.

59. Superintendent of Education, *Biennial Report, 1935-1937*, p. 15.

60. Superintendent of Education, *Biennial Report, 1941-1943*, p. 9.

61. Superintendent of Education, *Biennial Report, 1943-1945*, p. 50.

62. *Ibid.*

63. *Ibid.*, pp. 66-67.

64. On March 10, 1967, Tubb announced his intention not to seek reelection; when his term ended in January 1968, he had served longer than any predecessor.

65. Superintendent of Education, *Biennial Report, 1947-1949*, p. 18.

66. The department's publications included the following: a manual of administration, a manual for teaching health, a manual for teaching physical education, a school library handbook, a handbook for elementary teachers, a business education syllabus, a syllabus for Negro schools, education and teachers' directories, and elementary school regulations. It also suggested lists of elementary and high school library books, lists of science equipment, and lists of maps, globes, and charts.

67. William P. McLure, *Let Us Pay for the Kind of Education We Need,* Report of a study of state and local support of Mississippi's schools (University: Bureau of Educational Research, University of Mississippi, 1948).

68. File of materials collected by the Citizens' Council on Education, located at the Mississippi Education Association, Jackson.

69. *Ibid.*

70. *Ibid.*

71. Recess Education Committee, *A Report to the Mississippi State Legislature* (Jackson: The Committee, March 1953), p. 5.

72. *Ibid.*, p. 51.

73. Superintendent of Education, *Biennial Report, 1947-1949*, p. 14.

74. Superintendent of Education, *Biennial Report, 1949-1951*, p. 15.

75. *State Times* (Jackson), March 17, 1961, sec. 3A.

76. Thomas C. Jones, comp., *The Joy of Words* (Chicago: J. G. Ferguson Publishing Co., 1960), p. 34.

BIBLIOGRAPHY

Public Documents

Mississippi. *Constitution* (1817, 1832, 1869, 1890).

——*House Journal* (1870).

——*Journal of the Constitutional Convention* (1868).

——*Laws of the Extraordinary Session* (1865, 1917, 1947, 1953, 1954, 1955).

——*Laws of the Regular Session* (1864-1960).

——*Senate Journal* (1865, 1876, 1916).

——*Teachers Directory, 1966-1967.*

——*The Official and Statistical Register, 1908-1968.*

Books

Bettersworth, John K. *Mississippi: A History.* Austin, Tex.: The Steck Co., 1959.

Bond, Willard F. *I Had a Friend.* Kansas City, Mo.: The Author, 1958.

Broom, Knox M. *History of Mississippi Public Junior Colleges, 1928-1953.* Raymond, Miss.: Keith Press, 1954.

Butts, Alfred Benjamin. "Public Administration in Mississippi." *Mississippi Historical Society Publications* Vol. XII. Jackson: The Society, 1912.

Fant, Mabel, and Fant, John C. *History of Mississippi.* Jackson: The Mississippi Publishing Co., 1924.

Garner, James W. *Reconstruction in Mississippi.* Gloucester, Mass.: Peter Smith, 1964. Reprint. New York: The Macmillan Co., 1901.

Guyton, Pearl Vivian. *Our Mississippi.* Rev. ed.; Austin, Tex.: The Steck Co., 1959.

Hamilton, Peter J. "British West Florida." *Mississippi Historical Society Publications,* Vol. VII. Jackson: The Society, 1903.

Jones, Thomas C., comp., *The Joy of Words.* Chicago: J. G. Ferguson Publishing Co., 1960.

Lowry, Robert, and McCardle, William H. *A History of Mississippi.* Jackson: R. A. Henry and Co., 1890.

McLemore, Richard Aubrey, and McLemore, Nannie Pitts. *The Mississippi Story.* Atlanta: Laidlaw Brothers, 1964.

McNeily, J. S. "Climax and Collapse of Reconstruction in Mississippi, 1874-1876." *Mississippi Historical Society Publications,* Vol. XII. Jackson: The Society, 1912.

Mayes, Edward H. *Education in Mississippi.* Washington, D.C.: Government Printing Office, 1899.

—— *L. Q. C. Lamar, His Life, Times, and Speeches, 1825-1893.* 2d ed. Nashville: Publishing House of the Methodist Episcopal Church, 1896.

Noble, Stuart G. *Forty Years of Public Schools in Mississippi.* New York: Columbia University, 1918.

O'Shea, Michael V. *Public Education in Mississippi.* Jackson: Jackson Printing Co., 1926.

—— *A State Educational System at Work.* Washington, D.C.: Bernard B. Jones Fund, 1927.

Percy, William Alexander. *Lanterns on the Levee.* New York: Alfred A. Knopf, 1941.

Riley, Franklin L. *School History of Mississippi.* Richmond, Va.: B. F. Johnson Publishing Co., 1900.

Rowland, Dunbar. *Encyclopedia of Mississippi History.* Madison, Wis.: S. A. Brandt, 1907.

—— *History of Mississippi: The Heart of the South.* 4 vols.; Chicago: S. J. Clarke Publishing Co., 1925.

Sydnor, Charles S., and Bennett, Claude. *Mississippi History.* Richmond, Va.: B. F. Johnson Publishing Co., 1939.

Timberlake, Elsie. "Did the Reconstruction Regime Give Mississippi Her Public Schools?" *Mississippi Historical Society Publications,* Vol. XII. Jackson: The Society, 1912.

Weathersby, William H. *History of Educational Legislation in Mississippi from 1798 to 1860.* Chicago: University of Chicago Press, 1921.

Reports

McLure, William P. *Let Us Pay for the Kind of Education We Need.* Report of a study of state and local support of Mississippi's schools. University: Bureau of Educational Research, University of Mississippi, 1948.

Moffitt, M. E. *Twenty Years of Progress of Public Education, 1910-1930.* Research Bulletin No. 1. Jackson: Department of Education, 1931.

Recess Education Committee, *A Report to the Mississippi State Legislature.* Jackson: The Committee, 1953.

Superintendents of Education. *Annual Reports.* Jackson: Department of Education, 1870-76.

—— *Biennial Reports.* Jackson: Department of Education, 1876-1965.

Periodicals

Jackson Daily News. August 11, 1935; June 27, 1962.

State Times (Jackson). March 17, 1961, sec. 3A.

The Weekly Clarion (Jackson). April 5, 1876.

Unpublished Material

Butt, William Gibson. "A Documentary History of the Mississippi State Department of Education." Unpublished Ph.D. dissertation, University of Mississippi, Oxford, 1953.

Easom, Percy H. "Public School Legislation in Mississippi, 1860-1930." Unpublished Ph.D. dissertation, George Peabody College for Teachers, Nashville, Tennessee, 1937.

Humphrey, George Duke. "A History of the Public School Funds of Mississippi." Unpublished master's thesis, Department of Education, University of Chicago, 1931.

—— "Public Education for Whites in Mississippi." Unpublished Ph.D. dissertation, School of Education, Ohio State University, Columbus, 1939.

Other Sources

Brown, Albert Gallatin. "Message to the Legislature on January 6, 1846," Jackson, Mississippi.

File of materials collected by the Citizens' Council on Education, located at the Mississippi Education Association, Jackson.

Appendix A

MISSISSIPPI CHIEF STATE SCHOOL OFFICERS

1869-74	Henry R. Pease
1874-76	Thomas W. Cardozo
1876-77	Thomas S. Gathright
1877-78	Rev. Joseph Bardwell
1878-85	James Argyle Smith
1885-95	James R. Preston
1896-98	Andrew A. Kincannon
1898-1907	H. L. Whitfield
1907-14	Joseph N. Powers
1914-16	W. H. Smith
1916-35	W. F. Bond
1936	J. T. Calhoun
1936-45	J. S. Vandiver
1945-68	J. M. Tubb
1968-	Garvin H. Johnston

Appendix B

Chart I.--MISSISSIPPI DEPARTMENT OF EDUCATION, 1946

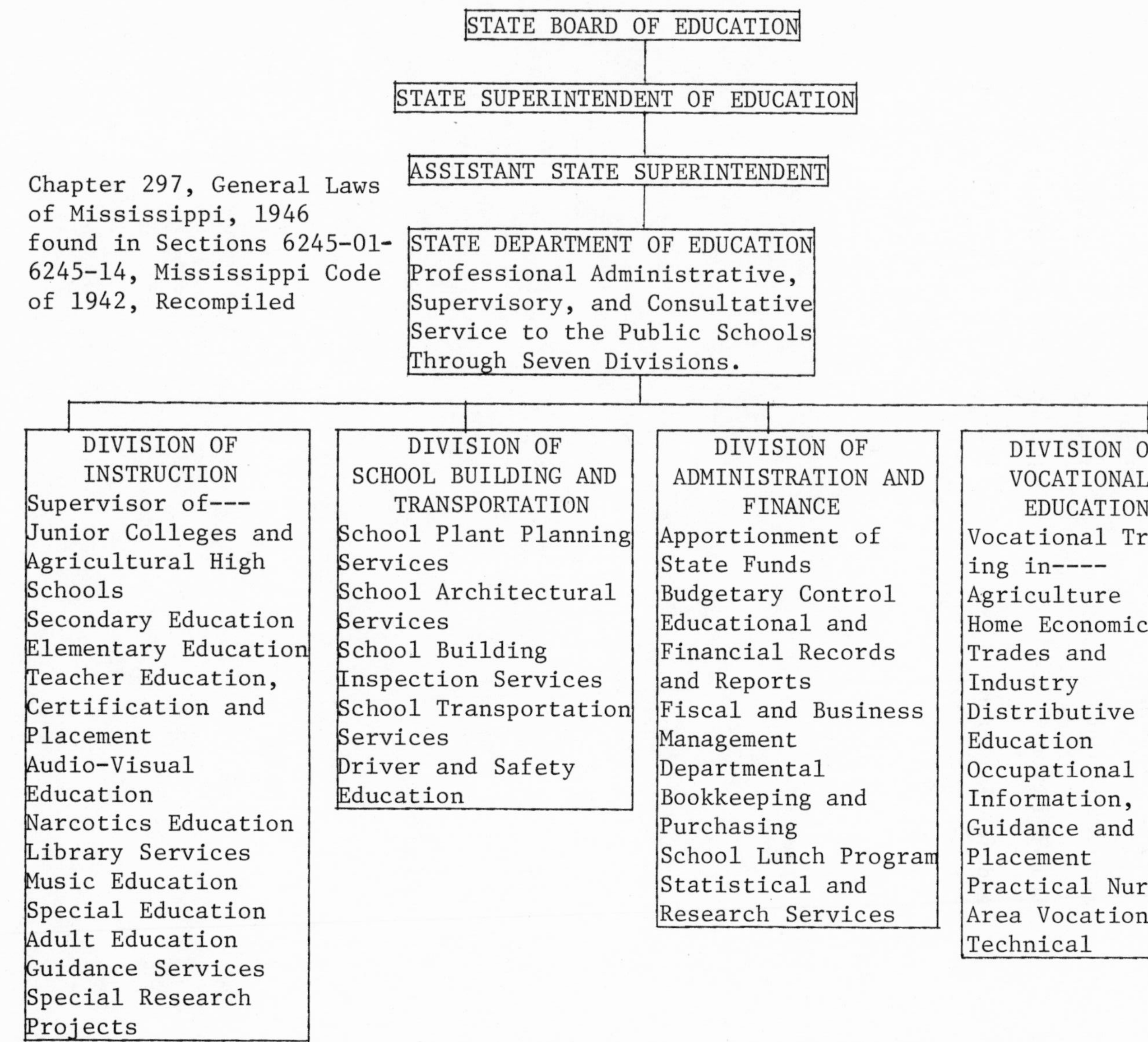

Appendix B

Chart I.--MISSISSIPPI DEPARTMENT OF EDUCATION, 1946 (Continued)

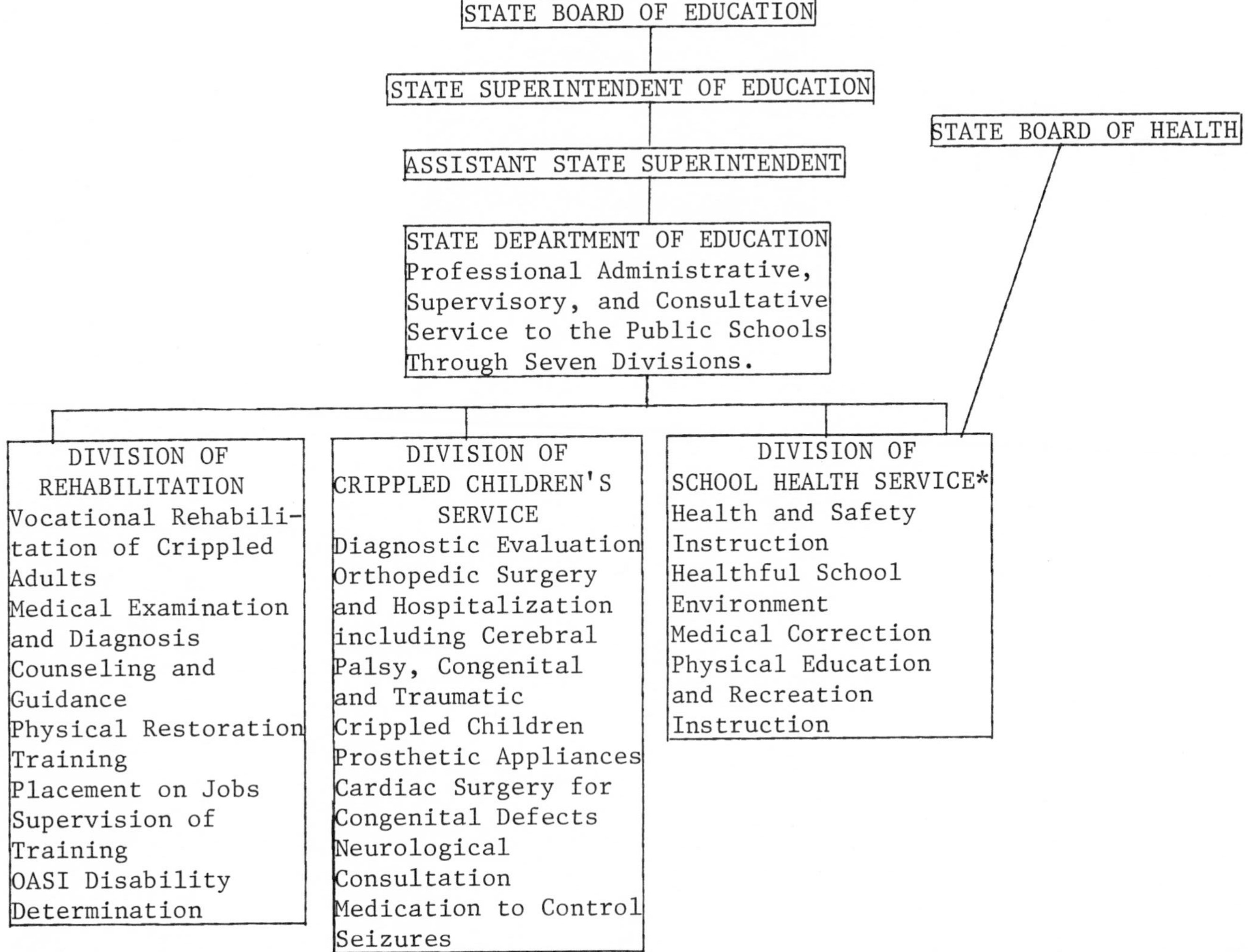

*The Division of School Health Service is administered jointly by the State Department of Education and the State Board of Health. Educational Director and Medical Director are equally responsible for the administration of this program.

Appendix B

Chart II.--MISSISSIPPI DEPARTMENT OF EDUCATION, 1964

STRUCTURE AND FUNCTIONS

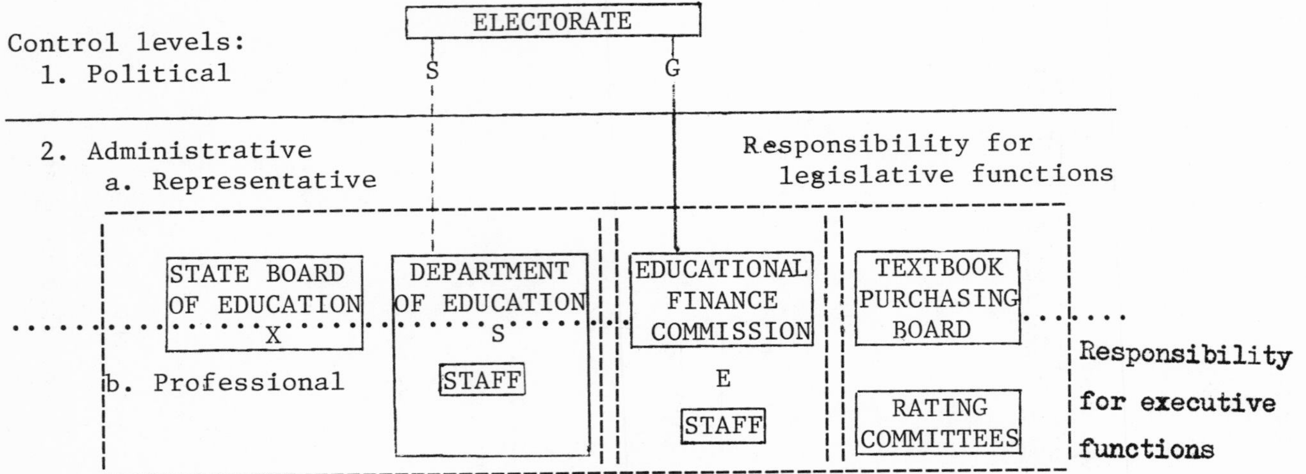

G. Governor
S. Superintendent of public education
X. All members serve ex officio
E. Executive secretary, educational finance commission

ORGANIZATION CHART

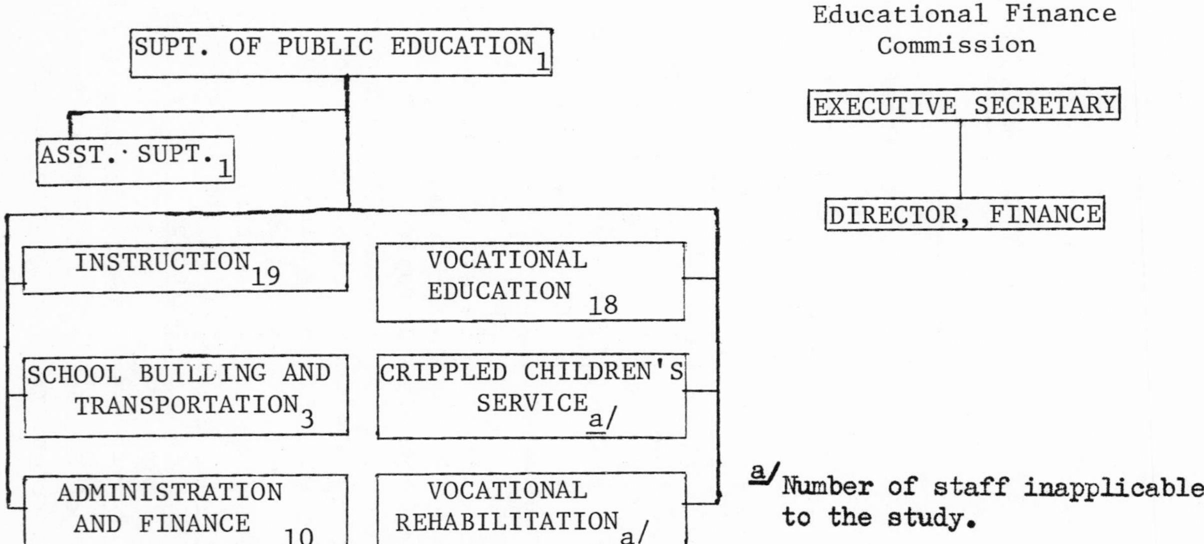

a/ Number of staff inapplicable to the study.

From Robert F. Will, State Education: Structure and Organization, Department of Health, Education, and Welfare, Office of Education, OE 23038. Washington, D.C.: Government Printing Office, 1964. pp. 90-91.

Appendix B

Supplement 1.--POSITIONS ADDED TO THE MISSISSIPPI DEPARTMENT OF EDUCATION, 1869-1945

State Superintendent of Education - 1869

State Board of EdUcation - 1869

Supervisor of Rural Schools - 1910

Supervisor of Negro Schools - 1916

Assistant State Superintendent of Education - 1916

Director of Vocational Education - 1918

Supervisor of Vocational Agriculture - 1918

Supervisor of Homemaking Education - 1918

Supervisor of Trades and Industrial Education - 1918

Supervisor of High Schools - 1919

Assistant Negro Rural School Supervisor - 1920

Supervisor of Civilian Rehabilitation - 1920

Assistant Supervisor of Trades and Industrial Education - 1921

Supervisor of Industrial Rehabilitation - 1921

Supervisor of Agricultural High Schools - 1924

Supervisor of Public School Music - 1924

Director of Information and Statistics - 1926

Director of School Building Service - 1928

Supervisor of Agricultural Education for Negro Schools - 1930

Director of Teacher Training and Certification - 1933

Supervisor of Crippled Children's Services - 1936

Supervisor of Alcohol and Narcotics Education - 1938

Supervisor of School Transportation - 1938

Assistant Director of Information and Statistics - 1939

Director of Civilian Rehabilitation - 1939

Coordinator of Adult Education - 1940

Supervisor of Adult Education - 1940

Supervisor of Distributive Education - 1949

School Health Services - coordinated - 1942
(Embracing several new staff members)

Appendix B

Supplement 2.--MISSISSIPPI DEPARTMENT EXPANDS WITH ADDED SECTIONS

1907 High School

1909 Elementary; Agriculture

1911 Home Economics

1912 Teacher Certification

1916 Negro Schools

1918 Vocational Trades and Industries

1925 Reference and Service

1929 Library

1934 Music

1935 Health and Physical Education

1937 Distributive Occupations, Safety

1939 Business Education

1940 Higher Education

1941--1965 Civil Defense, Finance, Administration and Research, School Lunch, Data Processing, School Transportation, School Attendance, Audio-Visual Aids, Veterans Education, Adult Education, Federally Financially Assisted Programs, Materials of Instruction, Guidance, Industrial Arts, Manpower Development and Training, Trade and Industrial Education

Appendix C

Table 1.—SYNOPSIS OF STATISTICS FROM BEGINNING OF PUBLIC SCHOOL SYSTEM

NUMBER OF PUPILS ENROLLED

		White	Colored	Total
Reports from 52 counties	1871	66,257	45,429	111,688
Reported as an estimate	1872	.....	......	148,000
A fractional part of year, 8 mos.	1873	.....	.....	80,000
Reports from 70 counties	1874	.....	.....	154,229
	1875	78,404	89,813	168,217
Reports from 50 counties	1876	76,026	90,178	166,204
Reports from 65 counties	1877	84,374	76,150	120,524
	1878	101,201	104,177	205,978
	1879	105,957	111,796	217,753
	1880	112,944	123,710	236,654
Reports from 73 counties	1881	111,655	125,633	237,288
Reports from 66 counties	1882	104,451	109,630	214,081
Reports from 71 counties	1883	125,598	141,398	266,996
	1884	129,203	149,373	278,576
	1885	142,177	154,430	296,607
	1886	129,203	152,530	281,743
	1886-87	126,919	143,825	270,734
	1887-88	147,817	162,304	310,121
	1888-89	148,435	173,552	321,987

AVERAGE ATTENDANCE

Years	No. counties reporting	No. days taught	White	Colored	Total
1871	52	110	.....	.....	90,000
1872	74	115	.....	.....	125,000
1873	...	80	.....	.....	50,500
1874	70	...	.....	.....	108,647
1875	74	100	40,380	66,514	106,894
1876	50	80	65,384	68,580	133,964
1877	65	77	52,672	44,627	97,302
1878	74	79½	64,318	71,658	135,976
1879	74	77½	66,381	72,592	138,973
1880	74	74½	72,881	83,880	166,761
1881	73	78	76,647	85,417	162,064
1882	59	79	61,738	73,578	145,316
1883	63	76	68,946	85,517	154,463
1884	74	77½	85,294	99,127	184,421
1885	74	78	84,347	101,038	185,385
1886	74	74	84,884	99,134	184,018
1886-87	74	84	77,868	85,996	163,864
1887-88	74	84	89,815	92,627	184,018
1888-89	74	85	90,716	101,710	192,426

	AVERAGE MONTHLY SALARIES			NO. TEACHERS EMPLOYED		
		White	Colored	White	Colored	Total
1871	$50.00			.....	.....	3,600
1872	51.32			.....	.....	4,800
1873	50.00			.....	.....	1,800
1874	46.92			.....	.....	3,845
1875	55.47			2,859	2,109	4,968
1876	39.87			2,973	1,005	3,978
1877	29.20			2,669	1,459	4,128
1878	27.85			2,948	1,813	4,761
1879	30.26			3,255	2,112	5,367
1880	30.05			3,250	2,314	5,564
1881	30.07			3,414	2,644	6,058
1882	30.03			2,910	2,272	5,182
1883	32.68			3,598	2,793	6,391
1884	28.73			3,873	2,933	6,816
1885	28.74			4,215	3,124	7,339
1886	28.18	$31.37	$27.40	3,840	3,012	6,852
1886-87	30.37	34.44	25.24	3,421	2,692	6,113
1887-88	30.07	34.52	24.05	3,776	2,790	6,566
1888-89	29.16	33.97	24.16	3,557	3,558	7,115

AMOUNT EXPENDED

1871	$ 950,000	
1872	1,136,987	
1873	492,500	for ¾ year
1874	890,072	
1875	985,600	
1876	417,760	(50 counties)
1877	481,215	(65 counties)
1878	592,805	not full reports
1879	641,548	not full reports
1880	830,704	
1881	757,757	
1882	610,284	(66 counties)
1883	803,875	(71 counties)
1884	799,932	
1885	840,776	(73 counties)
1886	802,476	
1886-87	839,797	
1887-88	962,263	
1888-89	1,117,111	

Source:

Report of J. R. Preston, state superintendent of education, to the Legislature for the years 1888-89.

Appendix C

Table 2. – NUMBER AND AVERAGE SALARIES OF CLASSROOM TEACHERS, 1944-65

Year	White teachers		Negro teachers		Total teachers	
	Number	Average salary	Number	Average salary	Number	Average salary
1944-45	7,421	$1,018.01	6,337	$ 407.81	13,758	$ 736.95
1945-46	8,087	1,108.34	6,034	398.73	14,121	805.12
1946-47	8,138	1,234.49	6,168	459.06	14,306	900.16
1947-48	8,343	1,637.30	6,333	599.12	14,676	1,189.30
1948-49	8,366	1,731.05	6,164	659.49	14,530	1,276.47
1949-50	8,451	1,805.69	6,332	710.56	14,783	1,336.61
1950-51	8,581	1,865.02	6,401	918.14	14,982	1,460.47
1951-52	8,708	1,943.20	6,405	978.92	15,113	1,534.53
1952-53	8,744	2,109.38	6,480	1,153.66	15,224	1,702.58
1953-54	8,701	2,176.55	6,421	1,244.08	15,122	1,780.61
1954-55	8,732	2,447.64	6,550	1,814.99	15,282	2,176.48
1955-56	8,928	2,609.31	6,540	2,010.20	15,468	2,356.04
1956-57	9,105	2,681.28	6,590	2,115.86	15,695	2,443.87
1957-58	9,553	2,838.48	6,929	2,264.46	16,482	2,597.17
1958-59	9,662	3,362.61	6,775	2,677.50	16,437	3,080.21
1959-60	10,247	3,427.84	7,193	2,829.62	17,440	3,181.09
1960-61	10,542	3,689.27	7,537	3,141.02	18,079	3,460.61
1961-62	10,849	3,742.39	7,757	3,236.75	18,606	3,531.58
1962-63	11,016	3,767.88	7,959	3,298.64	18,975	3,571.05
1963-64	11,264	4,010.06	8,074	3,565.54	19,338	3,824.48
1964-65	11,456	4,320.64	8,385	3,895.24	19,841	4,140.86
1965-66	11,576	4,357.98	8,574	4,016.19	20,150	4,212.58

Appendix D

ANNUAL REPORT OF STATE SUPERINTENDENT H. R. PEASE TO THE LEGISLATURE OF THE STATE OF MISSISSIPPI FOR THE YEAR ENDING DECEMBER 31, 1871

To His Excellency, the Governor, and the Honorable Legislature of the State of Mississippi:

GENTLEMEN–In submitting the annual report required by law from the Superintendent of Public Education, permit me, first, to call your attention to a general view of the present condition of Public Education exhibited in the following summary, which has been carefully prepared from the reports of school officers, and such information as I have been able to obtain from other sources:

Number of civil school districts	75
Number of public schools	3,450
Number of graded schools	100
Number of high schools	80
Number of evening schools	60
Number of normal or training schools	2
Number of universities	2
Number of teachers employed in the public schools	3,600
Number of pupils enrolled in the public schools	117,000
Number of youth of legal school age	304,762
Number of students under tuition in normal schools	100
Number of private schools	460
Number of pupils enrolled in private schools	7,050
Average attendance in the public schools	90,000
Average length of school term	5 mos. 10 days
Number of superintendents	70
Number of school directors	450
Whole number of school officers (including treasures and secretaries)	659
Number of schoolhouses (including buildings rented)	3,450
Number of schoolhouses built since the inauguration of our school system, about	600
Total value of public school property	$800,000

SCHOOL FUNDS

Amount of the common school fund (including the funds appropriated under the Act of 1859, Chickasaw and sixteenth section funds, regarded as available)	$1,950,000
Amount of revenue received and paid into the treasury from the various sources provided by the constitution and laws enacted since its adoption, accruing to the common school fund	529,464
Amount of revenue by special county tax collected and paid into the county treasury–reported	683,784
Amount of the common school income fund, apportioned to the several counties	172,550
Average monthly salaries of teachers	50

EXPENDITURES

Amount expended for superintendents' salaries	$35,073
Estimated amount expended for salaries and mileage of school directors	50,000
Estimated amount expended for salaries of secretaries of the Boards of Directors	6,500
Total cost of the Boards of School Directors, estimated at	58,000
Estimated cost, including expenditures of all kinds	950,000

Appendix E

MISSISSIPPI HISTORICAL SOCIETY

LAW OF 1846

This law provided for—

1. A General School Commissioner whose duties shall be to keep all statistical matters pertaining to educational conditions of the state in his office and make a semi-annual report of this.

2. County superintendents who shall have the general supervision of the county schools and render an annual report to the General Commissioner. (Note: this was a special act passed in 1848, and applied only to Hinds Tunica, Jefferson, Wilkinson, and Amite counties.)

3. County school commissioners, five in each county, appointed by the Board of Police. They were to serve for one year, to hold quarterly meetings, elect a president and a secretary, adopt by-laws, decide what schools, issue licenses, employ teachers, etc.

4. A Board of Police to levy a special school tax, not more than one-fourth of the state tax, provided the majority of the heads of families gave their consent in writing.

5. Funds arising from sale or lease of sixteenth sections to be placed in the hands of Commissioners for school purposes.

6. All escheats, fines, forfeitures and all monies arising from licenses for the sale of spiritous liquors, or for licenses granted to peddlers, hawkers, brokers, etc., to be set apart for school purposes.

LAW OF 1870

This law provided for—

1. A State Superintendent of Education whose duties shall be to keep reports from various counties, make an annual report to the legislature, and have general supervision of all school interests of the state.

2. County superintendents, who shall have general supervision of county schools, make an annual report embracing certain information required by the State Superintendent regarding the number of educable children, the amount of school fund, etc.

3. Boards of school directors, consisting of six members. These were appointed by the Board of Supervisors and each held office for six years. The county superintendent was ex officio president of the board and the clerk of the Circuit Court was an ex officio secretary. They were to meet quarterly; to make all needful by-laws; to divide school districts into subdivisions where necessary; to secure school grounds, establish graded schools, etc.

4. A Board of Supervisors to levy a special tax as estimated by the County School Board, provided it was not more than fifteen mills.

5. Management of sixteenth section land by County Board and the appropriation of proceeds to school purposes.

6. All fines, forfeitures, and monies for licenses, as well as gifts for school purposes to be placed in the hands of the State Board.

Source:

Mississippi Historical Society Publications, XII, 85.

25 Missouri

DEPARTMENT OF EDUCATION

Raymond A. Roberts

Contents

IN THE BEGINNING, 1812-21

The Missouri Territory became a chartered subdivision of the "Louisiana Purchase" territory in 1812, and Congress granted land to the territory for the benefit of public education. During this early period, however, the schools were all church supported. They were financed by charities or operated as "subscription" schools on a "rate bill" basis, with the tuition set according to the number of a family's children attending school. The income from the land grants was used only to pay the tuition of the indigents and orphans. Since the church and the individual family were responsible for education, the Bible and the three R's constituted the curriculum.

The "rate bill," legalized by the territory, provided for a local trustee to contract with teachers, set and collect the rate bill, and pay all expenses incurred for education in the township. This mild form of taxation, the first school tax, was on the child rather than property. The school code or law of 1853 permitted taxation by a vote of the people who would pay the tax, but it did not provide for a school board or trustee to levy a tax. Therefore, the rate bill form of taxation continued in most schools until 1865. At this time, the Legislature passed an act giving the township trustees, appointed by county courts, the right to levy a tax for educational purposes.

If some parts of this chapter appear to be limited in comparison to others, it is a matter of value judgment, since the organization, selection of content, and personal observations were left largely to the discretion of the writer. Every attempt has been made to treat each period fairly and objectively within the limitations of time and space.

The bibliography reflects the main sources of references; however, much was gained by personal interviews with department personnel and other educators of long tenure in Missouri. I am particularly grateful for the personal knowledge and observation shared by Oscar G. Shupp, supervisor of statistics, Missouri State Department of Education, for the past 25 years. His help and counsel have been invaluable. I am indebted to Commissioner Hubert Wheeler for the opportunity to develop this paper; it has been one of the most interesting personal experiences in my career as an educator.

Under the Banner of Early Statehood, 1821-54

The act of Congress authorizing territorial authorities to frame a constitution for admission to statehood included provisions for an educational system to preserve school land from waste and establish public schools as soon as practical and possible. Anxious for statehood, the first Missouri constitutional convention, in 1820, incorporated all such ideas into the constitution. As stated by Carrington, "the state had accepted a responsibility. It knew not what" (1).

Legislation enacted in 1825 provided for one or more school districts per township, and for township trustees, appointed by county courts, to care for and preserve school lands and establish the schools.

The first semblance of a state school system emerged from several laws the Legislature enacted in the 1830's. The first, in 1835, provided for three trustees in every district, assigned specifically to employ teachers, to operate school for at least 6 months, and to approve the subjects taught. The 1837 Legislature established a $400,000 permanent school fund, and in 1842 the first state school money was apportioned from permanent funds interest. An act passed in 1839 provided for a state superintendent of schools to handle fiscal matters and license teachers.

The Governor appointed Peter Glover the first state superintendent of schools in 1839, and he served until the General Assembly abolished the office 2 years later. In 1841, the assembly assigned the superintendency's limited duties to the secretary of state, who performed them until 1854. The three men serving as secretary of state during this period did an excellent job in promoting public education. E. B. Ewing, who served the last 4 years, from 1850 to 1854, was particularly interested im improving property taxation for operating the public schools. Evidently, he was instrumental in the 1853 legislation that reestablished the office of state superintendent the following year.

Vacillation to Stabilization, 1854-75

In 1854, the Governor appointed John W. Henry, a lawyer, to be state superintendent of schools for a 2-year term. He resigned after a few months because he believed the office should be held by a "school man." The Governor then appointed an educator, E. C. Davis, who served 2 years.

Davis was replaced by W. B. Starke, who served from 1856 to 1861, when the Legislature again abolished the office as a war measure. However, in 1859, Superintendent Starke was responsible for distributing the first elementary course of study. Superintendent Starke also was largely responsible for replacing the log schoolhouses with what he termed the box-car frame schoolhouse, usually 24 feet by 30 feet in dimension—generally known as the "little red school house." The Civil War forced most of the schools to close; however, Starke's influence for a graded school system and box-like structure continued to be felt in some areas during the war.

After the Civil War, such buildings became the accepted structure and continued to be used until after World War I. (The writer attended school in such a structure and began his teaching career in a building of this kind in 1927.)

The 1865 constitution provided for reestablishing the Office of State Superintendent of Schools. The Governor appointed T. A. Parker as state superintendent in 1866, and he served 5 years. Superintendent Parker, a progressive educator, prompted the 1866 and 1867 Legislatures to deviate from the status quo. Carrington wrote, "It tore up the past and substituted too many new things at once .... The returned soldiers want peace in their old homes and schools carried on as they left them" (2).

Among the most important changes effected by the 1866 revised school law was the requirement that free schools be maintained in every inhabited portion of the state and that there be an equalization of the taxation burden upon all persons and property for support of schools. It stated that the supervision of schools would be dictated by the course of instruction. Not only would grade schools be established, but there would be free education for the state's colored children.

Although there was resistance to the progressive, farsighted Parker administration, it made considerable progress in new buildings, obtained additional financial support, and improved certification and instruction. Parker's demands on the Legislature and general public for better support of the public school system resulted in large measure from an increase in the school population by over 170,000 from 1865 to 1867, much of which was due to immigration.

Ira Divoll, a former superintendent of the St. Louis public schools and an attorney, succeeded Parker. Superintendent Divoll was forced to resign after 1 year in office because of his health, and the Governor appointed John Monteith, a minister and teacher from Iron County, to complete the 4-year term. Monteith's policies were the opposite of Parker's aggressiveness, and he assumed a pastoral attitude and a "soft" approach.

From all indications, at this time a renewed system of state public education emerged and was reaffirmed as a state function. Superintendent Monteith gave evidence of this in 1874, when he wrote:

> I would do violence to my own feelings were I to fail to acknowledge the hearty cooperation of the teachers and school officers of the State, and the kind courtesies of two General Assemblies, in the discharge of the pleasant but arduous duties which three years have imposed (3).

The Monteith administration did work arduously. When a constitutional convention was called in 1874, public education demanded prominent and careful consideration. A "new law" regarding colored schools and a civil rights bill added to the complexities of his administration. In 1874, he wrote:

> The new law, like the old, is very stringent in its requirements of school directors to establish colored schools where in any district the number of children exceeds fifteen, or where the whole enumeration in the township reaches that number. Further than this, the law provides that the combination of children may be made across township lines, or in any manner in which the directors may expend the public fund for the object for which it is set apart. For the failure to provide suitable accommodations for the colored children, school directors may be subjected to a fine of from fifty to five hundred dollars. To provide a remedy for the children in case of such failure, the law gives the State Superintendent the full power of local boards to levy tax, build school houses, and perform any other duty necessary to accomplish the desired end .... It may be well to soothe our excited feelings by carefully considering what the natural results of the passage of this bill would be unaided by any purposed effort.
>
> Is it conceivable that the interests of 700,000 white school population could be sacrificed by any attempt to give forced prominence to the interests of 38,000 colored school population? If such a result could be conceived it would involve an astonishing infraction of that law of evolution or natural selection which in the progress of civilization has ever given the victory to the strongest. The first effect of the civil rights mixed school bills would be to arouse an intense hostility to the blacks in every portion of this State; and so far from entering the white schools, it is reasonable to believe that they would be driven to a closer aggregation and to more strictly separate schools under the sting of an offended public sentiment. The bill therefore would leave the white schools about as they are now, and result in a very serious crippling of the colored schools, if not in their extinction.

> The best interests of the colored people lie in the direction of separate schools established by law. But if this separate system is continued, it is well for every community to reflect that it can only succeed upon the basis of equal advantages to both classes (4).

John Monteith wanted to continue in office, but in 1875, Dr. R. D. Shannon received the appointment. Dr. Shannon, an educator from St. Joseph, Missouri, with a master's degree in education, also had a degree in medicine. The son of a Missouri university president, Dr. Shannon was serving at the time of his selection as private secretary to Governor Silas Woodson, his brother-in-law.

Shortly after he assumed office, Superintendent Shannon helped the 1875 constitutional convention change the school law. When the Legislature threatened to abolish the state teacher colleges during his administration, he staunchly defended the colleges and persuaded the public to continue them. He also proposed legislation to give adequate taxation for public education. Dr. Shannon was noted for his ability to use groups to solve current problems in education.

The following excerpts give evidence of his unyielding efforts for good education.

> The apportionment of State school money has been made in exact proportion to the enumeration of school population reported to this office. There can be no compact system without unison of effort . . . . There can not be cooperation without clearly defined and simple laws . . . . The people of the State will remain ignorant to needs until their school officials are rigidly required to perform their whole duty . . . . On taking charge of public school interests there was committed to me a trust, by courtesy called a system . . . . It was a system without a system (5).

Dr. Shannon was an honest, able administrator. In fact, he even took to the county grand juries the matter of inaccurate reporting and the refusal of district clerks to report to his office. The circuit judges tended to support him in rectifying the apathetic attitudes of the district clerks.

It is evident that the radical action of Parker, the pastoral approach by Monteith, followed by the fearless administrative ability of Shannon, all contributed equally to the stabilization of a vacillating state system of education previous to, during, and following the first test of national unity–the Civil War.

A Statewide System Emerges, 1875-98

The adoption of a new constitution in 1875 marked a new epoch in the history of Missouri and proved to be beneficial to a state system of education–still under the direction of Dr. Shannon. The office of state superintendent became stabilized by a legal directive of this constitution. The constitution directed that the state superintendent of schools continue to be elected for a 4-year term as were other state elective officials and that the General Assembly appropriate one-fourth of general revenue annually for school purposes, out of which the State Department of Education was to be supported. Heretofore, the Legislature decided the amount of funded moneys every 2 years.

Dr. Shannon wrote:

> The New Constitution just adopted contains some objectionable features, it has made some commendable advances, and places our public school system upon a surer basis than any on which it has ever before rested. The article on education in the new is a decided improvement on the same article in the old, or the Constitution of 1865. The last named instrument left much to the discretion of the legislature; such as providing for the support of schools out of the general revenue, etc. The New Constitution directs such support. In nearly every feature in which the old was permissory and under which an inimical legislature might seriously cripple our school interests, the present Constitution is mandatory, and leaves the legislature no hurtful power (6).

In the second half of his 8 years of tenure in rather difficult times, Superintendent Shannon optimistically reported to Governor John S. Phelps in January 1879 that–

1. A more general interest in State education had been manifested by the people;
2. A more cheerful feeling and better attendance prevailed;
3. More diligence to manage schools according to law was evident;
4. A greater number of qualified teachers caused improved education; and
5. A revival of interest on the part of teachers in associations and institutes prevailed (7).

The administration of Superintendent W. E. Coleman began in 1882. Coleman continued Dr. Shannon's struggle to clarify and coordinate the school laws. He wrote in 1888: "The entire school law should be revised . . . for fifteen years the laws have been patched, amended and repealed. Teachers, school officers and taxpayers are bewildered" (8). He also spoke out frankly about poor financial accounting, hiring of the "cheapest" teacher, lack of county school supervision, terms of less than 6 months, apathy of teachers, and the teaching of German or French as the first language. His two terms represented a sincere effort to improve public education.

In 1890, L. E. Wolfe, superintendent of Moberly public schools, took office as state superintendent with the intent of improving the elementary schools. At this time, the state had approximately 10,000 elementary school districts, and fewer than 100 schools in them offered a graded school course. Evidently, strong prejudices still existed against uniformity in public education.

Wolfe began by developing a much-needed graded course of study for the elementary schools and encouraged its implementation. This 1892 course of study for the elementary schools constituted a first in Missouri. Wolfe also emphasized the value of school libraries as a means of improving instruction. He developed a Teachers' Reading Circle program, which required that teachers read a certain number of books in psychology, pedagogy, science, history, geography, and literature as a part of an in-service training program. The books were purchased and circulated by the Missouri State Teachers Association. This cooperative program not only benefited the teachers but placed L. E. Wolfe in high professional standing. He evidently was a better educator than he was a politician. The Democratic convention selected, instead of Wolfe, W. T. Carrington, superintendent of schools at Mexico, Missouri, to run for state superintendent on the Democratic ticket. But a split still occurred in the Democratic party. As a result, Carrington was defeated by a good friend and college classmate, John R. Kirk, a Republican (a lawyer turned educator, superintendent of schools at Westport, now a part of Kansas City). John Kirk was the first Republican to be elected to a state office in 22 years in Missouri (9). He struck a new note in the educational campaign of the state.

It was reported by G. A. Theilmann "that it was apparent from the time Kirk took office that his aim was to make the highest possible use of existing instrumentalities" (10). From his reporting and public addresses, it is evident that he possessed a very broad viewpoint regarding state education. His interest and activities ranged from sanitation in the schools to improved school architecture, from improving elementary education to better teacher training at the college and university levels, from better methods of instructing the normal child to encouraging special education for the estimated 3,000 atypical children known at this time, and from proposing a college preparatory course to courses such as agriculture for work-bound pupils. He even proposed centralization of schools, free pupil transportation, and free textbooks in this early day. He was defeated for reelection by Carrington in 1898—the Democrats had got together again. (Carrington later worked for Kirk's appointment to the presidency of Northeast Missouri State Teachers College at Kirksville, Missouri.)

In Kirk's last report to the General Assembly in 1898, he ended by stating, "Competent judges of educational progress agree that education in Missouri is steadily assuming a more highly organized form" (11). No doubt he was disappointed in his defeat for the second term, but a review of his record as president of the Kirksville State Teachers College (1899-1925) indicates that his contributions to the progress of education far exceeded what he could have accomplished as state superintendent. Mr. Kirk, as he was called even by his friends, was always a gentleman and scholar, and he was highly motivated by his many interests in education and the welfare of the masses.

TURN OF THE CENTURY, 1898-1911

At the turn of the century, leadership of the state school system remained in the hands of W. T. Carrington. It is apparent from his writings and addresses that he intended to carry on the policies and philosophy of his predecessor, John Kirk. His campaign slogan became his basic aim when elected: "A school for every child—every child in school, good teachers, higher salaries, better schools, equal taxation, and equal opportunities for all children" (12).

The State Board of Education permitted Superintendent Carrington to employ a deputy and clerk in addition to his own clerk. Carrington exercised considerable leadership in improving and expanding education, and he gained substantial aid from various lay groups. The Missouri Federation of Women's Clubs, for example, united to support a kindergarten movement. (The first public school kindergarten in the nation was established in St. Louis in 1874.) The interest and work of this organization finally resulted in the first compulsory school attendance law enacted by the General Assembly in 1905. (It is interesting to note here that a permissive kindergarten law was finally passed by the General Assembly in 1967.) The General Assembly of 1901 passed a law authorizing the state superintendent to classify public high schools and to improve the grading of the rural school. The University of Missouri supplied a part-time high school inspector. The superintendent and his chief clerk inspected the rural schools. Carrington and his staff also developed a state course of study, grades 1-12, with subject matter outlined by weeks and quarters.

In 1901, Carrington wrote:

> Culture, discipline, information and utility are duly united in these courses. Isolation of both subjects and purpose has given way to unity in both theory and practice .... Everywhere students of pedagogy and supervisors of instruction have gradually seen the necessity of adjusting the work of the school to the child, rather than adjusting the child to a preconceived notion of what school should be (13).

The 1901 General Assembly, on the recommendation of Superintendent Carrington, passed legislation authorizing county boards of education, traditionally called commissioners, with certain supervisory powers: conducting teacher examinations, granting certificates, grading and classifying schools, and conducting teacher institutes. It was evident from the beginning that the county boards elected would not be qualified to perform such duties effectively. Carrington, therefore, recommended that the boards be authorized to hire a competent county supervisor or superintendent—the county unit form of school organization.

This phase of the legislation was rejected, apparently because of the people's fear of one-man rule. It is obvious, however, that Carrington's emphasis resulted in some county boards' employing a county supervisor to carry out their duties.

Superintendent Carrington wrote:

> Nine Missouri counties have supervision. Within the past three years I have made a close study of the school work in these counties and have made comparisons with counties similarly situated not having supervision. I am quite certain that the rural schools in counties having supervision are more uniformly well classified and graded. There is more definiteness of purpose, the teachers work with better spirit, the pupils are more regular and prompt in attendance, and the people manifest more concern for the general educational welfare (14).

Carrington's interest continued, and 4 years later he again urged efficient supervision of rural schools. He recommended that the Legislature provide every county with a school supervisor, with at least one assistant in large and populous counties. He stated that it should fix high qualifications and safeguard the selection so as to put only trained and experienced teachers in this position. He argued that it was better not to have it than to fill it with time servers and persons lacking scholarship, leadership, and pedagogical training. He wrote:

> Fix the salary high enough to commend the best talent and demand results. Make the duties more administrative and pedagogical than clerical. Give the supervisor authority to nominate teachers and transfer them for cause, such as is given to city superintendents. Constitute a special county board composed of business men to employ a supervisor on merit, as one who would build a good house would employ an architect to make plans and superintend its construction. Do not shift the responsibility to the people to determine whether they want such position. It should not be treated as an office. It should be filled by the employment of an expert to perform technical duties (15).

During this period, the state department was financed by apportionments by the General Assembly from the state school fund, which constituted one-fourth of the state general revenue. In the 1900 *State Blue Book*, an official state publication issued biennially by the secretary of state, Superintendent Carrington wrote that Missouri enjoyed the eminent distinction of having the largest available public school fund of any state in the American Union. The fund amounted to more than $12 million. There is no valid evidence on record to support this statement, but the photostatic copy from the Fiftieth Missouri Report of Public Schools, 1899, does support the statement of the funds available in Missouri.

Table 1. – GENERAL STATISTICS

SCHOOL FUND

State certificates of indebtedness at 6 percent	$ 2,909,000.00
State certificates of indebtedness at 5 percent	249,000.00
Cash in treasury	973.40
Total amount of state school fund	3,158,973.40
Seminary certificates at 6 percent	122,000.00
Seminary certificates at 5 percent	1,112,839.42
Cash in treasury to credit of seminary fund	1,181.46
Total seminary fund	1,236,020.83
Permanent county public school funds	4,296,035.23
Permanent township public school funds	3,678,254.07
Permanent special district funds	87,959.11
Total county, township, and district funds	8,052,248.41
Total school funds	$12,447,242.69

The state fund can be increased only by grant, gift, devise, or direct appropriation by the General Assembly.

The county public school fund is increased annually by the net proceeds of fines, penalties, forfeitures, estrays, and the sale of swamp lands.

The township school fund is annually increased by the sale of such part of the sixteenth section as yet remains in the market and is held in trust by the township.

Special district funds are such as have been secured to a district by a grant, gift, devise, or special legislation.

Superintendent Carrington left the office to assume the presidency of Southwest Missouri State Teachers College, Springfield, in 1907. He was succeeded by his chief clerk, Howard A. Gass.

Superintendent Gass entered the office with a working knowledge of public education in Missouri, since he had served as Carrington's chief clerk in two former administrations. During his administration, the General Assemblies enacted legislation placing more responsibility on the department for supervision of instruction and also appropriated funds for additional department personnel. Legislation in 1907 required that a county superintendent be elected in each county to replace the heretofore ineffective county board or county commissioners. A sum of $400 annually was appropriated from the state school fund as a part of the county superintendent's salary. It was recognized that this office was basically responsible for county supervision, but it also proved to be of aid and support to the state department in regulatory and supervisory functions and in statewide reporting.

A law was passed in 1907 on uniformity of county textbook adoption. This law directed that (a) a county commission of three persons be appointed to select books for the county schools–the state superintendent was authorized to appoint one member, and (b) the state department file a report of all textbooks sold in Missouri. A filing fee, listing of prices, performance bond, and contract were required of all companies doing business in Missouri. Additional department personnel were not provided for by the law for its implementation.

The following statement written by Superintendent Carrington indicates that he, rather than Gass, established the political climate for the enactment of a state textbook law; however, it should be noted again that Superintendent Gass was formerly Superintendent Carrington's chief clerk and received support from the Carrington factions.

> Settle the textbook question and if possible settle it permanently. The present situation is very unsatisfactory. It is as bad as it was two and four years ago, when there was strong demand for relief from the use of a few objectionable books that had been on the list many years. The last General Assembly acted wisely in repealing all laws regulating textbook adoption rather than let a law stand that fastened for an indefinite time the use of out-of-date and objectionable books. Teachers and people are practically unanimous in demanding uniformity. They differ somewhat as to whether adoptions should be by State, county or local authority. You perhaps know public sentiment better than I; yet, I am quite positive in the belief that a large majority of both teachers and patrons prefer State uniformity for rural and village schools. I am more positive in believing it best for the schools and in the interest of economy (16).

In the implementation of the new textbook law, Superintendent Gass explained that it provided for county uniformity of textbooks to be selected by a county commission. In counties not having supervision, this commission would be composed of the county board of education (in counties having supervision, of the county superintendent), one member appointed by the county court, and one appointed by the state board. Before a book could be considered for adoption by any such commission, it had to be filed, together with sworn agreements as to the price, to the fact that books equal in quality to the one filed would be furnished Missouri schools, affidavits as to the ownership of the publishing house and as to any interests held by the publishing house or its shareholders in other publishing houses, affidavits setting forth that no agreement to control the price of books had been entered into, and a bond for the faithful execution of all contracts. Up to December 1907, there had been filed under the provisions of this law 3,585 separate volumes.

Gass pointed out that the law also stipulated that a filing fee of $10 was required for each book or series of books filed. Series having many volumes, such as several series of classics with as many as 200 or 300 separate volumes, would be filed upon payment of one fee. The Legislature's purpose in requiring this filing fee was not to exclude any book from consideration, but to provide some revenue to pay the expenses connected with the filing and care of the books. Up to December 1907, these fees amounted to $6,150. Gass concluded:

> The law does not entirely fulfill the expectations of its friends. Its opponents have much fault fo find with it. But it is the law governing the selection and use of textbooks in this State, and all good citizens will unite in carrying out as nearly as may be the intent of the Legislature, and in making the law as effective as possible (17).

Since the enactment of this law, each successive superintendent apparently has applied the law as a service to public school administrators and to textbook companies doing business in Missouri. During the past 12 years, the writer has administered this law but feels that it has served its purpose and day. Fewer than 10 districts in the state (out of about 800 total districts) have made inquiry regarding the fulfillment of the law by textbook companies. It is reported, by those old enough to recall, that the enactment was actually passed to prevent some companies from selling at a lower rate to the larger city districts than to the village rural districts. It is a "nuisance" law today and serves no particular purpose.

Superintendent Gass reported in the Sixty-First Missouri Report of Public Schools in 1910 that additional office equipment had been purchased–four stacks of filing cases, one multigraph, one adding machine, one typewriter, one clock, and three office chairs; total cost was about $1,500.

The new multigraph made it possible to send thousands of circular letters to school board members, teachers, patrons, and organizations regarding the improvement of public education. Reporting during this period indicates that this represented the first concentrated effort to enlist by mailings the cooperation of agencies and organizations in solving educational problems.

Gass was defeated in 1911 by an excellent educator, William E. Evans, from St. Louis. The administration of Superintendent Evans is most noted for placing teacher training in the high schools and for apportioning public school funds on the basis of teacher training and school attendance rather than on the basis of school enumeration. The practice of state school surveys or descriptive research was begun at this time. The Carnegie Foundation was asked by the State Board of Education to make a study in 1911 for the purpose of upgrading teacher training and certification. As a result of this survey, sponsored by the state board and teachers colleges, changes in the teacher-training programs were made to meet the needs disclosed by the study. The study revealed that the majority of the teachers had not taken training beyond the high school level. The college training program also was modified to provide training more appropriate for rural teachers.

All reporting and accounting forms were prepared by the state department—38 different forms were prepared—and 1 million copies of various materials were distributed annually. (Sixty years later the department has its own printing room, fully equipped and staffed to print and distribute all printed material with the exception of bound books and curriculum guides. In comparison to the 38 forms printed in 1911-12, the department printed and distributed 278 different forms in 1965.)

The Forty-Sixth and Forty-Seventh General Assemblies passed legislation placing additional responsibility on the state department without making provisions for additional personnel. For instance, a 1911 law required transportation at public expense of schoolchildren living more than 2 miles from school. Another 1911 law limited the amount of state aid on the basis of less than 14 pupils average daily attendance, and the assembly also passed a school consolidation law. At the same time, the assembly provided state aid of $750 annually for first-class high schools offering teacher training—167 high schools—and $2,000 for agriculture, buildings, and auditoriums. The following year, in 1912, it passed a free textbook law for grades 1 through 8 and raised teacher certification requirements. Another law provided for the county school boards to hold an annual conference—all expenses paid.

In 1912, the General Assembly permitted state school money to be invested in approved drainage bonds which were sold to provide funds for draining the river bottoms, thus enhancing their value. It then appropriated one-third of the general revenue of the state for public schools. Money for the operation of the department came from this source and also constituted the first time an amount above the one-fourth required by law had been appropriated. (The practice of appropriating additional moneys over one-fourth was continued until 1945. A 1945 constitutional change directed that one-third of the general revenue be appropriated annually.)

Superintendent Evans' statement in the Sixty-Second Annual Report to the General Assembly in 1911 reflected additional participation by department members in summer school sessions and county teacher fall institutes. Evans apparently continued the practice of his predecessor in soliciting the support of existing organizations interested in education—the Grange Mothers, Rural Life Commission, Parents and Teachers Cooperative Clubs, P.E.O. Clubs, and the Women's Federated Clubs were approached.

Superintendent Evans ended his administration as a supporter of the county unit, a state educational tax, equalization in apportioning school moneys, vocational education, school consolidation, additional rural schools for Negro children, state aid for school libraries, improved school architecture, and practice teaching performed in public schools.

The 4-year tenure of Superintendent Evans could be described as an interval of change in state school administration; however, political influence of the existing educational "establishment" of Carrington and Gass continued to be felt. The educational climate remained favorable in general, and worthwhile innovations previously mentioned were accepted by the people. Writings of the time, however, indicate that the Legislature (Democrat majority—Evans was a Republican) failed to reflect the enthusiasm of the people and the professionals so as to cause the department to become a more effective division of the state government. The issue of local versus state control was reflected in the legislative records.

In the final analysis, the legislative action was typical of times to follow—vote for change but resistance to funding for full implementation. Evans was apparently a political accident. He was evidently elected by the enthusiasm of large-city voters and the apathy of rural voters in an off-year election—the state had joined the Republican ranks.

The organizational plan of the State Department of Education during this time remained basically the same as the 1907-14 plan. (See Appendix B.)

WORLD WAR I, REORGANIZATION, AND A "NEW" EDUCATION, 1912-23

The educational "establishment" prevailed in Missouri during the First World War. Former State Superintendent Gass ran against Evans in 1915 and was again elected. He died 9 months after taking office. Uel W. Lamkin, county superintendent of schools, Clinton, Missouri, was appointed by Governor Elliott Major to serve the remainder of the term. Superintendent Lamkin had served as W. T. Carrington's chief clerk in 1907-1909 and was noted to be a man who possessed the qualities of a "progressive" and had the courage to support his convictions. He recognized, in assuming the duties of the office, that the urgencies of the war should be given priority over innovative ideas in education; however, as the war efforts lessened in the latter part of his administration, his foresight and support of better educational opportunities for children and youth became evident.

He obtained state funding in 1918 for the implementation of the Smith-Hughes Act of 1917, which provided matching funds for vocational education. This constituted a first in education in Missouri—a particular phase of the school program supported by federal funding. There was little if any opposition to the passage of the Missouri Vocational Bill enacted by the General Assembly in 1918.

The heat of patriotism and evidence of the lack of vocational training of World War I inductees prevailed.

In a report to the General Assembly, Lamkin wrote:

> From a State viewpoint, the question of revenue to meet the grants of the National government for education is a serious one and should challenge the careful attention of the Legislature. The grants should be matched by State or local funds (18).

The issue of state versus federal control appeared on the horizon. From all indications, then as now, matching federal grants were questioned by those who represented state and local autonomy concepts, but the majority of the districts complied.

In a letter to Superintendent Lamkin in June 1918, Governor Frederick D. Gardner requested that a study of rural schools be made by the department. Acting on the counsel of the state board, Lamkin planned and administered the first state rural school survey. Abner Jones, an authority in rural education, was hired to direct this first research study of rural education. Jones died during the formative stages of the study. The study was then conducted by A. G. Capps of the University of Missouri at Columbia, who later became a nationally recognized authority on rural education. The data compiled served as the basic information in the study and research for future legislative acts pertaining to all phases of state education. The major recommendations were as follows:

1. That the State Board of Education be composed of five, seven, or nine men and women of broad scholarship, appointed by the Governor. Their powers and duties were also described.
2. That the state superintendent be appointed by the board.
3. That county superintendents be appointed by a county board of education.
4. That the tax burden for educational purposes be more equally distributed.
5. That a system of supervision of school building be established at the local and state levels.
6. That rural teachers receive salaries comparable to village and city teachers.
7. That the compulsory school laws be better enforced at the rural level.
8. That state courses of study continue to be developed to ensure attainable standards in all subjects.
9. That a countywide system of standardized testing be developed.
10. That the school term be extended beyond the present term of 8 months.
11. That a plan for reorganization of school districts be developed (19).

Had the fortunes of politics—the state again joined the Republican ranks, and Lamkin was a Democrat—not prevented Lamkin from continuing his work as superintendent, it is quite possible that many of the reforms recommended in the study would have become a reality one generation sooner. Lamkin was a fearless innovator.

Superintendent Lamkin ended his administration in a prophetic manner. In his last annual report to the General Assembly in 1918, he wrote: "If, and when a new constitution for Missouri is written, a State Board of Education, appointed by the Governor, should have the power to name the State Superintendent of Schools" (20). He further advocated reorganization of the school districts, legislation to equalize the financing of public education, and extension of vocational education as an integral part of the high school curriculum.

Lamkin continued to support his beliefs during his long tenure as president of Northwest State College from 1921 to 1946 and lived to see each of his major recommendations enacted upon by successive General Assemblies. His administration constituted the beginning of contemporary state education in Missouri from the standpoint of structure, organization, and philosophy.

A "New" Education, 1919-23

Sam A. Baker, formerly superintendent of Jefferson City public schools, defeated incumbent Uel W. Lamkin. Theilmann wrote: "Superintendent Sam A. Baker was conservative enough to please the most cautious and boldly aggressive enough to put forth a wise educational policy which the spirit of the times most willingly accepts" (21).

Baker wrote under the topic of "new education" in his report to the General Assembly in 1921:

> The new education is not merely stuffing the mind with facts, but it is the use of the mind in accomplishing a worthy deed. Do the thing and you will have the power. The gap of discouragement that lies between the close of a school course and the successful entrance into the work of life is fast being eliminated. The preparation of the schools is forming an easy path to join hands with the practical world . . . . Filling the mind with facts is only a small part of education. Thinking by use of these facts is only a small additional gain of power. The full value of true education first blooms out when thoughts are verified by material accomplishment. The plowing of a field, the building of a house, the making of a garment, the construction of a machine, require the true processes of education. The word "deed" spells education (22).

Superintendent Baker's idealistic approach to state education coincided with reality and the spirit of the times—Missourians were ready to move forward in education. His legislative program for improvement of education was successful in part because his predecessor, Lamkin, had set the stage for contemporary education through studies and committee reports.

New Laws Enacted

During Superintendent Baker's administration, the Legislature of 1921 passed many progressive school laws. The Missouri School of the Blind and the Missouri School of the Deaf were classed as educational institutions. Lincoln Institute was made a university. Instruction on care and hygiene of teeth was made compulsory. High school training was provided for Negro children, and a Negro inspector of schools was to be appointed by the state superintendent. State aid for teacher-training high schools was increased 100 percent; maximum wages and state aid for rural schools were increased 50 percent. Free county libraries could be established by law. A 4-year high school course was required for all teachers, and all teachers were required to secure a health certificate from a reputable physician. Ninth and tenth grades could be taught in local districts. A law provided for the rehabilitation of injured persons, and a physical education law was passed (23).

Although Lamkin and Baker represented different political parties, they had one thing in common—great personal appeal. They recognized and emphasized the economic and social factors involved in the progress of public education. Each believed in equal educational opportunity for all pupils. Each recognized the political power structure (political factions centered in the two larger cities) as an effective factor in school legislation.

A switch from a Republican to a Democratic administration in 1923 ended Baker's career as state superintendent. He was defeated by Charles A. Lee, superintendent of Butler public schools. The Baker administration had achieved effective growth of the department as a state service agency. Six new sections were added to the department during Baker's tenure: Negro education, vocational agriculture, vocational home economics, vocational trades-industries, physical education, and rehabilitation.

Superintendent Baker was the first and only superintendent to be elected Governor. His interest and influence in education were sustaining and were reflected in the progress of the public schools during his term as Governor, from 1925 to 1929. It should be noted that his opponent for superintendent in 1925, Lee, a Democrat, was reelected during Baker's term as Governor. A cooperative spirit between the two men was reflected in obtaining school legislation.

THE COMING OF CONTEMPORARY STATE EDUCATION, 1923-47

Lee was the first state superintendent to occupy the office for three elective terms, 1923 to 1935. His tenure provided many opportunities for continuity in planning that were heretofore impossible. Many recommendations and projections of former state superintendents became a reality through his dynamic leadership.

This period marked a turning point in the method of financing education in Missouri—the first major change since 1900. After extensive research and study, the 1931 School Law was enacted by the General Assembly. Basically, this law provided for an equalization method of financing the public schools and further provided for county redistricting boards to lay out optional, enlarged districts.

The 1931 School Law had its origin in a series of conferences called by Lee, beginning in 1923 and continuing through 1928—a professional committee, an advisory lay committee, and a conference of the presidents of state educational institutions. Their statewide study was financed by the Missouri State Teachers Association. A staff was employed, and priority problems were identified by the committees. Among the five basic problems were school support and educational needs. The individual committees and staff, working under the direction of department personnel, were concerned basically about the relation of wealth and income to all kinds of expenditures, including education in different classes and size of schools, and sources of revenue—state, federal, and local. The state department provided excellent leadership and implemented follow-through procedures to enactment of the law.

Legislative enactment also strengthened the county superintendent's office by requiring higher qualifications. Superintendent Lee and his staff were responsible for a major curriculum revision including the revision of all subjects—elementary and secondary—as a cooperative enterprise with the university. The services of the state department were extended through the addition of staff.

After the enactment of the 1931 School Law, Lee directed the writing of an extensive annual report to the General Assembly in 1932. This publication was the first and only such report that included narrative and statistical reporting of all schools in each of the 114 counties—the report contained 1,656 pages. Such reporting was beneficial at the time in bringing about a consensus of support of the 1931 law and its ramifications, as well as stimulating greater interest in the state's educational system. Radio education also served as a means of informing the people about educational problems and progress. This medium also was used in many schools as a new method in the classroom. Superintendent Lee inaugurated, in 1928, an official *Department of Education Bulletin*, which was issued monthly. This bulletin included educational announcements, professional writings, regulatory dates for reporting, new laws, and statistical information.

Lee embraced national trends and applied them to the state. He was a man of conviction, commitment, and involvement. His professional behavior was reflected in local school administration during his tenure. Progress in education during this era in Missouri was largely due to Lee's leadership. He was first an educator and second a politician. Although he was dependent on the political aspects as an elected official, he never confused the two on the platform.

After his tenure as superintendent, Lee continued to affect education in Missouri as professor of education at Washington University, St. Louis, for almost 30 years. His influence on education—12 years as the chief school officer—is still often recalled by present-day educators as the coming of contemporary education in Missouri.

Lee ran for a fourth term against Lloyd King, superintendent of schools, Monroe City, Missouri, in the 1934 primary and was defeated. Here, again, the political power structures of the two larger cities renewed their factional struggle and affected the election of the superintendent.

The tenure of Superintendent King, 1935 to 1943, included reconstruction programs following the Depression of the thirties and the involvements of World War II. His term encompassed education for economic stability, wartime problems, and education for the peace to follow. Such societal changes required a cooperative effort of all institutions. King unified the various educational agencies and organizations through the establishment and utilization of advisory committees of lay and educational leaders. The following advisory committees reflected this unifying effort:

Educational Conference (presidents of all state colleges and universities)

County superintendents (14 county superintendents)

City superintendents (12 city superintendents)

Educational research (5 leading research people in the state)

Vocational education for war production (14 leading lay citizens, WPA Educational Program)

School board members (12 leading board members)

Education for Negroes (50 members—educators and laymen)

Curriculum development (committees at all levels and subjects; membership of each including teachers, administrators, and college and university personnel).

The committees aided in the development of educational research studies, a most extensive development of courses of study, and educational bulletins at all levels during the forties—"Missouri at Work on the Curriculum" became a well-known theme in curriculum development and remains as a present-day guideline.

The following, a partial listing of publications, reflects the results of this cooperative effort:

Wartime Program for Missouri Schools

Guidance Handbook (the first in Missouri)

Victory Garden Program for Missouri Schools

Speech Education for Missouri–Forum Education

Missouri Schools and National Defense

Foreign Languages

Elementary Course of Study (1,319 pages–respectfully referred to by teachers as the "King's Bible," notably because it resembled the Bible in shape and size)

Wartime Training Program for Business Executives

Radio Education

In addition to these, over fifty other educational publications were developed and distributed. A new monthly official department publication, *Missouri Schools,* was inaugurated in 1935 by King. This periodical remains today as the official department publication.

Superintendent King introduced a system of school-district financial accounting of all school funds. It was in 1942 that the 1931 School Law's principle of equalization was fully financed at the first level.

During this period, the State Board of Education was again designated by the General Assembly to act as the board to administer federal laws on behalf of the state and was authorized to incur expenses for the administration of federal programs. The Works Progress Administration education program and other such programs were implemented in the schools under this enactment.

The state department made giant strides under the skillful leadership and cooperative spirit of Superintendent King in its progress toward becoming one of the most important divisions of the state government.

In his final report to the General Assembly in 1942, Superintendent King wrote:

> If the school of the future is to play an important role in American society, it must offer a dynamic program of education and be able and willing to play an important role in social engineering. The school must train its students in the practice of democracy to insure a lasting peace (24).

Superintendent King was defeated in 1942 for a third term by his Republican opponent, Roy Scantlin, county superintendent of Newton County. The political power structure of the larger cities again affected the election of a superintendent. A relatively unknown, untried candidate defeated a well-known, effective school administrator. There was a "rumble" among Missouri educators to get education in Missouri out of politics. It never reached the proportions of being a slogan like that during the good-roads program in the twenties—"Get Missouri out of the Mud"—but the feeling and fever never subsided. This feeling affected the changes made in the 1945 constitutional convention.

The emergencies and involvements of World War II were increasingly felt in the schools during the Scantlin administration—in certification of teachers, inadequate replacement of teaching equipment and materials, replacement of transportation, and building facilities. It was a time when innovations in education could only be anticipated and previous gains held under very adverse conditions.

The General Assembly in 1944 voted to call a constitutional convention, the first since 1875. When the convention was called, it was immediately recognized that the school laws would constitute one of the major changes. The convention asked Superintendent Scantlin and his staff to assist in the revision of 243 sections of law and to aid in the writing of the new proposals regarding the office of state superintendent. Scantlin exhibited excellent leadership in this process.

Scantlin, being of a rural background in personal and professional experience, deemed it advisable to conduct a follow-up study of the first rural education study. He appointed A. G. Capps, professor of education at the University of Missouri and director of the earlier study during Lamkin's administration, to direct the 1943 study.

As a result of the 1943 follow-up study, the 1945 General Assembly enacted major changes in the 1931 school finance laws. This study also served later as a basis for the 1947 School District Reorganization Law.

As the adverse conditions to education ended with the close of World War II, a new epoch in education came into being—education was at last out of politics.

The 1945 constitution provided for a State Board of Education appointed by the Governor and confirmed by the Senate (eight members, bipartisan). The chief state school officer was to be hereafter selected by this board. Superintendent Scantlin ended his tenure of one term of 4 years with the distinction of being the last elected superintendent.

Historically, the concept of the appointment of a chief state school officer had its origin in the 1918 annual report to the General Assembly by State Superintendent Lamkin, who had said that when a new constitution is written, a State Board of Education, appointed by the Governor, should have the power to name the State Superintendent of Schools (25).

This concept was again emphasized by the 1929 Missouri School Survey Committee in its report to State Superintendent Lee and the General Assembly:

> There are two elements in the situation, as affecting the administration of the public schools of the State, that need to be revised. It is not possible to secure from an ex officio board the same attention to the needs of the public school system of the State as might reasonably be expected from a board appointed for this purpose alone. The experience of many states has led to the development of state boards of education appointed by the Governor. These boards are given full responsibility for carrying out the mandate of the constitution and the acts of the legislature with respect to the development of the public school system of the state. The survey staff believes that in the State of Missouri the cause of public education would be served by the provision of a state board of education of seven members, to be named by the Governor, each to serve seven years and, after the initial appointment of the board, no more than one member to be appointed in any one year except in case of death or resignation. As important as is the selection of a state board of education which shall have the interests of the public school system as their sole responsibility, it is even more important that the State Superintendent of Schools be chosen because of his professional fitness and without reference to his ability to secure a majority at the polls. Students of educational administration are agreed that the state board of education should be given authority to select the State Superintendent of Schools or Commissioner of Education and to fix his salary. He should serve at the pleasure of the Board (26).

STATE EDUCATION AGENCY, 1947 TO PRESENT

Following the acceptance of a revised constitution by vote of the people on February 27, 1945, the General Assembly faced a most difficult task of implementing the new provisions of the constitution. Laws relating to the superintendent and the department were repealed and new ones were enacted, setting out the powers and duties of the newly created bipartisan State Board of Education, the Division of Public Schools, and the state commissioner of education.

The 1945 constitution stated in part:

> The supervision of instruction in the public schools shall be vested in a state board of education, consisting of eight lay members appointed by the Governor, by and with the advice and consent of the Senate; provided that at no time shall more than four members be of the same political party . . . . The board shall select and appoint a commissioner of education as its chief administrative officer, who shall be a citizen and resident of the state, and removable at its discretion. The board shall prescribe his duties and fix his compensation, and upon his recommendation shall fix their compensation (27).

Thus, the State Board of Education became a constitutional body and the state commissioner of education a constitutional officer.

In selecting the first commissioner, the board reviewed the qualifications of many Missouri educators. The usual process of screening was applied, and five Missouri school administrators were invited for a personal interview with the board. After due time, a committee from the board chose Hubert Wheeler, superintendent of the Marshall, Missouri, schools. He was one of the younger men interviewed and had exhibited sound administrative leadership and progressive ideas on teaching. Wheeler also had been active in the Missouri State Teachers Association and was serving as a member of the association's executive committee at the time of his appointment. He has served as commissioner for more than twenty years. The progress of education in Missouri during his administration confirms the judgment of the first State Board of Education in their selection. His policies and procedures have proved conservative enough to please the cautious and aggressive enough to support the progressive.

Efforts have been made to return the office of the chief school officer to an elective status. However, in each attempt, during the successive sessions of the General Assembly, Commissioner Wheeler kept out of the controversy and continued to promote sound educational practices and policies. The provisions of the 1945 constitution pertaining to education were defended successfully each time by the Missouri State Teachers Association and other interested lay and professional groups. Commissioner Wheeler once remarked in a staff meeting:

> We have nothing to trade but the education and welfare of the children and youth of Missouri, and I am certain that even those in favor of returning the office to an elective status also consider this commodity much too precious to use as a political pawn; therefore, we will continue our work in a nonpartisan manner and in the interest of the child.

Evidently the people of Missouri, lay and professional, have generally favored the policies and plans of the Division of Public Schools under the combined leadership of a bipartisan board and their appointed administrative officer.

The state department in Missouri has been affected over the past 20 years by state and federal legislation. Time and space will permit only a listing of the major sequential acts. This listing could also serve as a guide to anyone interested in doing a future study of any one of the acts or of the whole. Major state legislation that affected the structure, organization, and function of the Division of Public Schools from 1947 to 1965 is as follows:

1. Special education for the atypical child, 1947
2. School District Reorganization Law, 1948
3. Government surplus property utilization, 1947
4. School lunch program, 1947
5. Foundation financing program, 1955
6. Schools (operated by state board) for trainable retarded, 1958
7. Provision for the formation of junior college districts, 1961.

The following acts of Congress also have affected the structure, organization, and function of the Missouri Division of Public Schools from 1947 to 1965:

1. 1944 GI Bill of Rights—veterans' education
2. National Defense Education Act, 1958
3. Broadened Vocational Act, 1946
4. Civil Defense Adult Education Act, 1962
5. Vocational Education Act, 1963
6. Adult Basic Education Act, 1965
7. Elementary and Secondary Education Act, 1965.

State and federal laws and board of education policies resulted in the following major achievements of the administration from 1948 to 1958.

1. Adoption of a system of classification and accreditation of schools (study and development made by a statewide advisory committee in 1947 and adopted by the board in 1948).

2. School District Reorganization Law of 1948 (number of districts reduced from 8,422 to 2,629).

3. Upgrading of teacher qualifications and certification (see 10-year progression illustrated by following tables).

Table 2. – ELEMENTARY TEACHER PREPARATION IN COLLEGE SEMESTER HOURS, 1947-58

Year	Total elem. tchrs[a]	Number of elem. tchrs below 120 hours	Percent of elem. tchrs below 120 hours
1947-48	16,975	10,232	60.3%
1948-49	17,172	9,836	57.3
1949-50	17,330	9,355	54.0
1950-51	17,642	8,673	49.2
1951-52	17,751	7,923	44.6
1952-53	17,947	7,250	40.4
1953-54	18,299	6,793	37.1
1954-55	18,912	6,375	33.7
1955-56	19,582	6,055	30.9
1956-57	20,102	5,181	25.8
1957-58	20,934	4,761	22.6

[a]Includes elementary teachers, principals, supervisors, and kindergarten teachers.

Table 3. – HIGH SCHOOL TEACHER PREPARATION IN COLLEGE SEMESTER HOURS, 1947-58

Year	Total H. S. tchrs[a]	150+ hours	120-49 hours	Below 120 hours	Percent below 120
1947-48	6,410	2,749	3,212	449	7.0%
1948-49	6,443	2,895	3,201	347	5.4
1949-50	6,532	3,112	3,165	255	3.9
1950-51	6,794	3,394	3,217	183	2.7
1951-52	6,916	3,669	3,083	164	2.4
1952-53	7,114	3,933	3,031	150	2.1
1953-54	7,298	4,094	3,047	157	2.2
1954-55	7,411	4,175	3,069	167	2.3
1955-56	7,757	4,462	3,119	176	2.3
1956-57	8,257	4,831	3,274	151	1.8
1957-58	8,576	5,070	3,361	145	1.7

[a]Includes secondary school teachers, principals, and supervisors.

4. Extended implementation of the Special Education Law for the atypical child.

Table 4. – PROGRESSION OF SPECIAL EDUCATION, 1948-58

	Number of pupils	
	1948-49	1957-58
Orthopedic	750	492
Blind and partially seeing	72	107
Deaf and hard of hearing	171	247
Mentally retarded and deficient	1,212	10,979
Speech defectives	4,702	19,106
Home teaching	143	1,270
Total number of pupils	7,050	32,201
1965 total		40,073

5. School lunch services. Participating schools in 1948, 1,356; in 1958, 3,087. (In 1965, there were 2,966 schools–decline due to school district reorganization.)

6. School building facilities. New and improved building facilities became the component of school district reorganization. School building expenditure in 1948, $6,711,000; in 1958, $61,488,000.

7. School transportation (another component of school district reorganization). There were 103,939 pupils transported in 1945; 306,329 pupils in 1958; 458,813 pupils in 1965.

8. The state board authorized a Missouri Citizens Commission for study of all significant aspects of education in Missouri in 1950. As a result of this study, two bound volumes were printed and distributed: *Missouri Plans for Better Schools,* 1952, 72 pages; and *Better Schools for Missouri's Children,* 1952, 227 pages.

9. A follow-up study by a Joint Legislative Committee, completed and reported in 1955. All major recommendations of this committee have since been enacted into law.

10. A foundation financing program, 1955. This new program of financing public education in Missouri constituted the first change in financing education since 1931. It was not fully financed the first year. Financing in full would have required $83,040,679. During the school year 1955-56, an appropriation of 37.5 percent, a departure from the traditional 33.3 percent of the general revenue, was passed by the General Assembly.

11. Revision of the total school curriculum–K-12–a cooperative enterprise. This study and development program involved a total of nearly 1,000 people–teachers, principals, superintendents, college trainers, and department personnel served on 35 statewide committees appointed by the commissioner. Each study and production committee developed a curricular guide for teachers. This constituted the first departure from the traditional courses of study.

12. The additional use of automation. Additional equipment and personnel in this area facilitated the compiling of statistical data, apportionment of state school funds, and research activities.

13. Additional programs and services in all phases of vocational education. In keeping with technological changes, vocational education was emphasized through placing the directorship on an assistant commissioner status and was made an integral part of the Division of Instruction.

14. Numerous cooperative statewide and regional conferences of administrators, principals, and teachers. Such conferences are held annually for the purpose of interpreting educational problems and innovations.

Since 1958, the structure, organization, and services of the department have been radically affected by the implementation of the National Defense Education Act of 1958 (NDEA), the 1963 Vocational Education Act, and the Elementary and Secondary Education Act of 1965 (ESEA).

It would first appear that additional funds, regardless of source, would be beneficial to any state agency. However, it is now evident that the federally funded programs have also created adverse effects. For instance, they have increased regulatory services in comparison to increased supervisory services, and office space is now overcrowded. In the past, there was close cooperation among divisions and sections, contrasting to a present emergence of "separateness" and repetitious services. There is an uncertainty in budgeting for personnel services and equipment; thus, the department has been forced to engage in short-range planning instead of the long-range, stable planning that marked earlier operations. There is some fear that instead of strengthening the department as a state agency, it is being strengthened as an "arm" of the federal government.

Public education during the decade 1955-65 constitutes one of the largest growing businesses in Missouri. During the past 5 years, more than $50 million has been spent annually for new school buildings. The school transportation system is perhaps the largest transportation system in the state—292,000 miles are traveled daily to transport 458,813 pupils, with an overall expenditure of $17,700,000. The total expenditures for all public school services amounted to $473,260,268 in 1964-65. It is reported that school plant investment now exceeds $955 million.

During the school year 1964-65, there were 938 operating school districts—512 high school and 426 elementary; 922,027 pupils; and 37,627 teachers. Average per-pupil cost was $419.73; average annual teacher's salary, $5,631; average administrative salary, more than $9,000 annually.

It is evident that the provisions of the Constitution of 1945 removed many traditional obstacles to continuous progression and continuity in planning for improvement in public education at the state and local levels. These provisions, coupled with state and federally funded education programs, have fostered rapid strides in education—perhaps the greatest in the history of public education in Missouri. The sincere efforts, the sound administration policies and practices of the State Board of Education and Commissioner Hubert Wheeler, the cooperative spirit of all staff members cannot be discounted in the continuous progression of public education during the past 20 years. The spirit of cooperation between the department and district school administrators has also been sustaining and consistent throughout this administration. Kirk's "new note" in education, Baker's "new education," Lee's "contemporary education," King's "curricular innovations," and Scantlin's "follow-up study" of Lamkin's rural education study all served as excellent prologues to the present.

SUMMARY

It is not possible to analyze periodic progression on the basis of comparisons, because each era represented a particularly different set of circumstances. Readiness for improvement as well as apathy toward change were reflected in a greater or lesser degree during each period. It was evident that all administrations had one common intent—service to the schools of the state. It was also evident that the intent of all administrations was to improve the quality of procedures in keeping with quantity—additional personnel and funds.

It all began with two professionals and two secretaries in 1900; the 278 professionals and 226 secretaries in 1965 indicate the growth in quantity and the possibilities for additional services. The department's organizational structure is also an indication of quality services, but at no one period during the 65 years could it be said that the organizational plan provided the highest degree of efficiency, mainly because of a lack of adequate funds for personnel and physical facilities.

The past gave each succeeding administration lessons of courage, endurance, and achievement. The prospect of the future lured each administration on to unforeseen accomplishments. In most periods, societal changes prompted the unforeseen. It can be stated, without qualifications, that Missourians have experienced outstanding educational leadership at the state level during the first 65 years of the twentieth century.

The Missouri Department of Education seems to be in a transitional period in performing its leadership, regulatory, and supervisory services. The statement by Superintendent Kirk in 1898, "We are now working in a more highly organized form of education than thus far experienced," is, no doubt, truer now than it was at the turn of the century. The actions of the State Department of Education during the remainder of the century must be exemplary and in keeping with societal change—its knowledge and values. We must continue to exhibit courage, flexibility, and imagination to innovate as the times require.

In the fretful fever of the space-nuclear age, in the whirling passion of earnest endeavor, in the severe sixties, let us pause to ready ourselves for the most difficult era in education in Missouri—1968 to 2000—a period promising constant flux and restless discontent, the modern-day components of change, the only evident certainty during this period.

This brief history of the Missouri State Department of Education has been divided into such parts as "New Education," "Contemporary Education," and "Education Out of Politics." The coming period, 1968-2000, may be recorded by the educational historians as "Education for Survival."

FOOTNOTES

1. W. T. Carrington, *The History of Education in Missouri* (Jefferson City: Stephens Publishing Co., 1931), p. 34.

2. *Ibid.*, p. 39.

3. Superintendent of Schools, *Twenty-Fifth Missouri Report of Public Schools* (1874), p. 21.

4. *Ibid.*, p. 18.

5. Superintendent of Schools, *Twenty-Sixth Missouri Report of Public Schools* (1875), pp. 4-12.

6. *Ibid.*, pp. 5-6.

7. Superintendent of Schools, *Thirtieth Missouri Report of Public Schools* (1879), p. 5.

8. Superintendent of Schools, *Thirty-Ninth Missouri Report of Public Schools* (1889), p. 8.

9. Paul O. Selby, *The Board of Regents of Northeast Missouri State Teachers College* (Kirksville: Northeast Missouri State Teachers College, 1963), p. 46.

10. G. A. Theilmann, "A Century of Missouri Schools, 1821-1921," *Seventy-Second Missouri Report of Public Schools* (1921), p. 36.

11. Superintendent of Schools, *Forty-Ninth Missouri Report of Public Schools* (1898), p. 5.

12. Theilmann, *op. cit.*, p. 36.

13. Superintendent of Schools, *Fifty-Second Missouri Report of Public Schools* (1901), pp. 9-10.

14. Superintendent of Schools, *Fifty-Third Missouri Report of Public Schools* (1902), p. 9.

15. Superintendent of Schools, *Fifty-Seventh Missouri Report of Public Schools* (1906), p. 5.

16. *Ibid.*, p. 6.

17. Superintendent of Schools, *Fifty-Eighth Missouri Report of Public Schools* (1907), p. 32.

18. Superintendent of Schools, *Sixty-Ninth Missouri Report of Public Schools* (1918), p. 32.

19. *Ibid.*, pp. 37-118.

20. *Ibid.*, p. 15.

21. Theilmann, *op. cit.*, p. 38.

22. Superintendent of Schools, *Seventy-Second Missouri Report of Public Schools* (1921), pp. 44-45.

23. *Ibid.*, p. 49.

24. Superintendent of Schools, *Ninety-Third Missouri Report of Public Schools* (1942), p. 40.

25. Superintendent of Schools, *Sixty-Ninth Missouri Report of Public Schools* (1918), p. 15.

26. Superintendent of Schools, *Eightieth Missouri Report of Public Schools* (1929), p. 23.

27. Missouri, *Constitution* (revised 1945), art. 9, sec. 2.

BIBLIOGRAPHY

Public Documents

Missouri. *Constitution* (1945).

--*School Laws* (1900-66).

--*Official Manual, State of Missouri.* Jefferson City: Office of Secretary of State, 1899-1922.

Books and Bulletins

Carrington, W. T. *The History of Education in Missouri.* Jefferson City: Stephens Publishing Co., 1931.

King, Lloyd. *Meet Your State Department of Education.* Jefferson City: Department of Education, 1936.

Selby, Paul O. *The Board of Regents of Northeast Missouri State Teachers College.* Kirksville: Northeast Missouri State Teachers College, 1963.

Viles, N. E. *The Office of State Superintendent of Schools: A Brief History.* Jefferson City: Department of Education, 1938.

Williams, Walter. *The State of Missouri.* Jefferson City: Stephens Publishing Co., 1904.

Periodical

Missouri Schools (September-May 1935-65).

Reports

Department of Education. *Missouri School Directory.* Jefferson City: The Department, 1913-65.

Superintendent of Schools. *Missouri Report of Public Schools.* Jefferson City: Department of Education, 1874-1965.

Theilmann, G. A. "A Century of Missouri Schools, 1821-1921." *Seventy-Second Missouri Report of Public Schools.* Jefferson City: Department of Education, 1921.

Other Source

Wheeler, Hubert. Speech made by Commissioner Wheeler at the annual meeting of Council of Chief State School Officers, Santa Fe, New Mexico, 1960.

Appendix A

MISSOURI CHIEF STATE SCHOOL OFFICERS

State Superintendents

1839-41	Peter G. Glover
1841	Office abolished.
1841-54	Secretary of State served ex officio.
1854	John W. Henry
1854-56	Edwin C. Davis
1856-61	William B. Starke
1861	Office abolished.
1866-71	T. A. Parker
1871	Ira Divoll
1872-75	John Monteith
1875-82	Richard D. Shannon
1882-90	W. E. Coleman
1890-95	Lloyd E. Wolfe
1895-99	John R. Kirk
1899-1907	W. T. Carrington
1907-11	Howard A. Gass
1911-15	William E. Evans
1915-16	Howard A. Gass
1916-19	Uel W. Lamkin
1919-23	Sam A. Baker
1923-35	Charles A. Lee
1935-43	Lloyd King
1943-47	Roy Scantlin

State Commissioner

1947-	Hubert Wheeler

Appendix B

Chart I.--MISSOURI DEPARTMENT OF EDUCATION, 1900-1906

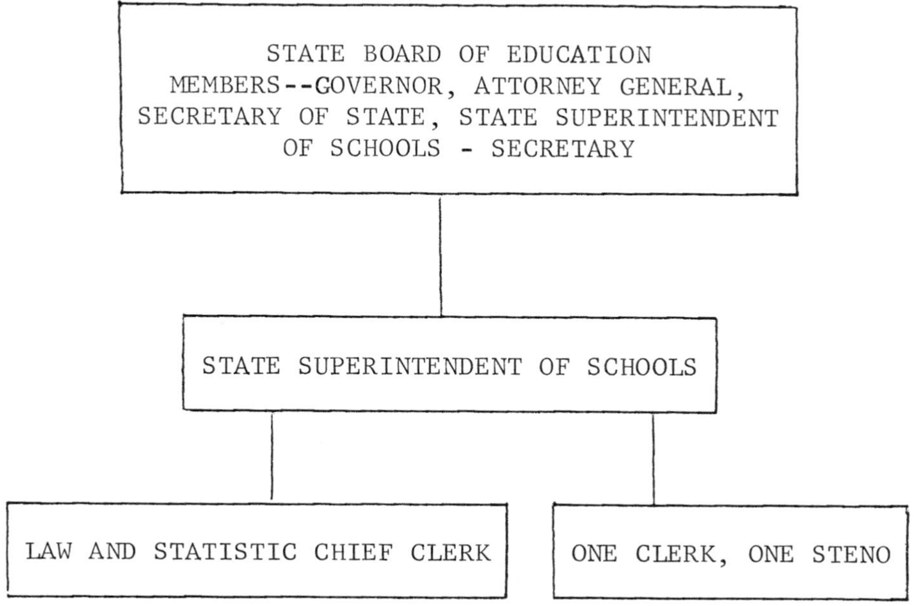

Chart II.--MISSOURI DEPARTMENT OF EDUCATION, 1907-14

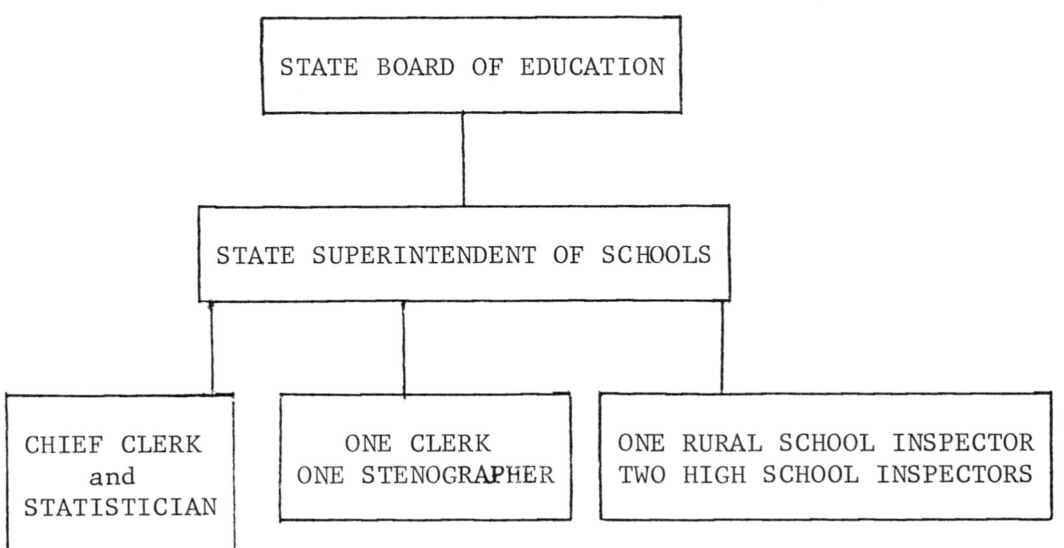

Appendix B

Chart III.--MISSOURI DEPARTMENT OF EDUCATION, 1915-18

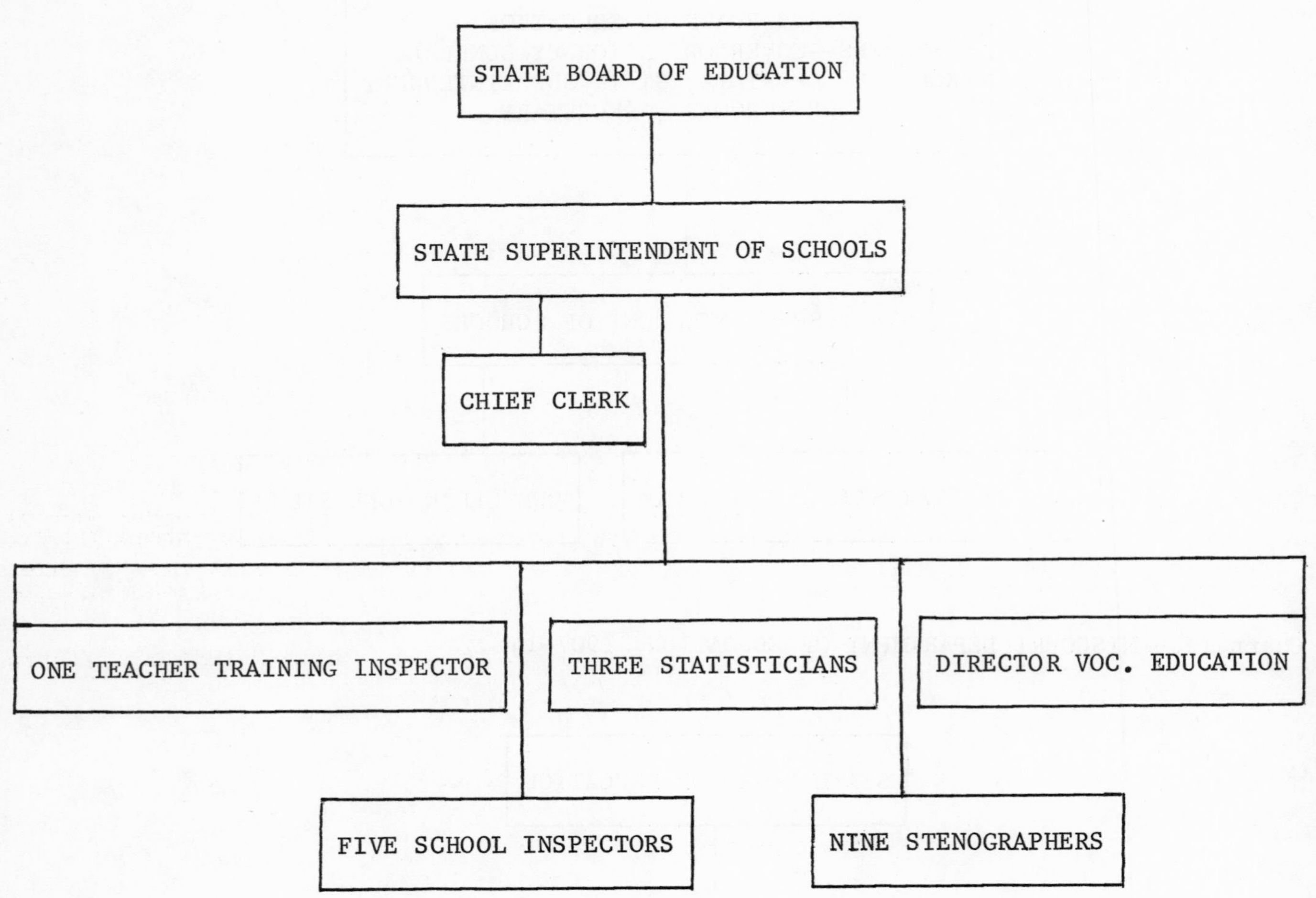

Appendix B

Chart IV.--MISSOURI DEPARTMENT OF EDUCATION, 1919-23

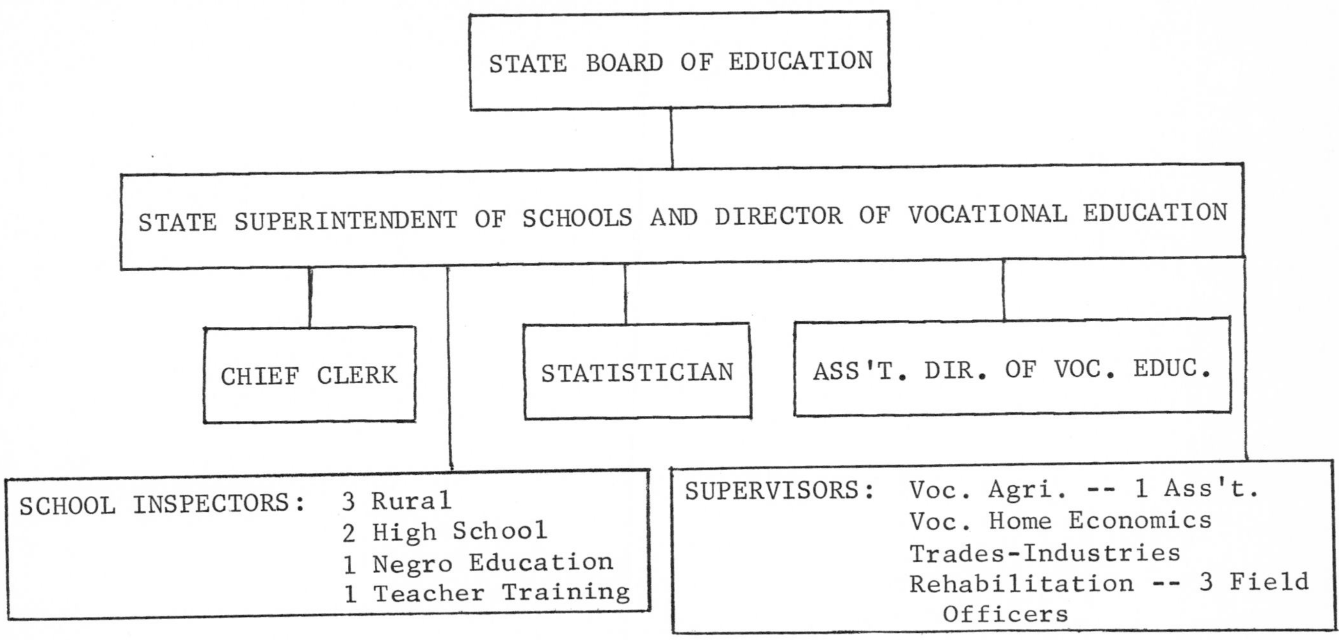

Chart V.--MISSOURI DEPARTMENT OF EDUCATION, 1930-34

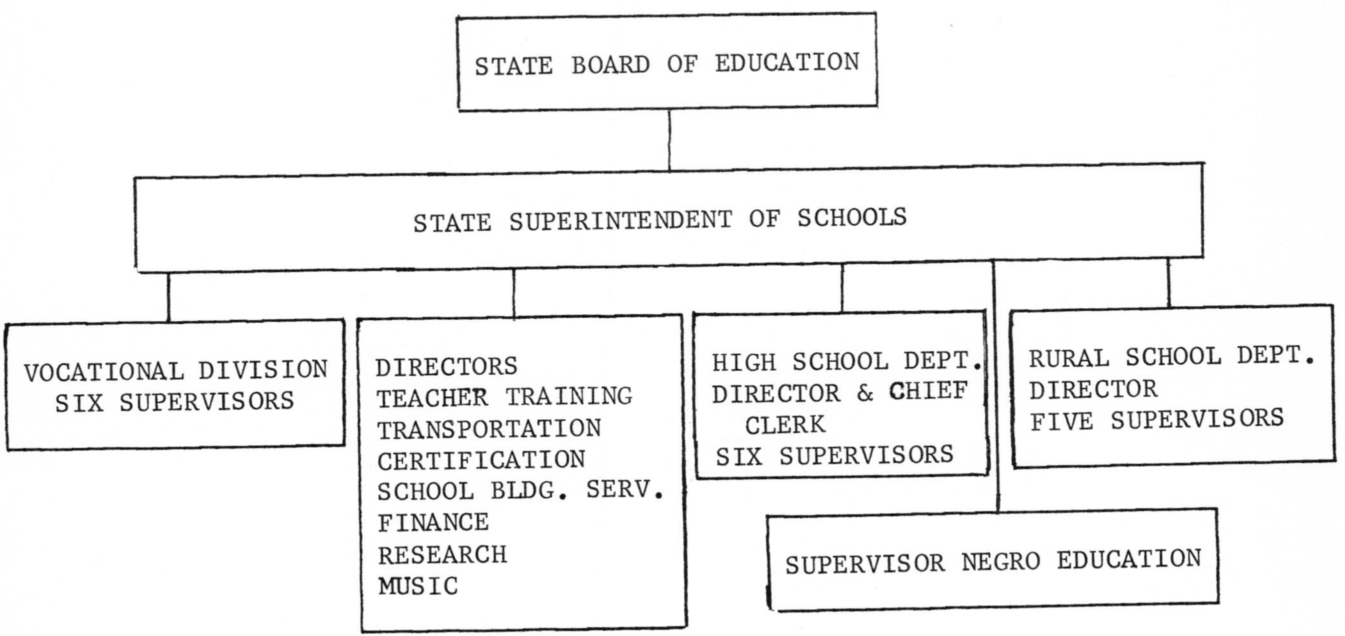

Eleven stenographers, a mailing clerk, and a janitor were employed.

Appendix B

Chart VI.--MISSOURI DEPARTMENT OF EDUCATION, 1935-46

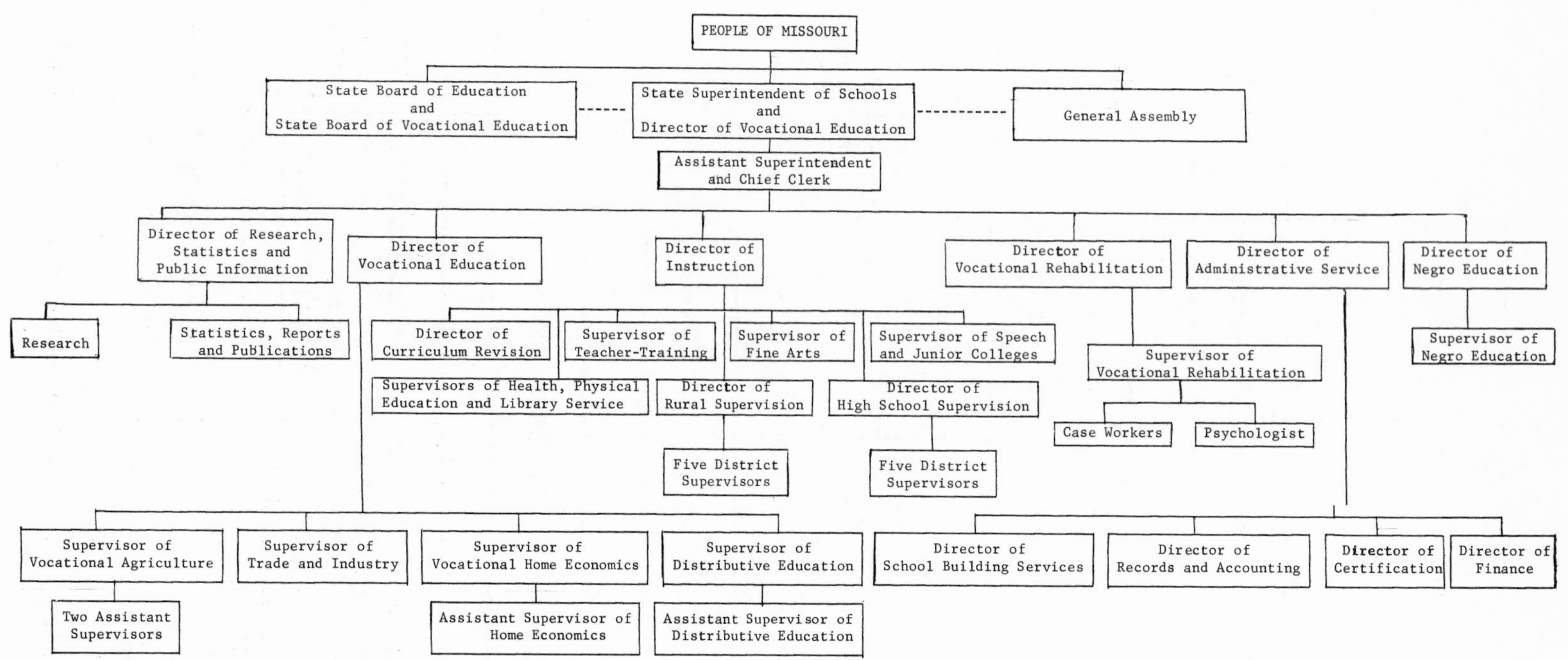
PEOPLE OF MISSOURI
State Board of Education and State Board of Vocational Education
State Superintendent of Schools and Director of Vocational Education
General Assembly
Assistant Superintendent and Chief Clerk
Director of Research, Statistics and Public Information
Director of Vocational Education
Director of Instruction
Director of Vocational Rehabilitation
Director of Administrative Service
Director of Negro Education
Research
Statistics, Reports and Publications
Director of Curriculum Revision
Supervisor of Teacher-Training
Supervisor of Fine Arts
Supervisor of Speech and Junior Colleges
Supervisors of Health, Physical Education and Library Service
Director of Rural Supervision
Director of High School Supervision
Five District Supervisors
Five District Supervisors
Supervisor of Vocational Rehabilitation
Case Workers
Psychologist
Supervisor of Negro Education
Supervisor of Vocational Agriculture
Two Assistant Supervisors
Supervisor of Trade and Industry
Supervisor of Vocational Home Economics
Assistant Supervisor of Home Economics
Supervisor of Distributive Education
Assistant Supervisor of Distributive Education
Director of School Building Services
Director of Records and Accounting
Director of Certification
Director of Finance

Appendix B

Chart VII.--MISSOURI DEPARTMENT OF EDUCATION, 1950

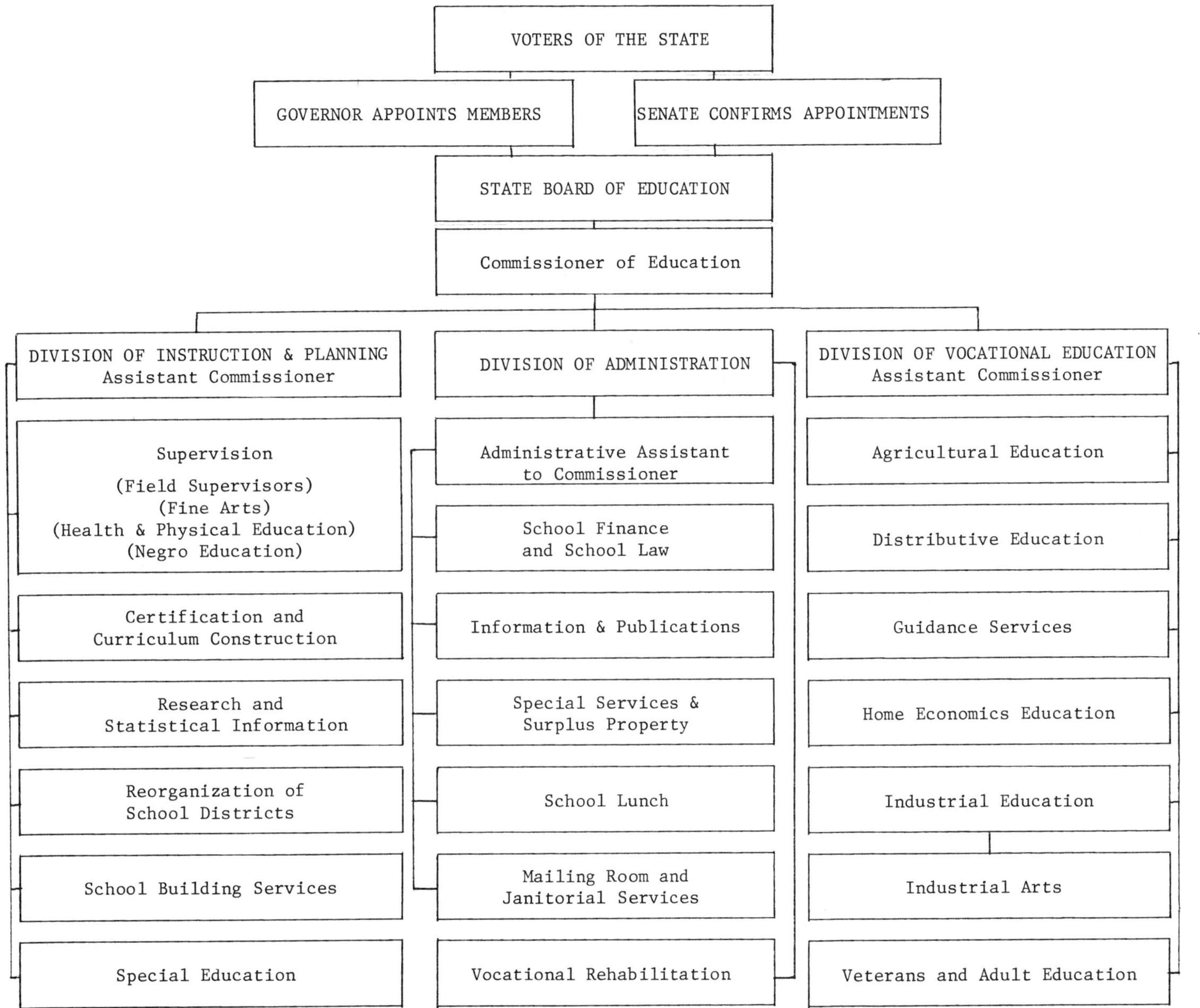

VOTERS OF THE STATE
GOVERNOR APPOINTS MEMBERS
SENATE CONFIRMS APPOINTMENTS
STATE BOARD OF EDUCATION
Commissioner of Education
DIVISION OF INSTRUCTION & PLANNING
Assistant Commissioner
Supervision
(Field Supervisors)
(Fine Arts)
(Health & Physical Education)
(Negro Education)
Certification and
Curriculum Construction
Research and
Statistical Information
Reorganization of
School Districts
School Building Services
Special Education
DIVISION OF ADMINISTRATION
Administrative Assistant
to Commissioner
School Finance
and School Law
Information & Publications
Special Services &
Surplus Property
School Lunch
Mailing Room and
Janitorial Services
Vocational Rehabilitation
DIVISION OF VOCATIONAL EDUCATION
Assistant Commissioner
Agricultural Education
Distributive Education
Guidance Services
Home Economics Education
Industrial Education
Industrial Arts
Veterans and Adult Education

Appendix B

Chart VIII.--MISSOURI DEPARTMENT OF EDUCATION, 1960

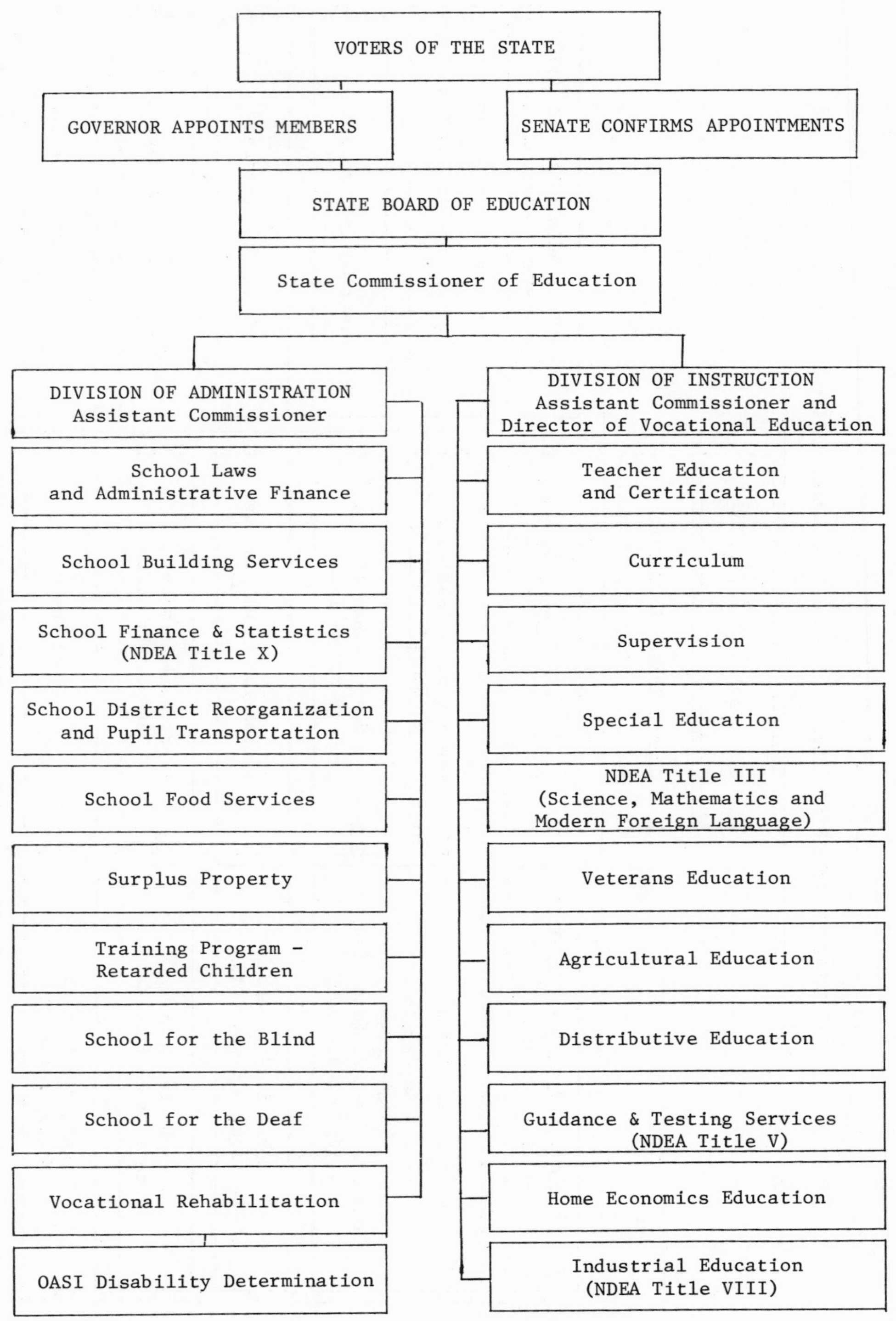
VOTERS OF THE STATE
GOVERNOR APPOINTS MEMBERS
SENATE CONFIRMS APPOINTMENTS
STATE BOARD OF EDUCATION
State Commissioner of Education
DIVISION OF ADMINISTRATION
Assistant Commissioner
School Laws and Administrative Finance
School Building Services
School Finance & Statistics (NDEA Title X)
School District Reorganization and Pupil Transportation
School Food Services
Surplus Property
Training Program - Retarded Children
School for the Blind
School for the Deaf
Vocational Rehabilitation
OASI Disability Determination
DIVISION OF INSTRUCTION
Assistant Commissioner and Director of Vocational Education
Teacher Education and Certification
Curriculum
Supervision
Special Education
NDEA Title III (Science, Mathematics and Modern Foreign Language)
Veterans Education
Agricultural Education
Distributive Education
Guidance & Testing Services (NDEA Title V)
Home Economics Education
Industrial Education (NDEA Title VIII)

Appendix B

Chart IX.--MISSOURI DEPARTMENT OF EDUCATION, 1962

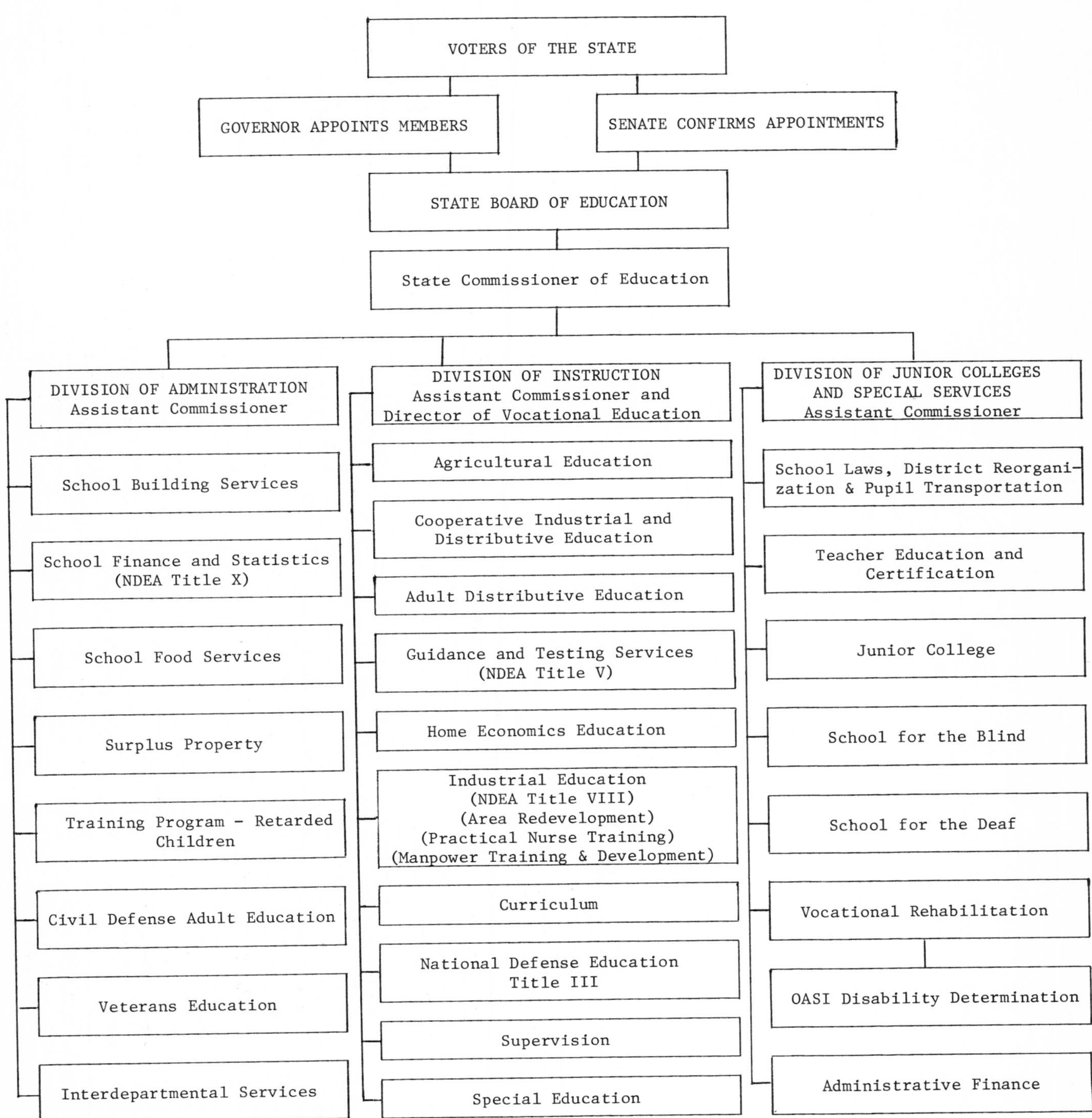
VOTERS OF THE STATE
GOVERNOR APPOINTS MEMBERS
SENATE CONFIRMS APPOINTMENTS
STATE BOARD OF EDUCATION
State Commissioner of Education
DIVISION OF ADMINISTRATION Assistant Commissioner
School Building Services
School Finance and Statistics (NDEA Title X)
School Food Services
Surplus Property
Training Program - Retarded Children
Civil Defense Adult Education
Veterans Education
Interdepartmental Services
DIVISION OF INSTRUCTION Assistant Commissioner and Director of Vocational Education
Agricultural Education
Cooperative Industrial and Distributive Education
Adult Distributive Education
Guidance and Testing Services (NDEA Title V)
Home Economics Education
Industrial Education (NDEA Title VIII) (Area Redevelopment) (Practical Nurse Training) (Manpower Training & Development)
Curriculum
National Defense Education Title III
Supervision
Special Education
DIVISION OF JUNIOR COLLEGES AND SPECIAL SERVICES Assistant Commissioner
School Laws, District Reorganization & Pupil Transportation
Teacher Education and Certification
Junior College
School for the Blind
School for the Deaf
Vocational Rehabilitation
OASI Disability Determination
Administrative Finance

Appendix B

Chart X.--MISSOURI DEPARTMENT OF EDUCATION, 1966

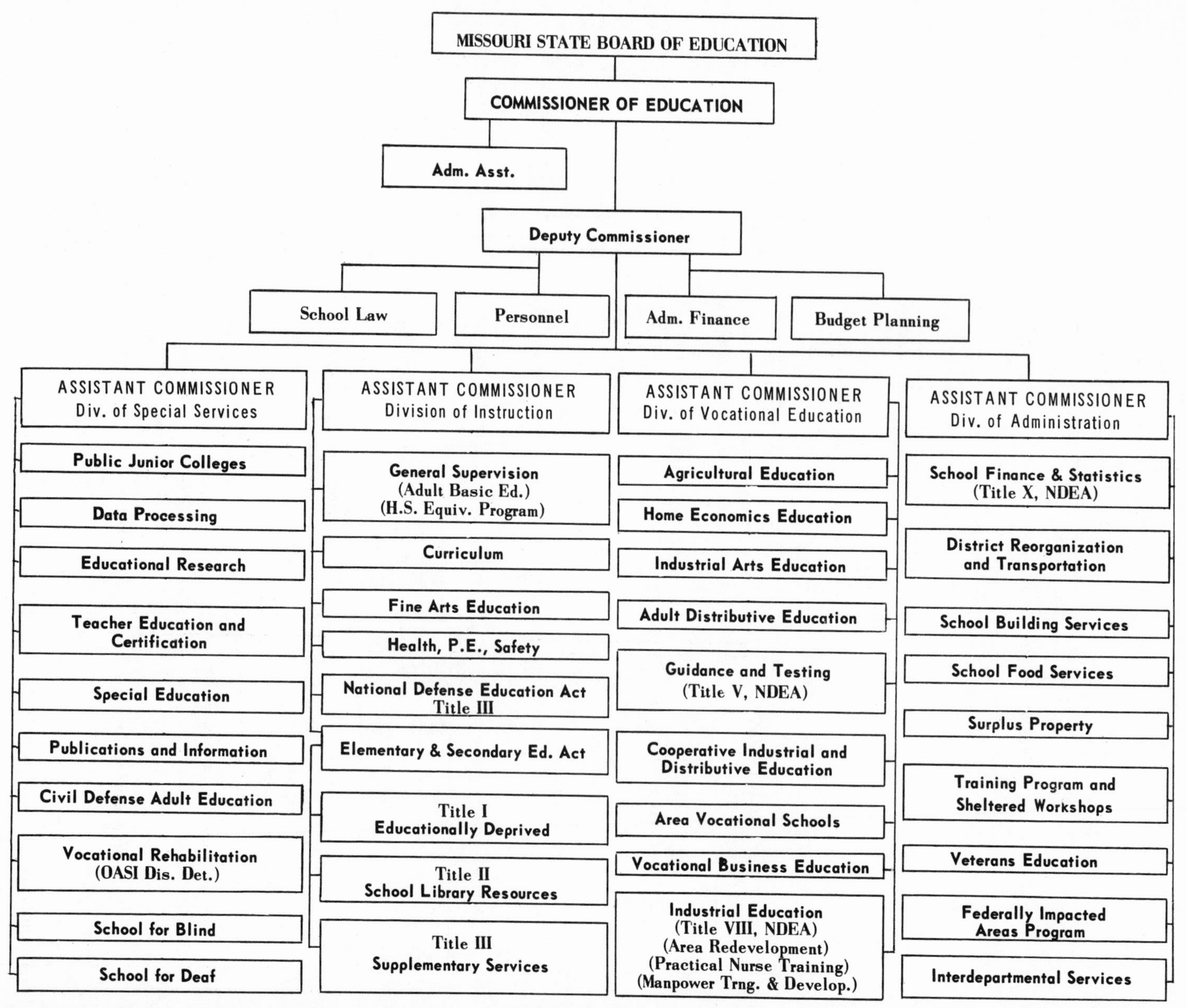

26 Montana

DEPARTMENT OF PUBLIC INSTRUCTION
Lyle L. Berg

Contents

FROM TERRITORY YEARS TO EARLY STATEHOOD

Early Educational Patterns

When Montana's first Territorial Governor, Sidney Edgerton, named the first superintendent of public instruction in 1864, no funds were available for his salary or office expenses. The appointment of Thomas J. Dimsdale (1), then a private school teacher in Virginia City, presaged problems that were to beset education in Montana for the next 100 years. This perhaps explains why Dimsdale prepared no reports, made no recommendations, and left nothing on record to show that he had even occupied this first post. Dimsdale continued to pursue his major interests in teaching and writing. His book entitled *The Vigilantes of Montana* was the first to be published in the territory.

While the Montana Territory was plagued by inadequate educational funds at this early period, the citizens certainly did not lack spirit or good educational intentions. Their enthusiasm was reflected in Governor Edgerton's message to the first Legislative Assembly, which convened at Bannack in December 1864: He asked for legislation to provide a common school system and thereby take advantage of federal grants. He was referring to the federal Organic Act of 1864, which established Montana as a territory and set apart two sections of land (16 and 36) in each township for the establishment of a school fund; the principal was to remain inviolable, and the interest was to be divided among all the school districts in the territory, proportionate to the number of pupils between the ages of 4 and 20 years enrolled in each district. In December 1864, the legislative school committee, appointed by the territorial council president, introduced Council Bill 38, "an act establishing a common school system for the Territory of Montana" (2); in January 1865, the bill passed the Legislature and became the first school law of Montana upon approval by the Governor.

The same year, an editorial appeared in the *Montana Post,* published at Virginia City, that clearly sounded the call and perhaps set the stage for Montana education in the years ahead. Certainly it showed the public's desire for further educational development from the private schools of itinerant professors and the early religious schools established by the Jesuit fathers to a more uniform and widespread system of free public education. "There is one question," the *Post's* editorialist argued—

> That can never remain in abeyance, as long as a particle of true parental feeling remains among us, or as long as the American conception of what a man or woman ought to be shall have enough of vital reality about it to necessitate its practical illustrations through the instrumentality of the noble school system, which is at once the pride and the salvation of this great Republic. Here, among the eternal hills that upheave their vast peaks in silent testimony of the goodness of their Creator, elevating within the grasp of man treasures that would otherwise be buried far beyond his reach—we feel that the development of our material prosperity has small worth, if the mind, the stature of the man, is dwarfed and stunted by neglect or apathy on the part of those to whose care its nurture and culture rightfully belong. The people of Montana have a good School Law, and ample provision for its effective working. Shall this become useless for good, by lying dormant? Or shall the energy of the people give the dry bones life, and constitute Education the tutelary genius of our Territory? In every inhabited spot, let schools be erected. Humble and deficient in many respects they must be, at first; but in a marvelously short time, if the endeavors of the mothers and fathers of Montana are persistent and well directed, a school system shall arise in our midst, worthy of our name and station, and the riches our children will inherit will fall into hands fitted to receive them, and to apply them intelligently for their own good and the welfare of the lands of their birth. Let school meetings be called; let the County Superintendents do their duty, supported by the sympathy and labours of the people, and we shall have to bless the Legislature for one good action in giving us a school law which shall stand a monument to their everlasting honor, like a good deed in a naughty world, in bright contrast to the authorization of chartered robbery and legal stultification (3).

In 1872, Cornelius Hedges, superintendent of public instruction, submitted to Governor Benjamin F. Potts what he called "the first regular report upon the public free schools of Montana," although Superintendent A. M. S. Carpenter in 1867 and Superintendent Campbell in 1868 had submitted brief reports to Governor Green Clay Smith and to Acting Governor James Tufts that undoubtedly were the first official reports of their kind in the territory. Nevertheless, Superintendent Hedges believed his report to be the first comprehensive report submitted, as indeed it was:

> It would have been personally a matter of pride and pleasure to have been able to present a fairer showing but it is necessary that a beginning be made, however unfavorable it may look, and as no former report exists with which to compare our present one, and ascertain whether any relative improvement has taken place, I will state, from personal observation, that such improvement has been most decided and gratifying (4).

The First County Superintendents

During this period, county treasurers were designated as county superintendents of schools, a post not often eagerly accepted, and the early biennial reports consisted of statistical information submitted to the state superintendent. The early state superintendents lamented publicly that the county reports were not being submitted promptly, if at all. The situation evidently became critical, and the Legislature passed a law making failure to submit required reports punishable by deduction of $100 from the salary of the county superintendent (today the penalty is loss of 2 months salary). The effectiveness of this action was doubtful, as the state superintendents for the next decade continued to complain of this dereliction of duty on the county superintendents' part. Meanwhile, the county superintendents would transfer the blame to the school district officers, and there the matter would rest.

While the early county superintendents were not particularly attuned to the needs of the educational community, they were expected to provide local leadership to the district schools; visit each school at least once a year; distribute all forms, circulars, and reports for school officers that they received from the state superintendent; apportion school funds to the district; pay all bills of county school districts; examine all persons who might wish to become teachers; and keep records and report to the state superintendent.

Early Reports of State Superintendents of Public Instruction

The superintendent of public instruction published in his annual and biennial reports to the Governor the statistics furnished by the county superintendents. In addition, he wrote on the public schools, listing present conditions as well as future aims, and reporting such general information as useful statistics and other comments he felt to be of interest. For example, Superintendent Hedges, one of the most insightful men to occupy the post of superintendent, expounded on government aid for the schools, courses of study, textbooks, teachers, schoolhouses, districts, and compulsory education and made general recommendations for the benefit of the schools.

The early statistics were a summary of miscellaneous information on the number of districts, public schools, male and female students, children of African descent, the total enrolled in public schools, the average number of days of school, the number of private schools and pupils, and the number of students not attending any school. One report in 1880 said that 51 children of African descent lived in the territory, the average school term was 96 days, and the territory had 9 brick schoolhouses and 84 log schoolhouses. (See Appendix D for typical curriculum.)

Superintendent Hedges, in defense of his textbook selection for the public schools, cited the work of the teacher as being greater than that of the author of any textbook and stated that a good teacher without any textbook at all could conduct a very successful school. He also stated that "object teaching" was winning its way to prominence and recommended that all school districts speedily supply themselves with charts and other "ingenious apparatus." However, at the same time he cautioned that the good teacher would not wait or rely solely on such modern conveniences, but would make constant use of the blackboard and slate, and that a complete and quick-witted teacher would never be at a loss for means of illustration.

Superintendent Hedges reported on the poor opportunities for teachers in the territory by pointing out that of the 91 districts in the territory only 3 or 4 held school longer than 6 months. This necessitated the teachers' seeking other employment for the remaining months. He realized that the territory should have a normal school to help supply good teachers to the public schools, but he recognized that "it would be folly to expect such facilities in the near future" (5).

The Creation of New Districts

One great concern at this time was that new school districts could be created by petition of five heads of families. Superintendent Hedges had opposed the enactment of this legislation, a stand that has since been justified, as today school districts are attempting the Herculean task of reorganizing and consolidating many small, inefficient school districts into larger ones. Montana today faces a formidable task that, because of its political implications, has been avoided by the Legislature and chief educational officers throughout the state. Consolidation and reorganization is not likely to make rapid progress until the Legislature imposes mandatory regulations and obligations on the people who continue to support their small individual schools. Such legislation does not seem to be in the immediate future.

The 1958 "Peabody Report" published data which stated that in 1948-49 Montana had 1,422 districts (of which 327 were nonoperating), and in 1957-58 this number had been reduced to 1,160 (with 207 listed as nonoperating) (6). State Superintendent Harriet Miller, in her report of 1966, stated that there were then 775 operating districts and 76 nonoperating districts (7). Obviously, a substantial number of schools have consolidated or closed since 1948. This voluntary consolidation has been brought about in part by the fact that many very small districts have been plagued by a perennial shortage of teachers and funds to carry on a suitable educational program.

State Department Leadership

The superintendent of public instruction provided the early leadership in three important aims of public education: compulsory education, improved teacher qualifications, and longer school terms. Superintendent Hedges saw the merit of these aims and the problems involved in achieving them: "Our population is too scattered; our school houses deficient in accommodation, rare, and widely separated; school terms too short, and teachers deficient in qualifications" (8). Concerning longer terms, he made a plea for federal help:

> We must have more means from some source to sustain longer terms of schools. If we can by no means obtain help from the National Government, if we must be left, in the days of our poverty and struggles to subdue a wilderness, to depend only on ourselves, I hope our people will awake to the hard necessity, and be willing to bear even greater burdens of taxation to serve the first necessity of any community--education for its youth. Better than the richest mines of precious metals, better than unnumbered herds and flocks, of farms groaning beneath the weight of harvest, is the wealth of the mind that waits to be set free by the inspiring touch of education (9).

Hedges took his post of territorial superintendent seriously and with single-minded purpose. He saw that the schools needed leadership and assumed the responsibility for providing it. His biennial reports are filled with both general and specific recommendations to the Governor and thence to the Legislature for the improvement of the public schools. He deserves to be remembered for his many contributions to Montana education, brought about by his aggressive action in pointing out areas needing improvement as well as his ability to look to the future needs of the modest educational establishment he headed.

For example, during his term as superintendent, 1872 to 1878, he chided the lawmakers for not authorizing the printing of more copies of his report, giving his reason as follows: Members of the Legislature might see the practical workings of the law and best learn of defects which required their attention; the people would see what had been accomplished by other counties and districts and be incited to generous rivalry; and by distributing the report throughout other states and territories, Montana could influence immigration of the most desirable character. Hedges understood well the value of general public education and saw in his report a chance to reach the people directly. He recommended changes in school law on teachers' certificates, the establishment of teachers institutes for in-service training, regulation of changes in textbooks, building of schools, school age, federal aid, and the establishment of a normal school for the training of teachers.

The Quest for Professional Standards

Superintendent Hedges was concerned with continually improving the school law. He pointed out that the law in many cases was incongruous with realities. For instance, the annual census was not taken before November 20 of each year, while the county superintendents' reports were to be submitted to the state office by November 1. Hence the number of students reported was necessarily that of the previous year.

Again, only one class of teacher certificate existed, issued by the county superintendent for a 2-year period. Each county superintendent fixed the standards for certification himself. The results were often bewildering, as graduates of normal schools with years of experience were required to pass a county superintendent's examination and were given the same certificate as the most poorly prepared teacher in the district. Teachers who met qualifications in one county might be unqualified in another. Hedges recommended that a simple remedy—

> Would be to fix a time once or twice in each year, when teachers desiring certificates might present themselves in their several counties, and in the presence of the county superintendent, assisted by two teachers, be subjected to an examination upon questions prepared by the territorial superintendent (10).

In this way, there would be some semblance of uniformity, and teachers would be qualified in all districts at once.

Hedges also recommended that teachers institutes be held regularly to elevate the standard and equality of instruction and that teachers' attendance should be obligatory.

An Instrument of Aid—School Law

The law allowed the resident voters of each district to vote taxes for building schools but did not authorize the district to incur any indebtedness for construction. For this reason, districts often had to build uncomfortable and inconvenient log schools that were erected by subscription or joint personal labor. Hedges recommended that each district be allowed to issue bonds to provide funds for immediate school construction and to pay the interest plus one-tenth of the principal each year during the 10-year term of the bonds.

Clark Wright, territorial superintendent from 1878 to 1879, called attention to the fact that–

> During the past year a school was taught containing only two scholars, and owing to a previous contract with the Trustees of the District, the teacher drew pay from the school fund, refusing to relinquish the school. The law at present allows the establishment of a school on the petition of five families, but does not designate the number of scholars requisite to entitle the teacher to a share in the school fund (11).

Superintendent Wright recommended that schools with fewer than 10 pupils not be entitled to a share of the school fund.

Evidence that an attempt was being made to keep school law abreast of the superintendent's requirements is shown by the fact that during 1878 district trustees could be fined $25 for not filing a school report with county superintendents. The law also provided for the territorial superintendent to hold annual teachers institutes of 2 to 5 days in length. School was to be adjourned during these sessions, and the cost of the institutes was to be borne by the counties.

The territorial superintendency had progressed, not always smoothly perhaps, but with high purpose and unalterable direction, to a point where districts could turn to it for leadership and direction. In 1877, the superintendent's report, for example, listed the adopted textbook titles for use in the territory; contained 10 printed forms for district use concerning leases, elections, and agreements; and asked that 6 months of school be considered the minimum. Ten years before Montana became a state, Superintendent W. Egbert Smith wrote in his report of 1879 that sparsely settled rural districts, short school terms, and small but costly schools prevented the territory from making a better educational showing. He pointed out the advantage of graded schools in reducing teacher load and inducing rivalry. "Grading," he said, "is an application to schools of the principle of 'division of labor' applied to all great business affairs" (12). In 1879, there were 99 schools in the territory, the school valuation was $99,345, and school attendance had shown a 72-percent increase from 1873. Enrollment had now reached almost 4,000. However, the superintendent pointed out that only 47.5 percent of school-age children were in school, and he advocated a compulsory attendance law. He also pointed out the obvious advantages of consolidation with the following table:

> Three small schools of 12 pupils each would cost about as follows:

3 cheap teachers at $50 each per month	$150.00
3 fires, 2 cords of wood each at $5 per cord	30.00
Cost of tuition and fuel per month	$180.00

Better education at less cost would result under the following budget:

1 good teacher at $100 per month.	$100.00
1 fire, 2 cords of wood at $5 per cord.	10.00
Cost of tuition and fuel per month	$110.00

Superintendent Smith was the first to make public the inadequacy of school supervision and reporting. He observed that "our present system amounts to no supervision." Partly to blame, he felt, was the county superintendents' lack of special qualifications for the job. This led in turn to a situation in which "there is always a class of good-for-nothing-else teachers who are ready to take advantage of such conditions and 'keep school' as a make shift . . . . Civilized nations are learning, but have not yet fully learned, that poor unqualified teachers are dear at any price" (13). Smith recommended the formation of a Territorial Board of Education to certify teachers as he agitated for professional qualifications for county superintendents of schools.

The public school system of the Territory of Montana at this time (1879) was organized as follows:

Officers

Territorial Superintendent of Public Instruction
County Superintendents
District Boards of Trustees, three members each
District Clerks

Schools

Ungraded District Schools
Graded Grammar Schools
City Graded and High Schools

Other Agencies

County Teachers Institutes
District and City Teachers Associations

Statehood

The closing years of Montana as a territory saw superintendents of public instruction preoccupied with similar problems of quality teachers, in-service institutes, school laws, and compulsory attendance. One superintendent wrote: "A 'quack' in our sick-rooms to prescribe for us medicine is sounder in philosophy and better in economy than the scapeling [sic] in our school rooms to prescribe education for our youth" (14). Seemingly, nothing was considered too small or insignificant to escape their attention. Another report mentioned the installation of two basement furnaces at a cost of $400 in the new school at Billings. The superintendent of that year wrote in praise: "But the greatest benefit of all would be the introduction of the heat at the level of the floor where it would warm the feet instead of the head" (15). Evidently all this was not accomplished without the usual amount of criticism, Cornelius Hedges, in seeking his second term in 1884, defended his position by stating in his report: "A word to teachers, school officers, and parents—it is made the duty of the territorial superintendent to suggest means of improving our schools . . . " (16).

With the arrival of statehood in 1889, the post of territorial superintendent of public instruction changed from an appointive position filled by the Governor to an elective one, as provided for by the State Constitution. There were 10,597 students enrolled in public schools of Montana, with an additional 1,260 enrolled in various private schools. Frame buildings had largely replaced log or adobe structures, and the superintendents' reports at this time were more detailed, showing increased valuations, districts, enrollments, and new buildings. Large sections were devoted to school laws, and many of the recommendations made by previous superintendents were now being enacted into school law, although many of the more pertinent ones were still neglected.

In 1889, John Gannon, the first elected superintendent, petitioned the Legislature to furnish him a clerk "as the pressure of his office and his frequent removal demanded more help." He continued: "The work is increasing and will continue to do so, while the change from a territorial form of government to that of statehood imposes duties upon the superintendent not contemplated by present statute" (17).

Gannon reported in 1891 that 20,787 students were enrolled in the state's public and private schools and that there were 5,534 volumes in the school libraries. The 1892 school valuation was totaled at about $1 million.

The subsequently elected superintendents from 1892 to 1900 were plagued with problems common to such state agencies across America—establishing colleges and universities; providing the best means of supporting public education; shaping the educational pattern; coping with the multiplying student body; certifying teachers; expanding the school facilities; and improving the teaching materials and curriculum.

Montana had particular problems. Her state capitol followed the gold strikes and consequently moved from Bannack to Virginia City, and thence to Helena, where it resides today, as rich lodes were struck in each of these areas. This meant that the miners and their families moved frequently, and a thriving community painfully getting its roots started with homes, stores, churches, and schools could suddenly find itself deserted as the "strike" died out and news of fabulous gold discoveries came in from elsewhere in the state. Today both Virginia City and Bannack are ghost towns, whereas they were once among the largest communities in Montana. Especially hard hit were the children of farmers and ranchers who had settled comfortably close to populated areas only to find themselves isolated as the miners and their families, together with stores and schools, decamped for richer areas.

The Question of Legality

Superintendent Gannon was the first to publish reports of the attorney general of Montana regarding legal school questions submitted to the superintendent. Besides his clerk and the attorney general, Gannon had no aides to help with the myriad school problems that came at the turn of the century.

It was extremely difficult to collect school taxes from unmarried men who resisted school taxation and were on the move constantly; part of the problem was undoubtedly due to the apathy or ignorance of local school trustees toward alleviating the problems by necessary action. To the everlasting credit of the territorial and state superintendents, they, almost without exception, published the deplorable conditions and continually placed before the Governor and the Legislature a mandate to improve educational opportunity in Montana. They took their responsibilities seriously, and, because they were politically attuned to the Governor and the Legislature and represented a majority of the citizens after 1889, their demands were most often heeded. Superintendent E. A. Carleton wrote in 1900: "It is refreshing to note the marked improvement in the public schools of the state . . . . We have come to learn the great lesson that school is not merely 'a preparation for life,' but that it is life itself" (18).

At least four forces were at work in the organization of Montana's early educational system: Federal stimulation helped to create common schools; a titular head of the common school system was recognized as necessary to devise courses of study and textbook lists, to supervise and give direction, and to collect and disseminate information to lawmakers about schools; the citizenry desired and worked to have free public schools; and the superintendent's annual report was used as an instrument to provide needed change by prodding the Legislature.

FROM EARLY STATEHOOD TO THE MODERN ERA

Youth and Maturity

During 1916, educational progress in Montana was a matter of considerable pride, and Superintendent H. A. Davee reported that in comparison with older states Montana "could find abundant reason for felicitation . . ." (19). This judgment was passed in the face of rapid growth in Montana schools, as the 1910 federal census listed the state's population as 376,053 with a school census of 85,126; and by 1916 the school population had risen to 147,374 (20).

Davee further reported that his department had a deputy superintendent, a rural inspector, a stenographer, and a clerk. "With the exception of the rural inspector," Davee stated, "the entire force was needed to take care of routine office duties" (21). Consequently, Davee requested two additional assistants–one to administer the teacher retirement fund and another to work principally in the field. The "routine office duties" produced valuable assistance to Montana's education, as evidenced by the list of publications being issued by the department: school laws, elementary and high school courses of study, school bulletins, and educational directory, library lists, school registers, a pioneer pamphlet, an Arbor Day manual, a special day bulletin for teaching patriotism, 64 different blanks, pension blanks, teachers examination questions, and eighth-grade questions.

By 1918, 14 communities in Montana were classified as cities (population 2,500 or over). Such cities and many smaller towns had modern schools of brick and stone and operated 9 months. They were adequately staffed with qualified teachers and were well supervised. However, many rural schools were still plagued with attendance problems (many averaged only 4 or 5 months), poor facilities, and poorly qualified teachers. A survey revealed that in one county only 1.3 percent of the teachers in rural schools had had training beyond high school, while in town schools in the same county 93 percent of the teachers were normal school graduates, and 100 percent had had *some* normal school or college training (22). Pay for rural teachers was smaller than for town or city teachers, which led to a critical teacher shortage in the rural areas. As a temporary measure to meet this emergency, rural-teacher-training courses were established in high schools.

The rural school situation was complicated by the fact that Montana is a large state, and early, crude transportation, especially during the winter months, made it almost impossible to transport children very far to attend school. Some parents solved this problem by moving to the school during the winter and living in earthen dugouts until the school term ended, and then returning to their farms in the spring. But many families could not afford this "luxury," and untold hundreds of youngsters were denied even rudimentary education. Nor was this problem soon solved, for letters to the state superintendent during the 1920's continued to plead for school facilities in remote areas. Typical letters on the subject describe the conditions:

> I have been trying hard for over 3 years to get school for my children. The members of the school board is at one side of the district and they don't seem to care whether the country children get school or not. If nothing can be done I will have to keep my children at home until we are able to send them. (December 1919)
>
> We are all agreed with the county superintendent about having two schools in our district, but how? We can hardly support one. It seems a shame not to have any school at all as there are some families in here of almost young men and women with no education whatever. (November 1920)
>
> We are denied school when there was $2,200 in the treasury of the district. The teachers we get are always relations of the clerk. There are always teachers to be found for school for the trustees' children, also the clerk's. (February 1920)
>
> I am a mother of 3 children. Two are of school age. We have 4.5 miles to our school. The school board promised us a school wagon when the school was being built, but they say now that they have not enuf money. It makes me feel so bad to think our 9 year old girl don't know anything. We are poor, for we don't have a crop for two years. If the school board would pay us just $20 a month I could move to town, which is 12 miles from our claim. Then I could pay rent. Then they could go every day. Oh, please help me. (October 1920) (23).

In 1916, Davee wrote that the state had 141 accredited high schools (including 17 county high schools) and 1,801 districts. Most of these schools were 4-year high schools, but 1-, 2-, and 3-year high schools were not uncommon. The class of 1918 graduated 40.6 percent of the first year's enrollment.

Montana had made steady progress toward improved educational programs, facilities, supervision, and learning opportunities, as exemplified in part by Superintendent May Trumper's report that "in 1917-18, $1.58 was spent on the public schools of the state for each $100 of wealth. In 1910 the Russell Sage Foundation study showed that Montana spent twenty-eight cents–the twelfth lowest in the United States" (24).

World War I

The entire nation was shocked to discover in World War I that there were 700,000 male illiterates between 21 and 31 years of age and that 29 percent of the total number of men examined for military service were rejected because of physical unfitness. Superintendent Trumper accepted these facts as a further challenge to Montana education, saying, "The problem of combating ignorance and physical defects is one of education–education for all" (25).

In 1917, Congress had passed the Smith-Hughes Vocational Act designed to promote agriculture, home economics, and trades. During that same year, the Montana Legislature moved to meet the appropriation requirements of the act. The vocational work emphasized in the Smith-Hughes Act was well under way in a number of high schools by 1918. The biennial report of that year listed 13 high schools participating in the program and showed that the federal funds involved were over $5,000 (26). Governor S. V. Stewart declared in a proclamation of 1918:

> Being deeply impressed with the imperative necessity of adequately meeting the situation when it comes, I, S. V. Stewart as governor of the State of Montana, do hereby appeal to the people of our state to do all within their power to maintain our schools at their pre-war point of efficiency and, wherever possible, to improve them; to the most desirable end that no boy or girl, no young man or young woman within our state may in future chide us with the accusation that because of the war he or she was deprived of opportunity to prepare and train for the full utilization of every faculty . . . (27).

The Ayres Report

In her biennial report of 1920, Miss Trumper referred to a survey that was to impede Montana's educational progress for the next few years. "During 1919," she stated, "Dr. Leonard P. Ayres, one of the foremost statisticians in America, and director of the Russell Sage Foundation, made a study of state school systems" (28). Dr. Ayres gave every state a numerical rating based on such factors as the population of children of school age in school, length of school term, amount of money spent for the support of school, salaries of teachers, etc.

The Ayres survey revealed that Montana ranked first of all the states when five financial components were averaged. Montana citizens felt jubilant about the state's educational showing, and the Ayres report was widely quoted. The survey failed, however, to account for such factors as schoolchildren with no opportunity to attend school, retardation, educational requirements for teachers, supervision, or methods of raising or distributing school funds. Moreover, in 1924, 46 percent of Montana schoolchildren were enrolled in rural districts (districts with a population of less than 1,000), which were commonly the poorer districts. For example, one Montana county had, in terms of wealth behind each teacher, a district with a figure of $225,000 and a second district with less than $25,000 (29).

The concept of the comprehensive high school was firmly established in Montana during the 1920's. The superintendent's biennial report of 1924 lists the following major divisions of study offered by high schools in Montana: English, foreign languages, mathematics, science, history, social studies, business, manual training, agriculture, home economics, normal training, and physical education. In addition, many high schools offered such miscellaneous subjects as music, vocations, public speaking, journalism, spelling, secretarial training, and penmanship.

The Phillips Report

The startling information that Montana had dropped to thirtieth place in national rank for the same 10 points in which Dr. Ayres in 1919 had ranked it first was revealed by Superintendent Trumper in her 1926 report, when she listed the new ranking of states by Frank M. Phillips of George Washington University (30). The Phillips report caused thoughtful concern among many Montana citizens, as evidenced by the following statement written by Miss Trumper in 1928.

> For the past two years there have been evidences of a serious purpose on the part of many individuals and organizations, and of some newspapers, to face the facts and to solve the problem of providing better educational advantages in Montana's public schools (31).

And, because the Phillips report had shown that Montana had ranked poorly in part because of financial support,

> The Legislative Assembly of Montana at its session in 1927 took a step which appears to be a definite effort to carry out the mandates of the State Constitution . . . . The establishment of a state equalization fund, even though it is not large, and even though it is derived from funds previously distributed to all of the schools of the state, has definitely provided for the past two years for more uniformity in school support than Montana has ever previously had (32).

School economy following World War I caused the discontinuance of kindergartens, which had been springing up rapidly in the state. In 1928-29, there were six school systems having kindergarten programs in the entire state. Progress has been slow, as today scarcely a dozen kindergartens are operating in the public schools of Montana.

The year 1929 marked the advent of a teacher certification law carrying a prerequisite of 4 years of high school preparation, or its equivalent, and 48 quarter-hours of approved academic or professional preparation. Consequently, at the end of 1931, all high schools in Montana were forced to close their normal training departments because their programs did not meet the new standards.

In 1930, Superintendent Elizabeth Ireland stated that the common school equalization fund was making it possible for "21,714 school children to be benefitted by a nine months term of school, who otherwise would have been denied this privilege. Practically 90 percent of the schools of Montana now have terms nine months long" (33).

In the early 1930's, vocational agriculture and home economics were emphasized in Montana high schools. The Depression made it impossible for the districts to match the federal funds of the Smith-Hughes Act, and at one time the federal government was furnishing $3 to every dollar of district money. Courses in trade and industry were offered in the evenings to adult students; methods of instruction involved a "laboratory" and project assignment. Curtailment of district expenditures made such programs unavailable in many districts, and enrollment in all phases of the program was approximately 1,200 students and adults in 1930. In contrast, by 1938, 6,139 were enrolled (34).

The Depression years caused a drastic setback in Montana education. Especially hard hit were many teachers who were forced to take large discounts on salary warrants when insufficient tax collections caused a shortage of funds. At times, the discounts amounted to nearly 50 percent, which reduced low salaries even further.

World War II

Superintendent Mary Condon, in her biennial report of 1950, summarized the problems which World War II thrust on Montana education:

> The situation brought about by the war years was such as to throw the entire school system into turmoil in many respects. With thousands of our trained teachers going into service and war industries, Montana found itself in a place where the shortage of qualified teachers became so acute that it was necessary to accept those who had very little, if any, training beyond high school. While a teacher was paid an average of $1,200 per year, she found she could go into war work and make two, three or four times that amount. It was necessary during these years to grant emergency certificates to unqualified teachers to such an extent that at the war's end 22 percent of all certificates issued were emergencies (35).

The increased birthrates from 1941 on meant that thousands of youngsters were ready to begin school in 1948 when facilities which had not been replaced or extended during the war years were in poor condition to receive them. Coupled with the problem of increased enrollment, there was also a demand for additional courses in Montana high schools, such as vocational, adult, and veterans training programs.

Miss Condon reported that the new finance law passed by the Legislative Assembly of 1949 provided for increased state support and the distribution of county and state funds on the basis of need. Aid for the public schools was increased from $1,647,427 in 1941 to $7,265,609 in 1949-50. "The whole program was pointed toward equal educational opportunity for every boy and girl in Montana no matter where he resided" (36), according to Miss Condon.

Following the war, the rise in the cost of running Montana schools was substantial, with the records showing an average property levy for each county for school purposes going from 29.43 mills in 1941 to 43.86 mills in 1949 (37).

The Fifties

The 1950's were concerned with catching up with the burden placed on Montana education by the postwar years. Miss Condon did a remarkable job in reporting critical educational needs of the state to the public. To her able leadership can be credited substantial improvement in state aid to school districts and greater educational opportunity for Montana youngsters.

In 1950, Congress passed Public Law 815, which provided for a survey in every state to determine the condition of school buildings and to outline future needs. Montana received $11,200 for this survey, and the state department discovered that 40 percent of all schools in Montana were from 31 to 50 years old and that more than half of the buildings were combustible (38).

Miss Condon was very effective in bringing such conditions to the attention of the public in a forthright and courageous manner that promoted improvement. Her biennial reports not only pointed out conditions as they were, but also effectively urged the necessary remedies. She was especially skilled in causing people to look at all facets of public education. Her reports were knowledgeable and extensive about school boards, superintendents of schools, finance, and teaching conditions, and expounded a philosophy of education regarding the curriculum as well. Educators and laymen may not have always agreed with her views, but there was no mistaking where she stood:

> The fundamentals are taught much better than they were 30 and 40 years ago. Then they were taught for knowledge of them, now they are taught for knowledge and use of them . . . . The reading rate and comprehension of servicemen between World Wars I and II rose four grade levels. Tests in spelling and language given in one of our large city systems showed pupils in every grade to be 1 to 2 grades above those taking the same test in 1919 (39).

In 1952, Miss Condon had 25 supervisors and directors in her department to help her carry out educational duties.

The period following World War II saw a need for increased financial support, more school construction, a broader tax base, salary increases, and curriculum improvement. Few would deny that Miss Condon met the challenge purposefully and well.

The present superintendent, Harriet Miller, has carried on the modern, complex role of the state superintendent in like fashion. At times direct and forceful rather than persuasive, she has worked diligently for the improvement of education in Montana. One creditable accomplishment has been the establishment of certification requirements, which resulted in well-qualified, professional teachers for Montana schools. The instructional services division was established in 1960 as part of a program to reorganize the Department of Public Instruction's functions for more effective administration and service.

Miss Miller's biennial report of 1966 lists 31 specific recommendations that she deemed necessary for legislative action. Among them were such vital issues in the improvement of Montana education as repealing the requirement that 40 percent of the voters must vote in a school election in favor of a simple majority; expanding vocational-technical programs; using federal funds for educational television (ETV); providing education for children under 6 years of age; and simplifying laws on school district boundaries to encourage voluntary consolidation (40).

DEPARTMENT OF PUBLIC INSTRUCTION CONSTITUTIONAL AND LEGAL DEVELOPMENTS

The Federal Organic Act

The Organic Act, passed by Congress in 1864, established a temporary government for the Territory of Montana and also provided for the support of a public school system in Section 14:

> And be it further enacted, That when the lands in said territory shall be surveyed under the direction of the Government of the United States, preparatory to bringing the same into market, sections numbered sixteen and thirty-six in each township in said territory shall be, and the same are hereby, reserved for the purpose of being applied to schools in said territory, and in the states and territories hereafter to be erected out of the same (41).

The first law to provide for a common school system in Montana was passed by the territory's first Legislative Council in 1864. While no provisions were made for the Office of Superintendent of Public Instruction, the Governor lost no time in creating the position by appointment.

In 1866, "A Bill to define the duties of Superintendents of Public Instruction and fix their salaries" (42) specified that a territorial superintendent was to be appointed by the Governor with the consent and advice of the council and was to receive an annual salary of $500. Although Acting Governor Thomas Francis Meagher felt the salary was inadequate, he signed the bill into law in April 1866. Consequently, after one appointee declined and another resigned, the Governor appointed A. M. S. Carpenter the first active superintendent of public instruction under the terms of the new law. However–

> The law creating the office of Superintendent of Public Instruction, enacted at the Session of 1866, came under the sweeping condemnation of Congress, together with the entire proceedings of the session, which was declared null and void by the amendment to the Organic Act. The fourth session of the legislative assembly in 1867 was required to again pass upon the creation of the office. The new bill provided that the "Superintendent of Public Instruction be elected by the Legislative Assembly, in joint convention assembled, to be commissioned by the Governor, who shall hold office until the general election in the year A.D. 1869" (43).

Montana School Law of 1872

In 1872, Montana enacted a new school law which stated that the superintendent of public instruction be appointed by the Governor for a period of 2 years. Although the law of 1867 referred to a general election in 1869, no superintendent was ever elected by the people until statehood came in 1889. The new law outlined the duties of the superintendent but failed to set forth any professional or educational requirements for the appointee, thus making the post absolutely political in nature.

The law required the superintendent to execute a bond of $2,000 pending the complete and faithful discharge of his duties and empowered him and ordered him to adopt a course of studies and rules and regulations for the public schools in the territory. He was to report annually to the Governor (biennially to the Legislative Assembly) and to have printed 700 to 1,000 copies of his report. It also required that he show in the report the conditions of the public schools, with full statistical tables by counties. He was to supply the county superintendents, teachers, and school officers with suitable forms for making reports, diplomas, certificates, and school registers, and maintain his office in a town in which there was a post office.

He was also to travel to the district schools, to meet with county superintendents, and to address public assemblies on subjects pertaining to the schools. For these duties he was to receive a salary of $2,000. Traveling expenses of $300 per year, with a similar amount set aside for rent, fuel, postage, and printing, were provided. In 1873, at an extraordinary session, the superintendent's salary was reduced to $1,200 (44).

Enabling Act and State Constitution

The Enabling Act made it possible for the Territory of Montana to gain admission to the Union as a state. Following passage of the act, a constitutional convention was held in Helena which adopted the constitution. After ratification by the people in October 1889 and fulfillment of other qualifications, Montana became a state in November 1889.

Article XI of the State Constitution is titled "Education." Section I states: "It shall be the duty of the legislative assembly of Montana to establish and maintain a general, uniform, and thorough system of public, free common schools" (45). Subsequent sections, as required by the Enabling Act, provided for establishment of a public school fund, sale of school lands, establishment of a state board of land commissioners, taxation procedures, age of educable children, use of public money for sectarian purposes, nonpartisan requirements for admission to public educational institutions, elections, and establishment of a State Board of Education to preside over the state educational institutions. The membership of the state board was to include the Governor, the state superintendent, and the attorney general as an ex officio member. The eight other members were to be appointed by the Governor, subject to the confirmation of the Senate. The third Legislative Assembly passed an act providing for the appointment, terms of office, powers, duties, and compensation of the state board.

Additional sections of the State Constitution provided for the state superintendent to be elected by the people. Women were given the right to hold office as county superintendents and the right to vote in school elections.

From the time when John Gannon pleaded for a clerk to aid him in the discharge of his duties as the first elected superintendent, the state superintendency has grown to the present organization of 97 full-time staff members (including clerical personnel), 19 workers serving part time in one position while serving in one or more other positions, supervision, and programs. (See Appendix B.)

Modern Status of the State Superintendent

The rise in status of the superintendent of public instruction as a duly elected official of the people provided even more impetus than usual for frequent demands for changes in school law to better accommodate educational needs. From a humble beginning—less than a dozen legal assignments spelled out by law—the state superintendency has progressed through the years to the point where the *School Laws of Montana, Annotated,* prepared and published by Superintendent Miller in 1961, list 117 duties of her office as prescribed by law (46).

Some of the major duties include serving as a member of the executive department of the state government, the State Board of Land Commissioners, and the State Board of Education; supervising the public schools and the state agency for surplus property; verifying school budgets and enforcing school budget laws; preparing a course of study for all elementary and high schools and courses of instruction in identifying and educating handicapped children in cooperation with the State Board of Health; formulating regulations for the issuance of all certificates for teaching; keeping complete data about school equalization aid; advising county superintendents on school matters and prescribing rules and regulations for financial accounting by boards of trustees; apportioning the state interest and income money among the counties and participating in programs under Public Law 88-452; administering federal funds; addressing public assemblies on public school subjects; enforcing textbook licensing provisions; printing school laws; reporting to the Governor biennially; and performing other duties pertaining to the operation of the department and the fulfillment of provisions of Section 75-1302, which requires "the general supervision of the public schools of the state" (47).

MONTANA SCHOOL FINANCE

Sources of Finance

The territorial government of Montana provided for the financing of district schools from several sources: A county tax was to be levied by the board of county commissioners, collected by the county treasurer, disbursed on trustees' warrants, and apportioned to each district pro rata to children over 4 years of age. This tax was to be used for establishing and maintaining public schools.

A second source of revenue was a local or district tax to be voted by the people, at special district meetings, for buildings, teachers' wages, or other purposes.

Fines arising from the breach of penal laws of the territory were to be added to the school fund and disbursed in the same manner as other school money.

In addition, all funds deriving from the sale of town lots under territorial laws were to be used for financing district schools. Such money was to be held by the county treasurer for the district in which the town was situated and was to be used for building and furnishing schools, but could be used for special school purposes if voters of the district so decided at a special election.

Finally, all money and the interest thereon coming from the sale of school lands granted by Congress was to go into a school fund. The principal was to be irreducible, but the interest was to be divided annually pro rata according to the population of schoolchildren over 4 years of age. The territory received no funds under this provision.

To be entitled to public money, districts had to maintain at least 3 months of school during the year, and all public schools had to be taught in English, with reading, writing, spelling, arithmetic, geography, and grammar as prescribed studies, plus other subjects as trustees deemed expedient and necessary. Thus the territorial laws set certain standards which local school systems were required to meet before they could receive funds.

From 1900 to 1923, income from school lands distributed by the State of Montana to schools was fractional, averaging only 7 percent of the total school sources of income. In reality, state funds from school land could not be classified as state financial aid as these lands were set aside by the federal government when Montana became a state. In 1923, special revenues collected by the state, such as gasoline and inheritance taxes, along with a newly enacted metal mines tax, provided "an amount probably equivalent to about $1.50 per child on the census list"(48).

In 1920, Superintendent Trumper listed state funds, county funds, and special district taxes levied on the districts as the three sources of school revenue. She said: "Montana's state school funds are derived entirely from the income from funds received from the sale of school lands and from the leasing of school lands. Montana has never provided a state tax for public schools .... State school funds are slowly increasing . . ." (49).

A 6-mill county tax was distributed to the schools on the census basis, a method of apportionment that Miss Trumper declared to be grossly unfair, as it placed a heavy burden on districts with few children.

Miss Trumper pointed out that—

> The district system has been replaced by the county unit system in three counties, but the district tax for schools continues to yield more than one-half of the money raised to support public elementary and high schools.
>
> Our system of taxation for educational purposes does not provide even fairly equal financial burdens for all patrons and taxpayers or equalized educational opportunities for all children of all the people.
>
> Two districts out of ten paid less than 6 mills special levy in 1919-20, while three out of ten paid from 11 to 40 mills (50).

Miss Trumper urged that changes in the constitution be made to permit larger support from the higher units of government for the Montana school system.

The constitution now permitted district bonding to a maximum of 5 percent of the amount of taxable property, but districts were hard pressed to dispose of their bonds because bonding companies and the State Land Board were placing most of their money in farm loans. This meant that districts had to go back to the earlier practice of providing school buildings from the general school budget, requiring a special levy, or closing inadequate schools.

In 1924, Miss Trumper again pointed out the lack of state revenue support for Montana schools. Her biennial report listed revenue sources as shown below:

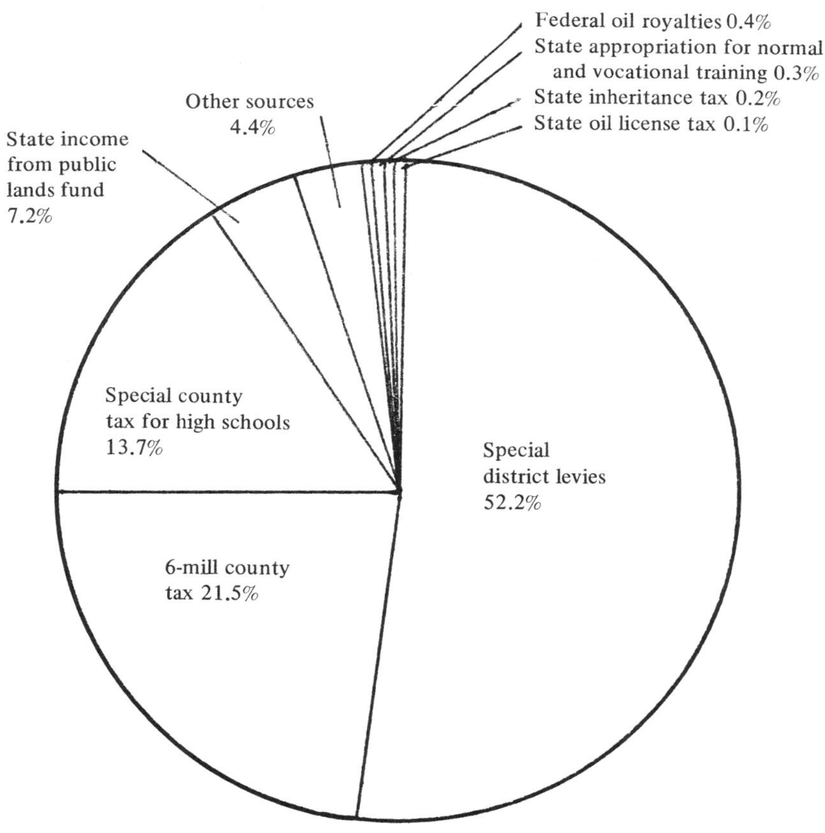

Minimum Foundation Program Law of 1949

In 1949, the method of support for Montana public schools was modernized to better meet the growing financial needs of the districts and to bring state aid in line with what was being done nationally. Each child was to be guaranteed a basic educational opportunity based on equality of financing.

The foundation law provided that after all districts and counties in the state had made the same financial effort to support their educational program, the state would supply the balance needed for minimum programs up to a point determined by law. These minimum foundation programs were based on a teacher unit for small elementary schools. For larger schools, including all high schools, the program was based on the number of pupils in the calculation known as "ANB" (average number belonging), determined by dividing the total days present and absent for all pupils by 180. Consecutive days absent over 3 were not counted toward the ANB. The ANB used for the school budget was computed on the attendance figures from the previous school term.

The uniform effort to be made by districts and counties for their elementary schools was a 5-mill district levy and a 10-mill countywide levy. For high schools, a 10-mill countywide levy was required. Elementary schools were entitled to raise funds on the district up to 20 percent of the foundation program without a vote of the people. High schools could use the permissive levy without a vote of the people up to 15 percent of the foundation program. Additional funds required above this amount necessitated a vote of the people. The 1950-52 report shows the percentages raised to 30 percent for elementary schools and for high schools with 100 or fewer students, and 25 percent for high schools with more than 100 students.

Recent Changes

The 1963 Legislature established the county levy at 25 mills for elementary schools and 15 mills for high schools as the basic foundation effort and raised the foundation limit from 50 percent to 75 percent of the maximum budget allowable without a vote of the people.

> Although the Foundation Program Law was substantially changed in 1963, the basic principles remain much the same .... The local district has been removed as the first level of basic Foundation Program support for elementary schools. The taxes from county-wide levies now constitute the basic support level for both elementary and high schools .... Broadening of the support base makes possible a greater degree of sharing of taxes from all property wealth within a county by all schools within a county (51).

The 1963 law sets forth a schedule that specifies the maximum amounts that may be budgeted per pupil without voter approval. This schedule is based on the amount actually budgeted for 1962-63 in the middle-cost schools of each size-group. "The maximum amount which a school board is permitted to budget for a school's general fund without seeking voter approval is determined by multiplying the school's ANB by the appropriate rate as set forth in the law" (52).

The law further provided that no elementary or high school could receive more than 75 percent of its maximum permissive budget from equalization funds.

> As each school determines its Maximum Schedule, it computes 75 percent of this as its foundation program. The equalization financing, in which the state aid is used, applies *only toward the Foundation Program portion* of the budget. The 25 percent of the Maximum Schedule *above* the Foundation Program is financed by a *permissive district levy.* Surplus cash-on-hand, tuition, and federal funds are applied to reduce the district levy (53).

Of special note is the fact that the foundation program schedule has increased biennially since 1949, its year of origin.

The current mill rate is set at 24 mills for elementary schools and 14 mills for high schools as basic foundation effort, and the foundation limit is 80 percent of the maximum budget allowable without a vote of the people.

The law did not guarantee that the state would meet its total obligation. If the equalization funds do not equal 100 percent of the foundation program, the state deficiency must be made up by a district levy in the elementary schools and a county levy in the high schools. One source (1961) points out:

> Since the Foundation Program was enacted in 1949 there have been only four years in which there were sufficient State funds available to equalize the full state obligation. In other years the State has provided only enough money to equalize from 90 percent to 95 percent of the amount necessary to meet all Foundation Programs. This State deficiency in equalization money becomes a responsibility of the local district and is raised by a property tax on the district (54).

By 1967, there were 7 years in which sufficient state funds were available to equalize the full state obligation.

Presently there are two levels of equalization money—the county and the state. The state's sources of revenue foı educational purposes are legislative appropriations from the state general fund, 25 percent of individual income tax revenues, 25 percent of corporation license tax revenues, U.S. oil and gas royalties, and interest and income from school lands (elementary disbursement only). The counties rely heavily on property tax for their revenue.

In general, the foundation program has made possible great improvements in educational opportunity in Montana schools.

> Prior to its enactment there were many low-valuation districts in which it was impossible to finance an adequate school program without confiscatory tax levies. In many of these districts tax levies are still below the level required in the years before the Foundation Program was enacted. In other districts levies are far below the level that would be required without the Foundation Program financing. This has been made possible because *state equalization dollars have taken the place of local property-tax dollars* (55).

Two features deserve special comment when Montana's foundation program is considered:

1. The State Board of Education set a minimum program of requirements that Montana schools had to meet before qualifying for state equalization funds. Included in the minimum standards were guidance, curriculum, length of school term, courses of study, libraries, administration, and teacher preparation. In most cases, the citizens have elected to tax themselves further to provide additional improvement over the minimum requirements.

2. The public has not been miserly in providing financial support for Montana's educational programs. In 1960, Montana's effort placed it third nationally in percent of per-capita personal income spent for public education:

Table 1. – ABILITY AND EFFORT TO SUPPORT EDUCATION, 1960 (56)

State	Personal income per pupil enrolled		Percent of personal income for public schools	
	Amount	National rank	Amount	National rank
California	$12,069	11	3.8	25
Nevada	11,330	15	3.2	44
Washington	10,379	19	4.5	11
Oregon	9,959	22	4.5	10
Colorado	9,925	23	4.4	13
Montana	9,306	26	5.0	3
Wyoming	9,037	31	4.6	8
Arizona	8,171	34	4.4	12
New Mexico	7,216	39	4.1	15
Idaho	7,172	40	4.0	17
Utah	6,980	42	5.5	1
NATION	$10,670	. . .	3.7	. . .

Further comparison with the Western states shows Montana ranking second in dependence on local-level taxation, with 69.4 percent of its school revenue collected from local sources (57). Montana obviously places great dependence on the property tax for school revenue.

In a tabulation for 1966-67 that includes the 50 states, Montana is ranked fifteenth in expenditure per pupil, thirty-fourth in average salary for classroom teachers, and twenty-eighth in per-capita personal income (58).

EFFECT OF FEDERAL PROGRAMS ON MONTANA EDUCATION

The National Defense Education Act of 1958 (NDEA) and the Elementary and Secondary Education Act of 1965 (ESEA) brought swift changes to the State Department of Public Instruction in Montana. In 1956-57, for instance, the state department had about 67.6 full-time equivalency employees; in 1966-67, this number had increased to 117. According to one state official (59), about 25 percent of this increase was a direct result of ESEA.

The districts, too, were required to respond in a positive manner. First, they had to turn to the state department for interpretation and materials to take advantage of various programs and to seek qualification and support. Second, this in turn forced them to examine in detail their requirements and the specific needs of their students. In trying to accomplish this, they frequently discovered areas that hadn't been given much attention before. ESEA made it possible for the districts to do something about the physical reasons why "Johnny can't read"—the need for eyeglasses or other physical causes that could keep a child from learning.

Another example of meeting the needs of the child rather than of the school is the $100,000 program for migrant children in the state. Educators have long known that these children needed special help, but outside of the classroom there was little equipment or funds to be brought to bear on the problem. The recent federal program to aid these children will run during the summer in those counties that have large numbers of such pupils in an effort to help them catch up with other children.

Federal programs have enabled Montana educators to look at educational aids that were once thought too expensive: instructional materials centers, language laboratories, TV facilities, and audiovisual equipment for each teacher. As a result, teachers have had to learn how to use new materials and devices and, in doing so, in many cases have improved their instructional techniques.

Such programs have had an impact on educational languages, as educators speak of "hardware" and "software" items—hardware referring to computers, electronic learning gear, and other "hard" items of equipment and apparatus; and software referring to services, personnel, or instructional programs being developed locally.

Title III of ESEA has impelled Montana educators to think in experimental terms; the emphasis in many cases had been on unique, imaginative, and innovative educational program development.

Title V encouraged and brought together lay and professional groups to examine educational problems. A recent eight-state project exemplifies such educational cooperation and offers great promise for eventual improvement of education throughout the Western states involved.

Title IV has established regional laboratories to study educational problems of all kinds and offer solutions. The Rocky Mountain Regional Laboratory, with headquarters at Denver, is presently studying small schools and problems common to them. Barbara Longmaid, executive assistant to Superintendent Miller, is currently serving as one of the board members of the laboratory. Other board members are selected from area superintendents.

A Large School

It is not difficult to find concrete examples of the impact that federal aid has had on schools in Montana. Most of this aid has been in the form of helping the districts provide needed equipment or services on a matching-fund basis. Library books, laboratory equipment, reading materials, audiovisual equipment, and similar objects were among the first evidences of federal aid. What was in the beginning a mere trickle quickly turned into a flood as almost every school, regardless of size, submitted its plan to upgrade its scientific program or increase its learning opportunities.

Today there is evidence that more sophisticated plans for improving the learning situation are under way. A large Montana high school, for example, has a federal planning grant to create a countywide resource center designed to cross over educational boundaries and to help all schools in the county implement promising educational innovations. The resource center will provide materials and leadership to help the smaller schools share in the latest resources designed to upgrade educational programs throughout the county. The federal government is expected to provide most of the funds necessary to carry out the program. This same high school also has a federal program that provides Saturday biology classes offering actual experience in the field. Federal aid provides transportation, materials, and teachers for biological field work on several hundred acres of forest service land.

A Small School

A small school in northern Montana has used NDEA funds to purchase needed teaching equipment and to improve the guidance department. ESEA funds have enabled this district to initiate a reading improvement program with special materials and a teacher; to select 33 students for a special summer academic improvement program; and to concentrate on the concept of an instructional materials center with necessary equipment, materials, and a librarian's aide. When the superintendent of this district was asked if the above would have been accomplished without federal aid, he answered, "Probably not! Federal aid has created an atmosphere where the board of trustees is willing to go ahead. It creates a logical next step" (60).

Other Factors

One complaint frequently heard concerning federal aid is that the applications have laid a burden on the average small district superintendent who already has his hands full. Large districts in some instances have been able to designate specialists to handle the paper work involved in federal aid programs. At present, at least five full-time directors of federal programs are employed by districts in the state. This number will increase as even small districts consolidate to hire the services of such specialists.

The average Montana citizen has not escaped the impact of federal aid. Missoula citizens recently agreed to match a $500,000 federal grant to establish a vocational-technical school in Missoula to serve a seven-county area. Such facilities are badly needed, as students now have to leave the state to get most post-high school vocational training. Without the matching federal funds, it is highly doubtful that the voters would have reacted so favorably, as a district special levy was rejected by the voters at the same time the funds were voted.

Missoula is not an isolated example. For example, there is a program called "Upward Bound," in which over a hundred youngsters who were not working to their capabilities and expectations are brought to college campuses to study for the summer months in an effort to "turn them on" academically and get them interested and directed toward higher education (61). The State Department of Public Instruction has a similar program designed to stimulate high school dropouts to return to school.

However, the federal programs have not been an educational panacea for Montana schools. Some of the money spent on hardware has been wasted on educational gadgetry which the teachers in many cases did not want or did not understand how to use. A statewide check would undoubtedly uncover many such objects gathering dust in numerous school districts. The desire to purchase was often spurred by the fact that there was only so much federal money allocated to Montana, and the districts who filed applications early had the best chance of getting it. Districts that took more time to discover their educational needs in depth often discovered that the funds had all been allocated or that the percentage of matching funds had been reduced for that year. A newspaper article in March 1967, commenting on federal aid across the nation, said:

> Some districts are getting only half of what they were told to plan on while others are getting more than expected, an Associated Press Survey showed. . . [recently].

> But in every state there are districts facing a shortage of money to pay bills they contracted for in the belief the federal government stood behind them (62).

"Red tape," says Superintendent Miller, "is giving a black eye to the present system of federal aid to education." Miss Miller, in an address, referred to the fact that the federal aid program is based on "categorical" funding methods which result in short-term planning and large regional offices. She accused the U.S. Office of Education of using confusing procedures, refusing to give "definite answers" to questions from the states, requiring needless paper work, and tying up the entire program in red tape. Miss Miller philosophically supports general aid but reserves the right to Congress to support specific areas of education of its choosing. "The real problem," Miss Miller believes, "is how do you put the brakes on the U.S. Office of Education?" (63).

Similar criticism can be heard in Montana regarding the type of federal aid which should be offered. The executive secretary of the Montana Education Association feels that "control should remain with state and local school districts, with emphasis on local districts, and not in Washington, D.C." (64).

Many small districts are beginning to ask about federal aid to help alleviate current educational problems such as replacing or extending educational facilities and getting and keeping qualified teachers. Because of the present dollar-thin tax base and spiraling costs, available money for general education and construction of facilities is becoming difficult to obtain. General federal aid might provide a more realistic solution in such districts, argue many Montana educators.

Another major problem has been the size of Montana in relation to the money allocated to the state department for administration. Administrative funds for Title I programs have been based on 1 percent of the total allocation. The state department has received $75,000 to administer its Title I programs, but with its many districts covering a wide area, the money has not been adequate to successfully administer the programs. It takes just as much work, paper, and time to process an application submitted by a small district representing 60 students as to handle the same form representing several thousand students. States with about the same number of districts as Montana but with many times the population receive substantially more money for administration of federal programs. Texas, for example, had an allocation of $775,251 for administration purposes in 1966, or $510 per school district, while Montana averaged only $87 per school district for state administration of Title I programs (65). The allocation procedure put a strain on states such as Montana with their limited population and great distances to cover. Since Montana has approximately one state department employee for every seven operating school districts, one of the problems federal aid has caused in Montana is administrative: how to service the large area with the limited personnel and finances available.

Adding to this burden is the fact that many small districts have part-time clerks and administrative officers, making proper applications and material purchase and use extremely difficult. One promising approach which the state department is urging is the consolidation of several small districts into larger cooperative projects to provide more service and leadership and to save administrative costs. The state department has experienced a fair amount of success with this method. Extremely helpful for Montana will be the current federal law which sets a minimum project value of $2,500 on Title I projects.

The superintendent's 1966 biennial report shows over $7 million in federal funds distributed to Montana's counties. In contrast, the biennial report of 1950-52 reported that federal money representing Indian, vocational, lunch, veterans-on-farms, Taylor grazing, U.S. oil and gas royalties, and federal forest programs amounted to slightly over $2 million.

In 1965-66, Montana had 521 Title I projects representing $3.4 million. As of April 1967, 119 projects had been approved this fiscal year, representing almost $2.3 million. It is expected that when the fiscal year ends, total approved projects will equal the amount of money allocated to the state for Title I projects.

Federal aid to education has vastly improved the quality of education in Montana. Teachers institutes, held at university campuses during the summer, increase teaching quality; the various programs have provided equipment, materials, personnel, and facilities for improved learning-teaching opportunities; special programs for the underprivileged and the handicapped have enabled them to attain more equal footing with their normal peers; and the districts in northwestern Montana being affected by the influx of workers and their children in the 3-year construction of the multimillion dollar Libby Dam Project are receiving federal aid in terms of newly constructed classrooms to meet the immediate needs of the impacted areas.

SUMMARY

The history and development of public education in Montana have not been dissimilar to those experienced by her sister states. The need for greater educational effort sprang into being at the grass-roots level and blossomed into a state system of direction and leadership based on the needs and aspirations of the localities. The effort to increase educational opportunity in Montana has always been a cooperative one, with the local districts and the state actively participating. The laws have been amended to meet the needs as they arose, and the study of Montana school law is a study of the development of Montana education and its leadership—from a single concept in several paragraphs to a complicated array of thousands of items to aid the schools in providing common educational experiences for man to move into the twenty-first century with honor, compassion, and understanding.

The next decade will be a critical one for the state departments of education and the local districts, as they search for answers to educational problems and seek to define new roles of educational responsibility. Montana's State Department of Public Instruction has steadily progressed during the last decades in its ability to satisfy the leadership requirements placed on it. Curriculum study guides have been prepared and distributed in major subject areas; numerous professional and lay committees have studied educational problems and made worthwhile recommendations; needed supervisors and departments have been created at the state level; and excellent handbooks, documents, and bulletins have been distributed to districts throughout the state. These efforts have strengthened the role of the state department and suggest that Montana education will be prepared to face new challenges in the future.

However, the requirements ahead call for bold and advanced thinking about such problems as—

1. *Finance.* Due to the sparseness of population, limited industrial development, and heavy reliance on property tax to support schools, the problem of how Montana will finance her educational requirements in the years ahead is a critical one. Many school districts today find that increased costs of instruction and building construction have placed them in an untenable position with the taxpayers. Their ability to legally bond themselves, for example, does not equal their educational need. Schools have been built like fortresses, and districts are extremely reluctant, and sometimes find it economically impossible, to raze the old structures and provide new spaces to house current innovations and practices. The old spaces do not lend themselves readily to modern teaching methods which place more emphasis on inquiry, independent study, large- and small-group instruction, and resource centers.

Providing new facilities, preparing for increased technological equipment and services, and maintaining a qualified professional staff will continue to be an increasingly expensive undertaking. New methods of financing educational requirements will have to be uncovered if Montana is to balance aims with means and still remain justifiably proud of its educational system.

2. *Organization.* The isolated school will continue to be a part of the Montana educational scene for many years ahead and will probably be justified and supported, but schools which operate within a 40-minute bus ride from each other cannot long afford to duplicate educational programs and buildings. Regrouping and reorganization of schools and districts is something Montana must face now if it is to cope successfully with educational problems in the future. To wait until such organization is voluntarily accomplished is too costly both in time and in financial resources.

3. *Control.* The federal government will doubtlessly have an increasingly larger role to play in future American education. Cunningham, writing on leadership and control in education, remarks:

> The responsibility for education will continue to rest with the states, although it appears that there will be a contest over this obligation involving the large cities and the federal government. The contest will become severe unless states can improve in their ability to satisfy educational needs (66).

A contest involving local as well as state and federal control would not be in the best interests of Montana education. To minimize such conflict will require vitality, courage, and resourcefulness on the part of educational leaders throughout the state as they call for moral and financial support of quality education in a responsible and forthright manner.

Cunningham summarizes neatly:

> There is little doubt that changes in the environment of the schools will be reflected in the leadership and control of American education. The citizen of the future will have more to say about schools, and so will teachers and students. Demands for participation will lead to alterations in the structures through which schools have been governed and administered. The traditional . . . [leadership and administrative roles] . . . will be modified but they will survive. The challenges are substantial but so is the nation's capacity to respond (67).

FOOTNOTES

1. Professor Thomas J. Dimsdale, an Englishman, was at one time a student of Oxford University. He taught a private school in Virginia City, Montana Territory, in 1863-65. He was the editor of the *Montana Post* and author of *The Vigilantes of Montana,* both published by D. W. Tilton and Co. in Virginia City. The book was published in 1865.
2. Emmet J. Riley, *Development of the Montana State Educational Organization, 1864-1930* (Washington, D.C.: Catholic University of America, 1931), p. 5.
3. Editorial, *Montana Post,* September 9, 1865. This edition is on file in the archives of the State Historical Library, Helena.
4. Territorial Superintendent of Public Instruction, *Biennial Report, Together with Montana School Law and Forms* (1873), p. 5.
5. *Ibid.*, p. 18.
6. W. D. McClurkin, *Public Schools of Montana: A Report to Montana Taxation-Education Commissions*

(Nashville, Tenn.: Division of Surveys and Field Services, George Peabody College for Teachers, 1958), p. 15.

7. Superintendent of Public Instruction, *Biennial Report* (1966), p. 27.

8. Territorial Superintendent of Public Instruction, *Biennial Report* (1873), p. 19.

9. *Ibid.*, p. 20.

10. Territorial Superintendent of Public Instruction, *Biennial Report* (1875), p. 12.

11. Territorial Superintendent of Public Instruction, *Biennial Report* (1878), p. 5.

12. Territorial Superintendent of Public Instruction, *Annual Report* (1879), p. 7.

13. *Ibid.*, p. 26.

14. Territorial Superintendent of Public Instruction, *Annual Report* (1880), p. 10.

15. Territorial Superintendent of Public Instruction, *Fifth Annual Report* (1883), Foreword.

16. Territorial Superintendent of Public Instruction, *Sixth Annual Report* (1884), p. 40.

17. Superintendent of Public Instruction, *Eleventh Annual Report* (1889), p. 6.

18. Superintendent of Public Instruction, *Sixth Biennial Report* (1900), p. 1.

19. Superintendent of Public Instruction, *Fourteenth Biennial Report* (1916), p. 6.

20. *Ibid.*

21. *Ibid.*, p. 7.

22. Superintendent of Public Instruction, *Fifteenth Biennial Report* (1918), p. 28.

23. Superintendent of Public Instruction, *Sixteenth Biennial Report* (1920), pp. 100-101.

24. Superintendent of Public Instruction, *Fifteenth Biennial Report* (1918), p. 102.

25. *Ibid.*, p. 125.

26. *Ibid.*, p. 78.

27. "Proclamation by the Governor of Montana," *The Inter-Mountain Educator,* XIV (September 1918), 24.

28. Superintendent of Public Instruction, *Sixteenth Biennial Report* (1920), p. 5.

29. Superintendent of Public Instruction, *Eighteenth Biennial Report* (1924), p. 25.

30. Superintendent of Public Instruction, *Nineteenth Biennial Report* (1926), p. 7.

31. Superintendent of Public Instruction, *Twentieth Biennial Report* (1928), p. 7.

32. *Ibid.*

33. Superintendent of Public Instruction, *Twenty-First Biennial Report* (1930), p. 23.

34. Superintendent of Public Instruction, *Twenty-Eighth Biennial Report* (1938), pp. 90-96.

35. Superintendent of Public Instruction, *Biennial Report* (1950), p. 6.

36. *Ibid.*, p. 6.

37. *Ibid.*

38. Superintendent of Public Instruction, *Biennial Report* (1952), p. 38.

39. *Ibid.*, p. 21.

40. Superintendent of Public Instruction, *Biennial Report* (1966), pp. 1-4.

41. Superintendent of Public Instruction, *School Laws of Montana, Annotated* (1961), p. 1.

42. Montana, *House Journal, 1866,* pp. 11, 75, 114.

43. Riley, *op. cit.*, p. 15.

44. Montana, *Laws, Extraordinary Session (1873),* p. 63.

45. Superintendent of Public Instruction, *School Laws of Montana, Annotated* (1961), p. 5.

46. Superintendent of Public Instruction, *Biennial Report* (1966), Appendix II, pp. a-g.

47. Superintendent of Public Instruction, *School Laws of Montana, Annotated* (1961), p. 96.

48. Superintendent of Public Instruction, *Eighteenth Biennial Report* (1924), p. 8.

49. Superintendent of Public Instruction, *Sixteenth Biennial Report* (1920), p. 106.

50. *Ibid.*, pp. 110, 112, 114.

51. Montana Education Association, *Here's How It Works: An Explanation of Montana's Equalization Foundation Program* (Helena: The Association, 1964 ed.), p. 3.

52. *Ibid.*

53. *Ibid.*, p. 4.

54. *Ibid.* (1967 ed.), p. 3.

55. *Ibid.*, p. 5.

56. School Foundation Study Committee, *Montana's School Foundation Program* (Helena: The Committee, 1962), p. 10.

57. *Ibid.*, p. 11, Table 18, "Percentage Distribution of Public School Revenue Receipts from Federal, State, and Local Sources, 1961-1962."

58. National Education Association, *NEA Research Bulletin* (Washington, D.C.: The Association, March 1967), p. 10.

59. Personal interview with Ralph G. Hay, director of services development, Montana Department of Public Instruction, March 15, 1967.

60. Personal interview with Roger Ranta, superintendent of schools in Eureka, Montana, August 22, 1967.

61. The "Upward Bound" project is at the University of Montana in Missoula. The federal government has provided the money to bring high school junior students who are underachievers to university campuses in an effort to "turn them on academically." Funds have provided teachers, materials, and a small stipend to each student. The students are expected to attend for two summer sessions during their junior and senior years.

62. *The Daily Missoulian,* March 21, 1967.

63. *Ibid.,* July 16, 1967.

64. *Ibid.*

65. Personal interview with Ralph G. Hay, March 15, 1967.

66. Luvern L. Cunningham, "Leadership and Control of Education," *Implications for Education of Prospective Changes in Society.* Designing Education for the Future: An Eight-State Project (Englewood Cliffs, N.J.: Citation Press, Scholastic Magazines, 1967), pp. 194-95.

67. *Ibid.,* p. 195.

BIBLIOGRAPHY

Public Documents

Montana. *Constitution* (1889).

—— *House Journal, 1866.*

—— *Laws* (1879, 1893).

—— *Laws, Extraordinary Session* (1873).

Superintendent of Public Instruction. *School Laws of Montana, Annotated* (1961, 1965).

Books

Cunningham, Luvern L. "Leadership and Control of Education." *Implications for Education of Prospective Changes in Society.* Edited by Edgar L. Morphet and Charles O. Ryan. Designing Education for the Future: An Eight-State Project. Englewood Cliffs, N.J.: Citation Press, Scholastic Magazines, 1967.

Riley, Emmet J. *Development of the Montana State Educational Organization, 1864-1930.* Washington, D.C.: Catholic University of America, 1931.

Reports

McClurkin, W. D. *Public Schools of Montana: A Report to Montana Taxation-Education Commissions.* Nashville, Tenn.: Division of Surveys and Field Services, George Peabody College for Teachers, 1958.

Montana Education Association. *Here's How It Works: An Explanation of Montana's Equalization Foundation Program.* Helena: The Association, 1961 and 1964.

National Education Association. *NEA Research Bulletin.* Washington, D.C.: The Association, March 1967.

School Foundation Study Committee. *Montana's School Foundation Program.* Helena: The Committee, 1962.

Superintendent of Public Instruction. *Early Schools in Montana.* Helena: Department of Public Instruction, 1964.

Territorial and State Superintendents of Public Instruction. *Annual and Biennial Reports.* Helena: Department of Public Instruction, 1873-1966.

Articles and Periodicals

Editorial, *Montana Post* (Virginia City), September 9, 1865. This edition is on file in the archives of the State Historical Library, Helena.

Montana Post (Virginia City), 1864-68.

"Proclamation by the Governor of Montana." *The Inter-Mountain Educator,* XIV (September 1918), 24.

The Daily Missoulian (Missoula), March 21 and July 16, 1967.

Other Sources

Hay, Ralph G. Personal interview with Hay, director of services development, March 15, 1967.

Ranta, Roger. Personal interview with Ranta, superintendent of schools, Eureka, Montana, August 22, 1967.

Appendix A

MONTANA CHIEF STATE SCHOOL OFFICERS

Territorial Superintendents of Public Instruction (Appointed by Governor)

1865	Thomas J. Dimsdale
1866	Peter Ronan (declined to serve)
1866-67	A. H. Barrett
1867-68	A. M. S. Carpenter
1868-69	Thomas F. Campbell
1869	James H. Mills
1869	S. G. Lathrop
1872-78	Cornelius Hedges
1878-79	Clark Wright
1879-81	W. Egbert Smith
1881-83	R. H. Howey
1883-85	Cornelius Hedges
1885-87	William W. Wylie
1887-89	Arthur C. Logan

State Superintendents of Public Instruction (Elected)

1889-93	John Gannon
1893-97	Eugene A. Steere
1897-1901	E. A. Carleton
1901-1905	W. W. Welch
1905-13	W. E. Harmon
1913-17	H. A. Davee
1917-29	May Trumper
1929-37	Elizabeth Ireland
1937-41	Ruth Reardon
1941-49	Elizabeth Ireland
1949-57	Mary M. Condon
1957-68	Harriet Miller

Appendix B

Chart I.--MONTANA DEPARTMENT OF PUBLIC INSTRUCTION, 1926

Superintendent
Deputy Superintendent
Two Rural Supervisors
One High School Supervisor

Chart II.--MONTANA DEPARTMENT OF PUBLIC INSTRUCTION, 1950

State Superintendent
  Deputy Superintendent
  Administrative Assistant

High School Supervisor
Rural School Supervisor
Music Supervisor
Supervisor of Visual Education
Director of School Lunch Program

Supervisor of Physical Education, Health, and Recreation
Supervisor of Indian Education and Transportation

Director of State Correspondence School

Director of Certification
Textbook Librarian
Nutritionist
State Director of Vocational Education
Supervisor of Vocational Agricultural Education
Assistant Supervisor of Vocational Agricultural Education
Supervisor of Apprenticeship Training
Supervisor of Home Economics
Supervisor of Occupational Information and Guidance
Supervisor of Distributive Education
Supervisor of Donable Property Program

Fiscal Accountant
Three Field Supervisors
District Supervisor
Fireman Trainer
Assistant Fireman Trainer
Director of Job Safety and Training Program

Appendix B

Chart III.--MONTANA DEPARTMENT OF PUBLIC INSTRUCTION, 1966

SUPERINTENDENT OF PUBLIC INSTRUCTION AND EXECUTIVE OFFICER OF VOCATIONAL EDUCATION

Deputy Superintendent

Executive Assistant

Division of Instructional Services

Director
- Coordinator, NDEA III and V-a
  - English
  - Foreign Languages
  - Guidance Services
  - Humanities and the Arts
  - Mathematics
  - Reading and Language Arts
  - Science
  - Social Sciences

Director, Vocational Education
- Agricultural Education
- Business and Distributive Education
- Home Economics Education
- Manpower Development and Training Act
- Technical Education
- Trade and Industrial Education
  - Fireman Training
- Vocational Guidance
- Work Study Program

Special Services
- Adult Basic Education
- Aviation Education*
- Driver Education
- Indian Education
- Library Services (ESEA II)
- Music
- Special Education

Division of Financial, Statistical and Information Services

Director
- Aid Distribution
  - P. L. 815 and P. L. 874
  - Transportation
  - State Equalization
  - Interest and Income
  - ESEA III
- Statistics
- Data Services
- Coordinator, Federal Programs
  - Accounting
- School Finance Specialist
- Information Services
  - Editing and Publishing
  - Documents
  - Information Dissemination

Division of Administrative Services

- Budget Control
  - Accounting
  - Purchasing and Inventory
- Personnel
- Staff Services
  - Office Services and Facilities

Division of General Services

Director
- Accreditation
  - Elementary
  - Secondary
- Audiovisual Library
- Certification
- General Educational Development Testing
- School Lunch
  - Nutrition Consultant
- Surplus Property
- Textbook Registration
- Veterans' Education and Training

Research and Development Group

- Division of Services Development
  - School District Consulting Services (ESEA I)
- Eight-State Project
- New Programs
- Research Coordinating Unit
- Special Projects
  - ESEA IV

---

* By arrangement with Montana Aeronautics Commission.

Appendix C

Table 2. – STATISTICAL DATA, MONTANA PUBLIC SCHOOLS, 1868-1962

Date	No. of census children	Recorded school enrollment	No. of school districts	No. of schools	No. of teachers employed	Aver. monthly salary of teachers	Aver. length of school term	Value of school property
1868	1,359	...	25	15	27	...	...	...
1872-73	3,517	1,881	91	51	99	$ 68.41	...	$ 21,192
1874-75	3,837	2,498	96	76	99	61.45	...	48,009
1876	4,271	2,734	99	83	110	63.50	...	56,080
1877	4,561	2,625[a]	103	87	110	61.02	...	55,485
1878	5,315	3,277	105	88	116	59.70	...	88,285
1879	5,885	3,909	...	99	145	58.45	...	99,345
1881	9,479	5,112[a]	144	132	177	62.50	110 days	140,250
1882	10,482	6,054	155	143	191	66.26	125 days	235,708
1883	12,485	...	180	160	226	58.80	...	197,300
1884	15,515	...	216	198	292	67.00	...	335,371
1885	16,626	...	249	249	337	71.00	...	377,766
1886	20,198	...	272	250	377	70.00	...	437,588
1887	23,165	...	289	266	394	65.50	...	548,367
1888	27,600	...	316	305	442	62.50	...	646,670
1889	36,803	...	344	419	507	66.56	...	698,798
1890	27,821	...	361	314	531	60.10	...	994,378
1896	41,201	...	565	549	953	51.16	...	1,447,581
1900	57,210	...	696	700	1,214	59.67	...	2,531,942
1905	70,814	48,386	817	907	1,663	83.00 (men)	6.1 months	...
1910	88,805	66,141	994	1,188	2,250	112.24	7.9 months	...
1961-62	205,729	163,857	1,018	1,157	7,504[b]	[c]	180 days	218,678,866

Source:

Annual and biennial reports of superintendents of public instruction of the Territory and State of Montana, 1881-1962.

[a]Not all counties reporting.

[b]Includes teachers, librarians, guidance and supervisory personnel, and administrators.

[c]Average annual salaries: elementary, $5,321; high school, $5,930.

Appendix D

A STUDY OUTLINE FOR STUDENTS IN MONTANA UNGRADED (RURAL) SCHOOLS, 1882*

Studies for Pupils in First Reader

1. Reading - First Reader
2. Spelling words in reading lesson
3. Writing on slates, using script speller
4. Read and write numbers to 100. Addition and subtraction by 1's, 2's, 3's, and 5's to 25.

Studies for Pupils in Second Reader

1. Reading - Second Reader
2. Spelling - oral, written, and phonic, words used in reading lesson
3. Writing - on slates, or using copybook, writing with pencil
4. Numbers - addition and subtraction tables to 12's
   Reading and writing numbers to 10,000
   Roman numbers to 100; multiplication tables to 6's.

Studies for Pupils in Third Reader

1. Reading - Third Reader
2. Spelling - oral, written, and phonic; use Swinton's Word Book
3. Reading and writing numbers of two periods; add, subtract, multiply, and divide; begin Robinson's First Book in Arithmetic and complete one-half
4. Geography - oral - Geography of Montana, and draw map of same
5. Writing.

Studies for Pupils in Fourth Reader

1. Reading - Fourth Reader
2. Spelling - Swinton's Word Book
3. Writing - Spencerian Copy Book
4. Geography - Monteith's Elementary
5. Grammar - Ginn & Heath's Elementary Lessons in English.

Studies for Pupils in Fifth Reader

1. Reading - Fifth Reader and History of the United States
2. Spelling - Swinton's Word Book
3. Writing - Spencerian Copy Book
4. Geography - Sill
5. Arithmetic - Robinson's Complete
   Declamation and composition throughout the course.

---

*Superintendent of Public Instruction. *Early Schools in Montana.* Helena: Department of Public Instruction, 1964. pp. 3-4.

27 Nebraska

DEPARTMENT OF EDUCATION
Ginger Jensen

Contents

EDUCATION PRIOR TO 1900

The Territorial Period

When the Nebraska Territory was organized in 1854, the 2,723 settlers were so scattered that it was difficult for them to establish schools except in a few villages and towns. These pioneers, accustomed to the Eastern woodlands and an abundant rainfall, spent so much time wresting a livelihood under the alien conditions of the Great Plains that cultural institutions had to play a secondary role. Building materials were scarce, and it was difficult to find teachers, textbooks, and other supplies.

Even though education had to take a back seat, the Territoral Legislature recognized its importance. During its first session in 1854, it created the Office of Territorial Librarian with the additional duty of superintendent of public instruction. More important at that time, it provided for county superintendents with the responsibility of dividing the land into convenient school districts, arranging elections, and generally supervising the schools.

The federal Enabling Act of 1854 set aside sections 16 and 36 in each township for the support of common schools. This land, amounting to 2,797,520 acres (1), was to be held in trust by the U.S. Congress until Nebraska achieved statehood. The Territorial Legislature passed an act in 1858 creating a common school fund from the land's proceeds. However, as railroads, homesteaders, and purchasers were acquiring acreage rapidly, Librarian-Superintendent John H. Kellom recommended quickly substituting better lands for sections 16 and 36 before they were sold or disposed of. The Legislature did not immediately respond.

The law of 1858 also provided for a territorial commissioner of common schools to be elected on a partisan basis. The following year, William E. Harvey defeated Kellom in the first election. Although Harvey was not an educator, he well understood the needs of the schools and attempted to make them more efficient. He strongly advocated classifying pupils by grades, providing at public expense textbooks suited to pupils' abilities in each grade, and requiring compulsory attendance. He continued the fight to secure better lands for the school fund. It was not until 1862, however, that the acting secretary of the interior notified the territorial land commissioner that he could select alternate lands in lieu of sections 16 and 36 if these had already been settled (2).

In the meantime, the common school fund was threatened at the local level. The Territorial Legislature in 1860 passed an act empowering the commissioner of common schools to investigate county superintendents, particularly their handling of funds. Few county treasurers actually remitted school funds to the territorial treasurer; if they sent any at all, it was only those amounts in excess of apportionment. Commissioner Harvey offered recommendations, but they were not adopted, and charges of mismanagement continued.

Despite repeated efforts to strengthen Nebraska's educational system from 1861 to 1866, there was little progress. In 1861, the commissioner's office was abolished and his duties assigned to the territorial auditor. The territorial auditor (librarian and school commissioner) lacked adequate funds and staff. The people did recognize education as a territorial function, however, and provided for establishing schools at the local, county, and territorial levels. This recognition influenced future Legislatures.

In 1866, the Legislature passed a joint resolution directing that a constitution for the proposed state of Nebraska be prepared and submitted to the people in an election on June 2. The adopted constitution, hastily drafted and weak in many respects, included an article on education which provided that the proceeds from all school lands should constitute a perpetual school fund and that this income, together with taxes levied by the Legislature, should be used to secure a thorough and efficient system of common schools throughout the state.

On March 1, 1867, President Andrew Johnson issued a proclamation declaring the admission of Nebraska into the Union, thus ending the territorial period.

School Lands and Funds

Governor David Butler, Nebraska's first Governor, called a special session of Legislature in May 1867. At this time, a statute was passed providing for the selection and management of state lands and specifying that the auditor should be made land commissioner in charge of administering them. County commissioners were to name three people to appraise the lands, which would be offered for sale to the highest bidder. No land was to be sold for less than its appraised value or for less than $7 per acre. The purchaser could pay one-tenth cash on prairie lands and one-half cash on all others, with the remainder financed by loans bearing interest at 10 percent annually. In case payments were not made, the lands reverted to the state, together with any improvements. Those lands not sold were to be offered for rent for a period of 25 years by the county commissioners in the county in which they were located.

All money received as principal from the sale of public land was paid to the state treasurer and invested by this officer, the Governor, and the land commissioner in federal or state securities bearing 6-percent interest. The interest from notes given in payment for school land constituted a temporary school fund to be distributed each year to the counties on the basis of the school census.

John Gillespie, the state's first land commissioner, favored amending the 1867 law to dispose of school lands at private as well as public sales and to place the administration of these sales directly in the hands of the land commissioner instead of the county commissioners. Although the Legislature did not agree to this at the time, 2 years later it changed the laws. These Acts of 1869 stipulated that the appraisers could not be holders of lands they were appraising, that unsold or unleased land would be offered annually for sale, and that funds from such sales could be invested in government securities or "other good and sufficient securities." This meant that many of the funds were loaned to friends and political allies at low-interest rates. Shortly after the enactment of the permanent fund, there was a default in interest on some of the loans, and the legal proceedings to recover the losses cost the public schools a substantial amount of revenue.

The air was soon heavy with charges, particularly that Governor Butler had lent some $40,000, which was supposed to be invested only in U.S. or state securities, to friends with inadequate security. It also was charged that he had speculated illegally in Lincoln lots and had accepted bribes from contractors, railroads, and private individuals. As the Governor campaigned for a third term in 1870, strong impeachment sentiment in the Legislature culminated in the creation of a joint committee to investigate all of the public activities of the capital commissioners.

Butler declared that the stories were merely gossip, and he considered the appointment of the committee solely the work of political enemies out to destroy him. Although he did not deny that he had exceeded instructions, he declared that at all times he had acted in the best interests of the state. U.S. bonds were depreciating rapidly, he argued, and the individuals to whom he lent the money provided better security. Besides, he said, it was for the state's interest to use the money to keep business flourishing.

The committee's report generally absolved the Governor and his associates of evil intent. The people apparently accepted the Governor's explanation, for he was reelected to a third term. Butler's enemies were not so easily satisfied. When the Legislature convened the following year, he was asked to account for funds collected from the federal government for school lands sold prior to the state's admission to the Union. The Governor replied that he had collected $16,881.26, which he had deposited with the state treasurer. When neither the treasurer nor the auditor's books showed the transaction, the Governor admitted that he had not deposited the money but had borrowed it for his own use. He assured the Legislature that it was adequately secured in mortgages on Pawnee County land.

Although influential voices argued that it would be expensive and cast great discredit on the new state, the House of Representatives, on March 6, approved 11 articles of impeachment against Governor Butler. The first charge, and the only one on which the Senate voted to convict him, was that the Governor appropriated school funds collected from the federal government for his own use. The trial revealed an incredible laxity in the handling of the state's financial affairs. As a result, the auditor was impeached for malfeasance but was not convicted. The state treasurer was severely criticized but not impeached. On June 1, 1871, the Senate convicted the Governor of misappropriating the state's funds, with the only penalty being removal from office. After a number of unsuccessful attempts, in 1877, Butler's friends in the Legislature finally expunged the impeachment proceedings from the record (3).

In 1875, a convention wrote a new constitution for Nebraska. The state superintendent of public instruction, whose office was reestablished in 1869 when the offices of auditor and school commissioner were divided, was specifically listed as one of the executive officers of the state. At the same time, the Constitution of 1875 forbade investing the permanent school funds in other than U.S. or state securities or registered county bonds of Nebraska. This resulted in a major portion of the funds' being invested in county bonds for the next 20 years.

Again, irregularities developed. The permanent school fund money, deposited in banks selected by the state treasurer, was highly profitable to the banks, and they willingly paid interest on it. The constitution denied the treasurer the right to receive money from the use of his office beyond his salary, but in some cases banks paid an interest on these deposits to a friend of the state treasurer. Thus, powerful interests organized to name the state treasurer. These groups provided the bond for the treasurer and divided the profits from the interest on the deposits of state money. Not only did this violate the law, but it blocked any possibility of a wider field for safely investing the state school funds.

Land speculators often took advantage of the laws by purchasing lands, never expecting to complete the payments, and then selling them at a large profit to someone who could. In other cases, speculators obtained a lease for a few cents an acre, thus gaining legal control over large tracts, which they then exploited for their own financial gain.

These practices brought serious criticism against the Board of Public Lands and Buildings' administration of the school lands. Many charged that it had permitted these lands to be leased at an appraised value of only 25¢ per acre before being offered for sale. Others criticized the board for not appraising the school lands every 5 years. Charles H. Gere, editor of the *Nebraska State Journal,* and many others ardently supported a proposal written in 1882 that the sale of school lands be stopped and that they be held in perpetual ownership by the state.

In January 1883, the Legislature amended the school land law to require that all school lands under lease be reappraised at once and each 5 years thereafter upon order of the Board of Public Lands and Buildings. It reduced the minimum rate of interest on the appraised value for leasing from 8 percent to 6 percent. Lessees in default of interest payments could have their leases or sales contracts forfeited after 6 months notice (4).

Charges continued to circulate, and 2 years later, in 1885, the Legislature appointed a committee of three Republicans and three Democrats to investigate state school land practices. The majority reported no evidence of misconduct, but the minority report censured the Board of Public Lands and Buildings and the land commissioner for permitting speculators to gain control over school lands under the guise of law. The Legislature then passed a law limiting the holdings of any one person to 640 acres (5).

Immediately following the Panic of 1893, with the dearth of private deposits, the banks found it necessary to use public funds—especially the public school fund—for their speculations. When the political campaigns revealed that over $1 million of the permanent school fund had not been invested, rumors began to circulate that it had been loaned in questionable speculations and would never be recovered. In part, this resulted in the election of a Populist Governor in 1894.

In the 1895 Legislature, a resolution was introduced calling upon the attorney general to bring action against the state treasurer of the preceding decade to recover approximately $500,000 interest on the $1 million uninvested school fund. This resolution, referred to a committee, never came to a vote. But 2 years later, Addison Sheldon introduced a bill replacing the old school land law with a new one prohibiting the further sale of school lands and substituting a system of perpetual leasing. This bill became law in April 1897.

In the same legislative session, Sheldon introduced and was successful in getting passed a resolution for investigating the state treasurer's office. The investigation revealed that payments on half of the land – about $1.3 million – were delinquent an average of 6 years; 720,000 acres were declared forfeited (6). The former state treasurer, who had been defeated in the election of 1896, could not account for $537,762, mostly from the permanent endowment funds. Although he was sentenced to 20 years in prison, the funds were never recovered. The treasurer's friends, however, maintained that much of the money had been lost before his term. Powerful political and financial interests combined to have him released, and he was eventually pardoned in January 1902. The investigation resulted in improved financial practices by the Board of Public Lands and Funds and in later safeguards through improved legislation.

Improving Education

There were many efforts to improve education before 1900. As early as 1860, the Territorial Legislature granted a charter for establishing a college-level school in the village of Peru. Reverend Hiram Burch and William Daily first solicited funds for such a school, and a female seminary was ultimately opened in September 1866. The following fall, the school was offered to the Methodist Conference; when the offer was rejected, it was offered to the 1867 session of the Nebraska Legislature. In accepting the school at Peru, the Legislature not only created Nebraska's first state normal school but also established the third teacher-training institution west of the Missouri River (7).

The University of Nebraska opened its doors in 1871, with the state superintendent of public instruction an ex officio member of the Board of Regents. Four years later, the Institute for the Blind was established, and in 1885, the School for Feeble-Minded Youth was opened. The services of the state normal school in Peru were improved, and the University of Nebraska cooperated in developing a course of study for high schools.

In 1867, the Nebraska State Teachers Association was established "for the purpose of elevating the profession of teaching, and promoting the interests of schools in Nebraska" (8). Whether the association functioned as a strong and influential lobbying organization or whether the recommended changes would have been accomplished anyway are moot points. The fact remains that between 1867 and 1900, many of its requested organizational and philosophical changes did come into being. These covered a wide and complex spectrum, including school records, finance laws, curriculum, textbooks, administration, teacher training, certification, and fringe benefits. Through the years, the association continued to strive for improved educational opportunities for children.

The 1895 Legislature was truly a busy one. It extended to private colleges and universities the privilege of issuing teacher's certificates; amended laws governing school district boundaries and the attendance of children in schools near their homes; and passed the first free high school attendance law, which permitted nonresident students who had satisfactorily completed the eighth grade to attend a Nebraska high school at county expense.

Thus, by the end of the century, Nebraska had improved its teacher preparation and its schoolhouses, enforced compulsory attendance laws, provided free textbooks, and improved the courses of study and school district organization.

Although Nebraska's last state superintendent of the nineteenth century, William R. Jackson, was unsuccessful in securing the enactment of his major recommendations into law, he did arouse interest by an official decision relating to Bible reading in the public schools. In November 1899, Jackson sent a directive, which was widely quoted across the nation, to the director of a school board near Beatrice in which he favored the use of the Bible, not as a sectarian book, but as part of the great literature of all time. In this he was sustained by the State Supreme Court.

DEVELOPING A STATE SYSTEM, 1900 TO 1930

Until 1891, when the Legislature finally authorized the state superintendent to appoint a permanent deputy, the office operated basically as a one-man department (9). But during the three decades beginning in 1870, the number of counties had increased from 32 to 90, the number of districts from 797 to 6,708, the number of schoolhouses from 298 to 6,733, and the number of children enrolled in school from 12,719 to 288,227. Thus, the responsibilities of the state superintendent became constantly heavier.

When William K. Fowler became state superintendent in January 1901, he reviewed the office's accomplishments and forecast what should be done in the twentieth century. He was supported by the Legislature, which passed an act directing the superintendent and the faculty of the state normal school to set up an examination procedure for admission to the school. The Legislature also rewrote the compulsory education law, clarified its operation, and continued the penalties for violating the law.

The 1901 Legislature passed a free high school attendance law which created an "adjunct" district of the nonhigh school districts in a county and provided that these districts levy a tax sufficient to pay the high school tuition of any pupils who qualified. In 1907, the Legislature passed a new free high school attendance law providing payment of tuition by the district in hope of establishing the law's constitutionality. It was tested in 1907, and Judge L. M. Pemberton of Beatrice held the law to be constitutional and reasonable.

Despite this progress, Superintendent Fowler realized there were still many problems. He saw the rural schools as largely unchanged through three generations while the city school systems were advancing because of fine supervision. It was incomprehensible to him that these two widely divergent kinds of schools could exist under the same laws. Thus, he issued 32 recommendations for urgently needed amendments to the school laws to advance consolidation of school districts, centralization of schools, and public transportation of pupils.

In 1905, State Superintendent Jasper L. McBrien, who assumed the office in January of that year, agreed with Fowler that consolidation was necessary. He had the support of the Nebraska State Teachers Association, which in 1905 made school consolidation one of its 12 programs (10). Superintendent McBrien cited 29 advantages from consolidating school districts, and he even argued that existing laws could be used if new ones were not forthcoming. In fact, several school districts did consolidate, and this encouraged other districts to follow.

The thirty-first session of the Nebraska Legislature changed the election laws so that certain judicial and educational personnel, including the state superintendent, were not to be nominated, endorsed, recommended, censured, criticized, or referred to in any manner by a political party, political convention, or primary. In other words, these candidates were to be nominated only by petition and voted upon on a nonpartisan ballot. However, the law was found to be invalid, and the state superintendents continued to be elected on a partisan basis.

Superintendent Edward C. Bishop, who assumed office in January 1909, made notable advances in consolidation. State Superintendent Augustus O. Thomas convened a statewide conference in Lincoln in September 1916 to study educational problems, at which he pointed out that 4-year high schools and 49 3-year high schools, all accredited by the university.

The state superintendents continued to advocate consolidation. State Superintendent Augustus O. Thomas convened a statewide conference in Lincoln in September 1916 to study educational problems, at which he pointed out that some 3,390 of the state's 6,571 districts enrolled no more than 12 children. Only about one-fourth of the eighth-grade graduates were entering high school. Thus, Thomas launched an intensive campaign to improve the preparation of rural teachers, establish standards for rural schools, develop a system of rural high schools, and strengthen the schools through consolidation.

It was 1919, however, before the Legislature passed an act to combine school districts within a county to create high school districts. Before new boundary changes could be effected, elections had to be held, and the superintendent was given the responsibility of refereeing any disputes arising from the act's operation. The Legislature did provide a small amount of state aid to districts consolidating under the law. Unfortunately the act proved to be defective; more than forty cases were appealed to the State Supreme Court.

The 1919 law was amended in 1921, and schools continued to consolidate. This required the state superintendent to devote a considerable amount of time to his duty as referee when disputes arose. Again, despite consolidations, the number of school buildings increased during the twenties. Moreover, Superintendent John M. Matzen reported in 1927 that 21 sod and 16 log school buildings were still in use.

Though imperfect, the law for school consolidation attempted to remedy a defect in the educational system that had existed from earliest times. Despite the small reduction from 7,264 districts in 1920 to 7,244 a decade later, the furor aroused by consolidation acquainted many people in Nebraska with the problem. Private denominational and parochial schools came under some measure of state supervision.

Upgrading the Teachers

One of the serious problems facing Nebraska schools at the turn of the century was a lack of competent teachers. During the nineteenth century, the Legislature had recognized the importance of workable laws governing teacher certification, but the several revisions still failed to entice the teachers so desperately needed. In 1901, the Legislature permitted three agencies besides the State Department of Education to issue teacher certificates: the University of Nebraska and other colleges, the county superintendents, and the boards of education in first-class cities. The state superintendent published a certification digest, but confusion continued to exist (11).

The 1901 Legislature authorized the University of Nebraska and other incorporated colleges and universities to award first-grade certificates valid for 3 years; after 3 years of successful experience, these were valid for life. The act directed the state superintendent to examine programs in the colleges and universities, other than the University of Nebraska, seeking to train teachers and to ascertain that their programs were comparable to those in the university. Confusion as to which colleges and universities might be recognized as having teacher education programs and should be eligible to grant first-grade teacher certificates prompted the Legislature of 1903 to amend the law by specifying the criteria by which the state superintendent could make his decision.

Also in its 1903 session, the Legislature provided for a new state normal school for central Nebraska at a site to be selected by the Board of Education of the State Normal School. The board, faced with many communities wanting the new school, chose Kearney on the one-hundred-eleventh ballot.

At the same time, the need for additional teachers prompted a law establishing junior normal schools in Alliance, McCook, Valentine, North Platte, and Holdrege. These junior normal schools operated in the city high schools during the summer, under the immediate supervision of the respective boards of education but under the general supervision of the state superintendent. Credits earned could be transferred to the State Normal School. New programs were later started at Alma, Broken Bow, Geneva, and O'Neill.

In its 1905 session, the Nebraska Legislature completely rewrote the teacher certification laws. It prescribed requirements for each of the three new classes of certificates and provided for three classes of county certificates, valid in the counties where issued. No changes were made in the kinds of certificates or requirements for city certificates, nor those issued by the State Normal School, the University of Nebraska, or the other colleges approved to issue teachers certificates. Since all examination questions and the subjects required for these teacher certificates were prepared and corrected in the state superintendent's office, this added materially to his work. The Legislature did provide for a State Board of Examiners, consisting of three people, to check the qualifications of those applying for life certificates. The state superintendent also could request the State Board of Examiners to assist him in comparing the educational programs in the colleges and universities with those of the University of Nebraska.

Prodded by recommendations from both the state superintendent and the Nebraska State Teachers Association, the 1907 Legislature raised standards for teaching in the rural schools from an eighth- to a twelfth-grade education and required the baccalaureate degree for all high school teachers. At the same time, it established normal training programs in Nebraska high schools and charged the state superintendent with administering them and paying subsidies to finance services of those schools deemed eligible. Those selected from the many applicants depended on the geographic distribution, staffing, program of studies, and numerous other details stipulated in the law. Within 2 years, more than 100 high schools had qualified for normal training and were enrolling more than 1,800 students, with nearly one-half qualified to teach in the rural schools upon graduation. A year later, in 1910, 107 high schools were offering normal training programs.

With two normal schools and eight junior normal schools in operation, the Legislature decided to replace the Board of Education of the State Normal School with one board, the Normal Board of Education. This new board consisted of five members appointed by the Governor, with the state treasurer and the state superintendent ex officio members. However, the act was found to be unconstitutional because of a technicality in its wording. Thus, the old board was obligated to continue operating under the 1867 law.

The state continued to expand its teacher education. In the spring of 1908, the University of Nebraska Board of Regents established a teachers college, which later became the university's largest single division. In 1909, the Nebraska Normal College, which had been established at

Wayne in 1891, became the state's third normal school. The 1909 Legislature then created a fourth normal school in the northwest part of the state. The board selected Chadron for its location and the following year accepted a gift of 85 acres for the site.

In its 1911 session, the Legislature abolished the State Normal School entrance examinations and authorized the Board of Education of the State Normal School to establish qualifications for entrance. It also amended the Normal Training Law to extend the program to some high schools not qualifying under the former law.

In 1911, the Governor appointed a School Code Commission to study the state's education. Contrary to the Nebraska State Teachers Association, which proposed that state and county superintendents be elected to long terms on nonpolitical ballots, the commission recommended abolishing the Office of Superintendent of Public Instruction and creating a State Board of Education with the authority to appoint a commissioner of education. It further suggested that the state's constitution be amended to prohibit further sale of school lands. It proposed a revised code of the school laws, including changes in the date of the annual school meeting, a requirement that county superintendents recommend a panel of qualified teachers from which school board officers might employ teachers, a requirement that all schools be graded according to the course of study, and elimination of the third-grade elementary county certificates. It also recommended that the state superintendent and the county superintendents hold valid teacher certificates. (Since 1919, state law has required the superintendent of public instruction to hold a valid teacher certificate of the highest grade issued by the office.) In addition, it was proposed that the state superintendent approve all school building plans and that the county sheriffs be designated as truant officers. The foresight of this commission must have been acute, as in a few short years the vast majority of its recommendations became reality.

One of the Nebraska State Teachers Association's 1911 recommendations received legislative sanction in 1917, when a law was passed providing for the nonpartisan nomination (by petition) and election of the state superintendent of public instruction and other educational and judicial officers. William H. Clemmons, who assumed the state superintendency in January 1917, won election in 1918 as the first candidate for the office without a political party designation.

Clemmons faced many problems resulting from the United States' participation in World War I. His reports indicate an awareness of long-range problems, but in those trying times he had little opportunity to solve them and found it difficult to keep existing programs operating. For instance, in 1919, it was necessary to revise the certification laws because of the severe shortages of properly qualified teachers. The city certificates were abolished, aliens were prohibited from teaching, and the state superintendent was authorized to issue "emergency" 1-year certificates.

In the 1918 general election, the people approved a proposal to elect members to a convention to revise the state's constitution. The constitutional convention, which met from December 2, 1919, until March 25, 1920, before recessing until October 19, proposed 41 amendments and submitted them to the electorate at a special election held on September 21. All passed, and these amendments became effective on January 1, 1921.

The new constitution, like the old one, named the superintendent of public instruction as an executive officer of the state, with a term of 4 years. It stipulated that all executive officers must maintain office in the state capitol and, except for the lieutenant governor, reside at the seat of government during their respective terms of office. The Governor could appoint officers to fill vacancies, all state officers were to report biennially to the Governor and Legislature and to post bond of not less than $50,000. There was no effort to elaborate on the superintendent's duties, beyond naming him to certain boards and commissions and requiring periodic reports from his office. But increasing his salary and doubling his term contributed significantly to the prestige and service of the office.

It was necessary for the Legislature to rewrite several statues to make them conform to the newly adopted Constitution of 1920. In 1921, it passed an act requiring all organized counties to have county superintendents with 4-year terms. The state normal schools were redesignated as state teachers colleges. At the same time, it reduced the number of county certificates to two, defined the certificates which could be issued by the state normal schools and other colleges, and required that all other certificates be issued by the state superintendent. It also expanded the examinations for issuing several of the lower-level certificates, which added to the responsibility and work of the state superintendent's office.

In 1925, the Legislature again rewrote the teacher certification laws and required that all teachers in public, private, denominational, and parochial schools hold valid certificates issued by the state. The law reduced the number of different levels of certificates and prescribed the requirements for each. This law defined the school year, required the registration of certificates in the county superintendents' offices, defined the examination procedures and costs, and provided for the revocation of teacher certificates for cause and with due process of law. Several amendments enacted in 1927 defined the certificates which the state normal schools could issue and their requirements. In 1929, the Legislature added to the list a "special music certificate" that could be issued by the state superintendent to those meeting his requirements.

Upon assuming office in 1927, Superintendent Charles W. Taylor improved the department's efficiency by establishing a central filing system staffed with trained clerks. More important, his reforms included reorganizing the office to include a secondary education and teacher training division, staff members of which would visit high schools and inspect their qualifications for accreditation and for special aid funds. The division prepared a high school manual in cooperation with the faculty of the University of Nebraska and offered to help the high schools solve their problems. Taylor also was responsible for initiating the junior high school program.

Financing Education

When Nebraska became a state, the federal government gave it about 2.8 million acres of land. The money derived from the sale of this land was placed in a permanent school fund for investment. The fund also received annually a percent of the severance tax on gas and oil and the proceeds from the sale of escheat estates. Only the interest from the permanent fund could be used, and this was placed in a temporary school fund, to be distributed to the school districts annually. In the period immediately following 1900, it became necessary for the land department to reclaim more than a million acres of land, because the contracts had been declared forfeited since 1897. At the same time, the school lands were reappraised at an evaluation increased from $1.5 million to more than $3 million. The rents from these school lands increased from $92,573 in 1898 to $175,829 in 1908.

In 1907, two significant measures, one by the state and one by the federal government, affected Nebraska's educational financing. In its thirtieth session, the Legislature voted a subsidy of up to $120 a year from state funds to those school districts unable to maintain 7 months of school after levying the maximum tax permitted by the statutes. This law, commonly referred to as "aid to weak districts," started with an initial appropriation of $50,000, distributed by the state superintendent. Two years later, the appropriation was increased to $75,000. Although the law failed to ensure a minimum 7-month school in all districts, it enabled most eligible districts to provide at least 5 months of school. To improve its effectiveness, in 1913 the Legislature clarified the law, extended the benefits to some schools not previously covered, and raised the maximum aid to $385. However, during the late 1920's, few schools were able to qualify for the aid, and although the act still remains a part of the Nebraska school laws, each year the number of eligible districts decreases.

The federal government passed in 1907 the Federal Forest Lands Act, by which it refunded to the state 25 percent of the gross receipts received from the sale of timber, seedlings, and other items raised on forest reserve lands. Five Nebraska counties qualified for revenue under this act, and the state statutes stipulate that one-fifth of the revenue shall be allocated to the county road fund, one-fifth equally to all school districts in the counties, and three-fifths to all school districts according to pupil population. Although the money received was not of great importance, it was the first federal aid to education received by Nebraska.

In the period beginning about 1910, a political movement developed to repeal the Sheldon Law of 1897 and thus to permit sale of school lands. Under the Sheldon Law, the leasing policy held that rentals should be a little lower than those of private landowners, to encourage leaseholders to improve their lands. This would give them security in its use while increasing the school fund income as population moved in and land values rose. In 1912, the outgoing state treasurer, the land commissioner, and the Governor all recommended that the educational lands again be offered for sale. But newly elected Governor John H. Morehead took the opposite view and argued that the lands should be retained by the state. Two bills introduced into the 1913 Legislature to sell the lands were killed before coming to a vote.

In 1915, the land sale proponents launched a fresh campaign, but the bill was defeated after a bitter debate. When the Legislature met again in 1917, another bill failed to pass by a single vote in the House of Representatives. A similar bill passed in the Senate, but it also was defeated in the House.

At the same time, there was considerable debate on the subject of reappraising the lands. Sentiment definitely favored reappraisal, but the controversy over the method defeated the proposals, and Sheldon's School Land Law of 1897 continued. The Junkin Amendment in the Constitutional Convention of 1919 ended an attempt to repeal the Sheldon School Land Law by prescribing disposal of the state school lands at public auction. Would-be purchasers did not want to take a chance on losing the land altogether to a high bidder (12).

The 1920 constitution created a board of commissioners to sell, lease, and generally manage the school lands and funds. This was an executive board, but it did not include the superintendent of public instruction (13). The new constitution did cause the 1921 Legislature to change the formula for distributing the semiannual appropriation of the temporary school fund to allow payment in lieu of taxes to counties which had tax-exempt school lands.

During Superintendent Charles Taylor's administration, the department was confronted with a major lawsuit when it refused to distribute the annual apportionment to District No. 6, Cedar County, because it appeared to be operated as a parochial school. The court sustained Taylor. He remained active in his fight for more favorable investment of the permanent school fund and a greater return from the leases of school lands. He succeeded in promoting a constitutional amendment giving him membership on the important Board of Educational Lands and Funds.

Vocational Education

As early as 1909, the Nebraska Legislature passed an act permitting county high schools to include programs in manual training, domestic science, and agriculture. In 1911, the Nebraska State Teachers Association recommended that state aid be granted for specialized courses in agriculture, home economics, and industrial training.

The state continued its support, and in 1913, the Legislature passed the Shumway Act, authorizing the state superintendent to aid rural schools up to $50 and high schools up to $1,250 to offer such courses. The state superintendent also was authorized to appoint an inspector of agricultural training, subject to the concurrence of the chancellor of the University of Nebraska. However, as late as 1919, schools eligible under this act were slow to take advantage of the funds available.

More popular was the Mallery Act passed in 1917, which entitled rural high schools and consolidated high schools offering classes in agriculture, home economics, or other industrial and vocational subjects to receive from $250 to $550 annually, depending on the number of rooms used and the amount expended for equipment. This fund continued until the 1955-56 biennium, when appropriations for this aid ceased to be granted by the Legislature.

World War I gave real impetus to vocational education. The U.S. Congress passed the Federal Vocational Education Act (commonly referred to as the Smith-Hughes Act) in February 1917. Its purpose was to prepare teachers in vocational subjects and to train workers in agricultural, trade and industrial, homemaking, and service occupations other than professional fields. In the same year, in order to participate in the program, the Nebraska Legislature created the Board of Vocational Education, consisting of the Governor as chairman, the state treasurer as treasurer, and the superintendent of public instruction as secretary.

In 1919, Congress rewrote the Vocational Education Act to clarify and improve the regulations and authorizations for training these teachers. At the same time, it clarified the authority and duties of the State Board of Vocational Education. The previous year, Congress had passed the Smith-Sears Vocational Rehabilitation Act, and in 1921 the Nebraska Legislature directed the state board to cooperate with the federal government in implementing its provisions in Nebraska. It also was authorized to appoint the necessary staff.

DEPRESSION, WAR, AND POSTWAR, 1930 TO 1955

The Depression

Like most agricultural states, Nebraska suffered severely during the Depression. Many communities dismissed part of their teaching staff and dropped courses. Buildings went unrepaired, and replacements, for the most part, were out of the question.

State Superintendent Charles W. Taylor fought hard against unreasonable retrenchments and appropriation cuts, and he attempted to bring about desirable changes in the laws affecting education generally. He reopened issues that had been dormant for many years by advocating more favorable investments of the permanent school fund and a greater return from school land leases. Finally, in 1938, the Legislature proposed an amendment to the Nebraska Constitution of 1920 creating a board of commissioners for managing the school lands and investing the funds. The amendment failed in the election that year (14). But 2 years later, the voters approved another amendment designating the Governor, secretary of state, treasurer, attorney general, and superintendent of public instruction as the Board of Educational Lands and Funds.

Taylor cooperated in several national surveys during these years. For instance, in 1932, the department participated in completing the Nebraska section of the National Survey of Secondary Education. It reported on the organization of the high schools, studying the advantages and disadvantages of "general" and "special" high schools, and studying high school enrollments. It also surveyed problems involving curriculum, homogeneous grouping, provisions for atypical children, and various instructional techniques.

The State Department of Education cooperated in completing Nebraska's portion of the American Council on Education's survey of secondary schools. Taylor stimulated guidance services in the high schools and encouraged the use of criteria developed by a Cooperative Study of Secondary School Standards for Self-Evaluation. There was an effort to lengthen the high school recitation periods, reduce class size, and restore courses dropped because of the Depression. There was an increased emphasis on preprofessional training as well as vocational aspects of normal training. In 1939, the superintendent established the Nebraska High School Improvement Program, which resulted in more than a dozen excellent reports on various aspects of secondary education.

The state superintendent used every means at his disposal to improve rural education and give it prestige. For one thing, he encouraged county boards to allow the county superintendents to hire clerical help and secure professional supervisory assistance. He expanded the standardization of schools and offered to designate districts which could qualify for 95 points on a 100-point scale as "superior schools." The superintendent also encouraged the formation of rural parent-teacher and county school associations. Furthermore, the department produced two excellent courses of study, one in 1929 and the other in 1936.

In 1933, to implement the law requiring schools to offer character education, the department created a character education division to bring together the various programs. This division, in close cooperation with the rural education and secondary education division, developed materials promoting virtues set forth in the law. It produced a course of study on character education and another on scientific temperance instruction. The division promoted the organization of character-building clubs and good citizens clubs in the schools and helped organize Junior Red Cross clubs. It administered the Knighthood of Youth organization in the state, which was essentially a character education program promoted by the department. Many elementary schools, especially rural schools, conducted this program for which a syllabus was provided by the department. It cooperated in planning programs for the state's 4-H Clubs and encouraged expansion of the Boy Scout and Girl Scout programs. This division remained active throughout Taylor's administration, and although it does not exist today as a separate division of the department, its philosophies of character education are as forceful as they were during the thirties.

Superintendent Taylor also led a drive to equalize educational opportunities. He pointed out that the property values in Nebraska did not coincide with the school population centers. Thus, he suggested that a statewide tax be enacted and that revenues be distributed by a legislative formula to correct the inequities and unfairness in the taxation program.

During the Depression, when there were more teachers looking for jobs than were available, it was possible to upgrade certification. The Legislature completely rewrote the laws in 1937, providing that as of September 1938 all certificates would be issued by the superintendent of public instruction upon the recommendation of the governing and administrative officers of institutions approved to prepare teachers. Grades of the new certificates and their requirements were listed. The law abolished the Board of Examiners for life certificates, but established a new Board of Educational Examiners to advise the superintendent of public instruction as to which colleges, other than the University of Nebraska and the state teachers colleges, were eligible to recommend candidates for certification.

Again, during a national emergency – a period of chaotic economic conditions – the federal government assisted states with specific educational programs. In 1933, Nebraska's State Department of Education received aid under the Federal Emergency Relief Administration Act to provide services for rural schools, teaching of adults to read and write, vocational education, rehabilitation of disabled persons, and general adult education, and later for setting up nursery schools.

The federal government also came to the aid of the states with the Works Progress Administration and the Public Works Administration, enabling Nebraska to renovate numerous school plants. As many as 250 workers were employed on these projects at one time. These federal funds also made it possible for a number of communities to build new school buildings.

World War II

The United States's entrance into World War II continued to make it difficult for communities to build new school plants or even renovate old ones, as there were shortages of both materials and labor. But more unfortunate was the constant shortage of teachers that plagued every state in the Union. The Nebraska Legislature gave the state superintendent authority to extend the term of certification for any teacher who possessed a valid certificate when he enlisted or was inducted into the armed forces. The 1947 Legislature did make an exception to the law prohibiting the certification of alien teachers by permitting the superintendent of public instruction to issue a temporary certificate to an authorized "exchange" teacher from a foreign country.

When Superintendent Wayne O. Reed assumed office in January 1943, he faced an acute shortage of teachers and was forced to issue hundreds of temporary certificates each year. Initially, oral and written exams were arranged for the candidates, but later the examination method was discontinued. He continued the policy of extending teacher certificates when the holders were serving in the armed forces. Although teacher certification had been greatly simplified by this time, many old certificates remained in effect to complicate matters.

In one of his first acts, Superintendent Reed reorganized his office into two major divisions: administrative assistance and supervisory assistance. An assistant superintendent of public instruction headed each division. Reed had campaigned for office with the slogan, "locally controlled, locally administered, community-centered schools," and throughout his administration he directed the department with this idea in mind.

One responsibility of the administrative division was ruling on problems arising from the operation of the school laws. Properly interpreting these school laws had always been difficult. Frequently, superintendents' decisions were referred to the attorney general's office for further opinions concerning the legislative history and intent.

The state superintendent also assigned the administrative division the tasks of conducting educational research and compiling and publishing school statistics. It issued teacher certificates, handled the disposing of federal surplus properties to the schools, and administered the bureau of education and registration of nurses. It became responsible for administering the school lunch program, approving and certifying educational programs for veterans, distributing various state-federal aid funds, reorganizing school districts, and carrying out school building surveys and services.

In 1944, through the impetus of a grant from the W. K. Kellogg Foundation of Battle Creek, Michigan, the

Nebraska State Department of Public Instruction and the Nebraska State Department of Health inaugurated a cooperative experiment project for improving school health education and health services. The foundation granted additional money in 1945 and 1946 to continue this Nebraska school health project.

The Kellogg grant and the aroused interest of individuals, schools, public and private health agencies, and teacher education institutions prompted numerous moves to improve school and community health. In March 1947, the State Department of Assistance and Child Welfare joined the Departments of Health and Public Instruction to officially sponsor "A Proposal for an Extended Nebraska School-Community Health Program." This new 3-year proposal centered the program in the six larger tax-supported teacher education institutions under the administration of the Department of Public Instruction and requested partial subsidization from the W. K. Kellogg Foundation. The foundation approved the program to run from July 1947 to July 1950 and allocated funds for its development (15).

Postwar Problems

Veterans Programs. In 1944, the U.S. Congress passed the Servicemen's Readjustment Act, commonly known as the GI Bill. That June, the Governor designated the Office of the Superintendent of Public Instruction as the appropriate state agency to approve the educational and training institutions, agencies, and services in Nebraska. All accredited universities, colleges, junior colleges, and high schools were immediately approved and the necessary facts submitted to the Veterans Administration. When the war ended, the phase of the veterans education program related to on-the-job training in business and industrial establishments expanded tremendously.

Congress approved another act in August 1946 to establish the first definite standards for approving applications from businesses and industries offering on-the-job training. The state department appointed a committee consisting of representatives of labor, veterans organizations and management to study all applications received after that date. In every case of a rejected application, the firm was advised of the reason for rejection and given an opportunity to revise the application.

Under the agreement with the Veterans Administration, the department was reimbursed for salaries and travel expenses of its staff, who were obligated to make annual inspections or supervisory visits to each approved business. The Veterans Administration asked the department to consider for recertification prior to January 1, 1947, all business firms and institutions previously approved to offer on-the-job training. The VA and the department maintained a close liaison with the chief of the VA's training facilities section cooperating with the department's director of veteran education and training.

The department was very active during the 1945-47 biennium assisting veterans with their educational problems. It established a program whereby high school diplomas could be granted to veterans on the basis of a satisfactory performance on the General Education Development Tests, published by the American Council on Education. These examinations were administered locally by high schools and returned to the department for scoring and recommendations. The tests were available in engineering, drawing, commercial correspondence, American history, English, Gregg shorthand, chemistry, first- and second- year algebra, and business English.

Veterans returning to high schools and colleges could claim credit for basic military training, courses completed with the Armed Forces Institute, service schools, and other special courses of instruction. At the request of the high schools, the state department evaluated these courses for credit on the basis of recommendations published by the American Council on Education.

For several months, the department conducted the Veterans Educational Information Clearance Service sponsored by the U.S. Office of Education. This made available information concerning vacancies in all institutions of higher learning, which was compiled and sent to these institutions for guidance purposes. These reports were exchanged monthly with other states and given to the county service officers and U.S. employment officers until November 1946. The following year, this service was reestablished on a semester and summer-term basis.

In 1947, the agriculture education division prepared a contract to cover institutional on-the-farm training for veterans, which was approved by the State Board of Vocational Education and the Veterans Administration. Under its provisions, local schools, with the assistance and supervision of the State Department of Vocational Education, established training programs and reimbursed approved instructors. Semiannually, the local school claimed a reimbursement from the State Department of Vocational Education. Thus, the handling of federal funds to local schools was kept in the hands of the regularly constituted state educational agencies.

When Congress passed the Veterans Readjustment Assistance Act of 1952, the Governor designated the Department of Public Instruction as the state approval agency for institutional education and training. This meant that the department had the same approval relationship with schools in matters pertaining to the education of Korean War veterans that it exercised under the law for World War II veterans. When the World War II educational program closed in 1956, the Veterans Readjustment Assistance Act of 1952 continued, but the Veterans on-farm training program terminated in April 1962.

Surplus Property. In November 1945, the Surplus Property Administration of the federal government announced that its regulation, effective 2 days earlier, was designed to channel surplus goods, on the basis of need, to nonprofit school systems, libraries, universities, research institutions, hospitals, and medical or sanitational institutions. The administration requested the Federal Security Agency to assist in distributing the surplus property to eligible educational and health institutions and other nonprofit agencies. The Federal Security Agency, in turn, delegated to its U.S. Office of Education the task of administering the program for educational institutions.

The Legislature or Governor of each state was requested to designate an agency to represent its own institutions to cooperate with the Office of Education, and Governor Dwight Griswold requested State Superintendent Wayne Reed to provide such an agency for Nebraska. Deputy Superintendent F. B. Decker, as executive officer of the state educational agency for surplus property, immediately invited all types of institutions to assist in working out ways of implementing the program. This gave all state educational institutions an opportunity to share in acquiring surplus property.

The War Assets Administration, as the principal selling agency for surplus property, allowed a discount from the listed fair value to properly certified educational institutions. These institutions could participate in bid sales conducted either by a selling agency or an owning agency, but in this case no discount was guaranteed. Through national sales and special programs, the schools were able to purchase specialized types of equipment and acquire property at discounts as high as 100 percent.

In 1950, Congress amended its surplus property regulations to authorize all federal agencies to donate property for educational purposes, thus making surplus donations a permanent service to educational institutions. In the same year another law extended the service to include tax-supported and nonprofit public health institutions, along with schools, colleges, and universities. The state law stipulated that the program should be operated under one agency.

In 1955, Congress again changed the Federal Property Administrative Services Act of 1949. Under the old act, the federal government could sell federal surplus property to private bidders. The law now contained a provision whereby all federal surplus property that had been screened by federal agencies was donable to educational and public health institutions. As a result, the Nebraska schools, universities and colleges, and hospitals not primarily for domiciliary care received a much greater quantity and improved quality of property.

Expanding the Department's Services

Imbued with the philosophy of "locally controlled, locally administered, community-centered schools," Superintendent Reed organized numerous conferences and institutes of professional and lay groups to study the educational programs of Nebraska and published many of their findings and recommendations. He also appointed committees with wide representation to revise both elementary and high school courses of study. Of great importance, he inaugurated an accelerated teacher-training program for rural and elementary schools.

In 1946, representatives from Nebraska's colleges and universities offering state-approved teacher education programs, the public schools, and organizations interested in the improvement of teacher education and professional standards set up the Nebraska Council on Teacher Education to serve as an advisory body to agencies and institutions responsible for teacher education and certification.

The council proved to be a most effective organization. The department cooperated with it and its component organizations in conducting a campaign to encourage young people to enter teaching as a career. It also encouraged boards of education to compile policies for their own guidance, as well as for school employees and their communities.

It is well that the citizens of Nebraska had become interested early in securing quality teachers, because the national shortage continued to grow. By 1954, the U.S. Commissioner of Education warned that the nation would need at least 100,000 new elementary school teachers the coming year – nearly three times as many as completed their preparation in teacher education institutions that spring. The State Department of Education carried in its 1955 annual report a statement by the Nebraska Council on Teacher Education that thousands of Nebraska children were being taught by teachers with no college preparation, and thousands of others by teachers with only one summer of college education. More than 1,200 substandard certificates were issued in 1954-55. Although the best schools consistently retained their good teachers, many communities had little holding power, and their teachers left the state for better opportunities elsewhere. The council stated:

> Nebraska needs to achieve in the near future a minimum certification standard of 2 years of college preparation for all elementary school teachers. When this standard is achieved, steps should be taken, as soon as possible, to raise the minimum of preparation to a college degree. Twenty-seven states now have this minimum standard of a college degree for all teachers. Of the remaining 21 states, 16 have a minimum standard of at least 2 years of college preparation for all teachers (16).

The School Lunch Program. The National School Lunch Act, enacted by Congress in June 1946, stipulated that the Governor of each state should appoint a state agency to administer the program in all schools. That August, the Governor of Nebraska appointed the superintendent of public instruction's office as the state agency. A special session of the Legislature provided for funds, stating that –

> The sum of $10,000 or so much thereof as may be necessary is hereby appropriated to the Superintendent of Public Instruction from the State general fund for the payment of salaries, wages, maintenance, supplies, traveling, and other expenses of administration and disbursement of funds received from the United States under the National School Lunch Act, for the biennium ending June 30, 1947 . . . (17).

Congress appropriated money to a state according to the number of children between the ages of 5 and 17 enrolled in school and the state's per-capita income in relation to that for the country as a whole. Ten percent of Nebraska's share was allocated to the parochial and nonprofit private schools, whose programs were administered by the state's production and marketing office, a division of the U.S. Department of Agriculture. This arrangement prevailed because state agencies in Nebraska are prohibited by law to pay tax moneys of any kind to private, parochial, or denominational schools.

Local schools interested in the school lunch program applied to the department. The department then signed a contract with the local sponsor, which could be the school, the local board of education, the PTA, or any interested local group. The law required that lunches be available without discrimination to all children in the school, regardless of ability to pay.

By 1947, so many new schools wanted to participate in the lunch programs that the State Department of Public Instruction, in cooperation with the State Department of Health and the state teachers colleges, employed two field consultants in nutrition to visit various schools and advise them in setting up new programs. In December 1954, when Congress made available an additional $50 million of Commodity Credit Corporation funds for a special school milk program, the Nebraska schools enrolled immediately.

Nebraska continued to participate in both the school lunch program and the special milk program. All funds disbursed by the department for these services are federal money, although the state pays for administering the program on the state level.

District Reorganization. In 1949, Superintendent Reed was successful in securing legislation giving the department complete responsibility for accrediting and approving school systems. He appointed an advisory committee to review the findings of the department's supervisory staff and to act on their recommendations. The state accreditation committee then carefully developed and adopted criteria for approving public elementary and high schools and specific standards for rural schools, private schools, and junior colleges.

The Nebraska Legislature enacted its first school district reorganization law in 1949. It established a six-member State Committee for Reorganization of School Districts, with the Governor appointing two from the teaching profession and three laymen, with the state superintendent a nonvoting member. By law, the committee functioned in an advisory capacity. County committees, elected in 92 of the 93 counties, carefully studied their district organizations, proposed reorganization plans, and worked with the state committee in submitting their plans to the electorate.

Superintendent Reed resigned in July 1950 to assume the presidency of Nebraska State Teachers College at Peru, and Governor Val Peterson appointed Otto G. Ruff to complete his term of office. When Ruff decided not to seek election, Freeman B. Decker assumed the office in January 1951.

Decker intensified the program of school district reorganization. To speed up consolidation, he recommended amending the law to give the State Committee for Reorganization of School Districts more authority, but the Legislature refused to act.

The Office of State Superintendent Abolished

The department's 1951 annual report proposed a constitutional amendment abolishing the Office of Superintendent of Public Instruction and establishing a State Board of Education. This board, consisting of six lay persons elected from the state's supreme court districts, would determine policy and appoint a commissioner of education. In turn, the commissioner would become the board's executive officer and head the State Department of Education. A bill was introduced to reorganize the department in this way and to abolish the position of superintendent of public instruction upon completion of the incumbent's term of office. The electorate then approved the amendment in 1952 to change the educational organization at the state level.

During the 1953 session, most of the Legislature's work was devoted to enacting new laws and corrective amendments to old laws to implement the constitutional amendment. In January 1955, the Office of State Superintendent of Public Instruction terminated. The Board of Education then appointed Decker as the new commissioner, and he remained in office until 1962.

The 1955 Legislature abolished the State Board of Vocational Education, established to enable Nebraska to participate in the Smith-Hughes Act of 1917, and transferred its duties to the newly created State Board of Education (18). As the new vocational education governing body, the elected State Board of Education scheduled meetings on the same date but at different times and kept a separate set of minutes for its two different functions. As the vocational board, it was responsible for administering federal and state funds and disbursing them to the local schools, providing training of teachers, and assisting local school boards and officials in setting up vocational departments and courses, planning programs, and securing instructors.

The 1955 Legislature did relieve the vocational education board from its responsibility for the rehabilitation division, which it had administered since the program began in 1921, and transferred it to the Department of Education.

From 1947 to 1962, the vocational board contracted annually with the Veterans Administration to administer and supervise the institutional on-farm training program. This program served nearly 20,000 World War II and Korean veterans, with a peak enrollment of 9,315 in 296 public school systems.

Since 1941, the State Board of Vocational Education had administered the Nebraska State Trade School, which the Legislature had established in the former Nebraska Soldiers and Sailors Home at Milford. The school offered 10- to 20-month courses in 12 different trades, and it provided dormitory and cafeteria facilities on a cost basis. During the 1956-57 school year, it operated with a maximum capacity enrollment of approximately 400 students. By 1965, the enrollment was up to 700 students.

A DECADE OF JET-AGE PROGRESS, 1955-65

Expanding Federal Programs

During the entire post-World War II period, there was an acceleration in programs offering federal money to education, and Nebraska had not been remiss in securing this aid for its boys and girls. A number, such as the vocational education and school lunch programs, have been mentioned. In 1948, the department received $47,125 to distribute to districts financially handicapped because they contained tax-exempt Indian lands. The department contracted with the Bureau of Indian Affairs to supervise schools enrolling students with one-quarter or more Indian blood residing in these districts. The program expanded the following year to include transportation and lunch funds, and it continued to expand so that by 1965, 687 eligible Indian pupils were being helped.

In 1950, Nebraska received funds under the Flood Control Act and under the provisions of Public Law 874, by which the federal government alleviates the financial burden of local schools due to the impact of federal activities on their communities. By 1966, 48 Nebraska school districts were receiving $4,033,919 compensation for additional pupils. Public Law 815, passed by Congress in 1951-52, defined the conditions under which districts could apply for adequate school plant facilities for children in federally affected areas. The department serves as an agency of the federal government in processing applications for financial assistance under this law, and as a consultant to the applicant school districts.

During the 1955-56 school year, Nebraska sold certain submarginal lands in Sioux and Dawes Counties under the Bankhead-Jones Farm Tenant Act. This land, referred to as the Pine Ridge Utilization Project, was to be retired from cultivation. The federal law stipulated that one-fourth of the income was to be returned to the counties where the land was situated to maintain the schools or roads, or both, as decided by the county board of commissioners. In the same year, under the Migratory Bird Conservation Act, the federal government provided money for schools or roads to counties in which wildlife refuges were located. And in 1956, Congress enacted the War Orphans Educational Assistance Act to provide scholarship aids to children of servicemen who died as the result of disability or disease incurred in the line of duty during World Wars I and II and the Korean conflict.

Civil Defense Adult Education. Early in 1958 the director of the Office of Civil and Defense Mobilization (OCDM) delegated to the U.S. Office of Education the responsibility of cooperating with state and local school authorities in teaching adults the principles of personal and family survival. The following March, the U.S. Commissioner appointed a director of Civil Defense education as a member of his staff. Nebraska, because of its strategic location, was one of the seven initial states selected to carry out a Civil Defense adult education program. The state superintendent, who was responsible for the program, in July 1960 appointed a coordinator and two consultants for Nebraska's program.

The state department certifies teachers who complete their training as Civil Defense adult educators. These persons are then qualified to teach Civil Defense courses in their communities under the auspices of local administrators. Teachers and the state staff are paid from federal funds, and the federal government supplies instructional materials. In July 1965, radiological monitoring training, funded by the federal government, also came under the CDAE program.

The National Defense Education Act of 1958. The National Defense Education Act of 1958, passed by Congress to strengthen instruction and provide increased educational opportunities to students in critical subject areas, brought new resources and encouragement to Nebraska public schools at a time when financial help was needed more than ever before. The U.S. Office of Education officially approved the Nebraska plan for participation in NDEA Title III in February 1959. These funds were to be used on a matching basis by the local school districts to strengthen public elementary and secondary school offerings in science, mathematics, and modern foreign language. The money could be used by local schools for equipment, materials, and minor remodeling. Funds also were available for the department to improve its supervisory program, and in the 1962-63 school year, it added a science supervisor and an audiovisual supervisor to its staff under this portion of the program. Since October 1964, Title III has been amended to include five additional subject matter areas: history, civics, geography, English, and reading.

Under NDEA's Title V, school districts could receive compensation for expenses in testing, materials, and counseling, though not specifically for administering the tests. The guidance and counseling areas had to conform to the state department standards to qualify for financial support. The state plan for testing, counseling, and guidance became effective in January 1959, and federal funds were received. Because of certain legal technicalities, the expenditure had to be limited only to testing during fiscal year 1958-59. As additional federal funds became available in subsequent years, the Nebraska program was expanded to include all three areas of testing, counseling, and guidance.

The State Board of Education approved a plan for area vocational-technical schools in December 1958 to receive funds immediately available under Title VIII of the NDEA. The state board approved Omaha Technical High School and the Nebraska Vocational-Technical School at Milford as area vocational schools to train highly skilled technicians for national defense. Under the law, the instruction had to be of less than college level.

The Nebraska program was developed through 1- and 2-year post-high school courses and/or as short unit extension courses for presently employed journeymen or technicians. The Nebraska Vocational-Technical School was at that time operating seven approved courses on a less than 12-month basis. The school began operating on a yearly basis during the 1965-66 school year and was offering 11 approved courses.

Under Title X of the federal assistance program, Nebraska could secure up to $50,000 per year in federal funds to match an equal amount of state funds for improving statistical services in the department. The Nebraska plan was approved in June 1959, revised in October, and again the following July.

The Manpower Development and Training Act. In November 1962, shortly after Congress passed the Manpower Development and Training Act, the state department initiated an occupational training program subsidized by these funds. Gradually, the program became centralized in the public schools of Omaha, Lincoln, and Sidney (Sioux Ordinance Base Facility), and at the Nebraska Vocational–Technical School at Milford. It was found that large centers could better provide the necessary equipment, facilities, and training personnel, so students were gradually moved to these primary centers from throughout Nebraska and neighboring states.

During 1965 and 1966, the Department of Education's vocational education division conducted MDTA training in agriculturally related occupations, business education, distributive education, trades and industry, and health occupations. Guidance and counseling services and basic education were available, as were programs especially designed for the severely disadvantaged.

Congress changed the Manpower Act by an amendment in 1965, limiting federal support of these projects to 90 percent. The 1965 Nebraska Legislature appropriated $50,000 to continue the program.

Rehabilitation and Economic Opportunity Acts. The Nebraska State Department of Education's Division of Rehabilitation Services obtained funds in 1962 from the Woods Charitable Foundation and the Vocational Rehabilitation Administration of the Department of HEW for a research and demonstration project to rehabilitate severely disabled people who were receiving benefits from the Bureau of Old Age and Survivors Insurance. Nebraska was one of 11 states taking part in this 3-year program (Project 965). The purpose of the project was to increase, intensify, and improve methods of rehabilitating severely disabled individuals and to determine how, when, and which cases would respond to effort and why.

Workers in this field had been frustrated for a long time because they could not give needed services to a great many people with severe and complex physical or mental disabilities. It was hoped that this program would devise new methods and patterns of administration, comprehensive rehabilitation centers, work adjustment centers, and other medical units that could be coordinated to meet the problem. It also included a study of the effect of subcultural and economic factors on the rehabilitation process in urban, semirural, and rural areas.

Out of 2,351 cases reviewed, the project selected 413 and referred them to counselors. Personal interviews and thorough investigations eliminated 69 percent, and effort was concentrated on the remaining 31 percent. When the project ended in 1965, 15 persons undergoing treatment continued to receive needed rehabilitation services through the division's regular program.

It was learned from Project 965 that the average cost of rehabilitating the severely disabled did not differ significantly from regular programs. Thus, the researchers recommended that part of the funds these people would be eligible to receive from the Trust Fund of the Old Age and Survivors Insurance Program be used for rehabilitation. It also was learned that physical restoration, preferably through a vocational rehabilitation center, was the most utilized service. The project concluded that job placement specialists should be added to the rehabilitation team. But perhaps the most valuable fact learned was that a state-operated, comprehensive rehabilitation center could increase the number of clients helped. Such a center could provide for mentally retarded and psychiatrically disabled individuals.

In June 1963, the department initiated a program, financed in part by the Vocational Rehabilitation Administration of the Department of HEW, to provide intensive, comprehensive vocational rehabilitation services to selected groups of handicapped individuals, who would apply for benefits from the two largest county public welfare offices. These groups included people receiving three categories of public assistance: families with dependent children, the permanently and totally disabled, and people receiving general assistance. The department hoped to create an effective interagency relationship to ensure that every possible effort was made to help these individuals return to gainful employment.

The coordinator-counselor of the project was located in the Lancaster County Department of Public Welfare, while Douglas County was served by a counselor in its department of public welfare. From June 1963 to the end of February 1965, 239 persons were referred to the project. When it terminated, there were 132 disabled persons in either a referred or an active case status. Of these, 85 were receiving vocational rehabilitation services, and decisions regarding acceptance were pending in 47 cases. The project did find that many "hard-core" welfare people could be rehabilitated and returned to employment.

Due to the Economic Opportunity Act, Nebraska, in 1965, began administration of a statewide program of adult basic education. Authorized by Title II-B of the act, the program is the responsibility of the adult basic education section of the state department. During its first year in operation, approximately 327 adults with less than an eighth-grade education received instruction under this program in three school districts of the state.

The Elementary and Secondary Education Act of 1965. President Johnson signed the Elementary and Secondary Education Act on April 11, 1965. To many this was an educational dream come true. It authorized more than $1.3 billion in federal funds to improve the education of young Americans.

Title I of ESEA provides federal grants to local public school districts for programs designed to meet the needs of educationally deprived children. Local school administrators, teachers, and selected lay people identify these children in low-income areas, establish the priority of their needs, and design a project. These projects may include supplementary and remedial instruction, guidance and counseling services, or health and welfare services. The state education agency is responsible for administering the program.

Title II provides federal funds to states for school library resources, textbooks, and instructional materials such as tapes, films, and slides. In Nebraska, since current emphasis was on raising each attendance center's library collection to a basic or minimum standard, no Title II funds were spent in 1965 for textbooks. The districts ascertain their most critical needs, and local school administrators, assisted by librarians and teachers, select the materials. The state department then reviews and approves the project. Again, the department's staff visits schools having Title II projects to provide assistance in improving libraries and instructional materials.

Title III, Projects to Advance Creativity in Education (PACE), attempts to stimulate local districts to reap the benefits of research and channel them from the educational laboratory into the classroom. A local committee, widely representative of the community, determines the priority of educational needs and plans a project to meet them. These projects are submitted to both the U.S. Office of Education and the State Department of Education. The state department may recommend approval or change, but funding is directly from the U.S. Office of Education.

Title V provides federal funds to state departments to improve educational planning through evaluation of programs, data collection and interpretation, curriculum materials, research, and teacher preparation. It provides funds to local school districts to provide consultative and technical assistance. The funds under Title V have enabled the Nebraska state department to make unprecedented progress. The addition of highly skilled specialists has had an impact on Nebraska's schools.

Financing Education

Until 1967, state aid to education in Nebraska could easily be classified as "piecemeal." Not only was there no foundation or equalization program for state aid, but there was no sales or income tax. Approximately 92 percent of the revenue of Nebraska public school districts came from local sources. The remaining 8 percent was derived from educational lands and funds, and state and federal aid. State appropriations were made for vocational and special education for handicapped children.

The state temporary school fund included rentals for use of school lands, interest earned on the investment of the permanent school fund, and a small amount of liquor and itinerant merchant license fees. The annual division of the temporary fund among the school districts was known as school apportionment. A fractional part of a tax levied on insurance premiums in lieu of a tax on intangible property of insurance companies was distributed statewide each year. None of these was of any sizable amount.

The permanent school fund consisted of money derived from the sale of school lands, a 2-percent severance tax on gas and oil, and proceeds from the sale of escheat estates. Only the interest earnings of this fund could be used, creating the above mentioned temporary school fund, which was distributed annually.

An amendment of the constitution in 1954 provided that the general management of all lands and funds and the investment of school funds be administered by a board of five members appointed by the Governor. The law was changed the following year, so that the Governor appointed one member from each of the four congressional districts and one from the state at large. Original terms were staggered, and reappointments for 5-year terms were prescribed (19).

The 1964 distributable sum of the school fund was larger than the usual annual amount because about 2,300 new leases on school land were written in 1963, representing about one-half of the total number of leases written on all school land in the state and also representing about one-half of the total acreage of school land. Rents on school land were customarily payable in semiannual installments, but on new leases the first annual payment was required. This brought an extra half-year's rent on 0.8 million acres to the income of the fund in 1963 for distribution in 1964. In addition, a bonus payment on a new lease was payable in its total amount when the lease was consummated. These two conditions increased collections in 1964, which were in excess of $6 million instead of the usual $3 million.

The following year, in 1965, over the objections of the Governor, the Legislature enacted a law requiring that all school lands be offered for sale as the leases expired. Thus, during 1966 the sale of 1,356 acres brought a total of $142,218 to the school fund (20). The fight still continues in each legislative session as to whether these lands shall be sold or held in trust for future generations.

Local school districts in Nebraska finance their public schools mainly by property taxation. In 1964-65, the school district taxes contributed $102,516,658 to the total revenue receipts of $134,645,338. The property taxes also provided $7,144,314 to pay high school districts for the tuition of pupils who resided in Class I districts. Additional revenue came from a tax on gross revenue derived by public power districts from retail sales, less the in-lieu-of tax paid by the agencies on the physical plant. The schools also received funds from such sources as police court fines and local license fees.

Revenue provided by the counties comes mainly from fines imposed in county courts and fees for operating licensed businesses outside incorporated cities and villages. This amounted to about $1,328,635 in 1964-65.

District Reorganization

The tax structure, and the financial inequities resulting from it, presented one of the major barriers in reorganizing school districts. In 1956, Nebraska, for the first time in 70 years, had fewer than 5,000 school districts. School district reorganization continued to be a constant and perplexing problem.

The State Committee for Reorganization of School Districts proposed that the Legislature require all land in the state to be in districts offering kindergarten through twelfth grade (K-12) by June 30, 1960. This proposal would dissolve any K-8 district that failed to become a K-12 district and would attach it to an existing K-12 district. Although educators and interested laymen heartily endorsed this proposal, it failed to become law.

Commissioner Freeman B. Decker pointed out in his annual report for 1960 that well-planned school district reorganization, making possible stronger financial support, had resulted in a broader and better curriculum in many schools, with special attention to highly important areas such as English, science, mathematics, history, and government. Schools could offer more electives and increase greatly their holding power.

In January 1962, Commissioner Decker resigned. From that time until the state board appointed his successor, Stanley L. Hawley served as acting commissioner. Hawley, a long-time member of the department staff, had served as deputy commissioner under Decker. In April 1962, the state board appointed Floyd A. Miller as the state's third commissioner of education. The new commissioner, a veteran staff member of the department, had been assistant commissioner for instructional services before being appointed.

During his first year, Commissioner Miller held a series of 11 meetings throughout the state to discuss Nebraska's educational program and prepare school district reorganization legislation. His suggestions resulted in a coordinated effort by educational organizations to introduce a reorganization bill. Numerous local citizen groups and community boards of education cooperated in forming educational study committees.

In 1962 and 1963, the State Board of Education took a firm and courageous stand on three of the most unpopular problems facing the state's educational progress: school district reorganization, a broader tax base, and state aid to education. Concerning reorganization, it stated:

> We believe that our commitment to quality education requires us to work vigorously toward adequate school district organization. Just to rearrange districts is not enough. A school district should have sufficient pupils and financial resources to make possible a quality program of general, special and vocational education for all children from kindergarten through high school. As a Board we accept the challenge of bringing about reorganization through both educational and lay leadership. We also believe that this demands the type of budget support which permits an adequate Department staff to provide the necessary leadership (21).

Even though the 1964-65 Legislature passed acts of far-reaching importance to Nebraska education, school district reorganization remained unsolved. It was extremely difficult to get county committees to prepare comprehensive reorganization plans for their people to vote on. The department attempted to provide local communities with as much help as possible in organizing citizens committees and developing sound plans. The department used every available opportunity to help the public understand that adequate, unified school districts could provide better education for the same amount of money.

Expanding Educational Opportunities

Nebraska's citizens continued to show considerable interest in educating exceptional pupils, including both the handicapped and the gifted. Parents, teachers, school board members, and administrators were interested in seeing that each child was given a program that met his individual needs, regardless of his ability or physical condition. Of three bills introduced in the 1957 session of the Legislature, two established educational services for the severely mentally retarded or "trainable" child, and the third provided special education for the gifted.

In 1961, the county chapters of the Nebraska State Society for Crippled Children financed a program of testing the hearing of both public and parochial school children throughout the state. The department administered the program, and a state consultant from its office of special education assisted the counties in the testing.

The department's responsibilities were further expanded when it assumed responsibililty in 1960 for administering the Nebraska School for the Deaf and the School for the Visually Handicapped. In 1961, it began administering the Experimental School for Trainable Mentally Retarded Children at Cozad, which had 30 children attending regularly at the time.

Under the auspices of the Cozad State School and the State Department of Education, Nebraska held its first camp for trainable mentally retarded children in Lexington, Nebraska, in 1963. Forty-seven children and sponsors were involved in a variety of camping activities designed specifically to meet the needs of the children.

Upgrading Instruction and Curriculum. Perhaps one of the most significant factors in improving education in Nebraska was the department's development and refinement of "committee evaluation" of the school systems. Actually, the Nebraska state department was one of the pioneers in developing the use of self-evaluation. In 1957, the department planned for committees to visit, review, and develop recommendations. This resulted in a realistic and efficient long-range program for classified schools, based on the strengths and weaknesses found in the total school program. Thus, a requirement for self-evaluation has become part of the accreditation procedure in Nebraska, and it has now been adopted by the North Central Association of Secondary Schools.

The department also has developed the practice of inviting local boards of education to meet with members of the state department when the school is being visited for evaluation. These contacts help local citizens develop a clearer understanding of the aims and objectives of school systems and how to meet these goals.

The 1959 Legislature permitted the State Board of Education to accredit privately owned business and trade schools domiciled in Nebraska that could meet standards set by the Committee for the Accreditation of Private Schools. In the same year, the Legislature required all privately owned correspondence, business, and trade schools to be licensed and bonded.

The state board continued to emphasize school classification as well as school district reorganization to ensure a minimum educational program. Superintendent Miller and his staff assisted people in various communities to organize grass-roots studies of available educational opportunities.

In 1965, the Legislature divided the state into 19 multicounty areas to provide supplementary educational services to local school districts. A county could ask to be excluded from these services if at least 5 percent of the voters in each of three-fifths of the county's school districts signed a petition requesting that exclusion be voted on at the next general election. These petitions were filed in 79 of the 93 counties. For this reason, the continued existence of many units would not be determined until November 1966.

Eighteen educational service unit boards, with the help of the state department, held meetings during the first year (1966) to develop a budget and explore what services to provide.

Teacher Certification. In 1957, the Legislature reduced the types of initial and renewal certificates for teachers from 68 to 12 (22). For renewals, the law required the applicant to take 8 semester hours, including 3 in education. If the certificate was based on a degree the renewal hours had to apply toward a master's degree or be approved by a recognized college as most suitable for the teacher.

At this time, 1957, a State Board of Education Examiners, appointed by the superintendent of public instruction, evaluated the teacher education programs of the colleges and universities by comparing them with the programs offered by the University of Nebraska. The Council on Teacher Education recommended that the approval of teacher education programs be transferred to the State Board of Education, with the stipulation that the board would perform this function through an advisory committee. The seventy-third session of the Legislature did shift to the State Board of Education the responsibility for establishing requirements, with the assistance of an advisory committee of 22 persons appointed by the board. The state board immediately adopted a policy of strengthening teacher education on the premise that all Nebraska teachers should have a liberal education, based on not less than a baccalaureate degree.

The Nebraska State Board of Education approved rules for issuing certificates and permits to teach, counsel, supervise, and administer, effective January 1, 1964. The rules required that the institution, as well as its teacher education program, be approved by the state board. Perhaps the outstanding feature of these new rules was a provision for recognizing successful teaching experience as one of the criteria for an advanced certificate. New rules and regulations effective in 1965 further provided for eliminating all new nondegree certificates, except the Provisional Rural Elementary, based on 60 college hours, and valid in Class I and II schools only. All certificates based on an approved teacher education program with a baccalaureate degree were valid from kindergarten through grade 12.

The state board appointed an official College Approval Committee consisting of the director of teacher education, the assistant commissioner of instructional services, the assistant commissioner of vocational education services, and representatives of the public school teachers, school administrators, college teachers, college administrators, and guidance and library specialists. This committee represents the State Board of Education and the commissioner of education in evaluating the colleges' and universities' education training programs. It then makes its recommendations to the State Board of Education.

Since this evaluation process was designed to supplement and not duplicate the efforts of existing accrediting agencies, the degree-granting institutions were required to hold regional accreditation to be eligible to offer a teacher education program. Thus, in Nebraska, the North Central Association of Colleges and Secondary Schools assumes major responsibility for evaluating staff, finance, facilities, library, administration, and academic competence. This enables the Advisory Committee on Teacher Education to concentrate its efforts on the programs themselves.

THE DEPARTMENT TODAY, 1965-67

State Aid to Education

In 1967, the State Board of Education again took a hard look at its philosophy and beliefs. On May 12, the board adopted the following statement: "We are committed to the principle that there be substantial state funds allocated to the school districts of the State to be distributed on the basis of total enrollment of all the children in all of the public and nonpublic school systems" (23).

At this time, Nebraska had not had a general state aid program since 1907, and it was estimated that it ranked near the bottom of all states in the amount of tax dollars appropriated to public elementary and secondary schools. But a number of unrelenting educational leaders and lawmakers were working continuously to change this. After numerous attempts to enact a bill for increased state tax dollars, in July 1967, the legislators voted 39 to 7 to approve one, despite adamant opposition. The bill was not perfect, and it needed legal clarification, but it was a step in the right direction.

Specifically, the new act included foundation aid based on average daily membership, incentive payments based on college preparation and the summer school program, and an equalization fund calculated on the assumed need of each local school district. Equalization aid is distributed so as to give districts with low valuation per pupil proportionally more assistance in order to equalize tax levies and educational opportunities. Foundation aid is allocated to a district in an amount equal to \$12.50 per kindergarten pupil, \$25 per pupil in grades 1 through 6, \$30 per pupil in grades 7 and 8, and \$35 per pupil in grades 9 through 12, based on average daily membership.

To qualify for equalization aid, Class I districts must provide local property tax support amounting to at least 10 mills. The minimum qualifying levy for Class II, III, IV, and V districts is 16 mills and must total at least 7 mills in Class VI districts. The law ensures each school district financial support amounting to one of the following two criteria, whichever is smaller: (1) \$250 per kindergarten pupil, \$450 per pupil in grades 1 through 6, \$500 per pupil in grades 7 and 8, and \$550 per pupil in grades 9 through 12; or (2) 108 percent of the district's per-pupil cost for the preceding year multiplied by average daily membership.

Bonus assistance is provided for school districts in counties with sparse population density amounting to less than four persons per square mile, and to all districts with special programs for gifted or culturally and educationally deprived children. School districts are eligible to collect bonus assistance for transportation costs for K-8 pupils residing in the district who live over 4 miles from school and high school students who live more than 8 miles. Additional incentive payments include \$350 for each classroom teacher holding a doctorate degree, \$250 for each teacher who has completed a 6-year college program or earned a master's degree, \$150 for each teacher holding a bachelor's degree, and 20¢ per student hour for each student participating in summer school programs.

Under the new law, a district is not eligible for state aid when, together with other financial support, it increases per-pupil expenditures more than 8 percent over the previous year or by an annual average of more than 8 percent over the previous 5-year period, whichever is larger. Districts which may suffer "undue financial hardship" from these limits may petition the State Board of Education for relief.

The law states that in the event the program is not fully funded, state aid will be distributed proportionally among the school districts. During the 1967-69 fiscal biennium, per-pupil financial aid was to be fully funded first, with the second priority going to incentive payment, and the third priority to equalization assistance (24). When the program is fully funded, the state will pay nearly one-half all local school costs. This will require about $67 million per year.

The Legislature made the state board, and consequently the state department's financial and statistical section, responsible for administering the law. To facilitate this administration, the department, in December 1967, added to its staff a director of state aid to public schools.

School District Reorganization

In October 1966, there were 2,346 school districts in Nebraska compared to 6,734 in 1949, when the Legislature passed the state's first school district reorganization law. Even though the 1966 total was a reduction of 182 from the previous year, this still left Nebraska with a greater number of school districts than any other state in the nation and a greater number than the combined total of 23 states. In other words, for the most part the 182 districts dissolved during the year represented little more than a rearrangement of boundary lines (25).

At least, the importance of school district reorganization was becoming more apparent. Citizens, local boards of education, and county reorganization committees were planning for better school district structures. The Department of Education's reorganization staff gathered data for these groups and assisted them in organizing their committees.

With only one full-time and one part-time staff member assigned to school district reorganization, it was not possible for the department to fulfill all the requests for assistance from the 93 county school district reorganization committees, local school officials, and citizens. Because of the increased need for field consultants to work with the locally organized study committees, the staff was greatly enlarged in 1967. Members of the State Committee for Reorganization of School Districts visited and advised community groups on their problems and met in 12 regular monthly sessions to review election plans and petition proposals.

The State Departments of Education in Iowa, Missouri, Nebraska, and South Dakota undertook in March 1966 an interstate project of school district organization, the Great Plains School District Organization Project, funded by the U.S. Office of Education until June 30, 1968. The Nebraska state department serves as the administrative agency for the project, which gives these states an opportunity to take a long, hard look at a problem that has plagued the region for many years. It is hoped that the research, discussion, and planning activities will help the participating states see their problems more clearly and provide a basis for developing acceptable units for administering education.

Accreditation

To upgrade the schools, the State Board of Education has continued to adopt new rules and regulations for approving nonpublic as well as public schools. During the years 1965-67, new regulations were adopted with penalties for violations. The citizens of many school districts fought them, particularly a rural-oriented organization dedicated to the status quo, ironically called the Nebraska School Improvement Association. The public hearings held by the state board often erupted into stormy sessions. Finally, in March 1967, the board adopted new rules and regulations for accrediting both public and nonpublic school systems.

To be sure that these rules and regulations were professionally sound, the board had submitted them to 14 different boards of education work conferences and to school personnel throughout the state. Individuals unable to attend the various meetings wrote in suggestions. It was emphasized again and again, before the state board approved them, that these rules and regulations did not apply to Class I school districts or to any other school districts or systems that did not voluntarily seek to be accredited. A school district or system did not have to be accredited to qualify for state funds. However, if the school district operated both a high school and an elementary school, it had to meet all the rules and regulations for those particular types of schools. Only entire school districts and/or systems were accredited; separate attendance areas or schools part of a school district or system were not individually accredited.

Teacher Certification and In-Service Training

In 1967, Nebraska again took a giant step forward when the state department added a special services certificate, providing a means for recognizing people who perform school services but are not actually involved in teaching. For instance, this certificate can be issued to nurses, speech therapists, librarians, and media specialists. Student teaching certificates also were added to the list, to be issued on a 1-year trial basis to student teachers recommended and assigned to the Lincoln City Schools by the University of Nebraska, Nebraska Wesleyan University, Union College, and Doane College.

To improve the quality of teaching, it is important to offer in-service training as well as preservice training; each is inadequate without the other. While preservice education is almost completely the responsibility of the colleges and universities, in-service education is primarily the task of the local school districts. However, the funds available from NDEA and ESEA have expanded considerably the State Department of Education's role in the in-service education of teachers. The department's acquisition of consultants with specialities has added a new dimension to this program since 1965.

During the 1966-67 school year, the department organized and promoted five workshops on "totalitarianism versus democracy" that attracted 220 teachers. The University of Nebraska and the department sponsored a summer workshop which brought together 25 outstanding K-12 social studies teachers to begin work on the state's first major social studies curriculum overhaul in a decade. The department also organized 25 English workshops for 2,000 K-12 English and language art teachers; and it sponsored a successful reading workshop for 541 teachers. It conducted 23 workshops to orient elementary teachers to the new art curriculum guide, copies of which were distributed to nearly 4,000 teachers. It also selected eight schools to organize in-service programs for elementary science.

One of the new services offered by the department is the library-media mobile unit, operated under ESEA Title II funds. It provides equipment, produces instructional materials such as transparencies, and offers book selection aids and catalogs of sources of nonprint materials such as filmstrips, films, and recordings. It enables specialists to give demonstrations in the production, utilization, and operation of instructional equipment to entire faculties. This mobile in-service training unit was displayed at many Nebraska schools during the 1966-67 school year and is available on request to any school or organization wishing to use it.

Model demonstration center libraries for elementary schools have been established at Omaha and Grand Island with ESEA Title II funds. Model demonstration libraries for secondary schools were opened at Waverly and Bellevue during the second semester of the 1967-68 school year. The department has urged administrators, teachers, school board members, and citizens interested in improving their school library programs to visit these centers. The Nebraska State Department of Education also has received money under NDEA and ESEA to produce curriculum materials and teacher handbooks which should greatly enrich the in-service program. The lack of funds has limited distribution of these materials in the past; but from 1965 to 1967, curriculum guides were planned for subject areas in which the teachers felt there was greatest need. Committees comprised of selected teachers and supervisors were assigned the task of producing the guides in art, health education, reading and language arts, English, and other fields.

Special Programs

Gifted Children. After the 1957 bill for educating Nebraska's gifted children failed to pass the Legislature, it was a decade before further legislation was introduced, despite the strong interest of many citizens. In 1967, the Legislature passed two bills that were important to this field. One was a section of the historic State Aid to Education bill, which provided special programs for both gifted children and culturally and educationally deprived children. The second bill enabled the state department to employ a consultant in special education.

Western Nebraska Vocational-Technical School. The federal government deeded to Nebraska a tract of land at Sidney known as the Sioux Army Depot, which contained approximately 1,000 acres with 111 buildings including 85 double apartments and equipment. In 1965, the Legislature established the Western Nebraska Vocational-Technical School on this tract, the acquisition value of which was nearly $750,000. The purpose was to offer post-high-school-level training in drafting, automotive technology, electricity and electronics technology, building construction technology, diesel and tractor mechanics, and air frame and power plant mechanics for the aircraft industry.

As of fiscal 1967-68, the enrollment was approximately 130, but it was anticipated that some 250 students would attend in 1968-69. It is estimated that this school can accommodate up to 2,000 students.

Vocational Rehabilitation. In March 1966, the Legislature established a vocational rehabilitation unit at Hastings State Hospital to rehabilitate individuals who might otherwise spend the rest of their lives in an institution. The unit began with 40 staff members, including some hospital personnel who were assigned to do vocational rehabilitation work under the administration and technical supervision of the state department's rehabilitation services division. Thus, the program was a cooperative effort between the division, the hospital, and the federal vocational rehabilitation administration, which provided matching funds for its operation.

The staff, multidisciplinary, consisted of both physicians and special personnel, such as a psychiatrist, psychologist, psychiatric social workers, a psychiatric nurse, a psychiatric technician, and an industrial therapist. Other positions included a coordinator of work preparation and a vocational instructor for the mentally ill. Housed in a modern four-story building within the hospital complex, the VRU accommodates 60 clients.

Also during 1966, another vocational rehabilitation unit was planned for the Norfolk State Hospital. Instead of being housed in one building, however, the 50 staff members were deployed throughout the institution, and clients remained in the various treatment units while undergoing rehabilitation. This decentralized type of VRU will provide a comparison with the centralized unit at Hastings. Perhaps it can be discovered what techniques and methods are best adapted to treating various types of mental disabilities.

Impact of Federal Funds

National Defense Education Act. Nebraska revised its plans for NDEA Title III funds in 1967 to add three new subject matter areas: the humanities, arts, and economics, and soon after, industrial arts. In December 1967, it amended reimbursement procedures so that state-operated public schools, which had been prohibited from participating in Title III programs because of state agency administrative procedures, could now secure funds.

In May 1965, the Nebraska State Board of Education approved a new state plan for guidance, counseling, and testing under Title V of NDEA. The U.S. Office of Education approved it in July. This change made it possible for elementary schools as well as secondary schools to receive moneys for approved guidance-counseling programs.

During the 1965-66 school year, a state advisory committee adopted progress criteria to evaluate counselor preparation and the counselor-student ratio in determining the amount of reimbursement to which a school is entitled under the NDEA programs.

In July 1967, Congress made the greatest change in the National Defense Education Act since its inception. Title X funds, which had been available to state departments of education to assist in statistical reporting and data processing, were shifted to Title V of the Elementary and Secondary Education Act. Title III NDEA supervisory funds were also shifted to Title V of the ESEA. Remaining NDEA title programs were left intact, including the section of Title III allocating funds to local public school districts for strengthening specified subject matter areas and assisting local schools in acquiring equipment, materials, and minor remodeling necessary for educational programs.

Elementary and Secondary Education Act. Congress reaffirmed the nation's commitment to quality education for all of America's youth by revising and extending the program to June 30, 1970. In 1966, Title VI was added, authorizing a 4-year program for handicapped children, including those with multiple handicaps. It also established in the U.S. Office of Education a National Advisory Committee on Handicapped Children and a Bureau for the Education and Training of the Handicapped. A Nebraska state plan was approved, effective October 1967, allowing the department to administer the Title VI program. Nebraska's 1968 allocation was set at $100,364.

Congress, in Title IV of the ESEA, named the Mid-Continent Regional Educational Laboratory (McREL) as one of 20 regional laboratories directed to take bold and imaginative steps to expedite application of educational research findings to solution of the nation's school problems. McREL, a nonprofit corporation, with more than 300 members representing public and private schools, colleges, and special institutions, primarily served major parts of Kansas, Missouri, Nebraska, and Oklahoma. However, due to a lack of appropriations, Nebraska's offices at Kearney, Omaha, Wayne, and Lincoln were closed in 1967. The state research projects in Omaha and the University of Nebraska continued to be administered by McREL's Kansas City regional headquarters.

Of special importance to Nebraska was an amendment to ESEA in 1967 that doubled the minimum allocation to state educational agencies for administering Title I programs. The state's allocation of $75,000 was now raised to $150,000.

One Title III revision by the Ninetieth Congress provided for state educational agencies to administer 75 percent of appropriated funds in fiscal 1969, with the U.S. Office of Education administering the remaining 25 percent. Previously, these funds had been administered solely by the USOE. In fiscal 1970, the states will assume administrative responsibility for all Title III funds except those necessary to complete projects begun in prior years.

Vocational Education. Great strides have been made in vocational education since the Vocational Education Act of 1963. By 1967, agricultural enrollment had increased 5.2 percent, distributive education 38 percent, health occupation 135.2 percent, home economics 4.5 percent, and technical education 61.7 percent. Secondary education expanded its vocational enrollment by 54 percent, post-secondary by 200 percent, and adult education by 12.1 percent. Comparing 1967 with 1966, new programs, such as diversified occupations, had increased 182.7 percent, office occupations by 50.1 percent, and special needs by 80 percent.

For the first time, it was possible for Nebraska to help local boards establish special needs programs for youngsters handicapped in various ways who could not benefit from regular programs of vocational education. This new program had developed training facilities in Nebraska schools for over 7,000 boys and girls. A home economics-related occupations program enables the schools to conduct vocational training for those preparing for gainful occupations involving knowledge and ability in the general area of home economics instead of just for work in the home.

Unfortunately, Nebraska's three newly developed area vocational-technical schools are not adequately financed from available federal money. It is now estimated that the need for additional federal funds for the 1968-69 school year will total between $1 and $2 million.

Special Education. Through continuing expansion, the State Department of Education has strengthened its special education program to serve the speech handicapped, acoustically handicapped, homebound physically handicapped, orthopedically handicapped, visually handicapped, educable mentally handicapped, and trainable mentally retarded.

During the 1966-67 school year, 8,914 handicapped children were served in 147 approved special education programs in 94 public school districts. Of these, 638 received speech and hearing diagnoses and psychological testing services under the direction of 338 teachers and therapists.

Conclusion

It has often been said that "the job makes the man." In Nebraska, the job has made the State Department of Education. From a small beginning, when the state superintendent's duties were performed by the territorial librarian (1855-59), the department has grown in service, size, and responsibility. There has been a spurt in recent years as a result of increased public interest in education and liberalized federal financial assistance.

Few, if any, of Nebraska's chief state school officers were content merely to perform the duties imposed on the office by law. The earlier ones were concerned with establishing schools and operating them, which in most cases involved applying and enforcing laws already on the statutes. But their concern about the qualifications of the persons who served as teachers led to plans for teacher education and certification. They sought to lengthen school terms and to publish better courses of study for elementary schools. Their early interest in constructing schoolhouses, sites, equipment, apparatus, supplies, and textbooks later was extended to include adequate provisions for heating, ventilating, lighting, and sanitation.

Nearly all the state superintendents offered plans for improving school finance. They saw the inefficiency of thousands of small school districts and recommended consolidation into larger districts.

The state superintendents led in efforts to adjust school programs to meet changing needs, advocating improvement of instruction in the "basic" subjects, addition of vocational courses and fine arts subjects, and experiences relating to improving citizenship. They advocated free high school privileges, a teacher retirement system, strengthening of the State Department of Public Instruction (later the State Department of Education), increases in services to local school districts and officers, and improvement of state educational programs. Their public pronouncements and recommendations for new laws and amendments were reported in newspapers and magazines and appeared in their annual and biennial reports. Thus, the amount of progress in the state educational system was dependent in large measure on the leadership and public relations programs of the chief state school officers.

The development of state school administration in Nebraska has been affected by economic fluctuations and by the Legislature's attitude toward school programs. Fortunately, as the public became more interested, it has increased its demands upon the state department for expanded and improved educational services. Thus, the department today had taken on a stature it has never had before. But if it is to meet its new responsibilities effectively, the state must be willing to see that it is properly financed, adequately staffed, and not constrained by constitutional, statutory, and political limitations.

Throughout the period covered by this study, state appropriations for the support of the State Department of Education were minimal and in no case entirely adequate. The same is true of special aid funds distributed by the department to eligible schools.

Nebraska took one of its most important steps when it established a policy-making State Board of Education, which in turn appoints the state commissioner of education. This brings greater unity to the statewide program of education.

Today, the department's stature is indicated not simply by its many responsibilities, but by the appreciation so frequently expressed by teachers, administrators, and supervisors for its quality of work and tireless efforts to provide assistance. The department is giving leadership through long-range planning and professional guidance. This leadership has strengthened local programs of education. At the same time, the department has recognized that local educational freedom is of surpassing importance in our American system. Although federal funds have enabled the State Department of Education to do a much better job for Nebraska's children, the department believes that these funds should lose their identity at the time of appropriation and become subject to management expenditure by the state and local boards of education.

FOOTNOTES

1. Addison Erwin Sheldon, *Land Systems and Policies in Nebraska* (Lincoln: Nebraska State Historical Society, 1936), p. 210.
2. *Ibid.*, pp. 217-18.
3. James C. Olson, *History of Nebraska* (Lincoln: University of Nebraska Press, 1955), pp. 150-52.
4. Sheldon, *op. cit.*, p. 232.
5. Elmer H. Mahlin, "History of Educational Lands in Nebraska," *Forty-Third Biennial Report of the Board of Educational Lands and Funds* (Lincoln: The Board, 1962), p. 5.
6. Sheldon, *op. cit.*, pp. 255-59.
7. *Nebraska Blue Book* (Lincoln: The Legislative Council, 1966), p. 555.
8. *Nebraska Education News*, Special Centennial Section (April 1967), p. 6.
9. A deputy was authorized in 1873, but his office was abolished 3 years later.
10. In 1905, the NSTA advocated (a) high standards for entrance into the teaching profession; (b) tenure for teachers; (c) creation of juvenile courts; (d) workable free high school attendance law; (e) child labor laws; (f) state aid for weak districts; (g) strengthening of the compulsory education laws; (h) increase in junior normal schools; (i) a library in every school district; (j) an emphasis on character education; (k) con-

solidation of schools; and (l) a general survey of the state's resources.

After 75 years as the Nebraska State Teachers Association, a World War II offensive to replace "Teachers" with "Education" was launched. In December 1942, the organization thereby changed its name to the Nebraska State Education Association, the name it is still known by today.

11. Six years later, when the Legislature rewrote the certification laws, it set up three classes of certificates but did not reduce the number of agencies permitted to issue them. Not until 1938 was teacher certification placed entirely in the hands of the State Department of Education.
12. Sheldon, *op. cit.,* p. 245.
13. Otto G. Ruff, "The Development of State School Administration in Nebraska" (unpublished Ph.D. dissertation, University of Nebraska, Lincoln, 1959), p. 176.
14. *Ibid.,* p. 196.
15. Superintendent of Public Instruction, *Annual Report* (1951), p. 40.
16. U.S. Commissioner of Education, *Annual Report* (1955) pp. 15-19.
17. Superintendent of Public Instruction, *Annual Report,* (1947), pp. 27-28.
18. The superintendent of public instruction had always served on this board. In 1941, the composition of the board was changed to include a member of the Board of Control, to be appointed by the Governor; two other persons appointed by the Governor; the dean of the University's College of Agriculture, and the superintendent of public instruction. Two years later, the Legislature named the Governor to the board as chairman, the state superintendent of public instruction as the executive secretary, and the presiding judge of the workmen's compensation court. In 1951, it was again changed to include the Governor, the superintendent of public instruction, the state treasurer (ex officio), and three additional persons to be appointed by the Governor—one in agriculture, another in industry, and a third representing skilled labor.
19. Mahlin, *op. cit.,* p. 5.
20. *Nebraska Blue Book* (Lincoln: The Legislative Council, 1966), p. 429.
21. Board of Education, *Annual Report* (1963), pp. 17-20.
22. The list of teaching certificates now included third-grade elementary, general elementary, junior elementary, Nebraska elementary, rural elementary temporary, elementary temporary, elementary substitute, Nebraska secondary, secondary temporary, secondary substitute, Nebraska administrative and supervisory, and miscellaneous (including special music permits).
23. Board of Education, *Annual Report* (1967), pp. 18-20.
24. *The Lincoln Star,* July 20, 1967.
25. Of the 182 school districts abolished, 14 were Class II or Class III (K-12) districts, while 168 were Class I (K-8) districts.

BIBLIOGRAPHY

Public Documents

Nebraska. *Constitution* (1875, amended 1920).

—— *Nebraska Law.* 77th Session, 1967. Legislative Bill 448, Sec. 8. p. 3.

—— *Nebraska Law.* 77th Session, 1967. Legislative Bill 266, Sec. 11. p. 1.

Books

Nebraska Blue Book. Lincoln: The Legislative Council, 1936, 1956, 1966.

Olson, James C. *History of Nebraska.* Lincoln: University of Nebraska Press, 1955.

Sheldon, Addison Erwin. *Land Systems and Policies in Nebraska.* Lincoln: Nebraska State Historical Society, 1936.

Reports

Board of Education. *Annual Reports.* Lincoln: The Department of Education, 1956-68.

Commissioner of Education. *Annual Report.* Lincoln: Department of Education, 1955.

Mahlin, Elmer H. "History of Educational Lands in Nebraska." *Forty-Third Biennial Report of the Board of Educational Lands and Funds.* Lincoln: The Board, 1962.

Superintendents of Public Instruction. *Annual Reports.* Lincoln: Department of Education, 1869-1965.

Periodicals

Nebraska Education News. Special Centennial Section (April 1967). Lincoln: Nebraska State Education Association, p. 6.

The Lincoln Star. July 20, 1967.

Unpublished Material

Decker, Freeman Bernard. "The Development of the Nebraska Common School Lands and Funds." Part I. Unpublished Ph.D. dissertation, University of Nebraska, Lincoln, 1959.

Nebraska League of Women Voters. "Government in Nebraska." Lincoln, 1961. (Mimeographed.)

Ruff, Otto G. "The Development of State School Administration in Nebraska." Unpublished Ph.D. dissertation, University of Nebraska, Lincoln, 1959.

Seidel, Paul E. "Financial Support of Education in Nebraska." Lincoln, Department of Education, 1963-64, pp. 8-13. (Mimeographed.)

"The Nebraska Council on Teacher Education: Its Organization, Purposes, and Accomplishments," Lincoln, 1967. (Mimeographed.)

Appendix A

NEBRASKA CHIEF STATE SCHOOL OFFICERS

Territorial Librarians, Superintendents of Public Instruction

1855	James S. Izard (8 months)
1855-57	H. C. Anderson
1857-59	John H. Kellom

Territorial Commissioner of Common Schools (to 1861) and Territorial Auditor (Librarian and School Commissioner) 1861-69

1859-65	William E. Harvey
1865-69	John Gillespie

State Superintendents of Public Instruction

1869-71	Samuel D. Beals
1871-77	John M. McKenzie
1877-81	S. R. Thompson
1881-87	William W. W. Jones
1887-91	George B. Lane
1891-95	A. K. Goudy
1895-97	Henry R. Corbett
1897-1901	William R. Jackson
1901-1905	William K. Fowler
1905-1909	Jasper L. McBrien
1909-11	Edward C. Bishop
1911	James W. Crabtree (8 months)
1911-15	James E. Delzell
1915-17	Augustus O. Thomas
1917-20	William Clemmons
1920-27	John M. Matzen
1927-43	Charles W. Taylor
1943-50	Wayne O. Reed
1950-51	Otto G. Ruff
1951-55	Freeman B. Decker

State Commissioners of Education

1955-62	Freeman B. Decker
1962-	Floyd A. Miller

NOTE:
A constitutional amendment, approved at the election of 1952, established a State Board of Education and a State Department of Education, with an appointive commissioner of education. The position of superintendent of public instruction was abolished upon the completion of the incumbent's term of office. From that time until the present, the commissioner of education has been appointed by the State Board of Education.

Appendix B

Chart I.--NEBRASKA DEPARTMENT OF EDUCATION, 1964-65

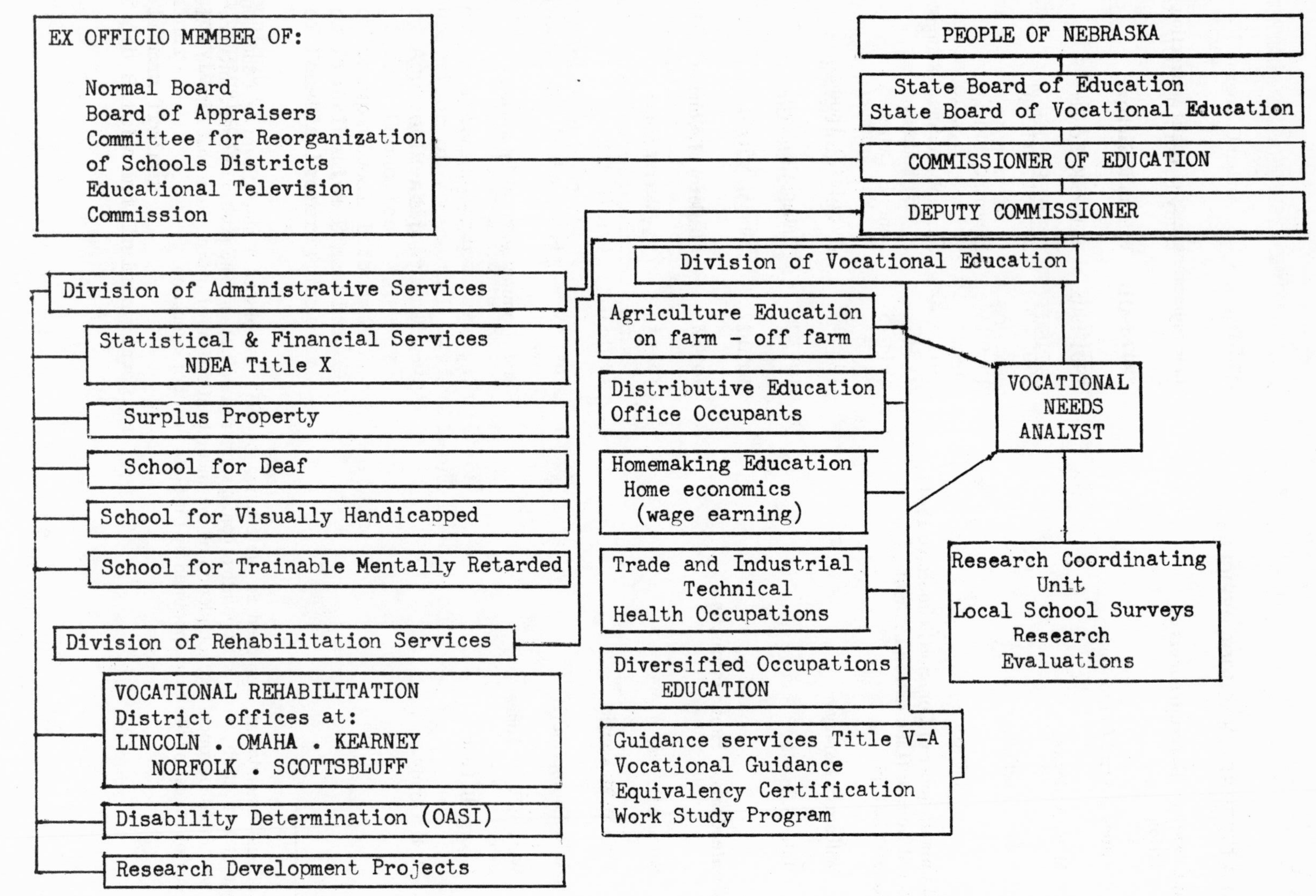

Source: The annual Report, 1964-65.

Appendix B

Chart I.--NEBRASKA DEPARTMENT OF EDUCATION, 1964-65 (Continued)

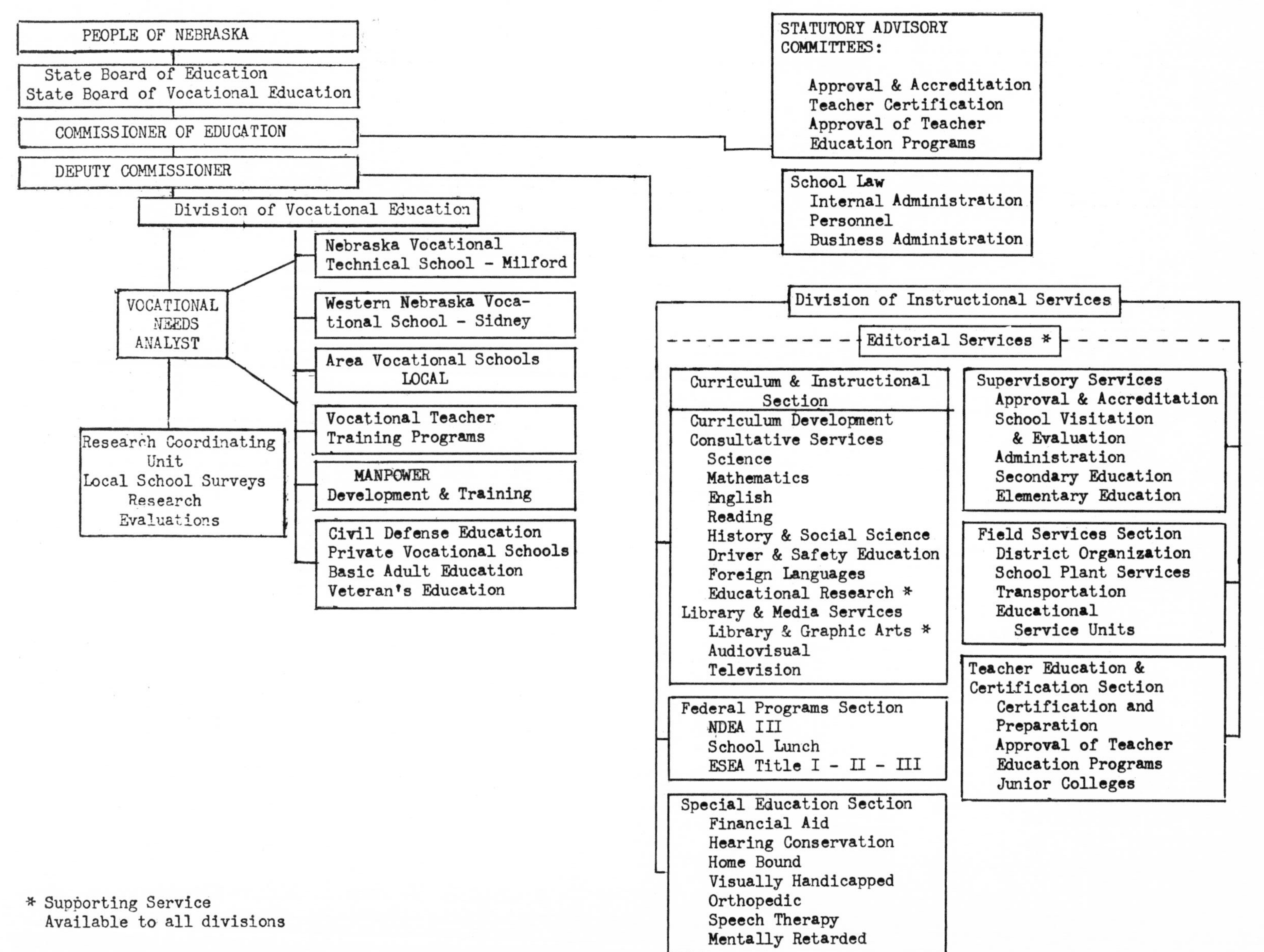

* Supporting Service
Available to all divisions

Appendix B

Chart II.--NEBRASKA DEPARTMENT OF EDUCATION, 1967-68

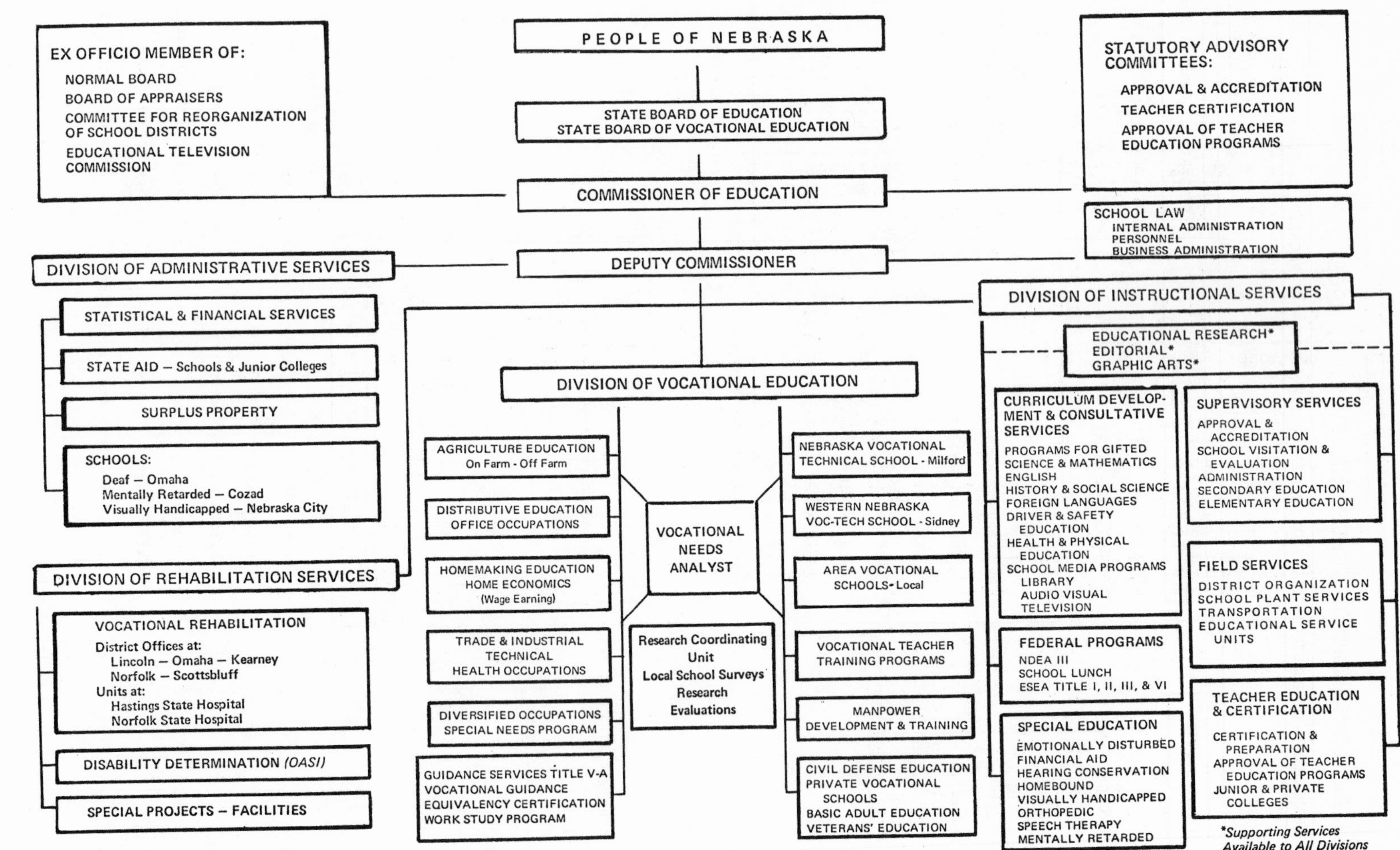

Appendix C

Table 1.--APPROPRIATIONS FOR NEBRASKA DEPARTMENT OF EDUCATION, 1869-1965

Years	State Supt. (1)	Salaries		Maintenance		Normal Training (6)	Fixed Charges Aid (7)	Aid to Weak Dist. (8)	Junior Normal Schools (9)	High School Inspec. (10)	Instr. of Deaf Child. (11)	Adult Immig. Instr. (12)	Tuition Service Pers. (13)	Relief of Sch. Dist. (14)
		Deputy (2)	Other (3)	Office (4)	Deficiency (5)									
1869 - 1870	4,000	...	...	...	185.30	...	...	...	...	...	...	...	...	...
1871 - 1872	4,000	...	...	800	...	...	...	...	...	...	...	...	...	...
1873 - 1874	4,000	1,500	...	7,640	...	...	...	...	...	...	...	...	...	...
1875 - 1876	4,000	1,500	...	2,000	...	...	...	...	...	...	...	...	...	...
1877 - 1879	4,500	...	...	3,278	...	...	...	...	...	...	...	...	...	...
1879 - 1881	4,000	...	...	4,600	...	...	...	...	...	...	...	...	...	...
1881 - 1883	4,000	...	...	4,750	...	...	...	...	...	...	...	...	...	...
1883 - 1885	4,000	...	...	10,700	...	...	...	...	...	...	...	...	...	...
1885 - 1887	4,000	...	...	11,800	...	...	...	...	...	...	...	...	...	...
1887 - 1889	4,000	...	...	11,650	...	...	...	...	...	...	...	...	...	...
1889 - 1891	4,000	...	...	8,775	...	...	...	...	...	...	...	...	...	...
1891 - 1893	4,000	3,000	...	13,339	...	...	...	...	...	...	...	...	...	...
1893 - 1895	4,000	3,000	1,600	9,925	...	...	...	...	...	...	...	...	...	...
1895 - 1897	4,000	3,000	1,600	10,350	883.55	...	...	...	...	...	...	...	...	...
1897 - 1899	4,000	3,000	1,600	11,160	...	...	...	...	...	...	...	...	...	...
1899 - 1901	4,000	3,200	1,600	9,400	...	...	...	...	...	...	...	...	...	...
1901 - 1903	4,000	3,000	1,680	10,000	246.16	...	...	...	...	...	...	...	...	...
1903 - 1905	4,000	3,400	1,680	11,000	150.00	...	...	...	12,000	...	...	...	...	...
1905 - 1907	4,000	3,600	1,680	10,000	1,000.00	...	...	...	15,000	...	...	...	...	...
1907 - 1909	4,000	3,600	1,680	13,000	1,163.26	50,000	...	50,000	15,000	...	...	...	...	...
1909 - 1911	4,000	3,600	1,680	14,500	2,108.00	75,000	...	75,000	20,000	...	...	...	...	...
1911 - 1913	4,000	3,600	1,680	17,000	...	100,000	...	75,000	20,000	...	...	...	...	...
1913 - 1915	4,000	3,600	1,680	17,000	...	125,000	15,000	75,000	14,000	...	...	...	...	...
1915 - 1917	4,000	3,600	7,480	10,000	...	125,000	30,000	50,000	...	...	...	...	...	...
1917 - 1919	4,000	3,600	13,760	13,000	...	118,000	20,000	50,000	...	...	...	...	...	...
1919 - 1921	4,000	3,600	35,000	16,500	50,479.63	154,000	30,000	20,000	5,000	...	...	...	...	...
1921 - 1923	10,000	INCL.(3)	48,800	20,000	...	224,725	50,000	100,000	...	...	...	...	...	...
1923 - 1925	10,000	5,280	46,370	20,000	...	210,000	110,000	...	...	20,000	...	...	...	...
1925 - 1927	10,000	5,280	48,800	20,000	...	205,000	110,000	...	...	20,000	6,500	...	...	...
1927 - 1929	10,000	5,280	48,800	20,000	...	195,000	100,000	INCL.(7)	...	20,000	10,000	19,200	...	...
1929 - 1931	10,000	5,280	56,600	20,000	...	195,000	100,000	...	...	20,000	10,000	19,200	...	...
1931 - 1933	10,000	5,280	56,600	20,000	...	175,000	110,000	...	...	18,000	9,000	19,200	...	...
1933 - 1935	10,000	5,280	45,880	17,000	...	100,000	100,000	...	...	8,000	8,000	...	...	...
1935 - 1937	10,000	5,280	48,880	17,000	...	100,000	100,000	...	...	10,000	9,000	3,000	...	...
1937 - 1939	10,000	5,280	45,880	17,000	...	100,000	100,000	...	...	10,000	9,000	3,000	15,000	30,000

Continued on following page

Appendix C

Table 1.--APPROPRIATIONS FOR NEBRASKA DEPARTMENT OF EDUCATION, 1869-1965 (Continued)

Years	(1)	(2)	(3)	(4)	(5)	(6)	(7)	(8)	(9)	(10)	(11)	(12)	(13)	(14)
1939 - 1941	10,000	5,280	43,060	16,000	...	94,000	94,000	...	...	9,000	5,600	...	15,000	...
1941 - 1943	10,000	5,280	38,060	16,000	...	94,000	94,000	...	...	9,000	9,000	...	20,000	...
1943 - 1945	10,000	6,600	40,000	16,000	...	75,000	83,000	...	...	32,000	5,000	...	...	...
1945 - 1947	10,000	INCL(3)	63,980	16,000	...	120,000	95,000	...	...	76,440	11,000	...	12,000	...
1947 - 1949	10,000	...	91,415	INCL(3)	...	122,000	109,000	...	...	84,500	12,000	1,500	...	...
1949 - 1951	10,000	...	130,000	...	...	115,765	75,000	...	...	158,800	6,000	6,000	32,000	...
1951 - 1953	13,000	...	153,420	...	...	70,830	28,000	...	...	180,050	INCL(18)	20,000	40,000	...
1953 - 1955	9,809	...	132,500	...	...	45,000	25,000	...	...	180,000	...	20,000	131,000	...
1955 - 1957			258,000			25,000	...	...	...	160,000	...	20,000	110,000	...
1957 - 1959			271,000			8,000	...	...	...	182,000	...	20,000	133,603	...
1959 - 1961			515,000			INCL(3)	...	...	...	INCL(3)	...	7,500	...	...
1961 - 1963			435,000			...	...	...	...	...	...	...	...	...
1963 - 1965			564,211			...	...	...	...	...	...	...	...	...

Beginning with the biennium (1939-41), 14 additional items were added to the appropriations.

Years	High School Manual (15)	School Lunch (16)	Veteran Education (17)	Special Education (18)	Reorg. School Dist. (19)	Reserve Teachers (20)	Match. Funds TitleIII (21)	School for Blind (22)	School for Deaf (23)	School for Men. Rtd. (24)	Division of Voc. Ed.: Salaries & Maintenance (25)	Division of Voc. Ed.: State Aid to Voc. Ed. (26)	Division of Voc. Ed.: Nebr. Trade School (27)	Rehab.: Rehab. Service (28)
1939 - 1941	7,500	...	...	...	...	...	...	...	...	...	...	...	...	...
1941 - 1943	7,500	...	...	...	...	...	...	...	...	...	...	...	...	...
1943 - 1945	7,500	...	...	...	...	...	...	...	...	...	...	...	...	...
1945 - 1947	INCL(10)	...	...	...	...	...	...	...	...	...	...	...	...	...
1947 - 1949	...	19,000	20,000	...	...	...	...	...	...	...	...	...	...	...
1949 - 1951	...	21,250	INCL(3)	250,000	26,750	...	...	...	...	...	...	...	...	...
1951 - 1953	...	30,330	...	428,160	14,170	...	...	...	...	...	...	...	...	...
1953 - 1955	...	INCL(3)	...	515,000	INCL(3)	...	...	...	...	...	...	...	...	...
1955 - 1957	...	...	...	528,000	...	...	...	...	...	...	127,000	215,000	315,000	215,000
1957 - 1959	...	...	...	591,940	...	308,000	...	...	...	...	136,438	248,648	325,000	300,000
1959 - 1961	...	...	...	625,000	...	...	INCL(3)	160,933	300,000	...	150,000	262,280	350,000	313,500
1961 - 1963	...	...	...	790,000	...	80,000	...	425,000	770,000	96,474	160,000	272,000	475,000	340,000
1963 - 1965	...	...	...	1,219,076	...	484,453	...	430,507	854,964	96,677	197,875	272,000	543,851	400,230

Appendix C

Table 2.–PUBLIC SCHOOL STATISTICS, 1869-70 TO 1964-65

Year	No. of counties	No. of districts	No. of schoolhouses	No. of children ages 5 to 21 years	No. of children enrolled in school			No. of districts K-12	No. of teachers[a]	Total wages paid to teachers[a]
					Public	Other	Total			
1869-70	32	797	298	32,589	12,719	---	---	20	536	$ 57,738
1879-80	64	3,132	2,701	142,348	92,549	---	---	70	4,100	549,200
1889-90	89	6,243	5,937	232,243	240,300	---	---	250	10,555	2,076,790
1899-1900	90	6,708	6,733	377,791	288,227	---	---	448	9,463	2,624,712
1909-10	92	7,071	7,157	376,477	278,936	---	---	534	11,099	4,568,423
1919-20	93	7,264	7,655	392,592	311,821	---	---	749	13,789	10,907,630
1929-30	93	7,244	7,565	423,602	325,216	---	---	940	14,400	15,209,877
1934-35	93	7,216	7,553	415,834	312,355	---	---	861	13,852	10,037,590
1939-40	93	7,192	7,511	369,154	276,188	---	---	836	13,759	10,900,654
1940-41	93	7,186	7,498	354,787	267,103	---	---	808	13,619	10,951,913
1941-42	93	7,009	7,440	342,145	257,664	---	---	720	13,397	10,948,395
1942-43	93	6,998	7,360	328,923	253,856	---	---	729	12,990	12,354,892
1943-44	93	6,986	7,379	318,714	237,603	---	---	736	12,503	13,986,768
1944-45	93	6,975	7,358	312,330	230,666	---	---	665	12,184	16,258,308
1945-46	93	6,956	7,277	308,662	230,147	---	---	651	12,125	17,803,457
1946-47	93	6,923	7,147	309,396	225,692	---	---	661	11,902	19,541,584
1947-48	93	6,864	7,136	314,610	225,525	---	---	654	11,857	22,055,957
1948-49	93	6,807	7,135	315,828	225,516	---	---	642	11,816	25,149,484
1949-50	93	6,734	7,008	317,850	227,879	---	---	647	11,948	26,856,628
1950-51	93	6,604	6,794	319,782	231,618	---	---	648	11,942	27,604,726
1951-52	93	6,466	6,611	327,339	233,031	---	---	640	11,905	29,849,304
1952-53	93	6,276	6,393	336,204	242,267	---	---	654	12,085	32,453,836
1953-54	93	5,983	6,071	343,428	249,920	---	---	660	12,413	35,161,005
1954-55	93	5,631	5,836	354,830	259,305	---	---	693	12,692	37,872,601
1955-56	93	5,340	5,067[b]	358,554	259,160[c]	---	---	462	13,142	40,069,841
1956-57	93	4,966	4,753[b]	363,690	262,142[c]	---	---	453	13,209	42,223,848
1957-58	93	4,660	4,340[b]	372,323	267,649[c]	45,608	313,257	439	13,290	44,661,108
1958-59	93	4,403	4,193[b]	383,333	278,130[c]	48,041	326,171	431	13,500	47,978,736
1959-60	93	3,777	3,953[b]	394,156	284,740	51,258	335,998	394	13,753	51,514,811
1960-61	93	3,529	3,748[b]	406,502	296,213	54,481	350,694	393	13,316	55,001,670
1961-62	93	3,278	3,567[b]	421,799	306,091	56,529	362,620	386	13,354	59,493,955[d]
1962-63	93	3,099	3,413[b]	433,966	315,216	57,887	373,103	380	14,050	71,253,447[d]
1963-64	93	2,927	3,253	442,359	332,493	58,386	390,879	396	14,985	76,258,817
1964-65	93	2,701	3,111	449,838	329,586	59,362	388,948	389	15,205	83,316,679

[a]Classroom teachers. Does not include principals and supervisors.
[b]Publicly owned school plants.
[c]Net figures as compared with numbers prior to 1955-56 which included reenrollments.
[d]Includes salaries of principals and supervisors.

Source:
Nebraska Blue Book, "Public School Statistics," 1966. pp. 552-53.

Appendix C

Table 3.–PUBLIC SCHOOL STATISTICS, 1869-70 TO 1964-65

Year	Value of school property	Receipts	Expenditures	Indebtedness	State apportionment from endowments	Total population of state
1869-70	$ 177,082	$ 120,806	$ 143,535	$ 31,657	$ 138,841	133,993
1879-80	2,064,768	1,134,039	1,108,617	1,008,799	257,623	---
1889-90	6,613,464	3,639,116	3,499,300	2,648,224	586,270	1,058,910
1899-1900	9,591,134	4,410,400	4,403,222	3,373,691	693,205	1,066,300
1909-10	16,290,412	8,971,991	7,454,215	4,640,590	692,357	1,192,214
1919-20	42,145,280	20,062,926	19,563,064	15,070,715	985,579	1,296,372
1929-30	85,303,692	27,733,859	27,853,595	35,121,274	1,025,162	1,377,963
1934-35	80,311,120	18,623,392	18,343,159	30,716,938	940,965	---
1939-40	82,361,854	20,549,162	20,427,683	26,740,166	984,696	1,315,834
1940-41	83,369,193	20,739,024	20,505,922	26,090,194	1,001,569	---
1941-42	84,869,351	21,123,277	20,991,682	24,622,082	1,015,568	---
1942-43	82,356,338	23,367,394	21,753,011	23,306,671	1,055,169	---
1943-44	82,961,309	24,829,968	23,845,259	21,183,850	1,171,807	---
1944-45	84,897,201	27,509,381	28,349,732	19,764,472	1,004,454	---
1945-46	86,373,538	30,173,401	29,530,870	16,813,203	982,719	---
1946-47	89,345,751	33,850,770	33,983,117	17,811,655	1,136,188	---
1947-48	92,718,617	39,103,901	38,988,347	18,060,934	1,321,974	---
1948-49	99,598,126	44,364,036	43,044,290	20,183,394	1,548,212	---
1949-50	112,612,541	48,577,379	46,544,048	22,120,221	1,561,307	---
1950-51	122,872,697	52,349,009	52,786,583	20,355,687	1,960,455	1,325,510
1951-52	134,895,474	64,267,780[a]	55,067,746[b]	30,850,045	2,934,602	---
1952-53	147,045,609	63,707,719[a]	61,771,696[b]	37,971,548	5,587,386	---
1953-54	160,798,629	65,400,718[a]	65,799,029[b]	41,884,241	1,988,331	---
1954-55	185,859,668	80,342,150[a]	74,232,625[b]	56,697,831	2,388,289	---
1955-56	239,225,587	71,007,239	72,617,107	83,014,567	3,040,758	---
1956-57	229,265,849	75,308,292	74,895,238	86,667,495	2,676,535	---
1957-58	236,131,810	78,599,979	78,102,027	89,816,495	2,719,752	---
1958-59	252,447,184	84,610,724	83,858,894	96,398,451	3,002,356	---
1959-60	293,436,124	92,946,748	83,988,931	102,464,631	3,079,681	---
1960-61	291,713,419	98,891,999	90,316,949	107,845,919	3,629,810	1,411,330
1961-62	312,545,519	102,922,342	101,296,532	110,290,573	3,246,468	---
1962-63	342,783,639	109,274,020	108,829,582	156,511,470	6,358,613	---
1963-64	387,445,810	120,417,898	116,787,415	160,015,447	2,610,274	---
1964-65	531,099,112	125,631,864	128,571,192	164,407,346	3,391,732	---

[a]Does not include money on hand at the beginning of the year nor the money received for the Veterans Education Program.
[b]Does not include money expended for the Veterans Education Program.

Source:

Nebraska Blue Book, "Public School Statistics," 1966. p. 553.

Appendix D

CONSTITUTIONAL AND LEGAL CHANGES IN STATUS OF NEBRASKA CHIEF STATE SCHOOL OFFICERS, 1854-1965

A. Title

1) Territorial Librarian-Superintendent of Public Instruction	1855 - 1859
2) Territorial Commissioner of Common Schools	1859 - 1861
3) Territorial Auditor (Librarian and School Commissioner)	1861 - 1869
4) State Superintendent of Public Instruction	1869 - 1955
5) State Commissioner of Education	1955 -

B. Term

1) Two years	1855 - 1871
	1875 - 1921
2) Four years	1871 - 1875
	1921 - 1955
3) Indefinite	1955 -

C. Educational Qualifications

1) Hold highest certificate authorized to issue	1919 -

D. Salary, per year

1) $ 200.00	1854 - 1858
2) $1,000.00	1858 - 1860
3) $ 600.00	1860 - 1864
4) $ 900.00	1864 - 1866
5) $1,000.00	1866 - 1867
6) $ 800.00	1867 - 1869
7) $2,000.00	1869 - 1877
8) $2,500.00	1877 - 1879
9) $2,000.00	1879 - 1921
10) $5,000.00	1921 - 1935
11) $3,400.00	1935 - 1937
12) $5,000.00	1937 - 1951
13) $6,500.00	1951 - 1953
14) $4,904.62	1953 - 1955
15) Set by the state board of education	1955 -

28 Nevada

DEPARTMENT OF EDUCATION
Harold Brown

Contents

ORGANIZATION OF THE STATE DEPARTMENT OF EDUCATION, 1864 TO 1900

The State of Nevada

Nevada, with an area of 110,540 square miles, ranks seventh among the states in size. All of the New England states can be contained within its borders, Massachusetts and New Hampshire within Nye County in central Nevada, and Connecticut within Washoe County, whose county seat is Reno. This great expanse, now populated by approximately four persons per square mile, had but one person per square mile as late as 1930. About two-thirds of the entire population live in Washoe and Clark Counties, represented by 14 of Nevada's 20 state Senators. Vast areas of the state remain uninhabited.

One writer aptly sums up the setting for education in the state:

> About 85 percent of the land is in the public domain; that is, it is still controlled by the federal government and not owned by private individuals. It serves the miner, the livestock owner, the sportsman, or the tourist at times, but most of it is of little use for the general public.
>
> Although much of Nevada is a "desert waste," the history of the state is a living example that the unwanted land of one era may be most valuable to a later age. Much of our story will be related to the fact that men have been able to extract valuable minerals from the Nevada mountains, making important contributions to the commerce and technology of modern society. The desert has many important advantages and possibilities as a playground and recreation center in a country where open space is becoming more difficult to find. Besides, our Nevada desert is becoming an important world laboratory in man's quest to reach the stars: It provided the nuclear rocket-testing grounds in the southern part of the state.
>
> Much of Nevada history, then, shows Nevada's desert is not really a "waste land" but a challenge and opportunity for civilized man (1).

The early history of Nevada is for the most part an account of its mining towns, such as Virginia City, Gold Hill, Austin, Aurora, Hamilton, Pioche, and later Tonopah and Goldfield. Fortunes were made quickly in these towns, which too often evaporated into "ghost" communities of empty, deteriorating buildings. The state's recent history includes the development of agriculture, its ranges, industry, education, and tourism, as well as its mining.

But Nevada is still truly the land of "the sage and the pine." While much of the state is occupied by sagebrush, better grades of pine are found along the western slopes. There are numerous rivers with fertile valleys, beautiful lakes, superhighways, fine churches, and excellent schools.

Statehood, 1864

Mormons, interested in the agricultural potentialities, were the first to establish a settlement in what became the Nevada Territory. In 1854, Brigham Young sent his people into the Carson, Walker, Washoe, and Truckee Valleys, where they built farming communities modeled on those that had proved successful in the Salt Lake region. Three years later, a Mormon colony was started in Las Vegas, but trouble with the U.S. government caused Young to pull his settlers back into Utah.

Prospectors and other farmers began to trickle into the Nevada country, but it was the discovery of the Comstock Lode in 1859 that brought a horde of miners into what was then a county of Utah. These were followed by saloon keepers, dance hall operators, gamblers, gunfighters, lawyers, capitalists, and men who were more interested in making money by selling to the new settlers than in mining. By 1860, while still a part of the Utah Territory, Nevada had a population of 6,857.

Nevada had little law and no effective government for its first few years, and claims were jumped and counter-jumped. During most of the mining period, the people were dependent on California for foodstuffs and other supplies, and Nevada was little more than a colony of California.

Despite the isolation and small population, the Nevadans frequently petitioned Congress for territorial status separate from Utah or suggested that California extend its dominion over them. A few farsighted citizens attempted to establish local governments, but they found little popular support. It was the approaching Civil War that forced Congress to accede to Nevada's request for independent territorial status. On March 2, 1861, two days before retiring from the presidency, James Buchanan signed the Organic Act creating Nevada as an independent territory.

As the Lincoln Administration took the reins of office, several congressional leaders were already suggesting statehood for the Nevada Territory. Gold and silver were needed to raise and equip federal troops, and pro-Union votes were badly needed in both the Senate and House of Representatives. Congress approved the first Enabling Act for statehood, but the territorial voters rejected the proposed constitution. In February 1864, another Enabling Act passed, and this time the new State Constitution was approved. The Territorial Legislature sent a certification of Nevada's loyalty, the first message sent over the Western Union Telegraph Company's new transcontinental wire, and President Lincoln proclaimed Nevada's statehood on October 31, 1864.

Nevada's swift progress to statehood in large measure resulted from pressure to get additional congressmen who could be counted on to vote for the Thirteenth Amendment, which excluded slavery from the United States and any place in its jurisdiction. The proposal had been defeated in the House the previous June. On February 1, 1865, the day Nevada's two Senators and one Representative were sworn in, the Thirty-Third Congress officially proposed this amendment to the Legislatures of the states.

By 1870, 6 years after statehood, Nevada's population had risen to 42,491. As in most other mining states, population fluctuated, depending on the discoveries both in the state and in other mining areas. In 1900, the census showed 42,335 people in the state—slightly fewer than 30 years earlier.

Establishing a State School System

The constitution adopted by Nevada in 1864 did not actually provide for a State Department of Education, but it did state that the people would elect a superintendent of public instruction for a 2-year term beginning the first Monday in January 1865. The members of the constitutional convention recognized the importance of education and included a provision for–

> A uniform system of common schools, by which a school shall be established and maintained in each school district for at least six months in every year . . . [and] in addition to other means provided for the support and maintenance of the university and common schools, the Legislature shall provide for their support and maintenance by direct legislative appropriation from the general fund . . . (2).

Three other sections of the State Constitution specifically stated that no sectarian instruction should be tolerated in any school or university established under the constitution.

In 1865, during its first session, the Legislature enacted a law establishing a State Board of Education composed of the Governor, the state superintendent of public instruction, and the surveyor general as ex officio members (3). These officials were responsible for investing the state school fund, later known as the state permanent school fund, and adopting all textbooks for school use (4). The board exercised its power to adopt textbooks until the Legislature created a State Textbook Commission in 1907. As members of the State Board of Education comprised a majority of the new commission, the board still had final control over the adoption of all textbooks and supplementary books used in the state (5).

Until 1885, county boards of examiners handled practically all teacher certification in Nevada. As in most states, these examinations covered the elementary school subjects for first-, second-, and third-grade certificates. The county boards certified teachers in each of the counties, which meant that a teacher could be certified for one county but not for another. The 1885 Legislature stated that it was the duty of the State Board of Education–

> To adopt a uniform system of rules for the State and County examinations; to grant, first, life diplomas, second, State Educational Diplomas, valid for six years, and all other types of elementary and high school certificates; also, certificates to graduates of Nevada State Normal School; to revoke any State Diploma or State or County Certificate (6).

In 1893, the state board was empowered to prepare teacher examinations for all the counties in Nevada, and in 1907, it became the sole teacher-certificating agency in the state. It adopted the courses of study, approved the books for public school libraries, and invested the state school fund. The board also appointed and removed the state deputy superintendents under the reorganization that occurred in 1907. But the minutes of the state board show that teacher certification continued to be the major theme of its meetings and one of its main functions up to 1966. The board at first considered each individual application for certification separately, but by 1965, it had become a matter of approving the recommendations of the state superintendent of public instruction.

Of the first four state superintendents, three – A. F. White, A. N. Fischer, and S. F. Kelley – were clergymen; but D. R. Sessions, who had resigned from the presidency of the University of Nevada (located at that time in Elko), was a professional educator (7). The terms of service for all of these men were marked by attempts to strengthen the authority of the office, to correct organization problems within the state, and to change through legislative action the method of distributing state funds to the several school districts. Superintendent Fischer, in his biennial report for 1868-70, first recommended a change in the method of the distribution of state school funds, stating that a pro-rata plan of apportionment was unfair to the small school districts.

Despite three such biennial recommendations from Fischer, the apportionment of state school funds on the basis of school population continued until 1877. The administrative problems centered largely on the inability of county school superintendents, often ill-equipped for their responsibilities, to fulfill the statutory requirements of making meaningful reports to the state superintendents. They were required also, according to the Statutes of Nevada, 1864-65, to make quarterly apportionments with public school moneys from the county treasury among the various school districts in proportion to the number of white children between the ages of 6 and 18 years; to visit each school in the county at least once each year; to distribute all blanks, forms, and copies of the school laws furnished by the state superintendent to school district trustees; to conduct teachers institutes annually at a cost not to exceed the sum of $100; to file reports from boards of school trustees, teachers, and census marshals; to fill vacancies of school trustees in school districts within the county; to draw warrants on the county treasurer for the purchase of textbooks for indigent children; to subscribe for school journals for each teacher and each member of the various boards and school trustees; and to give such aid as might be desirable to boards of school trustees, teachers, and school census marshals.

The state superintendent was faced with not only an inequitable distribution of available funds, but also an inadequate tax base. The state school tax was 5¢ on each $100 of taxable valuation, and remedial legislation was years late. The inequities among the counties are well illustrated in the biennial report of 1884 by C. S. Young in which he raises some interesting questions.

> Why is it that some of Nevada's offspring, with a scanty three months in school, must struggle to obtain from a cheaply paid teacher the elements of a primary education, while others can, for ten months annually, under the tuition of normal school and college graduates, enjoy the privileges of the grammar school and the high school? . . . Is there any rational explanation of the fact that while Storey County has an average of ten months of school, White Pine County has an average of four and one half months? . . . Have we a state system at all or is it not rather a county or district system? (8)

Yet, by the time Young had ended his tenure in 1886, he discerned a more favorable attitude toward the Office of State Superintendent of Public Instruction. He wrote:

> The duties of the executive state officer are more arduous than is generally supposed. His service is appreciated by but few. However, within the past two or three years this office evidently has been growing in favor with the people. Whereas a few years ago there was a general newspaper attack upon the office, it being charged that the office was useless and should be abolished, more recently it has received no words of censure from any source, but rather words of encouragement and commendation (9).

W. C. Dovey, elected in 1886, traveled 20,000 miles and made 250 visits to schools (at a cost to the state of $763) during the first year of his administration. His successor, Orvis Ring, elected in 1890, produced Nevada's first state course of study 3 years later. Despite its brevity, Superintendent H. C. Cutting, who served from 1895 to 1898, reported that this outline for each grade filled a great need in the schools.

The 1864-65 Legislature provided for county superintendents to be elected for 2 years. The county commissioners fixed the salaries of these officials with the proviso that such salary would be "at least sufficient to pay all necessary traveling expenses incurred by him in the performance of his duties" (10). The Legislature evidently did not consider visiting schools, apportioning public school moneys, and reporting to the state superintendent as professional, because the annual salaries of these county superintendents ranged from only $393 in 1868 to $449 in 1872. In 1879, the Legislature fixed the salaries to be paid at a minimum of $75 per year in Lincoln County and a maximum of $900 in rich Storey County, the home of Virginia City.

All of the early state superintendents, and especially Sessions and Young, felt keenly that the legal specifications of duties of the office prevented the exercise of genuine professional leadership. Office routine, clerical work, and other minutiae prevented the full exercise of the office in the best sense of the word. Both of these men made strenuous efforts to increase the strength of the office. In his 1882 report to the Legislature, Sessions insisted that –

> As long as the State Office of Superintendent of Public Instruction is continued in existence, it should be vitalized. The incumbent should be vested with some authority at the present; officially, he is a man of straw. The most conspicuous thing that he has to do is to visit schools (11).

State Superintendent C. S. Young likewise felt that the office should have greater executive power. Despite Young's failure to persuade the Legislature to remove the limitations of the office, he felt toward the end of his term, as we have seen, that the stature and favor of the office had advanced in the eyes of the public and the press.

A precedent was established in 1883 when the county clerk of Washoe County was named the ex officio county superintendent of schools. In an economy move 4 years later, the legislators designated Nevada's district attorneys ex officio county superintendents beginning January 1, 1889. Ben Curler and Patrick McCarran, one to become a Reno district judge and the other a U.S. Senator, were serving as district attorneys, and they pointed out that since no additional salary was provided, they generally did not relish the extra work. Their wives helped collect statistics, but little else was accomplished (12). As a result, during the years from 1887 to 1907, when the district attorneys were responsible for the county school administration, very little was done for the schools.

Up to the year 1907, then, the state was laboring to develop a satisfactory system of public education under almost insuperable handicaps. A series of able state superintendents of public instruction operated with little real authority. The county superintendents, elected officials, and the multitude of county and district school board members constituted a capricious and politically oriented power structure that, in effect, placed the development of education in Nevada in the hands of those characterized by C. S. Young, in an address to the Nevada State Teachers Institute in Virginia City, December 29, 1884, as–

> Merchants, and miners, and butchers and ranchers . . . though too illiterate to read or write his own name . . . yet such a man may attain the office of greater power in our educational system . . . . In our temple of learning there may sit enthroned accepted ignorance, before whom intelligence must bow in abject humiliation (13).

Despite pointed comments and astute political maneuvering by many of the able men who occupied the position of state superintendent of public instruction, and despite the almost general recognition of the futility of the district system by able educators, it remained entrenched in the state. Any suggestion to abolish it aroused cries of outrage from those who benefited from it the most. It was not until 1906 that the winds of change blew hard enough to shake the structure.

THE PERIOD FROM 1907 TO 1931

The Reorganization Act of 1907

Legislation enacted in 1907 ushered in a new era of public education in Nevada. This legislation effected a general reorganization of the school system resulting in a real plan of supervision. The Reorganization Act of 1907 was the culmination of over 20 years of discussion and agitation on the part of school officials who realized the need for more efficient school administration. Among these officers, Superintendents W. C. Dovey (14), Orvis Ring (15), and H. C. Cutting (16), many of whose early recommendations were written into law, should be credited with outstanding work. Romanzo Adams, professor of education and sociology at the University of Nevada, formulated the final plan of reorganization. Together with State Superintendent Orvis Ring, he ably led the movement which resulted in the adoption of the reorganization plan by the Nevada Education Association in 1906. After the widest possible publicity, a bill incorporating the provisions of the plan was presented to the Legislature and passed in March 1907.

The plan that evolved located state deputies at Elko, to supervise Elko County; at Eureka, to supervise Lander, Eureka, and White Pine Counties; at Winnemucca, to supervise Humboldt and Churchill Counties; in Reno, to supervise Douglas, Esmeralda, Lyon, Ormsby, Storey, and Washoe Counties; and at Tonopah to supervise Nye and Lincoln Counties. Three additional counties were established after 1907 (17). With the approval of the state board, the superintendent conferred upon the deputies the power and authority to act in his name, and in reality they were representatives of the state superintendent, serving as intermediary officers between the local schools and the state department at Carson City. Since the district attorneys, who had acted as county superintendents from 1889 to 1907, considered any work connected with the public schools secondary to their main duties, the 1907 act specifically stipulated that the deputies would devote full time to their positions.

The deputies had many and varied duties: to visit each school in their educational districts at least twice each year; to advise teachers about organization, management, and teaching methods; to inspect school buildings and equipment; to examine the records and observe the work of each school; to confer with school trustees; to hold teachers meetings; to act as deputy examiners at teachers examinations; and to report in writing regularly to the state superintendent. These reports comprise an interesting portion of the history of Nevada education. The law definitely specified that to hold this office the deputy must hold a Nevada teacher certificate of high school grade and have not fewer than 45 months of successful teaching experience, including 9 in Nevada.

Other Changes Under 1907 Reorganization Act

The Reorganization Act of 1907 created for the first time a commission authorized to adopt both elementary and secondary textbooks. Prior to this, the State Board of Education had this responsibility, but in actual operation local school principals, teachers, and superintendents always selected the high school textbooks. The Textbook Commission consisted of the State Board of Education, plus five additional members, one from each of the five educational supervision districts. All of these appointed members were required to be elementary school employees.

The Reorganization Act also added to the state superintendent's duties. Since 1864, he had been responsible for reporting annually to the Governor, visiting each county at least once per year, convening a state teachers institute annually, prescribing and preparing for school registers, and apportioning school moneys to the counties (18). He was now responsible for apportioning state aid, calling county teachers institutes when necessary, convening state teachers institutes biennially in the even-numbered years and district teachers institutes in odd-numbered years, and appointing school trustees where districts failed to elect. He also was required to nominate deputies for appointment by the state board and perform such other duties as might be prescribed by law (19).

Superintendent Ring died in 1910, and John Edwards Bray, appointed to fill his term, stayed in office until 1919. Bray urged the Legislature to compel school districts to levy a tax for the schools, but this was not to come until 1955. It was during his administration that Congress passed the Smith-Hughes Act early in 1917. This act called for the Governor to appoint a State Board of Vocational Education until legislative provisions could be made for it. The appointees were Superintendent Bray, the state director and supervisor of agriculture education, the supervisor of home economics education, and the supervisor of trades and industries.

Vocational Education

As early as 1910, vocational education received attention from the State Department of Education. For example, the Nevada high school course of study for the year 1910 outlined a complete agricultural curriculum. The state superintendent's 1909-10 report contained many references to course work in industrial training and domestic science in the high schools. Thus, it is not surprising that, when the Smith-Hughes Act passed, Nevada became one of the first states to accept its benefits by its Legislature's passing an act accepting its benefits within a few weeks. The Nevada law stated—

> That the State of Nevada does hereby accept the benefits of an act passed by the Senate and House of Representatives of the United States of America in Congress assembled entitled "An Act to provide for the promotion of vocational education; to provide for cooperation with the states in the promotion of such education in agriculture and the trades and industries; to provide for cooperation with the states in the preparation of teachers of vocational subjects; and to appropriate money and regulate its expenditure," approved February 17, 1917, and will observe and comply with all the requirements of said act (20).

In the same act, the Legislature designated the State Board of Education as the board for administering the act. It also appropriated $30,000 for the 1917-19 biennium as its share of the matching funds.

In 1923, the Legislature passed an act requiring the State Board of Vocational Education to be comprised of the three members of the State Board of Education, plus two appointed members. Four years later, another law made the state superintendent of public instruction the state director of vocational education.

THE THIRTIES TO THE PRESENT

In 1931, the Legislature altered the membership of the State Board of Education to include the Governor, the state superintendent of public instruction, and one elected representative from each of the five educational supervision districts. The president of the University of Nevada no longer was a member. At the same time, the Legislature authorized the position of secretary of the bureau of certification and added the public school teachers retirement-salary fund board to the state department. It expanded the State Board of Vocational Education to consist of the seven-member State Board of Education, plus one representative each from labor and agriculture, to make a total of nine. A director of vocational rehabilitation and a "local supervisor" to supervise industrial education in the White Pine County area were added to the vocational education staff.

State Superintendent Mildred Bray placed the schools of Nevada on a wartime footing soon after World War II began in December 1941 (21). During the war period, the schools became involved in the "Defense Stamp and Bond" campaign, the organization of students as officers in fire-alarm or air-raid drills, and the sacrifice of social activities to allow pupils and teachers to invest in government securities. There were wartime concerns in connection with most school functions and new problems for all schools.

The impact of the war on Nevada centered around the revival of mining, the establishment of air bases and radar facilities, and the expansion of training and testing facilities already in existence. The influx of service personnel and their families led to the anticipation of a serious teacher shortage. This problem was solved in part through the issuance of war emergency certificates, which permitted teachers who were otherwise qualified but who lacked recent professional training to reenter the teaching profession. Subsequent wartime bulletins from the state superintendent reflected the drain in national manpower on the schools and lesser problems such as tire and gasoline procurement for school transportation and the impact of the gasoline shortage on athletics.

Once the trying and harrowing period of World War II was over, the schools faced the almost equally difficult days of transition.

The state superintendents' reports from 1932 to 1950 show no major changes occurring in the state department, but a period of great progress began when Glenn A. Duncan, one of Nevada's great chief school executives, took office in January 1951. By the end of 1952, the department could list the following additions: a certification bureau, a retirement clerk and statistician, a supervisor of Indian education, a state supervisor of the school lunch program, a supervisor of occupational information and guidance services, and a state director and counselor of vocational rehabilitation. During the next biennium, the department added a supervisor of distributive and business education, a medical consultant to the vocational rehabilitation staff, and a supervisor for OASE disability determination.

More important than the department's expansion, the state superintendent was able to provide for a survey of Nevada public schools. In answer to suggestions from school administrators from many sections of the state, and upon State Superintendent Glenn Duncan's request, Governor Charles Russell, in the summer of 1953, appointed 28 prominent Nevada citizens representing all geographical areas of the state to a State School Committee. The group met at Carson City on November 5, 1953, and was given two specific responsibilities by the Governor: first, to investigate the financial conditions of schools throughout the state and, upon the basis of such investigation, recommend as to whether a special session of the Legislature was necessary; second, to carry on a survey of school conditions during 1954 and report the results of their survey at the 1955 session of the Legislature.

The committee represented many fields of industry and professional life of Nevada. At the first meeting, M. E. Lundberg of Elko, a prominent citizen of Nevada, was made chairman. Subcommittees were appointed to direct immediate investigations, and a second meeting of the entire committee was called for December 18. At this meeting, a resolution was presented calling for a special session of the Legislature to consider urgent school needs.

The Legislature met in special session in the spring of 1954 and authorized the Governor to appoint a fact-finding committee and provided for the appropriation of $30,000 from the state general fund for that purpose. Upon the recommendation of Superintendent Duncan, the Governor's School Committee assigned that responsibility to the George Peabody College for Teachers of Nashville, Tennessee. At the same time, the Legislature of 1954 indicated that a written report of the results of the investigation should be made to the Governor not later than January 15, 1955. During the period from March to December of 1954, a survey team moved into the state with 11 members headed by W. D. McClurkin, director of the Division of Survey and Field Services, George Peabody College. Among those who came to Nevada on this survey team were D. Harold Benjamin, then chairman of the Division of Social Foundations of Education, and Henry Harap, associate director of the Division of Surveys, both of George Peabody, and Charles Bursch, assistant division chief, School Planning, of the California State Department of Education.

The survey staff started its work in March 1954, visiting an extensive number of schools before the end of the school year. On the basis of observations in the schools, numerous conferences with parents, teachers, and other citizens, and analysis of school records and questionaires, the survey team was able to make recommendations late in the fall of 1954. These recommendations went to the State School Committee. The Peabody survey report under the title, *Public Education in Nevada,* was adopted by the Governor's committee with minor alterations. Since there were on the committee representatives of industrial concerns, such as the Kennecott Copper Company, it was not surprising that its report paid close attention to financial aspects. A feature of the report which the Governor's committee especially favored was that whereas in the past there had been several superintendents of schools in a county, there would henceforth be but one.

It was immediately evident that the Peabody report, calling for basic foundation funds, would demand additional expenditures. Something like an additional $4 million in funds per year would be necessary. The state sought new sources of income and settled on the introduction of a sales tax.

The Sales Tax

For several years prior to 1955, school administrators requested legislation that would provide additional funds from the state treasury. Repeatedly, the legislators assured them that they would be happy to provide additional funds for schools if there were any available. In response to such answers, the school administrators presented to legislative committees figures to show what a 1¢ gross sales tax would realize and what a 2¢ tax would realize. It was estimated before the bill was passed that assessment of a 2¢ sales tax would provide approximately $6 million in revenue. When a 2¢ sales tax was passed, many Nevada voters favored the bill thinking that it was earmarked for public schools. Such was not the case. (Later, in 1963, when there was an effort to pass a 3¢ sales tax in Nevada, by referendum vote, many of those who previously voted for the 2¢ tax voted against and defeated the passage of the 3¢ measure, feeling that they had been misled previously.) The sales tax, however, became effective July 1, 1955, and provided about $7 million in the first year of its operation.

Many voters in the state disliked the idea of the sales tax. This sentiment was particularly noticeable in the southern part of the state, where a petition was presented to put the 2¢ sales tax up for a referendum vote in the fall of 1956. State Superintendent Duncan urged defeat of the referendum to repeal the 2¢ sales tax, as unless the schools got additional funds, the operation of the formula recommended by the Peabody survey team would be impossible. The referendum calling for its repeal did fail, and the 2¢ sales tax remained on the books.

Basically, the Peabody formula for financing education, as passed in 1955, was as follows: State minimum requirements would be calculated by multiplying the average daily attendance of pupils in grades 1 through 12 by $80, kindergarten pupils in average daily attendance by $40, the number of certified teachers employed by $4,000, and adding the results. From this figure a 70¢ tax on the county's assessed valuation would be subtracted. The remainder would constitute the state's contribution. Changes in the per-pupil and per-teacher allotments from 1955 to 1966 greatly increased the state appropriation.

In the school year 1966-67, the last year of state distribution of school funds under the Peabody formula, the law provided that the state minimum requirements should consist of the sum of the following: the number of elementary and secondary school pupils in average daily attendance multiplied by $100, the number of kindergarten pupils in average daily attendance multiplied by $50, the number of handicapped pupils in average daily attendance multiplied by $500, the number of teacher entitlements multiplied by $5,100, and one-half the cost of transportation.

Other Results of the Peabody Survey

The Peabody survey provided not only for a new method of distributing state funds, but also for far-reaching changes in state school administration. After 92 years of "local" school districts, when as many as six kinds of districts were recognized by law and allowed to organize with five resident children and to exist with but three, Nevada was now to have 17 countywide school districts, each with its own administrative unit. This eliminated from 175 to 200 "local" school districts. The law stipulating that county superintendents be appointed by county boards of school trustees greatly simplified Nevada school administration by making countywide school districts directly responsible to the state department and eliminating intermediate school officials in Nevada.

The 1955 reorganization also streamlined the State Board of Education and the State Board of Vocational Education along lines recommended by the Peabody team: that each consist of identical membership, six lay members elected from the six educational supervision districts and one representative each from agriculture and labor, both selected by the six selected members. This is the composition of today's State Board of Education. In 1967, the state board again assumed final authority in selecting textbooks for the schools. Thus, with the power to determine *who* should teach and *what* should be taught, the state board is the most important educational agency in Nevada.

Under previous laws, there could be a superintendent of the county or district high school when there were 10 teachers employed, and an elementary school superintendent with a like number of teachers. Two entirely different philosophies of education might exist in the same geographical area, one pertaining to the secondary school and one to the elementary. Similarily, secondary and elementary education were financed by entirely different methods. Henceforth, there would be but one Board of Education, one superintendent of schools in an entire Nevada county, and one method of financing education.

Vocational Education

The state continued to increase its expenditures for vocational education (see Appendix C, Table 1, column 3). Expenditures increased from $33,150.99 in 1920 to $654,397.33 in 1965. The directory for the Department of Education in 1966 shows the State Vocational-Technical Advisory Committee consisting of nine members, and the State Vocational-Technical and Adult Education Division consisting of 16 members. At present, state and local sources are providing about $3 for every $1 received from the federal government for this program. In 1967, the Legislature transferred the Vocational Rehabilitation Division from the State Department of Education to the Department of Health and Welfare, now designated as the new Department of Health, Welfare, and Rehabilitation.

Other Important Changes

Prior to the administration of Glenn Duncan, there had been periodic efforts made to amend the Nevada constitution to allow the position of state superintendent of public instruction to be appointive rather than elective. Duncan, although an elected superintendent himself, continued to urge this change. It was, ironically, in the November 1956 election, 6 months after Duncan's untimely death, that the proposed amendment passed. Governor Charles H. Russell appointed Byron F. Stetler, Elko County superintendent, to serve until the next general election. In this election, which was the same one in which the constitutional amendment was passed making the office appointive, Stetler stood for election and was successful. He served as an elected superintendent until the State Board of Education, designated by the Legislature as the agency to appoint the state superintendent under the new constitutional amendment, selected him to continue in office on December 19, 1958. He thus became the first appointed state superintendent in Nevada's history.

One of the most interesting and curious changes brought about by the School Code of 1956 was the legal recognition of the Nevada State Department of Education. The document begins: "A State Department of Education is hereby created" (22). Over a period of years, as the state superintendency had developed and as various supervisors and deputies had been added to the department, the agency had grown out of necessity but with no legal basis.

There had been frequent references to the "State Department" in the statutes, in issues of the *Nevada Education Bulletin,* and in other state documents, but the department had indeed existed without legal status. In the narrowest sense, the history of the State Department of Education as a legal entity begins in 1956.

1959 Legislation

The county school authorities, school trustees, school administrators, and the deputy school superintendents themselves all felt that the deputy superintendents should be eliminated as supervisors of public instruction in the schools throughout the state (23). Consequently, the 1959 Legislature amended the law so that deputies might be located where the state superintendent and State Board of Education desired and that their functions henceforth would be primarily of a statewide nature, such as certification, administration, federal subsidies, transportation, and driver training. The new law provided that there would be only as many deputies as the state superintendent and the state board thought necessary and that these would be located where the state superintendent recommended. At present, all except one, an "area administrator" for the southern part of the state, stationed at Las Vegas, are located at the state capitol in Carson City. Since both county and state school administrators sanctioned the change, the new legislation encountered little resistance in the Legislature.

THE PRESENT STATUS

The Nevada Plan of Distributing State Funds

Despite the fact that there was not much opposition to the Peabody formula by the Nevada school administrators, a bill was presented to the 1967 Legislature which would alter considerably the method of distributing state school funds. Known as the Nevada Plan, it would require an additional 1¢ sales tax collected by the state to be returned to the counties in the same amount as collected from each county. Needless to say, whereas large sums of money were previously supplied from the state general fund to support the schools, now the county would be responsible for contributing much more than under the Peabody formula. Because many voters felt that the 3¢ sales tax was unconstitutional, the Nevada Supreme Court acted on its constitutionality soon after its passage in 1967; it declared it constitutional. Without the additional 1¢ sales tax, the new Nevada Plan would have been completely inoperative.

The Nevada Plan as passed provides basically as follows: To find state minimum requirements for a county school system, the weighted average daily attendance of pupils in grades K-12 is multiplied by the average cost per child in the county. To determine "local funds available" these figures are added: proceeds of a 70¢ countywide tax on assessed valuations, 25 percent of funds from Public Law 874 (the federal act providing funds for impacted areas), and proceeds of a 1¢ local (sales) school tax. From the figure attained by finding state minimum requirements the amount of "local funds available" is subtracted. The result represents the state's appropriation to a county's school fund.

The success of the Nevada Plan is yet to be determined. However, Lyon, White Pine, and Lincoln Counties, hit by strikes of miners that caused a decrease in school enrollment, have voiced opposition to a plan which distributes state aid solely on a per-pupil basis.

Recent Reorganization

In 1966, the State Board of Education contracted Thomas T. Tucker, Jr., chairman of the Department of School Administration, and J. Clark Davis, professor of education and administration, both of the University of Nevada, to make a study of the state department which might ultimately result in a new organization. In December 1966, the new organizational pattern of the Nevada State Department of Education was presented to the State Board of Education (24). As expressed in the proposals, the philosophy of the reorganization plan was that form should follow function. The plan dealt in the main with questions pertaining to (a) legislative enactments necessary to implement the recommendations; (b) recommendations concerning the type and number of consultants that the department should provide to service the various public school districts; (c) recommendations concerning the phasing-in of the proposed organization chart for administering the State Department of Education; and (d) the development of educational facilities for a new State Department of Education.

In respect to item (a), the consultants recommended that new legislation be drafted to the effect that the State Department of Education would be declared by law an educational institution with legislative autonomy of operation under the State Board of Education similar to that enjoyed by the University Board of Regents. In respect to item (b), after developing instruments to gain information from superintendents of the county school districts concerning many phases of state school administration, such as federal programs, special education, and adult education, the consultants recommended that the state board cause the state department to differentiate between the type and quality of services to be provided to the heavily populated counties, Clark and Washoe, as contrasted with the type and quality of services to be provided to the remainder of the 14 less populated counties. The consultants further recommended that the State Department of Education change from the practice of staffing with subject matter specialists to a plan whereby personnel would possess "area qualifications," i.e., elementary curriculum, secondary curriculum, etc. It also recommended that the state department employ, as soon as practical, specialists for the following areas: elementary education, secondary education, vocational-technical adult education, central services, and school administration.

In respect to item (c), in which recommendations were made for the phasing-in of the new organizational chart, the committee urged the establishment of the following positions: deputy superintendent and coordinator of divisions; associate superintendent of the operations division; associate superintendents of educational services; associate superintendent of administrative services; and administrative assistant to the state superintendent of public instruction (office to be established in Clark County).

In respect to item (d), pertaining to facility planning for the state department, the consultants recommended that the new facility be designed primarily for utility, but that the design evolve aesthetically from the architect's solution to the needs of the state department. The Department of School Administration of the University proposed these and many other recommendations of a similar nature. The state board has approved the proposals and is now taking measures to implement the organizational plan. It will probably take several years, perhaps 5, for proper adjustment to the organizational proposals.

The chart in Appendix B shows the approximate divisions with the functions and responsibilities to fall under each division. This is essentially the Tucker-Davis Plan.

State Distributive School Fund

In conclusion, some further comment is in order on the state department's participation in public school finance. Throughout its history, the state government of Nevada, in comparison with many states, has contributed generously to public school support. Never in its history has the state government through the State Department of Education failed to provide a sizable fraction of total public school budgets. In addition to federal funds, for instance, apportionments for vocational education have been made from the state distribution school fund, the main source of which is the state general fund.

Table 2 in Appendix C reveals the growth in this fund. Prior to 1947, when a law was passed providing for state support of high schools, only small amounts had been allotted for this purpose. The figures for 1961 and 1966 include not only the increases necessary to meet Nevada's great growth in population, but also the increases necessary to meet the legal requirements of teacher and pupil apportionments under the Peabody formula.

SUMMARY

Nevada has made progress since 1864 in public school education. Throughout its history the state has always supplied funds for elementary schools and since 1947 for high schools. Under the Peabody formula, in effect from July 1, 1956, to July 1, 1967, the state has contributed annually more than 50 percent of the total public school budgets. The county government, before and since 1956, when all "local" district schools were consolidated into 17 county school districts, has been a main source of school support. Prior to 1956, local school districts contributed but a small fraction of the total of public school budgets, and prior to 1906 no school district had derived as much as 10 percent of its support from this source. As late as 1912, Superintendent John Edwards Bray complained that "approximately three-fourths of the districts in the State have never raised any money locally for the support of their schools, . . ." (25).

In the school year 1927-28, fewer than 40 percent of the school districts levied a local tax. In 1955-56, the year before the adoption of the Peabody report, calling for countywide school districts, no local school district might levy more than a 25¢ tax (on $100 of assessed valuation) for school purposes, and district taxes accounted for less than 20 percent of total operating funds for elementary and high school education.

The adoption of countywide school districts has at least lessened greatly the disparities in educational opportunities among the schools within a county, and a state school system financed mainly by state and county support has tended in Nevada to equalize opportunities throughout the state. Under the Nevada Plan of 1967, where a 1¢ sales tax is part of the county's contribution to school support, the county will now contribute vastly more than the state to school operations.

FOOTNOTES

1. James W. Hulse, *Nevada Adventure: A History* (Reno: University of Nevada Press, 1965), p. 2.
2. Eleanore Bushnell, *The Nevada Constitution: Origin and Growth* (Reno: University of Nevada Press, 1965), pp. 47-48.
3. See Appendix E for the membership of the State Board of Education for different periods.
4. The board's participation in the investment of the state school fund is described in the minutes of the State Board of Education, found in the Office of the State Superintendent of Education, Carson City. For instance, the entry for January 11, 1879, reads: "The state board met in extra session to instruct the State Treasurer to reinvest the amount of the Nevada State School Fund." The State Board of Education continued to perform this duty until 1919, when the Legislature turned it over to the State Board of Finance.
5. See Appendix E for list of powers and duties of the State Board of Education by selected dates.

6. Nevada, *Statutes* (1885), ch. 91, sec. 4, pp. 81-82.
7. See Appendix A for a list of Nevada's state superintendents of public instruction.
8. Superintendent of Public Instruction, *Biennial Report* (1884), p. 4.
9. Superintendent of Public Instruction, *Biennial Report* (1886), p. 7.
10. Nevada, *Statutes* (1864-65), ch. 145, sec. 2, p. 418.
11. Superintendent of Public Instruction, *Biennial Report* (1882), p. 4.
12. Personal interviews with Judge Ben Curler and Senator Patrick McCarran, July 25, 1934.
13. C. S. Young, "Address to the Nevada State Teachers Institute," Virginia City, December 29, 1884.
14. Superintendent of Public Instruction, *Biennial Report* (1890), p. 46.
15. Superintendent of Public Instruction, *Biennial Report* (1894), pp. 32-34.
16. Superintendent of Public Instruction, *Biennial Report* (1896), pp. 5-11.
17. Clark, Mineral, and Pershing Counties were later carved from the original 14 in 1909, 1911, and 1919, respectively.
18. See Appendix D for a list of the state superintendent's powers and duties by selected dates.
19. Nevada, *Statutes* (1907), ch. 182, sec. 2, pp. 379-80.
20. Nevada, *Statutes* (1917), ch. 212, sec. 1, pp. 399-400.
21. "The Superintendent's Message," *Nevada Educational Bulletin,* January 1942, p. 2.
22. Nevada, *School Code* (1956), ch. 1, art. 1, sec. 1.
23. A sixth deputy had been added in 1955.
24. Thomas T. Tucker, Jr., and J. C. Davis, *A Plan for Organization and Administration of the State Department of Education* (Reno: Department of School Administration, University of Nevada, 1967); Thomas T. Tucker, Jr., and J. C. Davis, *A Report to the State Board of Education* (Reno: Department of School Administration, University of Nevada, 1966).
25. Superintendent of Public Instruction, *Biennial Report* (1912), p. 7.

BIBLIOGRAPHY

Public Documents

Nevada. *Constitution* (1864).

--*1947 School Code as Amended 1951 and School Laws Relating Thereto.* Carson City: State Printing Office, 1947.

--Nevada. *School Code* (1956, 1961).

--Nevada. *Statutes* (1864-1967).

Nevada Assembly. *Journals.* Carson City: State Printing Office, 1865-99.

Nevada Assembly and Senate. *Appendix to Journals.* Carson City: State Printing Office, 1899-1965.

Nevada School Law. Carson City: State Printing Office, 1935-65.

Nevada Senate. *Journals.* Carson City: State Printing Office, 1865-99.

Books

Bancroft, Hubert Howe. *History of Nevada.* Vol. XV. The Works of Hubert Howe Bancroft. San Francisco: The History Co., 1890.

Bushnell, Eleanore. *The Nevada Constitution: Origin and Growth.* Reno: University of Nevada Press, 1965.

Hulse, James W. *Nevada Adventure: A History.* Reno: University of Nevada Press, 1965.

Articles and Periodicals

Brown, Harold N. "Teachers Examination." *Nevada Historical Society Quarterly,* I, No. 1 (September 1957), 32-36.

Nevada Educational Bulletins, 1919-60.

Reports

McClurkin, W. D. *Public Education in Nevada: Survey Report.* Nashville, Tenn.: Division of Surveys and Field Services, George Peabody College for Teachers, 1954. A complete account of the Peabody survey team that reported to the Governor's Committee on Education in 1954.

Nevada State Controller. *Annual Reports.* Carson City: State Printing Office, 1866-1966.

Superintendents of Public Instruction. *Annual and Biennial Reports.* Carson City: Department of Education, 1866-1966.

Tucker, Thomas T., Jr., and Davis, J. C. *A Plan for Organization and Administration of the State Department of Education.* Reno: Department of School Administration, University of Nevada, 1967. This is the plan which led to the reorganization of the state department in 1967.

Tucker, Thomas T., Jr., and Davis, J. C. *A Report to the State Board of Education.* Reno: Department of School Administration, University of Nevada, 1966. Contains proposals for implementing the plan of reorganization by the same authors.

Unpublished Material

Brown, Harold N. "History of Elementary Education in Nevada, 1861-1934." Unpublished Ph.D. dissertation, University of California, Berkeley, 1935.

Gazelin, Emile J. "The Intermediate School Officer in Nevada." Unpublished master's thesis, University of Nevada, Reno, 1945.

Gray, R. Guild. "A History of Public School Finance in Nevada, 1861-1948." Unpublished master's thesis, University of Nevada, Reno, 1948.

Miller, John R. "Historical Background and Present Development of Vocational Education in Nevada, 1861-1951." Unpublished master's thesis, University of Nevada, Reno, 1952.

Other Sources

Curler, Judge Ben. Interview at his office in the Washoe County Court House, Reno, Nevada, July 25, 1934.

McCarran, Senator Patrick. Interview in the Riverside Hotel, Reno, Nevada, July 25, 1934.

State Board of Education. Minutes. 1879-1966.

Young, C. S. "Address to Nevada State Teachers Institute, Virginia City," December 29, 1884.

Appendix A

NEVADA CHIEF STATE SCHOOL OFFICERS

1865-66	Rev. A. F. White
1867-74	Rev. A. N. Fischer
1875-78	Rev. S. F. Kelley
1879-82	D. R. Sessions
1883-86	C. S. Young
1887-90	W. C. Dovey
1891-94	Orvis Ring
1895-98	H. C. Cutting
1899-1910	Orvis Ring
1910-19	John Edwards Bray
1919-26	W. J. Hunting
1927-34	Walter W. Anderson
1935-37	Chauncey W. Smith
1937-50	Mildred Bray
1951-56	Glenn A. Duncan
1956-66	Byron F. Stetler
1966-	Burnell Larson

Appendix B

Chart I.--NEVADA DEPARTMENT OF EDUCATION, 1966

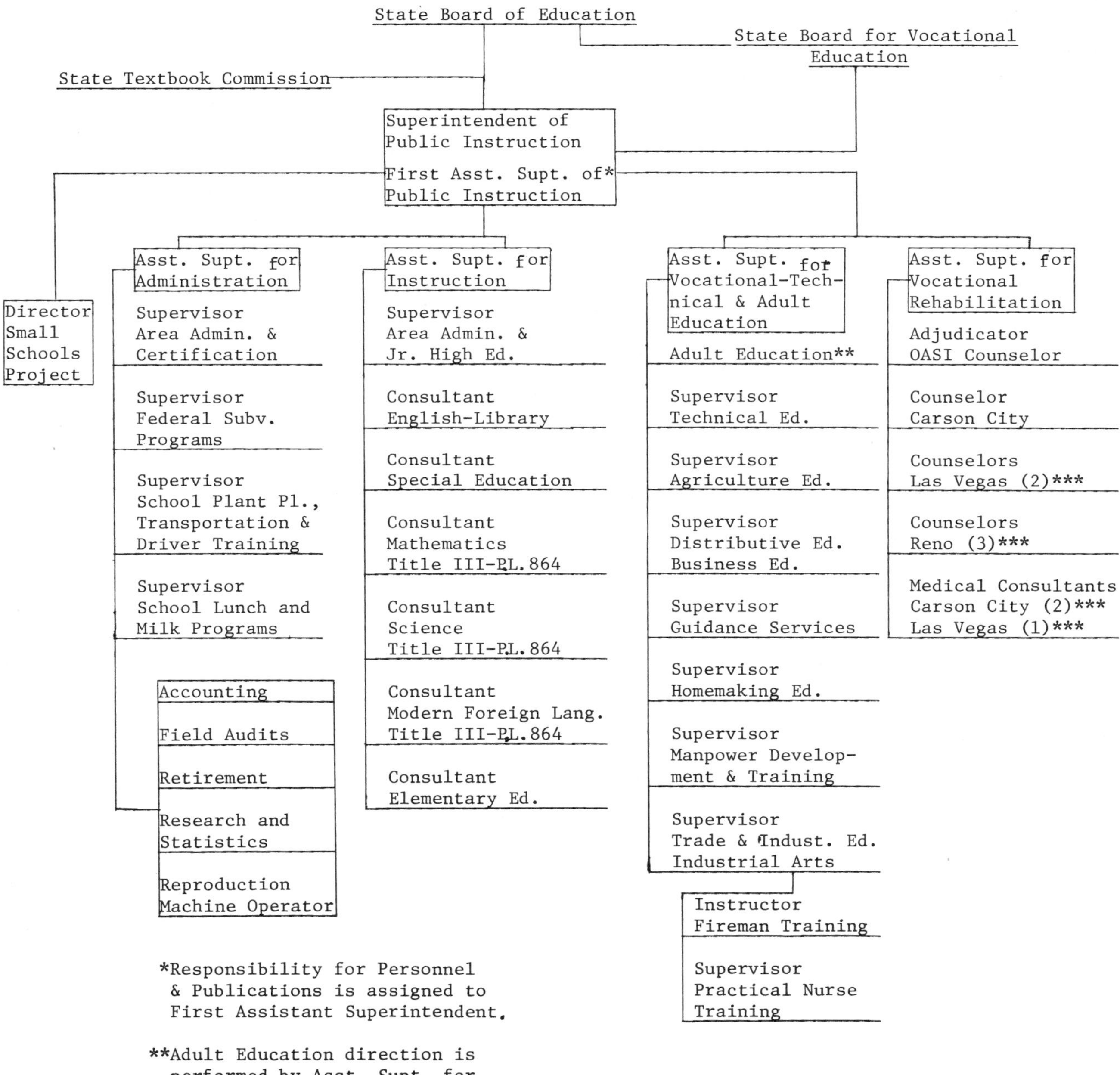

*Responsibility for Personnel & Publications is assigned to First Assistant Superintendent.

**Adult Education direction is performed by Asst. Supt. for Vocational-Technical Education.

***Figures shown in circles represent number of employees of title in office.

Appendix B

Chart II.--NEVADA DEPARTMENT OF EDUCATION, 1968

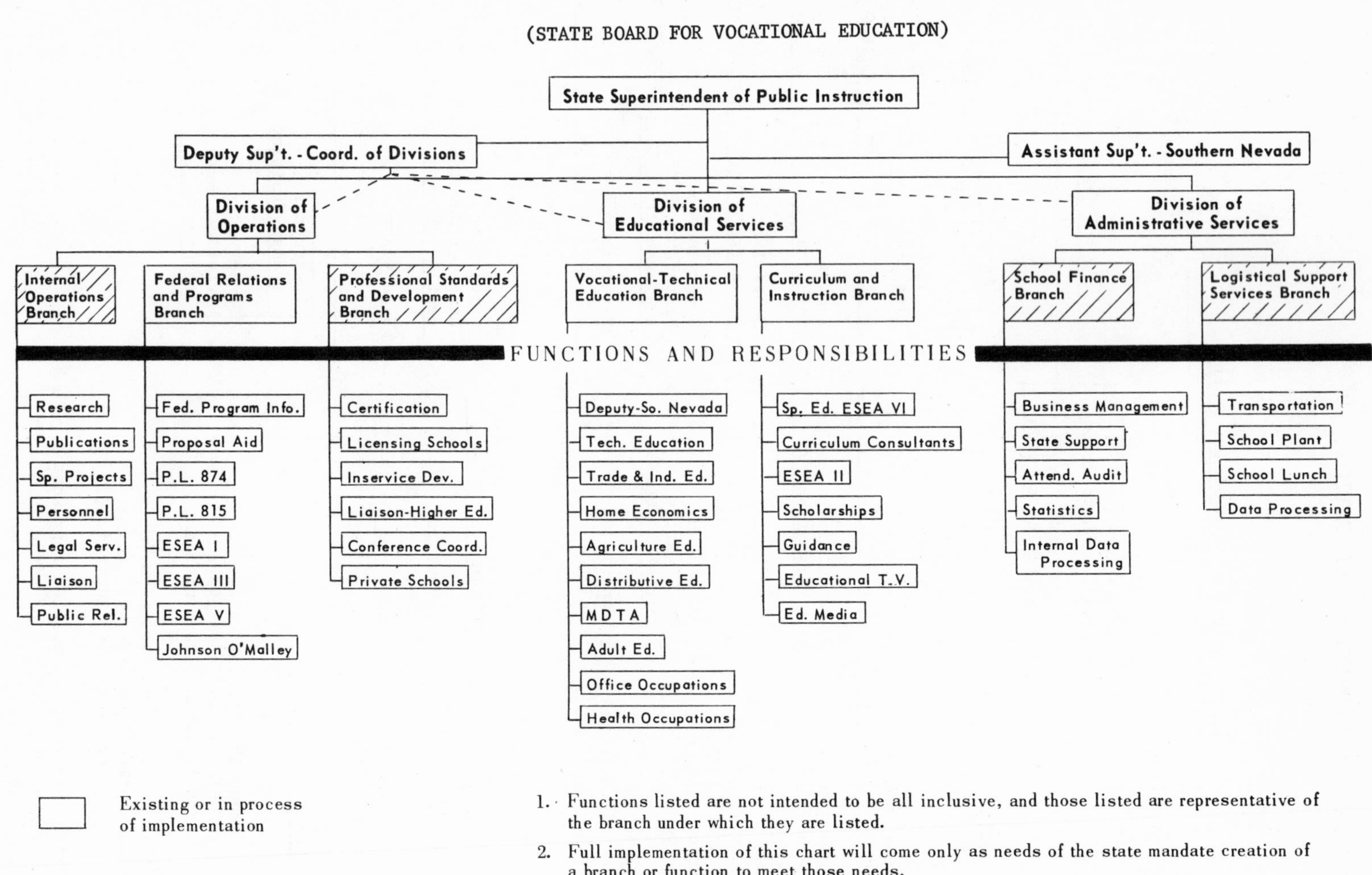

1. Functions listed are not intended to be all inclusive, and those listed are representative of the branch under which they are listed.
2. Full implementation of this chart will come only as needs of the state mandate creation of a branch or function to meet those needs.
3. Branches, sections and functions are subject to change as new and different needs of education develop within the state.

Appendix C

Table 1.–GROWTH OF STATE DEPARTMENT OF EDUCATION AS REVEALED BY EXPENDITURES FOR SELECTED YEARS

Year ending June 30	Expenditure for State Department of Education	Expenditure for vocational education by state	Department of Education retirement contribution	NDEA state's contribution	Totals
1900	$ 2,253.25	$ . . .	$ . . .	$ . . .	$ 2,253.25
1905	3,881.10	. . .	. . .	. . .	3,881.10
1910	3,857.35	. . .	. . .	. . .	3,857.35
1915	13,463.64	. . .	. . .	. . .	13,463.64
1920	19,215.54	33,150.99	. . .	. . .	52,366.53
1925	19,523.53	28,509.95	. . .	. . .	48,033.48
1930	28,265.25	38,453.13	14,412.43	. . .	81,130.81
1935	32,967.02	50,284.41	9,852.39	. . .	93,104.82
1940	33,807.89	75,066.14	20,868.13	. . .	129,742.16
1945	36,580.40	63,652.68	27,457.89	. . .	127,690.97
1950	68,326.83	121,237.49	123,672.09	. . .	313,236.41
1955	116,086.85	182,860.26	401,536.38	. . .	700,483.49
1960	228,792.03	349,707.53	773,492.29	53,212.07	1,405,203.92
1965	324,801.94	654,397.33	1,957,134.98	121,459.66	3,057,793.91

Appendix C

Table 2.– GROWTH OF STATE DEPARTMENT OF EDUCATION AS REVEALED BY STATE AID TO NEVADA'S PUBLIC SCHOOLS FOR SELECTED YEARS

Fiscal year ending	Amount of state distribution school fund
1865	$ 5,075.72
1875	36,783.55
1885	56,320.99
1895	109,786.58
1901	126,306.21
1911	214,330.15
1921	342,609.10
1931	414,276.90
1941	439,976.14
1951	2,692,440.46
1961	15,118,819.14
1966	29,177,631.52

Appendix D

DUTIES AND POWERS OF STATE SUPERINTENDENT OF PUBLIC INSTRUCTION

The *Statutes* of 1864–65 list five:

1. To make annual report to Governor
2. To visit each county once a year
3. To convene a state teachers institute annually
4. To prescribe, prepare, and distribute forms and school registers
5. To apportion school moneys to counties.

The *Statutes* of 1907 list ten:

1. To visit each county
2. To apportion state aid
3. To apportion county aid
4. To report to the Governor biennially
5. To prescribe rules and regulations for making reports and keeping the school register
6. To convene state teachers institutes biennially in even-numbered years and district teachers institutes in odd-numbered years
7. To call county teachers institutes when necessary
8. To appoint school trustees
9. To nominate deputies
10. To perform such other duties relative to the public schools as may be prescribed by law.

The *School Code* of 1935 lists eight:

1. To visit each county in the state at least once a year
2. To apportion the state distributive school fund
3. To apportion the county school funds
4. To report to the Governor biennially
5. To prescribe rules and regulations for making reports
6. To convene state teachers institutes biennially in even-numbered years
7. To call county teachers institutes
8. To perform other duties relative to public schools.

The *School Code* of 1947 lists the following:

1. To visit each county at least once a year
2. To apportion the state distributive school fund
3. To apportion the county school fund
4. To report to the Governor biennially
5. To prescribe rules and regulations
6. To convene a state teachers conference and five district teachers conferences
7. To perform other duties relative to the public schools
8. To prepare and supply printed materials to school trustees and teachers
9. To act on appeals
10. To be a member and secretary of the State Textbook Commission
11. To fill vacancies in school boards in accordance with law.

The 1965 *Code*, in its opening sentences, reads as follows:

As executive head of the State Department of Education, the superintendent of public instruction shall perform duties prescribed by law and also–

(a) Execute, direct, and supervise all administrative and technical activities of the department in accord with the policies prescribed by the State Board of Education;

(b) Employ such personnel as are approved by the State Board of Education and as are necessary for efficient operation of the department;

(c) Be responsible for organizing the department in a manner which will ensure efficient operation and service;

(d) Be responsible for maintaining liaison and coordinating activities with other state agencies exercising educational functions.

In addition to these more general statements, the *Code* also lists the following:

1) Execute, direct, and supervise all administrative and technical activities of the department

2) Employ such personnel as are approved by the State Board of Education

3) Be responsible for organizing the department

4) Be responsible for maintaining liaison and coordinating activities with other state agencies

5) The superintendent of public instruction shall perform such other duties relative to public schools as may be prescribed by law.

Appendix E

POWERS AND DUTIES OF STATE BOARD OF EDUCATION

1865

1. Invest the state school fund
2. Adopt elementary school textbooks.

1885

(Added to powers of 1865)
1. Participate in certification of teachers, a joint responsibility with county boards of examiners.
2. Life diplomas are authorized.

1893

(Added to previous powers)
1. State board empowered to prepare teachers' examinations to be given in the 14 counties of Nevada.

1907

1. Sole teacher-certificating agency in Nevada
2. Adopt courses of study
3. Appoint and remove state deputy superintendents of public instruction
4. Approve books for public school libraries
5. Invest permanent school fund.

1919

1. Power to invest the permanent school fund removed from State Board of Education and placed with State Board of Finance.

1955

1. Life diplomas discontinued 1/1/56.

1956

1. Public school year should consist of 180 days taught.

1957

The superintendent of public instruction shall be appointed by the State Board of Education, but any person elected to the office of superintendent of public instruction prior to the effective date of this section shall continue to hold such office until the expiration of the term for which he may have been elected.

1958

Appointed first state superintendent of public instruction to take office the first Monday in January 1959.

1967

State Board of Education to assume final authority in selection of textbooks for Nevada's public schools.

Appendix F

MEMBERSHIPS OF STATE BOARD OF EDUCATION BY PERIODS

1865–95

Ex officio membership: the Governor, the state superintendent of public instruction, and the surveyor general.

1895–1931

Ex officio membership: the Governor, the state superintendent of public instruction, and the president of the University of Nevada.

1931–55

Governor, state superintendent of public instruction, and five elected lay members, one from each of the five educational supervision districts.

1955

Eight lay members—six to be elected, one from each of the six educational supervision districts, and two to be appointed by the elected members of the board. Of these two, one would represent the interests of agriculture, the other the interests of labor.

1966

Board the same as in 1955.

29 New Hampshire

DEPARTMENT OF EDUCATION
William H. Mandrey

Contents

EARLY ATTEMPTS AT ORGANIZATION, 1820-1900

"Live free or die," the state motto, typifies the spirit of the early settlers who founded this tiny state. It expresses a revolt against centralized authority—a determination to satisfy their own needs, meet their own problems, and survive or perish with no assistance, guidance, or domination from any outsider. Perhaps this explains in large measure their strong insistence on local control in most matters, including education. Early New Hampshire laws reveal a concern in the state for a common school program, but the individual towns were left to initiate the programs, build the schools, and hire teachers from their own resources. Since the state exercised no effective authority in education, the common schools developed unevenly, their progress depending on the interest and will of local parents and officials. By 1827, the Legislature, noting failures in the town system, voted to create the district system, whereby progressive residents in a section of the town could establish and administer their own school and support it by whatever taxation they agreed to impose on themselves.

The three decades following the Revolution saw a marked increase in New Hampshire's population. In 1790, the state had 141,885 residents, but in 10 years the number increased to 183,858, a gain of almost 30 percent. Most of the newcomers settled in rural areas until about 1820, when industry and business began to spur the development of urban centers and become a vital factor in their economies. When the State Legislature sought in 1828 to increase financial support to the district schools being formed in these growing cities, rather than taxing its citizens directly for this aid, it turned over to them money from the Literary Fund (1) established in 1812 through an annual levy of one-half of 1 percent on the capital stock of banking corporations. In fact, from 1812 to the present, the state has resorted to various stratagems to aid education—from a corporation levy to the sweepstakes—without attempting to impose a direct tax on the people. A tax earmarked for education would have been violently opposed by the local forces. Even today, this opposition is clearly expressed by rejection of any broad-base tax proposals. Certainly, until 1900, the fate of the common schools depended almost entirely on local initiative and control. Although education was assumed to be a state responsibility, no state program or system of education existed until the outstanding legislation of 1919 was enacted.

The state did not attempt to exercise direction of the schools until 1846, when a law was passed creating the Office of Commissioner of Common Schools. The commissioner was to be appointed annually by the Governor and his Council. However, he never had control over the local superintending school committees, and the office was abolished in 1850. Seven years later, the Legislature established a Board of County School Commissioners, one member for each county. This first attempt at a state board of education certainly took little unified action and provided little centralized direction during its 17 years of existence. In 1867, the Legislature tried again, this time providing for a superintendent of public instruction, who would report to a Board of Education composed of the Governor and his Council (2). The loss of revenue during the panic of 1873 forced the Legislature to temporarily dissolve the superintendency, which, in turn, nullified the Governor's and Council's control. The Office of Superintendent of Public Instruction was reactivated the next year, but, until 1919, when the Office of Commissioner of Education and a State Board of Education were established, state direction of education rested on one man, responsible not to the Governor and Council, but only to the Legislature.

In the meantime, certain significant developments had taken place. In 1840, the Legislature granted districts permission to organize graded schools to eliminate the common, but unfortunate, practice of one person teaching all the children. Responding to a growing demand for secondary schools, the Legislature in 1845 acted to permit two or more contiguous districts to form a union to establish and maintain a high school. Three years later, with the enactment of the Somersworth Act, special school districts were allowed to open and maintain high schools independent of the towns. Yet, despite examples of genuine effort, dissatisfaction with progress under the district system (3) was growing and culminated in the Legislature's passing an act in 1875 making each town responsible for the education of its children and abolishing all districts with the exception of those maintaining high schools.

Another indication of the people's growing concern for the quality of their public schools was the passage of legislation in 1868 directing that each county hold an annual teachers institute at the expense of the state. Two years later, the Legislature established a normal school for the preparation of teachers, to be financed by the state and controlled by a board of trustees responsible to the Legislature. Not until years later, however, did the Legislature provide for a system of teacher certification and permit two or more towns together to hire a superintendent. Unfortunately, towns ignored the certification requirements and showed little interest in engaging competent school supervisors, though the normal school was preparing a modest number of trained teachers. To help correct these problems and encourage professional direction of the schools, the Legislature in 1899 agreed to pay half of superintendents' salaries and appropriated a modest sum to help poorer towns engage trained men.

Briefly, this is the situation as it existed in 1900. The picture was not a pleasing one. With the exception of the larger towns, where education was taken seriously, most of the teachers were not only untrained but had a limited education; schoolhouses left much to be desired in sanitation, neatness, and comfort; school boards were more concerned with the local tax rate than they were with the welfare of the children; supplies and texts were severely limited; and professional supervision was seldom seen. Transportation, where furnished, was poor; there was no requirement for the number of days schools were to be in session; and compulsory attendance was unknown.

It is true that the high schools were frequently well treated, since they were a source of local pride. Teachers were better paid and better prepared, and buildings were of more recent construction, but the curriculum and the teaching aids (libraries and laboratories) were very limited. Many towns refused to provide tuition, and so parents were forced to provide both the funds and transportation to the school. Many able youngsters were deprived of a high school education because their families couldn't afford to send them. A decline of population in the state from 1880 to 1900, about 22 percent, was undoubtedly due in part to the movement of people away from the countryside in the hope of securing better employment opportunities in the growing industrial centers of the East, where their children could attend better schools. It was a period of rapid decline in agriculture; many farm families, weary of the struggle with New Hampshire's stony soil, left to try their luck in the more fertile fields to the west. Only in the last quarter of the century did the state show any sense of financial responsibility for its schools; until this time, the normal school had been given inadequate funds, and the Legislature (as evidenced by its voting record) was in no mood to help the towns with their fiscal burdens.

1900 TO 1919

1899-1900 Report

In Superintendent Channing Folsom's biennial report for 1899-1900, it is evident that the office was primarily a one-man operation with quarters in the State House for Folsom, possibly a secretary, and a clerk to handle his correspondence and help collect statistics. The report is interesting because it makes no reference to salaries paid or expenditures made by the superintendent. It does indicate that he was to be assisted by the local directors of the school system, the eight superintendents in the larger towns and cities, and a supervisor in each of the three supervisory unions. It also contains a report from the trustees of the normal school urging the Legislature that "greater liberality be shown in your appropriation to the State Normal School" (4). It gives a detailed account of the superintendents' activities, as well as abundant statistics: attendance by teachers at the institutes and the number of pupils, schools, and local expenses for education. A questionnaire sent to all school boards on the subject of transportation revealed that a considerable number of towns opposed closing the one-room schools and transporting children to a central school, but the majority that had adopted the program reported that transportation cost less than maintaining the small schools and that the children received a better education.

Superintendent Folsom himself was a dedicated and able educator of considerable experience, who labored tirelessly to improve his state's schools. In addition to his other duties, a law was passed in 1897 which made the superintendent the regent of the State Board of Medical Examiners, responsible for admitting candidates, conducting the examinations, and issuing licenses to practice to those who in the judgment of the board were qualified. Nevertheless, he traveled the length and breadth of New Hampshire urging greatly increased state aid to education, a longer school year, higher standards and salaries for teachers, elimination of inefficient one-room schools, and more and better high schools. He sought help from organized groups such as the Grange and committees of the state teachers association.

His aggressiveness led to his dismissal in 1904. Superintendent Folsom worked hard to secure passage of the Grange Bill, an act giving $25,000 in special state aid to rural school districts. His efforts antagonized representatives from the cities and some members of the Governor's Council. When the Governor nominated him for reelection to another 2-year term, politicians in the Legislature defeated the recommendation, ending the career of this faithful public servant.

The new superintendent, Henry C. Morrison, was a trained, progressive schoolman who was not deterred by the clamor that led to the downfall of his predecessor. For 14 years, he unhesitatingly grappled with one problem after another. He was a skillful analyst and a clear thinker, who advanced a definite program of attack on each problem. His carefully prepared reports, while including the usual statistics, were devoted largely to presenting the issues. Armed with facts and a knowledge of what other states were doing, he fearlessly pointed out the steps New Hampshire had to take to gain a decent standing with its neighbors. He spent little time in the office; day after day he visited the schools and the normal school, talking with teachers and school boards, addressing institutes and innumerable public meetings, conferring with legislators, council members, and the Governor. He persuaded the Legislature to relieve him of his duties as regent of the medical examiners' board so that he could devote all of his energies to the schools.

Superintendent Morrison emphasized two basic needs: adequate state support for education and the improvement of schools through expert supervision and well-trained teachers. His inspections had uncovered weaknesses in the teaching programs and the lack of professional preparation and control. He pointed out time and again that one normal school was completely inadequate for the state—at least two were needed to supply a sufficient number of well-trained teachers in the rural schools. His campaign succeeded. In 1909, the Legislature voted to establish and maintain a second normal school at Keene to serve the southern part of the state. He also insisted on a better certification program with higher standards. To improve school attendance, he obtained authorization to investigate child labor, and, as a result, in the following session a more stringent Child Labor Act was passed which furnished him with two factory inspectors as well as an attendance agent. At the same time, he convinced the Legislature that not only was more state aid needed but the system of aid was the most inadequate where the funds were most needed, thus securing passage of the Equalization Act, which provided a much better distribution of additional state aid.

The 1913 legislative session revealed a greatly increased interest in education on the part of its members. Three deputy superintendents, responsible to the superintendent and charged with specific functions, were added to the staff. This permitted the superintendent to amass an array of evidence concerning conditions in the schools, because the deputies were expected to devote the major part of their time and energy in the field. They gathered facts about the health standards of the schools and the health of the children. As a result of their comprehensive study, the Medical Inspection Act was passed, and, though it did not yield the immediate improvement hoped for, it opened the way for better health for schoolchildren. Armed with the facts about the need for better supervision, the superintendent persuaded the education committee of the Legislature to recommend a bill calling for a system of professional supervision for the entire state. The bill was introduced and defeated by a very slim margin, but the issue had been placed squarely before the public and the legislators.

Two years later, the Legislature, impressed by the facts gathered by the attendance agent and the factory inspectors, passed a Mother's Relief Act and designated the Department of Public Instruction as the agency to give financial aid to widows and destitute mothers whose children were forced to leave school to help maintain the family. A Teachers Pension Fund was passed but failed to operate effectively because of an insufficient appropriation. The act established a Teachers Employment Bureau to check the loss of able teachers to other states and to attract out-of-state teachers to positions in New Hampshire. Two other acts were passed: one requiring better sanitary conditions in schoolhouses, the other a more workable and effective medical inspection service. At the same time, Superintendent Morrison persuaded the General Education Board to grant the department $5,500 to establish a bureau of research, primarily for making studies and publishing bulletins dealing with the curriculums of the elementary and secondary schools.

The State Board of Education in Connecticut had watched with interest the progress that had been made in New Hampshire as a result of Superintendent Morrison's militant efforts. In 1917, the board invited him to come to Connecticut as deputy commissioner of education at a substantial increase in salary. He accepted. Morrison had accomplished much and laid a sound foundation for the progress which was to be made a few years later. Fortunately the new superintendent, former deputy Ernest W. Butterfield, was an equally dedicated educator.

World War I

At this point we might do well to note certain factors that were to exert a great influence upon developments within the next few years. Possibly the greatest of these was America's entry into World War I. This global conflict, which called for new techniques in the conduct of modern warfare, placed a high value on education as an important factor in waging war. Modernized equipment, new weapons, and production problems in industry all demanded greater skills from the workers and a high degree of intelligent planning from those chosen to lead us to victory (5). The effort of providing better medical and social services for our fighting men accentuated the need for well-trained doctors, nurses, and social workers. The obsolete tactics of the Civil War and the brief war with Spain no longer were effective. Warfare had changed from individual to mass conflict, demanding a higher degree of intelligence on the part of both civilians and combatants. The draft required all citizens to be physically able and mentally alert.

It was the draft statistics that condemned common school standards as obsolete regarding our military preparation for modern warfare. The state and nation were shocked at the high percentage of young men being declared unfit for service for both physical and mental reasons. People asked. "Is this the best our schools can produce?" Many young Americans, most of them newcomers to our shores, were unable to read or write English and had little understanding of the true meaning of being an American. A nationwide demand for change under the name of Americanization swept the country, and state committees were organized to study the situation. The New Hampshire group soon found much to be done and challenged the schools to improve their programs. Many teachers left the classroom to enter the service, work in munition plants at better wages, or, as educated individuals, offer their services to their government in this emergency, thus creating a serious shortage of teachers.

Several organizations, notably the Grange and the teachers association, felt they must arouse the people to action to guarantee better schools. They were supported by the press, and the new superintendent, Butterfield, seized the opportunity to preach the gospel of better teachers, more state aid, and a stronger statewide program. He urged that an advisory committee of citizens be appointed to study the needs of the public schools, and in Governor-Elect Bartlett he found a sympathetic listener.

Advisory Committee Appointed

In November 1918, the Governor-Elect named eight outstanding citizens to such a committee (6). Since the Legislature convened in January, the committee had to move swiftly. Within 6 weeks, it had completed its task and reported to the Governor, who not only approved the substance of the report but promised to give it priority in the forthcoming legislative session. On March 13, the House of Representatives' Committee on Education recommended passage of the proposed act. The public's sense of pride in their state had been hurt; the people had been surprised to learn that their schools were not adequate and demanded immediate attention. Sensing this sentiment and hearing demands for drastic change from various groups, the Legislature passed the bill, effective the opening of the school year that September.

The salient points made by the Advisory Committee on Education were as follows:

1. The present state system is antiquated and out of touch with present-day needs. Most of the statutes are ineffective and actually impede progress; moreover, there is no strong central authority to enforce them. Excessive local control has worked harm, especially in rural areas, where conditions are deplorable.
2. Education is insufficiently financed. The state has failed to meet its responsibilities and what limited state aid has been given has been poorly distributed.
3. The normal schools and the program of teacher preparation and certification should be under the supervision and administration of a strong central authority.
4. The entire state program should be organized under an effective supervisory union law, thus ensuring professionally trained administrators to direct the public schools.
5. Schools should have a standard curriculum and should be in session for at least 34 weeks. Adult evening schools must be established to further the Americanization program, and the state must assume responsibility for an effective educational program in the "unorganized places" (7).

All this required that the government, as well as education, be reorganized to ensure the maintenance of an intelligent citizenry. Children must be housed in a satisfactory schoolhouse, given a proper curriculum, and taught by competent teachers working under professional direction. Where necessary, mothers must be adequately subsidized in order that all children might benefit. Federal funds should be sought to develop a good vocational program, and sufficient revenue must be levied to ensure an effective system of state aid.

Three general principles prompted the above recommendations:

1. When parents cannot or will not protect their children, the state must. Children then become legally, socially, and economically wards of the state.
2. Education must be divorced from politics and conducted on a sound business basis. To achieve this requires a strong, central governing board with powers and duties similar to those of the directors of a corporation.
3. An executive officer is needed, responsible to the board and authorized to hire a competent staff. Local district employees should be removed from positions of authority when the best interests of the state require such action.

The Great School Law of 1919

The Law of 1919, frequently referred to as the Great School Law, gave the state the momentum it needed for forward progress. Now a central agency existed with authority to make rules and regulations and to enforce school law while rendering true professional service to all pupils, teachers, and school boards. For the first time it could be said that New Hampshire had a state system of education;

no longer did all progress in education depend on the uncertain action of independent school districts. Under the act (8), the Governor and Council appointed a nonpartisan state board of five members, none to be professional educators, for 5-year terms. The Governor was an ex officio member of the board. Any appointed member could be removed for just cause and a successor appointed. They were to have the same powers and duties as the trustees of a corporation, with full authority to make rules and regulations for all facets of the educational program. They were to take over the responsibilities of the Americanization Committee, assume all powers vested in the superintendent of public instruction, the trustees of state normal schools, and the State Board for Vocational Education (created in 1917), and they were to administer federal funds.

One of the board's chief duties was to appoint an executive, the commissioner of education, who would serve for an indefinite period and could be removed from office when circumstances warranted it. It was to fix his salary, prescribe his duties, and appoint four deputy commissioners nominated by him. It also was authorized to prescribe the qualifications and duties of superintendents, assistant superintendents, teachers, and the employees of the state department.

The state board members were assigned the task of organizing the state into supervisory unions and establishing schools in the unorganized places or furnish tuition and transportation or board at a suitable and approved school for these resident pupils. They also were responsible for submitting budgets for the operation of schools, checking expenditures, preparing a biennial report on the schools' progress, and recommending further changes in the school laws. In consultation with local boards, they were to employ superintendents and, where necessary, assistant superintendents, whose salaries would be paid by the state and the supervisory unions. They were authorized to employ the necessary staff, confer with superintendents and teachers, and prepare courses for the schools. Also, they were given discretionary authority to employ competent persons "to examine and care for the health of pupils" (9), unless such activity was opposed by a parent or guardian.

To meet the costs of statewide supervision, districts were to pay annually to the state $2 for each pupil enrolled. Superintendents were given the sole authority to nominate teachers for employment by the local board members and to remove teachers, subject to their right of appeal to the commissioner. They also were required to report any violations of the law.

An investigation conducted by the Committee on Americanization revealed that a large number of children attending private schools conducted by a church group were being instructed in a foreign language. The new law required that all instruction in all schools, both public and private, be in English. A foreign language could be used by a private school purely for devotional purposes and could be taught in an elementary school provided that all subjects required by law were given proper time allotments.

Persons between the ages of 16 and 20 who could neither speak nor write English were to attend evening or special classes until they completed the minimum course of studies. Every district having twenty or more persons above the age of 21 or fifteen or more persons between the ages of 16 and 21 unable to speak or write English was required to teach them the language. The law forbade industry from employing such persons unless they could produce certificates from the superintendent of schools showing that they were attending schools or had been excused from the requirements. Employers failing to comply with this requirement could be fined up to $50 for each offense. These rigid regulations concerning non-English-speaking persons reflect the deep concern over persons who were not willing or anxious to learn how to think and speak like Americans, perhaps a natural part of the civic efforts undertaken under the stress of war (10).

The statistics gathered over the years by the superintendent clearly indicated that where children were *able* to go to school the attendance record was unusually high: The problem of poor attendance was confined almost entirely to rural areas. The lack of a state-enforced statute requiring a minimum number of days or weeks of schooling and the inability of children in isolated places to get to school were largely responsible for the poor record of the country schools.

The members of the commission unhesitatingly applied a remedy. The act not only called for a minimum school year of 36 weeks, but it also stipulated that transportation be furnished to all children below the ninth grade who lived more than 2 miles away from their schools. If transportation was not available, the pupils could be boarded in a suitable home at the expense of the district with the parents' consent. However, if a district could present evidence proving that a 36-week school year was unreasonable or impractical and that the school tax levied under the act would be insufficient, the state board could reduce the time requirement and adjust the tax rate to meet the situation.

Just how was this ambitious program to be paid for both on the state and local level? In addition to the $2 per pupil to be paid to the state by the towns for the support of supervision, section 29 stipulated that the income from the Literary Fund should be used to implement the act. Locally, the selectmen were obligated to assess "an annual tax of $3.50 on each thousand dollars of the value of the ratable estate taxable therein" (11).

If a district's obligations were not satisfied by a tax of $5 per $1,000 assessed valuation, the state would supply the difference. In such a situation, the state, acting through local school boards, would administer all the funds and make an accounting annually of all expenditures. In the unorganized places, the state treasurer would annually assess a tax of $3.50 per $1,000 of ratable property values for the support of public education.

The concept of furnishing equal educational opportunity to all children implied that common standards should apply to all schools, thus challenging the act's authors to define a "standard school." Section 24 leaves no doubt as to the requirements a school would have to meet before it could satisfy the conditions for state assistance. It states (12):

> A standard school as that term is used in this Act is one (1) maintained for at least 36 weeks in each year, (2) in a suitable and sanitary building, (3) equipped with approved furniture, books, maps and other necessary appliances, (4) taught by an approved teacher, (5) directed and supervised by an approved superintendent, (6) with suitable provision for the care of the health and physical welfare of all pupils.

Elementary schools under the act were schools teaching the first eight grades. The upper grades could be organized as a junior high school. Attendance at approved private schools was permitted.

The act also stated the amount of money available for the next 2 years, the sources of these funds, and the specific uses to which they would be put. For the first biennium the state was required to appropriate $558,200, with the act's provisions becoming effective September 1, 1919; but any unexpended appropriation from the first fiscal year would be available for use the following year (13).

The Law of 1919 gave New Hampshire a state system of education and abolished variant, uncoordinated, purely localized practices which had prevailed for nearly 300 years. It would be a mistake to conclude that all this came about spontaneously. It did not; rather, it was the effort of many concerned citizens who had worked for better schools over a period of years, an effort which was accentuated by the impact of World War I.

Nor can the influence of the Vermont School Law of 1915 be ignored. With a generous grant from the Carnegie Foundation for the Advancement of Learning, leading citizens and educators of that state joined forces to study the condition of the schools. The result was the Law of 1915, which produced sweeping changes in the organization of the state's school system. Since this law was widely publicized in New Hampshire, it served as a guide for the study commission and the members of the education committee, who cooperated in a study of methods of improving local schools. With a neighboring state forging ahead in a determination to improve its schools, state pride urged New Hampshire to take action—what Vermont could do, New Hampshire could do, too, and in fact, might do better.

Objections to the Law

Naturally there were doubting Thomases and critics. It was foolish, they said, to believe that the rural districts of the north country would ever be able to enjoy the opportunities available to the children of Manchester, even with state aid. And why, indeed, should the citizens of Manchester contribute to a state tax to help the schools of the north country? And who would believe for a moment that the private schools, particularly the numerous parochial schools organized by the Roman Catholic Church, would submit for one moment to the standards set by a State Board of Education? Surely the sprawling parochial system with schools in 19 large communities enrolling some 19,000 pupils in the elementary grades would not permit any interference with its established program and organization.

And how could children in the mountains be transported in all kinds of weather? Would not superintendents employed by the state serve as inspectors, continually harassing local boards to make improvements and spend more money? What was going to happen to the cherished heritage of the local control under which each district cared for its own? And what legislator, sent to Concord to protect the interests of his own district, would vote to spend such a huge sum to establish a bureaucracy to run the schools?

In addition to the specifications of the law itself, the state board was to be given broad powers to make its own rules and regulations controlling the conduct of superintendents, teachers, and even school board members. This, the dissidents maintained, was the final death blow to local independence and freedom of action.

All this was sheer speculation. The facts gathered by the proponents of the new order, widely disseminated by a progressive press and presented at public meetings of citizens and at hearings before the education committees of the House and Senate, could not be denied. The problems confronting the schools of the state and the best methods of solving them were clearly presented to the people. The time for temporary expedient measures had passed. A bold advance had to be made—the people demanded prompt action, and got it.

THE PERIOD FROM 1919 TO 1947

Organization of the First State Department of Education

The responsibilities of the various officials of the first State Department of Education are worth noting (14). The commissioner's chief functions were the interpretation and enforcement of school laws, the program of the normal schools, and the improvement of teachers, child welfare, and the other needs of the schools. He was expected to hold frequent conferences with his staff, direct their activities, and advise the members of the state board on the needs and progress of the schools under the new law. The deputy in charge of elementary schools was responsible for the program of supervision, distribution of state aid, condition of schoolhouses, the health program, and child labor. The deputy in charge of secondary schools was assigned the tasks of inspecting and approving high schools, representing the state in the development of the Smith-Hughes program, and conducting high school examinations. The Americanization program was the responsibility of the deputy in charge of school extension, who also inspected and approved private and parochial schools. Statistics, certification of teachers, registration of nurses, compilation of an educational directory, and the supervision of office correspondence and routine activities were the duties of the deputy in charge of office organization. The commissioner and the four deputies jointly prepared policy statements for the state board's approval.

It is quite obvious that much needed to be done, and the successful inauguration of such an ambitious reorganization of functions and powers called for men who would proceed, not as though armed with authority and power, but cautiously and diplomatically. This plan got off to an auspicious start, due largely to the caliber of the five men appointed to the board and to the common sense solutions to problems applied by the commissioner and his deputies. The fact that the law was passed by popular demand did not guarantee that those who had previously controlled the schools were going to surrender their authority willingly and embark on a policy of immediate cooperation. Delaying tactics and evasion of obligations were employed in several instances in recalcitrant areas, to be overcome in time by the calm, yet determined, approach of the state officials. The transition from the former organization to the new was accomplished by their patience, tact, and diplomacy, not by force or arbitrary action, so that great credit is due to those tolerant men who put the law into operation and the spirit of cooperation found so frequently in town and district officials.

The law's critics anxiously awaited the state board's rules and regulations. The board did not keep them in suspense for long, issuing a call for a "joint business conference on October 16 to be attended by the members of the board, the state department, and the superintendents and members of local school boards" (15). In his opening remarks, the chairman made it clear that the board's only purpose was to help local officials with their problems and that it wanted information which would help determine sound policies and methods of procedure. Rule making was to be a cooperative effort. The board clearly indicated that it intended to proceed by a rule of common sense and not be strictly tied to the letter of the law. The rules and regulations finally adopted were quite flexible and subject to change. The first concerned the board itself, clearly indicating its responsibilities. This was followed by two important statements, one dealing with the powers and duties of school boards and the other outlining the powers and duties of superintendents. The board wanted to clearly define the areas of authority between lay and professional control.

Rules and Regulations of the State Board of Education

It is not possible to discuss in detail all 22 sections of the rules and regulations which covered every facet of school activity. Certification of teachers and qualifications of superintendents and teachers were considered at length. The board urged that teachers councils be formed to arrange conferences on school problems among staff members, school boards, and superintendents in the hopes of developing a cooperative spirit and improving the effectiveness of the school program. Based on the Program of Studies for Elementary Schools accepted in 1916 and the Program of Studies for Secondary Schools approved in 1919, minimum curriculum standards were established for public, private, and parochial schools. Since so much concern had been expressed over our young men's fitness for service following the findings of the draft boards, considerable effort was devoted to setting up health and physical welfare standards for pupils and sanitary and health standards for school buildings. The rules and regulations further held that textbooks and supplies were to be selected by the superintendents within budgets established by local school boards. They also provided for a director, nominated by the commissioner, to manage the normal schools and outline the standards for admission and graduation, tuition payments, and the conduct of summer sessions and model schools.

A careful analysis of the rules and regulations, along with the law itself, clearly indicates the extent to which control shifted from local authorities to the State Board of Education through the state department and the superintendents who served communities as agents of the board. However, though the rules and regulations greatly emphasized the program and direction of the elementary and normal schools, they paid little attention to secondary schools other than making provisions for inspection and approval by the deputy commissioner in charge of secondary education, and decreeing that the curriculum was to follow the program of studies recently endorsed. Little had been said about secondary schools and the preparation of their teachers because most of the teachers were either college graduates or had completed their education far beyond that of the elementary teachers. The limited attention given to secondary schools was the outstanding weakness of the 1919 reorganization. It was hardly a surprise to many when, after a decade of secondary school inspections, some of the poorest teaching was found in these schools.

Postwar Activity

Even after the war was over, patriotic fervor was still at a high pitch, and some of the problems uncovered by the war still had to be faced. For instance, universal use of English was of paramount importance. Thus, the 1919 statute transferred the program of the Committee on Americanization (established in 1918) to the state department, and Deputy Commissioner Brooks was instructed to proceed at once to speed up the work begun by community groups and form special day and evening classes for adults. The extension of the school program to include Americanization classes met with almost no public resistance.

The schools had been drawn into many wartime programs. At the end of the war, some of these projects, such as the first aid courses, the thrift programs, and home economics programs, were continued. Local community groups cooperated closely with the schools: Banks conducted the thrift programs, industrial leaders organized classes for their employees and took much more active interest in what the schools were doing, labor unions passed resolutions supporting education for workers and began to take more interest in the development of the practical arts programs. The schoolhouse was no longer an isolated unit. All of these activities continued to be a concern for the state department. Some even took on greater significance due to the demand for better programs in vocational-technical education, industrial arts, and business practice. In August 1921, the Smith-Hughes program was adopted for secondary education in New Hampshire, a joint federal-state project which was desperately needed (16).

The Americanization program also reached the private and parochial schools. A great many pupils in these schools, especially the French-Canadians, were children of recent immigrants who wished to preserve their tradition and language and conducted these schools in their native tongue. A majority of the citizens denounced this practice as divisive, claiming that American ideals and knowledge of the political and social structure could only be transmitted to the children in English. It wasn't a matter of trying to downgrade or destroy a culture or tradition; most of the citizens simply felt that education for these children should break the barriers which were dividing the social order. Once this was understood by the private schools, there were few problems. The 1919 act required that English be used in all the schools. Implementation of the law proceeded smoothly, thanks largely to the talents of four outstanding leaders.

Much of the credit for leading the way to accepting the new order must be given to the Rt. Rev. Bishop Guertin, a progressive man with a broad understanding of social problems, who was the one recognized official head of the Catholic school system. In November 1918, he assured the people that he was willing to cooperate and appointed a liberal clergyman, Rev. P. J. Scott, diocesan superintendent of parochial schools. Bishop Guertin issued the instructions, and Father Scott saw to it that the Catholic schools complied. Great credit goes to Wilfred J. Lessard, a member of the state board and a Catholic of French-Canadian descent, who, as executive officer of the diocesan board, served as a liaison officer and worked closely with Bishop Guertin and Father Scott. Deputy Commissioner Brooks must be applauded for his patience, tact, and wisdom in representing the state department.

These four men succeeded largely because of the support given by the Association Canado-Américaine, the large Franco-American fraternal order which endorsed the entire program of the Americanization Committee and urged all Catholics to support their bishop in his liberal stand. In fact, with approximately 20,000 of the state's 90,000 enrolled in parochial schools, it would have been extremely difficult to implement the statute if the leaders of the church and the French-Canadian group had not worked for prompt compliance with the law. The parochial system now cooperates with the public schools in all matters of curriculum building and teacher preparation.

Financial Problems

The most serious problem that developed in New Hampshire is the one that usually plagues education–insufficient funds. The Legislature, committed then as now to a strict pay-as-you-go fiscal policy, was unwilling to appropriate enough money to meet the budget presented by the State Board of Education, because it had no prospects for securing the necessary revenue.

The 1920 commissioner's report included the following summary of expenditures of the state board:

Payments to districts	*Percent*
For equalization of opportunity	75.28
For maintenance of teacher training	11.89
For administration of the department	7.97
For Mothers Aid	4.86

Funds were needed for new buildings, cadet training centers, and extension courses, but the requests were repeatedly denied. Keene and Plymouth were woefully inadequate to meet the needs for professionally trained teachers, and the teacher shortage was becoming serious. Teachers received such low salaries that they soon left for other states where they could make more money and enjoy better teaching conditions. Four members of the state board and a deputy commissioner resigned in 1921, frustrated at the Legislature's failure to make necessary appropriations. In the meantime, other states were abandoning the 2-year normal school programs and instituting 3-year and 4-year courses for the preparation of junior and senior high school teachers, and it was obvious that New Hampshire would have to follow the trend as soon as the legislators could be convinced to finance such programs. It was 1927 before the new 2-year, 3-year, and 4-year curriculums were approved by the state board and 3 years later before the first bachelor of education degrees were conferred.

When Ernest W. Butterfield became commissioner, he knew full well the difficulties facing him in securing funds to implement the new state program. He labored to convince board members, the professionals, and the public that it deserved their full support. Employing diplomacy and yet being firm with those who opposed a centralized system of education, he consistently and doggedly hammered toward his objectives. Without his determined devotion and the support of his staff, the state board, and the teaching profession, the new organization would have been ineffective.

The state department gave major consideration to improving what went on in the classroom – curriculum, supervision, and the teacher. Not only was there a serious shortage of trained teachers, particularly in the rural areas and small towns, but standards of certification were much too low, facilities for teacher preparation were inadequate, and the curriculum at the normal schools needed to be improved. Courses usually centered on the textbook, and even here, fortunate indeed was the classroom that had a supply of good books. To meet this situation, the department decided to make the most of the existing training schools at Keene and Plymouth, expand them as rapidly as possible, initiate good summer schools and extension courses, and organize efficient practice schools as part of the training programs. In spite of the prevailing low salaries, the period of preparation was to be increased to 3 and 4 years, with more stringent certification requirements. At the same time, the department attempted to develop closer cooperation with the University of New Hampshire, hoping to gain more teacher preparation courses and additional extension courses for in-service training. Frank Spaulding, a New Hampshire native who was professor of education at Yale, accepted the commissioner's invitation to help develop a suitable curriculum for the schools.

Though supervision became a state responsibility, not all the supervisors were professionally competent. They, too, had to be given training. Though they were tied up with many administrative details, the superintendents were directed by the commissioner to make teacher improvement and better classroom performance their major concern. Institutes and conferences for teachers and supervisors were convened regularly.

The local school board, once the all-powerful unit in district affairs, still retained much authority and, unless guided in making the transition from the old to the new order, could retard progress considerably. Consequently, the department organized statewide conferences for school board members and superintendents. To help those boards whose progress was being undermined by apathy or outright opposition at the annual district meetings, it called numerous public meetings to stimulate local interest. In particular, it tried to interest the people in providing better health services, lighting, heating, and sanitation in the local school buildings. Progress did come, but slowly. Many of the one-room schools were closed; the students were transported to larger centralized schools with superior buildings, programs of study, and teachers. The public finally became convinced that this paid off for their children; and with better highways being built, transportation was no longer the serious obstacle it had been earlier.

The Columbia University Teachers College Report

Educators throughout the country had watched with great interest the daring step forward taken by New Hampshire in 1919 that had given the state so much authority and control over education. In particular, some of the faculty at Teachers College, Columbia University, had read the law carefully. Though they agreed it was a fine piece of legislation, they were skeptical as to how it would actually function. Thus, in 1927, 8 years after the law had been in operation, they sent a Ph.D. candidate, E. A. Bishop, to New Hampshire to make a careful check of the state's accomplishments during this period. His dissertation, published by Teachers College in 1930, said: "It has secured highly desirable results. It has secured them with a reasonable degree of economy. Surely this is the proper outcome of a meritorious system of educational organization, administration and support" (17).

Bishop found that all schools met or exceeded the 36-week year, and attendance was up from 91.3 percent to 94.6 percent. Health and sanitation conditions were greatly improved, now that the authority to condemn school buildings had been transferred from the State Board of Health to the State Board of Education. Previously, only 30 percent of the children had been given medical examinations, while nearly all in the state were now receiving them. The turnover of teachers had been greatly reduced, statewide standards had been raised, and more teachers were being trained than ever before. Perhaps part of this was due to the greater control the state had over professional administrators.

The report, widely distributed and discussed in college classrooms, supported the contention that progress can be made when there is a capable, centralized administration, legally empowered to give direction to local education. In fact, a system of local independent units developing at their own pace was vigorously condemned. However, progress calls for fiscal support. No matter how capable and dedicated the administration might be, regardless of the amount of authority given to a board or department by law, insufficient funds weaken the administrative process and slow down progress. New Hampshire had a good organization in motion, but the money to support this commendable legislation was not forthcoming. That has been New Hampshire's basic problem from 1919 to present.

Because the Legislature refused to appropriate the funds necessary for equalization aid to local districts, this vital part of the 1919 program failed, resulting in a serious setback to education. More money than previously was spent on education by the state and local districts, but it was still insufficient to meet the needs. Local boards presented annual budgets only to have them voted down at the district meetings. Firmly ingrained in the fiscal philosophy of "pay-as-you-go," the people's representatives at the state level followed suit. Now and then, the seriousness of the educational situation impressed the legislators, and they were willing to put out money for buildings to accommodate the normal school students and vote capital outlays for school buildings that were bursting at the seams. Teachers' salaries, however, increased very slowly. The legislators evidently felt that the appalling situation that had existed up to 1919 had now been corrected. They even strongly opposed accepting federal funds on a matching basis.

When Commissioner Butterfield resigned in July 1930 to become commissioner of education for the State of Connecticut, he was replaced by his deputy commissioner, James N. Pringle. Having served in the department since its reorganization, Dr. Pringle endorsed the policies and practices of his predecessor and made little change in the program. He expanded the efforts to get better teachers, more effective training programs at Keene and Plymouth, and better professional supervision, and to eliminate the ineffectual one-room schools. He worked as closely as possible with the school boards and the local communities. He also sought the help of newly formed lay organizations interested in public education, along with the Congress of Parents and Teachers, the Education Committee of the Grange, and groups of parents interested in handicapped children.

Depression and World War II

Federal participation in state programs greatly increased during the 1930's and 1940's, not because the people had a change of heart, but because of two great events affecting the entire nation – the Depression and the entrance of the United States into World War II. During the Depression, New Hampshire, like other states, turned to the national government for help. Programs were needed to assist youth, to help the unemployed in both the professions and labor, and to stimulate the local economy. The people of New Hampshire began to realize that the federal government must play an important role in meeting grave social and economic emergencies. This gradual acceptance of federal aid was first apparent in highway improvement, social services, and various forms of economic development; it was a necessary forerunner to a general acceptance of the principle that federal aid could and should be employed to improve local education. A few critics still raised the cry about wasted funds and clamored against bureaucratic control, but most people were too pleased with the overall results to listen.

The Japanese attack on Pearl Harbor aroused the nation to declare war, but America had already been working furiously for 2 or 3 years to provide the allied nations with weapons and war supplies. During this period, New Hampshire's industry was busy, and a number of educational programs were set up for training mechanics to tool the new weapons. In 1945, the Legislature voted to establish two state trade schools and several area vocational programs for high school students. Federal crash programs to improve standard courses in elementary and secondary education were not developed, however – certainly a difference from World War I. The Depression and World War II projects were largely economic in nature rather than educational.

The war also had an adverse effect on the schools of the state. A general manpower shortage soon developed, and many teachers went into lucrative fields in industry. Many attracted by good salaries never returned to the classroom. A shortage of all kinds of materials and supplies hurt the schools, and supply-economy measures were commonplace. Fighting for survival, the nation felt it could give few priorities to education. On the positive side, World War II, like World War I, reemphasized the importance of health and physical fitness, clearly demonstrated the need for more and better education for all levels of society, and ushered in a new age of technological and vocational education growing out of the experiences and the lessons learned in all fields during this national emergency.

Though the war effort did slow educational progress in the state, the demand for economy closed many ineffective one-room schools, fostered a decided improvement in transportation, and reduced the number of supervisory unions from 64 to 48. Greater interest was taken in deaf and other handicapped children due largely to the cooperation of private organizations with the state department. Local districts had to assume much of the increased cost of education, because the Legislature continually failed to appropriate the necessary funds for effective state aid. Though the state department made persistent efforts to improve the equalization formula and submitted carefully prepared budgets biennially for legislative action, state aid failed to keep pace with the steady growth of the school system. The fiscal situation became critical.

Finally realizing that something had to be done, the Legislature in 1945 appropriated $10,000 for an Interim Study Commission "to study the state educational system and to make a report of its findings and recommendations for the use of the 1947 legislature" (18). By the following May, the study group had been named and it in turn appointed A. D. Simpson of the Harvard Graduate School of Education to direct the study. Instead of surveying all facets of education, Dr. Simpson wisely limited his investigation to three critical areas: finances, the organization of the state department, and relationships with higher education. Guided largely by his findings, which were supplemented by other studies, the interim commission submitted its report to the 1947 session of the Legislature in February.

Commissioner Fuller

In the meantime, Dr. Pringle ended his 48 years of educational service, retiring in December 1945. He was replaced in February by Edgar Fuller, professor of education at the Harvard Graduate School, who had earned a doctorate of law at the University of Chicago and a doctorate of education at Harvard. The new commissioner had served as a high school teacher, principal, superintendent, junior college president, college instructor, and as acting chief of the aviation education division of the Civil Aeronautics Administration. Since it would be his responsibility to act on the recommendations of the commission, Dr. Fuller applied himself diligently to the great mass of material and information that had to be digested in less than a year if the commission's report to the Legislature was to be of value. He and his staff assisted the commission in every way possible, laboring to supply it with information of all kinds.

Commissioner Fuller was convinced that no matter how well the commission's report was prepared, effective action would not follow unless the people of the state were made aware of the seriousness of their school situation. As in 1918, much had to be done in a comparatively short time. To enlist the support of prominent laymen and professional leaders, he organized the Lay-Professional Educational Council in May 1946. Its sole function was "to study the educational problems of the state" (19). The organizational pattern was unique. The state would be divided into 12 regions, each region furnishing 36 members to the council; of this membership, one-third would be lay citizens, one-third professional educators, and one-third school board members. The regional councils would then meet regularly, and, in the majority of school districts, local meetings would be organized to include as many interested citizens as possible. Thus, all phases of elementary and secondary education were carefully discussed and debated in a sincere effort to find solutions.

This carefully planned campaign to secure the cooperation of the people was highly successful, confirming the commissioner's conviction – along with that of his department and the state board – that "given full opportunity to consider the facts about public education, the people of New Hampshire will make the right decisions about it" (20). To keep the issue alive at the local level, he took steps to organize the New Hampshire School Boards Association to utilize the special interests and talents of the local school officials.

Dr. Fuller felt that there was too much centralization of authority and that local school boards should assume more initiative and direction of their schools. Two decades after the state had made necessary changes by assuming the major role and enforcing statutes and exercising regulatory and investigating functions, it was time for the state department to change character, namely, to be more of a service agency. Dr. Fuller hoped that with the 1919 law operating quite effectively, with better supervision, and with a program of studies conducted by better trained teachers, the department could relax its controls and devote its efforts to helping school boards, superintendents, and teachers build stronger local school systems. This service function has been consistently developed and refined during the past 20 years.

In July 1947, the state department published the recommendations of the council in a bulletin entitled *Lay-Professional Council Report to the People of New Hampshire for the Youth of New Hampshire* (21). The report urged the establishment of kindergartens, stressed the importance of mastery of the basic skills and recognition of individual differences in grades 1 through 6, endorsed a comprehensive curriculum for all secondary schools including vocational training (thereby improving the "holding power" of the senior high school), and recommended changes in the teachers colleges to ensure better teacher preparation. It pointed out the need for a statewide guidance program directed by a specialist on the staff of the state department. Local school districts, the teachers colleges, and the university were urged to conduct adult education programs. The report stated that the council would make two special studies during the next biennium – one on the supervisory union as an administrative unit, the other on the financing of public education by local districts and the state. Unhappily, the council's zeal for these studies waned, and it published no reports. The well-known jingle "For want of a nail, etc." probably offers the best explanation of why the lay-professional movement suddenly collapsed. Commissioner Fuller had been the sparkplug that kept the project going. When, unfortunately, he resigned in July 1948, "the leader was lost," and with his departure "the cause was lost."

Report of the Interim Commission, 1947

After 9 months of intensive work, the Interim Study Commission completed its report for the Legislature. Its findings and recommendations were presented in seven sections: a general summary of the survey, financing education, personnel policy, educational structure of the state school system, the state board and education department, institutional relations with higher education, and nurse education. Of particular importance to history is Section V, which dealt with the state board and the education department:

> The State Board of Education represents in this state one of the oldest and most effective organizations in our country. If every state had such a board and board organization, educational progress on a nationwide basis might be assured. New Hampshire should take pride in the long history of good state educational organization and effective work on the part of the State Board of Education (22).

The commission added: "The key purposes of a State Department of Education – that is, the purposes looked at more broadly than as the execution of law and rules – are three in number: (1) guidance and leadership, (2) service, and (3) research and planning" (23).

Specific recommendations for improving the work of the state department were based not only on its findings, but on a modern philosophy of the function of any state government agency. The commission gave attention to the relationship between state and local authority and responsibility, pointing out that the state department was responsible for organizing a sound statewide educational program, but that encouraging local initiative and responsibility for good schools should also be a major concern of the state. It should cooperate more in supplying specialists to advise and guide local officials in their efforts. One of the great needs the commission found was for a research and planning division that would produce facts and statistics on which programs could be launched and evaluated. Instead of having divisions for elementary, secondary, and vocational education, the report recommended that five divisions be established: instructional service, administrative service, research and planning, personnel administration, and personnel improvement. In each case the emphasis was on service to local communities by staff specialists. The commission felt that a specialist should be engaged temporarily to improve citizenship education and that the supervision of nursing service could be improved by placing it under professional direction. In addition to urging adequate salaries for specialists and a doubling of the physical facilities available to the department, the commission praised Dr. Fuller's efforts in establishing the lay-professional council and his desire to bring the schools closer to the people by encouraging a greater local participation by school boards and citizens.

The interim commission's grave concern about the lack of state aid, the teacher shortage, and poor pupil transportation, and its conviction of the need for further study prompted it to recommend six legislative proposals: a new state aid formula, a state council on teacher education, a \$1,500 minimum salary for teachers, a certification council to advise the state board on the certification of all personnel, a \$200,000 annual appropriation for pupil transportation, and a special grant of \$2,000 to establish an interim commission to study the government structure of the state educational system and report its findings to the 1949 Legislature. After hearings on the above proposals the Legislature rejected all six.

Legislation of 1947

However, the 1947 Legislature did take enough positive action for Commissioner Fuller to state: "The General Court [state legislature] of 1947 passed the most fundamentally important educational legislation since 1919" (24). Publication of the interim commission's report, the activities of the lay-professional council, and the cooperation of the press and various organized groups in alerting the people to the critical state of public education produced sufficient pressure for the legislators to pass several important bills.

One of the most significant new laws, passed with little opposition, appropriated \$2 million annually from 1947 to 1949 according to a formula developed by the state department. No doubt the legislators were influenced substantially by the widely publicized report prepared by the lay-professional council, which censured the the state for giving less than 5 percent in state aid to the school districts, but certainly the bill received favorable consideration because of a sizable surplus in the state treasury.

At the same time, other fiscal action was taken to help the districts. In order to have a reserve fund for capital outlays, districts were permitted to lay aside annually .005 percent of their assessed valuations, and the local debt limit was increased from 2 percent of assessed valuation to 5 percent, and it could go up to 8 percent if the board of investigation, the Governor's Council, and the Governor all approved. But despite the interim commission's strong recommendation that local boards and districts be fiscally independent of town and city governments, the Legislature refused to act. Impressed, however, by the commission's strong case for larger administrative units that could guarantee better educational opportunity for all children, the lawmakers permitted districts to unite as "co-operative" school districts under a single administration. The act did not provide for incentive aid from the state.

To hold good teachers and to attract candidates from other states, the Legislature, following the example of other progressive states, passed a compulsory Teacher's Retirement Law that liberalized the provisions of the old permissive retirement system. Recognizing that many children needed psychiatric study and treatment, the General Court established a Childrens Study Home and Clinic in Concord, a big step forward in the movement to give special care to problem children. Prompted by the recommendations of the U.S. Public Health Service, which were included in the interim commission's report, it created the Office of Director of Nursing Education in the State Department of Education and provided state financing for better supervision and services for the nursing schools.

Though the action taken by the 1947 Legislature was of great significance, the state could not sustain the pace of progressive legislation and soon returned to the old practice of compromising on appropriations far below the amounts requested and needed. But a start in many directions had been made: new services in physical education, the fine arts, and the professional supervision of guidance and mental health. Local districts were freer to invest in educational programs. The GI Bill of Rights and other programs for World War II veterans brought new federally supported projects to the state and greatly increased the amount of federal aid it accepted.

The chart in Appendix B shows how the department was organized as of 1948. The development and progress that took place during the 29 years can best be appreciated by comparing this with the 1919 organization chart in Appendix B. The department now has four divisions, including the two teachers colleges, both completely under the supervision of the state board. Instead of 4 deputy commissioners, it has 1; there are 2 chiefs, 9 directors (including 1 for nursing education), 14 supervisors, 13 inspectors, and a consultant. In 1919, the department had one lone agent of industrial education; note the number directing vocational activities 28 years later, supported either all or in part by federal funds. The central office now has 23 secretary-clerks instead of 5. The accounting staff has increased from one accountant to a principal accountant, a director of educational finance, and three junior accountants. This chart of the expanded department does not include the staffs of the teachers colleges and trade schools.

THE RECENT PERIOD, 1948-68

Four commissioners of education have ably served the state since 1948. Commissioner Hilton C. Buley (1948-54) strove to improve education by recommending the reorganization of school districts into larger administrative units, thus providing a broader basis for increased financial support, and by emphasizing construction of modern schools with better equipment and facilities.

It was during the administration of Austin J. McCaffrey (1954-57) that attention was focused on the necessity for full implementation by the state of the Foundation Aid Act and provision by the Legislature of state aid for the education of physically handicapped, mentally retarded, and emotionally disturbed children.

Commissioner Charles F. Ritch, Jr., (1958-63) stressed the importance of the state's participation in federal aid programs under the NDEA Act and emphasized the need for expanded vocational education on the secondary and postsecondary school levels. He also secured passage of the act establishing minimum standards for secondary education.

The efforts of these leaders bore fruition during the administration of Commissioner Paul E. Farnum (1963-68), who skillfully engineered the expansion of larger administrative units, legislation for all handicapped children, greater vocational education opportunities, wider participation in NDEA and other federal aid programs, and implementation of rapid growth in school district and supervisory union reorganization. On July 1, 1968, Commissioner Farnum retired and was succeeded by his deputy commissioner, Newell J. Paire, an experienced former superintendent of schools.

Transfer of Division of Teacher Education

The department does not have the same responsibilities in all areas it did in 1948. For instance, it no longer contains a division of teacher education. The 1963 Legislature created the University of New Hampshire, a single corporate body under its own board of trustees. This board includes the commissioner of education and the presidents of the state colleges, now liberal arts institutions called Keene State College and Plymouth State College. This was in keeping with the nationwide trend, based on the idea that teachers needed broader preparation with less emphasis on methodology and more attention to subject matter. Enough time has not elapsed to evaluate the effectiveness of this administrative change.

Transfer of Youth Employment

Another of the department's functions that was transferred to a different agency was the handling of youth employment. The 1951 and 1953 Legislatures passed bills directing the commissioner of labor instead of the commissioner of education to be responsible for enforcing child labor laws.

The service activities of the department have increased greatly during the last decade and a half and have shifted in emphasis in the areas and types of services. Two stand out: vocational-technical education and special education. What the organization chart (25) does not show is the dramatically increased involvement of the federal government and the amount of federal money now available to the state. The State Board of Education intends to make greater use of federal funds under existing statutes in an effort to expand its services. Another development which should be pointed out is the increased concern for public school administration at the local level. In 1948, there were 48 superintendents and 7 assistant superintendents; in 1965, there were 46 superintendents, 19 assistant superintendents, 12 teacher consultants, and 3 business administrators.

Technical-Vocational Education

The marked increase in facilities for technical-vocational education is due to several factors. First, there was a substantial population increase during the last decade and a half: In 1950, 70,448 pupils attended public schools in the state; in 1965, the public schools enrolled 127,558, an increase of 44.9 percent.

New Hampshire is the second most industrialized state in New England and can boast the lowest unemployment ratio in the nation. With no sales or income tax to pay, manufacturers of electronics products, plastics, and small precision instruments moved into the state. Many were compelled to find employees in neighboring states because of a local skilled worker shortage. The state trade schools were unable to supply the demand. The manufacturers voiced their concern about the situation. Earle Little, chief of the division of vocational-technical education, capitalized on the situation. With the active support of the industrial leaders of the state, he engaged in a vigorous campaign to put an ambitious program for technical-vocational institutes before the 1963 Legislature. The overflow hearing before the education committees of the House and Senate was dominated by lay industrialists who pleaded the cause of a modern technical-vocational program. When the legislation passed, it inaugurated a new era in technical-vocational education. Within 2 years, a new technical institute was in operation, the two trade schools had been expanded, a third school was under way, and plans for two more postsecondary technical-vocational schools are on the drawing boards.

In an effort to make full use of the state's manpower, the department has begun an extensive program of vocational rehabilitation. In 1948, the vocational education division directed its attention to the war veteran, giving special emphasis to job training, guidance, and placement. The division staff included a director of vocational rehabilitation, two supervisors, and a medical-social consultant. By 1965, the department also had a codirector of Civil Defense adult education and an assistant coordinator, and it operated a vocational rehabilitation division, headed by a chief, with a professional staff of 12 assistants. This program, organized as a special division of the education department, was largely the result of the initiative and financial support of the federal government. New Hampshire has accepted federal assistance for its public school programs since Congress passed the Vocational Education Act in 1917.

Service to Handicapped Children

For years, advocates of special but separate education for the physically handicapped, mentally retarded, and emotionally disturbed had introduced bills in the Legislature but had always had inadequate support. James O'Neil, chairman of the House education committee, introduced a bill that focused legislative attention and support on a single total program with professional guidance responsible for its success. This was a decided step forward.

The Special Education Act of 1965 declares it "to be the policy of the state to provide the best and most effective education possible to all handicapped children in New Hampshire" (26). It placed responsibility for the program squarely on the state board and education department, empowering them to appoint personnel, submit an approved plan to school districts, set standards, and see that the tuition adjustments and transportation facilities were provided. The act stipulated that the program was to be established within the funds appropriated or available. Unfortunately, the department has never had enough money for a total attack on the problem.

The 1965 Legislature went a step further in its effort to establish a program of special education: It authorized the department to make a study of the education of gifted children. This was to be an intensive study over a 2-year period, and a full report was to be submitted to the Legislature.

The Junior College Movement

New Hampshire has no publicly supported junior college. Since the middle 1950's, civic, educational, social, and business organizations have stressed the need for such a program, mainly because such a large number of in-state pupils have been rejected by the colleges due to higher academic standards. In 1963, the interim commission recommended that such a program be added. Two years later, the Governor's Conference on Education again strongly recommended a junior college program. This time, the Legislature responded by creating a Junior College Commission to study the problem and submit recommendations to the Governor. A major question now is whether the state board or the trustees of the university should organize and operate the junior colleges. The commission report favors "adding a comprehensive curriculum to the programs of the Institutes" (27). If this is voted by the Legislature, the state board will assume the responsibility.

Recent Federal Programs

The successful launching of Sputnik by the Russians unleashed a storm of criticism of public education. Goaded into action, Congress passed the National Defense Education Act of 1958 (NDEA) to meet the charge that our schools were too weak in mathematics, science, and foreign languages.

The purpose was to stimulate state action by making grants (some on a matching basis) to state governments and holding the departments of education responsible for supervising the local programs within the framework of federal guidelines. New Hampshire lagged behind in demanding federal money and more federal participation in public education. Its leaders pursued a rather cautious policy, partly because of the state's poor showing in its support of education and partly because of strong opposition to federal aid per se. Historically, the burden of supporting schools had fallen on the local government.

As Congress voted additional millions – the Elementary and Secondary Education Act of 1965 (ESEA) – and as the government's program for education became more and more involved in social and economic problems such as the War on Poverty, employment, youth services, and rehabilitation, it affected all sectors of the population. If these needed programs are to continue, local and state revenues will be insufficient to maintain them, and federal aid is essential. Many conservatives have now accepted the fact that federal aid is here to stay and have decided they must go along with the trend.

Many organizations deserve credit for the part they have played in furthering the cause of education in New Hampshire. Parents organizations pushed for schools for handicapped children; several groups promoted educational television; and industrialists, concerned with better facilities for vocational and technical education, worked actively to secure state support for their projects. The state department staff welcomed the support of these citizens, cooperating by supplying necessary facts, serving on committees, and speaking at public meetings. In many instances, the state department has been the continuing influence behind their efforts.

In 1958, three representatives from each of the following New Hampshire organizations – the Congress of Parents and Teachers, the Council for Better Schools, the School Boards Association, the State Teachers Association, the Association of School Superintendents, and the State Department of Education – formed a joint committee to study the needs of New Hampshire education to inform citizens and legislators about the state's educational program. The state department supplied the basic facts, and the group held public meetings to outline the need for action at hearings conducted by the Legislature. The committee was responsible for putting in motion two Governor's Conferences on Education.

In all of these activities to stimulate citizen interest and action, the state department played a vital role. By working through and with these citizens groups, the state board has been able to secure helpful legislation. This strategy has been most successful, especially in dealing with the Legislature and public officials. It seems that the best way to block educational legislation in New Hampshire is for someone to introduce a bill sponsored by the state board. On the other hand, if a group of citizens introduces the bill and actively supports it, the chances for success are greatly enhanced.

Growth of Larger Administrative Units

A small state composed of many independent districts is bound to have many small high schools, especially in sparsely settled rural areas. Small high schools (attendance of less than 100) with their limited curriculum and excessive teacher turnover have hampered efforts to achieve quality education. Among elementary schools, a number of one-room schools disappeared with the rapid increase in good highways and a satisfactory transportation program.

Two towns successfully petitioned the Legislature as early as 1927 for special legislation to incorporate in a single school district. Thus began the cooperative school plan, creating a single administration with a larger tax base for its support. For more than 50 years, the state department has been working for the establishment of larger administrative units, convinced that more opportunities are possible if larger financial backing is made available. In the beginning, the state gave no financial aid to the project, and progress was slow. And many small districts were so imbued with local pride that they have fought any change in the operation of their own small high school.

In the midfifties, a committee of citizens and educators was appointed to study the state's high schools and recommend to the state board reasonable "minimum standards" it should employ for certifying "approved secondary schools." The board accepted and published the *Minimum Standards for Secondary Schools.* Then, in 1959, the Legislature passed an act defining in specific terms the standards a high school would have to maintain to qualify for state aid. Many school officials, realizing that they would not be able to meet the minimum standards, gave serious consideration to joining another district or districts. Certainly this boosted the cooperative movement. In 1963, two important acts were passed: the Cooperative School Act and the Authorized Regional Enrollment Act (AREA schools) which gave even greater impetus to the cause of larger administrative units through state incentive financial aid.

By 1965, 15 cooperative school districts were in operation, with two more commencing in 1966. Also, four AREA schools are open, with a fifth likely to be added. These larger schools naturally added considerably to the superintendent's duties, so the state department has added more assistant superintendents (28). To handle the financial operations of these larger units, five business administrators were hired by the districts. And since the superintendent could no longer spend the time to serve as a supervisor, a 1961 statute permitted district officers to employ a teacher consultant with specific duties; within 2 years, 12 teacher consultants were hired. The services and guidance of the state department staff are readily available to all these administrators.

Despite great strides in the work of the State Department of Education during the past 65 years, many problems remain. The chief of these is revenue; the department is always short of money. The local districts still bear the brunt of taxation and carry too much of the tax burden. New Hampshire is near the bottom of the list of states in the percentage of state aid given to education. This is likely to be true as long as the state seeks revenue chiefly from levies on alcohol, tobacco, the race track, and the sweepstakes. The solution is to draw from a broad-base tax, either sales or income. More and more people are aware of this, and in a matter of a few years it must certainly be voted for education. As compared with the 1900's, the people have become education conscious; good schools are given priority in the mind of the average citizen. The state has a fine education department responsible to a state board, fortunately separated from politics. Though money is not the only answer, it is the vital and critical factor if the state is to have a strong educational system striving for excellence.

Federal, State, and Local Relations

Financial considerations will be the determining factor in the future development of public education in New Hampshire. Education, like national defense, will become a vital issue, for in the present unstable world, education will be considered a powerful weapon of national defense. The federal government, in the national interest, will become more and more involved in education, particularly at the state level. More millions for education will be voted by Congress, not with the thought of nationalizing the schools, but because of its conviction that maintaining the highest standards of education for *all* our people is vital to the success of a democratic society. Federal aid, therefore, will exert a greater influence.

The federal government, respecting the principle established by the Constitution that education is a state responsibility, will function largely through state boards and departments of education. It will seek a partnership with the states to raise the standards of education. Millions of dollars will be funneled, not directly to local communities, but through state departments operating as agents of the national government. The state will distribute these funds to local school districts according to guidelines mutually acceptable to the state and federal governments. This will result in stronger state departments of education. The passage of Title V of ESEA clearly indicates the desire of the federal government to develop strong state departments. States that refuse federal funds will find themselves increasingly becoming targets for criticism by local school officials and citizens who want good schools.

Not all citizens will be happy over this mutual effort of the states and federal government. Some fear federal cutbacks in spending that will force the state and the local communities to carry the financial burden. Among this group are those who oppose any federal aid on a matching basis, claiming that once a program has been initiated the federal money will stop coming, thus creating a serious financial crisis for state and local governments. Recently, a group of New Hampshire citizens organized themselves as the Public Schools Association in opposition to the acceptance of federal and state participation in schools. Demanding more local control of education, they plan to alert the public to the dangers of centralized authority.

The cost of conducting good schools will continue to increase. With more federal funds dispersed through the state education agency, there will be greater reliance on the state and on the federal government for leadership and guidance in both programing and administration. The development of larger administrative units will call for closer cooperation between local and state governments. To meet the increasing complexity of problems, local boards must draw up effective written policies, develop new techniques in working with teachers and administrators, and keep their fellow citizens better informed about modern education. Should they fail in these vital areas, local control will become a mere formality.

FOOTNOTES

1. The Literary Fund was created to provide funds for a state college. The project was abandoned because of limited interest in public support of higher education.
2. During this period, two superintendents, Amos Hadley (1867-68) and James W. Patterson (1881-93), stand out as effective leaders in education.
3. Under the district system, in a given township a district with more taxable wealth had better schools than the district with limited assessed valuation. This inequality of educational opportunity was the cause of grave public concern and dissatisfaction. Professor Hiram Orcutt and other members of the Dartmouth faculty were instrumental in having town control replace the district system.
4. Superintendent of Public Instruction, *Biennial Report, 1899-1900.*, pp. 43-45.
5. It was at this time that federal aid to public secondary education was introduced. Fifty years earlier, the state college had been founded under the Land Grant College Act. Now Congress passed the Smith-Hughes Act of 1917 to further the technical and vocational training of our youth.
6. Much credit is due to the initiative and determination of Governor J. H. Bartlett (1919-20) for the passage of the Great School Law of 1919. "Governor Bartlett made it his premier issue. The Governor laid down the principle that public school education should no longer be dependent on the resources of each locality, that the state owed a duty to children to equalize school opportunities for the poor and rich towns alike." John H. Bartlett, *A Synoptic History of the Granite State* (Chicago: M. A. Donohue and Co., 1939), p. 107.
7. In the isolated, sparsely settled mountainous areas of the state, township boundaries were established, and the various sections were given a town name. However, no formal governmental organization was established by the widely scattered settlers; in fact, in many cases no school districts were created. These areas were referred to as "unorganized places."
8. New Hampshire, *Acts of 1919*, ch. 106, sec. 1 *et seq.*
9. *Ibid.*, ch. 106, sec. xxvii.

10. This type of law was being passed all over the country by a society swept up in a war hysteria.

11. New Hampshire, *Acts of 1919,* ch. 106, sec. 23.

12. *Ibid.,* sec. 24.

13. The Legislature also voted that there should be a codification of the statutes and that any laws inconsistent with the act be rescinded. This codification was achieved in 1921.

14. See Appendix B.

15. Chairman Frank S. Streeter sent out invitations to a meeting at the State House on October 16, 1919. Minutes of the State Board of Education, meeting of September 5, 1919.

16. The agent of industrial education, added to the state staff by the 1919 law, not only directed the agricultural projects for all schoolchildren during the war years but continued to expand the Smith-Hughes programs in the secondary schools.

17. Eugene A. Bishop, *The Development of a State School System: New Hampshire* (New York: Teachers College, Columbia University, 1930), p. 145.

18. New Hampshire, *Public Laws and Joint Resolution of the Legislature of 1945,* ch. 233, sec. 1.

19. Mrs. Carroll Reed, *Lay-Professional Council Report to the People of New Hampshire for the Youth of New Hampshire* (Concord: State Department of Education, July 1947), p. 9.

20. *Ibid.,* p. 5.

21. *Ibid.*

22. Commission To Study the State Educational System, *Public Education in New Hampshire* (Concord: Granite State Press, 1946), p. 179.

23. *Ibid.,* p. 180.

24. *Concerning Public Education in New Hampshire, Seventy-Third Report of the State Board of Education* (Concord: n.p., 1948).

25. See Appendix B.

26. New Hampshire, *Special Education Act of 1965,* ch. 186-A, sec. 1.

27. New Hampshire Junior College Commission, *Report* (Nashua: Sanders Associates, June 1966), p. 14

28. At present there are 19 assistant superintendents.

BIBLIOGRAPHY

Public Documents

New Hampshire. *Acts of 1919.*

-- *Constitution* (1874).

-- *Public Laws and Joint Resolution of the Legislature of 1945.*

-- *Revised Statutes Annotated (RSA) Relating to Public Schools* (1955).

-- *Special Education Act of 1965.*

Books

Bartlett, John H. *A Synoptic History of the Granite State.* Chicago: M. A. Donohue and Co., 1939.

Bishop, Eugene A. *The Development of a State School System: New Hampshire.* New York: Teachers College, Columbia University, 1930.

Bush, George Gary. *History of Education in New Hampshire.* Washington D.C.: Government Printing Office, 1898.

Charlton, Edwin A. *New Hampshire As It Is.* Part III. Claremont, N.H.: Tracy and Co., 1855.

Council of Chief State School Officers. *The State Department of Education: Legal Status, Functions and Organizations.* Washington, D.C.: The Council, 1963.

Long, Isaac. *New Hampshire Laws.* Title 92 on Schools. Concord: Luther Roby, 1830.

Pillsbury, Hobart. *New Hampshire: A History.* Vol. IV. New York: Lewis Historical Publishing Co., 1927.

Article and Periodical

Butterfield, Ernest W. "History of New Hampshire's Schools and School Legislation." *The Granite Monthly,* XLVII (January 1925).

Reports

Commission To Study the State Educational System. *Public Education in New Hampshire.* Concord: Granite State Press, 1946.

Concerning Public Education in New Hampshire, Seventy-Third Report of the State Board of Education. Concord: n.p., 1948.

Cusick, Margaret. *The Upper Quarter.* Concord: New Hampshire Council for Better Schools, January 1960.

Department of Education. *Educational Directory.* 1948-49, 1965-66.

-- *Reports of the Superintendents of Public Instruction and the Commissioners of Education.* 1876-1965.

Interim Commission on Education. *Report of the Interim Commission on Education.* 1963.

New Hampshire Junior College Commission. *Report.* Nashua: Sanders Associates, June 1966.

Reed, Mrs. Carroll. *Lay-Professional Council Report to the People of New Hampshire for the Youth of New Hampshire.* Concord: State Department of Education, July 1947.

Unpublished Material

Minutes of the New Hampshire State Board of Education, 1919-68.

Appendix A

NEW HAMPSHIRE CHIEF STATE SCHOOL OFFICERS

Superintendents of Public Instruction

1899-1904	Channing Folsom
1904-17	Henry C. Morrison
1917-19	Ernest W. Butterfield

Commissioners of Education

1919-30	Ernest W. Butterfield
1930-45	James N. Pringle
1946-48	Edgar Fuller
1948-54	Hilton C. Buley
1954-57	Austin J. McCaffrey
1958-63	Charles F. Ritch, Jr.
1963-68	Paul E. Farnum
1968-	Newell J. Paire

Appendix B

Chart I.--NEW HAMPSHIRE DEPARTMENT OF EDUCATION FOLLOWING PASSAGE OF THE SCHOOL LAW OF 1919

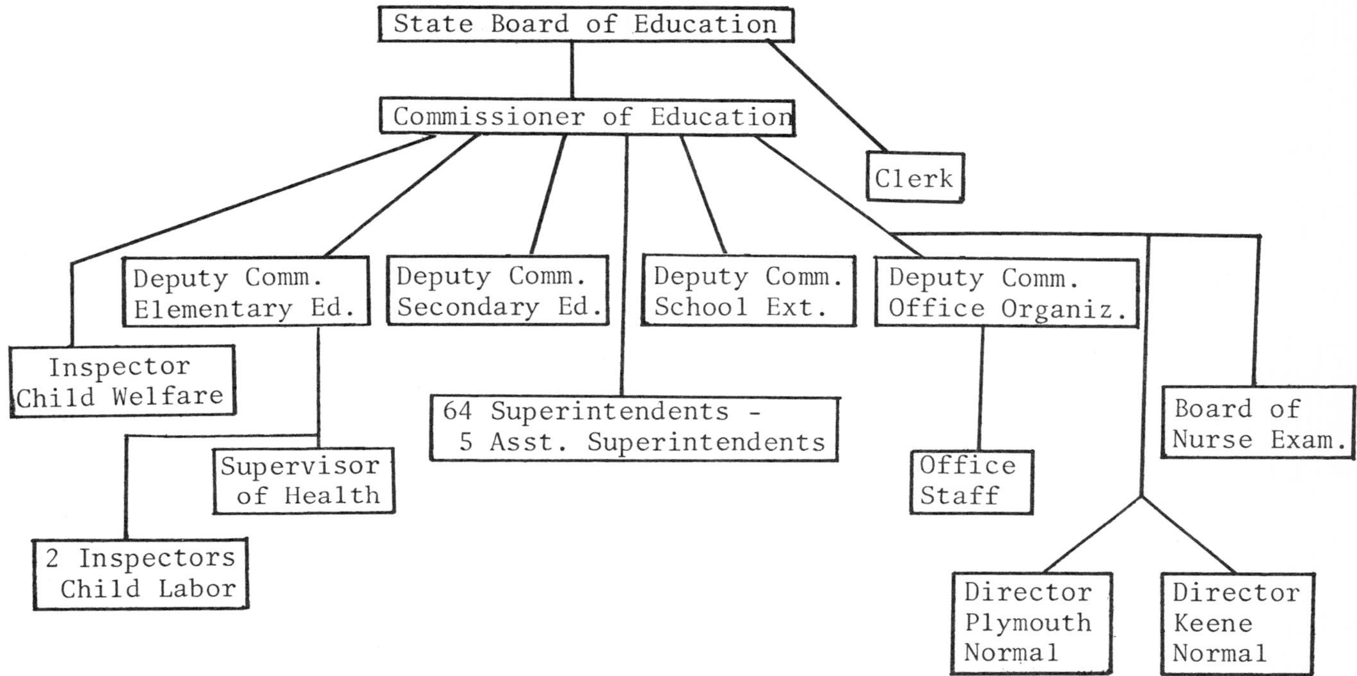

The office staff was to include: a secretary to the commissioner; four stenographers, one for each deputy; an accountant; a registrar; and an information clerk. An agent of industrial education in charge of all Smith-Hughes activities worked with the commissioner and the three deputies in charge of elementary schools, secondary schools, and school extension.

Appendix B

Chart II.--NEW HAMPSHIRE DEPARTMENT OF EDUCATION FOLLOWING THE LEGISLATION OF 1947*

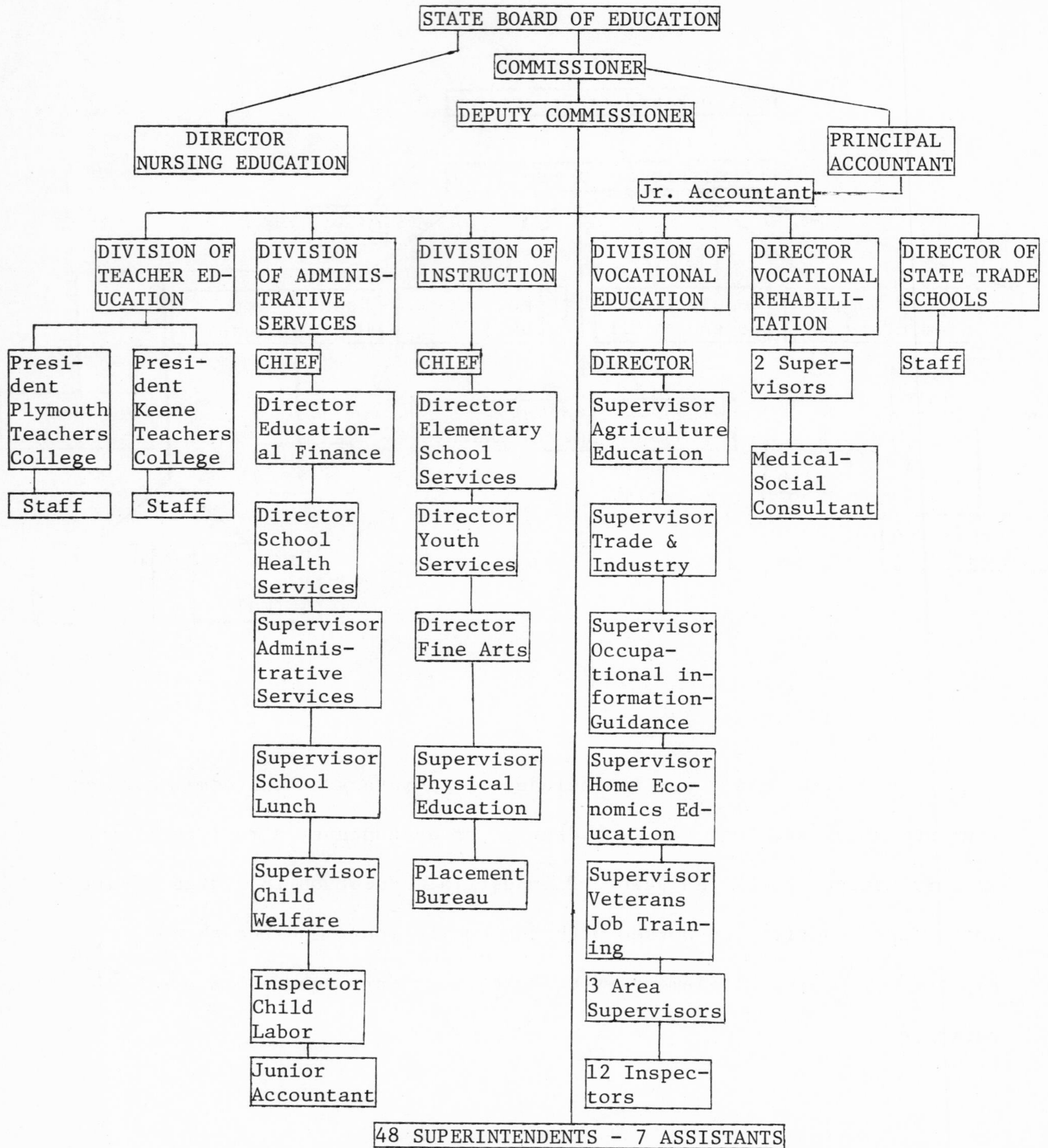

*From the Educational Directory 1948-49. Annual publication of the State Department of Education.

Appendix B

Chart III.--NEW HAMPSHIRE DEPARTMENT OF EDUCATION FOLLOWING LEGISLATION OF 1965*

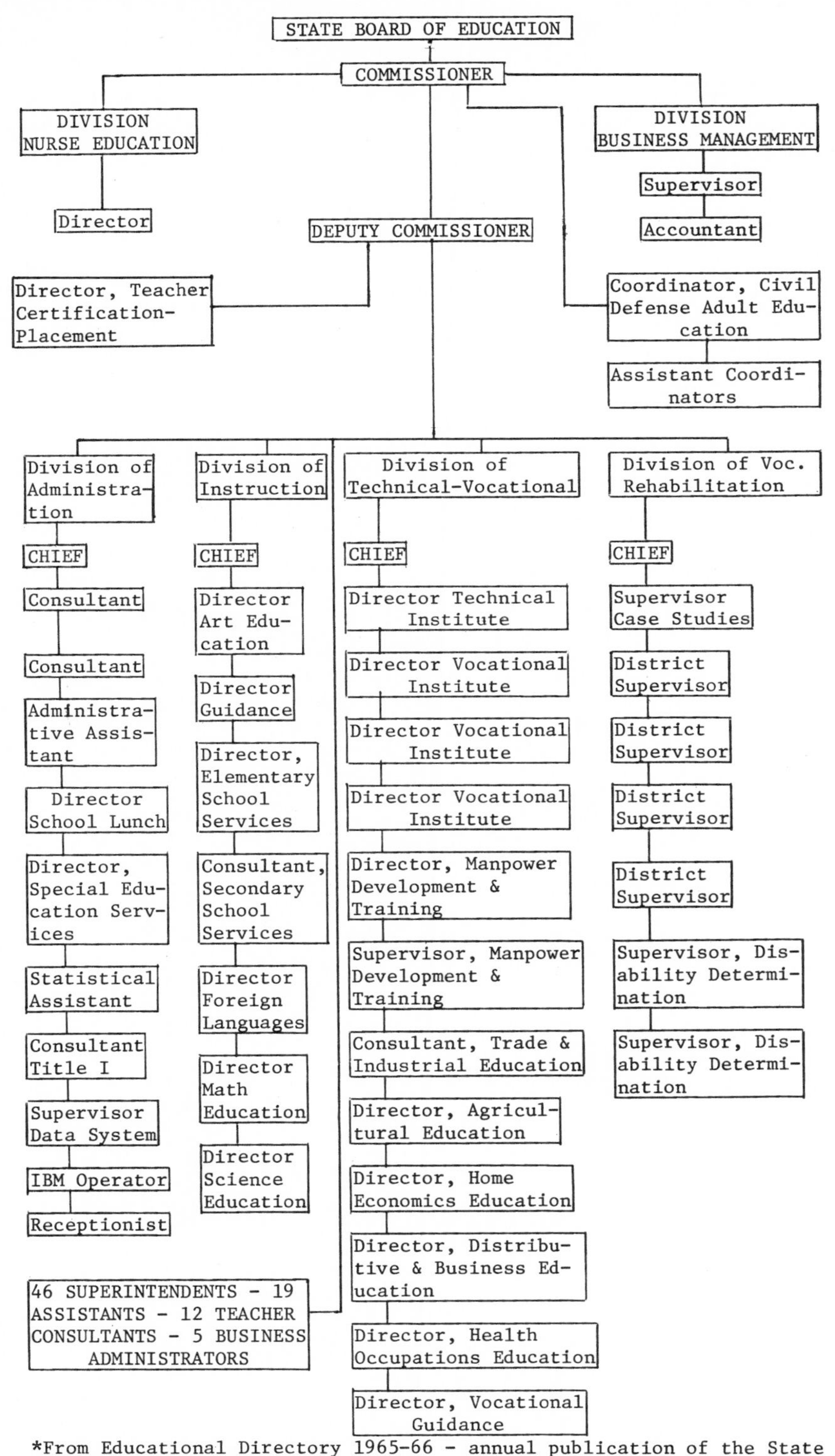

*From Educational Directory 1965-66 - annual publication of the State Depatment of Education.

Appendix C

Table 1. – GROWTH IN POPULATION AND ENROLLMENT AT PUBLIC AND PAROCHIAL SCHOOLS, 1900-66

Year	Population [a]	Public school enrollment [b]	Parochial school enrollment [b]
1900	411,588	51,031	9,827 (est.)
1910	430,572	54,966	13,990
1920	443,082	64,205	20,404
1930	465,293	73,707	21,735
1940	491,524	74,568	21,118
1950	533,242	73,314	23,313
1960	606,921	104,392	28,115
1966	679,090 (est.)	131,138	29,390
1900-60	47%	103%	183%

Table 2. – AMOUNT OF STATE AID AND THE PERCENT IT REPRESENTS OF TOTAL OPERATING COSTS OF PUBLIC EDUCATION, 1920-65 [c]

Year	State aid	Total operating expenses of public elementary and secondary schools	State's share of total operating expenses
1920	$ 336,060	$ 4,028,520	8.3%
1930	358,727	7,960,224	4.5
1940	386,908	8,888,513	4.07
1950	633,919	15,537,329	4.10
1960	2,252,692	35,813,488	6.3 [d]
1965	7,325,896	58,039,584	12.6 [e]

[a] U.S. Bureau of the Census.

[b] Statistics from the State Department of Education.

[c] Statistical division of the State Department of Education.

[d] Includes school building aid.

[e] Includes sweepstakes, aid to "needy districts," special aid to retarded children, and debt service.

30 New Jersey

DEPARTMENT OF EDUCATION
Robert F. Palmer

Contents

INTRODUCTION

The New Jersey State Department of Education has had a somewhat checkered history. The struggle to create an effective state system of education and to build and maintain public support for the system and the schools has moved ahead in spurts. New Jersey has been among the leading states of the nation in recognizing its educational needs, but not always among the first to take action to implement the necessary programs. It is to the everlasting credit of the many farsighted and dedicated leaders who, with the determined support of educational organizations, overcame numerous obstacles to advance the development of the state system and make possible the establishment of today's strong and viable department.

New Jersey was somewhat slow – slower, at least, than some of its fellow states – to enact the necessary legislation to establish a functioning state system of free public schools. But once the foundation was laid – a century ago, in 1867 – it was done carefully and thoroughly so that a dynamic and responsive Department of Education has emerged and flourished.

In the last century, the operation of the state school system has been marked by a steady and rewarding attempt to put together the best of a sound tradition with the imaginative adaptations necessary to the education and advancement of the individual and of society. The nature and scope of the department's activities have changed greatly over the years. As the state's population soared and became more urbanized – New Jersey is the nation's most urban state today – the philosophy of education and the concept of the state's role were continually revised accordingly.

It has not been easy to add the new and scrap the old as the times and needs required. But, as the result of a carefully laid foundation, New Jersey has managed to meet its educational responsibilities. Its school programs both for college-bound and vocationally oriented youngsters compare favorably with the best in other states, and its special programs for the physically and mentally handicapped, for preschool children, and for adults have been cited as among the best in the country.

Education in New Jersey is a state responsibility. The Legislature is mandated by the State Constitution to provide for the maintenance and support of a thorough and efficient system of free public schools for the instruction of all the children in the state between the ages of 5 and 18 years.

That constitutional clause has been the cornerstone of the development of an efficient and effective public education system in New Jersey since 1876. It was written as an amendment to the State Constitution of 1844, which had recognized the need for free public schools but had not set forth the state's responsibility. New Jersey retained the clause when its constitution was rewritten in 1948.

LAYING THE FOUNDATION

The early settlers in New Jersey brought with them a deep conviction of the importance of schooling and saw to it that schools were formed in the settlements.

The state's first residents were of various origins, and they brought with them different ideas about education. Some of the settlers were Dutch from New Amsterdam, some New Englanders from Long Island and Connecticut, some Swedes from the lower Delaware; others, English, Scotch, and Scotch-Irish from England, Scotland, and Ireland; and still others, Quakers from England and the neighboring colonies. Schools were established largely in communities settled by members of one of four Protestant denominations – Dutch Reformed, Congregationalists, Presbyterians, and Quakers. Many of the settlers had already acquired a liberal education and were determined to provide educational facilities for their children, under the direction of their own church leaders. This heterogeneity of population naturally deterred the establishment of any uniform state school plan, in sharp contrast to Massachusetts where almost every colonist was an English Puritan from England, with the result that church and state, with the same plans and purposes, could direct educational procedure uniformly.

New Jersey's first schoolmaster was Engelbert Steenhuysen. He set up shop in 1662 in the village of Bergen, now Jersey City, which had been settled by the

Dutch in extending their territory across the Hudson from New Amsterdam. Steenhuysen contracted to keep the school and to serve as church clerk. A log building erected about 1664 was used as both a schoolhouse and a church.

In these Dutch schools, the Dutch Reformed Church examined the teachers, enforced subscription to the creed, and largely determined the appointments (especially in the elementary schools), although legal support and control were apparently vested in civil authorities. In addition to the elementary subjects (reading, writing, spelling, and arithmetic), these schools taught the principles of Christianity and the catechism and prayers of the Reformed Church. Immigrants from New Sweden settled on the east side of the lower Delaware River and, like the Dutch, brought with them their elementary schools dominated by the Lutheran Church. These settlements were soon taken over by the Dutch and later included in the English territory (1).

Immigration from New England to New Jersey stepped up with the English conquest of New Netherlands in 1664. Numerous settlements came into being, including Elizabethtown, Rahway, Piscataway, Woodbridge, and Newark. The Congregational Church dominated most of the educational activities. All children were taught reading, writing, and arithmetic.

In 1668, New Jersey Governor Philip Carteret granted the Bergen Dutch immigrants a charter which stipulated that all persons should contribute according to their estates and proportions of land for the keeping of a free school to educate the youth.

This edict was received with less than unanimous acceptance. Balky citizens of surrounding villages objected to making payments to support the schoolmaster. As a result, the magistrates took what has become known as the earliest legal action in the state for the support of public education and declared in an order issued in December 1672 that all should pay their share for the schoolmaster's support.

At this time in history, immigrants were beginning to reach New Jersey's shores in large numbers from England, Ireland, and Scotland. Among them were Scotch Presbyterians seeking escape from persecution during the period of the Stuart Restoration (1660-89). Their religious customs and educational ideas are described by David Murray in the *History of Education in New Jersey:*

> Education was scarcely less essential to these hardy immigrants than religion. They followed the example of their native land and their native church in providing for the education of their children. Each family saw to it that the little ones were taught the rudiments of learning. Even without schools, and when the children were too young to be sent to school, they were taught by their mothers and older sisters to read and write. So that in such a community, where the adults were intelligent and educated, it was impossible that the children should grow up ignorant. In all the church organizations it was the custom and the authorized method of administering the affairs of the congregation to have a school for the better training of the young; of course, the main end aimed at in all these church schools was to learn to read the Holy Scriptures and to be able to commit to memory the catechism of the church. The clergymen were often, in these early times, themselves the teachers in the schools connected with their churches, and for this purpose the Presbyterian clergymen of the central regions of New Jersey, being mostly from the best parts of Scotland and Ireland, were especially well adapted (2).

The English Quakers, who settled in West Jersey, first in Salem in 1675 and then in Burlington in 1677, made sure that a school was attached to every meetinghouse. In 1682, the Assembly of West Jersey gave to Burlington the island of Matinicunk in the Delaware River for the maintenance of a school and the education of youth. This was the earliest grant of land in New Jersey for public education (3).

The second Assembly of the Pennsylvania Quakers outlined the plan of education for Quaker children at Philadelphia in 1683. The program provided for fundamental education in reading and writing for all until age 12, for trade education, and for the levying of a fine of £5 against parents who neglected their children's education.

In East Jersey, the General Assembly passed laws in 1693 and 1695 authorizing the inhabitants in any town to elect three men to handle such school matters as selecting a schoolmaster and designating a convenient place for a school. If any one refused to pay his assessment of school tax, these laws provided that his property should be sold in sufficient amounts to pay the tax.

When East and West Jersey were united as a royal province in 1702, their population totaled about 14,000. East Jersey contributed 10,000 inhabitants, largely New Englanders, Quakers, Scotch Presbyterians, and some Dutch; West Jersey had about 4,000, for the most part Quakers, an increasing number of Scotch, and a few Swedes and Germans (4).

Among the settlers coming from Scotland, Ulster, England, and Germany in large numbers from the 1680's until the time of the Revolution were many redemptioners or indentured servants. These persons, in order to pay their passage to America, had sold their services for a term of years (frequently 7) and thus became a sort of slave for that time. Upon completion of their term of service, New Jersey redemptioners received 50 acres of land to cultivate in their own right and became free citizens. During this period, the presence of so many redemptioners made social and educational problems in the state more difficult.

The churches maintained schools in areas where they could be afforded, and some made special provisions for the poor. Changes took place in educational procedures, but there was no organized plan in operation for the education of all children and youth of the colony. The period of royal government saw little legislation in regard to education.

Several grammar schools were in operation, but there was a need for a college to train men for the ministry. The Presbyterians won approval in 1746 to establish the College of New Jersey (now Princeton), and it opened in 1747 in Elizabeth. In 1776, the Dutch Reformed Church established Queen's (now Rutgers) College.

Little attention was available for schooling in the Revolution years. Schools closed or operated intermittently. The two colleges were hard hit. Uncertainty and depression for the schools continued for many years after establishment of the national government in 1789. Politics and political change were the absorbing interest. For some three decades following adoption of the federal Constitution, New Jersey gave few indications of any serious interest in public education. There was continued action toward making sure the very poor were given some education, and there were the private schools for those who could afford them. But there was not much attention for the large proportion of children between the two extremes (5).

Most citizens were opposed to taxation for schools. They felt that schools and schooling were a responsibility of the churches, or of individuals, or of families – not the responsibility of the state.

But there were some leaders, notably James Parker of Perth Amboy, a member of the State Assembly, who recognized the need for some state support for education. Thomas Jefferson had introduced a school bill in the Virginia Legislature in 1779 providing for tax-supported free schools within a state education system, and, even though his plan was not approved at that time, it had some impact on Parker and others in New Jersey. In 1809 and again in 1813, Parker tried unsuccessfully to introduce legislation to establish a state fund for public schools. He finally succeeded in February 1817, when the Legislature created a state school fund for the support of free schools.

The fund consisted of U.S. bonds and stock held by the state in the Newark Turnpike Road, the Trenton Banking Company, and the Cumberland Bank, which at the time totaled $113,238. The interest was to be used for the benefit of schools. In 1818, the Legislature created a board of trustees for the fund consisting of the Governor and other officers of the state. The trustees sought to expand the base of revenue for the fund before attempting to put it to use. In 1824, the Legislature provided that one-tenth of all state taxes should be added annually to the fund.

During this time, with the amount in the fund considered inadequate to meet its designated purpose, the Legislature took steps to encourage municipalities not to rely solely on state funds. In 1820, New Jersey authorized its townships to raise money for public schools. In 1828, they were empowered to raise money locally for the purpose of building and repairing schoolhouses. An act passed that same year added to the school fund all the taxes received from banking, insurance, and other incorporated companies in the state.

In 1829, a dozen years after the fund was created, the Legislature finally put it to use. Annual appropriations were begun as part of the state's first comprehensive school law.

Common School Crusade

New Jersey's first attempt to legislate some kind of a state public school system stemmed from a general movement in the state that began in 1828 and became known as the Common School Crusade. The leaders of this movement, notably Professor John Maclean of the College of New Jersey, who later was to become president of the college (now Princeton), felt that establishment of a system of public schools was required if New Jersey was to overcome its apparent educational shortcomings. At this time, more than a third of New Jersey children were without schooling of any kind.

In January 1828, Maclean delivered an address before the Literary and Philosophical Society of New Jersey at Nassau Hall, Princeton, on "A School System for New Jersey." Presenting a series of recommendations for legislative action, he said that townships should be authorized to raise money to build and operate schools, with the support of state funds apportioned to the necessities of the townships. He urged that provision be made for the education of teachers.

Professor Maclean recommended establishment of a State Board of Education which would be authorized to appoint a state superintendent of schools. He also advocated examining committees for the several counties to examine all persons seeking to become teachers. He issued a plea to the Legislature to enact measures as speedily as possible to afford all youth the means of obtaining a good education.

Many of Maclean's proposals were subsequently adopted by the Legislature. Among other things, a teacher-training institution was established, of which Maclean became a trustee. A State Board of Education was created, and he became a member. Maclean's proposed state school tax also finally came to be, although not until 1871.

Professor Maclean was a key member of a committee named by the New Jersey Missionary Society in 1828 to work toward establishment of schools in destitute parts of the state. The committee appointed Rev. Robert Baird as its agent to bring educational opportunity to areas lacking it. Rev. Baird visited every county and held public meetings to set forth the advantages of a good system of common schools. He also wrote and published numerous essays on the subject (6).

Rev. Baird's efforts did much to produce a popular sentiment in favor of a system of public schools. Various organizations and agencies were working toward that objective. The numerous petitions and communications which came to the Legislature from all parts of the state were referred to a committee.

After a study, the committee issued a report stressing the importance of a well-regulated system of common school education that would permit equal opportunity for all citizens to enjoy the benefits of education. The committee found that nearly 15,000 persons over 15 years of age in New Jersey were unable to read or write and that nearly 12,000 children under 15 were deprived of the means of obtaining even the rudiments of an education. The deplorable state of education, the committee said, called for the aid of the Legislature in establishing common schools. The committee declared it was time to put the school fund to use.

Acting on the report, the 1829 Legislature passed the first comprehensive school law in New Jersey. The law appropriated $20,000 annually from the school fund, which at the time amounted to $245,204 and was producing an interest of about $23,000. The money was to be apportioned to the counties in the ratio of the state taxes paid by them. The county board of freeholders was then to apportion the money to the townships. The legislation required each township to vote an additional sum for school purposes, or otherwise state aid would be withheld. Each township was authorized to elect a school committee to designate convenient school districts, to examine and license teachers, and to arrange for creation of a board of trustees for each district. The trustees were to provide a schoolhouse and a teacher and to compile a list of all children in the district between 4 and 16.

As soon as the law was enacted, however, the foes of the common schools, led by powerful private school interests, organized a crusade in opposition (7). They succeeded in 1830 in prevailing upon the Legislature to repeal the section providing for election of township school committees. This meant that the various committee duties in operating schools could no longer be performed.

The following year, the acts of both 1829 and 1830 were repealed, and another was passed. Although the same amount of money was appropriated from the school fund as before, its use was changed markedly. Whereas the public school money apportioned to the townships, together with that raised by township tax, had been used exclusively for schools established by the township committee or district trustees, these funds could now be used for the benefit of all schools, whether public, private, or parochial. This change was made in obedience to the demands of the religious denominations in the state (8). The money was distributed among all schools in proportion to the number of children taught, thus serving to dissipate the annual apportionment. The act allowed for a local vote to determine whether the money should be apportioned in accordance with the number of indigent poor in each school, rather than the total enrollment. The act contained no provision for forming school districts or for examining and licensing teachers.

Although dismayed by the turn of events, the friends of the common schools were not discouraged and continued to fight. But several years were to pass before prejudices were overcome and the general plan of a state system of schools was finally accepted.

With increasing agitation for legislation to change the 1831 school law, Governor William Pennington declared in his message of January 1838 that public sentiment and public interest alike demanded a thorough revision of the school system. He said the system was defective in that the common schools were not giving the mass of the population a sound education. The system, he said, should be revised without delay (9).

A convention of friends of the common schools assembled in Trenton later that month and declared the school laws defective. It recommended appointment of a state superintendent of common schools. The convention named a committee to issue an address to the people. The address said, in part:

> Every free State must provide for the education of all her children. Tax yourselves for the support of common schools, and you will never be in danger of taxation from a foreign power. You will need less taxation for the support of pauperism and the punishment of crime. Look to your school houses. See that they are convenient of access; that they are comfortable; that they are neat and tasteful. Look to the teachers. See that they are taught themselves and apt to teach – men that fear God and love their country. See that they are well accommodated, well treated, and well remunerated. Respect them and they will respect themselves, and your children will respect them. Look well to the scholars. Remember, you are to grow old among them. Remember, you are to die and leave your country in their hands (10).

In response to this expressed will of the people, the Legislature in 1838 repealed the acts of 1831 and enacted a law that restored many of the features of the act of 1829. The new legislation provided that township school committees again were to be elected, townships were to be divided into school districts, and district trustees were to be elected. Also, the bill increased the annual appropriation from the school fund to $30,000, fixed the maximum of school money that could be raised by the townships at twice the amount received from the state, authorized the board of freeholders to elect boards of county examiners for teacher licenses, and raised the minimum age of children to be included in the school census from 4 to 5. A feature of the 1831 law that was retained in the new law was that authorizing certain religious organizations to draw a portion of the public funds for the support of schools under their care.

Sentiment for public education continued to increase, and the movement drew strength from the establishment of a professional organization at New Brunswick in 1843 called the Society of Teachers and Friends of Education in New Jersey. About the same time, Newark gave birth to a group known as the Newark Educational Society, and in 1845 a Society for the Improvement of Common Schools was established (11).

Feeling was widespread for complete reorganization of education and establishment of a state system comparable to those being established in other states, including a state superintendent and provision for training and certification of teachers.

In keeping with a democratic reawakening among the people and largely through the efforts of James Parker, the new Constitution of 1844 (replacing the Constitution of 1776 which was then the oldest among the states) included the assumption of responsibility by the State of New Jersey for free public schools. It declared:

> The funds for the support of free schools and all money, stock and other property which may hereafter be appropriated for that purpose or received into the treasury under the provision of any law hereafter passed to augment the said fund shall be securely invested and remain a perpetual fund, and the income thereof, except so much as it may be judged expedient to apply to an increase of the capital, shall be annually appropriated to the support of public schools, for the equal benefit of all the people of the state; and it shall not be competent for the legislature to borrow, appropriate or use the said fund or any part thereof, for any other purpose under any pretense whatever (12).

This provision, however, could hardly be realized until attendance at public schools was made free by prohibiting tuition charges and by making arrangements for state and local financial support, as the Legislature of New Jersey did in 1871. Schools may have been free in theory under the 1844 constitutional provision, but they seldom were in practice; it was the custom to charge tuition for public schools as well as for private schools. Townships might refuse to raise money for schools, or they could raise a minimum of twice the amount received from the state school fund. State money was returned to the counties and townships on the basis of taxes paid – in other words, on the basis of wealth, not on the basis of the number of children to be educated. Consequently, the poorer sections of New Jersey received little state money, and at the same time there was little or no money raised by taxation for schools in these townships. Further, parents in these sections could hardly afford to pay tuition for the schooling of their children. The result was that schools in some districts remained closed or were open but for a short time – 2 or 3 months during the year (13).

Governor Daniel Haines in his legislative message of 1845 urged revision of the school law, declaring that it was a great shame that New Jersey, without any state debt, should suffer such neglect in the means and blessings of common school education. Later that year, the Legislature authorized the trustees of the school fund to appoint a superintendent of public schools. His authority was limited to the Counties of Essex and Passaic, but other counties wanting to come under his supervision could do so through their boards of freeholders. In April 1846, this authorization was superseded by a comprehensive law extending the jurisdiction of the superintendent over the whole state and designating the office as state superintendent of public schools, to be named by the school fund trustees.

The act of 1846 made obligatory the licensing of teachers, either by the county examiners or by the township superintendent. No teacher was entitled to a salary unless he possessed a certificate. Under the act, the townships were required to raise school money in an amount at least equal to that received from the state, and not greater than twice such amount. The townships were authorized to elect town school superintendents to perform the duties formerly assigned to the township school committees. These officers were allowed $1 a day for their services. The town superintendents were required to visit schools at least once every quarter, to examine and license teachers, to hold school moneys, to apportion and pay out the same, and to make an annual report to the state superintendent.

Filling the Office

The year 1846 saw the appointment of New Jersey's first state superintendent, Dr. Theodore F. King, a physician intensely interested in public education. In his first report as state superintendent, he said that the general feeling in regard to the common schools was dull and dormant and needed awakening. Dr. King traveled widely throughout the state and visited many schoolhouses. Although he found many shortcomings, which he duly reported, the superintendent put the greatest emphasis on the good facilities he found, citing these as examples to foster the spirit of improvement he was determined to lead. The doctor served 6 years in the job and in that time did much to focus attention on the need to upgrade the teaching profession. He urged formation of teacher associations and establishment of a training school for teachers. The first teachers institute was held in Somerville in June 1849.

Prompted by Superintendent King, Governor George Fort in his inaugural address in 1851 emphasized the need for a more complete system of free public schools. The Legislature of that year responded by increasing the state appropriation from the school fund to $40,000 and appropriating an additional sum of $40,000 out of the state treasury, making the annual school appropriation

$80,000. This act changed the basis of apportionment of the state appropriation. It was made to the counties in the ratio of population and to the townships in the ratio of the school census. No longer could the wealthy sections of the state receive the greater portion of state aid. The age range of schoolchildren was changed to 5 through 18. The maximum amount of school money that could be raised by the townships was set at $3 per child. The public money was to be used, as long as it lasted, in maintaining free schools. The remaining portion of the year, the schools were to be supported by tuition fees.

In 1852, the school fund trustees elected Dr. John H. Phillips state superintendent of public schools. Like his predecessor, he was a physician concerned with public education. In October 1853, Dr. Phillips issued a call for an educational convention in Trenton. The convention urged liberal state appropriations for education in the state, recommended formation of associations of friends of education, and advocated establishment of an educational journal in New Jersey to spread information among the people and to promote in various ways the cause of common school education (14).

The teachers at the convention called for a meeting to organize a state teachers assocation. December 28, 1853, was the date decided upon for this meeting, and on that day in New Brunswick's Bayard Street School, the organization now known as the New Jersey Education Association was formed. The association named its first state agent, Dr. Christopher Columbus Hoagland, the following year; like Dr. King and Dr. Phillips, this man was a physician who had abandoned the medical practice to become an educator. The association was to have a major role in advancing public education in the succeeding century by securing significant legislation affecting operation of the schools and by bolstering the teaching profession and the welfare of its members.

In 1854, teachers institutes were first established by law. The state appropriated $100 for each institute of not less than 40 teachers of common schools, in any county or in two or more adjoining counties of the state, who desired to assemble for that purpose for not less than 5 working days. The organization of any such institute, its place of meeting, and its general management were to be under the control and direction of the state superintendent.

Although educators in New Jersey were among the first in the country to advocate establishment of schools for the professional training of teachers in the 1820's, it was not until 1855 that one was actually established. By that time, four other states had founded normal schools. The legislation for the establishment and support of a normal school in New Jersey appropriated $10,000 for its support and provided for a board of trustees to locate and operate a state normal school. State Superintendent Phillips, by virtue of his position, became a member and secretary of the board. Choosing among several site offers, the board selected Trenton. The school opened with 15 students in a temporary building in October 1855.

The close working relationship between the state superintendent's office and the State Teachers Association in the early years was shown in 1860 when the school fund trustees elected the association president, Frederick William Ricord, as state superintendent. Ricord had conducted a private school in Newark from 1845 to 1847, was a member of the Newark Board of Education from 1852 to 1869, and was president of the teachers association in 1860 when he became superintendent. He proved to be a superintendent who liked to observe classroom work first-hand, as shown in this report he made in 1863:

> While riding on official business through a well-settled and beautiful country district, I stopped my horse in front of a neat and newly built school house, prompted by a desire to see if matters within corresponded with appearances without. The teacher politely offered me a seat but proceeded with an arithmetic lesson. A small urchin seated at the end of one of the forms commenced the old fashioned recreation of snapping flies with a bit of whalebone. The amusement did not, to be sure, occasion much disturbance, but it was a breach of decorum, to say nothing about the feeling of the flies. The teacher, who was at the moment standing in the middle aisle making some explanations to the class, moved slowly toward the young Negro, and without changing her voice, or ceasing to speak, raised him gently from his seat by the aid of one of his ears, and still continuing her explanations to the class, opened a closet, thrust him in, buttoned the door, and returned as if nothing had happened (15).

In 1864, the school fund trustees named Caleb M. Harrison state superintendent. A movement was under way among education leaders in the state and members of the Legislature to create a State Board of Education. Commenting on the proposal in 1865, Harrison said: "When New Jersey enacts that the interests of public instruction shall be placed in the hands of a State Board of Education, we may confidently look forward to the early dawn of a brighter era in our educational history" (16).

A Functioning System

The years 1866 and 1867 were active ones for education legislation in New Jersey, effecting significant changes in the administration of public education. Enabling legislation was enacted early in 1866 to create the first State Board of Education. The board consisted of the trustees of the school fund and the trustees of the normal school.

At its first meeting, in March 1866, the board elected 29-year-old Ellis A. Apgar as state superintendent at an annual salary of $3,000. A former professor of mathematics at Trenton State Normal School, he was widely known for his ability as an educator and for his intense interest in improving public education.

Near the end of the 1866 session of the Legislature, the section of the school law providing for distribution of a portion of the public money to schools under the management and control of religious denominations was repealed, and all the school moneys have since been reserved for the exclusive support of public schools (17).

In his first year as superintendent, Apgar realized that there was a need for more comprehensive legislation. As it was, his duties were limited, there were no powers spelled out for the board, and no public system was defined. He felt that the state school system should be better organized, with county school superintendencies established to afford liaison between the municipalities and his department. He long had felt that the weak feature of the state school system was its supervision by town superintendents. There were 230 town superintendents in 1866. They could not be brought together for consultation or instruction, nor could any uniformity in the performance of their duties or in the educational work of the state be secured by correspondence. Apgar also considered a number of these men incompetent.

In 1866, he recommended a change in this cumbersome system, stating his argument as follows:

> Let the State secure the constant services of 21 active, intelligent and right-principled men to look after and superintend the education of her children, and no one acquainted with the importance of proper school supervision can doubt the happy results. The provisions of the law and the instructions of the State Board of Education can be carried out; harmony of action on the part of all school officers can be secured; the standard of qualification of the teacher's profession will be elevated; county institutes will be better organized and better attended; statistics will be more readily and accurately reported; the provisions of the school law can be made known and explained to school officers and patrons; trustees and teachers will be made familiar with their duties and required to make accurate school reports; public attention will be aroused to the importance of encouraging and sustaining the educational enterprises of the day; the school finances of the State will be carefully looked after and faithfully reported; valuable suggestions occurring to any one in the performance of his duties will be made known to the rest; and unity of design and harmony of action will be secured by the facility with which they can meet and consult each other's views (18).

A bill embodying this change was submitted and made part of "An Act To Establish a System of Public Instruction" enacted by the 1867 Legislature in March 1867, to be effective immediately. The act included several revisions in the 1866 law, mainly toward enlarging the powers and duties of the State Board of Education. The board was given the authority to appoint county superintendents whose yearly salaries were to be 10¢ per child in the county between 5 and 18, provided the salary be not less than $500.

The 1867 legislation abolished the office of township superintendent, but the townships were required to raise by tax every year, in addition to the amount apportioned to their use, an amount of money not less than $2 nor more than $4 for every child in the township between the ages of 5 and 18. City districts were retained. The school districts of the townships under the supervision of the new school official for the county received much more definite and specific control through their school trustees. The state board was required to make rules and regulations for carrying out the provisions of the school laws and for examining and licensing teachers. It also was given authority to hear and decide appeals from decisions of the state superintendent.

The law of 1867 provided for state, county, and city boards of examiners. Without proper certification, teachers could not receive salaries. The legislation authorized the county superintendent to supervise the public schools of his county, with the exception of cities having a city superintendent of schools. The county superintendent heard all controversies arising under the school laws, with the provision that appeals from his decision could be made to the state superintendent.

The law of 1867 also created the State Association of School Superintendents for county and city superintendents, the president to be the state superintendent; increased state appropriations from $80,000 to $100,000 annually ($60,000 from the revenue of the state and $40,000 from the income of the school fund); specified that no school district could receive any part of state aid if that district did not maintain a public school for at least 5 months; and forbade corporal punishment in all public schools.

State Superintendent Apgar in his report for 1869 praised the soundness of the 1867 law but noted two defects: It did not make the public schools truly free, and it did not ensure adequate financial support. He rallied public opinion to his plea for necessary revisions, and in 1871 the Legislature enacted "An Act To Make Free the Public Schools of the State." The act contained the features suggested by the superintendent and made all the public schools of the state entirely free. The uncertain township tax was replaced by a uniform state school tax of 2 mills per $1 assessed valuation. The public schools were to be in session 9 months each year. If the money for schools from state and other sources was not sufficient to maintain the schools for 9 months in any township, then that township was to levy a tax to meet the deficiency. School trustees were prohibited from charging tuition fees.

In 1874, New Jersey passed its first compulsory school attendance act, requiring children between 8 and 13 to attend some school for at least 12 weeks in the year, including 6 consecutive weeks. Securing compulsory attendance had been one of Apgar's initial proposals when he took office. Reports from county superintendents showed that, despite increasing enrollment, a substantial percentage of children of school age was not enrolled. The 1874 law provided for an annual census in July to determine the number of absentee children (19).

In 1876, the state ratified amendments to its constitution barring appropriation of state money for the use of any society, association, or corporation whatever and mandating the Legislature to provide for the maintenance and support of a thorough and efficient system of free public schools for the instruction of all children between 5 and 18.

Thus, by 1876, Ellis A. Apgar saw virtually all his basic concepts of the needs of education embodied into law. These concepts have stood the test of time, and he has been called "the man who may rightfully be considered as the father of the state system of education in New Jersey" (20). In his 20 years as New Jersey's state superintendent, Apgar was the leader in planning and carrying out the revamping of education in New Jersey and the establishment of the foundation of a system that has remained fundamentally unchanged.

Apgar was succeeded by Edwin O. Chapman, who had compiled a varied yet impressive record as teacher, high school principal, colonel in the Union army, superintendent of Jersey City schools, member of the Jersey City Board of Education, member of the State Assembly, and an editor with the American News Company.

Chapman was appointed state superintendent by the State Board of Education in March 1885. He had no way of knowing that before the end of his service as chief state school officer, in 1892, he would become involved in one of the most unusual and intriguing chapters in New Jersey's education history. It was midway in Chapman's service that, as the result of a political hassle, the power of appointing the state superintendent was shifted from the Board of Education to the Governor, where it has remained ever since.

When Chapman's 3-year term expired in March 1888, the board appointed Charles W. Fuller to replace him. This action was somewhat unusual because, at the time, Fuller was a Republican leader in the assembly and the majority of board members were Democratic. Furthermore, Fuller, a lawyer, had had no experience as a working schoolman, although he had served on the Bayonne school board and the state board itself. His appointment was made possible because a Democratic member of the board agreed to support Fuller in the hope the Republican-dominated Legislature would then confirm his reappointment as a judge.

As it turned out, the judge was not reappointed, but Fuller had gained the superintendent's chair. He was unseated, however, after serving less than a year, as soon as the Democrats gained control of the Legislature in 1889. They decided the quickest way to oust Fuller would be to enact legislation giving the Governor power to appoint the superintendent, effective immediately. The bill passed in the State Senate on February 11 and in the assembly on February 13. Democratic Governor Robert S. Green signed it on February 14. The Governor rounded out the legislation annulling Fuller's appointment by nominating Chapman to a 3-year term on February 20. The Senate confirmed Chapman on February 28, and he returned to work for a second term. The Democratic newspapers of the day considered it a triumph of justice, but the Republican newspapers thought the removal of Fuller in this fashion was a dastardly deed (21).

In 1892, the Governor named Addison B. Poland, who had been superintendent of schools in Jersey City and president of the State Teachers Association, as state superintendent. In that year, the State Normal School and the School for the Deaf were placed under the jurisdiction of the State Board of Education.

The Township Act of 1894 consolidated all the small districts into one district with a board of education for the township; township boundaries were also to be the district boundaries. The act was followed by the appointment of supervising principals in many townships. Many small districts previously had not had such principal positions. City and borough districts were not changed by the act.

As a direct result of the 1894 act, the number of school districts in the state fell sharply from 1,408 in the 1893-94 school year to 374 in the fall of 1894. Children who lived in remote areas could be transported to and from school at public expense, with the necessary funds to be raised by a special tax the school districts were authorized to impose.

The State Board of Education was reorganized in 1894 to include two members from each congressional district. Members were to be appointed by the Governor for 5-year terms.

The Free Textbook Act, passed in 1894, provided free textbooks to all pupils enrolled in public schools.

High schools came late in New Jersey partly because of the opposition of private academies and partly because of the long period consumed in the establishment of the common schools. There was a well-established belief, held chiefly by an ultraconservative group, that more advanced education was a privilege of the "better class" and should not be extended to the children of the masses. This element was critical of the idea advanced by the progressives that public high schools should be expanded throughout the state. A principal obstacle to high schools appeared when the taxpayer realized that he was required to pay taxes for the support of the common schools and also was compelled to provide funds for the maintenance of a high school, to which he strenuously objected. It was not until 1895 that legislation was enacted establishing high schools in the larger counties. This meant that New Jersey, despite its geographic location, its resources, and its wealth, was late in adopting a complete system of education (22).

As the nineteenth century drew to a close, New Jersey had accepted its responsibility for a free public school system, had become really conscious of its educational problems, and was making a praiseworthy effort to solve them.

TWENTIETH-CENTURY SPURT

The dawning of the twentieth century seemed to awaken a new spirit in New Jersey to move more rapidly and more decisively to strengthen and upgrade the state system of public education. The Legislature enacted measures in 1900 to ensure adequate supervision, more modern facilities, and a sounder structure.

Having accepted its constitutional mandate to provide free public schools for all children between 5 and 18, New Jersey decided in 1900 to go even further. Schools were made free for children between 7 and 12, instead of between 8 and 13, and no child under 15 could be employed unless he had attended some public or private school within the preceding 12 months.

The state passed legislation making the kindergarten an integral part of the public school system in March 1900, and many districts wasted little time in forming such classes.

In his report for the year 1900-1901, Charles J. Baxter, who had become state superintendent in 1896, stated that the number of children going into kindergarten classes during the year was a substantial 15,006. This was the first official record of the kindergarten enrollment in New Jersey schools. Baxter said in his report:

> Other things being equal, pupils who have had the advantages of kindergarten invariably outstrip their classmates in the higher grades who have not had such training. When the kindergarten and the high school shall become conveniently available to every child in the State and the kindergarten spirit shall pervade all school work, our school system will then make a much closer approach to present ideals. Still higher ideals then will arise and the struggle toward the genuinely ideal will ever continue (23).

A most significant statistic concerning education in New Jersey at the turn of the century was that in 1901 there was a decrease of 63 in the total number of private schools compared with 1900. This reflected the growth of the public system. In that same year, 30 new public schools were built and 69 public schools enlarged. As Baxter commented in his report,

> This is the very natural result of the increased efficiency of our public schools. . . . The public school should be so well-equipped, its instruction so excellent, its moral tone so pronounced, and its environment so attractive that no child, save for exceptional reasons, will be sent elsewhere (24).

There were 336,432 pupils enrolled in New Jersey public schools in the 1900-1901 year, and the size of the average class was 44 pupils, with some classes up to 50 and 60. In commenting on the size, Baxter was most pleased that it had gone down from the figure of 46 in the previous year. He said:

> This is a most encouraging advance on right lines. No teacher should be given more than 40 pupils and he could accomplish far more for the community and the State if not required to teach more than 30. The greater the number of pupils placed under the instruction of one person, the greater the amount of force expended in maintaining order and the less his teaching power; also the greater the tendency to make use of formal and cumbersome school machinery which consumes valuable time in its operation and the more rare the opportunity to assist and encourage the individual pupil. Boards of Education that permit an enrollment of 50 or 60 pupils in one classroom really do economize in the expenditure of school funds, but, in so doing, are reprehensively wasteful of far greater values – the teacher's health and vitality and the pupil's most precious years (25).

The average annual salary of teachers in 1900-1901 was $543.62. The state school tax for that year was $2,317,825, based on $5 for each of the 457,479 school-age (between 5 and 18) children reported in the census. Average daily attendance was 207,947, less than half the number of eligible children counted in the census. Added to the state school tax for apportionment among the counties, also on the basis of the census, was the sum of $200,000 from the state school fund. All of the 389 school districts operating at the beginning of the 1900-1901 school year voted a school tax to supplement the state aid.

Under legislation enacted in 1900, local boards of education were authorized to appoint supervising principals, and, to encourage their use, any district employing a superintendent or a supervising principal full time was to receive a state appropriation of $600.

Other legislation in 1900 required that the state supervise schoolhouse planning, construction, and repair. County superintendents were delegated the responsibility of noting the condition of school buildings and sites and advising boards of education regarding school construction, heating, ventilating, and lighting.

In summing up the condition of public education at the time, Baxter declared in his report for the year 1900-1901:

> The first year of the new century finds New Jersey ably maintaining her educational rank among the

sisterhood of states. Our most liberal, intelligent and progressive citizens were never so interested in the public schools, never so deeply impressed with their importance to the Commonwealth, and never so helpful in the effort to establish a correct educational sentiment throughout the State. A higher standard of qualification and better salaries for our teachers, more thorough and effective instruction, more advanced and rational courses of study, and more adequate and sanitary school accommodations are the demands of the times, and to these the people are ably and generously responding. Progress is the watchword (26).

During the early years of the twentieth century, Charles J. Baxter continued to press for the legislation he felt was needed to widen the benefits of an education program to reach a greater proportion of the population and to ensure better teacher salaries.

Legislation enacted in 1903 authorized school boards to establish kindergartens for children between 4 and 7, authorized evening schools for persons over 12, set up the first statewide minimum salary schedule for teachers and administrators (the teacher minimum was $408 and the maximum ranged from $1,200 for females and $2,400 for males), required teachers to keep school registers, authorized business managers for city school districts and established the Teachers Retirement Fund

The State Board of Education in 1904 created the state inspector of high schools office and appointed Louis Bevier to the post. During the 5 years he was inspector, the number of approved high schools increased from 67 to 133, and the enrollment in public schools increased more than 50 percent and the number of teachers more than 60 percent. After the state, in 1907, began to reimburse districts without high schools 75 percent of the transportation costs for pupils attending high schools outside these districts, the number of such pupils increased from 1,817 that year to 3,151 in 1909. From 1904 to 1909, the amount of money expended for high schools in New Jersey was more than doubled. Dr. Bevier worked for agricultural high schools in rural communities and manual training high schools in cities and towns.

New Jersey passed its first teachers tenure of service act in 1909. This gave tenure to teachers, principals, and supervising principals completing three years of "good behavior and efficiency" in a district. The legislation resulted from continuing efforts by the State Department of Education and the teachers association to strengthen the professions and thereby benefit education generally. Salaries were improving. Teachers were staying on the job longer; the average teaching experience increased from 4 years in 1896 to 9 years in 1908. Teachers were better trained; in 1910, two-thirds of the teachers in the public schools were graduates of either normal schools, city training schools, or colleges (27).

REORGANIZATION OF 1911

A movement to reorganize the State Department of Education took shape between 1907 and 1909. Much legislation involving the operation of the public schools had been enacted since establishment of the state system in 1867. Enrollment had increased fourfold in that period, compared with a population increase of hardly threefold. Various education groups and social organizations began to express concern that the state department as it was then constituted lacked sufficient size and power to direct the continued expansion of educational services in the state. The department was little more than a business office for gathering data and compiling reports. There was no adequate machinery by which the state superintendent could exercise a leadership role in giving direction to efficient teaching and efficient school organization. The groups seeking a reorganization of the department prevailed upon state legislative leaders to set the legal wheels in motion (28).

With the support of Woodrow Wilson, then Governor of New Jersey, a resolution was adopted by the State Senate in April 1909, authorizing its president to name a committee of three Senators, together with the members of the State Board of Education, to study the education system and make recommendations.

The Senate directed the committee to investigate the methods and practices, expenses and disbursements of the free public schools of the state and to determine what, if any, amendments should be made to the present school laws for the purpose of securing greater economy in school expenses without decreasing the efficiency of the public school system.

In March 1911, nearly 2 years after the committee had been named, the Senate received the report on the educational survey. The report recommended a reorganization of the Department of Education, including establishment of a new Board of Education and new machinery for the operation of schools, with stronger state supervision and control. The major proposals were enacted by the Legislature in April 1911, to become effective in July of that year.

The reorganization abolished the State Board of Education with its 20 members and replaced it by a board with 8 members. The board was authorized to appoint an inspector of buildings who was to visit the schools and make reports, and an inspector of accounts to examine the accounts of the local school districts. The board also was to prescribe a compulsory, uniform, and simple bookkeeping system for districts.

The state superintendent of public instruction's office was abolished and replaced by that of commissioner of education to be appointed by the Governor for a term of 5 years. The reorganization plan authorized the commissioner to appoint four assistant commissioners, with the advice and consent of the board. The assistants were designated specifically to supervise secondary education, elementary education, and industrial education, respectively, and to hear controversies and disputes.

Authority vested in the commissioner also included the prescribing of minimum examinations throughout the state for graduation from grammar schools and for admission to high schools, and of a minimum course of study for the elementary schools and for the high schools.

The reorganization also provided for county superintendents to be appointed by the commissioner for terms of 3 years and required them to hold the highest teacher certificate issued in New Jersy. It further established special classes for the blind and the deaf and also for pupils 3 years or more below the normal, who were to be placed in classes of between 10 and 15 pupils.

The teacher-licensing system was changed to a single state system, thereby doing away with some 22 standards for the certification of teachers and replacing them with a single state standard. The state established four forms of certificates: provisional, limited, permanent, and special.

New legislation specified that plans and specifications for school building construction were to be submitted to the state board for approval, instead of only for suggestions and criticisms as in previous legislation.

In 1911, Governor Woodrow Wilson appointed Calvin N. Kendall as the new commissioner of education.

Former Indianapolis school superintendent, Mr. Kendall organized the department in three divisions—educational, law, and business—and assigned his assistants to definite positions within the three divisions, at the same time freeing himself of detailed work in order that he might have time as "the general advisory and supervisory officer of the state educational system." The commissioner and his assistants, working with the county superintendents, did much field work inspecting the public schools in various sections of the state (rural and urban) and talking with teachers and others employed in the schools, with members of boards of education, and with other residents of the school districts. Thus were Kendall and his assistants not only to obtain firsthand information about school conditions and school support, but also to assist directly in furthering remedial or constructive measures for the schools and in strengthening public support (29).

The year 1913 witnessed significant revisions of New Jersey's educational statutes. A compulsory school attendance act passed that year required all children ages 7 through 15 to attend school (30). County superintendents were made direct field representatives of the state department and required to devote full time to their duties. While some of their powers were transferred to assistant commissioners of education, the duties of the county superintendents in general administration and in supervision were greatly increased. The requirement that their appointment be approved by county boards of freeholders was eliminated.

The Legislature authorized establishment of vocational schools at the local and county levels. The law provided that, subject to the approval of the commissioner and state board, the board of any district, or two or more districts, might establish and maintain industrial, agricultural, and household arts schools. Each such school was to receive a $10,000 annual state appropriation. Response to the new legislation was slow at first. The act encouraged some big-city high schools to add vocational programs, but no statewide rush developed to give vocational education to the state's children. One result of the act was the growth of agriculture and home economics courses at high schools in rural areas.

Vocational education programs grew markedly with the passage by Congress in 1917 of the Smith-Hughes Act to promote vocational, agricultural, and industrial education. The act made federal aid available for the salaries of teachers, supervisors, and directors and for the training of teachers of vocational subjects. New Jersey was one of the first states to accept the federal funds. The allotment for New Jersey in 1918 was $42,550, but this amount increased annually until it reached $200,000 in 1926 and succeeding years. The act provided for distribution of the federal funds through the state department.

Throughout Kendall's occupation of the chief state school position (1911-21), he devoted much of his time and energy to bolstering the quality of instruction in the schools of New Jersey—particularly in the rural areas—and in boosting the image of the county and local school administrators.

In 1915, he observed:

> The public does not sufficiently realize how much the efficiency of a system of schools depends upon the character of the leadership. A high-minded, courageous, industrious, intelligent, trained superintendent of schools is a great educational asset. Nor does the public realize the differences that exist in different systems of schools in the same state and in different schools of the same city. Why these differences? They are due to the quality of the work of the superintendent and the supervising principals in charge of the respective systems and schools (31).

In that year, the state established a certificate for supervising principal requiring 1 year of experience as principal or supervisor and a passing mark on examinations in school organization and school law.

The role of the state department in providing help and advice to upgrade the effectiveness of teaching and the quality of education generally in the rural areas gained considerable strength in 1916 when county superintendents were authorized by legislation to appoint helping teachers. The act was passed on recommendation of the state department after a year's successful experiment involving the use of a teacher to assist in supervision of the rural schools in Hunterdon County.

The helping teachers quickly proved the value of the legislation by the assistance they gave in the numerous one- and two-room schools that existed throughout the state. At the time, New Jersey was encouraging consolidation of the small schools into larger units to enable more effective instruction and to provide additional services. An important influence was the assumption by the state of 75 percent of the expenditures for the transportation of pupils to approved public schools outside the home district and, in addition, a portion of the tuition charges.

The country's involvement in World War I had a distinct impact on New Jersey schools. The Legislature in 1917 directed that a course in physical training be taken by all pupils, excepting kindergartners, in the public schools. The poor physical condition of many young men who were called for military service at the time of this war was largely responsible for this law (32). In 1918, an act directed that each high school offer a course in community civics and a course in problems of American democracy. In 1919, the Legislature mandated a course for elementary grades in geography, history, and civics of New Jersey. Under these acts, the required courses were to be prepared by the Department of Education, which had the effect of strengthening the department's interest and voice in curriculum developments in the schools.

As a result of the increased attention from the state department, improvements were going ahead rapidly both in school facilities and in instructional programs. Courses in music, painting, shop and craft work, sewing, and cooking were being added to the curriculums in most high schools. And auditoriums, libraries, science laboratories, and gymnasiums were found in many high schools. The state was preparing and distributing guides for elementary school programs.

The upsurge in education in the state gained national recognition. In 1919, the Russell Sage Foundation ranked the schools of New Jersey fourth in efficiency of all the states of the Union, first among the states east of the Mississippi (33).

During this period, changes also were taking place in arrangement of grades. The New Jersey commissioner and his assistants had spoken out for the 6-year high school, or some modification of it, as early as 1912. Some districts by then already were combining the seventh, eighth, and ninth grades into separate schools. By 1925, junior high schools had been established in many cities. The junior high movement was accompanied by a greater attention in the schools to individual differences, to music, art, literature, leisure time activities, manual arts, and a better understanding of occupational life in industry, agriculture, commerce, and the home.

With the expansion of the public school system, the need for additional teachers was becoming all-important. Two state normal schools were in operation–Trenton and Montclair (the latter established in 1908)–when Commissioner Kendall in 1912 recommended that training be provided for teachers in service and that at least two additional state normal schools be established.

The majority of New Jersey's teachers at that time was being supplied from normal schools outside the state. In 1913, the Newark Normal School, built by the City of Newark, was taken over by the state. The Legislature of 1913 appropriated $14,000 for summer schools for the training of teachers. Courses for in-service teachers sprang up at Rutgers, where the education courses were directed by Charles H. Elliott from 1915 until he became state commissioner of education in 1927.

In 1923, Glassboro State Normal School was established, and Paterson City Normal School became a state normal school. Jersey City Normal School joined the ranks in 1929. These six normal schools–Trenton, Montclair, Newark, Glassboro, Paterson, and Jersey City–subsequently became state teachers colleges. In 1958, the word *teachers* was dropped as the schools began to develop into multipurpose institutions. They remain today as New Jersey's six state colleges. The six normal schools had been under the direct control of the State Board of Education until 1926 when the Legislature vested control and management in the commissioner.

Commissioner Kendall was succeeded in 1921 by John Enright, who had enjoyed a highly varied career as a teacher, county superintendent, president of the State Teachers Association, and assistant commissioner in charge of controversies and disputes. Enright served 4 years as commissioner and was followed by two Rutgers professors, John H. Logan (1925-27) and Charles H. Elliott (1927-43).

Until 1929, the general control and management of public education in New Jersey–elementary, secondary, and higher education–were vested in the State Board of Education. Then the Legislature created the State Board of Regents consisting of eight members appointed by the Governor. Its duties were to determine the state's needs regarding higher education and also to exercise custody over existing state property and facilities for higher education. Higher education then was lagging in facilities and financial support. (It should be recalled that from the time of the early settlers, a considerable proportion of New Jersey's college students attended institutions outside the state. The greater proportion of the state's population for many years lived in what might be called for all practical purposes the suburbs of New York City and Philadelphia and became accustomed to the advantages of higher education available there.)

In response to a growing demand, the Legislature in 1929 permitted the operation of school cafeterias. In 1931, school boards were authorized to establish kindergartens for children between 4 and 5 and required to establish kindergartens for children between 5 and 6.

The Depression brought severe problems in financing the schools. Teachers were released, class sizes increased, appropriations curtailed, the yearly supply of textbooks reduced almost to the vanishing point, the annual increment unpaid, special services eliminated, and teachers asked to accept a 10-percent reduction in salary. Everywhere was heard the cry of more economy until, in numerous instances, education was reduced to a mere skeleton (34).

Economic conditions were such that many worthy youth were denied the opportunity of higher education. To solve this problem, eight emergency junior colleges were organized during 1933 and 1934, with approval of the State Board of Education. These institutions had the dual purpose of preparing for advanced standing in college, if and when the family economic conditions improved, and of providing a terminal course. Federal relief aid was secured to reduce the costs of operation of these colleges, which operated in high school buildings from 4 to 10 p.m. The teaching staff consisted of college professors who, because of retrenchments in many colleges due to decreased enrollment, were willing to accept a position which barely provided necessary living expenses. The Legislature created a supervisory board for the junior colleges, and a staff member of the state department was appointed to work with the board. Most of these junior colleges were discontinued at the close of the Depression (35).

Enrollment in secondary and vocational schools increased greatly during the Depression. Federal funds were made available for new structures and additions, as well as for adult day and evening classes under the direction of the public school authorities. With municipal financial resources hard hit, a state public school fund was created in 1935 for the support of New Jersey's public schools and the equalization of educational opportunity. The state established a foundation program allotting a minimum aid to each district of $13 per elementary pupil and $22 per high school pupil and equalization aid of the excess of the actual cost over a 4.75-mill local tax. The total state aid was to be not less than $57 per elementary pupil or $98 per high school pupil. The money for this fund was to come from the railroad property tax, income from the state school fund, interest on the federal surplus revenue fund established in 1837, and other funds to be appropriated for the public schools by the Legislature.

Between 1911 and 1944, public education in New Jersey changed considerably in scope, content, and procedure. Some of the subjects and activities prescribed by law for the public schools of the state were physiology and hygiene (including special attention to the nature and effects of alcoholic drinks and narcotics), geography, history, and civics for advanced grades or intermediate schools; problems in American democracy for senior high school grades; and certain instruction in fire and accident prevention, and physical training (36).

There were periods of uncertainty and drifting when it seemed that the people of New Jersey were very doubtful about assuming responsibility for public education. The state was very late in assuming its full responsibility for free public schools. But it managed to make provisions for state and local boards and officers to supervise and direct a changing and frequently expanding education program (37).

The New Jersey population was changing from mostly rural to mostly urban. This had great influence on the nature of the curriculum in the schools, especially toward expansion of vocational offerings.

CONSOLIDATION OF 1945

New Jersey created a new State Department of Education in 1945 through the enactment of legislation consolidating and reorganizing numerous boards and agencies whose functions concerned the educational and cultural services of the state. The movement leading to the reorganization had started early in 1944 with conferences among the State Board of Education, the State Board of Regents, and Commissioner John H. Bosshart (38). The regents for a number of years had urged that their board be abolished and its duties in higher education transferred to the State Board of Education to achieve coordination of all public education in New Jersey under a single agency.

In February 1944, the commissioner and the two state boards sent a joint statement urging consolidation to the Commission on State Administrative Reorganization, headed by Charles R. Erdman, Jr. The commission concurred in the move, and bills designed to consolidate all the numerous educational and cultural services of the state were introduced in the 1944 session of the Legislature. The consolidation was planned to bring together—in addition to the Board of Education, the Board of Regents, and the commissioner of education—the Department of Public Instruction, the State Library, the Public Library Commission, and the State Museum into a single State Department of Education and to designate Rutgers University as the State University of New Jersey. The bills were widely studied by the people of the state, and 82 interested groups approved them in principle.

The 1945 Legislature saw the reintroduction and passage of the consolidation bills. The acts abolished the State Board of Education, which had 10 members (39), replacing it with a 12-member board to be appointed by the Governor for terms of 6 years instead of 8 years as previously. The Board of Regents was abolished and its functions transferred to the State Board of Education with expanded responsibilities in the field of higher education. The commissioner was directed to appoint a sixth assistant commissioner as supervisor of higher education. The State Board of Education fell heir to the State Library and the State Museum, which were made separate divisions in the department.

The 1945 bills also created a division against discrimination in the department to enforce compliance with laws intended to eliminate discrimination because of race, color, creed, or national origin (40). Rutgers University was designated as the State University of New Jersey, recognizing the historic relationship between Rutgers and the state. The legislation empowered the state to approve appropriations and thereby, in effect, to contract with the university for educational services.

The 1945 reorganization directed the commissioner to appoint directors, inspectors, and assistants for inspection of buildings and accounts, research, supervision of health education, issuance of academic qualifying certificates, supervision of adult education, supervision of teacher training, and supervision of special classes for subnormal, blind, deaf, and physically handicapped children; and such other services as the State Board of Education may deem necessary.

The reorganization strengthened the Department of Education's ability to face demands being made on the schools as a result of World War II. There were problems in providing facilities and establishing programs for returning servicemen and in meeting public pressure for curriculum changes to keep pace with scientific developments and social and economic conditions. The department coordinated the formation of special school programs for veterans. In the 1946-47 school year, New Jersey secondary schools cared for more than 14,000 veterans. This number was in addition to the more than 7,000 veterans in apprentice and on-the-job training programs who were given related instruction in vocational programs. The number of community adult schools in New Jersey tripled in 3 years, rising from 24 in 1945-46 to 75 in 1947-48.

Commissioner Bosshart noted in his report for the 1948-49 year that the concept of the educational responsibility of the state was expanding. Opportunities for adult education, requested and financed largely by the adults themselves, were being fostered by the department. Plans for the licensing of correspondence schools, to be required by law after July 1, 1950, aimed at the improvement of service available from those schools. More than 300 private nursery, child care, and prekindergarten schools had been licensed under the supervision of the department, ensuring safe, sanitary housing and education adjusted to the children's needs.

Early in the summer of 1949, the State Departments of Education and Conservation jointly established a School of Conservation for Teachers, whose purpose was to help teachers and other community leaders understand that conservation of human and material resources was a most urgent social and economic problem. The conservation school stressed that soil erosion, forest fires, lessening of the water supply, waste of minerals, and destruction of wild life were endangering society's future. The school was established in Stokes State Forest in northwestern New Jersey, where it has operated ever since.

John H. Bosshart continually spoke out on the importance of providing "appropriate" education for all the people, in the best interest of both the individual and the state. In his annual report for 1949-50, he said:

> Education has two basic functions. The first is to serve the needs and interests of the society which establishes and supports it. The second, without which the first cannot satisfactorily be achieved, is to provide, for the individual, growth opportunities appropriate to his particular abilities, needs, interests and aspirations. When an individual obtains an education appropriate to him, to an immeasurable extent, the welfare of the State is enhanced. The state that contains a people who individually have had their worthwhile potentialities developed to the highest possible extent can rightfully classify its people as a limitless resource. Its citizens will be varied in the contributions they can render. They will be deeply imbued with a consciousness of their own individual worth and dignity, which is the foundation of self-respect. They will be freer from the frustrations which warp personalities and impair the pursuit of happiness. The state which amply succeeds in providing appropriate education for its individual citizens will inevitably be strong in achievement, rich in character, powerful in influence, enterprising in nature, blessed with prosperity, infused with wisdom, and vigorous with the loyalty of capable people (41).

HIGHER EDUCATION CONTROVERSY

The historic shortage of higher education facilities in New Jersey became a matter of growing concern for the State Department of Education following World War II. There was the problem of accommodating returning servicemen in college. There was the increasing demand for post-high school courses to meet the needs of industry and the professions. And there was the prospect of a rising birth rate and consequent population explosion. Commissioner Bosshart foresaw the need for action as early as 1948 when he called for establishment of both 2- and 4-year public institutions of higher learning within commuting distances of students' homes. He urged the development and expansion of graduate courses, the establishment of professional schools, great increase in the state colleges, and a doubling of the facilities of the state university. In 1950, Bosshart said that a system of junior colleges should be created to offer 2-year terminal courses in technical areas and 2-year academic courses leading to transfer to a senior college.

When Frederick M. Raubinger (42) became commissioner of education in 1952, he took up the call for a vast expansion of public higher education facilities. Aware of the impact the postwar "baby boom" would eventually have on the state colleges, Raubinger and the state board in 1955 undertook a study of future space requirements. This was to become the first in a series of studies aimed at convincing the public and the legislators of the necessity for sharply increased capital appropriations for college facilities. Funds subsequently made available, largely through bond issues, fell far short of meeting the demonstrated needs.

Although expansion of the public college campuses was moving ahead, the lack of funds in the amounts sought by Raubinger and the state board meant that the expansion was not keeping pace with the rising demand for space. Controversy began to develop over reasons for New Jersey's continuing shortage of facilities. The department became the center of the controversy and was accused of failing to develop adequate plans for higher education. The department insisted that the necessary plans had been prepared but that insufficient funds had been appropriated to implement their recommendations. The Governor appointed a Committee on Higher Education in 1963 as a fact-finding committee, with Carroll V. Newsom, former president of New York University, as chairman. The Newsom committee reported in December 1964 and recommended a revamping of the higher education system in the state, including the removal of control of higher education from the state board.

The Newsom proposals were not acted upon, but they formed a part of the background for even more drastic proposals made in May 1966 by the Citizens Committee for Higher Education in New Jersey. Robert F. Goheen, president of Princeton University, chaired this committee. Its declared purpose had been to describe the college expansion required and then to win public support for an all-out campaign. After making a preliminary recommendation to strengthen the higher education division within the existing department, the Goheen committee, in a revised proposal, advocated transfer of control of higher education to a new state department of higher education.

Commissioner Raubinger and the Board of Education opposed the separation proposal, declaring that the single, unified system of public education, as established in the 1945 consolidation, should be maintained. The board presented its own proposal for restructuring the higher education system, keeping it under the board's control.

A bill embodying the plan for a separate state department of higher education as proposed by the Goheen committee and supported by the administration of Governor Richard J. Hughes was introduced in the Legislature May 31, 1966. A series of four lengthy and sometimes bitter hearings on the bill took place in the Senate that July. The Senate heard some 80 witnesses, including Commissioner Raubinger and State Board President George F. Smith, who repeated their opposition. The majority of the witnesses, including 25 members of the Goheen committee, favored the separation plan. In December 1966, the Legislature enacted the "Higher Education Act of 1966." The new law removed control of higher education from the board and established a new State Board of Higher Education to oversee a new State Department of Higher Education headed by the cabinet office of chancellor, to become effective July 1, 1967 (43). The act also created individual boards of trustees for the state colleges.

It was during the controversy over higher education in 1966 that Commissioner Raubinger handed in his resignation. He said only that he had accepted an offer to become a professor of education at the University of Illinois. He left New Jersey in August 1966.

Although New Jersey's facilities for higher learning remained well short of what both Raubinger and his critics desired, the rate of expansion of the public institutions of higher education, including 2-year colleges, was rapid.

The record shows that public higher education in New Jersey experienced unprecedented growth under the 22-year stewardship of the state department, from July 1945, when the State Board of Education assumed control from the Board of Regents, to July 1967, when responsibility passed to the newly created Board of Higher Education. The six state colleges, Rutgers University, and Newark College of Engineering expanded their physical facilities and upgraded their educational programs. Between 1945 and 1967, funds contributed annually by the state for operating expenses at the eight public institutions of higher learning increased from $3 million to $59 million. Student enrollment, full-time equated, rose from 9,000 to 52,000.

Capital appropriations during the 22-year period totaled $163 million, some $121 million of which came from bond issues. The top salary paid to full professors rose from $6,000 to $14,863, with supermaximums to $18,867. The six state colleges grew from small normal schools to multipurpose institutions with liberal arts offerings and strong graduate programs.

Five major studies carried out by the Board of Education between 1955 and 1965 spelled out the need for expansion of New Jersey's system of higher education to meet rising college enrollments. One of the studies, made in 1960, blueprinted the legislation (enacted effective in 1963) to help county governments establish 2-year public colleges. In the first 4 years after the law took effect, 17 of the 21 counties took positive action toward establishing such a college. Four opened in 1966 and two in 1967, with five more scheduled to open in 1968. A sixth study on New Jersey's higher education needs was initiated by the state board in 1967 when a consulting firm was engaged with federal funds to draw a master plan.

In late 1964, the Legislature approved purchase of the physical assets of the Seton Hall College of Medicine and Dentistry, and on July 1 of the following year, the institution was reconstituted as the New Jersey College of Medicine and Dentistry.

Working with representatives of New Jersey's private colleges, the Board of Education made recommendations leading to establishment and improvement of the State Scholarship Commission and the State Student Loan Program. The State Scholarship Program in 1966-67 was assisting 14,000 students, approximately 1 of every 11 New Jersey youth studying in or out of the state, in private or public colleges.

As of June 30, 1967, outstanding loans numbered 31,877 and were valued at $28 million.

The state created the New Jersey State Commission for the Higher Education Facilities Act of 1963 in that year to gain maximum benefits from federal financial aid programs. Between 1963 and 1966, New Jersey colleges, both public and private, shared $29 million in federal funds distributed through the state under the federal act.

The New Jersey Educational Facilities Authority, popularly known as the "Dormitory Authority," was established in 1966 to provide funds through the issuance of revenue bonds to build college dormitories and service-related facilities, thereby reducing the demand on the state for capital funds.

PRESSURES ON THE SCHOOLS

During the 1950's and 1960's, while the concerns over higher education were receiving the greatest discussion, the State Department of Education found itself involved also in a continuing struggle to meet the problems brought about by changing the nature of the public school system. Pupil population was soaring, and the districts were hard pressed to provide the required increases in instructional personnel and classrooms. There was pressure also to revise the educational programs in keeping with far-reaching scientific and technological developments.

Faced with the prospect of a rapidly increasing high school population, the department moved in the 1950's to spur the creation of regional high schools and thereby avoid the establishment of small, inefficient high schools. Legislation enacted in 1954 provided greater financial incentive for regionalization. In the period since 1931, when the first permissive regionalization legislation was passed, only five regional high schools had been established. After 1954, however, the number of regional high school districts grew rapidly, and by 1967 there were 56 in operation. The department's regionalization drive has given New Jersey a strong public high school system, with most of the high schools large enough to offer broad educational programs.

The dispute over the structure of the higher education system was not the only area in which Commissioner Raubinger was involved in controversy. He fought with vigor what he termed "the growing pressures toward impersonality, uniformity and rigidity in our schools." He declared his vehement opposition to proposals being made in the early 1960's for a higher degree of centralized control of education by the federal government, and he lashed out hard at the idea of a national curriculum commission. He became known nationally for his battle against outside control of the schools.

The greatest strength of American education on the elementary and secondary as well as on the college and university levels, Raubinger said, has been its diversity, its flexibility, its adaptability. He declared that this country has long maintained its conviction that its educational system controlled by its states and localities was one of its great democratic strengths. His premise was that program improvement should rest principally with the professional staff of the schools in cooperation with the local board of education, parents, and other able and interested citizens, under the general leadership and guidance of the state.

The U.S. Supreme Court's 1954 decision banning segregation in schools considerably widened the State Department of Education's leadership role. Even before the decision, the department had been active in seeing that enforced segregation—confined largely to some 50 elementary schools in southern New Jersey—was ended in compliance with a provision in the new State Constitution of 1947. When the 1954 ruling declared that "de facto" school segregation resulting from racially segregated neighborhoods was unconstitutional, Commissioner Raubinger moved quickly to urge districts to make plans to comply. His decisions in cases involving Orange, Plainfield, and Englewood established as New Jersey law the proposition that a school board must take appropriate action to eliminate de facto segregation where it could reasonably be accomplished. Raubinger declared that the mere existence of racial imbalance in a school, whether intentional or not, constituted an educational handicap to the pupils. He said that New Jersey law required school boards to provide "suitable" facilities and that segregated facilities were not "suitable." The commissioner's position, upheld by the State Board of Education and the courts, now provides clear-cut guidelines for the local school boards of the state.

One of the most nagging, most persistent problems that have faced the State Department of Education in the post-World War II period has been that of financing the expansion of the public schools. Historically, the state depended largely on local property taxes to operate the schools, with state aid meeting only a small portion of the costs. The New Jersey State School Aid Act of 1954 provided a fundation program on a permanent basis to assist all districts "in the maintenance and support of a thorough and efficient system of free public schools." The distribution formula was based on school operating costs, school enrollments, and community wealth, using a foundation program of $200 per pupil, with minimum aid of $50 per pupil and equalization aid added. In 1956, the school building aid act provided state funds for acquiring, constructing, and maintaining school facilities.

Commissioner Raubinger in the early 1960's declared flatly that the $200-per-pupil foundation program was meaningless. He urged greater state funds to relieve local real estate taxes and to maintain equal educational opportunity for all children. In 1964, he reported that during the previous 10 years enrollment had increased 70 percent, per-pupil costs had climbed from an average of $250 to an average of $420, a total of $850 million had been spent on facilities, and the outstanding school debt had risen from $162 million to more than $800 million. In that decade, support from local property taxation had increased from $153 million to $430 million, while state support had gone from $25 million to $96 million.

The pleas of the Department of Education and numerous education organizations for greater state financial assistance were finally heeded by the Governor and the Legislature. New Jersey enacted its first broad-based tax, a 3-percent sales tax, in 1966. As a result, $95 million, representing more than half of the sales tax revenue, was appropriated as school aid, thereby increasing the state's share of the total school costs to some 28 percent. The Legislature revised the equalization formula to provide a $400-per-pupil foundation program, with minimum aid of $75. About half of the 590 school districts received the minimum aid of $75; the average for all districts was figured at $130. The state's six largest cities were granted an additional $27 per pupil.

Although the state's share of school costs had increased substantially to 28 percent, the department did not relax its efforts to boost it even further. Joseph E. Clayton, the deputy commissioner who became acting commissioner upon Raubinger's departure in August 1966, appeared before the State Aid to School Districts Study Committee in November 1966 and recommended that the state aid be increased gradually over several years until the state furnished about 40 percent of the local districts' education expenditures. He pointed out that the nationwide average of state support was 39 percent.

While New Jersey ranks low among the states in percentage of school costs paid by state aid, it ranks high in per-pupil expenditures as a result of the great amount of local support. In 1967, the per-pupil expenditure in New Jersey exceeded $600.

Nearly 12 months elapsed between the date of Dr. Raubinger's departure and the appointment of a new education commissioner. Clayton was called upon to lead the department through the 1966-67 school year. Although working in an "acting" capacity, Clayton nevertheless moved to improve the state school system. Long recognizing the problems and inefficiency resulting from the state's great number of school districts, Clayton appointed a committee of educators in November 1966 to study the next steps in regionalization of districts and to make recommendations. He felt that the educational program would be enhanced if districts operating separate high school districts or separate elementary districts could be regionalized into full K-12 programs. He suggested that the state provide incentive aid to accomplish this.

If New Jersey has been behind other states in the total state financial aid for the schools, it has been ahead of most states in several other significant areas of aid. There has been considerable legislation in New Jersey in recent years to support the schooling of the handicapped. A 1954 law "mandated public schools to provide special education services and facilities for children classified as mentally retarded or physically handicapped." In 1959, child study teams were authorized in the counties and in individual districts to coordinate special education services. In 1966, legislation required school districts to identify and classify all handicapped pupils and to provide services for them. Under this legislation—considered the most comprehensive law in special education in the nation—the state pays one-half the cost of the education of children in special education categories. The education department's staff was expanded to provide the additional supervision and guidance required.

By 1967, New Jersey was paying three-fourths of the transportation costs for both public and private school pupils living far from their schools. Also, the state was assuming the burden of paying the employer's share of Social Security and other fringe benefits for the teachers at a cost, in 1967, of $90 million. In summary, by 1967, the state was paying some $300 million toward the school districts' total annual expenditures of more than $1 billion.

Accompanying the increase in state aid in the 1960's was a sharp hike in federal aid programs which have had a great impact on New Jersey schools. A new dimension was added to the work of the department in approving and overseeing the vast array of federal programs. During fiscal year 1967, New Jersey effectively utilized more than $76 million in federal funds made available for education programs operated through the State Department of Education. The money was used to carry out educational innovations, to develop remedial and compensatory programs, and to provide additional personnel and services—all directed toward effecting equality of educational opportunity for all children. Some $32 million of the total was allocated to the state under the Elementary and Secondary Education Act. There were 66 innovative projects under way in the state under Title III of the act. Approximately $15 million in federal funds was being spent on vocational education in the state, and other federal funds were being used for adult education, school lunch programs, and implementation of the National Defense Education Act.

New Jersey broadened considerably the services of its state department in the 1960's to guide the local districts in coping with society's changing needs and demands. In 1967, the department staff prepared booklets to provide the schools with data on establishing sex education programs, handling the problem of drug abuse, conducting experiments with live animals, and using bibliographies to aid in the teaching of the Negro's role in American history. The department expanded educational programs for the children of migrant workers. A Center for the Humanities was formed to provide the leadership and services required to implement the department's expanding programs in the humanities and the arts and to provide a more intensive focus for cultural concerns. In vocational education the development of a master plan was under way, and committees were formed to work toward greater cooperation with industry. A report was prepared to spell out improvements in student-teaching programs, especially for the urban schools.

Carl L. Marburger, who was in charge of education programs for the U.S. Bureau of Indian Affairs, assumed the office of New Jersey state education commissioner in July 1967, following his appointment by Governor Richard J. Hughes. The new commissioner had a background in urban education, and he set out at once to increase the department's services to the urban areas and to provide a stronger degree of state leadership in helping solve their problems. Marburger visited many of the older cities of the state, offering the education department's help. He formed an urban task force to provide department assistance to cities that had been beset by civil unrest in the summer of 1967. He organized an Urban Education Corps as a means of recruiting effective, dedicated teachers to the cities.

The corps, formed in the summer of 1967, channeled many teachers with a Peace Corps kind of spirit into inner-city schools for the 1967-68 year. Plans were made to use a federal grant to finance a program to recruit and train in the summer of 1968 some 500 outstanding college graduates to teach in New Jersey's most difficult schools.

The new commissioner expressed a determination to bolster the public schools in several problem areas. He announced his intention to secure additional funds to spur construction of school buildings, especially in the older cities where financial problems were severe, with statutory debt limits nearly exhausted. "The state," he said repeatedly, "must assume a greater responsibility for solving the education problems of its cities."

Marburger continued the movement for school district reorganization. "The 590 school districts seem to be too many," he observed. "There are many small districts and some with great inequities. I want a totality of education for each and every child." He also spoke out for continued efforts by the districts to effect racial integration of the schools wherever possible. "We must face the most critical issue of our times," he declared. "We can't give up on our cities" (44).

In an address to the professional staff of the Department of Education in December 1967, Commissioner Marburger said that he planned to establish innovative centers throughout the state "as a direct outreach to the local superintendents." The aim, he said, would be to help the local districts plan the most effective programs for all types of pupils, to help them assess the "hardware and software" the schools are being asked to use, and to make available through research projects and demonstration schools the latest data on how children learn and how they can best be taught. The education department, he said, must continually assess its operations to make sure it is giving the most effective service possible to the public schools of the state, their 1.3 million pupils, and their instructional force of 60,000 teachers and 10,000 supervisors and administrators.

Organization and Administration of the New Jersey State Department of Education

The New Jersey State Department of Education is a principal department of the executive branch of the state government. It is composed of the State Board of Education and the commissioner of education, with such divisions, bureaus, branches, officers, and employees as are necessary.

The Board of Education has 12 members, who serve without pay for overlapping terms of 6 years. Restrictions on appointments are that not more than one member can be appointed from any one county and that at least three members must be women. Regular meetings are held in Trenton on the first Wednesday in each month. The commissioner of education is secretary to the board.

The state board is a policy-making and regulatory body whose rules have the force of law when so designated by legislation. Examples of such regulation are rules for certification of teachers, school accounting procedures, school building guide requirements, approval of secondary schools, and establishment of standards in special education of handicapped children.

The commissioner of education is the chief state school officer. He is appointed by the Governor, by and with the advice and consent of the Senate, for a term of 5 years, commencing July 1, and until his successor is appointed.

As chief executive and administrative officer of the Department of Education, the commissioner is the budget and fiscal officer. He makes all appointments of personnel, subject to the approval of the state board and to Civil Service laws, and assigns their duties. He supervises all schools of the state receiving any part of the state appropriations.

The functions of the department can be described in four separate areas, the primary one being that of service to school districts throughout the state. New Jersey's 21 county superintendents, who are appointed by the commissioner, are field agents for the department to advise all those within the field of public education and to provide the services necessary to meet the needs of the schools in their counties.

The second area of responsibility is that of regulation. The department is charged with certification of teachers, approval of secondary and nursery schools, distribution of federal funds, and—through the county superintendents—all pupil transportation.

Another function of the department is adjudication. The commissioner is the first court of appeal and must render a decision before a case is carried to the State Board of Education or the courts.

The department also has an executive function in such matters as the dispensing of state aid and the administration of the State Library, the State Museum, and the State School for the Deaf.

Key staff members of the department are the deputy commissioner, who is in charge of the Division of Administration, and four assistant commissioners, who are in charge of the Divisions of Business and Finance, Controversies and Disputes, Curriculum and Instruction, and Vocational Education. The Library and Museum divisions are headed by directors.

The State Department of Education offices are located in the new State Education Building at 225 West State Street in Trenton. The department moved into the new building May 27, 1963, after 16 years in cramped quarters in an ancient brownstone. The building is part of a new New Jersey State Cultural Center which also includes the State Museum and State Library divisions of the education department. The Cultural Center complex, which adjoins the State Capitol buildings along the banks of the Delaware River, was completed in 1964 as part of New Jersey's tercentenary celebration.

FOOTNOTES

1. Ira T. Chapman, "Education in New Jersey," *The Story of New Jersey,* I (New York: Lewis Historical Publishing Co., 1945), 246.
2. David Murray, *History of Education in New Jersey* (Washington, D.C.: Government Printing Office, 1899), p. 14.
3. Chapman, *op. cit.,* p. 431.
4. *Ibid.,* p. 431.
5. *Ibid.,* p. 442.
6. Board of Education and Superintendent of Public Instruction, *Annual Report* (1879), p. 43.
7. Arthur L. Johnson, *History of the County Superintendency in New Jersey* (Trenton: Department of Education, 1952), p. 8.
8. Board of Education and Superintendent of Public Instruction, *Annual Report* (1879), p. 47.
9. Chapman, *op. cit.,* p. 452.
10. Murray, *op. cit.,* pp. 162-63.
11. Johnson, *op. cit.,* p. 11.
12. Chapman, *op. cit.,* p. 457.
13. *Ibid.,* p. 458.
14. Murray, *op. cit.,* pp. 166-72.
15. Superintendent of Public Schools, *Annual Report* (1863), p. 14.
16. Superintendent of Public Schools, *Annual Report* (1865), p. 377.
17. Board of Education and Superintendent of Public Instruction, *Annual Report* (1879), p. 55.
18. Board of Education and Superintendent of Public Instruction, *Annual Report* (1866), p. 435.
19. Johnson, *op. cit.,* p. 21.
20. *Ibid.,* p. 17.
21. *Newark Daily Journal,* February 11-28, 1889.
22. Johnson, *op. cit.,* p. 23.
23. Board of Education and Superintendent of Public Instruction, *Annual Report* (1901), p. 25.
24. *Ibid.,* p. 22.
25. *Ibid.,* p. 16.
26. *Ibid.,* p. 13.
27. Chapman, *op. cit.,* p. 487.
28. Johnson, *op. cit.,* p. 42.
29. Chapman, *op. cit.,* p. 495.
30. The law was amended in 1965 to require school attendance for all children from age 6 through age 15.
31. New Jersey School Development Council, *Chronicle of Selected Educational Highlights in New Jersey* (New Brunswick: Graduate School of Education, Rutgers University, 1965), p. 19.
32. Chapman, *op. cit.,* p. 511.
33. Board of Education and Commissioner of Education, *Annual Report* (1920), p. 25.
34. Johnson, *op. cit.,* p. 80.
35. *Ibid.,* pp. 80-82.
36. Chapman, *op. cit.,* p. 511.
37. *Ibid.,* p. 519.
38. John H. Bosshart, who had been supervising principal in the South Orange-Maplewood school district, was named state commissioner in 1943. The title of supervising principal was changed to superintendent in 1952, and the number of superintendents in the state increased from 45 to 251.
39. The number of members of the State Board of Education had been increased in 1921 from 8 to 10.
40. The Division Against Discrimination was redesignated as the Division on Civil Rights in 1960. This division was

transferred to the State Department of Law and Public Safety in 1963.

41. Board of Education and Commissioner of Education, *Annual Report* (1950), p. 155.

42. Frederick M. Raubinger had been superintendent of Ridgewood schools before becoming commissioner.

43. The transfer of higher education functions from the Board of Education to the new board did not include two offices which had been part of the old higher education division. The offices of teacher education and certification and adult education and academic credentials were retained in the State Department of Education.

44. Commissioner Marburger's views on the direction and goals of New Jersey's schools were spelled out in an address to the New Jersey Association of School Administrators on September 28, 1967, in Atlantic City.

BIBLIOGRAPHY

Public Document

New Jersey. *Constitution* (1947).

Books

Bole, Robert D., and Johnson, Laurence B. *The New Jersey High School: A History.* Princeton, N.J.: D. Van Nostrand Co., 1964.

Burr, Nelson, R. *Education in New Jersey, 1630-1871.* Princeton, N.J.: Princeton University Press, 1942.

Chapman, Ira T. "Education in New Jersey." *The Story of New Jersey,* Vol. I. New York: Lewis Historical Publishing Co., 1945.

Cubberley, Ellwood P. *Public Education in the United States.* Boston: Houghton Mifflin Co., 1919.

Johnson, Arthur L. *History of the County Superintendency in New Jersey.* Trenton: Department of Education, 1952.

Murray, David. *History of Education in New Jersey.* Washington, D.C.: Government Printing Office, 1899.

New Jersey School Development Council. *Chronicle of Selected Educational Highlights in New Jersey.* New Brunswick: Graduate School of Education, Rutgers University, 1965.

Walling, W. Donald. "Public Education." *New Jersey Almanac.* Upper Montclair, N.J.: The New Jersey Almanac, 1963.

West, Roscoe L. *Elementary Education in New Jersey: A History.* Princeton, N.J.: D. Van Nostrand Co., 1964.

Reports

Board of Education and Commissioner of Education. *Annual Reports.* Trenton: Department of Education, 1911-33 and 1946-65.

Board of Education and Superintendent of Public Instruction. *Annual Reports.* Trenton: Department of Education, 1866-1910.

Commissioner of Education. *Annual Reports.* Trenton: Department of Education, 1934-45.

Superintendent of Public Schools. *Annual Reports.* Trenton: Department of Education, 1846-65.

Periodical

Newark Daily Journal, February 11-28, 1889.

Other Source

Marburger, Carl L. "Address to the New Jersey Association of School Administrators," on September 28, 1967, Atlantic City.

Appendix A

NEW JERSEY CHIEF STATE SCHOOL OFFICERS

State Superintendents Appointed by Trustees of State School Fund Under Act of 1846

1846-52	Theodore F. King
1852-60	John H. Phillips
1860-64	Frederick W. Ricord
1864-66	Caleb M. Harrison

State Superintendents Appointed by State Board of Education Under Acts of 1866 and 1867

1866-85	Ellis A. Apgar
1885-88	Edwin O. Chapman
1888-89	Charles W. Fuller

State Superintendents Appointed by Governor Under Act of 1889

1889-92	Edwin O. Chapman
1892-96	Addison B. Poland
1896-1911	Charles J. Baxter

State Commissioners of Education Appointed by Governor Under Act of 1911

1911-21	Calvin N. Kendall
1921-25	John Enright
1925-27	John Logan
1927-43	Charles H. Elliott
1943-52	John H. Bosshart
1952-66	Frederick M. Raubinger
1966-67	Joseph E. Clayton (acting)
1967-	Carl L. Marburger

Appendix B

Chart I.--NEW JERSEY DEPARTMENT OF EDUCATION, 1950

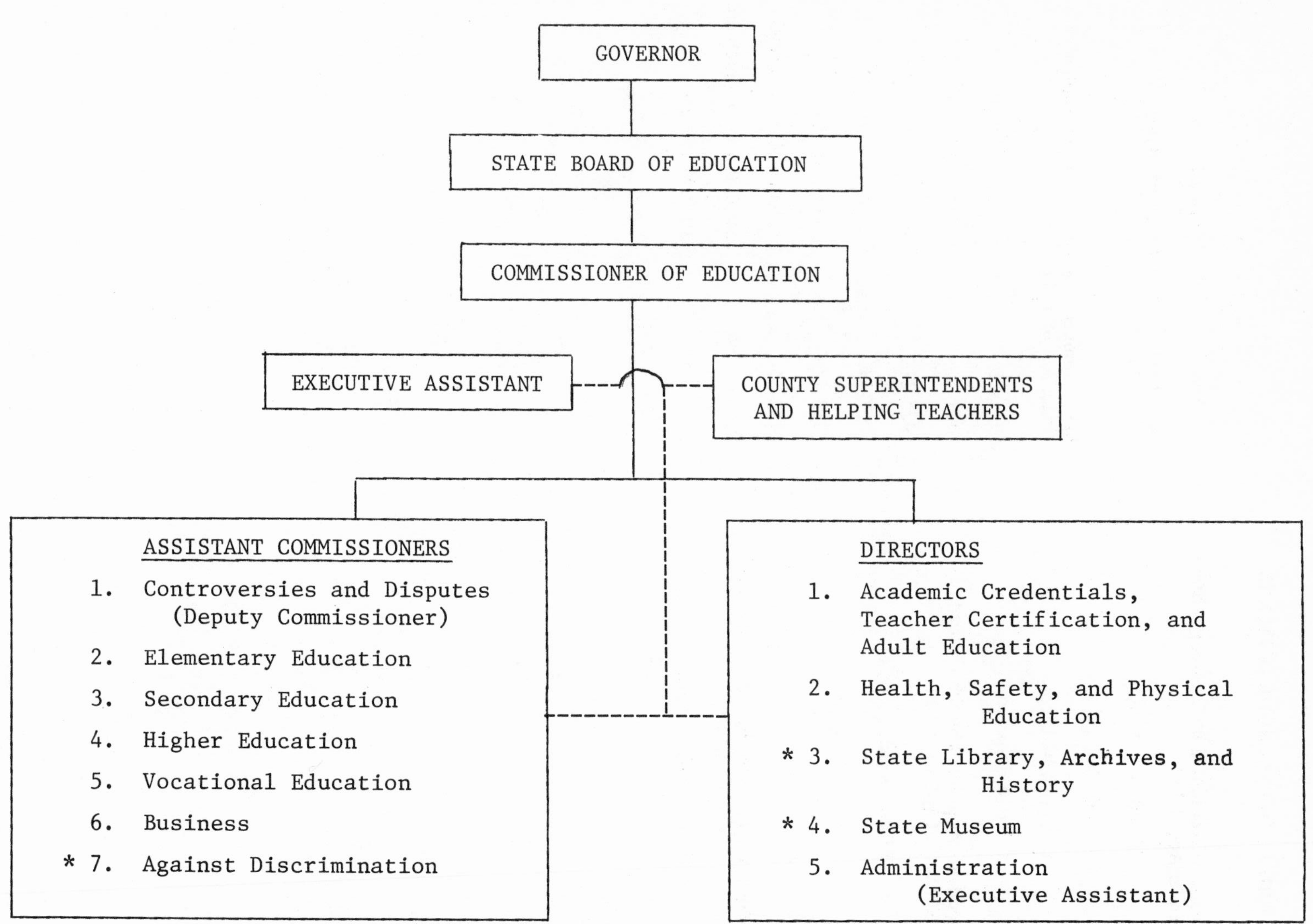

* This division is assisted by an advisory council.

Appendix B

Chart II.--NEW JERSEY DEPARTMENT OF EDUCATION, 1962

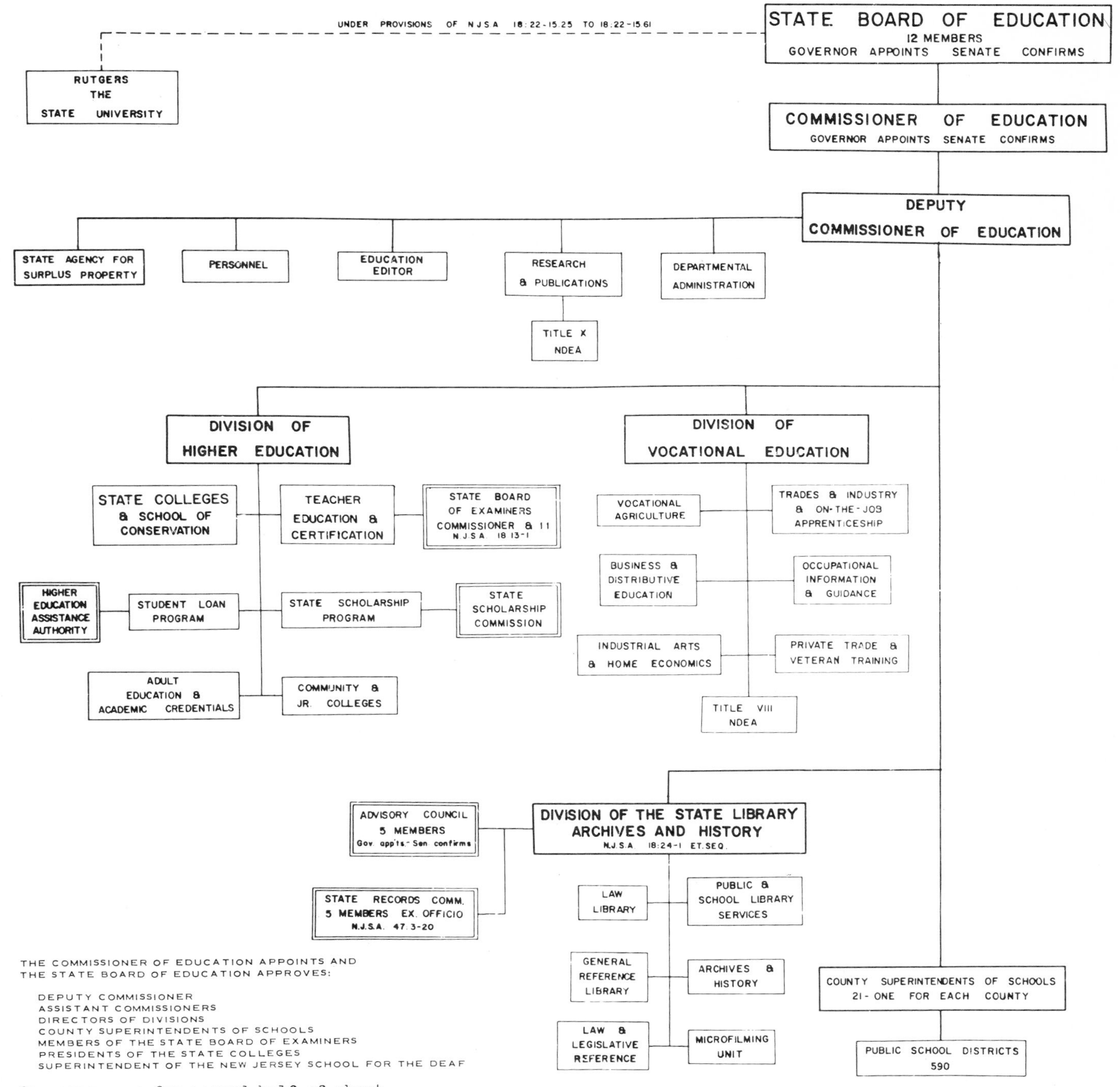

See next page for second half of chart.

Appendix B

Chart II.--NEW JERSEY DEPARTMENT OF EDUCATION, 1962 (Continued)

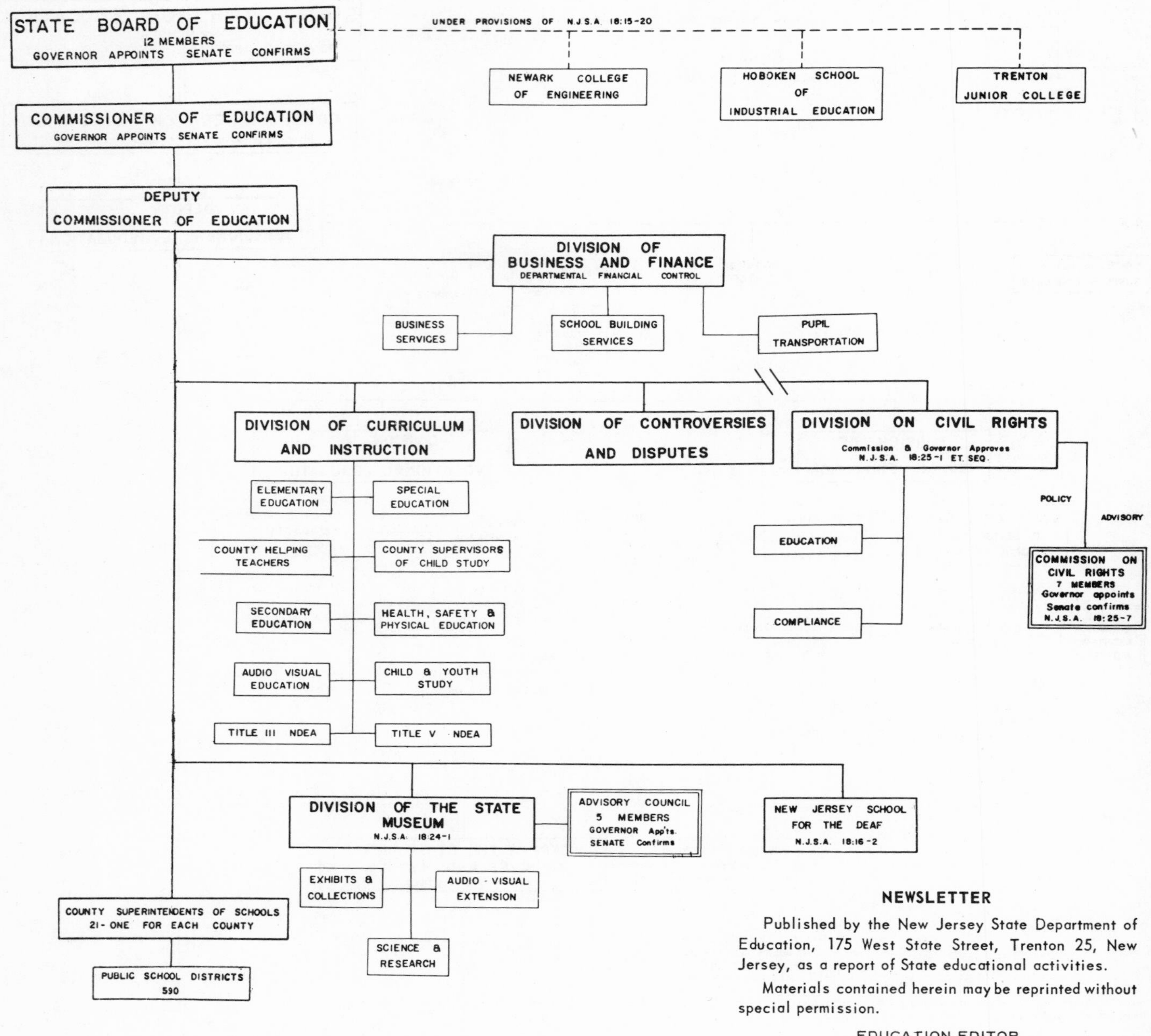

Appendix B

Chart III.--NEW JERSEY DEPARTMENT OF EDUCATION, 1968

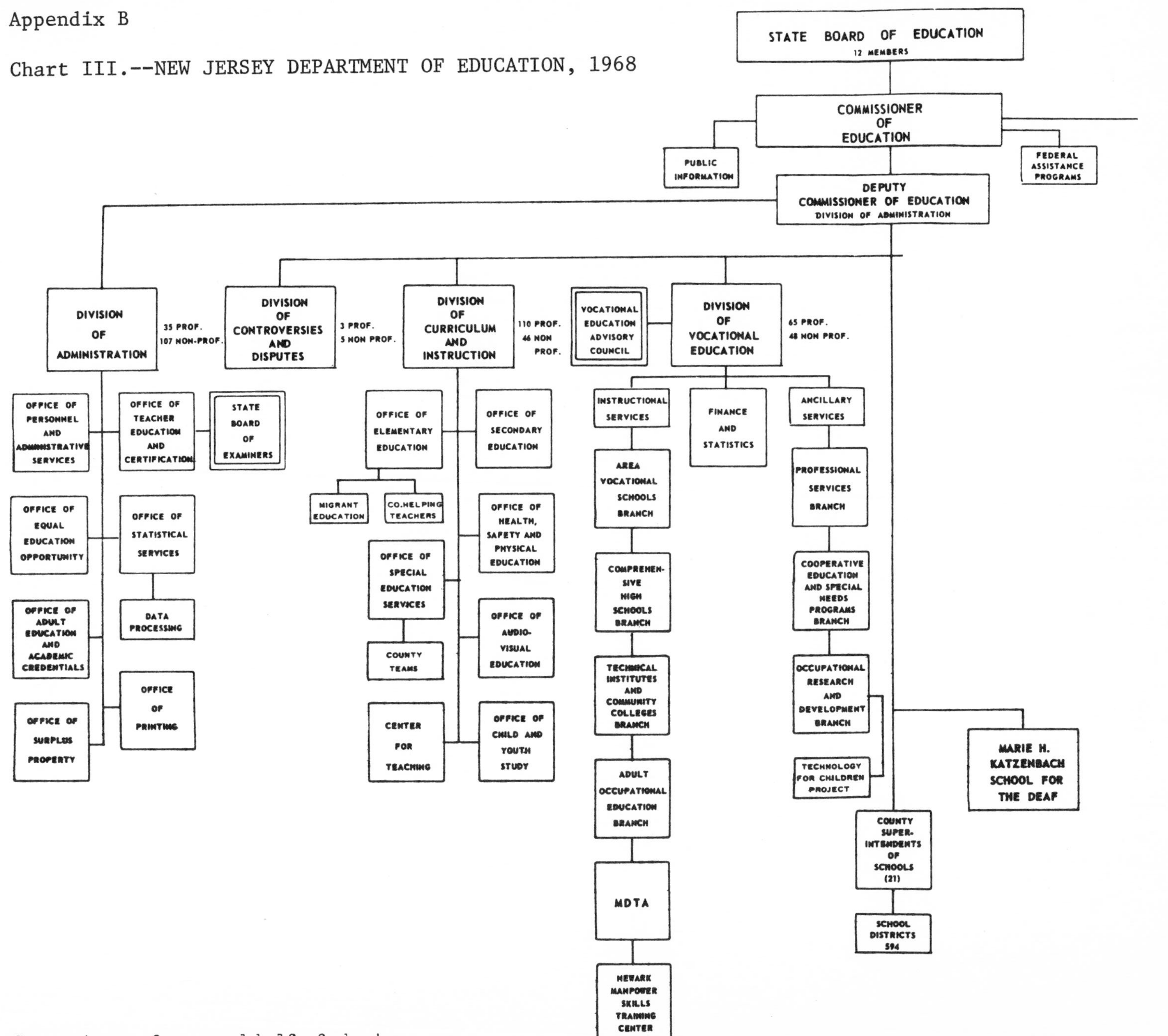

See next page for second half of chart.

Appendix B

Chart III.--NEW JERSEY DEPARTMENT OF EDUCATION, 1968 (Continued)

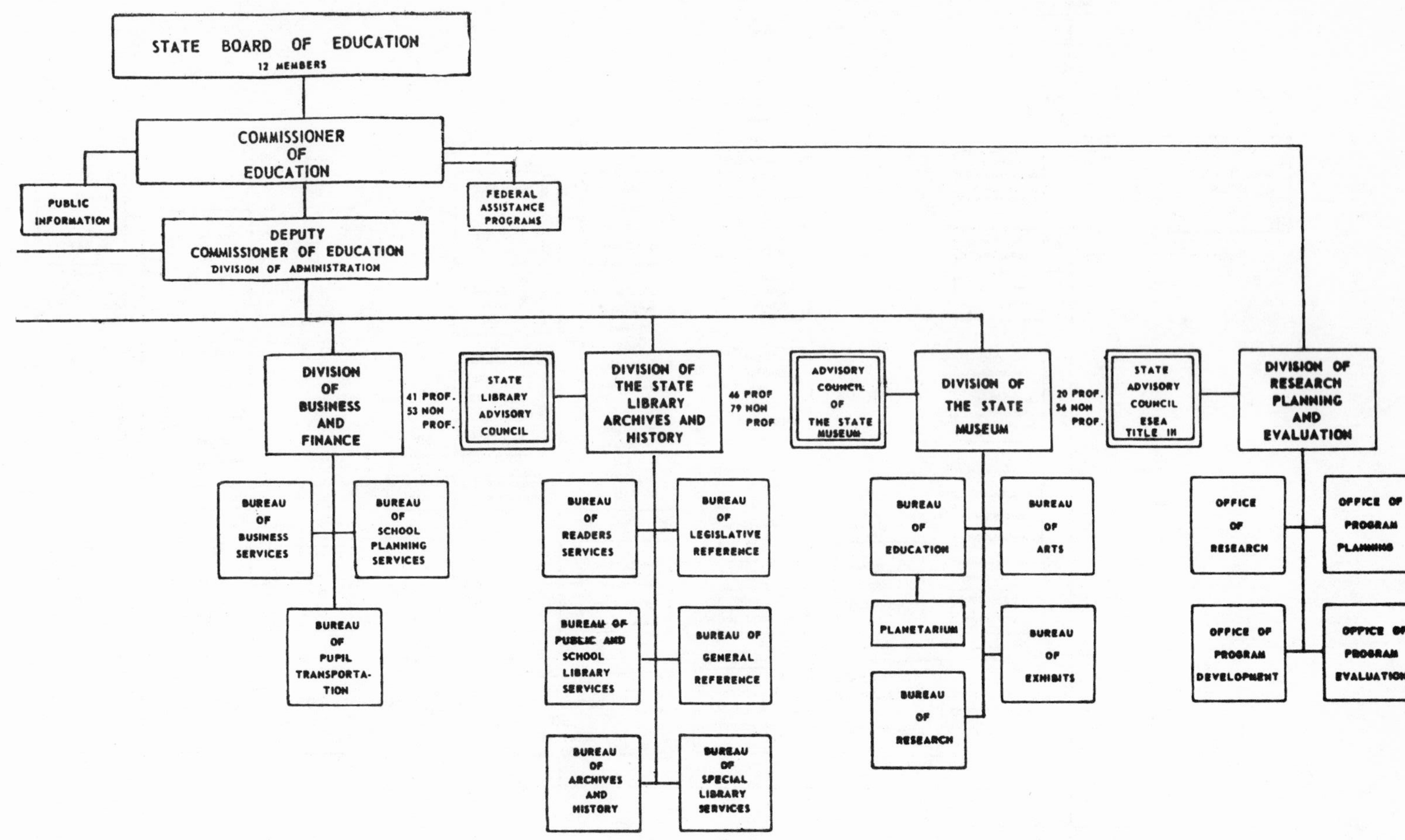

31 New Mexico

DEPARTMENT OF EDUCATION
Tom Wiley

Contents

INTRODUCTION

New Mexico was first explored by the Conquistadors more than a half a century before the Pilgrims landed on the East Coast. Today, little Spanish villages, interspersed along the Rio Grande and hidden in deep mountain canyons, have lived under the flag of the United States only little over a third as long as they did under the Spanish and Mexican flags. Indian villages basking under the sun have not changed greatly over the past 500 years. Navajos and Apaches roam their vast reservations and, until quite recently, have isolated themselves from any consequential contacts with the outside world.

Intermingled with these cultures in the late nineteenth and early twentieth centuries were a relatively few migrants from Eastern states, who lived in the towns and on the farms and ranches. It was a land of almost endless space and silence, broken now and then by the dust of a cattle drive or the lonely whistle of a locomotive.

Parts of New Mexico were dramatically changed from the moment the first mushroom of an atomic explosion "blossomed" over White Sands in southern New Mexico. The erection of scientific and military installations during the 1940's initiated a population explosion that caused tremendous economic and social changes, particularly in such cities as Albuquerque, Alamogordo, Clovis, Los Alamos, Las Cruces, and Roswell.

Today, New Mexico is a blend of the past, the present, and the future found in few other states. It is a long way from the lonely hogans of Shiprock to the scientific laboratories of Los Alamos.

SPANISH COLONIALISM, 1536 - 1820

When Cabeza de Vaca, the first Spaniard to see New Mexico, entered the Rio Grande Valley in 1536, he discovered the cliff houses or large communal dwellings constructed by the Pueblo Indians and became convinced that they held treasures. Francisco Vasquez de Coronado, one of the world's greatest explorers, who followed in 1540, found a flourishing culture but not the gold that had lured him into these deserts and mountains. Although disappointed at not uncovering sudden wealth, the Spaniards did appreciate the resources that had attracted the Pueblo Indians into settling this region and, under the leadership of Don Juan de Oñate, established the first town of San Gabriel in 1598.

Since the Spanish government considered it just as important to Christianize and educate the Indians to be good Spanish subjects as to raise crops and practice animal husbandry, 10 friars, including Alonso Martiniz, accompanied Oñate. During the next 11 years, they established missions and schools as they moved northward up the Rio Grande Valley. These friars and their successors made a valiant though not very successful attempt to teach agriculture, reading, writing, simple mathematics, singing, tailoring, shoemaking, carpentry, blacksmithing, metal working, weaving, music, and painting.

The Pueblo uprising in 1680 halted the development of missions for approximately 11 years, but when Don Diego de Vargas reconquered the Indians, he began rebuilding, though there was not as much zeal in maintaining the schools as earlier (1). The Spanish king gave specific orders in 1717 to reopen them, but apparently no aggressive attempt was made to obey this command by either church or state officials (2). Education continued to decline. Decrees issued in 1777 and 1813 to found a college at Santa Fe again showed good intentions, but because there were no resources to carry out the decree, it never opened.

The revolt of 1820 ended almost three centuries of Spanish rule. Within the first year, the Mexican government ordered the town councils to establish schools as soon as possible. Supported by half the tithes collected in New Mexico, schools were maintained at Santa Fe, Albuquerque, San Miguel, Belen, Taos, and Santa Cruz (3). A deputation, serving as a school board for the entire territory, further strengthened the schools by designating the teacher at Santa Fe as the chief teacher and passing a compulsory school attendance law.

A struggle went on during these years between those who wanted free public schools and those who preferred private schools. In 1833, the private school proponents succeeded in getting the upper hand and persuaded the Mexican government to order that tithes collected by the church be placed at the disposal of the bishop. The struggle continued, and 3 years later the government decreed that all public and private schools be abolished and reestablished under government supervision, supported by heads of families, with all children between 5 and 12 attending. Despite this effort to generate a public school system, it failed to materialize, and formal education was virtually nonexistent during the last years of Mexican control.

THE TERRITORIAL PERIOD, 1846 - 1912

Mexican rule over New Mexico ended with Kearny's occupation of the territory during the Mexican War and with the treaty of Guadalupe Hidalgo. Despite repeated pleas for aid and money, the Spanish-Americans and many Anglo-Americans, particularly the business groups and wealthier families who controlled the Territorial Legislature, fought taxation for a public school program and remained the opposing power structure for many years. This is quite understandable considering that one of the basic traditions of the New Mexicans who had lived under the flags, culture, and language of Spain and Mexico for almost three centuries involved the sacredness of property ownership and an inherent hatred of property taxation. Demonstrations protesting taxation similar to that of the Boston Tea Party are a matter of record in New Mexico.

In 1855-56, the Territorial Legislature attempted to establish regulations and financial support for a public school system. Every male whose property value did not exceed $250 was to pay a tax of $1, and males whose property exceeded $250 were to pay $1 on each additional $1,000 of its value. However, the counties of Rio Arriba, Santa Ana, Taos, Valencia, and Socorro were influential enough to secure exemptions for their residents whose property value did not exceed $50, and they forced through a provision allowing them to decide by popular vote whether they would be subjected to these laws. The vote was 37 for and 4,053 against public schools supported by taxation. As a consequence, in December 1856, the laws were repealed for the rest of the territory, only 10 months after they had become effective.

Despite efforts by the 1860 and 1863 Legislatures to require schools in all communities, financial support continued to be the insurmountable problem. During the 1870's, several laws forced culprits to pay for their misdeeds and at the same time support the schools with their fines for such crimes as burying the dead on Sunday, marrying "close relatives," and engaging in certain Sunday sports like cockfighting. Property owners obviously were determined not to be taxed. The great landowning Spanish patrons and the newly arrived businessmen from the East combated taxes for education by playing on the fear that public schools were an American scheme to wean the Spanish-American people away from the traditions and beliefs of their parents (4).

While most of the settlers from the East wanted public schools, many Spanish-Americans preferred parochial schools, which were well established by the midnineteenth century. As more and more Anglos settled down in the region, their demand for public schools grew stronger and louder. Governor L. B. Prince gave the latter his backing, and when a group of educators organized in the New Mexico Education Association in 1886 to lobby for better schools, he encouraged them. Soon, the association had gained considerable influence with the Legislature and in 1891 finally mustered sufficient strength to pass an act giving substance to an 1863 statute creating a Board of Education and the Office of Territorial Superintendent. At this time, the old board composed of the Governor, the secretary of state, the judges of the supreme court, and the bishop of New Mexico was replaced by one consisting of the Governor, the superintendent of public instruction, and the presidents of the University of New Mexico, the Agricultural College, and Saint Michael's College. The new board operated until statehood in 1912 (5).

To allay the apprehensions of the Spanish-Americans, Governor Prince appointed Amado Chavez, a Spanish-American, as territorial superintendent. An intelligent man, Chavez was sincere in his convictions about the need for public education. The 1891 statute proved to be an important turning point in New Mexico education. Not only did the superintendent exercise strong leadership, encouraging communities to found new schools and construct suitable buildings, but the law itself provided for bond issues for this construction, for levying local taxes, and licensing teachers. The latter was badly needed. It was 1889 before the Legislature had dared proclaim that anyone unable to read or write sufficiently to keep his records in Spanish or English should not be hired to teach, and the archives show signatures of both teachers and school directors written as X's. The new laws also provided for courses of study to be developed through elementary school and required attendance for the entire school year. As a result, the attendance figures increased from 18,315 in 1891 to 61,022 in 1911, and school expenditures jumped from $50,259 to $954,407 (6).

Unfortunately, no subsequent territorial superintendents exerted strong leadership until 1905, when Governor Miguel Otero appointed Hiram Hadley. Hadley had been president of the New Mexico Agricultural College (now New Mexico State University) in Las Cruces from 1890 to 1894 and vice-president of the University of New Mexico until 1897. Convinced that the power and influence residing in his office was "the most important factor" in developing a satisfactory school system (7), and despite being 72 when he was appointed, he traveled nearly 18,000 miles during the 2 years he served, vigorously attacking problems he found in nearly every community. State Superintendent John V. Conway paid the following tribute during a memorial service in his memory, December 10, 1922:

Hiram Hadley was regarded as the Father of Education in New Mexico, and it was during his term as Territorial Superintendent of Public Instruction that the first steps were taken toward the establishment of progressive educational laws, that have brought about the advancement we now have (8).

Despite considerable progress, New Mexico schools continued to have major weaknesses. In particular, the development of the county school administration followed a strange pattern because the statutes of 1866 called for the county probate judges to act as county school superintendents, and the justices of the peace in each precinct to appoint the teachers. Attempts to improve the system often merely added to the chaos. In 1884, the Office of County Superintendent was made elective, with three directors to be elected for each school district, the candidates running on a partisan ticket. The district judge appointed the county boards.

Since there were no minimum professional requirements for the county superintendent whose maximum term was set at 4 years, counties had a transient, political administration which was often in conflict with the municipal superintendent. Also, there were a large number of small, weak districts with few students and unqualified teachers. The district boards of directors, who were elected and served as advisers to the county superintendents in matters relating to the district schools, were often the chief opponents to district consolidation because from their point of view this meant centralizing power in the hands of a virtually alien board.

The appointment of able territorial superintendents did not lessen the opposition to taxes. Big corporations, such as the railroads whose trains crossed New Mexico, owned about 30 percent of the assessed property in the territory. Understandably, their outlook was the same as that of the large landholders. Local railroad tax agents also had little sympathy for the state's needs as a whole because the roads were completely transcontinental connections between the East, the Pacific, and Mexico; local districts were interested in taxing the rights-of-way to gain railroad property wealth, which in many instances meant better school buildings and indoor restrooms for their children in contrast to outhouses and coal stoves in other rural schools (9).

STATEHOOD

Given the problems suffered during the territorial period, a severely inadequate public school system was inevitable when statehood finally came in 1912. The teachers were poorly qualified, many buildings were unfit, and the school terms were irregular in length. Even as late as 1930, New Mexico ranked third from the lowest among the states in literacy. But the most damaging heritage of the earlier period was the attitude of the people who felt that education was a luxury and perhaps a waste rather than an investment. As a school historian pointed out, "the prudential considerations, with emphasis upon economy, greatly overshadowed the humanitarian values which cried out for an adequate educational program for every boy and girl" (10). There was a deliberate separation of budget-making authority from those responsible for the educational program, which meant that educational needs were too often measured in terms of an expedient support structure.

Not trusting the New Mexicans to provide for adequate education, Congress imposed regulations which placed the process of developing the new state's constitution under its close supervision. A number of New Mexican leaders favored the congressional Enabling Act section providing for public schools for all children, free from sectarian controls, and conducted in English, but they resented the congressional restrictions. Limitations had been placed on other territories seeking statehood, so the Congressmen felt they were doing their duty in protecting the vast acreage of trust lands and permanent school fund. The 1912 Enabling Act as passed set aside four sections (sections 16 and 36, sections 2 and 32) amounting to 12,100,000 acres and detailed the provisions for disposing of them. The proceeds were to go into the permanent fund; only the interest could be used.

Under these conditions, the constitutional convention was called with the encouragement of President Taft, who strongly favored admission of the territory to statehood. The 100 representatives who met to write the constitution included 32 attorneys, 20 stockmen, 14 merchants, 7 farmers, 6 general businessmen, and 4 saloon keepers, with a sprinkling of newspaper editors, territorial officers, physicians, bankers, and one college president.

Certainly the ranch, railroad, and mining interests were in a position to shape the new constitution. But, despite the fears of the *Albuquerque Journal* and many New Mexican educators, the convention did write a document that had considerable merit. For instance, Section 1 of Article XII makes it the duty of the Legislature to establish an adequate and uniform system of education open to all children of school age. It does not limit the ages or restrict the school system, leaving the details to the Legislature. Section 3 of this same article safeguards against the use of school funds for denominational or private schools, colleges, or universities. Other sections prohibit religious tests as a condition of admission to public schools; prevent students or teachers from being required to participate in religious services; provide a basis for compulsory education, for investing the permanent school fund, and for training teachers to be proficient in both English and Spanish—a provision that is particularly appropriate in New Mexico.

There were handicaps imposed by the constitution. Instead of providing for a state superintendent to serve as the State Board of Education's executive officer, it prescribed his election by popular vote to no more than two consecutive 2-year terms, the same as the other state office holders, and left to the Legislature determination of his power, duties, and compensation. The state superintendency as well as the other offices were probably made elective because the people were determined to swing as far as possible from the appointive officials of the long territorial period. Indeed, the citizenry continued to be most jealous of its prerogative of controlling officials through election and was no doubt responsible for the defeat of several amendments proposed at later dates to make the superintendent's office appointive.

The Board of Education under the new constitution was to be composed of the Governor and the state superintendent as ex officio, and five additional members appointed by the Governor, including a county superintendent, the head of a state educational institution, and at least one other person connected with schoolwork. In practice, except for rare exceptions, the Governor appointed all five persons connected with "educational work." While the constitution stated that the state board should "have the control, management, and direction of all schools" (11), it limited its power by such regulations as might be provided by law. When the statutory regulations were adapted in 1923, this new school code conferred two major powers on the state board.

One was the responsibility to "determine qualifications of persons teaching or desiring to teach in any of the public elementary and high schools of the state and to that end promulgate, from time to time, a system of classification of teachers" (12). These standards could be established by either examinations or credentials, such as institutional credits. Moreover, the board determined the ability of institutions to train teachers for certification. For example, in 1922, the board took official action to accredit the University of New Mexico for summer teacher education with the same standing as the state normal schools.

The second major responsibility given to the board was to establish minimum standards of instruction (13) and approve the textbooks. The 1923 code required certain basic curriculums:

> In such grades as the state board of education shall prescribe, the following subjects shall be taught in the public schools of the state: Reading, writing, arithmetic, spelling, geography, language and grammar, Spanish, New Mexico history, United States history, including the Declaration of Independence and the constitution [sic] of the United States and New Mexico, and other branches of learning as may seem expedient may be prescribed by the State Board of Education (14).

Specifically, the Legislature required courses on the effects of narcotics and alcoholic drinks and made teacher certification dependent on a knowledge of U.S. and New Mexico history, these subjects to be taught throughout the public schools. It further required that courses of study include manual training, domestic science, the elements of agriculture, and commercial science.

Textbook adoption has continued to be under the board's jurisdiction. For the past 20 years, a system of multiple adoption has been in effect, the board merely giving various publishers permission to persuade local boards that their texts should be purchased. It protects the board from pressure by the publishing companies. The state department accounts for textbook funds, seeing to it that no local administrative unit obligates itself for textbooks beyond its allocation or for books not included on the adopted list.

FINANCIAL CONTROLS

Three years after the constitution had been approved, the Legislature authorized school directors to estimate the funds they would need within their districts each year. The directors gave these estimates to the county superintendents, who transmitted them to the county commissioners. It granted the same authority to municipal boards of directors, but their estimated costs were given directly to the county commissioners. The rural district directors' authority was further weakened by the requirement that the county superintendent had to approve their warrants before payments could be made.

The current school fund provided by the constitution is primarily derived from land leases and interest from the permanent school fund, supplemented by court fines and proceeds from a statewide property tax. This money is then distributed to the districts on the basis of the school census. Provision also was made for an equalization factor to be applied in districts unable to maintain a 5-month school term when a tax was "levied to the limit allowed by law" (15).

When the Legislature wrote the School Code in 1923, it stipulated that county commissioners should levy and collect annual taxes of one-half mill on all taxable property for the current school fund, a part of which was to be designated as a reserve. If the county superintendent could verify to the state superintendent that his finances from a 15-mill local levy, plus the census proration, were insufficient and that not more than $300 had been spent for each schoolroom in the district during the full 5 months, he could requisition an allotment from the reserve to be paid by the state treasurer. The school district special property tax could not exceed 15 mills except in incorporated cities, towns, and villages where the maximum was 20 mills (16).

The New Mexico Education Association has played a significant role in pressing for improved education since its formation in 1886. In 1915, the Parent-Teachers Association became a part of the power structure, and these two were joined the next year by another organization, the New Mexico Taxpayers Association, which acted as a counter balance to the older two. The taxpayers association took the position that proposed expenditures were based on an overoptimistic forecast of income. So as New Mexico sought a solution of its educational problems, a power struggle over the distribution of money played an important part in shaping the legislation.

The influence of the economy-minded taxpayers association was evident in the 1923 School Code. Even the newspapers, echoing its demands for more returns from educational dollars, commented on the association's dominance in the Santa Fe power structure. But newer towns were aggressively demanding certain improvements, and to finance them they were talking about taxing property. The railroad and mining representatives, the ranchers, and the industrialists, alarmed at such "subversion," sought to smother their zealousness and, in particular, to keep the idea of taxing property from spreading to rural areas.

Thus, it was no coincidence that recommendations appearing in the *New Mexico Tax Bulletin,* published by the taxpayers association, were identical to the code adopted by the Legislature. For instance, it advocated that –

1. A strong tax commission should be provided.
2. Local and state budgets should be controlled and prepared by the state comptroller, the educational budget auditor to serve under his supervision.
3. Substantial reductions should be made in the educational budget, since schools cost more than any other agency; specifically,
   a. Teachers should be paid only "what they were worth";
   b. A schoolroom should not be provided for less than 10 pupils;
   c. School terms should be reduced to 7 or 8 months (except through local support);
   d. The county-unit property tax should be distributed to the units within the county on the basis of average daily attendance;
   e. School districts should be consolidated wherever feasible; and
   f. Transportation should be limited to bare necessity.
4. A limitation on tax levies should be established.

The association even admitted its potency, stating:

> At the regular and special sessions of the Legislature during the past six years, the Director of the Taxpayers' Association has been afforded every opportunity to assist the Governor and the Legislature in ascertaining needs of state departments and institutions in the preparation of the appropriation bills (17).

The association used the 1921-22 recession as a justification for some of its recommendations. For example, the January 1923 *Bulletin* reported that property assessment fell from $405 million in 1920 to $330 million in 1922 and that tax delinquency had reached $5 million (18). So, the code contained a limitation of 40.5 mills on the property tax.

Since the method by which budgets are made in New Mexico lies at the heart of many of the state's educational problems, to appreciate them it is necessary to understand how these budgets are determined. In each county the commissioners appoint two resident taxpayers to serve as the local budget commissioners. The educational budget auditor, appointed by the Governor, visits each county in the spring and with the two local budget commissioners forms the commission which sets the allowances for the schools, passing on each budget item by item.

> The thing that is surprising to one from outside the state is the power the Budget Commission, the State Budget Auditor, and later the State Tax Commission has to deny any item to a school district. Another interesting feature of this system is the obligation the county budget commission is under to divide funds between rival districts and between districts whose interests are well and poorly represented (19).

Many local school board members were treated as if they were intruders at budget hearings for their districts. At best, they were little more than observers at their own budgetary-approval proceedings, too often dominated by agents of large taxpaying groups.

The position of "educational budget auditor" has not changed, although the title has become "chief of the school finance division" (20). In other words, since 1923, the State Board of Education has operated efficiently and effectively in the areas of teacher standards and instruction but has little official power in the area of financial control, even though education is heavily supported at the state level. Under such a system, criticized severely by educational leaders throughout the state, it is no wonder that local school boards were forced to look toward Santa Fe, because here was the source of a large part of their revenue and all of their permission to spend it. As former State Superintendent Tom Wiley has pointed out,

> The budget auditor with the mark of a pencil could vacate classrooms, overload classrooms, and relocate, extend or reduce school bus routes. He might tailor the educational cloth in any pattern he desired, as long as he did not displease the Governor (21).

Quite likely, the far-reaching implications of these provisions were not realized by the state department officials. Because the proper role of the department in New Mexico was not blueprinted as it was in a number of other states, there was no tradition to follow. Also, it was generally agreed in the early part of the century that academic matters should be handled by educators but that the educational purse should be under the stewardship of laymen, who were considered more practical in matters of business. No available evidence indicates that educators opposed this division of powers; in fact, there is at least meager corroboration for the contention that a few powerful local superintendents who operated their systems like federal barons were fully aware of the situation and condoned the division because it weakened school power at the state level.

In specific areas, the State Board of Education *has* been given financial prerogatives. The transportation director, who holds a position created within the department in 1936, has jurisdiction over bus routes, minimum standards for buses, consummation of contracts for routes, and general administration of the distribution formula, most of the money coming from legislative appropriations (22). The state board also exercises financial control over the school lunch program—the entire federal allotment of funds, the minimum standards for lunches, and the post-audit of funds for these purposes all being part of its responsibilities. The same is true for vocational education. By statute, the state board is the vocational board and the state superintendent is its executive officer. Thus, the department controls the funds for trades and industry, vocational agriculture, home economics, distributive education, and vocational rehabilitation. A staff employed particularly for this purpose administers the National Defense Education Act allotments. The department must also approve local projects and request appropriations from the U. S. Office of Education before funds can be granted under Public Laws 815 and 874 of 1950 and Public Law 89-10 of 1965.

THE DEPRESSION

Like most other states, New Mexico was severely hurt by the economic chaos that befell the nation in 1929. The schools, as well as other government agencies, lacked the money to continue. The struggle to reduce the tax burden, centering around a proposed constitutional amendment limiting property taxation to 20 mills, involved most of the state's newspapers, educational leaders, ranchers, and businessmen. The taxpayers association, supported by the *Albuquerque Journal,* complained that too much had been spent on educational frills and charged that real property was bearing an undue share of the financial support. On the other side, the education association and The New Mexico American Legion, while admitting that real property was probably taxed too heavily, argued that the already crippled schools would become ineffective if the amendment passed without new revenue proposals.

State Superintendent Georgia Lusk predicted that 3,000 teachers would be out of jobs, that schools would be idle, and that 141,000 children would be denied an education. University of New Mexico Professor George I. Sanchez denounced the taxpayers association for misrepresenting the new amendment by claiming that laws could authorize additional taxes if the people so voted. He pointed out how difficult it would be to put such a law in operation, since the Legislature met only once every 2 years.

The issue was hotly debated throughout the summer of 1933. The New Mexico American Legion finally passed a resolution supporting the state education association's position, arguing that the children would be unable to secure an adequate education unless some means was found to finance the schools. The Central Labor Union took the same position, but it probably hurt the association's position more than it helped, since it was engaged in a series of unpopular coal strikes in the Gallup area at the time and some of the newspapers apparently tied the two issues together. Moreover, the *Albuquerque Journal* reported that all seven former Governors of New Mexico still living had endorsed the 20-mill limit and editorialized that the Chicago schools were to be commended for stripping down their educational program to operate within their income.

Banner headlines in the *Albuquerque Journal* announced on September 20 that the 20-mill limitation amendment had passed the previous day, carrying a majority of the counties. The Governor immediately called a special legislative session for April 9, 1934, to provide substitute taxation to make up for the revenue reduction. The Joint Tax Committee of the New Mexico Federation of Taxpayers Associations, a prestigious group of important men answerable directly to the Governor, recommended that money from new sources be placed in the public school funds, since the schools would bear most of the loss. It advocated a gross-receipts tax to be distributed on an average daily attendance basis; it also recommended that the laws be revised to give equality of property assessments between individuals in the counties and among the counties.

The emergency session finally passed a 2-percent "privilege tax" on gross receipts, exempting all societies and agencies not operated for gain. Rural power evinced itself in exemptions on "proceeds from the sale of poultry and products of the farm, ranch, grove or garden, when made by the grower or producer thereof, and of livestock or any growth or product derived therefrom. . ." (23). The executive secretary of the New Mexico Education Association complimented the Governor and the Legislature and expressed his pleasure that this "business" tax, by spreading the burden over a wider area, would be more equitable and satisfactory than heavy dependence on the property tax. New Mexico, like most other states, was forced to look for new sources of revenue during the Depression years.

Almost immediately, an argument began that has continued to rage for more than 30 years concerning the proper division of state funds. Since the Legislature had never trusted the people with the power to exert local initiative on behalf of their schools beyond the 7.25 mills established by tradition after the 20-mill limitation amendment, there was no willingness on the part of the Legislature now to supplement the difference with local effort, and the effect was stifling to education. Most tax authorities agree that state limitations on local taxation are of dubious merit, contending that taxpayers are not effectively protected and that such limitations obstruct sufficient financial support. Still, the proceeds of the new tax were earmarked for school purposes, the beginning of designating specific sources of revenue for the schools, at least fulfilling a genuine need for a statewide stabilized source of revenue. For the 29 years that this type of financing remained in operation, the state resources amounted to about three-fourths of the total revenues for education.

In 1934, a plan for distributing the new state funds was hurriedly drawn that called for the distribution of funds on the ratio of each county's school budget to the sum of all budgets within the state and used figures for previous years as a basis for the computation. The plan obviously favored the wealthier counties and immediately drew the fire of Dr. Sanchez. He argued that the 1933-34 budgets could not be accepted as a measure of educational need because drastic, inconsistent, and erratic reductions of already unsound budgets had made them the poorest and most inequitable measurement that could be conceived. The New Mexico Education Association's executive, legislative, and finance committees recommended a classroom-unit plan developed by Paul R. Mort of Teachers College, Columbia University, which finally was accepted. Along with it, however, a basic allowance was guaranteed for each county equal to the amount budgeted in 1934; this figure was then converted into classroom units, the high schools being weighted at four-thirds the cost of elementary schools. The plan remained in effect until 1941. As long as tax sources were earmarked, the taxpaying groups tended to go along with the school people in their arguments and recommendations.

With the Depression bearing heavily on the state, the New Mexico Education Association predicted at least $700,000 additional funds would be necessary by 1940. Yet, schoolmen complained about the misappropriation of the money available, charging that 13 counties suffered shortages while 18 enjoyed a comparatively favorable financial condition. It was not so much the complications in the formula, but the basic guarantee—a concession forced by the more powerful and wealthy counties—which "robbed" growing counties by overappropriating funds to those that were losing population. Under the formula,

> The state guaranteed counties an appropriation equal to the "basic allowance," regardless of whether they actually contained the number of classroom units indicated in the "basic allowance." In other words, a county could *officially* have more, but never fewer, classroom units than indicated by the basic formula (24).

The 18 "wealthy" counties followed the lead of Raymond Huff, superintendent of the Clayton public schools and president of the State Board of Education from 1931 to 1954, who quietly but effectively allied himself with the state's Governors throughout his long career. Since the Governor made appointments to the state board, to a large degree the members were answerable to him, and Huff used this relationship on many occasions to influence the Governor and the Legislature on educational matters. Quite naturally, he showed considerably more interest in the rural districts.

The 13 "poor" counties were defended by John Milne, the Albuquerque superintendent of schools for 45 years, and president of the state board from April 1928 until Huff succeeded him in 1931. Milne could be classed as an influential "feudal baron" in the field of education who worked capably behind the scenes with the dominant local political group. As superintendent of the largest school system in New Mexico, he had influence approximately equal to that enjoyed by Huff as state board president. At times, the two men clashed over issues involving the distribution formulas for school revenues, such contests ending in a deadlock or compromise. On many issues they agreed, however, and, when this was the case, they seldom lost a legislative battle.

In the conflict raging over the 1935 distribution plan, George I. Sanchez entered the list as champion of the poor "northern" counties, and quite by accident under the same umbrella as Albuquerque. He had been one of the stalwart supporters of the 1935 plan and stoutly defended the merits of the formula properly applied, but he challenged the state board's administration of it. He actually threw down the gauntlet in behalf of the northern counties and exhibited proof that the funds were not distributed according to the formula, thus disconcerting Huff and the board, who contended that the funds had been distributed in a "practical" manner to keep the schools open. Milne was not seriously disturbed because, according to Sanchez's study, he had lost an insignificant amount by the "practical" distribution. The northern counties were the real losers. Sanchez claimed that giving them the amounts due them under the formula would have taxed the earmarked funds to the extent that Albuquerque would not have benefited financially and that the "eastside" counties would have lost instead of actually benefiting as they did from the allocation. In short, neither Milne nor Huff agreed with Sanchez, and in the power struggle which ensued, the "eastside" and the "big population" centers were careful not to play into the hands of the "northern" counties.

A Citizen-Taxpayers Committee, appointed by Governor John E. Miles in 1940 to study the situation, recommended a new formula for distributing funds based upon "average daily attendance," weighting 1.75 for high school students in comparison to the elementary pupils. The victory went to the heavily populated areas with a considerable financial gain for those having a large ratio of high school students, to the disadvantage of the sparsely settled areas. The "eastside" sparsely settled areas did exercise sufficient power to secure a preferential position for financing transportation from earmarked sources of school revenue. During a meeting on the recommendations in the spring of 1941, Milne predicted transportation would get an appropriation even if the schools had to close because of insufficient funds to pay teachers. At his insistence, a provision was passed setting a maximum of 20 percent for transportation costs from state funds (25).

The age of "educational feudal barons," when Milne and Huff wielded great power with most superintendents following in their train, essentially disappeared following their retirement in the middle fifties. However, there were still a few powerful individualists in the state reigning in their own bailiwicks. One of the best examples of this kind of baron was T. C. Jaramillo, superintendent of the La Joya school system 50 miles south of Albuquerque, who ruled his community with an iron hand and defied attempts to usurp his power. When the state board tried to consolidate La Joya with the Socorro school district in 1953, Jaramillo was a member of the State Senate. He thundered in the Senate chamber that "the hierarchy that coerces the schools" should be trimmed of its power (26). Since the state board had a great deal of discretion in ordering district reorganization at the time, Senator Jaramillo followed his denunciations with a bill, which he forced through the 1954 session, reducing its authority substantially.

Jaramillo successfully defied the state board in a number of its efforts to consolidate his small district with adjoining districts. For instance, in 1962, pursuant to a law requiring the state department to survey all small, independent districts and recommend a suitable reorganization, it advocated that La Joya merge with the Belen school district. Though Jaramillo was no longer a member of the State Senate, he organized the boards of all affected small districts, and under his leadership they became so aggressive that the Legislature rescinded its mandate in 1963, passing a statute forbidding the State Board of Education to survey small districts for reorganization unless their boards requested it to do so. Jaramillo retired from his superintendency in 1964, and a few months later La Joya was consolidated with the Belen system. But while he had ruled his tiny "kingdom," it had remained unchanged.

By 1966, all of the "barons" had departed. Leaders such as Earl Nunn, superintendent in Las Cruces, and Joe Otero, the Taos superintendent, are very influential, but they work mainly as members of a team along with the state superintendent.

COURT DECISIONS AND STATUTORY PROVISIONS

The Church and State Issue

Many Catholic nuns accepted teaching positions in the public schools of New Mexico, particularly in the economically poor districts of Mora, Taos, and Rio Arriba Counties. Some of the public schools could not have existed had these nuns or others not taught with missionary zeal rather than for the monetary rewards the districts could afford. After the passage of the Equalization Act in 1935 making state funds available for all school districts, however, it was possible to employ teachers for fair salaries even in the poorer counties, which in turn made available a reasonable supply of lay teachers.

In 1948, a number of citizens complained about nuns' teaching in the public schools of Dixon, a small Rio Arriba community which was one of the strong Presbyterian missionary centers in the state. Out of this opposition emerged the Dixon Case (27), which the court decided with the following significant stipulations:

1. One hundred thirty-nine nuns were specifically barred from teaching in the public schools.
2. The State Board of Education and all local boards were prohibited from holding tax-supported school classes in buildings having religious emblems.
3. The state board was restrained from adopting special textbooks for use by religious orders.
4. The state board was restrained from allowing children state-furnished transportation to parochial schools.

Although the decision favored the plaintiffs, they appealed to the supreme court for more general prohibitions against religious involvement in the public schools.

When the state board passed a resolution prohibiting public school teachers from wearing religious garb and declared that church property should not be used for public school purposes early in 1951, Archbishop Byrne of the Santa Fe Archdiocese directed that all nuns leave the public schools at the end of that term. The outcome was an effective and definite separation of church-school relations. No longer did schools sponsor baccalaureate exercises except when attendance was on a voluntary basis or when various churches inaugurated services for their graduates. Undoubtedly, the quality of teaching deteriorated in some schools because it was difficult to replace the nuns, who were often qualified and effective teachers, but in a few years the schools were operating satisfactorily with a lay teaching corps. The eastern section of the United States had separated the public schools from the church some years earlier; New Mexico had only recently become a state and as a territory had not felt the impact from the other states until late in the nineteenth century.

The Integration Issue

In 1954, the U.S. Supreme Court ruled segregation to be illegal and notified the Governors that integration must commence at the beginning of the following term unless they requested and were granted a special reprieve. Governor Edwin L. Mechem, after consulting with the state superintendent and the state board, notified the court that such an extension would not be necessary in New Mexico. The very next year, Clovis, Hobbs, Lovington, Las Cruces, and Gadsden integrated their schools with only a few minor incidents. A teacher in Las Cruces, discharged because she would be teaching white as well as Negro children, did appeal, and the State Board of Education ruled that her tenure had been unlawfully violated and ordered the school to reinstate her (28). In another case, Negro children transported from the Gadsden school district to a segregated high school in Las Cruces demanded entrance to the Gadsden high school. The local board appealed to the state superintendent who, with the advice of the attorney general, ruled that they should be admitted to the high school within their own district.

ORGANIZATION AND FUNCTIONS OF THE STATE DEPARTMENT OF EDUCATION

Since its creation, the state department has been organized primarily as an agency for (a) regulation and control, (b) service and leadership, and (c) research. The time given to each of these factors has varied considerably over the past 50 years, shifting with the times as well as the administrations. In the beginning, supervisors were considered to be little more than inspectors who searched out weaknesses in the local schools but did very little to help correct them—too often the tragic history of understaffed departments in poor states. It was not until after the Council of Chief State School Officers initiated its study of departmental functions in 1950 that New Mexico began to operate under the theory that "for every control there should be a corresponding service" (29).

In 1959, the department set forth its new approach as a "partnership concept" along nine fronts: curriculum and instruction, finance, school business administration, personnel, transportation, school plant facilities, school district organization, special services, and state-federal relationships. Instead of spending so much time on enforcement, the department gradually placed major emphasis on encouraging and sponsoring in-service training. Sometimes this was accomplished by the department's supervisors; at other times it was done in cooperation with universities and colleges. The first extensive effort along this line developed in the early fifties when the department sponsored a cooperative program for education administration with funds partially furnished by the Kellogg Foundation (30). Other programs followed, such as the bus drivers institute held each summer on the New Mexico Western College campus. Supervisors organized workshops in arts and crafts, mathematics, language arts, and social studies in cooperation with and often sponsored by other state universities and colleges. Many guides were published and distributed on teaching Spanish, music, the social studies, and other subjects.

As was the case in many other states, New Mexico's department was weak on research. Dr. Sanchez, who served as director of research statistics for the department, inaugurated its first significant study in the early thirties of the underprivileged children of Spanish descent in northern New Mexico. With a grant from the Rockefeller Foundation, the department initiated intensive research in teaching English as a second language, assisted by the University of New Mexico and the Bernalillo County public schools. Directed by L. S. Tireman and Marie Hughes, this study did not terminate until 1937 and in large measure converted the school into a force in the community.

Although the actual findings were not organized and disseminated effectively, the outstanding product was the development of teachers who succeeded to supervisory positions and who for many years exercised a wholesome influence on education. Perhaps more could have been done if the funds had not been terminated and if the results had been published and distributed statewide.

Two other major projects conducted by the department should be mentioned, one relating to Navajo schoolchildren and the other to small schools. Virginia Keehan, director of guidance, accomplished the former in the early fifties with a grant from the Field Foundation. Sponsored cooperatively with Colorado, Arizona, Utah, and Nevada, the study in the Small School Area commenced in 1960 and is still in progress. Certainly more research is needed, and the U.S. Office of Education is to be commended for its recent efforts to strengthen the departments in this area.

RELATIONS WITH OTHER ORGANIZATIONS

The position of the state department within the structure of the Santa Fe scene is difficult to assess. Generally speaking, the chief of the school finance division stands for economy while the New Mexico Education Association urges more expenditures, specifically for teachers' salaries. The department's position is somewhat between these two, at times throwing its influence closer to one and then the other. It is rare when all three of these powerful agencies are in complete agreement, so a triangular situation seems almost inevitable, since the issue of school finance is one of "high tension."

The agency least vulnerable to direct pressure by the state's officialdom is the education association, because its budget is not subject to government review and control. Its chief foe is the taxpayers association and its subsidiaries, which claim in essence that the education association has no regard for economic factors. On the other hand, the education association continues the perennial contest, accusing the taxpayers association of caring less for human values than for a well-balanced fiscal climate. The state department has often attempted to be the mediator, at times with dismal results and at others with fair success.

For many years, public school men had done little more than guard earmarked sources against inroads by other agencies, persuading the Legislature to "leave alone" the sales tax and three-fourths of the income tax, which had been the major revenues assigned to education since 1934. While this income had been adequate in the forties and had even enabled a large surplus to develop, by the end of the next decade it dwindled so much that by 1960 the schools were in financial trouble. In short, the earmarked sources could no longer supply the funds to carry the educational load. Since there was a 7.25-mill tax limit on property (usually assessed at a very low average rate), there were no leeway for local initiative and no alternative but austere budgets. For the first time in many years, school leaders appeared before the Legislature to request additional sources of revenue. Accustomed to viewing the fiscal structure as permanently suitable, the legislators were alarmed; before the situation was solved, they as well as many schoolmen suffered traumatic experiences.

The Mort Report

The Legislature reacted by requesting a study of the situation. The department responded by bringing in Paul Mort to conduct an all-inclusive survey of the financial condition of the state's public education. Following a painstaking examination, Dr. Mort recommended that the Legislature guarantee a base appropriation for each pupil and stop earmarking sources. He advised the state to make a supplementary appropriation over and above this support, based on the ability and effort of each district, the matching ratio to be determined by the true taxing power of the district. In other words, a district would be free to raise as little or as much as it desired, but the state's proportion would be determined by the ability rating of the district.

Mort also pointed out that the local tax base should be developed, (a) permitting the schoolboard of the administrative units to vote a tax beyond the 20-mill limit, (b) raising assessment levels on an equalized basis, and (c) transferring the state property-tax levy to local school units, or authorizing a local school surtax on income at the local level, collected along with the state income tax and returned to the unit. He further recommended that hindrances to efficient local management should be removed by paying the state appropriation directly to the school administrative units, making the 5-mill county maintenance tax a school district tax, and eliminating the earmarking of maintenance and direct-charge taxes.

He felt that the State Department of Education should continuously study this new system and report any weaknesses to the Legislature. His report recommended using the average daily membership rather than average daily attendance in computing the financial ability of the unit, and weighting the schedule for small schools at both the elementary and high school level. To assist the poor municipal government, already spending heavily for other services, he recommended a reduction which would "apply to any school district in which the local burden of non-educational government exceeds" (31) the average for all communities under 20,000 population.

Mort suggested a graduated system whereby administrative units which demonstrated maturity in supporting and operating their schools would be freed from state control in their budget making. Other units, less alert, would be supervised in preparing their budgets by state agencies, preferably the education department. Thus the report embodied recommendations that (a) the state maintain a substantial base support, (b) the state reward local units on the basis of local funds raised, and in inverse proportion to their true ability and tax-raising power, and (c) the district be given more judgment in school taxation and budget making.

Legislative Reaction

The Legislature called a special session in February 1962 for the exclusive purpose of enacting emergency school legislation. Mort's recommendations were introduced in Senate Bill 27 and gained immediate support. In the meantime, Governor Mechem requested John Gott, chief of the school finance division, to withdraw from the study committee and come up with a plan. Gott, who had worked closely with Mort and the committee, was in an embarrassing position. He finally recommended all features of the Mort plan except the partnership aspect for supplemental state assistance, one of its vital elements. However, Gott testified that his proposal was an "interim recommendation" and expressed hope that the full Mort formula would become law at a later date. In his appearance before the Legislature in February 1962, Mort testified that Gott's proposal was "exactly the same thing that I thought in 1924 and I have learned a lot since 1924" (32).

The New Mexico Education Association officials compounded the confusion by proposing that no changes should be made in the distribution of state funds. Legislative leaders and Governor Mechem rejected this and endorsed the Gott-recommended portion of the Mort plan, introduced as House Bill 15. The school administrators and the State Board of Education finally conceded that the

Senate bill carrying the full Mort plan did not have sufficient support, but many of its provisions were accepted and the law enacted. The unit for distributing state funds was changed to "average daily membership" from "average daily attendance," the weighting system now took into account administrative-unit size, and state funds as well as countywide taxes were to be allocated on a new formula basis instead of being distributed to the counties as in the past. Although the federal mineral lease fund and the current school fund were assigned to education, the law abolished earmarking the sales tax and income tax, stating that the "distribution shall be made within a limit set by the Legislature . . . using the support figure. All funds remaining in the equalization fund at the end of each fiscal year shall revert to the general fund" (33).

A year later, the state board presented a program for state-level support calling for a slight change in the weighting formula, the support figure to be increased from $270 to $280 per weighted pupil and a minimum guarantee per pupil. This guarantee would amount to $45, the state to supply any deficiency after taking credit for 75 percent of non-state-derived funds, allowing 25 percent of local or federal funds for leeway at the administrative-unit level. In other words, the full minimum guarantee under the board's plan would be $325 per pupil, the first $280 being the base support, any difference within the remaining $45 after credit had been taken for 75 percent of nonstate resources to be filled from state revenue.

Politically powerful Senator Albert Greer introduced a second plan which included a formula based on detailed slide-rule calculations using as a source the "line of best fit." Drawn on graph paper, it indicated the pupil-cost for each school attendance unit in the state which involved a cost figure for elementary, junior, and high school levels. It was computed for school size, carrying 28 weighting intervals, beginning with schools having less than 20 pupils up to schools with 1,500.

Education leaders reacted sharply to the Greer formula, and on February 5, in a fiery hearing before the Joint Finance Committee, State Superintendent Tom Wiley and representatives of the State Board of Education faced members of the committee who challenged the role of the board in the area of school finance. One old-time Senator asked the question, echoed by several satellites, "Why in the hell are you recommending a finance plan? That should come from the Chief of the School Finance Division!" (34). This expressed the general attitude that the state board had very little prestige in the area of finance. Greer used every means possible to carry his plan into effect, and a few days later, the bill carrying the board's proposal was scuttled. However, House Bill 364, which was almost identical to it, was introduced with Governor Jack Campbell's approval. It met with heavy opposition, and John Gott, who was appointed by the Governor to defend it, was hard pressed at the hearings.

In the meantime, Democratic Floor Leader Austin Roberts appealed to New Mexico Education Association officials to work with Senator Greer for some kind of an agreement on his proposal. After several meetings the Senator finally agreed to modify some of his plan's objectionable features, one in particular relating to an exceptionally light "weighting" of pupils in the large high school bracket. This was a necessary modification, because despite the fact that he used the "line of best fit" up to a certain point in plotting his weighting scheme (35), by his own admission he had deliberately tipped it toward the lower-cost side of the graph at the level of the larger high schools, claiming that "if the Roswell high school can operate at a low pupil cost level, so can all of the others" (36). With this compromise, the plan was reluctantly accepted by educational leaders, and the Legislature passed it.

For the first time, the Legislature provided a minimum-support clause. It had no real significance, however, because it concluded: "In the event the appropriation for this section is insufficient to permit all districts to meet the minimum level established by the legislature, the Chief shall make an appropriate reduction in the minimum support level" (37). Along with this, the Legislature resurrected the system of budget commissioners which it had abolished in 1962. This meant that local school board members who for the past year had been serving as local budget commissioners no longer could do so; budgetary review once more became the province of two local budget commissioners appointed by the county commissioners.

During this period, strong power plays were in motion. One major reason the state board contracted Paul Mort as a consultant during the 1961 financial dilemma was the feeling that if the state department exercised leadership, it could wrest control of school finances from the chief of school finance and give it to the superintendent of public instruction. Despite a strong effort, the tradition of 40 years prevailed, and there was no fundamental change. Again, 6 years later (1967), the state board formally resolved that this control over finances should be under the agency responsible for education standards, the state department. Whether it succeeds or not, it will serve as a defensive measure against those who would transfer to the chief of the state finance division the department's present power to distribute federal funds.

CHANGE IN STRUCTURE

As early as 1929, there had been a futile effort to change the state superintendency to an appointive position. The Legislature again attempted to change it in 1935 by submitting a constitutional amendment to the people, only to see it voted down. For the third time, New Mexicans rejected an appointed superintendency in a special election 11 years later. The Congress of Parents and Teachers, its sizable membership always posing great potential political strength but seldom exerting it, finally became militant. It was determined to pass a state-reorganization amendment introduced in the 1957 legislative session which would establish an elected State Board of Education, one member from each judicial district, with the power to appoint the state superintendent. Despite severe attacks against the reorganization, the amendment did pass in the 1958 general election.

On January 2, 1959, Governor John Burroughs appointed the first interim state board under the new provision. Two days later, the board organized and named as superintendent the individual elected at the time the amendment passed, although it was not mandatory that it do so. Four of the originally appointed members were elected to the board in 1960, and in their first meeting all 10 members drew lots to decide the length of terms: three drew 2-year terms; three, 4-year terms; and four, 6-year terms. Two years later, after the 1962 election, only three of the originally appointed board members remained.

There were definite improvements following the reorganization: The board no longer served at the pleasure of the Governor, and the superintendent no longer was restricted to two consecutive terms totaling 4 years. As an appointed officer, he served at the pleasure of the new board–a board essentially composed of laymen elected from judicial districts. The new system has aroused criticisms, particulary because board members are elected in a partisan manner, running on party tickets at primary and general elections.

This does not imply political manipulations on the part of the board, the real objection being that educational issues and candidates are virtually lost in the lengthy ballots and general campaign confusion. The result has been a heavy turnover of board members, in part because incumbents have fallen victim to the popularity of upper-echelon candidates of the opposing party carrying the entire slate to victory. Also, the judicial districts from which the candidates run are not geared to the county or state power structure, nor do they make allowance for adequate representation from heavily populated areas. For example, one district with a population of over 300,000 and another with less than 30,000 each elect one, and only one, state board member. Fortunately, several strong personalities have capably represented the state's educational interests (38).

Perhaps one of the most significant decisions the state board faced in its first year concerned teacher certification. Due to considerable agitation from a few legislators who felt that "professional education" courses were unnecessary prerequisites for certificates, the Senate passed a memorial requesting the state board to eliminate them. During the board meeting in 1959, Dean Chester Travelstead of the University of New Mexico's College of Education, Dean Donal Roush of New Mexico State University's College of Education, and John Aragon, assistant executive secretary of the New Mexico School Boards Association, defended the prevailing requirements. After a lengthy discussion, one member abstained, five voted against and four in favor of a motion to abolish the requirement.

IMPACT OF FEDERAL PROGRAMS

The Smith-Hughes Act marked the first traces of federal influence on the department's budgets and services. The State Board of Education was designated as the board for vocational education which had to be in operation before the state could receive the funds from the government. With the state superintendent as the executive officer, the department employed supervisors of vocational agriculture, trade and industry, home economics, and vocational rehabilitation. The appropriations finally reached the point in 1964 where it was necessary to name a director of vocational education.

Despite the long period of federal aid to education, the U.S. Office of Education's influence on New Mexico's programs was negligible until the state acquired funds under Titles III, V, VIII, and X of the National Defense Education Act passed in 1958. Within 6 years, approximately one-fourth of its employees were connected in some way with the services extended through federal appropriations. When the Elementary and Secondary Education Act (Public Law 89-10) funds became available in 1966, nearly one-half of the employees were federally connected through appropriations and categorical services.

The department struggles to maintain a service attitude toward the local districts and at the same time retain as much autonomy as possible, but there is no doubt that its activities are "Washington oriented." It bustles with activity, processing and administering federal contracts; large department divisions and substantial staffs work under the various titles (39) and the 1963 Vocational Education Act. In 1962-63, federal funds comprised only 30 percent of the department's operating budget, but 5 years later (1967-68) the national government furnished 50 percent of the budget. It appears that the state departments of New Mexico and other states are to a much larger extent than might be supposed becoming "clearinghouses" for the U.S. Office of Education.

OBSERVATIONS

In theory, the State Board of Education should properly interpret the financial needs of the schools for the Governor and the Legislature, but it is vulnerable for several reasons. First, as long as school budgets are controlled by the chief of the school finance division or by any other noneducational agency, it is reasonable to assume that the state board will be considered an intruder or at least a second-level authority if it takes a militant stand on school finance. This is the record thus far. The board was effectively relieved of fiscal responsiblility in 1923 when the Legislature created the office of educational budget auditor. Changing the state superintendency to an appointed position only cured half the difficulty. Few people seem to have discerned that as long as budgetary control is held by another agency, the department cannot be strong or effective regardless of how the superintendent is selected. John Gott sums up the situation well:

> Most people recognize that theoretically the proper residence of educational leadership is the State Department of Education. All too often these same persons criticize that agency for lack of leadership, little noting that the legal division of authority on certain phases and aspects of education leaves the Department of Education completely incapable of assuming the role that is theoretically its prerogative (40).

If the Legislature begins to feel pressure from the state board, it can immediately attack the internal-operating budget, an old but effective trick. It has been said—with too much truth—that "special treatment of legislators and legislative committees is automatic and axiomatic within the bureaucracy. Requests of legislators are handled swiftly and with special care" if the agency is not willing to face a budgetary attack (41). And the state superintendent is in a very peculiar position. To gain the schoolmen's respect he must be an educational statesman, not a politician, but if he is to enter the legislative area as a public official, he must be able to speak in terms understood and appreciated by politicians. The Governor who runs and serves as an out-and-out political official is in a much stronger position, even after discounting his veto power.

Another reason for the state board's vulnerability is its built-in rivalry with the New Mexico Education Association, a rivalry which developed in part because the association desires to create its own council and has tended to resent leadership from the state agency. Neither wants to be accused of following the other's lead. But the state department operates in a unique atmosphere. It cannot claim a direct effect on the education of boys and girls because its operations are once removed from the pupils, and it has no alumni to rally to its legislative aid as do local schools, colleges, and universities.

Legally, education is a state responsibility, but the average parent or man on the street is not aware of this, if indeed he gives it much thought at all. When pressed, a parent will say, "The education of my child is my responsibility. A part of this job I delegate to the local school." Note that he will say "the local school"; most parents do not admit that their children's education is controlled by an individual or board in some far-away place, such as the state capital, because, historically, education has been a local responsibility. The point is simple: The school must be administered in such a place and manner that its management is accessible to its patrons. Observation of nonlegal groups such as the parent-teachers association indicates a determination on their part to have an active and continuing voice in school matters. If parents are dissatisfied or distrustful, they will storm the local school board's citadel to break through oppressive administrative controls with informal or nonofficial approaches if necessary, and not wait until the next board election for a solution.

How does this affect the state board and the state superintendent? History indicates that departments of education have evolved or are in the process of evolving through several stages. The early state superintendent's chief duties were to tabulate and edit the few reports demanded of local divisions, to advise about the law, and to apportion the meager state aid as the Legislature provided. Gradually, these duties included vocational education and approval of minimum standards.

Minimum standard signifies a level of education below which no district should operate, but to the laymen it too often connotes a different standard of education. The state superintendent usually thinks in terms of larger school plants, better equipment, and a more efficient per-capita investment, which means a consolidation of schools, while the patron of the small school thinks in terms of individual attention bestowed on his child, school spirit, proximity of the school to his home, and its identification with the community.

Often the people in the rural districts are inherently suspicious of city people and feel that consolidation significantly diminishes their voice in school matters. When they appeal to the state board or superintendent, they are rightly told that they should discuss their troubles with the local board, a board which does not seem local to them since they do not live in the same neighborhoods as the board members. Often they contend that they have appeared before the local board without receiving a satisfactory reply. This is not too far wrong because every minority group tends to desire state control until it becomes a majority and controls the local situation, at which point it regards state control as meddlesome and obnoxious.

This leaves the state agency in a peculiar position. People fundamentally desire and believe in local control, yet they realize (more clearly in times of crisis) that there should be a governing body at the state level. Argue as they will that education can be governed in the same manner as all other government agencies, when education is subjected to the authority of any other agency than the State Board of Education, its unique features become evident, and the need for a strong state board appears. The question arises, "How can the state board function effectively where there is a firm belief in local control on one hand and the implicit need for state direction on the other?"

One solution is that the state should do for the local community only what the community cannot do as well or better for itself, thus encouraging local maturity. There should be a feeling of gain rather than loss when a local board and superintendent go beyond the point of needing supervisory assistance from the state department. Although the department should know of important deviations from standard procedures, it should respect and encourage local units to inaugurate educational research and projects and to develop innovations. One school authority stated that "essential needs must be recognized by those who are aware of these objectives and at the same time in close association with boys and girls" (42).

Encouraging superior schools, both large and small, to serve as "lighthouses" to others is an important function of state departments, which should also assume the responsibility for making the results of these local research projects and innovations available to all schools. Mort, in discussing the considerable lag between beneficial educational discoveries and the general consciousness of them, made a serious charge: "The lag in permissive legislation may be due partly to fear on the part of local administrators that to bring the adaptation to the attention of the state department of education would be to awaken opposition" (43). Where such a climate exists, it borders on the "cat-and-mouse" concept of state-local relationships rather than that of a partnership.

A partnership carries with it more controversy and peril than is noticeable at first glance. Many legislative leaders who believe that the state department should operate as an inquisitorial agency—one that constantly challenges local districts in their expenditures—may not realize that this destroys a working relationship between the department and local units which obligates mutual judgments on important problems. Too many critics have construed "partnership" as "connivance," unable to perceive that the department should be a facilitator of local progress. Needless to add, the safe position would be for the state department to "nest" in the security of legislative approval by taking a dim and suspicious view of local procedures. Fortunately, mainly through the professional leadership of the Council of Chief State School Officers, there has been a trend away from the inquisitoral approach during the past 15 years.

Perhaps the state department could realize its most significant potential by taking the lead in an evaluation of educational philosophy. To be successful, this would require wide participation of leaders of local groups and organizations, as well as of skilled specialists from institutions of higher learning.

> The quality and form of an educational system is dependent upon the value judgements made by those in a position to affect the system; therefore, it behooves us, as educational leaders, to be as certain as possible that this direction is as valid as we can possibly make it (44).

This is no insignificant task, because it involves taking account of objectives and aims of individual pupils, teachers, and citizens from the community level, the state level, through the national and international levels. There is a sense of urgency as we rocket into the latter decades of the twentieth century to develop a philosophy we can use, but it can and must be accomplished. Neither methods nor curriculum are sacred if changes are necessary for progress.

Perhaps this situation is dramatically illustrated by the federal government's two-booted jump into the educational arena. The emphasis—a part of the pattern—has been legally established at the national level ever since the Russians first ventured into space. It is reflected in the high school vocational education programs and the post-1958 emphasis on science, mathematics, and language. Recent appropriations are guiding the course of education, but it is difficult to define the long-range effects, particularly on the Department of Education.

Will the state departments become subdivisions of the U.S. Office of Education, to a great extent, merely following the "big cookbook" that details the recipes for using funds appropriated by Congress? Can the departments maintain an independent voice in dealing with the local school administrations, or will they eventually be forced to play supporting roles with the federal government controlling them? The answers are just now unfolding, but in New Mexico as in many other states the department is attempting to maintain its independence to the fullest extent possible. And although the task of settling these baffling problems must be shared by many groups and agencies, a greater responsibility must rest with the educational system. It cannot be done by retreating into the past, but by using the past as a launching pad for advancing beyond the present in establishing clear goals for the schools. The state department is in the most favorable situation to exercise leadership and bring about a meeting of minds which could launch such ventures. And although its activities are often viewed with a jaundiced eye, they are essential, and most thoughtful people recognize this. Education, as set forth in the constitution, is a state responsibility, and vigorous leadership by state departments to give directions in the coming years is absolutely necessary.

FOOTNOTES

1. For further information see Frank D. Reeve, *History of New Mexico* (New York: Lewis Historical Publishing Co., 1961), p. 81.
2. Bishop Lamy in the midnineteenth century made the first significant move toward establishment of schools.
3. Thomas B. Bailey, Jr., "Designing Education for the Future: Some Significant Events and Trends in the Development of Education in New Mexico" (unpublished mimeographed manuscript, May 1966, Department of Education, Santa Fe), p. 2.

4. Since the public school idea was entirely new and brought in by the "gringos," a great many of the people were suspicious, afraid that these newcomers were determined to change the ideas and ideals of their children. Tom Wiley, *Public School Education in New Mexico* (Albuquerque: Division of Government Research, University of New Mexico, 1965), p. 25.
5. New Mexico Territory, *Session Laws* (1863), p. 52; (1891), p. 25.
6. Bailey, *op. cit.*, p. 5.
7. S. P. Nanninga, *The New Mexico School System* (Albuquerque: University of New Mexico Press, 1946), pp. 9-11.
8. Anna R. Hadley, C. H. Allen, and C. F. Allen, *Hiram Hadley* (n.p: The Authors, 1924), p. 95.
9. Wiley, *op. cit.*, p. 27.
10. *Ibid.*, p. 28.
11. New Mexico, *Constitution* (1912), art. 5, sec. 1.
12. New Mexico, *Session Laws* (1923), ch. 148, sec. 105. A most successful cooperative effort between the State Board of Education and the New Mexico Education Association is in the field of teacher certification standards. The Teacher Education and Professional Standards Commission, an affiliate of the association, brought its first recommendations before the state board in 1954. Since that time, a number of far-reaching proposals have been presented for its action by the standards commission. In practically every instance, the board has adopted these proposals.
13. Jennie Gonzales, who had been a teacher in the San Jose Training School, pioneered as a qualified state supervisor of elementary education in the early thirties. Mary Watson, an expert in elementary education, served as elementary school supervisor in the State Department of Education during three periods: 1937-38, 1943-46, and 1951-54. Through her perseverance and skill, she exerted a lasting influence on the instructional program of the state's elementary schools.
14. New Mexico, *Session Laws* (1923), ch. 148, sec. 1418.
15. New Mexico, *Constitution* (1912), art. 12, sec. 4.
16. New Mexico, *Session Laws* (1912), ch. 51.
17. *New Mexico Tax Bulletin* (January 1922).
18. *Ibid.* (January 1923).
19. New Mexico Educational Survey Board, *Public Education in New Mexico* (Nashville, Tenn.: Division of Surveys and Field Services, George Peabody College for Teachers, 1948), p. 226.
20. New Mexico, *Session Laws* (1957), ch. 249, sec. 7.
21. Wiley, *op. cit.*, p. 45.
22. J. T. Reese served as director of transportation from 1936 to 1966. Through his efforts, minimum standards of safety were established; he was instrumental in organizing the school bus drivers institute which was held annually in cooperation with one of the state's higher institutions of learning.
23. New Mexico, *Session Laws* (1934), ch. 7, art. ii, as quoted from Wiley, *op. cit.*, p. 51.
24. Wiley, *op. cit.*, p. 55.
25. The author was present at the meeting of the school officials when this item was discussed with the Governor's committee.
26. The author personally attended these sessions.
27. Officially, Zellers *v.* Huff, 55 N.M. 501; 236 P. 2d 949 (1951). Lydia Zellers was a resident of the community, and Raymond Huff was the president of the State Board of Education.
28. The tenure law passed in 1937 allows classroom teachers a hearing at the local level with the right of appeal to the state board. Many cases have been appealed, and the local boards have been upheld in about one-half of them.
29. Department of Education, *A Guide for State-Local Relationships in Education* (Santa Fe: The Department, 1959), p. 5.
30. Frank Angel, an outstanding teacher in the Nambe Community School Project of which Mary Watson was principal (1939-42), later served as supervisor of rural schools in Bernalillo County. He joined the staff of the state department in 1951 and served through 1954. His outstanding contribution has been his leadership as director of the New Mexico Cooperative Program in Educational Administration. He has been a member of the University of New Mexico faculty since 1958 and served as a consultant on many important state department committees relative to state-local relations and finance while Tom Wiley was superintendent of public instruction.
31. Paul R. Mort, *Toward a More Dynamic Fiscal Policy for New Mexico Schools,* a report to the Board of Education (Santa Fe: Department of Education, 1961), p. 15.
32. *Albuquerque Journal,* February 15, 1962.
33. New Mexico, *Session Laws* (1962), ch. 21.
34. Question addressed to Tom Wiley by Senator P. M. Carr.
35. After plotting the actual per-capita cost by school size, Senator Greer attempted to run a line of average relationship between per-capita cost and size of attendance units.
36. Tom Wiley heard Senator Greer make this statement in February 1963.

37. New Mexico, *Session Laws* (1963), ch. 310, sec. 4.
38. A few persons who can serve as examples of efficient state board members include Virgil Henry of Hobbs, president of the board since 1961; K. I. Langley of Tucumcari; Edward Jory, Mary Wilson, and Fred Comstock, who have served successively from Albuquerque; Billie Holder of Alamogordo, who served a 2-year term; and Beverly Agnew from the northwest area of the state.
39. Mildred Fitzpatrick, with a supervisory and principalship background in Curry County, New Mexico, joined the staff of the state department in July 1959 and served most capably as supervisor of elementary education until 1965, when she was appointed the department's director of Title I under Public Law 89-10. Dr. Fitzpatrick is presently serving in that capacity and has been instrumental in creating a harmonious, cooperative climate between the U.S. Office of Education and the local school districts.
40. John Gott, "Public School Finance in New Mexico" *New Mexico School Review,* XLIV (September 1964), 23.
41. Herbert A. Simon, Donald Smithburg, and Victor A. Thompson, *Public Administration* (New York: Alfred A. Knopf, 1959), p. 402.
42. Paul R. Mort and Donald Ross, *Principles of School Administration* (New York: McGraw-Hill Book Co., 1957), p. 201.
43. *Ibid.*
44. John T. Zepper, "Administrators, School Boards and Educational Purposes" (unpublished mimeographed paper, University of New Mexico, Albuquerque, 1963).

BIBLIOGRAPHY

Public Documents

New Mexico. *Constitution* (1912).

—— *Session Laws* (1915-63).

—— Territory. *Session Laws* (1863-1903).

U.S. Congress. *Enabling Act for New Mexico* (1910).

Zellers *v.* Huff, 55 N.M. 501; 236 P. 2d 949 (1951).

Books

Department of Education. *A Guide for State-Local Relationships in Education.* Santa Fe: The Department, 1959.

Donnelly, Thomas C. *The Government of New Mexico.* 2d ed. Albuquerque: University of New Mexico Press, 1953.

Hadley, Anna R.; Allen, C. H.; and Allen, C. F. *Hiram Hadley.* n.p.: The Authors, 1924. A copy is available in the University of New Mexico Library, Albuquerque.

Hodgin, C. E. *Early School Laws in New Mexico.* Albuquerque: University of New Mexico, 1906.

Mort, Paul R., and Ross, Donald. *Principles of School Administration.* New York: McGraw-Hill Book Co., 1957.

Nanninga, S. P. *The New Mexico School System.* Albuquerque: University of New Mexico Press, 1946.

Reeve, Frank D. *History of New Mexico.* New York: Lewis Historical Publishing Co., 1961.

Sanchez, George I. *Forgotten People.* Albuquerque: University of New Mexico Press, 1940.

Seyfried, J. E. *Costs and Methods of Financing Education in New Mexico.* Santa Fe: New Mexico Education Association, 1932.

Simon, Herbert A.; Smithburg, Donald; and Thompson, Victor A. *Public Administration.* New York: Alfred A. Knopf, 1959.

Wiley, Tom. *Public School Education in New Mexico.* Albuquerque: Division of Government Research, University of New Mexico, 1965.

Reports

Mort, Paul R. *Toward a More Dynamic Fiscal Policy for New Mexico Schools.* Report to the State Board of Education. Santa Fe: Department of Education, 1961.

Murphy, Irvin P. *Analysis and Evaluation of the New Mexico School Code: A Report to the Legislature, 1962.* Microfilm available, University Microfilms, Inc., 313 N. First Street, Ann Arbor, Mich.

New Mexico Educational Survey Board. *Public Education in New Mexico.* Nashville, Tenn.: Division of Surveys and Field Services, George Peabody College for Teachers, 1948.

Sanchez, George I. "Future Legislative Program for Financing Public Education in New Mexico: A Conference Report on Financing Public Education in New Mexico." *University of New Mexico Bulletin* VIII, No. 3 (September 15, 1932), 97, 98.

Articles and Periodicals

Albuquerque Journal, September 20, 1933, and February 15, 1962.

Carlsbad Current Argus, 1961.

Deming Headlight, 1910.

Gott, John. "Public School Finance in New Mexico." *New Mexico School Review,* XLIV (September 1964), 23.

Las Cruces News Sun, 1961.

New Mexico School Review. Vols. XIII, XX, XXVII, XLIV (1921, 1928, 1931, 1950).

New Mexico Tax Bulletin (January 1922, 1923).

Santa Fe Weekly New Mexican, 1874.

Santa Fe New Mexican, 1940, 1961.

Seyfried, J. E. "Analysis and Evaluation of New Mexico School Laws." *The University of New Mexico Bulletin,* VI, No. 2 (1932), 39 ff.

— — "Public School Budgetary Procedure." *The University of New Mexico Bulletin,* VI, No. 1 (July 1, 1932), 10.

Unpublished Material

Bailey, Thomas B., Jr. "Designing Education for the Future: Some Significant Events and Trends in the Development of Education in New Mexico." Unpublished mimeographed manuscript, May 1966, Department of Education, Santa Fe.

Moyers, Robert A. "A History of Education in New Mexico." Unpublished Ph.D. dissertation, George Peabody College for Teachers, Nashville, Tennessee, 1941.

Zepper, John T. "Administrators, School Boards and Educational Purposes." Unpublished mimeographed paper, University of New Mexico, Albuquerque, 1963.

Other Sources

Board of Education. Minutes of the meetings held in Santa Fe, New Mexico, in 1920, 1926, 1938, 1939, 1941, 1948, 1949, 1961.

New Mexico Education Association. Minutes of the Executive Committee and Council meetings in Santa Fe, New Mexico, 1933, 1948.

Appendix A

NEW MEXICO CHIEF STATE SCHOOL OFFICERS

Appointed by Territorial Governors

1891-96	Amado Chavez
1897	Placido Sandovel
1898-1902	Manuel C. DeBaca
1904	Amado Chavez
1905	Hiram Hadley
1911	James E. Clark

Elected at General Election

1912-16	A. N. White
1917-20	Jonathan H. Wagner
1921-22	John V. Conway
1923-26	Esabel Eckles
1927-29	Lois Randolph
1929-30	A. Montoya
1931-34	Georgia Lusk
1935-38	H. R. Rodgers
1939-42	Grace Corrigan
1943-46	Georgia Lusk
1947-50	Charles Rose
1951-54	Tom Wiley
1955-58	Georgia Lusk

Appointed by the State Board of Education

1959-63	Tom Wiley
1963-	Leonard De Layo

Appendix B

Chart I.--NEW MEXICO DEPARTMENT OF EDUCATION, 1967-68

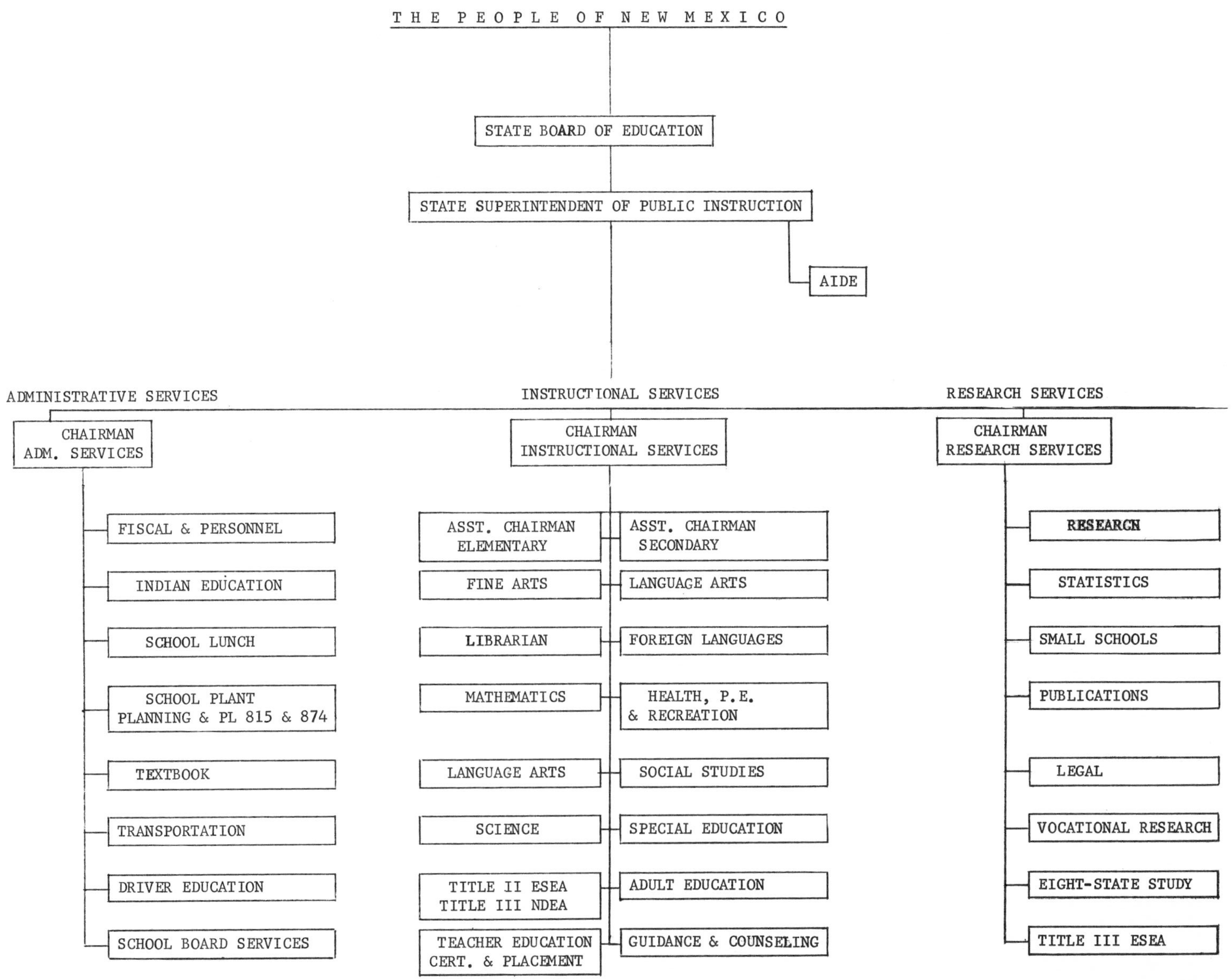

THE PEOPLE OF NEW MEXICO

STATE BOARD OF EDUCATION

STATE SUPERINTENDENT OF PUBLIC INSTRUCTION

AIDE

ADMINISTRATIVE SERVICES

CHAIRMAN ADM. SERVICES

- FISCAL & PERSONNEL
- INDIAN EDUCATION
- SCHOOL LUNCH
- SCHOOL PLANT PLANNING & PL 815 & 874
- TEXTBOOK
- TRANSPORTATION
- DRIVER EDUCATION
- SCHOOL BOARD SERVICES

INSTRUCTIONAL SERVICES

CHAIRMAN INSTRUCTIONAL SERVICES

- ASST. CHAIRMAN ELEMENTARY
- FINE ARTS
- LIBRARIAN
- MATHEMATICS
- LANGUAGE ARTS
- SCIENCE
- TITLE II ESEA TITLE III NDEA
- TEACHER EDUCATION CERT. & PLACEMENT
- ASST. CHAIRMAN SECONDARY
- LANGUAGE ARTS
- FOREIGN LANGUAGES
- HEALTH, P.E. & RECREATION
- SOCIAL STUDIES
- SPECIAL EDUCATION
- ADULT EDUCATION
- GUIDANCE & COUNSELING

RESEARCH SERVICES

CHAIRMAN RESEARCH SERVICES

- RESEARCH
- STATISTICS
- SMALL SCHOOLS
- PUBLICATIONS
- LEGAL
- VOCATIONAL RESEARCH
- EIGHT-STATE STUDY
- TITLE III ESEA

See next page for second half of chart.

Appendix B

Chart I.--NEW MEXICO DEPARTMENT OF EDUCATION, 1967-68 (Continued)

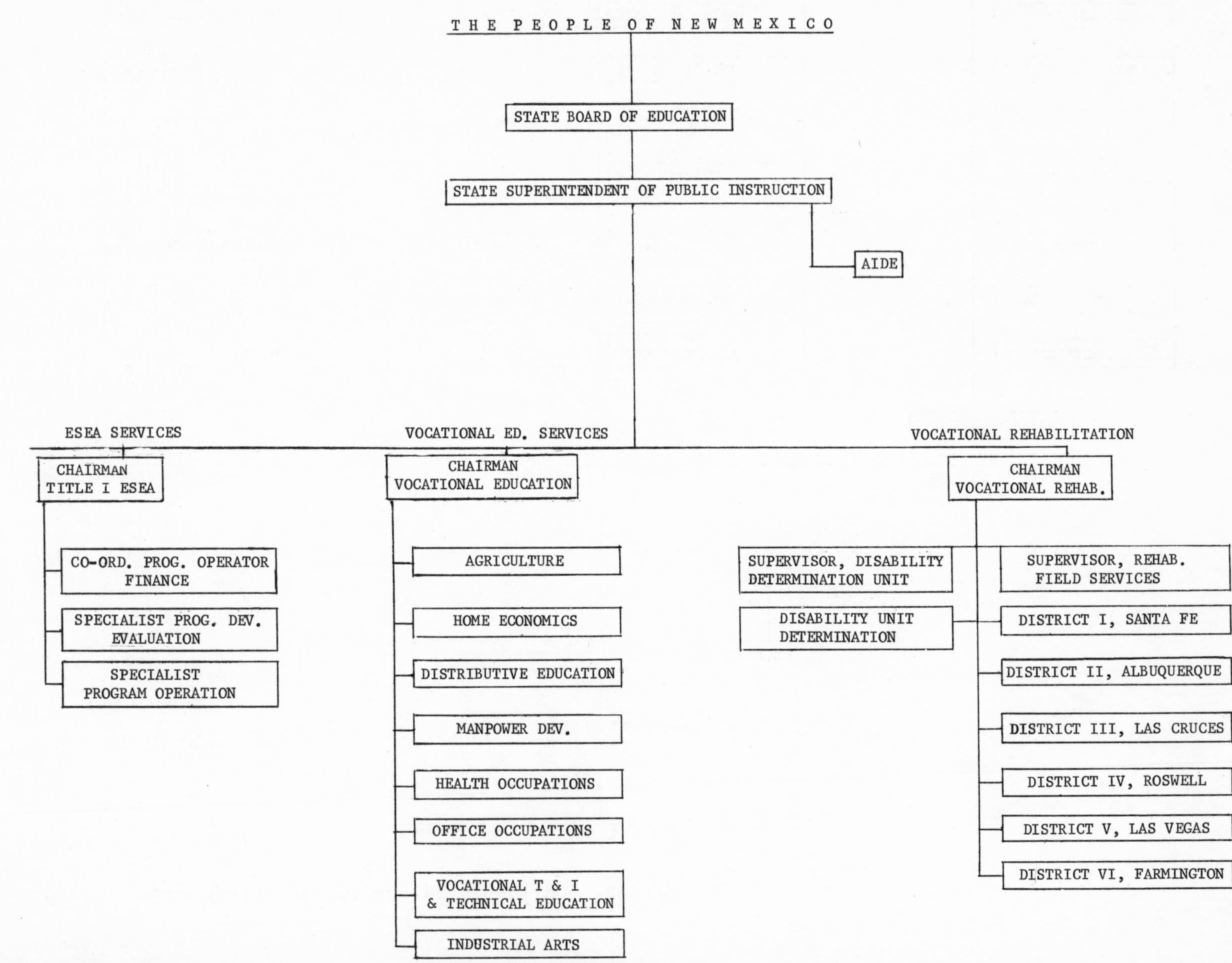

32 New York

STATE EDUCATION DEPARTMENT

Edmund H. Crane
Esther C. Smith
Kathryn Sue Updike

Contents

THE EARLY YEARS

The New York State system of education is inherited partly from the Dutch, and partly from the English, who wrested the colony from Holland in 1664. The Dutch and English concepts of education were essentially different. Primarily trades people, the Dutch were concerned with providing widespread general education and established tax-supported elementary schools under the control of church and state in all of their colonies. Under the English, who were more concerned with the education of the elite at the secondary level and beyond, the common school system of the Dutch all but disappeared, a system of private and church-supported academies developed. The year 1754 witnessed the opening of the private Kings College in New York City to cater to the special needs of the well-to-do.

After the Revolutionary War, one of the first problems to which the new state government gave its attention was education. In 1784, before adoption of the first State Constitution and within 6 months of the time that British troops evacuated New York City, the State Legislature created the corporate body of the Regents of the State of New York to act as a governing body of Kings College, later renamed Columbia College. Three years later, the state authorized the Board of Regents to charter new colleges and gave the board broad powers of supervision over them. At the same time, it was charged with the general supervision of all academies and authorized to charter new ones. The state empowered the regents to grant financial aid—direct monetary grants and land grants to colleges and, in small amounts, money grants to academies. Later the Board of Regents was relieved of direct operating responsibility for Columbia College and became solely a state control agent. Thus, secondary and higher education continued in the colonial pattern of church and private local control, but under general state governance and with state support.

The Board of Regents had no responsibility for elementary education, but it recognized the state's need for a strong elementary program as early as 1787, when it reported to the Legislature that the building of public schools for teaching reading, writing, and arithmetic was of great importance which should not be left to the discretion of private individuals but should be promoted by public authority.

Although the Board of Regents and other groups continued to urge the establishment of common schools, New York took no action until 1795, when, partly in response to Governor George Clinton's message to the Legislature urging that common schools be established throughout the state, the Legislature enacted a bill appropriating $100,000 a year for each of the next 5 years to encourage the establishment and maintenance of common schools. The same legislation required that to qualify for state funds, the local school must raise a sum equal to half again as much as the allotment for which it qualified. Thus were initiated two of the principles that have appeared in all legislation relating to public school support—state support and a mandated local contribution.

After the 5-year period of the 1795 legislation, its terms were not renewed, and for a decade the state made no further effort to encourage public education. Evidence indicated that the lack of action was due not to lack of interest, but to disagreement over what should be done and whether the common school program should be placed under the control of the Board of Regents.

Finally, under persistent and growing pressure, the Legislature passed the Common School Act of 1812, laying the groundwork for the pattern of public school control that exists in the state today. This act divided the towns of the state into school districts which became the bases for today's centralizations and consolidations. It provided for the local control of schools by boards of trustees, who serve as state agents. It established a system of support similar to that in the early Dutch colonies: The board of trustees was empowered to levy a tax to build and maintain schools; the state contributed to the payment of teachers' salaries; additional costs were to be covered by an assessment against the parents of pupils. To govern the public elementary school system, the Legislature created the Department of Public Instruction, headed by the state superintendent of schools, thus marking the first organization of the elementary schools in any state into a common system under the jurisdiction of an appointed officer.

In 1853, the Union Free School Act extended public support of education to the secondary level. The immediate intent of this law was to permit cities and other populous places to consolidate their many common school districts into a single district and to organize public high schools under the control of boards of education.

Thus, all through the nineteenth century, there were two state educational authorities: The regents had general control of colleges and universities and of the private academies; the state superintendent of schools was in general control of elementary education. Both authorities claimed control of the public high school. An inevitable conflict for jurisdiction over the high schools arose between the two and lasted until after the turn of the century.

The nineteenth century was a period of evolutionary but solid growth toward a state educational system, the legal status of which was founded on legislative acts. In the constitutional convention of 1894, however, an education article gave education a constitutional foundation—culminating the effort of 250 years of campaigning for a system of free public education. It also directed that the corporation created in 1784 as the Regents of the University of New York State be continued under the name of the University of the State of New York and that not less than nine regents should govern the body and discharge its functions which may be changed by the Legislature.

This short article provided a firm base for state support and general control of education in the state. Because it left all details as to the allocation of responsibilities, establishment of state-local relationships, standards, and finance to legislative decision, it has given the state system great flexibility and enables it to adjust quickly to changing needs and conditions.

The nineteenth century saw also the birth of the State Library (1818); the State Museum (1836); and the Board of Regents control of the professions of medicine (1890), dentistry (1895), veterinary medicine (1895), and certified public accounting (1896).

THE TWENTIETH CENTURY: ORGANIZING FOR QUALITY EDUCATION

The twentieth-century history of the New York State Education Department properly begins with the important legislation of 1904. During the nineteenth century, there had evolved two separate educational authorities—the regents and the state superintendent of schools—and there had been a considerable area of overlapping authority and consequent dispute and conflict. The Unification Act of 1904 settled the relevant issues by joining the two authorities into one organization with the Board of Regents as its governing board and the state superintendent of schools, retitled state commissioner of education, as the chief executive officer of the Board of Regents and chief administrative officer of the State Education Department. Thus all educational institutions—public and private, elementary and secondary, colleges and universities, libraries and museums—were placed under the general supervision and governance of a single control board, the Regents of the University of the State of New York.

The Board of Regents has broad powers of governance and control over all educational institutions in New York State, public and private, from the elementary to the university level. It has sweeping power over public schools and lesser but still highly influential power over private schools through its right to charter and register (which implies the right to establish requirements for a charter) and its right to visit and to require periodic reports from the institutions. The board continues, through the powers vested in it earlier, to license and regulate specified professions, to maintain and operate the State Library, and to charter and have general governance of public and private libraries in the state. The 1904 legislation also transferred to the Board of Regents the responsibility for maintenance and operation of the State Museum and Division of Science.

Members of the Board of Regents are elected by vote of the joint Houses of the Legislature. The constitution provides that there shall not be fewer than nine members. There are now 15, 1 from each of the state's judicial districts and 4 at large, serving 15-year overlapping terms. Each year, one member is elected, in addition to any unplanned vacancies which might occur. The members meet monthly for a 2-day session. They are nonsalaried but are reimbursed for expenses in connection with their office.

The Board of Regents appoints the commissioner of education, who is chief administrative officer of the Education Department. As chief executive, he enforces the school law and the regulations approved by the regents. With the approval of the Board of Regents, he makes and enforces regulations concerning the schools, including the establishment of standards and the certification of teachers and other professional personnel in schools; prescribes examination procedure; and makes regulations governing other selected professions. These regulations have the effect of law. Responsible for long-range educational planning and development of appropriate educational programs, the commissioner allocates state funds to state-supported educational institutions and administers a broad program of supervisory and consultative services to the schools and colleges. Aside from his responsibilities as chief executive officer of the regents, he has the judicial authority, originally held by the state superintendent of schools, to settle disputes in the schools.

The Education Department of New York State is unique in its relationship to state government. The Governor does not appoint the head of the department, the Board of Regents, or its chief administrative officer, the commissioner of education. This gives the department a greater degree of autonomy than is enjoyed by other state departments of education. Nevertheless, it should be pointed out that the Legislature has the power to increase, modify, or decrease the authority of the regents. It approves the department budget. And it can and does legislate with respect to such educational matters as minimum salaries for teachers and district organization.

The administrative offices of the University of the State of New York, including the State Education Department, are located at present in the State Education Building in Albany. Authorized by a law passed in 1906, the building is the first in the world to be erected and devoted exclusively to the administrative educational work of a commonwealth.

At the time of unification in 1904, in addition to the State Library and State Museum and Division of Science, the department was organized into seven bureaus: examinations, accounts, attendance, inspections, law, records, and statistics. The three general divisions, each headed by an assistant commissioner, were elementary, secondary, and higher education. In 1912, when the department moved into the newly erected Education Building, its staff numbered 250. (See Appendix B.)

Developments in education—and in the Education Department—during the twentieth century have not proceeded in an orderly way toward the attainment of established goals but rather have reflected the forces of change in society in general. The 1904 Unification Act provided the legislative base for the department, and Andrew S. Draper, New York's first commissioner, guided its organization. Until the mid-1930's, although the department expanded, the basic administrative structure remained unchanged. In 1937, partially as a reflection of recommendations made by the "Regents Inquiry into the Character and Cost of Education in New York State," a major reorganization of the department took place. The state made broad programs the responsibility of the several associate commissioners and assigned more specifically defined areas to the directors and bureau chiefs. (See Appendix B.)

Elementary and Secondary Education

Examinations administered under the authority of the Board of Regents have played an important role in developing and maintaining the high standards of instruction in New York's secondary schools. At their inception in 1865, the examinations were a series of specific end-of-course tests which were used as entrance examinations for the academies and colleges and to ensure the maintenance of standards. As changes in society led to changes in the function of high school education, the regents modified the examinations so they would serve as broad evaluation instruments. Today the regents examinations are a comprehensive system of end-of-course high school achievement tests prepared and rated by teachers. They are offered in January, June, and August and include 25 different high school subjects. The public high schools of the state are required to make general use of regents examinations; their use is optional in the private high schools.

From 1913 to 1944, regents examination grades determined the winners of state scholarships. In the early 1940's, the State Examination Board explored alternate methods of granting awards, culminating in 1944 with the development of the regents scholarship examination which has, since that time, determined scholarship winners and also served a general college guidance function. Since 1962, the regents scholarship examination has also been used as a qualifying examination for distribution of scholar incentive awards.

The most recent testing service is the pupil evaluation program, established in the fall of 1965 to provide teachers, schools, and the State Education Department with an annual inventory of pupil achievement in arithmetic and reading in grades 1, 3, 6, and 9. The tests used in the program are standardized tests of achievement, based on New York State courses of study and are administered at the beginning of each school year to pupils in every school in the state. The test advisory service provides consultative help to the schools in selection and use of all published standardized tests and aids in improvement of teacher-prepared classroom tests.

Education in 1904 consisted of many small schools, meagerly trained teachers, secondary programs designed for the academically able pupil only, and supervision in the form of inspections by Education Department personnel. There were 690 union free school districts and 9,961 common school districts staffed by 37,954 elementary and secondary teachers, the majority of whom had no more than a year's training beyond high school. The school commissioners, most of whom had no professional training, were supposed to supervise these scantily trained and widely dispersed teachers. The commissioners devoted most of their time to administrative supervision and detailed reporting of school conditions and activities.

The department had, in addition to assistant commissioners for elementary and secondary education, a division or bureau (the term seems to have been used interchangeably) of inspections. The assistant commissioners were expected to be generalists, to settle controversies wherever practicable, and to promote the interests of schools in every feasible way. Apart from a stenographer and a messenger, an assistant commissioner had no staff. When he wanted an inspection he called on the Division of Inspections, which carried one out and reported the results to him. The 15 employees of this division investigated universities, colleges, technical and professional schools, normal schools, training classes, academic institutions, and common schools. Apparently not specializing, they were expected to be so conversant with schoolwork as to be fairly able to judge its quality at any level and in any area.

Growth and development in the educational system have occasioned very different supervisory needs. After 1914, and especially after the Central School Act of 1925, there was a steady diminution of one- and two-room schools as larger schools were formed. Concurrent with the changes in district organization was a slow but constant rise in the level of teacher training. The trend away from the strictly academic started with the introduction of agriculture and home economics in the rural high schools established under the Central School Act—expanded to include business and distributive education, agriculture, home economics, vocational-technical subjects, art, and music, each taught by a teacher specialist. During and after the 1930's, there was a steady growth in the point of view that supervision, if it was to produce better teaching, should not be of the inspectorial, rating, and reporting type, but rather should be an advisory and supporting activity. Such a trend may be observed superficially in changes in titles: For example, local supervisors were retitled consultants and helping teachers. Less frequently, it has resulted in a complete separation of the rating and reporting function (for tenure, promotion, and, in some cases, salary decisions) and the instructional improvement function.

Changes in the nature and organization of supervision in the state department have paralleled changes in the schools. As teachers became more specialized, supervision necessarily became specialized, too. The appropriate assistant commissioners organized supervisory units staffed by specialists. With the expanding work, first in the vocational fields and later in the academic fields, bureaus or units with bureau status replaced the individual specialist. Early instructional supervision, in the form of classroom visits, continued for some years. As state supervisors used group meetings, conferences, and workshops to aid in supervision, improved local leadership lessened the necessity for supervision at the classroom level.

Initiation in 1961 of a new supervisory device, the cooperative review service, marked the beginning of a new relationship between the department and the local school. To date, some 100 school districts have been reviewed under this system. A review focuses on the overall school program and the development of a plan of action to solve the most serious problems of an individual school district. Although the initial request for a cooperative review must come from the local school board, both local and department personnel are involved in its completion. After local authorities complete a preliminary review of practices and policies and administer a series of prescribed tests, a team of department specialists visits the school to examine its practices. Finally, the results of the two reports are correlated, and recommendations are made.

The years since 1904 also have seen important and far-reaching changes in curriculum. In 1910, the Education Department issued a 256-page syllabus for elementary schools that made definite provision for an elementary course of 6 years and an intermediate course to cover the work of grades 7 and 8. At the sêcondary level, the specialists in the inspections division, which had come under the direction of the assistant commissioner for secondary education and whose members were becoming academic specialists, prepared course outlines. The Smith-Hughes Act of 1917 and the Vocational Law of 1918 spurred curriculum writing in the vocational subjects, and the department wrote outlines which would conform to federal requirements.

In 1933, the department issued a *Prospectus for Rural Teachers.* It suggested the division of subject matter into five broad areas: language arts, social studies, arts, science, and mathematics. A radical departure from the former rather limited and specific skills organization, this *Prospectus* initiated a new trend in curriculum organization which eventually led to today's emphasis on development of concepts. Following World War II, social and economic factors and new knowledge placed great pressure on curriculum writers for new and different materials. A trend toward moving materials downward in grade level left room at the top for more advanced courses for which materials had to be prepared. Science, which had not been widely taught in the elementary schools, was voluntarily taught in many districts after World War II and was made mandatory in 1958. Advances in technology opened up new occupations for which training programs had to be written. Child development principles were more deeply examined as a guide to curriculum organization, and the viewpoint was being strongly presented that school programs should place less stress on remembering and greater stress on reasoning and the development and application of principle.

As a result, there was a great upsurge of curriculum work in the Education Department. New programs were written that expressed the new points of view in learning, suggested new materials and methods, and incorporated new technical devices for teaching. The department also conceived advanced courses and programs for groups with special needs. As materials for secondary level use were prepared, the plan writers followed up on what had been done in elementary education in 1938 by breaking down discrete subject walls. For example, they molded algebra, geometry, and trigonometry into a comprehensive mathematics course. And, for the first time, they wrote the program in basic subjects—language, social studies, mathematics, and science—and art and music as full 12-year sequences without the traditional break between elementary and secondary level.

The present procedure for revising curriculum involves experts in the various curriculum areas and key teachers and instructional supervisors from public, parochial, and independent schools of the state. New curriculum publications are prepared, and usually 100 to 150 cooperating schools representative of the various regions of the state try them out experimentally.

The period from 1965 to 1968 brought several significant changes to the New York State Education Department. The department developed a new performing arts program involving about 1.5 million students. Activities include in-school performances, attendance at summer matinee performances at the Saratoga Performing Arts Center, visits to the Lincoln Center and museums in New York City, as well as a series of workshops for professional personnel. A Division of Humanities and the Arts, formed in 1967, includes the new bureaus of music and art education and is responsible for the supervision of humanities programs in elementary and secondary schools.

Prekindergarten programs have become a major concern for the public schools in New York State. These programs receive support from the Office of Economic Opportunity under Project Head Start (which began in 1965), Title I of the Elementary and Secondary Education Act, and a special state-aid fund established by the 1966 Legislature for experimental prekindergarten programs for disadvantaged 3- and 4-year-olds. The 1968 Legislature approved $5 million for continuing these programs.

In February 1967, the department organized an office of science and technology to coordinate the activities of elementary and secondary schools, colleges, and other agencies—both public and private—trying to solve a wide variety of problems facing society. Surveys are providing information on facilities and personnel in higher education for teaching and research in order to establish long-range objectives. The office has special interest in the role of state government in the development of science and in the unique and specific roles of a state education department in the field of science education.

Qualifying Examinations

In 1904, a Division of Examination, administratively responsible directly to the commissioner of education, was responsible for administration of the regents examinations, teacher examinations as a basis of certification, and preliminary examinations for entry into normal and professional schools. As certification of teachers by examination ground to a halt in 1924, this part of the division's responsibilities ceased. Expanding its testing program to include elementary and secondary tests of a standardized type, the department renamed the division the Division of Examinations and Testing. Continually increasing responsibilities, due to the development of scholarship tests and fellowship tests for professional study, led in 1961 to a further reorganization of the division as the Regents Examination and Scholarship Center under an assistant commissioner. Within the center are three bureaus: elementary and secondary educational testing, higher and professional educational testing, and pupil testing and advisory services.

In 1904, there were assistant commissioners of education for elementary and secondary education, both without a staff. Soon thereafter, the inspections division came under the direction of the assistant commissioner for secondary education and, in 1938, was renamed the Division of Secondary School Supervision. That same year, the state established a Division of Elementary Education.

A medical inspections bureau came into being in 1923 to administer the mandated health examinations. Its responsibilities expanded, and in 1930, the state established a Division of Health and Physical Education which had the added duty of encouraging and supervising health instruction and physical education programs.

From the time of their inception, these divisions grew continuously, with the specialists becoming a group of specialists of bureau status. In 1963, a major reorganization of the State Education Department recognized this growth and made a distinction between instructional supervision and supervision of administrative and organizational arrangements.

The state appointed an associate commissioner for educational supervision in 1937. In 1963, he was retitled associate commissioner for elementary, secondary, and continuing education. Responsible to him are assistant commissioners for instructional services (general education), educational administration and supervision, occupational education, and pupil personnel services and continuing education.

Districting

Sparsely populated agricultural and forest areas contrast sharply with the large metropolitan centers in New York, to produce a very unevenly distributed population. In 1904, the state had 10,651 school districts, as set up by the 1812 Common School Law, and the majority of its population lay in rural areas. In order to bring professional leadership to rural districts and strengthen the program of the rural schools, the Legislature in 1912 created the Office of District Superintendent of Schools and divided the counties of the state into 207 supervisory districts. Local school commissioners elected the district superintendent from among candidates who qualified under state regulation. The district superintendent thereafter was a state intermediate officer, through whom information flowed between the schools and the Education Department. In 1923, the state formed a rural education bureau to supervise the rural schools and provide district superintendents with a direct contact in the department.

By 1933, education leaders saw that the process of centralization was having a dual effect on the district superintendency. Centralization was bringing a higher level of professional leadership to the local districts at the same time that it was reducing the number of local units under the district superintendent's supervision. Therefore, the state authorized the commissioner of education in each case where a superintendency was vacated to review the situation and, where advisable, discontinue the superintendency, annexing its territory to one or more adjoining superintendencies. As a result, the number of district superintendencies had, by 1965, been reduced to 70.

Further attempts to improve rural education were made through the creation of stronger local units. A 1914 Central School Law permitted rural districts to consolidate to form more efficient units. Because it carried no reward features, the legislation was largely ineffective. Three years later, the Legislature enacted a bill to join into one administrative unit all of the common school districts in each town. This bill aroused such vigorous opposition that it was repealed.

In 1925, studies of rural education needs carried out by the Committee of 21, composed for the most part of representatives of farm organizations, resulted in passage of a revised Central School Law. The law provided that a central district would receive all the state moneys to which it would be entitled as a union free district and, in addition, those moneys the former constituent districts would have received, and a building and transportation quota. Under the highly favorable terms of this act, centralization advanced rapidly. As it did so, however, two sources of potential danger surfaced. The state had left formulation of districts and district boundaries to local initiative. Some districts were too small to be effective units, and between the centralized districts intervening spaces had been left that never could become effective units.

The year 1942 found a total of 5,857 school districts in New York State including 295 central districts formerly comprising 3,991 districts. That year, the state formed a joint legislative committee on the state education system which, in 1946, presented a master plan for the reorganization of school districts. This master plan would guide the commissioner of education in laying out new central districts when voters of uncentralized areas expressed a desire for reorganization.

The master plan recognized that small districts, inadequate in size and financial base, are wasteful of personnel, facilities, and money. By 1965, the total number of school districts in New York State was 997. When the master plan for school district organization has been fully implemented, the total number of districts should be approximately 500.

Development of the master plan also focused attention on the fact that there were many districts contiguous to cities where social and economic ties were essentially cityward. In 1952, the Legislature passed a law enabling such districts to consolidate with the city district, thereby forming enlarged city school districts. Under this legislation, the state extended the school district boundaries of 35 cities to include a total of 365 neighboring districts.

In the late 1930's and early 1940's, it became obvious to educational leaders that local districts in thinly populated areas would not be able individually to meet the variety of needs of rural youth in a highly mechanistic and mobile society. The Council on Rural Education and the State Education Department undertook joint studies, and in 1948, the Legislature passed the Intermediate District Law. Under this act, a sufficient group of central and union free districts could combine to provide to all of the schools of the area those kinds of educational services that the individual districts could not provide.

A provision of the Intermediate District Law of 1948 made it possible for each supervisory district, later two or more contiguous supervisory districts, to form a Board of Cooperative Educational Services (BOCES) to provide services to the local districts. BOCES received state aid and generally had the powers granted intermediate districts except that they could not levy taxes or own real property. BOCES proved an acceptable form of organization, and in 1965 there were 69 boards covering almost the entire rural areas of New York State.

In recent years, with the pressure for increased education brought on by scientific and technological advances, there have been renewed efforts to strengthen education through area schools. In 1964, legislation was introduced to permit the establishment of Area Centers for Cooperative Educational Services (ACCES). ACCES schools would serve relatively large areas of the state and build and operate schools to provide vocational-technical education and other services that local schools could not provide. An ACCES bill passed both Houses of the Legislature in 1964 but was vetoed by the Governor. Introduced again in 1965, the bill failed passage. It is anticipated that interest in such legislation will be sustained in the future and that these enlarged districts will be allowed to build and operate facilities.

Urban School Problems

The greatest area of concern in recent years has been city schools, where slightly over 50 percent of the state's children attend school. The city districts have long been hampered by financial stringency and, in recent years, by the growing resentment of minority groups isolated in a particular school or area.

Accompanying the financial problems of the city schools are the problems of equalizing educational opportunities for all children. In 1961, Commissioner James E. Allen, Jr., in a speech, showed concern about the growing evidence that segregated schools are detrimental, psychologically and educationally, to students and pointed out the relevancy of the problem to the stability and vitality of our democratic society.

In order to identify the extent of the problem of segregation and determine how best to solve it in New York State, the State Education Department conducted a census of the racial characteristics of its schools in the fall of 1961 and in their meeting of March 19-20, 1964, the State Board of Regents issued a statement against de facto segregation in which they stressed the various conditions among communities and the need for localities to devise solutions according to their individual needs. The regents pointed out that legislation restricting community choices would hamper local initiative and determination.

New York State formulated plans to increase assistance to its urban school system. In May 1965, Commissioner Allen stressed that the problems of urban education are inseparable from those of the urban community and that the decline of the school has paralleled the decline of the central city. The department established an Office of Urban Education to strengthen services to larger city school districts.

Twenty-six school districts will share $52 million during the 1968-69 school year for community education centers and equality incentive projects. Three factors used to select participating school districts were low student scores on statewide achievement tests, the number of participants in the aid to dependent children program, and school enrollment. The grants will range from $44.5 million for New York City to $14,000 for Fulton.

New Programs

At the beginning of the twentieth century, the state's program of public education was rigidly structured and primarily academic. The state examination system, which then covered every subject in grades 4 through 12, set a single, inflexible standard. Pupils conformed to the program and met the standard, or they were eliminated. An indication of the difficulties encountered is the 1904 records which show that 1 in 16 pupils completed a 4-year high school program.

Although some of the forces which led to changes in school programs in this century came from within the educational establishment, many were the result of outside influences. For example, farm and rural organizations urged programs that would prepare students for effective rural living. Similarly, labor organizations insisted on preparatory programs for business and industrial occupations. Developments in the field of educational measurement led to the wider recognition and better understanding of individual differences in the needs, purposes, and abilities of school children.

At the same time, there was growing acceptance of the principle that education is not the privilege of the more able. In a democracy, it is a social and economic requirement and the birthright of all.

These developments led, first, to the extension and broadening of programs. They also led to the acceptance of new responsibilities by the schools: the responsibility for seeing, as far as possible, that children come to school in good enough physical and psychological condition to benefit from instruction and that they are not denied an equal opportunity for education because of personal limitations.

In 1904, schools provided instruction in physiology and hygiene with special reference to the effects of alcoholic drinks, stimulants, and narcotics on the human system. In 1910, this program was expanded to include the health value of proper dental care, and, in 1918, a full-time dentist was appointed to coordinate the program of dental care required by the 1910 legislation. Today, a school district may appoint a dentist and/or dental hygienist; it is not required to do so.

The New York State Education Department has been a pioneer among the states in developing school medical and physical education services. In 1913, legislation transferred school medical inspection, then largely a check of sight and hearing, from the State Department of Health to the State Education Department and made annual medical examinations mandatory in all schools except those in New York City, Buffalo, and Rochester. Although the program aimed at the control of communicable diseases, such as diphtheria and scarlet fever, it was based on the philosophy that no child should suffer unnecessary retardation or maladjustment in school through physical handicaps or defects which could be corrected. The first state school medical inspector took office in 1915. Gradually the staff increased, and the state created a bureau under the chief of medical inspection in 1923. And also, new services were added to the superivision of medical inspection throughout the state, and the bureau eventually included among its services the conservation of sight and hearing, the elimination of tuberculosis among schoolchildren, the development of a better understanding of the services that can be rendered by psychiatry, the improvement of oral hygiene, and school nursing services.

The year 1916 witnessed the birth of the physical education bureau as part of the state military commission. Three years later, it became a bureau in the State Education Department.

When the United States entered World War I, the physical examination conducted under the National Selective Service Act showed that a very large percentage of prospective draftees had physical defects sufficient to bar them from service. Legislation immediately following made physical education compulsory for all children over 8 years of age. In 1920, the regents authorized the assistant commissioner for elementary education to coordinate the work of the physical education and the medical inspection bureaus and in 1928 created the health and physical education division.

At the time of World War II, there still was a high prevalence of physical defects among draftees, and the physical education requirement was expanded by regulation to 5 hours of physical education per week. At the present time, the commissioner's regulations indicate that school districts should provide daily instruction in physical education of up to 120 minutes per week in grades 1 through 6, and up to 300 minutes per week in grades 7 through 12, of which 90 minutes per week must be class instruction. Over the years, the department has developed a series of tests to evaluate programs and measure physical fitness.

In 1951, the assistant commissioner for instructional services continued the instructional phases of health and physical education in the Division of Health, Physical Education, and Recreation. The health service aspects of the program—the supervision of medical, dental, and school nurse services—were assigned to the Bureau of Health Service in the newly created Division of Pupil Personnel Services, under the charge of an assistant commissioner for pupil personnel services and continuing education.

The 1967 Legislature authorized an allocation of $250,000 a year for 5 years to the Education Department to revise the entire elementary and secondary health syllabus. A five-strand syllabus is being prepared to include physical health, sociological health, mental health, environmental and community health programs, and education for survival. The emphasis is on a broad coverage of material designed to enable students to make intelligent decisions about such matters as smoking, drinking, and use of drugs.

Compulsory Attendance

At the time of unification, the state had a compulsory education law requiring attendance in school of all children from 8 through 14 years of age. In the Education Department, the attendance division had the responsibility for child accounting and enforcement of the law. Local attendance officers were law enforcement officers, and their attitudes toward absentees were legalistic and authoritarian. They regarded truants as incorrigibles. Over the years, attitudes and practices changed from punishment to remediation. The title "attendance officer" was changed to "attendance supervisor" in 1939, and schools were urged to employ persons with appropriate training. In 1955, legislation became effective which required professional preparation for full-time attendance personnel.

Although the state enacted legislation in 1908 that required an annual census of all children between the ages of 5 and 18 (large cities were exempt from this requirement) to provide a firmer basis for the enforcement of attendance, other factors were increasingly recognized as having an effect on attendance.

In 1941, the state reassigned the responsibilities of the attendance and child accounting division—the child accounting functions went to the bureau of statistical services, and attendance supervisory services went to the bureau of guidance. After 1943, no reference to arrests for truancy is found in departmental reports.

EXTENDING EDUCATIONAL OPPORTUNITIES

Handicapped Children

Attention to the needs of the physically handicapped at the time of unification was offered in special schools. Ten such schools were operating in 1910. With the exception of the New York State School for the Blind, Batavia, these institutions were private corporations, all subject to visitation and supervision by the State Education Department.

Legislation enacted in 1917 required cities and union free school districts to take a census of physically handicapped children and to establish special classes for such children. In 1923, the state established a Special Schools Bureau, under the direction of the assistant commissioner for secondary education, to supervise the schools for the handicapped, Indian schools, and reform schools. Six years later, the state transferred the bureau to the direction of the assistant commissioner for vocational education. Supervision of the blind and deaf was a responsibility of the bureau from the time of its creation until 1936.

Additional legislation in 1917 required that the schools identify all pupils who were 3 or more years retarded in school, thus focusing attention on the mentally handicapped. This was followed by legislation requiring districts with ten or more mentally handicapped children to maintain special classes for them. In 1918, two specialists, a psychiatrist and a supervisor, joined the staff of the mental hygiene bureau in the medical inspections division to administer this law. Two years later a psychologist was added, and in 1923, these duties were assumed by the newly created Bureau of Educational Measurements when the mental hygiene bureau was discontinued.

In 1925, the Legislature made provision for state aid for the physical and educational needs of physically handicapped children. In 1926, the Board of Regents established the Bureau of Physically Handicapped Children to administer state aid under the supervision of the assistant commissioner for vocational education. The bureau gradually assumed the responsibilities relating to the handicapped which had been performed by other units. In 1936, the department transferred supervisory duties relating to residential schools for the blind and deaf to the physically handicapped children bureau. Services pertaining to the mentally retarded children were assumed in 1941. In 1946, the bureau became responsible for supervising the education of delinquent children.

Two years later, the department placed the physically handicapped children bureau under the supervision of the assistant commissioner for instructional supervision, changing its name to the Bureau of Handicapped Children. In response to a need for closer coordination, the bureau in 1950 became part of the newly created Division of Pupil Personnel Services. Its purpose is to supervise educational services for physically, mentally, and emotionally handicapped children. In 1962, further specialization resulted in the creation of the Division for Handicapped Children, including the physically handicapped children bureau, mentally handicapped children bureau, State School for the Blind, and State School for the Deaf.

Emotionally disturbed children were also being brought to the attention of educators, and in 1959, the state enacted legislation to permit school districts to establish services for these children. This type of program has become mandatory under the direction of the Division for Handicapped Children.

Educational activities on behalf of handicapped children during the past 10 years have focused on extending educational opportunities to disability categories such as brain-injured children, emotionally disturbed children, and children with multiple handicaps who before this time had not been provided with adequate educational opportunities in our public schools. Approximately 95,100 handicapped children were being served in public schools during the 1964-65 school year.

Educational and Vocational Guidance

The early years of the twentieth century witnessed a period of intense concern for the educational needs of children not adequately served by the traditional academic program. At the time the first Central School Act was passed in 1913, labor organizations were urging the expansion of vocational education.

The period 1904 to 1920 marked the beginning of the scientific movement in education. In 1903, the Society of Educational Research was organized in New York City to carry out educational measurement. During the next few years, scales for measuring handwriting, spelling, and fundamental operations in arithmetic were developed. At the same time, methods of measuring intelligence and achievement were being developed, and psychological testing methods were being applied to the study of problems of delinquency and retardation. In 1920, the department employed a specialist in educational measurements and 3 years later organized the Bureau of Educational Measurements. The function of this office was to encourage and provide instruction in the use of standardized test materials in the schools.

Legislation in 1933 required the large cities of the state to organize and maintain local bureaus of educational and vocational guidance. In the same year, the Education Department employed a supervisor of guidance to encourage and direct the growth of guidance in the schools. In 1937, the state formed a Bureau of Guidance under the direction of the assistant commissioner for vocational and extension education. Its functions included the general supervision of the guidance programs maintained by local school authorities; the assisting of local school authorities in development of guidance bureaus and special guidance and counseling programs; and the preparation of courses of study.

During the first half of the century, all of the special services to children—the health services (including the services of the school nurses and the dental hygienists), guidance and psychological services, and special services for the handicapped—grew rapidly throughout the state system. Within the department, they were directed by units quite separate from each other organizationally. The state saw the need for their close coordination and, in 1950, appointed an assistant commissioner for pupil personnel services. The state attached the health services, guidance, and handicapped children bureaus to the division.

The services continued to grow. In 1955, legislation made permissible special classes for the severely mentally handicapped (trainable but not educable), and 1961 legislation made these classes mandatory. That year also witnessed the formation of the Bureau of Psychological Services. Also in 1961, Project STEP (School to Employment Program), aimed at the prospective school dropout, was developed under the direction of the guidance bureau. Toward the end of this period, plans were under way to bring together in one bureau the attendance and school social work functions of the pupil personnel services division. A program for special classes for the emotionally disturbed became mandatory in 1966 under the direction of the physically handicapped children bureau.

Adult Education

In the early twentieth century, New York State's adult education program was directed toward meeting the special needs of immigrants. The state provided instruction in the common branches, in high school subjects needed for employment or for entrance to technical or professional schools. In 1915, a supervisor was appointed in the Education Department to give general supervision to evening schools and classes.

World War I saw the program much broadened with new vocational training programs organized to meet the needs of war industry; and in 1917, the state created an educational extension bureau to promote adult vocational classes. In 1931, it was renamed the Bureau of Adult Education and placed under the direction of a newly created assistant commissioner for vocational and extension education.

The Depression of the 1930's brought about another surge in adult education with stress on consumer education and vocational retraining, resulting in 1937 in the creation of the adult education bureau in the Division of Adult Education and Library Extension.

In 1945, the Legislature amended the Education Law to provide special financial aid to schools maintaining adult classes. With this encouragement, the program continued to grow with the main objectives of training adults for more effective citizenship, greater earning power, improved home and family life, and enrichment of their lives as individuals. A departmental reorganization in 1949 transferred adult education from the jurisdiction of the assistant commissioner for vocational education to that of the new assistant commissioner for pupil personnel services and adult education.

The state reduced the amount of its special state aid for adult education in 1958 and discontinued it in 1962 when a revision of the state formula greatly increased general aid. Although adult education programs managed to meet new needs as they arose, problems of the developing retirement plans, retraining for supplemental income, and planning interesting leisure time activities became areas of great concern. The rapid technological changes of the time, too, were changing employment needs, and adult education in many places was undertaking the task of retraining workers. The federal Manpower Development and Training Act of 1962 brought new financial resources for the retraining of unemployed and underemployed workers. In addition, a massive drive to reduce adult illiteracy continued with greater advances being effected by the Vocational Education Act of 1963 and provisions of the Economic Opportunity Act of 1964. With the continuing growth and broadening of programs for adults and out-of-school youth, New York has reconstituted the adult education bureau as the Division of Continuing Education with three bureaus.

The department inaugurated a new program of college proficiency examinations in 1963. Under the program a series of examinations is given to enable persons to earn some college credit and meet certain teacher certification requirements without attendance at regular college courses. The tests are open to all persons who believe they have competence in a subject, and scores are sent to colleges which can decide whether or not to award college credit.

Civil Defense

After World War II and the development of the nuclear bomb by other world powers, much concern evolved as to the possibility of nuclear warfare and the extreme vulnerability of schools and communities in case of nuclear attack. Schools were urged to plan what they could do to provide shelter against all but a direct hit during attack and to avoid the effects of fallout. In 1951, a coordinator of Civil Defense was appointed in the Education Department. His function was to work with schools and colleges on the development of bomb and fallout shelters and to train children to respond to a warning signal. He also worked with leaders in adult education and in cooperation with the State Civil Defense Commission to help communities train local leaders and develop community defense plans.

Vocational Rehabilitation

Between 1916 and 1920, as a result of strong pressures to meet the needs of injured workers and disabled veterans of World War I, the federal government engaged in broad-scale studies of the problems of the handicapped. Passage of legislation providing rehabilitation services for veterans gave impetus to the drive for similar services for the civilian population, and, in June 1920, the first federal Vocational Rehabilitation Act, providing grants-in-aid to states for programs for vocational rehabilitation of handicapped persons, became law. During this same period, several states similarly were studying and considering the development of services for handicapped persons, especially for injured workers. New York was one of 12 states which passed legislation regarding vocational rehabilitation prior to the passage of the federal law.

The New York State law designated the Board of Regents as the State Board of Vocational Education and placed the rehabilitation program under the jurisdiction of the board; it created an advisory commission consisting of the commissioner of education (as chairman), the commissioner of health, and the industrial commissioner; and it directed the commissioner of education to designate, within the Education Department, a director for the new program who would serve also as the executive secretary of the advisory commission.

The program got under way in July 1921 with the establishment of a Bureau of Rehabilitation under the general direction of the assistant commissioner for vocational and extension education. Offering a broader program than that provided by the federal act, the New York State law authorized services to render a physically handicapped person fit to engage in a remunerative occupation. In its early years, the state program followed the pattern of the federal legislation, devoting its attention primarily to persons injured in industrial accidents and concentrating on provision of prosthetic appliances and counseling, training, placement, and follow-up services.

Since its inception, the vocational rehabilitation program has continually increased the number of handicapped persons served annually and the scope of its program services. A major revision of the federal Vocational Rehabilitation Act in 1943 was followed by revision of the state law in 1944 which made medical, surgical, and psychiatric treatment available to the disabled in the program. In 1945, the state broadened the law to include the mentally handicapped and those disabled by epilepsy.

Further growth followed passage of the revised federal Vocational Rehabilitation Act of 1954 which increased financial support and broadened coverage of the program. This revision empowered state rehabilitation agencies to make project grants to voluntary community agencies for development of rehabilitation facilities and services.

In 1955, the New York State agency approved the first of many such project grants which have enabled it to maintain leadership in the availability of rehabilitation facilities and services. The 1954 federal act also provided the first authority and funds for the training of professional rehabilitation counselors, and the New York State agency was the first state agency to benefit from these provisions by establishing an organized rehabilitation counselor intern training program with the help of a federal training grant.

Vocational Preparation

Prior to 1904, half a dozen cities of the state had seen the introduction of home economics instruction. The regents, in 1895, had authorized a syllabus for a course entitled Home Science which they designated an academic program. Its principal curricular subdivisions were food, home nursing, household science, and public hygiene.

Legislation enacted in 1910 permitted school districts to establish schools or classes to teach vocational homemaking and courses in "household arts" specifically classified as general education courses leading to the development of two parallel paths in the study of home arts. In 1912, the state appointed a supervisor of home economics. The central school movement, which required the teaching of home economics in all centralizations, gave impetus to home economics teaching, and, in 1928, the state established a Bureau of Home Economics under the assistant commissioner for vocational and extension education.

Private business schools in New York State were the first to recognize the need for courses which would prepare youth for office employment. The regents recognized business education as an approved part of the secondary school program in 1897.

In 1905, pupils could qualify for a state business or stenography diploma or a state business or stenography certificate, the certificates being granted for less than the full 4-year course. After 1910, the state discontinued the state certificates and granted only an academic diploma in commercial subjects. The major objective of the early commercial education program was vocational–to prepare youth for employment in various kinds of office work, especially after World War I increased the demand for office workers.

In 1925, a syllabus organized business content into courses and suggested teaching methods and supervisory procedures. In 1934-35, the state developed 2- and 3-unit sequences in business subjects to meet the major and minor requirements for its general (nonvocational) diploma. That same year, the state introduced outlines for an approved office practice course and, the following year, saw a syllabus written for a secretarial practice course.

The Education Department created the Bureau of Business Education in 1937. The following year saw development of a distributive education program to meet the requirements for federal aid from the George-Deen Act.

During the World War II years, a variety of changes rendered programs more effective as vocational preparation. The state made subjects such as secretarial practice, office practice, and advanced courses in bookkeeping and shorthand double-period subjects. Since that time, the program has advanced rapidly, and the department has introduced new course materials to meet modern conditions. The new course materials have included machine transcription, office practice, business data processing, preparatory distributive education, and twelfth-year vocational business practice.

In 1904, there was strong pressure, particularly from labor organizations, for secondary programs that would (a) hold pupils in school longer and support the drive against child labor and (b) have direct occupational objectives and content. Only one year after unification, in 1905, the Technical High School of Buffalo opened its doors.

The Vocational Education Act of 1917 gave incentive to the establishment of vocational programs in the public schools. Under this legislation, school districts could receive partial reimbursement for the cost of a program. In the same year, to administer federally aided programs and to give leadership to the development of vocational education, the state created the Division of Agricultural and Industrial Education in the department.

This became, in 1920, the Division of Vocational and Extension Education, and its functions included the organization and supervision of all forms of education under public supervision and control of less-than-college-grade education planned primarily to prepare persons for definite vocations. Included were the areas of technical and industrial education. In response to the need for persons with both teaching and work experience, the state established a scholarship fund at Oswego specifically for training trade and industrial teachers. The Bureau of Vocational Curriculum Development and Industrial Teacher Training, established in the industrial education division in 1948, derived from this early work. The greatest emphasis on industrial teacher training came in the early 1940's as a result of World War II.

Continued growth in this area culminated in 1927 in appointment of an assistant commissioner for vocational education and placement of the renamed Bureau of Vocational Education under his jurisdiction. The bureau has held still other names in the interim, being known from 1944 to 1949 as the Bureau of Industrial and Technical Education and, from 1949 to the present, as the Bureau of Trade and Technical Education.

Vocational education expanded rapidly during World War II when over a million persons were trained for war industry in New York State. The national emergency preceding the entrance of the United States into World War II found exceedingly little trained manpower for industrial plants. Acts of Congress at this time authorized emergency defense production training. The schools of New York State rapidly expanded their training programs to meet defense and war production training needs. Training was initiated through joint action of the department and local boards of education, with the advice of industrial leaders and labor representatives. The federal government bore the total cost of instruction, while the local schools contributed the equipment.

In rural areas, cooperative organizations provided vocational training more efficiently. The state passed a law permitting the formation of boards of cooperative educational services in 1948, allowing the districts to establish and provide many types of programs as a cooperative venture.

Paralleling this expansion of facilities was creation of a Division of Industrial Education which included the bureaus of trade and technical education, industrial arts education, occupational extension and industrial services, private trade schools, and vocational curriculum development and industrial teacher training.

Industrial arts education grew out of the manual training and manual arts programs of the nineteenth century. Original courses in woodworking, metal working, and painting aimed at developing understanding of tools and materials rather than perfecting salable skills.

In 1908, the department added a supervisor of drawing and industrial training. Although the general education values of industrial arts found ready acceptance, programs in the early part of the century were limited largely to the city and other large systems. Centralization and the junior high school movement gave a strong impetus to industrial arts in the following years.

As a result of a survey conducted in 1931, the state placed emphasis on the use in industrial arts shops of the materials most widely utilized in its industries—woodworking, textiles, printing, electricity, ceramics, and metal. However, industrial arts continued its general education characteristics and objectives. In 1935, the Legislature amended the Education Law to provide a legal basis for establishment of industrial arts subjects. This legislation specifically defines the program as general education.

The increase in the industrial arts programs throughout New York State resulted in 1950 in creation of the industrial arts education bureau under the assistant commissioner for vocational education (now occupational education).

No established courses of instruction in agriculture existed in New York State schools at the time of unification in 1904. However, leaders in agricultural organizations—the State Grange, the Dairymen's League, the American Farm Bureau Federation—were advocating such courses, and in response to their demands the state added a Division of Trade and Agricultural Education in 1908. Local high schools began instruction in agriculture 2 years later. At this time, a supervisor of agricultural education was employed in the Education Department.

The year 1914 saw incorporation of a full program for training agricultural teachers in the Department of Rural Education at Cornell. Legislation established agriculture as a secondary subject throughout the state in 1917. By 1937, programs were so numerous that the state formed a separate agricultural education bureau. Following World War II, attention began to focus on the agriculturally related occupations and their training needs. Trends since World War II have been toward development of programs in which at least 2 years are specialized and in the provision of cooperative instruction, as through BOCES, to provide the larger student groups necessary for specialization.

To meet economic, sociological, and educational challenges in New York State, trade and technical educators have initiated, expanded, and enriched training programs to serve both in- and out-of-school youth and adults. The shortage of public trade and vocational educational facilities in the early part of the century encouraged the establishment of private trade schools and correspondence schools in many vocational areas. The Education Department appointed a supervisor in the Division of Vocational Education with the special responsibility of inspecting these schools.

After World War II, when educational and training grants were available to returning veterans, there was a tremendous upsurge in the number of private occupational schools. A bureau of private trade and correspondence schools was established in 1952 in the vocational education division to meet the demand for more supervisors in that area. Following passage of the federal Manpower Development and Training Act in 1962, the state established the bureau of manpower development and training to coordinate all of the department's efforts in the area of manpower development and training. Creation of this bureau in 1963 reflected the regents' and the department's concern with the technologically unemployed, the underemployed, the dropout, and the graduate with no salable skills. In 1964, the state formed a Division of Special Occupational Services to include the bureaus of occupational school supervision and of manpower development and training and to administer the vocational work-study program for high school youth.

EXPANDING RESPONSIBILITIES

Finance and Management Services

In 1904, the State Education Department had none of its units assigned solely and specifically to finance and management services, but it soon recognized the need for specialization in these services. However, several grants or quotas—such as teacher quotas, district quotas, and grants through the literature fund—provided state aid equivalent to about 11 percent of school costs. In fact, the first quarter of the twentieth century might be called the quota period in New York's school finance. In the department, the Division of Statistics carried out the work connected with apportionment of state aid.

After 1904, there was a steady increase in the amounts of state aid given schools, mostly from granting new quotas established for special areas. As a result of an increase in the work in connection with apportionment, the department created a Division of Finance, under the assistant commissioner for elementary and secondary education in 1921 and transferred to it all apportionment responsibilities from the statistics division.

The number of quotas continued to increase so that, by 1925, there were no less than 25 quotas or grants through which state aid was provided to the districts. No sound underlying principle governed the rapid growth in the number of different kinds of quotas the state was distributing, and it was generally recognized that a more scientific plan was necessary. During the 1920's a number of studies reviewed, among other things, the need for revised financial methods.

In 1920, the U.S. Commissioner of Education called a Citizens Conference on Education, and, as a result, the American Council on Education undertook an extensive inquiry concentrated on certain states, among which was New York. The findings of the council, reported in three volumes dealing with general problems of financing the state schools and of dealing with the costs of elementary and secondary schools, had a powerful influence in shaping the policies of New York with respect to state aid for public education. These reports clarified the principle of equalization of educational opportunity and support.

The Committee of 21 on Rural Schools (1921-22), the Educational Finance Inquiry Committee (1923), the Legislative Committee on Taxation and Retrenchment (1924), and the Friedsam Commission on Educational Finance (1926) pointed up the need for three significant adjustments: (1) a higher level of state support; (2) recognition of the equalization principle in apportioning aid; and (3) a method, more scientific than the multiple-quota method, of allocating state aid. The study of the Committee of 21 called particular attention to the differences in the ability of local communities to support schools. These studies resulted in state aid formulas that, with only minor revisions, served the state adequately until after World War II.

The New York State Joint Legislative Commission accepted the principle of equalization of support as classified and defined by the above studies. In 1925, proposed legislation included this principle in the Cole-Rice Law, which recognized that, in order to give equal educational opportunity to all the children of the commonwealth, the wealth of the entire state must be made to contribute to the support of educational need wherever and in whatever proportion such need exists. Although it provided more generous apportionment to small districts which combined into a larger central district, the Cole-Rice Law did little to alleviate the financial problems of the city districts.

The Friedsam Commission in 1926 presented a plan for greatly increasing the amount of state aid as a means of providing local tax relief.

Following World War II, increasing costs and decreasing value of the dollar necessitated further revisions, particularly as related to a measure of the cost of a minimum or foundation program.

All through the 1950's, soaring enrollments and mounting costs were among the more serious problems facing education in New York State. Study of state aid continued. In 1960, the Joint Legislative Committee on School Financing came into being and led to the first state aid overhaul since 1925. The new law, effective July 1, 1962, substituted for the principle of foundation aid the new principle of shared costs and incorporated numerous special aids heretofore in existence. The new formula provided aid in four areas: operating expenses, school facilities, pupil transportation, and size correction.

The increasing complexities of financing education in the state are reflected in the changing structure within the department. In 1929, the state appointed an assistant commissioner for finance and transferred the finance division to his jurisdiction. Among its responsibilities is that of allocating federal funds to local educational agencies.

The year 1946 saw creation of the school lunch section and an educational agency for surplus property. In 1964, the finance division was divided into two sections: one to administer state aid funds, the other federal aid funds, including the school lunch program. In the same year, the state appointed an associate commissioner for finance and management services and transferred the function of research in educational finance to its finance division.

During the later 1920's, the finance division began to extend its activities to include the apportioning of funds. The division added an associate in educational finance to advise local authorities on subjects affecting administration and to make occasional audits on request.

The state established a Bureau of Field Services (finance) in 1937 to supervise budgeting, financing, and business methods in schools; assist in the improvement of business management; make special studies of financing and business practices; and provide advisory services to local school officials. The bureau was placed under the jurisdiction of the assistant commissioner for finance.

In 1941, the state gave the bureau responsibility for administering the school transportation program; the next year, it made the bureau responsible for recommending whether small school districts should be discouraged from continued operation by a curtailment of state aid. When, in 1951, New York State granted fiscal independence to its 56 cities with population under 100,000, it also extended the bureau's service responsibilities to more and larger school districts. The Bureau of Field Services became the Division of School Business Management in 1957.

In 1904, the personnel of the inspections division carried out all school visitations and inspections, including the inspection of physical facilities.

Legislation enacted in 1910 required the approval by the commissioner of sites and school construction plans in all districts except in cities over 50,000 in population, causing the inspections division to concentrate primarily on physical facilities. Six years later the regents renamed the division the Bureau of School Buildings and Grounds.

Postsecondary Education

New York State historically placed its reliance for higher education on a system of private universities, colleges, and professional schools. The 1904 annual report of the State Education Department gives a count of 78 such institutions in operation, all under the general governance and control of the Board of Regents. In addition, there were 1 public teachers college preparing secondary teachers and 11 (1 was later discontinued) normal schools preparing elementary teachers. These were under operational control of the Board of Regents, their budget appearing as part of the department budget.

In 1904, the regents created the Office of First Assistant Commissioner of Education and soon thereafter retitled him assistant commissioner for higher and professional education. This subdivision was the slowest to form specialized operational units. Not until 1926 was any operational unit recognized by name in the annual reports. That year's annual report identifies the Division of Higher and Professional Education.

The position of associate commissioner for higher and professional education came into being in 1937. Under this man were an assistant commissioner for higher education and an assistant commissioner for professional education.

Under the assistant commissioner for higher education is the higher education division, which is responsible for evaluating and registering general-purpose undergraduate and graduate curriculums in higher institutions. It makes recommendations relative to the chartering of new institutions and assists with the development of special collegiate programs and projects.

Responsibilities imposed on the department as a result of new federal programs led to a reorganization within the higher education division, including the formation of three new bureaus. The Bureau of College Evaluation concerns itself with the accreditation of colleges and changes. The Bureau of 2-Year College Programs administers the higher education aspects of the Vocational Education Act of 1963 and Title V of the National Defense Education Act. The Bureau of Special College Programs administers graduate fellowships awarded by New York State and provides consultative services to colleges and universities on financial aid available to students. It also serves as liaison with the College Committee on the Disadvantaged.

Teacher Training and Certification

At the turn of the century, there were many ways in which teachers could be certified to teach. Elementary teachers could be certified on completion of a course in one of the state normal schools, on completion of a training class course in an academy or public high schools, or on passing a superintendent's examination or a state examination. The State Normal College at Albany trained secondary teachers. The private college system prepared teachers of all grades. Control of this diversified system by the Education Department was divided. The first assistant commissioner (higher and professional education) supervised teacher programs in the private institutions, the second assistant commissioner (secondary education) supervised the teacher-training program of the State Normal College, and the third assistant commissioner (elementary education) supervised the several ways of preparing elementary teachers. Finally, in 1925, the state created a teacher training and certification bureau to effect better supervision over teacher education programs and be directly responsible to the commissioner of education. In 1932, the state established the Office of Assistant Commissioner for Teacher Training and Certification.

Concurrent with changes in the administration of teacher training and certification in the department, changes were occurring in the schools which prepared teachers. In 1923, the normal schools, which had been providing 2-year training programs, lengthened their programs to 3 years. The state discontinued all forms of teacher certification based on 1 year of training by 1924; 2 years of training by 1925; and 3 years of training by 1936. Except in New York City and Buffalo, certification by examination was continued in 1926, and in all but some vocational subjects, 4 years of training are now required for temporary certification, 5 years for permanent.

In 1942, the state placed the Division of Teacher Training and Certification under the assistant commissioner for higher education. Following World War II, a strong effort was made to improve the quality of teaching. The division worked with college and local authorities to develop in-service training programs, especially in mathematics and science, and to adopt revised objectives in other courses, such as modern foreign languages. Over the years certification has become much more specific. In the place of the early all-purpose life certificate, there are now specific certificates for various grade levels and subjects, and for administrators, student personnel workers, and teachers of special subjects.

The Teachers Reserve, started in April 1967 to alleviate teacher shortages, recruits and trains prospects interested in entering or reentering the profession. Refresher courses at Syracuse University, Long Island University, and the State University Colleges at Cortland and Plattsburgh have been given to more than 600 former teachers, primarily mid-career women who interrupted teaching careers because of family responsibilities, to prepare them to reenter the classroom. A system of partnership teaching has been devised whereby two persons teach one class, each on a half-time basis. This has proven particularly effective in bringing teachers back to the classroom at the elementary school level.

In its efforts to recruit teachers, the Teachers Reserve has also looked for people outside the profession. Long Island University and Syracuse University conduct training programs designed to qualify liberal arts graduates for teaching. More than 150 former members of the Peace Corps have been placed in teaching positions in New York State schools, and approximately 100 others were assisted by the Teachers Reserve office in securing placement.

Future plans for the Teachers Reserve include a comprehensive canvas to locate former teachers who might be persuaded to return to the classroom and the establishment of more university-based programs to involve all qualified teachers who are not presently teaching.

Licensing the Professions

At the time of unification, the Board of Regents determined the requirements for licensing the professions of medicine, dentistry, veterinary medicine, pharmacy, nurse training, and public accounting. In 1926, the state formed the higher and professional education division, including a professional examinations bureau. In 1931, the professional licensing bureau was born.

The year 1941 saw the establishment of the position of assistant commissioner for professional education. The state created a Division of Professional Education and assigned to it all of the responsibilities connected with ensuring a high level of professional service in the state: qualifications for entry into training, professional examinations, licensing, and control of professional practice. The state also transferred, from the higher education division, the functions of evaluating and registering the curriculums of professional schools and evaluating foreign credentials. In 1942, the Division of Law Enforcement was formed.

The Division of Professional Education has responsibility for the development and application of curriculum registration standards for all educational programs relating to the licensed professions, the evaluation of charter applications, relations with advisory councils, and the improvement of licensing examination content. Close liaison is maintained with the office of the assistant commissioner for planning in higher education in the evaluation of needs in professional education.

The Division of Professional Licensing Services is responsible for the evaluation and processing of applications for admission to the licensing examinations, for endorsement of out-of-state licenses, for final confirmation of qualifications, for analysis and processing of petitions to the regents relating to licenses, and for the biennial registration of all licenses.

The Division of Professional Conduct functions in relation to matters involving alleged unprofessional conduct on the part of all professions except pharmacy (which is the responsibility of the Board of Pharmacy) or unlawful practice in any profession. It carries out necessary investigations, cooperates in the presentation of facts before disciplinary bodies, and handles related enforcement duties.

State Master Plan

In 1959, Governor Rockefeller and the Board of Regents appointed a committee to study higher education needs in New York State. The committee reported in 1960 and recommended (a) wide availability and diversity of educational opportunity to students with various intellectual capabilities and of all income classes in the state; (b) a strong system of public as well as private education, including strong public universities; and (c) the attainment of excellence in academic instruction and research in all the institutions of higher learning in the state.

New legislation required the Board of Regents to prepare a state master plan for the development of higher education, to be presented in 1964 and every 4 years thereafter. The master plan was to coordinate the institutional plans of the State University of New York, City University of New York, and private institutions.

In 1962, the state formed an Office of Planning in Higher Education to gather, analyze, and interpret the necessary data from public and private institutions and prepare for the regents materials in relation to a statewide plan for the development and expansion of higher education. An Office of Assistant Commissioner for Higher Education Planning was created in 1965. The assistant commissioner is responsible directly to the associate commissioner for higher and professional education.

Administration and Foreign Affairs

In 1961, the state created in the Education Department an Office of Administrative Services in Higher Education. It helps institutions secure the maximum value from funds expended in administrative, business, and academic areas. It gives consultative services on such topics as space planning and utilization, student registration procedures, admission procedures, long-range planning techniques, machine accounting, and long-range budgetary planning. It also helps in the development of interinstitutional cooperation projects.

The nation's involvement with emerging nations in Asia, Africa, and the established but turbulent nations of South America sparked a growing recognition of a need on the part of Americans for greater knowledge of the history, culture, and problems of many national groups. Up to this time, these groups had been largely ignored or treated superficially in our educational programs. The State Education Department's recognition of this need resulted in 1961 in creation of the Office of Foreign Area Studies, charged with the responsibility of advising and assisting schools and colleges in developing programs of study and intercultural exchanges.

Birth of the State University

The State University of New York came into being in 1948 during the administration of Governor Thomas E. Dewey. Although New York was the forty-eighth state to establish a state university, the idea of a decentralized institution consisting of colleges of various types in every part of the state had nowhere been tried on so large a scale. The institutions brought together under the aegis of the State University of New York included teachers colleges, agricultural and technical institutes, and specialized programs at private universities.

Just as the establishment of the normal schools in the nineteenth century was accompanied by controversy and opposition, there were many citizens in the 1940's who saw no need for a state university. However, others believed that the state's provisions for higher education were not sufficient. In 1946, Governor Dewey appointed a commission to study the need for a state university. After 2 years, the commission proposed formation of a university which would preserve the geographically decentralized pattern already established. A subsequent legislative act made all state-controlled colleges and institutions parts of a state university governed by a board of trustees appointed by the Governor. In the fall of 1964, the State University of New York included 30 public 4-year institutions, 6 state supported 2-year schools, and 28 community colleges.

Financial Assistance

New York State has a long history of generous public support for higher education. The total state program of financial assistance is broad and comprehensive, comprising an extensive network of low-tuition public colleges, scholarships for outstanding high school graduates, scholar incentive assistance in the form of tuition grants to all students with college potential, and state-guaranteed loans to college students.

At the present time, New York State's financial assistance program to postsecondary students is the largest of all the states, with a $70-million program serving 200,000 students. New York State instituted its first scholarship awards in 1865 when the Cornell University scholarships were established. They were designed as full-tution scholarships for 4 years at Cornell. The first awards of $100 per year were made in 1868.

The period between 1865 and 1965 witnessed a dramatic growth of direct financial grants to college students in New York State, in both amounts awarded and numbers of students served. The Legislature established the Regents College Scholarship Program, the first such program in any state. The program provided an annual stipend of $100 a year to 750 students each year. Despite the growth in secondary and college enrollments and increased college tuition, the number and stipends of the regents college scholarships remained unchanged from 1913 to 1946. In 1946, the first step was taken to increase both the number of awards and the stipends.

Accompanying the growth in the number of scholarships and in the stipends was the introduction of a requirement that family financial ability be considered in determing the size of the award granted an individual. Financial need has been a consideration since 1958. Current range of the stipends of the regents college scholarship awards is $250 to $1,000 per year.

Financial aid for students at the graduate and professional level was initiated in New York State in 1949 with establishment of a program of medical and dental scholarships. A fellowship program for college teaching began in 1958, to be followed by regents graduate fellowships in arts, sciences, and engineering, and the Lehman fellowships in social sciences and public affairs. Scholarships for undergraduate study are restricted to use in approved public and private colleges in New York State.

Cultural Education

The cultural education services, under the control of the regents and the department, include the informal educational opportunities and services made available to the general public, such as libraries, museums, and historic places in the state. As of 1965, the organization under the associate commissioner for cultural education included the assistant commissioner, State Museum and Science Service; state librarian and assistant commissioner for libraries; director, Division of Educational Communications; state historian, Archives and History; administrator, Division of Intercultural Relations in Education; and director, Division of Motion Pictures.

State Library. In the early 1900's, the State Library comprised a law library, a medical library, an education library, a general reference library, and an extension library. It had especially rich collections in American and state history and in genealogy. Heading the library was a director of libraries and home education, directly responsible to the commissioner of education. Shortly after 1904, the state created a school libraries division to provide advisory and supervisory services to libraries in public schools. These functions remained under the jurisdiction of the State Library until 1921, when they were transferred to the secondary education division.

In 1912, the state formed a library extension division to provide reference services and to supplement, on a loan basis, the collections of local libraries. It was primarily concerned with supplementing school library collections.

The State Library was transferred in 1937 to the jurisdiction of the assistant commissioner for higher education. Further changes occurred in 1947, when the state moved the home education responsibilities of the director of the State Library to the adult education division under the assistant commissioner for vocational and extension education. In 1948, to make internal operation more efficient, New York State established a new technical processes section to order, bind, catalog, and shelve library collections, and to plan a library rehabilitation program.

The New York law requires all the free libraries serving the public, whether supported from tax funds or not, to be chartered subject to the will of the regents. The existence of regional systems and their contracts with member libraries must be approved. In addition, the library certification law requires that systems libraries and registered public libraries employ only certified librarians with public funds. Thus the coming into existence of new libraries and the consolidation of existing ones are under the control of the State Library.

With the availability of federal funds and new developments in modern equipment adaptable to the needs of libraries throughout the state, the need to strengthen the division of library development became more apparent. The department established two new units, the Bureau of Academic and Research Libraries and the Bureau of Public Library Services, to provide the necessary leadership in this area.

State Museum and Science Service. Another of the state's long-established educational services is the State Museum and Science Service. In 1904, under the reorganization brought about by the Unification Act, the department grouped all the scientific interests in a separate division termed the Division of Science, with trained scientists in archaeology, botany, entomology, genealogy, paleontology, mineralogy, and zoology. The State Museum functioned in this connection as the depository of the materials acquired by the scientific corps. The Division of Science functioned at this time under a director of science and state museums.

In the 1937 reorganization of the department the state made the State Museum and Science Service responsible to the assistant commissioner for higher education. Legislation passed in 1945 redefined the functions of the State Museum and Science Service when the entire staff of the two services was placed under the director. The state empowered and directed the newly created Science Services to make its services available to all departments of the state government and to the citizens of the state. It was authorized to engage in continued scientific research and to cooperate with scientific units of other states, federal government educational institutions, and industry in the discovery, analysis, and dissemination of scientific information.

In line with other departmental changes in 1954, the position of assistant commissioner for the State Museum and Science Service was established. Later, in 1958, an associate commissioner for cultural education was appointed, and the State Museum and Science Service was then transferred to his jurisdiction from that of the associate commissioner for higher education.

The State Museum attracts approximately 225,000 visitors each year, including many delegations of teachers and schoolchildren from all parts of the state. It is also responsible for publishing reports, bulletins, special studies, and other materials.

State History. In 1911, the state transferred the office of the state historian from the Executive Department to the Education Department, thus bringing all governmental units concerned with state history under one control board. The transfer accomplished, the Legislature authorized the regents to create a Division of History and a Division of Public Records, responsible directly to the commissioner of education. Four years later, the regents united the two divisions into the Division of Archives and History with the state historian as director. Archives is actually a misnomer, as the state historian has never collected public documents for archival purposes. His responsibility in this field has been confined to records management and advisory services.

Legislation in 1913 made the state historian responsible for ensuring the safety of official records of all kinds relating to history in the state and all of its subdivisions. Susbequent legislation, in 1919, provided for the appointment of a local historian in every city, village, and town in the state and gave the state historian the responsibility for advising and assisting the local historians in their duties. The administration of historic sites was added to the duties of the state historian in 1944.

Records in local offices of government are the responsibility of the Education Department, and the commissioner's statutory authority is exercised through the state historian. Nearly 4,000 offices of local government are serviced in this program.

In 1937, the state transferred the archives and history division to the jurisdiction of the assistant commissioner for higher education. In 1958, it was moved from the jurisdiction of the then associate commissioner for higher and professional education to that of the associate commissioner for cultural education and special services.

Further reorganization resulted in the rank of assistant commissioner for the state historian.

A New York History Museum is in the process of development. Collections have been arranged, recorded, and made available for research, exhibits, and loans. Extensive planning has been undertaken for a proposed historical museum in the cultural center of the South Mall, a complex of governmental and cultural buildings being developed in Albany.

Visual Aids. In 1904, the state established a bureau of visual instruction in the Education Department. It had the responsibility to advise and assist schools in the selection and use of maps, globes, and all other types of visual aids. As more technical devices for visual instruction came into being, there was a tendency to concentrate more on these, gathering and maintaining collections of slides for loan to schools, and later evaluating and recommending motion picture films. In 1937, the state renamed it the Bureau of Audio and Visual Aids and incorporated it into the school administrative services division. Two years later, the bureau discontinued the loan of slides and other materials and redefined its functions in terms of research, experimentation, and consultation. In 1950, the state placed the bureau directly under the supervision of the assistant commissioner for instructional services.

Reflecting departmental interest in television as an educating medium, the state employed in 1956 a consultant on educational television, directly responsible to the deputy commissioner of education, to make investigations and advise on the most effective ways of using television in instruction.

In 1958, New York formed an educational communications division and placed it under the jurisdiction of the associate commissioner for cultural education with the audio and visual aids bureau, retitled in 1960 the Bureau of Classroom Communications. It established a mass communications bureau in 1964 within the Division of Educational Communications, with responsibilities for educational television and radio.

Since 1927, the Board of Regents had been charged with reviewing and licensing motion pictures for showing in New York State theaters. To accomplish this, the regents had created a motion picture division, directly responsible to the commissioner of education. The division operated under the statutory right granted the regents to reject films which they found to be indecent, inhuman, immoral, sacrilegious, or tending to incite crime or corrupt morals.

The division operated for many years to the apparent satisfaction of both the public and the motion picture industry. Its imprimatur came to be accepted by many states. Over the years, however, court decisions narrowed the area of regulation to the point where restrictive powers were almost nonexistent. In 1965, the state abolished the Division of Motion Pictures.

Racial Inequalities

Passage in 1948 of the Educational Practices Act forbidding discrimination by educational institutions on the basis of race, creed, or color led, in the early 1950's, to a growing concern as to whether the members of minority groups were being accorded full and equal opportunity for education. By 1955, widened interest led to the appointment of an administrator of the Educational Practices Act to the Education Department staff. His office, under the jurisdiction of the associate commissioner for higher education, was at the beginning primarily concerned with discriminative practices in admission to higher institutions.

In 1957, the state charged the Division of Intercultural Relations in Education to deal with problems related to racial, religious, and ethnic factors at all levels of education. The division administers antidiscrimination legislation, assists in the development of programs designed to achieve integration, and provides consultative services to local school boards. It has worked closely with the commissioner's advisory committee and was the agency which carried out the ethnic census in the public schools.

During the 1960's, the division has become heavily involved in problems of integration in the local schools and in providing materials designed for integrating information about the Negro into daily teaching. Other resources are being prepared, and attempts are being made for the use of various media in teacher education, classroom instruction, and community enlightenment.

OPERATING A GROWING DEPARTMENT

Departmental Advisory and Administrative Services

The Board of Regents is legally charged with long-range planning and policy making with respect to education in New York State; the commissioner of education, with advising the regents in policy formulation and decision making. As chief executive officer of the Board of Regents, the commissioner has responsibility for administering the State Education Department. Those units and offices in the department whose prime responsibility is concerned with the policy-making function and with departmental management can readily be conceived as staff, as opposed to line, units.

Legal Services

Immediately after unification, in 1904, the regents created a Law Division, headed by a chief or director, immediately responsible to the commisssioner of education. A few years later, he carried the title of chief of the Law Division and counsel to the university. Up to the present, the counsel has continued to be directly responsible to the commissioner of education.

In 1919, the state empowered the commissioner of education to designate an assistant commissioner or the counsel to the university as deputy commissioner to perform specified duties and to exercise the functions of the commissioner in case of absence or disability of the commissioner of education. The counsel to the university was so designated, and, with a short interlude in 1926-28, he served the double function and carried the dual title of deputy commissioner and counsel until 1940, when the two offices were separated.

Responsibilities of the counsel are to act as legal adviser to the regents, the commissioner of education, and the department; prepare legislative bills for introduction to the Legislature when requested; perform such legal services as are required in the administration of the education system; and represent the regents and the commissioner of education in all matters and proceedings to which they are a party.

In addition to the responsibilities listed, the state gave the counsel added duties ex officio. In 1921, legislation made him legal adviser to the State Teachers Retirement System. He took on further responsibilities in 1944 when he was made counsel for the State Dormitory Authority, a corporation created to facilitate increased higher education construction. In 1958, the state made him counsel to the Higher Education Assistance Corporation, a legal corporation which, with the cooperation of banks, lends money to students enrolled in higher education institutions to cover their educational costs.

The growing responsibilities of the Law Division led to an increase in staff. In the latter 1950's, an internal reorganization took place. The state created three sections: the higher and professional education section, the elementary and secondary education section, and the department operations section. It added the federal matters section in the 1960's.

Financial, Administrative, and Related Services

One of the divisions established by the regents after unification in 1904 was the Division of Accounts which had charge of all departmental financial records, certified all expenditures, and looked after departmental payrolls. The regents also authorized appointment of a secretary to the commissioner of education who was really the business officer of the department. He kept all departmental personnel records and supervised those not attached to the established divisions. He was in charge of publications, building maintenance, mail service, and similar departmental operations.

Because of growth of the administrative functions, the state created an administration division in 1907. This supplanted and absorbed both the accounts division and the Office of the Secretary to the Commissioner of Education. There were no recorded subdivisions within the division, but note is made of a cashier's office and an editor, the latter newly appointed to the department.

During the following years, the groups engaged in each of the several activities charged to the division became identified, at least semiformally, as the following sections: personnel, planning and procedures, business management, office services, accounts, building and ground maintenance, and publications.

Departmental publications had so increased by 1923 that the Bureau of Publications became a subunit in the administration division. In 1932, as a result of continued growth, the state made the director of the division the assistant commissioner for administration. In 1935, it retitled him assistant commissioner for personnel and public relations. Although the new title appears more limiting to the administrative activities and adds public relations, there seem to have been no substantive changes in his responsibilities. When the special public relations office was created in 1950 in the department, the assistant commissioner became assistant commissioner for business management and personnel. As of 1965, the title was assistant commissioner for administrative services. (See Appendix B.)

Continued growth of the department and new responsibilities resulted in 1961 in the raising of several of the sections of the business management and personnel office to bureau status, as follows: finance, personnel, and planning and procedures bureaus. The state added a Division of Electronic Data Processing in 1962.

Statistical Services

In 1904, the State Education Department had, as one of its operating units, a statistics division responsible for gathering, tabulating, and aiding in the interpretation of educational data. In the years immediately following, a widespread interest developed in scientific measurement as a means of improving teaching and learning. The use of intelligence and psychological examinations in World War I increased interest in standardized testing, and, in 1920, the department added a specialist in educational measurements, his responsibility being to advise school authorities on the selection and use of standardized tests. During the same year, the state established an educational measurements bureau.

Following its formation, the educational measurements bureau began to make studies of the characteristics of pupils and of the factors affecting their educational welfare. In 1928, it became the Division of Research, directly responsible to the commissioner of education and charged with the responsibility of conducting surveys and research as a basis for educational planning.

The Regents Inquiry into the Character and Costs of Education (1938) recommended that research be the focal point of the reorganization of the State Education Department as a basis for establishing new policies and for leadership. An assistant commissioner was given jurisdiction over the research division and the Bureau of Statistics.

In a statement of 1939, the regents pointed out the future direction of research. They planned to conduct inquiries and studies to evaluate current programs and to formulate new policies to be used as the basis for educational planning. Correspondingly, the state expanded the program to cover, as the need arose, all facets of the program from elementary school through the college level.

With the great growth in college enrollments after World War II, the state appointed a temporary Commission on the Need for a State University to make studies relative to the need for and organization of public higher education facilities. Staff members of the research division were assigned to work with the commission. After the creation of the State University of New York, this same staff continued to work, on loan, for the university. In 1957, they were recalled, and a Division of Research in Higher Education, under the assistant commissioner for research, was created in the department.

The postwar years were characterized, also, by a tremendous increase in the cost of education. In 1957, the state created a finance studies section in the research division to make studies of the financial needs of education and to devise equitable methods of distributing costs. This unit expanded and 3 years later became the Bureau of Educational Finance Research.

The state reorganized the research offices in 1964 to provide greater specialization of activity. It also transferred the Bureau of Educational Finance Research to the jurisdiction of the associate commissioner for educational finance and management services. The state created four new bureaus in the former research offices under the retitled associate commissioner for research and evaluation.

That same year, a Center on Innovation was established in the office of the commissioner. The center was the outgrowth of departmental concern about how the educational system might best be organized to discover new ideas and accelerate their adoption in the schools. In response to this concern, Commissioner Allen appointed a consultant, Henry M. Brickell, to make a study of education experimentation in the state and to recommend a plan for action. The analysis of the dynamics of instructional change accompanied by recommendations for the adoption of changes appeared in *Organizing New York State for Educational Change,* a 1961 publication of the department. The center has concerned itself with innovations that promote quality education and the abolition of educational inequity associated with race or economic class.

Information Center on Education

In 1966-67, the department created an Information Center on Education to be responsible for identifying, implementing, and operating data systems in all areas of education and coordinating all data-collection procedures within the department. The information center's first major endeavor was to develop a Basic Educational Data System (BEDS) to streamline the procedures by which data from the public schools were reported and processed. In the fall of 1967, New York State teachers spent approximately half a day completing machine-readable forms to satisfy many of the department's information needs for the entire school year.

The relative decentralization of data collection within the department had resulted in schools' receiving multiple requests for the same information. Under BEDS, there has already been a sharp reduction in the number of requests for the same information. In addition, liaison with other educational agencies means that surveys can be completed more readily and effectively. The system enables the department to summarize data within weeks after receipt and provide a current and updated view of education across the state.

Public Relations

Beginning in 1935, public relations activities had been carried out in the offices of the assistant commissioner for personnel and public relations. No specialized unit had been developed for this service, but, in 1950, Commissioner Francis Spaulding recognized that the issues of public education were assuming new and increased importance for the citizens of the state and that not only parents but all public-minded citizens desired and had a right to know what the state educational program was, what it needed, and how it worked. Acting upon the commissioner's recommendation in 1950, the regents created the Office of Public Relations with a special assistant for public relations. This special assistant is directly responsible to the commissioner of education. It is his responsibility to analyze public relations needs, to advise the commissioner and the regents on public relations matters, and to develop and coordinate an ongoing public relations program.

THE EDUCATION PICTURE

The legal and administrative structure for education in New York State continues to be the state's greatest asset in accomplishing educational objectives. Within this framework New York has succeeded in developing a closely knit progressive and efficient system of education extending from the prekindergarten to the adult level. A network of higher education facilities, including public and private, 2-year, 4-year, technical, and professional institutions, has been chartered. The aegis of the Board of Regents has been extended over a wide variety of educational and quasi-educational activities, such as the supervision of libraries, museums, sites famous in history or science, historical records, survey and research projects, and licensing of the professions. The schools have adjusted their goals and programs to meet every type of ability and vocational need, and to assist mentally, physically, and emotionally handicapped pupils. An education through and beyond high school is accessible to every young New Yorker with ability whether he lives on an isolated farm or in a crowded tenement.

BIBLIOGRAPHY

Public Documents

New York. *Constitution* (1894).

——"Education Law." *McKinney's Consolidated Laws of New York 1947-1967,* Book 16.

——*Regulations of the Commissioner of Education of the State of New York.* Albany: The University of the State of New York, State Education Department, 1942-64, with addenda to date.

New York Secretary of State. *Manual for the Use of the Legislature of the State of New York, 1965-66.* Albany: Williams Press, 1965.

Books

Graves, F. P. *History of the State Education Department.* Vol. IX of *History of the State of New York.* 10 vols. New York: Columbia University Press, 1937.

Hodge, D. E., and Hodge, L. F. *A Century of Service to Public Education.* New York: State Teachers Association, 1945.

Horner, Harlan H., ed. *The University of the State of New York.* Albany: The State Education Department, 1954.

Stoddard, A. D. "Department of Education." *Story of State Government, State of New York.* Albany: Association of State Civil Service Employees of the State of New York, 1945.

Reports

Abbott, F. C. *Government Policy and Higher Education: A Study of the Regents of the University of the State of New York 1784-1949.* Ithaca, N.Y.: Cornell University Press, 1958.

Brickell, Henry M. *Organizing New York State for Educational Change.* Albany: University of the State of New York, State Education Department, 1961. Reprinted 1966.

Department of Public Instruction. *Annual Reports* (1854-1903).

Joint Legislative Committee on the State Education System. *Master Plan for School District Reorganization: New York State.* Legal Document No. 25. Albany: Williams Press, 1947.

State Education Department. *Annual Education Summary 1963-64.* Albany: University of the State of New York, State Education Department, 1965.

——*Annual Reports* (1904-68).

——*Experimentation and Innovation.* A 7-year report. Albany: University of the State of New York, State Education Department, 1965.

——*Handbook on Examinations and Scholarships.* Albany: University of the State of New York Press, 1966.

——*Proceedings of the Dedication of the New York State Education Building.* Albany: The Department, 1913.

——*Proceedings of Eighty-Seventh Convocation of the University of the State of New York.* Bulletin No. 1436. Albany: University of the State of New York, State Education Department, 1955.

——*Proceedings of Eighty-Eighth Convocation of the University of the State of New York.* Albany: University of the State of New York Press, 1956.

——*Regents Examinations: 1865-1965. 100 Years of Quality Control in Education.* Albany: University of the State of New York, State Education Department, 1965.

——*The Regents Statewide Plan for the Expansion and Development of Higher Education, 1964.* Albany: University of the State of New York, State Education Department, 1965.

——*The Regents of the University of the State of New York, 1754-1959.* Albany: University of the State of New York, State Education Department, 1959.

State Education Department and the Educational Research Association of New York State. *Instructional Improvement Through Research 1963-64.* Proceedings of the New York State Convocation on Educational Research. Albany: University of the State of New York, State Education Department, 1965.

State University of New York. *Crucial Questions About Higher Education.* Albany: The University, 1955.

Articles and Periodicals

"Dr. Allen Speaks to School Boards." *Bulletin to the Schools,* XLVIII, No. 4 (December 1961).

Monypenny, Phillip. "Survey of Library Functions of the States." *Journal of the American Library Association,* LV (October 1961).

State Education Department. *Bulletin to the Schools.* 1922-65.

Unpublished Material

Allen, James E., Jr. "Goals and Plans for Education in New York State." Memorandum from the Commissioner of Education to the Board of Regents, August 1961.

Center for Urban Education. "A Plan for Accelerating Quality Integrated Education in the Buffalo School System." Prepared under contract with the New York State Education Department, August 1966. (Mimeographed.)

Furney, Oakley. "Industrial Arts and Vocational Industrial Education of Secondary School Grade." Albany: New York State Education Department, August 7, 1938. (Mimeographed.)

Other Source

"Organizations, Services, Functions." Chart issued annually by the New York State Education Department.

Appendix A

NEW YORK CHIEF STATE SCHOOL OFFICERS

Superintendents of Education

1813-21	Gideon Hawley
1821-54	Secretaries of state served as superintendents during this period after the office of the superintendency was abolished by the Legislature in 1821.
1854-57	Victor M. Rice
1857-61	Henry H. VanDyke
1861-62	Emerson W. Keyes
1862-68	Victor M. Rice
1868-74	Abram B. Weaver
1874-83	Neil Gilmour
1883-86	William B. Ruggles
1886	James E. Morrison
1886-92	Andrew S. Draper
1892-95	James F. Crooker
1895-1904	Charles R. Skinner

Commissioners of Education

1904-13	Andrew S. Draper
1913-21	John H. Finley
1921-40	Frank Pierrepont Graves
1940-42	Ernest E. Cole
1942-46	George D. Stoddard
1946-50	Francis Trow Spaulding
1950-55	Lewis A. Wilson
1955-	James E. Allen, Jr.

Appendix B

Chart I.--NEW YORK STATE EDUCATION DEPARTMENT ORGANIZATION, 1904

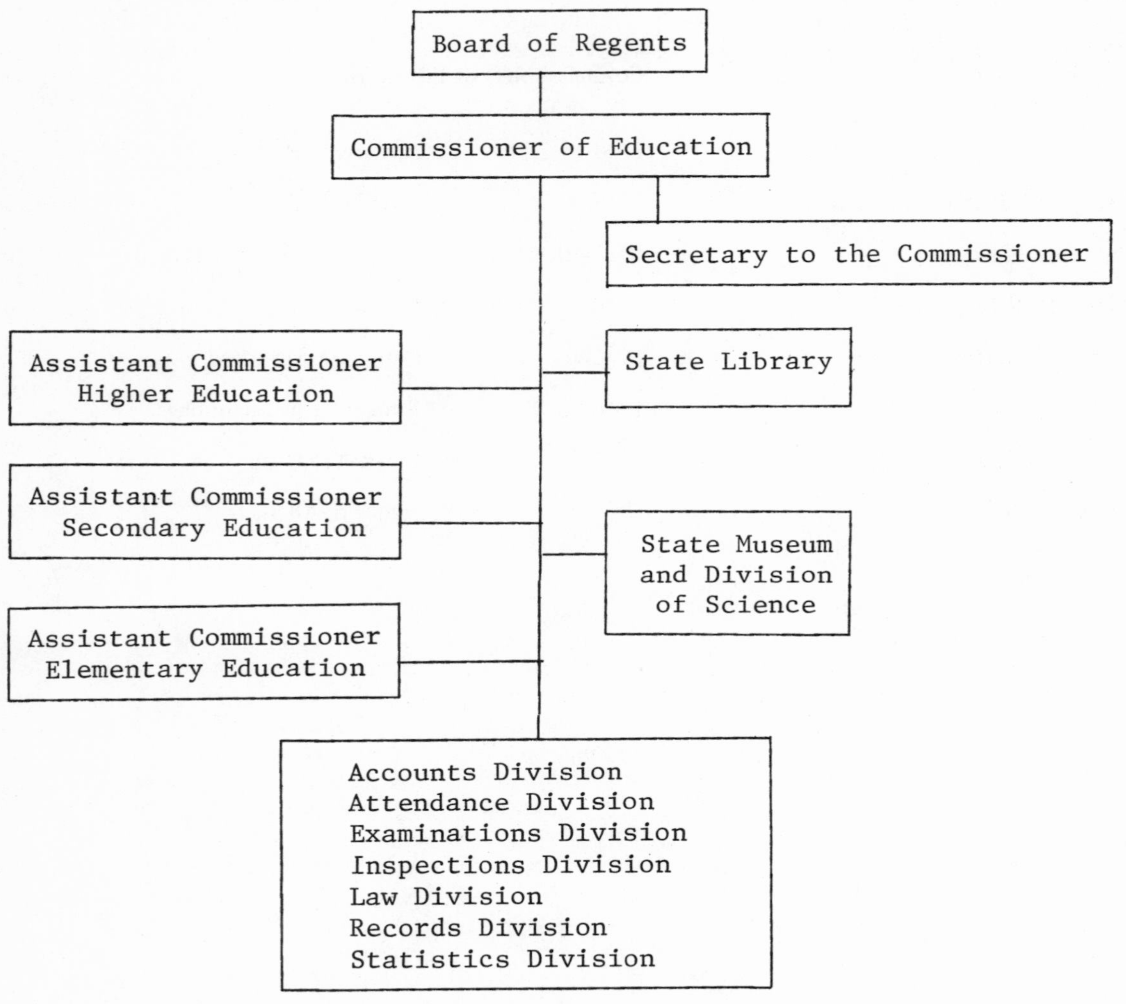

Number of Employees: 224

Appendix B

Chart II.--NEW YORK STATE EDUCATION DEPARTMENT, 1937

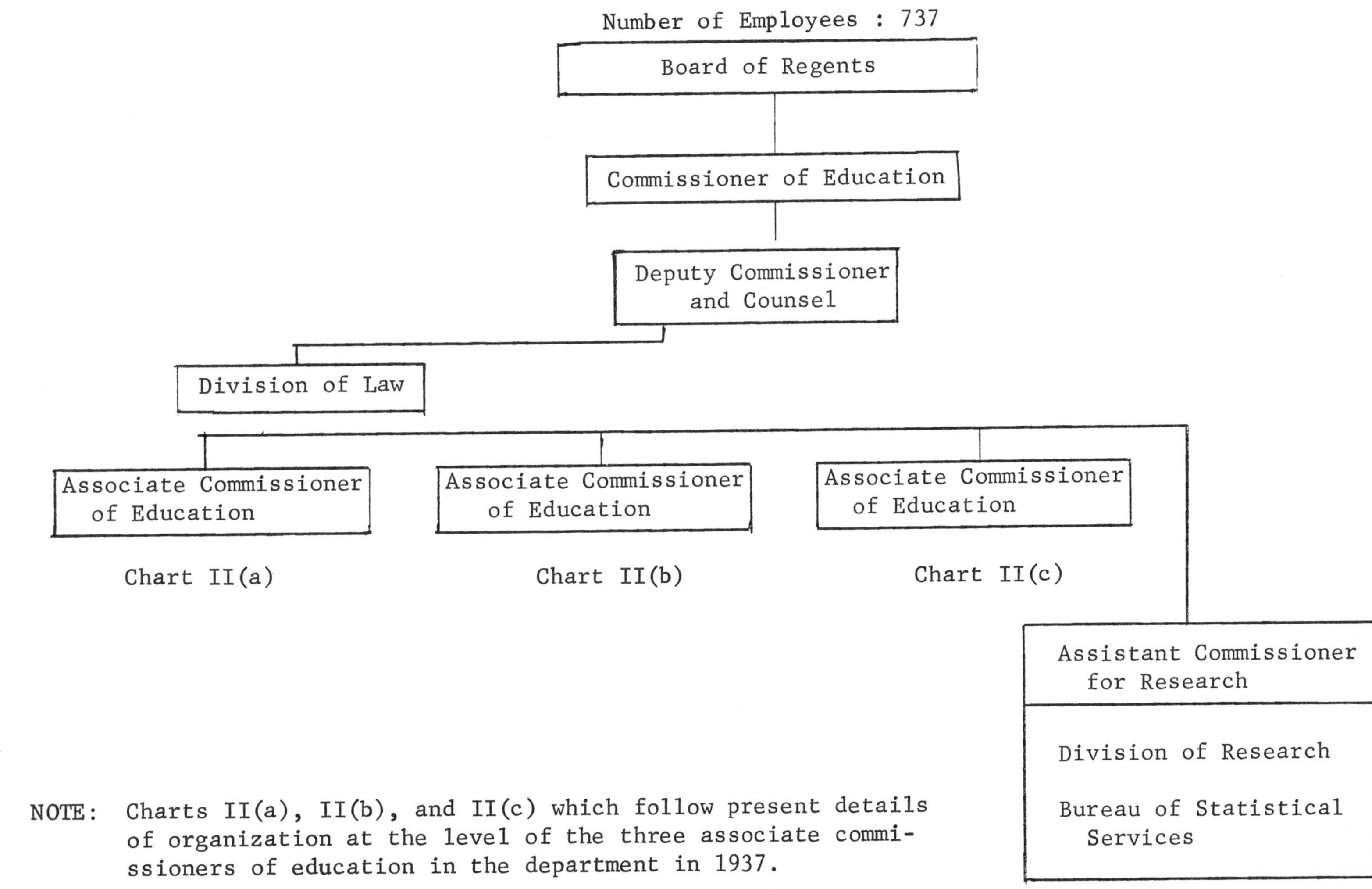

NOTE: Charts II(a), II(b), and II(c) which follow present details of organization at the level of the three associate commissioners of education in the department in 1937.

Appendix B

Chart II(a)

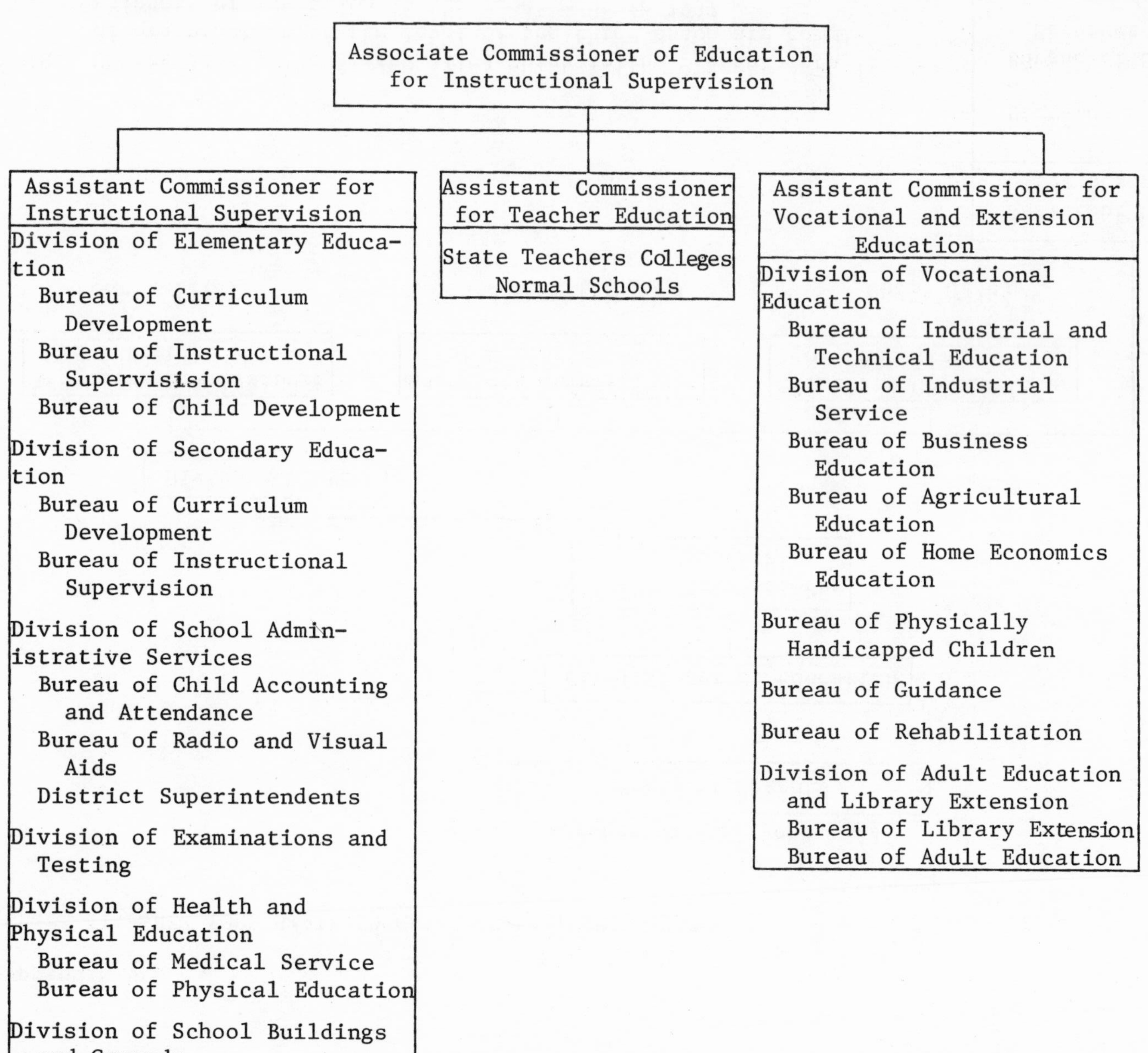
Associate Commissioner of Education for Instructional Supervision
Assistant Commissioner for Instructional Supervision
Division of Elementary Education
Bureau of Curriculum Development
Bureau of Instructional Supervisision
Bureau of Child Development
Division of Secondary Education
Bureau of Curriculum Development
Bureau of Instructional Supervision
Division of School Administrative Services
Bureau of Child Accounting and Attendance
Bureau of Radio and Visual Aids
District Superintendents
Division of Examinations and Testing
Division of Health and Physical Education
Bureau of Medical Service
Bureau of Physical Education
Division of School Buildings and Grounds
Assistant Commissioner for Teacher Education
State Teachers Colleges
Normal Schools
Assistant Commissioner for Vocational and Extension Education
Division of Vocational Education
Bureau of Industrial and Technical Education
Bureau of Industrial Service
Bureau of Business Education
Bureau of Agricultural Education
Bureau of Home Economics Education
Bureau of Physically Handicapped Children
Bureau of Guidance
Bureau of Rehabilitation
Division of Adult Education and Library Extension
Bureau of Library Extension
Bureau of Adult Education

Appendix B

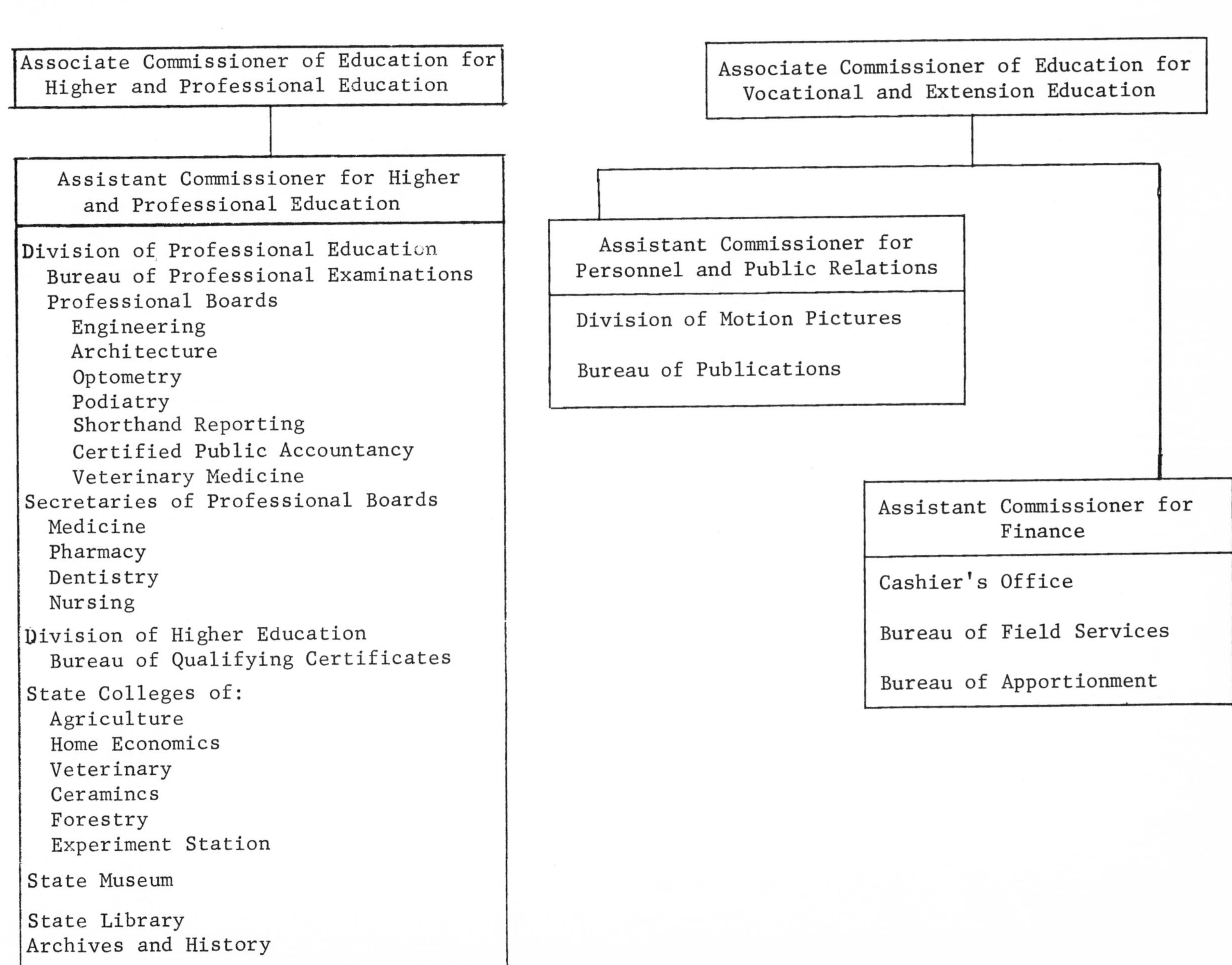
Chart II(b)
Associate Commissioner of Education for Higher and Professional Education
Assistant Commissioner for Higher and Professional Education
Division of Professional Education
Bureau of Professional Examinations
Professional Boards
Engineering
Architecture
Optometry
Podiatry
Shorthand Reporting
Certified Public Accountancy
Veterinary Medicine
Secretaries of Professional Boards
Medicine
Pharmacy
Dentistry
Nursing
Division of Higher Education
Bureau of Qualifying Certificates
State Colleges of:
Agriculture
Home Economics
Veterinary
Ceramincs
Forestry
Experiment Station
State Museum
State Library
Archives and History
Chart II(c)
Associate Commissioner of Education for Vocational and Extension Education
Assistant Commissioner for Personnel and Public Relations
Division of Motion Pictures
Bureau of Publications
Assistant Commissioner for Finance
Cashier's Office
Bureau of Field Services
Bureau of Apportionment

Appendix B

Chart III.--NEW YORK STATE EDUCATION DEPARTMENT, 1965

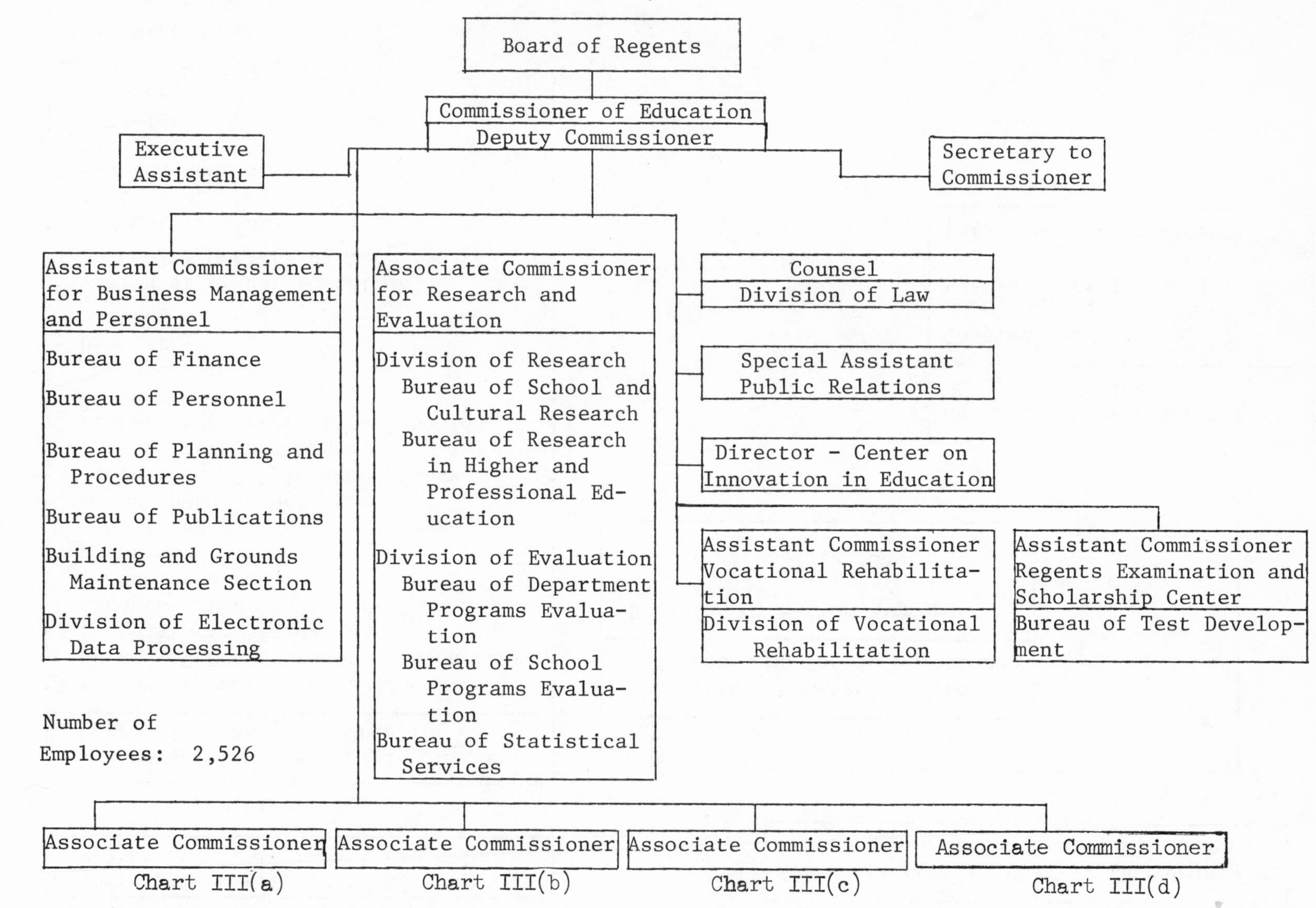

Note: Charts III(a), III(b) and III(c) which follow present details of organization at the level of the four associate commissioners of education in the department in 1965.

Appendix B

Chart III(a)

Associate Commissioner
Elementary, Secondary
and Adult Education

Assistant Commissioner
Instructional Services
General Education

Curriculum Development Center
- Bureau of Elementary Curriculum Development
- Bureau of Secondary Curriculum Development
- Bureau of Continuing Education Curriculum Development

Academic Subject Units
- Academic Subject Specialists in Art, Music and School Libraries
- Bureau of English Education
- Bureau of Foreign Language Education
- Bureau of Mathematics Education
- Bureau of Science Education
- Bureau of Social Studies Education

Division of Health, Physical Education and Recreation
- Bureau of Health and Safety Education
- Bureau of Physical Education

Assistant Commissioner
Instructional Services
Vocational Education

Division of Industrial Education
- Bureau of Trade and Technical Education
- Bureau of Industrial Arts Education
- Bureau of Occupational Extension and Industrial Services
- Bureau of Private Trade and Correspondence Schools
- Bureau of Manpower Development

Bureau of Business and Distributive Education

Bureau of Agricultural Education

Bureau of Home Economics Education

Assistant Commissioner
Pupil Personnel Services
and Adult Education

Bureau of Adult Education

Division of Pupil Personnel Services
- Bureau of Guidance
- Bureau of Health Service
- Bureau of Psychological Services

Division for Handicapped Children
- Bureau for Phsyically Handicapped Children
- Bureau for Mentally Handicapped Children
- State School for the Blind at Batavia
- State School for the Deaf at Rome

Civil Defense Schools

Assistant Commissioner
Educational Administration and Supervision

Division of School Supervision
- Bureau of Elementary School Supervision
- Bureau of Secondary School Supervision
- Bureau of Child Development and Parent Education

Bureau of School District Organization

District Superintendents

Appendix B

Chart III(b)

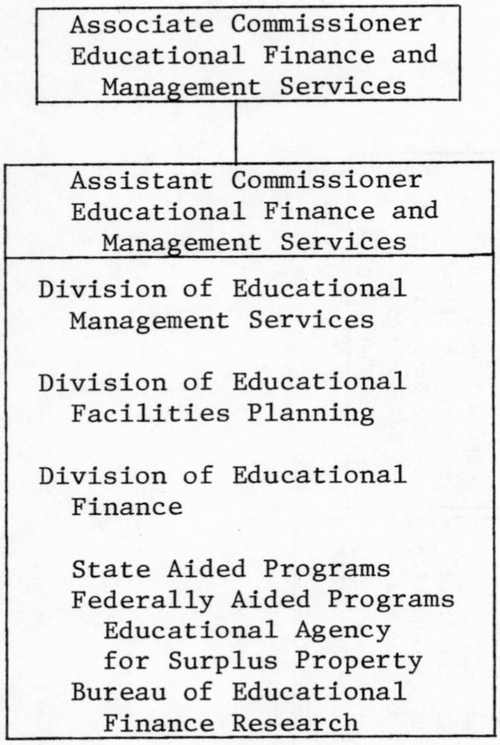

Associate Commissioner
Educational Finance and
Management Services

Assistant Commissioner
Educational Finance and
Management Services

Division of Educational
Management Services

Division of Educational
Facilities Planning

Division of Educational
Finance

State Aided Programs
Federally Aided Programs
Educational Agency
for Surplus Property
Bureau of Educational
Finance Research

Appendix B

Chart III(c)

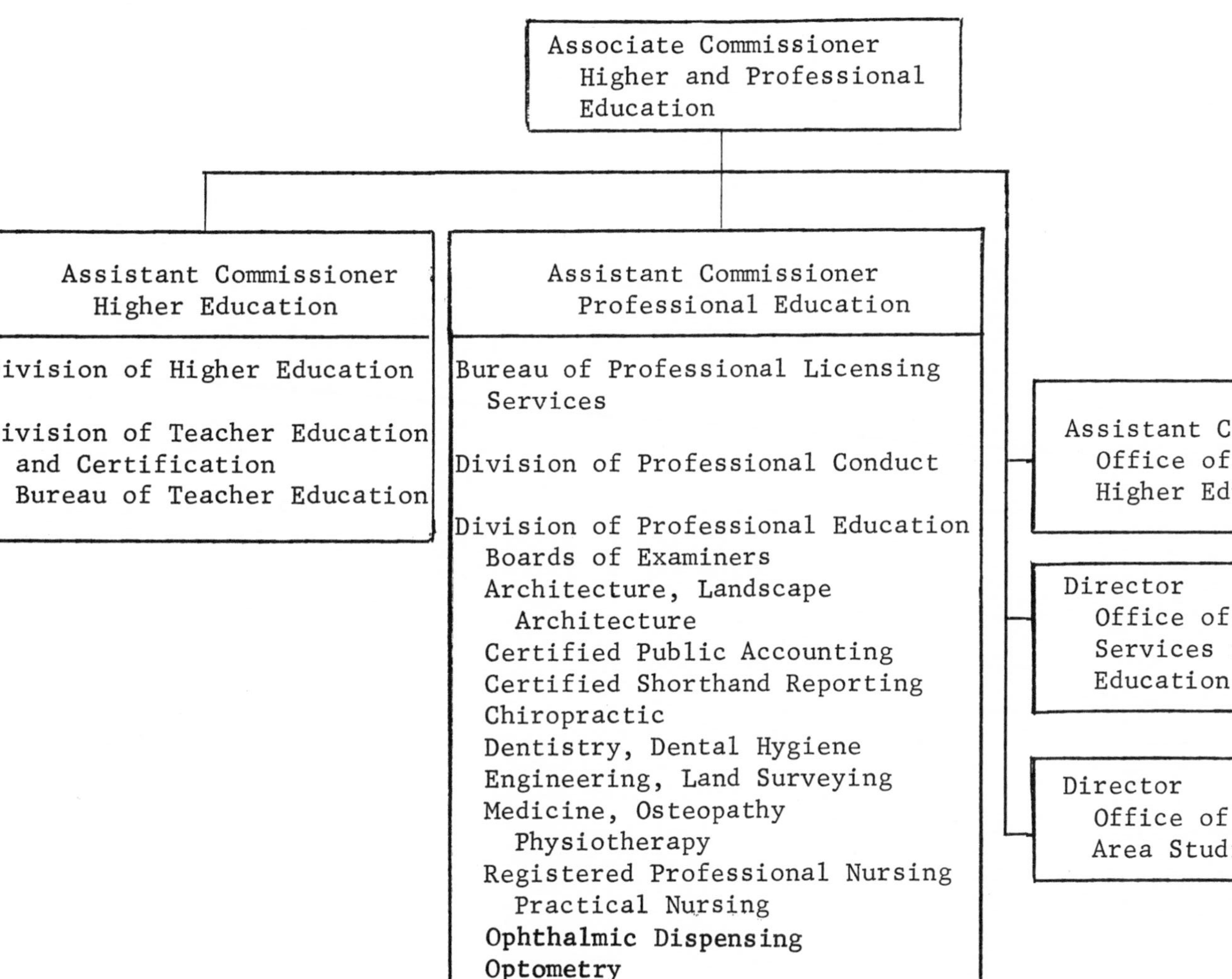

Appendix B

Chart III(d)

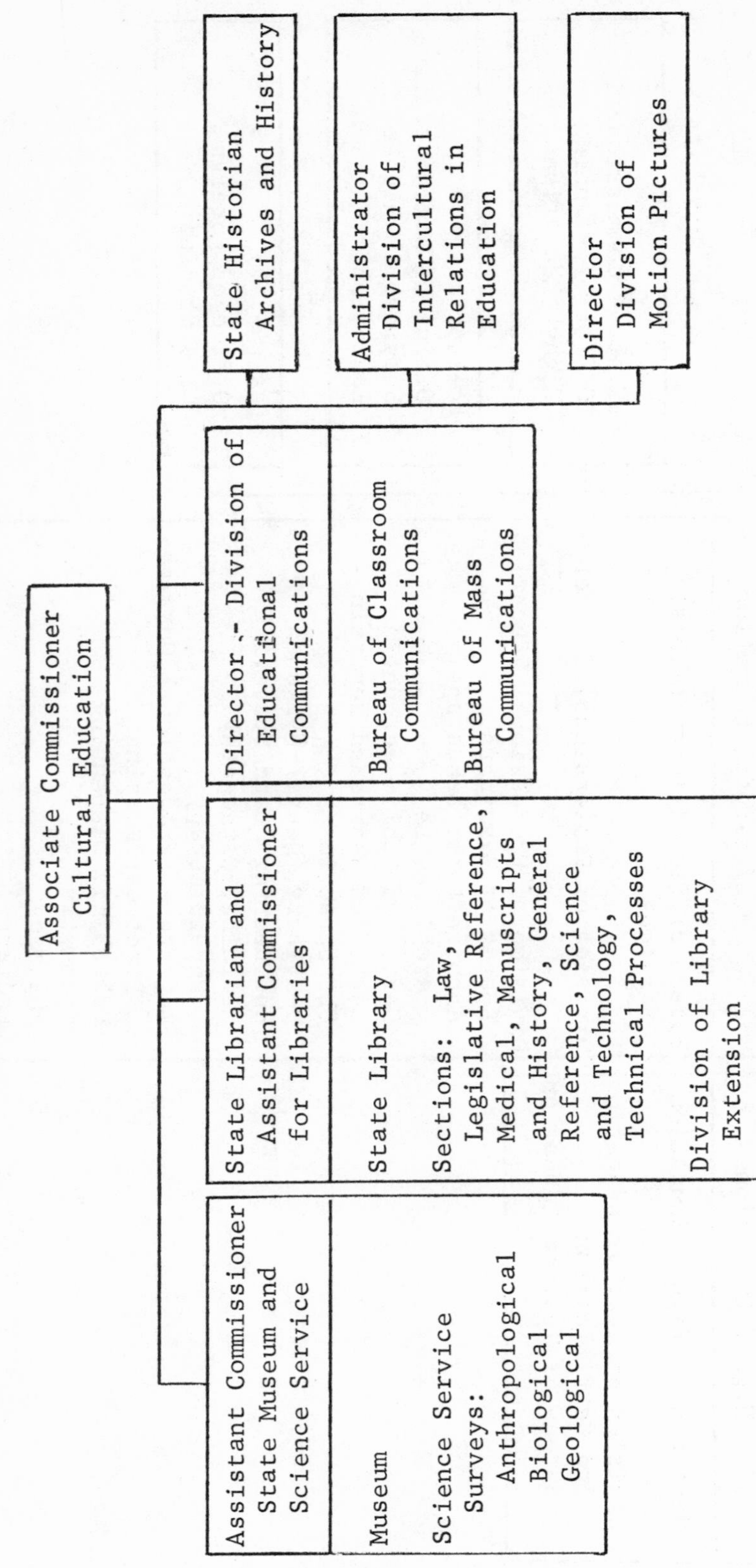

Appendix C

IMPORTANT DATES IN THE HISTORY OF EDUCATION IN NEW YORK STATE, 1904-68

1904 The Unification Act, bringing all education in the state under one responsible control board, the Board of Regents of New York State.

1904 Pharmacy established as a profession under the regents.

1907 Osteopathy established as a profession under the regents.

1908 Optometry established as a profession under the regents.

1908 State legislation provided for the organization of a system of general trade and industrial schools.

1909 Creation of education law.

1911 Certified shorthand reporting established as a profession under the regents.

1911 Office of School Commissioner abolished and that of District Superintendent created.

1912 State Education Building completed and dedicated.

1912 Podiatry established as a profession under the regents.

1913 Passage of law establishing 3,000 university scholarships throughout the state.

1913 Adoption of law providing for medical inspection of schoolchildren.

1913 Creation of Office of President of the University.

1913 Central Rural School Act passed.

1915 Architecture established as a profession under the regents.

1915 Dental hygiene established as a profession under the regents.

1916 Physical training law enacted.

1917 Establishment of city school districts.

1917 Establishment of tenure system for teachers in city school districts.

1917 Legislation required that all physically handicapped be identified in the school census.

1917 Legislation required that schools identify all pupils who were 3 or more years retarded in school, focusing on the mentally handicapped.

1917 Legislation established agriculture as a secondary school subject.

1918 Continuation school law passed.

1919 First teachers' mandatory salary increase passed.

1919 First junior college chartered.

1920 Professional engineering established as a profession under the regents.

1920 Land surveying established as a profession under the regents.

1921 Committee of 21 on Rural Schools.

1923 Normal school course increased.

1923 Educational Finance Inquiry Committee.

1925 Centralization law revised to encourage centralization through special fiscal aid.

1925 First equalization quota for apportionment of school funds established by statutory enactment.

1926 Friedsam Commission on Educational Finance.

1926 Physiotherapy established as a profession under the regents.

1927 Framing of the cardinal principles of education.

1935 Education law amended to give legal basis for the establishment of industrial arts subjects.

1938 Extension of tenure system for teachers employed in "village superintendencies."

1938 Normal schools changed to teachers colleges and the course changed from 3 to 4 years.

1938 Licensed practical nursing established as a profession under the regents.

1944 Regents propose new institutes of arts and sciences.

1945 Extension of tenure system to all school districts employing eight or more teachers.

1945 State aid voted to local public schools for adult education.

1946 Ophthalmic dispensing established as a profession under the regents.

1946 State scholarship stipend raised from $100 to $350 a year.

1947 Master Plan for School District Reorganization (Joint Legislative Committee on the State Education System).

1948 Creation of State University of New York.

1948 Community colleges authorized by law.

1948 Act to prohibit unfair educational practices with respect to admission to educational institutions.

1948 Intermediate District Law passed.

1949 Number of state scholarships doubled.

1949 Scholarships established for medical and dental students.

1950 First community college established at Jamestown.

1951 Grant of fiscal independence and responsibility to the 56 smaller city school districts.

1951 Regents' Statement on Moral and Spiritual Training in the Schools.

1952 Law passed for instruction in the schools about the nature and effect of narcotics and habit-forming drugs.

1952 Regents apply for educational TV channels.

1954 Abolition of separate schools for Indian pupils.

1956 First state-supported closed-circuit TV programs.

1956 Legislative action materially increasing teachers' salaries and state aid to schools.

1956 "Need factor" in awarding state scholarships established by the regents.

1956 Psychology established as a profession under the regents.

1957 Higher Education Assistance Corporation created to guarantee loans to students attending higher institutions.

1958 Legislature mandated science one of common subjects for elementary education.

1961 Special classes for the severely mentally handicapped mandated by law.

1961 Cooperative Review Service, a new supervisory device.

1961 Office of Foreign Area Studies established.

1961 Advisory Council on Financial Assistance to College Students established.

1962 New York State scholar incentive program began.

1962 Regents college teaching fellowships for advanced graduate study established.

1963 Board of Regents for the first time issued a position paper on methods of instruction in one of the Three R's, *The Teaching of Reading, a Position Paper, 1963.*

1963 College proficiency examination program began.

1963 Law provided for the licensing of chiropractors by the State Education Department.

1964 Legislation introduced to encourage special classes for the emotionally disturbed.

1965 Prekindergarten programs were coordinated with Head Start projects.

1965 A new performing arts program was begun by the department.

1965 The Office of Urban Education was formed to aid large cities.

1966 A new Information Center on Education was established.

1966 The department began extensive experimental programs for children ages 3 and 4.

1967 The New York Legislature made a 5-year appropriation to revise the elementary and secondary health syllabus to include physical, sociological, mental, and environment health, and education for survival.

1967 The Teachers Reserve was organized to bring additional persons into teaching.

1967 The Office of Science and Technology was organized.

1968 The Legislature voted state funds to expand prekindergarten programs.

33 North Carolina

DEPARTMENT OF PUBLIC INSTRUCTION
Vester M. Mulholland

Assisted by Associates
in the Department

Contents

BEFORE 1900: TOWARD A STATE ADMINISTRATION OF SCHOOLS

Creating the State Superintendency

The evolution in North Carolina of the position of a chief state school office, a state board of education, and a state department of education was the natural result of the need in state government for receiving and editing local school reports and, on the basis of these, for distributing funds to local schools. Although the first common school law of North Carolina, the legal authority for the beginning of a system of public schools, was enacted in 1839, it was in 1852 that the first specific statute was passed that virtually guaranteed the creation of a state department of public instruction. It was in 1868, however, that the first semblance of a department staff was in evidence.

The first official reference to the state administration of public education occurred in 1817, when State Senator Archibald D. Murphey of Orange County, later known as the father of North Carolina's common schools, presented an elaborate report to the General Assembly designed to stem emigration and to increase North Carolina's wealth. The report outlined a comprehensive plan for public education, including primary schools, academies, a state university, a course of study, provisions for the education of the poor, an asylum for the deaf and dumb, a state school fund, and a state board of education. Although a bill incorporating Murphey's plan did not pass, the assembly did enact legislation in 1825 similar to that of six other states, providing a literary fund to establish public elementary schools and a board to manage the fund. This fund for establishing the common schools consisted of the following:

> The dividends arising from the stocks then held or afterwards acquired by the State in the banks of New Berne and Cape Fear, the dividends arising from the stocks owned by the State in the Cape Fear Navigation Company, the Roanoke Navigation Company, and the Clubfoot and Harlowe's Creek Canal Company, the tax imposed by law on license to retailers of spirituous liquors and auctioneers, the unexpended balance of the agricultural fund, all moneys paid to the State for entries of vacant lands, and all the vacant and unappropriated swamp lands of the State, together with such sums of money as the Legislature may hereafter find it convenient to appropriate from time to time (1).

As North Carolina parted with its public domain in 1790, when Congress requested it as a means of paying the public debt incurred by the 13 original states in their struggle for independence, it had surrendered what would have yielded a magnificent school fund under this legislation of 1825. This was in marked contrast with Connecticut, which had not contributed her public lands to paying the common debt but had held her "western reserve" for her own uses and thus laid the foundation of her school fund.

At the General Assembly's request, the president and directors of the literary fund—in reality a state board of education—drew up another report in 1838 emphasizing the urgent need for a central administrative authority for the common schools. It outlined the function and duties of a proposed "superintendent of common schools," functions and duties later to be carried out by the Department of Public Instruction. The following year, the assembly enacted many of the main features of the report, but it made no provision for an executive head or administrative officer.

This 1839 law, although weak in several respects, did set forth certain basic principles that have been fundamental in operating the North Carolina public schools. The first section, for example, permitted the people to vote *for* or *against* taxes to support the schools. For every dollar such a tax would yield, the state literary fund furnished $2, thus establishing the precedent of school support based on a combination of state and local funds, a principle found in varying degrees in all subsequent school legislation. The law also contained the germ of the current concept of county boards of education. But it was silent about teachers' qualifications and employment, the length of school terms, subjects to be taught, and a chief state school officer.

In 1840, there were 632 public primary schools with 14,937 students, and about 140 academies with 4,398 students (2). As the school system was growing rapidly, Governor John M. Morehead in 1842, Governor William A. Graham in 1846, and Governor Charles Manley in 1850 urged the General Assembly, on behalf of the literary board, to provide for a superintendent; the assembly failed, however, to make such a provision. J. B. Cherry, with Calvin H. Wiley's support, introduced a similar bill that became law in December 1852. This act provided for a general superintendent of common schools, defined his duties and functions, and indicated that he was to be elected by the General Assembly for a 2-year term and that he was to be paid $1,500 per year from the literary fund.

Although a Whig, Wiley was elected by the Democratic Legislature as first superintendent of schools the same month the bill became law; he assumed office in January 1853. This date also marks the beginning of a state department of public education; for, in actuality, the first superintendent performed many of the duties and services that were assigned to the Department of Public Instruction in 1868.

Wiley, a reformer at heart, labored with determination and patience during his 13 years in office to develop an enthusiastic interest in education, to unite the people in a common effort, and to reorganize the state's entire educational program. He devoted himself unselfishly and constructively to the improvement of teacher training, teacher certification, classroom instruction, the preparation and distribution of printed materials—especially textbooks, the publication of school statistics, and procedures for textbook adoptions.

Early in 1857, Wiley pointed out that when he took office 4 years earlier, a work on general education in the United States had classified North Carolina at the bottom of the list and spoke of its educational statistics as "startling." But, "now the last publication of this kind, the *Educational Year Book,* published in Boston, a few weeks ago alluded to our progress as 'unparalleled' " (3). He admitted that while North Carolina was not altogether undeserving of the harsh sayings, it was entitled to the complimentary ones, and he asked the people to do their duty and work toward the goal of universal education of the people. He pointed out that the common schools, once considered charity schools only for the poor, now were regarded as one of the greatest and most honorable interests of the state.

By the time the Civil War erupted in 1861, Wiley's resourcefulness, versatility, and indefatigability had produced one of the best school systems in the South. The number of public primary schools had increased to approximately 4,000 with 160,000 students, and the number of academies had risen to 350 with approximately 15,000 students.

Although some schools remained open during the Civil War, the public school system as a whole suffered a tremendous setback. When the state was forced to repudiate its Civil War debt, the literary fund was wrecked, and the common schools were left without adequate state aid. The Thirteenth Amendment presented an equally serious problem relative to the social status of the freemen. In addition, the office of state superintendent was vacated and the position abolished.

When North Carolina adopted its Constitution of 1868, it created the Office of Superintendent of Public Instruction in lieu of the superintendent of common schools. The Republicans controlling the state government immediately appointed the Reverend Samuel Stanford Ashley, a carpetbagger from Massachusetts, as the new superintendent. The records indicate that Ashley was an earnest man of some ability; but he possessed pronounced prejudices, traits which made him impudent and reckless. He favored mixing the races, a concept intolerable to most of the state's citizens. The State Board of Education, authorized by the new constitution, appointed a Negro from Connecticut, J. W. Hood, as its agent and assistant superintendent of public instruction. Ashley, Hood, and three clerks constituted the actual beginning of the Department of Public Instruction in North Carolina.

The Constitution of 1868 guaranteed that public instruction in North Carolina would be at public expense for all the children without regard to race, condition, or color. In its declaration of "rights," it affirmed the right of every citizen to be educated and the duty of the state to furnish the advantages of education. But when State Superintendent Ashley spoke in August 1869 at the tenth session of the National Teachers Association at Trenton, New Jersey, he stated:

> We have in North Carolina, 300,000 children between six and twenty years of age, and they are scattered over a territory of 50,000 square miles; we have few adequate school houses. These two difficulties seriously obstruct our work. Most of the old school houses are log shanties; often without doors, with entrance for light made by removing a log or two from the side, and destitute of furniture. In fact, in that great State, while there are many very good private school buildings, there are whole counties, and populous counties, too, which have no public school houses such as you would regard as worthy of the name of a school house.
>
> We have, therefore, to build our school houses in cities, towns and villages. At least $2,500,000 are needed to put us in possession of comfortable houses (4).

He also pointed out that there were few teachers and no normal schools; academies were giving some normal instruction, but there were no teachers in regular training.

To open the schools, North Carolina raised money partly by a "capitation tax" on every man between the ages of 21 and 50 years. Seventy-five percent of this tax was earmarked for public instruction. The Legislature appropriated $100,000 from the general treasury, and with the $250,000 expected from the tax, it hoped to open 1,000 schools within the first 12 months. Although the $350,000 appeared meager, Ashley pointed out that this was a great thing for the Legislature to do when there was a debt of $30 million resting upon the state.

Building a State School System

The General Assembly of 1869 virtually reenacted the Law of 1839, with the addition of a general school tax, a definitely prescribed school term, provisions for educating the Negroes, and new responsibilities for the state superintendent. The task of rebuilding the state school system was staggering in the face of widespread poverty, inexperience, ignorance, prejudice, and the fear of mixed schools. The task was further complicated when the conservative assembly, reacting against the Republican administration, abolished the state superintendent's staff in 1870, reducing the office to a little more than a poorly paid clerkship. In spite of the fact that the General Assembly of 1873 further enlarged the state superintendent's responsibilities, particularly in the areas of schoolhouse planning and publications, it was almost impossible for the department to function. Although most of its efforts to improve education were largely ineffectual, the department did devote attention to supervising Negro schools and training Negro teachers.

Many individuals supported the department's efforts to assist the Negroes. In three of the largest towns in North Carolina, the graded schools for both races were managed by the same white superintendent. One of the state's prominent physicians instructed a class of Negro medical students at Shaw University in Raleigh, and the son of a prominent clergyman of the Southern Presbyterian Church was instructing Negroes at Biddle University in Charlotte. The principal of one of the most successful private schools took charge of the Negro normal school at New Berne (5).

In 1885, in accordance with the constitution of the state, the General Assembly established a "normal department" in the University of North Carolina. It was open to young men preparing to teach, tuition free, on condition that they sign a pledge to teach at least 1 year after leaving the institution. A total of 13 normal schools were active in the state during this period: 8 for whites and 5 for Negroes. The annual appropriation for the Negro normal schools was double that for the whites. White normal schools were in the nature of teacher institutes and were held at convenient points for 1 month during the summer. Negro normal schools were established at fixed points and were regularly in session 8 or 9 months of the year. These efforts were clearly effective in supplying more and better teachers (6).

Despite such progress, however, the public schools still suffered from the effects of the Civil War. Superintendent Sidney M. Finger, who took office in 1885, summed up the dilemma clearly and bluntly:

> The State has done well in the revival of her public schools, and she will continue to struggle on, carrying her burden, earnestly looking forward to the time when the Congress of the United States will open the doors of the Treasury and extend aid. North Carolina and other Southern States gave to the United States vast domains which were used to pay a common debt, a debt of the original thirteen States, and in the course of events it turns out that the United States frees the slaves of the South, and makes them citizens and voters while in a condition of extreme ignorance. . . . Surely the Government that could find warrant in the Constitution to free the Negroes and make them citizens can also find authority to distribute from its overflowing Treasury funds to educate them for the proper discharge of the duties of freemen and citizens (7).

According to legislation enacted in 1890, students were limited in what they could study since the laws stated that no branches should be taught in the public schools except spelling, defining, reading, writing, arithmetic, English grammar, geography, elementary physiology and hygiene, and the history of the state and the United States. The General Assembly of 1891 added a new subject to the curriculum, "the nature of alcoholic drinks and narcotics and special instruction as to their effect upon the human system "(8).

In 1897, the Fusionist-dominated Legislature created the State Board of Examiners as an agency of the State Board of Education, with the superintendent of public instruction as its chairman. The Legislature gave this board the authority to define and grant first-grade life certificates, to furnish annual examinations to supervisors, and to prepare and recommend a course of reading and professional study for teachers (9).

Superintendent Charles H. Mebane

In 1898, Charles H. Mebane (10), who served as state superintendent from 1897 to 1901, prepared the most comprehensive biennial report (895 pages) ever assembled by a superintendent. Replete with photographs, it traced historical developments; gave sketches of academies, colleges, and private schools in North Carolina; included the official records of Calvin H. Wiley; explained the major school laws; and detailed the course of study for teachers drawn up by the State Board of Examiners. Mebane, a Fusionist, tried desperately to keep the schools out of politics (11). He recommended to the 1899 assembly that textbooks be adopted by the board of examiners rather than by the county boards of education; that a tax be placed on the earnings of railroads, telegraph, telephone, express, and insurance companies; and that the assembly enact some form of compulsory attendance.

He also advocated that "civil government" be added to the subjects taught in the schools. The General Assembly of 1899, controlled by the Democrats, not only repealed much of the legislation of 1897, which was passed by the Fusionists, but it refused to act on a majority of Mebane's recommendations. This assembly, however, did pass an act, recommended by Mebane, appropriating $100,000 to the public schools to be distributed to the counties on the basis of their population (12). With the Democrats in full power, Mebane was not reelected in 1901 (13).

During the latter part of the nineteenth century, the department was little more than a statistical bureau and the superintendency little more than a clerkship (14). Since the department had limited authority and personnel, improvement of instruction was a matter for local authorities. The department assumed practically no responsibility for the preparation of teachers, for the improvement of Negro schools, or for teacher examination and certification. On a much smaller scale, however, the department prepared and distributed printed matter essentially as it does today.

THE DEPARTMENT OF PUBLIC INSTRUCTION, 1900 TO 1931

The Educational Ground Swell

The development of the department from a minor bureau in 1900, consisting of only the state superintendent and his clerk, into a strong state agency in 1921, made up of nine divisions, began in the political campaign of 1900. The Democrats, preoccupied with consolidating their gains after Reconstruction and the period when Negroes had dominated the state's politics, had passed only a few laws for the public schools and the Department of Public Instruction. Charles B. Aycock, the Democratic nominee for Governor, realizing that his party's campaign for white supremacy might boomerang, changed it into a crusade for universal, popular education.

The major obstacles to an organized, strong Department of Public Instruction had been the apathy of the people, the lack of support in the General Assembly, and the indifference of state officials. But when James Y. Joyner became state superintendent in 1902, a great educational revival was sweeping the state. Joyner, who had taught in the public schools, was charming, likable, and passionately interested in the schools. A former professor of English in the State Normal and Industrial College at Greensboro, he proved to be an expert politician capable of uniting practically everyone in an effective campaign for universal public education. Joyner predicted that within the next 25 years, every country and city child would have access to a complete system of education, which he described with eloquence and precision:

> This system will include elementary and high schools adequately equipped with comfortable houses, ample grounds, and trained teachers. The schools will be efficiently supervised by competent superintendents, maintained for eight or ten months in the year by state, county, and district taxation. Every child will be required to secure at home in the elementary school a mastery, at least, of the rudiments of learning that constitute the foundation of all education and of all preparation for intelligent citizenship and efficient service. Every child who has the desire and capacity will be afforded opportunity to secure near home, in county and township high schools, fuller preparation for college or for life, through courses of study shaped to meet the needs and natural adaptations of all for literary, professional, commercial, and industrial life.
>
> These elementary and high schools, planted in the rural districts within reach of the rural population, will become the centers of a new social, intellectual, civic, industrial, and agricultural life. They will elevate to a higher plane of intelligence, labor, and service the great masses of the country people and prevent the degeneration of this biggest and best part of our population into an Old-World peasantry (15).

Grass-roots enthusiasm for better schools in this period received much of its impetus from the political parties, the Governor's office, the state superintendent, the colleges and universities, and outstanding educators and businessmen across the state. But its most powerful motivating force grew out of direct discussions with people at the local level, which were made possible by funds from the Southern Education Board. The Central Campaign Committee for the Promotion of Public Education in North Carolina planned systematic campaigns for local taxation, for consolidating school districts, for building and equipping better schoolhouses, and for providing longer school terms and larger salaries for teachers. Various committees collected, wrote, and distributed weekly articles about better schools to every newspaper in the state. They even wrote to all ministers requesting that they preach sermons on public education at least once a year.

This enthusiasm was specifically reflected in the activities and growth of the state department during the first two decades of the century. Superintendent Joyner made intensive efforts to prepare and certificate teachers, to improve Negro education, to bring new quality to supervision, to extend education in the local communities, to prepare and distribute more useful material for public school personnel, to improve schoolhouse planning, and to supervise more effectively school finance and records.

Superintendent Joyner also stressed publications as a major means of improving all facets of education throughout the state. Between 1902 and 1908, the department published 31 bulletins. A division of publications was established in 1909, when the General Assembly gave the superintendent specific authority to print at state expense "such educational bulletins as he shall deem necessary for the professional improvement of teachers and for the cultivation of public sentiment for public education . . ." (16). Under this authority, the department issued 70 bulletins between 1909 and 1912. In 1915, the General Assembly appropriated $18,000 biennially to be used for the department's printing.

Preparation and Certification of Teachers

In 1903, at the request of Superintendent Joyner and the State Board of Examiners, the seven normal schools for Negroes were reduced to four by the State Board of Education. The following year, Charles L. Coon, superintendent of the Salisbury schools, became the "superintendent of the Colored Normal Schools." When the General Assembly expanded his duties in 1909 to include supervision of the training of all teachers, the first definite step was made toward the formation of a division of teacher training. The department attempted to improve instruction by requiring teachers to attend 2-week county institutes, 30 of which were held in 1909 and 66 in 1910, enrolling a total of 6,551 teachers. The department also organized institutes for Negro teachers in the majority of counties, most of which were taught by Negro schoolmen.

The state department encouraged colleges and universities to develop summer school sessions as another step to improve teacher preparation. Beginning in 1910, it required that teachers attend either a biennial county institute or an accredited summer school or else be debarred from teaching in the public schools until they had met this requirement (17).

Another method of teacher training, designed to furnish a carefully selected course of reading, was the North Carolina Teachers' Reading Circle, organized in 1909. Although membership in this group was optional, the department requested county superintendents to give preferences in positions and salaries to teachers who participated in it.

Until 1915, the state department's examination was the only basis for initial certification, but in this year it was agreed that academic and professional credits from approved institutions of higher learning might be accepted in lieu of an examination. In 1917, the General Assembly abolished the State Board of Examiners, which it had created 20 years earlier. A new system of certification and training was instituted under a reorganized State Board of Examiners and institute conductors, with the superintendent as chairman. During the period of certifying teachers by examination only, stimulation for professional improvement came from the examinations themselves, from the reading circles, or from the normal school programs.

In 1920, the State Education Commission reported that the state's certification system was grossly inadequate (18). The following year, a teacher training division was established. A. T. Allen, the first director of this division, was succeeded by James E. Hillman in 1923, when Allen became state superintendent. His interest and understanding of conditions prompted Superintendent Allen to recommend in 1926 that 20 normal schools be established throughout the state over a period of 10 years to provide prospective teachers with at least 2 years of training beyond the high school. In 1927, the information and statistics division conducted a comprehensive study of teacher training, findings of which indicated the need for higher standards and more teachers. It was 1929 before the teacher training division instituted these changes and promulgated new certification requirements and possible standards for practice teaching in the colleges (19).

Negro Education

In each of his biennial reports from 1902 to 1912, Superintendent J. Y. Joyner strongly recommended improvements in Negro education. He especially emphasized the need for training Negro industrial and agricultural teachers. With money from the Jeanes Fund, the department employed its first state supervisor for Negro schools, N.C. Newbold, in 1913. Newbold coordinated the work of the county supervisory teachers employed through the Jeanes and the Slater Funds, and he encouraged the counties to hold institutes for Negro teachers. He instigated the preparation of a course of study and training for rural Negro teachers and urged the assembly to appropriate $10,000 annually for county industrial-teacher training schools, industrial supervisors for Negro rural schools, and institutes or summer schools for Negro teachers. The assembly, however, took no action on this recommendation.

Mrs. Annie W. Holland, employed as the state Jeanes Teacher in 1916, assisted Newbold in his work with the county supervisors (20). She organized Negro women and children into clubs for instruction in gardening, cooking, canning, sewing, home sanitation, and other practical household activities.

Throughout the twenties, the Division of Negro Education continued to promote better interracial relations, to assist Negro schools with educational problems, and to supervise the three state Negro normal schools and the Indian normal school. It also administered funds donated by private foundations: By 1929, the Negro education division was responsible for spending about $450,000 donated by the General Education Board, the Jeanes Fund, and the Rosenwald Fund. The General Education Board, through the Jeanes Fund and without department assistance, paid the salary and expenses of the director of Negro education, beginning in 1913.

Supervision of Instruction

Prior to the twentieth century, only State Superintendent Ashley (1868-71) had a staff member for supervising instruction, an assistant who could give only limited supervision to the Negro schools. In his biennial report of 1902, Superintendent Joyner requested five deputy superintendents or state supervisors of education who might focus attention on improving instruction; bringing reasonable uniformity to the state's educational system; collecting more accurate information on school conditions; aiding the county superintendent; preparing courses of study and reading for superintendents and teachers; assisting schools in instituting graded courses of study; stimulating county boards by their personal visits; and aiding in the collection of fines and forfeitures belonging to the school fund. It was 1907, however, before North Carolina's first public school law required the addition of a competent person to the state department's staff to inspect the general condition pertaining to the high schools "to see that suitable arrangements have been made for giving high school instruction" (21). In the same year, Superintendent Joyner appointed N. W. Walker, professor of secondary education and agent for high schools at the University of North Carolina, as the first inspector of public high schools in North Carolina (22).

The state superintendent appointed L. C. Brodgen, superintendent of the Kinston graded schools, as supervisor of rural elementary schools in 1909. Not only did he work with county superintendents on problems of tardiness, increasing enrollments and attendance, grading and classifying pupils, and preschool work, he also conducted a study concerning the feasibility of consolidating one-teacher elementary schools and transporting pupils at public expense.

As early as 1910, Superintendent Joyner advocated vocational education. In his president's address to the NEA convention in 1910, he said:

> But 95 per cent of the people of the United States make their living by industrial pursuits. Scarcely 5 per cent of our population ever reach the college or the university. It was, therefore, but another natural evolution of democracy, but another inevitable demand of the common man, that the courses of instruction in the secondary schools should be adapted to the needs of the 95 as well as of the 5 per cent, should lead into life as well as into college, and into industrial pursuits instead of away from them (23).

In 1903, the General Assembly required schools to offer "Elements of Agriculture." The 1911 assembly appropriated funds for county farm-life schools (24) and continued to expand this program in subsequent years. When the Smith-Hughes Act passed in 1917, the assembly immediately created a State Board of Vocational Agriculture to administer the program and supervise the work the schools were already doing in this field. The board named T.E. Browne as director of vocational education and in 1919 added supervisors for agricultural education, trade and industrial education, and home economics. Since the status of these supervisors was not clearly defined in the Vocational Education Act of 1919, the State Education Commission of 1920 recommended abolishing the State Board of Vocational Education and consigning its power and authority to the State Board of Education. The result was that a new vocational education division was created under the department with T. E. Browne as its director. By 1923, the division had a staff of 16 persons.

Throughout the twenties, the vocational education division continued to supervise agricultural education and trade and industrial education (25). Since this division provided supervision only in specific areas, Superintendent Eugene C. Brooks created the supervision division in 1921 to bring together the state inspector of high schools, the state supervisor of rural elementary schools, and the director of schools for adult illiterates. The director of schools for adult illiterates was the only one provided by state funds (26). In 1927, the supervision division was renamed the Division of Elementary Instruction.

Community Education

Superintendent Joyner became genuinely concerned when the 1910 census ranked North Carolina third in the nation in its percentage of native-born white illiterates. In 1914, the department inaugurated a statewide plan for promoting community improvement by designating Community Service Week as a cooperative effort of the State Department of Education and the extension service of Agricultural and Mechanical College at Raleigh. The success of this venture prompted Superintendent Joyner to suggest that it become permanent. The following year it was expanded, and November was designated as "Moonlight School Month," a period in which more than 5,000 public school teachers volunteered to teach adult illiterates in the community schools.

In 1917, the General Assembly appropriated $25,000 to be used on a matching basis to organize "moonlight schools" throughout the state, under the general supervision of the state superintendent. Two years later, the assembly made these schools a part of the school system by providing for their support from the state's public school funds and for the county superintendents to administer them. The state department prepared a reader and other textbooks for these schools.

The success of the adult illiterate program caused many people to declare that community service should be expanded and made permanent. In 1916, this general enthusiasm culminated in the formation of a state bureau of community service, cooperatively supported and directed by six state organizations, including the state department. During the following year, the General Assembly passed an act for further improving the social and educational conditions of rural communities through a series of motion pictures to be provided by the superintendent of public instruction. This popular and successful motion picture service and the bureau of community service were combined at Superintendent Joyner's request, and in 1920 this combination became a bureau in the state department.

Schoolhouse Planning

The School Law of 1869 stated that the superintendent of public instruction should make "such suggestions on school architecture as he may deem useful with such woodcuts and plans of schoolhouses as he may be able to obtain" (27). From that time, state superintendents displayed considerable interest in schoolhouse planning and gave much assistance to local schools. In October 1902, the state board authorized Superintendent Joyner, who was particularly interested in improving school buildings, to contract with an architect to prepare plans, specifications, and cuts for building new schoolhouses. Superintendent Joyner explained that these plans were prepared "to prevent waste of money on barnlike and improperly constructed houses, and to suggest more convenient, sanitary, and beautiful schoolhouses at reasonable costs . . . " (28).

In 1903, the new state literary fund set up a loan fund that enabled the state board to help school districts erect or improve their buildings. The board required that all schoolhouses built or improved by these funds be constructed in accordance with plans approved by the state superintendent; by 1908, the department had published a bulletin on "Plans for Public Schoolhouses." Although granted this authority by both the assembly and the state board, the superintendent was unable to enforce this requirement until 1920, when the state board appointed a director of schoolhouse planning. In a special session, August 1920, when the General Assembly appropriated $10,000 for schoolhouse planning, State Superintendent Eugene C. Brooks appointed a "Supervisor of the State Loan Fund and the Building of All New Buildings," thus creating a Division of Schoolhouse Planning.

The assembly strengthened the new division in 1925 and 1927 by acts providing for a special loan fund of $5 million for school buildings with two stipulations: no loans could be made for repairing or erecting a building with fewer than seven rooms; and no loans could be made until the building plans were approved by the state superintendent. This division helped the county boards of education with their plans for organizing schools on a countywide basis and gave assistance to other department divisions in working out county school surveys and plans.

Governmental and Departmental Reorganizations

Throughout the 1920's, both Superintendents Eugene C. Brooks (1919-23) and A. T. Allen (1923-34) led a movement to make the county the unit of administration under the control, supervision, and direction of the state. Since they regarded the state's responsibility as one of furnishing leadership and expert assistance to the counties, there was a greater need than ever before for a strong state department. In 1919, the General Assembly attempted to implement this countywide idea by requiring that the state public school fund's apportionment be administered to encourage district consolidation and the elimination of small schools. The assembly went still further in 1924 by passing an act forbidding the county boards of education to create, abolish, or consolidate school districts except in accordance with the county plan outlined in the act.

The financial support for this plan would come from both the county and the state. Those counties unable to provide the 6-month school term required by the constitution would be aided from a $3.25 million equalizing fund, established by the General Assembly in 1927 to provide equal educational opportunities throughout the state. Following the recommendations of the commission for the county boards of education, the assembly also established an equalization state board and a uniform system of accounting and fiscal procedure. By the 1929-30 school year, the assembly had increased the equalizing fund to over $5 million.

As the department attempted to streamline school administration through the county unit plan, its staff and duties increased. From 1920 to 1924, the department was organized into 10 divisions (29). In 1920, it consisted of the superintendent, 13 professional specialists, and 5 stenographers; 3 years later it included 53 professional plus clerical staff members. Changes continued to take place as new divisions were created and as old divisions were combined, separated, renamed, or abolished.

As efforts continued to organize the department most efficiently to accommodate rapid growth and progress, overlapping and some illogical grouping of responsibilities resulted. For instance, the school inspection division, responsible for some of the same general activities at the high school level as the supervision division, was established in 1925 with funds appropriated by the General Assembly. Comparable efforts had been supported by the General Education Board since the first statewide high school law of 1907.

During these years, the department was fortunate in receiving money from several foundations with which to supplement its state money. The General Education Board of the Rockefeller Foundation, for example, provided the funds for the countywide school planning. It also subsidized many specific positions, such as the director of Negro education; in addition, divisions were granted special funds in the areas of schoolhouse planning, supervision, rural elementary supervision, and high school inspection. In 1926, the General Education Board gave the department $7,500 on an indefinite annual basis to establish an information and statistics division, whose function was to conduct research studies and compile research information and statistics for publication by the department.

The first activity of this division was a study of teacher training for the State Education Commission. Published in 1929 as "Teacher Training in North Carolina," this study was the first bulletin of the new division, which was headed by M. C. S. Noble, Jr. During the 1927-28 school year, the division was involved in 136 programs, projects, and research studies; in 1928-29, there were 380; and in 1929-30, the director collected data on almost 600 studies. In 1929, the General Education Board of the Rockefeller Foundation offered to give the state department $6,500 annually for 4 years to help the schools improve their libraries. The following year, this money was used to employ a director and a stenographer.

In 1929, the General Assembly authorized another educational commission to study the school system primarily to promote efficiency and prevent overlapping. Responsibility for the study was turned over to the Brookings Institution. After a 4-month intensive study of the state government, the commission issued a report in 1930, which read in part:

> The Department as now organized consists of twelve divisions. Under these conditions it is difficult to maintain consistent approach to the field or to obtain unity of purpose and activity in the Department's contacts with local school officials. It often happens that the separate divisions, acting in their advisory capacities, give conflicting and diverse opinions on educational matters. This, of course, leads to criticism.
>
> There is also a tendency for each division to build around itself impregnable walls and to divest itself of all interest other than its own field of endeavor. This situation renders it impossible for the Department to function effectively because of the lack of wholesome cooperation which is so vitally important (30).

The report recommended that the department be organized into five bureaus: administration, supervision, information and statistics, Negro education, and vocational education.

The assembly also authorized another study by an educational commission in 1929, primarily to devise a more economical plan of administration. The report of this commission in 1930 paved the way for legislation enacted the following year that changed the entire philosophy of state and county responsibilities for education (31). The report did not, however, alter the department itself.

DEPRESSION AND WAR, 1931-46

Divided Authority

The Depression had a profound impact on North Carolina education. Actually, the creation of the State Board of Equalization in 1927 marked the turning point in transferring control from the county unit to that of the state. But in 1931, the General Assembly gave the board the power to decide the number of teachers to be allotted to each county as well as the authority to make all necessary rules and regulations regarding the transportation of children at public expense (32). In view of the state's financial situation, this assembly also disallowed separate increments in the state's salary schedule for 2 succeeding years and reduced all salaries up to 10 percent. Powers given to the board were so broad and significant that by 1933 it was virtually the dictator of the state's educational system. The assembly assumed complete responsibility for supporting public school education for a term of 8 months. This meant that most local taxes for supporting schools were abolished and that the state would support most of the costs of public education by levying a statewide sales tax.

State control followed state support. The state equalization board not only forced the schools to abide by its decisions, but it also began to bring other state boards and educational agencies within its sphere of influence. Following the recommendation of the Brookings report, the General Assembly abolished the board in 1933; but instead of transferring its duties to other departments as recommended, it created in its place an even more powerful agency, the State School Commission. Its authority and responsibility altered in many ways the work of the Department of Public Instruction. State Superintendent Clyde A. Erwin, a former school superintendent in Rutherford County who succeeded Allen in 1934, praised the assembly's work. He stated that a desperate financial situation had been saved and that the assembly's action had laid the foundation for one of the soundest educational systems among the states.

When the State Board of Education was established in 1868, it was the only state agency concerned with the administration of the public schools. Over the years, the General Assembly created others, so that by 1940 there were five state agencies directly involved: the State Board of Education, the State Board for Vocational Education, the State Textbook Commission, the State School Commission, and the State Board of Health. In 1942, Superintendent Erwin pointed out that although his office was authorized by law to "direct the operations of the public schools and enforce the laws and regulations thereto . . . " (33), subsequent legislation had transferred specific duties to these other state agencies. He called attention to the confusion existing among the local school superintendents as a result.

In an effort to bring some order to school administration at the state level, the General Assembly passed an act in March 1941 permitting the people to vote on an amendment to the constitution that would place the supervision and administration of the public school system and its funds entirely in the hands of the state education board. The amendment passed in November, and the changes became effective in April 1943. The 1943 General Assembly then abolished the State School Commission, the State Textbook Commission, the State Board for Vocational Education, and the State Board for Commercial Education, transferring their duties and powers to the State Board of Education. At the same time, it extended the school term from 8 to 9 months.

In 1945, the General Assembly appointed a controller for the state board with responsibility for all matters pertaining to budgeting, allocation of personnel, accounting, certification, and disbursing of public school funds. In effect the controller's office replaced the school commission. The same legislation charged the superintendent with carrying out the board's instructional policies and with organizing and administering the department, other than financial affairs. A total of five divisions were set up under the controller's direction: auditing and accounting, plant operation, teacher allotment and general control, textbooks, and transportation.

Improving the Schools' Instructional Programs

In an effort to organize the state's public schools into a unified system from the first grade through high school, the department in 1932 merged its school inspection and elementary education divisions to form the Division of Instructional Services. Two years later, the Division of School Libraries was placed in this division, and the state assumed all responsibility for this service, including the director's salary formerly paid by the General Education Board. The federal Civil Works Administration assisted libraries throughout the state from 1933 to 1935, thereby enabling the number of librarians to increase from 88 to 282.

To improve the schools' instructional programs in all subjects, the instructional services division sponsored regional 1-day conferences and institutes in music, child development, character education, language arts, reading, commercial education, social disease control, mathematics, art, safety, physical education, science, and social studies. Recognized authorities in these subject areas and representatives from textbook publishers often assisted in these conferences and institutes. At the same time, the division continued to inspect the schools, supervise elementary and secondary schools, supervise the accreditation of schools, and prepare courses of study and special bulletins.

Curriculum Revision

The department created a Division of Curriculum Instruction in 1934 to prepare a new state course of study; the division, financed in part by the General Education Board, was abolished when the task was completed. Superintendent Allen appointed James E. Hillman, director of certification, to direct this comprehensive curriculum study. Members of the department, teachers, lay citizens, summer school participants, and special consultants cooperated in publishing an outstanding bulletin entitled "Courses of Study for the Elementary and Secondary Schools in North Carolina, 1935." Following this study and the publication of this bulletin, Hillman assumed the directorship of the new Division of Professional Services, formerly the Division of Certification.

In 1941, the assembly adopted the recommendation of the education commission of 1939 for 12 years of instruction in the public schools. In the fall of the same year, Superintendent Erwin announced that the 12-year program would be planned primarily by two study groups: the Central Curriculum Committee and the Lay and Professional Study Group. These committees studied the nine general subject areas offered by the schools and recommended that the additional grade be placed in the elementary school. They also recommended changes in almost all elementary school subjects, but few in the high school course of study.

Improving Teaching

During the Depression, there were more teachers looking for jobs than there were jobs available. Since improving instruction also involved upgrading the teaching staffs and the preparation of teachers, the department took this opportunity to increase its requirements. By 1941, all beginning teachers were required to be graduates of standard 4-year colleges, and the state board ruled that those who were not would have to obtain a degree by September 1943 or be dropped to the certificate of the next lower class.

From 1936 to 1940, Superintendent Clyde A. Erwin worked diligently to upgrade standards for teachers. Although not a college graduate himself, Erwin was an astute politician and excellent speaker, who could communicate with all groups. His close association with the North Carolina Education Association made him a favorite among the state's educators. Erwin recommended time and again that the school law be amended to require all newly elected superintendents of schools to hold a certificate authorized by the state board. He also requested an annual appropriation of $250,000 to be used for "master's certificates" for teachers who had earned graduate credits and who were known for their outstanding teaching ability. Erwin also requested $750,500 for the 1941-43 biennium to bring the state salary schedule for Negro teachers in line with that for white teachers.

After the United States entered World War II, it was necessary to lower the certification requirements in order to replace those teachers who went into the armed forces or war industry. The first graduate certificates became effective in July 1941, and the first principals' certificates in July 1942. Beginning in 1942, it was necessary to issue "war permits" to those having at least 60 semester hours of college credit. As the war extended into the 1944-45 school year, certification requirements had to be relaxed still further.

Negro Education

During the Depression, the Division of Negro Education operated primarily as a coordinating agency between the Negro schools and the other divisions of the department, with particular emphasis on improving organization and instruction in the elementary schools. The division lost three of its staff members between 1929 and 1933, leaving only one person to supervise the organization and instruction of all the state's Negro elementary schools. The division worked closely with the Jeanes supervisors for Negro schools in 26 counties; it attempted to organize and supervise the teacher training program in the 12 Negro colleges; and finally it prepared and revised courses of study to be used in the colleges for training both elementary and high school teachers. Throughout this period, the Negro education division also supervised the accreditation of colleges and normal schools, as well as public and private schools. It encouraged and assisted schools in consolidating their programs, secured new buses for Negro schools, sent representatives to the countywide teachers and PTA meetings, met with local boards of education in behalf of the Negro schools, and promoted conferences on race relations. It also helped Negro schools secure the libraries and equipment required for accreditation.

In December 1943, the state board authorized the division to make a comprehensive study of Negro education in the state. N. C. Newbold and his staff produced a report in which a long-range program for improving public school facilities was recommended. The state board adopted this report in January 1945. Recommendations also were made for reorganizing and consolidating Negro schools under plans approved by the state department and for making further surveys to determine the future needs of Negro schools. The report also pointed out that vocational education should be expanded in the Negro schools, that there should be more supervisors for the Negro elementary schools, and that these schools should receive a larger appropriation for equipment and supplies (34). The 1945 General Assembly, however, took no action on these recommendations.

Vocational and Adult Education

Adult Education. Although the department had operated vocational educational programs for school-age students since the passage of the Smith-Hughes Act in 1917, it was the Depression and funds from the Civil Works Administration that prompted the organization of a Division of Adult Education in the early thirties. At its inception this program was primarily a relief effort and secondarily an educational program. During the 1933-34 school year, approximately 900 unemployed teachers were paid $50 per month with these federal funds to work in adult schools. The adult program received funds from the U.S. Office of Education in 1936; and in 1937 and 1939, the General Assembly voted funds to guarantee continuance of the program.

The schools for teaching adults established in 1937 varied from unit to unit; but, for the most part, they emphasized adult elementary education to combat illiteracy, Americanization programs for the foreign born, home management, health and hygiene, homecraft, public speaking, and the practical principles of economics. In the 1937-38 school year, more than 43,000 adults were enrolled in these community schools.

In 1940, Superintendent Erwin requested an annual appropriation of $145,000 to establish adult educational programs entirely financed by state funds in 20 counties, and on a matching basis in 80 counties. The adult education division continued to cooperate with the WPA until 1943, when the division was discontinued to avoid duplication of effort in other divisions.

Vocational Education in the 1930's. Federal aid enabled the department to expand its vocational education division during the thirties. For example, the number of staff members increased from 17 in the 1929-30 school year to 25 in the 1939-40 year. During this same period, the 154 schools enrolling 5,300 students in vocational agriculture increased to 412 with 18,965 students in 1940-41. The Civilian Conservation Corps began providing instructors for evening classes in agriculture in the 1937-38 school year. At the same time, the CCC cooperated with the schoolhouse planning division to promote the construction of home economics cottages in connection with the high schools. At the end of the twenties, only six schools enrolled 227 girls in home economics; but at the end of the next decade, 286 departments were enrolling 21,247 girls. There were 384 classes with 12,122 students.

The War Years. The Division of Vocational Education worked closely during the war years with the state National Youth Administration director, John A. Lang. In January 1941, the department employed a supervisor of NYA education. Shortly thereafter, he employed an assistant, six other staff members to work in the state's three NYA districts, and one supervisor for the program for Negroes. By the end of the 1940-41 school year, there were 10,509 out-of-school youth enrolled in the NYA education program, and 447 resident and nonresident centers under the supervision of the vocational education division. When the NYA funds were cut drastically, enrollments dwindled during the next year to approximately 4,000 in 144 centers. The program was discontinued in June 1942. A new program, Vocational Training for Defense, assumed the functions of the NYA program.

The U.S. Office of Education allotted funds for training people in national defense, and the department began such a program in July 1940. The vocational education division set up seven training centers throughout the state to instruct students in shipbuilding, aircraft production, and other related industries. When the United States entered the war in 1941, this program was expanded and strengthened. In July 1942, the NYA program was replaced by a dual program: vocational training for war production workers and rural war production training. By June 1945, more than 48,000 persons had been trained for work in 92 war industries. When the war ended, the program was changed from war production to training for the textile industry.

The department also modified its vocational agriculture program so that specific efforts might be directed toward the needs resulting from the war. It attempted to strengthen the Future Farmers of America, to introduce courses in mechanical operations for out-of-school rural youth, to acquire positions both in the defense industries and for mechanical jobs on the farm, and to develop programs on rural war production. During the 1943-44 school year, 4,011 classes enrolled 57,862 students in these defense training programs, and at the same time more than 29,000 North Carolina farm people were being trained in 250 school community canneries.

The occupational information and guidance section, which had been added to the vocational education division in 1939, proved to be invaluable during the war as more and more people were drained into the service. Although the guidance service itself suffered from the loss of key counselors, this section continued to contribute positively to the realization of department goals throughout the forties (35).

Under the terms of the Emergency Relief Administration Act of 1935, the U.S. Office of Education sponsored a significant study of local school organization and administration in 10 states, including North Carolina. This "Study of Local School Units in North Carolina, 1937" recommended that the vocational education division be enlarged to include a supervisor of distributive occupations as well as a director of vocational guidance. The George-Deen Act of 1937 enabled the department to employ a state supervisor of distributive education in 1939. Particularly useful during the war years, this program emphasized special courses for preparing new workers to replace those who went either into the service or into war industries. It attempted to familiarize experienced salespeople with wartime regulations and new merchandise, as well as to provide information on government regulations and laws for managers and owners of retail businesses. In addition, it provided instruction for executives in supervising employees.

Even before the war, the department's vocational rehabilitation work had expanded. For instance, in the 1929-30 school year the program had rehabilitated 72 persons, whereas in 1940-41 it had served 402. During the war, there were many applications for rehabilitation services from men rejected by Selective Service, and many more were served who were referrals from the State Employment Commission and the American Red Cross. The emphasis was on short training courses in order to prepare these people for essential war industries (36). Long-range rehabilitation and training had to be delayed until the end of the war.

In 1939, the State Board of Health and the State Department of Public Instruction received financial assistance from the Rockefeller Foundation to prepare teachers for assuming responsibility for a large share of the health instruction. As a joint operation they organized the division of school health coordinating service in July 1939, not only to instruct but to simplify and facilitate health services for all youth. The state department supplied three health and physical education advisors who worked as staff members in the school health coordinating service beginning in 1944. Two years later, Superintendent Erwin recommended that the General Assembly appropriate $50,000 annually to the state board to initiate a program for preparing personnel to render health services to youth and to correlate health work in the schools with other agencies engaged in remedial health aid.

Physical Facilities

Schoolhouse Planning. North Carolina was the first and virtually the only state to profit from the approximately $300,000 in federal relief funds available in 1932. During the next 2 years, the Division of Schoolhouse Planning gave all possible assistance to school administrators in survey work, preparation of plans, and applications for CWA and PWA projects. It assisted in selecting building sites and in supervising construction; finally, it inspected the completed buildings.

During the 1935-36 school year, the department, in cooperation with the Julius Rosenwald Fund, sponsored a statewide contest in school plant rehabilitation and beautification. With additional aid from the Rosenwald Fund, it also established a 3-year demonstration in school plant maintenance in Nash County. State Superintendent Erwin recommended that the assembly increase the literary fund to $3 million so that the amount available for school building loans could be increased from $300,000 to $500,000.

In 1939, the director of schoolhouse planning and the director of vocational education were authorized to select rural communities in which vocational buildings could be built and equipped from funds appropriated by the General Assembly to the North Carolina Rural Rehabilitation Corporation, established in 1935. The schoolhouse planning division prepared building plans and then distributed them to units unable to employ an architect. In 1940, the director reported that the division had cooperated with the WPA in planning and erecting school buildings costing $13 million.

Until the United States entered the war, school plant construction proceeded in a normal manner. Beginning in 1942, when labor and materials required for building purposes were deemed essential to the war effort, the chief objective of the schoolhouse planning division was to maintain the status quo (37). The division was engaged, however, in a study of school plant needs in preparation for construction in the postwar period; in addition, it prepared a bulletin on planning modern school plant facilities, also for use by local school units at the conclusion of the war. During this period the federal government, under provisions of the Lanham Act, provided assistance in the erection of school plant facilities in war-impacted areas of the state, such as the city of Wilmington and the counties of New Hanover, Onslow, and Craven. Curtailment of building activities during the war years was followed by a tremendous construction program that caused the staff and functions of this division to be greatly increased.

Textbooks

Prior to 1935, the state took no active part in distributing textbooks to the public schools, even though the state board was authorized to adopt the texts. In 1935, the General Assembly passed an act providing for a state textbook purchase and rental commission to operate as a part of the state department. Two years later, the assembly amended the 1935 law, authorizing the textbook commission to supply free textbooks to all elementary school pupils and to continue the rental system for supplementary readers in the elementary grades and for basal textbooks in the high schools. By 1939, the commission abolished this system of establishing a rental fee for each textbook by creating a flat fee system whereby all students paid one fee to cover the cost of renting all high school textbooks (38).

School Lunch Program

The school lunch program evolved as a result of the urgencies created by the Depression and World War II. From 1935, North Carolina schools operated some school lunch programs by using WPA and NYA labor along with food products donated by the Surplus Commodities Corporation. When the WPA and NYA programs were discontinued in March 1943, the lunchroom programs declined. But, as a part of the nation's food program during World War II, a child-feeding program was developed; this program became a part of the vocational education division in August 1943. Governor Melville Broughton issued an executive order transferring $13,114, previously allocated to the department of charities and public welfare, for supervising these WPA school lunchrooms.

At the time this program was organized, the staff consisted of a state supervisor and three other persons, but by June 1946 it had grown to 11. The supervisors visited various schools, sponsored conferences for lunchroom workers, issued bulletins, and cooperated with the schoolhouse planning division in drawing up plans for school lunchrooms. When Congress passed the National School Lunch Act in 1946, the program was put on a continuing basis.

Publications

The Division of Publications continued to be concerned with compiling, editing, publishing, and distributing printed materials during the thirties. "State School Facts," issued since 1924 as a semimonthly five-column paper to keep the people informed about public education, became a monthly in 1930.

In October 1936, the department also began publishing a 24-page mimeographed pamphlet, the "North Carolina Public School Bulletin," which by the following year was being distributed to 5,500 individuals, organizations, and institutions. The "Bulletin" became a printed paper of eight pages in September 1939, and in September 1941 it was increased to 12 pages. After May 1941, "State School Facts" became a regular feature of the "Bulletin."

A PERIOD OF NOTABLE GROWTH, 1946-65

Changes Within the Department

In 1947, the General Assembly appropriated $50,000 to supplement $100,000 donated by the Knapp Foundation for the State Education Commission to make a study of North Carolina's educational system. In its 1948 report (39), the commission was highly critical of the administrative system that the General Assembly had established in 1945. The law creating the office of controller had resulted in a division of authority and an overlapping of duties with the state superintendent. Although the commission strongly recommended that the assembly clarify the lines of authority and make the state superintendent the sole executive officer of the State Board of Education, the assembly failed to act.

The commission recommended that the staff of the Department of Public Instruction be increased and that its name be changed to "State Department of Education." It indicated that the department should be brought together into not more than five major divisions, with each division being headed by a person with education equivalent to a doctor's degree. It did not recommend that the organization be fixed by law, but it did suggest that the state superintendent be given the authority to organize the department with the approval of the state board.

When Superintendent Erwin died in 1952, Governor Kerr Scott appointed Charles F. Carroll as state superintendent of public instruction. Prior to his appointment, Dr.

Carroll had been superintendent of the High Point City Schools and was widely known as a genteel, level-headed individual, who possessed a remarkable understanding of education in North Carolina. Under his leadership, the department continued to expand, and by 1956, four new divisions–research and statistics, vocational rehabilitation, school health and physical education, and special education–had been added to the six that had existed a decade earlier (40). The department also added a general assistant state superintendent, an administrative assistant, an assistant state superintendent of instruction, and a coordinator of teacher education. In 1945-46, the department's annual budget was $133,366, but by the 1955-56 school year, the budget had grown to $361,341. Along with these administrative changes and new legislative appropriations, division services had been expanded to embrace many new areas.

This tremendous expansion continued to accelerate from 1956 to 1965 as the entire state manifested a widespread desire to improve education. Although part of this enthusiasm for quality education was spawned by a national trend, there were notable experiences in North Carolina that led to significant educational progress. Governors of the period indicated strong interest in education and exercised outstanding initiative to bring about improvements. Governor Terry Sanford, who had campaigned on a platform of improving education, was active on behalf of education throughout his term of office and worked diligently to bring quality education to all of North Carolina's youth (41). There was also a new era in the state superintendent's dealings with superintendents, principals, supervisors, teachers, and the lay public (42).

This healthy climate for better education resulted in a number of critical evaluations of both the state department and the public schools as a means of improving education. There were efforts to develop state accreditation standards within the department, to supervise self-studies of local schools, and to formulate effective teaching guides. Emphasis on helping all youth in North Carolina achieve to the best of their abilities was reflected in refined and expanded programs at all levels. These efforts to improve education were strongly supported by organized groups within the state, particularly the United Forces for Education, which endorsed many legislative proposals for more effective services. This organization was composed of the North Carolina Congress of Colored Parents and Teachers, Congress of Parents and Teachers, American Association of University Women, North Carolina Education Association, Federation of Music Clubs, Federation of Women's Clubs, State Grange, North Carolina Teachers Association, and State School Boards Association.

In this atmosphere for improving education at all levels, the state department engaged in experiments and innovations. Emphasis on planning and educational leadership became increasingly apparent. Working relationships with other organizations and agencies were broadened, and the department assumed constructive leadership in effecting provisions of the Civil Rights Act of 1964. Federally sponsored or cosponsored programs, along with foundation projects, became one of the major aspects of the department's overall responsibility.

Although the department in recent years had operated through 10 divisions, the number was reduced to 5 during the 1958-60 biennium, as the state education commission had recommended several years earlier. This reorganization, designed to coordinate services and facilitate efficiency, still left several former divisions as staff services: publications and central services, educational research, statistical services, NDEA administration, school athletics and activities, teacher merit study, and the North Carolina fund project. The controller's office continued to be organized in seven divisions: auditing and accounting, insurance, personnel, plant operation, teacher allotment and general control, transportation, and textbooks.

Expanding Instruction

The department continued to add staff members as it expanded its general supervision of elementary schools and high schools. During the summers of 1947 and 1948, it organized special courses in the teaching of safety and driver education for teachers at the University of North Carolina. Through private funds (43), the department was able to employ a director of safety education in 1948; and in 1949, the General Assembly appropriated funds to continue this program. Teacher-training courses in driver education increased to 4 in 1952, 8 in 1953, and 12 in 1955. The General Assembly passed legislation providing for teaching safety and driver education in the public schools in 1953, and during the following year the department added two additional staff members for this program. It also prepared a curriculum guide in driver education and a manual in safety education in the spring of 1954.

Following a request by Superintendent Erwin, the General Assembly enabled the department to employ a supervisor of music education in 1950. Within 3 years, interest in music education had become so extensive that the assembly, with widespread organized encouragement throughout the state, primarily from the home demonstration clubs of North Carolina, voted the funds to employ six music supervisors. These consultants not only held area workshops with classroom teachers but also cooperated in an advisory capacity with teacher-training institutions. In 1955, the assembly withdrew funds for three of the six supervisors.

Resource-use education, with emphasis on the conservation an development of natural, social, and human resources in schools and communities, also received emphasis in this period. Governor Gregg Cherry appointed a commission of 50 persons, representing all interests in the state, to explore the need for comprehensive resource-use programs. The General Education Board provided funds to employ a staff for 2 years to initiate this experimental program. Richard L. Weaver, the program director, first had offices at the University of North Carolina but was eventually transferred to the Department of Public Instruction. In 1949, the state decided to support resource-use education as a permanent part of the instructional services division.

Special Education

In keeping with its objective of giving quality education to all students, the General Assembly of 1949 amended the law of 1947 to authorize the state board to use public funds to establish a special education program in accordance with rules and regulations which the board might prescribe. This permitted the schools to include special classes for children with physical and mental handicaps. In 1949, the department established the Division of Special Education.

One of the first problems faced by this division was that of working with the children who were recovering from poliomyelitis contracted during the epidemic of 1948. School centers were established in four hospitals to which the state assigned 11 teachers. Functioning as continuation schools, these centers served 182 students until they were able to return to school or home, where they came under the "homebound" phase of the special education program.

By 1954, special education had expanded to the point that the state superintendent requested an additional supervisor in the area of mental retardation. The General Assembly of 1955 took no action on this request. In 1963, the assembly authorized the department to staff and equip a curriculum library in the area of mental retardation for use by teachers, administrators, and other professional and interested lay persons.

Negro Education

N. C. Newbold, a member of the department since June 1913 and the director of the Division of Negro Education since its organization in 1921, retired in 1948. He was replaced by G. H. Ferguson. Between 1950 and 1960, much emphasis was placed on expansion of plants, consolidations, and transportation facilities. Beginning in 1957, many Negroes were granted student loans through the Prospective Teachers Scholarship Loans, a program which was initiated at that time.

The Negro education division was merged into the instructional services division in 1960. By 1965, this division included seven professional staff members who were Negroes, each of whom worked in the areas of elementary and secondary education and that of library services. Increasingly these staff members rendered services on a nonracial basis. Primary emphasis throughout these years, as many accomplishments were realized, was on the achievement of status through educational attainment (44).

Teacher Certification

Biennially for 16 years, the North Carolina General Assembly passed legislation to extend the life of certificates held by teachers who could not meet the state board's certification requirements. Early in this period, James E. Hillman, director of the Division of Professional Services, advised teachers that renewal credit would be required by September 1948.

In 1948 the State Education Commission recommended that the professional services division be provided with at least one additional highly trained consultant in teacher education and that the staff of the division be expanded to render additional services in guidance and leadership in the selection and recruitment of teachers, in administration and supervision of an enlarged and expanded program of supervised student teaching, and in administration and supervision of scholarship aid and placement services for teachers. The 1953 General Assembly made provisions for the department to employ a coordinator of teacher education.

Four years later, the assembly created a scholarship loan fund for prospective teachers. Administered by the state superintendent, the fund included provisions for 300 regular scholarship loans of not more than $350 each for the first year of the 1957-59 biennium and $600 for the second year. The program was extended in 1959 and again in 1961. By 1962, students utilizing this fund were enrolled in 51 North Carolina colleges and universities, and 3 years later they were studying in 56 institutions. More than 300 teachers had repaid their obligations by teaching in the state by 1965, and approximately 1,000 at that time were teaching and simultaneously repaying their financial obligations.

In August 1959, the state board passed rules and regulations governing the use of a 3-day extended term of employment for academic teachers. In July 1961, the department extended the terms of academic teachers to 5 days in order to offer 180 full days of instruction and to provide the instructional staff with an opportunity to perform the duties essential to the opening and closing of school. The 1961 and 1963 sessions of the General Assembly further attempted to upgrade and update the subject matter knowledge of classroom teachers by appropriating $150,000 annually for in-service education.

The 1959 General Assembly authorized the state board to make a study of "teacher evaluation, rating, and certification." The board named an advisory committee to implement the study, and by December it had appointed a director. The state department cooperated with the director throughout the 2-year study in collecting and interpreting all data relative to the subject.

In the final report adopted by the state board emphasis was placed on the continuing use of the National Teacher Examination by the teacher preparation institutions of the state as a means of improving the preparation of teachers and not as a basis for rating.

> It seems important now for the Board of Education to assist the various teacher education institutions in improving the quality of the program in the various units by stimulation, guidance, and understanding. Testing will measure one important phase of preparation and should be continued under State Board supervision (45).

The State Board of Education accepted in principle an approved program approach to teacher education and certification in January 1961. In September 1962, the board adopted standards and guidelines, developed by committees and subcommittees involving more than 1,000 educators, which placed a greater share of responsibility on the teacher preparation institutions in determining the necessary certification qualifications. This meant that the institutions were responsible for recruiting, selecting, and retaining only those persons displaying genuine promise. It placed emphasis on the appropriateness of the institution for teacher education in such areas as faculty, personnel policies, resources, and facilities.

During this period of rapid growth, the 1961 assembly authorized the state board to conduct an experimental program in merit pay for teachers, the third such study within a period of 20 years; the 1963 assembly voted to continue the program for an additional 2 years. This $400,000 study involved approximately 1,200 teachers in three administrative units. In spite of the excellent inservice experiences the experiment afforded teachers, the final report to the 1965 assembly recommended that a uniform, statewide merit pay program not be introduced. It declared, however, that merit programs should be encouraged at the local level as specific conditions conducive to their success were found to exist. The study also prompted other recommendations for the continuing improvement of instruction. The assembly took no action on this report or any of its recommendations.

School Health and Physical Education

In 1949, the General Assembly began appropriating $440,000 annually to the state board for school health work, including the diagnosis and correction of chronic remedial defects of indigent children. It was the responsibility of the school health coordinating service to plan the program and administer these funds. Two years later, the service moved from the Board of Health Building to the Education Building, and the following year the department organized it as a separate division of school health and physical education and school health coordinating service. This new division was to work not only with health instruction and physical education, but also with safety, healthful environment, mental hygiene, and health services to the public schools.

In 1952, the state board adopted uniform standards of health, safety, and eligibility for schools operating athletic programs. The department appointed a consultant in health and physical education to integrate athletics with the total program of physical education.

Vocational Education

In 1945, the assembly designated the department as the approval agency for the funds Congress appropriated for training World War II veterans. By the end of 1946, there were 51,765 North Carolina veterans in institutional, on-the-job, and veteran farmer training; 3 years later, there were 70,539. The vocational education division's trade and industrial section supervised the on-the-job training, which included 17,508 veterans in December 1946, 18,605 in 1947, and 3,219 in January 1956. The vocational agriculture section employed five district supervisors and one supervisor for Negro schools to conduct a program of 200 hours of group instruction plus 100 hours of individual on-the-farm instruction per year. There were 6,530 veterans in this program in December 1946 and 24,098 by the end of 1949; but by January 1956, there were only 2,606.

Both the guidance services and the industrial rehabilitation programs continued to grow during the postwar period. Of the state's 933 high schools in 1956, scheduled time for student guidance was available in 323. In the same year, the industrial rehabilitation operation had expanded to such an extent that it was set up as a separate division and spent more than $1.25 million during the 1955-56 school year in treating 7,097 cases.

Improving Physical Facilities

Schoolhouse Planning. At the end of World War II, Superintendent Erwin reported that a survey directed by the state board revealed the need for $100 million of new school buildings in North Carolina. This 1946 report, approved by the board, proposed that the state distribute $25 million to local administrative units over a 5-year period. The 1947 General Assembly, occupied with many other postwar problems, took no action on this recommendation. The next year, again with the support of the state board and this time with the backing of the State Education Commission, Superintendent Erwin reported to the Governor and the assembly that at least $100 million was urgently needed to provide up-to-date school facilities. Moreover, the commission recommended that the department employ nine people at the schoolhouse planning division—which had only a director at the time—and that it expand its advisory services to all administrative units.

In April 1949, the General Assembly passed an act appropriating $25 million for the state board to allocate to the counties for school buildings and authorized a bond election for an additional $25 million. The act also authorized the board to deduct up to one-fourth of 1 percent of the amount allocated to each county to be used for surveys and construction plans, improvements, or repairs of school buildings. The department then created a survey section in the schoolhouse planning division, and by 1951, it had added two additional staff members.

North Carolina received $93,520 from the federal government, which it matched with state funds in 1951, to initiate a statewide survey of school facilities. The first step—collecting information concerning the condition of buildings, facilities needed, and the financial resources available—was incorporated into a report submitted to the U.S. Office of Education. The second phase of the survey involved a long-range study to determine the need, location, building sites, type, and size of individual school plant projects in each administrative unit. On the basis of this information the department developed a statewide master plan for school construction.

With the urgent recommendation of Superintendent Charles F. Carroll, the 1953 General Assembly voted to hold a statewide election for issuing $50 million in school construction bonds. In October, the citizens voted in favor of the bond issue, and the building program was continued. By the end of June 1956, the state board had approved 1,040 school projects amounting to more than $77 million.

School Lunch Program

During the postwar decade, the school lunch program continued to expand. When it began in 1943, there were only 4 people on the staff with 549 schools participating; by the end of 1948, the staff had increased to 18, and 1,422 schools were serving lunches. Two supervisors for the Negro school lunch program were added to the state office in 1949. During the 1955-56 school year, 1,628 schools participated in the school lunch program. In 1963-64, a total of 2,040 of the 2,154 public schools in the state provided meal service, with over 90 percent of these schools participating in the National School Lunch Program.

NEW AND EXPANDED SERVICES, 1956-65

As the department initiated new services, it became responsible for certain "new" areas in curriculum, assumed responsibility for operating federally inspired programs, and launched a number of experiments throughout the state. Its personnel increased from approximately 230 in 1956 to almost 500 in 1965. The office of the controller employed an additional 140.

Enriching Instruction

During this period there was widespread emphasis on standardized testing in the schools of the state. The percentage of students tested annually, grades 7 through 12, increased from 60 percent in the 1961-62 school year to 68 percent in 1963-64. Slightly more than two-thirds of this testing was made possible through Title V of the National Defense Education Act.

In an effort to insist that all students stay in school as long as possible, for the first time in the history of North Carolina state funds were allocated during the 1962-64 biennium to aid county and city administrative units in enforcing compulsory attendance laws. Attendance counselors, operating in 46 of the 159 administrative units, worked in every possible way with potential dropouts and chronic absentees in an effort to encourage these people to remain in school. Reports indicated that these counselors had a considerable impact in improving school attendance and in preventing dropouts.

For those who dropped out of school, the department established a high school equivalency program that covered five broad areas of knowledge. As the program evolved, it was extended to qualified prison inmates and to members of the armed forces who met residence requirements. Applications for these tests increased each year until approximately 12,000 certificates had been issued by the end of 1965.

One of the most significant programs of this period was that for educating the disadvantaged, made possible through federal funds allotted under the Elementary and Secondary Education Act of 1965. The department disseminated information about the program to all school administrative units and interpreted the guidelines and regulations concerning the program that were issued from the U.S. Office of Education. This was accomplished in part through numerous personal conferences with local school personnel. The department organized a series of regional conferences early in 1966 to evaluate the projects that had been approved. It appointed coordinators for each of the several titles of the ESEA and assigned virtually all staff members certain responsibilities for implementing the provisions of this act.

From 1958 to 1963, the North Carolina public schools spent more than $14 million in federal and local funds for improving instruction under Title III of the National Defense Education Act of 1958. All administrative units in the state participated under Title III at least 1 year during this period. As a result, science laboratory facilities increased in quantity and quality throughout the state. Through the use of additional teaching aids, schools were able to increase interest and improve instruction in mathematics. The audiolingual approach to teaching modern foreign languages also improved instruction in this area. North Carolina's progress under the NDEA program attracted national attention during this period.

Another program designed to improve instruction, sponsored by the U.S. Office of Education through the Goldsboro city schools and the state department, was inaugurated in the 1964-65 school year. Under the Cooperative Research Study, a project in first-grade reading was developed for the 751 children in all of the Goldsboro schools' 28 first-grade classes. The major purpose of the project was to compare three approaches to teaching first-grade reading: a traditional basal reader approach, an approach using basal readers plus intensive phonics, and an approach using the above methods plus sensory experiences. Findings indicated that no approach to the teaching of reading will necessarily reach all children, but that the sensory experiences approach is more beneficial than either of the other two.

Since the statutes of North Carolina declare that the state superintendent is responsible for the education of all children within the state, the department during this decade provided a consultant for its 170 nonpublic schools and issued three publications on the subject. The first full-time coordinator for nonpublic schools was appointed in 1961-62, and he and his successors worked with the more than 700 kindergartens throughout the state. State Superintendent Charles Carroll urged the 1963 and 1965 Legislatures to establish statewide kindergartens, beginning with certain experimental and pilot programs. By the end of 1965, however, no funds had been appropriated for public kindergartens, although the 1965 Legislature had given Orange County permission to experiment in this area for a period of 3 years with money offered by the Ford Foundation.

With grants from the Richardson Foundation of Greensboro, the state board in November 1957 authorized a special curriculum study, which was initiated in April 1958. In 1961, the General Assembly made the curriculum study and research department a permanent agency under the state board's supervision. The general objective of the agency was to provide the board with information and recommendations needed in its policy-making decisions on curriculum and other matters of educational concern. Specifically, it was—

> To sponsor new experiments designed to produce high-quality education in the public schools; to disseminate information about new developments in education and to adapt these developments to public school needs in North Carolina; and to promote the adoption of successful new educational developments . . . (46).

The agency was terminated in June 1965.

One other program sponsored under Title III of the Elementary and Secondary Education Act, known as Projects To Advance Creativity in Education, was designed to assist schools in establishing a variety of supplementary educational centers and services. The state superintendent appointed a planning and review committee for Title III, with the chairman serving as the acting coordinator. Fifty-four school systems submitted 58 proposals during the first three application periods, 16 of which were approved with budgets totaling approximately $660,000. Eight of these projects were for comprehensive, supplementary educational centers and services; two were for fine arts programs; two, for purposes of planning new curriculum approaches; and one each for a marine science center, a center for Latin American studies, a model school unit, and a guidance program for delinquent youth.

In July 1962, the state board made provisions for a new staff service in the state department known as "School Athletics and Activities." This official action was paralleled by the issuance of a policy statement by the state board concerning the protection of school time necessary for a quality curriculum, with emphasis on a proper balance between subjects and activities. In February 1965, a student activities handbook, unique among the states, was published. In this significant bulletin, "Student Activities, North Carolina Public Schools," emphasis is placed on objectives, policies, and legal responsibilities. The publication was intended not only for teachers and administrators but for school board members as well.

Provisions for further in-service education of teachers were made by the 1961 and the 1963 assemblies when $150,000 was appropriated annually to provide for upgrading and updating the subject matter knowledge of classroom teachers. In 1964-65, through the transfer of funds secured by the state board, opportunity was made available for approximately 8,000 elementary teachers to participate in a televised course in mathematics.

Materials

In March 1960, the state board established a vocational materials laboratory to collect, evaluate, develop, and distribute new materials and suggest new techniques for vocational education teachers. Attention was focused on materials in trade and industrial education, as expansion in this area had been so rapid that printed materials often were outdated soon after publication.

The curriculum library in mental retardation—organized, staffed, and equipped in 1963—quickly became an up-to-date center for comprehensive materials on mental retardation. Materials and services available through this center were available not only to department staff members but to teachers, administrators, and other professional and lay personnel interested in mental retardation.

The department also established a general professional library in 1965 for its staff members. With both state and federal funds, these materials and services were expanded in such a comprehensive manner that almost any materials needed in relation to the staff's professional responsibilities were available, including those through interlibrary loans.

In cooperation with the University of North Carolina and the Ford Foundation, the state department initiated an in-school TV experiment in 1957. The General Assembly appropriated funds for the 1959-61 biennium to supplement the Ford support. The success of this experiment prompted the state board to agree that TV education should be incorporated into the North Carolina public school program. The first supervisor, appointed in 1961, was assisted by a consultant and four studio teachers. Funds were appropriated by the General Assembly in 1961, 1963, and again in 1965 to finance a statewide program of TV instruction under supervision of the department. At the end of the 1961-62 school year, approximately 30,000 students were receiving TV instruction in one or more courses.

Beginning with the 1962-63 school year, the department, with state and Old Dominion Foundation funds, coordinated 60 statewide presentations of professional dramatic productions. Theatre-in-Education, Inc., a New York equity company, presented excerpts from Shakespearean dramas to approximately 50,000 students in the first year. The success of this venture prompted similar productions in subsequent years and in as many different schools as possible. The state board assumed full responsibility for financing these presentations after the first year, except in 1965-66 when a group of North Carolina banks underwrote the project.

Through the Vagabond Players of the Flat Rock Playhouse, North Carolina's oldest professional theater, another effort in live theater for students was initiated in 1964-65 with 60 performances of *The World of Carl Sandburg*. These productions, financed through arrangements with the Northwestern Bank and the State Board of Education, also were presented to audiences of approximately 50,000 each year. Follow-up evaluations by teachers and students indicated that the productions were eminently worthwhile, both educationally and as entertainment.

Exceptional Children

In its effort to give every child in North Carolina an opportunity to develop to his fullest extent, the state board initiated a short-term, residential school for gifted and talented students during the summer of 1963. This experimental school, known as the Governor's School of North Carolina because Governor Terry Sanford was influential in starting it, was financed by the Carnegie Corporation and by businesses and foundations of Winston-Salem.

The school served 400 gifted and talented high school students in each of its 8-week sessions with a minimum duplication of students from summer to summer. The curriculum was designed to enrich the knowledge of each student and to encourage creativity in his particular area of interest, such as English, mathematics, natural science, social science, foreign languages, art, choral music, orchestra, dance, drama, and piano. In addition, all students participated in special discussion groups, forums, and lectures under the supervision of instructors from the various academic disciplines. The school attempted to examine the content and instructional methods appropriate for gifted and talented students. Results of the experiment, including the findings of several broad research projects, were made available to the schools of the state so that they might profit from what was learned.

The department was indirectly involved in an experimental residential school for underachieving eighth-grade boys from all sections of the state during this period, with Superintendent Carroll serving on its board of directors. Financed by grants totaling $3.5 million from the Carnegie Corporation, the State Board of Education, and the U.S. Office of Education, the North Carolina Advancement School was founded in November 1964 as a research project of the Learning Institute of North Carolina. Its purpose was to develop and test ways effectively to educate underachievers. It had the unique advantage of operating annually four separate sessions of 3 months each, with nearly 1,000 boys participating. This arrangement permitted a large number of experiments and a great number of comparisons in a short time.

The Advancement School, utilizing experimental as well as established methods and materials, attempted to devise and evaluate new ways of teaching and learning that might be adopted in all classrooms throughout the state. The testing of methodology was conducted in selected experimental classes throughout the state as well as in the Advancement School itself. The school also was designed to give selective groups of classroom teachers a working knowledge of new approaches to the understanding of student problems and motivation. The especially designed counseling program encouraged continuing achievement on the part of the students after they returned to their home schools.

The Comprehensive School Improvement Program, financed by the State Board of Education and the Ford Foundation through the North Carolina Fund, was initiated in October 1963 as a field-oriented project and was coordinated by the State Department of Public Instruction. In its efforts to improve methods of teaching reading, writing, and arithmetic, emphasis was placed on team-teaching, multigrade organizational patterns, use of college consultants, use of teacher aides, extensive use of instructional materials and audiovisual aids, and visits to other schools.

Consideration in this program also was given to reorganization of the school day, redesign of the curriculum, redeployment of the teaching staff, more effective use of television and other technological resources, in-service education of teachers, and improved communication between teachers and pupils and between teachers and parents. At the end of 1965, the program involved 228 schools, 398 teaching teams, and approximately 25,000 students, 900 teachers, and 100 college consultants from 28 colleges.

Leadership Training

In North Carolina the state board has been responsible for making personnel allotments for superintendents, assistant superintendents, supervisors, teachers, principals, and attendance counselors. The department first received funds from the General Assembly in 1961 to provide assistant superintendents, and in that year, it allotted 44; during the 1965-66 term, it provided 95.

State-allotted supervisory positions in North Carolina, according to board policy, must first be used to ensure competent instructional leadership for general studies common to all students. After this supervision has been provided at both the elementary and secondary levels, special services may be given in specific areas, such as library and instructional materials, guidance and counseling, and the fine arts. In the 1965-66 school year, there were 304 state-allotted supervisors, although others were employed locally.

North Carolina allots teaching positions to meet minimum standards only; the department, however, encourages local communities to provide financing beyond state allotments for ensuring maximum efficiency. From 1956 to 1965, these allotment procedures were liberalized at the state level, thereby permitting more and more state-allotted personnel to local administrative units. In 1965, the assembly appropriated funds for reducing the teacher-pupil ratio in grades 1 through 3.

Members of the state department, especially the superintendent, the assistant superintendent, the directors of divisions, and special consultants, are called on frequently for advice, counseling, and assistance in planning. This was particularly true after the schools became involved in federal programs, many of which were new and untried. Throughout this period of rapid growth and expansion, the state department acted on the premise that it had a primary leadership responsibility for planning, executing, and evaluating area conferences and workshops that might be of value to educators throughout the state. For example, in 1958, after Congress passed the National Defense Education Act, the department arranged a series of conferences concerning the acceptable way to prepare projects, request materials and equipment, and evaluate projects. The department also held area conferences concerning the implementation of the Vocational Education Act of 1963 and the Elementary and Secondary Education Act of 1965.

Throughout this period, the department gave leadership to classroom TV teachers each year in helping them evaluate their work and make plans for the coming year. The state department in this decade planned four state conferences for beginning principals and similar conferences for all principals. It arranged leadership conferences to introduce new publications, to discuss their contents, and to share suggestions on how best to use these publications.

Similarly, the department gave increasing assistance to schools during this period in planning self-studies; it also formulated study guides in various areas and arranged for state and Southern Association accreditation. The state department's leadership had an impact on all curriculum programs—including those which were federally financed—and on all programs pertaining to school activities in athletics, publications, research, school libraries, testing, audiovisual education, and the school lunch program.

Even before Congress enacted the Civil Rights Act of 1964, North Carolina had already desegregated 274 of its 2,135 public schools. During the 1964-65 school year, 84 of the 169 school units were integrated, compared to 45 the preceding year; 3,054 Negroes were attending white schools in 1964-65 as compared to 1,519 in 1963-64. There were 47 teachers and 180 white students in predominantly Negro schools in 1964-65, compared to 5 teachers the previous year.

State Superintendent Carroll and Assistant Superintendent J. E. Miller worked individually and in groups with local superintendents, school board members, board attorneys, and others in interpreting the Civil Rights Act. In this area, as was commonly true, North Carolina's educational leadership assumed intelligent initiative and mustered effective cooperation throughout the state in understanding and implementing the provisions of the act. The changes that occurred in this critical period were effected with the dignity typical of a state accustomed to obedience to law and respect for all races.

FOOTNOTES

1. Charles Lee Smith, *The History of Education in North Carolina*, Bureau of Education Circular of Information No. 2, 1888, part of *Contributions to American Educational History*, ed. by Herbert B. Adams. (Washington, D.C.: Government Printing Office, 1888), p. 167.
2. Edgar W. Knight, *Public School Education in North Carolina* (New York: Houghton Mifflin Co., 1916), p. 163.
3. C. H. Wiley, "An Address to the Officers and Friends of the Common Schools in North Carolina," *North Carolina Education Journal*, XXIII (January 1957), 23, 66, 69. Reprinted from *North Carolina Common School Journal*, I (March 1857).
4. Henry Barnard, ed., *Proceedings of the National Teachers' Association: The National Education Association from Its Foundation in 1857 to the Close of the Session of 1870* (Syracuse, N.Y.: C. W. Bardeen, 1909), p. 709.
5. Robert Bingham, "The New South," *The Journal of Proceedings and Addresses of the National Education Association, Session of the Year 1884, at Madison, Wisconsin* (Boston: The National Education Association, 1885), p. 94.

6. Smith, *op. cit.*, pp. 174-75.

7. *Ibid.*, pp. 175-76.

8. North Carolina, *Public Laws and Resolutions of the General Assembly* (1891), ch. 199, sec. 42.

9. The Department of Public Instruction did not assume the functions and duties of the State Board of Examiners until 1921, when the Division of Certification was created by the General Assembly.

10. Mebane was a native of Guilford County, a graduate of Catawba College, and a schoolteacher of some years' experience. He was earnest and enthusiastic, and under him the office of state superintendent became a new educational agency. Mebane showed a clear grasp of the state's educational problems and he won the respect of the school forces. A live wire, he has been called one of the great campaigners for universal education in North Carolina, *News and Observer* (Raleigh), December 16, 1926; R. D. W. Connor, *North Carolina: Rebuilding an Ancient Commonwealth, 1584-1925*, II (New York: The American Historical Society, 1929), p. 449.

11. Having taken no part in politics, unlike his predecessors, he expressed the hope that the time would soon come when public opinion would forbid any superintendent from taking an active part in political campaigns.

12. North Carolina, *Public Laws and Resolutions of the General Assembly* (1899), ch. 637. This was the first direct appropriation by the state for public schools. The General Assembly of 1869 had appropriated $100,000 for schools out of any surplus in the state treasury; but as there was never any surplus, this was only a paper appropriation.

13. Although elected on the Fusion ticket in 1896, Mebane had administered his office without a trace of partisanship. He was so acceptable to many Democrats that they urged their party to take this opportunity to divorce the schools from politics. The majority of the convention, however, was determined to make a clean sweep of the Fusion group. Thomas F. Toon, with an honorable Confederate Army record to his credit, was nominated and succeeded Mebane in office in January 1901.

14. Actually, the state superintendent and a clerk, Major John Devereaux, who was assigned to the office in 1881, comprised the entire staff of the department until a stenographer was added in 1901.

15. Knight, *op. cit.*, pp. 372-73.

16. North Carolina, *Public Laws and Resolutions of the General Assembly* (1909), ch. 525, sec. 2.

17. *Ibid.*, sec. 6.

18. The State Education Commission reported that the teachers in North Carolina were "as a body, ill prepared, inexperienced, and unstable" primarily because of "low salaries, a poor certification system, and inadequate teacher training institutions." *Public Education in North Carolina: A Report by the State Education Commission*, prepared under the direction of the commission by the General Education Board (Raleigh: State of North Carolina, 1920), p. 57. Concerning the problem of certification, the commission stated that the prevailing way of certificating teachers had contributed to the present unpreparedness of the teaching body. "With salaries low, with little distinction in pay or otherwise between the trained and the untrained, with teachers scarce, our certificating authorities have been able to do little to foster teacher training, while the conditions under which certificates were issued minimized even the little they could do." *Ibid.*, p. 49.

    The commission pointed out that the state system of certification set up under the State Board of Examiners and institute conductors was incomplete and ineffective because the city and county superintendents still issued second- and third-grade certificates. Each of these 236 superintendents was a law unto himself, setting up his own standards for the certification of the more than one-third of the teaching force of the state who held these certificates. To provide an effective statewide system of certification, the commission recommended a change in the certification law and a change in the organization for certification.

19. James E. Hillman, who replaced Allen as director of the Division of Teacher Training in 1923, was responsible for initiating these changes; and he prepared a booklet setting forth these new standards and certification requirements.

20. Mrs. Holland, whose salary was paid by the General Education Board and by the Jeanes Fund, was responsible to N. C. Newbold, who directed her itineraries and her efforts throughout the counties.

21. North Carolina, *Public Laws and Resolutions of the General Assembly* (1907), ch. 280, secs. 1, 3, 4. Although the General Assembly of 1864-65 had passed a graded school law to provide instruction in public schools beyond the common schools, no schools went into operation because of the collapse of education during the closing months of the Civil War. High schools were operating in 1907 in the towns and cities of the state by special acts of the General Assembly, but these were maintained by local taxation with no help from the state and were not a part of the state public school system.

22. Walker served from 1907 to 1920. His position at the University was made possible by the funds from the General Education Board, and until 1917 the General Education Board paid for his services to the state department. After 1917, the General Assembly allowed the State Board of Education to reserve $500 out of the appropriation for high schools to be used in defraying part of the necessary expense in connection with the inspection and supervision of rural high schools. North Carolina, *Public Laws and Resolutions of the General Assembly* (1917), ch. 285, sec. 4.

23. James Y. Joyner, "Some Dominant Tendencies in American Education," *Journal of Proceedings and Addresses of the National Education Association,* Inaugural address at Boston (Winona, Minn.:The Association, 1910), p. 80.

24. The 1911 General Assembly appropriated $25,000 annually to establish a maximum of 10 farm-life schools each year in connection with the best county high schools. It was agreed that only one farm-life school might be established in a county and that the county had to provide $25,000 for buildings and equipment and $2,500 annually to maintain the school.

25. In 1921, North Carolina matched funds available under the Smith-Bankhead Act of 1920 to provide vocational rehabilitation of disabled citizens.

26. Salary for the state inspector of high schools was furnished by the General Education Board; salary for the state supervisor of rural elementary schools, by the Peabody Fund.

27. North Carolina, *Public Laws and Resolutions of the General Assembly* (1868-1869), ch. 184, secs. 22, 69. Two sections of the law of 1869 may be interpreted as steps toward the functions of the Division of Schoolhouse Planning in plans and estimates for building a schoolhouse were to be approved by the superintendent and State Board of Education. Another section of the law required the superintendent of public instruction to distribute plans of schoolhouses and suggestions on school architecture. These were the first legal requirements for schoolhouse planning at the state level, and the initial move toward the functions of a Division of Schoolhouse Planning.

28. Superintendent of Public Instruction, *Biennial Report, 1900-1902*, p. 15. This was the first step toward a Division of Schoolhouse Planning since 1869, when Superintendent Ashley had issued a collection of plans for school buildings.

29. Each of the assigned functions had previously been delegated to individual staff members, or they were new functions assigned by the General Assembly.

30. The Brookings Institution, *Report on a Survey of the Organization and Administration of the State Government of North Carolina* (1930), p. 169.

31. Heretofore, the counties had provided the money for the constitutional 6-month school term, with some aid from the state treasury in an increasing equalization fund. Hereafter, the state was to take over all provisions for the 6-month school term with aid from the counties.

32. In 1923, for the first time in North Carolina's history, state funds ($30,000) were provided for pupil transportation. From 1923 until 1927, the state board distributed these funds for the various administrative units. But in 1927, the State Board of Equalization was given the authority to determine the amount of money any single administrative unit might receive for pupil transportation.

33. Superintendent of Public Instruction, *Biennial Report, 1940-42*, Part I, pp. 61-62.

34. White and Negro teachers were paid on the same salary schedule for the first time in the 1944-45 school year. North Carolina was the first state with two different salary schedules to make them equal.

35. North Carolina was the second state in the nation to have a full-time coordinator of counseling and guidance services.

36. The program was administered from Raleigh through five district offices, with three district supervisors working out of each office.

37. Priorities and permits were granted for the construction of essential buildings destroyed by fire or other causes; but no other new construction was allowed except for new lunchrooms, cafeterias, vocational buildings, and canneries which were approved by the federal government as essential even in wartime.

38. All books submitted by publishers for particular subjects were evaluated by the textbook commission, which was composed of teachers, principals, supervisors, and superintendents. The textbooks were then purchased and distributed to the county and city units by the textbook division.

39. The report, *Education in North Carolina Today and Tomorrow: The Report of the State Education Commission* (1948), was published in its entirety by the United Forces for Education after obstacles had been met at the state level for printing more than a summary of its recommendations.

40. See Appendix B for organization of the department in 1955-68.

41. In his campaign speeches throughout North Carolina, Sanford, the youngest Governor since Aycock at the turn of the century, pleaded for "massive education, not massive resistance." In his inaugural address he forcibly declared that "quality education is the foundation of economic development, of democracy, of the needs and hopes of the nation."

    Sixty days later, he outlined his program of quality education to the General Assembly and asked for the elimination of practically all exemptions from the state's 3-percent sales tax. This meant tax on food, and the critics cried loudly about unfairness and "High Tax Terry." In one of his public answers to the critics, he stated, "If we tax bread, we also will be taxing cake. If we tax fatback, we also will tax caviar. If we tax corn meal, we will also tax filet mignon. No one is going to go hungry because of this tax. But the children of North Carolina will go thirsty for quality education if we do not enact this program for better schools."

    While Sanford was in office, a network of community colleges was established; three new senior colleges were created; teachers' salaries were increased approximately 22 percent, an experimental school for talented youth was established; the North Carolina School of the Arts came into being; a residential school for underachievers was founded; the Learning Institute of North Carolina, a research organization, was organized; a retraining program for dropouts was initiated by the North Carolina Bankers Association. Nearly 3,000 additional teachers were employed under Sanford's program, as well as 44 assistant superintendents and additional supervisors. Clerical assistants were added to the schools; library allotments were doubled; funds were provided for in-service education; 300 additional prospective teacher scholarship loan funds were provided; college salaries were increased; TV services were expanded; and a Department of Curriculum and Research was established.

42. In addition, other forces of statewide importance were at work during this period. The Legislatures, through their appropriations, their extension of staff services in the State Department of Public Instruction, their educational study commissions, evidenced a strong interest in improving public schools. The State Board of Education continued to establish forward-looking policies; pronouncements of the state superintendent were increasingly forthright, realistic, and dynamic; priorities established in the state department, with special emphasis on local self-studies, were conducive to improved education; organized efforts of informed laymen were felt throughout the state; and federal assistance, through appropriations and guidelines for effecting educational improvements, alerted state and local officials to ways of making education more productive at all levels.

43. The North Carolina Association of Insurance Agents, Inc., offered funds and encouragement for the department's first director of safety education.

44. Between 1921 and 1960, Negro high school enrollments increased from 16,817 to 68,255; because of consolidation the number of schoolhouses decreased from 2,442 to 996; the number of accredited high schools increased from 7 to 208; the number of high school graduates increased from 59 to 10,837; and the number of teachers, principals, and supervisors increased from 4,556 in 1924 to 10,137 in 1960. In 1921-22, the average training of the Negro teacher was 3.51 years of high school; by 1959-60, the training was approximately 4.33 years of college. G. H. Ferguson, "Some Facts About the Education of Negroes in North Carolina, 1921-1960," unpublished manuscript, prepared as a historical document for the State Department of Public Instruction, 1962.

45. North Carolina State Board of Education, "Report-National Teacher Examination," 1961. (Mimeographed.)

46. North Carolina, *The Budget,* Vol II: *"B" Budget Recommendation, "A" and "B," Budget Summaries, and Statements for Biennial, July 1, 1961 to June 30, 1963, Fiscal Years 1961-62 and 1962-63* (January 3, 1961), p. 219.

BIBLIOGRAPHY

Public Documents

North Carolina. *The Budget.* Vol II: *"B" Budget Recommendation, "A" and "B," Budget Summaries, and Statements for Biennial, July 1, 1961 to June 30, 1963, Fiscal Years 1961-62 and 1962-63* (January 3, 1961).

--*Constitution* (1868).

--*Public Laws and Resolutions of the General Assembly* (1891-1965).

Books and Pamphlets

Adams, Herbert B. *The Study of History in American Colleges and Universities.* Bureau of Education Circular of Information No. 2. Washington, D.C.: Government Printing Office, 1887.

Barnard, Henry, ed. *Proceedings of the National Teachers' Association: The National Education Association from Its Foundation in 1857 to the Close of the Session of 1870.* Syracuse, N.Y.: C. W. Bardeen, 1909.

Bingham, Robert. "The New South." *The Journal of Proceedings and Addresses of the National Education Association, Session of the Year 1884, at Madison, Wisconsin.* Boston: The National Education Association, 1885.

Connor, R. D. W. *North Carolina: Rebuilding an Ancient Commonwealth, 1584-1925.* 4 vols. New York: The American Historical Society, 1929.

Dabney, Charles W. *Universal Education in the South.* 2 vols. Chapel Hill: University of North Carolina Press, 1936.

Hamilton, J. G. de R. *North Carolina Since 1860.* 3 vols. New York: The Lewis Publishing Co., 1919.

Joyner, James Y. "Some Dominant Tendencies in American Education." *Journal of Proceedings and Addresses of the National Education Association.* Inaugural address at Boston, 1910. Winona, Minn.: The Association, 1910.

Knight, Edgar W. *Public School Education in North Carolina.* New York: Houghton Mifflin Co., 1916.

Mitchell, Memory F., ed. *Messages, Addresses, and Public Papers of Terry Sanford, Governor of North Carolina, 1961-1965.* Raleigh: Council of State, 1966.

Sanford, Terry. *But What About the People?* New York: Harper and Row, 1966.

Smith, Charles Lee. *The History of Education in North Carolina.* Bureau of Education Circular of Information No. 2, 1888, from *Contributions to American Educational History.* Edited by Herbert B. Adams. Washington, D.C.: Government Printing Office, 1888.

Teacher Education in North Carolina: A Cooperative Approach. Raleigh: North Carolina Board of Higher Education, 1961.

Articles and Periodicals

North Carolina Public School Bulletin. Raleigh: State of North Carolina, selected issues.

News and Observer (Raleigh), December 16, 1926.

North Carolina. *State School Facts,* selected issues. Raleigh: State of North Carolina.

Wiley, C. H. "An Address to the Officers and Friends of the Common Schools in North Carolina." *North Carolina Education Journal,* XXIII (January 1957). Reprinted from *North Carolina Common School Journal,* I (March 1857).

Reports

Brookings Institution. *Report on a Survey of the Organization and Administration of the State Government of North Carolina.* Washington, D.C.: Brookings Institution, 1930.

Bureau of Community Service. *Biennial Report, 1918-1920.* Raleigh: The Bureau, 1920.

State Education Commission. *Education in North Carolina Today and Tomorrow.* Raleigh: United Forces for Education, 1948.

--*Public Education in North Carolina.* Prepared under the direction of the General Education Board. Raleigh: The Commission, 1920.

--*Report.* Raleigh: The Commission, 1920.

Superintendents of Common Schools. *Annual Reports.* Raleigh: Department of Education, 1853-65.

Superintendents of Public Instruction. *Annual and Biennial Reports.* Raleigh: Department of Education, 1868-1965.

Unpublished Material

Board of Education. "Report—National Teacher Examination." Paper may be obtained at the Board of Education, Raleigh, North Carolina. Written in 1961.

Ferguson, G. H. "Some Facts About the Education of Negroes in North Carolina, 1921-1960." Prepared for the Department of Education, Raleigh, North Carolina.

Prince, David Hyde. "A History of the State Department of Public Instruction in North Carolina, 1852-1956." Unpublished Ph.D. dissertation, University of North Carolina, Chapel Hill, 1959.

Appendix A

NORTH CAROLINA CHIEF STATE SCHOOL OFFICERS

State Superintendents of Common Schools

1853-66	Calvin H. Wiley
1866	Office abolished

State Superintendents of Public Instruction

1868-71	Samuel Stanford Ashley
1871-72	Alexander McIver
1872	James Reid (died before taking office)
1872-74	Alexander McIver
1874-76	Stephen D. Pool
1876-77	John Pool
1877-85	John C. Scarborough
1885-93	Sidney M. Finger
1893-97	John C. Scarborough
1897-1901	Charles H. Mebane
1901-1902	Thomas F. Toon
1902-19	James Y. Joyner
1919-23	Eugene C. Brooks
1923-34	Arch Turner Allen
1934-52	Clyde A. Erwin
1952-68	Charles F. Carroll

Appendix B

Chart I.--NORTH CAROLINA PUBLIC SCHOOL SYSTEM, 1955

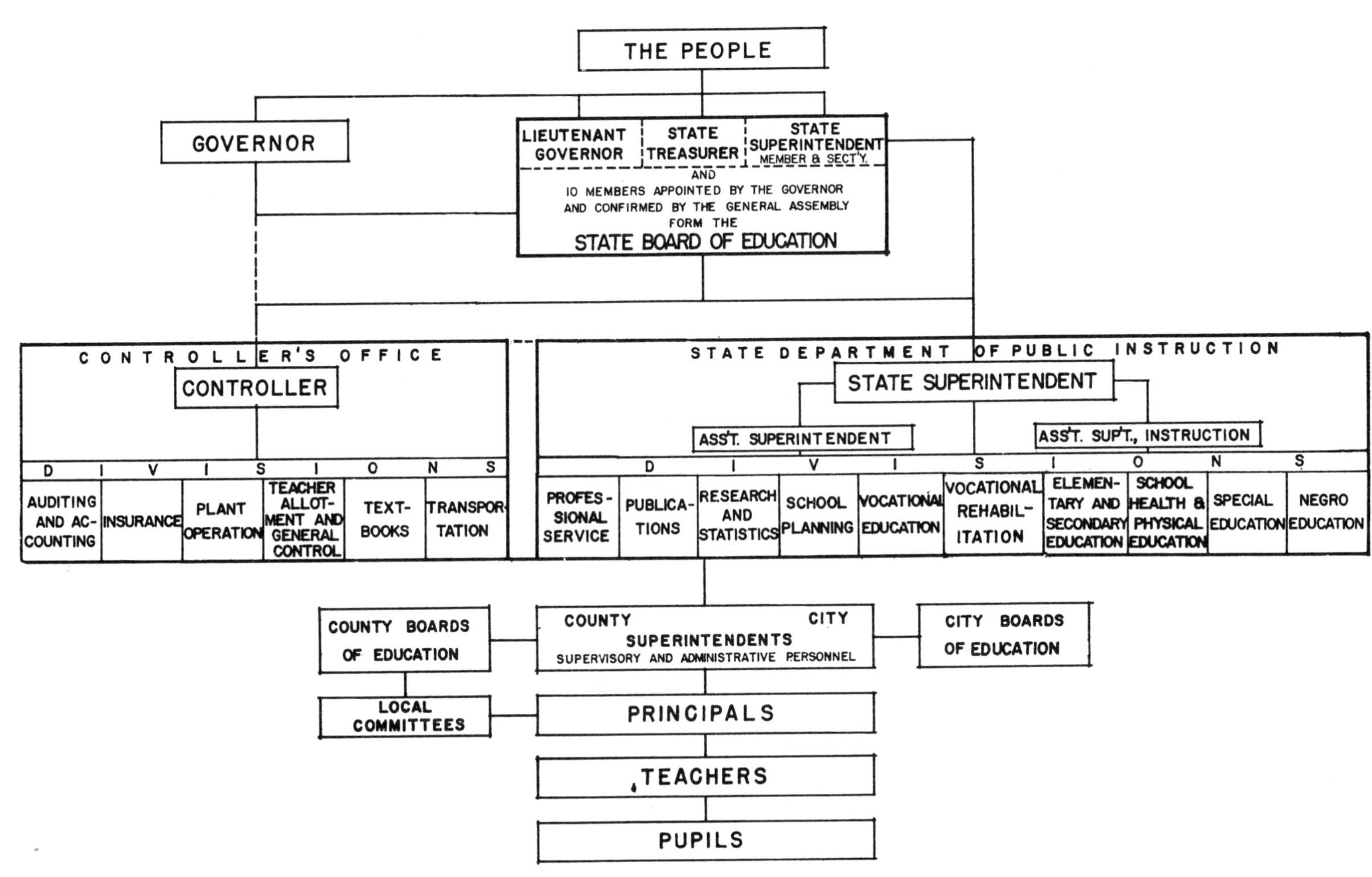
THE PEOPLE
GOVERNOR
LIEUTENANT GOVERNOR
STATE TREASURER
STATE SUPERINTENDENT MEMBER & SECT'Y.
AND
10 MEMBERS APPOINTED BY THE GOVERNOR AND CONFIRMED BY THE GENERAL ASSEMBLY FORM THE
STATE BOARD OF EDUCATION
CONTROLLER'S OFFICE
CONTROLLER
DIVISIONS
AUDITING AND ACCOUNTING
INSURANCE
PLANT OPERATION
TEACHER ALLOTMENT AND GENERAL CONTROL
TEXTBOOKS
TRANSPORTATION
STATE DEPARTMENT OF PUBLIC INSTRUCTION
STATE SUPERINTENDENT
ASS'T. SUPERINTENDENT
ASS'T. SUP'T., INSTRUCTION
DIVISIONS
PROFESSIONAL SERVICE
PUBLICATIONS
RESEARCH AND STATISTICS
SCHOOL PLANNING
VOCATIONAL EDUCATION
VOCATIONAL REHABILITATION
ELEMENTARY AND SECONDARY EDUCATION
SCHOOL HEALTH & PHYSICAL EDUCATION
SPECIAL EDUCATION
NEGRO EDUCATION
COUNTY BOARDS OF EDUCATION
COUNTY CITY SUPERINTENDENTS
SUPERVISORY AND ADMINISTRATIVE PERSONNEL
CITY BOARDS OF EDUCATION
LOCAL COMMITTEES
PRINCIPALS
TEACHERS
PUPILS

Appendix B

Chart II.--STATE SERVICES OF THE NORTH CAROLINA PUBLIC SCHOOLS, 1965

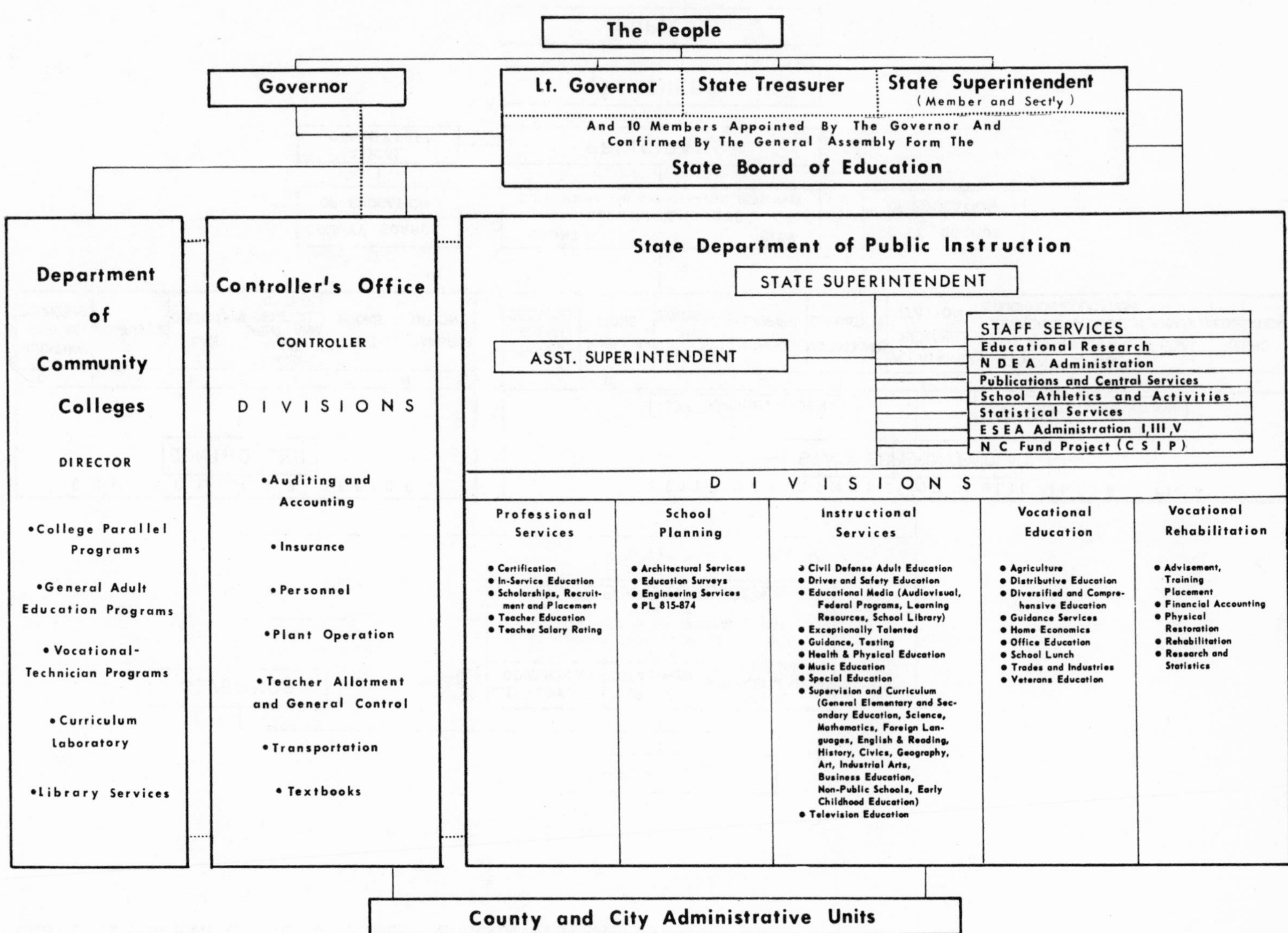

The People
Governor
Lt. Governor
State Treasurer
State Superintendent (Member and Sec'ly)
And 10 Members Appointed By The Governor And Confirmed By The General Assembly Form The
State Board of Education
Department of Community Colleges
DIRECTOR
•College Parallel Programs
•General Adult Education Programs
•Vocational-Technician Programs
•Curriculum Laboratory
•Library Services
Controller's Office
CONTROLLER
DIVISIONS
•Auditing and Accounting
•Insurance
•Personnel
•Plant Operation
•Teacher Allotment and General Control
•Transportation
•Textbooks
State Department of Public Instruction
STATE SUPERINTENDENT
ASST. SUPERINTENDENT
STAFF SERVICES
Educational Research
N D E A Administration
Publications and Central Services
School Athletics and Activities
Statistical Services
E S E A Administration I, III, V
N C Fund Project (C S I P)
DIVISIONS
Professional Services
• Certification
• In-Service Education
• Scholarships, Recruitment and Placement
• Teacher Education
• Teacher Salary Rating
School Planning
• Architectural Services
• Education Surveys
• Engineering Services
• PL 815-874
Instructional Services
• Civil Defense Adult Education
• Driver and Safety Education
• Educational Media (Audiovisual, Federal Programs, Learning Resources, School Library)
• Exceptionally Talented
• Guidance, Testing
• Health & Physical Education
• Music Education
• Special Education
• Supervision and Curriculum (General Elementary and Secondary Education, Science, Mathematics, Foreign Languages, English & Reading, History, Civics, Geography, Art, Industrial Arts, Business Education, Non-Public Schools, Early Childhood Education)
• Television Education
Vocational Education
• Agriculture
• Distributive Education
• Diversified and Comprehensive Education
• Guidance Services
• Home Economics
• Office Education
• School Lunch
• Trades and Industries
• Veterans Education
Vocational Rehabilitation
• Advisement, Training Placement
• Financial Accounting
• Physical Restoration
• Rehabilitation
• Research and Statistics
County and City Administrative Units

Appendix B

Chart III.--STATE SERVICES OF THE NORTH CAROLINA PUBLIC SCHOOLS, 1968

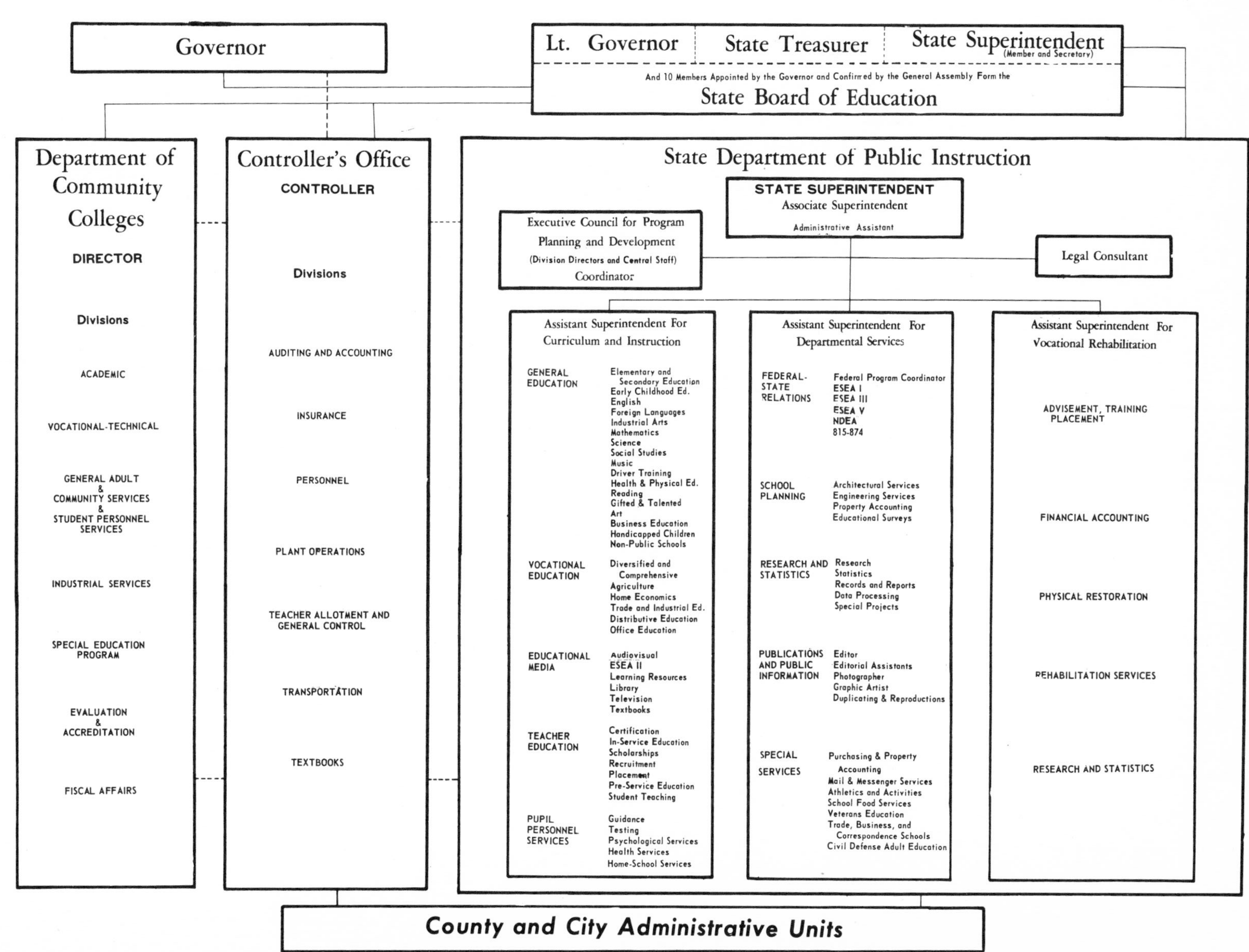
Governor
Lt. Governor
State Treasurer
State Superintendent
(Member and Secretary)
And 10 Members Appointed by the Governor and Confirmed by the General Assembly Form the
State Board of Education
Department of Community Colleges
DIRECTOR
Divisions
ACADEMIC
VOCATIONAL-TECHNICAL
GENERAL ADULT & COMMUNITY SERVICES & STUDENT PERSONNEL SERVICES
INDUSTRIAL SERVICES
SPECIAL EDUCATION PROGRAM
EVALUATION & ACCREDITATION
FISCAL AFFAIRS
Controller's Office
CONTROLLER
Divisions
AUDITING AND ACCOUNTING
INSURANCE
PERSONNEL
PLANT OPERATIONS
TEACHER ALLOTMENT AND GENERAL CONTROL
TRANSPORTATION
TEXTBOOKS
State Department of Public Instruction
STATE SUPERINTENDENT
Associate Superintendent
Administrative Assistant
Executive Council for Program Planning and Development
(Division Directors and Central Staff)
Coordinator
Legal Consultant
Assistant Superintendent For Curriculum and Instruction
GENERAL EDUCATION
Elementary and Secondary Education
Early Childhood Ed.
English
Foreign Languages
Industrial Arts
Mathematics
Science
Social Studies
Music
Driver Training
Health & Physical Ed.
Reading
Gifted & Talented
Art
Business Education
Handicapped Children
Non-Public Schools
VOCATIONAL EDUCATION
Diversified and Comprehensive
Agriculture
Home Economics
Trade and Industrial Ed.
Distributive Education
Office Education
EDUCATIONAL MEDIA
Audiovisual
ESEA II
Learning Resources
Library
Television
Textbooks
TEACHER EDUCATION
Certification
In-Service Education
Scholarships
Recruitment
Placement
Pre-Service Education
Student Teaching
PUPIL PERSONNEL SERVICES
Guidance
Testing
Psychological Services
Health Services
Home-School Services
Assistant Superintendent For Departmental Services
FEDERAL-STATE RELATIONS
Federal Program Coordinator
ESEA I
ESEA III
ESEA V
NDEA
815-874
SCHOOL PLANNING
Architectural Services
Engineering Services
Property Accounting
Educational Surveys
RESEARCH AND STATISTICS
Research
Statistics
Records and Reports
Data Processing
Special Projects
PUBLICATIONS AND PUBLIC INFORMATION
Editor
Editorial Assistants
Photographer
Graphic Artist
Duplicating & Reproductions
SPECIAL SERVICES
Purchasing & Property Accounting
Mail & Messenger Services
Athletics and Activities
School Food Services
Veterans Education
Trade, Business, and Correspondence Schools
Civil Defense Adult Education
Assistant Superintendent For Vocational Rehabilitation
ADVISEMENT, TRAINING PLACEMENT
FINANCIAL ACCOUNTING
PHYSICAL RESTORATION
REHABILITATION SERVICES
RESEARCH AND STATISTICS
County and City Administrative Units

34 North Dakota

DEPARTMENT OF PUBLIC INSTRUCTION

E. J. Taylor, Jr.

Contents

INTRODUCTION

Sir Richard Livingston has stated that the most searching question that can be asked concerning any individual or nation is: "Whom has he taken for master and how faithful is his service?" (1). He suggests that excellence might be accepted as the master. North Dakota has been blessed with more than its share of leaders who have served the cause of excellence with vigor and fidelity.

A bountiful sufficiency of educational statistics on North Dakota can be found in the references listed in the bibliography of this chapter. Information regarding the men and women who made these statistics is not so plentiful. It is the intention of the writer to emphasize the careers of some of the leaders who developed public education in North Dakota from a log cabin to a well-organized and highly regarded department of education in less than a century, thereby introducing the chronological events for which they usually were responsible.

So many people have been helpful in furnishing material that it is impossible to recognize them here. However, a special acknowledgment must be made to Bertha Palmer, whose *Brief History of the Department of Public Instruction, 1860–1932* (2) is a gold mine of information. It was obviously prepared prior to the fire which destroyed the North Dakota capitol and most of the educational records of the state.

TERRITORIAL DAYS

As was the case in most Midwestern states, early settlement of Dakota Territory and North Dakota followed the rivers. Steamboats appeared early on the Missouri. In 1832, when the steamer "Yellowstone" reached Fort Union, located near the present boundary between North Dakota and Montana, the event was noted even in European newspapers. In the late 1850's, small settlements sprang up at Sioux Falls, Vermillion, and Yankton, all located in what is now southeastern South Dakota. About the same time, French-Canadian fur traders appeared at Pembina and at St. Joseph, a mission established by Father Belcourt on the site of present day Walhalla, North Dakota. The largest house, 28 by 50 feet, served as chapel, school, and residence for the religious. Ministry was primarily to the métis (3). In 1853, the U.S. Commissioner of Indian Affairs gave $500 in support of the school. It was Sir George Simpson, governor of the Hudson Bay Company, who made the settlement a hinterland of St. Paul, Minnesota. Simpson encouraged business and mail connections with St. Paul, and his enthusiasm prompted the construction of the first steamboat on the Red River of the North (4) in 1859.

President Buchanan signed a bill creating Dakota Territory on March 2, 1861. At that time, there was only one school in all the area comprising the present States of North Dakota and South Dakota plus portions of Montana and Wyoming. Organized in the summer of 1860 at Bon Homme, South Dakota, this school met in a log cabin. Emma Bradford was the teacher for its nine pupils.

The first territorial officers were appointed by President Lincoln. Provision for public schools was made by an "Act for the Legislation and Support of Common Schools," which was passed by the first Legislative Assembly and approved in May 1862. That summer, when the people were alarmed by the Santee Sioux uprising, practically all inhabitants abandoned the territory, except those in the Yankton and Pembina settlements. Most of the settlers who abandoned their homes never returned.

The first Territorial Legislature also declared that schools should "at all times be equally free and accessible to all white children over five and under twenty-one years." It is doubtful that discrimination was intended. In any case, the word *white* was deleted by 1868 and has never reappeared (5).

The next school legislation was an act approved in January 1863. The law created a territorial Board of Education comprised of the territorial Governor, secretary, and treasurer, and required an annual meeting at the capitol. The board was to appoint a superintendent of public instruction, whose duties were specified by the law and who would serve as clerk of the board (6). Superintendent W. H. H. Beadle, who was one of the best territorial superintendents, later stated, "This provision was retained many years and ought never to have been abandoned" (7). The members of the first Board of Education were Newton Edmunds, Governor; John Hutchinson, secretary; J. O. Taylor, treasurer; James S. Foster, clerk and ex officio superintendent of public instruction. The first meeting was in December 1863, in the office of Governor Edmunds in Yankton.

The first school building in what is now North Dakota was built in 1875. Although it was in use for only 6 years, it is still standing in Pembina, complete with the original blackboards.

An act approved in February 1879 was drafted by A. W. Barber, superintendent of Yankton County, who introduced several practical improvements based on his experience. While there had been little or no agitation for women suffrage, this act authorized women to vote at school district meetings. In 1881, several amendments were made, one of which authorized women to hold the office of county superintendent.

Superintendent Beadle secured passage of the act approved in March 1883, which was an almost entirely new law. It required the organization of school districts by township lines in all but 18 of the older counties; in these, each board of county commissioners was authorized to put the law in force. The boards in two counties did so, and it went into operation in all new counties. The old districts remained in 15 counties, of which Cass, Grand Forks, Walsh, Pembina, and Barnes are now in North Dakota.

Congress enacted the Homestead Law in 1862. One of its by-products was the organization of a colony called the Free Homestead Association at Syracuse, New York, with James S. Foster as secretary. Before he came to Dakota, Foster had been engaged in educational work in central New York. It was natural that he should become the first superintendent of public instruction in Dakota Territory. He proved to be an excellent man and almost single-handedly organized the first Department of Education. Mr. Foster ascertained by interview and letters that there were about 600 children of legal school age in the territory. After his retirement as superintendent of public instruction in 1868, he became the first commissioner of immigration for the territory.

From 1869 to 1879, five different superintendents struggled to get schools going in the territory. The short periods of time each was in the office did not allow great accomplishment. Most of them left the office when greener pastures beckoned.

When Ulysses S. Grant was President of the United States, he chose W. H. H. Beadle as surveyor-general of Dakota Territory. Beadle was a citizen of Grant County, Wisconsin, and it is said that he was appointed due to the influence of a Congressman who feared that Mr. Beadle would be a successful candidate against him at the next election. Whatever the reason for Mr. Beadle's appointment, it was a most fortunate one for Dakota. For over 20 years, he dominated affairs in Dakota Territory. A picture of Beadle indicates that he was a distinguished-looking gentleman. It is said that he was not ostentatious in his public duties and did not appear to realize that he was doing any more or carrying any more than his share of a citizen's duties. However, the record shows that he took part in almost every necessary and commendable work. He frequently wrote for publication in journals and newspapers and often gave public lectures regarding the vast and useful resources of the territory. He was a member of various boards and councils to the Legislature, churches, schools, and colleges, all of which substantially benefited from his capable assistance. The first real promoter of Dakota, he is best remembered for his labors to the benefit of educational matters, including the conservation of school lands. In 1879, he was nominated superintendent of public instruction by the Governor and confirmed by the legislative council for an indefinite period. He held office until 1885.

In 1881, Beadle published a review of statehood questions, including division of the territory into two states. Touching school lands, his article says:

> We have an intelligent people. Let the state be formed by them intelligently, deliberately, and wisely. . . . The chief material interest the convention will handle will be the school, university, and other state lands. The welfare of the people, the honor of the state and its future character are involved in the handling of the school and university lands. . . . They are reserved for the permanent common welfare. Their full value should be secured to this end (8).

Beadle is credited with the responsibility for those sections in the Enabling Act dealing with lands for the support of public schools and educational institutions, which read in part:

> Upon the admission of each of said states into the Union, sections numbered 16 and 36 in every township of said proposed states. . . are hereby granted to said states for the support of common schools . . . . All lands herein granted for educational purposes shall be disposed of only at public sale, and at a price not less than $10.00 per acre, the proceeds to constitute a permanent school fund, the interest of which only shall be expended in the support of said schools. But said lands may. . . be leased for periods of not more than five years . . . . Shall not be subject to preemption, homestead entry . . . but shall be reserved for school purposes only . . . (9).

This provision, which apparently was opposed by some citizens of Dakota Territory, has proved to be one of the wisest of the Enabling Act and of the constitution of North Dakota. Beadle was appointed by the Secretary of the Interior to make the selection of the lands donated by Congress. The people of North and South Dakota owe him a debt of gratitude for the preservation of the school lands which still form a handsome endowment (10).

A remarkable statement appeared in the annual report of the U. S. Commissioner of Education for 1884–85, giving statistical information of value to the reputation of the Territory of Dakota. The commissioner found that Dakota led 22 of the states in the amount it expended for educational purposes. He also found that Dakota had a schoolhouse for every 151 people within its borders. In the value of permanent school property, Dakota outranked 15 states; and in the number of teachers employed, 14 states (11).

From 1885 to statehood in 1889, three men occupied the office of state superintendent. None served long enough to have much influence on the permanent development of the schools of the territory. It should be noted that the Legislature in 1887 provided for a Board of Education to be appointed by the Governor, with the superintendent of public instruction as president. Eugene A. Dye was the first president as ex officio superintendent of public instruction. The other members of the first board were Frank A. Willson and George A. McFarland, who was secretary of the board. McFarland was the young superintendent of schools at Scotland, South Dakota, who had come West 3 years before. A graduate of Hiram College of Ohio, he was destined to have an important influence on education in North Dakota for many years. In 1889, he became instructor in history and psychology at the state normal school at Madison, South Dakota. In 1892, he became principal of the state normal school at Valley City, North Dakota, where he served as principal and president until 1918. He became president of the State Teachers College at Minot in 1922 and remained there until his death in 1938.

No organization can be better than the persons comprising it, and certainly this applies to the education profession. As today, territorial administrators cried for more and better prepared teachers. This much we may be sure of: Few persons entered the profession unless they were unselfish and dedicated to the task of educating the children placed under their care. Most had the knack of getting along with children, and a goodly number were natural teachers with the ability to inspire their young charges.

Two examples of early Nelson County teachers are worth recounting. When a blizzard threatened one afternoon in 1888, the teacher of a one-room country school, not much older than some of her pupils, kept the children at school and kept them marching all night. The next day all were found safe. These remarkable women brought their own brand of courage to the territory.

Rachel Tyndall taught at Mapes in the late eighties and early nineties. She was a well-educated woman, who with her mother was proving up on a homestead. They lived in a sod house that was lined with tapestries to make a comfortable abode. One of Miss Tyndall's pupils, who is still living in North Dakota, remembers her as a cultured lady who inspired her charges and taught them well.

STATEHOOD

The constitution of the new State of North Dakota provided for the election of the superintendent of public instruction. The first election was held in October 1889, at the same time that the State Constitution was ratified by the people. The officers, including William Mitchell, who had been elected superintendent of public instruction, qualified for office immediately after November 2, 1889, the date President Benjamin Harrison signed the bill that admitted North Dakota to the Union.

Mitchell, who was always known as Captain Mitchell, had served in the Civil War as an officer in an Ohio regiment and had been superintendent of schools in Columbus, Ohio. He came to Fargo in 1883 and was elected superintendent of Cass County schools in 1887. He was a first-class executive and administrator and a fine lecturer. Captain Mitchell presented to the Legislative Assembly a comprehensive plan for a system of free public schools for enactment into law under the mandate of the State Constitution, which read:

> The legislative assembly shall provide at its first session after the adoption of this constitution for a uniform system for free public schools throughout the state, beginning with the primary and extending through all grades up to and including the normal and collegiate course (12).

There was considerable controversy regarding the existence of a dual system of public schools created under widely differing general school laws. There was the "district" system and the "township" system, plus a heterogeneous mass of special school districts that had grown up in territorial days. It might be said that the territorial school system was entirely devoid of system; it had to be unified. The department decided to promote township organization without doing violence to existing districts, and it wisely formulated a plan whereby all future changes of school district boundaries should be made to conform with civil township boundaries.

Superintendent Mitchell died in March 1890. His educational bill providing for a uniform system of free public schools was enacted into law and approved by the Governor soon after his death.

To fill Mitchell's unexpired term, the Governor appointed William J. Clapp, who was then followed in 1891 by John Ogden. Prior to the Civil War, Ogden had been principal of the state normal school at Winona, Minnesota. Something of his character may be found in his letter of resignation, which was presented to the school's governing committee on December 14, 1861.

> Gentlemen: I hereby tender you my resignation of the principalship of the institution intrusted to my care, thanking you most sincerely for the generous support

and council [sic] you have given me. In taking this step it is proper that you and the public should understand the reason that impells me to it.

My distracted and dishonored country calls louder for my poor service just now than the school does. [sic.] I have, ever since our national flag was dishonored, cherished the desire and indulged the determination that – whenever I could do so without violation of a sense of duty – I would lay aside the habiliments of the schoolroom and assume those of the camp, and now I am resolved to heed that call and rush to the breach, and with my life, if necessary, stay, if possible, the impious hands that are now clutching at the very existence of our free institutions. What are our schools worth? What is our country worth without these? Our sons and daughters must be slaves. Our beloved land must be a hissing and a by word among the nations of the earth? Shall this fair and goodly land, the glorious Northwest become a stench in the nostrils of the Almighty, who made it so fair and so free? No, not while there is one living soul to thrust a sword at treason. I confess my blood boils when I think of the deep disgrace of our country.

My brethren and fellow-teachers are in the field. Some of them – the bravest and best – have already fallen. Their blood will do more to cleanse this nation than their teaching would. So will mine. I feel ashamed to tarry longer. You may not urge me to stay . . . . With these feelings, I am with very great respect,

Your most obedient servant,

John Ogden (13)

Ogden had a most unusual career as an officer during the war and after. He was the first principal of Fisk University at Nashville, Tennessee, and Mrs. Ogden trained the first Jubilee Singers sent out from there. Later, the Ogdens went to Worthington, Ohio, where Ogden was principal of a normal school and Mrs. Ogden organized the first kindergarten teacher-training class west of the Allegheny Mountains. They became interested in the pioneer settlement of Dakota and in 1887 moved to McIntosh County where he became a homesteader, an institute conductor, an educational lecturer, and the author of several professional books. In 1891, Ogden promulgated the following salutation to the flag, which was adopted and generally used by the public schools of North Dakota until World War I, when the current Pledge of Allegiance came into use: "I give my head [touching the right hand to the head], my heart [placing the right hand over the heart], and my hand [extending the hand forward, palm upward] to my country, – one country, one language, one flag [pointing the hand to the flag]" (14).

Superintendent Ogden's report dated November 1, 1892, submitted to Governor Andrew H. Burke (the drummer boy of Chickamauga), was a volume of 805 pages!

Two state normal schools at Mayville and Valley City were organized and began to function. A joint Board of Directors was created by law, which was afterwards established as the Board of Regents, with control of all state educational institutions. The superintendent of public instruction was chairman, and the deputy superintendent was secretary of the joint Board of Directors of Normal Schools.

The North Dakota Education Association was organized in 1890. One of its first projects was promotion of the Teachers' Reading Circle, which was subsequently recognized by enactment of a law making provision for certifying the completion of reading courses by teachers and for reporting the results to the department. A state educational library, including a circulating library, was established.

Unfortunately, a new state superintendent was chosen at every election until 1904. This did not allow any long-term policies to be formulated and put into effect. All the state superintendents were excellent men and women, and all did their duty. During this time, the Board of University and School Lands, with the superintendent of public instruction as ex officio secretary, was organized, and it handled the school lands well.

The constitution provided that women be granted suffrage on school matters, thus making them eligible for election as state and county superintendents of schools. In 1893, Laura J. Eisenhuth was elected superintendent; 2 years later, Emma F. Bates was chosen for 2 years. Both these women were of high character and dominating personality. Both were of unusual mental attainments, deeply religious, positive, and fearless. With reluctance it must be recorded that part of the reason education did not advance faster was petty political jealousy between otherwise capable and efficient persons. For example, Mrs. Eisenhuth and Miss Bates were not on speaking terms. When Miss Bates was ready to assume the office of state superintendent, she sent a messenger to her predecessor to get out, as she was coming! Amusing, but not conducive to an efficient turnover of the office.

The ladies were followed by two interesting gentlemen, John G. Halland and Joseph M. Devine. Halland particularly interested himself in preparing a uniform course of study, and he did much to standardize the common schools. Under his leadership, the state high school board adopted regulations for required and elective subjects. Summer schools were organized with the aid of state funds for training teachers in service. Halland's recommendations for improving the common schools through supervision of teaching and careful selection of teachers were far in advance of the practice in 1900. Unfortunately, Halland had neither the time nor the personality to carry out his fine plans.

In 1900, Joseph M. Devine was elected superintendent of public instruction. Devine had already been Governor of North Dakota, as he had completed the unexpired term of Governor Frank Briggs, who died in office.

Devine, who attempted to grade the rural schools, stated in his report:

> The greatest difficulty encountered was the inability of the teachers to interpret the course of study for the reason that they had no previous training in graded schools and, therefore, were wholly unfamiliar with the plan and scope of the course of study (15).

He predicted the exchange of the little red schoolhouse for the consolidated school. His successors struggled for years to carry out some of the policies he first advocated. After retiring from elective office, Devine served as superintendent of the state training school.

During this period of relative instability in the Office of Superintendent of Public Instruction, a group of young men began coming into the state. They were to have a marked effect on education in North Dakota for many years to come. We have already mentioned George A. McFarland, who arrived in Dakota Territory in April 1887 and became principal of the state normal school in Valley City in 1892. He was destined to serve North Dakota well for the rest of his life.

THE GOLDEN AGE

Walter Lincoln Stockwell was graduated from the University of Minnesota in 1889. He came to North Dakota as principal of the school at St. Thomas, and in 1892 he became superintendent of the city schools of Grafton, where he served until he was elected superintendent of public instruction in 1902. He chose for his deputy Edwin James Taylor, who had been superintendent of Grand Forks County. Taylor succeeded Stockwell in 1911 and continued in office until 1917. Bertha R. Palmer spoke of this period as the "Golden Age of Education" (16) in North Dakota. The long period of continuity was sufficient to establish the school system of the state, and many of the policies initiated at that time continue to the present day.

Stockwell was noted for the zeal, youthful vigor, energy, and enthusiasm that always characterized his work. Over and beyond his educational duties, he was intensely interested in the development of the state and gave freely of his time, energy, and money for the building of the communities in which he lived. Largely through his efforts, the first Carnegie Library in North Dakota was established in Grafton. He was an outstanding leader in education, an eloquent and inspiring public speaker, and a progressive and forceful thinker. He was author of the law providing aid to schools secured from a statewide tax. The measure was a most progressive one at the time it was enacted, and it resulted in material improvements in those schools that met the requirements. Much was done during his administration to make the high school system more effective, including the appointment of the first high school inspector. He made a most valuable contribution to education by creating widespread favorable sentiment toward the public schools. After his retirement in 1911, Stockwell became grand secretary of the Masonic bodies of the state. In this office he continued to contribute his influence to the development of the public schools.

In January 1911, Stockwell was succeeded by Edwin James Taylor, who had served as deputy during the entire preceding administration. Taylor was well prepared to build on the gains already accomplished.

In 1890, two weeks after his graduation from St. Lawrence University, Taylor arrived at Grand Forks, North Dakota. It was his intention to seek admission to the North Dakota bar, and he accomplished this aim. It was frequently the custom of young would-be lawyers to teach school while preparing for the bar examinations. He followed that course and taught school at Emerado, North Dakota. The measure of the 20-year-old schoolmaster became apparent in the one-room country school. According to Chief Justice William L. Nuessle of the supreme court of North Dakota, Taylor was a strict disciplinarian and a stern taskmaster. When he left Emerado for Grand Forks, he took with him five boys from that one-room rural school whom he encouraged to enter the new state university. One became chief justice of the supreme court; another, John Hancock, had a successful career in Wall Street and became a benefactor of the university. The other three became president of Kentucky State Agricultural College, president of a bank, and a respected grain elevator superintendent.

When he was just past his twenty-second birthday, Taylor was elected county superintendent of the Grand Forks County schools. He himself became a benefactor of the struggling new university when he contributed a month's pay to help keep the university alive as the Legislature had failed to appropriate sufficient funds. He inspected his schools on horseback, and once he had a narrow escape when caught in a blizzard.

Taylor and another Lawrentian, John Haig, for many years superintendent of schools of Ramsey County, were due to have great influence on education in North Dakota. As a youth, Haig had been injured by a horse and as a result had lost a leg. This did not affect his mobility or his fine sense of humor and marvelous personality. He once made the statement that he recognized the loss of his leg as a blessing of God, as he realized that he would never have had the opportunity to go to college had he been able-bodied and fit for work on the farm. When he visited Bismarck, he was invariably the overnight guest at the home of the state superintendent. Among their mutual interests from the time they were young men was the organization and building of an education association in North Dakota. Taylor became president of the new organization at the age of 25 (17).

What kinds of teachers were available in North Dakota prior to World War I? The reports of every state superintendent mentioned this problem and suggested remedies. Higher certification standards were advocated and adopted. Salaries were raised, even though they remained pitifully small by present-day standards. Every superintendent cried for more and better teachers. This does not mean to imply that there were few good teachers in North Dakota. On the contrary, there were many excellent and devoted ones. In the one-room country school, the high-quality teacher was likely to be a farmer's wife and the mother of one or more children. She usually had a reasonably good education, and her principal motivation was to see that her own children received the best possible education. Some superior teachers could be found, usually in the towns, who would compare favorably with the best found anywhere.

Shortly before World War I, county superintendents exchanged their horses and buggies for Model T Fords – the kind that had to be cranked. Mrs. Senner Nertrost Whipple, superintendent of Wells County from 1915 to 1922, recalled the Model T as a great time-saver and an improvement over the horse and buggy, although it did succumb to mud holes and sand dunes. Newspapers, old gunny sacks, and Sears-Roebuck catalogs usually exerted enough traction to jar it loose! She regularly visited 90 rural, 3 county consolidated, and a dozen small town schools in this manner.

Another big problem was enforcing rural school attendance, especially during the seeding and harvest seasons. Mrs. Whipple found one 9-year-old lad ploughing with a team of four horses. When his mother was asked about this, she replied: "Oh, that's nothing, all he has to do is hold the lines, and he will have plenty of time to go to school!" School lunch programs were unknown. Once Mrs. Whipple surprised a gopher invading a lunch pail in the school entry! (18).

In 1909, the Legislature created a commission to revise the school laws of North Dakota. The commission consisted of five members, two ex officio and three appointed (19). The commission made its report and recommended repeal of almost all existing school laws. It drafted a comprehensive bill, which was passed by both Houses of the Legislature and approved by the Governor. The law became Chapter 266 of the Session Laws of 1911. The most pronounced change in the law was that governing the issuance of teachers' certificates. A board of examiners was created which had full charge of the certification of teachers. The superintendent of public instruction was ex officio secretary (20).

Other important educational legislation enacted in the 1911 session provided for the organization of county agricultural and training schools, as well as for the appointment of an officer to be known as the "inspector of rural and graded schools." It made an appropriation for state aid to such rural and graded schools as met the requirements prescribed by the superintendent of public instruction. Under the provisions of this law, N. C. Macdonald, who was then superintendent of the Mandan schools, was appointed inspector, which office he held until January 1917, when he became superintendent of public instruction.

One of the reasons for the high state of morale of the teachers of North Dakota at that time was the knowledge that the superintendent of public instruction was deeply concerned in their interests and was working for them. The most important educational law of 1913 was the creation of the teachers insurance and retirement fund. The retirement fund, with modifications, is a monument to a deep concern for the welfare of teachers.

Another important accomplishment of the legislative session of 1913 was the creation of a State Board of Education to consist of the president of the university, the president of the agricultural college, the superintendent of public instruction, a normal school principal, an industrial school principal, the high school inspector, the rural school inspector, a county superintendent of schools, and a male citizen of the state not engaged in educational work. This board took over the work of the high school board, the boards of management of the county agricultural and training schools, the board of examiners for teachers' certificates, and the classification of rural, graded, consolidated, and high schools. During this period, the start was made toward consolidation of rural schools.

The advent of the Model T Ford gave a glimmer of the possibility of transporting pupils for considerable distances. As the roads of that day were poor, or sometimes almost nonexistent, little was accomplished. Nevertheless, the foundation was laid for rapid consolidation once school buses and good roads were available.

Cultural problems were enormous in North Dakota during the first part of the twentieth century. In 1910, with settlement practically completed, North Dakota had eight persons per square mile. The United States had 31 persons; the middle Atlantic states, 193; and Ohio, 117. In North Dakota, only 11 percent of the population lived in centers of 2,500 or more. The sparseness of population, living mostly on farms and in small villages, made difficult the support of churches, schools, libraries, and other social institutions. North Dakota needed these institutions, but the scarcity of people increased the per-capita cost. In North Dakota, as in all the semi-arid West, space itself became a social cost (21). Nevertheless, there were leaders who not only recognized the cost and were willing to pay it but were willing to sell their fellow citizens on the matter. The problem was aggravated by the large portion of first-generation immigrants from Europe. In 1910, more than 27 percent of North Dakota's adult residents were foreign born. With their children (one or both parents foreign born), they made up 71 percent of the population. The remainder, except for about 6,000 Indians, were largely persons of older American stock. About 21 percent of North Dakota's residents were Norwegian, 20 percent German (about half of them from Russia), 12 percent English and Celtic (Irish,

Scottish, and Welsh), 5 percent Swedish, 12 percent other newer Americans, and the balance older Americans. During the period 1910 to 1920, there was a substantial increase in the number of Germans and Russians, who by 1920 made up about 22 percent of the population (22).

While the immigrant groups were widely scattered throughout the state, the Norwegians and German-Russians tended to hold distinct sections of the state. The Norwegians settled principally in the Red River Valley and westward along the main line of the Great Northern Railroad in the northern part of the state. The English and Scotch were fairly well concentrated in the northeastern part of the state near the Canadian boundary. The German-Russians settled in a large triangle in the central part of the state, with some Austrians in the southwestern portion. The Norwegian group was fairly easily assimilated. There was very little illiteracy among them, as they valued education. Their children were sent to the public schools and rapidly learned the English language. They seemed to develop a bent for politics, and as time went on the Norwegian group became a strong political factor in the state.

The German-Russians were a peculiar problem, which came to a head during the early part of the twentieth century. In July 1763, Catherine the Great, Empress of Russia, invited people to Russia to settle in the vast districts along the Volga River and the Ural Mountains. Catherine, who had been a German princess, desired to further the spread of Western civilization started by Peter the Great. She hoped to have the German colonists mingle with the Russian peasants and thus aid her goal. She promised land and liberal loans to build homes and purchase farm implements and animals. Both Catholics and Protestants were promised freedom of religion, and it was further stipulated that the settlers were not to interfere in the religion of the Russian people. Most important, they would forever be exempted from military service. The Germans in Russia were never considered by the Russian populace nor by the government as first-class citizens. Since they enjoyed more rights and privileges than the Russian people, they became an object of envy and jealousy. At first the children were taught only the German language, but in time they learned the Russian language as well. Unfortunately, a dialect grew up among them, and the problems of communication can well be imagined.

According to the manifesto of July 22, 1763, the German colonists invited by Catherine II to come and settle in Russia were forever to be free from military service. Czar Alexander II introduced an era of internal reform. In 1861, he abolished serfdom in his empire. In 1876, the duty of military service was extended to embrace the nobility of Russia, the merchants' guild, and at the same time the German colonists were also deprived of their exemption. However, the Russian government gave them the choice of either leaving Russia or serving in the armed forces of their country. Thousands of descendants of colonists in the Volga region decided to emigrate (23). Starting about 1874, the inhabitants of many of the German-Russian colonies emigrated to various parts of the world, the first of them moving to Kansas and later Nebraska. Later, considerable groups migrated to what is now North Dakota. The German-Russian groups had their own schools in Russia, and, in general, the people were determined to have schools and see that their children were not illiterate. This situation continued when the colonies migrated to the United States and to North Dakota in particular. Unfortunately, their schools too frequently were conducted in a German-Russian dialect into which a certain amount of English was absorbed – an almost impossible dialect developed.

The situation was delicate but had to be met head on. E. J. Taylor was not the man to shrink from the task. He found a good ally in Rt. Rev. Vincent Wehrle, a pioneer missionary priest, who became the first abbot of Assumption Abbey at Richardton, North Dakota, and later first bishop of Bismarck. Superintendent Taylor's insistence that only teachers qualified to teach standard English be employed met with some resistance but with ultimate success. The popular TV star and band leader Lawrence Welk is a product of one of the schools in which English superseded the German-Russian dialect.

The report of the state superintendent for the biennium ending in June 1912 has a joyous note. Optimism is evident. The new codification of school laws had become effective July 1, 1911. The board of examiners for certification of teachers had been hard at work, and the results of its labors seemed to be "beneficial in the extreme." Consolidation of rural schools seemed around the corner. In the year ending June 30, 1911, there were 114 consolidated schools with an enrollment of about 19,668 pupils, with about 117,000 pupils enrolled in 4,732 one-room schools. During that year, 113 one-room schools had been done away with. Parts VIII and IX of the report consisted of some ninety pages of a special report on rural, graded, and consolidated schools. It was obviously prepared to sell members of the Legislature and responsible citizens on the benefits of consolidation. Little did Superintendent Taylor know that it would require half a century to accomplish his goal.

During the period from 1911 to 1916, inclusive, all school laws were revised, the attendance laws strengthened, qualifications of teachers increased, state aid to rural schools provided, a teachers retirement fund created, county agricultural and training schools organized, the election of county and state superintendents provided for on a no-party ballot, salaries of county superintendents and deputies increased, and the health of pupils safeguarded.

An important survey of the state educational institutions was made by the U.S. Commissioner of Education, who appointed three educators to do the work and published the report in a national bulletin which appeared in 1916.

At the close of 1916, the records of the office were up-to-date, and the files in excellent order. Unfortunately, most of them were destroyed when the capitol burned in December 1930.

WAR AND DEPRESSION

In the fall of 1916, a political revolution occurred in North Dakota, when the nonpartisan league gained control of the state. Neil C. Macdonald, who had been the rural school inspector, was elected superintendent of public instruction. He offered as his major policy "equality of opportunity for all the children of the state to attend good schools."

Superintendent Macdonald was followed by two ladies, both of whom served long enough to define and put into effect substantial policies. Moreover, both ladies were in close accord regarding their policies, so the schools enjoyed another period of sustained leadership. Minnie Jean Nielson was elected superintendent of public instruction in 1918 and continued in office until January 1927. Miss Nielson had a strong, aggressive personality, an energetic and untiring physique, and a broad, far-reaching vision. She was a natural publicist, and during the years of her leadership "school was news."

The legislative session of 1919 created the State Board of Administration with five members: three on salary, to be appointed by the Governor, plus the commissioner of agriculture and the superintendent of public instruction as members ex officio. The new board superseded and took over the duties of three boards: the Board of Educational Examiners, in charge of certification; the Board of Regents, in charge of normal schools, colleges, and the university; and the Board of Control, in charge of penal and charitable institutions. The State Board of Administration also was designated as the State Board for Vocational Education by the Legislature, which enacted in 1919 an acceptance of the Smith-Hughes Vocational Education Act of 1917.

A measure was initiated at the primary election of June 1920 which returned to the superintendent of public instruction the preparation of the course of study and the certification of teachers. Moreover, it gave the superintendent charge of all high school examinations, which before 1919 had been directed by the president of the university.

Miss Nielson was followed by Bertha R. Palmer, who was elected in the fall of 1926 and took office in January 1927. Miss Palmer had become assistant superintendent of public instruction in 1919, so she was familiar with the policies and problems when she took office. She was well aware that the weak spot was the one-teacher school, where more than one-half of all the teachers in the state were employed and where more than one-half of all the children of legal school age attended. Much progress was made during her administration, which continued through 1932. Unfortunately, most of the records of her administration, as well as preceding ones, were lost in the fire of December 1930.

In 1916, Arthur E. Thompson, recently graduated from St. Olaf's College, Northfield, Minnesota, arrived in North Dakota to become superintendent of the city schools in Washburn. He was destined to have great influence on the schools of North Dakota. In 1917, he entered the Army and served about 18 months in France with the Rainbow Division. After the war, he returned to Washburn and resumed the position of city superintendent of schools from 1919 to 1922. In that year, he was elected McLean County superintendent, which office he held until he became state superintendent in January 1933.

Thompson's administration, from 1933 to 1946, covered a most difficult period (24). The drought in North Dakota and the Depression played havoc with the schools. Taxes were not being paid, and the Legislature was compelled to make severe budget cuts. Superintendent Thompson, at the request of the Governor, reduced his request drastically and later had difficulty in getting the Legislature to increase the budgets to their former size.

Among the special duties that fell to the new superintendent was participation in a new state capitol commission, where he rendered excellent service. The functional design of an architecturally beautiful capitol, which was constructed at minimum cost, is a lasting memorial to the members of this capitol commission.

For 14 months, Thompson also was a member of the Federal Economic Recovery Administration Committee, which met evenings and helped set up projects that would give relief where it was most needed. It was well that the superintendent was a member of this committee, for many school districts would not have been able to operate had federal funds not been made available to them. The situation was particularly acute in September 1934, when many telephone calls came to the desk of the superintendent requesting information concerning what school districts should do when there were no funds to pay teachers or otherwise operate the schools. Characteristically, Mr. Thompson always answered, "Open anyway." He did not know how funds would be obtained, but he succeeded in getting sufficient federal funds to keep the schools going. The permanent state school fund, even in the depth of the Depression, yielded over a million dollars per year for distribution on the basis of the school census.

Perhaps the outstanding accomplishment of Superintendent Thompson, legislative or otherwise, was the establishment of the state school equalization fund, which he designed to help distressed school districts. The concept of a state fund to give state aid and equalize aid to districts gradually developed. Support for this idea was given by members of the education association, the parent-teacher association, and the Department of Public Instruction. When it was proposed to Governor Moses, who was ill at the time, he promised his support and did help. The basic principle was to finance the school fund with a sales tax. The law was passed by the 1933 session of the Legislature. While the amount first allocated was inadequate, it was the basis for support of the needier schools. The Sales Tax Law of 1933 was referred to the voters and defeated. Nevertheless, the idea remained. In 1935, efforts again were made to set up the fund. The sales tax was again referred, and this time upheld by the people. The principal argument by its proponents was that the sales tax would replace local taxes.

The 1935 Equalization Act proved a success. Certain emergency features in the original law were changed when prosperity returned to North Dakota. Ever since that time, equalization has been a major feature of the educational structure of the state. It has kept many schools in operation and maintained others above minimum program status.

Around 1942, a teacher shortage developed, which was met by calling back to the classroom many retired teachers and by an intensive recruitment program to induce high school graduates to go into the teaching profession.

Throughout his entire time in office, Thompson had acute political problems, all of which he handled skillfully and to the advantage of the schools of North Dakota. But for his wise leadership, the situation might have become chaotic. His ability to get along with people was well illustrated by the fact that, despite heavily divided political opinions in the state, he was regularly reelected. He was unopposed for reelection in 1946 but chose to resign from office in order to campaign for the office of U.S. Senator.

As previously mentioned, the legislative session of 1919 had enacted a law creating the State Board of Administration. At the state primary election held in June 1938, a constitutional amendment, known as Article 54, was approved, establishing a State Board of Higher Education, with seven members appointed by the Governor and confirmed by the Senate. The Governor must appoint from a list of names submitted by a committee consisting of the president of the education association, the chief justice of the State Supreme Court, and the superintendent of public instruction. Should the Governor not approve any of the names submitted, he has the right to request the committee to submit additional names. Other than this, the superintendent of public instruction has no control over the state institutions of higher learning. The board appoints its own commissioner and operates separately from the Office of the Superintendent of Public Instruction.

POST-WORLD WAR II

In September 1946, Governor Aandahl appointed Garfield B. Nordrum superintendent of public instruction to succeed Thompson. Nordrum had been director of the equalization fund in the Department of Public Instruction from 1942, and in 1946 he had been promoted to deputy superintendent. Thus, it was felt, there would be a continuity of policy provided Nordrum was elected at the impending statewide election. Because of the late resignation, no names were printed on the no-party ballot. This was the first and only state "sticker" election held in North Dakota.

Nordrum was chosen by the people from several candidates and reelected in 1948 and in 1950. In spite of the many immediate postwar problems with which he had to cope – a teacher shortage, new building construction, and school finance – his administration was a progressive one. He secured passage of the countywide 10-mill levy law, which provided assistance in financing public elementary education. In 1949, high school tuition payments were extended to include all students in high school. To assist in the recruitment of qualified teachers, a state scholarship law was enacted. Other important laws included a school building code, provision for permanent school building funds, and one which provided for reorganization of school districts so as to increase the tax base. Superintendent Nordrum recognized the need and the state's responsibility for the education of handicapped children. He was tireless in promoting legislation that provided for special education for exceptional children, which was enacted into law by the 1951 Legislature.

In order to force reorganization of school districts, the 1947 Legislature set up a special Committee on School District Reorganization, which was intended to hurry the abolition of the one-room country school (25). However, the committee moved too fast, and opposition developed. In 1951, the Legislature abolished the committee and placed the responsibility for reorganization in the hands of the state superintendent, setting certain requirements that made the task more difficult. However, reorganization went forward, and today the one-room rural school is a thing of the past in North Dakota except in a few isolated places.

In January 1951, Nordrum resigned to accept a position as chief of party, responsible jointly to the Institute of Inter-American Affairs and to the Diplomatic Mission of the Department of State. Governor Norman Brunsdale appointed M. F. Peterson, who had been deputy state superintendent from July 1947. He continues in office to the present time – 1968. Thus, another long period of continuity of general policy came about.

The first problem confronting the new state superintendent was that of legislation, as he came into office at the beginning of the 1951 session of the Legislature. Several important laws for improvement of public education in North Dakota were passed by that Legislature. Two are referred to above. The county tuition fund law was amended to provide payments to small schools employing two, three, or four elementary teachers.

For many years, school districts located on the borders of the state that offered no school facilities or high schools had been a pressing problem. The Legislature authorized reciprocity between North Dakota and its three bordering states – Minnesota, Montana, and South Dakota. The bill allowed the state superintendent to enter into reciprocal tuition agreements, a plan that has worked quite satisfactorily. The Legislature levied a countywide tax of 1 mill to establish a county equalization fund for high schools, and this tax was increased by the 1953 Legislature. This law has been of great value in equalizing the support of high school education. The same Legislature also amended the county tuition law so that school districts which closed their schools and made agreements with neighboring districts for the attendance of their pupils and also provided transportation for these pupils to the neighboring schools would receive the same amount of money from the tuition fund that they would receive if their schools were in operation. This has been an important factor in closing inefficient and uneconomical schools. Another step forward that year was the elimination of the second-grade elementary certificate.

The 1955 legislative session took action to correct some of the problems created by the growing complexities of scope and function posed by the State Board of Administration. It created a State Board of Public School Education, consisting of the Governor as chairman, the attorney general, the state superintendent of public instruction, a member to be selected by the North Dakota Education Association, and a member to be selected by the North Dakota School Officers Association. The state superintendent of public instruction was designated by the law as the executive director and secretary of the board. The State Board of Public School Education was designated as the State Board for Vocational Education and given responsibility for all federal-state programs of vocational education and vocational rehabilitation. It also took over the functions of the state board of equalization, the emergency fund board, the board for school district reorganization, the state board of teaching scholarships, the advisory council on special education, the state school construction fund, and other elementary and secondary education funds. It assumed responsibility for the high school correspondence division, which had been operating under the higher education board.

SPECIAL PROGRAMS

Vocational Education

The report of the superintendent of public instruction dated November 1, 1912, stated that agricultural education was receiving a good deal of attention and was being emphasized throughout the state. The superintendent expected that in the election to be held a few days later several counties would take action regarding establishment of county agricultural training schools under provisions of Chapter 265, Session Laws of 1911. He further stated that the state high school board, acting under the provisions of Chapter 40, Session Laws of 1911, had designated five high schools as agricultural high schools. It was noted that all first-class high schools were offering manual training and domestic science and most of them agriculture. He felt that the state would greatly benefit from this teaching if properly done and the pupils taught the dignity of work. However, county agricultural schools did not develop as had been anticipated, and the 1966 report of the superintendent of public instruction indicates that only the Walsh County school still exists.

The 1955 legislative session created the State Board of Public School Education and further designated it as the State Board for Vocational Education to administer all reimbursable vocational education in North Dakota. This program has been developed in conformity with the provisions of the Smith-Hughes Act, the George-Barden Act, and the Vocational Education Act of 1963. It is designed to promote and develop vocational education programs for persons of all ages and in all parts of the state. By 1966, the vocational agriculture program in North Dakota had grown to 4,456 pupils enrolled in 65 schools. The same year, 13,291 were enrolled in various home economics programs and 2,077 in other programs.

Indian Education

Since 1868, all schools legally have been equally free and accessible to all children. The integration of Negro children has never been a problem in North Dakota, and Indian children always have been accepted. Although the education of Indian children was long considered a "federal problem," this should not be construed to mean that Indian children were ever excluded from the public schools of North Dakota. Statistics regarding Indian schools first appeared in the report of the superintendent of public instruction in 1940. They indicated that 2,150 pupils, both day and boarding, were enrolled in federal schools in North Dakota and that 228 tuition-paid Indian children were in the public schools during the 1939-40 fiscal year. Reports after 1940 contain increasing amounts of valuable data, including tribes represented and degrees of Indian blood. From names given, it is apparent that some Indian teachers were being used.

The Johnson-O'Malley Act of 1936 marked the beginning of a new policy in Indian education. The superintendent of public instruction's report of 1954 mentioned that receipts from Johnson-O'Malley funds equaled only 40 percent of the average cost per pupil. It also mentioned that despite overcrowding, communities in the neighborhood of Indian reservations deserved commendation for their acceptance of these pupils into their schools and communities. The report for the biennium ending June 30, 1962, indicates that 20 to 30 percent fewer Indian pupils graduated from high school than non-Indian pupils. It was believed that special guidance would partially alleviate this problem.

Only a year later, the director of Indian education reported that integration of Indians in the public schools was proving beneficial to all concerned. He cited the attendance of Lucky Mound pupils at Parshall as an example and stated that use of Johnson-O'Malley funds for the guidance program at the Maddock High School had proven beneficial. However, he mentioned that failure of Indian students to receive proper training for job placement was the greatest problem on our Indian reservations.

RECENT YEARS

This seems a good point to summarize the evolution of the administration of the educational system of North Dakota since statehood.

The first state educational institutions to be organized were the university, the agricultural college (now North Dakota State University), and two normal schools, one at Valley City and the other at Mayville. Both of the latter are now 4-year state colleges. Each institution had its own board of trustees. The boards of the two normal schools met jointly once a year, under the chairmanship of the state superintendent of public instruction, for formal ratification of faculty appointments.

In 1891, Webster Merrifield, who had just become president of the University of North Dakota, called a conference of high school men (26) to consider organizing a state high school system. This conference resulted in a system of high school examinations to be conducted by the university and a determination to secure legislation regarding the high school system. In 1895, the Legislature created a state high school board with power to classify schools. The first appropriation for state aid to high schools was made in 1899 and increased by succeeding Legislatures until the establishment of the equalization fund in 1935.

The 1911 legislative session created two state boards: the State Board for Normal Schools and the State Board of Examiners, with the state superintendent as president. The latter was charged with the duty of examination and certification of teachers. The same Legislature changed the personnel of the already existing high school board, replacing the Governor with the president of the agricultural college. Changes followed rapidly. The State Board of Education, which embodied both the board of examiners and the high school board, was set up in 1913, with the superintendent of public instruction as president. The State Board of Administration, established in 1919, took over the administrative duties of the three existing boards. Reference has already been made to this powerful board. When the Smith-Hughes vocational education act became effective, the State Board of Administration also became the State Board for Vocational Education.

At the primary election held in June 1938, a constitutional amendment was approved establishing a State Board of Higher Education. The 1939 legislative session enacted a bill into law placing the administration of the extension division under the higher education board, designating it as the State Board for Vocational Education.

In 1955, the Legislature established virtually what existed prior to the enactment of the State Board of Administration Law. It set up a State Board of Public School Education which, with the Board of Higher Education and the Board of Administration, seemed a logical division of responsibilities. This organization, with certain modifications to be discussed below, remains to the present day.

As mentioned above, M. F. Peterson became state superintendent in 1951 and continues in office today, having served longer than any of his predecessors. Superintendent Peterson is well prepared for the position. His undergraduate training was received at Concordia College, with graduate work at the University of North Dakota. Prior to becoming deputy state superintendent in 1947, he was teacher, principal, and city superintendent.

Due to Mr. Peterson's work, the 1959 Legislature increased requirements for and stabilized accreditation of high schools. The same Legislature also enacted a far-reaching bill setting up a state foundation program for financing public elementary and secondary schools, repealing the former equalization levy. More important legislation followed. In 1963, the Legislature changed the personnel of the Board of Public School Education, which also continued to serve as the vocational education and vocational rehabilitation boards. The Legislature prescribed that the board should consist of seven members, six of whom were to be appointed by the Governor for 6-year terms, one from each of the judicial districts of the state. The seventh member is the superintendent of public instruction, who is ex officio director and secretary of the board. He is a voting member of the board (27).

The people of North Dakota expressed their confidence in the state school administration by adopting in 1964 a constitutional amendment increasing the terms of the state and county superintendents to 4 years. In 1965, another milestone was achieved when the Legislature decreed that after July 1, 1969, no teacher certificates will be issued to anyone with less than 4 years of college education. All certificates will be first-grade but will be divided as to elementary or high school, and the high school certificates will specify the field.

There is little question that this law will present problems, but they promise to be the problems of growth and progress. Help will come from the North Dakota School Boards Association (28) and the North Dakota Council on Education, two fine organizations which have been in existence for many years. The association, which has been active for over 42 years, was given official recognition in 1967.

The council, with over 22 years of service to North Dakota, is composed of interested professionals and laymen and offers a splendid channel for communication between schoolmen and the public.

This account closes on an optimistic note. In 1966, the Council of Chief State School Officers chose Superintendent M. F. Peterson as its 1967-68 president, the first North Dakotan to hold that office. Growth continues on all fronts. Funds to support a statewide study, evaluation, and plan for educational development for North Dakota from 1967 to 1975 were provided by the Legislature, by the federal government under provisions of Title V, Elementary and Secondary Education Act of 1965, and by the University of North Dakota. The study was made by a staff under the leadership of Kent G. Alm, and a preliminary report or "Overview" was recently published. The "Overview" sounds a bugle call for dramatic improvements in education in North Dakota over the next 8 years. The cost seems within reasonable expectations. North Dakota is still marching forward.

FOOTNOTES

1. Sir Richard Livingston, *Some Tasks for Education* (New York: Oxford University Press, 1946), p. 47.
2. Bertha R. Palmer, *A Brief History of the Department of Public Instruction, 1860–1932* (Bismarck: Department of Public Instruction, 1932).
3. Métis refers to a person of mixed blood, especially French and North-American Indian.
4. The Red River of the North flows northward toward Winnipeg, Manitoba.
5. Palmer, *op. cit.,* p. 4.
6. There were revisions and changes to the above mentioned law by the Territorial Legislature in 1866, 1867, 1869, 1877, 1879, and 1881.
7. Palmer, *op. cit.,* p. 4.
8. George W. Kingsbury, *History of Dakota Territory,* II (Chicago: S. J. Clarke Publishing Co., 1915), p. 1651.
9. U.S. Congress, *Enabling Act of 1889,* 50th Cong., 2d sess., Title XXV, secs. 10–11, p. 676.
10. After leaving the Department of Public Instruction, Beadle served as president of the state normal school at Madison, South Dakota. He died in 1915. A statue of him stands in the capitol at Pierre, South Dakota.
11. Kingsbury, *op. cit.*
12. North Dakota, *Constitution* (1889).
13. Palmer, *op. cit.,* p. 26.
14. *Ibid.,* p. 25. The words *one language* had real meaning for North Dakotans in those days.
15. Superintendent of Public Instruction, *Biennial Report,* 1902–1905, p. 31.
16. Palmer, *op. cit.,* p. 48.
17. John Ogden was the organizing chairman. Homer B. Sprague was the first president. Other early leaders included William Mitchell, M. A. Shirley, A. L. Woods. J. M. Devine, George McFarland, and Joseph Kennedy.
18. Letter from Mrs. Senner Nertrost Whipple, April 24, 1968.
19. The ex officio members were Andrew Miller, attorney general, and E. J. Taylor, then deputy superintendent of public instruction. Governor John Burke appointed Dean Joseph Kennedy of the School of Education of the University of North Dakota, Dean Arland D. Weeks of the School of Education of the State Agricultural College, and Professor R. M. Black, a member of the faculty of the State School of Science.
20. Appointed members of the first Board of Examiners included Dean Kennedy, Professor Black, Superintendent W. E. Hoover of Fargo, and Superintendent P. S. Berg of Dickinson.
21. Elwyn B. Robinson, *History of North Dakota* (Lincoln: University of Nebraska Press, 1966), p. 281.
22. *Ibid.,* p. 282.
23. Msgr. George P. Aberle, *From the Steppes to the Prairies* (Bismarck: Bismarck Tribune Co., 1963).
24. The school population (ages 6 to 21) of North Dakota reached an all-time high of 224,169 in 1932. It fell until 1948, when it approximately equaled that of 1911. Since 1948, it has climbed steadily.

Year	School Population	Total Enrollment	Enrollment One-Room Schools
1911	159,353	136,668	117,000
1936	216,233	152,554	54,900
1946	160,335	114,591	33,007
1956	165,211	124,608	24,735
1966	200,667	154,854	3,368

25. The members of the special committee included S. E. Halpern, chairman; Carl C. Swain, president, Minot State College; Mrs. Oliver Nelson; Harley R. Swanson; A. C. Van Wyk; Arthur H. White; and Superintendent G. B. Nordrum, ex officio member and secretary. The committee employed T. S. Grimsrud, superintendent of the Lisbon city schools, as director.
26. Among those present were Superintendent W. L. Stockwell of Grafton, Superintendent Darius Stewart of Fargo, County Superintendent Joseph Kennedy of Traill, and Mrs. Mattie Davis, principal at Casselton.
27. In 1967, the State Board of Public School Education was split into two boards: the State Board of Public School Education, and the State Board for Vocational Education. The superintendent of public instruction is ex officio secretary of both boards. The board members are appointed by the Governor from three

recommendations submitted by a committee consisting of the president of the North Dakota Education Association, the president of the North Dakota School Boards Association, and the president of the North Dakota Bar Association. The Governor may request the committee to submit additional names if none submitted are satisfactory to him. At the present time (1968), the same persons are members of both boards. Both these boards must meet at least once a year with the State Board of Higher Education.

28. D. B. Allen, for many years secretary of the North Dakota School Boards Association, is spoken of as being the "father" of the organization. He was recognized as the 1967 "Layman of the Year" by the North Dakota Council on Education.

BIBLIOGRAPHY

Public Documents

North Dakota. *Blue Book.* Bismarck: Secretary of State's Office, various years.

--*Constitution* (1889).

U.S. Congress. *Enabling Act of 1889,* 50th Cong., 2d sess., Title XXV, secs. 10–11, p. 676.

Books

Aberle, Msgr. George P. *From the Steppes to the Prairies.* Bismarck: Bismarck Tribune Co., 1963.

Kingsbury, George W. *History of Dakota Territory.* Vol. II. Chicago: S. J. Clarke Publishing Co., 1915.

Livingston, Sir Richard. *Some Tasks for Education.* New York: Oxford University Press, 1946.

Palmer, Bertha R. *A Brief History of the Department of Public Instruction, 1860–1932.* Bismarck: Department of Public Instruction, 1932.

Piper, Marion J. *Dakota Portraits.* Mohall, N. Dak.: By the Author, Box 98, 1964.

Robinson, Elwyn B. *History of North Dakota.* Lincoln: University of Nebraska Press, 1966.

Rolfsrud, Erling Nicolai. *Extraordinary North Dakotans.* Alexandria, Minn.: Lantern Books, 1954.

Thompson, Arthur E. *Our Public Schools in North Dakota.* Fargo: North Dakota Congress of Parents and Teachers, 1936.

Reports

Alm, Kent G., *et al. Educational Development of North Dakota, 1967–1975: An Overview.* Grand Forks: University of North Dakota Press, 1967.

Gamble, William A., *et al. Survey of the Public Education System in North Dakota.* No. 2609. Bismarck: North Dakota Work Progress, 1941.

Superintendents of Public Instruction. *Biennial Reports.* Bismarck: Department of Public Instruction, various years.

Article and Periodical

"N.D.E.A. Diamond Anniversary." *North Dakota Teacher,* XLII, No. 4 (December 1962), 18-19.

Unpublished Material

Erickson, Edward. "Boards Established for the Administration of the Educational System of North Dakota Since Statehood." Bismarck, Office of the Superintendent of Public Instruction, 1955. (Mimeographed.)

Nordrum, Garfield B. Personal files, 1949-67, Bismarck.

Peterson, M. F. Untitled brochure on the history of the State Department of Public Instruction in 1954. No. A64 in the North Dakota Historical Society files at Bismarck, 1955. (Mimeographed.)

Taylor, Edwin J. Personal files, 1890-1955. North Dakota State Historical Society, Bismarck. (Typewritten.)

Other Source

Whipple, Mrs. Senner Nertrost. Letter dated April 24, 1968.

Appendix A

NORTH DAKOTA CHIEF STATE SCHOOL OFFICERS

Territory of Dakota, 1864–89

1849-69	Territorial ex officio board of education: Newton Edmunds, Governor; John Hutchinson, secretary; J. O. Taylor, treasurer; James S. Foster, clerk and ex officio superintendent
1869	T. McKendrick Stuart
1869-72	J. W. Turner
1872-75	E. W. Miller
1875-77	J. J. McIntyre
1877-79	W. E. Caton
1879-85	W. H. H. Beadle
1885-87	A. Sheridan Jones
1887-89	Territorial board of education: Eugene A. Dye, president; Frank A. Wilson, vice-president; George A. McFarland, secretary
1889	Territorial board of education: Leonard A. Rose, president; A. T. Free, vice-president; C. M. Young, secretary

State of North Dakota, 1889–1968

1889-90	William Mitchell
1890-91	W. J. Clapp
1891-93	John Ogden
1893-95	Laura J. Eisenhuth
1895-97	Emma F. Bates
1897-1901	John G. Halland
1901-1903	Joseph M. Devine
1903-11	Walter L. Stockwell
1911-17	E. J. Taylor
1917-19	Neil C. Macdonald
1919-27	Minnie Jean Nielson
1927-33	Bertha R. Palmer
1933-46	Arthur E. Thompson
1946-51	Garfield B. Nordrum
1951-	M. F. Peterson

Appendix B

Chart I.--NORTH DAKOTA DEPARTMENT OF PUBLIC INSTRUCTION, 1925

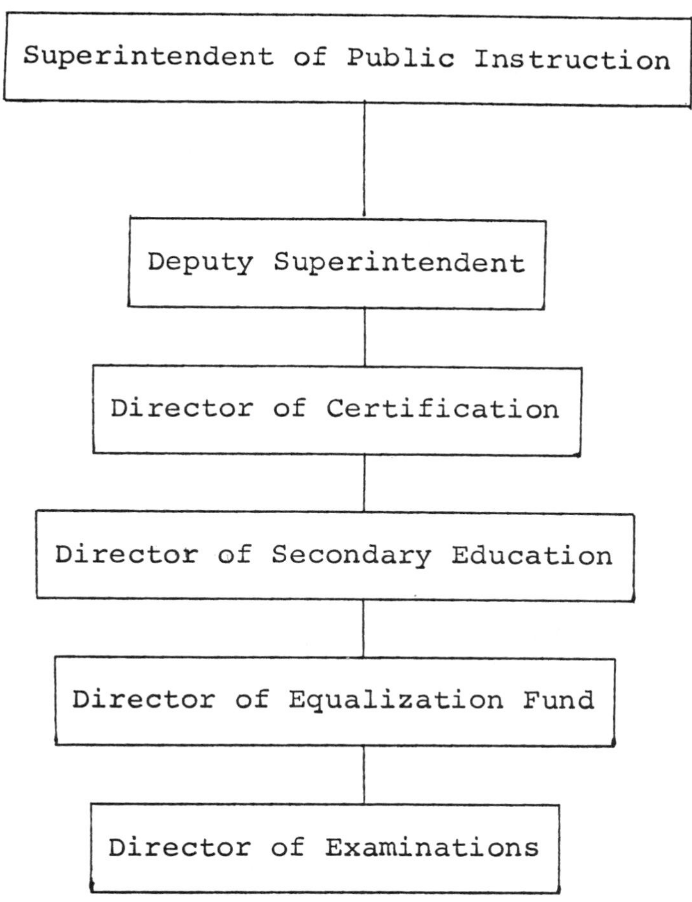

Appendix B

Chart II.--NORTH DAKOTA DEPARTMENT OF PUBLIC INSTRUCTION, 1951

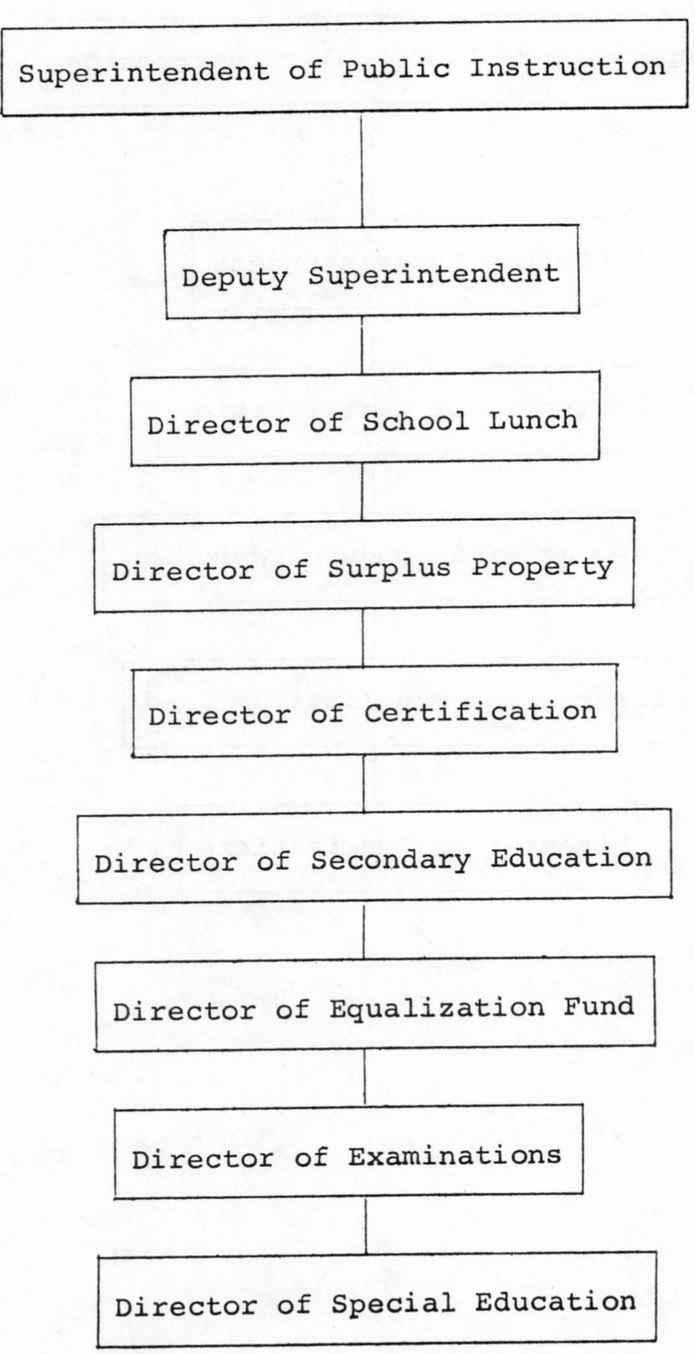

Appendix B

Chart III.--NORTH DAKOTA DEPARTMENT OF PUBLIC INSTRUCTION, 1965

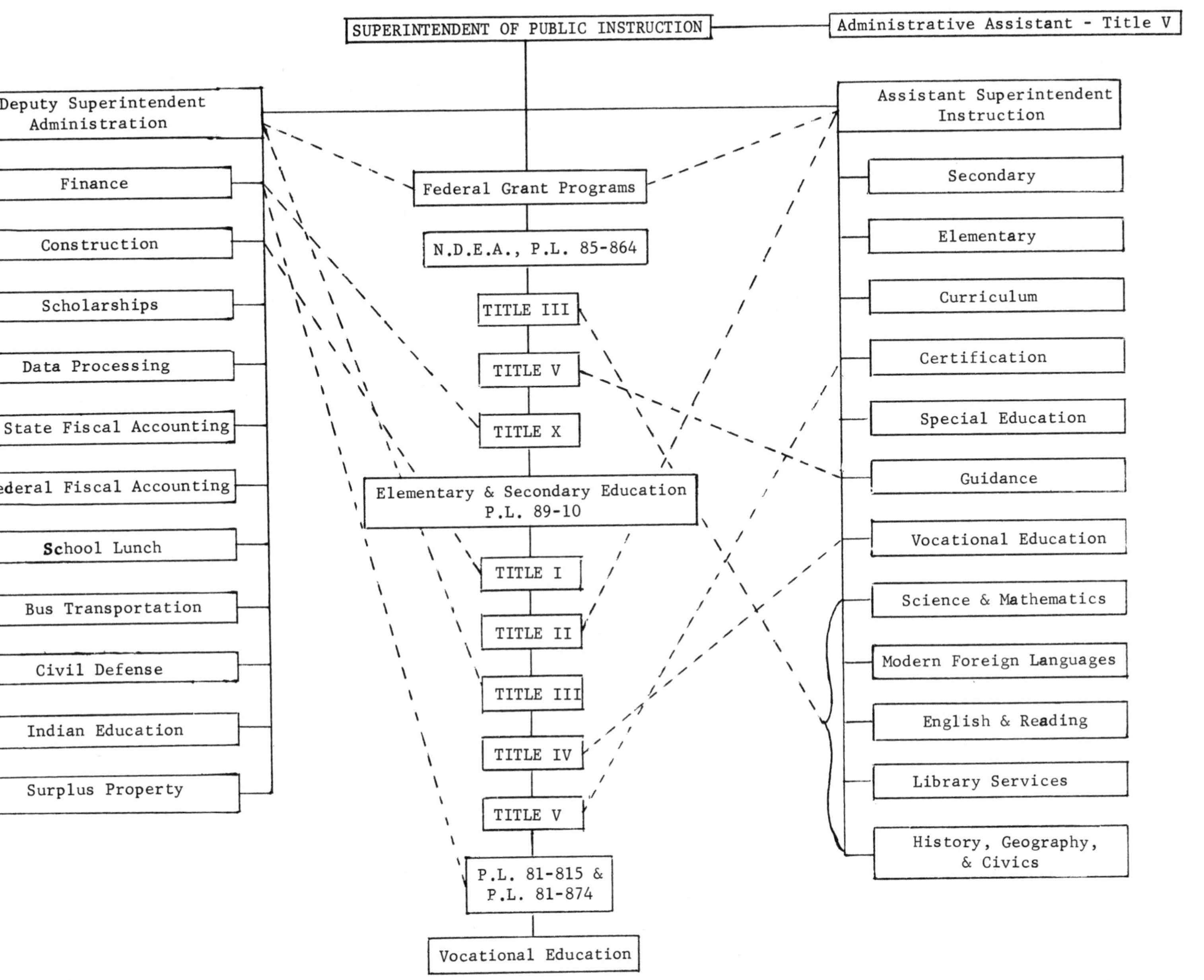
SUPERINTENDENT OF PUBLIC INSTRUCTION
Administrative Assistant - Title V
Deputy Superintendent Administration
Finance
Construction
Scholarships
Data Processing
State Fiscal Accounting
Federal Fiscal Accounting
School Lunch
Bus Transportation
Civil Defense
Indian Education
Surplus Property
Federal Grant Programs
N.D.E.A., P.L. 85-864
TITLE III
TITLE V
TITLE X
Elementary & Secondary Education P.L. 89-10
TITLE I
TITLE II
TITLE III
TITLE IV
TITLE V
P.L. 81-815 & P.L. 81-874
Vocational Education
Assistant Superintendent Instruction
Secondary
Elementary
Curriculum
Certification
Special Education
Guidance
Vocational Education
Science & Mathematics
Modern Foreign Languages
English & Reading
Library Services
History, Geography, & Civics

35 Ohio

DEPARTMENT OF EDUCATION
R. Merle Eyman
Earl Metz

Contents

INTRODUCTION

Ohio was admitted to statehood on February 19, 1803 (1), and was, thus, the first state to be admitted to the Union from the Northwest Territory and the first state to which the grant of section 16 for school purposes was made. In its early statehood, Ohio was a frontier community, settled by a class of people who were compelled to be self-reliant and to solve their own problems, educational as well as others. It was a heavily timbered area, where means of communication were lacking or extremely difficult at best. Because of these natural conditions, it would have been a difficult task to establish any general system of control or supervision over education in the early period even if there had been a wholehearted desire to do so.

By the time means of communication had become simplified through a system of public roads and canals, the people had become accustomed to attending to their own educational needs and were somewhat resentful toward any outside influences or suggestions. Furthermore, the settlers in Ohio had no common educational background. They came from New England, from Virginia, Maryland, and Kentucky, and, in fact, from nearly all of the older states (2).

From the very first, the traditions of Ohio were against centralization or consolidation of power or authority. The first State Constitution was formed soon after the bitter political struggle between Jefferson and Adams and at a time when the arbitrary domination of the Territorial Governor, Arthur St. Clair, had prejudiced the people against centralized executive power. Nowhere was this prejudice against centralized administration better illustrated than in the field of educational legislation.

The tendency, during this early period of Ohio history, was to depend largely on local initiative and control. The encouragement of public education by legislative provisions as specified in the constitution was interpreted by the Legislature to mean the passing of a large number of acts to meet the special needs or desires of particular districts, or, even in the case of school lands, the desires of certain individuals. The general laws passed at that time may be said to have pointed out methods of organization and control instead of devising any efficient system of supervision or of inflicting any penalties in order to bring about specific educational results. They were largely permissive in nature, often leaving the initiative to the discretion of the local communities. In its customs and ideals, each area reflected the current thought and practice of that part of the country from which its settlers came. In no field was this more evident than that of education.

After Ohio was admitted as a state, its population increased with astonishing rapidity. In the years from 1810 to 1840, the transformation from a thickly wooded frontier to a settled farming community had largely taken place. The following census figures from 1800 to 1850 give some idea of this transformation (3):

Year	Population of Ohio	Increase	Percentage increase
1800	45,365	. . .	. . .
1810	230,760	185,395	408.67%
1820	580,434	349,674	151.53%
1830	937,903	357,469	61.58%
1840	1,519,467	581,564	62.00%
1850	1,980,329	460,862	30.33%

The state was divided into a number of separate tracts such as the Western Reserve, the Ohio Company's Purchase, the Symmes Purchase, the Virginia Military Lands, and the U.S. Military Lands. The early settlements in these sections usually were made up of people who came into the wilderness together from one or another of the older states of the Union.

The Ohio Company's Purchase and the Western Reserve were, at first, largely settled by colonists from New England. Marietta, dating from 1787, and Cleveland, from 1796, were respective centers of influence in these two separate areas.

Three colonies were established in the Symmes Purchase in 1788: the one at Losantiville, later rechristened "Cincinnati" by Governor St. Clair, was destined to be, in many ways, a leader for the entire state as well as for the Miami Valley. Many of the early settlers here, as at Marietta, had seen service in the Revolutionary War. Although the early settlers came from many localities, men from New Jersey figured quite prominently, aided by settlers from several other middle states. Later, there were many settlers from Virginia, Maryland, Pennsylvania, New York, and New England.

The Virginia Military Lands section, located between the Little Miami and the Scioto Rivers, received its first settlers from Virginia and the South. General Nathaniel Massie and Duncan McArthur founded Chillicothe, on the Scioto River, in 1796, the first colony on this tract.

On the eastern ridge of the state, south of the Western Reserve, the first settlers were largely from Pennsylvania. Many were of German stock, with a considerable number of Scotch, Irish, and Scotch-Irish.

The U.S. Military Lands seem to have had no homogeneous group, but drew settlers from practically all of the older states. There was also a considerable settlement of French at Gallipolis and a sprinkling of French all along the Ohio River. From 1830, there was considerable German influence from the influx of German immigrants that had begun at about that time (4).

As these data suggest, attempts to establish a state system of public education encountered many problems in the early days of Ohio history. There was no agreement as to the means of financing any general system of education, nor, indeed, any real agreement as to the need for such a system at all. The educational traditions were quite different in different portions of the state.

The first state superintendent, Samuel Lewis, stated in his second annual report in 1838: "The people have not heretofore followed any particular system. The directors of each district have done that which was right in their own eyes, and generally adopted, as far as they could, the particular system of the state from which they came" (5).

Those from the South brought with them the traditions of the private school and parental responsibility for education. The New England settlers brought the idea of a public school system with taxation and public control, but unfortunately for Ohio's subsequent educational history, the New England migration came at a period when the public school sentiment in Massachusetts and other New England states was at a comparatively low ebb, and when the decentralization tendency that gave Massachusetts the district school legislation of 1789 was at its time of greatest influence.

The New England settlers in Ohio favored the public school idea, but the district system with which they were familiar was a highly decentralized one. The common school (locally supported and controlled), as a district school, and the academy, as the secondary school, were two fundamental concepts in the minds of practically all of those who were active in securing Ohio's early school legislation.

Prior to 1825, support of public education in the rural areas of Ohio depended largely on the proceeds from land grants, such as section 16 and section 29 in each township.

A broad indifference to education prevailed in many sections of the state. Apparently, it was often considered educationally sufficient for a boy to be able to write, to read the Bible or an almanac, and to calculate the value of a load of hay or other farm produce involved in common financial transactions. Indeed, many people believed that an education tended to destroy a boy's capacity for manual labor and that a girl did not need to learn to write.

Before canal transportation opened a market for farm produce, it was difficult for families to earn a living, and the development of brawn appeared to be more important than the acquiring of knowledge.

In 1879, the first school was established at Belpre. It was operated in a log cabin, which an ancestor of one of the founders of the Battelle Memorial Institute donated for the purpose. In most places, a church or an abandoned log hut was considered adequate for a school building. Ink was made at home from oak bark or poke berries, pens were made of quills, and textbooks were sewed from linen thread. At best, the school term was short and the schools primitive.

The first schoolhouse in Ohio was built at Columbia, now Cincinnati, and supported by subscriptions, as were most other schools of this period. Because subscriptions for educational purposes were generally quite meager, the Ohio Company added $160 to implement the funds to provide instruction for children at Marietta, Belpre, and Waterford.

EDUCATION PRIOR TO 1906

The recognition in Ohio that public education is a state function and responsibility developed through the influence of the Ordinance of 1785, the Ordinance of 1787, the Constitution of the United States, and the Ohio Constitution.

Ordinance of 1785

The Ordinance of 1785 was known as the ordinance "for ascertaining the mode of disposing of lands in the Western territory" (6). It reserved section 16 in each township "for the maintenance of public schools within the said township." This provision was the inception of the rule for the reservation of certain sections of land for school purposes. This grant set aside for the use of the schools an amount of land equal to one square mile or 640 acres for each surveyed township of 36 square miles.

The first action in accord with this provision occurred when Manasseh Cutler, an agent for the Ohio Company, completed the bargain for the lands acquired by the company at the mouth of the Muskingum River (7). Not only did Cutler obtain a reaffirmation of the provision for the grant of section 16 for school purposes, but, in addition, he obtained a grant of section 29 in each township for the support of religion and also an added grant of two sections for the support of a university. It was this bargain of the Ohio Company that put into actual operation the provisions of the Ordinance of 1785 concerning school lands. This was followed immediately by the Symmes Purchase between the Miami Rivers, and both sections 16 and 29 were similarly reserved.

These statewide grants directed the attention of settlers in all parts of the state and from all parts of the United States to the purpose for which the grants were made, namely, the operation of schools.

It was evidently the original opinion of many of the settlers in Ohio, and, perhaps, even the design of Congress, that these land grants, if properly managed, would support public schools without a tax on the citizens. It soon became evident, however, that this one source of income would be inadequate.

Ordinance of 1787

The Ordinance of 1787 for the Northwest Territory stated that religion, morality, and knowledge, necessary for good government and the happiness of mankind, and schools and the means of education should forever be encouraged. However, the financial encouragement offered at that time consisted of reserving one section—namely, section 16—out of each township in the Northwest Territory, the proceeds from the lease or sale of these lands to be used for the maintenance of public schools.

Although the early Governors congratulated the state on this provision which had been made for the "encouragement" of schools, it soon became evident that funds in amounts sufficient to operate the schools could not be derived from the proceeds of school lands alone and that the granting of lands for purposes of education was therefore not sufficient encouragement to guarantee "good government and the happiness of mankind."

Having thus encouraged education in the Northwest Territory, Congress left to the territories and to the states the tremendous task of actually providing schools. However, the early pioneers were too busy clearing the land and building homes to give much serious attention to establishing schools. Meanwhile, the estate of the schools as provided by the Ordinance of 1785 was gradually becoming dissipated. Much of the land was being sold at a figure considerably below its true value, and, consequently, much less was being derived from the sale of lands than what had originally been expected.

The Constitution of the United States

Public education as such is not mentioned in the Constitution of the United States. However, Ohio, like other states, received its authority and responsibility for supporting public education through the enactment of the Tenth Amendment to the U.S. Constitution. This amendment states that the powers not delegated to the United States by the Constitution, nor prohibited by it to the states, are reserved to the states respectively or to the people.

Therefore, public education in Ohio may be considered as one of these powers *reserved* to the states. Consequently, public education in the governmental structure is essentially a matter of state responsibility. Provision for public education is now contained in the constitution of all of the states.

The Ohio Constitution

The constitution adopted in 1802, when Ohio became a state, remained in force until 1851. It made no specific provisions for education, but, following the pattern established by the Ordinance of 1787, stated that—

> Religion, morality, and knowledge, however, being essential to good government, it shall be the duty of the General Assembly to pass suitable laws to protect every religious denomination in the peaceful enjoyment of its own mode of public worship, and to encourage schools and the means of education (8).

Also, the Constitution of 1802 contained the following provision:

> No law shall be passed to prevent the boards in the several counties and townships within this state from an equal participation in the schools, academies, colleges, and universities within this state which are endowed in whole or in part from the revenue arising from the donations made by the United States for the support of schools and colleges; all doors of said schools, academies and universities shall be opened for the reception of scholars, students and teachers of every accord, without any distinction or preference whatever contrary to the intent for which said donations remain (9).

Further constitutional provisions for education required that the principal of all funds granted or entrusted to the state for educational and religious purposes should forever be preserved inviolate and undiminished; and the income arising therefrom should be applied to the specific objects of the original grants or appropriations. It also stated that no religious or other sect or sects should ever have any exclusive right to, or control of, any part of the state's school funds.

Sections 3 and 4 of Article VI of the Ohio constitution, adopted September 3, 1912, stated:

> Provision shall be made by law for the organization, administration and control of the public school system of the state supported by public funds; provided that each school district embraced wholly or in part within any city shall have the power of referendum vote to

determine for itself the number of members and the organization of the district board of education, and provision shall be made by law for the exercise of this power by such school districts.

A superintendent of public instruction to replace the state commissioner of common schools shall be included as one of the officers of the executive department to be appointed by the Governor, for a term of 4 years, with the power and duties now exercised by the state commissioner of common schools until otherwise provided by law, and with such other powers as may be provided by law (10).

Inasmuch as the Constitution of Ohio makes it a state duty and responsibility to establish and maintain a system of common schools, education is a matter of state concern, and the system of public education in Ohio is the creature of both the State Constitution and statutory laws (11).

The policy of the Ohio Legislature and of the state from the beginning of its existence under the first constitution has been to encourage schools and to foster education in every reasonable way. Also, insofar as the laws do not conflict with the constitution, the courts have no responsibility or authority to question legislative wisdom or policy relating to the management and control of the school system. The courts are limited to interpreting the provisions and enforcement of such laws that may conflict with the constitution (12).

Early Legislation in Ohio

The first legislation concerning schools involved efforts to work out a method of handling the school lands, and during Ohio's early statehood these efforts remained one of the most persistent incentives to educational legislation and a constant reminder of the need for a state school system.

The first general school act for Ohio, which was passed in January 1821 (13), did little more than legalize means by which the settlers in the townships could lay off districts and establish schools. It made no provision for taxation and organized no definite system. It was, however, important as the first recognition by the state of a system of common schools. Since the Law of 1821 was obviously inadequate and ineffective, a campaign was immediately launched for a more effective law.

The Legislature appointed a committee of five to investigate the schools and school lands, but problems of hegemony with the trustees of the school lands prevented the committee from being very effective. However, the committee's recommendation to the Governor that seven commissioners be appointed, charged with the duty to "devise a system of law for the support and regulation of common schools" (14), resulted in the first active steps toward state regulation of education. These seven commissioners, through the media of addresses, pamphlets, and the press, awakened public interest in the financial support of schools. The Legislature of 1825 enacted a compulsory county tax levy of 0.5 mill, the first state legislation designed to improve the common schools. This tax was raised to 0.75 mill in 1829, 1 mill in 1834, and to 2 mills in 1838. It was reduced to 0.4 mill in 1847.

In 1827, the principle of using fines for the support of schools first appears. These fines were assessed for various offenses, such as allowing Canada thistles to mature, keeping a breachy or unruly animal, engaging in medical malpractice of various kinds, or disregarding court orders in quo warranto procedure.

Following the Act of 1824, the law underwent numerous modifications and amendments, but the system of administration remained essentially unchanged until 1838. The Law of 1824 had made no provision for centralized control and had created no adequate machinery for uniting into a true state system the various schools and school districts already established. There were no state, county, or township supervision; little actual knowledge; and no control of what various communities were doing educationally. While the law had established the fundamental principle of taxation for schools, the actual system remained disjointed, decentralized, and ineffective.

The first suggestion for reform came from the friends of education in Cincinnati. A group of teachers and other earnest advocates of popular education had organized a voluntary organization known as the College of Teachers or Western Academic Institute. Partly as a result of a demand from this group for a better organization, a bill was introduced in 1837 to create the Office of State Superintendent of Common Schools. It met with determined opposition but finally passed the House by a vote of 35 to 34 and became a law in March of that same year when the Senate cast a decisive vote in its favor.

The movement for a state department of education and a state superintendent had grown rapidly after 1824 and culminated in 1837 when, by a joint resolution of both Houses of the General Assembly, Samuel Lewis of Cincinnati was elected as the first superintendent of common schools in Ohio and was commissioned by the Governor. Ohio thus became the seventh state in the Union to make provision for a chief state school official.

The duties of the first state superintendent in Ohio were mostly clerical in nature and subordinated to the Office of the Secretary of State. Statistics concerning the schools were to be gathered and submitted to the Legislature with suggestions for the betterment of the schools within the framework of existing funds (15).

The same Law of 1837 provided for a township superintendent of common schools, who was to be the township clerk, and a county superintendent of common schools, who was to be the county auditor. The duties of each were clerical only, rather than administrative and regulatory. At least, the schools of the state were now more closely linked through the offices of township, county, and state superintendents than ever before.

The Law of 1838 was a direct result of the work of Samuel Lewis during his first year as state superintendent and his report of the needs and conditions of the schools as he saw them while touring the state, visiting the schools, and addressing meetings, in an attempt to arouse people to an active interest in the need for better school conditions. In this work, he visited more than 300 schools, traveling on horseback over 1,200 miles over the rough country roads, visiting schools by day, addressing public meetings by night, and everywhere preaching the gospel of a better school system and a free education for every Ohio boy and girl.

His report for the year 1837, based on his own observations and such statistics as he could gather from the county auditors, gave the first assembled information about the common schools of the state. The report found the Legislature in a receptive mood, and the Law of 1838 was passed with but little opposition.

The essential feature of this new law was that it was the first one to give a degree of organization and some headship to the system. The new code not only retained the state superintendent of common schools office but made it a "permanent" office. The Act of 1837 had created the office but had done nothing to change the other school laws or to establish any machinery of administration. The new law made the county auditor in each county also the county superintendent of schools and, as such, responsible to the state superintendent of common schools in all educational affairs. Similarly, the township clerk was made the township superintendent of schools in each township, subordinate to the county superintendent.

An organization had thus been effected, by means of which an authorized state officer could reach out into the most remote district of the state, either to give help or information or to see that the law was obeyed. If equipped with sufficient assistance through a department of education, Ohio, through this law, had the mechanism for effective educational administration.

The real strength of the system rested in the person of the state superintendent. Mr. Lewis filled the office for 3 years and, in those 3 years, did the same kind of work for Ohio that Horace Mann had been doing in Massachusetts. Unfortunately for Ohio, and its subsequent educational history, Mr. Lewis, because of failing health, gave up the office after 3 years of tireless service. Because some opposition had developed, the Legislature transferred the work to the Office of the Secretary of State. This office was given $400 additional for clerical assistance, and the work became almost entirely the collection of statistics and making reports, instead of the administration of a statewide school system.

Permanency in the area of political life and political enactments is often impossible. The Office of State Superintendent of Common Schools created "permanently" by the Act of 1838 was abolished by another act and by another General Assembly in 1840. Apparently, the action was taken to effect a savings of $800 in the superintendent's salary. The secretary of state was made ex officio superintendent. In an amendment to this latter act, the title of "township clerk" was substituted for that of township superintendent, and "county auditor" was substituted for county superintendent. Duties, clerical in nature, were changed only slightly, and some semblance of the connections among the township, the county, and the ex officio superintendent continued to be maintained (16).

The general educational legislation passed between 1840 and 1850 was concerned only with the district school. No general legislation was enacted to establish secondary or higher education institutions as a part of the state system, and it was not until 1847 that any legislation was passed to make provision for town and city schools and a graded system other than that found in a few special town and city charters. The Akron Act was passed in 1847, and in 1849 the provisions of this act were extended to all municipalities having 200 or more inhabitants.

In 1850, the Legislature passed another act which again created the office of state superintendent, but in an entirely different form than the former law. This law never actually became operative because the General Assembly, which was the appointing body, allowed it to lapse through its failure to appoint the officers provided for in the law.

Briefly, this law provided for a State Board of Public Instruction consisting of five members, appointed by the General Assembly. The first members were to be appointed for terms from 1 to 5 years. After that, one member was to be appointed each year for a 5-year term. Each member, during the last year of his term, was to receive the title of state superintendent of common schools and was to perform the duties of that office. The duties were limited mainly to the collection of statistics and making reports. The board was to divide the state into four districts, and each member would serve as a district superintendent in one of these districts. The salary of each district superintendent was to be $1,000, and the salary of the state superintendent was to be $1,200.

However, this law never came into effect because the General Assembly passed an act providing for "the reorganization, supervision, and maintenance of common schools" (17).

This law reestablished the office of state superintendent but changed the title to state commissioner of common schools. The provisions of this law served as the basis for the regulation of the public schools of Ohio for nearly 50 years.

While public education in Ohio has always been considered the responsibility of the state, the abdication of this responsibility by the state to the local schools and school districts in the early 1800's resulted in a slow growth in state responsibility and administration of its schools. It was not until about 1861 that the growing power, authority, and responsibility of the state began to be apparent. The acts and laws–however ineffective–passed by the Legislature from 1861 to 1900 portray the evolution of state responsibility for administration of the education of youth and the regulation of the schools.

An act which was indicative of the developing authority of the state commissioner was one passed in 1861 that required the officers of the teachers institutes to furnish the state commissioner of common schools an account of the money received, from what sources it came, and how it was expended.

An Act of 1865 requested the commissioner to gather information concerning "the organization and results of the best normal school in this country, and the probable cost of establishing one or more efficient normal schools in this state" (18).

The Law of 1873 required a codification of the school laws relating to the commissioner of common schools. A summation of the powers and duties of the state commissioner of common schools indicates that even though many clerical duties still remained, these aspects were slowly changing to that of power, influence, and prestige (19).

The commissioner was required by law to furnish forms for the reports of boards of education, and these boards were required to report to him on demand. Probate judges and clerks of city and county boards were required to make reports to him, as were officers of seminaries, academies, and private schools. The commissioner was required to publish and distribute copies of the school laws to school officials and to make an annual report to the Governor and to the General Assembly. He was mandated to be a member of the State Geological Board, now known as the Ohio Archaeological and Historical Society. Many other memberships, later mandated by law for the state commissioner, required such a tremendous amount of time and energy on his part that, eventually, he had very little time to devote to his real job, namely, leadership in the field of education. Some of these memberships mandated by law were the State Library Board, the State Teachers' Retirement Board, the Ohio Records Commission, the boards of trustees of the state universities, and the War Orphans' Scholarship Board.

He was required by law to appoint a State Board of Examiners; to hold or order teachers institutes to be held; to countersign life certificates issued by the board of examiners; and to have supervision of the state school fund.

Cost of Textbooks Standardized

A law passed in 1890 standardized the cost of textbooks, and a law in 1891 required boards of education to make their selection of textbooks from the list as prepared by the state commissioner of common schools. Cost of books was not to exceed 75 percent of the publisher's list price. Commissioner Charles C. Miller reported in 1891 that, in his opinion, this provision would reduce the cost of textbooks to parents in the sum of $1 million (20).

Commissioner Miller further stated that there was a growing belief among educators that the state should supply all needed textbooks free of charge.

Important acts of the Legislature between 1891 and 1906 give further evidence of more duties and responsibilities being assigned to the commissioner of common schools. Important acts passed by the General Assembly during the tenure of Commissioners Charles C. Miller, Oscar T. Corson, and L. D. Bonebrake provided for uniform teachers examinations under the direction and control of the commissioner, and authorization of day schools for the instruction of the deaf under the supervision of the State Department of Education. In fact, the Law of 1898 establishing the day schools for the instruction of the deaf is the first reference made by law in Ohio to a department of education. Although the State Department of Education was not officially defined until the enactment of Section 3301.13 R.C. in 1956, it has always been considered to be the administrative unit and organization chosen by the superintendent to assist him in his duties and responsibilities in connection with public education in the state. The department consists of a staff of such professional, clerical, and other employees as may be necessary to perform the duties and to exercise the required functions of the department.

While there appears to be no definite record concerning the exact number of employees in the state commissioner of common schools office in the period prior to 1906, evidence indicates that the number was quite small. The first reference in this respect is found in an act passed in 1900 which made an appropriation for a chief clerk, a statistical clerk, and a stenographer. Again in 1902, the Legislature made an appropriation for a corresponding clerk. The state commissioner was required to prepare Arbor Day exercises for use in the schools, and during this same year the law required him to prepare questions for certain examinations in the schools.

From 1837 to 1906, 18 commissioners of common schools served a total of 55 years, averaging a tenure of approximately 3 years. During this span of 69 years, the secretary of state performed the duties of the commissioner from 1840 to 1854. The first superintendent, Samuel Lewis, was appointed to the office by a joint resolution of both Houses of the General Assembly. All of the others, known as state commissioners of common schools, were elected to office by the qualified voters of the state.

In 1906, the General Assembly of Ohio provided by law that the state commissioner of common schools should be elected biennially at a salary of $4,000 per year. This was an increase of $2,000.

EDUCATION IN OHIO FROM 1906 THROUGH 1940

This period in the educational history of Ohio extends through World War I, the Depression, and to the eve of World War II. It includes a period when the public schools of Ohio experienced the greatest financial difficulties ever encountered. Teachers received lower salaries, at times they were paid in script, and for long periods they received no payment of any kind. Reductions were made in supplies and equipment, schoolrooms were overcrowded, and school terms were shortened. It is to the everlasting credit of the school administrators, teachers, and other school employees that, during this crisis, they accepted larger classes, additional duties, and less money, thus riding out the storm with fortitude.

During this period, several things occurred which tended to give the state commissioner of common schools more authority and responsibility in the administration of the public schools. This trend probably resulted, at least in part, from the existing crisis rather than from any real desire of the citizens to give up local autonomy. In order to clarify what took place during this period, the following sections will discuss some of the responsibilities shifted to the state commissioner.

Financial Aid for Financially Weak School Districts

From 1906 to 1940, there were five legislative enactments dealing with state financial support for schools. Three of these acts were favorable, because they assisted in the financial support to schools, and two were unfavorable, because they, at least indirectly, had the opposite effect.

The 1906 law, commonly known as the State Aid System for Weak School Districts, remained in effect until its repeal in 1935, when the State Equalization or Foundation Program Law replaced it. Under the provisions of the State Aid Law, the state commissioner of common schools was charged with the responsibility of administering the fund according to law and on approval of the state auditor. In the early years, school districts were reluctant to apply for state aid, partly because of the stigma attached to being a "financially weak" school district and partly because of the fear of state control. In the first year, only $82,000 was distributed, and even 10 years later, the amount was only $173,000. However, in later years (1918 to 1935), between one-third and one-half of the school districts in the state were receiving aid, the total average amount for the last 3 years being $6 million.

It appears that in the later years of the existence of this State Aid Law, certain legislators brought political pressure on the state commissioner and state auditor to promote aid for certain districts in their legislative districts. This pressure led to some questionable aid (21).

In spite of this shortcoming, one former state commissioner who had experience with the administration of this law contended that this act was really the *only true state aid system* for financially weak school districts. This former state commissioner contends (and many people agree) that the State Foundation Program Law enacted in 1935 and amended several times thereafter provides financial assistance to the *rich* school districts as well as the *poor* districts even though it is not needed in the rich districts (22).

The contention of the former state commissioner is substantiated in part, at least, by an article in the *Ohio Schools,* entitled "State Aid up to Now" (23).

An article, written by an Ohio assistant attorney general, bemoans the fact that, under the foundation program, some of the wealthiest districts in the state have received state aid. It appears to him (a) that the policy of the state should have continued as it was expressed in the 1906 law which provided for the equalization of educational advantages throughout the state, (b) that districts having ample taxable property valuation locally and the means of defraying the costs of educating their children should be required to provide the support locally, and (c) that the state ought not to be called upon to assist except in certain districts which are known as permanent state aid districts and in which taxable property is not sufficient to raise adequate revenues for school purposes.

Three incidents occurred after 1928 which seriously affected the 1933 school districts financially.

In 1929, legislation was enacted which exempted much tangible personal property from the tax duplicate and also lowered the rate of assessment on the remaining tangible personal property.

In the early 1930's, the worst economic collapse in Ohio's history brought additional reductions in the tax duplicate. Between 1929 and 1935, the total tax duplicate in Ohio dropped from $13.7 billion to $8.7 billion. In addition to this, delinquent taxes were mounting each year.

The third reduction occurred in November 1933 when the electorate voted into the constitution a tax-limitation amendment which reduced from 15 mills to 10 mills the maximum which could be levied without a vote of the people for the support of all forms of local government in any local taxing subdivision.

B. A. Stevens, director of research, Ohio Education Association, reported in an article in the *Ohio Schools* that as early as the school year 1930-31, many school districts were feeling the effect of diminishing tax collections. In a significant number of cases, retrenchments in operating costs were being made. School operating costs had declined steadily from a peak of expenditures of nearly $113 million in 1931-32 to budgeted expenditures of approximately $74 million for 1932-33.

During the school year 1931-32, one-third of the city school districts of the state were forced to shorten the school term. In a number of cases, the full term was completed only because the teachers taught from 1 to 4 weeks without pay. The close of the school year 1932-33 found an accumulation of a deficit for the school districts of the state of approximately $22.5 million.

Dr. Stevens, research director of the OEA, collected statistics from the superintendents of schools in the state concerning the number of months schools could operate with resources available for the 1933-34 school year. He received reports from all of the city districts and from 85 percent of the exempted village and county school districts in the state.

He found that three cities, two exempted villages, and seven local districts in the county systems did not have enough money in sight to keep their schools open for even 1 month during the school year. Only 3 cities, 1 exempted village, and 47 local school districts had sufficient money available to keep the schools open for the full 9 months. Medians for the three classes of school districts were strikingly uniform. The typical district of the state had only enough money in sight for the year to keep the schools open for 4 or 5 months at most during the year.

During the years 1932 to 1935, part of the financial burden of school support in Ohio was shifted from the local school district to the state. In the Ninetieth General Assembly, an effort was made to secure tax support for a state foundation program and an equalization method of distributing state funds. However, both programs failed by a few votes in the closing moments of the regular session. However, 1¢ of the liquid fuel tax was appropriated for schools, the money to be distributed on a straight per-pupil basis without reference to need.

In a special session late in 1934, the Legislature passed a sales tax of 3 percent, which, together with the liquid fuel tax and what remained of the intangible tax, furnished sufficient state funds to supplement the revenue available from local sources to support a meager educational program in 1934 and 1935.

It finally became evident to the General Assembly that the tax base would have to be broadened in order to avert a financial collapse of the schools and local subdivisions of government. By this time, the state's share of the total operating costs of the public schools had dropped to as low as 4 percent.

Governor George White authorized B. O. Skinner, director of education, to appoint a commission to make a survey of the financial situation of the public schools of Ohio. The Ohio Education Association pledged its financial support to the commission for the survey.

Paul R. Mort of Columbia University was employed as director of the commission, and L. L. Rummel, field editor of the *Ohio Farmer,* was chosen as secretary.

The secretary of the commission gave a summary of its report in the *Ohio Schools* for December 1932. The commission discovered that in the poor districts, salaries of teachers had been reduced in many cases 20 percent to 40 percent and that building programs were well nigh impossible. The commission observed that Ohio schools had suffered more in this time of economic distress than those in nearby states.

The commission discovered that the appraisal of real estate caused a decline of taxes from 10 percent to 20 percent and that the return from personal property under the new law was less than that anticipated by the lawmakers. Tax delinquency assumed unprecedented proportions. Moreover, Ohio schools faced a bonded indebtedness above $238 million, and these bonds, plus the interest on them, had to be paid at face value prior to anything else. Many school districts expended from 20 to 30 percent of their revenue for interest and debt retirement.

The commission report noted that in formulating its program for public education, Ohio had placed responsibility on the local district and forced property to bear nearly all the tax burden, which amounted to almost 97 percent of the cost of education. Only about 4 percent was paid from the state treasury.

It stated further that schools are a state institution, just as roads are; that 12,000 miles of roads in the state highway system are built and maintained largely by the motorists through a gasoline tax and license fees earmarked for roads. It said that the state should assume a greater responsibility in financing education and guarantee to every child equal educational opportunities to a certain prescribed minimum standard.

The commission explained what type of minimum educational program the state should demand and support. The school districts in Ohio had an average operating expenditure per child amounting to $60 for elementary pupils and $102 for high school students. Half of the districts spent more, and half of the school districts had a lower level. The lower level of 800 state-aid districts averaged only $40 annually for elementary pupils and $68 for high school pupils. If a $60 minimum were established in Ohio, it would immediately require $8 million in additional revenue.

The director of research, Dr. Mort, decided that it would be wiser to take the level of state-aid districts as the starting point for equalization—$40 per pupil. This minimum program would include all current operating expenses but not capital outlay, interest on indebtedness, or bond retirement. Administration, supervision, salaries, textbooks, library books, wages of janitors and engineers, fuel, water, light, power, supplies, promotion of health, transportation, school lunches, playgrounds, insurance, and other incidentals all were included in the recommended program of $40 per pupil, or of $1,200 per year for a classroom of 30 in average daily attendance.

State Foundation Program. The report of the new commission was named the *Mort Plan for the Equalization of Education Through the Medium of Financial Support for*

Financially Weak School Districts. The state superintendent of public instruction and the teaching profession took the leadership in trying to gain support for the Mort plan. Some of the various organizations throughout the state that endorsed the plan were farm bureaus, Kiwanis Clubs, local American Legions, Federations of Women's Clubs, county boards of education, farmers institutes, local Granges, parent-teacher organizations, the Ohio Pastors' Association, some local county taxpayer leagues, and also some local chambers of commerce. Rural organizations were strongly in favor of the plan.

Opposed to the plan were the cities and some of the financially poor school districts. The latter believed that they would receive more support under the old equalization plan than they would under the new.

The former were certain that they would have less money to run their schools and that, indirectly, it would be an additional cost to them.

Superintendent Skinner and other educational leaders spent a prodigious amount of effort in getting the plan enacted into law. Renamed the *State Foundation Program of School Support,* it was introduced in the General Assembly in the year 1933, embodying the recommendation that $29 million of state money be appropriated. When the program failed to be enacted, another attempt was made to pass it at a special session. This time, the program failed to pass by four votes.

When a new Legislature convened in January 1935, the foundation program was submitted again. Although the Foundation Program Bill passed the House with a splendid vote on April 2, 7 long weeks of struggle followed before the House put on the finishing touches by concurring in the Senate amendments. During this time, there were behind-the-scene efforts to introduce aid for private and parochial schools, but on June 5, 1935, the Traxler-Kiefer-Matthews Bill was signed by Governor Davey, and a great milestone had been passed.

The Foundation Program Law enacted in 1935 established a per-pupil foundation of $22.50 for kindergarten, of $45.50 for elementary school, and of $67.50 for high school.

Schools with fewer than 180 pupils were granted a weighted scale of enrollment, since, if their existence was recognized as necessary, an adjustment needed to be made in their favor. For example, a high school of 45 pupils needed as many teachers as one enrolling 90 pupils.

The foundation program of transportation was included, subject to the approval of the director of education. An approved budget of tuition cost was included to pay for the attendance of the district's children who were assigned to the schools of another district.

The funds necessary to meet a foundation program were derived from a levy of 3 mills on the tax duplicate of the school districts and a uniform payment by the state to every district amounting, on a 9-month basis, to $15.30 per kindergarten pupil on average daily attendance, $30.60 per elementary pupil, $49.50 per high school pupil, and $36 per part-time continuation and evening school pupil. This flat distribution from the state public school fund represented the state's full obligation to all districts where the total of the 3-mill levy and the uniform payment equaled the total foundation program as described above. In cases where the 3-mill levy and the state's uniform per-pupil payment did not provide enough money to meet the approved foundation program, the state was obligated to provide additional aid so that the district would not have less than the foundation program.

The guiding principles of the law remain in effect in much the same way today, but the details of the program have been amended by law continuously since 1935.

Consolidation and Centralization of School Districts

Consolidation of school districts in Ohio can be divided arbitrarily into about three distinct eras that stand out in the history of public education in Ohio. The first began in 1912 following the adoption of an amendment to Article VI of the constitution. The second began in 1937, and the third in the 1960's.

Centralization and consolidation of schools was practically nil prior to 1906. As early as 1872, the state commissioner of common schools, Thomas W. Harvey, stated in his report to the General Assembly and to the Governor that—

> Something must be done soon by way of redistricting the townships, or for providing for centralization of the schools in Ohio. Our townships have from six to nine sub-districts in many instances, and very many of these schools are run during the summer months with from 3 to 8 scholars. The winter schools also are proportionately small (24).

Harvey said that, with this state of affairs, no person could create any real enthusiasm in his schoolwork, and the school authorities did not feel that, in these cases, they could pay the wages which qualified teachers would demand. Harvey added that he was satisfied that some method of collecting children of the rural districts could be devised by which they could have all the advantages of the graded schools.

Twenty-eight years later, Commissioner Lewis D. Bonebrake, in his report, bemoaned the fact that there had been practically no consolidation or centralization of schools. He reported that, in 1892, just 20 years after the recommendation of Commissioner Harvey, one school district was consolidated in Kingsville, Ashtabula County. He said that the Kingsville Township Board of Education, confronted with the necessity of providing a new school building, boldly undertook to solve the complex problem. Realizing that Kingsville schools were small and the per-capita expense was unduly large, the board finally decided to transport the children of the township to a village school. In order to make the centralization legal and to provide for the cost of transportation, a special bill applying only to Kingsville Township was introduced into the General Assembly, and it became law in 1894.

In 1898, Commissioner Bonebrake was instrumental in obtaining permissive legislation which would permit any township to change the boundaries of subdistricts, to suspend the school in such districts, and to provide for the conveyance of said pupils to another district or districts as might be most convenient for them and providing that the cost of such conveyance would be paid out of the contingent fund of the district.

Thus, the groundwork was established for consolidation of school districts, but no great progress in that direction was made until about 1916 when the recommendations of the 1913 School Survey Commission and the resulting New Rural School Code began to be effective.

Table 1. – TREND IN THE NUMBER OF OHIO SCHOOL DISTRICTS, 1910-41

School year	City districts	Exempted village districts	Township or rural districts	Total number of districts
1910-11	69	0	2,274	2,643
1911-12	81	0	2,566	2,647
1912-13	80	0	2,582	2,662
1913-14	80	0	2,582	2,662
1914-15	80	0	2,594	2,674
1935-36	109	62	1,765	1,936
1936-37	109	67	1,592	1,768
1937-38	109	71	1,547	1,727
1938-39	109	77	1,520	1,706
1939-40	109	79	1,502	1,690
1940-41	109	83	1,481	1,673

Source:

R. M. Eyman, *History of County School Districts in Ohio*, Columbus: Ohio Education Association, 1962, p. 28.

The State School Survey Commission of 1913 and the New Rural School Code

The Fourth Constitutional Convention of Ohio, which convened in Columbus in January 1912, submitted to the people a proposal to amend Article VI of the constitution as follows: "Provision shall be made by law for the organization, administration and control of the public school system of the state supported by public funds" (25).

This proposal was adopted at the special election held in September 1912. James M. Cox, who was elected Governor the following November, was keenly conscious of the great importance of the movement to organize rural life, a subject which, broadly speaking, was at that time gaining more public attention than any other. He realized that a school system commensurate in efficiency with the importance of rural life and its industries was necessary and fundamental to the progress and consummation of such a movement; that the country boys and girls were not getting a square deal because the so-called system then in use was inadequate to their needs, purposes, and interests and failed to reveal to them the possiblities of rural life and rural activities (26).

In his first message to the General Assembly, Governor Cox made a number of recommendations. He called attention to the fact that Ohio had no uniform school system and that it did not rank with the best states in the Union. He suggested that investigation should precede legislation. He called further attention to the fact that other states had found it necessary to withhold distribution of the state common school funds to districts until these had fully complied with minimum standards.

In response to the suggestions and recommendations of Governor Cox, the General Assembly passed an act, which became law in March 1913, to create a commission to conduct a survey of the public schools and the normal schools of the state. The survey, which extended into every county of the state, gave particular attention to the "common schools" in the county districts. This policy grew out of "the apparent need of a thorough awakening of the rural communities."

The letter of transmittal from the commission to Governor Cox stated that laws for improvement must come from the people of the state and that an "awakening" was necessary.

The report moved Governor Cox to action, and he sought to create an "awakening" immediately. He issued a proclamation to the people suggesting that every school district in Ohio observe Friday afternoon and evening, November 14, by assembling at the "shrine of the local schoolhouse" in observance of School Survey Day, and urging action and support for legislative action. "Let it be a day of 'genuine awakening,' " he said. He promised speakers and literature so that all might know the true conditions and prescribed remedies. He suggested further that an Educational Congress be held in Columbus on December 5 and 6, inviting every community to send delegates (27).

A 1913 survey disclosed the following discouraging facts:

1. Less than half the teachers in the rural schools were graduates of high school, and 18 percent had no education beyond elementary school. Sixty percent of the teachers in high schools in such districts had no college training, and one-fifth of them were not even high school graduates.

2. Sixty percent taught 5 years or less (rural). In the one-room township elementary and high schools, half the teachers were first-year teachers.
3. Nearly half the teachers in the schools surveyed had no professional training whatever.
4. Teachers taught from the book exclusively, gave leading questions, and were guilty of unnecessary talking.
5. Furniture and equipment, if any, were inadequate and inappropriate.
6. The physical plant was woefully inadequate, as were the playgrounds.
7. Practically no attention was given to the health of the pupils.
8. There was no uniformity as to records and reports.
9. Many boards of education were not enforcing the compulsory law (28).

Governor Cox called the General Assembly together, explaining to the members that rural communities were entitled to the same educational advantages as the cities. He made clear that the Ohio Survey Commission laid stress on consolidation, supervision, and the training of teachers. He pointed out that a state as rich as Ohio could take hold of the conditions, pass laws permitting and encouraging consolidation of districts, and institute proper supervision of teachers with the state paying half the cost, which was its constitutional responsibility.

The General Assembly, in response to Governor Cox, enacted what was commonly known as the "New Rural School Code." The new code created a county school district, a county board of education, and a county superintendent, with proper educational qualifications. Certification requirements were increased, and the county board was given power to consolidate school districts and to divide the county district into supervision districts for the purpose of improving instruction.

Vernon M. Riegel, assistant director of education under F. B. Pearson, gathered and published in 1920 all the data he could obtain from county superintendents who had consolidated school districts on what consolidation did to improve education. As a result of his efforts and those of county superintendents, many second- and third-grade high schools either merged with schools of higher grades or built new ones. This was the first concerted movement in Ohio toward consolidation in a period when dirt roads exceeded paved roads.

The second movement toward further consolidation had its origins in 1935 when the Works Progress Administration provided funds to the U.S. Office of Education for studies of school organization in 10 states. E. L. Bowsher, director of education, explained that Ohio was one of the 10 selected because of the state's need for school reorganization and the probability that the results of the study would be used in connection with the reorganization provisions of the school foundation program of the state. (The State Foundation Program enacted in 1935 stated that any school district with fewer than 180 pupils could have the state's share of funds prorated on a schedule somewhat less than that for larger schools.)

The first school district to be created in Ohio at the conclusion of the survey was Jefferson-Union in Jefferson County, largely, if not completely, with the efforts of County Superintendent Delbert Woodford. A modern high school was built. Sixty percent of the cost of construction was funded by the WPA.

Beginning of Increased Emphasis on Secondary Education

The latter part of the nineteenth century and the early part of the twentieth century occupy a unique place in the history of secondary education in Ohio. Independent academies and seminaries reached the peak of their rapid development in 1851. Shortly thereafter, the influence of the seminaries and academies began a steady decline, which was still in progress 75 years later. The publicly supported secondary school was almost unknown prior to the middle of the nineteenth century. After the year 1850, the interest in secondary education began to center about the public high school.

The earlier secondary schools were independent academies and seminaries, which were dependent on the initiative and interest of the individual parent or community for their existence and sustenance.

It was to these schools that the children had to look for educational opportunities beyond the elementary grades. The constitution had made provision for private groups to organize schools of secondary rank. Beyond this constitutional provision, nothing had been done by the state to encourage the growth of secondary education.

The story of the development of the tax-supported, free public high school in Ohio belongs particularly to the period from 1851 to 1925. Its numerical growth has been most rapid since 1900. At the beginning of the year 1851, Ohio had no general law concerning tax-supported, free secondary schools. A few of the more forward-looking communities had passed legislation establishing high schools similar to the academy in organization and support. The earliest high school of this nature in Ohio was chartered in Elyria in 1830, to be followed the next year by the Woodward High School of Cincinnati. By the year 1851, 14 such high schools had been chartered in Ohio, and the sentiment in favor of free high schools steadily gathered momentum from that time forward.

Ohio's first general law providing for the establishment of high schools passed in 1853 was permissive in character. By the terms of this law, boards of education were authorized to establish schools of higher grades than primary, to be called central or high schools. More than one of these could be established where the school boards deemed them necessary. When the board of education had decided on the need of one or more high schools, the voters of the township were authorized to vote on the question of the cost and location of the schools.

Ohio's legislation concerning high schools for this period is not commensurate with the growth or importance of these schools. Following the passage of the first general law in 1853, high school legislation was confined to the details of district organization and support. The early legislation was, at all times, permissive in character.

In an era of dirt roads and horse-drawn vehicles, it is understandable that a township could have two or three high schools and make consolidation or centralization a problem for the future. This is exactly what happened. From a very few high schools in Ohio in 1850, the number reached 836 in 1900, 1,475 in 1920, and 1,275 in 1925.

Teacher Education and Certification

In the period between 1906 and 1940, the state commissioner of common schools and his staff, now known as the Department of Education, began to assume real authority and responsibility for the preparation and certification of teachers.

In order to more fully understand the progress made during this period, some explanation must be made concerning the situation with respect to these matters prior to 1906.

In 1821, the district school committee was authorized to employ "competent" teachers, with no mention being made of certification. Four years later, the principle of county certification appeared and remained until 1850. The Law of 1825 provided for the appointment of three examiners of common schools in each county by the court of common pleas, who should examine and certify teachers and visit and examine schools.

In 1827, the court of common pleas was allowed to appoint such number of examiners as they might deem expedient, not to exceed one for each organized township in the county. The evident intent of the law was to allow single examiners to examine within the township. Four years later, in 1831, the examiners were directed to give the certificate in the branches in which the teacher was found qualified to teach, and no certificate was to be granted unless the candidate could teach reading, writing, and arithmetic (29).

In 1838, the county became the unit for certification, and the mode of appointment of three examiners was by the court of common pleas (30). No teacher in any common school was permitted to teach a subject not named in the certificate. In 1849, English and geography were added to the requirements for certification.

The power and control of the commissioner of common schools over teacher education and certification was slow in developing. The first act indicative of his growing power was in 1861 when a legislative act required the officers of teachers institutes to report to the commissioner "thirty days after every meeting giving an account of the moneys received, from what sources, and how expended by them, and such other matters relative to the institute as the Commissioner might require" (31).

In 1864, the commissioner, for the first time, was given some control over inspection of teacher education. The county examiners were required to report to the commissioner all details of their certification activities and the moneys received. One year later, the state commissioner was given authority to appoint a board of three examiners to have jurisdiction over the issuance of life certificates which had to be "countersigned by the Commissioner" (32).

State control of teacher preparation had its beginning in 1865 when the Legislature, by an act, passed a resolution requesting the commissioner to gather information concerning "the organization of the best normal school in this country and the probable cost of establishing one or more efficient normal schools in this state" (33). It was not until 1893 that legislation was enacted aimed at setting up more uniform standards for teachers. This law provided for a uniform system of examination for teachers in the state specifying that "the secretary of the State Board of Examiners and Commissioner of Common Schools should prepare a series of questions, and print and distribute the same to the examiners in the several counties of the state" (34). The grading of the examinations, however, remained with the county examiners. All of this had happened prior to 1906.

An act passed in 1910 provided for some standardization of teacher education. This act granted the commissioner the power to approve normal schools, teachers colleges, or universities as teacher education institutes.

From about 1920 to 1935, the directors of education sought to upgrade the education of teachers by obviating teachers examinations for those who obtained a stipulated minimum amount of education at approved institutions of teacher education. Under Vernon M. Riegel, director of education, and E. B. Hawes, Division of Examination and Licensing, a pamphlet of laws and regulations relating to teachers certificates was published for the first time in the school year 1921-22. The superintendent of public instruction could grant a 4-year provisional elementary certificate without examination to an applicant who had graduated from a first-grade high school and had completed a full 2 years academic and professional course at any approved normal school or college. He could grant a 4-year provisional secondary certificate without examination to an applicant who possessed a diploma from a first-class high school and had completed a full 4-year academic and professional course in an approved institution (35). For the first time, the State Department of Education entered into the granting of provisional certificates issued by the superintendent of public instruction to qualified applicants.

A subsequent publication was issued in 1930 for the purpose of further interpretation of rules and regulations for certification. The State Department of Education was now regulating the renewal of certificates issued by local examiners by requiring a graduated scale of additional training for each renewal (36).

In September 1935, a new law went into effect which abolished the local boards of examiners and centralized the issuance of all certificates in the hands of the state director of education and five-member State Board of Examiners. The Law of 1935 also mandated the state director to prescribe standards for the approval of institutions of higher education engaged in the preparation of teachers. The Division of Teacher Education and Certification was established and charged with preparing standards for both certification of teachers and teacher education institutions.

The 1935 law provided for four grades of certificates—temporary, provisional, professional, and permanent—and nine types of certificates. The laws and regulations were not published in printed form until 1939. The regulations were the work of Harold J. Bowers, who became the division director in 1937, remaining in this position until 1958 when he was appointed assistant superintendent of public instruction, in which post he served through 1966, when he was appointed deputy superintendent of public instruction. The professional employee of the state department who has a longer tenure than any other person, Dr. Bowers has played an important role in all changes of certification laws and regulations since 1936.

During this period from 1906 through 1940, 11 chief state school officers administered the public schools of Ohio through the State Department of Education, their average tenure being 4 years. Four were voted into office by the electorate, and, after the constitutional amendment in 1912, seven were appointees of the Governor.

The period closed on an optimistic note, described in *Ohio Schools* for June 1939. It said, in part, that considerable progress in developing the state educational program had been made; that, during the regular session of the General Assembly, no legislation evidencing an unfriendly or a reactionary attitude toward the public schools had been proposed. Legislatively, it had been a period of progress on all state educational fronts.

During these earlier years of the state superintendency, school legislation was rarely concerned with the duties of the state superintendent or the state education agency. Kennneth Ray, former state superintendent of public instruction (1941-45), stated that the development of the state educational system had been slow and laborious. Dr. Ray summarized the activities of the state superintendent between 1837 and 1912 as follows:

> In the first half century after Ohio finally made permanent provision for a chief state school official, the annual reports (of the superintendent) are largely discussions of educational theories, practices, and recommendations rather than of educational achievements. This is perhaps understandable because firm foundations are usually slow in shaping. It took almost forty years to establish the office of chief state school official; then after only three years of existence, it was discarded for sixteen years before being re-established . . . . In 1911, the Commissioner of Common Schools was still seeking some means of making the state school reports more accurate and speedy (37).

The reorganization directed by the 1921 code formally established the State Department of Education. The educational program at the state level experienced a rapid growth during the 1920's. In 1921, administrative action established the position of assistant director of education. Between 1920 and 1930, the following agencies and divisions of the Department of Education were created: vocational rehabilitation, special education, high school supervision, visual education, teacher training, music, child accounting, adult education, examining and licensing, scholarship tests, health and physical education, guidance, and radio education.

In 1927, the state schools for the blind and deaf were transferred from the Department of Public Welfare to the Department of Education. The rapid growth of the state department was temporarily checked in the 1930's by the Depression. With the enactment of the first State School Foundation Law in 1935, the department assumed major responsibilities in the calculation and allocation of state school aid.

EDUCATION IN OHIO SINCE 1940

The State Department of Education in Ohio has been marked by several contrasting periods of development. Between approximately 1840 and 1920, the growth of the department was extremely slow in terms of organization and personnel. From 1920 to 1930, the growth was fairly rapid, and then, as has already been mentioned, it was considerably retarded between 1930 and 1940 by the Depression. Since 1940, each succeeding decade has witnessed a more rapid growth for the department.

The present organizational structure of the state department includes most of the agencies or divisions which were created between 1920 and 1940, although some consolidations have been made and division titles have been changed in some cases. Attempts have been made to coordinate the work of the various divisions by placing them under the supervision of assistant superintendents of education. One deputy superintendent and four assistant superintendents now assist the state superintendent of public instruction in his work. Since 1955, several new divisions, such as research and development, computer services and statistical reports, publications, and guidance and testing, have been established in the department.

The need for increased financial assistance, minimum standards, and advisory services from the state level has been increasing each year in the local school districts. The increase in the appropriation for school assistance from $200,000 in 1837 to the biennial appropriation for 1967-69 of $922,838,686 gives one measure of the state's participation in the operation of the schools.

The history of the State Department of Education from 1940 to 1968 was marked by increased cost of school operation, a steadily increasing shortage of the number of qualified teachers, accelerated birthrate, and teacher salary problems.

The Ohio School Survey of 1954 and the creation of the State Board of Education in 1956, which occurred during this period, probably had tremendous effects on the future progress of public education in Ohio.

The Ohio School Survey

Not since 1913 had state authorities made a thorough attempt to appraise the public schools of the state. The One-Hundredth General Assembly of Ohio enacted Sections 103.41 to 103.43 of the Ohio Revised Code providing for an 11-member Ohio School Survey Committee, charged with the responsibility of making a comprehensive study of the public school system of the state.

Organized in the fall of 1953, the committee approached its task in the firm belief that public education should not be studied from the viewpoint of the professional educator alone, or any other special group.

The committee organized six study committees in the fields of instruction, personnel and teacher education, state educational organization, local district organization, housing and transportation, and finance. Each committee was composed of lay and professional people of all races and creeds from all sections of the state. Each committee had a highly qualified out-of-state consultant, as well as a staff assistant provided by the six state universities.

Before formulating their recommendations, the study committees collected and analyzed a mass of information from official records, personal interviews, and questionnaires. During School Visitation Week the members of these committees, the survey committee, and the consultants visited a cross section of schools in 66 of the 88 counties of the state.

The following are some of the findings made by the survey committe:

Only two-thirds of Ohio's school districts operate high schools. In other districts, the older pupils have to go outside the district to attend high school on a tuition basis. Only about 55 percent of the high school pupils attending schools have a satisfactory program, as determined by the research staff.

It is difficult to secure enough qualified teachers to keep pace with increasing enrollments. Teaching loads are generally heavy throughout the state. The quality of instruction varies greatly from school to school. In general, guidance and counseling receive too little attention, and many schools do not provide adequately for exceptional children.

Ohio ranks high in financial ability and low in financial effort to support public schools. Because of high costs and existing debt limitations, many boards of education are unable to provide enough classrooms and other necessary school building facilities.

It is impossible to determine satisfactorily how Ohio schools compare with those in other states. However, the following listing gives some idea of Ohio's standing:

Factor considered	Ohio's rank among the states
Years of schooling completed by persons over 25 years of age	17
Percent of draftees who passed armed forces qualification test in 1950	27
Current expenditure per pupil in average daily attendance	35
Average salaries of teachers	16
Average value of public school property per pupil	15
General state tax revenue per capita of total population	35
Percent of income spent for schools	43
Financial ability as measured by income payments per capita	8

Increased school populations will inevitably result in increased costs for public education in Ohio. Approximately twice as many children were born in Ohio in 1953 as in 1939. During the same 14-year period, the public school enrollment increased approximately 250,000.

The enrollment increase from 1953 to 1956 will probably be as great as during the preceding 14-year period, and from 1956 to 1960, it is expected to be even greater. Estimated increase in school population required by 1960 at least 17,000 additional teachers and approximately that same number of new classrooms.

Ohio schools range in quality from excellent to very poor. Evidence indicates that some excellent teaching is found in nearly every community, but a large proportion of the teaching in many communities is not satisfactory. Some of the unsatisfactory teaching is due to faulty organization and administration; some, to limited supplies and equipment. It may be the result of overcrowded classes, obsolete buildings, or lack of community interest or cooperation.

In a number of communities, the financial resources are too limited to permit the employment of well-trained teachers or the development of good school programs. In most communities, schools give too little attention to the development of exceptional children or to meeting the individual needs of other children. Ohio schools should continue efforts to secure better teachers and better teaching.

Practically all Ohio high school teachers are college graduates, and one-third have master's degrees, but about half of Ohio's elementary teachers are not college graduates.

Practically all Ohio teachers have some professional training in addition to general college work, but, except in a few special fields, the amount of time devoted to professional courses is not excessive.

School authorities and citizens are well satisfied with the quality of teaching done by most teachers. There is, however, substantial dissatisfaction with the performance of some teachers, and teachers themselves recognize the need for improvement.

A good school district is one which has enough pupils and a large enough tax base so that it can (a) offer at least 12 years of schooling; (b) attract and hold a competent staff; (c) employ supervisors, teachers of special classes, guidance counselors, and other specialized professional personnel; and (d) provide a broad educational program and the necessary staff, teaching supplies, and building facilities to make it effective. It is difficult to provide a satisfactory program with fewer than 240 pupils in the high school, and a total enrollment of at least 1,200 pupils in the school district. (Recommended minimum standards later were established as 500 pupils in high school, grades 9-12, and a total enrollment of 2,500 to 3,000 pupils in grades 1-12.)

Ohio has too many small school districts and too many small high schools. In October 1953, Ohio had 1,337 school districts. By counties they ranged from 4 to 40. Eight counties had more than 25 school districts, and 12 had fewer than 10 districts.

Three-fourths of the high schools of the state had fewer than 500 pupils, and 58 percent had fewer than 300 pupils. One-third of the school districts had no high school at all.

About 45 percent of Ohio high school pupils were in schools which did not have a satisfactory program. Only one district in six had as many as 1,200 pupils in total enrollment. One-tenth had fewer than 100 pupils, and one-fourth had fewer than 200.

State financial aid is now distributed to school districts in a way which discourages the combining of small, inefficient schools. Ohio school districts vary in tax valuation from $1,500 to $255,000 per pupil. The richest district has 170 times as much ability to support schools as the poorest.

Ohio has a shortage of school buildings. Furthermore, although there are many excellent school buildings in Ohio, there are also many which are old, unsafe, and unsuitable for today's educational programs. It would cost $61 million to replace them and approximately $84 million to make needed repairs on existing school buildings which are otherwise suitable for continued use.

Schools throughout the state are overcrowded. Ohio should spend $89 million at once for added capacity for pupils already in school. It needs to build eight new classrooms a day at a cost of an additional $340 million to house anticipated enrollment increases by 1960.

If all Ohio school districts needing buildings were to borrow up to the 8-percent legal debt limit, about 20 percent would fall short of their immediate needs. The total shortage would be at least $37 million. This shortage would increase as enrollments grow and would reach a cumulative total of $153 million by 1960. Boards of education now have no legal means available to raise necessary funds.

The present plan of financing public education is unsatisfactory and should be completely overhauled. The proposed foundation program (to be financed from state and local funds) would permit the following educational services for all children:

A competent teacher for every 30 pupils, in both elementary and high schools. Necessary small schools, classes in vocational education, and classes for exceptional children would require smaller classes. Additional principals, supervisors, librarians, and other special instructional personnel would be needed in proportion to the number of teachers.

All services needed for administration, operation, and maintenance of the schools would be based on the number of classroom units; transportation would be based chiefly on the number of pupils transported and the area served.

In an attempt to guarantee that each school district would have sufficient funds to provide a reasonably satisfactory program of education, the survey committee recommended a new foundation program plan for financing public schools.

In 1955, the Ohio General Assembly enacted a new foundation program law based on the recommendations of the Ohio Survey Commission. The steps in computing the program were as follows:

Step 1. Find the cost of the foundation program for each school district as follows:

(a) Determine the salary allowance by multiplying the number of classroom units by an allotment ranging from $3,000 to $4,100, depending on the training level of the teachers, and add 10 percent for retirement and sick leave. (b) Multiply the number of classroom units by $1,300 to get the amount to be included for all other current expenses except transportation. (c) Determine the transportation cost by a formula yet to be established.

Add the above three items to determine the total cost of the foundation program to be financed from state and local funds.

Step 2. Find for each district the amount which would be available from a 10-mill levy on the assessed valuation. This is the required local contribution.

Step 3. For each district, subtract the yield from the 10-mill levy (Step 2) from the cost of the foundation program (Step 1). The difference is the amount to be provided from state funds, except that no district is to receive less than $1,750 per classroom unit (approximately the amount now received) from state funds.

The program has been amended by the General Assembly in practically every session since 1955, but the basic principles remain much the same as those originally recommended by the commission.

Another recommendation of the Ohio School Survey Commission was to have an elected State Board of Education composed of lay citizens serving staggered terms of 6 years.

The Creation of the State Board of Education in 1956

The concept of a State Board of Education was not new to Ohio or to the nation. In 1838, the first state superintendent of common schools had recommended to the Legislature that a state board be established. In 1850, the General Assembly passed an act providing for the creation of a State Board of Education. The bill stipulated that state board members were to be elected by the Legislature. This bill never became law because the General Assembly failed to carry out the election before adjournment.

In nearly 90 years, Ohio had never come as close to obtaining a State Board of Education as it had in 1850. Between 1850 and 1939, periodic attempts were made in the Legislature to establish a state board. Although several Governors and numerous state superintendents of public instruction had advocated the creation of a state board, only six bills pertaining to this subject were introduced in the Legislature during this period of time. None of these bills succeeded in passing both Houses of the Legislature.

Pursuant to a recommendation of the Governor, the Legislature, in 1939, adopted a resolution proposing an amendment to the Ohio constitution. The proposed amendment would have included a State Board of Education and a director of education, appointed by, and whose term of office and compensation would be fixed by, the state board. The amendment was voted on by the electorate in November 1939 and was defeated by a 3 to 2 margin.

Despite the 1939 defeat of the proposal for a state board, the proponents of such a measure were encouraged by the new interest which was aroused for a state board. During the next 14 years, there was more activity in support of a state board than there had been in the entire preceding 100 years. Professional educators and educational organizations were in the forefront in stressing the need for a State Board of Education. Consequently, again in 1953, the General Assembly adopted a resolution to amend the Ohio constitution. The proposed amendment was similar to the one which had been defeated in 1939 and contained the following language:

> There shall be a state board of education which shall be selected in such manner and for such terms as shall be provided by law. There shall be a superintendent of public instruction, who shall be appointed by the state board of education. The respective powers and duties of the board and of the superintendent shall be prescribed by law.

The "yes" vote was 298,460; the "no" vote, 213,337 (38).

Consequently, the Legislature, which met in January 1955, was faced with the task of enacting legislation to provide for a state board and a state superintendent of public instruction appointed by the state board. The amendment did not specify the number of board members and the method of election. The sponsors of the amendment recommended a board of nine members, one member to be elected from each of the nine judicial districts in the state. The bill passed the House with those provisions but was amended in the Senate to consist of 23 members, one to be elected from each of the 23 congressional districts as they existed on January 1, 1955. The General Assembly meeting in 1967 amended the law to provide for a board of 24 members, one to be elected from each of the 24 congressional districts as they existed in 1967. Consequently, Ohio has the largest membership of any State Board of Education in the country.

As mandated by the constitutional amendment (Section 4 of Article VI), the 1955 Legislature prescribed the powers, duties, and responsibilities of the State Board of Education and of the state superintendent. The Ohio Revised Code contains a major portion of these statutory powers and duties. In general, the powers and duties of the state board are in the realms of policy making, and the powers and duties of the superintendent are executive in nature.

More than 100 sections in the Revised Code pertain to functions of the State Board of Education. The board has the general power and duty to—

1. Exercise general supervision over the system of education.
2. Formulate policy, plan, and evaluate functions pertaining to public schools and adult education.
3. Exercise leadership in the improvement of public education.
4. Administer the educational policies of the state relative to public education.

5. Provide consultative and advisory services to school districts.

Its many specific powers and duties fall into five major categories: finance, operation of the Department of Education, curriculum and instruction, school district organization and administration, and miscellaneous.

The Ohio constitution also requires that the powers and duties of the superintendent of public instruction be prescribed by law. The General Assembly, meeting in 1955, enacted Sections 3301.11 and 3301.12 of the Ohio Revised Code, which gave a general description of his duties and responsibilities. In general, the superintendent is authorized to—

1. Serve as executive and administrative head of the State Board of Education in its administration of all educational matters and functions placed under its management and control.

2. Execute, under the direction of the State Board of Education, the educational policies, orders, directives, and administrative functions of the board, and direct, under rules and regulations adopted by the board, the work of all persons employed in the State Department of Education.

3. Provide technical and professional assistance and advice to all school districts in reference to all aspects of education including finance, buildings and equipment, administration, organization of school districts, curriculum and instruction, transportation of pupils, personnel problems, and the interpretation of school laws and school regulations.

4. Prescribe forms and require the preparation and filing of such financial and other reports from school districts, officers, and employees as are necessary or proper.

5. Prescribe and require the installation by school districts of such standardized reporting forms and accounting procedures as are essential to the businesslike operations of the public schools of the state.

6. Conduct such studies and research projects as are necessary or desirable for the improvement of public school education in Ohio, and such as may be assigned to him by the State Board of Education.

7. Prepare and submit annually to the state board a report of the activities of the state department and the status, problems, and needs of education in Ohio.

8. Supervise all agencies over which the board exercises administrative control, including schools for education of handicapped persons.

In November 1955, the 23 members of the state board were elected to office (one from each congressional district as they existed at that time), and at the first meeting of the board in January 1956, the board members chose by lot their length of terms according to law (39).

However, in 1967, the General Assembly amended the Ohio Revised Code to provide for 24 members of the state board to coincide with the newly redistricted 24 congressional districts. Consequently, in November 1967, the entire membership of 24 was elected to office. Again, in January 1968, these 24 members drew length of terms by lot—8 for 2 years, 8 for 4 years, and 8 for 6 years. Presumably, in 1969, and in each succeeding 2 years, 18 members will be elected or reelected for 6-year terms.

Voting statistics on the election of state board members indicate that if the board reflects voter desires, it does so in a very limited sense. Election results indicate that voter interest concerning state board elections has apparently declined in the 13-year period in which these elections have been held. The issue of an elective versus an appointive board is still a matter of concern throughout the state.

Appointment by the Governor is the most frequently mentioned alternative method of selecting state board members. Several arguments are commonly voiced in support of gubernatorial appointment. The Governor is able to select members of the highest caliber who could give considerable prestige to the education program at the state level. Many years of experience with gubernatorial appointment of trustees for Ohio's state universities indicate that these appointees are quite often persons who have received national recognition in academic, business, and governmental fields.

Nevertheless, despite all the shortcomings of the elective method, Ohio was fortunate in securing high-caliber membership on its first state board, although the majority had never previously served on any board of education. Of the 23 members, 21 were men and 2 were women. Eleven were practicing attorneys. The turnover of membership on the board has not been large, although of the 23 original members elected in 1953, only 6 remain on the board at this time (1968).

Upon its establishment in 1956, the State Board of Education in Ohio immediately encountered many problems. The law permitted the board to continue to employ any person holding any position or office in the state department which was in existence immediately prior to January 3, 1956, until such time as appointments of personnel were made under the provisions of the Ohio Revised Code (40).

In order to prevent a complete disruption of the educational program, the state board, at its first meeting on January 3, 1956, took action to continue the employment of all of the members of the department who were on the staff at that time. In fact, the superintendent of public instruction, R. M. Eyman, and his assistant, W. D. Darling, who were in office at that time, continued to serve in those same positions until April 1957, when E. E. Holt became the first state superintendent of public instruction selected by the State Board of Education. Both Eyman and Darling were then made Holt's assistants.

In November 1956, the board announced the appointment of a superintendent to take office in July

1957. However, in February 1957, the board rescinded the appointment made 3 months earlier, because the constitutionality of the appointment was questioned on the ground that the person selected for the superintendency was not a resident of Ohio. According to the constitution, "no person shall be elected or appointed to any office of this state unless possessed of the qualifications of an elector . . ." (41).

When Eyman retired in July 1958, his position was filled by Harold J. Bowers, who had served as director of the Division of Teacher Education and Certification since 1936. Holt retired from office in July 1966, and Darling retired in September 1966. M. Byron Morton was appointed as an assistant superintendent in 1958 and served in that capacity until he retired in 1967.

Martin Essex was elected state superintendent of public instruction to succeed Holt and took office July 1, 1966.

Dr. Bowers was appointed to a newly created position, that of deputy superintendent. Wayne Carle and Paul Spayde were appointed assistant superintendents in 1966, and Thomas Quick was appointed as an assistant in 1967. Robert Greer was appointed assistant superintendent in 1968.

After the first State Board of Education had completed its organization, its first task was to adopt policies. Previously, the director of education, as state superintendent of public instruction, was the policy-making official as well as the executive officer who executed the policies.

The law enacted by the General Assembly in 1955 attempted to transfer all policy-making functions from the superintendent of public instruction to the state board. Consequently, the board spent considerable time during the first several months of its tenure in reviewing policies which were already in operation in the department in relation to the schools, and either adopting these same policies, amending and then adopting the amended policy, or formulating and adopting completely new policies to replace some of the old ones.

As soon as some of these routine matters could be properly handled, the board gave its attention to some problems which had been pointed out by the 1955 Ohio Survey Committee. These specific problems involved improvement of instruction, teacher education and certification, and school district organization, each of which will be discussed in the following sections.

Improvement of Instruction. In February 1957, the board adopted the elementary school standards which it had been studying for a year. These standards became effective in April 1957. The board then considered high school standards, and these became effective in January 1958.

The staff of the Division of Elementary and Secondary Education was increased so that schools could be visited by a representative of the department more frequently. Previously, because of the limited number of general supervisors in the division, many schools had not been visited for 7 or 8 years, although the department was responsible, according to law, for chartering high schools and for revoking charters when schools did not measure up to state standards.

Programs of instruction are now being broadened continuously, and more attention is being given to specialized courses. Vocational education, special education, guidance and testing are being emphasized to a greater extent.

One of the problems facing the state board was the number of high schools (most of them with small enrollments) which were not meeting the Ohio high school standards. Between the years 1934 and 1948, the state superintendents had revoked only 15 high school charters. In 1949-50, the General Assembly established a high school board consisting of five staff members in the state department. In accordance with the legislation, the superintendent was required to revoke charters upon recommendation of the high school board. In slightly less than 4 years (1949 to 1953), 121 charters were revoked. The high school board was officially dissolved by the Legislature in 1955. The State Supreme Court had made the high school board somewhat inoperative in 1953, when it ruled that the Administrative Procedure Act must be followed in the future and that an unlawful delegation of legislative power had been made to an administrative agency.

By adopting new high school standards and following the Administrative Procedure Act, the state board was again able to revoke the charters of high schools which did not meet these standards. Table 2 on page 967 gives a picture of high school charters revoked during the 25-year period 1934-35 to 1959-60.

Teacher Education and Certification. In 1957, the State Board of Education adopted another revision of laws and regulations which became effective in 1959. Elaborate committees representing a cross section of all segments of the teaching profession, both public and private, conducted research and made recommendations to the Board. Both subject matter people and personnel from the colleges sought significant increases in semester hour requirements for their respective disciplines. At the somewhat stormy public hearing in September 1957, conducted by the board, which hearing was required by the Administrative Procedure Act, the professional educators attended en masse. Some members of the state board were opposed to what they called excessive hours of professional preparation for teachers and wished a reduction, but although the board finally approved the substantial increase in semester hour requirements for certification in most of the subject matter fields, it left the professional semester hour requirements substantially unchanged.

Table 2. – NUMBER OF HIGH SCHOOL CHARTERS REVOKED BY THE OHIO DEPARTMENT OF EDUCATION, 1934-1960

School year	Number of charters revoked	School year	Number of charters revoked	School year	Number of charters revoked
1934-35	2	1943-44	0	1952-53	34
1935-36	0	1944-45	1	1953-54	0
1936-37	1	1945-46	1	1954-55	0
1937-38	1	1946-47	0	1955-56	0
1938-39	0	1947-48	1	1956-57	0
1939-40	0	1948-49	3	1957-58	0
1940-41	0	1949-50	8	1958-59	22
1941-42	5	1950-51	25	1959-60	35
1942-43	0	1951-52	54		

Total number revoked, 193

Source:

A Ohio Legislative Service Commission, "Organization and Methods of the Ohio Department of Education," Staff Research Report No. 43. December 1960, p. 48.

The board adopted one more significant change in certification in December 1961, which affected the certification of superintendents. Acting on a request which stemmed largely from leadership of the American Association of School Administrators, the board adopted a prescribed curriculum for the certification of superintendents which required a minimum of 60 semester hours of graduate credit, at least 10 semester hours of which were to be completed while in full-time residence.

School District Organization. The issues raised by school district reorganization have been numerous and difficult. Local pride in maintaining small school districts (many of which were inadequate with respect to revenue resources and educational standards) has been a difficult and understandable roadblock to school district reorganization. During the period 1954-55 to 1959-60, the number of school districts in Ohio was reduced to a greater extent than in any other 5-year period, as shown in Table 3.

The State Board of Education, through the State Department of Education, has exerted considerable influence in the reorganization of school districts in Ohio by formulating and adopting certain policies. Board policy has prohibited some school districts from submitting bond issues in excess of 6 percent of the assessed tax valuation of the district. The constitution forbids a district to submit a bond issue which would make the net indebtedness exceed 6 percent of the assessed valuation of the district without approval of the state board. Other regulatory actions of the state board have encouraged consolidation of school districts. Prior to 1968, the state board had little or no authority to mandate consolidation. It had authority to conduct studies and propose consolidations where there was evidence of need for consolidation. Four such studies

Table 3. – NUMBER OF SCHOOL DISTRICTS IN OHIO, 1941-68

School year	City	Exempted village	Local	Total number
1941-42	113	83	1,462	1,658
1943-44	113	85	1,439	1,637
1945-46	113	86	1,423	1,622
1947-48	113	87	1,393	1,593
1949-50	113	89	1,397	1,509
1951-52	135	71	1,222	1,428
1953-54	135	74	1,131	1,340
1955-56	136	80	1,049	1,265
1957-58	137	78	875	1,090
1959-60	140	77	757	984
1961-62	153	68	608	829
1963-64	157	66	577	800
1965-66	160	61	510	731
1967-68	163	54	479	696

Source:

Ohio Department of Education.

were conducted in 1965-66, and several have been conducted since that time. However, the electors in the territory affected have the right by referendum to accept or reject the proposal (42).

The General Assembly of 1965 mandated the state board to prepare and submit to the assembly, not later than January 1967, a master plan for the organization of school districts in Ohio. This study was conducted under the direction of Ralph D. Purdy of Miami University. The Master Plan, which was submitted to the next General Assembly, established, as a primary objective, the creation of school districts as administrative units, each of which could economically provide and financially support an educational program sufficiently broad to meet the various post-high school needs of its students, including those entering college, those entering the labor market, and those entering other post-high school careers.

Even though endorsed by the State Board of Education, the Master Plan failed to be enacted into law.

Due in large measure to the dynamic, aggressive leadership of State Superintendent Martin Essex and of members of his staff, this General Assembly did, however, enact numerous laws which form the basis for "An Educational Renaissance in Ohio." This legislative program includes the following highlights:

The major increase in state funding for schools in the 1965-67 biennium, the largest thrust for elementary and secondary education in Ohio history, represented an unprecedented 39.2-percent increase over the previous biennium–$260,010,156 in additional dollars and a total of $922,838,686 in state support that is nearly three times the state's $363,346,189 investment a decade ago (1957-59). It brings needed relief to the mounting pressure on local property taxes, producing an amount for schools, statewide, equivalent to a 3.8-mill levy.

These funds are helping Ohio schools compete for needed teachers. They have raised teacher salaries to the range of the upper one-fourth of the states. The new statewide pay scale, which will encourage the employment of qualified and experienced persons in poorer districts, is the highest schedule of its kind in the nation.

The educational purchasing power for instruction, books, utilities, and other operating costs has jumped 38 percent, from $290 to $400 per pupil in the poorest districts.

This appropriation is also making possible the following:

Largest expansion of vocational education in history for 85,000 students in vocational classes

Largest growth ever of classes and other services for 200,000 mentally and physically handicapped children

The Midwest's first state-supported programs to improve the educational status of disadvantaged children in urban centers and rural pockets of poverty

Major extension of instructional TV programs for schools

A special state subsidy to make driver-training classes available to every Ohio youth

The first state funds to match federal funds for a million-dollar basic education program for the retraining of unemployables

Funds to make auxiliary services, such as audiovisual aids and television, available to nonpublic school pupils on the same basis as in public schools

Tuition assistance to local boards of education for payments for mentally retarded children

The chartering of school districts to ensure emphasis on good elementary, as well as secondary, schools.

Major reforms in the voting of school funds, the more equitable funding of pupil transportation, improvement of all state pension benefits, and provision for employee insurance plans have been among more than forty other significant enactments.

Truly, Ohio schools have been brought to the threshold of a new era, with a mighty thrust to improve the supply of suitable teachers, to extend and expand vocational education, to bring special services to the handicapped and disadvantaged, and to finance better education for all pupils.

FOOTNOTES

1. U.S. Department of Commerce, Bureau of the Census, *Statistical Abstracts of the U.S., 1910,* XXXIII (Washington, D.C.: Government Printing Office, 1911), 21.
2. Caleb Atwater, *A History of the State of Ohio* (Cincinnati: Glazen and Shepard, 1838), p. 351.
3. U.S. Department of Commerce, Bureau of the Census, *Statistical Abstracts of the U.S., 1911,* XXXIV (Washington, D.C.: Government Printing Office, 1912), 40.
4. Samuel Peters Orth, *The Centralization of Administration in Ohio* (New York: Columbia University Press, 1903), p. 164.
5. Ohio, *Documents, 1838,* Doc. No. 32, p. 30.
6. *U.S. Laws, 1789-1815,* Vol. I, ch. 32.
7. Aaron Burke Hinsdale, *The Old Northwest* (New York: n.p., 1888), p. 268.
8. Ohio, *Constitution* (1802), art. 1, sec. 7.
9. Ohio, *Constitution* (1802), art. 1, sec. 25.
10. Ohio, *Constitution* (1912), art. 6, secs. 3, 4.

11. Ohio, *Constitution* (1912), art. 6, sec. 2. Also see State *ex. rel.* Steinle *v.* Faust, Ohio 55 Ohio App. 370, 9 N.E. 2d 912 (1937).
12. Methodist Children's Home *v.* Board of Education, Ohio (1922).
13. Ohio, *Laws* (1821), XIX, 21.
14. Atwater, *op. cit.*, p. 254.
15. Ohio, *Laws* (1837), XXXV, 82.
16. Ohio, *Laws* (1842), XL, 49-50.
17. Ohio, *Laws* (1853), LI, 421.
18. Ohio, *Laws* (1865), LXII, 614.
19. Ohio, *Laws* (1876), LXXIII, 225-46.
20. Commissioner of Common Schools, *Thirty-Eighth Annual Report* (1892), p. 13.
21. Interview with E. L. Bowsher, Superintendent of Public Instruction (1935-37), on November 15, 1967.
22. Interview with Vernon M. Riegel, Superintendent of Public Instruction (1920-27), on November 13, 1967.
23. Wilbur E. Benoy, "State Aid up to Now," *The Ohio Schools,* IV (April 1926), 115-16.
24. Commissioner of Common Schools, *Nineteenth Annual Report* (1873), p. 163.
25. Ohio, *Constitution* (1912), art. 6, sec. 3.
26. Vernon M. Riegel, *A Study of Rural School Conditions in Ohio* (Columbus: The F. J. Heer Printing Co., 1920), p. 5.
27. *Ibid.*, pp. 6-7.
28. *Ibid.*, p. 12.
29. James J. Burns, *Educational History of Ohio* (Columbus: Historical Publishing Co., 1905), p. 54.
30. *Ibid.*, p. 120.
31. Nelson L. Bossing, *The History of Educational Legislation in Ohio, from 1821 to 1925* (Columbus: The F. J. Heer Printing Co., 1931), pp. 12-18.
32. Commissioner of Common Schools, *Twelfth Annual Report* (1865), p. 156.
33. Ohio, *Laws* (1865), LXII, 214.
34. *Ibid.*, 192.
35. Bossing, *op. cit.*, pp. 124-47.
36. Kenneth C. Ray, "The Evolution and the Reorganization of the State Department of Education" (unpublished Ph.D. dissertation, Ohio State University, Columbus, 1943), p. 67.
37. *Ibid.*, p. 42.
38. Robert S. Drury, *Drury's Ohio School Guide,* Title XXXIII (3d ed.; Cincinnati: W. H. Anderson Co., 1954), p. 402.
39. Ohio, *Revised Code* (1955), sec. 3301.25.
40. Ohio, *Revised Code* (1955), secs. 3301.08, 3301.13, 3301.04.
41. Ohio, *Constitution* (amended 1953), art. 11, sec. 4.
42. Ohio, *Revised Code* (1955), secs. 3311.37, 3311.38.

BIBLIOGRAPHY

Public Documents

Methodist Children's Home *v.* Board of Education, Ohio (1922).

Ohio. *Constitution* (1802, 1851, 1912 amended in 1953).

-- *Documents, 1838.*

-- *Laws* (1821-1890).

-- *Revised Code* (1955).

State *ex. rel.* Steinle *v.* Faust, Ohio 55 Ohio App. 370, 9 N.E. 2d 912 (1937).

U.S. Department of Commerce, Bureau of the Census. *Statistical Abstracts of the U.S.,* Vol. XXXIII and Vol. XXXIV. Washington, D.C.: Government Printing Office, 1910 and 1911.

U.S. Laws, 1789-1815, Vol. I.

Books and Pamphlets

Atwater, Caleb. *A History of the State of Ohio.* Cincinnati: Glazen and Shepard, 1838.

Bossing, Nelson L. *The History of Educational Legislation in Ohio, from 1821 to 1925.* Columbus: The F. J. Heer Printing Co., 1931.

Burns, James J. *Educational History of Ohio.* Columbus: Historical Publishing Co., 1905.

Drury, Robert S. *A Brief History of the State Board of Education of Ohio, 1956-1966.* Columbus: Columbus Blank Book Co., 1967.

-- *Drury's Ohio School Guide,* Title XXXIII. 3d ed. Cincinnati: W. H. Anderson Co., 1954.

Eyman, R. M. *History of County School Districts in Ohio.* Columbus: Ohio Education Association, 1962.

Hinsdale, Aaron Burke. *The Old Northwest.* New York, n.p., 1888.

Orth, Samuel Peters. *The Centralization of Administration in Ohio.* New York: Columbia University Press, 1903.

Randall, E. O. *Ohio Centennial Anniversary Celebration 1903.* Columbus: The F. J. Heer Printing Co., 1903.

Reeder, Ward G. *The Chief State School Official.* Washington, D.C.: Government Printing Office, 1924.

Riegel, Vernon M. *A Study of Rural School Conditions in Ohio.* Columbus: The F. J. Heer Printing Co., 1920.

Reports

Commissioner of Common Schools. *Annual Reports.* Columbus: Department of Education, 1851-1967.

Manahan, William. *Report of the Ohio State School Survey Commission.* Columbus: Department of Education, 1955.

Miller, Frank W. *Report of State School Book Commission.* Columbus: Department of Education, 1915.

Ohio Legislative Service Commission. *Organization and Methods of the Ohio Department of Education.* Staff Research Report No. 43. Columbus: Department of Education, 1960.

Articles and Periodicals

Benoy, Wilbur E. "State Aid up to Now." *The Ohio Schools,* IV (April 1926), 115-16.

Miller, Edward A. "The History of Educational Legislation in Ohio." *Ohio Archaeological and Historical Society Quarterly,* XXVII, No. 1 (January 1918) and No. 2 (April 1918).

Unpublished Material

Ray, Kenneth C. "The Evolution and the Reorganization of the State Department of Education." Unpublished Ph.D. dissertation, Ohio State University, Columbus, 1943.

Other Sources

Bowsher, E. L. Interview with Bowsher, Superintendent of Public Instruction (1935-37), on November 13, 1967.

Riegel, Vernon M. Interview with Riegel, Superintendent of Public Instruction (1920-27), on November 13, 1967.

Appendix A

OHIO CHIEF STATE SCHOOL OFFICERS

State Superintendents of Common Schools

1837-40	Samuel Lewis
1840-54	Duties performed by secretary of state

State Commissioners of Common Schools
(Elected by Electorate)

1854-57	Hiram H. Barney
1857-63	Anson Smythe
1863	C. W. H. Cathcart
1863-66	Emerson E. White
1866-69	John A. Norris
1869-71	William D. Henkle
1871-75	Thomas W. Harvey
1875-78	Charles C. Smart
1878-81	James J. Burns
1881-84	C. F. DeWolf
1884-87	Leroy D. Brown
1887-89	Eli T. Tappan
1889-91	John Hancock
1891-92	Charles C. Miller
1892-98	Oscar T. Corson
1898-1904	Lewis D. Bonebrake
1904-1909	Edmund A. Jones
1909-11	John W. Zeller
1911-13	Frank W. Miller

State Superintendents of Public Instruction
(Appointed by Governor)

1913-16	Frank W. Miller
1916-20	Frank B. Pearson
1920-21	Vernon M. Riegel

Directors of Education and Superintendents of Public Instruction
(Appointed by Governor)

1921-27	Vernon M. Riegel
1927-31	John L. Clifton
1931-35	Beverly O. Skinner
1935-37	E. L. Bowsher
1937-41	E. N. Dietrich
1941-45	Kenneth C. Ray
1945-54	Clyde Hissong
1954-57	R. M. Eyman

Superintendents of Public Instruction
(Appointed by State Board of Education)

1957-66	E. E. Holt
1966-	Martin W. Essex

Appendix B

Chart I.--OHIO DEPARTMENT OF EDUCATION, 1940's

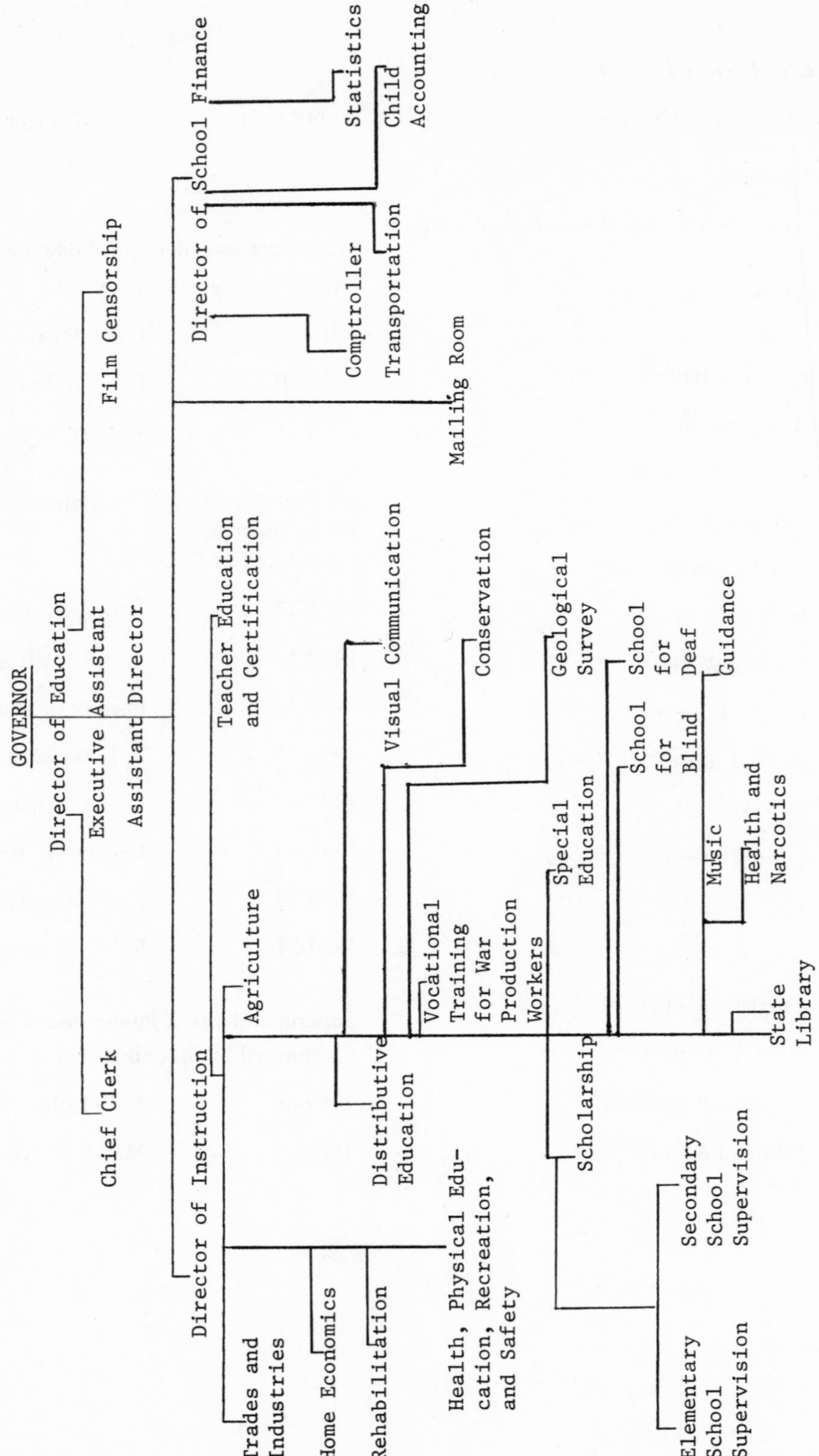

Appendix B

Chart II.--OHIO DEPARTMENT OF EDUCATION, 1960

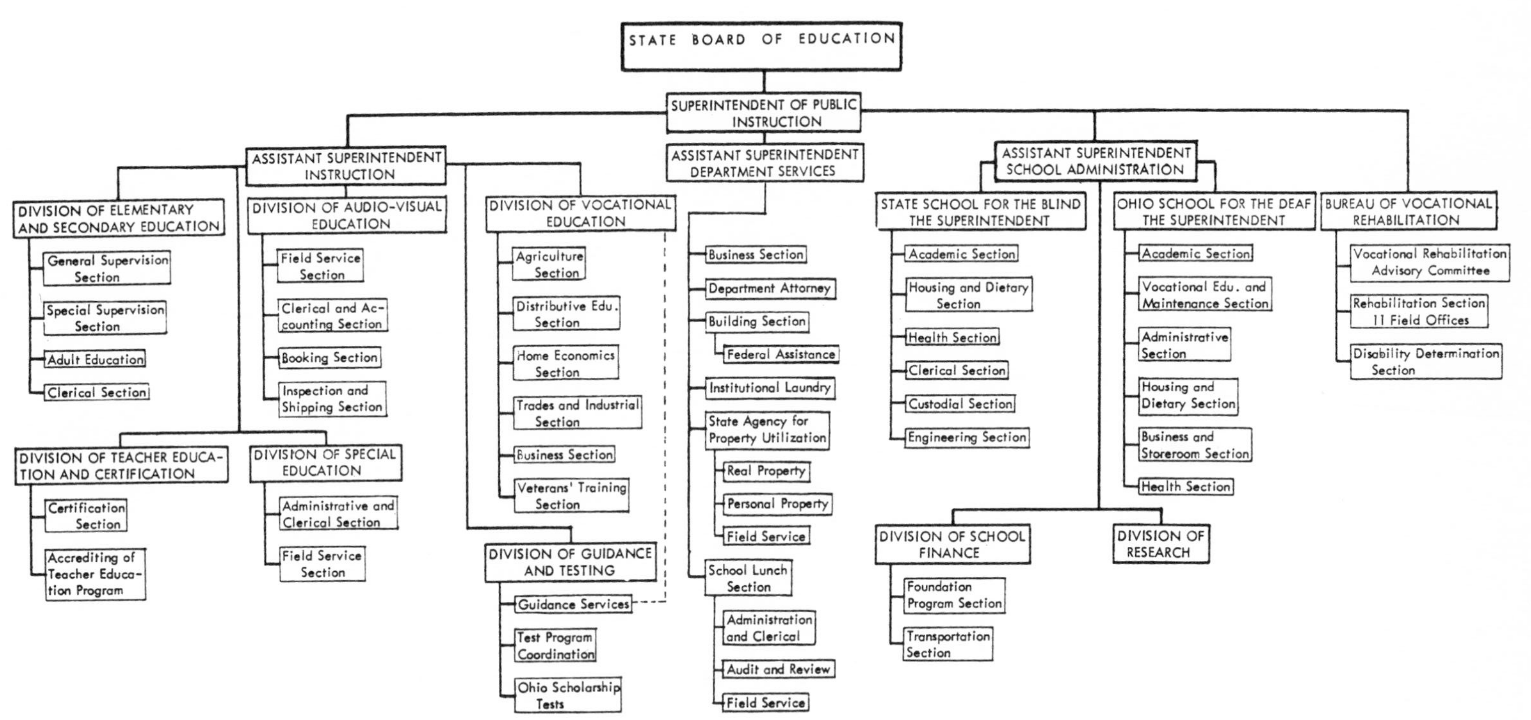

Appendix B

Chart III.--OHIO DEPARTMENT OF EDUCATION, CIRCA 1967

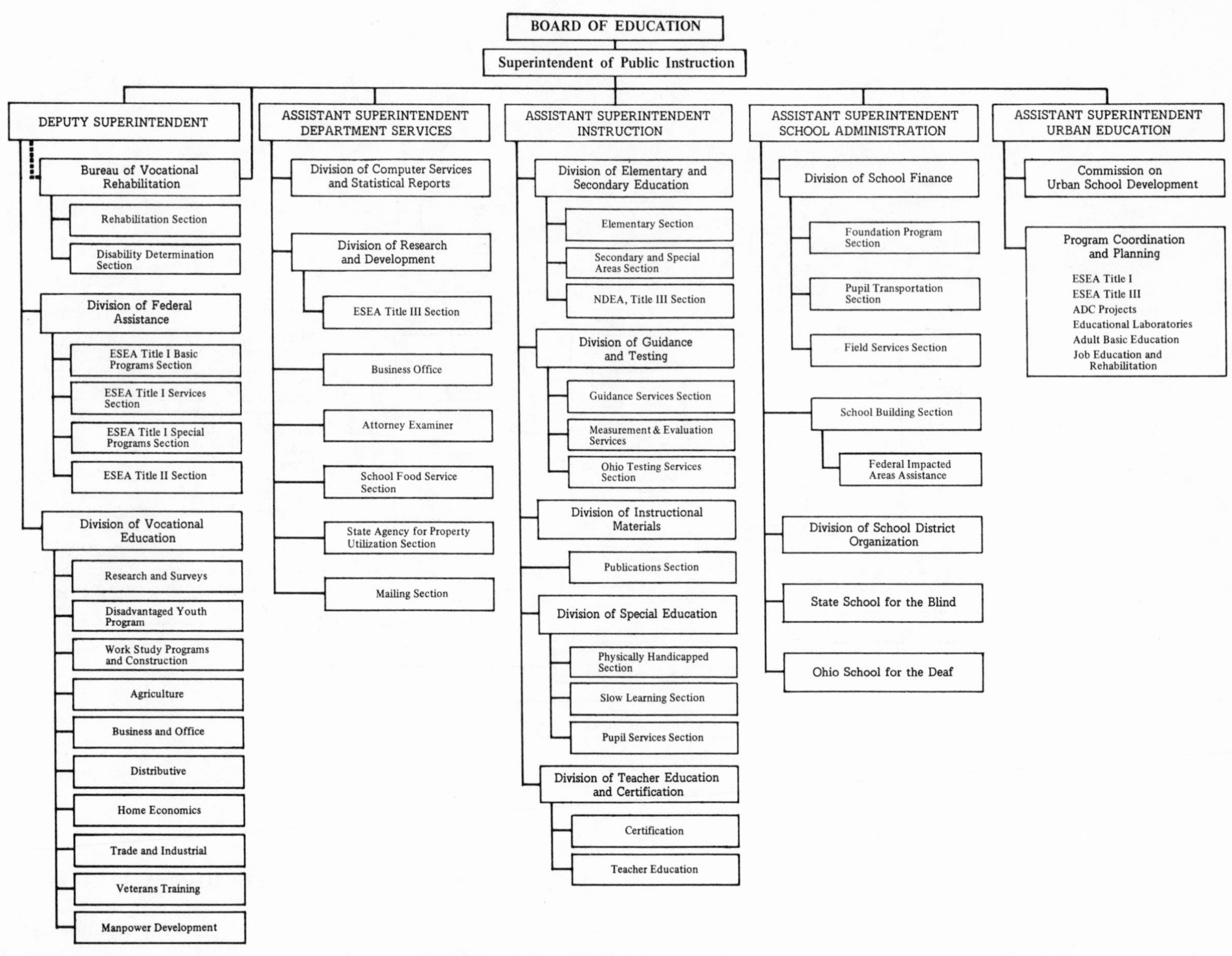

36 Oklahoma

DEPARTMENT OF EDUCATION
Guy H. Lambert
Guy M. Rankin

Contents

CREATING A SCHOOL SYSTEM

The Indians

Until the early nineteenth century, Indians roamed across the tall, lush grasses of the prairies, hunting the abundant buffalo and other game, or tilled the soil in the rich river bottoms. When the Louisiana Purchase in 1803 made this land a part of the United States, American explorers began mapping the Oklahoma Territory. After the War of 1812 and the acquisition of Florida, Southerners harassed by frequent Indian uprisings eyed these newly acquired western lands as a place to which they could banish the Indians.

Indian removal treaties sent the five civilized tribes—the Cherokee, Chocktaw, Chickasaw, Creek, and Seminole—over the "Trail of Tears" to eastern Oklahoma, where the soil and climate were much more favorable than in the plains of western Oklahoma, where dry land farming had to be developed.

Oklahoma became a haven of refuge for Indian tribes from all areas. The newly located Indians were allotted areas for settlement and given land. They eventually established governments of their own and became nations with capitals and elected officials. Aided by missionaries and to a lesser degree by the United States, they built schools and churches.

Since the Indians who became involved in the Civil War were usually on the side of the Confederacy, this often was used as an excuse for abrogating treaties and taking their land. To protect the Indian lands, the U.S. government established military posts in eastern Oklahoma, which was this country's western frontier at the time. These forts became centers for negotiating with the Plains Indians, who still lived in central, northern, and western Oklahoma and roamed from Texas to the Dakotas. Plains Indians began settling on the reservations after 1867. The invention of the repeating rifle, which resulted in the slaughter of the buffalo by white hunters, destroyed nature's balance and thus the economic basis of the Plains Indians' way of life. Their anger at the white man, who had reduced them to dependency, was vented in occasional uprisings until about 1875.

In the meantime, Texans began driving their cattle north to the railway terminals in Kansas, and this resulted in many grazing leases on Indian land in the central and northern part of the state. Railroad building caused an influx of many other white men; and the discovery of coal in eastern Oklahoma in the 1870's lured still more white people into the lands of the Indians.

The Creek and Seminole tribes ceded a large area in the western part of their nations to the United States. Many white people were attracted to these government-owned "unassigned lands" by the agricultural opportunities and put pressure on the government to open this fertile area for settlement. In 1889, Congress passed legislation authorizing the opening of these unassigned lands.

Land Openings

On April 22, 1889, some 50,000 homeseekers and adventurers lined the borders of the unassigned land, each with his dreams, either confident of a better life on his own land carved from the new territory or with hopes of staking a choice spot which could be turned for a quick profit. At noon, a gun sounded the signal, and horses, carriages, wagons, and men on foot moved in a wave to begin the first race into this virgin country, devoid of fences, with few highways and few bridges (1). By nightfall, hundreds of settlers mingled in new towns that were miraculously springing to life, and thousands of tired families camped on new homesteads of 160 acres each. Because even the climate was inhospitable to the family-enterprise economy to which these settlers were accustomed, they endured many hardships before their dreams could be realized.

At the end of the opening day rush into Oklahoma's "promised lands," six counties were born: Oklahoma, Logan, Cleveland, Canadian, Kingfisher, and Payne. Beaver County was added in 1890. On September 22, 1891, the second run took place, this time into the Shawnee Reservation.

In 1893, the government established the Dawes Commission to negotiate with the Indian tribes for their surplus land. It offered them allotments and then reached an agreement for purchasing large tracts around them. Three other runs followed, from 1892 to 1895, into the Cheyenne-Arapahoe Reservation, the Cherokee Outlet, and the Kickapoo Reservation, opening an additional 9,868,976 acres to settlement. On August 16, 1901, the Kiowa Comanches' lands were opened by lottery. In 1906, sealed bids opened an area known as the Big Pasture.

Territorial Schools

It took little time to establish law and order and the departments and agencies necessary to carry on the functions of government in these newly opened lands. Congress designated Oklahoma a territory under an Organic Act passed in May 1890. This act set up executive and judicial branches of government and provided for a delegate to Congress, a Territorial Legislature, and schools. It also provided for an appointed territorial superintendent of public instruction and county superintendents.

When the new Territorial Legislature held its first session in 1890, what is now the State of Oklahoma was still divided into Indian Territory and Oklahoma Territory. Although it adopted the school laws of Kansas (with a few modifications) as the school laws for the Oklahoma Territory, the responsibility for educating the children fell mainly on each locale. The settlers made every effort to organize one-room, one-teacher, eight-grade schools within walking distances of every rural family—which for the most part were inadequate for the society at that time. Since most homesteaders were young parents with growing families, these schools often overflowed with 50 or more pupils.

There was no serious effort to provide more than an eighth-grade education, as not many farm boys or girls were serious about pursuing studies beyond this point; for most, it was terminal. In 1908, one county with nearly 5,000 children in 74 schools graduated only 42 from the eighth grade (2). A letter from the files of a former county superintendent describes one of these typical territorial schools:

> Our first school was held in Edd Coyle's old house in 1896. There were sixty-two pupils enrolled, desks were not available and the pupils had logs to sit on.
>
> Sylvia Fairbanks was the first teacher. Her salary was $15 per month; however, she did not receive her pay until two years later.
>
> Two months of school was the average term and school opened in November and closed in December. The district got its own district owned school house in 1898 and it was built by patrons of the district who donated their labor (3).

Teachers' salaries, too often little more than those paid unskilled labor, were so low that many communities found it difficult to attract good teachers. In its first session, in 1890, the Legislature wisely established a territorial normal school to prepare teachers for these rural schools, which did alleviate the situation to a considerable degree. Until statehood, each county superintendent was responsible for certifying his own teachers on the basis of examinations prepared by the Territorial Department of Education.

Fortunately, hundreds of enthusiastic and self-sacrificing individuals scattered throughout the state dedicated a major portion of their lives to developing Oklahoma's greatest asset: its wealth of boys and girls. And despite short terms, crowded and inadequate buildings, little or no equipment, and poor lighting and heating facilities, all real handicaps to educating students, the success of many outstanding citizens who attended these schools attests to the ability of some people to overcome handicaps and even thrive on adversity.

The white population in Indian Territory continued to increase, and many of these children were deprived of even the most rudimentary education. Under the Curtis Act of 1898, the federal government assumed control of the schools in this area and appointed a superintendent for Indian Territory. The tribes were hesitant to surrender control of their institutions, but since the Secretary of the Interior controlled their funds, they had to acquiesce. Former leaders were left in administrative positions, however.

The federally appointed superintendent set up summer normal schools and certified teachers. Joe C. Jackson, who surveyed education in eastern Oklahoma, stated:

> Under Federal control, funds were made available to expand and increase the number of day schools in the Territory and opened them to whites. Consequently by 1907 there were 996 day schools in the region, most of which were available to white children.
>
> Along with this program of increasing educational opportunities for rural children, the Government broadened the curriculum of the academies to the end that vocational work replaced or supplemented much of the liberal arts; intensified and broadened the program of the summer normals; raised teacher standards; made it possible for towns to incorporate; vote bonds; levy taxes and thus provide schools through legal channels; minimize graft and corruption; and generally laid the groundwork for the state educational system that was to come (4).

Statehood

The Indian nations struggled to remain independent of Oklahoma Territory. In 1905, they held a convention and adopted a constitution for an Indian state of Sequoyah, but their effort to gain separate statehood failed. The following year, President Theodore Roosevelt signed an Enabling Act combining the Indian Territory and Oklahoma Territory into a single state. A convention adopted a constitution in July 1907, and the people ratified it 2 months later. Oklahoma was declared a state on November 16, 1907.

The new constitution Alabama had adopted greatly influenced the convention that drew up the state's basic law, and some of its provisions appear in the Oklahoma document. It also decided that the laws enforced during the territorial period "at the time of the admission of the state into the Union, which are not repugnant to this constitution and which are not locally inapplicable, shall be extended to and remain in force in the state of Oklahoma until they expire by their own limitations or are altered or repealed by law" (5).

The constitution framers stipulated that "until otherwise provided by law, the Governor, Secretary of State, and Attorney General shall be ex officio members, and with the Superintendent, compose said Board of Education" (6). Obviously, by adding "until otherwise provided by law," they recognize that the original state board, composed of ex officio members, could not for long spend sufficient time to meet the needs of the public school system.

The new constitution stated specifically that "the legislature shall establish and maintain a system of free public schools wherein all of the children of the state may be educated" (7). Statutes now specifically list the powers and duties of the State Board of Education, designating it as the governing board of the State Department of Education. It lists the qualifications and duties of the state superintendent, an elected official, who serves as the state board's executive officer.

> No person shall be eligible to nomination, appointment, or election to the office of State Superintendent of Public Instruction unless he (1) holds at least a Master's Degree in school administration from a college recognized by the state board of education; (2) is a qualified elector of the state of Oklahoma; and (3) meets the requirements to qualify for an administrator's certificate. Provided further, that no person shall be allowed to file as a candidate for nomination or election to the office of State Superintendent of Public Instruction nor shall the name of any person appear on any election ballot as a candidate for such office unless he then has the qualifications herein prescribed (8).

The 1907 constitution provided for the state to be divided into counties, and eastern Oklahoma was divided into 40. Each county was to elect a superintendent with the authority to establish and largely control the local schools. The first county superintendents divided the counties into school districts; in the first year of statehood 2,142 school districts were formed in what had been Indian Territory.

At first, local rather than state officers were responsible for renovating old buildings, constructing new facilities, and certifying and finding competent teachers. The financial burden proved to be more than the local units could bear, however, and Congress responded with a $300,000 special appropriation to provide rural schools for Indian Territory.

At the start, both the county superintendents and federal supervisors were involved in teacher training and certification. Conflict soon developed because there was strong sentiment for complete local control. Congress appropriated $300,000 each year until 1913, when it stopped federal aid to county schools (9).

In November 1907, E. D. Cameron, who had served as territorial superintendent from May 1893 to May 1897, became the first elected state superintendent of public instruction. He presided over the 1909 convention of the Oklahoma Teachers Association in Oklahoma City, which urged the establishment of rural high schools throughout the state. As president of the convention, Superintendent Cameron asked for civil service for teachers and seven-month minimum school terms, arguing that "the occupation of the teacher should be made more secure and less uncertain" (10).

LEGAL CHANGES

R. H. Wilson, a native of Scotsville, Kentucky, who came to Oklahoma in 1903, taught school 7 years, served as the Grady County superintendent of schools from 1907 to 1911 and became state superintendent in January 1911. In his first year in office, the Legislature changed the school laws and created the State Board of Education as it is known today. The Legislature decreed that the Governor should appoint six members to the board. The superintendent of public instruction was its constitutional president.

Although the State Department of Education is the administrative agency for the State Board of Education, it is not subject to its governing board's initiative alone. The department itself must be sensitive to the needs of a dynamic society—completely flexible. On many occasions it must take the responsibility to initiate necessary changes, subject, of course, to the board's or Legislature's approval.

The seven-member board was organized in March 1911, with Leslie T. Hoffman of Oklahoma City as its secretary and R. H. Wilson as president. The new law continued to make the office of state superintendent elective for a 4-year term, and it stipulated that the salary would be $2,500 per annum. No person was eligible to the office except a male person of more than 30 years of age, who had been a qualified elector of this state for 3 years before his election (11).

State Superintendent R. H. Wilson pointed out that the state board strongly favored the consolidation of rural school districts, as provided for by the state's laws. He agreed wholeheartedly that farm boys and girls should have the same or equivalent advantages of education as the boys and girls in the towns. He believed this could be brought about only by grading the country schools more effectively, providing more efficient teachers, securing better supervision, and providing additional instruction above the eighth grade as needed.

Superintendent Wilson believed that forming larger districts from smaller ones would accomplish this, since this had already happened in a number of the progressive states, as well as in more than a score of schools in Oklahoma. Wilson stated: "So far as this Board is advised, not one of these schools, either in other states or in our own state, has reported that it would be willing to go back to the old system" (12).

The State Aid Law of 1911 permitted the superintendent and the state board to use the union graded consolidated district fund to assist in constructing school buildings for consolidated districts. The law read as follows:

> Whenever a school district of not less than twenty-five (25) square miles in area shall have been established and conducted for a period of not less than six months under the terms of existing laws with reference to the consolidation of schools, and a building containing not fewer than three rooms, suitably constructed, equipped and furnished shall have been built, and a graded school employing not less than three teachers shall have been conducted for a term of not less than six months, upon making proof of compliance with the foregoing provisions approved by the State Superintendent of Public Instruction shall have drawn a warrant in favor of the district treasurer as provided in Section 5 of this act (13).

Superintendent Wilson continued to serve as chief state school officer and president of the State Board of Education until 1922, when he decided to become a gubernatorial candidate. During this time, the department grew in both size and prestige. The number of teachers in Oklahoma increased from 10,282 to 17,274, and the general fund expenditures for public education increased from $8,957,568 to $26,973,599 (14).

Progress Under State Superintendent M. A. Nash

M. A. Nash, secretary of the Oklahoma Education Association, won election to the state superintendency in 1922 and assumed office in January 1923. Extremely able, he was the first Phi Beta Kappa to hold the state superintendency. He worked hard to standardize the rural schools throughout the state, using a "model school score card." About 500 districts qualified as "model schools" in 1924; 1,500 the following year; and 2,000 in 1925.

Nash also emphasized both the teaching of reading and health education. He added two additional rural school supervisors to his staff at the close of 1926 and, with the cooperation of every health agency in the state, improved this phase of the schools' work considerably. In this same year, he made a number of important recommendations that became the basis for many later statutes that today constitute the program for public education in Oklahoma.

Dr. Nash specifically recommended increasing the minimum school term from 3 to 9 months and the enactment of a full-time school attendance law. He recommended a plan for state financial aid to guarantee more equality of educational opportunity, with specific procedures for bringing this about. Superintendent Nash asked the Legislature to give the State Board of Education sole responsibility for issuing teacher certificates. He also requested an appropriation to help provide county supervisors of instruction, and he cooperated with The American Legion in promoting an adult education program to eradicate illiteracy (15).

Oklahoma lost a farsighted state superintendent when Dr. Nash resigned in April 1927 to become president of Oklahoma College for Women at Chickasha.

The Better Schools Amendments

Approval of the Better Schools Amendments in the general election of 1946 constitutes a landmark in the state's educational history. These amendments increased state aid to school districts and allowed teachers a wider preference in choosing textbooks, a measure supported by teachers and administrators for many years. In fact, the Oklahoma Education Association presented the amendments and financed most of the campaign for their adoption. The OEA was joined by the State School Boards Association and the Oklahoma Congress of Parents and Teachers, whose officers and members contributed much time and energy. The presidents of these associations spoke on the radio several times to ask people to support the amendments. Local parent-teacher groups telephoned and passed out literature urging voter approval, and they even stood in the rain to hand out materials on election day.

Taxpayer groups, especially the Oklahoma Chamber of Commerce, strongly opposed the Better Schools Amendments. The proponents also had to overcome a natural tendency by many to leave the situation alone. This was the first time in the state's history when significant amendments to the constitution were approved in a general election with the silent vote counted as a negative vote.

Dire predictions—an integral part of most opposition campaigns—failed to scare the voters, who were willing to vote a feasible program for improving the schools. And with the successful campaign to pass the amendments began the close cooperation among the OEA, State Schoolboards

Association, State Congress of Parents and Teachers, and the State Department of Education, which still exists today.

Textbook Law

When Oklahoma wrote its 1907 constitution, it provided for what was then considered the most progressive method of choosing a textbook: the one-book, exclusive adoption method at the state level, by a commission composed of laymen and schoolmen. It stated that "the legislature shall provide for a uniform system of textbooks for the common schools of the state" (16). The Oklahoma Education Association, the Oklahoma Congress of Parents and Teachers, the State School Boards Association, and other groups supported the 1946 amendment, which made educators assume the entire responsibility for selecting and adopting textbooks. This constitutional change stipulated that the state would provide funds for purchasing the books, and it gave the teachers an opportunity to select from multiple lists. The constitution, as amended in the general election of 1946, now reads:

> The Legislature shall provide for a system of textbooks for the common schools of the State, and the State through appropriate legislation shall furnish such textbooks free of cost for use by all pupils therein. The Legislature shall authorize the Governor to appoint a committee composed of active educators of the State, whose duty it shall be to prepare official multiple textbook lists from which textbooks for use in such schools shall be selected by committees composed of active educators in the local school districts in a manner to be designated by the Legislature (17).

The Legislature in 1947 then directed the state department to organize a textbook division and appoint a director, when vitalizing the constitutional provisions.

The School Code of 1947

The Legislature enacted one of its most important measures for education since statehood when it approved the Oklahoma School Code in 1947. Educators and legislators had long recognized the necessity for repealing or clarifying these numerous laws; many were obsolete, contradictory, and unsuited to the needs of modern schools, and actually hindered the educational process. The code not only repealed some outdated and unworkable statutes, but it grouped all pertaining to particular subjects in a convenient manner and improved the administration of the system considerably. Perhaps the best proof that this code was wisely written and satisfied a real need in the state is that subsequent sessions of the Legislature have not changed it except for minor revisions, and the state's administration of public schools has encountered fewer difficulties than before.

SCHOOL FINANCE

The Territorial Period

As stated earlier, during the territorial period (and early statehood) school terms were generally short, ranging from 3 to 8 months, and the funds for maintaining them and paying the teachers were hard to collect. In one county, carved from the Cherokee strip in 1893, a contract for the 1895-96 school year shows that a teacher was employed for a 3-month term with a salary of $20 per month in cash. It also was very difficult in those days to turn school district warrants into cash. But, at the same time, a man with a shovel or pitchfork could demand the magnificent wage of $1 per day.

During this territorial period, all districts were authorized by law to levy a maximum of 10 mills if a majority of the school district electors voted to do so. In addition to the amount this levy raised for the schools, each district was entitled to prorate part of a county 2-mill levy and to receive a share in the funds from the public school land leases, which in turn was based on its enumeration. In the few independent districts, the city council could levy a maximum of 15 mills for school purposes.

When Congress opened the unassigned lands to settlement, it reserved sections 16 and 36 for the public schools. By 1900, the revenue from these lands amounted only to $1 per enumerated pupil; thus, if a district had 60 students, it received a total of $60. One reason these sections did not produce more revenue was the fact that until a settler proved his claim and received a deed, no tax could be levied on the land itself. The Indian lands were not subject to ad valorem duties, leaving only personal property upon which school levies could be applied. It is no small wonder that the schools had only the bare necessities: short school terms, inadequate buildings, few supplies, and poorly paid teachers.

In an effort to keep the schoolhouse within walking distance of every child, the regional school districts were based on the township, and each township was divided into four parts, allowing 9 square miles to a school district. Since these homesteads were widely scattered, it was necessary to create many districts, so that in the first school year (1907-1908) the new state had a total of 5,656—slightly over 3,400 in Oklahoma Territory, and a few over 2,000 in Indian Territory. We cannot be too critical of these early day schools because they were the best this young territory's settlers could afford.

The Permanent School Fund

When Oklahoma was admitted to statehood in 1907, its constitution permitted each district to allocate its income from a 5-mill local tax for current expenses, and if a majority of the people approved, the district could make an excess levy of 10 mills. At the same time, the public school lands that Congress had set aside in the territory were turned over to the new state, and in lieu of the school lands not reserved in the Indian Territory, Congress gave Oklahoma $5 million. It was the revenue from this trust fund and the public school lands which became the state's permanent school fund. The constitution provided for the care and distribution of earnings from this fund, and though it has been carefully preserved through the years, it still does not produce a large amount of revenue in comparison to the overall financing. For instance, in the school year 1964-65, it amounted to only $3,000,461–less than 1.5 percent of the school's total revenue.

One serious problem that afflicted the state's financial structure was the wide variance in the wealth evaluation of the counties and school districts. In the fiscal year 1961-62, a rural two-teacher school of Delaware County, a northeastern Oklahoma school district containing restricted Indian lands, had a total net evaluation of $15,276. In the same year, a school district maintaining a one-teacher rural school in a county in central Oklahoma had a net evaluation of $993,262. While a southeastern county had an assessed evaluation of only $1,000 for each enrolled pupil, a northwestern county's evaluation exceeded $10,000 per student (18).

Providing for Equalization

The unequal distribution of wealth made state aid imperative for Oklahoma's schools. From 1907 to 1933, school districts participated in the distribution of a 0.25 mill statewide levy, but the Legislature discontinued it during the Depression to give relief to the ad valorem taxpayers. The state also has utilized other sources of revenue, such as county mortgage taxes, gross production taxes, and auto and farm truck licenses. But these additional sources did little to equalize the school districts' ability to provide adequate educational programs for all students. The Legislature appropriated $100,000 to help pay current expenses of financially weak schools in 1919, and succeeding Legislatures increased it fivefold within 6 years.

When M. A. Nash resigned, the Governor appointed John Vaughan, a Tennessean who had served as superintendent of schools at Kingston and Wapanucka and as a member of the Oklahoma State Senate from 1917 to 1921. At the time of his appointment, he was dean, registrar, and acting president of Southeastern State College at Durant. In part as the result of Superintendent Vaughan's leadership, the 1927 Legislature earmarked one-fourth of the revenue from a gross production tax to create a state equalization fund, stipulating that not more than $1.5 million could be so apportioned during a school year. Two years later, the Legislature supplemented this fund by $250,000, by another $175,000 in 1931, and by $600,000 in 1933. Although these were the Depression years, state aid to schools had increased from $1,489,762 in 1927-28 to $8,180,000 in 1935-36, when Vaughan resigned to become president of Northeastern State College at Tahlequah.

The chief weakness of these early efforts was that no objective method had been designed for distributing the funds. The state department put forth every effort to make an equitable distribution but too often allowed the loud wails of the needy districts to be the measure of bare necessity. Undoubtedly, some districts received more than their share while others, equally deserving, got little or, in some cases, no state aid.

Just before Vaughan's resignation became effective, the 1937 Legislature passed its first real state aid bill by appropriating $8,180,000 from the general revenue fund for each year of the biennium–really a milestone in the history of Oklahoma education. Governor E. W. Marland appointed A. L. Crable, the director of correspondence study at Oklahoma A & M, to complete the term of office which had begun in January 1935. It was in part Crable's leadership, in cooperation with other educators and associations in the state, that prompted the Legislature to increase its appropriation to $12,800,000 for each year of the biennium. This law also extended the high school year to 9 months and greatly increased the number of approved junior and senior high schools. Crable received specific funds from the Legislature to establish the position of director of curriculum in the state department.

The Program of State Aid Today

With modifications, the program of state aid established in 1935–supplemented by additional funds from larger appropriations or from additional sources of revenue in successive legislative sessions–is the program of state aid that Oklahoma followed for the next 30 years. These legislative appropriations have never been easy to procure, but the state superintendent and the department have consistently cooperated with the Oklahoma Education Association, the Oklahoma Congress of Parents and Teachers, and the State School Boards Association in presenting the schools' needs as clearly and fairly as possible.

The competition for revenue funds remains a permanent condition. Generally, earmarked funds have not benefited all segments of public education, because in many instances funds raised for the public schools have been placed in the state's general revenue fund and appropriated for other purposes. In the 1964-65 school year, the grand total available for the public schools was $217,595,744. Of this amount, $87,336,525 (about 40 percent) came from state sources, and $48,522,031 represented the Legislature's appropriation paid to school districts as state aid (19). The following year, state aid increased to $65,540,880.

When the separate or segregated schools provided for in the original constitution were discontinued, the 4-mill levy—a countywide levy apportioned to school districts on an average daily attendance basis—reserved for these segregated schools was now continued by law for the use of all public schools. By certifying the need, a district may also have a levy of 20 mills, and if a majority of electors vote, an excess levy of 5 mills. In addition to these levies, a district may vote to authorize an additional 10 mills as a local support levy. Funds from all of these levies go into the general operating fund of the school districts. Schools may also authorize a building fund levy of 5 mills. But public school finance is not permanently solved, because there are so many variables within the framework, and the future will undoubtedly bring additional needs.

Federal School Funds

From territorial days, Oklahoma has benefited from federal money. Since federal law exempted Indian lands from taxation, the government had to assume responsibility for supporting local schools. The Oklahoma State Department of Education has found federal money helpful and necessary, and it has little complaint about bureaucracy in its administration.

State Superintendent Oliver Hodge pointed out that the state department had been responsible for allocating and disbursing $21 million in federal funds under various special acts. This does not include school lunch money or Indian education funds and does not include vocational education aid disbursed by the State Board for Vocational Education through the department's vocational education division. Dr. Hodge added:

> In appropriating these millions, Congress reaffirms the principle and declares that states and local communities have, and must retain, control over the primary responsibility for public education. However, when Congress appropriates such sums, it expects that they be accounted for, and it is interested in the worth of such programs. It therefore behooves all recipients to (a) use the funds for the purposes they are intended, (b) invest them in the most efficient and effective manner, and (c) properly account for every penny received (20).

When Congress passed the National Defense Education Act of 1958, it originally provided for funds under Title III to be matched by school districts who wished to acquire materials and equipment to improve instruction in science, mathematics, and foreign languages. Title III was expanded in October 1964 to include history, geography, civics, English, and reading. Oklahoma's allocation for 1965-66 under Title III was $1,153,000. All but two high school districts participated in the program 1 or 2 years, but districts failing to make the required local financial effort did not receive these funds. Over an 8-year period, this program has used more than $14 million in state federal funds, and the present requests are greater than the funds available.

Title V-A of NDEA provides federal funds for testing and counseling guidance where properly certified personnel are available to administer the program. In 1958-59, only 67 programs were approved and 15,634 ninth-graders tested. In 1966, the eighth year of its operation, tests were given to 37,563 ninth-graders. The state plan has been amended now to provide for elementary school guidance.

Title X of NDEA, now supplemented by Title V of the Elementary and Secondary Education Act (ESEA) of 1965, provides funds for improving state department programs for gathering, compiling, analyzing, and disseminating educational data. The state department has planned to install terminal data-processing equipment to serve a network of many centers established by school districts and other subagencies throughout the state.

Title V of ESEA provided $231,000 to strengthen the state department, enabling it to purchase equipment and employ additional personnel. It already has been of assistance to the department's curriculum division; finance division; instruction division; certification and teacher education; special education; and health, safety, physical and driver education. It has provided assistance for the guidance, informational services, and school lunch divisions, and it has enabled the department to expand its special professional library. It would be difficult to overestimate the value of this program.

Title I of ESEA provides funds for improving and increasing the education of the educationally deprived and disadvantaged youth. In 1965-66, Oklahoma was allotted $17,393,688 for these purposes. By March 1966, some 697 projects from 748 school districts had been approved to spend $50,843,705. These programs have enabled the school districts to employ additional teachers, administrative assistants, clerks, health workers, psychologists, and teacher aides. Also, districts have purchased equipment and materials and have organized in-service training programs so as to more effectively implement this program.

Title II of ESEA supplements present expenditures for books, library, and educational materials for pupils and teachers. The state department receives 5 percent of the funds allocated for administering the program. The law provides for loaning these materials to private schools, but the Oklahoma attorney general ruled in September 1965 that neither state nor school districts can legally make these loans (21). Thus, the U.S. Commissioner of Education contracts directly with other agencies, and $1,266,000 is held from the Oklahoma allotment to provide this service.

There has been considerable prejudice against the state's receiving money from the federal government, and many people and a large part of the press for years have regarded it a capital sin to recommend any kind of a new tax. Despite this, the State Department of Education and the Oklahoma Education Association have worked together to secure more finances for education. The issue between the two has been what financing is necessary to provide competitive teachers' salaries, proper teacher-student ratios, and adequate facilities to give the children of the state the quality of educational services considered minimal for today's world.

A considerable part of this outcry against federal money and taxes has come from far-right extremists, who are well financed and organized in the state. They have neatly packaged their economic doctrines against federal financing with the emblem of the cross and the flag.

Despite the prejudices of many Oklahomans and the fulminations of the far right, the state increasingly needs to use federal funds on the local level to support education. Explosions in knowledge and population have given us a heritage undreamed of at the beginning of this century. It is conservatively estimated that more than 50 percent of the value of our resources today lies in the field of intangible knowledge (such as technical know-how). Local political boundary lines have less significance in the geography of everyday life. Thus, the political fiber and fabric of our country must respond to changes in the economic body, regardless of political partisanship, and the state must rely on these new federal programs to meet the challenge of this changing world.

It is not unusual in this century for an individual to have had more than $50,000 in public and private funds invested in his education. He starts out in life "affected with public interest," and it is our schools which will pass a greater part of our heritage from generation to generation. A properly educated individual may easily have an earning potential of $250,000 or even millions of dollars. In our affluent society, instantaneous prosperity may well come to a man brought up in poverty, if the man is properly educated and placed where his knowledge and skills have the greatest value.

The idea that high purpose and productive initiative must be limited to individual and local dimensions went out with the development of modern transportation, communication, and industrial techniques. Regardless of political partisanship, the economic laws of private enterprise will determine the use of federal instruments in many areas which were previously considered local.

SCHOOL DISTRICTS AND CONSOLIDATION

Early Efforts To Consolidate

The Territorial Legislature enacted a law in 1891 to organize school districts in the western lands opened by homesteaders, squared 3 miles on each side (one-fourth the size of a township) or 9 square miles per district. On admission to statehood 16 years later, Oklahoma Territory contained 3,441 school districts with only 185 high schools, all in cities or towns. Forty new counties had been created in Indian Territory or the eastern part of the state, and these were divided into 2,200 school districts in 1908 (22). For the most part, these eastern school districts were much larger than those in Oklahoma Territory.

The law permitted the county superintendent to organize districts, and the Department of Education worked closely with these officials during this early period. But in his first biennial report, the state superintendent wrote that he found a number of school districts too small and with too few children to justify schools with even a minimum grade school curriculum, to say nothing about opportunities for high school education.

The Legislature passed an act in 1895 enabling two or more districts to unite to offer instruction in the higher grades at a central school while maintaining the district schools. Four common school districts with territory in Payne and Pawnee Counties formed the first consolidated district at Quay in 1903. But for the most part, this plan was not successful, and though the law was modified, only a few districts were organized as union graded districts during the next 15 years. The poor roads and bridgeless creeks that handicapped transportation presented one of the major barriers.

It was obvious by 1908 that students in many small districts should travel greater distances to larger schools. Stating his position plainly in his first annual report, State Superintendent E. D. Camerson said: "In some of these districts, we will put into operation the plan of conveying the children to and from school every day. We favor this plan of large districts, graded schools and conveying children to and from school every day" (23). The report continued: "If an average of four districts would unite in this way to run one school, our state would soon be filled with rural district schools doing good work in the higher grades, and our district schools would be as good as any in the world" (24).

In the meantime, the problem was becoming more acute due to a shift in population; Oklahoma was no longer strictly rural. New methods of farming, the tractor, and other mechanized operations were causing thousands to leave farm communities for industrial areas. In effect, the process of urbanization gradually pulled people away from localities so that schools could no longer be supported and were no longer needed, though the buildings stood for years as monuments to the earlier days.

As mentioned earlier, State Superintendent R. H. Wilson secured support from the new State Board for Reorganization, and the State Aid Law of 1911 enabled this board and Wilson to consolidate school districts. Nevertheless, by 1914, the number of school districts had increased to 5,880. The 1919 Legislature attempted to reduce the number of schools by giving county superintendents arbitrary power to annex school districts, and it allowed them to disorganize districts with fewer than eight children by annexing to adjoining districts. But county superintendents were elected officials, reluctant to close schools the communities wanted to keep, so little progress was made in abolishing local districts.

Period of Active Consolidation, 1915-30

By the time Oklahoma was admitted as a state, it had gradually solved its transportation problems with a fair system of dirt roads stretching across the territory and bridges spanning most of the larger streams. The state had constructed some permanent highways in 1915, and it was at this time that public school consolidation really gained its impetus. In 1918, 86 consolidated districts were providing transportation, and 2 years later, this number had increased to 184. Motorized vehicles gradually replaced the horse-drawn wagons, so that the Legislature legalized them for transporting pupils in 1919. Local districts generally paid for this transportation until the General Equalization Aid Law of 1935 made transportation a part of the minimum program for Oklahoma public schools.

State Superintendent R. H. Wilson wrote in 1916 that "the records in some counties have been carelessly kept and county superintendents are unable to give complete information concerning the consolidated and union graded districts in their counties" (25). Several districts, after voting for consolidation, had not voted bonds for central buildings and had been forced to disorganize. Both the state board and the Legislature made several attempts to bring about reforms. For instance, the board published a bulletin in September 1911 entitled *Rural School Consolidation*, outlining the requirements and procedures for consolidation, as well as a survey of progress up to that time.

Two years later, in 1913, the Legislature tried to help newly organized districts and at the same time give an impetus to consolidation by appropriating $100,000 for buildings. The Legislature required the following: that (a) new school buildings be located centrally, (b) the consolidated districts have an area of 25 square miles each, and have a minimum evaluation of $500,000, and (c) transportation be provided for students living 2 or more miles from schools. It failed to appropriate funds for this purpose in 1915 but in later sessions continued to aid buildings, and this undoubtedly promoted consolidation.

By 1920, the cost of transportation still appeared to be the major problem in creating large central schools; 98 consolidated districts reported that they spent 20 percent of their entire operating costs for this purpose. This delayed consolidation, particularly in those areas where evaluations were extremely low and it was impossible for them to meet this additional expense.

The most active period of consolidation occurred from 1915 to 1930, during the superintendencies of R. H. Wilson, M. A. Nash, and John Vaughan. Fortunately, they served with boards composed of men with vision and initiative, whose chief aim was to make high school education accessible to every boy and girl in the state. It was during this period that terminal education moved first to the high school and then beyond to college and the university. This could not have been accomplished without the dedicated efforts of numerous able county superintendents. It is impossible to name every superintendent in the 77 counties who contributed so greatly to improve the state's education through consolidation, but particularly outstanding were H. H. Porter of Jackson County and Milton C. Butler of Greer County.

Transportation Solved

Consolidation brought all school-age children to central buildings. The union graded school provided for the lower grades to remain in the district's original buildings, while the upper-grade students were transported to the central location where suitable facilities and curriculums could be provided. This enabled the districts to pay higher teachers' salaries, follow a higher standard of maintenance, and provide transportation. Each morning, in every community, buses with similar equipment and personnel line up in front of the local schools to begin the day's run. This takes place routinely throughout the school year. The state department has carried heavy responsibilities in developing and administering this important program, and it represents one of the significant factors in the increased cost of education.

From 1935 to 1945, hundreds of school buses rolled over all-weather roads built from material obtained locally, such as sand, gravel, crushed rock, and in more fortunate communities, asphalt. And since World War II, Oklahoma has constructed thousands of miles of first-class roads. By 1945, many rural schools no longer were operating but were transferring their elementary as well as high school pupils and providing transportation routes through the districts. And by this time, the state was helping districts transport all of their transferred pupils.

The 1947 Law

The Legislature finally enacted a stronger law in 1947 to bring about school district reorganization. This law stated that any district not maintaining its school for 1 year would be annexed, and if the average daily attendance fell below 13 in any elementary school district, it would be annexed unless it could be declared an "isolated" district (26). It also provided for a reduction in the number of small and uneconomical high schools.

By September 1, 1950, the total number of school districts had been reduced to 2,177, from 4,450 in 1946, and more than 1,100 of these were not maintaining home schools. Many other districts were hard-pressed financially and suffered from inadequate standards in both their elementary and secondary schools. By the 1964-65 school year, the districts were reduced to 1,118, and by September 1, 1966, the finance division reported only 998 school districts in the state. The Oklahoma State Department of Education has attempted to administer the annexation laws fairly and, at the same time, provide proper and adequate educational opportunity for all.

SPECIAL PROGRAMS

Vocational Rehabilitation

As a direct result of World War I, Congress enacted "an Act for the promotion of the vocational rehabilitation of persons disabled in industry, or otherwise, and their return to civil employment." Passed on June 2, 1920, it was known as the "civilian rehabilitation program" to distinguish it from a veterans program organized the previous year. One of the most far-reaching pieces of social legislation of the day, it established one of the first national grant-in-aid programs designed to give financial support to a state-administered operation (27).

Oklahoma initiated its own program when the Tenth Oklahoma Legislature enacted Senate Joint Resolution No. 39 in March 1925, accepting the terms of the federal act and pledging the good faith of the state in carrying it out. Unfortunately, it did not provide an appropriation for its support, but the state board accepted the responsibility and operated it for almost 2 years with funds contributed by civic clubs and interested individuals, matched dollar for dollar by the federal government. The Eleventh Oklahoma Legislature then voted an emergency appropriation of $5,000, effective in March 1927, for the remainder of the first biennium, and an appropriation of $19,267 for each year of the following biennium. Two years later, in September 1929, the Legislature made the program a division of the State Department of Education.

The rehabilitation program experienced a slow but constant growth during the next few years, expanding to include persons with hidden disabilities, such as lung and cardiac conditions, as well as those suffering from emotional and mental illnesses, mental retardation, and character disorders. This development can best be seen through a comparison of figures from 1929 to 1965 (28).

Biennium	Number rehabilitated	Total caseload	Expenditures
1929-30	188	348	$ Not given
1939-40	762	1,566	$ 223,271
1949-50	2,040	5,057	$1,157,717
1959-60	3,240	8,019	$3,526,624
1965 (single year)	2,402	10,974	$3,238,238

The figures given above adequately dramatize this dynamic national movement as it affected Oklahoma, but they do not tell the entire story. The state's financial investment has been recovered many times over, the most important result being the reclamation of thousands of disabled men and women who subsequently enriched their communities and the State of Oklahoma.

Special Education

The Legislature passed the first special education law in 1945 to provide for individual children whose handicaps made it impossible or impractical for them to benefit from regular school programs. Subsequently, it has amended the law a number of times and now authorizes the districts to organize classes for children who are mentally retarded, mentally handicapped, physically handicapped, and emotionally disturbed. Since it is not practical for every district to organize such classes, the law provides for reimbursing districts for transportation or boarding costs up to but not exceeding $450 per year if children are transferred for placement in special classes.

The Legislature placed the Children's Memorial Hospital in Oklahoma City under the state board's control in 1957, and in 1965 it was placed under the supervision of the Division of Special Education. The department also provides counseling and job placement services for students through its Division of Vocational Rehabilitation. The cooperation and coordination of these two agencies has provèd to be a major factor in providing a successful and realistic educational program for handicapped children.

The U.S. Office of Education's spot surveys have found that more than 10 percent of our nation's schoolchildren are handicapped, but Oklahoma discovered these figures to be very conservative when it conducted surveys in its own communities. Despite the problem of providing educational programs to meet the needs of handicapped youngsters, the department continues to strive to live up to its philosophy that all children are entitled to an education, and this is becoming more of a reality in Oklahoma year by year.

School Lunch Program

Congress placed the school lunch program on a permanent basis on July 4, 1946, by voting funds to assist in providing nonprofit lunches to both public and private schools of high school grade or under. The U.S. Department of Agriculture is responsible for carrying out the provisions through the state departments of education. In Oklahoma, as in several other states, the State Department of Public Welfare has handled the commodity distribution, but the State Department of Education's school lunch division handles the functions of the program. This division has two primary objectives: to increase the consumption of food in order to develop a better domestic market for agricultural commodities, and to assist local communities in developing, maintaining, operating, and expanding a program to provide from one-third to one-half of the nutritive requirements of schoolchildren.

The state matches each dollar paid by the federal government with $3 from its own resources as long as its per-capita income equals or exceeds the average per-capita income of the United States. Oklahoma, participating on a limited basis with a small number of schools in 1943, now serves 225,000 pupils daily. From 1947-48 to the 1963-64 school year, the total number of meals served children grew from 16,706,247 to 37,289,730. The local communities contributed more than $11,700,000 to the lunch program in 1963-64 to pay for lunches, labor, and equipment.

The state appropriated $150,000 for the fiscal year beginning June 30, 1965, to administer the National School Lunch Program, but the state had provided no funds up to this time to reimburse schools as had several other states. The state furnishes supplies each month to the schools and mails a monthly newsletter with a list of foods in plentiful supply, menus, and recipes. The newsletter also emphasizes the contractual responsibilities so that schools are posted on items affecting the program's operation. Workshops for food service personnel are held on college campuses during summer months, and approximately 1,000 register for this one-week training program each year. The school lunch division maintains liaison with the State Department of Public Health, the State Department of Public Welfare, the Oklahoma and National School Food Service Association, as well as the Department of Education's other divisions and architects who design school buildings (29).

Indian Education

From 1830 to 1840, a number of mission teachers accompanied the tribes when they were removed to Indian Territory and established schools, usually separating the boys' schools from the girls'. Each of the five civilized tribes provided facilities for educating its own young people. The bicameral Legislature of the Western Cherokees passed the first school aid law in 1832 to provide for five schools and to employ Sequoyah at an annual salary of $400 to supervise the teaching of his syllabary.

In recent years, the Oklahoma State Department of Education, through its Indian education division, has been able to assist in the education of Indian children under a contract with the U.S. Department of the Interior's Bureau of Indian Affairs, based on the Johnson-O'Malley Act of 1936. Prior to 1947, the Indian bureau administered the entire program, but since then the State Department of Education has supervised it.

In general, the Indian children have a good attendance record in the public schools, staying on through graduation from the eighth grade and even from high school. During the 1964-65 school term, there was an increase of 71 pupils in the eighth grade and 159 graduates over the previous year. These students are taking an increasing interest in post-high school training, and large numbers of them are seeking placement in both vocational schools and colleges.

Obtaining free school lunches is an ever-increasing problem for the Indian child, especially if his family resides inside the city limits of an incorporated town or city of 500 or more, because, according to the Oklahoma plan, he is not eligible for the aid. Also, each individual school district and its board has the sole responsibility for determining who is indigent. Many who need aid are not receiving it at present, but there were 425 districts with 426 schools in 60 counties (of the state's 77 counties) participating in the program during the 1963-64 school year, with 12,634 Indians included in a total of 165,270 pupils (30).

At present, there are two area offices administering Indian educational affairs, one in eastern Oklahoma at Muskogee and the other at Anadarko in the western part of the state. There were 338 schools enrolling 9,912 Indian pupils in Muskogee and 75 schools enrolling 2,955 in Anadarko in the 1964-65 school year.

RELATIONS WITH OTHER ORGANIZATIONS

The Curriculum Improvement Commission

The Oklahoma Secondary School Curriculum Improvement Commission was organized in 1952 by the Oklahoma Secondary Principals Association. In 1955, the name was changed to the Oklahoma Curriculum Improvement Commission, and the sponsors now are the Oklahoma Association of School Administrators, the Oklahoma Secondary School Principals Association, the Oklahoma Department of Elementary School Administrators, the Oklahoma Department of Classroom Teachers, and the Oklahoma Association for Supervision and Curriculum Development. The membership of the commission is selected from these sponsoring organizations and from the 12 geographical districts of the Oklahoma Education Association.

A unique organization, the Oklahoma Curriculum Improvement Commission is incorporated under the laws of the state and is financed by dues paid by constituent members. All school systems receive curriculum guides, which the commission produces free of charge. This self-perpetuating commission has about 35 members, chosen from all sections of the state and from all levels of instruction. A plan of rotating membership ensures a steady but orderly revision of the roster. It has written, published, and distributed 30 curriculum guides, including revisions. Generally, the vertical approach (kindergarten through twelfth grade) has been followed in preparing each guide.

The director of the curriculum division of the State Department of Education is the executive secretary of the commission, and the department furnishes secretarial assistance, office space, and equipment. The commission is an extension of the curriculum division and supplements its program in a definite and satisfactory manner. It helps to organize and promote meetings, conferences, and workshops designed to improve in-service training in most of the subject matter fields. Each year, the commission completes a volume of *Successful Ventures in Contemporary Education* and sends free copies to schools within the state.

The Oklahoma Commission on Educational Administration

The Oklahoma Association of School Administrators (OASA) created the Oklahoma Commission on Educational Administration (OCEA) for the specific purpose of promoting better educational administration. The commission incorporated a state committee as its policy-making body in November 1955, as a nonprofit corporation under the provisions of the state's laws. This committee holds a minimum of six regular meetings each year and collects dues from school systems, individuals, and groups to finance its activities and the work of the commission.

The committee's scope and importance have grown to the point that it has broadened its membership to include representatives from other organizations of professional school personnel and those with allied interests. At present, in addition to the OASA, the state committee consists of representatives from the State School Boards Association, the Oklahoma Congress of Parents and Teachers, the Oklahoma Association of Secondary School Principals, the Oklahoma Association of Elementary School Administrators, the State Department of Education, colleges of education, and coordinators appointed by the state chairmen to represent the Oklahoma Education Association districts.

The purpose of the commission is to help improve all phases of public school education in Oklahoma. It cooperates with other agencies in a wide variety of specific projects and activities, jointly sponsored by both educators and laymen. OCEA has financed the publication of an impressive list of documents and research studies designed specifically for use in Oklahoma and has distributed them without charge (31). The State Department of Education furnished secretarial assistance, office space, and necessary equipment at the state capitol.

Most of the publications by the OCEA's affiliated groups are shared. Copies of newsletters are exchanged, and each has permission to use this material. Many of these newsletters and bulletins are received by the same people, but each has its own mailing list. Publications also are distributed at the state committee's regular meetings.

At each meeting, representatives of the groups affiliated with the state committee report on projects and activities in progress and those planned for the future. Members are thus able to render assistance whenever it is needed.

STATE SUPERINTENDENT OLIVER HODGE

Oliver Hodge filed for the Office of State Superintendent of Public Instruction in 1946, while he was county superintendent of schools in Tulsa County. He won nomination over the incumbent and led his ticket in the November election. A former classroom teacher, principal, athletic coach, and graduate instructor at the University of Oklahoma, he led the department during the period of its greatest change. The year he took office, the new school code was enacted. The U.S. Supreme Court decision on school integration made him responsible for implementing it. Hodge outlined a dignified and successful program to accomplish this, and it has been activated.

The shortage of teachers during this period vied with the problem of upgrading professional qualifications; but with the philosophy that quality comes first, 99 percent of the public school teachers employed in recent years have had at least a bachelor's degree. This has placed Oklahoma at the head of the nation in this category for a number of years (32). It was also under Hodge's leadership that the unworkable, exclusive one-book adoption was changed in 1947 to a system of multiple selections.

The State Department of Education carries many responsibilities of which some of its citizens are unaware. For instance, the Legislature passed a law in 1963 authorizing annual workshops for newly elected school board members (33). The statutes assign many similar responsibilities to the State Board of Education (34). The total state expenditure from the general fund in the school year 1946-47 was $46,181,682; by the school year 1964-65, it had increased to $182,744,540 (35). The state department is a big business operation and must have the best leadership that Oklahoma can offer.

Dr. Hodge died in January 1968, during his sixth 4-year term. An editorial in the *Daily Oklahoman* paid one of the many tributes to Hodge. It said in part:

> In the death of Dr. Oliver Hodge, the state has lost not only the head of its public school system but a genuine leader in education . . . .
>
> Holding a political job, Dr. Hodge was less politician on the surface than almost any other elected official during his career. He was an idealist in education and although there were legal restrictions that somewhat limited his activities, many improvements can be laid to his influence and quiet balancing of the possible with the impossible . . . (36).

To fill the unexpired term, Governor Dewey F. Bartlett appointed D. D. Creech, superintendent of schools in Pryor, Oklahoma, who took office as state superintendent in April 1968. A native Oklahoman, Dr. Creech had held superintendencies at Fargo, Arnett, and Velma, before going to Pryor in 1960.

With the addition of federal money and state matching funds, the schools of Oklahoma will continue to attempt to meet the challenge of educating young people for a complex, technological world community. There are few educators in the state as qualified to face this challenge as Dr. Creech. How well he succeeds will depend not on his own ability and that of his staff, but on the people of Oklahoma—legislators, teachers, school board members, interested laymen, administrators, and parents.

IN CONCLUSION

Twentieth-century Oklahoma has a nineteenth-century heritage that is unique in many ways. Its roots go back to the pioneer period, but its history is relatively short. However brief chronologically, this history is conterminous with the greatest revolution or explosion of knowledge our world has known. This has meant an extremely rapid adjustment to changing conditions. Some of the pioneers still living have seen the state's educational opportunities grow from 6-month terms in one-room county schools to terms of 180 days in centralized, modern, consolidated schools and great universities.

During the first 15 years of this century, Oklahoma was largely a rural agricultural society, consisting of a family enterprise system in which each family farmed a homestead of 160 acres. The family produced the greatest part of its food supply on its own land. When drought, hail, flood, or grasshoppers ravaged the land, there was much privation. Under these conditions, eighth-grade grammar school education was more adequate than a bachelor's degree today.

The development of revolutionary means of transportation and communication produced new conditions. For example, when better highways were built, it was no longer necessary to have a school within walking distance of every child. The ability to transport students quickly and safely gave the annexation and consolidation movement impetus; the one-room school became obsolete and was replaced by larger and newer schools with modern facilities.

The 5,580 school districts in 1914 were reduced to approximately 900 by January 1965 and to 856 by May 1968, as the state became rapidly urbanized. A concentration of large numbers of students in one school is not only sociably desirable but makes it possible to offer a better curriculum and adopt the new educational media. It also makes it economically feasible to institute a school lunch program.

FOOTNOTES

1. There were several land openings. The opening of the "unassigned" lands, or Old Oklahoma, was the first, April 22, 1889.
2. Superintendent of Public Instruction, *Second Biennial Report* (1908), pp. 80-81, 107-108.
3. Personal files of Guy H. Lambert, former county superintendent of Noble County.
4. Joe C. Jackson, "Survey of Education in Eastern Oklahoma, 1907-1915," *Chronicles of Oklahoma*, XXIX (1951), 200-21.
5. Oklahoma, *Constitution* (1907), Schedule 2.
6. *Ibid.*, art. 13, sec. 5.
7. *Ibid.*, art. 13, sec. 1.
8. Oklahoma, *School Laws* (1967), art. 1, secs. 5b, 5c.
9. Federal aid has come into Oklahoma in many forms since statehood, but the administration of these funds has followed different patterns.
10. Superintendent of Public Instruction, *Third Biennial Report* (1910), pp. 30, 32.
11. Oklahoma, Secretary of State, comp., *Oklahoma Red Book*, Vol. II. Oklahoma City: Office of the Secretary of State, 1912.
12. Board of Education, "Rural School Consolidation Bulletin, 1911," p. 5. Bound in a collection of miscellaneous bulletins in the Professional Library, Department of Education, Oklahoma City.
13. *Ibid.*, p. 29.
14. "Comparable Data, 1909-1910, and 1964-1965," *Twenty-Ninth Biennial Report* (Oklahoma City: Department of Education, 1962), pp. 292-93.
15. Board of Education, *Eleventh Biennial Report* (1926), pp. 7-9.
16. Oklahoma, *Constitution* (1907), art. 13, sec. 6.
17. Oklahoma, *Constitution* (1907 as amended in 1946), art. 13, sec. 6.
18. Department of Education, *Twenty-Ninth Biennial Report* (1962), pp. 117, 242.
19. Department of Education, *Thirty-First Biennial Report* (1966), pp. 252-54.
20. Oliver Hodge, "Oklahoma's Federal School Funds," *Oklahoma Teacher,* XLVII, No. 8 (April 1966), 12-15.
21. Attorney general's opinion in file of deputy state superintendent of schools, September 16, 1965.
22. Clay W. Kerr, "Development of the Legal Structure and the Program of High Schools in Oklahoma" (unpublished Ph.D. dissertation, University of Oklahoma, Norman, 1956), p. 78.
23. Superintendent of Public Instruction, *First Biennial Report* (1908).
24. *Ibid.*
25. Department of Education, *Sixth Biennial Report* (1916), pp. 16-17.
26. Oklahoma, *School Code* (1949), art. 7, secs. 1-3, and Superintendent of Public Instruction, *Annual Bulletin for Elementary and Secondary Schools,* No. 113-N

(Oklahoma City: Department of Education, July 1967), p. 12. If pupils live 16 miles or more from their school, the district would be declared an "isolated" district.

27. Interview with Voyle C. Scurlock, former director of the Division of Vocational Rehabilitation of the State Department of Education.

28. *Ibid.*

29. Department of Education, *Thirty-First Biennial Report* (1966), pp. 132-37.

30. Department of Education, *Annual Report of Indian Education Division, 1967.* In compliance with its contract, one year the state spent $64,126 for instruction, $11,231 for transportation, $330,912 for lunches, and $12,145 for other services.

31. For example, Guy Lambert and Guy Rankin, *An Outline History of the State Department of Education, 1900-1965* (Oklahoma City: Oklahoma Commission on Educational Administration, 1968).

32. National Education Association, Research Division, *Rankings of the States* (Washington, D.C.: The Association, 1959), p. 17; (1962), p. 24; and (1963), p. 27. Oklahoma ranked first in the nation with the number of teachers with a bachelor's degree or better. National Education Association, Research Division, *Teacher Supply and Demand in Public Schools 1967,* research report R18 (Washington, D.C.: The Association, 1967), p. 61. This ranks Oklahoma 99.9 percent.

33. Oklahoma, *School Laws* (1963), secs. 47a, 47b, 47c, pp. 38-39.

34. Oklahoma, *School Laws* (1967), art. 2, pp. 23-29.

35. See Appendix C, Table 1.

36. Editorial, "Good Public Servant," *Daily Oklahoman,* January 16, 1968.

BIBLIOGRAPHY

Public Documents

Oklahoma. *Constitution* (1907, as amended to January 1, 1968).

——*School Code* (1949).

——*School Laws* (1963, 1967).

——Secretary of State, comp. *Oklahoma Red Book.* 2 vols. Oklahoma City: Office of the Secretary of State, 1912.

——*Statutes* (1961 and 1967 Supplement).

Books

Dale, Edward Everett, and Wardell, Morris L. *History of Oklahoma.* Englewood Cliffs, N.J.: Prentice-Hall, 1948.

Department of Education. *Oklahoma Educational Directory.* Oklahoma City: The Department, 1917-68.

Lambert, Guy, and Rankin, Guy. *An Outline History of the State Department of Education, 1900-1965.* Oklahoma City: Oklahoma Commission on Educational Administration, 1968.

McReynolds, Edwin C.; Merriott, Alice; and Faulconer, Estele. *Oklahoma, The Story of Its Past and Present.* Norman: University of Oklahoma Press, 1961.

Superintendent of Public Instruction. *Annual Bulletin for Elementary and Secondary Schools.* No. 113-N. Oklahoma City: Department of Education, July 1967.

Reports

Board of Education. *Biennial Reports.* Oklahoma City: Department of Education, 1908-66.

Department of Education. *Annual Report of Indian Education Division, 1967.* Oklahoma City: The Department, 1967.

National Education Association, Research Division. *Rankings of the States.* Washington, D.C.: The Association, 1959, 1962, 1963.

——*Teacher Supply and Demand in Public Schools.* Research report R18. Washington, D.C.: The Association, 1967.

Superintendents of Public Instruction. *Biennial Reports.* Oklahoma City: Department of Education, 1908-66.

Articles and Periodicals

Chronicles of Oklahoma. A quarterly publication of the Oklahoma Historical Society, Historical Building, Oklahoma City.

Davidson, Oscar W. "Early History of Oklahoma Education." *Chronicles of Oklahoma,* XXVII (1949), 354-72.

——"Education at Statehood." *Chronicles of Oklahoma,* XXVII (1950), 63-80.

Editorial, "Good Public Servant." *Daily Oklahoman,* January 16, 1968.

Hodge, Oliver. "Oklahoma's Federal School Funds." *Oklahoma Teacher,* XLVII, No. 8 (April 1966), 12-15.

Jackson, Joe C. "Survey of Education in Eastern Oklahoma, 1907-1915." *Chronicles of Oklahoma,* XXIX (1951), 200-21.

Oklahoma School Herald. Published prior to publication of *Oklahoma Teacher* in 1912. Bound volumes in Oklahoma Historical Society Building, Oklahoma City.

Oklahoma Today. Published quarterly in Oklahoma City by the Industrial Development and Park Department.

Unpublished Material

Attorney general's opinion in file of deputy state superintendent of schools, September 16, 1965.

Board of Education, "Rural School Consolidation Bulletin, 1911." Bound in a collection of miscellaneous bulletins in the Professional Library, Department of Education, Oklahoma City.

Drain, Myrtle. "History of Education of Choctaws and Chickasaws." Unpublished master's thesis, University of Oklahoma, Norman.

Jackson, Joe C. "History of Education in Eastern Oklahoma, 1899-1915." Unpublished Ph.D. dissertation, University of Oklahoma, Norman, 1950.

Kerr, Clay W. "Development of the Legal Structure and the Program of High Schools in Oklahoma." Unpublished Ph.D. dissertation, University of Oklahoma, Norman, 1956.

Other Sources

Board of Education. Complete file of minutes from territorial board to present.

Interviews with M. A. Nash, W. T. Doyel, Ella Hunt, A. L. Crable, Oliver Hodge, Voyle C. Scurlock, and others.

Lambert, Guy H. Personal files.

Appendix A

OKLAHOMA CHIEF STATE SCHOOL OFFICERS

Territorial Superintendents of Public Instruction

In 1890, the date of the first Territorial Legislature, provision was made for the appointment of a territorial superintendent of public instruction. This superintendent, together with the county superintendents, constituted the Territorial Board of Education.

1890-92	J. H. Lawhead
1892-93	J. H. Parker
1893-97	E. D. Cameron
1897-98	Albert O. Nichols
1898-1901	S. N. Hopkins
1901-1907	L. W. Baxter
1907	J. E. Dyche (Jan.-Nov.)

State Board of Education–Nov. 15, 1907, to Mar. 6, 1911

When Oklahoma Territory and Indian Territory merged to form the present State of Oklahoma, no specific legislation was passed creating the State Board of Education, and the Territorial Board of Education became the temporary State Board of Education. The State Board of Education during this interim consisted of the Governor, secretary of state, attorney general, and the state superintendent of public instruction.

State Superintendents of Public Instruction

1907-11	E. D. Cameron
1911-23	R. H. Wilson
1923-27	M. A. Nash
1927-36	John Vaughan
1936-47	A. L. Crable
1947-68	Oliver Hodge
1968-	D. D. Creech

Appendix B

Chart I.--OKLAHOMA TERRITORIES PRIOR TO STATEHOOD

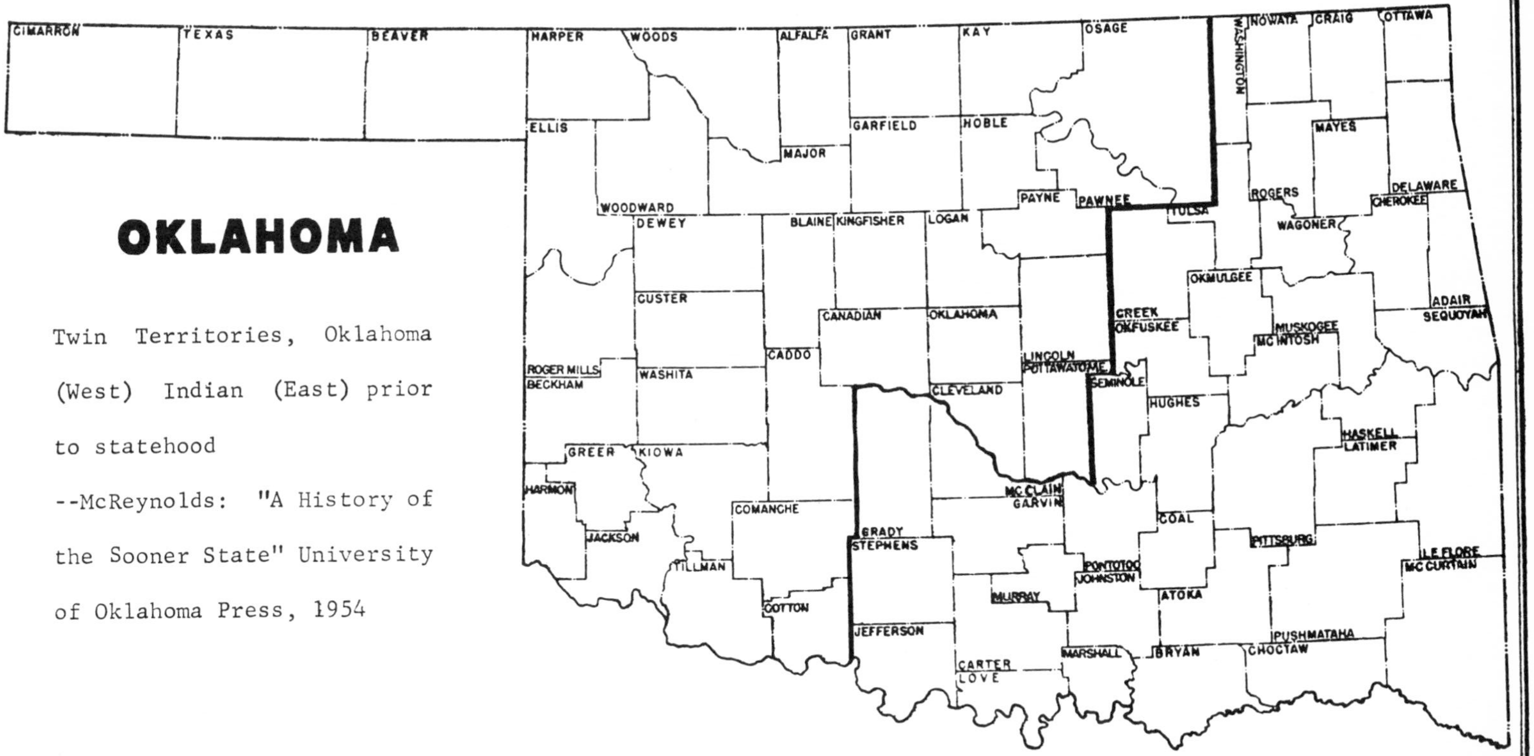

OKLAHOMA

Twin Territories, Oklahoma (West) Indian (East) prior to statehood

--McReynolds: "A History of the Sooner State" University of Oklahoma Press, 1954

Appendix B

Chart II.--OKLAHOMA DEPARTMENT OF EDUCATION, 1959

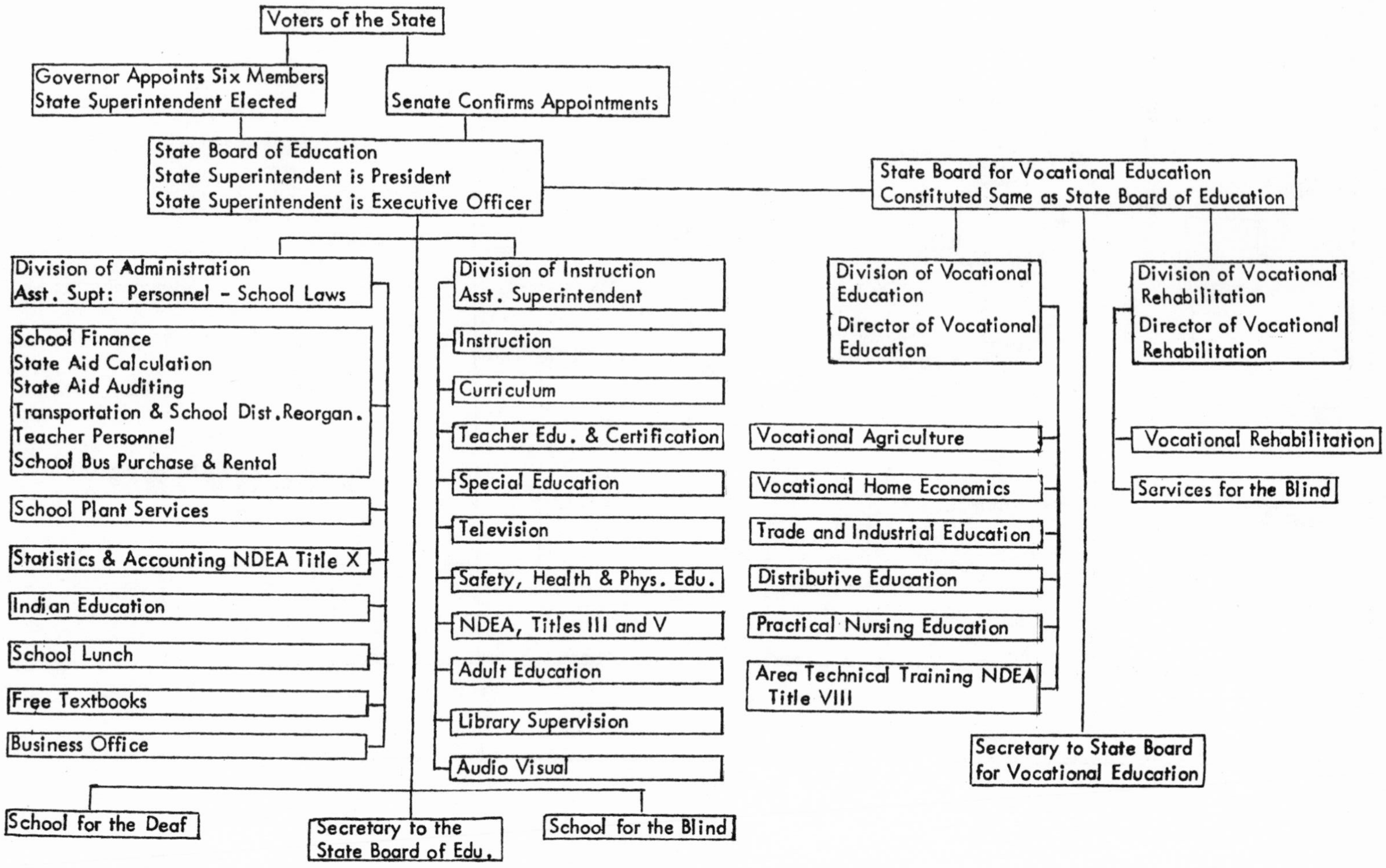

Voters of the State

Governor Appoints Six Members
State Superintendent Elected

Senate Confirms Appointments

State Board of Education
State Superintendent is President
State Superintendent is Executive Officer

State Board for Vocational Education
Constituted Same as State Board of Education

Division of Administration
Asst. Supt: Personnel - School Laws

School Finance
State Aid Calculation
State Aid Auditing
Transportation & School Dist. Reorgan.
Teacher Personnel
School Bus Purchase & Rental

School Plant Services

Statistics & Accounting NDEA Title X

Indian Education

School Lunch

Free Textbooks

Business Office

Division of Instruction
Asst. Superintendent

Instruction

Curriculum

Teacher Edu. & Certification

Special Education

Television

Safety, Health & Phys. Edu.

NDEA, Titles III and V

Adult Education

Library Supervision

Audio Visual

School for the Deaf

Secretary to the State Board of Edu.

School for the Blind

Division of Vocational Education
Director of Vocational Education

Vocational Agriculture

Vocational Home Economics

Trade and Industrial Education

Distributive Education

Practical Nursing Education

Area Technical Training NDEA Title VIII

Secretary to State Board for Vocational Education

Division of Vocational Rehabilitation
Director of Vocational Rehabilitation

Vocational Rehabilitation

Services for the Blind

Appendix B

Chart III.—OKLAHOMA DEPARTMENT OF EDUCATION, 1966

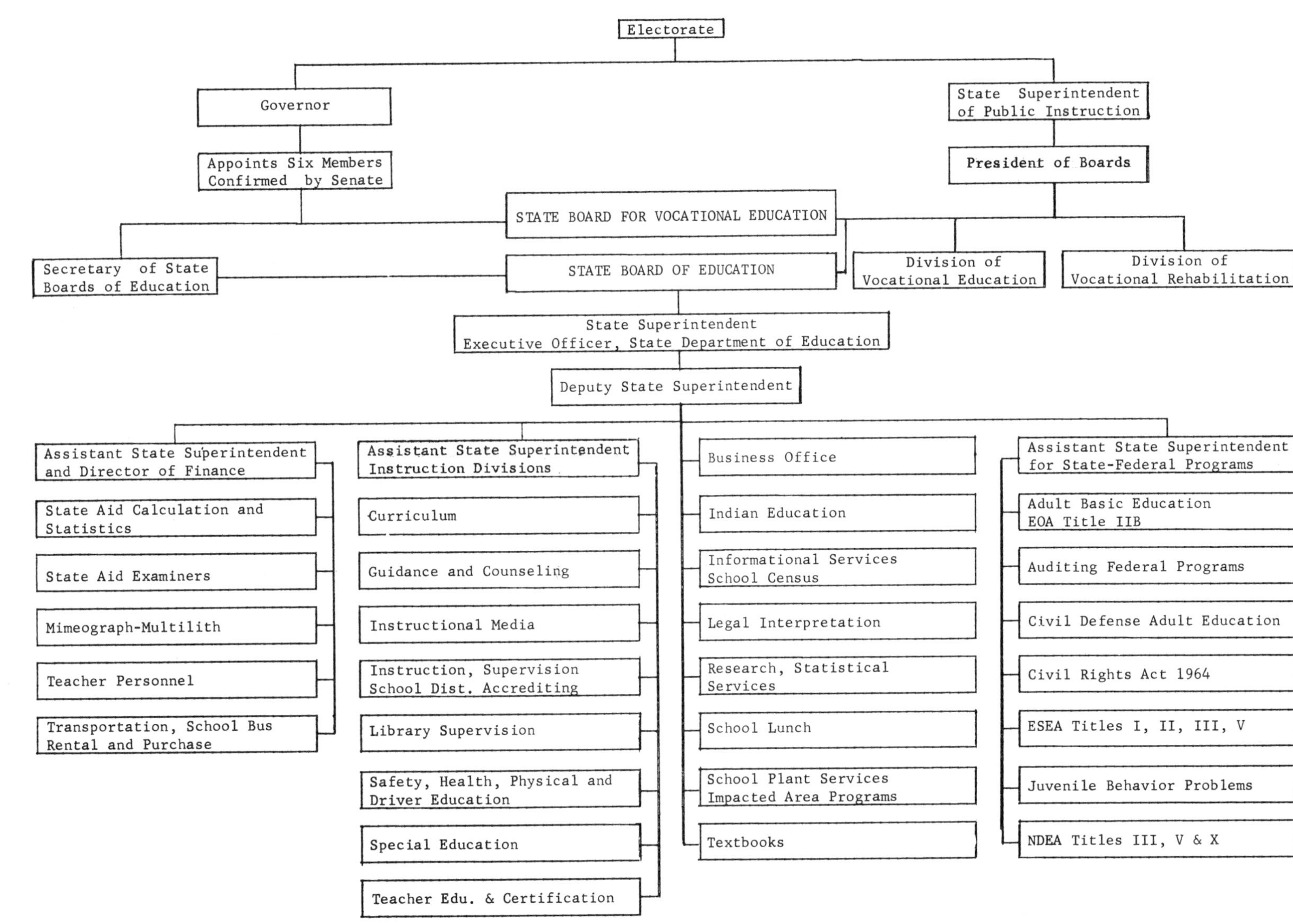

Appendix C

Table 1. – COMPARABLE DATA CONCERNING THE PUBLIC SCHOOLS OF OKLAHOMA BEGINNING WITH 1919-20

School Year	Total A.D.A.	No. of teachers employed	Average annual salary	State aid	Total current expenditure[a]	Per cap. based on A.D.A.	State total net valuation
1919-20	355,998	15,711	745	100,000	$ 22,826,950	$ 64.12	$1,695,797,187
1920-21	390,596	16,611	990	285,000	26,477,161	67.79	1,739,835,008
1921-22	431,519	17,274	1,010	200,000	26,973,599	62.51	1,671,753,031
1922-23	441,037	17,988	1,005	650,000	29,503,560	66.90	1,686,187,934
1923-24	427,345	18,404	1,001	650,000	31,701,334	74.18	1,665,566,451
1924-25	457,413	18,390	1,001	500,000	28,506,483	62.32	1,674,826,952
1925-26	444,905	18,393	1,032	500,000	27,885,900	62.68	1,697,364,213
1926-27	432,086	18,813	1,022	500,000	29,540,764	68.37	1,729,432,830
1927-28	457,983	19,130	991	1,489,763	31,262,378	68.26	1,791,424,587
1928-29	461,808	19,565	1,041	1,489,250	33,574,956	51.04	1,829,674,641
1929-30	470,090	20,146	1,096	1,754,882	31,995,433	68.06	1,851,602,103
1930-31	492,864	19,978	1,120	1,792,522	31,692,896	64.30	1,753,690,249
1931-32	493,244	19,842	1,071	1,398,416	28,272,859	57.32	1,409,663,561
1932-33	491,464	19,510	901	1,491,009	23,105,974	47.01	1,232,731,121
1933-34	492,022	19,300	784	1,412,630	21,081,200	42.84	1,258,686,473
1934-35	501,890	19,617	860	2,810,565	23,158,076	46.14	1,232,928,286
1935-36	497,974	19,858	982	8,180,000	28,077,299	56.38	1,221,659,918
1936-37	498,753	20,459	976	8,454,000	29,034,401	58.21	1,099,735,872
1937-38	492,907	20,874	1,061	12,233,733	32,414,918	65.76	1,103,189,782
1938-39	502,561	20,938	1,083	12,737,945	33,307,502	66.28	1,070,560,468
1939-40	485,290	20,980	1,040	11,436,321	31,507,591	64.93	1,054,067,835
1940-41	463,763	20,276	1,069	11,359,758	31,343,562	67.59	1,061,983,422
1941-42	439,238	19,391	1,140	8,208,443	32,015,748	72.89	1,092,050,565
1942-43	413,205	18,084	1,284	7,555,055	31,798,188	76.95	1,248,906,651
1943-44	386,061	17,272	1,418	8,717,239	34,684,381	89.84	1,302,573,500
1944-45	383,028	16,931	1,506	9,542,543	36,083,921	94.21	1,315,052,379
1945-46	391,337	17,863	1,815	15,524,922	44,244,242	113.06	1,391,238,021
1946-47	405,667	18,312	1,837	17,086,149	46,181,682	113.84	1,423,516,463
1947-48	399,966	18,097	2,209	18,764,958	57,368,768	143.43	1,554,090,583
1948-49	395,631	18,447	2,306	18,092,215	62,656,628	158.37	1,402,276,751
1949-50	401,931	18,885	2,776	25,611,082	74,774,461	186.04	1,485,096,011
1950-51	409,191	19,244	2,808	24,782,979	78,834,478	192.66	1,547,017,095
1951-52	404,767	19,477	3,113	28,224,464	87,424,082	215.99	1,647,726,019
1952-53	411,430	19,411	3,237	27,132,130	90,274,234	219.42	1,724,215,669
1953-54	425,425	19,695	3,502	30,568,973	97,416,867	228.99	1,806,078,557
1954-55	447,394	20,075	3,570	30,443,402	100,382,127	224.37	1,854,873,584
1955-56	453,173	20,512	3,768	30,328,425	108,639,187	239.73	1,930,985,725
1956-57	460,146	20,683	3,943	29,646,372	115,930,959	251.94	2,009,607,374
1957-58	460,385	20,698	4,272	31,531,572	124,347,106	270.09	2,082,262,809
1958-59	476,489	20,858	4,646	38,416,359	136,902,684	287.32	2,147,193,171
1959-60	485,559	21,530	4,792	42,547,117	144,845,480	298.26	2,234,900,180
1960-61	495,123	21,983	4,904	43,468,203	151,508,111	306.00	2,355,709,113
1961-62	503,671	22,466	5,069	45,408,599	158,937,206	315.56	2,497,133,560
1962-63	518,872	23,026	5,257	49,288,292	168,509,664	324.76	2,597,915,409
1963-64	532,781	23,687	5,302	50,972,242	176,699,792	331.66	2,681,355,608
1964-65	541,367	24,377	5,312	48,522,031	182,744,540	337.56	2,803,158,819
1965-66	545,611	25,380	5,894	65,540,880	230,333,636	422.16	3,053,210,944

Source:

Department of Education, *Thirty-First Biennial Report* (1966), pp. 271-73.

[a] **1964-65 and prior years include only general fund expenditures.**

Appendix C

Table 2. – NUMBER OF SCHOOL DISTRICTS IN OKLAHOMA, BY YEARS, BEGINNING WITH STATEHOOD

Year	Districts	Year	Districts	Year	Districts
1907-1908	5,656	1927-28	5,024	1947-48	2,664
1908-1909	. . .	1928-29	4,978	1948-49	2,338
1909-10	5,725	1929-30	4,933	1949-50	2,332
1910-11	5,820	1930-31	4,869	1950-51	2,177
1911-12	. . .	1931-32	4,836	1951-52	2,100
1912-13	5,861	1932-33	4,825	1952-53	1,989
1913-14	5,880	1933-34	4,816	1953-54	1,888
1914-15	. . .	1934-35	4,791	1954-55	1,802
1915-16	5,843	1935-36	4,760	1955-56	1,738
1916-17	5,838	1936-37	4,738	1956-57	1,643
1917-18	. . .	1937-38	4,697	1957-58	1,468
1918-19	5,716	1938-39	4,646	1958-59	1,372
1919-20	. . .	1939-40	4,644	1959-60	1,322
1920-21	5,414	1940-41	. . .	1960-61	1,274
1921-22	. . .	1941-42	4,518	1961-62	1,232
1922-23	5,190	1942-43	. . .	1962-63	1,180
1923-24	5,159	1943-44	4,448	1963-64	1,160
1924-25	5,142	1944-45	. . .	1964-65	1,049
1925-26	5,103	1945-46	. . .	1965-66	998
1926-27	5,078	1946-47	4,450		

Source:

Department of Education, *Thirty-First Biennial Report* (1966), p. 274.

37 Oregon

DEPARTMENT OF EDUCATION
Jesse V. Fasold

Contents

THE DEPARTMENT AS A CLERICAL ARM OF THE SUPERINTENDENT, 1849-1925

The early development of Oregon's public schools was the responsibility of the superintendent of public instruction, the State Department of Education existing only as his clerical help. As late as 1925, the department consisted of the superintendent, two professional assistants, and a handful of secretaries. The early superintendents carried out most of their business personally, answering letters and collecting reports entirely on their own. Sometimes they dug into their own pockets for expenses.

Initial Legislation, 1849-72

Oregon's administrative authority for education began in 1849, when the Territorial Legislature authorized the Governor to appoint a superintendent of common schools every 3 years (1) and established an educational fund to be distributed according to population. Since no organized common school system actually existed, the Legislature abolished the office in 1851, and it was not until 8 years later, when Oregon became a state, that the public school concept again assumed importance.

A statewide public school system was still not fully established when Oregon's constitution was adopted in 1859, so it contained a provision that the Governor serve as the superintendent of public instruction for the first 5 years of statehood (2). This arrangement was prolonged for the first 13 years, however, with four Governors–Whiteaker, Gibbs, Woods, and Grover–holding the office. With so many other demands on their time and a rapid turnover in the Legislature, these men did little to develop legislation for a public school system. Gibbs did pay out of his own pocket to finance the first state reports on the public schools. And his successor, Governor Woods, claimed that he found the schools still "disorganized and unsatisfactory" and pressed for legislation that would allow him to appoint a state school official who could devote his entire time to education (3).

The constitution stated: "It shall be competent for the legislative assembly to provide by law for the election of a Superintendent of Public Instruction, to provide for his compensation, and to prescribe his powers and duties" (4). The Legislature elected a superintendent in 1870 but 2 years later made the office part of the general election and set the salary at $1,500 (5). The constitution did not specify whether "election" in Article 8 referred to a popular or a legislative election. The Legislature decided early that it could assign the election to the public, but it remains a controversial issue today.

The 1872 legislation also outlined the responsibilities of state, county, and local educational administration. The State Board of Education, comprised of the Governor, secretary of state, and superintendent of public instruction, was to meet semiannually to authorize textbooks, provide for school government, and grant teaching certificates. This state board and the Office of Superintendent of Public Instruction thus constituted the beginning of state administration of education. The State Department of Education, not defined by law until 1951, evolved from the superintendent's need for assistance rather than from a specific legislative program. The early history of the department is actually no more than a record of the activities of the state superintendents and their professional and clerical help.

Early State Superintendents, 1873-1900

Simpson and School Statistics, 1873-74. The law provided for the superintendent to be elected by the joint ballot of the House and the Senate, but so much legislation had to be crowded through in the last session that the Legislature failed to choose anyone. Consequently, the Governor exercised his constitutional power to fill state offices and appointed Sylvester C. Simpson. In the 20 months he served, Professor Simpson accomplished two important tasks: He initiated a system for supplying school statistics, beginning with the first biennial report; and he organized a plan for acquiring a uniform series of textbooks for the entire state. When he took office, "he found not only different textbooks being used in several schools throughout the state for the teaching of the same subject, but teachers actually conducting classes where pupils were following different texts in the same room" (6). His plan–

> Was not accomplished without considerable dissatisfaction on the part of parents who were forced to buy new texts, some teachers who did not like the new texts, and some who complained against the "school book monopoly." However, once established, the opposition to the series has appeared to have died out rapidly (7).

Superintendent Powell reported that the authorized texts were being used exclusively by 1880.

Rowland and Powell–A Stable Public System, 1874-82. When Professor Simpson chose not to serve another term, his co-worker and professor at the Willamette University Medical School, L. L. Rowland, was elected in 1874. From study at Virginia's Bethany College to the presidency of Christian College in Monmouth, he had gained the rich educational background necessary to carry on the development of a common school system. At the end of his 4-year term, the number of districts had increased 34 percent, public school enrollment 29 percent, the number of teachers 72 percent, and the total value of school property 50 percent (8).

Perhaps the most important task entrusted to the state superintendent during the terms of Dr. Rowland and his successor, L. J. Powell, was establishing annual teacher institutes in each judicial district according to the 1872 law. Otherwise, their main duties consisted of gathering educational data and certifying teachers with the State Board of Examiners. The clerical assistants, the only semblance of a department, were often paid by the superintendents themselves to gather statistics and negotiate teacher certificates. Both Rowland and Powell spent much of their time establishing a system of authorized textbooks chosen by the state board from a list provided by the local districts.

McElroy and Teacher Improvement, 1882-95. E. B. McElroy, educated at the State Normal School in Pennsylvania, taught several years on the East Coast and was a county school superintendent in Oregon for 4 years before becoming state superintendent. He devoted most of his 13-year term to improving the teaching staff. After securing the State Board of Examiners' approval, he persuaded the 1882 Legislature to "recognize" the state normal schools at Monmouth and Ashland. Recognition implied that the schools would receive financial support, but appropriation laws failed to pass in several sessions. Three other normal schools met the state standards during the following 7 years, greatly improving their ability to upgrade standards for teachers.

In 1887, the Legislature enacted a law providing free education to all residents under age 21. It passed a Compulsory School Attendance Act 2 years later requiring all Oregon residents from 8 to 14 years of age to attend public schools a minimum of 12 weeks each school year, at least 8 of them consecutively (9). This law was revolutionary for the time, and the citizens reacted strongly against the state's assuming so much authority. The superintendent received a large share of the public's criticism. Three years later, McElroy wrote: "The law has proven to be very defective... the very name 'compulsory' seems to be offensive to many people of the state" (10).

Irwin and High School Development, 1895-99. When George M. Irwin became superintendent, the country was still in the grip of the depression that followed the panic of 1893. The excitement over Cuba and free silver also diverted public attention from local issues. Not only were times unfavorable for educational expansion, but the new superintendent himself was conservative. Educated at Ohio Wesleyan University, he had served as a Methodist Episcopal pastor and as superintendent of the Chemawa Indian Training School. High schools increased in both number and importance during this period, and Irwin did attempt to continue the policies established by his predecessors for improving the quality of both teachers and normal schools.

New Responsibilities for the State Superintendent, 1900-25

Before 1900, the state superintendents spent most of their time on correspondence. They continually had to train new county superintendents for these low-paying, frequently vacated jobs. They had to present the biennial report to the Legislature, and gathering data with little clerical help used up much of their time. The Legislature finally recognized their problems and in 1899 provided the superintendent with an assistant and $1,500 for clerical help to answer questions about teacher certification. This meager appropriation marked the birth of the State Department of Education. For some time after 1900, when the state superintendent's authority was extended to include the controlling boards of higher education and ex officio membership in the Oregon Library Commission, this clerical allowance remained the same.

Before the higher education department was placed under a single separate board, the members of the State Board of Education served ex officio as regents of various state colleges and universities. For a time, each school had its own board of trustees, appointed by the Governor with the consent of the Senate, and including the state board members, but this was abolished by a law which went into effect in July 1931. By the end of 1932, a newly created Board of Higher Education integrated the schools into a single cohesive unit (11).

John H. Ackerman, 1899-1911. John Ackerman taught in three states and was a principal in the Portland schools and school superintendent of Multnomah County before becoming state superintendent. His administration became one of the most important in the state's history. During his first 3 years as superintendent, the school law was largely rewritten. The Daly Bill of 1899 established the first uniform statewide curriculum for grammar schools and an eighth-grade examination to help standardize instruction. Two years later, a newly established State Textbook Commission consisting of five members appointed by the Governor was given the responsibility for selecting textbooks. Although the textbook law was amended in 1907, 1921, 1923, and 1951, the basic principle of selection has not changed.

The Legislature inaugurated the state system of high schools by passing a "Grades Above the Eighth" bill in 1901, allowing counties to establish high schools when the district voted to do so. Six years later, it passed an additional law allowing two or more contiguous districts to form a union high school. The public normal schools were closed during Ackerman's administration, and the school at Monmouth was reestablished with a different method of support.

During his 12 years as state superintendent, Ackerman did much to raise the standards for preparing teachers, to improve the educational record systems, to improve school buildings, and to make the teachers more sensitive to their professional opportunities and obligations. The county institutes, in their prime at this time, were the principal means for providing in-service training. Since each wanted the state superintendent to be one of its speakers, Ackerman performed near miracles in getting to three widely scattered meetings in three consecutive days, driving all night over bad roads after each engagement. Fortunately, he had tremendous physical energy and always gave a forward-looking, optimistic talk.

In spite of his enthusiasm, his definite ideas, and his perseverance, Ackerman was big enough to allow persons to differ with him. He was an administrator enough to know how to delegate tasks and then refrain from interfering, giving full blame or credit when it was completed. By utilizing his staff's special abilities and preparations, he enabled them to perform their jobs more efficiently and, at the same time, was free to work at tasks which he could do more efficiently than others.

E. S. Evenden, professor of education, Teachers College, Columbia University, had this to say of John H. Ackerman:

> He did things that got results by the best means at his command though he paid the usual price of arousing opposition from persons who differed with him in the ends he sought or the means he used to obtain those ends. He had hosts of friends who knew his idealism, students who were loyal to him... and citizens who appreciated his championship of their schools . . . (12).

Alderman and Vocational Education, 1911-13. Lewis R. Alderman assumed the superintendency in 1911 during a time of growing interest in vocational education. In 1913, the Legislature appropriated $6,000 per year to begin developing a vocational education division in the state department and authorized the superintendent to hire two assistants to travel around the state promoting studies in agriculture, manual training, home economics, and industrial programs. Before resigning to become chief administrator of the Portland public schools, Alderman asserted that the vocational program and, surprisingly, the temporary reopening of the state normal schools were among the most significant developments of his 2 years. In a review he stated:

> A deep and widespread interest in the study of agriculture, domestic science and manual training, a steady increase in the number of high schools, a vigorous attempt on the part of the state to bring the school and home into closer relationships by the home credit plan, and the securing of a firm and permanent position in our education system for a State Normal School are some of the most interesting signs of progress in our public schools (13).

Churchill and the First School Standards, 1913-26. Julius A. Churchill, superintendent of schools in Baker City since 1891, was appointed to fill the vacancy created by Alderman's resignation. He continued to work in vocational education, attracting national attention by establishing a program of extracurricular industrial training which enrolled 12,000 children in clubs that gave them practice in sewing, poultry raising, cooking and baking, crop growing, and similar skills.

Perhaps Churchill's outstanding contribution was the improvement of school building standards. The county superintendents and the State Board of Education adopted the first set of regulations for rural and village school buildings in 1913. These, plus more stringent standards established in 1920, sought to regulate lighting, heating, ventilation, condition of the grounds, water sanitation, and even teacher qualifications. Although the state could not offer monetary rewards for schools that complied, the office did send visiting committees to the various schools to try to enforce the standards. Less than a third of the rural schools were able to meet the standards between 1923 and 1934. Not until 1947, when the superintendent threatened to withhold funds from the Basic School Support Law unless the minimum standards were fulfilled, were all of the building regulations enforced. On the other hand, the state board adopted standards for high schools in 1915, and 5 years later visiting committees reported that most schools could meet them.

World War I widely affected Oregon schools. For example, Superintendent Churchill spent considerable time directing the sale of saving bonds stamps. Also, vocational agriculture was reemphasized, and a State Board for Vocational Education was established by Governor Withycombe under emergency circumstances in 1917 to administer funds from the new National Vocational Education Act (Smith-Hughes Bill). The following year, the Legislature made the board permanent. It consisted of the State Board of Education and four persons appointed by the Governor. The superintendent of public instruction served as executive officer. This board, administering a separate budget of about $80,000 a year including federal funds, remained a separate agency under the state board and state superintendent until it was officially incorporated into the State Department of Education in 1951 (14).

The war also revealed the poor physical condition of many young men. Superintendent Churchill appointed a committee in 1919 to investigate how the schools could promote physical exercise and training. The committee produced a series of pamphlets detailing the exercises and activities suitable for pupils at each grade level through high school.

One problem faced by the superintendent after the war stemmed from a popular initiative measure enacted in 1922 that required all children to attend public schools only. Hill Military Academy and other private institutions challenged the law, and 3 years later the U.S. Supreme Court ruled it unconstitutional.

Another problem arose in 1923 when a group of concerned citizens pressed the Legislature to require the schools to teach the federal Constitution. Perhaps they were sensitive because other states regarded their initiative and referendum as evidence of radical tendencies, and they felt they should reassert their regard for the ancient hallmarks of federal government. People were seeking a pre-World War I "normalcy" and rejecting anything that threatened to disturb the status quo. Actually, civics, with an emphasis on the federal Constitution, had been taught in both the elementary and high schools since the beginning of state supervision. Nevertheless, the act passed in 1923. Except for a few changes in wording, it is still in effect, stating:

> In all public and private schools located in the State of Oregon commencing with the school year next ensuing after the passage of this act, there shall be given regular courses of instruction in the Constitution of the United States. Such instruction in the Constitution of the United States shall begin not later than the opening of the eighth grade, and shall continue in the high school course, and in courses in state colleges, universities, and the educational department of state and municipal institutions to an extent to be determined by the Superintendent of Public Instruction (15).

Also, in 1925, the state board appointed five people to serve as a Commission of Americanization, which was added to the adult education program.

Summary: The First Half-Century of State Administration

During the early years of the state's involvement in education, the superintendent of public instruction, at first a mere researcher for statewide reports, became responsible for supervising teacher certification, establishing a uniform curriculum, and standardizing school facilities. He also administered the distribution of federal funds from the National Vocational Education Act and programed physical education courses.

But the state superintendent was able to do little about the most serious educational problem during this period: providing sufficient funds for school support. The Oregon constitution directed the state treasurer to distribute money from the irreducible school fund received from the sale of federal lands, but this was insufficient and was not state support in the usual sense (16). A voters pamphlet for the May 1920 election pointed out that Oregon was one of seven states not using state revenues to support its schools, which in turn usually meant low teachers' salaries. As a result of the publicity, the Legislature, by a three-to-one vote, established the elementary school fund. Money was to be derived from a statewide tax of nearly $2 million, levied by each county, and was to be distributed to each elementary district according to the number of elementary teachers in the district. While this bill promoted the principle of state support, it was far from sufficient because it excluded the secondary schools and provided only 12.5 percent of all school revenue. The public and the Legislature frequently discussed additional state support, but no new legislation was passed until 1942, af first because of the Depression and later because of our entry into World War II.

Progress in education during these first 50 years resulted primarily from the superintendent's personal initiative and interest. After 1925, it came from external forces. The first sizable federal grant had already created a vocational education board which was subsidiary to the department, but had more personnel and a larger budget. The Depression and World War II brought more federal projects requiring state administration. Thus, during the next 25 years, the department's growth resulted more from external demands such as national emergencies, economic necessities, and population growth than from the personal efforts of the chief state school officer.

The budget for state and county administration was $10,000 in 1872; by 1924, it had increased to $41,850 for the state alone, with an additional $40,000 allotted to the vocational education board. Yet, by 1920, the education department consisted of only two professional members, including the superintendent, and a handful of clerical workers. Over the next 40 years, it increased to 340 employees with a budget of more than $250 million (17).

THE STATE DEPARTMENT AS PROFESSIONAL STAFF, 1925-50

The period from 1925 to 1945 is not particularly important for legislative or organizational changes. Problems and responsibilities created by the Depression and World War II, such as school enrollment fluctuations and federal education projects, challenged the department to attempt additional projects of its own. The state superintendent from 1927 to 1937, C. A. Howard, recognized the department's organizational difficulties and made corrective recommendations in his biennial reports. Despite his early diagnosis, most of the problems were not corrected until after World War II.

Legislative Changes, 1929-31

Two changes of some significance took place in 1929 and 1931 affecting the organization and responsibilities of the department. First, the Legislature established the State Board of Higher Education as a separate organization (18), making Oregon colleges and universities "in no way subject to the authority of the superintendent of public instruction" (19). Since that time, higher education has operated under an authority separate from the elementary and secondary schools. Second, a free textbook act was passed, requiring districts to budget funds annually to purchase books used by the elementary (but not the secondary) schools. By further acknowledging the state's duty to supervise school finance, this law established a principle that became increasingly important after World War II.

State Responsibility During the Depression, 1930-40

Federal Programs. The department's largest single task between 1933 and 1940 was operating the emergency education programs established with federal funds. For instance, during the 1933-34 biennium, the Federal Emergency Relief Administration authorized funds for emergency vocational, adult, and rural education programs. These required no additional staff members except for a few secretaries who received federal relief funds. The programs operated under the direction of the department until 1936 (20). They were then transferred to the Works Progress Administration officer for Oregon, E. J. Griffith, who appointed his own staff and incorporated the programs into the scope and organization of his other projects, depicted in Figure 1 (21).

By the 1939-40 biennium, the state department employed five supervisors, who directed projects and were spending about $340,000 in 17 different areas for the WPA education and recreation programs. In the 1935-36 biennial report, Griffith had commended the state department:

> The WPA education and recreation program of the State Department of Education is effectively rendering two important services: first, giving employment to needy, qualified persons throughout the state, and second, extending to the people of Oregon certain educational and recreational opportunities which heretofore they have not been able to obtain. The state department of education, as sponsor for this program, has given time and energy unsparingly and has constantly maintained cooperation and sympathetic understanding to the end that the objectives of the program might be effectively achieved (22).

Figure 1. – WPA EDUCATION AND RECREATION PROGRAM OF DEPARTMENT OF EDUCATION, 1933-34

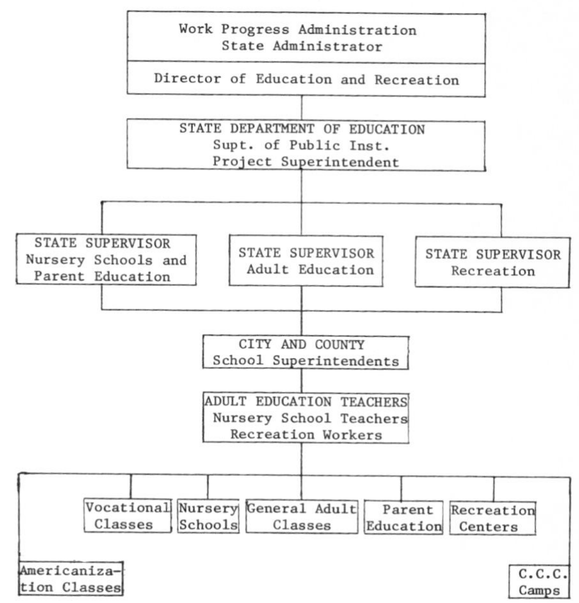

High School Development, 1930-38. With no jobs available for children who would normally have dropped out of school, the Depression years saw an overwhelming increase in high school enrollments. As early as 1930, the new standards adopted by the state board had emphasized practical subjects, such as general mathematics and business, and had placed less stress on purely academic or cultural studies. This "commercial" trend continued during these years, and even the smaller schools were offering bookkeeping and typing, according to a 1938 survey (23). But the many small high schools created a special problem: They were least capable of handling the extra students and had the poorest equipment to meet the demand for vocational courses. They also suffered from rapid teacher turnover and limited funds. The biennial reports continually restated the need for a separate administrator for secondary schools, but they also showed that other demands on the department were too heavy to allow it to create such a specialized position.

The high schools did receive federal assistance between 1935 and 1940. Stimulated by aid from the Civil Works Administration and the Public Works Administration, a wave of high school building construction spread throughout the state, resulting in 52 new high schools, 27 new gymnasiums, and 33 new building additions (24). At the end of this active period, the WPA inspected all rural and some first-class districts, selected model buildings as guides for future construction, and prepared a statewide map of district boundaries and school locations (25).

Recognition of the Department's Problems, 1926-37

Superintendent C. A. Howard recognized the weaknesses in the state administration and strongly recommended changes that eventually became law, but not until after his retirement. Numerous small schools and 2,200 separate districts, many unable to meet education costs, created a major obstacle to statewide standardization. Howard reported:

> There is a growing tendency in other states toward more centralized responsibility and control with resultant higher efficiency in value received for correspondingly fewer tax dollars. It is becoming obvious that the acceptance by the state of a larger participation in school support will also yield fruits of efficiency and economy (26).

In relation to this, he recommended in his 1935 report that the state establish a larger school-support fund. Oregon was providing only 2.3 percent of the state's annual education costs, the second lowest rate in all 48 states. Howard maintained that although state responsibility for education had been firmly established by all states, Oregon was delegating too much of the financial burden to county and local governments.

Superintendent Howard found that Oregon had the second smallest department of education in the nation and repeatedly asked for a larger budget and staff, particularly for a secondary education administrator and a special budget for publications. But the Depression and strong competition from other state agencies nullified the effect of these requests. The department only increased from two in 1926 to six in 1942, plus an additional staff of five professionals under the WPA project. The staff of the vocational education department, thanks to the Smith-Hughes and George-Reed Acts, equaled that of the education department and the WPA combined.

Repeated requests for a more centralized school system, a larger percentage of state support, and an enlarged education department to supervise the system went unheeded while public attention was given to the war effort in the first half of the forties. During the term of Rex Putnam, who took office in 1937, the public did vote in the most important piece of school legislation since the turn of the century: a Basic School Support Fund Law with an appropriation from the state general fund to be allotted to all public elementary and secondary education in Oregon.

World War II, 1940-45

From 1940 to 1942, Oregon teachers, responding to a need for more workers trained for war industry, worked through the summer to create programs for more than 75,000 persons. The department organized nursery schools and extended-care plans for schoolchildren of working mothers. Both the department and individual schools organized programs to register people for rationing, collect scrap materials, sell defense bonds and stamps, and recruit volunteers for Civil Defense. As the biennial report for 1941-42 stated, "Because schools are natural centers for all communities, . . . are staffed with able and willing persons, and because they generally have public confidence, the government turned to them for help in various war efforts" (27).

In 1943, the vocational rehabilitation department enlarged its program to include the mentally disabled as well as the physically handicapped. It was removed from the vocational education board to become a separate agency and finally was incorporated back into the Department of Education in 1951. It is the only division in the state education complex that administers direct instead of advisory services. Although the vocational rehabilitation division has the largest operating budget and number of employees of all the divisions, it is actually the least involved with matters immediately pertaining to public schools.

The war brought to the state department many new problems and responsibilities. It had to issue emergency certificates when qualified teachers went into the service or accepted defense jobs. The state's urban schools were overcrowded because of congestion in defense plant areas, while many rural schools were almost empty because of high school dropouts and population shifts. The school year had to be shortened to allow children to harvest crops. And school buses could not be replaced as they deteriorated.

During the upheaval of the war years, the state department was officially defined for the first time. The 1941-42 biennial report acknowledged the department's responsibility to coordinate public education:

> The State Department of Education has general administrative and supervisory responsibility for the operation of public schools of the state. In performing this function it works with the county school superintendents in the counties and the local administrators and teachers in the school districts. This cooperative relationship is the necessary and desirable procedure to make a statewide program move forward and to give initiative and responsibility to local districts (28).

This report also pointed out that the state department was serving as a mediator between federal project administrators and their executors on the lower level. In the first year of the war, the superintendent requested the U.S. Office of Education to channel federal funds through the state department to local areas because too much "delay and bureaucratic red tape" resulted when other methods were employed. So many new and important responsibilities had been thrust on the department by federal grants—the enlarged vocational education board, the WPA projects, and the school building programs of 1935-40—that it logically envisioned one of its functions to be liaison between federal and local agencies.

Post-World War II

Finance Revisions, 1942-47. The state school support fund, created in 1942, was the first major move to increase state aid to local districts. Prior to this, a kind of state aid trickled down from the irreducible school fund and the elementary school fund, but the new law ordered the surplus from state tax funds distributed to school districts to complement special school tax levies, thus putting into practice the principle of state support. It supplied $5 million per year to public education until 1945 when the amount was increased to $8 million.

In 1947, the Legislature passed a revolutionary new law, the basic school support fund, which not only guaranteed each district a minimum level of state support but provided extra funds for transportation and special programs, equalized the state's share of school district taxes, and provided for periodic studies of the school system. One provision, that local districts would not be able to obtain state funds unless they met the state standards, greatly increased the state department's influence on local districts. Revised and adopted by the state board, these standards established minimum requirements for school buildings, staff, organization, curriculum—in fact, all important phases of the school system. According to the biennial report,

> Through the enactments of the 1947 legislature and subsequent amendments, the legal provisions for the state standardization program have become a part of the Basic School Support Fund Act, and the failure to maintain standard conditions within a school district is now cause for the school district's ineligibility for the receipt of state school fund allotments. The Basic School Fund is based upon the concept of the foundation program which may be considered as a state responsibility and a minimum program of education below which no school district should be permitted to fall (29).

It is significant that the state support funds of 1942 and 1947, both largely responsible for creating a strong state authority in Oregon education, were enacted by the "initiative." After similar recommendations had languished in the Legislature for almost a decade, the petition and ballot of private citizens, led by the Oregon Education Association and local parent-teacher associations, won a stronger, more active State Department of Education.

The moneys were distributed in 1947 as follows:

Emergency conditions	$ 250,000
Handicapped children's program	450,000
Gifted and mentally retarded programs	40,000
Transportation	1,700,000
State institution schools	100,000
Flat grants and equalization	30,000,000
Administration (including standardization)	140,000

New Programs. The department assumed the operation of a handicapped children's program in 1941, when the Legislature made its first appropriation for special education. Beginning with a budget of about $5,000 for the first year, the program was expanded to a $200,000 budget with 10 additional employees during the next 4 years. The Legislature also appropriated $26,000 to the state department in 1945 to improve health and physical education instruction. Three federal programs also began in 1947: The Legislature placed the school lunch program under the department so it could administer the funds available under the National School Lunch Act; the department, under a contract with the U.S. Bureau of Indian Affairs, assumed full responsibility for educating Indian children and received limited federal funds for a state director; and the department agreed to operate for Oregon the education clauses in the "GI Bill of Rights" for returning war veterans (30).

Summary: State Department Growth During National Crises

The need for a centralizing agency in state education was constantly reasserted during the thirties and early forties, although few legal or financial provisions were enacted to help stabilize the department. The superintendent and his staff were invaluable to local districts when the Depression and World War II created demands for rapid reorganization. The department also provided extensive services to the federal government by operating special programs necessary to stabilize the economy.

The department gained its greatest influence through the legislation of 1947, initiated by citizens dedicated to the principle of state responsibility for finance and standards in public education. The basic school support fund made it possible for the state office to develop and enforce minimum standards for all public schools and created a guaranteed budget for some of the department's special functions.

The many programs added during the forties demonstrate the department's growth as the centralized agency for public schools in Oregon. Not only did various federal projects call for new professional positions, but, even more important, the Legislature began making regular appropriations for special educational services. From 1925 to 1950, the department's professional staff increased from 2 to 26, presaging the much greater expansion that would occur in the fifties and sixties.

THE DEPARTMENT AS A LEGALIZED CENTRAL AGENCY

Commissioned by the 1949 Legislature to survey public education in Oregon, T. C. Holy presented a report that resulted in a vast reorganization of state administrative policies as well as the formal recognition of the State Department of Education. The office now assumed full responsibility as a centralized agency. Its professional staff distributed state and federal funds to local school districts, supervised teacher certification, and enforced the minimum state standards for education, in addition to administering many specialized programs in research, curriculum development, and other areas. The standardization program alone required many additional employees after 1947.

Appropriations from state and national agencies have enabled the department to expand the staff to carry on exciting experimental programs in classrooms and administrative procedures. New professional positions are being created to efficiently use increasing federal grants, such as those under the Elementary and Secondary Education Act. At present, the possibilities for the department's growth seem unlimited.

Recommendations for Reorganization, 1950-66

The Holy Report. While the 1949 Legislature recognized that no legal basis had ever been created for an agency called the State Department of Education, such a department had already assumed several important functions. So that progress would not be hindered by obsolete laws, the Legislature appropriated $55,000 for a study of the major revisions needed for a unified, strong system of state education. It was to cover the following:

> The public elementary and secondary schools of the state and any questions relating to the improvement of the public school system of Oregon, including particularly a study with a view toward making recommendations on the state organization and supervision of schools, the equalization of education opportunities, the reorganization of local administrative units, the financing of schools from the state and local level and its effect on taxation, the effect of the basic school fund, transportation, simplification of school laws, financing school buildings, and building requirements (31).

The advisory committee selected T. C. Holy, director of educational research at Ohio State University and a nationally known authority on education, to execute the study and submit recommendations to the 1951 Legislature. Dr. Holy completed his report in 1950, and the Legislature used it to make major reorganizations in certain aspects of school administration as outlined below.

Figure 2. – OREGON DEPARTMENT OF EDUCATION, 1951

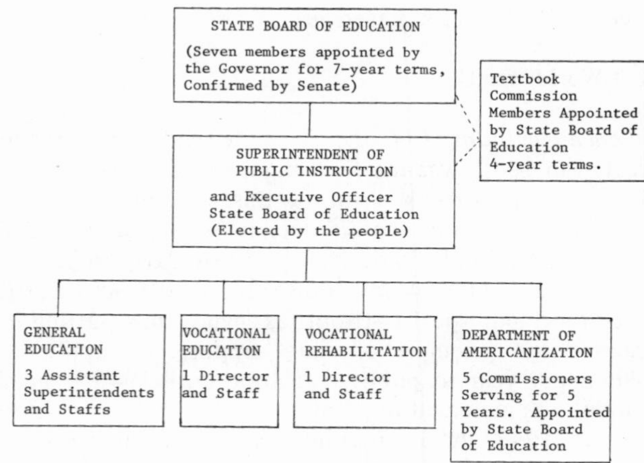

As created by Chapter 169, *Oregon Laws,* 1951.

The department was placed under the direction and control of the State Board of Education, comprised of seven members appointed by the Governor for 7-year terms, one from each congressional district and the remainder from the state at large. These state board members could not be engaged in school teaching, administration, or operation. The law also said:

> As executive head of the Department of Education, the Superintendent of Public Instruction performs duties prescribed by law and executes, directs, and supervises all administrative and technical activities of the department in accordance with the policies prescribed by the State Board of Education (32).

During its first 16 years of formal existence, the department issued many statements of its operating philosophy. The first, from the "Holy Report" of 1950, emphasized the development of strong leadership at the state level but with sufficient flexibility to encourage local initiative. It deplored any attempt to operate or control local school programs but promised to see that the districts were properly organized to develop programs that best met their needs. It added that–

> The chief responsibility of the central education agency, . . . should be to provide competent leadership. In the final analysis, the provision of such leadership will be the best assurance that needed improvement will be made in the state school program (33).

As a result of large increases in federal grants between 1950 and 1965, mainly through the National Defense

Education Act and the Elementary and Secondary Education Act, the department was again forced to think seriously about its purposes and its relations with the U.S. Office of Education. A 1965 proposal by the Oregon department to the USOE declared that it was imperative that the departments of education be strengthened if they were actually to improve education through the increases in financial support. The proposal stated that the federal government was calling on state administrators "to organize creatively in such a way as to bring additional human and financial resources to bear upon the identification of problems in education and the development of useful concepts that lead to solutions to these problems" (34). Although this proposal was not developed, it shows that creative leadership and maintaining a proper balance among state, federal, and local school administrations have been the department's constant concerns (35).

Administrative Changes in the State Board and Superintendency. The "Holy Report" labeled the State Board of Education obsolete because it consisted of four gubernatorial appointees with three ex officio members: the Governor, the secretary of state, and the state superintendent. Holy felt that this was contrary to the general practice in more effectively organized states, where state boards were elected by and responsible to the people, and he recommended popular election for Oregon's board. The 1951 reorganization made these positions elective. Holy also criticized the election of the state superintendent by popular vote, because he believed that qualified educators might pass up an office requiring a political campaign, but the Legislature refused to change the procedure.

Rex Putnam, who had served as superintendent for 24 years, resigned in the middle of a term in 1961. His administration had been distinguished by many progressive changes in school financing, evaluation, and organization. Among the significant changes were state support for special education and curriculum improvement, establishment of dual teacher-training institutions, extension of the period for preparing both elementary and secondary teachers, certification of school administrators, school district reorganization, federal funds for general education, and the beginning of the Oregon Program with foundation grant funds. Under his guidance, the department gained appropriate recognition and influence as the centralized agency for the school system.

The assistant superintendent, Joy Hill Gubser, describes him as a humble man without boast and pretention, a gentle and kindly man who knew none so bad but he could find good in him. He delighted audiences with his stories and shared his homely and practical philosophy with his staff, reminding them often that the state department did not have answers to all of the problems of education. He felt strongly that there was much to be gained by sharing in educational effort with the schools and colleges of the state.

Governor Mark O. Hatfield appointed Leon P. Minear to replace Dr. Putnam. Leon Minear's 5 years in office saw many statewide programs initiated to improve education, the Oregon Program among the most important. During Minear's first year, the Legislature made the state superintendency subject to election by the state board. This action was challenged 2 years later, and the Oregon Supreme Court ruled it unconstitutional in April 1965. The people have twice since defeated an amendment to the constitution providing for an appointed state superintendent.

Dr. Holy's "Report Card," 1966. Dr. Holy returned to Oregon in 1966 to evaluate the progress achieved during the 16 years since his study and made up-to-date recommendations that are still bringing changes. For instance, in 1950 he had vigorously attacked the state for permitting the existence of 1,250 school districts, many of them overlapping or inactive, which resulted in inefficient administration. The 1957 School District Reorganization Law reduced the number of districts to 478, including 91 new administrative districts. Today, there are 390, and the state department can better communicate.

Holy's "Report Cards" for 1950 and 1966 show that he considers school finances to be in even worse shape today. In 1950, Oregon ranked twenty-eighth in percent of school revenue provided by the state; in 1960, it ranked fortieth. Holy pointed out that the intent of the basic school support fund had not been fully realized because the Legislature failed to increase the fund proportionally with the educational system's growth. His finding has prompted the department to make a comprehensive study of the state's school support.

Figure 3. – A REPORT CARD (36)

Results of Holy 1965-66 Study of Oregon Education

	Comparative Scores	
	1949-50	1965-66
Local school organization	F	C
State organization	C	B
School finance	B	C
School buildings	C	B
Elementary schools	B	B+
High schools	B	B+
Community colleges	(2)	B
Teachers, administrators	B	B+
Textbooks, libraries, visual aids	D	B
Vocational training	B	B
Student guidance	C	B
Special education	B	B
Health, physical education	B	C
Adult education	D	C
School lunch program	B	B
Pupil transportation	D	B

Dr. Holy's first report claimed that the Oregon Textbook Commission gave teachers very little voice in selecting materials. The law was amended in 1951 to require a multiple selection of textbooks in all subjects, as initially suggested by committees of teachers. It allowed for local adoptions if the books met the standards laid down by the commission.

These evaluations of Oregon education undoubtedly have had a strong progessive influence on the state department. Holy was not an easy grader. But the state department could cite with pride improvements in all of the 16 areas except school finance and health and physical education. Perhaps the greatest advances have been made in local school organizations, instructional materials, and pupil transportation. Based on his 1966 study, Holy's legislative recommendations, supplemented by specific plans from the department, include provisions for state-aided kindergartens, state school support reorganization, a state subsidy for gifted children, and further school reorganization. Undoubtedly they will influence the 1967 Legislature to make additional changes.

New State-Funded Programs, 1950-66

When the department incorporated the vocational education and rehabilitation division, its staff size immediately doubled. But greater state and federal appropriations for special programs were a more important influence in increasing the number of employees—from 26 in 1950 to about 340 in 1966. The development of community colleges, one of Oregon's most ambitious programs, resulted in the addition of a new assistant superintendent and several professionals.

Community Colleges, 1951-66. The Holy survey found that the state needed community colleges and, along with a special study in 1950, recommended the development of three post-high school institutions offering mainly vocational-technical training. The permissive legislation of 1951 and the funding laws of 1957, 1959, and 1961 established standards for community colleges and created a plan for developing a statewide system of 2-year, post-high school institutions, perhaps the most important single development in public education in Oregon since the basic school support fund of 1947. The Legislature outlined the requirements but did not provide enough funds for rapid growth of community colleges until 1961. At present, there are 11 (37), with an enrollment of nearly 30,000 students during 1966-67. They offer more than 200 lower-division collegiate, vocational-technical, and adult education courses, with approximately 65 percent of the students taking occupational and related courses (38). Dr. Holy called this 15-year growth "northing short of phenomenal."

Gifted and Mentally Retarded Children, 1951-63. Following Dr. Holy's recommendations, the 1951 Legislature initiated studies and pilot programs for both gifted and mentally retarded children. Four years later, it ended the pilot operation and established a permanent program for mentally retarded children offering three types of services: (1) special classes, (2) referral to the Outpatient Diagnostic Clinic at Oregon Fairview Home (via the state department), and (3) consultant services to school districts. The retarded child program was expanded in 1959 and now receives about $1.2 million a year.

The Legislature did not vote extensive funds to help gifted children until 1957, after Sputnik. It reviewed this appropriation in 1963 and reduced its support to the point where the state department could no longer afford to staff the program. Apparently, the Legislature's intent had been to provide stimulative rather than supportive funds. The appropriation provided districts with 3 years of funds on a diminishing, phase-out basis, intending for local funds to take up the program in each district that wanted to continue it. In his 1966 evaluation, Dr. Holy strongly criticized the state for not having special programs for gifted children.

Adult Indian Education and Training Programs, 1955-61. The department contracted with the Bureau of Indian Affairs in 1955 to take over the adult Indian education program, which included formal education and college training, on-reservation vocational training, and general information about the withdrawal of federal supervision of Indian property. The department employed six staff members in this program at its peak but reduced the staff to two when several projects were completed in 1961.

Curriculum Improvement and Driver Education, 1957. The department initiated a bill in 1957 to provide state funds to local school districts to upgrade their curriculums. Local superintendents were so involved with the problems of finance, staff, and facilities growing out of the post-World War II population explosion that they needed extra help in stimulating schools to enrich their offerings. The resulting Curriculum Improvement Fund Law marked the beginning of an emphasis—a show of real concern—in this area. Efforts in curriculum improvement have since been accelerated through additional support from the National Defense Education Act and the Ford Foundation and through the creation in 1963 of the Oregon Council for Curriculum Instruction.

Along with the Curriculum Improvement Fund Law, the Legislature authorized a statewide reimbursement program for high school driver education. The secondary education section was given the responsibility for counseling local districts on driver education and making it part of the regular standardization and visitation program.

New Cooperative Operations, 1963-66. The department began two experiments in 1963 that emphasized cooperation between different levels of organization. The new

Oregon Council for Curriculum Instruction units organized a cooperative effort between state officials and special committees from regional areas, and the Governor's Education Improvement Advisory Commission encouraged a series of direct contacts between the state administration and the citizens. Finally, the launching of "Project Springboard" in 1966 marked the beginning of a cooperative venture among the department, local districts, and major industries, involving varying levels of education and crossing county lines. This placed the department in a unique position, compared with many other states that usually concentrate on working through single administrative units.

The Council for Curriculum Instruction is composed of 10 regional units especially designed to identify local curriculum problems and make necessary changes, and more specifically to improve curriculum instruction, provide extra in-service teacher training, and increase instructional materials services. The department provides a state coordinating committee and a general field consultant for each of the 10 regions to encourage the systematic study and solution of regional curriculum problems.

The Governor's Education Improvement Advisory Commission. The Governor appointed this commission in 1962 to inform citizens about current education programs. Within three years, it had prepared 10 pamphlets on problem areas, each with an attached opinionnaire on possible solutions (39). In the 1965-66 school year, it presented a series of "Public Conversations on Education" dinners, presided over by Governor Mark Hatfield, which disseminated its reports to community leaders, such as members of school boards, PTA's, and service clubs. These people in turn were asked to complete the questionnaires and pass on the information to their own service and business organizations. The reactions culled from the questionnaires were then compiled by the state department as the basis for possible legislative recommendations. There is little doubt that the commission has greatly improved relations between educators and the general public and that, by basing action on prevailing attitudes and promoting interest and discussions, it will have a major impact on educational issues in the future.

"Project Springboard." By developing 10 schools as state-coordinated audiovisual demonstration centers, this project is the nation's first professional partnership among a state department, local schools, and a dozen major audiovisual companies. Each school has collected a comprehensive array of audiovisual materials which the department and commercial firms are training teachers to use. Purchases of the latest technical equipment are made possible by matching funds from these commercial firms and the local districts. The demonstrations, which will begin in 1968, are expected to attract visitors from throughout the nation.

New Nationally Funded Programs, 1950-65

The almost hysterical concern for education that followed Russia's success with Sputnik in 1957 prompted Congress to pass the National Defense Education Act of 1958. Seven years later, it enacted another major government program for education, the Elementary and Secondary Education Act. Both of these programs have created many new functions for state departments of education, such as planning proposals for obtaining the funds and acting as liaison between the U.S. Office of Education and local districts. Oregon's department employs more than 25 professionals whose salaries are paid out of these two grants. In 1962, the state department used its own initiative to obtain \$3.5 million from a private, nonprofit corporation, enabling it to add an entirely new division. Other federal legislation such as the Vocational Education Act of 1963 and the Economic Opportunity Act of 1964 also expanded the department's specific services.

National Defense Education Act, 1959-66. The department created the Instructional Services Section in April 1959 to coordinate the state's participation in the National Defense Education Act. With Title I funds, the department developed the instructional materials centers, regional pools of audiovisual equipment serving nearby school districts. The Jackson County service provides the most outstanding example of progress in this area, growing from a "package set" of 50 motion pictures to a \$600,000 collection including every audiovisual medium. The department has used Title V funds to stimulate guidance services in elementary schools. As a result, 44 schools have added full-time counselors, and 20 others, part-time counselors. These funds also have been used to furnish approved guidance services in high schools since 1959, many under the direction of the department's consultants. Title X supplied funds to improve the state's statistical services, allowing for a complete overhaul of reporting forms and accounting procedures. The department's data-processing service, an extensive IBM complex, was also initiated under this title and was expanded with Elementary and Secondary Education Act funds a few years later.

The National Defense Education Act, originally providing consultants in science, mathematics, and modern languages, was extended in 1964 to include English, geography, history, and civics. The department thus was able to employ special consultants in many of these areas, providing leadership and improving instruction. The National Defense Education Act funds fostered the biggest growth in the department's staff since 1947.

The Oregon Program, 1961-66. The Legislature appropriated \$35,000 in 1961 to plan a proposal for a 4-year educational improvement program to be financed by the Ford Foundation. The following year, the foundation granted Oregon $3.5 million, mainly to improve instruction through additional teacher training and experiments in modern teaching methods. Specifically, the program was designated to accelerate change through such experiments as team teaching and flexible scheduling, a teacher-intern program, and exploration of the latest instructional materials and techniques.

Under this program, the education department employed two full-time staff members in teacher education to mediate among colleges, universities, and the school districts receiving interns. It also established an education development division in 1962, composed of specialists who analyze problems and develop corrective proposals. Along with these projects, the department planned annual summer workshops for teachers and administrators, inviting educational authorities from throughout the nation to present the latest information on school organization, team teaching, learning theory, education for the disadvantaged child, and reading and writing instruction.

Vocational Education Act of 1963. This act provided matching funds to improve vocational agriculture training for people of all ages. The Legislature approved a study of vocational information procedures to establish data-gathering instruments for continually assessing human resources and work opportunities. The department received funds to create a model for guidance in vocational agriculture at high school and post-high school levels, mainly in counseling students in realistic terms and helping them get jobs. The number of new vocational classes supported by these federal funds has increased greatly.

Economic Opportunity Act of 1964. This act has had a limited effect on the department because it established its own administration. But the War on Poverty immediately affected Oregon schools through preschool training programs, supplementary remedial aid for schoolchildren, special education for children of migrant farm laborers, and work-study programs for disadvantaged children. The department employs a liaison officer to work with the Office of Economic Opportunity and help local schools with their proposals. The preschool training programs held in Oregon during the summer of 1967 have strongly influenced the legislators in considering the department's proposals for state-supported kindergartens in the 1967 legislative session.

Growth Under the Elementary and Secondary Education Act, 1965. Since most of the provisions of this legislation were created on a 5-year basis, the programs are still in the developmental phase and have not yet exerted their full influence on the department. But several staff members have been added to the department to help process proposals for Elementary and Secondary Education Act funds from the local districts. A large group is engaged in examining programs for the special education of culturally deprived children under Title I, and others are inspecting proposals under Title III for special services instruction before passing them on to the U.S. Office of Education for approval. But Title V has had the greatest impact by allotting money for strengthening state leadership. Various divisions have added several employees, but the greatest number has gone to the new Communications Material Center, which provides the department with a research library and librarian, a graphic artist, a photographer, and a program coordinator. These should greatly increase the quality and variety of state department publications.

Summary: The State's Education Under State Department Leadership, 1966

The major developments under the Oregon Program, the National Defense Education Act, and the Elementary and Secondary Education Act occurred under the able leadership of Superintendent Leon P. Minear. At the close of the 1965-66 school year, he cited the following evidence of Oregon's superior school system:

General Statistics. Ninth-graders remaining in school until graduation have increased from 63.8 percent in 1952 to 82.6 percent in 1965, with half of this increase occurring since 1960.

Selective Service statistics for 1965 show that Oregon had the lowest number of draftees failing the mental ability test of any state; the failure rate was 1.9 percent compared to a high in one state of 46.8 percent.

The education department, local school districts, and the colleges and universities have cooperated in a 4-year, $3.5-million Ford Foundation-supported effort to update and upgrade public school programs; to reduce the gap between actual classroom instruction and new knowledge in subject fields, teaching, and learning; and to improve teacher training.

Subject Matter Achievement. Oregon children's basic skills in reading, writing, and arithmetic were 1.5 years above the national standards when Science Research Associates conducted the last statewide sample testing in 1962.

Oregon's colleges and universities report a high median score for entering students on the 1965 Scholastic Aptitude Tests in English and math, and superior achievement scores on the College Board Entrance Exams.

The state has been a leader in developing elementary and secondary courses in economic understanding. Three school districts, the education department, and the Oregon Council on Economic Education are participating in a $2.5-million nationwide developmental economic education program. The schools are demonstrating how to teach economics at varying degrees of complexity at all elementary and secondary grade levels.

The President's Council on Physical Fitness cited Oregon as one of the top three states in the nation in its support of physical fitness programs. Six schools served as national demonstration centers for outstanding physical education programs this past year. Extensive research and development is currently under way to improve the quality of vocational education programs and to make such programs available to all students.

Special Education. These programs have been expanded to enable 20,000 mentally and physically handicapped children to attend public schools. These facts, combined with Dr. Holy's "Report Card" of 1966, indicated that Oregon is providing mature leadership and that great gains and improvements *can* be made in the quality of education. The local districts, for their part, seem to be confident that the State Department of Education will cooperate with them while attaining greater quality and strength as the centralized agency for state school administration.

The incentive for much of the progress made in Oregon's schools since 1961 came from Superintendent Leon P. Minear. Born in Texas, educated and employed in California, Colorado, and Oregon, Dr. Minear brought a spirit of pioneering and "ground-breaking" to state school administration that is highly essential in this age of unprecedented social and technological change.

His wide variety of interests and intense concern for the welfare of children in terms of the learning experiences that can be provided for them gave Dr. Minear his strength as an educator. His amazing ability to grasp "the big picture" and relate its parts provided him with the administrative skill to head the education department staff and a 23,000-teacher school system.

On April 1, 1968, Superintendent Minear accepted a position in vocational and technical education in the Office of Education in Washington. Deputy Jesse V. Fasold served as the interim chief state school officer until June 30, when Dale Parnell was appointed to serve until the election in November 1968, which will determine the person to serve the remainder of the 4-year term ending in January 1971 to which Minear was elected in November 1966.

In Oregon, the change followed a 1965 decision of the Oregon Supreme Court, which found a technical mistake of wording in the Oregon State Constitution: The words *elect* and *election* were held to refer to selection by the people rather than by the State Board of Education (40). This decision removed the power to appoint the chief state school officer that had been exercised by the State Board of Education during the period 1961-65 and forced the state superintendent who had been appointed by the board to run for reelection After his reelection, the decision continued to raise many question about the authority of major elements of the Oregon state system of education.

The charts in Appendix B show these changes, including that resulting from the decision of the Oregon Supreme Court in July 1968 which restored the general authority of the State Board of Education, leaving the state superintendent a constitutionally elected officer and the executive officer of the board without substantial authority of his own.

FOOTNOTES

1. For further information, see Robert G. Raymer, "A History of the Superintendency of Public Instruction in the State of Oregon, 1849-1925" (unpublished Ph.D. dissertation, University of Oregon, Eugene, 1926), p. 9.
2. Oregon, *Constitution* (1859), art. 8, sec. 1.
3. Raymer, *op. cit.,* pp. 20-24.
4. Oregon, *Constitution* (1859), art. 8, sec. 1.
5. There were few records on the first superintendent's 2-year term. The new law went into effect in the 1874 general election. Oregon, *Laws* (1872), p. 145.
6. Raymer, *op. cit.,* p. 54.
7. *Ibid.,* p. 57.
8. *Ibid.,* p. 43.
9. For the complete law, see Oregon, *Laws* (1889), Title VIII.
10. *Biennial Report of the Superintendent of Public Instruction, 1891-1892,* p. 149.
11. Morris S. Isseks, *History of State Administrative Agencies in Oregon, 1843-1937,* published as a report under the auspices of the Works Progress Administration (Salem: Oregon State Planning Board, 1939), pp. 132, 127-55.
12. E. S. Evenden, "The Education of Teachers in Oregon," *Elementary Education Bulletin,* No. 2 (March 1936), pp. 3-4. This was an address originally delivered by Evenden on the occasion of the dedication of the J. H. Ackerman Training School, Eastern Oregon Normal School, La Grande, on January 27, 1936.
13. *Biennial Report of the Superintendent of Public Instruction, 1911-1912.*
14. Although vocational education development will be followed throughout this report, the State Board of Education is not included in departmental statistics until after the organizational change of 1951.
15. Oregon, *Laws* (1923), ch. 7.
16. For the description of this provision see Oregon, *Constitution* (1859), art. 8, sec. 2.
17. See Appendix C, Tables 1 and 2.
18. Oregon, *Code* (1930), Title XXXV, ch. 45.
19. Superintendent of Public Instruction, *Biennial Report, 1929-1930,* p. 11.

20. Roben J. Maaske, a state department employee, directed the program from 1934 to 1936.

21. Superintendent of Public Instruction, *Biennial Report, 1935-1936,* p. 37.

22. *Ibid.,* p. 42.

23. Superintendent of Public Instruction, *Biennial Report, 1937-1938,* pp. 23-28.

24. Superintendent of Public Instruction, *Biennial Report, 1939-1940,* p. 27.

25. Six of the 154 persons employed by the WPA survey were from the State Department of Education. For a more detailed report, see Superintendent of Public Instruction, *Biennial Report, 1938-1940,* p. 52.

26. Superintendent of Public Instruction, *Biennial Report, 1931-1932,* p. 10.

27. Superintendent of Public Instruction, *Biennial Report, 1941-1942,* p. 17.

28. *Ibid.,* p. 13.

29. Superintendent of Public Instruction, *Biennial Report, 1947-48,* p. 27.

30. See Appendix C for more detail on the growth of personnel and funds.

31. T. C. Holy, *A Study of Public Elementary and Secondary Education in Oregon* (Salem: Board of Education, 1950), p. *v*.

32. Department of Education, "The Organization, Function, and Staff of the Offices of Education in Oregon," Department of Education, Salem, 1950. (Mimeographed.) Organizational charts of the department for other periods are shown in Appendix B.

33. Holy, *op. cit.,* p. 72.

34. This came from a rough draft of this proposal.

35. A more complete statement of the department's operational philosophy, written in 1965, is contained in Appendix B, Supplement 1.

36. T. C. Holy, "Comparative Data from the 1949-1950 and 1965-1966 Reports with Recommendations" (unpublished rough draft, Department of Education, Salem, 1966).

37. The Oregon community colleges operating in 1966 are Blue Mountain Community College, Pendleton; Central Oregon Community College, Bend; Clackamas Community College, Oregon City; Clatsop Community College, Astoria; Lane Community College, Eugene; Mt. Hood Community College, Gresham; Portland Community College, Portland; Salem Technical-Vocational Community College, Salem; Southwestern Oregon Community College, Coos Bay; Treasure Valley Community College, Ontario; and Umpqua Community College, Roseburg.

38. Robert Halton, state department director of community colleges, supplied these figures.

39. Governor's Education Improvement Advisory Commission, *Reports of the Commission Nos. 1-10* (Salem: Department of Education, 1965 and 1966).

40. State *ex rel.* Musa *v.* Minear, 240 Oregon 315 (1965).

BIBLIOGRAPHY

Public Documents

Oregon. *Code* (1930)..

--*Constitution* (1859).

--*Laws* (1872, 1881-1965).

State *ex rel.* Musa *v.* Minear. 240 Oregon 315 (1965).

Books

Holy, T. C. *A Study of Public Elementary and Secondary Education in Oregon.* Salem: Board of Education, 1950.

Isseks, Morris S. *History of State Administrative Agencies in Oregon, 1843-1937.* Salem: Oregon State Planning Board, 1939.

Legislative Interim Committee on Education. *Oregon's Public Schools: Curriculum, Quality, Personnel, Organization:* Salem: The Committee, December 1960.

Reports

Department of Education. *A Report on Oregon Schools.* Salem: The Department, 1960.

--*The Oregon Program: A Design for the Improvement of Education.* Salem: The Department, 1964.

--*The Oregon State Department of Education: Organization and Functions.* Salem: The Department, 1954.

--*What Convictions Lead Us?* Salem: The Department, 1966.

Director of the Budget. *State of Oregon Biennial Budget.* Salem: Department of Finance and Administration, 1943-67.

Education Subcommittees of the Governor's Committee on Children and Youth. *Programs, Progress, Projections in Education: A Report.* Salem: The Committee, 1962.

Governor's Education Improvement Advisory Commission. *Reports of the Commission, Nos. 1-10.* Salem: Department of Education, 1965 and 1966.

Superintendents of Public Instruction. *Biennial Reports.* Salem: Department of Education, 1881-1965.

University of Oregon, School of Education. *A Study of the Basic School Support Fund in Oregon.* Eugene: The University Press, 1954.

Article and Periodical

Evenden, E. S. "The Education of Teachers in Oregon." *Elementary Education Bulletin,* No. 2 (March 1936).

Unpublished Material

Baker, John L. "Powers and Duties of the Oregon State Board of Education." Unpublished master's thesis, School of Education, University of Oregon, Eugene, 1951.

Department of Education. "Goals of the State Department of Education." Salem, The Department, 1961. (Mimeographed.)

——"The Organization, Function, and Staff of the Offices of Education in Oregon." Salem, The Department, 1950. (Mimeographed.)

——"Policies and Procedures of the State Board of Education, Oregon." Salem, The Department, 1960. (Mimeographed.)

Edwards, J. W. "Review of Department Practices and Services." Memorandum to Dr. Leon P. Minear. April 22, 1964. (Mimeographed.)

Holy, T. C. "Comparative Data from the 1949-1950 and 1965-1966 Reports with Recommendations." Unpublished rough draft, Salem, Department of Education, 1966.

Raymer, Robert G. "A History of the Superintendency of Public Instruction in the State of Oregon, 1849-1925." Unpublished Ph.D. dissertation, University of Oregon, Eugene, 1926.

Sheldon, Henry D. "A Critical and Descriptive Bibliography of the History of Education in the State of Oregon." Education Series, Vol. II, No. 1, Eugene, bound by the University Press, 1929. (Typewritten.)

Other Source

Halton, Robert. Personal interview with Halton, director of community colleges, Oregon State Department of Education, 1967.

Appendix A

OREGON CHIEF STATE SCHOOL OFFICERS

State Superintendents of Public Instruction

1873-74	Sylvester C. Simpson
1874-78	L. L. Rowland
1878-82	Leonard J. Powell
1882-95	E. B. McElroy
1895-99	G. M. Irwin
1899-1911	J. H. Ackerman
1911-13	L. R. Alderman
1913-26	Julius A. Churchill
1926	R. R. Turner (Oct. – Dec.)
1927-37	Charles A. Howard
1937-61	Rex Putnam
1961-68	Leon P. Minear
1968	Jesse V. Fasold (Apr. – June)
1968-	Dale Parnell

Appendix B

Chart I.--OREGON DEPARTMENT OF EDUCATION, 1920

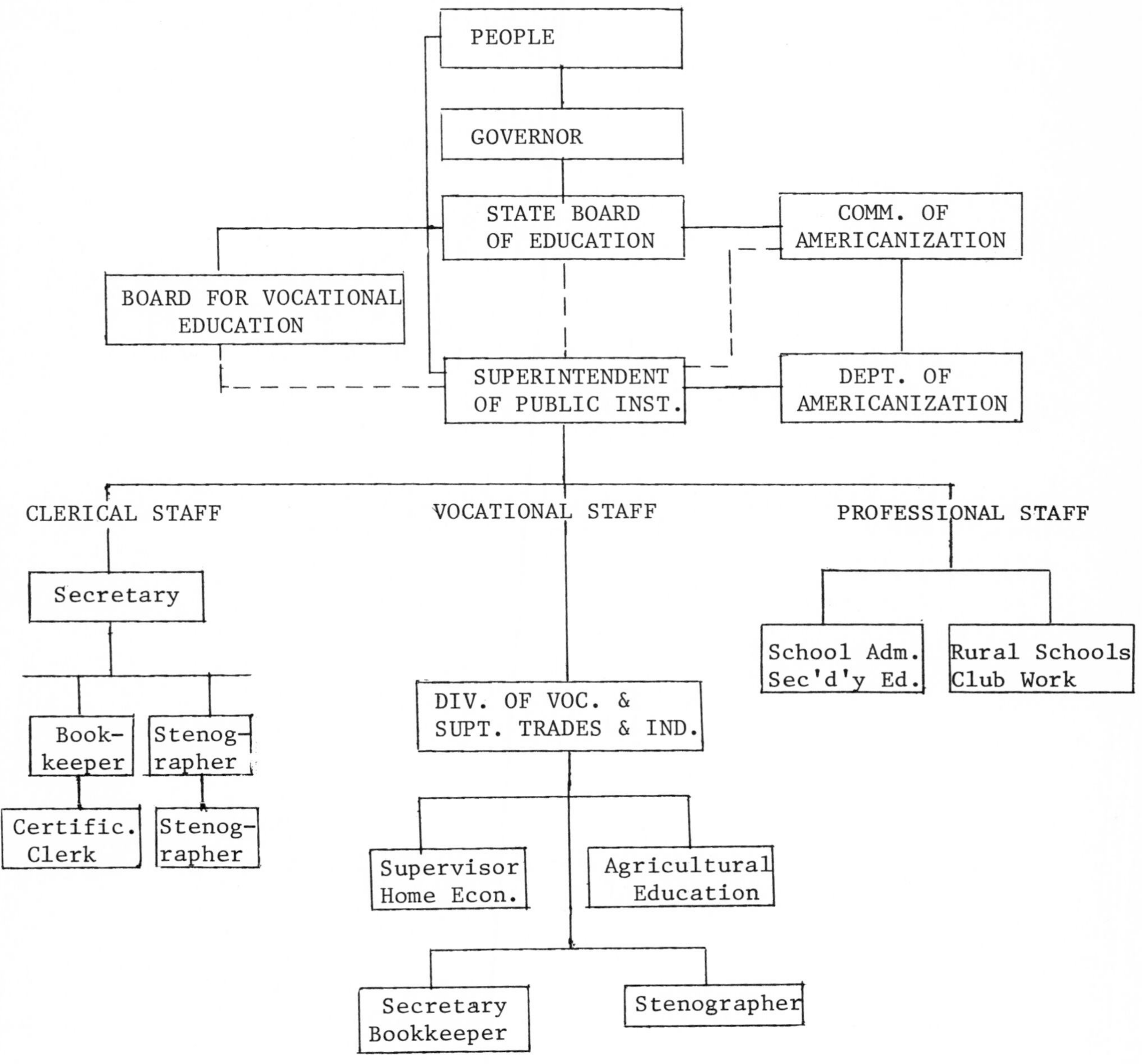

Appendix B

Chart II.--OREGON DEPARTMENT OF EDUCATION, CIRCA 1935

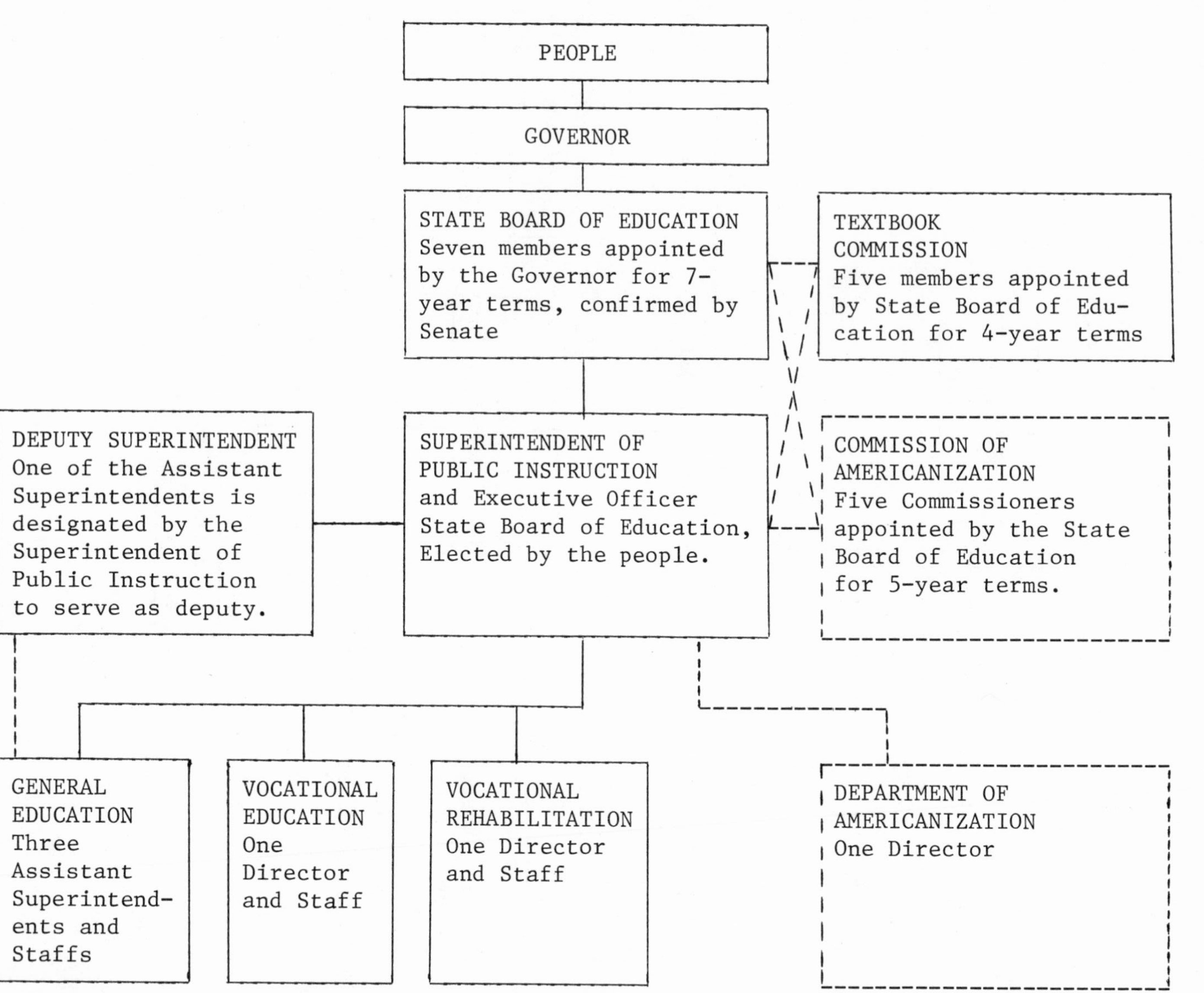

Appendix B

Chart III.--OREGON DEPARTMENT OF EDUCATION, 1950

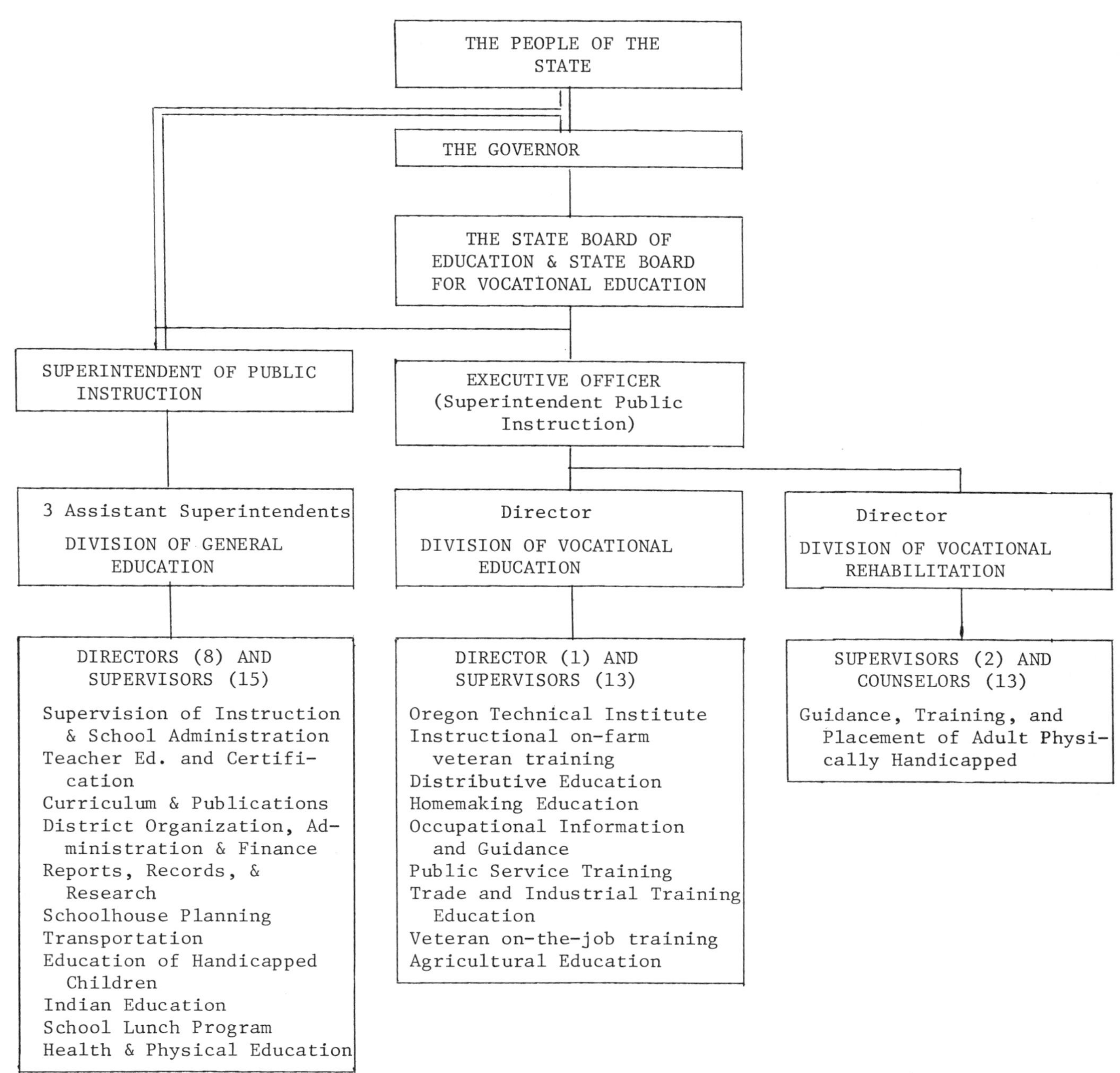
THE PEOPLE OF THE STATE
THE GOVERNOR
THE STATE BOARD OF EDUCATION & STATE BOARD FOR VOCATIONAL EDUCATION
SUPERINTENDENT OF PUBLIC INSTRUCTION
EXECUTIVE OFFICER (Superintendent Public Instruction)
3 Assistant Superintendents
DIVISION OF GENERAL EDUCATION
Director
DIVISION OF VOCATIONAL EDUCATION
Director
DIVISION OF VOCATIONAL REHABILITATION
DIRECTORS (8) AND SUPERVISORS (15)
Supervision of Instruction & School Administration
Teacher Ed. and Certification
Curriculum & Publications
District Organization, Administration & Finance
Reports, Records, & Research
Schoolhouse Planning
Transportation
Education of Handicapped Children
Indian Education
School Lunch Program
Health & Physical Education
DIRECTOR (1) AND SUPERVISORS (13)
Oregon Technical Institute
Instructional on-farm veteran training
Distributive Education
Homemaking Education
Occupational Information and Guidance
Public Service Training
Trade and Industrial Training Education
Veteran on-the-job training
Agricultural Education
SUPERVISORS (2) AND COUNSELORS (13)
Guidance, Training, and Placement of Adult Physically Handicapped

Appendix B

Chart IV.--OREGON DEPARTMENT OF EDUCATION, 1961-66

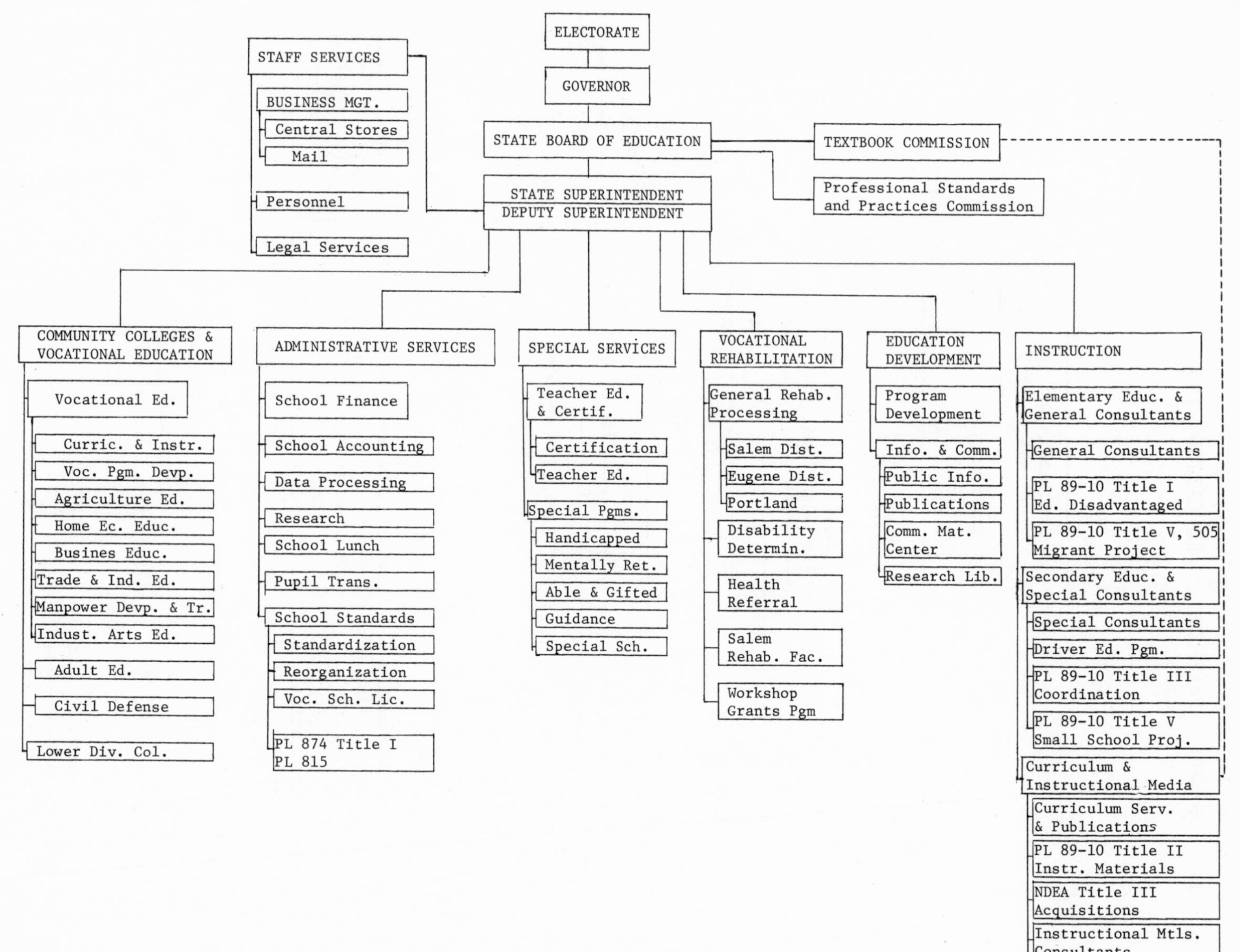

Appendix B

Chart V.--OREGON DEPARTMENT OF EDUCATION, 1966-68

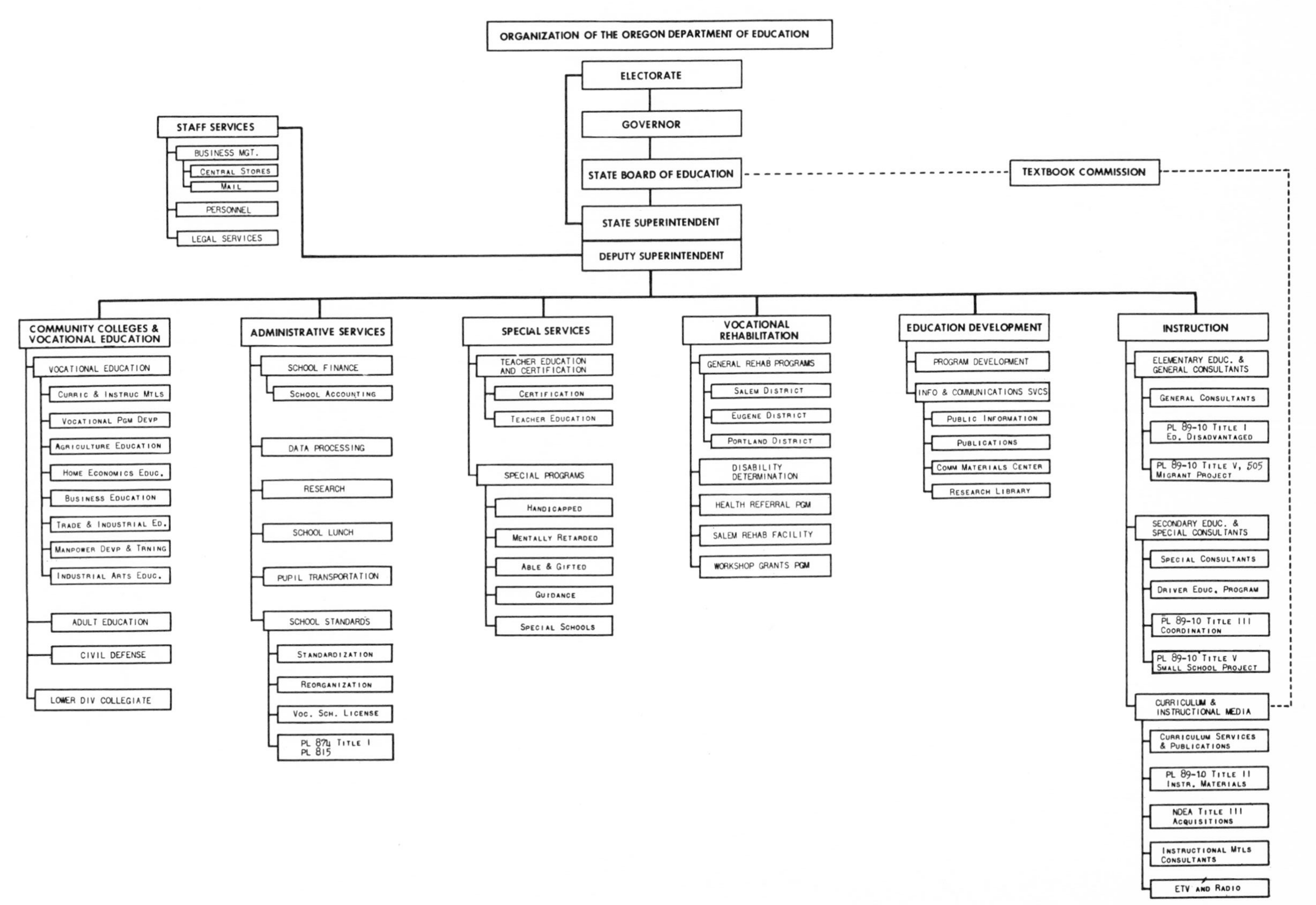

Appendix B

Chart VI.--OREGON BOARD OF EDUCATION, July 1968

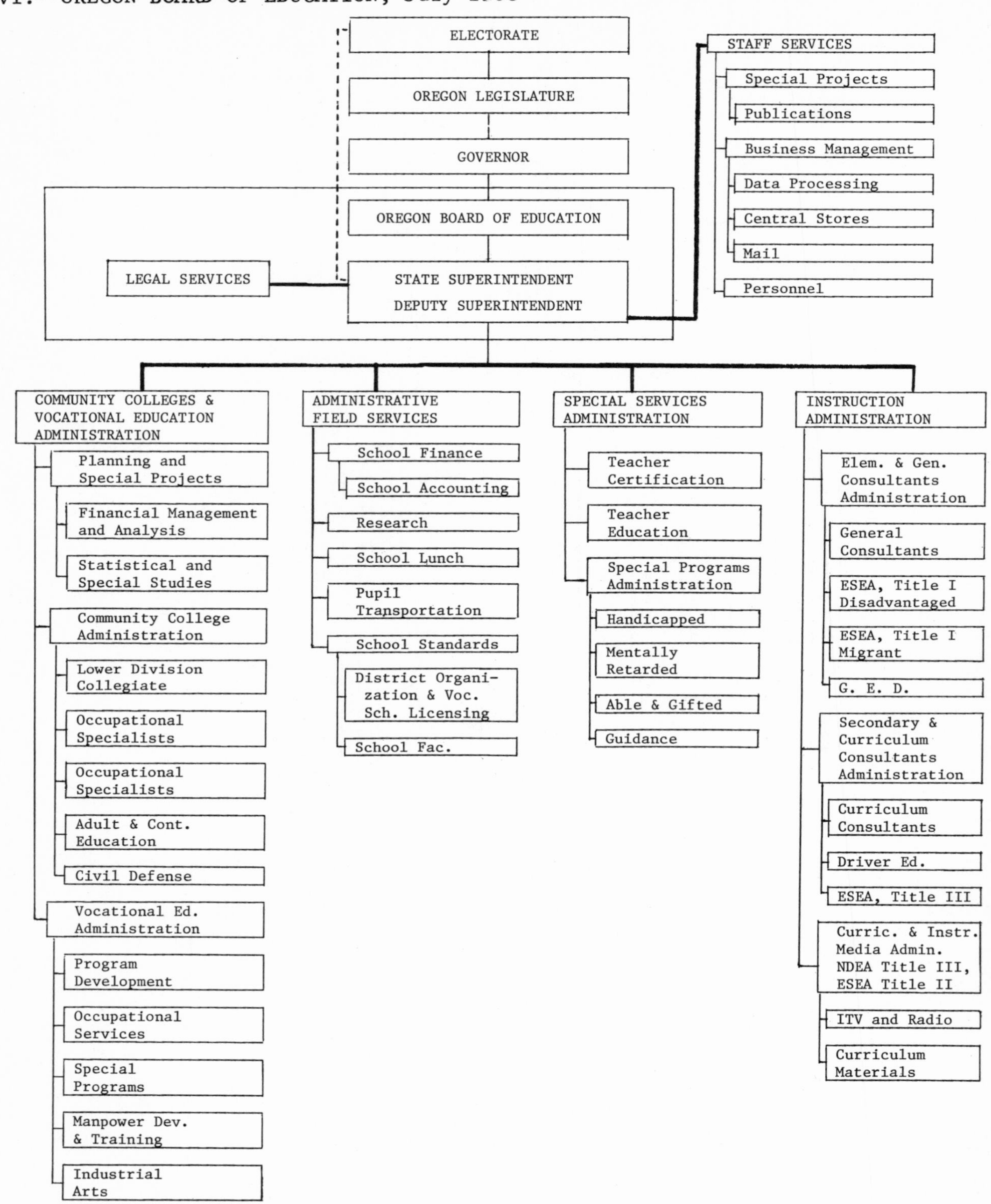

Appendix B

Supplement 1. — OPERATIONAL PHILOSOPHY OF THE STATE BOARD OF EDUCATION

The Oregon Constitution directs the Legislative Assembly to provide by law for the establishment of a uniform and general system of common schools. Laws relating to the Oregon public school system provide that the administrative functions of the state relating to supervision, management, and control of schools which are not conferred by law on some other agency shall be exercised by the Department of Education under direction and control of the State Board of Education. The Superintendent of Public Instruction, an elected official, exercises, under the direction of the Board, a general superintendence of school officers and the public schools. He has certain other educational duties and powers conferred upon him by statute, and it is provided that he shall be the administrative officer of the Board and executive head of the Department. Thus, the State Board of Education, the Office of Superintendent of Public Instruction, and the Department of Education act in concert in carrying out the constitutional mandate and the legislative program relating to public schools in Oregon.

The State Board of Education has five basic functions—regulatory, executive, evaluative, and those related to policy-making and leadership. The two major areas of Board Responsibility are in regulation and leadership.

In exercising the regulatory functions provided by law, the State Board of Education establishes standards, rules, and regulations applicable to the Department of Education; the public elementary and secondary schools of the state; and in certain instances, private schools. Board regulations and standards exist to ensure that the instructional and educational program of the Oregon public school system adheres to a minimum basic program in scope, quality and efficiency. Standards established by the Board are minimum and not maximum requirements.

It is the policy of the Board that standards and regulations be developed cooperatively between the professional staff in the Department of Education; local school officials; and whenever possible, lay citizens. It is the intent of the Board to encourage local administrative units to develop sound educational programs which at least meet the Board's minimum requirements and exceed them whenever possible. Unless otherwise provided by statute, however, administration and control of the local educational program is vested in the local administrative unit.

In addition to the general field of public education, the State Board of Education is responsible for regulation and administration of programs of vocational rehabilitation in Oregon, under both federal and state laws. This it does through the Division of Vocational Rehabilitation, a part of the Department of Education.

The Board exercises leadership to improve education and vocational rehabilitation at both the local and state level. Leadership services from the Department of Education should be available to local school districts, colleges and universities in the state, the legislature, the governor, other state agencies with programs bearing on education and vocational rehabilitation, and to the public generally. The leadership responsibility of the Board entails planning and research, consultant services, coordination, public relations, and in-service.

Planning involves identification of problems and purposes and determination of ways to resolve and attain them. Continual planning is required for each of the operating divisions of the Department of Education and for the total state program of education and vocational rehabilitation. In planning, the Board uses the services of the entire professional staff of the Department of Education. It also enlists the participation of representative groups and individuals outside the Department. The purpose of the Board in all educational planning is to stimulate and encourage initiative and responsibility at the local district level.

Research provides the basis for policy formulation and long-range planning. The Department should maintain research activities of its own and should collaborate with the research activities of other organizations and groups interested in education and vocational rehabilitation. The Department of Education should also serve as a channel for the exchange of ideas and for the dissemination of data accumulated through research.

The Department assumes leadership responsiblities with schools at the local and community level in the administration and improvement of the state educational program. The Department should be staffed with specialists able to translate ideas for education development into action; it should become the major communication and service center of education, linking schools to each other and to the state, and the state to the nation. The regulatory authority of the Department is exercised only when it is required by statute or when local responsibility has not been assumed and discharged. The Department shall be judicious in its use of authority and shall recognize the control over education that is vested in the district school boards.

The State Board of Education recognizes that an increasing portion of the burden of financing education is being assumed by the federal government, and this will continue if all individuals are to have equal opportunities through education and training. The Board will continue to accept federal funds and to cooperate with federal programs, but neither the funds nor the programs will be permitted to serve partisan interests or allowed to lessen state or local control and responsibility for education. Federal programs must operate within the framework established by Oregon statutes and rules and regulations of the State Board of Education.

Source:

Division of Education Development, Oregon Department of Education. *Biennial Report,* 1965-66. pp. 1-2.

Appendix C

Table 1.–STATE DEPARTMENT OF EDUCATION PERSONNEL, 1920-66

A. Professional Staff for the State Department, 1920-50

	1920-21	1930-31	1940-41	1945-46	1949-50
General education	1	2	3	6	20
Special education	...	...	...	3	6
Vocational education	...	...	9	10	12
Voc. rehabilitation	...	...	4	7	17

B. Professional Staff for the State Department, 1950-66

	1950	1952	1954	1956	1958	1960	1962	1964	1966
State superintendent	1	1	1	1	1	1	1	1	1
Deputy supt.	1	1	1	1	1	1	1	1	1
Instruction Division									
Assistant superintendent	1	1	1	1	1	1	1	1	1
Elementary & gen. cons.	4	6	6	5	8	8	7	7	9
Migrant program	...	...	...	...	...	1	1	...	...
ESEA I and III	...	...	...	...	...	...	...	...	3
Secondary & spec. cons.	1	3	4	4	6	8	9	12	9
Small school cons.	...	...	...	...	...	...	...	...	1
Curr. & inst. materials	2	3	3	3	3	4	4	4	7
Health & phys. ed.	2	2	2	2	2	2	2	1	1
Staff Services Division									
Business management	...	...	...	...	...	1	2	2	3
Personnel	...	...	...	...	...	1	1	1	1
Legal	...	...	...	...	...	...	...	1	1
Community Colleges & Vocational Educ. Division									
Assistant superintendent	1	1	1	1	1	1	2	1	1
Lower division coll.	...	...	...	...	...	...	...	...	1
Civil Defense	...	...	...	...	...	...	2	2	2
Adult education	...	...	...	...	...	...	...	...	...
Vocational educ.	...	...	...	...	...	...	...	3	3
Agriculture	4	4	3	3	3	3	2	2	2
Home economics	2	3	3	3	2	2	3	2	2
Industrial educ.	3	3	3	2	3	4	4	3	3
Bus. & dist. educ.	1	1	1	1	1	1	1	1	2
Public serv. trng.	1	1	1	1	1	4	3	1	1
Manpower devel.	...	...	...	...	...	...	...	1	1
Administrative Serv. Division									
Assistant superintendent	1	1	1	1	1	1	1	1	1
School finance	1	1	1	1	1	2	2	1	2
School accounting	...	...	...	...	...	...	1	1	1

See next page for second half of table.

Table 1.–STATE DEPARTMENT OF EDUCATION PERSONNEL, 1920-66 (Continued)

B. Professional Staff for the State Department, 1950-66 (Continued)

	1950	.1952	1954	1956	1958	1960	1962	1964	1966
Data processing	...	...	...	...	...	...	...	3	4
Research	...	...	...	...	...	...	2	3	3
School lunch	2	2	2	2	3	4	5	5	5
Transportation	1	1	1	1	2	3	3	2	2
School standards[a]	...	...	...	...	...	...	1	2	2
Reorganization	...	...	1	1	1	1	1	...	...
Priv. voc. sch. licng.	...	...	...	1	1	...	...	...	1
P.L. 874 & 815	...	...	...	...	...	...	...	...	...
Sch. planning/facilities	1	1	1	1	1	1	2	1	1
Indian education	...	...	...	6	2	2	...	...	...
Special Services Division									
Assistant superintendent	1	1	1	1	1	1	1	1	1
Teacher educ. & cert.	2	2	2	2	2	2	3	3	3
Special educ. programs	5	5	6	6	6	6	10	10	10
Guidance	1	1	2	2	2	2	2	3	3
Education Development									
Assistant superintendent	...	...	...	...	...	...	1	1	1
Publications	...	...	...	...	...	...	1	1	3
Curr. Mat. Center	...	...	...	...	...	...	1	1	1
General	...	...	...	...	...	...	2	2	3
TOTAL	39	45	48	53	56	68	85	88	103

[a] Prior to October 1962, standardization functions were handled by elementary and secondary consultants in the Division of Instruction.

Appendix C

Table 2.–SOURCES OF REVENUE, 1955-67

Source	1955-57	1957-59	1959-61
Fees & licenses	$ 508,000	$ 484,000	$ ---
Gifts & grants	---	---	20,000
Federal funds	2,161,000	2,612,000	4,204,000
School districts	---	---	242,000
Motor Vehicle Dept.	---	861,293	1,000,000
General fund approp.	3,118,000	4,041,000	2,412,000
Basic sch. sup. fund	71,521,000	96,140,000	107,632,000
Community coll. const.	---	---	---
Vocational rehab.	---	---	---
Total	$ 77,260,000	$102,760,000	$114,540,000

Source	1961-63	Est. 1963-65	Est. 1965-67
Fees & licenses	$ ---	$ ---	$ ---
Gifts & grants	1,010,000	1,990,000	594,000
Federal funds	5,110,000	7,125,000	10,402,000
School districts	315,000	304,000	332,000
Motor Vehicle Dept.	1,006,000	1,063,000	1,115,000
General fund approp.	4,678,000	11,593,000	15,073,000
Basic sch. sup. fund	127,239,000	126,351,000	146,569,000
Community coll. const.	---	1,390,000	3,610,000
Vocational rehab.	---	156,710	39,200,000
Total	$137,530,000	$151,383,000	$178,000,000[a]

[a]Actual employment in September 1966 showed approximately 340 full-time positions in the department. The approved budget for 1967-69 is $269,856,240. This budget is still subject to the approval of the 1967 Legislature.

38 Pennsylvania

DEPARTMENT OF PUBLIC INSTRUCTION
Patricia L. Rosenbaum

Contents

EDUCATION BEFORE 1900

The first mention of a working schoolmaster appears in the official records for 1679 of what is now the Commonwealth of Pennsylvania. In March of that year, teacher E. Draughton sued Dirck Williams for payment promised him for teaching Williams' children to read the Bible. It was a forecast of things to come, for Pennsylvania, in spite of its historic role as one of the 13 original colonies, lagged far behind Massachusetts and New York in the development of public education. To understand the staggering problems which faced those who sought to build a centralized system of public education in the Keystone State, it is necessary to go back almost 300 years to explore the diversity of elements that went into the Commonwealth at its birth.

The great Quaker, William Penn, following the tenets of his faith, founded his Commonwealth as a "Holy Experiment" in civil liberty and religious freedom. But this act, noble as it was, sowed the seeds of friction which continued to haunt the supporters of public education 150 years later.

This history of Pennsylvania's Department of Public Instruction has been a responsibility of J. R. Rackley, superintendent of public instruction, who appointed a committee of department staff members to coordinate the research. A. G. Breidenstine, deputy superintendent of public instruction, was named chairman of the committee. Other members were Herbert E. Bryan, Neal V. Musmanno, George W. Hoffman, and Warren E. Ringler. As secretary of the committee, Warren Ringler supervised the project for the department and was appointed to the Study Commission of the Council of Chief State School Officers which cooperated in its early development.

Severino Stefanon, secretary to the State Board of Education, worked with the department committee during its planning phase and suggested Patricia Rosenbaum to do the research and prepare the manuscript for the department. She was assisted in her work by contributions from many present and former staff members in the department and others working for education in the Commonwealth of Pennsylvania.

Penn dreamed of a free and universal public school system for his colony. In fact, the first *Frame of Government* he drew up in England stated that "the Governor and Provincial Council shall erect and order all public schools, and encourage and reward the authors of useful sciences and laudable inventions in the said Province" (1). Another article directed that "all children within this Province of the age of twelve years, shall be taught some useful trade or skill, to the end that none may be idle, but the poor may work to live, and the rich, if they become poor, may not want" (2). Penn's ideas in education, as in other fields, were far in advance of his time.

After Penn returned to England to remain for 14 years, his Provincial Council did not press the development of a school system. Continuing quarrels between the Governors who succeeded Penn and the Provincial Assembly, the diversity of the new settlers, and the Commonwealth's geography all contributed to a loss of interest in the founder's dream. Gradually, control of education slipped into the hands of private and religious groups.

Other colonies attracted more or less homogeneous groups—Catholics flocked to Maryland and Puritans to New England. But Penn's doctrine of tolerance and religious freedom and the Quaker tradition of noninterference in others' affairs attracted an impressive mixture of nationalities and creeds: English Quakers, German Pietists, Scotch-Irish Presbyterians, Dutch and Swedish Lutherans, and Catholics from England, France, Holland, and Germany. For instance, the German Pietists, like the Quakers, fled from persecution in their homeland. Suspicious of central authority, asking only to be left in peace to practice their faith and follow their traditions, the various sects settled into communities speaking their own language and provided the education they alone deemed necessary for their children. This was also true of other national and religious groups of immigrants.

The Quakers, who exercised the strongest influence in the infant colony, provided good common-school or elementary education for their own children and, in many cases, for the children of the poor. They were not equally interested in higher education, mainly because they did not believe it was necessary for spiritual leadership. More important, they would not impose their own concern for education on others, since to do so would violate their belief in individual freedom. Nor did they encourage the development of a strong central government; their problems were settled in Meeting, and they considered any outside authority unnecessary. The Quakers' hands-off attitude toward the affairs of others, their lack of interest in a strong central government, and their general lack of interest in education beyond religious training, together with the isolationism of the German Pietists, made Penn's vision of a system of public education an impossibility (3).

The state's geography also discouraged cooperation. Although the eastern part is fairly level, northern and western Pennsylvania are cut by mountain ridges into narrow valleys and small fertile plains. With transportation depending on rivers or rough trails, communication was difficult. The national and religious groups gathered into communities to protect old heritages and folkways and became largely self-sufficient entities.

In the late eighteenth century, the Whiskey Rebellion in western Pennsylvania amply demonstrated this self-sufficiency and resistance to central authority. The predominantly Scotch-Irish farmers, still living under frontier conditions, resisted with muskets the government's attempts to collect a tax on whiskey. A few years later, in 1799, another attempt to levy taxes precipitated the Fries' Rebellion of the Pennsylvania Germans in the eastern part of the state.

The Commonwealth's tolerant atmosphere diminished the threat to the early settlers' religious beliefs, and the hard frontier life had brought no new need for schooling. On the contrary, the average man had little time for niceties. Thus, there was little demand for common schools and even less for secondary and higher education. At the outbreak of the Revolutionary War, education generally was in a decline except in Philadelphia, then the intellectual center of the colonies.

Although a few leaders realized the need for public schools, it was difficult for them to persuade others. For instance, although the State Constitution of 1776 carried a requirement that the Legislature open a school in each county, it was more than 50 years before a single elementary school was founded. Ten years later, in 1786, the Legislature set aside 60,000 acres of state lands to endow public schools, but in the following years most of the state's financial efforts were directed toward private education at the secondary or college level in an attempt to to develop a supply of teachers.

When the constitution was rewritten in 1790, the first article of the section on education read: "The Legislature shall, as soon as conveniently may be, provide by law for the establishment of schools throughout the state, in such a manner that the poor may be taught gratis" (4). This brief statement, plus one on promoting the arts and sciences in one or more institutions, were copied into the 1838 constitution and remained the sole constitutional provisions for education until the constitution was again rewritten in 1873.

Throughout the early nineteenth century, most of the Governors and a majority of the legislators supported better public schools, while the conservative rural voters generally opposed them. In particular, the Germans still considered public education a threat to their language and customs, an alien creation of a distrusted central authority which would demand increased taxes of them. When the Legislature, at the request of Governor Thomas McKean, passed a law providing free elementary education for paupers' children in 1802, it was never applied. Two years later, the Legislature passed a similar law, to similar effect, and passed a third version in 1809.

However, sentiment in favor of the public schools was rising. The Pennsylvania Society for the Promotion of Public Schools was organized in Philadelphia in 1827. Two years later, the workingmen's organizations in Philadelphia asked each candidate for office for his views on public schools.

The Free School Act of 1834

The winner of the gubernatorial campaign of 1829 was regular Democratic candidate George Wolf of Northampton County. A lawyer and early follower of Thomas Jefferson, Wolf had served three terms in the lower House of the Legislature and three terms in Congress before retiring to run for Governor. During his two terms, Governor Wolf's major accomplishment was establishment of a free public education system in the Commonwealth. Although other Governors had given their support to the idea of free public education, he was the first to make it an avowed purpose of his administration. In fact, his ardent advocacy of free public schools contributed to his defeat when he ran for a third term in 1835–perhaps the first time, but not the last, that a political career has risen or fallen on an education issue.

The actual author of the legislation creating a system of free public schools for the Commonwealth was State Senator Samuel Breck of Philadelphia. A native of Massachusetts, a man of wealth and education, Breck had already served in the State Senate and the U.S. Congress when he agreed to run again for the Senate in 1833, primarily to promote public education. He was named chairman of the Senate Education Committee for the 1834 session, and through his efforts a joint committee on education was appointed. Under his guidance as chairman, the bill to establish free public schools passed both Houses of the Legislature with very little opposition and only four dissenting votes (5).

Although somewhat cumbersome, the Act of 1834 was a milestone in the state's educational progress. It directed every county to organize a school division, with every political subdivision down to the ward level forming a school district. It authorized the county commissioners to levy county taxes for school support. If no taxes were levied, the county could receive no financial assistance from the state, thus setting a pattern for future relations between the districts and the state and for the expansion of educational services. It provided for boards of school directors with specific duties and powers and charged them with inspecting the schools. The secretary of the Commonwealth was named the superintendent of common schools. The Legislature appropriated $75,000 to pay the state's share of the educational costs.

The ease with which the bill passed the General Assembly was deceptive. When, according to the act, the notices of election of school directors were posted, opposition began to mount. At least 4,000 schoolhouses had been built in the state by volunteer contributions; the teachers' salaries and maintenance costs were paid through tuition charges. "Why build free schools?" people asked. In the more densely settled communities, church schools were established with the local minister in charge, frequently teaching as well as preaching; many religious denominations believed that secular education should be closely tied to religious instruction. German-speaking citizens feared the destruction of their traditions and language, and opponents of central government and taxation also rallied to resist the public schools. Others argued that "free schools would furnish the hot-beds wherein idle drones too lazy for honest labor would be reared and maintained" (6).

The fight over elections to the General Assembly was bitter, and feelings ran high. One historian wrote:

> Party and even church ties were for a time broken up, the rich arrayed themselves against the poor and the business and social relations of whole neighborhoods were greatly disturbed .... Enmities were created between individuals and families that outlasted the lifetime of those concerned (7).

It appeared at first that the enemies of the free school bill had won the day, and, as the new assembly convened, most people had little doubt that the act would be repealed. More than 500 petitions came in, most in opposition—including 66 who signed their names by marks—from the mass of Pennsylvania Germans who lived in the southeastern counties.

The Senate quickly passed a repeal bill, but since the foes of public education could not command a clear majority in the House, a vigorous struggle ensued. The cause of public education seemed lost until Thaddeus Stevens, representing Adams County, delivered a brilliant speech supporting the Free School Act (8). His fervor and the undisputable facts moved the House to pass a measure strengthening the act, and the Senate approved it just before adjourning. Although it was years before free public schools were a reality for all, the principle of state control of the system was finally established.

Much to the surprise of many people who had supported Joseph Ritner in his campaign to succeed Wolf as Governor, once in office Ritner became a strong supporter of public education. He appointed Thomas Burrowes, a political figure, secretary of the Commonwealth; thus, under the terms of the Free School Act, Burrowes also served as superintendent of common schools. During his administration, the School Act of 1836 corrected some of the weaknesses of the 1834 legislation. At the same time, the Legislature passed a special law permitting central high schools to be established Almost immediately, the Central High School opened in Philadelphia, and the rest of the state gradually began to develop an interest in secondary education. Other laws were passed during the 1840's, but perhaps the most important was the 1849 act which eliminated the "permissive" features of the 1834 and 1836 Free School Acts and made the state directives mandatory. The progress and interest in education sparked during this period continued throughout Burrowes' life.

Generally, this was the pattern of Pennsylvania's development of education. Educators, concerned citizens, and legislators would urge an innovation; the assembly would enact a measure permitting but not requiring it, with varying amounts of financial support; then progressive districts would inaugurate the new program. Its success would bring increasing public pressure to make it comprehensive, and sooner or later this would culminate in mandatory legislation with a state subsidy. The Department of Public Instruction (established in 1873) would be involved in persuading districts to cooperate, suggesting standards and procedures, supervising distribution of the subsidy, and finally administering the standards and financial support when the program became mandatory. The speed with which the program would be accepted depended on the organized power of the local resistance to change, the traditional distrust of centralized authority and taxation, the strong rural conservatives in the Legislature and the apportionment of legislative seats tending to give this element a disproportionate influence, and the character and interest of the incumbent Governor and superintendent of public instruction.

An Act Creating County Superintendents

Pennsylvania took another big step forward when William Bigler became Governor in 1852. After working closely with a number of the state's leading educators, his administration got from the Legislature the Act of 1854, which created the position of county superintendent of schools, strengthened the powers of school boards, and eliminated as districts the subdistricts and wards of cities. The law also involved the state more closely in local administration of schools, providing a channel for distributing state funds to the districts. The county superintendent was empowered to examine and certify teachers, a move in the direction of uniform statewide standards, not fully to be achieved until the next century. This county supervision of schools was to be replaced by a network of larger "intermediate units" in July 1968.

Various groups reacted violently against the law creating county superintendents. The anti-free-school element—the mass of conservative, tax-fearing, change-resisting citizens still smarting from their defeat in 1834—was joined by school directors, who resented what they viewed as an attempt to limit their authority, and by teachers, who feared they would not qualify under the new law. Once again, a controversial education issue influenced political fortunes: Governor Bigler was defeated for re-election in the fall of 1854. However, his successor, Governor James Pollock, not only defended the Act of 1854 but boldly advocated increasing appropriations for education and opening normal schools for training teachers. He also strengthened the cause of public education by appointing Andrew G. Curtin secretary of the Commonwealth and superintendent of public schools and Henry C. Hickock as his deputy superintendent (9).

Strengthening Public Schools

For more than 15 years, educational leaders had been contending that by separating the offices of the secretary of the Commonwealth and superintendent of public schools, the public education program would gain efficiency and prestige. In 1857, the Legislature did separate the two offices. Deputy Hickock became the first superintendent of common schools to head a separate department of education. Later the same year, the Pollock administration answered another appeal that educators had been making for years by securing a law establishing normal schools. As early as 1825, the principal of the Germantown Academy had urged that such schools be established. The new county superintendents' reports starkly revealed the deficiencies in the preparation and qualifications of teachers. But the schools created by the 1857 legislation were to be privately owned, again amply demonstrating the fear of state control and the prevailing emphasis on local authority and initiative. The state would only give them aid.

The Civil War diverted the public's concern from education; when peace returned, changing social conditions brought new challenges to the public schools. Industrial production boomed; the cities were growing, and workingmen were organizing at an increasing rate. This industrial urban growth did not affect Pennsylvania as much as it did other states at this time, for many of the state's young farmers returned from the war to their farms and stayed there. In spite of the lure of the cities, farm crops and acreage under cultivation increased in the state, and the conservative rural population remained to influence the course of education during the next few years.

Legislation in 1867 strengthened the authority of the county superintendents, raised the requirements for teacher certification, and gave school boards the right of eminent domain, but not until 1874 was the superintendent of common schools, James P. Wickersham (10), able to report that free public schools were operating in every district. That this was 40 years after passage of the law requiring them illustrated a common weakness in the state's educational legislation: the lack of penalties to enforce compliance. For instance, the Free School Act required schools to be established but provided no enforcement beyond withholding state subsidies. If a district had no schools, it did not need the subsidy, so 23 districts with six or seven thousand school-age children had still not provided public schools by 1866. It was financial incentives in the form of retroactive payments that brought all of the lost sheep into the fold by 1874.

Pennsylvania adopted a new constitution in 1873, the one it operates under today, which enlarged the educational provisions of the 1838 constitution and changed the name of the educational agency to the Department of Public Instruction—its present title (11). At the time, the department consisted of six persons: the superintendent, his deputy, three clerks, and a messenger. The constitution placed the superintendent of public instruction at the head of the department and prescribed his term of office to preclude his being arbitrarily dismissed by the Governor (12). The constitution made definite provisions for the education of "all children of the Commonwealth above the age of six years" and firmly shut the door to further appropriations of state funds to sectarian schools. Women were given equality under the school laws, making them eligible for any office or position.

Secondary education, which was mainly in private hands until the end of the nineteenth century, developed slowly in Pennsylvania in part because the state gave financial support to the private colleges and academies. Directors were given the authority to form "joint high schools" in 1854, but few did. It was 1887 before the Legislature permitted city and borough districts to establish high schools; 8 years later, it allowed every district to do so.

The movement gained ground, stimulating the growth of the Department of Public Instruction and receiving encouragement from it. The state education association, organized in 1852, set up a high school section in 1905. Three years later, the position of high school inspector was created, the first professional staff position beside the superintendent and his deputies.

PUBLIC EDUCATION IN THE EARLY 1900'S

State Superintendent Nathan C. Schaeffer

At the beginning of the twentieth century, Nathan C. Schaeffer was serving as superintendent of public instruction. A native Pennsylvanian, Dr. Schaeffer was ordained as a minister in the German Reformed Church, served on the faculty of Franklin and Marshall College in Lancaster for 8 years, and then became principal of Kutztown Normal School, a post he held for 16 years. Governor Robert E. Pattison had asked him to be superintendent of public instruction in 1893. Even though he was a Democrat appointed by a Democrat, he was reappointed by Republican Governors until his death in 1919, achieving the longest tenure of any superintendent.

Under Schaeffer's supervision, the department continued to encourage high school growth, worked to raise the level of teacher preparation, and had the responsibility for inaugurating the first compulsory free textbook law in 1893. It was also during his administration that the Legislature passed the first compulsory attendance law in 1895. A man generally of conservative tendencies, he viewed the department's role as one of mediation between the old and the new. In an editorial he wrote for the *Pennsylvania School Journal,* he stated his desire "to abolish the defects of the present without sacrificing the heritage of the past . . ." (13).

As the new century began, Superintendent Schaeffer was seriously disturbed over the low state of the teaching profession. The basic requirement for teachers was a high school education offered by the normal schools or the public high schools; both offered 2-, 3-, or 4-year programs, and a high school diploma was not necessary for admission to the normal schools. Teachers completing the program were then certified through examinations given by the county superintendents according to the Act of 1854. This, plus the fact that private corporations controlled the normal schools and, thus, teacher education, made it difficult for Dr. Schaeffer to do little more than urge better salaries and higher qualifications.

The State Teachers' Association became the Pennsylvania State Education Association in 1900, with its constitution and bylaws modeled after those of the National Education Association. Schaeffer now had an ally in his efforts to raise the standards for teachers, and cooperation between the department and the association on standards, salaries, and working conditions proved to be the rule. Many professional people served in both organizations; the present executive secretary of PSEA, Ralph Swan, was once the acting state superintendent.

Schaeffer, the PSEA, and others believed that improving the quality of teachers would improve the public high schools. Unfortunately, local control was so strong that the department could not play a leading role in the high schools' steady growth during the first decade of the century. The Legislature first offered state support for township high schools in 1901. Two years later, school directors of districts without high schools were permitted to pay tuition for their students to attend high schools in other districts; this became mandatory in 1905. The department was able to exercise more influence after the Legislature approved salaries for two high school inspectors in 1908—the first professional expansion of the department since it had become an independent agency—particularly since the department had to approve a high school before it could be paid state subsidies.

The state had attempted to consolidate districts and eliminate wards and subdistricts as early as 1854, but this confronted localism head-on (the conflict has not ended to this day). When the first centralization law passed in 1901, authorizing the establishment of central high schools in townships, with pupils transported at public expense, no districts took advantage of the law.

Another of Superintendent Schaeffer's most vexing problems was the dilemma over the 1895 compulsory attendance law and the regulation on vaccination. No law existed requiring vaccination, and parents could not legally be forced to have their children protected against smallpox, but school attendance *was* mandatory, and vaccination was required for admittance.

The 1911 Code. The increasing body of education legislation and the resulting contradictions and confusions prompted the Legislature to request Governor Edwin S. Stuart to create an educational commission to draw up a school code. Appointed in 1907 (14), the commission did more than simply compile the existing legislation into a single document. The code it presented to the Legislature in 1909 was a comprehensive bill embodying all the principles of previous legislation in a harmonious whole. After a stormy session in which many amendments were tacked on to it, Governor Stuart, a strong supporter of educational progress, decided to veto the bill because the amendments made it "more than doubtful whether an approval of the bill would be of any benefit to the cause of education in the State" (15).

Discouraged but not defeated, the commission members continued to meet at their own expense to work out a new version of the code. It finally appeared in the July 1910 *Pennsylvania School Journal,* the same issue which carried the Governor's veto of the original code. The General Assembly passed the revised code in 1911, and it was signed into law by Governor John K. Tener. It not only codified existing legislation but included new provisions which (a) classified high schools and districts as first, second, third, and fourth class by population; (b) established a six-member board of education to oversee the system and equalize educational advantages throughout the Commonwealth; and (c) specified the qualifications for various types of teaching certificates and the minimum salaries for each. It also listed procedures whereby the Board of Education could purchase the state normal schools outright.

The 1911 code increased the size of the departmental staff in order to aid the development of secondary education. Within 2 years, four high school inspectors were employed, along with expert assistants in agriculture, industrial education, and drawing–a new high school curriculum interest. Two supervisory bureaus also were added (16). The department also had begun to publish advice to local schools on curriculum, and the state board was issuing suggested school building plans and specifications.

Vocational Education. William Penn had expressed concern "that all children within this Province . . . shall be taught some useful trade or skill," but the real impetus for formal vocational education did not develop until after the Civil War. In 1887, the Legislature authorized Governor James A. Beaver to appoint a five-member industrial education commission to study the desirability of developing technical and industrial education. It was this commission's report that encouraged the growth of manual training schools in the cities and larger towns. Perhaps the popular exhibit by the Russian railway apprentices at the 1876 Philadelphia Centennial Exhibition, as well as the work being done in the schools of France and Germany, suggested the need for such training. Pennsylvania's postwar industrialization made such a program doubly attractive.

Pennsylvania, with its prosperous agriculture, suffered a shortage of adult industrial workers; thousands of children were thus employed in industry in the early decades of the twentieth century. Many groups, including educators, social reformers, and labor unions, opposed child labor and were strong enough to bring about the Coxe Child Labor Law in 1915, which required minors between 14 and 16 to attend school for a certain number of hours per week. This provided an additional opportunity for developing vocational programs as well as basic instruction.

General agriculture was already a part of the regular curriculum, but the Showalter Act of 1913 set up a statewide vocational program in agriculture, trade and industrial education, and home economics. This effort was formalized 2 years later in an official vocational education bureau, which contained agricultural and industrial divisions. In 1917, the Legislature voted to allow the state to apply for federal Smith-Hughes funds for programs in the skilled trades, handicrafts, and agriculture. By the following year, the Bureau of Vocational Education had a professional staff of 18, illustrating dramatically the impact of federal money on state services. This federal support proved a mixed blessing, however, as vocational education's independent finances encouraged it to be independent in action, and the superintendent had problems controlling it from time to time (17). A vocational, technical, and continuing education bureau still administers some of the programs begun in the early twentieth century, along with a host of new ones.

Teaching standards and working conditions improved significantly during and after World War I. For instance, the state enacted minimum salary laws and in 1917 established the Public School Employees' Retirement Fund. All 13 of the normal schools had been purchased by 1920, and the Cheyney Training School was added in 1921 to prepare Negro teachers. World War I undoubtedly acted as a catalyst on the expansion of these teacher-training institutions and, since there was a real shortage of teachers, brought about further improvements in status and conditions. The department did everything possible to lure young people into the field, while the emphasis on industrial growth was bringing about new opportunities in vocational education.

Superintendent Thomas E. Finegan

When Dr. Schaeffer died in office, Governor William C. Sproul (18) appointed Thomas E. Finegan, then deputy commissioner of education for New York, to succeed him. A native of New York, Dr. Finegan had been a teacher and administrator in the public schools before joining the New York department as supervisor of examinations in 1892. By 1915, he had advanced to deputy commissioner, and his departure from the state was lamented by his fellow educators (19). Governor Sproul was assailed for going outside Pennsylvania to choose his superintendent, but the Governor did not waver in supporting Finegan and his programs throughout his term. This partnership formed by an interested Governor and a vigorous superintendent resulted in marked educational progress.

Dr. Finegan first reorganized the department into a businesslike, service-oriented organization staffed with qualified professionals. Indeed, the reorganization was so thorough that it might better be called a reconstruction. From Dr. Schaeffer's 3 bureaus–vocational education, professional education, and medical education and licensure–Dr. Finegan made 10: administration, attendance, health education, preprofessional and professional credentials, rural education, school buildings, school employees' retirement, special education, certification and training of teachers, and vocational education. The conservative elements in the department who disapproved were soon outweighed by the new staff brought in to administer the new structure.

Dr. Finegan then established the Education Congress, a 2-day meeting which brought local school people from all parts of the state to Harrisburg to review old problems and discuss new developments. The congress has been held regularly since Dr. Finegan's time and remains an important feature of the current program.

Consolidation. The General Assembly did not act on Finegan's legislative program until 1921, but it did pass the Sweitzer Act during its 1919 session, requiring all schools with ten or fewer students to close unless special permission to continue operation was obtained from the Board of Education. Two years later, to sweeten the proposition, it voted a $200 subsidy to the districts for each closed school. Rural people were slowly realizing that their children were suffering educationally from the one-teacher schools. Most had inadequate buildings, outdated textbooks, unspeakable sanitary facilities—schools which were little more than training grounds for new teachers. The conservative nature of the Pennsylvania Germans, however, made it painful for them to relinquish these local institutions. As late as the 1926-27 school year, 486 were still operating, and by the spring of 1934, 237 still were open.

More than 30 years passed before all one-teacher schools in Pennsylvania finally closed their doors. As they declined, the rural consolidated schools increased. In the 1918-19 school year, there were 115, most founded as a result of smaller schools' closing; by the end of the 1932-33 school year, 780 approved consolidated schools enrolled some 180,000 pupils (20).

To meet a teacher shortage, the Legislature passed the Woodruff Salary Act and increased state aid for salaries. Teacher certification became an important element in determining state reimbursement, the law providing a minimum of $60, $70, and $80 per month for various categories of certification. On the basis of standard teacher certificates, the act offered the districts $5 per month for provisional, $12.50 for professional or normal school, $20 for others, with an additional $5 per month for rural teachers. The remainder was still paid on a 50-50 basis on teachers and pupils.

The Edmonds Act. Finegan's program was presented to the General Assembly in more than one hundred bills. The House and Senate Education Committees condensed them to one omnibus bill covering 72 specific laws, which the General Assembly passed as the Edmonds Act, named after the chairman of the House Committee. This act provided the legal and financial basis for sweeping changes in the department and in public education itself for the next 24 years. It replaced the State Board of Education with a State Council of Education, the superintendent remaining the chief executive officer. The College and University Council, created by the Legislature in 1895 to grant charters to institutions of higher education, was eliminated and its functions turned over to the state council, which now had the power to coordinate all educational policy at the state level.

One of the principal weaknesses in Pennsylvania's educational system was the low standard for beginning teachers. The Edmonds Act made the class of school district, the division or organization, and the grades of teaching certificate the bases for state subsidies to encourage higher salaries and higher certification levels. Although the act established a statewide minimum standard, it took the power to issue teacher certificates from the county superintendents and vested it in the State Council of Education and the superintendent of public instruction. The state now had control of all teacher training and certification.

Another part of the act defined elementary and secondary education systems and made the junior high school an official part of the system. It gave the state council the right to prescribe high school studies, the beginning of a responsibility for curriculum requirements that has increased through the years. Libraries were required in all new secondary school buildings, mainly because the Middle States Association of Secondary Schools and Colleges required them for accreditation. Elementary school libraries have received the same attention only recently.

With the strong support of Governor Sproul, the Emonds Act passed the Legislature against relatively little opposition. The increased centralization of authority resulting from the act again mobilized all the forces defending local control. Previous laws had not disturbed local authority to a great extent, but the Edmonds Act brought the power of the state into every district. Specific attacks centered on the certification requirements—now in the hands of the state—the increase in salaries, and the state's interference in such administrative matters as attendance, sanitation, and construction. The Pennsylvania Grange led the sortie against both the legislation and Dr. Finegan personally, calling him a "czar" and a "carpetbagger." Despite these efforts, the Legislature was not disposed to repeal its work, and the Edmonds Act remained in force until the next great educational upheaval in 1945.

Both gubernatorial candidates supported Dr. Finegan's program in the 1922 Republican primary campaign (21) when Gifford Pinchot, one of Pennsylvania's outstanding Governors, was elected to his first term (22). Despite Pinchot's endorsement of Finegan's program, friction soon developed between the two men. Whatever its nature, political or personal—the records are not clear—the Governor refused to reappoint Dr. Finegan on the expiration of his term unless Finegan agreed to submit in advançe an undated resignation which the Governor could accept at his pleasure. Dr. Finegan refused.

Although he was not reappointed, Finegan deserves the credit for creating the department's modern structure, which stresses services to local districts. Under his administration, Pennsylvania moved toward the gradual achievement of William Penn's dream of providing education for every child. When the Second Education Congress in 1920 focused on the Ayres Report of the Russell Sage Foundation, it revealed, to the consternation of Pennsylvania educators, that the state had dropped from tenth place in 1890 to twenty-first in 1918. But by 1922, the director of statistics for the Russell Sage Foundation reviewed the state's progress and announced that it had advanced to a rank comparable to the second-ranked state in the 1918 report.

J. George Becht

Governor Pinchot appointed J. George Becht, first deputy superintendent and former secretary of the board of education, to replace Dr. Finegan. Born in Lycoming County, Dr. Becht began teaching at the age of 15; in 1893, he was appointed superintendent of Lycoming County schools. He became a teacher at West Chester State Normal School in 1903 and 2 years later was principal of Clarion State Normal School. When the Board of Education was organized in 1912, he became its secretary and remained in that position until the board was replaced by the state council, at which time he became the first deputy under Finegan (23).

One of the Pinchot administration's first acts was to develop an administrative code for the entire state government. Clyde King, lured from the University of Pennsylvania to the Governor's office, wrote most of this code, which significantly strengthened the department's role as the chief executive agency for the state's educational policies. The code brought all agencies concerned with education under the department's umbrella: 14 professional examing boards; the state library and museum; the school employees' retirement board; the historical commission; the board of censors; four state institutions—the state oral school, the Home for Training in Speech, the Soldiers' Orphans School, and the Thaddeus Stevens Industrial School. In June 1924, the department's reorganization showed five divisions with more than 20 bureaus. The state council's role was also enlarged to include supervision and development of standards for all institutions supported wholly or in part by state funds and not supervised by public school authorities.

The Legislature passed an act in its 1919 session allowing local districts to carry out programs for physically and mentally handicapped children, replacing the system whereby each district paid for institutional programs arranged by families. In its 1925 session, the Legislature not only made the extension schools an integral part of the public education program but also authorized state subsidies for districts operating classes for physically and mentally handicapped children. This was an important step in the state's efforts to offer a chance for education to all children.

An act in 1923 considerably advanced consolidation by authorizing transportation subsidies to be paid districts on the basis of their wealth. At the same time, the 1923 Edmonds Act took into consideration the wealth of a district as a factor in reimbursement, thus enlarging its equalization philosophy. It was beginning to offer proportionately larger shares of support to poorer districts to enable them to offer an education program comparable to that in the wealthier districts (24).

State Superintendents Haas and Keith

Not in the best of health when he assumed office, Dr. Becht died in 1925, the strain of the position undoubtedly having hastened his death. Governor Pinchot selected his second deputy, Francis B. Haas, to complete his term. Born in Philadelphia, Dr. Haas had been a teacher and school administrator in his home city until he came to the department in 1920 as assistant director of the teacher bureau. He received his doctorate of education (then called pedagogy) from Temple University in 1927. His term was short because when the Senate refused to confirm his appointment, he resigned in January 1927 to permit incoming Governor John S. Fisher to name his own superintendent. Haas did organize a kindergarten and elementary education division and changed the state normal schools into state teachers colleges during his short term. He was again appointed superintendent 12 years later and served with distinction for 16 years.

Governor Fisher, himself a former teacher and supporter of the first minimum salary bill, appointed the former principal of the Indiana (Pennsylvania) State Normal School, John A. H. Keith, superintendent of public instruction. Dr. Keith was born in Illinois and had taught in public and normal schools in his own state until he became president of the state normal school in Oshkosh, Wisconsin, in 1907. Ten years later, he moved to Indiana, Pennsylvania.

The department's services and programs changed little during his administration. The General Assembly did authorize construction of an education building in the capitol complex in Harrisburg in 1929. Pennsylvania was only the second state to provide a headquarters for its state education agency, and the cornerstone was laid in November 1929, with great enthusiasm and high hopes.

DEPRESSION AND WAR

Tight Budgets

The onset of the Depression halted progress immediately. Almost a million men were unemployed in Pennsylvania by 1931, and Governor Pinchot, serving his second term, was locked in battle with the Legislature to provide relief measures. Pennsylvania was harder hit than most parts of the nation; with 8 percent of the population it had 10 percent of the unemployed.

Since most people's attention was turned to other concerns than the public school system, educators simply fought to survive. The 1931 Legislature appropriated about $93 million for education support but reduced it in a 1932 special session to about $89,300,000, decreasing the department's funds by more than 10 percent. The state had to assist financially distressed districts, however, and the department's school business bureau administered these funds. The Legislature voted additional emergency legislation in 1933 allowing districts to cut teachers' salaries to 90 percent of mandated minimums, with an additional 10-percent reduction if the superintendent approved. Thus, Pennsylvania's schools tightened their belts and weathered the storm. It was the superintendent's boast that not one Commonwealth school disbanded from 1931 to 1935, although throughout the rest of the country, 20,000 schools closed their doors during this same period.

By concurrent resolutions in 1929 and 1931, the Legislature created the Sterling Committee, which launched a study of the state government's organization in 1935 (25). Mainly concerned with economy and cost reductions, its report recommended an extensive reorganization of the department, reducing the number of bureaus and the staff's salaries. For instance, it suggested that the visual education division be scrapped and called for a 25-percent reduction in the professional licensing division's staff. It recommended that the school districts reorganize into larger, more economical units; that two state teachers colleges close immediately, with the possibility that two more would be closed; and that the boards of trustees of the state teachers colleges be discarded. It also suggested that the department charge nominal fees for teaching certificates. The department heeded part of the report and reorganized into a three-bureau structure in the following years.

Despite serious financial problems brought on by the Depression, a law passed in 1931 allowed districts to establish kindergartens as integral parts of their school systems. The new education building, begun so optimistically in the twenties, was dedicated in 1931 and is the home of the department today.

Superintendent Keith's term expired in 1931, and his poor health removed him from consideration for another term. Governor Pinchot appointed James N. Rule as acting superintendent and later as full superintendent. As a member of the department since 1921 and the deputy superintendent since 1923, Dr. Rule had directed much of the department's activity during Dr. Keith's illness. A native of Manchester, Iowa, he was educated at Washington and Jefferson College in Pennsylvania and taught in the Washington, Pennsylvania, schools before becoming assistant principal of the Washington and Jefferson Academy. He became the academy's principal in 1907, went to Pittsburgh 5 years later as principal of Central High School, and then to Schenley High School. He came to the department in 1921 as the first director of science, became second deputy for secondary education in 1923, and first deputy under Dr. Becht. In 1925, he became the first executive secretary of the State Council of Education.

During the early years of the Depression, Dr. Rule was limited by the Legislature's overriding concern with economy and cost reduction. In 1934, he called a meeting of educators and interested citizens to consider ways in which these problems could be met—an appropriate celebration for the centennial of the free public school system. More than 2,000 attended this "Citizen's Conference on School Recovery in Pennsylvania" to hear the superintendent outline the "Three R's of School Recovery": Restoration of the instruction program, Reorganization of school districts, and Revision of the system of school support.

The final "R" was a cause of mounting concern. The Legislature, besieged by hard-pressed citizens, found the schools an increasing problem, with educational organizations calling for more funds and different ways of distributing them. Almost every year, a committee was appointed to study the problem (26). However, some sound legislation resulted, and it was a little more than a decade before another change was made in the system by which the state supported public education

The emergency legislation on teachers' salaries expired in 1935 and was not reenacted; the state reverted to the provisions of the Edmonds Act. Federal-state emergency relief programs in adult education were supervised by the department and included courses in academic education, art, English, citizenship, guidance, handicrafts, music, nursery schools, parental education, recreation, social science, vocational education, and workers education. Federal aid was becoming available for school buildings, and the tone of official reports indicated that public education might be returning to a more normal condition.

State Superintendent Lester K. Ade

Dr. Rule's term expired in 1935, and he was succeeded by Lester K. Ade, president of the Connecticut State Teachers College at New Haven, and the first superintendent to hold a Ph.D. degree. Dr. Ade, a native Pennsylvanian, began teaching in the Williamsport (Pennsylvania) public schools, became supervising principal of the Muncy (Pennsylvania) schools, and finally principal of the Muncy Normal School. He left Muncy to become dean of West Chester (Pennsylvania) Teachers College and in 1928 took the position in New Haven.

Dr. Ade, vitally interested in improving the quality of teacher education, appointed an Advisory Committee on Minimum Standards in 1936 to review certification requirements. The following year, the Legislature enacted the Mundy Tenure Act and gave the superintendent power to withhold state subsidies from districts failing to award the mandated minimum teacher salary increments.

Convinced that the department needed a strong public relations program, Dr. Ade established monthly staff conferences, prepared many publications, and encouraged frequent meetings between his professionals and the public. He also inaugurated training programs for firemen and building custodians; this service expanded to the present independent Public Service Institute, which offers a variety of training programs to government and municipal employees.

The legislators again turned to consolidation in 1937, passing an act which provided for the merger of smaller districts. To their disappointment, it proved to be no more attractive than the provisions for union districts. Although there were now three ways by which districts could be organized into larger units, it was the late 1940's, when the mandatory reorganization law passed with its financial incentives, before notable consolidations occurred (27). The 1937 legislation offered state aid for transportation and created boards of school directors with powers to merge and reorganize districts, but it, too, was mainly "permissive" and was thus ignored (28).

During Dr. Ade's superintendency, the 1937 Legislature expanded the special education program by permitting mental hygiene clinics to be established for children and requiring local authorities to appoint county supervisors of special education within 2 years. Two years later, it gave the superintendent the power to make these appointments where districts failed to do so.

Governor Arthur H. James appointed Deputy Superintendent Clarence E. Ackley as acting superintendent when Dr. Ade's term expired in 1939. Several months later, Dr. Francis B. Haas resigned as president of Bloomsburg State Teachers College to accept his second term as Pennsylvania state superintendent. Elected president of the Pennsylvania State Education Association, Dr. Haas had gained an enviable reputation in education circles since his first term.

The War Years

Vocational Education. The threat of war forced the government to place considerable stress on vocational education and training for vital wartime industries. The Governor's Job Mobilization Committee had already stirred interest in industrial training programs when the National Defense Vocational Education programs began in the summer of 1940. By the following year, the department's staff included a state director of vocational training for defense workers, who supervised three types of programs: specific training in and for industry, the National Youth Administration vocational programs, and essential instruction for young people out of school. Dr. Haas was especially proud of the aviation education program; beginning with the Pennsylvania State School of Aeronautics in 1942, it is still part of the state's curriculum.

Educational guidance, especially for developing and preparing skilled workers for vital industries, became important as wartime production demands increased drastically. The Division of Occupational Information and Guidance, established in 1943, handled most of these activities. Academic and psychological guidance is a relatively recent development; state guidance activities were first designed to meet wartime industrial needs.

School Building. The federal Lanham Act of 1940—the predecessor of the present-day aid to impacted areas—provided financial assistance for school building construction in areas heavily affected by defense industries and the war effort. Two years later, the federal Community Facilities Act enlarged the program and authorized the superintendent to approve school sites and buildings. Unfortunately, these acts did little to alleviate the sad conditions found in most communities where so many school buildings dated from the previous century. The Depression era restrictions and the wartime halt to civilian building turned the schools into one of the state's worst war casualties (29).

Financing Postwar Needs. As early as 1943, the Legislature looked forward to Pennsylvania's postwar needs by appointing study committees to check into the distribution of school costs between local and state sources. A wartime industrial boom had put Pennsylvania's finances in good shape, and a surplus had accumulated sufficient to permit Governor Edward Martin to retire the General State Authority bonds, amounting to nearly $48 million. This time the committee's report resulted in the approval of a new subsidy play in 1945.

The Hare-Lee-Sollenberger Act offered state aid to school districts on the basis of local ability to pay for basic education programs (30). In general, the state set a figure which it estimated as the basic amount necessary to educate a roomful of schoolchildren identified as 30 elementary or 22 secondary students. In 1945, it set this figure at $1,800, but by 1959 it was up to $5,800. The state guaranteed that each district would have at least that amount for each teaching unit that met the state's regulations and standards.

Most of the districts were willing to comply. The amount they actually received from the state depended on the wealth of the district measured per pupil in taxable property. It was calculated by a complicated process, using a "reimbursement fraction" for each district, applied to the total amount, to determine the state's share. It was possible for the state to pay as much as 95 percent of the $5,800 amount guaranteed to a poor district in 1959, and as little as the $1,000 minimum to a wealthy one. Of course, there was no limit to the amount which the district could spend if its resources permitted. The state's schools had suffered from a severe teacher shortage, and the state had been forced to issue emergency certificates by 1943. Cost-of-living salary increases attracted a few teachers, but by the end of the war the schools were still understaffed. The new legislation helped the situation to some extent by including a new single salary schedule for teachers, with an additional increment for the master's degree.

During the war, the department was given the power to regulate private trade schools. In the postwar years, this regulatory function expanded to include private academic, business, and correspondence schools founded to meet returning veterans' demands for educational opportunities, thus giving the public some protection against fraudulent operations.

POSTWAR EXPANSION

The war had encouraged many educational programs outside the standard high schools, and these created problems for students who had participated in them. The 1945 Legislature authorized the department to set up procedures to grant high school diplomas for this "equivalent experience." The department then turned over the task of rating credits earned in these special study programs to a newly formed Division of Secondary Education Evaluation, which issued equivalent diplomas when merited. At the same time, however, the department lost some of its administrative responsibilities when the historical commission and the state museum and archives division merged into an independent State Historical and Museum Commission.

The department began a general reevaluation and revision of the school curriculum on its own initiative in 1946. The war years had brought a tremendous increase in scientific and technical knowledge, which had to be incorporated into what was being taught. More important, very little work had been done in curriculum revision during the Depression and war years. The 1947 Legislature backed the department's efforts and requested that it make a thorough study of the curriculum regulations as a basis for updating them. The superintendent also appointed an Advisory Committee on Secondary Education.

The new subsidy program and the curriculum regulations marked the beginning of an outpouring of education legislation by the 1947 General Assembly. Everything seemed outdated—the shadow of the postwar population explosion loomed just as the knowledge explosion from the wartime discoveries in science and technology was becoming apparent.

As mentioned above, the school buildings were in a pathetic state. To help districts meet their construction costs, the assembly created the State Public School Building Authority. It then amended the Municipal Authority Act to include school construction. Because of the constitutional limit on the debts that municipalities could incur, Pennsylvania pioneered the authority method of construction for all manner of public buildings (31).

In other legislation, the General Assembly increased teachers' salaries along with the basic school subsidy. It established a State Tax Equalization Board to help determine local wealth for school tax purposes. The benefits of special education were enlarged to include cerebral palsied children, and the extension programs were expanded to include recreational and social services for school-age children.

Perhaps the most important accomplishment of the 1947 Legislature was in the field of school district reorganization. Act 361 (32) for the first time mandated a general reorganization rather than simply permitting it. It directed county boards of school directors to prepare plans for mergers and the reorganization of county districts according to the state council's standards. It was by no means a complete success, because it did not penalize the directors for failing to comply and did not impose rigid standards. Until the Legislature offered subsidies for jointures, mergers, and unions in 1951, comparatively few districts consolidated (33). But even these reorganizations did not fully meet most educators' standards for consolidation, and reorganization has remained a hotly contested item in the state's education program.

The Legislature and the State Department of Education pushed ahead during the next few years in the fields broken by the 1945 and 1947 legislative landslides. The 1951 Municipal Authority Act was further enlarged to permit school districts to set up their own authorities. The state's share of rental payments was made more liberal, and the state participated in a federally sponsored national survey of school facilities which resulted in the publication of a report entitled *Pennsylvania Surveys Its Public School Facilities* (34).

The department continued its curriculum revision and published a number of guides for elementary and secondary school programs. Audiovisual services, enriched by techniques developed during the war, expanded; by the end of 1952, 17 audiovisual service centers had been established, partly with funds appropriated by the George-Barden Act. In 1952, the Board of State Teachers College Presidents asked the State Council of Education's permission to offer graduate programs leading to the master of education degree; although these colleges had expanded their facilities and curriculums, this request was not granted until 1957.

Higher Education

Beyond its administration of the state teachers colleges, the department had little authority in the field of higher education. The state council could only grant charters to colleges and universities and approve their teacher education programs. It reported every year on the funds given to certain colleges and universities, but the funds themselves were provided by direct legislative grants, and the department had no control over them (35).

Public interest in higher education increased in the postwar years, resulting in a rising number of inquiries to the state council. These were usually passed on to the teacher education bureau. By 1951, this procedure had become so unsatisfactory that the Legislature authorized the department to create a Bureau of Higher Education headed by a deputy superintendent. This program has since grown tremendously, and the need for an expanding staff in this bureau has been one of the outstanding characteristics of the department's postwar expansion (36).

Special Education

The 1951 Legislature further extended the state's special education program One act allowed districts to establish speech and hearing centers, and another allowed them to establish day-care training centers for mentally retarded children who could not be served by the regular schools. But this legislation was still permissive, stating that only districts wishing to provide these services were to receive state funds–none could be compelled to provide them.

When Dr. Haas retired in 1955, the newly elected Democratic Governor, George M. Leader (37), appointed Deputy Superintendent Ralph C. Swan as acting superintendent. At one time, Governor Leader had hoped to become a teacher himself, and he was especially interested in education for handicapped children. Establishing a mandatory program for these children became one of the early priorities of his administration; the program passed in the 1955 session, with an accompanying act providing funds for transporting the children to school–almost 30 years after the state passed the first permissive legislation in special education.

Two years later, in 1957, the department organized a Bureau of Special Services for pupils to supervise the special education programs. The next year, the assembly again expanded special education by mandating that programs be established for all "exceptional children." The bureau now supervises instructional programs for the gifted, the physically and mentally handicapped, and the emotionally and socially disturbed–one of the most comprehensive special education programs in the country.

Departmental Reorganization and Expansion

Another in the long line of governmental surveys to bring economy to state government was made by the Chesterman Committee in 1953 (38). Its report on education recommended that a lay Board of Education be created to formulate policy and recommend candidates for the state superintendency. It further recommended that the department's professional staff be covered by Civil Service and that the department be reorganized to eliminate some of its administrative responsibilities that were not truly educational. In particular, it called for a reorganization of the school districts to abolish the financially distressed districts still receiving subsidies begun during the Depression. The report advised closing half the state teachers colleges. The superintendent implemented whatever recommendations he could by administrative action, but the major ones required legislative action, and they were not approved.

When the National Defense Education Act of 1958 provided funds for guidance and testing, the department created a Division of Guidance and Testing to handle all of these functions except occupational counseling. Another expansion occurred in 1961, when the department set up a Division of Testing to administer the state scholarships, the secondary school equivalency diplomas, the preprofessional and high school testing programs, and the examinations for special teaching certificates.

EDUCATION FOR THE SPACE AGE

Charles H. Boehm

Departmental Expansion. In 1956, Governor Leader chose Charles H. Boehm to replace Swan, the acting superintendent for the previous 17 months. Dr. Boehm, who had started as a teacher in the Woodbridge, New Jersey, schools, became a supervising principal and then a high school principal in Pennsylvania. He was first the assistant superintendent and then superintendent of the Bucks County schools, where he grew up. He was a great admirer of Thomas Finegan and tried to pattern his own administration after his.

Perhaps the new superintendent's strongest interests were in the fields of research and curriculum development (39), at a time when a combination of factors aided in making these fields matters of serious public concern. The 1955 Legislature collided with the Governor over a tax program (40) but finally approved a statewide sales tax devoted solely to education. Russia orbited Sputnik late in 1957, and the ensuing shockwaves jarred the public's complacency about the superiority of American schools.

Taking advantage of the public's demand to "do something" about education, Governor Leader called a Conference for the Improvement of Instruction, which met in Harrisburg in January 1958. Civic leaders and educators from all parts of the state spent 2 days discussing ways of improving the quality of the Commonwealth's education. The same year, the Pennsylvania State Education Association's Committee of Fifteen recommended a broad expansion in program and financial support. The publicity from both the conference and the PSEA's recommendations stimulated more public interest.

NDEA poured money into the schools for programs in mathematics, science, languages, guidance and testing, and increased research. This federal aid, which allowed the department to expand its services and staff, meshed with the superintendent's keen interest in developing a curriculum for the space age. Dr. Boehm won national recognition for instituting programs in earth and space science. He also set about establishing such innovations as regional instructional and audiovisual centers throughout the Commonwealth and a network of educational TV channels. To handle these responsibilities, he created a Bureau of Instructional Materials and Services.

Higher Education. The rising interest in education could not help having an impact on higher education; in particular there was pressure to improve teacher education. Over the years, the state teachers colleges had grown individually, with no overall comprehensive planning. One of Dr. Boehm's concerns was to develop a master campus plan. He set about acquiring sites and started one of the nation's largest college construction programs, at the same time laying plans to develop the individual specialties in each college.

After they strengthened their curriculums to include liberal arts, the state teachers colleges became state colleges. In 1961, they received permission from the state council to offer more than teacher education programs, and 4 years later they were authorized to become universities after meeting the necessary qualifications. At the same time, in 1965, Indiana State College became Indiana University of Pennsylvania.

Investigations and Recommendations. The year 1959 saw the department the target of a legislative investigation. The state director of vocational education had been pursuing an independent course—he received funds from federal and state appropriations, not from the general departmental appropriations. Dr. Boehm was determined to exercise control over this program and, with the consent of the State Board for Vocational Education, eventually maneuvered the director out of his job by abolishing it. Its functions were turned over to the director of the vocational education bureau. Controversy naturally resulted, and from it came charges of misuse of funds by the superintendent.

The Republican-controlled State Senate appointed a special committee to investigate charges that excessive sums had been spent for redecorating the superintendent's office suite, particularly the ultramodern, electronically equipped conference room. When the committee could find no proof of the charge, it abandoned the inquisitional character of its investigation to examine the department's total program. The department took full advantage of this opportunity to tell its story to what had become basically a sympathetic audience. The committee exonerated the superintendent of any charge of wrongdoing, but in the end its report had little impact on the progress of education in Pennsylvania. Its brief exploration of departmental programs, however, encouraged the legislators to request further studies.

Late in 1959, the House asked the Governor to appoint a blue-ribbon study commission to thoroughly assess public education and make recommendations for the future. In response, Governor David L. Lawrence appointed a Governor's Committee on Education under the chairmanship of Lieutenant Governor John Morgan Davis. This committee made one of the most exhaustive and detailed studies of education on record, publishing nine research monographs during the evaluation (41). Its report and recommendations, presented to the Governor in 1961, lit a fire under Pennsylvania public education which is still burning.

The committee noted: "Equality of educational opportunity may be the law, but it is not the fact" (42). It recommended changes, improvements, and expansion in every area, and Dr. Boehm ordered his staff to put into effect all that could be implemented without legislative or executive order.

A campaign was undertaken to secure the remaining recommendations by legislative action. The first two bills passed reorganized the school districts and established a system of community colleges. The community college proposal was not new; Governor Leader had made a similar recommendation in 1957, but it had been defeated. This 1961 proposal, based on the recommendation of the Governor's Committee, never even came to a vote in the Legislature. But the need was still there, and in the next session the Legislature passed a bill which not only permitted the establishment of community colleges but committed the state to generous financial support for them. Perhaps this was due in large measure to support from the newly appointed Governor's Committee of 100 for Better Education. This committee, composed of most of the Governor's Committee on Education and many Commonwealth leaders, waged an active campaign for reorganization and for community colleges.

A sweeping reorganization bill (Act 561) to achieve the ends the department had sought for years passed in the 1961 session, despite storms of protest. The proponents of local control again marshaled their forces. Led by the Pennsylvania Grange, the Pennsylvania Association of Township Supervisors, the school board directors, and the citizens and schoolmen who believed the legislation posed a threat to their jobs and influence over school affairs vigorously campaigned against the legislators who had voted for it. As a result, a number of legislators lost their seats.

Although Act 561 was repealed in the 1963 session, the forces supporting reorganization were too strong to be defeated completely (43). They were able to put through a new act that seemed less sweeping, though its effect was much the same as the previous one. It contained an additional requirement that the state board (44) study ways of measuring educational quality as a factor in district reorganization.

In the meantime, the department, urged by the superintendent's interest and stimulated by the Governor's committee report, continued to move ahead in its curriculum experiments. It created the Office of Curriculum Research and Development to foster experiments as well as encourage the adoption of proven innovations. Area curriculum centers were set up at the state colleges. The schools added a course in world culture to the curriculum, and NDEA grants continued to encourage better teaching in science, mathematics, and languages.

In his 1962 report, the superintendent noted that nine regular broadcasting councils had been added to the state's educational TV network. With the assistance of an NDEA grant, the superintendent had appointed a special committee to study the use of teaching machines and programed learning—the first such study in the country. The department reorganized the higher education bureau and began preparing a 5-year plan based on the recommendations of the Governor's committee for state colleges. The department also focused attention on development of a master plan for higher education throughout the Commonwealth.

The General Assembly's 1963 session was very productive for education. It passed a district reorganization bill, created the Pennsylvania Higher Education Assistance Agency to offer state-guaranteed loans to young people wanting to attend college, and allocated $2.5 million for planning and design of state colleges. Although two area technical schools were opened in the previous school year, it passed a State Vocational Education Act to encourage the development of other such schools with federal money.

Criticism of the State Council of Education had been growing louder year by year. President Eric Walker of Pennsylvania State University and the official representative of the Pennsylvania Association of Colleges and Universities, among others, complained that the council was slighting higher education and urged the creation of a separate policy-making body. The Governor's committee report also had included a strong recommendation that the council be reorganized to give a bigger voice to higher education and to remove it from the superintendent's direct control.

In response, the Legislature, with Governor William W. Scranton's endorsement, followed the Governor's Committee of 100 for Better Education report and created a State Board of Education as the top policy-making body in state education. The state superintendent became its nonvoting chief executive officer. The board was divided into two seven-member councils—one for basic education, one for higher education—plus three members serving at large. Each council was held responsible for action in its own area, though the board was to make all final decisions. The State Board of Education, like the State Council of Education before it, also serves as the State Board for Vocational Education (45).

In subsequent legislation, the assembly directed the state board to make studies and specific recommendations in five areas of education: measurements of quality of education, a master plan for higher education, a study of state vocational-technical education, a plan for community colleges, and a subsidy system for support of public schools. Authorized to develop standards for school district reorganization, it completed its task in less than a month. The vigor and ability of the board members were amply demonstrated; not only did they complete this task quickly, but during the same period they adopted standards for community colleges. The board sponsored a study in the administration and organization of state colleges and completed an overall review and revision of all curriculum regulations.

The department continued its work in curriculum development throughout 1963, adding economics and world cultures to high school graduation requirements. It also added 4 years of language study and earth and space science to the elementary school curriculum. Under a grant from the Ford Foundation, the office of curriculum, research, and development began an experimental program on the dropout problem. Several prekindergarten classes were operating before Congress inaugurated the national Head Start program. Pennsylvania became the first state in the nation to adopt a program for intergroup and human relations education, and the department received national acclaim and the Freedoms Foundation George Washington Medal Award for a teacher's guide on this subject.

Dr. Boehm resigned as superintendent early in 1964 to accept a position as an educational consultant for the federal government. A controversial figure, he had greatly expanded the department's functions in curriculum development and higher education. The department's staff had grown to 1,000 persons, and the number who held doctorates increased from two to over forty-five. Education now accounted for over half of the state's annual budget.

J. R. Rackley

Deputy Superintendent George W. Hoffman served as acting superintendent for 18 months, until Governor Scranton appointed J. R. Rackley in October 1965. Dr. Rackley, vice-president for resident instruction at Pennsylvania State University, was born in Oklahoma and taught history and social studies in the Oklahoma City schools before teaching in colleges in Tennessee, Connecticut, and Oklahoma. He joined the U.S. Office of Education as deputy commissioner in 1955, served for a short term as acting commissioner in 1956, and became dean of the College of Education and professor of education at Pennsylvania State University that September. He became vice-president of the university in 1962 (46).

At the time Rackley took office, education costs were steadily mounting, and there were increasing demands for new programs to meet the space age. The 1959 Governor's committee had noted that since the beginning of state aid for public education, the state's share of the cost had increased to nearly 50 percent, and it recommended that this percentage be maintained as a matter of principle. A joint study committee, appointed by the Governor to consist of legislators and the newly appointed state board members, pointed out these concerns to the 1965 General Assembly, which responded by passing a new subsidy plan that preserved the philosophy of equalization of educational opportunity, as well as the 50-50 division of cost. At the same time, it attempted to give help to heavily populated areas experiencing the problems peculiar to urban societies.

A LOOK AT THE FUTURE

Pennsylvania's public education programs have shifted gradually from an intense local control to a state and local partnership during the century. The state's desire throughout these years has remained constant: to offer equal educational opportunity to all children. Alternatively it has tried to gain cooperation by offering money and advice and to compel it by law. The department's and the state superintendents' continuing concerns have been to consolidate districts and improve teaching standards, two vital elements in a successful educational program. Their success has always depended on a variety of factors: their own enthusiasm and drive, the interest of the legislative and executive branches, the support of public opinion, and the climate of the times.

A look at the future indicates an ever-increasing state responsibility—both financial and administrative—especially in the areas of post-high school and higher education. A growing partnership with the federal government seems inevitable, as it, too, becomes more deeply involved in educational support and planning. The 1965 Pennsylvania school subsidy program promises a deepening emphasis on the problems of the urban schools and the children who attend them.

FOOTNOTES

1. William Penn, *Frame of Government* (1682), art. 12, p. 52.
2. *Ibid.*, p. 61.
3. For further information, see Louise G. Walsh and Matthew J. Walsh, *History and Organization of Education in Pennsylvania* (2d ed.; Indiana, Pa.: State Teachers College, 1928), p. 55.
4. Pennsylvania, *Constitution* (1790), pp. 372-74.
5. Walsh, *op. cit.*, p. 117.
6. Department of Public Instruction, *100 Years of Free Public Schools in Pennsylvania* (Harrisburg: The Department, 1934), p. 17.
7. James P. Wickersham, *Educatiбn in Pennsylvania* (Lancaster, Pa.: Inquirer Publishing Co., 1886), p. 318, as quoted in Walsh, *op. cit.*, pp. 120-21.
8. Thaddeus Stevens, born in Vermont in 1792, was active for many years in Pennsylvania politics before achieving national prominence as an abolitionist and member of Congress immediately before and during the Civil War. He was the acknowledged leader of the House until his death in 1868, a fanatic opponent of slavery. Although his national reputation rests on his work in this cause, much of his prewar career in state politics concerned the strengthening of the free school movement.
9. According to one historian, Andrew Curtin was the moving spirit behind the educational advances of the Pollock administration. A dynamic and gifted man, Curtin later served as "War Governor" of the state and continued in public life until his death in 1894. Wayland F. Dunaway, *History of Pennsylvania* (2d ed.; New York: Prentice-Hall, 1948), pp. 345-50.
10. James P. Wickersham, a native Pennsylvanian, was a leading figure in the early days of the free public schools. He was the first county superintendent of Lancaster County and one of the founders of the oldest state normal school, now Millersville State College. He served as head of the State Department of Education from 1866 to 1881, a period which included the change from the Department of Common Schools to the Department of Public Instruction. He helped organize the Lancaster County, Pennsylvania State, and National Education Associations and served as president of each. His *History of Education in Pennsylvania* (Lancaster, Pa.: Inquirer Publishing Co., 1886) is a treasury of source material.
11. The available source material indicates no public controversy over this change. It seems to have developed because of a rising interest in secondary education; the constitution now referred to "public schools" instead of "common schools." The general trend was to expand education beyond the elementary level. Superintendent Wickersham indicated that the constitutionality of state support for secondary education might have been raised in the following sentence in his annual report for 1874: "No constitutional objection will hereafter stand in the way of the establishment of schools of the highest grade. . . ." p. xvi.
12. In 1886, Governor Robert E. Pattison attempted to remove Superintendent E. E. Higbee by requesting his resignation on a charge of mismanagement of the Soldiers' Orphans School, but Dr. Higbee refused to resign. When Governor Pattison was elected for a second, nonconsecutive term, he tried to remove David J. Waller, the incumbent superintendent,

appointed by his predecessor, in favor of Z. X. Snyder. The matter was carried to the State Supreme Court, which decided in Dr. Waller's favor.

13. Walsh, *op. cit.*, p. 201.

14. The commission, chaired by Dr. Schaeffer, was composed of Martin G. Brumbaugh, David B. Oliver, William Landel, John S. Rilling, James M. Coughlin, and G. M. Phillips as secretary. Brumbaugh was perhaps the most influential member of the commission. A native Pennsylvanian, he was superintendent of schools in Huntingdon County, president of Juniata College, and finally superintendent of schools in Philadelphia when named to the educational commission. He later served as Governor of the Commonwealth from 1915 to 1919, and his administration supported many educational developments, including the child labor laws and the creation of the Bureau of Vocational Education. He appointed Dr. Schaeffer to the superintendency for Schaeffer's last term.

15. Governor Stuart's veto message as quoted in Walsh, *op. cit.*, p. 402.

16. These were the Bureau of Medical Education and Licensure and the Bureau of Professional Education. The former, mainly responsible for approving medical education programs, was the first of a number of professional licensing boards which came under the department's jurisdiction. The latter approved programs in preprofessional education for medicine, dentistry, and pharmacy; it was the first of many efforts to set standards for various types of professional training.

17. A legislative investigation in 1959 had its origins in the efforts of the superintendent to exercise more control over the Bureau of Vocational Education.

18. Governor William C. Sproul, a native of Lancaster County, was a newspaperman and businessman before being elected to the State Senate in 1896. He served in the Senate for 22 years prior to being elected Governor. His administration played an important role in education through his firm support of Dr. Finegan and his program. Dunaway, *op. cit.*, p. 485.

19. A tribute to Finegan by William McAndrew, assistant superintendent of the New York City schools, refers to "his fine quality of brains" and "his considerate heart" and notes the "personal bereavement" of a "great company of public school workers" because he was leaving the state. Walsh, *op. cit.*, p. 404.

20. Department of Public Instruction, *100 Years of Free Public Schools in Pennsylvania* (Harrisburg: The Department, 1934), pp. 41-42.

21. From 1861 to the present, Pennsylvania has had only four Democratic Governors: Robert E. Pattison, 1883-87 and 1891-95; George H. Earle, 1935-39: George M. Leader, 1955-59; and David L. Lawrence, 1959-63. After the Civil War, Pennsylvania politics were controlled by the Republican machine headed first by Simon Cameron; then by his son Donald; later by Matthew Quay; and finally by Senator Boise Penrose. After Penrose's death in 1921, no single man or machine held complete control, but the Republican party still dominated the state. Consequently, in most cases it was the party primary and not the general election which determined who would be Governor. The Governors usually were men of good quality, but they remained protégés of the machine which named the candidates; the law forbidding the same man from serving consecutive terms made it impossible for them to develop any real power while in office.

22. Gifford Pinchot, one of the most colorful figures in Pennsylvania politics, was a progressive Republican who won the nomination for Governor as a reform candidate in the confusion following Boise Penrose's death in 1921. The first American to make forestry his profession, he had served as chief of the U.S. Forest Service under President Theodore Roosevelt. Pinchot was defeated in 1926 for the Republican nomination by Philadelphia boss William S. Vare (whom the Senate refused to seat) and was reelected Governor in 1930.
Pinchot's principal interests as Governor were conservation, reorganization of state government, highway development, and opposition to the public utilities. Pennsylvanians still refer to him as the man who "got the farmer out of the mud." He was also an ardent "dry," and this was an issue in his campaigns.

23. According to veteran educators and department staff members, Dr. Becht was the choice of the education community to succeed Dr. Schaeffer. Governor Sproul refused to appoint him, however, because he was strongly disliked by one of the Governor's political allies. While secretary of the state board, Dr. Becht had vigorously pursued the task of purchasing the state normal schools from the private corporations, and since the Governor's friend held an interest in one of these corporations, he opposed the state's taking over.

24. This concept of the state's responsibility in education grew until, in 1945, a new subsidy program was enacted clearly expressing this idea.

25. These investigative committees can be divided into three basic types. First is the study committee appointed by the Legislature—the Sterling Committee is an example—with membership drawn from either or both Houses or the outside; it investigates and recommends legislation in a particular area. The second type is the study committee appointed by the Governor at the Legislature's request or on his own initiative. The third type is appointed by the superintendent to advise and help in developing standards and procedures in such areas as teacher certification and curriculum.

26. In 1927, the Legislature appointed an educational commission on subsidies which made recommendations, but the Legislature did not act. Another

study committee on subsidies was appointed in 1930. The superintendent appointed the Committee for the Study of Educational Problems in Pennsylvania in 1931 to revise the School Code; its efforts were unsuccessful. The Sterling Committee made its study the following year. In 1933, a legislative committee was appointed to investigate the cause of the increasing costs of education and ways to reduce them. The next year, Superintendent Rule held his Citizen's Conference on School Recovery. The Legislature created another Educational Costs Survey Committee in 1935, and 3 years later the Pennsylvania State Education Association appointed a study committee on school costs. The Legislature appointed a committee to study state and local participation in school costs in 1943, and its recommendations resulted in the 1945 Hare-Lee-Sollenberger Act.

27. The three methods of reorganization available to school districts were union, as provided in the 1911 Union District Act (revised in 1921); merger, as provided in the 1937 legislation; and jointure, or joint board organization, which had been permitted since 1854. In merger and union, the districts involved actually ceased to exist individually and formed a new district; these methods required approval from the voters. Jointure was a contractual agreement among a group of districts to conduct joint schools. The districts retained their individuality and their own boards; in fact, several districts were part of two jointures at different educational levels.

    None of these methods was widely used until the 1947 mandatory reorganization act. Jointure, because of its simplicity–it could be arranged by school boards without a popular vote–became the most common. Few districts created in this way were large enough, however, to meet educators' standards for efficiency and financial resources. For a study of reorganization, see Governor's Committee on Education, *E Pluribus Unum,* Educational Research Monograph Series (Harrisburg: Department of Public Instruction, 1960).

28. Throughout the 1920's and 1930's, the Department continued to coax districts into larger, more efficient units. Lee Driver, first director of consolidation projects and later head of the Bureau of Rural Service, toured the state tirelessly, speaking to Granges, rural groups, and various citizens associations. His lectures, illustrated by lantern slides which were a curiosity then, drew large crowds and won him a reputation as the "Magic Lantern" man.

29. Governor's Committee on Education, *Johnny Gets a Schoolhouse,* Educational Research Monograph Series (Harrisburg: Department of Public Instruction, 1960).

30. According to an interview in May 1967 with Harvey E. Gayman, retired executive secretary of the Pennsylvania State Education Association and member of the department staff from the early 1920's to 1928, the National Education Association recognized Act 403, the Hare-Lee-Sollenberger Act, as the best law of its kind in the country at the time.

31. Under the Pennsylvania constitution, all municipalities (including school districts) are limited in the amount of debt they may incur to a percentage of their assessed valuation. This has resulted in the development of authority financing, except where districts have sold general obligation bonds to cover the construction costs and are still within the debt limit. The Legislature authorized municipal authorities in 1925, but not until 1947 was the law amended to allow these authorities to finance school buildings. The State Public School Authority was created to assist districts, but the real impetus to school building came in 1951, when school districts were empowered to establish their own authorities, with state support. Governor's Committee on Education, *Johnny Gets a Schoolhouse,* Educational Research Monograph Series (Harrisburg: Department of Public Instruction, 1960).

32. The 1938 extra session of the Legislature passed three acts embodying the Thompson School Building Program. These acts would have provided a broad school building program generously financed by the state, with the department approving the plans and proposing more efficient district reorganization. Details for making the money available were never worked out, however, and the program was never put into effect.

33. In the 1949-50 school year, there were 11 union districts, no merged districts, and 190 joint boards in a total of 557 districts. By the 1959-60 school year, there were 71 union districts, 60 merged districts, and 436 joint boards, covering 1,875 districts. Governor's Committee on Education, "The Report and Recommendations to the Governor's Conference on the Improvement of Instruction, December, 1960, by Task Force 2." Harrisburg, Department of Public Instruction files. (Mimeographed.)

34. Department of Public Instruction, *Pennsylvania Surveys Its Public School Facilities* (Harrisburg: The Department, 1954).

35. Beside the state colleges, 15 institutions of higher education received financial support from the state in the 1958-59 school year. These included the Pennsylvania State University, University of Pennsylvania, Temple University, University of Pittsburgh, Lincoln University, three medical schools, Dickinson Law School, Drexel School of Technology, Philadelphia College of Osteopathy, and four other technical institutions. Governor's Committee on Education, *Crisis in Academe,* Educational Research Monograph Series (Harrisburg: Department of Public Instruction, 1961).

36. The reorganization of the department approved on October 17, 1966, provided for a deputy superintendent to be the chief administrative officer for

the superintendent. A commissioner for basic education is supported by an assistant commissioner and director of staff services for the Council of Basic Education, an assistant commissioner for programs and services, and an assistant commissioner for school administration. A commissioner for higher education is supported by an assistant commissioner and director of staff services for the Council of Higher Education.

37. George M. Leader, the third Democrat to serve as Governor since the Civil War, had turned to chicken farming when he was selected to follow his father, Guy Leader of York County, in the Senate. He served one term before he was chosen by party leaders to run for Governor in 1954.

    After its lean years, the Democratic party was discouraged and weakened; experts gave Leader little chance for victory. Young, vigorous, intelligent, and attractive, he waged an energetic campaign that contrasted favorably with that of the inarticulate and relatively colorless Republican candidate. His victory by nearly 280,000 votes carried with it Secretary of Internal Affairs Genevieve Blatt and a majority in the House. A liberal and champion of good government, Leader is sometimes called "the Democrats' Pinchot." He was defeated in his try for the U.S. Senate in 1958 and has not held public office since. Sylvester K. Stevens, *Pennsylvania, Birthplace of a Nation* (New York: Random House, 1964), p. 292.

38. No real governmental reorganization had taken place since the Pinchot administration, but increasing pressures forced Governor John S. Fine to appoint this committee, headed by Francis J. Chesterman, retired Bell Telephone executive, and composed mainly of men from the business and financial world.

39. In Dr. Boehm's official biographical sketch, prepared while he was superintendent, his specific activities were divided into the categories of curriculum development, research and development, and higher education, indicating the order of importance he placed on each.

40. Governor Leader had promised in his campaign that he would repeal the 1-percent sales tax levied by his predecessor, Republican Governor John S. Fine. He kept his promise but then had his own proposal for a classified income tax flatly opposed by the Republican-controlled State Senate. No compromise was possible, and after a record 17-month session, the Governor was forced to accept a 3-percent sales tax earmarked entirely for education.

41. These were: *Keystone High–Fifty-Nine, One End of the Log, The Chance To Learn, Johnny Gets a Schoolhouse, E Pluribus Unum, The Noble Investment,* all in 1960; *A Respect for Talent, Crisis in Academe, Our Standing Among the States,* all in 1961. The committee also published *Facts and Figures on Education in Pennsylvania* and *The Fourth "R."*

42. Governor's Committee on Education, *Final Report* (Harrisburg: Department of Public Instruction 1961), p. 5.

43. The Governor's Committee of 100 for Better Education and the PSEA were active in this fight, both strongly supporting the principle of reorganization. The committee authored *Recommendations for Legislation Leading to an Improved Program of Education in Pennsylvania* and *Community Colleges for Pennsylvania* (Harrisburg: Department of Public Instruction, 1963) as well as *Facts and Figures on Education in Pennsylvania* (rev. ed.; Harrisburg: Department of Public Instruction, 1962).

44. The state board replaced the State Council of Education in 1963.

45. The reorganization of the department, completed in 1966, matches the organization of the State Board of Education.

46. Dr. Rackley announced his resignation as of June 1967 to return to Pennsylvania State University as the Provost, and David H. Kurtzman was named to succeed him on September 1, 1967. A. G. Breidenstine served as acting superintendent during the interim.

BIBLIOGRAPHY

Public Documents

Commonwealth of Pennsylvania. *Constitution* (1790, 1873 as amended).

-- *Pennsylvania Manual* (1965-66), sec. 8.

Penn, William. *Frame of Government* (1682).

Books and Pamphlets

Bureau of Special Services for Pupils, Department of Public Instruction. *Services and Special Programs.* Harrisburg: The Department, 1962.

Department of Public Instruction. *Curriculum Regulations.* Harrisburg: The Department, 1962.

-- *Pennsylvania Today.* Harrisburg: The Department, 1962.

-- *100 Years of Free Public Schools in Pennsylvania.* Harrisburg: The Department, 1934.

-- *The Three R's of Public School Recovery.* Harrisburg: The Department, 1934.

Dunaway, Wayland F. *History of Pennsylvania.* 2d ed. New York: Prentice-Hall, 1948.

Governor's Committee of 100 for Better Education. *Community Colleges for Pennsylvania.* Harrisburg: Department of Public Instruction, 1963.

--*Facts and Figures on Education in Pennsylvania.* Revised edition. Harrisburg: Department of Public Instruction, 1962.

Governor's Committee on Education. *The Chance To Learn.* Educational Research Monograph Series. Harrisburg: Department of Public Instruction, 1960.

--*Crisis in Academe.* Educational Research Monograph Series. Harrisburg: Department of Public Instruction, 1961.

--*E Pluribus Unum.* Educational Research Monograph Series. Harrisburg: Department of Public Instruction, 1960.

-- *Facts and Figures on Education in Pennsylvania.* Harrisburg: Department of Public Instruction, 1961. (Revised, 1962).

--*The Fourth "R."* Harrisburg: Department of Public Instruction, 1961.

--*Johnny Gets a Schoolhouse.* Educational Research Monograph Series. Harrisburg: Department of Public Instruction, 1960.

--*Keystone High–Fifty-Nine.* Educational Research Monograph Series. Harrisburg: Department of Public Instruction, 1960.

--*The Noble Investment.* Educational Research Monograph Series. Harrisburg: Department of Public Instruction, 1960.

--*One End of the Log.* Educational Research Monograph Series. Harrisburg: Department of Public Instruction, 1960.

--*Our Standing Among the States.* Educational Research Monograph Series. Harrisburg: Department of Public Instruction, 1961.

-- *A Respect for Talent.* Educational Research Monograph Series. Harrisburg: Department of Public Instruction, 1961.

Haas, Francis P. *The Superintendent Speaks.* Harrisburg: Department of Public Instruction, 1953-54.

PSEA Committee of Fifteen. *Education in Pennsylvania: Today and Tomorrow.* Harrisburg: Pennsylvania State Education Association, 1958.

Pennsylvania State Education Association. *Student PSEA.* Harrisburg: The Association, 1966.

State Board of Education. *State Board of Education.* Harrisburg: Department of Public Instruction, 1967.

Stevens, Sylvester K. *Pennsylvania, Birthplace of a Nation.* New York: Random House, 1964.

Walsh, Louise G., and Walsh, Matthew J. *History and Organization of Education in Pennsylvania.* 2d ed. Indiana, Pa.: State Teachers College, 1928.

Wickersham, J. P. *Education in Pennsylvania.* Lancaster, Pa.: Inquirer Publishing Co., 1886.

Reports

Department of Public Instruction. *Pennsylvania Surveys Its Public School Facilities.* Harrisburg: The Department, 1954.

Governor's Committee of 100 for Better Education. *Recommendations for Legislation Leading to an Improved Program of Education in Pennsylvania.* Harrisburg: Department of Public Instruction, 1963.

Governor's Committee on Education. *Final Report.* Harrisburg: Department of Public Instruction, 1961.

Proceedings of the Citizen's Conference on School Recovery in Pennsylvania. Harrisburg: Department of Public Instruction, 1934.

Proceedings of the Forty-Third Education Congress. Harrisburg: Department of Public Instruction, 1964.

Report of the Pennsylvania Committee on State Finances (Sterling Committee). Harrisburg: Commonwealth of Pennsylvania, 1933.

Report of the State Government Survey Committee (Chesterman Committee). Harrisburg: Commonwealth of Pennsylvania, 1953.

Superintendents of Public Instruction. *Annual and Biennial Reports.* Harrisburg: Department of Public Instruction, 1900-62.

Unpublished Material

Leech, Charles D. "Implications for Public Education in Pennsylvania Resulting from Federal Control of Certain Subsidized Programs." Unpublished Ph.D. dissertation, Pennsylvania State University, University Park, 1959.

McCoy, Eugene M. "History and Development of the Pennsylvania Department of Public Instruction to 1945." Unpublished Ph.D. dissertation, University of Pennsylvania, Philadelphia, 1959.

Proceedings of the State Council on Higher Education, 1921-63. State board files.

"Report of the School Finance Survey Committee, 1964." State board files.

"Report of the Special (Legislative) Committee To Investigate the Department of Public Instruction, 1959." State board and Department of Public Instruction files.

"Reports on Quality Education, Master Plan for Community Colleges, and Vocational Education, 1966." State board files.

Governor's Committee on Education. "The Report and Recommendations to the Governor's Conference on the Improvement of Instruction, December,1960, by Task Force 2." Harrisburg, Department of Public Instruction files. (Mimeographed.)

Robinson, R. W. "History and Development of Public School Transportation, Chronology of Consolidation and Transportation, 1897-1947." Harrisburg, Department of Public Instruction files.

Tinney, James J. "Development and Control of State Support of Public Education in Pennsylvania from 1925-1957." Unpublished Ph.D. dissertation, University of Pittsburgh, 1958.

Other Source

Gayman, Harvey E. Personal interview in the State Department of Public Instruction offices, May 1967.

Appendix A

PENNSYLVANIA CHIEF STATE SCHOOL OFFICERS

Superintendents of Commonwealth and Common Schools

1834-35	James Findlay
1835-38	Thomas H. Burrowes
1838-42	Francis R. Shunk

Secretaries of Commonwealth and Superintendents of Common Schools

1842-43	Anson V. Parsons
1843-45	Charles McClure
1845-47	Jesse Miller
1847-50	Townsend Haines
1850-52	Alexander L. Russell
1852-53	Francis W. Hughes
1853-55	Charles A. Black
1855-57	Andrew G. Curtin

Superintendents of Common Schools

1857-60	Henry C. Hickok
1860-63	Thomas H. Burrowes
1863-66	Charles R. Coburn
1866-74	James P. Wickersham

Superintendents of Public Instruction

1874-81	James P. Wickersham
1881-89	Elnathan E. Higbee
1889-93	David J. Waller, Jr.
1893-1919	Nathan C. Schaeffer
1919-23	Thomas E. Finegan
1923-25	J. George Becht
1925-27	Francis B. Haas
1927-31	John A. H. Keith
1931-35	James N. Rule
1935-39	Lester K. Ade
1939-55	Francis B. Haas
1955-56	Ralph Swan (acting)
1956-64	Charles H. Boehm
1964-65	George W. Hoffman (acting)
1965-67	J. Ralph Rackley
1967-	David H. Kurtzman

Appendix B

Chart I.--PENNSYLVANIA DEPARTMENT OF PUBLIC INSTRUCTION, 1966

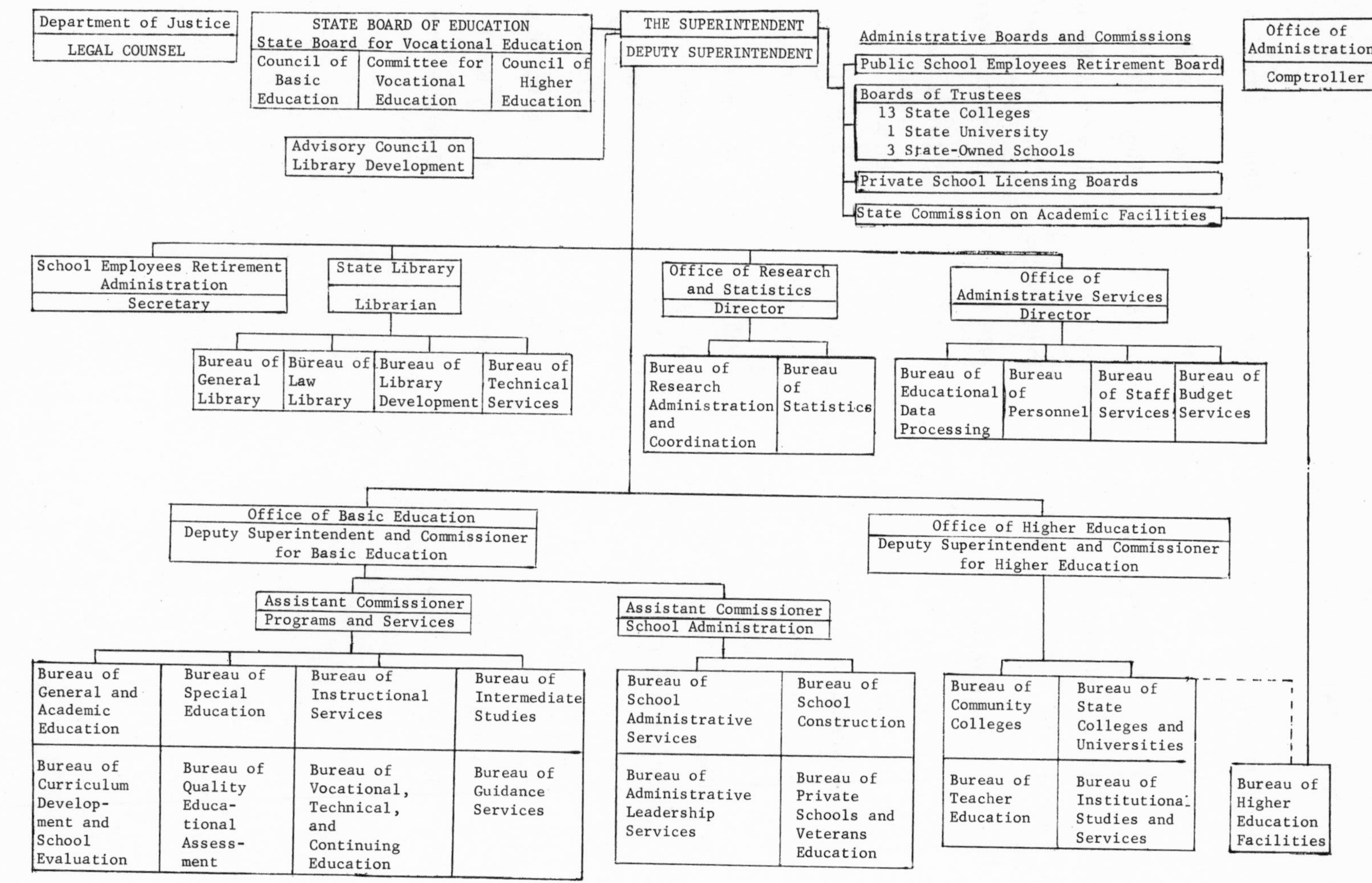

Appendix B

Supplement 1.–DEVELOPMENT OF PENNSYLVANIA DEPARTMENT OF PUBLIC INSTRUCTION

1900

Superintendent
Two deputy superintendents
- Financial clerk
- Recording clerk
- Statistical clerk
- Messenger
- Stenographer-typist

1905

Addition of:
- Stenographer-typist

1908

Addition of:
- Two high school inspectors

1911

(Reorganization following passage of School Code)

Superintendent
Two deputy superintendents
- Financial clerk
- Recording clerk
- Statistical clerk
- Messenger
- Two stenographer-typists
- Four high school inspectors
- Expert assistants in agriculture, industrial education, drawing

Bureau of Medical Education and Licensure
Bureau of Preprofessional education

1913

Addition of:
- Two stenographer-typists

1915

Creation of:
- Bureau of Vocation
  - Agricultural Division
    - Staff of six, including expert assistant in agriculture
  - Industrial Division
    - Staff of seven, including expert assistants in industrial education and drawing

1916

Addition of:
- Supervisor of home economics in Agricultural Division
- Supervisor of music and drawing in Industrial Division

1918

Addition of:
- Supervisor of homemaking
- Supervisor of school gardens in Agricultural Division
- Supervisor of household arts education
- Supervisor of continuation schools in Industrial Division

1920

(Reorganization by Thomas E. Finegan)

Ten service–oriented bureaus:
- Administration
- Attendance
- Health education
- Preprofessional and professional credentials
- Rural education
- School buildings
- School employees' retirement
- Special education
- Certification and training of teachers
- Vocational education

Departmental staff included supervisors of:
- Art education
- Child study
- Continuation schools
- English
- Gardens
- High school inspection
- Home economics
- School libraries and juvenile literature
- Social studies

1924

(Reorganization following passage of the Administrative Code)

Superintendent
Executive assistant
Chief accountant and budget officer
Director of research and statistics

Five divisions, each headed by a deputy superintendent:

I. Secondary education
Extension education

Appendix B

Supplement 1.–DEVELOPMENT OF PENNSYLVANIA DEPARTMENT OF PUBLIC INSTRUCTION (Continued)

Special education
Teacher bureau
State normal schools
Institutions for teacher preparation
Institutions for special education

II. Rural service
Consolidation processes
Curriculum services
Art
Elementary and kindergarten education
English
Geography
Health and physical education
Mathematics and science
Music
School libraries (departmental library)
Social studies
Visual education
State Board of Censors (motion picture)

III. Vocational education
Agricultural education
Continuation schools and vocational guidance
Home economics
Industrial education
State Library and Museum
Institutions for vocational education
Pennsylvania Historical Commission

IV. Public School Business Bureau
Child help and accounting
School buildings
Public School Employees' Retirement Fund

V. Credentials Bureau
Professional examing boards
Institutions of higher learning

1926

I. Normal schools
Secondary schools
Special and extension education
Certification of teachers
Teacher instruction
Library

II. Legal relations and services to school districts
School business
Child help and accounting
School buildings

III. Vocational education
Vocational agriculture
Vocational home economics
Industrial and continuation school education

IV. School visitation, conference, and advice
Rural service
School visitation
Art
Kindergarten and elementary education
Health and physical education
Visual education
Music

V. Service to professional examining boards and higher education
Credentials
Examinations
Real estate licensing

VI. State Library and Museum
General library
Library extension
Law library
Archives and Historical Commission
Museum

Director of statistics and research
Comptroller
Department services

1933

(Reorganization according to recommendations of the Sterling Committee)

Superintendent
Two deputy superintendents
Executive assistant
Editor
Bureau of Curriculum
Extension education
Kindergarten and elementary education
Secondary education
Special education
Agricultural education
Art
Music
Health and physical education
Home economics
Industrial and continuation education

Bureau of School Administration and Finance
School business
Fiscal control

Appendix B

Supplement 1.–DEVELOPMENT OF PENNSYLVANIA DEPARTMENT OF PUBLIC INSTRUCTION (Continued)

Child accounting and statistics
Rural schools
School buildings
Institutional
District
Bureau of Professional Licensing
Teacher certification
Elementary
Secondary and placement
Preprofessional credentials and examination
Law enforcement
Issuing
Professional Examining Boards Advisory Committee
(Listed as separate agencies)
State Library
State Museum
Public School Employees' Retirement Board
State Council of Education
Board of Motion Picture Censors
Historical Commission
State teachers colleges and trade schools
State-owned schools

1936

Superintendent
Deputy superintendent
Executive assistant
Editor
State Council of Education
Bureau of Administration and Finance
School law
Child accounting and research
School plant
Consolidation and transportation
Bureau of Teacher Education and Certification
Bureau of Instruction
Elementary
Secondary
Special
Extension
Agriculture
Home economics
Guidance
Tests and measures
Industrial
Business
Vocational rehabilitation
Health and physical education
Art
Music
Conservation
Curriculum construction
State Library and Museum
Bureau of Professional Licensing
Personal examination
Law enforcement
Preprofessional credentials
Registration and renewal
Boards of state teachers colleges
Board of presidents of state teachers colleges
Public School Employees' Retirement Board
Pennsylvania Historical Commission
State Board of Motion Picture Censors
Professional Examining Boards

1938

Changes:
Two deputy superintendents
Public Service Institute under the Bureau of Instruction

1940

Changes:
Division of Business Education in Bureau of Instruction
Public Service Institute becomes independent agency

1944

Addition of:
Regulation of private trade schools, highway safety, preinduction training, and school lunch under Bureau of Instruction

1945

Creation of:
Division of Secondary Education Evaluation, Historical Commission, Museum and Archives combined in Museum and Historical Commission; made an independent agency

1947

Addition of:
State Board of Private Business Schools; Division of Private (Academic) School Registration
Farm and home safety under Bureau of Instruction

1950

Superintendent
State Council of Education
State-aided institutions
School law
Comptroller
Publications and Public Information
Public School Employees' Retirement Board
Credentials Evaluation Division

Bureau of School Administration

Appendix B

Supplement 1.–DEVELOPMENT OF PENNSYLVANIA DEPARTMENT OF PUBLIC INSTRUCTION (Continued)

Child accounting and research
Consolidation and transportation
School business
School plant
Bureau of Teacher Education and Certification
State Teachers Colleges
Bureau of Professional Licensing
State Library
Bureau of Instruction
Elementary
Secondary
Curriculum revision in secondary schools
Art
Audiovisual
Health and physical education
Music
School lunch and nutrition
School nurse
Special education
Agriculture
Aviation
Business
Distributive
Extension
Farm and home safety
Highway safety
Home economics
Junior historian
Occupational information and guidance
Trade and industrial
Public Service Institute
Veterans training program
State Board of Private Academic Schools
State Board of Private Business Schools
State Board of Private Correspondence Schools
Private trade school registration
Division of Free Food Distribution
Surplus property
Education library
State-owned schools

1952

First deputy
Comptroller
Publications and public information
School law
State Council of Education
Public School Employees' Retirement Board
Deputy for higher and teacher education
Bureau of Higher Education
Credentials evaluation
Accreditation of training facilities for veterans
State-aided educational institutions
Teacher education and certification
State teachers colleges

Bureau of School Licensing and Special Services
State Library
State Board of Motion Picture Censors
Third deputy
Bureau of School Administration
School business
Child accounting and research
Consolidation and Transportation
School planning
Bureau of General Education
Art
Aviation
Elementary
Health, physical education, and recreation
School nursing
Highway safety
Junior historian
Music
School library
Secondary
Special education
Bureau of Adult, Vocational, and Practical Arts Education
Agriculture
Audiovisual
Business
Free food distribution
Distributive
Extension
Farm and home safety
Federal surplus property
Homemaking
Industrial
Occupational information and guidance
Public Service Institute
School lunch and nutrition
Fourth deputy
Professional licensing
Professional library
State-owned schools

1956

Superintendent
Executive Bureau
Administration
Research
Public information and publications
Program development and leadership services
Bureau of Curriculum Administration
Adult extension
Agriculture
Business
Distributive
Occupational information and guidance
Farm and home safety

Appendix B

Supplement 1.–DEVELOPMENT OF PENNSYLVANIA DEPARTMENT OF PUBLIC INSTRUCTION (Continued)

Homemaking
Practical nursing
Trade and industrial
Bureau of Curriculum Services
Instructional aids and materials
Highway safety
Bureau of School District Organization
Bureau of School Business Services
Bureau of Higher Education Credentials Evaluation
Bureau of Private Schools and Veterans Education
Bureau of School Buildings
Public School Employees' Retirement Board
Bureau of Professional Licensing
Bureau of Curriculum Development
Public Service Institute
Bureau of Teacher Education and Teacher Certification
State Library

1957

Creation of:
Bureau of Special Pupil Services

1962

Superintendent
Office of Curriculum Research and Development Projects
Bureau of Special Services for Pupils
Exceptional children
Guidance and counseling
Testing
Bureau of Instructional Materials and Mass Media
Planning and development
Bureau of Curriculum Development
Bureau of Curriculum Administration
Bureau of Curriculum Services
Bureau of Higher Education
Planning and development
Professional and graduate education
Special services
Undergraduate education
State colleges
Staff services
Coordinator of NDEA
Bureau of School Business
Bureau of School Buildings
Bureau of School District Organization
Bureau of Research and Statistics

1965

Superintendent
Executive deputy
Public information
Legal relations
Public School Employees' Retirement Board
State Library
Deputy for research and development
Research
Statistics
Curriculum planning
Instructional materials
Teacher education
Deputy for school administration
County and district affairs
Federal and state affairs
School construction
School district organization
Distressed schools
Deputy for instruction
Evaluations coordinator
General and academic education
Vocational, technical, and continuing education
Special education
Deputy for higher education
Community colleges
College and university coordination
Academic standards and services
Higher education facilities
State college coordinator
Private school licensing boards
State-owned schools
Director of administrative services
Comptroller

1966

(Reorganization initiated in 1965 and approved in October 1966)

Superintendent
Deputy superintendent
Career development
Federal programs
Legislative services
Public information
Publications
School Employees' Retirement Board
State Library
General library
Law library
Library development
Technical services
Office of Research and Statistics–Director
Research administration and coordination
Statistics
Office of Administrative Services–Director
Educational data processing
Personnel
Director
Staff services
Budget services

Appendix B

Supplement 1.–DEVELOPMENT OF PENNSYLVANIA DEPARTMENT OF PUBLIC INSTRUCTION (Continued)

Commissioner for basic education
  Assistant commissioner and director of staff services
  Assistant commissioner–programs and services
    General and academic education
    Special education
    Instructional services
    Intermediate unit services
    Curriculum development and school evaluation
    Quality educational assessment
    Vocational, technical, and continuing education
    Guidance services
  Assistant commissioner–school administration
    School administrative services
    School construction
    Administrative leadership services
    Private schools and veterans education
Commissioner for higher education
  Assistant commissioner and director of staff services
    Community colleges
    State colleges and universities
    Teacher education
    Institutional studies and services
    Higher education facilities
Legal counsel
Comptroller's Office

Appendix C

Table 1.–STATE APPROPRIATIONS FOR PUBLIC SCHOOLS IN PENNSYLVANIA, 1899-1900 THROUGH 1964-65

Year ending	Total	Year ending	Total	Year ending	Total
1900	$ 5,500,000	1922	$12,895,179	1944	$ 54,183,760
1901	5,000,000	1923	17,488,417	1945	57,050,427
1902	5,550,000	1924	26,044,267	1946	61,654,771
1903	5,550,000	1925	19,699,856	1947	75,890,256
1904	5,262,500	1926	21,957,004	1948	91,318,346
1905	5,262,500	1927	22,846,138	1949	95,918,562
1906	5,312,500	1928	24,750,237	1950	105,979,252
1907	5,312,500	1929	24,987,383	1951	120,564,543
1908	7,125,000	1930	28,266,214	1952	138,445,060
1909	7,125,000	1931	27,731,627	1953	165,815,169
1910	7,125,000	1932	32,645,259	1954	185,616,164
1911	6,950,581	1933	29,017,936	1955	197,834,364
1912	6,998,537	1934	30,633,931	1956	199,785,600
1913	7,004,212	1935	26,913,756	1957	280,446,360
1914	6,977,927	1936	35,122,996	1958	287,174,162
1915	7,096,077	1937	34,784,694	1959	336,346,493
1916	7,102,857	1938	33,890,753	1960	362,288,352
1917	7,472,093	1939	34,263,510	1961	356,963,251
1918	7,410,759	1940	37,768,769	1962	375,478,412
1919	7,814,252	1941	30,644,753	1963	374,734,433
1920	10,832,703	1942	46,544,147	1964	430,090,969
1921	8,850,346	1943	42,910,325	1965	468,467,017

Source:

Bureau of Statistics, Department of Public Instruction, Commonwealth of Pennsylvania, September 1966.

39 Puerto Rico

DEPARTMENT OF EDUCATION
Angel M. Mergal

Contents

INTRODUCTION

Upon the signing of the Treaty of Paris on December 10, 1898, which ended the Spanish-American War, the Island of Puerto Rico ceased to be a Spanish colony and became a possession of the United States. The final paragraph of Article IX says: "The civil rights and political status of the native inhabitants of the territories hereby ceded to the United States shall be determined by Congress" (1). The United States ratified the treaty February 6, 1899, and 2 months later, on April 11, President William McKinley proclaimed its ratification by both nations. General G.W. Davis then issued Military Order No. 132, allowing Spanish citizens born in Spain 1 year to declare their intention of retaining their Spanish citizenship "in default of which declaration they shall be held to have renounced it and have adopted the nationality of the territory in which they may reside" (2). This same Article IX left the declaration of citizenship of the Puerto Ricans "to be determined by Congress."

The acquisition of overseas colonies was something inconceivable to most Americans. The debates in the press and in Congress indicate the resulting confusion. In an article for the *New York Daily Tribune,* Attorney General James H. Hoy enthusiastically placed McKinley on the same level as George Washington, declaring: "Washington, Father of the Republic; Lincoln, the Saviour of the Republic; and McKinley, the *Pathfinder* of the Republic" (3). But both Houses of Congress showed a disorientation very foreign to a pathfinder. The citizenship of the Puerto Ricans and the status of the island were converted into moot questions that remain so today. The Foraker Act made them citizens of Puerto Rico; the Jones Act made them citizens of the United States; but still, in 1927, 1934, and 1938, amendments were introduced on citizenship, and today Puerto Ricans are discussing whether the Congress, which voted for American citizenship in 1917, has the power to take it away. The U.S. Supreme Court has never made a clear and definitive decision on this point.

Three days after landing in Guánica, General Nelson A. Miles issued from Ponce a proclamation "to the inhabitants of Puerto Rico" as to the purpose of the invasion, in which he said:

> They (the Americans) come bearing the banner of freedom. . . . They bring you the fostering arm of a nation of free people, whose greatest power is in justice and humanity to all those living within its fold. The chief object of the American military forces will be . . . to give to the people of your beautiful island the largest measure of liberty. We have come to bestow upon you the immunities and blessings of the liberal institutions of our Government (4).

Justice and fair play have always been essential characteristics of the United States, but their manifestations sometimes seem obscure.

Miles's promise is what the Diffies called, in 1931, *A Broken Pledge* (5). On February 3, 1928, when Colonel Lindbergh flew to Puerto Rico as an ambassador of peace, José Tous Soto, Speaker of the House, read a legislative resolution welcoming the Colonel as a symbol of the United States. He added a reminder of Miles's promise:

> The good wishes of Porto Rico will go with you to the land of the brave and the free, and to your country and to your people you will convey a message of Porto Rico not far different from the cry of Patrick Henry—Liberty or death! . . . Grant us the freedom that you enjoy . . . which you have promised us (6).

The people were not crying for independence, but for freedom—the kind of creative freedom symbolized by the American flag.

This kind of freedom has been pursued and is being achieved, basically, in the schoolrooms. It is the story of 67 years of hard, sacrificial, and intelligent effort. It is the effort that a commission from Columbia University called "the wonder of a century" (7). The purpose of this chapter is to trace a brief outline of this "wonder." The full story would take several hundred pages more.

Puerto Rico is the highest peak of a submerged mountain range forming the Archipelago of the Caribbean and extending from the southern part of Florida to Trinidad, north to Venezuela. All the islands of the Archipelago are called Antilles. Puerto Rico, about the size of Long Island, is the smallest of the larger islands, and Cuba is the largest. Including the small neighboring islands of Vieques, Culebra, Santa Cruz, Monito, and Desecheo that form part of Puerto Rico, the area is 3,435 square miles with a population of 2,349,544, according to the census of 1960. There are more than 687 persons per square mile.

Up to 1950, Puerto Rico had practically no industries; it was a rural county, "a government of poor people for poor people," said Governor Jesús T. Piñero. The principal problems for education were excess population and lack of resources. Although federal aid has ameliorated the situation to some extent since 1950, then and today the island faces additional problems caused by rapid urban growth.

In 1898, with less income and the same territorial expanse, the island had a population of 857,660 inhabitants and a school population of 397,912 children between 6 and 16 years of age. The 1960 census revealed a school population of 859,982 children between the ages of 6 and 18. In 1898, the illiteracy rate was 85 percent, and in 1965, it was only 15 percent. In his report to General Davis for 1899-1900, General John Eaton, the first commissioner of education under the military government, wrote:

> The indications of educational sentiment were extremely interesting. I had rarely been situated in a way to hear education more universally commended. It was good for everybody, and everybody wanted it. All classes talked about it. The need of improvement was admitted on all hands. Americans and Porto Ricans were prolific with plans. The General (Davis) promised to give free passage on Government transports to both teachers and pupils who should go to the States for educational purposes . . . . Every source of information disclosed the inadequacy of instruction. Clearly education must be revolutionized (8).

From this moment to the present, the history of Puerto Rico has been the story of *The Quiet Revolution*—in a much deeper sense than Homer Page (9) realized—and reform has been the perpetual feature of its education. Faith in public education continues to be as great as it was before the turn of the century.

During the period prior to 1898, the schools were not graded; each teacher classified his pupils according to his own ideas. Generally, the teacher himself taught the pupils in the first and second classes (the most advanced); and advanced pupils, as assistants to the teachers, had charge of the third and fourth (or beginners) classes. The pupils learned by heart the lessons in textbooks written in the old way with questions and answers. The pupil who recited the lessons without omitting any of the words received the highest mark. Object lessons were entirely unknown.

The *alcalde* and the *párroco* (priest) were the only members of the school board who visited the schools and exercised any supervision over them. The teachers obtained their schools through competitive examinations before an examining board appointed by the Governor. Thus, "the teacher obtained his school for life. He was the proprietor of his school . . . . In fact, it can be said that there was no real organization in the public schools of Puerto Rico, every teacher being the ruler of his own school" (10).

After General Nelson A. Miles took official possession of the island in October 1898 from the Spanish Governor, General Ricardo Ortega, he left for the States and turned over his command to General John R. Brooke, the first American military Governor. Brooke left Puerto Rico in December, and General Guy V. Henry became the second military Governor. General G.W. Davis, the third and last military Governor, took charge in May 1899.

At the time General Miles took possession, the island was governed by an autonomic charter granted in November 1897 by the Queen Regent of Spain, María Cristina, mother of the child King Alfonso XIII. General Macías inaugurated the new system in February 1898. The autonomic cabinet, composed of six members, included Manuel F. Rossy as the secretary of instruction.

Governor Henry issued a military order abolishing the cabinet and creating four departments: state, justice, treasury, and interior. Education was established as a bureau under the head of the interior department. But when General Davis found that local political strife made it impossible to work through civil officials, he dismissed all the heads and replaced them with military officers.

On May 1, 1900, in pursuance of orders from the Secretary of War, the military Governor transferred control of civil affairs to Charles H. Allen, the first civil Governor of Puerto Rico (11).

THE FOUNDERS, 1899 TO 1907

The first four commissioners of education, two under military government and two under the first civil charter (the Foraker Law), founded the Puerto Rican Department of Education. The President sent to Puerto Rico the best he could find in the States, and all four proved to be excellent choices. (See Appendix A.)

General John Eaton, who had been U.S. Commissioner of Education, was recommended for the job by his successor in Washington, D.C., W. T. Harris. When the President created the Military Geographical Department of Puerto Rico October 1, 1898, the Adjutant-General's office directed Major General John R. Brooke to assume command. Eighteen days later, by Order No. 1, General Brooke assumed command of the Headquarters Department of Puerto Rico and began his duties as military Governor. That same day, he raised the American flag on the island. But on December 9, General Brooke was recalled to the States, and when Dr. Eaton arrived early in January, General Guy V. Henry was in command as Governor (12). About the middle of January 1899, Victor S. Clark joined Eaton as his assistant.

Early in February, as mentioned earlier, Governor Henry reorganized the administrative departments of the insular government and formally organized the bureau of education under the interior department. As head of the bureau, Commissioner Eaton made two tours of inspection, visiting all the large towns, while his assistant visited about one-fourth of the smaller municipalities.

Eaton had to develop an educational system from scratch. Whatever buildings were left from the Spanish system were badly damaged by San Ciriaco, a tropical cyclone that swept over the island in 1899, causing 3,000 deaths and $20 million in damage. The coffee plantations were ruined for many years to come.

Dr. Eaton, however, was encouraged by the people's tremendous enthusiasm for education. Two years after the American flag had been raised at La Fortaleza (Governor's Palace), a number of distinguished citizens met in the San Juan Theater. Their first petition was for teachers and schools, and they expressed their desire in written resolutions. They wrote that "the best means of advancing the people would be kindergartens and normal schools as established in the United States. Our elementary and superior schools should be transformed and graded according to modern pedagogical methods" (13).

Federico Degetau, head of the interior department and Eaton's superior, wanted to introduce in Puerto Rico the practices of the famous Spanish scholar and educator Francisco Giner de los Ríos, who had been Degetau's professor of law in the Central University in Madrid. For instance, he wanted to found a pedagogical museum and a Spanish-American university. Eaton knew that under the circumstances this was a dream. Giner himself had worked in the face of tremendous opposition and difficulties, including imprisonment. "The rule of this people by Spain," wrote Eaton, "was one of both suppression and oppression" (14). Beside this, the cyclone had worsened the financial condition of several municipalities. He pointed out:

> There are towns where there literally has not been a cent in the treasury since the cyclone. The actual amount expended upon the schools is nothing. . . . The American teachers are in some cases teaching in bar rooms without so much as a table or chairs or benches, simply with a reading chart and books, with the little children seated on boxes or little chairs which they bring from home. . . (15).

Yet, the people still had hope in the *Americanos.* The American nation had been to the Puerto Rican the synonym of all that was just and grand and righteous. They hoped their island could be made into a twentieth-century Garden of Eden, "in which the native, trained in the new methods of freedom, may for the first time in three centuries enjoy the sweets of liberty" (16).

As a result of his surveys, Eaton began preparing a code of school laws. Governor Henry promulgated in May 1899 the first 10 General Orders, making them effective immediately. They provided and defined the duties for an insular board and local or municipal boards, and for the election of municipal school trustees. Thirteen additional orders were to go into effect July 1. These abolished the fee system, made education absolutely free to all residents between 6 and 18 years, limited the school year to 9 months, and established a graded system of schools. They also determined the legal qualification of teachers and provided for their certification.

Despite the many changes and trials so soon after the war, Eaton felt that General Henry showed great singleness of purpose and devotion to the public interest, and his vigorous enforcement of the law had been combined with great personal kindness. True, there had been many personal disappointments, but when it was known that he was leaving the command, the officers of the Society for the Benefit of the Children conferred with the teachers and invited both General Henry and General Davis, who would assume office as the third military Governor in May 1899, to meet with them. The teachers then had a beautiful farewell ceremony for General Henry and a welcome for General Davis, described in part as follows.

> The singing of Columbia by the young ladies of the Normal College was nicely rendered. . . . The band of the Beneficencia (Charities) assisted by playing the "Star-Spangled Banner" and "America." The speeches in English were made by two pupils of Mr. Timothee, 22 Sol, and the same in Spanish by two pupils of Mr. Saavedra, Santurce (17).

When General Henry embarked, the multitudes gathered on the wharf for a further manifestation of regret and word of parting. As his vessel touched at Ponce, there was a similar demonstration by all classes of citizens, but especially by those who had cooperated in plans of improving the place and in efforts for promoting the American School at Ponce (18).

In May 1899, the same month Governor Henry relinquished his command, Commissioner Eaton was forced by ill health to give up his work in Puerto Rico and return to the United States. He was succeeded by his assistant, Victor Clark.

In July 1899, Governor Davis introduced a new feature in the educational system by appointing an insular Board of Education composed of five members, of which Victor S. Clark was president. A month later, he issued a General Order providing for municipal elections and the election of five school trustees for each municipal board. General Davis' school code defined the term, power, and organization of these boards and divided the island into six school districts.

The internal political turmoil and the failure of the local boards forced greater centralization. In October 1899, Davis ordered that not more than three of the local trustees could belong to the same political party, and the power to appoint teachers was transferred to the president of the insular board.

Victor S. Clark, president of the board, received an order from the Headquarters Department to summarize Henry's General Orders concerning education. Dated February 26, 1900, Clark's report, entitled *Laws Governing Public Instruction* and published first in the official *Gazette,* contains a report of the 16 district supervisors then at work in the island.

The new board also produced a bilingual *Teacher's Manual for the Public Schools of Puerto Rico* (19)–595 pages, with hundreds of photographs and illustrations. This gave teachers and school officials a brief account of the educational thought, literature, and system of school organization prevailing in the United States. The *Manual* proved to be very influential in Puerto Rico.

Following two surveys by Eaton and Clark, occasional surveys by commissions and American experts developed as a general trend of education in Puerto Rico. The Institute (high school established before 1898) and the normal school for girls were investigated by Professor J. G. Meyers, former instructor at the Massachusetts Institute of Technology. Both were found wanting.

The following March, Dr. Clark resigned his position as president of the board and was succeeded by George G. Groff, one of the original board members, who had been vice-president of Bucknell University. Groff held the position until the civil regime took over on May 1, 1900, when he was appointed acting commissioner of education, pending the permanent organization of the new civil government.

As acting director of public instruction and president of the insular board, Groff visited the schools. He described the results:

> We visited a school during school hours and found the teacher in bed taking a *siesta*; other teachers were away attending store. In another case we found a teacher who was running a rum shop. Teachers went around the schoolroom in untidy and insufficient attire and the demand of the neighborhood calls upon the time of the teachers left him less than the required time for instructing the pupils (20).

An insular (survey) commission, composed of Kennedy, Watkins, and Curtis, came to this same conclusion after visiting the schools early in spring 1899. They reported:

> The schools we visited are simply pretensions to education and in the United States would not be regarded as being worthy of the name. The books most generally found in those schools are a primer, a catechism, and a mental philosophy, and the system of education consists almost entirely of memorizing alone (21).

The misery of the people was so great and the teachers' salaries so ridiculously small that it is no wonder these deplorable conditions existed. However, there were private schools, such as Timothee's in San Juan, Saavedra's in Santurce, and Huyke's in Arroyo, that were exceptions to the rule and where English was very well taught.

Martin Grove Brumbaugh

President McKinley appointed Martin Grove Brumbaugh, head of the department of pedagogy at the University of Pennsylvania, as the first civil commissioner of education in June 1900. A graduate of Harvard with an M.A. and Ph.D. from the University of Pennsylvania, Brumbaugh had taught in both the public schools and college, had written several books, and at the time of his appointment was editor of the Lippincot Educational Series (22).

When Brumbaugh assumed office on August 6, there was great confusion and practically no system of education. Unqualified persons had received teachers licenses, and there was practically no supervision of their work. The municipalities, most of them in debt, could make no appropriations to the local boards. Under these conditions it seemed necessary to further centralize education.

The bicameral Legislature, as established by the Foraker Act, consisted of an Executive Council of 11 members appointed by the President and a 35-member House of Delegates elected from seven districts created by the council. The President was required to appoint to the council five native Puerto Ricans, plus, ex officio, the secretary, attorney general, treasurer, auditor, commissioner of the interior, and commissioner of education.

Since the commissioner of education also was a legislator, he had the opportunity to design the first educational law in Puerto Rico and give his office the authority necessary to bring some order to this situation. In January 1901, the Legislature passed the school law that is still the legal foundation for the Puerto Rican educational system. Because of his wide experience in educational matters, Commissioner Brumbaugh was able to correct the errors made by General Henry, Dr. Eaton, and Dr. Clark. One of the island's educational historians wrote:

> In contrast with the military orders where administration of schools was in the hands of local Boards, there is now a high degree of centralization. . . . The tendency has generally been to extend more and more (the Commissioner's) powers and duties, to centralize the system more and more (23).

The commissioner received absolute authority in some cases. For instance, the local school boards could select and recommend teachers to the commissioner, but only he had the power to appoint them. The law also stipulated that the commissioner would select the teachers of English. To handle these duties, it was necessary to staff a central office of 10 persons, thus creating a Department of Education. Besides the commissioner, there were an assistant commissioner, a disbursing officer, a secretary, two stenographers, a bookkeeper, a shipping clerk, a messenger, and a janitor.

At first, the department was burdened with a tremendous mass of details. For instance, it distributed the following quantities of books and materials: 524 reading charts, 18,000 first readers, 10,400 second readers, 7,680 third readers, 800 fourth readers, 700 fifth readers, 6,000 song books, and 2,440 elementary and 100 advanced geography books. It also distributed 10,720 elementary arithmetic books, 1,690 advanced arithmetic books, 4,960 language lessons, 3,460 U.S. history books, 7,800 elementary language books in both languages, 800 Spanish-English dictionaries, and tons of other teaching materials. Although the commissioner realized that the department should not be obliged to handle all of this, he "thought best to assume all these obligations of detail in order that a compact and consistent organization of the system of education should be wrought out from the beginning" (24).

At the time Brumbaugh took office, there were 508 schoolhouses used by the public schools, only two belonging to the government and the rest rented from private parties by the municipalities. Brumbaugh was able to persuade the President to allot to public school construction $200,000 from the trust fund for public works created from custom duties collected on Puerto Rican products, according to Public Law 69, approved by the U.S. Congress April 12, 1900. By the end of his first year in office, he had constructed two new schoolhouses and was in the process of building 27 others.

In June 1901, there were 33,854 pupils attending the public schools, with 771 teachers in the regular schools, 16 in the high schools and normal school, and 16 supervisors. Puerto Rican statesman Luis Sánchez Morales introduced a bill granting scholarships for 20 Puerto Rican students to study in the United States. The Legislature enacted it, and the program ran for 12 years, supported by Puerto Rican funds.

It was necessary for the state government to pay most of the expenses of education, because not less than 10 percent nor more than 20 percent of all moneys received by the municipalities was set aside for the schools. The department's records were destroyed by fire in July 1900, but in his first annual report Commissioner Brumbaugh stated that since that date the government of Puerto Rico had spent $331,791 on public education.

Samuel McCune Lindsay

In December 1901, President Theodore Roosevelt appointed Samuel McCune Lindsay to replace Brumbaugh, who had resigned because of ill health. A native of Pittsburgh, this distinguished sociologist had attended the Universities of Pennsylvania, Vienna, Rome, and Paris, and earned his Ph.D. from the University of Halle in Germany. He assumed the office of commissioner of education in February 1902 and became the first chancellor of the University of Puerto Rico. It was unfortunate that the tropical Eden, rife with diseases, political unrest, and unsanitary conditions, was not favorable to scholars like Brumbaugh and Lindsay, who were unable to carry out their 4-year terms.

During Lindsay's first year in office there were 1,115 schools, both public and private, with 70,216 pupils in 717 separate buildings, but the highest daily attendance averaged only about 40,000 pupils. All classes were conducted in English in approximately 30 schools, although English as a subject was taught in every school on the island. In fact, there were 150 American teachers of English in Puerto Rico.

To accommodate all of the pupils who should have been attending, the island desperately needed new schools and buildings. This condition was only partially relieved when 19 agricultural-rural schools and two industrial schools (the first at San Juan and the second at Mayagüez) opened before the end of 1902. Two more industrial schools were projected, one in Arecibo and the other at Ponce, where a Spanish-Renaissance style building was under construction at a cost of $25,000. In all, the government had set aside $250,000 from the trust fund for erecting school buildings.

All the schools offered 8-year courses, except the island's only high school, established in San Juan in 1899. In its fourth year, the high school enrolled 235 students (both graded and secondary), with an expected graduating class of 5 students. Commissioner Lindsay was confident its work was "going forward and producing results that those who observe it at close range have scarcely dared to expect" (25).

Lindsay argued that Puerto Rico needed immediately a number of well-trained native teachers. The salary paid to an American teacher of English, the best salary in the island, was $50 a month for 9 months, plus an allowance by the local school board amounting to from $54 to $135 per year, or a total annual income of about $504. The rural teachers of the first class received $35 monthly, those of the second class $30, and those of the third class, $25. Graded teachers of the first class received $55 per month, the second class received $50, and the third class, $45. Principals earned from $70 to $80, depending on the class of the school.

During the summer vacation of 1899, 48 native teachers were sent to the United States at government expense to study English in American schools. Selected youth from the public schools also were sent to preparatory schools in the states, and by the summer of 1901, 219 pupils had taken advantage of this program under the supervision of the commissioner. Many of these students became excellent educators. But there was an urgent need to establish other programs to educate people who would teach. Lindsay wrote in his report for 1902 that the "demand for the establishment of an institution of college grade, which in time will lead to the development of a great Antillean

University as part of the public schools system of Porto Rico, is likely to increase as the years go on" (26). The University of Puerto Rico was formally organized in June 1903. The university's first building was a normal school, erected at a cost of $21,000 from the extra trust fund of $150,000 approved by the President (27).

Besides founding the university, Lindsay also continued the practice of teacher excursions to the United States for professional improvement. In 1904, he made arrangements with the presidents of Harvard and Cornell Universities for 500 teachers to study on their campuses during a 6-week summer session. The War Department offered transportation at $1 per day, and the teachers left June 26. One transport went to Boston and the other to New York, and at the close of the summer school, they left for Philadelphia and on to Washington, D.C., where they were received by Roland P. Falkner, who already had been appointed to succeed Dr. Lindsay. President Theodore Roosevelt received them at the White House with the following words:

> I wish to greet you with all my heart at the national capital. It is my earnest wish, as it was the wish of my lamented predecessor, and it is the wish of the people of the United States, that only an unmixed good shall come to the people of Puerto Rico because of their connection with this country. I greet you with peculiar pleasure and interest, because this body and those like you, that are engaged in the work of education in Puerto Rico, are doing that work which more than any other is vital to the future of the Island (28).

Summary

By the time Commissioner Lindsay left office in October 1904, the first commissioners of education had performed a Herculean task (29).

During these first 5 years of American occupancy, 914 schools had been opened—a gain of 134 over the previous year (1901)—and by 1903, there were 1,014 schools. By April 1903, 1,097 teachers were coping with about 377,200 boys and girls from 5 to 18 years of age, compared to 322,393 in 1899. But total enrollment during the 1903 school year was only 64,039 pupils, with 6,177 in the special schools, or an estimated 19 percent of the school population and 7 percent of the 1,000,907 total population. The special schools included 10 kindergartens, 44 night classes, 6 industrial classes, 23 high school classes, 2 practice school classes, and 4 normal classes.

The total yearly expenditures for education from insular appropriations amounted to $545,106. The municipal governments contributed an additional $149,917, and insular funds provided $1,038 for two training classes for professional nurses and $14,865 for educating Puerto Rican students in the United States. There were 45 Puerto Rican students in the states, 20 receiving $250 each per year and the remainder receiving $400. One of these students, José Padín, later became commissioner of education. Altogether, the total expenditures for education amounted to $817,815, as compared to $577,585 the previous year. The average cost of the common school per pupil amounted to $7.97.

The highly centralized school system worked so satisfactorily that the Legislature favored even more centralization. It enacted a new school law, approved by the Governor in March 1903, which included the first provisions for compulsory attendance in elementary school.

The President of the United States set aside for Puerto Rico $2 million in trust funds, mainly collected by the federal government in custom duties on Puerto Rican products entering the United States. Most of it, $1,400,000, went to the public roads, and $447,500 went into school buildings. In Mayagüez, a newly erected 16-room brick building was named Roosevelt Industrial School after Miss Alice Roosevelt, and a cornerstone was laid during her visit to Puerto Rico during the 1903 winter season. Lindsay recommended at least $100,000 annually to construct schools and encouraged the municipalities to build their own.

During these 5 years, a number of distinguished American educators came to the island to contribute to the Propaganda Conferences—short seminars for the in-service training of teachers. These included Charles J. Skinner, U.S. Congressman; State Superintendent Mason S. Stone, of Vermont; and Professor W. F. Phelps, of Minnesota. Charles de Garmo, head of the School of Education at Cornell University, and James Earl Russell, dean of Teachers College at Columbia University, both outstanding educators, served as professors at the conferences, meeting in different parts of the island, usually for 8 days, with as many as seven meetings each day. Brumbaugh pointed out that about 300 teachers and at least 3,000 of the leading citizens interested in education attended these conferences.

De Garmo, in a letter to Dr. Lindsay, stated that he was somewhat skeptical before he visited the island regarding the efforts to teach all of the people a new tongue—still one of the most important single issues in education in Puerto Rico today. De Garmo did conclude that there should be better publicity and better public relations for Puerto Rico in the States. Governor Hunt, on the other hand, responded that "the insular Legislature and insular authorities respond to every demand the Department of Education makes for legislation or aid and any other kind in building up or strengthening the school system" (30).

Sarah W. Dagget, State Regent of the Daughters of the American Revolution in Massachusetts, established a school at her own expense as a memorial to her father. Major R. H. Pratt, the superintendent of the Indian School at Carlisle, Pennsylvania, offered scholarships, and Juan José Osuna started his American studies at Carlisle as a Puerto Rican Indian boy. W. T. Harris, U.S. Commissioner of Education, "was watchful to furnish every aid in the power of his office" (31).

THE STRUGGLE: FROM SAN CIRIACO TO SAN CIPRIAN, 1905 TO 1932

The successors to Commissioner Lindsay and Governor Hunt did everything possible to build an excellent educational system, but they struggled in the face of many odds. San Ciriaco and the new regime's commercial laws crippled the coffee industry for many years, making it necessary to develop the tobacco and sugar industries (32).

Then came World War I and its aftermath, with the influenza epidemic, the earthquakes, and the tobacco crash caused by the economic depression in the nation. Then on September 13, 1928, another cyclone caused 300 deaths and $50 million in losses. Under the New Deal, there was a painful recovery (33), but when Rexford G. Tugwell arrived to govern the island in September 1941, he perceived it still to be "a stricken land" (34).

The Language Problem

The years from 1904 to 1915 were marked with progress, the main aims being to reduce illiteracy by increasing the enrollment, provide additional classrooms, and train more teachers. The major educational problem, however, remained that of language. Educators, in appraising the cultural status of the islanders, committed the usual mistake of judging the cultural level only by the wretched conditions of public education. For instance, Commissioner Victor S. Clark states:

> There does not seem to be among the masses the same devotion to their native tongue or to any national ideal that animates the Frenchman, for instance, in Canada . . . . Another important fact that must not be overlooked is that the majority of the people of this Island do not speak pure Spanish. Their language is a patois almost unintelligible to the natives of Barcelona or Madrid. It possesses no literature and little value as an intellectual medium. There is a bare possibility that it will be nearly as easy to educate this people out of their patois into English as it will be to educate them in the elegant tongue of Castille (35).

Apart from the fact that Catalonian and not Spanish is spoken in Barcelona, that the elegant tongue of Castille is not pure Spanish, Clark shows himself completely ignorant of the Puerto Rican cultural reality. But, in 1930, he corrected himself by writing that—

> The teaching of two languages not only increases the cost of instruction, but it encroaches upon the time available for other subjects . . . . However, the members of the present Survey incline to the opinion that the teaching of English in the elementary grades should be continued (36).

This opinion, in itself, was carefully conditioned.

Commissioner Brumbaugh, who was more cautious on the language question, stated that the children should use both languages, and he formulated the policy that has governed language teaching to the present. N. C. Shaeffer, state superintendent of public instruction in Pennsylvania, wisely remarked that a man is as many times a man as he has languages in which to think. Thus, American teachers received instruction in Spanish, and the Puerto Rican teachers learned English. But, as one observer wrote, these Puerto Rican teachers "have large schools, crowded daily, . . . and although they have never been given a good professional training, they are so hard-working" that he wished "all the teachers might take example from them" (37).

Perhaps one of the most dramatic illustrations of a talented boy's efforts in the new school language program appears in Commissioner Lindsay's annual report of 1902:

> It is true I am in a position with the San Juan Light and Transit Company, but I can do little that scarcely it is not sufficient for me to address myself. I have prepare myself to can be a teacher. The next time for being not able to pay one who could give lessons to me. This letter will not be correct but it is a sign of my progress in the English language. I wait for a satisfactory answer, for I go every time forward and forward . . . . At the end of September I will be 16 years old (38).

Commissioner Falkner made English the official language of the schoolroom and the medium of instruction in all subjects except Spanish itself. He had boundless enthusiasm. In 1907, he reported that "so great an impetus has been given to this work that the time seems not far distant when the graded schools will be taught exclusively in the English language" (39). The whole curriculum of the school system was thus leveled so that it could be adapted to the deficiency in language of both pupils and teachers.

In order to accommodate more children of school age, in 1907, Falkner introduced the double enrollment and increased the number of rural schools to 614. The urban schools were already well organized with a school population of 354,721, but still a great deal had to be done. The industrial schools were closed this year, and in the following year, 1908, the agricultural program was eliminated, because the Legislature failed to appropriate the necessary funds, and there were not enough trained teachers.

The only school at the secondary level, the Model and Training School, burned down on July 1, 1900. The following November, the English and Graded School of San Juan was established and offered high school work. In its fourth year, 1904, and the first year of Falkner's term as commissioner of education, it graduated its first class. At the same time, another one had begun in Ponce, one more had been started in Mayaguez, and a fourth had been planned for Fajardo.

When Edwin G. Dexter succeeded Falkner as commissioner in August 1907, he stepped up instruction in English. Pauline Rojas, director of the English program under Villaronga, writes: "With the exception of Dexter, no Commissioner of Education ever attempted to teach everything in English" (40). Even though half the first grades were receiving instruction in English, Dexter seemed to ignore this and instituted his new course for graded schools, which went into effect at the beginning of the 1909-10 school year. Dexter wrote that, in this way—

> English has been made the medium of instruction in practically the entire graded school system . . . enrolling 35,000 pupils—89.7 percent the preceding year; 9.9 percent were taught partly in English; and 0.6 percent had English taught as a special subject (41).

Commissioners Dexter and Bainter, 1907 to 1915

Commissioner Dexter found that of the 68,828 enrollment, only 44,218 were attending school; the census of 1910 reported 390,640 children of school age. Since his aim was "to provide instruction for all children of school age" (42), he found himself compelled to introduce the double enrollment practice, prevalent in some parts of the United States. When he resigned in 1912, the enrollment had reached 160,657 pupils, but he also left the problem of double enrollment that even today is a challenging one.

Brumbaugh's law in 1901 provided for night schools, and Dexter decided these must be extended. During his first 2 years, the adults attending these night schools were in the majority, but by 1906, of the 2,846 night pupils in the urban areas only 23 percent were adults. Dexter also established night schools in the country, so that, by 1912, there were 139 urban and 209 rural night schools, with a rural enrollment of 8,594. The following year, the urban schools increased to 150 with 7,430 pupils, and the 149 rural schools enrolled 5,157.

In the 1909-10 school year, 18 municipalities opened first- and second-year continuation schools beyond the eighth grade. These extended rapidly, and several developed into full-fledged high schools: Arecibo in 1912; Humacao in 1913; and Bayamón, Yauco, Guayama, Aguadilla, Fajardo, and Caguas in 1916.

Dexter also encouraged higher education and professional schooling by providing student aid. In 1907, the Legislature empowered local boards to use not more than 5 percent of their income to aid students from rural schools who wanted to obtain their common school diplomas. The commissioner was given the power to grant these students scholarships amounting to $108 to continue their high school education. Scholarships ranging from $40 to $100 also were granted to candidates for teaching agriculture. The program was extended so that students could be granted scholarships of $280 for attending the normal school at Río Piedras, and the commissioner could grant $250 and $500 annual scholarships for students to study in the United States.

The teachers themselves were vitally interested in helping the island progress educationally. In June 1911, 516 teachers met at Ponce to organize the Teachers Association of Puerto Rico (AMPR). Its main purpose was to cooperate with the government to improve the schools, offer creative criticism, and oppose practices that seemed unjust, inadequate, or improper. Although the association has received criticism, it has performed its work admirably well, particularly after it was reorganized in 1949. All persons holding a teacher license are eligible to join, and it is governed by a constitution and bylaws registered with the Puerto Rico Department of State.

Edward M. Bainter, who succeeded Dexter in July 1912, was fortunate in having more money with which to work for improving schools. In his January 1913 message to the Legislature, Governor George R. Colton stated that in Puerto Rico there were over 390,000 children between 5 and 18 years of age, while the school enrollment was only 160,657 and the average daily attendance 125,000 pupils. He blamed the situation on a shortage of funds. And although the islanders were Puerto Rican citizens, they received no federal grants except from Morrill Land Grant funds and special appropriations.

Colton laid the groundwork, but it was Governor Arthur Yager, who entered office in November 1913, who was able to get the Legislature to pass the Big Budget that gave the schools an economic bonanza in 1913. A former schoolteacher, Yager was sympathetic toward education and in his January 1915 message expressed his concern that only 50 percent of the school population was actually enrolled (43).

As early as 1902, Commissioner Lindsay had stated that there was no more important forward step in the educational work in the island than to get the proposed industrial and trade schools established on a solid foundation. Three were opened at San Juan, Mayagüez, and Ponce, but the solid foundation was lacking; there was only $20,000 appropriated and $25,000 from trust funds. These industrial schools and the agricultural-rural schools did the pioneer work in vocational education; however, the industrial schools eventually failed, due to lack of funds and well-trained teachers.

Commissioner Bainter, a specialist in vocational and prevocational education, emphasized manual training, home economics, and agriculture as subjects essential to the curriculum. Beginning in 1913, manual training was required in grades 6 through 10. Since an average of 3,181 boys were enrolled in these manual training classes, Bainter appointed a general supervisor for this field. Although home economics was equally emphasized, it was not until 1919 that Commissioner P. G. Miller appointed Elsie Mae Willsey as special supervisor for this subject.

The problems continued to mount, however. By 1914, Puerto Rican school enrollment reached 207,101, the largest up to that time, despite the fact that only 50 percent of the school-age population was enrolled. By 1915, it jumped to 419,282, and there were 1,473 schools and 2,535 teachers. This meant an average enrollment per teacher of 81, and in one rural school an 18-year-old girl taught 250 pupils!

One development that benefited the children of a few schools was the initiation of a school lunch program by a rural school teacher in Manatí in 1914-15. The following year, the teachers of Ponce made arrangements with a local restaurant to furnish lunches for 8 children, and each teacher took one child home so that 24 children were given lunches. San Germán and Juncos followed, and soon the practice became general.

Commissioner Bainter was very interested in developing a physical education program. In 1913, he appointed a general supervisor with instructions to develop playgrounds and athletics. Two years later, there were 68 towns with playgrounds, operating at a cost of $59,000, compared with the 27 towns with playgrounds in 1909, at an expense of $3,000 per year (44). All of the subsequent commissioners have given attention to health and physical education.

In his 1914 report, Bainter stated that he was giving special attention to the Spanish language because the people desired to conserve their mother tongue in all its purity. Since English was being used as a medium of instruction in practically all branches of the curriculum for the graded schools, many thought that Spanish was not receiving due attention. As a result, the Legislature created the position of general supervisor of Spanish, and Bainter appointed Manuel G. Nin. The 1914 report stated that—

> The instruction in the graded school system is given in the English language in all subjects, with the exception of Spanish, nature study, and the first year's work in hygiene and sanitation . . . . The Spanish language is taught as a special subject, beginning with the first grade and continuing to the end of the course (45).

The Miller Decade, 1915 to 1925

Paul G. Miller had entered Puerto Rico with the invading army, and by 1902 he was chief of the Division of Supervision and Statistics and in charge of English examination of Puerto Rican teachers under Commissioner Lindsay. His office attempted to encourage a more rapid acquisition of the English language, especially by Puerto Rican teachers, by holding an annual examination in elementary English, open to all teachers on the island, to check their progress and attendance. Local school boards were advised to select those who scored best in the examination. In fact, the examination was required of all new candidates for teacher certificates of whatever grade.

The results of the examination seemed to be worthwhile. In Commissioner Lindsay's 1903 report, Miller wrote:

> Although this Circular was criticized in the Island press . . . under the pretense of defending the rights of the teachers . . . and by a limited number of teachers who had underestimated the importance of English . . . I am glad to say that the vast majority of teachers immediately began to prepare for this examination (46).

Manuel G. Nin of Yauco received a prize for a 96.6 mark. Gerardo Sellés Solá from the Humacao District got a 95, but no prize. Both men later made great contributions to education in Puerto Rico.

Together with Albert Martínez, secretary of the department and former supervisor of the San Juan District, Miller accompanied Commissioner Lindsay, Dr. de Garmo, and E. T. Divine on an inspection tour of the island. He acted as interpreter for public addresses and frequently spoke to the audiences in Spanish. Thus, Miller understood the educational problems when he became the commissioner of education in August 1915.

Miller's term as commissioner was very creative and eventful. He began during the economic crisis that followed the Big Budget, and it was not until 1919 that the economy began to recover. Puerto Rico sent 17,000 men to World War I, but there was no economic boom as after World War II. Instead, the difficulties of 1918 were followed by an influenza epidemic which closed the schools for several months. By the end of the decade, the island had suffered a tobacco crash and the San Felipe cyclone.

It was only a year after Miller had assumed office as commissioner of education that the first disaster hit: the great statesman Luis Muñoz Rivera died in November 1916. He had been able to keep the island's politics under control since 1904, and his death signaled the beginning of new agitation which did not stop until his son, Luis Muñoz Marín, won in 1944.

But the following year, 1917, there was great rejoicing on the island when the Jones Act, the new Organic Charter granting American citizenship to the islanders, became effective on March 2. According to the new statute, the Executive Council consisted of seven members to be appointed by the President of the United States, including the commissioner of education. However, the council had no legislative power.

The new act defined the powers of the commissioner as follows:

> The Commissioner of Education shall superintend public instruction throughout Puerto Rico; all proposed disbursements on account thereof must be approved by him, and all courses of study shall be prepared by him, subject to disapproval by the Governor if he desires to act. He shall prepare rules governing the selection of teachers, and appointments of teachers by local school

boards shall be subject to his approval, and he shall perform such other duties, not inconsistent with this Act, as may be prescribed by law (47).

This law was the end result of a 19-year trend toward absolute centralization of power in the head of the department of education.

At the time Miller became commissioner, the population of Puerto Rico was estimated to be 1,200,000, out of which 419,282 were of school age (between 5 and 18 years) and 211,588 of compulsory school age. But the enrollment was only 151,582, including private schools, or 35.8 percent of the total school age population. The problem persisted. In the 1920 official census, the total population was 1,299,802, with a school-age population of 438,743, but the total enrollment of 193,269 had increased to only 43.1 percent of the total. By the time Miller left the office in 1925, the total enrollment was 230,120.

Miller established professional reading courses for his teachers, which included such works as Bagley's *Classroom Management,* Earheart's *Types of Teaching,* Thorndike's *Principles of Teaching,* and Strayer's *A Brief Course in The Teaching Process.* The supervisors conducted weekly discussions and exercises and required a written work in English at the end of the year. In all, 924 urban and 138 rural teachers participated in these courses.

In 1919, Commissioner Miller made a genuine effort to determine how well the English language was being taught in the schools by requesting José Padín, then subcommissioner of education, to make a study. Padín concluded that the program was failing because of poor teaching and the imposition of methods and materials suitable in the States but not in Puerto Rico.

The commissioner immediately adopted a new plan of using Spanish as the medium of instruction in the first four grades, making a transition to English in the fifth and sixth, and from the seventh to the eighth using English as the medium of instruction. He assigned General Superintendent Pedro P. Arán the task of writing the Spanish course and Joseph Morin that of developing a method for introducing the new plan in the elementary schools. José González Ginorio, who became general superintendent of Spanish in 1919, worked out a method similar to that developed by Morin. For many years, both Ginorio's and Morin's methods were in use.

In 1919, the Legislature revised the school law to replace the local school boards with a director of education, elected as a member of the municipal assembly. Miller also suggested a general survey of education, but this was not accomplished until a few months after he left office in 1925. He suggested that the 6–3–3 system be used, and this was later carried out by a man who succeeded him more than a decade later.

In the same year, 1919, Commissioner Miller attended one of the most productive meetings held in 25 years. The commissioner called a meeting of the supervisors of schools and the municipal directors to be held at the same time and then arranged for both joint and sectional meetings. This promoted goodwill, mutual understanding, and a new point of view on educational problems.

Huyke and Consolidation, 1925 to 1930

When Juan B. Huyke succeeded Miller as commissioner of education in October 1925, he became the first Puerto Rican to hold the position. His father, Enrique Huyke, was the founder of Colegio San Bernardo and was a member of the first two insular boards of education. Huyke, who was born in Arroyo, progressed from classroom teacher to general superintendent under Dexter. In 1911, he graduated in law and was president of the lower House from 1912 to 1920. From 1918 to 1920, he was Acting Governor of Puerto Rico and was practicing law when he was appointed commissioner of education in June 1925.

Huyke's term coincided with the survey of the public educational system of Puerto Rico, directed by the International Institute of Teachers College, Columbia University, under an appropriation of $25,000, voted by the Legislature in March 1925. Although Huyke did not mention it in his annual report for 1925-26, he was a member of the survey committee (48). The report, published the following year, covered the historical, economic, and social aspects of education, along with the measurement of results, teachers, administration, supervision, financing, and the work in both elementary education and the university. It concluded that educational progress during the previous 27 years was "a great achievement, without parallel in the United States" (49).

According to the Columbia University survey, the general aims of education in Puerto Rico had served to reduce illiteracy, to increase enrollment, and to improve democratic citizenship. It pointed out that the two most difficult problems to be faced were double enrollment and bilingual instruction. The report went on to analyze various other shortcomings and to make suggestions that the rural schools be consolidated and that there be a diversification of schools and curriculums and a broadening of the aims of education beyond the linguistic. It put special emphasis on vocational education.

In regard to centralization, the survey stated: "In few other school systems is the administration so completely in the hands of a single person as in Puerto Rico. Responsible only to the President of the United States, the Commissioner of Education is absolute in his authority" (50). It recommended that the central office be reorganized into two divisions, technical and adminstrative, and that English be taught as a separate subject up to the fourth grade and from then on used as a general medium of instruction. It also proposed that education be compulsory at 6 instead of 8 years and that rural school teachers be trained in the Mayagüez College of Agriculture. It proposed that the post of municipal school director be abolished, that the school boards be reinstated, and that a long-term program of education be planned.

Despite the fact that the Department of Education disregarded most of the 15 items in the survey recommendations, Governor H. M. Towner made a lengthy commentary in his fifth message to the Legislature in February 1927. He wrote:

> The Department of Education must organize a Division of Technical Research dedicated to the study of the educational program and to carry on experiments relating to it. A Division of Health and Physical Education must be established. . . .The local Boards of Education must be reinstated instead of the School Director. The Legislature should establish a permanent fund for educational extension. Forty per cent of the total budget for education should be distributed equally among all municipalities, according to their needs (51).

He then analyzed the convenience of the 6-3-3 plan and reemphasized the reduction of the 40-percent illiteracy then prevailing. No other Governor's message had ever given so much space to education.

Commissioner Huyke, however, had already decided to put his emphasis on consolidation. He considered it necessary to bring together several one-room schools into a larger unit if these rural schools were to be turned into something more than agencies to combat illiteracy. After consolidating more than 200 rural schools, he created a series of second units to bring several rural one-room schools together. Grades 6 to 8 were placed on a vocational curriculum with emphasis on agriculture, manual arts, home economics, and trades. The purpose of this second unit was to raise the standard of living of the rural community, to improve the productive capacity of the island, to carry out a program of social and health instruction based on the needs of the people in the rural centers, and to improve the life and home conditions of the people.

Convinced of the possibilities of these second units, the Legislature voted $25,000 to establish them. Six were established in 1928: Carolina, Arecibo, Lares, Aguadilla, Utuado, and Corozal. During the 1929-30 school year, the Legislature voted more money to increase the number to 14, and they have continued to grow.

By 1939, there were 83 second units enrolling 9,522 pupils, and in 1945-46, there were 130 units operating as junior high schools with an enrollment of 14,368 pupils. They have proven to be very successful. Not even San Felipe was strong enough to stop their growth. In fact, this is perhaps one of the most important single features of education in Puerto Rico.

Huyke also campaigned to improve teacher training, with the slogan: "A high school diploma for every rural teacher." He recommended that a rural traveling library be created, although this was not done until years after his term, and that a 6-3-3 organization of schools be adopted. In 1926, the Central High School in Santurce was dedicated, the largest and most beautiful high school building in the island.

Huyke's language policy followed the traditional slogan of "acquisition of English and conservation of Spanish." Grades 1 through 4 were taught in Spanish with English as a subject, the first and second grades following the oral approach. The fifth grade was transition, half and half; from there on English was the medium of instruction. He declared the aim of this arrangement to be in harmony with the racial traits of the Puerto Ricans.

San Felipe caused considerable damage, and the First Church of Christ in Boston sent $1,035 to replace damaged books. A total of $136,371 was being used for school lunches for 11.5 percent of the total attendance. By this time, according to Huyke's last annual report in 1928-29, there were 220,940 pupils studying under 4,478 teachers, and the island's budget totaled $4,197,657, plus $1,625,785 from municipal funds.

THE REFORMERS, 1930 TO 1945

The years from the cyclone in 1928 (San Felipe) to the one in 1935 (San Ciprián) constitute a transitional period in the history of Puerto Rico. In fact, from 1928 to 1944, still suffering birth pangs, the island experienced economic, political, and cultural turmoil. This cyclonic period has been succeeded, from 1944 to the present, by a creative revolution.

Depression and Cyclone

President Hoover appointed José Padín commissioner of education for Puerto Rico early in 1930, and he took office in January. In turn, he appointed Pedro A. Cebollero as his subcommissioner, and these very capable men accomplished a lot under severe conditions to advance education on the island. Padín himself had received his early education during the period of the founders and as an outstanding student was sent to various states on a scholarship. He received his B.A. from Haverford, which also granted him an LL.D. in 1931; he earned his Ph.D. from Dartmouth in 1934. He served as teacher of English and assistant supervisor in Guayama from 1908 to 1909, and supervisor in Arecibo until 1912. From 1912 to 1913 he was general supervisor of English, undercommissioner in Miller's administration from 1916 to 1917, and at the time Hoover appointed him commissioner he was working as an editor for D. C. Heath Company. Following his resignation as commissioner in December 1936, he returned to work with the D. C. Heath Company.

Because Padín had the mind and outlook of an educator, as well as the titles, his work was creative and influential beyond the bounds of his term of office. Puerto Rico had not recovered from the damage caused in 1928 by San Felipe when San Ciprián swept over the northeast, killing 257 people, injuring 4,820, destroying 42,431 buildings, and damaging 32,446 dwellings. The losses amounted to $40 million, and 76,295 families were ruined. The effect on the schools was devastating: 893 schoolrooms were destroyed, and it was estimated that 46 municipalities were seriously affected.

Governor J. R. Beverly appointed an executive committee of aid and rehabilitation to be presided over by Padín. The insular government still had $164,258 left over in the emergency fund created for San Felipe, and this, together with an appropriation of $74,988 by the Legislature for immediate relief of the victims, was used to initiate reconstruction. The government then floated a loan of $5.5 million for a long-term reconstruction program.

Puerto Rico was to suffer another calamity. The tobacco crash, caused by the limitations of the American market, seriously hurt Puerto Rico as the Depression in the States struck the island. Coffee plantations were destroyed once more by the cyclones. But President Roosevelt's New Deal also began to operate in Puerto Rico, and it brought about some relief. In 1934, Carlos E. Chardón, chancellor of the University of Puerto Rico, Rafael Méndez Ramos, commissioner of agriculture, and Rafael Fernández García, professor of agriculture at the university, were called to the states to help plan the economic reconstruction of the island. After several months of hard work they presented a reconstruction program known as Plan Chardón. Under the management of Ernest Gruening, head of the Division of Territories and Insular Possessions, Puerto Rico's Economic Reconstruction Administration began to put the plan into operation, with Dr. Chardón serving as Gruening's local assistant (52).

Commissioner Padín had a sharp and profound mind and a very broad understanding of history and contemporary culture. He took advantage of the surveys and writings of his predecessors to get a complete picture of the educational situation at the time he took office.

Surveys of Conditions. In particular, the commissioner relied on a report prepared by Victor S. Clark, the former commissioner of education under the military government, who served as director of a committee to investigate the island for the Brookings Institution. This report pointed out that two dissimilar cultures were in the process of assimilation on the island. Clark wrote that its people constituted a relatively small and isolated community, vividly conscious of its individuality and correspondingly jealous of its special character and privileges. This essential feature of the Puerto Rican, called *insularismo* by Antonio S. Pedreira, one of the island's most distinguished university professors, imparts a sort of ambivalence to the collective personality which is very difficult for outsiders to understand. Padín himself showed his inability to appreciate it when he asked the question, "Where are we going?" and answered, "We do not know but it seems that we know the way" (53).

The situation in the rural communities was nothing short of deplorable. According to the 1925 survey, approximately 97 percent of the urban children between 5 and 14 years of age were on the school registers, but only 40 percent of those in the country districts were registered. And about two-thirds of the rural schools operated on the double enrollment system, whereby the children attended only half a day. Furthermore, between the first and fourth grade there was about an 80-percent dropout rate; for every 100 first-graders, only 20 went beyond the fourth grade. However, the school lunch program inaugurated a little after the survey did improve this situation, although it was not extended to the whole island until 1940.

In March 1931, President Hoover visited Puerto Rico, and Luis Sánchez Morales, president of the Senate, delivered a welcome address at a joint meeting of the Legislature. He pointed out that the islanders had been asking for some of the federal laws to be applied to Puerto Rico to improve and extend public instruction. He added: "That aid is needed more than ever in the midst of the great crisis that weighs on us, due mainly to the hurricane of 1928, made worse by the disastrous economic conditions now prevailing. . . . We are unable to educate half of our children. . ." (54). In December 1933, President Franklin D. Roosevelt sent Ernest Hopkins, president of Dartmouth, to survey the educational situation in the island and report to him personally. Hopkins wired Roosevelt the following message: "I arrived here this morning and found myself immersed in the question at issue almost immediately. There is more politics to the square rod down here than to the square mile at home. . . ." He added that he thought Governor R. H. Gore "is probably the worst blunderer that ever came along" (55). Despite Gore's opposition, Padín was reappointed commissioner of education for a second term in February 1934. The following month, President Roosevelt himself visited the island.

Padín faced intelligently and squarely the problems of double enrollment, school mortality, industrial education, the need of federal aid by legislation, and the equalization of educational opportunities for the rural as well as the urban areas. He also pushed for the 6-3-3 plan and strengthening of the second unit. He urged that the island establish a governmental development agency (Fomento) for industrialization, but this was not accomplished until 20 years after his term of office.

In agreement with the Columbia survey and the Brookings report, Padín got approval in April 1931 for an act improving vocational education. At least this was a start. In an "Address on Vocational Education," delivered to the graduating class of the Mayagüez College of Agriculture, he pointed out that there were many ups and downs in establishing industrial and vocational education in Puerto Rico despite the efforts of his administration and those of his predecessors.

The Language Issue. Padín had clearly expressed his philosophy for Puerto Rican education in 1930 in an address in which he said:

> For thirty years we have been hesitant and anguished without knowing with certainty what are we educating our country for. I assert that we must educate Puerto Rico for living its own life in its fullness. Its own life, because Puerto Rico is conscious of itself, because its personality is already clearly defined. We must replenish the Puerto Rican personality with vigorous and healthy nourishment (56).

In 1945, in a graduation address at the University of Puerto Rico, he again stated that "the Fatherland is not made by royal decree, nor by the mercy of a sovereign. It is created from the spiritual substance of its offspring" (57). These are the ends to which he dedicated his years of service.

In August 1934, Commissioner Padín issued Circular Letter No. 10, stating that all subjects in the elementary schools would be taught in Spanish except the classes in English. He pointed out that the time given English had increased 100 percent in the upper grades so that intensive instruction could be given. In his report for the 1934-35 school year, he wrote: "Since the beginning of my term of office, I have been trying to attack the problem of teaching English to the people of Puerto Rico along pedagogical lines. . ." (58).

In the face of criticism from Governor Blanton Winship, before taking a strong stand on the language issue Commissioner Padín invited William S. Gray, an eminent educator from the University of Chicago, to visit the island and evaluate his program. Dr. Gray arrived in the spring of 1936 and after a careful survey reported to Padín that he approved the change from English to Spanish as the sole medium of instruction in the elementary grades. The value of English as a subject in the curriculum was still receiving full recognition.

Again, in 1936, the commissioner brought Michael West, an English educator and expert on bilingualism, to inspect the matter. In his report to the commissioner, West stated the following:

> There is essentially no bilingual problem in Puerto Rico. Devote English periods of Grade I and II to reading in the mother tongue, and begin English reading when the children have got a sound foundation of reading ability in their own tongue . . . . Learning in the school subjects is considerably impeded by the use of textbooks in English (59).

In June 1937, José M. Gallardo replaced Padín as commissioner of education. Born in San Germán, he received his Ph.D. from the University of North Carolina in the spring of 1937. At the time President Roosevelt appointed him, he was professor of modern languages at the College of Charleston, South Carolina (60).

Looking at Padín's administration, Gallardo found enough educational issues in Puerto Rico to challenge any young man. Padín had perhaps boiled it to a head when asked the crucial question, "Where are we going?" The facetious answer, "We don't know, but we know the way," is only a symptom of perplexity, and this was the real challenge to Gallardo, although he perhaps did not realize it. It was the task of the reformers to pull Puerto Rico out of this perplexity.

Almost immediately the President wrote to the new commissioner:

> I desire at this time to make clear the attitude of my administration on the extremely important matter of teaching English in Puerto Rico . . . . It is regrettable that today hundreds of thousands of Puerto Ricans have little and often virtually no knowledge of the English language . . . . It is an indispensable part of the American policy that the comming [sic] generation of American citizens in Puerto Rico grow up with a complete facility in the English tongue . . . (61).

Commissioner Gallardo's Accomplishments

Gallardo's attempt to solve the language problem was not acceptable to most of Puerto Rico's leaders, nor was it acceptable to the federal policy makers. Nevertheless, he was responsible for two important accomplishments: introducing the junior high school to Puerto Rico and framing a philosophy of education for the island. The 6-3-3 plan had been considered by his predecessors and had been recommended by the Columbia survey, but it was not accepted until Gallardo introduced it in July 1942. Today, it is the structure of the system of public instruction.

Before Gallardo's term as commissioner ended in August 1945, he had created 1,000 additional teaching jobs and new classrooms, largely from $3 million contributed by the United States. He also had established professional norms for selecting teachers and had eliminated the system of classifying them. Teachers were paid for 12 months instead of 10 months for the school year, and Commissioner Gallardo established a scale of salaries according to professional qualifications. In other words, the salaries of rural and urban teachers were equalized. Secondary schooling was introduced into the rural zones, and there was a special emphasis on vocational and prevocational education in both rural and urban areas. Musical and art education were emphasized, visual education was established, and there was an expansion of extension and adult education. It is also to his credit that he improved the School of the Air and created a Division of Research and Evaluation.

In January 1938, Gallardo inaugurated a Bureau of Adult Education; by September, it operated 132 schools with 8,502 students. Its growth has been steady, and by 1944 it was ready to cooperate with the Veterans Administration.

At the very beginning of World War II, the vocational schools contributed 400 trained workers to the Army and Navy shops. War veterans were later enrolled in the vocational schools and rehabilitation centers. Under Gallardo's leadership, the public schools sold $883,768 in war bonds and stamps during the year 1943-44 and $1,871,387 during the year 1944-45.

After Gallardo's resignation in August 1945, Herbert A. Martin served as acting commissioner until the appointment of Mariano Villaronga. Martin organized the educational services to enlisted men and veterans that expanded greatly during Villaronga's period. In the year 1945, 78 diplomas were granted to veterans, and 131 certificates and 2,500 units of high school credit were approved.

Gallardo's language policy was very complicated. At the very outset of his term, he called a meeting of his supervisory staff at Arecibo to intensify the teaching of English, according to his commitments with President Roosevelt. First and second grades were to be taught in Spanish; third and fourth, two-thirds in Spanish; fifth and sixth, one-half in Spanish. For the seventh and eighth there were three alternatives: (1) one-third of the time devoted to instruction in Spanish; (2) all instruction in English, with 90 to 100 minutes daily devoted to Spanish; (3) Mondays, Wednesdays, and Fridays, instruction all in English; Tuesdays and Thursdays, all in Spanish.

This plan was discontinued very soon, as it was not practical. The following year the plan was modified, and again in the year 1940-41, after 4 years of experience. In Circular Letter No. 1, July 1942, another modification was introduced. English was to be taught as a subject from the first to the sixth grades and Spanish was the medium of instruction. Harold L. Ickes, Secretary of Interior with Roosevelt, was quite displeased with the outcome of Gallardo's plans. In February 1943, Gallardo had a hearing before the Subcommittee on Territories and Insular Affairs meeting in San Juan, and in March 1943, he received a cable from Secretary Ickes expressing regret that he had paid little attention to specific instructions from the President to teach English in the Puerto Rican schools and stating that he would not have been appointed if he had not assured Ickes that this would be the keystone of his school policy.

Now it was Gallardo's turn to be displeased. He answered Ickes in respectful, informative, and strong terms in May 1943. Gallardo's policy, however, did not have more approval in Puerto Rico than in Washington. It was followed by Villaronga's policy, which has been continued with improvements until the present.

THE QUIET REVOLUTION, 1946 TO THE PRESENT

Mariano Villaronga

In December 1944, in an interview for *El Mundo*, the elected resident commissioner for Puerto Rico in Washington, D.C., Jesús T. Piñero, stated: "In ten years many things and many experiences in the life of our country have changed: governments, men, and parties. The attitudes of our people toward life and destiny have changed almost radically" (62).

This change really began in 1940, the year Theodore Brameld has called "a year of destiny." Brameld points out that during the thirties the Roosevelt administration encouraged a mood of social change in Puerto Rico, and Rexford Tugwell, a leading New Dealer, served during World War II as a vigorous Governor. The Popular party achieved its first success at the polls in 1940; 4 years later, Luis Muñoz Marín was elected president of the Senate by a large majority. In 1946, President Truman appointed Jesús T. Piñero as the first Puerto Rican Governor; 2 years later, Luis Muñoz Marín was the first Puerto Rican Governor elected at the polls. It was not until 1952 that the Commonwealth of Puerto Rico framed its own constitution.

Parallel to the political developments, Chancellor Jaime Benítez led a reform at the University of Puerto Rico. From an enrollment of about 4,000 students, the university has now grown to about 25,000. The School of Medicine, created in 1952, measures up to the highest standards of the American Medical Association. Thus, as the economic structure of the island changed, the social and cultural milieu completely changed with it, to bring about the "quiet revolution."

Mariano Villaronga, after receiving his M.A. from Harvard, had been involved in the turmoil of these creative years as principal of the Ponce High School. He shared in the university reform as professor and personal consultant to the chancellor. Then in November 1946, President Truman appointed him commissioner of education, and as commissioner he was president of the university's board of trustees. In the meantime, subcommissioner Francisco Collazo, a graduate of Columbia and professor of education at the University of Puerto Rico, acted as commissioner from July 1947 to the end of 1948. But when Governor Muñoz Marín was elected, he appointed Villaronga his secretary of education. Villaronga assumed office on January 1, 1949 (63).

As a member of the Governor's cabinet and as president of the university board, Villaronga was very influential during this revolutionary period. In part, this was because he had the foresight to develop close collaboration with the Puerto Rican Teachers Association and the university.

Since Padín's time, the Puerto Rican Teachers Association had been agitating for educational reform and had actively called for a new philosophy of education. When Villaronga assumed office, one of his main purposes was to "bring the school more in touch with the social reality of Puerto Rico" (64). The cultural and social realities had changed at such a vertiginous rhythm that it was all the department of education could do to keep pace. The change from an agricultural to an industrial economy and the subsequent concentration of population in the urban zones brought new administrative problems, not to mention the rapid changes in the political structure. In the wake of World War II, Villaronga had the tremendous task of making it possible for the public schools to accommodate the veterans who wanted to study under the GI Bill of Rights.

Villaronga also was interested in promoting reform. Top educators, both local and from abroad, had been lecturing in every annual convention held by the Puerto Rican Teachers Association, and Gallardo had included Villaronga on a committee with a number of these distinguished educators to work out future plans. When he assumed the post of secretary of education, Villaronga got the Legislature to approve an appropriation of $75,000 for the second Columbia survey, which was conducted during the 1948-49 school year and published in 1950 (65). Villaronga's wide and intensive program was guided by the approach, research, and findings of this survey. Since it also served as a guide for the succeeding secretary, and since a great number of leading Puerto Rican educators are graduates of Columbia, it has been very influential on the island.

One of the most important contributions of Villaronga's administration as secretary of education was the definite proclamation by law that Spanish was to be the official language of instruction for all levels and subjects, except English. The subject of English was accorded a preferential position when the department created a special section just to guide, intensify, and improve by all possible means English teaching. Professor Charles C. Fries, from the University of Michigan, served as a consultant and produced the world-famous Fries English Series. A program for training field supervisors is still under way.

Villaronga also instituted an accelerated program to increase the teaching personnel and the school enrollment. This greatly reduced illiteracy but forced the government to accept many teachers who could not meet the earlier standards. The vocational high school was created, and its high school diploma was accepted as an entrance requirement by the university.

By Act No. 76, ratified in March 1946, the Legislature approved a united budget, transferring to the state budget the expenses that had been paid by the municipalities up to this time, and all the school property belonging to the municipalities was transferred to the insular government. Equalization of finances in the school districts has been a moot question since the department's beginning. The school planning office, created by Villaronga, still works under the Insular Planning Board. The law concerning the certification of teachers was revised and approved by the government. And the department created an education press for producing textbooks and other teaching materials. The magazine for the schools, *Escuela*, commenced publishing three different editions, one for each school level, to be used as teaching materials and as a supplement for the too few textbooks. Although the constitution states that textbooks are to be provided as one of the marks of free education, during Villaronga's time there still were not enough textbooks.

The centralization so important to the early commissioners was now partially discarded. For instance, the appointment of teachers was decentralized and vested in local school authorities. At the same time the secretary's office assumed the additional responsibility of operating the government's broadcasting station (WIPR) and expanding the School of the Air. This period brought an increased budget for scholarships and student aid, and an expansion of cooperative education. The department obtained more federal grants and established a Division of Research and Statistics. The Legislature also approved the organization of a Division of Community Education and drafted the Morovis Plan for self-instruction in adult education.

The Morovis Plan, intended for towns like Morovis, with no high school or transportation, was a system of free studies, with a student center for lectures, library with reference books, films, projector, and scientific apparatus for experiments and demonstrations. Each center had three teachers, one for languages and humanities, one for science and mathematics, and one for clerical work. The extension office gave examinations three times during the year, December 8 to 10, March 1 to 3, and May 23 to 28. In forthcoming years, the plan was extended to Rincón, Hormigueros, Cidra, and Las Marías. It was discontinued when high schools or transportation were provided for all towns.

Efraín Sánchez Hidalgo, 1957 to 1960

Upon the resignation of Mariano Villaronga on account of illness, Governor Luis Muñoz Marín appointed Efraín Sánchez Hidalgo as secretary of education. A professor of educational psychology at the University of Puerto Rico, Dr. Hidalgo was a veteran of World War II and earned his Ph.D. from Columbia University (66).

Governor Muñoz Marín was very much concerned with the role of education in his economic and political programs. The economists supplied by "Fomento," the Puerto Rico Development Agency, had presented their ideas, and he had discussed them with Everett Reimer, secretary of the Committee for Human Resources, who was his personal adviser on education (67). The Puerto Rico

Planning Board, organized by Governor Tugwell in 1942, had become a successful brain trust and had increased its power and functions year by year. The Governor attempted to collect all the information necessary to make long-term plans for education.

In September 1957, the lower House of the Legislature passed a resolution ordering its public instruction committee to make an evaluation of the school system. Two months later, in a meeting of the Governor's cabinet, with the secretary present, it was agreed that his office would also make investigations and prepare recommendations to attack vigorously the problems of student retention. These recommendations would include information on schoolrooms, transportation, scholarships, teachers, and all other factors that would lead to keeping students in the schools. Beresford L. Hayward, a young member of Chicago's planning board, was brought to the department as planning consultant, and he submitted his report to Secretary Hidalgo in August 1958. This proved to be a very thorough study and is the beginning of what may be called the period of scientific educational reform.

One of the projects Dr. Hidalgo initiated almost as soon as he took charge of the department was known as a "Consultation of the People." All public schools worked through the consultation to take the necessary measures to meet the needs pointed to in the survey. The secretary was able to offer preliminary optimistic results of this consultation in his annual report for 1957-58, but he resigned before he could apply the findings of the project to the reform itself.

In the fall of 1958, through the mediation of Professor Carl J. Friedrich, Governor Muñoz Marín contracted to bring three distinguished European professors to make another general survey and give advice and counsel to the secretary. The three distinguished educators, Christian Caselmann of the University of Heidelberg, Lamberto Borghi of the University of Florence, and Morten Bredsdorff of Teachers College of Vordinborg, Denmark, submitted their final report in May 1959. But these men continued to be vitally interested in the island's education. Carl Friedrich delivered the university's lectures in January 1958, published as a study of the political and juridical structure of the Commonwealth (68). Dr. Bredsdorff returned to Puerto Rico twice, during the summer of 1960 and during the summer of 1967.

In the meantime, in September 1958, the Legislature's public instruction committee signed a contract with the Superior Council of Education (the University of Puerto Rico Board of Trustees) to make a survey of education in Puerto Rico, as ordered by the resolution it passed the previous year. Directed by Ismael Rodríguez Bou, a prolific writer and scholar and the permanent secretary of the "Consejo Superior de Enseñanza" (CSE), the council made one of the most thorough studies of education to this time. The report was published in three volumes by the University of Puerto Rico Press in June 1962 (69). Although this was the best work of its kind peprared in Puerto Rico, Rodríguez Bou continued to carry out many additional surveys (70).

Hayward's survey, the one by Rodríguez Bou, and the European reports proved to be of paramount importance for the reform that has continued to be carried on under the present administration of Angel Quintero Alfaro. As Governor Muñoz Marín stated in his State of the Commonwealth message to the Legislature for 1960, he was proclaiming 1960-70 to be the Decade of Education.

Cándido Oliveras, 1960 to 1965

Cándido Oliveras succeeded Hidalgo in May 1960. Although he had been an instructor at the university, he was an economist and a public administrator rather than an educator. At the time of his appointment, Oliveras was president of the Planning Board and had held many important administrative positions in the government. He chose for his undersecretary a distinguished young professor of humanities, Angel Quintero Alfaro, a graduate of the University of Chicago and dean of the College of General Studies at the University of Puerto Rico.

The secretary and his assistant were reformers by nature and came to the department with the intention to carry through the reforms suggested by Hayward, the European professors, and the Superior Council. These recommendations would mean a complete overhaul of the system of public education in Puerto Rico. For instance, it would mean taking measures to retain students in the schools and continuing the work of improving and retaining teachers, fostering better community relations, instituting a program of scholarships, and building school facilities. It would require the use of teaching aids, such as machines and programed instruction, to build a program of quality education.

Of great importance in the reform of Puerto Rico's educational system was the idea that there should be an equalization of educational opportunities in rural and urban areas, as well as an effort to include more of the population. For instance, this would mean establishing nursery schools and kindergartens, improving the community education and adult education programs, and adding programs for retarded and gifted students. It also would cover increases in salaries and pensions, along with other marginal benefits, for the teachers. There would be a renewal of the second unit, and looming over all would be the language issue. The reform also would include administrative decentralization, with the establishment of local school boards. Many of these ideas had been advocated for years by the teachers association.

To carry out these reforms, Oliveras, backed and counseled by his undersecretary, Quintero Alfaro, instituted in September 1961 a series of meetings in the central office, beginning with a discussion of a philosophy of education for Puerto Rico. This first meeting was held in two sessions of about 3 hours each, with the Governor present along with most of the leading educators on the island. The subsequent meetings, all held in one session each, discussed topics such as the curriculum, the student body, teachers, planning, organization, and community education.

Within 2 months after the discussions had been started, Secretary Oliveras held one of the most interesting and helpful seminars on language teaching in the history of the island. Many distinguished scholars from abroad came to Puerto Rico (71). These men, in cooperation with the University of Puerto Rico professors and program directors of the Department of Education, have been very influential in improving language teaching. Professor Wallace Lambert of McGill University returned later to work in the department for a short time.

The secretary also inaugurated two other outstanding activities: the establishment of exemplary schools and the regionalization of administrative and supervisory functions. These have been continued and improved upon since Oliveras' term of office and are still in progress.

Fortunately, the secretary was strongly backed in all of his efforts by Governor Muñoz Marín. In his message to the Fourth Legislative Assembly in February 1964, the Governor raised the issue of the purpose of the Commonwealth and dedicated a long section to education. He stated that the Puerto Rican purpose should transcend party lines and should be affirmed by the people. He continued: "The vitality of a people is the vitality of its collective purpose . . . . Material abundance, without moral and spiritual excellence is not enough. Neither can the will of the people be limited to the service of intangible concepts at the cost of material well being."

In his speech, the Governor went on to explain six points to implement the purpose, and the first was education. "Our attitude toward education and the teacher must change in a revolutionary way . . . . The country's education needs a basic guide. No other more comprehensive and simple than the Preamble to our Constitution" (72). He stated that no child should be without school nor a school without a complete curriculum or enough well-trained and well-motivated teachers. A second goal should be an education so personalized as to consider individual differences. And third, he stated that education was a vital, never-ending process. It must include libraries, museums, good television, good radio, good cultural institutions, excellent and abundant books at low prices, and all possible forms and means for improving everybody's understanding, as well as their life and their work for its sustenance.

Governor Luis Muñoz Marín stepped down in January 1965, after handpicking his successor, Governor Roberto Sánchez Vilella. On February 1, 1965, the new Governor appointed Angel Quintero Alfaro to succeed Oliveras as secretary of education. Director Quintero then selected as his subsecretary Pedro José Rivera, also a Ph.D. from the University of Chicago and at the time dean of students at the University of Puerto Rico. A good team, Quintero and his subsecretary agreed wholeheartedly with the message on education expressed by the former Governor and have attempted to put it into practice.

To make universality a reality, the secretary has attempted to expand opportunity from nursery schools to adult and community education. He has organized work camps, especially for dropouts of high school age, and rehabilitation has been intensified and improved. A TV program, added to the WIPR broadcasting station during the term of Secretary Sánchez Hidalgo, has been expanded and used to full advantage.

Quintero also has attempted to bring about more continuity in education by testing new techniques and organizations to bridge the gaps between the different levels of the system from elementary to college, and also between schools and the community. This has meant developing a flexibility so as not to limit the development of the gifted students and perhaps will mean dropping the 6-3-3 organization for an alternative, such as the 6-6. It also means utilizing the advanced placement plan.

Secretary Quintero agreed wholeheartedly with the purpose of improving the quality of teaching in Puerto Rico. This has meant installing modern teaching aids, such as teaching machines and programed instruction. A psychologist himself, the secretary is quite interested in the application of new methods and technical devices evolving from psychological research and experimentation. Teacher education has been improved and coordinated with the schools of education at the university and the colleges. Seminars have been organized, and the department has arranged travel abroad for teachers, directors, and supervisors. Top educators have come from abroad. The department also has eliminated the double enrollment, increased the exemplary schools, and used to best advantage the regional offices, curriculum centers, centers of study and supervision, and organizational guiding districts.

To ensure diversification, the department attempted several projects to individualize training according to the potential and ambition of each student from nursery to college, including the retarded and the gifted. There also was an effort to bring about equalization of facilities and opportunities for the rural and urban zones, as well as an equalization of opportunity for all. To implement these programs, Dr. Quintero used all personnel and economic resourses at his command–insular, federal, and private foundations–as well as all means and forms of instruction. He disposed of a number of obsolete practices and created and/or introduced new ones. In June 1965, commenting on all aspects of his educational ideas, he stated: "A lot depends on our resources . . . and also on the methods we employ . . . . If we use our imagination it (the problem of double enrollment) can be solved in a decade" (73). He stated that the goals of his administration would be won with better organization and improved communication between the teacher in the classroom and the department. He also hoped to upgrade the position of the teacher and to persuade more people to enter the profession. And, of course, he said he hoped for more and better materials and a greater use of facilities.

In projecting future plans, Dr. Quintero stated that he expects an itinerate principal to be available in every rural area as a nucleus for the more isolated schools, each nucleus including a second unit up to the ninth grade. He praised the exemplary schools as one of the outstanding projects, with more than 30 such schools constantly improving through tested materials, programs, and methods. There were already 9 secondary schools with 1,623 students and 13 vocational schools serving 18,000 students. There are vocational programs for young adults outside the school and special courses for commerce and industry enrolling 35,000 students annually.

The undersecretary, Pedro José Rivera, also has analyzed the advance in quantity and quality of the island's schools. He has stated that the goals cannot be accomplished if the educational program follows the traditional patterns and that the department must help the schools break obsolete forms of work, generate more successes in operations, and incorporate more stimulating ways of educational action to bring about offerings of a higher quality. This is being done and is now under trial.

The last statement of Quintero Alfaro concerning his educational policy is his Memorandum, April 23, 1968, addressed to all his teaching, supervisory, and technical staff. In this document, a summing up of the educational conference held in San Juan from April 8 to 10, he summarized not only his accomplishments, but also his projects to 1980.

The most important of his long list of recommendations concern preschool education (Head Start and education in the cradle) and postsecondary education, which means a widening of the program to embrace all the life of the citizen.

For the preschool period the secretary contemplates organizing a *first cycle* of education without grades, individualized by groups of teachers, for pupils between 4 and 8 years. The main purpose of this cycle is the global development of the child; his adaptation to the school environment; and the strengthening of his imagination, creativity, and liking for education. A thorough study of child rearing should be undertaken in three or six communities for ages 3 to 6 to guide preschool education.

The benefits of high school and postsecondary education should be extended to the rural zones. For these purposes the rural high school should be also a community center. A curriculum commission should be created composed of both educators and qualified citizens that will revise continually the educational program, from the second year of the child to postsecondary education.

These accomplishments and projections would never have been possible without federal support. For the year 1966-67, out of a total budget of $204,557,248, the federal sources contributed $40,238,450. For the year 1967-68, this contribution was increased to $44,769,701 (74).

Out of 46 possible activities using federal funds, 40 have been organized, among them six Job Corps in Vieques, Río Grande, Arecibo, Guayama, Juana Díaz, and Mayagüez. Also, a Center of Educational Opportunities has been operating in San Juan, with combined federal and insular funds, for dropouts of high school age. Up to the present, this center has been very successful. Federal resources have been of paramount importance in elimination of double enrollment, training of teaching personnel, strengthening of vocational education and rehabilitation, library service, production and distribution of textbooks and educational materials, the Head Start centers, utilization of mechanical aids and teaching machines, and courses for Civil Defense.

FOOTNOTES

1. *Treaty of Paris* (1898), Art. IX.
2. Governor General, *Report* (1900), p. 1492.
3. *New York Daily Tribune,* March 4, 1900.
4. G. W. Davis, *Military Government of Porto Rico* (Washington, D.C.: Government Printing Office, 1902). A 1932 amendment to the Organic Act of 1917 changed the name of Porto Rico to Puerto Rico.
5. Bailey W. Diffie and Justine W. Diffie, *Porto Rico: A Broken Pledge* (New York: The Vanguard Press, 1931).
6. A. G. Dana, *Porto Rico's Case* (New Haven, Conn.: Tuttle, Morehouse & Taylor Co., 1928), p. 7.
7. International Institute, Teachers College, Columbia University, *A Survey of the Public Educational System of Porto Rico* (New York: Bureau of Publications, Teachers College, Columbia University, 1926), p. 53.
8. J. Eaton, *Education in Porto Rico* (Washington, D.C.: U.S. Bureau of Education, 1901), ch. 4, p. 227.
9. Homer Page, *Puerto Rico: The Quiet Revolution* (New York: The Viking Press, 1963).
10. Governor General, *Annual Report* (1902), p. 231. Enrique Landrón, the principal of San Juan, wrote a very interesting report to Commissioner Brumbaugh describing education in Puerto Rico prior to 1898. José Padín, commissioner of education from 1930 to 1936, in "Una Escuela de Antes" (An Old-Time School), gave another description of education to 1898, published in Ismael Rodríguez Bou, *Problemas de Lectura y Lengua en Puerto Rico* (San Juan: Superior Council on Education, University of Puerto Rico, 1948), pp. 167ff.

11. Puerto Rico, *Documents on the Constitutional History of Puerto Rico* (Washington, D.C.: Office of Puerto Rico, 1st ed., 1948), pp. 3-6; 2d ed., 1964.

12. Eaton, *op. cit.,* p. 221. Also see Governor General, *Military Report* (1902), p. 124.

13. *Ibid.,* p.252.

14. Eaton, *op. cit.,* pp. 233-34.

15. *Ibid.*

16. *Ibid.,* p. 252.

17. *San Juan News,* as quoted by Eaton, *op. cit.,* pp. 233-34.

18. Perhaps the most touching indication of the Puerto Ricans' affection and gratitude to General Henry occurred when the news of his death reached the island. His illness was brief, and he died in New York City on October 27, 1899. Hundreds of telegrams and letters of sympathy were received by his widow from all parts of the island, and from many Puerto Ricans who were in the States.

19. Victor S. Clark, *Teacher's Manual for the Public Schools of Puerto Rico* (New York: Silver, Burdett and Co., 1900), p. vii.

20. Davis, *op. cit.,* p. 122.

21. *Ibid.*

22. James H. McLeary, *First Annual Register of Puerto Rico* (San Juan: Press of the *San Juan News,* 1901), p. 49.

23. Juan José Osuna, *A History of Education in Puerto Rico* (San Juan: University of Puerto Rico Press, 1949), p. 140.

24. Governor General, *Annual Report* (1901), p. 350.

25. Governor General, *Annual Report* (1902), p. 255.

26. Governor General, *Annual Report* (1902), p. 238.

27. Governor General, *Annual Report* (1902), p. 235.

28. Governor General, *Annual Report* (1904), pp. 20-21.

29. Governor Allen had already written in his *Annual Report* (1901), p. 93: "Perhaps no member of the Executive Council has a more difficult task to perform than the Commissioner of Education. . . .The work of initiating a system of education here which will supply primary instruction to 400,000 ignorant boys and girls by whom we are surrounded is a herculean labor."

30. Governor General, *Annual Report* (1903), pp. 21, 157, 285.

31. Governor General, *Annual Report* (1900), p. 268.

32. An insight into Puerto Rico's economy during these years can be found in Dana, *op. cit.,* and in Diffie and Diffie, *op. cit.*

33. Thomas Mathews, *Puerto Rican Politics and the New Deal* (Gainesville: University of Florida, 1960).

34. R. G. Tugwell, *The Stricken Land* (New York: Doubleday & Co., Inc., 1947).

35. Juan José Osuna, *op. cit.,* p. 341.

36. Brookings Institution, *Puerto Rico and Its Problems* (Washington, D.C.: The Institution, 1930), pp. 80-81.

37. Governor General, *Annual Report* (1902), p. 352.

38. Governor General, *Annual Report* (1902), p. 33.

39. Governor General, *Annual Report* (1907), p.382.

40. Pauline M. Rojas, "Talk to the Rotary Club of San Juan," originally a speech made in San Juan, Puerto Rico, on September 28, 1954.

41. Governor General, *Annual Report* (1910), p. 7.

42. Governor General, *Annual Report* (1912), p. 202.

43. Nestor Rigual, *Mensajes de los Gobernadores de Puerto Rico* (San Juan: Superior Council on Education, University of Puerto Rico Press, 1967), pp. 106, 116, 138.

44. Osuna, *op. cit.,* pp. 185, 226, 240, 336.

45. Governor General, *Annual Report* (1914), pp. 364, 559.

46. Governor General, *Annual Report* (1903), p. 289.

47. Jones Act, P. L. 64-368, c. 145, 39 Stat. 951 sec. 17 (1917).

48. The survey committee included Huyke, Antonio R. Barceló, José Tous Soto, and Juan José Osuna. The survey commission consisted of Paul Monroe, S. P. Gapen, J. F. Jenkins, Samuel McCune Lindsay, former commissioner A. B. Meredith, Harold Rugg, W. Carsen Ryan, H. F. Schwartz, L. M. Wilson, and G. N. Works.

49. *A Survey of the Public Educational System of Puerto Rico* (New York: Columbia University, 1926), p. 2.

50. *Ibid.,* p. 49.

51. Commissioner of Education, *Annual Report* (1928), p. 10.

52. For an excellent essay on the New Deal and its impact on Puerto Rico, see Mathews, *op. cit.*

53. José Padín, *Personas Sobre Cosas* (San Juan: Biblioteca de Autores Puertorriqueños, 1951), pp. 54-65; also "La Doctrina del Nuevo Trato," pp. 186-205.

54. Luis Sánchez Morales, *De Antes y de Ahora* (Madrid: Centro Editorial Ruben Darioa, 1936), p. 82.

55. Mathews, *op. cit.,* pp. 83-86, 106-109.

56. Padín, *op. cit.,* pp. 44-53.

57. Padín, *op. cit.,* p. 209.

58. Commissioner of Education, *Annual Report* (1935), pp. 1-2.

59. Osuna, *op. cit.,* pp. 372-75.

60. At present he is in charge of the office of resident foreign students at the University of Puerto Rico.

61. Osuna, *op. cit.,* p. 376.

62. *El Mundo* (San Juan), Dec. 3, 1944.

63. The title of commissioner was changed to secretary by Law No. 76, Sec. 1, March 19, 1946, and incorporated into the Puerto Rico Constitution, Art. I, Sec. 1, July 25, 1952. *Leyes de Puerto Rico Anotadas* (1946), Title 3, sec. 141, I, 494.

64. Secretary of Education, *Report* (1947), p. 27.

65. International Institute, Teachers College, Columbia University, *Public Education and the Future of Puerto Rico: A Curriculum Survey* (New York: Bureau of Publications, Columbia University, 1950).

66. At present, he is again professor of educational psychology at the University of Puerto Rico.

67. Everett Reimer, "Educational Implications of Economic Development," *Revista Educación* (January 1961), p. 15.

68. Carl J. Friedrich, *Puerto Rico: Middle Road to Freedom* (New York: Rinehart and Co., 1959).

69. Ismael Rodríguez Bou, *Estudio del Sistema Educativo de Puerto Rico* (3 vols.; Rio Piedras: Superior Council on Education, University of Puerto Rico Press, 1962).

70. See bibliography for several of his publications.

71. These scholars included men such as Charles Ferguson, Professor Américo Castro, Professor Maurice Swadesh, Professor Dell H. Hymes, Theodore Anderson, W. Nelson Francis, Warner Rice, Professor Ralph Long, Professor Robert Lado, Professor Wallace Lambert, Professor Uriel Weinreich, Professor Federico de Onís, Professor Angel Rosenblat, and Professor Dennis Girard.

72. Luis Muñoz Marín, *Mensaje a la Cuarta Asamblea Legislativa* (San Juan: Departamento de Instruccion, 1964), pp. 12-14.

73. *San Juan Review* (June 1965), p. 73.

74. Instrucción Pública en Puerto Rico, Departamento de Instrucción, 1968, p. 72. y Resumen de Aportaciones Federales al Sistema de Instrucción Pública del Estado Libre Asociado de Puerto Rico y la Utilización de las Mismas, June 1957. (Unpublished.)

BIBLIOGRAPHY

Public Documents

Puerto Rico. *Constitución* I (Julio 26, 1952), Título 18, sec. 1.

—— *Documents on the Constitutional History of Puerto Rico.* Washington, D.C.: Office of Puerto Rico, 1st ed., 1948; 2d ed., 1964.

—— Estado Libre Asociado de Puerto Rico. *Leyes de Puerto Rico, Anotadas* (Marzo 19, 1946), Título 3, sec. 141, Ley Num. 76.

Jones Act, P.L. 64-368, c. 145, 39 Stat. 951 sec. 17 (1917).

Treaty of Paris (1898), Art. IX.

Books

Brameld, T. *The Remaking of a Culture.* New York: Harper and Brothers, 1959.

Brookings Institution. *Puerto Rico and Its Problems.* Washington, D.C.: The Institution, 1930.

Bunker, H.F. *Cartas a los Maestros Asociados.* San Juan: Asociación de Maestros de Puerto Rico, 1956.

Cebollero, P. A. *La Política Linguístico-Escolar de Puerto Rico.* Río Piedras Superior Council on Education, University of Puerto Rico, 1945.

Clark, Victor S. *Teachers' Manual for the Public Schools of Puerto Rico.* New York: Silver, Burdett & Co., 1900.

Dana, A. G. *Porto Rico's Case.* New Haven, Conn.: Tuttle, Morehouse & Taylor Co., 1928.

Departamento de Instrucción de Puerto Rico. *Conferencia Sobre la Enseñanza de la Lengua.* San Juan: Departamento de Instrucción, 1965.

Diffie, Bailey W., and Diffie, Justine W. *Porto Rico: A Broken Pledge.* New York: The Vanguard Press, 1931.

Fernández Méndez, E. *La Identidad y la Cultura.* San Juan: Ediciones "El Cemi," printed by Editorial Cultura, Mexico, 1959.

—— *The Sources on Puerto Rican Culture History: A Critical Appraisal.* San Juan: Ediciones "El Cemi," printed by Editorial Cultura, Mexico, 1967.

Fife, R. H., and Manuel, H. T. *The Teaching of English in Puerto Rico.* San Juan: Department of Instruction, 1951.

Friedrich, Carl J. *Puerto Rico: Middle Road to Freedom.* New York: Rinehart and Co., 1959.

Géigel Polanco, V. *El Despertar de un Pueblo.* San Juan: Biblioteca de Autores Puertorriqueños, 1942.

Hartzell, C. *Register of Puerto Rico.* San Juan: Press of Louis E. Tuzo & Co., 1903.

Hayward, Beresford. *Toward Comprehensive Educational Planning in Puerto Rico.* San Juan: Department of Education, 1958.

Lugo-Silva, E. *The Tugwell Administration in Puerto Rico, 1941-1946.* Río Piedras: The author, University of Puerto Rico, 1955.

Mathews, Thomas. *Puerto Rican Politics and the New Deal.* Gainesville: University of Florida, 1960.

Mergal, A. M. *Puerto Rico: Enigma y Promesa.* San Juan: Club de la Prensa, 1960.

McLeary, James H. *First Annual Register of Puerto Rico.* San Juan: Press of the *San Juan News,* 1901.

Miller, P. G. *Historia de Puerto Rico.* New York: Rand, McNally & Co., 1922.

Morales Carrión, A. *Ojeada al Proceso Histórico de Puerto Rico.* San Juan: Departamento de Instrucción Pública, 1965.

Osuna, Juan José. *A History of Education in Puerto Rico.* San Juan: University of Puerto Rico Press, 1949.

Padín, José. *Personas Sobre Cosas.* San Juan: Biblioteca de Autores Puertorriqueños, 1951.

Page, Homer. *Puerto Rico: The Quiet Revolution.* New York: The Viking Press, 1963.

Pedreira, A. *Insularismo.* Madrid: *Tipografía Artística,* 1934.

Picó, R. *Puerto Rico: Planificación y Acción.* San Juan: Banco Gubernamental de Fomento, 1962.

Porrata, O. E. *Retardation in the Elementary Urban Schools of Puerto Rico.* San Juan: University of Puerto Rico Press, 1933.

Quintero, A. G. *La Instrucción Pública en Puerto Rico.* San Juan: Department of Instruction, 1968.

Rigual, Nestor. *Mensajes de los Gobernadores de Puerto Rico.* San Juan: Superior Council on Education, University of Puerto Rico, 1967.

Rodríguez Bou, Ismael. *El Analfabetismo en Puerto Rico.* San Juan: Council on Education, University of Puerto Rico, 1945.

—— *Estudio del Sistema Educativo de Puerto Rico.* 3 vols. Río Piedras: Superior Council on Education, University of Puerto Rico, 1962.

—— *La Deserción Escolar en Puerto Rico.* San Juan: Council on Education, University of Puerto Rico, n.d.

—— *Problemas de la Educación en Puerto Rico.* Río Piedras: Superior Council on Education, University of Puerto Rico, 1942.

—— *Problemas de Lectura y Lengua en Puerto Rico.* San Juan: Superior Council on Education, University of Puerto Rico, 1948.

—— *Seminario Sobre Radiodifusión en Puerto Rico.* Río Piedras: Superior Council on Education, University of Puerto Rico, 1951.

Sánchez Morales, Luis. *De Antes y de Ahora.* Madrid: Centro Editorial Rubén Darío, 1936.

Tugwell, R. G. *The Stricken Land.* New York: Doubleday and Co., 1947.

Articles and Periodicals

Arroyo, M., y Estrada, A. "Teachers Association of Puerto Rico," *San Juan Star,* October 17, 1967.

El Mundo (San Juan), December 3, 1944.

Fernández García, R. "La Educación en Puerto Rico," *El Mundo* (San Juan), December 27, 1934.

Miranda Archilla, G. "Reorientación de la Filosofía Educativa de Puerto Rico," *El Mundo* (San Juan), 26 de Mayo de 1946.

New York Daily Tribune, March 4, 1900.

Padín, J. "Relación de la Isla con Estados Unidos," *El Mundo* (San Juan), April 3, 1954.

Quintero, A. G. "Interview." *San Juan Review* (June 1965).

—— "Las Escuelas Ejemplares." *Revista Educación* (Marzo-Abril 1961).

—— "La Orientación del Estudiante de Talento Superior." *Revista Educación* (Abril 1963).

Reimer, Everett. "Educational Implications of Economic Development." *Revista Educación* (Enero 1961).

San Juan Review (June 1965), p. 73.

Reports

Carroll, Henry K. *Report on the Island of Porto Rico.* Washington, D.C.: Government Printing Office, 1899.

Caselman, C.; Borghi, L.; and Bredsdorff, M. *The Educational System in Puerto Rico.* San Juan: Department of Education, 1959.

Collazo, F. *Informe Anual del Departamento de Instrucción, 1946-1947.* San Juan: The Department, 1947.

Commissioner of Education (later Secretary of Education). *Annual Reports.* Washington, D.C.: Government Printing Office, 1900-67.

Davis, G. W. *Civil Affairs of Porto Rico.* Washington, D.C.: Government Printing Office, 1900.

—— *Military Government of Porto Rico.* Washington, D.C.: Government Printing Office, 1902.

Departamento de Instrucción. *The Puerto Rican Child in His Cultural Context.* San Juan: El Departamento, 1966.

—— *La Escuela Pública en Puerto Rico: Normas de Supervisión y Administración Escolar.* San Juan: El Departamento, 1954.

Eaton, J. *Education in Porto Rico.* Washington, D.C.: U.S. Bureau of Education, 1901.

Governor General. *Reports.* Washington, D.C.: Government Printing Office, 1900-67.

International Institute, Teachers College, Columbia University. *Public Education and the Future of Puerto Rico: A Curriculum Survey.* New York: Bureau of Publications, Columbia University, 1950.

—— *A Survey of the Public Educational System of Porto Rico.* New York: Bureau of Publications, Teachers College, Columbia University, 1926.

Junta de Planificación. *Indices Seleccionados de Progreso Económico y Social, 1939-1966.* San Juan: La Junta, 1966.

—— *Anario Estadístico, 1961-1962.* San Juan: La Junta, 1962.

Muñoz Marín, Luis. *Mensaje a la Cuarta Asamblea Legislativa.* San Juan: Departamento de Instrucción, 1964.

Quintero, A. G. *Evaluación y Proyecciones de la Situación Educativa en Puerto Rico.* San Juan: Departamento de Instrucción, 1965.

—— *La Instrucción Pública en Puerto Rico.* San Juan: Departamento de Instrucción, 1968.

Rodríguez Pacheco, O. *Some Aspects of Educational Planning in Puerto Rico.* San Juan: Department of Education, 1963.

Unpublished Material

Carrión, Z. "Desarrollo de la Educación Secundaria en los Ultimos 16 Años, 1948-1964." Departamento de Instrucción, San Juan, 1964. (Mimeographed.)

—— "Desarrollo de la Escuela Superior en los Ultimos 12 Años." Departamento de Instrucción, San Juan. (Mimeographed.)

—— "El Currículo de la Escuela Superior en Puerto Rico Durante los Ultimos 12 Años." Departamento de Instrucción, San Juan, 1962. (Mimeographed.)

—— "Efforts To Improve the Quality of Instruction in Secondary Schools During the Years 1961-1964." Departamento de Instrucción, San Juan, 1964. (Mimeographed.)

Departamento de Instrucción. "Ciclo de Conferencias Sobre el Sistema de Instrucción Pública de Puerto Rico," Sept. a Dic. de 1961. (Mimeographed.)

—— "Programa Especial de Escuela Superior." Departamento de Instrucción, San Juan, 1963. (Mimeographed.)

—— "Escuela Secundaria, Documentos." Departamento de Instrucción, San Juan, 1966. (Mimeographed.)

—— "Plan de Desarrollo Currícular." Departamento de Instrucción, San Juan, February 9-12, 1966. (Mimeographed.)

—— "Seminario de Educadores." Departamento de Instrucción, Puerto Rico, 1966- . This seminar continues to meet.

Gallardo, J. M. "Filosofía Educativa." Carta Circular Num. 1, July 1, 1942. San Juan, Bureau of Supplies, Printing, and Transportation, Department of Instruction. (Mimeographed.)

Hamill, C. O. "The Achievement of Eleventh Grade Special High School Project Students in Grades Ten and Eleven." Departamento de Instrucción, San Juan, April 1964. (Mimeographed.)

—— "Estudio Comparativo de Resultados de la Prueba de Aptitud Académica del College Entrance Examination Board Entre las Escuelas Superiores que Participaron en el Proyecto Especial de Enriquecimiento del Currículo." Departamento de Instrucción, San Juan, February 1967. (Mimeographed.)

Leavitt, José A. "Historical Sketch of Adult and Extension Activities." Unpublished paper in the Department of Education, San Juan, 1949.

Maurás, J. M. "El Desarrollo de la Educación Elemental en Puerto Rico Durante los Años de 1948-1964." Departamento de Instrucción, San Juan, Febrero de 1965. (Mimeographed.)

—— "Síntesis del Origen y Desarrollo de la Escuela Intermedia en Puerto Rico." Departamento de Instrucción, San Juan, 1961. (Mimeographed.)

Quintero, A. G. "Palabras al Prestar Juramento." Departamento de Instrucción, San Juan, Febrero de 1965. (Mimeographed.)

—— "Mensaje a la Asamblea de la AMPR." Departamento de Instrucción, San Juan, Diciembre 1966. (Mimeographed.)

Rivera, P. J. "La Oficina Regional Como Estructura Dentro del Departamento de Instrucción Pública." Departamento de Instrucción, San Juan, Agosto 1966. (Mimeographed.)

—— "Nuevos Programas y Enfoques del Sistema de Instrucción Pública de Puerto Rico." Departamento de Instrucción, San Juan, Agosto 9, 1967. (Mimeographed.)

"Resumen de Aportaciones Federales al Sistema de Instrucción Pública del Estado Libre Asociado de Puerto Rico y la Utilización de las Mismas." June 1957. (Unpublished.)

Roca, P. "El Futuro de la Educación en Puerto Rico: La Responsabilidad del Estudiante." 17 de Abril de 1958. (Mimeographed.)

Villaronga, M. "The Teaching of English in Puerto Rico." Department of Education, San Juan, 1947. (Mimeographed.)

Other Sources

Brunet, V., y Rivera, J. J. "Estado de la Educación y Situación de los Educadores en Puerto Rico." VI Congreso Americano de Educadores, Montevideo, Uruguay, 1957.

Fisher, C. L. "Activities of the Division of Research and Statistics." Unpublished records of the Department of Education, Second Annual Convention Association meeting of April 6-7, 1956.

Rojas, Pauline M. "Talk to the Rotary Club of San Juan," on September 28, 1954.

Appendix A

PUERTO RICO CHIEF SCHOOL OFFICERS AND OTHER EXECUTIVES

Presidents of the United States		Governors of Puerto Rico		Chief School Officers of Puerto Rico	
1897-1901	W. McKinley	1898	Gen. J.R. Brooke (Oct.-Dec.)		
		1898-99	Gen. G. W. Henry	1899	John Eaton (Jan.-May)
		1899-1900	Gen. G. V. Davis	1899-1900	Victor Clark
1901-1909	T. Roosevelt	1900-1901	Ch. H. Allen	1900-1902	M. G. Brumbaugh
		1901-1904	W. H. Hunt	1902-1904	S. M. Lindsay
		1904-1907	B. Winthrop	1904-1907	R. P. Falkner
		1907-1909	R. H. Post	1907-12	Edwin G. Dexter
1909-13	W. H. Taft	1909-13	G. R. Colton	1912-15	E. M. Bainter
1913-21	W. Wilson	1913-21	A. Yager	1915-25	P. G. Miller
1921-23	W. G. Harding	1921-23	E. M. Reiley		
1923-29	C. Coolidge	1923-29	H. M. Towner	1925-30	J. B. Huyke
1929-33	H. C. Hoover	1929-32	T. Roosevelt, Jr.	1930-36	J. Padín
		1932-33	J. R. Beverly		
1933-45	F. D. Roosevelt	1933-34	R. H. Gore		
		1935-39	Gen. B. Winship	1937	H. A. Martin (Jan.-June)
		1939-40	Adm. W. A. Leahy	1937-45	J. M. Gallardo
		1941	G. J. Swope (Jan.-June)		
		1941-46	R. G. Tugwell	1945-46	H. A. Martin
1945-53	H. S. Truman	1946-49	J. M. Piñero	1946-47	M. Villaronga
		1949-65	L. Muñoz Marín	1947-48	F. Collazo
				1949-57	M. Villaronga
1953-61	D. D. Eisenhower			1957-60	E. Sánchez Hidalgo
1961-63	J. F. Kennedy			1960-65	C. Oliveras
1963-68	L. B. Johnson	1965-68	R. S. Vilella	1965-68	A. G. Quintero

Appendix B

Chart I.--DEPARTAMENTO DE INSTRUCCION PUBLICA DE PUERTO RICO, 1900-20

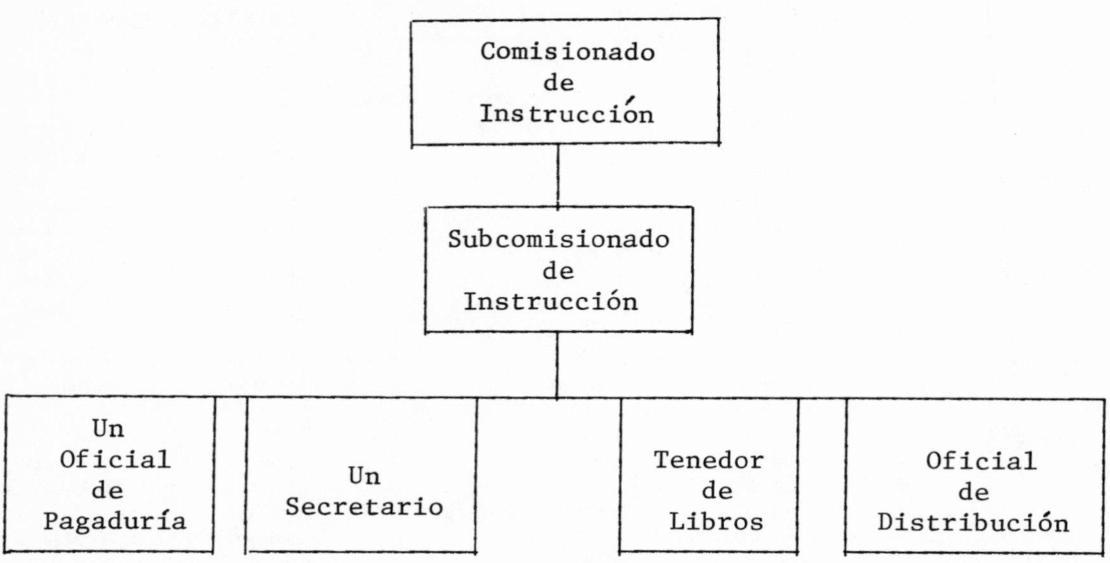

Chart II.--DEPARTAMENTO DE INSTRUCCION PUBLICA DE PUERTO RICO, 1920-30

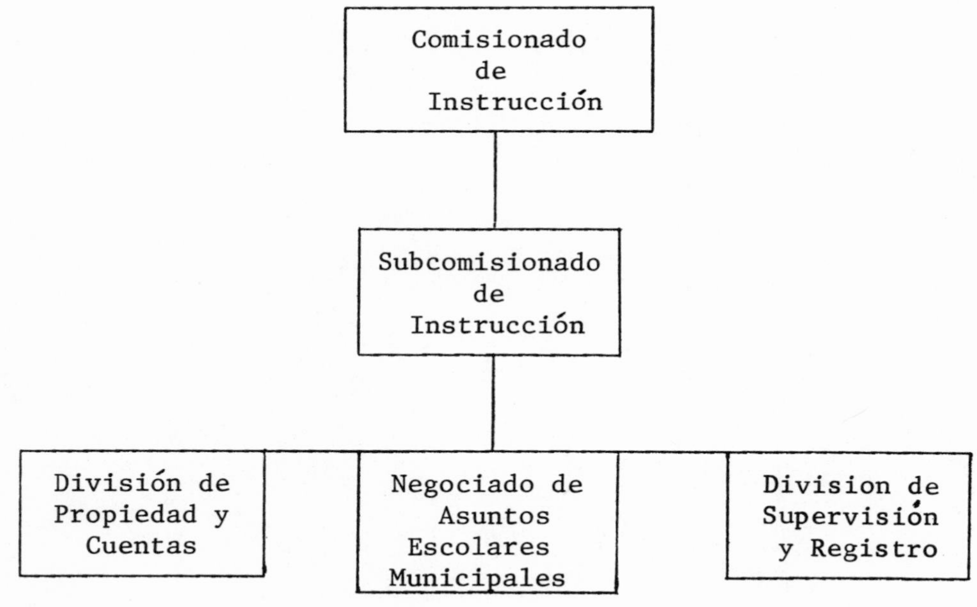

Appendix B

Chart III.--DEPARTAMENTO DE INSTRUCCION PUBLICA DE PUERTO RICO, 1945-48

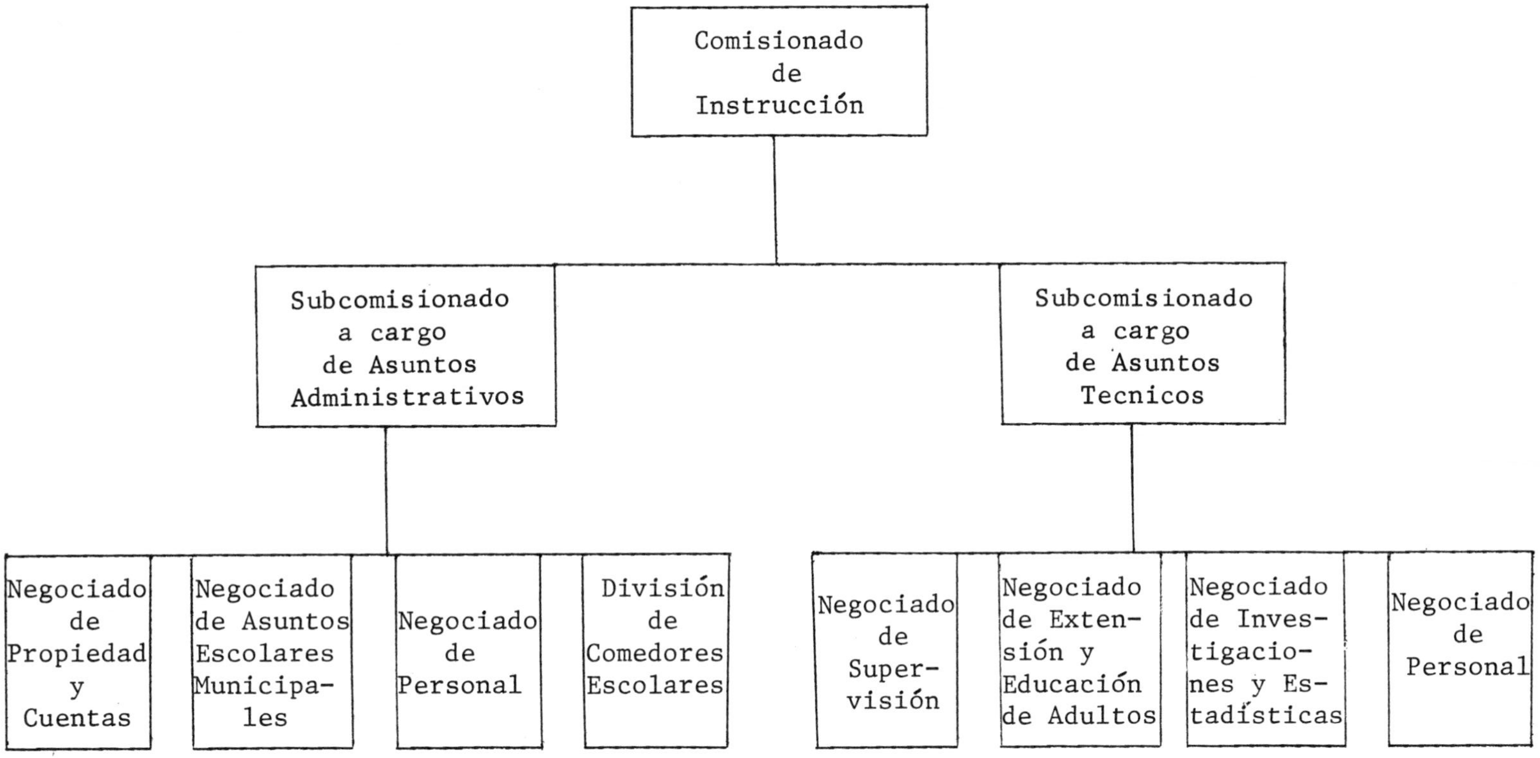

Appendix B

Chart IV.--DEPARTAMENTO DE INSTRUCCION PUBLICA DE PUERTO RICO, 1966

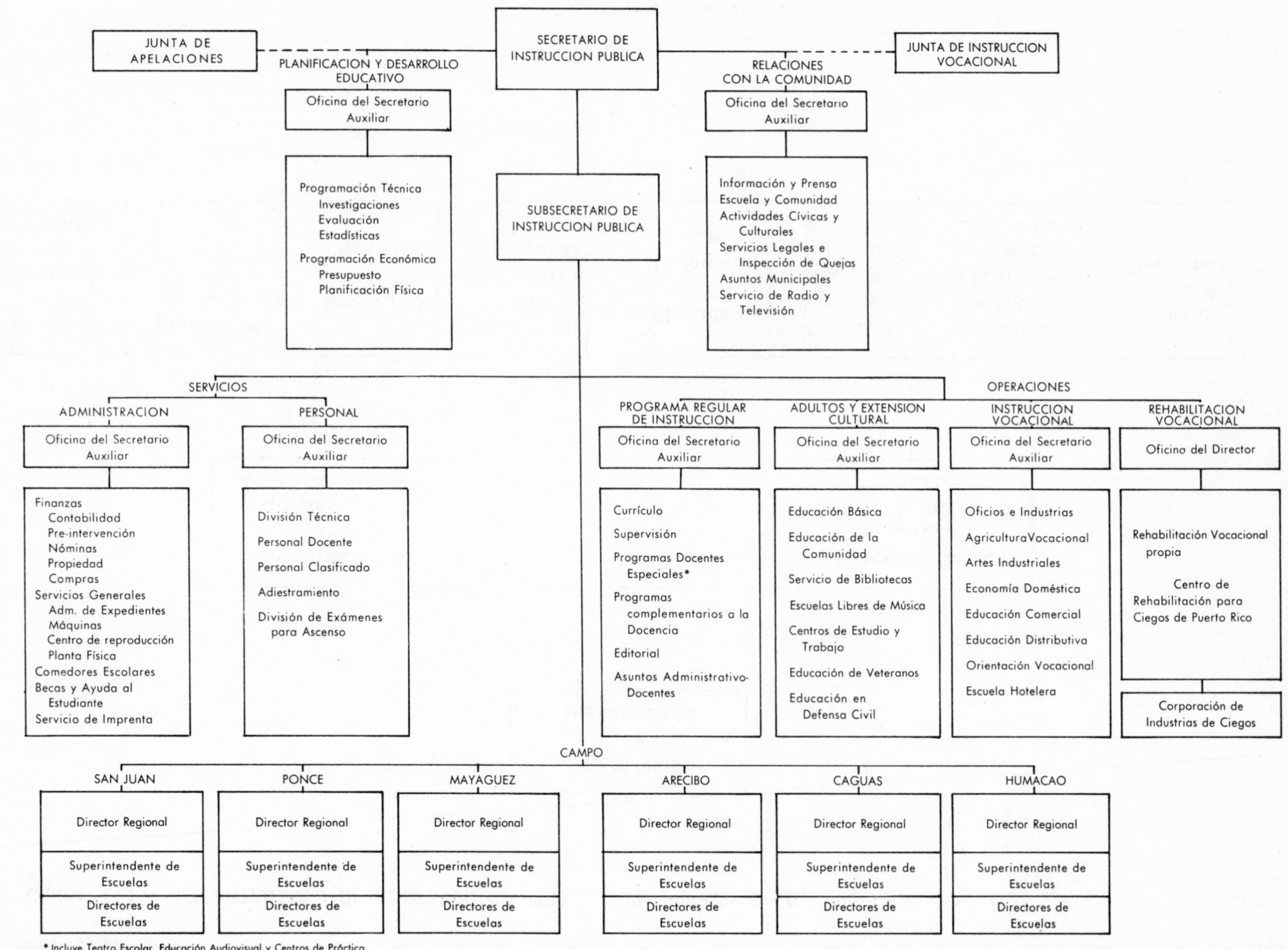

* Incluye Teatro Escolar, Educación Audiovisual y Centros de Práctica.

40 Rhode Island

DEPARTMENT OF EDUCATION

Arthur R. Pontarelli

Contents

INTRODUCTION

Although Rhode Island is the smallest state in the Union – 200 Rhode Islands can be swallowed up in the massive State of Texas – it does bear, ironically enough, the longest official name: *Rhode Island and Providence Plantations.* And although its highest point (Jerimoth Hill) is only 812 feet above sea level, Rhode Island's geographical dimensions do not diminish one whit its spirit and vision, for the history and heritage of Rhode Island are as rich and varied as its people and as solid and deep as the actual bedrock on which it stands. The long chronicle of Rhode Island men and women, of events and utterances and achievements, is an enduring testimony of its special endowments: Roger Williams, Anne Hutchinson, John Clarke, Nathanael Greene, Oliver Hazard Perry, Ambrose Burnside, Henry Barnard, Moses Brown, Samuel Slater, Gilbert Stuart, Nelson Aldrich, Theodore Francis Green, George M. Cohan, "Gabby" Hartnett, and "Nap" Lajoie are but a few of the worthies of the State of Rhode Island who have left their impress on the history of this state and nation. Even our little rooster, the Rhode Island Red, symbolizing the activity and the vitality of the state, has gained national renown.

Thus, as the history of education in Rhode Island is reviewed, there will be expressions of "firsts" which are made, not in the spirit of boastfulness, but in the spirit of forgivable pride, for the educational achievements of this state are fitting measurements of its historic and persistent eagerness to explore new avenues, new ideas, and new techniques. And as we attempt to present the development of education from 1900 to 1968, the hallmarks of education in Rhode Island prior to 1900 must be clearly identified mainly because the great body of legal structure established during this early period was to lay the foundation for future development.

EARLY COLONIAL PERIOD

The Charter of 1663 granted by King Charles II of England to the "English Colony of Rhode Island and Providence Plantations in New England in America" declared the intent of the colony "to hold forth a lively experiment that a most flourishing civil state may stand and best be maintained with a full liberty in religious concernments" (1). Three centuries later, one looks at these words now inscribed above the Rhode Island State House entrance and realizes with what penetrating prophecy they were to proclaim the story of this state.

As one notes the key role this state was to play in the establishment of an independent nation; in the development of a highly industrialized country; in the guarantee of religious freedom to all; in its contribution to art, to the theater, to sports, and in its leadership in the field of education, it is evident that Rhode Island has fulfilled its promise of a "lively experiment."

Rhode Island did not follow the traditional pattern exhibited in other colonies where local units complied with laws on mandating schools that the various colonies had enacted. In this state, the towns and corporate groups established their own schools, and state legislation followed some years later. For example, the first statewide legislation in education did not appear until 1800; yet, as early as 1640, a public school system was being established in Newport. Indeed, Charles Carroll, author, historian, and educator, recorded Newport's free public school as the first such system in all English America (2).

During the early colonial period, three basic types of schools were in operation in Rhode Island. The first kind was public schools supported wholly or in part by the individual towns through such practices as land grants for school sites; house lots for the schoolmaster; and tracts of land, the income from which provided support of the schools. In some communities, the town built the schoolhouse and leased or rented the facility to the schoolmaster. In still other districts, the town paid the schoolmaster wholly or in part to provide instruction to the children. Town records indicate that around 1750 Barrington, Bristol, Middletown, Newport, Portsmouth, Providence, and Warwick maintained public schools.

A second and more common type of school in the early colonial period was the private school. These schools were in the most part church-affiliated: Congregationalist

Episcopalian, Baptist, Society of Friends, Jewish. Societies or individuals established and supported others.

The student of school law interested in the matter of public funds to support sectarian schools will find it worthy of mention that as early as 1790 the school committee of the town of Providence recommended that the town pay to the Society of Friends a share of the public school money for tuition purposes. However, there is no record that an appropriation was made to implement this plan.

A third type of school was the Dame School, an educational pattern derived from the English system in which, for a small fee, a woman of the neighborhood would give instruction in the fundamentals of reading, writing, arithmetic, and some "finishing" subjects to young children. It is only natural to assume that in this period many children of the wealthy familes were instructed on a private tutorial basis.

First Statewide Legislation

To John Howland – barber, soldier with Washington at the Battle of Trenton, Providence town treasurer, member of the school committee, leader of civic and social groups – must go the major credit for the initial statewide legislation for public schools. As a leader of the Providence Association of Mechanics and Manufacturers, John Howland used the influence of this powerful organization to advocate free public schools. While Providence and a few other communities maintained free public schools around 1800, support and maintenance of the schools varied widely around the state, and the cry of unequal educational opportunity was not uncommon even in those days.

The extent of the state's involvement in support of schools at that time was to exempt school property from taxation, to grant charters, and to permit local communities or groups to hold lotteries for construction and maintenance of schools. As early as 1764, permission was granted to hold a lottery to establish Rhode Island College in Warren. This institution moved to Providence in 1770 and developed into one of the nation's greatest institutions of higher learning – Brown University.

A petition drafted by Howland and presented to the General Assembly in 1799 expressed concern –

> That numbers of the rising generation whom nature has liberally endowed, are suffered to grow up in ignorance, when a common education would qualify them to act their parts in life with advantage to the public and reputation to themselves.
>
> That in consequence of there being no legal provision for the establishment of schools, and for want of public attention and encouragement, this so essential part of our social duty is left to the partial patronage of individuals, whose cares do not extend beyond the limits of their own families, while numbers in every part of the state are deprived a privilege which it is the common right of every child to enjoy (3).

In Rhode Island, unlike the newly formed states of the Northwest territories (which enjoyed federally supported educational endowments), the traditional system of government existed for two centuries before public education was recognized as a general responsibility of the state (4).

Education received little public support before 1800. The schools were supported by individuals who leagued together for the common purpose of promoting education. It was more than a century and a half after the charter of Rhode Island was granted before the General Assembly assumed any degree of responsibility to promote public education through tax support (5).

In 1800, a law was passed making "free" schools mandatory and making local taxes permissive. In an attempt to make this new approach to education more palatable to the towns, the General Assembly provided state aid by remitting one-fifth of the taxes paid by the respective towns to the state. Apparently it was a tasteless dish, since few towns other than Providence and Smithfield showed any real effort to raise tax money for their schools. The law was repealed in 1803.

Still, the advocates of free schools, supported by the local press and key members of the General Assembly, continued to press for statewide legislation. It was not until 1828 that the assembly effected enduring legislation. It avoided mandating public schools, but it did permit the taxes for this purpose, limiting the amount that could be raised locally (6). This law provided "that the town meeting shall appoint a school committee to have the power to locate schools and make necessary rules and regulations" (7). What the General Assembly did, in effect, was to create state government machinery–the town school committe–and set it in motion, supplanting the interested groups that had formerly, and voluntarily, espoused the cause of education. Subsequently, Rhode Island adopted a constitution which, for the most part, made the General Assembly "a state school committee to promote for the whole State those functions which the law of 1828 had assigned to the new governmental agency, the town school committee" (8).

A school bill was enacted in 1828, but the final compromise produced not "free" schools but "public" schools. Public schools, while open to all children of the district, made certain charges, such as for tuition, books, and even maintenance of school property. The bill made provisions for an annual appropriation ($10,000) for support of public schools and for a permanent school fund.

A survey made by educator Oliver Angell in 1831 shows the effects of the Law of 1828. Some significant indications of improvements in this short period included the fact that the total number of schools had increased from 294 to 504, that the number of children receiving public school instruction had increased from fewer than 1,400 to approximately 14,000, and that more than half the towns in the state (17 of 31) made local appropriations to supplement state assistance. It appears that the School Act of 1828 had made some notable improvements even though its critics bemoaned the fact that the legislation included no provision for collection of statistics or measurement of educational progress.

The period from 1828 to 1842 has been described as a critical period of adjustment in Rhode Island education, for the schools found themselves in strong competition with the industrial expansion. The textile industry, initiated through Samuel Slater's development of the first cotton spinning mill in America, was quick to recruit older boys and girls for service in the mills. The need for child labor laws was evident if school enrollments were not to stagnate. It should be of interest to school historians that Providence at this time conducted school on a year-round basis and that Providence, in 1839, appointed a professional superintendent of schools, Nathan Bishop, whom Gleeson described as "the first superintendent of schools to be appointed in America" (9).

In 1841 and 1842, Rhode Island found itself beset with political troubles as Thomas Wilson Dorr led a "people's revolt" against the "landholders" to establish a new constitution. Dorr's efforts to take over the state government were unsuccessful, but his agitation did produce a new constitution in 1842, which provided in Article XII:

> Of Education
>
> Section 1. The diffusion of knowledge, as well as of virtue, among the people being essential to the preservation of their rights and liberties, it shall be the duty of the General Assembly to promote public schools and to adopt all other means which they may deem necessary and proper to secure to the people the advantages and opportunities of education (10).

The Constitution of 1842 has prevailed to the present day with few revisions, although a constitutional convention assembled in 1967 to modernize the previous document.

A State System Established

In 1843, Wilkins Updike, a representative from South Kingstown, made a stirring plea before the General Assembly for a survey to be made of the schools of the state. Updike attacked the physical condition of schools, inadequacy of instruction, lack of uniformity of textbooks, and poor preparation of teachers. As a result, Governor James Fenner appointed Henry Barnard, fresh from his position as secretary of the school commissioners of Connecticut, to be state agent to perform the survey. Substantially, the plan underscored two principal considerations: an appraisal of the public schools and an awakening of public interest to promote better education. The study bore fruit, for the resultant Law of 1845, commonly called the Barnard Law, included measures for the improvement of education and for a state system of administration.

The Barnard Law provided for the appointment of a commissioner of public schools whose duties required him to "wear many hats" as an educational expert or adviser to the General Assembly, a publicity agent for maintaining public interest, an efficiency agent for projects for improvement of schools, an amiable counselor of school officials, the dispenser of state aid, a state superintendent of schools, an agent for training teachers, a school statistician, and a judicial officer. Because of the excellent survey Barnard made and the resulting rapport established with the General Assembly, it was only natural that this man, often called the "outstanding American educational reformer of the nineteenth century" (11), was appointed commissioner of public schools in 1845.

With the passage of the Barnard Law, the General Assembly had instituted a state system for administration and supervision of education. It provided, further, for the compulsory support of schools by towns, expanded authority of school committees, certification of teachers, a minimum school year, school reports, and other measures for strengthening the quality of education, such as restriction on the size of classes. However, the law was not without its defects, as time would prove. The statute called for the creation of trustees in school districts, which was to bring about conflicts of authority. Also, the law made no provisions for compulsory attendance or an appropriation to train teachers. Giant strides had been made, nevertheless, in establishing the foundations for a state system of education that has carried to the present day.

Barnard's tenure of office lasted to 1849, at which time he resigned for reasons of ill health, but he was to earn the undying gratitude of a most appreciative state. Barnard later went on to even greater endeavors culminating with his selection as the first U.S. Commissioner of Education in 1867.

Elisha Reynolds Potter, who had been Henry Barnard's assistant and associate, succeeded to the position of commissioner in 1849. A resourceful and experienced lawyer and public officer, Commissioner Potter, in rewriting the Barnard Law in 1851, recast it into legal language, a change that tended to make the legislation more effective. Potter ably promoted the theories and general policies of Commissioner Barnard.

Through his efforts, after two unsuccessful ventures in private normal schools, a state-supported normal school for preparing teachers was established in 1854. He repressed agitation that might have precipitated a religious conflict in public education and that might have provoked as serious a controversy in Rhode Island as elsewhere. He was keenly aware of the significance of the commissioner's judicial authority and did much through exercise of this power to win prestige and to establish dignity for his office. Subsequently, as associate justice of the Supreme Court of Rhode Island, Potter wrote the opinion of the court in the Cottrell case, a decision which laid down the rule for the appellate jurisdiction of the commissioner. Realizing the importance of a close affiliation with the General Assembly as the repository of power through law to advance public education, he recommended in 1855 the establishment of a State Board of Education. He further advocated free schools, or the abolition of tuition (rate bills), and also free textbooks. During the Potter administration, which lasted until 1855, the state appropriation was increased from $25,000 to $50,000.

The decade from 1845 to 1855 was indeed one of phenomenal achievement and progress. The contributions of Barnard and Potter in establishing and fortifying the state system of education were to endure to the present time. The vision of Barnard and the judicial ability of Potter combined to establish a firm foundation on which was to develop a sound educational system.

A Period of Consolidation

The 15-year period, 1855 to 1869, might best be described as a plateau period during which gains were consolidated. One explanation for the lack of new advances might be that the commissioners in these years were not as successful as their predecessors in promoting legislation and securing its passage.

Reverend Robert Allyn of East Greenwich succeeded Commissioner Potter and served from 1855 to 1858. His most significant service was an investigation of school enrollment, attendance, finance, and a detailed statistical report to the General Assembly. Reverend Allyn further sustained the judicial authority and made recommendations for free schools and free textbooks.

John Kingsbury served as commissioner in 1858-59. In his year of service, he visited schools and reported on conditions as he found them, thus affording a basis for comparison of schools with Barnard's report.

Joshua B. Chapin was commissioner from 1859 to 1861 and again from 1863 to 1869. Henry Rousmaniere was the interim commissioner from 1861 to 1863. Chapin strongly advocated the abolition of tuition and was rewarded when, in 1868, the General Assembly passed legislation to this end. It was Dr. Chapin who, fighting for equal status for women teachers, noted that "females have peculiar talent, and when properly educated, have greater power over the manners, morals, and minds of children" (12).

New Horizons

When Thomas W. Bicknell succeeded Dr. Chapin as commissioner in 1869, he restored vigorous leadership to the position. He immediately directed his efforts to the need for a State Board of Education, and the General Assembly responded in 1870 with such legislation. This new State Board of Education was made up of the Governor, lieutenant governor, and six members of the General Assembly, two from Providence County and one each from the other four counties. The board was empowered with "the general supervision and control of the public schools. . .with such high schools, normal schools, and normal institutions as are or may be established and maintained wholly or in part by the state. . ." (13). With Commissioner Bicknell as its counselor, the newly created state board was successful in achieving mandatory supervision, town appropriations to equal state appropriations, truancy legislation, support for evening schools, and free public libraries. Among Commissioner Bicknell's most active campaigns at the time of his resignation in 1875 was his fight for the eradication of illiteracy.

Thomas B. Stockwell served as commissioner from 1875 to 1905, a period equal to the combined terms of all his predecessors. Supported vigorously by the state board, Stockwell continued the campaign against illiteracy. Fighting for compulsory attendance laws, Commissioner Stockwell, following the axiom of Horace Mann that every child has a right to education, advocated that society had a right to demand that every child be educated. His efforts led to a gradual succession of truancy laws, child labor laws, and, finally, compulsory attendance statutes.

During his tenure, Stockwell also was instrumental in securing legislation in the areas of school census, state support for secondary schools, free textbooks, increased supervision of schools, consolidation of schools, and state certification of teachers. A telling piece of legislation, passed in 1904, abolished the practice, instituted by the Barnard Law of 1845, of establishing multiple school districts in a community and centralized the control and operation of schools under school committees. Five years after the passage of the Barnard Law, there were 322 school districts in Rhode Island, and final abolition of this fragmentation of school control was slow in developing. The Rhode Island College of Agriculture and Mechanic Arts, the Rhode Island Institute for the Deaf, the Rhode Island School of Design, and the State and Home School all were founded during Stockwell's tenure. Among Stockwell's noteworthy achievements was his publication of *A History of Public Education in Rhode Island,* which has served as a work of reference to students of early Rhode Island history.

In summary, this chapter has attempted to outline the major developments leading to the establishment of a state system of administration of free public education through a State Board of Education, a commissioner of public schools, local school committees in charge of town systems, and school superintendents.

As of 1900, the state board and the commissioner of public schools had the following responsibilities:

Board of Education

- To maintain general supervision and control of the public schools of the state
- To prescribe and cause to be enforced all rules and regulations necessary to carrying into effect the laws in relation to public schools
- To serve with the commissioner of public schools as a board of trustees, to manage the Rhode Island Normal School, admit students thereto, and pay the traveling expenses of students
- To elect the commissioner of public schools
- To supervise the education of deaf, blind, and imbecile children of school age
- To examine teachers and issue certificates of qualification and eligibility to teach
- To approve courses of study in high schools and standards for high schools as conditions precedent to paying state aid to high schools.

Commissioner of Public Schools

- To visit as often as practicable every town in the state for the purpose of inspecting the schools and diffusing as widely as possible—by public addresses and personal communication with school officers, teachers, and parents—a knowledge of the defects and desirable improvements in the administration of the system and the government and instruction of the schools
- To apportion the state's appropriation of teachers' money
- To provide teachers institutes
- To hear and decide appeals in disputes arising under school law
- To supervise the public schools generally
- To direct courses of study prescribed by town school committees
- To serve as ex officio secretary of the State Board of Education
- To report annually to the State Board of Education
- To serve as a member of the board of trustees of the Rhode Island Normal School.

Clearly it is evident that a strong foundation for free public education has been established through the administrative echelons of authority, local and state financial assistance to public schools, free tuition, free textbooks, preparation and certification of teachers, and compulsory attendance laws.

DEVELOPMENT OF TWENTIETH-CENTURY EDUCATION

At the turn of the century, the 37 local governmental units in the state employed approximately 2,000 teachers and provided free public education to slightly over 70,000 pupils. Total expenditures for schools amounted to $1.5 million. While public secondary education had not as yet been mandated, 19 public high schools were in operation. In addition, the private and parochial school enrollments totaled approximately 15,000. A number of private academies and private schools, such as the Moses Brown School, LaSalle Academy, East Greenwich Academy, St. Mary's Seminary, Elmhurst Academy, and Lapham Institute, provided secondary education.

The population of the state at this time numbered 428,556, of whom approximately 30 percent were foreign-born. Rhode Island was indeed a melting pot, giving haven and opportunity to thousands of Irish, Italians, French-Canadians, Poles, Portuguese, and others, most of whom were absorbed into the labor force of the rapidly expanding industries of the state. The ethnic diversity of the state can best be characterized by a statement of Stuart Hale, the Providence *Journal-Bulletin* staff writer:

> Take a staid, industrious Yankee town. Add a full measure of sturdy Italian stock and blend in liberal amounts from the Emerald Isle (remove the brogue, but slowly). Sprinkle with honest Polish faces (leaving in the polkas), and the sons and daughters of French Canada. Spice with the products of Portugal, Greece, Armenia, and other warm lands. Stir well and serve. . .that's Providence (14).

In such a rich milieu, it was only natural for the schools to play a meaningful role in providing a basic education to the growing population. However, the problems of the schools of the state were many. Among the most pressing were the problems of school finance; the extension of free education to all through the secondary grades; the many problems involving teacher welfare, such as salaries, tenure, pensions, and professional improvement; the extension of the school year; the need for a drastic reduction of school districts; and provisions for the safety and health of schoolchildren.

The Ranger Era: 1905-35

As was noted in the previous section, the district system within towns was abolished, and the centralization of school management under one school committee was accomplished by Commissioner Stockwell in 1904. His successor, Walter E. Ranger, led the way to a new era of school improvements. Walter E. Ranger came to Rhode Island from Vermont, where he had served as state superintendent of schools. His strong background and experience in school administration brought to this state expert leadership at a time when many programs needed to be developed. In his first year of service, Commissioner Ranger undertook a general survey of schools. In his second year, he produced a monumental report recommending pensions for teachers, a state system of traveling libraries, a state home and school for the feeble-minded, state certification of superintendents, extension of high school education, industrial and trade education, improved school sanitation, reasonable tenure for teachers, and a summer school for teachers. During the course of the term of his office, Commissioner Ranger was able to see these vital educational matters and many other recommendations he had proposed enacted into law.

Concern for the improvement of teachers' professional preparation and economic status resulted in legislation dealing with state certification, pensions, minimum salary, and professional improvement programs. The "uniform high standard" Act of 1898, which was the culmination of an extensive state board report on education in the state as requested in a 1906 General Assembly resolution, had placed the authority of certification in the State Board of Education instead of in districts, school committees, and teacher-training institutions. The board established four grades of certificates and moved gradually toward the upgrading of teachers through higher standards.

In 1903, the commissioner of public schools was granted authority to withhold an amount of state school money equal to the wages paid by any town to a teacher without a state certificate, thereby permitting strict enforcement of the certification statutes. Through a succession of revisions of standards over the years – with major revisions in 1909, 1923, 1938, 1951, and 1964 – the level of teacher standards has increased to the stage where at the present time all teachers at both elementary and secondary levels must obtain a master's degree within a period of 6 years following receipt of the provisional certificate. (Chart I of Appendix B shows in graphic form the dramatic upgrading of preparation of teachers from 1900 to 1960.)

Rhode Island has been among the leaders in the certification movement throughout the years and has eagerly participated in reciprocity compacts as established in 1948 among 8 states in the Northeast and later expanded to a total of 11 states for the purpose of easy mobility of teachers across state lines. The department has sought and cooperated in the NCATE movement to extend this same philosophy even beyond the 11-state boundaries and looks hopefully toward the most recent efforts of establishing a policy of reciprocity for all 50 states.

As a companion measure to certification standards, Ranger advocated extension education of teachers through courses at the Rhode Island Normal School and the Rhode Island School of Design, and through the Graduate Department of Education at Brown University. In 1916, a study of state normal schools by the National Bureau of Education gave special commendation to the normal school for its excellent undergraduate program for preparation of teachers. In 1920, Rhode Island Normal School developed a full 4-year program and changed its name to the Rhode Island College of Education; in 1959, it attained its current status as Rhode Island College.

Concern for teacher welfare prompted Ranger to advocate teacher pensions and minimum salary laws. In 1907, legislation was enacted providing for pensions of up to $500 per year to any person 60 years old who had been a teacher for 35 years, 25 of which had to be in the public schools of the state. Modifications in later years were to provide for disability pensions and less stringent requirements to qualify for a pension. The notable feature of this pension program was that it was supported wholly by the state.

Minimum salary for teachers was one of the original 10 points recommended by Ranger in his report to the General Assembly in 1906. While this recommendation had been made by several of the previous commissioners, no legislation was enacted until 1909 when the assembly provided that "the annual salary of a teacher regularly employed in any public school of the state shall not be less than $400" (15). (The average salary at that time was $681.) It further provided state reimbursement to towns on a matching basis for the expense of meeting this requirement.

This statute was instrumental in lengthening the school year because in some communities the school committees determined that the increasing of annual salary need not increase the weekly wage and construed the statute to justify a lengthening of the school year. At the time of the Barnard Law in 1845, the school year varied throughout the state from 4 months in some communities to a full year in Providence. The Barnard Law established a minimum of 4 months of school, and in 1872 the minimum was increased to 6 months. In 1871, the average school year in Rhode Island was 35 weeks, the longest in New England. In 1895, it reached 189 days, and by 1915 it was 195 days. In 1914, the minimum school year became 36 weeks, and in 1917 it became 180 days.

At the recommendation of Commissioner Ranger, the General Assembly in 1909 increased state aid to communities providing secondary schools and mandated that any town not maintaining a high school must make provision at the expense of the town for the free attendance of its children at some approved high school or academy. This statute made it obligatory to provide a high school education. In 1914, the state board established minimum requirements for approval of high schools in order to qualify for state aid. It also appointed an inspector of high schools to visit and examine the schools. The criteria for approval included a school calendar of at least 38 weeks; a faculty of three or more teachers, with a ratio of at least one teacher for every 30 students; a teacher load of not more than 5 hours of instruction time excluding other duties; proper certification of teachers; a minimum of 15 units of study in a 4-year course; adequate instructional equipment; a well-equipped library; and proper standards of admission, instruction, and discipline.

With the mandating of secondary school education, the state had now developed a full span of public-supported elementary, secondary, and college education. As was noted earlier, the Rhode Island Normal School was established in 1854 to provide for the preparation of teachers in the state schools. The school's present teacher preparation program dates back to 1871, as established under a board of trustees made up of the state board and the commissioner of public instruction. At the turn of the century, the enrollment of the school numbered 218 students.

The Rhode Island College of Agriculture and Mechanic Arts in Kingston provided for public education in the fields of agriculture, mechanical engineering, civil engineering, electrical engineering, 4-year teacher courses in applied science and home economics, and 2-year courses in agriculture and domestic science. This institution, established in 1892 with assistance from the Morrill (land grant) Act, was controlled by a board of seven members – the commissioner of public instruction, one member appointed by the State Board of Agriculture, and five members appointed by the Governor. In 1909, this institution, with an enrollment of 250, became the Rhode Island State College.

While the above data might indicate that attention during this period focused only on the development of a system of preparatory education for college, nothing could be further from the truth. The General Assembly in 1910 requested the commissioner of public schools to determine the status and needs of the state in respect to industrial, vocational, and agricultural education and to recommend improvements in these areas. Commissioner Ranger responded with a 100-page report indicating the status of such programs and recommended the establishment of and state support for vocational education not only in regular day programs but also in adult evening schools. When the General Assembly responded with legislation providing financial assistance, Pawtucket, Central Falls, Warwick, and Westerly were among the first communities to avail themselves of it. When the federal Vocational Education Act was passed in 1917, the recommendations of Commissioner Ranger and the action of the General Assembly placed Rhode Island in an advantageous position, because the machinery was already operational to implement its provisions.

The effect of the federal legislation in vocational education on the department structure is readily apparent as one notes the reorganization of the education department in 1930, which called for a commissioner of education (title changed in 1920) and abolished the position of assistant commissioner established in 1910. It established a vocational education division, an adult education division, and a research and studies division. The function of the last division was to audit financial accounts of school systems, to collate and summarize statistical reports, to direct research studies, and to survey school systems. The establishment of an adult education division can be attributed to Commissioner Ranger's efforts to promote Americanization and literacy classes as well as general adult educational improvement.

In 1922, a report made by a commission established to study educational problems led to the enactment of the Peck bill, which provided for financial support to local school districts on the basis of the number of schools, classrooms, and $1.50 per capita in average daily attendance. Among other provisions of this bill were the prohibition of commercial activities in schools and the approval of private schools by the state board instead of by local school committees. The proposal created considerable controversy and became an issue in the general state elections in that year. Although the legislation was enacted, the issue was far from dead, and in 1925 the power to approve or disapprove private schools was restored to the local school committees.

In his desire to improve the school environment and health services to schoolchildren, Commissioner Ranger successfully advocated state aid for medical inspections, dental inspections, physical education, sanitation standards, and safety measures. Coupled with new compulsory attendance measures, these recommendations resulted in substantial improvements in school conditions throughout the state.

In concern for the welfare of its adults as well as its youth, the State Board of Education, acting in its capacity as the State Board for Vocational Education, undertook a program of industrial vocational education in 1919 for the purpose of rehabilitating adults. Rhode Island thereby became one of the first states in the nation to undertake such a program. In 1920, federal legislation was introduced providing for vocational guidance and counseling services, vocational training, and maintenance and support for individuals qualifying for such services. When federal funds became available in 1921, a joint federal-state effort was established that has continued to the present day. Indeed, this state has developed such an extensive program of vocational rehabilitation that it ranks among the top six state agencies in the country in the percent of individuals restored to gainful self-sufficiency. In 1935, when the Board of Education was abolished, a separate Board for Vocational Education was created to meet the requirements of federal rehabilitation statutes.

On October 30, 1930, Commissioner Ranger was honored with a banquet on the completion of 25 years of service to this state. At this occasion, John J. Tigert, formerly U.S. Commissioner of Education, discussed the achievements of the Ranger era.

> Reviewing the record of the Commissioner of Education of Rhode Island for this epoch in education, his administration parallels, if it does not transcend, the progress made in a national way . . . . He has been among the leaders, and in no one of the progressive measures

accomplished throughout the country has he ever failed to keep abreast in his home state . . . . It is not possible to enumerate all the legislative measures that have been adopted in Rhode Island during this time . . .

Minimum employment age for children raised to 14 years
Enactment of the first teachers' pension law
A minimum salary law for teachers
State aid for medical inspection of school children
Compulsory school attendance for children up to sixteen years of age, unless the child is fifteen years old and employed
Physical education made mandatory.

Along the line of equalizing educational opportunities and the promotion of guidance and vocational work, Dr. Ranger has always interested himself in the success of these movements. He has made a notable contribution through his support of the Federal-State College at Kingston . . .

He secured also the establishment of the Exeter School for Feeble Minded . . . .

He procured state aid for traveling libraries.

. . . the certificate law was extended to superintendents.

Other measures which have aided administration have been: the extension of the school census to cover ages four to twenty-one instead of five to fifteen years; the authorization of the survey of state school finances and administration, followed by a complete report and a division of survey and research established in the State Department of Education. Mention was made of the fact that training for citizenship has come to be a paramount objective in American education. So far as I know, Dr. Ranger was one of the first to lay stress at this point, and I am sure there is no one who has given more unstintedly of time and effort to promote the teaching and training of good citizens. He secured legislation which required the principles of popular and representative government to be taught in all the schools of the state.

During his administration appropriations for schools have increased approximately 150 per cent. State aid has been greatly increased for high schools, and towns have been required to provide high school instruction. Appropriations have been secured for the provision of free state scholarships for post-graduate courses at Brown University, at Rhode Island School of Design, and in the Rhode Island College of Pharmacy. School committees of towns have been authorized to spend money at a rate established by preceding appropriation if the town meeting fails to appropriate for school purposes.

The name of the Rhode Island Normal School has been changed to the Rhode Island College of Education and larger appropriations have been secured. He has been a prime factor in the securing of new buildings for the Rhode Island College of Education and for the State College at Kingston (16).

Truly, Walter E. Ranger served Rhode Island well. He retired in 1935.

Rhode Island in the Depression

The stock market crash of 1929 and the consequent Depression created acute economic problems in Rhode Island. However, although many small businesses failed, the state's banks did not suffer any permanent failures (17).

In Rhode Island, as well as other parts of the country, federal agencies, such as the National Recovery Administration (NRA), the Works Progress Administration (WPA) and others, were organized and established to assist in the care and welfare of the unemployed.

With characteristic vigor, the state board struck a chord of municipal support of public schools in its annual report (1931) to the General Assembly. Despite economic depression, the statements and the sentiments of the board's report and those that followed it were consistently responsive to the needs of the schools. The report noted that the state had ample reason for legitimate pride in the fact that, while school budgets had been prepared with considerably more care than ever before, there had been little disposition to enforce a retrenchment at the expense of public education (18). The report particularly stressed the fact that curtailments in the field of education were unwise if for no other reason than the obvious one that educational losses [were] "irretrievable" (19). The report concludes with a rather incisive philosophical and practical observation that clearly exemplifies the fact that, even in the midst of such unsettled times as the Depression, the purpose and the dedication of those entrusted with the vital matter of the education of its youth stood unshaken: "There remains only a remote possibility, an almost certain impossibility, that a child's loss of opportunity for education can be recouped. No community can afford to save money at the expense of the education of the rising generation" (20).

According to the report made at the end of the fiscal year 1931-32, Rhode Island was one of only a very few states which remained able to report in a roll call of the states, "all schools open, and all school terms maintained" (21). Furthermore, although the rate of increase had lost the acceleration of earlier years, Rhode Island still could report a slight gain in expenditures for current maintenance of school (22). The report also noted, however, that Rhode Island was not without its dislocations and curtailments in the educational crisis that had gripped the nation during those dark days after 1929. Rigid cutbacks in a program of new buildings were effected, and major reductions in expenditures were realized at the expense of teachers, maintenance of plants, textbooks, and educational supplies. The report lamented the facts of the reductions as being "wholly inconsistent with sound educational policy" (23). The report further observed that "teachers [were] courageous, generous, self-sacrificing in continuing cheerful service under depressing conditions which [had] included in several towns and cities long waits for the payment of salaries after the latter had been reduced in amount" (24).

The board viewed these conditions as "unbearable and intolerable" (25). It recommended that the State of Rhode Island assume a larger share of responsibility for the support of the public school system and urged that the General Assembly establish a revised state program that would include –

1. A large increase in state appropriation for public education to be apportioned to towns and cities;
2. A decrease in the burden imposed by statute upon towns and cities;
3. A readjustment of taxation for school support whereby school taxable property would be relieved in part and more of the burden of school support would be transferred to general taxation of the type from which the state derived its revenue;
4. Ample assurance from continued adequate financial support of public school programs to prevent the ills which attend delayed payments of salaries particularly;
5. A renewed construction program to be made possible in part by the relief of property from taxation for general maintenance and a readjustment of capital outlays (26).

The board concluded its annual report by reflecting on the fact that "its position [was] justified by the imposition in the last year of an exaction of $425,000 on 4,000 public school teachers in the name of alleged economy" (27).

During the Depression, voices spoke for and against certain educational policies in Rhode Island. An anecdote can well illustrate both the support for and criticism of education in many quarters of the state during those bleak days.

Superintendent Deering of West Warwick carried the fight for his teachers into a town meeting, shoring up a defense of their meager salaries by vigorously resisting a budget reduction for the school system of that town. The proposal, if passed, would have resulted in even smaller pay envelopes for the teachers. Deering cited the high qualifications required for appointment as a teacher and pointed out that the salaries paid in West Warwick were already lower than in several nearby municipalities. A citizen then rose to state that no group had done more for the town of West Warwick than the teachers. A rejoinder to this by an exponent of the proposed budget cut drew loud opposition when he remonstrated, saying, "Are the school teachers so much more intelligent and discerning than their sisters employed in the mills or the wives of men struggling to get a living or mothers of children who want something to eat?" (28).

One teacher, pleading her own case, pointed out that she had spent 16 years in preparation for teaching school and received an annual salary of $1,100, which amounted to little more than $21 per week (29).

In its final vote, the town meeting supported Superintendent Deering's position.

A NEW ORDER

On January 1, 1935, Governor Theodore Francis Green, who had taken over the gubernatorial reins of Rhode Island in 1932, engineered the enactment of a reorganization statute that completely restructured the entire government of the state. In the field of education specifically, the State Board of Education was abolished after 65 years of existence, and the Office of Commissioner also was abolished after 90 years of existence. The reorganization of public education service set up a State Department of Education with a director of education succeeding to the powers and functions of both the state board and the commissioner. James F. Rockett, superintendent of schools in Woonsocket, Rhode Island, was appointed director of education and assumed office in March 1935. At the same time, a promotion and supervision division was created within the new department to assist in the functions of the director of education. Charles Carroll was appointed to this position.

The reorganization statute also abolished the board of trustees of Rhode Island College. A board of regents within the state department was established to govern the state institutions. Further, all library activities were transferred from the State Department of Education to the library division under the secretary of state. The Bureau of the Blind was transferred from the public welfare division to the Department of Education, and the School for the Deaf was placed under the director of education, with the assistance of an advisory board.

In compliance with federal regulations, the State Board for Vocational Education was established, consisting of the directors of education, of agriculture and conservation, and of labor. This board, functioning also as the state agency for vocational rehabilitation, was increased to five members in 1939 by the addition of two members appointed by the Governor.

The termination of a State Board of Education in 1935 ended the participation of lay leaders as policy makers in the education field from that time until 1951, when Governor Dennis J. Roberts established a new education board. The contributions of the individual board members from 1870 to 1935 would be too numerous to mention. However, the service of certain individuals merits documentation. Probably without peer in length of service was Frank Hill, representative from Hopkinton, whose tenure on the board for over 36 years commenced in 1867. Others distinguished for their lengthy service are Frank Thompson, 33 years (1890-1923); George T. Baker, 26 years (1894-1920); E. Charles Francis, 24 years (1909-33); and Samuel H. Cross, 24 years (1870-82 and 1885-97).

As mentioned earlier, the new director of the State Department of Education, appointed by the Governor with the consent of the Senate, assumed all powers and duties of the previous board and the commissioner. The state appropriations for education remained practically unchanged.

Among Director Rockett's first recommendations made to the General Assembly were requests for additional state aid in the form of equalization aid. It had been clearly established that the local school departments were handicapped by the failure of the state to modernize its tax system and to balance the burdens between the property tax and other tax bases. The property tax still remained as the sole source of support for local operations. With economic growth developing at uneven rates, serious consideration was required of the state to develop a plan for taking into account the varying abilities of communities to support schools at a minimum level of effectiveness.

The policy of state support by general appropriations allocated with some concern for relative need was approximately a century old in Rhode Island. The cry of the education community then became one for equalization of educational opportunity through a program of tax equalization. With this background, the General Assembly in 1936 enacted the McEntee-Kiernan bill, which appropriated $200,000 for the purpose of equalization of educational opportunities in the several cities and towns. This aid took into account the relative abilities of the communities to support a basic program of education and provided for grants of $2.50 per pupil in average daily attendance. It further required a minimum level of support by a school district to qualify for such aid. With the passage of the McEntee-Kiernan bill, the state took a significant step forward in assuming its constitutional role as the agency with prime responsibility for the education of its children. Of greater importance, however, was the major objective in attempting to establish the principle of equal educational opportunity.

A further extension of the compulsory attendance law was enacted in 1937, when the age limits for school attendance were fixed at 7 to 16 years of age with no exemptions whatever because of employment. It is interesting to compare enrollment and attendance figures for Rhode Island with those for the United States as reported by the U.S. Office of Education, 1930-32 (30).

	R.I.	U.S.
Percent of total enrollment in high school	20.5	19.6
Percent of attendance on enrollment	86.0	84.7
Annual expenditure per pupil enrolled (1930)	$98.35	$81.36
Per-capita cost of pupils in average daily attendance	$109.30	$87.67
Average value of school property per pupil in average attendance	$372.00	$205.00

The matter of school transportation received the attention of the General Assembly in 1937 when it enacted legislation requiring school committees to provide –

> Suitable transportation to and from school for pupils attending public schools of elementary and high school grades who reside so far from any public school as to make their regular attendance at school impracticable and for any pupil whose regular attendance would otherwise be impracticable on account of physical disability or infirmity.

The statute further indicated that "for pupils attending private schools of elementary and high school grades, except such schools as are operated for profit, the same rights and privileges as to transportation to and from school as are provided for pupils attending public schools" (31). In light of the many problems that attended the implementation of such legislation, Director of Education Rockett issued the following memorandum to school administrators in August 1937:

> Many inquiries have come to the state department of education regarding various interpretations and rulings of the above act. Inasmuch as several legal technicalities were involved, the approval of the following interpretations was requested and secured from the Attorney General:
>
> The matter of suitable transportation is a mandatory legal requirement and must be furnished wherever necessary in the same manner as school maintenance, books, supplies, instruction, etc.
>
> By "suitable transportation" is meant either the furnishing of a suitable conveyance or the furnishing of sufficient funds to allow transportation for the pupil through means of a suitable conveyance.
>
> Such suitable transportation must be furnished for two groups of pupils: first, those pupils who reside so far from any public school as to make their regular attendance at school impracticable, and second, those whose regular attendance would be impracticable, in the absence of such transportation, on account of physical disability or infirmity.
>
> "Who reside so far from any public school" is to be interpreted as beyond a reasonable walking distance to

be determined by the school committee after giving consideration to age of children, local conditions, and hazards involved. . . (32).

This interpretation has served as a general guideline to the present time in the matter of resolving disputes on transportation.

In 1939, legislation was passed creating a separate Board of Trustees of State Colleges, which assumed the powers, duties, and functions of the board of regents formerly within the state department. This new corporate board assumed control over the Rhode Island State College and the Rhode Island College of Education. The board, composed of the director of education (ex officio) and six other members, has continued to the present time as the governing body of the public-supported institutions of higher learning with only a slight expansion in the board composition, which now totals nine members.

In December 1939, Director of Education Rockett, in a communication to Senator Charles T. Algren, chairman of the Legislative Council, made an urgent request for a commission to study the "educational hoge-podge of laws" and to make recommendations to unify and coordinate the laws governing education. A number of categorical aid programs had developed over the years which indeed needed reevaluation. A few of these statutes provided aid for support of superintendents' salaries, promotion of health, support of public schools, reference books and apparatus, evening schools, manual training and household arts, vocational education, Americanization classes, consolidation of schools, equalization aid, and transportation. For some of these programs, the support to the individual communities amounted to $200 (reference books) or $250 (health). The General Assembly, convinced of the need for a review of the statutes, authorized the establishment of such a commission.

The Commission on the Legal Structure of Rhode Island Public Education, with Dr. Rockett as its chairman and Paul R. Mort of Columbia as the director of studies, conducted an extensive study of all phases of elementary and secondary education in the state. It made recommendations, in a two-volume report, which were to serve as guides for legislation in the years to come. Among its chief provisions were recommendations regarding state-operated vocational training, state-operated programs for handicapped children, state-operated Americanization education, continuing census by school departments, employment of visiting teachers rather than truant officers, minimum salary schedule for teachers, adequate tenure legislation, supplementary retirement plan, testing and selection of prospective teachers by the State Department of Education, changes in election of school committee members, delineation of powers of superintendent and school committee, changes in business and fiscal operations, appointment of a State Board of Education, legislative functions of school committee, reorganization of school districts, equalization of burden of school support, and recodification of school laws (33).

The above are but a sampling of the 66 general and specific recommendations made by the commission over a 15-month period from September 1940 to December 1941. The foresight and wisdom of Dr. Mort were reflected in recommendations which, 25 years later, still have great relevance and significance. Although the report did not produce sweeping legislative programs, the study and recommendations have served as a base of reference for a number of separate educational statutes over the years. Director Rockett had established a solid foundation from which to promote new legislation.

Teacher tenure, one of the above-mentioned areas, was of growing concern to Rockett, to the Rhode Island Institute of Instruction, and to the teachers themselves. While some communities, such as Pawtucket, had provided for some measure of job security, it was clearly established that to provide real and effective tenure would require legislation mandating school committees to guarantee that security. After several vigorous campaigns, the General Assembly enacted such legislation in 1946.

In 1945, the minimum salary of teachers employed on a full-time basis was raised to $1,200. As noted earlier, the first minimum salary statute as enacted in 1909 established a base of $400 per annum. In 1922, this level was raised to $650 and remained as such until the 1945 legislation.

Another interesting piece of legislation enacted during Rockett's administration called for the establishment and maintenance of the Rhode Island Nautical School under the aegis of the director of education. It provided for the instruction of students in the science of navigation, for the acquisition of a suitable vessel, and even for a schedule of cruises. The school never materialized, as no appropriation was provided. The legislation, however, still exists in the current education laws.

In 1947, after a long and illustrious career in public education, James Rockett was succeeded by Michael F. Walsh. Walsh had served as dean, assistant superintendent, and acting superintendent of schools in Newport, Rhode Island, and also served as a member of the study commission under Rockett. Familiar with the recommendations of that commission, Director Walsh set out to improve teacher welfare and strengthen the State Department of Education.

The General Assembly of 1947 responded to the need for teacher salary increases and established a state salary grant of $600 to every teacher regularly employed by any city or town. This grant was earmarked specifically for teachers' salaries and was designed to supplement rather than to supplant existing salary schedules. In effect, it also raised the minimum salary schedule to $1,800 per year. A state sales tax was initiated to support this grant. The state appropriation in support of this act was $2,340,000 for the fiscal year 1947-48, and a similar amount was appropriated for the fiscal year 1948-49. This became the largest state appropriation for any single educational purpose in the history of the state up to that time.

The $600 salary grant was followed in 1948 by a statewide retirement program for teachers which significantly expanded the benefits afforded teachers under the prior pension system. Optional annuity, nonduty and duty disability, and insurance clauses were provided within the retirement plan. The amount payable is equal to 1.7 percent of "average compensation" for each year of credited service not exceeding 45 years. Thus, the maximum allowance is 75 percent of average compensation.

The 1947 General Assembly also enacted legislation that provided for the establishment, maintenance, and operation of nonprofit school lunch programs in the public and nonpublic schools of the state. From this legislation developed the only state-operated school lunch service in the United States. Initially staffed with only a few people, the school lunch services division has grown to a force of over 650 under department control and in 1965 served 4.2 million balanced meals in the schools of 36 cities and towns.

In May of 1947, Walsh, in a letter to U.S. Commissioner of Education John W. Studebaker, requested the Office of Education to make an appraisal of the organization and functions of the department and "to outline a program for the development and improvement of the services of the department with a view of meeting the long-term post-war educational needs of the state." A team of USOE specialists, headed by Fred Beach, reviewed the existing operation (see Chart III, Appendix B) that provided for a director of education and three assistant directors – one for vocational education, one for administration, and one for instruction.

The recommendations of the committee included recodification of all state education laws; educational programs, including vocational, at grades 13 and 14; guidance, testing, and counseling services; research and statistical services; teacher certification services; and supervisors in academic areas. It was felt that these recommendations would enhance the principal department functions of leadership, planning, research, and advisory service to local education agencies. This 1947 study, in essence, became a reaffirmation and reinforcement of the 1942 study, which had previously made strong recommendations for department restructuring, state financing, school district reorganization, creation of a State Board of Education, broader state services to local school districts, and recodification of education laws.

The establishment of the professional position of supervisor of teacher certification is an example of the enhancement of the department role and services. The acquisition in 1948 of William P. Robinson, Jr., to serve in that capacity led to full-time evaluation of credentials, teacher education service to colleges and universities, counseling of prospective teachers, increased certification standards, and Rhode Island's involvement in such compacts as the 8-state reciprocity certification agreement in 1949 and its extension to 11 states in 1956.

Reestablishment of a State Board of Education

As previously noted, the studies and surveys of 1942 and 1947 had reaffirmed the need for a lay group to serve as a policy-making body to the director of education. The two principal reasons for creating such a board were, first, that the delegation of legislative power to a single individual was particularly open to question and, second, that prudence and experience always dictate, whenever policies are being established, that they can best be developed by the involvement of a number of persons.

There had been some community ground swell from various civic and professional groups for the establishment of a State Board of Education during the 1940's, but it was not until 1951 that the General Assembly enacted legislation creating such a board consisting of seven members to be appointed by the Governor.

On June 25, 1951, Governor Dennis J. Roberts swore in the members of the State Board of Education. An organizational meeting was conducted in the Governor's chamber, at which the Reverend Cornelius B. Collins was elected chairman and Michael F. Walsh was appointed commissioner of education. Dr. Walsh had served from 1947 as director of education.

The several responsibilities of the board indicate that it shall have general supervision and control of public schools, be the policy-forming and planning agency for the public school system of the state, determine and adopt policies for the more efficient operation of any phase of public school education, and review the educational needs of the state. (See Powers and Duties of the Board, Appendix C.)

Among the duties and responsibilities of the commissioner of education, as spelled out in the statute, are to carry out the policies and programs formulated by the Board of Education, to approve and distribute state funds, to interpret school law, to have general supervision of the Department of Education, and to appoint the several officers and employees of the department. (See Duties of the Commissioner, Appendix C.)

Mindful of its mandate, the board proceeded to promulgate new certification standards; scholarship programs for teachers, undergraduates, nurses, and special education personnel; and a program for the education of retarded children. It initiated a detailed study of the state aid laws in 1953, which culminated in the enactment in 1955 of the foundation program.

This legislation was a reassuring and cardinal step in improving the financial condition of the schools, for it made provision to assist those communities having financial difficulties because of a relatively small tax base. This principle, commonly known as the equalization principle, assured every child the opportunity of obtaining at least an acceptable minimum education. The impact of this legislation is revealed by the fact that the statute brought 15 percent of the total money provided by the act to the education of the 10 percent of the children in communities most handicapped by lack of taxing ability. It also established a minimum salary scale of $3,200 to $5,200 for certified teachers, as well as pupil-teacher ratios. The board recommendation for a tax equalization board was also accepted.

The matter of providing vocational education programs adequate to the needs of the youth and industries of the state received considerable deliberation by the state board. Spearheaded by board member Edwin C. Brown, surveys and needs of the state were developed, and recommendations were prepared for legislative action. Although the board recommended at least $4 million to initiate state-operated programs, the General Assembly's initial approval amounted to only $600,000. On the basis of this legislation, a state-operated vocational-technical school was established in 1954. The school became operational in 1958 on a small scale, but efforts of the state board had been recognized in that this legislation was to establish the basis for further statewide vocational-technical programs in the 1960's.

Further improvements in the late 1950's were the recodification of education laws in 1956, the establishment of programs for the education of gifted children (1958 enactment with a $60,000 appropriation), and a study commission on higher education. In April 1959, Governor Christopher Del Sesto approved the State Board of Education's recommendation for a departmental reorganization. This reorganization provided for a commissioner of education; a deputy commissioner and two associate commissioners, each of whom headed a major division; and four chiefs, each of whom headed a minor division. (See Chart IV, Appendix B.)

The reorganization of the department incorporated the establishment of the instruction division, which had been recommended by the 1942 study, as a department function to assist local school districts in the various instructional fields. This was made even more imperative because of the 1958 federal legislation commonly identified as NDEA. Department specialists in mathematics, science, modern foreign languages, and guidance would not be available to local education agencies.

As was noted earlier, a commission had been appointed in 1957 to study higher education and to report to the General Assembly the suggested measures to meet the needs of the future. The commission made several recommendations, among them being significant expansion of the University of Rhode Island and Rhode Island College facilities; development of a state junior college system; and a state scholarship program. While the first and second recommendations were to be developed by the Board of Trustees of State Colleges, the latter recommendation was placed under the commissioner of education. Rhode Island thus became one of the first six states to establish a state scholarship program for qualified college-bound youth of the state. Grants ranging from $250 to $1,000 per year are made to 5 percent of the total of the graduating class (public and nonpublic) to attend the college of their choice.

In its role of advising the General Assembly and Governor of needed educational legislation, the State Board of Education, in its 1959 recommendations for legislative action, indicated its goal –

> To assure quality education for all Rhode Island youth. That is, at least an adequate minimum education for every child in the state and at the same time encourage the citizenry of Rhode Island through their local communities and through guidance from the Department of Education to improve upon this minimum in every way possible (34).

Although the 1955 foundation act had provided an initial step in realigning the fiscal posture of education in the state, a stronger state-local partnership was required. The 1965 act establishing a state equalization board, a 1967 amendment to the foundation act, and the 1958 permissive legislation for school district reorganization were additional steps in promoting this joint responsibility. The board's recommendation for new school operation and a schoolhousing legislation included several interesting features: a guaranteed minimum of 25 percent of the full cost of education to all communities; an equalization factor to assist the less affluent school districts; an "education improvement fund" available to the state board to encourage local innovation and experimentation; the elimination of 12 categorical aid statutes; incentives (increased aid) to encourage small school districts to regionalize; and a new minimum salary scale for teachers ($4,000-$6,000).

A truly encouraging feature of these recommendations was the open-end proposal that the state would share, not just in the minimum amount, but in all expenditures at whatever level the local school district chose for both operational and capital outlays.

With the concerted effort of many education-minded groups, Chapters 26 and 27 of the Public Laws of 1960 were enacted by the General Assembly and signed by Governor Del Sesto. Rhode Island thus became the first state to provide open-end state support for school operations and construction. The enactment of this statute, and its subsequent amendment in 1964 increasing the state's share, have greatly enhanced the opportunity for all school districts to provide a quality education. This legislation has been nationally acclaimed for its goal of genuinely making the state and local education agency partners in the education enterprise.

EMERGENT CHALLENGES FOR THE STATE EDUCATIONAL SYSTEM

The period of the 1960's can best be described as one in which the State Board of Education has made a serious appraisal of the role and responsibilities of the board and the department and, convinced of the leadership functions of these agencies, has moved with conviction and vigor to fulfill its duties. After its reestablishment in 1951, the board provided a number of rules, regulations, and standards (see Appendix D). For example, in the areas of teacher certification, education of handicapped children, approval and accreditation of secondary schools, school libraries, and vocational education, the board established new standards or higher standards where they were deemed necessary.

Early in 1963, Commissioner Walsh was forced to retire because of ill health. William P. Robinson, Jr., deputy commissioner, who had been serving as acting commissioner during Walsh's absence, was appointed commissioner in February 1963. Familiar with the educational problems of the state, Commissioner Robinson in September 1963 outlined specific areas of special concern both for the board and the General Assembly. Among the most pressing issues identified were future development of vocational education in the state; increased financial assistance for school districts; special assistance to economically depressed areas; de facto segregation; dropout problem; school district reorganization; special education; and department staffing.

The matter of vocational education had become a statewide issue with the advent of the federal vocational act of 1963 and the availability of $10 million of state funds through bonds and appropriations. After much debate and discussion, the state embarked on a program of secondary vocational-technical programs in area-comprehensive high schools and a postsecondary vocational-technical program as a joint venture with the Board of Trustees of State Colleges as part of the junior college system. It was finally determined to establish a separate vocational high school in the Blackstone Valley in response to the requests of educational, civic, and legislative leaders of the area. Few educational topics in recent years have received as much wholesome and heated debate as the issue of statewide vocational-technical education. In any event, the department staff has been significantly strengthened to perform the statewide mandate by the addition of a new position of associate commissioner for vocational-technical education and a number of consultants in research, technical, distributive, and business education, and in curriculum development.

The commissioner recommended increased state aid with special consideration to the problems of the larger urban communities because of their greater financial burden, larger numbers of economically and culturally deprived children, and, as in the case of Providence, the problem of de facto segregation. The state board was indeed sensitive to these problems and developed recommendations for legislative action in an attempt to ameliorate these conditions.

In the matter of school district reorganization, the board's desire to develop the most efficient and effective school organizational pattern led it to seek out department and consultant studies. As noted throughout this chapter, the matter of proliferation of separate, inadequate, and expensive school programs was a constant concern of commissioners and state boards. The problem is further complicated as the state considers the cost effectiveness of providing additional state aid to provide equal educational opportunity. Recommendations have been proposed ranging from a single state-operated school system to varying numbers of regionalized systems.

Of continuing and growing concern to the board has been the matter of department organization and staffing to meet the challenge of the new era in education. Buttressed with the recommendations of the commissioner and previous department studies, the board has made this item a priority in its recommendations to the Governor and to the General Assembly.

Generous outlays and fresh programs of the federal government have stimulated the vigor of the State of Rhode Island and its public officials. According to one report, in 1966, state departments, collectively, administered approximately $3 billion. In addition, from 1961 to 1966, federal programs have increased from 10 to 20 and "the size of appropriations has increased substantially in recent years" (35).

The emergence of a number of federal programs of the magnitude of the Elementary and Secondary Education Act of 1965 has placed an even greater responsibility for leadership and consultative services on the shoulders of the department. The implementation of the Title V provisions of ESEA has brought a significant growth in personnel and services in the state agency. As the board seeks to develop a statewide information data system and to automate department processes, the Title V legislation has been of great assistance. Rhode Island indeed welcomes this growing federal concern for the education of all its citizens.

Another program which has been of special interest to this state has been the development of the nationwide Compact for Education. Governor John Chafee has been among those early leaders in attempting to develop a common interest and pool of information among the states as they study the important matters of education. Rhode Island expects the compact to be a catalyst for many new and exciting innovations as the states move closer to each other in developing new concepts in education.

FOOTNOTES

1. Paul F. Gleeson, *Rhode Island: The Development of a Democracy* (Providence: Oxford Press, 1957), Frontispiece.

2. Charles Carroll, *Public Education in Rhode Island* (Providence: Board of Education, 1918), p. 14.
3. *Ibid.,* p. 78.
4. Commission on the Legal Structure of Rhode Island Public Education, *Schools for Our Children,* II (2 vols.; Providence: The Commission, 1942), 37.
5. *Ibid.*
6. *Ibid.,* p. 38.
7. *Ibid.*
8. *Ibid.,* p. 39.
9. Gleeson, *op. cit.,* p. 211.
10. Elmer J. Thompson, *A Study of the Constitution of Rhode Island and Providence Plantations* (Providence: Board of Education, 1956), p. 41.
11. Carroll, *op. cit.,* p. 129.
12. *Ibid.,* p. 184.
13. Rhode Island, *Acts and Resolves of the General Assembly* (1871).
14. Rhode Island Development Council, *This Is Providence, Rhode Island* (Providence: The Council, 1941), p. 3.
15. Rhode Island, *Acts and Resolves of the General Assembly* (1909).
16. "Annual Report of the Institute of Instruction," *Quarterly Journal of the Rhode Island Institute of Instruction,* IV (January 1931), 10-11. The Institute of Instruction was established by Henry Barnard in 1845 and was the forerunner of the present Rhode Island Education Association. It is the oldest professional organization of teachers and school administrators in the United States.
17. Gleeson, *op. cit.,* p. 60.
18. "Annual Report of the State Board," *Quarterly Journal of the Rhode Island Institute of Instruction,* V (April 1932), 5.
19. *Ibid.*
20. *Ibid.*
21. "Annual Report of the State Board," *Quarterly Journal of the Rhode Island Institute of Instruction,* VII (April 1934), 10.
22. *Ibid.*
23. *Ibid.*
24. *Ibid.*
25. *Ibid.*
26. *Ibid.*
27. *Ibid.*
28. "Annual Report of the State Board," *Quarterly Journal of the Rhode Island Institute of Instruction,* VI (July 1932), 6.
29. *Ibid.*
30. "Annual Report of the State Board," *Quarterly Journal of the Rhode Island Institute of Instruction,* VIII (January 1935), 6.
31. Rhode Island, *General Laws, as Amended* (1956), Title XVI, ch. 21, secs. 1-2.
32. Edward M. McEntee, *Laws of Rhode Island Relating to Education* (Providence: Oxford Press, 1948), p. 23.
33. Commission on the Legal Structure of Rhode Island Public Education, *Schools for Our Children,* I (2 vols.; Providence: The Commission, 1940), 11-15.
34. Department of Education, *Financing Tomorrow's Schools Today* (Providence: The Department, 1961), p. 22.
35. Nicholas Masters, "The Expanding Roles with Implications for State Education Departments," *The Emerging Role of State Education Departments,* ed. by Dick C. Rice and Powell E. Toth (Columbus: Ohio State University, 1967), p. 321.

BIBLIOGRAPHY

Public Documents

Rhode Island. *Acts and Resolves of the General Assembly* (1871, 1909).

—— *Constitution* (1843, with revisions).

—— *General Laws, as Amended* (1956).

Books and Pamphlets

Bicknell, Thomas W. *The History of the State of Rhode Island and Providence Plantations.* New York: American Historical Society, 1920.

Butts, R. Freeman. *A Cultural History of Western Education.* New York: McGraw-Hill Book Co., 1955.

Carroll, Charles. *Public Education in Rhode Island.* Providence: Board of Education, 1918.

—— *Rhode Island: Three Centuries of Democracy.* 3 vols. New York: Lewis Historical Publishing Co., 1932.

Commission on the Legal Structure of Rhode Island Public Education. *Schools for Our Children.* 2 vols. Providence: The Commission, 1940, 1942.

Department of Education. *Financing Tomorrow's Schools Today.* Providence: The Department, 1961.

Gleeson, Paul F. *Rhode Island: The Development of a Democracy.* Providence: Oxford Press, 1957.

McEntee, Edward M. *Laws of Rhode Island Relating to Education.* Providence: Oxford Press, 1948.

Masters, Nicholas. "The Expanding Roles with Implications for State Education Departments." *The Emerging Role of State Education Departments.* Edited by

Dick C. Rice and Powell E. Toth. Columbus: Ohio State University, 1967.

Providence Governmental Research Bureau. *Public Education in Rhode Island.* Providence: The Bureau, 1941.

Rhode Island Development Council. *This Is Providence, Rhode Island.* Providence: The Council, 1941.

Rhode Island Tercentenary Commission. *Rhode Island's Historic Background.* Providence: The Commission, 1936.

Stockwell, Thomas B. *A History of Public Education in Rhode Island, 1636-1876.* Providence: Board of Education, 1876.

Tanner, Earl C. *Rhode Island: A Brief History.* Providence: Board of Education, 1955.

Thompson, Elmer J. *A Study of the Constitution of Rhode Island and Providence Plantations.* Providence: Board of Education, 1956.

Reports

Board of Education. *Annual Reports.* Providence: The Board, 1932-60.

—— *The Financing of School Buildings.* Staff Study No. 4. Providence: The Board, 1955.

—— *Improving Education in Rhode Island.* Providence: The Board, 1947.

—— *Legal Arrangements Governing Educational Offerings and School Operation.* Staff Study No. 5. Providence: The Board, 1955.

—— *Levels of Local Support and Vigor of Local Taxation in Rhode Island Towns and Cities.* Staff Study No. 2. Providence: The Board, 1955.

—— *State and Local Financing of School Operation.* Staff Study No. 3. Providence: The Board, 1955.

—— *The Status of Public School Support in Rhode Island.* Staff Study No. 1. Providence: The Board, 1955.

Commissioner of Education. *Annual Reports.* Providence: Board of Education, 1960-68.

Institute of Instruction. *Annual Report.* Providence: The Institute, 1931.

Periodical

Quarterly Journal of the Rhode Island Institute of Instruction. January 1928 to 1955. Published by the Rhode Island Institute of Instruction, Providence, now the Rhode Island Education Association.

Appendix A

RHODE ISLAND CHIEF STATE SCHOOL OFFICERS

Commissioners of Public Schools

1845-49	Henry Barnard
1849-55	Elisha R. Potter
1855-58	Robert Allyn
1858-59	John Kingsbury
1859-61	Joshua B. Chapin
1861-63	Henry Rousmaniere
1863-69	Joshua B. Chapin
1869-75	Thomas W. Bicknell
1875-1905	Thomas B. Stockwell
1905-20	Walter E. Ranger

Commissioner of Education

1920-35	Walter E. Ranger

Directors of Education

1935-47	James F. Rockett
1947-51	Michael F. Walsh

Commissioners of Education

1951-63	Michael F. Walsh
1963-	William P. Robinson, Jr.

Appendix B

Chart I.--CHANGING SCHOOL STANDARDS IN RHODE ISLAND

F A D I N G

EARLY 20th CENTURY

MASS INSTRUCTION METHODS PREDOMINANT. LITTLE OR NO RESPONSIBILITY IS ASSUMED BY TEACHERS FOR THE LEARNING OF INDIVIDUAL CHILDREN.

CHILDREN TESTED FOR REJECTION IS CENTRAL STRATEGY OF THE SCHOOL.

VERY LIMITED OPPORTUNITY FOR THE UNUSUAL CHILD, PARTICULARLY IN LOWER GRADES. DROPOUT RATE OFTEN OVER 50%.

LITTLE OR NO COMMUNITY PARTICIPATION IN SCHOOL ACTIVITIES.

TEACHING MATERIALS AND EQUIPMENT SPARSE.

DISCIPLINE: TRAINING TO ACT IN ACCORDANCE WITH ARBITRARY RULES.

D O M I N A N T

MIDDLE 20th CENTURY

MASS METHODS OF INSTRUCTION DOMINATE BUT WITH VARYING DEGREES OF IDENTIFICATION OF INDIVIDUAL DIFFERENCES AND LEARNING NEEDS.

EMERGENCE OF SPECIAL GROUPS (RETARDED, HANDICAPPED, GIFTED) FOR EMPHASIS ON INDIVIDUAL LEARNING IN SMALL CLASSES.

BROADENING CURRICULUM AND OPPORTUNITIES FOR THE UNUSUAL CHILD.

DROPOUT RATE OVER 30%.

E M E R G I N G

LATE 20th CENTURY

RESPONSIBILITY FOR INDIVIDUAL LEARNING OF ALL CHILDREN IS THE CENTRAL STRATEGY OF THE SCHOOL. MASS METHODS OF INSTRUCTION NOT DOMINANT. CHILDREN GROUPED FOR INSTRUCTION BUT TAUGHT AS INDIVIDUALS.

OPPORTUNITY FOR THE UNUSUAL CHILD IS EXTENSIVE, PARTICULARLY IN THE LOWER GRADES. CHILDREN TESTED FOR DIAGNOSTIC PURPOSES RATHER THAN FOR REJECTION.

DROPOUT RATE NEGLIGIBLE.

EXTENSIVE COMMUNITY PARTICIPATION IN SCHOOL ACTIVITIES.

ADEQUATE TEACHING MATERIALS.

DISCIPLINE: ORDERLY GROWTH OF THE INDIVIDUAL THROUGH INCREASED RELIANCE ON ONE'S SELF AND ONE'S OWN POWERS.

TYPICAL CLASS SIZE RANGES FROM 30 TO 45 PUPILS.

4 - 6 PROFESSIONAL PERSONNEL PER 100 PUPILS

SALARIES ARE NINE-TENTHS OF TOTAL COSTS.

SALARY RANGES:
MIN. $4,000 TO $4,500
MAX. $6,000 TO $6,500

TYPICAL CLASS SIZE RANGES FROM LESS THAN 15 PUPILS IN SPECIAL CLASSES TO 35 IN REGULAR CLASSES.

5 - 7 PROFESSIONAL PERSONNEL PER 100 PUPILS

SALARIES ARE THREE-FOURTHS OF TOTAL COSTS.

SALARY RANGES:
MIN. $4,500 TO $5,000
MAX. $6,500 TO $8,000

S C H O O L P A T T E R N

NO TYPICAL CLASS SIZE. "CLASSES" RANGE FROM ONE PUPIL TO OVER 100 PUPILS.

6 - 8 PROFESSIONAL PERSONNEL PER 100 PUPILS

SALARIES ARE TWO-THIRDS OF TOTAL COSTS.

SALARY RANGES:
MIN. $4,500 TO $5,000
MAX. $7,000 TO $12,000

Costs Per Child $300 $400 $500 $600 $700 $800

Source: Division of Research and Planning.

Appendix B

Chart II.--RHODE ISLAND, 60 YEARS OF IMPROVING TEACHER TRAINING

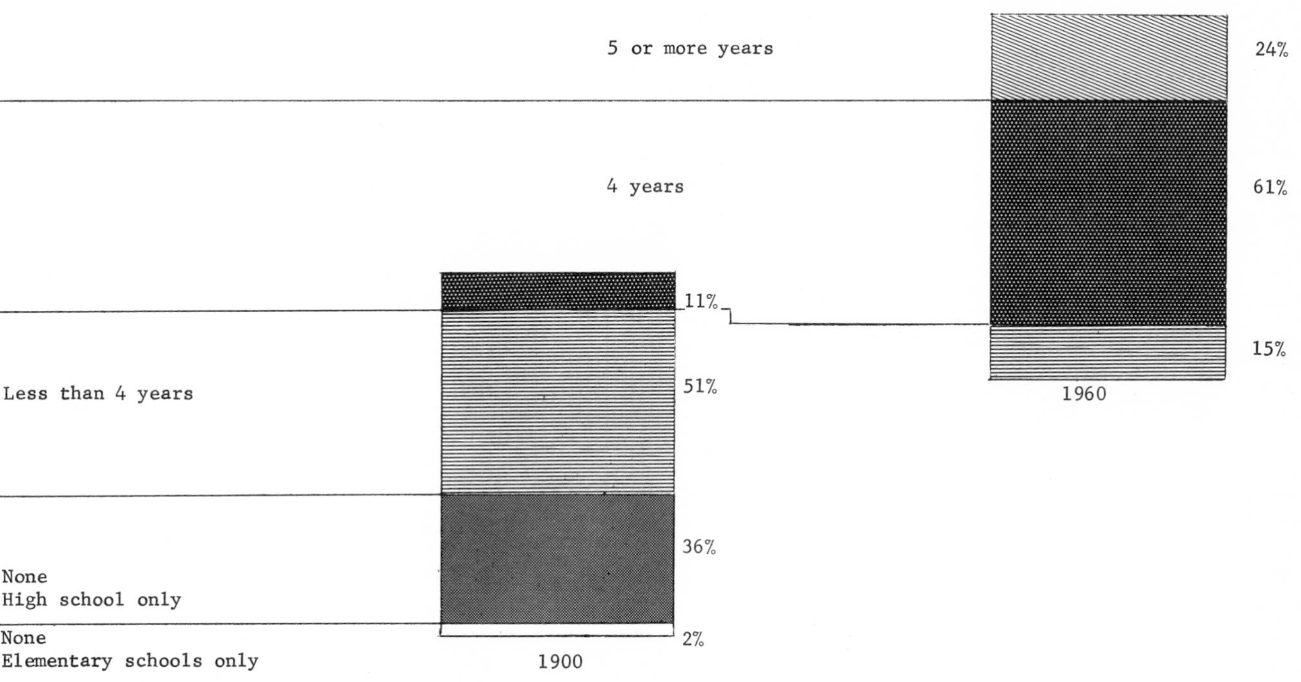

Source: Division of Research and Planning.

Appendix B

Chart III.--RHODE ISLAND DEPARTMENT OF EDUCATION, 1947

Director of Education

Assistant Director for Vocational Education	Assistant Director for Administration	Assistant Director for Instruction	Principal, Rhode Island School for the Deaf
Supervisor, Home Economics Education	Supervisor, School Plant and Transportation	Supervisor, Secondary Education	Staff of the School
Supervisor, Trade and Industrial Education	Supervisor, Research and Statistics	Supervisor, Elementary Education	
Supervisor, Vocational Agriculture Education	Fiscal and Personnel Officer	Supervisor, Adult Education	
Supervisor, Adult Vocational Education	Certification Officer	Supervisor, Health, Physical Education and Recreation	
Supervisor, Distributive Occupations		Supervisor, School Lunches	
Supervisor, Guidance Services*		Nutritionist	
Supervisor, Rehabilitation		Operating Staff	
Assistant Supervisor			
Three Counselors			
Two Instructors			

*Guidance service was placed in the Vocational Division because Federal vocational funds are available to pay one half the supervisor's salary. Since Guidance includes but is not limited to vocational education, the supervisor might work more effectively if placed in one of the other divisions when such are established. Moreover such action would not now affect availability of Federal funds.

Chart IV.--RHODE ISLAND DEPARTMENT OF EDUCATION, 1965

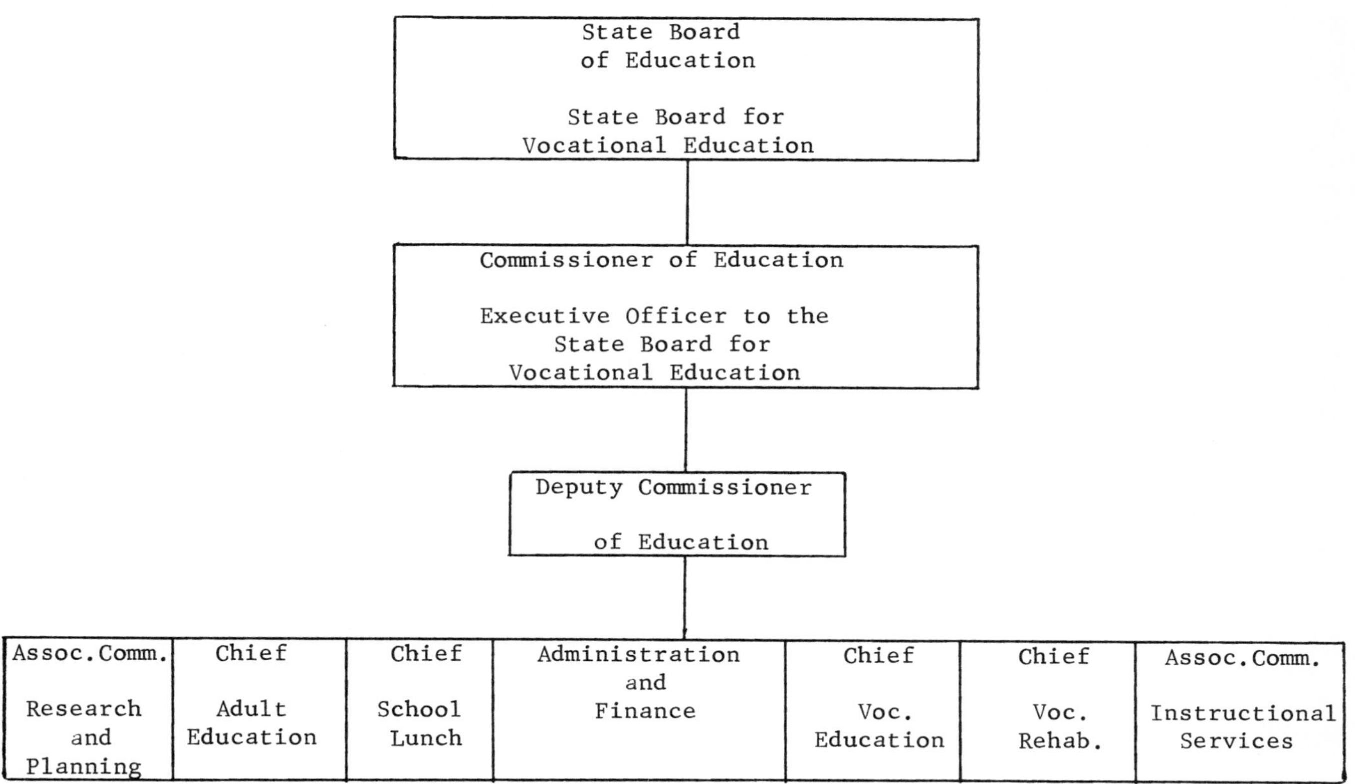

Education is a responsibility of the state as prescribed in the state constitution. By legislative act, this state responsibility is placed in the Department of Education headed by a Board of Education. The Board formulates and adopts all basic educational policies which are executed by the Commissioner of Education. The powers and duties of the Board and the Commissioner are established by law.

In April of 1959, the Department was reorganized by the Board as shown above, and the organization was approved by the Governor as required by law. It provides for the Commissioner a staff composed of a Deputy Commissioner, two Associate Commissioners, each of whom heads a major division, and four chiefs, each of whom heads a minor division.

Appendix C

Table 1.–SALARY SCALE FOR THE YEARS 1966-67 AND 1967-68 (MONTHLY)

Categories	Lowest			Intermediate			Highest
Normal	$235	$255	$275	$295	$315	$335	$350
B.A.	300	320	340	360	380	400	420
M.A.	370	390	410	430	450	470	490
Ph.D.	475	495	515	535	555	575	595

Table 2.–SALARY SCALE FOR THE YEARS FOLLOWING 1968-69 (MONTHLY)

Categories	Lowest			Intermediate				Highest
Normal	$250	$270	$290	$310	$330	$350	$370	$370
B.A.	325	350	375	400	425	450	475	500
M.A.	400	425	450	475	500	525	550	575
Ph.D.	525	550	575	600	625	650	675	700

Appendix D

STATE BOARD OF EDUCATION

Powers and Duties of the Board – (General Laws (1956), 16-14, Vol. III, p. 495)

The State Board of Education shall have the power and shall be required –

To be responsible for the formation and adoption of state educational policies.

To adopt standards and qualifications for the certification of teachers and to provide for the issuance of certificates.

To establish rules for the approval and accrediting of secondary schools.

To review the subjects and courses of study to be taught and instructional standards to be maintained in the elementary and secondary schools.

To be responsible for the distribution of state school funds.

To study, review, and make recommendations for the design, construction, and location of school buildings when so requested by any school authority.

To recommend standards for school libraries and to provide school library services.

To make recommendations relative to the transportation of pupils, school bus routes, time schedules, and other matters pertaining to pupil transportation, together with the right to cause every city and town school department to submit its respective school bus routes, schedules, and other matters pertinent hereto.

To enforce the provisions of all laws relating to schools and education.

To decide appeals from decisions of the commissioner.

To prescribe forms for the use of local school committees and local officers.

To adopt and require standard accounting and auditing procedures for local school officers.

To provide for the organization of the State Department of Education and to establish divisions, bureaus, or other administrative units within the department with the approval of the Governor.

THE COMMISSIONER OF EDUCATION

Duties of the Commissioner – (General Laws (1956), 16-1-5, Vol. III, p. 497)

It shall be the duty of the commissioner of education –

To carry out the policies and program formulated by the State Board of Education.

To evaluate credentials of applicants for certificates, to verify that the certification of teachers is in accordance with law and established standards, and to issue such certificates at the direction of the board.

To certify the approval of accredited schools.

To recommend to the board an outline of the subjects and courses of study and the instructional standards for elementary and secondary schools.

To approve the distribution of state school funds in accordance with law and the regulations of the board.

To verify that school sites and school building plans are in accordance with law and regulations.

To exercise supervision over school libraries and library services.

To certify that school bus routes and schedules and all contracts for pupil transportation conform with provisions of law and the rules and regulations of the board.

To require the observance of all laws relating to schools and education.

To interpret school law and to decide such controversies as may be appealed to him from decisions of local school committees.

To prepare and recommend standard forms for the use of local schools.

To prepare, with the assistance of the department of administration, a manual of standard financial records and procedures for local school officers.

To have general supervision of the State Department of Education and to appoint the several officers and employees of the department subject to the provisions of the state merit system act.

41 South Carolina

DEPARTMENT OF EDUCATION
Frank M. Kirk

Contents

DEVELOPING A SCHOOL SYSTEM

The Free Schools

Pauper Schools. Some time before 1696, a private citizen, Richard Morgan, left money for founding a free school in South Carolina (1). The Free School Act of 1710 stated, however, that such legacies had not been put to proper use, which was one of the reasons for its passage.

The Society for the Propagation of the Gospel in Foreign Parts, incorporated in 1701 in London under auspices of the Church of England, sent missionaries to teach in the province the following year. Since this group attempted to fill the needs of the Negro and Indian slaves as well as those of the wealthy landowners, it was rebuffed by the aristocracy (2). Despite this antipathy, private schools were established and did flourish, mainly to provide a Christian education. "The knowledge of grammar and the latin and greek languages, and of mathematics, could be obtained in Carolina at any time after 1712, or the 42nd year subsequent to the settlement of the province" (3).

The Free School Act of 1710 stated in its preamble:

> John Douglas should be preceptor or teacher of said school; and that on his ceasing to be so the commissioners should appoint his successor who should be of the religion of the church of England, and capable of teaching the latin and greek languages—that the teacher should have a salary of £100 per annum, to be paid out of the public treasury, and the use of lands and buildings belonging to the school, for which he was to teach twelve scholars, to be nominated by the commissioners, free of expense; and for all others he was to receive at the rate of £4 per annum (4).

The reference to free tuition for those nominated by the commissioners tells the story of the state's educational program for more than two centuries. South Carolinians did not like the free education because of their prejudice against "pauper" schools. The wealthy continued to send their children to private schools, followed by the grand tour of Europe; the "poor but proud" either sent their children to tuition schools for a limited time or they did not send them at all, and only the paupers attended the free schools. "The first public school in America, in the accepted sense, existed in Charleston, at least as early as 1743" (5). One author describes these schools as follows:

> The Church of England . . . conceived public education, aside from collegiate education, as intended for orphans and children of the poor, and as a charity which the State was under little or no obligation in providing. All children of the middle and upper classes of society attended private or church schools or were taught by tutors in the home, and for such instruction paid a proper tuition fee. Paupers and orphans, in limited numbers and for a limited time, were provided with some form of useful education at the expense of the Church and of the State (6).

By the end of the Revolution, there were 11 public schools, 3 charitable grammar schools, and 8 private schools in the state's 24 parishes and districts. Most of the 200 teachers were from England.

It was not until 1811 that Stephen Elliott introduced into the Legislature "an act to establish free schools throughout the state." Thus, Elliott became known as the "father of the first public school system in South Carolina" (7). The Legislature appropriated $300 a year for each school and provided for all pupils to receive elementary instruction free of charge, preference being given to poor orphans and children of indigent parents. The act bore as little fruit as the provincial act 100 years earlier, probably because it favored paupers.

Reverend Thrummel of All Saints Parish in 1829 expressed the state's view of public education as a charity:

> It is bounty intended for the poor. The rich will not avail themselves of it, since they do not need it, while the poor will rather keep their children at home altogether, rather than by sending them to free schools, attach to them, as they think and feel, the stigma of being poor and of receiving an education as paupers (8).

The primary detriment to the free public school system was "that its need was not felt by the people" (9).

The will of John De La Howe in 1796 provided for the first school to teach manual labor in the United States. The following year, an agricultural or farm school opened "to receive and train free of charge neglected and dependent children" (10). For many years, the Agricultural Society of South Carolina operated it but later gave title to the Legislature, and in 1918, it was operated directly under the Legislature. In November 1937, a fire completely destroyed the school. It has been rebuilt and now is state-supported.

C. G. Memminger and the Charleston Schools. Despite the popular prejudice against public schools, free schools were accepted in Charleston. In 1855, Christopher Gustavus Memminger instituted a plan for improving the city schools that lasted until February 1865, when the last call for troops to fight on the side of South Carolina in the Civil War took every white male from 16 to 60. "Under his wise and progressive leadership the common school system of that city, with the Charleston College, Citadel Academy, Orphan House and High School, had given to Charleston the educational distinction it now holds among the large cities of the Southern States" (11).

In 1803, the year Memminger was born in Württemberg, Germany, his father died; his mother emigrated to America 4 years later with her parents. Mrs. Memminger died shortly after reaching Charleston, and the grandparents left for Philadelphia, leaving the boy in the Orphan House in Charleston. When he was 11, he was adopted by Thomas Bennett, later a Governor of South Carolina, and applied for citizenship in 1824. Memminger became an outstanding attorney and served as secretary of the treasury of the Confederate states.

In 1834, together with W. J. Bennett, son of the Governor, Memminger made a study of South Carolina's schools. He made many trips to the North, especially to the New England states. As a result, he was instrumental in having the Legislature pass an act permitting the Charleston municipal government to levy a special tax for educational purposes. By 1856, the Charleston school system, patterned on the New York plan, was well established, with heads of the schools brought in from the North.

The first training school for teachers in South Carolina, the Memminger Normal School, was established in 1859 in Charleston. It was organized to train female teachers for the state, and student teaching was offered in the elementary schools of Charleston for a period of 8 weeks. Certificates were awarded at the end of a 3-year course. The course was based on the Lancastrian, or monitorial, system where abler pupils helped with instruction, and was along classical lines although students learned the theory and practice of teaching.

At this time, there was a new spirit toward the state's educational institutions. Before the American Revolution, many of South Carolina's youth had been educated in Great Britain. But now the feeling was different—Great Britain no longer was the mother country. There was a marked increase in the academies, and the records of the graduates indicate that the training was excellent.

In 1855, at the invitation of the Governor, Henry Barnard of Connecticut visited Charleston and aroused the people's interest in educational conditions by his earnest and eloquent presentation of the school system he had developed in the North. Memminger took advantage of this interest to petition the Legislature to establish a common school system for the city. For the first time, the Legislature passed an act giving the commissioners power to impose a local tax on property, in addition to the state fund.

In July 1856, C. G. Memminger gave a masterly explanation of the new law at the inauguration of the common school system for Charleston. He pointed out that the old system of 1811 could not be improved as long as a confession of pauperism was required. Teachers were brought in from the North, and the schools were graded according to the Massachusetts plan. By 1860, there were 4,000 pupils in the Charleston schools.

Many serious-minded people, though engaged in the more critical issues of the time, recognized the importance of public schools. When a bill appropriating funds for a State Department of Education, to promote the development of a system of free schools, was introduced in the Legislature in 1861, an eloquent speech in support of the measure by James H. Carlisle, a young Spartanburg teacher, convinced the lower House to pass it immediately. The Senate, however, considered the measure an unwarranted extravagance and defeated it.

Thus, the history of the free school movement in South Carolina from 1811 to 1865 illustrates the difficulty of establishing a system of universal education in an aristocratic state. One observer reported: "In no country or Commonwealth has there been witnessed so remarkable a spectacle of unanimity of purpose among the leaders of public opinion on the subject of popular education, with almost utter failure of results, as in South Carolina" (12).

South Carolina endured the ordeals of war and entered the Reconstruction period with the state controlled by the Republicans through a carpetbagger government. It was during Reconstruction that this Republican government adopted a constitution which first recognized free public education in the state. Thus, this Constitution of 1868 marked a decided era in South Carolina's educational history: It laid the organizational basis for public education enterprise which has survived to this day.

The First State Superintendent, J. K. Jillson

The man largely responsible for these provisions was Justus Kendall Jillson, a delegate to the constitutional convention, who had been persuaded by the Massachusetts Freedman's Bureau to teach in a Negro school in Camden, South Carolina. He was responsible for the constitution's article on education, providing for a state superintendent and a State Board of Education; property and poll taxes earmarked for education; a free public normal school to train teachers; educational institutions for the blind; a state reform school; and a state university. The constitution also included compulsory school attendance for all children between the ages of 6 and 16 years, but it is probable that a compulsory attendance law was never actually in effect. The constitution stated that no law to that effect should be passed until a system of public schools "has been thoroughly and completely organized," and facilities made available to all inhabitants for the free education of their children. There is no evidence that such an organization was ever completed, nor is there evidence that facilities for a free education were afforded to all.

Jillson himself, who had become State Senator and chairman of the Senate's Committee on Education, was nominated for the state superintendency by the Republican state nominating convention and defeated his Democratic opponent, J. A. Leland. Although a Massachusetts carpetbagger, Jillson was never touched by the scandals that tainted many in the Reconstruction government. Described by a Charleston paper in 1869 as "puffy, fat, broad, wordy, and well informed" (13), he was scrupulously honest and devoted to education. Even Jillson's political enemies acknowledged that he labored as hard and conscientiously as any state officer to perfect a plan that would be acceptable to the public and fulfill the purposes of his department.

Despite his efforts and contributions, Jillson struggled against insuperable odds. Although he was still a member of the Senate, the new state superintendent could not get the assembly to fulfill the terms of the 1868 constitution by introducing legislation to establish free schools throughout the state until February 1870. Even the Charleston paper expressed its regrets that this admirable bill had failed.

When the "Act To Establish and Maintain a System of Free Common Schools for the State of South Carolina" finally did pass, Superintendent Jillson found he did not have sufficient money to run the schools. Despite his urgings, the Legislature in 1870 appropriated only $50,000 for school purposes, less than 25 cents per pupil (14). By 1873, the annual school appropriation was up to $300,000, and the school population had increased by more than 33,000 pupils. But the unpaid balances of state school appropriations for the previous 3 years amounted to over $322,000, and most teachers had been waiting that long to receive their salaries (15). By the end of Jillson's term in 1876, the school system was on the verge of collapse. This was attributed in large measure to the Reconstruction government's squandering these appropriations for other purposes and to the incompetent, dishonest, and overpaid country commissioners' absorbing a large part of the available funds (16).

Jillson faced other frustrations in his earnest efforts to build a good state school system. As a strong abolitionist, he had been responsible in large measure for the constitution's including the following provision: "All the public schools, colleges and universities of this State, supported in whole or in part by the public funds, shall be free and open to all the children and youths of the State, without regard to race or color" (17). Mixed schools were a practical impossibility. The majority of the superintendents reported that Negro as well as white parents preferred separate schools. The entire body of trustees and faculty resigned from the School for Deaf, Dumb, and Blind when it was ordered to receive Negro students in the same classes and tables as the whites. When no others could be found to take their places, the school was closed for 3 years.

Jillson reported to the General Assembly that probably no state in the Union was so cursed with poor teachers as was South Carolina. He charged that the county boards of examiners granted certificates to people with poor moral attributes. He asked that the teaching profession be regarded equal in dignity, honor, and importance to that of theology, medicine, or law. But the General Assembly ignored his pleas.

Hugh S. Thompson Established a State System

Jillson was not renominated on the Republican ticket in 1876, the year marking the fall of the Radical regime (18). The Republican candidate, John R. Tolbert, was defeated by the Democratic nominee, Hugh S. Thompson. Thompson, a native Charlestonian from one of the oldest families in the state, was a Southern gentleman of culture, modesty, noble bearing, and attractive manners. His background for this position was excellent. He graduated from South Carolina Military Academy and taught in that institution until 1861. After serving in the Confederate Army in the defense of Charleston, he became head of the Classical School at Columbia (19). When he took office in 1877, along with the newly elected Governor, General Wade Hampton, it was possible to begin carrying out the 1868 constitution.

Thompson and his clerk comprised the entire working force of the department when, on May 1, 1877, he took the first steps actually to establish a state public school system. He faced some of the same problems as his predecessor, such as incompetent county commissioners, the almost total absence of teachers in the country districts, quarrels over locating schools in partially settled neighborhoods, and the extreme poverty of the people. On top of this, his predecessor's efforts increased the old opposition to the public schools. A large part of the money collected from the poll tax the first year had to be used to pay school debts of the previous administration.

But with the hardy support of Governor Hampton, Thompson set about gathering the ablest schoolmen in the state to help him formulate a new school law. He studied the laws then in force and noticed glaring deficiencies, particularly in duties and powers of county school commissioners and local trustees. He studied laws of other states and made his recommendations in his first annual report in 1877. The Legislature passed the new school law in December 1877, but it did not go into effect until the following year.

Under the 1878 law, the State Board of Examiners, composed of the state superintendent and four persons appointed by the Governor, became the central authority. The board had the authority to interpret school laws, to set up rules for examining prospective teachers, and to adopt a uniform set of textbooks, and had other powers and duties as are held by the present State Board of Education.

By assisting Thompson in checking plunder and incompetency, it enabled him to lay the foundations for a system of public schools in the state. It established and graded the elementary schools for both races and started normal institutes and schools to train teachers.

It was very difficult to induce the people to levy the necessary taxes to provide good teachers. However, several followed Charleston's example and adopted plans of local taxation. One by one, the towns and counties fell into line, until finally voluntary taxation became almost statewide, and the people wrote provisions for a local tax into the Constitution of 1895. In 1878, the General Assembly levied a 2-mill tax for school purposes, which, with the poll tax, remained the sole support of the public schools. The Legislature made no appropriations except for the State Department of Education.

Superintendent Thompson and the board, as one of its first acts in May 1878, commended the white teachers in the Negro schools and took steps to secure better teachers. A series of summer institutes was initiated. These, in part, prompted the University of South Carolina to offer teacher-training courses in 1882; 5 years later, it opened a statewide normal school. In his 1878 report, Thompson stated: "Teachers' Conventions, Teachers' Institutes, and Normal Schools are powerful agencies which, if properly employed, will raise the profession of teaching to the dignity to which, by its importance, it is entitled" (20).

In his last annual report, Thompson pointed out that the schools had increased from 2,493 to 3,183, and the number of teachers from 2,674 to 3,413. By comparing the number of schools to teachers it is evident that the majority were one-teacher schools. Attendance had increased from 102,396 to 145,974, which was the largest number of pupils ever attending the state's public schools. The average school term was 4 months. In assessing Thompson's contribution, one historian states:

> In the face of political and social chaos, with the white people opposed to public schools, afraid of Negro domination, disgusted and angry; and with the Negroes suspicious and sullen, the whites very poor and the Negroes all paupers, Thompson undertook the task of building a system of schools on the basis of the original provision in the constitution formed by the hated Reconstruction government. It took splendid courage and far-seeing statesmanship to do this. With firmness, tact, and patience, by earnest teaching and wise action, Thompson succeeded in six years in inducing the people of South Carolina to accept his plans for universal education. He will always stand as one of the wisest, strongest, and most devoted men of that troubled period (21).

Asbury S. Coward succeeded Thompson in 1882 and served 4 rather uneventful years. It was during this time and that of his successor, James Henry Rice, that Benjamin R. Tillman led a movement of the "plain people" against the "aristocrats." Tillman, afterwards Governor and Senator, and his farmers were primarily interested in agriculture and industrial education, and they awakened the people to their importance.

Designating Authority

W. D. Mayfield was elected state superintendent in 1890, and the 8 years he served were the longest term of any superintendent up to that date. It was during his term that the Constitution of 1895 was adopted, the one under which South Carolina has continued to operate. Although many people had lamented the Constitution of 1868 when it was adopted by a Radical group, nothing had been done about a new constitution for 28 years, 18 of them when Democrats were in power. Actually, the Constitution of 1895 made no essential changes in the provisions for public education, but it did provide for separate schools for the white and Negro races and authorized a 3-mill tax in every county for school purposes.

The following year, the General Assembly passed an "Act To Declare the Free School Law of the State" (22). Although the law was slightly amended 4 years later, it remained a fundamental law until further revisions in 1964 (23). This act defined the duties, responsibilities, and powers of the superintendent, the state board, the county board, and the trustees. It further provided that if the 3-mill tax, the poll tax, and the net income from the alcoholic beverage tax should not yield sufficient revenue for the schools, the Legislature could levy additional taxes as necessary.

In 1898, John J. McMahan became state superintendent. Although little occurred during his one term in office, his reports do throw some light on the conditions at the time. In 1900, he complained:

> It is a misnomer to say that we have a system of public schools. In the actual working of the great majority of schools in this State, there is no system, no orderly organization. Each County supports its own schools with practically no help from the State as a whole. Each District has as poor school as its people will tolerate–and in some Districts anything will be tolerated (24).

In his report of 1902, he stated—perhaps with justification—"the errors in the County Superintendents' reports almost destroy one's beliefs in the truth of statistics" (25).

THE ADMINISTRATION OF O. B. MARTIN

The Awakening of the Public to Education

A change in attitude toward public education as the responsibility of citizens was being felt more and more strongly with the beginning of the new century. The idea, prevalent for more than two centuries, that "free schools" were pauper schools and that those who could afford it should patronize private tutors and academies was changing toward one of public support. Previously, little or no thought was given to the masses and their educational needs, except by the Reconstructionists.

In 1853, James H. Thornwell (26) had written a much publicized letter to Governor John L. Manning detailing the importance of the college and its leadership in all educational matters. In his first annual report, the new state superintendent refers to this letter and quotes much of it. He strongly defends "common schools" and argues the cause of public education. He includes this quotation from Dr. Thornwell's letter: "If we must dispense with one or the other (public schools or colleges), I have no hesitation in saying that on the score of public good alone it were wiser to dispense with the schools. One sun is better than a thousand stars" (27). This philosophy was not restricted to Dr. Thornwell, but was typical. Dr. Thornwell, however, did believe in public education and supported the schools strongly.

Superintendent Martin was sensitive to the public sentiment and realized it was ready for change. Accordingly, in one of the early acts of his administration, he called an educational conference which met in the Senate chamber in Columbia on April 11, 1903. The invitation included a number of educators and those interested in the schools to discuss some of the problems facing education, particularly the need for more funds. The Southern Education Foundation, along with the Peabody Fund, showed keen interest in the education welfare of the Southern states and agreed to underwrite the meeting. The conference, the first on record of its kind to be held in the state, was well attended. Described at length in the Charleston *News and Courier*, and other newspapers, it received wide publicity.

Within a week, Winthrop College called a second conference to be held in Columbia from April 14 to 16, this time for county superintendents. Martin, delighted with both meetings, stated:

> To my mind, the Conference in Columbia and the Conference of County Superintendents at Winthrop College the following week, are among the most important meetings ever held in the State . . . . Both meetings were unanimous in the belief that the most immediate and pressing need is the development of the rural schools, and they further resolved to contribute all possible aid to that end (28).

Educators stressed the importance of rural schools, which, from that time, received increasing support from the Legislature. Although the need was widespread, Martin is responsible for publicizing it and should be given credit for much that was accomplished. Thus was born the "educational campaign," as it was known, mentioned in subsequent annual reports.

The General Assembly reacted quickly during the following session and passed two items of legislation, both designed to improve rural schools. In February 1904, the assembly enacted "An Act To Encourage the Establishment of Libraries in the Public Schools of the Rural Districts" (29). The following month, the State Board of Education adopted rules and regulations to implement the new law, and in his 1905 report Martin reported that 600 libraries had already been established under the act.

The same session of the assembly adopted legislation that inaugurated state aid for building schools in South Carolina. The law, strictly limited to rural schools, reimbursed county boards $50 for each $100 raised, but no school was to receive more than $350. Martin said the act was one "which I think will encourage the establishment of many new schoolhouses with better equipment" (30). But the law actually spawned many small, inadequate schools, which could be eliminated only by consolidation 50 years later.

Superintendent Martin expressed an interest in consolidation as early as 1905. Many educators were concerned because too many little schools were being constructed, and they believed that a number of districts should merge. Local interests prevented such consolidations, and schools already established hesitated to merge with newer institutions.

The state had instituted a uniform adoption of textbooks in 1882, but with only one text for each subject or grade. The law permitted a 10-percent markup over list price, and sometimes the markup was on both a county and local basis. As a result, people were paying prices that varied considerably from the list prices. Martin suggested that the state establish a central depository (31).

With so much attention focused on education, the General Assembly was amenable to new ideas. In 1906, there was organized at Winthrop College the School Improvement Association, which accomplished much in strengthening rural schools and improving plants and facilities. Formed by Winthrop and the State Department of Education, the association became a part of the department and remained active for 20 years, financed by an annual appropriation from the Legislature.

At the same time, in 1906, the Kindergarten Association of South Carolina organized to secure legal recognition of kindergartens, particularly to secure legislation similar to that enacted in Florida. Despite its efforts, this association accomplished little as the state was not yet ready to assume the burden. It is still not ready, for although there is permissive legislation allowing districts to form kindergartens (32), there is no state aid for them, and financial support remains the responsibility of the districts. The movement is still under way, with the South Carolina Education Association and other groups exerting pressure on the Legislature. A number of kindergartens have been organized and are functioning under the Elementary and Secondary Education Act of 1965, but these are limited to the underprivileged.

A third movement should be mentioned: the continuation of summer schools and summer institutes for teachers. Begun during Thompson's administration, they received greater emphasis during Martin's term. The summer schools were well staffed and attracted many teachers. Unquestionably they greatly improved the competency of teachers and brought new ideas into the state.

The High School Act of 1907

After Martin's election, there was a growing interest in public high schools, particularly where there were none. Municipalities, willing to levy taxes for their support, had established high schools, but the state's emphasis was on rural high schools. Education leaders had carried on an active campaign in the General Assembly to establish and improve the state's high schools. Finally, the assembly passed the High School Act in February 1907, although appropriations were not made until the following July. Fifty-eight new high schools were established under this law during the first 5 months of the 1907-1908 school session.

The first state appropriation (renewable annually) for public schools in South Carolina amounted to $50,000, but only $28,000 was expended the first year. The State Board of Education also was designated as the State High School Board, and for the first time the State Department of Education added an employee (although part-time), when W. H. Hand, of the University of South Carolina, was named state high school inspector.

The high schools were categorized according to 4-year, 3-year, and 2-year terms. Under the law and according to the rules of the state board the state furnished financial assistance only to those schools having a minimum enrollment of 25 pupils, taught by at least two teachers.

Some of the schools started industrial and commercial education at the turn of the century, but Superintendent Martin addressed a letter to county superintendents in October 1907, urging that all schools include the teaching of agriculture as soon as possible. The Act of 1909 strengthened the High School Act of 1907 by including city high schools in its provisions and by removing some of the limitations, particularly the restrictions on communities with less than 1,000.

The High School Act focused on rural high schools. It paid little attention to curriculum and did not adopt a state-approved course of study. Teachers were poorly trained, and there were no true certification requirements. As a result, the preparation varied widely for the few who attempted college. The rapid increase in the number of small high schools compounded problems that were long in solving. Yet a start had been made.

Martin's Final Annual Report

Superintendent Martin's 1907 report pointed out that between 1869 and 1907 enrollment increased from 28,409 to 314,399 and the number of teachers from 528 to 6,228. Expenditures of $77,949 in his first year in office rose to $1,853,572 during his final year, while the number of schools increased from 630 to 4,995–mostly rural, one- and two-teacher schools.

THE ADMINISTRATION OF J. E. SWEARINGEN

The Man and His Times

Capitalizing on the new mood of the people towards the public schools and their willingness to support them, Martin's successor, J. E. Swearingen, carried on his movement with vigor. Swearingen inherited the new schools established under the High School Act of 1907 and did much to strengthen them during his 14 years in office. During this time, legal changes developed rapidly, and there were the beginnings of state school administration. He was at the helm during World War I and the 1920-21 depression, which also saw the emergence of the dreaded boll weevil. This period also saw the beginning of compulsory attendance and the start of the tremendous impact of federal aid to education.

Swearingen, totally blind from an accident in his youth, had made a brilliant record as a mathematics major at the University of South Carolina. His uncanny memory enabled him to amass an incredible amount of information that he could recall instantly. As state superintendent his secretary would read to him the correspondence, which he would file in order in his pocket. He would dictate his answers from memory concisely and without error. The annual reports also show this remarkable ability to acquire, retain, and transmit detailed information stored in memory.

There are many stories about Superintendent Swearingen's keen memory and touch. For instance, on one occasion he walked into a supervisor's office where a county superintendent stood whose home Swearingen had visited several years before. The county superintendent remarked that he had brought his wife along. Swearingen greeted her and then remarked that she had put on some weight. The astonished woman admitted she had and asked him how he knew it. "Oh," he replied easily, "by the feel of your palm."

He insisted that all office doors remain open and checked each morning to see who was late. On one occasion a supervisor came in quite early to do some work and closed the door behind him for privacy. As usual, Swearingen felt his way to each office and, finding the supervisor's door closed, was heard to say quite audibly, "Damn him, he is late."

While Swearingen took every opportunity to ask and even demand needed legislation, he was quick to give the General Assembly full credit for enacting good educational laws. Perhaps it was his ability to recognize sound legislation that kept him in rapport with the lawmakers. His opening statement in the report for 1910 was succinct: "The legislative session of 1910 was emphatically educational" (33). Statements of a similar nature are found frequently among his other annual reports.

Legal Changes in Finance

The Constitution of 1868 had placed the responsibility for education squarely on the county, and this was repeated in the Constitution of 1895. With the development of schools in the larger cities and towns, townships gradually became the administrative unit instead of the counties, and they requested legislation permitting special taxes.

Commencing with the passage of the High School Act of 1907, counties were split into districts, and it was these districts which gradually became the administrative unit of state finance. Although the Constitution of 1895 attempted to outlaw special legislation, it was powerless to control what happened during the years that followed.

Districts were created in such rapid order that by 1922 the reports listed 1,993 in the state. However, 46 of these districts were located in two counties and consequently are reported twice; the actual number of administrative districts in the state was 1,947. Consolidation gradually reduced the number of districts to 1,220 by the year 1947. This reduction came about chiefly by dissolution of districts without schools. Through the efforts of the State Department of Education and the Educational Finance Commission (created by the 1951 Legislature), the number was drastically reduced to 107 (34).

In his 1910 report, Swearingen pointed out that the most significant act passed by that General Assembly was No. 585: "A Joint Resolution To Provide for a Commission To Examine and Revise the School Law of the State and To Recommend Changes in the Same" (35). The resolution passed unanimously in both the House and the Senate, although it had met with scant consideration the previous year before the legislators had studied it.

Ten years later, nothing had been done to revise the school law, although the assembly had appointed a committee to draft a new school code. "Unfortunately this recommendation [to draft a new school code] was not approved. The need is still unsupplied" (36). Finally, the General Assembly passed Act No. 292: "A Joint Resolution To Create a Committee To Make a Continuous Study of the Educational System of the Public Schools of the State" (37). This committee was a continuation of the committee authorized by the General Assembly in 1963 under Concurrent Resolution H1651. The assembly appointed the committee, and it is studying the school law. The committee will recommend a new school code in 1968.

In 1916, the state supplied barely a twelfth of the funds expended in its public school education (38). All other moneys were raised from local taxation, which varied greatly by district. In 1965, state aid funds for public schools amounted to 60 percent, local taxes to 34 percent, and federal funds accounted for the remaining 6 percent. There is still a wide variation in the sums local districts appropriate for schools.

With the growth of the state's share came a corresponding increase in state school administration. Swearingen wrote in 1920: "The multiplication of local school laws is becoming a serious problem. A few general laws would be far simpler and far more effective than the hundreds of local acts now scattered through the Statutes" (39). This is still a serious problem.

The assembly revised the High School Act of 1907 several times, as well as the acts providing state aid for construction. The Aid to Weak Schools Act, first introduced in 1909, was revised a number of times (40).

The Mill Schools

Textile mills gradually became more and more important in South Carolina, replacing agriculture as the chief industry. The mills were reluctant to accept some of the local taxes to support the schools, many preferring to build and maintain their own and pay teachers' salaries. As a result, in 1915, the General Assembly created the Office of State Supervisor of Mill Schools in the State Department of Education.

The mill schools supervisor's first report in 1916 states: "I have yet to discover why mill children should be separated from the other white children of the state and enrolled in different schools" (41). The same remark is to be found in subsequent reports. Actually, some of the so-called mill schools were partially financed by the state. The supervisor in his 1919 report classified these mill schools in three categories: regular public schools drawing state and county aid through public taxation and regularly supervised by state and county authorities; schools supported in part by public funds and in part by the mill (many schools in this class were under the control of the regular school authorities); and schools owned and controlled entirely by the mill.

The schools owned and maintained by the mills had no tax levies, except the constitutional tax collected from the county "in a more or less legal way" (42). The supervisor reported that their biggest difficulty was insufficient space, and it was not uncommon to find 50 to 75 children in one classroom. The schools also had trouble with attendance, and one report mentioned that many first- and second-graders were not enrolled, thus ignoring the compulsory attendance law. Most of the schools operated double sessions daily, and the supervisor made one of the earliest references to a 12-month session when he suggested that mill schools operate on a year-round basis. Many of the mills constructed imposing buildings, some of which are in existence today.

Changes in taxation laws gradually obviated the need for these schools, and they do not appear in the reports after 1925 (43).

Compulsory Attendance

Regular school attendance had always been a problem. Not only had the state long attempted to enroll those who should be in school, but it was also concerned about the high rate of dropouts and ensuing illiteracy. Night classes and adult education attempted to cut the illiteracy rate, but it still remained high.

Jillson strongly believed in compulsory attendance, and it was largely through his insistance that it was introduced in the Constitution of 1868. Unfortunately, it was not enforced. The Constitution of 1895 eliminated compulsory attendance, and the state remained without an attendance law for two decades. For years, many tried to get the Legislature to pass a regular attendance law, but they were unsuccessful until 1915, and then over the objections of Governor Cole L. Blease. In his annual message to the members of the General Assembly in January 1914, Governor Blease stated that "people do not need and they do not want compulsory education; what they need and what they want and what they demand, and what they are going to have is adequate school facilities" (44). The law required attendance at school of children between the ages of 8 and 14, but its weakness lay in the fact that it was a "local option compulsory attendance law" (45).

Most of the districts did not accept its provisions, and the law remained rather ineffectual. In 1937, the assembly passed the Regular Attendance Law stipulating that children between the ages of 6 and 16 should enroll in school and maintain regular attendance. It also provided for attendance teachers in each county, whose salaries were to be paid by the state. The law further required an annual census of all school-age children. Most important, this was not a "local option compulsory attendance law"—it was applicable to all (46).

The Legislature strengthened the Regular Attendance Law in both 1955 and 1961 by making more specific the duties of the attendance teachers, or attendance supervisors as they were renamed in 1955.

The U.S. Supreme Court decision of 1954 caused considerable uncertainty and confusion. Actually, South Carolinians feared integration and the complete breakdown of segregation as practiced in the state for many years. As a result, the Legislature in 1955 repealed sections of the attendance law providing for regular school attendance. Two years later, the Legislature attempted to give more importance to the work of attendance supervisors. The Regular Attendance Law of 1937 was not strictly enforced, nor was the 1957 act. Thus, in reality, the state has no compulsory attendance law although sentiment is rapidly developing for it at present.

Vocational Education

As early as the 1908-1909 school session, the state superintendent asked schools to introduce home economics, or courses in cooking and sewing as they were called at the time. Five years later, some schools were offering such courses (47). At the same time, several larger high schools offered industrial arts programs and a few business courses. Courses in agriculture were introduced in Darlington County during the session of 1914-15 (48), but the real beginning of agricultural education commenced with the Toole Act of 1916 (49).

When Congress passed the Smith-Hughes Act in 1917, South Carolina acted quickly to come under the law. President Woodrow Wilson signed the act on February 23, 1917, and 3 days later the state accepted its provisions. This funded programs in agriculture, trade and industrial education, and home economics. Although agriculture and trade and industries were already common, home economics did not get a real start until 1920 (50).

In his 1918 report, Swearingen stated that "South Carolina must enlarge the scope of her colleges by introducing vocational instruction at Clemson, Winthrop and the State College" (51). The institutions of higher learning accepted the challenge and promptly started vocational courses. Today, there is practically no field not covered.

The federal Smith-Hughes Act was implemented by the George-Reed Act of 1929, the George-Ellzey Act of 1934, the George-Deen Act of 1936, and the George-Barden Act of 1946 (52). The Vocational Education Act of 1963 provided the final impetus. Now vocational areas include not only agriculture, home economics, and trade and industries, but also distributive education, industrial arts, manpower, office occupations, and health occupations. The state maintains two area trade schools at present and plans more than 50 area vocational centers.

World War I

The World War I years placed a strain on the schools in two ways. First, South Carolina had made a real beginning in building schools, but now construction halted abruptly. A rapid recovery followed, however, and according to the 1921 report, progress was evident. Second, there was a serious shortage of teachers. Swearingen had reported:

> Every Department of Education has been affected by the war . . . . Hundreds of our best young men have left the teacher's desk to don the uniform. Many young women have also left the classroom to take up the work and business of the men who have gone into the Army. It has been far more difficult to run the school this year than usual. The shortage of teachers will become even more pressing in the future (53).

This was one of the first references to women's leaving the classroom for work and business.

The South Carolina Association

The South Carolina Education Association has played a prominent part in educational progress, particularly during the last 30 years. It has been active in affairs affecting teacher welfare, especially salaries, and has lent its full support in many other ways to such programs as teacher retirement, certification, and the twelfth-grade movement.

First known as the Teachers Association, when formed in 1850 at the request of Governor Whitemarsh B. Seabrook, it languished during the 30 years that followed. Attempts to revive it in 1870 during Reconstruction failed. In 1881, about 125 teachers met in Greenville and organized a permanent State Teachers Association, renamed in 1924 the South Carolina Education Association.

During Swearingen's last year in office, in 1922, E. S. Dreher, then president of the association, formed departments of classroom teachers, superintendents, etc., which became important to its success. A full-time secretary-treasurer was elected in 1924. Today, the organization has some 25 departments, with permanent committees and commissions, and 28 employees.

In 1906, the Negro Teachers organized the Palmetto Education Association. Together, the Palmetto Education Association and the South Carolina Education Association have a total membership of approximately 27,000, and there are indications at present that the two organizations will merge.

Swearingen's Final Report

In the last year of Superintendent Swearingen's tenure, South Carolina suffered from both the depression of 1920-21 and the boll weevil. Swearingen reported in 1922:

> Unfortunately, owing to the hard times of the past two years, the State appropriations have been insufficient to take care fully of all applications meeting the requirements. This failure, and the fact that payment of taxes has been slow throughout the State, have worked in many instances real hardship on teachers, schools, and county superintendents. Many country teachers have failed to get their salaries for the last month or two of their school terms, which has tended to discourage them in their work (54).

In this final report, Swearingen showed a total enrollment of 479,309 compared to the 314,399 at the beginning of his term 14 years earlier, and teachers had increased in number from 6,228 to 10,814. Expenditures had increased from $1,853,572 to $9,517,968.

THE ADMINISTRATION OF JAMES H. HOPE, 1922-46

Superintendent James H. Hope began his administration while the state was recovering from the depression following World War I, and it continued on through the Depression and World War II. He maintained his office consecutively for 24 years, the longest on record. "It was during the administration of James H. Hope, State Superintendent of Education from 1922 to 1946 . . . that public education was accelerated and many of the fine services provided by the State were inaugurated" (55).

Fortunately, when Hope took office the Legislature was generally sympathetic and responsive to the public's genuine interest in education. At the end of his first year, he stated:

> In submitting to you this report of school activities for 1922-23 and financial receipts and disbursements for the fiscal year just closing I am impelled to say that never in the history of the State have the schools had more loyal support in their several activities than they have had at the hands of this present General Assembly (56).

This and subsequent Legislatures enabled Hope to bring about improvements, including a new state law (the 6-0-1 Law), the addition of the twelfth grade, upgrading of certification and teacher education, a teacher retirement law, and the Textbook Law.

The 6-0-1 Law

In his 1923 report, Hope analyzed in detail his plan for a new state aid law in keeping with his philosophy that "the money should be taken from where it is, to educate the children of the State where they are" (57). Such a measure had long been urged by both the State Department of Education and the State Teachers Association. The following year, the General Assembly enacted the act, which was known as the "6-0-1 Law."

Superintendent Hope had argued that there were "so many state aid laws for schools on the statute books that very few school officials, to say nothing of the masses, understand their operation" (58). These included the Term Extension Law, Rural Graded School Law, Equalizing Law To Guarantee a Seven-Month Term, Law To Establish and Maintain High Schools, Law To Relieve Overcrowding of Elementary Grades of Approved High Schools, and the Law To Encourage the Erection of Adequate School Buildings. The new law wiped out these previous acts and provided the following:

> After requiring each county to use a three-mill constitutional tax and to levy a four-mill ad valorem tax, the state supplements these two sources of revenue by direct state appropriation and pays the salary of all public school teachers under a given schedule for the first six months, provided the district or county runs its school or schools an additional month (59).

The new state aid law resulted in higher teachers' salaries, better buildings and equipment, longer school terms, and greatly simplified methods of accounting in the State Department of Education. Although it reflected the will of the people as well as that of the department and the teachers association, the law was not entirely satisfactory. All counties were required to pay the 7-mill tax, which became the state fund for equalization. Yet, counties varied widely in the money each could raise to supplement the fund. This disparity still exists.

Certification and Teacher Education

From the founding of the Memminger Normal School in 1859, there was considerable interest in educating teachers for South Carolina. After the War Between the States, public appeals to the Legislature for state normal schools failed because the government lacked the funds. But, in 1883, South Carolina College (now the University of South Carolina) offered the first college courses designed for teachers. In the meantime, beginning in 1880, the state established summer institutes for teachers, and, in 1904, the Legislature appropriated $1,000 for a state summer school.

David B. Johnson, superintendent of schools in Columbia, so impressed the Legislature with the small training school for teachers he had started that it decided to establish a state normal and industrial school. In 1886, this school became Winthrop College. Five years later, the institution became a state-supported college as the South Carolina Industrial and Winthrop Normal School. In 1920, the name was changed to Winthrop College, the South Carolina College for Women.

By 1918, 15 institutions of higher learning had added to their curriculums normal courses patterned after the course of study at the university. In 1921, the state department published its first rules and regulations for the certification of teachers graduated from these colleges. These requirements were revised many times, and it was not until 1945 that student teaching was made compulsory for every prospective teacher. Today, 22 colleges and universities offer student teaching in South Carolina.

Teachers were certified by a board of examiners, beginning in 1897, and this continued until 1945. Conscious of the need for an improved program of teacher education and certification, the State Board of Education authorized a study of the qualifications of South Carolina teachers (60). The South Carolina Education Association and other interested groups strongly supported the survey. The publication of the results (61) became the basis for state board action in 1944, when it adopted new certification regulations providing for a professional single salary schedule based on education, experience, and grade on the National Teacher Examination. These new regulations were revised the following year and remain in effect as a qualification for the distribution of state aid for teachers' salaries. (South Carolina is the only state which requires the National Teacher Examination for certification. The state also requires that the examination be given in the state under state administration.)

Vocational Rehabilitation

The Smith-Bankhead Act, passed by Congress in 1920, required the states to match federal appropriations. Since South Carolina could not find the matching funds, it was 7 years before it participated in the vocational rehabilitation program. In March 1927, the General Assembly passed a joint resolution "authorizing the State Superintendent to accept allotments of Federal Aid available for rehabilitation and to set up this service in South Carolina" (62). The department employed a supervisor of vocational rehabilitation that year, but it was not until 1935 that the assembly approved the program item in the department's appropriation.

The Vocational Rehabilitation Act of 1943 superseded the Smith-Bankhead Act and changed the annual appropriation to a permanent program. At this time, the emphasis shifted from vocational education to physical restoration. Although the program remained in the department for 30 years, its impact was not really educational.

In 1955, Congress passed legislation permitting vocational rehabilitation to become a separate agency. The assembly removed the program from the department 2 years later and established it as a separate agency.

School Lunch Program

The state department organized the School Lunch Improvement Association in 1920 and directed its activities for 6 years. The association began serving hot lunches in schools and aroused considerable interest in the program. Although it was dissolved in 1926, the schools continued serving lunches. When federal funds became available in 1932 for employing labor for this purpose, the entire program received considerable encouragement.

In 1933, in the heart of the Depression, the Reconstruction Finance Corporation allocated funds to develop a statewide program as a relief measure. The program was expanded by the Civil Works Administration and by the Emergency Relief Administration in 1935. The objectives were to establish useful work projects for needy persons and to feed well-balanced meals to malnourished children. The program also encouraged the production and canning of foods for lunchroom use.

The Emergency Relief Administration was discontinued in 1943, but that same year the Legislature passed a School Lunch Act which enabled the state department to continue the program, employing a state director and a supervisor for each county. Thus, the program continued without interruption. In 1943, the U. S. War Food Administration reimbursed schools for lunches served, and 3 years later, Congress passed the School Lunch Act. It has been revised and improved by subsequent acts (63).

Of pupils in average daily attendance in 1966, approximately 75 percent received lunches. The total cost of the program exceeds $28 million and is expected to continue increasing. For instance, breakfasts are planned for the disadvantaged, as well as feeding programs for pupils attending summer schools. South Carolina is justly proud of its efforts in this area.

Textbook Commission

As stated earlier, O.B. Martin suggested a central depository for textbooks in his annual report for 1905. Evidently, Martin did not realize that a depository had been in operation since 1893 (64). However, since counties and many bookstores stocked the books, it was not until 1925 that full use was made of the central depository.

The State Board of Education, formerly responsible for a uniform adoption of textbooks, continued to have responsibility under the new legislation. A 1936 act transferred the duty to administer provisions of the textbook law to a new agency, the Textbook Commission, and made the state superintendent of education a member of the commission.

The Textbook Commission's chief purpose was to provide pupils with a system of rental textbooks. Under the law, the state owns books which it rents to pupils at an amount "in its discretion." The original amount set was one-third of the list price, but the rent was subsequently reduced on some texts as finances permitted. The law also permitted library books and audiovisual equipment to be furnished. One interesting section of the law that will undoubtedly create future legislation reads: "The State Schoolbook Commission shall waive rentals for as many of the grammar and high school grades as available funds will permit, to the end that textbooks shall be supplied to the school children of the State without charge at the earliest possible date" (65).

The state board started the practice of multiple adoptions in 1941, and it continues to the present. Since single adoptions restricted the curriculum, the schools responded enthusiastically to the multiple adoptions.

One section of the textbook law states that "provisions of this section shall not apply to any school district that provides free schoolbooks to the value of twenty thousand dollars or more to the children of such school district" (66). Another section stipulated that "school districts enrolling five thousand or more pupils shall have the right to set up rental or free textbook systems and choose and purchase their own textbooks" (67). School districts were quick to take advantage of these provisions and claim the many exceptions. This has, of course, invalidated the theory of uniform adoptions (68). The 1964 General Assembly made it mandatory that the commission give up its independent status in 2 years and become a division in the State Department of Education.

Twelve-Year School Program

Alone among the states, South Carolina continued to graduate students from the eleventh grade, although tests indicated that students were at a disadvantage compared to those who attended school a year longer (69). The Legislature's reluctance to adopt a proposal for a 12-year system stemmed in part from the finances required and in part from a skepticism of something new. However, the doubts were overcome, and in January 1944 "the General Assembly passed unanimously a Concurrent Resolution requesting the State Board of Education to proceed at once with plans for setting up a twelfth grade within the school system of the State" (70).

The state board responded the very next day by making the twelfth grade an integral part of the state's public school system. The board acted on the basis that the twelfth grade was not an additional grade to be placed on top of the eleventh grade nor the insertion of a grade somewhere along the educational ladder, but rather an extra year to be employed throughout the total public school system to strength and enrich the whole program.

A series of workshops and study conferences were held to study the problems brought by the new law and determine how best to implement it. Until the twelfth grade was fully effective, students were permitted to follow courses leading to an eleventh-grade or twelfth-grade certificate. The last eleventh-grade certificates were issued in 1948.

Adult Education

Despite its long history and rich cultural heritage, South Carolina continues to rank distressingly low in literacy. The state is on the bottom of the list in the percent of Selective Service draftees passing preinduction and induction mental tests, forty-ninth in the percent of population 14 years old and older classed as illiterate, and tied for last place in median school years completed by persons who are 25 years old and older (71). This condition has always existed.

The state's efforts have reduced illiteracy. From 1900 to 1910, there was a reduction of 7 percent of the illiterate white population, and from 1910 to 1920, there was a total reduction of 22 percent. "South Carolina outranked every other state in the Union in per cent reduction of illiteracy and per cent gain in school attendance" (72). And this was before the department added a supervisor of adult education, who inaugurated more vigorous efforts to combat illiteracy.

The Opportunity School, founded in 1921 as a summer session at the Daughters of the American Revolution school at Tamasee, was operated on various college campuses until the state acquired a former army air base in 1946, which was in part deeded to the school. The school remained under the State Department of Education until 1957, when the Legislature created an autonomous board to operate it. The Legislature names a majority of the trustees and gives it an annual appropriation.

The Opportunity School is unique. The minimum age for enrolling is 16, but there is no maximum age. Its purpose is to provide an education for those who were denied one, by offering room and board and an academic course of study. It affords an opportunity for anyone to earn a South Carolina certificate of high school equivalency or the school's diploma. Through its regular session, summer school, and special courses it reaches about 500 pupils annually.

The Depression and War Years

South Carolina schools were hit hard during the early thirties, although the U. S. government plugged many holes punctured by the Bank Holiday. Salaries of teachers sank to a lob ebb. During the 1932-33 session, the state could not meet aid demands and in desperation resorted to promises to pay or "script." Under this system, all but the wealthier districts were forced to pass this script on to teachers, and to get cash the teachers were forced to discount them where they could. Schools operated on austere budgets, and many services were curtailed.

On the state level, programs in agriculture, home economics, trade and industries, and many others faced limited appropriations for equipment. The lack of funds prevented the development of any new experimental courses. On the local level, science laboratories suffered because supplies could not be replaced and it was impossible to purchase new equipment. Few schools had libraries, and all lacked the funds to purchase needed books.

Gradually, government spending and prewar activities restored the economy. Then the state, along with the rest of the nation, faced the necessities of World War II. Schools met the new demands with courage but some uncertainty. The state department's vocational division, particularly trades and industries, was called on by the military for training programs at defense and military installations. The department cooperated with the schools' agriculture and home economics departments to develop such programs as home gardens and canning foods. The military's use of audiovisual and visual equipment in training programs had a powerful impact on education.

As in World War I, there was a staggering loss of teachers. The schools later lost students as boys flocked to the colors despite the department's stress on the importance of completing their education. Schools took part in food stamp programs, in war bond drives, and some inaugurated military programs. Finally, in 1945, education faced an atomic peace and many dramatic changes.

Retirement

Perhaps no legislation has done more for teacher morale than the Retirement Law of 1945. Those who faced an uncertain future with dread now had something to look forward to when their teaching days were over. In his final report, Hope said: "The desire to reward long and faithful service, and offer security to the capable efficient teacher is in process of fruition through the Retirement Law" (73).

The need for a retirement program had been obvious for a long time, and as early as the 1936-37 school year, the South Carolina Education Association had spearheaded a drive for one. The association quickly secured support from the State Employees Association, the State Congress of Parents and Teachers, and other groups interested in teacher welfare. However, a number of legislators were unwilling for the state to take on this financial burden, and many did not understand the estimates of actuaries or the operations of a retirement system. The profession itself was indifferent, especially those under retirement programs in larger school systems. At the same time, many private citizens questioned setting up a retirement system for what they considered a select group. And when World War II erupted, most efforts were subordinated to it.

The association continued to hold meetings in every county and hearings before committees of the Legislature. Gradually, it overcame opposition and indifference, and the Legislature enacted the Retirement Law in 1945. Two years later, it placed the state retirement system under the State Budget and Control Board. Its membership is not restricted to teachers, and all state employees are members.

The Completion of Twenty-Four Years

Although recognizing the many unfavorable educational comparisons between South Carolina and other states, Hope stated: "The only fair evaluation of progress is in comparison between actual situations as they exist within the State at any given times, rather than emphasizing our relative position in regard to other states where conditions may be wholly unrelated" (74). His 1946 report presented exhaustive statistics to show the progress made during his administration.

During this period of progress, the State Department of Education grew considerably. Swearingen left a staff of 24, 6 of them on loan from colleges and 5 paid by the General Education Board. Hope had on his staff 133, part of the salaries and travel of 2 paid by the General Education Board. There was also a growth in federal aid. In 1923, the state received $71,366 under the Smith-Hughes Act. In 1924, federal funds for vocational education amounted to $5,595,323, and $2,175,000 in federal aid came for school lunch and emergency war programs. Hope remarked at the end of his term of office that there was abundant evidence that the great State of South Carolina had gone into the school business in earnest.

ADMINISTRATION OF JESSE T. ANDERSON, 1946-66

Reorganization of the State Department of Education

State Superintendent Jesse T. Anderson,who was to retire in December 1966, served 20 consecutive years–longer than any of his predecessors, next to Hope. In carrying out Hope's programs and beginning others, his administration reflected the many changes occurring in education.

The first problem Anderson faced was to reorganize the state department and put it on a firmer basis. From its founding in 1868 until 1947, the department had not been organized. In fact, there was little need for organization in the early days–state funds were not appropriated for a department, and the staff was small. In one of his first acts, Anderson grouped his employees into five divisions, effective July 1, 1947. At his request, the Legislature appropriated additional funds to add personnel. The Legislature also acceded to his request for 14 area teacher helpers, one for each judicial circuit, but in all succeeding sessions the General Assembly failed to allocate funds for this purpose. Anderson did continue to change the pattern of the department to meet changing needs and conditions.

State Legislation

Early in 1947, the Legislature authorized the Peabody Survey to study the statewide organization of schools. The committee reported to the Legislature in 1948, calling for a county-unit organization and a foundation program for education. The legislators did not accept the report because they thought it too expensive to implement. But, the following year, near the close of the session, the assembly, by a joint resolution, directed county boards of education to appoint committees to study school district organization.

The same year, 1949, the House of Representatives appointed the Hollings Committee to study the needs of the schools (75), and the State Department of Education made members of its staff available to the committee. It investigated school construction and transportation in a number of states and reported to the General Assembly early in 1951. This, in part, resulted in the assembly's creating a State Educational Finance Commission and enacting a 3-percent sales tax.

For a number of years prior to the Supreme Court decision of 1954, there had been fears regarding desegregation. Mixed with these fears was the late realization that there was not true equality of schools and that Negro schools were definitely inferior. These feelings were frustrated with the realization that under the existing tax structure a building program to meet needs of Negro students was impossible.

The Educational Finance Commission. James Francis Byrnes, inaugurated Governor in 1951 (76), realized the plight of South Carolina education and was determined that adequate schools for Negroes would be constructed as one way of preventing desegregation. It was largely because of his interest that the assembly accepted the Hollings Committee recommendations and in 1951 passed the 3-percent sales tax and established the State Educational Finance Commission.

Although the Legislature created separate agencies for textbooks (1936), school building and transportation (1951), educational television (1960), and technical education (1961), both the state superintendent of education and the Governor were appointed members of each commission. The Governor also served as a member of the State Board of Education until a new board took office January 1, 1954. The State Department of Education influenced each of these commissions and the State Educational Finance Commission; the state superintendent played a significant role in policies affecting school construction, district reorganization, and transportation.

The powers and duties of the new finance commission were enormous: It was charged to set up a school construction program and a state-owned transportation system, and to conduct as soon as practicable a survey of the entire school system. Accordingly, in 1951, the commission made an exhaustive survey of the entire state. Numerous teams sought to discover building needs and how districts could best be reorganized and consolidated. The 1951 act granted counties construction aid on the basis of certain criteria, principally that a district should have a high school for each race and that a high school's minimum enrollment should be an anticipated 250. The Legislature did not mandate the criteria, and the reorganization was not perfect. Yet, it resulted in consolidating 1,220 districts to 107 between 1951 and 1956.

Districts were given construction aid on the basis of $15 per pupil enrolled (77). Under the terms of the law, 20-year bonds were issued, enabling the state to inaugurate a construction program in 1952. This resulted in mergers among many small schools. At the same time, the powers, duties, and responsibilities of the state department's schoolhouse planning section were transferred to the commission.

Similarly, the transportation section of the state department was transferred to the commission in 1951. Since 1928, counties or districts had owned their school buses, or else transportation was done by contract. The 1951 law made the state responsible for transporting all pupils who lived over 1.5 miles from their schools; thus South Carolina purchased and operated the buses. The State Highway Department fueled and maintained all buses until the commission took this over. At present, it operates regional maintenance shops throughout the state. After a thorough course of instruction, students were hired as drivers.

Educational Television. The Legislature became convinced that television could be used to enrich the curriculum and strengthen courses. In 1957, it adopted a concurrent resolution requesting that a legislative committee study the use of television in the public schools. The following March, the committee recommended that a pilot project be set up in one of the schools in Columbia. During the summer of 1958, in a studio built at Dreher High School, the project began with two subjects, French and geometry. The following summer, the program expanded to include algebra and was extended to five area schools in Columbia.

In 1960, the General Assembly created the South Carolina Educational Television Commission, which inaugurated a program of videotapes on closed-circuit television. The new commission expanded rapidly and in 1963 had two open-circuit stations, with plans for open-circuit programs to reach every school in the state.

Technical Education. In its 1961 session, the assembly created the Technical Education Commission to implement a statewide system of technical education. To meet funding requirements established by Congress under the Manpower Development and Training Act of 1962, the commission was placed under the advisory supervision of the state department in 1963. Thus, the commission administers the Manpower Development and Training Act as well as the Special Training for Economic Progress (STEP) launched in 1964.

The law gave the State Committee for Technical Education the following responsibilities: technical training of high school graduates; "crash" training of persons for jobs in new or expanding industries; increased emphasis on industrial arts programs and basic industrial vocational programs within existing high school curriculums; and upgrading and updating of employed workers. The committee has become deeply involved with all of these except vocational education in the secondary schools, which remains in the state department.

Reorganization of the State Board of Education

In accordance with the provisions of the Constitution of 1895, the State Board of Education consisted of seven members appointed by the Governor, with the Governor ex officio chairman and the state superintendent of education ex officio secretary. The South Carolina School Boards Association and the South Carolina Education Association concluded, however, that the state should have a new state board, with the authority to appoint a superintendent of education. These two groups campaigned successfully, and, in 1962, the Legislature permitted referendums on both issues. The proposed state board would be composed of one representative elected from each judicial circuit by the county legislative delegations of each circuit.

The following November, the first referendum passed, but the second, calling for appointment of the state superintendent of education was rejected. This rejection may be partly due to a general feeling that the State Board of Education was not truly elective and could become political.

The new State Board of Education took office January 1, 1964. The act ratifying the 1963 referendum authorized the General Assembly to define the duties and responsibilities of the new board. Although this has been done, it is expected to be charged with more duties and responsibilities as new needs arise.

Federal Aid

Traditionally, South Carolina has distrusted federal aid; legislative leaders and many others warned that it would lead to control. But historically, the state has accepted funds from the government as a welcome relief from more taxation and to enrich the state's programs. South Carolina accepted federal funds from many programs, such as those dealing with the GI Bill of Rights, vocational education, adult education, the National Defense Education Act of 1958, Public Law 815 and Public Law 874 of 1950, and the Elementary and Secondary Act of 1965. These funds were always accepted, however, with a wary eye for any controls such aid might bring. There were still warnings from those who feared federal aid, particularly when federal aid bypassed the State Department of Education in such legislation as the Lanham Act and the Works Progress Administration.

Despite the opposition, most people clearly saw the advantages of rapidly expanding federal activities in education and entered each program willingly as federal aid expanded beyond vocational assistance and rehabilitation. South Carolina accepted the National Defense Education Act of 1958 and its subsequent expansion. But, although many districts accepted the matching provisions of Titles III and V, there were many that would not or could not match the equalizing funds. As a result, in no year since the program began has South Carolina used all of its allocations.

The Vocational Education Act of 1963 doubled the allocations spent in this area, and the state matched all funds. The Lanham Act of 1941 and the subsequent provisions of Public Laws 815 and 874, financially assisting areas where the impact of federal activities results in a severe drain on school districts, particularly aided South Carolina because of its many defense installations. Public Law 815 grants funds for construction, and Public Law 874 gives financial help to districts where the government has acquired property and its activities result in an influx of new students. Assistance to adult education will undoubtedly be of tremendous value in the state's fight against illiteracy.

The Civil Rights Act of 1964 revived fears of federal control. Yet, the state accepted its provisions, and most districts have indicated that they intend to comply. There was not one incident of violent opposition, thus sparing South Carolina the misfortunes of some states.

The Serviceman's Readjustment Act, more popularly known as the GI Bill of Rights, enacted by Congress in June 1944, was implemented when the Governor designated the state department as the certifying agency in South Carolina. It provided vocational readjustment and restored lost educational opportunities to those whose careers had been interrupted or impeded by active military service. The bill also extended the opportunity of a higher education to those who might not otherwise be able to afford it.

The original GI Bill of Rights has been amended and the benefits extended a number of times. The Veterans' Readjustment Benefits Act of 1966 replaces the 1944 Serviceman's Readjustment Act and makes the benefits available to those who have seen service since January 1, 1955. In September 1947, the department entered into an agreement to become the agent of all schools operating the institutional on-the-farm training programs for veterans. Prior to this, the Veterans Administration had contracted directly with the individual schools.

The GI Bill of Rights has been the largest adult education program in the state. Thousands have been able to secure a college education; thousands have returned to high school and earned diplomas; many others have received special training in various fields. Since the program's inception, of the 146,000 who have received benefits under the bill, 90,000 entered college.

It is difficult for many younger people to appreciate fully the changes that have occurred with the growing impact of federal aid, but not for those whose memories extend back to the prewar days when federal programs were extremely limited. Today, there is hardly a phase of education, either on the local or state level, that is not affected by governmental activity.

School lunches are now generally accepted by even the harshest critics of federal aid. Categorical help in many areas has strengthened curriculums. Vocational assistance has developed courses undreamed of earlier and has extended specialized training beyond school age. The National Defense Education Act of 1958 has instilled new life into practically every field and has revolutionized teaching. Federal aid to impacted areas has helped solve problems once thought insoluble. Adult education programs have brought hope to many and are challenging illiteracy. The Elementary and Secondary Education Act of 1965 has uncovered many submerged problems and provides opportunity for long-needed experimentation.

With all these advances, however, one problem remains and grows larger with each program: How far shall the U.S. government go? Should federal aid remedy weaknesses that were once considered to be problems for local agencies and the state to handle? These questions are not yet answered.

Summary

Jesse Anderson's administration epitomized the advances public education has made in South Carolina since it was founded as a colony in 1670. The stigma attached to public schools for almost three centuries has gone. Although about 20,000 students are still enrolled in private schools, the old idea that free schools are "pauper" institutions has given way to pride in public education and a determination to give it support. Perhaps this is the most significant change, as we see statewide taxation both expected and encouraged.

Jillson's determination that education should be integrated has taken 100 years to become real; but the Civil Rights Act of 1964 is the law of the land, and a gradual phasing out of the state's dual system is inevitable. Similarly, his ardent desire for compulsory education also is destined to become the law of the land.

There was dissatisfaction when a 1955 act took regular attendance off the statutes, and there are indications that compulsory attendance will be restored. Anderson best expressed this desire to extend the benefits when he said that "public education should provide education opportunities that [would] give every boy and girl the privilege of developing his or her greatest potential" (78). Practically every state superintendent since Jillson has realized that education provides an opportunity to do something tangible for the great majority who are not college-bound. With today's stress on vocational education, that opportunity is realized.

Almost one-quarter of a billion dollars has been spent on school construction during the last 20 years. With demands for more schools for an expanding population and with demands for additional facilities to meet changing needs, it is dubious that all requirements will ever be met. The building program has ended the trend begun in 1907 by the High School Act. No longer is there proliferation of small, inadequate schools–the trend is toward larger schools, adequately financed, offering broad courses of study. There are now 1,383 elementary and secondary schools, a reduction of more than 1,600 during the last two decades. The once common one-teacher schools all have been abandoned.

South Carolina has achieved striking progress in consolidating school districts, reducing almost 2,000 to 108. Much of this resulted from the construction program and criteria established by the State Educational Finance Commission. Consolidation of small inadequate schools into larger units would not have been possible if transportation to larger centers had not been provided. Today, more than 5,000 buses transport almost 350,000 children daily. This has improved attendance and kept young people in school for more years than ever before.

Anderson takes great pride in the school's holding power–more students are staying in school until graduation. Attendance is now 90 percent, and a drive is underway to reduce further the number of dropouts. In 1967, 44 percent of those who started the first grade 12 years before were in their last year of school. The number of dropouts remains distressingly high, but the percentage of those who remain in school has doubled in a decade. Along with the improved attendance by whites, the number of Negroes remaining 12 years increased by almost 300 percent. Better schools and better programs, as well as improved transportation, have contributed to the increased enrollment and greater holding power. There were more than 12,000 Negro seniors in 1966, compared to 4,000 in 1951, and only 300 some 20 years ago.

For many years, high schools have had to meet certain standards before receiving accreditation. Elementary schools, on the other hand, had no standards and no official guidelines until 1961, when purely voluntary standards were developed. More and more schools have officially adopted the voluntary standards.

The State Department of Education expanded and reorganized to keep up with the increasing tempo of the times. When Anderson took office, his departmental staff numbered 133; he left a staff of 865, which had increased by 500 when the State Educational Finance Commission and the Textbook Commission merged with the department in 1966. There are indications that more personnel will be added to meet the growing needs resulting from increasing federal aid.

Much happened during Anderson's administration–probably more than during any comparable period since the State Department of Education was organized almost a century ago. But there are still questions unanswered and problems to be solved to challenge Cyril B. Busbee, who became state superintendent of education in January 1967.

The new State Board of Education, which took office on January 1, 1964, worked hard to formulate a philosophy, establish policies, define its role, and clearly establish relationships with the superintendent. The latter is important because under the present law relationships between a newly established board and a new superintendent can be secured only by mutual cooperation. Establishing this relationship also becomes a responsibility of the new superintendent.

In April 1967, the State Board of Education finally adopted a philosophy statement, setting out its responsibilities for planning, regulating, upholding, and improving education. It recognized that the state superintendent and the department were responsible for administrative functions. But it agreed that there should be a minimum quality of education below which no school district should be allowed to fall. And this would require a system of state financial aid.

The board stated that there should be an annual evaluation of educational quality in each school district in the state. To correct weaknesses, the state superintendent should develop a 5-year plan, which the board would approve after open hearings and reevaluate and update annually. Each local school district should have a 1-year plan within the long-range master plan. The board recognized, however, that a number of local districts were too small to offer a high-quality level of education and should be consolidated with neighboring districts. Thus, the board will make consolidation recommendations where pertinent.

The state board's statement of educational philosophy emphasized the importance of local control. South Carolina has jealously guarded her autonomy in education and has respected the right of districts in determining local policy, even though this has changed in recent years, and federal programs have affected local interests. The new superintendent must take these changes into serious consideration.

FOOTNOTES

1. South Carolina, *General House of Commons* (1703), pp. 70-71. A copy can be found in the Archives Department in Columbia and at the Charleston Library Society.
2. For further information, see Gertrude Foster, "Documentary History of Education in South Carolina" (unpublished Ph.D. dissertation, University of South Carolina, Columbia, 1932).
3. David Ramsay, *The History of South Carolina,* II (2 vols.; Charleston, S.C.: David Longworth, 1809), 354.
4. *Ibid.*
5. Charles William Dabney, *Universal Education in the South,* I (2 vols.; Chapel Hill: University of North Carolina Press, 1936), 221.
6. Ellwood P. Cubberley, *State School Administration* (Boston: Houghton-Mifflin Co., 1927), p. 4.
7. Henry T. Thompson, *The Establishment of the Public School System in South Carolina* (Columbia: The R. L. Bryan Co., 1927), p. 5.
8. Robert Means Davis, "A Sketch of Education in South Carolina," *Hammonds Hand Book of South Carolina, 1883* (Charleston, S.C.: Walker, Evans & Cogswell, 1883). Reprinted by The Steering Committee, University of South Carolina, 1944.
9. *Ibid.*
10. *Historical Sketch of the John De La Howe School,* reprinted from the seventh annual report (1931) of the "orphan section" of the Duke endowment, with supplement. (Anderson, S.C.: Anderson Printing Co., 1950), p. 11.
11. U.S. Commissioner of Education, *Annual Report, 1899-1900,* I, 467.
12. A. D. Mayo, "Common Schools in the South, 1830-1860," *Report of the United States Commissioner of Education, 1899-1900,* I (Washington, D.C.: Government Printing Office, 1901), p. 468.
13. Charleston *Daily Courier,* Nov. 27, 1869, as quoted in Richard L. Towers, "The 'Carpetbagger' Who Was South Carolina's First State Superintendent of Education," *Education Report*, X (December 1967), 2.
14. "Centennial of a Seer," *South Carolina Schools,* XIX, No. 4 (Summer 1968), 6-7. According to a South Carolina state census in 1871, there were 209,376 children between the ages of 6 and 16 years in the state at the time.
15. Towers, *op. cit.,* p. 2.
16. "Centennial of a Seer," *South Carolina Schools,* XIX, No. 4 (Summer 1968), 7.
17. South Carolina, *Constitution* (1868), art. 10, sec. 10.
18. Evidently Jillson did not seek renomination. He returned to Springfield, Massachusetts, and worked as a book agent of sorts. Despondent and suffering from acute rheumatism, he committed suicide on December 8, 1881.
19. He later served as Governor of the state, Assistant Secretary of the Treasury, a member of the U.S. Civil Service Commission, and comptroller of a leading insurance company in New York City.
20. Superintendent of Education, *Annual Report, 1878,* pp. 55-56. In this report, Thompson quoted from a speech by the Reverend B. Sears, general agent of the Peabody Educational Fund. Like other advocates of in-service training of teachers, it had a "modern approach":
    The great fault with untrained teachers is that they do little but teach the words and formulas of books. A normal graduate teaches things, principles, thoughts; every point is examined orally, and subjects are sifted by the exercise of the judgment as well as the memory. The pupil is made to see with his own eyes and to rely on his own observations. Books are a mere syllabus, a skeleton, to be clothed with flesh by the teacher and pupil. Practical knowledge of almost every kind is worked in continually with the subjects of study. All the common objects of sight, such as flowers, plants, trees, rocks, birds, insects, tame and wild animals, forms, colors and dimensions, manners, morals, laws of health, gymnastic exercises, drawing and the cultivation of the voice, receive special attention. This common sense knowledge of useful things is a vital part of popular education. Instead of this, how often are the poor children wearied with the endless repetition of mere words, the dry and stale lumber of the books.
21. Dabney, *op. cit.,* I, 236-37.
22. South Carolina, *Acts and Joint Resolutions of the General Assembly* (1896).
23. The 1964 revisions amended the composition of the State Board of Education and were more specific in the duties and responsibilities of the board and the superintendent of education.
24. Superintendent of Education, *Annual Report, 1900,* p. 19.
25. Superintendent of Education, *Annual Report, 1902,* p. 11.
26. James H. Thornwell was born in 1812 and died in 1862. An 1831 graduate of the University of South Carolina (then known as the South Carolina College), he was ordained to the Presbyterian ministry, but 4 years later he returned to his alma mater, where he served as professor and president for 25 years .
27. Superintendent of Education, *Annual Report, 1903,* pp. 7-8.
28. *Ibid.,* p. 9.
29. Superintendent of Education, *Annual Report, 1904,* p. 71.
30. Superintendent of Education, *Annual Report, 1905* p. 54.

31. This discussion is continued later under "The Administration of James H. Hope, 1922-46."
32. South Carolina, *School Laws* (1962), pp. 109-10. This legislation dates back to 1913.
33. Superintendent of Education, *Annual Report, 1910,* p.1.
34. An account of the State Educational Finance Commission and the consolidation of districts also may be found in this chapter.
35. South Carolina, *Acts of the General Assembly* (1910), p.9.
36. Superintendent of Education, *Annual Report, 1920,* p. 40.
37. South Carolina, *Acts of the General Assembly* (1965), p. 516.
38. Superintendent of Education, *Annual Report, 1916*, p. 8.
39. Superintendent of Education, *Annual Report, 1920,* p. 39.
40. These acts were changed considerably by legislation in 1924 and 1951; this paper will explain these changes later.
41. Superintendent of Education, *Annual Report, 1916,* p. 109.
42. Superintendent of Education, *Annual Report, 1919,* p. 170. This comment was made by the supervisor of mill schools.
43. The General Assembly of 1920 was particularly active in school legislation. A pamphlet of statewide laws dealing with the subject is included in the Superintendent of Education, *Annual Report, 1919.* Among laws enacted were "An Act To Provide an Equalization Fund for Needy Schools and Repeal an Act Entitled 'An Act To Guarantee Adequate Facilities and Teaching Corps in Needy School Districts.' " This act gave more support to needy school districts. Also enacted were "An Act To Establish and Maintain High Schools," and "An Act To Relieve the Overcrowding of Pupils in the Elementary Grades of State-Aided High Schools." The same assembly passed "An Act To Encourage the Erection of Adequate School Buildings," and another act permitting school districts to levy special taxes up to 15 mills. This same year, the Legislature passed "An Act To Require Levy of a Three Mill Constitutional Tax for Schools." These laws all were designed to improve the tax structure of school districts. Of particular importance was passage of the 6-0-1 Law of 1924, which superseded most of the school aid bills previously passed and was chiefly responsible for the demise of the mill schools.
44. South Carolina, *Journal of the House of Representatives* (1914), p. 13.
45. Superintendent of Education, *Annual Report, 1917,* p. 17.
46. South Carolina, *Acts of the General Assembly* (1937), act 344, p. 556.
47. *Thirty-Three Years of Vocational Education in South Carolina, 1917-1950* (Columbia: Department of Education, n.d.), p. 10.
48. Superintendent of Education, *Annual Report, 1915,* p. 16.
49. South Carolina, *Acts of the General Assembly* (1916), act 503, p. 878. This provided an annual state appropriation of $5,000 for "consolidated schools doing practical classroom and field work in agriculture."
50. Department of Education, *Thirty-Three Years of Vocational Education in South Carolina, 1917-1950* (Columbia: The Department, n.d.), p. 21.
51. Superintendent of Education, *Annual Report, 1918,* p.11.
52. Hollis P. Allen, *The Federal Government and Education* (New York: McGraw-Hill Book Co., 1950), pp. 72 ff.
53. Superintendent of Education, *Annual Report, 1917,* p. 26.
54. Superintendent of Education, *Annual Report, 1922,* p. 123.
55. Elizabeth Ketchen, "Eighty-Two Years of Progress in Education" (unpublished manuscript in the files of the South Carolina Department of Education, 1956), p. 5.
56. Superintendent of Education, *Annual Report, 1923,* p. 1.
57. *Ibid.*, p. 23.
58. *Ibid.*, p. 33.
59. Superintendent of Education, *Annual Report, 1924,* p. 17. In 1935, the term was extended to 8 months, and in 1943, to 9 months.
60. For full information about the investigation, see University of South Carolina, Steering Committee, *The Investigation of Educational Qualifications of Teachers in South Carolina, Directory, Purposes and Plans* (Columbia: The Committee, January 1942).
61. J. M. Daniel, *Excellent Teachers, Their Qualities and Qualifications: A Report of the Investigation of Educational Qualifications of Teachers in South Carolina* (Columbia: The Steering Committee, University of South Carolina, 1944).
62. Superintendent of Education, *Annual Report, 1927,* p. 34.
63. *South Carolina Education News,* II, No. 6 (February 1946), 1.
64. The R.L. Bryan Company is the central depository for the state. Arthur St. J. Simons, chairman of the Board of Directors, states that his company has been the central depository since 1893. Other sources corroborate the statement.

65. South Carolina, Department of Education, *School Laws* (1962), p. 93.
66. *Ibid.*, sec. 21-476, p. 91.
67. *Ibid.*, sec. 21-456, p. 89.
68. For a closer understanding of the Textbook Law, see South Carolina, *Code of Laws* (1962), p. 86.
69. Superintendent of Education, *Annual Report, 1945*, p. 97.
70. *Ibid.*, p. 95.
71. National Education Association, Research Division, *Rankings of the States, 1968* (Washington, D.C.: The Association, 1968), pp. 27-28.
72. Superintendent of Education, *Annual Report, 1927*, p. 26.
73. Superintendent of Education, *Annual Report, 1946*, p. 42.
74. *Ibid.*, p. 19.
75. The committee was named after Ernest F. Hollings, a member of the House of Representatives. Hollings, in 1954, was elected Lieutenant Governor, Governor in 1958, and Senator in 1966.
76. James Francis Byrnes, South Carolina's most distinguished citizen, served 14 years in Congress, two terms as Senator, Associate Justice of the U.S. Supreme Court, Director of Economic Stabilization, Director of War Mobilization, and from 1945 to 1947 Secretary of State under President Truman.
77. In 1953, this was raised to $20, and in 1967, to $25.
78. Superintendent of Education, *Annual Report, 1966*, pp. 16-17. This statement is found in many of Anderson's speeches and reports.

BIBLIOGRAPHY

Public Documents

South Carolina. *Acts and Joint Resolutions of the General Assembly* (1896-1965).

—— *Code of Laws of South Carolina and School Laws of South Carolina* (1962).

—— *Constitution* (1868, 1895).

—— *General House of Commons* (1703).

—— *Journal of the House of Representatives* (1914).

Books and Pamphlets

Allen, Hollis P. *The Federal Government and Education.* New York: McGraw-Hill Book Co., 1950.

Capers, Henry D. *The Life and Times of C.G. Memminger.* Richmond, Va.: Everett Waddey Co., 1893.

Carlisle, J. H., Jr., ed. *Addresses of J. H. Carlisle, 1825-1909.* Columbia: The State Co., 1910.

Carroll, B.R. *Historical Collections of South Carolina.* 2 vols. New York: Harper & Bros., 1836.

Cubberley, Ellwood P. *State School Administration.* Boston: Houghton-Mifflin Co., 1927.

Dabney, Charles William. *Universal Education in the South.* 2 vols. Chapel Hill: University of North Carolina Press, 1936.

Dalcho, Frederick. *An Historical Account of the Protestant Episcopal Church in South Carolina.* Charleston, S.C.: E. Thayer, 1820.

Daniel, J. M. *Excellent Teachers, Their Qualities and Qualifications: A Report of the Investigation of Educational Qualifications of Teachers in South Carolina.* Columbia: The Steering Committee, University of South Carolina, 1944.

Davis, Robert Means. "A Sketch of Education in South Carolina." *Hammonds Hand Book of South Carolina, 1883.* Charleston, S.C.: Walker, Evans and Cogswell, 1883. Reprinted by The Steering Committee, University of South Carolina, 1944.

Department of Education. *The Palmetto State: A Handbook of Information About South Carolina for Teachers and Students.* 12th ed. Columbia: The Department, 1967.

——*Standards for Accredited Elementary Schools of South Carolina.* Columbia: The Department, 1967.

——*Standards for Accredited High Schools of South Carolina.* Columbia: The Department, 1968.

——*Thirty-Three Years of Vocational Education in South Carolina, 1917-1950.* Columbia: The Department, n.d.

Historical Sketch of the John De La Howe School. Reprinted from the seventh annual report (1931) of the "orphan section" of the Duke endowment, with supplement. Anderson, S.C.: Anderson Printing Co., 1950.

Johnson, Joseph. *Traditions and Reminiscences of the American Revolution.* Charleston, S.C.: Walter & James, 1851.

Joyner, Judith R. *Public Schools in South Carolina.* Columbia: University of South Carolina Press, 1969.

Joynes, Edward Southey. *A Midsummer Ramble.* Columbia: Bryan Printing Co., 1890. Address before the Teachers' Institute, Florence, S.C., July 1890, published at the request of school authorities of Florence.

——*Personal Recollections of Teachers' Institutes and of Teachers of South Carolina.* Columbia: South Carolina University, 1914.

Knight, Edgar Wallace, ed. *A Documentary History of Education in the South Before 1860.* 2 vols. Chapel Hill: University of North Carolina Press, 1949.

McCrady, Edward. *Education in South Carolina Prior to and During the Revolution.* Charleston: South Carolina Historical Society, 1883. An address made before the South Carolina Historical Society, August 6, 1883.

Meriwether, Colyer. *History of Higher Education in South Carolina with a Sketch of the Free School System.* Washington, D.C.: Government Printing Office, 1889.

Ramage, Burr James. *Local Government and Free Schools in South Carolina.* Baltimore, Md.: Johns Hopkins University, 1883.

Ramsay, David. *The History of South Carolina.* 2 vols. Charleston, S.C.: David Longworth, 1809.

Reynolds, John Schreiner. *Reconstruction in South Carolina, 1865-1877.* Columbia: The State Co., 1905.

Sims, William Gilmore. *The History of South Carolina.* Charleston, S.C.: S. Babcock Co., 1842.

Stoddard, James Alexander. *Backgrounds of Secondary Education in South Carolina.* Columbia: Extension Division, University of South Carolina, 1924.

Swanson, Ernst W., and Griffin, John A., eds. *Public Education in the South: Today and Tomorrow.* Chapel Hill: University of North Carolina Press, 1955. This is a statistical survey based on studies by John M. MacLachlan, Truman M. Pierce & Associates, and Ernst W. Swanson.

Swearingen, Mrs. John E. *A Gallant Journey: Mr. Swearingen and His Family.* Columbia: University of South Carolina Press, 1959.

Thomas, Albert Sidney. *A Historical Account of the Protestant Episcopal Church in South Carolina, 1820-1957.* Columbia: The R. L. Bryan Co., 1957.

Thomason, John Furman. *The Foundations of the Public Schools of South Carolina.* Columbia: The State Co., 1925.

Thompson, Henry T. *The Establishment of the Public School System in South Carolina.* Columbia: The R. L. Bryan Co., 1927.

Wallace, David Duncan. *The History of South Carolina.* 3 vols. New York: The American Historical Society, Inc., 1934.

—— *History of the S.C. Teachers' Association, 1924.* Columbia: The State Co., 1924.

Watson, Ebbie Julian. *Handbook of South Carolina.* 2d ed. Columbia: The State Co., 1908.

Reports

National Education Association, Research Division. *Rankings of the States, 1968.* Washington, D.C.: The Association, 1968.

Superintendents of Education. *Annual Reports.* Columbia: Department of Education, 1878-1966.

U.S. Commissioner of Education. *Annual Report, 1899-1900.* Washington, D.C.: Government Printing Office, 1901.

University of South Carolina, Steering Committee. *The Investigation of Educational Qualifications of Teachers in South Carolina, Directory, Purposes, and Plans.* Columbia: The Committee, 1942.

Articles and Periodicals

"Centennial of a Seer." *South Carolina Schools,* XIX, No. 4 (Summer 1968), 6-7.

South Carolina Education News, II, No. 6 (1946), 1.

Towers, Richard L. "The 'Carpetbagger' Who Was South Carolina's First State Superintendent of Education." *Education Report,* X (December 1967), 1.

Unpublished Material

Foster, Gertrude. "Documentary History of Education in South Carolina." Unpublished Ph.D. dissertation, University of South Carolina, Columbia, 1932.

Ketchen, Elizabeth. "Eighty-Two Years of Progress in Education." Unpublished manuscript in the files of the South Carolina Department of Education, 1956.

Woodall, Michael Vance. "Justus K. Jillson: South Carolina's First Superintendent of Education." Unpublished paper, University of South Carolina, Columbia, 1966.

Appendix A

SOUTH CAROLINA CHIEF STATE SCHOOL OFFICERS

State Superintendents of Education

1868-76	J. K. Jillson
1876-82	Hugh S. Thompson
1882-86	Asbury Coward
1886-90	James Henry Rice
1890-98	W. D. Mayfield
1898-1902	John J. McMahan
1902-1908	O. B. Martin
1908-22	John E. Swearingen
1922-46	James H. Hope
1946-67	Jesse T. Anderson
1967-	Cyril B. Busbee

Appendix B

Chart I.--SOUTH CAROLINA DEPARTMENT OF EDUCATION, 1910

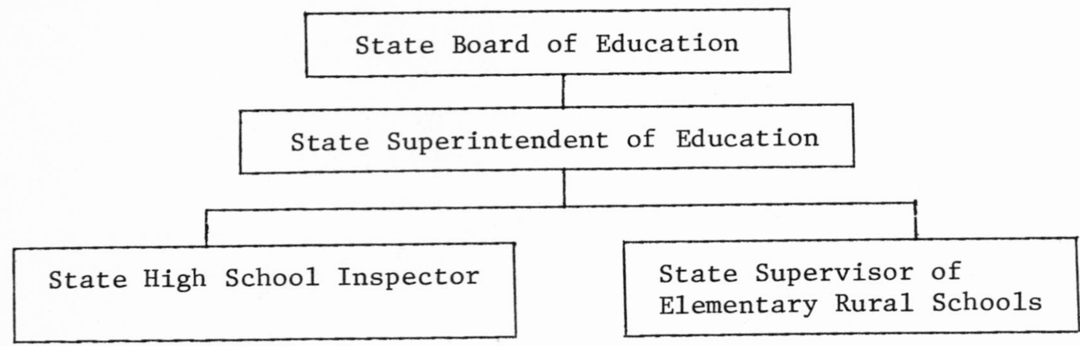

Prior to 1947 the State Department of Education was not organized into divisions and the charts through 1940 are approximations of the services rendered.

Chart II.--SOUTH CAROLINA DEPARTMENT OF EDUCATION, 1920

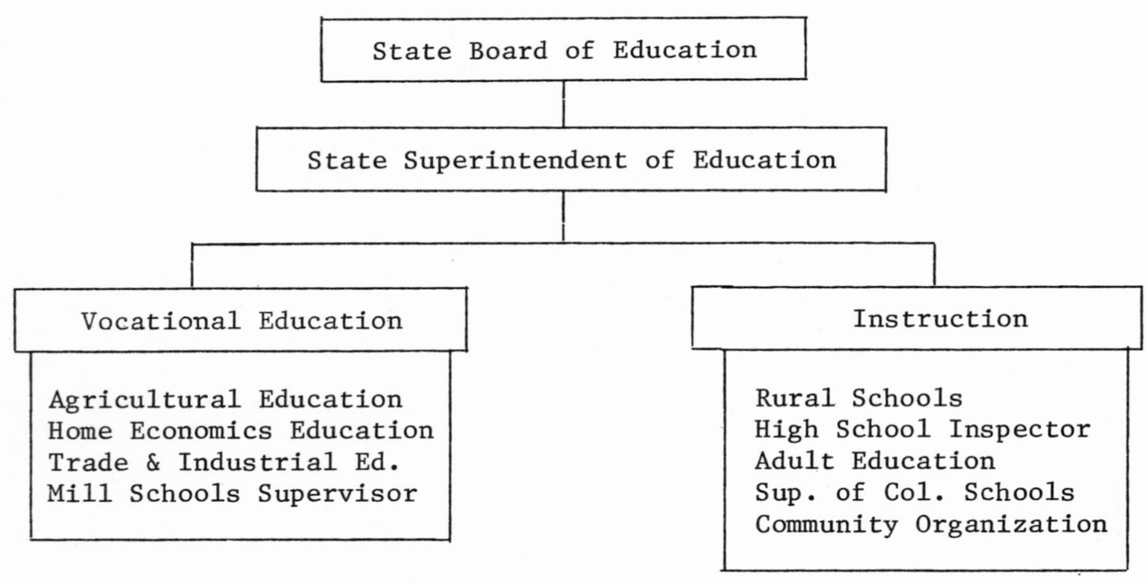

Appendix B

Chart III.--SOUTH CAROLINA DEPARTMENT OF EDUCATION, 1930

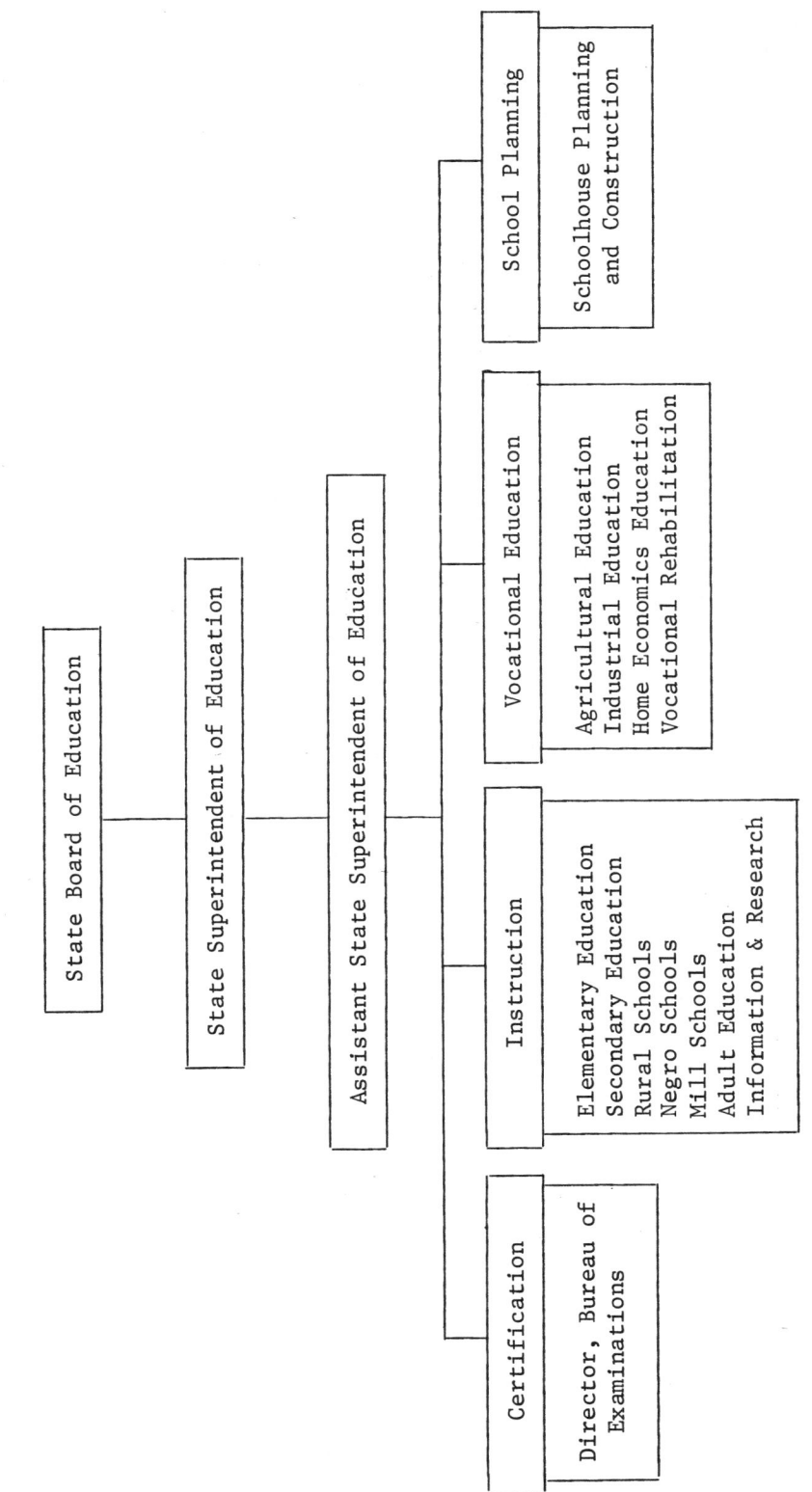

State Board of Education

State Superintendent of Education

Assistant State Superintendent of Education

Certification

Director, Bureau of Examinations

Instruction

Elementary Education
Secondary Education
Rural Schools
Negro Schools
Mill Schools
Adult Education
Information & Research

Vocational Education

Agricultural Education
Industrial Education
Home Economics Education
Vocational Rehabilitation

School Planning

Schoolhouse Planning and Construction

Appendix B

Chart IV.--SOUTH CAROLINA DEPARTMENT OF EDUCATION, 1940

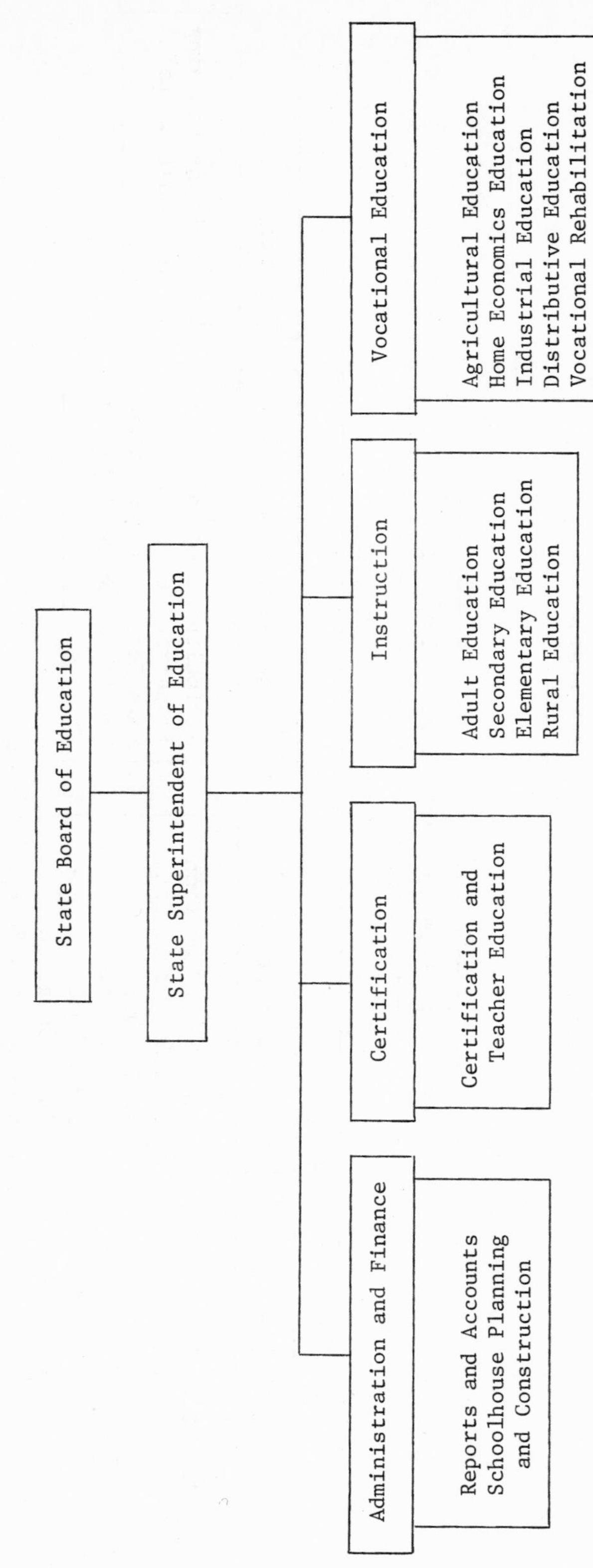

Appendix B

Chart V.--SOUTH CAROLINA DEPARTMENT OF EDUCATION, 1950

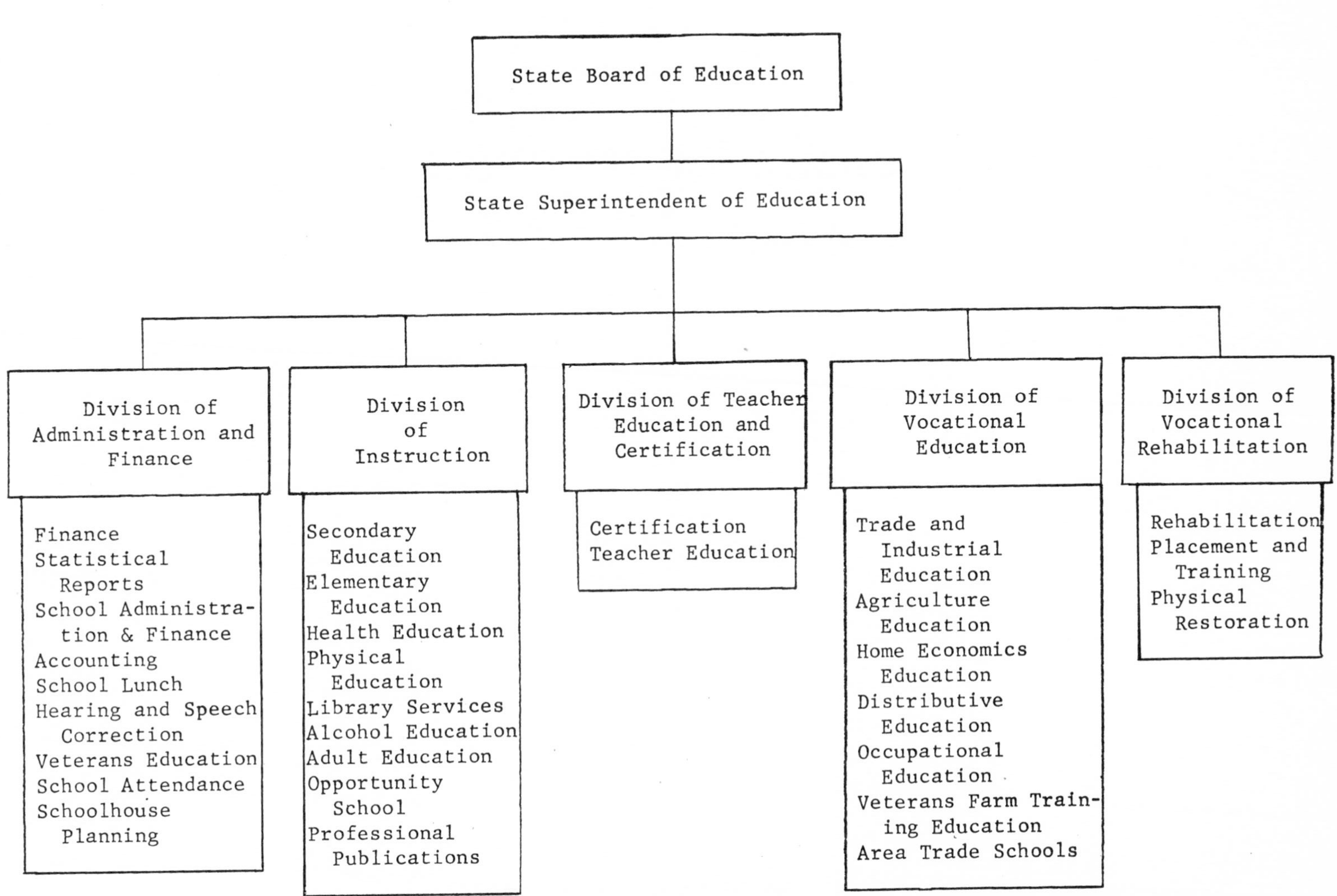
State Board of Education
State Superintendent of Education
Division of Administration and Finance
Finance
Statistical Reports
School Administration & Finance
Accounting
School Lunch
Hearing and Speech Correction
Veterans Education
School Attendance
Schoolhouse Planning
Division of Instruction
Secondary Education
Elementary Education
Health Education
Physical Education
Library Services
Alcohol Education
Adult Education
Opportunity School
Professional Publications
Division of Teacher Education and Certification
Certification
Teacher Education
Division of Vocational Education
Trade and Industrial Education
Agriculture Education
Home Economics Education
Distributive Education
Occupational Education
Veterans Farm Training Education
Area Trade Schools
Division of Vocational Rehabilitation
Rehabilitation
Placement and Training
Physical Restoration

Appendix B

Chart VI.--SOUTH CAROLINA DEPARTMENT OF EDUCATION, 1960

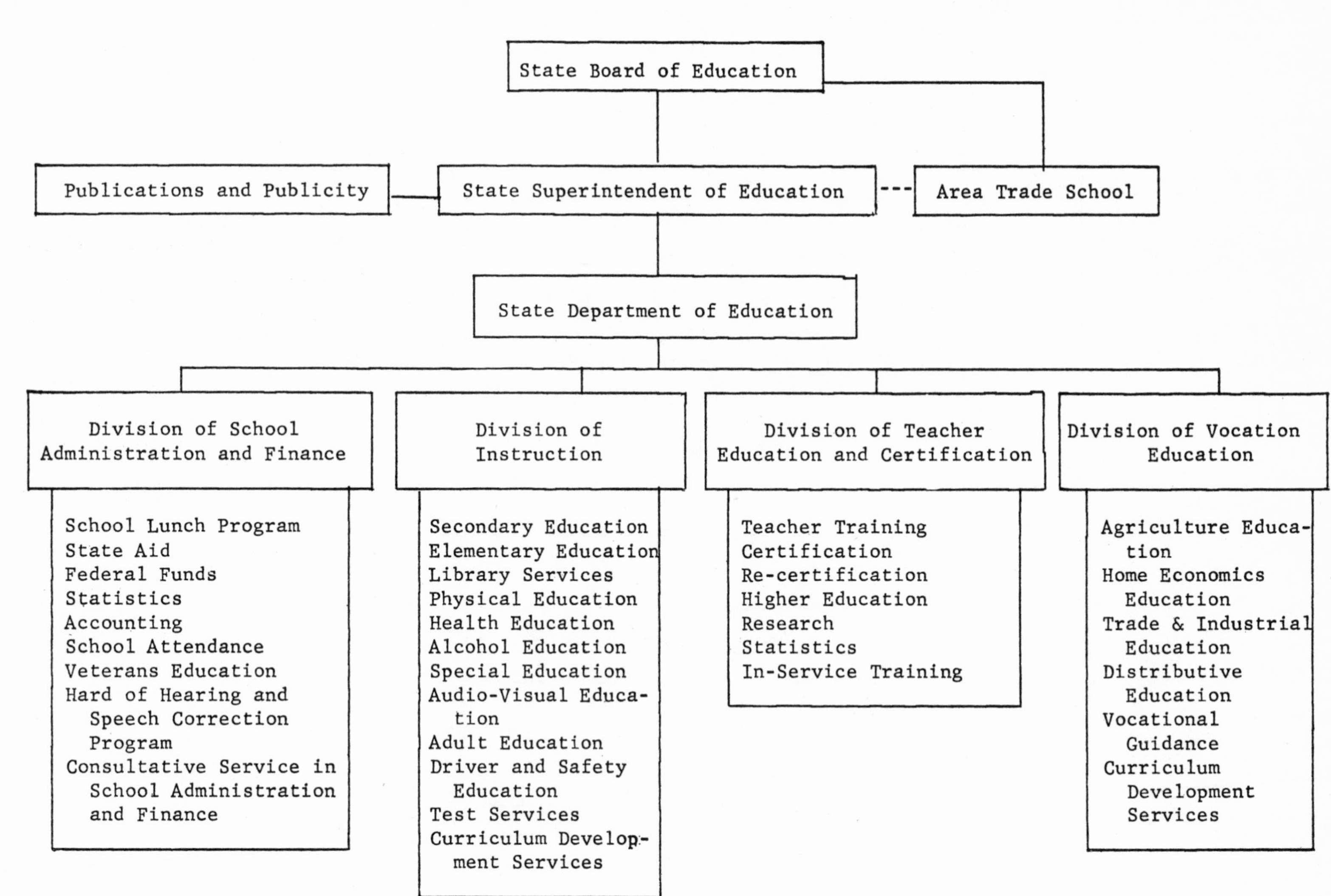
State Board of Education
Publications and Publicity
State Superintendent of Education
Area Trade School
State Department of Education
Division of School Administration and Finance
School Lunch Program
State Aid
Federal Funds
Statistics
Accounting
School Attendance
Veterans Education
Hard of Hearing and Speech Correction Program
Consultative Service in School Administration and Finance
Division of Instruction
Secondary Education
Elementary Education
Library Services
Physical Education
Health Education
Alcohol Education
Special Education
Audio-Visual Education
Adult Education
Driver and Safety Education
Test Services
Curriculum Development Services
Division of Teacher Education and Certification
Teacher Training
Certification
Re-certification
Higher Education
Research
Statistics
In-Service Training
Division of Vocation Education
Agriculture Education
Home Economics Education
Trade & Industrial Education
Distributive Education
Vocational Guidance
Curriculum Development Services

Appendix B

Chart VII.--SOUTH CAROLINA DEPARTMENT OF EDUCATION, 1966

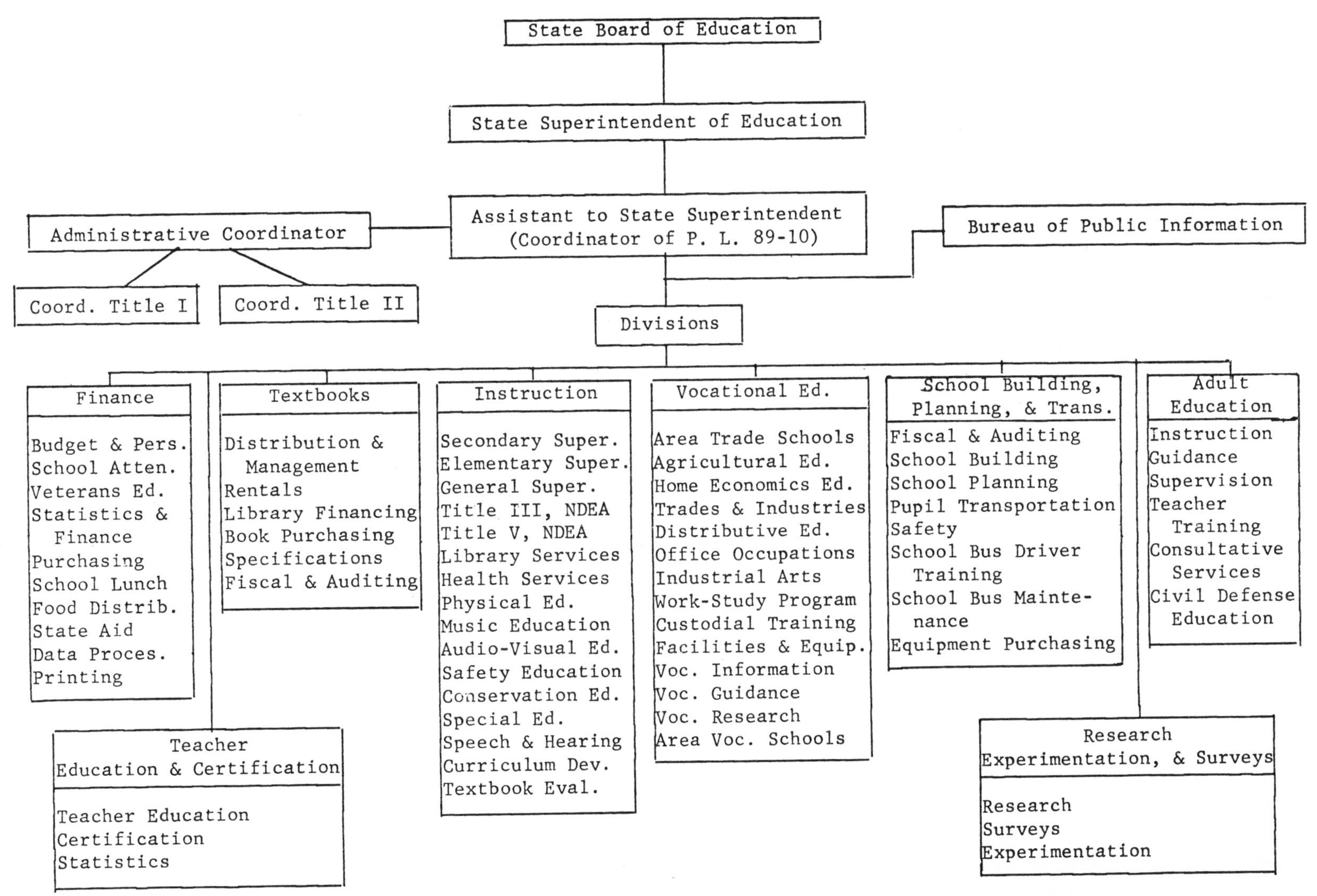

Appendix B

Chart VIII.--SOUTH CAROLINA DEPARTMENT OF EDUCATION, 1968

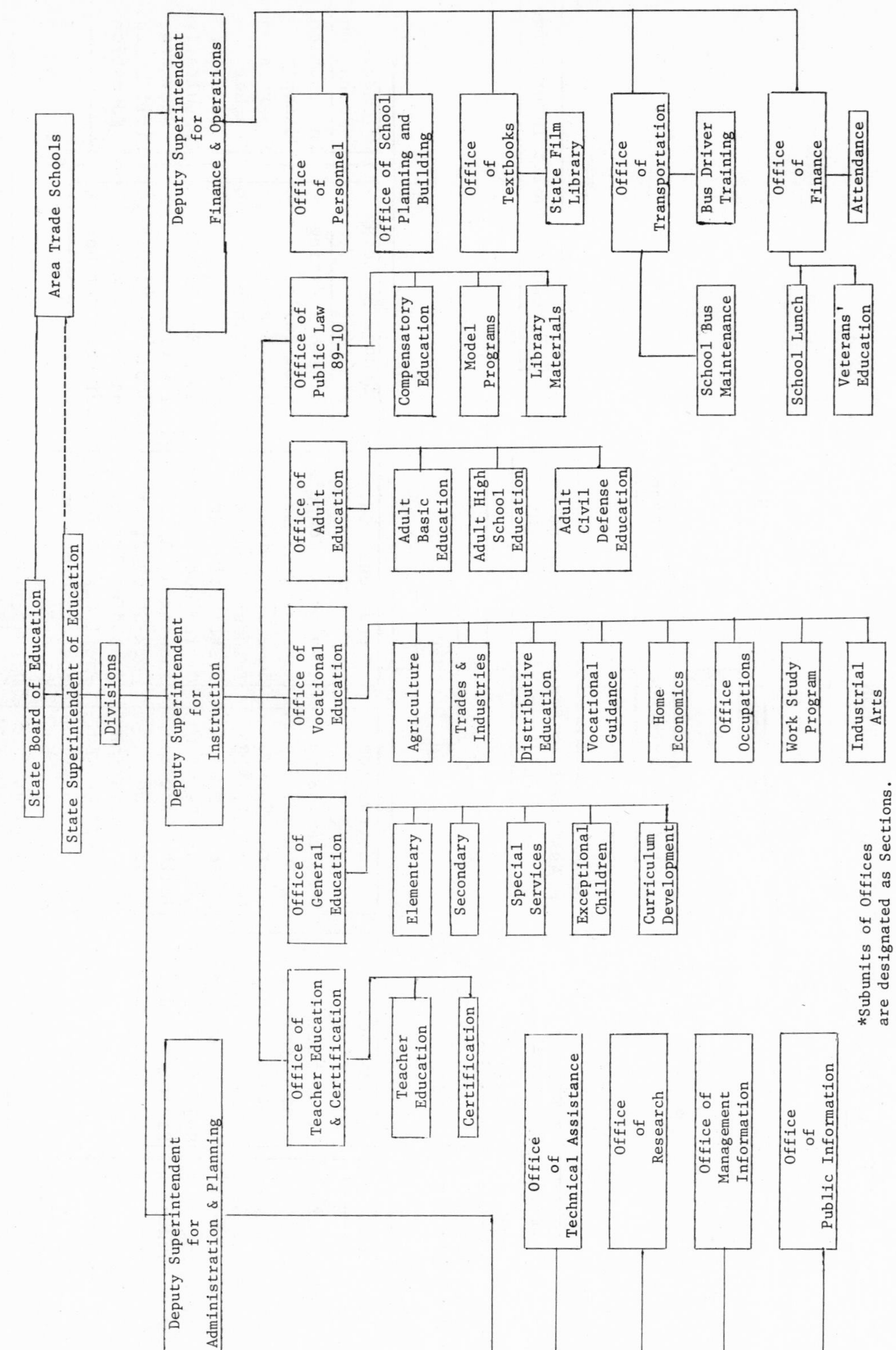

42 South Dakota

DEPARTMENT OF PUBLIC INSTRUCTION
James C. Schooler

Contents

EDUCATION IN SOUTH DAKOTA PRIOR TO 1900

In 1862, the Dakota Territorial Legislature established a board of education composed of the Governor, the treasurer, and the secretary of the territory and authorized the appointment of a superintendent of public instruction who would also serve as the board's secretary (1). The board would recommend revisions in the school law, make reports to the Legislature, and select the textbooks for the common schools. The members of the board and the superintendent were to be paid $3 a day while on duty, plus an allowance for travel. Two years later, in 1864, the board formally organized, and it appointed James S. Foster as the first superintendent of public instruction. The superintendent was directed to keep a record of the board's official acts and to promote high standards of education in the territory. His duties also included visiting schools, conferring with the county superintendents, and distributing to them blank forms for collecting statistics. He was responsible for reporting annually to the board about the condition of the territory's common schools, for listing their expenditures, and for suggesting how they might improve their organization and methods of instruction.

Superintendent Foster, born in Salisbury, Connecticut, had come under the influence of the great New England educator, Horace Mann. He was a man of ability, and his reports reflect his knowledge and zeal. When the 1865-66 Territorial Legislature abolished the position of secretary to the board and created an elective board of education, the new members in 1866 appointed Foster as superintendent of public instruction (2).

When Foster took office, the Dakota Territory had no schools except a few private ones and had passed no official acts; therefore, his first report in December 1864 consisted chiefly of recommendations, such as the fundamental necessity of a regular levy to support the schools. In his 1867 report, Foster cautioned that to avoid future trouble, it was necessary that the territory's first districting be done with care to reduce the need for redistricting. He urged the Legislature to pass a law providing for an equitable division of property when the districts were created. The superintendent also pointed out the need for a normal school in this new region, "especially of the propriety of federal provision for such a school" (3).

In 1867, no one qualified for the education board, so it was dropped – the last board in the territory until 1887, when the Legislature revived it on the recommendation of Superintendent A. Sheridan Jones. The 1867 Legislature provided for an elected superintendent who would serve a 2-year term. In addition to his other powers, the superintendent was granted the authority to approve all textbooks used in the public schools, regulate the certificates to teach issued by the county superintendents, conduct territorial teachers institutes, discourage the use of sectarian books in the public schools, and assist in selecting books for libraries. The law ordered him to furnish copies of school laws to district officers, hear the appeals of county superintendents, and render interpretations of these laws. The superintendent's salary was established at $4 per day, plus an allowance for materials.

In 1869, T. M. Stuart was appointed state superintendent. Stuart served only a few months, and Foster was appointed to fill out his 2-year term. J. W. Turner was appointed superintendent in 1870. The 1870-71 Legislature had authorized the superintendent to appoint a deputy, and Foster, although busy with other matters, agreed to serve in this position (4).

During these years, the superintendents devoted most of their efforts to improving teaching and school management by developing courses of study and conducting institutes for teachers. They counseled with county superintendents and school district board members on the operation and fiscal management of the school districts. Unfortunately, the state superintendents had meager funds to carry out their duties. The lack of funds for printing may be one of the reasons why the official reports are virtually nonexistent from 1867 to 1884 (5).

The early superintendents were paid inadequately for the many responsibilities of their office. For instance, in 1873 the salary was fixed at $600 per year, and then changed in 1875 to $5 per day for the time actually devoted to school business. The $600 was restored in 1877 – the same as it had been 4 years earlier.

The state superintendency assumed considerable importance when William H. H. Beadle accepted the position in 1879. His work during the 6 years he held office was of great value to the territory and later to the state in developing and systemizing a plan of public instruction. His efforts in saving the school lands of the Dakotas, and indirectly the school lands of other states, have been widely acknowledged. After a study of other states, he became convinced that the township system of school district organization as practiced in Indiana was the best for Dakota, and, in 1883, he convinced the Legislature to make the township the legal unit for school operation. By 1886, it had been adopted by 68 of the territory's 83 organized counties. These 68 counties consisted of only 365 school districts, while the 15 older counties, where the smaller unit district system was firmly entrenched, had 1,150 districts (6). Even after the township system was abolished, the township school districts remained the basic unit in many counties.

The Legislature again changed the state department's structure in 1887 by delegating all of the superintendent's duties to the Territorial Board of Education. In addition, the board was given the authority to revoke teacher certificates, prescribe a course of study for common and high schools, adopt and furnish schoolhouse plans, and specify the duties of the deputy superintendent. The superintendent was now an administrator, responsible for the full management and supervision of the schools. His most important responsibilities involved deciding controversies and disputes according to the laws or the board's rules and regulations. He kept then—as now—the books, maps, charts, and plans for school buildings in his office.

When South Dakota became a state in 1889, its constitution provided for a superintendent of public instruction to be elected for a term of 2 years at a salary of $1,800 per year. The new state's Legislature, in its first session in 1890, abolished the education board and transferred its powers and duties to the superintendent. Except for tinkering with the laws as they applied to operating schools in the counties, townships, and districts, the Legislature made no more changes in the state's educational system until 1901. During this period, the department was apparently a one-man operation.

EDUCATION IN SOUTH DAKOTA, 1900-65

In 1901, the South Dakota Legislature undertook a complete revision of the school laws. The superintendent's duties were changed very little, but he was given responsibility for supervising all common and high schools. For the first time, the superintendent was provided with an office at the state capitol and was directed to file his papers, reports, and the public documents received from the county superintendents so that they could be inspected by the Legislature at any time. His salary remained at $1,800 per year, but he was given $200 for expenses incurred while traveling on the business of the department. The superintendent also was authorized to appoint a deputy at a salary of $1,200 per year.

The Legislature passed a compulsory attendance law in 1905, but the superintendent's biennial report for 1906-1908 indicates that the pupils in the rural districts attended on an average only 85 days per year while those in the independent districts attended 131 days. About 69 percent of the pupils attended schools in rural districts where the eighth grade was the highest offered; 31 percent were enrolled in the independent districts – 5 percent in the high schools and 26 percent in the lower grades. Unfortunately, although the law required every child between 8 and 14 to attend school, too often the school officials were hesitant to enforce it. Since in many schools the teachers and administrators preferred to expel mischievous children, Superintendent H. H. Ustrud recommended that the attendance law be enforced by a juvenile court.

At the end of the first decade of the twentieth century, many improvements had taken place in curriculum and school buildings, but the schools still found it difficult to secure qualified teachers. There was a growing interest in instruction in manual training, domestic science, and agriculture, but teachers with the proper training were scarce, and those already teaching were trying to do too much without adequate apparatus and laboratories. However, Superintendent Ustrud stated that he was particularly pleased that in many places modern school buildings had replaced the old box-shaped schoolhouses with cross lights and poor ventilation and heating, erected with no thought for the welfare and comfort of the children. But he added:

> This condition is too often the exception and not the general rule. In the march of progress in the educational world the country school is lagging behind. Over two-thirds of the children of school age in our state are attending the country schools, and in their behalf I would plead for a square deal (7).

Superintendent Ustrud called for an educational awakening. He challenged the people to put their schoolhouses in good condition and pay enough to attract the best teachers so that they could build something they would be proud of. He stated: "The time is now for a concerted action on the part of all our citizens for better educational facilities for our children. In the sparsely settled communities I would recommend that state aid be provided for the buildings of schoolhouses" (8).

To carry out his recommendations, Ustrud urged that the county superintendents be given more authority over local school boards in selecting teachers and spending public funds. He contended that in a number of cases school officers were employing uncertified teachers. He recommended that the certificates required by law for the county superintendents should require bookkeeping and accounting so they could assist school officers with their accounting and reporting.

C. G. Lawrence, a former Lincoln County superintendent, became state superintendent in January 1911. His staff consisted of a deputy, a clerk responsible for issuing teaching certificates, a statistical clerk, and one stenographer. The superintendent conferred with the county superintendents, attended various school officers and teachers meetings, visited the high schools, and gathered the statistics for a biennial report to the Governor and the general public. He worked closely with the South Dakota Education Association and the county superintendents in developing recommendations for legislation to improve the schools.

Superintendent Lawrence was particularly interested in improving the quality of teaching in South Dakota. He estimated that each year approximately 1,500 inexperienced teachers without training in professional education – and many who had completed only 1 or 2 years of high school – were being employed in the rural schools. Although they had passed the state's examination for certificates, he felt that "they have not been properly prepared for undertaking the difficult work of teaching." He contended that "the only remedy for this weakness in our educational system is the establishment of normal training in our high schools to supplement the work of our regular normal schools" (9). He proposed that the Legislature authorize financial support for normal training departments in the high schools; such a plan had been adopted by the Kansas Legislature in 1909, and it had proven extremely popular.

A committee composed of city superintendents, high school principals, and a representative from the state department drafted recommendations for legislative action authorizing additional normal training courses in certain high schools. No action was taken, however, until State Superintendent Fred L. Shaw included these recommendations in his biennial report of October 1918. The Legislature approved the bill the following year and appropriated $30,000 in 1919 and $60,000 for 1920 to aid high schools approved by the state superintendent to "maintain a normal department for the training of teachers with special reference to work in the rural schools of the state." The state superintendent was authorized to "prescribe the conditions of admission to the normal training classes, the course of instruction, and the rules and regulations under which such instruction shall be given" (10). The annual financial assistance per school ranged from $500 to one enrolling from five to ten pupils in normal training classes to $1,000 to schools enrolling over twenty in such classes.

Superintendent Lawrence also took up school consolidation as a solution to the problem of the many small rural schools. In 1913, the Legislature passed an act providing for reorganization to reduce the number of rural schools. The department prepared for public distribution five bulletins covering general education problems, one of which was designed to assist voters when the question of consolidation was put before the various communities.

Superintendent Lawrence resigned in September 1914 to return to Lincoln County as superintendent of the Canton city schools. He was replaced by Charles H. Lugg. Superintendent Lugg agreed that consolidation offered a solution to the rural school problem, but he warned that "it must not be accepted without a clear understanding of the experience of other communities that have tried it, and the knowledge that it is not suitable for all conditions" (11).

When it became apparent that the United States would be involved in World War I, a number of people demanded that the schools do their "patriotic duty" by dismissing the students early to speed up agricultural production. France and England, having tried this, warned that it was a mistake from both a patriotic and an economic standpoint to cripple the schoolwork of those who would eventually have to assume the burden of the present struggle. The warnings were not heeded, however, and students and teachers withdrew from their classrooms to the extent that those who remained lost their enthusiasm and spirit. The federal government finally began a campaign to keep the schools running at full efficiency.

In South Dakota, a number of neighborhoods were comprised of immigrants who could not read or write English and in some cases could not speak it. Many fell prey to anti-American propaganda. In 1918 the Legislature met in an extra session and passed an act "forbidding the use of any foreign language as the language of instruction in any schools or educational institutions of the state, either public or private, except as it may be necessary in teaching the foreign language itself as one of the subjects of study in our secondary and higher institutions" (12). At the same time, the teaching of German was suspended in all educational institutions for the duration of the war.

These conditions, along with the fact that in many cases the majority of electors in some school districts did not believe in education—even to promote literacy—caused the schools to be looked upon as nuisances interfering with the right of parents to force their children to labor whenever they needed them. Some of the school buildings were in such bad condition that they hampered students in their work. These factors prompted the 1919 Legislature to enact the Americanization Act, with its main aim to disseminate propaganda and maintain strong schools.

In July 1919, M. M. Guhin assumed the position of state director of Americanization and immediately began a campaign to explain the need, purpose, and spirit of his program. Night schools were established in the many foreign-language-speaking communities – the most successful being in the one-room country schools. A number of teachers worked without compensation except for the many expressions of appreciation from their students for helping them learn to read and write. As a result, "the real process of naturalization began taking place – a process involving attitude and emotional response to America" (13).

Many of the native-born citizens suffered from near illiteracy rather than absolute illiteracy. For instance, it was common to receive letters like the following:

> Dere Ser;
>
> Rescevd; I will led you no that I cand go to sccul. I paist the fourd grad and some other higher grads. I whout send you my report card bout I cand find it no more. Ill teall the trought thads onosto good (honest to God) Im twenty two years old (14).

The older people who attended the night schools became convinced of the importance of education. After the first few years, many of the evening schools had served their purpose, so they were discontinued, and the day schools offered the citizenship training. The Americanization and vocational rehabilitation programs were combined in 1927, but since the need for the former had diminished, the 1931 Legislature repealed the Americanization Act and drastically reduced the appropriation. As the money dwindled, the Americanization program came to a close, but not before it had established the principle that every child in South Dakota should grow up with the opportunity to attend a public school in his own community and learn to read and write the English language.

Superintendent Lugg realized that his predecessors had suffered many frustrations in dealing with the Legislature on items of a professional and technical nature. The South Dakota schools had been surpassed by the schools in the adjoining states despite the efficient work the school system had done in the past. He stated that it was time for the Legislature to confine itself to determining fundamental issues and not consider the details of school regulation. He added:

> Practically every legislature since statehood has been called upon to consider a vast array of bills pertaining to educational matters, many of which were well advised while many were not. A deep-seated prejudice has sprung up in the minds of many of our best and most experienced legislators against any legislation pertaining to schools – a condition that is most unfortunate (15).

Lugg recommended that the Legislature create a State Board of Education to regulate matters that were purely professional and technical, such as the details concerning teachers institutes, certification of teachers, courses of study, and school reports. He also contended that a board was needed because the department's functions were increasing and all of the responsibilities that he would turn over to the board were now unjustly placed on the state superintendent's shoulders. Neither the public nor the Legislature was willing to accept this recommendation for a state board for another 40 years, but many board proponents after Lugg continually repeated his arguments.

The Legislature did create a vocational education state board to take advantage of the Smith-Hughes Act passed by Congress in 1917, but no funds were appropriated to administer the act. The State Board of Regents loaned the superintendent two instructors from the colleges to serve as inspectors of the high school programs initiated under the provisions of the Smith-Hughes Act.

The Legislature also created a commission to study South Dakota's educational problems and ordered it to report to the Governor prior to July 1, 1918. Under the chairmanship of Harold M. Foght of the U.S. Bureau of Education, the commission offered many helpful suggestions for administering and reorganizing the public educational system. Although the 1919 Legislature implemented none of the major recommendations, when Fred L. Shaw was appointed state superintendent in September 1918 to complete Lugg's unexpired term, he immediately began a vigorous campaign to improve the department's status. He found that the South Dakota department's appropriation was the smallest of any state in the Union.

Perhaps the survey commission's report contributed to his success in obtaining the legislation he desired. The Legislature appropriated \$20,600 each for the 1920 and 1921 fiscal years to take full advantage of the funds available for vocational education under the Smith-Hughes Act. It authorized the State Board of Vocational Education to approve high schools recommended by the state superintendent for departments of vocational agriculture, home economics, and trade and industrial education, and to appoint officers and assistants to administer the vocational education program. This was important legislation because it lodged the vocational education program within the Department of Public Instruction instead of placing it in another agency as in a number of other states.

The Legislature also increased the appropriations for the department. This enabled Superintendent Shaw to add an assistant superintendent, a high school supervisor, a rural school supervisor, a supervisor of home economics, and a director with two assistants to supervise the adult education and Americanization program. For the first time, the department was in a position to perform many of the supervisory and inspection duties assigned to the state superintendent.

Superintendent Shaw was equally concerned about the general status of education and the quality of instruction in the schools. He campaigned for authorization to add field superintendents in the county superintendents' offices who could visit and counsel with teachers in the rural communities. He supported legislation requiring all districts to provide free textbooks for their pupils rather than the previous system, whereby books were furnished only when a majority of a district's electors petitioned the school board to provide them.

Superintendent Shaw reorganized his state department into four "departments" or sections in addition to himself and his deputy. The high school department consisted of the high school supervisor, the vocational agriculture supervisor, and the home economics supervisor; the rural education and Americanization department included a director, three assistants, and a truant officer; the rehabilitation department consisted of a director; and the certification department was made up of the chairman of the board of examiners, an examination clerk, and a credentials clerk. Six stenographers were employed for all departments.

During Shaw's second term, considerable progress was made in the local school systems in both the urban and rural districts. Many buildings were constructed, and a number of old buildings were remodeled. Teachers took advantage of the normal training programs established in some 60 high schools; at the end of this period, approximately 25 percent of the state's teachers had an equivalent of 2 or more years of work at the college level above a 4-year high school education, and 50 percent of the teachers held first-grade or higher certificates. The state course of study for the elementary and secondary schools was thoroughly revised and reorganized. Most of the high schools followed the new course, which emphasized a curriculum adapted to the various needs of the community along vocational lines.

The rural schools remained a problem. They still employed many inexperienced teachers, and too often local school boards failed to provide the proper tools and working conditions. In 1919, the Legislature attempted to solve the problem in part by appropriating state aid to standardize the rural schools. Shaw was later convinced that this financial assistance did indeed improve education in many rural districts, and he encouraged its continuation in the face of considerable opposition. In his 1922-24 report he referred to this campaign against state aid:

> Perhaps the most notable happening during the last three years has been the persistent campaign of propaganda against the public schools which is being carried on by organizations under sinister and un-American influence. All efforts to meet the financial demands of the public school system have been suppressed with the utmost skill and the minds of many well meaning people have been poisoned by prejudices against all forms of public school support except the limited local support derived from a property tax which is recognized as the least effective and most unfair means of raising public revenue (16).

The rural schools also were helped by a free high school tuition law passed in 1921, which provided an opportunity for every boy and girl in South Dakota to achieve a high school education at public expense. This placed an increasing demand on the high schools to provide facilities and teachers for expanding enrollments. At the same time, progress continued to be made in consolidating the rural schools, which in many cases were now providing 12 full years of education.

Superintendent Shaw repeatedly recommended separating the educational system from partisan politics and asked that the Legislature submit to the people a constitutional amendment creating a State Board of Education. He further suggested that the state board of regents and superintendent of public instruction offices be abolished and these functions be assumed by a State Board of Education consisting of three members elected on a nonpartisan ballot. He felt that this would remove the schools from the vicissitudes of politics and would enable the state to adopt a permanent, forward-looking educational program. The Legislature seriously considered the proposal from time to time, but its proponents failed to gain sufficient support to win approval.

The 1923 Legislature enacted a law permitting the schools to release time for religious instruction despite Shaw's attitude that it was unnecessary. He felt that it relieved the teacher from the responsibility of presenting broad ethical and moral instruction in the classroom. He admitted that there was a need for religious instruction and that the average child received practically none. But he believed that the solution should be in the home and church rather than the responsibility of the state. He contended that the church was not doing all it should to revive the religious atmosphere of the home, because in far too many cases the religious atmosphere of the church was also wanting. Thus, if any legislation should attempt to further religious instruction, Shaw argued that it should be designed to encourage a revival of the religious spirit both in the church and the home, with the emphasis on the responsibility of these institutions. He concluded that no matter how much formal instruction might be given, the result in terms of developing a religious spirit would be an absolute failure. He stated:

> The condition of the Jewish race at the time of the coming of the Messiah is a striking example that a nation may have a thorough knowledge of the Scriptures and be very punctilious in the matter of religious performance without having very much religious spirit. This is a matter of great importance upon which the Legislature will be called to act but must not act hastily, or with prejudice (17).

The growth and development of the department and the improvement in the quantity and quality of educational opportunities during Superintendent Shaw's 6-year administration are evidence of one of the brighter periods in the educational history of South Dakota. His forward-looking philosophy, coupled with his enthusiastic, energetic leadership and practical approach to the problems confronting education, affected the Legislature and the general public. It is true he was aided in large measure by the favorable economic situation that emerged after the stringent war years, which created an environment for accepting new ideas and changes in educational methodology and techniques. The conservative element of society, which had mainly controlled educational purse-strings since the state's beginnings, was momentarily overcome by the glittering promises of the bright future pictured for the 30-year-old state. Although Shaw strived to maintain the momentum created in the early years of his administration, the golden era was short-lived. The conservative philosophy returned to dominate the educational scene during the waning months of his term, and the fortunes of the Department of Public Instruction deteriorated rapidly.

C. G. St. John was elected superintendent of public instruction in the fall of 1924 and assumed the office the following January. St. John attempted to reverse the conservative trend by pleading that the existing services and support for the rural schools be maintained. In his first report to the Governor in December 1926, he stated:

> Our rural schools must not be handicapped by any plan of retrenchment in expenditures. They are the foundation of liberty and progress. A depression in the schools today will be felt in the industry and progress of tomorrow. The children from every farm and fireside are calling to us – challenging us as to what we will do for them and their future welfare. We can not turn a deaf ear to this challenge. We must promote schools, equip them with the best that we can afford, and see that every person who is entrusted with the care and training of our children must be especially prepared for her work. The future intelligence of our citizenship of tomorrow is too important to be left to the possibility of chance, so we must know when we issue a certificate to a teacher that she has the proper training to present the subject matter to her pupils in a scientific manner. Let us do this for our children and they will rise up and bless us (18).

Despite St. John's efforts, his term saw the inauguration of a period of retrenchment that curtailed the prestige, activities, and effectiveness of the department for the next 16 years. The Legislature decreased education appropriations to such a level that by the end of St. John's 4-year tenure, only six professional people remained besides the state superintendent and his deputy. This eliminated the two rural school supervisors and the high school supervisor and abolished the rural education and Americanization department; these duties were assigned to the supervisor of rehabilitation. The supervisor of agriculture and the supervisor of home economics were retained as well as the chairman of the board of examiners and the credentials clerk. In effect, the professional staff of the department was reduced to the size and effectiveness of the period prior to 1920.

Superintendent St. John made recommendation after recommendation, most of them completely unheeded by the Legislature. He labored strenuously to preserve the state support plan for the rural schools, but he had to acknowledge that the state was –

> Passing through a period of financial stress, owing to poor crops and bank failures, and school finances have been considerably handicapped. . . .The schools also are receiving their share of criticism as their cost is a large part of the public expense (19).

In his report to the Governor in December 1926, he pointed out that his records proved beyond any doubt that the small amount appropriated for state aid had been a "wonderful source" for improving the rural schools; about one-fourth could now meet the qualifications set by the department for standard schools.

St. John reported that many rural schools still needed buildings with modern equipment for lighting, heating, and ventilating; library books; up-to-date sets of maps, globes, and charts; and teachers with training and experience. He pointed out that a 1925 department survey found that in the 50 counties reporting, 9.9 percent of the pupils in the eighth grade failed in the standard schools, and 24 percent failed in the nonstandard schools. Since it cost $98 per pupil to keep a child in school, it was evident that a great saving of both time and cost could be made if he did not have to repeat a course.

Even though the superintendent agreed to taking a slight reduction in the amount necessary to maintain the aid program by eliminating the schools that had received financial support for 10 years and proposed a small tax on incomes above $5,000 to provide the funds, his pleadings fell on deaf legislative ears.

The rural schools, always laboring under serious handicaps, suffered severely from this loss of revenue. The financial support decreased about 30 percent in the standard rural schools, and a slackening in the enforcement of the compulsory attendance law resulted in the rural districts' losing students. The superintendent charged that the Legislature's refusal to appropriate the $360,000 in state aid provided by law was probably the greatest cause for a loss in both standards and attendance. About 40 percent of the state aid had come from taxes levied against railroads, telegraph and telephone lines, and city property, but now all of the money had to come from the local farm property if the districts were to maintain standard schools. Many of the rural schools needed painting and repairs that could not be done if left to the resources of the local boards.

Before he left office, Superintendent St. John recommended an amendment to the state constitution that would change the method of electing the county superintendent and the state superintendent so that these offices could be removed from politics. He believed that these officers should be selected because of their fitness for the positions. However, this proposal was not accepted for another decade.

E. C. Giffen, a rural school supervisor under St. John, became superintendent of public instruction in January 1929. An increase in the budget enabled the department to add a supervisor of elementary education and a supervisor of secondary education (20), bringing the total professional staff to eight, not counting the superintendent and his deputy. The position of assistant superintendent was eliminated and replaced by the office of executive secretary of the Young Citizens League.

The Young Citizens League, organized mainly in the rural schools, sponsored worthwhile activities for the homes, schools, and communities. The department encouraged this work by distributing 5,000 copies of a monthly eight-page paper, *The Young Citizen*, consisting in part of contributions from boys and girls. The organization also gave music instruction in schools throughout the state. A special committee developed a prospective music course especially adapted to the rural schools, and 7,500 copies of it were distributed free to the teachers. Superintendent Giffen stated: "Out of this has grown South Dakota's Young Citizens League program. The program began with one county and has grown until last year approximately forty counties successfully organized a County Chorus" (21).

Superintendent Giffen shared much of the philosophy of his predecessor and continued most of his programs. The department developed a new course of study for the elementary and secondary schools, which combined history, geography, civics, and some phases of science and health into a social studies course. The new curriculum also included reading, literature, language, grammar, spelling, and handwriting in the language arts. But the most significant accomplishment of Superintendent Giffen came in his second term – the recodification of the school laws by the 1931 Legislature, which markedly changed the statutes relating to transportation, tuition, and certification, and implemented a uniform accounting and reporting system in the school districts. The new 1931 code completely revised and raised the certification and training standards for teachers. Teachers in all high schools were required to have a baccalaureate degree, and elementary teachers had to have a 2-year certificate (a certificate backed by 2 years of college).

A number of schools were now demanding the extremely popular vocational education program. Adult farm organizations cooperated with the agriculture program, providing information on cooperation, land utilization, marketing, and taxation. A survey showed that 50 percent of the students who had taken vocational agriculture courses in high school were engaged in work closely related to it. The homemaking program was expanded, and interest grew in the trades and industrial education programs.

When the budget for the Americanization program was cut to one-half the amount requested in 1931, the department decided to curtail the aid paid to the schools and to use the balance of the funds to match federal money available for training disabled persons. Thus, when the Americanization program ended, the rehabilitation program became more significant. Approximately 90 persons were in training, and over 100 requests for assistance were on file.

The Depression caught many school districts heavily in debt, and the financial assistance the state should render continued to be one of the most perplexing and complex problems. The state superintendents during this period continually urged more state support for the public school system. Superintendent Giffen reported as follows:

> In 1916 the total indebtedness of school districts was only $5,000,000. In 1920, the amount was $8,500,000. In 1924, the indebtedness had reached $19,500,000. By 1926 school districts had reached the peak of outstanding indebtedness and at that time owed a total of $20,200,000. Since 1926 there has been a slight tendency to decrease the indebtedness until now (1932) the outstanding indebtedness of the school districts amounts to approximately $17,000,000 (22).

The superintendent stated that he knew the debts had to be paid, and at the same time there had to be some relief from the burden of taxation for school purposes. This could be done either by closing many schools until the obligations were met or by completely revising the system of taxation to bring in new sources of revenue to the depleted school treasuries. But, he pointed out, the constitution clearly stated that the state must provide equal educational opportunities for every child of school age, and equal educational opportunities had never existed and never could be established until the provisions of the constitution were carried out as the framers intended.

The superintendent contended that the tremendous tax burden for public education should not be entirely a local affair, but that the state had to assume its responsibilities. He concluded:

> My plea to the legislature is to maintain the present standard of public schools for the children of the state. When the legislature begins to cut public expenditures, it should not begin with the schools. It should begin with the least necessary political jobs and offices and with the further construction of highways and public buildings. The education of the children of our state is of far greater importance than material construction of any kind. We recognize that many retrenchments must be made until economic recovery is obtained. Let us,

therefore, make our cuts in the direction of material construction where recovery can be made later, when conditions warrant such recovery.

Complete information concerning the problem of school finance of this state is contained in this report and should serve as the basis upon which to formulate legislation with a view to bringing about a solution of the problem of school support (23).

I. D. Weeks assumed the Office of Superintendent of Public Instruction in January 1933, when the Depression was at its worst. Agricultural states were particularly hard hit, and the situation was made worse by a continuing drought and grasshopper infestation. The 1933 Legislature dusted off Superintendent St. John's recommendations to the 1927 Legislature and passed a tax on gross income, with 50 percent of the proceeds allocated to the public schools, 45 percent credited to the Interest and Income Common School Fund and distributed to districts on the basis of the school census, and 5 percent allocated to the distressed school districts by a prescribed formula.

At the same time, the Legislature reduced the department's annual budget from approximately $76,000 to $27,000 (24). Despite this reduction, Superintendent Weeks was able to continue all the major activities of the department and assumed the administration of all relief projects connected with elementary and secondary education, including the distribution of the 5-percent gross income tax fund. He was able to add a supervisor of trades and industrial education and a supervisor of adult education, but financial assistance for home economics instruction was virtually eliminated. Federal funds enabled him to expand the vocational rehabilitation program.

The inequalities of educational opportunity offered by the small high schools became increasingly deplorable during this period. Many were forced to reduce their staffs substantially. The department attempted to help the students by initiating a correspondence course, which offered them a greater opportunity than did their schools' limited faculties. To further assist these small high schools, the department established an "approved list" of those doing acceptable work on a limited scale and whose school officials were cooperating with the state department, even though they were unable to meet the requirements for regular accreditation.

Representatives of numerous lay organizations held a statewide conference in February 1934 to discuss the educational crisis and agreed to appoint a citizens committee to prepare recommendations for legislation. To facilitate the work of this committee, R. W. Kraushaar, the department's supervisor of secondary education, conducted extensive studies of the school system's financial support, curriculum, buildings, and administration. While the Legislature was slow to respond to the committee's suggestions and recommendations, many of Kraushaar's suggestions were eventually enacted into law.

The 1935 Legislature proposed two constitutional amendments, both of which the voters approved in the general election of 1936. These provided for the election of the state superintendent and the county superintendents on a nonpolitical ballot and removed the 4-year limit on the county superintendents' tenure. Despite the claims of its proponents, this change appears to have had little effect on the prestige and fortunes of the department or on the educational group's recommendations to the Legislature. The Legislature increased the department's budget a mere $1,300, and this was spent for some much needed office equipment, such as typewriters and filing cases.

The 1935 Legislature enacted a 2-percent sales tax and designated 8 percent of the proceeds for the distressed school districts. This reduced the local property tax levy by an amount equal to that received from the state. But, by the end of 1936, the financial condition of most districts was critical, with over 25 percent operating on registered warrants.

From the beginning of the Depression, the Permanent School Fund (25) had been the target of various schemes to support the state's staggering economy, and it became the concern of various educational groups and leaders to defeat these proposals. Fortunately, the commissioners of school and public lands, who have been custodians of the school lands since statehood, had always received the hearty and spontaneous cooperation of the South Dakota Education Association. When various groups tried to shift deficits in farm loans, which many counties had acquired through defaulted payments during the Depression, onto the Public Lands Fund, Commissioner Ben Strool successfully staved off the threat.

The forces favoring the change then proposed constitutional amendments to this effect, but these were defeated by the combined efforts of the SDEA, the Beadle Club (26), the PTA, and aroused citizens. Superintendent Weeks cautioned those proposing a change in the administration of the Permanent School Fund: "This fund in South Dakota is one of the largest in the nation. It must be kept inviolate. . ." (27). The Permanent School Fund was preserved, and today it annually provides approximately $2.5 million in interest and income for the public schools, thanks to the foresightedness and perseverance of these dedicated educational leaders and citizens.

The Depression period did emphasize the importance of a state support program for public education. Even though many school districts reduced their indebtedness substantially, the reduction was often accomplished by budget cuts that seriously affected the efficiency of the schools. The 1939 Legislature began appropriating a stipulated amount for state support rather than a percentage of the state sales tax. At the same time, the Legislature assigned the superintendent the task of distributing the state aid, and he retained this duty until 1959, when it was transferred to the Department of Public Instruction.

Public school enrollment decreased approximately 15 percent during the 1930's, and the teaching force was reduced 10 percent. The teachers were better prepared than ever in the state's history, but low salaries, lack of equipment, and poor building maintenance caused many of the best trained ones to seek employment elsewhere. Although the agricultural economy of the state improved substantially during the early 1940's, many people left the state for jobs in industry as the nation prepared for an all-out war effort against Japan and Germany. This exodus included many teachers and prospective teachers, so the teacher shortage became acute. Because of transportation difficulties stemming from tire and gas rationing, a number of rural schools were reopened, creating a demand for more rural teachers.

Superintendent J. F. Hines requested increased aid for distressed school districts and direct aid to the schools to alleviate some of these problems, but the 1941 Legislature turned a deaf ear. It even reduced the department's annual budget to $20,000. Again, in 1943, he recommended that the distressed school appropriation be increased from $150,000 to $250,000 and the general aid to all districts be not less than $1.5 million. He also included a request for a $6,000 increase in the department's budget to maintain his present staff and support an additional deputy or assistant superintendent. The 1943 Legislature increased the department budget to $30,050 annually but failed to provide for the assistant superintendent.

Teachers continued to leave the profession and the state to join the armed forces or to work in the war plants or at other private jobs. Superintendent Hines commented:

> While the war itself has been the primary cause we cannot ignore the fact that security, better salary schedules and retirement have contributed their share. School districts cannot compete with industry and teachers are mindful of the extremely low salaries offered during the depression (28).

To meet this severe shortage, certificates were reinstated without additional college credits, and high school graduates were encouraged to take the examination for second-grade certificates. In his report to the Governor and the 1947 Legislature, Superintendent Hines recommended that a minimum salary law and a teacher tenure law be enacted and that the certification laws be amended to permit enough flexibility to meet the changing times.

Incredible as it seems, the superintendent himself was still receiving a salary of only $1,800 a year—the salary set by the Constitution of 1889. In 1946, a constitutional amendment was approved giving the Legislature the authority to fix the salaries of any constitutional officers by two-thirds vote in each house. The 1947 Legislature increased the salary of the superintendent of public instruction to $4,800 per year.

By the end of the war, although the number of department staff members remained the same, their duties had shifted, and they had assumed many new responsibilities. For instance, the high school supervisor had taken over the responsibility for occupational information and guidance services, and a director had been appointed for a new division in curriculum and research. To meet these new responsibilities, Superintendent Hines asked the 1947 Legislature for an increase in the department's budget. He pointed out that more and more was expected of the department each year and that to give this service, it needed the best-trained personnel. During the war, both vocational rehabilitation and vocational education had become increasingly important, and these were in dire need of funds when the peace came. Hines also asked for more authority to decide school questions.

But the appropriations for the 1946-48 biennium continued to be far below the department's needs. The director of curriculum and research resigned, and his duties were taken over by the distributive education officer, thus reducing the staff to eight professional people in addition to the superintendent and his deputy.

At the close of the 1946-48 biennium, Superintendent Hines retired. He had served 2.5 years as deputy and 13.5 years as superintendent during the most difficult and frustrating period in the department's history. A capable administrator and a dedicated educator, he had surrounded himself with an efficient, talented, and dedicated staff. His pleas for funds to improve conditions and expand programs had fallen mainly on unsympathetic ears. The teaching force had reached new heights both numerically and professionally, but it had rapidly declined during the Depression as the population dwindled due to the drought and the economic circumstances. In quantity and quality, the teaching force had reached an all-time low. Economic conditions improved after 1940, but the frugality of the school boards and the Legislature during the previous 10 years had become so firmly entrenched that the shortage of professionally trained and qualified teachers – even under reduced professional requirements – continued for another two decades.

Harold S. Freeman was elected state superintendent in the fall of 1948 and assumed office in January 1949. He obtained a small increase in the department's appropriations and established a number of new positions, including a school lunch director, an additional rehabilitation officer, a supervisor of Indian education, and a surplus commodity supervisor, all related to federal programs. The professional staff now numbered 13 in addition to the state superintendent; although the position of deputy was still authorized by law, it was not filled.

Finances were still precarious in a majority of districts operating high schools, because the tax base and mill-levy limit were not sufficient, and these districts were accumulating large debts. The rural schools still had a teacher shortage. In his recommendations to the 1951 Legislature, Superintendent Freeman stated:

> Our State Department of Public Instruction has the least number of professional employees of any state in the United States. If this department is to assume the leadership which should rightly be expected of it, additional personnel will be necessary in order to offer the services expected of it by the schools of the state. In the meantime we are offering extended service as time, personnel, and finances will permit. We believe that the State Department of Public Instruction is a service organization for the schools of the state and shall strive to operate it on that basis to the best of our ability (29).

In 1950, a U.S. Office of Education study of all state departments revealed that South Dakota claimed to offer services in 28 areas, but that of the 156 man-months of professional staff time devoted to department services, 151 were spent in only 7 of the 28 areas: guidance, 6; instructional services, 18; research and statistics, 6; school lunch, 13; teacher certification, 24; vocational education, 48; and vocational rehabilitation, 36. The remaining 21 areas of service received an aggregate of only 5 man-months of service. The study also revealed that 68 percent of the department's time was devoted to federally subsidized programs of guidance, school lunch, vocational education, and vocational rehabilitation (30).

The 1951 Legislature yielded to Superintendent Freeman's requests and appropriated funds to improve and increase the department's services. Four new positions were created: a consultant on school law, finance, and accounts; a consultant on school buildings and facilities; a consultant on school district reorganization; and a statistician. The high school supervisor was relieved of his responsibility for vocational guidance, and a separate position was created for this service. The supervisor of education was no longer responsible for the Young Citizens League as an executive secretary was again employed for this organization. One director was placed in charge of both commodity distribution and the school lunch program. The total staff now consisted of 19 professional persons plus the superintendent.

The financial resources were still inadequate to meet the needs of many schools. The 1951 Legislature decided to follow a recommendation Superintendent Freeman had made in his first biennial report and enacted a school district reorganization plan to increase the size and tax base of many districts. The act proved to be cumbersome and time consuming, and despite the efforts of the department's personnel little was actually accomplished. Twenty-four counties established county planning committees, but there was no real reduction or enlargement of the school districts.

The School District Reorganization Act was really a long-range program; special appropriations were still needed to support current operations. The 1951 Legislature appropriated $100,000 for the 1951-53 biennium to establish a plan for educating crippled and physically handicapped children, and a supervisor of special education was hired. It also authorized a vocational rehabilitation division, and the State Board of Education also became the State Board of Vocational Education. The vocational rehabilitation division was created within the board and headed by a director responsible for the administration of the vocational rehabilitation program. Other personnel in the division were to be appointed by the superintendent of public instruction on the recommendation of the director and approval of the board. The department also hired a director and three assistants to administer the Veterans' Readjustment Assistance Act of 1952 – commonly referred to as "institutional-on-farm training" – passed by the Eighty-Second Congress.

Another study by the U.S. Office of Education in 1952 showed that 86 percent of the department's professional staff devoted their efforts to federally subsidized programs – only 14 percent were connected with strictly state-sponsored functions and services. The study also revealed that the highest salary paid in the department was not over $4,999, and although the state required at least a bachelor's degree for the position of supervisor, two supervisors did not have degrees.

Most independent school districts continued to be plagued by low assessed evaluations and limited mill levies. Increased costs for maintenance caused many districts to operate with a deficit and with no hope of balancing the budget from current revenues. The county elementary school equalization fund enacted by the 1953 Legislature gave considerable relief to a majority of the common (rural) school districts, enabling them to become financially solvent.

At this time, South Dakota had a large number of common school districts (authorized to operate only an elementary school program) that did not operate schools and often had few expenses due to the fact that they contained few or no resident children of school age. The property owners in these districts enjoyed extremely low tax rates. The purpose of the county elementary school equalization fund legislation was to levy at least one-half of the cost of operating the elementary schools in the county over all of the property located in the common school districts in the county. The receipts of this levy were prorated back to the districts on the basis of their individual expenses. This had the effect of causing all of the property to support at least a portion of the educational program of the state.

The 1953 Legislature decided that the State Board of Education should be composed of seven members, all appointed by the Governor for 7-year overlapping terms; none could be a professional educator. The superintendent was named as the ex officio president without power to vote. The board was authorized to consult and advise the superintendent concerning matters relating to elementary and secondary education in addition to its duties relating to vocational education and the vocational rehabilitation program. For the first time, the members of the board were authorized to receive a salary of $10 per day when in session in addition to mileage and hotel expenses.

The school law was still badly in need of revision and recodification, so the state board directed the department's school law consultant to coordinate this task. E. V. Morrill, an attorney with considerable experience in school law and past chairman of the Senate education committee, was employed as a legal adviser and, with the assistance of a representative from the attorney general's office, drafted a bill to present to the 1955 Legislature. They patterned the composition and powers of the State Board of Education and the powers and duties of the superintendent and Department of Public Instruction – where the state constitution permitted – on the recommendations of the National Council of Chief State School Officers as presented in its 1952 publication, "The State Department of Education." The Legislature enacted these changes in 1955.

Under the new laws, the duties of both the state board and the superintendent were greatly extended. For instance, in addition to its duties relating to vocational education and vocational rehabilitation and its power to consult and advise the superintendent concerning elementary and secondary education, the board was given the power to appoint and affix the salaries of the department's professional staff (except the deputy superintendent) on the superintendent's recommendation. The board was to formulate policies and adopt rules necessary to carry out its functions, hear all appeals arising from its rules and regulations, recommend to the Governor and Legislature laws necessary for the state's educational needs, publish the laws relating to education, set minimum standards for school districts, and reject or approve all master plans for reorganization. It was given the authority to prescribe the requirements for teacher certificates, adopt a state course of study, and establish the standards for classifying, approving, and accrediting public and nonpublic schools.

The state superintendent, in addition to his other duties, was to keep the state board advised as to the status of the public schools, delegate and administer executive functions to the department's personnel, examine the high schools and all elementary grades, and accredit the high schools to institutions of higher education. He was to prepare and submit to the state board the courses of study, and classify, approve, and accredit public and nonpublic schools.

In analyzing the effect of these legal changes, the Legislative Research Council stated:

> It marks the first time that the Legislature (1) made the Superintendent of Public Instruction directly responsible for the conduct of many of his duties to the State Board of Education; (2) recognized that the professional staff of the Department of Public Instruction was more than the office staff of the Superintendent by placing control of such staff's appointments and salaries with the State Board of Education; (3) authorized the State Board of Education to act in more than a merely advisory capacity in matters other than vocational education and vocational rehabilitation; and (4) directed the superintendent to delegate his ministerial and executive duties to the professional staff of the Department of Public Instruction (31).

The 1957 Legislature changed the board's structure and substantially amended the powers granted to it in 1955. The new law made appointments to the board subject to the Senate's approval and provided for the Governor to fill the vacancies so that each supreme court district was represented. The terms were limited to 5 years, and no appointed member could succeed himself. Instead of spelling out all the duties and powers in great detail, the 1957 amendment repealed many of these subsections and provided that "the State Board shall be responsible for the adoption of all policies for carrying out educational functions as relate to elementary and secondary schools, or as may be vested in the State Department" (32). The board's power to establish standards for approving building plans was limited to suggesting standards, and it could do no more than consult with the superintendent about school district reorganization.

The 1957 Legislature directed the state board to transfer to the superintendent three functions: publishing laws relating to education, prescribing a uniform system for gathering educational data, and accepting and distributing commodities, moneys, goods, and services available from the state or federal government.

Superintendent Freeman died in May 1957, and Deputy Superintendent W. G. Elliot served as "acting superintendent" until M. F. Coddington assumed office in June 1958, following his appointment by the Governor. The department's services and program had substantially improved and expanded during Freeman's tenure. The professional staff had increased from 8 in 1948 to 30 in 1958, almost a 300-percent increase (33). While much of this expansion was related to programs sponsored or financed by the federal government, the educational program for exceptional children, which had added a psychologist and a teaching consultant during the previous biennium, was primarily supported from state appropriations. The school law had been completely revised, and a State Board of Education had been created that was responsible for elementary and secondary education, including the certification of teachers. The state legislative appropriations increased from $1.5 million in 1949 to $2.5 million in 1958. (Despite this increase, the state appropriations were barely able to keep pace with the increasing costs of the local administrative units.)

The State Board of Education agreed in December 1958 to accept responsibility for administering Title III of the National Defense Education Act (NDEA) passed by Congress earlier in the year to strengthen elementary and secondary instruction in science, mathematics, and foreign languages. In the following session, the Legislature failed to provide an administrator for the program, so the deputy superintendent assumed this responsibility. NDEA also partially financed the Iowa Tests of Educational Development for grades 9 through 12 in all South Dakota high schools during the 1959-60 school year. The University of South Dakota supplied the balance from its research funds. Many schools were able to inaugurate programs or expand their services for handicapped children because the Legislature appropriated over $500,000 for special education in the 1958-60 biennium.

The secondary education division completely revised standards for accrediting the high schools; they were now classified on the basis of the quantity and quality of their program. By the end of 1962, 98 public schools and 14 nonpublic schools were classified as first-class accredited schools, and 150 public and 11 nonpublic schools received second-class accreditation. Over 74 percent of all high school students were enrolled in the first-class accredited schools.

By 1960, the state board had adopted certification requirements for counselors in the vocational guidance division. The guidance and special education divisions were then merged in July 1961 to form the pupil personnel services division. The department also established a school administration and law division in July 1960 by combining the former school law, finance, and accounts division and the research, records, and reports division. School buildings, school district reorganization, and transportation comprised a third division. The surplus commodities distribution program was merged with the school lunch and special milk program, and both came under the administration of a single director. The practical nurse education program was combined with the trade, industrial, and distributive programs. The vocational rehabilitation department established four district and two subdistrict offices. In summarizing the accomplishments of his second term, Superintendent Coddington stated:

> In numbers only, the increased participation in such areas of vocational rehabilitation, school lunch, and service to the retarded stands out. Improvement of the physical plants among the schools, an increasing number of school buses, more school district reorganization, new modernized courses of study in several fields, added science equipment encouraged by and assisted with the National Defense Education Act, more adequate Indian Education Programs, increased state aid, an upgrading of certification requirements for teachers and improved scholastic opportunities for more high school students also present more definite achievements based on sound foundations set up in former years (34).

With funds from Title X of NDEA, the state board created the statistical services division in July 1963. Some electronic data-processing equipment was obtained, and the division began compiling the data used by the department's various divisions. This equipment was especially helpful in the distribution of state aid to school districts.

In 1963, the Legislature appropriated $7,500 to finance a survey of the possible advantages of educational television (ETV). The 1965 Legislature accepted the survey group's recommendations and created a board of directors, separate and apart from the State Board of Education, except that the state superintendent was a member, to establish policy and exercise control over the proposed state ETV network (35).

Since 1917, when the Legislature voted to accept the Smith-Hughes Act aid, the state superintendent had served as the director of vocational education. When Congress enacted the Vocational Education Act of 1963, it became apparent that a full-time director for the vocational division was needed, and the State Board of Vocational Education created this position in March 1964. The board also appointed a director for the vocational rehabilitation division created by the 1951 Legislature. This officer was governed by the rules and regulations established by the State Board of Vocational Education and was responsible to the state superintendent only in appointing personnel.

When policy relating to vocational rehabilitation was considered at regular or special meetings, the board convened as the State Board of Vocational Education. It met as the State Board of Education when considering policies, rules, and regulations relating to the other aspects of elementary and secondary education.

In the 1965 session, a small group of legislators expressed dissatisfaction with certain features of the state's plan for utilizing federal funds under the Vocational Education Act. They succeeded in getting a bill passed creating a vocational education division under the State Board of Vocational Education (the State Board of Education). The board was directed to adopt policy for promoting and coordinating vocational training in technical education, to approve or disapprove state plans submitted to federal agencies, and to make recommendations to the Governor and Legislature. It was also made responsible for distributing funds appropriated by the Legislature and granted by federal agencies to the public secondary, postsecondary, trade, and technical schools for state plans approved by the board.

The 1965 law also stipulated that the Governor would appoint the director of the vocational education division on recommendation of the board. He would have to have a master's degree with special training in vocational education from an accredited institution of higher learning. His salary was set at not more than $12,000, the actual amount to be determined by the Governor, who had the power to remove him at any time for cause. The director was to serve as the division's chief administrative officer and have general control and supervision over all vocational training and technical education in the public schools. He was to select the staff personnel under the direction of the board, which would set the qualifications while he would set the salaries subject to the board's approval. He was required to keep the board advised of the status of the programs, administer all of the policies adopted by the board, prepare the state plans for board approval, submit the courses of study to the board, prescribe uniform systems of gathering and reporting data on vocational training and technical education, conduct research and compile statistics relating to the training, and establish a system of fiscal control and fund reporting.

At the same time, the State Board of Vocational Education decided to appoint a full-time director of vocational education in 1964. Superintendent Coddington organized the State Department of Instruction into a division of instruction and a division of administration, each headed by an assistant superintendent. The lines of authoritative communication to the sections assigned to each of these divisions existed more in fancy than in fact. The two assistant superintendents continued serving as section directors, one for secondary education and the other for school district reorganization, school buildings, and transportation, which left them little time to devote to the supervision of the other sections in their divisions. The long-standing practice of each section director's reporting directly to the state superintendent contributed to the assistant superintendents' frustrations. Nevertheless, the personal relationships continued on a cordial, professional, and cooperative basis. When additional personnel were hired to relieve the assistant superintendents of some of their routine duties, the new plan began to function.

THE DEPARTMENT TODAY

Organization

As of June 1967, the state education administration in South Dakota consisted of the State Board of Education, the superintendent of public instruction, and the Department of Public Instruction. (See Appendix B.) The state board consists of seven members appointed by the Governor, subject to the approval of the Senate, for 5-year overlapping terms (36). The board is responsible for adopting all policies governing the department and for carrying out the functions relating to elementary and secondary education vested in the department. The state board also serves as the State Board of Vocational Education and formulates policies for the vocational education and vocational rehabilitation divisions.

The superintendent of public instruction, elected on a nonpartisan ballot for a 2-year term, is a constitutional officer in the executive branch of the state government. His salary is determined annually by the Legislature. The superintendent is the executive secretary and the executive officer of the State Board of Education and is responsible for executing and administering all policies promulgated by the board. He has the power to appoint and prescribe the duties of a deputy and is chairman of the State Library Commission, chairman of the Teachers Retirement Liquidation Board, a member of the Indian Commission, a member of the State Planning Commission, and an appointed member of the Governor's Traffic Safety Council.

The Department of Public Instruction is unique in the executive branch of the state government. Although numerous references are made to it in the laws, it has never heen expressly established and is not clearly identified in the statutes or the constitution. Nevertheless, it is commonly considered to consist of the superintendent of public instruction and the professional and clerical personnel under the direct jurisdiction of his office and the state board. The majority of its functions are those the Legislature has assigned to the superintendent. In fact, one of the duties of the superintendent is to delegate ministerial and executive functions to the staff of the department. In a few instances, the Legislature has specifically directed that a particular function, such as the distribution of state aid to school districts, be performed by the department. But no true distinction exists between the powers and duties of the superintendent and those of the department.

The general administration of the department is vested in the office of the superintendent and his immediate staff, which consists of an executive assistant and the comptroller. The comptroller is responsible for departmental internal services, including personnel and fiscal management, and he reports directly to the superintendent. As directed by the state board, he maintains a working relationship with the state budget officer and the employment division.

The department is divided into two general areas—instruction and administration—each under the supervision of an assistant superintendent. Under the assistant superintendent for administration are the divisions of school district reorganization, transportation, school buildings, statistical services in NDEA Title X, research and public information, school administration and legal services, and school lunch and food commodity distribution. He is also responsible for the Great Plains School District Reorganization Project and the Midwestern States Educational Information Project.

The Great Plains School District Reorganization Project is a cooperative, comprehensive 2-year study of the school districts in the Great Plains area conducted by the education agencies of Nebraska, Missouri, Iowa, and South Dakota. This project is administered through the Nebraska education department by a steering committee composed of representatives of each participating agency and the project director. A state director stationed in each state constitutes the professional staff of the project, which is funded by a Title V grant of $355,000 under the Elementary and Secondary Education Act of 1965 (ESEA).

Thirteen states have embarked on a Midwestern States Educational Information Project to develop and implement a unique educational information system pertaining to pupils, staff, instruction, finance, and facilities. Since Iowa is the contracting state, the central staff is located in Des Moines. Each of the cooperating states, including South Dakota, is represented on the policy committee or governing body by one person at the administrative level. The coordinating committee and five subcommittees, one for each of the five basic areas of concern, each composed of a representative from each participating state, constitute the organization. A state coordinator financed by the project is located in each state to assist staff members with their assignments.

Under the assistant superintendent for instruction are the divisions of elementary education, secondary education, curriculum, pupil personnel services, NDEA Titles III and V, teacher education and certification, Indian education, adult basic education, ESEA Titles I and II, and the instruction and subject area specialists. The assistant superintendents report to the superintendent on the activities of their areas.

Federal Programs

The state-federal programs and legal services division is unique in that its head reports directly to the superintendent. It supplies up-to-date information on federal educational programs, and the coordinator occasionally assumes administration of these under the state board's jurisdiction until an administrator is appointed. Under the federal impact law (P.L. 81-874), this division distributes approximately $3 million in funds annually to school districts.

Under NDEA, Title III, funds are provided to strengthen instruction in science, mathematics, modern foreign languages, and other critical areas in schools through grants approved by the state department. It provides for laboratories and other special equipment, including audiovisual and printed materials other than textbooks. It also provides some funds for remodeling space for such equipment and materials. The department also has received a grant for expanding supervisory services in specified areas of instruction and for administering the state's plan. Under ESEA Title III, four educational planning centers have been established and funded from an allocation to South Dakota of approximately $1,100,000.

The state board created an adult basic education division in 1967 to administer approximately $50,000 annually for adult education, expected to be available to South Dakota under Title III of P.L. 89-750, Elementary and Secondary Education Act Amendments of 1966. Studies indicate that the adult basic education program is needed by the reservation Indians and in the larger cities.

The Indian education division is concerned mainly with the administration of the Johnson-O'Malley Act, a federal program designed to provide funds for school districts based on the percent of nontaxable Indian land, the ratio of Indian to non-Indian enrollment, the financial need, and the quality of the educational program. It also reimburses the districts for lunches and milk given free to needy Indian children.

The department's school lunch division serves as a state agency for the programs administered on a national level by the food distribution division of the U.S. Department of Agriculture, such as the National School Lunch Program, the Special Milk Program, the child care centers, and summer camps; the commodity program for needy persons in the counties and on the Indian reservations; the institutional commodity programs; and the commodity program for summer camps. New programs in connection with the War on Poverty and the Child Nutrition Act of 1966, which offers a pilot breakfast program and additional food services, will undoubtedly create more duties and responsibilities for this division.

The state department helps local districts take advantage of federal money under Title I of ESEA to develop special programs for educationally deprived children in areas where low-income families are concentrated. The grants under this title are made directly to the school systems from funds available to the state, as there are no matching requirements. With more than 2,000 school districts, South Dakota has had considerable difficulty using the money available under this title because of many small individual allocations and the lack of local personnel to implement the projects. During its first year, the state approved projects to spend only 68 percent of the funds available; only three other states were below this percentage. The unused funds cannot be reallocated without the approval of the U.S. Commissioner of Education. There is no doubt that the multiplicity of small districts unable to use these grants is causing a hardship and loss of money, since the larger districts could readily use these funds.

An analysis of the projects approved in 1966 reveals that the major concern of school administrators is to provide educationally disadvantaged children with the basic skills to ensure their success in later years. This means that the greatest emphasis is being placed on remedial work in reading. But the state has had difficulty administering and implementing this title because of Congress' failure to pass an appropriations bill in time for local educational agencies to plan effectively for using the funds.

South Dakota also receives funds under Title II of ESEA to supplement state and local funds for school library resources and other printed instructional material. The allocation within the state is on the basis of need, justified by the quality and quantity of library resources available in the elementary schools compared to those available in the secondary schools.

The Civil Defense adult education division was created in May 1963 to administer and operate a personal and family survival training program and a radiological monitor training program (RAMONT). Under contract from the U.S. Office of Education, the department offers 12-hour courses for personal and family survival in times of nuclear and man-made disasters. The department has trained a number of certified teachers as personal and family-survival instructors. The purpose of RAMONT is to train radiological monitors for the stations operated by the local Civil Defense directors.

The department's pupil personnel services administer funds available to South Dakota from the federal government to provide materials from the American Printing House for the Blind to partially sighted children in the elementary and secondary schools. It also administers the $46,000 available for training professional personnel for educating handicapped children and this money has had a marked effect on the quality of instruction. The division also expects to take advantage of any funds available under ESEA Title VI by adding a speech and hearing specialist, more psychological services, and consultants in special education.

Federal funds provide 68.44 percent of the basic support program for vocational rehabilitation, 75 percent of the extension and improvement grants, and 90 percent of the funds for in-service training programs in this field. The vocational rehabilitation division also operates an old-age and survivor's insurance (OASI) disability determination program under contract with the U.S. Department of Health, Education, and Welfare, financed entirely by federal funds.

The vocational education division's major responsibility has been to administer the federally aided vocational education programs. Under the Smith-Hughes and George-Barden Acts, the federal government allots approximately $380,000 to South Dakota each year for programs in agriculture, distributive education, home-making, trades and industries, practical nurse training, and technical education. These funds are matched by state and local funds; the administrative and teacher-training costs are considered an administrative responsibility. The remaining amount after matching the administrative costs is distributed to the local districts on a 50-percent federal and a 50-percent state and local matching basis to reimburse the school boards for the various programs.

The federal Vocational Education Act provided funds to supplement those available under the Smith-Hughes and George-Barden programs and, in addition, provided funds for business and office education and health occupations. Under the Manpower Development and Training Act and the Area Redevelopment Act, special training courses for the unemployed and the underemployed are entirely federally financed. The South Dakota Legislature provides an annual appropriation of $100,000 to the vocational education division.

RELATIONSHIPS WITH OTHER AGENCIES AND ORGANIZATIONS

Department of Finance

The State Board of Finance, consisting of the Governor, the state treasurer, the secretary of state, the state auditor, the attorney general, the commissioner of school and public lands, the superintendent of banks, and the secretary of finance, carries on advisory supervision of all funds received by the state treasury and general supervision of the State's fiscal affairs. All departments and agencies are subject to the rules and regulations adopted and administered by the State Board of Finance. Thus, before the Department of Public Instruction can purchase any item or order any printing work, it must have the approval of the finance department's purchasing and printing division.

The education department must abide by the finance board's rules and regulations relating to the employment of personnel, compensation plans, and salary schedules, and the board approves payrolls and allocates office space for all state agencies housed in the capitol building and the city of Pierre. The employment division keeps annual leave, sick leave, and time records for all state employees and approves monthly payrolls. The state travel commission is responsible for all state-owned vehicles, and the capitol supply service provides office supplies and materials to the various departments operating in the capitol building and its various annexes. A microfilming service maintained by the central services division has been of considerable benefit to the education department in controlling and storing its records.

The finance department is also responsible for keeping a complete inventory of all property owned by the state. Each agency must submit to the department an annual inventory showing what is on hand, the disposition of any property transferred or discarded, and the addition of any new property since the last report.

Office of the Budget

The Legislature created the Office of the Budget to promote economy and efficiency in the fiscal management of the state government. Each agency must prepare and submit an annual budget to the budget board, which reviews the requests and makes its recommendations. The Governor and the budget director submit these requests, together with the recommendations of the budget board, to the Legislature. After the appropriations are made, the operating budgets for all state agencies are then submitted to the Office of the Budget for approval.

Committee for Education

State Superintendent J. F. Hines and a small group of city superintendents organized the Committee for Education in 1942 to promote desirable school legislation. During its early years, it served primarily as a vehicle for soliciting funds to employ a lobbyist during the legislative sessions. It had no constitution and no committees. The South Dakota Education Association and the South Dakota School Boards Association contributed to the fund, along with a number of the larger school districts and interested individuals.

Even though the organization was conceived and led by a dominant and forceful educator, Charles Dalthorp, superintendent of the Aberdeen City school system, its early efforts were not very successful. The membership base was too small and its effort involved only a few people, the majority being educators. Though it championed worthy causes, it was handicapped because the group was considered to be an "educator's pressure group" and not truly representative of the public.

Other statewide organizations were invited to join the Committee for Education in 1946. A constitution was adopted, committees were appointed, and the organization was incorporated under the laws of South Dakota. Its membership consisted of the Associated School Boards of South Dakota, the American Association of University Women (South Dakota state division), the South Dakota Congress of Parents and Teachers, the South Dakota Education Association, the Department of School Administration, the Department of Higher Education, the County Superintendents' Association, and the South Dakota Federation of Women's Clubs.

With these changes, the Committee for Education became an action group. It published a "Report to the People," the first in a series of bulletins carrying carefully documented statements portraying the condition of the state's educational system and from four to six specific legislative proposals. These bulletins were circulated to the membership, to the legislators, and to the general public. The committee secured some legislation in the 1947 session and continued to grow in membership and influence. By 1958, 17 statewide organizations claiming a combined membership of around 75,000 had affiliated.

The committee's efforts have been directed at four main concerns through the years: to increase state support for the schools (since 1958, through a minimum foundation program), to increase salaries for the state superintendent and his staff, to secure additional services to the schools by the Department of Public Instruction, and to achieve school district reorganization. All of these have been accomplished in varying degrees. Many fine pieces of school legislation have been proposed by the committee and ultimately enacted, including increased mill-levy limitations for local school districts (1947), state funds to administer the school lunch program (1949), state support of education for the physically and mentally handicapped (1951), and the creation of an education board for elementary and secondary education (1953 and 1955). The committee also was instrumental in getting the Legislature to pass teacher tenure laws and retirement legislation in 1951, a school district reorganization law in 1951 and 1955, and a raise in the constitutional debt limit for school districts from 5 to 10 percent of the assessed valuation in 1954.

Perhaps the greatest test of the committee's sincerity and resoluteness occurred in 1955, when the Legislature completely revised the school laws to include a number of suggestions proposed by the committee. A well-organized opposition group, claiming that the new code would force school district reorganization against the will of the minority, that it would violate the long-standing tradition of local control, and that it would infringe on the parents' freedom to select the school for their children, attempted to refer the new code to a vote of the people in the 1956 general election.

Referendum petitions were circulated and filed with the secretary of state in time to prevent the new code from becoming effective on the usual date, July 1, 1955. The committee, desiring to avoid a long struggle and anxious to get on with the improvements included in the code, empowered its president, Mrs. George Headley, to act in its behalf as plaintiff and employed attorneys to examine the petitions. They succeeded in proving to both the circuit and state supreme courts that a substantial number of technical errors in the petitions reduced the total number of acceptable signatures to below the number required. The new code then became the school law in South Dakota on September 9, 1955. Subsequent minor amendments forced through the Legislature at the insistence of the opposition eroded some of its effectiveness, but the main tenets of the new code remained in effect.

The Associated School Boards of South Dakota, one of the original members at the time of incorporation, withdrew its membership from the committee in 1960, but not its moral support. This association had become well organized and well financed, and its board of directors felt it could be more effective with the Legislature as an independent agency with its own lobbyist. The South Dakota Farm Bureau Federation withdrew its membership in 1963, due to some of its local organizations' opposition to the committee's stand on the 12-year school district proposal.

These two losses have been offset by the addition of other groups, thus maintaining a membership level of some eighteen statewide organizations, the majority related more or less to education.

The South Dakota Education Association

Territorial Superintendent W. H. H. Beadle, urged by several county superintendents to organize a state teachers association, called a meeting in July 1884 and founded the South Dakota Education Association, which adopted its constitution in 1886. General Beadle, elected its first president, held office for three consecutive annual terms. E. A. Dye succeeded Beadle as territorial superintendent and served as president of the SDEA in 1887. Superintendents G. L. Pinkham, M. M. Ramer, C. H. Lugg, G. W. Nash, C. G. Lawrence, I. D. Weeks, and H. S. Freeman all served in both capacities, but, except for Pinkham, not at the same time. Thus, a cordial professional relationship has existed between the superintendent of public instruction and the SDEA since its beginning. In fact, the early biennial reports by the superintendents usually included convention programs and resolutions adopted at the annual meetings of the SDEA.

The organization's executive committee was enlarged in 1922, and the superintendent of public instruction automatically became a member of the board of directors, the governing body of the association. This relationship has continued to the present and has proven to be mutually beneficial, as the SDEA almost invariably supports the proposals for educational progress sponsored by the State Board of Education, the superintendent, and his staff.

Associated School Boards of South Dakota

SDEA, recognizing the need for an organization of school board members, provided them the opportunity to create one at its annual convention in 1906. On the 1906 convention program of SDEA, the meeting was designated as the "School Board Department." The organization was not officially recognized as a department in the constitution, however, until its revision in 1912. The "School Board Department" was deleted in the 1953 revision of the constitution.

The 1949 Legislature created the Associated School Boards of South Dakota and authorized it to adopt a constitution and bylaws (37). It authorized membership dues and the use of school district funds for a delegate to attend the state convention and other meetings. The association was directed to report annually to the superintendent of public instruction and later to the state board "any matters which pertain to an increase in the efficiency of the public school system" (38). The secretary-treasurer of the association was required to prepare a complete financial report for its membership.

D. B. Doner, the registrar at South Dakota State College in Brookings and a member of the school board of the Brookings Independent School District, served part time as the secretary-treasurer until 1954, when the membership adopted a dues schedule sufficient to permit the hiring of a full-time executive secretary. J. W. Deacon became the first executive secretary in February 1955 and served for a year before he resigned. He was succeeded by William G. Elliot, who resigned after a few months to become deputy superintendent of public instruction. Gordon Nelson, the present executive secretary, was hired in October 1957 and established a permanent office for the Associated School Boards in Huron.

Relationships with the department, the superintendent of public instruction, and the state board have been maintained at a high professional level over the years. The Associated School Boards has worked closely with the State Board of Education promoting legislation. It keeps school board members informed through its conventions, workshops, and publications. The organization's major legislative activity in recent years has been directed toward increasing state financial support for public schools and improving the method of distribution; increasing the effectiveness of the local school districts through appropriate reorganization; and strengthening the state department through increased appropriations for salaries and improved office accommodations and working conditions for the professional and clerical staff.

South Dakota High School Activities Association

The South Dakota High School Athletics Association was organized at a meeting of school superintendents and high school principals at the SDEA convention at Brookings in December 1905. Its purpose was to regulate interschool athletic competition and supervise the state championship tournaments. A five-member board of control, consisting of four superintendents and/or high school principals and one athletic coach, representing the various sized schools, acts as the governing body and establishes the policies, rules, and regulations. A full-time executive secretary has been employed since 1937.

The association's early efforts were directed toward protecting the true value of athletic competition, too often sacrificed because of local pressure to win. It also hoped to keep inflated athletic values from jeopardizing those that should be expected from the academic and other nonathletic school activities.

Parallel associations for other types of school activities involving interschool competition, such as forensics and music, were formed from time to time, but many of these had a difficult time because they produced no revenue. After an intensive study by the South Dakota Association of School Administrators and the High School

Principal's Association, the High School Athletics Association was enlarged in 1960 to include all high school activities. The name was then changed to the South Dakota High School Activities Association, and the membership of the board of control was limited to superintendents and high school principals. In 1964, the board of control was enlarged to include a school board member representing the Associated School Boards.

All accredited public high schools were eligible for membership, as were the federal Indian schools and private and parochial high schools if their applications were supported by two-thirds of the membership. The federal Indian schools were accepted, but the private and parochial schools consistently failed to receive the necessary two-thirds vote. This prompted the Legislature to prohibit the association from excluding private and parochial schools, and after 2 years of litigation the supreme court upheld the legislation. Since July 1966, all accredited high schools in the state are eligible for membership.

The South Dakota High School Activities Association now coordinates and supervises all interschool activities at the high school level, except such organizations as the Future Farmers, Future Homemakers, and Future Teachers organizations. A good working relationship exists between the administrative personnel of the association and the division of secondary education in the Department of Public Instruction.

State Library Commission

> The efforts to establish a free library commission date back to 1905 when Mrs. Stella Marie Stutenroth of Watertown, chairwoman of the legislative committee of the South Dakota Federation of Women's Clubs, caused to be introduced into the legislature a bill which would have established such a commission (39).

This was an era of bad roads, poor transportation, and no radio or television. People read for recreation, so reading materials were in great demand. Few public libraries were operating in the state, and there were practically none in the rural areas. Women's clubs envisioned a central library supported by state funds from which whole libraries of from 20 to 50 books could be sent to an area for a certain length of time, distributed, and then returned to the central location to be exchanged for a new "traveling library." The club women developed a small system of traveling libraries—eventually aided by the South Dakota Library Association—until the pressure was sufficient to force the Legislature to create the "State Free Library Commission."

The Federation of Women's Clubs attempted to organize a library association as early as 1904. But it was not until 2 years later at a meeting in conjunction with SDEA at Sioux Falls that the South Dakota Library Association was founded. The association was nearly an extra-governmental organization from 1906 to 1913. It compiled a statistical analysis of the condition of *The Libraries of South Dakota* in 1908, 1910, and 1912. In 1912, the association set out to convince the Legislature that the state needed above all things to enact legislation reducing its library provisions to a single system and make arrangements for the traveling libraries.

The 1913 Legislature did establish a Free Library Commission. Free libraries were defined as the Supreme Court Library; the State Library; the free public libraries of several cities, towns, townships, and school districts; and the state-owned traveling libraries for which the law provided. However, the Supreme Court Library remained under the management of the supreme court; and the city, town, township, and school district libraries remained under the control of their respective boards of trustees or boards of education. Thus, only the State Library and the traveling libraries were placed under the Free Library Commission (40).

The commission consisted of five members: the Governor, the superintendent of public instruction, the state librarian, and two appointees chosen by the State Library Association and the State Federation of Women's Clubs to serve 3-year terms. The law provided for the superintendent of public instruction to serve as president of the commission and as state librarian. The commission was to maintain its offices in the State Library at the capitol.

The commission's first regular meeting was held at the State Library in April 1913. The 1915 Legislature changed the law to make it permissive instead of mandatory for schools to purchase only books found on the list published by the commission. Two years later, the Legislature created a board of county library trustees, and while this did not directly affect the commission, it did expand the scope of its organizational, promotional, and assistance duties to a fairly large degree. The State Library was kept totally separate from what was called for many years the "Commission Library," but cooperation between them continued for a long time. In 1920, it was reported that "by mutual consent, neither the Free Library Commission nor the State Library duplicate unnecessarily any of the material contained in the library of the other department" (41). In 1943, the Legislature abolished the State Library and the office of the state librarian; the director of the Free Library Commission took over these duties.

In 1953, the duties of the commission were again defined. Its name was changed to State Library Commission, and it was—

> Designated as the State agency to apply to and receive from any private agency or the federal government or any agency thereof such gifts or funds as are granted or allotted for promoting library services as now or hereafter may be available to the state of South Dakota or any political subdivision or agencies (42).

This later caused several problems in administering funds available to South Dakota school districts for improving school libraries and other provisions under Title II of ESEA. Both the commission and the State Board of Education felt that they had the primary responsibility for administering these funds. A cooperative arrangement was agreed to by both agencies for administering the funds during the 1965-66 and 1966-67 school years. But to clarify the situation and definitely fix the responsibility, the 1967 Legislature amended this section with following sentence:

> The provisions of this section shall not apply to funds or gifts which are granted or allotted to the State of South Dakota or to local public school districts for the purpose of acquiring library books or other library resource materials for local public school districts (43).

In 1957, the membership of the commission was increased to five appointed members serving 5-year overlapping terms. Two new appointments were to be made from nominations presented to the Governor by the South Dakota Junior Chamber of Commerce and the Associated School Boards of South Dakota.

Because of the close relationship between the state superintendent and the State Library Commission, both in the statutes and in practical operation, the commission has been the agency over the years to establish standards and provide supervision for school libraries. As a result of the controversy over the federal funds under Title II, the 1967 Legislature directed the state board to have full and complete supervision over school libraries. A cooperative working relationship continues between the State Library Commission and the Department of Public Instruction on the administration and supervision of school libraries. School librarians are invited to attend workshops conducted by the director, and many school administrators continue to take advantage of the services offered by the library commission in the development and maintenance of school libraries.

FOOTNOTES

1. Dakota Territorial Legislature, *Session Laws* (1864), ch. 41.
2. The first board of education was composed of Territorial Governor Newton Edmunds, Secretary of the Territory Jon Hutchinson, and Treasurer J. O. Taylor. The first elected board in 1866 consisted of J. W. Turner, S. A. Bentley, and William Walters.
3. Superintendent of Public Instruction, "History of Education in South Dakota," *Fourteenth Biennial Report, 1916-1918,* pp. 19-20.
4. No information is available as to why the Legislature began appointing superintendents in apparent contradiction to the law of 1867.
5. From 1878 until 1884, only one report can be found, and this is in double columns covering only a few pages. In 1882, Superintendent William H. H. Beadle addressed a report to all school officers, carefully noting that this was done at his own expense. Superintendent of Public Instruction, "History of Education in South Dakota," *Fourteenth Biennial Report, 1916-1918,* pp. 19-20.
6. Ralph V. Hunkins, *SDEA: History of the South Dakota Education Association* (Pierre: South Dakota Education Association, 1959), pp. 7-8.
7. Superintendent of Public Instruction, *Tenth Biennial Report, 1908-1910,* pp. 2-3.
8. *Ibid.*
9. Superintendent of Public Instruction, *Eleventh Biennial Report, 1910-1912,* p. 8.
10. South Dakota, *Session Laws* (1919), ch. 182.
11. Superintendent of Public Instruction, *Twelfth Biennial Report, 1912-1914,* pp. 10-11.
12. Superintendent of Public Instruction, *Fourteenth Biennial Report, 1916-1918,* p. 11.
13. Superintendent of Public Instruction, *Fifteenth Annual Report, 1918-1920,* p. 14.
14. *Ibid.,* p. 17. The person writing the report probably added the "(honest to God)".
15. Superintendent of Public Instruction, *Twelfth Biennial Report, 1912-1914.* pp. 11-12.
16. Superintendent of Public Instruction, *Seventeenth Biennial Report, 1922-1924,* p. 6.
17. Superintendent of Public Instruction, *Sixteenth Biennial Report, 1920-1922,* p. 12.
18. Superintendent of Public Instruction, *Eighteenth Biennial Report, 1924-1926,* p. 7.
19. *Ibid.,* p. 5.
20. R. W. Kraushaar was appointed supervisor of secondary education in 1929 and served for 8 years. During his first 2 years, he directed a committee of educators in preparing an administrative handbook for the South Dakota schools and made a study of the South Dakota school law for the recodification committee. He was also responsible for preparing a system of financial accounting that guided the school system for more than a quarter of a century.
21. Superintendent of Public Instruction, *Twentieth Biennial Report, 1928-1930,* p. 5.
22. Superintendent of Public Instruction, *Twenty-First Biennial Report, 1930-1932,* pp. 8-9.
23. *Ibid.*
24. The 1933 Legislature also changed the composition of the State Board of Education to include one representative each from labor, homemaking, and agriculture, and a superintendent or principal of an independent school district. The Governor was to appoint all four to 4-year terms.

25. The Permanent School Fund is composed of proceeds from the sale of the state school and public lands. Income from the investments of the fund plus the income from rents on the land is distributed annually to the school districts on a per-capita (school census) basis. The school census includes all resident persons from age 6 through age 20 as of November 1.

26. This was an organization named after former Superintendent William H. H. Beadle, founded in March 1934 to "honor men who have done outstanding work in the cause of education in South Dakota" and to "perpetuate the contributions to education of General Beadle, and to honor his name." Its main purpose has been to protect the school lands and the Permanent School Fund. Hunkins, *op. cit.*, pp. 65-67.

27. Superintendent of Public Instruction, *Twenty-Second Biennial Report, 1932-1934,* p. 7.

28. Superintendent of Public Instruction, *Twenty-Seventh Biennial Report, 1942-1944,* p. 7.

29. Superintendent of Public Instruction, *Thirtieth Biennial Report, 1948-1950,* p. 8.

30. For further information, see State Legislative Research Council, "Organizations and Functions of the State Department of Public Instruction," *Staff Background Memorandum* (Pierre: The Council, 1965), p. 6.

31. *Ibid.*, pp. 8-10.

32. *Ibid.*

33. The institutional on-farm training staff was fading out and was reduced to one supervisor at the end of the 1958-60 biennium. Eleven of the 29 professional staff members were hired by a vocational rehabilitation division. An accountant, a statistician, and a consultant on school business administration were added to the research division.

34. Superintendent of Public Instruction, *Thirty-Sixth Biennial Report, 1960-1962,* p. 2.

35. For further information, see South Dakota, *Session Laws* (1965), ch. 67.

36. The Legislature in 1959 amended the law relating to the state board by eliminating two provisions: that a city superintendent of schools could not be a member of the board and that members of the board could not succeed themselves. State Legislative Research Council, *op. cit.*, pp. 8-10.

37. For further information, see South Dakota, *Session Laws* (1949), ch. 1968.

38. South Dakota, *Session Laws* (1955), ch. 41.

39. South Dakota Free Library Commission, *Eleventh Biennial Report* (1932), p. 5.

40. For further information, see South Dakota, *Session Laws* (1913), ch. 217.

41. South Dakota Free Library Commission, *Fourth Biennial Report* (1920), p. 15.

42. South Dakota, *Session Laws* (1953), ch. 175.

43. South Dakota, *Session Laws* (1967), ch. 37.

BIBLIOGRAPHY

Public Documents

Dakota Territorial Legislature. *Session Laws* (1864-67, 1887-89).

South Dakota. *Constitution* (1889).

—— *Session Laws* (1913-67).

Book

Hunkins, Ralph V. *SDEA: History of South Dakota Education Association.* Pierre: South Dakota Education Association, 1959.

Reports

South Dakota Free Library Commission. *Biennial Reports.* Pierre: The Commission, 1916, 1920, 1930, and 1932.

State Legislative Research Council. "Organizations and Functions of the State Department of Public Instruction." *Staff Background Memorandum.* Pierre: The Council, 1965.

Superintendents of Public Instruction. *Biennial Reports.* Pierre: Department of Public Instruction, 1906-66.

Appendix A

SOUTH DAKOTA CHIEF STATE SCHOOL OFFICERS

Territorial Superintendents

1864-68	James S. Foster (ex officio)
1869	T. McKendrick Stuart
1869-70	James S. Foster
1870-71	J. W. Turner
1872-74	E. W. Miller
1875-76	J. J. McIntire
1877-78	W. E. Caton
1879-85	W. H. H. Beadle
1885-87	A. Sheridan Jones
1887-89	Eugene A. Dye
1889	Leonard A. Rose

State Superintendents

1889-91	Gilbert L. Pinkham
1891-95	Cortez Salmon
1895-99	Frank Crane
1899-1903	E. E. Collins
1903-1906	George W. Nash
1906-1907	M. M. Ramer
1907-11	H. H. Ustrud
1911-14	C. G. Lawrence
1914-18	Charles H. Lugg
1918-25	Fred L. Shaw
1925-29	C. G. St. John
1929-33	E. C. Giffen
1933-35	I. D. Weeks
1935-49	J. F. Hines
1949-57	Harold S. Freeman
1958-67	Merrill F. Coddington
1967-	Gordon A. Diedtrich

Appendix B

Chart I.--SOUTH DAKOTA DEPARTMENT OF PUBLIC INSTRUCTION, 1920

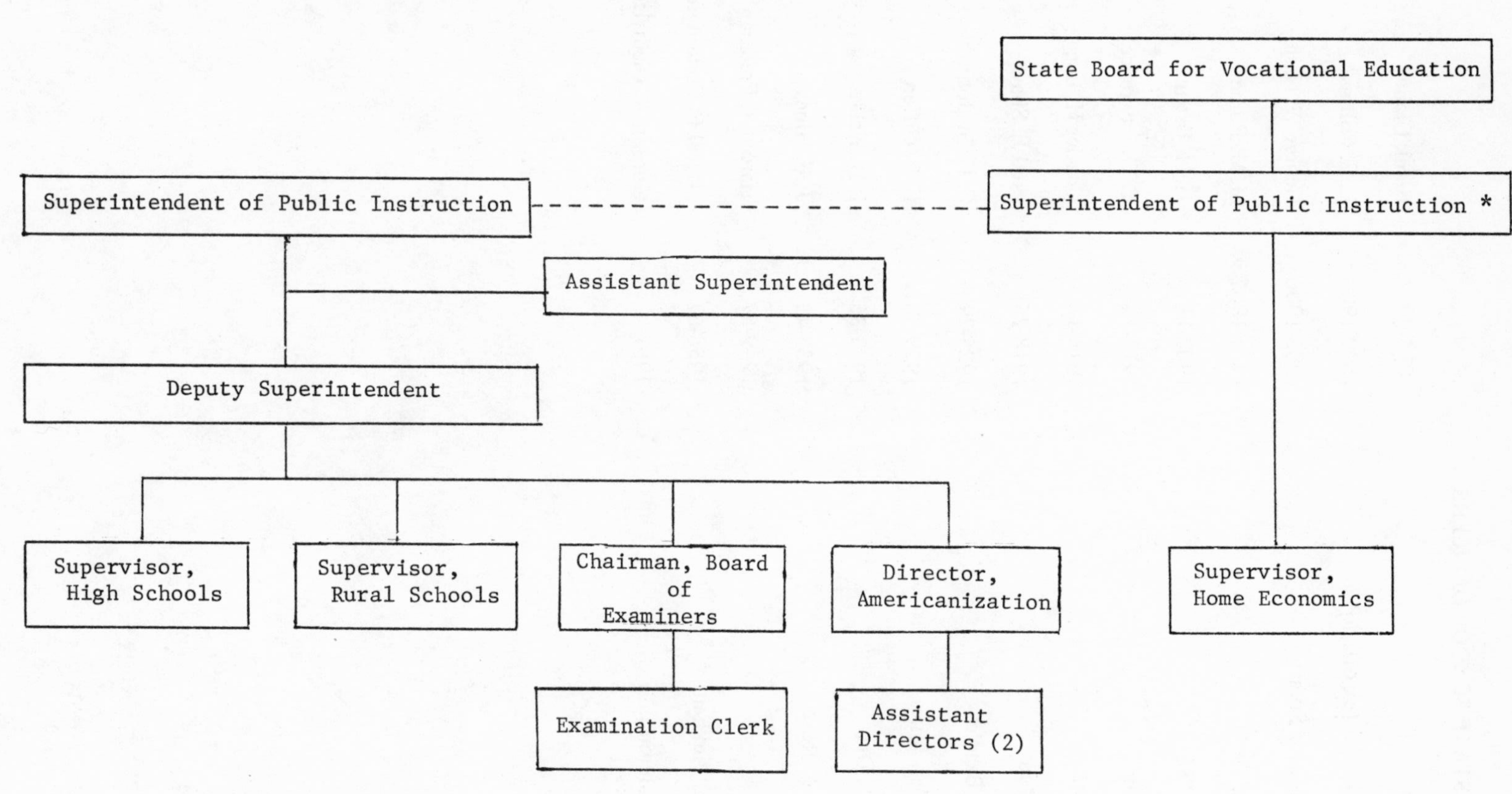

*Also a member of and President of the State Board for Vocational Education

Appendix B

Chart II.--SOUTH DAKOTA DEPARTMENT OF PUBLIC INSTRUCTION, 1952

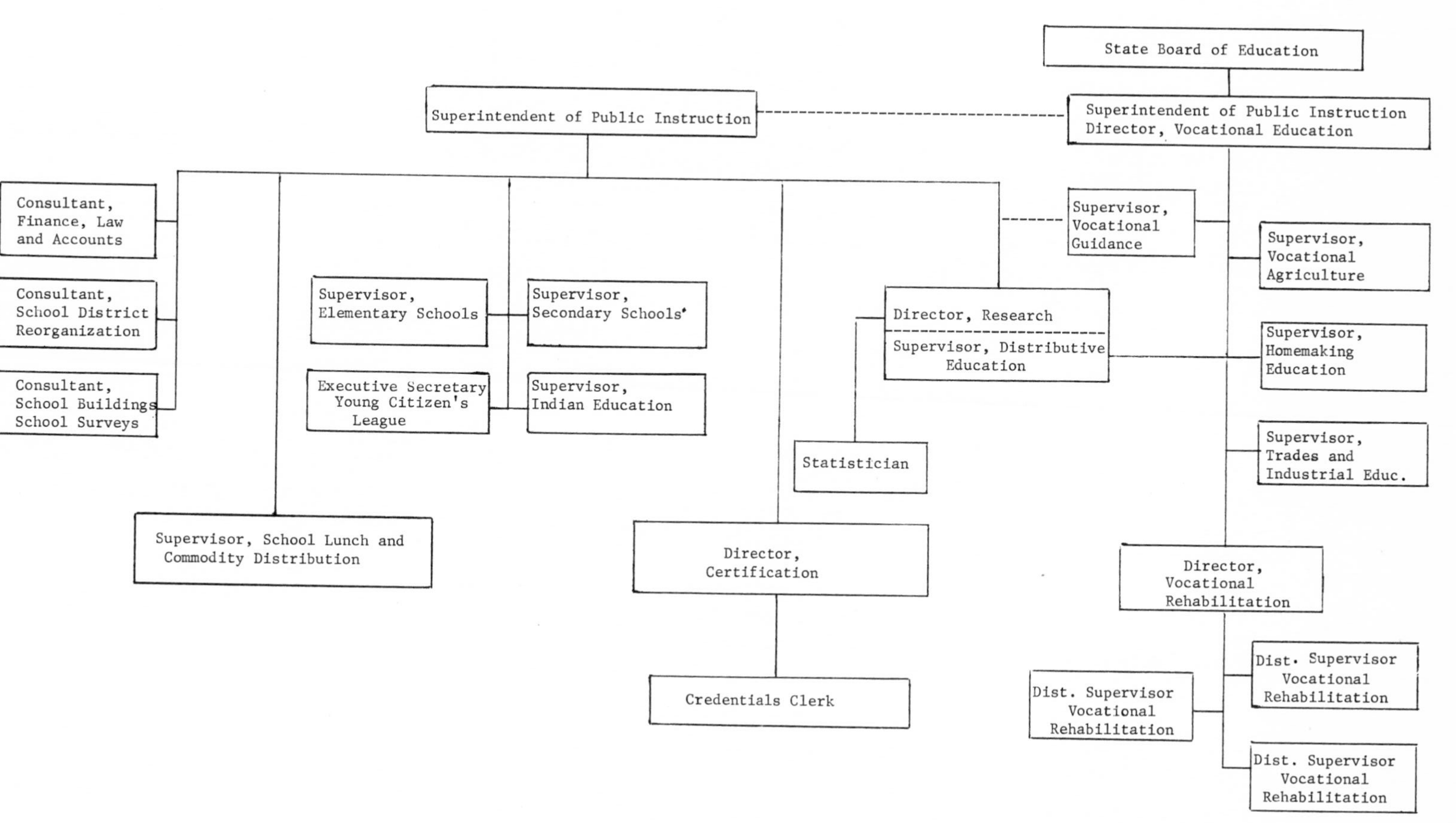

Appendix B

Chart III.--SOUTH DAKOTA EDUCATION STRUCTURE, 1966-67

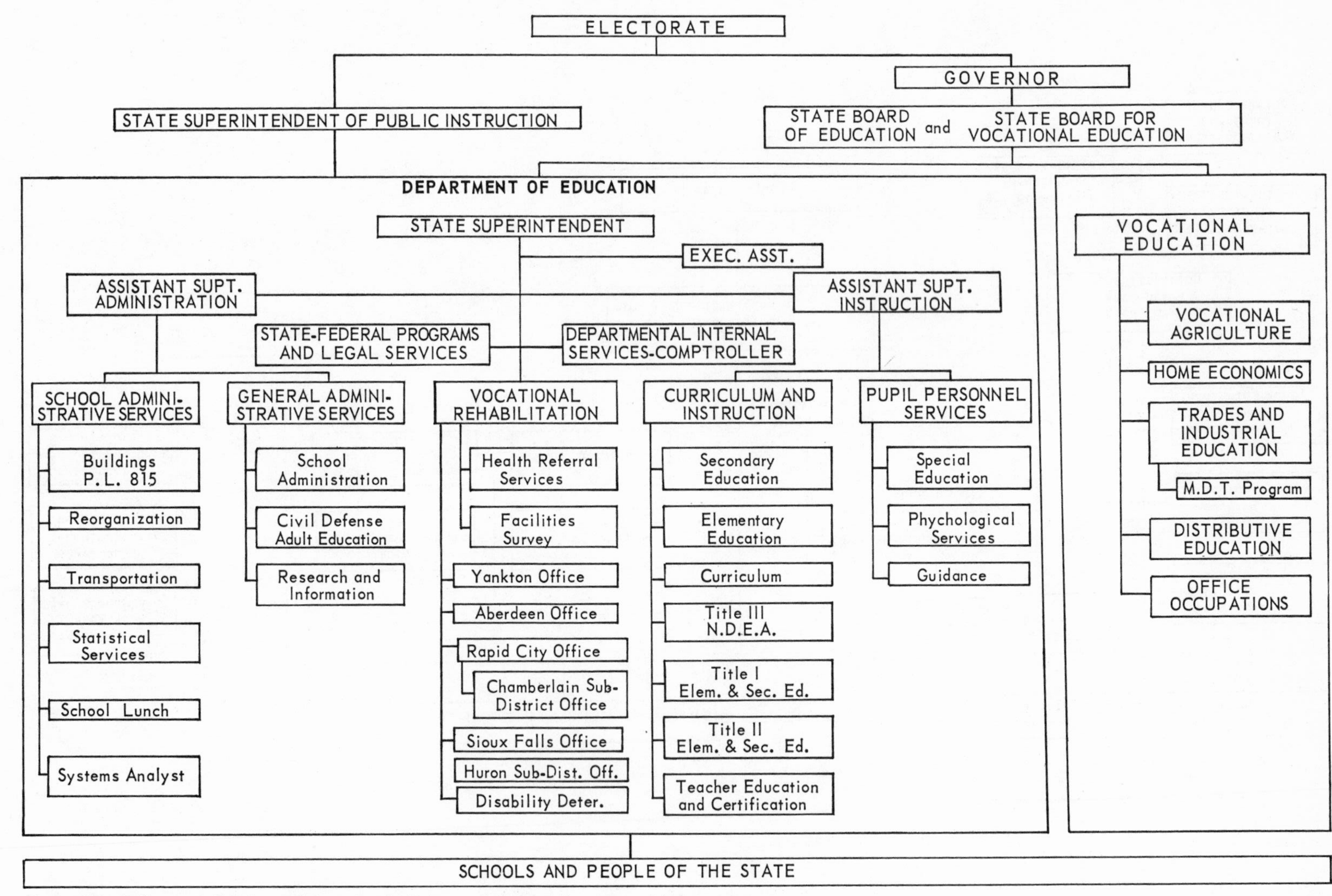

From The Role and Policymaking Activities of State Boards of Education, a special research study under Title V of P. L. 89-10, prepared and edited by Dean M. Schweickhard, September 1967.

Appendix C

Table 1.–EXPENDITURES OF THE SOUTH DAKOTA DEPARTMENT OF PUBLIC INSTRUCTION, FISCAL YEAR 1966

Part I. Expenditures made from state funds

	Salaries	Operation & maintenance	Travel	Grants & aid	Total
Certification	$ 20,410.84	$ 2,532.81	$ 1,417.58	---	$ 24,361.23
Curriculum	26,664.52	1,328.87	2,603.33	---	30,596.72
Title III NDEA	8,017.86	244.08	311.85	---	8,573.79
Title V Guidance	---	---	---	---	---
Reorganization	22,875.33	905.73	2,066.01	---	25,847.07
Title X Research	15,435.81	5,342.41	298.01	---	21,076.23
School law & admin.	13,002.87	4,018.31	3,937.68	---	14,918.64
School lunch	38,182.59	4,018.31	3,937.68	---	46,138.58
Secondary education	14,366.55	1,180.46	644.72	---	16,191.73
Special education	35,141.86	4,319.05	6,055.82	---	45,516.73
Special Education Ad. Com.	---	---	275.37	---	275.37
State supt.	11,711.23	2,110.98	1,814.12	---	15,636.33
State board	20,755.72	244.49	3,457.38	---	5,777.59
Voc. education	30,303.53	5,886.18	4,980.25	$ 31,511.88	72,681.84
Voc. Adv. Com.	---	---	---	---	---
Consultants	555.00	---	---	---	555.00
Fiscal	15,221.68	4,111.84	228.72	---	19,562.24
Title I, ESEA	2,851.88	692.87	346.63	---	3,891.38
Phy. Ed. Adv. Com.	15,221.68	96.33	581.31	---	677.64
Subtotals	$ 256,817.27	$ 34,299.33	$ 29,649.63	$ 31,511.88	$ 352,278.11
Commodity distrib.	14,483.35	386.68	5,676.03	---	20,546.06
Y. C. L.	150.00	441.68	400.41	---	992.09
State gen. rehab.	---	---	---	169,302.88	169,302.88
Spec. ed. for hdcp. children	---	---	---	409,989.08	409,989.08
Total state funds	$ 271,450.62	$ 35,127.69	$ 35,726.07	$ 610,803.84	$ 953,108.22

See next page for second half of table.

Table 1.- EXPENDITURES OF THE SOUTH DAKOTA DEPARTMENT OF PUBLIC INSTRUCTION, FISCAL YEAR 1966 (Continued)

Part II. Expenditures made from federal funds

	Salaries	Operation & maintenance	Travel	Grants & aid	Total
NDEA III	$ 14,772.03	$ 20,947.32	$ 7,893.84	---	$ 43,613.19
Title III reim.	---	---	---	$ 171,769.09	171,769.09
Title V	15,058.82	3,621.87	2,411.08	74,726.47	95,818.24
Title X	10,255.09	6,014.84	759.10	---	17,029.04
Indian education	21,179.45	4,360.59	1,590.41	487,421.31	514,551.76
Institute	---	---	---	20,198.89	20,198.89
Federal sch. lch. & milk	---	---	---	968,766.68	968,766.68
Fed. public instruction					
NDEA III	---	730.50	---	---	730.50
NDEA V	---	9,936.18	534.25	6,123.66	16,594.09
NDEA X	---	---	---	---	---
Adult basic education	---	---	---	12,700.00	12,700.00
M.D.T.A. program	$ 19,801.96	$ 3,741.21	$ 7,094.58	$ 565,681.54	$ 596,319.29
Fellowships	296.98	---	---	46,705.52	47,002.50
Civil Defense	17,260.78	3,674.37	1,851.25	3,951.48	26,737.88
A.R.A. program	---	---	---	6,847.26	6,847.26
Iowa Project	781.50	479.79	84.45	---	1,345.74
D.D.U.	43,761.17	5,865.57	1,196.46	25,197.94	76,021.14
State spec. rehab.	---	---	---	267,332.21	267,332.21
Fed. misc. rehab.	144,322.84	30,571.28	11,013.05	436.792.90	622,700.07
George-Barden Act	16,921.29	822.55	2,053.84	306,656.19	326,453.87
Smith-Hughes Act	2,156.02	---	---	40,783.98	42,940.00
Voc. Act of 1963	11,277.13	4,207.29	3,075.83	91,786.64	110,346.89
Fed. Elem & Sec. Ed. Act	---	---	---	600,000.00	---
(does not include obligated construction)					
Title I	30,570.38	12,064.76	6,796.80	3,994,579.88	4,044,011.82
Title II	1,174.71	2,527.81	99.60	---	3,802.12
Title V	26,653.22	34,170.38	6,833.58	---	67,657.18
Total federal funds	$ 376,243.37	$ 143,736.32	$ 53,288.12	$7,528,021.64	$8,101,289.45
Total federal and state funds expended	$ 647,693.99	$ 178,864.01	$ 89,014.19	$8,138,825.48	$9,054,397.67
Percent of federal funds	58.09%	80.36%	59.86%	92.50%	89.47%

Source:

State Superintendent of Public Instruction, *Thirty-Eighth Biennial Report, 1964-1966*, p. 9.

43 Tennessee

DEPARTMENT OF EDUCATION
Sam Smith

Contents

EARLY HISTORY

The people of Tennessee accepted the basic ideas and principles of public education only after bitter public debate. That a democracy had a duty to ensure equal educational opportunity for all its youth was a concept at issue in this state—as in most others—throughout the nineteenth century. The European dogma that the education of all was dangerous to society and that it was not one man's responsibility to help educate the child of another continued to be held by the wealthy and privileged classes of Tennessee throughout most of the century.

Tennessee's first constitution, in 1796, had been silent on the question of education; thus, by implication it left the task of educating youth to private initiative by individuals or religious groups. One religious group, the Scottish Presbyterians, had been the leading educational thrust in the old Southwest Territory and continued its outstanding work after Tennessee achieved statehood.

Samuel Doak, a Princeton graduate and Presbyterian minister, was Tennessee's first teacher. He opened his home in Jonesboro to use as a school in 1781. In steady succession after this, Martin Academy (later Washington College), Davidson Academy (successively the University of Nashville and George Peabody College for Teachers), Greeneville College (later Tusculum), and Blount College (later the University of Tennessee) were established by Presbyterian ministers before 1800. Private academies and colleges were thus the first educational establishments in the state and became the foundation of the educational structure in Tennessee. Most of these institutions were financially undernourished, depending primarily on tuition for continued operation. (Tuition was advertised in 1829 by the Nashville Female Academy at $70 for a 5-month period to include board, washing, firewood, candles, and servant hire.) Other forms of financing attempted were the lottery (first used in 1801 as a device to raise funds for educational institutions in New York State and North Carolina (1), sale of stock, and personal gifts from wealthy patrons. Academies generally were considered college preparatory schools and were attended by only a small minority of school-age pupils. From a peak of several hundred academies demies chartered in Tennessee, the number declined sharply after the Civil War. The last one was chartered in 1889.

Legislators and other public figures gave little more than lip service to public schools in the early nineteenth century. Older states, like Tennessee, did not share in the congressional land grants for public education to the degree which did states created later. Consequently, Tennessee turned in 1806 to the device of a permanent public school fund to support its early efforts in public education. This method never had the desired effect, however, because it was a relatively small amount and because it checked any tendency to raise school taxes locally. In addition, careless management of the fund over the years severely damaged the image of public education in the state.

Election of Tennessee's Andrew Jackson as President of the United States in 1829 symbolized the end of the old class order centered in the Northeast and Tidewater areas of the nation. His enunciation of "confidence in the virtue and good sense of the people," and the sum of his actions as President eventuated in a democratic revolution which promoted the development of public education across the country (2).

New York, in 1812, was the first state to create an office to exercise general supervision of public education. Tennessee waited, however, for the impetus from Jacksonian democracy to establish its first state position of educational leadership. The General Assembly created the Office of Superintendent of Public Instruction in 1836, requiring the person in this position to control the common school fund and to formulate plans for the advancement of public education.

Robert H. McEwen became the first state superintendent, but his gross mismanagement of the fund (much of which he lent to friends and relatives who were caught by the Panic of 1837) placed him under such a cloud that he was barely able to finish two terms of office (3). Subsequent investigation of this matter severely damaged the prestige of his office and the concept of public schools, and, for the next 4 years, those who served as state superintendent did so only as figureheads. The office was abolished in 1844.

In 1853, a new Governor of Tennessee ascended the steps of the almost completed state capitol building. This man was Andrew Johnson, who—despite his total lack of formal education—was later to become President of the United States. The dynamic new Governor was anxious to provide for the youth of his era a free public school education, an opportunity which he himself had been denied. The 1850 census had shown that a substantial portion of the total white population over 20 years of age could neither read nor write. Johnson therefore recommended to the Legislature that a property tax be levied on the people of the whole state in order to infuse "life and energy to our dying or dead system of common school education" (4). Under his leadership, Tennessee passed the first property tax for public education in the state's history, an action which almost doubled the amount of funds available for that purpose.

The state did not have long to enjoy its new status, for the people soon found themselves in the unrelenting grip of the Civil War. And with the coming of this tragedy, public school progress during the Johnson administration ground to a halt.

In the immediate postwar South, no system of public education was to be found. Private schools reopened for children of privileged Southern families, and until 1872 the educational activities of the Freedman's Bureau continued among Southern Negroes. Yet the majority of Southern white children were growing up in illiteracy because of the lack of opportunity for an education.

In 1867, the Radical Legislature passed an effective act for the reorganization of public schools which provided for a structure of organization and authority—and included an appropriate system of taxation to support the measure. However, these tax funds were almost completely diverted to the payment of interest on state bonds issued to aid railroad construction. The effectiveness of this measure was thus largely compromised.

John Eaton, Jr., a New Hampshire-born minister who had served with Ulysses S. Grant as a chaplain during the Civil War, became state superintendent during the period 1867-69. A man of considerable talent and energy, Eaton toured the state in 1869 for a personal view of school conditions, after which he prepared a comprehensive survey of Tennessee's educational needs. In his report, he cited a need for sharply increased funds and substantial changes in program including the establishment of normal schools for training of teachers and equal opportunities for Negroes (5). This report, however, shared the same fate as other work of the Radical regime: The reorganized Conservative state government of 1870 repealed practically all the legislation of the immediate postwar period.

Like other Southern states, Tennessee waited upon Northern philanthropy and the activities of a concerned citizenry for the impetus to establish a public school system which would take root and grow.

Early in the 1870's, there emerged on Tennessee's public forum a man who was representative of the concerned citizenry and whose voice became more eloquent and compelling than any other state figure of his time in the support of public education. This man was Joseph Buckner Killebrew—farmer, educator, journalist, author, orator, and one of the most distinguished public servants that Tennessee has produced. Born in Montgomery County near Clarksville, Killebrew struggled against great odds to gain an education. His talent was so apparent, however, that a generous benefactor underwrote his outstanding career at the University of North Carolina. After the war, Killebrew embarked on a decade of public service in Tennessee which included the office of assistant state superintendent of public instruction and agent for the Peabody Fund.

Throughout 1871, as Killebrew wrote an agricultural column for the Nashville *Union and American* and made speeches around the state on the problems of the farmer and other matters at public issue, he spoke frequently in support of education. "The idea of public education," he said, "is one too deeply imbedded in the spirit of the age to be successfully resisted" (6). He argued with all of the logic and appeal at his command that the material interests of the state demanded an effective system of public education:

> We may inveigh against the principles of taxing one man to educate the children of another; we may declaim against the interference of the State in matters that concern mostly the parents of children; we may ascribe unworthy motives to the friends of public schools, yet after all the great truth stares us in the face, that we cannot have an increase of population and resist this dominant idea of the age, and we cannot be prosperous without an increase in population (7).

But opposition to this "dominant idea of the age" was both sizable and powerful. In Tennessee, as in other Southern states, it was the former slaveholding planter who opposed direct taxes on his property for the maintenance of public schools and, indeed, the principle of public education itself. Early in 1871, William G. Harding, eminent proprietor of Belle Meade Plantation in Nashville, spoke out against universal education at a meeting of the Davidson County Farmer's Club. "I cannot believe," he said, "that we have yet reached the period and perhaps never will, when the drudgery of plantation and household work will require intelligent and educated minds" (8). Arguing primarily against education for the Negro, he projected his argument to include all manual labor. His plea was that education was neither necessary nor desirable for all men.

In spite of such opposition, however, the tide of sentiment for an effective system of public education ran forward, encouraged by Northern philanthropy. In June 1872, Barnas Sears, former president of Brown University and then general agent for the Peabody Fund, in his report to the Peabody Fund trustees, discussed the unfortunate change in the public school law in Tennessee which had taken place in 1870. He stated, however, that a reaction had set in against the inadequate public school system and that sentiment in the state was already changing toward better schools. To support his statement, he cited a request received the previous December from the State Teachers' Association for $1,500 to support an agent who would work with interested organizations and state officers of the association in creating sentiment favorable to public schools. The result of granting this request, he said, was that a "highly intelligent and influential gentleman" was appointed agent of the fund; and in January 1872 he was made the assistant superintendent of public instruction (the state treasurer at this time still maintained the ex officio title of state superintendent of public instruction), a fact which in itself showed the merit of the appointment (9). This new agent for the Peabody Fund in Tennessee was Killebrew.

Just seven weeks after assuming his positions with the Peabody Fund and with the Department of Public Instruction, Killebrew delivered an important and memorable report to the Legislature. His report outlined the conditions of the existing public school system county by county, including statements on the amount of taxes voted for support of schools, the number of school commissioners elected, the number of schools in operation, the number of months in operation annually, and the number of pupils enrolled. Killebrew prefaced his report with an impressive argument for the establishment of an effective system of public instruction, an argument based primarily on economic considerations. He stated that the greatest obstacle to be overcome was the prevalent idea that education should be a matter of private initiative. Killebrew quickly discounted this line of reasoning by stating that this conception could just as easily be used to apply to police systems, courts, penitentiaries, and other public institutions. Public schools, he said, were a public responsibility in the same way as were these other institutions (10).

In concluding his report, Killebrew pleaded for the appointment of a full-time state superintendent of public instruction who would direct the state educational system; he also recommended the appointment of county superintendents who would serve a function on the local level analogous to that of the state superintendent. Dr. Sears, in a report to the trustees of the Peabody Fund, complimented Killebrew's report, calling it "most valuable . . . , of the most elevated character . . . , and well adapted to awaken the people from their lethargy" (11).

Supporters of the public school system continued their efforts to arouse sentiment for its establishment throughout 1872 in preparation for the Thirty-Eighth General Assembly. They were so successful that Governor John C. Brown, in an address to the assembly, urged the adoption of a state educational system which would include a full-time state superintendent and a State Board of Education. He pointed out the fact that Tennessee ranked third highest of the states of the Union in illiteracy and that the prosperity and permanence of the state government depended on the intelligence of the people. He therefore advocated that the Legislature act accordingly and remedy this serious educational deficiency (12).

The result of this dedicated activity by Killebrew, the State Teachers' Association, the Peabody Fund, and Governor Brown's administration was the passage in 1873 of "An Act To Establish and Maintain a Uniform System of Public Schools in Tennessee." This act has remained until the present time the basic framework of the state system of education in Tennessee.

The act, in brief, provides for a state superintendent of public instruction, county superintendents, and district school directors with the state superintendent having central responsibility for ensuring that the state school laws are faithfully executed. The legislation also stipulates that the superintendent see to the collection and dissemination of statistical and other information related to the schools.

The permanent school fund was fixed at $2,512,500 with 6-percent interest on the state indebtedness to be paid annually to the schools. In addition, every male was taxed $1 (a poll tax), and a 1-mill tax on the property tax dollar was established, both for the support of public education.

Thus the sentiment for public education seemed partially won in Tennessee, and over the whole South there were encouraging signs of an awakening interest in the subject. Sears felt able to report to the Peabody Fund trustees in October 1874 that "the public mind in nearly all these states of the South is more and more imbued with the doctrine of free schools; and nothing in the future is more certain than the acceptance of that principle by the people at large" (13). Events in Tennessee, however, revealed that Sears's optimism was premature.

To be sure, there was some immediate improvement in the state system after the passage of the 1873 act. In contrast to the conditions prevalent at that time, illustrated in Killebrew's report—one-fifth of the state's population had no opportunity for any sort of education, in many counties there were no schools of any sort, and fewer than one-third of the counties had levied any supplementary tax for educational purposes (14)—the next few years witnessed some improvement in the system. By 1879, two-thirds of the counties had levied some sort of supplementary tax for schools, and the great majority of Tennessee's counties had established schools. From a low point of $89,000 in 1871, total annual expenditure on education had risen to $815,000 by 1879 (15). Also, through the interest and influence of Barnas Sears and the Peabody Fund, a normal school was joined to the University of Nashville in 1875 as the first teacher-training institution in the state (16).

Despite these encouraging developments, Tennessee's school system continued until the end of the century to languish in relationship to its needs. Reports of the state superintendent of public instruction show conclusively that, in spite of tremendous efforts by concerned citizens, there was little real improvement in the condition of public education in Tennessee before 1900. Although some system of public schools was established in a majority of the counties by the turn of the century, the average length of the school term did not exceed 4 months and often was less. The average daily attendance of pupils did not exceed two-fifths of the scholastic population. Average teacher pay was less than $35 a month, and total expenditure for schools in the state averaged no more than $1 million a year. Many counties levied no tax to supplement state support for schools, and the number of teachers did not at any time exceed 8,000, with the result that the average teacher-pupil ratio was approximately 1 to 49 (17).

The basic reason for this lack of progress was an economic one. Agriculture, in which 80 percent (18) of the people were engaged in the post-Civil War South, was in an increasingly depressed state from 1870 until the end of the century. The loss of the slave labor system upon which the plantation economy had depended was a blow from which Tennessee and the South were slow to recover. Soil exhaustion and erosion were daily burdens with which the farmer labored. Rising costs and declining returns continued as constant factors in the agricultural picture for three decades after the war. Thus the estimated value of farm products in the state fell from $86,472,847 in 1870 to $55,194,181 in 1890 (19). Therefore, real progress in public education in the state was to wait until the twentieth century and final recovery from the severe economic loss and dislocation of the Civil War and Reconstruction.

As the century drew to a close, the South's economy slowly began to improve. Cotton, which in 1898 brought 6¢ per pound, brought 9.5¢ in 1902 (20). Industrial prospects became brighter, and large infusions of new philanthropy for Tennessee and the South loomed on the immediate horizon.

A review of the nineteenth-century progress in public education development shows that much had been done to gain support of the concept. An organizational structure had been brought into being through the Act of 1873, and this was undergirded by legislation in 1875 forming a State Board of Education. Finally, in 1899, a State Textbook Commission was created to establish uniform texts for the public schools. The state had neared the threshold of breaking the barrier to permanent progress in public education.

THE EDUCATIONAL CAMPAIGN PERIOD AND AFTER: 1900-45

The period from 1903 to 1913 has been described by one authority as "the most intensive and extensive educational crusade in the history of the state" (21). Indeed, at this time, a bevy of talented, well-trained, and concerned men were available to begin their work. Led by Philander Priestly Claxton, they were to cover the state for a decade preaching the cause of public education and ensuring the passage of the important legislations of 1909 and 1913.

P.P. Claxton was the most brilliant and best trained of this competent group, which included Charles Dabney, president of the University of Tennessee, and Seymour Mynders, Robert L. Jones, and John W. Brister, all superintendents of public instruction from 1903 to 1913. The Governors of this era also were educationally minded.

The acknowledged leader of the educational forces, Claxton was born in 1862 in Bedford County, Tennessee. He graduated with high honors from the University of Tennessee in 1882, matriculating for only 2.5 years. Later in his life, he wrote that one evening while attending the increasingly famous Johns Hopkins Graduate School, he was walking through the streets of Baltimore when "a certain streak of altruistic enthusiasm" caused him to decide to devote his life to the improvement of education in the Southern states (22). Thus, after several months of study in Germany, he returned home to fulfill this vision. For a time he worked in the school systems of North Carolina as a teacher, as county and city superintendent, and later as professor of pedagogy and German at Greensboro Normal and Industrial School. In 1897, he began to publish the *North Carolina Journal of Education* in which he advocated such progressive educational measures as 10-month schools which would be compulsory and free to all, school consolidation, transportation of students at public expense, establishment of kindergartens, improved curriculums, and higher quality of instruction.

Northern philanthropy had established an interest in the cause of improving the quality of Southern education at its Conference for Education in the South, first held in West Virginia in 1898. This interest was made effective in the formation of its executive arm, the Southern Education Board, which was gradually merged into a larger, more comprehensive, and more richly endowed organization—the General Education Board, a body which became largely underwritten by the Rockefeller family. The union of these two organizations was consummated in 1915. Charles Dabney served on the Southern Education Board and with its consent called Claxton to Knoxville in 1902 to become chief of the investigation and information bureau of the board. In a short while, Claxton was publishing statistics on the deficiencies of Tennessee's school system which would be used as background for the upcoming educational campaign years. During this same time, Dabney asked him to initiate a summer school for teachers to be called "Summer School of the South," which was to be underwritten by the board. This work Claxton did so successfully that total enrollment during the first summer of 1902 comprised 2,019 teachers who came from 28 states and 1 territory (23). During this year, he also was asked to establish and become head of the first Department of Education at the university, a task which he performed with his usual competence. Throughout the next few years, he worked very closely with the superintendents of public instruction in ordering the drive for improved public education.

As the campaign era moved successfully toward its end, Claxton accepted appointment as U.S. Commissioner of Education, a post which he occupied from 1911 to 1921. He was sometimes called the "Horace Mann of the South" (24), and Dabney once stated his belief that when Claxton's work was known, he would be ranked as one of the foremost school reformers of the country (25).

James B. Frazier was elected Governor of Tennessee in November 1902. A graduate of the state university, he had attended the Conference for Education in the South and had visited and lectured before the Summer School of the South in 1902. His message to the Legislature in January 1903 established his vital personal concern for education and its improvement: "Universal education," he said, "is the only safeguard for universal suffrage. It is the very bedrock of our civilization as well as our prosperity; . . . it has come to be universally conceded in all the American Commonwealths that public education is a function of the State" (26). He stated that the first imperative need was money with which to improve the public schools of the state. He recommended that the surplus left in the treasury at the end of the school year be distributed to the schools and that counties be allowed to increase taxes for school purposes to enable them to maintain public schools for at least 6 months of each year. He recommended school consolidation and the making of school districts coextensive with civil districts. He suggested that state aid to Peabody College as a teacher-training institution be continued and that the state university be given necessary aid. This address was probably the most important any Governor of Tennessee had made on matters of education to this time.

Governor Frazier wisely appointed an able man, Seymour A. Mynders, superintendent of public instruction. A graduate of the University of Tennessee, Mynders had been a teacher and an administrator in various divisions of the public school system. He possessed both warmth and tact in dealing with everyone.

Mynders immediately began to work with Claxton and others in organizing a systematic campaign for better schools in Tennessee to be underwritten by the General Education Board. The campaign consisted of sending out speakers to canvas the state in behalf of public education. Commencements, religious meetings, meetings of farmers, and even picnics were chosen as fertile fields to be cultivated. Ministers were asked to speak on education, and newspaper editors, to write on educational topics. Even women's clubs and labor unions heard speakers on education. Claxton wrote that—

> Usually these rallies lasted all day with picnic-dinners. The best of them had wagonloads of watermelons . . . . At these we spoke to more than 100,000 people during the year. In many places the attendance ran up to two, three, or four thousand and once to six thousand. In a political campaign year . . . we had much larger attendance at our educational meetings than the political speakers had (27).

At these meetings with the citizens of the state, the campaign speakers bore down hard on seven points:

> More money for elementary schools with per capita distribution; special help for weak schools in poor counties; school library needs; state appropriation to supplement salaries of county superintendents; state appropriation for county high schools; three normal schools for the preparation of white teachers and one for Negro teachers; and a larger appropriation to the University of Tennessee (28).

Throughout these biennial campaigns, Claxton worked with Mynders, Jones, and Brister toward their common goal. With one exception, the superintendent's headquarters in Nashville was campaign headquarters, and during each legislative session Claxton was constantly on Capitol Hill proving to be an excellent lobbyist for the cause of education.

Robert L. Jones, state superintendent from 1907 to 1911, was, like his predecessor, a competent educator. Born in White County and graduated from Burritt College, he had done additional work at the University of Chicago. Jones had been a teacher, principal, county and city superintendent, and college president before coming to the superintendency. He had been president of the State Teachers' Association in 1905 and had served on the State Textbook Commission.

The general education bill of 1909 was to a great extent a monument to Jones's talents. This important act expressed the need to improve, unify, and extend the public education system of Tennessee by providing state revenue to support all levels of public education. Twenty-five percent of the gross revenue of the state was allocated to education under this legislation. The bulk of this support went to the counties, apportioned on the basis of scholastic population with an equalization clause and a special effort to promote the development and maintenance of high schools. A considerable portion also went to establish three normal schools for the training of teachers in each grand division of the state and an agricultural and industrial normal school for Negroes. Important amendments to the general education act provided for a change of the local administrative unit from the school district to the county and an allowance for school consolidation in the interest of greater effectiveness.

John W. Brister, who attended Peabody College, the University of Chicago, and had taught at Montgomery Bell

Academy, entered the superintendency of public instruction in 1911 with some handicap. He was without the broad public school acquaintance which his immediate predecessors had enjoyed. Also, he emerged on the scene as Claxton was leaving Tennessee and just as the state political atmosphere was heating up again between the prohibitionists and those who favored legal liquor. As if these disadvantages were not enough, he was only Governor Hooper's compromise choice for the position (29).

That Brister was able to secure a positive legislative program during his tenure of office was thus greatly surprising and was a substantial tribute to his competence. His monuments were the various educational measures of 1913 which increased the general school fund from 25 percent to 33.3 percent of the state's gross revenue, established compulsory school attendance for all children 8 to 14 years old for 80 consecutive days, provided for uniform examination and certification of teachers, and gave additional authority to county boards to consolidate schools and provide transportation for pupils.

Although coming to an end with Brister's ouster, this crusading period was one of substantial accomplishment. Many county high schools were established, four normal schools were built at Johnson City, Murfreesboro, Memphis, and Nashville (and another was to be added at Cookeville in 1915), some school consolidation was initiated, school libraries were given a modicum of support, teacher training was improved, and, finally, a formula was developed to guarantee a certain level of state support for public education across the state.

Albert Williams, a former high school supervisor and a competent, aggressive, and popular young man, assumed the position of superintendent of public instruction in 1919. He was immediately successful in adding to the financial base of public education by securing a small property tax for this purpose, and in strengthening the compulsory school attendance law. Under his leadership, the State Teachers' Association was reorganized into an effective body, the Public Schools Officers' Association was strengthened, and at Williams' invitation Claxton was asked to preside over a Citizens' Conference on Education held at Monteagle in August 1920. This conference opted for minimum 8-month school terms, adequate support of high schools, support for the university and the normal schools, and sufficient funds to place the state in an improved educational position nationally. By the end of Williams' term of office in 1921, the state equalization fund had climbed to $570,000 from a $73,000 point in 1913.

The primary educational breakthrough of this era came during the administration of Governor Austin Peay (1922-27). Peay appointed as his educational leader Perry L. Harned, who, like himself, was from Montgomery County.

Harned had one of the richest backgrounds of any person yet to assume the position of superintendent of public instruction. He had been a member of the State Board of Education since 1901 and had served as its chairman. He had been a member of the textbook commission. He was the first high school inspector under the educational act of 1909 and had also served as state elementary supervisor. He had been a leader of the Public School Officers' Association and the State Teachers' Association. Harned also was a political figure, having served as county and state campaign manager for former Governors. His opposition to A.H. Roberts' successful candidacy in 1918 was said to have caused the Governor to gain repeal of the law allowing the state board to elect the state superintendent (30). Henceforth after 1919, the Governor himself would have this power of appointment.

In the first few years of Peay's administration, Harned and proponents of public school progress convinced Peay that education was one of the most important responsibilities of the state. Together, these men brought into being a series of measures undergirding education which were to help make this administration one of the most important in the history of the state. As a part of his reorganization of the state government, Peay changed the name of the superintendent of public instruction to commissioner of education and gave him cabinet status. In addition, he codified all the school laws in the great Act of 1925 which, among other things, provided for an equalization fund guaranteeing 8-month school terms for all counties which would ensure certain local financial support; repealed numerous pieces of cumbersome local legislation; initiated an improved method of licensing teachers, supervisors, and superintendents; devised a uniform system for the promotion of elementary school children; and increased the school fund by levying a tobacco tax, most of which was earmarked for public education. In addition, the normal schools were converted into teachers colleges, and an extensive building program was undertaken for rural schools and for all units of higher education. Two new institutions made their appearance as a result of the 1927 legislation. These were Austin Peay Normal College at Clarksville and a junior college at Martin, a part of the University of Tennessee system.

Peay's administration undergirded Harned's educational program to the fullest degree. And while these progressive years did not bring a millennium to Tennessee public education, they did provide a solid plateau from which to continue the upward ascent. This progress, however, was interrupted by the Depression years which represented a difficult time for public education in the state. In 1933, appropriations for higher education were cut 66.6 percent, secondary schools 28 percent, and elementary schools 19.5 percent. Throughout the period of Depression and World War II, retrenchment or hold-the-line fiscal philosophy prevailed in state government. Continued progress therefore awaited the conclusion of World War II and more favorable administration attitudes toward public education.

FURTHER DEVELOPMENT OF PROGRAM AND LEGISLATION: 1946-68

The advent of World War II hit hard at the public schools of Tennessee. Throughout the state public schools suffered severely with the influx of so many of its teachers, both men and women, into the armed forces. With the conclusion of the war, however, and with the election of Jim Nance McCord as Governor in 1944, prospects for educational improvement brightened considerably. The Tennessee Education Association launched during this period an intensive campaign for better schools, but it was apparent to everyone that new tax sources would have to be found before substantial improvements were made.

In 1945, the General Assembly passed a law requiring Burgin Dossett, the commissioner of education, to undertake a survey of public education in the state and report his findings to the 1947 assembly (31).

Under Dossett's able guidance, this study estimated the adequacy of the state's public educational effort and found it deficient in many important areas. It pointed up, for example, that only 46 of 100 Tennessee children finished high school (32). It showed that the majority of school plants were of insufficient size and were poorly equipped, and that the local financial structure in the support of schools was wholly inadequate. It found that Tennessee ranked tenth among Southern states in the assessed valuation of property per child of school age, and it found a great variation in financial ability of counties to support public education. For example, one county in the state had 12 times the resources of the poorest county, and thus there was an obvious need for considerably greater equalization. It found that Tennessee's support of public education was low when compared with other Southern states, with only 33.9 percent of the state tax revenue going to public schools. It recommended a single tax fund for elementary and high school programs to guarantee an adequate equalization program for grades 1 through 12 with an assurance of a certain level of local effort. It also called for one policy-making body, a State Board of Education, to formulate policies for all phases of the state educational program—elementary through the university levels—and advocated that this board be composed of nine members, appointed by the Governor, serving for 9-year terms. It advocated that the chief administrative officer—the commissioner of education—be appointed by the State Board of Education on the basis of professional qualifications for an indefinite term. It also advised that the personnel of the state department be placed under Civil Service.

As a result of this survey, Governor McCord asked for a 2-percent sales tax from the 1947 General Assembly with the bulk of the proceeds to go for education. This act began a new era for schools across the state. It appropriated $24,870,932 for public elementary and secondary schools in its first year and ensured that local governments would contribute no less than $19,500,000 per annum. Perhaps the most important aspect of this measure was the reorganization of aid to local school units. The old equalization programs were poorly financed and conceived. Yet, since very early in this century, there had been some degree of equalization pointing directly toward the elementary school level. Following closely the recommendation of the study report, a new minimum foundation program was initiated at this time, including grades 1 through 12 and incorporating all facets of the local educational program except capital outlay, which was brought into the program in 1949. The establishment of this program surely must rank high in the record of public school progress in this century.

The year 1955 brought forth an economic index as a basis for determining local relative ability to match equalizing funds. Such factors as retail sales tax collections, automobile registration payments, value of agricultural products sold, and the number of gainfully employed nongovernmental workers were all weighed to estimate closely the actual resources of a county. From 1947 to 1967, the local contributions to the equalization fund have declined from $19.5 million to $17.5 million, whereas the state share has risen over these years from $25 million to approximately $165 million. Thus the state share of the equalization fund in 1967-68 is nearly 90 percent.

Governor McCord's support of the sales tax for public schools cost him a third term, but he rested on a job well done. Under the administrations of Governors Gordon Browning, Frank Clement, and Buford Ellington, education has continued to move forward in Tennessee. Governor Clement supported a 3-percent sales tax in 1955 in behalf of education, and educational funds thus reached a new high level (33). Although many persons questioned the wisdom of using the basically regressive sales tax to finance state public education, the various gubernatorial administrations worked under the handicap of a state constitution which prohibited the passage of a state income tax. A sales tax seemed, therefore, to be the most expedient way to raise large sums of money to support the expanding public education system. This method of state financing has continued to be followed throughout the decade of the 1960's. In 1963, the General Assembly passed a local option sales tax, enabling local governments to add 1 percent to the present 3-percent state tax. One-half of the revenue from this source was earmarked for educational purposes.

Federal Aid

With the passage of the National Defense Education Act in 1958, the Higher Education Facilities Act of 1963, and the Elementary and Secondary Education Act of 1965, Tennessee gained a new source of much needed funds for education.

Tennessee had a favorable attitude toward federal aid to education dating from an earlier period. The General

Assembly in 1945 made the first gesture on the part of the state to encourage such aid. It passed a joint resolution which stated in part that since World War II had pointed up the great difference in educational opportunity in various regions of the nation and since Tennessee had found itself near the top of the list of states whose men were rejected for the armed services because of educational deficiencies, there was a great need for the passage of federal legislation to relieve this inequality. The resolution continued by asking the Tennessee congressional delegation to support the various bills regarding federal aid in Congress.

Although this aid has not been received unquestioningly or with unanimous acclaim, the vast majority of Tennesseans have felt that there were ample constitutional safeguards which thus enabled the state to receive this help in true partnership with the federal and local governments, out of a mutual interest in the advancement of public education at all levels.

Desegregation

The decade of the 1960's has been in every sense a revolutionary one for public education in Tennessee. In addition to enormous increases of funding at all levels of government, desegregation of the public schools has made substantial progress.

Tennessee moved slowly toward some compliance with the landmark U.S. Supreme Court decision of Brown *v.* Topeka in 1954. On the whole, the state's response to this decision was moderate. One of the state's leading newspapers, the Memphis *Commercial Appeal*, in an editorial on May 18, 1954, said that, "the main thing now is for the American people to face this thing squarely as an accomplished fact and work out our destiny for the general good and the greater glory of the nation" (34). Because of the skillful handling of this matter by Governor Frank Clement, Tennessee remained completely free of state legislation designed to preserve segregation in schools and also was free from any public school closing which other Southern states experienced. The first public school to be integrated in Tennessee was at Clinton, Anderson County, in September 1956. Here a notorious agitator, John Kasper, created considerable disturbance before Governor Clement, opting for the preservation of law and order and seeking to preserve the peace and carry out the law, sent in the state guard to quell the disturbance. The second school to be integrated in the state was the Nashville Hattie Cotten Elementary School in September 1957. Again, Kasper was on the scene agitating—and the result was a bomb explosion which destroyed much of the school. For his role here, Kasper served a prison term (35).

On the whole, however, Tennessee's movement toward integration was relatively peaceful, if slow. The percentage of Negroes in integrated schools was only 1 percent by 1960 and 2.7 percent by early 1964. With the coming of the Civil Rights Act of 1964, however, the pace was to quicken substantially since this law contained a clause which forbade the use of federal funds by any public agency (including schools) which practiced racial discrimination. Very quickly the percentage of Negro students attending desegregated schools began to rise—to 6 percent in 1965, to 16 percent in 1966, to 29 percent in 1967, and to 34 percent by early 1968 (the second highest percentage of desegregation of all 11 Southern states for all of these years), figured on the basis of the state's kindergarten through twelfth-grade program. At this writing, there are only 2 of the state's 151 systems which are out of compliance with the Office of Education regulations. The State Department of Education has set a tentative deadline of the 1969-70 school year for total abolishment of the dual racial structure of schools.

Personal Legacies

Through the years, there have been key professional staff members of the department who deserve special recognition for their contributions over long periods of dedicated service. Such men were George Freeman, whose name was synonymous with vocational education for four decades; James B. Calhoun in the school plant area; Roy Vance in secondary work; and Lee Thomas in the elementary area. Still active are Clarence A. McCanless, who has one of the longest tenures in the Department of some 35 years in fiscal and legal matters; Wesley Pickel, who has spent most of his long years in school plant and construction and dispenses gentle wisdom along with his technical advice; and William E. Turner, whose concerned and selfless work with the General Education Board and later the State Department of Education in upgrading the quality of Negro schools helped so much to promote the understanding and goodwill which the majority of Negro and white Tennesseans have displayed in this era of change.

During the last two decades, the various commissioners who have served have been able and dedicated. Burgin Dossett, Jack Smith, James A. Barksdale, Quill Cope, and Joe Morgan all were gentlemen of the highest order who brought professional competence and integrity to the department.

Throughout this period of profound change in the 1960's, however, the state department has had at its head a man of unusual strength and resourcefulness. J. Howard Warf came to this position in January 1963, from an educational and a political background. Although he has never been without opposition in both professional and political circles, he nevertheless has conducted affairs of the department in regard to matters of school desegregation and the handling of large-scale federal financing in a strong, statesmanlike way. Throughout these years, he has upheld the laws of the land firmly and without equivocation. His success in doubling the state appropriation for education

Table 1.– PROFESSIONAL AND CLERICAL STAFFING LEVELS, OFFICE OF CHIEF STATE SCHOOL OFFICER, 1910-67

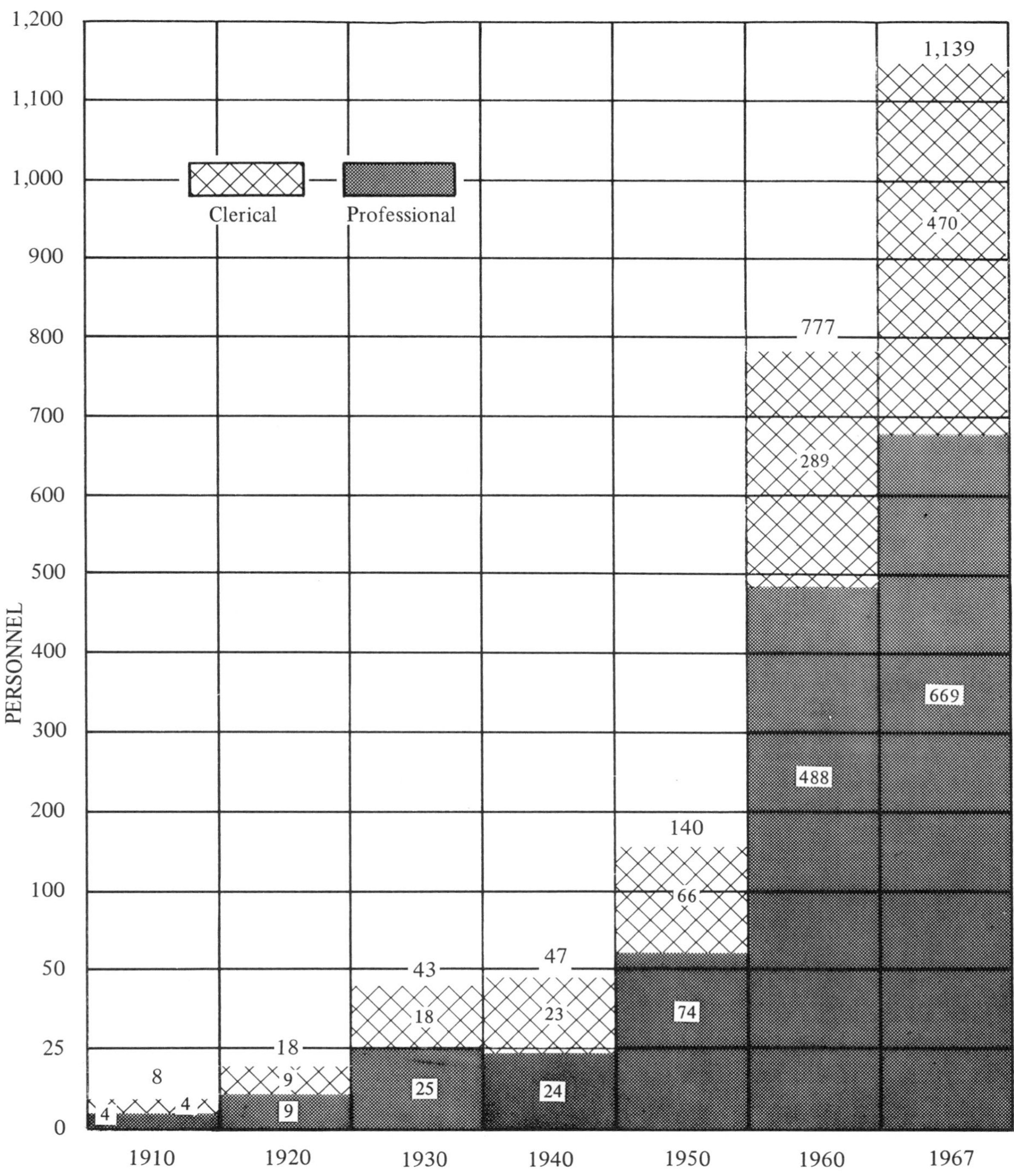

Source:

Annual Statistical Reports of the State Commissioner of Education, 1910-1967; State Personnel Records, 1910-1967.

during his years of office is also noteworthy. Undoubtedly, his administration will be judged one of the stronger ones as the history of the department is further written.

THE DEVELOPMENT OF THE STATE DEPARTMENT OF EDUCATION

The State Department of Education in Tennessee is primarily a twentieth-century institution. It has been said that this unit of state government was more a result than a cause of the educational revival of the early part of the twentieth century. Indeed there was a permanent superintendent of public instruction's office from 1873 on, but it was not until 1891 that a clerk was provided to cope with some of the clerical detail. Under Mynders' administration (1903-1907), the department had three persons with one stenographer having been added. During the Jones administration (1907-11), there were added an elementary school inspector, a high school inspector, and a school improvement organizer. In 1913, a director of libraries and a supervisor of certification were brought in, and the following year a supervisor of rural Negro schools and a supervisor of industrial work were added. During 1920, a supervisor of Smith-Hughes work, an associate high school inspector, and a supervisor of physiology and hygiene were added, and in 1921, the supervisor of teacher training joined the department. Over the years there has been a steady increase in the number of personnel on the staff of the state department as the programs of service to the schools have increased in number and depth. Table I traces the growth of the department from 8 staff members in 1910, to 43 in 1930 and, as a result of considerable growth after World War II, to 140 members in 1950. With the tremendous growth in state concern for education during the 1950's, combined with a new interest in education by the federal government, the department grew to 777 persons by 1960. In 1967, primarily as a result of the enormous impact of federal programs on the state department and on local education which amounted to $70 million annually, the number of state department personnel had grown to 1,139, including 669 professional and 470 clerical positions.

This growth in staff is also wholly correlated with an increase in state funding for educational purposes. Table 2 shows that from an initial appropriation of $15,000 in 1875, the state's educational interest grew to the point 50 years later that it contributed $1.2 million to education by 1925. A quarter of a century later in 1950, the state appropriation for education was $58.3 million. Within the next decade, this figure almost tripled. By 1960, the appropriation was $142.3 million, a figure which itself was to more than double in 8 short years. The fiscal 1968-69 state appropriation for all public education purposes is $313.2 million.

The state department is constitutionally founded through Section 49-101 of the Tennessee Code Annotated which states that "there is established a system of public instruction" (36). This system is further defined in Section 49-102 as being composed of the commissioner of education, the State Board of Education, the county superintendents, and the county and city boards of education.

The state department has as its basic function the provision of leadership in planning, research, consultative services, public relations, and in-service education. In addition, the regulation of such matters as the establishment and maintenance of certain standards, a guarantee of educational opportunities to all persons, the protection of life and health in the schools, the safeguarding and use of public school funds, and the coordination of the operations of state and local education agencies are all of concern and active interest for the department.

The commissioner of education is the chief state school officer in Tennessee and is by virtue of his office chairman of the State Board of Education. His duties within this framework have grown with the department's general expansion to the point that this position is one of the most demanding and highly pressured in state government. For example, he has responsibility for the expenditure of almost 50 percent of the state budget. He is responsible with the state board for 6 state universities, 5 community colleges, 4 special schools, 24 area vocational-technical schools, 3 technical institutes, and various vocational rehabilitation centers over the state, the educational TV network, and the galaxy of new federal programs, all of which relate to public education. He also is a member of numerous boards and commissions which demand some degree of time and attention. All of this work is in addition to the routine responsibility which has been traditionally identified with the department and its operation as the central office in relationship to public schools.

Within the framework of the expansion of the department, it is revealing to view through Table 3 some statistical comparisons of growth and progress in the public schools over the last 35 years.

Two reorganizations of the state department also should be noted. The first was under Quill Cope in the mid-1950's which established the positions of coordinators (see Appendix B), and the second was under J. Howard Warf, which established the positions of assistant commissioners of education (see Appendix B).

CURRENT PROGRAMS AND ACTIVITIES

Public education in Tennessee today is a program of vast proportions. The complex work and vital programs are presented, in brief, below.

Special Schools

Tennessee has four schools known as special schools which are operated directly by the State Board of Education and

Table 2.–STATE APPROPRIATIONS FOR EDUCATION, 1875-1968

Year	Amount	Year	Amount
1875-76	$ 15,000	1922-23	$ 506,500
1876-77	15,000	1923-24	619,000
1877-78	46,500	1924-25	619,000
1878-79	46,500	1925-26	1,227,060
1879-80	43,600	1926-27	1,227,060
1880-81	43,600	1927-28	1,282,000
1881-82	60,100	1928-29	1,282,000
1882-83	60,100	1929-30	8,042,000
1883-84	52,500	1930-31	8,042,000
1884-85	52,500	1931-32	6,166,000
1885-86	206,200	1932-33	6,160,000
1886-87	206,200	1933-34	5,727,000
1887-88	204,100	1934-35	5,727,000
1888-89	204,100	1935-36	6,087,000
1889-90	217,000	1936-37	6,087,000
1890-91	217,000	1937-38	10,245,000
1891-92	203,600	1938-39	10,245,000
1892-93	203,600	1939-40	10,864,800
1893-94	226,900	1940-41	10,864,800
1894-96	226,900	1941-42	11,338,000
1895-96	225,000	1942-43	11,338,000
1896-97	225,000	1943-44	13,106,000
1897-98	222,000	1944-45	16,138,000
1898-99	222,000	1945-46	16,897,000
1899-1900	247,000	1946-47	16,897,000
1900-1901	247,000	1947-48	33,408,000
1901-1902	218,000	1948-49	33,408,000
1902-1903	218,000	1949-50	58,251,000
1903-1904	239,000	1950-51	58,333,000
1904-1905	239,000	1951-52	66,344,000
1905-1906	271,000	1952-53	67,561,000
1906-1907	271,000	1953-54	77,020,000
1907-1908	217,400	1954-55	79,269,000
1908-1909	217,400	1955-56	89,075,000
1909-10	187,000	1956-57	93,642,000
1910-11	187,000	1957-58	110,467,000
1911-12	172,500	1958-59	115,941,000
1912-13	172,500	1959-60	128,868,000
1913-14	198,000	1960-61	142,379,000
1914-15	198,000	1961-62	144,671,000
1915-16	197,000	1962-63	153,652,000
1916-17	197,000	1963-64	178,644,000
1917-18	199,000	1964-65	190,923,000
1918-19	199,000	1965-66	216,155,200
1919-20	484,000	1966-67	247,118,000
1920-21	484,000	1967-68	292,342,300
1921-22	506,500	1968-69	313,194,300

Table 3.–SOME STATEWIDE STATISTICAL COMPARISONS BETWEEN THE SCHOOL YEARS 1932-33 AND 1966-67 IN TENNESSEE PUBLIC EDUCATION, GRADES 1-12

Item	Approximate number, amount, or percent for the school year 1932-33	Approximate number, amount, or percent for the school year 1966-67
Total average daily attendance, grades 1 through 12, in the public schools	507,000	828,100
Total number of teachers in the public schools	18,600	34,960
Percent of teachers in the public schools who held bachelor's degree or above	25%	88.6%
Total number of public schools	6,800	2,000
Number of one-teacher public schools included in the total number of public schools	3,000	50
Total number of vehicles used to transport children to the public schools	900 "trucks" and 200 "wagons"	4,600 school buses and other motor vehicles
Total number of pupils enrolled for transportation in the public schools	42,000	414,150
Total expenditures for current operation of the public schools	$17,500,000	$312,581,200
Amount spent for current operation, per pupil in average daily attendance in the public schools	$35	$377
Average annual salary of all teachers in the public schools	$743	$5,755
Total amount spent for capital outlay and capital improvements in the public schools	$600,000	$70,504,435
Total number of pupils graduated from public high schools	11,000	46,780 (regular diploma) 2,790 (equivalency diploma)

its chairman, the commissioner of education. These are the School for the Blind located near Nashville, which dates from 1844 as a state institution and had 225 pupils in residence in 1968; the School for the Deaf in Knoxville, founded in 1845 and with 325 students in residence; the Tennessee Preparatory School in Nashville, which became a state institution in 1885 and as a residential school focuses on the needs of dependent children of which there are 750 presently enrolled; and finally, York Institute located by legislative enactment at Jamestown in 1925. This latter institution operates as a county high school enrolling 650 pupils and is maintained by the state in honor of Sergeant Alvin C. York in commemoration of his valor and heroism in World War I.

Field Services

This area was established recently to provide the commissioner of education direct liaison with the county superintendents and with the Legislature.

Informational Services

This unit also has developed quite recently from Title V of the Elementary and Secondary Education Act with responsibility for such publications as a departmental newsletter and a sleek informational magazine designed to tell the story of the work of the department. In addition, this unit handles news releases, does supportive research for speeches by department members, handles routine correspondence for the department, and develops documentary films.

Equal Educational Opportunity

Under the requirements of federal guidelines and the increasingly strict enforcement proceedings of the U.S. Office of Education and the federal courts, it has seemed advisable to offer every assistance possible to superintendents and local boards of education in their desegregation problems—especially in negotiating their desegregation plans with the USOE. For this purpose, the state commissioner of education established in 1965 the Division of Equal Educational Opportunity which is financed by an ESEA Title IV grant. From the beginning this unit has attempted to ensure that public school systems of Tennessee are in approved compliance with the Civil Rights Act where at all possible so that they might continue to be eligible to receive federal funds under the several categories authorized by Congress.

Teacher Certification

In 1951, the General Assembly gave to the State Board of Education complete authority for setting requirements for certification of teachers, supervisors, principals, and superintendents and for the issuance of certificates. Subsequent to this delegation of authority, the state board appointed an Advisory Council on Teacher Education and Certification composed of representative educators to make extensive studies in regard to teacher education and certification. Over the years, this council has made significant reports to the state board and has adopted the "Approved Program" approach, whereby the board approves separately the teacher education program of each institution.

Educational Loan Corporation

The Tennessee Educational Loan Corporation has, since it was established in 1963, guaranteed 10,684 loans to 7,782 worthy Tennessee students in a total amount of $7,915,000 to further their education beyond the high school level.

Higher Education

The Division of Higher Education has existed in the State Department of Education for several years. It was reorganized, however, in August 1963, when a new position of assistant commissioner for higher education was created with responsibility for carrying out the administrative, academic, financial, research, planning, and coordinating functions in the development, evaluation, and improvement of college and university programs for which the state board and the state department have responsibility. This coincided with granting of use of state bond authority for institutions of higher education for the financing of structures which were revenue producing and thus could repay the bonds. And also, it coincided with the Higher Education Facilities Act which aided construction.

The state board serves as the governing body for six state universities—Austin Peay State University, East Tennessee State University, Memphis State University, Middle Tennessee State University, Tennessee Agricultural and Industrial State University, and Tennessee Technological University; in addition, it has the responsibility for three new state-community colleges already operating in Columbia, Jackson, and Cleveland and for two additional ones at Tullahoma and Dyersburg slated to open in 1969.

The division also serves in a consultative role for the state board and the state department in the evaluation of teacher education programs and as liaison with other institutions and agencies in the general areas of higher learning.

Statistical Services

This unit, which dates from 1959, has responsibility for computer services and statistics and operates basically under Title I of NDEA and Title V of ESEA. At this point, it works with the annual statistical report of the state department and aids in collection and dissemination of educational data in all areas. It has been particularly successful in automating school lunch reports and in placing the total vocational rehabilitation client file on the computer. The full potential of effective use of the computer for the department, however, has not been reached as yet.

Educational Television

Educational television had its beginning in Tennessee with the appointment in 1953 of the first Educational Television Commission, which was instrumental in having an engineering site survey made of the state and in securing the assignment of eight channels for educational purposes. The General Assembly in 1955 created the first permanent Educational Television Commission composed of the Governor, the commissioner of education, and one other citizen selected by the Governor.

The first fully operative station in the state was WKNO-TV, Channel 10, Memphis, which went on the air in June 1956. It was followed by station WDCN-TV, Channel 2, Nashville, which began telecasting in September 1962.

In 1963, the State Board of Education became the primary authority for operating educational television in Tennessee and started work to operate an educational TV network so that each public school in the state might ultimately be within receiving distance. In July 1963, the State Board of Education, through its chairman, created the Division of Educational Television in the State Department of Education and began to employ staff personnel for the division.

Plans for construction of the Sneedville educational TV station on Short Mountain began in mid-1965, and station WSJK-TV, Channel 2, officially went on the air in March 1967, with temporary studio facilities located at the University of Tennessee in Knoxville. Construction of permanent studio facilities at East Tennessee State University in Johnson City and at the University of Tennessee are expected to be completed in July 1968 and September 1969, respectively.

In July 1966, the State Board of Education received a construction permit from the Federal Communications Commission to activate Channel 45 in Chattanooga. It is anticipated that by 1970 the Tennessee educational TV network will be completed with a single-channel system providing educational programs to every school system within the state. This network will consist of six stations interconnected by microwave so that programs may originate from any one of five production centers.

Finance and Administrative Services

This division has the responsibility of distributing state funds for educational purposes in conformity with the laws, rules, and regulations governing this distribution. Over the years, as state funds for educational purposes have increased rapidly and with the enormous federal contribution to local education, the various superintendents and school boards in the state have requested assistance from the state department in establishing accounting systems; in initiating methods of keeping necessary records; in interpreting the laws, rules, and regulations; and in completing the many reports and forms necessary to disperse the funds properly. To handle these requests, Tennessee has established a system of supervisors over the state, with each supervisor expected to make periodic visits to the administrative offices of every school district and to offer whatever assistance is needed.

This division is also responsible for ensuring that local units maintain the level of financial effort required by law. It also makes projections of needed increases in teacher salaries, costs of the minimum foundation program, sick leave, and textbooks for the commissioner of education and the state board to use in preparing each budget.

School Food Service Program

After the National School Lunch Act was passed in 1946, there was little major change in this basic legislation until 1962 when the apportionment formula was changed. The change provided for substantially greater amounts of reimbursement money which Tennessee received because of its relatively high participation rate. In addition, the Special Commodity Assistance Program and the Special Cash Assistance Program for especially needy schools joined with the School Food Service portion of ESEA Title I to provide substantial growth of this outstanding program.

During 1966-67, two new additions were added to the basic School Food Service Program. One was a pilot breakfast program provided in school for children either from economically deprived families or who rode long distances to school. The second portion of this important addition was a provision through the Child Nutrition Act for needed equipment to prepare lunches and breakfasts.

Division of Instruction

This unit of the state department has grown out of the work of early elementary and high school inspectors. Today, its responsibility covers the whole instructional program of public schools. In addition, it has assumed some authority over ancillary services and advises the commissioner of education and the state board in a number of ways. In the area of curriculum and supervision, this unit issues high school and equivalency diplomas to the youth of Tennessee and works closely with the study councils of principals, supervisors, teachers, and superintendents in seeking solutions to problems confronting Tennessee school systems. It provides consultative and supervisory services to local school systems in the areas of health and physical education, health services, art, and music; it also renders services to local systems in developing plans for curriculum improvement, for in-service education of teachers, and for the implementation of experimental programs. Through its seven major offices across the state, the area of curriculum and supervision also provides supervisory, regulatory, and consultative services of a general nature.

This division also offers consultative services and workshops on audiovisual aids. It distributes funds for the purchase of instructional materials and offers advice in the use of textbooks. It constantly seeks to upgrade and administer new acts which reflect this effort. It offers guidance and counseling services, a program which has expanded greatly since 1958 when there were 7 qualified counselors in Tennessee to a point where there are now 700 such persons with varying degrees of qualifications.

Psychological service for the public schools is a relatively new area of interest for the state department, and this program, too, has been substantially expanded over the few years of its operation.

A new program of adult basic education began in 1965 and is directed primarily to those persons who have less than a fifth-grade education. Civil Defense adult education also is operated by this division.

Shortly after its inception in 1958, Title III of NDEA was placed under this division for administration. The purpose of this important act is to provide substantial assistance in various forms to individuals and to states and their subdivisions to ensure trained manpower of sufficient quality and quantity to meet the national defense needs of the United States. Title III authorizes matching grants of federal funds to states and loans to nonprofit private schools to help equip and remodel laboratories and classrooms; it also offers other grants to assist states in expanding their supervisory and related services in science, mathematics, and foreign languages. Tennessee began to participate in this act in 1959 and was pleased to see additional subject areas such as history, civics, geography, English, and reading added to Title III in 1964. Economics joined the list in 1965 and industrial arts in 1966. Supervisors have been employed to administer the various units of this act, and, on the whole, staff members have assumed leadership roles in curriculum matters pertaining to their respective subject area speciality.

In 1955, Tennessee established the area of special education in the Division of Instruction. During that year, there were 1,000 handicapped children receiving instruction in public schools across the state. By 1967, this service had been included in the minimum foundation school program, and the scope of its effort had been considerably broadened. Now, children who are physically handicapped—either orthopedically, visually, or linguistically—can participate in this program. Those who are psychologically handicapped by mental retardation or emotional disturbances can also be included. Since 1959, almost 1,000 new teaching positions have been added in the area of special education in Tennessee.

This division also administers Title I of the Elementary and Secondary Education Act of 1965. Title I is by far the most significant portion of this law insofar as the amount of money involved and the type of assistance it provides is concerned. Offering financial aid to school systems to educate America's economically deprived children, this is one of the major pieces of social legislation of our time. Under this law, each state receives federal aid for its schools commensurate with the number of children ages 5 through 17 in the state who fall within the legal definition of economically deprived. Virtually all of this money, however, is spent by the local educational agencies.

In the first 3 years of the operation of this title, over $95 million was granted to Tennessee to provide compensatory education for children from economically destitute families. This money also stimulated a vital and new activity in the state-supported schools for delinquent, neglected, handicapped, and migrant children. Also, corrective and remedial reading, health and nutrition, physical education, mathematics, science, and social studies have all been areas of focus in this program.

School Plant and Pupil Transportation

The Division of School Planning officially became a separate unit of the state department in 1929. The division did not at this time, however, have the authority to establish or administer school building standards. Substantive legislation in this regard did not appear until 1955 when an act was passed providing that the state board had the authority to establish minimum standards for school sites, school attendance centers, construction of buildings for school purposes, major repairs of buildings for school purposes of a capital outlay nature, and equipment for buildings for school purposes. The act specifically forbade school districts to obligate or expend school funds of a capital outlay nature which did not conform to standards adopted by the state board.

Since 1947, 24,070 teaching stations, 435 libraries, 322 shops, and 609 gymnasiums have been built. In addition, the state has constructed 355 gymnatoriums, 1,501 cafeterias, 136 cafetoriums, 349 multipurpose rooms, and other auxiliary rooms. During the fiscal year 1966-67, there was more money spent on public school construction than at any other time in the history of the state—$55 million.

In the last few years, substantial achievement has been made in upgrading the maintenance of vehicles and in improving the caliber of driver personnel. In fiscal 1966-67, the state transportation maintenance and operation allocation was $10.4 million, excluding capital outlay.

Special Services

The Tennessee Educational Agency for Surplus Property began operation in early 1946 as a division of the state department. The objective of this agency was to assist educational institutions in the state to obtain federal surplus property.

In the latter part of 1958, a new warehouse was constructed, and a few years later, an IBM accounting and inventory system was inaugurated for this program. By 1968, the amount of property which had been transferred was in the neighborhood of $125 million, figured at acquisition cost to the federal government.

Library and Archives

For many years, this unit had encompassed the state regional library extension service, archival preservation of the state's records, and the State Library reference service. Since 1958, it has operated under the State Department of Education whose commissioner is advised in the conduct of its programs by a seven-member Library and Archives Commission.

State Museum

The State Museum dates from 1920 when it was established to house the relics and mementoes of World War I. After World War II, it was expanded to include the same kinds of materials from this war. Over the years, it has come to house not only items of a military nature, but also archaeological exhibits, natural history objects, and exhibits of state resources, as well as Civil War and Spanish-American War materials.

Vocational-Technical Education

In 1917, the Congress of the United States recognized the need for vocational education programs which would prepare youth and adults for employment in a growing economy resulting from the industrial development taking place in the United States and the demands for an improved agriculture. The Smith-Hughes Act, or National Vocational Education Act, was signed by President Woodrow Wilson in February 1917. The first Vocational Education Act appropriated, on a permanent basis, federal funds to the states for training in agriculture, home economics, trades and industry, and teacher education. The Tennessee General Assembly, in session at the time, passed an Enabling Act in March 1917 to allow the state to take full advantage of the federal funds and designated that the State Board of Education should also serve as the State Board for Vocational Education.

Prior to this act and only 2 days after the signing of the Smith-Hughes Act, one of the first vocational agriculture programs in the nation got under way at Grove High School in Paris, Tennessee. During the remainder of 1917, four additional agriculture programs were initiated. During that year, 340 students were enrolled in these five programs.

Over the past 50 years, Tennessee has enlarged its program of vocational-technical education to offer instruction in distributive education, office occupations, technical areas, and health occupations in high schools, area vocational-technical schools, and technical institutes.

One of the most significant developments which have allowed growth, expansion, and innovation in Tennessee's program of vocational-technical education was the passage of the Vocational Education Act of 1963. Appropriations by this act are not designed specifically for a given service or program and may be spent where there is a need for job-type training. The act requires that training be organized to serve all persons who want, need, and can profit from vocational-technical education.

Tennessee has gradually shifted from an agricultural to an industrial economy. This industrial growth has brought to the state sophisticated industry which performs exacting manufacturing and engineering operations. Occupational training programs in the state have thus been forced to expand in order to provide training demanded by these new employment opportunities. To provide a steady supply of trained and capable employees, Tennessee has set up a statewide system of area vocational-technical schools, basing training needs on present and prospective occupational needs of the area served and the state as a whole. The legislation creating these schools was passed by the General Assembly in 1963.

The first construction contract for new facilities was awarded in April 1964 for the Shelbyville State Area Vocational-Technical School. Twenty-two area schools are now in operation, and construction on two more will begin during 1968. These schools, cooperating closely with industrial development agencies in providing training for new and expanding industries, have become increasingly important to industrial growth in the state. Most of these schools which have operated for at least 1 year have extensive waiting lists.

In addition to this available training, three vocational-technical institutes have been approved; two are in operation now, and one is soon to be completed. These institutes have primarily a postsecondary focus and are located in the major metropolitan centers of the state.

Vocational-technical education in Tennessee has as its controlling purpose the training of individuals for useful employment. It is designed to meet the needs of persons 14 years of age and over who are preparing for or who have already entered various kinds of careers.

Vocational Rehabilitation

The federal Vocational Rehabilitation Act of 1920 was designed as legislation for the aid of persons who were injured in industrial accidents or who were otherwise unable to be employed. This legislation followed closely the passage of the Soldier Rehabilitation Act of 1918 which had a similar purpose.

Tennessee was one of the first states in the nation to join with the federal government in implementing this newly passed act. An executive order was issued establishing the first state-federal rehabilitation program within a few days after the passage of the federal act. Tennessee's rehabilitation program, however, is traditionally measured from 1921, when the Legislature passed an act establishing it at the state level. This program has operated from the beginning under the vocational education board. It has always been a grant-in-aid program with state funds being matched with federal funds. During the year ending June 1922, the first full year of the division's operation, the program rehabilitated 26 handicapped persons at an average cost of $38.58 each.

A major expansion of the program came in 1954 when Public Law 565 greatly improved the federal government's ability to make grants to the states and also established a system of grants for projects and for training.

Additional expansion came in 1965 when Public Law 89-333 made additional funds available and included behavorial disorders as a handicapping condition eligible for rehabilitation services. Federal funds available to Tennessee in 1968-69 are more than $18 million. At current level, the state is taking advantage of less than one-third of the funds available for both of its public programs for handicapped people, the Division of Vocational Rehabilitation in the State Department of Education and the Rehabilitation Services for the Blind in the Department of Public Welfare.

In general, the vocational rehabilitation division sponsors such programs as an intensive treatment-rehabilitation center for juvenile offenders at Jordonia in cooperation with the Department of Corrections; a correctional rehabilitation center for adult public offenders at the state prison; a special education-rehabilitation work study program in cooperation with the Division of Instruction; 14 vocational training centers for the mentally retarded and other physically disabled persons in areas throughout the state; a rehabilitation facility at Central State Hospital in cooperation with the Department of Mental Health; an out-patient rehabilitation facility in Memphis in cooperation with Les Passes Club, the City of Memphis, and Shelby County; a disability determination section operated by contract with the Social Security Administration; and a health referral program operated by contract with the U.S. Public Health Service.

Any person of work age who has a physical or mental disability or a behavioral disorder resulting from educational, social, environmental, or economic deprivation whose disability constitutes a barrier to employment is eligible for the services of the Division of Vocational Rehabilitation, provided there is a reasonable chance that the services of the agency can make the person employable.

CONCLUSION

From an embryo in 1873, the Tennessee State Department of Education has grown to a full-fledged educational body. Growth was slow, however, until the early twentieth century, when it began to have a significant staff and an influence in the development of public education in the state. During the Peay administration, the department was elevated in official importance, and the commissioner of education became a member of the administrative cabinet for the first time.

It was not until the post-World War II period, however, that the department began to grow toward the dimension of size and influence which it now occupies. Enormous increases in state funding plus the recent entrance of the federal government into large-scale public education financing have determined the department's development in the last quarter century.

With this expansion and growth, it is natural that many problems have developed as new programs are initiated before older ones are yet consolidated. Nevertheless, the department, with its great number of concerned and dedicated persons, insists that it will continue to move forward to meet the needs of the individual child and youth wherever he is found in the state. This would seem to be at once its challenge and its responsibility.

FOOTNOTES

1. Edgar W. Knight, *Education in the United States* (New York: Ginn and Co., 1951), p. 247.
2. *Ibid*., p. 184.
3. Stanley J. Folmsbee, Robert E. Corlew, and Enoch L. Mitchell, *History of Tennessee* (New York: Lewis Historical Publishing Co., 1960), I, 437-38.
4. Tennessee, *House Journal,* 30th General Assembly (1853-54), pp. 455-57.
5. Superintendent of Public Instruction, *First Report of the Superintendent of Public Instruction* (Nashville: George E. Grisham, 1869), pp. 38-45.
6. Joseph B. Killebrew, "Address on the Farming Interests," p. 16, given in most counties in the state, 1871. State Library Section, Tennessee State Library and Archives, Nashville. (Typewritten.)
7. *Ibid.*
8. *Union and American,* Nashville, February 5, 1871, p. 5.
9. *Proceedings of the Trustees of the Peabody Education Fund From Their Original Organization on the 8th of February, 1867,* printed by Order of the Trustees (6 vols; Boston: John Wilson & Son, 1875), I, 1-3, 324-25. The Peabody Fund was an endowment made by an early philanthropist, George Foster Peabody, for the purpose of promoting and encouraging "intellectual, moral and industrial education among the young of the more destitute portion" of the Southern region.
10. *Report of the Assistant Superintendent of Public Instruction in Report of Superintendent William Morrow*

(ex officio) to 37th General Assembly (Nashville: Jones, Purvis and Co., 1872), pp. 25-72.

11. *Proceedings of Peabody Trustees, op. cit.*, I, 325-26.

12. Tennessee, *Senate Journal,* 38th General Assembly (1873), pp. 14-16.

13. *Proceedings of Peabody Trustees, op. cit.*, I, 404-405.

14. *Report of the Assistant Superintendent* (1872), p. 7.

15. Joseph B. Killebrew, "Address on the Importance of Levying a Tax for the Support of Common Schools," p. 2. Available in State Library Section, Tennessee State Library and Archives, Nashville. See also "Annual Report of the Superintendent of Public Instruction," *Appendix to House Journal* (1875), pp. 8-9; "Annual Report of the Superintendent of Public Instruction," *Appendix to Senate Journal* (1879), pp. 5-9.

16. University of Nashville Minute Books, I, 1852-1906, 334-45. Manuscript Section, Tennessee State Library and Archives, Nashville.

17. "Annual Report of the Superintendent of Public Instruction," *Appendix to House Journal* (1875), pp. 8-9; *ibid., Appendix to Senate Journal* (1879), pp. 5-9; *ibid., Appendix to Senate Journal* (1881), pp. 5-9; *ibid., Appendix to Senate Journal* (1891), pp. 8-10.

18. Andrew D. Holt, *The Struggle for a State System of Public Schools in Tennessee, 1903-1936* (New York: Columbia University, 1938), p. 5.

19. U.S. Department of Commerce, Bureau of the Census, *Eleventh Census of the United States, 1890,* Vol I.: *Agriculture* (Washington, D.C.: Government Printing Office, 1891), p. 92.

20. U.S. Department of Commerce and Labor, *Statistical Abstracts of the United States* (Washington, D.C.: Government Printing Office, 1903), p. 453.

21. Holt, *op. cit.*, p. viii.

22. Charles Lee Lewis, *Philander Priestly Claxton, Crusader for Public Education* (Knoxville: University of Tennessee Press, 1948), p. 43.

23. *Ibid.*, pp. 127-34.

24. *Ibid.*, p. 292.

25. *Ibid.*, p. 160.

26. Charles William Dabney, *Universal Education in the South* (2 vols.; Chapel Hill: University of North Carolina Press, 1936), II, 362.

27. *Ibid.*, p. 365.

28. *Ibid.*

29. Holt, *op cit.*, pp. 127-29.

30. *Ibid.*, p. 340. See also Tennessee, *Acts.* Sixty-First General Assembly (1919), pp. 37-38.

31. Tennessee, *Acts,* Seventy-Fourth General Assembly (1945), pp. 376-77.

32. Department of Education, *A Study of Tennessee's Program of Public Education* (Nashville: The Department, 1948), p. 21.

33. Tennessee, *Acts,* Seventy-Ninth General Assembly (1955), pp. 167-74.

34. Editorial, *Commercial Appeal* (Memphis), May 18, 1954.

35. Hugh Davis Graham, "Desegregation in Nashville: The Dynamics of Compliance," *Tennessee Historical Quarterly,* XXV (Summer 1966), 135-54.

36. *Tennessee Code Annotated* (1966), secs. 49-102.

BIBLIOGRAPHY

Public Documents

Tennessee. *Acts.* Sixty-First General Assembly, 1919; Seventy-Fourth General Assembly, 1945; Seventy-Ninth General Assembly, 1955.

——*Constitution* (1870).

——*House Journal.* Thirtieth General Assembly, 1853-54.

——*House Journal: Appendix.* Twenty-Ninth General Assembly, 1875.

——*Senate Journal.* Thirty-Eighth General Assembly, 1873.

——*Senate Journal: Appendix.* Forty-First General Assembly, 1879; Forty-Second General Assembly, 1881; Forty-Seventh General Assembly, 1891.

Tennessee Code Annotated (1966).

U.S. Department of Commerce. Bureau of the Census. *Eleventh Census of the United States, 1890.* Vol I: *Agriculture.* Washington, D.C.: Government Printing Office, 1891.

U.S. Departments of Commerce and Labor. *Statistical Abstracts of the United States.* Washington, D.C.: Government Printing Office, 1903.

Books

Dabney, Charles William. *Universal Education in the South.* 2 vols. Chapel Hill: University of North Carolina Press, 1936.

Folmsbee, Stanley J.; Corlew, Robert E.; and Mitchell, Enoch L. *History of Tennessee.* New York: Lewis Historical Publishing Co., 1960.

Holt, Andrew D. *The Struggle for a State System of Public Schools in Tennessee, 1903-1936.* New York: Columbia University, 1938.

Knight, Edgar W. *Education in the United States.* New York: Ginn and Co., 1951.

Lewis, Charles Lee. *Philander Priestly Claxton, Crusader for Public Education.* Knoxville: University of Tennessee Press, 1948.

Articles and Periodicals

Graham, Hugh Davis. "Desegregation in Nashville: The Dynamics of Compliance," *Tennessee Historical Quarterly*, XXV (Summer 1966), 135-54.

Commercial Appeal (Memphis). May 18, 1954.

Union and American (Nashville). February 5, 1871.

Reports

Commissioners of Education. *Reports.* Nashville: The Department, 1923-68.

Department of Education. *A Study of Tennessee's Program of Public Education.* Nashville: The Department, 1948.

Proceedings of the Trustees of the Peabody Education Fund. 6 vols. Boston: John Wilson & Son, 1875.

Report of the Assistant Superintendent of Public Instruction in Report of Superintendent William Morrow (ex officio) to the 37th General Assembly. Nashville: Jones, Purvis & Co., 1872.

Superintendents of Public Instruction. *Reports.* Nashville: The Department, 1873-1923.

Other Sources

Killebrew, Joseph B. "Address on the Farming Interests." 1871. No other publishing information available. State Library Section, Tennessee State Library and Archives, Nashville.

——"Address on the Importance of Levying a Tax for the Support of Common Schools." 1872. State Library Section, Tennessee State Library and Archives, Nashville.

University of Nashville Minute Book. Vol. I, 1852-1906. Manuscript Section, Tennessee State Library and Archives, Nashville.

Appendix A

TENNESSEE CHIEF STATE SCHOOL OFFICERS

The Office of State Superintendent of Public Instruction was created in 1836 and was abolished in 1844. The following superintendents were elected by the Legislature:

1836-40	Robert H. McEwen
1840-41	Robert P. Currin
1841-44	Scott Terry

From 1844 to 1867, the state treasurer was ex officio superintendent of public instruction. In 1867, the office was again created. The following superintendents were elected by the people and served for the respective periods shown below:

1867-69	John Eaton, Jr.
1869-71	A. J. Tipton

In 1870, the office was again abolished, and the duties developed upon the state treasurer, who was made ex officio superintendent of public instruction.

In 1873, the office was recreated, and the following officers, appointed by the Governor and confirmed by the Senate, have served the terms shown below:

1872-73	Joseph B. Killebrew (asst. supt.)
1873-75	John M. Fleming
1875-81	Leon Trousdale
1881-82	W. S. Doak
1882	Julia A. Doak (Apr.–July)
1882-83	G. S. Crawford
1883-87	Thomas H. Paine
1887-91	Frank M. Smith
1891-93	W. R. Garrett
1893-95	Frank M. Smith
1895-97	S. G. Gilbreath
1897-99	Price Thomas
1899-1903	Morgan C. Fitzpatrick
1903-1907	Seymour Mynders
1907-11	R. L. Jones
1911-13	J. W. Brister
1913-15	S. H. Thompson
1915-19	S. W. Sherrill
1919-21	Albert Williams
1921-23	J. B. Brown

Under the reorganization bill of 1923, the State Department of Public Instruction became the State Department of Education. The title of the chief state school officer was changed to commissioner of education.

1923-33	P. L. Harned
1933-37	Walter D. Cocking
1937-38	W. A. Bass
1938	J. M. Smith (Jan.–Sept.)
1938-39	Halbert Harvill
1939-45	B. O. Duggan
1945-49	Burgin E. Dossett
1949-50	J. M. Smith
1950-53	J. A. Barksdale
1953-58	Quill E. Cope
1958-63	Joe Morgan
1963-	J. H. Warf

Appendix B

Chart I.--TENNESSEE DEPARTMENT OF EDUCATION, 1955

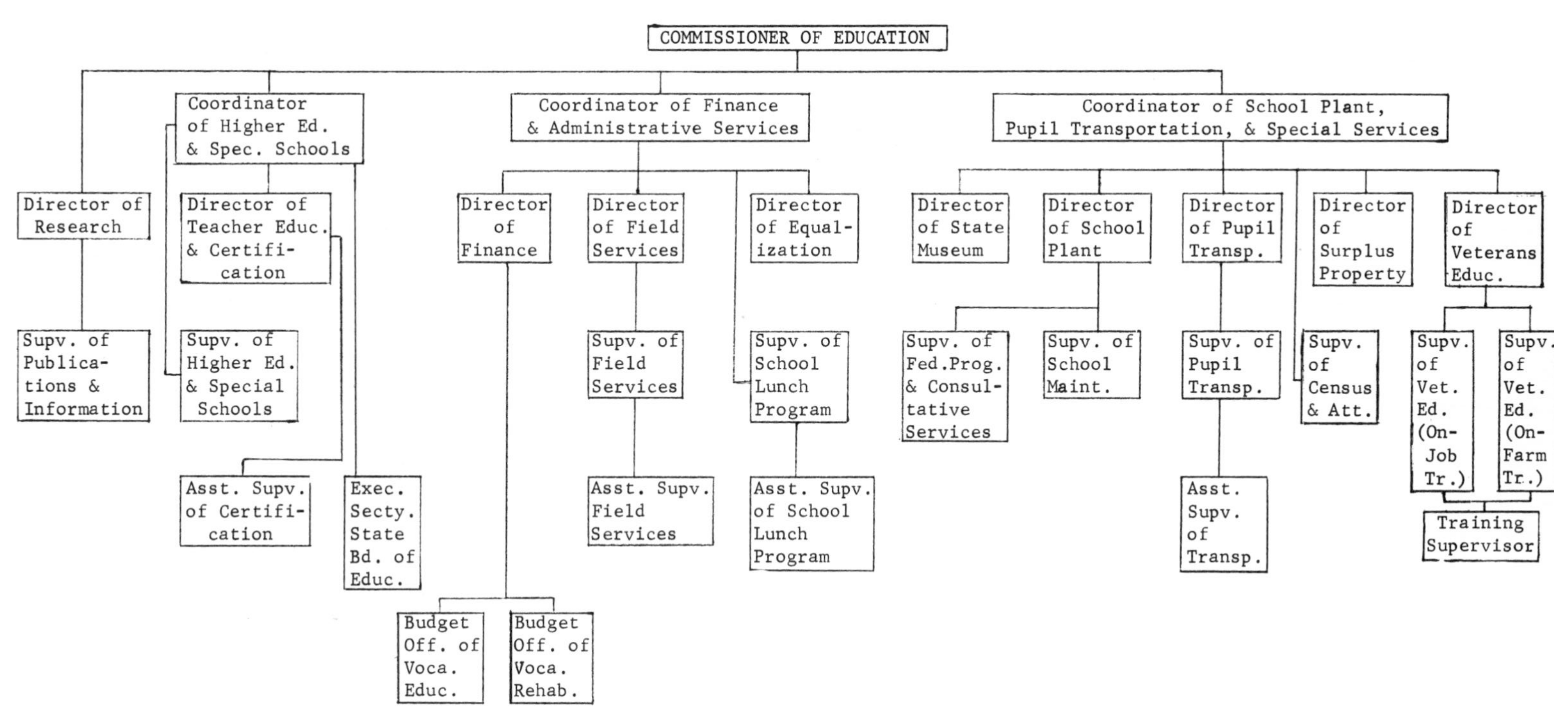

See next page for second half of chart.

Appendix B

Chart I.--TENNESSEE DEPARTMENT OF EDUCATION, 1955 (Continued)

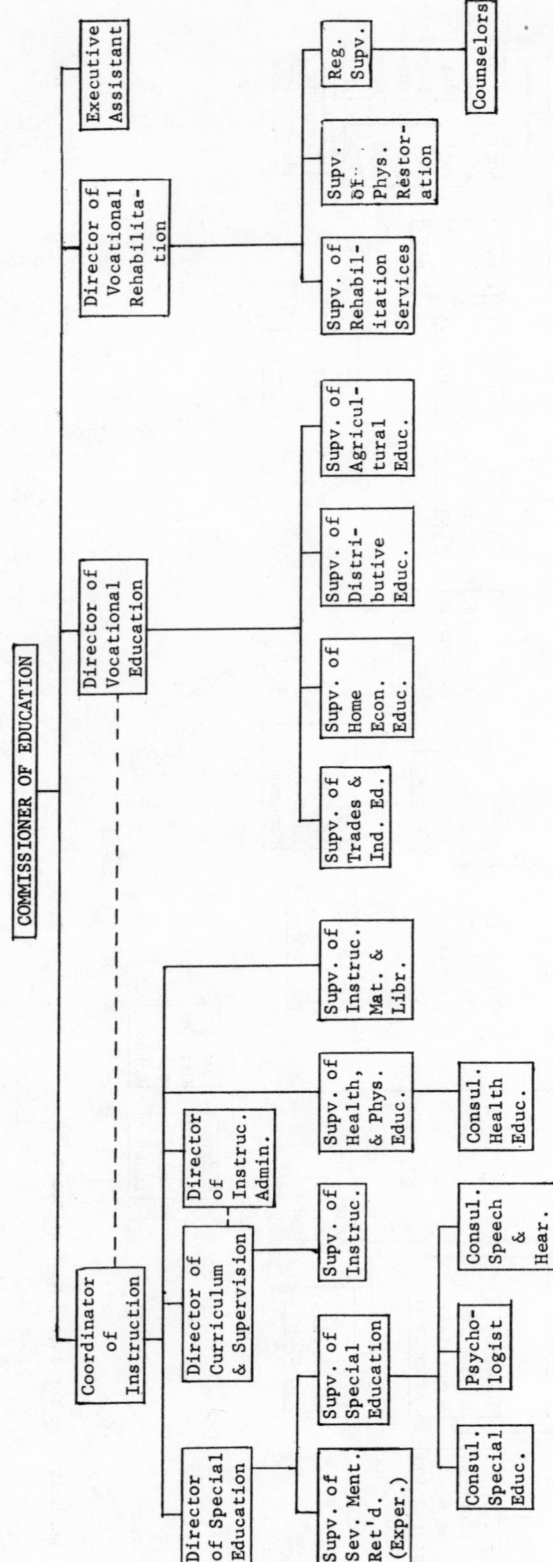

Appendix B

Chart II.--TENNESSEE DEPARTMENT OF EDUCATION, 1968

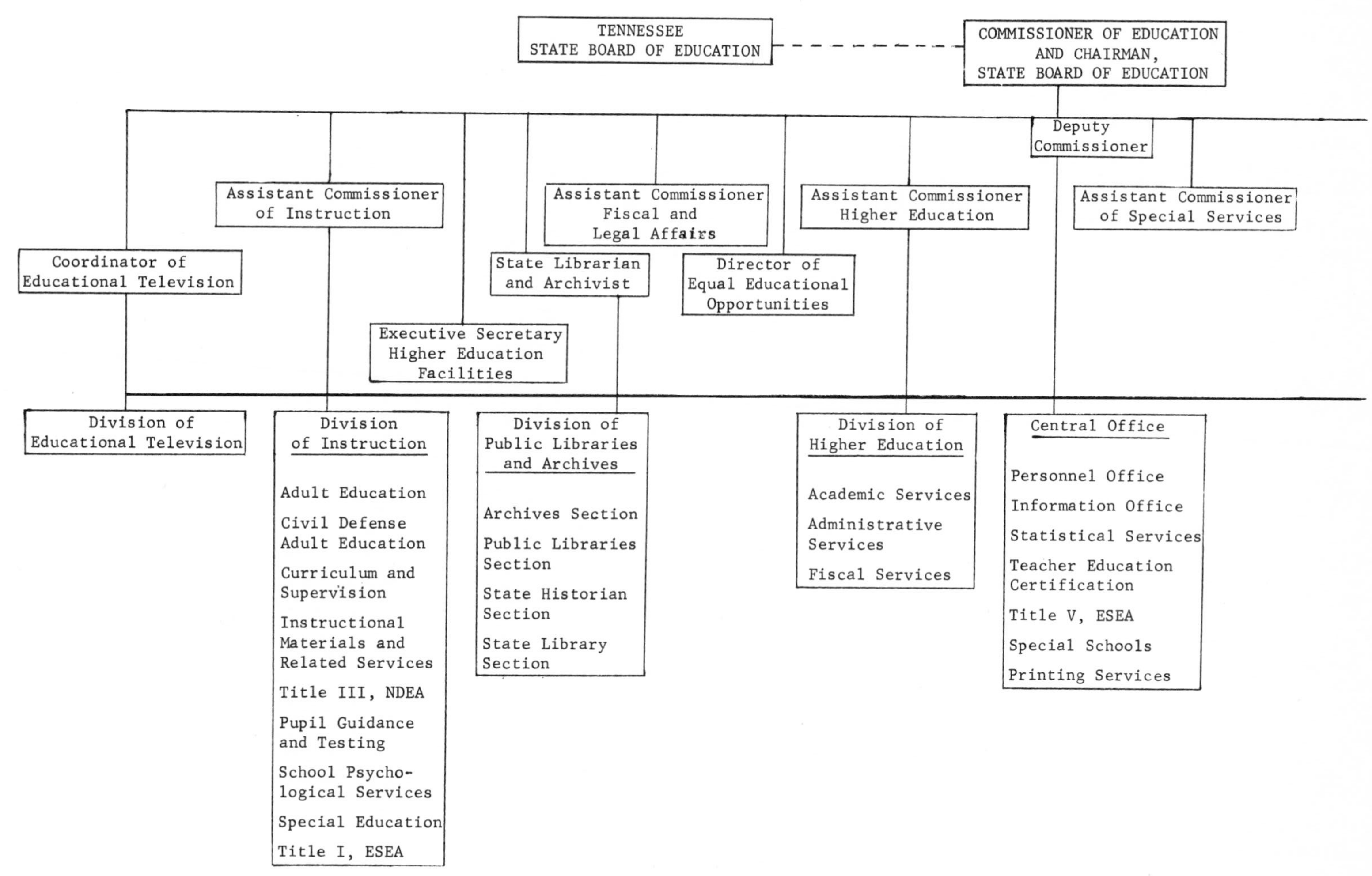

See next page for second half of chart.

Appendix B

Chart II.--TENNESSEE DEPARTMENT OF EDUCATION, 1968 (Continued)

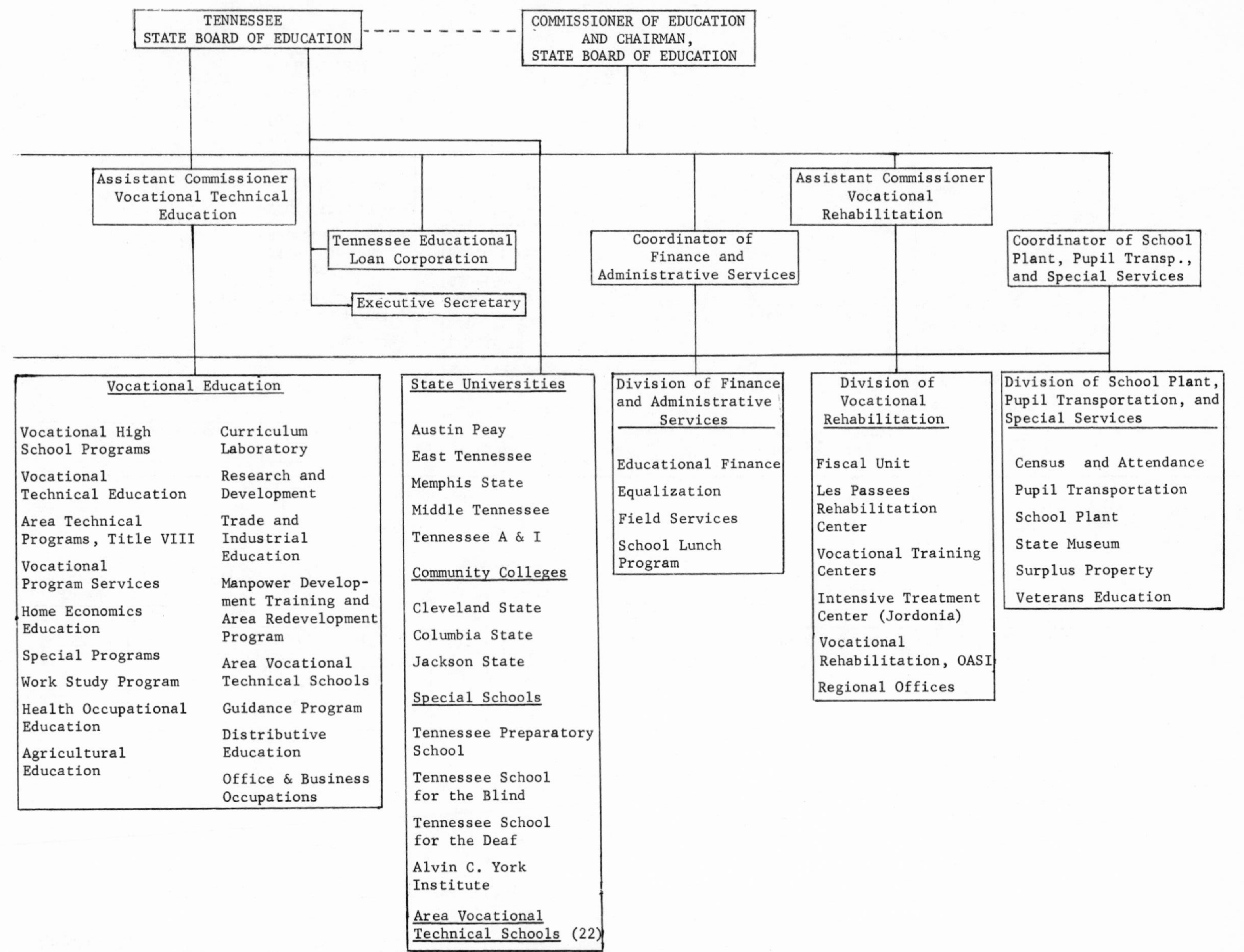

44 Texas

TEXAS EDUCATION AGENCY

E. D. Yoes, Jr.

Contents

EDUCATIONAL PATTERNS BEFORE 1900

The Republic

Among the reasons enumerated in the Texas Declaration of Independence of 1836 for severing political ties with Mexico was that the Mexican government had "failed to establish any public system of education, although possessed of almost boundless resources (the public domain) . . . " (1).

However, when the fathers of the republic came to write their own constitution and provide for public education, they found that the use of the public domain to finance adequate schools was easier said than done.

The first Anglo-American public school law in Texas was that of 1840, providing for the surveying and setting aside of four leagues (17,712 acres) of land in each county which could be sold by the county commissioners for the purchase of necessary endowments, one half for the use and benefit of an academic school of each county, and the remainder distributed equally among the various common school districts. The county judge and his associates were the school board, empowered to establish districts, administer teacher certificates, and supervise the schools. Provision also was made for two universities.

The Texians (2) were applying the ideas that lay behind the Northwest Ordinance of 1787, the academy system, and the English tradition of the common school. Counties were the largest unit of educational administration they contemplated, and there was no provision for state school taxation.

In fact, the Law of 1840 never had much effect; home instruction continued to be the rule and itinerant schoolmasters the exception to that rule until after the Civil War. The republic, when it gave specific attention to public education, did so by issuing charters to seminaries and academies, colleges and universities, most of which were private or denominational schools that prospered for a time and then, with a few notable exceptions, failed (3).

The State

A new state constitution in 1845 provided that one-tenth of the annual state tax revenue be set aside as a perpetual fund for the support of free public schools. This established a policy of assisting the people in private and community educational enterprises.

The Constitution of 1845 marked the acceptance, in principle, of general taxation for education and an end to the dream of financing public schools solely out of the limitless supply of land (4).

The tithe of state revenue and the county lands together, however, proved insufficient. By 1850, the facts were distressingly obvious: Only 15 percent of the state's children were being instructed to any purpose. An ingenious solution, in the School Law of 1854, set apart $2 million of the $10 million in 5-percent U.S. Indemnity Bonds received in settlement of Texas' boundary claims against the United States as a permanent school fund. Loaned to railroad companies at 6 percent, this fund was expected to provide income sufficient to pay teachers' salaries.

Provision was made for free tuition of the indigent and orphans out of the tithe of annual state revenue, but there were never actually any pauper schools in Texas. Nearly all children were recipients of the state bounty, while the poor for the most part preferred ignorance with pride to the humiliation and taunts that accompanied a pauper's child to school.

The 1854 law also permitted the patrons of any school to employ the teacher of a primary department of any college or academy, and convert the primary department of that institution into a common school. As a result of this, the state found itself subsidizing religious and private schools on a larger scale than before. Only in two or three counties populated by German refugees of 1848 were actual public common schools formed. Elsewhere, the private school interests triumphed, even forcing the abandonment of the districting provision of the 1845 constitution.

The larger communities led the way to better schools. A free public school promoted by the German population made its appearance in San Antonio in 1853. This was the beginning of the ultimately enormous differential between urban and rural education.

The various Protestant denominations also were active in establishing schools, yet often left the connection between the school and the church that had founded it deliberately vague, lest patronage be limited to only one denomination. The Texas Grand Masonic Lodge appointed a superintendent of education, chartered schools, and aided community school boards by furnishing buildings and making loans.

Reconstruction

The Civil War left Texas industrially prostrate. Agriculture was revolutionized by Emancipation, and a whole new social order had to be developed before prosperity was again possible. The railroads, whose repayments and interest were the source of school funds, defaulted or paid in depreciated and unacceptable currency, while much of the balance of the school fund was diverted to other purposes, being reduced to virtually nothing by 1865. Private schools and universities were decimated.

In 1866, a new constitution was drawn up, closely resembling in its educational provisions the School Law of 1854. The Radical Republicans quickly set aside this constitution, and Reconstruction began. Overnight, so to speak, Texas went from one form of education to another. The Carpetbag Constitution of 1869 required free public schools for all inhabitants from 6 to 18, established a state superintendent of public instruction, laid off all counties into school districts, made attendance compulsory for 4 months of the year, set up the permanent school fund again, put all county school lands under state control, made one-fourth of all annual revenues from general taxation a source of school support, established a poll tax of $1 on every voter as another source of school moneys, and demanded local taxation sufficient to build a school in every district and operate it for 10 months a year. It provided every necessity for administering a completely modern school system except public support.

The provisions of this "infamous" law do not look so infamous today and might have worked to the benefit of the state had they not aroused intense opposition. The reaction they evoked, in the form of hatred for compulsory attendance, education of Negroes, alleged extravagance, and Northern textbooks, was to have long-lasting harmful effects on education.

When the disputed Hayes-Tilden election of 1876 permitted the South in general to escape all vestiges of Reconstruction, the carpetbag school law in Texas was overthrown, leaving public education in a state of chaos.

The Constitution of 1876

The only things upon which Texans could generally agree when Article VII of the new state constitution was written were that there must be separate schools for white and Negro children and that the permanent school fund must never again be diverted to any extraneous purpose. All other points caused intense and protracted dispute. As finally adopted, Article VII abolished the state superintendent's office and all supervisory functions, ended compulsory attendance and districting, made the school age 8 to 14, rendered local taxation for schools impossible, returned county lands to the respective counties, and restricted the proportion of state general revenue for support of schools to one-fourth or less of the state occupation and ad valorem taxes. In addition, 45 million acres of public domain were set apart for public school support, and the permanent school fund derived therefrom invested in bonds. With amendments from time to time to correct some of its defects, this is the constitution "enjoyed" by Texas until the present.

The school law was rewritten in 1876 to conform to the new constitution. The so-called community system, unique to Texas, was the result. Parents organized themselves into school communities and submitted to the county judge—ex officio superintendent—a list of children to be schooled. The judge in turn appointed three trustees to hire teachers and oversee the school. At the end of the year, a report of attendance was made, after which reimbursement was made from the state available school fund.

This system had some advantages—chiefly those related to the sparsely settled and rapidly growing character of a frontier state—but disadvantages were numerous and abuses frequent.

By 1879, it was obvious that the community system was not working. In that year, Governor O.M. Roberts vetoed the general appropriation bill, charging that annual revenues were insufficient to meet expenses of government, pay the Reconstruction debt, and permit the allocation of one-fourth of all state moneys for schools. Schools were instead allotted only one-sixth, an action that provoked a second bitter fight over free public schools.

In 1883, the first amendment to Article VII of the 1876 constitution was passed by a small majority (5). It provided one-fourth of the revenue derived from the state occupation tax, the poll tax, as before, and an ad valorem tax of such amount, not to exceed 20¢ on the $100 valuation, as would suffice to maintain public free schools for 6 months a year.

In 1884, the school law was again rewritten. The Office of State Superintendent was re-created; all counties were redistricted except 53 in East Texas and the Rio Grande Valley, which continued the "community" system; local taxation up to 20¢ on $100 valuation was permitted if two-thirds of local voters approved it; the state ad valorem tax was affirmed; and the permanent school fund was to be invested in county and other bonds to increase the amount of interest it earned.

Inadequate though it may have been, the School Law of 1884 was the last time that changes in the structure of public education occasioned bitter struggle and sweeping reversals of policy. Changes in the schools proceeded in a more orderly manner during the last 15 years of the nineteenth century.

The Independent School District

A series of laws gradually granted cities and towns more freedom in the development and administration of their schools. Thus was born and grew the independent school district. By 1900, there were 526 of them; in these independent districts the high school displaced the earlier academy. The common schools, on the other hand, continued to be ungraded, disorganized, staffed by poorly paid or unpaid teachers, and housed in barns, church buildings, Masonic temples, and county jails.

The contrast between the quality of these two kinds of schools began to lead to demands for change, and the needs of the independent districts began to generate improvements.

For example, with the introduction of grading the need for standardization of textbooks became obvious. In 1897, the Legislature established a uniform textbook law, with provision for a state textbook adoption board.

A system of accreditation was created in 1885 when high schools sent selected test papers for examination by the faculty of the newly founded (1883) University of Texas. If found satisfactory, the high school sending the exhibit was considered to be affiliated with the university, and its graduates were admitted without entrance examinations.

At the close of the century, State Superintendent Kendall advised the Legislature to authorize the State Board of Education to invest the permanent school fund in the building bonds of independent school districts. Such districts had been having difficulty selling bonds, which they had been permitted to do only since 1895 (6). When the permanent school fund began to be used to underwrite them, school district bond issues started to build school buildings, and common schools suddenly began to see some advantages to becoming independent districts.

THE EARLY TWENTIETH CENTURY

Superiority of the Urban School

As the new century arrived, the superiority of the urban schools and independent districts over rural and common schools ranged from 30 to 50 percent no matter what index was chosen: expenditure per child, length of term, value of school property, or teachers' salaries. Complacency about Texas' general educational posture was high, however, for did not the state have the largest permanent school fund in the Union and the largest income from this source?

W. S. Sutton, professor of education and dean at the University of Texas, issued a bulletin in 1904 containing what he called "Some Wholesome Educational Statistics" chosen to puncture complacency. These were comparative national rankings which showed that Texas stood thirty-seventh in the amount spent per capita, forty-second with respect to length of school year, and thirty-eighth in percent of scholastic population enrolled in school.

The Conference for Education

In 1907, the Conference for Education was formed through the initiative of Dr. Sutton, State Superintendent R. B. Cousins, and H. C. Pritchett, president of Sam Houston Normal Institute. At a meeting in Austin, officers of the conference were selected from among the laymen and educators present (7). A public information campaign was begun. Annually, for about 5 years, a mass meeting was held to discuss public school problems; information bulletins were published; agitation was conducted for the passage of two constitutional amendments.

The first amendment, passed in 1908, permitted use of school tax funds to buy equipment for common school buildings, abolished the rule that two-thirds of the voters had to concur to permit local school taxes, and increased the limit on local taxation from 20¢ to 50¢ on the $100 valuation. The second, in 1909, permitted formation of school districts that crossed county lines.

A large number of small contributions from Texas schoolteachers and a few large sums from lay sponsors financed the Conference for Education; after 1912, the State Department of Education, the Extension Division of the A&M College, and the PTA (then known as the Congress of Mothers) assumed its functions.

Birth of Rural Aid

In 1911, as a result of further agitation by the conference, a rural high school law was passed which established county boards of education, authorized the State Department of Education to classify county (common) schools according to the number of teachers employed, permitted creation of rural high schools and the consolidation of common school districts, and arranged for free tuition (8). The State Board of Education was allocated $50,000 to aid rural districts in equipping new schools.

If this law did not provide sufficient money to accomplish all it permitted, it did open the door for communities with funds to do what had never been possible before, thereby making the inequities of rural education still more conspicuous.

In 1915, a special state aid bill for rural and small town schools was passed, which appropriated $1 million for the task. The operation of this law was to have far-reaching consequences for the structure and development of education in Texas.

Entitled an Equalization Aid Law, it was familiarly known as rural aid. Although the formal title gives an indication of the feelings which prompted the measure, it is a misnomer nevertheless, because it was not really designed to erase the inequalities between rural and urban schools. The law's express purpose was to inspire rural school districts to efforts at self-improvement and to provide a source of funds for lengthening the school year (9).

Many school buildings in rural districts were mere shanties, or worse; the chief effort of the rural aid law in its beginnings was directed to the construction of modern, sanitary schoolhouses. Any district could receive aid once only without meeting any conditions. To receive it more than once, a district had to show that each school ground was at least 1 acre in extent and that each building met state specifications, had equipment prescribed in the state course guide, and subsisted on a local school tax of at least 50¢ on $100 valuation.

Originally, aid was given only to schools with fewer than 200 students, and payments to any given school could not exceed $500 per annum. But both these provisions were gradually broadened; by 1949, any school with less than 1,500 students qualified, and the sums allocated were far greater than $500.

Rural Aid and State Department Reorganization

One of the first effects of the rural aid law was to oblige the reorganization of the State Department of Education. Properly speaking, there was no such department in Texas before 1915, because the state superintendent had little money and less staff. Under R. B. Cousins, for example, in the years 1907-1908 there were a chief clerk, a teachers' certificate clerk, a statistics clerk, a mail clerk, an audit clerk, a stenographer, a porter (10).

This tiny band labored to produce the 600-page biennial report, a pamphlet on Texas school laws, a textbook circular listing all adoptions, an apportionment circular, a public school officer's guide, the *Course of Study for the Public Free Schools of Texas* (86 pages, 20,000 copies—enough for every teacher to have one), and "fifty thousand circulars in the interest of the Amendment" (11).

"There is urgent need of additional clerical help," Cousins wrote in 1909. "Not a man has been added to the force in ten years, and the work has more than quadrupled" (12).

More help did not arrive until the operations of the rural aid law compelled a complete reorganization of the state department in 1916. The Smith-Hughes law followed in 1917. The institution then emerged with a professional staff of 29 and a structure of nine divisions (13). The duties of the high schools division included the conduct of visits and the making of reports on the accreditation status of high schools. While the rural schools division administered rural aid with a director and two assistants, the high schools division required the services of a chief supervisor and five supervisors (14).

Accreditation of High Schools

When the State Department of Education assumed the burden of accrediting high schools, fewer than half the pupils in Texas had access to that form of education. The high schools division accordingly made it its business not only to examine applicant schools for standards, but to promote the establishment of more high schools (15).

By the mid-1920's, it had become the paramount purpose of every Texas community to have its own high school. Administrative excellence thereby came to be identified with the securing of full state accreditation in all subjects within 2 years of setting up a new high school. Accreditation was by subject; a school might be accredited in math but not in English. The method of determining fitness was to read pupils' examination papers. This method was better than none, but it had serious flaws which quickly came to light.

With college enrollments climbing sharply during the third and fourth decades of the century, the pressure to get accredited was intense. Weaker schools throughout the state began to complain, because they could never quite make it across the line to fully accredited status, and their graduates had difficulty entering good colleges.

As early as the mid-twenties, some supervisors in the high schools division began filing accreditation reports that dealt with the amount and kind of instructional supervision, the economic health of the district, and the adequacy of the school system as a whole rather than solely with the quality of examination papers. Two parallel standards of accreditation gradually evolved. Not until the reorganization of the whole educational structure of Texas in 1949-50 was the system of accreditation subjected to thorough study. The state board adopted new standards for accreditation in 1954, and the granting of accreditation by subject was abandoned (16).

State Purchase of Textbooks and Compulsory Attendance

As early as 1888, State Superintendent Oscar Cooper recommended provision of free state-adopted textbooks to public school pupils in Texas and cited the advantages that accrued to pupils in California as a result of that state's establishment of a textbook printing house. In 1891, the first bill directed at promoting uniform adoption of textbooks passed the Legislature, but memories of the Radical Republican school law and its Northern textbooks remained strong. Not until 1897 did a second uniform textbook bill become law, setting up a State Board of Textbook Adoption (17).

The 1897 Uniform Textbook Act was still a long way from a plan of state purchase. Adoption of such a plan depended, as events revealed, on the operation of a compulsory attendance law.

In 1903, the state's first child labor law, enacted under the nationwide stimulus of progressivism, forbade the employment of children under 15 in certain forms of labor, with exceptions for agriculture.

In the cities, the child labor law evoked sentiment in favor of compulsory school attendance, and the Conference for Education, the Congress of Mothers, and the Texas State Teachers Association began agitating for enactment of a compulsory attendance law, at first without much success. The principal opposition arose from memories of Reconstruction.

In 1910, the University of Texas established the Interscholastic League, an association of secondary schools for encouragement and regulation of athletic competition. In 1911, declamation contests and debates were added to the roster of events; in 1914, the subject chosen for debate in all league meets in Texas was: "Should Attendance in the Public Schools Be Compulsory?"

By means of these debates, public attention was at last directed to the rational arguments for compulsory attendance and diverted from further fruitless brooding on the melancholy past. In 1915, the Legislature passed a compulsory school attendance law requiring 60 days of school. During World War I, the duration of attendance was raised to 80, then 100 days.

Passage of compulsory attendance confronted school administrators with the problem of providing textbooks for all. It was manifestly impractical to compel children to attend schools that lacked sufficient books. In 1915, therefore, the Legislature authorized local option in the provision of textbooks without charge to pupils. In many cases, city schools purchased books for the lower grades; poor and rural schools could not provide books in the same way. The visible inequity of the situation led to demands for its correction.

In 1917, the Legislature submitted to the people a proposed amendment to the constitution increasing the state ad valorem tax from 20¢ to 35¢ per $100 and setting aside from this increase sufficient sums to purchase state-adopted texts. The amendment passed by a very large majority.

Gradual Expansion of Rural Aid

In 1915, the rural aid bill appropriated the sum of $1 million for the program of incentives to rural schools. Over the years that followed, the appropriations grew larger as the administrators of rural aid found ways to expand its original goals and means.

For example, the twenties were a period of road building and improvement that began with paving on only a tiny portion of more than 18,000 Texas miles of dirt roads and ended with more than one-third of the state's highways rescued from the mud. It was natural that bus transportation should appear an excellent solution to the problems of providing equal educational opportunity to rural children. Soon after the great surge of highway improvement began, funds for school buses began to be included in rural aid. By the mid-thirties, it proved economical to centralize all bus purchasing and supplies in the state department.

Rural aid also soon included "ample provision for the payment of high school tuition for such students as are compelled to leave their home districts to secure high school instruction" (18).

The largest portion of rural aid, however, came to be expended for teachers' salaries, with the intention of guaranteeing a minimum salary for teachers in eligible districts.

In 1918, for example, a teacher holding a permanent certificate was entitled to be paid a maximum of $85 out of state per-capita money, and a holder of a certificate of the second grade could earn $60. Then as now, wealthy schools paid their teachers more than this state maximum; but since nothing constrained poor schools to pay their teachers as much as that, they often paid considerably less.

Modification of rural aid to incorporate salary aid was intended to guarantee a minimum salary. It did not work as hoped, however, for two reasons: The salary aid was not extended automatically, eligible districts had to request it, and the district had to match the aid funds dollar for dollar. Many districts were reluctant to pay teachers as much as $85 per month lest they then earn more than clerks in stores and thereby undermine the established social order. In spite of this reluctance, the salary aid component of rural aid appropriations grew until it was larger than bus funds and tuition payments combined (19).

The School Survey of 1925

Texans thought their state had made progress in education as a result of the reforms instigated by the Conference for Education and by professional and parent associations from 1908 onward. Although there had been improvements in actual terms, in relative terms the state stood almost exactly where it had when the century began, as shown by the 1920 *Index Number for State School Systems*, published by L. P. Ayres of the Russell Sage Foundation. Texas ranked thirty-ninth.

The friends of education in Texas had organized a Better Schools Campaign to pass the constitutional amendment raising the ad valorem state tax to provide free textbooks. In the spring of 1920, the Better Schools Campaign was again mobilized with the announced purpose of promoting an amendment whereby all school districts would be granted the power to vote for their schools such support as they deemed necessary, thereby removing "all constitutional limit on the rate of tax" in school districts (20).

Texas teachers assessed themselves to raise a war chest of about $4,000 with which the Better Schools Campaign, led by Annie Webb Blanton, state superintendent, organized a May 1 "tag day." The proceeds of tag day were $24,000 for a state campaign fund and an equal sum for county campaign funds. The amendment passed by a large majority (21).

In 1921, the Legislature established a Committee on the Survey of the State Institutions of Higher Education, headed by Oscar H. Cooper, former state superintendent from 1887 to 1890. This committee reported that no investigation of colleges and universities was possible without a parallel inquiry into the public schools. In response to this report, the Legislature in 1923 appointed a large and representative commission with a mandate to conduct a general study of the school system of Texas. The commission engaged George A. Works of the College of Agriculture at Cornell to be director of the study. Despite all kinds of niggling obstacles, such as statewide floods and no advances for travel or per diem, the *Texas Educational Survey Report* was completed and published in 1925.

The Texas Educational Survey Report

The survey, at that time one of the most extensive investigations of the operation of a state's schools and department of education ever made, pointed out a number of facts:

Rural children did not have much chance for a high school education; fewer than 1 percent of the common school districts maintained 4-year high schools.

Thirty-three percent of all white pupils and 70 percent of all colored pupils attended school less than 6 months. Half of all white pupils were 1 year overage in their grade by Texas standards, to say nothing of standards in other states. Seventy percent of all Negro pupils were 1 year overage, and half of all Negro pupils were 2 years overage.

There was no standard method of taking the school census, upon which the state apportionment of per-capita money was based. No uniform plan for assessing property values was followed.

The ex officio State Board of Education, composed of the Governor, the comptroller, and the appointed secretary of state, lacked money and time to meet.

The state superintendent's functions were vague and were assigned by the ex officio board rather than prescribed by law. As the result of changes and reforms, the State Department of Education, consisting of some 56 professional people, had grown too big for the scattered rooms it occupied in the pink granite capitol, yet remained too small for the task it was supposed to be doing.

The Smith-Hughes Act had already begun to prove inadequate, particularly at meeting the needs of rural schools and those in smaller cities. Other states had begun to supplement the act, and the survey strongly implied that Texas should do likewise if it wished to crawl out of thirty-ninth place.

The organization and development of junior high schools required more attention because many students were in need of better terminal education. In 1925, only Beaumont and San Antonio operated such schools.

Extensive reorganization of higher education was necessary. A properly financed and administered junior college program was needed, as was some unified administration of senior institutions.

Some of the recommendations of the survey report were followed, others were not, and still others were eventually effected by gradual changes in demographic patterns.

For example, the number of independent school districts had grown from about 500 in 1910 to 805 in 1920. By 1930, there were approximately 1,000 of them, a figure which remained relatively constant thereafter, fluctuating only about 5 percent. While not all independent districts provided superior educational opportunities, they were more likely to do so than the small common schools. Common school districts had numbered more than 8,000 in the first decade of the century; their number shrank to about 7,000 in 1930, to about 5,000 at the outbreak of World War II, and to 3,516 in 1949 on the eve of administrative reorganization. Such changes in relative numbers of kinds of districts were partly the result of deliberate policies of the state, including incentives toward reorganization which were part of rural aid bills from the 1920's onward, and partly the result of rural population decline.

At the same time, however, very little progress was made with respect to the difference between Negro pupil attendance and white pupil attendance. The general average was lowered by the low levels maintained in Negro schools. Negro per-capita money was used to operate the white schools for 8 or 9 months, leaving the Negro schools to operate 6 months or less.

Reforms were not slow in coming with regard to the organization of the State Department of Education and the duties of the state superintendent of education, but they came under circumstances that generated a certain bitterness and introduced for a time a definite bias into the administration of public education in Texas.

The position of state superintendent, when restored reluctantly in 1884, was that of an elective functionary with a term of 2 years. Only three state superintendents served longer than 4 years in the period from 1884 to 1924. There was little continuity in the policies of successive superintendents, and administrative continuity depended greatly on the succession of chief clerks who carried on the real work of the office. No one was more aware of these facts than S. M. N. Marrs, state superintendent from 1923 to 1932 (22).

Marrs was convinced that the state superintendent ought to hold a position analogous to that of a local superintendent of schools—as the executive for a board of concerned laymen. With the report of the Texas Educational Survey as an authoritative reference, he worked to convince the Legislature and the people that Texas needed a State Board of Education with time to devote to the creation of a continuous program of development and improvement of education. His efforts bore fruit with the passage of an amendment to the constitution in 1929, which created a nine-member appointed State Board of Education (23).

The Office of State Superintendent Changes

S. M. N. Marrs died suddenly in the spring of 1932, and Governor Ross Sterling appointed C. N. Shaver, former superintendent of Huntsville, to serve out his remaining term of office.

Through the years, the people of Texas had gradually come to regard the office of state superintendent as essentially nonpolitical, even though elective. Campaigns for the office were frequently unopposed races in which the candidates sought to inform rather than harangue the voters and to mobilize support for new educational programs rather than simply to garner votes for himself (24). Miss Blanton's campaigns were good, if untypical, examples of this procedure, marked as they were by the same evangelical appeal that had been applied to votes for women and the call for national prohibition.

In 1932, however, the incumbent found himself opposed. L. A. Woods of Waco stumped the state presenting a program of action for education, enlisting personal support, making promises, and playing politics. The character of the campaign represented a sharp break with tradition. Politics, Texas style, were introduced into the campaign for chief state school officer.

One of the charges Dr. Woods brought against the incumbent, for example, was that the State Department of Education was too remote from the people, and geared to do everything for the city schools, nothing for rural ones (25).

This contained enough truth to hurt: The high schools division *was* large, and high schools were found principally in urban areas. Far from neglecting rural schools, however, the state department in the twenties had done much to help them by increasing the per-capita allotment, encouraging consolidation, and promoting free tuition.

But the Depression was bearing down hard everywhere, and Texas faced deficits that threatened to reduce promised per-capita apportionment below levels previously reached and to force it to renege on obligations to aid rural schools to the amount of more than $800,000.

The electorate was more conscious of the smarting of these wounds than of the steady progress made in the preceding decade.

The state was not the only political unit having difficulty financing its share of public education. Local school districts had been hit hard at the beginning of the thirties by the adoption of a homestead amendment that resulted in a loss of ad valorem revenue totaling more than $9.6 million in 1932, or nearly one-third of the state's available school fund (26).

Nor was that all. Taxpayers associations were springing up all over Texas with the announced objective of suspension or elimination of property taxes, which they claimed no longer could be paid. In some localities, these groups succeeded in wreaking havoc with local property valuations (27).

The financial straits in which public education lay gave validity to another of Dr. Woods's election charges—that the pedagogical experimentation of the twenties had produced an extravagant expansion of scholastic programs. Dr. Woods urged the electorate to demand that a process of deflation be applied to Texas schools as well as to other elements of government.

Dr. Woods urged that school overhead be reduced and in paid newspaper ads used the slogan, "Not More Money for the Schools, but More Schools for the Money." In a corollary to that slogan, the reserved and academic tone of the State Department of Education was to be changed. In particular, the vocational education components of education were to be brought into new prominence and expanded in scope.

In response to the financial pressures of the Depression, the districting plan of Texas schools was becoming a chaotic scramble to annex the most valuable revenue-bearing properties. Though all schools were suffering, the rich schools were not suffering as much as the poor (28).

To cope with this inequity, Dr. Woods proposed that the state department take a more prominent role than before in the districting of schools (29). After he took office, he created a research division, which became responsible for educational surveys designed to document the need for consolidation where necessary.

THE ADMINISTRATION OF L. A. WOODS

Dr. Woods and His Opponents

If Dr. Woods waged a thoroughly political campaign, the times provided ample excuse for it. That his administration also was steeped in politics was the natural consequence of the campaign. Nevertheless, many people never forgave him for the way he said and did what was necessary in the circumstances. The educational world in Texas was soon divided into his supporters and his opponents.

Among his first opponents were some members of the State Department of Education—a natural result of some of the campaign accusations. The new superintendent tried to surround himself with people loyal to him, but he found that there were some established patterns of administration that lay beyond his control. In particular, some professional personnel were paid not by the state but by the various philanthropic foundations active in education (30). In addition, certain earmarked funds placed restrictions on expenditures. In spite of such checks, however, the new state superintendent complied with the customs of the time and with the tradition of patronage in politics. A new slate of personnel was installed.

A second and more enduring set of opponents consisted of the appointed nine-member State Board of Education (31). Dr. Woods felt that the state board cramped his style. For its part, the board regarded the state superintendent as neither a politician-educator nor an educator-politician, but simply as a politician. This point is made in the following excerpt from a board report:

> Leaders in the field of public education in Texas have endorsed the idea of selection of the State Superintendent of Public Instruction by the State Board of Education on the basis solely of educational qualifications and administrative experience. Accession to this office should not be controlled by current non-educational, political issues.
>
> Appointment of the State Superintendent of Public Instruction would enable that officer to devote more time to the functions of the office than is possible under the present set-up which calls for much political "fence building." Legislation providing appointment of the State Superintendent is respectfully recommended (32).

The state board itself was open to the charge of "politics," since its members were appointed rather than elected. Woods's reply to the board's animadversions was more succinct than their statement: "It is hereby recommended that the State Superintendent's office be kept as far as possible out of politics; therefore the State Superintendent should continue to be elected by the people of the State" (33).

Neither party to the feud could conquer or subdue the other; the state superintendent had his supporters well organized, as will be shown subsequently; the State Board of Education had its own budget, with which it produced its own biennial report to the Legislature in a manner completely independent of the state department (34).

Woods and His Supporters. True to his campaign promises, Woods set out to "bring the State Department of Education close to the people" by doing everything possible for rural and small town schools—a popular move with the rural-dominated Legislature.

In his second term of office, he established the post of deputy state superintendent as a way of bringing the department closer to the schools of the vast state. Twenty-four deputies were responsible, in regions ranging in size up to twenty-five or more counties, for checking on the eligibility of schools for rural aid, and for helping schoolmen prepare rural aid budgets for their districts.

Although the job of deputy state superintendent paid only $3,600 per annum (35)—a small salary even in those times—the post was eagerly sought, for it was viewed as a path of advancement for ambitious school administrators.

The deputies were frequently called to Austin to receive and relay information or to participate in planning conferences, especially when new legislative proposals were to be offered or new school legislation implemented. They thus constituted a vital link of communication between the needs of the schools and the decision-making apparatus of the state. Their efforts enabled the State Department of Education to raise the per-capita apportionment higher each year. They also helped reelect Dr. Woods, for in addition to maintaining contact with his supporters in schools and communities around the state, the deputies cultivated personal acquaintances with members of the Legislature, thus giving the superintendent a rapport with lawmakers that must have done much to sustain his political longevity.

Role of the Educational Foundations

In spite of being understaffed and overcommitted, the State Department of Education in Texas during the thirties and forties was not merely the toy of social, political, and technological forces. From time to time, it managed to originate or skillfully adapt methods for assistance to the public schools.

Some credit for the creative vigor of the department probably belongs to the various philanthropic educational foundations, such as the General Education Board of the Rockefeller Foundation, the Carnegie Foundation, the Jeanes Fund, the Julius Rosenwald Fund, and the Peabody Foundation.

The effects of these philanthropies were quite substantial in view of the minor sums of money they bestowed; indeed, many people without intimate understanding of education have been baffled by how such relatively small amounts could be any help at all in such vast fields of need.

For example, in 1902, a special investigating committee appointed by the Texas Legislature to look into the operations of the educational philanthropies reported that the Peabody General Agent had dispensed $4,000 to Sam Houston State Teacher's College, $1,000 in support of "summer normals," $800 to North Texas State Teacher's College, and $600 to Prairie View College during the biennium. The investigating committee accordingly termed the Peabody Fund a farce, and scornfully said that "it would do as much good to throw it at a bird or give it to a railroad conductor" (36).

Not so, replied State Superintendent Arthur Lefevre in his biennial report. The value of these moneys lay in the fact that they were not subject to the laws and regulations governing ordinary state expenditures for the administration of public schools and so could be used for whatever purpose the state superintendent might choose.

In former times, lack of sufficient funds severely limited the planning function of the state department. Leadership, in modern education, depends largely on planning. Before the advent of federal programs intended to promote planning, funds for any planning that was done were often discretionary money from philanthropic foundations, used to pay the salaries of professional personnel who were trained for certain specific new tasks.

For example, the General Education Board financed a year of study at Teachers College of Columbia University for a member of the staff who became, on his return to Texas, director of research and finance, and concurrently director of studies for the State Board of Education (37). The General Education Board also paid the salaries and the operating expenses of a school plants division until 1935, at which time the Legislature transferred support of the division to state funds.

The Jeanes supervisory services provided a handful of professional personnel who worked with Negro teachers to improve their limited skills and train them in new elements of curriculum such as vocational subjects.

In the State Department of Education, the General Education Board financed a Negro education division. When this support terminated in 1942, after 20 years, the superintendent requested that it be taken up by the state.

Similarly, in 1946, the state assumed the burden of supporting a health and physical education division, maintained for 6 years by the Kellogg Foundation (38).

Thus, indirectly, philanthropic support supplied impetus to the adoption of new modes of dealing with problems and to a greater consciousness of needs.

Woods's Accomplishments

When the waves of curriculum reform reached Texas schools in the early Depression years, the response of the state educational leadership was commendable. The Texas State Teachers Association began the movement by adopting a resolution at its statewide meeting in November 1932 calling on the state board and the state superintendent to sponsor broad-scale curriculum revision.

Woods honored the resolution by calling together in 1933 a group of recognized experts in curriculum (39). Under the leadership of Henry Otto of the University of Texas, this team of consultants devised a five-track plan which set up certain definite objectives in terms of desirable qualities of citizens in a democratic society, rather than simply outlining pages of textbooks in various subjects as had been the custom.

In following up this plan, curriculum consultants of the state department, in conference with representatives of subject teachers, wrote units for practically every offering in the state guide. Then representatives of schools and curriculum areas from all over Texas were called together to criticize the plans and units. More than 30,000 teachers participated before the revisions were concluded.

When all agreed-upon changes had been incorporated in the units, they were published and urged on teachers. To provide a continuing reinforcement for the new curriculum plans, the textbooks division became the curriculum and textbooks division, headed by J. Carl Mathews. The state superintendent requested permission from the Legislature to "adopt whatever books are needed for the development of a well-rounded educational program" (40).

The practice of multiple adoptions of textbooks, begun during the twenties with reference to high school subjects, was thus extended to apply to elementary curriculum as well.

Another innovation of Dr. Woods's was the introduction of public school music supervision and the promotion of public school music programs. The list of state-adopted texts included music books and materials.

In 1936, the Texas School of the Air, a pioneering effort at using the mass media of communication for curriculum enrichment and some direct instruction, was launched.

The Woods administration also saw the beginning of various new techniques of communication within the professional community, such as the Midwinter Conference of Public School Administrators and the issuance for a time of a monthly information bulletin, "With the Public Schools," by the information and statistics division.

But by far the greatest accomplishments of those years were the sixfold increase in the appropriation for rural aid and the reduction by half or more of the number of common school districts, with the consequent improvement in the quality and quantity of educational opportunity for rural children.

The expansion of rural aid and a concomitant growth in per-capita apportionment for schools were both responses of the state to the fact that local tax support of schools shrank during the thirties from a decline in taxable values and widespread delinquency in tax payment.

The reduction of the number of common schools was also partly a result of the Depression and partly a result of skillful development of administrative techniques for facilitating consolidation, such as the formula which permitted small districts to transfer their pupils to the tutelage of larger ones without losing their identity.

The virtues and defects of Dr. Woods's administration were closely linked. In his fence building, the state superintendent sometimes sacrificed long-range educational improvements for short-run political advantage. And the concentration on problems of rural and small town schools led to a situation in which the large urban school systems were left to work out their own problems—which were not small, only different—strictly alone. Such a policy had to change under the pressure of demographic shifts such as those brought by World War II.

DEVELOPMENT SINCE WORLD WAR II

The Coming of Gilmer-Aikin

At the end of the war, it was obvious to everyone in public education that a number of problems—some longstanding, some new—stood in need of immediate solutions. The crop of war babies would soon reach school age and tax further the already overcrowded physical plant. Dilapidated buildings, inadequate equipment, and a shortage of qualified teachers were at the head of the list of priorities for schools. During the war, the budget of the state department omitted the school plants and structural safety division, because no one had had materials with which to construct other than temporary classrooms and because the professional staff of the division had been called into military service (41).

The superintendent recommended that the Legislature increase teachers' salaries to provide a minimum of \$2,000 for those with degrees or the equivalent and an annual increase of \$200 for holders of master's degrees (42).

Then, at the regular session of the Fiftieth Legislature, Representative Blankenship of Dallas introduced a bill incorporating the plan of the Texas State Teachers Association (TSTA) for raising teaching salaries—a bill whose language did not differ in any major way from the recommendation of the state superintendent except proposing that "if the available (school fund) failed to provide \$55 per capita (the amount required to finance the salary increase), then the amount necessary to make this payment should be transferred from. . .the omnibus tax bill. . ." (43).

Legislators had no objection to giving the teachers more money, but some of the more conservative ones took alarm at the proposal to finance the pay increase—no matter to how small an extent—out of the general revenue fund of the state. About the middle of the session, therefore, Senator Taylor and Representative Gilmer introduced a conservative counterplan for financing higher salaries for teachers.

The conservative bill set up the same minimum salary schedule as the Blankenship bills but provided that the state should contribute aid above per capita only to those schools which could show need. This would have resulted in no extra state money for the richer school districts, including some in the large cities. Moreover, the counterplan called for a biennial appropriation bill which would have meant that most Texas schools would be forced to operate on a 2-year plan subject to the will of all future Legislatures (44). The TSTA promptly criticized the Taylor counterplan, charging that it was "a serious effort (by) the South Texas Chamber of Commerce and other special interest groups . . . to defeat the objectives and needs of the schools of the State" (45).

Soon, the public school teachers regarded Senator Taylor and Representative Gilmer not only as the chief enemies of the public schools but also as the personification of all the evils implied in the words *special interests.* Both men were novices in the field of school financing and somewhat taken aback at the intensity of the rejection their plan received, but they thought that if a group of interested people gave the problem thorough study, a feasible way to replace the per-capita method of financing could be found (46).

In March 1947, therefore, Representative Gilmer introduced House Concurrent Resolution 48, calling for an 18-member study committee to tackle all questions relating to the improvement of the public school system of Texas (47). In the Senate, Senator Aikin, a longtime friend of education and ally of the TSTA, sponsored the resolution—a fact which mollified that association somewhat. The TSTA had already concluded that the committee, if appointed, would accomplish little and therefore that the matter was not worth contesting (48).

The committee was provided \$25,000 of House contingency funds with which to operate. It was known as the Gilmer-Aikin Committee after the sponsors of the resolution and at its first meeting elected Senator Taylor its chairman—a move which did nothing to convince Texas teachers of its disinterested character (49).

The Gilmer-Aikin Committee spent 1947 deciding what it would work on. In December came a very important turning point—when Edgar L. Morphet, nationally known authority on educational finance, met with the committee and suggested some tested techniques for selling a program of modernized public education to the people. Morphet—

> Made it perfectly clear that success in Florida, [where he had been executive director of the Citizens' Committee that had secured educational reform] was attained primarily through citizens' organizations operating throughout the state and working with the main committee (50).

The Gilmer-Aikin Committee acted on this advice and proceeded to organize as the Floridians had done. It hired L. D. Haskew, dean of the School of Education at the University of Texas, as its technical adviser. Five statewide advisory committees were chosen to work with the existing subcommittees of the Gilmer-Aikin Committee. Wherever possible, county committees of lay and professional people also were formed. H. A. Moore, a member of the committee, was appointed executive director (51).

By September 1948, the subcommittee reports were sufficiently advanced to permit circulation of a tentative draft of proposals. After the proposals had been scrutinized by all the advisory committees, they were published as a booklet, *To Have What We Must*. Among the 33 specific recommendations were those calling for a minimum foundation program of education that would combine state and local support with the state underwriting costs above a reasonable uniform effort. Others called for the establishment of local administrative units designed for most efficient school management, the redesign of state administrative machinery, a minimum state salary schedule for teachers, and such administrative and legal changes as were necessary for consistency (52).

The committee handled public relations ably but nevertheless failed to get its proposals presented to a special session of the Legislature because of growing opposition from both the state board and the state superintendent of public instruction (53). The Gilmer-Aikin Bills had to be presented during the regular session of 1949.

To write the proposals of the Gilmer-Aikin Committee into the language of bills, Senator Taylor called on the officers and legislative committee of the TSTA for assistance, an invitation that had the effect of thawing the coolness the association had felt toward the committee (54).

As finally cast in the form of bills, the committee's proposals provided for reorganization of the state administration of education through consolidation and rationalization of existing educational divisions of the state into one central education agency—the Texas Education Agency—composed of the State Board of Education, a commissioner of education chosen by the board (Senate Bill 115), and a State Department of Education; establishment of a minimum foundation program for education, including setting up of formulas for financial allotments, and the payment of the difference between program costs and the combination of local funds and state per-capita payments from the special Foundation School Fund (Senate Bill 116); and a plan of automatic financing to eliminate the need for biennial appropriations by the Legislature (Senate Bill 117) (55).

Dr. Woods was aware of the advantages of a minimum foundation program and favored the plan for automatic financing, but he opposed the reorganization of the State Department of Education, especially the plan of having the state board appoint the commissioner of education.

If he had chosen to oppose only the reorganization bill (Senate Bill 115) while giving support to the other two, Dr. Woods might have been the first commissioner of education chosen by the newly constituted state board. Instead of adopting a position from which to bargain, however, the state superintendent took a completely intransigent stand (56).

Members of the appointed State Board of Education also opposed Senate Bill 115 because it provided that board members should be elected. Their opposition was not so overt, however, as that of the State Department of Education (57).

Other opposition came from a small group of representatives of textbook publishing companies, who disliked a provision of Senate Bill 115 that called for multiple adoption of textbooks in elementary grades (58).

By February 1949, the Texas State Teachers Association had decided, however, that the bills contained no hidden clauses but were in fact what they purported to be—a design to improve education in Texas. The association therefore began using its full weight in support of the bills. Three or four days each week, Charles Tennyson, public relations director of the association, invited various House members and Senate and House sponsors to lunch with him and members of the TSTA legislative committee (59).

In addition, close contacts were maintained with school people known to favor the bills, and they in turn brought influence to bear on their representatives. Many meetings were held around Texas to rouse the enthusiasm of school people and to discuss the issues. A new pressure technique seldom used with previous Legislatures was employed extensively—the filling of the galleries with supporters of the program both at committee hearings and throughout the House debate. This had a wholesome effect in keeping members in line with their pledges to support the bills. The proponents used every legitimate device that could be devised (60).

The state superintendent employed every means at his disposal, from radio talks to form letters to city and county superintendents and school boards, and pamphlets. He attacked Gilmer-Aikin in the newspapers, warning that passage of the bills would be disastrous to equal educational opportunity for youth in rural areas and small towns. A substitute bill designed to undermine the Gilmer-Aikin proposals was introduced in the House, and Dr. Woods was quite active in its support (61).

The attempt to arouse public interest was highly successful on both sides of the measure, but the proponents had organized earlier and more thoroughly and managed their bills very skillfully in committee and on the floor. In the final days of the legislative session of 1949, the three bills passed.

The Minimum Foundation School Program Evaluated

Passage of the Gilmer-Aikin Bills was widely hailed as victory in Texas for modern concepts of educational administration. Yet, in the opinion of some experts, the foundation school program which emerged from the new law was an expedient rather than a true plan for educational excellence—an expedient, furthermore, which was substantially altered by the Legislature in the process of passage (62).

The intent of the measures was to put a fiscal floor under poor schools (which wealthy ones could exceed if they so desired) while making certain that no district was able to substitute state support for local taxes. However, under the foundation school laws it is still advantageous for a district to be small, i.e., to make the state minimum the school's maximum and so escape the necessity for increasing local taxation (63).

Moreover, instead of proceeding to regularize the assessment of property taxes from county to county, the Legislature has permitted wide variations to persist, thus making the complex formulas in the Gilmer-Aikin proposals for securing equitable allotments somewhat ineffective.

Despite these criticisms, however, the foundation school program has enabled Texas to come much closer than ever before to providing equal educational opportunity for its children.

In the interim period during the summer of 1949, the Governor appointed L. P. Sturgeon to act as commissioner of education pending the appointment of a permanent executive by the elected State Board of Education (64).

For its part, the state board spent several months interviewing a large number of competent school administrators before settling on J. W. Edgar, whose membership on the Gilmer-Aikin Committee had made him reluctant to permit consideration of his name (65).

Dr. Edgar was a member of Texas Association of School Administrators, composed of superintendents of schools in cities of 100,000 population or more. Some interpreted his appointment as indicating a swing in the direction of policies favorable to big city schools. This was a justifiable presumption, but a mistaken one. There was to be no continuation of the political atmosphere that had existed in the previous two decades.

J. W. Edgar Emphasizes Professionalism

The most important new policy the new chief state school officer cultivated was one of asking rather than telling. Keeping himself very much in the background, he tried to assume the role that S. M. N. Marrs had envisioned for the office by assiduously promoting cooperative planning and thorough preliminary studies. By declining to impose solutions of his own devising, he tried to let the state board perform its function of reaching informed policy decisions, however tedious such a procedure might often be. He attempted to bring about harmony between the large-school and small-school administrators associations and succeeded in involving these organizations in some cooperative planning. He cultivated a greater degree of local autonomy of decision making in schools.

The new law prohibited the State Department of Education from making any overt efforts to secure school district consolidations, but Edgar himself met from time to time with local boards of trustees in an attempt to set forth clearly the exact facts about the true cost of a high-quality educational program (66).

To help small schools desirous of maintaining their identity, Dr. Edgar caused to be launched a Small Schools Study aimed at discovering better ways to assist districts with less than 500 average daily attendance. From this study grew the establishment of a Texas Small Schools Project in the administrative services division.

As redesigned in 1950, the State Department of Education consisted of four departments: school administration and finance, agency administration, instructional services, and vocational services.

An assistant commissioner or a deputy commissioner headed each office. Under the Office of Instructional Services were grouped, for example, the curriculum development, professional standards (including both certification and accreditation functions) and special education divisions. The last named moved after 1960 into a new vocational rehabilitation and special education department.

Cooperative Planning and Advisory Committees

Immediately after it came into office, the State Board of Education called for a careful study of teacher certification as the first step toward improvement of professional standards as the Gilmer-Aikin Act directed.

Under Dr. Edgar's leadership, the appropriate associations were involved in establishing a planning committee to develop procedures for a statewide study (67). This was followed by a statewide conference on teacher certification in July 1950, at which some tentative proposals for new requirements were formulated and subsequently issued as a bulletin, *Toward Professional Competence for Teachers.*

During the 1950-51 school year, thousands of study groups were formed among professionals and laymen, who submitted reports which were compiled for a second statewide conference in July 1951. This conference decided that certification requirements should be formulated to support desired teacher-education programs.

A steering committee of 19 assumed the responsibility of publication, continued study, and the writing of revised proposals. As a result of its labors, a second publication, *Proposed Standards for the Certification of Texas Teachers,* was issued in 1952. It was duly disseminated and critiqued; its recommendations were revised after much testimony.

The resulting consensus became the basis for changes in the certification requirements in Texas. The procedure followed in this particular instance may be taken as broadly typical of the procedure in other cooperative planning ventures under the minimum foundation school act as administered by Commissioner Edgar (68).

In addition to reliance on advisory committees and study commissions, the State Department of Education under the leadership of Dr. Edgar began, during the fifties, to place greater emphasis on formal in-service training for staff members.

In 1950, under the leadership of Warren Hitt, deputy commissioner, a special program of staff development was organized. It was affiliated with the School of Education of the University of Texas at Austin and provided 3 hours of credit in educational administration. During the first year it was conducted, the course analyzed problems of state educational administration and explored techniques of operation. During its second year, the course analyzed leadership opportunities. "One technical skill emerged as important . . . arranging conferences, clinics, workshops, area meetings, etc., and performing in group situations" (69).

This staff in-service program was part of a larger project in action-research in administrative techniques, funded by the Kellogg Foundation, which lasted from 1950 to 1956 (70).

A part of the responsibility assigned the State Board of Education under the minimum foundation school laws was evaluation of the outcomes of the new program. In 1953, the Texas Research League, a nonprofit research organization, was engaged to conduct an objective study of the administration and financing of the foundation program.

The league report found that the foundation school program had "contributed substantially to the progress of public school education in Texas" (71). It also identified certain defects in the program, including a failure to carry out planned reorganization of school districts, inefficient methods of calculating the current classroom teacher and operating allotments, inequities in the measurement of local capacity for program cost sharing, and a loophole or two in the modes of calculating local district fund assignment. The report recommended that the state available school fund be apportioned among districts on the basis of average daily attendance rather than scholastic population and that the annual scholastic census be conducted biennially and in a standard sampling manner (72).

Acting on these recommendations, the state board made legislative recommendations designed to promote desirable changes in the statutes. Some of the recommendations met with approval, and others did not (73).

Through the leadership of the state department, various technical improvements were made in the operation of the system of textbook selection and approval, and recommended refinements in the management of the permanent school fund were secured.

More Attention for Spanish-Speaking Children

During the course of World War I, when xenophobia rose in the United States and when the German Empire attempted to capitalize on Mexican resentment of U.S. expansionism, mutual distrust between the nationalities in Texas created a demand for educational policies that would enforce acculturation of minorities. The existence of a large group of Spanish-speaking people within the borders of Texas was viewed for the first time as a "problem." Legislation was enacted making English the only "language of instruction" in Texas schools.

The Texas Educational Survey Report of 1925 devoted an entire chapter to the subject of teaching Mexican-American children and made a number of recommendations, such as the following:

> In the opinion of the Survey Staff, they should be segregated in the first two or three grades, when they are unable to speak English . . . . This recommendation has been made with some reluctance, as the . . . practice varies from community to community. In some instances it has been used for the purpose of giving to Mexican children a shorter school year, inferior buildings and equipment and poorly paid teachers (74).

Segregation, whether for instructional purposes or for other reasons, remained the rule in many schools until the period after World War II, when agitation for reform began to make itself felt, resulting in at least two court decisions that struck down separate instruction for Spanish-speaking pupils.

In 1958, Felix Tijerina of Houston, national president of the League of United Latin American Clubs, conceived the idea of setting up schools outside the public schools to attempt to equip Spanish-speaking pupils with a minimum English vocabulary before their entry into public school. This "Little School of the 400" (400 English words) was successful in leading to establishment by the Texas Education Agency of a preschool program for non-English speaking children. There followed in 1963 the establishment of the Texas Project for the Education of Migrant Children (by far the greatest number of whom are Mexican-American), which attempted to benefit the children whose parents follow the crops by compressing the school curriculum into 6 months through lengthening of the school day. These projects developed new methods of teaching Spanish-speaking children and thus facilitated a trend, now under way, toward the cultivation of bilingual instruction.

National Defense Education Act

The availability of funds under NDEA brought both direct and indirect changes to the structure and programs of the State Department of Education.

In direct fashion, the advent of NDEA led to the addition of staff in several parts of the state department, particularly consultants in the curriculum areas of interest to the U.S. Congress: mathematics, science, and foreign languages. As NDEA was subsequently broadened, the staff of the program development division in the office of instruction continued to expand, and program approval of applications for NDEA funds to support guidance and counseling and library materials became a new function of the office of administration.

Indirectly, NDEA led to other kinds of expansion. In 1959, the National Education Association secured a grant under the act to set up regional conferences throughout the nation to plan for the establishment of research and dissemination projects in instructional media.

The following year, Texas representatives attended two of these regional conferences. The delegation of 18 persons from all components of the educational enterprise returned home to become an advisory committee on instructional media, which requested the Texas Education Agency to submit a proposal to the U.S. Office of Education for a dissemination project contract under Title VII of NDEA.

To carry out the initial phases of the project, the instructional media division was organized within the office of instruction. Its four professional personnel recruited and trained a staff of 24 demonstration teachers and employed suitable means to publicize the project (75).

NDEA funds also made possible the establishment of an electronic computer and the hiring of personnel to process statistical and research data (76).

In 1965, the Elementary and Secondary Education Act ushered in an entirely new era in public education in Texas, as in other states. The effects of this legislation and funding cannot be historically assessed, for the changes brought about as a result of Title I, Title III, and Title V are still under way, and the outcome of many projects started under the various titles is not yet known. Not merely the magnitude of funds available, but the purposes to which those funds were to be directed, were in many cases unprecedented.

One result of the massive infusion of funds (more than $180 million for Texas under Title I alone) was of course an increase in the sheer size and number of functions of the State Department of Education, bringing with it new problems of coordination and control, reorganization, and redirection of effort. Revisions in structure are still being made in an effort to cope with the changes. One significant change occurred in 1966 with the inauguration of an office of planning as part of the commissioner's office, financed with funds from Title V of ESEA. This office was instrumental in the introduction of new concepts of internal communication and cooperative planning for instructional purposes, and in the creation of a new educational entity in Texas—the Regional Education Service Center—of which there are 20, each with its staff of specialists responsible for providing schools with services and assistance they could not otherwise obtain. The centers are not intermediate units of administration, but service organizations only; nonetheless, they are likely repositories of certain functions of the State Department of Education that have heretofore been concentrated in the state capital. It therefore appears that one indirect result of the largest and most recent federal aid program is a decentralization and rationalization of the State Department of Education. It also seems likely that a prime result of federal aid programs is an accelerated adoption of more modern techniques of management and planning by the state department.

As it was once with private philanthropy, so now it appears to be with federal aid. A program begun with the help of outside funds is quite likely to be continued in some form after those funds are withdrawn, if it should be. The changes wrought in the State Department of Education by the intervention of federal aid are irreversible. Their significance is quite disproportionate to the relative size of federal (8 percent) and state (48 percent) expenditures for public education in Texas. If federal aid should cease tomorrow, the changes it has brought would be likely to endure.

FOOTNOTES

1. Texas, *Declaration of Independence,* adopted in Convention at Washington-on-the-Brazos, March 2, 1836.

2. The earliest Anglo-American settlers of the region used the word *Texian,* now archaic, to refer to themselves. It has come to mean only the culture and the people of prestatehood times.

3. Some survivors of the period are Baylor University, founded in 1845; Austin College, founded 1849; and Southwestern University at Georgetown, originally Rutersville University, in 1840.

4. The term *free schools* meant charity institutions to the advocates of private and church education and free tuition to the advocates of free schools for all children—an artful compromise of which the constitution writers were proud.

5. Governor Ireland, the Texas State Teachers Association, and many political leaders of the state backed the amendment. Behind these supporters lay the persuasive activities of Barnas Sears, general agent for the Peabody Fund, which had been active in Texas as throughout the South since 1869 with small but judicious grants to establish exemplary schools, subsidize the travel allowance of the secretary of the ex officio State Board of Education, and promote the establishment of normal institutes and summer training programs for teachers.

6. Superintendent of Public Instruction, *Ninth Biennial Report* (1895).

7. The executive board included Clarence N. Ousley, chairman, publisher of the *Fort Worth Record;* H. H. Harrington, vice chairman, president of A&M; A. N. McCallum, recording secretary, superintendent of Austin public schools; W. S. Sutton, corresponding secretary, dean of the School of Education, University of Texas; and E. P. Wilmot, treasurer, president of the Austin National Bank. Clarence Ousley was also chosen chairman of the Executive Board, whose

members included David F. Houston, president of the University of Texas; H. C. Pritchett, president of Sam Houston Normal Institute; Oscar H. Cooper, state superintendent from 1887 to 1891; R. B. Cousins, state superintendent; and J. L. Long, superintendent of the Dallas public schools. As its general agent the conference hired F. M. Bralley, former chief clerk of the State Department of Education and later state superintendent.

8. The classification of common schools and the accreditation of high schools by the state department did not begin until 1917, when the University of Texas completed phasing out of affiliation procedures.

9. In 1915, approximately 70 percent of the state's population lived in the country, and about one-third of all labor on farms was that of school-age children. The school term in rural districts was 4 months or less. About 18 percent of city children attended high school; only 7 percent of rural children did. About 1 percent of all Texas students graduated from high school.

10. Superintendent of Public Instruction, *Biennial Report* (1909), p. 57.

11. *Ibid.*

12. *Ibid.*

13. The divisions were administration and law, high schools, rural schools, audits and accounts, statistics and reports, examinations (for teaching certificates), certification, mail and supplies, and vocational education. The last, in Texas as elsewhere, included subdivisions of agriculture, home economics, and industrial arts.

14. Superintendent of Public Instruction, *Biennial Report* (1918), p. 38.

15. *Ibid.*, p. 31.

16. W. R. Goodson, "The Program of School Accreditation in Texas" (unpublished typewritten report of the director, Division of School Accreditation, Texas Education Agency, 1962), p. 3. Dr. Goodson also writes:

> During this time (the period 1917-1952) more than 2,000 regulations were made having to do with all aspects of the elementary and secondary school programs. The influence of the committee was one of the most powerful forces in Texas education. An example of this is found in the fact that the State did not have a certificate law during this time that ensured a teacher holding a college degree, but accreditation regulations had this requirement and about 97 per cent of Texas teachers had degrees by 1950.

17. The bill establishing this body and defining its functions was first passed in 1891, but when it came to the secretary of state's office it was discovered that opponents of the measure had secretly caused the enabling clause to be excised from the bill after passage and engrossment. Hence the 1891 bill never became effective. Superintendent of Public Instruction, *Twenty-Third Biennial Report* (1925), p. 25.

18. Superintendent of Public Instruction, *Twenty-First Biennial Report* (1921), p. 12.

19. From the $1 million of the 1915-17 biennium, rural aid grew to $3 million in the mid-1920's, to $6 million in the early Depression years, then to $11 million in 1936-37, doubling approximately every 6 years. P.E. Hutchinson, legislative accountant, "Report to the Joint Legislative Committee, Fiftieth Legislature" (unpublished typewritten report in Mr. Hutchinson's personal files, March 1947).

20. Superintendent of Public Instruction, *Twenty-Second Biennial Report* (1924), p. 12. Constitutional limits were lifted, but statutory ones were still imposed.

21. Miss Blanton, a noted feminist and founder of Delta Kappa Gamma—a sorority for women in education—aroused strong loyalty and a crusading spirit on behalf of better schools among women teachers.

22. Starlin Marion Newberry Marrs had been a teacher and county school superintendent in Texas from 1885 to 1889, chief clerk of the state department from 1889 to 1890, superintendent of schools at Terrell until 1919, chief supervisor of high schools in the reorganized state department from 1919 to 1923, and successor to Miss Blanton as state superintendent.

23. The State Board of Vocational Education and the State Board of Education were combined in the same body by this legislation, and vocational rehabilitation was taken out of the charge of the eleemosynary institutions and placed under the State Board of Vocational Education—a plan unique to Texas which has worked efficiently and smoothly ever since.

24. Because Texas was a one-party state, the campaign for state superintendent was actually one between rival Democrats in an all-white primary rather than a contest in the general election. In the 1932 primary in July, Woods charged that C. N. Shaver had never completed high school, let alone attended Columbia Teachers College, the University of Chicago, or the University of Texas, as the incumbent claimed. *Austin Statesman*, July 17, 1932, p. 4.

25. Candidate Woods was asked to address a gathering at Comanche "protesting educational administrative policies and arbitrary methods and expenses." This meeting was said to be indicative of the feelings of small town and rural people at the time. *Austin Statesman,* July 13, 1932, p. 2.

26. "As a result of the adoption of the homestead amendment—a commendable step toward relieving real estate of its disproportionate tax burdens—the schools face a loss . . . of from one-fourth to one-third of the present state available school fund." Superintendent of Public Instruction, *Twenty-Seventh Biennial Report* (1932), p. 12.

27. N. S. Holland, *A Brief History of the Texas Association of School Administrators* (Chicago: Nystrom & Co., 1953), p. 42. In San Antonio, where approximately $2.6 million in unpaid taxes was owed to the city and school district, teachers were sent out during the summer of 1932 to call personally on the 250 biggest delinquents in hopes of collecting sufficient funds to pay the more than $500 million in back salaries owed them. *Austin Statesman*, July 4, 1932, p. 3.

28. Dr. Woods, as organizer and principal of the first rural high school in Texas (at Mart), was confident of his ability to come to the aid of the poor districts. He had also served as a county superintendent (McLennan Co.). He claimed to be, however, "in no sense a politician or even politically minded." *Austin Statesman*, paid political advertisement for Woods, July 3, 1932, p. 2.

29. Virtually every biennial report during Dr. Woods's administration emphasized the need for fewer small, inefficient units of administration and hailed the reduction in numbers of Texas districts.

30. The General Education Board of the Rockefeller Foundation financed the training of a specialist in research; the Jeanes Fund and the Julius Rosenwald Fund were supporters of supervisors of Negro education.

31. "It was said that Dr. Woods came to Austin with a bill in his pocket to abolish the State Board." Interview with Ruth Huey, director of homemaking education (retired), June 27, 1967.

32. Board of Education, *Fifth Biennial Report, 1936-1938* (1938), p. 15.

33. Superintendent of Public Instruction, *Twenty-Ninth Biennial Report* (1937), p. 23.

34. The state board could and did pursue independent courses of action, such as launching a second statewide survey of education in 1936 with the help of WPA funds. This survey disclosed little new information; the same old problems and inequities were again identified. It did, however, draw up the first atlas of school district boundaries ever made in Texas, thereby throwing the districting muddle into high relief.

35. The state superintendent himself earned only $5,000. Department of Education, "Payroll Summaries for 1948." (Unpublished report bound in looseleaf binder, in custody of F. M. Coffee, director of office services, Texas Education Agency.

36. As quoted by the Superintendent of Public Instruction, *Tenth Biennial Report* (1902), p. 33.

37. This was Henry F. Alves, later a division head in the U.S. Office of Education and director of the Kellogg Foundation's five-state project in educational administration.

38. Superintendent of Public Instruction, *Thirty-Fourth Biennial Report* (1946).

39. The group included such people as Sam Culpepper, E. L. Galyean, S. D. McAlister, R. H. Rhodes, Bascom Story, Tom Spence, Edgar A. Wilson, and Cecil Yarborough.

40. Superintendent of Public Instruction, *Twenty-Ninth Biennial Report* (1938), p. 21.

41. Superintendent of Public Instruction, *Thirty-Fourth Biennial Report* (1946), p. 22. The feud between Dr. Woods and the State Board of Education was still in progress, also; the State Board of Education had elected someone other than the state superintendent (its ex officio secretary) as executive secretary of vocational education—an action that had the effect of separating the operations of vocational education from the Department of Education for a brief but aggravating time. *Ibid*., p. 23.

42. *Ibid*., p. 23.

43. Rae Files Still, *The Gilmer-Aikin Bills* (Austin: The Steck Company, 1952), p. 13.

44. *Ibid*., p. 14.

45. *Ibid*.

46. *Ibid*., pp. 15-16.

47. Members of the committee coming from the House were Representative Claude Gilmer; Representative Ottis Lock, former superintendent of schools; and Mrs. Rae Files Still, chairman of the House Education Committee and a former classroom teacher. Members appointed by the Speaker were R. L. Thomas of Dallas; Peyton L. Townsend of Dallas; and J. C. Peyton of El Paso, director of the Texas Manufacturers' Association. From the Senate were Senator A. M. Aikin; Senator James E. Taylor; and Senator Gus Strauss. The president of the Senate (then lieutenant governor, later Governor) Allan Shivers appointed C. B. Downing, superintendent at Albany; J. W. Edgar, superintendent at Austin and later commissioner of education; and H. A. Moore, superintendent at Kerrville. The Governor appointed Beauford Jester; H. W. Stilwell, superintendent at Texarkana; B. F. Pittinger, former dean of education at the University of Texas; Nan Proctor, a teacher; Mrs. J. G. Smith, former president of the Texas PTA; J. Turrentine, former dean of education at Texas State College for Women; and Wright Morrow, Houston lawyer and National Democratic committeeman. *Ibid*., p. 19.

48. *Ibid*., p. 17.

49. Frederick Eby, professor emeritus of education at the University of Texas, testified later that he had been asked to serve on the committee but had declined because of his doubts about its impartiality. *Ibid*., p. 19.

50. *Ibid*., p. 23.

51. *Ibid*., pp. 24-25.

52. *Ibid*., pp. 28-33.

53. *Ibid*., pp. 34-35.

54. *Ibid.*, p. 40.

55. *Ibid.*, pp. 2-10.

56. The reason he did so is not precisely known, but the opinions and desires of some of his principal subordinates heavily influenced Dr. Woods's decision. *Ibid.*, p. 43.

57. *Ibid.*, p. 82.

58. *Ibid.*, p. 83.

59. *Ibid.*, p. 70.

60. *Ibid.*, pp. 71-73.

61. *Ibid.*, pp. 74-77.

62. Interview with Bascom Hayes, professor of educational administration, University of Texas, April 3, 1967.

63. Interview with Bascom Hayes, April 3, 1967.

64. Sturgeon is currently executive director of governmental and public relations with the Texas State Teachers Association. At the date mentioned, he was superintendent of New Boston, Texas, schools.

65. During World War II, Edgar had been superintendent at Orange, Texas, acquiring valuable experience as local administrator of the Lanham Act, the first "Federal Aid to Impacted Areas" school aid measure. From Orange, he became superintendent at Austin, then a city of more than 100,000. His experience was thus very broad, indeed unique, if one takes into account his service with the Gilmer-Aikin Committee.

66. One alternative any small district faces is consolidation, but often, after hearing the whole story, a school board will choose to increase its taxes rather than consolidate. The rate of voluntary consolidation remains about the same as it was during the thirties.

67. The Texas State Teachers Association, the Texas Vocational Association, and the Texas Council on Teacher Education all were conducting or about to begin studies of their own. The conference was attended by representatives of every professional education organization and school-related group in the state, from the PTA to the Texas Association of School Boards.

68. Through the 10 years from 1954 to 1963 the State Board of Education authorized 37 advisory commissions. They met for a mean period of approximately 1.5 years. Only 10 of them met for more than 2 years before completing their task and being disbanded. One of the 10 long-term commissions was on school accreditation and has been in existence continuously since 1918. Other than this commission, only the advisory commissions on administration of vocational education, on utilization of school facilities and personnel, on the project in teacher recruitment and education by television, on coordination of special education and vocational rehabilitation, and on state text selection took more than 3 years to reach closure.

69. Henry F. Alves, ed., *Five-Year Review of the Southwestern Cooperative Program in Educational Administration* (Austin: University of Texas, 1957), p. 44.

70. Warren Hitt and Henry F. Alves, *Educational Leadership: The Emerging Role of State Departments of Education* (Austin: University of Texas, 1953). This project also raised the status and effectiveness of the various voluntary associations of school administrators: Texas Association of School Boards; Texas Association of School Administrators; Texas Association of Supervisors and Curriculum Directors; and the Texas Association of Secondary School Principals.

71. Texas Research League, *Texas Public Schools Under the Minimum Foundation Program—An Evaluation, 1949-1954,* authorized revision and short version of the league's report (Austin: Texas Education Agency, 1954), p. 1.

72. *Ibid.*, pp. 2-14, passim.

73. Recommendation to redefine a scholastic as a child in average daily attendance was presented to the Texas Legislature in 1957, 1959, 1961, 1963, 1965, and 1966 without result. On the other hand, a recommendation that school districts be eligible for consolidation incentive aid payments was adopted by the Fifty-Eighth Legislature without benefit of recommendation. Successive recommendations are in *Recommendations for Legislative Consideration on Public Education in Texas* (Austin: Texas Education Agency, 1957, 1959, 1961, 1963, 1965, and 1966). These are short pamphlets prepared prior to each regular legislative session by the Texas Education Agency and distributed to legislators. They vary from 16 to 32 pages in length.

74. George Works, ed., *Texas Educational Survey Report*, Vol. I (Austin: Texas Educational Survey Commission, 1925), p. 241. This is an eight-volume report: Vol. I, *Organization and Administration*; Vol. II, *Financial Support*; Vol. III, *Secondary Education*; Vol. IV, *Educational Achievement*; Vol. V, *Courses of Study and Instruction*; Vol. VI, *Higher Education*; Vol. VII, *Vocational Education*; and Vol. VIII, *General Report.*

75. Bill Kinniell, ed., "Use of Teacher Demonstration Teams by a State Department of Education To Disseminate Information on New Educational Media," report of project under Title VII-B, NDEA, Austin, Texas, 1963, ERIC Document No. 003123, available from ERIC Document Reproduction Service, 4936 Fairmont Avenue, Bethesda, Maryland.

76. Texas Education Agency, *Forty-First Biennial Report* (Austin: The Agency, January 1959), p. 70. Among other tasks, the computer was used to develop Texas and local school norms for a statewide achievement and ability test program inaugurated in 1958.

BIBLIOGRAPHY

Public Documents

Texas. *Constitution* (1845, 1861, 1866, 1869, 1876 as amended).

—— *Declaration of Independence* (1836).

Books

Alves, Henry F., ed. *Five-Year Review of the Southwestern Cooperative Program in Educational Administration*. Austin: University of Texas, 1957.

Hitt, Warren, and Alves, Henry F. *Educational Leadership: The Emerging Role of State Departments of Education*. Austin: University of Texas, 1953.

Holland, N. S. *A Brief History of the Texas Association of School Administrators*. Chicago: Nystrom & Co., 1953.

Still, Rae Files. *The Gilmer-Aikin Bills*. Austin: The Steck Company, 1952.

Texas Education Agency. *Recommendations for Legislative Consideration on Public Education in Texas*. Austin: The Agency, 1957, 1959, 1961, 1963, 1965, and 1966.

Reports

Board of Education. *Biennial Reports*. Austin: The Board, 1936-68.

Kinniell, Bill, ed. "Use of Teacher Demonstration Teams by a State Department of Education To Disseminate Information on New Educational Media." Report of project under Title VII-B, NDEA, Austin, Texas, 1963. ERIC Document No. 003123. Available from ERIC Document Reproduction Service, 4936 Fairmont Avenue, Bethesda, Maryland.

Superintendents of Public Instruction. *Biennial Reports*. Austin: Department of Education, 1895-1968.

Texas Research League. *Texas Public Schools Under the Minimum Foundation Program–An Evaluation, 1949-1954*. Austin: Texas Education Agency, 1954.

Works, George, ed. *Texas Educational Survey Report*. 8 vols. Austin: Texas Educational Survey Commission, 1925.

Periodical

Austin Statesman. July 3, 4, 13, 17, 1932.

Unpublished Material

Department of Education. "Payroll Summaries for 1948." Unpublished report bound in looseleaf binder, in custody of F. M. Coffee, director of office services, Texas Education Agency.

Goodson, W. R. "The Program of School Accreditation in Texas." Unpublished report of the director, Division of School Accreditation, Texas Education Agency, 1962.

Hutchinson, P. E. "Report to the Joint Legislative Committee, Fiftieth Legislature." Unpublished typewritten report in Mr. Hutchinson's personal files, March 1947.

Other Sources

Hayes, Bascom. Interview with Hayes, The University of Texas in Austin, April 3, 1967.

Huey, Ruth. Interview with Miss Huey, director of homemaking education (retired), June 27, 1967.

Appendix A

TEXAS CHIEF STATE SCHOOL OFFICERS

Superintendents of Public Instruction

1866-67	Pryor Lea
1867-71	Edwin M. Wheelock
1871-74	Jacob C. DeGress
1874-84	O. H. Hollingsworth
1884-87	B. M. Baker
1887-90	O. H. Cooper
1890-91	H. C. Pritchett
1891-99	J. M. Carlisle
1899-1901	J. S. Kendall
1901-1905	Arthur Lefevre
1905-10	R. B. Cousins
1910-13	F. M. Bralley
1913-19	W. F. Doughty
1919-23	Annie Webb Blanton
1923-32	S. M. N. Marrs
1932	C. N. Shaver (Apr.–Oct.)
1932-33	L. W. Rogers
1933-51	L. A. Woods

State Commissioner of Education

1951-	J. W. Edgar

Appendix B

Chart I.--TEXAS EDUCATION AGENCY, 1962

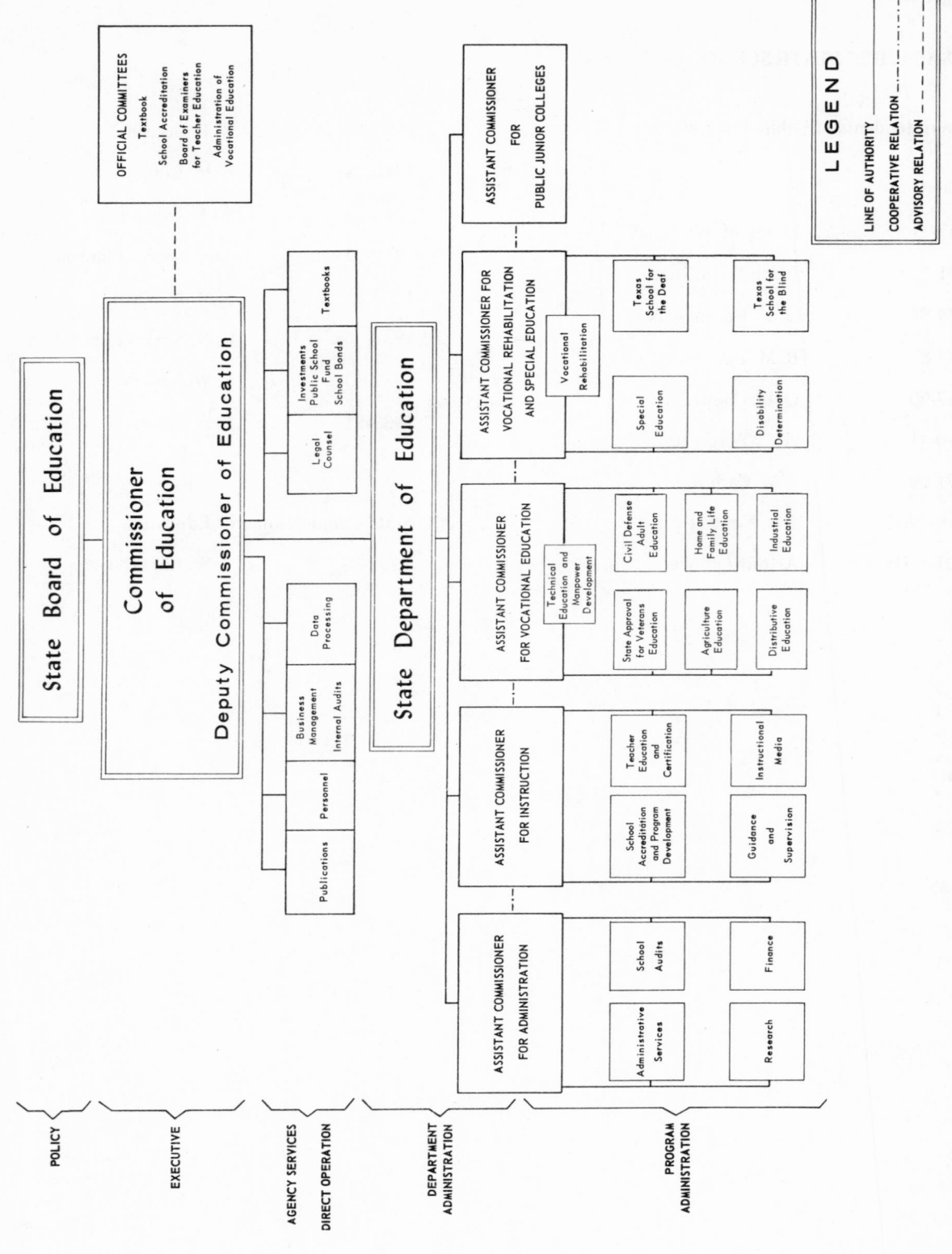

Appendix B

Chart II.--TEXAS EDUCATION AGENCY, 1968

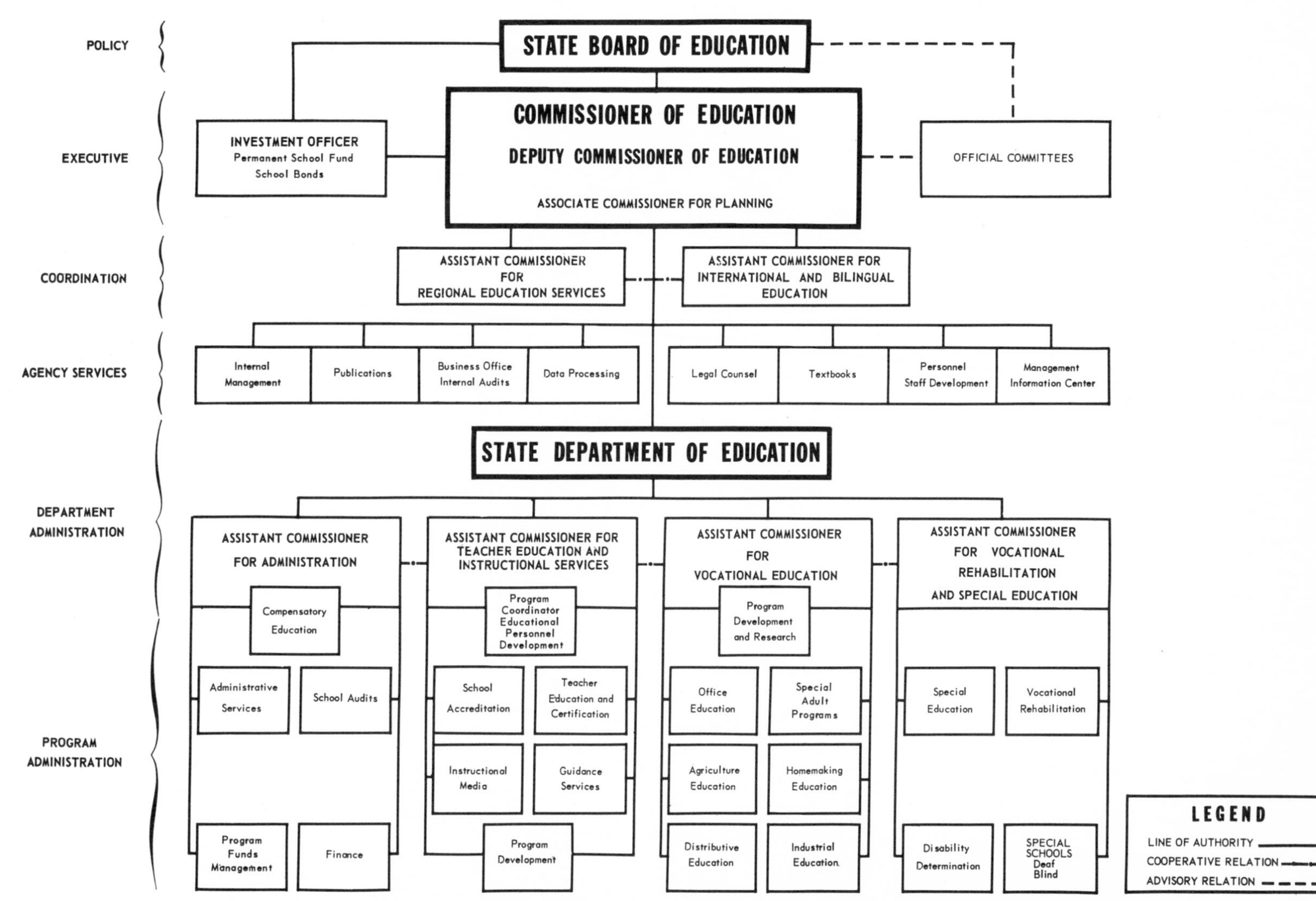
POLICY
EXECUTIVE
COORDINATION
AGENCY SERVICES
DEPARTMENT ADMINISTRATION
PROGRAM ADMINISTRATION
STATE BOARD OF EDUCATION
COMMISSIONER OF EDUCATION
DEPUTY COMMISSIONER OF EDUCATION
ASSOCIATE COMMISSIONER FOR PLANNING
INVESTMENT OFFICER
Permanent School Fund
School Bonds
OFFICIAL COMMITTEES
ASSISTANT COMMISSIONER FOR REGIONAL EDUCATION SERVICES
ASSISTANT COMMISSIONER FOR INTERNATIONAL AND BILINGUAL EDUCATION
Internal Management
Publications
Business Office Internal Audits
Data Processing
Legal Counsel
Textbooks
Personnel Staff Development
Management Information Center
STATE DEPARTMENT OF EDUCATION
ASSISTANT COMMISSIONER FOR ADMINISTRATION
Compensatory Education
Administrative Services
School Audits
Program Funds Management
Finance
ASSISTANT COMMISSIONER FOR TEACHER EDUCATION AND INSTRUCTIONAL SERVICES
Program Coordinator Educational Personnel Development
School Accreditation
Teacher Education and Certification
Instructional Media
Guidance Services
Program Development
ASSISTANT COMMISSIONER FOR VOCATIONAL EDUCATION
Program Development and Research
Office Education
Special Adult Programs
Agriculture Education
Homemaking Education
Distributive Education
Industrial Education
ASSISTANT COMMISSIONER FOR VOCATIONAL REHABILITATION AND SPECIAL EDUCATION
Special Education
Vocational Rehabilitation
Disability Determination
SPECIAL SCHOOLS Deaf Blind
LEGEND
LINE OF AUTHORITY
COOPERATIVE RELATION
ADVISORY RELATION

45 Utah

BOARD OF EDUCATION
Lerue W. Winget

Contents

DEVELOPING A PATTERN OF CENTRALIZED CONTROL OF EDUCATION PRIOR TO 1900

Education Fundamental to Mormonism

For 46 years preceding its admission as a state on January 4, 1896, Utah had been a territory, and 3 years prior to this a religious colony. During this time basic patterns were established, so an understanding of the educational views and efforts of the Mormon founders of the public school system, the acts of the territorial assembly, the regents' plan of control, and the area's social, economic, and religious problems is necessary for interpreting the organizational development and functions of the Office of State Superintendent of Public Instruction.

The first company of Mormon settlers who entered Salt Lake Valley in July 1847, like many who followed, had migrated from Illinois. Mormonism had come into existence when six original members founded a church in upstate New York in 1830. Building a membership and propagating their theological concepts made education especially important, and church leaders constantly encouraged it. To live the creed, the members had to be conversant with it. Members had to prepare themselves for effective proselyting if others were to accept the principles of the doctrine. Indeed, if the purpose of Mormon life was to be fulfilled, certain beliefs had to be understood and observed, all of them indicating that things of lasting value depended upon education: "Seek not for riches, but for wisdom" (1); "The glory of God is intelligence" (2); "Whatever principle of intelligence we attain unto in this life, it will rise with us in the resurrection" (3).

Territorial Superintendents Increase Centralization

These Mormon pioneers brought centralized control of education with them, and this has continued to be a basic characteristic of educational organization and administration in Utah, despite shifts and adaptations through periods of religious, economic, social, and political change. For instance, those who founded the University of Deseret in 1850 intended the board of regents to do more than organize and operate an institution of higher learning. In effect, the regents were to operate very much like a territorial education board, giving overall control and supervision to education throughout the territory. With the help of the university, the regents would provide a plan for administering the common schools throughout the proposed state. Governor Brigham Young gave additional impetus to a centralized plan of supervision and a uniform program in 1851 in a message to the Legislative Assembly:

> A Superintendent of Public Instruction, with a fixed salary, might be of incalculable benefit, at this early period of our national existence, in the formation of a uniform system of common schools, as well as an introduction system of public instruction . . . " (4).

The Legislative Assembly enacted into law the Governor's recommendations in October 1851, strengthening the authority of the chancellor and regents by authorizing them "to appoint a Superintendent of Primary Schools, for the Territory of Utah, under their supervision and discretionary control . . ." (5). Three years later, it amended the law, making it mandatory for the chancellor and regents to appoint a superintendent of common schools who would hold his office at the pleasure of the board.

Another basic law with respect to the common schools was enacted by the Territorial Legislature in 1852. This law initiated the establishment of local districts and trustees. The board of regents recommended this legislation in an attempt to make education available for all the people of the territory. The powers of local districts were limited, and the superintendent of the common schools was required to make a full and complete report, including enrollments, funds collected and expended, and the length of the school year. These new duties, combined with the individual leadership that the territorial superintendents displayed, gave them a significant role in developing a more centralized control of education.

Duties of Superintendents

The board of regents appointed Elias Smith as the first territorial superintendent of common schools in 1851, and he served until replaced by William Willis in 1856. Although the law was still vague and made superintendents responsible to the board of regents, the most difficult task for these early superintendents was to establish an effective relationship with the local districts. The local schools were under the direction of three local trustees, until an 1860 law created the office of county superintendent. The law listed the county official's duties, the most important being "to make an annual report to the territorial superintendent of common schools . . . stating the particulars contained in the trustees' and teachers' reports" (6). This provided a complete structure for school organization and administration, giving the territorial superintendent a line of administrative relationships extending down through county and local administrative officers to the teacher and, in effect, establishing the superintendent as the head of the territorial school system.

An 1890 law provided the territorial superintendent the legal basis for operating as the chief executive for the school organization, giving him almost the same authority as he has today. It allowed him to develop strong leadership as he labored for a uniform system of public schools. Superintendent Jacob S. Boreman stressed adequate reporting, rating of schools, the advantages of uniform textbook adoption, the necessity of carefully selecting and training teachers, the need for legislative action to provide uniform teachers' examinations, and the desirability of placing teacher certification within the central agency. The superintendent has had, since 1890, the legal responsibility of giving written answers to all questions concerning school law requested by local authorities. And he was charged by the same law with the business operation of the district schools and management of the revenues appropriated for their support (7).

The territorial superintendents were usually effective in recommending legislation. For instance, the compulsory attendance law passed in 1890, which required parents of children between 8 and 14 years to send them to school at least 16 weeks each school year—with a penalty for failing to do so—was devised by Superintendent Boreman. The law also required superintendents to visit schools. Although the laws had not previously required visits, superintendents had directly contacted districts and provided supervision, rendering invaluable service. In fact, by 1878, the superintendent found it necessary to enlist a few other people to help him check the progress of pupils and teaching methods during these visits. Sometimes he gave demonstrations and held conferences with the teachers and trustees. After the 1890 law made visiting mandatory, one superintendent reported: "The results of this experience, which the law requires me to give, have been most gratifying . . ." (8). Like other duties assumed by or thrust on superintendents, under their leadership this program of supervision contributed to the pattern of centralized control which developed prior to statehood.

Non-Mormons Influence Education

Most of the early Mormon pioneers were New Englanders who had endured persecution and hardships for their faith and were searching for a place where they might live their creed without interference. In establishing themselves in Utah, they took on a cultural oneness. After the completion of the transcontinental railroad in 1869, newcomers increasingly intruded on their haven. Also, the discovery of various mineral deposits throughout the territory brought capital and labor from the outside. In contrast to the particularly agrarian philosophy and life style of the Mormons, more and more "gentile" commercialists established themselves in Salt Lake City (9). This shift in the population's religious and social composition during the latter quarter of the nineteenth century brought friction between the Mormons and the non-Mormons. The non-Mormon newcomers were not willing to subject their youngsters to an education influenced by Mormon church leaders and objected to "paying taxes for maintenance of school buildings unless a public body established by civil law, and not the church, held title to the ground and schoolhouse, thereon . . ." (10).

The result was an interdenominational balance of common schools run by the Mormons and private schools operated by other Christian denominations. The Episcopal Church organized the first private school in 1867. In 1884, President Chester A. Arthur reported to Congress:

> The denominational schools now number 79 with an average of nearly 6,000 pupils in average daily attendance, many of whom are the children of Mormon parents. These schools are distributed as follows—Episcopalian, 5; Methodist, 10; Congregational, 26; Presbyterian, 35; Baptist, 2; Catholic, 1 (11).

Establishing a State Board of Education, 1896

When Utah was admitted to statehood in 1896, the constitution stated: "The general control and supervision of the public school system shall be vested in a State Board of Education, consisting of the Superintendent of Public Instruction, and such other persons as the Legislature may provide" (12). The Legislature followed this mandate with an act in April 1896 stating:

> The State Board of Education shall consist of the State Superintendent of Public Instruction, the president of the State University, the principal of the State Agricultural College and two other persons of large experience and eminent professional standing to be appointed by and with the consent of the Senate for a period of four years. The State Superintendent of Public Instruction shall be Chairman of the State Board . . . (13).

The board met for the first time in June 1896 in the office of the first state superintendent of public instruction, John R. Park.

The State Superintendent's Major Functions, 1896-1900

In addition to duties that had developed during the territorial period, the new state superintendent took on two additional functions of major significance. One was to develop a uniform statewide system of administration and supervision by consolidating districts and county units. Many years before he became state superintendent, Park had advocated a law providing for the consolidation of all school districts into county school districts except in cities of more than 5,000 population. Such a bill was introduced in 1888, but it failed, and no similar legislation was proposed until after statehood (14). A year after Park took over the state superintendency, he explained in detail in his first report a proposed county-unit system, carefully pointing to its advantages. Courageously, he stated: "I urge at this time that the adoption of this plan be seriously considered for our schools, to be known to us as the county or county district plan, as the county is the lowest available civil unit for us" (15). His proposal attracted increasing support, but no action took place before his death in 1900.

The second major function assumed by the state superintendent was teacher certification. When the 1896 Legislature created the superintendent's office and the State Board of Education, it specifically authorized the board to issue state diplomas and state certificates. During these early years, the primary concern of the board was teacher certification, and it is entirely possible that this problem, earlier the focus of numerous recommendations by territorial superintendents, was a strong factor in the creation of the board itself. Certainly it had been a major reason for the chartering of the University of Deseret, and territorial superintendents had complained for years about the confusion in the existing system of teacher examinations and certificates under the 1852 law, which allowed county boards of examiners, consisting of three men appointed by the county court, to issue certificates. With no legal standards, a wide variety of practices had developed. Although the 1890 Legislature gave the territorial commissioner authority to issue certificates valid in any county, it also gave cities the right to certify their own teachers, and the appointed county boards of examiners also continued to grant certification.

DEVELOPING THE OFFICE OF THE STATE SUPERINTENDENT OF PUBLIC INSTRUCTION

The administrative arm of the state board is the Office of the State Superintendent of Public Instruction, consisting of all the employees who assist the board in providing general control and supervision of the public school system. Through the years, the office has been referred to in official documents, superintendents' biennial reports, and the statutes by many names, such as "state school office staff," "office of the state superintendent," and "state department of education." Currently, it is referred to as the Office of the State Superintendent of Public Instruction, or simply the office.

The development of its structure and organization was inevitably aligned to the changing structure and organization of the state board, since the state superintendent was both chairman of the board and head of the office from the beginning of statehood until 1951. Before 1896, the territorial superintendent had served either under the board of regents of the University of Deseret or with no board at all, the latter case holding true a major portion of the time. The composition of the board remained fairly constant from 1896 to 1915, when the number of members increased from five to nine, the Governor appointing six instead of two, which increased lay participation in forming policy for the state school system. Appendix B, Supplement 1, summarizes the evolution of both the superintendent and the state board, pointing up some of the changes whereby one affected the other.

Despite the increased lay support, the board was much criticized. For one thing, the Governor traditionally appointed two educators to the board along with the three ex officio educators; thus, five of the nine members were engaged in educational work. In 1926, a survey group recommended that the Governor appoint all nine members, who would then select the superintendent and set his salary without specific legal restrictions. No legislation resulted, but the agitation continued. Seven years later, another commission conducted another study and ended with similar recommendations.

In his 1934 biennial report, Superintendent Charles H. Skidmore strongly recommended that the state pass a constitutional amendment eliminating the state superintendent from the ballot and providing for the board to be appointed by the Governor or elected by the people. The House had passed such a bill in the previous session with little opposition, but it failed by one vote to get the necessary two-thirds majority in the Senate. With the platforms of both major political parties favoring such legislation, it seemed certain that it would be passed by the 1935 Legislature. A law did pass which adjusted the method of selecting the board, a method followed for the next 16 years, but did not change its relationship to the superintendent. Why the Legislature did not act favorably on the superintendent's recommendation is something of a mystery. Skidmore failed to give the reasons in his next report, but it could be that local school district personnel and board members effectively lobbied for the law that passed.

The issue did not die. The Legislature authorized the Governor to appoint a fact-finding commission to study the school system and state educational institutions in 1939; the commission's report the following year again advised that the state board select the state superintendent. Ten years later, the National Education Association conducted another survey at the request of the state board and came to the same conclusion.

From 1928 to 1949, nearly every superintendent's biennial report, supported by every survey but two since 1926, recommended that the board be made an elective body with the authority to appoint the state superintendent. Despite the efforts of strong spokesmen like Superintendent Skidmore and his predecessor, Superintendent C. N. Jensen, it was E. Allen Bateman, a tall, strong-willed man, who provided the leadership needed to finally achieve success. In stating his case, Dr. Bateman made the following claims:

> No state which has its chief state school officer appointed by the State Board of Education has ever changed this method of appointment.
>
> To permit the people of the state to control the state public school system, they should elect the members of the State Board of Education. To permit the State Board to be responsible for the proper execution of policies and procedures which it adopts, the Board should appoint its chief administrative officer. The members of the State Board of Education should be elected by the people, probably by judicial district areas, as at present, and by a non-partisan method of election. The present conventions of school board members should be used as nominating conventions, with the right of supplemental nomination by petition, and election should be held in December at the time of the regular district school board election (16).

As recommended by Dr. Bateman, the necessary constitutional amendments were submitted to the people in the 1950 general election, and they passed. The constitution now reads:

> The general control and supervision of the public school system shall be vested in a State Board of Education, the members of which shall be elected as provided by law. The board shall appoint the State Superintendent of Public Instruction, who shall be executive officer of the board (17).

When the 1951 Legislature failed in its regular session to enact the legislation demanded by the amendments, a special session called that June passed a law providing for a nine-member elected board which would appoint the state superintendent—the climax of a 25-year effort.

Changes in Size and Structure of the Office, 1896-1950

Figure 1 shows that from statehood until the outbreak of World War II, the office changed very little in size. In fact,

Figure 1. – PROFESSIONAL AND CLERICAL STAFFING LEVELS, OFFICE OF THE STATE SUPERINTENDENT OF PUBLIC INSTRUCTION, 1910-66

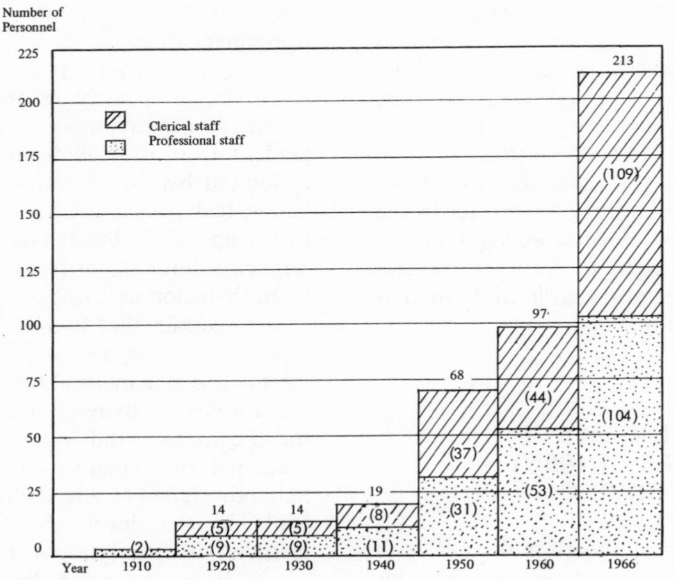

Source:
Biennial Reports of the State Superintendent of Public Instruction, 1910-60; *Personnel Records,* Office of the State Superintendent of Public Instruction, December 31, 1966.

the professional staff consisted of only the state superintendent and his deputy until 1910, increasing to only 11 professional people during the next 30 years. These positions were established by statute until 1921, when the state board was given authority to appoint its own staff. Most of the expansion from 1910 to 1940 resulted from federal support of state vocational educational programs and the addition of full-time directors for secondary schools, elementary schools, health and physical education, teacher certification, and research and statistics. Four of the nine professional positions added during this period were in the area of vocational education, supported in part by federal funds.

The number of professionals nearly tripled from 1940 to 1950, expanding to 31. The secretarial staff increased even more, jumping from 8 to 37. This growth was due primarily to the office's becoming involved in federally aided programs in national defense, veterans' training, vocational rehabilitation, and the school lunch program. By 1950, 71 percent of the office's 68 employees were working in federally supported activities (18).

Examples of patterns of organization followed by the office prior to 1950 are found in Appendix B.

Growth from 1950 to 1965

The office has had its greatest expansion since 1960. It had earlier increased in staff from 68 to 97 (43 percent) between 1950 and 1960. Staff size has more than doubled since then, and it now stands at over 200. The office not only initiated new programs but expanded and diversified its responsibilities in almost every area. From 1951 to 1966, elementary, secondary, and vocational education, special educational services, research and planning, and finance and publications received considerable boosts, attributable in large measure to the National Defense Education Act of 1958, which especially influenced elementary and secondary curriculum staffing. Table 1 shows systematic staff growth in research and planning, finance and publications, vocational education, and special educational services. A rather startling expansion of the vocational rehabilitation staff during these years was due to the integration of services for the visually handicapped with the general rehabilitation program in 1964.

The rapid increase in the office's personnel in the areas of elementary and secondary education, instructional media, research and planning, finance and publications, and vocational rehabilitation has caused concern among legislators, others holding political office, and local school district personnel. The latter in particular are apprehensive about the possibility of additional state control as well as an increase in federal control.

To cope with its expanding responsibilities, the office has had to make organizational adjustments as shown in Appendix B. A second deputy superintendent was appointed in 1962 in a realignment of responsibilities under the deputies; prior to this, directors and heads of institutions reported directly to the state superintendent. The 1964 chart reflects Superintendent T. H. Bell's efforts to redeploy his staff and consolidate smaller, closely related units into larger divisions. Those services having to do primarily with instruction carried out in local districts for grades K-12 and on the adult level were to be administered through divisions grouped under a deputy superintendent for instruction. A deputy for administration was given jurisdiction over services not primarily instructional and those having to do with post-high school or special institutions. The 1966 chart shows the addition of a third deputy superintendent with responsibility for post-high school institutions formerly assigned to the deputy for administration. An administrative assistant also has been added.

Table 1. – STAFF CHANGES IN STATE DEPARTMENT OF EDUCATION BY MAJOR ORGANIZATIONAL UNIT, 1951 THROUGH APRIL 1966

Organizational unit	Number of personnel			
	1951	1961	1965	April 1966
Administrative	4.0	6.0	6.0	8.0
Elementary & secondary education	4.0	14.6	15.3	23.0
Vocational education	20.0	14.0	21.0	18.5[a]
Special educational services	.0	4.8	7.5	16.0
Instructional media	.0	.7	2.2	10.0
Teacher personnel	4.0	5.8	6.0	7.0
Research & planning	.0	2.0	8.5	13.0
Finance & publications	6.0	9.5	16.5	25.0
School food services	5.0	6.0	7.5	6.5
Rehabilitation	19.0	39.0	90.0	114.0
Special projects	.0	1.0	2.0	2.0
Total	62.0	103.4	182.5	243.0

Source:
Fiscal records of the Utah Department of Education for the years indicated.

[a]Figure for April 1966 adjusted to exclude personnel supported by vocational education funds but assigned to other divisions.

PROGRAMS AND SERVICES

The Office of Public Instruction conducts the services and programs for which the state board is responsible and which are essential to the general control and supervision of the public school system. As in other state education agencies, it helps the board perform two roles: (a) as a regulatory agency for the public elementary and secondary schools, and (b) as a governing agency for several special programs operated on a statewide basis.

The office assumed responsibility early in its history for establishing a teacher certification program, developing a uniform statewide system of administration and supervision by consolidating school districts under county boards, providing direction for the high school movement, interpreting laws, disbursing school funds, and giving leadership to the instructional program. Services required in the early years of statehood were relatively simple in nature. Today, in our rapidly changing society, both education and the services required of the office are increasing in number and complexity.

The Impact of Federal Assistance Programs

In recent years and particularly since 1958, federal aid programs affecting education have proliferated, forcing changes in both the nature and scope of the office's services. Relatively large sums are now available to the office under the National Defense Education Act of 1958, the Manpower Development and Training Act of 1961, the Vocational Education Act of 1963, the Economic Opportunity Act of 1964, and the Elementary and Secondary Education Act of 1965. This has placed the office in a strong leadership-regulatory role by involving it in program planning and in processing, approving, and distributing federal money to local school districts.

In 1965, under Title I of ESEA, the state approved district projects and distributed over $2.8 million and rendered consultant services for programs designed to help the educationally disadvantaged child. Programs for instructional media resources, vocational education, manpower development and training, statistics, equipment and materials for subject areas termed critical for national defense, and guidance and counseling have demanded new or expanded administrative and consultant services, placing the office's personnel in an evaluative role and increasing their contacts and communications with the local school districts.

Although most federal programs have changed and strengthened the role of the office, there are two exceptions: ESEA Title III and the Manpower Development and Training Act. Title III, which supports the establishment of innovative demonstration centers, is administered by the U.S. Office of Education directly with local districts. Project approval rests with the Office of Education and not with the state superintendent, although the state's recommendations are solicited. Funds under the Manpower Act are channeled through the U.S. Department of Labor. Although the need, type, and location of programs are worked out in cooperation with the state superintendent, they are ultimately determined by the U.S. Employment Service.

On the other hand, some federal programs have increased the office's capabilities with 100 percent grants for administering the acts or specifically for strengthening selected service areas. All federal programs administered by the office provide funds for state administration and supervision or for program strengthening. Two that are specifically geared to fortify the office's management and leadership roles are Title X of NDEA and Title V of ESEA. Title X permits the office to strengthen its data-processing management, programing, management operation, keypunch, pupil, staff, and property accounting functions. Title V has enabled the office to employ an administrative assistant to the state superintendent; a chief accountant; an administrator for the instructional media division; specialists in audiovisual materials, education of the physically and mentally handicapped, and art and music instruction; a specialist in teacher certification and training; a specialist in school accreditation; and a publications editor and typist for curriculum development. It also financed an outside management study and provided $40,000 for special curriculum development projects in 1966.

The impact of these federal aid programs on the office's service capabilities are illustrated by Table 2. As of

Table 2. – PROFESSIONAL POSITIONS IN THE OFFICE OF THE STATE SUPERINTENDENT OF PUBLIC INSTRUCTION IN RELATION TO METHOD OF FINANCING, APRIL 1966[a]

Position level	Total pos.	State funds	Match. funds	Fed. funds	Priv. funds
Office of state superintendent	4	3	. . .	1	. . .
Division administrators	9	5	3	1	. . .
Coordinators, specialists, counselors, teachers, managers	121	19	85	16	1
Total	134	27	88	18	1
Percent	100%	20%	66%	13%	1%

Source:

Division of Finance and Publications, Office of the State Superintendent of Public Instruction.

[a]Excludes personnel employed by the institutions controlled by the State Board of Education.

April 1966, 106 (79 percent) of the 134 professional positions were subsidized in full or in part by federal funds; only 27 positions (20 percent) were supported entirely by state funds. Anticipated federal and private expenditures for the 1966 fiscal year accounted for more than 53 percent of the office's total, compared to approximately 31 percent in 1950.

Actions Stimulating the Office's Educational Leadership

The Legislature has recently moved to help the office develop its leadership capabilities and supervisory services. For example, it has earmarked over $100,000 in mineral-leasing funds annually for research projects approved by the office. It has increased state aid to school districts, particularly for vocational education, special education, libraries, and extended-year and summer programs, and has placed additional responsibilities on the office for setting standards, approving and distributing grants, and providing consultant services.

State superintendents themselves, recognizing the increasing demands on public education, have taken steps to improve and extend staff leadership in service capabilities. They have made concerted efforts to recruit outstanding persons with advanced degrees and wide experience. The state board has released time to professional personnel for advanced training. The office has developed new and meaningful relationships with such organizations as the Society of Superintendents, the Utah School Boards Association, and the Coordinating Council of Higher Education. And it has assigned supervisory responsibilities to local school districts for certain facets of the new bilevel teacher certification program. A recent survey by a management consultant firm found that 29 of 38 responding districts rated the office's staff either "above" or "well above" average. No district ranked the staff below average.

Post-High School and Special Institutions

The state constitution charges the state board with controlling and supervising the public school system, which is defined as kindergartens, common schools, high schools, institutions for the deaf and blind, an agricultural college, a university, and such other schools as the Legislature may establish. In practice, however, the state board has never attempted to exercise control over the universities, the Utah State Industrial School, or the Utah Training School, although it did serve as the governing board for the public junior colleges for many years.

Utah has no locally controlled, public, post-high school educational institutions. The College of Eastern Utah (formerly Carbon Junior College) is a branch of the University of Utah; Snow Junior College is a branch of Utah State University; and the three other 2-year post-high school institutions–Dixie Junior College, Utah Trade Technical Institute at Provo, and Salt Lake Trade Technical Institute–are controlled by the State Board of Education. The Coordinating Council of Higher Education coordinates these five along with all other public higher education institutions. Snow College was a state school from 1932 until 1951. On the other hand, the Salt Lake Trade Technical Institute and Utah Trade Technical Institute at Provo have been operated by the state board since their establishment.

During the early 1960's, the control of these institutions received considerable attention. The Coordinating Council of Higher Education sponsored legislation introduced in 1965 to create a junior college commission to govern them, but it was fought strenuously by the state board, its staff, and the institutions under its control. The bill passed the Senate but failed in the House.

A School for the Deaf was established in connection with the University of Utah in 1884. Along with the School for the Blind, established on the campus in Ogden 12 years later when Utah became a state, it is under the direction of the state board. The 1896 law stated that these schools were to develop self-respecting, self-supporting individuals who, in spite of their handicaps, could sustain themselves in competition with so-called normal members of society.

Traditionally, the presidents of the post-high school institutions under the state board's control and the superintendent of the schools for the deaf and blind have brought their agendas to the state board for approval monthly. Prior to 1961, each reported directly to the state superintendent to work out his agenda. From 1961 to 1965, they reported to the deputy superintendent for administration, and since 1966, to the new deputy superintendent for institutions.

Adult Education

In 1934, in the nadir of the Depression, the Legislature authorized every district board of education to raise and appropriate funds to establish classes in general adult education and appropriated $20,000 to the state board to assist them. This state support was reduced to $15,000 for the 1937-39 biennium, and to only $10,000 per biennium in the years after World War II, distributed on a basis of $51.50 to each class, approved by the state superintendent. This state support to the school districts continued to diminish until it ceased altogether.

The state board had appointed a supervisor of family life for adults in 1945, but it was the 1958-59 school year before the first full-time director of general education, supported by a grant from the National Association of Public School Adult Educators, was appointed to the office. When the grant expired and the director accepted a position at the University of Utah, a part-time director replaced him. In 1965, another full-time specialist was appointed, half of his salary coming from Title II-B of the Economic Opportunity Act of 1964 for adult basic education programs.

By the 1965-66 school year, 32,067 persons were enrolled in 1,565 classes, with 12,061 completing requirements for graduation from adult high schools in 503 classes. An additional 1,240 were enrolled in the adult basic education programs funded by Title II-B. Most of the funds for adult education were coming from fees paid by the enrollees, which, of course, kept many who needed the program from signing up. The school districts supplied some funds, and about $29,000 was appropriated by the Legislature to support general adult education for the 1965-67 biennium.

Communication and Public Relations

Too often the public has not been aware of the importance and the activities of the state superintendent's office, despite its publications and its efforts to build public relations. Eighteen newsletters are mailed to members of the education profession today, prepared somewhat sporadically by various divisions. Most of these started in the late 1950's or early 1960's, but the "News Letter of the Division of Health, Physical Education and Recreation" began as early as 1929. Of special interest are the office's official policy statements titled "Items to Superintendents," which are mailed to all district superintendents only "when something happens." They usually contain administrative procedures, statistical information from the finance division, or information about programs administered by other divisions. The content is approved by the administrative staff.

To inform employees about meetings, administrative policy and practices, and other personnel items, the office has published an interior newsletter called "The Education Courier" since 1962. In September 1966, it became a weekly publication.

In the near future, regular monthly news bulletins, containing information of more general interest to educators than the smaller, more specialized newsletters, will be prepared by the modern, well-equipped publication section, possibly replacing a number of the smaller ones. A full-time staff member is now in charge of public relations and dissemination of information, and it may be that the office eventually will distribute a weekly column to newspapers across the state. The office also will use radio, television, and regular announcements to help explain its functions to the public.

Curriculum and Instruction

One of the office's central concerns is the quality of instruction in the schools—the learnings planned for students, the broad objectives to which these should lead, and the performance of teachers. This concern has manifested itself in such activities as suggesting educational objectives to the schools; developing courses of study; evaluating textbooks; recommending, and in some cases approving, expenditures for materials and equipment; encouraging or actually setting forth guidelines for organization, accreditation, and quality of education; promoting new curriculum programs; encouraging and directing the development of library and media services, and approving expenditures of special state and federal funds in this area; and providing supervisory and consultative services to assist program improvement, in-service development, and innovation.

Objectives. The office has always been concerned with establishing objectives of education, but in a rather informal way prior to 1953, when the Legislature mandated that the state course of study committee define the aims, purposes, philosophy, and objectives of the public elementary and secondary schools. With the office's leadership, educators and laymen throughout the state worked out a statement which was finally approved by the state course of study committee in 1956 (19). It has served as a guidepost for curriculum development in Utah since that time.

Course of Study. Prior to statehood, textbooks and the teacher's personal judgment largely determined the content of subjects taught in the schools. But in 1894, a detailed course of study—characteristic of this period, when formalism and standardization held sway across the nation—was published for the common schools, grades 1 through 9. The purposes were to (a) help develop and systematize the schoolwork, (b) serve as an outline specifying the textbook pages to be covered per period of time, and (c) stimulate improvement by suggesting desirable teaching methods and philosophies.

Following the recommendation of the state superintendent, the 1907 Legislature ended the old method of voluntary course of study development by providing for a state course of study committee. Under the leadership of State Superintendent A. C. Nelson, the committee developed a course of study for each subject the following year, obviously influenced by the concepts of John Dewey, G. Stanley Hall, and others. State Superintendent E. G. Gowens initiated a greater effort to relate curriculum to live situations and to develop courses of study that would see curriculum making and teaching as one extended process. In 1916, he helped devise a uniform minimum curriculum, providing the opportunity, at the district and school levels, for adaptation to local needs, using the 6-6 plan of organization as a basis.

For the next 30 years, courses were infrequently reviewed, but in 1946, the office provided for continuous review. Curriculum committees were organized in each elementary and secondary subject field to help the office and the state course of study committee. The composition of these curriculum committees was altered in 1959 to ensure a more orderly procedure for adopting courses of study.

Currently, specialists in the office work with curriculum committees continuously involved in developing courses of study. Teachers, administrators, supervisors, and college faculty cooperate with the office staff to produce curriculum guides for each subject area. Financing these committees has proven difficult; until recent federal legislation brought financial relief, committee members had to be subsidized by their local districts.

Textbook Adoption. Although the territorial superintendents had led many efforts to bring about uniformity in textbooks almost from the time of the first settlements, the constitution gave neither the Legislature nor the state board the power to prescribe them for the schools. Until the State Textbook Commission was formed in 1909, the state superintendent called conventions of district superintendents to adopt textbooks.

In the early years of statehood, there was little correlation between course of study development and textbook adoption. As time passed, the relationship changed, at least in theory, from textbook domination of the course of study to a situation in which the textbook was adopted as a tool in teaching a course. Actually, adoption developed as a highly centralized program, because until 1935 only one book was adopted for each course. A trend toward multiple adoptions began in that year. Provisions were made in 1941 to combine the membership of the course of study committee and the textbook commission, thus facilitating correlation between courses of study and textbooks.

Even more flexibility has developed during the past two decades. In recent years, the same committee that develops curriculum guides has evaluated the textbooks, and its recommendations are acted on by the State Course of Study Committee-Textbook Commission. New textbooks are evaluated and considered for adoption each year, with the official adoption list distributed annually to those who need it. Adoption is for four years.

Standards, Accreditation, and Quality. The first standards for high schools, established in 1911, were largely quantitative—such as requiring a 9-month school term. Periodic revisions were frequently the result of new programs for financial support. In 1926, when the office was making a vigorous effort to secure accreditation from the Northwest Association of Secondary and Higher Schools, a new state accreditation program was developed for upgrading high schools. Gradually the association replaced the state, accrediting 84 of the 93 public and private high schools in 1966.

After the city of Ogden inaugurated the first junior high program in 1910, curriculum and instruction naturally oriented around its pattern as the junior high school movement spread rapidly. A statement of evaluative criteria gradually developed and, when published in 1960, drew considerable attention across the nation. When the state board approved a voluntary program of state accreditation for junior high schools 3 years later, these criteria were used as a part of the process. By the end of the 1965-66 school year, 17 junior high schools were accredited.

From the first decade of the century, occasional efforts were made to establish standards for elementary schools. When the board devised a voluntary program for accrediting junior high schools, it also approved one for the elementary schools. But because no adequately developed criteria and procedures had been devised, actual accreditation was delayed until after the close of 1965.

The office has attempted to improve the quality of instruction throughout the state in a number of ways. Periodically, it has secured the board's approval to upgrade high school graduation requirements and programs of study, the most recent major revisions occurring in 1957 and 1958 (see Appendix C). It also carried out a school merit-rating program from 1953 until the 1961 Legislature declined to appropriate further money for the program. Utah has never had a prescribed statewide standardized testing program, but the office does list recommended tests and requires that only approved tests be used if the users claim reimbursement under Title V of NDEA. All districts conduct their own testing programs with consultant help from the office.

In keeping with its long-held interest in quality education, the office has given leadership to curriculum enrichment and expansion. For instance, during World War I, when the nation found itself industrially unprepared and many of its young men physically unfit for military service, it gave special attention to vocational education and health education. Agriculture, home economics, trade and industrial education, distributive education, and health and physical education all were added to the curriculum.

The rapid technological changes and the social, economic, and political stresses of the period since World War II have demanded more and better education for an enlarged population. This has challenged the office to further enrich and expand the curriculum, resulting in further additions such as driver education and programs for the disadvantaged. Title III of NDEA, ESEA, and the Vocational Education Act of 1963 have been a major influence in stimulating richer offerings in vocational subjects, science, mathematics, foreign languages, social studies, English, and reading. Another new curricular emphasis that has influenced most of the subject areas was that of a state-sponsored effort to strengthen America through education.

Instructional Media Services. As early as 1911, the Legislature delegated the responsibility for promoting new and better libraries to the state board. Howard R. Driggs, the first man assigned to the task, visited libraries, called conventions of librarians, and arranged for librarianship courses at the University of Utah. Through the years, the office exerted efforts to bring about greater cooperation between public and school libraries; improve library management; hold annual conventions for librarians; and recommend standards, methods, and booklists. The County Library Law enacted in 1917, encouraged and supported by the state superintendent and his staff, improved the state's library picture considerably. Following directly on county consolidation, this county library system was very effective in establishing libraries, in promoting after-school education, and in supplementing the activities of the schools in general. For many years, the office carried out these library activities in a commendable way, although little staff time seems to have been provided for them between 1946 and 1964.

Following the enactment of a federal library law in 1957, the Legislature established a State Library Commission to oversee the public libraries and to cooperate with the schools and other agencies in carrying out its work. Although the library commission had professional librarians on its staff, it was not until 1965 that the state superintendent's office could budget for a professional librarian to give leadership to school library work. The Legislature provided special funds for the libraries in the districts, and Title II of ESEA allotted money for library resources; both of these acts, coming at a time when school libraries were at a low ebb, were welcomed with open arms despite federal red tape.

The office became interested in educational television when the Federal Communications Commission allocated Channel 7 to Utah for this purpose in 1951. Superintendent Bateman, anxious to take advantage of this action, persuaded the Legislature to enact a bill in 1953 establishing a Utah Educational Television Foundation, only to have Governor J. Bracken Lee veto it after the Legislature had adjourned. The very next year, an interested group formed a nonprofit corporation, also named the Utah Educational Television Foundation, which established a broadcasting station for Channel 7 in cooperation with the University of Utah on its campus and commenced operating on a limited basis in 1957. When the office received an appropriation for ETV the following year, it appointed a specialist to provide statewide leadership. More assistance was ensured when the Joint Committee on Educational Television, consisting of state board members and the Coordinating Council of Higher Education, was organized in 1961.

With money from ESEA, the office established for the first time an educational media division, bringing under one head library services, audiovisual services, ETV, and related services. In addition to supplying leadership, this division approved district applications for special state and federal funds and for library services and materials.

Kindergarten and Preschool Education. Although the constitution included kindergarten as a part of the public schools, Dr. Park, the first state superintendent, took a strangely negative view toward making kindergarten an integral part of the system. His successor, Emma J. McVicker, the only woman state superintendent in Utah's history, took the opposite view. Following her urgings, several laws were passed in 1902 promoting kindergarten for children from 4 to 6 years old. By the 1910-11 school year, over 11,000 children were enrolled. To further this progress, the State Federation of Women's Clubs strongly urged the state board to send another message encouraging all districts with the required 2,000 population to establish kindergartens. Today, all districts have kindergartens, most of them operating the full year. Since 1921, the office has provided for the kindergarten program, working closely with local districts, and since 1964 has cooperated with local representatives of the Office of Economic Opportunity in encouraging Head Start programs for preschool children.

Summer and Extended-Year Programs. Prior to 1964, most of the public school programs were limited to 9 months, the exceptions being summer kindergartens and summer programs for vocational agriculture and homemaking. Through the combined efforts of local districts and the office in 1965, the Legislature was persuaded to provide $800,000 for conducting minimum programs, including basic and enriched courses, curriculum development, and in-service activities for teachers. The state board was responsible for the standards for these programs. The results after the first year were good, and there was every indication that the program would continue, since practically every district participated.

Educational Opportunity for Exceptional Children. The Legislature initiated its first special education programs for handicapped children in 1953 by authorizing state financial assistance for districts operating classes for such children. The state board then approved both general and special standards for children who were mentally retarded, those needing speech and hearing correction, those needing remedial help, those who were deaf or hard of hearing, those who were blind or partially seeing, and those who were hospitalized or homebound. By the 1965-66 school year, 652 special classes were serving 17,546 children.

The state superintendent received permission from the board in 1957 to establish a committee that would advise the districts on how to educate gifted children. Following a tentative report 3 years later, the committee turned in a final report in 1962 which evoked such diverse reactions that the board could not agree to approve it. Some members were concerned that intellectual snobbishness would be encouraged. Finally, the board did approve an advanced placement program for faster students, worked out in cooperation with higher education institutions and assisted by a Ford Foundation grant. The program has developed rapidly.

Legal Services

In 1890, the Legislature passed an act with the following provisions:

> The state superintendent shall advise with superintendents and with school boards and other school officers upon all matters involving the welfare of the schools. He shall, when requested by superintendents or school officers, give them written answers to all questions concerning the school law. His decisions shall be held to be correct and final until set aside by a court of competent jurisdiction or by subsequent legislation (20).

This statute is generally regarded by students of school law to be well designed, since it is unsound to require the courts "to answer a purely educational question as distinguished from a purely legal one. . ." (21). It has not been challenged but has been discussed by lawyers, judges, and school people. In a court case decided by the Utah Supreme Court, the justice who wrote the opinion in which the majority concurred referred to it as "an unusual statute, where one not an attorney may act in that capacity . . ." (22). He did not challenge the law, but advised the defendant to seek the legal counsel of the state superintendent.

State Superintendent C. N. Jensen wrote to the attorney general in 1924 asking for an opinion on a question raised by a member of a local district board of education and passed along the board member's letter. The attorney general, considering this a request from an individual and not an official request from the board of education, advised Jensen as follows:

> It is the policy of this office not to advise individuals relative to matters of this kind and I believe you will be safe in following the same policy. You, by law, are the legal advisor of school boards and in this instance the school board has not asked you for advice or an opinion. You should hold yourself in a position to advise the board, should they so desire, and not attempt to advise individuals on questions involving the powers and duties of the board. By following this policy I find it avoids friction and is the safer policy to pursue, under the conditions (23).

Attorney General Joseph Chez issued an opinion to Superintendent Charles H. Skidmore in March 1933 on the state superintendent's rendering opinions to public school officers, concluding that since a local board of education "is not a legal part of or subdivision of the county, but rather an independent corporation, [that] the county attorney is not the official legal advisor to the local board of education" (24). He further distinguished between the legal advice given by the attorney general to state officers and the answers furnished local school superintendents by the state superintendent, concluding that—

> This section of the Constitution [the section which deals with the Attorney General] provides, and the law also further provides that the Attorney General is adviser for the Superintendent of Public Instruction, thus the several Boards of Education seek legal advice from the Attorney General's office through the State Superintendent of Public Instruction.
>
> It is my opinion that the several Boards of Education can seek the legal services they wish, so long as the services pertain to school matters, from the Attorney General's Office, through the Department of Public Instruction (25).

Over the years, the state superintendent has been called on many times to render opinions concerning the schools. Believing that these opinions carry the weight of law "until set aside by a court of competent jurisdiction or by subsequent legislation" (26), he has not been reluctant to interpret these legal questions. In fact, with increasing enrollments and a proliferation of new responsibilities over pupils and public welfare, he issues a written opinion to some district almost weekly. "Off-the-cuff" legal advice is given daily over the telephone and through personal consultations. The subjects are as diverse as the problems confronting the local administrators, so the superintendent is required to have a knowledge of the state's laws as well as court cases decided daily across the nation. Since he does not maintain a legal staff, he must rely on the attorney general's office staff for advice. With the help of these competent attorneys and his own staff's understanding of educational administrative problems, the state superintendent will continue to answer legal questions concerning the operation of the public schools.

Organization of Effective Local District and Attendance Units

From the time Utah became a state, Dr. Parks and other state superintendents worked to establish a county-unit plan. School and civic leaders repeatedly pointed to the shortage of high schools and protested to both state officials and legislators the lack of graded, effective elementary school programs which could not be corrected without a legally ordered consolidation of districts. Permissive consolidation was granted in 1905, and 10 years later consolidation became mandatory for all counties.

The high school movement demonstrated that lack of consolidation was a barrier to establishing and improving high schools. The High School Law of 1911 established a state high school fund and required the state board to set the standards and the length of school year that high schools would have to achieve before obtaining payments. It adopted a 36-week minimum school year and set the standards for the number of years of high school to be offered, the employment of certified teachers, the course of study to be followed, and graduation requirements. Professor Mosiah Hall, the state's first high school inspector, served with distinction, visiting the schools and reporting on their condition, and making a significant contribution to their growth and improvement. The swift increase in enrollments following enactment of the 1911 law, as noted in Table 3 , somewhat parallels the national picture, where the number of high school students nearly doubled every decade from 1890 to 1930. Between 1900 and 1920, however, the rate of increase in Utah far outstripped that for the nation. Just as interesting is the rapid shift in comparative enrollment percentages among public high schools, Latter-Day Saint secondary schools, and other denominational secondary schools between 1890 and 1925, as shown in Figure 2.

Actually, consolidation in Utah preceded the national consolidation movement, the state essentially having what is called a county-unit pattern of organization since 1915. There are currently 40 school districts and 29 counties. Cities of the first and second class (a total of five) are school districts in themselves by constitutional authority and cannot by legislative action be consolidated with any segment of the county in which they exist.

Table 3. – TREND IN HIGH SCHOOL ENROLLMENT (GRADES 9-12) FOR UTAH AND THE NATION, 1890-1930

Year	Utah [a]	United States [b]
1890	. . .	202,963
1900	1,139	519,251
1910	3,899	915,061
1920	14,130	2,181,216
1930	29,711	4,299,422

[a]From several biennial reports of the state superintendent of public instruction, 1900-1930.

[b]Leslie L. Chisholm, *The Work of the Modern High School* (New York: Macmillan Co., 1953), p. 32.

State superintendents, students of school administration, and legislative councils have suggested during the past few decades that Utah might further reduce the number of

Figure 2. – GROWTH OF PUBLIC HIGH SCHOOL ENROLLMENT, 1890-1925

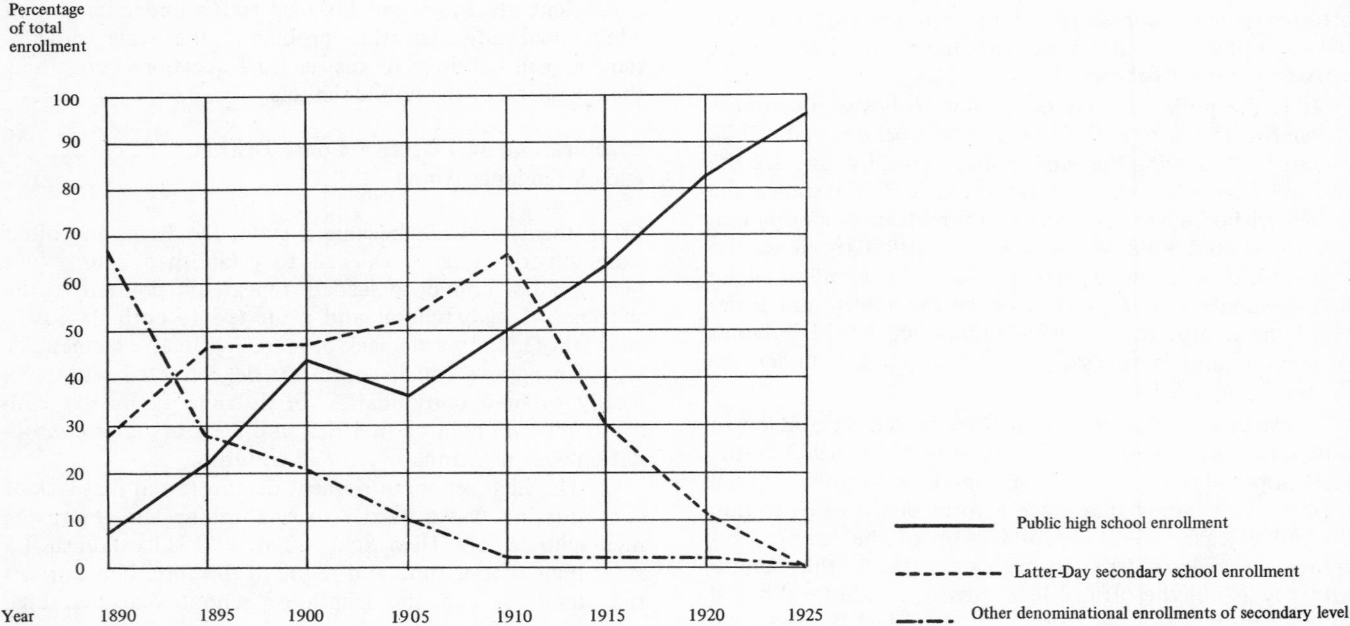

Source:

M. Lynn Bennion, *Mormonism and Education* (Salt Lake City: Deseret News Press, 1939), p. 177.

local districts. For instance, one county contains three very small districts, one of which is a city district and the other two comprehending the remainder of the county. A bill to form one district from the three failed in the 1965 session because these districts vigorously opposed it. Indications are that further legislative action will be sought in the next session, the Utah Legislative Council studying the problem during the interim. Anticipating such legislation, the three district boards requested early in 1966 that the office make a survey to determine the best plan for implementing the impending consolidation, and it is currently under way.

In addition to developing the county-unit plan and influencing interdistrict consolidation, the office also sought to encourage in-district reorganization of schools wherever it seemed possible to improve educational programs at equal or lower per-pupil costs. Because the state is sparsely populated, with districts covering large areas, and because consolidated districts were established early, many believe that the potential for improving by consolidation is greater through in-district reorganization than through interdistrict reorganization. So many schools have small enrollments. Of 169 secondary schools operating in 1965, 25 had fewer than 50 students graduating; of 406 elementary schools, 111 had fewer than 7 teachers.

For many years, the finance program has given the state board the authority to grant additional distribution units (approximately $8,590 per 27 students in average daily attendance during the 1965-66 school year) for schools that must necessarily be small. But as social, economic, and transportation conditions change, so must the criteria for determining which schools should continue operations. In recent years, to promote in-district reorganization, the office has withheld special school status from some schools that had previously been granted additional distribution units. Walter D. Talbot, the deputy superintendent for administration, proposed a new set of criteria in 1966 for determining which schools should receive special status and special distribution units (27). Currently, it is being studied by various educational groups and the state board.

Through participation in such programs as Title III of ESEA and growing recognition by small local districts that they cannot on their own adequately provide such services as special education and supervision, local officials in consultation with the state superintendent are exploring ways of providing additional services on a regional or interdistrict basis. Legislation was to be sought in 1967 to assist with this.

Public School Finance

Utah has run the gamut of known methods for financing public schools. In the beginning, teaching was exchanged for produce; later, schools received only private financing; finally, they were supported by public funds. The Legislative Assembly levied taxes to support the public schools shortly after the beginning of education in Utah, but it was not until 1874 that it "passed an act that initiated a trend that has prevailed from that time to the present in attempting to make education free" (28). Prior to 1874—and for some years to follow—taxes were permissive rather than mandatory. This, coupled with the facts that districts were fiscally dependent on several agencies and that the federal government refused to appropriate money for territorial schools, made the financial problems more difficult.

Development of Finance Programs for Maintenance and Operation. Each biennial legislative session from 1874 to 1880 amended and enlarged the revenue law. The drive to secure an adequate financial base for the public schools was climaxed by passage of an act in 1890 designed to make public schools free to all people. Instead of raising school revenue only by district taxes, territorial taxes, school taxes, tuition fees, donations, and rent, this new law—and subsequent legislation—granted the trustees much greater latitude.

The Free School Act was amended in 1903 to require boards of education to furnish, free of charge, textbooks and supplies to all but high school students. Also, now that Utah was no longer a territory, other states' experiences in finance were brought to bear to induce the state to establish state revenues for local districts that complied with certain minimum standards. A law was passed 2 years later permitting local districts to apply for state money to employ teachers at a minimum salary of $300 if local taxes were insufficient to meet the standard. In other words, this standard established the salary of teachers as the criterion by which state money could be obtained. This remained a working principle for a number of years, although the teachers' salaries increased to $450 in 1909, to $525 in 1915, and to $600 in 1917. The time a school district would employ a teacher increased from 28 to 32 weeks in 1917, thus increasing educational opportunities for students.

Although the elementary schools generally could be run without charging tuition, the high schools up to 1909 were suffering from a lack of funds. The Legislature proposed a constitutional amendment to increase maximum taxation for a high school fund. The voters approved it, the 1911 Legislature implemented it, and the money was apportioned to the districts. The Legislature increased the levy 3 years later, at the same time voting to give local boards the authority to levy a local tax for initiating and maintaining high schools.

Yielding to pressure from many people and organizations, the Legislature ordered consolidation in all counties which had not already organized county high school districts. The law made it mandatory that all county school districts consolidate, with a few exceptions.

The consolidation undoubtedly helped the financial picture considerably, but there were still wide differences in per-capita wealth among districts, causing many people to demand greater state support for education through an equalization program. These efforts culminated in 1919, when the voters ratified a constitutional amendment resulting in greater school revenue. The Legislature acted 2 years later to establish the "$25 School Fund" under which the state paid the districts $25 for each school-age person as determined by the school census. Not only did this fail to meet the "equalization" goal (although it brought in more money for operation), but it widened the disparity between rich and poor districts. A survey commission pointed out these gross inequities in 1926, and, after constant urging by state and Utah Education Association officials, the 1929 Legislature finally proposed a constitutional amendment calling for "an equalization fund which, when added to other revenues provided for this purpose by the legislature, shall be $5.00 for each person of school age as shown by the last preceding school census" (29). This plan to place more state money at the disposal of the districts was completed in 1931—not without additional state control, however. One educational historian wrote:

> The legislature passed an "act creating and defining a uniform program of public school education in the State of Utah, creating a state equalization fund and providing for the apportionment of any revenue made available for an equalization fund." The act provided new minimum educational requirements and gave the state board of education full power to administer the fund. The law provided that "Districts not approved by the State board of education . . . shall not participate in the equalization fund" (30).

The new law instituted several important concepts in educational finance. It was weighted in favor of high school students, recognizing that their education cost more; it gave consideration to the increased cost of transporting children; it made allowance for one- and two-room schools in districts requiring additional money to achieve equality; it considered the ability of districts to finance education; and it provided a "cost of living" increment by adjusting the amount per student each year until a maximum was reached in 1936-37. Along with the fiscal independence (except at the state level) won earlier, these provisions promised to adequately care for school needs for some time to come.

Unfortunately, the nation's and state's economic futures were still uncertain, the recovery from the Depression breaking sharply in 1937 to bring additional problems in school finance. Again in 1938, the Legislature proposed further amendments which would increase tax money available for a uniform school fund. As it was finally put into effect, the law established the principle of the distribution unit, defined the unit, and set aside $1,655 to be allocated to each unit from local taxes and the state. The principle of equalization was retained in the provision that "no school district having a per capita assessed valuation of $4,000 or more per census child shall receive more from the $5.00 equalization fund than such district received in 1936-37" (31).

For some strange reason, the Legislature amended the 1937 law 2 years later to provide for the distribution of funds on a per-student basis as practiced earlier. The amendments which apportioned the uniform school fund money provided for several new practices: (a) Expenses were authorized for the state board to investigate special and unequal conditions in the districts; (b) funds were provided, not to exceed $75,000, for the board to make payments to districts to equalize education and improve educational practices; and (c) funds were added to the revenues from the state district school fund, the high school fund, the equalization fund, and a local levy of 10 mills on the assessed valuation of tangible property in each district, to equal $86 per student in average daily attendance.

World War II and the inflation that followed created acute problems with teacher salaries. By 1943, it was necessary for the Legislature to act again. At first, it appeared that for the second time in history the lawmakers would tie the apportionment of state funds directly to teacher salaries. They appropriated $658,000 from the general fund to the uniform school fund, $175,000 to be used exclusively for teachers' salaries, the remainder to be "apportioned and distributed on a per capita basis of the number of full-time employees during the school year, 1942-43, of the local boards of education . . . and . . . used solely and exclusively for the payment of salaries and wages of employees" (32). At the same time, the Legislature appropriated an additional $2,632,000 for the biennium beginning July 1943 to pay salaries of employees. The law also specified that after 1942-43, no district could receive this money unless it paid the following salaries:

> (a) To certificated teachers who do not hold a degree, not less than $840.00 per annum.
>
> To certificated teachers who hold a bachelor's degree, not less than $960.00 per annum.
>
> (b) There shall be an increase in salary of teachers in excess of the minimum salaries above mentioned to teachers who maintain their legal certification . . . $50.00 per year for the first six years of experience . . . and shall average an increase of not less than $45 per year for at least sixteen years of experience inclusive of the first six years.
>
> -
>
> (d) The board of education of each district shall prepare and adopt annually a schedule of the salaries of clerks, stenographers, custodians, janitors, bus drivers and other employees and file the same with the state board of education and no payments may be made in excess of said schedules (33).

The cost of education increased rapidly during the war. Again, in 1945, the Legislature found it necessary to raise the taxation limit for school districts to raise more money. Significantly, Utah returned to the distribution-unit formula containing the equalization feature of a guaranteed minimum program per unit for a minimum levy of 10 mills at the local level. The figure was increased, however, to $3,000 per unit. It retained the $5 equalization figure and the high school fund, appropriating $500,000 for transportation payments on the basis of the number of students transported 2.5 or more miles to school.

At a special legislative session called in 1946, it was proposed that the constitution be amended to restrict the state's contribution to no more than 75 percent of the total cost of a minimum school program, with no more than 75 percent of the state's portion to come from a state property tax levy. The following year, the law perpetuated the distribution-unit principle, setting its value at $3,300, setting the classroom unit at each 30 weighted pupils, the secondary students receiving weights of 1.5, and elementary, 1.0. It also increased the transportation appropriation to $675,000, retaining the principle of a flat grant.

The report of a survey committee established in 1951 to study school building conditions and the need for new buildings stirred considerable discussion during the 1953 legislative session, resulting in an act whereby the state supported construction more directly. But it required a special session to complete all of the business for the schools. The Legislature increased the value of the distribution unit to a maximum of $4,050, at the same time giving the districts an option of qualifying for a basic program on a sliding scale (based on the number of mills levied by the district) from $3,450 to $4,050. It also provided for a supplemental state-supported program not to exceed 12 percent of the basic program. A new concept in financing transportation was enacted, based on $19 per pupil regularly enrolled in kindergarten through grade 6 and actually transported 1.5 miles each way between home and school, and 2 miles or more for grades 7 through 12. Unfortunately, the Legislature specified that "in no event [could] more than three-fourths of the total actual transportation cost" (34) be paid from state funds.

In each biennial session from 1953 to 1963 (excluding 1955), the Legislature amended the uniform school program. In 1957, it increased the distribution unit from $4,050 to $4,800 on a sliding scale for the basic program, plus a supplement not to exceed 12 percent of the basic. Two years later, the unit was again increased to $5,150, and the supplemental program to 15 percent of the basic. Finally, a dramatic increase was enacted in 1963 to a distribution-unit value of $6,850 for a local levy of 16 mills, the supplemental program increasing to $437 per distribution unit or an amount provided by local levy of 4 mills, whichever was greater. The leeway program, which had started at 25 percent of the basic program in 1957, was now 16 percent of the basic program. Transportation payments, $20 per student in 1957, were now based on $2 per mile annually for the average number of miles traveled per day by each student eligible for transportation (35).

Public school support continued to increase, so that by fiscal 1967, the value of the basic program distribution unit had reached $7,250, and the supplemental or "board leeway" program $140 per distribution unit per mill. The voted leeway program was changed drastically to allow a guaranteed program of $100 per distribution unit per mill for fiscal 1966, and $110 for fiscal 1967. The levy requirements at the local level remained at 16 mills for the basic program, increasing from a mandatory 4 to a permissive 11 mills in 1966 and 12 mills in 1967 for the board leeway program; the voted leeway program increased 10 mills as a local option on a vote by the people. In addition, transportation allocations were increased to $2.50 per average daily pupil mile, annually. Efforts to increase activity in library programs and summer and extended-year programs received a state appropriation of $700,000 in fiscal 1966 and $800,000 in fiscal 1967 (36).

The tradition of local districts' being solely responsible for financing school construction ended in 1951. Superintendent Bateman had been instrumental in introducing a bill in 1949 which would have authorized state funds to help local districts erect needed buildings. The bill failed, but a similar one passed 2 years later providing state financial assistance from a $2 million appropriation to qualified districts, establishing another milestone in the state's educational history. This aid, continuing since 1951, had an appropriation for the 1965-67 biennium of $6 million.

The principle of state aid for capital outlay was further strengthened by the enactment of the continuing school building program in 1959. This went beyond the concept of state emergency aid or aid on a supplemental basis for an indefinite period, establishing the equalization concept at the state level for school construction. While the appropriation was not sufficient to solve all problems and state supplemental aid continued to be necessary, it did provide long-range assistance which the office had long deemed necessary.

Pupil Personnel Services

Pupil personnel services had their beginning in both Utah and the nation in the vocational education movement that emerged during the first and second decades of the twentieth century. The Smith-Hughes Act of 1917 not only stimulated the growth of vocational education, but also recognized the need for helping young men and women with their vocational decisions, in turn giving rise to the guidance and counseling movement. Administrators from Salt Lake City, Jordan, Granite, and the Grand Districts recognized their responsibility in this new area and were

Table 4. – RATIO, NUMBER, AND FULL-TIME EQUIVALENT GUIDANCE PERSONNEL, 1948-66

	Elementary			Secondary	
Year	No. of personnel	Full-time equivalent	Ratio	Full-time equivalent	Ratio
1948-49	83	...	...	27.00	1 to 871
1958-59	183	...	...	133.00	1 to 645
1959-60	256	...	...	180.00	1 to 517
1960-61	275	...	...	206.00	1 to 483
1961-62	318	27.05	1 to 5,348	252.00	1 to 398
1962-63	323	26.43	1 to 5,676	274.00	1 to 416
1963-64	363	21.79	1 to 7,223	317.00	1 to 352
1964-65	381	32.10	1 to 5,151	308.91	1 to 381
1965-66	396	39.90	1 to 4,167	321.59	1 to 374

among the first to provide these services in an organized fashion.

Leadership on the state level emerged from a whole complex of factors and influences, taking definite form when a supervisor of guidance was appointed by the office in 1943. Despite his contributions, the position was not filled for a long period after he left until NDEA initiated a new era for these services, with a new state director appointed to head an independent division. The money available through Title V of NDEA, though small in amount, stimulated guidance programs considerably, and the results can be easily observed. In 1964, the Division of Pupil Personnel Services became a section along with special education and adult education, within a consolidated Division of Special Educational Services.

Utah has promoted the concept of "pupil personnel services" in contrast to the more restricted term *guidance services.* Under this heading, the specific areas are identified as psychological services, psychometric services, guidance, school social work, school health programs, pupil accounting, and identification and diagnostic services for special education. This section attempts to provide leadership throughout the state in all of these areas through the supervisory and consultative services it brings to local district personnel. (See Table 4.)

Research

In the early history of the office, the research section was combined with the finance division, its main duties centering on collecting data from districts on costs, salaries, enrollments, days of school, transportation, and similar statistics. Financed by a uniform school fund allocation for research, its personnel assisted with surveys and other research when time and money permitted.

Research was given a bit more status when an assistant director was assigned primarily to research during the 1944-46 biennium. But from 1946 to 1950, despite the recognized need for research in many areas, research meant mainly gathering and interpreting statistical data in school finance. When Governor J. Bracken Lee vetoed a $20,000 appropriation to the research office, a bitter battle followed between the board and the Governor, which undoubtedly impaired relations for many years (37).

During the next few years, numerous grants from public and private agencies formed the basis for important research, particularly the Kellogg Foundation's support for research in administration during the 1950-52 biennium. In keeping with its new status, the research division was separated from the finance division. Almost immediately, it reactivated the Utah Educational Research Council originally organized in 1946, which published its first bulletin (continued on a yearly basis since that time) in 1952–a listing of graduate studies completed in Utah institutions. The council also published research on pupil transportation and was of considerable help in developing a new formula for financing Utah schools. Revised into a nonprofit organization with the office's director of research as its executive secretary and treasurer, the council solicited considerable funds from various industries and funding organizations. Thus, it was able to initiate a school building survey and several studies in curriculum and instruction.

Of particular significance was a series of studies sponsored in cooperation with the office and financed by the Kennecott Copper Company. The Utah Secondary School Principals Association also cooperated with the office in sponsoring studies in the general area of new procedures in the utilization of staff in the secondary school, financed through private foundation grants. A full-time director of research was employed during the 1958-60 biennium, and the research division became a clearinghouse for all questionnaires and requests regarding information and statistical data. It also undertook two major projects: (a) the follow-up of Utah students attending out-of-state colleges or universities, and (b) an investigation of the relationship between teacher competency and teacher turnover.

The Legislature gave a considerable boost to educational research in 1961 by earmarking an annual percentage of revenue from the federal Mineral Leasing Act. This led to a vast expansion in research activities and to experiments in the utilization of staff and facilities in such areas as American values—the center of much attention and funds. With the aid of a Ford Foundation grant, the office was able to participate in the launching of the Western States Small Schools Project and appointed a director for the Utah portion. The research division also cooperated with the university's economic education centers and in the development of the Utah Council on Economic Education, which was to serve in an advisory capacity for research and studies in economics.

The percentage of money allocated from the Mineral Leasing Fund was increased in the 1962-64 biennium. A new Division of Research and Planning was established, with sections on small-school improvement, statistics, curriculum, research, and school plant planning. This work continues to be important in improving the quality of education in the state.

School Food Services

Even prior to the Depression years, a few schools had inaugurated some type of supplementary food program. But it was the Works Progress Administration that gave impetus to the school lunch movement in 1935 with a program whose purposes were (a) to feed needy and undernourished school children, (b) to create employment, and (c) to create a noncommercial outlet for agricultural surpluses. The "school lunch" proved to be such a success and received so much school and community support that, starting in 1943, Congress voted to continue it on a year-to-year basis. The program was finally revised and put on a long-term permanent basis in 1946, and it is under this law that the national program operates today.

The office of the superintendent has administered the school lunch program since 1943, acting as an agent for the federal government and cooperating with the federal workers who in the early stages of the program dealt directly with local school districts in all its phases. The Legislature set a tax of 4 percent (amended to 8 percent in 1965) on the retail price of wines and liquors and allocated $20,000 per year (increased to $45,000 in 1965) of the resulting revenue to the state board for administering and supervising the program and the remainder to the school districts according to the number of lunches served. Revenue from this liquor tax increased from $393,000 in 1943 to $1,273,000 for the 1965-66 fiscal year. Table 5 shows these details. In 1944, 282 school lunch units in 36 of the 40 school districts fed 31,800 students daily. At the beginning of the 1966-67 school year, 481 schools in 39 districts were serving approximately 125,000 students daily.

With passage of the 1946 National School Lunch Act, the federal government ceased maintaining a staff of workers to deal directly with local school districts in all phases of the program. The superintendent's office took over the administration, and the positions of canning supervisors were abolished as garden growing and canning programs initiated by the Works Progress Administration were discontinued. The present staff consists of a program administrator, three specialists, three clerical personnel, and one supervisor of commodity distribution.

Perhaps supervision has had more effect on the nature and direction of the school lunch program than any other factor, serving as a means of communication among school districts. It is an instrument for maintaining high standards and aids the local units through personal contacts, letters, publications, workshops, conferences, demonstrations, and TV programs. Food workers, managers, and supervisors also are helped by spot-checks by the nutritional and administrative survey to determine as accurately as possible the status of local programs and the areas where the office can be of greatest assistance.

Through the years, since the school lunch program's humble beginnings in the early 1930's, a new set of objectives has evolved. The program is no longer geared only to helping the needy child; it is now directed toward improving the nutritional status of all children. No longer is the program interested in just feeding the child; it is now interested in helping him to learn, and the program is designed to provide "lunch schoolrooms" as well as "school lunchrooms."

School Plant Planning

The office's responsibility for coordinating school plant services was a part-time duty assigned to a member of the staff until the Legislature enacted a law in 1951 appropriating $2 million for emergency aid (aid provided by the state to assist districts that could not meet building needs with their own resources) to local districts. This immediately forced the office to assign a man full time to handle these new responsibilities. At first, this director's activities involved working with two commissions created by the 1951 act: the School Building Survey Commission, which appropriated emergency funds for school construction, and the Public School Survey Commission. Due to the Depression and war conditions, for 20 years preceding the passage

Table 5. – FINANCIAL GROWTH OF THE UTAH SCHOOL LUNCH PROGRAM, 1943-66

Receipts

Year	Sales	State fund	Federal fund incl. spec. milk	Bd. of Ed. and other	Total	Value of commodities
1943-44	. . .	$ 393,000	. . .	. . .	$1,142,000	. . .
1953-54	$1,896,000	538,000	$ 959,000	$ 71,000	2,829,000	$ 918,000
1963-64	5,385,000	722,000	1,149,000	128,000	7,384,000	2,273,000
1965-66	6,196,000	1,273,000	1,404,000	104,000	8,976,000	1,718,000

Expenditures

Year	Food	Labor	Equipment	Other	Total
1943-44	. . .	. . .	. . .	. . .	$ 891,000
1953-54	$1,533,000	$ 938,000	$ 150,000	$189,000	2,810,000
1963-64	3,613,000	2,893,000	328,000	547,000	7,382,000
1965-66	4,513,000	3,490,000	347,000	541,000	8,890,000

Participation

Year	Total meals
1943-44	4,504,970
1953-54	10,442,543
1963-64	22,379,377
1965-66	25,585,876

of this act school building construction had been seriously curtailed.

The state board adopted standards for school construction during the 1952-54 biennium as the law required. But in its January 1953 report to Governor Lee, the temporary School Building Survey Commission stated that in its opinion the standards for the emergency program were too high, considering the minimum standards mentioned in the new law. Although the Governor asked the Legislature in both its regular session and its special session in December 1953 to look into these charges, it did not see fit to make a formal investigation, but reenacted the provisions of the 1951 law for another 2 years. The following year, the Governor requested that the Legislative Council investigate. During the summer, the council's educational committee held informal hearings at which the state board presented a brief general defense of its procedures with a request that the temporary building survey commission present written, specific reasons why it felt the emergency standards were too high. The Governor immediately ordered all funds frozen and requested the attorney general and the state auditor to investigate the commission's charges. Fortunately, the freeze was soon modified to permit construction to proceed.

The Legislature passed the Continuing School Building Act in 1959, requiring all districts to file a comprehensive program of their construction plans for a 5-year period. The districts estimated their total needs at $106,357,000. The Legislature appropriated $4 million in 1961, and during the 1962-64 biennium the office approved construction of 19 new elementary schools, 8 new secondary schools, and additions and modifications of 29 elementary and 19 secondary schools. During the next biennium, the school plant planning division merged with statistics and research in the Division of Research and Planning, and construction proceeded at a greater rate. State construction aid increased to $5,700,000 in the 1962-64 biennium and $6 million to 14 participating districts in the following biennium. By the end of 1964, total expenditures stood at $66,850,000.

The school planning division did more than just allocate funds. As early as 1954, it began publication of a series of guides devoted to planning facilities for food services, industrial arts, vocational agriculture, and mechanics. After 1956, new guides were published to assist in planning for elementary schools, secondary schools, physical education facilities, homemaking facilities, educational specifications, and a long-range program of school construction. These guides were revised and updated in 1964. The program of property accounting instituted during the 1962-64 biennium to get current information on all capital equipment has resulted in a manual on physical facilities and equipment and a start on a second manual on property accounting.

It has been recognized in recent years that the services of the division need expanding, and some steps have been taken. For example, a basic record system has been planned which will accumulate the data in usable form to greatly simplify future surveys. The data should allow at any time the study and evaluation of practices in school construction and of the services rendered by the division.

Under the current law, the state superintendent has the power to prepare a code of standards for any school construction in excess of $20,000. He can enforce compliance because contracts cannot be let until he signs his approval to the plans and specifications.

Supervisory and Consultant Services

From the early history of the office, the board and the state superintendent were charged with the general control and supervision of the public school system and with responsibilities stipulated in specific programs that allowed the office to provide supervisory and consultant services to the extent budgets permitted. As the staff grew from two professional members in 1900 to over a hundred in 1965, the office had many lean years in trying to exercise this leadership. A considerable amount of help has come recently from federal funds.

The early development of the county-unit plan helped the office considerably in providing supervisory services at the district and school level, reducing the need for so many visits by office personnel. Very gradually, these services shifted from an emphasis on classroom visits to (a) providing leadership in arranging meetings for groups of teachers in subject matter areas and grade levels; (b) working with groups of superintendents and administrators; (c) holding regional and state in-service workshops; (d) making team in-service visits and team evaluations of schools and programs; (e) publishing bulletins, guides, newsletters, and recommended lists of materials; (f) sponsoring in-service telecasts. Consultant services were being provided in a wide range of areas by 1965, including finance, transportation, research, food services, and curriculum and instruction.

A questionnaire sent to local superintendents during 1965-66 revealed that the outlying rural areas were quite concerned because they were not in close enough contact with the state superintendent's office. They tended to favor regional offices in one or more areas, which would enable them to obtain more immediate assistance. A major concern expressed by many staff members has been the need for additional supervisory and nonteaching professionals at the district level.

Teacher Education and Certification

During the early years of statehood, the state board and the superintendent concerned themselves primarily with teacher certification, considering each applicant individually. But they constantly struggled with a great dilemma: a need for more teachers and the desire to hire teachers with more formal education. Beginning with territorial Superintendent Campbell in 1866, the office solved the problem in part by granting scholarships to selected students desiring to teach. As Utah followed the trend toward substituting credits and courses for examinations, the office shortly after the turn of the century found itself spending more and more time adopting teacher preparation curriculums and inspecting teacher education programs.

The board's duties increased greatly as it assumed more control over certification, so that in 1913 it established a certification committee to act for it in clear-cut cases. Within 2 years, the board required all beginning elementary teachers to have 1 year beyond high school and required high school teachers to have college degrees. No longer limited to certifying county teachers as in early years, the board and the office controlled the examination and certification of all teachers within county districts by 1915. Legislation in 1919, 1925, and 1929 completed the process, making the board responsible for certifying superintendents and city teachers and expanding its duties in certifying other teachers. These laws further stipulated that no person was entitled to teach, supervise, or act as superintendent unless he was properly certified.

The requirements were continually upgraded after 1922 so that by World War II beginning elementary teachers had to have the same 4 years of training as secondary teachers. Further strengthening of requirements took place in 1946 (38). After several years of discussion between State Superintendent T. H. Bell and teacher-training institutions and the Utah Education Association, on Bell's recommendation the state board approved a new two-level certification program to begin in 1966. Teachers completing an approved 4-year preparation program could be issued a basic professional certificate; those who had taught successfully for 3 years and took an approved fifth year of training could qualify for the professional certificate. Administrators were required to have 2 years of training beyond the bachelor's degree. Teacher educational programs were to be reevaluated at 5-year intervals.

Like many other states, Utah issued letters of authorization on an emergency basis to employ teachers with less than standard training during major wars and other periods of teacher shortage. It is satisfying to note that for the 1965-66 school year, more than 98.8 percent were properly certificated.

Transportation

Transportation became an important item on the Legislature's agenda following the consolidation legislation of 1915 and the Compulsory School Attendance Act of 1919, particularly in the larger county districts. In 1931, the Legislature enacted one of the state's more important education provisions (still appearing in the current minimum school program law), stipulating that all pupils living more than 2.5 miles from school were to be transported to and from their classes, or a reasonable arrangement was to be made toward such transportation. This act was little modified until 1961, when state support was changed to an amount equal to $2 per mile annually for the average number of pupils actually in grades K - 6 who traveled 1.5 miles or more each way daily and for each secondary school student, grades 7 - 12, who traveled 2 or more miles each way. The Legislature increased the allowance to $2.50 per mile in 1965 and at the same time agreed to transport students going to school under "hazardous conditions" when the state board approved.

During the 1965-66 school year, 83,296 pupils were transported to and from school, including 9,000–at district expense–eligible under the 1.5-mile and 2-mile limits, and 2,400 due to hazardous conditions; districts transporting pupils because of hazardous conditions were reimbursed at the rate of $2.50 per annual average mile. This meant that Utah districts employed the full-time equivalent of 442 persons at a cost of $3,300,000 in 1965-66, including $2,900,000 for maintenance and operation and $363,000 for capital outlay. The state reimbursed the local districts for about 69 percent of the cost of maintenance and operation.

Vocational Education

Since the 1870's, when Brigham Young established Brigham Young College in Logan, the schools have taught vocational education. But the real impetus came with the Legislature's acceptance of funds under the Smith-Hughes Act of 1917, aiding programs in vocational agriculture, homemaking, business and trade, and industrial training. The Legislature voted an appropriation for this purpose in 1919, designating the State Board of Education as the State Board for Vocational Education. The law states:

> The State Board of Education is hereby designated as the State Board for Vocational Education, and the State Superintendent of Public Instruction is hereby designated as its chief executive officer.
>
> The State Board for Vocational Education shall have all necessary authority to cooperate with the United States Office of Education in the administration of the said Act of Congress, to administer any legislation enacted pursuant thereto by the State of Utah and to administer the funds provided by the Federal Government and the State of Utah for the promotion and maintenance of vocational education in agricultural subjects, trade and industrial subjects, business and distributive education subjects, home economics subjects, and education in health, civic and patriotic service (39).

Additional federal funds were accepted by the board under the George-Reed Act of 1929, the George-Ellzey Act of 1934, and the George-Deen Act of 1936 (for distributive education). Until passage of the George-Barden Act of 1946, which increased federal funds by nearly 400 percent, most vocational training was at the high school and adult levels; it now became possible to establish postsecondary preparatory programs in the junior colleges. At the same time, the state board established the Salt Lake Area Vocational School in Salt Lake City and the Central Utah Vocational School in Provo.

Although most postsecondary vocational education has been in the trade and technical areas, the Practical Nurse Education Act of 1955, NDEA, and the 1963 Vocational Education Act added new dimensions. They inaugurated new programs in health occupations, technician training, office occupations, home economics "for gainful employment," and appropriate classes for the academically and socioeconomically disadvantaged, and made funds available to encourage more effective teacher training, occupational guidance, and local and state supervision. The office has also been concerned with other vocational programs since 1940. For instance, during World War II, over 65,000 persons were enrolled in a Vocational Education for National Defense program, while others were trained in food production under the Student Youth Act. Over 30,000 veterans participated in veterans' institutional on-the-farm and on-the-job training from 1945 to 1957. The Manpower Development and Training Act has retrained and upgraded the skills and abilities of more than 1,500 persons since 1962. Table 6 provides partial details.

Advisory committees, composed of representatives from labor, management, the farm, and the home, aid in

Table 6. – VOCATIONAL ENROLLMENTS BY YEARS FOR FISCAL YEAR ENDING AS INDICATED[a]

Vocational section	1925	1935	1945	1950	1955	1960	1965
Agriculture	1,142	2,202	2,713	6,935	4,726	4,169	4,291
Homemaking	2,393	3,926	5,257	13,052	12,176	13,804	18,413
Trades & industries	222	922	1,878	6,466	6,381	5,550	7,763
Distributive education	. . .	. . .	4,198	6,528	4,780	4,016	2,400
Office occupations	. . .	. . .	. . .	. . .	. . .	. . .	16,356
Health occupations	. . .	. . .	. . .	. . .	. . .	247	422
Technician training	. . .	. . .	. . .	. . .	. . .	644[b]	1,398[b]
War production and defense training	. . .	. . .	29,713	. . .	. . .	. . .	. . .
Veteran training	. . .	. . .	376	10,906	848	. . .	. . .
Manpower training	. . .	. . .	. . .	. . .	. . .	. . .	885

[a]Enrollments as shown by reports to the U.S. Office of Education. Programs in which enrollments are not listed were not in operation during the years as listed.

[b]Number trained under Title III, George-Barden Act.

determining the training needs of youth and adults. The Legislature appropriates money for a number of vocational categories, and for every dollar of federal funds spent in 1965 state and local funds contributed an additional $3. Thirty-eight of the 40 school districts and eight post-secondary schools conducted vocational training in 1966. Thus, the agricultural, business, and industrial growth of Utah is inseparably tied to vocational education financed by both the national government and the state and administered by the office's staff.

Vocational Rehabilitation

Congress first showed interest in the rehabilitation of civilians when it passed the Smith-Sears Act in 1918. Together with the Vocational Rehabilitation Act of 1920, the program was placed on a more or less experimental basis. Appropriations were meager, granted from one Congress to another until 1935, when the program was put on a permanent basis in the federal Social Security law.

Until 1943, the program amounted to little more than vocational guidance, training, the provision of prosthetic appliances, occupational adjustment, and placement. Amendments passed in 1943, known as Public Law 78-113, liberalized the program considerably, extending services to the mentally disabled (including the mentally retarded), and provided medical, surgical, and psychiatric services, hospitalization, training, maintenance, and occupational tools. Generously financed, the program shifted from a scholarship to a needs-of-the-client basis. The law was amended again in 1954, further expanding the financing, providing for rehabilitation facilities and centers throughout the country, and setting up training grants and traineeships to attract personnel with graduate and specialized training in rehabilitation.

The act was again amended in 1965, this time to create workshops, rehabilitation centers, and other rehabilitation resources; to remove the requirement of economic need for some services; and to provide for grants to states to undertake comprehensive, in-depth planning projects so they could serve all who needed them by 1975. It supplied more money but put all states on an equal matching ratio.

RELATIONSHIPS WITH OTHER STATE AGENCIES AND ORGANIZATIONS

Inherent in the Governor's office are broad appointive powers, and with his veto power, his responsibility for formulating biennial budgets, and his membership on the State Board of Examiners, he exercises considerable control over public education. The superintendent's office must work with the Governor as well as with the attorney general, the Legislature, and the Legislative Council. The 13-member council, established in 1947 as a research and investigating body for the Legislature, has spent much time in recent years trying to solve educational problems. Since the office depends on the attorney general for legal assistance, such functions as purchasing land, writing contracts, and providing legal opinions asked for by districts all require a close working relationship between the two agencies.

The office maintains many other relationships, and practically every professional staff member has numerous contacts with outside groups. Some are official, such as dealings with the state personnel division, the state finance department, and the State Board of Examiners. Memberships in the Exchange Club, the Utah Vocational Association, the League of Women Voters, and others are often informal and voluntary. But all are vital. Without dynamic and cooperative interaction with other state agencies and organizations, the office could not carry out its constitutional mandate to provide general control and supervision over the public school system. Although all contacts are important, this section will deal with the relationships of major significance to the overall work of the office (40).

Coordinating Council of Higher Education

The Legislature created a Coordinating Council of Higher Education in 1959, endowing it with advisory powers to coordinate the services and programs of all publicly supported post-high school institutions. As mentioned earlier, it was at first composed of nine members, six appointed by the Governor and three representing the board of regents of the University of Utah, the board of trustees of Utah State University, and the State Board of Education (41). Subsequently, two persons were added, one representing the board of trustees of Webber State College and the other representing the College of Southern Utah (now a 4-year institution with a separate board). The Governor appoints the members of each higher education board while the members of the state board are elected by popular vote (42).

The statute establishing the coordinating council requested it to exercise leadership and give direction to statewide planning of public and post-high school education, define the role and program of each public post-high school educational institution, establish criteria for the budget, study new methods of instruction and new techniques for increasing efficiency, and define the standards and regulations for recruiting and admitting students. The state board has had a representative on the council since its inception and has worked with it to provide leadership in cooperative planning and coordination of services and programs. The council advises the Governor, the Legislature, and the governing boards of higher education institutions on statewide policies in program development and financing.

Several problems and issues existing since the council was created are still unresolved. The major one involves the membership of the council itself—specifically, the objectivity of the five members representing the controlling boards toward state needs versus institutional needs. Also, there are pressures from many areas to create new institutions of higher learning. Following a study, the council recommended the creation of a junior college board, but legislation to implement it was defeated in 1965. The council itself disagrees as to its own role. Should it be a fact-finding body gathering data for Legislatures without evaluating these data, or should it use the data as a basis for making recommendations? More and more, it tends to both evaluate and recommend. Its power and jurisdiction have been unclear—ranging from little, if any, to recommendations which would change it into a "super board" controlling all institutions of higher learning in the state. Certainly, the political climate has influenced both the power and jurisdiction of the council. Some college administrators and their boards, protective of their own rights and authority, have been fearful of the council's power.

Joint Committee on Educational Television

The emergence and growth of educational television in Utah has been dramatic. Several attempts were made to provide a structure for coordinating ETV, but it was the indication that federal financial assistance might be available that brought this effort to a climax. Fear that there would be no authorized central agency to coordinate and receive federal funds led to the establishment of the Joint Committee on Educational Television. The committee, consisting of four members each from the State Board of Education and the Coordinating Council on Higher Education, serves as a forum for discussion of mutual problems. It receives and administers federal funds and, in consultation with the Utah Television Foundation, makes recommendations to the Legislature.

State Board of Examiners, Department of Finance, and State Personnel Office

The State Board of Examiners' power over education resides in the state constitution, which stipulates that the Governor, the attorney general, and the secretary of state—

> Shall constitute a Board of Examiners, with power to examine all claims against the State, except salaries or compensation of officers fixed by law, and perform such other duties as may be presented by law; and no claim against the State, except for salaries and compensation of officers fixed by law, shall be passed upon by the legislature without having been considered and acted upon by the said Board of Examiners (43).

A perusal of the minutes of the State Board of Education gives examples of these controls. The Board of Examiners forced Superintendent E. Allen Bateman to go without salary for nearly a year in 1951-52, and the Board of Education was able to secure payment to him only by going to court. In May 1954, the Board of Examiners refused salary increases for 15 Board of Education employees.

The finance department and its personnel office also exercise budgetary and other controls over the state board and its institutions. They have the power to approve or disapprove job positions, determine the number of jobs as related to salary, and write salary schedules for all state employees. Since the Board of Education is constitutionally charged with controlling and supervising the public school system, and its members are elected by the citizens, it would seem that, once the Legislature has appropriated money, the board should be entrusted to spend it wisely, unfettered by red tape or additional controls other than reasonable reports and audits. Such an agency needs the freedom to employ the staff necessary to give leadership for its policies and to use its discretionary power in setting salaries. Yet, the truth is that it has been denied such power by the personnel director, the finance director, and the Board of Examiners. In this regard, the state board has less authority than a local board of education or universities which by law have a similar relationship to the Board of Examiners. As long as this condition exists, the state board will be inhibited from fully carrying out the tasks for which it was established; only when it is given the freedom to make expenditures within its approved appropriations and budgets will it achieve the stature necessary to render the educational leadership so urgently needed in Utah today.

State Course of Study Committee and Textbook Commission

Both the committee and commission, created in 1907 and 1909 respectively, have been described earlier. Since 1941, the personnel of the two have been one and the same. Membership consists of the state superintendent, who serves as chairman, the dean of the College of Education at the University of Utah, the dean of the College of Education at Utah State University, three district superintendents appointed by the state board, and five lay citizens appointed by the Governor. The deputy superintendent for instruction serves as secretary.

This committee has the responsibility to establish aims, purposes, objectives, and a philosophy of education to guide the schools, and to approve courses for all districts. The textbook commission adopts textbooks with regard to these objectives and courses. The state board then executes the directives of these official agencies, and an examination of the minutes reveals that they have worked in close harmony with the office, getting assistance from its instructional staff.

State Department of Health and State Department of Welfare

The office has long enjoyed a harmonious relationship with these departments, working with them in such areas as special education, Indian affairs, day-care centers, mental health, mental retardation, Civil Defense, health education, and training programs for welfare clients. Since passage of ESEA, the need for greater cooperation has been recognized, and in recent months a joint committee has been meeting periodically.

State Land Board

It is highly important that school lands be well managed, since they have contributed substantially to Utah education in the past and offer considerable potential support for the future. Membership of the State Land Board managing them consists of the state superintendent (or whomever the state board designates) and five other persons appointed by the Governor with the advice and consent of the Senate, all holding 6-year terms (44). This board directs, manages, and controls all lands granted to the state by the U.S. government or others, and land lying below the water's edge of any lake or stream to which the state is entitled, except in the case of lands used or set apart for public purposes or occupied by public buildings. It may sell or lease these lands in the best interests of the state in accordance with the law, depositing all money collected in the state treasury. Certain funds are earmarked for the public elementary and secondary schools, the University of Utah, Utah State University, and other specific educational uses.

State Library Commission

This commission, composed of nine members appointed by the Governor with the advice and consent of the Senate for 6-year overlapping terms (45), was created in 1957. It operates a State Library and is empowered to provide for its housing and to promote and develop public library services throughout the state in cooperation with the state municipal libraries, schools, or other agencies. It employs the necessary staff, sets the rules and standards, and distributes books and materials. Its bookmobiles have become very popular in the rural areas. The office of the state superintendent has always worked closely with this commission.

State School Boards Association

This association was officially recognized in 1959 as "an organization and agency of the school boards of Utah and representative of members of said school boards" (46). It holds annual conferences, works to keep its members informed of educational happenings, helps sponsor legislation, and makes other attempts to upgrade the public school system. The office has worked closely with the association in many instances to seek answers to common problems, and all members of the state board are members of it.

Utah Education Association

Although it was not until 1870 that the territory's teachers organized to meet twice each year in Salt Lake City, a number of early educators who became territorial superintendents were active in local associations. The association's first president, territorial Superintendent Robert L. Campbell, joined with his successors, such as John R. Park and Karl G. Maeser, to promote its work. It has flourished, and by 1965, it could boast of 12,286 members (47).

Historically, the office and the Utah Education Association have enjoyed a cooperative, wholesome relationship, especially in teacher education and certification and the development of school legislation. Staff members from each organization have served on the other's committees. During the last decade, however, frictions have developed, and although they are ameliorated at present, they should be noted for the sake of historical accuracy.

In the months following Sputnik, the state board considered lengthening the school year. Officials of the UEA requested that the board initiate additional action "to provide classroom conditions which will permit a substantial increase in the *quality* as well as the *quantity* of the school program" (48). After considerable discussion, the board increased the minimum days in the school year from 172 to 177, beginning in the fall of 1958. At the same time, it agreed that improvements were needed in many areas, including curriculum, teacher qualifications, salaries, and school buildings, but it was of the opinion that "all of these objectives cannot be achieved at one time" (49). The board expressed its intention to further lengthen the school day to approximately the same as the average in other states.

Several months later, on Superintendent Bateman's recommendation, the board adopted a motion placing the schools on a minimum of 180 days, beginning with 1959. This prompted a vigorous protest from association officials who criticized the action in an issue of the *Utah Education Review,* contending that the board and state superintendent had not given the teachers' viewpoints adequate consideration. The board reviewed the entire matter in its May meeting and charged that the UEA had been unfair, but took no further action.

More friction developed in 1964. Over a period of several years, there had been considerable debate between school groups and the political structure over the need for improving the quality of education, the rate of expenditure per pupil, and teachers' salaries compared to those in the other Rocky Mountain states. Open conflict developed between the association and Governor George Dewey Clyde, and when the Governor refused to accept the recommendations of a study committee jointly agreed to by him and the UEA, the association declared a 2-day work recess. In a special session the first day of the recess, the state board directed State Superintendent T. H. Bell to request the attorney general to immediately petition the court to serve a temporary restraining order on the UEA leadership so that it could not interfere in any way with the teachers' contractual obligations. A majority of the UEA members failed to show up at their schools during the recess. The restraining order was served but removed less than a week later when it became clear that further violations of contracts would not be recommended or approved by the UEA leadership.

Both the UEA and its parent organization, the National Education Association, placed sanctions on Utah, and opening the schools in the fall of 1964 proved difficult. A change in Governors and favorable legislation in 1965 apparently eliminated the conflict, although scars remained. Relationships between the office and the association were very good at the close of 1966.

FOOTNOTES

1. Church of Jesus Christ of Latter-Day Saints, *Doctrine and Covenants* (Salt Lake City: Deseret News Press, 1950), sec. 6: verse 7.
2. *Ibid.*, 99:36.
3. *Ibid.*, 130:18.
4. Brigham Young, "Governor's Message," *Journal of the Joint Sessions of the Legislative Assembly of the Territory of Utah, 1851-1876,* p. 5.
5. Utah Territory, *Acts, Resolutions and Memorials: Passed by the First Annual and Special Session of the Legislative Assembly of the Territory of Utah* (1851), p. 257.
6. Utah Territory, *Acts, Resolutions and Memorials: Passed by the Legislative Assembly of the Territory of Utah During the Ninth Annual Session* (1860), sec. 3. pp. 22-26.
7. For further information on the duties and responsibilities given the territorial superintendent by the 1890 law, see Utah Territory, *Laws* (1890), ch. 72.
8. Territorial Commissioner of Schools, *Biennial Report, 1894-95,* p. 5.
9. For an analysis of the factors causing a shift in the composition of the population, see LaVerne C. Bane, "History of Education in Utah, 1870-1896" (unpublished Ph.D. dissertation, Stanford University, Palo Alto, 1940), pp. i-ii.

10. John C. Moffitt, *The History of Public Education in Utah* (Provo: By the Author, 1946), p. 51.
11. U.S. Congress, House, *Executive Document 153,* 48th Congress, 1st sess. May 6, 1884.
12. Utah, *Constitution* (1896), art. 10, sec. 8.
13. Utah, *Laws* (1896), ch. 130, secs. 1-9.
14. E. Allen Bateman, *Development of the County-Unit School District in Utah* (published Ph.D. dissertation, New York : Teachers College, Columbia University, 1940), p. 17.
15. Superintendent of Public Instruction, *First Annual Report, 1896,* p. 18.
16. Superintendent of Public Instruction, *Twenty-Seventh Annual Report, 1958,* p. 6.
17. Utah, *Constitution* (Amended November 4, 1950), art. 10, sec. 8.
18. Taken from records available in the Office of the State Superintendent of Public Instruction.
19. For a complete statement, see Department of Public Instruction, *Curriculum Framework for Utah Schools* (Salt Lake City: The Department, 1964), p. 24.
20. *Utah Code Annotated* (1953), V, 570.
21. Robert R. Hamilton and Paul R. Mort, *The Law and Public Education* (2d ed.; Brooklyn: The Foundation Press, Inc., 1959), p. 22.
22. Conover *v.* Board of Education of Nebo School District, 1 Utah 2d 375, 267 P 2d 768 (1954).
23. Utah, *Attorney General's Opinion: High School-Weber County Controversy* (August 18, 1924).
24. Utah, *Attorney General's Opinion: County Attorney Not Legal Advisor of the Board* (March 3, 1933).
25. *Ibid.*
26. *Utah Code Annotated* (1953), V, 570.
27. For further information, see Walter D. Talbot, "Study of the Extent to Which Further Consolidation Is Feasible and Desirable Within Selected School Districts in Utah," (unpublished Ph.D. dissertation, Utah State University, Logan, 1966), ch. 4.
28. Moffitt, *op. cit.,* p. 130.
29. *Ibid.,* p. 145.
30. *Ibid.,* pp. 145-46.
31. *Ibid.,* pp. 152-53.
32. Utah, *Laws* (1943), p. 14.
33. *Ibid.,* pp. 115-16.
34. Utah, *Laws* (1953), p. 68.
35. In 1959, the value of the distribution unit went from $4,650 to $5,150 on a sliding scale, and the supplemental program was increased from 12 percent to 15 percent of the basic. Utah, *Laws* (1959), pp. 158-63. In 1961, the value of the distribution unit increased to a solid figure of $5,400, the supplemental program to $775, with the districts required to impose 12 mills to qualify for a guarantee on the supplemental program. Utah, *Laws* (1961), pp. 361-67.
36. The basic program distribution unit of $7,250 was the amount guaranteed by the state in 1967 for every 27 students in average daily attendance in the regular program, grades 1-12. Districts received the same guarantee for every 50 students in average daily attendance at the kindergarten level. Still different requirements were in force with respect to special education programs and small isolated schools. Utah, *School Laws* (1965), Title 53, ch. 7, defines the various terms in detail and explains how these amounts are determined.
37. For further information, see Minutes of the Utah State Board of Education, April 29, 1949, pp. 1746-47; October 7, 1949, pp. 1804-1807. (Mimeographed.)
38. The requirements for certification of administrators, supervisors, teachers, school librarians, and counselors were strengthened in 1946 by board action.
39. Utah, *School Laws* (1965), Title 53, ch. 16, secs. 2, 5, p. 51.
40. Since the relationship with the U.S. Office of Education has been discussed in the section on programs and services, it is given no explanation here.
41. The representatives for the board of regents of the University of Utah and the board of trustees of Utah State University also represented their branch colleges.
42. Dixie Junior College at St. George, the Salt Lake Trade Technical Institute, and the Utah Trade Technical Institute of Provo are the institutions of higher learning under the control of the State Board of Education.
43. Utah, *Constitution* (Amended November 4, 1950), art. 7, sec. 13.
44. For purposes of appointment, the state is divided into five districts.
45. One member is appointed on recommendation from each of the following agencies: the Office of the State Superintendent of Public Instruction, the Law Library Board, the Legislative Council, and the State Historical Society Board. At least two of the other five members must be appointed from rural areas. The secretary of state serves as an ex officio member of the commission.
46. *Utah Code Annotated* (1953), Supplement (1959), Title 53, ch. 1, sec. 15.
47. An extensive historical account of the association, its development and service, has been written by John C. Moffitt and is available from the Utah Education Association headquarters in Salt Lake City.
48. Minutes of the Utah State Board of Education, January 31, April 4, 1958, pp. 4003-4005. (Mimeographed.)
49. *Ibid.*

BIBLIOGRAPHY

Public Documents

Conover *v.* Board of Education of Nebo School District, 1 Utah 2d, 375, 267, P 2d 768 (1954).

U.S. Congress. House. *Executive Document 153.* 48th Congress, 1st sess. May 6, 1884.

Utah. *Attorney General's Opinion: County Attorney Not Legal Advisor of the Board* (March 3, 1933).

—— *Attorney General's Opinion: High School-Weber County Controversy* (August 18, 1924).

—— *Constitution* (1896, as amended).

—— *Laws* (1896, 1905-11, 1919-65).

—— *School Laws* (1965).

—— *Utah Code Annotated* (1953).

Utah Territory. *Acts, Resolutions and Memorials: Passed at the Several Annual and Special Sessions of the Legislative Assembly* (1851-55).

—— *Acts, Resolutions and Memorials: Passed by the Legislative Assembly of the Territory of Utah During the Ninth Annual Session* (1860).

—— *Laws* (1890).

Young, Brigham. "Governor's Message." *Journals of the Joint Session of the Legislative Assembly of the Territory of Utah, 1851-1876.*

Books and Pamphlets

Bateman, E. Allen. *Development of the County-Unit School District in Utah.* New York: Teachers College, Columbia University, 1940.

Bennion, M. Lynn. *Mormonism and Education.* Salt Lake City: Deseret News Press, 1939.

Campbell, Jay J. *Historical Perspective on Major Education Changes in Utah, 1847-1966.* Salt Lake City: Utah State Board of Education, 1966.

Chisholm, Leslie L. *The Work of the Modern High School.* New York: Macmillan Co., 1953.

Church of Jesus Christ of Latter-Day Saints. *Doctrine and Covenants.* Salt Lake City: Deseret News Press, 1950.

Department of Public Instruction. *Curriculum Framework for Utah Schools.* Salt Lake City: The Department, 1964.

Hamilton, Robert R., and Mort, Paul R. *The Law and Public Education.* 2d ed. Brooklyn: The Foundation Press, Inc., 1959.

Moffitt, John C. *The History of Public Education in Utah.* Provo: By the Author, 1946.

—— *A Century of Service.* Salt Lake City: Utah Education Association, 1961.

National Education Association of the United States. *An Inquiry into the Organization and Administration of the State Educational Agency of Utah.* Washington, D.C.: National Commission for the Defense of Education Through Education, 1950.

Reports

The Fact Finding Body. *Public Education in Utah.* Report of the Fact Finding Body appointed in 1939 by the Governor of the State of Utah. Salt Lake City: The Fact Finding Body, 1940.

Investigating Committee of Utah Governmental Units. *Report,* 1933. Salt Lake City: The Committee, 1933.

Superintendents of Public Instruction and Territorial Commissioners. *Reports*, 1894-1967.

Territorial Commissioners and Superintendents of Public Instruction. *Annual and Biennial Reports.* Salt Lake City: Education Department, 1894-1968.

U.S. Bureau of Education. *Survey of Education in Utah,* No. 18. Washington, D.C.: Government Printing Office, 1926.

Periodical

Utah Educational Review. LII (May 1959).

Unpublished Material

Bane, LaVerne C. "History of Education in Utah, 1870-1896." Unpublished Ph.D. dissertation, Stanford University, 1940.

Minutes of the Utah State Board of Education, 1896-1965. (Mimeographed.)

Talbot, Walter D. "Study of the Extent to Which Further Consolidation Is Feasible and Desirable Within Selected School Districts in Utah." Unpublished Ph.D. dissertation, Utah State University, Logan, 1966.

Winget, Lerue. "Local Practices in the Selection of Textbooks from the State Approved List in Utah." Unpublished master's thesis, University of Utah, Salt Lake City, 1950.

——"The History of the State Board of Education in Utah with Particular Emphasis upon the Instructional Program." Unpublished Ph.D. dissertation, University of Utah, Salt Lake City, 1962.

Appendix A

UTAH CHIEF STATE SCHOOL OFFICERS

Territorial Superintendent of Primary Schools

1851-56 Elias Smith

Territorial Superintendents of Common Schools

1856-62 William Willis

1862-74 Robert Campbell

Territorial Superintendents of District Schools

1874-77 O. H. Riggs

1877-81 John Taylor

1881-87 John Nuttall

Territorial Commissioners of Schools

1887-89 P. L. Williams

1889-94 Jacob S. Boreman

1894-96 T. B. Lewis

State Superintendents of Public Instruction

1896-1900 John R. Park

1900-1901 Mrs. Emma J. McVicker

1901-13 A. C. Nelson

1913-15 A. C. Matheson

1915-19 E. G. Gowans

1919-20 G. N. Child

1920-21 L. J. Muir

1921 George Thomas (Jan.-July)

1921-33 C. N. Jensen

1933-45 Charles H. Skidmore

1945-60 E. Allen Bateman

1960-62 Wilburn N. Ball

1962 Marsden B. Stokes (Apr.-Aug.)

1962-63 Marion G. Merkley

1963- Terrel H. Bell

Appendix B

Chart I.--UTAH DEPARTMENT OF EDUCATION[(a)], 1910-40

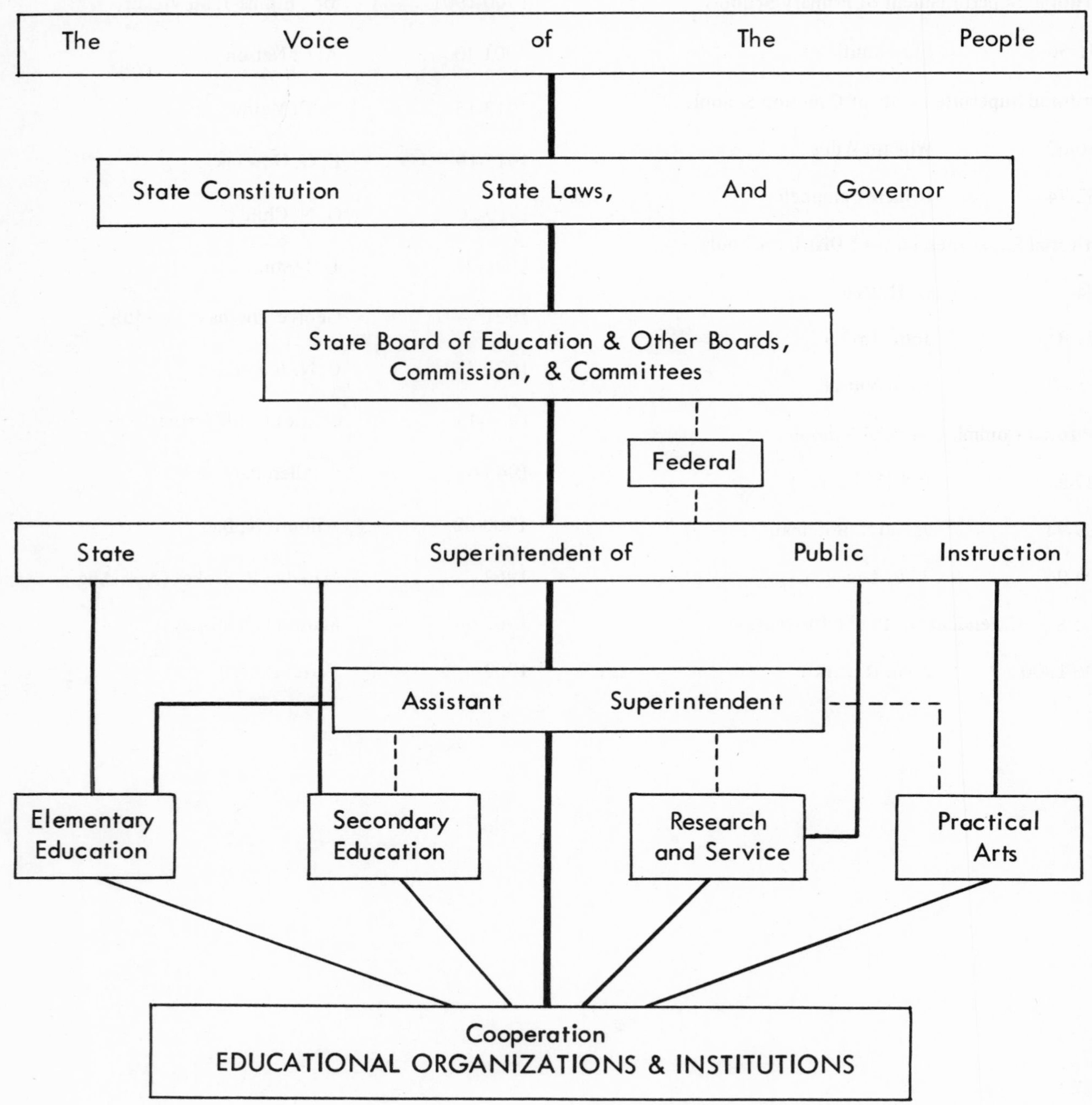

(a)From Biennial Report of the State Superintendent of Public Instruction, 1932-34, p. 34

Appendix B

Chart II.--UTAH DEPARTMENT OF EDUCATION[a], 1942-44

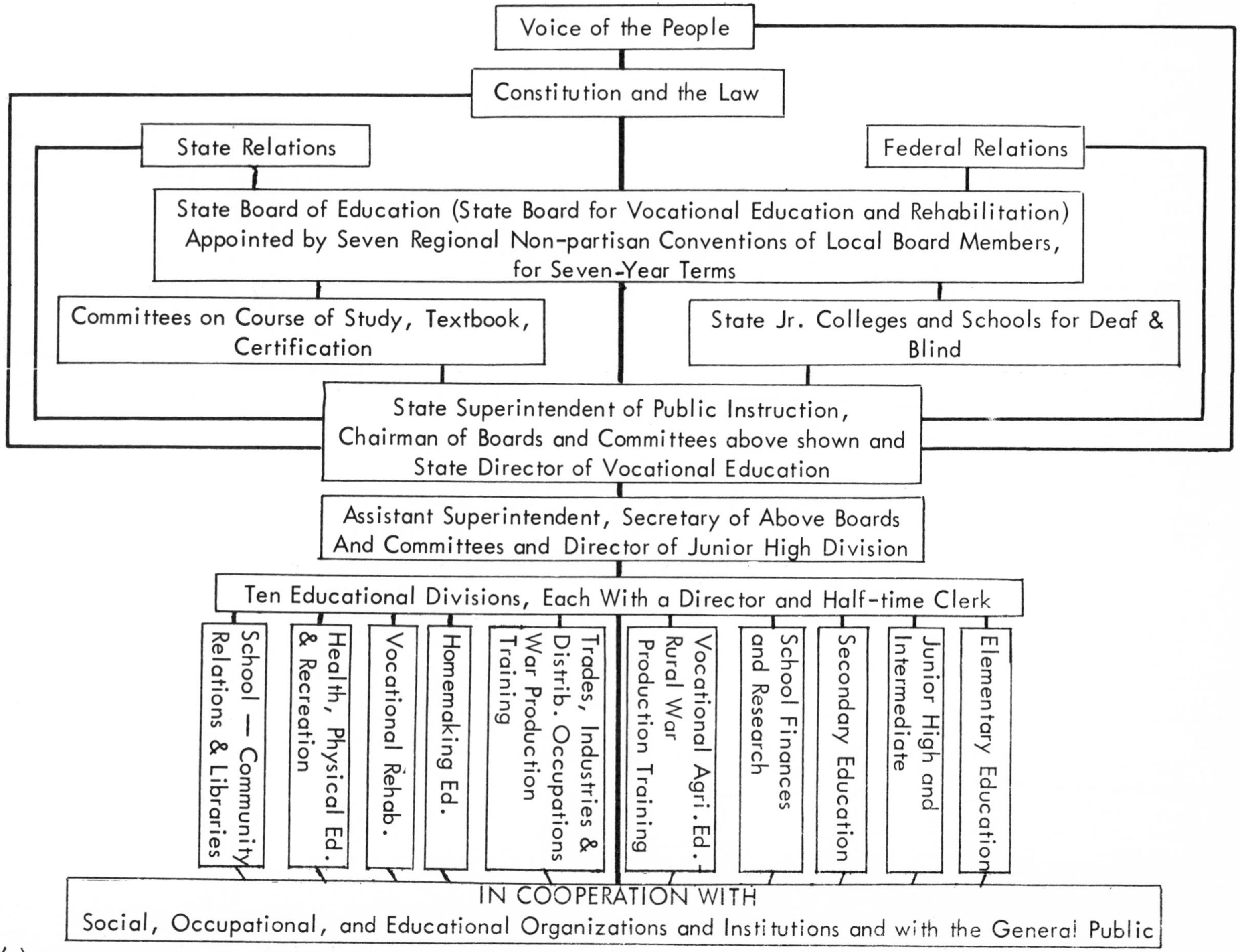

(a)From Biennial Report of the State Superintendent of Public Instruction, 1942-44, p. 19.

Appendix B

Chart III.--UTAH DEPARTMENT OF PUBLIC INSTRUCTION,[a] 1962

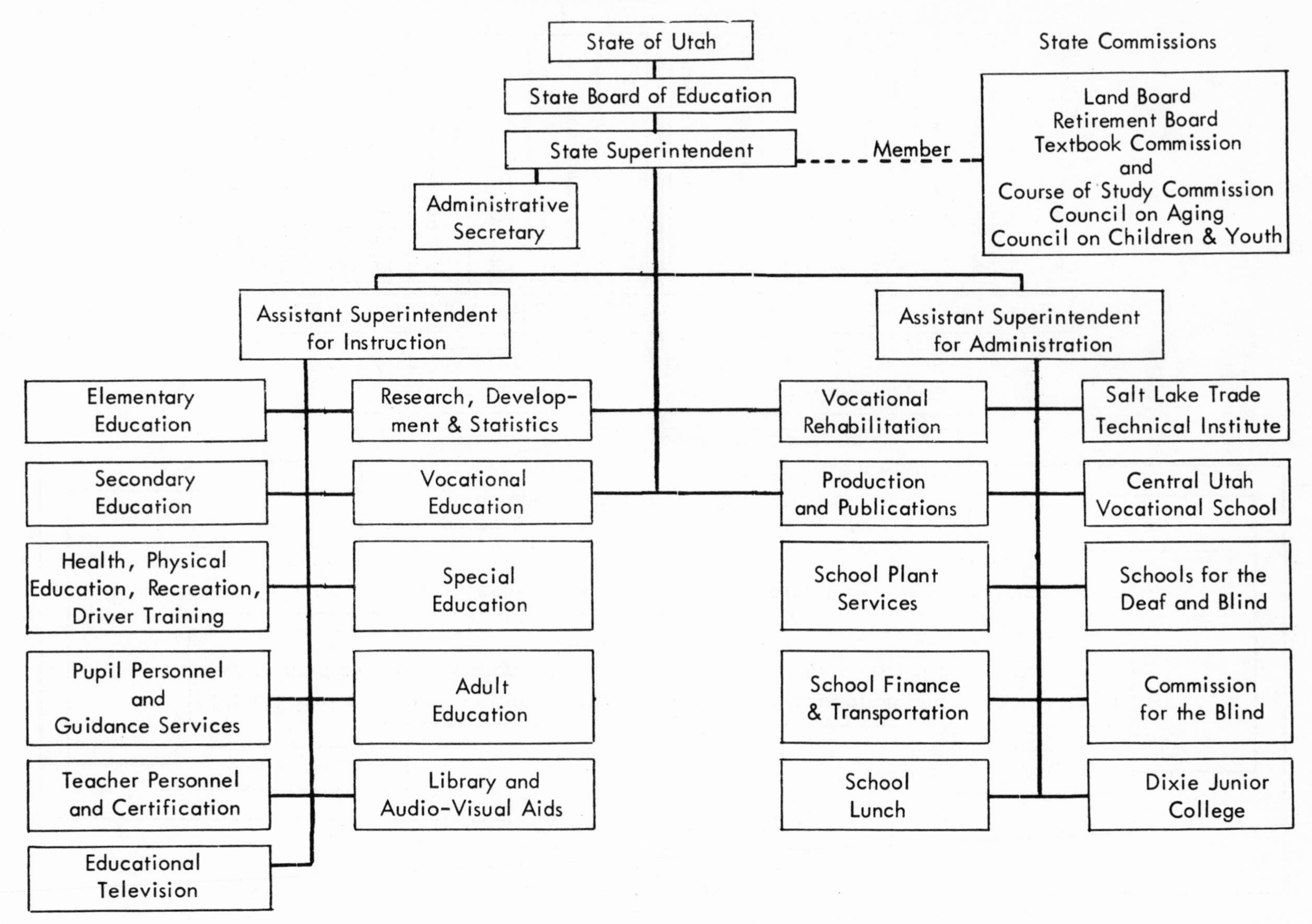

(a)Winget, op. cit., p. 347

Appendix B

Chart IV.--UTAH DEPARTMENT OF PUBLIC INSTRUCTION[a], 1964

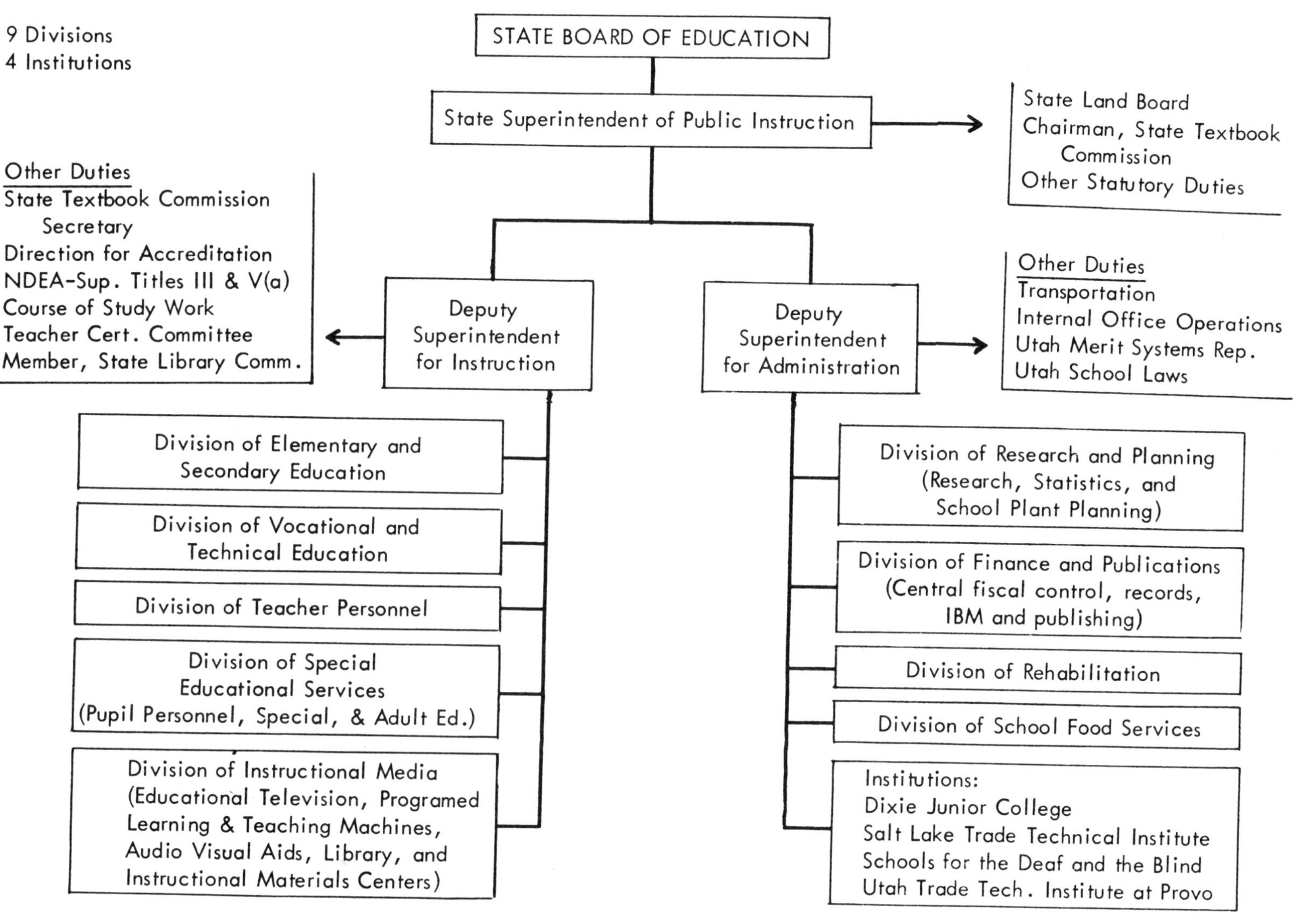

(a) From E. T. DeMars, Utah School Organization & Administration (Salt Lake City: College of Education, University of Utah, 1964), p. 136.

Appendix B

Chart V.--UTAH STATE BOARD OF EDUCATION, 1966

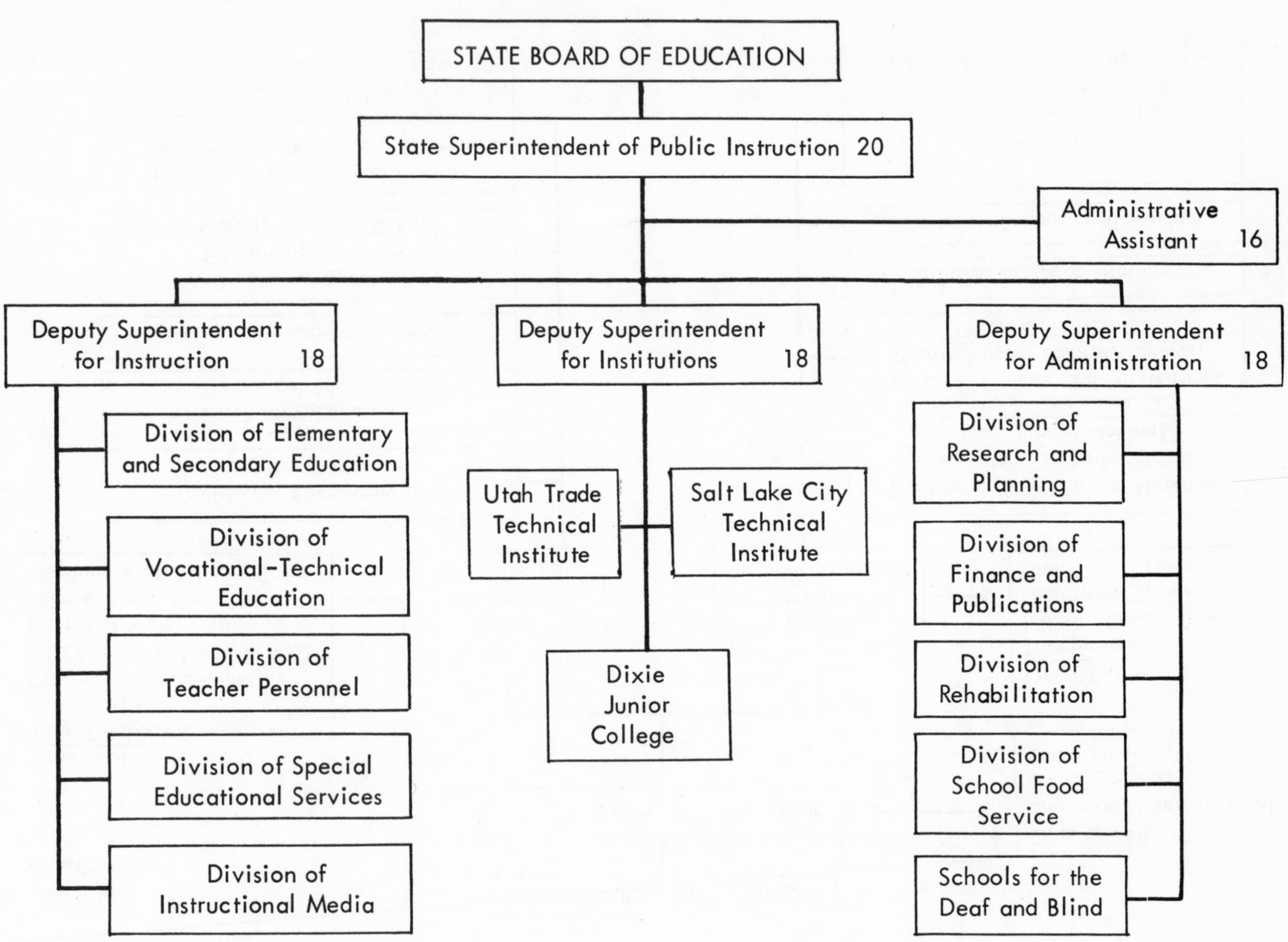
STATE BOARD OF EDUCATION
State Superintendent of Public Instruction 20
Administrative Assistant 16
Deputy Superintendent for Instruction 18
Division of Elementary and Secondary Education
Division of Vocational-Technical Education
Division of Teacher Personnel
Division of Special Educational Services
Division of Instructional Media
Deputy Superintendent for Institutions 18
Utah Trade Technical Institute
Salt Lake City Technical Institute
Dixie Junior College
Deputy Superintendent for Administration 18
Division of Research and Planning
Division of Finance and Publications
Division of Rehabilitation
Division of School Food Service
Schools for the Deaf and Blind

Appendix B

Supplement 1. – SUMMARY OF THE DEVELOPMENT OF THE STATE BOARD OF EDUCATION AND THE OFFICE OF STATE SUPERINTENDENT IN UTAH[a]

Year	Composition of board	Nomination and selection of board members	Selection of superintendent
1850	Twelve members: board of regents, University of Deseret	Chosen by vote of both Houses of the General Assembly	
1851	Same		Appointed by board of regents, University of Deseret
1862	Authority of board of regents began to wane		Elected by Legislature
1876			Elected by popular vote of people
1887			Appointed by territorial supreme court
1896	State superintendent (chairman), president of the State University, principal of the Agricultural College, and two other persons	First three named were ex officio; other two appointed by the Governor, with the consent of the Senate; 4-year terms	Elected by popular vote of people; to have been a resident citizen for 5 years just preceding his election
1915	Same as 1896, except six appointed persons instead of two	First three ex officio; six appointed by Governor, with consent of Senate; 6-year terms	Same
1935	State superintendent (chairman), and nine other members	State superintendent ex officio; nine appointed by seven regional school board conventions, on a staggered basis; vacancies filled by Governor; 7-year terms	Same
1951	Nine members; chairman to be selected by group from their membership	Nominated by seven regional nominating conventions open to all qualified registered electors, and by petition; elected on nonpartisan ballot on a staggered basis; vacancies filled by appointment by regional school board conventions; 6-year terms	Appointed by board; to have been a resident citizen for 5 years just preceding his appointment
1953	Same	Same, except term shortened to 4 years, making it possible to change a majority of the board every other election	Same, except salary fixed at $8,000
1957	Same	Same	Same, except salary fixed at $10,000
1959	Same	Same	Same, except statutory limitation of $14,000 on salary
1961	Same	Same	Same
1963	Same	Same	Appointed by board, without residency requirement on statutory limitation on salary
1965	Same	Regular election and nominating convention procedures remained same, but provision made for primary election and the number of signatures required for nomination by petition increased from 50 to 100 qualified and registered electors.	Same

[a] Taken from Utah territorial and state laws for the years indicated.

Appendix C

PROGRAM OF STUDIES FOR UTAH SECONDARY SCHOOLS[a], IN EFFECT AFTER 1958

Subject[b]	7th Grade	8th Grade	9th Grade	10th Grade	11th Grade	12th Grade
Language Arts[c]	1[d] R	1 R	1 R	1 R	1 R	R
Foreign Language[e]				1 O →	→	→
Social Studies[f]	Utah Hist. 1/2 R	U.S. Hist. 1 R	World Geo. 1/2 R	World Hist. O or R	Am. Hist. & Gov't. 1 R	Am. Social & Econ. Probs O or R
Mathematics[g]	Arithmetic 1 R	Arithmetic 1 R		1 R →	→	→
Science[h]		General Science 1 R →	→	1 R →	→	→
Health[i]	1/2 R →	→		1/2 R →	→	→
Physical Education[j]	1/2 R	1/2 R	1/2 R	1 R →	→	→
Homemaking, Girls[k]	1 R →	→	→	2 O →	→	→
Industrial Arts[k]	1 R →	→	→	2 O →	→	→
Art	1/2 R →	→	→	O →	→	→
Music	1/2 R →	→	→	O →	→	→
Typing, I and II				O →	→	→

Appendix C

PROGRAM OF STUDIES FOR UTAH SECONDARY SCHOOLS[a], IN EFFECT AFTER 1958 (Continued)

[a]Bateman, "Items for Superintendents, State Program of Studies for Secondary Schools and High Schools Graduation Requirements, as Amended," April 10, 1958, pp. 29-33.

[b]Any secondary school, on a personal guidance basis, may exempt any students from meeting any one unit or its equivalent of these requirements provided the number does not exceed 5 percent of the class enrollment, and any student may be exempted from meeting two units of the requirements, provided the number of students so exempted does not exceed 2 percent of the class enrollment.

[c]Remedial programs may be substituted for basic language arts courses at any level. At least two units of the last three must be English. There may be substituted for either eleventh- or twelfth-grade English, one unit from among the subjects offered in grades 10-12 in the general area of language arts. One unit of foreign language may be substituted for ninth-grade language arts or for a unit of English in the senior high if the substitution was not made in the ninth grade.

[d]The "1" indicates the number of "contact" units (representing 50 minutes multiplied by the number of days in the school year for the senior high and a class period held each day all year long for the junior high). "R" indicates that the subject is required. "O" indicates that the subject must be offered in the school. An arrow indicates the condition noted is to take place somewhere within the grades covered by the arrow.

[e]Provided the high school has an enrollment of at least 350 students, grades 10-12.

[f]One unit in addition to American history and government is required in grades 10-12. The unit may be from one or a combination of the following: world history, one unit; America's social and economic problems, one unit; sociology, one-half unit; world geography, one-half unit; or economics, one-half unit.

[g]Algebra, geometry, second year algebra and consumer mathematics must be offered.

[h]One additional unit is recommended for the junior high. At the senior high level this requirement must be filled by either biology, botany, zoology, physiology (if not substituted for health), agricultural science, physics, chemistry, senior physical science, or a combination of any two of the biological science courses. Biology and physics, chemistry or senior physical science must be offered.

[i]One-half unit physiology may be substituted for the health requirement.

[j]This work shall be taken on a half-unit basis in any two of the grades 10-12.

[k]It is recommended that one-half unit be required in each of grades 7 and 8, although one unit in grades 8 or 9 will fulfill the requirement. It is recommended that a full year elective be offered in grade 9.

46 Vermont

DEPARTMENT OF EDUCATION
Marshall True
Judith Cyronak

Assisted by Leon H. Bruno

Contents

INTRODUCTION

The advocates of better schools at an Arlington, Vermont, town meeting were trying to persuade their fellow citizens to replace the meager one-room district school and two-room village schools with a modern school. The problem was a universal one; the town had little money. Opponents of the new school—as Dorothy Canfield Fisher, Vermont author and longtime resident of Arlington, remembers—had had the best of the meeting, concentrating their arguments on what they called "hard facts." The need, they said, was for other things—especially bridges, which are important to a town surrounded by streams, as Arlington is.

The sense of the meeting shifted abruptly, however, when the town grocer remarked, "What we are being told here is that if we keep up our bridges, we won't have money enough to run decently good schools for our children. If that is so . . . then I say, LET THE BRIDGES FALL DOWN." The grocer then put the real question to his fellow citizens: "Which would you rather have, forty years from now in our town—dumb ignorant people that can't earn a decent living to take care of their children, going over good bridges? Or folks with well-trained brains who know their way around? Such people can build their own bridges" (1). Arlington voted to build a better school.

The dilemma expressed in Dorothy Canfield Fisher's anecdote has been a real one in Vermont. As residents of a small, predominantly rural, and invariably poor state, Vermonters have been forced to pick their improvements gingerly. Despite a strong commitment to educational improvement, they have not always been able to do what they would like for their schools. State Superintendent of Education Mason S. Stone's comment of 1908 wryly captures the essence of this dilemma:

> The penal institutions in Vermont are in excellent condition, and within a few years, the State has erected a splendid hospital for the insane. Now that the State has its criminals and insane well housed and cared for, it would be well to devise means for improving its schools, and thus prevent as far as possible patronage upon those other institutions (2).

Despite a lack of adequate revenues, Vermont has consistently made an impressive and continuing effort to provide the best education possible (3). One of the major forces in providing the best possible education has been the Vermont Board of Education, which has, in cooperation with the state commissioner of education, provided educational leadership for the state since 1915.

The board's task has not always been an easy one. In addition to inadequate finances, it has had to cope with problems arising out of Vermont's continuing ruralism. Unlike most states, Vermont did not experience a major population growth in the first half of the twentieth century; its problem has been the continuing decline in the population of its rural communities (4). The result of this population shift has been a relative decline in the property values of many Vermont communities and a subsequent unwillingness on the part of these communities to foot their education bill. Another result has been that the distribution of Vermont's population has tended to concentrate the wealth of the state in a few of its larger towns and place on these towns an inequitable tax burden. Because its population has remained relatively stable, Vermont has only recently had to face the problems of urban schools and the population explosion which forced many states to adopt double sessions in already crowded schools while they sought desperately to solve educational problems.

Continuing on the positive side of the ledger, the state board in Vermont has not been the political football it has been in other states. Since the legislation of 1915 (to be discussed below), Vermont has enjoyed the advantages of having a professional department of education reasonably unbuffeted by the winds of political change. To be sure, politics in Vermont have affected education—it would not be realistic to view Vermont education as being free of politics—but political corruption, e.g., the buying and selling of educational posts, which has occurred in some states, has not been much a part of Vermont education. The board has also benefited from Vermont's until recently unblemished Republicanism, which ensured that the vagaries of party politics, and the consequent insidious spoils system, would not dominate Vermont educational policies.

As a result of the board's professionalism and stability, educators in Vermont have displayed commendable willingness to innovate and experiment in education. Vermonters in Washington, from Senator Justin Morrill, sponsor of the Land Grant College Act of 1862, and Senator Carroll S. Page, one of the leading advocates of the Smith-Hughes Act of 1917, to the incumbent Senators, George Aiken and Winston Prouty, have consistently advocated programs of federal aid to education (5). On the state level, the commissioners of education have prided themselves on keeping abreast of national trends in education. Francis L. Bailey, a former teacher in Carleton Washburne's well-known Winnetka, Illinois, school system and an Ed. D. from Teachers College, Columbia University, prides himself on having played an active role in the National Education Association and keeping up with the latest innovations (6).

A. John Holden, Jr., commissioner of education from 1948 to 1965, spent a *Wanderjahr* in Germany studying rural education and returned to Vermont to try to put some of his ideas to work in the one-room Morse School in East Montpelier. Dr. Holden, who recalls his teaching at the Morse School as "a single-handed effort to do something radical with the one-room school," was trying to utilize what he saw as some of the inherent advantages of the one-room school (7).

This spirit of trying to make the best of difficult circumstances has been an important influence in Vermont education. It has encouraged Vermont educators to struggle against their twin problems of poverty and population shifts.

NINETEENTH-CENTURY BACKGROUND

The Carnegie Commission for the Advancement of Teaching, which conducted a thorough survey of the Vermont school system in 1912, recognized that the state had never assumed a constructive responsibility for public educational policy. This was due, the commission said, to "the sturdiness and independence of local communities [in Vermont, the] isolation of . . . geographic sections of the state . . . and the absence of any dominating city centers of population" (8).

The commission believed that the absence of a positive state policy in education explained the lack of an appropriate machinery for administration, supervision, and inspection of the state school system. Throughout the nineteenth century, the state had experimented with various methods of school administration and had apparently found no system completely adequate.

Early settlers in Vermont, attracted to the lumber industry and a growing potash trade, followed the Connecticut River Valley northward. The river became their chief connection with the outside world. Logs and sawed lumber were shipped downriver to Hartford, Connecticut; upstream by pole boats came necessities of living, rum, and molasses. Residents on both sides of the river, including Dartmouth College President Eleazer Wheelock, became advocates of a "Valley State" that would include towns on both sides of the river. Wheelock and others hoped that Hanover, New Hampshire, home of Dartmouth, would serve as the state capital (9).

As a result of this situation, Vermont's early political history presents a welter of moves and countermoves regarding Vermont's political future. Proposals ranged from giving Vermont the territory east of the Connecticut and west to the Hudson to dividing Vermont between New York and New Hampshire along the ridge of the Green Mountains. Naturally enough, this political confusion retarded the development of a common school system in Vermont. Despite some earlier abortive proposals, it was not until after Vermont was admitted to the Union in 1791 that the State Legislature required towns to provide schools to teach English, writing, and arithmetic. Educational development proceeded slowly until the election of Cornelius Van Ness as Governor in 1823. In his inaugural address, Governor Van Ness suggested, "Knowledge and virtue are the main pillars of a free government; and the only foundation on which they can stand is education." Governor Van Ness saw "no injustice in compelling the rich to contribute to the education of the poor," and he, therefore, recommended revision and strengthening of Vermont's education laws (10). His successor, Ezra Brooks, persuaded the Legislature to consider some of Van Ness's proposals. In 1827, the Legislature set up a Board of Commissioners for common schools. This first State Board of Education was abolished 6 years later, chiefly because it prescribed texts to be used in the common school.

Vermont's strong tradition of localism also contributed to its inability to establish any kind of effective central administration of the schools. In 1845, the Legislature established the Office of State Superintendent of Schools to supervise educational policy more efficiently; in 1851, however, not agreeing to the need for such an officer, the Legislature refused to appoint a superintendent. In 1856, the Legislature once again apparently saw the need of some central direction for the schools and established another State Board of Education, consisting of the Governor, the lieutenant governor, and three others to be appointed by the Governor. This awkward agency administered education for 18 years. Then it was abolished because, in the eyes of the legislators, it was too aggressive and officious for men who possessed mere academic knowledge of conditions and schools. In 1874, the Legislature revived the Office of State Superintendent of Schools. Thus for most of the nineteenth century, educational administration in Vermont was varied and complex. Educators and the Legislature shifted administrative responsibility from state to town and town to state with great frequency and with little regard for educational efficiency. Not until 1892, when Mason Stone was elected state superintendent of schools, was the modern movement toward a more centralized state educational system begun (11). Historically, Vermont has maintained that education is a local affair and has accepted regionalization reluctantly.

MASON STONE AND EARLY EDUCATIONAL REFORM

At the turn of the century, Vermont entered an era of educational reform which culminated in the school legislation of 1915. The reform bill was based on the recommendations of the Carnegie Foundation in 1912, but the initial reform impulse began earlier. One of the prime contributors to this drive toward more active state leadership in education was Mason S. Stone. A native of Waterbury Center, Vermont, and a graduate of the University of Vermont, Stone served as state superintendent of education from 1892 to 1916. Except for a 3-year interlude, 1902 to 1905, when the U.S. government sent him to the Philippines to help set up a school system for that newly acquired territory, Mason Stone dominated Vermont education. He came to the superintendent's office with a good deal of experience in educational administration: he had been principal of Williston Academy, Bristol High School, and People's Academy in Morrisville, Vermont. He had spent 2 years as supervisor of schools for Orleans County and a year as superintendent of schools in Southampton, Massachusetts.

Unlike many educators—before and since—Stone delighted in the political maneuvering inherent in the election of a superintendent. He took pride in knowing each of Vermont's 246 legislators personally and almost always had a majority of them favorably disposed toward him. One senses without being able to document it that Stone's delight with the politics of his office enhanced his role as an educational leader. Every new Legislature required that Stone reformulate and reargue and consequently strengthen his educational program. Former Commissioner Ralph E. Noble, who knew Stone quite well, remembers best his "black, bright and very intelligent eyes" (12).

Surveying the problems of Vermont education in 1900, Stone recognized that the schools, especially in rural areas, were suffering from lack of adequate financial support and of skilled supervision. He believed that the inequities that grew out of this situation could only be resolved through skilled supervision at state expense. Like many of his contemporaries, Stone realized that the district school system, controlled by local boards of education, was becoming increasingly inadequate to meet modern educational needs. Society's demands on education were becoming more specialized, and educational methods were going to have to be more sophisticated and scientific. Stone recognized that educational administration would have to be a full-time professional occupation.

> Inefficiency is not the fault of the superintendents; it is the defect of the system. The superintendents are the appointees of the local school boards, and they are without question the most capable persons available in the various towns. But as school affairs are adventitious to their regular trade, business or profession, the supervision of the schools is a matter of secondary importance. Frequently, too, the persons called to the supervision of the schools are less informed in the educational matters than the teachers (13).

Stone recommended that towns be combined into supervisory units, over which a professional supervisor would be placed for each supervisory union district. The salary of this supervisor should be paid by the state and should be large enough to attract a person "who, on account of his character and power, will be recognized in the various towns as a public-speaker, businessman and educator" (14).

Some of Stone's aims were realized in 1906 when the General Assembly passed an education bill that provided for the voluntary union of towns for the purpose of school supervision. The salaries of the union superintendents were to be subsidized by the state. In addition, the act provided for a permanent school fund, consolidation of rural schools, school transportation, and standardization principles for high schools.

Stone, continuing his crusade for a better school system, declared that teacher training and vocational training were the state's two biggest remaining problems. He insisted that the state had an obligation to provide adequate teaching if it made education compulsory. He shared the concern of many educators with practical education. He recognized that the complex needs of a growing industrial society were going to require a new approach to education. In the 1908 *School Report,* Stone outlined the vocational needs of Vermont and the existing attempts to meet those needs through state-supported vocational education. The chief occupation of Vermont was agriculture, and Stone felt that the agricultural future of the state depended on how well the educational system could prepare Vermont's youth to take their place in this field. "Apparently Vermont's future success in agriculture will depend upon the opportunities the state affords for preparation for intensive farming. Today Vermont has done scarcely anything in this direction" (15).

Aside from the State Agricultural College, which had an enrollment of 79 students in 1912-13 (16), the state had done little to further educational opportunities in vocational areas. In 1908, the Legislature authorized annual state aid of $250 for any elementary school that included vocational education in its curriculum, but by 1912, only four schools were receiving such aid (17). In 1910, when the Randolph State Normal School was discontinued, the Randolph State School of Agriculture took its place. It was the only real trade school in the state that was exclusively a state effort.

The school legislation of 1910 realized more of Stone's plans for educational progress. For example, medical inspection of schoolchildren was made mandatory, and teacher-training courses in high schools were instituted.

Significant progress was made under Stone's leadership, but in 1912, there was still no centralized administrative agency to coordinate educational activities. The year 1912 marked a turning point in Vermont educational history. A conference of school superintendents and principals had recommended a more centralized school system, and in 1912 the Legislature provided for a State Board of Education, to be appointed by the Governor. One of the board's chief responsibilities was the appointment of the state superintendent of education, who had been elected up to that time by the Legislature.

The board also was charged with the responsibility of determining qualifications for union superintendents and teachers. In 1913, the board agreed on standards for these positions: Union superintendents were required to possess a college degree or 4 years of normal school training, at least 2 years of teaching experience, and knowledge of the history of education, educational psychology, school administration, and methods of teaching; the requirements for a teaching certificate were a satisfactory teaching record, a college degree or 4 years of normal training, and academic background in the areas of history and principles of education, psychology of education, methods of teaching, and school administration (18). These standards reflected an increasing concern with the professionalization of education.

The most significant event marking 1912 as an educational turning point was the election of Republican Governor Allen M. Fletcher. In the election, which was decided by the Legislature because no candidate received a majority vote, Fletcher campaigned on a platform that was every bit as progressive as that of the Progressive party, which had split the Republican party in half. The campaign was heavily influenced by national issues, for the state platforms were practically identical (19). The Vermont Republican party in 1912 was concerned with administrative reform and more specifically with the consolidation of commissions and departments and with economy in state spending. Fletcher apparently saw educational reform as a part of the overall administrative reform that he had promised Vermont's voters. It was on his recommendation that the General Assembly of 1912 passed a resolution calling for him to create a nine-man commission—such as he had earlier requested—to study the state school system.

THE CARNEGIE SURVEY AND ITS AFTERMATH

Vermont's appointment of an educational commission was a reflection of a national educational mood. Progressive educators, in their attempt to professionalize the nation's school systems, were beginning to use scientific tools for evaluating them. The school survey was one such method that was gaining increasing national acceptance in the second decade of the twentieth century (20).

The Vermont Educational Commission in 1912 engaged the Carnegie Foundation for the Advancement of Teaching to conduct a complete educational survey of the state. The Vermont commission held that it was necessary to employ a body of experts in order to conduct the survey properly and to ensure the objectivity of the results and recommendations. "The Commission wanted the facts: to hew the line and let the chips fall where they would in its seeking after the truth of the educational conditions of the state" (21).

In its final report, the Carnegie Foundation complimented Vermont on its progressive activity. It pointed out that this inquiry represented the first comprehensive effort on the part of any state to study its school system as a whole from the elementary school to the university. It also stated that the Foundation assumed that educational institutions in Vermont were not unrelated agencies, but formed parts of one educational system, whether controlled by the state or not.

Guy Potter Benton, president of the University of Vermont in 1913, praised Governor Fletcher and the commission in a speech in which he claimed that this investigation was the most important of all such studies in the nation because it was so comprehensive. He added: "We have an educational commission in this state which is unique in the history of such commissions and a sure guarantee of unselfish and patriotic service which will put Vermont in the vanguard of educational progress in this country" (22).

The State Board of Education, which was appointed in 1912, voted in 1913 to instruct the superintendent of education to cooperate with the Carnegie survey staff in its study of educational conditions (23).

The Carnegie commission's recommendations, which were reviewed by the Vermont commission and submitted in the form of a bill, ranged from elementary school curriculum to the financing of higher education. The emphasis of the report and the resulting legislation, however, were administrative in nature. The commission was convinced that no substantial progress could take place unless Vermont adopted a clear policy in educational matters and a centralized administrative agency to guide the state. The administrative system was the focal point in the recommended reform program. Without an effective state-controlled administrative system, no other reforms were possible.

The Carnegie survey team clearly supported the trend toward state-controlled administration that was gaining acceptance across the country. The report stated that the once widely accepted plan of electing the superintendent by popular vote or by legislative election was being replaced by a plan which placed control with a small, appointed Board of Education, composed of layment who served without pay. Vermont had adopted this method in 1912, but the survey recommended felt that the board's powers should be increased so that it would have general control of the entire educational system of the state. The commissioner of education, to be appointed by the board, was to be a man "of such breadth of education, of such special training, of such varied educational experience, and with such a record of successful performance as will entitle him to be entrusted with the important responsibilities of the Board" (24). Public educational policy would be determined by the Legislature and executed by the Office of the Commissioner, which was to receive guidance from a small, public-spirited Board of Education. The typically progressive ideal of freeing education from political interference, yet making it responsive to popular will, is evident in the survey team's recommendation. General principles of progressive education seem to have had as much influence on this reform measure as did the specific needs of the State of Vermont.

Another major reform, adopted by the Legislature in 1915, also was an attempt to centralize the state's educational system. School unions had been optional since 1906, and the Carnegie Foundation recommended the extension of union supervision. The Vermont commission, convinced that the experiment in union supervision was producing beneficial effects, recommended to the Legislature that union supervision be made mandatory.

The legislation was passed in 1915. It included, in addition to the administrative reforms mentioned above, provisions for curriculum revision, transportation and board, vocational education, courses in teacher training, and examination and certification of teachers. In order to receive the benefits of the act, which included state subsidies for union supervision, teachers in rural communities, and courses in teacher training and vocational education, the towns were required to raise a percentage of their school finances through local taxation and to meet qualifications to be established by the state board.

One very significant recommendation of the Carnegie report that was not included in the legislation was the elimination of state support to all institutions of higher education in the state in favor of one state-supported university. The relationship of the state to the University of Vermont, Middlebury College, and Norwich University was unusual: It corresponded neither to the typical New England college supported by endowment nor to the state university owned by the state. All of these institutions were controlled by private trustees, but the state contributed to their costs of operation. In view of the state's primary responsibility to elementary and secondary education, the survey recommendation was that state aid to Middlebury College and Norwich University be terminated. This issue was hotly contested by the interested parties, and the Legislature finally refused to take the action recommended by the commission.

Another significant recommendation on which the Legislature did not act was the establishment of a central, state-owned teacher-training college to replace the inefficient normal schools at Johnson and Castleton. The Legislature did authorize the board to establish, at no expense to the state, a teacher-training college. However, the project was not given serious consideration until 1921.

The 1915 school law marked the culmination of an era of progressive innovation in the state. Under Mason Stone's leadership, Vermont had made a concerted effort to launch its school system into the twentieth century. Stone, however, was less than pleased with the eventual outcome. He resigned his post as superintendent in June 1915 and was only persuaded to accept the office of commissioner on the condition that he be replaced as soon as the welfare of the state permitted (25). Stone had not anticipated that the reform impulse he had so diligently nurtured would result in what he called a paternalistic and bureaucratic educational system.

> With centralization of people came centralization of government and with centralization of government came more officials, more autocratic power, and more expense. And so a state of mind was automatically prepared and the swollen and arbitrary school law of 1915 found a congenial atmosphere in which to flourish, operate, and perpetuate itself (26).

To Mason Stone, the legislation was bureaucratic; to his contemporaries, it was progressive. To be progressive in 1915 was to be right.

In 1915, the state board, under the leadership of the disappointed Mason Stone, was faced with the enormous task of implementing the new school legislation. Stone's dissatisfaction was not an auspicious beginning for a task of this magnitude. Its accomplishment was to face even greater difficulties in the future, in the form of statewide reaction against the new legislation and finally against the board and its policies.

The first job tackled by the newly constituted board was the reorganization of supervisory unions in accordance with the principle of mandatory supervision. The board determined principles by which the reorganization should take place. The territory of existing districts was to be preserved; county lines would be observed as far as possible; districts would be composed of towns closely associated commercially and politically; and contiguous towns and topographic conditions would be taken into consideration. The advice of the towns was solicited. The board requested that the towns already organized in unions evaluate their systems and make recommendations. The remainder of the towns were asked to decide what other towns they would like to become affiliated with (27). The board then turned to determining qualifications for the position of union superintendent. The existing superintendents were given priority, and qualifications were quite general. A union superintendent should have "good personality, good habits, good industry, good health and good sense" (28). The board was concerned with professional supervision, but qualifications had to remain broad and flexible because of the state's inability to hire a sufficient number of candidates who could meet the requirements of extensive background and education (29).

The board accepted Mason Stone's resignation in 1916, and Milo Hillegas, associate professor at Teachers College, Columbia University, and former member of the Carnegie commission, was invited to fill the position of commissioner of education. Born in Plattsburgh, New York, Hillegas received a Ph. D. from Columbia in 1912 and had a varied background in teaching and school administration. He had taught high school in Fort Dodge, Iowa, from 1898 to 1900 and served as principal of schools in Schuylerville, New York, from 1902 to 1904. From 1904 to 1908, he was principal in Chatham, New York, and then served as editor-in-chief for the U.S. Bureau of Education from 1910 to 1911.

As commissioner, Hillegas faced the difficult problem of implementing the 1915 legislation. There was some feeling in the state that the board should have chosen a Vermonter to fill this important position. The rural press stated quite frankly that they were watching Mr. Hillegas carefully, although they would give the man a few months before beginning to criticize his methods and plans (30). "Undaunted by criticism, and with a firm resolution to effect the improvements intrusted to his administration, Dr. Hillegas vigorously attacked the problem of reorganizing Vermont's educational affairs" (31).

One of Hillegas' most pressing problems was the shortage of teachers, caused in part by the country's entry into World War I and in part by the state's lack of funds. In a competitive market, Vermont could not afford to keep its teachers by raising their salaries. In spite of this problem, the board under Hillegas' leadership continued to raise professional standards for teachers and teacher-training institutions. The board was particularly concerned that teachers understand the conditions of rural life and its relationship to educational methods. In a further attempt to provide trained teachers for the rural schools, the 1915 legislation included a state subsidy program to aid the towns in paying a minimum wage to teachers.

Normal school standards also were upgraded in this period (32). Applicants were required to possess a high school education, and the course of study included principles and methods and psychology and ethics as well as the standard subject matter. In order to meet the heavy demand for rural elementary school teachers, the "lower course" of study was retained. Only 2 years of high school were required for this 1-year course. The board had also recommended in 1913 that normal school principals be asked to consult the U. S. government reports on rural education in the formulation of their curriculums. It was further recommended that instruction be provided in rural sociology and economics, schoolhouse construction and sanitation, rural schoolhouse organization, and use of the educational resources available in a rural community (33).

The acts of 1912 and 1915 had established state subsidies for vocational education programs in high schools. The board had reviewed and approved 16 of these by 1914. A considerable boost was given to Vermont's vocational education program by the passage of the federal Smith-Hughes Act of 1917. The first bill of its kind, the Smith-Hughes Act provided money for vocational education in high schools through a matching program with the states. The money could be spent in paying salaries of teachers, supervisors and directors of agricultural projects, and teachers of industrial subjects, and in the preparation of teachers of agriculture, trade, and home economics. Vermont's share of the original appropriation was $15,000; the state added $45,000 to that sum. The bulk of the total was spent on training teachers of vocational subjects, and the remainder was used to pay teachers' salaries.

Hillegas felt that World War I offered Vermont schoolchildren an opportunity for public service and educational experience. The Public Safety Committee financed the establishment of the Green Mountain Guard, a group of boys and girls from the public schools who worked in gardens and on farms. The children performed a public service while learning many valuable principles. In his annual report he stated: "The schools of Vermont have been strengthened during the period of the war because boys and girls have been led to work with a purpose such as did not exist earlier. They have been keen to understand current events and to do their share in helping win the war" (34).

Hillegas resigned at the end of his 5-year leave of absence from Columbia University, and Clarence H. Dempsey became commissioner of education in 1921. Born in Washington Mills, New York, Dempsey was educated at Boston University and Norwich University in Vermont. He had studied at the Universities of Munich and Berlin from 1896 to 1898. A former St. Johnsbury, Vermont, school superintendent, Dempsey was hailed as a Vermonter returning to the state. With this auspicious beginning, Dempsey should have had an easier experience than Hillegas, but he had to survive a heated controversy about the state's normal schools and a period of reactionary legislation.

Under the pressures of wartime, the student body at the state's normal schools declined. Hillegas had recognized that this was a nationwide phenomenon. Nevertheless, in 1919, the Legislature refused to extend the charter of the

Johnson and Castleton normal schools. As of August 1920, the state had no normal schools for the training of teachers. The board was faced with a *fait accompli* and was not happy with the situation.

The board faced both a long- and a short-range problem. It was on this authority that the board acted. Provisions had to be made for those students currently enrolled in the normal schools, and the future of teacher training in the state had to be planned. First, the board arranged for students to complete their course of study at the University of Vermont, which provided a special course, with tuition paid by the state, for students of Johnson and Castleton. It then proceeded to the larger problem of future plans.

The board had been authorized by the 1919 Legislature to provide, at no cost to the state, a single centralized teacher-training institution. In the 1920 *Biennial Report,* the board recommended that the state take advantage of a Carnegie Corporation offer of $100,000 for the purpose of constructing a single teacher-training college in Burlington. The University of Vermont would contribute $200,000 to the project, and the school would be affiliated with the university. The state would be required to appropriate $100,000 annually for the maintenance of the institution.

The proposal was introduced to the 1921 Legislature with the strong support of Commissioner Dempsey and the state board. The board's public endorsement of this proposal was unprecedented in Vermont educational history. Commissioner Dempsey, speaking to the Legislature, urged the state to take responsibility for the establishment of the institution on the grounds that a collegiate-level teacher–training school was a fundamental necessity for an adequate school system (35). There was, however, strong opposition to the plan. Representative Stearns of Johnson introduced a bill which would reopen the normal schools and extend teacher-training courses in the high schools. Stearns claimed that a central collegiate-level institution would tend to provide the kind of education that would lure teachers away from rural school teaching. He also maintained that the university, not the state, would benefit from the institution. "The state," he claimed, " is not being given one dollar. It is being given to the University of Vermont and the University is going to let the State Board come down there and run a teachers college in connection with the University" (36). The state board was accused of representing the private interests of the university. Needless to say, Mr. Stearns also was accused of representing the private interests of Johnson, Vermont. The *Burlington Free Press* claimed that: "The Johnson-Castleton education bill is misnamed. It should be entitled 'An Act To Keep Vermont as It Is.' Instead of providing new facilities for the training of teachers, it takes the old facilities, regroups them, stamps a strange name on them and says, here is the panacea for Vermont's educational ills" (37).

One other interesting charge deserves mention. Mr. Stearns, addressing the Legislature, said, "Some of you have seen a short gentleman for the last two weeks who has been lobbying here for this [centralization] bill " (38). Stearns was referring to Mason Stone, who was back on the educational scene. Mr. Stone, Stearns alleged, had a private motive for his endeavor. He was supposed to have said in 1910 that his greatest ambition was to see the creation of a centralized normal school with himself at its head. Whatever the motives of Stearns, the board, or Mason Stone, the Vermont House of Representatives rejected the board's proposal and adopted the Stearns bill.

The normal school controversy was but a prelude to an even more bitter controversy over the very nature of educational progress in the state. Increasingly, local school officials had become critical of the reforms of Hillegas and the Carnegie commission. Commissioner Dempsey was the doubtful beneficiary of a political mood that had become fatigued with change and reform. Political attitudes had been well expressed in a *Burlington Free Press* editorial on Governor Proctor's views on education. Proctor, according to the *Free Press,* believed that "our schools have reached a high standard which must be retained . . . we should avoid experimentation in education; we can economize by cutting down overhead" (39). One later commentator on Vermont education noted that "the legislature retained the high standards by jettisoning the most important phase of the state education plan, namely the compulsory union supervision" (40).

A reactionary mood had begun to affect educational policy as early as 1919. The Legislature in that year revoked the board's authority to appoint union superintendents and returned this power to local school officials. In 1923, the whole supervisory system collapsed. The legislation of 1923 reduced the State Board of Education from five members to three, eliminated compulsory supervision, and reduced the staff of the State Department of Education. In place of compulsory supervision, each town was empowered to select one of three methods of school supervision: (1) hire a town superintendent, (2) hire a supervising principal, or (3) form a union with other towns and hire a union superintendent.

Professional positions in the state department were abolished, and in their place the board could hire as many deputy commissioners and helping teachers as were required, but with a total salary limit of $20,000. Two deputy commissioners and two helping teachers were actually appointed. Despite this turn of events, Commissioner Dempsey noted ruefully in the fifth *Biennial Report* of the state board and commissioner of education that "reasonably adequate and prompt service has been rendered" (41).

One positive feature of the act is that it empowered the state board to establish minimum standards for state approval and state aid. Minimum essential standards were established by 1924, and the board also issued suggestions for improving the schools. Standard courses were required in 4-year high schools, senior high schools, junior high schools, and 2-year high schools. Special provisions were made for one- or two-teacher high schools, which were justified only if qualified teachers and suitable equipment were provided.

The years following the legislation of 1923 were, on the whole, quiet ones in Vermont. Educators seemed to breathe a sigh of relief; the reform pressure no longer existed. The familiar routines prevailed once more. The state department had not lost its enthusiasm for action; Dempsey reported critically in 1924 that "the state is in the peculiar position here of doing less for its superior young people that are devoting themselves to the training and education of the youth of Vermont than it is for its insane and criminal charges" (42). What had happened, however, is that the state and the public had ceased to listen to the educational innovators. Dempsey could report the problems facing Vermont education, and he did–telling the public about the problems of the rural schools, which were losing nearly one-third of the school directors every year–but little was done.

One significant reform movement that the department was able to maintain was its drive for the standardization of rural schools. The board sought to ensure that every school building be maintained in excellent repair. It declared through manifestos and visiting committees that schools should be attractive, grounds suitable for play and exercise, classrooms properly lighted, heated, furnished, "cheerful, clean and pleasing," and that there be adequate sanitation facilities and ample supplies of books and other educational materials (43).

The board had hoped that state aid could be used as an inducement to the towns and communities to operate standardized schools; obviously, with the mood of the Legislature, this was not forthcoming. But the drive to maintain good standards for the schools was aided by the generosity of private benefactors, notably former Governor Redfield Proctor and Miss Emily Dutton Proctor, who offered annual prizes to the rural school in each county that showed the greatest improvement between March and September. The drive to standardize the schools was quite successful. In 1920-21, a survey of Vermont schools had revealed *no* satisfactory school facilities in the state. By 1922, there were 16 standard and 8 superior schools; by 1924, 60 standard schools and 41 superior schools. Four years later, 242 schools were in the standard and superior categories (44).

Commissioner Dempsey's achievements in the face of a general mood of public indifference were impressive, and it seemed in 1930 that the tide was about to turn in his favor, when he ran into trouble. Apparently an influential legislator had a daughter who was interested in being a teacher. The girl was not qualified, and Commissioner Dempsey refused to certify her to teach in Vermont. The result was that the legislator, lobbying among his colleagues, managed to get enough votes to pass a bill cutting Dempsey's salary. As soon as the salary cut was passed in June 1931, Dempsey resigned to take a job as superintendent of schools in Arlington, Massachusetts, at a considerably higher salary (45).

REORGANIZATION AND REFORM IN THE 1930'S

Meeting in Rutland, Vermont, in September 1931, the State Board of Education elected Francis L. Bailey as commissioner of education. One of 42 candidates the board interviewed, Bailey had recently taken a doctorate at Teachers College, Columbia University, and was recommended by the faculty at Teachers College. Although Bailey was young enough to be called the "boy commissioner" by his fellow superintendents at national and regional conferences, he brought an interesting and varied educational experience to his new position in Vermont. Born and reared in Michigan, Bailey had studied at the University of Michigan, receiving his B.A. in 1921. On graduation he accepted a position as high school principal at Harbor Springs, Michigan. After 3 years in this position, he returned to study for a master's degree at the University of Michigan.

In the spring of 1924, one of Bailey's professors asked for a volunteer to go to hear "that great American educator, Carleton Washburne," who was speaking in a nearby community. Bailey volunteered and, impressed with Washburne's account of his educational experiments in the Winnetka, Illinois, school system (46), talked with Washburne after the meeting. Washburne, apparently impressed with the young man, offered him a job with the Winnetka school system. As head of the science department, Bailey involved himself deeply in Winnetka's plan of individualized instruction and found the system to his liking. In 1928, Bailey returned to graduate work at the University of Chicago and then at Teachers College. After 2 years at Teachers College, he accepted the state commissioner's position in Vermont (47).

The state board welcomed the young man, and Bailey found the members of the board to be "very cordial and cooperative." Despite the spirit of cordiality, Bailey's work was complicated by Vermont educators' struggle to maintain reasonable standards of education despite a desperate shortage of funds produced by Vermont's determination to survive the Depression by severe austerity measures. Bailey had the unpleasant task of telling the local schools that the state could not help them weather the financial crisis, which the state board blamed on Franklin Roosevelt's "bank holiday." Bailey, himself, was forced to accept a 20-percent cut in his salary. It is a tribute to his energy and skill that anything at all was accomplished during the depths of the Depression, when it was a day-to-day question whether the schools could remain open for the requisite number of weeks (48).

Shortly after Bailey took office, the board authorized him to make a study of the status of teaching in Vermont schools. The board also discussed the educational recommendations of the Vermont Commission on Country Life, which had been published in 1931 (49). Two of the more interesting sections of the report dealt with state aid to education and state supervision of education (50). The commission had suggested that state aid to education would be spent far more efficiently if the Legislature could be persuaded to return to the more consistent school supervision procedures of the pre-1923 period. Thus the state could cut down administrative expenses in the name of reform.

In the spring of 1933, Governor Wilson appointed Mortimer Proctor and Howard Rice, chairmen of the appropriations committees of the House and Senate respectively, to a committee to study Vermont education. The Proctor Committee was instructed to economize on state aid to education. The committee, which turned much of its work over to a retired educator, Don C. Bliss, studied the reports of the Vermont Commission on Country Life, talked with high school principals around the state, and decided that a threefold reform program was necessary. First, the state should grant an immediate increase of 50 percent for state aid to education; second, a more efficient system of school supervision should be established for Vermont's schools, returning them to a system similar to that which had existed prior to 1923; third, the Legislature should approve the establishment in the state department of a number of positions that would contribute to the increased professionalization of Vermont school administration. Among the new positions recommended by the committee were a director of guidance and research, a director of health and physical education, a state supervisor for high schools, and additional state helping teachers. These recommendations—coming but a year after the Governor had talked with leading educators about the possible necessity of closing some of Vermont's schools—revealed that Vermonters were willing to tackle their educational problems even during the Depression.

The Legislature of 1935 received the committee's recommendations favorably, enacting them into law virtually unchanged. One recommendation called for the redistricting of the state into more efficient supervisory units. The state passed the legislation in the early spring and charged Commissioner Bailey with carrying the redistricting by July 1, 1935, but provided no instructions on how it should be done (51).

Commissioner Bailey, who carried out the redistricting with Carl Batchelder, his deputy commissioner, remembers the spring of 1935 as one of almost continuous meetings at which he was charged with the delicate chore of persuading reluctant school committees to hire qualified superintendents to replace the existing supervising principals. Bailey, a gentle man with firm convictions, was convinced that replacing casual supervision with professional supervision was an absolute prerequisite for improving Vermont schools. He was faced with hostile principals who resented the "autocratic" power the Legislature had placed in the hands of the commissioner, whom some of them nicknamed "Emperor" Bailey.

Bailey often achieved his objectives by exhausting the opposition. He remembers one particularly long and arduous session in Bennington that did not get down to business until midnight and then only resolved on a superintendent when dawn was approaching. Bailey also brought candidates for the superintendency to these meetings, so that the instant the school committee decided it would have a superintendent, they could get down to selecting a man for the position (52).

By June 1936, Bailey could proudly report that the number of supervisory units had been cut from 88 to 62. There were only nine supervisory principals remaining. That 79 school committees were persuaded to join supervisory unions testifies to the energy and determination of the commissioner. Bailey also reported that the average union district consisted of five towns and an average of 47 teachers.

The other important part of the legislation of 1935 provided for a dramatic increase in state aid to education. In calling for increased aid, the Proctor Committee's report insisted on the principle that the state had an obligation to maintain equal educational facilities throughout the state, just as it had an obligation to construct highways and provide for common defense (53).

In attempting to equalize the schools, the state board was simply recognizing that local districts varied widely in their ability to support their schools. The new law on state aid to education guaranteed that poorer districts, defined as those with a tax list of $10,000 or less, would receive sufficient state money to provide $15 per pupil. The law also provided that richer districts, those having a tax list greater than $10,000, would have their percentage of state aid reduced (54). As a result of the new law, Commissioner Bailey was able to report that "the new method of computing state aid has resulted in a much fairer distribution than formerly, and it is now possible to increase materially the aid to the poorer districts and to do much to lessen their load" (55).

Bailey saw a number of other significant changes in the state department during his tenure. He was authorized, for example, to appoint a director of secondary and vocational education, a position which its first occupant, Ralph E. Noble, less pretentiously called "high-school supervisor." Bailey later recalled that Noble did "a marvelous job," setting up committees throughout the state that revised, updated, and improved high school curriculums. In conjunction with Deputy Commissioner Batchelder and Noble, Bailey also extensively revised qualifications of superintendents, principals, and teachers. Throughout, the intention of the board and the commissioner was to upgrade and improve the quality of both administration and instruction in Vermont schools. For the first time, for example, superintendents were required to be college graduates with a minimum of 24 hours of professional education courses and 5 years of secondary school teaching experience. This forced "the lot of superintendents who were farmers' wives" out of the superintendencies that they held and contributed to the increased professionalization of Vermont schools.

In line with these other changes, Bailey's office began to spearhead a drive to make the state normal schools 4-year colleges. Bailey saw that Vermont faced an acute teacher shortage that could not be met by stopgap measures but required a comprehensive study of Vermont's teacher needs. Much of the information and evidence needed to provide a comprehensive picture was obtained by Bailey himself in the course of preparing his book, *A Planned Supply of Teachers for Vermont,* which was published by Columbia University in 1939. He discovered that by 1936-37, it had become necessary to employ approximately one-third of all beginning teachers from outside the state. He was convinced that it was impossible for Vermont to continue to obtain teachers this way. Thus, during his commissionership, the position and function of the state normal schools became once again a live issue—one which was still very much alive in 1968.

Another development during Bailey's term of office was a relatively constant expansion of the state department staff. When Bailey took office in 1931, the commissioner was assisted by an executive clerk, two deputy commissioners (56), a secretary, and a certification clerk. By 1938, the staff had been expanded to include a director of secondary and vocational education, a director of educational research and guidance, a director of vocational rehabilitation, two state helping teachers, seven state supervisors (57), an executive clerk, a draftsman, and three stenographers. While part of this expansion was due to Vermont's recovery from the Depression, it also undoubtedly reflected the increasing demands made on the department and its increasingly professionalized response to these demands.

During his commissionership, Bailey also moved to break down the isolation that had traditionally characterized Vermont towns. Under his prodding, four regional state school director's groups were formed in 1935. These groups had two objectives. First, through conversations and professional meetings, superintendents and principals were encouraged to think of themselves as channels through which educational suggestions could be offered to the Legislature. Second, the groups were regarded as agencies for improving state and local cooperation. The commissioner clearly realized that if a sense of shared goals and purposes existed, state and local officials would cooperate with one another far more readily.

From the perspective of a quarter century, former Commissioner Bailey is pleased with his work in Vermont. What he remembers are the pleasant associations and the congenial conversations and the lasting friendships. By 1939, however, Bailey was growing weary of the unending round of conferences, state principals meetings, visits to schools, school boards, and PTA's and talks with teachers. When officials of Gorham State Teachers College in Maine offered him the presidency of that school, he accepted, welcoming the opportunity to spend more time at home with his wife and son.

INNOVATION AND INCREASED RESPONSIBILITIES

When the board asked Bailey about candidates to succeed him, he unhesitatingly recommended his supervisor of high schools, Ralph E. Noble, who had just been appointed superintendent in Springfield, Vermont. In September 1940, Noble became commissioner of education. Noble had entered the state department in August 1935, after resigning as superintendent of schools in Barre, Vermont, and had been actively involved in efforts to upgrade the quality of high school instruction in the state. Since he had been with the department for 5 years prior to assuming the commissionership, he had an excellent understanding of the workings of both the board and the department.

Noble also had been one of the most important figures in one of Bailey's chief innovations. As supervisor of high schools, Noble had been charged with drawing up a directory of approved academies and high schools, a traditional function of the department. To this, he added the regular collection of annual data on the high schools: statistics on enrollments, different kinds of students, grade distribution, number of teachers, and the number of students they were responsible for. This reasonably sophisticated data collection was an essential prerequisite for the statewide planning with which the state department had become increasingly involved.

Noble's term as commissioner was one of consolidation. He conceived of his role as executive and administrative head of the state board, whose role was legislative and advisory. In Noble's mind, the only question that was likely to become critical was that of money, and, as Judge Horatio Luce, a member of the board, once remarked in his presence, "Ralph always has the money to do what he wants" (58). Despite his knowledge of the intricacies of board politics and his concept of the commissioner as chief executive, Noble's administration accomplished little of the kind of innovation that had taken place during Bailey's term (59).

Noble's administration was not without its excitement, however. When the schools opened in 1940, America faced a strained and foreboding outside world. Another war in Europe was imminent. Out of this uneasiness and tension arose a controversy over the use of the textbooks of Harold O. Rugg in Vermont's schools. The opening salvo of the controversy was fired in the fall of 1940 by the *Burlington Free Press,* which accused Rugg of arguing "that the American way of life is obsolete and should be scrapped in favor of a new social order of a collectivistic type patterned after Marxian socialism" (60). As public concern over the *Free Press* accusations deepened, Noble found himself under pressure to act against the use of the Rugg texts in Vermont schools. Noble told inquirers, "I personally should be very much opposed to a state adoption of textbooks since I think that is just the sort of undemocratic procedure to which we are all opposed. The governments of totalitarian states tell their communities what instructional material to use" (61). Fortunately, Vermont tradition upheld Noble, and in October 1940, the State Board of Education announced its policy to the newspapers:

> Since 1833, one hundred and seven years ago, when the first Board of Education was legislated out of office for prescribing textbooks, for the public schools throughout the state, no Vermont State Board of Education or Commissioner of Education has had jurisdiction over the selection of books to be used in any schools (62).

The Rugg textbook controversy raged intermittently for the next 13 years, but the state board did not waver in its conviction that textbook selection was a matter for local determination.

Noble was convinced that the state had an obligation to increase its support for education. In October 1940, the board reported its opinion "that no money could be appropriated to better advantage than that for increasing 'state support' for education, in view of the fact that it not only would further extend equal educational opportunities, but also help to relieve the tax burden in some towns" (63).

The commissioner's term of office was adversely affected by the outbreak of World War II. In Vermont, as elsewhere across the nation, educational innovations, whether in new school construction or in the introduction of new programs, came to a virtual halt. Commissioner Noble spent a great deal of his time during the war years trying to cope with a desperate teacher shortage, when thousands of Vermont men left the state to fight and many women left teaching to go into defense plants. Noble was forced to adopt the expedient of granting special war emergency certificates to teachers who were, for a variety of reasons, no longer eligible for regular certification in Vermont (64). The department also was forced to employ upper-class students from the three state normal schools to teach regular classes in the schools. It was only through efforts of this sort that Vermonters were able to keep many of their schools open at all. One major complicating factor was teachers' salaries, which were increasingly unattractive in a period of rising prices and rising wages (65).

Commissioner Noble, acting under instructions from Governor William H. Wills, also turned his attention to the problems of planning for postwar schools. Politicians and educators alike were aware that peace would bring formidable problems when veterans who had interrupted their education would return to finish it. Given the initial shortage of teachers that confronted him daily, it is not surprising that Commissioner Noble emphasized teacher training and recruitment in his analysis of the problems Vermont education might face after the war. To get a sufficient number of good teachers, Vermont needed a wage comparable to that offered in other fields of endeavor. Noble called for "the establishment of a minimum salary of not less than $1,000 per year for the elementary teachers." Without something of this sort, Noble suggested, "the children of our state are bound to lose their just right to a good education" (66). In addition to raising teachers' salaries, he also suggested that the state department actively recruit teachers by visiting secondary schools. Noble saw the task of recruiting teachers as the duty of society—clubs, parent-teacher organizations, and individuals interested in the schools.

The growth in the department continued during the postwar years. The state normal schools at Johnson, Castleton, and Lyndon were made state teachers colleges in 1947.

The war and the U.S. Army's widespread use of training films persuaded many of the educational value of films; in April 1947, the board approved a visual education plan which created a Vermont Film Pool "to supply visual education films and instructional help to the schools" (67).

Also in the immediate postwar years, the board began to function as an accrediting agency for all state schools. This authority was conferred on the board in 1940 by the secretary of state but was little exercised during the war years, when standards of accreditation were stretched to include any school that could stay open. After the war, however, the board evolved a policy toward accredited institutions. The board's requirements for accreditation were such that the "lower courses" of study in the normal schools had to be eliminated. In 1948, the board decided that "with the fall of 1949 no teachers college students could be enrolled for less than the full four year course . . ." (68).

After the war, Vermonters became increasingly concerned about federal aid to education. The hot lunch program and aid to vocational education, the latter provided to the states under the Smith-Hughes Act, had been accepted in Vermont and were generally regarded as smooth operations. There existed, however, widespread conviction that federal aid would bring about federal control of the schools. This sentiment was well expressed in Commissioner Noble's *Vermont's Public Schools:*

> If the State shirks its responsibility . . . those who place the education of Vermont's children ahead of governmental theories will seek out and ultimately obtain federal aid. This would bring federal control which we do not want. Whether the state or the Federal government improves our schools, the State will pay the bill (69).

Yet, as the federal government began to concern itself with education, Vermont and the state board were faced with a dilemma: They badly needed the money that federal largesse would provide, yet they were fearful that the federal government would dictate how their schools should be run. Ultimately, of course, Vermont's needs won out over theories of government.

In February 1948, the board announced that it accepted "the principle of federal aid as a sound and necessary supplement to local and state taxation for public school support." Vermonters, however, do not abandon principles easily, and the board's statement continued: "It [the Board] believes that such federal funds as Congress may make available to the states should be free from any controls interfering with the educational policies established and administered by the state through its legally established bodies." The board further declared its conviction that "all federal aid directed toward the welfare of children not attending tax supported schools should be confined to non-educational services" (70). The board then repeated this article of faith stating:

> It believes strongly however that federal aid distinctly designed to aid the process of education itself should be confined to the development of a system of tax-supported public schools to which this nation has long been committed—a nation which is still in a process of struggling to overcome the economic barriers which still hinder the achievement of a free and equal educational opportunity for all children wherever they may live (71).

Commissioner Noble remembers that this policy was reached easily: He formulated it and wrote the statement, and the board approved it. These principles governed Vermont's attitudes toward federal aid in the late forties, and, despite heavy incursions caused by massive doses of post-Sputnik federal aid, Vermonters still maintain a firm devotion to the independence of their schools.

Noble also was one of the leaders in the postwar establishment of the Vermont Higher Education Council, which has served as a valuable evaluator, critic, and friend of higher education in Vermont.

In May 1948, Dr. Noble submitted his resignation in order to become president of Vermont Junior College in Montpelier. His tenure of office had been during a rocky period for Vermont education. His achievements, in view of the obstacles he faced, were impressive.

Unlike Bailey, who had urged Noble's appointment to succeed him, Noble remained aloof from the board's search for his successor. The leading candidate was John C. Huden, president of Castleton State Teachers College, longtime Vermont educator, and author of *The Development of State School Administration in Vermont* (72), a valuable contribution to the history of education in Vermont. Huden, however, was clearly identified with the existing educational establishment in Vermont, and those who advocated educational innovation cast about for a different candidate. Huden's chief opposition came from A. John Holden, Jr., longtime career educator, a Vermonter, who was then in the Department of Education at Geneseo State Teachers College in New York State. Huden also was unpopular with the proponents of local schools. In his book, Huden spends a good bit of time castigating proponents of localism in Vermont education who failed to see the virtue of centralized administration for the state. Holden, while certainly every bit as strong an advocate of an efficient central administration for Vermont schools, had been less conspicuously outspoken on the subject than John Huden.

The board interviewed both candidates in October 1948 and the next day offered the commissionership to Dr. Holden, who accepted. Holden brought an impressive educational background to the commissionership. An engineering student at Harvard, he had taught in Vermont elementary schools, spent a year abroad studying European systems of education, had been a superintendent of schools in Danville, Vermont, for 7 years, and had, after receiving his Ed.D. from Teachers College, Columbia University, in 1943, served as a professor of education at Middlebury College and as a member of Middlebury's school board. He had moved to Geneseo in 1947, just 2 years before he became commissioner of education for Vermont.

Dr. Holden spent just over sixteen years in the commissioner's office—from 1948 to 1965. Under his leadership, both the quantity and kind of services required from the State Department of Education were expanded, especially in the areas of planning, curriculum development, and information gathering. The kind of contributions that the department would be asked to make in the years to come were suggested in an administrative reorganization of the department, which took place shortly after Dr. Holden took office. Directorships of health and physical education and educational planning were established. The latter post, to which Winn L. Taplin was appointed, is the significant one; it was no longer enough for the state department to administer and care for the existing educational structure; it now also had the specific responsibility for planning Vermont's educational future. This high regard for planning grounded in reasonably sophisticated information was also reflected in Holden's conviction regarding school construction that "good business dictates that no building should be erected until a careful study has been made as nearly as possible (of) the probable educational program that building should have *twenty years* in the future" (73).

This matter-of-fact devotion to planning characterizes Holden's administration. Rather than proceeding from preconceived educational theories, the commissioner tried to build an empirical case and then decide what was likely to be the best move for the educational future of Vermont.

As Vermont approached midcentury, it was becoming increasingly evident that it had not been keeping pace with its educational needs and that Holden's talents for planning and proceeding empirically would be useful. Population growth, which had been relatively static up to World War II, had begun to accelerate. The total population, which had actually decreased slightly during the decade 1930-40, began to climb upward.

Also, Vermont's population began to take on a new character. It was no longer true that "Vermont was 51 percent Republican and 49 percent cows, and both Republicans and cows live in the country or in small towns" (74). Vermont's large towns were getting larger while the small towns dwindled. This meant, as Commissioner Holden pointed out, "that life in Vermont is more varied than it was fifty years ago, that there are more different kinds of people with more different kinds of occupations and many more different kinds of educational needs" (75). This change held a threat for Vermont schools. The state obviously needed new school facilities to accommodate increasing numbers of students. Between September 1945 and September 1949, Vermont's first-grade population increased significantly, and estimates of future growth predicted that the increase in population would continue. This meant that Vermont towns would increasingly face the pressure of an expanding school population with an educational system that was barely adequate to meet present needs.

Vermonters faced the challenge to build more schools. The Legislature in 1949 had granted the state board the authority to "accept, use, disburse and account for" federal funds for building construction. Also, under the terms of this act, the state board had been authorized to make a survey of Vermont's school needs. The School Housing Survey of 1950 estimated that the state would need to construct 106 new school buildings between 1950 and 1962 and to renovate and modernize 150 more. This, the survey estimated, would cost close to $25 million. Faced with this staggering task, Vermonters once again became concerned with their schools. Education in the 1950's became a live public issue.

Responding directly to the problem, groups of citizens and educators from 43 towns began to study the possibility of more effective and more economical education through their combined efforts. They were encouraged in these efforts by the School Survey of 1950, which reported that the average per-pupil cost in high schools of less than 100 was $242.89, and in schools over 200, $207.68 (76). Yet it was not only a question of dollars and cents. Travel, especially in the winter months, is difficult in Vermont. Many parents objected to having small children carried several miles to school each day. Also, neighborhoods were often fearful that closing the neighborhood school would result in a diminished social life for the community.

Despite the fact that most Vermonters wanted to move ahead, they also felt a comparably intense wish to conserve "that face-to-face human feeling which Vermonters so justly cherish" (77). The state board was obviously feeling the public pulse when it announced in September 1949:

> The State Board of Education is definitely and unanimously of the opinion that no one pattern of local school organization—consolidation or decentralization—would under the present conditions be good for the State of Vermont as a whole. But though no one pattern may be good for the whole state, each locality is faced with the necessity of working out its own pattern of school organization (78).

To help Vermonters plan for their schools, the state department offered itself as a resource for information, planning assistance, and educational guidance. It published a pamphlet entitled "A Guide of Citizens Action for the Public Schools" to help "local citizens to improve their schools while keeping them the people's schools" (79).

The Vermont assembly took action on the question of school construction with Act No. 256 of the 1953 Legislature, by which the state authorized state aid for school building construction. During the first year of operation, the state spent $303,811 for new construction in 20 districts and $1,430,927 in "retroactive" aid to 55 school districts out of the total 1953 appropriation of $7,880,000 (80). This amount, despite an additional increase of $1,800,000 in 1957, was by 1958 clearly not sufficient. In fact, an estimate in that year suggested that Vermont would have to spend at least another $8 million on state aid for school construction. Although school construction did not go as rapidly as many would have liked, by 1960, significant progress had been made and the state was "definitely gaining in its effort to provide safe, healthful and educationally efficient buildings for all Vermont school children and their teachers" (81).

Like his predecessor, Holden faced considerable problems in getting and keeping enough teachers to staff Vermont schools. Despite the effectiveness of Commissioner Noble's efforts to attract students for Vermont's teachers colleges (82), Vermont still faced a severe shortage of teachers, particularly on the elementary level. Part of this shortage was due to increasing enrollment; part was due to low salaries; another part was due to poor facilities at the state teachers colleges.

Holden reported:

> The young prospective teachers want and are entitled to colleges which can compare favorably in program and facilities with other colleges. Not one of our teachers colleges has a trained librarian. Not one of our teachers colleges has a gymnasium. The new dormitory at Castleton is a step, but a very small one, in the direction of supplying facilities *worthy of a college.* It must be followed up by further planned improvement at Castleton and at any other colleges which are designated for development as permanent teachers colleges (83).

By 1957, the board had decided that future needs would demand that all three facilities be kept open and, in early 1957, recommended that–

> It should be the policy of the state to develop improved facilities at all three teachers colleges and introduce more varied programs in order to help to provide opportunity for education beyond the high school to the greatly increased number of young people who will be seeking it within the next few years (84).

The Legislature approved this policy by voting funds for expansion and staff increases. Vermont's commitment to the state teachers colleges, which had been wavering for 50 years, was now solid. Concern over the fate of the teachers colleges did not end with the 1957 legislation, however. It took another direction, and increasingly the Legislature was pressured to take control of the state colleges away from the board and vest it in the hands of a separately constituted body. This drive ended only in 1961, when the Legislature established the Vermont State College Corporation to govern the state colleges. Direction of, and consequently the future of, the state colleges is an issue which has dotted the pages of Vermont newspapers in recent years.

Slow progress was made toward providing Vermont with an adequate supply of teachers during the fifties. The most effective device for encouraging men and women to teach in Vermont was, naturally, raising the minimum salary, which was consistently increased through the fifties and into the sixties. Vermont, however, still pays teachers poorly. The 1966 *Biennial Report* of the state department suggests: "Teacher recruitment is an area that needs urgent attention. The shortage of qualified teachers and educational specialists appears to grow more serious each year" (85).

Another significant development in Vermont's efforts to meet the challenge to education in the middle of the twentieth century was the drive to establish union or consolidated schools. The School Facilities Survey of 1951 had revealed that larger schools were more efficient in terms of pupil cost. But the building, organization, and supervision of the larger schools posed problems in state and local relations. The state board therefore felt obliged to go slowly. Commissioner Holden, who was very much aware that he could not be "high-handed in his dealings with local school officials," was, however, deeply committed to the principle that "the education of all of the children of the state is the responsibility of all the people of the state " (86). But he also wisely recognized that all the people of the state could not be coerced into educating all the children. Therefore, Holden proceeded by persuasion and argument; in area after area, the state department provided information, consultation, and guidance to citizens groups seeking means of consolidation. The department also provided guidelines for the establishment of union schools and for the kinds of services that the union schools should provide.

In many ways, Vermont had the nucleus of a union high school system before the establishment of the first union high school district in Bennington in 1952. Very few of Vermont's high schools were strictly home-town schools: the vast majority educated tuition pupils from other communities. Most Vermont high schools were regional schools in the sense that they served not one town but a group of towns. Existing informally, however, this system had two distinct disadvantages. The people who sent their children to high school in another town had no voice in the policies and operation of the school. The town that maintained the school operated at a disadvantage because it could not appeal to the other towns or to the state for help with the cost of additional construction.

The State Board of Education sought in the early fifties to take advantage of the spirit of cooperation that existed in many regions of Vermont to create union schools that would better meet changing educational needs. This has not always been an easy task; local interests have prevented the formation of some union schools, while other attempts have bogged down in a financial and bureaucratic morass. The trend toward union high schools has been supported by the State Department of Education and the Legislature. Since the basic law governing the establishment of union school districts was enacted in 1953 (amended in 1955 and 1961), 16 union districts have been established in Vermont. Commissioner Holden reported in 1964 that the evidence indicated that they were successful in providing a broader and more effective range of opportunity for young people of secondary school age. Presumably, the success of existing union schools will make the formation of new ones more desirable.

Another significant modern development in Vermont education has been the diminishing effect of Vermont's rural isolation. Better highways, improved communication facilities, increasing numbers of what Vermonters are fond of describing as "permanent summer residents," and a variety of other factors have contributed to a more widespread willingness of Vermont communities to consider themselves part of the state and nation. A factor that has also contributed to this increasing cosmopolitanism, at least in education, has been the active drive of the board and the department to encourage citizens of Vermont to find out what is going on in their schools.

One of the most interesting contributions made by Holden to publicizing Vermont's educational progress and problems was his experiment "Operation Listen." Operation Listen consisted of 13 meetings, held throughout the state, at which various members of the board met with local citizens to exchange views and information on Vermont education. These meetings were a success. The discussions were vocal, excited, and tremendously educational both for the public and for members of the state board, the commissioner, and his staff. As Holden reported in a memorandum to the board: "It was clear at most of these meetings that people wanted to know more about the state's educational system, its status and its problems" (87). Also, Commissioner Holden and the board were able to learn what concerned the public and what they wanted done. Chief among the concerns of the public were educational standards, curriculum development, local supervision, and state aid to education. As a result of Operation Listen, the state department intensified its efforts in these areas.

While Operation Listen has not been repeated, it did have valuable effects on both professional educators and the citizens of Vermont. One of the interesting developments resulting was a mimeographed newsletter entitled "Vermont Future," which dealt with educational developments in Vermont and was a conscious effort on the part of Holden to keep the public informed. The newsletter later had to be abandoned for lack of staff and funds. It was Commissioner Holden's personal vehicle from the beginning; he wrote most of the articles and edited the newsletter. This alone was a formidable task which was made more burdensome by the fact that every word of the newsletter had to be approved by the State Board of Education (88). Ultimately, "Vermont Future" became just too time-consuming, and Holden had to give it up despite its obvious educational value.

RECENT DEVELOPMENTS

Dr. Holden retired in September 1965. His successor was a young educator from Pennsylvania, Richard A. Gibboney. Dr. Gibboney regarded himself as an innovator and immediately took steps to increase the tempo of educational change in Vermont.

Gibboney's innovation plans for Vermont education were aided by the passage of the federal government's Elementary and Secondary Education Act of 1965 (ESEA). The state department, under Gibboney's direction, quickly took advantage of the federal government's offer of money; in 1965, the department sponsored two Title V projects. The first of these was a study of audiovisual education in Vermont. The second was a Student Advisory Conference, at which high school students throughout the state aired *their* views on education.

In 1966, Gibboney's initiative sparked work on a Title III project entitled "Planning for Education Innovation in a Rural State." This project became a model for a systematic study of Vermont teachers and classrooms. The project's goals were, of course, improving instruction. This project came to maturity in January 1968, when the federal government provided funds for three Regional Action Centers in Vermont. Two more centers were approved in April 1968 and were operating by that summer, thus completing the statewide plan for the systematic improvement of instruction in Vermont. The plan will be carried out by action center personnel working in cooperation with local school superintendents, and the program will be financed in part by ESEA Title III funds and in part by funds from participating local school districts.

Gibboney also reorganized the state department on the basis of plans drawn up by Arthur D. Little and Company of Boston. Reorganization included establishing a research and development unit, hiring a program coordinator to do liaison work among branches of the department, and a number of other administrative changes.

The atmosphere of Gibboney's administration was one of action. The Montpelier *Times Argus* reported just before Commissioner Gibboney's resignation that the state department was involved in over 135 separate major educational programs. Not all Vermonters, however, were convinced that the sense of motion around the commissioner's office was purposive or necessary. Rumblings appeared in the press about "change for its own sake." Finally, Gibboney, recognizing what one board member called an unresolvable impasse which inhibited the leadership he could bring to education in Vermont, submitted his resignation in July 1967.

Gibboney's deputy commissioner, Daniel G. O'Connor, was named acting commissioner of education and served competently in this capacity until Harvey B. Scribner of Teaneck, New Jersey, was appointed commissioner in December 1967.

Increasingly in this century, Vermont has become convinced of the truth of what educators had long argued—that "our educational system has become the most important public function of our nation and our state. It is in our Vermont schoolrooms and in the schoolrooms all over our country . . . that the future of our country and our world will be determined" (89). In 1968, prodded by the post-Sputnik national controversy over education, stimulated by increasing amounts of federal aid to education, and more conscious of public interest in their schools, Vermont educators faced a challenging future. Most of the foundations for a truly excellent educational system existed in Vermont in 1968. The problem was to build on them. As the State Board of Education commented in 1966,

> These are exciting days in education. Never has there been as great an opportunity to continue past efforts in

the slow progress of renewing our schools to meet today's needs while carefully beginning new efforts for improvement so that youngsters now in school may compete successfully in the unknown and somewhat frightening world of the twenty-first century—now only half a life time away (90).

FOOTNOTES

1. Dorothy Canfield Fisher, "Let the Bridges Fall Down" (unpublished manuscript in the Wilbur Collection, Bailey Library, University of Vermont).

2. Superintendent of Education, *School Report* (1908), p. 18. In 1916, the *School Report* was changed to the *Biennial Report of the State Board of Education.*

3. Within the framework of Vermont's revenues, the state has done reasonably well by its educational system. The reader should also bear in mind that "education is only one service of government. If state expenditures for non-educational services, say highways or welfare, are inordinately high because of special circumstances, should the state be blamed for spending less on education than other states in which non-educational expenditures are lower?" This qualification, raised by Stephen K. Bailey, *et al., Schoolmen and Politics: A Study of State Aid to Education in the Northeast* (Syracuse, N.Y.: Syracuse University Press, 1962), p. 17, should be remembered. It also should be remembered that local taxes in Vermont, which go in large measure to the schools, have been high. Vermont's per-capita expenditure on education is above the national average now and has been close to the national average throughout the century.

4. From 1900 to 1950, Vermont registered a population increase of only 9.9 percent, compared to New Hampshire's 29.6-percent increase and the national increase of 98.3 percent. Six of Vermont's counties showed a population increase while the remaining eight declined. The rural population declined by 27,675.

5. John A. Neuenschwander, "Senator George D. Aiken and Federal Aid to Education, 1941-1949" (unpublished master's thesis, University of Vermont, Burlington, 1965). Neuenschwander convincingly demonstrates Senator Aiken's little known contributions to the cause of federal aid.

6. Interview with Francis L. Bailey, Gorham, Maine, November 26, 1967.

7. Interview with A. John Holden, Jr., Newton, Massachusetts, November 18, 1967 (hereafter referred to as the Holden Interview).

8. Carnegie Foundation for the Advancement of Teaching, *A Study of Education in Vermont* (New York: The Foundation, 1914), p. 148.

9. The authors are indebted to John Nelson for his research on the history of Vermont education. Nelson's work has proved an excellent source of information and an invaluable guide to additional sources. His unpublished work was made available through the State Department of Education.

10. Board of Education, "Development of the State Educational System of Vermont: Historical Sketch," *Biennial Report of the State Board of Education* (1920), p. 21.

11. *Ibid.*

12. Interview with Ralph E. Noble, Montpelier, Vermont, November 16, 1967.

13. Superintendent of Education, *School Report* (1906), p. 10.

14. Superintendent of Education, *School Report* (1900), p. 10.

15. Superintendent of Education, *School Report* (1908), p. 37.

16. Carnegie Foundation for the Advancement of Teaching, *op. cit.*, p. 164.

17. *Ibid.*, p. 128.

18. Board of Education, Minutes of the March 19, 1913, meeting.

19. Lester F. Jipp, "The Progressive Party in Vermont in 1912" (unpublished master's thesis, University of Vermont, 1965).

20. R. Freeman Butts and Lawrence A. Cremin, *A History of Education in American Culture* (New York: Henry Holt and Company, 1953), p. 433.

21. *Report of the Commission To Investigate the Educational Systems and Conditions of Vermont* (Montpelier: The Commission, 1914), p. 2.

22. Guy Potter Benton, "The Educational Challenge to Vermont," an address to the Unity Club, mimeograph in the Board of Education Minutes for the meeting of March 28, 1913.

23. Board of Education, Minutes of the April 7, 1913, meeting.

24. Carnegie Foundation for the Advancement of Teaching, *op. cit.*, p. 150.

25. Board of Education, Minutes of the June 19, 1915, meeting.

26. Mason S. Stone, *History of Education: State of Vermont* (Montpelier: Capital City Press, 1935), p. 327.

27. Board of Education, Minutes of the June 19, 1915, meeting.

28. *Ibid.*

29. Lyman W. Bole, *Development of Professional Supervision of Vermont Public Schools,* pamphlet published for the Vermont School Superintendent's Association (Brattleboro: Colonel Press, 1964).

30. John C. Huden, *Development of State School Administration in Vermont* (Montpelier: Vermont Historical Society, 1944), p. 203.
31. *Ibid.*, p. 205.
32. Board of Education, Minutes of the July 1915 meeting.
33. Board of Education, Minutes of the April 16, 1913, meeting.
34. Board of Education, *Biennial Report* (1918), p. 26.
35. *Burlington Free Press*, Feb. 10, 1921.
36. *Ibid.*, Mar. 11, 1921.
37. *Ibid.*, Jan. 28, 1921.
38. *Ibid.*, Mar. 11, 1921.
39. *Burlington Free Press*, January 5, 1923, quoted in Huden, *op. cit.*, p. 246.
40. Huden, *op. cit.*
41. Board of Education, *Biennial Report* (1924), p. 1.
42. *Ibid.*, p. 20.
43. *Ibid.* See also the report of Dorothy Canfield Fisher's committee to study rural schools, in the Board of Education Minutes for the June 29, 1921, meeting.
44. Board of Education, *Biennial Report* (1928), p. 23.
45. John E. Nelson, "Seesawing in Vermont Education, 1777-1966" (unpublished manuscript in the files of the Department of Education, Montpelier), p. 5.
46. Lawrence A. Cremin, *The Transformation of the School: Progressivism in American Education, 1876-1957* (New York: Alfred A. Knopf, Inc., 1961), pp. 295-297.
47. Interview with Francis L. Bailey, November 26, 1967.
48. Board of Education, Minutes of the April 6, 1933, meeting. For a general picture of Vermont during the Depression, see Duane Lockard, *New England State Politics* (Princeton, N.J.: Princeton University Press, 1959), pp. 38-48.
49. Board of Education, Minutes of the December 31, 1931, meeting. See also Two Hundred Vermonters, *Rural Vermont: A Program for the Future* (Montpelier: Vermont Commission on Country Life, 1931), especially chap. 14, which deals with education.
50. The committee on education had been headed by Katherine M. Cook of the U.S. Office of Education. Her committee criticized Vermont's reliance on local taxation to support the schools and demonstrated the virtual impossibility of smaller towns' effectively providing for education without substantial state aid designated to equalize the schools. Her committee also was critical of the lack of staff resources in the State Department of Education and dismayed at the ineptitude of large numbers of Vermont's town superintendents and supervising principals.
51. Vermont, *Public Act No. 86* (1935), sec. 7. This act provided that "The State Board of Education through the Commissioner of Education, acting as the executive officer of the Board, shall as soon as possible combine the several school districts of the State into supervisory unions each approximating fifty teachers with districts grouped in the interest of convenience and efficiency . . . . "
52. Interview with Francis L. Bailey, November 26, 1967.
53. Board of Education, *Biennial Report* (1936), p. 8. In accepting the "foundation formula" that state aid to education was primarily concerned with supporting "public education at a level deemed essential to children in all parts of the State," Vermonters had recognized the "creative work" of a small group of professors from Teachers College, Columbia University, who had since World War I tried "to devise a means of superseding a hodge-podge of patently inequitable state quota grants, and for using state resources to upgrade generally the quality of public education – especially in rural areas." For a good discussion of this point, see Stephen K. Bailey, *op. cit.*, pp. 17-19.
54. Board of Education, *Biennial Report* (1938), p. 11.
55. *Ibid.*, p. 14. It should be noted, however, that the State Board of Education had no authority to determine the amount of its tax dollar a local district could spend on its schools, and consequently disparate school systems continued to develop. This crucial question of local willingness to pay was not a real consideration in 1934.
56. In 1933, Bailey was deprived of one of the deputy commissionships—a position not reestablished until World War II. Board of Education, *Biennial Report* (1936).
57. State supervisors included one for health and physical education, two for agriculture, two for home economics, and one for trade and industries. Board of Education, *Biennial Report* (1938).
58. Dr. Noble, at least, remembers it this way. He also commented that Commissioner Bailey had had "some tough fights" and that his own tenure of office was a good bit smoother. Interview with Ralph E. Noble, November 16, 1967.
59. *Ibid.*
60. Burlington Free Press, *Why Partisan Opinionated Textbooks for Vermont School Youngsters?* (Burlington: Free Press, 1940), p. 5. This is a collection of the paper's editorials from its September and October 1940 issues.
61. Letter, Ralph E. Noble to the Reverend J. Edward Carothers, September 18, 1940, State Department of Education files, Montpelier.
62. Board of Education, Minutes of the October 18, 1940, meeting.
63. *Ibid.*
64. In 1941-42, Vermont issued 7 of these emergency certificates; in 1942-43, 294; in 1943-44, 452; and in 1945-46, 642.

65. Board of Education, *Biennial Report* (1946).

66. Ralph E. Noble, *Vermont's Public Schools* (Montpelier: Department of Education, 1943), pp. 42-44.

67. Board of Education, Minutes of the April 10, 1947, meeting.

68. Board of Education, Minutes of the May 13, 1948, meeting.

69. Ralph E. Noble, *Vermont's Public Schools* (Montpelier: Department of Education, 1943), pp. 14-15.

70. Board of Education, Minutes of the February 10, 1948, meeting.

71. *Ibid.*

72. Huden, *op. cit.*

73. Board of Education, Minutes of the September 15, 1949, meeting.

74. Stephen K. Bailey, *et al., Schoolmen and Politics: A Study of State Aid to Education in the Northeast* (Syracuse, N.Y.: Syracuse University Press, 1962), p. 13.

75. Board of Education, *Biennial Report* (1950), p. 3.

76. Department of Education, "School Facilities in Vermont, 1951," Wilbur Collection, University of Vermont, p. 42. (Mimeographed.)

77. Board of Education, *Biennial Report* (1950), p. 13.

78. Board of Education, Minutes of the September 15, 1949, meeting.

79. Board of Education, *Biennial Report* (1952), p. 8.

80. Board of Education, *Biennial Report* (1954), p. 8. Since the act gave the state board the authority to approve of "new construction for wards of state assistance," the board from this point on was greatly involved with resolving questions about what district should get what money and when. Also, this authority gave the board considerable leverage in its drive to standardize at least the physical quality of Vermont schools.

81. Board of Education, *Biennial Report* (1960), p. 7.

82. Enrollment in Vermont's teachers college increased 26.9 percent between 1948 and 1949, compared to a national increase of 8.5 percent.

83. Board of Education, *Biennial Report* (1952), p. 15.

84. *Ibid.* (1958), p. 40.

85. Board of Education, *Biennial Report* (1966), p. 43.

86. Board of Education, *Biennial Report* (1952), p. 29.

87. A. John Holden, Jr., "Memorandum to State Board of Education," December 8, 1959.

88. Former Commissioner Holden reports that the board was generally very fair-minded but that occasionally the meticulousness of its criticisms could be irksome. In one instance, the board insisted that he revise the phrase *instructional anarchy* to read *instructional chaos.* Holden remembers in this instance that he meant anarchy; he did not mean chaos, and to a sensitive reader the words have different connotations.

89. Board of Education, *Biennial Report* (1962), p. 17.

90. Board of Education, *Biennial Report* (1966), foreword.

BIBLIOGRAPHY

Public Documents

Vermont. *Acts, 1900-1966.*

--*Constitution* (1793).

-- *Public Act No. 86* (1935), sec. 7.

Books

Anderson, W. A. *Population Change in Vermont.* Burlington: Vermont Department of Agriculture, 1955.

Bailey, Francis L. *A Planned Supply of Teachers in Vermont.* New York: Bureau of Publications, Teachers College, Columbia University, 1939.

Bailey, Stephen K.; Frost, Richard T.; Marsh, Paul E.; and Wood, Robert C. *Schoolmen and Politics: A Study of State Aid to Education in the Northeast.* Syracuse, N.Y.: Syracuse University Press, 1962.

Bole, Lyman W. *Development of Professional Supervision of Vermont Public Schools.* Brattleboro, Vt.: Colonel Press, 1964.

Burlington Free Press. *Why Partisan Opinionated Textbooks for Vermont School Youngsters?* Burlington, Vt.: Free Press, 1940. This is a collection of the paper's editorials from its September and October 1940 issues.

Butts, R. Freeman, and Cremin, Lawrence A. *A History of Education in American Culture.* New York: Henry Holt and Company, 1953.

Cremin, Lawrence A. *The Transformation of the School: Progressivism in American Education, 1876-1957.* New York: Alfred A. Knopf, Inc., 1961.

Huden, John C. *Development of State School Administration in Vermont.* Montpelier: Vermont Historical Society, 1944.

Lockard, Duane. *New England State Politics.* Princeton, N.J.: Princeton University Press, 1959.

Noble, Ralph E. *Vermont's Public Schools.* Montpelier: Department of Education, 1943.

Stone, Mason S. *History of Education: State of Vermont.* Montpelier: Capital City Press, 1935.

Woodward, Florence M. *The People of Vermont: Population Patterns and Trends Since 1940.* Montpelier: Vermont Development Commission, 1958.

Reports

Board of Education. *Biennial Reports*. Montpelier: The Board, 1916-66.

Carnegie Foundation for the Advancement of Teaching. *A Study of Education in Vermont*. New York: The Foundation, 1914.

Report of the Commission To Investigate the Educational Systems and Conditions of Vermont. Montpelier, Vt.: The Commission, 1914.

Superintendents of Education. *School Reports, 1900-1916*. This was published in various cities by different publishers from time to time.

Two Hundred Vermonters. *Rural Vermont: A Program for the Future*. Montpelier: Vermont Commission on Country Life, 1931.

Articles and Periodicals

Burlington Free Press. January 28, February 10, and March 11, 1921.

Norman, Albert. "Vermont State Colleges: Historical Approach to a Contemporary Problem." *Vermont History* (July and October 1964), pp. 121-53 and 184-212.

Unpublished Material

Department of Education. "School Facilities in Vermont, 1951," Wilbur Collection, Bailey Library, University of Vermont, Burlington. (Mimeographed.)

Fisher, Dorothy Canfield. "Let the Bridges Fall Down." Unpublished manuscript in the Wilbur Collection, Bailey Library, University of Vermont, Burlington.

Jipp, Lester F. "The Progressive Party in Vermont in 1912." Unpublished master's thesis, University of Vermont, Burlington, 1965.

Nelson, John. "Seesawing in Vermont Education, 1777-1966." Unpublished work, Department of Education, Montpelier.

Neuenschwander, John A. "Senator George Aiken and Federal Aid to Education, 1941-1949." Unpublished master's thesis, University of Vermont, Burlington, 1965.

Other Sources

Bailey, Francis L. Interview, Gorham, Maine, November 26, 1967.

Benton, Guy Potter. "The Educational Challenge to Vermont." An address to the Unity Club of Burlington, mimeograph in the Board of Education Minutes of the March 28, 1913, meeting.

Board of Education. Minutes of the March 19, 1913, through the September 15, 1949, meetings. (Typewritten.)

Holden, A. John, Jr. Interview, Newton, Massachusetts, November 18, 1967.

——"Memorandum to State Board of Education," December 8, 1959.

——Letter to The Reverend J. Edward Carothers, September 18, 1940, State Department of Education files, Montpelier.

Noble, Ralph E. Interview, Montpelier, Vermont, November 16, 1967.

Appendix A

VERMONT CHIEF STATE SCHOOL OFFICERS

Superintendents of Education

1892-1902	Mason S. Stone
1902-1905	Walter Rauger
1905-15	Mason S. Stone

Commissioners of Education

1915-16	Mason S. Stone
1916-21	Milo B. Hillegas
1921-31	Clarence H. Dempsey
1931-39	Francis L. Bailey
1940-48	Ralph E. Noble
1948-65	A. John Holden, Jr.
1965-67	Richard A. Gibboney
1967-68	Daniel G. O'Connor (acting)
1968-	Harvey B. Scribner

Appendix B

Chart I.--VERMONT DEPARTMENT OF EDUCATION, 1900

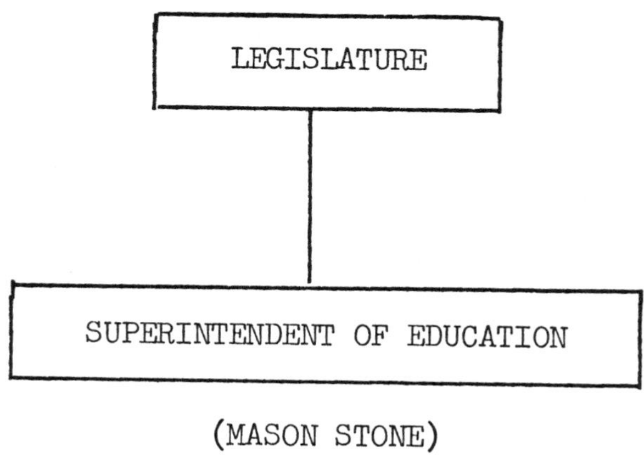

Appendix B

Chart II.--VERMONT DEPARTMENT OF EDUCATION, 1965

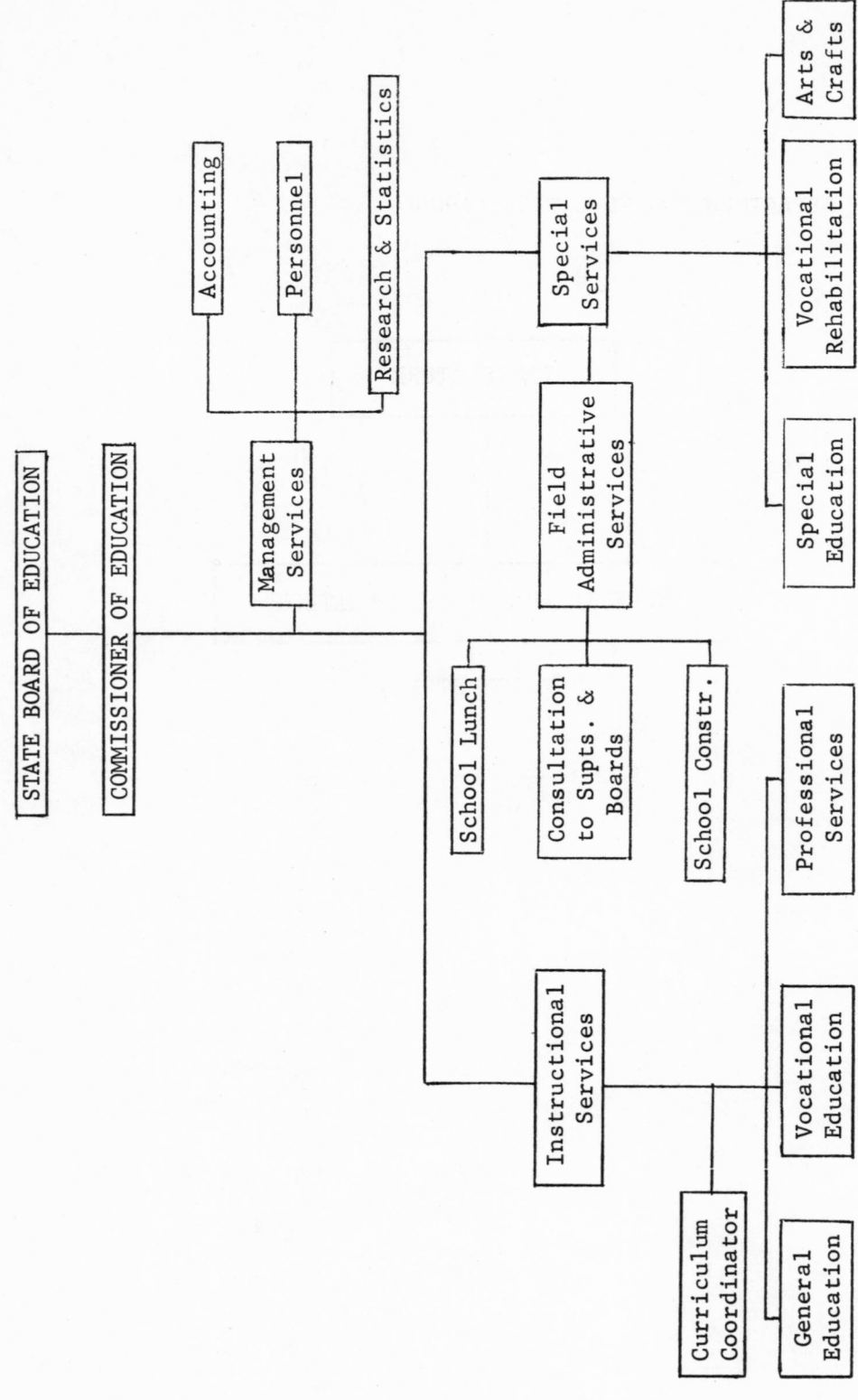

- STATE BOARD OF EDUCATION
  - COMMISSIONER OF EDUCATION
    - Management Services
      - Accounting
      - Personnel
      - Research & Statistics
    - Special Services
      - Special Education
      - Vocational Rehabilitation
      - Arts & Crafts
    - Field Administrative Services
      - School Lunch
      - Consultation to Supts. & Boards
      - School Constr.
    - Instructional Services
      - Curriculum Coordinator
      - General Education
      - Vocational Education
      - Professional Services

Appendix B

Chart III.--VERMONT DEPARTMENT OF EDUCATION, 1968

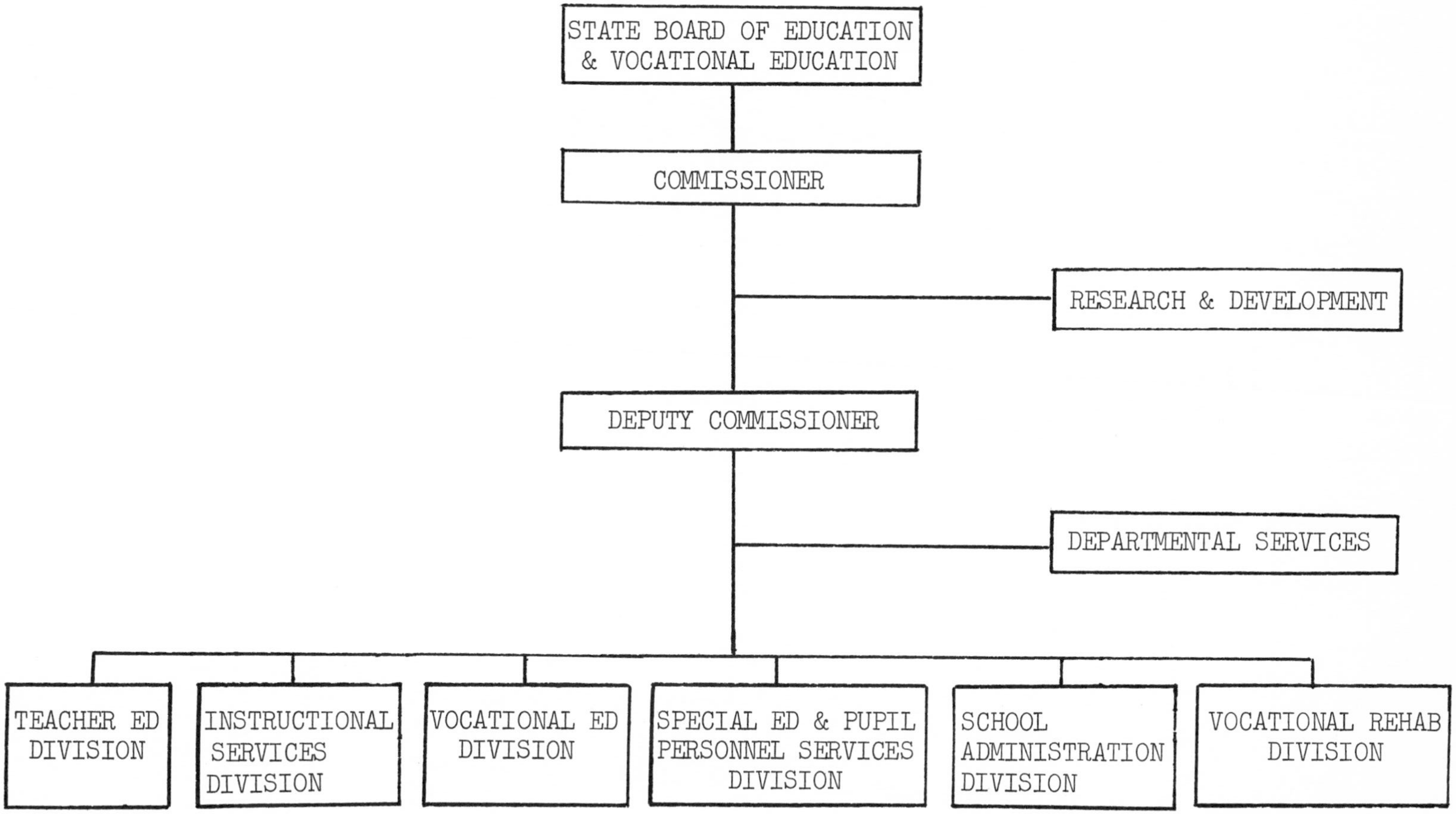

STATE BOARD OF EDUCATION & VOCATIONAL EDUCATION

COMMISSIONER

RESEARCH & DEVELOPMENT

DEPUTY COMMISSIONER

DEPARTMENTAL SERVICES

TEACHER ED DIVISION

INSTRUCTIONAL SERVICES DIVISION

VOCATIONAL ED DIVISION

SPECIAL ED & PUPIL PERSONNEL SERVICES DIVISION

SCHOOL ADMINISTRATION DIVISION

VOCATIONAL REHAB DIVISION

47 Virginia

BOARD OF EDUCATION
Fendall R. Ellis
Harry L. Smith
C. J. Watkins

Contents

BACKGROUND AND BEGINNING, 1607-1900

The Virginia Colony, established at Jamestown in 1607, was a commercial enterprise of the London Company. Unlike the Pilgrims, who fled to the New World to escape an autocratic church and state, the Virginia colonists sought to extend English rule in America. Whereas the settlers at Plymouth voluntarily agreed to govern by vote of the majority, those at Jamestown followed the less democratic practices of England. A majority of the first settlers were members of the English aristocracy. The system of land grants favored this group, which emerged as a strong upper class, holding most of the land and political and economic power for generations. Large numbers of immigrant laborers, indentured servants, slaves, and artisans followed to make up a second social class, which was markedly lower. A strong middle class did not develop for nearly two centuries.

Large plantations held by the aristocracy were the centers of an agrarian economy. The plantation order was mainly a decentralized society, for roads were poor and distances between plantations were relatively great.

Beginnings of Education

The colonists' institutions (political, religious, social, and educational) generally paralleled those of England. The values, ideals, and ambitions of the two peoples were similar. The colonial belief that education was a private rather than a governmental function corresponded to the English system. Governor William Berkeley characterized this educational policy as "the same course that is taken in England . . ., every man according to his ability instructing his children" (1). The gentry could afford private tutors; the only "public" schooling was in the form of charitable aid for orphans and indigents.

Since the first settlers in Virginia were all adults, the colonists had no need for any sort of schooling prior to 1619. In that year, 100 orphans from England arrived with the stipulation that their masters should teach them a trade. This development influenced the pattern of education in Virginia for more than two centuries. Apprenticeship laws enacted in 1643, 1646, and 1672 paralleled the famous apprenticeship and poor laws of England and attempted to provide some vocational, educational, and religious training for orphans, indigent children, and other minors without guardians. Emphasis was on trade apprenticeship, and academic training generally was limited to learning to read and write. A general law of 1705 provided that masters were to be "compelled" to teach orphans in their charge to read and write. This is believed to be the first legislative requirement that reading and writing be taught in the New World (2).

Early Schools

Virginia's first schools were established to aid the colony's sizable group of orphaned and needy children and to supplement the rudimentary educational provisions of the apprenticeship legislation. A short-lived "free school" was established at Charles City in 1620, primarily because of the efforts of Patrick Copeland, a ship's captain. A second school of this type, believed to be the first effective provision for free education in America, was established in 1634 in Elizabeth City County (now the city of Hampton) by the will of Benjamin Symms, a wealthy landowner. Symms bequeathed "200 acres of land and the milk and the increase from eight cows" for the support of this school (3). Other similar schools followed. By 1671, when Governor Berkeley uttered the now famous words, "I thank God that there are no free schools in Virginia, "there were in fact several such schools being operated in the colony as a result of endowments (4).

Community/private schools were established during the colonial period, usually as cooperative ventures among neighbors. They were often known as "Old Field" schools, because they were frequently located in fields which were no longer used for farming. Tuition fees, agreed on by the teacher and parents, financed these schools. In some cases, however, schools were organized and begun by teachers, many of whom were clergymen attempting to supplement their incomes. Other teachers were semi-itinerants who relocated frequently, often because of financial uncertainty or lack of community acceptance. Thus, the quality of schools and teachers was uneven. The community schools generally were local, private, free-enterprise operations.

For the most part, the planters, merchants, and other well-to-do people employed private tutors for their children. In the beginning, these tutors, mostly local clergymen, gave the church a marked influence on instruction. But this influence waned when most of the clergy returned to England at the start of the Revolution. In general, the private tutors were more competent and learned men than were the teachers in community and free schools.

Grammar schools and academies, patronized by the gentry, constituted the other principal types of early schools in Virginia. These were primarily private secondary schools that often included elementary and college level programs. The College of William and Mary, founded in 1693, was the center for higher education.

The pattern established by Virginia's early schools continued to 1860 with few major changes. The academies flourished and formed the backbone of a strong private school system. Free schools, aided after 1820 by the Literary Fund, were charity institutions.

Jefferson's Plan for Public Education

Thomas Jefferson held that public education was vital to democratic government and essential for an informed electorate. He expressed this view in a letter to George Washington: "It is an axiom in my mind that our liberty can never be safe except in the hands of the people themselves and that too with the people of a certain degree of instruction. This is the business of the state to effect and on a general plan" (5).

In 1779, Jefferson introduced in the Legislature "A Bill for the More General Diffusion of Knowledge." The proposal called for a vertical state system of elementary schools, secondary schools, and colleges, crowned by a state university. All white boys and girls would attend free elementary schools for 3 years of 10 months each. Such schools would be located in each ward or "hundred" of every county and would be supported by local taxation. The most able students who completed elementary school would be selected to attend a secondary school at public expense. And the outstanding boys who completed the secondary program could continue for 3 years in one of nine colleges. Boys not selected for education at public expense could continue their schooling if their parents bore the cost.

The Legislature enacted portions of the law, including a clause providing for election of local aldermen, to initiate the plan in each county. However, county courts were made responsible for holding elections of aldermen, and this they failed to do in every instance.

In 1796, the Legislature established a system of primary schools as outlined by Jefferson. Again, however, the county courts were required to take the first steps. Of the outcome, Jefferson said in 1816:

> The experience of twenty years has proved that no court will ever begin it. The reason is obvious. The members of the court are the wealthy members of the counties, and as the expenses of the schools are to be defrayed by a contribution proportioned to the aggregate of other taxes which everyone pays, they consider it a plan to educate the poor at the expense of the rich (6).

Jefferson was to achieve only part of his plan—that of founding the state university. For nearly half a century, he attempted to establish a state public school system. The failure of his efforts was due partly to the fact that too much was left to local initiative with too little centralization of authority at the state level. Probably this was a result of Jefferson's well-known distrust of a strong central government.

The Literary Fund

When the General Assembly created the Literary Fund in 1810, it established a basis for supporting free public schools. Control of the fund was assigned to a corporate body consisting of the Governor, lieutenant governor, treasurer, president of the court of appeals, and their successors. Initial financial support was provided by "escheats, confiscations, fines, penalties and forfeitures, and all rights accruing to the state as derelict." The principal was invested with income to be used for "providing schools for the poor in any county of the State" (7). Disbursements were to be made only after the fund's income reached $45,000 annually, and they were to be distributed on the basis of population in the counties. The fund was increased considerably in 1816, when it was assigned $1,210,550 repaid by the federal government for money borrowed from Virginia during the War of 1812.

In the beginning, the Literary Fund was used to support higher education, such as tuition scholarships to private schools and aid in establishing the University of Virginia. It was 1822 before disbursements were made for the original purpose—providing primary schooling for those unable to afford a private school education. A total of 8,531 poor white children attended the supported schools in 1823, at an average annual cost of $5.12 per child; 14,169 attended in 1829, at an average yearly cost of $2.82; and 47,320 attended in 1840, at a cost of $1.51.

The fund's local operation was assigned to commissioners appointed by the courts. The commissioners sought out indigent children, aided in organizing the schools (often in abandoned buildings), and disbursed funds for their operation. Use of the moneys for buildings or equipment was not allowed until the Legislature passed the District School Law of 1829. This act empowered the school commissioners to establish district free schools and made local residents responsible for 60 percent of the building costs and 50 percent of teachers' salaries, with the balance chargeable to the Literary Fund. However, the maximum rate available from the fund was 4¢ per pupil for each day of school attendance.

Major efforts to strengthen the system were made in 1846, 1851, and 1853. In 1846, the General Assembly provided for the establishment of a local school system under a county school superintendent, with commissioners from each district constituting a county school board. This act attempted to build on the existing local school commissioner system; however, it left the matter of local tax support entirely to local initiative and, for this reason, was slow and uneven in becoming effective. In 1851, the assembly added 50 percent of the capitation tax to the Literary Fund; in 1853, it earmarked the entire tax proceeds for this purpose.

These acts established the principle of direct tax support for public education. The fund's effectiveness, however, was hampered for many years because public school disbursements were limited to $45,000 annually. Also, moneys were periodically diverted to colleges and academies. Despite these handicaps, attendance rose from 50,000 in 1850 to 85,455 in 1860.

In 1860-61, the principal of the Literary Fund was $1,877,365, an increase of $316,666 that year, with $298,870 spent primarily for operating a system of primary schools for indigent children. The total expenditures did not include local funds. By 1861, each of the 149 counties had a superintendent and a local board of school commissioners.

The Legislature diverted income from the fund to the defense of the state in 1861, and part of the principal was invested in Confederate bonds. This loss, together with other investment losses since 1810, amounted to $440,837. In 1871, the fund totaled $1,596,069.

Although the Literary Fund was a limited and inadequate basis for a public school system, it did provide educational opportunity for many children and was the only state assistance for education prior to 1871. It established the principle of public money for public schools, provided a rudimentary public school system, and aided in developing the concept of education as a state responsibility. Unfortunately, the fund reinforced the existing idea that public schools were for the needy, and the negative implications of "schools for the poor" persisted. The concept of the public school as a charitable institution was slow to die in Virginia.

The Underwood Constitution of 1869

A state public school system, differing in detail but similar in spirit to one first proposed by Jefferson a century earlier, was established with ratification of the Underwood Constitution in 1869. This Reconstruction measure aroused vigorous opposition, much of which centered on the provisions establishing a public school system. The state had been a battlefield for 4 years; people were weary. Social and commercial institutions had collapsed, and property resources were severely depleted. Many people felt that the cost of a public school system, which would also serve the newly liberated Negroes, comprising about 30 percent of the population, was an unwarranted, unrealistic, and probably unbearable financial burden. Further, many thought that the convention was not representative of the people, since a majority of the members were either Negroes or natives of other states or foreign countries. Convening under the authority of a military government, the convention was not without elements of duress, both implied and real.

The Underwood Constitution provided for a state superintendent of public instruction to be elected by the General Assembly. It also set up a State Board of Education, consisting of the Governor, attorney general, and chief state school officer, that would have the authority to appoint and to remove county superintendents and district school trustees, to manage the school funds, and to regulate all matters involving the administration of the school system. The General Assembly was authorized to adopt compulsory attendance laws and to levy taxes for the support of schools.

Following the convention's adjournment, an anti-constitutional or conservative party formed to advocate rejection of the constitution by the electorate. In a heated campaign the conservative forces were defeated; the constitution was ratified in July 1869 and remained in effect for 30 years.

Beginning of the Public School System

Following ratification of the Underwood Constitution, the General Assembly moved promptly to elect the first state superintendent of public instruction. William H. Ruffner, who had the support of General Robert E. Lee, was chosen from 15 applicants. He was a son of Henry Ruffner, former president of Washington College (now Washington and Lee University), who had long struggled to establish an adequate public school system.

The constitution required the state superintendent to submit a plan for the organization of the state's public school system within 30 days. Aware that any plan for public schools would cause bitter opposition in eastern Virginia, Dr. Ruffner moved rapidly, completing his task within 25 days. His plan outlined in general the duties of the superintendent of public instruction in relation to other officers of the public school system, and the duties of the county superintendent and the district trustees. It also stipulated that the cost of the system should be paid by funds from the state treasury, the county treasuries, and taxes levied by the school districts. It further required the public schools to provide free education to all persons between 5 and 21 years of age.

With few modifications, the plan was approved by the Legislature on July 11, 1870, described by Ruffner as "a day which marks an epoch in the history of Virginia" (8). The State Board of Education began appointing school officials to operate the system and in 3 months had appointed the necessary 1,400 county superintendents and district trustees. These officials now had to provide buildings, take the school census, select teachers, and organize for work. Dr. Ruffner was anxious to begin at least a few schools in each county as soon as possible; consequently, public schools were open in all counties in November 1870. At the close of the school year, 130,000 pupils were attending 2,900 schools, with 3,000 teachers. The beginning, although long delayed, was an auspicious one.

The system Ruffner had conceived survived strong opposition and the severe financial burdens of Reconstruction for 30 years, until the more favorably received Constitution of 1902 reaffirmed the principle of a state-supported public school system.

William H. Ruffner's Administration

The state was indeed fortunate to have Dr. Ruffner as the first state superintendent. A man of integrity, energy, and ability, he was completely devoted to the cause of education. He attacked the problems with enthusiasm, noting in January 1871 that "the public school work moves on with a vigor which is surprising in view of the fact that not a dollar of the public money has yet become available for the support of the system" (9).

Dr. Ruffner was determined that the people would have better schools than ever before. With this in mind, his communications to superintendents placed great emphasis on the importance of employing capable teachers. In his second annual report he wrote: "As is the teacher, so is the school. School laws, taxes, offices, buildings, apparatus, books, grading, are all in vain without good teachers" (10).

He also used his office to enhance the leadership role of the superintendency. In this connection he said: "This officer has charge of the entire school interest within his territory. His supervision extends over every subject . . . . His cares are boundless, his labors unending. He is the principal of the whole set of schools and the patron of education in his county or city" (11).

During the early years of his administration, Ruffner faced two major problems–winning acceptance and support for the public school system, and preventing funds earmarked in the constitution for public schools from being diverted to other governmental obligations.

As the instigator of what his opponents called the "Yankee system," Ruffner was under constant attack. The most voluble and able of his opponents was R. L. Dabney from eastern Virginia. Ruffner was categorized as the great "leveler," his scheme was called the "leveling policy," and his opponents freely acknowledged "the hope that the whole system may be wrecked at an early date" (12).

Fearing a mixture "of the children of the decent and the children of the vile," alarmed by the extreme poverty of the state following the Civil War, and opposed to an institution that had its origin in the North, Dabney and his colleagues sought to sow the seeds of dissension in all sections of the state (13).

As one observer said,

> Surely, it took a great heart and a persistent determination to face the old time combination of political, social and religious agitators who had thwarted Jefferson's most favorite contention, that had beaten to the wall for more than a century a system of state education, and that was ready to deal the fatal blow to Ruffner's cherished plan (14).

Ruffner, however, was a formidable opponent. Armed with sound logic and knowledge of political economy, he successfully refuted the claims of his opponents. His biographer stated:

> From 1876 he became the leading educator in his state. He had risen as the champion of education, he had borne every kind of insult, he had braved the fury of his opponents, he had conquered; and now, when the significance of his work had become apparent throughout the state, he was heralded with epithets far different from those with which he was greeted only a few years before. The Virginia free school system was recognized as a permanent affair, and, whatever had been its deficiencies in the past, it had a promising future (15).

Perhaps even more difficult than winning acceptance and support for the public school system was retaining funds earmarked in the constitution for public schools from being diverted to other purposes. Early in Ruffner's administration, the state auditor found the state income insufficient to maintain the government, support the schools, and pay interest on the public debt. Consequently, from 1870 through 1879, amounts ranging from $12,000 to $238,000 annually were diverted from the school funds to those other needs (16).

Dr. Ruffner vigorously opposed this practice. In his 1878 annual report, he devoted 72 pages to attacking it and marshaling his facts against it. His eloquent statement covers the place of education in the development of a free people and its relationship to culture, morals, religion, crime, pauperism, and property.

Although opposed by Governor James L. Kemper, Dr. Ruffner's cause was aided in 1877 by the election of a Legislature pledged to restore the school funds. Finally, 2 years later, the Legislature passed the Henkel Bill, setting up a plan requiring the auditor to set apart for the use of the schools those funds required for this purpose under the constitution. Over a period of years, all diverted funds were restored to the schools.

In view of these difficulties, the achievements of Ruffner–sometimes referred to as the "Horace Mann of the

South"—in establishing the public school system in Virginia and in guiding it successfully during its first 12 years are little short of phenomenal.

Farr, Buchanan, and Massey

R. R. Farr succeeded Ruffner as state superintendent (1882-86). John L. Buchanan followed (1886-90), and then John E. Massey (1890-98). During these administrations, the number of pupils and teachers increased, and the patrons and citizens developed greater confidence in the system. Acceptance of the public school system became well established during their administrations, and there was gradual growth without major innovations or difficulties. In 1880, 220,730 pupils were taught by 4,873 teachers, expenditures totaled $1,086,718, and school property was valued at $1,177,544. By 1900, 370,595 pupils were taught by 8,954 teachers, expenditures totaled $1,942,531, and school property was valued at $3,536,293.

The major developments between the close of Dr. Ruffner's administration and the end of the nineteenth century were the addition of programs of instruction in the upper grades and the development of normal school programs for training teachers. The farsighted recommendations made by Superintendent Massey included establishment of a State Board of Examiners, repeal of legislation which based teachers' salaries on pupil attendance, preparation of courses of study, and increased tax support for schools. Massey also sought to provide financial aid for library programs and for increasing the salaries of superintendents. Since most of these progressive measures were carried out within the next few years, Massey's efforts undoubtedly laid the groundwork for their later attainment.

AN EDUCATIONAL AWAKENING, 1900-18

After enduring the severe burdens of Reconstruction, the people of Virginia began to take more interest in public affairs, including those related to education. Between 1900 and 1918, a number of significant developments shaped the growth and influenced the direction of public education in the state. Chief among these were the adoption of the Constitution of 1902, the celebrated "May Campaign" of 1905, and the movement to establish high schools.

Constitution of 1902

By 1900, Virginians were ready to consider a new constitution to replace the unpopular Underwood Constitution of 1869. The disillusionment which followed the Civil War had been replaced by a keen interest in education and government, due in large measure to a group of public-spirited men and women who conducted a vigorous statewide campaign to bring about a constitutional convention.

James W. Southall, appointed state superintendent of public instruction in 1898, welcomed the convention as an opportunity to change certain conditions about which he had repeatedly expressed concern. He was particularly anxious to improve and consolidate rural schools, increase state and local financial support for schools, provide higher salaries for teachers, and establish a State Board of Examiners to handle teacher certification. Southall immediately called a meeting of Virginia educators in July 1901 to make recommendations for constitutional provisions pertaining to public education.

The new State Constitution, ratified to become effective in 1902, gave a mandate for public education by providing that "the General Assembly of Virginia shall establish and maintain an efficient system of public free schools throughout the State."

While the Constitution of 1902 retained the existing structure of public education, it made several significant revisions. For instance, it expanded the State Board of Education to include (in addition to the Governor, attorney general, and chief state school officer) three experienced educators elected by the Senate and two division superintendents selected by the board. Thus, it created an eight-member board. The new constitution also changed the method of selecting the state superintendent of public instruction by transferring his election from the General Assembly to the people. It stipulated that he must be an experienced educator. Further, the constitution authorized the board to divide the state into school divisions, each to contain not less than one county or city; the magisterial districts within the counties retained their separate school boards.

The "May Campaign" of 1905

The leadership and foresight exhibited by Southall before and during the constitutional convention of 1902 were reflected in other developments during his term. The highlight of his administration was the May Campaign of 1905. A series of conferences aimed at improving the South's public education stimulated an already growing interest. Distinguished educators from both the North and the South participated in these meetings, three of which were held at Capon Springs, West Virginia. Among the participants were Edwin A. Alderman, later president of the University of Virginia; J. L. M. Curry of the Peabody Fund; George Foster Peabody of New York; and Samuel C. Mitchell of Richmond College.

The state's division superintendents held a 3-day conference in Richmond in January 1902, which was financed by the General Education Board. The 110 superintendents who attended (out of 117) discussed such topics as taxation, consolidation and transportation, industrial training for Negro schools, Negro education, preparation and selection of teachers, compulsory education laws, and supervision in rural schools. Dr. Southall concluded that "it was the opinion of all who attended this conference that it was the most important educational meeting they had ever known to be held in Virginia, and its stimulating effects have been visible in almost every department of school work" (17).

The General Assembly, the State Board of Education, the University of Virginia, and leading business, civic, and educational associations invited the Sixth Annual Conference for Education in the South to hold its 1903 meeting in Richmond. Scholars and philanthropists from the New England, Middle Atlantic, South Atlantic, and Gulf states participated in the discussions, which embraced all branches of school work from the kindergarten to the university.

Superintendent Southall stated:

> It is impossible to overestimate the value and influence of such meetings on the educational, social and material interests of the country. Mr. Robert C. Ogden, the wise and large-hearted president of the conference, deserves well of the entire country for the able and unselfish service he had given to make this organization a power for good in the restoration of fraternal relations between the once estranged sections and in the upbuilding of the educational interests of the southern states (18).

These conferences and meetings continued to build interest and spark action, culminating in the May Campaign. Summarizing the impact of the campaign, Southall said:

> In assuming the duties of this office, now nearly eight years ago, I emphasized the importance of waging an educational campaign for the improvement of our public schools. Funds for this purpose were not then available, but the formation of local educational associations and later of the Virginia Cooperative Education Commission made this dream capable of realization, and finally issued in the splendid movement known as the May Campaign of 1905, in which more than a hundred of the leading citizens of Virginia delivered educational addresses in nearly every city and county of the Commonwealth. More than this, the pulpit, the press, and all other agencies that make for the common good have been enlisted in the noble work . . . intended to improve our public schools, and thus afford the children of the Commonwealth better preparation for the active duties of life . . . . That we have at last waked up to the importance of this truth is illustrated by the fact that in the recent campaign for State officers and members of the General Assembly such matters as the improvement of the public schools and the public highways were the chief issues at stake. When public discussion begins to play freely around things that need improvement or reform, the day of improvement and reform is in sight (19).

The whole state was involved in the cause of education. At 100 meetings, Governor A. J. Montague and other leading public figures delivered 300 addresses. They distributed more than 200,000 pages of educational literature and organized 50 citizen groups, all within 30 days! This increased public interest in education laid the groundwork for constructive measures adopted during the administration of Southall's successor, Joseph D. Eggleston, the first elected superintendent.

In 1903, Governor Montague, Hollis B. Frisell, head of Hampton Institute, Samuel C. Mitchell of Richmond College, Robert B. Frazer of Warrenton, and Eggleston met in Richmond "to perfect an organization that would carry forward some definite plan by which the people of Virginia would realize the necessity for more democracy in education" (20). Thus, they organized the Cooperative Education Association, one of the important groups that campaigned for better schools.

The association's 1904 platform consisted of eight planks: 9 months of schooling for every child; high schools within reasonable distance of every child; well-trained teachers; agricultural and industrial training; efficient supervision; promotion of libraries; schools for the defective and dependent; and a citizens education association in every county and city.

The May Campaign resulted in far-reaching legislation during the administration of Joseph D. Eggleston, including part of that advocated by the Cooperative Education Association. For instance, the Mann High School Bill, passed in 1906 after a struggle and close vote in the Legislature, authorized funds for high school programs where the localities furnished adequate buildings and teachers' salaries. The Legislature increased the appropriation of $50,000 to $126,000 in 1909, and to $133,000 in 1910.

The Strode Bill of 1908, combining several educational programs into one act, authorized new state normal schools at Harrisonburg and Radford; permitted localities to increase salaries of division superintendents; appropriated $25,000 to encourage the replacement of one-room schools with graded elementary schools; established construction requirements for school buildings to provide more adequate space, light, ventilation, and sanitary facilities; and required that pupils' sight and hearing be tested.

The Legislature also enacted the Williams Loan Fund Bill in 1908, permitting district boards to borrow from the Literary Fund for school building construction if the department approved the plans. This requirement was extended later to all public school buildings.

Development of High Schools

Before 1900, opportunities for high school education were severely limited. Most of the private academies (for which the state had been noted before 1860) did not survive the Civil War and Reconstruction. Although the exact number of high schools in 1900 is not known, Superintendent Massey reported 60 in 1897, which probably included limited high school programs offered in elementary schools. Only 10,210 white students and 1,031 Negro students, representing 4 percent of the whites and seven-tenths of 1 percent of the Negroes enrolled in the public schools, were studying "the higher branches" (21).

Early in his administration, Superintendent Southall urged the establishment of more county or district high schools:

> We need these high schools to articulate the common schools with the University of Virginia and the other higher institutions of learning. We need them also to prepare teachers for the common schools. The proportion of college and normal school graduates who are teaching in the public schools is very small (22).

An act passed at the extra session of the General Assembly in 1903 reaffirmed the 1875 law providing for secondary education under regulations prescribed by the State Board of Education. A fee, not exceeding $2.50 per month per pupil, could be required. The state board established minimum requirements for the course of study and for teachers in high schools in 1904, the first step in developing standards for high school accreditation.

A comprehensive program of high school accreditation began in 1912 when the Southern Association of Colleges and Secondary Schools established a Virginia Commission on Accredited Schools, with which the public instruction department issued annual joint reports on high schools from the 1912-13 school year until 1929. In his introduction to the first report, Superintendent R.C. Stearnes (1913-18) referred to the accreditation program as—

> The first serious effort to apply some definite and uniform standard of measurement to the work of all the secondary schools of the State. On the part of the State Inspectors, including the Secretary of the State Board of Education, this has meant several months of careful investigation and days crowded with painstaking efforts to secure accurate reports . . . . The division superintendents have given material aid both in securing good reports and in reinforcing the visitorial work of the State Officers (23).

The Department of Public Instruction issued a new course of study for high schools in 1915, superseding the rudimentary first course published in 1910. It consisted mainly of college preparatory work but included subjects in business, agriculture, and homemaking. Aided by the Smith-Hughes Act (passed by Congress in 1917) vocational education programs were expanded still further. Instead of being limited primarily to agriculture, emphasis was now given to trade and industry, business, home economics, and other areas of instruction.

Further efforts to strengthen the secondary education program in 1917 included establishing requirements for a standard 4-year high school, including organization, teaching staff, and program of studies. The number of schools increased rapidly, and by the 1917-18 school year, there were 522 high schools enrolling 27,107 students.

Other Developments

In 1904, the General Assembly authorized the State Board of Education to appoint a board to examine teachers and inspect schools on a statewide basis. A board of five members was appointed the following year with the examination of teachers as the first task on its agenda. Although uniform examinations had been introduced in 1891 to reduce the multiplicity of examinations, each superintendent had continued to grade the examinations taken by teachers in his division, so that considerable variation in grading standards continued. The State Board of Examiners took full charge of certificating teachers and organizing a grading system which applied uniform standards to all examination papers.

The Board of Examiners' second major function was to inspect schools. Each member was made responsible for approximately 15 counties. Although their primary duty was to visit and inspect schools, the staff soon expanded their work to include other activities. In cooperation with local officials, teachers, and patrons, they helped plan school buildings, consolidate schools, train teachers, and secure additional support for the schools.

In 1908, the General Assembly appropriated $2,500 to match local contributions for establishing school libraries. It increased the appropriation periodically and thus developed a statewide library program which continues today.

Several private philanthropic organizations made noteworthy contributions to public education during this period. The Anna T. Jeanes Foundation, established in 1908, contributed funds for local school boards to employ Negro supervisors and improve instruction in Negro schools. The Jeanes supervisors aided in making shopwork, homemaking, and other vocational skills an integral part of the curriculum in the schools for Negro children. Their efforts were appreciated, and this program continued successfully for 40 years to become a Virginia tradition. The John F. Slater Fund, established before 1900, aided Virginia to develop facilities for Negroes. The Julius Rosenwald Fund, established in 1917, contributed substantially to the erection of better schools for Negroes. Two other private philanthropic organizations making major continuing contributions to public education in Virginia were the General Education Board, which administered funds provided by John D. Rockefeller, Sr., and the George Peabody Fund.

During its 1916 session, the General Assembly passed legislation authorizing the State Board of Education to establish educational qualifications for division superintendents. The regulations that the state board adopted required the superintendents to participate in educational work for 10 years prior to their appointments and specified that they be college graduates with at least two 3-hour college courses in education or 3 years additional experience as a teacher, principal, or supervisor. This established professional standards for division superintendents and helped considerably in upgrading the quality of school administration in the state.

During this period, the first course of study for elementary schools was published in 1907, and a revised edition was issued in 1909. High school courses of study were published in 1906 and 1910. The latter publication listed minimum requirements in subjects and units for three grades of high schools: first, second, and third. Requirements for first-grade high schools included 12 required units: English, 4 units; mathematics, 3 units; history, 3 units; and science, 2 units. Five elective units were to be selected from the following subjects: Latin, German, French, Spanish, history, physical geography, agriculture, manual arts, botany and zoology, physics, chemistry, and mathematics. The development of these early courses of study indicated a trend toward state-level leadership and guidance in improving classroom instruction.

GROWTH AND DEVELOPMENT, 1918-31

In 1918, Harris H. Hart succeeded Stearnes as state superintendent. Elected by popular vote, he possessed outstanding qualifications for his high office. The Governor had appointed him to the State Board of Examiners when it was established in 1905. He had served as a teacher, principal, superintendent of Roanoke, and member of the State Board of Education.

During Hart's superintendency, from 1918 to 1931 (the longest term to the present date), public education made considerable progress. His administration abolished the cumbersome district system, conducted two major statewide educational surveys, reorganized the structure of public education, improved teacher certification procedures, expanded and strengthened the department, and established a fund for equalizing educational opportunity. It was indeed a period of growth and development.

Dr. Hart, a man of unusual administrative ability, was able to identify the most important problems and to isolate factors necessary for their solution. While many of these problems were not subject to terminal solution (indeed, some remain quite relevant today), he brought them into focus and initiated improvements.

Progressive Measures

During his first year in office, Superintendent Hart initiated a campaign to strengthen the public school system by (a) eliminating the district system, (b) enacting a statewide compulsory school attendance law, and (c) providing free textbooks.

In his first annual report, Dr. Hart discussed these measures:

> It is of the highest importance . . . for the machinery of local administration to be much simplified and made more responsive to intelligent public demands. You are aware of the fact that in each county there is a trustee electoral board, composed of the county school superintendent, the Commonwealth's Attorney, and a citizen appointed by the court. This board has the dual function of appointing school trustees for each school district, and also of hearing cases appealed from the local board of trustees. Each local district board is organized with a chairman and a clerk; is a corporate body, and under the laws of the state operates the schools of the district unit. This gives the State of Virginia five hundred twenty-three separate units of operation. In my opinion the first serious step to take in producing uniform efficiency in the school system of Virginia is to establish at once county uniformity. To my mind, the schools should unquestionably be operated on the basis of the county rather then the district unit with a county school board composed of one member elected from each magisterial district. The number of school trustees would be reduced by sixty-six and two-thirds percent. The school affairs of the county would be viewed in the light of a common unified undertaking. Purely artificial differences in terms, teachers salaries, etc., which now prevail inside of many of our counties, would naturally give place to uniform endeavor.
>
> If the schools fulfill their real function in the State, they must reach all of the boys and girls and provide adequate facilities for their training. The number of children in Virginia who are now not attending school at all, and the number who are attending school with such irregularity as to make proper training impossible, form an alarming per cent of the total number of children . . . . Nothing short of compulsory education and adequate facilities for its proper execution will make the schools thoroughly effective.
>
> A necessary adjunct to compulsory education is to furnish textbooks free to pupils as soon as the State's finances will justify . . . . Several considerations point to the wisdom of having the State purchase textbooks at wholesale prices and lend them to pupils rather than continue the present arrangement of having pupils purchase their own books at retail prices (24).

Two of Dr. Hart's recommendations were adopted in 1922, when the General Assembly enacted the county unit law and a statewide compulsory attendance law. Although free textbooks were not approved, the assembly passed a new textbook law permitting local school boards to purchase directly from publishers at wholesale prices.

The county unit law was the greatest single administrative improvement since the establishment of the public school system in 1870. It made the county the unit of administration, rather than the district, with each county school board replacing several independent district boards. During the first year of operation, the law reduced the administrative units from about 700 to approximately 150; it reduced the number of local school board members and school officials from about 2,000 to less than 500. This resulted in greater administrative efficiency, simplified action, and achieved more uniformity in policy and method. It also encouraged school consolidation and larger enrollments. Dr. Hart, who was responsible for this far-reaching improvement, may well have been the first superintendent to recognize its importance; certainly he was the first to campaign strongly for it.

The compulsory attendance law served to reduce illiteracy, increase attendance, and strengthen the public school system. The Legislature repealed this law in 1959 during the desegregation crisis, but it was reenacted in 1968.

Statewide School Surveys

Two major statewide surveys were conducted during Superintendent Hart's administration. The first was initiated in 1918, when the General Assembly appointed a commission to "study the educational affairs of the State." Superintendent Hart served as commission chairman, and Alexander Inglis of Harvard directed the study, aided by an outstanding professional staff and consultants. One of the first state studies of its kind, the Inglis survey of 1918-19, which conducted a comprehensive pupil-testing program, was notable for its scope and thoroughness as well as for the professional stature of the participants.

The commission not only recommended the three measures emphasized by Hart in his initial program, but also made other recommendations for: a revision of the State Board of Education; the appointment of the state superintendent of public institution; changes in the distribution of state school funds and the levying of local school taxes; a longer school term; lowering of the school entrance age from 7 to 6 years; strengthening of teacher-training programs; raising of qualifications and salaries of division superintendents; and increase of funds for high schools and rural schools. Perhaps the strongest recommendation was for increased financial support, both state and local, with particular emphasis on the need for higher teachers' salaries.

The 1927 General Assembly appointed another statewide survey commission as a part of Governor Harry F. Byrd's "short ballot" program to simplify state government. M.V. O'Shea of the University of Wisconsin directed this survey aided by a staff of 28 persons, including prominent educators and experts in public finance. Although the staff had only 4 months in which to complete its work, it issued a comprehensive report containing recommendations concerning the entire structure of public education in Virginia.

The Inglis and O'Shea surveys were valuable objective analyses of education in Virginia and influenced important constitutional revisions in 1928. One of these provided for a State Board of Education of seven members, appointed by the Governor for 4-year staggered terms, subject to confirmation by the General Assembly. Another called for the Governor to appoint the state superintendent of public instruction for a 4-year term. Also, responsibility for selecting and appointing division superintendents was transferred from the state board to the local school boards. Superintendents were, however, to be chosen from a list of professionally qualified candidates maintained by the state board. These procedures of appointment have continued with only slight change to the present time.

Teacher Certifications

In his 1927 study, "Certification of Teachers," Thomas D. Eason identifies four periods in the history of teacher certification in Virginia. Division superintendents handled teacher examination and certification from 1870 to 1905; the State Board of Examiners, from 1905 to 1911; and a state school inspector, from 1911 to 1918. The fourth or modern period began with Superintendent Hart's administration.

In 1919, the State Board of Education made major revisions in teacher certification practices by replacing the existing 28 types of certificates with 7 new classifications: collegiate professional, collegiate, special (for high school subjects), normal professional (for junior high school subjects and elementary school), elementary, first grade, and second grade. At the same time, it established professional standards for the renewal of certificates. These revisions simplified certification and raised the standards.

Further efforts to strengthen the certification program were undertaken during Hart's administration. Certification on the basis of examination was discontinued in 1925. First-grade certificates were not issued after 1926; holders were required to earn higher certificates by 1931 or lose their licenses to teach. The special certificate was not issued after 1929, and the second-grade and elementary certificates were discontinued in 1931. Thus, the 28 types of certificates available in 1918 were reduced by 1931 to three types: collegiate professional, collegiate, and normal professional. Local permits, which authorized schools to employ noncertificated teachers when conditions required it, continued in use although the Hart administration issued them reluctantly and reduced the numbers significantly. Requirements for renewing normal professional certificates were raised, and collegiate certificates were made nonrenewable; holders were required to earn a collegiate professional certificate within 4 years.

In summary, the teacher certification system was reorganized, simplified, and strengthened during Hart's administration. Standards were raised from a level where applicants who had completed only the eighth grade could be certificated to teach by passing an examination to one where no applicant who had completed less than 2 years of college could be certificated. This was the beginning of Virginia's modern period of teacher certification, and the system which was developed at that time has required few changes to the present.

Attempt To Measure Efficiency

In his report for the 1918-20 biennium, Dr. Hart described a plan "to ascertain as nearly as can be the ratio between the efficiency of the school work and the financial investment; and . . . to discover the relative position of each county and city with reference to certain aspects of educational work" (25).

Patterned after the Ayer's Index plan for comparing state school systems, Hart's scheme included five "financial" and five "academic" factors. By designating a rating of 100 as satisfactory, the various counties and cities could be ranked in the order of their efficiency according to these 10 factors.

The "academic" factors used were percentage attendance of school-age population (100 percent as the goal); percent of teachers holding first-grade and higher certificates (100 percent as the goal); length of term in days times one-half (200 days as the considered goal); percent of total enrollment in high school times 10 (10 percent as the goal); percent of all pupils in grades represented by seventh grade times 10 (10 percent as the goal).

The "financial" factors were average annual salary of teachers times one-tenth ($1,000 as the goal); percent of local funds for teachers' salaries times 2 (50 percent as the goal); total cost per room times one-fifteenth ($1,500 as the goal); per-capita cost of instruction based on enrollment times 4 ($25 as the goal); total per-capita cost of maintenance and instruction times 3 ($33.33 as the goal).

Dr. Hart's annual report for the 1919-20 school year ranked the counties and cities on the index scale. The low for the counties was 36; the high, 85. The low for the cities was 73.5; the high, 117. The average for the counties was 61, and for the cities, 92. The comparative ranking continued to be reported through the 1927-28 school year.

Although Hart recognized the shortcomings of his plan in measuring "the quality of instruction," the plan did help local school authorities to point up the greatest weaknesses in their systems. It also underscored the great diversity in the adequacy of the state's educational program.

First Equalization Fund

The educational disparities in the counties and cities revealed by Dr. Hart's "efficiency" ratings pointed up the need for equalizing educational opportunity throughout the state. Dr. Hart made the first attempt to initiate such a program. In his 1928-29 annual report, Dr. Hart pointed out:

> It is now pretty well agreed that some form of equalization of educational opportunity should be established in Virginia, although there appears to be some division of opinion as to the method of approach. It is urged on one hand that a large equalization fund of, say, a million dollars should be set up for the proper assistance of those counties not economically able to support an adequate system of training. A second plan is to use the entire State appropriation for the purpose of guaranteeing minimum basic educational facilities all over the State using a relatively small equalization fund to supplement the local appropriations in certain counties for this purpose. It appears that in the present circumstances in Virginia the latter method gives promise of better results (26).

Contrary to Dr. Hart's recommendation, the General Assembly adopted the first plan for "a large equalization fund" when it appropriated $500,000 as an equalization fund for 1930-31. Fortunately, the state board was given wide latitude in distributing the fund. According to Hart, the distribution plan agreed upon required an 8-month term and used a "sliding scale of appropriation from the State based upon the qualifications of the teachers employed by the county, with the amount to be paid by the county remaining a constant sum" (27). The plan did not adequately take into account the factors of local ability and effort, probably because such data were not available at the time; however, the poorer counties received the larger part of the fund.

Strengthening the Department of Education

The title "Department of Education" replaced that of "Department of Public Instruction" during the first year of Hart's administration. In some respects, this change was symbolic of the forthcoming development of a modern state education department.

At that time, the department consisted of the chief state school officer, secretary to the state board, eight state school supervisors, an auditor-statistician, six stenographers, and a shipping clerk. The supervisory function developed gradually from the original State Board of Examiners and inspectors, which had assumed such responsibilities over the years, to the creation of supervisory positions in the department. During 1918-19, the department's efforts centered on adopting accreditation standards for institutions of higher learning, establishing new minimum standards for accrediting high schools, developing vocational education programs under the Smith-Hughes Act, and measuring educational efficiency in the county and city school divisions.

The department added a director of a teachers bureau in 1919-20. The following year, for the first time, Dr. Hart listed in his annual report nine supervisory staff members by specific assignments: home economics, agriculture, secondary education (two), teacher training, Negro education, physical education, rural education, and trade and industrial education. The department also initiated a program for rehabilitating the physically handicapped by assigning a supervisor this responsibility.

The department continued to expand to meet increasing needs. It increased the staff to 13 supervisors in 1921-22 and added new services in textbooks, school libraries, and school buildings. The school buildings service developed standard plans which were widely used, aided in selecting sites, and supervised school construction. Departmental services continued to emphasize field work and supervisory assistance to localities.

When the county unit law of 1922 prompted the consolidation of districts, Hart turned his attention to consolidating the many small high schools established under the district system. In 1923, he cited data showing that per-pupil cost was much higher in the small high school, often requiring a diversion of funds needed in the elementary program. Although significant progress in school consolidation awaited the development of improved highways and pupil transportation, a beginning was made at this time.

The department's staff increased to 16 by 1925-26, including 1 member in a new research service. The following year, the department established a research and surveys division. Its initial activities included conducting school surveys, giving experimental tests to high school seniors in selected counties, making statistical studies, and preparing reports on acceleration and retardation.

The department's supervisory services were listed by classifications for the first time in the annual report for 1928-29. Including 19 professional staff members, these classifications were accounting and statistics, agricultural education, civilian rehabilitation, home economics education, Negro education, physical education, research and surveys, rural education, school buildings, school libraries and textbooks, secondary education, teacher training and certification, and trade and industrial education. The following year, a program in vocational and educational guidance was established so that the schools might "give more serious attention to the study of pupils rather than devote time almost exclusively to the study of subject matter" (28).

This period was one of the truly significant eras in public education in Virginia. Under Dr. Hart's dynamic leadership, notable achievements were made which provided a foundation for future improvements.

A DECADE OF CURRICULUM REVISION, 1931-41

Sidney B. Hall succeeded Hart in January 1931. A young man with a broad background in educational theory and practice, Dr. Hall had been a high school principal, state supervisor of secondary education, and professor of secondary education at George Peabody College for Teachers. He also had observed and studied education in Europe.

Hall's appointment coincided with the Depression of the 1930's, which had serious repercussions on public education. The state's overall financial position at the beginning of the Depression had been favorable, since its predominantly agrarian economy was less affected at first than the economy of the more highly industrialized states. Tax income from both state and local sources declined sharply, however.

In spite of decreased state and local revenue, which resulted in curtailed budgets, Hall reported that most of the counties and cities maintained 8-month school terms during 1932-33. In his annual report, he explained:

> It should be pointed out that the full term was realized, not because there was sufficient money, but, because, when the money which was available was exhausted, the teachers in the various school systems volunteered their service in order that the schools might not have to close and thus deny to the children of the State the educational opportunity that was theirs. Too much credit cannot be attributed to the teaching force . . . for this type of loyalty. When it is pointed out that the teachers of the State have suffered a reduction in salary to the extent of 21 per cent, and when it is realized that, in addition to this reduction, they have actually given many weeks of their service free of charge, it is not too much to say that a comparable situation in any other vocation or profession is almost not to be found (29).

In 1933-34, the Governor, with authorization from the General Assembly, reduced state school appropriations 30 percent. This sharp cut was reflected in the average annual salary of teachers, which declined from $909 in 1930-31 to $692 in 1933-34. Hall estimated early in the year that even with this salary reduction, approximately $655,000 would be needed for 62 counties to maintain a normal and legal school term. After Hall's figures were questioned and sharply criticized, Governor John Garland Pollard instituted a separate study. The Governor's study concluded that only $165,000 would be needed. But at the end of the year, the state superintendent's figures were vindicated when it was found that it had been necessary to secure $710,000 in federal aid to enable 72 counties to operate 8-month terms.

Despite the serious problems, Hall pointed to sustained teacher morale, increased enrollments, school consolidations, and advances in teacher preparation, which he attributed to "the sacrificial services of the teachers, principals, and superintendents. . . " (30).

Curriculum Revision

At the beginning of his administration, Hall was disturbed to find that many children of school age were not enrolled in school and that the average daily attendance for the state was only 83 percent. He envisioned the need for an intensive program to improve instruction, chiefly through curriculum revision. The goal was to provide children with "enriched and more meaningful experiences in the classroom" (31), thereby increasing enrollment and attendance and improving the "holding power" of the schools.

To carry out and coordinate an improved program, Superintendent Hall reorganized the department into six divisions–research and finance, higher education, instruction, vocational education, school buildings, and school libraries and textbooks. The agency also was enlarged to include a total of 28 staff members. The newly created Division of Instruction unified the supervision of secondary education, elementary education, Negro education, and health and physical education under the leadership of a director of instruction. The superintendent assigned this division primary responsibility for initiating and developing a program to improve instruction.

The department directed its initial efforts toward a broad concept of curriculum revision (see Appendix C). In an organizational bulletin issued in March 1932, the department defined the curriculum as "all the experiences which children have at school under the guidance of their teachers" (32). The bulletin stressed the teacher's role in planning such a curriculum:

> It becomes obvious from this concept of the curriculum that teachers and pupils together actually make the curriculum, and that all teachers in the State of Virginia are engaged in curriculum construction whether or not they recognize it as such. The State Curriculum Program then is undertaking to assist teachers to develop a more adequate curriculum to the end that the instruction which children receive will be improved (33).

Within the next 2 years, more than 10,000 of the state's 17,000 teachers participated in curriculum planning workshops and seminar groups, for which state and local supervisors served as advisors and discussion leaders. In carrying out their leadership roles, the department's staff stressed the need for cooperation with local lay and professional groups and respected local freedom and responsibility, while attempting to stimulate initiative. The department appointed an additional staff member to strengthen its elementary education supervisory services.

In 1934, the department published a new course of study for elementary schools that included a variety of experiences, activities, and projects intended to stimulate learning. The program challenged the teacher to involve the pupils in selecting and planning experiences best suited to their interests, abilities, and needs. The courses were not organized into fixed patterns or units, but were designed to promote a flexible learning environment.

In secondary education, the department centered its efforts on developing a core curriculum plan to supplant the traditional, strictly academic program of required subjects with courses of study emphasizing problem solving and the development of needed skills and appreciations. It stressed the need for imaginative and ingenious teaching methods to implement such programs. Like the new elementary program, it avoided rigid organization of subject matter. The department issued core curriculum courses of study for the eighth grade in 1934 and for each of the four high school grades from 1937 to 1941. It issued a manual of administration for high schools in 1937.

An important part of the program's philosophy emphasized the need to consider curriculum revision as a continuing process of improvement and expansion. During 1937-47, the department made frequent appraisals of the program and conducted major evaluations from 1939 to 1941. These evaluations included 27 regional conferences and many additional meetings for study and discussion, involving an estimated 20,000 participants.

In his study of curriculum development programs, J. Galen Saylor described the Virginia program as follows:

> The program is evolutionary rather than revolutionary. It is a continuous widespread effort with one dominating purpose–the improvement of instruction in the classrooms of the State. The program is a cooperative undertaking with all the educational forces of the State, teachers, supervisors, principals, superintendents, staffs of teacher training institutions, members of the State Department and the lay public participating. Widespread participation prevails. Participation is entirely voluntary even to use of courses of study.
>
> The program is comprehensive, covering all levels of school organization and being concerned with all major factors related to instruction, such as teacher pre-service and in-service training, books and supplies, materials to guide curriculum development, evaluation of the outcomes of instruction, teaching procedures, and the like. An enlightened supervisory program, guided and directed by the State Department, constitutes the chief method of carrying forward the program from a State standpoint (34).

The enthusiasm the program aroused outside Virginia was matched by opposition from some of the leading educators within the state. The most frequent criticisms were that the fundamental skills of reading, writing, and arithmetic were not sufficiently emphasized, that too much attention was given to the "whims" rather than the "needs" of students, that achievement standards were ignored, and that the program was indefinite in its aims and not explicit in its content. In 1955, reaction against certain aspects of the new curriculum caused Governor Thomas B. Stanley to order its withdrawal from use.

With the exception of curriculum revision, the Depression years were not noted for major changes or innovations. This does not mean, however, that no significant advances were made during this period. For example, Virginia effectively used federal funds from the Public Works Administration and the Works Progress Administration to provide needed schoolhousing.

The department conducted special studies, including school building surveys in many counties, to identify the most critical housing needs and to suggest long-term building programs. It made efforts to use federal funds, largely to consolidate high schools into larger centers and to reduce the number of one- and two-room elementary schools.

The 1935-36 annual report revealed that there were approximately 400 accredited high schools in the counties, and an additional 100 offering 1 or more years of high school work. Each of the 400 schools served an area of approximately 100 square miles. The report suggested that a high school could serve an area of at least 200 square miles without subjecting students to unreasonable travel distances on school buses. It called attention to the advantages of the large high school from the standpoint of program offering and per-pupil costs.

The state spent approximately $17.5 million on new school buildings between 1930-31 and 1940-41. During the same period, the value of buildings increased from $62 million to $80 million. The total number of buildings decreased from 5,618 to 4,892, and the one-room schools decreased from 2,764 to 1,923.

Progress continued throughout the Depression years. In 1934-35, the requirements for division superintendents were raised to include the master's degree, training in administration and finance, and a minimum of 3 years experience as supervisor or principal. Three years later, the department initiated a state music program with a supervisor of music. In 1938-39, the department established a Division of Rehabilitation and Special and Adult Education which was to have far-reaching effects on the state's educational program. The division included a director and four supervisors of rehabilitation education, two supervisors of special education, and a supervisor of adult education.

In 1940-41, a supervisor of distributive education was assigned to the Division of Vocational Education, and a supervisor of audiovisual education was added to the Division of Libraries and Textbooks. The department's expansion during the late 1930's and early 1940's reflected improvements in the economy.

THE WAR AND POSTWAR YEARS, 1941-57

The period from 1941 to 1957 was marked by many educational problems growing largely out of the war and postwar years. A serious shortage of teachers developed at the beginning of the war and remains an unresolved problem today in certain rural areas. The gap between building needs and new construction widened as a result of materials shortages, building restrictions, and inflation. The U.S. Supreme Court decision in the desegregation case of 1954 caused uncertainty as to the future of public education itself.

Three state superintendents served during this period: Dabney S. Lancaster (1941-46), G. Tyler Miller (1946-49), and Dowell J. Howard (1949-57). Dr. Lancaster had served previously as state supervisor of agricultural education, secretary to the State Board of Education, and dean of students at the University of Alabama. Dr. Miller had been a division superintendent of schools in Warren and Rappahannock counties and in the city of Charlottesville. Dr. Howard had served as supervisor of agricultural education and as assistant superintendent of public instruction.

World War II

The department was expanded during 1941-42 with the appointment of an assistant superintendent of public instruction and the establishment of a defense training division, responsible for preparing defense industry workers. During the next 3 years, more than 77,000 people received such training.

In addition to continuing the regular school program during the war years, the department emphasized physical fitness, war production, conservation and distribution of essential goods and services, skills in mathematics and science, effects of inflation, air-mindedness, international relations, and mobilization of students and teachers. It provided child-care centers for children of working mothers before and after school hours and during vacation periods. It gave special attention to health and physical fitness, emotional stability, and home-school-community relationships. To help in the war effort, children collected scrap metal, worked in victory gardens, and bought and sold savings bonds and stamps.

As the war progressed, its impact was reflected in declining enrollments as students were inducted into the armed forces or found jobs in industry. Teachers added to their work load by participating in rationing, Selective Service registration, Civil Defense, and other war-related activities. As war activities increased in Virginia, many teachers left their classrooms to work in war production plants. Even more distressing was the fact that the number of students preparing for the teaching profession decreased by almost 50 percent between 1940 and 1945.

Despite the handicaps caused by the war, some forward steps were taken during this period. The department initiated visiting-teacher and conservation education programs, increased emphasis on guidance, and started a statewide testing program. The state appropriated in 1945 approximately $1 million to help local school systems purchase audiovisual equipment. It made considerable progress toward equalizing the salaries of white and Negro teachers, and it attained equal salary scales for elementary and high school teachers in nearly all divisions. A special appropriation in 1944 provided for employing school principals for 12 months rather than the customary 9 or 10 months. There was a gradual transition from an 11-year to a 12-year school program, which became statewide when Nelson County added the twelfth year in 1960.

The Teacher Shortage

The shortage of qualified teachers that developed at the outbreak of World War II became increasingly severe, and by the end of the war it was critical. "Drastic action is needed," State Superintendent Lancaster said in 1946, "to hold fast to our best teachers and to fill the ranks with the ablest minds and finest characters that the Commonwealth produces" (35).

Lancaster called attention to the fact that approximately 3,000 teachers with less than 2 years of college training were employed in public schools, as compared with 1,000 in 1941. "Relatively few young people are preparing to teach and it seems clear that in spite of all the gains of recent years, Virginia faces a critical teacher situation" (36), he said.

The widely held belief that most of the absentees would resume teaching after the war proved to be a false hope, for the number returning was insignificant compared to the serious deficiency. Inflation continued into the postwar period and pay increases voted by the General Assembly did not make teacher salaries competitive with those in other states or with those paid by private industry. Recruitment of new teachers became increasingly difficult as enrollments in teacher-training colleges declined.

Several new developments served to accentuate the need for more teachers. These included the increased birthrate following the war, improved holding power of the schools, and the change to a 12-year system. Broader curriculum offerings and the need to readjust the heavy pupil loads carried by teachers during the war further aggravated the situation.

To combat the teacher shortage, the state initiated a scholarship program in 1947, providing loans up to $300 per year for undergraduates preparing to teach. It made scholarships not exceeding $100 per summer session available to teachers who were not fully qualified. Although these scholarship loans bore interest at the rate of 3 percent, both principal and interest could be canceled by teaching in the state's public school. Undergraduate participation was limited initially to juniors and seniors taking preparatory courses to teach in the elementary schools. In 1948, however, the General Assembly extended eligibility to students in all 4 years of college as well as to those preparing to teach high school subjects for which qualified teachers were not available. During the first year of the program, 205 undergraduate students received scholarships, as did 111 teachers taking summer work. By 1957, 7,139 undergraduates and 8,590 teachers had benefited from the program. This plan which has been expanded and liberalized periodically, continues to play a major role in preparing teachers for the public schools.

To make the profession more attractive to prospective teachers, the state established in 1942 an actuarially sound retirement system for teachers and other state employees, and 6 years later it appropriated funds for a sick leave plan for teachers. The 1952 session of the General Assembly appropriated $19.5 million to increase teachers' salaries and establish a statewide minimum salary scale, ranging from $2,000 to $3,200 for college graduates.

Legislative Studies

Beginning in 1944, the General Assembly conducted an extensive 7-year appraisal of public education. Major studies were made by five separate groups: the Denny Commission (1944), the McCue Committee (1946), the Moses Commission (1947), the Gray Commission (1948), and the Moore Commission (1951). In no period in the state's history was more time given to the study of the school system. The basic problems centered on the need for sufficient funds to attract and hold competent teachers and to provide buildings and other facilities.

The Denny Commission, headed by George H. Denny, was instructed to study all facets of the school program, including curriculum, training of teachers, and other matters deemed essential to the improvement of the public school system. It held meetings throughout the state to give citizens the opportunity to express their views. The consensus expressed at these meetings included dissatisfaction with the standing of Virginia's schools compared with other states; the need for greater emphasis on the three R's and vocational education; higher salaries for teachers; stricter enforcement of the compulsory attendance law; and a desire to bring the management of the schools closer to the people.

The Denny Commission's recommendations, many of which were never implemented, covered all areas of the school programs. Included were recommendations that the governing body in the counties be elected at a time different from that of other county officials and on the basis of an educational platform, that free textbooks be provided, and that a sound equalization program be established. Other recommendations called attention to the need for greater emphasis on the three R's, consolidation of schools, improvements in Negro education, strengthening of teacher-training programs in state institutions, and increased efforts to improve home-community relationships. Recommendations were adopted to increase state support for libraries, to provide a limited increase in equalization funds for poorer counties, and to help equalize educational opportunities for Negroes.

The McCue Committee, headed by delegate Edward O. McCue, Jr., studied the advisability of further subsidizing the training of prospective teachers, providing sick leave for teachers, and instituting a minimum salary schedule. This committee recommended that scholarships of $300, available previously only to college juniors and seniors, be extended to selected freshmen and sophomores who were preparing to teach, that the number of scholarships awarded annually be increased, and that sick leave be extended to teachers as well as to other state employees. These recommendations were adopted. The committee opposed the idea of establishing minimum salaries for teachers, stating that it "would tend to destroy flexibility in the handling of personnel problems" and was not feasible in view of the unpredictability of "the course of economic events" (37). The report blamed the State Department of Education for the teacher shortage and other problems and recommended that a full-time paid chairman of the State Board of Education take over the management of the business affairs handled by the state superintendent of public instruction. This recommendation was not adopted.

The Moses Commission, headed by State Senator Charles T. Moses, made a thorough study of school needs and held five public meetings throughout the state. It recommended higher teacher salaries, more money for needy counties, expanded vocational programs, transportation improvements, liberalized retirement benefits, and sick leave for teachers. It also estimated that the recommended programs would cost an additional $39 million, a large part of which was appropriated by the General Assembly.

A commission on state and local revenues and expenditures, of which State Senator Garland Gray was chairman, was directed by the General Assembly—

> To make an intensive and thorough examination and study of all state and local taxes and revenue, and receipts and all state expenditures, allocations and grants-in-aid (both in general and special funds), the propriety thereof and the sources from which the revenues are or may be derived (38).

The Gray Commission recommended the appointment of school board members in the counties by the boards of supervisors, a statewide testing program, increased equalization moneys for the poorer counties, greater financial school support by the localities, modification of school building regulations, continued emphasis on the fundamental subjects, and other measures.

A commission under the chairmanship of Delegate E. Blackburn Moore issued a report in 1951 entitled "A Foundation Education Program for Virginia." It found that the state board and the state superintendent of public instruction were giving increased emphasis to the teaching of the fundamental subjects as recommended by previous studies, that the greatest impediments to effective teaching were an insufficient number of properly trained teachers in the elementary grades and too heavy teacher loads, and that methods of financing had not equalized educational opportunities in the school systems of the state. This commission recommended increasing the number and amount of teacher-training scholarships, eliminating salary differentials between elementary and high school teachers, delaying further curriculum expansion until the present program was adequately financed, and making additional funds contingent on reducing class size and equalizing educational opportunity in the school systems.

The "Battle Fund" for School Construction

The state entered the war and postwar period with a tremendous backlog of school building needs, for the Depression had created a serious gap between needs and construction despite increased construction for several years prior to 1941. War priorities allocated manpower and materials to the defense program and forced a suspension of new school construction "for the duration." Also, much of the normal maintenance, repair, and improvement of school plants was deferred. Thus, these years of hard use shortened the life of the buildings, many of which were already outmoded in design.

Postwar efforts to meet the critical shortage of buildings encountered serious difficulties. Residential, commercial, and industrial construction needs also had been deferred during the war, resulting in postwar competition for labor and materials, as well as soaring costs. Not only did the schools suffer from inflation, but the availability of materials and equipment often was uncertain, and delays in construction were common. Rising interest rates and inaccurate cost estimates added to the difficulties. And all of this occurred at a time when additional classrooms were needed to accommodate rapidly increasing enrollments during the early 1950's.

A department study in 1948, utilizing data from the division superintendents to project the state's school building needs for the next 10 years, estimated the cost of needed facilities to be $401 million. A private accounting firm, authorized by the General Assembly to make a similar study, estimated construction needs at $279.5 million. Subsequent developments proved both estimates too low.

The 1950 session of the General Assembly convened after one of the most closely contested gubernatorial elections in the state's history. Public education was a major issue in the campaign, and the candidates made strong commitments to improve the public schools. Shortly after his election, Governor John S. Battle carried out his campaign promise by recommending that $75 million in state aid be given to localities for school construction. The General Assembly approved his proposal; in addition, it transferred $11 million from the sinking fund to the Literary Fund for school construction loans to localities.

Consolidation of Schools

Beginning with the administration of Superintendent Hart, greater attention has been given to establishing consolidated schools of sufficient size to offer comprehensive education programs at reasonable per-capita cost. Progress, which has depended on the development of improved highways and pupil transportation, has been made during the tenure of each succeeding superintendent.

Consolidation was accelerated during World War II and the postwar years. In 1942, the Legislature provided $500,000 to aid local school divisions in meeting the cost of pupil transportation, and it increased this appropriation to more than $3.5 million in 1950. A pupil transportation service was established in the department in 1946 with the appointment of a supervisor and an assistant. These efforts culminated in dramatic gains in consolidation as shown by the following data: In 1940, there were 340 high schools with fewer than seven teachers; in 1950 there were 173. In 1940, there were 284 high schools with seven or more teachers; in 1950 there were 383. In 1940, a total of 624 high schools enrolled 122,073 pupils; by 1950, 556 high schools enrolled 148,389 pupils. In 1957, a total of 417 high schools enrolled 227,314 pupils, and only 39 of these schools had fewer than 7 teachers. The trend toward fewer schools and larger enrollments has continued to the present time.

The Gray Commission

In August 1954, Governor Thomas B. Stanley appointed a legislative commission on public education, composed of 32 members of the General Assembly, to determine the effect on public education of the 1954 U.S. Supreme Court decision in the school segregation cases. Senator Garland Gray was selected to serve as chairman. Following two interim reports, the commission gave its full report in November 1955.

The plan developed by the Gray Commission attempted to prevent extensive school closings and at the same time avoid compulsory integration. It recommended a tuition grant program to permit pupils to attend nonsectarian private schools and public schools outside the locality were they resided, the state paying a maximum of $125 per school year for a pupil attending an elementary school and a maximum of $150 for a pupil attending a high school.

Although the voters approved the tuition grant program, the plan was shelved during a period of "massive resistance" to the desegregation decision. However, its main provisions were revived in 1959 following recommendations of the Perrow Commission during the administration of Governor J. Lindsay Almond, Jr.

QUALITY EDUCATION FOR THE SPACE AGE, 1957-68

Although many factors affected the course of public education in the decade beginning in 1957, two major developments cast their shadows over the public school system during this period. One grew out of the U.S. Supreme Court decision on school desegregation, and the other out of the launching of Sputnik by the Russians in 1957.

Davis Y. Paschall, who became superintendent of public instruction in March 1957, called his first full year in office "a year of crisis in public education" and referred to "the explosive series of events related to integration suits emanating from the Supreme Court decision of 1954, and the birth pangs of a space age that turned critically to education as a determiner in the sudden warfare of ideologies for the capture of the minds of men" (39).

Commission on Public Education

The 1958 General Assembly, reflecting the public concern generated by Sputnik, enacted legislation providing for a commission to evaluate the curriculum, teacher training and certification, "and related matters" in the public schools in Virginia.

The commission, headed by State (now U.S.) Senator William B. Spong, Jr., endorsed the state department's efforts to strengthen teacher education and the high school curriculum. Its report also emphasized the need for improving the quality of teaching in the following statement:

> No matter how fine the buildings or how broad the scope of the curriculum, in the final analysis the excellence of education is primarily dependent upon the quality of teaching . . . . We are acutely aware that the higher curriculum requirements adopted by the State Board of Education cannot be effective if they are beyond the present capabilities of our teachers (40).

The report stressed the necessity of strengthening program offerings in science, mathematics, foreign languages, and English. But at the same time, it recommended a balanced curriculum in the following terms:

> Although we are stressing the teaching of science in high school, it is vital that the curriculum be kept in balance as science is only one of the fields in which children need to be educated . . . the scientist lacking skills in the communication arts cannot transmit his knowledge effectively . . . . This Commonwealth, the birthplace of Washington, Jefferson, Madison, and the other founders

of the Republic, cannot overlook the humanities and thus turn her back upon our great heritage (41).

To upgrade the quality of public education, the General Assembly appropriated funds for various special programs to be administered by the state department. These included teacher institutes in mathematics, science, foreign languages, guidance, and U.S. and Virginia government, with emphasis on the relationship of basic principles to our economic way of life; state aid on a matching basis for the purchase of mathematics, science, and foreign language equipment; state aid for the employment of guidance counselors in high schools; and a general scholarship and loan program for needy but able Virginia students attending state institutions of higher learning.

The Desegregation Crisis

Dr. Paschall, who had broad experience in public school work and who had held the position of director of elementary and special education before he became superintendent of public instruction, found the state confronted with a major crisis that had been building up since the desegregation decision of the U.S. Supreme Court in 1954. White high schools were closed in Norfolk, Front Royal, Charlottesville, and Prince Edward County following the federal court order to desegregate. The city schools reopened during 1958, but schools in Prince Edward County remained closed until the fall of 1964. During the controversy involving the state's public school system, Paschall reminded Virginians that—

> Unprecedented tides of recurring crises have swept the shores of public education in this Commonwealth during the past three and one-half years. Its survival and advances have been due to the great faith of the people and the superb leadership of those who possessed a deep sense of educational stewardship (42).

Caught between the federal court decisions on the one hand and the state's laws against integration on the other, Governor J. Lindsay Almond, Jr., appointed in 1958 a special commission on public education to recommend to the General Assembly the steps the state should take to deal with the school crisis. Mosby G. Perrow, Jr., of Lynchburg, at the time a member of the State Senate and later president of the State Board of Education, was named chairman of the commission, which presented its recommendations to the General Assembly the following year. Two of the key proposals approved by the Legislature were repeal of the state's compulsory attendance law in favor of a "local option" statute, and a tuition grant program to make state funds available for parents of children attending private nonsectarian schools or public schools in localities other than those in which they normally would be enrolled. The local option statute existed until early in 1968, when the General Assembly passed a statewide compulsory attendance law.

Moving to strengthen public education in this period of turmoil, the State Board of Education approved major changes in the high school curriculum. A "Statement of Policy for High Schools," which became effective in September 1959, increased the number of units required for graduation from 16 to 20, based on a 5-year high school program. Qualified eighth-graders were encouraged to earn credits in Latin or a modern foreign language, algebra, and advanced science. During Paschall's administration, the state board also upgraded certification regulations for teachers, revised requirements for school building construction in order to give more flexibility to the localities, and made changes designed to strength accreditation standards for high schools.

When Paschall resigned as state superintendent in August 1960 to become president of the College of William and Mary, he left behind a record of progress in public education during an extremely difficult period.

Paschall's successor, Woodrow W. Wilkerson, also was selected from the State Department of Education, where he had served as director of secondary education immediately before his appointment as superintendent. During the administration of Dr. Wilkerson, a man of energy, vision, and determination, the rate of progress in public education has been accelerated.

As the State Board of Education stepped up its improvement efforts, it asked to be relieved of the responsibility for serving as the governing board for Longwood, Madison, and Virginia State Colleges, and for the vocational rehabilitation program. The General Assembly approved the board's request and passed legislation to provide separate governing boards for the three institutions and for the rehabilitation program, effective July 1, 1964. The Virginia State School at Hampton, the last of the institutions left under the board's control by the 1964 Legislature, was placed under a separate board in 1966.

In order that the state superintendent might devote his full energies to his work as chief executive of the public school system, the General Assembly upon recommendation of the Governor relieved him of the responsibility of serving as ex officio member on the boards of the state-supported educational institutions.

Instructional Emphasis on the American Form of Government and Economic Way of Life

The development of materials and guidelines for instruction in economic education began in 1959, when the state board authorized the superintendent of public instruction to appoint a committee to work with the Division of Secondary Education to develop a unit on basic principles of the American form of government and economic way of life.

An outline for the unit was prepared for incorporation in the senior high school course in Virginia and U.S. government and was distributed to school divisions during the 1960-61 school year. As a further step in strengthening economic instruction, the board requested the preparation of materials contrasting communism and the American system of freedom under law.

During 1962-63, a guide entitled *Communism in Contrast with the Principles of American Freedom* was distributed, and regional meetings were held throughout the state to discuss its use.

A third publication, *An Instructional Guide for Virginia and United States Government*, was issued in November 1964 to give teachers suggestions for selecting, organizing, and presenting content to further the study of the American political and economic system in contrast with totalitarianism, especially communism.

"This publication," Dr. Wilkerson said, "is unique in its extensive incorporation of an instructional emphasis on the basic principles and beliefs undergirding our economic system and the contrast in depth of the American system of freedom under law with communism" (43).

Upon recommendation of the state superintendent and with the board's approval, the program was refined and expanded to include a guide for the required course in Virginia and U.S. history, a guide for the elective course in civics in grades 8 and 9, a guide to stress economic education in the elementary grades, and revisions of teacher certification regulations to provide a stronger background in economics education.

A 33-member State Advisory Council, composed of lawyers, businessmen, industrialists, Virginia legislators, and educators, was appointed by Wilkerson in April 1965 to serve in an advisory role in the continued planning and development of the economic education program.

A guide entitled *Elementary School Economics,* which offers teaching suggestions in the areas of natural and human resources; production, distribution, and consumption of goods and services; money; taxes; and free enterprise economy, is being used by teachers in grades 1 through 7 in the public schools.

Work also has been completed on a guide for high school teachers of Virginia and U.S. history.

New certification standards for teachers, which became effective July 1, 1968, require that an applicant seeking endorsement in elementary education must complete a course in basic economics and that an applicant seeking endorsement in history, geography, government, or sociology at the secondary level also must complete a course in basic economics.

At the request of the State Board of Education, the 1966 General Assembly substantially increased the funds available for in-service education of teachers. The state board directed that top priority be given to in-service courses in basic economics.

Vocational Education

The decade beginning in 1957 was a period of growth for vocational and technical education programs for high school students and for adults, reflecting Virginia's rapid industrial development. Enrollment in vocational classes doubled during this period, and new programs were initiated. This increasing interest culminated in a study made by a legislative commission appointed in 1962.

After an extensive review of Virginia's vocational needs, the commission made broad recommendations for improving vocational and technical education in the public schools and at the post-high school level. As a result of these recommendations, the 1964 General Assembly made a special appropriation of $3 million for vocational and technical education for the biennium beginning in July 1964 to establish new programs and to expand and upgrade existing programs. It gave special attention to experimental programs for youth with special needs, upgrading technical institutes and area vocational-technical schools, vocational guidance institutes, vocational training centers for high school youth and adults, and establishment of a program of technical education to be administered by a new technical education board.

Progress in this field continued as Virginia inaugurated the Manpower Training Program in 1963 and established an additional service in the department's Division of Vocational Education to coordinate and plan construction of local vocational centers. New vocational facilities have been constructed and equipped in both rural and urban areas. Fourteen vocational centers (five in the Appalachian region) have been completed to provide facilities for educating high school youth and adults in business and office occupations, industrial and technical occupations, agriculture, distributive occupations, and wage-earning occupations in home economics.

Increased Federal Aid

Two new federal programs—the Vocational Education Act of 1963 and the Elementary and Secondary Education Act of 1965—substantially increased federal aid for public schools in the state. The Vocational Education Act has provided approximately $6 million annually for construction of area vocational schools; for purchase of equipment for high school and adult programs; for programs for persons with special needs; and for ancillary services, such as teacher training, development of instructional materials, innovative programs, and research.

The Elementary and Secondary Education Act has channeled approximately $35 million annually into the state for programs for disadvantaged children, library resources, innovative programs in education, and for strengthening the state department. In 1966-67, more than 180,000 children in 1,177 target schools participated in Title I classes conducted during the regular or summer sessions.

The increased federal funds came at a time when some school divisions were engaged in a controversy with the Department of Health, Education, and Welfare (HEW) over certain features of the civil rights program. Controversy centered on two major aspects of HEW's school desegregation policies. Some school administrators contended that HEW was unlawfully requiring "racial balance" in public schools and that in promoting staff and faculty desegregation the federal agency was exceeding its authority in the area of employment practices. Because of differences over the Civil Rights Act, funds administered through HEW were cut off for seven counties and one city and deferred for new federal programs in five other counties.

Nine-Point Program

In an effort to improve the quality of education in Virginia, Dr. Wilkerson recommended and the state board approved a nine-point plan in 1965. This plan called for (1) upgrading the minimum qualification requirements for teachers, (2) upgrading the salary schedule, (3) providing more teaching scholarships (recruitment program), (4) expanding the in-service training program, (5) improving library services and materials, (6) expanding special education, (7) establishing a uniform reimbursement rate for all state aid positions, (8) encouraging extended use of educational television, and (9) providing more time for teachers to devote to planning instructional activities. The 1966 General Assembly made record appropriations for public education, approving those proposals of the board that required additional funds.

The General Assembly inaugurated in 1966 a new era in public education when it adopted a 2-percent state sales tax and provided that one-half the gross revenue produced by the tax be returned to the localities to be used for public school purposes. An additional 1-percent tax became effective in 1968. The sales tax bill also empowered the cities and counties in the state to levy a 1-percent sales tax for their own use.

The 1966 General Assembly also appropriated money for the first time to help localities conduct summer school programs. This aid made it possible for more students to take courses they could not schedule during regular school terms and enabled more students to move toward graduation on an accelerated basis.

Kindergarten Education

The State Board of Education in 1966 recorded its support for state aid for kindergarten classes operated as part of the public school program in Virginia.

In the same year, the General Assembly approved the principle of state aid for public school kindergartens. Two years later, it appropriated $15 million for the 1968-70 biennium to aid localities operating kindergartens as part of their public school programs.

In preparation for the full-scale operation of kindergartens, the State Board of Education, upon recommendation of the superintendent of public instruction, adopted in 1967 the first regulations in the state's history governing the operation of public school kindergartens. These regulations established standards for certification of kindergarten teachers, length of the school day, and size of classrooms. In-service education regulations were amended by the board to make it possible for applicants recommended by division superintendents to take courses leading to an endorsement in kindergarten education.

In January 1968, a curriculum guide for kindergarten education was approved by the board. This guide was prepared by a committee, appointed by the state superintendent, composed of kindergarten teachers, college teachers of early childhood education, superintendents, principals, a director of elementary education, a consultant of the National Education Association, and members of the elementary education service of the State Department of Education.

Accreditation of Elementary Schools

As a major step in the program to improve public education, the state superintendent recommended in January 1967 that the accreditation program be expanded to include elementary as well as high schools. In requesting state board approval for appointment of a committee to make a study and, if feasible, to prepare a plan for accrediting elementary schools, Wilkerson noted that the development of standards for the elementary schools was directly related to efforts to raise the level of public education in the state.

The state board gave its approval for the study, and in May 1967, an 18-member committee was named by the state superintendent to carry out this assignment which he described as "one of the most significant ever taken in the field of elementary education in Virginia" (44).

Teacher Certification

To upgrade the quality of teaching in the public schools, the certification requirements for teachers were revised in 1960 and again in 1968. This action was taken in both instances after many months of intensive study by committees representing the public and private schools of the state, teacher-training institutions, and the department.

The 1960 standards reflected greater emphasis on excellence in scholarship and a broad, basic education of all teachers as an essential part of their preparation. The requirements in basic education for high school teachers were increased from 36 to 48 semester hours, and for elementary teachers from 36 to 59 semester hours. Substantial increases in semester hours were required for those preparing to teach the following basic subjects in high school: English, mathematics, biology, chemistry, physics, general science, history and social science, and foreign languages. In addition, specific content in several fields, including mathematics and science, was established for elementary teachers.

The 1968 standards represent a further increase in the depth and range of subject matter required for certification in each teaching field. Following are some of the major changes:

The collegiate professional certificate will be issued initially for a period of 5 years from the date of qualification and is renewable for 5 years. (This certificate was previously issued for a period of 10 years and was renewable for 10 years.)

General education requirements provide that all applicants must possess a baccalaureate degree with a background of 48 semester hours in general education, including a minimum of 12 semester hours of humanities courses, 12 hours of social science, 12 hours of laboratory science and mathematics, and 4 hours of health and physical education. The remaining 8 hours must be from the humanities, social science, and laboratory science and mathematics. (The revised regulations also recommend that all teachers take a course in speech and in basic economics to satisfy in part the general education requirements.)

Not less than 120 clock hours of student teaching are required with a minimum of at least 90 clock hours given to actual teaching.

For an endorsement in elementary education, grades 1-7, the applicant must complete a total of 60 semester hours in specific subjects, including a required course in American history and a course in basic economics.

The revised regulations increase the number of semester hours required for an endorsement in art, distributive education, driver education, English and speech, English and journalism, English and dramatics, foreign languages, health and physical education, history and social science, mathematics, music, science, and special education. (An applicant for endorsement in history, geography, or sociology is required to complete a course in basic economics.)

A new industrial education certificate will be issued to qualified applicants in vocational industrial education. This certificate will be based in part on successful work experience and in part on college credit courses.

Raising the Quality of Public Education

Governor Mills E. Godwin, Jr., sounded the keynote of his administration in his inaugural address in 1966 when he said:

> We can take no rest until all our public schools–not just some–will compare with any in the nation; until all our colleges and universities–not just some–can hold up their heads in any company; until all our sons and daughters–not just some–have the same chance to train their minds and their skills to the utmost (45).

Following through on this theme, the Governor called a statewide Conference on Education in Richmond in October 1966. This historic meeting was attended by 1,900 people, who heard the state's chief executive and other leading Virginians call for more rapid improvements in education at all levels, and especially the elimination of disparities between public school programs in different sections of Virginia. The Governor said:

> This [conference] is not a time nor a place for looking back for it is the future we are concerned with here.
>
> It is a time instead to examine education as we never have before, to find its weakness and its strength, to assess its needs in the light of the Virginia which is taking shape around us, and of her place in a nation speeding to new heights.
>
> It is time to look within ourselves, to ask what we really mean when we say that education must come first among our public and our private obligations (46).

Backed by prominent citizens and educators, the campaign was carried throughout the state in a series of regional and local conferences, focusing attention on the most critical needs in each locality of the state.

Dr. Wilkerson acclaimed the Governor's statewide conference and the regional conferences as epoch-making events for education at all levels.

Meanwhile, the State Board of Education attacked the "quality education" problem on another front. In 1967, the board authorized the state superintendent of public instruction to appoint a committee to develop a plan to effect substantial improvements in public education, particularly in those localities where the needs are greatest. The 15-member committee, headed by William M. Turner of Petersburg, consisted of school superintendents, school board members, state legislators, locally elected officials, and state department personnel. Its attention was concentrated on staff and in-service education, curriculum and instruction, instructional aids and services, buildings, financial support, and evaluation. Its final report was presented to the board in April 1967, and some of its recommendations were put into effect almost immediately.

The Board of Education's 1968-70 budget requests reflected other recommendations. A key proposal contained in the report and approved by the board was the recommendation that visiting teams be assigned to evaluate programs for school divisions having the greatest educational needs. These teams work with superintendents, school board members, and members of local governing bodies to formulate plans for effecting substantial educational improvements. This program became effective in July 1968.

The committee on raising the level of public education made several other major proposals. For instance, it recommended that the department determine those localities in greatest need of fully certified teachers and give top priority to provide money for adequate in-service training. It suggested giving priority to applicants for loans from the Literary Fund to those school divisions needing improved physical facilities the most. It further recommended that the department assist in planning and conducting special education programs on a regional basis in those localities having the greatest need.

The committee also recommended a study of "ways and means" to effect the consolidation of small school divisions and a study of the formula for distributing state aid to public schools. Special legislative commissions were to make both studies.

Strengthening the State Department of Education

Between 1957 and 1968, the leadership and supervisory responsibilities of the State Department of Education were expanded to improve the public school program throughout Virginia.

Impetus was given to this effort by the report of the commission on public education in 1960, which recommended the employment of subject supervisors in English, science, foreign languages, mathematics, and social studies (history, government, geography, economics) to assist in improving instructional programs, particularly in the smaller high schools. Following the commission's recommendations, subject supervisors were added to the staff of the Division of Secondary Education. This supervisory program is being extended to include subject field supervisors in the Division of Elementary and Special Education.

Funds from Title V of the Elementary and Secondary Education Act of 1965 have been used for the employment of additional professional personnel to strengthen programs in elementary and secondary education, research, special education, and other areas. The position of special assistant for federal programs was established in the department in July 1965. Consultants also have been employed for seminars and workshops for department personnel.

In an effort to better acquaint the people of the state with progress, needs, and problems in public education, a public information service was established in 1959. As a further step in this direction, the department began publication in 1965 of a quarterly news magazine which is distributed to public school personnel, representatives of business and industry, school boards and local governing bodies, and various organizations interested in public education.

A Division of Educational Research was established in 1963, with these major functions: to conduct research studies requested by the state board and the state superintendent of public instruction; to encourage and assist local school divisions in designing and conducting pilot studies; to coordinate educational research in the state; and to provide a two-way flow of educational data between local school systems and the state department.

Data-processing procedures, involving a computer and other electronic equipment, are being used by the department to increase its capacity to collect, process, and disseminate information more rapidly and efficiently. This program provides a reservoir of basic information about public education. These data constitute a framework for decisions aimed at improving the quality of public education in the state.

The department's central office staff was reorganized in 1967 to relieve the state superintendent of numerous administrative responsibilities and enable him to devote more time to major needs and problems of the public school system. The state board established new positions of deputy superintendent (formerly assistant superintendent), assistant superintendent for administration and finance, assistant superintendent for instruction, and special assistant for evaluation and planning.

The discharge of citizenship responsibilities in an extremely complex era, the unprecedented expansion of knowledge, the increasing selectivity of college admission requirements, the impact of advances in technology on education and job opportunities, the high priority accorded education by business and industry, and, finally, the aspirations of parents for their children—all underscore the urgency of constant efforts to further strengthen the public school program.

Public interest in improving educational opportunities for youth and adults has reached new heights. This upsurge of interest and the quickened pace in pursuit of excellence in education hold great promise for the future of the public schools in the Commonwealth of Virginia.

FOOTNOTES

1. Cornelius J. Heatwole, *A History of Education in Virginia* (New York: The Macmillan Co., 1916), p. 10.
2. *Ibid.*, p. 33.
3. W.W.Hening, *Statutes at Large*, VI (13 vols.; New York: G. P. Putnam's Sons, 1910), 350.
4. Heatwole, *op. cit.*, p. 37.
5. Paul Monroe, *Founding of the American Public School System* (New York: The Macmillan Co., 1940), p. 713.
6. A. J. Morrison, *The Beginnings of Public Education in Virginia, 1776-1860* (Richmond: Board of Education, 1917), p. 9.

7. Heatwole, *op. cit.*, p. 105.
8. Superintendent of Public Instruction, *Annual Report, 1870-71*, p. 4.
9. *Ibid.*, p. 5.
10. Superintendent of Public Instruction, *Annual Report, 1871-72*, p. 63.
11. *Ibid.*, p. 78.
12. Early Lee Fox, "William Henry Ruffner and the Rise of the Public Free School System of Virginia," *John P. Branch Historical Papers*, Vol. III, No. 2 (Ashland, Va.: Randolph-Macon College, 1910).
13. *Ibid.*
14. *Ibid.*, p. 139.
15. *Ibid.*, p. 142.
16. Superintendent of Public Instruction, *Annual Report, 1882-83*, p. 129.
17. Superintendent of Public Instruction, *Biennial Report, 1901-03*, p. 35.
18. *Ibid.*, p. 36.
19. *Ibid.*, Introduction.
20. Heatwole, *op. cit.*, p. 313.
21. Superintendent of Public Instruction, *Biennial Report, 1897-99*, p. 7.
22. Superintendent of Public Instruction, *Biennial Report, 1899-1901*, p. 33.
23. Superintendent of Public Instruction, *Biennial Report, 1912-14*, Introduction.
24. Superintendent of Public Instruction, *Annual Report, 1917-18*, pp. 14, 17, 18.
25. Superintendent of Public Instruction, *Biennial Report, 1918-20, p. 13.*
26. Superintendent of Public Instruction, *Annual Report, 1928-29*, p. 16.
27. *Ibid.*
28. Superintendent of Public Instruction, *Annual Report, 1929-30*, p. 15.
29. Superintendent of Public Instruction, *Annual Report, 1932-33*, p. 13.
30. Superintendent of Public Instruction, *Annual Report, 1933-34*, p. 14.
31. Board of Education, *Tentative Course of Study in Virginia Elementary Schools, Grades 1-7*, Bulletin XIX, No. 5 (Richmond: The Board, 1937), p. 11.
32. Board of Education, *Organization for Virginia State Curriculum Program* (Richmond: The Board, 1932), p. 2.
33. *Ibid.*, p. 5.
34. J. Galen Saylor, *Factors Associated with Participation in Cooperative Programs of Curriculum Development* (New York: Teachers College, Columbia University, 1941), p. 72.
35. Superintendent of Public Instruction, *Annual Report, 1945-46*, p. 17.
36. *Ibid.*
37. Virginia Legislative Advisory Council, *Virginia Public Schools*, (Richmond: Commonwealth of Virginia, 1947), p. 14.
38. Virginia, *Journal of the Senate, 1948*, p. 523.
39. Superintendent of Public Instruction, *Annual Report, 1958-59*, p. 23.
40. Commission on Public Education, *Report of the Commission*, Part II (Richmond: Department of Purchases and Supplies, 1960), p. 28.
41. *Ibid.*
42. Superintendent of Public Instruction, *Annual Report, 1959-60*, p. 28.
43. Board of Education, *An Instructional Guide for Virginia and United States Government*, Vol. XLVII, No. 5 (Richmond: The Board, 1964), preface, p. i.
44. Woodrow W. Wilkerson, Statement to State Board of Education, January 1967.
45. Mills E. Godwin, Jr., *Inaugural Address* (Richmond: Virginia Department of Purchases and Supply, Senate Document No. 3, 1966).
46. Mills E. Godwin, Jr., "Keynote Address," *Governor's Conference on Education* (Richmond: Office of the Governor, October 1966), p. 6

BIBLIOGRAPHY

Public Documents

Virginia. *Constitution* (1902).

––*Journal of the Senate, 1948.* Richmond: Virginia Division of Purchase and Printing, 1948.

Books

Adams, James Truslow. *The Living Jefferson.* New York: Charles Scribner's Sons, 1936.

Andrews, Matthew Page. *Virginia, The Old Dominion.* New York: Doubleday and Co., Inc., 1937.

Board of Education. *An Instructional Guide for Virginia and United States Government.* Vol. XLVII, No. 5. Richmond: The Board, 1964.

––*Organization for Virginia State Curriculum Program.* Richmond: The Board, 1932.

––*Regulations of the State Board of Education.* Vol. XLI, No. 7. Richmond: The Board, 1963.

––*Standards for Accrediting of Secondary Schools.* Vol. XLII, No. 7. Richmond: The Board, 1965.

——*A Statement of Policy for Public Schools in Virginia.* Richmond: The Board, 1961.

——*Tentative Course of Study in Virginia Elementary Schools, Grades 1-7.* Bulletin XIX, No. 5. Richmond: The Board, 1937.

Bruce, Philip Alexander. *Institutional History of Virginia.* New York: G. P. Putnam's Sons, 1910.

Buck, J. L. Blair. *The Development of Public Schools in Virginia, 1607-1952.* Richmond: Board of Education, 1917.

Dabney, C. W. *Universal Education in the South.* Vols. I, II. Chapel Hill: University of North Carolina Press, 1936.

Fox, Early Lee. "William Henry Ruffner and the Rise of the Public Free School System of Virginia." *John P. Branch Historical Papers.* Vol. III, No. 2. Ashland, Va.: Randolph-Macon College, 1910.

Good, H. G. *A History of American Education.* New York: The Macmillan Co., 1956.

Heatwole, Cornelius J. *A History of Education in Virginia.* New York: The Macmillan Co., 1916.

Hening, William Waller. *Statutes at Large.* Vol. VI. 13 vols. New York: G. P. Putnam's Sons, 1910.

Johnson, James G. "The Examination, the Certification and the Training of Teachers for the Public Free Schools of Virginia." *McGuffey Reader.* Vol. III, No. 8. Charlottesville, Va.: The Michie Press, 1938.

Knight, Edgar W. *Public Education in the South.* New York: Ginn and Co., 1922.

Maddox, William Arthur. *The Free School Idea in Virginia Before the Civil War.* New York: Bureau of Publications, Teachers College, Columbia University, 1918.

Monroe, Paul. *Founding of the American Public School System.* New York: The Macmillan Co., 1940.

Morrison, A. J. *The Beginnings of Public Education in Virginia, 1776-1860.* Richmond: Board of Education, 1917.

Saylor, J. Galen. *Factors Associated with Participation in Cooperative Programs of Curriculum Development.* New York: Bureau of Publications, Teachers College, Columbia University, 1941.

Reports

Commission on Public Education, William B. Spong, Jr., chairman. *Report of the Commission.* Richmond: Virginia Department of Purchases and Supplies. Part I, 1959, and Part II, 1960.

Commission on Public Education, Garland Gray, chairman. *Report of the Commission.* Richmond: Virginia Division of Purchase and Printing, 1955.

Commission on Public Schools, Charles T. Moses, chairman. *Report of the Commission.* Richmond: Virginia Division of Purchase and Printing, 1947.

Commission on State and Local Revenues and Expenditures, Garland Gray, chairman. *Report of the Commission.* Richmond: Virginia Division of Purchase and Printing, 1948.

Commission To Study the Curricula and the Teaching of Certain Matters in the Secondary Schools, Lloyd C. Bird, chairman. *Report of the Commission.* Richmond: Virginia Division of Purchase and Printing, 1948.

Commission To Study the Virginia Public School System, Lloyd M. Robinette, chairman. *Report of the Commission.* Richmond: Virginia Division of Purchase and Printing, 1940.

Educational Commission of Virginia, M. V. O'Shea, director. *Report of the Commission.* Richmond: Virginia Division of Purchase and Printing, 1944.

Governor's Conference on Education. Richmond: Office of the Governor, October 1966.

Stauffer, William H. *Report on the Finances of Public Free Schools in Virginia.* Richmond: Virginia Division of Purchase and Printing, Senate Document No. 4, 1934.

Superintendents of Public Instruction. *Annual and Biennial Reports.* Richmond: Department of Education, 1870-1968.

Virginia Advisory Legislative Council, Mosby G. Perrow, Jr., chairman. *Report of the Council.* Richmond: Virginia Division of Purchase and Printing, 1957.

Virginia Commission on Education, Mosby G. Perrow, Jr., chairman. *Report of the Commission.* Richmond: Virginia Department of Purchases and Supplies, 1959.

Virginia Education Commission, George A. Denny, chairman. *Report of the Commission.* Richmond: Virginia Division of Purchase and Printing, 1944.

Virginia Education Commission, Alexander Inglis, director. *Report of the Commission and Survey Staff's Report.* Richmond: Virginia Division of Purchase and Printing, 1919.

Virginia Education Commission. *Report of the Commission.* Richmond: Virginia Department of Public Printing, 1912.

Virginia Education Facilities Committee, M. M. Long, chairman. *Report of the Committee.* Richmond: Virginia Department of Purchases and Supplies, 1959.

Virginia Legislative Advisory Council. *Virginia Public Schools.* Richmond: Commonwealth of Virginia, 1947.

Article and Periodical

Lancaster, Dabney S. "Distribution of School Funds." *University of Virginia Newsletter* (January 1947).

Unpublished Material

Board of Education. "Projected Enrollment in Virginia Public Schools, 1966-1967–1981-1982." (Mimeographed.)

——"Virginia's Supply of Teachers, a Report for the Year 1966-1967." (Mimeographed.)

Boitnott, John W. "Secondary Education in Virginia, 1845-1870." Unpublished Ph.D. dissertation, University of Virginia, Charlottesville, 1935.

Bowman, Raymond P. G. "Secondary Education in Virginia, 1870-1886." Unpublished Ph.D. dissertation, University of Virginia, Charlottesville, 1938.

Helmer, James McKinley. "The Development of a State System of Teacher Certification in Virginia, 1820-1950." Unpublished master's thesis, College of William and Mary, Williamsburg, 1950.

Meade, Richard Andrew. "A History of the Constitutional Provision for Education in Virginia." Unpublished Ph.D. dissertation, University of Virginia, Charlottesville, 1941.

Phippins, Calvin H. "Legislation Affecting Secondary Education in Virginia from 1619 to 1845." Unpublished Ph.D. dissertation, University of Virginia, Charlottesville, 1932.

Sisson, Francis W. "The Role of State Leadership in Helping Local Schools Improve Instruction Better To Meet the Needs of Youth in Virginia." Unpublished Ph.D. dissertation, Teachers College, Columbia University, 1952.

Wilkerson, Woodrow W. "The Employment of Supervising Principals on a Twelve Month Basis in Virginia." Unpublished Ph.D. dissertation, University of Maryland, College Park, 1952.

Addresses

Byrd, Harry Flood. *The Educational System of Virginia.* Address of Governor Byrd to General Assembly. Richmond: Virginia Division of Purchase and Printing, Senate Document No. 6, 1928.

Godwin, Mills E., Jr. *Inaugural Address.* Richmond: Virginia Department of Purchases and Supplies, Senate Document No. 3, 1966.

——"Keynote Address." *Governor's Conference on Education.* Richmond: Office of the Governor, October 1966.

Other Source

Wilkerson, Woodrow W. Statement to State Board of Education, January 1967.

Appendix A

VIRGINIA CHIEF STATE SCHOOL OFFICERS

1870-82	William H. Ruffner	1918-31	Harris Hart
1882-86	R. R. Farr	1931-41	Sidney B. Hall
1886-90	John L. Buchanan	1941-46	Dabney S. Lancaster
1890-98	John E. Massey	1946-49	G. Tyler Miller
1898-1906	James W. Southall	1949-57	Dowell J. Howard
1906-13	Joseph D. Eggleston, Jr.	1957-60	Davis Y. Paschall
1913-18	R. C. Stearnes	1960-	Woodrow W. Wilkerson

Appendix B

Chart I.--STRUCTURE OF PUBLIC EDUCATION IN VIRGINIA, 1964-65

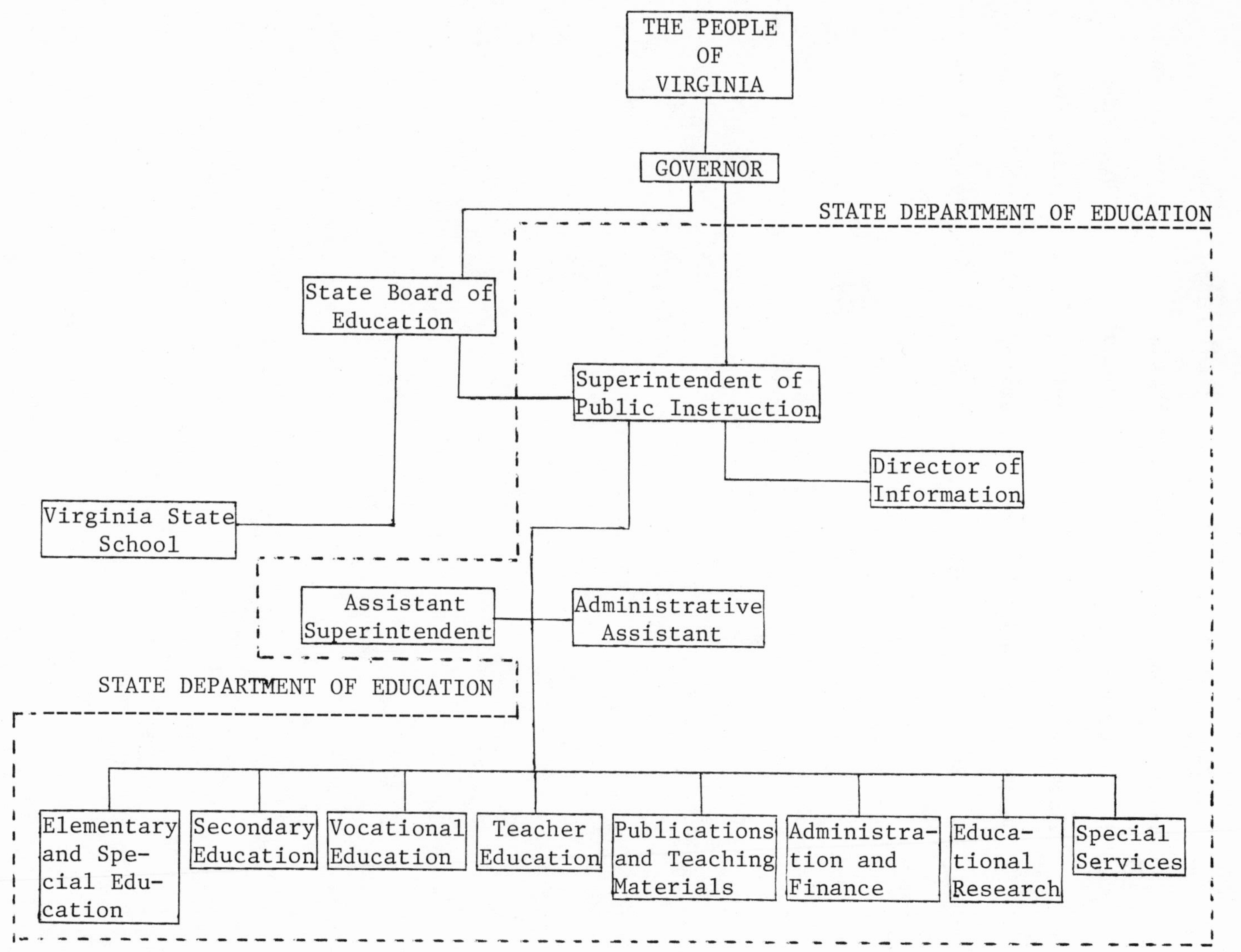

Appendix B

Chart II.--INTERNAL ORGANIZATION OF THE VIRGINIA DEPARTMENT OF EDUCATION, 1968

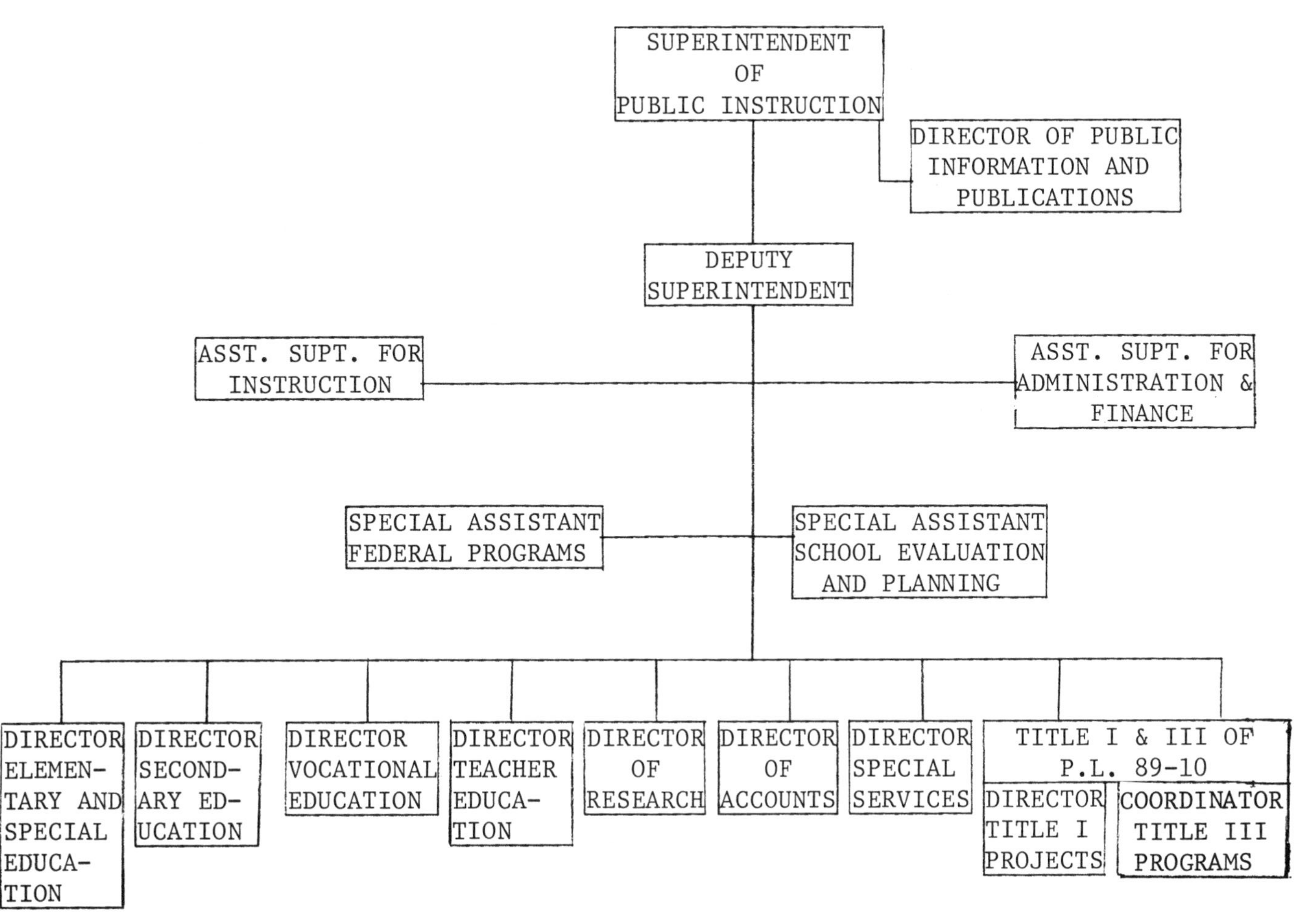

Appendix C

STATE ORGANIZATION FOR VIRGINIA PROGRAM TO IMPROVE INSTRUCTION, 1931-41

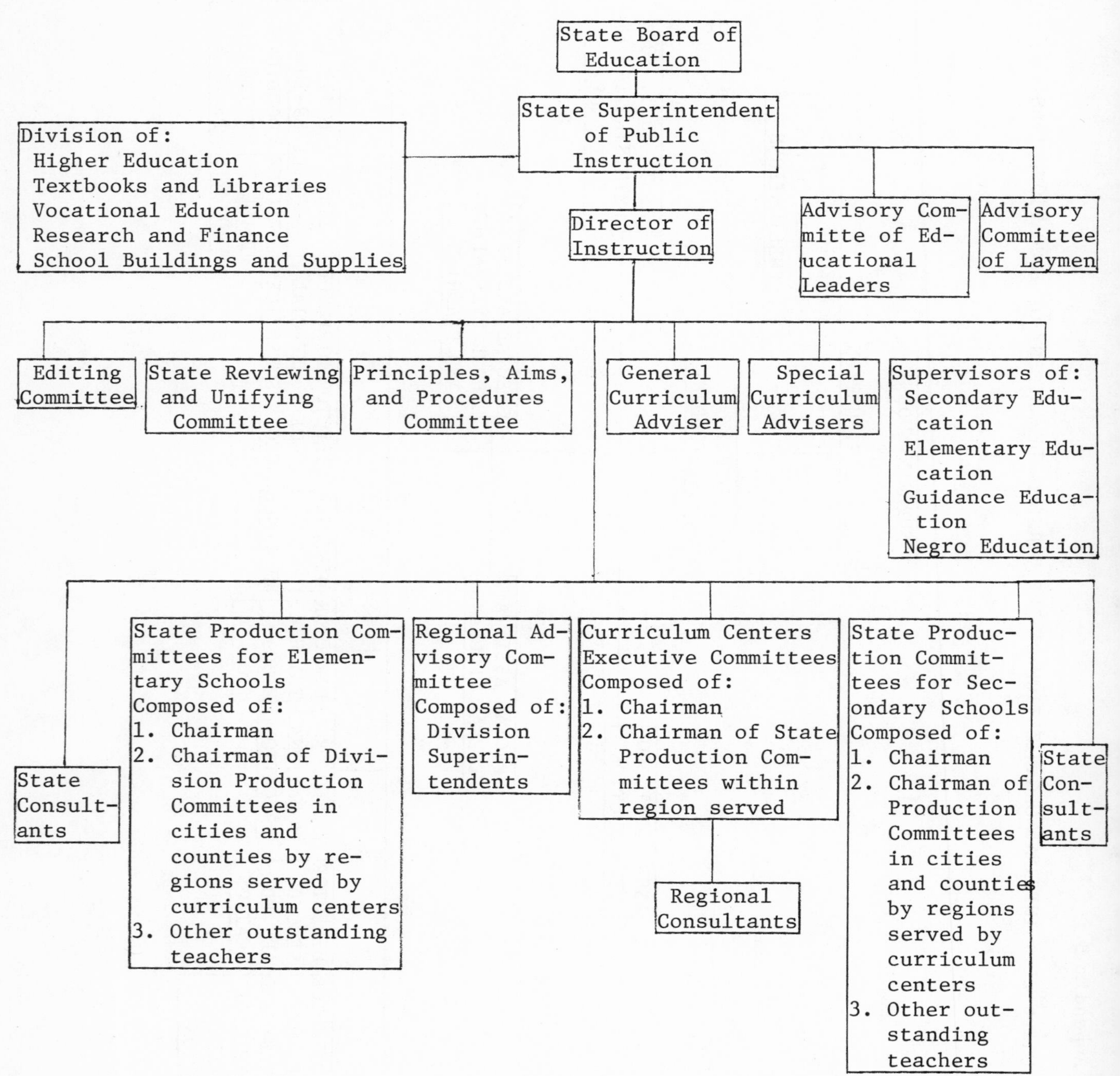

48 Washington

OFFICE OF THE SUPERINTENDENT
OF PUBLIC INSTRUCTION
Robert G. Wark

Contents

TERRITORIAL DEVELOPMENTS

First Schools

Fur trappers and missionaries began moving into northern Oregon, as Washington was then known, in the 1830's. But it was not until after the Oregon Treaty of 1846, whereby Great Britain relinquished its interest south of the forty-ninth parallel, that a steady stream of settlers began moving into the territory. An unofficial census in 1849 found 304 people north and west of the Columbia River, and a year later the official census listed a population of 1,049. In addition to the school operated at the Hudson Bay Company's Fort Vancouver headquarters since 1832, three more had been established. The census did not show the school that Spokane Garry, later chief of the tribe from which he took his first name, had started around 1830 on the site of present-day Spokane; and there is no mention of the missionary schools that opened in eastern Washington during the 1840's.

These pioneers had little use for the officials who governed them from the territorial capitol at Salem. The feeling was shared by the longtime settlers of Oregon's Willamette Valley, who considered their northern neighbors a lot of rowdies. By mutual agreement, the Washington Territory was created from the Oregon Territory by President Fillmore's signature in March 1853.

In establishing the Oregon Territory, Congress had for the first time granted two sections of every township, rather than one, for the support of education. In framing the Organic Code, which served as the new territory's constitution for 36 years, Congress was as generous to Washington as it had been to Oregon. Thus, even in the beginning, Washington's schools benefited from federal expenditures to a greater degree than most states, just as the state's economy in later years can trace much of its development to federal involvement in electric power production, agricultural development, military bases, and aircraft production.

The school lands were of little use during the territorial days. Surveying was a time-consuming task; but, more important, the land commissioner ruled that funds from any sales would not be available until statehood. Nevertheless, the people were interested in building a school system for their children. Governor Isaac I. Stevens, in his first message to the Territorial Legislature, strongly supported education:

> The subject of education already occupies the minds and hearts of the citizens of this Territory, and I feel confident that they will aim at nothing less than to provide for a system which shall place within the means of all the full development of the capacities with which each has been endowed. Let every youth, however limited his opportunities, find his place in the school, the college, the university, if God has given him the necessary gifts. Congress has made liberal appropriations of land for the support of the schools, and I would recommend that a special commission be instituted to report on the whole system of schools (1).

Early Laws

In April 1854, the Territorial Assembly passed an act establishing a common school system. It was similar in many respects to the Oregon law, developed through an evolutionary process from Iowa, which in turn owed a lot to Michigan law, which was based on New England law. There was one unfortunate difference between the Oregon and Washington school laws: Washington lawmakers, sensitive to their constituents' pioneer distrust of central authority, decided not to provide for a territorial superintendent or any other form of centralization.

The Law of 1854 called for the proceeds of the land donated by the government to go into a permanent school fund, with the interest only to be used for education. The schools were to receive money for teachers' salaries from a 2-mill tax levied by the county commissioners on the county's taxable property. Fines for breach of the penal code were to go to the schools. School districts were required to match the county fund through tax levies or otherwise. The law empowered school districts to vote additional taxes to raise buildings, repair them, and buy books and equipment. This arrangement, with periodical increases in the maximum levy, financed the schools until 1895.

The 1854 law also provided for the election of a county superintendent for a term of 3 years. He was to set district boundaries, examine teachers, issue certificates, visit all schools annually, apportion school funds to districts on the basis of the number of children from 4 to 21, and make an annual report. For this he was to receive no less than $25 a year; but if the county commissioners thought he deserved it, they could pay him as much as $500. The law further provided for three school directors for 3-year terms. Except for slight modifications, this law remained largely intact until 1877.

The Dark Era

The lack of central authority made the schools a system in name only. Few county superintendents were seriously interested in their jobs; the difficulties of travel prevented many from making the required annual visits, and few submitted annual reports. The records of this period are nearly nonexistent. Many children attended private schools, some good, some not. One educational historian has called these first 20 years of the territorial period the "dark era" in education (2).

Although they were interested in education, the settlers had many other serious concerns, such as a series of Indian wars and the Civil War. Further, D. R. Bigelow, framer of the Law of 1854 and later Thurston County (Olympia) superintendent of schools, pointed out:

> They [the settlers of New England] came to make homes and surrounded them with all that make homes desirable; whereas in our case, a majority of our citizens, who have been best able, both in talents and money, to build up the country's moral and educative interests, have been adventurers; their citizenship in the Territory depending on some contingency; and consequently they have not felt that interest in the education of the country, either of the present or future generations as to induce them to make any adequate effort to accomplish it (3).

First Superintendent

The schools languished until 1861, when the Legislature established the Office of Territorial Superintendent of Schools. Reverend B. C. Lippincott, a Methodist minister and president of Puget Sound Institute of Olympia, was appointed the first superintendent by the Legislature. Charged with reporting annually to the Legislature and recommending improvements, Superintendent Lippincott requested in first report in 1862 that the county superintendents be required to report to his office annually and that his office be allowed to issue teacher certificates good in any county. Unfortunately, he also devoted much of his report to questioning the need for the new territorial university—opened in November 1861—when the common schools were in such poor straits. He boldly stated his opinion that there was not a single youth in the territory capable of passing the college entrance examination. As the university had considerably more friends than enemies in the Legislature, it was voted to abolish the Office of Territorial Superintendent. So the common schools struggled through the dark era for another 10 years.

The Legislature reestablished the office in January 1872 and appointed Nelson Rounds as territorial superintendent. His salary of $300, one-tenth of the Governor's, was also to cover office rent, stationery, printing, travel, and incidentals. The law did not prohibit the superintendents from moonlighting, and at least one operated a newspaper throughout his term. This was made easier because there was no requirement that the superintendent's office be located in the territorial capital at Olympia, only that he reside where there was a post office. So the seat of territorial education shifted from Olympia to such towns as Goldendale, Waitsburg, Garfield, and Port Townsend.

Dr. Rounds, a Methodist minister and president of Willamette University before assuming the superintendency, presented in January 1873 the first statistical data on education in the territory. They showed that there were 144 schoolhouses, 222 school districts, 157 schools in operation, and 3,828 children attending out of 8,290 of school age (4).

Beginnings of a System

John P. Judson, the third territorial superintendent, deserves much of the credit for leading the schools out of the frontier era and welding them into a system. Judson was responsible for the Law of 1877, which developed from his unique method of organizing the first territory-wide teachers institutes. Judson held three such meetings to write the 1877 law. This method established a precedent, so that for many years Washington's school law was largely the result of professional educators' deliberations.

The 1877 law established a Territorial Board of Education and empowered it to adopt uniform textbooks, issue teacher certificates, prepare examination questions for county superintendents, and set the rules for governing the schools. The law expanded the duties of the territorial superintendent, requiring him to visit schools, address the public on educational matters, hold annual territorial teacher institutes, and help establish county institutes. To compensate for these extra duties, the superintendent's salary was doubled to $600 per year, plus up to $300 more for expenses. With the approval of the Legislative Council, the Governor would appoint the superintendent for a 2-year term.

The new law stimulated the growth of grade schools by permitting single districts to establish them, and two or more districts to set up a union or grade school by vote of the residents affected. Children from 8 to 16 in towns with a population of over 400 were required to attend school for at least 6 months each year. The county tax levy was raised to a minimum of 3 and a maximum of 6 mills. County boards were established to conduct semiannual examinations of potential teachers. The law also ensured adequate statistical reports by stipulating that county superintendents would forfeit $100 of their increased salaries for failure to report to the territorial superintendent as required.

The Board of Education

The newly established Board of Education consisted of two laymen, one from each judicial district, and the territorial superintendent serving as the ex officio president (5). In its first year of operation, the board established regulations for governing the common schools and examining teachers. It complied with the new law requiring uniform textbooks by selecting A. S. Barnes and Company's "Independent Series of Standard Textbooks" for the specified 5-year period, thus ending the "promiscuous use of all kinds of text books" (6), one of the territorial school system's major problems. The board adopted a complete course of study for the graded schools and for 2 years of high school, although the legality of high schools remained in doubt for several years. The senior year curriculum included "geometry and history throughout the year. Botany and the Constitution of the United States, first half; chemistry and astronomy, second half. Rhetorical exercises throughout the high school course" (7).

When Judson's outstanding administration ended in 1880, Washington was entering its greatest period of change. The completion of a transcontinental railroad terminating in Tacoma in 1883 signaled the start of a 14-year boom that saw the territory achieve the nation's highest growth rate for the decade. Between 1887 and 1889 alone, 95,000 people settled in Washington, a figure higher than the total population in the previous census. No outstanding changes were instituted in the schools throughout the remainder of the territorial period; for the most part, Judson's successors built and expanded on the foundation he had provided.

Jonathan S. Houghton, who took office following Judson, noted that between 1878 and his 1881 report the number of school districts had doubled in some eastern parts of the territory. He lobbied for greater appropriations because of the travel required to visit these districts. Dr. Houghton traveled 4,000 miles and held three territorial institutes during his 2-year term, partly in an effort to raise teachers' professional standards.

Last Territorial Superintendents

Superintendent Charles W. Wheeler, who took office in 1882, was concerned about the professional training of Washington teachers. Wheeler succeeded in getting the Legislature to amend the law to require all teachers to attend annual institutes in counties having more than 10 districts. He was probably the first superintendent to advocate a territorial normal school. The schools were expanding, and the territory needed more teachers. For instance, during the biennium from 1884 to 1886, Superintendent R. C. Kerr reported that 189 schoolhouses were built, 267 new districts were formed, the graded schools increased from 15 to 24, and the number of teachers increased from 490 to 1,040.

John C. Lawrence, who served as superintendent from 1886 to 1888, continued Wheeler's demands for a state normal school and emphasized teacher institutes. He was successful in getting a course of study adopted for ungraded schools. Lawrence was probably the first superintendent to recommend free textbooks. He favored statehood for Washington so that the school lands could be sold to the highest bidder, estimating that they would bring $5 million. How surprised he would be to learn that today timber sales from these lands contribute more than $7 million annually to the common school fund.

The last territorial superintendent, J. H. Morgan, concluded that the greatest need was for more efficient teachers. As the territorial era closed, there were 1,161 school districts in Washington, 1,044 schoolhouses, 49 graded schools, 46,751 children enrolled out of 72,723 of school age, and 1,349 teachers. The 536 male teachers were earning an average of $47.66 per month, while 813 female teachers averaged $39.67, teaching an average school year of 4.6 months. Morgan pointed to considerable progress during the past 50 years and was confident about the future prospects for the schools under statehood, because more money was expected from the school lands to increase teachers' pay, to build better schools, and to obtain better furniture, more apparatus, and school libraries.

STATEHOOD

Legal Foundations

Western settlers had long chafed under the "colonialism" of territorial government, and pressure grew through the 1880's as the railroads brought more and more people to the Western states. The Omnibus Bill, or Enabling Act, signed by President Cleveland on Washington's Birthday, 1889, paved the way for statehood for Washington, Montana, and the two Dakotas.

The act required Washington to provide a system of public education open to all children and free of sectarian control. Sections 16 and 36 of each township were again set aside for the common schools, with a provision that these lands would not be sold for less than $10 an acre. Revenue from the sales was to become part of the permanent school fund, and only the interest could be spent for school support. Five percent of all public land sales in the state was to go into the school fund. The act confirmed the 1854 grant of 90,000 acres for the university and set aside 90,000 acres for an agricultural college, 100,000 acres for a scientific school, 100,000 acres for support of state normal schools, and 200,000 acres for charitable, penal, and reformatory institutions. Congress again had provided well for education and for the state.

The 1889 Constitution. The constitutional convention of 1889 included among its 75 delegates 11 who had been connected with education in some way. Perhaps they were in part responsible for including the following:

> It is the paramount duty of the state to make ample provision for the education of all children residing within its borders, without distinction or preference on account of race, color, caste or sex.
>
> The legislature shall provide for a general and uniform system of public schools. The public school system shall include common schools, and such high schools, normal schools, and technical schools as may hereafter be established. But the entire revenue derived from the common school fund and the state tax for common schools shall be exclusively applied to the support of the common schools (8).

These statements continue today to be the foundation of Washington's school system. They provide the impetus to equalize financial support for all of the state's children–an elusive goal which state superintendents have strived to reach ever since. The constitution stipulates that the principal of the common school fund shall remain permanent and irreducible. It specifies the sources of the fund as well as the manner in which lands may be sold and restricts the method of investing the fund.

The constitution designated the superintendent of public instruction a member of the executive department; like all members of the executive, he is elected popularly every 4 years without restriction as to the number of terms. His duties are to supervise all matters pertaining to public schools and perform other duties as prescribed by law. The constitution also set the superintendent's salary at $2,000–half the Governor's–to a maximum of $4,000 (9). The constitution did not provide for a State Board of Education, an oversight that was to cause some difficulty over half a century later.

First State Superintendent. In the election of October 1889, Washington voters ratified the constitution and elected Robert Bruce Bryan the first state superintendent of public instruction. He was elected for three terms in all, 1889 to 1892 and 1900 to 1908, but he died in the last year of his final term. Born in Ohio in 1842, Bryan was wounded in the Battles of the Wilderness and Spottsylvania during the Civil War. After the war, he took teacher training, taught in Kansas, and worked on a newspaper before coming West. He was superintendent of schools in Montesano, Washington, from 1886 until his election to the state superintendency. He drafted the state's first code of public instruction and was working on a revision at the time of his death.

Superintendent Bryan observed that the new Legislature repealed the old school law and adopted a new one without radical change. In his first term Bryan was mainly concerned with two problems: The average daily attendance was but 42 percent of the school census, and Washington lagged behind other states in the average length of its school year. These problems were principally rural and due in large measure to the inequalities of school financing. The superintendent pointed out that the county commissioners provided funds ranging from $15.54 per child in Clallam County down to $3.50 in Skamania County because of variations in the value of taxable property and the rate of levy. He was convinced that a state tax should be enacted which, when added to the income from the permanent school fund, would yield not less than $10 per pupil annually.

Barefoot Schoolboy Law. Bryan's concern for school support was taken up by his successor, Charles W. Bean, former superintendent of Whitman County. John R. Rogers of Puyallup, later to become Governor, introduced the legislation for a state school tax in 1895. The act became Washington's famed Barefoot Schoolboy Law. It provided for a state levy of up to 4 mills annually which, when added to the income from the permanent school fund, would produce $6 for each child between 5 and 21. This law introduced into American education the new principle that it was the state's responsibility to guarantee every child a basic education.

The new tax vindicated Superintendent Bryan's insistence that it would help solve the problems of low enrollment and a short school year. By 1898, enrollment had jumped to over 82 percent of the census, and the average school year had increased by more than a month. But the law did not provide equality of school support throughout the state; today's administrators continue to wrestle with the problem.

High Schools. During Superintendent Bean's administration the Legislature clarified the legal status of high schools for the first time. The constitution appeared to exclude high schools from the proceeds of the common school fund; some statutes seemed to provide for them, others did not. Seattle neatly ducked the issue in 1893 by "abolishing" its high school and renaming it the senior grammar school. The 1895 Legislature took care of the matter by empowering the State Board of Education "to prepare a course or courses of study for the primary, grammar and high school departments of the common schools" (10).

Despite their questionable status, high schools had grown. A private school in Olympia taught high school subjects as early as 1856. The territorial university, more high school than university for several years, offered secondary courses from 1861 to 1895. But the first formal public high school probably was the one opened by Dayton in 1880. Twelve years later, the state had five 4-year high schools, four 3-year high schools, and one 2-year course. The 1895 legislation stimulated their growth, and by 1900 there were 47 high schools.

Bean presented to the Legislature a number of constructive recommendations on school support, certification, free textbooks, unification of curriculum, district organization, and qualifications for county superintendents.

Law of 1897. In 1896, Frank J. Browne was elected state superintendent. Born in Ohio, Browne had taught in Tacoma, been superintendent of the Port Townsend schools, and principal of Columbia City (now part of Seattle) schools. Browne's annual reports markedly departed from custom by containing few recommendations and consisting almost entirely of state board reports, examination questions, statistics, the board's new course of study for common schools, and manuals of exercises for observing special days—including the gala Washington's First Bird Day.

During his first year, Superintendent Browne's principal contribution was the School Law of 1897, which legislators of the day considered the nation's best. For the first time state aid was apportioned on the basis of total days' attendance, with each district given a minimum credit of 2,000 days. Previously apportionment had been according to the number of children residing in the district. Two years later, following Browne's recommendation, the Legislature raised state aid from \$6 to \$8 per child and provided for a 5-mill limit.

The 1897 Legislature reorganized the State Board of Education to consist of the superintendent of public instruction and four persons appointed by the Governor, two of whom were to be active teachers holding life certificates. The 1897 school law vested the state board with the total authority to grant teacher certificates; county superintendents retained only the responsibility for conducting examinations. The Legislature also created a State Board of Higher Education consisting of the State Board of Education and the heads of the five state institutions of higher learning. The operations of the two boards confused high school accreditation for the next 12 years.

Bryan's Return

Robert Bryan returned to office for his second term in 1900. Both he and his successor, Henry B. Dewey, gave outstanding leadership in a period when the schools were expanding their horizons and, as Dewey noted, "the people as a whole are taking a more sustained interest in the welfare of the boys and girls of the state" (11). During the first decade of the twentieth century, the number of children enrolled in school doubled, the number of high school graduates quadrupled, and the average school year increased from 6 to 7.7 months.

To encourage the growth of union high schools, the 1901 Legislature passed an act to have the superintendent give a \$100 bonus for each grade above the grammar grades maintained by a union district. Bryan pointed to a number of imperfections in the law—mostly relating to the means by which certain districts were circumventing its intent to obtain the bonus. The 1903 Legislature closed these loopholes to Bryan's satisfaction.

Bryan, regarded as the father of education in Washington, appeared to his deputy, Henry Dewey, as "a man of strong convictions, untiring energy and forceful personality" (12). However, at times he showed a somewhat sarcastic sense of humor. For instance, in his 1904 report, he stated:

> The idea bored itself into the brains of a few leading educational people in this state, that the whole school system is being damned by the fact that the state superintendent and all county superintendents are elected in just the same manner that all other state and county officers are elected. It had not occurred to me before this excitement sprang up; but I am now astonished to think that I have not felt mortified and chagrined to think that I was elected by practically the same process that Wm. McKinley was elected, and by exactly the same process by which my colleagues in the State Capitol building were elected. I am now happy to think that I now have a good and sufficient reason for being unhappy during the remainder of my life, and it should be a sufficient and just cause to make all county superintendents in this state wretched, to reflect upon the fact that they, too, were nominated and elected in the same manner as were their associate county officers (13).

Code of 1909. Undoubtedly Bryan's greatest contribution to education was the Code of 1909, a complete recodification of the first state law of 1897, which he had also drafted. The 1907 Legislature appointed the code commission, which contained among its membership three state superintendents: Bryan, Dewey (after Bryan's death), and Noah D. Showalter, who would become superintendent in 1928. When Bryan died in 1907 while still working on the revision, Governor Mead appointed Dewey to fill the unexpired 9-month term, and Dewey directed the completion of the code commission's report.

The code commission responded to Superintendent Dewey's request that an additional assistant superintendent position be authorized, bringing the staff to two assistant superintendents; one deputy, who doubled as inspector of schools; a stenographer; and the Board of Examiners, who served part-time. Dewey, the first superintendent to refer to the budget and staffing of his office, based his request for the additional staff members on the "numerous and important duties" that had been added, such as certification, inspection of schools, eighth-grade examinations, and the requirement that the superintendent attend school directors annual meetings in every county.

The Code of 1909 contained nearly all the prescribed duties of the state superintendent as they exist today. In addition to the constitutional authority to supervise all matters pertaining to the public schools, they included (a) writing the biennial report to the Governor; (b) arranging for the preparation and distribution of blanks, forms, registers, courses of study, rules and regulations for the government of common schools, examination questions for teachers, and all else necessary for teachers and officials to discharge their administrative duties; (c) attending education meetings, visiting schools, and consulting county superintendents and other school officers; (d) providing the state auditor a monthly statement of travel expenses; (e) printing and distributing to school officials forms and instructions for execution of the laws relating to public schools; (f) acting as ex officio president of the State Board of Education; (g) holding an annual convention of the county superintendents; (h) filing all papers, reports, and public documents transmitted to him by school officers; (i) obtaining an annual report from the president, manager, or principal of every educational institution in the state; (j) keeping in his office a directory of all boards of regents and trustees of state educational institutions, their faculties, and all teachers receiving certificates to teach in the common schools; (k) issuing certificates as provided by law; (l) keeping records of his office's business and the meetings of the state board; (m) deciding all points of law submitted by county superintendents and appeals of their decisions; (n) administering oaths and affirmations; (o) delivering all records, books, maps, documents, and papers of his office to his successor; (p) preparing and revising from time to time a state manual; and (q) performing such other duties as might be prescribed by law.

The 1909 law abolished the State Board of Higher Education and restructured the State Board of Education to consist of the superintendents of public instruction, the presidents of the state university and the state college, the principal of one of the normal schools, a superintendent of a first-class district, a county superintendent, and the principal of a fully accredited 4-year high school. This settled a controversy of several years as to whether the education board, and later the higher education board, or the state college and university were to accredit high schools. Sole authority to accredit high schools was assigned to the State Board of Education by the 1909 law.

The Law of 1909 required the county commissioners to levy a tax sufficient to produce the sum of $10 for each school-age child residing in the county, up to a limit of 5 mills. This brought the county fund into equality with the state fund. County support remained at this level until 1933.

The 1909 code included a new certification law. With its elaborate system of certificates it remained the basic law for many years, and elements of today's law trace back to it.

Henry B. Dewey

Henry B. Dewey, appointed Bryan's deputy superintendent in 1905 and superintendent on Bryan's death, won the office himself for the 1908-12 term. A graduate of the University of Michigan in 1890, he had served as superintendent of Shiawassee County, Michigan, and Pierce County, Washington. An enthusiastic booster of Washington education, Dewey was one of the ablest officers in the state's service. His reports, lively and interesting, were the first to contain details on physical education, athletics, and the need for playgrounds. To encourage standardization, he advocated employing a high school inspector, which the 1911 Legislature authorized.

Most of Dewey's major concerns would hardly seem out of place today. He centered his department's activities on expanding vocational training, adopting a flexible course of study, and giving more attention to civic and moral instruction. He also advocated greater cooperation among teachers, parents, and the public (he approved of the rapid growth of the PTA movement), and more use of the school plant by the community. He probably is best remembered for his contributions to the progress of rural education.

In his last biennial report, Dewey highlighted accomplishments of his administration. He had appointed a rural school expert as deputy superintendent, instituted sex hygiene instruction in state normal schools, and required industrial training in grammar school grades and agriculture in the eighth grade. He and the department had given increased attention to the needs and capacity of individual students. Night school, first authorized in 1907, had increased dramatically. Moving pictures were more generally used; there was widespread use of the Victrola and a variety of musical instruments; warm lunches were served in many rural and city schools; and the State Board of Health banished the common drinking cup from public schools (14).

In 1921, the Republican party nominated Dewey to run for one of two newly created congressional at-large seats. Although he finished second in the primary, two Progressives, who had not run in the primary, won in the general election, with Dewey a close third among six candidates. Houghton Mifflin Company hired him as a representative, and he later became their managing editor.

The Preston Era

Washington experienced another boom during World War I. From 1914 to 1919, the number of wage earners doubled; Seattle's work force jumped from 11,000 to over 40,000. After the postwar depression, growth resumed, but less spectacularly. Nevertheless, during Mrs. Josephine Corliss Preston's superintendency, from 1912 to 1928, secondary schools and colleges increased almost 400 percent, high school graduates increased from 2,512 to 21,587, and the cost of schools tripled to $33 million (15).

Mrs. Preston received her education and initial teaching experience in Minnesota, but for the 9 years prior to her election as state superintendent, she had served as superintendent of Walla Walla County schools. A member of the War Emergency Education Commission, one of seven division chairmen of the first World Conference on Education, and national president of both the National Education Association and the Council of State Superintendents and Commissioners of Education, she achieved national prominence during her four terms as state superintendent. In Washington she endeared herself to multitudes of parents and children by sending personal letters of congratulation, signed in her own handwriting, to every child promoted from eighth grade. A large, positive person, with an approach to people and problems bordering on the puritanical, she was known (behind her back, to be sure) among staff members as the Duchess.

Rural Problems. Mrs. Preston's chief concern as state superintendent was the quality of rural education and the welfare of rural teachers. In 1924, she wrote:

> Rural education is the greatest problem in American education today . . . . The greatest need is for teachers with initiative, leadership, high ideals, strong character, broad sympathy and superior professional training and education who are willing to go into the country to teach (16).

She believed that most rural teachers were quitting because they had to room and board with families whose children they were teaching all day. Her solution was to convince the Legislature to provide teachers' cottages.

The 1913 Legislature passed an act authorizing school directors to make school property more available for community purposes. This cleared the way for two of Superintendent Preston's favorite causes: It encouraged schools to become centers of community social and intellectual life, and it authorized directors to provide suitable dwellings and accommodations for teachers, supervisors, and their assistants. Thus, by 1924, she could proudly announce that more than 400 teachers' cottages had been erected in Washington, and this move to improve living conditions for teachers was sweeping the country (17).

Even before she succeeded in obtaining rural teacher housing, Mrs. Preston had made considerable progress in upgrading rural education. In 1917, in an effort to standardize rural schools, she printed the first standard rating cards. She also continued the department's support for the standardized rural school plans and specifications Dewey had instituted in 1911. In describing the benefits, she stated:

> It is no uncommon thing to be traveling along a road right through the forests in the western part of the state and to come suddenly upon a modern one-room school house, with ample playground and well-kept outbuildings; or in the eastern part of the state to come upon such a building in traveling through the rural districts. It is hard to measure the valuable results which have come from the supplying of plans and specifications by this department for one, two, and three-room school buildings (18).

Mrs. Preston gave considerable attention to consolidation and transportation as means of improving rural education. In 1922, she advocated enlarging school districts to coincide with "natural" neighborhood centers, which she believed would reduce the number of districts from 2,400 to 600. The "natural" units consisted of communities and the surrounding rural areas which were tied to the community economically and socially as well as educationally. Her financial advisor, L. D. Burris, prepared a map based on a study of 800 "natural" community units. Mrs. Preston was convinced that this was in keeping with the national trend toward larger school units but would not deprive Washington's citizens of their cherished local control. She believed local control would suffer if the state adopted the county unit plan then in vogue and recommended by Governor Hart's 1921 code commission.

Neither Mrs. Preston's community center plan nor the county unit plan was adopted, but the consolidation movement did progress carefully and intelligently. Before the end of her last term as state superintendent, the number of consolidated districts increased from 130 to 400. But the State of Washington has not yet succeeded in achieving what educators consider a satisfactory school district organization.

School Support. School support was no less of a problem to Superintendent Preston than it has been to every superintendent. She continually sought better pay for county superintendents and teachers. In 1920, considering the shortage of teachers a crisis, she pushed through a special legislative session the so-called 20-10 law, which increased state aid from $10 to $20 per census child but retained the $10 county aid. Two years later, however, Mrs. Preston found herself in the unhappy position of having to oppose an initiative measure to raise state aid another $10 per child. She stated:

> I regret to find myself differing from many people who are sincerely interested in education, but I feel that much of sentiment in favor of the bill is based on a misunderstanding of its real effect. Any thoughtful person will know that as Superintendent of Public Instruction I am deeply and unselfishly interested in the civic and school welfare of the children of this state. It is my business to be interested if I had no other urge or impulse. My experience and contact with our schools convinced me that the 30-10 measure will not be for the best interests of education (19).

She did not believe that there was an emergency demanding such a change, and she felt that the proposed changes in the distribution of funds–in the name of equalization–would be harmful. Although convinced that true equalization could never be achieved through a general distribution system, as early as 1922 she advocated a state equalization fund to give special help to certain one-room and needy grade schools. Both Houses of the Legislature passed an equalization fund measure by more than four to one in 1928, but the Governor vetoed it.

Despite these financial problems, Washington's teacher standards continued to progress, enabling the state to maintain its high rank in certification. Mrs. Preston noted that beginning in 1917 all candidates for certificates had to graduate from high school and complete 9 weeks of training in a normal school. A decade later, 2 years of normal training was the minimum. From 1913 to 1924, teachers with diplomas and certificates from the state's five institutions of higher learning increased from 563 to 5,000.

Vocational Education. Vitally interested in vocational education, Mrs. Preston formed a vocational education commission and an advisory board in 1914. When the 1917 Smith-Hughes Act provided federal aid for vocational education, the Legislature designated the State Board of Education as the State Board for Vocational Education and named the superintendent as its chief executive officer. She appointed a director of vocational education in 1917 and a supervisor of agricultural education the following year.

Vocational education accounted for part of the increase in the superintendent's staff during Mrs. Preston's tenure. In her 1916 report, she noted that the office had grown from territorial days, when the superintendent virtually carried it around in his pocket, to a staff consisting of nine regular assistants, a State Board of Examiners, associate assistants, and additional stenographers part of the time. By 1924, four staff members were assigned to vocational education alone.

By 1928, the staff of the superintendent's office numbered 24, plus the Board of Examiners. The superintendent's duties had been increased by law to include ex officio membership on the Country Life Commission, State Humane Bureau, State Library Committee, Archives Committee, Voting Machine Committee, and designation as president of the board of trustees of the State Teachers' Retirement Fund (enacted in 1922). Despite the greater responsibilities and increased staff, the State Bureau of Inspection testified that the office was most efficient and reflected much credit on Mrs. Preston's business ability.

Mrs. Preston helped create much of Washington's present system of education. In 1917, the Legislature authorized kindergartens, with the provision that apportionments were to be paid out of state funds. Hot school lunches became a widespread practice, and the school transportation system took on major proportions. She encouraged the development of junior high schools, and the first junior college was opened in 1925. To crown her many years of service to Washington education, the April 1926 issue of the *American School Board Journal* announced that "Dr. Frank Phillips, Chief Statistician of the U.S. Bureau of Education and Professor in George Washington University, ranks Washington first on his ten point scale for the school year of 1923-24."

He ranked all the states on the following 10 points: (1) percentage of illiteracy among the 10 years of age and over in 1920; (2) ratio of number of children in average daily attendance to number of children aged 5-17, inclusive; (3) percent of enrollment in high school; (4) average number of days attended by each child enrolled; (5) average number of days schools were in session; (6) ratio of number of students taking teacher-preparing courses to number of teachers employed; (7) percentage of high school graduates continuing education next year; (8) total cost, excluding salaries, per pupil in average daily attendance; (9) average annual salary of teachers, principals, and supervisors; and (10) total amount expended per child of school age (20).

Washington voters, however, are not noted for rewarding long service by public officials, meritorious or otherwise. In the only upset in the 1928 Republican primary, Mrs. Preston was defeated by Noah D. Showalter. Since no Democrat filed for the office, Showalter was essentially elected in the primary.

THE DEPRESSION YEARS

Noah D. Showalter

Noah D. Showalter was already highly regarded in Washington education circles when he was elected state superintendent. A graduate of Lewiston (Idaho) State Normal School, he had been a summer student at Columbia and Stanford and had earned B.A. and M.A. degrees at Washington State. In 1920, the College of Puget Sound conferred on him the honorary doctor of laws degree.

Showalter had been a teacher, county superintendent, and head of the rural department of the State Normal School at Cheney before being named principal (later called president) of that institution in 1910. He had been a member of the state code commission in 1907-1908, and as principal of Cheney he had served a term on the State Board of Education. During the 17 years Showalter headed the Cheney Normal School, he raised standards, organized the curriculum, collected a more capable faculty, and met the demand for better trained teachers. He resigned in 1926 because the Governor vetoed an appropriation he believed necessary to conduct an effective program.

N.D., as he was called by close friends, was a gentleman and a scholar in the true meaning of the words. Lincolnesque in appearance, he is remembered by those who knew him as a man well informed on any subject and highly respected across the state. A specialist in rural education, in 1920 he wrote *A Handbook for Rural Officers* (21) and was credited with being the first Northwest educator to establish rural demonstration schools.

Effects of Depression. The Northwest suffered more severely in the early years of the Depression than some other regions, and education was not spared. The number of pupils in average daily attendance dropped for the first time in the state's history. The number of teachers employed fell from 12,022 in 1931 to 10,990 in 1934, and their average salaries declined from $1,525 to $1,217. An obvious reminder that Showalter's 8-year incumbency encompassed the Depression period is the fact that he published only one report (1936) to cover the four biennia.

Showalter was convinced that the state should assume half the operating cost of the schools if they were to continue doing an adequate job. In the face of lower tax collections and mounting costs, he sponsored a program to provide 25¢ a day in state aid for each pupil in attendance. The bill failed to pass the 1929 Legislature, so he proposed a similar program in 1931. This plan included his recommendations for a county unit organization, with a county superintendent appointed by an elective county board of education. Governor Hartley, advocating retrenchment and fearing that the Showalter plan would raise costs, vetoed the bill.

The Showalter Bill. For 2 years, school finances grew steadily worse. The 1933 Legislature, recognizing the need for more state support, finally passed the Showalter Bill or New Barefoot School Measure. This established the principle of basic state support of 25¢ a day per pupil in attendance.

But Showalter and the schools still were not out of the woods, because the previous year the voters, by initiative, had imposed a 40-mill limit on property taxes. To bail them out of sure disaster, the same Legislature (1931) enacted a business tax to provide at least $6 million of emergency revenue for the schools. It actually only raised two-thirds of the money needed to meet the 25¢-a-day level, so the 1935 Legislature enacted a revised business and occupation tax, a 2-percent retail sales tax, and a series of taxes on public utilities, admissions, cigarettes, fuel oil, and other services and commodities. For the moment the schools were saved, but the 40-mill limit and the patchwork of taxation of the 1930's has become the plague of the schools in the 1960's.

Junior High Arrives. The 1933 Showalter Act also legalized junior high schools and ensured their support by allowing them 30¢ of state aid per day per pupil. Mrs. Preston had encouraged their development, and the state board had set some standards for them in 1930, but until 1933 the junior high schools existed mainly as departments of elementary schools.

The junior high schools were organized on the 6-3-3 plan. The state board set up a curriculum of core courses for the 3-year period, which included health, English, social science, mathematics, and science in grades 7 and 8, and electives from these subjects in grade 9. Time was provided for guidance, auditorium, club, and homeroom activities. By 1936, two-thirds of the state's 56 fully accredited junior high schools were in separate buildings; but in smaller districts, laboratories, auditoriums, gymnasiums, and cafeterias were used in common. There were 29,572 children attending these schools in 1936.

Transportation. School transportation also benefited from the 1933 Showalter Act by a provision whereby the state agreed to pay approximately half the cost. Since the turn of the century, school directors had been authorized to provide and pay for students' transportation to and from school. In 1911, when Superintendent Dewey published the first report on school transportation, 62 districts were furnishing transportation to 1,855 students. The typical "school bus" was a lumber wagon with board seats and a canvas top. A few luxury models had springs and coke-fired foot warmers. By 1933, 840 districts were transporting 67,500 students over 2,448 route miles at a cost of over $1.3 million a year.

Expansion. Showalter completely reorganized the Office of Superintendent of Public Instruction during his administration. He established a director of research and statistics and appointed L. D. Burris, the only holdover from Mrs. Preston's administration. The position of high school inspector was dropped, but he added two high school supervisors, a junior high school supervisor, and an elementary supervisor.

The Showalter Bill and federal aid available through the George-Reed Act of 1929, the George-Ellzey Act of 1934, and the George-Deen Act of 1936 enabled vocational education to increase its staff to nine members, and a separate division was established. When federal matching funds were offered for vocational rehabilitation in 1933, three more were added to the division.

A new Division of Indian Education, with a three-man staff, was created. This partially resulted from the belated bestowal of American citizenship on the Indian, thus obligating the state to provide for his education. It resulted in part from the 1934 Johnson-O'Malley Act, which permitted the Secretary of the Interior to enter into a single contract with a state for the education of all its Indian students. Previously, individual superintendents of Indian agencies contracted with local school districts.

Rise of the Individual

Perhaps Showalter's most significant contribution to Washington education was in shifting emphasis from standardization to recognition of the individual. The superintendents during territorial and early statehood days were trying to organize the struggling and widely scattered elements of pioneer education to build a solidly based system of public schools. This could best be accomplished by standardizing textbooks, plans for buildings, rules for students' and teachers' behavior, and curriculums.

By the time Superintendent Showalter took office, the common school system had been firmly established, and he could turn to the more intellectual aspects of education. He proclaimed this modern philosophy:

> Just as individuals vary in mentality, they vary in interests, in abilities, and in emotional life. Children and adults work most effectively and with the greatest satisfaction when motivated by their own interests. When skillfully aroused, these furnish tremendous driving power. It becomes the responsibility of the school to locate and direct these interests . . . .
>
> Time was when the teacher was a classroom performer and occupied the center of the stage. Classroom activities represented the interests and purposes of the teacher; pupils were expected only to memorize and absorb knowledge. Today's pupil is encouraged to discover his own problems, and to set about solving them . . . .
>
> Curriculum content should be centered about child interests under adult guidance . . . . Subject matter should be introduced to develop and broaden experience. Attitudes, habits and skills should be woven into the total pattern and developed simultaneously with the solution of problems (22).

Showalter criticized the 1930 curriculum as "a subject-matter curriculum." Under his leadership, the state board appointed a statewide curriculum commission of 16 members to work steadily on revision. The 1937 Legislature was urged to provide an adequate budget to continue the work.

School Library

In line with his belief in the individualization of instruction, Showalter emphatically endorsed school libraries. Although the first territorial board enacted a uniform system of textbooks, even at that early date a few dissenters urged that there be less textbook teaching and more instruction based on a variety of books. But the first published biennial report of 1879, under the brave heading *The Number of Libraries*, found only *one* each in Jefferson and Mason Counties.

School libraries grew, however, and in 1930, the state board established minimum standards: 500 books and a teacher-librarian with at least 7 quarter hours of training in library science for schools with enrollments under 100. It set higher requirements for larger schools. The requirements prescribed library credentials for all teacher-librarians after 1934, and the same year the board adopted minimum library standards for elementary schools. By 1936, Showalter was able to state:

> Today a well-organized, well-equipped, properly housed library is as essential to educational progress as the electric motor is to industry or the automobile to transportation. Next in importance to the employment of an enthusiastic, well-qualified, thoroughly successful teaching staff in a well-managed school is the provision of an adequate library. The most efficient teacher can give only meager service when she has to work with inadequate tools (23).

The last year state superintendents were elected on a partisan basis was 1936. Had the Legislature acted earlier or later, Showalter might have extended his illustrious career longer than two terms. Despite the high regard of Washingtonians for Showalter, he was a Republican, and no Republican survived the 1936 Roosevelt landslide.

When the victorious candidate, Stanley F. Atwood, publicly announced that he was going to clean out the office, Showalter found jobs for every member of his staff before relinquishing office in January 1937. Atwood assumed an empty office. The new superintendent then tried to discharge the vocational education staff so he could appoint people of his choice. But he could make appointments as chief executive officer of the State Board for Vocational Education only with the board's approval. The board refused its approval, and the staff remained. The 1939 Legislature then gave the vocational board the right to select its own chairman and appoint its own executive officer.

Stanley F. Atwood

Superintendent Atwood was graduated from the State Normal School at Ellensburg and the University of Washington, served as teacher and principal at several schools, and was teaching history at West Seattle High School when elected. Very liberal in his politics, he served only one term. He published two reports—one covering the first biennium and the second covering his entire term.

Atwood was beset with financial problems immediately on assuming office. The 1933 Showalter Bill had gradually increased school revenues to a 1936-37 high of $29,211,579. The following year, they declined by over $1 million. The state's income enabled payment of only 22.35¢ a day per pupil in 1937-38 and 20¢ the next year. The 1937 Legislature finally passed an equalization bill to provide funds for poor districts, as recommended in 1922 by Mrs. Preston; but because of shrinking tax receipts and miscalculation, only $600,000 was appropriated out of $4 million needed.

The 1939 Legislature rescued the schools by appropriating enough money to raise state aid back to 25¢ a day. The superintendent reported that for the 1939-40 school year, the schools would receive $29.5 million, the state providing 61 percent and county and local sources the remainder. The federal government would provide an additional $350,000 to $400,000 for vocational and Indian education.

But Superintendent Atwood continued to press for a better equalization formula. Like previous superintendents, he pointed out that the state continued to violate its constitution by discriminating against children who lived in counties with poor taxable resources. He proposed to form a single fund from the amount all districts could raise by a 10-mill tax, the income from a maximum county tax levy and county equalization, and the legislative appropriations. The state would then distribute the funds according to attendance by "classroom units." The measure was not adopted.

Federal Building Funds

Though federal assistance in school operations had been felt only in Indian education and vocational education, it was becoming a factor in school construction. In his quadrennial report, Atwood stated:

> Through the help of the Public Works Administration, the Works Progress Administration, and the State Department of Social Security, an unusually large number of new buildings have been erected . . . . The buildings constructed have generally been of high quality and most of them of the more permanent types of construction.
>
> The generosity of the Federal government in its work-creating activities has given the school systems of the state of Washington approximately $13 million worth of new buildings at a comparatively small cost to the school districts. Very few of these buildings involved any bond issues on the part of the school districts (24).

Included in this construction were a number of new high schools. On Washington's fiftieth anniversary, Atwood reviewed the "phenomenal growth" of high schools during that period: Attendance had grown from 320 to over 105,000—from 1 student for every 1,100 inhabitants to 1 for every 15. He stated that in proportion to total school enrollment, the state enjoyed the largest high school enrollment in the nation. This growth no longer permitted adequate inspection by the superintendent's small staff. Atwood instituted a new program of self-evaluation, which the state superintendent's office continues to recommend today.

Curriculum Change

The high school curriculum changed during Atwood's term. In his report, he commented:

> Gradually, although tardily, the curriculum is being modified to minister to the needs of the pupil and the welfare of the state. The narrow confines of the college preparatory courses, which served a very limited number and favorite few, are giving way to a broader and more functional program (25).

Atwood attempted to speed the progress by installing a curriculum director, but the position was not created until later. The state curriculum commission, recommended by his predecessor and approved by the state board, did not receive support from the Legislature. But the Washington Education Association, which helped create the commission, convinced the school districts to finance it through subscription.

For the first time, classroom teachers became involved in curriculum study along with administrators. The *Washington Curriculum Journal*, first published in May 1937, became the clearinghouse for their experiments and studies. This became the *Washington State Curriculum Journal* and was published by the superintendent of public instruction beginning in 1941.

Certification

During his first 2 years in office, Atwood appears to have been at considerable odds with the state board over teacher certification. Backed by a number of opinions rendered by the attorney general, he stated:

> In assuming the powers as indicated in this article, the State Board of Education has not only set aside every legal provision in regard to the certification of teachers and set itself up as a legislative board in excess of authority delegated to it by the Legislature, it has by its actions also attempted to repeal or amend section 4542, Remington's Compiled Statutes, which prescribes the requirements for the certificates to be issued by the teachers' colleges; section 4557, Remington's Compiled

Statutes, which among other items grants to the regents of the University of Washington the right to issue teachers' diplomas according to certain specified requirements; and section 4599, Remington's Compiled Statutes, which grants to the regents of the State College of Washington the authority to issue teachers' diplomas according to standards defined by law (26).

Atwood recommended repealing the certification standards, setting up new ones, and designating the state department as the authority for determining types and kinds of certificates. Two years later, he attacked the inconsistency of the laws which permitted a high school graduate with 3 years of normal schooling to teach at the elementary level but prohibited a 4- or 5-year education graduate of the state college or university from doing so until he had completed an additional year of normal training. Quite logically, he pointed out that this oddity in the law robbed the schools of many potentially excellent teachers from inside and outside the state.

On the teachers' behalf, Atwood fought a move to repeal the minimum teacher salary law enacted by the 1937 Legislature and lobbied for teacher tenure. Tenure for Washington teachers had failed to pass in 1929, 1935, and 1937, although it was in effect in about half the states.

The 1937 Legislature provided for special education classes for the physically and mentally handicapped in second- and third-class school districts and gave the state board authority to develop details for operating these schools. Previously, special education had been limited to first-class districts. On the state board's recommendation, the University of Washington pioneered the training of teachers for remedial programs.

Atwood, for the first time, encouraged the use of radio in education. In 1939, the department organized and sponsored a round-table program entitled "What People Think," which was carried by stations in Seattle, Spokane, and Wenatchee.

In Washington, a prime requisite for election to the state superintendency is usually the support of the educational "fraternity." Atwood apparently lacked this essential in sufficient quantity for, in 1940, a group of school superintendents met in Seattle's Meany Hotel to decide on a new candidate. They concluded that the best vote-getter would be Pearl A. Wanamaker, who had proven her political acumen in three terms as a State Representative and two as a State Senator. The superintendents organized a caravan of 50 cars and drove to her home to persuade her to run.

At 41, Pearl Wanamaker was a small, attractive woman with platinum hair (later to become a distinguished white) and bright blue eyes. An educator of considerable experience, she had served as an elementary school teacher, principal, high school teacher, and county superintendent. Possessed of an informal charm, she was to become famous as the toughest legislative fighter the state education system had ever seen. A national magazine called her ruthless whenever a penny-pinching Legislature tried to cut her school budget or shortchange the children. One discomfited Senator complained: "She drives right into your home town and tells your constituents you're voting against their kids" (27). In keeping with the new nonpartisan status of her office, Superintendent Wanamaker stated: "I have been accused of playing politics. I have. But I absolutely will not play partisan politics" (28).

During the campaign, a caravan terminated in an informal potlatch where Mrs. Wanamaker sat on a log with her two small children and discussed issues and answered questions (29). In the Roosevelt landslide of 1940, she defeated Stanley Atwood 462,145 to 322,123 and began the first of four terms. Atwood's staff had vacated by the time she took office.

THE WANAMAKER ERA

During her administration, Superintendent Pearl A. Wanamaker became a national and international figure. She was elected president of the National Education Association and the Council of Chief State School Officers, and first vice-president of the American Association of School Administrators. She received the Matrix Table Award, the National Press Woman Award, and the American Education Award. She was one of 27 educators selected to advise General Douglas MacArthur on overhauling Japan's schools, and one of five sent back in 1950 to see how the system operated.

Throughout her superintendency she fought for higher teacher salaries, better teacher training, improved certification, more support for schools and construction, and school district reorganization. Certainly, they were needed. During the last 10 years of her incumbency, school population rose 50 percent while the total population increased only 19 percent.

World War II

Educational adjustments to World War II faced Mrs. Wanamaker almost immediately. School dates and schedules had to be changed to accommodate young laborers, particularly those in agriculture. Emergency certification and statewide in-service training programs had to be instituted to combat the teacher shortage. School transportation had to be curtailed because of the equipment and fuel shortage.

The state department undertook many programs to aid the war effort. For instance, the schools agreed to provide over 12,000 aircraft recognition models for the Navy. They acted as registration agencies to inaugurate food and gasoline rationing programs. With aid from federal funds, the department established an extensive nursery school program and conducted scrap and war savings drives.

New federal programs greatly boosted vocational education. Nearly 11,500 students were enrolled in the Food Production War Training Program, and over 300,000 people were trained under the War Production Training Program. Citizenship training for aliens took on a new importance, forcing a great expansion in the department's responsibilities for adult education. Where 15,848 were enrolled in night schools in 1936-37, 58,902 attended in 1941-42–not including vocational students.

As the war came to a close and emergency programs were no longer necessary, others rose to take their place. War production training gave way to veteran education. The superintendent had to set up administrative machinery for acquiring surplus property.

Many of the war-born problems remained to plague the state's school system, particularly those stemming from the population increase and inflation. Mrs. Wanamaker summed up the situation:

> The postwar period for which we had planned was suddenly upon us. But we soon learned that America could not shift quickly to a peacetime economy and many of our problems have become more acute since the end of the war.
>
> There is no prospect of relieving the acute teacher shortage for several years . . . . A substantial part of the population influx of the war years has remained in the state since the close of the war. The annual number of births during recent years has been more than double the number of births in 1933. Enrollment increases in the elementary schools are reflecting these basic population trends.
>
> School building construction was curtailed sharply during the depression years and was limited to the most urgent conditions in war industry areas during the war years. Hence, a large accumulated deficiency in school housing exists . . . . Relatively, the ability of local school systems to finance the rehabilitation of school plants has been reduced by fifty per cent . . . . The return of war veterans to our schools has seriously overcrowded facilities at the institutions of higher learning, the public junior colleges and vocational training schools (30).

School Construction

From 1933 to 1941, state and federal funds appropriated for makework programs were used to build schools; the need for the buildings was not a primary factor. The 1941 Legislature, for the first time, voted state aid for construction as a distinct program. Applications were to be submitted to the state superintendent of public instruction, who approved them if he decided there was a need for the building.

The 1947 Legislature established the principle of state matching funds for construction with a sliding scale of support, depending on the local district's ability to pay. The law designated the state board as the agency for allocating grants and setting rules for administering them. The act required the superintendent to conduct studies to determine the need for facilities, recommend action on the applications, and guide local districts as to design, maintenance, operation, and planning of building projects.

Between 1941 and 1947, the Legislature appropriated nearly $15 million in state aid for school construction. It authorized a $20-million bond issue for emergency construction in 1947 and established a School Emergency Construction Board consisting of the state superintendent, a member of the State Board of Education, and three persons appointed by the Governor. From 1947 to 1957, over $15 million in state aid was allotted for school construction, and the voters approved $90 million in statewide bond issues for emergency construction. One of Mrs. Wanamaker's major accomplishments was the construction of 875 school buildings during her administration.

The state had received federal assistance for school construction since the Depression. However, Public Law 815, which took effect in 1951, was the first comprehensive program for determining the impact of federal activities on local schools and an equitable distribution of funds for building. Within a year and a half, over $20 million was allocated for state school construction under Public Law 815.

Operating Funds

As enrollment increases outstripped population gains, the demand for more operating funds became as important as the need for construction funds, and Mrs. Wanamaker constantly battled for more school support. From the beginning of statehood, school districts had been permitted to raise a 10-mill tax without a vote of the people; she was able to get the limit raised to 14 mills. But since local tax sources were inhibited by the 40-mill limit, she gained increases in state aid until the state was financing 70 percent of school operating costs in 1946.

State funds were apportioned on the basis of attendance at the time Mrs. Wanamaker took office. To bring about a reduction in teacher loads, she obtained a major change so that state aid would be apportioned partly on the basis of the number of certificated employees. She succeeded in raising basic state support from 25¢ to 40¢ per day per pupil, plus $1,190 for each certificated employee. She obtained increases in equalized county support from 5¢ to 17¢, and in equalized local support from 15¢ to 43¢ per day. The transportation reimbursement was raised from 50 percent to a maximum of 90 percent of the cost. Special credits were employed to encourage the development of libraries, guidance, health, and remedial programs.

By the end of her administration, Mrs. Wanamaker was probably the first Washington state superintendent who could say: "Washington has made marked advances in providing equalized educational opportunities for all children" (31). School district receipts had increased from over $38 million to nearly $185 million. The average teacher salary jumped from $1,669 in 1940 to $4,467 in 1956. She noted, however, that Washington's rank among the states in regard to teachers' salaries, which had risen from fourteenth to third highest during the war, had fallen to thirteenth by 1956.

Not only did she attempt to raise salaries, but she also constantly worked to improve teacher education and certification in her efforts to solve the war-born teacher shortage. The most important change in education and certification came in 1949, when the Legislature authorized all five state institutions of higher learning to train teachers for any "grade, level, department or position of the public schools of the state, provided that the courses offered in all of the aforesaid training are approved by the state board of education" (32). Previously, elementary teacher training had been delegated to the normal schools (now state colleges) and secondary education to the state college and university.

Following the legislative action, the state board made Washington the first state to adopt the general certificate, which permitted a professionally competent teacher to teach any grade from 1 to 12. The new program required all teachers to complete 4 years of college or university education, followed by 1 year of carefully supervised teaching, and then a fifth year of college or university work.

Federal Aid

During World War II, as the influx of war workers forced a number of school districts to hire additional teachers, Congress appropriated funds to assist the schools. Federal aid grew substantially, from less than 1 percent of school district total receipts in 1940–when federal funds were limited to Indian and vocational education–to nearly 5 percent in 1956.

Many state schools were already serving hot lunches to students in 1943 when the National School Lunch Act was passed. Under the state superintendent's direction, 326 school districts were soon taking part in the new hot lunch program. By 1956, Washington was receiving $755,242 from the government for school lunches, $1,605,879 in donated commodities, and $822,023 for the new Federal Special School Milk Fund.

As stated above, federal funds had bolstered Washington's school construction programs–particularly after the enactment of Public Law 815 in 1950. Public Law 874, a companion measure to Public Law 815, brought order to federal grants for school maintenance and operations. Second in the nation in the number of federal projects within its boundaries, Washington has fared well from these laws. Over $7 million in federal aid was received under the two acts during Mrs. Wanamaker's last year in office.

Vocational rehabilitation began to outstrip vocational education in the receipt of federal finances during these years. By 1956, both were accounting for around $.5 million in government funds. All of these, together with $315,898 for Indian education, brought Washington State nearly $27 million from Washington, D.C., during Mrs. Wanamaker's last biennium.

Organization

Under permissive rulings, school districts had been gradually reduced from a high of around 2,700 in 1910 to 1,609 in 1937. A 1937 reorganization act reduced the number to 1,323 by 1941. Between 1941 and 1946, as a result of 1941 legislation, the number dropped to 672. But Mrs. Wanamaker still did not consider the situation satisfactory. She called for the "enactment of a new, comprehensive, and forward looking school district organization law to replace existing statutes governing the formation of new districts and the alteration of boundaries of existing districts" (33). The Legislature responded by passing new laws in 1947, 1953, and 1955. Under these acts, the number of districts was reduced to 498.

Curriculum

In 1942, Mrs. Wanamaker appointed a state director of curriculum to coordinate the work of the various agencies involved in curriculum improvement, thus establishing a new division. The department had the previous year taken over publication of the *Washington State Curriculum Journal,* and in 1942, the superintendent's office assumed the sponsorship of the state curriculum commission. In the following 2 years, the department published a number of curriculum guides; with a few exceptions, none had been published since 1930.

Under Mrs. Wanamaker's direction the supervisory program developed its present form. The department staff attempted to assist local administrators and teachers in building an educational program to meet the needs of the individual child in the community. State supervisors visited classrooms, met with individual teachers, and took part in faculty meetings. The staff supplemented these visits with statewide and regional teacher conferences.

The superintendent's instructional staff worked with committees of teachers and school administrators in preparing study guides and developing curriculum, the curriculum commission serving in an advisory capacity. The department's professional and curriculum library made materials available to educators throughout the state. An instructional materials service was established, and Mrs. Wanamaker employed a consultant to assist local districts. Curriculum and instruction were major topics of a series of annual summer meetings she instituted for school administrators from all over the state.

Mrs. Wanamaker expanded the curriculum in many ways. In addition to reading, writing, arithmetic, history, science, art, music, and citizenship, increasing emphasis was given to health and physical education, safety education, recreation, and guidance. The department sponsored a drivers education workshop and sought ways to extend driver training to all eligible students. A number of schools began maintaining forest plots, and in 1955, the superintendent encouraged others to follow suit by establishing an advisory committee on conservation education. Washington became one of the leading states in developing programs for conservation and outdoor education.

Superintendent Wanamaker gave special emphasis to the education of handicapped children during her administration. She held the controversial view that they should be educated alongside normal children so they could better adjust to the normal world in which they would live. She said that placing the handicapped in institutions was "just another kind of segregation" (34). Between 1942 and 1956, the number of children receiving special education increased from 5,824 to over 25,000 with more than 77 percent enrolled in regular elementary and secondary classes.

Junior Colleges

In 1941, the Legislature made the junior colleges, which had been founded by individual communities, public institutions and provided them with state aid. During the 1942-43 school year, the eight junior colleges had a combined enrollment of 1,056. In 1945, they became an official part of the public school system, and the state board assumed responsibility for their curriculum. At the same time, the 1945 law permitted junior colleges to provide a 2-year general program of post-high school study in addition to terminal vocational education and college preparatory courses. By 1956, 22,000 students were enrolled full or part time in the state's 10 junior colleges.

Superintendent's Staff

In 1952, the Legislature placed the professional and nonprofessional employees of both the superintendent of public instruction and the State Board for Vocational Education under Civil Service. At this time, the department staff numbered 52 and was organized in four divisions: administration and finance, teachers' education and certification, central services, and instruction. The 49-man vocational education staff was subdivided as follows: vocational agriculture, trades and industries, vocational rehabilitation, distributive education, and home economics.

Lay State Board

Acting on Mrs. Wanamaker's recommendation, the 1947 Legislature reorganized the State Board of Education into its present-day form of two directors from each congressional district elected by local school district directors. Board members are elected for 6-year terms, staggered so that two terms expire each year. The Legislature prescribed the duties for the new lay board to include preparing courses for study in the common schools and approving programs for preparing teachers. It was made responsible for certifying teachers, accrediting all secondary schools, and accrediting colleges and universities preparing teachers for certification. The state board also was made responsible for classifying high school districts and non-high school districts and for establishing standards, rules, and regulations governing apportionment of the current state school fund, state school building funds, and funds for special services. It approves preparatory requirements for admission to the state-supported institutions of higher learning. The board decides appeals by teachers from the state superintendent's decisions on the revocation of certificates. It prescribes rules for the general government of the common schools, and it districts the state.

Like most superintendents in recent years, Mrs. Wanamaker recommended that the state board appoint the state superintendent, but this recommendation has not been accepted.

Libel from the Right Wing

Late in 1955, radio commentator Fulton Lewis, Jr., in an attack on the White House Conference on Education, broadcast that close relatives of Mrs. Wanamaker were associated with communism. He then admitted the charges were not true and broadcast a retraction 3 days later. Mrs. Wanamaker filed a libel suit against Lewis and won judgments totaling $25,000 in Washington and Oklahoma. A third trial in Baltimore resulted in a deadlocked jury. She and Lewis then agreed that the case should be settled for all states and the District of Columbia in the Federal District Court for the District of Columbia. In 1959, this trial brought a ruling of libel per se by the judge and a jury verdict of $145,000 for Mrs. Wanamaker. The judge later set the verdict aside as excessive, but by agreement of both parties the final amount of the settlement was not made public (35).

As pointed out previously, Washington's voters are noted for their reluctance to maintain office holders for numerous terms. Governors are usually limited to two terms; one made it three times, but not consecutively. The record for state superintendents thus far is four terms.

Without a doubt, Mrs. Wanamaker had been the state's most illustrious superintendent; the schools were consistently ranked among the nation's best. In her zeal to get the best for Washington's children, however, she made enemies—particularly in the Legislature. It was rumored that she might run for the Office of Governor, but she chose to seek reelection to the office she had held longer than any person except Mrs. Preston.

In the 1956 primary, Mrs. Wanamaker received the most votes; but in the general election, Lloyd Andrews apparently received the votes that had gone to a third primary candidate. To the dismay of the state's educators, he defeated Mrs. Wanamaker by nearly 160,000 votes. Today she remains active in education as the Northwest regional representative of *Scholastic* magazine.

THE SPUTNIK ERA

Lloyd Andrews

Superintendent Lloyd Andrews had been graduated from Washington State College, served as a State Senator, and taught high school before entering the Navy in World War II. Since he had operated a successful apple orchard and shipping business near Spokane after the war, educators did not consider him a member of the fraternity. He was not popular with them, particularly in the first years of his term.

Like Superintendent Atwood in 1937, Andrews soon ran into conflicts in authority between the superintendent and the state board that had evolved over the years. Authority of the state superintendent rests in the State Constitution, that of the Board of Education does not. The Legislature had assigned various duties and responsibilities to the board, both policy making and administrative, and had empowered the board to employ assistants to carry them out. At one point the State Supreme Court even ruled that a member of the board was an executive officer of the state with certain legal executive functions.

When Andrews took office, the board passed a resolution to make clear that its 12-man staff would carry out the duties the Legislature had assigned to the Board of Education. This made it impossible for the superintendent to remove the board's staff members and appoint others responsible to him. In fact, separate budget requests were prepared by the state board and the state superintendent.

In 1959, the state board resolved the conflict by designating the superintendent its chief executive officer and giving him the responsibility to carry out its decisions and supervise its staff. The Legislature helped by making one appropriation for both the superintendent and the board.

Sputnik. In 1957, the year Superintendent Andrews assumed office, the Russians launched Sputnik. This resulted in American education's becoming a critical public issue. Subject matter and teaching methods came under increasing scrutiny. The state superintendent gave particular attention to curriculum studies. Staff members worked with various teachers committees in preparing and distributing new curriculum guides for all basic subject areas from grade 1 through 12. They gave more attention to science and mathematics and to special courses for gifted, average, and slow learners.

The department launched a research study on educational opportunities for the gifted and conducted other studies on junior and senior high school instruction. Staff members undertook a study of audiovisual materials, equipment, and services in local districts and county offices, which resulted in the selection of a statewide committee to prepare administrative procedures for strengthening the program. Superintendent Andrews employed a part-time staff member to make special studies on the possibilities of extending the school year, on teacher-pupil and administrator-pupil ratios, and on the use of school buildings.

Andrews' business background served him well in matters of administration and finance. He directed a complete revision of school accounting procedures; and with the assistance of the state auditor, educational administrators, and business people, he published a school accounting guide. The publication followed closely the pattern set forth by the U.S. Office of Education and made possible a better system of accounting for local districts. He conducted short- and long-range studies of school building costs, maintenance, and use in an effort to stretch construction dollars in the face of rising building costs.

Merit Pay. In 1958, Superintendent Andrews appointed five teachers and school administrators and six lay people to study the feasibility of a teachers merit pay system. The committee concluded that, ideally, able teachers should receive additional pay so long as such an incentive program would be reflected in a larger rather than a smaller salary budget. It advised that a valid measurement of teacher competence and classroom performance posed difficult problems. The committee found that adopting a statewide merit pay system would not be feasible without a revision of school support laws and regulations. Thus, merit pay programs in Washington have continued to be matters for local determination.

Andrews asked the state board to revise and strengthen the regulations for establishing extended secondary programs and adult evening courses in high schools. The board did issue new regulations to prevent unnecessary duplication of these programs and to encourage economic development and operation of postgraduate programs offered in the high schools.

The superintendent also reported that the state board had conducted a study of the organization and operation of the state's junior colleges in hopes of establishing uniformity in their finances and operations. Andrews declared this would make it possible to draw conclusions about the cost of junior college programs and the most effective way to operate them. He pointed out that there was increasing pressure to establish more junior colleges—especially in the urban counties of King, Pierce, and Spokane.

The enactment of the National Defense Education Act by the Eighty-Fifth Congress brought nearly $650,000 to Washington in the 1959-60 school year and enabled the state superintendent to add more staff.

In 1960, the state's Republican party was determined to unseat Democratic Governor Albert D. Rosellini. Recalling Superintendent Andrews' sound defeat of Mrs. Wanamaker, a proven vote-getter, the Republicans backed him as their candidate for Governor. Andrews and Rosellini engaged in the newly popular sport of televised debates; although Andrews was technically the better speaker, he apparently could not get his message across to the independent voter. The election was close, but Rosellini retained his office.

Louis Bruno and the 1960's

Meanwhile, a group of school officials had approached Superintendent Louis Bruno of Pullman and, because of his experience at all levels of education, asked him to run for state superintendent. "Really, it didn't make much sense, me running," Bruno recalled later. "I was making more money in Pullman than I could as state superintendent" (36). But he agreed to run.

The first truly nonpartisan candidate for the state superintendency, Republican or Democrat, Bruno called on both party headquarters whenever he campaigned in a new town. He won handily.

Bruno was not unfamiliar with Olympia; he had served a term on the State Board of Education prior to World War II and a year and a half on the state superintendent's staff before beginning his 12-year stint at Pullman. The son of immigrant parents who prized the education they had been denied, Bruno worked his way through Washington State to an education degree. He taught at Raymond High School, then served as its principal from 1931 to 1941.

Tall and impressive in appearance, he commands respect naturally. Yet his warm, informal manner, his friendly smile, and his genuine interest in each individual have made him greatly admired by his staff. Clerks and division heads, alike, have become accustomed to having the superintendent pop into their offices for a few pleasantries. Bruno has been known to express concern that the rapid growth of the superintendent's office has made it impossible for him to know every member of the staff by first name within the first few days of employment.

A tireless speaker on education, Bruno drives nearly 50,000 miles a year to meet with educators, businessmen, and taxpayers. Perhaps his popularity with Washington citizens can be explained in part by his distaste for the fancy words so dear to many educators. The superintendent's public information officer claims to be under threat of instant dismissal should words such as "in-depth," "overview," or "paraprofessional" creep into a departmental release or publication. A firm believer in communication, Bruno installed the department's first full-scale public information program.

Bruno was the only state superintendent appointed by President Johnson to the National Advisory Council on Education of Disadvantaged Children. He has served as a member of the board of the Council of Chief State School Officers. In 1966, Seattle Pacific College awarded him an honorary doctor of laws degree.

Age of Education. Superintendent Bruno assumed office in time to preside over a revolution in education—the dawn of what he calls the Age of Education. Vast changes in curriculum and methods were made to enable the schools to meet the challenge of a runaway technology. The problems of urban education, the dropout, and the disadvantaged assumed major proportions. Students were tasting a new independence. Population growth and shifts brought new dimensions to the ever-present problem of school support.

Against this onslaught of change, Bruno has continually reminded his constitutents to keep social and technical revolution in proper perspective:

> Does it ever occur to you that the schools are the only agency to which the government can turn in the face of these monumental emergencies? Or that the community colleges, the 4-year colleges, and the universities comprise the one indispensable source for trained leadership for almost every segment of society?
>
> Technological and scientific advances are fascinating, but intrinsically they are meaningless unless man becomes their master instead of their slave. I would like to suggest that in my opinion the mightiest achievement of the next hundred years will be man's ability to place technology in its proper relationship to his universe (37).

To ensure that this will happen, Bruno urges the schools to teach children to learn how to learn. Rote memorization will not provide the foundation youngsters will need to cope with the future, he says, because half the jobs they will fill as adults haven't been invented yet.

Bruno believes the state's schools are meeting their responsibilities, and he gives much of the credit to Washington's teachers. "Since 1949, no state in the nation has had higher requirements for teacher certification than the State of Washington," he proclaims, "but we also have, in our classrooms, some of the finest teachers anywhere" (38).

Federal Relations. Superintendent Bruno does not expect the federal government to do the job of the state and community in providing for education. Whatever position is taken on state-federal-local relationships, he declares, the debate about federal aid to education is now as outdated as last year's hemline. He realizes that the federal government wants a job done, will insist that it can be done, and if necessary will establish the machinery to do it. Therefore, he feels that it is the responsibility of the State Office of Public Instruction to obviate any criticism by the federal government that the State of Washington is not doing its job.

Bruno does express concern that a national testing program conducted by the federal government could lead to a national curriculum at the expense of local interests and regional problems. He has spoken out against federal legislation that tends to bypass state and local educational agencies to deal directly with local institutions. However, he credits such federal legislation as the Vocational Education Act of 1963 and the National Defense Education Act of 1958 with considerable success in specific areas of curriculum.

Curriculum Change. Superintendent Bruno has stated that despite considerable talk about curriculum change for the past 30 years, until recently we have been doing business on much the same old basis. He points out, however, that since the early sixties fantastic changes have occurred in curriculum content and methods that will result in curriculum improvement. He says research shows that curriculum change in Washington schools occurred four times faster in 1965 than in 1958.

Bruno thinks the state has made good progress in introducing new courses in science education that emphasize the student as an active participant rather than a spectator. In fact, Washington has attained one of the nation's highest ratings for introducing new science curriculums; but Superintendent Bruno wants more improvement at the elementary and junior high school levels. He estimates that 50 to 70 percent of the elementary schools and 60 to 80 percent of the high schools have introduced new mathematics curriculums. In a different area he is particularly proud of a project he sponsored in cooperation with the Northwest and Joint Councils for Economics Education which has resulted in economics study at all grade levels.

Taking note of the general dissatisfaction with present programs in English, Superintendent Bruno looks for a major breakthrough in reading, writing, spelling, and composition. Foreign languages, he insists, must be learned well enough to communicate. Washington's vigorous language program now employs 1,000 instructors who are teaching 10 different languages in grades 7 through 12.

He is concerned with spotty developments in health and physical education courses, noting that some parts of the state have fine programs while others have none at all. The superintendent believes that the state can never be truly successful until every boy and girl has the finest program of physical education and health available from kindergarten through high school.

Bruno has also given strong support to vocational education. Although Washington ranks first among the 50 states in the percentage of people enrolled in vocational programs, he wants better programs with greater emphasis on the importance of technical training. He realizes that enrolling in a strictly vocational program appears to have some sort of stigma, but he believes that better guidance programs can do much to assist students in making wise choices relating to their interests, abilities, and capabilities. The superintendent has instituted one of the nation's most ambitious programs for elementary school guidance counseling in the hope that learning problems can be detected and remedied early.

Office of Public Instruction. To keep up with the vast changes that have characterized society and education in the sixties, the Office of Public Instruction has undoubtedly undergone its greatest change under Bruno's direction. On assuming office, he consolidated the services available to the state's schools and established six divisions under assistant superintendents for curriculum and instruction, administration and finance, teacher education and certification, community colleges and adult education, vocational education, and vocational rehabilitation. This organization remained largely intact until the 1967 Legislature created a separate board for community colleges and a coordinating council for vocational education and rehabilitation.

At Bruno's request, the 1961 Legislature provided for a research director and a statewide research program. The staff has conducted studies in such areas as dropouts in the metropolitan Seattle area, the 12-month school program, new teaching methods, use of remote computer facilities, preparation of teachers, and a variety of programs in curriculum. At the same time the research office was created, the department established its educational data-processing center.

The National Defense Education Act has enabled the department to create new supervisory positions in science, mathematics, foreign language, guidance and counseling, libraries, and audiovisual services. Title V of the Elementary and Secondary Education Act is providing funds for a learning resources center and laboratory. (With a staff of 217, the Office of Public Instruction now operates with a budget in excess of $2.5 million a year.) But the explosive changes in public schooling which have brought about the transformation of the superintendent's staff have continued to plague him with the problem of finding more resources to keep up quality education.

School Support. In discussing the taxpayer's obligation to the children of the state, Superintendent Bruno points out that—

> Economic studies have shown that for each dollar invested in tangible capital, a 5-percent rate of return to

society can be expected. On the other hand, each dollar invested in the *education* of its citizens brings a rate of return to the state of over 10 percent (39).

In answering those who ask if the taxpayer receives his dollar's worth for school support, he points out that while Washington enjoys a school system consistently among the nation's best, the state ranks eighteenth in per-pupil expenditure. He is concerned that the state has slipped to eighteenth among the states in educational expenditure, and he warns that the effects of lagging investment in education will be felt for years.

Superintendent Bruno expresses alarm at the dangerous trend of Legislatures to reduce the state's share and increase the local share of school support. State support has dropped to 55 percent. With the state's constitutional prohibition on income tax and the 40-mill limit on property tax, school people must depend on "special" levies to raise local taxes above the 40-mill limit and meet increasing school maintenance and operating costs. Most first-class districts ask for an annual "special" levy for up to 25 percent of their operating funds. Originally intended to meet emergencies, the levy is an unreliable source of funds because of the limitation requiring a 60-percent yes vote from 40 percent of the turnout in the previous general election. It is also expensive and inhibits effective planning. The superintendent, the Governor, civic groups, and countless citizens have fought to reform the state's patchwork tax structure and establish a positive school finance program, but state legislators continue to duck this responsibility.

Post-High School Education. The chief reason for the rising cost of Washington schools has been the growing demand for post-high school education. In 11 years, from 1955 to 1966, the number of juniors and seniors desiring education beyond high school jumped from 35 to 90 percent. During Bruno's administration, the number of community colleges built or authorized has doubled. Full-time enrollment jumped 70 percent in a 3-year period and at the same time enrollment in the state's seven vocational technical institutes increased by 3,000. These factors, plus retraining, rehabilitation, and greater interest in general adult education, have in large measure increased school appropriations from $435,300 in the 1961-63 biennium to $626,700 in the 1965-67 biennium.

The state has had to construct 500 to 700 new classrooms each year to house annual enrollment increases of 20,000 to 30,000 children. A 1966 constitutional amendment facilitated construction financing by allowing the interest and income from the permanent school fund to be used for amortizing school construction bonds. About three-fourths of the original school lands remained unsold in 1957, when the state adopted the policy of retaining them and managing the property for maximum income. The permanent school fund is now over $108 million, and the interest accounts for more than $3.5 million a year.

Washington has come a long way since 1887, when Superintendent John C. Lawrence expressed the fervent hope that the territory would soon become a state, since the sale of school land would bring $5 million which, at a "low" interest of about 7 percent per annum, would yield $350,000 for school purposes.

Ranked Number One

In a national index of education strengths and weaknesses, Superintendent Bruno can proudly point to Washington's rank as number one in the nation with the lowest failure rate among those taking the Armed Forces Mental Qualifications Test in 1966. Washington ranks among the leaders in the median number of school years completed by persons 25 years or over, low illiteracy rate, and low dropout rate between the high school freshmen and senior years (40).

This is the kind of school system Washington pioneers anticipated in writing a constitution that made paramount the state's duty to provide ample education for every child. It is the kind of system that could not have happened without strong central leadership. The pioneers learned this lesson through the trials and errors of territorial days and provided constitutionally for a state superintendent who would be truly a leader and not a record keeper. It is the kind of system that has evolved through the cumulative efforts of a succession of strong and dedicated superintendents.

In a dynamic era, it is a system of schools that must continue to improve. As Superintendent Bruno says,

> We must try to provide every class with a good teacher, a good library and good guidance. If we do that, maybe my fondest wish could be a reality—to make sure every child had an equal chance for an education that would fit his personal needs. Right now, we are simply not reaching every boy and girl. No state system is. We have much work left to do (41).

This is the challenge for tomorrow's chief state school officer.

FOOTNOTES

1. Territory of Washington, *House Journal* (1854), p. 21.
2. Thomas W. Bibb, *History of Early Common School Education in Washington* (Seattle: University of Washington, 1929), p. 73.
3. *Weekly Echo* (Olympia), December 8, 1870.
4. *Puget Sound Courier* (Olympia), January 10, 1873.
5. Although the organization of the board has changed several times, the state superintendent continues to hold the position of ex officio president.

6. Territorial Superintendent of Public Instruction, *Report, 1877-1879,* p. 31.
7. *Ibid.,* p. 22.
8. Washington, *Constitution* (1889), art. 9, secs. 1, 2.
9. The twentieth amendment in 1948 removed executive salaries from the constitution.
10. Washington, *Laws* (1895), ch. 150, sec. 1, p. 375.
11. Superintendent of Public Instruction, *Twentieth Biennial Report, 1908-1910,* p. 5.
12. Superintendent of Public Instruction, *Nineteenth Biennial Report, 1906-1908,* p. 201.
13. Superintendent of Public Instruction, *Seventeenth Biennial Report, 1902-1904,* pp. 195-96.
14. The Department of Public Instruction's budget for the 2 years ending April 1, 1913, was $13,050, exclusive of printing costs.
15. Frederick E. Bolton and Thomas W. Bibb, *History of Education in Washington,* Bulletin 1934, No. 9 (Washington, D.C.: Government Printing Office, 1935), p. 116.
16. Josephine Corliss Preston, "School Teachers Must Live," *Success* (Christmas 1924).
17. The communities benefited as much as the teachers, as the cottages enabled them to take greater interest in clubs and community projects. See the Superintendent of Public Instruction's *Twenty-Fourth Biennial Report, 1916-1918,* p. 89.
18. Superintendent of Public Instruction, *Twenty-Second Biennial Report, 1912-1914,* p. 19.
19. Superintendent of Public Instruction, *Twenty-Sixth Biennial Report, 1920-1922,* p. 19.
20. Superintendent of Public Instruction, *Twenty-Third Biennial Report, 1922-1924,* pp. 15-22.
21. Noah D. Showalter, *A Handbook for Rural Officers* (New York: Houghton Mifflin Co., 1920).
22. Superintendent of Public Instruction, *Report, 1928-1936,* pp. 13, 62.
23. *Ibid.,* p. 18.
24. Superintendent of Public Instruction, *Report, 1937-1940,* pp. 15-16.
25. Superintendent of Public Instruction, *Biennial Report, 1936-1938,* p. 31.
26. *Ibid.,* p. 27.
27. Dan C. Fowler, "Education's No. 1 Saleswoman," *Look,* October 19, 1954, p. 54.
28. "Fighting Lady," *Time,* February 6, 1956, p. 61.
29. Mary C. Wark, personal interview with Mrs. Gertrude Ellis at Olympia, Washington, in August 1967.
30. Superintendent of Public Instruction, *Thirty-Eighth Biennial Reports, 1944-1946,* p. 13.
31. Superintendent of Public Instruction, *Forty-Third Biennial Report, 1954-1956,* p. 13.
32. Superintendent of Public Instruction, *Education in Washington* (Olympia: Office of the Superintendent, May 1950), p. 4.
33. Superintendent of Public Instruction, *Thirty-Eighth Biennial Report, 1944-1946,* p. 63.
34. Fowler, *op. cit.,* p. 56.
35. Edgar Fuller, "Report from Washington," *Nation's Schools,* LXV, No. 3 (March 1960), p. 106.
36. *Daily Olympian,* September 8, 1963, p. 1.
37. Louis Bruno, address to "Youth Looks to the Future" award ceremony, Spokane, Washington, on May 26, 1966.
38. "Louis Bruno, State Superintendent of Public Instruction," *Public Affairs Profile* (Seattle: Pacific Northwest Bell, 1967).
39. Superintendent of Public Instruction, *Education Fact Sheet* (Olympia: Office of the Superintendent, 1965), p. 5.
40. Richard de Neufville and Caryl Connor, "How Good Are Our Schools?" *American Education,* II (October 1966), 9; National Education Association, Research Division, *Rankings of the States* (Washington, D.C.: The Association, 1968), pp. 27-28.
41. "Louis Bruno," *op. cit., Public Affairs Profile.*

BIBLIOGRAPHY

Public Documents

State of Washington. *Constitution* (1889).

—— *Laws* (1895), ch. 150, sec. 1.

Territory of Washington. *House Journal* (1854).

Books and Pamphlets

Babcock, Chester D., and Babcock, Clare Applegate. *Our Pacific Northwest.* New York: Webster Publishing Division, McGraw-Hill Book Co., 1963.

Bibb, Thomas W. *History of Early Common School Education in Washington.* Seattle: University of Washington, 1929.

Bolton, Frederick E., and Bibb, Thomas W. *History of Education in Washington.* Bulletin 1934, No. 9. Washington, D.C.: Government Printing Office, 1935.

Bowden, Angie Burt. *Early Schools of Washington Territory.* Seattle: Lowman and Hanford, 1935.

Hazard, Joseph T. *Pioneer Teachers of Washington.* Seattle: Seattle Retired Teachers Association, 1955.

Johansen, Dorothy O., and Gates, Charles M. *Empire of the Columbia.* New York: Harper and Brothers, 1957.

Showalter, Noah D. *A Handbook for Rural Officers.* New York: Houghton Mifflin Co., 1920.

Stewart, Edgar I. *Washington Northwest Frontier.* 2 vols. New York: Lewis Historical Publishing Co., 1957.

Superintendent of Public Instruction. *Educational Services for the Public Schools.* Olympia: Department of Public Instruction, 1963.

--*State Manual of Washington.* Olympia: Department of Public Instruction, 1960.

--*Facts About Education.* Olympia: Department of Public Instruction, 1964.

Webster, D. H.; Campbell, E. H.; and Smith, G. D. *Washington State Government.* Seattle: University of Washington Press, 1962.

Articles and Periodicals

Daily Olympian. September 8, 1963, p. 1.

"Fighting Lady." *Time,* February 6, 1956, p. 61.

Fowler, Dan C. "Education's No. 1 Saleswoman." *Look,* October 19, 1954, p. 54.

Fuller, Edgar. "Report from Washington." *Nation's Schools,* LXV, No. 3 (March 1960), 106.

"Louis Bruno, State Superintendent of Public Instruction." *Public Affairs Profile.* Pamphlet used in Pacific Northwest Bell's employee information program. Seattle: Pacific Northwest Bell, 1967.

Neufville, Richard de, and Connor, Caryl. "How Good Are Our Schools?" *American Education,* II (October 1966), 9.

Preston, Josephine Corliss. "School Teachers Must Live." *Success* (Christmas 1924).

Puget Sound Courier (Olympia). January 10, 1873.

State Curriculum Commission. *Washington Curriculum Journal,* 1937-41. Seattle: The Commission.

Superintendent of Public Instruction. *Education in Washington,* 1941-54. Olympia: Office of the Superintendent.

-- *Washington State Curriculum Journal,* 1941–. Olympia: Office of the Superintendent.

-- *Your Public Schools,* 1961–. Olympia: Office of the Superintendent.

Weekly Echo (Olympia). December 8, 1870.

Reports

Interim Committee on Education. *Education in Washington.* Report of Washington State Legislature. Olympia: The Committee, 1960, 1962, 1964, and 1966.

National Education Association, Research Division. *Rankings of the States.* Washington, D.C.: The Association, 1968.

Strayer, George D. *Public Instruction in Washington.* A report of the survey of public education in the State of Washington. Published by the author, 1946.

Superintendents of Public Instruction. *Annual and Biennial Reports.* Olympia: State of Washington, 1879-1966.

-- *Budget Request for the Public Schools,* 1963-65, 1965-67, 1967-69. Olympia: State of Washington.

-- *Education Fact Sheet.* Olympia: Office of the Superintendent, 1965.

Territorial Superintendent of Public Instruction. *Report, 1877-1879.* Olympia: Office of the Superintendent.

Other Sources

Bruno, Louis. "Youth Looks to the Future." Address at award ceremony, Spokane, Washington, May 26, 1966.

Burris, L. D. Personal interview with L. D. Burris by Mary C. Wark, August 1967.

Ellis, Gertrude. Personal interview with Mrs. Gertrude Ellis at Olympia, Washington, by Mary C. Wark, August 1967.

Appendix A

WASHINGTON CHIEF STATE SCHOOL OFFICERS

Territorial Superintendents

1861-62	B. C. Lippincott
1872-74	Nelson Rounds
1874-80	John P. Judson
1880-82	Jonathan S. Houghton
1882-84	Charles W. Wheeler
1884-86	R. C. Kerr
1886-88	John C. Lawrence
1888-89	John H. Morgan

State Superintendents

1889-92	Robert B. Bryan
1892-96	Charles W. Bean
1896-1900	Frank J. Browne
1900-1907	Robert B. Bryan
1907-12	Henry B. Dewey
1912-28	Josephine Corliss Preston
1928-36	Noah D. Showalter
1936-40	Stanley F. Atwood
1940-56	Pearl A. Wanamaker
1956-60	Lloyd Andrews
1960-	Louis Bruno

Appendix B

Chart I.--OFFICE OF THE WASHINGTON STATE SUPERINTENDENT OF PUBLIC INSTRUCTION, 1936

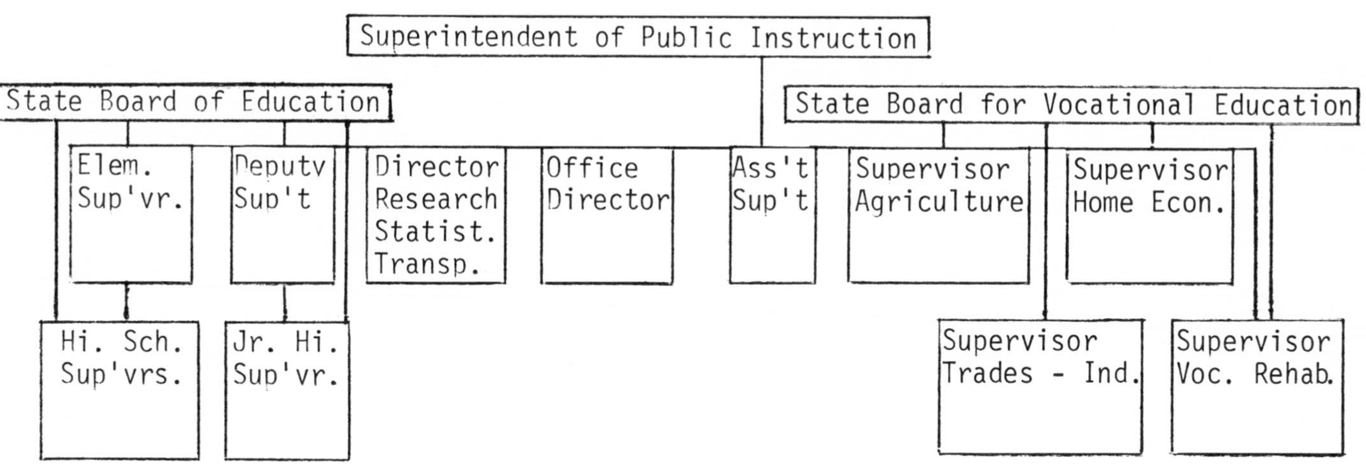

Appendix B

Chart II.--OFFICE OF THE WASHINGTON STATE SUPERINTENDENT OF PUBLIC INSTRUCTION, 1952

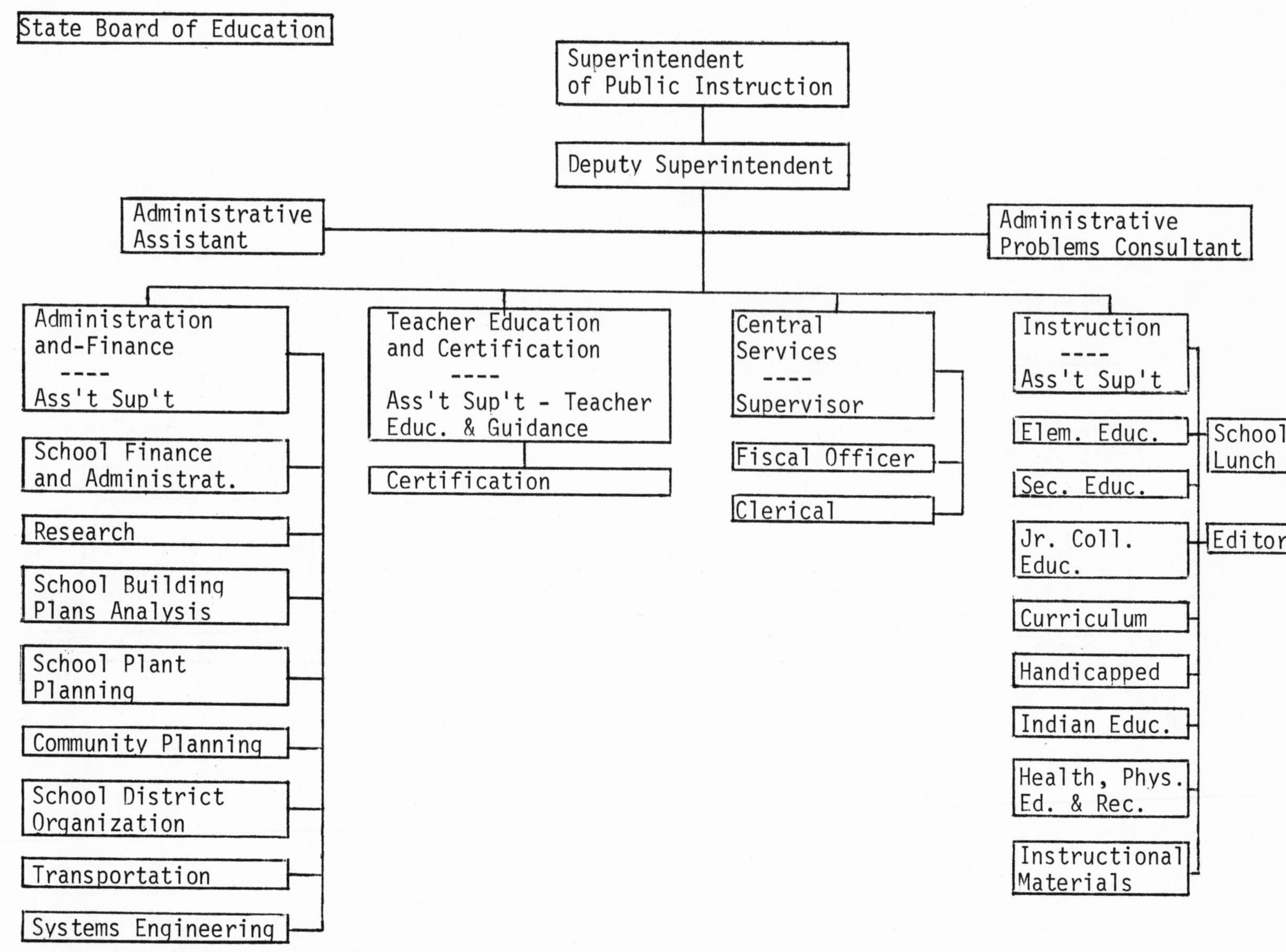

Appendix B

Chart II.--OFFICE OF THE WASHINGTON STATE SUPERINTENDENT OF PUBLIC INSTRUCTION, 1952 (Continued)

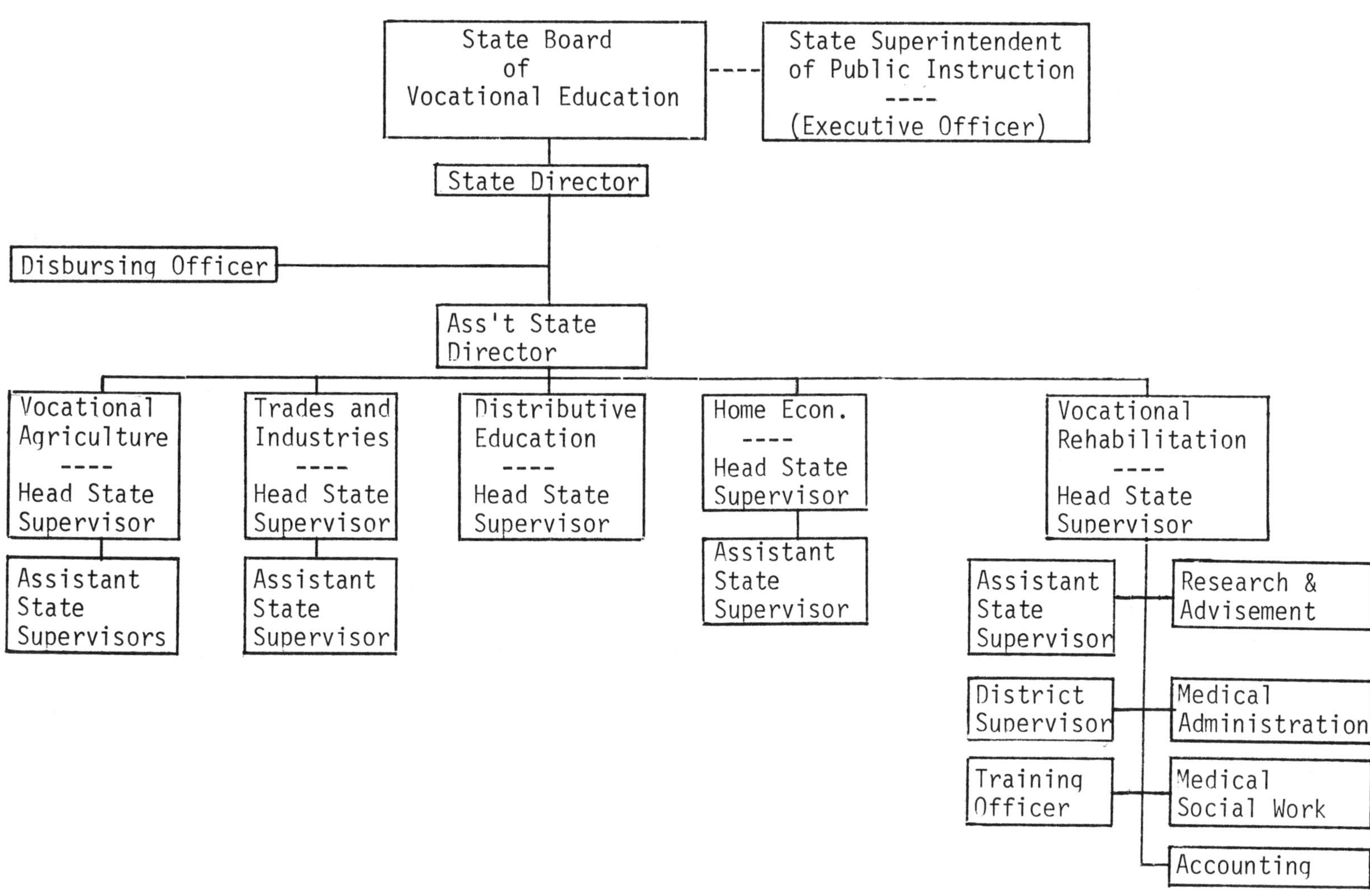

Appendix B

Chart III.--OFFICE OF THE WASHINGTON STATE SUPERINTENDENT OF PUBLIC INSTRUCTION, 1968

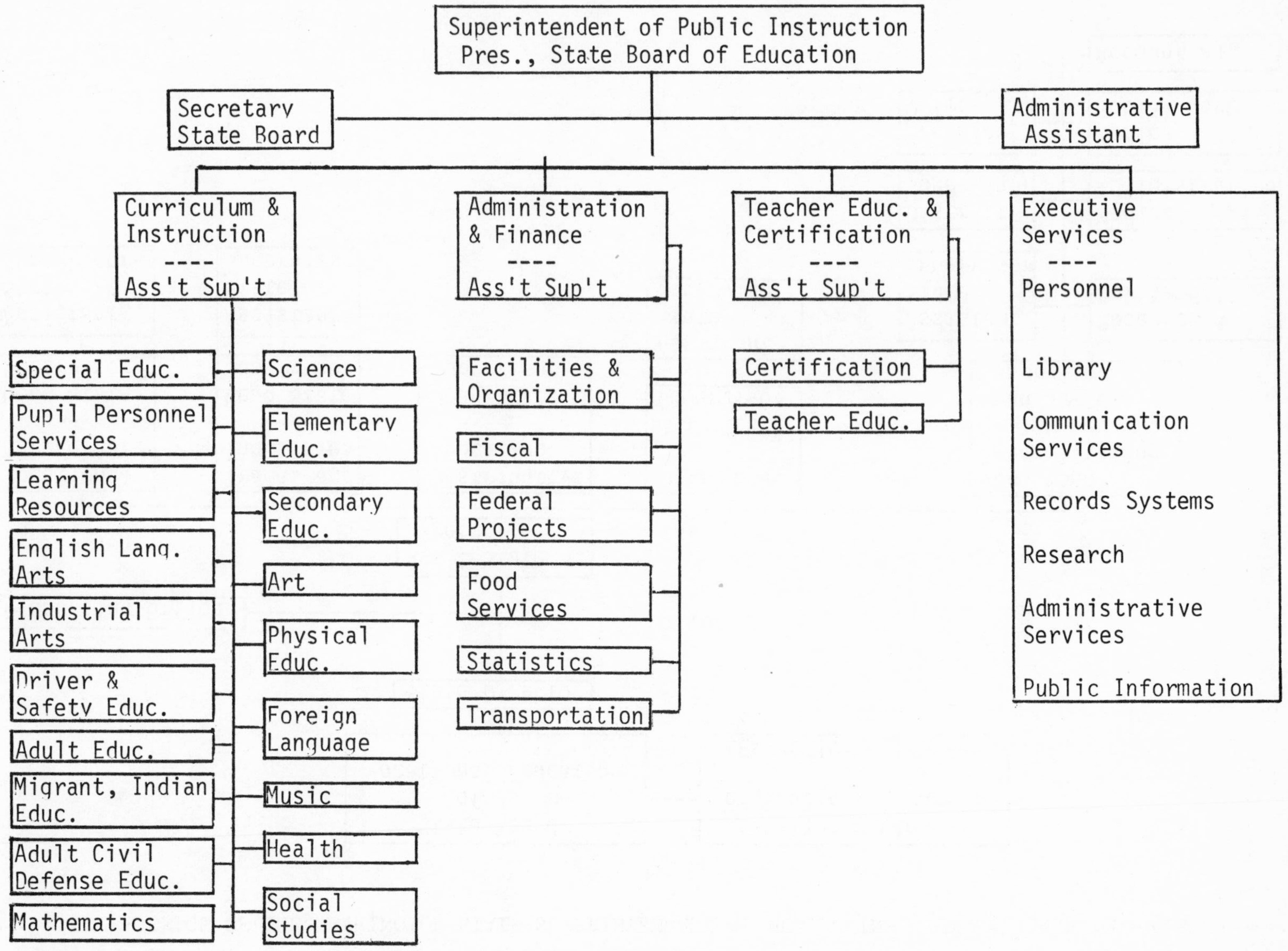

Superintendent of Public Instruction
Pres., State Board of Education

Secretary
State Board

Administrative
Assistant

Curriculum &
Instruction

Ass't Sup't

Special Educ.
Pupil Personnel Services
Learning Resources
English Lang. Arts
Industrial Arts
Driver & Safety Educ.
Adult Educ.
Migrant, Indian Educ.
Adult Civil Defense Educ.
Mathematics

Science
Elementary Educ.
Secondary Educ.
Art
Physical Educ.
Foreign Language
Music
Health
Social Studies

Administration
& Finance

Ass't Sup't

Facilities & Organization
Fiscal
Federal Projects
Food Services
Statistics
Transportation

Teacher Educ. &
Certification

Ass't Sup't

Certification
Teacher Educ.

Executive
Services

Personnel

Library
Communication Services
Records Systems
Research
Administrative Services
Public Information

49 West Virginia

DEPARTMENT OF EDUCATION

Prepared by the Department Staff

Contents

NINETEENTH CENTURY

The Public School Prior to 1863

Colonial Virginia limited its control of education to certain provisions for orphan and indigent children and to the certification of teachers. Tutors employed by the wealthy planters often taught the children of the overseers and artisans and in some instances the children from neighboring plantations. On many plantations, school buildings were provided. Following these plantation schools, private schools and common schools—later called Old Field Schools—developed. The latter, usually "subscription schools," existed in the West Virginia territory as early as 1748, and they expanded due to a spirit of cooperation among the German and Scotch-Irish frontiersmen.

Dislocations caused by the Indian and Revolutionary Wars coupled with the state's sparse population kept many communities from forming schools, and, where they did exist, the quality of education was at a low level.

In 1817, Virginia enacted a measure dividing the state into districts with sole responsibility for establishing and supporting public schools, except for state allocations for educating poor children. However, the districts failed to implement the act. Thus, in 1829, the General Assembly passed a district free school act authorizing state subsidies to district schools, yet permitting a major degree of local authority. That same year, the first free public school in Western Virginia was established under the act in Monroe County. Despite this beginning, the act was not generally effective in either the eastern or the western parts of Virginia.

In 1841, the General Assembly called upon the members of its Literary Fund to present a plan for a reorganized school system. The result was a series of educational conventions throughout the Commonwealth. The convention at Clarksburg placed the western counties firmly on the side of free schools of higher quality for all white youth, local levies to supplement state and federal subsidies, more centralization through a state superintendent, and other reforms. Legislation embodying some of these features, but retaining "moderate tuition fees" and rejecting uniformity and educational quality for sparsely settled areas, failed to pass the following year, and the western counties lost their most effectively planned campaign and much of their momentum.

One of the "Twin Acts" of 1846 provided for districting counties and for electing a county superintendent but retained the indigent tuition feature. The second provided for free schools for white children following a favorable two-thirds vote by the district. Later acts removed most of the barriers to free district schools by 1850.

During the following 13 years, only three counties actually founded free district schools. This was due in large measure to a sparsity of population in large areas of the state. But perhaps of equal importance, the ministers and editors who had formerly led the fight to establish free schools became more conservative.

Statehood, 1863-1900

Of the issues on which the eastern and western counties of Virginia strongly disagreed before the formation of West Virginia in 1863, that of "free schools" was prominent. Strong pleas for improved free schools by western delegates had been unsuccessful in the constitutional conventions of 1829-30 and 1851, although the assembly had made some progress. But the first West Virginia Constitution, ratified in March 1863, mandated a thorough and efficient system of free schools. It also created an invested fund to provide income to supplement the moneys from both state general taxes and local property taxes to establish and support the schools. The constitution further provided for county school superintendents and township school officials and, at the state level, for the election of a general superintendent of free schools.

The Legislature convened on June 20, 1863, the day the State of West Virginia came into existence. Six months later, in conformity with the provisions of the constitution, it established a system of free schools and constituted every township a school district; it provided for the election of a general superintendent by the joint vote of the two Houses of the Legislature for a term of 2 years at a salary of $1,500 per year. The superintendent's duties included disbursing school funds by signing requisitions for the auditor to approve for payment to the county treasurers for the free schools which were entitled to receive them.

The history of the Department of Schools for the next 37 years was very much the history of the activities of one man–the state superintendent. During this entire period he had no professional assistants. In fact, the first superintendents had no assistants of any kind–later ones were able to employ a clerk, or clerks, and stenographers.

The reports of the state superintendents are significant in depicting the status of the free school system at this early period in West Virginia. In 1866, for example, the state superintendent stated:

> School houses are "few and far between." Some of the buildings called by that name are almost in ruins, others are cheerless and comfortless log structures, prisons to both teacher and pupils. . . . The people exhibit a willingness to shoulder the burden, heavy as it is, of displacing these relics of an effete social and political era by such buildings as should be an index of their appreciation of education. . . . The people are clamoring for schools and school houses. . . . The small number of teachers is not commensurate with the educational wants of the state–indeed the demand largely exceeds the supply. A special condition of their demand is a hopeful sign–the call for *good* teachers. . . . The present mode of granting certificates is subject to several objections. There is no uniform standard of merit (1).

The number of schoolhouses reported by the superintendent in 1870 was as follows (2):

	Total	Increase over last year
Frame buildings	1,124	188
Stone buildings	17	7
Brick buildings	68	10
Log buildings	904	290
Total	2,113	495

Also included in the superintendent's report of 1870 were these comments:

> This great increase of log houses indicates that the system is gaining firmer foothold than it has heretofore had in the back counties, where but a few other houses are built and where the system has met with the strongest opposition. . . .
>
> The General Superintendent is now required to do office work without a clerk, and also to travel in the state at large–rather difficult things to be done at the same time by one person. . . . The question arises, whether the Superintendent should not have a clerk, relieving his duties of the incongruity and enabling more and better service to be performed (3).

By 1870, a political realignment in the state resulted in the call for a new constitutional convention to be held in 1872. Although it was feared the convention might do away with the requirement that the state establish and maintain a free school system, this did not materialize. A strong effort to eliminate the requirement for a state superintendent of schools was defeated, but he was made a part of the executive branch. No professional qualifications were listed for either the county or state superintendents.

The second West Virginia Constitution, passed by the convention in April 1872, and ratified by popular vote in August 1872, contained the following statement in Section 1 of Article XII; "The Legislature shall provide, by general law, for a thorough and efficient system of free schools"(4). In Section 2, it stipulated that "the State Superintendent of Free Schools shall have a general supervision of free schools and perform such other duties in relation thereto as may be prescribed by law"(5). His travel expenses were limited to $500 per year. Although the state superintendent also served as adjutant general and quarter master general from 1871 to 1877, he was able to devote his primary attention to schools.

Section 4 of the new constitution continued the school fund created by the Constitution of 1863 and established the Board of School Fund, composed of the Governor, state superintendent, auditor, and treasurer. Section 6 continued the same school districts. Except for the creation of independent school districts, the magisterial school districts remained until 1933, when the county became the school district.

The 1872-73 Legislature amended the school law by providing for the election of the state superintendent for a term of 4 years and charged him with the supervision of all county superintendents and free schools of the state. It also created the General School Fund for the support of free schools, including the salary of the state superintendent and the expenses of his office, and specified its sources of revenue.

A review of the superintendent's reports from 1863 to 1900 indicates that the problems confronting the state superintendent and the public school system were not notably different from those at present: school finances, school building, teachers, teacher certification, textbooks, county and district supervision, courses of study, libraries, and high schools. These early superintendents gave considerable attention to teachers institutes, teachers reading circles, examinations, and Arbor Day. Even though by 1900 the state department consisted only of the state superintendent, one or two clerks, and a stenographer, it had exerted considerable influence in developing West Virginia's public school system.

Teacher Preparation and Certification

By 1864, the problem of obtaining properly trained teachers had resulted in holding various kinds of county institutes. A meeting called in 1865 by State Superintendent William R. White emphasized this form of teacher preparation. Their immediate success prompted White to encourage more county institutes and to provide an organizational format.

This leadership resulted in White's election as president of the state teachers organization in 1865 and established a precedent for electing the state superintendent to this position until 1904. This, in turn, placed the state superintendent in the editorship and proprietorship of the *West Virginia Journal of Education* from 1881 to 1904. Since the *Journal* was considered to be the property of each state superintendent, he established it as the official publication of his office as well as that of the teachers organization. Each state superintendent sold the publication to his successor until Thomas C. Miller, for unspecified reasons, discontinued the state superintendent's role as president of the statewide organization and owner-editor of the *Journal.* Thus ended an era in which the state superintendent had been the principal voice and direct leader of the teachers of the state as well as the officially elected head of the state school system.

In 1873, the Legislature provided for five grades of a 1-year certificate to be issued by a county board of examiners as normal school certificates. At the same time, it established a board consisting of the state superintendent and two teachers appointed by the Governor to examine teachers and issue professional or life certificates. In 1879, it reduced the grades of certificates obtainable by examination to three, and examinations for holders of professional and normal certificates were made optional with local boards of education. Two years later, the Legislature further diminished the quality of certification by eliminating the normal school certificates.

In 1887, the State Board of Examiners was created, along with grades of state certificates for 6 and 12 years. Four years later, in 1891, the Legislature again discontinued the professional certificate. In 1903, by a uniform examinations act, it transferred the preparation of questions, grading of tests, and granting of certificates to the state superintendent, although the county and state examining boards were retained. The act authorized three grades of certificates, with the stipulation that the lowest grade could be issued only once to a person.

County and state meetings, usually called institutes and organized largely for teacher-training purposes, continued to increase. Local organizations for other purposes, centering around regional round tables, originated about 1899 and predominated until formation of the county unit system in 1933. (These are still represented in the seven regional organizations of administrators sponsored by the education department.) These meetings—especially the statewide ones—usually gave some attention to legislative and other major issues but rarely were effective. They confined their action for the most part to responding to attacks on education.

Summer Normals

From 1880 to 1910, the summer normal, a sort of nondescript institution offering both elementary and secondary courses, provided educational opportunity for many who could not afford to go to college or even to a state normal school. Many of these normals were taught by county superintendents with the aid of one or both of the other members of the county examining boards. A legislative act of 1910 forbade this practice and thus dealt the summer normals an all but fatal blow.

The normal offered five courses. The preparatory covered the common school branches except bookkeeping, civil government, and general history. The other four included a teacher-training course; a business course with instruction in bookkeeping, shorthand, etc.; music for beginners; and a liberal education course for college preparation. Although the average summer normal was little more than a "cramming" institution to help teachers pass written examinations, these schools served a useful purpose in the transitional period between the academy and the development of the high schools.

The summer normals were not progressive, and by 1909, teachers were beginning to desert them for more professional training. In other words, teaching was becoming a profession.

County Institutes

The teachers county institute was, at best, an extended normal providing information, enthusiasm, and a smattering of professional training. In fact, as an itinerate teacher-training institution, it provided about all of the professional training teachers received. At its worst, it was a compulsory five-day ordeal.

Although all active teachers, beginning in 1877, were required to attend at least one county institute annually, prior to 1879 the Legislature made no appropriation to maintain them. Between 1879 and 1895, their total annual state allowance amounted to only $500. As this was wholly inadequate, county institutes would have been abandoned but for aid from the Peabody Fund, which, prior to 1879, financed them entirely. In an effort to improve the quality of the personnel, they were gradually supplemented by Peabody institutes concerned primarily with the training of institute instructors and financed entirely by the Peabody Fund.

The Legislature increased the annual allowance to $1,000 in 1895 and to $3,000 in 1899. After 1895, however, the Peabody Fund gave decreasing sums, and beginning in 1903 this money was used by the state superintendent largely as a reserve to pay special lecturers.

Compensation tended to be standardized at $25 per week for each instructor, and the total cost for any county was limited to $100.

Following an 1877 act abolishing district institutes, the teachers county institute entered its heyday and remained highly popular where county superintendents and institute instructors were zealous and capable. The annual attendance increased from 4,410 in 1881 to a peak of 9,936 in 1899.

"The graded course of institute work," covering a 2-year period in both academic and professional subjects, was almost as important as the institute itself. Under an 1879 act, the state superintendent was required to prescribe a course of study for all institutes. It was mainly academic for the first dozen years, but in 1891, the Legislature prescribed that it be a professional course embracing "history of education, school management, methods of teaching, and educational psychology." This, seemingly, put the legislators and the politicians in advance of the educators in this respect.

By the turn of the century, a number of factors were contributing to the declining influence of the county institute. Most important, there was a scarcity of both instructors and a high quality of instruction. Reflecting a national trend, teachers wanted instruction that was more specialized and readily transferable to their classrooms. They also objected to institutes held in midsummer. In 1901, the Legislature passed an act that not only required county superintendents to organize and conduct district institutes, but also paid teachers to attend them. A number of counties began organizing district institutes during the 1901-1902 school year, and these, supplemented by round tables, were increasingly favored.

Curriculum

Since instruction was organized primarily around textbooks, their selection was of great importance. From 1863 to 1865, elementary school textbook selection was the responsibility of the county superintendent, who was required to obtain uniformity "as far as practicable." This proved to be most difficult, however, and criticisms of constant changes in textbooks and the resulting expense prompted the Legislature to require the state superintendent to "prescribe a series of textbooks to be used in the free schools." Superintendent White complied, but too often local schools ignored the statute. An attempt to make noncompliance a misdemeanor was rejected as interference with parental authority.

In 1873, the Legislature itself prescribed a uniform series of textbooks. Six years later, it modified the act to authorize the state superintendent to contract for the prescribed list for 5 years and to ensure that the quality and cost would be maintained. The basic features of this act are still in force. In 1882, maximum prices were fixed for some textbooks, and in 1885, school boards were required to purchase and keep available a reasonable supply of textbooks.

In 1895, the practice of supplying textbooks through local merchants was replaced by a statewide depository system. Under provisions of this act, the Governor appointed a commission to select and contract for needed texts when no acceptable contracts with publishers could be made. Unfortunately, this resulted in such confusion that it strengthened the hand of those who favored adoption by local units. Two years later, in 1897, textbook selection was returned to a bipartisan board appointed by the county court, consisting of the county superintendent, three active teachers, and four nonteaching freeholders. This system also proved to be fallible as charges of favoritism and corruption became prevalent.

County Superintendent Alexander L. Wade of Monongalia County published a graded course of study and graduating system for county schools in book form in 1881, and, with modifications, it was adopted immediately by many states as well as by several counties in West Virginia. It was not, however, authorized on a statewide basis in West Virginia until 10 years later. This 1891 legislative act required the state superintendent to prescribe "a manual and graded course of primary instruction" for county and village schools, to arrange the order of study of the several branches and the time to be devoted to each, and to provide for the advancement of pupils from grade to grade and their graduation upon the successful completion of the course. At the same time, the law required bookkeeping and civil government to be taught after July 1892, along with courses in orthography, reading, penmanship, arithmetic, English grammar, U.S. history, general history, state history, and physiology and hygiene.

State Superintendent Virgil A. Lewis, in his efforts to establish a state system as contemplated in the constitution, put the new system into effect with zeal and resourcefulness. Despite the fact that the free public schools had functioned for more than a quarter century, no effort had been made to standardize them except through the use of common textbooks. Thus, there had developed about as many different practices as there were teachers. Superintendent Lewis attempted to remedy this in part by publishing in 1894 a *Manual and Graded Course of Study for County and Village Schools.* It was immediately popular and in general use by 1896.

Uniformity was achieved in part by extending the school term and requiring attendance. The school month, which had varied from 20 to 22 days, was standardized at 20 days in 1887. Eight years later, in 1895, the 4-month minimum school term was raised to 5 months, although local voters could elect to have a longer term.

The state's first compulsory attendance law, enacted in 1879, proved disappointing. Not only did it contain inadequate definitions, but since the law could be suspended by 60 percent of the voters of any school unit, considerable overt resistance nullified it in many areas.

High Schools

In 1865, the Legislature gave boards of education authority to establish graded schools offering courses of study equivalent to those of the best high schools. This law was considerably strengthened in 1873 when the Legislature gave district boards of education specific authority, with the approval of three-fifths of the voters, to establish high schools and lay special levies not to exceed 30¢ on each $100 valuation for their support and maintenance. This authority was extended in 1889 to include a provision which permitted joint high schools to be established, gave more authority to boards of education in respect to high schools, and required county superintendents to report any information about them as requested by the state superintendent.

Despite these efforts, the high school, officially considered to be in 1885 "a factor of transcendent importance in the education of the people" and described as "the crown and completion of the free school system"(6), was lagging in growth behind that of many surrounding states.

In 1897, West Virginia had only 24 "so-called high schools" and was "one of the very few states without a first class high school" in the amount of work offered (7). By 1906, the number had increased "in name" to 50 or more, but in reality the few that were operating properly were in the larger towns and cities, thus perpetuating the inequalities that existed on the lower levels. Unfortunately, there were enough high schools and state-maintained secondary schools to all but kill off the old-time academies in the state, thus placing West Virginia in a worse position with respect to secondary education than other Southern states, particularly Virginia and North Carolina.

Inasmuch as high schools were then generally admitted to be the sine qua non of educational progress, reasons for their failure to develop in West Virginia are fundamental to an understanding of the state's educational history. Perhaps most important was a traditional aversion by the people to higher education, going back to a time when it was considered a patriotic duty to oppose such a system financed by them in eastern Virginia for "nabobs."

Although the growing industrialization stimulated the growth of high schools in many areas of the country, the immediate impact was just the opposite in West Virginia. Instead of completing high school, the boys accepted positions which the new economic order made available.

Undoubtedly, the graded schools contributed to the retardation. In 1904, there were more than 600, offering courses which may have extended from the kindergarten through the twelfth grade. After 1891, the required use of the graded course of study brought a degree of uniformity in the primary and elementary work, and the additional offerings, except in a few places, were considered by local citizens and boards to meet their needs and abilities. For a public accustomed to mistaking form for substance the so-called high schools were good enough.

West Virginia contained six state normals, which for the most part were only academies, and three preparatory schools for the state university. Each county had one or more private or select schools taught in the summer by the county superintendent or by persons preparing teachers for examinations, and other private schools operating actively during the school year. These schools tended to bypass the high schools and thus contributed to the failure to establish high schools which resulted in retarding the state's educational progress.

Financing secondary education was a continual problem. Before the school fund was limited and rededicated to the primary and elementary schools in 1902, its annual increments offered a possible means for constructing and maintaining high schools. By the time this source was eliminated, high schools had won increasing favor with the county providing their support. When the counties failed, the people began turning to the district units, but the financial problem remained unsolved. Whether the proposed high schools should be financed entirely by local units or be subsidized in part by the state continued to be a hotly debated question.

Summary

Throughout the nineteenth century, leadership was shifting to persons educated by public free schools, and legislative experimenting to adjust them to a society wracked by Civil War and its aftermaths culminated in a somewhat distinctive system. Under the leadership of State Superintendent William R. White and County Superintendent Alexander L. Wade, in some respects, the new state led the entire country in educational progress during Reconstruction. In 1900, Thomas C. Miller, a schoolman with a professional viewpoint and purpose, was elected to the state superintendency. Therefore, failure to keep the state in the forefront of educational progress was not due primarily to a lack of interest in popular education. More than anything else perhaps, it was a maladjustment to the Industrial Revolution. During this industrialization, progress was largely a matter of corporate initiative and control with chief interest in material gain. Unfortunately for the state's educational interests, the corporate control of its industrial economy was largely nonresident. In only a few instances did the leaders, either resident or nonresident, oppose public free schools, but the schools were of secondary rather than primary interest, as in the pre-Civil War and Reconstruction periods.

In the period beginning about 1890, there was a change in the character and technique of those who took over control of the schools. For the most part they had all been born after the Civil War, and many were followers of N. M. Butler and John Dewey. Generally, they believed that good teachers were not born to their profession and could be trained. Admittedly, natural aptitude was helpful, but it was not, as in the former period, a sine qua non. With few exceptions, their common goal was a state educational system embracing all public-supported institutions. Taking their cues from the business world, the new leaders generally believed that education could and should be administered and financed scientifically. The greatest difficulty was that it was not an immediate and obvious dividend-paying investment.

Shortly after 1880, unification of the state educational system became a common objective among the leaders. Although such a system was implied in the constitution, attainment was first proposed by State Superintendent Benjamin S. Morgan. As the absence of secondary schools was generally conceded to be the weakest link in the system, his plan included establishing public high schools throughout the state and a strong academic department in each of the state normals, thus temporarily forfeiting the legal right of the latter to become either teacher-training institutions or colleges.

As a result of the discussions on unification and teacher-training programs, two schools of thought developed: One called for a "new education"; and the other, the old school, claimed to be based on the lessons of experience. The old school generally held that teachers were born, whereas the new school believed that they could be made, even out of fishermen. In other words, the old school emphasized knowledge and aptitude, whereas the new school emphasized knowledge and teacher training. The pros and cons of each occupied the major portion of the educational journals and divided teachers and administrators into two semihostile camps. Although the old school dominated at the end of this period, the new school had gained a secure foothold.

Legislation to prevent the employment of children under 12 years of age in mines, factories, workshops, or in agriculture during the regular school session, first requested in 1887, went unheeded for two decades. In 1907, boys under 14 years of age and girls of any age were forbidden to work in coal mines.

There was a growing realization of the need for vocational education and kindergartens. In 1899 the Legislature authorized towns and villages of 1,000 or more population to establish kindergartens without the approval of the voters. Of some significance is the fact that by 1900 the number of Negro women teachers exceeded the number of men; and five years later white women teachers exceeded the number of men.

At the turn of the century, Wheeling, with 38,878 inhabitants, was the only city in West Virginia having a population more than 25,000, and 11 communities were over 4,000. Out of a state population of 958,800, 753,099 were classified as rural, 94,662 as semirural, and 111,039 as urban (defined as living in a community of over 4,000) (8). With over 75 percent of the population patronizing rural schools, it is easy to understand why there was an emphasis on agriculture education during the early 1900's.

In March 1901, at the time A. B. White succeeded George Wesley Atkinson as Governor, Thomas C. Miller replaced James Russell Trotter to become the twelfth state superintendent of free schools. In his first biennial report, he pointed out that of 312,124 youth in the state, only 235,191 were enrolled in the schools, and the average daily attendance was 150,017. There were 5,854 single-room schools, 262 graded schools, and 40 high schools, of which 5,510 were frame, 309 log, and 176 brick and stone (9).

THE DEPARTMENT'S CHANGING STRUCTURE 1900 TO 1965

The State Superintendent, 1900-19

Although the Legislature did not give the state superintendent express authority to employ assistants and other employees until 1919, he did hire a few such persons. By the end of 1904, the state department consisted of the state superintendent, two clerks, and one stenographer (10). The following year, the Legislature created a State Board of Examiners of four members, appointed by the state superintendent, to hold examinations and issue teacher certificates. He was further assisted when in 1908 the Legislature replaced this board with a State Board of Education. This board, which was composed of the state superintendent and five persons engaged in educational work appointed by the superintendent, not only performed the examining duties of the State Board of Examiners, but also prescribed courses of study for the public schools.

The number of persons in the state department remained almost constant during the first decade despite the growing number of schools. In 1910, however, with help from the Rockefeller Foundation, the Southern Education Board, and the Legislature, the state department reorganized and established new divisions of high schools, rural schools, examinations, publications, and institutes. At the same time, an assistant state superintendent was added to the staff.

The Southern Education Board provided the funds to employ the first rural school supervisor, L. J. Hanifan, who commenced his duties in July 1910 (11). For the next several years, this division concerned itself with problems of consolidation, standardization of rural schools through the use of an "efficiency score card," and district supervision. It published manuals and conducted conferences and workshops for teachers.

The Rockefeller Foundation paid the salary and expenses of the supervisor of high schools from 1910 to

1925. At the beginning of this period, there were forty 4-year high schools, twenty 3-year high schools, twelve 2-year high schools, and nine schools offering 1 year of secondary work (12).

In 1911, the Legislature divided the high schools into three classes. The law stated that it "shall be the duty of the state superintendent of schools to classify all of the high schools of the state in accordance with the provisions of the act"(13). The high schools division assumed the responsibility for making the classifications.

This division's responsibilities increased dramatically in 1926, when West Virginia's colleges and secondary schools affiliated with the North Central Association of Colleges and Secondary Schools. The inspections, correspondence, reports, and general supervision required to bring the schools to association standards involved considerable work.

When the National Vocational Education Act (Smith-Hughes) was passed in 1917, the Legislature immediately accepted its provisions and designated the State Board of Regents to be in charge of this program. This board, created in 1909 to exercise full control over the educational departments of several state institutions, appointed an administrative and supervisory staff to incorporate vocational programs into the educational system.

The 1919 Reorganization

In 1919, the Legislature passed an act which had a tremendous impact on both the State Department of Education and the public schools. The law specifically provided for assistants by stating:

> For carrying into effect the provision of this chapter the State Superintendent of Schools shall maintain a department of public schools at his office in the State Capitol, and shall have authority to employ assistants and such other employees as may be necessary, including a state supervisor of colored schools (14).

The 1919 law required the state superintendent to prescribe and print forms necessary for carrying out the details of the school systems and distribute them to school officers. He was to prepare and publish course of study manuals and to see that minimum standards were maintained in the several grades of the public schools. He was made responsible for preparing and publishing a list of books suitable for school libraries, copies of the school law, as well as those reports, circulars, and bulletins that he believed would promote the best interest of the schools. Since the Legislature met every 2 years, the state superintendent was to report to the Governor—and thus to the Legislature—biennially (15).

The Act of 1919 abolished the State Board of Regents, the State Board of Education, and the State School Book Commission, and it created a seven-member Board of Education, with the state superintendent a member ex officio and its chief executive officer. The other six members were appointed by the Governor.

The Department's Growth, 1920-68

By 1920, the state department consisted of the state superintendent, assistant state superintendent, supervisor of rural schools, supervisor of high schools, assistant supervisor of high schools, supervisor of Negro schools, supervisor of examinations, director of vocational education, supervisor of vocational agriculture, supervisor of home economics, supervisor of trade and industrial education, and supervisor of mining education, along with essential clerical staff. Because the Legislature had not provided state funds for administering and supervising vocational education, the secretary of the state board served as director of vocational education, and the four supervisors were "borrowed" from the faculty of the West Virginia University (16).

During the following decade, the state department added the following staff: supervisor of physical education, supervisor of certification, supervisor of teacher training, director of educational research, statistician, assistant director of vocational education, supervisor of vocational agriculture, assistant supervisor of vocational agriculture, supervisor of home economics, and supervisor of trade and industrial education. After 1938, instead of being listed by title only, the members were listed by divisions. The divisions in 1940 included general administration, high schools, elementary schools (until 1933, rural schools), certification, research, Negro schools, vocational education, and vocational rehabilitation. By 1950, divisions had been added in school transportation, school plant planning, school lunch, and veterans education and training.

The 1933 Legislature enacted one of the most far-reaching laws in the history of West Virginia education when it established the county unit plan of organization. The school law was amended to read: "A school district shall include all the territory in one county. Existing magisterial school districts and sub-districts and independent districts are abolished"(17). These two sentences of the amendment abolished 54 independent school districts and 344 magisterial school districts, replacing them with 55 county school districts—one for each county in the state.

Beginning in 1952, the state inaugurated an extensive study of the educational program and its relation to the people in three pilot counties—Greenbrier, Marion, and Mercer. With a limited grant from the W. K. Kellogg Foundation, the study was conducted under the auspices of the West Virginia Association of School Superintendents and the West Virginia Committee of the Cooperative Program in Educational Administration, the latter composed of representatives from the state department, the institutions of higher education, and the state's professional associations. The Southern States Cooperative Program in Educational Administration and the boards of education of the three counties involved supplied the consultative services.

At the end of 5 years, the West Virginia Continuing Program in Educational Leadership assumed all projects being conducted by the West Virginia Cooperative Program in Educational Administration. Supported by a second grant from the W. K. Kellogg Foundation, the state committee, together with the state department, continued to sponsor the study.

In June 1955, the West Virginia Department of Education entered into an agreement with the Kellogg Foundation whereby the state superintendent would serve as the executive officer to receive grants from the Kellogg Foundation, which, in turn, would provide him with an office and a secretary for the director. The grants received were to be distributed under the direction and supervision of the West Virginia Executive Committee for the Cooperative Program in Educational Leadership.

A change of major and far-reaching significance occurred in the state superintendent's office in 1958, when an amendment to the constitution provided that—

> The general supervision of the free schools of the state shall be vested in the West Virginia Board of Education which shall perform such duties as may be prescribed by law. The Board shall consist of nine members to be appointed by the Governor by and with the advice and consent of the Senate (18).

The State Board of Education was given the responsibility of appointing the state superintendent of free schools, and he was removed as a member of the board. He did, however, retain his membership on the Board of Public Works. This amendment helped to ensure that future state superintendents would be professionally qualified and would be partially insulated from political pressures. It also reduced the opportunity for conflict between the state superintendent and the state board.

Financing Education

The first West Virginia Constitution, ratified in 1863, provided for a School Fund to be set aside from all money accruing to the state from the proceeds of forfeited and delinquent lands; lands sold for taxes; grants, devices, and bequests; corporate taxes; money paid as exemption from military duty; and sums appropriated by the Legislature. Under regulations prescribed by law, this fund was to be invested in interest-bearing securities of the United States and West Virginia; this interest was to be used for no other purpose than the support of the free schools.

Under a new constitution ratified in August 1872, the 1872-73 Legislature created a Board of the School Fund, composed of the Governor, the state superintendent of free schools, the auditor, and the treasurer, to administer the fund. This board was given the responsibility for investing the money in bonds, but if such securities were not available it could purchase other solvent interest-bearing securities. By 1900, the School Fund was receiving annually from $45,000 to $56,000.

A constitutional amendment ratified in 1902 limited the School Fund to $1 million, which remained the limitation in 1965. During the Depression years of the 1930's, there were losses in the fund due to bankruptcy, but it was built back to the $1 million mark in later years. In the 1965-66 school year, the fund received $55,700, which was transferred to the General School Fund.

The 1872-73 Legislature also created the General School Fund as an added source of revenue for the public schools. Its money was derived from a state tax of 10¢ on each $100 valuation of all real and personal property of the state, interest on the invested School Fund, confiscations and fines accruing to the state, the proceeds from the annual capitation tax, and interest on investments in U.S. bonds. In subsequent years, funds from many other sources were deposited in the General School Fund, including those allotted by the federal government to the state for educational purposes.

The General School Fund supplied the salary and other expenses of the state superintendent, as well as other sums he found necessary to expend. After these deductions, the state auditor certified the net amount to the state superintendent, who in turn annually distributed these moneys to the cities and counties on the basis of school enumeration.

Along with the School Fund and General School Fund, the schools were supported by local levies voted by boards of education of magisterial and independent school districts, which went into separate accounts referred to as the Teachers Fund and the Building Fund. In 1908, the Legislature authorized the Board of Public Works to divert $50,000 of the General School Fund to supplement the salaries of teachers in districts which could not maintain minimum terms under the existing maximum levies. The following year, it increased this supplementary fund to $75,000 for teachers and $15,000 for buildings. To cover these items, together with additional expenditures of the State Department of Education and a contemplated increase in the county superintendents' salaries in 1909, the Legislature fixed the General School Fund at $750,000. At the same time, it directed the Board of Public Works to transfer the necessary state funds to keep it at that figure.

The General School Fund remained at this level during the next decade, although the Legislature added about $75,000 in case of need. The $75,000 supplementary aid to teachers and the $15,000 supplementary aid to the Building Fund did not change. However, the demands for additional funds for teachers' salaries, district supervision, and standard schools prompted the 1921 Legislature to add $1 million to the General School Fund.

From 1921 to 1931, the General School Fund ranged from $2 million to $2.5 million. It was used to pay the expenses of the state department and the salaries of the county superintendents, to supplement teachers funds and maintenance funds in districts unable to meet the minimum requirements with their maximum levies, to aid the high schools, and to help magisterial school districts maintain standard schools. The remainder—and larger sum—was distributed to the school districts on a per-pupil basis.

The state superintendent continued to allot the General School Fund to school districts until the Legislature created the Board of School Finance in 1939. This board, composed of the state superintendent of free schools (chairman), the state tax commissioner, and the director of the budget, assumed the responsibility for allotting and distributing state aid.

Prior to the tax limitation amendment in 1933, the distributable amounts paid to local school boards from the General School Fund provided about 5 percent of the total cost of elementary and secondary education in West Virginia. The loss of local revenues after 1933, the heart of the Depression, forced the state to increase its aid to county boards of education. The state continued to assume an ever-increasing share of the public school costs, so that by 1965, it was providing approximately 53 percent of the total.

VARIOUS DEPARTMENTAL FUNCTIONS

Teacher Certification

Legislation relating to uniform examinations for teachers enacted by the 1903 session of the Legislature had placed the responsibility for preparing and grading examinations and granting certificates with the state superintendent. To discharge this function the state department established a Division of Examinations in 1910, primarily to conduct the uniform examinations for teachers, grade the manuscripts, and issue certificates. That year, there were 12,792 applicants for these examinations. Of this number, 280 were issued No. 1 certificates, 2,143 were issued No. 2 certificates, 2,833 were issued No. 3 certificates, and 327 certificates were renewed. This means that 5,970 failed and 1,239 were not issued. The state superintendent also issued 251 uniform certificates to graduates of the state normal schools and the state university. The three types of certificates were based on the scores made on the uniform examinations with those making scores in the upper bracket receiving the No. 1 certificate, those in the next bracket receiving the No. 2 certificate, and those receiving scores in the lowest passing bracket receiving the No. 3 certificates.

At the end of the following decade, in 1920, out of 4,710 applicants in the uniform examinations, 3,475 received certificates. At the same time, 568 received certificates upon graduation from schools maintaining approved normal school courses, of which 295 were from state schools, 55 from private and denominational schools, and 218 from teacher-training high schools.

In 1924, the Division of Examinations became the Division of Teacher Training. Two years later, it was changed to the Division of Certification, as it was now mainly concerned with certifying teachers based on graduation from approved schools and raising the professional standards for teaching. By 1930, only 977 certificates were issued through the uniform examination.

During the period from 1930 to 1940, teacher preparation programs were generally based on course and semester hour requirements. Courses were required which were generally thought to provide certain competencies essential for teaching success. The relationship between teacher preparation and teacher certification was not clearly defined, and teacher certification was often regarded as a mere counting of courses and credit hours. In 1941-45, the department participated in a study of standards for teacher preparation and certification. Other participants in this study were representatives of the state's institutions of higher education and of the public schools. The study resulted in new minimum standards for teacher preparation and certification adopted by the State Board of Education in 1945. These standards were generally limited to the completion of a prescribed number of semester hours in an approved college or university with a minimum number of hours specified in general education, professional education, and subject or area specializations.

One of the distinctive developments resulting from this study was the creation of a so-called "single curriculum" for teachers in grades 1 through 12. However, as the institutions of higher education were not generally enthusiastic about this concept, it did not enjoy widespread use. This study resulted also in a clearer understanding of the relationship of teacher preparation to teacher certification, and the two functions were consequently combined in the Division of Teacher Preparation and Professional Standards.

During the decade 1950-60, consideration was given to reducing the number of types of teaching certificates. The result was the adoption of the professional certificate with endorsement appropriate to a particular level or area of specialization consistent with the program completed.

The standards developed in the 1941-45 study, with certain modifications, remained in effect until a new study was undertaken under the leadership of the Division of Teacher Preparation and Professional Standards in 1960. This latter study resulted in an "approved programs" approach to teacher preparation and certification. This pattern called for the adoption by the state board of minimum standards for institutional training programs; the development of programs by institutions approved by the state board; and institutional recommendation of candidates for certification. By 1965, practically all the colleges and universities in the state were approved under such programs, and the others were in the process of preparing programs eligible for state board approval.

The approved programs approach placed greater emphasis on a close working relationship between the department in its teacher preparation function and the preparing institutions. It proved difficult for one person to administer the certification process and have adequate time to work effectively with the colleges and universities. The Division of Teacher Preparation and Professional Standards was, therefore, divided in 1968 into two divisions—the Division of Teacher Preparation and the Division of Teacher Certification. Both divisions remained in the Bureau of Instruction, but, in view of the volume and importance of their work, consideration was being given to the creation of a separate bureau composed of these divisions.

Textbooks

"The fifty-fifth section of our school law prescribes a fixed series of school books to be used in the free public schools in the state—and a particular textbook is prescribed for each branch of study to the exclusion of all others"(19). Thus it was from the inception of the public school system in 1863 until the selection of textbooks by the county adoption system, enacted in 1897. So much criticism arose that in 1904 the state superintendent reported a strong trend in favor of state uniformity. It was 1909, however, before the Legislature created a State Textbook Commission, consisting of the state superintendent and eight citizens, five of whom were required to be active educators. The commission was authorized to adopt one book or a series of books for each subject to be used for 5-year periods. The independent districts or towns of 3,500 or more population were granted the right to make their own selections. In 1919, the commission's duties were transferred to the state board.

Despite earlier experiences, the West Virginia Education Association had pressed, for several years prior to legislative approval, for resumption of local adoptions on the grounds that no one textbook was appropriate for all counties. It believed that state adoption of a multiple list of textbooks would ensure quality as well as diversity at the local level.

The profession finally prevailed, and the law was changed in 1953. With subsequent slight modifications, this is the procedure in effect today (20). State committees of educators recommend the books to be included on the multiple list for each subject to the state board, and, after adoption, county committees of teachers select their texts from the state list. The books are adopted for 4 years on a rotating plan, which results in some subjects' being considered each year.

County boards of education in West Virginia have been authorized to supply free textbooks since 1903. In 1935, Governor H. Guy Kump placed $1 million in the biennial budget for publicly owned textbooks written by persons employed by the state, but the funds were diverted by the Legislature for teachers' salaries and school maintenance.

Since 1939, county boards have been required to supply free textbooks to public schools for pupils whose parents cannot afford to purchase them, and they may supply state-adopted textbooks for pupils in private schools under similar circumstances. At the same time these statutes were enacted, the Legislature established an appropriation of $150,000.

Interest in a free textbook program has not been maintained at the state level as the appropriation has generally been unchanged. There is now a growing belief that the program is an integral part of a free school system, but implementation of this concern has been left to the counties.

Pupil Transportation and Driver Education

Although the state department collected data from county school systems, such as the number of pupils transported, the number of buses in use, and transportation costs, it was not until the 1936-37 school year that state supervision was provided. The department revised standards, established regulations, and sent out report forms. It commenced holding county conferences on the organization and administration of pupil transportation and checking all bids submitted to county boards for the purchase of buses.

In the 1942-44 biennium, the first full-time state supervisor of school transportation was appointed. At the same time, safety was given a special emphasis. The State Board of Education adopted new minimum standards for design and equipment of school buses which became effective the following year. These standards were revised in 1961 and again in 1965. In recent years, emphasis of the Division of School Transportation has been directed toward improvement in uniformity of transportation practices and equipment; relief of overloads on buses; safety practices; improved scheduling for equalizing the school day for transported pupils; and training of drivers and supervisory personnel.

During the early 1940's, the Department of Education cooperated with the Department of Public Safety in encouraging and promoting driver education in the public schools. In 1945, the two departments presented *A Course of Study in Driver Education for Secondary Schools* (21), and interest continued to grow. By 1948 the program justified employing a full-time director.

Under the leadership of the state director, the first statewide conference on driver education was held at Jackson's Mill in April 1950. This resulted in a revision of the earlier *Course of Study*. At a workshop conference in 1957, the course was again revised as *A Course of Study in Driver and Traffic Safety Education for West Virginia High Schools* (22).

Research and Surveys

From 1900, the department had staff members responsible for carrying on educational research, collecting and tabulating school statistics, and publishing the results. The name of the section changed at different times, but it was officially established as the Division of Investigation and Statistics in July 1926. The General Education Board of the Rockefeller Foundation paid the salary of the director, his traveling expenses, and the expense of a stenographer for a period of 7 years.

In 1927, the Legislature appropriated $20,000 to employ experts in various educational fields to make the first survey of West Virginia's public schools. Under the direction of L. V. Cavins, a member of the state department, the survey was conducted during 1928 and 1929. The results, published in four volumes, covered organization, administration, and finance; educational achievements; school buildings; and institutions of higher education (23).

State department staff members have not been involved directly with the remaining three surveys, but they have provided statistics and other information the survey staffs have needed. George D. Strayer directed a survey published in 1945 as *A Report of a Survey of Public Education in the State of West Virginia* (24). Under Project Director E. L. Lindman, the Division of Surveys and Field Services of George Peabody College for Teachers conducted a survey in 1956 (25), and E. K. Feaster directed another survey that was published the following year (26).

Since the above studies dealt with different facets of the state's educational enterprise, recommendations resulting from them showed varying emphases. Some of the more significant recommendations which emerged from one or more of the studies advocated further school consolidation, added emphasis on vocational education, initiation of a state-supported system of kindergartens, more adequate guidance services in the high schools and junior high schools, better physical facilities, and allocation of functions among the higher education institutions of the state through a reorganization of the administrative structure.

The regular session of the Legislature in 1955 authorized a survey of higher education which was conducted under the direction of John E. Brewton at the invitation of the Joint Committee on Government and Finance, Commission on Interstate Cooperation, and the Citizens Advisory Committee. Published in 1956 under the title *Public Higher Education in West Virginia*, this study related principally to the organization and control of higher education, enrollment projections, teacher education, and financing public higher education in the state.

The 1966 session of the Legislature authorized a study of higher education to emphasize the allocation of functions among the various colleges and universities to be made by a Committee on Higher Education composed of the membership of the State Board of Education, the Board of Governors of West Virginia University, and the State Association of College and University Presidents. This committee reported its recommendations to the Legislature in late 1966, recommending a complete reorganization of higher education under a board of regents. Bills embodying these recommendations were introduced to the 1967 session of the Legislature but were not enacted, and further study of the organization of higher education is continuing.

Publications

Since the nineteenth century, the state department has published materials that have had an impact on the schools either directly or through the Legislature. Some have been required by law, such as the reports of the state superintendent mentioned earlier. The state law also required the state superintendent to print copies of the school law in sufficient quantities for distribution to school officials and other citizens. State Superintendent Thomas C. Miller printed the first copies in 1903.

In 1904, a *History of Education* (27) was prepared under the direction of the state superintendent for distribution at the Louisiana Purchase Exposition at St. Louis, Missouri, and throughout the state, particularly to the school libraries. A revised edition was issued in 1907, when 2,500 copies were published for distribution at the Jamestown, Virginia, Exposition.

From time to time the state department issued bulletins on particular subjects. In 1934, it began the monthly publication of an educational bulletin. The first three numbers were mimeographed, but subsequent issues were printed. Once each year a special statistical number was issued, and other "specials" have appeared from time to time. The department terminated the regular monthly or bimonthly publication of this bulletin in 1958.

The state department has published courses of study for high schools, junior high schools, elementary schools, and one- and two-room rural schools. It has issued requirements for certifying school personnel, administrators, supervisors, and teachers; rules and regulations of the state board regarding school transportation and schoolhouse construction; and standards for classifying schools. It also has published handbooks and songbooks for teachers institutes and source books for teachers in most subjects at the various grade levels.

The department has issued school directories up to the present, listing the state and county school personnel. Although earlier ones did not list persons below principals, later ones list all administrators, supervisors, and teaching personnel employed by boards of education. Probably the most significant current publication of the department is the annual report of the state superintendent.

In the last decade, the work of the publications office has shown a dramatic increase in volume. It would be impractical to attempt to list all of these publications, but reference to some of them is made in other sections. Much of this volume had consisted of curriculum guides for use by local school systems. Typical of these publications are curriculum guides in science, mathematics, music, and foreign languages (28).

The School Lunch Program

In the early 1930's, a few West Virginia schools established school lunch programs. Later, with aid from the Food Distribution Administration and supervision by the Works Progress Administration after 1935, these school lunch programs expanded considerably. The WPA even took over the supervision of the programs of gardening and canning along with the school lunches, while the Food Distribution Administration provided the surplus food for the lunches.

In March 1942, the WPA relinquished supervision of all projects. To assist counties in continuing these programs after the WPA's withdrawal, the state department obtained an appropriation of $18,000 from the Legislature for the remainder of the fiscal year. For the following year, 1944-45, the Legislature appropriated $100,000 to aid the counties and $6,500 for the state department to employ a state supervisor of school lunch and to pay other expenses for a new School Lunch Division.

In June 1946, Congress passed Public Law 396, which appropriated funds to help schools maintain school lunch programs. The funds allotted to West Virginia were channeled through the state department. As the responsibilities of the School Lunch Division increased, the state appropriation increased until it was able to take over the complete supervision of the lunch programs in 1947-48. By this time, the division had four assistant supervisors and additional clerical help.

In 1954, following an act by Congress making federal funds available to the states for promoting the use of whole milk in the public schools, this special program became an important phase of the West Virginia school lunch program. The state school lunch staff was responsible for its promotion.

Beginning in 1947, the division inaugurated a series of workshops for county supervisors, teachers, cooks, and other county personnel working in the program. These workshops became an annual activity. In-service and preservice training programs designed to improve the professional level of all school food service personnel were developed in cooperation with county boards of education during the period 1960-65. During the 1966-67 school year, the school lunch branch worked with the Bureau of Vocational Education in developing and initiating adult education programs for school food service personnel (29).

School Plant Planning

During the 1942-44 biennium, the state department employed John E. Marshall as supervisor in the Division of Surveys and Schoolhouse Planning. By the next biennium, he was director of the Division of Research and Schoolhouse Planning, which in 1949 was divided into research and school plant planning. A publication entitled *Standards for Schoolhouse Construction* (30) was published in 1945 and revised for distribution in January 1951.

The state department did not have a specialist in school plant planning from 1955 to 1958, when the National Defense Education Act enabled it to employ a director in this capacity.

In 1960, the state department published the *Handbook on Planning School Facilities* (31). In 1962, the division cooperated in a federally sponsored inventory of the state's school facilities. The data gathered by this study formed the basis for a perpetual inventory of school plant property which has since been maintained.

During the school year 1966-67, the division renewed its participation in the annual Interstate Building Conference conducted by George Peabody College for Teachers.

As required by state law, the division continues to approve plans for school building, construction, and repair throughout the state. The extent of this work is reflected in the fact that during 1966-67, 97 sets of plans and specifications for new construction, additions, or renovations were reviewed and approved.

Surplus Property

In July 1945, the state department created a Division of Surplus Property to locate and obtain surplus property from the armed forces for the state's schools. During the following biennium, the division secured surplus property valued at $1,718,000 for the vocational and high schools in 55 counties, the colleges, and other eligible organizations.

The Legislature enacted a law, effective in June 1949, designating the State Department of Purchases as the sole agency in West Virginia authorized to receive and distribute property available for educational purposes. Thus, in June 1950, the Division of Surplus Property ceased to exist. But during the period from July 1945 to June 1950, the division had distributed surplus property valued at nearly $4 million.

VARIOUS EDUCATIONAL PROGRAMS

Vocational Education

In February 1917, President Woodrow Wilson approved the first National Vocational Education Act (Smith-Hughes), and in May 1917, the West Virginia Legislature passed an act accepting its provisions and benefits. The acceptance act designated the Board of Regents–after 1919, the Board of Education–as the State Vocational Board to carry out the Smith-Hughes Act in West Virginia.

From 1900 to 1946, the state superintendent served as president of the State Vocational Board; after 1946, he was a member of the board and its executive officer. Thus, from the beginning, there was a legal connection between the state board and the state department through the state superintendent. This connection was not always a close one, depending on how the state superintendent, the board, or the vocational personnel viewed the association.

The Smith-Hughes Act appropriated funds to enable the states to promote the study of agriculture, home economics, trade and industrial education, and for training teachers in these fields. Subsequent additional appropriations by Congress for vocational education, such as the George-Barden Act of 1946 which added distributive education, resulted in considerable expansion of vocational education programs. Thus, the state board appointed a director of vocational education, supervisors in the different fields, and office personnel to help it carry out its responsibilities.

The first allotment of federal funds to West Virginia, $21,722, came in the 1917-18 school year. Four members of the West Virginia University faculty agreed to help the state board inaugurate classes for adult farmers, tradesmen, homemakers, and other adults.

Beginning in the year 1921-22, the Legislature appropriated $25,000 for vocational education and increased the amount until it was $970,067 for 1964-65, including $500,000 for the area vocational education program.

As more federal and state funds for vocational education became available, the duties and responsibilities of the Division of Vocational Education increased proportionately. From time to time, special funds became available–adding to the personnel's work load–for food preservation, training war production workers, and various training programs for World War II and Korean veterans.

The George-Barden Act of 1946 added distributive education as an area qualifying for federal support. The most significant recent development in vocational education resulted from the National Vocational Act of 1963. This act focused attention on the needs of individuals such as (a) the unemployed youth, (b) the high school dropout, (c) the disadvantaged individual, and (d) the displaced worker.

By 1964, vocational education was administered by the Bureau of Vocational, Technical, and Adult Education, reflecting the Vocational Education Act of 1963. In addition to the bureau head, this bureau also employed supervisors of trade and industrial education, technical education, vocational agriculture, vocational home economics, and distributive education as well as supervisors of area vocational programs and area redevelopment training.

The 1967 Legislature authorized a study of vocational, technical, and adult education by the Joint Committee on Government and Finance. This study was prepared under the direction of the Bureau of Vocational Education and Joseph T. Nerden of the Department of Industrial and Technical Education of North Carolina State University. The report was completed in 1968 for presentation to the 1969 session of the Legislature. It projected the need for vocational education throughout the state and recommended, among other things, a considerable expansion of vocational education at the secondary school level; occupational education for post-high school youth; creation of a coordinating council for all aspects of vocational education in the state which would be advisory to the West Virginia Board of Education; an increase in adult basic education programs; and additional emphasis on the development of a statewide system of area vocational and technical schools (32).

Vocational Rehabilitation

In April 1921, the Legislature provided for cooperation with the U.S. government in the vocational rehabilitation of the physically disabled citizens of the state. The law authorized the state board to organize a Division of Rehabilitation. The following year, in 1922, the division was organized within the State Department of Education with State Director J. F. Marsh assisted by five special agents.

From 1922 to 1933, Marsh served as director, being replaced in that year by the assistant state superintendent of schools, who remained in that position until 1945 when the Legislature passed a vocational rehabilitation act making the organization a separate unit of the state board instead of a division of the state department.

Veterans Education

During the 1944-46 biennium, the state department established a Division of Veterans Education with H. L. Duncan as director. It was charged with the responsibility of assisting school administrators, supervisors, and teachers in organizing their programs to give maximum opportunity to returning veterans who wanted additional education and training. It also was required to approve establishments offering on-the-job training to returning veterans.

In 1946, 16 field representatives were employed to handle the inspection, approval, and supervision of on-the-job training. In the same year, D. F. Cronin became state supervisor of the program.

The education and training program for World War II veterans ended July 1956. However, in 1952, the Korean GI Bill had been enacted by Congress, and, as in preceding years, the Division of Veterans Education and Training was the approval agency under contract with the Veterans Administration.

The work of this division increased dramatically under the impact of the Vietnam conflict, which resulted in the passage by Congress of Public Law 90-77 relating to education of veterans of this war. In 1968, the Division of Veterans Education and Training, in addition to the director, was employing three field representatives to supervise the education of Vietnam veterans.

Special Education

The state department inaugurated a program of teaching homebound crippled children in 1941. The Legislature appropriated $22,500 for 106 teachers to care for 320 children in 32 counties. By the end of 1946, the number of homebound children taught was 278, and in 1951 it was 530, including a small group of mentally handicapped. There were then 19 full-time and 176 part-time teachers employed in 40 counties, and the state appropriation of $60,000 was insufficient to meet the demand.

The 1955 Legislature appropriated $100,000, including the salary of a state supervisor of special education, for programs for exceptional children. The programs initiated or continued during the years immediately following included the physically handicapped and mentally retarded children placed in special classes and home instruction services for children too handicapped to attend classes. The department, in 1956, held a series of workshops for teachers of the deaf and blind, the physically handicapped, and for the mentally retarded. By 1960, 48 counties were participating in special education programs. Programs provided included psychological evaluations, special class programs organized according to need, home instruction programs, a telephone instruction program, a program for the blind and visually handicapped, and an excess cost program which provided special equipment not ordinarily found in regular classrooms.

Title I of the Elementary and Secondary Education Act, which was implemented in the state in 1966, provided additional funds for special education. During that year, 32 new special classes for mentally retarded were added to those already in operation under other funding. In addition to programs previously mentioned, county systems were providing 17 speech and hearing therapists or correctionists, and the department was administering a grant program for preparation of professional personnel in the education of handicapped children under the provisions of Public Law 85-926 and Public Law 88-164.

The Comprehensive Educational Program

During the period 1955-1960, the department designed a proposal to encourage local school systems to go beyond minimum requirements in the provision and operation of educational programs. This proposal, designed to stimulate greater financial effort by the counties and referred to as the "Incentive Plan," was presented in a report to the Governor and Legislature in 1958 (33). The basic feature of this plan provided for state matching of local funds raised for education over and above those which could be secured by applying the regular levy rates to existing valuations. The proposal sought to stimulate higher property valuations. To qualify, a local educational agency would be required to present a 5-year plan of program improvement contemplated with these added funds. Implementation of the proposal required a legislative appropriation of $12 million in addition to the regular appropriation of school aid under the formula then in effect.

Although the Incentive Plan was never implemented by the Legislature, the incentive concept remained very much alive. State department personnel, as well as many county school administrators, were convinced of the necessity for some such approach of raising the quality of local educational programs. With the enthusiastic support of the county school superintendents, the department designed a somewhat similar proposal known as the Comprehensive Educational Program, which was submitted to the 1965 Legislature.

This proposal received a more favorable reception. The 1965 Legislature amended the code by adding a new section relating to a comprehensive educational program and providing financial support for it. Essentially, this was an innovative incentive program providing funds of $1 million for upgrading, diversifying, and broadening county educational programs beyond minimum requirements. The law stated the following:

> The State Board of Education, through the State Superintendent of Schools, shall establish standards and criteria especially designed to guide the development of plans for a comprehensive educational program, or programs; to provide for their evaluation and approval; and for the allocation and distribution of State funds which may be appropriated to assist county school systems to meet additional costs of development and operation of such programs (34).

The law further required the state superintendent to provide assistance to counties in developing and preparing their plans for a comprehensive education program to ensure that every county would have the opportunity to fully participate and receive its maximum share of the available funds.

The state department assigned this program its top priority to fulfill the responsibility placed upon it by the law. By 1966, 65 subject or service area plans had been approved or were on file in the state department committing counties to progress toward the Comprehensive Educational Program goals. Much of the state department's work was in helping local administrators and teachers implement their plans.

The department continued to request greater financial support to permit complete implementation of the Comprehensive Educational Program, but through 1968 the level of funding remained at $1 million annually.

EMERGING ROLES OF THE DEPARTMENT

Administration–Services–Leadership

The preceding sections indicate that the West Virginia Department of Education has evolved from a one-man operation to an organization large enough to be divided into a number of divisions, each with a professional staff consistent with its responsibilities. While this evolution has occupied approximately a century, it has accelerated rapidly in recent years. For example, the professional members of the department numbered 19 in 1946 (35); by 1961, members had been added requiring a reorganization into bureaus (36); and by 1966, the department listed 86 professional positions, although some of them were vacant (37). A number of factors are responsible for this transition, among them an increase in school population, the consolidation of school districts in 1933, and the rapid shift in financial support for education from the local district to the state level. This shift stemmed largely from a constitutional amendment voted in 1932 which limited the tax rate that could be levied on all classes of property.

It is probable, however, that the most significant developments in the department have resulted from changes in philosophy as to the role which the department should play in the overall educational operation of the state.

In general, the department, during the first 50 years of its existence, was concerned with discharging administrative and regulatory functions. These included such activities as collecting data for the state superintendent's annual report, distributing state funds which were negligible when compared to current state financial support, certifying teachers, interpreting legislative acts and state board regulations, and making sure that local school agencies complied with them.

It was not until the period from 1920 to 1930 that the department began to devote significant amounts of time to the service function. In this period, teacher certification by examination showed a rapid decline, and the department began working much more closely with the colleges in developing procedures for certificating their graduates. In this decade also, the first broad survey of public education was conducted by the department. In the decade 1930-40, supervisory services from the state level were provided in the school lunch and pupil transportation programs, and the first regular department bulletins were issued. Departmental services in the areas of school plant planning and surplus property administration were not initiated until after 1940.

Although the department gradually devoted an increasing proportion of its time and energy to service activities, it continued to discharge its administrative and regulatory functions. This assumption of an expanding service role naturally resulted in the addition of departmental personnel and some revisions in departmental structure which are reflected in the personnel listed for the department in the reports of the state superintendent from about 1925 to 1950.

Even while the service function was assuming a dominant position in the work of the department, a third category of departmental activities was beginning to emerge. Naturally, from its inception the department had been discharging some functions which involved leadership, but real emphasis on the assumption of a leadership role is not apparent until about 1950. The first actual evidence that the department recognized leadership as a major rather than an incidental function appeared in the 1961 report of the state superintendent (38). Recent developments indicate that the department, while continuing to discharge its administrative and regulatory functions and to assume an increasing load of service responsibilities, now considers its primary role to be that of educational leadership. This recognition may be illustrated best by recent trends in selected departmental activities such as regional organization, supervision and curriculum development, administration of federal programs, and educational planning.

Regional Organization

To ensure closer contact with the counties, the department encouraged county superintendents and their staffs to meet in regional groups which would facilitate the maintenance of a face-to-face relationship with department members. This movement began to operate on a somewhat informal basis in the decade 1930-40. By 1948, county supervisors of instruction were meeting in six regional groups (39); and by 1951, secondary school principals also were beginning to meet on a regional basis (40).

About 1958, the department, the state-supported colleges and universities, and the county superintendents agreed on a regional organization based on seven regions, each of which would include at least one of the state-supported colleges. Each of these regions was provided with a coordinator whose salary was paid jointly by the institution and by the department (41). This plan was not completely implemented in the first 2 or 3 years of its existence because of the difficulty in attracting properly qualified personnel.

These coordinators provided liaison among the department, the colleges, and the public schools and were particularly concerned with in-service education of teachers and project planning with emphasis on federally supported programs. Working with the coordinator in each region after 1965 was a specialist for projects under Title I of the Elementary and Secondary Education Act.

Supervision and Curriculum Development

A survey of reports of the state superintendent indicates that the department has been concerned over a long period of time with supervision and curriculum development. As counties employed additional staff to provide supervisory services, the department initiated two statewide workshops per year to give in-service experiences for such personnel. One of the products of these workshops, which began about 1945, was the establishment of standards for graduate preparation for supervisors. These workshops also devoted considerable time to curriculum development. Emphasis during this period was on the concept of a grade 1-12 continuum, and the curriculum materials developed reflected this concept.

During this period, the department did not have adequate staff to provide more than nominal supervision from the state level. Significant supervisory services by the department did not materialize prior to 1958, when the National Defense Education Act was passed by Congress. Title III of this act financed supervisory services for science, mathematics, and foreign languages.

The Comprehensive Educational Program previously referred to, which became effective in 1965, along with the Elementary and Secondary Education Act enacted in the same year, provided opportunities to expand supervisory services at both the state and local levels. Although subject area specialists had been employed on a limited basis as early as 1958, the number of such personnel expanded substantially after 1965, until the services of 12 such specialists were available on a statewide basis in 1968. A list of the curriculum materials prepared and distributed in any one of a number of recent years reflects the contribution of federal support to the supervisory services offered by the department (42).

Administration of Federal Aid to Education

Reference was made in a preceding section to the significant impact of the National Defense Education Act on instruction in science, mathematics, and foreign languages under Title III of the act. Title V provided for expanded guidance and testing services, and the department took full advantage of these provisions. At the end of the first year of operation under this title, 1960, two assistant supervisors had been added to assist the guidance director. Staff activities during that year included the implementation of county plans for guidance services, publication of professional materials, coordination of a statewide testing program, and conducting of college orientation and related programs (43).

Title X of NDEA was concerned with the development and improvement of statistical services in state departments. Financed by state funds and by federal funds available under Title X, a study of statistical services of the department was authorized in 1956 and completed in 1961. This study was conducted by the Bureau of Educational Field Services of Miami (Ohio) University (44). As an outgrowth of this study, a Division of Data Processing was organized and a supervisor employed in 1961 (45). This division was concerned initially with teacher education and a certified list of teachers, and the high school testing program. The department secured a computer in 1966 and initiated a 5-year plan to establish a broad educational data base to meet the demand for information required for effective planning and decision making (46).

The Elementary and Secondary Education Act was implemented by the department in 1966. It was found necessary to expand the staff significantly to administer Titles I, II, and III, the last of which was on a regional basis under a state department director. The categorical nature of these titles required extensive leadership and direction by department staff in the development of acceptable programs by local agencies and in the approval of educational materials to be purchased. Directors for Titles I, II, and III were employed in the school year 1966-67 (47). A director for Title VI was hired in 1968.

Some of the more significant developments in the department resulting from the Elementary and Secondary Education Act were made possible by Title V, which had as one of its purposes the strengthening of state departments. Under the provisions of this title, three new staff positions, responsible directly to the state superintendent, were created. These were a director of educational planning, director of educational research, and coordinator of higher education and public schools. A fourth new position, responsible to the assistant superintendent for instruction, a coordinator of student teaching programs, also was financed under Title V. In addition to these new positions, staff or equipment was added to strengthen the school plant planning, data processing, publications, educational television, audiovisual education, and professional library services divisions (48).

Educational Planning

The Office of Educational Planning, which was created and staffed in 1966, was given as its first assignment an examination of the structure of the department in relation to its administrative, service, and leadership roles. During the initial year of its operation, this office carried out this assignment and, with the help of all units in the department, produced a plan for departmental organization, administration, and services. This tentative plan was discussed in detail by members of the planning office with administrators in selected counties, and their reactions to the work of the department were noted. These reactions became the basis for recommendations to the state superintendent relating to changes in departmental structure and activities.

The planning office in 1967 participated in a multistate study (administered by the state department of Utah) of comprehensive educational planning by state departments and produced a model structure for the planning process. During the same year, the Governor appointed a statewide planning committee, and the Office of Educational Planning participated in the work of this committee, especially with respect to educational planning.

The department, under the leadership of the planning office, initiated in 1967 a study of educational goals for the state. This study resulted in the formulation of a list of 23 general goals. To assess the present status of the state in regard to each goal, the office contracted with the Human Resources Research Institute of West Virginia University to reduce these general goals to their component parts in performance terms. It was expected that this process would require some months but, once completed, would provide the framework for much of the functioning of the data-processing division. The department regarded an accurate assessment of the present status as essential for long-range planning of programs in general and for state administration of Title III of the Elementary and Secondary Education Act and of the Education Professions Development Act in particular.

On the basis of the educational goals established, the self-evaluation of the department, the reactions of the county administrative staffs, and the assessment of status, the department in 1968 prepared a series of proposals to be presented to the 1969 session of the Legislature.

A FORWARD LOOK

Seen in historical perspective, the present status of the State Department of Education seems to make it reasonably certain that the work and structure of the department will continue to experience change although not necessarily at the accelerated rate of recent years. It is much more difficult to judge the nature and direction of changes which the future may bring. But discernible trends which show no sign of abating make certain predictions reasonably safe. Other developments may occur because of economic and sociological pressures even though no trend has been established. Some of the areas in which future developments seem most likely to affect the work of the department are (a) size of administrative units, (b) relationship with other governmental agencies, (c) span of the individual's life for which educators must plan, (d) the nature and organization of the curriculum, (e) the impact of federal participation, and (f) staff administration.

Size of Administrative Units

The fact that there are only 55 school districts in West Virginia has enabled the state to provide programs and services not available to many students before the adoption of the county as the unit of school administration. Yet, the fact remains that there are too many small schools operating in the state to permit the most effective programs. The political boundaries represented by county lines are not consistent with economic boundaries and often inhibit desirable school consolidation and the improved educational programs which larger units make possible.

It was to provide better services to counties that the state department encouraged the voluntary cooperation of county school systems through regional centers. In many respects, these regional operations have proved quite satisfactory, yet there is a limit to what can be accomplished on a voluntary basis, and legal restrictions make the financing of regional projects quite complex.

Some responsible public figures have gone so far as to advocate the amalgamation of county school units into one state-financed and state-controlled system. In view of the traditional attitude favoring local control of and participation in educational policy making, it is not likely that a statewide system will develop in the foreseeable future. Yet, there seems to be a growing sentiment for legislation which would create larger units, and the department has consistently encouraged this concept. When and if such a development occurs, the department will need to exert strong leadership in the development of programs appropriate to the larger units.

Relationship with Other Governmental Agencies

The necessity for a closer working relationship with other governmental agencies has become increasingly apparent. One of the key words in education today is "planning." Effective educational planning cannot take place in isolation: It requires information in regard to projected economic developments, demographic studies, public health figures, and communications data. Not only must educational plans consider developments in these areas, they will be affected and conditioned by them and predicated upon them. Even now, it is difficult to distinguish between education and public welfare in the administration of Title I of the ESEA or between education and public health in the administration of Title VI.

Another factor which will necessitate a closer working relationship with other agencies of government is the rising cost of public services. The tax dollar can be stretched only so far, and educators must keep an open mind toward duplication of services where such duplication can be effectively and economically eliminated. The sharing of facilities, equipment, and even personnel is a possibility which the various agencies cannot afford to ignore and which must be considered in long-range planning.

Span of the Individual's Life for Which Educators Must Plan

The traditional concern of the department has been limited primarily to programs for grades 1-12. There has been increasing public interest in state-financed programs for preschool children, and there is good reason to believe that the next Legislature will endorse at least pilot preschool programs in each county of the state.

At the other end of the continuum, programs of adult basic education are being expanded, as are programs of vocational, technical, and adult education for the non-college-bound person, and the schools are increasingly accepting responsibility for retraining the unemployed.

These developments have tremendous implications for the department in regard to developing programs for training teachers for preschool and adult education programs, for supplying adequate supervision, and especially in regard to the effect that financial support of these added segments will have on the support available for the more traditional grades 1-12 programs.

The Nature and Organization of the Curriculum

While curriculum studies seem to be in operation almost continuously, the number of basic curricular changes scarcely seems proportionate to the volume of such studies or the time and effort which have been involved. The projected development of preschool education programs will doubtless call for some curricular revision. But the major changes will probably concern the somewhat unbalanced relationship between general or cultural education on the one hand and vocational education on the other. Studies already conducted indicate the desirability of more vocational offerings at the high school level in view of the percentage of high school graduates who do not enter college.

The organization of the curriculum is also being questioned on many fronts. Few educators have been satisfied with the product of the junior high school, and such deviations as the middle school are being studied. There is also much difference of opinion as to the most desirable organization of post-high school programs. Some favor state-supported junior colleges, some advocate state-supported area vocational schools, and others feel that the operation of thirteenth-and fourteenth-year programs as a part of the county school system is the best approach. This is an area in which hard decisions have been postponed, and the department will need to give leadership when the day of decision arrives.

The Impact of Federal Participation

Participation in state and local educational programs by the federal government through the provisions of the National Defense Education Act, the Elementary and Secondary Education Act, and the National Vocational Education Act has already produced significant changes in state department administration. The categorical nature of these acts has doubtless served worthy purposes which were concerns of Congress, but it has resulted in a heavy work load for state departments in the preparation of state plans and projects and in the financial accounting required.

There is little question that federal aid to education is here to stay. The real questions for the future relate to the nature of federal programs and the extent to which Congress may be willing to underwrite them. While there has been considerable expression from school administrators in favor of general rather than categorical federal support, belief in the philosophy of categorical aid is strong in the minds of many Congressmen. There is much reason to believe that the federal aid of the future may be based on a combination of general and categorical programs. Either approach will require the services of a substantial segment of the department's staff, but the categorical approach may hold more promise of financial support for departmental operation.

Staff Administration

The tendency of the state department staff to expand, which has been particularly strong since the advent of large-scale federal aid programs, is likely to continue. Continued growth will demand a more sophisticated system of staff administration than has been necessary in the past.

It is likely that a separate bureau or division of personnel administration will eventuate. This unit will find it necessary to anticipate personnel needs in the light of developing programs and to engage in an aggressive and systematic program of recruitment. The unit also must be concerned with in-service training programs consistent with the administrative, service, and leadership roles of the department.

The personnel administration unit naturally will be concerned with the establishment and maintenance of personnel standards, staff organization, promotion policies, and the whole field of staff welfare and benefits. It goes without saying that the staff of this personnel unit must be trained and experienced in personnel administration.

FOOTNOTES

1. Superintendent of Free Schools, *Second Annual Report* (1866), pp. 5, 6, 10.
2. Superintendent of Free Schools, *Seventh Annual Report* (1870), p. 47.
3. *Ibid.*, pp. 15, 43.
4. West Virginia, *Constitution* (1872), art. 12, sec. 1.
5. *Ibid.*, art. 12, sec. 2.
6. Superintendent of Free Schools, *Twenty-Second Annual Report* (1885), p. 7.
7. Superintendent of Free Schools, *Biennial Report* (1898), pp. 16, 19.
8. U.S. Bureau of the Census, *Twelfth Census of the United States Taken in 1900*, Vol. I (Washington, D.C.: The Bureau, 1901), pp. 645 et seq.
9. Superintendent of Free Schools, *Biennial Report* (1903), pp. 7, 13, 15, 16.
10. Superintendent of Free Schools, *Biennial Report* (1903), p. 6. See also Superintendent of Free Schools, *Biennial Report* (1905), p. D.
11. Superintendent of Free Schools, *Biennial Report* (1911), p. 78.
12. *Ibid.*, pp. 92, 93.
13. West Virginia, *Acts* (1911), ch. 68, sec. 30-C, p. 162.
14. West Virginia, *Acts* (1919), ch. 2, secs. 17-26, pp. 49-52.
15. West Virginia, *Constitution* (1872); Amendment (1954), art. 6, sec. 18.
16. Superintendent of Free Schools, *Biennial Report* (1920), p. 59.
17. West Virginia, *Acts* (1933), ch. 8, art. 1, sec. 3, p. 76.
18. West Virginia, *Constitution* (1872); Amendment (1958), art. 12, sec. 2.
19. Superintendent of Free Schools, *Eighth Annual Report* (1871), p. 51.
20. West Virginia, *Acts* (1953), ch. 76, art. 2a, pp. 232-37.
21. Department of Education, *A Course of Study in Driver Education for Secondary Schools* (Charleston: The Department, 1945).
22. Department of Education, *A Course of Study in Driver and Traffic Safety Education for West Virginia High Schools* (Charleston: The Department, 1957).
23. L. V. Cavins, *Survey of Education in West Virginia* (4 vols.; Charleston: Department of Education, 1929).
24. George D. Strayer, director of survey, *A Report of a Survey of Public Education in the State of West Virginia* (Charleston: Legislative Interim Committee, 1945).
25. George Peabody College for Teachers, Division of Surveys and Field Services, *West Virginia Public Schools: A Survey Report,* E. L. Lindman, project director (Nashville, Tenn.: The College, 1956).
26. Legislative Interim Committee, *A Survey of the Educational Programs of West Virginia Public Schools*, E. K. Feaster, director (Charleston: The Committee, 1957).
27. Thomas C. Miller, *A History of Education* (Charleston: Tribune Printing Co., 1904).
28. Superintendent of Free Schools, *Fifty-First Report* (1964), pp. 26-29.
29. Superintendent of Free Schools, *Fifty-Third Report* (1966), p. 50.
30. Department of Education, *Standards of Schoolhouse Construction* (Charleston: The Department, 1945; rev. 1951).
31. Department of Education, *Handbook on Planning School Facilities* (Charleston: The Department, 1960).
32. Bureau of Education, and Joseph T. Nerden, consultant, "Report to Sub-Committee on Education, Joint Committee on Government and Finance, Legislature of West Virginia," The Department of Education, Charleston, 1968, pp. 227-51. (Mimeographed.)
33. Superintendent of Free Schools, *Forty-Seventh Report* (1960), pp. 12-16.
34. West Virginia, *Acts* (1965), Regular Session, ch. 57, art. 2, sec. 23, pp. 251-52.
35. Superintendent of Free Schools, *Thirty-Seventh Biennial Report* (1946), p. 57.
36. Superintendent of Free Schools, *Forty-Eighth Report* (1961), p. 29.
37. Superintendent of Free Schools, *Fifty-Third Report* (1966), pp. 7-12.
38. Superintendent of Free Schools, *Forty-Eighth Report* (1961), p. 14.
39. Superintendent of Free Schools, *Thirty-Ninth Biennial Report* (1950), p. 18.
40. Superintendent of Free Schools, *Fortieth Biennial Report* (1952), p. 33.
41. Superintendent of Free Schools, *Forty-Sixth Report* (1959), p. 18.
42. Superintendent of Free Schools, *Fifty-Second Report* (1965), pp. 34-36.
43. Superintendent of Free Schools, *Forty-Seventh Report* (1960), p. 18.
44. *Ibid.*, p. 19.
45. Superintendent of Free Schools, *Forty-Eighth Report* (1961), p. 25.
46. Superintendent of Free Schools, *Fifty-Third Report* (1966), pp. 18-19.

47. *Ibid.*, pp. 52-58.

48. *Ibid.*, pp. 59-60.

BIBLIOGRAPHY

Public Documents

U.S. Bureau of the Census. *Twelfth Census of the United States Taken in 1900.* Washington, D.C.: Government Printing Office, 1901.

West Virginia. *Acts* (1911, 1919, 1933, 1953, 1965).

—— *Constitution* (1872, with amendments of 1954 and 1958).

Books and Pamphlets

Ambler, C. H. *A History of Education in West Virginia.* Huntington, W. Va.: Standard Printing and Publishing Company, 1951.

Cavins, L. V. *Survey of Education in West Virginia.* 4 vols. Charleston: Department of Education, 1929.

Department of Education. *A Course of Study in Driver and Traffic Safety Education for West Virginia High Schools.* Charleston: The Department, 1957.

—— *A Course of Study in Driver Education for Secondary Schools.* Charleston: The Department, 1945.

—— *Handbook on Planning School Facilities.* Charleston: The Department, 1960.

—— *Standards of Schoolhouse Construction.* Charleston: The Department, 1945; revised 1951.

Legislative Interim Committee, E. K. Feaster, director. *A Survey of the Educational Programs of West Virginia Public Schools.* Charleston: The Committee, 1957.

Miller, Thomas C. *A History of Education.* Charleston: Tribune Printing Company, 1904.

National Council on Schoolhouse Construction. *Guide for Planning School Plants.* Washington, D.C.: The Council, 1958.

Trent, W. W. *Mountaineer Education.* Charleston: Jarrett Printing Company, 1960.

Reports

George Peabody College for Teachers, Division of Survey and Field Services, C. L. Lindman, director. *West Virginia Public Schools: A Survey Report.* Nashville, Tenn.: The College, 1956.

Strayer, George D., director of survey. *A Report of a Survey of Public Education in the State of West Virginia.* Charleston: Legislative Interim Committee, 1945.

Superintendents of Free Schools. *Annual and Biennial Reports.* Charleston: The Department, 1866-1968. At times these reports have been published in Wheeling, W. Va., and in Beckley, W. Va.

Unpublished Material

Bureau of Education and Nerden, Joseph T., consultant. "Report to Sub-Committee on Education, Joint Committee on Government and Finance, Legislature of West Virginia," The Department of Education, Charleston, 1968. (Mimeographed.)

Appendix A

WEST VIRGINIA CHIEF STATE SCHOOL OFFICERS

State Superintendents of Free Schools

1863-69	William R. White	1893-97	Virgil A. Lewis
1869-70	H. A. G. Zeigler	1897-1901	James Russell Trotter
1870-71	Alvin D. Williams	1901-1909	Thomas C. Miller
1871-73	Charles S. Lewis	1909-21	M. P. Shawkey
1873	William K. Pendleton (Jan.-Mar.)	1921-29	George M. Ford
1873-77	Benjamin W. Byrne	1929-33	William C. Cook
1877-81	William K. Pendleton	1933-57	W. W. Trent
1881-85	Bernard I. Butcher	1957-61	R. Virgil Rohrbough
1885-93	Benjamin S. Morgan	1961-	Rex M. Smith

Appendix B

Chart I.--WEST VIRGINIA DEPARTMENT OF EDUCATION, 1901-1902

State Superintendent of Free Schools
2Clerks
Stenographer

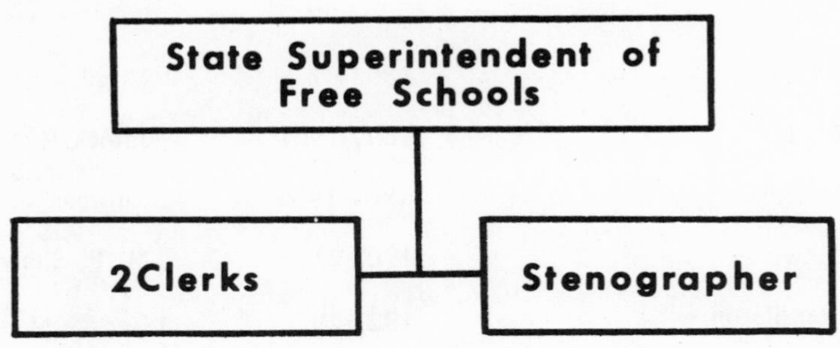

Chart II.--WEST VIRGINIA DEPARTMENT OF EDUCATION, 1919-20

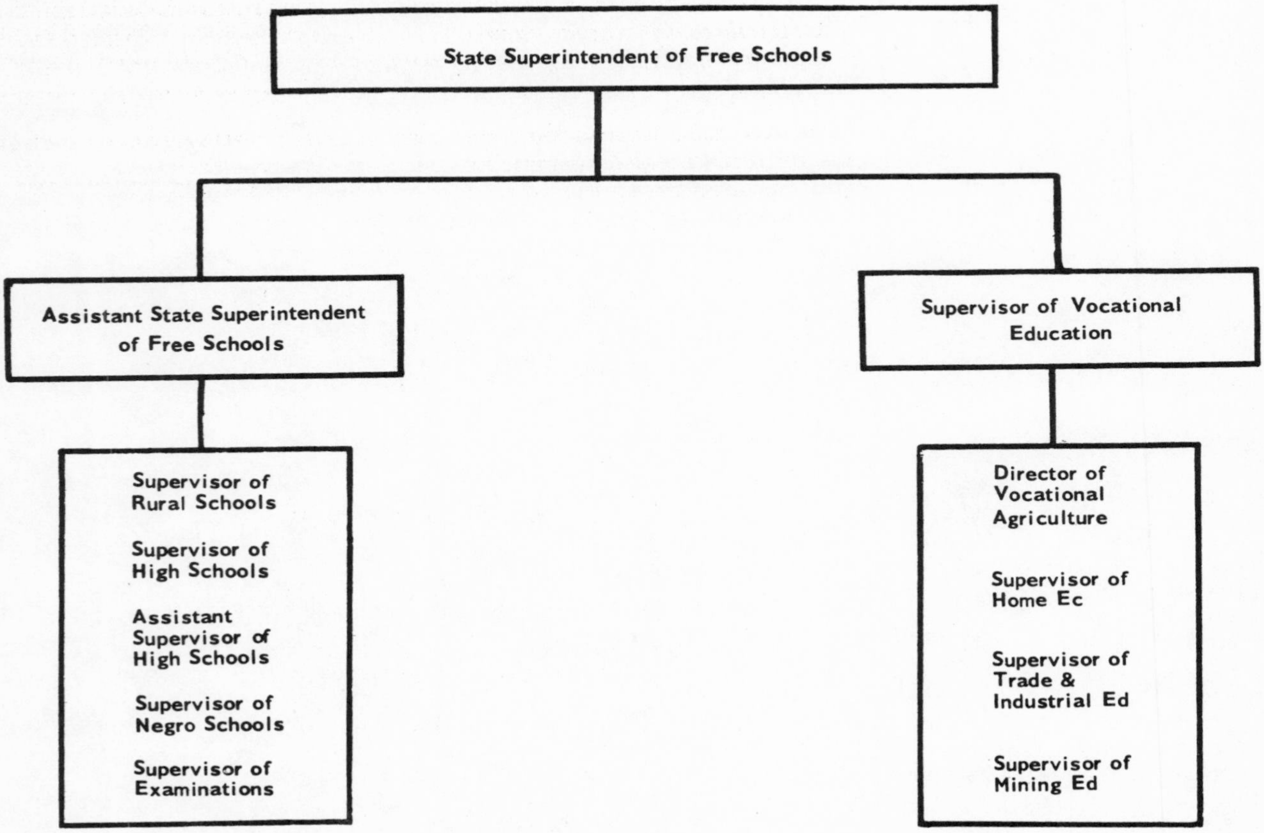

State Superintendent of Free Schools
Assistant State Superintendent of Free Schools
Supervisor of Vocational Education
Supervisor of Rural Schools
Supervisor of High Schools
Assistant Supervisor of High Schools
Supervisor of Negro Schools
Supervisor of Examinations
Director of Vocational Agriculture
Supervisor of Home Ec
Supervisor of Trade & Industrial Ed
Supervisor of Mining Ed

Appendix B

Chart III.--WEST VIRGINIA DEPARTMENT OF EDUCATION, 1938-40

State Superintendent of Free Schools
Assistant Superintendent of Free Schools
Administrative Secretary
Statistical Clerk
Division of High Schools
Supervisor
Division of Elementary Schools
Supervisor
Assistant Supervisor
Division of Certification
Supervisor
Division of Research
Supervisor
Division of Negro Schools
Supervisor
Division of Vocational Education
Director (State Superintendent)
Assistant Director
4 Supervisors
Vocational Agriculture
Home Ec
Technical & Industrial Ed
Distributive Ed
3 Assistant Supervisors
Vocational Agriculture
Home Ec
Technical & Industrial Ed
Teacher Trainer
Division of Vocational Rehabilitation
Director
Assistant Director
4 Field Agents

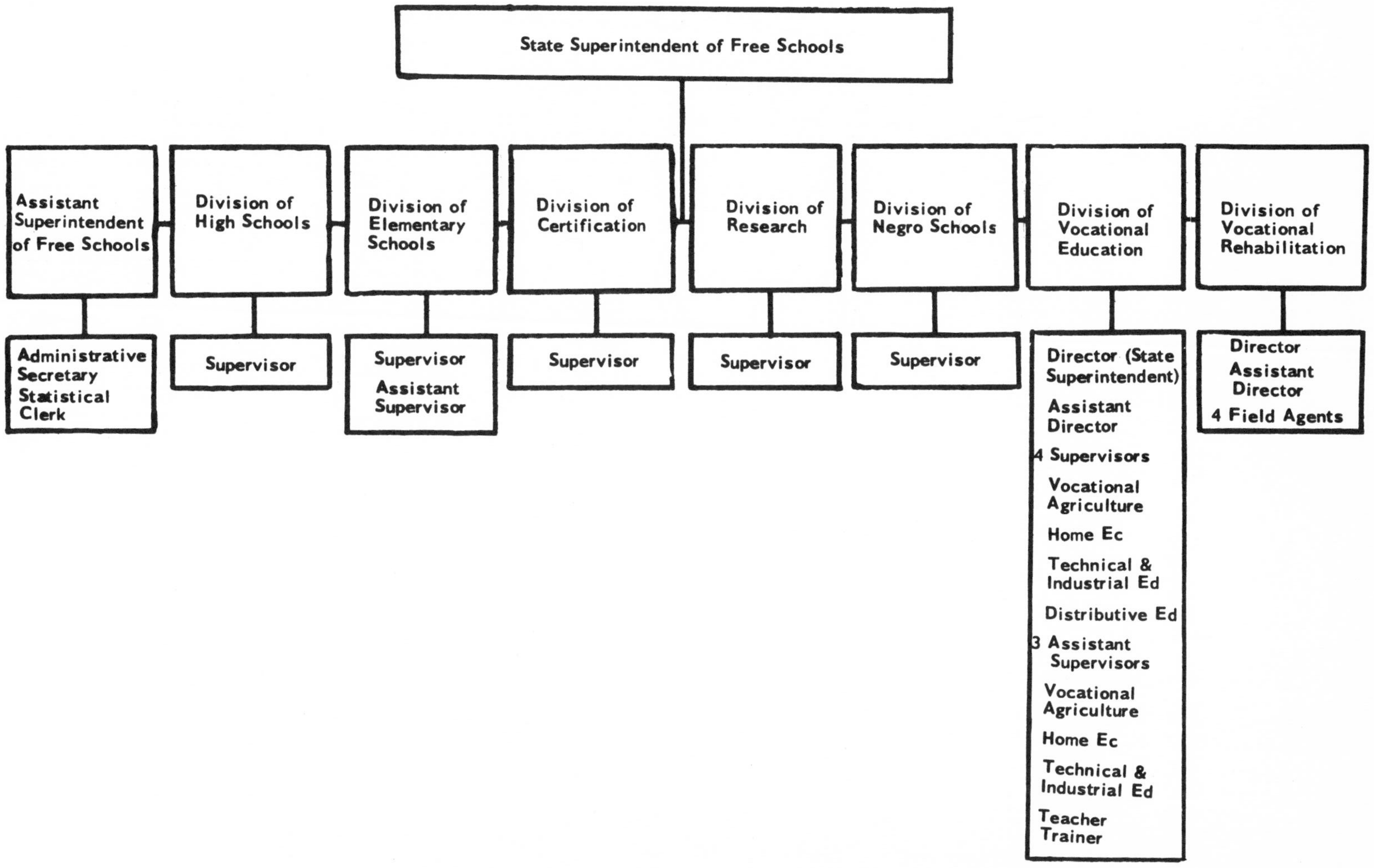

Appendix B

Chart IV.--WEST VIRGINIA DEPARTMENT OF EDUCATION, 1966

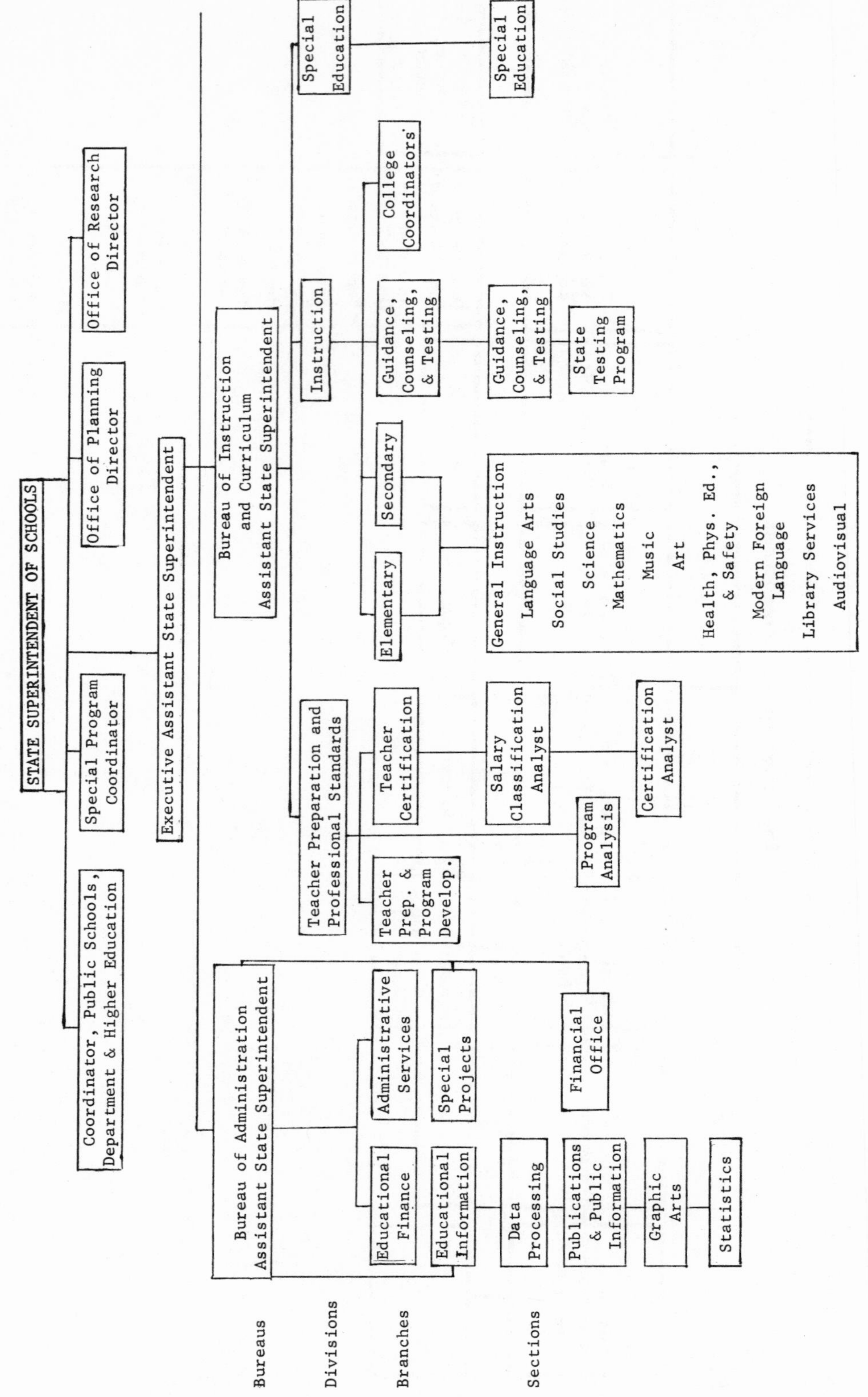

Appendix B

Chart IV.--WEST VIRGINIA DEPARTMENT OF EDUCATION, 1966 (Continued)

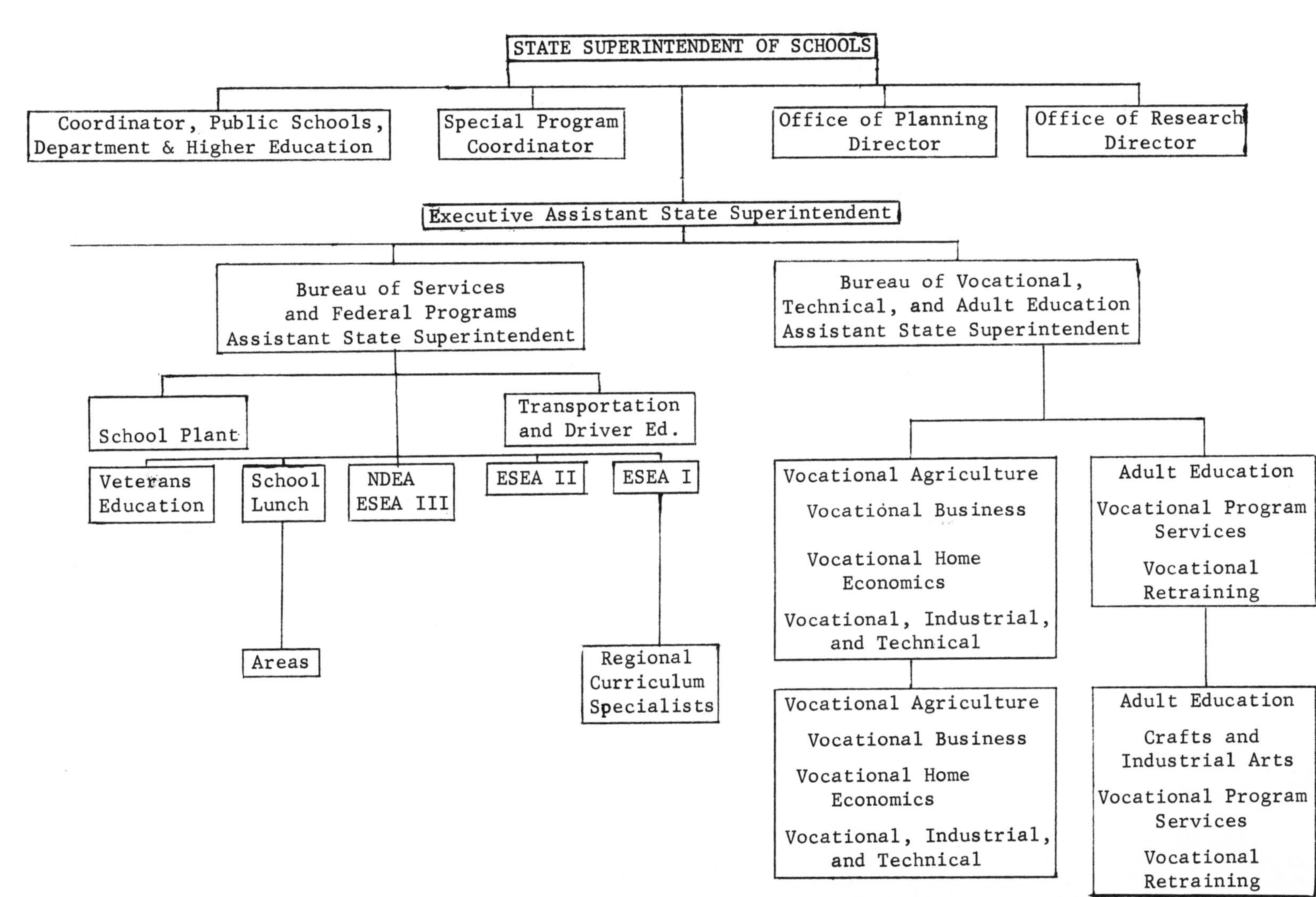

50 Wisconsin

DEPARTMENT OF PUBLIC INSTRUCTION
Walter B. Senty
Robert C. Van Raalte

Contents

FROM TERRITORIAL DAYS TO 1900

The first legislation to affect education in what later became Wisconsin was the Ordinance of 1787, passed by Congress to guide the establishment of the new Northwest Territory. The document contained the now famous statement: "Religion and knowledge being necessary for good government and the happiness of mankind, schools and the means of education shall be forever encouraged"(1). Actually, education was already important to the people who settled in Wisconsin; even before the Northwest Territory was formally organized, the pioneers had built schools in several communities scattered throughout the region.

These early attempts to provide education for Wisconsin's youngsters were entirely local and reached only a small number. Anyone who could be induced to teach was pressed into service. The buildings can only be described as rustic; they usually were constructed of logs, though a few were built of brick or stone. Curtainless windows frequently were placed so high that only the teacher could see out—at least eliminating one source of distraction for the pupils. State Superintendent Azel P. Ladd described the typical schools of 1853 as—

> Mean murderous things. Often I have found them located in close proximity to a swamp or marsh, where the children, in the summer session, could recreate themselves in the two-fold and interesting employment of catching tadpoles and the fever and ague (2).

The Wisconsin Territorial Legislature enacted in 1839 the first law relating specifically to the organization of common or elementary schools in Wisconsin, patterning it after the school laws of Michigan. Wisconsin had been part of the Michigan Territory until 1836, and when Michigan entered the Union, the new Territory of Wisconsin kept many of the provisions that had been in effect in Michigan.

As the territory's population grew, chiefly as a result of the discovery of valuable lead deposits in the southwest, a patchwork quilt of local autonomous schools developed. The need for some kind of supervision and coordination among these independent schools was obvious. The Territorial Assembly discussed the possibility of creating a central board of education to solve this problem, and a bill was finally introduced "to establish a state board of education and the office of state superintendent of public instruction and to prescribe their duties"(3). It passed the lower House but was defeated in the Council (the upper House) by a single vote.

Michael Frank, the assemblyman who had introduced the bill, still hoped to establish a free public educational system for the entire territory and asked the Legislature to allow him to try out the idea in Southport, his home community. In 1845, the Legislature authorized the village of Southport—now the city of Racine—to collect taxes for the support of a public school, provided the citizens of the community voted in favor of the plan. In an effort to defeat Frank's proposal, the antipublic-school forces, especially the large property owners in the Legislature who favored private schools and academies, persuaded the Legislature to set the date of the election only 2 months ahead. Frank fought back, working diligently to convince his Southport neighbors that the school was needed. He editorialized in his paper, the *Telegraph;* he wrote and distributed pamphlets; he made speech after speech. In the end, his dedication and work paid off: The referendum passed in April 1845 by 11 votes, and the territory had its first free public school (4).

Three years later in 1848, when Wisconsin entered the Union as the thirtieth state, its new constitution stipulated:

> The supervision of public instruction shall be vested in a state superintendent and such other officers as the legislature may direct. The state superintendent shall be chosen by the qualified electors of the state in such manner as the legislature shall provide. His powers, duties, and compensation shall be prescribed by law. Provided, that his compensation shall not exceed $1,200 annually (5).

Although the constitution did not deal specifically with the question of a statewide board of education, its requirement that the state superintendent be elected by the citizens reflected the people's basic conservatism in matters of education, arising in large measure from a history of nearly 200 years of independent and locally controlled schools.

When the first State Legislature convened, it decided that the state superintendent should be elected on a partisan basis for a 2-year term at a salary of $1,000 per year, should have general supervision over the common schools, and should apportion financial aid to the various schools. The responsibility for distributing funds grew in the twentieth century to be one of the superintendent's most important powers, for as education became more elaborate and expensive, schools needed more money to improve their offerings. By 1900, various laws allotting state aid to education made the granting of such aid conditional on whether the school's educational program met the requirements of the state superintendent. All Wisconsin laws passed since 1910 bearing on educational programs or financial aid to schools have tied the allotment of aid to the superintendent's approval of a school's program. Thus, by controlling the purse strings, the state superintendents have played a decisive role in inducing Wisconsin's schools to improve themselves.

The public schools in Wisconsin initially were supported by a common school fund sustained by the proceeds from land sales. According to an act of Congress in 1825, the sixteenth section of each township was set aside when a state entered the Union and the money realized from its sale used to support the public schools. This netted Wisconsin 66,731 acres in 1848 when it became a state. In addition, the federal government had granted over 700,000 acres of land to the state in 1840 and 1841, making a total of nearly 2 million acres (6). The income from this fund was distributed to the towns and cities "in just proportion to the number of children and youth residing therein between the ages of four and twenty years"(7). In turn, the communities were required to collect taxes equal to the amounts they received from the common school fund.

Unfortunately, the administration of the school finance program had many failings. Because of greed, graft, mismanagement, and simple ignorance, in many years the amount available for distribution was less than 50¢ per child. However, in the early 1850's, each pupil could be educated for only $2.26 per year, according to the state superintendent's financial report for 1855. The common school fund still exists today, and the interest from it is used to buy books and supplies for the public school libraries.

From the time of statehood until 1900, the state superintendents gradually gained influence and became more effective in dealing with the schools. The office also accumulated a professional staff, which comprised the State Department of Public Instruction, to help handle the myriad problems that developed during these 50 years.

Town superintendents originally were entrusted with the task of certificating teachers, but by a law passed in 1861, the Legislature turned this responsibility over to the county superintendents. This resulted in a certain amount of centralized authority over the quality of teaching, but the trend did not continue to a point where certification became efficient. The state had 71 counties, none of which accepted a certificate issued in any other county. Since the requirements for certification varied at the discretion of the county superintendent and generally were far from rigorous, the problem of differing requirements also plagued teacher training. Thus, despite the change from local to county certificating, teacher certification was still unwieldy and confusing.

The Legislature passed an act in 1875 authorizing public high schools to be established with aid from the state up to a maximum of $500 per year. The result was a rapid increase in the number of high schools throughout the state. Unfortunately, standards for certificating high school teachers had not been set, and in some counties it was possible for a person with no more than an eighth-grade education to teach high school students. By 1900, the situation had improved somewhat, for the state superintendent had been given the power to deny state aid to schools that employed a principal or an assistant principal who did not have a state certificate or a diploma from a college, university, or normal school. But teachers in the high schools still were not required to hold such diplomas or certificates.

Furthermore, no provisions had been made for supervising the high schools. Although the responsibility for inspecting the schools and determining which ones were entitled to state aid fell to the state superintendent, the Legislature refused to allot sufficient funds to enable him to do the job. However, the lawmakers finally stipulated that the superintendent could "call to his assistance in the work of inspection and supervision of free high schools, the professor of theory and art of teaching in the University"(8). The University of Wisconsin had earlier abolished this position, but it realized the advantages of being able to supervise state high schools and quickly named a man to the vacant professorship. The university continued to inspect, supervise, and accredit high schools until 1913, even after funds had been appropriated for the superintendent to employ a high school inspector in his department.

In addition to the problems of building quality schools and training qualified teachers, the state faced several special situations before the turn of the century. One of these was the question of sectarian instruction in the public schools. It had been the custom ever since territorial days to read portions of the Bible as a regular part of the daily program. A problem arose when the parents of several Catholic children in the town of Edgerton objected to use of the King James version of the Bible on the grounds that it was sectarian education. The case eventually came before the State Supreme Court, which decided that Bible reading as it was being practiced at that time was in violation of the constitutional provision for separation of church and state—no matter what version of the Bible was used.

Another area of concern was education for handicapped children. As early as 1885, the Legislature gave the state superintendent power to authorize any village or city board of education to set up and maintain a school for handicapped children. At the same time, a private school for the handicapped in Milwaukee was incorporated into that city's public school system. By the turn of the century, the state superintendent finally was given the authority to employ an inspector of public day schools for the deaf and blind.

THE NEW SUPERINTENDENCY

In general, the development of the Wisconsin Department of Public Instruction can be separated into two distinct and contrasting periods: the first from 1848 to 1903, and the second from 1903 to the present. The turnover in men holding the office of state superintendent indicates the difference in these two periods. During the first 53 years, 16 different men held the office; during the following 62 years, only 4 served as superintendent.

The change resulted from an amendment to the state constitution, ratified by the voters in 1902, that completely revised the section dealing with education. This amendment provided that the state superintendent should be chosen at the spring election on a nonpartisan basis for a 4-year term. Previously the office was a partisan one, and the term was only 2 years. Now, once elected, the superintendent would have sufficient time to develop programs and to leave the imprint of his philosophy and personality on the state's education.

The amendment also directed the Legislature to prescribe the superintendent's powers and duties and define his qualifications. Another important provision gave the Legislature the authority to determine the superintendent's salary—which had remained for 50 years at $1,200 per year, the level fixed in the constitution (9). This placed the emphasis on talented educators rather than talented politicians and allowed the state to offer a salary competitive enough to attract leading educators to the office.

L. D. Harvey, a forceful leader first elected state superintendent in 1898, was the person most responsible for the constitutional amendment. He was primarily interested in bringing some order and efficiency to the vast number of independent schools and school districts scattered randomly throughout the state. Harvey tried to consolidate school districts, but he was greatly handicapped by the meager funds allotted the department. In fact, his entire staff in 1900 consisted of four professional workers, a chief clerk, and a library clerk. Consequently, he was severely limited in establishing a working relationship with educators in all parts of the state. For the most part, he had to restrict his interchanges to the section in the *Wisconsin Journal of Education* set aside for the state superintendent to express his views. The Legislature had at least consigned sufficient funds to send one copy of this journal to each school district, in this way enabling Harvey to explain his program to the schools.

Superintendent Harvey seized every opportunity to promote a greater uniformity in Wisconsin's school systems. When the Legislature appropriated $14,000 in 1901 for the county school superintendents to improve their summer teacher-training institutes, Harvey saw his opportunity. He called the 191 institute directors to Madison for 5 days of instruction, thus ensuring some similarity in the way each county conducted its summer program. In addition, the 1901 Legislature finally granted the funds Harvey had requested for his small department to develop a statewide course of study for all the public schools in Wisconsin.

The 1901 Legislature also passed the first important legislation encouraging school districts to combine into multiteacher schools. Harvey had fought hard for this law, which stipulated that any school with two teachers would get an extra $200 in state aid, and each school with three or more teachers would receive $300.

Encouraged by the support he was now receiving from the lawmakers, Superintendent Harvey declared war on the one-room schools. He stated his case in a report to the 1902 Legislature:

> This age is rightly termed the age of progress. We see evidence of it on every side. In rural communities the crude log houses have given way to comfortable and commodious dwellings. The ramshackle buildings in cities have been replaced by stately stone mansions and towering edifices filled with offices and stores. The self-binder and reaper have taken the place of the sickle and scythe. Steam and electricity are annihilating distances and bringing to our doors the favorite products of other countries and other climes.
>
> In education, also, the last few decades have witnessed great progress. The high school, the people's college, is firmly entrenched in the hearts of the American people. Today we have 222 free high schools in Wisconsin. In this one phase of education alone, progress has not kept pace with the improvements in other directions. I refer to the district school. While improved conditions exist as to books, apparatus, and to some extent in buildings, yet on the whole, the rural school ranks very much lower in comparison with other educational institutions than it did 30 years ago (10).

Unfortunately, battles are not won with words alone, and since the superintendent was ahead of his time, he made only slight gains in consolidation.

Harvey's accomplishments reached a climax when his fellow citizens ratified the far-reaching constitutional amendment he had sponsored at the general election in

November 1902. At the same time, they voted for a state superintendent of schools under the old provisions of the constitution, and it is ironic that Harvey was not on the ballot; he had failed to get his party's nomination.

YEARS OF CONFLICT

C. P. Cary, the most colorful and controversial man ever to hold the office, won the election and became the new superintendent of schools. A fighter, he was engaged in stormy conflict during most of the 18 years he served, and several of these battles had considerable influence on later events in education. Even before his first term ended in 1905, Cary had provoked a number of people and had gained several enemies. Many people urged Harvey to run for state superintendent once again, but he declined, saying: "I am sure that if I am a candidate, powerful influences will be brought to bear through political organizations to control the action of voters at the polls"(11). Harvey added that he felt it was more important to establish the principle of a nonpartisan superintendency than for him to be again elected to the office.

Although Cary was not especially concerned with consolidation, which had been Harvey's prime objective, he did support during his term a bill offering state aid to school districts that closed their schools and transported pupils to other districts. Wisconsin needed to expand and develop its high schools from 1900 to 1920, so Cary found it necessary to devote considerable time and effort to this problem. The first real controversy erupted in 1909 following the introduction of a bill designed to give the state superintendent exclusive jurisdiction over the supervision of the state's high schools. Cary was strongly opposed to the University of Wisconsin's role in supervising and accrediting high schools, and he actively backed the bill. But the Legislature refused to accede to his wishes—perhaps in part because one of the legislators most enthusiastic about the proposal died before it could even be voted out of committee.

Undaunted by this setback, Cary continued to question the right of the university to exercise jurisdiction over the high schools. His perseverance and unremitting pressure were finally rewarded in 1913, when the Legislature appropriated funds for Cary to employ sufficient personnel to supervise the schools adequately. His biennial report for the 1914-16 period states:

> The [high] schools have fought themselves free, to a large extent, from college and university domination so that they are now able to study their own needs and to operate the schools as to be of largest benefit to the largest number, instead of making the one end and aim of the school preparation for college and university (12).

In the meantime, while Cary concentrated on gaining supervision over the high schools, another problem was developing. Although the number of high schools was increasing rapidly, a compulsory attendance law passed in 1907 gave them a great spurt in enrollment. Youth who had little desire for higher education and could never hope to attend college were now forced to attend high schools catering to the entrance requirements and dominated by the shadow of the University of Wisconsin. Educators and laymen joined to demand a better education for the vocationally inclined. As a result, manual training, home economics, and commercial subjects were introduced into the curriculum (13), and pressure from both business and labor leaders prompted the Legislature to pass a law allowing cities to establish trade schools. Milwaukee promptly took over a private trade school and became the first city in the nation to offer public vocational training.

By 1909, there was even a greater need for a more adequate industrial education program, so the Legislature appointed a study commission to recommend improvements in its legislation. Two years later, the commission presented its report, and it was written into a bill. Since the bill would create a separate State Board of Industrial Education, Superintendent Cary was seriously disturbed by it and managed to influence the form in which it finally passed. The compromise version gave the state superintendent the authority to appoint the director of the board, and the wily Cary designated one of the assistants in his own office as the director, thereby remaining in control of the state's vocational education program (14).

The industrial education board and Cary constantly fought until finally, in 1917, the Legislature amended the law to allow the members of the board to select their own director and set their own policies. This only added fuel to the fire, and the incessant struggle set the stage for the dual system of public education that exists in Wisconsin today. Cary was particularly vitriolic in his statements concerning the board: "America is not ready for a peasant class of schools, or for separate and independent schools for laboring classes. . . . They [the board] want a caste system"(15). He elaborated his views before the National Society for the Promotion of Industrial Education in 1919: "I have always contended that a board of education in anything larger than a city . . . is entirely incompetent and inadequate to deal with the situation"(16). He claimed the members of the industrial education board "did not know whether they were afoot or on horseback"(17).

Since Cary's day, the type of student enrolling in the vocational schools has changed greatly, but the schools have remained under the supervision of an independent board of adult, technical, and vocational education.

Meanwhile, Cary had found a new opponent. In 1915, the Legislature created the State Board of Education to control the financial affairs of all state educational agencies. Cary recognized the threat this board posed to the superintendent's traditional control over the state's educational purse strings. He took the position that it had no jurisdiction over the state superintendent, a constitutional officer, and refused to comply with any of the board's requests for information.

This lack of cooperation between the state superintendent and the secretary of the state board was particularly unsettling. When the secretary, Edward Fitzpatrick, wrote to Cary asking for "long-range suggestions for the educational program in Wisconsin"(18), Cary refused to furnish any details and replied: "When the proper time comes I shall be glad to give such support as lies in my power to any proposed legislation by the State Board of Education that seems to me at that time to be worthwhile"(19). The differences that developed between these two men were one of the reasons Cary was defeated for reelection in 1921, but he did not suffer his loss of prestige alone—the state board itself was abolished 2 years later (20).

Cary had used the statewide curriculum initiated by Harvey as a tool to strengthen the superintendent's control over the schools of the state. Since all legislative acts after 1910 that dealt with curricular offerings or state funds made the receipt of aid dependent on whether the school met requirements outlined by the state superintendent, a school that wanted to receive financial assistance would have to comply with the guidelines set up by the state department.

But there were other problems. In 1899, a law had been passed establishing county normal schools to train elementary teachers. A few years later, the Legislature enacted a law that offered aid to school boards in counties without normal schools to create teacher-training courses in the high schools on approval of the state superintendent. So by 1913, Wisconsin had state normal schools, county normal schools, and high school teacher-training departments, all preparing students to be elementary teachers. It was clearly a case of furnishing quantity rather than quality, especially for the one-room rural schools. The courses of study in these state and county normals and in the high school training departments varied greatly, each school appearing to be a law unto itself. With such diversity, supervision and coordination of teacher preparation were badly needed.

In 1915, Cary's staff included only five elementary supervisors—two assigned to inspect state graded schools (21), two to supervise city schools, and one to inspect rural schools. Comfortable classrooms were still in the future, and the supervisors had to emphasize the importance of such physical and tangible aspects of the school as heating, lighting, sanitary conditions, water supply, and adherence to the course of study prepared by the department. But as early as 1917, evidence appeared of a change in emphasis toward more intangible factors influencing teaching and learning when the department issued a bulletin entitled *Agencies of Supervision,* intended as a guide for local administrators and supervisors in carrying out effective administrative programs.

In 1915, the Legislature passed a law that set the stage for marked improvement of education in the rural and village schools of Wisconsin. It provided for a statewide system of county supervising teachers and required each county superintendent of schools to employ a supervising teacher. The state agreed to reimburse the county for this teacher's total salary and travel expenses.

In spite of the conflicts that characterized Cary's tenure as state superintendent, the department was stronger, more effective, and more influential when he left than when he assumed office. The department consisted of only 4 professional workers when Cary was first elected; it numbered 23 when he was defeated (22). His regime had seen the enactment of the first teachers retirement and pension system in the nation, and the department had been placed on a formal budget for the first time in its history.

BEGINNINGS OF CONSOLIDATION

Cary's years in office came to an ironical end—even as had his predecessor's. The man elected superintendent in 1921 was John Callahan, Cary's old nemesis, the former director of the vocational education board. In spite of the personal animosities that might have continued as a result of the Cary-Callahan differences, the department ran smoothly under its new leader. All members of the department's staff except the superintendent and his deputy are Civil Service employees.

Civil Service has been in effect in Wisconsin since 1905, one of many progressive acts initiated between 1901 and 1906, when Robert M. LaFollette, Sr., was Governor. A department head is often at a disadvantage in competing for able personnel under this system because the salary he can offer cannot exceed the limits approved by the Legislature. But there are advantages as well. The Civil Service is free from political influence or control, and it ensures continuity in the department's work; there is no complete personnel turnover when a new state superintendent takes office.

Since Superintendent Callahan had spent 3 turbulent years as director of vocational education, he was particularly anxious to develop harmonious relations between the Board of Vocational and Adult Education (as it was then called) and his department. It is to his credit that he accomplished this and much more.

In 1924, Callahan issued a report based on exhaustive surveys of the inequalities in wealth among school districts throughout the state (23). The report, presented to the Legislature, was largely responsible for the lawmakers' enactment of the Equalization Law of 1927, which came to be called the Callahan Equalization Law. At the time the

Legislature passed this bill, it apportioned the common school fund simply on the basis of school population, and although many amendments have been made to the 1927 law, its basic principle has been retained. For districts that had an equalized valuation of at least $250,000 per teacher employed, the state gave a flat grant based on the number of teachers in the district. For those districts having valuations of less than $250,000 per teacher, the state furnished equalization aid based on a formula that provided increasing amounts for the poorer districts. The money paid to low valuation districts was considered equalization money, and as such, no conditions or limitations on its use were to apply. It was the first such law to be passed by any state.

Despite Superintendent Harvey's efforts, after 1900, the state made little progress in reorganizing school districts. In fact, the situation actually deteriorated. Clever legislators recognized that since the equalization law gave every school district $250 in state aid and each received $250 in county aid—whether it operated a school in the district or not—there was nothing to prevent a local board from subdividing its district. The newly formed district would then send its children to the same school they had been attending all along, but both the new and old districts would be eligible for the grants. Local school officials were quick to take advantage of this loophole and created many nonoperating districts. The equalization law actually subsidized inefficiency and encouraged a proliferation of the already numerous school districts. The problem grew even worse when the rurally dominated Legislature authorized portions of any district outside the corporate limits of a village or city to withdraw and form one or more separate districts. By 1938, the state had 7,408 school districts, 5,809 of which operated one-room country schools.

It was 1939 before the political balance had shifted enough to enable the Legislature to pass bills favoring district reorganization. One such law denied districts the right to operate one-room schools averaging a daily attendance of less than 10 and still receive the equalization aid available to other low valuation districts. It actually provided for all regular state and county aid to the schools to be prorated on the basis of average daily attendance. A second act gave the state superintendent the power to attach districts with less than $100,000 assessed valuations to contiguous districts. Callahan immediately reduced the number of school districts to about 6,600 by this method, but he met stiff opposition at every step.

When the 1941 Legislature held public hearings on bills opposing district reorganization, hundreds of people from all parts of the state flocked to the capitol to express their views. During one of the hearings—conducted before an overflow crowd in the assembly chamber—the speakers, rallying to the support of the "little red schoolhouse," leveled vicious abuse at Callahan.

Callahan waited until both sides had been heard before rising to speak. Hisses and catcalls greeted him as he walked to the microphone. He calmly laid his pipe on the rostrum, looked at the audience, and said in a soft and subdued tone, "You folks have called me some nasty names. You called me a 'dictator,' a 'Hitler,' and said other rather unpleasant things about me. Now, my fellow citizens, you know that ain't so"(24). He went on to defend the legislators for enacting the laws encouraging reorganization and pointed out how these bills would provide better education for the children of Wisconsin. He even warned his opponents that he considered the legislation which had already been passed "only the beginning." And when he had finished, he was given a good round of applause. It was the beginning of the end for rural domination of the Legislature and the schools.

The state superintendent continued to emphasize the need for more school district reorganization. He presented facts both to the public and to the Legislature, showing the presence of a definite relationship between the size of a high school and the richness of its curricular offering. Through it all, he kept his sense of humor and the proper perspective. The joining of three districts by their town boards aroused considerable opposition, and an appeal was filed with the office of the superintendent. Callahan ordered a referendum, and the overall area favored consolidation; but one of the high school districts voted against the merger 100 to 1. Callahan accepted the total vote to create a new high school for the combined district.

Residents of the district that had opposed the proposition requested that the superintendent meet with them so they could register their protests. Callahan agreed, and about a dozen persons traveled to Madison to present some rather pertinent arguments against the merger. After all the representatives had spoken, Callahan told them that they were to be commended for their pride in their local high school. "I am sure that if I were a citizen of your community I would be sitting on the other side of this table," he said. "But I am the state superintendent of schools and it is my responsibility to do all I can to assure that all boys and girls of the state have a chance for a good education. My answer to you is no." The spokesman for the group got up and said, "Well, we rather expected that. Come along, John, and have dinner with us"(25).

While the state superintendent was fighting for consolidation and reorganization of school districts, equally important but less dramatic changes were taking place. As part of a program to help local schools improve their instructional methods, the department published 31 pamphlets between 1924 and 1926. These publications, such as *Reading Difficulties in Arithmetic* and *Study of Children's Interests,* were due in large measure to the efforts of C. J. Anderson, Callahan's able assistant.

Evolution also took place in the technique of supervising schools. More attention was being given to small conferences of administrators and selected teachers than to statewide meetings and general plans. During 1928, one of the department's publications, *The Teaching of English*, was used as a basis for many of the department's discussions with teachers and administrators (26). The questions listed for the conferences indicate that the department was attempting to stimulate original and creative thought, a radical departure from its previous stance, when it had encouraged all schools in the state to use a centrally prepared and prescribed course of study. No doubt the courses of study and teachers' manuals put out by the department had served a good purpose as long as teachers—especially on the elementary level—had very little professional training. But by 1929, under the influence of county teacher-training institutes and county supervising teachers, the quality of teachers was noticeably improved on all levels, and the prescribed study guides were obsolete.

While this trend to liberalize the schools was taking place, an old bugaboo reared its head: In 1929, the assembly's education committee proposed the creation of a State Board of Education. This was the year of the crash which ushered in our Depression, and although the cost of education remained constant, the money available to the state began dwindling. Forced to find new ways to cut expenses, the Legislature turned to organization of the school system. Cary's shadow still loomed over the proceedings, however, and the bill to create a state board was defeated. But before the 1929 session ended, the lawmakers appointed an Interim Committee on Education to thoroughly study the educational problems facing the state. The committee, composed of three senators and four assemblymen, took the job seriously. They met for 80 full-day sessions, conferred with education officials from Ohio, Pennsylvania, Virginia, Maryland, New York, Connecticut, and Massachusetts, and held discussions with several authorities from Columbia University and with the U.S. Commissioner of Education.

In 1931, the committee presented its report to the Legislature (27). It advocated condensing the lines of educational authority by creating a State Board of Education to replace eight existing major boards and four minor ones, and recommended changes in the appointing powers of some 30 other boards and commissions. Although the committee's suggestions were not then put into effect, the report did focus attention on Wisconsin's educational problems and exercised considerable influence on later legislation.

In 1937, one of the committee's recommendations was heeded when the separate state schools for the blind and the deaf were transferred to the State Department of Public Instruction by executive order. Shortly afterward, they were placed in the department's newly organized bureau for handicapped children. This enabled the state to coordinate and improve its efforts to provide education for all handicapped children, regardless of their disability.

Streamlining was also needed in another area: A truly chaotic condition had developed in teacher preparation and certification. In 1939, the Legislature granted the state superintendent of schools exclusive authority to certificate teachers and the responsibility for setting up certification standards. Not only were the city and county school superintendents stripped of their power to certificate teachers, but this act brought a semblance of order to the teacher-training programs offered by numerous state institutions.

With his new authority to establish qualifications for certification, Superintendent Callahan began reviewing teacher-training courses in all institutions. Those offering programs approved by the department could guarantee their graduates certification, while those offering training without approval could give no such assurances. Thus Callahan and his department applied all possible pressure to force the teacher-training institutions to comply with the standards.

Along with these efforts to upgrade teacher training, a new concept of curriculum planning emerged emphasizing local and regional initiative and control. This trend began in 1939 under the leadership of J. F. Waddell, one of Callahan's assistant superintendents. Waddell and his staff arranged many curriculum conferences and formed study committees, all involving both educational and lay leaders from throughout Wisconsin.

The most extensive and far-reaching of these grass-roots programs started in 1943. Known as the Wisconsin Cooperative Curriculum Planning Program, it was under the direction of Professor Gordon MacKenzie of the University of Wisconsin School of Education. In order to finance the various committees' traveling expenses, the Wisconsin Education Association appropriated $7,500 for the first year and $11,500 for the second. The department's supervisory staff, specialists from the university, faculty members from the state universities, and teachers, supervisors, and administrators from all parts of the state participated on the committees organized to look into the problems of curriculum planning.

By 1947, 20 committees had completed reports, which were published and distributed to the schools. The titles of some of their bulletins, indicative of the scope of the studies, included *The Task of the School, Cooperation in the School and Community*, and *Art in the Total School Program*. Meanwhile, several other committees were preparing bulletins using the problems approach to curriculum planning, and they turned out such publications as *Guidance to Curriculum Building* for both kindergarten and junior high school levels (28).

It is difficult to point to any one event or year as being responsible for the change in the state's attitude that resulted in an increased permissiveness and more local autonomy. Its educational philosophy was influenced by a number of factors: an increase in the professional training of teachers, supervisors, and administrators; the liberalizing influences of the state teacher-training institutions, especially the University of Wisconsin; and the success of the annual curriculum workshops and institutes and the broad participation of teachers on curriculum planning committees.

Another significant development was the introduction of team supervision, which was in extensive use by 1947. Elementary and secondary supervisors began visiting schools jointly, often accompanied by specialists in music, physical education, or libraries, making it possible to work with the total school program at one time. The visits were scheduled in advance so that local teachers and administrators could prepare the discussions and conferences. At the conclusion of their tour, the supervisors presented the school with a written evaluation, which included reports on the staff, school philosophy, administration, curriculum, and school plant.

Pressure exerted by leading educators of the state and by several members of the state department during the midforties finally prompted Callahan to overhaul the department in 1947. The department had become strong and active and enjoyed considerable influence and control over the state's educational establishment. The superintendent's office, with its staff of 37 professional workers, was now responsible for completely supervising the elementary and secondary schools, certificating teachers, setting standards for teacher-training courses, educating handicapped children, and dispensing state funds to the educational institutions of Wisconsin.

CONSOLIDATION CARRIED THROUGH

G. E. Watson succeeded Callahan in the superintendency in 1949. Both Watson and his first assistant, Russell F. Lewis, were able educators and administrators, and the department's effectiveness and leadership increased during the 12 years Watson held office. As a result of this steady growth and strong leadership, the department finally developed into a truly efficient agent for molding public education.

Superintendent Watson decided the time was ripe to launch an aggressive program to enlarge and consolidate school districts into more manageable administrative units. He judged correctly. Perhaps his single greatest achievement as superintendent resulted from his tireless effort to develop a favorable attitude on the part of Wisconsin's citizens toward reorganizing and enlarging school districts. He personally sparked an all-out campaign against the one-room schools.

In the fall of 1950, Watson scheduled a series of meetings in various sections of the state to discuss plans for reorganizing school districts. They were well attended by persons cognizant of the many educational advantages of reorganization, but the audiences also included officers and members of the State Rural School Boards Association, a conservative group firmly opposed to all consolidation on the grounds that the one-room school was the last refuge of freedom and democracy in America.

At a meeting in Waupaca County, during the few minutes left for questions following Watson's address, the president of the Rural School Boards Association stood up and in a very sarcastic tone asked whether he was correct in interpreting the superintendent's statement to mean that he was opposed to the one-room school. Watson retorted:

> Yes, you understood me correctly, but let me repeat that you interpreted my statement as I had intended, and so that there will be no misunderstanding by anyone in the audience, I again say to you that this is one time when you are absolutely right. I am launching a movement which I hope will eliminate the one-room school and the small high school (29).

The factor that helped Watson most in his campaign was a revision of the state aid program the year before he was elected that provided for an annual classification of school districts into two categories. Districts offering an improved curriculum and services were given an "integrated" status and were rewarded with a higher level of state aid; districts not having an acceptable program were designated "basic" and received a lower level of aid. The desire for more state money induced the districts to form administrative units having more students and a greater tax base, as only then could they afford to provide a program which would qualify as "integrated." Also, since the supervisory division of the state superintendent's office assigned the classifications (on the basis of compliance to standards established under the new law), the department's consultative services were more effective and in greater demand. In all, the law was a real stimulus to school district reorganization and greater educational efficiency.

A study of one-room schools initiated by Watson also stimulated the reorganization movement. The Legislature found this firsthand information most useful during the sessions, when school district reorganization was a hot issue. One section of the report of the study stated:

> An interesting finding in one county was that a redistribution of pupils so that each teacher would have 25 pupils would have resulted in the need for 42 fewer teachers! At an average salary of $3,000, this would have resulted in a saving of $126,000 (30).

The report revealed that many one-room schools had pitiably inadequate physical facilities; too frequently they lacked indoor plumbing, running water, dictionaries, encyclopedias, atlases, and other reference works. The conditions uncovered by the study shocked many legislators and educators, and the superintendent capitalized on this surprise and dismay to push his cause.

Watson's campaign received another important boost from James B. Conant, one of the nation's most respected educators. In November 1958, in a speech at Madison sponsored jointly by the Wisconsin Association of School Boards, the University of Wisconsin, and the department, Dr. Conant declared to the state's school officials and administrators that in order to provide the variety and quality of education necessary to meet the challenges of the twentieth century, a high school should have at least 500 pupils. Smaller schools, in his opinion, were doomed to providing inadequate education simply because they were small. Résumés of Dr. Conant's speech were widely distributed, and the impact on the educational community was overwhelming. Watson received the backing he needed to complete his efforts to eliminate the small high school.

During the fifties, districts continued to be reorganized, leaving only as many elementary schools as were needed within a single administrative unit administered by a board of education, taught by one staff, and financed by a uniform tax. Most of these reorganizations can be attributed to Superintendent Watson's forceful personality and determination. He appeared personally at practically every legislative hearing on bills dealing with any phase of school district reorganization. He also addressed county boards, county school board conventions, PTA's, and many other groups to stress the benefits that would accrue to boys and girls as a result of larger schools. His dedication spurred every member of the department to help the superintendent attain his objectives.

Watson's efforts were rewarded when the 1959 Legislature passed a bill allowing two or more counties to join and share the services of a single county superintendent of schools and authorizing the state superintendent to initiate such jointure whenever a vacancy in a county superintendency occurred. Within 3 years, half the counties had taken advantage of this law. Additional action by the 1959 Legislature required the entire state to be divided into high school districts by 1962, and although some work remains to be done in eliminating the small, inefficient high schools, steps in this direction are being taken (31).

Although reorganization was certainly the most important objective of Watson's administration, the department made headway on other fronts as well. Taking over where Callahan had left off, Russell F. Lewis, the deputy state superintendent, attempted to achieve a closer integration between teacher preparation and teacher certification. Over a 2-year period, members of the department visited all of the teacher-training institutions in the state. The conferences and discussions following these visits resulted in revision of curriculums in the colleges as well as changes in the department's certification requirements.

Problems arose periodically concerning religion in education, particularly over the question of furnishing state aid and raising local taxes to support schools taught by nuns. This issue came to a head in 1951 in the Lima Consolidated School District. This district operated two schools: an eight-teacher school run by nuns and a one-room school to which most of the Protestant families sent their children. When the local school board closed the one-room school, several parents refused to let their youngsters attend the Lima Consolidated School and were brought into court by the county sheriff for violating the state truancy law. The court directed the state superintendent to testify about the status of the school. After a thorough investigation, Watson declared that the nuns were giving sectarian instruction, and it could not be considered a public school.

This Lima School decision put an end to the practice of offering state funds to schools taught by members of religious sects (32), but the line between public and private education was not precisely defined, and legal problems continued to arise. In 1962, the Legislature passed a bill legalizing the transportation of pupils to private and parochial schools at public expense, but in the same year the Wisconsin Supreme Court declared the law unconstitutional.

Watson's administration also made tremendous strides in increased services to children with special educational needs. New laws were passed which broadened the existing programs and increased the state's financial support to local districts for special education. In part, this exceptional progress was due to new attitudes toward handicapped children that were just emerging. The fields of genetics and psychiatry were clarifying the causes of handicaps. Understanding and sympathy were replacing fear and stigma. But part of the credit for increased educational opportunities for exceptional children must go to Governor Walter J. Kohler. Intensely interested in these children, the Governor used his influence with the Legislature to promote these measures. In 1947, the Legislature increased the money available to local schools for children enrolled in special classes from $55,000 to $325,000. Reimbursement was changed to a "cost-of-service" basis, which was sufficiently flexible to allow for variations among communities and among individuals in the same community.

The National Defense Education Act of 1958, passed during the nation's awakened concern over education after the Russian Sputnik, had wide repercussions in Wisconsin. The program was designed to help schools acquire facilities for science, mathematics, and language courses, and for testing and guidance services. But considerable opposition to the act was raised among educators, local school boards, and legislators who feared that the use of federal funds would lead to federal control of the schools. During the first year the NDEA program was in operation, many schools refused to participate. Objections gradually disappeared, and today only a handful of districts still decline federal funds.

NDEA is aimed specifically at certain subject matter areas, while over the years the department's policy had evolved toward more general and overall supervision. It is still too early to determine exactly what effect NDEA will have on Wisconsin's philosophy of school supervision. The federal funds have already had a considerable impact in many areas. They enabled the department to increase its personnel substantially (by 1962 the staff included 81 professionals) and to apply data-processing techniques to teacher certification.

Since the end of the feud between Cary and the University of Wisconsin, the relations between the department and the university have been cordial. In 1960, the department and the School of Education at the university initiated a teacher intern plan, one of their most important cooperative projects. It was agreed that teachers in training would become paid members of the public schools' teaching staff so they could participate directly and meaningfully in classroom experiences. Watson's assistant, Russell Lewis, in a move that would have been unthinkable during Cary's term 50 years before, left the department to join the university and take charge of the intern program.

During the early sixties, the department took steps to revise the social studies curriculum. By the end of 1961, more than 25 educators, representing all segments of the public school system, had agreed to serve on a study committee for this purpose. The complete results have not yet been reported.

THE DEPARTMENT TODAY

Most of the programs initiated by Superintendent Watson were continued by his successor, Angus B. Rothwell. Rothwell took office in July 1961 and appointed William C. Kahl as his deputy. With federal and foundation grants, the department was able to increase its staff to 128 by the end of Rothwell's term in 1966. During these years, foundation grants became increasingly important for conducting experimental programs and procedures. Many of these programs, such as developing a film for use in conservation education, were considered worthwhile but had been difficult to finance out of regular departmental budgets.

Until 1963, every attempt to persuade the Legislature to require 4 years of training for all elementary teachers met defeat. In that year, due to Superintendent Rothwell's influence, legislation did pass stipulating that a prospective teacher must have 4 years of preparation to obtain a license (33).

A trend which had been developing for more than 100 years finally culminated under Rothwell's leadership. The county superintendent of schools, one of the earliest and, for many years, one of the most important figures in Wisconsin public education, was becoming obsolete. Originally granted considerable power in making decisions concerning the schools, the county superintendent's authority had gradually eroded. In 1863, the Legislature had enacted a law that allowed cities to set up superintendencies independent of the county office. It was only a matter of time before district reorganization and the population flow to urban regions reduced both the areas and the enrollments under the jurisdiction of county superintendents. Their realms became almost exclusively one-room country schools. By the time Rothwell took office, less than 25 percent of Wisconsin's pupils were in districts still administered by county school officers.

After familiarizing himself with the situation, Rothwell requested the state's educational and lay leaders to study the county superintendency and recommend a solution to the problem. The investigation disclosed the need for some kind of agency between the local school district level and the department; it was clear that the local districts needed services they could not obtain on their own. The study group recommended abolishing the office of county superintendent and creating a regional service unit in its place. The Legislature followed this advice in 1965 and created the Cooperative Educational Service Agencies.

Each cooperative agency is responsible for supplying services to a cluster of school districts spread over an area comprised of at least two counties. A board of control, consisting of local school board members in the operating region, sets policy and governs each agency. Under this plan, control of the schools remains in the hands of locally elected officials. The board is responsible for hiring an agency coordinator, whose only task is to coordinate activities among the school districts in his agency. The coordinator plays no part in making policy decisions and, in fact, acts only on the independent school board's request.

Today, Wisconsin has a three-tiered system of school organization: local school districts, the 19 cooperative agencies, and the state department. Under this new approach, school district officials must look at problems on a regional basis, and they must cooperate with officials of other districts in developing educational programs for the area as a whole.

A second outstanding achievement during Rothwell's term was the founding of an English-Language Arts Curriculum Study Project. The department sponsored this study in collaboration with the Wisconsin Council of English Teachers and the University of Wisconsin, with funds provided by the U.S. Office of Education. The project was directed by Robert C. Pooley of the University of Wisconsin, one of the most highly respected authorities in the teaching of English in the United States. School systems throughout the state were invited to participate by adopting the experimental programs devised by the curriculum committees. In this way, the project leaders received a feedback to their proposals and reactions from the grass roots. The three bulletins published by the English-Language Arts Curriculum Study Project—*Teaching Literature in Wisconsin, Teaching Speaking and Writing in*

Wisconsin, and *Teaching the English Language in Wisconsin*—all have won national acclaim (34).

Rothwell again had to deal with the old problem of the state's relations to the parochial schools. A law which authorized parochial and private pupils to ride on public school buses had been declared unconstitutional by the State Supreme Court in 1962, so the only way to provide such transportation was to change the constitution itself. A bill was introduced in the Legislature, and the voters approved the amendment to the state constitution in April 1967. State-financed transportation of pupils to private and parochial schools is now permissible.

Superintendent Rothwell's administration continued to develop the vocational schools, which had been gradually adjusting their programs to meet the demands of a changing society. At present, 2 (in Madison and Milwaukee) of the 40 local vocational, technical, and adult schools have developed 2-year college programs, and both are approved by the North Central Association of Colleges and Secondary Schools. Since the state plans to establish technical institutes over the entire state through its vocational school system, it does not anticipate developing the community or junior college plan for post-high school education. The 1965 Legislature passed a bill requiring all areas of the state to be placed in a district operating a vocational, technical, and adult school. This parallels the history of elementary and high school education and perhaps foreshadows the availability of higher education for all Wisconsin students.

The 1965 Legislature also made the Coordinating Committee for Higher Education permanent by appropriating funds for a director and his staff. This committee, established 10 years earlier to oversee all post-high school educational programs and institutions, had never been able to function properly. Now it could implement its plans.

Superintendent Rothwell was reelected to a second term, but upon the completion of the first year, resigned to become the first executive secretary of the newly rejuvenated coordinating committee. The appointment gave recognition to his ability and his understanding of Wisconsin's major educational problems, as well as to his experience as a teacher and school administrator.

When William C. Kahl succeeded Rothwell in 1966, the state had an excellent base and organizational pattern for its educational program. All phases of elementary and secondary education were under the supervision of a mature state department which had adapted and grown strong enough to meet the challenges of the future.

FOOTNOTES

1. Conrad E. Patzer, *Public Education in Wisconsin* (Madison: Department of Public Instruction, 1924), p. 103.
2. James I. Clark, *Education in Wisconsin* (Madison: State Historical Society, 1958), p. 11.
3. Patzer, *op. cit.*, p. 17.
4. *Ibid.*
5. *Ibid.*, p. 29.
6. The State Constitution adopted in 1848 set aside the following sources of the common school fund: (a) proceeds of the sale of the 1,705,622 acres, plus 5 percent of the net proceeds from all public lands to which the state was entitled in 1848; (b) the clear proceeds from all property accruing to the state by forfeiture or escheat; (c) all money paid for exemption from military duty; (d) all fines collected in the several counties for breaking of penal laws; and (e) all moneys arising from any grant to the state when the purpose is not specified.
7. Patzer, *op. cit.*, p. 106.
8. *Ibid.*, p. 461. See also Wisconsin, *Laws* (1883), ch. 325; amended by Wisconsin, *Laws* (1885), ch. 243.
9. See Appendix C, Table 1, for a summary of departmental salaries from 1900 to 1966.
10. Department of Public Instruction, *Biennial Report of the State Superintendent of Public Instruction, 1901-1902*, pp. 41-42.
11. "L. D. Harvey, Not a Candidate," *Wisconsin Journal of Education*, XXXVII, No. 3 (March 1905), 58.
12. Department of Public Instruction, *Biennial Report of the State Superintendent of Public Instruction, 1914-1916*, p. 3.
13. Edgar G. Doudna, *The Making of Our Wisconsin Schools: 1848-1948* (Madison: State Centennial Committee, 1948), pp. 3-25.
14. Board of Education, *Wisconsin's Educational Horizon*, III, No. 2, Part I (December 1921), 3.
15. *Ibid.*, p. 17.
16. *Ibid.*, p. 7.
17. *Ibid.*, p. 19.
18. *Ibid.*, No. 3, Part I (December 1920), 26.
19. *Ibid.*
20. Patzer, *op. cit.*, p. 223.
21. The 1901 state laws encouraging districts to consolidate provided state aid to districts forming two-teacher schools and schools combining with three or more teachers. Thus, multiple-teacher elementary schools were always called "state graded schools."
22. See Appendix B for a summary of the department's organization and growth.
23. John Callahan, *Equalizing Educational Opportunity in Wisconsin* (Madison: State Department of Public Instruction, 1924), pp. 1-62.
24. *The Milwaukee Journal*, January 30, February 9, March 1, 1941; *The Capital Times* (Madison), January 30, 1941.

25. The author, a staff member, was present at the meeting in State Superintendent Callahan's office in July 1942.
26. Department of Public Instruction, *Biennial Report of the Superintendent of Public Instruction, 1928-1930*, pp. 17-19.
27. Wisconsin Interim Legislative Committee on Education, *A Plan for Reorganizing Wisconsin's System of Education* (Madison: The Committee, 1931).
28. Department of Public Instruction, *Guidance to Curriculum Building*, Bulletin No. 1 (Madison: The Department, 1947), and Bulletin No. 2 (Madison: The Department, 1950).
29. Interview with Robert C. Van Raalte, who was present at the meeting held in Washington High School, New London, Wisconsin, in November 1950.
30. Department of Public Instruction, *Biennial Report of the Superintendent of Public Instruction, 1953-1955*, pp. 25-27.
31. See Appendix C, Table 2.
32. William W. Boyer, Jr., "Sectarian Instruction of Public School Pupils," *Wisconsin Law Review*, Vol. 1953 (March 1953), 215-32.
33. See Appendix C, Table 3, for a review of the increase in teachers' professional training from 1943 to 1964.
34. Department of Public Instruction, *Biennial Report of the Superintendent of Public Instruction, 1963-1965*, pp. 60-62.

BIBLIOGRAPHY

Public Documents

Wisconsin. *Constitution* (1848).

—— *Laws* (1883, 1885, 1947, 1949, and 1965).

Books

Beery, George S., and Fowlkes, John Guy. *A Study of the Transportation of High School Pupils in Wisconsin: 1937-1938.* Madison: Department of Public Instruction, 1938.

Board of Education. *Wisconsin's Educational Horizon*, III, No. 3, Part I (December 1920) and III, No. 2, Part I (December 1921).

Bush, Maybell G. *Agencies of Supervision.* Madison: Department of Public Instruction, 1917.

Callahan, John. *Equalizing Educational Opportunity in Wisconsin.* Madison: Department of Public Instruction, 1924.

—— *The Financial Situation in Wisconsin High School Districts.* Madison: Department of Public Instruction, 1926.

Cary, C. P. *Bulletin Relating to Teachers' Meeting in City Schools.* Madison: Department of Public Instruction, 1916.

Cheney, Rosa; Comings, George; and McDonald, Ellen. *Social and Civic Work in Country Communities.* Madison: Department of Public Instruction, 1913.

Clark, James I. *Education in Wisconsin.* Madison: State Historical Society, 1958.

Department of Public Instruction. *Guidance to Curriculum Building.* Bulletins No. 1 and No. 2. Madison: The Department, 1947 and 1950.

—— *Self Evaluation Data Sheets for Basic or Integrated Studies.* Madison: The Department, 1966.

—— *Standards Affecting the Classification of Your School District.* Madison: The Department, 1966.

—— *A Study of the Public School System in Wisconsin Compared with Some National Trends.* Madison: The Department, 1945.

—— *Work in Advance of Grade Eight.* Madison: The Department, 1937.

Doudna, Edgar G. *The Making of Our Wisconsin Schools: 1848-1948.* Madison: State Centennial Committee, 1948. Reprinted from *Wisconsin Journal of Education*, LXXX, No. 5 (January 1948), 219-50.

—— *The Thirtieth Star.* Madison: Democrat Printing Co., 1948.

English Language Arts Curriculum Project. *Teaching Literature in Wisconsin.* Madison: Department of Public Instruction, 1965.

—— *Teaching Speaking and Writing in Wisconsin.* Madison: Department of Public Instruction, 1966.

—— *Teaching the English Language in Wisconsin.* Madison: Department of Public Instruction, 1967.

Patzer, Conrad E. *Public Education in Wisconsin.* Madison: Department of Public Instruction, 1924.

Articles and Periodicals

Boyer, William W., Jr. "Sectarian Instruction of Public School Pupils," *Wisconsin Law Review*, Vol. 1953 (March 1953), 215-32.

The Capital Times (Madison). January 30, 1941.

"L. D. Harvey, Not a Candidate." *Wisconsin Journal of Education*, XXXVII, No. 3 (March 1905), 58.

The Milwaukee Journal. January 30, February 9, and March 1, 1941.

Wisconsin State Journal, January 3, 1941, p. 2.

Reports

Department of Public Instruction. *Biennial Reports of the Superintendents of Public Instruction.* Madison: The Department, 1902-68.

State Commission on the Improvement of the Educational System. *Report of the Commission on Improvement of the Educational System.* M. G. Toepel, executive secretary. Issued in accordance with the directives of ch. 573 of the *Laws* (1947). Madison: The Commission, 1947.

Wisconsin Interim Legislative Committee on Education. *A Plan for Reorganizing Wisconsin's System of Education.* A report submitted to the Legislature of 1931. Madison: The Committee, 1931.

Wisconsin Supervising Teachers Association. *Wisconsin School Supervisors in Service.* Madison: The Association, 1949.

Other Source

Van Raalte, Robert C. Personal interview with Van Raalte, assistant superintendent of the Wisconsin Department of Public Instruction, in April 1967.

Appendix A

WISCONSIN CHIEF STATE SCHOOL OFFICERS

State Superintendents of Public Instruction

1849-52	Eleazor Root
1852-54	Azel P. Ladd
1854-55	Hiram A. Wright
1855-60	Lyman C. Draper
1860-64	Jostah Pickard
1864-68	John G. McMynn
1868-70	Alexander Craig
1870-74	Samuel Fellows
1874-78	Edward Searing
1878-82	William C. Whitford
1882-87	Robert Graham
1887-91	Jesse B. Thayer
1891-95	Oliver E. Wells
1895-99	John Q. Emery
1899-1903	Lorenzo Harvey
1903-21	Charles P. Cary
1921-49	John Callahan
1949-61	George E. Watson
1961-66	Angus B. Rothwell
1966-	William C. Kahl

Appendix B

Chart I.--WISCONSIN DEPARTMENT OF PUBLIC INSTRUCTION, 1920

1 - Assistant Superintendent
1 - First Assistant
1 - Second Assistant
2 - Supervisors, High School
3 - Supervisors, State Graded School
3 - Supervisors, City Grades
1 - Supervisor, Manual Arts
1 - Supervisor, Rural Schools
1 - Publicity Editor
1 - Supervisor of Libraries
1 - Ass't. Library Supervisor
1 - Supv. Tests & Measurements
1 - Assistant Psychologist
1 - Director Special Education
1 - Supervisor, Domestic Science
1 - Supervisor, Deaf & Blind
1 - Statistician

Chart II.--WISCONSIN DEPARTMENT OF PUBLIC INSTRUCTION, 1947

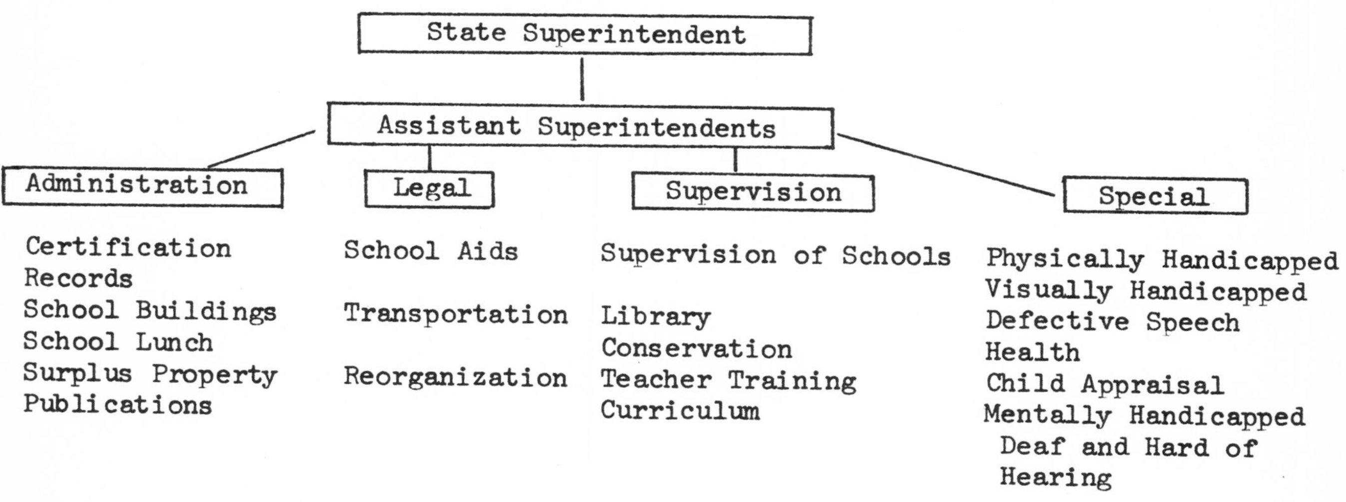

Appendix B

Chart III.--WISCONSIN DEPARTMENT OF PUBLIC INSTRUCTION, 1962

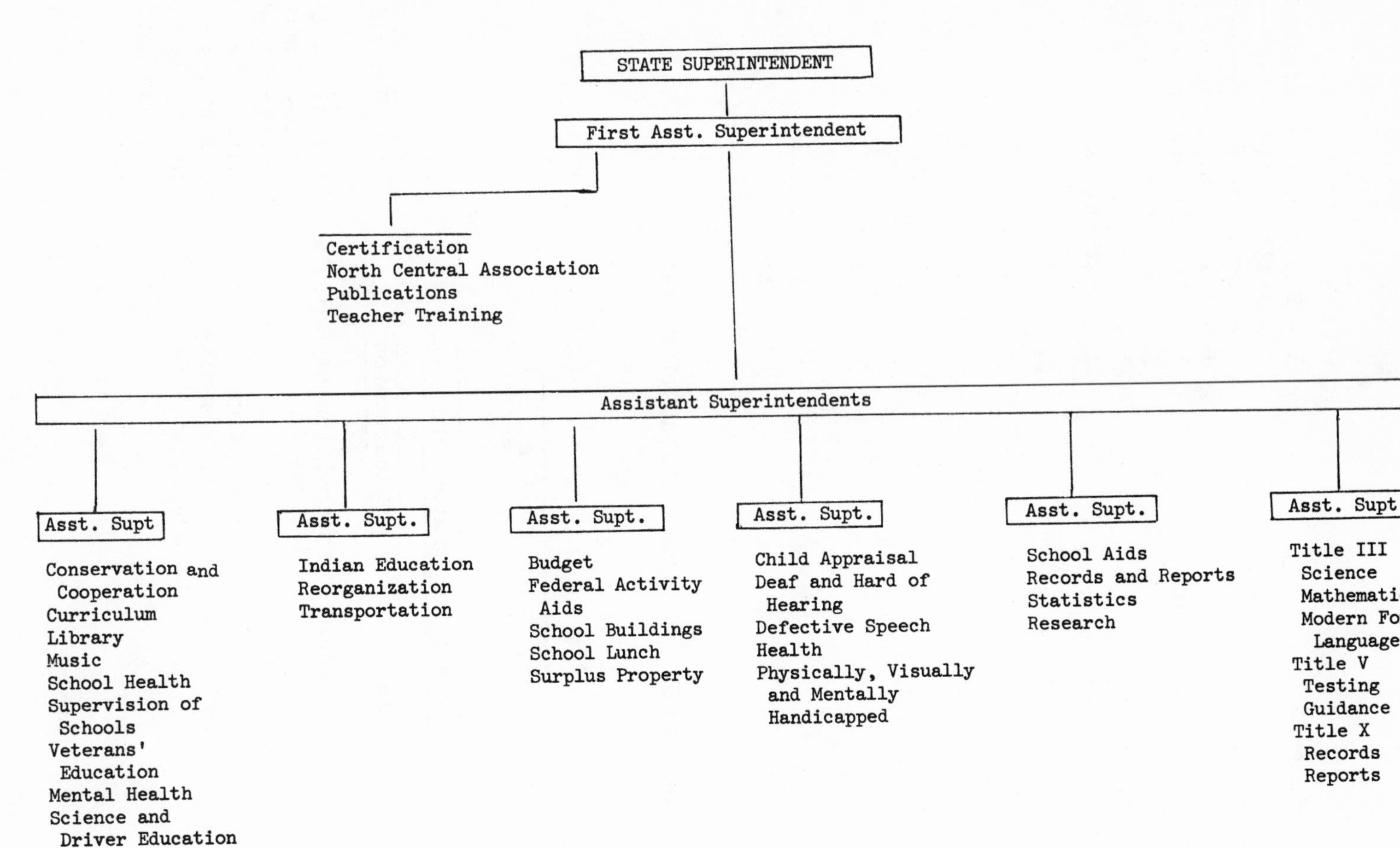
STATE SUPERINTENDENT
First Asst. Superintendent
Certification
North Central Association
Publications
Teacher Training
Assistant Superintendents
Asst. Supt
Conservation and Cooperation
Curriculum
Library
Music
School Health
Supervision of Schools
Veterans' Education
Mental Health
Science and Driver Education
Asst. Supt.
Indian Education
Reorganization
Transportation
Asst. Supt.
Budget
Federal Activity Aids
School Buildings
School Lunch
Surplus Property
Asst. Supt.
Child Appraisal
Deaf and Hard of Hearing
Defective Speech
Health
Physically, Visually and Mentally Handicapped
Asst. Supt.
School Aids
Records and Reports
Statistics
Research
Asst. Supt.
Title III
Science
Mathematics
Modern Foreign Language
Title V
Testing
Guidance
Title X
Records
Reports

Appendix B

Chart IV.--WISCONSIN DEPARTMENT OF PUBLIC INSTRUCTION, 1965

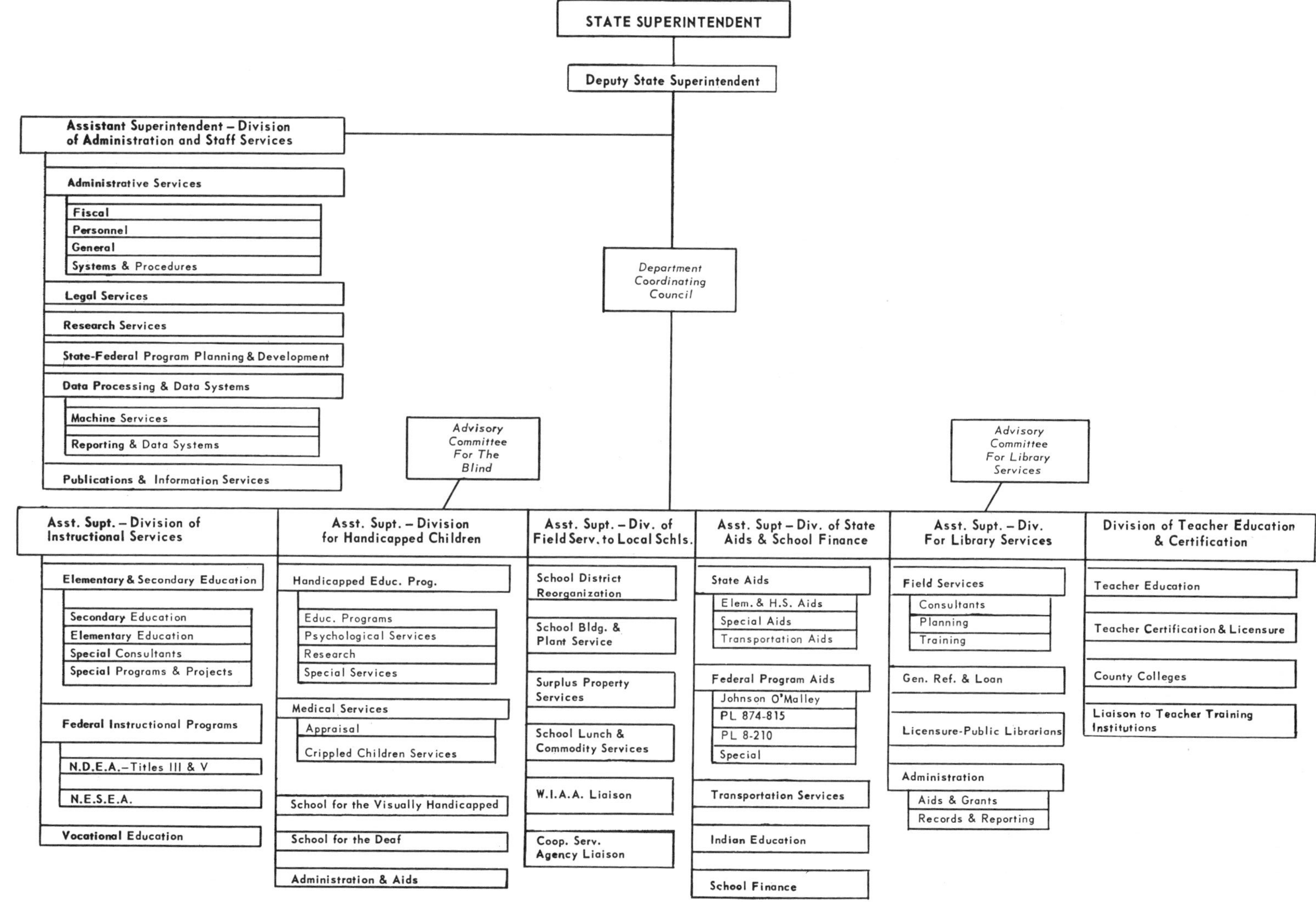

Appendix C

Table 1. – MONTHLY SALARIES OF PROFESSIONAL WORKERS, 1900-66

Year	State superintendent	Assistant superintendent	Secondary supervisors	Elementary supervisors
1900	$ 100.00	$ 150.00	$ 134.00	. . .
1905	416.66	209.00	209.00	$ 150.00
1910	416.66	208.00	208.00	150.00
1920	416.66	333 - 375.00	333 - 375.00	250 - 333.00
1930	500.00	333 - 375.00	333 - 375.00	250 - 333.00
1940	416.66	300 - 375.00	300 - 375.00	250 - 333.00
1950	808.38	510 - 610.00	440 - 510.00	440 - 510.00
1960	1,416.50	765 - 965.00	650 - 790.00	650 - 790.00
1964	1,416.50	974 -1,264.00	824 -1,069.00	824 -1,069.00
1966	1,750.00	1,270 -1,602.50	993 -1,258.00	993 -1,258.00

Source:

Files of State Bureau of Personnel.

Table 2. – SUMMARY OF DISTRICT REORGANIZATION, 1848-1965

	1848	1900	1937	1964	1965
Number of districts	1,430	6,529	7,777	695	572
One-room schools	. . .	6,185	6,155	95	41
Number of districts with high schools	1	209	444	396	395
Number of high schools	1	211	459	426	430
High school enrollment	. . .	17,442	148,275	249,146	265,207
Total public enrollment	33,174	386,221	546,316	806,668	859,101
Length of term in months	3.93	6-9	9.1	9.25	9.25

Appendix C

Table 3.–TEACHERS' PROFESSIONAL TRAINING, 1943-65

	1943-44	1950-51	1960-61	1964-65
STATE TOTAL	20,407	21,978	31,356	38,543
High school total	6,162	7,152	9,609	14,928
Elementary total	14,245	14,826	21,747	23,615
Degree high school	5,466	6,928	11,244	14,854
Nondegree high school	716	224	122	74
Degree elementary	4,145	6,298	12,740	18,483
Nondegree elementary	10,100	8,528	7,258	5,132

NOTE:

In the 1943-44 school term, 71 percent of the elementary teachers had no professional degree. By the 1964-65 term, this percentage had been reduced to 17 percent.

Table 4. – TRANSPORTATION, 1924-63

Year	Amount of state aid for transportation	Number of pupils transported
1924-25	$ 118,002.00	14,000 (est.)
1937	240,000.00	16,500 (est.)
1945	319,021.23	25,000 (est.)
1951	3,225,056.86	88,950
1959-60	4,893,668.25	226,813
1962-63	6,171,072.13	308,013

NOTE:

The first legislative act authorizing pupil transportation in Wisconsin was enacted in 1897. In 1927-28 only 1 out of 40 pupils was transported, but in 1962-63 more than 1 out of every 3 pupils was transported–an increase of more than 1,000 percent in about 35 years.

51 Wyoming

DEPARTMENT OF EDUCATION
Paul Graves

Contents

WYOMING EDUCATION PRIOR TO 1900

Historians have identified 1840 as the beginning of the era of immigration in America. Soon after that year, the Western trails were heavy with the traffic of immigrants bound for new lives in Oregon, California, or Utah. The most heavily traveled trail followed the North Platte River to Fort Laramie, situated at the junction of the North Platte and Laramie Rivers. A trading post had been established at that point in 1834, and it became an army post in 1849. The trail continued along the North Platte to the site of present-day Casper, where it then followed the Sweetwater River to the South Pass of the Continental Divide. From that point, the trail separated into several alternate routes. Many travelers preferred to continue southwestward to Fort Bridger, a trading post erected in 1842-43 by Jim Bridger, one of the much-written-about mountain men.

Few of these immigrants showed any desire to settle in the vast region that was later to be Wyoming, and most of them spent less than a month crossing the area enroute to other destinations. According to the census of 1860, there were about 400 permanent settlers in the area. Fort Laramie and Fort Bridger each had close to 150 residing in or near the forts. With the exception of a few wandering prospectors and trappers, the remaining population could be found on a few isolated ranches along the valley of the North Platte in what are now Platte and Goshen Counties.

Fort Laramie was the site of the first school in the area, which was established during the 1850's by the Reverend William Vaux. According to a letter reported to have been written by an army major at the post, Vaux was considered to be not only a poor teacher but a poor chaplain as well (1). It is believed that the children around Fort Bridger fared a bit better in their education. As early as 1860, William A. Carter, the sutler of the post, employed a teacher for his own children and invited the other children in the area to attend the private school.

In 1863, while Wyoming was still a part of Dakota Territory, statutes provided that in every school district should be taught orthography (spelling), reading, writing, English grammar (Latinized, no doubt), geography, and arithmetic. Early programs were dominated by literary and classical interests.

Population changed little from 1860 for the next 7 years. In July 1867, a party of nine settled at the site of present-day Cheyenne. The Union Pacific Railroad had been laying track at a feverish pace in its race with the Central Pacific to complete a rail line connecting the East and West. In early July, the tracklayers had progressed to a point approximately 75 miles west of North Platte, Nebraska. By the time the rails reached Cheyenne on November 13, 1867, the town had grown to a community with an estimated 200 business buildings and a population of 4,000 people (2).

Other towns continued to spring up ahead of the rail crews. The Union Pacific was responsible for the creation of a dozen towns across southern Wyoming, among which to survive were Cheyenne, Laramie, Green River, Rawlins, Rock Springs, and Evanston. As new towns were created, schools were soon provided. Cheyenne, by February 1868, had 114 children enrolled in school, with an average daily attendance of 86 (3).

Wyoming became a territory in July 1868, and little time elapsed before the need for an educational system was recognized. Provisions were made in the first session of the Territorial Assembly for the regulation and maintenance of education.

The Office of Superintendent of Public Instruction was created to be held in conjunction with other territorial offices. The territorial auditor, for example, was appointed as ex officio superintendent of public instruction in 1869, with his stipend for this service set at $500 per year. His duties included general supervision of the schools, distribution of school funds, recommendations relating to textbooks, and reports to the Legislative Assembly on the condition of the schools (4).

Elective county superintendents were provided and charged with dividing the settled areas into school districts, apportioning the county school tax, examining and certifying teachers, and generally supervising the schools. Each school was to be visited at least twice each term by the county superintendents.

District school boards also were created by the first Territorial Legislature. Each board was to have a chairman, a clerk, and a treasurer. District meetings were authorized in May and October to determine the number of schools needed, the length of the school year, the location of school sites, the courses to be taught, and other business required for the operation of the schools. In addition, the district boards were responsible for setting the district school tax, subject to the approval of the county commissioners. One power given the district boards was never enforced: In districts where 15 or more Negro children resided, separate schools could be established; no segregated schools were ever opened.

The territorial auditor's responsibilities in supervising education were short-lived, for he was relieved of his ex officio duties as superintendent of public instruction in 1871. Although the reason was never clearly indicated, disagreement seemed to center around a disparity in the length of school terms among the various schools and the inability to persuade the county superintendents to file reports relating to the condition of the schools.

The office of territorial superintendent was abolished for a time, and provisions were made for the county superintendents to make their annual reports directly to the Territorial Governor (5). This arrangement lasted about a year.

The last territorial auditor to serve as superintendent of public instruction was J. H. Hayford of Laramie, who in 1871, prior to the abolishment of the office, submitted the first report on public instruction. Dr. Hayford noted that good schools could be found in Albany and Laramie Counties, fair schools in Uinta and Carbon Counties, and neither superintendent nor schools in Sweetwater County (6). Records indicate that although the schools in existence at the time of the report were grade schools, plans were entertained to add high school departments in 1873. The first high school did not appear, however, until 1875 in Cheyenne, and only five others were established prior to the turn of the century (7). The first high school subjects taught (around 1878) included astronomy, intellectual philosophy, chemistry, Latin, Greek, and physical geography.

The legislative session of 1873 can be credited with laying the foundation for the present educational system. During that session, the whole matter of education was reviewed and generally resulted in the repeal of the provisions established in 1869. In addition, more explicit regulations governing the operation and control of schools emerged from that session. Further action saw the territorial librarian (an office created in 1871) made ex officio superintendent of public instruction, an alignment that continued until statehood was achieved in 1890. His duties were summarized as follows:

> The filing of all papers, reports, and public documents transmitted by school officers of the several counties.
>
> The general supervision of all the district schools in the state.
>
> Putting all schools into uniform operation.
>
> Preparing and printing suitable forms for all reports.
>
> Making a report to the legislative assembly the first day of each regular session on the condition of the schools.
>
> Placing one copy of all books, maps, charts, or school apparatus received from publishers, inventors, or manufacturers in the public library of the Territory.
>
> Granting certificates of qualification to teachers of proper learning and ability to teach. Regulating the grade of county certificates (8).

Much of the time of the territorial superintendent was devoted to the preparation of teacher institutes, which were provided for by the Education Act of 1873. These institutes were to be held in the county seats of each county in existence, with no less than 4 days nor more than 10 days to be devoted to the instruction and advancement of teachers. In 1883, $1,500 was appropriated to pay the travel expenses of teachers who attended such institutes. By 1887, teacher attendance was made mandatory by law (9).

Participants in the institutes devoted much of their time to designing curricular offerings for the territorial schools. Legislative attempts to influence the curriculum were not felt until 1886, at which time the Territorial Assembly provided that physiology and hygiene, especially the effects of alcohol and narcotics, be taught in all schools above the primary second grade and in all educational institutions supported wholly or in part by the territory (10).

The decade preceding statehood was one of rapid population growth in Wyoming. According to reports from the county superintendents, the number of schoolhouses increased from 39 in 1883 to 198 in 1890; the number of teachers grew from 89 to 259, with an average salary of $61.67 per month; school enrollment jumped from 3,352 to 7,875. However, the cost per pupil per month dropped from $2.87 to $2.78 during this period (11). With such rapid growth in such a short period, it is little wonder that schools were conducted in such places as a log building with a dirt roof, the upper room of a railroad section house, a rented building, the spare room of a ranch, the vacant office of a mining company, a blacksmith's shop, the basement of the town hall, and a sheep wagon (12).

An educational venture that received very little publicity during this period was the establishment in 1889 of the first school for the Indian children of Wyoming. Only 12 years earlier, federal troops had chased the last of the hostile Indian bands from Wyoming. By the fall of 1877, the last remaining Indians had been herded onto the Shoshonis' Wind River Reservation. For several years, the Reverend John Roberts, an Episcopal missionary, had been at work doing what he could to improve the lot of the Indians. In the middle 1880's, Reverend Roberts approached the Commissioner of Indian Affairs with a proposition. After explaining the need for a school for Indian children, he suggested that if the federal government would construct a school, the Episcopal Church would maintain and operate it at no further costs to the government. The proposition was accepted, and a school was erected at Fort Washakie in 1889 (13).

The Roman Catholic Church extended a similar offer in an attempt to establish a school near present-day Riverton, Wyoming, but the federal government did not see fit to finance the construction of another such school. However, this did not deter the Catholic missionaries. At church expense, St. Stephen's Mission School for Indian children was built and has remained in operation to this time.

The remaining years of the nineteenth century provided even more expression of the value of education. In 1886, Mrs. F. D. M. Bratten formed the Magic City Kindergarten in Cheyenne, charging a tuition fee of $4 per month (14). During the next 10 years, a number of other communities established kindergartens–all of which were privately owned. In 1895, the Legislature empowered the local trustees to establish free kindergartens for children between 4 and 5 years of age. These were to be supported from the special school fund, and only graduates of approved kindergarten training schools were to be employed as teachers. Records do not indicate the location of these training schools.

Other private ventures in education included the Wyoming Institute, a Baptist secondary school founded in 1870 by Reverend D. J. Pierce at Laramie (15). Within 2 years, its staff included four instructors–a man and three women. St. Mary's School, a Roman Catholic institution, was established in 1870 in the city of Laramie. Its growth was slow, but by 1881, it had 4 teachers, all women, and 73 pupils. The next year, the enrollment jumped to 110 pupils. In 1885, St. Mary's gave place to a larger and better Catholic school established at Cheyenne by the Society of the Holy Child Jesus. A large school building and convent were erected in 1885-86. At this time, there were also two branches of St. John's parochial school at Cheyenne, with about 250 pupils.

The Wyoming Collegiate Institute at Big Horn, a Congregational school, was started in 1894-95 with 3 teachers (2 men and 1 woman) and 56 pupils (34 boys and 22 girls).

After Sheridan High School started in 1893, the Wyoming Collegiate Institute declined and soon succumbed. By 1898, the enrollment dropped to 23 pupils. Sheridan College was founded in 1899 with 5 faculty members and an enrollment of 60 pupils. It soon suffered a decline which terminated in extinction.

Attention also was given to the need for higher education during this period. The Territorial Assembly created the university in March of 1886, with a tax of one-fourth of a mill on all taxable property established for its maintenance (16). In 1891, this was reduced to one-eighth of a mill in compliance with the Morrill and Hatch Acts. Although as early as 1893 reference can be found to accredited high schools whose graduates could enter the university without examination, the impact of the institution was slow in coming. According to Dean Justice F. Soule, "During the first twenty-five years, we never knew whether we should be there or not the next year"(17).

When Wyoming was admitted to the Union as a state in 1890, the sixteenth and thirty-sixth sections of land in each township were set aside for education. This was known as the Oregon-type land grant. The sale of these lands and the income from federal prospecting constituted the State Permanent School Fund. The earnings from invested funds, agricultural and grazing leases, and certain mineral prospecting leases on unsold school lands were placed in what is known as the Land Income Fund, which was to be distributed to the various school districts of the state on the basis of the school census, covering children from 6 through 20 years of age. In 1892, the Permanent School Fund amounted to $4,400, and the Land Income Fund was $3,141,842, or $30.48 per census child.

From the beginning of statehood, schools were supported by a general county school tax which guaranteed $300 per teacher and driver of a transportation vehicle–in some cases the transportation driver was to receive $450–but this tax was not to exceed 3 mills (18). In addition, districts levied taxes on their assessed valuations for the support of schools. The state support was the proceeds of the Land Income Fund distributed to the districts.

Stephen H. Farwell was elected the new state's first superintendent of public instruction. During his 4 years in office, much time was devoted to the need for a system of free textbooks. Schools had been required to use state-adopted textbooks under the provisions of the Session Laws of 1888 (Chapter 72, Schools, Chapter 4, Section 3, page 165). New adoptions were required each 5 years and were the responsibility of a group composed of the several county and city superintendents. As the State Constitution stipulated that "neither the Legislature nor the Superintendent of Public Instruction shall have power to prescribe textbooks to be used in public schools"(19), Farwell was apprehensive of calling the textbook selection group together, believing that such action may have been in conflict with the provisions of the constitution. Numerous letters to the attorney general requested legal opinions concerning this issue. The final opinion of the attorney general suggested that a legislative session was so close at hand that the Legislature should be requested to review the problem and enact a law in harmony with the constitution.

A great deal of time also was devoted to preparing an exhibit of Wyoming's educational system for display at the World's Columbian Exposition held in Chicago in 1893. Examples of pupils' class work, pictures of Wyoming schools, courses of study, as well as charts showing funds and revenues, school enrollment and attendance data, were collected for inclusion in the exhibit.

Although the state superintendent was responsible by law for teacher certification, Superintendent Farwell ducked the issue by referring to Section 3908 of the Revised Statutes, 1887. The law provided that the county superintendents examine all persons desirous of teaching in the public schools; if in their opinion such persons were qualified, a certificate was issued authorizing them to teach. The state superintendent considered issuance of certificates by his office as being superfluous.

Superintendent Farwell made three major recommendations to the Legislature. One called for a law providing for a school census to be made in January by the clerks of each school district and to be submitted to the state superintendent for compilation. It would then be the duty of the state auditor to compute a prorated list of funds to be distributed to the counties. The state treasurer would then prepare and transmit warrants to each of the county treasurers, who in turn would distribute the funds to the individual school districts. The state superintendent believed such a law was needed if there were to be any effective adherence to Article VII, Section 8, of the State Constitution, which dictated that "provisions shall be made by general law for the equitable distribution" of the income derived from the school lands "among the several counties according to the number of children of school age in each"(20). Section 3949 of the Revised Statutes defined school age as between the ages of 7 and 20 years inclusive.

A second recommendation called for creation of a commission of not less than five persons to revise the school laws of that day. Superintendent Farwell admonished that new laws "should not be such as will disturb, more than need be, existing laws"(21). His third major recommendation was for adoption of a state system of free textbooks.

All school laws presented for consideration by the first and second Legislatures failed to pass.

Farwell's successor was Mrs. Estelle Reel, who served during 1895-96. She immediately supported her predecessor's recommendation for free textbooks. During her administration, Mrs. Reel spent most of her time visiting teacher institutes, summer schools, and other meetings concerned with education. At every opportunity, she expressed the need for preparation of a standard course of study that would be suitable for all rural schools in the state. In support of her plan, she argued that it would systemize the work of the teachers and county superintendents and provide more equal schooling for the children. She also was a strong advocate of the importance of school libraries.

Elected to the state superintendency in 1897 was C. H. Parmelee, who served only 2 years. Records do not indicate accomplishments of much significance during this period. He, too, recommended revision of the school code and free textbooks. In his biennial report to the Governor, Superintendent Parmelee admitted that he did not have time to learn much about school problems during his 2 years of office.

Thomas T. Tynan, who had the honor of being the last state superintendent of the nineteenth century and the first of the twentieth, served from 1899 to 1907. Although many educators have criticized high schools for being too oriented for the college-bound, not many have been as critical of high schools as T. T. Tynan, when he commented:

> As statistics show that the great majority of pupils in our public schools do not go any further than the seventh and eighth grades, I believe that more attention should be given to the primary and intermediate departments of our schools. It is more important to have sufficient room and good teachers for the primary and intermediate classes than to have expensive high schools.

In his appraisal of the high schools, he stated, "The present system tends toward making the pupils' work superficial, and introduces that very obnoxious system called cramming"(22).

It is doubtful that the superintendent's evaluation of high schools was based on fact. By his own admission, he visited only two counties his first year in office. In 1900, he visited nine counties and spent a total of only 1 day in each. With this limited opportunity to observe schools in operation, it is difficult to assess his comments as valid. He attributed his lack of visits to limited funds.

The Legislature of 1899 enacted a law establishing a state system of free textbooks. Superintendent Tynan probably cannot be credited with the success of the legislation since he had been in office less than 60 days at time of its passage. Other legislation in 1899 included the creation of a State Board of Examiners to administer the program of examination of persons for the purpose of teacher certification. The board members were charged with preparing the test to be administered and grading the tests after they were received from the county superintendents. The state superintendent of public instruction granted certificates to those qualified by test scores.

The last decade of the nineteenth century was one of rapid growth for education in Wyoming. School buildings increased from 198 in 1890 to 372 in 1900. Enrollment rose from 7,875 to 14,512, teachers from 259 to 570. Teacher salaries, however, saw no increase. As a matter of fact, salaries declined from an average of $61.67 per month in 1890 to $48.09 per month at the close of the century (23).

THE LEGAL AND FINANCIAL FRAMEWORK FOR WYOMING EDUCATION

In November 1889, the people of the Wyoming Territory accepted a constitution drafted by the state constitutional convention. Admission to the Union followed in July 1890. The constitution and the first State Legislature virtually accepted the system of education in vogue during territorial days.

The State Superintendent of Public Instruction

The position of state superintendent of public instruction was one of the five top elective positions created by the State Constitution, and its duties, according to the constitution, were to be prescribed by law. Even today, a host of responsibilities outside the area of education make the job a difficult one and absorb approximately one-fourth of the state superintendent's time.

To enjoy tenure in office, the person filling the position must be politically as well as educationally oriented. Campaigning for reelection also detracts from the time needed to administer the state educational programs. As early as 1915, it was suggested that the chief state school officer be appointed rather than be elected by the people (24). Although the recommendation is still being voiced, reluctance to the change still continues. Several persons interviewed expressed the feeling that the main reason for not removing the position from partisan politics is that this office is authorized in the constitution as well as the statutes. Not only would it be extremely difficult to amend both the constitution and the statutes, but it would necessitate a subsequent addition of another elected official to keep the number of the executive council at five—thereby precluding split decisions in government policy action.

Several other reasons are given for not wanting the position removed from politics. People say that they are concerned about the direction and policy of education and that as long as education spends most of their tax dollars they want the opportunity to vote out of office the administrator who does not do a good job. Apparently, no thought is given to the possibility that an appointee to the position could be removed more quickly than the time required to wait until the next election rolls around. But even more significantly, the line of reasoning indicates the misconception that so often surrounds the authority and responsibility of the state superintendent. The fact is that he is directly responsible only for moneys spent in the state department—a small percentage of the tax dollars spent on education. It is the Legislature that determines the amount of money for education and how it is spent. The other education agencies (i.e., the university, the community colleges, and the local school districts) are directly responsible for their expenditures, and these represent by far the greatest amounts of expenditures on education by the state.

One can only marvel that constructive educational programs have emerged at all amidst the many pressures directed toward the state superintendent of public instruction. However, there are 21 other states that elect their chief state school officer on a partisan, political basis.

We find early reports of superintendents concentrating on county school reports, discussions and price lists of textbooks, the state university, and opinions of the attorney general relating to the powers of the state superintendent. Around the turn of the century, however, appeared reports containing such subjects as pupil enrollment, qualifications of teachers, assessed valuations of counties and mill levies, values of school properties, and records of state disbursements.

T. T. Tynan discovered soon after the turn of the century that the office of state superintendent enjoyed no immunity from pressure. His failure to submit a biennial report to the Governor and the Legislature for the years 1903-1904 did nothing to endear him to that group. The following is an excerpt from his biennial report for 1905-1906:

> You will also find appended the biennial report of said office for the two years prior, 1903-1904. Unfortunately I was unable to gather data and statistics of sufficient accuracy as to warrant the filing of said report two years ago in accordance with and at the time required by law, and deemed it best not to file a report under such circumstances, meekly submitting to the humility attending the dereliction of an officer to his superior and the consequent reporting of such offense by that officer in his message to the Legislature (25).

It was evident that the legislators did not agree with his decision, for in 1905 they reduced his contingency funds below what had been appropriated for a number of years. Tynan retaliated by calling their actions "malicious and in violation of their oath of office"(26). Apparently, he did not consider his failure to report a violation of his oath. Considering the friction that developed between the state superintendent and the Legislature, the results of the next election were not a surprise: A. D. Cook was elected to the post.

During Cook's administration, the Legislature of 1907 enacted a compulsory education law setting the compulsory school age as between 7 and 14 years inclusive (27). The Legislature also amended the law governing the State Board of Examiners, giving it the power to examine teachers for purposes of certification, which had been the responsibility of the county superintendents (28).

Cook's short tenure in office resulted more from economic conditions in the state than from the nature of his accomplishments. After the financial panic in October 1907, the state underwent a brief recession that extended into 1908. Although the economy of the state improved rapidly, many became disenchanted with the Republican party. The Democrats, feeling they had no one strong enough to defeat the Republican candidate for Governor, offered their nomination to Joseph M. Carey, a lifelong Republican. Carey, who had served as U.S. Senator from Wyoming and was abandoned by the Republicans when he sought reelection in 1895, accepted the Democratic nomination. His popularity resulted in his election, and he carried with him to victory two Democratic candidates: Frank L. Houx as secretary of state, and Rose A. Bird as superintendent of public instruction. These were the first state offices won by the Democrats since 1892.

Governor Carey proved to be one of the most progressive chief executives in Wyoming history. His success in mustering support for reform legislation in both the 1911 and 1913 sessions of the Legislature was astonishing, for in neither case did the Democrats have a majority in either House.

In 1913, the Legislature provided several pieces of legislation which helped strengthen the state school system. Provisions were made for transmittal of public funds for school support on a businesslike basis (29). Prior to 1913, school funds were distributed by the county superintendents and county treasurers to the district treasurers, with little concern for accurate record keeping. In most cases, the only records of transmittal were kept by the county officials. The new law required that duplicate remittance slips be issued with each remittal of funds. County officials were directed to send one copy to the district treasurer and one copy to the district clerk.

The quality of teacher-training institutes also received legislative attention. Most institutes had been conducted by the county superintendents and usually were considered to be of little value. Chapter 44 of the 1913 Session Laws provided that two or more districts could pool their funds to support joint institutes conducted by qualified instructors and lecturers. To provide adequate funding for the procurement of top-quality people, the Legislature directed each county to appropriate funds to defray the costs. The amount per county varied according to assessed valuation.

Chapter 52 of the Session Laws of 1913 was enacted to provide a fairer distribution of taxes to rural districts for support of their schools. Earlier apportionment of county funds had been according to the number of pupils in a district. The new law provided for the division of funds on the basis of the number of teachers employed for a period of at least 6 months.

Attention also was given to improving the elementary school curriculum. A law was enacted directing the state superintendent to prepare a uniform course of study for the elementary schools of the state (30). The law specified the subjects to be taught and charged the county superintendent with ensuring that all schools under his supervision followed the prescribed course of study. Schools with more than three teachers were permitted to adapt the curriculum to the environment of the local area.

An awareness of the problems that past state superintendents had encountered in gathering reports from school officials prompted the 1913 Legislature to enact a law in the hopes of correcting the situation (31). Stipulations were made that any school wishing to receive state funds had to maintain accurate records and submit reports when necessary. Failure to submit reports as requested would result in a fine against the school official responsible.

In her biennial report to the Governor in 1912, Superintendent Bird recommended that the power to establish or alter district boundary lines be removed as a responsibility of the county superintendent. Numerous incidents had been reported of district boundary changes' being made during school terms with no provisions for tax support for the newly formed districts. Many times, boundary disputes became so intense that the county commissioners and the state superintendent were called upon to resolve them. The Legislature, acting on the state superintendent's recommendation, enacted legislation providing for the establishment of district boundary boards composed of the county superintendents of schools and the boards of county commissioners (32). Although creation of the boards removed some of the pressure from the county superintendents, it did not eliminate disputes over boundary changes. Protests persist until this time and are as emotionally charged as they were prior to 1913. Perhaps the Legislature will have to assume the responsibility for such changes.

Under the leadership of Governor Carey, a number of solutions to Wyoming's educational problems were considered. T. A. Larson, in his *History of Wyoming,* appraised the administration of Carey as follows:

> One sees a frugal, well informed capable Progressive who was often unhorsed by the fractious majority Republicans. Nationally in this era, Progressives worked for political, humanitarian, and economic reforms. In comparison with other Progressive leaders, Carey was primarily interested in reforms designed to purify the political system, secondarily in humanitarian reforms, and scarcely at all in reforms calculated to circumscribe big business. Carey's accomplishments were noteworthy. When one considers the political circumstances, one must credit him with no mean achievement (33).

Governor Carey did not seek reelection in 1914 but chose to campaign for the Democratic candidate for

Governor, John B. Kendrick, a Sheridan County rancher. Kendrick was victorious, but all other Democratic candidates for the five top state offices were defeated, with the exception of the secretary of state. Mrs. Edith K. O. Clark was elected to the post of state superintendent of public instruction.

In 1915, at the request of the Legislature, Governor Kendrick appointed a school code committee to study the school system of the state and recommend new legislation relating to education. Further request was submitted to the Bureau of Education, a division of the U.S. Department of the Interior, for help in conducting the study. The bureau assigned A. C. Monahan, a specialist in agricultural education and rural school administration, and Katherine M. Cook, an assistant in rural education, to help make the study. Upon completion of their investigations, the committee, with help from the federal consultants, offered the following recommendations:

1. Provision for a State Board of Education as the responsible head of the educational system, the executive officer of the board to be the state superintendent of public instruction.
2. Reorganization of the State Department of Instruction by . . . clearly defining the duties of the state superintendent by legislative enactment . . . relieving the state superintendent from service on boards and commissions not connected with education . . . making the position appointive instead of elective . . . adding at least two efficient field agents to inspect secondary, vocational, and special schools receiving state aid . . . providing an annual state appropriation to be expended by the State Board of Education on the recommendations of the state superintendent . . . for purposes that may be authorized by law.
3. Nonpolitical school officers.
4. Provision for expert supervision of rural schools.
5. A County Board of Education.
6. Independent supervision of city districts.
7. A more equitable distribution of the burden of the support of education.
8. Requirements for a higher standard of general and professional education for teachers.
9. Provisions for professional training for teachers.
10. Reorganization of the plan of certification of teachers.
11. Provisions for vocational education.
12. Control of special state institutions by the state board (34).

The State Board of Education was created by the Legislature in 1917 (35). The composition of the board, the method of selection, and its relationship to the state superintendent of public instruction have been under constant attack from the start. The law provided for a seven-man board, which would include the state superintendent of public instruction as an ex officio member with voting rights. The six additional members were appointed by the state superintendent, with the approval of the Governor. No more than four of the members could be from the same political party. Two were supposed to be actively engaged in educational work. Critics, in most cases, have expressed the belief that such procedures of selection have placed the state board in the position of being nothing more than a tool of the chief state school officer.

Criticism concerning the system has never been confined to any particular group or groups but has emerged from all quarters. There was never any definite display of support for the method of selection after its initiation. The delay in change stemmed mainly from the inability of critics to combine their efforts in drafting legislation to effect the change. Not until the legislative session of 1967 were constructive efforts successful and the method of selection and composition of the board altered (36).

A second creation of the Legislature in 1917 was the provision for a commissioner of education to be appointed by the State Board of Education (37). The legislators of that day viewed the increased responsibilities of education as more than one man could cope with and a commissioner was to have provided assistance to the state superintendent. J. O. Creager, the first commissioner of education, served from 1917 through 1919. Critics have stated that in truth the commissioner was installed to run the education programs and to partially free the superintendent to accommodate the inherent political and state governmental responsibilities which are necessary to hold that position.

Perhaps a more honest appraisal of the reason for creating the post of commissioner centers around the noneducational responsibilities of the state superintendent. Wyoming has a unique government structure. All five of the elective state officers serve as an executive council. In the absence of the Governor, the other state officers, according to a prescribed order, serve in an acting capacity as Governor. In addition, the five state officers serve on a number of state boards and commissions. Article 18, Section 3, of the State Constitution stipulated that "the governor, secretary of state, state treasurer, state auditor, and superintendent of public instruction shall constitute a board of land commissioners." The constitution also provided for their service on a State School Land Board, and on a State Board of Charities and Reform.

Chapter 62, Article 1, of the 1927 Statutes broadened such responsibilities of elected officials. The law stated:

> The five elective state officers of the State of Wyoming shall comprise the membership of all state boards and commissions upon which two or more such officers are now serving by a provision of statutory law; provided, the terms hereof shall not apply to the board of university trustees.

However, the first Legislature after statehood placed the state superintendent of public instruction on the board of trustees of the university (38). At the latest count, the state superintendent serves on 16 different boards and commissions. The first week of each month is devoted to his fulfilling the duties of these extra responsibilities. These factors give strong support to the need for a commissioner.

The election of 1918 saw the son of former Governor Carey victorious in the gubernatorial race. Robert D. Carey was the Republican candidate, with the full support of his father, who had ended his feud with Francis E. Warren, longtime head of the Republican party.

Mrs. Katharine A. Morton, also a Republican, was elected as state superintendent. Mrs. Morton enjoyed the longest tenure in office of all holding the position before or after her election. Her years of service extended from 1919 to 1935.

By 1920, the state had grown, and the complexity of the state superintendent's job continued to increase. The 1919 Legislature indicated an awareness of the problem by passage of an act providing for additional staff, equipment, and space. Four new professional staff positions were immediately created. Assisting the state superintendent, in addition to the commissioner of education, were a state director of vocational education (receiving one-half his salary from federal funds), a state supervisor of vocational-agricultural education, a state supervisor of the Smith-Hughes Act home economics program (these two likewise partially paid by federal funds), and a state director of special education. All of these were ultimately responsible to the State Board of Education.

Federal funds for support of vocational education were provided by the Smith-Hughes Act. One of the conditions of the act called for the state to match each federal dollar with a dollar from state funds. In 1917, $15,000 federal money was allotted to Wyoming, but as the Legislature appropriated only $3,000 for matching purposes, a major portion of the federal funds was lost to the state. In 1918, the state appropriation still matched only one-fifth of the $15,000 available. Beginning with 1919, the federal allotment for Wyoming was increased to $20,000 per year, until 1923 when it was to rise to $30,000 annually. The 1919 Legislature, instead of improving the situation, reduced the state appropriation to $2,000 per year for the biennium. The following figures indicate the unfavorable support of vocational education in Wyoming in 1919, as compared with its neighboring states (39).

State	Federal funds	State funds
Wyoming	$ 20,000	$ 2,000
Colorado	31,950	41,340
Nebraska	44,521	50,000
Montana	21,145	21,500
Utah	20,187	50,000
Idaho	21,476	21,476

Because of the limited funds available, the Division of Vocational Education extended its services to only a few schools. This was done in the hope that each might receive enough to be of material benefit. Initially, vocational agriculture was given major emphasis. However, classes in industrial education increased from 2 in 1919 to 32 in 1922 (40). These were evening classes designed to improve the skills of workers already in industry and to provide them with new skills qualifying them for advancement. Practically nothing was done in the area of home economics until the Legislature increased the level of support. Prior to that time, no more than $2,000 per year was available from federal sources, and the Legislature had not seen fit to match even that small amount (41).

Although the first 10 years were extremely difficult for those involved with vocational education, perseverance of a few dedicated professionals established a base for what was later to become one of the most effective divisions of the state department.

Public interest for special training facilities for handicapped children had begun to mount about 1909 (42). Within 10 years, the pressure of interested citizens resulted in the passage of House Bill No. 92 in February 1919, which provided for the education and training of children afflicted with physical or mental handicaps. A Division of Special Education was created to administer the law, and $10,000 was appropriated for the first year's operation.

Interest continued to grow in support of special education. The 1920 Legislature increased the appropriation for development of such programs to $25,000 (43). Funds continued to increase as long as lay interest remained high. However, as citizen support for vocational education reached the point of effectiveness, interest in special education started to wane, and funds for its support began to diminish.

At no time during the 1920's was there sufficient money to support the size staff needed adequately to administer the new programs of the state department. In 1924, the department had the smallest administrative staff of any Western state (44). However, a professional staff was initiated.

Although the Depression resulted in overall cutbacks in funds for education, a Division for the Industrial and Educational Supervision of the Deaf and Blind was created in 1930 to implement a bill enacted by the 1929 Legislature. Chapter 160 of the Session Laws of Wyoming, 1929, was passed after much prodding of the Legislature by the Lion's Clubs of the state. The law called for accommodation of the needs of those not of school age who were deaf and blind.

Also added to the staff in the early 1930's were an assistant director for special education and a deputy state superintendent. Although the latter position was authorized by the 1899 Legislature, earlier state superintendents apparently did not see a need for an assistant other than the commissioner of education.

In 1930, the beginning of State Superintendent Morton's last term in office, much attention was directed toward the problems of school finance. Governor Emerson, serving his second term in office, called a meeting to study the problems of the financing and evaluation of Wyoming schools. Fortunately, the Governor had at his disposal two of the nation's most capable authorities in the area of school finance and evaluation: Paul Mort of Columbia University had been collaborating with Walter Reusser of the University of Wyoming in a pilot program of school evaluation. These two capable leaders were instrumental in developing a study that showed the need and the procedure for the distribution of state funds to school districts on the basis of equalization of educational opportunity and equalization of school support (45). Governor Emerson did not live to see the results of the study he proposed. During the 1931 legislative session, he died of pneumonia at the age of 48.

The Democrats made a clean sweep in the election of 1934, winning all five top elective positions and, for the first time in state history, a majority in both Houses of the Legislature. Jack R. Gage was elected state superintendent. In Professor Larson's words, "Best vote getter of all was Jack Gage, whose principal political stock in trade was a steady stream of jokes, mainly directed at himself"(46).

A state sales tax was adopted by the 1935 Legislature in preference to an income tax. Labor opposition to a sales tax was particularly strong in the House of Representatives, and only after a personal plea by Governor Miller was sufficient support mustered to ensure its passage (47).

The first equalization law also was passed by the Legislature in 1935, and $187,000 was set aside for equalization purposes from the newly enacted state sales tax (48). The equalization law provided for the computation of teaching units, for the determination of a minimum foundation program level, and for a local qualifying tax levy. Only somewhere between 25 and 30 percent of the school districts received equalization aid.

With Gage having been the top vote-getter in the election of 1934 and his own party in control of both Houses, one might have expected support for school legislation. However, the passage of the equalization law in 1935 was the last piece of school legislation of any significance during the 1930's. Party bickering destroyed the Democrats' chance of victory in the election of 1938. Control of both Houses of the Legislature was regained by the Republicans, along with the offices of Governor, state treasurer, and superintendent of public instruction. Esther L. Anderson won election as state superintendent and served in that position through 1946.

The 8 years under Mrs. Anderson's administration could best be described as a replay of the previous 8 years. Vocational education and vocational rehabilitation continued as the major thrust of the State Department of Education. Of the five new positions created during this period, four were additions to the vocational staff: a research specialist, two assistants in vocational rehabilitation, and a state fiscal agent for defense training programs.

Installation of a fiscal agent can be credited more to hindsight than foresight. In August 1941, Frank M. Treat, director of vocational education, presented two vouchers for approval to the state superintendent. Mrs. Anderson refused to approve the vouchers, which were payable to a Roy C. Conover, on the grounds that the class for which Mr. Conover was being paid had been closed since February 1941. An extensive investigation revealed that Mr. Conover had been relieved of his duties as a part-time instructor of trade and industry in 1932 but that Treat had kept Conover's name on the payroll and continued submitting vouchers for payment of his salary. Over a period of 13 years, Treat had cashed a total of 203 warrants after forging the names of the payees and signing his own name as endorsee. The total loss to the state was $45,805.15. The attorney general advised that in his judgment no one in the three previous administrations or in Mrs. Anderson's, other than Treat, was involved in the fraudulent scheme. Treat was tried and pleaded guilty (49). After this event, the hiring of a fiscal agent seemed a wise move.

In 1943, the Legislature established the Wyoming Teacher Retirement System (50). An executive secretary was employed to administer the program, and the education board was authorized to sit as the official teacher retirement board.

From all evidence, the major emphasis of the state department during the war years was directed toward the war effort. Many programs were initiated for the training of "Out-of-School Rural Youth," provided for by an act of Congress in 1940. Courses were offered in the operation and care of tractors, trucks, and automobiles; metalwork; woodworking; and elementary electricity. The courses were designed to provide preliminary training for defense industries, including agriculture.

Had it not been for an action by the State Board of Education in 1945, it would seem no schooling other than vocational any longer existed in Wyoming. In April 1945, the board created a Division of Elementary and Special Education (51), which 4 years later was to be renamed the Division of Elementary Education and Education of Handicapped Children. The action by the state board in 1945 was a promising sign. For 16 years, the state department had provided little leadership throughout the state except in the vocational area. What contacts were made with local districts placed the department in the role of inspector.

With the election of Edna B. Stolt in 1948 and the end of 16 years of national emergency–first economic and then war–Wyoming entered a new era in education. The change was not dramatic but the prosperity of the 1950's resulted in an almost continuous improvement in the services rendered by the state department.

In 1954, the Wyoming Citizens Committee on Educational Problems recommended that Wyoming should embark on a plan of state and local support of public schools based on a good foundation program of education made possible in all districts (52). A state-guaranteed program of education for every child, it was in a sense a minimum educational program for it allowed a local school district to exceed the minimum program to the extent that its constituents might desire and were able to support.

Such a plan was submitted to the 1955 Legislature and was passed with overwhelming support. The legislation provided the core and the framework for Wyoming's financing of its schools. It was recognized, even in 1955, that as times and educational needs changed, the foundation program also would need to be modified. The program has served Wyoming education well during the past years. Even though some improvements have been made, there is a continuous need to modernize it both in relation to program and to dollar value of the costs. Yet it represents a solid basis on which to finance the schools of today as well as those of tomorrow.

The demand for school construction, more teachers, higher salaries, and increased services all contributed to the rising costs of education during this period. As costs continued to mount, more and more demands were voiced for greater state support.

In the election of 1954, the Democratic candidate for state superintendent of public instruction, Velma Linford, emerged victorious. During her first 4 years in office, Superintendent Linford offered several ideas for improving the state department, one of which was that the position of commissioner of education no longer was needed. The statutory position was eliminated by the Legislature in 1959. A complete administrative reorganization of the department followed.

The new organizational structure included the State Board of Education, the state superintendent, the deputy superintendent, and three divisions, each under an assistant superintendent: administration, instruction, and vocational rehabilitation divisions. The several activities and services of the entire department were placed under one or another of these divisions. Under Miss Linford's leadership, the state department became better known throughout the state, and many of her ideas for improvement of Wyoming education were of merit. The revision of the procedures for the accreditation of schools should be recognized as one of her noteworthy contributions. Moreover, a program was designed to encourage continuous improvement of local school programs through a combination of self-analysis and committee evaluation. An evaluative instrument was prepared which identified the basic characteristics of good school programs in all areas of operation, and copies were distributed to local districts to guide them in their efforts at analyzing their individual programs. After the self-evaluation by the local districts, a team of state department personnel and professionals in the field visited each district to assist in developing plans for improvement. Under the new procedures, schools were not compared and rated against each other but were evaluated on the basis of the characteristics and needs of each individual community.

The year 1962 proved to be a good one for the Republicans as they swept all five of the state's elective officers, and Miss Linford was defeated by Cecil M. Shaw of Casper, Wyoming.

During the school year 1962-63, the department was again reorganized, this time into six divisions, each headed by an assistant superintendent: administration, business and finance, vocational education, vocational rehabilitation, special education, and instruction. In July 1965, a research division was added; soon afterwards, special education was transferred from the Division of Vocational Rehabilitation to the Division of Instruction. These divisions were envisioned as major areas of service carried on by the state department personnel, with each service placed in its appropriate division. The door was left open to future adjustment as experience indicated a need.

In 1966, there were 61 professional staff positions in the State Department of Education, including 32 in vocational rehabilitation, plus a substantial number in charge of administering federally financed programs. But more qualified service personnel were needed if the various programs necessary to meet the educational needs of the state were to be provided. Limited appropriations, of course, placed restrictions on addition of personnel.

PROBLEMS FACED BY THE STATE DEPARTMENT

Curriculum

At the heart of all education lies the curriculum; in a dynamic society, the curriculum must be in a state of perpetual flux, or it fails to meet the needs of the pupils pursuing it. Perhaps at no time in the past have demands for curricular progress been so urgent as they are today. A glance at the broader changes in curricular offerings throughout Wyoming's educational history will hint at what lies ahead.

Some expansion of curriculum took place after the turn of the century. However, until 1921, high schools generally confined themselves to a curriculum divided into a college preparatory program and one with a commercial emphasis. The curriculums were heavily weighted in favor of the college-bound, although only a small percentage of students ever attended college. Statements of many interested persons of the time reveal a concern with the segment of the student body not attending college. Implementation of the Smith-Hughes Act by the Legislature in 1917 started the ball rolling in agriculture and to some extent in home economics.

The year 1921 saw considerable expansion of curricular offerings in larger schools, which was fostered in part by a ruling of the state board that required schools to submit their programs of study to the commissioner of education before accreditation could be granted. Some leading schools offered college preparatory, general, stenographic training, bookkeeping, home economics, mechanical arts, and normal training courses. Size, then as now, naturally played an important part in this. Although curricular offerings were considered for accreditation in 1921, they represented only a small segment of the evaluative criteria.

Schools were rated on the basis of a 100-point scale. Points were awarded on the following basis:

I. The school plant	40 points
a. Accommodation for teachers	8 points
b. Location	3 points
c. Outbuildings	3 points
d. School buildings	15 points
e. Heating	2 points
f. Equipment and supplies	9 points
II. School efficiency	60 points
a. Community activities	12 points
b. Organization	15 points
c. The teacher	15 points
d. Educational progress	18 points

Elementary-level curriculums were receiving attention as well. In 1913, the Legislature provided an elementary school course of study which tended to make for more uniform instruction. Prior to this, Wyoming had been using curriculums from other states. A new rural curriculum adopted in 1924-26 streamlined and improved the course of study and better provided for pupil needs by reducing the number of classes taught by each teacher from 35 to 14.

But curricular study and development are not static. Curriculum revisions, additions, and studies have been the order of the day almost since the inception of education in Wyoming. Curriculum has had to adjust to the demands of a changing world. In 1940-42, for example, Wyoming high schools adjusted their educational programs to the needs of the war emergency program, with 32 high schools offering preflight aeronautics; some taught radio communications; and nearly all of them expanded programs in physical education, science, mathematics, and vocational education (53). Revision of curriculums in elementary mathematics was accomplished in 1949 and 1950 through teacher-principal workshops at the University of Wyoming. Driver education classes were introduced into high schools in 1951-52. Later, distributive education classes were added to certain high school curriculums. Within the state, workshops continue in all subject fields into the present day. In 1965, English teachers, working with university specialists in cooperation with the state department, wrote the first English curriculum guide in Wyoming history, and this, too, will need continuing attention and revision. So the story goes, in English, social studies, physical education, music, reading, conservation, the elementary field—all of these programs are currently receiving attention. Originally written by state department personnel or by one or two individuals, curriculum studies are now done cooperatively by teachers, administrators, and expert consultants in curriculum workshops.

Division of Vocational Education

Records and information relating to vocational education in Wyoming began with the passage of the Smith-Hughes Act of 1917, allocating federal money for the promotion and development of vocational home economics, agriculture, trades, and industry. The provisions of the Smith-Hughes Act were accepted by the 1917 Legislature, and an appropriation of $3,000 was made for administrative expenses (54).

In January 1918, J. R. Coxen was selected as half-time state director and half-time teacher-trainer in trades and industry. He served as state director of vocational education until 1925 and was succeeded by F. M. Treat, who held that position until 1941. Sam Hitchcock, state supervisor of agricultural education from 1935 to 1941, was named state director in 1941 and served in that capacity until his retirement in 1961. In the past 6 years, five persons have served short terms as state director.

Turnover of state supervisors has been slight. Only five persons have held the position of head state supervisor of home economics education, one of whom served 32 years. Prior to 1962, assistant state staff for home economics education were employed on a part-time or full-time basis for 22 years. Only eight persons have served as supervisor of agricultural education during the 50 years from 1917 to 1967. Assistant state agricultural education staff have been employed intermittently.

Wyoming, being a rural state, has concentrated on programs related to ranching and farming to a greater extent than it has to trade and industry occupations. Youth organizations designed to develop leadership and good citizenship have been an integral part of vocational education in home economics and agriculture for some 40 years.

A full-time state supervisor of trades and industry education was not employed by the state until 1967. Until that time, those responsibilities were assumed by staff members with other administrative responsibilities. Up to the present, five high school trades and industry programs have been developed, plus two postsecondary programs.

With the passage of the George-Deen Act in 1936, federal funds were available for distributive education. Records and information for this area are incomplete, but it is believed that approximately ten different persons have been designated to give state leadership to the programs intermittently. Since 1964, high schools conducting distributive education programs have increased from 4 to 12. One postsecondary program has been initiated, and a youth organization also has functioned in this area.

For several years prior to 1955, a full-time staff member was employed as supervisor of research and occupational information. Eight years later, in 1963, this position was staffed on a part-time basis to direct vocational guidance.

Quotes from the biennial report of the state superintendent, 1926-28, indicate that the goals for vocational education were much the same as they are today.

> The prime aim of vocational education is to train in habits of thinking and doing. It is especially for those who do not plan to go on with higher educational work. The courses in vocational education are so offered as to give actual experience to those partaking. Vocational education becomes a part of the experiences of any individual whereby he trains to carry on successfully any gainful occupation (55).

The Vocational Act of 1963 allocates federal funds to promote and develop programs to prepare and upgrade all persons, youth and adults, to achieve and maintain skills for occupations requiring less than a college degree. Additional professional leadership personnel at the state level has been limited.

Since 1962, staff members have been added to direct the federal programs of research, manpower development training, and adult basic education. Business and office, health, and women's occupations responsibilities were handled by the directors of distributive education, trade and industry, and home economics. State funds for vocational education, appropriated by the Legislature in 1967, have doubled–but they are still much less than is needed.

The status, needs, and challenges for increased vocational-technical education were reviewed in 1967 by a Governor's Committee on Vocational-Technical Education. Its findings and recommendations will give the people of Wyoming an opportunity to evaluate efforts toward meeting the rapidly changing employment conditions that exist today and those that are likely to take place in the near future.

Division of Vocational Rehabilitation

A story of apocryphal origin relates that two men were debating the merits of a mutual federal-state effort in the rehabilitation of physically and mentally handicapped when one of them, in an effort to carry the day, exclaimed, "Well, then, are we our brother's keeper?" "No," answered the other. "We are our brother's brother." This story expresses well the function and the record of federal-state cooperation in Wyoming. From tax consumers to taxpayers, the participants in Wyoming's rehabilitation programs find new usefulness, new independence, and new hope.

In June 1920, Wyoming, through its legislative authority, accepted the provisions and benefits of an act of Congress entitled "An Act To Provide for the Promotion of Vocational Rehabilitation of Persons Disabled in Industry, or Otherwise and Their Return to Civil Employment"(56). The State Board of Education was designated as the state board responsible for cooperating with the federal government in carrying out the provisions and purposes of this federal act.

The program that was carried on for the first 23 years was primarily educational. Accomplishments up to 1943 clearly fell far short of the needs of eligible vocationally handicapped persons because the existing law had a number of limitations that made a well-rounded vocational rehabilitation program impossible.

There was a statutory limit on the amount of funds available for state grants-in-aid; no physical restoration services, except prosthetic appliances, were included; no special services for the blind were provided; until 1939, federal funds could not be used to provide maintenance during rehabilitation. The services were limited for the most part to vocational counseling, vocational training, obtaining artificial appliances, and placement services. Experiences throughout these years proved beyond a doubt that under proper conditions handicapped men and women compete on an equal basis with so-called normal workers. Experience also showed that many vocationally handicapped persons were being declared ineligible because the provisions of the regulations pertaining to expenditure of funds limited the extent of services for which moneys could be expended for rehabilitation purposes. Realizing the inadequacies of this program, the Seventy-Eighth Congress passed Public Law 113, which made it possible to greatly expand the scope of the program.

Recognizing the value of this legislation, in 1945, Wyoming accepted the provisions of this law. The staffing of the program began with a meager number of dedicated individuals and has expanded to the present staff, in excess of 60. In addition to the regular rehabilitation districts, the agency is also represented in all of the state institutions (Wyoming State Training School, Wyoming Girls' School,

Wyoming Industrial Institute, and Wyoming State Penitentiary). A number of innovative projects have been initiated by the Division of Vocational Rehabilitation through the Division of Services for the Visually Handicapped, and these have become an integral part of the total rehabilitation program.

Today, vocational rehabilitation is limited only by lack of financial means to operate a program extensive enough to provide complete rehabilitation services to all eligible vocationally handicapped men and women in Wyoming.

Division of Certification and Placement

The state board is authorized to establish rules and regulations for administering the laws governing the certification of teachers (57). This has become an increasingly greater responsibility with the growth in the number of teachers and the raising of standards for certification. At one time, a graduate satisfactorily completing the high school "normal" training course could be certified to teach. In 1962, the bachelor's degree became mandatory as a requirement for the standard certificate. Issuance of certificates increased from 960 in 1935-36 to 1,898 in 1965-66. The approximate number of certified teachers in 1966 was 5,000.

Involved in the certification process are the collection of personal data and credentials for candidates and the evaluation of these data in terms of standards, rules, and regulations.

> The law passed by the Thirteenth Legislature, 1917, provides for the following classes of certificates: (1) elementary city school certificates; (2) rural school certificates; (3) high school certificates; (4) administrative certificates; (5) special certificates (58).

In 1948-50, 21 classes of certificates were recognized. The *Wyoming Teacher Certification Regulations, January 1, 1965,* provide for three basic certificates: the initial certificate, the standard certificate, and the professional certificate.

Closely related to the certification process is a placement service which was provided by statute in 1919 and operates without charge for the benefit of superintendents and trustees who desire to engage teachers. This service includes the collection and evaluation of reliable data concerning the qualifications of candidates for employment in the schools of the state.

Another related activity is the Wyoming Legislative Scholarship Program, created in 1959 and designed to stimulate and encourage interest in preparation for the teaching profession among high school graduates and undergraduate college students.

The state department staff responsible for performing the sundry and related certification and placement activities has, of course, varied from time to time. The staffing of the present Division of Certification and Placement includes the director and four highly trained assistants. The first assistant directs the general flow of all communications, including applications for certification and the processing of the certificates, and also handles the correspondence and other clerical work related to the legislative scholarships. A certification assistant carries the major responsibility for evaluating college transcripts and assists in handling personal inquiries relating to certification. A placement assistant handles all correspondence with applicants for employment, making a preliminary evaluation of personal credentials, contacting references, and handling referrals to prospective employing superintendents and school boards. A fourth assistant has primary responsibility for setting up folios for applicants for certification, for accumulating the necessary credentials materials, and notifying applicants of any additional materials needed. All assistants have joint responsibilities for general office routine, including preparation and processing of correspondence, processing of certificates, and filing of credentials and related records.

School District Reorganization

There is evidence of a desire to improve the quality of the public schools' educational program in Wyoming through the continued development of high standards for certification and placement of teachers. Present regulations provide for recognition of specialized preparation. The present staff is dedicated to the efficient processing of credentials, uniform and consistent interpretation of rules and regulations, and impartial application of the personnel requirements. The early elimination of all substandard permits is a goal.

At the outset of its educational history, Wyoming had a problem quite opposite to the one which was to plague it later: It had too *few* school districts! When Wyoming Territory was organized in 1869, it had five counties, each of which consisted of a common school district extending the width of the Territory. This vast size compelled change; and the first Territorial Assembly gave the county superintendents power to divide settled parts of counties into school districts and to alter and change boundaries as conditions required. But even this authority did little to avoid the formidable distances between school districts.

Districts began to multiply; by 1892, there were 190; by 1900, 205; and by 1910, 303. In 1913, legislation was passed creating district boundary boards which were composed of the county commissioners and the county superintendent. A standardization movement was begun to encourage upgrading of schools. This movement fostered some consolidation of school districts. After a high of 415 districts was reached in 1930, the number declined to 382 in 1940.

Many districts had consolidated, but many others found themselves unable to support a proper educational program. Educational opportunities needed to be made equal in all districts; public funds needed to be used more judiciously. The 1947 Legislature, made aware of this need, appointed committees to study and recommend reorganization plans and in 1949 established criteria to govern organization of school districts. In essence, these stipulated that (a) the district should be large enough to organize a school program from kindergarten through twelfth grade; (b) the district should be large enough to hold desirable administrative and teaching personnel and have a large enough number of pupils to make progress possible and reasonable; (c) the district should be small enough in area and population that people would be able to participate effectively in support and control, and in the social affairs of the schools; (d) the districts could, if necessary, transcend county lines; and (e) the reorganization of the school district does not have to mean consolidation or abolition of neighborhood schools, and the district should have sufficient wealth to carry its program adequately with state and local funds. This legislation helped, for consolidation of districts accelerated. From 382 in 1940, the number slid to 312 in 1950, and to 200 in 1963.

The 1960-62 biennial report of the state superintendent stated that only about 30 percent of Wyoming's districts met the minimum standard for the kind of district organization that could produce quality schools; that is, that a good district is organized to operate a K-12 program in which meaningful integration of the curriculum can be achieved.

The same report stressed great differences in the abilities of districts in Wyoming to raise funds because of variations of valuations for each child. And with regard to qualified personnel, the report states that only 95 of Wyoming's 204 districts employed fully qualified superintendents, that 89 employed no superintendent or principal, and that 20 employed a fully qualified principal or head teacher. Only 26 of the districts could provide guidance services, either full or part time, and only 15 of the districts having sufficient population to provide for the mentally handicapped in special education classes were doing so.

Education of Indian Children

There is little evidence indicating concern at the state level for the problems of educating Indian children during the first half of the twentieth century. There seemed to be a general willingness to leave such problems to the mission schools and to the Bureau of Indian Affairs. The schools operated by the Episcopal and Catholic churches were originally maintained as boarding schools. In the early 1930's, with some financial help from the federal government, provisions were made for day-school pupils.

As financial support began to dwindle, the educational programs for the Indian children began to deteriorate. Both of the Episcopal schools (Robert's Mission and St. Michael's) were forced to close in the middle fifties because of the lack of funds. The St. Stephen's school continued to operate, but it was forced to discontinue its high school program in 1965.

At the closing of the federally supported day schools, the Indian children in the Wind River Reservation area were integrated into the public schools. It was soon apparent that the public school teachers lacked the training necessary to cope with the special problems inherent in the education of Indian children.

In 1958, a contract was negotiated by the Bureau of Indian Affairs with the State Department of Education. Under the terms of the contract, the department was to provide guidance services and other assistance to the local districts in improving their programs to educate Indian children. Funds were made available by the Johnson-O'Malley Act and the contractual period extended from 1959 through 1963.

A guidance counselor was employed by the state department and based in Fremont County, where a majority of the Indian children attended school. The counselor spent the first 3 years working with the children, parents, and teachers, attempting to provide them with a better understanding of the necessity for and problems of getting an education. A great deal of time was devoted to testing to identify the extent of each child's ability and to determine those pupils most in need of placement into classes for the educable retarded.

Although high school attendance improved during the first 3 years of the contract, there appeared little evidence that school programs had been significantly improved. A decision was made to change the emphasis from direct guidance services to consultative services in guidance and instruction during the last 2 years of the contract.

The services of the Johnson-O'Malley special counselor were discontinued in 1965, and funds for support of Indian education were made available to the local schools through Public Law 874. The local districts now have total responsibility for the education of Indian children, and their relationship with the state department is the same as in other districts.

FEDERAL-STATE RELATIONSHIPS

During the 1950's, there was considerable opposition to accepting additional federal financial aid that would involve matching funds by the state for the support of public elementary and secondary education—but such opposition did not extend to the university or community college. The thought of accepting federal funds (to which strings might be attached) had for many years created controversy within the state.

Congress enacted the National Defense Education Act of 1958, and the issue was focused in Wyoming in the 1959 Legislature. That Legislature enacted a bill which stipulated that NDEA funds could be accepted providing the federal budget was in balance and funds were not available elsewhere.

Such a situation arose in 1960, when Superintendent Linford received official notice from the federal government that its budget was in balance. Through action of the state board, the state superintendent and the board went on record as having ascertained that funds were not otherwise available for certain educational efforts. The state board then decided to accept NDEA funds. However, the jubilation of the advocates of federal aid was short-lived.

Political opposition began to brew among some legislators who viewed with disfavor the actions of the state board and state superintendent. Opponents of federal aid to the public and elementary schools mustered their forces; and in February 1961, the Legislature enacted legislation to repeal the law it had passed in 1959 and to further prohibit the acceptance of such matching funds. By May, as a result of this legislation, Wyoming again became a nonparticipant in NDEA funds for the public elementary and secondary schools.

The fight over acceptance of federal funds for education continued in the 1960's. There was, however, a complete change of thinking by the 1965 Legislature, when it enacted legislation that permitted Wyoming to participate without qualification in the NDEA and subsequent federal legislation for education. The reasons behind this reversal are several:

1. The state was suffering economically; and outside money–including federal money–would stimulate the economy.

2. People realized that the university and the community colleges had benefited from such legislation and that the educational program of the schools could also benefit.

3. There was a general recognition that federal financial aid for schools was "a fact of life" and that Wyoming might as well use its own tax money rather than have another state use it.

Therefore, at long last, Wyoming became a full-fledged participant. As the last of the 50 states to enter the program, the state now was faced with staffing and other changes which accompany increased responsibilities. The first year's operation could perhaps be described as hectic, partially because local districts had little time to plan before application deadlines were upon them. The enactment of Public Law 89-10, the Elementary and Secondary Education Act of 1965, provided more problems for the still understaffed state department as well as for the local districts.

Considering the frustrations of the district superintendents faced with the flood of paperwork that was required for participation, interest throughout the state increased at a rapid rate in acquiring the federal funds. There was soon a definite recognition that many of the constructive programs that were developed would have never been possible without federal assistance.

Perhaps the greatest change in state department functions has been in the areas of instruction and planning. New staff have been added in a number of subject areas, thereby making it possible for the first time for attention to be given to the nonvocational subjects. One example of the emerging planning function–long-range planning–is that of a Title V, Section 505, project which has received much attention in the state and may perhaps point the direction of educational change for the future. This project, "Designing Education for the Future: An Eight-State Project," has drawn much support from both lay and educational leaders.

While some of the districts in the state still had refused up to 1965 to accept federal funds, the great majority have done much to improve their programs through funds available under NDEA Title III. Since the passage of the Elementary and Secondary Education Act of 1965, great strides have been made in improving educational opportunities for the disadvantaged through Title I funds. Many creative projects have resulted from participation in Title III, including a planetarium at Casper which has drawn nationwide attention.

The controversy in federal financial aid for Wyoming education has not died down completely. Discussion now seems to be centering around categorical aid versus general aid–not over the accepting or rejecting of federal funds.

Changes have indeed been made in Wyoming.

FOOTNOTES

1. Louisa C. Watson, "Fort Laramie, 1849-1869" (unpublished master's thesis, University of Wyoming, 1963).
2. *Cheyenne Leader,* November 2, 1867.
3. T. A. Larson, *History of Wyoming* (Lincoln: University of Nebraska Press, 1965), p. 44.
4. Wyoming, *Statutes* (1869), ch. 7, title 1, sec. 2.
5. Harrison C. Dale, *A Sketch of the History of Education in Wyoming* (Cheyenne: Department of Public Instruction, October 1916), p. 8.
6. Territorial Auditor, *Biennial Report* (1872).
7. Dale, *op. cit.*, p. 25.
8. Wyoming, *Laws, Memorials, and Resolutions* (1874), ch. 58, sec. 2f.
9. Wyoming, *Compiled Laws* (1887), secs. 3910, 3911.
10. Wyoming, *Compiled Laws* (1886), ch. 35, p. 75.

11. Superintendent of Public Instruction, *Biennial Report* (1892), p. 7.
12. Dale, *op. cit.*, p. 13.
13. All information regarding early Indian education in Wyoming was obtained from telephone interviews with Superintendent Hobbs of the Wind River Reservation at Fort Washakie, Wyoming.
14. U.S. Commissioner of Education, *Report* (1886), p. 171.
15. U.S. Commissioner of Education, *Report* (1874), p. 651.
16. Dale, *op. cit.*, p. 35.
17. Larson, *op. cit.*, p. 228.
18. Wyoming, *Statutes* (1890), ch. 67, sec. 3914, p. 141.
19. Wyoming, *Constitution* (1889), art. 7, sec. 2.
20. Wyoming, *Constitution* (1889), art. 7, sec. 8.
21. Superintendent of Public Instruction, *Biennial Report* (1892), p. 20.
22. Superintendent of Public Instruction, *Biennial Report* (1902), p. 6.
23. *Ibid.*, p. 17.
24. A. C. Monahan and Katherine M. Cook, *Educational Survey of Wyoming,* Department of the Interior, Bureau of Education, Bulletin No. 29 (Washington, D.C.: Government Printing Office, 1916), p. 96.
25. Superintendent of Public Instruction, *Biennial Report* (1906), p. 27.
26. *Ibid.*, p. 30.
27. Superintendent of Public Instruction, *Biennial Report* (1908), p. 8.
28. *Ibid.*, p. 10.
29. Wyoming, *Session Laws* (1913), ch. 15.
30. *Ibid.*, ch. 53.
31. *Ibid.*, ch. 92.
32. *Ibid.*, ch. 42.
33. Larson, *op. cit.*, p. 334.
34. Monahan and Cook, *op. cit.*, pp. 96-104.
35. Wyoming, *Statutes* (1919), ch. 127, art. 4.
36. Wyoming, *Statutes* (1967), ch. 96, art. 2.
37. Wyoming, *Compiled Statutes* (1920), secs. 2331-2346.
38. Wyoming, *Revised Statutes* (1891), ch. 1, sec. 3.
39. Superintendent of Public Instruction, *Biennial Report* (1920), p. 38.
40. Superintendent of Public Instruction, *Biennial Report* (1922), p. 51.
41. Superintendent of Public Instruction, *Biennial Report* (1924), p. 56.
42. Superintendent of Public Instruction, *Biennial Report* (1920), p. 41.
43. Superintendent of Public Instruction, *Biennial Report* (1922), p. 72.
44. Superintendent of Public Instruction, *Biennial Report* (1924), p. 11.
45. Superintendent of Public Instruction, *Biennial Report* (1932), p. 9. Much of the information relating to problems of school finance in Wyoming was gathered in interviews with Walter C. Reusser of Laramie, Wyoming.
46. Larson, *op. cit.*, p. 465.
47. *Ibid.*
48. Superintendent of Public Instruction, *Biennial Report* (1940), p. 105.
49. Superintendent of Public Instruction, *Biennial Report* (1942), p. 70.
50. Superintendent of Public Instruction, *Biennial Report* (1944), pp. 8, 63.
51. Superintendent of Public Instruction, *Biennial Report* (1946), p. 7.
52. Citizens Committee on Educational Problems, *Public Education in Wyoming*, a digest of the report of the Wyoming Citizens Committee on Educational Problems (Cheyenne: The Committee, November 1, 1954).
53. Superintendent of Public Instruction, *Biennial Report* (1942), p. 10.
54. Wyoming, *Session Laws* (1917), ch. 109, p. 144.
55. Superintendent of Public Instruction, *Biennial Report* (1928), p. 81.
56. Wyoming, *Statutes* (1957), 21-277, 21-282.
57. Wyoming, *Statutes* (1919), ch. 127, sec. 17.
58. Department of Education, *Certification of Teachers* (Cheyenne: The Department, 1917).

BIBLIOGRAPHY

Public Documents

Wyoming. *Compiled Laws* (1886, 1887).

—— *Compiled Statutes* (1920).

—— *Constitution* (1890).

—— *Laws, Memorials, and Resolutions* (1874).

—— *Revised Statutes* (1887, 1891).

—— *Session Laws* (1913, 1917).

—— *Statutes* (1869, 1890, 1919, 1927, 1957, and 1967).

Books

Dale, Harrison C. *A Sketch of the History of Education in Wyoming*. Cheyenne: Department of Public Instruction, October 1916.

Department of Education. *Certification of Teachers*. Cheyenne: The Department, 1917.

Larson, T. A. *History of Wyoming*. Lincoln: University of Nebraska Press, 1965.

Reports

Citizens Committee on Educational Problems. *Public Education in Wyoming*. A digest of the report of the Wyoming Citizens Committee on Educational Problems. Cheyenne: The Committee, November 1, 1954.

Monahan, A. C., and Cook, Katherine M. *Educational Survey of Wyoming*. Department of the Interior, Bureau of Education, Bulletin No. 29. Washington, D.C.: Government Printing Office, 1916.

Superintendents of Public Instruction. *Biennial Reports*. Cheyenne: Department of Education, 1892-1967.

Territorial Auditor. *Biennial Report, 1870*.

U.S. Commissioner of Education. *Reports*. Washington, D.C.: Bureau of Education, 1874, 1886.

Periodical

Cheyenne Leader, November 2, 1867.

Unpublished Material

Watson, Louisa C. "Fort Laramie, 1849-1869." Unpublished master's thesis, University of Wyoming, 1963.

Other Source

Telephone interviews with Superintendent Hobbs of the Wind River Reservation at Fort Washakie, Wyoming.

Appendix A

WYOMING CHIEF STATE SCHOOL OFFICERS

State Superintendents of Public Instruction

1890-94	Stephen H. Farwell
1895-96	Estelle Reel
1897-98	C. H. Parmelee
1899-1907	T. T. Tynan
1907-11	A. D. Cook
1911-15	Rose A. Bird-Maley
1915-19	Edith K. O. Clark
1919-35	Katharine A. Morton
1935-39	Jack R. Gage
1939-47	Esther L. Anderson
1947-55	Edna Stolt
1955-63	Velma Linford
1963-67	Cecil M. Shaw
1967-	Harry Roberts

Appendix B

Chart I.--WYOMING DEPARTMENT OF EDUCATION, 1968

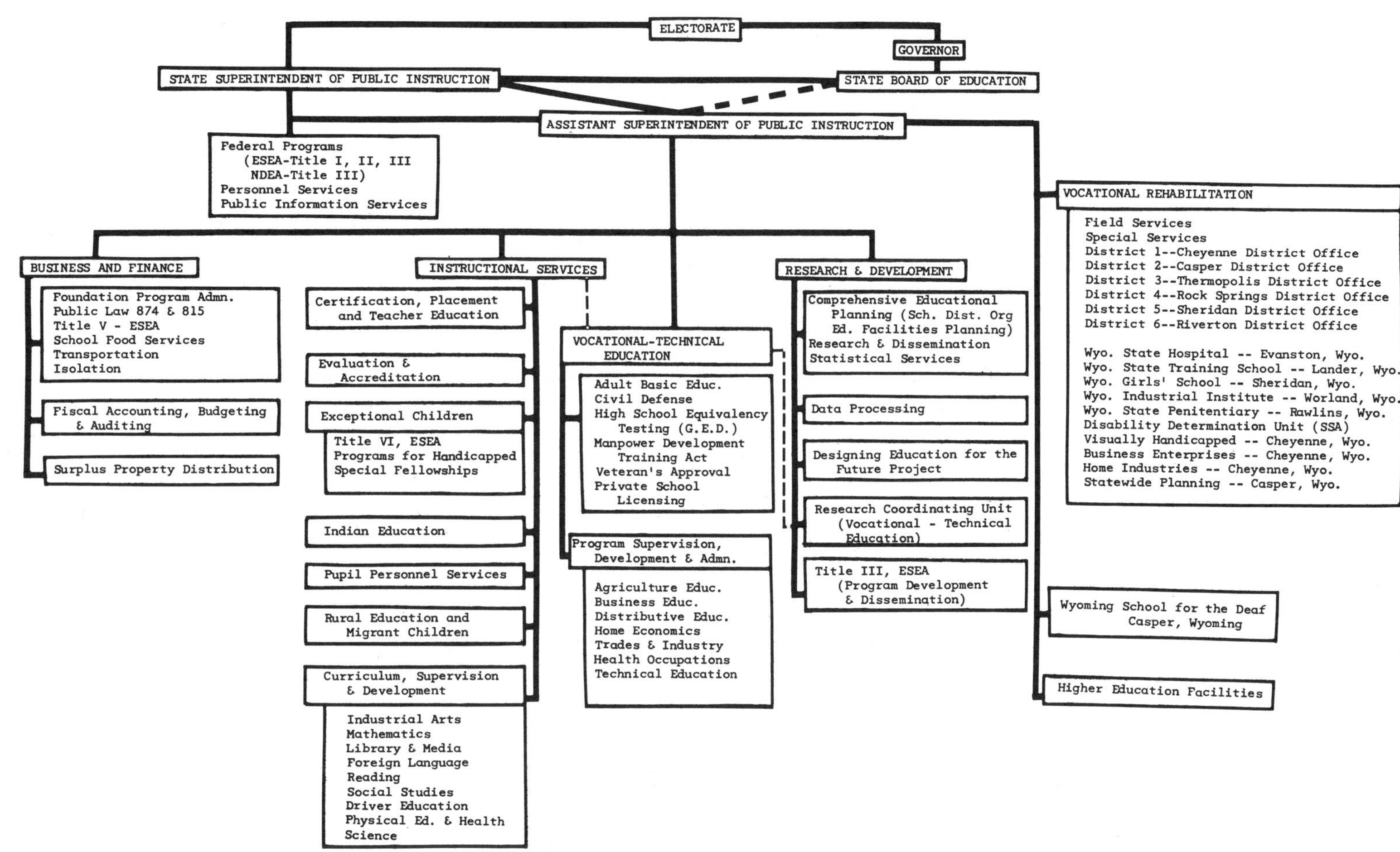

52 American Samoa

DEPARTMENT OF EDUCATION
William B. Banks

Contents

EARLY DEVELOPMENTS

Historical Background (1)

The origin of the first Samoan settlers has been lost in antiquity, although anthropologists agree that they landed more than 2,000 years ago. The islands were probably first discovered by Europeans when the Dutch explorer Jacob Roggeveen visited them in 1792. The United States' interests were first represented when an American explorer, Charles Wilkes, surveyed the islands in 1839. Great Britain appointed representatives to Samoa in 1847; the United States, in 1853; and Germany, in 1861.

After several years of disputes over possessions, Germany and the United States divided the archipelago in 1900, the portion of Samoa east of longitude 170° coming under U.S. jurisdiction (2). The Department of the Navy administered the territory until 1951; the Department of the Interior took over that year and continues to administer Samoa today.

1900 to 1911

The Navy was given the responsibility of administering these islands because it had maintained a coaling station in the Pago Harbor for a number of years. This adversely affected the development of Samoa's educational system, for despite the desire to do a good job, the Navy was not equipped or staffed for such a task. Moreover, it had to start from scratch, as the islands had only five schools worthy of the name. The London Missionary Society operated two well-established schools for boys at Fagalele and Ta'u in Manu'a, and a girls' school at Ataloma. The Roman Catholics ran a girls' school in Leone, and the Latter-Day Saints had an agricultural school at Mapusaga. All were private religious institutions, open only to very restricted groups of students and staff, and offering limited facilities and a narrow curriculum to a few students under unfavorable conditions. Even where teachers were qualified, their isolation and inability to keep up with the changes in the outside world soon diminished their effectiveness.

The London Missionary Society did maintain a large number of "pastor's schools" in connection with its churches. Taught by village clergymen whose educational experience scarcely qualified them as teachers, the schools were almost totally without equipment. But children did learn a little arithmetic and how to read and write in Samoan. There were no public schools, nor did the social structure provide for them.

Commander B. F. Tilley, commandant of the naval station at Tutuila and the island's ranking officer, regarded the missionary efforts as encouraging. But he realized that literacy in the Samoan language, desirable as it might be, would not prepare the people for the problems they would face as the new century increasingly made its way into the islands. With great foresight, Tilley saw that the Samoans needed an international language to bridge the technical and social barriers. They needed practical courses that would provide them with the ability to understand the world into which they were moving. Thus, he proposed that government-sponsored manual training schools be established at Tutuila and in the Manu'a group, and that domestic science courses for girls be offered in Tutuila. In all of these schools, learning English would take precedence over everything else.

After surveying the problems, Tilley's executive officer, E. J. Dorn, wrote to the Department of the Navy, suggesting that the commissioner of education, then a functionary of the Interior Department, be given the task of inaugurating an educational system for American Samoa. The Navy assented, and the commissioner surveyed the educational situation. He recommended that $347.50 be made available immediately for school equipment, especially for a number of new *McGuffey's Readers.* Despite the modesty of his proposal, which was the first request for federal funds for education in Samoa, the money was not immediately available, and the letter and recommendations were filed for future reference.

Tilley felt a strong sense of frustration. He could not achieve the objectives he felt were necessary with the 57 inefficient, church-operated village schools spread throughout the islands (3). Both Tilley and his successor made additional unsuccessful requests for funds. Finally, with the help of Father Bellwaldt of the Catholic Church and a subsidy from the territorial funds, a nonsectarian boys' school was established near Leone, the government's first venture in education.

In the following year, 1903, the government actually organized its first school, which consisted of one Samoan teacher and was located in Ta'u, Manu'a. At the same time, a number of non-Samoan residents clamored for a school in the Pago Bay area. A study revealed the advantage of having such a school, and, with a $1,000 appropriation from the Copra Fund, the second school was opened in Fagatogo in 1904 with two stateside teachers. These two instructors, along with the one in Manu'a, were the first public school teachers in Samoa. During the next 2 years, despite the evident need for schools and the requests for funds, naval authorities were unable to provide any additional help. Districts were forced to raise their own money and create schools, as did the people of Leone, who organized a boys' school in 1906. The school in Ta'u, Manu'a, was closed in 1906 when the teacher decided to leave the island.

First Efforts To Organize a System

Long before the Americans took over at Tutuila, intense rivalry had developed between the various missionary groups. Antagonisms carried over into the educational programs, and the subsidy granted the Catholics in 1903 aggravated the situation. By 1911, the atmosphere was tense, with little hope for improvement. The schools were uniformly deficient in many respects, including goals for the students, and showed little desire to cooperate to correct the deficiencies. Education was almost entirely dependent on agencies not subject to government regulation, and efforts to work through these agencies only increased the ill will and the failures.

The new commandant and Governor, W. M. Crose, greatly perturbed over these conditions, attempted a two-pronged attack. First, he invited all outlander teachers to a conference (only the Catholics did not attend) which passed a resolution calling for compulsory education. This in turn resulted in a new directive prepared by Crose entitled *Regulation To Enforce the Educational Right of Children,* to be put into effect in February 1912. Crose's second step entailed a complete survey of the territory's educational needs and deficiencies. He pointed to the inability of the island's economy to finance solutions to the serious educational problems he uncovered, and he requested federal aid. Submitted first to the Secretary of the Navy, the request was then turned over to the Department of the Interior, and finally to the U.S. Commissioner of Education, P. P. Claxton. The commissioner suggested that the size of the schools be increased and the number of schools reduced for more efficiency. He proposed an annual education budget of $20,000, which would include matching funds from the territory. He also recommended that a Department of Education be established with an American director and assistants and that a normal school to train Samoan teachers be founded. Exhilarated by the possibilities, Crose immediately obtained the $10,000 in territorial funds required, and it appeared that an adequate, publicly supervised system of education would emerge in the islands. He was severely disappointed when the federal funds were again denied.

The government's efforts were not completely wasted, for they created a new educational atmosphere in Samoa. Not only was Crose backed by a cooperative spirit among the residents, but he now had an organization through which to work; although purely voluntary, it was far better than anything thus far. Despite a lack of specific power to do so, he did name a school board to bring some order to the process of learning in the territory.

During the next 5 years, there was a settling down after the early excitement, and little improvement took place in the educational system. The Ta'u school acquired a stateside principal in 1914, but it was destroyed by a hurricane the following year and was not reopened until 5 years later. With the schools at Leone and Fagatogo (now called the Poyer School), which had moved into new buildings at the head of Pago Bay, there were still only three public schools operating at the end of the decade.

In summary, during the period from 1900 to 1920, the inability of the territorial government effectively to present its educational difficulties and needs to Washington, which was half the world away physically and even further culturally, defeated the hopes of several farsighted commandants. Some important steps had been taken, however. The three public schools could only care for a small proportion of the students, but this was a start. The Samoans, supporting the schools entirely from limited local funds, had demonstrated their desire for education. The Board of Education had been able to develop minimum standards, which were now accepted by the majority of educational institutions, and a gradually developing spirit of harmony laid the foundation for a real system.

THE BEGINNING OF A SYSTEM

The revolution in Samoan education began when Captain Waldo Evans became commandant and Governor in 1920. He appointed the naval station chaplain to the new Office of Superintendent of Education, establishing a practice maintained for the duration of naval stewardship of the territory. He then appointed a new Board of Education to replace the group formed by Crose and divided American Samoa into 15 school districts.

When the Samoan Legislature, the *Fono,* met in 1921, it followed the Governor's lead and imposed a school tax of $2 on each taypayer, which was, however, not nearly enough to support a satisfactory system. To meet the appalling shortage of qualified teachers, the *Fono* immediately inaugurated 6-week training courses or summer workshops. By the end of the year, six government elementary schools were operating. Although the school system had doubled its facilities, it still needed funds from the federal government, which did not fully understand the situation and remained unconvinced that a large investment in education for the Samoans would be of value.

Throughout the decade, growth was slow, the school budget increasing only from $9,000 in 1921 to $20,000 in 1930. Student enrollment in the six schools climbed from 737 in 1921 to 2,118 students in 24 schools by 1932, with formal education now extended through the ninth grade. In 1932, the Frederick Duclos Barstow Foundation for American Samoa provided Samoan education a new impetus. Young Barstow had spent considerable time in the islands; when he died, his parents established the foundation in his name for the people he had learned to love. At the foundation's expense, the University of Hawaii surveyed the territory's educational needs, finally recommending that the foundation build one good school so Samoans could see what quality education meant. The Feleti School, the nickname given to Barstow by the Samoans, opened in 1933 with Gordon Brown as its first director.

The Feleti School provided a fine model, but the other schools could not come up to its standards without more money. They were still below stateside standards, and conditions were deteriorating. When Benjamin O. Wist of the University of Hawaii was appointed advisor of public education for Samoa in 1935, he found approximately 2,000 students in the government schools struggling to learn the English language. It was not until 1938 that the first textbooks designed specifically for use in Samoa were printed.

World War II had an adverse effect on the already stagnant educational situation. As might be expected, little attention was paid to the schools during the war, the enrollment remaining about 2,000 in 1944, the same as a decade earlier (4). But immediately following the peace, a new emphasis was placed on education. For the first time, the Navy sent an officer with training and experience to act as director of education. Under his leadership, a high school was opened in October 1946, the first to provide an education for general public use beyond elementary school. The first principal, Harrison Matsinger, his wife, and three Samoan teachers had the responsibility of developing the curriculum from the ground up. They soon discovered, however, that their 108 pupils' earlier education had not prepared them to meet stateside high school standards. Though more effort and money for Samoan education first flowed into the high school, the trend was reversed by 1950, so that more was now spent improving elementary facilities.

The Department of Education gradually ceased to be the stepchild of the territorial government and began to take a definite form. In 1949, the system was placed under the control of an eight-member Board of Education consisting of three Samoans, the island's chief justice, and four naval officers. The chaplain still served as director of education, but a professional educator was employed as superintendent of instruction. All children from 7 to 15, inclusive, were required to attend school. The high school, now approved for veterans' training, enrolled more than 200 students. Perhaps more important, the aims of education had changed during these years. Basically, the schools had been organized to teach English to Samoans and to promote "Americanization," but these goals were no longer sufficient. The *Fono* expressed regret and concern that young people were losing respect and appreciation for Samoan customs. The native culture was losing ground because of the schools' philosophy, and this prompted many to want education deemphasized in Samoa.

From 1929 on, schools were concerned not so much with "Americanization" as with trying to fit into the pattern of Samoan life, reflect the natural socioeconomic environment, and train the people to deal with Samoan problems. When the general aims for education were established in 1935, they merely stated that the schools would attempt to preserve the best of the Samoan culture and, at the same time, provide the people with the necessary intellectual and social tools to meet the world into which they were moving. But stating aims and organizing schools to achieve them proved to be two different things; although the system had many accomplishments to its credit by 1951, neither of these general goals had been fulfilled. Only a few tools were available. These were elementary schools, still housed in *fales* (open, thatched huts), several junior highs, and a high school, all using Western-style structures, equipment, and supplies. Each village was responsible for its own elementary school. Samoan supervisors were visiting the schools and checking on the equipment and the teachers; the vocational training school provided job training for veterans; and in 1952, the Feleti School had been turned into a teacher-training institution. Progress had been achieved, but the total picture was still one of inadequacy.

THE MODERN ERA

In July 1951, the administrative jurisdiction of American Samoa was taken over by the Department of the Interior after 51 years of naval administration (5). Civilians replaced naval personnel in governmental positions, including those within the Department of Education. The director of education, the head of the department, was directly responsible to the Governor. The assistant to the director was placed in charge of personnel, buildings, and equipment for all junior high schools. Superintendents were placed in elementary and secondary schools, the vocational training program, and the teacher-training program.

The new government provided a stability unobtainable previously, but old problems continued to plague the system. A high birthrate produced an increasing number of students, threatening to overwhelm existing facilities. During 1952, 14 new schools were completed along with living quarters for 12 teachers, making a total of 51 public schools, including 4 junior highs and 1 high school. Of the 5,116 students in the territory, 3,861 were enrolled in the public school system. It was still difficult to obtain federal funds, and the local districts could not finance quality education. Like the Navy, the new civilian officials were forced to do their best with limited resources.

Early in 1952, the director of elementary education assumed control over the teacher-training program to coordinate it more closely with the actual operation of the schools. Since 156 teachers in the system were not nearly enough, it was necessary to fill the training program with high school seniors. They still represented an enormous improvement over the teachers in the field at the time. To further meet this teaching shortage, the director of education decided to change the Feleti School into the Feleti Memorial Teacher-Training School.

Gradually, the new civilian administrators adopted the official objectives for education which had been stated as early as 1933. In 1955, the department stated officially that the purpose of the curriculum would be to teach (a) both Samoan and English in the elementary schools; (b) the fundamental processes of reading, writing, and arithmetic; (c) science and health; (d) the social sciences; (e) vocational preparation; and (f) avocational pursuits. It declared that it would teach exclusively in English in the village elementary schools and the junior high schools. It would operate senior high schools for a select group of junior high graduates and offer college preparatory, commercial, and teacher training in 1-year postgraduate courses (6). The board resolved to continue the long-established practice of compulsory education for students age 7 to age 15, inclusive. It also hoped to provide scholarships and special training for qualified students in needed fields. The Governor reported:

> It shall be the policy to upgrade the entire school system as soon as possible, with initial emphasis being placed in the five junior high schools which feed into the high school and into the community a better trained group of young people at an early date (7).

Although the director of the Department of Education and his two assistants were from the United States, the administrative assistant, a consultant, a chief supervisor, and the eight supervisors responsible for general instruction were all Samoans. The assistant principal of the high school was a Samoan, as were 50 junior high and elementary principals. The director was responsible for the supervision and coordination of the school system, curriculum, organization, buildings, facilities, training programs, scholarships, budget submissions, and accreditation and certification. The department itself consisted of a Division of Elementary Education responsible for grades 1 through 9, and a Division of Secondary Education responsible for grades 10 through 12 and for the teacher training, vocational training, and adult educational testing programs.

Operating the island's educational system was extremely frustrating. True, there were advances, such as the dependents' school for children of stateside employees, the Feleti School for prospective teachers, the book rental agency for various Samoan communities, and a Samoan culture program concentrating primarily on writing books for the schools on Samoan culture and customs. But the teacher-training programs still had to depend on the Barstow Foundation for financing. The elementary schools of the open *fale* type were taught mainly by teachers who had little opportunity for schooling beyond the elementary level. Most of the junior high buildings, never adequate anyway, were deteriorating rapidly; the high school was still very selective, admitting only about 105 students each year, which allowed only 30 percent of the junior high graduates to attend high school. The adult education program was limited to providing information, when it should have been engaged in creative academic activities. It was small wonder that the 1959 budget of $323,211 fell far short of meeting the schools' real needs.

THE TURNING POINT

In 1961, when the Committee on Interior and Insular Affairs presented a report entitled "The Study Mission to Eastern (American) Samoa," a complete analysis of the island's economic needs and a survey of the conditions of the school system, Congress became thoroughly aware of Samoa's educational problems. The committee reported that educational standards were lower in Samoa than in any other territory under U.S. jurisdiction. It charged that the untrained, poorly equipped, and underpaid teaching force labored in unequipped, inadequate buildings which would be unrecognizable as schools in the States. It did praise the efforts of both Samoans and stateside administrators, giving them credit for the situation's being no worse than it was. The report pointed up a single truth: There had been a lack of resources to finance an adequate education system.

The committee found a prominent flaw to be the contradictory philosophy of education. It hailed the admirable attempts to preserve old Samoan traditions but concluded that they were not being adjusted to changing conditions. A desire for full citizenship was growing among Samoans, and the culture itself had drawn more and more toward the American way of life. Samoans were finding new opportunities to travel to the United States, and an ever-increasing number of people were moving into the islands, diminishing the influence of local traditions and customs.

The committee had little trouble finding prominent examples to reinforce its conclusions. The island had been fragmented into a number of inefficient, tiny districts. For instance, in the Leone area seven elementary schools operated within a radius of 1 mile, most of them within sight of the others. Poorer areas failed completely to provide schools, and their children received no formal instruction. The *fales,* housing half of Samoa's public schools, were open to the elements, had inadequate lighting—if any at all—and the meager equipment was usually makeshift and outmoded. The elementary schools had no libraries and little audiovisual equipment. The entire system operated on a shoestring, spending less than $50 per child per year, including teacher salaries, which were by far the largest item in the budget, low as they were. Only $5,000 had been allotted in the 1960 and 1961 budgets for teaching aids, and $4,800 for equipment.

The committee recommended that the village schools be consolidated into new, larger buildings and that salaries be increased to attract qualified stateside teachers. Real direction was needed to solve the contradiction of teaching the traditional Samoan culture while striving for a stateside standard program. But leadership depended as much on the Governor as on the Department of Education. The community's wishes were supposedly reflected by the Board of Education appointed by the Governor, but the board's powers had fluctuated through the years, at times being completely removed, and it now acted only in an advisory capacity. The history of change and conflicting ideas had left little in the way of policy, and now it was very difficult to implement long-range planning.

When Governor H. Rex Lee assumed office in 1961, he was appalled at the territory's educational structure. Armed with the committee's report, he spent the early part of 1962 outlining a 3-year rehabilitation program, a full, effective analysis that enlisted the strong support of the Department of the Interior. Congress and the Administration backed his proposals and appropriated $9.5 million for the program in October 1962.

With enough money, things happened quickly. The University of California at Berkeley helped recruit 40 new teachers. Three new high school buildings were constructed, and, for the first time, 100 percent of the junior high school graduates were able to enroll. But the Governor was still dissatisfied. Untrained teachers still staffed most of the elementary schools, and nothing had been done for the adults. Lee wanted to raise the entire educational level of the territory as rapidly and dramatically as possible.

After a great deal of deliberation, the Governor proposed that a dozen or so outstanding teachers bring the best in education to students in 300 classrooms through educational television. This would also provide adults with classes in everything from health to self-government. The Secretary of the Interior supported the proposal, and Congress appropriated funds for a survey to determine if it would be feasible. Under the direction of the National Association of Educational Broadcasters, a team headed by Vernon Bronson concluded its study with a strong recommendation for ETV. By the end of 1963, workers were constructing housing for new stateside personnel, erecting the transmitter and antenna, extending the capacity of the power plant, and installing power and TV equipment in the remote villages. At the same time, the department began working on a plan that would set up 26 consolidated elementary schools.

The new studio, christened the Michael J. Kirwan Educational Television Center, began broadcasting to the elementary students the next year and by 1965 carried complete secondary school programing. Using six channels, it presented materials in every subject area to all grade levels from 1 to 12. Presenting television as the *core* of a teaching program rather than as a supplement attracted worldwide attention. Visiting teams of educational experts flew in to study this revolutionary concept in action. It is still too early to make a final evaluation of its effectiveness, but there is general consensus that Samoan students are learning faster and better than ever before.

ADMINISTRATION AND SUPERVISION OF EDUCATION

From 1900 to 1965, the administration of the school system fluctuated mainly according to the different approaches of the various Governors. The Department of Education did not develop a firm pattern of functions and administrative responsibilities until the Navy's authority ended in 1951. From 1961 to present, the changes have been mainly sequential, growing naturally out of expansion and progress. Undoubtedly, gaps will continue to appear as the system develops, but the present organization seems to allow for expansion and problem solving (8). Because of the unique structure of the educational process as it evolved in Samoa, each of the organization's functions will be briefly described (9).

Director of Education

The director is responsible for the entire system of education, the only person qualified to answer the questions and requests of the Governor. He serves as ex officio chairman of the elementary curriculum advisory committee, the secondary curriculum advisory committee, and of the joint committee for the articulation of subject matter. Since the Department of Education performs one of the major functions of the territorial government and the director serves as a member of the Governor's board, he occupies a position of great responsibility in the government as a member of these committees.

The department has five assistant directors in the following areas: (1) the assistant director for administration, who is responsible for all department records, including budget and personnel records, for assigning housing, and for maintaining contractual obligations; (2) the assistant director for engineering services, who is a qualified, licensed TV engineer in charge of installing, maintaining, repairing, and replacing all technical equipment associated with television; (3) the assistant director for management of the Instructional Resource Center, who operates the center and coordinates its various activities; (4) the assistant director for elementary instruction, who supervises the TV teachers, research teachers, teacher training, and all other aspects of education in the elementary schools; and (5) the assistant director for secondary instruction, who supervises the TV teachers, research teachers, classroom instruction supervisors, the vocational and skills program, and all other aspects of education in the secondary schools.

The Department of Education has announced the following objectives (10): (a) To improve the technical and subject matter competency of the native Samoan teachers; (b) to prepare the great majority of Samoan children to live, work, and make better lives for themselves in Samoa; (c) to offer equality of educational opportunity to all the children in all the villages in all the islands in American Samoa; (d) to increase competency in the use of English to the point where language is no barrier to educational development; (e) to raise the level of learning opportunities to the point where those Samoan children who desire to go beyond high school may obtain a sound educational base to enable them to enter American colleges and universities and compete on an equal level with other American students; (f) to develop such manual skills and functional arts as will contribute to a better economic and social structure; (g) to provide opportunities for adults and out-of-school youth in language competencies, civic understanding, and vocational skills; and (h) to train native Samoan teachers and technicians to fill all positions within the department.

True universal secondary education for the children of Samoa, which began in 1964, brought about several changes in the educational system. Supplanting the traditional classroom situation with an imaginative system using television as the basic tool brought about modifications in class schedules, a substitution of large classes for the small ones, and new approaches to study. The new consolidated high schools included rooms designed to serve classes that could be supervised, directed, and motivated by a single teacher. Built especially for televised lessons, they have a maximum flexibility to accommodate individual study or small, special, intermediate classes without affecting the efficiency of regular instruction. In turn, they influenced the organization of the staff and faculty, as reflected in the Department of Education's new positions.

In the new system of cooperative instruction by television, an instructional team composed of the classroom teachers and those responsible for the televised presentations develops the scope, sequence, and goals of each course, subjecting them continually to criticism and modification. The role of the classroom teacher necessarily changes as he amplifies, relates, and reinforces the concepts presented on the screen. The actual operation of the cooperative team is depicted in the chart on the next page.

Schools

Basically, two types of elementary schools operate in the territory. In the least accessible villages, such as in Fagali'i and Asu, the old, open, *fale*-type structures still exist. These will be replaced in the near future by the other type, the new consolidated schools designed to fit the Samoan environment while providing the best instruction possible by television. Architecturally, the new buildings are similar to the oval Samoan *fale* but are built of concrete and supplied with all the materials and equipment usually identified with classrooms. The roofs are shingled to harmonize with the surrounding environment, and the grounds are attractively landscaped. Each school consists of approximately six buildings, each containing two classrooms with an appropriate number of TV receivers, desks, blackboards, and storage cabinets. One building is occupied by the principal's office, the cafeteria, and the teachers' room. A home for the stateside principal is built in each complex. The elementary schools have four regular levels of instruction, each encompassing two grades, and a fifth level equivalent to the eighth and ninth grades. At present, 5,053 students are enrolled in the 22 new consolidated elementary schools.

The territory has three high schools in operation, one on the site of the old High School of American Samoa in Utulei, another at Leone, and a third just opened in Manu'a. A new high school is being built on the eastern end of Tutuila. These new schools consist of groups of buildings of circular design, making possible the greatest utilization of space and televised instruction. They contain large classrooms, areas for individual study, and special instruction rooms, quite adequate for the present enrollment of 2,800 students.

The Dependents School, located at Utulei, is open to children of all contract employees as well as qualified Samoan children. It offers a standard stateside program of instruction for grades 1-12 and serves approximately 280 students.

Today, the teacher-training program is a 2-year course that includes classwork in methods and content, observation, and practice teaching. Occupying a portion of the Feleti Memorial Library in Utulei, it also offers a college preparatory program for high school graduates. Presently,

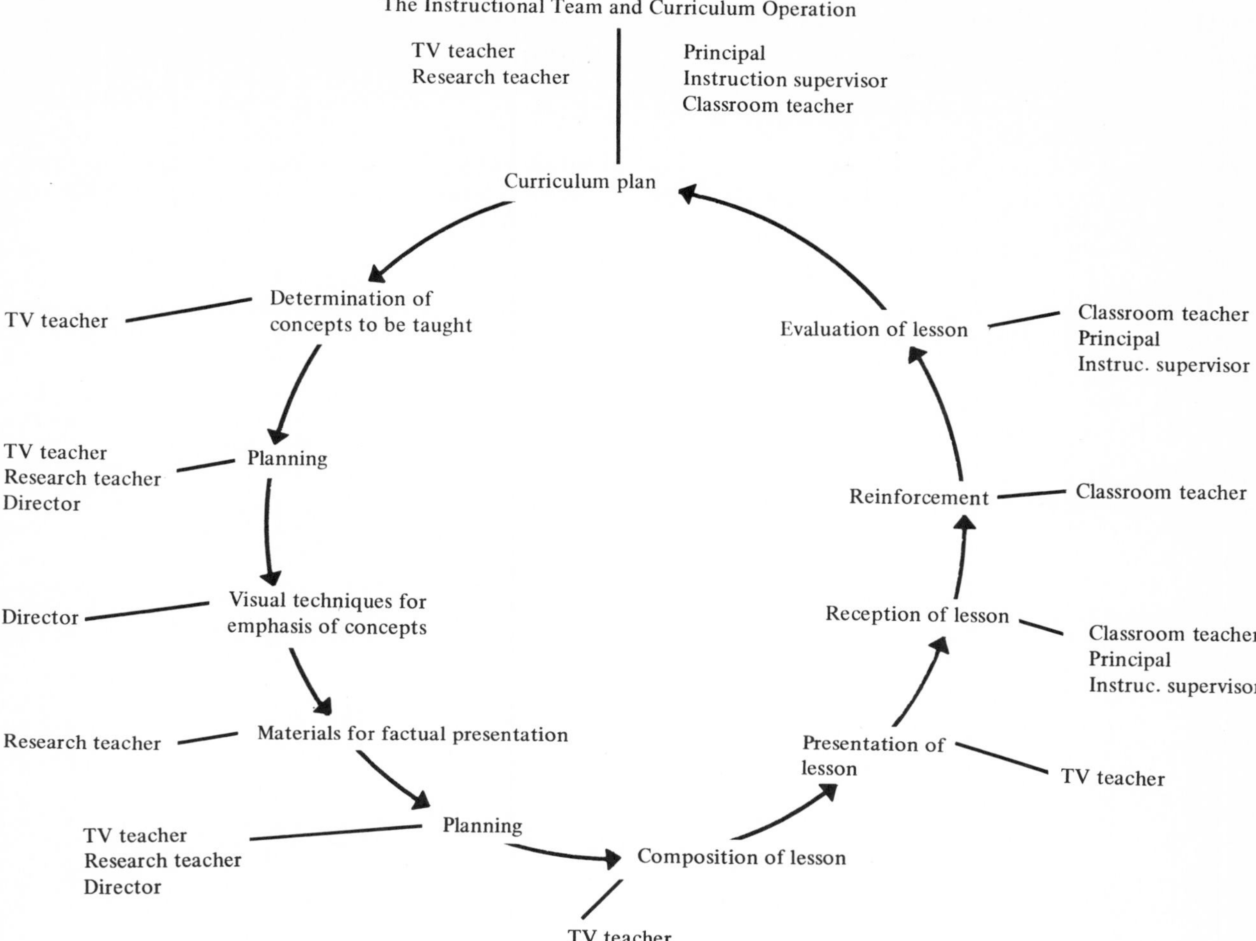

40 students are in teacher training and 20 in the post-scholarship program.

Other Department Functions

To upgrade the educational level of all the people, the islands need a strong adult education program. This is achieved partly through cultural, academic, and social programs on evening television. Also, the Instructional Resource Center and several schools offer regular academic programs for adults.

The Department of Education maintains its own publications department at the resource center in Utulei. Thus, it is able to furnish all printed materials for each lesson, as well as specially prepared books, readers, and other materials to supplement its programs.

The department supervises the Territorial Library, which provides professional services to the schools and the community. The library has 14,000 volumes in general circulation at present, in addition to an extensive reserve section.

The department also supervises the selection of students for the mainland scholarship program, at present giving 85 Samoans an opportunity to attend colleges and universities in the United States.

FOOTNOTES

1. For further information in summary form, see *Encyclopaedia Britannica*, 1964 ed., XIX, 921-22.

2. Sylvia Masterman, *The Origins of International Rivalry in Samoa* (London: George, Allen and Unwin, 1934).

3. In 1902, the churches sponsored the following number of schools: London Missionary Society, 40; Catholic, 13; Mormon, 3; Wesleyan, 1.
4. *Pacific Islands Yearbook* (Sydney, Australia: Pacific Publications, Ltd., 1944).
5. U.S. President, Harry S. Truman, "Transfer of Administration of American Samoa from the Secretary of the Navy to the Secretary of the Interior," Executive Order No. 10264, effective July 1, 1951.
6. Nurses were trained in the hospital, and medical or dental practitioners were trained at the Central Medical School in Fiji.
7. *Annual Report of the Governor of American Samoa to the Secretary of the Interior* (Honolulu: Fredrick Duclos Barstow Foundation, 1955).
8. There were 210 teachers in the system.
9. Appendix B outlines the entire organization of administrative functions.
10. Department of Education, *Staff and Faculty Manual of System and Organization* (Pago Pago: The Department, 1965).

BIBLIOGRAPHY

Public Documents

American Samoa. *Senate Proceedings*, 1921-51. Many records, some unpublished and unprinted, dating back to Navy days. Available in Pago Pago.

U.S. Congress. Senate Committee on Interior and Insular Affairs. *Economic Needs of American Samoa.* 1961.

U.S. President, Harry S. Truman. "Transfer of Administration of American Samoa from the Secretary of the Navy to the Secretary of the Interior." Executive Order No. 10264. Effective July 1, 1951.

Books

Coulter, John W. *The Pacific Dependencies of the United States.* New York: The Macmillan Co., 1957.

Department of Education. *Cooperative Instruction by Television in the Secondary Schools of American Samoa.* Pago Pago: The Department, 1964.

—— *Staff and Faculty Manual of System and Organization.* Pago Pago: The Department, 1965.

Grey, Robert. *American Samoa and Its Naval Administration.* Washington, D.C.: Government Printing Office, 1961.

Masterman, Sylvia. *The Origins of International Rivalry in Samoa.* London: George, Allen and Unwin, 1934.

Reports

Annual Report of the Governor of American Samoa to the Secretary of the Interior. Honolulu: Fredrick Duclos Barstow Foundation, 1952-64.

Bronson, Vernon. *Elementary Education in American Samoa.* An excerpt from a paper on procedure and policy in the development of education and instructional television. Pago Pago: Department of Education, 1964.

Emerson, Rupert, et al. *America's Pacific Dependencies: A Report on Conditions in the Island Dependencies in the Pacific Area.* New York: American Institute of Pacific Relations, 1949.

Schramm, Wilbur. "Educational Television in Samoa: A Study of the Development and Direction of Instructional Television in Samoa, and Its Potential for International Development." *New Educational Media in Action: Case Studies for Planners.* Edited by Phillip Coombs. Paris: International Institute for Educational Planning, 1966.

United Nations. *Non-Self Governing Territories.* 1951.

Articles and Periodicals

Pacific Islands Yearbook. Sydney, Australia: Pacific Publications, Ltd., 1944.

"Samoa." *Encyclopaedia Britannica*, XIX (1964).

Unpublished Material

Archives and Records of American Samoa, 1900-60. These are miscellaneous papers, many unpublished and unprinted, available in Pago Pago.

Other Sources

Multitauaopele, Chief Fiaui. Personal interviews with Chief Multitauaopele, advisor to the Department of Education. American Samoa, July-September 1965.

Tuiteleleapaga, Chief N.I. Personal interviews with Chief Tuiteleleapaga, assistant to the director of education for Samoan affairs. Pago Pago, American Samoa, July-September 1965.

Appendix A

AMERICAN SAMOA CHIEF SCHOOL OFFICERS

Directors of Education Under the Department of the Interior

1949-51	J. R. Trace	1957-63	M. J. Senter
1951-53	H. S. Spencer	1963-65	J. C. Wright
1953-55	L. M. Fort	1965-67	John W. Harold
1955-57	D. A. Rothschild	1967-	Roy D. Cobb

Appendix B

Chart I.--AMERICAN SAMOA DEPARTMENT OF EDUCATION PERSONNEL, 1965-66

DEPARTMENT OR AREA	SAMOAN	STATESIDE	TOTAL
OFFICE OF DIRECTOR	2	3	5
ADMINISTRATIVE OFFICE	22	4	26
ELEMENTARY:			
(TEACHERS)	221	0	221
(ADMINISTRATIVE)	12	38 (1)	50
SERVICE PERSONNEL	55	50	105
SECONDARY:			
(TEACHERS)	79	9	88
(ADMINISTRATIVE)	5	21 (2)	26
SCHOOL LUNCH PROGRAM	65	2	67
SAMOAN INFORMATION	8	4	12
DEPENDENTS SCHOOL	6	11	17
TOTAL	476	143	619

1- includes TV teachers

2- includes TV teachers

Appendix B

Chart II.--AMERICAN SAMOA DEPARTMENT OF EDUCATION, 1966

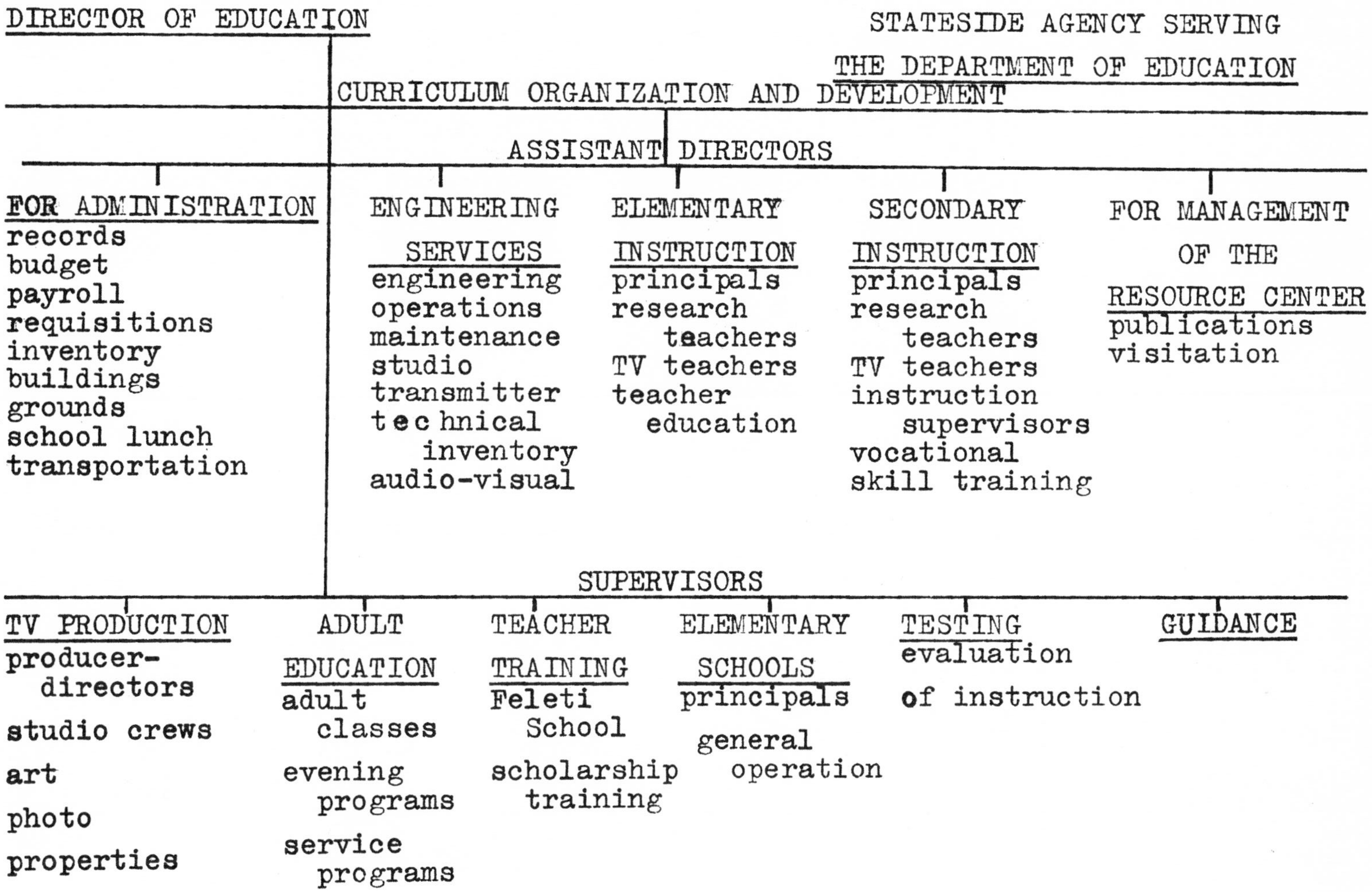

DIRECTOR OF EDUCATION

STATESIDE AGENCY SERVING THE DEPARTMENT OF EDUCATION

CURRICULUM ORGANIZATION AND DEVELOPMENT

ASSISTANT DIRECTORS

FOR ADMINISTRATION	ENGINEERING SERVICES	ELEMENTARY INSTRUCTION	SECONDARY INSTRUCTION	FOR MANAGEMENT OF THE RESOURCE CENTER
records budget payroll requisitions inventory buildings grounds school lunch transportation	engineering operations maintenance studio transmitter technical inventory audio-visual	principals research teachers TV teachers teacher education	principals research teachers TV teachers instruction supervisors vocational skill training	publications visitation

SUPERVISORS

TV PRODUCTION	ADULT EDUCATION	TEACHER TRAINING	ELEMENTARY SCHOOLS	TESTING	GUIDANCE
producer-directors studio crews art photo properties	adult classes evening programs service programs	Feleti School scholarship training	principals general operation	evaluation of instruction	

Appendix B

Chart III.--AMERICAN SAMOA SCHOOLS

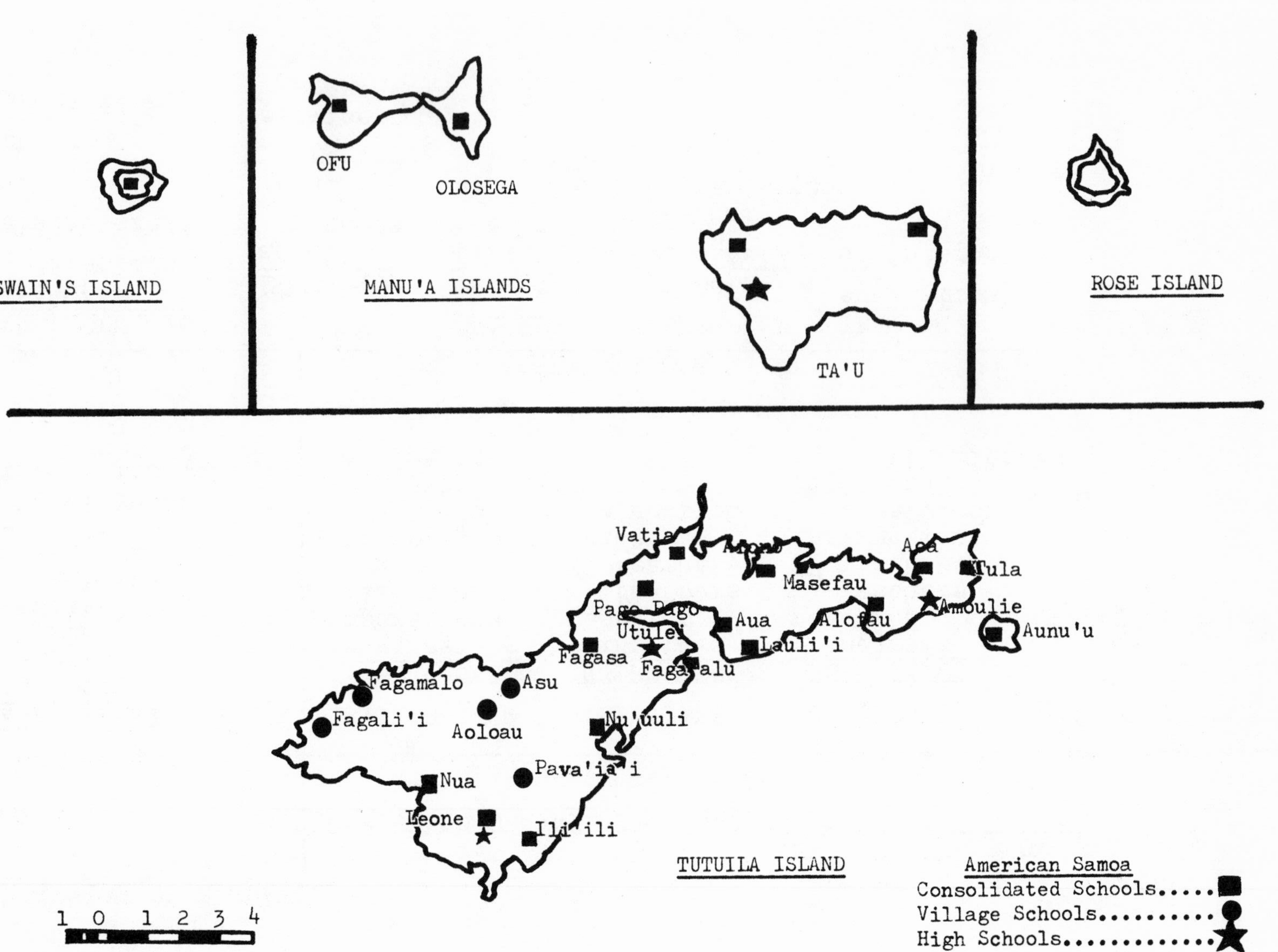

Appendix C

Table 1. – NUMBER OF SCHOOLS, STUDENT ENROLLMENT, AND BUDGET: SELECTED YEARS FROM 1921 TO 1965

Year	Schools	Pupils	Budget
1921	6	737	$ 9,600
1922	19	1,567	15,982
1926	19	1,800	20,218
1930	20	2,000	20,572
1932	20	2,118	
1934	20	2,208	19,428
1937	21	2,188	20,655
1940	35	2,770	22,516
1943	43	2,575	20,800
1944	32	2,054	26,000
1946	42	3,000	55,000
1952	. . .	3,500	250,000
1965	24	7,853	3,287,886

Table 2. – COST OF PUBLIC EDUCATION IN SAMOA

Type of cost	Amount in thousands	Per-capita cost	Number of pupils
(A) Non-TV costs			
Director's office	$ 51	. . .	. . .
Administrative office	63	$ 16	7,000
Dependents school	135	397	343
Elementary schools	737	141	5,197
Secondary schools	554	382	1,454
	Subtotal, non-TV costs $1,440		
(B) TV costs			
Operating costs	1,199	181	6,600
Capital charges	179	27	6,600
Interest	45	7	6,600
	Subtotal, TV costs $1,423		
		216	6,600
Total system costs	2,863	409	7,000

Source:

Schramm, Wilbur, *Educational Television in Samoa*, 1966, p. 43, Table 11.

Appendix C

Table 3. – COST OF THE TV SYSTEM

Type of cost	Amount in thousands	
A. Capital costs (to Jan. 1966)		
(a) Costs of transmission		
Transmitters, towers, antennas	$ 541	
Studio equipment	525	
Microwave	49	
Videotape recorders	314	
Translators	7	
TV building and installations	653	
Aerial tramway to transmitter site	195	
Subtotal transmission cost		$ 2,284
(b) Cost of reception		
Receiving systems	15	
Receivers and accessories	82	
Subtotal, reception costs		$ 97
Total, capital costs of TV system		$ 2,381
B. Operating costs (fiscal year 1966)		
(a) Production materials, etc.		
Production, general	89	
Engineering	102	
Administrative	19	
Subtotal, production materials		$ 210
(b) Production outlays, etc.		
Salaries (excluding teachers)	553	
Phone, electricity, rent	133	
Other services	18	
Subtotals, production outlays		$ 704
(c) TV teaching costs		
Elementary	120	
High school	105	
Printing and reproduction	60	
Subtotal, TV teaching costs		$ 285
Summary TV operating costs		
(a) Production materials	210	
(b) Production outlays	704	
(c) TV teaching costs	285	
Total, TV operating costs		$ 1,199

Source:

Schramm, Wilbur, *Educational Television in Samoa*, 1966, p. 38.

53 Guam

DEPARTMENT OF EDUCATION
Harley G. Jones
Trubee Joy Jones

Contents

INTRODUCTION

The actual history of the Department of Education of the Government of Guam may be considered as dating only from the passage by Congress in 1950 of the Organic Act of Guam. This act, which established Guam's governmental structure, provided for most of the island's present legislative self-government as an organized but unincorporated territory of the United States. Previously, what was called the Department of Education was merely an arm of the Naval Governor's administration and could not correctly be considered a State (or Territorial) Department of Education in the sense that it is today. Nevertheless, the post-1950 history of the department must be viewed in its relationship not only to the previous U.S. administration, but also to the unique historical background of the island, going back far earlier than when the United States took it over in 1898. Since Guam's Department of Education embraces both territorial and local agencies, the roles of individual schools and events not directly in the department's jurisdiction assume a greater importance in the department's development than might otherwise be the case.

Guam is the largest and southernmost of the Mariana Islands, located 5,100 miles west of San Francisco. In June 1966, 45,877 permanent residents and about 40,000 military personnel and dependents lived in this 225-square-mile area, which is 30 miles long and 4 to 9 miles wide (1). The entire island is surrounded by coral reef 20 to 700 yards wide. The climate is warm and humid, with temperatures ranging from 80 to 90 degrees. The average annual rainfall is 83 inches, but the weather pattern is punctuated from time to time by severe typhoons which do considerable damage. The farmers raise corn, sweet potatoes, taro, and cassava, as well as chickens, pigs, and cattle. The majority of Guamanians are Roman Catholic, but a number belong to various Protestant denominations.

The tapestry of Guam's educational history is woven of many threads. To untangle them is to unravel a story of migrations of peoples from prehistoric Asia, the Spanish conquest, English exploration, whaling, piracy, American independence and its entry into the role of landholder and protector, Japan's World War II Pacific empire, and the rehabilitation of a people torn from their natural heritage to face the problems of adapting to a complicated, alien culture.

THE SPANISH PERIOD

The island was left unclaimed by the West after Magellan's visit in 1521, until 1668 when the first Spanish colony arrived—Jesuits, led by Padre Diego Luis de Sanvitores (2). Christianity was introduced to the Chamorro people, and the first educational instruction was given. The hundred years following the landing of these first missionaries were years of turmoil and saw the end of the Chamorro people as a race. The Chamorros received the Jesuits with friendliness and courtesy at first but in time grew restive as their old ways of life were threatened by the new religion (3).

Spanish colonization continued, and the priests kept on with their work, interrupted by church burnings and ambushes by the now hostile Chamorros. The College of San Juan de Letran, started earlier and then closed because of wars between the Spaniards and the Chamorros, was reopened, as was a girl's school in Agana. In less than a century, Guam's old culture had been nearly wiped out by suppressive military Governors and by the new religion, Christianity. A new people was emerging to which the present-day Guamanians owe their origins. In spite of the turmoil of the seventeenth century, roads had been built and permanent sites for towns and villages established. Agana became the capital of the Marianas, and the religious education of the people was stubbornly continued.

During the eighteenth century, Guam became a nearly forgotten Spanish colony. The Jesuits were ordered out of the islands by the Spanish monarchy in 1769 and

Grateful acknowledgment is made to all who have generously assisted in the preparation of this history. Among those people are Ivan Ward Lasher, the former director of education, Government of Guam; Teresita Salas, assistant superintendent for curriculum and instruction, Department of Education; Scott Wilson, professor of anthropology at the College of Guam; and Emily Johnston.

were replaced by members of the Order of Saint Augustine. The College of San Juan de Letran and the useful handicrafts and fine ranches were neglected, cattle ran wild, and the people deteriorated into a state of near poverty.

In 1771, a new Governor, Don Mariano Tobias, arrived. He reintroduced animal husbandry and established two public schools (one for boys and one for girls) that emphasized reading, writing, arithmetic, and music. The nineteenth century saw little improvement in Guam's economic or educational situation. The Treaty of Paris in 1898 ended the Spanish-American War and ceded Guam, among other territories, to the United States.

Although this short review of Guam's pre-American history includes very little about the organization of the education of Guam, it does bear direct relationship to the Guamanians' attitude toward education and the fact that modern education is still in its infancy here. During the 300 years of Spanish rule, very little was done to educate Guam's people. Whatever was accomplished up to 1900 was done by the Jesuits and, to some extent, the Augustinians. This was mostly religious training, however. Education for the masses was limited to a speaking knowledge of Spanish. Little writing was taught. Also, what was taught in the schools seldom carried over to the home. (Guam's present-day educators still cite this as the major language-teaching problem, for English is used only within class at school, and it does not usually carry over into the home. English is always a second language for these children, as was Spanish under Spain's rule.) The minute school is out, Guamanians in school offices and the children leaving for home switch immediately to Chamorro. Among the students there is really no interest in English except as a convenience at school.

Most children receiving education during the Spanish rule were from well-to-do homes. Even this training was rudimentary—elementary arithmetic, reading, writing, and Spanish. Many of the ruling people felt that too much education of the masses would lead to trouble. (Later, even some American Governors were of this opinion, a lamentable problem of the ruled and ruling throughout history.)

However, the Roman Catholic Church *had* established schools in all the large towns and villages throughout the island by the time of the American takeover, including intermediate grades for boys and girls at the College of San Juan de Letran and the College of Las Niñas.

THE AMERICAN PERIOD

Thus education stood when Guam became a possession of the United States in 1898. The first specific American recommendation for the establishment of public schools on Guam is in a report prepared for the government by Lieutenant Vincendon L. Cottman, USN. Cottman's report indicated that almost everything would have to be done for Guam to get it on its feet. He wrote, "Establish Public Schools and compel all children to go to school and teach them English, having male teachers for the boys and women teachers for the girls" (4).

Because all of Guam was declared to be a naval station, its Governors were appointed by the Secretary of the Navy and commissioned by the President. The Governors were in complete charge of island life, which meant that, as under the Spanish, patterns of government changed with each new Governor. Still, the problems themselves remained the same, and paramount among them was education.

Lieutenant William Edwin Safford, USN, taught the first English class in Guam in 1899. He reported as follows:

> I myself have started a night school for teaching English three nights a week. I have about fifty pupils, ranging from the age of five to fifty years. Among them, besides the natives, are a number of bondsmen (Italians) and Chinese servants of the officers' mess. I usually begin by pointing to various objects and pronouncing the corresponding English names. My pupils repeat the words after me; then I teach a few adjectives, such as long, short, thin, thick, hard, soft, illustrating the meaning by objects having these attributes; then a few verbs, such as walk, sit, stand, fall, catch, see, hear, speak. Most of my pupils do pretty well but the youngest do the best (5).

Naval officers were placed in all positions of authority in the government. In spite of domestic problems, Captain Richard P. Leary, the first Naval Governor, and Lieutenant Safford succeeded in organizing public offices to such a degree that it was possible to see a pattern developing which could be set on paper. Among the new departments was the Department of Education, headed by the Governor.

In addition to the existing Spanish Catholic schools, three private schools were started in 1900 and 1901 for the teaching of English. Rose Custino, daughter of a Guamanian whaler, had earlier opened the first in 1900. Lieutenant Albert Moritz, chief engineer of the station ship *USS Yosemite,* began an English class; the first Protestant missionaries, under the auspices of the American Board of Missions, also began a school.

Lieutenant Safford found that most of the people could not even write their names, so the first compulsory education order was issued, called "General Order No. 13, requiring every adult resident of the island to learn to read, write and speak the English language" (6).

A general order issued by Captain Leary in January 1900 included these stipulations:

1. All necessary expenses for the maintenance of the public schools will be defrayed by the Government.
2. Religious instruction in favor of any particular church or creed is prohibited . . . .

3. All children between the ages of eight and fourteen years must attend school, unless excused therefrom by competent authority for good reasons that interfere with their attendance.
4. Instruction in the English language will be introduced in the public schools as soon as suitable teachers can be provided (7).

Commander Seaton Schroeder relieved Leary in July 1900. Schroeder, at least, had something more than a beginning from which to work. Among his first concerns was, of course, education, but the cost of rebuilding after a devastating typhoon hit the island in November 1900 reduced the small island treasury to almost nothing.

In spite of this, by October 1901, three schools with English instruction were started in Agana under the supervision of H. H. Hiatt, a graduate of Iowa State University, who was assisted by his wife and daughter. English and arithmetic were the principal subjects. Guamanians were so eager to obtain this education that the schools became overcrowded immediately, another problem unsolved to this day. Hiatt was able to stay only until 1902, when funds to pay his salary ran out. In September of that year, a severe earthquake almost totally destroyed Agana, including the schools. With the exception of a short-lived effort to restore one of the schools, all remained closed for the next 2 years. There were no funds to rebuild them.

Commander G. L. Dyer, the next Governor, reopened the schools in June 1904. His staff of teachers included three Guamanian girls, two American clerks, and a marine. Dyer had opened eight schools by the end of his administration. The enrollment, 297 students in Agana and 26 in Asan when he began his term, had grown to 1,592. Dyer asked, in his annual report for 1906, for $49,140 from the Navy to operate these schools. His request was denied.

Dyer was succeeded by Captain E. J. Dorn in December 1907. From his arrival, Dorn improved the schools considerably. Four more were opened, including Dorn Hall.

Yigo (pronounced Gee'-go) school was built in 1913. In 1914, a permanent school building went up in Umatac, and an intermediate school—called a high school—was built on the hill overlooking Agana near the present Governor's house. In 1915, a 53-pupil school was built at Yona (Jó-nya). In 1919, Saturday morning normal classes began for teachers; they studied mathematics, history, and other subjects. Emphasis was still on reading and speaking English, and educational supervision was still under the Navy.

The Governor delegated responsibility for education to his aide, and in the Governor's report for 1917, this officer is first officially referred to as a "head" of the Department of Education. After 1919, the Navy chaplains were required to administer the department. The duties of chaplain, along with the total welfare of Guam's educational system including an annual report to the Governor, presented an almost Herculean task. The chaplain was assisted by a trained American educator who acted as superintendent of public instruction. In 1933, this office was officially designated superintendent of schools, and assistant superintendencies were established in 1946. The title of superintendent was changed to director of education in 1952.

A Board of Education

A Board of Education was established in 1938. Members consisted of the head of the Department of Education and one elected representative each from the Guam Teachers Association, the Parent-Teachers Association, the House Council of the Guam Congress, and the House of Assembly of the Guam Congress. Members were chosen for a term of 2 years.

However, the people did not have an effective share in the control of education; their board's function was purely advisory, and its only power was to set its own time for meetings, draw up its own rules of procedure, and keep minutes of its meetings and activities. As far as teachers themselves were concerned, absolute obedience and uniformity of instruction were demanded of them, with the central office, under the Navy, in control.

Briefly, the growth of the schools from 1921 to 1931 was as follows (8):

	1921	1931
Number of schools	14	30
Number of teachers	47	130
Number of pupils	1,865	3,745
Total expenditures	$35,845	$62,281

In 1924, a special normal school was opened to train Guamanians as teachers.

Good health practices were strictly enforced in the schools, including vaccination, inoculation, and worm checkups. Practical classes in fishnetmaking, weaving, cooking, and sewing were established and continued up to 1941. The 4-H Club became popular (9).

Thomas Collins, appointed superintendent of schools in 1922, adapted the California school curriculum to the local system. In 1924, he reorganized the school system, tested and regraded the children, and began a new program for children from grades 1 through 8. He encouraged children to contribute through their schools to the *Guam Recorder,* as an incentive to increasing local interest in reading. Boys went to school in the morning and girls in the afternoon; a double session was instituted in 1939 because of overcrowding. The practice of holding a grand program for the closing day of school was inaugurated, with the closing days staggered in order that leading government officials might attend the different schools to observe the festivities.

Collins also directed the first teacher summer session, beginning in June 1932. He established a 2-year normal school with instruction in college-level subjects. "Attendance was compulsory for all teachers and candidates for teaching positions. The summer teacher's institute, as it was later called, has been a part of the inservice training of Guamanian teachers since that time" (10). These summer institutes were held until 1951.

Three days after Pearl Harbor was attacked (December 10, 1941), Guam fell to the Japanese, and for the first time an American possession was held by an enemy power. During the occupation all education came under Japanese control. The Japanese zealously built new schools and forced the attendance of the children during the day and adults at night. Reading, writing, arithmetic, Japanese history, and simple Japanese language were taught, patriotic songs and games were learned, and a rigid calisthenics program followed.

Because of shortages in the teaching staff, young Guamanian men and women were chosen as "volunteers" to attend Japanese training schools. From these they went into the school system as interpreters, assistants, and supervisors in agricultural projects. However, in spite of subjugation, Guam remained loyal to the United States.

During the 2 years following the Americans' return in 1944, Guam was under military rule. Nothing was left of the old island school system, and over a year passed before schools began to resemble anything like what they had been before the war. Again, the schools taught basic subjects and began to educate the people in practical and industrial arts. Under a welfare and education department, supervised by a Lt. Commander Votow, the schools slowly recovered. Simon A. Sanchez, superintendent of schools before the war, helped the department, and all those who formerly had had anything to do with education were assembled. By October 1944, five schools had been started.

Everything was makeshift. The pupils brought with them what they could. Classes often were held outside under the coconut palms. Chalk, paper, and pencils were supposed to be furnished, but one veteran teacher of this period recalls using all boards painted black on which writing was done with bits of broken pottery (11). When possible, materials were mimeographed, and every school book surviving the war was added to the meager libraries.

As new villages were begun and old ones rebuilt, temporary village schools also were built, and by 1946, 21 schools were in operation, with an enrollment of 7,150. School population soared with the natural increase of the native Guamanians, the influx of new military and civilian personnel, by a program inaugurated to bring Trust Territory students to the high schools, and by a Filipino colony. For example, the Department of Education's annual report for 1955 showed an enrollment of 8,726 pupils in grades 1-8 and 22 schools in operation (12).

The first postwar junior high school was opened in 1953. It was located in Agana; Pedro C. Sanchez was principal. The school served children in the seventh and eighth grades, with a ninth grade being added in 1954. By 1960, Agat and Inarajan also had junior high schools.

The first high school education in Guam began in 1917, when courses were offered in the Armesen Building, located beside the Governor's palace in Agana and taught by naval officers and a civilian, John A. Pearson (13).

In 1923, the first real high school was organized. Its enrollment was nine students. The school was discontinued in 1924, to be replaced by the Guam Evening High School. In 1928, the evening school graduated its first class of seven members; its graduates are among the leading citizens of Guam today.

The Seaton Schroeder Junior High School, Guam's first modern junior high, was opened in 1930, with Mrs. Agueda I. Johnston (sometimes called "the first lady of Guam") as principal. In 1931, 17 students comprised the first Schroeder graduating class.

In 1936, George Washington High School was opened. Mrs Johnston became its principal. A standard high school curriculum was used, and Stanford achievement tests were given to those applying for admission to the seventh grade; from thirty to fifty-five new students were admitted each year. Two classes graduated before the war, but the third class was interrupted by the Japanese occupation and could not complete its courses until 1945. Even before the war, overcrowding forced the schools to hold double sessions in a school year running from July to March.

At the end of the 1946 school year, Mrs. Johnston was transferred to the Department of Education, and most of the teachers who had started high school with her resigned for better positions or left teaching. Norbert Tabery became the new principal, with a staff of new teachers, including a number from the mainland. Tabery was principal for only 1 year and then assumed the position of director of education, the job of principal going to Christian P. Zeien, who held this position from 1948 to 1952. While Tabery was director, the high schools' curriculum expanded from a strictly academic program to include home economics and physical education, as well as teacher training.

Paul Gettys replaced Zeien in 1952. The North Central Association of Colleges and Secondary Schools accredited George Washington High School in May 1957.

With the continuing increase in enrollment and the awareness by the island people of the importance of education, the Guam Legislature appropriated $500,000 for a new, permanent high school. Various problems delayed construction until 1957, when the appropriation was increased to $1,500,000. Tumon Junior-Senior High School began operation in September 1957. Its name was changed to John F. Kennedy High School after President Kennedy's assassination. Albert Fain was principal of the new high school, which had 1,300 students, 55 teachers, and 6 administrative staff members. Tumon was accredited its first year (14).

Administration by Department of the Interior

In 1949, President Truman transferred Guam's administration from the Navy to the Department of the Interior and appointed Carlton S. Skinner as Governor of Guam, ending 50 years of Navy administration. In February 1949, "A Bill To Provide Civil Government for Guam and for Other Purposes" (arising out of the complicated matter of land claims on Guam) was introduced in Congress. It was passed by the House in May 1950 and by the Senate in July. In August 1950, the Organic Act of Guam was signed by President Truman, who declared it to be effective as of July 21, 1944, the date of the liberation of Guam in World War II. It granted the inhabitants of Guam the privileges of U.S. citizenship and a larger measure of self-government.

Certain sections of the Organic Act pertained to the education department of Guam. Executive authority was vested in the Governor, who was given responsibility for supervision of and control over all executive departments and agencies of the government. The Governor was empowered to appoint, with the advice and consent of the Legislature, the heads of all departments. In making such appointments, he was required by law to give preference to qualified Guamanians. He also could, in general, remove from office all department and agency heads. His appointment was for 4 years, and a Secretary of Guam, carrying the full powers of the Governor in case of a vacancy in that office, was appointed to serve in place of the Governor when he was "off island" and to assist him when he was in his office.

Ford Q. Elvidge was the second civilian Governor of Guam, following Skinner. During his term he tried to improve the island's school system. However, his efforts were not met with great cooperation from the Territorial Legislature, and he resigned in April 1953. Still, according to Carano and Sanchez,

> The Guam legislature consistently approved Department of Education requests for funds and in some instances actually increased the budget requests. The budget for fiscal year 1957, however, was an exception. That year, after public hearings, the legislature's Committee on Taxation and Finance recommended cuts of over $180,000. The proposed cuts were opposed by a group of legislators composed of Congresswoman Cynthia J. Torres and Lagrimas L. G. Untalan. All were veteran educators of both the prewar and the immediate postwar periods. After lengthy and heated debate on the floor of the legislature, most of the proposed cuts were restored (15).

Although sporadic attempts at adult education had been made before World War II, the majority of Guamanian adults had not had much opportunity for educational advancement. The few adult schools were evening schools, taught by interested military and civilian personnel, but constant changes in staff plus economic problems discouraged any real planned program. However, in January 1952, the Department of Education, realizing the vocational needs of the islanders, opened the Guam Evening Vocational School. Such courses as business English, shorthand, cabinetmaking, radio repair, appliance repair, motor repair, accounting, blueprint reading, bookkeeping, clerk-stenography, and office management were offered. Vocational training had been stressed from the time of the first American occupation in 1899, most of the Naval Governors realizing the need for more independent skills for the Guamanians. By 1930, agriculture had become an integral part of the public school system, and by 1941, vocational education had become equally important.

After the war, emphasis on vocational training was continued. Tabery, while principal of George Washington High School, introduced on-the-job training and later, as director of education, appointed Paul Carano vocational coordinator. Carano "supervised the apprenticeship training of 432 students in military, government, and civilian business establishments" (16). Attempts to get federal aid for this program were unsuccessful until 1958, when President Eisenhower signed into law an omnibus bill passed by Congress bringing aid to the program. George Washington High School established a regular vocational department in 1951 and recruited industrial arts teachers from the mainland. They worked under the supervision of Robert Moran, vocational consultant in the Department of Education.

Since then, educational opportunities for adults have increased rapidly, with an apprentice school at the naval station opened by the U.S. Navy in 1956, a trade school opened by the Government of Guam, and a night school program begun in 1960.

With the coming of the free, compulsory 12-grade school programs following World War II, the islanders wanted education. The 12th-grade graduate was a person of stature on the island, but for those with the ambition to continue their education, there was no place to go. Until the Organic Act of 1950, Guamanians were not free to travel off the island at will. Besides, most of them could not afford to. A few young Guamanians had been sent to the States for advanced training before the war, but even so, not many Guamanians held college degrees. By 1940, only two Guamanian teachers held degrees, and these teachers were employed part time. The first professionally trained Guamanian teacher in Guam's schools was Pedro C. Sanchez, hired in 1949 (17).

An attempt to start a normal school in 1946 at Adelup Point failed for lack of students. Following this, the University of Hawaii, during the summers of 1946, 1947, and 1948, sent as many as five instructors to Guam to conduct basic college preparation courses. No summer session was held in 1949 because of misunderstandings over housing and transportation.

At the Guamanians' request, the University of Hawaii considered starting a full-fledged college program for the territory. The financial uncertainties of such a venture caused university officials to decide against it, however.

The Guam Legislature authorized establishment of a territorial college in 1952. José R. Palomo, the first Guamanian director of education, contacted various educational institutions in the States to obtain advice on beginning a junior college. Ohio State University was willing to help. Palomo appointed Pedro C. Sanchez the first Guamanian dean of the college. Buildings went up at Mangilao, and in June 1952, the first session of the Territorial College of Guam began. The emphasis was on teacher training; 192 enrolled—110 regular students, the rest elementary school teachers taking in-service training.

John S. Haitema was director of education during the college's second year, and the emphasis continued to be on teacher training and the community college concept.

The college continued to grow, adding secretarial training, junior accountant training, junior college 2-year training for those wishing to continue toward a degree at some other college, government employee in-service training, and noncollege credit courses for adults.

In 1959, the Western College Association accredited the college for a 3-year period. In August 1961, with the passage of Public Law 6-40, the Territorial College became the College of Guam, a 4-year institution awarding the baccalaureate.

Dr. Sanchez was named its first president, and the college moved to its permanent location overlooking Pago Bay and the Pacific Ocean. Today, the college is separate from the Department of Education and is governed by a board of regents. It offers several 2-year technical courses, such as nursing, in addition to degree programs. Looking to the future, it plans to offer graduate degrees at the university level.

During the 1950's, members of the Legislature continually expressed great concern over education on the island. In July 1960, the Legislature passed a generous scholarship bill, authorizing more than 150 scholarships—

> For students wishing to study in mainland colleges and universities. Other scholarships were authorized for use in the Territorial College of Guam. The law on the free use of textbooks was amended so as to enable students attending private schools to benefit from the act. At the close of the first session in 1960 several congressmen showed concern over the matter of teachers' salaries. Two bills were introduced providing for salary increases for educational employees (18).

Guam's young population is swelling at an alarming pace, putting a great strain on the educational system. There is a great need for—

> Skilled, technical, and professional labor from within the local resident population while at the same time preparing our students for competition with those who are the products of other educational systems. The aims and purposes of education on the island today do not differ greatly from those of prewar Guam, with the exception that less emphasis is now being placed on agriculture (19).

Guam's greatest educational problem is developing students' proficiency in the English language. There is a subtle resistance toward English, principally among the older Guamanians. Chamorro is often spoken in government offices and in businesses, in spite of "Speak English" signs. And Chamorro is still the language of the home. This naturally causes a problem in communication and is the basis for much misunderstanding, not only on the part of the statesider who expects to be able to transact his business in English, but on the part of the Guamanian, who is sensitive to criticism concerning his language.

Much effort has been made recently to supplement the teaching of English in the classroom, doubtless impaired because of little carryover into private life. In March 1964, the Board of Education adopted the ungraded primary, to be used in place of grades 1, 2, and 3. Under this plan, each child's rate of learning is studied, his progress is recognized, and teaching is adjusted to give the child as much time as he needs. Both the slow learner and the gifted child are profiting from this.

Operation Head Start was inaugurated in Guam in 1965. Local educators hope that through Head Start and the ungraded primary, younger children will find English a more usable language and will carry their learning into the home.

The Brodie Memorial School for Exceptional Children, with a new school and all new facilities as of 1966, is increasingly able to care for the specialized needs of exceptional children. For older handicapped persons, the Division of Vocational Rehabilitation has a well-planned and improving program. Guam's high schools lost their accreditation in 1965, and additional consultants were added to the department, including one in audiovisual, in the start of the department's commitment to expand and develop its educational media resources. This was probably one of the department's most significant postwar decisions, in terms of its long-range impact on education.

Great strides have been made in recent years in adult education. Guam now has an excellent program, conducted mainly in the evening, and taught by trained teachers and vocational instructors.

To further advance the education of adult Guamanians, the College of Guam conducts night courses, not only at the college, but on the military bases. Scholarships are available for students to continue their higher education at the College of Guam and in the United States.

Many people have been involved in shaping the educational philosophy of Guam. H. H. Hiatt served as superintendent of schools from 1901 to 1913. Jacques Schnabel, an American resident and one of Guam's early teachers, took his place until 1922, when Thomas Collins replaced him, to be succeeded by Alice V. Wall in 1925. Following was Mrs. Esther M. Riddle. In 1927, Simon A. Sanchez became superintendent. He held the office until June 1959, when he retired. After Sanchez came, successively, Oscar L. Musgrave, Edwin Battiste, and Richard Tennessen. Teresita Salas served in an acting capacity at various times between appointments of superintendents.

The Directors of Education

George V. Hall, in 1947, began to reshape the department. However, the tenure of the directors of education was too short to allow them to carry out long-range plans. From 1947 to 1953, four directors and three acting directors served. In 1952, Dr. Haitema took office and served until July 1957, when John R. Trace of Ohio replaced him. Trace resigned in July 1962, to be replaced by Eric Dennard.

Because the Department of Education was under the complete control of the Governor, the Guamanians themselves had little voice until 1938, when the first Board of Education was formed. However, even this was controlled by the Governor, who appointed the members to 2-year terms and limited the board's power to "strictly advisory function to matters pertaining to buildings and grounds, material, equipment, new school districts, sessions and socioeconomic conditions affecting the school program" (20).

After the war, the board was reestablished by the Governor, with changes, and in 1949, the Guam Congress made further changes. The board was now composed of one member from each of the two Houses of the Guam Congress; three members elected at large; three representatives of the armed forces, appointed by the Governor; and one representative from temporary residents not members of the armed forces, also appointed by the Governor. The director of education and the superintendent of schools were ex officio members, without voting power. The board was still largely advisory until the passage of the Education Code by the first Guam Legislature in 1952. This code gave the board the power it needed to become a policy-making body, which helped improve the relations between the educational system and the legislative and executive branches.

Each year more tax moneys are needed to supplement the federal aid programs, placing greater strain on the people themselves. No end is in sight, as the birthrate soars and more and more schools, textbooks, and educational facilities are needed. Since no educational tax structure exists as yet, politics enter into the enacting and allotting of appropriations via the Governor's office and the Legislature, causing at times great delays in starting desirable education programs. Guamanians in general are not sophisticated enough in political matters to follow the maze of political maneuvering which must, as a matter of course, accompany this type of arrangement. Federal appropriations and tax revenues are beyond their understanding. They are apt to be indifferent to school board meetings and legislative hearings. They need more education in civic responsibility to become aware of the needs of their educational system and their potential contribution to it.

Guam's strategic importance today makes it vital that its children be well educated. It is inevitable that the future will bring more youth programs and more schools, both academic and vocational. More consistency and stability will be needed in administrative areas and school administrative areas, and school administrators will require more mainland training in order to keep Guam abreast of modern educational advances.

The policy of importing qualified teachers from off-island must be changed to an upgrading of Guamanian teachers themselves, thereby lessening the great teacher turnover each year. The cost of living on Guam is high. An urgent need of the moment, one on which the Department of Education is constantly working, is to increase salaries to such a point that island teachers will wish to return to Guam after leaving the island for their advanced degrees on the mainland.

On Guam, the challenge and possibility of fulfillment present themselves to any educator undertaking the task of teaching its youth. Guam's past, present, and future combine to make it a unique area where the educator can see the evolution of social change before his very eyes. Guam has the opportunity of meeting this challenge today and, for the first time, coming out on top; for it has, in the history of its educational endeavors, ably demonstrated that it has learned well the virtue of patience and the value of persistence.

FOOTNOTES

1. Agana is the capital with a population of 1,204, but Sinajana has a population of 4,246, Tamuning has 2,842, and Agana Heights has 2,304.
2. Charles F. Reid, *Education in the Territories and Outlying Possessions of the United States* (New York: Bureau of Publications, Teachers College, Columbia University, 1941), p. 299.
3. For further information, see Remedios L. G. Perez and Alice W. Wygart, "Guam: Past and Present," Department of Education, Agana, 1951, p. 54. (Mimeographed.)

4. Paul Carano and Pedro C. Sanchez, *Complete History of Guam* (Tokyo: Charles E. Tuttle Co., Inc., 1964), p. 182.
5. *Ibid.*, quoting Francis Lee Albert, "History of the Department of Education in Guam during the American Administration," *Guam Recorder* (Agana), VIII (October 1931), 373, 378-86.
6. Carano and Sanchez, *op. cit.*, p. 406.
7. *Ibid.*, quoting Naval Government of Guam, General Order No. 12.
8. Reid, *op. cit.*, p. 320.
9. *Guam Recorder* (Agana), I, No. 1 (September 1924), 9-10.
10. Carano and Sanchez, *op. cit.*, p. 413.
11. Victor Obermeier, who came to Guam to teach in 1949 for a 1-year stay and is still with the Department of Education as a personnel officer, had, in several personal interviews at the department in Agana, many such stories of early postwar education.
12. Carano and Sanchez, *op. cit.*, p. 418, citing Department of Education, *Annual Report* (1955).
13. *Ibid.*, p. 421.
14. Figures on the costs of school buildings, increases of costs per pupil, and teachers' salaries (compared to prewar wages of $.60 to $3.09 a day) can be found in Carano and Sanchez, *op. cit.*, pp. 418-21.
15. *Ibid.*, p. 421.
16. *Ibid.*, p. 427.
17. Carano and Sanchez co-authored the only up-to-date history of Guam, which was published in 1964. Portions of this chapter rely heavily upon that work.
18. Carano and Sanchez, *op. cit.*, p. 383.
19. Harley Jones, "Educational Policy, Legislation and Administration on Guam," prepared for UNESCO's *World Survey of Education*, V (Agana: Department of Education, March 1967), 2.
20. Carano and Sanchez, *op. cit.*, p. 435, quoting Laura Thompson, *Guam and Its People* (Princeton, N.J.: Princeton University Press, 1947), p. 219.

BIBLIOGRAPHY

Books and Pamphlets

Beardsley, Charles. *Guam: Past and Present.* Rutland, Vt.: Charles E. Tuttle Co., Inc., 1964.

Carano, Paul, and Sanchez, Pedro C. *Complete History of Guam.* Tokyo: Charles E. Tuttle Co., Inc., 1964. This is the most authoritative history of Guam at present, including all phases of its development and an excellent bibliography.

Clark, Blake. *Robinson Crusoe, USA: The Adventures of George R. Tweed on Jap-Held Guam as Told to Blake Clark.* New York and London: Whittlesey House, McGraw-Hill Book Co., 1945.

Department of Education. *An Invitation To Teach on Guam.* Agana: The Department, 1966. This is a teacher recruitment brochure.

Reid, Charles F. *Education in the Territories and Outlying Possessions of the United States.* New York: Bureau of Publications, Teachers College, Columbia University, 1941.

Safford, William Edwin. *The Useful Plants of the Island of Guam: With an Introductory Account of the Physical Features and Natural History of the Island, of the Character and History of Its People, and of Their Agriculture.* Vol. IX: *Contributions from the U.S. National Herbarium.* Washington, D.C.: Government Printing Office, 1905.

Searles, Paul J. and Ruth. *A School History of Guam.* Agana: Naval Government Print Shop, 1937.

Standish, Robert. *Bonin.* New York: The Macmillan Co., 1944. This is a historical novel about the Bonin Islands, but it presents an interesting description of the decadence of Guam immediately prior to the American occupation.

Thompson, Laura. *Guam and Its People.* Princeton, N.J.: Princeton University Press, 1947.

Reports

Department of Education. *Annual Reports.* These are mimeographed in Agana and sent on to be included in the Governor's Reports.

Governor's Annual Report to the Secretary of the Interior. Washington, D.C.: Government Printing Office, 1951-66.

Tudor Engineering Company. *Guam Harbor Development Study.* Contract NBy 51550 (A-E) TEC File 310. San Francisco: Tudor Engineering Co., 1964. This contains excellent background material on many aspects of Guam, including population and education.

U.S. Navy. *Annual Report to the Secretary of the Interior.* Agana: Naval Government Print Shop, 1901-41.

Articles and Periodicals

Grace, H. Ted, and Salas, Teresita. "Guam's Education Marches On." *Peabody Journal of Education,* XLIV, No. 1 (July 1966), 37-39.

Guam Daily News. Liberation Day Supplement Annual, 1953.

Guam Recorder (Agana). Vol. I (1924) through Vol. XVIII (1941). Files at the Nieves H. Flores Memorial Library, Agana, Guam.

Kahn, Ely J. "Stragglers." *The New Yorker* (3-part series, "Reporter at Large"), March 17, 24, and 31, 1962.

"Letter from Guam." *The New Yorker,* February 13, 1965, pp. 39-40ff.

Unpublished Material

Carano, Paul. "Historical Glimpses at the Development of Education in Guam, 1565-1961." Agana, September 1, 1961. (Mimeographed.)

Jones, Harley. "Educational Policy, Legislation and Administration on Guam." Prepared for UNESCO's *World Survey of Education,* Vol. V. Agana: Department of Education, March 1967. (Typewritten.)

Minter, Mahlon. "Educational Legislation of the Guam Legislature." College of Guam, 1967. (Typewritten.)

Perez, Remedios L. G., and Wygart, Alice W. "Guam: Past and Present." Department of Education, Agana, 1951. (Mimeographed.)

Other Source

Department of Education, Agana. Personal interviews with selected staff members. October 1966, through March 1967.

Appendix A

GUAM CHIEF SCHOOL OFFICERS

Directors of Education

1946-48	George V. Hall
1948-49	Norbert F. Tabery
1949-50	Orin Robinson
1950-52	José R. Palomo
1952	Herbert Spencer (acting)
1952	Pearl Heidarn (acting)
1952-57	John S. Haitema
1957-62	John R. Trace
1962	Cecil Willis (acting)
1963	Tom Rathbone (acting)
1963-65	Eric N. Dennard
1965-67	Ivan Ward Lasher
1967-	Larry P. Martin

Appendix B

Chart I.--GUAM DEPARTMENT OF EDUCATION, 1967

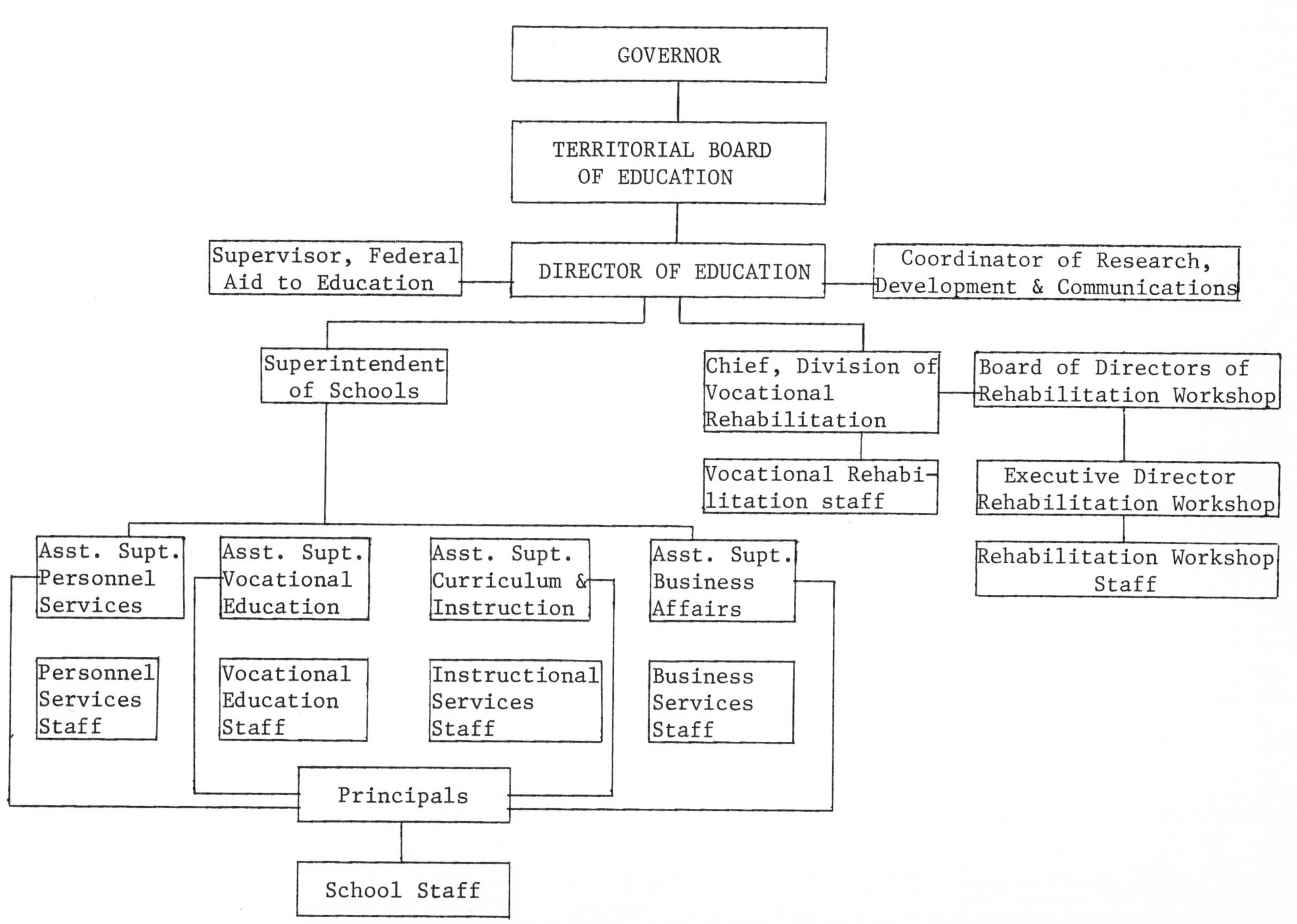

Appendix B

Chart II.--ISLAND OF GUAM

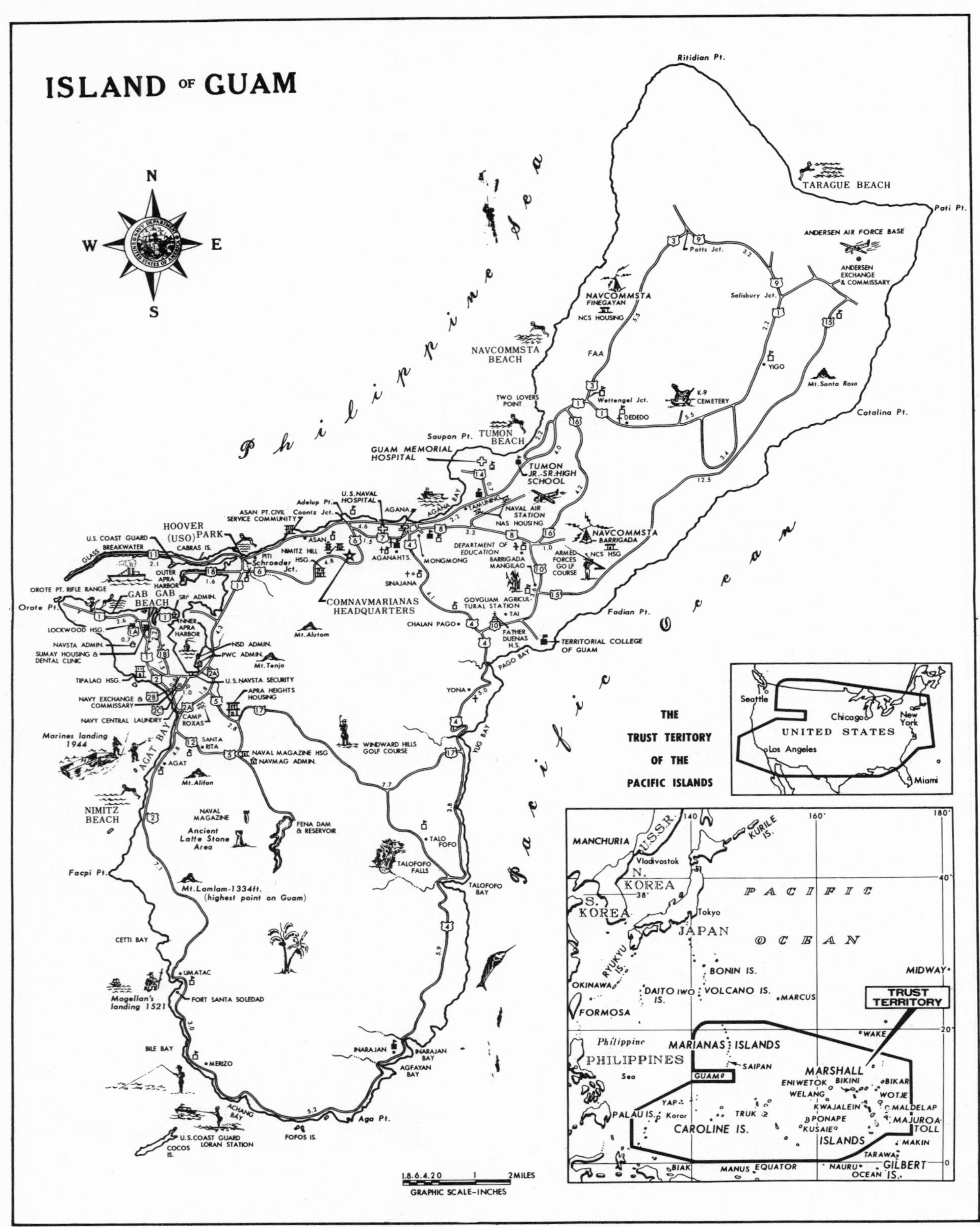

54 Panama Canal Zone

DIVISION OF SCHOOLS
Francis A. Castles

Contents

BEFORE THE "BIG DITCH"

During the time when the French were attempting to construct the Panama Canal, little effort was made to organize a system of public schools. The children were instructed usually at home or in private schools. But when the United States gained control of the Canal Zone in 1904, although President Theodore Roosevelt's major concern was to "make the dirt fly," the Isthmian Canal Commission authorized the establishment of a public school system. The following June, William Howard Taft, Roosevelt's Secretary of War, approved spending $30,000 for this purpose.

The first school in the Canal Zone opened at Corozal in January 1906, using borrowed tables and chairs, a few sample textbooks, and some other supplies collected on the isthmus. The Corozal school and those that followed were first supervised by the Collector of Revenues, but in May 1906 they were turned over to the Bureau of Municipalities. The Canal Zone's five municipalities immediately enacted ordinances making every person having legal charge or control of children between 6 and 14 years of age responsible for their attendance at the public schools for regularly prescribed terms. The ordinances stipulated that persons violating them would pay a $5 fine for the first offense and $10 for subsequent offenses (1).

Seven months later, the educational system had so expanded that it was made a separate division under the Department of Law and Government. David O'Connor, head of the department, was appointed the Canal Zone's first superintendent of schools. In 1907, schools for white children were opened at La Boca, Ancon, Pedro Miguel, Paraiso, Culebra, Empire, Cristobal, and Colón. The teachers for these schools were carefully selected from numerous applicants, with preference given to those with normal school training and previous experience in the United States. In fact, 14 of the 18 chosen were experienced teachers. But it proved difficult to hire colored teachers, so there was a delay in opening the schools for colored children at La Boca, Las Sabanas, Paraiso, Culebra, Empire, Gatun, Cristobal, and Playa de Flor. This continued to be a problem for several years.

The Canal Zone schools were divided into eight grades to conform to similar organization of elementary schools in the United States. The curriculum included reading, writing, spelling, grammar, geography, elementary physiology, and free-hand drawing. In addition, the English-speaking children were taught Spanish and the Spanish-speaking taught English. For American children who were too advanced for the elementary grades, high school classes were organized at Culebra and Cristobal, teaching algebra, geometry, Latin, Spanish, botany, physical geography, general history, rhetoric, and biology. All children of parents employed by the Isthmian Canal Commission could attend free, but children of parents who were not residents of the Canal Zone were required to pay a tuition fee of $2 per month for the elementary grades and $4 per month for the high school grades.

In 1908, Professor Henry Lester Smith, a graduate of Indiana State University and the supervising principal in Indianapolis, succeeded David O'Connor as superintendent of schools. During the first year of his administration, a new white school was constructed at Gorgona, and new colored schools were built at Cruces, San Pablo, and Mount Hope. A new school for white children was authorized at Corozal to replace the small, temporary school, that had been the Canal Zone's first. One half the 36 white teachers hired for the following year were graduated from university or normal schools in the United States. Twelve had B.A. degrees, and 11 held certificates from normal schools—all had 2 or more years of experience in the States or the Canal Zone.

As the students progressed through the grades, there was an increasing demand for high school classes. At the end of October 1908, 20 students were enrolled in the two high schools, 11 at Culebra, and 9 at Cristobal. The following year, high school courses were offered at Gatun. This was the only time in the Canal Zone's history that three white high schools existed.

The high school students usually carried four subjects, but if first- or second-year students had excellent marks, they were given permission to carry an additional subject. These students attended two terms of 4.5 months each for 4 years to earn a total of 32 credits. Eight credits were required in Latin, eight in mathematics, four in history, one in civil government, three in physical science, and eight in English. An optional course in Spanish was open to all students. Courses in French and German also were available to students capable of carrying an increased load, and because of a shortage of Latin books a number of students took German to avoid any delay. The schools attempted to set standards that would enable the students to enter American colleges or universities without difficulty–they were being prepared for the entrance examinations at Harvard and Vassar.

To overcome the disadvantage of requiring teachers to instruct in all departments, and to establish a good working library, the three high schools were consolidated at Cristobal at the end of the 1909 school year. School spirit increased immediately. Every student joined the school association or one of the two literary societies. The boys interested in baseball and basketball organized an athletic association; the girls reported once a week for baseball and calisthenics.

In July 1910, a consolidation plan for the elementary public schools for white children combined the schools at Colón Beach and Cristobal into one school at Cristobal. Las Cascadas was consolidated with the school at Empire, and the Empire school was doubled in size. The Paraiso school merged with the one at Pedro Miguel, and the Corozal school combined with the school at Ancon. A second floor was added to the building at Ancon, and it was decided that the students residing in Corozal and Balboa would be brought to the Ancon school for the first-year high school courses as a branch of the Cristobal High School, rather than getting a separate school. Finally, in 1910, the superintendent moved the new Cristobal High School to Gatun, so that the students would have less distance to travel from points along the railroad line running the 50 miles from Panama City.

The school at Cruces, 4 miles above the railroad bridge at Gamboa, was first held in an old church badly in need of repair. In 1910, it was decided to construct a new building. The new building had to be framed at Bas Obispo, transported on a flatcar to the dynamite storehouse near the Gamboa bridge, then moved about 150 feet to the river where the 24- by 36-foot frame was loaded onto a raft and towed upstream to Cruces (2).

There were constant checks on the children's health, and the teachers were instructed to detect and prevent communicable diseases. To ensure proper lighting and ventilation, recommendations by an inspection team of medical officers resulted in lowering the outer wall of many school buildings to within 5 feet of the floor and eliminating the screen verandas. Individual water cups were ordered for all schools, and the public drinking glass on railroad trains was abolished. The medical inspection team found health problems in 409 (46 percent) of the 887 children examined.

In June 1911, the chief justice of the Canal Zone Supreme Court delivered an address at a baccalaureate service at Gatun in honor of the first graduating class of a Canal Zone high school. The commencement exercises were held June 30 at the same location. Two students graduated: Blanche Marguerite Stevens of Gorgona and Maria Elise Johnson of Gatun.

By March 1912, 75 students were enrolled in the high school (3). These students had previously traveled an aggregate of 1.5 million miles to and from school without an accident, but to reduce operating costs and minimize this railroad travel, the superintendent of schools agreed to a reorganization in March 1912. The first- and second-year students at Gorgona, Culebra, and intermediate points were directed to attend the school at Empire. The first- and second-year students south of Culebra and all third- and fourth-year students in the Canal Zone were to attend the consolidated school at Ancon. Two new white schools for first, second, and third grades were opened at Toro Point. The upper-grade school at Culebra was discontinued, and the children in the fifth, sixth, seventh, and eighth grades were transported to Empire.

Thirteen of the 75 teachers employed in 1912 held degrees from colleges and universities, 19 held diplomas from standard normal schools, and 12 had at least 2 years of normal school teaching and training. During January and February 1913, the Division of Schools received an average of five applications daily for positions as teachers in the white schools. Over 1,500 applications were on file during March, and 500 were from teachers with at least 2 years experience, all highly recommended. The conditions afforded unusual opportunities for selecting and appointing only those who possessed the highest qualifications.

WORLD WAR I AND THE TWENTIES

As the canal neared completion, areas that had once been villages and townsites were flooded, forcing constant changes in the location of the schools. By the end of 1914, grades 1-12 were offered at Balboa Heights and grades 1-10 at Cristobal. Ancon, Corozal, Culebra, Las Cascadas, and Gatun offered grades 1-8, while Pedro Miguel offered grades 1-7 and Paraiso grades 1-4. Grades 1-8 for colored children, most of whom were dependents of West Indians who had come to the Canal Zone to work during the construction period, were opened at La Boca, Ancon, Paraiso, Gatun, Mount Hope, and Cristobal. However, the Mount Hope school for colored children was closed in December 1915. Due to a shortage of funds, it was decided that children of employees who were not citizens of the United States and not living in Colón or Panama could not be granted preschool privileges or entitled to attend the Canal Zone schools. This closed the Ancon colored school, and it was relocated in Panama City under new boundary jurisdictions.

When the "big ditch" was finally completed in 1914, the Division of Schools became a part of the executive department. The direct responsibility for administering the Canal Zone schools now rested with the superintendent of schools, who reported to the executive secretary of the Panama Canal. The Governor appointed Albert R. Lang superintendent of schools in 1913, and he served until 1922.

When the Corozal school closed in 1915, the few children had to be transported to the Balboa school. In fact, 1 out of every 10 white children and 1 in every 63 colored children were transported by train to school each day. These pupils traveled an aggregate of 2,400 miles per day, or 48,000 miles per month, at a cost of $300 per month—five-eights of a cent per mile. Seventeen stations were located along the railroad line, but only Cristobal, Paraiso, Empire, Gatun, Balboa, Pedro Miguel, and Ancon had sufficient population to justify establishing schools.

The distances between the schools resulted in the Zone's first athletic meet's, held in 1914, being performed on the respective schools' grounds and the results telephoned. By 1916, track meets were becoming popular, and the "telephone meet" was discontinued. For the second meet, a loving cup for the victor was ordered from the States by the editor of a Panama newspaper, but before it arrived, the Corozal school was closed, the physical education director in charge of the meet had returned to the United States, and the editor had died. No one would pay the express charges on the cup, and it was in the Colón express office when it burned to the ground in April 1915. To eliminate a recurrence, the Division of Schools decided to present a banner as a permanent trophy, which would be transferred each year to the winning school.

In 1910, 30 students in the Empire school for colored children had been given tools to cultivate a plot of ground 12 by 20 feet to discover the horticultural possibilities of the Canal Zone soil for giving the students training. The project was directed by a graduate of the Agricultural College of Kingston, Jamaica, whose major aim was to find out what fruits and vegetables could be raised at a profit. The original plan was to confine the gardening to boys, but the girls showed such an intense desire that permission was given to them to enter the classes.

In May 1917, the U.S. Commissioner of Education initiated a movement to have every boy and girl over 9 years of age cultivate a garden to alleviate the food shortage caused by World War I. Since the school gardens for colored children had been very successful, the Canal Zone schools had a head start on such a project. With cooperation from the supply department, the schools received the necessary seeds and commenced the first plowing. The produce was then sold by commissaries at the current price, and the profits were used to purchase pianos, victrolas, books, and pictures.

The war made it difficult for the schools to keep their buildings in proper repair, both in the Canal Zone and in the United States. The U.S. Commissioner of Education urged the schools to try to maintain their standards during the war and keep up regular attendance by the pupils. In a letter of May 1917 to the superintendents of schools, he said:

> Everywhere there seems to be fear lest our schools of all kinds and grades, and especially the public schools, will suffer this year because of conditions growing out of our entrance into the war. On the other hand, both for the present defense and for future welfare of our country, as well as for the individual benefits of the children, it is of the greatest importance that the schools shall be maintained in their full efficiency, both as to standards of work and attendance of children (4).

To provide the benefits mentioned in the letter, the supervisor of industrial training conducted a vacation school at the Balboa school shop during the summer of 1917. Morning sessions were attended by boys from the Balboa area, while the afternoon sessions admitted students who lived out of town. The 52 boys, ranging from sixth-graders to seniors in high school, needed little motivation, and the output of articles—ranging from library tables to tie racks—for the 3 months equaled that for an entire school year with only one-eighth as many class sections.

In 1918, night-school classes were opened for all U.S. citizens. The schools offered a commercial course, including typing, bookkeeping, and shorthand; a mathematics course, including algebra and geometry; and courses in Spanish and English. The participants paid $4 per month for each subject and attended two nights a week for 2 hours. Classes to accommodate those working night shifts were scheduled on Saturday afternoons.

The colored schools did not advance as rapidly as the white schools. The buildings were overcrowded, there was a waiting list of those wanting to enter, the equipment was inadequate, and the teachers were required to care for more children than they could possibly instruct. New schools at Cristobal and Gatun and the addition of seven new teachers in 1923 helped solve some of the problems, but schools were still overcrowded and often lacked textbooks. But when the Otis Classification Test was given to the sixth-, seventh-, and eighth-grade colored students, the results were considerably below those of students in the white schools and those in corresponding grades in the States. The results of the 1926 Otis Classification Test indicated that the average achievement of pupils in the white schools was decidedly superior to that in the corresponding grades in the States.

The white schools gradually increased in average daily attendance each year from 1915 to 1932, except for 1922 and 1928, while the colored school attendance fluctuated from year to year (5). The teacher-pupil ratio for the colored schools at times was 1 to 50, and in 1926 several hundred students did not receive any education. In 1928, over 1,000 students between the ages of 6 and 16 had no facilities.

The superintendent of schools made an effort to secure needed facilities for the colored students, but the funds appropriated by Congress were insufficient for this purpose. Congress did appropriate additional funds in 1927 to employ 13 more teachers and allow over 600 more colored pupils to attend school. Eight new classrooms were constructed at Silver City and Cristobal, and six additional rooms were constructed at Gatun. To relieve some of the congestion and improve the standards of work in the colored schools, the superintendent approved a 12-month school year for the 1927-28 fiscal year and added manual training to supplement the courses in the eighth grade. In 1929, the facilities were still not adequate for the colored children, so 22 rooms were added to the schools, and new eight-room wooden buildings were constructed at Silver City, Red Tank, and Paraiso. With all the inadequacies, the 1932 expenditures were still 15 times the $30,000 first appropriated in 1905.

In 1930, the superintendent of schools initiated a survey of the Canal Zone schools. It was conducted by N. L. Englehardt of Teachers College, Columbia University. His report revealed that the white children were well above the standards existing in the States, but it did criticize the lack of breadth and enrichment in the academic subjects. As a result, the Balboa High School revised its curriculum to include biology, Latin American history, theory of music, fine arts, and advanced courses in household arts. The Cristobal school added chemistry, theory of music, fine arts, and a year of advanced mechanical drawing. The Cristobal mathematics requirement was increased to one-half year of algebra and one-half year of trigonometry, giving its students the same full 4-year course in mathematics as offered at Balboa. The survey also resulted in four new supervisory positions' being established, including a director of research, a supervisor of art, and special teachers in art and music.

DEPRESSION YEARS TO REORGANIZATION, 1933-54

During the Depression, studies revealed that the professional fields were overcrowded but that semiprofessional positions, such as shop foremen, mechanics, accountants, draftsmen, and medical technicians, were open for young people with the proper vocational training. The bleak economic picture prevented many students from finishing regular 4-year college courses. The junior college movement was already popular in the United States, and during the twenties, some residents had begun advocating one for the Canal Zone. During the early thirties, there was an increasing demand that students be given access to a comparatively inexpensive college education.

The liberal local newspapers started a campaign to establish a junior college, contending that jobs were nonexistent in the Canal Zone and that further education was an economic impossibility for most students. But the official consideration of the junior college proposal hinged on finances. The administration was willing to start the college if the funds could be found, even though Balboa High School was underequipped and overcrowded, an equally pressing and important problem.

A detailed study of the feasibility of founding a junior college was started in 1932, but the necessary deliberations did not proceed fast enough to suit the public. An organization called the Pacific Civil Council devised a slogan for a junior college campaign: "A Junior College for the Canal Zone by October 1, 1932." Governor Harry Burgess voiced the administration's skepticism in a memorandum to the council's executive secretary: "I do not believe Congress will authorize the junior college until the United States finances are in very much better shape than they are likely to be in the next two years" (6).

With Congress in a miserly mood and the Budget Bureau holding tight to the purse strings, it was decided to charge tuition for a junior college's operating expenses rather than risk a request for additional appropriations. The $50,000 necessary for a frame building to be built next to Balboa High School and for laboratory equipment, furniture, books, and other items came from funds saved on the La Boca school and the new school at Cristobal.

In September 1933, the junior college opened on the third floor of the high school building with 65 students. Before the end of its first year, the new junior college was recognized by the American Association of Junior Colleges (7). The following year, its new quarters were ready. By 1935, the Canal Zone Junior College had graduated 24 students, and 17 of these wanted to continue their training. A study 2 years later showed that 55 students who had attended the junior college during the first 3 years were employed by the Panama Canal Company or the Panama Railroad.

In 1935, the Canal Zone again expanded its opportunities for higher education by opening a normal school to train teachers for the colored schools in the town of La Boca. Only about one-eighth of the applicants were accepted, but 37 of the original students completed a 4-year course and received diplomas. At the same time, the Canal Zone Junior College added extension courses in accounting, business, English, shorthand, typing, Spanish, mathematics, and industrial lubrication. Over 600 students enrolled for these courses.

In 1936, the Division of Schools took over the Panama Canal Astronomical Observatory adjacent to the

Miraflores Locks to provide training in astronomy (8). Instruction has continued at the observatory, and it is very popular during the dry season. Lectures are held two evenings a week, and average attendance is usually 75, not counting the lectures for special groups on other nights.

During the 1940's, many Army and Navy personnel returned to the United States, causing a decline in the school enrollments. The table in Appendix C reveals the fluctuation in the average daily attendance caused by the Depression, the entrance into the war, and the end of the war "baby boom."

When the second wartime school year (1942-43) opened, the superintendent made plans to adapt the secondary school curriculums and activities to meet the war needs. Preinduction courses were introduced in a number of fields, including electricity, automotive mechanics, and aeronautics. A Victory Corps, organized in the high school to assist in such things as bond drives and Civil Defense, served as a focus for student activities. Two special 1-year curriculums in commerce and engineering were established in the Canal Zone Junior College, but the Selective Service Act and many opportunities for wartime employment kept the junior college enrollments at a low figure.

The postwar baby boom prompted the construction of a 27-room elementary school at Fort Kobbe to take care of the children residing at Fort Kobbe, Howard Field, Farfan, Lacona, Rousseau, Rodman, and the Naval Ammunition Depot. The Bureau of Clubs and Playgrounds had started kindergartens, but in 1940 they became a part of the school program. A new kindergarten opened at Ancon in 1950. All sixth-grade pupils were transferred to the Balboa school when the administrative offices of the schools division were transferred from the third floor of the Balboa Elementary School to the Civil Affairs Building, thus adding four new rooms to accommodate the new students.

In addition to operating its normal school facilities, the Division of Schools operated an apprentice school for young American and Panamanian men who had won appointments to craft apprenticeships in the Panama Canal organization. Only a limited number of appointments were made each year, based on a competitive exam open to high school graduates. This program was administered under the direction of the apprentice committee appointed by the Governor and the superintendent of schools, who as a member of this committee was especially responsible for its overall management. The apprentice school was transferred in 1953 to the Electrical Division of the Panama Canal Company, which now has complete control of the program.

REORGANIZATION TO 1966

In 1954, following the demands from both individuals and groups within the Republic of Panama and the Canal Zone, the superintendent completed plans to reorganize the colored schools into Latin American schools, which would use a Spanish-language curriculum in place of the English offered previously. The conversion plan was based on the sound educational principle that the schools should be primarily concerned with preparing the child for an environment in which he would spend his adult life. An intensive training period was provided for all teachers not proficient in Spanish.

The change took effect from kindergarten through grade 6 when the schools opened in August 1954, with the conversion of the secondary grades planned for the 1955-56 school year. Since most of the older children had at least 3 or 4 years of Spanish-language classes, the change was smooth and efficient. Lower-grade children had no experience in Spanish, however, until the schools offered it in the fall of 1954. A difficulty arose over a lack of textbooks in Spanish. This was corrected, and the curriculum was soon patterned after the schools in Panama. Spanish was later incorporated into the curriculum of the American schools in grades 1, 2, and 3 providing a continuous Spanish program from grades 1 to 8. The entire changeover was completed by 1956, and the Latin American schools are now functioning normally.

In March 1954, an evaluation team for the Middle States Association of Colleges and Secondary Schools was favorably impressed with the schools and indicated that the system was intelligently administered for the welfare of the boys and girls. Its report further stated that the administration was responsible for two school systems: the American schools and the Latin American schools. Even though the community itself had no control over the administration of these schools, the evaluating team felt that everyone, from the Governor to the professional members of the staff, was sensitive to the needs of Canal Zone pupils.

The survey team recommended that the schools use audiovisual aids, pay more attention to health services, gradually give the students more responsibility for choosing their own programs, and establish similar programs jointly prepared by the pupils and teachers to use the abilities and skills of a great many students. It suggested that the superintendent install a follow-up program for students in college and in the world of work. It also pointed out the need for in-service training for the staff members, particularly since the Canal Zone was so far from the great centers of intellectual life.

Cristobal High School was praised for its varied and extensive program of studies despite its small enrollment. The student body possessed an average mental ability higher than that of schools of the United States, and 46 percent of its graduates attended institutions of higher learning. The ROTC and the English department received excellent ratings. It was recommended, however, that

Cristobal High School use extensive audiovisual aids and develop an art course.

The 220 teachers employed by the schools division in 1956 had received undergraduate training from 148 different colleges, universities, and institutions located in 38 states and the District of Columbia. Thirty-eight percent of these teachers received their education in the Eastern and Western North Central states, 24 percent in the Middle Atlantic states, 17 percent in the Eastern and Western South Central states, and 9 percent in the Mountain states. Nineteen were from Minnesota, the most from any single state.

Enrollments continued to increase, making it necessary to add new school facilities. A new Paraiso High School was officially opened in June 1956, constructed from a shell of a building used as a storehouse by the locks division. The classrooms and facilities, rivaling any of the American schools in the Zone, cost $125,000 and contained 10 regular classrooms, physical science and biology rooms, and a library. The library was designed to be used by the people in the community of Paraiso as well as by the students. The La Boca Elementary and Junior High Schools were vacated and their classes transferred to the more modern La Boca High School. The Latin American Junior College at La Boca also was discontinued, and the students who would have attended now enrolled at the University of Panama.

Handicapped children requiring special help had been permitted to attend regular classes if their presence did not unduly distract the other students and their mothers volunteered to work as orderlies and training assistants. At least the students benefited from social contact with other students. But in 1956, with 200 or more children in the Canal Zone needing special schooling because of physical or mental handicaps, the need for special training was brought to the attention of Governor William E. Potter. He responded:

> It is only reasonable that the Government should provide adequate educational facilities for the handicapped in this remote location, where no municipal or charitable institution, research center or private school or clinic is available to our Canal Zone population (9).

The staff for the handicapped program was carefully selected: Thirteen members of the Canal Zone school system were scattered from New York to California to take special training for teaching and working with the deaf, blind, or otherwise handicapped. These teachers received a regular salary while attending school, but all summer school expenses were their own responsibility.

The program for the handicapped began in 1958 for children suffering from cerebral palsy, postpolio effects, heart ailments, and handicaps in motor control. The students were given a series of standardized and informal tasks, and a differentiated program was then designed for each pupil. Five children with physical handicaps were organized as a special class at Gorgas Hospital. They were given a regular first-grade curriculum as well as special activities, such as changing the date on the calendar—a real ceremony each morning—and learning to tell the time from a cardboard clock.

Speech and hearing difficulties were most prevalent at the outset of the special program. A survey revealed that 970 pupils in the U.S. schools and 796 in the Latin American schools—about 10 percent—were found urgently in need of speech therapy. Three trained speech correctionists worked with children who stuttered, had difficulty with articulation, or simply possessed unpleasant voices. Three children had speech defects due to cleft palates, and a few were cerebral-palsied children whose speech problems stemmed from lack of muscular control.

A new world was opened to blind children through the use of braille. Sight-saving classes also were started under this program. The rooms were gaily decorated to reflect as much light as possible, and large easels were used for fingerpainting so that the children could relax and be expressive despite their impaired vision. During the next school year, 1958-59, the special education program was expanded to the Latin American schools, and a remedial reading program was inaugurated at all schools. A new special education room was constructed at Paraiso.

All of the schools continued to expand, so that by 1959 there were 11,000 students in the U.S. and Latin American Canal Zone schools (10). The schools included 12 kindergartens, 15 elementary schools, five junior high schools, four high schools, and the Canal Zone Junior College. They employed 400 teachers and principals. A number of new buildings had been added and older classrooms remodeled or added to.

Scholarships in varying amounts were available to graduates of the Canal Zone high schools and college. Some were offered by the colleges to students who wished to attend, and various fraternal and community groups, such as the Elks, the Order of Eastern Star, and the Lion's Club helped finance college educations. The Canal Zone's two college clubs offered scholarships and others were available through the National Science Foundation and the ROTC. The military academies also offered appointments. At the beginning of the 1959 school year nearly 50 students were attending colleges in the States on scholarships.

During the 1960-61 school year, the schools division was modernized, and two independent functional branches were established, one for the U.S. schools and the other for the Latin American schools. An assistant superintendent headed each branch and reported directly to the superintendent of schools, who was responsible for the overall administration.

There has been no set pattern for recruiting superintendents; several have been appointed from within the system while others have been appointed from outside.

The Canal Zone's Latin American schools were established to orient the student to his native Panama and to prepare him for his eventual obligations as a Panamanian citizen. By 1962, this objective had been accomplished to the point that the Latin American schools coincided closely to those of Panama. Spanish was the major language, with English listed only as a subject in the curriculum. The Panamanian teachers and professors were well qualified, with degrees from the University of Panama and the universities of other countries. The enrollment in the Canal Zone Latin American schools in Rainbow City, Paraiso, Santa Cruz, and Pedro Miguel totaled 3,886 students; the staff, 154.

Curundu Junior High School has just been completed on a 25-acre site with room for softball and baseball diamonds, a football field, and a track. The two academic buildings house 48 classrooms, 2 study halls, and 24 laboratories for general science, chemistry, art, language, household arts, and shop. There is an administrative suite between the two academic buildings with teachers lounges, two audiovisual rooms, and eight standard classrooms. The new school provides education for grades 7, 8, and 9; previously, grade 9 had attended Balboa High School. A geodesic cafetorium seats 700 students for dining and 1,450 students for assemblies. The Canal Zone schools have come of age in every respect.

FOOTNOTES

1. After a superintendent of schools was appointed, he was empowered to consider exceptions to the compulsory school attendance ordinance if the child was physically incapacitated or lived a distance more than 2 miles from the nearest school and had no free transportation.
2. In its early years, this school did not meet with much success because an English-speaking teacher was hired to instruct students who spoke only Spanish. In 1910, a Spanish male teacher from Peru was hired.
3. Students were enrolled from all states except Arizona, Montana, Oregon, South Carolina, South Dakota, and Wyoming.
4. Letter from the U.S. Commissioner of Education to all superintendents of schools in May 1917.
5. See Appendix C.
6. Memorandum from Governor Harry Burgess to the executive secretary of the Pacific Civil Council in February 1932.
7. Since November 1941, it has been accredited by the Middle States Association of Colleges and Secondary Schools.
8. The Panama Canal Astronomical Observatory was founded in 1930.
9. Statement made by Governor William E. Potter to a committee of parents interested in special education programs, Balboa, Canal Zone, in October 1956.
10. Only 400 of the 11,000 students were tuition students from Panama.

BIBLIOGRAPHY

Public Document

Ordinances and Resolutions Passed by the Municipal Council of Ancon, Canal Zone. Panama City: Press of Sosa and Paredes, 1906.

Books

Abbot, Willes J. *The Panama Canal.* New York: Syndicate Publishing Co., 1914.

Biesanz, John and Mavis. *The People of Panama.* New York: Columbia University Press, 1955.

Haskin, Frederick J. *The Panama Canal.* Garden City, N.Y.: Doubleday, Page & Co., 1913.

Padelford, Norman J. *The Panama Canal in Peace and War.* New York: The Macmillan Co., 1942.

Rolofson, Robert H. *Christian Cooperation at the World's Crossroads.* Mount Hope, Canal Zone: Mount Hope Printing Plant, 1950.

Ross, Walter G. *Historical Background of the Panama Canal.* Washington, D.C.: Panama Canal Society of Washington, D.C., 1947.

Article and Periodical

Johnson, Lawrence. "The Development of the Canal Zone Schools." *Pan-American Magazine* (September 1936), pp. 33-41.

Reports

Canal Record, Vols. I-IX. Mount Hope, Canal Zone: Canal Commission Printing Office, 1908-19.

Lang, Albert R. *A Résumé of the Canal Zone Public School System.* Balboa Heights: Panama Canal Printing Office, 1917.

Panama Canal Review, Vols. III-IX. Mount Hope, Canal Zone: Mount Hope Printing Plant, 1950-58.

Principals' Monthly Reports to the Superintendent, 1904-1932. On file in the Office of the Superintendent of Schools, Balboa Heights. (Typewritten.)

Other Sources

Letter from the U.S. Commissioner of Education to all superintendents of schools in May 1917.

Memorandum from Governor Harry Burgess to the executive secretary of the Pacific Civil Council in February 1932.

Statement made by Governor William E. Potter to a committee of parents interested in special education programs, Balboa, Canal Zone, in October 1956.

Appendix A

PANAMA CANAL ZONE CHIEF SCHOOL OFFICERS

Superintendents of Schools

1907-1908	David O'Connor	1925-27	John Grouried
1908-1909	Henry L. Smith	1927-48	Benjamin M. Williams
1909-13	Frank A. Gause	1948-53	Lawrence Johnson
1913-22	Albert R. Lang	1953-64	Sigurd E. Esser
1922-25	W. W. Wood	1964-	Francis A. Castles

Appendix B

Chart I.--CANAL ZONE GOVERNMENT, 1967

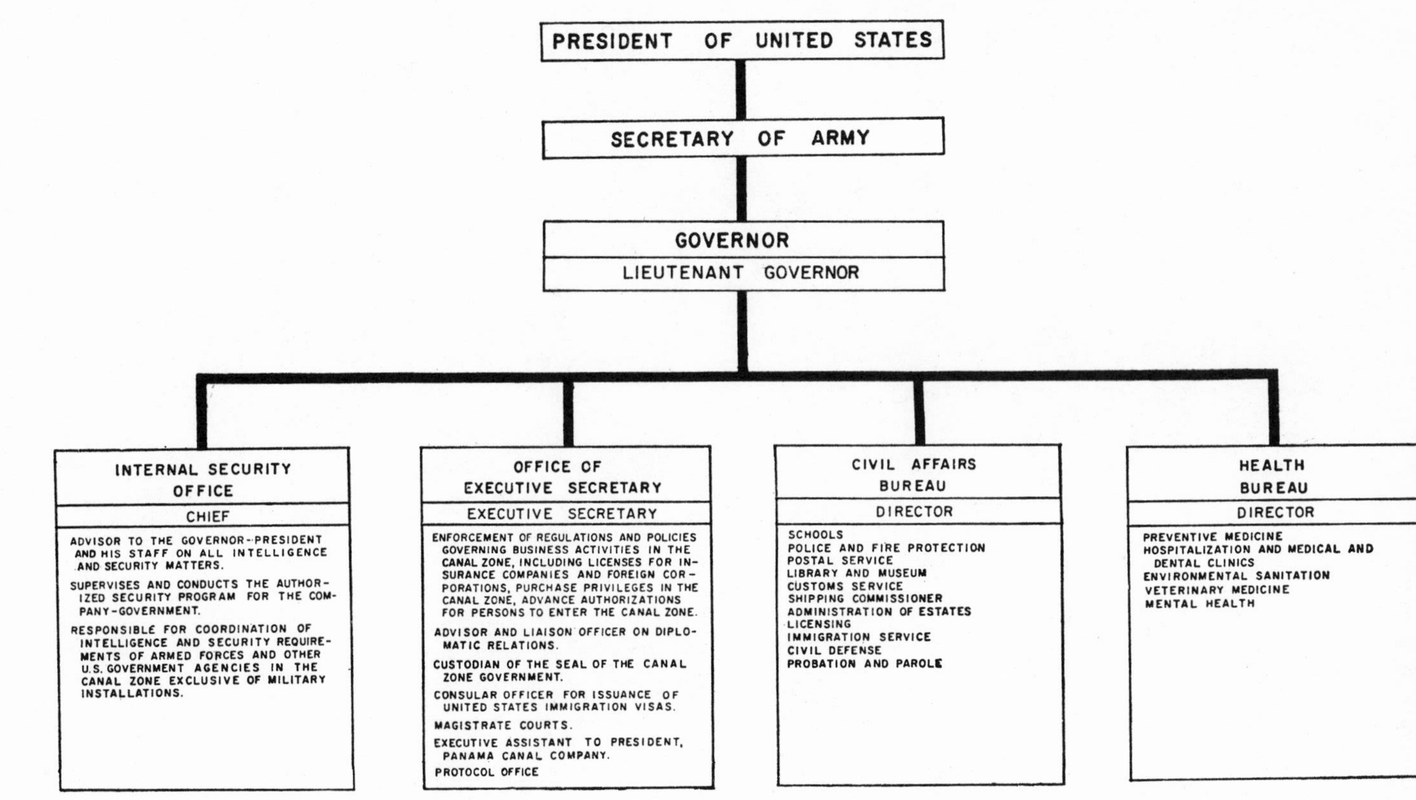

From Annual Report, Panama Canal Company, June 30, 1967

Appendix B

Chart II.--DIVISION OF SCHOOLS IN THE CIVIL AFFAIRS BUREAU, CANAL ZONE GOVERNMENT, 1967

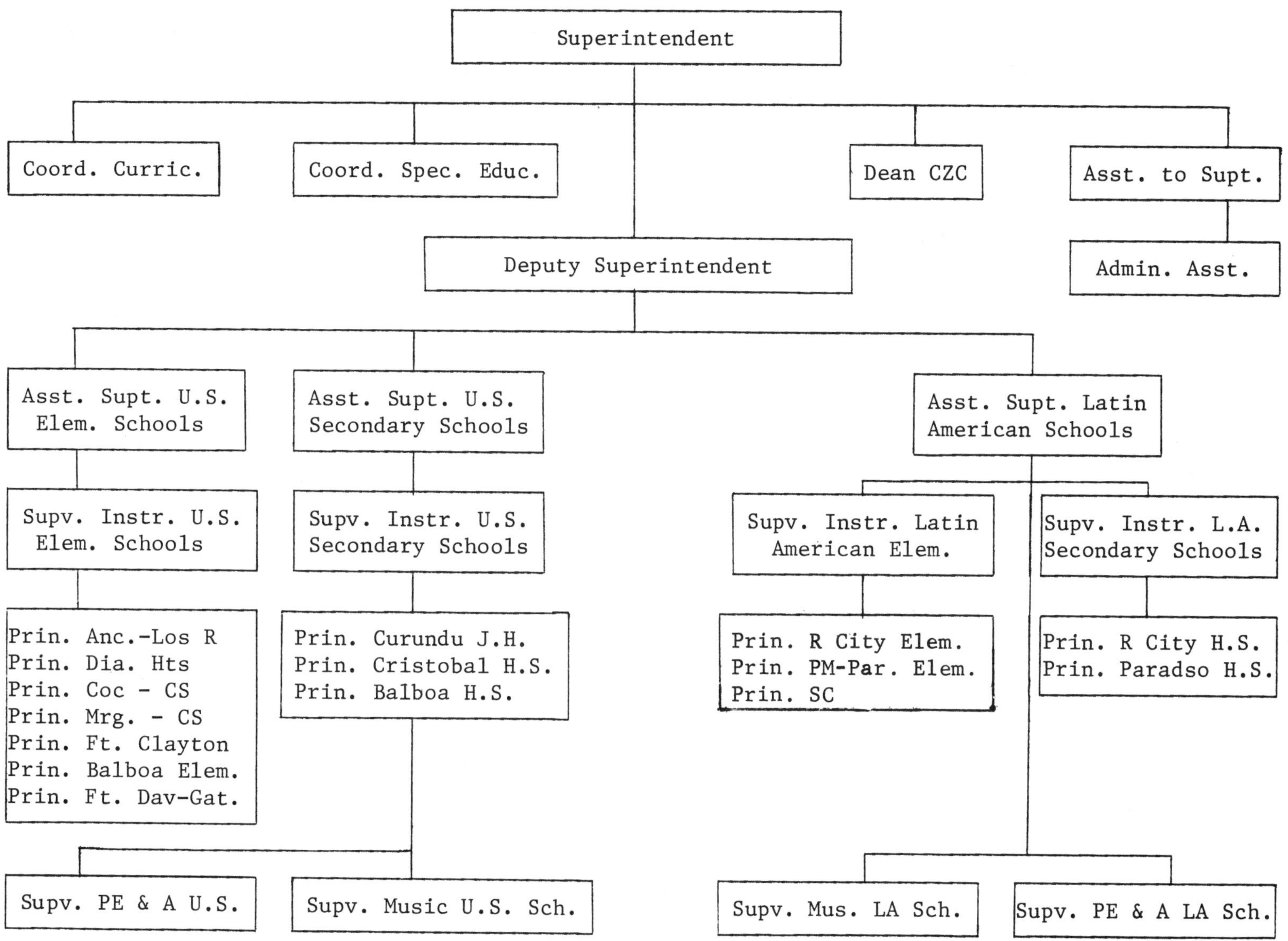

Appendix B

Chart III.--PANAMA CANAL ZONE

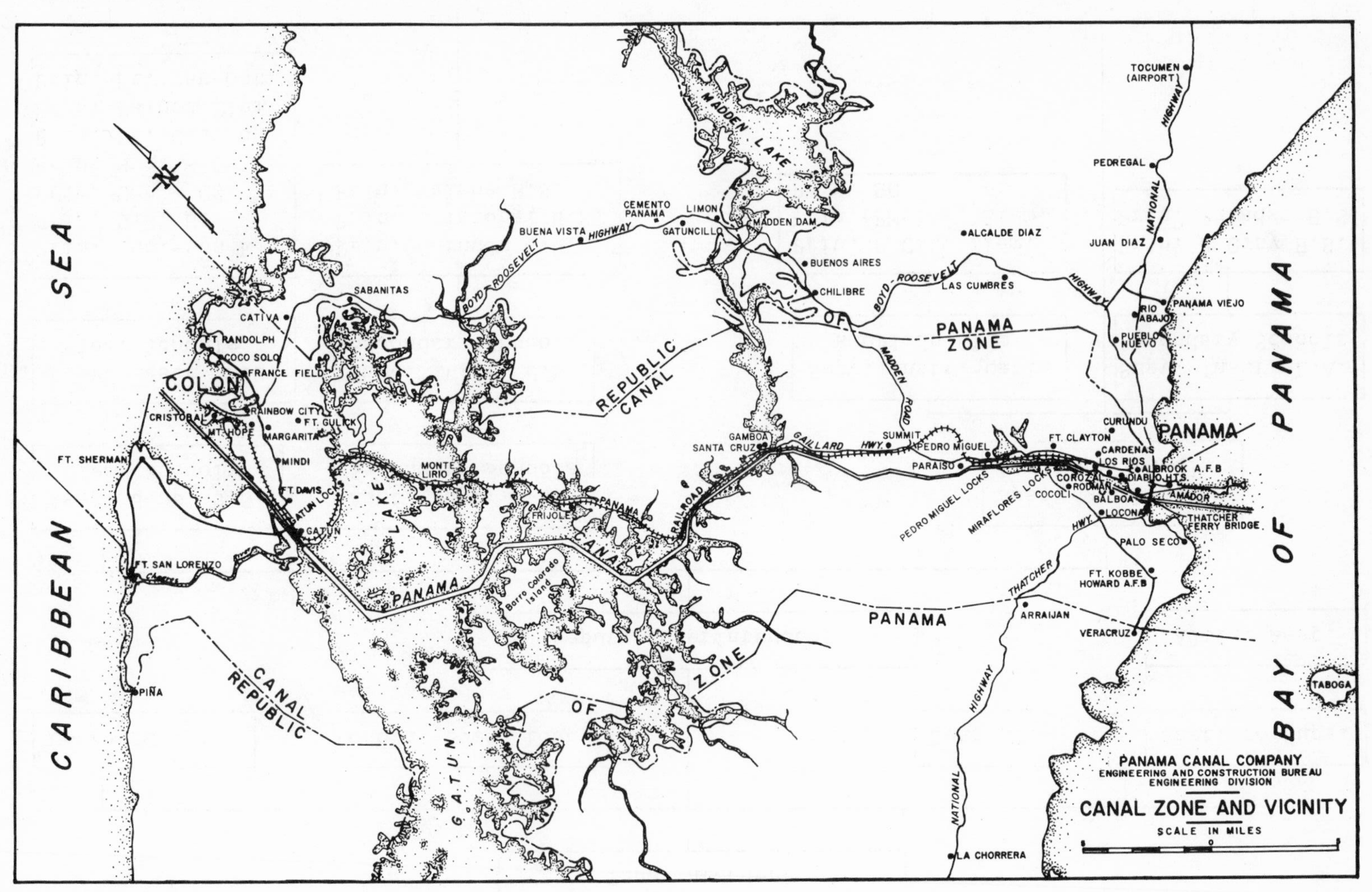

Appendix C

Table 1.–AVERAGE DAILY ATTENDANCE IN CANAL ZONE SCHOOLS, 1904-54

Year	White	Colored	Total
1904	---	---	---
1905	---	---	150
1906	107	1,000	1,107
1907	167	971	1,138
1908	385	765	1,150
1909	539	784	1,287
1910	682	577	1,259
1911	839	556	1,359
1912	980	734	1,714
1913	1,029	799	1,828
1914	968	715	1,682
1915	1,006	776	1,782
1916	1,065	436	1,501
1917	1,213	497	1,710
1918	1,323	640	1,963
1919	1,423	755	2,178
1920	1,589	865	2,459
1921	1,323	1,019	2,342
1922	1,519	1,343	2,862
1923	1,766	2,010	3,776
1924	1,764	1,529	3,293
1925	1,898	1,788	3,686
1926	2,052	1,977	4,029
1927	2,430	2,017	4,447
1928	2,263	2,593	4,866
1929	2,355	2,581	4,946
1930	2,510	3,559	6,069
1931	2,641	3,731	6,372
1932	2,737	3,619	6,356
1933	2,858	3,886	6,744
1934	2,790	3,586	6,376
1935	2,797	3,406	6,203
1936	2,717	3,186	5,903
1937	2,755	3,091	5,846
1938	2,765	2,881	5,646
1939	2,686	2,818	5,504
1940	2,798	2,686	5,484
1941	3,296	2,725	6,021
1942	3,144	2,802	5,946
1943	2,632	2,783	5,415
1944	2,828	2,748	5,576
1945	2,881	2,805	5,686
1946	3,130	2,636	5,766
1947	3,625	2,791	6,416
1948	3,978	2,846	6,824
1949	4,244	3,104	7,348
1950	4,335	3,245	7,580
1951	4,171	3,377	7,548
1952	5,181	3,915	9,096
1953	5,032	3,588	8,620
1954	5,485	3,824	9,309

Source:

Principals' Monthly Reports to the Superintendent.

55 Virgin Islands

DEPARTMENT OF EDUCATION
Alexander Henderson

Contents

PUBLIC EDUCATION PRIOR TO 1917

Columbus discovered the Virgin Islands on his second voyage to the New World in 1493 and named them "St. Ursula and the 11,000 Virgins," presumably because of the number of islands, islets, cays, and rocks he found. Danish, English, Dutch, and French voyagers visited the islands during the seventeenth century, but the English and the Dutch made the first recorded settlement on the island of St. Croix in 1625 (1). The Danes settled St. Thomas in 1666 and took possession 5 years later. In 1684, the Danes settled St. John and claimed it for the crown in 1717.

In 1685, the Danish West India and Guinea Company authorized a company of Brandenburgers to establish themselves in St. Thomas to carry on commerce—particularly the transportation and sale of African slaves. From that year to 1733, when the Danes purchased St. Croix from the French and organized the islands as the Danish West Indies, the number of slaves increased so rapidly that the European settlers became alarmed for their safety. To keep the slaves more docile, the whites decided to bring in Moravian missionaries to teach and preach to them, and the first of these landed in St. Thomas in December 1732.

As early as 1736, a missionary, Friedrich Martin, attempted to start a school for slave children. Over the following years, interest continued to grow in establishing an educational system in the Danish West Indies.

Several Lutheran missionaries arrived from Denmark to teach the slaves Danish and religion in 1756 and 1757, in hopes that they would eventually join the Danish-speaking congregation. But this idea was abandoned in 1771, and a separate Lutheran missionary congregation using the Creole language was established (2).

In 1781, the able and energetic Governor Peter Clausen issued a publication on the education of the youth, and that December a rescript called for selecting four of the best free Negroes from the Lutheran congregation to become schoolmasters and sextons. Children of poor slaves were admitted free to these Lutheran schools, but children of slaves who had accumulated property, free colored people, and other congregations paid a tuition.

In February 1785, King Christian VII resolved that free schools for white children should be established—one in St. Thomas and two in St. Croix at Christiansted and Frederiksted.

It was the Moravian Brethren, however, who brought free *compulsory* education to the islands. In 1774, King Christian VII had issued a special edict in their favor, which reduced the opposition to their work with the slaves and gained the cooperation of many planters. It was 1839, however, before Governor General Peter von Scholten signed an agreement in Germany with the authorities of the Moravian Church entrusting the church with the responsibility of starting free and compulsory education in St. Croix (3). The first school opened 2 years later at Estate la Grande Princesse, and within a year's time, with liberal contributions from the planters, seven other rural schools were started.

The instruction in these schools was first and foremost designed to improve the children's moral character and religious life. Spelling was taught principally with words found in the Bible, and reading consisted mainly of Biblical sentences. Lessons focused on incidents described in the Bible, and the morals were explained to influence the children's conduct.

At first, this free compulsory education did not extend beyond the child's eighth birthday. The obvious shortcomings of such a brief education were immediately recognized, and 2 years later a royal decree extended Saturday schools for children aged 8 to 11, and Sunday school for those from 10 to 14 years. A regulation issued in 1847 made the estate managers answerable for the school attendance of the children and liable to fines for noncompliance (4).

These schools were controlled by a school commission composed of the captains of the island's nine quarters and the judges of the Christiansted and Frederiksted jurisdictions. The director of education attended the board meetings and presided at required monthly teachers meetings (5).

The teaching staff was a combination of Europeans in key positions and British West Indians trained at the teachers training college founded by the Mico Charity in

Antigua, British West Indies. Promising students selected from each school assisted the appointed teacher by instructing younger children under the general supervision of the principal. The early teachers were all foreign men, but soon native men and women were sent by the government to Mico Institute and later to the Moravian Training College for Ladies, founded in Spring Garden, Antigua, in 1840. The first woman teacher began work in 1871.

The general outline of the system described above persisted well into the twentieth century. The only change worthy of note occurred in 1872, when the Moravian supervision of schools ended. In that year, the government assumed the right to appoint the school inspector.

In 1910, the last inspector, O. Rubner Petersen, was appointed. His tenure ended when the Danish West Indies were transferred to the United States in 1917 (6). Petersen attempted to break the system from its strong English tradition. Before taking up his duties, he visited Hampton and Tuskegee Institutes in the United States, and during his term he tried to introduce manual training and gardening for boys and housework for girls. Unfortunately, lack of funds prevented his plans from getting any further than the School Ordinance of 1912. Thus, little was accomplished to improve public education in the Danish West Indies from the turn of the century to the transfer of the islands in 1917.

GROWTH OF THE DEPARTMENT, 1917-65

When the United States assumed control of the Virgin Islands, the Navy was given the responsibility for administering them. In his annual report for 1917, the Governor, Rear Admiral James H. Oliver, declared: "The existing system of public education in these islands leaves about everything in the way of an adequate system to be desired" (7). He pointed out that more than anything else, the inhabitants needed instruction in the use of their hands, and this was not available. Not only was there no school where children could learn the trades and agriculture, but there were no normal schools in the islands, and since the natives were too poor to send their children to the United States for advanced instruction, they could not become school instructors even if they displayed natural abilities.

One of Governor Oliver's first steps to improve public education was to appoint Daniel R. Nase as director of education and Arthur E. Lindborg as assistant director. According to the School Law of 1921, Director Nase was empowered to "appoint clerks, messengers, etc. at such salaries as may be provided by budget" (8). The law placed all schools under the education department, outlined the director's duties and powers, and established a board of review for each of the two municipalities, St. Thomas–St. John and St. Croix.

In fiscal year 1929, the Colonial Council of the municipality of St. Thomas-St. John adopted legislation to convert its review board into a Board of Education with much broader powers. In one of its first acts, the Board of Education reclassified the public school teachers and extended summer vacations by one month. It also placed greater emphasis on instruction in mechanical arts, home economics, stenography, bookkeeping, practical agriculture, poultry raising, and beekeeping. It recommended that a Boy Scout movement be inaugurated and a scoutmaster be appointed to the staff of the Department of Education.

The Navy Department turned over the territory's administration to the Department of the Interior in March 1931, and Paul M. Pearson was appointed the first civilian Governor. Three years later, he reported that "the valuable recommendations made by the Hampton Survey Commission, in their Report of the Educational Survey of the Virgin Islands issued in 1929, have formed the basic principles of the administration's educational program" (9).

When the civil administration took over in 1931, George H. Ivins was appointed director of education (the Education Law of 1940 changed that title to superintendent of education). Throughout this period, there was considerable progress. In his 1937 report, Governor Cramer stated:

> Efforts were continued, but so far without success, to secure action by the local legislatures for the enactment of revised school laws based on the findings of a comprehensive survey of education undertaken in fiscal year 1936 . . . . In accordance with familiar American procedure [these revised school laws would allow] the election of school boards whose membership may be expected to create increasing local interest in and support for public educational activities. Clear and fixed standards of teacher training and promotion are established in them (10).

The 1939-40 Legislative Assembly enacted a new school law which superseded some portions of the Education Law of 1921, but though the law produced many positive results, the Legislature had not faced some of the territory's serious educational problems. For instance, the law did not provide for automatic increases in teachers' salaries based on length of service and satisfactory performance. It had no provisions for pensioning older teachers whose usefulness had declined. It did establish school boards with certain duties and responsibilities in line with the generally accepted practice of democratizing the control and direction of public education. Not until 2 years later did the municipality of St. Thomas-St. John adopt a standard for teachers' salaries and for the promotion of teachers on the basis of training and service.

The education department continued to expand. It hired an assistant superintendent and six supervising teachers in 1942. The next year, it added administrative and supervisory assistants in physical education, art, music, attendance, adult education, vocational training, preschool child development, and teacher training.

In 1951, an Insular Board for Vocational Education was created, and it immediately hired qualified personnel for each of the major fields of operation: trade and industry, home economics, and vocational guidance. Later in the year, a vocational agriculture program was started on St. Croix.

In July 1955, the Governor's Executive Order No. 9 abolished the education department for the two municipalities and created the Virgin Islands Department of Education under the direction of a commissioner of education (11). Control was vested in the Virgin Islands Board of Education, composed of seven members appointed by the Governor: three residents each of St. Thomas and St. Croix, and one of St. John. To run the islands' 31 schools, the Department of Education was divided into four divisions as follows: elementary school, including kindergarten; secondary school and college, including adult education; auxiliary services responsible for buildings, grounds, transportation, procurement, school lunch, and business; and vocational education and rehabilitation. The department also had three bureaus: recreation, which included playgrounds, parks, and beaches; library and museums; and special activities, which included out-of-school activities, testing, scholarships, certification, census, and attendance. The department changed its four divisions in 1960-61 to include administration, educational programs, community services, and miscellaneous grants.

The commissioner was aided by an assistant commissioner and 23 administrators, including directors, chiefs, supervisors, coordinators, and administrative assistants. In a reorganization during 1961-62, new positions were created for a deputy commissioner for St. Croix, a deputy commissioner for curriculum and instruction, a deputy commissioner for business and auxiliary services, three new directors, a coordinator of educational statistics, and an education officer for St. John. Other positions were added in subsequent years, but the recreation bureau was placed under the Department of Agriculture in 1965-66.

The Department of Education continues to grow, adding staff for additional services as the need becomes apparent and the money is available. The department is somewhat unique in that its functions are analogous to those of a state education department yet they include those that are performed by city or county agencies and local districts on the mainland (12).

DEVELOPMENT OF CURRICULUMS

The islands' school system was organized on a 6-3-3 plan by 1921. The primary and elementary schools used the courses of study developed for New Mexico's schools in 1919, and the junior high schools based their course of study on that developed by Utah.

The School Law of 1921 empowered the director of education to "establish, maintain and direct, when funds are available, in addition to the rural and urban graded schools, such special schools as night schools, industrial schools, high schools, reform schools, and kindergarten schools" (13). However, no public secondary education was available on the islands until instruction was extended to the eighth grade in 1920. In 1922, instruction was extended to the tenth grade, 2 years later to the eleventh, and in 1931 it was available through the twelfth grade and a class of four high school seniors graduated.

The Bureau of Efficiency sent a committee to the islands in 1921 and in its report to Congress, the bureau chief, Herbert D. Brown, recommended that full emphasis be given in the first 6 years to manual training for boys and home economics for girls. The committee believed that the seventh, eighth, and ninth grades should be organized as an agricultural and industrial school under a junior high school department. Waldo H. Evans, the last naval Governor, disagreed with the committee's recommendation that the last 3 years of high school be eliminated. He pointed out that stenographic and bookkeeping courses in the high schools helped supply the business personnel for the large commercial institutions and government departments. When Dr. Pearson became the first civilian Governor 2 years later, he stated to the Secretary of the Interior:

> An imperative need of the schools is that they should be modernized and made to meet the needs of the islands by training children to do and to become interested in what they can find to do in the islands. To accomplish this, the building up of an agricultural high school recommended by the Bureau of Efficiency is much needed. This school must be developed through the curriculum in the lower grades . . . . The program of development must begin with the teacher. In order that the teacher may know what and how to teach these subjects, means must be found for bringing all teachers into a summer school, the only normal instruction available to them. For that purpose I plan to bring to the islands the most experienced and efficient instructors for a summer school and a new Director of Education (George H. Ivins) who is in sympathy with the plans and experienced in promoting them (14).

This disagreement as to which type of education was best for the children was reflected in the islands' two municipal councils and separate boards of education. A vocational institute established on St. Croix in 1932 for the next few years placed an emphasis on agriculture and the trades. St. Thomas High School also gave an increasing amount of time to cooking, sewing, and home economics in general, and to carpentry, cabinetmaking, and other manual arts. It offered courses in rug making and basketry to assist these growing island industries. More vocational courses were added during the Depression.

In 1933, the National Recovery Act provided funds for a very successful program in adult education which trained the natives to work in the nursery schools it established in three large towns. The following year, St. Thomas High School introduced commercial courses in bookkeeping, shorthand, and typing; it established a vocational division in 1940.

The trend of adding commercial courses, arts, crafts, dressmaking, dramatics, foods, industrial work for girls, apprenticeships for boys in automobile mechanics, cabinet-making, and printing continued through the 1940's. St. Thomas started evening school credits in vocational courses in 1947.

On St. Croix, the Department of Education cooperated with business establishments to place seniors in jobs for working experience during the morning hours. In 1948, the department established a veterans program in elementary and secondary subjects that enrolled nearly 300 veterans. The following year, vocational courses were added in automobile mechanics, electricity, wood-working, plumbing, and pipefitting. The veterans program on St. Croix also offered courses in masonry, carpentry, mechanical drawing, mechanics, and other related sciences.

When Congress passed a bill in 1950 extending to the islands the provisions of the Vocational Education Act of 1946, they became eligible for a maximum grant of $40,000 per year on a 50-percent matching basis. This immediately enabled St. Croix to add agriculture to its high school curriculum. In 1952, St. Croix added a trades and industry program and a course in plumbing, and it extended its agricultural program to adults.

In 1960, the principals and department heads of the islands' high schools met to develop curriculum materials, course outlines, and study guides. During the year, there was a definite improvement in instruction and curriculum on the elementary level, in part due to the equipment, materials, and reference books obtained with National Defense Education Act (NDEA) funds. These funds also strengthened secondary instruction in science, mathematics, and foreign languages and enabled the schools to offer guidance programs to the majority of students. By 1962, three types of vocational education training programs were available: the in-school program, the adult all-day program, and an evening-school program. With funds from Public Laws 85-864 and 85-874, the two high schools installed speech laboratories for foreign languages. Title V of NDEA provided funds for starting a guidance and testing center, and the number of counselors was increased from two to four.

As a result of the department's reorganization in 1962, the curriculum and instruction division began holding regular meetings to plan, study, and evaluate curriculum changes. Teachers, supervisors, and principals on all three islands developed teaching aids and outlines for language arts in the elementary grades. On the secondary level, following a visit by a committee from the Secondary Commission of the Middle States Association of Secondary Schools and Colleges, the staff worked together to develop a comprehensive curriculum, standardize textbooks, and adopt uniform requirements for graduation. St. Thomas' Charlotte Amalie High School and Christiansted High School were accredited in 1964.

The department continued to expand its activities and staff. With federal assistance in 1965, it engaged in plans for operating Head Start programs for preschool children, a cultural enrichment program for educationally deprived children, a Neighborhood Youth Corps for potential dropouts, and an adult basic education program.

In particular, the vocational education program expanded. The Julius E. Sprauve School on St. John offered practical arts and home economics, including courses in carpentry, agriculture, masonry, electronics, auto mechanics, electricity, plumbing, practical nursing, hotel and restaurant training, mechanical drawing, sewing, and fancy needlecraft. The department rewrote the vocational education state plan to qualify for additional federal funds under the Vocational Education Act of 1963.

PLANNING FOR ADEQUATE CLASSROOMS

In 1917, Denmark turned over to the United States 20 schoolhouses of various sizes to accommodate the 2,267 students. Although the number of pupils increased 50 percent, to a total of 3,411, during the first 16 years of U.S. sovereignty, no new buildings were erected and no major repairs were made. Two buildings that formerly housed U.S. marines and a former residence were turned into schools to accommodate the increase, but there was still much overcrowding. During the 1934-35 school year, in the midst of the Depression, seven new buildings were completed, and the others received extensive repairs (15).

The Governor's report to the Secretary of the Interior for the 1944-45 school year stated:

> The need of a new high school and certain elementary schools, in addition to the remodeling of certain existing schools, continue to be the greatest handicap to the program of education in this municipality (St. Thomas and St. John). Present limitations of space have required the application of measures to restrict high school enrollment within the limits of the maximum capacity of classroom space . . . . The municipality of St. Croix, like the municipality of St. Thomas and St. John, is handicapped by the lack of suitable school buildings and equipment (16).

At the end of the 1948-49 school year, the Governor reported: "Enrollment in the public schools has increased over 30 percent in the last 10 years (to 4,401), but no additional accommodations have been provided" (17).

With federal funds available under Public Law 510 during the 1951-52 school year, plans were made to build two new high schools, an elementary school, and a new one-room rural school. Orme Lewis, the assistant secretary of the Department of the Interior, was the principal speaker at the groundbreaking ceremonies in 1953 for the new Charlotte Amalie High School and the one at Christiansted. He later stated that the significance could be "sensed only by those aware of the fact that at present with the exception of a few smaller units, schools are housed entirely in makeshift buildings never intended for school use" (18). The two new schools were in operation in school year 1954-55.

The department also planned for new elementary schools. Contracts were awarded, and by the 1953-54 school year, new elementary schools opened at Cruz Bay (subsequently named the Julius E. Sprauve School), at John's Folly on St. John, and at Christiansted on St. Croix. Consolidated schools were approved for Frederiksted and King's Hill, St. Croix, and these were ready in 1958. The former was named the Claude O. Markoe School, and the latter, the Charles H. Emanuel School—after two veteran educators.

Three years after the consolidated schools opened on St. Croix, 42 new elementary classrooms were ready on St. Thomas, the first since the mid-1950's: eight in the Nisky area, two in Frenchtown, and a large 32-classroom building on a 10-acre tract in the Sugar Estate area. This school was named the Lockhart Elementary School after the St. Thomas merchant philanthropist, Herbert E. Lockhart.

Three new buildings did not solve all the space problems. At the request of Governor Ralph M. Paiewonsky, the Legislature appropriated over $1.5 million for construction during the 1961-62 session. Two new three-classroom primary buildings were built the following year by Peace Corps volunteers as a part of the group's technical training for building similar schools in Africa. One was constructed on the site of the Charles H. Emanuel School, and the other at the Nisky School. By the end of the year, an additional three new elementary classrooms and nine vocational classrooms were nearly completed on St. Thomas. Plans also were completed for an eight-room elementary school at Estate Grove Place, St. Croix, and contracts were awarded for three gymnasiums, a music suite (band room and choral rooms), shops, and additional classrooms at several other schools.

During the period when the islands were acquiring additional high school and elementary space, the kindergartens were not neglected. A class in carpentry in St. Thomas built a kindergarten at Polyberg. The Paul M. Pearson Gardens Kindergarten opened in September 1957, and the Jane E. Tuitt School, named after a veteran educator and acting commissioner of education, opened later in the year at Savan, St. Thomas, for grades K-4.

In 1961, a kindergarten also was opened at Frenchtown.

Despite the rapid construction that had marked the previous years, the 1964-65 Legislature decided that a crash school construction program was necessary. It earmarked $4.2 million from a newly authorized bond issue to construct 130 classrooms: 45 for a new St. Croix Central High School, 40 for the new St. Thomas Wayne Aspinal Junior High School, 10 additional classrooms at the Charles Emanuel School, 10 for a new elementary school at Estate Tutu, St. Thomas, 10 for a new elementary school at Bourne Field, and an additional 5 classrooms, a new library, a teachers lounge, and a principal's office for the Julius E. Sprauve School. Most were expected to be ready by September 1966 to accommodate the 10,453 students enrolled at the end of 1965 (19).

TEACHERS—PREPARATION AND SALARIES

Summer Schools and In-Service Training

The Rules and Regulations effective November 1, 1921, for the Virgin Islands Department of Education said that any U.S. citizen in the Virgin Islands over 16 years of age known to be of good moral character and sound physical health was eligible to take the examinations to obtain a license as an assistant graded teacher, a graded teacher, or a principal teacher. "Special Teachers' certificates or licenses will be granted to those persons who possess diplomas from recognized normal schools, colleges, or universities, or who are specially fitted to teach some vocational or commercial subject" (20).

In the early 1920's, the department attempted to improve the quality of teachers by in-service training programs and summer schools. These continued through the 1930's, despite the Depression. In 1933, instructors from the Progressive Education Association came to the islands to conduct a summer demonstration school. The Teachers' Association of St. Thomas began a summer institute in 1936, which allowed teachers to earn subject credits. In the 1940's, generous gifts from the Carnegie Corporation made it possible for a number of teachers to attend the University of Puerto Rico.

In 1943, the St. Thomas Teachers' Institute began in-service training courses for teachers during the spring as well as the summer. Two years later, the Polytechnic Institute of Puerto Rico conducted extension courses on St. Croix enabling teachers to earn college credits. St. Thomas Teachers' Institute observed its tenth anniversary in the 1947-48 school year by sponsoring four extension courses offered by Polytechnic. New York University conducted a workshop in anthropology during the summer of 1950 for local teachers and 60 students from all over the United States.

Financed by the Fund for the Advancement of Education, the Hampton Institute-on-Island program offered four courses during the summer of 1955 and two during the school year. It held its 1957 summer sessions on St. Croix and then held classes in college algebra and tests and measurements during the school year. In the 1959-60 school years, its summer program was keyed mainly for elementary school teachers. During that summer, new branches of the Catholic University operating in the islands' Catholic high schools offered college-level courses.

Scholarships

By the early 1930's, several universities in the United States were granting scholarships to promising students and teachers who pledged to return to the islands to teach. Eleven scholarship students were on the mainland in 1934, and within 2 years nine had completed their training and had returned to the island's public school system. Not only did the schools themselves offer scholarships, but in 1936, the municipality of St. Thomas-St. John enacted an ordinance establishing a scholarship fund to assist two or three of the best qualified local high school graduates in going to college in the United States.

By 1940, both municipalities were providing scholarships so that teachers could attend summer school sessions at the University of Puerto Rico and regular sessions on the mainland. Governor Lawrence W. Cramer, in his report for the fiscal year ending June 1940, stated:

> With only a few exceptions all the teachers in the municipal school system are natives of the islands. The improvement in the educational status of teachers has been accomplished in part by the establishment of municipal scholarship funds created by ordinance in each municipality under which cash grants or loans are made to teachers or students who desire to go to the continental United States for higher education (21).

By the end of World War II, the municipality of St. Thomas-St. John adopted a plan whereby four teachers would be released annually to study on scholarships in the United States and Puerto Rico. In 1952, Alonzo Moron, a native of St. Thomas and president of Hampton Institute, proposed a plan whereby his institution would participate in a three-phase program involving teacher-training scholarships for graduate and undergraduate study, in-service courses for teachers on the islands, and leadership in studying education in the islands as proposed by a committee of consultants from the U.S. Office of Education in 1950.

The Department of Education put considerable emphasis on in-service training programs during the 1961-62 school year but still processed 135 applications for loans and financial assistance for students to attend colleges and universities throughout the United States. It entered into a contract with New York University to upgrade educational standards (22).

The in-service training programs and institutes, the summer extension courses, and scholarships improved the quality of teachers in the Virgin Islands. By 1942, 76 percent of all teachers of both municipalities held a high school diploma or certificate. Up to 1936, the median level of all teachers was the completion of the ninth grade, but by 1950, the level was completion of high school. By the spring of 1956–the first year under the reorganized Department of Education–of the 188 teachers employed, 62 were college graduates, 36 had 2 years or more of college work, 75 had completed 2 years of college, and 15 had other training. Five years later, 63 percent of the elementary classroom teachers still did not possess academic degrees, but 129 of the 255 teachers in the department were college graduates, 66 had completed 2 or more years of college, 23 had less than 2 years of college, and only 37 had no collegiate training.

During school year 1965-66, the department employed 454 professionals: 396 teachers and 58 administrators. Of this number, 74 were non-degree holders; 44 had been equated to the bachelor's level after serving 15 years or more; 246 held a bachelor's degree; 89 had earned a master's degree; and 2 had earned a doctorate.

Salaries

The Rules and Regulations of 1921 stipulated that an assistant graded teacher was to receive from $10 to $25 per month, a graded teacher from $25 to $50, and a principal-teacher from $50 to $75. The special teacher's salary was left to the discretion of the director of education. From 1918 to 1934, the average monthly salary of teachers rose from $16.23 to $48.24, and the number of teachers from 81 to 119. By the end of World War II, the average yearly salary of teachers in St. Thomas was $1,200 and in St. Croix $899.69. The elementary school teachers were being paid $2,569.27 and high school teachers $3,705.65 by 1956.

Salaries continued to increase, so that by 1960, the average salary for elementary teachers was $3,138.24 and that of high school teachers $3,997.80. Governor Paiewonsky recommended and the 1963 Legislature approved a new pay plan increasing salaries an average of $849 per person. The minimum for those holding a bachelor's degree rose from $4,000 to $4,600, while those holding a master's degree started at $5,400 instead of $4,800. The pay scale was again revised effective the following year, so that of the 454 professionals employed during the 1965-66 school year, those with a bachelor's degree received a base salary increase to $5,400 and those with a master's degree to $6,000.

Increases in Per-Capita Expenditures for Public Education

Connected with the increase in teachers' salaries was the amount of money the people in the islands were willing to pay for education. The lack of funds had prevented School Inspector Rubner Petersen from improving education in the Danish West Indies under the School Ordinance of 1912.

The government had budgeted only 15,637 Danish West Indian dollars (DWI) for education. In 1921, the amount set aside for education rose to 53,967 DWI dollars, a little over 28.5 DWI dollars for each of the 2,671 children enrolled in the public schools. The enrollment rose to 3,083 pupils in the 1926-27 school year, and only 27.12 DWI dollars were spent on each pupil. At the end of the Depression decade in 1940, the average was $33.73 per pupil (23).

By the end of World War II, the total budget for both municipalities rose to a high of $250,000. Since each municipality controlled its own fiscal affairs until the formation of a single Virgin Islands Department of Education in 1955-56, there was a difference in the average annual expenditure per child—$66.50 on St. Thomas-St. John and $52.40 on St. Croix. Eight years later, for the first time, St. Thomas-St. John spent over $100 annually ($105.12) to educate each child, while St. Croix was only slightly behind with $97.13.

During the first year of operation of the Virgin Islands Department of Education, the average annual expenditure amounted to $141 for each of the 5,886 pupils in the public schools. Three years later, the figure was $216.97, but, as dramatic as was this increase, the average for the 50 states on the mainland was $360 for the same period. In the spring of 1965, 9,399 pupils were enrolled in the public schools, and $4,689,633 in local funds were appropriated to give an average expenditure per pupil of $495 compared to $483 in the 50 states.

INTERAGENCY RELATIONSHIPS

The Department of Education has cooperated with and depended on many other agencies and institutions throughout its history. From the very beginning, the church and the state cooperated in getting public education started in the islands, and until 1872, the church administered the schools. Since 1917, agencies of the federal and local governments and colleges and universities outside the islands have cooperated in developing the system of public education through surveys, institutes, training programs, and scholarship grants. As stated above, Hampton Institute conducted the first important survey of education, and its findings, published in 1929, established the department's basic principles for the next few years (24). Jeanes teachers, supported by the Jeanes Fund to upgrade rural Negro schools, performed a valuable service in the estate villages of St. Croix during the Depression, and in 1935 the Carnegie Foundation gave $7,500 to the Slater Fund to maintain a Jeanes teacher on St. Thomas.

Funds contributed by the Golden Rule Foundation enabled the department to serve hot lunches to the needy children on St. Thomas. The health and education departments cooperated with the schools by conducting medical and dental examinations, treatments, and health training to correct unhealthy practices and diet.

From the beginning, the department has worked closely with the federal government. The Public Works Administration enabled the islands to repair and remodel schoolhouses, and funds from the National Recovery Act were used to inaugurate a program in adult education and a nursery school program. The hot lunch program, the precursor of the school lunch program, was largely financed by the Works Progress Administration, with the Agricultural Marketing Administration contributing free commodities. During the 1946-47 school year, the U.S. Department of Agriculture furnished cash grants and foodstuffs without charge to enable the department to serve 501,978 lunches. The National Youth Administration gave funds for education and training of youth.

Following World War II, the local government collaborated with the Veterans' Administration to establish educational programs. The federal government made over $100,000 available to local education for the 1948-49 school year, chiefly to support the veterans education program.

By 1955-56, the federal government was contributing $132,116 to public education in the islands. Three years later, the Department of Education acquired materials through NDEA and secured financial aid for federally affected areas under the provisions of Public Laws 85-874 and 85-815. During the 1960-61 school year, the U.S. Office of Education sponsored institutes and conferences on the mainland in foreign languages, mathematics, and science. Federal moneys were received from Public Laws 85-864 and 85-874 and Titles III, V, and X of the NDEA, as well as from federal programs for vocational education, rural libraries, school lunch, and vocational rehabilitation.

During the 1961-62 school year, Arthur A. Richards, the present commissioner of education, was selected, along with 19 other educators, by the U.S. Department of State to participate in an international seminar in Europe under a Fulbright program. Educators from the islands participated, for the first time, in the evaluation of mainland high schools for accreditation by the Middle States Association of Secondary Schools and Colleges. At the invitation of the commissioner, the association sent three teams in March 1963 to evaluate the islands' secondary schools.

In 1965, the department received $419,466 from the federal government, including funds from the NDEA, Titles III, V, and X; vocational education and rural library extension programs; school lunch; a special federal grant, Public Law 85-874; vocational rehabilitation; and manpower development and training. The local government contributed $4,679,633 to public education to make the total public school education budget $5,109,099. At the same time, the department sponsored three projects approved by the Economic Opportunity Act: Operation Head Start, a work training program to assist potential dropouts, and an adult basic education program.

During May 1965, the Christiansted High School Band performed at the New York World's Fair, playing everything from classics to calypso—including the new "Virgin Islands March."

The schools not only match the states in salaries, but can now take their regular part in all activities and be evaluated on the same basis as the stateside schools. They have truly come of age.

FOOTNOTES

1. The English drove out the Dutch in 1645; they were themselves ousted by the Spanish in 1650, who, in turn, were replaced by the French in 1651.
2. For further information, see Kay Black Fjeldsoe, "Education in the Danish West Indies, Especially St. Thomas and St. Jan," quoted in *The Teachers' Voice,* I No. 6 (February 12, 1917), 1.
3. It was Governor von Scholten who issued the famous Emancipation Proclamation in 1848.
4. For further information, see R.C. Forster, "One Hundred Years of Compulsory Education, St. Croix, V.I.," Christiansted, St. Croix, 1941. (Mimeographed.)
5. During the decade following the establishment of free compulsory schools in St. Croix, similar schools were started in St. Thomas, and what has been said of the St. Croix schools applies there also.
6. The United States began negotiation to buy the islands from Denmark shortly after the Civil War. Secretary of State Seward visited St. Thomas in 1866 and the following year offered $7.5 million for St. Thomas and St. Jan (St. John). The United States again tried to purchase the islands in 1902, 1911, and 1912. The formal transfer of the islands occurred on March 31, 1917.
7. Governor, *Annual Report* (1917), as quoted in Governor, *Annual Report to the Secretary of the Interior* (1940), p. 34.
8. Department of Education, *School Law for the Virgin Islands of the United States: Rules and Regulations of the Department of Education,* Bulletin No. 1 (St. Thomas: Kirtland Printing Co., 1921), p. 1.
9. The commission, composed of Thomas H. Dickinson and W. Carson Ryan, Jr., of Swarthmore College, W.T.B. Williams of Tuskegee Institute, and C.D. Stevenson of Hampton Institute, recommended improving the qualifications and salaries of teachers, improving the curriculum, improving school buildings, conducting an adult education program, conducting a nursery school program, and providing health and welfare work through the schools.
10. Governor, *Annual Report to the Secretary of the Interior* (1937), p. 14.
11. Department of Education, *Education Laws of the Virgin Islands* (Orford, N.H.: Equity Publishing Company, 1961). This included all amendments and changes enacted by the Legislature to July 1961. It was revised and expanded in 1965.
12. See Appendix B for the department's 1965 organization chart.
13. Department of Education, *School Law for the Virgin Islands of the United States: Rules and Regulations of the Department of Education,* Bulletin No. 1 (St. Thomas: Kirtland Printing Co., 1921), p. 2.
14. Governor, *Annual Report to the Secretary of the Interior* (1931), p. 6.
15. The public works department did the work, financed by PWA grants under the National Recovery Program. Governor, *Annual Report to the Secretary of the Interior* (1935), pp. 7,12.
16. Governor, *Annual Report to the Secretary of the Interior* (1945), pp. 7-8.
17. Governor, *Annual Report to the Secretary of the Interior* (1949), p. 8.
18. Governor, *Annual Report to the Secretary of the Interior* (1953), p. 16.
19. Due to construction delays, it was school year 1967-68 before Central High, Aspinal Junior High, and Tutu schools opened their doors.
20. Department of Education, *School Law for the Virgin Islands of the United States: Rules and Regulations of the Department of Education,* Bulletin No. 1 (St. Thomas: Kirtland Printing Co., 1921), p. 18.
21. Governor, *Annual Report to the Secretary of the Interior* (1940), p. 36.
22. The New York University—Virgin Islands project came into being in 1962-63, following a comprehensive survey of public school education by the university. Among other things, the university agreed to furnish executive training for six officials of the department and to conduct courses and workshops for principals, supervisors, and teachers. The project was successfully concluded in 1966.
23. The Danish West Indian dollar was pegged at $1.05 U.S. In 1934, U.S. money became the official currency in the islands.
24. Hampton Normal and Agricultural Institute, *Report of the Educational Survey of the Virgin Islands,* Thomas H. Dickinson, chairman (Hampton, Va.: The Press of The Institute, 1929).

BIBLIOGRAPHY

Public Documents

Department of Education. *Education Laws of the Virgin Islands.* Jane E. Tuitt, compiler. Orford, N.H.: Equity

Publishing Company, 1961. Revised and expanded in 1965.

—— *School Law for the Virgin Islands of the United States: Rules and Regulations of the Department of Education.* Bulletin No. 1. St. Thomas: Kirtland Printing Co., 1921.

U.S. Congress. *Joint Commission To Visit and Report on Conditions in the Virgin Islands.* Document No. 734, 66th Cong., 2d sess. Washington, D.C.: Government Printing Office, 1920.

Books

Blauch, Lloyd E., and Reid, Charles F. "Education in the Virgin Islands." *Public Education in the Territories and Outlying Possessions.* Advisory Committee on Education. Staff Study No. 16. Washington, D.C.: Government Printing Office, 1939.

Department of Education. *Course of Study for the Elementary Schools of the Virgin Islands of the U.S.A.* Bulletin No. 2. St. Thomas: Kirtland Printing Co., 1922.

Larsen, Jens. *Virgin Islands Story.* Philadelphia, Pa.: Muhlenberg Press, 1950.

Lindborg, Arthur E. *Education in the Virgin Islands.* U.S. Department of the Interior, Office of Education Leaflet No. 42. Washington, D.C.: Government Printing Office, 1932.

Reid, Charles F. *Education in the Territories and Outlying Possessions.* Contributions to Education No. 85. New York: Teachers College, Columbia University, 1941.

Reports

Center for School Services, School of Education, New York University. *The Virgin Islands, A Comprehensive Survey Completed at the Request of the Commissioner of Education.* New York: The University, December 1963.

Governor. *Annual Reports to the Secretary of the Interior.* Washington, D.C.: Government Printing Office, 1931-53.

Hampton Normal and Agricultural Institute. *Report of the Educational Survey of the Virgin Islands.* Thomas H. Dickinson, chairman. Hampton, Va.: The Press of The Institute, 1929.

Articles and Periodicals

"Aids Virgin Islands Summer School." *Porto Rico Progress,* XXXVII (July 18, 1929), 8.

"Auspicious Beginning of Virgin Islands Teachers' Association." *School Life,* X (January 1925), 99.

Chamberlain, Ernest B. "Education in the Virgin Islands." *Institute of International Education News Bulletin,* VIII (April 1933), 9-10.

"Education in the Virgin Islands." *School and Society,* VI (July 21, 1917), 79-80.

Fjeldsoe, Kay Black. "Education in the Danish West Indies, Especially St. Thomas and St. Jan." Quoted in *The Teachers' Voice,* I, No. 6 (February 12, 1917), 1.

Jarvis, J. Antonio. "A Brief Survey of Education in the Virgin Islands." *Opportunity,* VII (January 1929), 16-18.

Lane, Bess B. "Education in the Virgin Islands." *Journal of Negro Education,* XXII (January 1940), 16.

Pearson, Paul M. "Education in the Virgin Islands." *School Life,* XX (February 1935), 155ff; (March 1935), 162; (April 1935), 173.

"People of the Virgin Islands Desire Improved Educational Facilities." *School and Society,* L (December 30, 1939), 858.

Reid, Charles F. "Administration of Education in the Territories and Outlying Possessions." *World Education,* IV (January 1939), 71-73.

—— "Inequality of Educational Opportunity Under the American Flag." *Scholastic,* XXVI (May 11, 1935), 7.

"Summer Normal Schools for Teachers." *Virgin Islands Broadcaster* (St. Thomas), No. 4 (February 5, 1929).

"The Educational Survey of the Virgin Islands." *School and Society,* L (December 30, 1939), 858ff.

Unpublished Material

Forster, R. C. "One Hundred Years of Compulsory Education, St. Croix, V.I." Christiansted, St. Croix, 1941. (Mimeographed.)

Appendix A

VIRGIN ISLANDS CHIEF SCHOOL OFFICERS

Directors

1906	John T. Quinn
1906-17	O. Rubner Petersen
1917	Reverend Walter
1917-19	Henry C. Blair
1919-21	Otto C. McDonough[a]–Arthur S. Howe, assistant[b]
1921-23	Daniel R. Nase[a]–Arthur E. Lindborg, assistant[b]
1923-31	Arthur E. Lindborg[a]–Sarah Tate and Harold J. Benedict, assistants[b]
1931-34	George H. Ivins
1935-40	C. Frederick Dixon[a]–Raymond Thompson[b], Frederick D. Dorsch[b], and A. Thurston Child[b]

Superintendents of Education

1940-55	C. Frederick Dixon[a]–Mrs. P. Byrd Larsen[b]

Commissioners of Education

1955	Robert C. Cotton
1957-60	Andrew C. Preston
1960-61	Alonzo Moron
1961	Jane E. Tuitt (acting, May-June)
1961-63	Pedro C. Sanchez
1963-66	Jane E. Tuitt
1967-	Arthur A. Richards

NOTE:

The Education Law of 1940 changed the title from director of education to superintendent of education. In 1955, the Governor's Executive Order changed the title to commissioner of education.

[a] For St. Thomas and St. John.

[b] For St. Croix.

Appendix B

Chart I.--VIRGIN ISLANDS DEPARTMENT OF EDUCATION, 1965

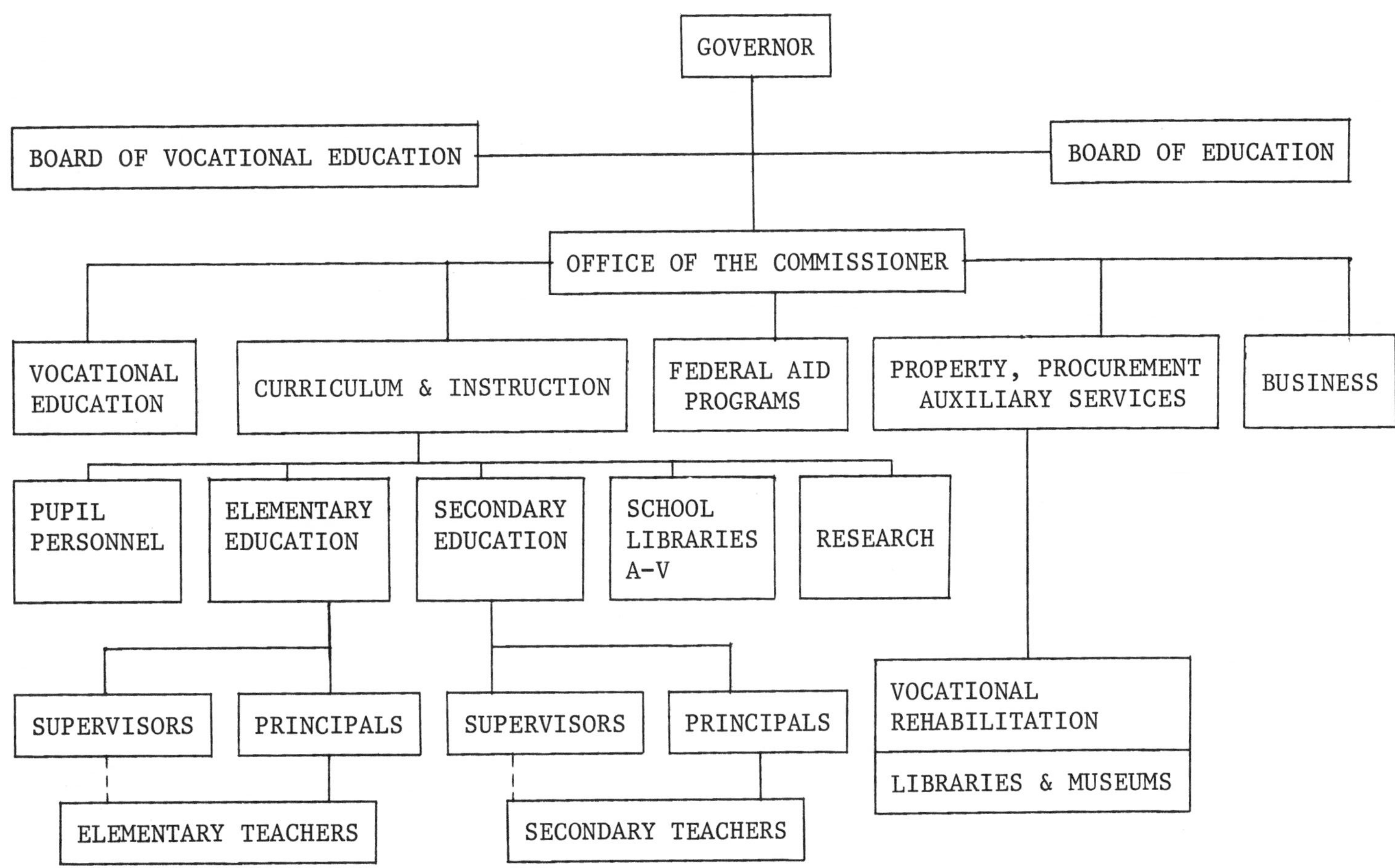